Father Ted

the complete scripts

Graham Linehan & Arthur Mathews

HAT TRICK

BOXTREE

First published 1999 by Boxtree
an imprint of Macmillan Publishers Ltd
25 Eccleston Place London SW1W 9NF
Basingstoke and Oxford

www.macmillan.co.uk

Associated companies throughout the world

ISBN 0 7522 1850 6

A CIP catalogue record for this book is available from
the British Library.

Picture credits

Hat Trick Productions Ltd: pages vii, 12, 29, 43, 62, 67, 90, 99,
118, 127, 144, 152, 171, 178, 196, 211, 229, 243, 261, 279,
290, 305, 322, 338, 352, 365, 368.

Designed by Dan Newman/Perfect Bound Design
Printed by Mackays of Chatham plc.

**The new Father Ted video (catalogue number VC6780)
is also available to buy from all good video outlets.**

dedications

I'd like to dedicate this book to my parents – Graham

To Paul Wonderful – Arthur

acknowledgements

We'd like to thank Geoffrey Perkins for making the first series ten times better than it would have been had we had our own way all the time . . . Mary Bell of Hat Trick for looking after us and looking after the show and realising that doing so amounted to the same thing . . . Denise O'Donoghue and Jimmy Mulville at Hat Trick for trusting us enough to never give us notes . . . Seamus Cassidy for having the guts to commission it after our first sitcom ended up filling the valued 3 a.m. slot on Channel 4 . . . Lissa Evans for being a great studio producer . . . Declan Lowney for not killing us while he was directing the first and second series . . . Andy de Emmony for not killing us while he was doing the third series . . . the ever-dependable crews in Ireland and England which were comprised of some of the best people in the world . . . the various people who worked in the production office, for their patience and hard work . . . the various visiting cast members for consistently 'getting it' . . . Ken Sweeney for his friendship and his sterling work as a sort of SuperExtra . . . John Fisher for his unusual hair . . . Neil Hannon for writing the music, especially the tune for 'My Lovely Horse' . . . the journalists who gave the show a chance . . . the journalists who were so obviously and amusingly enraged by its success . . . *Fawlty Towers*, *The Simpsons* and *Seinfeld* for their influence . . . Paul Wonderful for inspiring at least two characters and being generally hilarious . . . Patrick and Cheryl McCormack for the use of the Parochial House, and for not minding when we turned the front garden into The Somme . . . the fans of the show in Ireland, England and wherever else the thing ended up . . . Dermot Morgan, Ardal O'Hanlon, Frank Kelly and Pauline McLynn for being everything we hoped for and more . . . The Catholic Church . . . and finally, the Big Guy himself, without whom all this would have been a show about three firemen or something, and may not have worked quite so well.

contents

Introduction vii

SERIES 1

Episode 1:   Good Luck, Father Ted 8
Episode 2:   Entertaining Father Stone 22
Episode 3:   The Passion of Saint Tibulus 36
Episode 4:   Competition Time 50
Episode 5:   And God Created Woman 64
Episode 6:   Grant Unto Him Eternal Rest 78

SERIES 2

Episode 1:   Hell 92
Episode 2:   Think Fast, Father Ted 106
Episode 3:   Tentacles of Doom 120
Episode 4:   The Old Grey Whistle Theft 134
Episode 5:   Song For Europe 148
Episode 6:   The Plague 162
Episode 7:   Rock a Hula Ted 176
Episode 8:   Cigarettes and Alcohol and Rollerblading 190
Episode 9:   New Jack City 204
Episode 10: Flight Into Terror 218

christmas special

A Christmassy Ted 232

SERIES 3

Episode 1:   Are You Right There, Father Ted? 256
Episode 2:   Chirpy Burpy Cheap Sheep 270
Episode 3:   Speed 3 284
Episode 4:   The Mainland 298
Episode 5:   Escape From Victory 312
Episode 6:   Kicking Bishop Brennan Up The Arse 326
Episode 7:   Night of the Nearly Dead 340
Episode 8:   Going to America .354

introduction

We're great fans of script books, but too many of them seem to be transcribed from the screen by a third party rather than written by the original authors. With this in mind, we've decided to publish the next-to-last drafts of each episode of *Father Ted*, and so provide you with the extra characters and scenes and jokes that didn't make it into the final version for one or another reason. Now, what we've got here doesn't differ too wildly from what ended up on your TV screens, but there's the odd nice surprise. The process of making *Father Ted* was fun – we always had a great crew, and the cast exceeded our wildest expectations – but the process of writing it was even better. We rarely sweated over the scripts contained here – it was more like dropping by the Parochial House, turning on a tape recorder and seeing what happened next. If this book goes some way to illuminating that process, then it'll have done its job. On the other hand, if it just makes you laugh, it'll have done its job too. Enjoy yourselves. We certainly did.

Graham Linehan and Arthur Mathews, September 1999

Publisher's note: The footnotes contained in these scripts reveal significant changes that took place between this penultimate draft of the script and the final version that was broadcast. As well as anecdotal details, they highlight scenes that were deleted or inserted and large amounts of dialogue that was deleted (small amounts of dialogue are footnoted only when their insertion or omission had a marked influence on the development of the plot).

good luck, father ted

GRAHAM: There was an element of debate about which episode of *Father Ted* should be the first in the series. The choice was between this and *The Passion of Saint Tibulus*. In fact, neither was the first to be written; our initial proposal to Hat Trick was in the form of three scenes of what is now Episode Six. In the end we decided that this one should be first because all the central characters have moments where they step up and make their idiosyncracies known; Dougal, Mrs Doyle and Jack are basically just being themselves while the plot revolves around Ted. It's a good 'welcome to the band'. And, because we'd written the last episode first, we had a fair idea of who our characters were already.

We didn't realise we were doing it at the time, but aside from Ted, each central character seems to be a parody of popular perceptions of the Irish. We were certainly sick of the clichés about Ireland – even the nice ones – so it felt good to bend and stretch and exaggerate those stereotypes until they became caricatures. Mrs Doyle is a caricature of our alleged friendliness, Jack is a caricature of our supposed capacity for drink and Dougal is a caricature of our perceived hilarious and delightful light-headedness, God bless us.

In this particular episode I think we might have made a tactical error. Although I like the *Deliverance* joke with the banjo, I'm not sure that it should have been in the first episode. Given the way the rest of the series went, it seems uncharacteristically savage, an inappropriate calling card.

Both Arthur and I make an appearance now and again in the series, and my back makes an appearance in this episode. (I promise I'm only mentioning this because I like the joke.) There's a 'ride' hidden behind Jack and Dougal on the roundabout called 'Goad the Fierce Man' – you can see the fierce man on the ladder. That's me in the red jacket goading him.

ARTHUR: Actually, this isn't my favourite episode. In retrospect I would have preferred to open the series with *The Passion of Saint Tibulus* (now Episode Three), but it is still a good introduction. Ted's wish to appear on television is very much to the fore. He cares deeply about all the really superficial things that priests aren't supposed to care about – especially money – and he's utterly useless at hiding the fact. I also like the bit about Dougal comparing fortune telling to 'heaven and hell and everlasting life and that type of stuff'.

John and Mary O'Leary hate each other, they're stuck in this awful marriage, but they would just die if a priest saw them arguing. And they don't just stop fighting when they see a priest; they make this sudden switch to become this extraordinarily loving couple.

PART ONE

SCENE 1 INT./DAY 1
SET: PAROCHIAL HOUSE

We see Father Ted Crilly, a middle-aged, pleasant, well-meaning priest, looking at a large notebook. He is wearing a grey cardigan. We can see his clerical collar underneath it.

TED: Right, so that's Tuesday dealt with . . . now let's have a look at Wednesday.

Father Jack Hackett, an elderly, blotchy, ugly, ill-tempered priest, looks back at Ted with undisguised disgust from his ancient armchair. Father Jack looks about seventy years old. A cigarette with one long line of ash protruding from it dangles from his hand. An empty bottle of whiskey lies on his lap. His clerical clothes are stained horribly.

TED: Ah . . . the half seven Mass, I can take that . . .

Jack glares at him.

TED: And maybe . . . could you do the half eight at all — ?

He looks at Jack hopefully. Jack stares back.

TED: Right, I can take that as well. Now . . . the half past six evening on Sunday . . . ?

Jack says nothing. He takes a drag on his cigarette and blows the smoke out while still staring at Ted.

TED: The evening mass, now . . . too early for you . . .? (*No response from Jack.*) No problem . . . I can do that . . . just make a note . . .

He writes something in his notebook. A young, gormless priest, Father Dougal McGuire, enters the room. There are noticeable globules of shaving foam all over his face and in his hair.

DOUGAL: Morning, Ted.

TED: Morning, Dougal.

Ted looks up and notices the foam. He considers the sight.

TED (*pointing to just below his own ear*): There's . . . a little bit of shaving cream there . . .

DOUGAL (*looking closely at Ted*): No, there's not, Ted.

TED: No, on you, Dougal.

DOUGAL: Where exactly, Ted?

TED: Just . . . there below your ear . . .

DOUGAL (*wiping softly beneath his ear*): Here?

TED: Yes, and there's . . . there's a bit more . . .

Ted points to just below his own lip. Dougal wipes the foam from his lip.

DOUGAL: Gone?

TED: No, there's still just a tiny . . . Dougal, it's all over the place.

DOUGAL (*goes to mirror*): How on earth did all that get there? I didn't even shave this morning.

Ted just looks at him. Dougal wipes himself clean of the rest of the foam. Ted examines his notebook.

DOUGAL: So what are we doing today, Ted? Confessions and Mass and things like that, I suppose.

TED: Yes, Dougal. Things like that.

Dougal nods, smiling. He looks around. Pause.

DOUGAL: It's great being a priest, isn't it, Ted?

Ted doesn't say anything. He takes a sweet from a bowl beside the telephone. Dougal looks at Jack. Jack looks at Dougal with even more contempt than he displayed to Ted.

DOUGAL (*whispers*): Is Father Jack getting drained today?

TED: Tuesday.

DOUGAL (*looks out of the window*): It's lovely out.

Shot of the view outside the window. Storm-force winds batter the trees. Pause.

DOUGAL: Oh, wait'll I tell you! . . . Funland's coming to Craggy Island!

TED: This fairground thing? I wouldn't have much interest in that now, to be honest.

DOUGAL: They've got a spider baby.

TED: A what?

DOUGAL: A spider baby. It's like a freakshow thing. It's got the body of a spider, but it's actually a baby!

We see that Father Jack is drifting off to sleep.

TED: And how is it a baby? Does it have a nappy on or something?

DOUGAL: No.

TED: Does it have the head of a baby?

DOUGAL: Emmmm . . . no.

TED: Dougal, if it looks like a spider, and it doesn't gurgle at you or anything, how do you know it's actually a baby?

Pause.

DOUGAL: They keep it in a pram.

TED: Are you absolutely sure about this? You're not confusing it with a dream you had, or something?

DOUGAL: Yes, I saw it on the News. Honestly. I . . . oh, wait now . . . Eh, yes, actually, now that you say it, it was a dream, yes.

Ted sighs and lifts up a diagram. It has a drawing of an outline of a head. The space around the head is filled with a single word – 'reality'. Inside the head is the word 'dream'.

TED (*pointing at diagram*): Dougal. Have you been studying this like I told you to?

DOUGAL: I have, I have, Ted. Sorry . . . but we should go anyway, Ted. It'll be great! Last year I had a go at the horse riding and it was fantastic!

TED: I didn't know you could ride horses.

DOUGAL: Ah, it wasn't a real horse, Ted. It was an old lad with a saddle on him. God, he must have been eighty. He wasn't able to go very fast. I was lashin' him with the whip, but I couldn't get much of a response out of him.

TED: And how long were you up on him?

DOUGAL: I'd say it was about . . . an hour.

TED: So you were up on an eighty-year-old man, riding him around and whipping him for sixty minutes? (*Rubs his eyes.*) You realise that image is going to stay with me for the rest of my life now . . .

DOUGAL: Ah, it's great. We should go!

TED: No, I don't think I could take the excitement, to be honest.

Dougal nods, but still looks disappointed.

DOUGAL: See if there's anything on the telly, so.

Dougal switches on the television. As soon as he does so, it wakes Jack, who sits up with a start, grabs the whiskey bottle, smashes in the television screen and goes back to sleep. Ted gives Jack's prone figure a disapproving glance.

DOUGAL: Or, maybe I'll just go and study the old diagram.

He picks up the diagram and leaves the room. The telephone rings. Ted picks it up absent-mindedly.

TED: Hello, Father Ted Crilly speaking . . .

SCENE 2 INT./DAY 1
SET: OFFICE/PAROCHIAL HOUSE
The man on the other end of the telephone is a television producer. His name is Terry MacNamee.

TERRY: Hello, Father. Sorry to disturb you. My name is Terry MacNamee. I'm producing the programme *Faith Of Our Fathers* for Telly Eireann at the moment. We're doing a special about priests who work in isolated communities, and I was wondering if you'd be interested in talking to us . . .

TED: Oh! Well, that's . . . that's very exciting . . . *Faith Of Our Fathers* is my favourite programme.

TERRY: Well, you're the first person we thought of . . . (*He springs around on his chair and we see a chart with many, many priests' names on it, all of them crossed off. The only remaining one is 'Father Ted Crilly'.*) If you are interested, we could come over. We can also give you a small fee for your trouble.

SCENE 3 INT./DAY 1
SET: PAROCHIAL HOUSE/OFFICE
Dougal walks into the room behind Ted.

DOUGAL: Who's that, Ted?

Ted jumps with fright.

TED: Eh . . . it's no one, Dougal.

DOUGAL: No one?

TERRY: Hello? Father Crilly?

DOUGAL: It must be someone, Ted.

TED: Eh, just a second . . .

He puts his hand over the mouthpiece. He takes a sweet from a bag and throws it over to the other side of the room and Dougal runs for it. Ted continues his conversation with Terry.

TED: Sorry about that.

TERRY (*looking at charts*): Father, quick question. How do you get to Craggy Island, exactly? It doesn't seem to be on any maps.

TED: No, it wouldn't be on any maps, now, Terry, we're not exactly New York! The best way to find it is to head out from Galway and go slightly north until you see the English boats with the nuclear symbols on the side. They go very close to the island when they're dumping the old 'glow-in-the-dark'.

TERRY: Oh, one thing. Are there other priests living there with you? (*Looks at a sheet of paper.*) Our researcher doesn't mention anyone else.

TED: Oh, well, ah . . .

He looks at Dougal, who is having trouble unwrapping the sweet. Jack snores loudly, and Ted looks over at him. A line of spittle is falling from his mouth. It rises and falls as Jack snores.

TED: There's no one else here.

TERRY: Right, then. We'll see you Saturday. I'll ring when I get there.

TED: See you so! Bye . . .

Ted looks at Dougal. Dougal has finally managed to unwrap the sweet. He chews it slowly, a look of ecstasy on his face. Ted smiles at him. Jack belches.

SCENE 4 EXT./NIGHT 1
SET: ANT COLONY
Stock footage from a nature programme. We see close-ups of ants, chewing leaves, fighting and crawling all over each other. The sight is framed as if seen through binoculars.

SCENE 5 INT./NIGHT 1
SET: PAROCHIAL HOUSE
We see Dougal looking through a pair of binoculars. He lowers them from his face then brings them back up again.

SCENE 6 EXT./NIGHT 1
SET: ANT COLONY
More footage of ants.

SCENE 7 INT./NIGHT 1
SET: PAROCHIAL HOUSE
Dougal wraps the strap around the binoculars.

DOUGAL: The ants are back, Ted.

Ted is on the floor, removing parts from the smashed television. He lays them out to one side.

TED: Never put on the television when Father Jack's asleep, Dougal. You know how he is.

DOUGAL: But he's always asleep.

We see Jack asleep in his chair in exactly the same position as he was in previous scenes.

TED: Well, anyone who's worked as long as he has for the Church deserves a rest. It's actually quite an honour for us to look after him in his old age.

Father Jack opens his mouth and draws in breath in a noisy, violent way.

TED (*laughs softly*): Dreaming of past glories, no doubt.

We close-up on Jack's blotched face. The screen goes white.

SCENE 8 INT./DAY 2
SET: SCHOOL HALL
We see a nun addressing a hall full of schoolgirls.

NUN: Girls? Girls, pay attention. We've got a special treat today. Father Hackett has very kindly volunteered to take you all for volleyball practice.

Cut to a slightly younger Jack, who is smoking a cigarette nearby. He looks at the girls in a fixed, disconcerting way. He leans over to the nun and whispers something in her ear.

NUN: . . . Oh, right, Father . . . and he's just reminded me that it's very warm today, so there'll be no need for your tracksuit tops.

Jack smiles, worryingly.

SCENE 9 INT./NIGHT 2
SET: PAROCHIAL HOUSE
*We see Jack frowning, still asleep. Ted enters the
room, twiddling a screwdriver. He walks over to the
television and bends down to look at it. He unscrews
the front section and hands it to Dougal. Dougal
takes the frame and holds it in front of his face.*

DOUGAL (*addresses camera*): Hello, Father
Dougal McGuire here, and welcome to this
week's *Top of the Pops*. In at number 45 is
Father Ted Crilly with 'I've Got The Power'.
And still at number 17 for the sixteenth week
in a row is Father Jack Hackett with 'I'm A
Sleepy Priest' . . .

*Suddenly Jack wakes up with a start. He sees
Dougal in the television.*

JACK: How did that gobshite get on
television?

*The housekeeper, Mrs Doyle, enters. She carries cups
and saucers and a pot of tea on a tray.*

MRS DOYLE: Hello to you all! Oh, is the
television broken again, Father?

TED: It is. We had a bit of trouble with —

MRS DOYLE: Never you mind! There's
nothing wrong with it that won't be fixed with
a bit of 'you know what' in the head
department.

Ted smiles kindly at Mrs Doyle.

MRS DOYLE: Who's for tea, then?

DOUGAL: Me please, Mrs Doyle.

JACK: Tea! Feck!

TED: I'm fine, Mrs Doyle.

Pause. Mrs Doyle looks at Ted.

MRS DOYLE: You won't have a cup?

TED (*sighs*): No, honestly, Mrs Doyle, I won't
have a cup, I'm fine.

MRS DOYLE: You sure now? It's hot.

TED: No, I'm not in the mood thanks, Mrs Doyle.

MRS DOYLE: All right . . . ah, go on! Will you not have a drop?

TED: No, Mrs Doyle, thanks anyway.

MRS DOYLE: A small cup?

TED: I'm fine.

MRS DOYLE: I'll tell you what, Father, I'll pour a cup for you anyway.

TED (*places hand over cup*): No, seriously, Mrs Doyle —

Mrs Doyle pours anyway. It spills over Ted's hand.

TED: Aaaarrrrgghhh!

MRS DOYLE (*oblivious*): . . . And you have it if you want.

Ted rubs his hand and looks at her fiercely.

MRS DOYLE (*turning to Jack*): Now, Father, what do you say to a cup?

JACK: Feck off, cup!

She starts to pour a cup. Jack grunts and mumbles under his breath in Mrs Doyle's face.

MRS DOYLE (*to Ted*): He loves his cup of tea . . .

JACK: Feck off!

MRS DOYLE (*finishes pouring*): There we go!

She leaves the cup beside Jack and starts to walk towards the door. He throws the cup after her. It smashes on the wall beside her head but she doesn't notice. She turns suddenly.

MRS DOYLE: Oh, Father Crilly, I almost forgot. There was a 'phone call earlier from a Terry MacNamee.

TED (*suddenly alert*): Right!

DOUGAL: Who's that, Ted?

MRS DOYLE: He's something to do with . . . was it the television?

TED: Yes! He's the man who's coming to fix the television.

MRS DOYLE: Anyway, he'll be here tomorrow at twelve.

TED: Grand . . .

Mrs Doyle smiles again and leaves. Dougal walks up to the television, stepping around the parts on the floor. He presses the 'on' button a few times.

DOUGAL: Ah, yeah, it's good you called someone, Ted. It's still not working.

Reaction shot of Ted considering Dougal.

SCENE 10 INT./NIGHT 2
SET: TED AND DOUGAL'S BEDROOM
Dougal is in the bedroom, looking into the cupboard mirror. He is playing air guitar with a tennis racket. We notice that Ted's bed, the one nearest the door, has a 'Pope John Paul II, Ireland 1979' duvet cover. Dougal has a Jack Charlton duvet cover. He wears an Ireland jersey and boxer shorts.

DOUGAL (*singing*): . . . 'You're simply the best!' . . . Dow, dow, dow, dow . . .

Ted walks through the door. He wears normal striped pyjamas. He looks at Dougal.

DOUGAL: . . . Dow, dow, dow, dow . . .

TED: Ahem . . .

DOUGAL (*jumps*): Oh! Ted! You frightened me there!

TED (*amused*): You doing the old pop-star thing there, Dougal?

DOUGAL: I am! It was great being on television today, Ted. I think I've caught the old telly bug.*

TED: Well, get into bed now and go asleep. You don't want to get overtired.

DOUGAL (*climbing into bed*): D'yever want to get into television yourself, Ted?

TED (*slightly uncomfortable*): Ah, no. I wouldn't have any interest in that type of thing, really.

DOUGAL: Right . . . I can't imagine you'd be much good, actually.

TED: What? Why not?

DOUGAL: Ah, I don't know . . . You're a bit

---

* It's easy to miss, but in the actual episode, Dougal actually places his air 'guitar' back in its stand when he's finished playing.

serious. And your eyes are a bit crossed. They're a bit wonky. The cameras can pick that up, you know.

TED (*shocked*): I am not cross-eyed!

DOUGAL: Ah, you are a bit now, Ted. Half the time I don't know if you're talking to me or Father Jack.

TED (*angry*): Dougal, will you just . . . get some sleep.

DOUGAL: Fair enough, Ted! Just have to say the old prayers.

Dougal kneels down.

DOUGAL: Our Father, who art in . . .

Pause.

TED: Heaven.

DOUGAL: Right. Hallowed be thy . . .?

TED: Name. Listen, Dougal, you know you can praise God with sleep?

DOUGAL: Can you, Ted?

TED: You can. It's a way of thanking him for a tiring day.

DOUGAL: There's a lot of ways you can praise God, isn't there? Like when you told me to praise him by just, you know, going out of the room.

TED: That's a good one, yes.

Ted turns off the light. The two lie in bed, barely illuminated by the moon outside.

Pause.

DOUGAL: Ted? . . . Ted?

TED (*sighs*): Yes, what?

DOUGAL: Did you ever wonder if there were any other planets besides Earth?

TED: Goodnight, Dougal.

SCENE 11 INT./DAY 3
SET: PAROCHIAL HOUSE
We see Jack in his armchair, asleep. There is a sound of muffled conversation from the corner of the room. Jack's eye darts open and he fixes his gaze on something. We pan across to where he is looking. We see the cord of a telephone leading behind the curtain. Ted is there, on the telephone. He spots Jack

looking at him and wraps the curtain around him.

TED: Right! There we go! Sorry, Terry, go ahead . . . You made it, then?

SCENE 12 EXT./DAY 3
SET: TELEPHONE POLE ON THE ISLAND
Terry is telephoning from the island's sole telephone box – it's actually just a telephone on a pole by the side of the road. He seems totally unprepared for the ferocity of the weather on Craggy Island, and his brightly coloured tie dances madly around his face and neck. A camera team freeze nearby.

TERRY (*shouting over wind as he looks around*): I think so! There don't seem to be any indications that this is Craggy Island. There's no signs or anything!

SCENE 13 INT./DAY 3
SET: PAROCHIAL HOUSE
We see Ted behind the curtain.

TED: Is there a man looking at you with a T-shirt saying 'I Shot JR'?

SCENE 14 EXT./DAY 3
SET: TELEPHONE POLE ON THE ISLAND/PAROCHIAL HOUSE
Terry frowns at this question and looks around. He sees a large, strange-looking man staring at him with a fixed, gormless expression. He does indeed wear a faded T-shirt with 'I Shot JR' written on it. It's too small for him and his belly pokes out from under it.

TERRY (*taken aback*): Actually . . . there is.

TED: Oh, you're here, so!

TERRY: What? This line is very bad, Father. You're a bit muffled.

SCENE 15 INT./DAY 3
SET: PAROCHIAL HOUSE/TELEPHONE POLE ON THE ISLAND
Ted looks around at his self-made cave.

TED: Oh, yes, I'm . . . ah . . . I have a portable phone and you caught me by surprise when you called, you know? I'm . . . on the toilet.

Ted grimaces in embarrassment at what he has just said. In the background, out of the window, we see Dougal passing. He sees Ted and looks puzzled.

TERRY: Oh, right . . . ah . . . so, where can we meet up? Anywhere we can go and get some nice shots? Any local landmarks?

TED: No.

TERRY: What?

TED: No, there's no landmarks here now, Terry.

TERRY: None at all?

Dougal approaches the window. He looks at Ted, sees something offscreen and then seems to have an idea. He suppresses a laugh and disappears to the right.

TED: No. The island itself is a kind of landmark. For ships and that. The general rule is that if you're heading away from it, you're going in the right direction.

TERRY: Right, so, ah . . .

TED: There's the field.

TERRY (*putting on a brave face*): Oh, a field! Yes. That sounds . . .

TED: Well, it's not a field, really, but it doesn't have as many rocks in it as most places.

TERRY: Look, that's fine, Father. We'll meet at the field. How do I get there?

TED: Oh, just ask Tom there. He'll help you out.

TERRY: OK, then. Thanks, Father.

Terry puts down the telephone and looks over at Tom, the T-shirt man. A bird has landed on a post right beside him. Tom notices the bird, produces a shotgun and blows it to smithereens. Reaction shot of Terry, his face frozen. Tom looks back and smiles broadly. He has four teeth in total.

TOM (*points to where the bird was, and shouts*): Bird!

Terry exchanges a worried look with the camera team.

SCENE 16 INT./DAY 3
SET: PAROCHIAL HOUSE
Ted is still at the window. We see a grotto-sized statue of the Virgin Mary being raised into shot behind him. He turns around and sees it.

TED: Aaaaaaaaaaaaaaaaaaaaarrghh!

He falls back, bringing the whole curtain rail down with him. When the curtain falls, it reveals a cowed Dougal, holding the statue.

SCENE 17 INT./DAY 3
SET: PAROCHIAL HOUSE
Ted sits holding a cup of tea. He is trembling, staring ahead of him as if in shock.

DOUGAL: God, Ted, I'm so sorry. It was just a joke.

TED: T—t—try to avoid doing that again, Dougal. I thought it was really . . . Herself. That's the last thing I need.

TED: Anyway . . . it's time for Jack's walk. (*To Jack.*) Time for your walk, Father! Off around the cliffs!

DOUGAL: Can I bring him to Funland, Ted?

TED: No, he wouldn't like that, now. Bring him round the cliffs. And Dougal, if you're stopping near the edge, put the brakes on. He was just lucky the last time.

DOUGAL: You not coming, Ted?

TED: No, I think I'll stay here and pray for a while.

DOUGAL (*slyly*): O'ho! What're you after, Ted?

TED: I'm not after anything, Dougal! It's not unknown for members of the clergy to pray from time to time, you know.

Mrs Doyle enters the room pushing a wheelchair.

MRS DOYLE: Here we are, Father Crilly.

JACK (*sees the chair*): Gerraway!

MRS DOYLE: There's nothing Father Hackett likes better than to get out and about in the fresh air!

Jack is warding them off with a big walking stick.

JACK: Grrrrgaaaahhhhggghhh!

Dougal, Ted and Mrs Doyle try to grab him so they can lift him into the wheelchair. Jack suddenly goes limp, like a protester, but they eventually manage to drag him over. When they land him in the wheelchair, he slides down to the floor in one move. They drag him up again. Ted puts a blanket on his legs and starts to tuck it in.

TED: This'll keep you lovely and warm . . .

Jack slaps Ted in the face. Mrs Doyle wheels him to the door. Jack then leaps out of the wheelchair, runs back to his armchair, and wedges himself in again. Ted, Dougal and Mrs Doyle, breathing heavily, turn around to look at him.

SCENE 18 INT./DAY 3
SET: PAROCHIAL HOUSE
We see Jack being wheeled out of the house by Dougal. He has been tied to the chair at various places. He has one hand just about free and is holding a walking stick. With the hook of the stick, he drags a small table behind him. Ted removes it from the table as it comes through the door. Dougal and Mrs Doyle seem not to notice Jack's reluctance, and act cheerful.

TED: Bye, then! (*To Mrs Doyle as they leave.*) Every single day the same thing . . .

MRS DOYLE (*putting on hat and coat*): Ah, once he's out there he has a great time. He loves the old cliffs.

TED: Mmm . . .

MRS DOYLE: Well, I'll be off then, Father! What are you up to yourself?

TED: Oh, I think I'll stay here and have a bit of an old pray.

MRS DOYLE: All right, then! Enjoy the rest of the weekend!

Mrs Doyle leaves. Ted smiles in an excited, sneaky

way and closes the door quickly.

SCENE 18A INT./DAY 3
SET: PAROCHIAL HOUSE HALLWAY
TED (*rubs his hands*): Right!

He puts on a coat and goes the other way.

SCENE 19 INT./DAY 3
SET: PAROCHIAL HOUSE
From a distance, we see Ted leaving by the back door and running at full speed across the landscape.

SCENE 20 EXT./DAY 3
SET: FRONT GATE
We see Dougal looking around the gate at the house. He turns Jack's chair and wheels it in another direction.

END OF PART ONE

* * *

PART TWO

SCENE 21 EXT./DAY 3
SET: ENTRANCE TO FAIRGROUND
Ted has arrived at a gate set in a stone wall. A sign on the gate reads 'The Field' in professional lettering, while written underneath in thick, black marker-pen ink are the words 'Today, Funland'. Ted sees that Tom, still in his JR T-shirt, is sitting on the wall. We hear Wurlitzer music coming from inside.

TED: God, I didn't know this bloody thing was on here . . .

TOM: Hello, Father.

TED: Hello, Tom . . . ah, the Telly Eireann lads, did you get them here all right?

TOM: I did, yes, Father. They said they were going to film a bit of the island. They'll be back soon.

TED: Oh, no, they're not going near the cliffs, are they?

TOM (*shakes his head*): They headed off the other way.

TED: Thank God for that. (*Looking around.*) Right . . . so I'll wait in the field, so . . .

TOM: Father, I've killed a man.

TED (*looking around, not really listening*): Have you, Tom? I'll, ah . . . I'll talk to you about that later. (*Brightly.*) I'm doing an interview for the television!

Ted walks through the gate.

SCENE 22 EXT./DAY 3
SET: FAIRGROUND
Funland is the most pathetic fairground in the world. The names of the rides are written on flimsy cardboard signs: there is 'The Ladder', which is a ladder leaning against a wall. We see a young boy halfway up it while a surly youth wearing a large moneybag watches him. The surly youth has a very weak moustache.

SURLY YOUTH: Keep your hands on the sides.

We also see a sign for 'The Whirly-Go-Round – an experience unlike any other'. Cut to reveal four people going around very slowly on a flat, circular platform. Another moneybag-wearing youth occasionally walks across it for no clear reason. Then we see a sign with 'Car Ride' written on it. A group of people wait beside the sign. A beaten-up Ford Escort arrives, two children get out of the car and are replaced by a young man and his girlfriend. The car takes off again. Cut to a ride called 'The Gate of Hell', which is just a surly youth swinging a young boy back and forth on a gate. We also see a crane in the background. Then we see a stall that sells sweets. It is manned by Mr and Mrs O'Leary, a middle-aged couple.

MR O'LEARY: You stupid, ignorant, bitch!

MRS O'LEARY: Don't you call me a bitch, you bastard! You can't even get it up!

MR O'LEARY: You big, fat, smelly cow!

MRS O'LEARY: Titface! You've got a face like a pair of tits!

MR O'LEARY: Well, at least that's one pair between us.

Mrs O'Leary produces a knife and tries to stab Mr O'Leary. Mr O'Leary grabs the knife and gives Mrs O'Leary a karate chop on the neck. Ted walks into shot. The two stop fighting before he sees them. He turns around and notices them at last.

MR O'LEARY (*very cheerily*): Hello, Father!

TED: Oh, hello, John . . . Hello, Mary. Are you not in the shop today?

MRS O'LEARY (*puts a fond arm around Mr O'Leary*): Well, with Funland here, we decided to open a stall for a few days.

MRS O'LEARY: Will you have a packet of Toffos, Father?

TED: No thanks, Mary. I have to meet someone now. Actually . . . to be honest, I'm being interviewed for a television programme.

MR O'LEARY: Really? Oh, that's fantastic.

MRS O'LEARY: You know, Father, I think you'd be brilliant on television.

TED (*very flattered*): Well, thank you very much . . .

MR O'LEARY: You know, Father, I'd say you'd be more than a match for Gay Byrne or Terry Wogan, or any of them.

TED: Oh, it'll be a few weeks before I get to their level, I'd say . . .

MRS O'LEARY: John was just saying to me the other day, 'Wouldn't Father Crilly be brilliant on television?'

MR O'LEARY: I was. In fact, I think you could do anything you turned your mind to, Father. Television, acting in films, writing bestsellers . . .

TED: Oh, go on! I think you only see my good side . . .

MRS O'LEARY: You only have a good side, Father.

They all laugh good-naturedly. Ted looks at his watch.

TED: Anyway, I'd better go. I must try and track down this film unit. They'll probably want to do a few close-ups and mastershots and noddys and all that with me. I'll see you soon.

He moves out of shot. Mr and Mrs O'Leary wave after him.

MR O'LEARY: Good luck, Father Ted! (*Pause. He turns to Mrs O'Leary.*) Get those feckin' Crunchies out of the car!

Cut back to Ted, who looks at his watch anxiously. He looks up and his face freezes in horror. Cut to Dougal and Jack, who are having a ride on the Whirly-Go-Round. Jack is still in his wheelchair on the platform as it slowly turns. Dougal looks over and sees Ted. Ted turns and pretends to examine the wall behind him.

DOUGAL: Ted! Ted! Over here, Ted.

Ted is forced to turn around and acknowledge him. He makes his way to the ride.

DOUGAL: Ted, what are you doing here? I thought you weren't interested in this kind of thing . . .

TED: You're supposed to be taking Father Jack for his walk!

DOUGAL: . . . Well, ah . . . the cliffs were closed for the day.

TED: How could the cliffs be closed, Dougal?

DOUGAL: OK, no, it wasn't that. Ahem . . . They were gone.

TED: They were gone? The cliffs were gone? Dougal, how could the cliffs just disappear?

DOUGAL (*pause*): Erosion.

TED (*sighs*): Now, come off of that and off to the cliffs with you.

DOUGAL: There's just a few more turns to go, I think.

Ted stands beside the platform as it turns. Dougal and Jack pass by every couple of seconds. Each time they do, Dougal waves at Ted like a five-year-old waving at his parents. Ted waves half-heartedly back the first time, but after that he just glowers at them.

SCENE 23 EXT./DAY 3
SET: SOMEWHERE ON THE ISLAND
We see the camera team relaxing, having a smoke, etc., near a thatched cottage. The cameraman is facing a small bald boy who has a banjo. The cameraman starts playing a guitar, and the bald boy joins in on the banjo. They play 'Duelling Banjos' from 'Deliverance'.

SCENE 24 EXT./DAY 3
SET: FAIRGROUND
Dougal and Ted are wheeling Jack through the fairground.

TED: Now, you're to go straight home, do you hear?

Dougal sulks.

TED: I don't want to hear any more nonsense.

DOUGAL: Everyone else is here . . .

TED: Dougal, you're a priest! You have to show some decorum.

DOUGAL (*whispers*): Wish I wasn't a priest.

TED: Dougal! If Father Jack heard you say that!

DOUGAL: Sure, he told me once he doesn't believe in God!

TED: Dougal!

Ted walks Dougal out of shot. Jack is left alone. He scowls and makes strange noises. Some young girls pass by. He looks at them and then slowly follows them out of shot, pushing the wheels of his chair with all his might.

SCENE 25 EXT./DAY 3
SET: OUTSIDE TENT
Ted and Dougal walk into shot. A sign beside the tent reads 'Tarot Reading's – Fortune's Told'.*

DOUGAL: Ted, can I have a go on the 'Crane of Death'?

TED: The what?

DOUGAL: The 'Crane of Death'. It's called that because there was a fella killed on it last year.

TED: . . . Dougal, I'm sick and tired of —

DOUGAL: Ted! Ted, look! A fortune teller! Just give us one go here!

TED: You shouldn't waste your money on that stuff, Dougal.

DOUGAL: There might be something in it, Ted.

TED: It's a lot of rubbish. How could anyone believe any of that nonsense?

DOUGAL: Come on, Ted. Sure it's no more peculiar than that stuff that they taught us in the seminary. Heaven and Hell and everlasting life and that type of stuff. You're not meant to

---

*Evidence of our obsession with misplaced apostrophes which, of course, meant absolutely nothing on screen.

take it seriously.

TED: Dougal! You *are* meant to take it seriously!

DOUGAL: Are you? What? Heaven, Hell and everlasting life and all that?

TED: Of course.

DOUGAL: Tsch!

TED: Look, if I let you go in, will you go home straight after that?

DOUGAL: Oh, yeah! I promise.

TED: Right.

They enter the tent.

SCENE 26 INT./DAY 3
SET: TENT
Ted and a very excited Dougal enter the tent. An old woman sits at the table facing them.

WOMAN: Hello.

Dougal's smile dies. He looks at the woman, then turns and whispers to Ted.

DOUGAL: Ted, let's go.

TED: What's wrong, Dougal?

DOUGAL: I'm scared.

TED: Oh, for pity's — look, I'll do it and then you can watch.

Dougal just nods. Ted turns to the woman.

TED: Hello, there!

WOMAN: Sit.

TED: All righty . . .

WOMAN: First, you must cross my palm with silver.

TED: Silver? I don't carry huge bags of it around. I'm afr—

WOMAN: Give me a pound.

TED: Oh! Right!

The woman takes the money and fans out some cards.

WOMAN: You must choose, and I will interpret. One card at a time, please.

Ted turns over a card, giving Dougal a jokey

'spooked' look as he does so. The first card is the Grim Reaper. Ted turns, sees the card and jumps slightly.

TED: Can I pick another card? I wasn't concentrating.

WOMAN (*laughs*): No, no . . . this is a common misunderstanding. The Grim Reaper does not mean death in a literal sense. Rather, it may be the death of an old way of life and the beginning of a new one.

TED: Ahhh! I know what that is!

He remembers Dougal is behind him.

TED: . . . Probably about getting that new light for the bike . . .

WOMAN: Another card, please.

Ted turns over another card. Again, it's the Grim Reaper.

TED: Ah . . . is that good?

WOMAN: Well . . . that, ah . . . maybe it will become clear on the next card . . .

Ted turns over another card. Again, it's the Grim Reaper.

WOMAN: This is really weird. There's only supposed to be one in each pack . . .

Ted and Dougal exchange worried looks.

SCENE 27 EXT./DAY 3
SET: ENTRANCE TO FIELD
Tom is still sitting on the wall. He is reading a newspaper – 'The Craggy Island Examiner'. The headline reads 'Crazed murderer still at large'. The camera team arrive beside him.

TERRY: Hello again, Tom . . . Father Crilly around yet?

TOM: He is, yes. He's in there.

Terry notices a large scar on Tom's hand.

TERRY: Fffewww . . . nasty scar there, Tom. Where'd you get that?

TOM: Oh, I was . . . in an argument.

TERRY: Oh . . . I hope you won.

TOM: I certainly did. (*Pause.*) But that's nothin'. . . . I've had worse than that!

Tom quickly turns around, bends over and pulls down his trousers. We see the shocked faces of the camera team.

TOM: Would you believe me own dog did that to me?

One of the camera team puts his hand over his mouth and rushes off.

TOM: Doesn't it look like a face?

SCENE 28 EXT./DAY 3
SET: FAIRGROUND
Dougal and Ted are looking around anxiously.

TED: Where did he get to? You'll have to get him back home for his drink. It's nearly five . . . Listen, you go that way and I'll go this way. (*Cut to Jack on a metal seat, asleep. Cut to Ted looking around. He sees him and walks over. Back to Jack on the seat. Ted goes up and sits on the seat beside him. He starts shaking him softly.*) Father? Father? We'd better be off.

SCENE 29 EXT./DAY 3
SET: FAIRGROUND
Cut to Dougal wandering around looking for Ted and Jack. We hear an offscreen voice.

VOICE: Father! Father!

Cut to reveal the camera team beckoning to Dougal. Dougal goes over to them.

TERRY: There you are, Father. We got here at last.

Dougal looks confused.

SCENE 30 EXT./DAY 3
SET: CRANE CHAIR
Ted is still talking to Jack.

TED: Father, Father? . . . (*Fondly.*) Tsk . . . dead to the world . . . You don't know what's goin' on, do you . . .?

Jack wakes up.

JACK: Gin! Vodka!

TED: That's right, Father, time for your drink . . .

JACK: Thunderbird! Yellow packs!

Jack looks around in confusion, realising where he is.

TED: Come on, we'd better –

Ted moves to get out of the chair and almost falls into empty space. We see that the crane has lifted them high above the ground.

TED: Arrggghh!!! What the hell are we doing up here?!!!

Pause.

JACK: Drink!

SCENE 31 EXT./DAY 3
SET: FAIRGROUND
Dougal is with the television people.

DOUGAL: Are you from the television?

TERRY: Eh . . . yes . . .

DOUGAL: Great!

TERRY: We'll just ask you a few questions . . .

DOUGAL: Questions? I'm going to be on television?

TERRY: Eh . . . well, yes . . . We'll start off with the history of the island, move on to how life has changed in the last few years for the islanders . . . economically and culturally . . .

Terry's voice fades out as we close in on Dougal's face. He is open-mouthed and slightly vacant.

SCENE 32 INT./DAY 3
SET: DOUGAL'S MIND
Animation. We see the diagram with the silhouette of the head and 'dream' and 'reality' written on it. Question marks appear beside 'reality', then beside 'dream'. Then the words swap places. Then a few animated rabbits come into the scene and start hopping about.

SCENE 33 EXT./DAY 3
SET: FAIRGROUND
Dougal is now smiling gormlessly, a million miles away. We hear Terry's voice.

TERRY: . . . Aaaaand, action! Father, how would you say that people's religious beliefs here on Craggy Island have been affected by the advent of television and greater access to the media in general?

SCENE 34 EXT./DAY 3
SET: THE CRANE

Ted looks panic-stricken.

TED: I've got to get off!! My interview!! Oh, Jesus, my interview!

JACK: Drink!

TED (*sees something in the distance*): Oh, God! They're talking to Dougal! Nooooo!!!!!

JACK: Drink! Drink! Drink! Drink! Drink!

Jack starts rocking the chair back and forth.

TED: I've got to think of something . . . Come on, Ted, think!

Jack finally rocks the chair so much that Ted is tipped out of it. Ted falls without a noise.

SCENE 35 INT./NIGHT 3
SET: PAROCHIAL HOUSE
We see the floor beside Jack's chair. Bottles of rum and whiskey and wine and cans of beer litter the floor. Jack's callused hand drops lifelessly into view, a can of Castrol GTX rolling from it. Cut to a full view of him. His lap is covered with bottles and he is asleep. The camera pans around and we see a very excited Dougal staring at the television.

DOUGAL (*to someone on his right*): There I am! It's me! I'm on the telly! Look!

SCENE 36 EXT./DAY 3
SET: FAIRGROUND
Cut to the television. We see Dougal in an interview pose, the crane in the background.

DOUGAL (*on television*): . . . I suppose God is a bit like the Loch Ness monster. Not a lot of people have seen him, but there's the odd photograph . . . He doesn't look like a load of tyres though . . .

In the background we see an ambulance pulling up, blazing its lights and sounding its siren.

DOUGAL: . . . But, you know . . . does he exist? (*Shrugs.*) Who knows?

We see the ambulance pulling off.

DOUGAL: See over there? Just under that tree? I was hit by lightning there.

SCENE 37 INT./NIGHT 3
SET: PAROCHIAL HOUSE
Back in the Parochial House, we see Ted, sitting beside Dougal, covered from head to toe in a full-length cast. We can just see his eyes. He bangs his arm up and down in frustration, groaning loudly. Dougal turns to him.

DOUGAL: I know! It's great, isn't it?

SCENE 38 EXT./DAY 3
SET: FAIRGROUND
Cut back to the television Dougal.

DOUGAL (*on television*): . . . The spider baby . . . ah, yes. It's got the body of a spider, but the mind of a baby . . .

As Dougal talks on, the words 'Father Ted Crilly' appear beneath him.

SCENE 39 INT./NIGHT 3
SET: PAROCHIAL HOUSE
Cut to Ted, who is sobbing uncontrollably.

DOUGAL: I know! I can't believe it either! I'm on television!

Jack wakes up. He sees the television and gets a shock.

JACK: That gobshite again! He's never off the air!

He throws a bottle at the television.

THE END

entertaining father stone

ARTHUR: Our original idea about the titles was that they would all be in the vein of *Good Luck, Father Ted* and *Think Fast, Father Ted*, like the titles of the old 'Mister Moto' films, but we couldn't think of any more than two. In retrospect I'm glad, because it meant we could have more fun with them. This, for instance, is a fairly obvious reference to one of my favourite films, Joe Orton's *Entertaining Mr Sloane*.

The story was inspired by a 'friend' of friends of mine who used to visit them every summer. He was awful. Apart from the fact that he used to cheat at golf, he had this peculiar ability to dominate – and simultaneously ruin the atmosphere in – a room without really doing anything. One of those people who are just there. He wasn't quite as deathly silent as Father Stone, but he was on the way, apparently.

I love the silences – the quietness and calm of this episode. If I had to pick a favourite, this would probably be it. *Father Ted* can be quite frantic, perhaps too frantic on occasion, and this makes for a quiet interlude. We were really enjoying the fact that they were sitting around in silence having a truly terrible time, but after about fifteen pages we realised the episode had to go somewhere, it needed a twist – so we had Father Stone being struck by lightning. That, in turn, provides another indication of their attitude to religion. The only time we ever see Ted pray is when he's in terrible trouble and he calls on God in the last resort. But he always gets it wrong: he even offers God money to help them get rid of Father Stone.

I like the way it ends with Father Stone staying for ever. That's the beauty of sitcoms as opposed to drama: you can end one episode with something terrible happening and then not even refer to it in the next. But we did think of getting Stone back and having a running joke that he'd have a room in the house and stay there indefinitely.

GRAHAM: Initially, John and Mary were also going to provide a running joke through every episode, but I'm glad we dropped that idea. I don't think they would have worked in every episode as they're always exactly the same, fighting and then swooning over each other the moment they see a priest. It probably works better to only see them occasionally.

We also rather abandoned another joke after this episode: the weather. It was always in the back of our minds that the weather on Craggy Island would be constantly awful, pouring with rain literally all the time. Logistically, it would have been difficult to sustain, but that wasn't the real reason for losing it. Rather, we just seemed to forget about it . . . But I'm glad we did. It's not a good thing to paint yourself into a corner at the start of a sitcom series.

PART ONE
SCENE 1 INT./DAY 1
SET: PAROCHIAL HOUSE

DOUGAL: Ted, if you had three wishes, what would they be?

TED: Three wishes? . . . God, I don't know really. I suppose . . . world peace, that'd be the first one . . . then maybe an end to hunger . . . and . . . ah . . . (*We see a quick flash of Ted dancing with some girls in a nightclub.*) . . . more money for hospitals and that type of thing.

DOUGAL: Fair enough, Ted.

TED: And yourself, Dougal . . . What would your three wishes be?

DOUGAL: Oh, Lord. I dunno. I'm happy enough, really.

TED: You wouldn't want anything at all, Dougal?

DOUGAL: No, I don't think so. I can't think of anything, anyway.

TED: So you wouldn't even like . . . say, a big car to drive around in?

DOUGAL (*incredibly excited*): Eh? Oh, God, I don't know . . . I think that'd be fine. The car'd be fine.

TED: You wouldn't like to be . . . a big rock star or something? Like Elvis?

DOUGAL: Oh, God, yeah! That'd be great! I'd love to be a rock star! Like Elvis or something!

Pause.

TED: So, your third wish. If you had one . . .

DOUGAL: Oh, that'd be fine. If I had a big car to drive and I was Elvis . . . that'd be grand.

TED (*trying something out*): You wouldn't like . . . this cup?

He lifts up a cup from the table.

DOUGAL: Oh, God, yeah! I'd love that cup! If I had that cup and I was in a big car and I was Elvis! That'd be fantastic!

TED: You've never had much of an imagination, have you, Dougal?

DOUGAL: Oh, no, Ted, you're right there.

SCENE 2 INT./DAY 1
SET: PAROCHIAL HOUSE
The room is completely silent apart from the sonorous ticking of the clock. We see Ted sitting in an armchair, smiling politely at someone and drinking tea. Jack is asleep in his armchair. We see whom Ted is smiling at. It is Father Paul Stone, a serious-looking priest. There is a long, long pause. Ted keeps up a rigid, unconvincing smile.

TED: Would you like more tea, Paul?

STONE: I'm fine.

TED: Right . . . (*Pause.*) Will I turn on the television?

STONE: No, I'm fine.

Pause.

TED: Right, so . . .

Another long pause.

TED: Have you seen Father Shortall recently?

STONE: No.

TED: I was just thinking . . . what would he be? Would he be eighty now?

STONE: I suppose so.

Pause. We hear the front door opening outside. Dougal sticks his head in through the door.

TED (*immediately*): Dougal, you want to have a word with me? Fair enough. Won't be a moment, Paul.

Ted bounds to the door and yanks a confused Dougal out.

SCENE 3 INT./DAY 1
SET: PAROCHIAL HOUSE HALLWAY
Ted closes the door and takes deep breaths. With shaking hands, he lights up a fag.

DOUGAL: What's up with you, Ted? Who's that?

TED: God, I had to get out of there.

DOUGAL: Who is it, Ted?

TED: Now, Dougal . . . don't overreact.

DOUGAL: Fair enough, Ted.

TED: All right . . . (*Deep breath.*) It's Father Stone.

Dougal falls out of shot.

TED: Dougal! Get up!

DOUGAL: Oh, Ted, no, not him!

Ted lifts Dougal back into shot. Dougal looks as if he's just been stabbed.

TED: It's him all right.

DOUGAL: God almighty.

TED: I know —

DOUGAL: Why didn't you tell him not to come? You said you would! You promised after last time!

TED: I tried! But he did what he always does! I said, don't come, Father. It's not a good time for us, and he said, no, I will come, and then I said, no, Father, don't come, there's no room, and that still didn't put him off. God, I can't stand it! Those awful protracted silences!

DOUGAL: You could have lied to him!

TED: I told him all sorts of lies! I said there was a massive radiation leak and we were all dying of cholera and we were spending all our time throwing bodies into a mass

grave . . . But you know the way he is! He just shrugs it off.*

DOUGAL: Oh, God, Ted.

TED (*motioning him back to the living room*): Come on, Dougal. You've got to keep me company.

DOUGAL: No!!!

TED: Dougal!

He wrestles with Dougal for a moment or two. Dougal keeps trying to slide on to the ground through Ted's arms, but finally Ted manages to half-lift, half-drag him into the living room.

SCENE 4 INT./DAY 1
SET: PAROCHIAL HOUSE
Still struggling, Ted and Dougal burst into the room. As soon as they do so, they stand up straight and smile widely at Stone.

TED: Back again!

No response.

TED: Sorry, Paul, you remember Dougal?

STONE: Yes.

Pause.

TED: 'Course you do. Sure you must be coming here . . . how many years is it?

PAUL: A few, anyway.

Pause.

TED: Five. Yes . . . five years it is. Every summer . . . (*Pause.*) What time are you going back tomorrow?

PAUL: Ah, I might stay.

Pause.

TED: What?

PAUL: I might stay.

TED (*urgently*): How long?

PAUL: Don't know. A few weeks.

TED: A few weeks?

---

*For the final version we deleted the previous three sentences and inserted the following line: 'I told him all sorts of lies! Great big massive lies with fecking bells hanging off them!'

PAUL: Yeah.

Dougal falls out of shot again. He gets to his feet slowly.

DOUGAL: Sorry about that, Ted. Fell over.

TED: You don't have to get back to your parish, then?

STONE: No. Not for a while, anyway.

TED: Right . . . except . . . there's only one problem in that . . . Dougal and I were thinking of doing something that . . . Dougal, what were we thinking of doing?

DOUGAL: Oh, the thing there.

TED: Yes, the thing we were going to do together . . .

DOUGAL: Yes.

Pause.

TED: What was it again? That thing we were thinking of . . .

DOUGAL: Big thing it was, Ted. Eh . . .

TED: Eh . . . eh . . . eh . . . holiday . . . we're going on holiday!

STONE: That's fine. I'll mind the place.

TED (*to Dougal*): Wait, it wasn't that we were going on holiday at all. We were going to do something else that means that no one can stay in the house.

Pause.

TED (*biting his lip*): Ooooohhh . . . what was it again?

Pause. Dougal looks desperate. Ted snaps his fingers, desperately trying to come up with something.

TED: What were we going to do . . .? We were going to . . .

Pause. Ted is gesticulating wildly in order to bring forth an idea.

DOUGAL: . . . Have the paintings rehung . . .

TED: Brilliant! Brilliant . . . memory there, Dougal! Have you noticed? They're all crooked. Look at that one, there. (*Ted goes up to a painting and starts 'adjusting' it.*) God,

what type of angle do you call that?

DOUGAL: Ahh, it's a mad angle.

TED: So we can't stay here. Too dangerous. Can't be around when people are shifting paintings all over the place.

STONE: Where will you go?

TED: Eh, we'll be staying in a hotel, probably.

STONE: That's all right. I'll go with you.

Ted looks horrified. He looks at Dougal.

TED: Sorry, Paul, I just have to sort out something with Dougal.

He rises and motions Dougal to follow him. They go outside the door.

SCENE 5 INT./DAY 1
SET: PAROCHIAL HOUSE HALLWAY

TED: What are we going to do? Think, Dougal, think!

Dougal looks very blank.

TED: OK, I'll do the thinking. God, what'll we do?

DOUGAL: Ted . . . Jack.

TED: Oh, God, if he sees him! He'll . . . Christ almighty! I'll have to break it to him gently. You get Paul out of the house and I'll —

DOUGAL: You're not leaving me alone with him, Ted!

TED: Dougal!

DOUGAL: Sorry, Ted, but I have to say no. I just can't. There's no way.

TED: Right, so are you going to tell Jack?

DOUGAL: I'll get my coat.

They go back inside.

SCENE 6 INT./DAY 1
SET: PAROCHIAL HOUSE

TED: Paul, Dougal's going for a walk. Would you like to join him?

STONE: No, thanks.

TED: Will you not go? It's lovely.

STONE: No, thanks. I'm fine.

TED: Paul, he has to show you something. It's very important.

STONE: Is it?

TED: Oh, yes. Very important. This could be the most important thing you'll ever see.

STONE: Yeah?

TED: Oh, yes.

STONE: Right.

TED: So you'll go?

STONE: No, I'm fine. I'll see it again.

TED: OK, Paul, to be honest, Dougal doesn't want to show you anything. It's just . . . there's a fire in the house, and you'll have to leave.

STONE: A fire?

TED: Yes. I didn't want you to get into a panic because it's only a small fire. But it could spread. And if you died in it, I'd never forgive myself. You go out with Dougal, and I'll fight the blaze.

STONE: All right.

TED: You're going!?

STONE: Yeah, if there's a fire.

TED: Great!

Stone gets up. Dougal appears at the door in his coat. Dougal looks terror-stricken.

TED: Don't worry about me, now! Bit of water'll do the trick!

They leave. Ted looks at Jack with trepidation. He goes to the shelves and takes something off the top.

SCENE 7 EXT./DAY 1
SET: PAROCHIAL HOUSE
We see Dougal gently ushering Stone outside.

DOUGAL: Have you seen Father Shortall lately?

STONE: No.

DOUGAL: I suppose he must be about eighty now.

STONE: I suppose so.

SCENE 8 INT./DAY 1
SET: PAROCHIAL HOUSE
We see that Ted is wearing a crash helmet and protective shoulderpads. He approaches Jack.

TED: Father? Father, you awake?

Jack awakens in a slow, blinking, peaceful way. He looks at Ted glassily, still half-asleep.

TED: Father. (*Deep breath.*) We have a visitor.

SCENE 9 EXT./DAY 1
SET: PAROCHIAL HOUSE
Dougal and Stone are standing outside the house.

DOUGAL: So . . . how's everything then?

STONE: All right.

Just as Dougal is about to speak, a figure smashes through the window of the front room. It is Ted, who has obviously been thrown through it with some force. He stands up and brushes himself off. Inside the house, we just about hear Jack.

JACK (*distantly*): Not that bastard! You keep him away from me!

Ted calmly walks back to the front door of the house, giving Dougal and Stone a little wave.

TED: Bit of a backdraft! . . . Nearly out!

He walks through the door and into the house. Stone looks at Dougal.

SCENE 10 INT./DAY 1
SET: PAROCHIAL HOUSE
Ted and Dougal are sitting down, captive to the unearthly silence. Stone looks at them, his occasional blinking the only sign of life.

DOUGAL: Jack gone to bed, then, Ted?

TED: Yes, he was a little tired.

SCENE 11 INT./DAY 1
SET: JACK'S BEDROOM
We see Jack tied down to his bed, struggling mightily.

SCENE 12 INT./DAY 1
SET: PAROCHIAL HOUSE
Again, we see the three men sitting in silence. A very, very long pause.

TED: Well, I suppose my bath'll be ready by now.

He stands up. Dougal grabs hold of his arm and then his leg, both of which Ted wrestles free from.

SCENE 13 INT./DAY 1
SET: BATHROOM
Ted walks into the bathroom in his dressing gown. He closes the door, takes the dressing gown off and gets into the bath.

TED: Ahhhhhhhh . . .

Ted closes his eyes. He smiles and relaxes. He opens them to see Stone looking down at him.

TED (*Pause. He doesn't quite know what to say*): Can I help you, Paul?

STONE: I'm fine.

Pause. Ted moves his hand to cover his middle. There is another long pause.

TED: Ah . . .

Pause.

TED: Sorry, Paul . . . I . . . ah . . . I'm having a bath.

STONE: I just wanted to go to the toilet.

TED: Ah . . . all right, go ahead, Paul.

Paul walks to the toilet beside the bath, pulls down his trousers and sits down.

TED (*to himself*): Oh, for Jaysus' sake . . .

Ted covers his eyes.

SCENE 14 INT./EVENING 1
SET: PAROCHIAL HOUSE
Stone, Dougal and Ted are sitting in their usual chairs. The unearthly silence is reaching breaking point. Ted gets up.

TED: Right! Time for bed!

STONE (*looks at his watch*): It's only half seven.

TED: Yeah, but . . . I have to be up at eleven tomorrow. Dougal, you'd better get some rest, too.

Dougal stands up and runs out of the room at top speed.

TED: Goodnight, then!

SCENE 15 INT./EVENING 1
SET: TED AND DOUGAL'S BEDROOM
Ted and Dougal are in their beds, staring at the ceiling.

DOUGAL: I can't take much more of this, Ted.

TED: I know, I know . . .

DOUGAL: Six years. You'd think that by now he'd have got the message. Do you remember that year when we knew he was coming and we pretended to be on a retreat?

TED: That was amazing. Anyone else'd go, oh, fair enough, and just not come. God . . . five days hiding in the attic. No food, no water . . . rats everywhere . . . God, if only we'd thought of it this year . . .

DOUGAL: How'd you meet him in the first place?

TED: He was introduced to me by Father Jim Dougan. We were at a conference and Dougan came up, said, this is Father Stone, and then ran out of the building. Just ran out! I should have known something was up . . . So we started talking . . . Well, I started talking. You know how he is. Just to break the silence, I invited him to stay . . . just for something to say, you know? The next day, *the next day*, he arrived on the island. I wouldn't mind if he just said something. But he just sits there! I mean, what does he get out of it!

DOUGAL: I hope he's gone before your birthday party . . .

TED: Oh, God, he'll be gone long before then. What is it? Three weeks away?

SCENE 16 INT./NIGHT 2
SET: PAROCHIAL HOUSE (3 WEEKS LATER)
We see Stone sitting in what is by now his usual chair, wearing a party hat. We see that there are more guests sitting around, all wearing party hats,

all completely silent. Ted looks very embarrassed. Jack is getting drunk somewhere else in the room. The mood is that of a funeral. One guest, Father Billy Kerrigan, looks at his watch and stands up.*

BILLY: God, look at the time. Better get going, Ted.

TED: Oh . . . fair enough . . .

Another priest, Father Liam Fay, leans forward.

LIAM: Actually, I'd better be off as well. Can I get a lift from you, Billy?

BILLY: No problem. Anyone else need a lift?

Everyone puts their hand up. They all stand up and follow Billy out of the room. Dougal is one of them.

TED: Dougal . . .

Dougal turns and sits down again, looking miserable. Stone sits there, not saying anything. The three stare at each other. Jack falls off the table, drunk.

END OF PART ONE

* * *

PART TWO

SCENE 17 INT./NIGHT 2
SET: TED AND DOUGAL'S BEDROOM
It is very dark, but Ted is lit up by light. He is praying.

TED: Please, God . . . please get rid of him. I don't care how you do it. Just, please . . . please get rid of him. Do you want money? Anything you want. Name any charity. Just . . . please! Please get rid of him! . . .

He starts sobbing.

SCENE 18 EXT./DAY 3
SET: CRAZY GOLF COURSE
We see a sign saying 'Craggy Island Crazy Golf – £1.00, Members – 50p'. The sign is being lashed by wind and rain. There seems to be only one hole on the course. It is just a row of cement blocks with a windmill at the end of it. We hear thunder in the distance. Ted and Dougal are playing the hole. It is raining buckets. They look miserable.

DOUGAL: Maybe we should go home, Ted.

TED: Think about it, Dougal. Think about who's sitting in the living room.

Pause.

DOUGAL: I think it's clearing up a bit, anyway.

He lines up the putt. As he does so, the windmill is blown away by a gust of wind. Dougal is now aiming at an empty space.

DOUGAL: The windmill thing's blown away, there, Ted.

TED: Never mind. Just have your go.

Dougal lines up his shot. Just as he's about to putt, we hear a voice from nearby.

STONE: Golf, yeah . . .?

TED (*to himself*): God help us . . . (*To Stone.*) Ah, yes. Crazy golf, Paul . . . Not exactly the U.S. Masters!

STONE: No.

Pause.

TED: Will you have a go, Paul?

STONE: No.

TED: Ah, you will. It's great fun! Isn't it, Dougal?

DOUGAL: Oh, yeah. Fantastic, Ted.

TED: You'll have a go, Paul?

STONE: No.

TED: Go on! Sure it's even easier now the windmill has blown away!

Ted takes the club from Dougal and more or less forces the club into Stone's hands.

TED: There you go, Paul. Give it a real go! Sure what's the worst thing that can happen?

Stone raises the club slightly and is hit by a massive bolt of lightning.

STONE (*high-pitched*): Waiieeee!!!!

Ted and Dougal are gobsmacked. They look at each other.

DOUGAL: Uh-oh.

SCENE 19 INT./DAY 3
SET: HOSPITAL CORRIDOR
Ted and Dougal are sitting in a corridor, looking worried.

TED: Oh, God, Dougal, it's all my fault!

DOUGAL: Don't be silly, Ted. What'd you do, pray for him to be hit by lightning?

TED: No, no, of course not . . . Well, I asked him to intervene in some way, but this is a bit much. (*Looks up and addresses God.*) What were you thinking of?

DOUGAL: Who would have thought that being hit by lightning would land you in hospital . . .?

TED: What? What are you talking about? Of course it can land you in hospital!

DOUGAL: Well . . . it's not usually serious, is it, Ted? I was hit by lightning a few times and I never had to go to hospital.

TED: Yes, but . . . you're different from most people, Dougal. All that happened to you was balloons kept sticking to you. Most people do have to drop into a hospital after being hit by lightning. Just to be polite, you know? (*Pause.*) God, I hate hospitals.

DOUGAL: Did you ever notice that it's usually sick people who end up in hospital?

TED: Thank you, John Pilger.

DOUGAL: Oh, yeah, they all come here. (*Pause.*) Of course you're a goner the minute you walk through the door. I'd prefer to take my chances in the real world. No matter how sick I was, I'd never go under the hammer.

TED: Under the knife, Dougal. Under the hammer is auctioneering.

DOUGAL: Oh, right . . . (*Pause.*) Did you ever see that film, Ted, where your man has his head transplanted on to a fly, and the fly's head was transplanted on to the man?

TED: Oh, yes . . . what was it called . . .?

DOUGAL: *Out of Africa*, I think. Anyway, your man has the head of the fly and he's chasing his wife all over the place and she's hiding the jam and everything, so he won't get stuck in it . . .

TED: I'll have to stop you there, Dougal.

DOUGAL: Yes, Ted?

TED: No reason. I just have to stop you.

Suddenly, Jack is wheeled by on a trolley. A doctor follows behind.

TED: There he is. The weekly emergency. What is it today, Doctor?

JACK: Frig!

DOCTOR: We don't know. I think it's a combination of Babycham and Harpic.

The doctor moves off.

TED: Only things left after the party, I suppose . . .

DOUGAL: They've been in there a long time, haven't they, Ted?

TED: They have . . . God . . . What's going on?

DOUGAL: Do you think he'll die, Ted? He's been in there for a while.

TED: They're probably just doing tests.

DOUGAL: What type of tests? General knowledge?

TED: No . . .

DOUGAL: They won't be able to get much out of him in that condition.

TED: No, no, medical tests.

DOUGAL: Sure what would he know about that, Ted? He's a priest!

Jack suddenly runs by, holding his IV drip. Some doctors and nurses run after him.

TED: God, would you look at that! He can move when he wants to.

They see the shopkeepers, John and Mary O'Leary, approaching from the end of the corridor. Mr O'Leary has a bloodstained bandage around his head. Mrs O'Leary has her arm in a sling.

MRS O'LEARY: You stupid bastard. You've really, really done it this time.

MR O'LEARY: You started it, you bitch.

MRS O'LEARY: God, I should have finished the job. The next time I — (*She notices Ted.*). Ah, Father . . .

TED: Hello, John. Hello, Mary.

MR O'LEARY: Ah . . . well . . . What are you doing here?

TED: A friend of ours had an accident.

MRS O'LEARY: Oh, dear.

Pause. Ted looks at Mr O'Leary's bloodstained bandage.

TED: And what happened to you? That looks a bit nasty.

MR O'LEARY: Ah, it's nothing, Father. Just a headache. Don't know why I bothered coming, really.

TED: Is that blood there?

MR O'LEARY: No. God, no. I don't think so. I just got a slight nick with a knife while Mary was putting the bandage on. It's not a stab wound.

MRS O'LEARY: Sure, he's fine.

TED: You look like you've been in the wars yourself, Mary.

MRS O'LEARY: Ah . . . it's just a sprain, Father. It's nothing. I was lifting a bag of coal. It's not broken . . . (*Pause.*) Or if it is — sure what the hell!

TED: Ah, ha!

Pause.

MR O'LEARY: Anyway, I hope your friend gets better.

MRS O'LEARY: We'll be off. Goodbye, Fathers.

They move off, smiling, out of earshot of Ted and Dougal.

MRS O'LEARY: The next time, I'll make friggin' sure . . .

MR O'LEARY: Shut up, you batty old witch.

Cut back to Ted and Dougal.

DOUGAL: They're a lovely couple, though, aren't they? John and Mary?

TED: Ah, they are, all right . . .

As they talk, we see Mrs O'Leary kick Mr O'Leary in the groin. Mr O'Leary falls on the ground and starts holding his groin and moaning. Mrs O'Leary continues kicking him on the floor.

SCENE 20 INT./DAY 3
SET: HOSPITAL CORRIDOR
Ted and Dougal sit in the corridor. Ted looks tired and drawn, but Dougal seems as fresh as always.

TED: How much longer are they going to be . . .?

DOUGAL (*looks at his watch*): God, Ted, we hardly even know him, when you think about it. Does he have much of a family?

TED: The parents are still alive . . . and I think he has a brother, a doctor in America.

DOUGAL: A doctor. Wow.

TED: You wouldn't think it, would you? But that used to be common enough. The favourite son would become a doctor or something, and the idiot brother would be sent off to the priesthood.

Pause.

DOUGAL: Your brother's a doctor, isn't he?

TED: He is, yes.

A doctor comes out of the room. Ted and Dougal stand up.

TED: So, how's the patient?

DOCTOR: He's hanging in there. It's mostly shock, but . . .

TED: Great! Well, that's not serious!

DOCTOR: Well, it's quite serious. A bolt of lightning can do a lot of damage.

TED: Can it?

DOCTOR: Yes. His reactions are very poor at the moment.

TED (*slightly desperate*): Oh, he's always been like that. Very poor reactions. That's normal for him.

DOCTOR: Well, actually, he's not reacting at all to any stimulus.

TED: Again, no need to worry. That's always the way with him.

DOCTOR: Look, Father, I'm the doctor. And I know that it's not normal to fail to react to a stimulus.

TED: I'm sure it is. Watch this.

Ted throws a pen at Dougal. It bounces off Dougal's head. Dougal doesn't react.

TED: Y'see? It's a thing with priests. We have our minds on more spiritual things.

There's no need to worry.

DOCTOR: Well, no, I think I will worry about it . . .

TED (*defeated at last*)**:** Oh, God, OK, OK . . . Look, can we see him? I'd like to say a prayer.

DOCTOR: Yes, all right, Father. This way . . .

SCENE 21 INT./DAY 3
SET: HOSPITAL WAITING ROOM
We see Stone, standing in the same position, holding the golf club, his face frozen in a cross-eyed grimace. His hair stands on end. Beside him are IV drips, a heart monitor, etc.

DOCTOR: As you can see, we still haven't been able to remove the golf club.

TED: Why isn't he in bed?

DOCTOR: It's hard to get him in a comfortable position when he's in that stance. (*Looks at his watch.*) But you're right, he's been on his feet long enough.

DOUGAL: He looks like a trophy.

TED (*laughs slightly*)**:** You know, he does a bit!

There is a knock on the door. A woman sticks her head around it. She is Mrs Stone, Stone's mother.

MRS STONE: Sorry, I heard — Oh, no! Paul!

She runs over and hugs Stone, who teeters slightly. Stone's father, Mr Stone, enters, followed by Granny Stone, a tiny, fierce-faced woman.

DOCTOR: Come on, Mrs Stone, we have to put him into bed. Father, could you?

Ted and the doctor put him into bed. Dougal stands in front of the heart monitor, transfixed by the bleeping noise and the white dot. Mrs Stone hugs her husband, still weeping. She turns back just as Ted is finished.

MRS STONE: Oh! You must be Father Crilly.

TED: I am, yes.

MRS STONE: Oh, God bless you, Father. God bless you.

Mr Stone coughs lightly.

MRS STONE: Father, this is my husband, Dermot.

Mr Stone grabs Ted's hand with both of his and pumps it up and down many, many times.

MR STONE: Oh, God, Father, it's terrible, it's terrible, God, Father, forgive me Father, forgive me for using the Lord's name, Father, but, Jesus Christ, isn't it terrible, Father!

TED: It is, yes —

MR STONE (*still shaking Ted's hand*)**:** It is, it is, it is, it is, it's terrible, Father, it is, I couldn't have said it better myself, terrible is the word, terrible is . . . I tell you, terrible is too small a word, Father, God bless you, but it is, it's too small a word, Father. (*Turns to Stone's prone figure.*) Look at what you've done to your mother! You little bastard! You're useless! Get up out of that bed now!

TED: Now, Mr Stone . . .

MR STONE: I'm sorry, Father. Him causing you this trouble. God forgive me for saying this, but wouldn't it have been better if he'd been killed? And herself all upset. Jesus, what you must think of him. And us, for bringing him into the world . . .

TED: Now, Mr Stone . . .

MR STONE: I'm going out for a drink. Will you join me?

TED: Eh, no, I think I should stay here for the moment . . .

MR STONE: Fair enough. See you later, then.

He stops shaking Ted's hand and walks out.

MRS STONE: . . . And this is Mammy . . .

Ted turns to smile at the old woman but is met by a gaze of terrible, vicious suspicion from her. His smile dies immediately.

TED (*nervously*)**:** Hello!

The old woman, still looking very scary indeed, beckons Ted with her finger. Ted walks over to her.

TED: Yes?

He bends down to hear her.

GRANNY STONE (*whispers*): I know what you're up to.

Ted bolts upright, looking terrified. He is immediately grabbed by Mrs Stone.

MRS STONE: Oh, God, Father, you know . . . Paul thought the world of you.

TED: Ah, well . . .

MRS STONE: He did. He never stopped talking about you. It was Father Ted said this and Father Ted said that. He worshipped you, Father.

TED (*massively uncomfortable*): Really?

MRS STONE: He'd come back from Craggy Island and he'd be counting the days till he could come back. Literally. He had a chart and he'd mark the days as they went by. And just at the very bottom of the chart, Father, there'd be a photograph of yourself.

TED: Oh, God . . .

MRS STONE (*reaches into her bag*): He used to paint as well, Father. He did this one for you, but he was too shy to bring it himself.

She takes out the painting. It is a small, framed portrait, quite well done, of a smiling Ted and Stone, their arms around each other's shoulders in a lads' embrace.

TED (*aghast at this*): But, he never gave me any indication . . .

MRS STONE: And of course, he had this, Father.*

She shows him a medallion containing a lock of hair.*

MRS STONE: He said that he snipped that off when you were asleep, Father. He would have asked, but he was afraid that you'd say no to him. And that would have broken his heart. He wanted a memento of you to carry around with him wherever he was . . .*

Suddenly, we hear a loud bleeping noise.

MRS STONE: Oh, God!!!!

Ted runs over to Stone.

TED: Oh, God, what is it?!

MRS STONE: It's his heart! Do something, Father!

Ted pauses for a moment, looking desperate, then begins to pummel Stone fiercely on the chest. Stone jolts wildly with each punch. Cut to Dougal looking at his watch. He adjusts it and the wild bleeping sound stops. Ted and Mrs Stone look at Dougal. Dougal smiles at them gormlessly.

TED (*grits his teeth*): Dougal . . .

Ted looks at the old woman. She is still giving Ted the evil eye. The doctor enters.

DOCTOR: Mrs Stone, could you come with

* We deleted these lines from the final version.

me? I need you to fill out some forms.

MRS STONE: Will he be all right, Doctor?

DOCTOR: We're doing all we can. But he is quite ill. Just hope for the best.

Ted looks devastated.

MRS STONE: All right, Doctor. Come on, Mammy.

The old woman turns and gives Ted the evil eye again. The two women leave the room.

TED: She knows!

DOUGAL: What, Ted?

TED: The old woman! She knows! She knows it's all my fault!

DOUGAL: Sure how would she know that, Ted?

TED: Oh, they know, Dougal. They have ways. Old women are closer to God than we'll ever be. Why do you think they're always going to Mass? They get to that age and they have a direct line. They don't need the operator any more. Oh, she knows all right . . . But who could blame her for being angry with me? It's all my fault! I mean . . . Why did I do it?!

He falls to his knees beside the bed.

TED: Oh, Lord, please bring him back! I never wanted you to take him away. There was no need for the lightning! You know I

didn't mean that! That was just silly! Oh, God, please bring him back. Bring him back and I swear, I swear we'll look after him! He can stay as long as he wants —

DOUGAL: Ah, now, Ted —

TED: Shut up, Dougal! I swear, bring him back and I'll take care of him for the rest of my days! Please! Please do this one thing!!!!

Ted looks at Stone. No response. He looks up again.

TED: Ah, come on! Please! Please! I swear I'll . . . I'll . . .

He looks down. Stone is staring at him without expression. He is back to his former self.

TED: Paul! Paul, I don't believe it! You're back! Oh, Lord, thank you! It's a miracle! It's a miracle! DOCTOR! DOCTOR! Paul, are you all right? Can we get you anything?

Pause.

STONE: I'm fine, thanks.

SCENE 22 INT./DAY 3
SET: PAROCHIAL HOUSE
We see Ted, Dougal, Jack and Stone, all staring at each other. Pause. After a moment, the credits start to roll in silence. The silence is broken occasionally by slight coughs.

THE END

the passion of saint tibulus

GRAHAM: This episode was very easy to write – we just followed the course of certain events in real life. Whenever a provocative film stirs up controversy, it's a pleasure to watch all the moral guardians who try and protect us from it becoming unpaid, unwitting publicists for the film company. *Je Vous Salue, Marie* – Godard's updating of the Virgin Mary story – caused one hell of a storm in Ireland. A friend of mine went to see it in Trinity College and he was punched by a nun when he came out. She punched him in the face just for watching a film. These people still don't seem to understand the basic concept that the more fuss you make about a film, the more people will want to see it. Would anyone really have been desperate to see *Je Vous Salue, Marie* if it hadn't been banned?

We knew when we were plotting the episode that having Ted and Dougal stage a protest would provide lots of opportunities for jokes. That's how we generally plot an episode – we look for those kind of opportunities and string them together as believably as we can. I'm very happy with their ineffectual protesting in the cinema: 'That'll be enough out of you, now!' – all that stuff. I think Dermot and Ardal even threw in 'Ye dirty pups, ye!' during filming.

This was a contender for the first episode, because in it we explain why Ted, Dougal and Jack have been banished to Craggy Island. I think it actually works better being in Episode Three – it would have been too obvious to fill the audience in on the backstory (a word I use with much embarrassment, by the way) in the first episode.

Mrs Doyle is also beginning to show her true colours here, evolving into a psychotically hospitable character with her demented insistence on offering tca to the bishop. At first we really didn't realise the potential of her character, or of Pauline McLynn's phenomenal ability which I think, develops into tremendous physical comedy later in the series. We did try and give her one stand-out moment in each episode (sometimes, shamefully, failing – as in *Entertaining Father Stone*).

ARTHUR: Geoffrey Perkins, our producer, was an enormous influence at the beginning, making sure we didn't stray too far from the point. He also did the wonderful voice-over for Father Hernandez at the beginning of the episode. I really haven't a clue how we decided on having him speak Spanish, which, bizarrely, they understand, and having a translation for the viewers. But I think it works well because Geoffrey's enunciation is so droll.

Bishops being up to no good in the bedroom was still a relatively novel plotline at this point. It was certainly influenced by the news of Bishop Casey's affair, which was greeted with horror by older people in Ireland and unbridled joy by everyone else. It also coincided with the exposure of an affair between a priest called Father Michael Cleary and his housekeeper, but our take on all that was very light with Brennan prancing around with his mistress in full bishop's garb. I'm still not sure why, but we had to lose a shot of Brennan's child making bishop's hat-shaped sandcastles on the beach. This was a pity, because I think that image summed the situation up in one very simple gag.

PART ONE

SCENE 1 EXT./NIGHT 1
SET: PAROCHIAL HOUSE

Through the rain-streaked window of the Parochial House, we see Father Dougal McGuire, a young innocent-looking priest, staring out at the night. Occasionally his face is illuminated by flashes of lightning. From the noise, we can assume that the rain is pummelling the earth.

SCENE 2 INT./NIGHT 1
SET: PAROCHIAL HOUSE

We see Father Ted Crilly sitting at a table with a handsome, black-haired priest. This is Father José Hernandez, a Cuban. Whenever he speaks, his dialogue is dubbed (no one comments on this). His 'voice' is very deep and smooth; he sounds like a real lady-killer. The two priests are seated around a Cluedo board. They are drinking cups of tea. A large brown candle burns in the centre of the table. Father Jack Hackett, an elderly man whom we can't see clearly as yet, watches television in another part of the room. Cut to Dougal, who is still watching the torrential rain. We see more lightning and hear more thunder.

DOUGAL: Looks like rain, Ted.

Ted raises his eyes heavenward when he hears this.

TED: Dougal, come on. It's your go.

Dougal walks over and assumes his place at the table. He rolls some dice. Ted smiles at Hernandez.

TED *(brightly)*: I must say, Father Hernandez, it's been wonderful having you over. But I expect you're getting a bit homesick for Cuba by now.

JOSE *(dubbed)*: Si. Mi pais es muy hermoso.
[Yes. My country is very beautiful.]

JOSE *(dubbed)*: Pero, Ted, usted es un hombre muy afortunado. En Craggy Island tiene usted dos buenos amigos, el Padre Dougal . . .
[But, Ted, you have a great life here on Craggy Island. You have two good friends, Father Dougal . . .]

Shot of Dougal choking on something. He gags for a while and then takes one of the Cluedo pieces out of his mouth and looks at it quizzically.

JOSE *(dubbed)*: . . . Y claro, el Padre Jack.
[. . . And, of course, Father Jack.]

We see Father Jack's face for the first time. We hear the sound of flies buzzing. His mouth hangs open, and a thin line of drool hangs from his mouth. His teeth are blackened and broken. His nose is large, red and bruised. One of his eyes rolls up into the socket. A tooth sticks out of the corner of his mouth, pushing his lip up into a permanent sneer. One of his ears looks as if it has been badly burnt. When he breathes, he sounds like a sleeping animal.*

Mrs Doyle enters with more tea.

TED: Yes . . . yes, it's . . . it's great here. Although, I must say, sometimes I miss the noise and the lights and the . . . you know, the whole buzz of the big city.

JOSE *(dubbed)*: Usted estaba en Wexford, verdad?
[You were in Wexford, weren't you?]

TED: I was, yes. But, you know, Craggy Island has its charms. The west part of the island was beautiful. Until it drifted off, of course.

JOSE *(dubbed)*: Se desprendio?
[Drifted off?]

TED: Yes. There was a bit of a storm and it came loose. Now, of course, we don't have a west side. It's just north, south and east. But while it was there it was lovely.

JOSE *(dubbed)*: Sabe usted Ted . . . su ama de llaves es una mujer muy hermosa.
[You know, Ted, your housekeeper is a very beautiful woman.]

He smiles at Mrs Doyle. She doesn't know how to deal with this, and makes a hasty exit.

---

*Obviously, we reined ourselves in on some of this.

DOUGAL: Colonel Mustard, in the kitchen, with the candlestick?

TED: But you have Colonel Mustard! You showed him to me earlier! How could it be Colonel Mustard if you have Colonel Mustard?!!

Slight pause.

DOUGAL: Ohhh, right . . .

TED: Father Hernandez, your go . . .

JOSE *(dubbed)*: Si . . . Creo que fue el Reverendo Green . . . con el cuchillo . . . en la estancia.
[Yes . . . I think it was Reverend Green, with the knife, in the drawing room.]

TED: Those Protestants! Up to no good as usual!

Everyone laughs softly.

TED: What's Father Jack looking at?

Shot of Father Jack staring intently at the television.

JOSE: En ocasiones esto del celibato es muy duro para un hombre . . . je, je, je . . .
[Sometimes, this celibacy is hard for a man . . . heh, heh . . .]

TED: Oh, well . . . you have to take the rough with the smooth, I suppose. Bishop Brennan springs to mind.

JOSE *(dubbed)*: Ah si . . .?
[Oh, yes . . .?]

TED: Yes, Bishop Len Brennan. He's our . . . kind of boss, I suppose. He's the one who thought Dougal and Father Jack would be better off working here . . . on an island with, you know . . . a very small population. Anyway, the rumour is that his housekeeper caught him once, ah, 'in delicto flagrante'. They say, ah . . . they say the union was 'blessed' if you know what I mean.

JOSE *(dubbed)*: No! . . . Nino o nina?
[No! . . . boy or girl?]

TED: A boy, I think. Lives in America now, or so goes the rumour anyway!

DOUGAL: Was it . . . Colonel Mustard . . . in the kitchen . . . with the candlestick?

TED: What?

TED: What's that you're watching, Father?

JACK *(barks)*: What?!

TED: What film are you watching?

JACK: What?!

TED: Isn't that Keifer Sutherland?

JACK: What?!

TED: Is that *Flatliners* you're watching?

JACK: What?!

JOSE *(dubbed)*: El Padre Jack esta un poco mal de los oidos?
[Is Father Jack a little hard of hearing?]

JACK: What?!

TED: Well, he gets a kind of waxy build-up in his ears. Then we have to syringe them. It's not very nice.

JACK: What?!

JOSE *(cringing slightly)*: Mmmhmm . . .

JACK: What?!

DOUGAL: It's great, though, in a way, 'cause we're never short of candles, you know?

Dougal indicates the very large candle in the middle

of the table. Hernandez looks at it with something approaching horror.

JACK: What?!

TED: Yes, most of that was in his head last week. And up there . . .

He points to a row of candles on the mantelpiece.

TED: We've nearly enough for a papal funeral! He's a one-man candle factory! Aren't you, Father?

JACK: What?!

TED *(whispering to Hernandez)*: To be honest, though, he can hear well enough when he wants to. Watch this. *(Louder.)* Father Jack, would you like a glass of brandy?

JACK: Yes!

TED: You see? He's a terrible man!

JACK *(shouts)*: Brandy!

TED *(good-humouredly)*: All right! All right!

Ted gets the brandy and a large bowl-shaped glass and brings it over to Jack. He starts pouring.

TED: Say when . . .

JACK: What?!

TED *(still pouring)*: Say when . . .

JACK: What?!

TED: Tell me when you want me to stop pouring.

JACK: What?!

TED: Say when!

JACK: What?!

Jack's glass is full to the brim.

TED: Oh, right, that's it, is it? You sure you don't want more?!

JACK: Yes!

He grabs the bottle from Ted. Ted gives him a look and starts to move back to the table. The telephone rings, however, and he stops to pick up the receiver.

TED: Hello, Craggy Island Parochial House. Father Ted Crilly speaking. *(His face grows slightly fearful.)* Oh! Bishop Brennan! . . . How are you? Yes . . . No . . . All right . . . Yes, of course . . . Good, yes . . . All right, then . . .

Bye, so! *(He puts the telephone down.)* That was the boss. He's coming over. He says he wants to talk to us about something. *(More to himself.)* It must be important . . . he's had to come back early from his holidays.

Dougal is examining the Cluedo wallet where the killer, location and weapon card are hidden.

DOUGAL: Ted. Shouldn't there be some cards in here, or something?

He holds it up. It's empty.

SCENE 3 EXT./MORNING 2
SET: PAROCHIAL HOUSE HALLWAY
Hernandez is saying goodbye to Ted and Dougal. He shakes hands with them both.

JOSE *(dubbed)*: Nuevamente, no tengo palabras para expresar mi gratitud.

[Again, I have no words to say how thankful I am.]

DOUGAL *(whispers)*: That's a bit ungrateful, Ted.

TED *(ignoring Dougal)*: Don't you worry about it, Father!

JOSE *(dubbed)*: Sin embargo, lo que si tengo son algunos regalos que les manda la gente de mi pueblo.
[However, I do have some gifts from people of my village.]

He hands a package to Dougal.

JOSE *(dubbed)*: Por favor, no se vayan ustedes a reir de sencillez de este regalito. Es solo un ejemplo de artesania cubana.
[Please do not laugh at this simple gift. It is just an example of Cuban handicraft.]

Dougal unwraps the package like a ten-year-old boy.

DOUGAL: It's a video recorder!

JOSE *(dubbed)*: Si, lo lamento. Es un modelo muy basico. Solo tiene el sistema de pregrabado con tres semanas de anticipacion.
[Yes, I am sorry. It is a very basic model. It has only a three week pre-record facility.]

DOUGAL: No, don't worry about it! It's great!

He runs inside.

TED: Thanks very much, Father Hernandez. That's wonderful.

JOSE *(dubbed):* Y, en cuanto a usted Ted, tengo algo muy especial.
[And for you, Ted, I have something very special.]

He gives Ted a package. Ted opens it.

TED: You really didn't have to . . .

He sees that it is a hand-carved wooden sculpture of a male figure with a very large appendage sticking up into the air.

TED *(shocked):* . . . You really didn't have to . . .

JOSE *(dubbed):* Es un simbolo cubano de fertilidad. Espero que le traiga tanta suerte a used, como la que me ha traido a mi . . . si? . . . eh? Eh, mi buen amigo . . .?
[It is a Cuban fertility symbol. I hope it brings you as much luck as it brought me, yes? Eh? Eh, my friend?]

TED: Ha, ha, yes . . .

JOSE: Bueno, adios, Ted.
[Well, goodbye, Ted.]

He puts on a pair of designer sunglasses and walks out of shot.

SCENE 4 EXT./DAY 2
SET: PAROCHIAL HOUSE
Ted waves goodbye. Cut to Hernandez in a Ferrari. He waves and takes off at incredible speed.

SCENE 5 INT./DAY 2
SET: PAROCHIAL HOUSE
Dougal is down on all fours, messing around with the VCR. Ted is cleaning up the room.

TED: C'mon now, Dougal. The Bishop'll be here any minute.

DOUGAL: Oh, right.

TED: Now, do you remember what I told you?

DOUGAL: Eh . . .

TED: It's very simple. On no account mention what we were talking about last night.

DOUGAL: Right. *(Pause.)* What were we

talking about last night?

TED: You know . . . the rumours about the Bishop's little mistake.

DOUGAL: Right. *(Pause.)* What mistake was that, Ted?

TED: His son. His son in America.

DOUGAL: Oh, yes. *(Pause.)* He has a son in America?

TED: Yes! Well, so they say . . .

DOUGAL: Right, OK. *(Pause.)* That's news to me, Ted.

TED: We were talking about it last night, Dougal! To Father Hernandez.

DOUGAL: Who? Oh, right! The Cuban lad.

TED: But you remember now . . . not a word about the son . . .

DOUGAL: Oh, right!

TED: . . . Just . . . forget about all that, all right? Forget about it. Don't say a word. Have you got that?

DOUGAL: I have, Ted.

TED: I don't want you saying anything stupid.

DOUGAL: The lights are on, but there's nobody home, Ted.

TED: Are you sure?

DOUGAL: I am indeed, Ted. Don't worry about that at all.

TED: Grand. All right. I think that's everything.

He notices that Jack's hair is a little awry. He approaches him gingerly, producing a comb as he does so.

TED: Father . . . Father, do you think I could . . . ?

He holds the comb out towards Jack's hair, ready to put it back into place. As the comb approaches, Jack leans away from it, a very threatening look on his face. Ted keeps approaching. Jack starts growling softly but menacingly.*

TED: It's just for the Bishop. We should have you looking your best . . .

Jack looks like a cobra about to strike. Ted moves the comb forward again, then seems to think better of the whole thing.*

TED: Maybe it's fine. We'll leave it as it is. Let it settle.

We stay on Jack as Ted moves out of shot. Jack relaxes, and there is a pause. Then, from behind the seat, Ted's head slowly comes into sight. He raises the comb and moves it towards Jack's head. Jack shifts in his seat, oblivious to all this. Ted retreats, then goes to the arm of the chair. From here, he tries to blow Jack's hair into position. It works. Jack spins around, but Ted has gone. Mrs Doyle comes into the room.*

MRS DOYLE: Father Crilly, Bishop Brennan is here.

TED: Hell's bells! Right . . . Show him in. *(To Dougal.)* Dougal, please remember, whatever you do, not a word about the son. Honestly, this is the most important thing I'll ever ask you to do. Don't say a word.

DOUGAL: There's no danger of that whatsoever, Ted.

TED: OK.

Mrs Doyle brings in the Bishop. He is about fifty,

plump and very stern-faced.† He has a large leather carrier-bag.

TED: Ah, hello, Bishop Brennan! Are you well?

The Bishop barely acknowledges their presence. Jack, in turn, is oblivious to the Bishop's arrival. Dougal smiles happily.

TED: Your Eminence, sit down there beside Father Dougal. Mrs Doyle, could you make some tea for us?

MRS DOYLE: Certainly, Father.

The Bishop sits beside Dougal. Ted sits down in a chair opposite them both. On the little table beside Ted is the Cuban fertility statue. The Bishop stares at it. Ted doesn't know at first what he's staring at. He then turns and notices the statue. He tries to cover the appendage with his hand, but then he realises that he's touching it. He eventually knocks it on to the ground to get it out of sight. There is another pause. Dougal watches the Bishop closely. We hear a clock ticking. Dougal clears his throat ominously. There is a very, very long pause.

DOUGAL: How's the son?

The Bishop bristles visibly.

BISHOP: What?

TED *(panicking)*: The Son of God. How is the Son of God? Everything well in the world of religion?

BISHOP: What? The world of religion? What are you talking about, Crilly?

TED: You know . . . ah . . . Mrs Doyle! Is that tea ready?! Ha, ha!

Mrs Doyle enters, carrying a tray.

MRS DOYLE: Here I am! Here I am! . . . Ah, isn't this grand?

She hands a cup to the Bishop. He puts his hand out to stop her.

BISHOP: I'm fine, thank you, Mrs Doyle.

MRS DOYLE: Will you not have a cup of tea, Bishop Brennan?

BISHOP: No, no, I'm not staying long. I just want to get right to the point and get the hell out of here.

---

*These stage directions were deleted from the final version because it was too difficult to play.

† Played in the end by the very non-plump Jim Norton.

MRS DOYLE: Are you sure you won't have a cup?

BISHOP: Certain, thank you. *(To Ted.)* Now, I –

MRS DOYLE: Go on, have a cup.

BISHOP: I won't thanks. *(To Ted.)* Now —

MRS DOYLE: Everyone else is having a cup. Will you not have one yourself?

BISHOP: No. I don't have time. Crilly, I —

MRS DOYLE: You'll feel left out. You'll be Bishop Piggy In The Middle.

BISHOP: I'm fine, I'm fine.

MRS DOYLE: You sure you won't have a cup? Just a drop?

BISHOP: No! . . .

MRS DOYLE *(sings softly)*: Bishop Piggy In The Middle . . .

Ted leans over.

TED *(whispers)*: Actually, Your Eminence, just say yes. It's quicker, believe me.

BISHOP: All right, then.

MRS DOYLE *(pleased)*: Grand!

She gives him the tea and leaves. The Bishop addresses the three priests.

BISHOP: Well, I hope you're not doing too

much damage here. Jack, are you behaving yourself?

Jack is smoking a fag. He blows out some smoke contemptuously.

JACK *(under his breath)*: . . . Feck off!

BISHOP: What did you say?!

TED: Ha, ha! Anyway, Your Eminence, what brings you to the island? Are you thinking of letting us head back to our old parishes?

BISHOP: Fat chance! You're here until I tell you otherwise. Do you think I'd let Jack back into a normal parish after what he did in Athlone? Dressing up as a nun to get into a girls' school!* How do you think I felt when I had to explain that to Cardinal Daly?

TED: Well, yes, but . . . surely I'm all right . . .

BISHOP: No, no. You're here until every penny of that money is accounted for.

TED: I told you, that money was just resting in my account until . . .

BISHOP: Enough!

TED: I don't know where it went!

BISHOP: Crilly, I won't tell you again! And as for this . . . cabbage . . . *(Dougal looks very uncomfortable. Ted goes very quiet.)* . . . The mere idea of letting him back into the real world after The Blackrock Incident.

TED *(quietly)*: Yes, that was . . . unfortunate.

BISHOP: The amount of lives irreparably damaged . . .† The tourist industry shattered in a single blow . . . My God, do you know how many strings I had to pull to stop the Vatican getting involved?

Jack chuckles to himself. Dougal is ashen-faced.

BISHOP: I don't even want to talk about it. I just want to get this film thing over with.

TED: Film? What film?

---

*We deleted this sentence from the final version.

†The following lines were inserted in final version:

DOUGAL: They were only nuns.

BISHOP: Nuns are people too.

BISHOP: This . . . whatever it's called . . . film. *The Passion of Saint Tibulus.* His Holiness banned it, but because of some loophole the bloody thing's being shown here on this godforsaken hellhole.

DOUGAL: Oh, yes, that's right. Is it any good, do you know?

BISHOP: I don't care if it's any good or not! All I know is that we have to be seen to be making a stand against it. That's where you and Larry and Moe come in.

TED: What do you mean?

BISHOP: I know that normally you wouldn't be able to organise a nun-shoot in a nunnery, but it's up to you to make the Church's position clear. Make some kind of protest. Even you should be able to manage that.

DOUGAL *(touched)*: Thanks very much.

BISHOP: This is very important. Don't make a balls of it. I'll be in touch.

He gets up and starts to head out of the room. Ted tries to attract his attention.

TED: . . . Ah . . . ah, Your Eminence? This isn't really my area.

BISHOP: Nothing's your area, Crilly! You don't have an area! Unless it's a kind of play area with sandcastles and buckets and spades. Just do what you're told, all right?

He leaves the room, slamming the door. There is a quiet pause.

DOUGAL: Bye, then!

SCENE 6 EXT./DAY 2
SET: CINEMA
Establish cinema.

SCENE 7 INT./DAY 2
SET: CINEMA
The Ormonde is a once-natty but now slightly dilapidated old cinema. Ted and Dougal are finding some seats near the back. The only other cinemagoers are an old woman in peasant garb at the front and an old man with a dog. Ted and Dougal take their places.

TED: Look at this . . . This is silly . . . there's only one person in the cinema, for God's sake . . .

DOUGAL: Why wouldn't Jack come along, Ted?

TED: I asked him, he said he'd be along sooner or later . . . God . . . I don't see the point of this at all . . .

A middle-aged, well-dressed man, Michael Cocheese, comes out in front of the screen. He has fair, wavy hair and wears a bow-tie.

COCHEESE *(well spoken)*: Well, Ladies and Gentlemen, hello. I'm Michael Cocheese, owner of The Ormonde and film critic for *The Craggy Island Examiner*. I'm pleased to say we've got a bit of a treat lined up today for all you fans of French cinema.

The old woman sits up straighter when she hears this.

OLD WOMAN: Is this subtitled?

COCHEESE: Pardon?

OLD WOMAN: Is this subtitled or is it dubbed?

COCHEESE: Ah, it's subtitled.

The old woman, without a word, stands up and makes her way out of the cinema. Cut to Ted and Dougal, watching her go.

DOUGAL: Ted, should we start protesting now, or what?

TED: Yes, I suppose so.

DOUGAL: Or maybe we should wait 'til we see a bit of the film?

TED: No, we'll just get it over with . . .

DOUGAL: Maybe it's not so bad. It could be another *Commitments*.

TED: It doesn't matter whether it's good or bad, Dougal. It's just the morality that we don't agree with. Right, let's go . . .

They start booing in a terribly unconvincing way.

DOUGAL: Boo! . . . Boo! . . . Give it up, lads!

TED: Come on now, you!

We see Cocheese looking at Ted and Dougal, confused.

TED: That'll be enough out of you, now!

DOUGAL: Boo! . . .

TED: Terrible film . . .

COCHEESE: What? Who's that?!

We see the dog turn around and look at Ted and Dougal.

DOUGAL: Booo! . . .

TED: You dirty, filthy beggars!

Cocheese stands up and makes towards Ted and Dougal.

COCHEESE: Now, look, you! . . . Oh, Father Ted, Father Dougal. It's yourselves.

TED: Hello, Michael, how are you?

COCHEESE: Oh, I'm grand. How's Father Jack? I haven't seen him since we had *Caligula** on . . .

TED: Oh, he's grand. He was a bit tired so he didn't come along today.

COCHEESE: Right. But what are you up to, though? You're making a fair racket.

TED: Oh, it's a long story . . . We have the Bishop over, you know, Len Brennan . . .

COCHEESE: Ohhh, that gobshite.

TED: . . . And he's going mad because of the film.

DOUGAL: He told us to come down and kick up a fuss.

COCHEESE: Right. It's just, you're making a bit of a racket. Could you try to keep it down? You have to think about other people.

He indicates the empty cinema.

TED: No problem.

DOUGAL: You can count on us, Michael!

Cocheese smiles and starts to walk off.

TED: Michael! Michael!

Cocheese turns back. Ted grabs his elbow gently.

TED: Are we still OK for the old . . . *(He smiles*

---

*In the final version this became a 'Sharon Stone season' because we thought there was a risk people would have forgotten *Caligula*.

and points at his collar.) . . . half price?

COCHEESE: No problem at all. Enjoy the film.

TED *(jokingly)*: Boo!

COCHEESE: Now, you!

Ted and Dougal laugh good-naturedly.

END OF PART ONE

* * *

PART TWO

SCENE 8 INT./NIGHT 2
SET: TED AND DOUGAL'S BEDROOM
Ted and Dougal lie in their beds, looking at the ceiling, very confused looks on their faces. Dougal has a teddy bear with a clerical collar round its neck.

TED: What was all that about?

DOUGAL: You're asking the wrong person now, Ted. I couldn't make head nor tail of it.

TED: I know for a fact that Saint Tibulus wore more clothes than that. Sure wasn't he from Norway or somewhere? He'd have frozen to death.

DOUGAL: Do you remember the bit when Saint Tibulus was trying to take that banana off the other lad?

TED: That wasn't a banana, Dougal. Anyway, look, I'm going to sleep. Good night, Dougal.

Ted turns off the light. Pause. After a moment, Dougal starts mumbling in his sleep.

DOUGAL *(offscreen)*: I'll have a B, please, Bob . . . Beethoven . . . C, please, Bob . . . Carnivorous . . . F, please, Bob . . .

TED *(moans)*: . . . Not *Blockbusters* again . . .

DOUGAL: Fettuccine . . .

Ted puts the pillow over his head.

SCENE 9 INT./MORNING 3
SET: TED AND DOUGAL'S BEDROOM
The light shines through the window. Ted wakes up, blinking. He yawns and looks at the little novelty Pope-clock beside the bed.

TED: Oohhh, let's see . . . six a.m. . . . Oh, great, another eight hours' sleep . . .

DOUGAL: You awake, Ted?

TED: Mmmmhh . . .

DOUGAL: This is fantastic, isn't it, Ted? Another great lie-in for the lads.

TED: It is . . .

DOUGAL: Do you know what'd be terrible, Ted? Wouldn't it be terrible if Bishop Brennan came in and told us to go down to the cinema and start protesting again?

Suddenly, the door bursts open and the Bishop storms in like a force of nature. Ted and Dougal sit bolt-upright in their beds.

SCENE 10 EXT./MORNING 3
SET: CINEMA
Ted and Dougal stand outside The Ormonde carrying placards. They're cold and still half-asleep. The placards read 'Down With This Type Of Thing' and 'Careful, Now'.

TED: This is ridiculous. The flippin' place doesn't open for another seven hours.

DOUGAL: Ted . . . Ted, what about what the Bishop said? Didn't he want us to chain ourselves to the railings?

TED: How are we going to do that?

DOUGAL: O'Leary's might have something.

TED: Yeah, you go off and get something. I'll stay here and guard this closed cinema against anyone who might want to see a film that's not on for another seven hours.

Dougal moves off.

SCENE 11 INT./DAY 3
SET: PAROCHIAL HOUSE
The Bishop walks into the room. He sees Jack, sitting in his usual chair. The Bishop looks warily at him. Jack is eating something.

BISHOP: Jack, what are you up to? Why aren't you at the film?

JACK: . . . Feck off!

BISHOP: What?! What did you say?

Jack gives him a sarcastically innocent look.

BISHOP *(pause)*: Listen . . . did you see my bag, my travel bag?

Jack gives the Bishop a 'puzzled' look. He is still chewing.

BISHOP: Well, if you see it, give it to me. My bloody passport and everything's in there . . . all right?

Jack nods in a compliant sort of way, but when the Bishop leaves, he smiles evilly and reaches down beside his chair. He brings the Bishop's bag into view and opens the zip. He starts rummaging through the bag, grunting slightly like a foraging animal. He takes out a videotape and puts it to one side. We see 'Holiday '94' written on the side. He then takes out a passport, opens it and laughs nastily at the photo of the Bishop. We see it, too – it shows Brennan looking numbly at the camera, wearing his Bishop's hat. He rummages about a bit more and we then see, from his point of view, a plastic bag inside a pouch that has 'Duty Free' written on it. A blast of dramatic music plays as we see Jack's eyes widen. Cut back to the videotape with 'Holiday 94' written on it resting beside him.

SCENE 12 INT./DAY 3
SET: HARDWARE SHOP
We see Mr and Mrs O'Leary in the middle of a heated argument.

MR O'LEARY: Ahhh, ya fat old bitch!

MRS O'LEARY: Don't you talk to me like that, you big pile of shite! You ignorant prick!

MR O'LEARY: You watch that filthy mouth of yours!

MRS O'LEARY: I'll watch nothing! I'll stick this up your arse!

She holds up a huge knife. Suddenly, Dougal enters the shop.

DOUGAL: Hello, you two!

MR O'LEARY *(suddenly cheery)*: Father, how's tricks?

MRS O'LEARY: We haven't seen you in a while, Father. We were just going to have some tea, if you'd like a drop?

DOUGAL: Oh, no, I'm fine there, Mrs O'Leary.

MR O'LEARY: What can I 'do you for', Father?

DOUGAL: I was looking for a pair of handcuffs, actually.

Pause.

MR O'LEARY: A pair of handcuffs? What do you need them for?

DOUGAL: Oh, nothin' much. They're for me and Ted.

Pause.

MRS O'LEARY: You and Father Ted?

DOUGAL: Yes. We're just tryin' something out.

Pause.

MR O'LEARY: Well, actually, funnily enough, I think we have a pair. Sergeant Thornton left them here when he retired.

DOUGAL: Retired from what?

MR O'LEARY: From the police.

DOUGAL: The police? Was Sergeant Thornton a policeman?

MR O'LEARY: Em, he was, yes. Why did you think he used to wear the uniform?

DOUGAL: I thought he was just having a laugh.

Mr O'Leary has no idea what to say to this.

MR O'LEARY: Anyway, Father, here's the handcuffs.

He gives them to Dougal. Dougal hands over the money.

DOUGAL: Bye now!

Exit Dougal.

MR O'LEARY: Bye, Father! *(Pause.)* What are you doing standing there, you stupid bitch?!

MRS O'LEARY: Don't you call me stupid, you toerag! I'll friggin' kill you!

She lunges at Mr O'Leary. We leave them there, locked in combat.

SCENE 13 EXT./DAY 3
SET: CINEMA
Ted and Dougal are handcuffed to the cinema railings. Their placards are beside them. A constant stream of people is filing casually past them into the

cinema. Ted is protesting in an apathetic sort of way. A middle-aged farmer, Jim Halpin, passes by.

JIM: Hello, Father Crilly, Father McGuire.

TED: Hello, Jim.

JIM: I saw your picture in the paper.

TED: What?

JIM: Here. Have a look.

He gives the paper to Ted. Dougal reads it over Ted's shoulder. They are both highly excited. We can see a headline in the paper, which reads 'Priests protest against blasphemous film'.

JIM: So, it's a blasphemous film is it, Father?

TED: Oh, it is.

JIM: What type of thing is it?

DOUGAL: It's mad stuff.

TED: It's very immoral. You wouldn't like it, Jim.

JIM: Is it a type of nudey thing, Father?

TED: Oh, you wouldn't believe the amount of nudity in it.

JIM: Is it nudey men or women mostly? Or a bit of both?

TED: Oh, every type of thing.

JIM: And you see the lot, do you, Father? It's not just the top half you see?

TED: There's nothing left to the imagination, Jim.

JIM: Right. Well, I'll be off, then.

TED: Bye, Jim!

He walks straight into the cinema. Ted is amazed and disgusted. Two very meek old ladies, Mrs Sheridan and Mrs Glynn, pass by.

MRS SHERIDAN: Ah, hello, Fathers.

TED: Hello, Mrs Sheridan, Mrs Glynn.

MRS GLYNN (*reads poster*): *The Passion of Saint Tibulus.* What's that? Is it a musical or a western or what?

MRS SHERIDAN: We always go on Tuesdays. Gets us out of the house.

MRS GLYNN: We saw a great one a few

weeks ago. *The Crying Game.*

MRS SHERIDAN: Oh, that was brilliant.

MRS GLYNN: There's a great bit in it where there's this girl, and then you find out it's not a girl at all, but a man.

MRS SHERIDAN: Yes. He takes his lad out.

TED: What?!

MRS GLYNN: He takes his lad out. You only see it for a second, but you get the message!

MRS SHERIDAN: I didn't know what it was for a second! It's been so long since I've seen one!

MRS GLYNN: I thought it looked like your Billy's!

MRS SHERIDAN: No, Billy's is rounder at the top. Anyway, Father, bye!

They both go inside.

DOUGAL: Should we be stopping them going inside, or what, Ted?

TED: It just shows, doesn't it? No one takes a blind bit of notice of what the Church says any more.

Another old man, Pat Harty, passes by.

TED: Ah, hello, Pat.

PAT: Father Crilly, hello.

TED: Pat, how's your wife? I hear she hasn't been well.

PAT: She's dead, Father.

TED: Oh no! That's terrible! When did she . . .

PAT: Ah, a few hours ago.

TED: Really?

PAT: Yes. Anyway, that's just the way.

Pause.

PAT: What's the film like, Father?

TED: What?

PAT: Is it any good? I was reading about it in the paper.

TED: Now, Pat. I don't think you should be thinking about going to the film if your wife's just died.

PAT: Yeah, Yeah. It's just, ah . . . I was always a bit of a fan of Saint Tibulus.

TED: Well, now . . .

PAT: Sure, I might wander in. I'll contact you about the funeral details, Father . . .

He heads off into the cinema.

TED: . . . This isn't going too well . . .

Cocheese comes out of the cinema.

COCHEESE: Well, Fathers, I must say, this is extraordinary. This is the most successful film we've had since *Jurassic Park*. It's breaking all sorts of records due to all this publicity over your protest.

TED: Well, we certainly didn't plan it like that . . .

Cocheese looks up the road.

COCHEESE: Oh, look who it is!

TED: Oh, thank God, a bit of support.

It's Jack. He walks towards the three men, not acknowledging their presence.

TED: Fair play to you for turning up!

Jack walks straight past them and enters the cinema.

TED: Brilliant.

COCHEESE (*running after Jack*): Come on, Father, I'll get y'a seat right at the front . . .

Pause.

TED: Right. I've had enough. Dougal, we're leaving. Give us the keys.

Dougal looks very puzzled.

DOUGAL: Keys?

SCENE 14 INT./DAY 3
SET: PAROCHIAL HOUSE
Ted and Dougal sit beside each other, still chained to a big lump of railing complete with section of wall. They look exceptionally cowed. Jack sleeps noisily in his chair. Cut to the Bishop sitting at the table, poring over a map of the world that he has spread out in front of him.

TED: Ah . . . what's this now, Your Eminence?

When the Bishop talks, he is very, very, very calm.

BISHOP: Why am I looking at a map of the world? Well, how can I explain it . . .?

He sits down on the edge of the table.

BISHOP: Firstly, a resumé of the last few days. I don't know if you remember . . . I came in here and I had this idea about you mounting a dignified protest about this film. Do you remember that?

TED (*uncomfortably*)**:** Yes.

BISHOP: Good. Just to make the Church's opposition to the film clear. But, and this is the part that I think is interesting . . . you've actually managed to make it the most successful film that has ever been shown here! Isn't that great?

TED: Ah –

The Bishop gives Ted a look that shuts him up immediately.

BISHOP: People are coming from all over the country to see the film. They're even coming from Gdansk! And, this is wonderful . . . look at this . . .

He takes a poster from a tube and unfolds it. It's the promotional poster for 'The Passion of Saint Tibulus'. It features a photograph of Dougal and Ted tied to the railings, and a shot of Jack giving a thumbs-up in the cinema. The slogan on the poster reads 'The film they tried to ban!'.

BISHOP: Look. There's you, there's Forrest Gump. And there's Father Jack actually watching the film. What a turn-up for the books! Ha, ha! Right. Now, I think the best thing would be for you three to continue your careers as priests-cum-film promoters outside of my jurisdiction. Don't you think? Ted, I thought you might like to go to America. (*Looking at map.*) What part, do you think?

TED: Oh, ah . . . (*Hopefully.*) Las Vegas?

BISHOP: Oh, sorry, Ted, I meant South America! I tell you what, there's a little island off the coast of Surinam, and, ha, ha, there's a couple of tribes there . . . you'll like this . . . they've been beating the shit out of each other since 1907. We've never found the right man to bring them together in a spirit of Christian harmony. But I think you're the man.

TED: Well, thanks very much, but –

BISHOP: No need to thank me. One question. Do you know how to make arrows?

TED: Ah, no –

BISHOP: Never mind, never mind. It'll come in time. Anyway, Dougal . . . on to you. Isn't it funny how some of these places in the Philippines can keep on going without any sort of proper sewerage system?

DOUGAL: Oh, you're right there, Your Honour.

BISHOP: The amount of diseases that leads to. I read somewhere that they still have diseases over there that we got rid of in the eighteenth century. And of course the clergy aren't immune from all this. Their place is with their flock. Swimmin' about in the river with the rest of them.

He turns on the sleeping Jack.

BISHOP: Jack. Where can we stick you?

He notices Jack is asleep.

BISHOP: Jack! Wake up!

TED: I wouldn't do that, Bishop.

BISHOP: You shut up! Jack! Wake up!

He leans over and shakes Jack. We see a huge close-up of Jack's eye opening. We see only the white of his eye. Then, his pupil swings down from behind his eyelid and fixes on the Bishop. Cut back to the Bishop leaning over Jack.

JACK *(a roar from the very depths of hell)*: Feck off!

He punches the Bishop. The Bishop falls over. He stands up, adjusting his clothes. He has a bloody nose.

BISHOP: Oh, that's it, Jack. I've got you now. I've got all of you! You think this place is bad . . . Wait'll you see your new parishes. Wait'll you see!

He leaves the room and slams the door. Dougal and Ted look despondent. Jack is still just waking up.

TED: Well . . . that's it, then. I suppose . . . I suppose all we can do now is pack . . .

DOUGAL: I don't want to go to the Philippines, Ted . . . I can't even spell the Philippines . . . I know it begins with an 'F'.

TED: I know, I know . . . if only there were some way we could persuade the Bishop to change his mind. If only we had something we could bargain with . . . or . . . oh, I don't know . . .

Meanwhile, Jack has switched on the VCR.

TED: Did you get a film out, Father? I tell you, the last thing I want to see now is a film . . .

Nonetheless, Ted looks at the screen.

SCENE 15 EXT./DAY X
SET: BEACH
This is the video that Jack, Dougal and Ted are watching. We don't see anything interesting at first, but then we see the Bishop come into shot. He is laughing, running along the beach, wearing a pair of swimming trunks. We then see that he is chasing a young woman in a bikini, who is laughing and playfully putting the Bishop's hat on her head as she runs. He catches her and wrestles playfully with her as she tries to hold the hat out of reach. Cut to the Bishop lying on a deckchair looking proudly at something offscreen. The camera turns to reveal the Bishop's son making large arched sandcastles with the Bishop's hat.

SCENE 16 EXT./DAY X
SET: BEACH
Cut to the Bishop on a swing, this time in full regalia, the woman pushing him. The Bishop holds the boy in his lap. The film ends.

SCENE 17 INT./DAY 3
SET: PAROCHIAL HOUSE
Cut back to Dougal, Ted and Jack.

TED: Well . . . that was great!

DOUGAL: You're right there, Ted.

Pause.

TED: Will we 'phone him now or will we watch it again?

Pause.

TED: Ah, we'll watch it again.

They press 'play' on the video and settle back in their seats.

THE END

competition time

ARTHUR: The 'All-Priests' Stars in Their Eyes Lookalike' competition was inspired by the All Priests' Roadshow in Ireland, otherwise known as the Holy Show. Basically, it's a bunch of very good-natured priests who tour the country, singing and telling jokes and doing their various turns. Not by any means the strangest manifestation of faith in Ireland; I recently saw a film containing footage from an Irish newsreel of 1964. One item it contained was the Annual Blessing of the Jets at Dublin Airport. Priests were blessing jets on the runway. . .Even better was the Annual Blessing of the Scooters, when about 200 mods had their minds put to rest in the space of an afternoon. The competition host himself, Henry Sellers, is very much the Irish light entertainer abroad – the Henry Kelly/Terry Wogan/Eamonn Andrews type.

GRAHAM: The idea of having a trio of doppelgänger priests on a nearby island hit us like a bolt out of the blue. An idea like that is worth a hundred gags, because it dictates what you should be writing about. You set up the rivalry, involve them in a confrontation with high stakes and have lots of gloating at the end. That system also took care of the plots of *Song For Europe* and *Escape From Victory*. Oh, and just to set the record straight once and for all – Dick Byrne is not a sexual reference. If we had had any idea people would think that, we'd have changed his name immediately.

One thing that is puzzling about this episode is how Jack managed to get himself dressed up as Elvis at the beginning. I mean, it's a complete mystery how he did it. In fact, it's the sort of thing you don't really want to go into, so perhaps I shouldn't have brought it up. Just pretend I didn't say anything.

PART ONE
SCENE 1 INT./MORNING 1
SET: PAROCHIAL HOUSE
We see the door of the room. Ted is behind it, but we don't see him, or Dougal and Jack, to whom he is talking.

TED: All right, you ready?

DOUGAL: Ready when you are, Ted!

TED: You'll like this, Dougal. OK! One, two, three! Here I come!

He jumps into the room, facing the wall, his arms outstretched. His black leather jacket has 'Elvis' written on the back. He is dressed as Elvis circa 1968 – his 'guitar man' phase – black leather, greased black wig, pointed boots and a guitar. He spins around and the smile on his face immediately disappears when he sees Dougal and Jack. Cut to reveal that they are dressed in exactly the same way. Ted can't believe this. Pause.

DOUGAL: Who're you supposed to be, Ted?

TED: What do you think you're doing? You two can't go as Elvis!

DOUGAL: You . . . Wait a second, you're Elvis as well!

TED: Of course I'm Elvis! I've got 'Elvis' written on my back! I don't believe this —

DOUGAL: Bit of a coincidence, all right. Great minds think alike, I suppose.

TED: I've been saying for the last two weeks I was going as Elvis!

DOUGAL: Ahh! That's probably where I got the idea . . .

Ted walks over to Dougal. The leather creaks noisily whenever he moves.

TED: This is great, this really is. The first 'All-Priests' Stars In Their Eyes Lookalike' competition I thought I'd have a chance of winning. I don't believe it. Look! I even cleared a space for the trophy beside the one we got for coming third in the ludo championships.

We see a 'trophy' on the mantelpiece. It comprises four coloured discs – they look like ludo pieces – stuck to each other in a vertical line on a plastic base.

DOUGAL: You might still win, Ted, you never know.

TED: But what if you're on before me? I'll look like an eejit! Everyone'll think I copied the idea off you!

DOUGAL: Well, Ted, to be fair . . . it is a bit weird you happened to think of it as well.

TED: I thought of it first! It was my idea!

DOUGAL: I believe you, Ted. (*To himself.*) Thousands wouldn't.

TED: Forget it! Just forget it! You do whatever you want! I'll just have to be Mother Teresa again.

He sits down in a sulk. Jack, who has been watching him all this time, takes another drag on his cigarette and exhales. Pause.

JACK: Who're you supposed to be?

TED (*trying to suppress his anger. Pause.*): Elvis. I'm Elvis.

JACK: I'm Elvis!

TED: I know you are, Father! We're all Elvis! That's the problem!

Mrs Doyle enters the room.

MRS DOYLE: Tea, Fathers?

JACK: Feck off!!!

MRS DOYLE: There's nothing nicer than a cup of tea in the afternoon . . . (*She notices*

Ted's appearance.) . . . Oh, you look a bit different, Father. Have you had a haircut, or something?

TED: No, I'm Elvis Presley.

MRS DOYLE: Are you, Father? Well that's a turn-up for the books.

DOUGAL: It's for the 'All-Priests Lookalike' show tomorrow.

MRS DOYLE: Ah, now I see. Well, I must say I'm looking forward to that. Is Father Kiernan coming?

TED (*quietly*): He won't be, no.

MRS DOYLE: He's a great laugh. Always full of the joys of spring. I remember him last year, telling all his stories. He had me in stitches. It's true what they say about chubby men, isn't it? They are jollier than the rest of us. They have a way of looking at things —

TED: He shot himself.

MRS DOYLE: Did he? Oh, that's terrible. I suppose that's often the way with fat men. They laugh to hide the tears. But sure that's life. Happy one moment, then, I suppose, you just go . . . and shoot yourself, and . . . there you go. Anyway! Tea!

She starts pouring. She looks at Ted. Pause.

MRS DOYLE (*cagily*): Will you have a cup, Father?

TED: No, thanks. I'm fine.

MRS DOYLE: Go on!

TED: No, thanks . . . Well, actually . . . all right. Just a drop.

Pause.

MRS DOYLE: What?

TED (*holding his hand out for the cup*): I'll have just a little bit.

MRS DOYLE (*pulling cup away slightly*): Ah, now, you don't really want any, Father.

TED: No, I do!

MRS DOYLE: No, I'm forcing it on you, Father.

TED: No, you're not . . .

MRS DOYLE: No, I am. (*She slaps herself on the wrist.*) You're just a big dictator, Joan!* Can't take no for an answer!

TED: But I'm not saying no, Mrs Doyle.

MRS DOYLE: Ah, you're saying no with your eyes, Father.

TED: . . . I'll just have a little cup, Mrs Doyle.

Mrs Doyle wags her finger at him and smiles.

TED (*cannot believe this*): Please, Mrs Doyle . . .

MRS DOYLE (*to Dougal*): Cup of tea, Father?

The telephone starts ringing. Ted, shaking his head in wonder, goes to answer it.

TED (*picks up the telephone*): Hello?

SCENE 2 INT./DAY 1
SET: RIVAL PAROCHIAL
HOUSE/PAROCHIAL HOUSE
We see a middle-aged priest, Father Dick Byrne, on the telephone. In the background we see a housekeeper handing out tea to two other priests, a young simple-minded type, Father Cyril McDuff, and an old crotchety type, Father Jim Johnson. Cutting back and forth between Ted and Dick, we see that the action is identical on either side of the line.

DICK: Ted! How are you?! Dick Byrne here!

TED (*not too happy*): Ah . . . hello, Dick. How are things on Rugged Island?

DICK: Not so bad, Ted! You all set for tomorrow?

TED: The show? Em . . .

DICK: Looking forward to not getting your hands on the trophy again?

TED (*slightly angry*): Actually, I think the trophy's going to Craggy Island this year.

DICK: That'll be the day, Ted. What have you got planned?

---

*Oh, my God! Her first name! This is a very good example of the kind of information one carelessly flings about in the early days of writing a sitcom, without realising that it has the potential to be a lovely dark secret for years and years.

TED: Ah, now, I shouldn't say . . . it'd be giving you an advant—

DICK: Mother Teresa?

Furious pause.

TED: No!

DICK: I tell you what, keep it as a surprise. Actually, I'm only joking really. I do think you might be in with a chance this year, Ted.

TED (*calms somewhat*)**:** Oh, well . . . Do you really, Dick?

DICK: No.

Ted is so enraged that he misses the cradle when he puts the telephone down, and has to slam it a few times to get it into place. On the other end of the line, we see Dick sniggering to himself.

CYRIL (*very Dougal-like*)**:** Who's that, Dick?

SCENE 3 INT./DAY 1
SET: PAROCHIAL HOUSE
Ted is furious. He storms over to Dougal.

TED: I'm asking you one more time, Dougal! Don't go as Elvis!

DOUGAL: What?

TED: We have a chance, for once, of having the Lookalike championship trophy in this house. If we all go as Elvis, none of us will win!

DOUGAL: Can't I go as Elvis?

TED: Look, Dougal, I've been looking forward to this for ages. I know all the moves and everything! And remember who's judging this year!

DOUGAL: Who, Ted?

TED: Henry Sellers!

DOUGAL: No! He's coming here! Wow!

TED: I told you this, Dougal! Father Dunne is bringing him over.

DOUGAL: I've never met a celebrity before.

TED: You met the Pope.

DOUGAL: Did I?

TED: Don't you remember? When we went to Rome.

DOUGAL (*thinks*)**:** That was the Pope? The fella living in the art gallery?

TED: The Vatican, Dougal! It was The Vatican!

DOUGAL: All the same, Ted, I wouldn't say he's a 'celebrity' in the true sense of the word, you know?

TED: Dougal, the Pope is God's representative on earth.

DOUGAL: Huh! . . . You'd think he'd be taller.

TED: What, like a giant? A giant Pope, Dougal? Is that what you'd have preferred? Maybe next time they'll make Hulk Hogan Pope. Would that help you at all?

DOUGAL: Still, though, Henry Sellers, coming here . . . . Ha . . . . (*Pause.*) Aaaaaaaaaaaarrrrgghhhhhhhhhhh!!!!!!!

He starts running around in circles.

DOUGAL: Aaaaaaaaaaaaggghhhhhh!!!! Henry Sellers? *The* Henry Sellers?

TED (*puts his hands on Dougal's shoulders*)**:** Dougal, calm down. We have to concentrate on the Elvis problem. Look, why don't we toss for it? Whoever wins can be Elvis.

DOUGAL (*calming*)**:** . . . Yes . . . All right.

Ted takes out a coin and prepares to toss it.

TED: Right. Heads or tails?

Dougal pauses for a long time.

TED: Heads or tails, Dougal?

DOUGAL: Heads . . . (*Ted tosses the coin.*) . . . No, tails!

The coin falls to the ground.

DOUGAL: Heads! Tails! (*He bends down to the coin.*) Heads!

TED: Dougal! You have to give me a choice between the two!

DOUGAL: Sorry, sorry. Got a bit excited there, Ted.

TED: All right, we'll go again. Heads or tails?

DOUGAL: Heads.

TED: You sure now?

DOUGAL: Absolutely pos— tails.

TED: Right.

Ted flips the coin.

DOUGAL: No, heads! Tails! Heads!

TED: Dougal!

DOUGAL: Heads!

TED: Dougal, calm down.

DOUGAL: Tails! Heads! Tails! Heads!

Dougal is staring strangely. His head quivers in a weird way.

TED: Dougal! Dougal! Are you all right?

DOUGAL (*calming*)**:** I'm fine. Sorry, Ted. I'm not the best at making decisions . . . Or am I?

TED: Look, Dougal. You toss the coin, all right? I'll take . . . heads. Heads it is! Toss the coin, there.

DOUGAL: All right.

Dougal flips the coin straight at the ludo trophy. The top two pieces break and fall off. Ted looks as if he's about to explode.

TED: Right! Forget it! Forget it! Forget it!

Ted storms off. Dougal looks at the coin on the ground, then checks that Ted has left the room. He does an Elvis-style karate chop.

DOUGAL: Yesss . . .

SCENE 4 INT./NIGHT 1
SET: PAROCHIAL HOUSE
Ted is reading 'The Sunday Independent'. He makes a point of not looking at Dougal. Dougal is watching television. Jack sleeps. They are all dressed normally again. Ted is determinedly not looking at Dougal. Dougal looks at Ted with a worried expression.

DOUGAL: Ted, Henry's on. Ted?

Ted ignores him. We see the television.

SCENE 5 INT./DAY X
SET: QUIZ SHOW
Henry Sellers, the host of 'Morning Quiz', is interviewing a contestant, a very old woman who seems to be having trouble seeing him. She looks slightly to his left.

HENRY: So, back to you for a five-point question, Monica. The capital of England . . . is it New York, London or Munich?

Pause.

HENRY: I'll give you a clue. You live there.

Pause. Quick shot of Henry displaying a slight expression of weariness. We hear a 'ding-dong' sound.

HENRY: Jane, do you know?

Cut to the other contestant. She seems embarrassed.

JANE: I leaned on the button by mistake.

HENRY: All right, back to Monica . . .

Pause. Monica stares ahead.

SCENE 6 INT./NIGHT 1
SET: PAROCHIAL HOUSE
Cut back to Dougal watching the show.

DOUGAL: He's great, isn't he, Ted? Henry? And he'll be here any second! Are you excited, Ted? Henry Sellers! Look at him askin' the questions there.

Ted turns his head away. Dougal looks upset. Cut back to the programme.

HENRY: 'A stitch in time saves . . .' How many?

The 'ding-dong' noise sounds again. Henry turns to Jane.

JANE (*holding her hand up*)**:** Sorry!

Cut back to Dougal and Ted.

DOUGAL: Any idea why he left the BBC, Ted? (*No response.*) Probably just got fed up asking questions. I suppose we can ask him ourselves when he comes. I'll ask him. (*No response. We hear applause and end-of-show music from the television.*) Oh, it's over, Ted. Do you want to have a look at another one? (*Dougal holds another video. No response.*) I suppose it's not as much fun when you know the answers . . . (*Pause.*) Ted, look, why don't you be Elvis. Since you thought of it first I suppose it's only fair. I'll go as Mother Teresa.

Ted at last looks at Dougal. His expression softens.

TED: Ah, Dougal . . . no, no, I'm sorry. I'm being selfish. I'm sorry. You go as Elvis.

DOUGAL: No, Ted, it's not fair on you. You had your heart set on it.

TED: No, seriously, Dougal. You go.

DOUGAL: Really? Great! Thanks, Ted!

Ted looks a little put out at this, but he doesn't know what to say. Dougal puts in another video.

TED: . . . Unless you'd prefer to go as Mother Teresa . . .

DOUGAL: Ah, not really, Ted, no. Anyway, there's only one Mother Teresa, Ted, and that's you.

TED (*not meaning it*)**:** Thanks, Dougal. Oh, well . . . at least we've got the honour of taking care of Mr Sellers. And remember, it's very important that we be extremely nice to him. That'll increase the chances of us winning a hundred per cent. We'll fill him up with food and drink until it's coming out of his ears . . . (*Turns to Jack.*) You'll be nice to Mr Sellers, won't you, Father?

Jack is looking at Ted strangely. He seems confused and a little wary.

JACK: Wha . . .?

TED: Father, are you all right. You look —

Ted sees something on the floor.

TED (*picks up a bottle*)**:** Ah, no, Father! Not Toilet Duck! You know what that does to you!

Jack looks up at Ted with increased puzzlement and horror.

TED: You'll be seeing the pink elephants again! (*Holds up three fingers.*) How many fingers am I holding, up Father?

SCENE 6A INT./EVENING 1
SET: PAROCHIAL HOUSE
We see Ted from Jack's point of view. Ted's hand appears incredibly large, about the size of the fake hands you see at football matches.

JACK (*still frightened*)**:** Three?

TED: Well, you're not too bad. Maybe you're immune to it now.

The doorbell rings.

DOUGAL: That'll be him! That's Henry! Oh, God!

TED: Dougal, calm down! He's just a normal person like you or me. Well, like me, anyway.

Mrs Doyle sticks her head in.

MRS DOYLE (*very excited*)**:** He's here!

She steps back to allow Henry into the room. He is well dressed in a light blue suit. He walks up to Ted with his hand out.

HENRY: Hello, there! Henry Sellers!

TED: Hello, Mr Sellers. Father Ted Crilly. It's an honour to have you here!

HENRY: Well, it's lovely to be here. (*To Dougal.*) Hello Father . . .?

Dougal has gone rigid. He stares at Henry, unable to move a muscle.

TED: Sorry, Mr Sellers. This is Father Dougal McGuire.

Dougal continues to stare.

TED: Father Dougal . . . Say something to Mr Sellers!

Slight pause. Ted gives Dougal a little kick.

DOUGAL: Ow! How old are you?

TED: Dougal! Don't be asking Mr Sellers how old he is!

HENRY: Ha, ha, ha! That's quite all right. I'm thirty-seven, Father.

Ted muses on this for a moment and then brings him over to Jack.

TED: And over here is Father Jack Hackett . . .

Henry approaches Jack. We see this from Jack's point of view. Henry is bathed in a strange light, and he is dressed up as a garden gnome. Cut to Jack's terrified expression.

JACK: Aaaaaggghhhhhhhhh!!!!!!

Jack stumbles from his chair, trying his best not to go near Henry, and practically kills himself trying to get out of the room.

TED: Bye, Father! . . . (*To Henry.*) He's just gone out for his walk.

As Ted talks, we see a terrified Jack running past the window at top speed. Henry looks puzzled.

TED (*to Henry*): Can we get you anything at all, Mr Sellers?

HENRY: Call me Henry. Eh, if you'd have something to eat . . . Maybe a sandwich?

TED: Mrs Doyle, could you bring in some sandwiches . . .?

MRS DOYLE: Right, Father. How many, Father?

TED: Oh, ah, two hundred.

HENRY: Oh, honestly, I'm —

TED: Oh, you're absolutely right, Henry. Three hundred. Sure I might have one myself!

She leaves. Ted sits down. Dougal is looking in a very fixated way at Henry's 'hair'. Henry is looking straight ahead, but still seems very aware of Dougal's eyes.

DOUGAL: Is there something wrong with your head?

TED: DOUGAL!!!

DOUGAL: What? It's just his hair looks a bit . . .

TED: Dougal, shut up!!!

DOUGAL: Why? I didn't say anything. I just said that his hair looks a bit mad . . .

TED (*quickly changing the subject*): Is Father Dunne with you?

HENRY: He is. He's just bringing in the b— oh, here he is . . .

Father Barty Dunne, a jolly, good-natured priest, arrives, carrying some luggage. He holds out his hand to Ted.

BARTY: Ted!

Ted rises again.

TED: Barty, How are you? Sit down, there . . .

BARTY: Good to be on Craggy Island, again. God, I haven't seen you in ages. I remember the last time . . . ha, ha, we had that, ha, ha, funny incident, ha, ha, I suppose . . . ha, ha . . . you've forgotten all about it . . . HA! HA! It was the type of thing . . . ha, ha, ha, HA! HA!

HENRY: What's this . . .?

TED: Ah, the last time Father Dunne was here, Father Hackett lost his slippers . . .

BARTY: It was a bit of a . . . ha, ha, ha . . . He had us all lookin' for them . . . ha, ha, ha . . . Bit of a . . . ha, ha, ha, ha, ha . . . It was a bit like the type of thing . . . ha, ha . . . ha, ha, ha, ha . . .

TED: We found them after a while.

Henry nods, smiles kindly. He looks around, to see Dougal still rigid. Barty distracts him again.

BARTY: I suppose . . . ha, ha, ha . . . I suppose it's a bit like . . . ha, ha, ha, ha . . . I suppose it's a bit like . . . ha, ha, ha, ha . . . ha, ha, ha, ha, ha . . . It's a bit . . . ha, ha, ha . . .

TED: How long was the car journ—

HENRY (*immediately*): Four hours.

Ted nods understandingly.

END OF PART ONE

* * *

PART TWO

SCENE 7 INT./EVENING 1
SET: PAROCHIAL HOUSE
There is a mountainously huge pile of sandwiches on a tray on the table. Henry, Ted and Barty sit around the room. They each have a small plate, with half-eaten sandwiches on each one. Dougal is still dumbstruck.* Ted and Barty each have a glass of whiskey. Henry is drinking tea. Barty drones on, and the rest look very, very bored.

BARTY: . . . I suppose . . . in all honesty . . . ha, ha, ha, ha, ha, ha . . . with the thing there! . . . Oh! Ha, ha, ha, ha, ha! . . .

DOUGAL (*unable to speak*): Mmbrorlrorrr!!!

Henry smiles uncertainly at Dougal.

TED: So, Henry, what's it like being a TV star?

HENRY: Well . . .

BARTY: You must be, you must be, you must be . . . ha, ha, ha, ha, ha, ha, ha . . . I suppose you must be . . . ha, ha, ha, ha, ha . . . with the television . . . ha, ha, ha . . . with the way things are goin' . . .ha, ha, ha, ha, ha, ha . . . ah, Lord . . .

TED: I have to say again, Henry, we're just so delighted to have you here. Can I get you anything else?

HENRY: No, no, I'm fine.

TED: More sandwiches?

---

*We have a feeling Dougal is dumbstruck because we didn't know what to do with him.

HENRY: Hmmm? (*He turns and sees the sandwich mountain.*) Oh . . . you've . . . brought more in. No, really, I'm fine.

DOUGAL: Everything OK with your hair?

TED: Dougal, will you please stop talking about Henry's hair!!! I'm sorry Henry, it's just that your hair looks so natural, Dougal can't stop talking about it. It really is a beautiful head of hair . . . Anyway, what I was saying was . . . Anything you want at all, we can get it for you. There's no problem. And I mean that. Anything that you want. Anything that you want – that it would be at all possible for us to get you – just ask us. And I mean anything. (*Pause.*) There's no problem there at all. Anything.

HENRY: Well, I tell you what, I've been having a bit of difficulty getting the British papers over here. Would it be possible —

TED: Can't help you there, Henry. (*Pause.*) But anything else. Anything you want. Just ask. Except, obviously, the British papers.

HENRY: Well, I must say, your Craggy Island hospitality is very impressive. There must be something about priests and islands. Something in the air that makes them extremely generous and kind.

TED (*modestly*): Ah, well . . .

HENRY: Tell me, Father, do you know a Father Dick Byrne at all?

TED (*concerned*): What?

HENRY: Father Dick Byrne. He lives over there on Rugged Island. He's there with a . . . Father Johnson and a Father McDuff?

TED: What about them?

HENRY: Oh, they're always inviting me to come and stay with them. And they've sent me all types of presents and gifts. They're big fans of the show. I believe they're taking part in the Lookalike competition tomorrow . . .

TED: Hmmm . . . Well, to be honest, Henry . . . to be quite honest . . . and I don't know how to put this kindly, but . . . I think they're just buttering you up, there.

HENRY: What, for the competition, you mean? I'm sure they wouldn't do that.

TED: Well, you know . . . you should watch yourself with that lot.

HENRY: Their island's quite near this one, isn't it?

TED: Why? You're not thinking of visiting them, are you?

HENRY: Well, it is nearby, isn't it?

TED: Well, to be honest, Henry, you'd be making a mistake to visit them.

HENRY: Why is that Father?

Pause.

TED: They're lepers.

HENRY: They're what?

TED: They're lepers. The three of them. Rugged Island is a leper colony.

HENRY: You're not serious. A leper colony?

TED: Well, no. It's not leprosy. But there is something wrong with them. Did you never think how strange it was, three priests living on an island together?

HENRY: I suppose . . .

TED: No, there's something not quite right there . . . You'd be better off staying well away from them.

BARTY (*getting up*): Ted, where's the old . . . eh . . . ha, ha, ha, the old . . . eh . . . ha, ha, ha . . .

TED: The old? Oh, yes . . . you go upstairs and it's first on the left . . .

Barty leaves. Pause. Dougal is still looking at Henry's hair.

DOUGAL: It's a wig!!!

Ted stands up, grabs Dougal by the shirt collar and the seat of his pants and frogmarches him outside before he can say anything else. Henry looks on, very puzzled. Mrs Doyle enters with a tray. On it is a bottle of sherry and four glasses.

MRS DOYLE: Time for a little nightcap, everyone! Oh, and you're running out of sandwiches. I'll bring in some more . . .

Mrs Doyle starts pouring sherry into each of the glasses.

HENRY: I won't have one, thanks.

MRS DOYLE: Oh, now don't be silly! You will!

HENRY: No, really, I shouldn't.

Ted returns.

TED: Ah, go on. It'll help you sleep.

HENRY: . . . No, it's not a good idea. You go ahead.

TED: You've been saying no all day. A little drop won't do you any harm.

MRS DOYLE: The tiniest drop. Just a weeny, tiny bit.

She hands him the glass. He takes it reluctantly.

TED: The day a bit of sherry does anyone any harm is the day Ireland doesn't win the Eurovision!

They laugh at the idea.

MRS DOYLE: Ah, go on.

HENRY: No, I —

MRS DOYLE: Ahhhh, go on. Go on. Go on, go on, go on, go on, go on, go on, go on, go on —

HENRY: No, seriously . . .

MRS DOYLE: Go on. Go on. Go on, go on, go on, go on, go on, go on, go on, go on, go on, go on, go on, go on, go on, go on, go on, go on, go on, go on, go on, GO ON!!!!

HENRY (*jumps with the shock*): Well . . . Just a drop, then.

Henry smiles nervously. He puts the glass slowly to his lips. Fade to black.

SCENE 8 INT./NIGHT 1
SET: PAROCHIAL HOUSE
Fade back up to reveal that there are books strewn all over the floor, broken, overturned furniture and other indications that a disaster has occurred. Cut to Henry, who seems to have undergone a complete personality change. He is standing at the fireplace swigging sherry from the bottle, roaring and shouting his head off. Ted, Dougal and Barty are hiding behind the sofa.

HENRY: What a shower of BASTARDS!

BARTY (*to Ted, very concerned*): Oh, Lord, Ted, why'd you give him a drink?

TED: I didn't know this would happen!

BARTY: That's why he was sacked from that programme! He's a terrible alcoholic! He's been on the wagon for a year . . . My God, Ted!

TED: How was I supposed to know?!

HENRY: Sack me? Sack me?! I made the BBC! I made it!

He falls to the ground and starts sobbing uncontrollably. Ted makes a tentative move towards Henry.

TED: Henry? Maybe if you have a bit of a rest you'll feel better . . .

HENRY: Get away from me, priest!

TED: The thing is, I think it's time we should all head up to bed . . .

Henry walks over to the television and, with a single kick, smashes in the screen.

TED: Good man, Henry! There's never anything on, anyway. Sure I'll give it a kick myself.

He gives it a pathetic little kick.

HENRY: You want a fight?

TED (*looks nervously at his watch*): Well, y'know, I'd love a bit of an ould scrap, but . . .

HENRY: Bloody priests!

TED: O'ho!

HENRY: Bunch of sanctimonious bastards. Made my life a bloody misery . . .

TED: Well, sorry about that, Henry . . . Are you sure you wouldn't like to —

HENRY: Arrrrrrghhhh!

Henry turns over the table.

TED: Well, I suppose we could stay up a little longer if you want . . .

HENRY: I've had enough of you bastards! I'm off! Don't try to stop me!

TED: Well, Henry, it's a *bit* late . . . Ha, ha . . .

Henry takes a run-up to the window and leaps through it. We hear his scream dwindling as he disappears into the night. Ted and Barty run to the window and watch him go.

DOUGAL: It's true what they say, though, isn't it? You should never meet your heroes. You'll always be disappointed.

SCENE 9 EXT./DAWN 2
SET: NEAR WOODS

DOUGAL: God, Ted, imagine if we're not able to get him back. He'd be like Big Foot, except he'd be a BBC television presenter.

Ted and Dougal have joined Sergeant Deegan, a gruff, serious policeman. They hide behind some rocks.

DEEGAN: D'ye see him? There . . . by the trees . . .

He hands Ted a pair of binoculars. Ted looks through them and we see the woods from his point of view. At first we don't see anything. Then a figure in the distance, wearing a bright shirt and tie, runs from one entanglement of trees to another. It is a brief, dark, fleeting movement.

TED: Got him! There he is!

He passes the binoculars to Dougal. Dougal has a look.

TED: Sorry about all this, Sergeant.

DEEGAN: Oh, no problem, Father. I've been through this before . . . rock stars, actors, television personalities. They give up the drink and drugs and come over to places like this. The solitude can get to them. What happened to this fella?

TED: Well, he was fine one minute, and then he had a sip of sherry . . .

The sergeant laughs at Ted's naïveté.

DEEGAN: Relapse. That's when they're at their most dangerous. Right, y'ready? I want you two to bang these sticks together and shout a bit. That'll scare him out of the woods so I can get a clear shot.

He lifts a rifle into shot.

TED: You're going to shoot him?!

DEEGAN: A tranquilliser dart, Father. It'll just put him to sleep for a bit.

TED: Still . . . it seems a bit extreme.

DEEGAN: It's the best way, Father, believe me.

TED: Well, you know best.

DEEGAN: God . . . this reminds me of Vietnam.

TED: Were you in Vietnam, Sergeant?

DEEGAN: No, no . . . I mean, you know, in the films . . . All right . . . (*He takes quick, sharp breaths in quick succession.*) . . . Let's go!

The three come out of cover and walk towards the woods. Ted and Dougal bang sticks against tins.

TED: Come on, Henry! Out you come!

DOUGAL: Go on out of it, there!

They make some more noise. Suddenly, Henry, a distant shadowy figure, runs out of the woods to the side.

TED: There's nothing of interest to you in there now, Henry. (*Ted sees Henry.*) There!

DEEGAN: Got him.

Deegan raises the gun and fires. There is a 'phut' noise and Henry falls to the ground. Suddenly, another figure breaks from the woods and runs in the opposite direction.

TED: It's Jack!

DEEGAN: I've got a clear shot, Father! Do you want me to get him?

TED (*smiling kindly*)**:** No . . . let him go. He'll

make his own way back.

They watch as Jack runs off into the distance.

DEEGAN (*shakes his head*)**:** Look at him go. Beautiful.

SCENE 10 INT./DAY 2
SET: PAROCHIAL HOUSE
We see Henry asleep on the sofa. Ted and Dougal stand over him. Ted has a cup of tea in his hand. Henry makes a few grunting noises and then wakes up.

HENRY: Uhhhh . . . Oh, God, my head . . .

TED: Here you are Henry. A nice cup of tea.

HENRY: Where am I? Oh, my God. What? What happened last night? I remember having a sip of sherry . . .

TED: Nothing to worry about, Henry.

HENRY: I hope I didn't do anything to embarrass you, Father.

DOUGAL: Ha, ha, ha, ha, ha, ha, ha, ha!!!!

TED: Dougal! No, no, you were fine, Henry.

The telephone rings.

TED: Oh, no . . . that'll be Dick Byrne. I do feel kind of sorry for him, though. Marooned out there with those eejits and they've absolutely nothing in common.

SCENE 11 INT./DAY 2
SET: RIVAL PAROCHIAL
HOUSE/PAROCHIAL HOUSE
We see Father Dick Byrne talking to Cyril and Jim as he waits on the telephone for Ted to pick up.

DICK: . . . absolutely nothing in common. Ah, Ted! Hello!

TED: Hello, Dick . . .

DICK: Ted! We were just talking about you.

TED: Really?

DICK: Yeah, we were saying how great you were.

TED: Really?

DICK: No!!!!!

TED: Hilarious, Dick.

DICK: I was just calling to make sure you're going to turn up tonight . . .

TED: Why wouldn't I turn up?

DICK: Well, you know, it might be a little embarrassing to come last again.

TED: I won't be coming last, Dick. It'll be you who'll be coming last! In fact, I was wondering if you'd like to put a little bet on the show tonight. Raise the stakes a bit . . .

DICK: Put your money where your mouth is, Ted. What are we talking about here? A pound? Two pounds?

TED (*moves telephone to other ear*): Five pounds?

DICK (*pause. Moves telephone to other ear*): Five pounds?

TED: You're not scared are you, Dick?

DICK: Of course I'm not scared. Five pounds it is! See you tonight!

He puts down the telephone.

CYRIL: Who's that, Dick?

JIM: Drink!

Dick looks at the telephone, concerned.

SCENE 12 INT./DAY 2
SET: PAROCHIAL HOUSE
Ted puts his head in his hands. Henry is leaving the room.

HENRY: I'd better get cleaned up for tonight, brush my teeth . . . I've got this weird taste of raw meat in my mouth for some reason . . .

TED: Right you are, Henry! (*Henry leaves.*) Oh, what did I do that for? We haven't a hope in hell.

DOUGAL: Why can't we all go as Elvis, Ted?

TED: 'Cause we'll all look the same! Anyway . . . (*He looks at his watch.*) Jack should be back any minute for his afternoon drink.

We hear a crash outside the room.

JACK (*from outside*): Drink!

TED: There he is.

Jack comes into the room. He looks wrecked. Puffy, bloated and exhausted.

DOUGAL: God, Ted! He looks very rough! We'll have to get him sobered up if he's going to do the contest.

Dougal walks towards Jack. Ted stops him.

TED: Dougal. Wait . . . I've got an idea.

Cut to Jack looking at them both, breathing heavily.

SCENE 13 EXT./EVENING 2
SET: PAROCHIAL HALL
Establish hall.

SCENE 14 INT./EVENING 2
SET: PAROCHIAL HALL
A priest dressed as Ziggy Stardust is performing on stage. He has nearly finished his act. Henry is sitting at a small desk to the side of the stage, making notes.

PRIEST (*sings*): Ziggy played . . . geeetaarrrrrrrr . . .

Applause. He bows and walks off. Henry and Father Barty Dunne walk onstage.

BARTY: Fantastic! Father Harry Fitzpatrick, there. He looks a bit . . . ha, ha, he won't mind me saying this . . . ha, ha . . . ha, ha, HA, HA, HA!!!! Ah, no . . . Anyway, Henry . . . marks for Father Fitzpatrick?

HENRY: Very good. (*He holds up a card with a number on it.*) I'll give him seven out of ten.

Everyone applauds, except Father Fitzpatrick, who is watching in the wings.

FATHER FITZPATRICK: Bastard.

BARTY: O'ho! Not bad at all. 'Ziggy played guitar' . . . ha, ha . . . anyway, that means the lads from Rugged Island are still in the lead with nine out of ten! A big hand for Diana Ross and two of the Supremes!

We see Dick, Cyril and Jim all with blacked faces and wigs. They look absurd. They turn to each other and shake hands.

BARTY: Now, now, don't start celebrating yet! We've still got one more act to go! Ladies and Gentlemen, please welcome to the stage . . . aha, ha, ha, ha, ha . . . the lads . . . ha, ha,

ha, ha . . . I suppose, it's a bit like . . . ha, ha, ha, ha . . . Anyway, from these very shores, Father Ted Crilly, with Father McGuire and Father Hackett . . .

Applause. The light goes down. The stage is in complete blackness.

TED'S VOICE: Elvis Presley was a simple truckdriver from America. But one day in the 1950s, he invented rock 'n' roll!

The lights come up to reveal Dougal revealed as a young Elvis circa 1955, complete with pink jacket, guitar and blue suede shoes. He mimes to 'Hound Dog' for a short while. The music stops, the stage goes black and we hear Ted's voice again.

TED'S VOICE: Elvis became famous. Then

they forced him into the army. Then, he came out. Then, ten years later he came back with a comeback special.

The lights come on and Ted is revealed in his leather Elvis costume. He mimes 'Guitar Man'. The music stops, and the stage goes black once more.

TED'S VOICE: Elvis was back! From then until the end of his life he played in Las Vegas and became once again the 'King Of Rock 'n' Roll'!

The lights come on to the strains of 'My Way'. Jack is revealed in Las Vegas costume, sitting in an armchair, looking like a fat, bloated Elvis circa his death. He has a burger in his hand and is smoking. He looks around as if he doesn't know where he is.

TED'S VOICE: Ladies and Gentlemen, that was 'The Three Ages of Elvis' . . . Thank you!!

The audience applauds.

BARTY: Fantastic. Ha, ha . . . Lord God almighty! Three Elvises! Anyway, over to you Henry for the marks . . .

Cut to Henry. The atmosphere is tense. A smile slowly crosses his lips. He holds a card up slowly. We see that it is the maximum 'Ten'. There is wild applause. Cut to Dick, who looks disgusted. He gets up to leave and motions to Cyril and Jim to join him.

SCENE 15 INT./NIGHT 2
SET: PAROCHIAL HOUSE
Ted is being congratulated by Barty and Henry.

BARTY: Brilliant, Ted. It was fantastic. It was a bit like . . . ha, ha, ha . . .

TED: Thanks very much, Barty.

Dick and Cyril arrive. Dick hands over a fiver to Ted.

DICK (*very angry*): Five pounds, Ted!

TED (*taking the money*): Ah, Dick. Hard luck.

CYRIL: Did we not win, Dick?

TED: No, I'm afraid you didn't, Cyril. This year the trophy goes to Craggy Island! But you have every chance of winning next year.

DICK: Do you really think so Ted?

TED: No!!!

DICK: Come on Cyril. Let's go.

Father Jim wanders into shot holding an empty glass.

JIM: I'm out of feckin' whiskey.

DICK: There's plenty at home, Father.

The three priests leave briskly.

DOUGAL: That Cyril McDuff's an awful eejit, isn't he, Ted?

Mrs Doyle arrives with a tray of glasses.

HENRY: Well, I suppose since I didn't make a fool of myself the last time, I might have a drop of champagne. Cheers!

TED: Henry, no!

Too late. Henry downs the champagne.

HENRY: Don't worry yourself, Father. I'm fine. If I can't celebrate tonight, then when can I? The bastards! What the hell is going on?! The bastards! How dare they fire me! I'm Henry Sellers! I'm Henry Sellers!

He runs to the window and jumps out. Dougal walks up to Ted.

TED: Well, there he goes again.

DOUGAL: You're right there, Ted.

TED: Ah, we'll get him in the morning. Well done again, Dougal. How do you like the trophy?

They turn to look at it. We see them from the trophy's position.

DOUGAL'S VOICE: Ah, it's great. And it's all because of you, Ted!

TED'S VOICE: Put it there, Dougal!

Cut to the two of them standing on either side of the trophy. They shake hands. From this vantage point, we see that the trophy is absolutely tiny, about the size of a thimble. They turn to look at it again.

THE END

and god created woman

ARTHUR: This was a favourite among fans of more mainstream comedy, while people who were really keen on *Father Ted* were more ambivalent. It's not surprising really, as this is far less surreal than many other episodes. It's also something of a cliché, but we felt we had to do it. You can't really write twenty-odd episodes of *Father Ted* without using the Priest-Meets-Glamorous-Woman plotline.

Mrs Doyle's bad language speech gave us another aspect to Mrs Doyle's character – a kind of suppressed sexual obsession masquerading as disgust. We were beginning to discover things about Mrs Doyle ourselves here. Like the fact that she deeply distrusts any woman who isn't a nun and doesn't have a mole and a moustache. That made it easier to locate her attitude towards different women later on in the series. We should point out that 'Ride me sideways!' was Pauline's line – she threw it in during rehearsal. When Dermot closed the door on her, he was laughing so much that we had to cut away sharpish.

GRAHAM: I disagree very much with Arthur about this episode. I think it's a good mixture of surrealism (the blue card for Jack, the meeting with Tom, the incredibly quick Mass) and really nice observational comedy (Ted's attempts to appear literary and his inability to say goodbye to Polly at the start). The plot could have had a turn or two more, I suppose, and the part with the housewarming party didn't quite work as well as we thought it would, but I think it's the best ambassador for the first series.

The scene with the nuns interviewing Ted was inspired by Saturday morning television interviews with pop-stars, when children would ask the same questions every week about the stars' most embarrassing moments and what their inspirations were. The 'Zoe Ball' role is taken by Rosemary Henderson (Sister Assumpta), who is just one of the many fabulous comic actors in Ireland. We liked her so much we reinvented her character for *Cigarettes and Alcohol and Rollerblading*.

The joke about Ted not being able to say goodbye to Polly Clarke is based on our attempts to leave aftershow parties at places like the BBC. What happens is, you tend to meet someone you vaguely know (or maybe, like Polly, someone vaguely famous), have a nice, thorough chat with them and then say goodbye. Then about three minutes later you find yourself having to dredge up extra conversational nuggets when you meet them outside waiting for a taxi. That's why, I think, famous people always pretend they haven't seen you the second time. Or else it's my personality.

PART ONE

SCENE 1 INT./DAY 1
SET: BOOKSHOP

We see a poster inside the bookshop – a photograph of a glamorous, Edna O'Brien-type novelist underneath the words 'Polly Clarke', signing copies of her new book. A few well-dressed people stand around the bookshop, drinking glasses of wine. Some people are putting on their coats and leaving. We see Ted talking to Polly Clarke.

TED: . . . Now, I love a bit of Oscar Wilde, I suppose. He always does it for me.

POLLY: Ah, Wilde . . . 'The only thing worse than being talked about, is not being talked about.'

TED: Exactly! You know, I don't think Wilde could have put it better himself.

POLLY: Well, it was him who said that, actually.

Pause.

TED: Yes, but . . . he wouldn't have said it in that kind of ladylike way . . .

POLLY: Oh, you're a charmer, Father . . .

TED: Miss Clarke, I don't suppose you'd sign a copy of the latest for me?

POLLY: I'd be delighted.

TED (*as she writes*): Father Ted C— Just Ted Crilly, actually. Don't bother with the Father.

POLLY (*writing*): I envy you, really, Father. You must have great peace of mind being a priest. That's what I'd love . . . a feeling of serenity.

TED: Oh, I have serenity coming out of my ears. Too much serenity, really. A bit of excitement would suit me down to the ground. It must be great being a writer, though, jetting around the world, being interviewed, going on television . . .

POLLY: Don't forget writing, Father.

TED: Hmm? Oh, right . . . Well, thanks again for the autograph. I have to go – we've got some nuns coming to visit us on the island so we're all very busy . . .

POLLY: OK, Father . . . (*Someone hands her another book to sign.*) . . . Bye, bye!

TED: Goodbye now. Good luck with the book.

Ted moves off.

SCENE 2 INT./DAY 1
SET: LIFT

Outside a lift. Ted is looking at the page where Polly has signed the book. It reads 'To Father Curley, Best Wishes, Polly Clarke'. The lift doors open and Ted steps in.

TED (*quietly to himself*): Ah, feck . . .

Polly walks into the lift just as Ted says this.

TED: Ah, there you are again!

POLLY: Ah, Father Curley . . .

TED (*jokingly*): Going down? Ha, ha . . .

POLLY (*smiles*): Thanks . . .

The lift doors close. Slightly embarrassing moment. Ted opens the book and looks at the erroneous inscription.

TED: Eh . . .

Polly smiles at him. Ted looks at her but then chickens out.

TED: Thanks again for the autograph.

POLLY: You're welcome.

Pause. The lift doors open. They step out.

TED: Well . . .

POLLY: Ha . . .

TED: Good luck with the book again!

POLLY: Thanks very much, Father . . .

TED: Bye, then!

POLLY: Bye, Father!

They move off in opposite directions.

SCENE 3 EXT./DAY 1
SET: CAR PARK

Ted arrives beside his car. He puts his keys into the door. Polly arrives beside Ted. She takes out keys and puts them into the door of the car beside Ted's. She notices him. More embarrassment ensues.

POLLY: Well hello . . . again!

TED: Ah, hello!

POLLY: We're going to have to stop meeting like this!

TED: Ah, ha!

POLLY: Well . . . goodbye again!

TED: Bye! Good luck with the book!

They get into their respective cars. Ted waves from inside.

TED: Bye, bye.

They rev up their engines and move off, waving at each other.

SCENE 4 EXT./DAY 1
SET: TRAFFIC LIGHTS
We see Ted waiting at the traffic lights. There is one more car directly in front of him, another car beside that in the other lane. A car pulls up alongside his. Ted turns to see Polly Clarke in the neighbouring car. She turns at exactly the same time. They smile and nod at each other, but the scene is obviously fraught with embarrassment. Pause. Ted waves slightly.

TED (*mouths the words*): See you soon, then!

We see Polly smiling and nodding from the neighbouring car. Cut back to Ted, who turns to the lights again. He is very aware of Polly's presence beside him. Cut to the traffic lights, which are still red.

TED (*talking through clenched teeth*): Change . . . please change . . . for God's sake . . .

He turns again to Polly and smiles. He holds up the book.

TED (*mouths the words*): Good luck with the book!

He turns again.

TED: Please change. Please. Please change. God, please make the lights change. Hail Mary, full of grace, the Lord is with thee . . .

The lights change. Ted immediately slams his foot down on to the accelerator and the car lurches into the one in front. Ted is mortified.

TED: Oh, God almighty!!!

The man in front gets out of the car. He looks very angry. Polly doesn't notice the commotion and drives off.

TED: Oh, Christ!

The man gestures angrily at Ted. Ted rolls down the window to talk to him.

TED: Sorry about that.

The man comes into shot and blocks our view of Ted. He is a very broad-shouldered, beefy type. We see the man's arm coming back, then we hear a punch, and Ted's cry of pain and surprise.*

SCENE 5 INT./DAY 1
SET: PAROCHIAL HOUSE HALLWAY
Ted walks through the front door. He has a bloody nose. He walks towards the living room and steps inside.

SCENE 6 INT./DAY 1
SET: PAROCHIAL HOUSE
We see Polly sitting on the sofa. She is reading an issue of 'Cosmopolitan' magazine. Ted walks into the room. She looks up and sees him. He sees who it is and walks straight out again.

SCENE 7 INT./DAY 1
SET: HALLWAY
Ted looks up at the ceiling, addressing God.

TED: All right, what's going on?

He turns and walks into the room again.

SCENE 8 INT./DAY 1
SET: PAROCHIAL HOUSE
Ted walks into the living room. Polly looks very puzzled, but not displeased.

TED: Miss Clarke . . . ?

POLLY: Father, what are you doing here?

TED (*still dazed*): Oh . . . I'm the parish priest here.

POLLY: That's extraordinary. Looks like someone's trying to keep us together!

Ted looks befuddled.

POLLY: I've rented a cottage on the island, you see. But it's not ready yet. The builders suggested I stay here for the night. Is that OK?

---

*Our director, Declan Lowney, decided to speed all this action up, and consequently make it one of the funniest moments in the episode.

TED: . . . Yes, yes . . . This is amazing . . . God . . . we were both going the same way. But of course, you're very welcome to stay.

Mrs Doyle enters.

MRS DOYLE: Oh, hello, Father. You've met your visitor, then . . .

TED: Mrs Doyle, Miss Clarke will be staying the night. Could you show her where the spare room is?

MRS DOYLE (*coldly*): What?

TED: Could you show her to the spare room?

MRS DOYLE: Yes . . . it's just . . . I was going to make some tea . . .

TED: Well, you can do that later, Mrs Doyle. (*To Polly.*) I think tea is a bit common for Miss Clarke's tastes!

Ted and Polly laugh. Mrs Doyle does not appreciate this remark.

MRS DOYLE (*to Polly*): All right. Come on.

TED: Have a shower and . . . I mean, have a shower if you want . . . I don't want you to

have a shower, but . . . it might . . . you might want to get out of your clothes . . . Well, obviously, that's no concern of mine . . . but, ah . . . Mrs Doyle?

Mrs Doyle ushers her out. Ted sits down and looks at the issue of 'Cosmopolitan' left behind by Polly. He picks it up and flips through it. His eyebrows raise and we cut to see that he is looking at the 'Or are you just pleased to see me?' Wonderbra advertisement. He is looking at this as Dougal's head appears over the sofa directly behind him.

DOUGAL: Ted . . .

TED (*throws the magazine into the air*): Aaaaaaaaggghhhh!!!!!

Ted leaps into a standing position.

DOUGAL: Who was that, Ted?

TED (*clutching his heart*): For God's sake, Dougal!! What do you think you're doing?!

DOUGAL: I was hiding, Ted.

TED: Hiding from who?

DOUGAL: Hiding from yer one. I heard her coming in so I hid behind the sofa.

TED: Dougal, I'm still slightly confused . . . Why did you do that?

DOUGAL: Oh, I wouldn't know what to say to her. I thought I'd better wait until you got home.

TED: She's only a woman, Dougal.

DOUGAL (*very uncomfortable*): Oh, I don't . . . I don't know many women, Ted.

TED: What about your mother?

DOUGAL (*incredulous pause*): My mother? She's not really a woman, Ted. She's not like the women you see on the telly. Like The Gladiators. She wouldn't be one of them.

TED: Well . . . I . . . I'm sure that's their loss. But what about Mrs Doyle? She's a woman.

DOUGAL: Ah, Ted, come on . . .

TED: No, Dougal she is. She's just as much a woman as one of The Gladiators or the lady who runs Pakistan. You're just saying that because she's not conventionally attractive. You can't think like that anymore, Dougal . . .

DOUGAL: Mmm . . .

TED: . . . This is the twenty-first century, remember.*

DOUGAL: Anyway, who's that one you were talking to?

TED: She's a novelist. I've just been to her book signing. Apparently she's taken a cottage on the island . . .

We hear a scream from upstairs. Dougal and Ted look at each other, then run out of the room.

SCENE 9 INT./DAY 1
SET: SPARE BEDROOM
Polly stands in the room looking a little shaken. Mrs Doyle seems unsure what to do. Ted and Dougal enter and look at the bed. We see Jack lying on his back on the bed dressed only in socks, vest and underpants. He looks like a beached whale. There is a half-empty bottle of whiskey in his hand. He snores loudly. This is a fairly unsettling sight.

---

*Like computers that haven't been checked for the Millennium Bug, this joke will stop working the moment the calendar flips to 1/1/00.

POLLY: I'm sorry, Father. I just got a bit of a shock.

TED: Come on now, Father . . . (*He turns to Polly.*) This is Father Hackett. He gets a bit confused sometimes. (*To Jack.*) Come on, Father!

Jack rolls away from him.

TED: No, Father. Not your room! Not your room! No! Come on, now . . .

Jack moans and then lashes out at Ted, striking him across the face. Ted falls out of shot then immediately stands up again. Jack goes mad, thrashing about wildly.

JACK: Arse! Arse! Feck!!! Arse!! Feck!! Arrrgghhhh!!!

TED (*to Dougal*): Father!

Dougal doesn't respond to this.

TED: Dougal! Give us one of the cards! Quickly!

Polly turns to look at Dougal, who immediately averts his gaze. He moves past her, keeping his head fixed in this position. He stands by Ted, taking some cards out of his pocket and fanning them. We see they are all different colours.

DOUGAL: What colour, Ted?

TED: Blue, Dougal! Quickly!

Dougal gives Ted a blue card and immediately shows it to Jack. Jack continues screaming until he sees the card, when he suddenly calms and stops.

TED: There we go. (*To Polly.*) The old blue has a great calming effect.

They lift him out of bed and lead him past Polly.

JACK: Hehhh . . .

TED: That's right. That's Miss Clarke. Dougal . . .

JACK (*as he is led out of sight*): Woman!

TED: It *is* a woman, Father. You're right on the button.

Mrs Doyle and Polly are left behind.

MRS DOYLE (*smiles coldly*): Well . . . Have a lovely stay.

She leaves the room. Polly, as quietly as possible, closes the door and locks it.

SCENE 10 INT./NIGHT 1*
SET: TED AND DOUGAL'S BEDROOM
We see Ted reading 'Bejewelled with Kisses'. He looks up over his glasses at Dougal. Dougal is reading Polly's copy of 'Cosmopolitan', his eyes wide.

DOUGAL (*under his breath*): . . . Jaysus . . .

TED: It might not be a good idea reading that Dougal. You'll get confused.

DOUGAL (*pauses and, turns page*): God, Ted, Kim Basinger is forty.

He shows Ted a full-page photograph of a glamorous Miss Basinger.

DOUGAL: I hope I look this good when I'm forty. My God.

Ted starts to say something, then thinks better of it and returns to his book. He talks to Dougal absently while looking at it.

TED: So . . . what do you think of Miss Clarke?

DOUGAL: Oh, she's very nice. I think we hit it off.

TED: Dougal, you were hiding from her. I don't think that fits the definition of 'hitting it off'. She is very nice, though . . . It'll be great to have someone here on the island I can talk to . . . about books and films and poetry and so on . . .

DOUGAL (*a little hurt*): You can talk to me, Ted.

Ted looks at Dougal.

DOUGAL: Seriously, Ted. Let's talk about something.

TED: . . . OK. What do you want to talk about?

Long pause. Dougal looks at Ted vacantly.

DOUGAL: What?

TED: All right, I'll pick something . . . ehhhh . . . What's your biggest fear in life?

DOUGAL: I wouldn't like to be hit on the head with a football.

TED: You . . .

*We deleted this scene from the final version.

DOUGAL: I don't think about it all the time. Only when I'm passing by football pitches.

Pause. Ted doesn't know what to say.

DOUGAL: God! I'm glad I talked to you about that . . . I feel much better now.

TED: I . . . yes . . . I can understand . . . Anyway, I think I'll go to sleep. You'd better sign off yourself, Dougal. Big day with the nuns tomorrow. Put the magazine away, now.

DOUGAL: Right so.

Ted turns off the light. Pause.

DOUGAL: Ted?

TED: Yes, Dougal?

DOUGAL: What's female circumcision, Ted? . . . Ted?

Pause. After a moment, we hear Ted pretending to snore.

SCENE 11 INT./MORNING 2
SET: PAROCHIAL HOUSE
Ted looks immaculate. His hair is as smooth as plastic. His face is as smooth as a baby's bottom and he wears a blacker-than-black jacket. He checks himself in the mirror, then looks at his lapel badge. He rubs it, looks uncertain, then picks up a spray from the mantelpiece and sprays it. He shines it with his sleeve. He starts walking around the room, trying out various poses/ways of walking, etc. He mouths little phrases to himself, as if rehearsing a conversation. He laughs urbanely, practises a 'thoughtful look', etc. He keeps adjusting his jacket. He walks to a chair and leans on it in what he imagines to be a casual yet stylish way. He tries various poses here. Then he remembers something and goes to the bookcase. He starts taking down books and leaving them on the table. They are 'War and Peace', 'Crime and Punishment', 'The Odyssey' and 'The Commitments' by Roddy Doyle. He reconsiders the Doyle book and puts it back on the shelf. He leans on the chair again, tries a few poses and finally settles on one. The door opens and he opens his mouth in a smile. Dougal enters. Ted's smile disappears and he resumes his normal stance.

TED: Ah. Hello, Dougal.

DOUGAL (*looks at the books*): Ah, good idea, Ted. You throwing out the ones you couldn't get through?

TED: No, no, Dougal, I'm just . . . putting them in alphabetical order.

DOUGAL: Fair enough.

TED: You taking Jack for his walk, then?

DOUGAL: Suppose so, Ted. Do you want to come at all?

TED: No . . . no, I'd better . . . prepare for the nuns.

Mrs Doyle enters, pushing Jack in his wheelchair.

MRS DOYLE: Here we are, Father. It's a lovely day out.

JACK: My arse.

MRS DOYLE (*to Dougal*): Do you want him on automatic or manual, Father?

DOUGAL: Em . . . automatic, I think. Nice day . . . might as well take it easy.

TED: That's right, Dougal. You take your time.

MRS DOYLE: Fair enough.

Mrs Doyle produces a steel bar-like contraption and attaches it to Jack's wheelchair. It bends in the middle, and at its end, hanging from a piece of string, is a small bottle of whiskey. It hangs just in front of Jack, carrot-and-stick-like. Jack immediately starts pushing the wheels of the chair forward. Dougal casually walks after it. Mrs Doyle waves goodbye. She turns to Ted when they're gone, looking slightly disgusted.

MRS DOYLE: Well, Father, I never thought we'd have anyone like her staying here.

TED: Hmm? Oh, Miss Clarke? I know. It's very exciting, isn't it? A famous novelist!

MRS DOYLE: You haven't read any of her books, have you, Father?

TED: Well, actually, I'm a bit of a fan, Mrs Doyle. That's where I was the other day. At her book signing.

MRS DOYLE: Well, I'm surprised at that, Father. I didn't think you'd like that sort of thing. I read a bit of one of them once. God, I couldn't finish it. The language . . . unbelievable.

TED: It's a bit gritty, Mrs Doyle. But sure that's the modern world.

MRS DOYLE: It was a bit much for me, Father . . . 'Feck this and feck that' . . .

TED: Yes, Mrs Doyle.

MRS DOYLE: 'You big bastard' . . . Oh, dreadful language . . . 'You big hairy arse' . . . 'You big fecker' . . . Fierce stuff altogether. And of course, the F word, Father. The bad F word. Worse than feck. You know the one I mean.

TED: I do, Mrs Doyle.

MRS DOYLE (*pause*): 'F you!', 'F your effing wife!' Awful stuff. I don't know why they have to use that type of language. (*Pause.*) 'I'll stick this effing pitchfork up your hole!' That was another one.

TED: OK, Mrs Doyle. I see what you mean.

MRS DOYLE: 'Bastard' this and 'bastard' that. You can't move for the 'bastards' in her books. It's wall-to-wall bastards!

TED: Is it? Anyway —

MRS DOYLE: 'You big bastard'. 'You fecker.' 'You bollocks.' 'Get your bollocks out of my face.' . . . God, it's terrible, Father.

TED (*starts to usher her out*): Yes . . . you go and get ready for the nuns, Mrs Doyle . . .

Ted finally manages to slam the door shut. He leans against it, breathing heavily. Then he goes back to the books on the table and starts to pose around them again. He looks down and adjusts his fly. He pulls it down and then can't pull it up again. He turns and hops slightly as he tries to pull it up. Behind him the door opens and Polly comes in. She sees the books on the table and smiles. She picks one up and starts looking at it. Ted is still hopping up and down. He finally turns, pulling up the zip.

TED: Ahhhh . . . there you go . . . Aaaaghhhhh! (*Ted tries to assume his 'stylish' pose again. He has a little trouble with this.*) Hello there Miss Clarke! . . . Did you have a nice sleep?

POLLY: Oh, I slept like a log. It's so peaceful here . . . God, I need a bit of peace after the year I've had.

TED: I see . . .

POLLY: I've had quite a rough time of it recently. My husband left me for another woman. I suppose it was my fault. The sex was getting a little boring and I never did anything to spice it up.

TED (*massively uncomfortable*): Tcha! Isn't it always the way . . .

POLLY: Near the end I tried a few things. I'd dress up in some really revealing lingerie, and when he came through the door I'd just leap on top of him and have sex there in the hall.

Pause.

TED: So, you had a good sleep, then.

POLLY: Yes, I . . . Oh, God, sorry, Father! I probably shocked you!

TED: Oh . . . go . . . go away with . . . no, I've heard far more shocking things in confession down through the years.

He walks away from Polly in a very strange, uncomfortable way.

POLLY (*sighs*): Do you ever think of the future, Father?

TED: Oh, I used to think about it. The future. And then the future became the present, so I was obviously thinking about it a lot then. And now it's in the past, so I don't really think about it that often.

POLLY: The future is in the past?

TED: Well, it wasn't then, of course. It was the future . . . But when you're a priest, to be honest, the whole time is like a continual present, you know?

Polly smiles at him. She then looks down at the books on the table.

POLLY: Do you like Dostoevsky?

Ted smiles blankly. Polly smiles and holds up 'Crime and Punishment'.

TED: Oh! Oh, him? Oh, yes, that's one of my favourites, all right. I must have read that book . . . ten times.

POLLY: I see you're reading it again. There's a bookmark here on page seven.

Ted smiles and nods.

POLLY: Did you feel his sense of commitment wane towards the end?

TED: Well, yes.

POLLY: When did you feel that began to happen?

TED: Towards the end. (*Pause.*) Around the time he stopped writing about crime and went on to the punishment bit. It began to drag a bit there for me.

POLLY: I always felt that if Joyce, Keats and Lawrence were sitting in a room together and Dostoevsky came in, there'd be a bit of a fight for the last piece of pudding!

She laughs. Ted joins in, throwing his head back. He turns slightly and we see him pull a 'what the hell did that mean?' expression.

POLLY: It's great having someone to talk to about these things . . . My husband, there was a man who really was afraid of Virginia Woolf.

Ted nods.

TED: Was she following him or something?

POLLY: Ha, ha, ha, ha!!!

TED (*uncertain*): Ha, ha, ha, ha . . .

POLLY: Would you . . . I don't suppose you'd like to come up to the cottage later? For a drink? And maybe more book talk!

TED: Oh, that would be delightfug.

POLLY (*laughs*): Sorry?

TED: I'd be delightegetted.

POLLY: Right. See you later then, Father. About seven.

TED: Seven. Seven o'clock. Right.

She leaves. Ted smiles to himself, then looks up at the ceiling.

TED: It's just a drink!

END OF PART ONE

* * *

PART TWO

SCENE 12 INT./DAY 2
SET: PAROCHIAL HOUSE
We see a close-up of Ted, smiling in a fixed way. He sips from a cup of tea. Cut to a wide shot of the room. We see five nuns sitting on chairs together, smiling and looking at the ground. Pause.

TED: So! You had no trouble getting here.

ASSUMPTA: No, no. I drove Sister Julia in the Renault and Sister Margaret took the Mini.

TED: It's great having the old car, all the same . . . Any more tea at all?

The nuns talk as one, and do so as quietly as possible. We can't make out any words but the gist of it seems to be that they don't want any more tea.

TED: Sister Margaret, will you not have something?

Margaret goes bright red. All the other nuns turn exactly the same shade at exactly the same time.* Sister Margaret begins to speak as softly as possible.

MARGARET: . . . No, thank you, Father.

TED: Sorry?

ASSUMPTA: She's fine, Father. Ah, what time does the Mass tonight start, Father?

TED: Oh, at seven o'clock.

ASSUMPTA: That's grand. We don't want to be up too late.

TED: Well, seven isn't too . . . (*His eyes widen.*) Aaaargh!!

The nuns jump slightly with fright.

ASSUMPTA: Father! Are you all right?

---

*We were going to smother them in make-up to get this effect but in the end, we decided to leave it to the performances of the actresses.

TED: Yes . . . yes. Oh, dear, there's just . . . seven o' clock . . . I may have to leave early.

ASSUMPTA: During the Mass? Oh, you couldn't leave during the Mass, could you, Father?

TED: No, it's just . . .

A very old nun whispers something in Sister Assumpta's ear.

ASSUMPTA: Sister Julia says that you say a lovely Mass. She says that you said one of the nicest Masses she ever heard.

Another nun whispers something to Assumpta.

ASSUMPTA: Sister Teresa says she thought last year's Mass here was fabulous. She says she'd give it ten out of ten. And she's very hard to please. She's seen you do . . . what? Is it about fifty Masses since then?

Teresa nods. She looks very embarrassed.

ASSUMPTA: Show Father Crilly the photographs, Teresa. You'll like these, Father . . .

Teresa takes some photographs out of her bag. She hands them meekly to Assumpta, who shows them to Ted.

ASSUMPTA: There's you at last year's Mass here . . . and that's you doing the Mass the year before . . . And . . . what's that? . . . your sister-in-law's funeral . . . my personal favourite . . .

We see that all the photographs are incredibly dull shots of Ted saying Mass. They are all more or less identical, except for one, which has Ted sporting a ridiculous-looking, bushy beard.

ASSUMPTA: That's when you had the beard . . . Sister Julia was saying the other day that you're the best priest that she's ever seen saying Mass. And she's been to Mass about half a million times.

TED (*flipping quickly through the photographs*): Really?

ASSUMPTA: Actually, Father, you couldn't sign a few for us?

TED: The photographs?

ASSUMPTA: Yes.

TED: Ah . . . all right . . .

He produces a pen and starts signing them. We see that some of the nuns are putting their hands up.

ASSUMPTA: Could you put on my one, 'To Sister Assumpta'?

TED: Sure . . .

ASSUMPTA: Father, Sister Margaret wants to ask a question . . .

TED: Yes?

MARGARET: Where do you get your ideas for your sermons?

ASSUMPTA: Where do you get your ideas for your sermons?

TED: Oh, just . . . overheard conversations, the News, whatever. Listen, I have to be honest here . . . I mightn't be able to—

Two nuns have their hands up.

ASSUMPTA: Sister Julia, do you have a question?

JULIA: What's your most embarrassing moment saying Mass?

ASSUMPTA: What's your most embarrassing moment saying Mass?

TED: Well, I suppose it was the time I forgot my sister-in-law's name . . . That got me a bit hot under the collar.

Everyone laughs kindly.

TED: Anyway, listen . . . the thing is, I might not be able to say this evening's.

Very pregnant pause.

ASSUMPTA: What, Father?

TED: I have something quite important to do.

ASSUMPTA: Not more important than saying Mass, surely?

TED: It's just that someone I know very well is . . . dying.

ASSUMPTA: Oh dear. Is it serious?

TED: Yes. In this particular case, the person who's dying is quite seriously ill. It's a good friend of ours . . .

The door opens and Dougal wheels Father Jack in.

JACK: Nuns! Reverse! Reverse! Reverse! Reverse!

Dougal immediately wheels Jack back out through the doorway. After a moment, he returns.

ASSUMPTA: Hello, Father McGuire! Father Crilly's just been telling us about your friend dying.

DOUGAL: Who's that, Ted?

TED: Oh, old Jim.

DOUGAL: Is he dying? Poor old Jim. He won't like that.

TED: Oh, he's terribly down.

Pause.

DOUGAL: Wait a second . . . Jim Halpin?

TED: Yes.

DOUGAL: I was just talkin' to him and he didn't say anything about it.

TED: Oh, well, that's Jim. Brave is not the word.

DOUGAL: He's just outside. Hold on, I'll get him.

TED: What?! What's he doing outside? He . . . he should be home in bed.

DOUGAL: I met him earlier. He wanted a lend of some sugar. Jim! C'mere for a mo', will you?

TED: Dougal, at this moment, the man needs peace. Don't—

Jim enters the room.

TED: Hello, Jim.

JIM: Hello, Father. Hello, Sisters.

DOUGAL: Jim, you never told me you were ill.

JIM: What? I had a cold a few weeks back.

DOUGAL: A cold? Ted said you were dying.

JIM: Dying? Oh, no. I don't think so, anyway.

Everyone looks at Ted.

TED: Ah . . . well, I was talking to Doctor Sinnot the other day, and he said that you . . . that you might be dying. He wasn't a hundred per cent sure himself, now. So don't go worrying yourself unnecessarily.

JIM: God almighty! I'd better give him a call.

He moves towards the telephone.

TED: I wouldn't go calling him, Jim.

JIM: Why not?

TED: He can't use the phone. He's . . . gone deaf.

DOUGAL: Doctor Sinnot's gone deaf, Ted? That's terrible!

TED: It is, all right.

Dougal sees something through the window.

DOUGAL: O'ho, wait a second, Ted! There he is now!

Dougal opens the window.

DOUGAL: Doctor Sinnot! Doctor Sinnot! (*Turns to Ted.*) He heard that all right, Ted. Doctor! C'mere for a second!

TED: Actually, wait . . . I've just remembered. Jim's actually not dying, and Doctor Sinnot's not deaf. I was thinking of two completely different people.

ASSUMPTA: Oh . . . so you will be able to do the Mass tonight, Father.

TED: I will, yes. Thanks to Father Dougal for clearing up that little misunderstanding.

He puts a friendly arm around Dougal's shoulders. Pause.

DOUGAL: Ted . . . Ted, you're hurting me . . .

SCENE 13 INT./DAY 2
SET: SACRISTY
Dougal is helping Ted get into his vestments.

TED: All right, listen, Dougal, I'm going to have to go straight after this, so you'll have to take care of the nuns.

DOUGAL: Fair enough, Ted . . . What'll I do with them?

TED: Whatever you want . . . Just try not to kill them or anything.

DOUGAL: Ha, ha! No chance of that, Ted!

TED: Remember Sister Janita?

DOUGAL: Oh, right . . . That was a bit too close for comfort, all right.

TED: Well, just be careful this time. (*Looks at his watch.*) . . . Oh, God . . . Right, are they all in there?

Dougal looks through the door into the church.

DOUGAL: They are. Like peas in a pub.

TED: Pod. Right. See you later.

Dougal leaves the sacristy. Ted takes a deep breath, then walks out into the church. The door swings open wide, and then closes slowly. We see the door closing, and as we do, we hear Ted's muffled voice coming from without. Then we hear the nuns say something simultaneously. Then Ted says something. The door is just about to click shut when Ted opens it and comes charging into the sacristy, tearing off his vestments. He looks pleased and focussed.

TED: Right . . .

SCENE 14 EXT./DAY 2
SET: CHURCH
Ted exits the church at top speed, taking out his car keys as he does so. He runs towards his car, but as he approaches it, we see his expression change to one of horror. We see that the two cars belonging to the nuns are blocking his car at both ends, effectively stopping it from moving anywhere. He can't believe it, especially since there is tons of room all along the road. He gets in the car and starts the engine. We see him cursing like crazy. He turns around as if to reverse. We see the back bumper edging into the front bumper of the other car. He then edges forward into the other car. He turns the wheel around many, many times, edging the car backwards. Then he turns the wheel

just a little bit more. We hear a 'crack'. Ted stops. He turns off the engine, holds the wheel and spins it as easily as one would a bicycle wheel. We see Ted, but can't hear him, and he is clearly saying 'fuck' again and again. He gets out of the car, still repeating the word. As he opens the door, we can finally hear him.

TED: Flip! Flip! Flip! Flip! Flip! Flip!

Ted starts running down the road. After a while, he hears a vehicle in the distance behind him. He stops running and holds his thumb out. We see a Renault van in the distance. He adjusts his collar so that it's clear he's a priest. The van keeps approaching. Ted takes a deep breath.

TED: Please, please, please, please, please . . .

The van keeps coming down the long, straight road. This takes a minute or so. We see Ted in the foreground, the van in the distance, getting larger by the second – rather like Omar Sharif's appearance in 'Lawrence of Arabia'. After a while, the van runs straight into Ted and knocks him on to the hood. We see Ted with his face pressed against the windscreen. Inside the van we see Tom, looking shocked. He puts on the brakes, and Ted slides off the hood and on to the road. He lies there as we hear the car door opening. Tom runs around to the front of the car.

TOM: Sorry, Father! Didn't see you there!

TED (*from the ground*): No problem, Tom. Can you give me a lift?

SCENE 15 INT./DAY 2
SET: CAR
We see the two driving along at a 'brisk' pace. Ted is holding on to the dashboard. There is no suspension in the car and Ted is being thrown about wildly. A dog is beside Ted, barking his head off. Ted is constantly trying to bring a seatbelt down around him, but it extends only about half a foot before stopping.

TED (*very, very nervous*): Ho, ho!!!

TOM (*to dog*): Headcase! Shut up! Shut up, Headcase! Shut up! Will ya shut the feck up! Shut up! Shut up!

TED: Thanks again for the lift, Tom.

TOM: No problem, Father. I just have to stop at the post office for a moment.

TED (*looks at his watch*): Well it's just, I am in a

bit of —

TOM (*stopping the car*): Won't be a second, Father. Could you hand me that parcel?

Ted gives him a long parcel.

TED: It's just — I'm supposed to be meeting someone — God, that's heavy . . .

TOM: Back in a mo', Father. Shut up, Headcase!!

Tom unbuckles his buckle, which isn't attached to a seatbelt, and puts it on the dashboard.

SCENE 15A EXT./DAY 2
SET: POST OFFICE
He leaves the car and walks into the post office. The dog continues barking. We hear three gunshots and some muffled shouting. Tom comes out of the post office carrying a bag and the long parcel.

SCENE 15B INT./DAY 2
SET: CAR
He gets into the car, putting the seatbelt back in place.

TOM: Sorry about that, Father. Right! (*To the dog.*) You! Shut up!

TED: You're not up to your old tricks again, are you, Tom?

TOM: No, no, Father. It's my money, I just didn't want to fill out the forms.

The car rips off at top speed.

SCENE 16 EXT./NIGHT 2
SET: COTTAGE
Blackness. We hear Tom's van pulling up and a loud crash!!

SCENE 17 EXT./NIGHT 2
SET: COTTAGE
Ted appears at the doorway, looking fairly dishevelled. He tries to tidy himself as best he can. The door opens. Polly stands there, smiling. She looks devastating in a slinky, black, low-cut dress.

POLLY: Father Curley! You came!

Ted starts to reply, takes in Polly's appearance, and then can't say anything.

POLLY: C'mon and have a drink. What would

you like. Sherry? I think I've got everything you might want in here.

Ted can't say anything. He follows her into the living room, a huge smile on his face. When he gets in, however, his smile dies. In the room we see Dougal, Jack, the nuns and a few assorted guests milling about, drinking, etc.

DOUGAL: Ted, Ted! Over here!

Ted moves over to Dougal and the nuns.

DOUGAL: This is great, isn't it?

TED: What are you doing here?

DOUGAL: What? Well . . . you know, we were invited . . .

TED: Invited? . . .

DOUGAL: Same as you, Ted. Can't have a housewarming on your own, can you, Ted?

TED (*massively disappointed*): No . . . no, I suppose you can't . . .

Assumpta approaches Ted.

ASSUMPTA (*coldly*): Very short Mass tonight, Father. We were all a bit disappointed, weren't we, Sisters?

She looks at the other nuns. They all look very unfriendly, especially Teresa, who stares at Ted with a look of disgust.

ASSUMPTA: We mightn't be back next year. They say Father Clippit does a good long Mass. Three hours, he does, on a good night, since his stroke. That's value for money.

TED: Well, Sister, you see . . .

ASSUMPTA (*looks conspicuously at her watch*): Oh, sorry, Father. I'm in a hurry.

She walks off. Ted looks up to see Polly engaged in deep conversation with the old nun. Dougal is struggling with a huge bag of family-sized crisps.

DOUGAL: God, how do you get these open?

He crushes the sides of the bag and it explodes, showering a downcast Ted with crisps. Fade out.

SCENE 17A INT./NIGHT 2
SET: COTTAGE
We fade back in as everyone is leaving the party. Polly stands beside Ted. The nuns file out past them.

TED: I'll see you back in . . .

ASSUMPTA: Hrrmmphhh . . .

Jack walks past. He looks very strange, as if a rubber raft has inflated inside his jacket. Ted stops him.

TED: Now, Father . . .

Ted reaches inside Jack's jacket and starts to remove bottles of whiskey, six-packs, and some more bottles of various different types of alcohol. Ted puts the booty on a nearby table. Jack moves off grumpily and Ted starts to follow him out, when he is stopped by Polly.

POLLY: Father, before you go, could I have a quick word?

TED (*brightens*): Oh . . . right . . . (*To Dougal.*) Dougal, you go on ahead, I'll see you in a while . . .

DOUGAL: Right so, Ted.

Dougal leaves. Ted closes the door after him. He turns to see Polly sitting down on the sofa. She pats the space beside her and Ted sits down there.

TED: So . . .

POLLY: Would you like a drink, Father Curley?

TED: Oh, yes . . .

Polly goes to the drinks cabinet and pours them both drinks. She walks back to Ted and hands him his.

POLLY: It was nice talking to you today, Father.

TED: Well, if you can't talk to a priest, who can you talk to? We're taught how to listen. Not that we had 'listening classes' or anything! It's not as if we didn't know how to listen, already. Because that's just being there and someone talking to you . . . which is, you know, quite easy . . . unless you're deaf . . . not a lot of work involved there . . . no swotting for exams with the old listening . . .

POLLY: Father, remember I was telling you that I had reached a crossroads in my life.

TED: Yes, yes, I do.

POLLY: Well, what do you think I should do? I need advice.

TED (*puts on his 'caring priest voice'*): . . . Is it a busy crossroads at all?

POLLY: You, know, Father, that's interesting. I think one road leads back to where I was. And that's a busy road. A glamorous road. Overflowing with traffic and people and bright lights. And the other road is a quiet country road with serenity and peace and fulfilment.

TED: I see.

POLLY: Which one would you choose, Father?

TED: Ah, that's an easy one.

POLLY: Yes, Father. The choice is obvious . . .

TED: Bright lights! Glamour! Film premières! . . .

POLLY: Well, I was thinking . . .

TED (*smiling*): Parties! Cocaine busts! Las Vegas! . . .

POLLY: No . . . Father? Father?

TED (*smiling in a faraway manner*): Hmm? Sorry?

POLLY: Father, what I wanted to say was . . . I know I've made the right choice!

TED: I know you have, Polly! And I'm with you all the way!

POLLY: I'm going to become a nun!

Pause.

TED: Oh . . . feck!

POLLY: What, Father?

TED: Feck! Feck! Fecking great news! Just . . . fecking . . . marvellous!

POLLY (*continuing enthusiastically*): I was talking to Sister Julia earlier. She's ninety-seven years old. Did you ever wonder what it would be like to be a ninety-seven-year old nun, Father?*

TED (*can't think what to say*): No.*

POLLY: She's ninety-seven. She's deaf. She's half-blind, she's never been with a man in her life, and she's one of the most joyful people I've ever met.*

TED: Oh . . . yes. Although it's not obvious at first, I suppose. She's not exactly Mr Motivator.*

POLLY: Father, thank you.*

TED: Eh . . . *

POLLY: For helping to show me that the religious life is the one for me.*

Pause.

TED: Are you absolutely sure you're making the right decision? Don't you want to give that other road just a few more miles?*

POLLY: I'm heading off tomorrow, Father. I'm not going to leave it a day longer.*

TED (*very disappointed*): Oh . . . *

POLLY: I'll be sorry to leave Craggy Island. It's silly I know. I've only been here a day! But I'll always remember you. When I look into my Bible in twenty years' time, I'll probably still be thinking about . . . Father Ted Curley.

TED: Crilly.

POLLY: What?

TED: Father Ted Crilly. (*He offers her his hand.*) How are you? Now, I'd better be off.

He stands up and walks out of shot. Polly looks after him, confused.

SCENE 18 INT./NIGHT 2
SET: PAROCHIAL HOUSE
Ted comes into the room, looking at his copy of Polly's book. He lets it drop on to the table. Jack is laughing wildly at the sight of Dougal, who has his head stuck down the back of the sofa.

TED: Oh . . . Dougal, not again.

DOUGAL (*muffled*): Sorry, Ted. I was looking for change.

Ted sighs.

TED: Ah, well . . . back to the everyday grind . . .

He starts trying to pull Dougal out of the chair. Roll credits.

THE END

---

*We deleted these lines from the final version.

GRANT UNTO HIM ETERNAL REST

GRAHAM: This was the first episode to be conceived, and it contains the three scenes with which we presented *Father Ted* to Hat Trick. If I remember correctly, they were the scene where Ted enters the bedroom to find Jack dead, the scene with the monkey priest and the crying priest, and a portion of the mausoleum scene at the end. I always say that the reason Jack had so few words in his vocabulary is because he started off his life by being dead, so even 'Feck! Drink! Arse! Girls!' is quite chatty for him.

Now, I know how difficult this might be to believe, but it wasn't until the show was being edited that someone pointed out the similarity between Ted discovering Jack's body and a similiar scene in *Fawlty Towers*. It's terribly similar, but I swear it wasn't a conscious lift. Furthermore, if we were going to deliberately copy another show, I hope we wouldn't be stupid enough to plagiarise the all-time great British sitcom.

Perhaps because of it being the first one we wrote, Ted and Dougal behave in slightly uncharacteristic ways here. The reflective moment in the mausoleum when Dougal and Ted discuss their beliefs is unusual, especially when Ted recites James Joyce. And towards the end Ted and Dougal are on the verge of going out of character when they leave the room to buy floor polish, the substance that 'killed' Jack in the first place. In the early days of a sitcom, when you're still insecure about whether it's funny or not, it's always tempting to make someone behave out of character for the sake of a gag. It's not too bad, as these things go, but I hope I wouldn't do it now.

ARTHUR: This was quite an easy episode to write and was probably helped by the fact that it's a very old-fashioned idea: beneficiaries of a will having to do something unusual in order to inherit the money. Dougal's 'Last Rites' speech features references to Costacurta, Baggio and Roberto – Ardal and myself were big fans of Channel 4's coverage of Italian football. The character of the monkey priest was born entirely out of a desire to see a man walk into a room with another man, holding his hand limply and walking like a gibbon. Like Father Hernandez in *The Passion of Saint Tibulus*, he seems to be able to make himself understood. It's almost as if priests are a sort of species in *Father Ted*; it doesn't matter what they're doing or saying, other priests can always understand them.

PART ONE

SCENE 1 INT./MORNING 1
SET: PAROCHIAL HOUSE

Camera centres on Dougal, then pulls back to reveal him sitting beside a nun, Sister Monica. She is a youngish, respectable, Dana type. There is a slight, embarrassed pause.

DOUGAL: So, then. You're a nun?

Ted walks into the room.

TED: Right, Sister Monica, I've left your bags in the hall. I thought before we leave you to the boat, we might go and see the Holy Stone.

MONICA: The what?

TED: The Holy Stone of Clonrichert.

DOUGAL: Oh, great!

TED: Yes, it's good to go now 'cause there'll be no tourists. Although that's a pity in a way, 'cause when the tourists are here there's a van that sells ice-cream and fizzy drinks and all that. And sometimes the local shop gets in these magnificent souvenir combs.

DOUGAL: Yes, they're fantastic combs. (*He produces a comb.*) I got this one last year. You can see there they've written 'I Saw The Holy Stone of Clonrichert'.

The nun smiles politely and nods.

TED: The Stone's great, though. We've seen it, I think, about three hundred times.

MONICA: Well, why not. It'd round off the weekend.

TED: If you thought the ludo night was exciting, then this'll drive you over the edge! It's all been leading up to the Holy Stone . . .

MONICA: What's so holy about it anyway, Father?

TED: Ah, it's just a general kind of holiness. Father Dougal stood beside it for about ten minutes once and he got a marvellous sense of serenity.

DOUGAL: Yes, I got a great buzz off it.

MONICA: Why is it called the Holy Stone of Clonrichert? I thought Clonrichert was in Fermanagh . . .

TED: It is. The Stone used to be up there all

right, but apparently it wasn't doing great business. So! A treat in store for you!

MONICA: Yes . . . I . . . wonderful. I'll just freshen up.

She leaves the room. Dougal waits until she's gone, then turns to Ted.

DOUGAL: She'll be putting on make-up, I suppose. Impress the lads.

TED (*discreetly*): Ah, no. She's probably gone to the toilet or something.

DOUGAL: Aren't nuns great, though, Ted? It's good because you don't feel as nervous with them as you do with real women.

TED: Oh, you're right there.

DOUGAL: Even though I only got the courage to talk to her a minute ago it's nice to have a nun around. Gives the place a bit of glamour, you know?

TED: Yes . . . a woman's touch . . .

Dougal looks puzzled at this.

TED: Anyway, listen, I'll just go and rouse Jack, tell him we're off.

Ted leaves the room. Dougal takes out his comb, reads the inscription again and starts running it through his hair. Monica comes back in. Dougal smiles at her. There's a pause, as Dougal searches for something to say.

DOUGAL (*conversationally*): Ted says you were touching him.

Reaction shot of Monica.

SCENE 2 INT./MORNING 1
SET: JACK'S BEDROOM
Jack's bedroom is a mess. Dust and cobwebs everywhere, stains on the bedspread. Paintings on the wall covered in so much dust that you can't make them out. Clothes strewn here and there, etc. Father Jack Hackett sits in his chair, staring lifelessly at the wall. He may very well be dead. There is a knock on the door. Ted opens the door and marches in purposefully.

TED: Father Jack! Are you all right there? Ready for another day?

He walks into the room and absent-mindedly starts picking things up.

TED: You really should let Mrs Doyle clean up in here . . . Well, you're looking a lot better today, anyway. A good night's rest always does you the world of good, doesn't it?

He sits in a chair beside Jack and leans towards him.

TED: We're off with Sister Monica now, so when you get dressed, could you ask Mrs Doyle to have dinner ready for about five? We'll be back before then, anyway. Ah, but just in case the milkman calls, the money is under the statue of Our Lord being embarrassed by the Romans. All right, then?

He then walks into an adjoining room. The other door opens and Dougal comes in. He notices Jack.

DOUGAL (*quietly*): Morning, Father.

There is no response. As Ted talks, Dougal walks over to Jack and examines him closely. He waves a hand in front of his face, then steps back.

TED (*offscreen*): Would you like a cup of tea before I go? I know you won't mind us leaving you alone because Dougal got the new Al Pacino video for you, *Carlito's Way.** It's probably not as violent as the ones you usually like, but, well . . . give it a go.

Ted comes out of the room carrying a teapot.

TED: Dougal. What are you doing?

---

*Carlito's Way was changed to *Reservoir Dogs* in the final version. In fact, *Carlito's Way* is nowhere near a violent enough film for this joke to work. We think we picked it because we'd seen it the night before we wrote it!

DOUGAL: This looks very bad, Ted.

TED: What?

DOUGAL: He's very drunk.

TED: Still? He must've been at it all night . . . (*Looking around.*) Where does he hide it?

DOUGAL: I haven't seen him this bad since that wedding in Clones. Do you remember, Ted? Didn't he disappear off with Sister Concepta?

TED: Oh, God, yes . . . The Blue Nun.

DOUGAL (*notices something*): I think it's worse than that, Ted . . .

Dougal raises a bottle of floor-polish. He turns it over and shakes it. It's empty.

TED: Oh, Goddddd . . .

He holds the teapot out to Dougal.

TED: Hold this. (*To Jack.*) Now, Father, this is very bad. Do you not remember the last time? With the Windolene?

Dougal is holding the teapot not by the handle, but around the sides.

TED (*rousing him*): Father Jack. Father Jack, are you there?

DOUGAL: Ted . . .

TED: Imagine the damage floor-polish would do to you. Dear God . . .

DOUGAL: Ted . . .

TED: What is it?

DOUGAL: I'm in tremendous pain, Ted.

TED: Put it down, then! God, Dougal. Right, we'd better get him. Dougal, get him under the arms . . . Father Jack, come on now, we can't let Sister Monica see you like this.

They lift him out of the chair, and start to walk him around the room slowly.

TED: Come on, Father, big steps . . .

Suddenly, Monica comes into the room.

MONICA: What's the matter?

TED: Ah, Sister Monica, there you are. Ah, it just takes Father Jack's motor a little time to get going in the mornings.

MONICA: He doesn't look well.

TED: No, he's grand. We're just taking him on a little trip to the toilet. Will we go on a little trip to the toilet, Father?

MONICA: Put him down there in that chair and we'll have a look at him.

TED: Well, he doesn't like to be fussed over.

MONICA: I really think you should let me look at him.

Ted and Dougal settle Jack back in the chair. Monica picks up his wrist to feel his pulse.

MONICA (*alarmed*): Oh, Holy Mother of God . . . he's dead!

DOUGAL: What's the problem there, Sister?

MONICA: Father Jack, he's dead! There's no pulse, and he's stone cold.

TED: Ah, come on, Father Jack, you're not dead are you?

MONICA: He's very definitely dead.

TED (*sternly*): Come on now, Father! The joke's over!

MONICA: Father, he's gone. I think you should go and get help. Father Dougal here can give him the sacraments.

TED (*walking out*): Well, I'll call Dr. Sinnot, but I really think we're making a load of fuss over nothing.

Reaction shot of Dougal looking very worried. When he's gone, Monica blesses herself and bows her head. Dougal looks at her, then looks at the body, then at her again. She raises her head slightly, looks at Dougal. Dougal smiles at her, waves.

MONICA (*whispers*): The last rites, Father . . .

DOUGAL: Oh! Of course. Right. Shouldn't we wait for Ted . . . ?

MONICA: There's no need, really. Is there any anointing oil?

DOUGAL: No, I think himself drank it last week.

Reaction shot as Monica takes this in.

DOUGAL: You sure you wouldn't like to do the honours . . . ?

MONICA: What?

DOUGAL: No, of course you wouldn't. I suppose . . . I suppose I'm wearing the trousers as far as this goes . . .

He addresses Father Jack.

DOUGAL: 'We are gathered here today, to join two . . . people . . .' No, wait a second . . . that's not it . . .

Slight pause. Monica is pretending not to notice. Dougal looks very panicky. Finally, he goes for it.

DOUGAL: Well, Father. Best of luck. (*He looks expectantly at Monica.*) Oh. There's more. Of course . . . well, ah . . . sorry I didn't get a chance to see you off . . . I don't know whether I should be looking at you here or, or up there. I'll look up there . . .

Reaction shot of Monica. Dougal is now addressing the roof.

DOUGAL: Anyway, you're up there anyway. With Our Lord, and Stalin and Bob Marley and the rest of them. And of course my own parents. Actually I'd like to take this opportunity to say hello to them. Hello Mammy and Daddy. Hope they're looking after you up there.

MONICA: The Latin, Father . . .

DOUGAL: Oh, right! Of course . . . ah, totus tuus, minimus, cannus, costacurta, baggio, roberto et dino . . .

Ted comes back.

MONICA: Did you ring the doctor, Father?

TED: Yes. Well, it looks bad, all right. I gave Doctor Sinnot the symptoms over the phone, and he says he's probably dead, all right. The pulse not being there is bad enough, but the heart stopping is the real danger sign.

DOUGAL: That happened to my uncle and he was fine afterwards.

TED: His heart stopped? For how long?

DOUGAL: A week.

TED: A week? Really? And he was fine afterwards?

DOUGAL (*thinks a second*): Actually, no. Now I think of it, he died.

Pregnant pause. *

MONICA (*to Ted*): Ah, Father Dougal's just giving him the last rites.*

TED (*horrified*): Oh Jesus! Actually, maybe I should take over!*

Ted and Monica pray over the body. Dougal watches them, slightly impatient. He looks at his watch. *

DOUGAL: . . . Ted . . . the Holy Stone closes at three, Ted.*

TED (*fierce whisper*): Dougal!*

Pause. *

DOUGAL (*under breath*): . . . Jawohl, mein Führer . . .*

SCENE 3 INT./DAY 1
SET: PAROCHIAL HOUSE
The room is very quiet. About six priests stand around, slowly eating sandwiches and drinking tea. Monica is also present. The mood is solemn, but friendly. The priests are (1) a black 'Shaft' type priest who resembles an extra from a blaxploitation movie of the 1970s, with large handlebar moustache and huge Afro haircut; (2) a nervous priest who moves like a small bird; (3) an elderly priest who has no distinguishing characteristics; (4) another elderly priest; and, finally, Ted and Dougal. Mrs Doyle walks from cleric to cleric, a tray of tiny sandwiches in her hands. Her mood is sunny, as usual. In another part of the room lies Jack in his coffin. Meanwhile, Monica is talking to the Shaft priest.

MONICA: . . . is absolutely great to see. I mean the level of commitment amongst the African Church in bringing the faith to the people is just wonderful. It's marvellous, isn't it?

SHAFT PRIEST (*heavy accent*): Sure, I wouldn't know. I'm from Galway.

He walks away. Cut to Mrs Doyle offering the elderly priest – Father Paul Cleary – a tiny sandwich from her tray.

MRS DOYLE: Will you have a sandwich, Father?

---

* We deleted these lines from the final version.

CLEARY: No, thanks, Mrs Doyle, I'm fine.

MRS DOYLE: Have a try. They're tomato and jam.

CLEARY: No, no. Thanks, anyway.

MRS DOYLE: Ah, go on, have one. They're only small.

CLEARY: No, thanks, I'm grand.

MRS DOYLE: Are you sure you won't have one?

CLEARY: No, thanks, Mrs Doyle. I ate before I came.

MRS DOYLE: Would you like one for later? I can put one in a bag.

CLEARY: Ah, no, thanks —

MRS DOYLE (*produces a tiny plastic bag*): Here's a little bag you can take one home in. You can eat it later, or you can eat it now, if you want. Whatever suits you.

CLEARY: Well . . .

MRS DOYLE: Ah, you'll have it now!

CLEARY: Ah, sure, I might as well!

Cut to Ted beckoning to Mrs Doyle.

TED: Mrs Doyle!

Cut back to Cleary reaching for a sandwich, but Mrs Doyle has already set off in Ted's direction.

TED: I think Father Mackey wants a sandwich!

Cut to the second elderly priest hiding in a corner of the room. He is desperately trying to signal to Ted that he doesn't want Mrs Doyle to come over. Too late. She starts off towards him. We see the priest trying to hide behind his hand.

MRS DOYLE (*approaching him*): Father Mackey, will you have a sandwich? . . .

The door flies open and two men enter. The first, Father Jim Sutton, a man around the same age as Ted, has obviously been crying. The second, Father Fintan Fay, who has a limp grasp of Father Jim's hand, walks in a crouching position, like a monkey. The monkey priest is very old.

JIM (*close to tears*): I'm terribly sorry I'm late . . . Ted . . . the car . . . the car broke down . . .

TED (*quietly*)**:** That's all right. (*Taking the monkey priest's hand.*) Father Fay, how are you?

MONKEY PRIEST: Egghh, eghhh, ngaaa, egghhh.

TED: He did. It was very quick.

MONKEY PRIEST: Ngaaaa?

TED: Ah, yes, I suppose so . . .

JIM: Oh, Christ, Ted!

He falls into Ted's arms.

JIM: Why him, Ted? Why is it always the good ones?

He looks up to heaven and punches his fist into the air.

JIM: You Bastard!

TED (*very concerned*)**:** Now, Father Sutton . . .

Sutton falls to his knees and starts to weep uncontrollably.

JIM: He could have been Pope, Ted. The feckin' Jesuits, they have it all tied up . . .*

TED: Yes . . .

Ted leads Jim to the casket.

JIM: Imagine, Ted. A Polish Pope! It should have been Jack! But it's not what you know, is it? It's who you know.

TED: It's sad all right. Ah, but look at him. He looks so serene.

Shot of Jack in the casket looking as scary and ugly as ever. Sutton is still distraught.

JIM: Oh, God . . .

He starts banging his fists on the side of the coffin, becoming increasingly hysterical each time.

JIM: No! No! No! No! He's dead, Ted! We'll never see him again!

TED: Well, we'll see him in the next world . . .

JIM (*very sceptically*)**:** Oh yeah, sure.

Meanwhile, the monkey priest has climbed halfway up the bookcase.

JIM: Oh, God, no! Get him down, get him

down!

TED: There's nothing of interest to you up there, Father!

Scenes of chaos then ensue as the priests attempt to get the monkey priest down. He starts throwing books at them. They duck for cover. Fade out as the noise continues.

SCENE 4 INT./EARLY EVENING 1
SET: PAROCHIAL HOUSE
Dougal has just finished putting the last book back in its place. The room now looks back to normal. Dougal turns and notices Jack's empty chair. He looks at it nervously. Gradually, he edges towards the chair. He looks around, and then sits down gingerly in it. He smiles and surveys the room, pleased with himself. He then starts doing an exaggerated, childish, squint-eyed impression of Father Jack holding a glass and smoking.

DOUGAL: Ehhhh . . . give me lots of drink . . . ehhhh . . .

Ted and Monica enter the room while Dougal is thus engaged. Ted walks over to stand directly in front of Dougal. Dougal doesn't notice because his eyes are closed.

DOUGAL: Uhhhhh . . . Feck off, Ted! . . . You big fool . . . ehhh . . .

TED: What are you doing, Dougal?

DOUGAL (*jumping a mile*)**:** Whaaa!

TED: I don't think you should be getting up to that kind of nonsense. Now, come on, up you get.

Dougal stands up, looking sheepish.

---

* This is complete nonsense – another example of our painstaking research procedure.

TED: We should leave the chair idle for a while. (*He looks at the chair.*) Would y'ever look at that. The seat's completely bald. (*Rubbing it.*) Smooth as a baby's behind.

DOUGAL (*big smile*): You'd know all about that, Ted!

TED (*shocked*): What?

DOUGAL: When you're baptising them. The babies.

TED: Oh! I'm just going to give Sister Monica a lift to the boat.

MONICA: Thank you, Father.

TED: O'ho, no, it's the least we could do. You were always terribly good to Father Jack. It's the least we could do.

Mrs Doyle knocks lightly on the door before sticking her head in.

MRS DOYLE: Father Crilly? There's a woman here to see you.

TED: A woman, Mrs Doyle? You mean a nun.

MRS DOYLE: No, no, it's a woman. A young woman. Very well turned out.

DOUGAL: I'll be off then!

Before Dougal can escape, the woman in question strides confidently into the room. She looks like someone out of 'LA Law'. Her name is Laura Sweeney.

SWEENEY: Hello, Father Crilly?

TED: Yes?

SWEENEY: I'm from Corless, Corless and Sweeney.

TED: Oh, we're fine for coal, thanks.

SWEENEY: Oh, no, it's nothing to do with coal. My name is Laura Sweeney. (*She shakes hands with Ted.*) This must be Father McGuire!

Dougal stares at the floor, his face bright red.

DOUGAL: . . . Hhhhrhhhmm . . . uh . . . mmh . . .

SWEENEY: Anyway, I think you'd both better sit down. I've got a bit of a shock for you.

TED: Before you say anything, I just want to assure you that that was a routine relocation of funds . . .

SWEENEY: No, no . . .

TED: . . . The money was simply resting in my account for a while before I moved it on to—

SWEENEY: No, you don't understand. This is about Father Hackett. Please, sit down and I'll explain everything to you.

Dougal and Ted sit down. Miss Sweeney produces an official-looking document.

SWEENEY: It may come as a surprise for you to learn that Father Hackett left a will.

TED: Really? What does it say?

SWEENEY: Well . . . if I may . . .

As she reads from it, we stay on Ted and Dougal.

SWEENEY: 'I, Father Jack Hackett, being of sound mind and body, leave my entire fortune to Father Ted Crilly and Father Dougal McGuire to be distributed equally amongst them . . .'

TED: What?!

He stands up and reads over her shoulder. Dougal looks at Ted expectantly. Monica appears in the doorway, two heavy suitcases in her hands.

MONICA: Eh, I'll be off now, then . . .

No response.

MONICA: I'll make my way to the boat myself, then? . . .

TED (*without looking at her*): . . . Yeah, yeah . . .

MONICA: Bye, Fathers . . .

They don't hear her. Monica leaves, her suitcase weighing her down.

TED: Dougal! Look at this! He's left us some money!

DOUGAL: That's very nice of him. How much?

TED (*reads*): Half . . . half a million.

Ted faints and falls out of shot. Dougal grabs the paper before he does so.

DOUGAL: Half a million pounds!? Each?!! (*Disappointed.*) Oh . . . no, between us. It's only a quarter of a million each, Ted. Ted?

Dougal sees that Ted has fainted.

SCENE 5 INT./EARLY EVENING 1
SET: PAROCHIAL HOUSE
*Ted is lying on a sofa. Miss Sweeney and Dougal sit
on the other chairs in the room. Ted is pressing a
damp cloth to his head. Miss Sweeney is putting
papers into her case. Mrs Doyle is nearby,
pretending to dust some shelves so as to be able to
listen.*

SWEENEY: . . . So that's that. It looks like
you're going to be very rich men . . .

TED: Grand.

SWEENEY: There's just that sole requirement,
which I'm surprised Father Hackett didn't
discuss with you himself . . .

TED: Oh? . . .

SWEENEY: When is the funeral again?

DOUGAL: Again? Well, we haven't had the
first one yet. I didn't think there'd be two
funerals.

SWEENEY: No. Sorry, maybe I didn't make
myself clear . . .

TED: It's tomorrow morning.

SWEENEY: Right, well, you know about
Father Hackett's terrible fear of being buried
alive.

DOUGAL: There's no chance of that now, is
there? He's dead.

TED: Oh, God, yes, he was terribly frightened
of that. That's why he wouldn't do Confession
– he didn't like enclosed spaces. Of course, he
also just didn't want to do it . . .

DOUGAL: A load of people telling you their
sins . . . Who'd be bothered with that?

Ted looks at Dougal.

SWEENEY: Well, Father Hackett's fear was so
great that he stipulated that you two must
spend the night before the burial with him.
Just in case he wakes up.

TED: Well, that's hardly likely, is it?

SWEENEY (*chuckles*): Of course, but
nonetheless, it's in the will. In order to claim
the inheritance, you and Father McGuire have

to spend the night with Father Hackett.

TED: OK, OK. Right. Well, I suppose it's the
least we can do. Anyway, we can discuss it
with the solicitor.

A pregnant pause ensues.

SWEENEY (*testily*): I am the solicitor.

*Another pregnant pause. Ted smiles at Dougal, then
back at the solicitor.*

TED (*incredulous*): No, you're not . . .

SWEENEY: I'm sorry, but I am the senior
partner in Corless, Corless and Sweeney.

TED: Now, come on, now . . . just because
we're from the island, you think you can have
a bit of fun with us.

SWEENEY: I assure you —

TED: All right, all right, very funny. The big
thickos from the island. But we're not as thick
as we look. Eh? Are we, eh?

DOUGAL (*laughing*): No way, José!

SWEENEY: Wait a second – why do you
think I've been talking to you for the last hour
and a half?

TED: Look, you're a lovely girl, but I really
think we should talk to the solicitor.

DOUGAL: If you're a solicitor, then I'm Boy
George.

There is another frozen moment.

SCENE 6 INT./EVENING 1*
SET: PAROCHIAL HOUSE
*Dougal is filling a flask with hot water. He is
singing Culture Club's 'Karma Chameleon' to
himself. Ted enters the room with a rucksack and a
pile of candles. He has a bandage over his eye.*

TED: You ready yet, Dougal?

DOUGAL: Not yet, Ted. Be with you in a
moment. How's your head?

TED: Oh, not too bad. She was aiming for my
eye, I think. It's true what they say, though,
about these career women being aggressive.

---

*We relocated this scene to the crypt, glued
the next scene to it and lost the tea-in-the-
face gag in the final version.

DOUGAL: Yes, she was very aggressive, wasn't she, Ted?

TED: And the language out of her! You wouldn't hear that from a docker.

DOUGAL: Ah, you would, Ted. They use very bad language.

TED: Effing this, and effing that.

DOUGAL: It was worse than that, Ted. She was saying fu—

TED: Now, Dougal! But anyway, who would have thought Jack had half a million pounds?

DOUGAL: And he never said a word about it.

TED: . . . There it was, lying in a bank account all these years . . .

DOUGAL: But . . . explain to me again, where'd he get it in the first place?

TED: As far as I can understand it, he was just an astute saver. He tried to avoid giving money to charity, he wouldn't wear trousers in the summer, so that obviously saved a couple of bob on wear and tear, all sorts of little savings all over the place. It all adds up, you know.

Ted leaves the room. Dougal puts a teabag into the thermos, closes the lid and shakes it roughly. He

then opens the lid and searches for the teabag with a fork. He rattles the fork around.

DOUGAL: C'mere, y'bollicks . . .*

He slowly lifts the thermos up, looking into it as he does so. He continues to lift it, until suddenly a cascade of tea explodes into his face.

DOUGAL: Arrrrggghh!!!

END OF PART ONE

* * *

PART TWO

SCENE 7 INT./NIGHT 1
SET: CRYPT
Dougal's face is as red as a lobster. He and Ted sit on either side of an imposing coffin. Dougal looks at Ted, hoping for him to begin a conversation. Ted is deep in his own thoughts. Dougal thinks for a second. He then reaches in his pocket and takes out his comb. He reads the inscription again. Then he combs his hair. He puts the comb away. He looks to Ted again. No sign of life. He thinks for a second, then takes the comb out again.

TED (*absently*): I suppose, though, we only really knew him in his twilight years.

We can see Dougal in the background, trying to see whom Ted's talking to.

TED: But I think we saw the best of him. A really lovely man, a true Knight of the Church . . . gentle, lovely sense of humour, patient, good natured . . .

DOUGAL: Sorry, Ted, who's this now?

Pause.

TED : Who would you say I'd be talking about at this particular moment, Dougal?

DOUGAL: I'm not sure. I didn't catch the start.

TED: Father Jack, of course!

DOUGAL: Oh, right. Yes.

TED: A great priest.

*Note that this line is completely out of character.

SCENE 7A INT./DAY X
SET: PAROCHIAL HOUSE
Shot of a bolt-upright Jack, lying stiffly on his chair, unable to bend his body so that it fits its contours. He smokes a cigarette and in his other hand holds a glass of whiskey. Cut back to Ted and Dougal.

SCENE 7B INT./NIGHT 1
SET: CRYPT

DOUGAL: First priest to denounce The Beatles.

TED: That's right.

DOUGAL: He could see what they were up to.

TED: And he loved children, of course.

DOUGAL: He did, yes.

Pause.

TED: They were terrified of him, though.

DOUGAL: Well, he had that stick. He'd be waving that stick. Maybe they thought he'd hit them.

TED: I heard that when he was teaching in Saint Colm's he was a great believer in discipline.

FLASHBACK
SCENE 8 INT./DAY X
SET: SCHOOL
Shot of a young Jack, cigarette hanging from his mouth, viciously kicking a student who lies in a foetal position on the ground.

SCENE 9 INT./NIGHT 1
SET: CRYPT

DOUGAL: Would you say he was a good teacher?

TED: A friend of mine had him, Father Jimmy Rannable. He studied under him for a couple of years. He told me once, he said, no one, no one had such a huge effect on him as Jack did.

DOUGAL: Father Jimmy Rannable . . . Oh, yeah! Whatever happened to him?

TED: Do you remember the Drumshank Massacre?

DOUGAL: Yes . . . ?

TED: That was him.

DOUGAL: Oh . . .

Pause.

TED: Another thing about Father Jack . . . He loved a bit of competition. Great sense of fair play . . .

FLASHBACK
SCENE 10 INT./DAY X
SET: PAROCHIAL HOUSE
Shot of Jack playing chess with Ted. Jack scowls at Ted and the board in a very intimidating manner. Ted gingerly picks up a piece, thinks, and places it on another square. He then leans back and gives Jack a 'what-do-you-think-of-that?' kind of look. Jack looks at the board for a moment or two, then kicks it into the air. Then he leans over and punches Ted in the face.

SCENE 11 INT./NIGHT 1
SET: CRYPT

TED: . . . And a great traditionalist. Didn't really agree with a lot of the modern thinking within the Church.

SCENE 12 INT./DAY X
SET: CLASSROOM
Shot of Jack standing beside a blackboard. There is a sheet hanging over it. Jack is obviously shouting at the top of his voice. He whisks away the sheet to reveal the word 'Hell!'. Then he throws a match into a little pot that goes up in flames. He puts his fingers to the sides of his head and does an impression of the devil. We see a classroom of very young children, crying.

SCENE 13 INT./NIGHT 1
SET: CRYPT
Ted in reflective mood. Pause.

TED: Funny . . . one moment you're there, the next . . . Someone once said, Dougal, that life is just a thin sliver of light between two immensities of darkness . . . Makes you think . . .

DOUGAL: It does, Ted . . .

Long pause.

DOUGAL: . . . About what?

TED (*angrily*): About death, Dougal, about death.

DOUGAL: That's a bit morbid, isn't it? What started you off thinking about death?

Ted buries his face in his hands. He recovers after an instant and becomes reflective again.

TED (*sighs*): Ah, well . . . it's nice to have this time with him, though. Maybe sometimes we weren't as thoughtful as we could have been. At least now we're able to spend some time with him. Treat him with the respect he deserves . . .

DOUGAL: You're right there, Ted . . . (*Pause.*) Do you fancy an oul game of charades?

TED: Why not, I suppose?!

DOUGAL: All right, you go first.

TED: Right. (*He stands up.*) Right, I've got one. I'll start with an easy one.

He begins to mime 'a film'.

DOUGAL: Fishing. Gone fishing. Something to do with boxing? One-handed boxing?

TED: No, no, Dougal, it's a film.

DOUGAL: You're not supposed to tell me, Ted.

TED: OK, OK . . . (*He begins to mime again.*)

DOUGAL: Film. One film.

TED: No, one word.

DOUGAL: Ah, come on now, Ted. You're making it a bit easy for me . . . I'm not an eejit . . . Right, one-word film . . . can't be too many of them . . . *Salem's Lot*?

Ted shakes his head. He points to his teeth.

DOUGAL: Teeth. Mouth. Tongue. Is there a film called *Tongue? Tom Tongue.*

Ted starts pretending to swim, baring his teeth as he does so.

DOUGAL: Tongue fish. Swim tongue. *Swim, Tongue Fish!* Fish. *Attack of the Giant Killing Fish?* Tongue. Tonguefish. *The Deep. Piranha. Jaws 2*?

Ted nods and points desperately at Dougal.

DOUGAL: Ah, I'm close, then. *Ghostbusters 2? Superman 2. Batman Returns. Lethal Weapon 2* . . . ah . . .

TED: It's *Jaws!* You had it!

DOUGAL: No, I had *Jaws 2*. Different film. Very different film. Different shark.

Ted glowers at Dougal. Fade to black.

SCENE 14 INT./NIGHT 1
SET: CRYPT
When we fade up again, Dougal and Ted are lying in their sleeping-bags. Ted's eyes are closed. Dougal stares up at the ceiling, looking around in a nervous manner.

DOUGAL: Ted? . . . Ted? . . . Are you still awake?

TED: Yes, yes . . .

DOUGAL: Can I ask you a question?

TED (*sighs*): Oh, not again . . . Look, Dougal, when a man and a lady are very much in love . . .

DOUGAL: No, no, I wasn't going to ask that, Ted. I was going to ask . . . do you believe in an afterlife?

TED: Do I what?

DOUGAL: Do you believe in an afterlife?

TED: Well, Dougal, what would you say? Considering that for the last twenty years I've been walking round administering the sacraments and being a general type of spiritual light in people's lives . . .

DOUGAL: You're sort of uncertain?

TED: No, in fact, I'm actually the opposite of uncertain. Generally speaking, priests tend to have a fairly strong belief in the afterlife.

DOUGAL: I wish I had your faith, Ted.

TED: Dougal, how did you get into the Church? Was it, like, collect twelve crisp packets and become a priest?

DOUGAL: It's just that at times like this, you start thinking about things. Like maybe settling down. Finding the right girl . . .*

TED: Hold on. Now, hold on. This is obviously . . .*

DOUGAL: Sometimes you wonder if there's really a God . . .*

TED: Just hold it there, Father McGuire. Look, think about it a second. How do cars work? How does a record-player work?*

DOUGAL: Well . . . I wouldn't know, exactly . . .*

TED: Well, there you go – all these things are done by God.*

DOUGAL: But, if you're wrong, Ted . . . if there's no afterlife.*

TED: Look, of course there's an afterlife. Sure, if there was no afterlife our time here on earth would be completely meaningless. We'd be just going through the motions with no hopes, and no reason for living. We'd just be like isolated planets in a lonely Godless universe . . .*

DOUGAL (*cheerily*): I suppose you're right, Ted. I feel a lot better now. Thanks very much. Goodnight!*

*Dougal snuggles into his sleeping-bag and closes his eyes. Ted does the same, but after a moment opens his eyes again and stares at the ceiling, terrified.**

---

*We deleted these lines from the final version.

SCENE 15 INT./NIGHT 1
SET: CRYPT

A blue light is starting to creep through the one window in the crypt. Dougal and Ted are still in their sleeping-bags.

DOUGAL: . . . Ted?

TED: Dougal, please let me go to sleep. The birds'll be up in a second and they'll be screeching their heads off.

DOUGAL: Oh . . . all right . . .

TED (*sighs*): What is it, then?

DOUGAL: I was just wondering. What are you going to do with your share of the money?

Ted turns around and looks at the ceiling, suddenly interested.

TED: I . . . well . . . Luckily there's a lot of great charity organisations that are always grateful for money . . . Concern, Food for Africa, St Vincent de Paul . . .

Fade out as he speaks. We hear funky music and see Ted's soft-focus fantasy.

SCENE 16 INT./NIGHT 1
SET: NIGHTCLUB
Ted is wearing sunglasses and dancing in a club with some beautiful women. They laugh and hug him. Ted laughs and jokingly raises an admonishing finger. Cut to Ted at a craps table. He throws some dice and obviously gets a seven. He jumps with joy while the women at the table go crazy, hugging and kissing him.

SCENE 17 INT./NIGHT 1
SET: CRYPT

TED: . . . Maybe a few pounds for Comic Relief . . . What's the use of money if you can't use it for good, eh, Dougal?

SCENE 18 INT./NIGHT 1
SET: CRYPT
Cut back to Dougal in the crypt, licking his lips.

TED: So, some good'll come from Jack's death.

DOUGAL: It's hard to believe he's gone.

TED: You're right there . . .

SCENE 19 EXT./DAWN 2
SET: THE ISLAND
Assorted shots of the island. Everything looks bleak but somehow beautiful, rather like the closing moments of John Huston's 'The Dead'. Over all this, we hear Ted's voiceover.

TED (*offscreen*)**:** It's beginning to snow again. The flakes, silver and dark, are falling obliquely against the lamplight. It's probably snowing all over the island – on the central plain, on the treeless hills, falling softly on the graveyards, on the crosses and headstones, upon all the living . . . and the dead.

JACK (*offscreen*)**:** Will you shut the feck up!

SCENE 20 INT./DAWN 2
SET: CRYPT

Ted jumps up in the air with shock. He spins around and sees Jack standing next to him, his burial shroud around his shoulders. Jack is holding his head as if it's about to explode.

TED: Argggghghhhhhhhhhhhhh!!!!!!!!!

Ted faints. His scream has woken Dougal, however. Dougal stands up and rushes over to Ted's prone body.

DOUGAL: Ted! Ted! What's wrong? Father Jack, what happened to him? Ted! Did you see what happened, Father Jack? What—

Dougal realises whom he's talking to and immediately passes out.

SCENE 21 INT./DAY 2
SET: PAROCHIAL HOUSE

Unpleasant close-up of Father Jack's big, fat face. He is snoring, his eyes are squeezed shut – he even sleeps in a menacing way – and he is back in his old chair. Cut to Ted, watching him with a kind of awe.

TED: So . . . there is he, risen from the dead. Just like . . . ah . . . that fella . . . E.T. (*Pause.*) Your face is looking a lot better, Dougal.

Cut to Dougal. White flakes are peeling from his face. It is also horribly puffed-up and tender-looking.*

DOUGAL: Oh, really?

TED (*not terribly convincingly*): Mmm . . .

DOUGAL: Thanks, Ted.

Jack lets rip with another loud snore.

DOUGAL: There's one thing I'm a bit confused about, though.

TED: Yes?

DOUGAL: Is Jack dead, then? Or what?

TED: Apparently not. I think the floor-polish brought about all the symptoms of death . . . such as . . . no heartbeat, rigor mortis, decomposition. But he was lucky. The effects just seemed to wear off.

DOUGAL: Well . . . it's good to have him back, isn't it, Ted?

TED (*unconvincing nod*): Mm . . .

DOUGAL: Who needs half a million pounds, anyway?

TED: Yes, our life is the spiritual life.

DOUGAL: . . . Pity, though, to think of all that money just lying about.

TED: It is, actually . . . and I can't see himself putting it to much use.

DOUGAL: It could be doing good work, couldn't it? Couldn't it, Ted?

TED: It could.

Pause.

TED: But . . . to be honest, Dougal . . . I don't like talking about it, but . . . it's just a matter of time, really . . . he's not a young man and . . . you know . . . and I suppose it won't be so bad when he's gone. The money will be some kind of comfort to us, I suppose.

DOUGAL: Well, that's something.

TED: That's right. Now . . . (*He stands.*) will you come down to the shops with me? I think we need some more floor-polish.

They walk to the door.

DOUGAL: Yes. Maybe we should get a few different brands? Just to try them out?

TED: Yes, and we can leave them around the house. So they don't get lost.

They leave the room. We hear Dougal's voice fading as he gets further away.

DOUGAL: Or just put them in Jack's room, ask him to keep an eye on them . . .

They leave the room. Close-up of Jack. He wakes up suddenly.

JACK: Drink!

He realises that no one's around and looks surly. He looks directly at the camera and scowls. Pause.

JACK: Feck OFF!!!!!!!

THE END

---

*The hot tea, remember?

hell

GRAHAM: This episode was inspired partly by the dreadful holidays my parents would take me on when I was young. I don't know what was going through their heads but we went to some really terrible places, campsites with stinky outdoor showers and a whole new range of kids to be bullied by. There's a tradition in British comedy of going on holiday to really crappy places which goes way back to the early *Carry On* films right up to *Withnail and I* and beyond. Arthur showed me the *Likely Lads* movie which, like this episode, featured a terrible caravan holiday. As we always felt that *Ted* was a sitcom in the British tradition although it was set in Ireland, it seemed appropriate to try and follow that tradition.

There was a very simple structure in this episode; it revolved around the three 'moments'– the encounters with the romantic couple which were complicated further by the arrival of Graham Norton's character, Father Noel Furlong (Arthur's inspired casting, that). We also used one of our favourite devices – that of the unbelievably obvious expositional opening, which is used when Tom learns the basics of door-opening/sewage-unloading. One reviewer commented, 'It's embarrassingly obvious what's going to happen' – and missed the point brilliantly.

The scene where Dougal can't get to grips with the difference between a small cow and a faraway cow isn't in this draft because we thought of it on location. I think it's probably the all-time most-quoted joke of all three series. It replaced the rather fine noughts and crosses gag that was great on paper, but just didn't work when filmed.

ARTHUR: I'd never met Graham Norton but I'd heard him on the radio and thought he might add something to the character. We didn't see him as being camp at first; we just liked the idea of a priest who is simply incredibly excited to be around young people, so excited that he interprets their really quite sensible lifestyles as unbelievably dangerous and exciting. He's based on someone our good friend Paul Wonderful had met. Paul's a great performer and a very, very funny man and it was really his impression of this mad priest that led to Father Noel being created. To set the record straight once and for all, Noel is not having sex with the teenagers in his charge. A lot of people thought this, including Graham Norton, but take it from us, Noel's completely asexual.

Part of this episode *was* hell for the actors. The whole sewage plot at the beginning started as an in-joke on Dermot and then backfired on him and Ardal and all of us. We'd used a rain machine in the first series (in *Entertaining Father Stone*) and Dermot was standing under it, feeling miserable, when he said jokingly, 'What are you going to do to me next? Cover me in shit, I suppose.' So we spent the next few months wondering how we could cover Ted in shit . . .When the time came, the special effect liquid shit we ended up using was freezing cold. We didn't know this and we were trying to get a funny performance out of Dermot and Ardal and they were in agony, *blinded* by the cold. We felt terrible for them; they really were in shock afterwards.

PART ONE
SCENE 1 EXT./DAY 1
SET: ROADWAY

Pre-credit sequence. A man is speaking to Tom, who is still wearing his 'I Shot JR' T-shirt, as they stand at the door to a large articulated truck. The container behind the cab is silver and cylindrical and has 'Craggy Island Sewage Works' written on it. Tom watches the man with his usual expression of incredible concentration.

MAN: Now, Tom, this is the first time you've been trusted with such a large consignment of raw sewage. Are you sure you'll be all right?

TOM: I will, yeah. Don't worry about me at all.

MAN (*pointing into truck*): And remember, Tom, this is the button that opens the doors, and this is the button that makes the sewage shoot out.

TOM: Right. That one opens the doors, and that one makes the stuff come out.

MAN: No, no, no . . . the other way around.

TOM: Right y'are!

Cut to Tom gripping the wheel of the truck and starting to drive off. Opening titles roll. We see a close-up of a 'The Holy Stone of Clonrichert' day-by-day calendar. It reads July 18. A hand comes into shot and rips it away so that it reads July 19. Cut to Ted looking at the calendar, a puzzled expression on his face.

SCENE 2 INT./DAY 1
SET: PAROCHIAL HOUSE

TED: July nineteenth . . . why does that date strike me as important?

Dougal is sitting at the table playing magnetic fishing. He lifts a fish up out of the makeshift 'pool'.

DOUGAL: Yes! (*To Ted.*) Ah, July nineteenth . . . I wouldn't know, Ted, y'big bollocks.

TED: I'm sorry?

DOUGAL: I said, I wouldn't know, Ted, you big bollocks.

TED (*beat*): Have you been reading those Roddy Doyle books again, Dougal?

DOUGAL: I have, yeah, Ted. I read all of them this morning, you big gobshite.

TED: Well, that's all very well, Dougal, but you have to remember they're just stories. Normal people like us don't use that type of language. Remember, this is the real world.

DOUGAL (*reeling in one of the fish*): Oh, you're right there, Ted.

TED: Anyway, July nineteenth . . . any idea why that should be important?

DOUGAL: Would it be the day the Ice Age ended?

TED: No, I don't think they could be that precise about the Ice Age, Dougal.

DOUGAL: I'll look it up in the diary.

Dougal places his little fishing rod in a special holder so that it's still hanging out over the 'pool'. He checks the 'lines' on one or two other rods he has already placed there. He goes to the bookcase and grabs the diary.

DOUGAL: The nineteenth of July . . . 'On This Day' . . . 'Galway liberated from Indians' . . . 'Church condemns cars for first time' . . . Aha! Ted. 'Ice Age ends'.

TED: No, it's nothing to do with that type of thing, Dougal. It's something to do with us. Is it something we always do on July the nineteenth?

DOUGAL: Do we go to the shops?

TED: Well, we might. But that wouldn't be specific to July the nineteenth, Dougal. We'd tend to go to the shops a bit more often than that.

DOUGAL: What could it be, Ted? Maybe it's something to do with Jack?

TED: Maybe . . . it . . . Oh, God! It's not his bath is it???!!!

DOUGAL: Oh, God, Ted, no! It couldn't be!

TED: No, wait, wait, calm down . . . sure he only just had his bath. Remember? Just before Christmas?

DOUGAL: Oh, thank God for that . . . God almighty!

They stand there for a moment, breathing heavily, hands on their hearts. Mrs Doyle comes in.

MRS DOYLE: Time for tea, Fathers.

TED: Mrs Doyle, does anything strike you as important about July nineteenth?

MRS DOYLE: It doesn't matter what day it is, Father. There's always time for a nice cup of tea. Sure didn't Our Lord himself on the cross pause for a nice cup of tea before he gave himself up for the world?

TED: No, he didn't, Mrs Doyle.

MRS DOYLE: Well, whatever equivalent they had for tea in those days. Cake, or whatever. And speaking of cake . . . I have cake!

She holds up a container full of cake.

TED: I'm fine for cake, Mrs Doyle.

MRS DOYLE: Are you sure, Father? There's cocaine in it . . .

TED: There's what?

MRS DOYLE: Oh, no, not cocaine. What am I on about . . . I meant, what do you call them . . . raisins.*

---

* For the final version we inserted three pages of dialogue here about Mrs Doyle forcing cake on Ted and then keeping it back from him. Why we added it in, we don't know. It had the effect of making the first scene run on far, far too long.

TED: No, this date thing is bothering me now. July nineteenth . . . July nineteenth . . . July nineteenth . . .

The door opens and Jack enters. He is wearing a one-piece Victorian-style black bathing suit – possibly with dog collar? He stands at the doorway with a bucket and spade in his hand and a knotted hankerchief on his head. Ted, Dougal and Mrs Doyle stare at him for a moment.

TED: Aha! Holiday!

SCENE 3 EXT./DAY 1
SET: PAROCHIAL HOUSE
Dougal is throwing things into a small trailer attached to the back of the car, totally randomly – a toothbrush, a hurling stick, a sleeping-bag, a kettle, some snorkelling gear, skis, etc.

TED: C'mon Dougal. Better get moving. (*Dougal runs to the car and gets in the front seat. Jack is in the backseat.*) Right! Let's go!

He moves his hand to the ignition.

DOUGAL: Ted, where'll we go on holiday?

TED (*stops short*): Oh . . . God . . . I dunno . . .

DOUGAL: Pierson's?

TED: Pierson's? No, that's only up the road. Anyway, Mr. Pierson doesn't really like people staying with him on their holidays. It's not actually a guesthouse.

DOUGAL: Isn't it?

TED: No, no. Do you not remember the big argument we had with him last year? When we tried to stay the second week . . . Wait! Do you know where we'll go?! Father O'Rourke has that caravan. He said we could use it any time we wanted!

DOUGAL: Oh, God, Ted, not again. It's very small, that caravan.

TED: No, he got a new one! Apparently it's twice as big! Let's go!

He starts the ignition and begins to drive away. Jaunty 'holiday' music plays.

SCENE 4 EXT./DAY 1
SET: CARAVAN PARK
The car pulls up outside a huge, shiny, new-looking mobile home. Dougal sticks his head out of the window, impossibly excited.

TED: He said it's the one at the end.

DOUGAL: Ted! Ted! There it is! It's huge!

TED: Dougal, calm down. (*To Jack.*) We're here, Father!

JACK: Feck off!

They get out of the car. Ted stretches and looks around, then stares at the back of the car.

TED: Dougal . . .

DOUGAL: Yes, Ted?

TED: Where's the trailer? With all the stuff in it?

Cut to reveal that the trailer is, indeed, nowhere to be seen.

SCENE 5 EXT./DAY 1
SET: PAROCHIAL HOUSE
We see the trailer exactly where it was originally.*

SCENE 6 INT./DAY 1
SET: MOBILE HOME
Ted, Dougal and Jack walk in. Jack immediately goes to sit in a corner.

JACK: Drink!

TED: Yes, Father, I promise you. In a minute.

DOUGAL: It's great, isn't it, Ted?

TED: It's very nice, all right.

Jack lights up a cigarette. Ted stretches. Dougal sits forward in his seat excitedly. They are all grouped down one side of the mobile home.

---

* We inserted a new scene here which opened with Ted saying to Dougal, 'Next thing you'll be telling me you forgot to lock the front door', and was followed by a scene of the Parochial House being burgled.

SCENE 7 INT./DAY 1
SET: SHOWER UNIT
A small mini-shower-type thing. A man, Mr. Gleason, steps out, leaving a woman, Mrs Gleason, behind the frosted glass.

WOMAN: Wait a second, you have to do my back.

MAN: No, I'm wrinkling up like a raisin in there. See you in a sec.

The man walks out of the room, naked. He starts to dry his hair.

SCENE 8 INT./DAY 1
SET: MOBILE HOME
The man comes into the main part of the home, still naked. Ted and Dougal stop talking and look at him. Jack stops smoking his cigarette for a moment. The man walks, still towelling his head, with his bottom to the camera – he still hasn't noticed the three, and sits beside Ted. Ted just looks at him, confused. The man stops drying his hair and takes the towel away. He turns to Ted, Dougal and Jack and looks at them. They look back at him. There is a 'moment'.

SCENE 9 EXT./DAY 1
SET: CARAVAN PARK
Ted is talking to a policeman, who is writing something in a notebook.

TED: . . . Father Ted Crilly, Craggy Island Parochial House, Craggy Island . . .

We see the man and woman in their dressing gowns watching the priests with scowls on their faces. Cut to Dougal looking down at the ground nearby. Cut back to Ted at the police car, which is starting to drive away.

TED: Honestly, Officer, I can't apologise enough . . . (*The car drives off. Ted looks at Dougal.*) Oh, Ghodddd . . . that was so embarrassing . . .

DOUGAL: Ted, if that one's not our one, which is?

A caravan in the background pulls away to reveal a tiny, tiny caravan, slightly unbalanced to one side. Dougal and Ted look around, framing the caravan between them. We cut before they turn around to notice it.

SCENE 10 INT./DAY 1
SET: CARAVAN

Ted and Dougal are squeezing into a very small space. The caravan is absolutely tiny. Jack jumps in front of them and sticks himself into a corner. Ted and Dougal look around before sitting across from Jack. They are all very close to one another. Jack stares right into Ted's eyes in a disconcerting manner.*

DOUGAL: Sure this is great! It is bigger than last year's one. What do you want to do first, Ted?

TED: Well, we'll take it easy first. Don't want to go mad on the first day. I think we should just, you know, get settled in to the old caravan. (*They look around the caravan for a moment.*) Right. That's enough of that. Where'll we go?

DOUGAL: There's a booklet here, Ted.

TED: Right, let's see . . .

He picks up a tiny booklet that is incredibly small and bears the words 'Things to do in Kilkelly'. He looks at it briefly.

TED (*reading*): 'Places of interest' . . . 'Saint Kevin's Stump' . . . That sounds good . . . 'The Magic Road' . . .

He turns over another page, but sees that there are no more pages in the booklet. He tosses it away.

TED: Two places of interest. Still, that's one more than Craggy Island has.

DOUGAL: What's The Magic Road?

TED: It's one of these bizarre natural wonders where everything's gone haywire and nothing works the way it's supposed to. It's sort of like you, Dougal, except it's a road. There's a few of them around the country.

DOUGAL: I still don't understand. It's a kind of mad road?

TED: Yes. It's what's called a 'strange phenomenon'. If you stopped a car on it and took off the handbrake, it'd go uphill. And water would flow up it.

DOUGAL: That's almost as mad as that thing you told me about the loaves and the fishes.

TED: No, Dougal, that's not mad. That's when Our Lord got just one or two bits of food and turned it into a big pile of food and everyone had it for dinner.

DOUGAL: God, he was fantastic, wasn't he?

TED: Ah, yeah, he was *brilliant* . . . OK, let's try and find the magic road.*

Ted opens the door of the caravan. Outside it's pouring with rain. Ted closes the door.

TED: All right, come on . . . will we play some Scrabble?

DOUGAL: Yeah! Brilliant!

TED: Did you bring the Travel Scrabble, Dougal?

DOUGAL: I brought the normal Scrabble and the Travel Scrabble. The Travel Scrabble for when we were travelling and the normal Scrabble for when we arrived.

TED (*impressed*): Good man, Dougal . . .

DOUGAL: Oh, no, wait a second. Now I think of it, I didn't bring either of them.

TED: Right.

DOUGAL: God, I'm an awful eejit. I wish we had something else. They should have more 'travel' versions of games, shouldn't they, Ted? I mean I've got this great idea for golf in a car — †

TED: I don't want to hear the rest of this, Dougal.†

DOUGAL: No, I know it sounds mad, but if you got very small clubs —†

TED: No, I don't want to hear this . . .†

DOUGAL: No, all you need is a fairly big ball . . .†

TED: No, Dougal. No. All right? No, stop.

---

* We decided to abandon this idea of Jack staring at Ted for the final version.

* After this, we inserted a scene of them putting Jack to bed by putting a cardboard box over his head.

† We deleted these lines from the final version.

I'm going to set you on fire if you don't stop talking about playing golf in the car.[†]

Pause.[†]

DOUGAL: Oh, all right.[†]

TED: So . . . what are we going to do for the next two weeks? This isn't exactly Disneyland.

DOUGAL: God, no, it's not even *close*. Will I put on the kettle?

TED (*sighs*): Yeah, go on.

Dougal fills the kettle and turns it on. The three of them watch the kettle.

DOUGAL: That must be one of those ones that clicks off automatically.

TED: Yes. (*Pause. After a few moments, the water begins to steam slightly.*) Bit of steam there. (*Pause. He turns to Dougal.*) Incidentally, did you bring any teabags?

DOUGAL: No.

TED (*sighs*): Right . . .

Ted takes out a cigarette and watches the kettle.

SCENE 11 INT./DAY 1
SET: CARAVAN
The kettle is boiling. It clicks off.

DOUGAL: Kettle's boiled, Ted. Will I put a bit more water in and turn it on again?

Ted is lying with his head back. He looks very bored.

TED: No, I liked it best the first time . . . and it's sort of gone downhill from there.

Ted puts his head back again. Fade out.

SCENE 12 INT./DAY 1
SET: CARAVAN
Fade back. Ted has his hands over his eyes.

TED: . . . Ninety-nine, one hundred! Coming, ready or not! (*Cut to main part of the caravan. Dougal has put some cushions around him and has pulled the curtain over his head. Ted walks up to him. He seems very unexcited as he taps Dougal's shoulder.*) Found you.

DOUGAL: Gahhhhh!!!! All right, Ted. Your go!

Dougal runs out of shot.

DOUGAL (*offscreen*): One, two, three, four, five . . . (*Ted looks at where Dougal was, sighs, then arranges the cushions around him and puts his head behind the curtain.*) . . . six, seven, eight . . .

Fade down.

SCENE 12A INT./DAY 1*
SET: CARAVAN
Fade up. Ted is smoking, looking bored. Suddenly inspiration strikes.

TED: I know! Father Larry Duff!

DOUGAL: Ah, Larry!

TED: He often comes around this area when he gets a break. I'll give him a call on his mobile. I got him one for Christmas and he's always complaining that no one rings him on it.

TED: He must have it turned off.

Fade down.

SCENE 12B EXT./DAY 1
SET: ROAD
Cut to a priest driving a car. He hears a high-pitched bleeping noise and looks around in confusion. Then he turns back to the road and screams. Cut to stock footage of a car veering out of control and going over the edge of a huge cliff. Cut back to Ted still on the mobile phone.

SCENE 12C INT./DAY 1
SET: CARAVAN
Ted switches off the mobile.

---

* In the final version we inserted the faraway cow scene as follows:

Close-up of a bunch of toy plastic cows... the kind you'd get with a toy farm set. Pull back to reveal Ted and Dougal. Dougal frowns, puzzled.

TED: . . . OK, one last time. These are small and the ones out there are *far away*. Small . . . far away...

Dougal smiles and shakes his head, uncomprehending.

TED: Ah, forget it!

Ted throws them down in disgust.

Fade down.

Fade up.

Cut to wildebeest galloping across a plain – as though seen through Dougal's binoculars. Reveal Dougal looking through the window with binoculars. He turns to Ted.

DOUGAL: Ted, you know the way your eyes sometimes play tricks on you?

SCENE 12D INT./DAY 1†
SET: CARAVAN
Fade up. Ted is sitting beside Dougal. He has a black marker in his hand. He looks fairly vexed. Dougal looks puzzled.

DOUGAL: Wait . . . so . . . I put the thing here . . .

TED: No! No, no, no, you can't put the thing there! You have to draw one in where there isn't already one of mine . . .

Cut to reveal that they are looking at a game of noughts and crosses. Experimental crosses and noughts are placed randomly all over the paper. A hand comes into shot and points at a nought.

DOUGAL: So I put an X here . . .

TED: No! . . .

Fade down.

SCENE 13 INT./DAY 1†
SET: CARAVAN
Ted and Dougal are lying around in different parts of the caravan, bored, bored, bored.

TED: God . . . how long have we been here now?

DOUGAL: Ah, about twenty minutes. (*Pause.*) Will we have a bit of an old pray?

TED: No, I'm not really in the mood, Dougal.

DOUGAL: Ah, I suppose you're right. Sure

---

† We deleted this scene from final version.

we're on holiday! We can forget about God and religion and all that nonsense.

TED: Yes, Dougal.

Fade out.

END OF PART ONE

* * *

PART TWO

SCENE 14 EXT./DAY 1
SET: FIELD
Fade up to reveal Dougal and Ted standing around in a featureless field, apart from a large rock in the centre of it. Ted and Dougal are looking at a stump.

DOUGAL: Why is it called Saint Kevin's stump?

TED (*looks at brochure*): Doesn't say . . .

Pause. Ted and Dougal look bored.

DOUGAL: So, is this what all holidays are like, Ted?

TED: Actually . . . yeah. (*Pause.*) Anyway, we'd better get back to Jack.

DOUGAL: Ah, he's fine. He said he'd stay put by the cliffs.

TED: I'm always worried leaving him near the cliffs, Dougal.

DOUGAL: Ah, Ted, he's nowhere near the edge. Sure what could happen to him?

SCENE 15 EXT./DAY 1
SET: MAGIC ROAD
We see Jack on his wheelchair at the bottom of a path that extends behind him up a hill. He is asleep. He wakes up suddenly.

JACK: DRINK!

He starts beating his fists up and down. We see one of the wheels on the wheelchair starting to turn backwards slowly. Jack's chair then starts rolling backwards up the hill, away from the camera. We see a sign that reads 'The Magic Road' beside the path.

JACK: DRINK! DRINK! DRINK!

He continues to roll up the path.

SCENE 16 EXT./DAY 1
SET: FIELD
Ted and Dougal are still standing around.

DOUGAL: Can we walk up to the rock and back, Ted?

TED (*sighs*): Well . . .

DOUGAL: Come on, Ted, we're on holiday. Live a little.

TED: All right. But we'd better get back to Jack soon.

They start walking towards the rock.

SCENE 17 EXT./DAY 1
SET: MAGIC ROAD
From the same point of view that we saw earlier, we see that Jack is now heading towards the cliff at tremendous speed.

JACK: DRINK! DRINK! DRINK! (*He finally reaches the cliff edge and disappears backwards over it. Dwindling.*) DRINK! DRINK! DRINK!

We hear a distant splash.

SCENE 18 EXT./DAY 1
SET: FIELD
Ted and Dougal have just reached the rock.

TED: Well, here we are.

DOUGAL: Will we walk over to that fence now?

TED: No, we might just blow up with excitement if we do that now. Anyway, we should save something for next week.

Ted turns and tries to lift himself up on to the rock. He sticks his head over it, then Dougal does the same. We see, from their point of view, the couple from the mobile home kissing passionately, some picnic gear beside them. Mr. Gleason has his hand up Mrs Gleason's jumper. He pauses, sensing something, then looks up. Ted and Dougal look at him. There is a 'moment'.

SCENE 19 EXT./DAY 1
SET: CARAVAN PARK
Ted is talking to a policeman again. Dougal stands beside him.

TED: . . . Father Ted Crilly . . . Craggy Island Parochial House . . . sure you know all that . . .

DOUGAL: Ted, maybe we should tell him about Jack.

TED: No, Dougal.

POLICEMAN: What's that about?

DOUGAL: It's just we were with another priest, and he's gone missing.

POLICEMAN: Well, do you want to report it or not?

TED: Ah, no. He'll turn up.

DOUGAL: Should we not report it, Ted? Just in case?

TED: Ah . . . (*The policeman looks at him.*) It won't cost anything, will it?

POLICEMAN: No.

TED: OK, so the man you're looking for, even though there's no need to look for him because he'll turn up any second, is Father

Jack Hackett . . . Ah God, how would you describe him . . .

DOUGAL: Mid-fifties . . .

TED: . . . To mid-eighties . . . tremendous smell of vegetables off him, for some reason . . .

DOUGAL: . . . Angry man, very angry man . . .

TED: . . . Hates children . . . likes the odd drink . . . and, ah, if you find him, don't come up on him from behind. He won't like that at all.*

POLICEMAN: We'll look out for him. Right . . . anything else I can do for you while I'm here? Want to confess to any robberies or unsolved murders or anything?

TED: No, I don't think so, anyway . . . Dougal?

DOUGAL (*thinks for a second*): . . . No . . .

TED (*jokily*): No, we're fine for the old unsolved mur —

The policeman gives them a cold look. Ted shuts up. They wait for a moment, looking abashed, as the policeman moves away.

DOUGAL: What do you think's happened to Jack, Ted?

TED: I don't know, Dougal. God . . . some holiday this is turning out to be. C'mon. At least there'll be a bit more room in the caravan.

They move off.

SCENE 20 INT./DAY 1
SET: CARAVAN
We see four Aran-jumper-wearing individuals,

---

* It's always nice to come across an opportunity like this. The convention of giving a description to a policeman provides you with what we call, when we're drunk, a 'joke basket'– a chance to deliver a bunch of gags in an interesting manner and learn some fun new stuff about Jack in the process. We were just as interested as anyone else to discover that he had 'a tremendous smell of vegetables off him'.

quite young, two men and two girls. With them is Father Noel Furlong, a jolly priest who is about forty. Noel has a thing of being incredibly excited when he's around young people. Ted and Dougal enter. They're surprised, but not very happy. The kids and the priest are singing a rousing rendition of 'Ebony and Ivory'.

NOEL: Ted!

TED (*looking very crestfallen*): Noel . . .

NOEL (*friendly*): What in goodness name are you doing here?

TED: Well, this is our caravan, actually, Noel.

NOEL: Well, Father O'Rourke said we could use it.

TED: Well, that's what he said to us as well.

NOEL: I think he must say it to everybody. Sure that's the type of man he is. Generous to a fault, the fault being that he's too generous. Anyway, plenty of room for everyone. Sit down and we'll have a bit of an old song. What'll we sing? Will you sing one, Ted?

TED: No, I won't, thanks.

NOEL: Ah, you will!

TED: I'd rather not.

NOEL: Will you dance, then? Come on. Tony, stick on the *Riverdance* album.

TED: Honestly, Noel, I'm a little tired. I won't —

NOEL: What? Ah, maybe you're right. Actually, we're all a bit exhausted from the old singing. We had a great old session last night. And then of course, we had to go to the *local*. I mean it must have been about *nine*, but there's a few people around here who'd put *Oliver Reed* to shame. What? (*He looks at one of the singers.*) Gerry Fields knows who I'm talking about! Ah? What? Eh? (*The singer ignores him.*) Ho-ho! Anyway, we arrived back at, God, it must have been half ten, and some of us crawled in – *Janine Reilly* knows who I'm talking about there. Don't you?! Don't you?! (*The girl looks at him without interest.*) . . . And then of course some of the wild bunch started up! What!? Who's that I could be talking about? *Eh? Heh? Tony Lynch?* He knows! Ahhhhhhh, ha, ha, look at him there! All sweetness and light! Well he wasn't like that last night when he crawled into bed at *ten past eleven*!!!! (*He puts out his hand to Dougal.*) Hello. Father Noel Furlong. You're a fine young fella! What age would you say I am!? What age!? Go on, guess! (*Ted puts his eyes to heaven.*) Ted, don't tell him, you know! He knows! Look at him there dyin' to tell him! Go on! What age would you say?

DOUGAL (*thinks*): Forty?

NOEL (*face freezes, turns to red.*): Ted, haven't seen you for ages, how are you?

Ted opens his mouth to answer.

NOEL (*sings*): 'You saw the whole of the moon!' (*The Ceol Na Gael crowd immediately start singing along.*) 'I was grounded!' Come on, Tony Lynch, sing up! 'You saw the crescent . . .'

We see Ted, looking very, very tired indeed. Fade out. We come back as they are finishing.

NOEL (*very stridently*): 'Dirty old tooooooowwwwwwnnnnnn! Dirty old . . . towwwwwwn!' Oh, God, Ted, they have me worn out. They're a mad crowd. What time is it? (*He looks at his watch.*) Half ten! Oh, God. And I'll tell you, Nuala Ryan, I'm not going down to the pub with you! (*We see Nuala, asleep with her mouth open.*) No! I won't! Don't you give me that look! No, we should all go to bed. (*Tony goes out through the door.*) Where's Tony Fields off to? Probably to get some heroin!

TONY: No, I'm just going to the toilet, Father.

NOEL: Oh, right . . . Anyone need to go to the toilet? Nuala . . . are you OK?

NUALA (*waking up*): I'm fine, Father.

NOEL (*trying to be discreet*): Janine, do you need to go?

JANINE: No, I'm fine, thanks.

NOEL: Anyone else? Ted, Dougal, are you OK?

TED: We're grand, thanks Noel.

NOEL: Are you sure now? Ted? You don't need a little tinkle?

TED: I'm fine, Noel. I'll go again.

NOEL: There's no need to be embarrassed if you want to go. We all have to go sometime. There's no need to be ashamed of a thing like that.

TED: No, I'm not ashamed at all, Noel. I just don't want to go.

NOEL: There's no shame in it. You know that.

TED: Yes. Honestly, Noel, I'm fine.

NOEL: You're all like camels! Anyway, we'll get the sleeping-bags.

TED: Will it not be a bit cramped, Noel?

NOEL: Not at all! The more the merrier!

Shot of an unconvinced Ted.

SCENE 21 INT./NIGHT 1
SET: CARAVAN
We see the Ceol Na Gael crowd, Ted and Dougal and Father Furlong all in sleeping-bags in the caravan. It is incredibly cramped. Ted is trying to sleep. There is a foot jammed up against his face. Dougal is also completely squashed. In the background we hear Father Furlong talking away to the Ceol Na Gael crowd, who are all fast asleep. He, however, is as full of energy as ever.

NOEL: . . . Saint Colm's had a great old football team in the mid Fifties. There was the three-in-a-row team, and they won the Father Fitzgibbon Cup three years in a row. Father Fitzgibbon . . . thing about him was that he looked like a cup. Big ears. Like handles. TED, D'YE REMEMBER HIM? TED! TED! ARE Y'ASLEEP!? DO YE REMEMB—

TED: YES, I REMEMBER HIM, NOEL!

NOEL: Oooooohhhh hoooooo! Who's a bit of a Moaning Michael tonight? God almighty, it's very late. I think what we should all do now is TELL A FEW GHOST STORIES.

DOUGAL: Ted?

TED: Yes.

DOUGAL: I'm going mad.

TED: Yes, yes, let's get out of here. Let's go home.

Ted and Dougal extract themselves from their sleeping-bags and start to leave.

NOEL: Who's that now? Is that Gerry Fields heading off to the disco?

TED: Ah, no, Noel. It's only us. We might head out for some fresh air.

NOEL: Right so, Ted. Don't forget to bring us back some!

TED: Hah, right so! (*Under his breath.*) You big feckin' eejit . . .

SCENE 22 EXT./EARLY MORNING 2
SET: CARAVAN PARK
Ted and Dougal leave the caravan, Ted grabbing a carrier-bag on his way out. Outside Ted lights up a fag.

DOUGAL: What about Jack?

TED: Chances are he's gone back to Craggy Island. He's got an incredible homing instinct. Hmmmmm . . . I wouldn't be surprised if we opened the front door to find him there with a big smile on his face and his arms outstretched to welcome us back.

DOUGAL: What?

TED: Well, maybe not with the smile on his face or the outstretched arms. Or the welcome back. But he's probably there. Oh God.

He sees Mr. Gleason walking towards them with a towel around his waist. He hasn't seen them yet.

TED: Oh, God, it's your man! Dougal, quick, I don't want him to see us!

They duck into the small pre-fab toilet and listen at the door.

DOUGAL: Everything all right there, Ted?

TED: Give it another minute.

Cut to a full-on view of the pair. We see behind them the top half of Mrs Gleason, who is sitting on the toilet. Pause. They slowly turn around. Mrs Gleason looks at them. There is a 'moment'.

Ted and Dougal run out of the toilet and make towards their car. Mrs Gleason comes out after them.

MRS GLEASON: Gerry! Gerry!

We see Mr. Gleason, still wearing the towel. He turns and sees Ted and Dougal running away. He runs after them. Ted and Dougal get to the car. Ted tries to open the door.

TED: Open! Please open!

DOUGAL: You're all right, Ted. He's a fair bit away yet. (*We see Mr. Gleason running towards them.*) Might be worth speeding up there a bit, Ted.

Ted finally opens the door. They jump in and start the engine. Gleason jumps on to the bonnet.

TED: Sorry about that!

MR GLEASON: Bloody perverts!

SCENE 23 INT./DAY 2
SET: CAR
Ted and Dougal have obviously been driving for some time. They both look embarrassed. Hold on this for a moment. Then cut to reveal that Mr. Gleason is still sprawled over the bonnet, completely naked. He glowers at them through the windscreen. Dougal smiles back at him and gives him a little wave.

DOUGAL: Ted, maybe we should stop and let him off. He's probably very cold now that

his towel's blown off.

TED: I've been thinking about that for ages. It's just . . . I'm sure he'll start giving out to us.

DOUGAL: We could pretend we didn't see him.

TED: I don't think he'd believe us. I mean, we can hardly see the road with him spread all over the windscreen.

DOUGAL: Ah, Ted. We'd better let him off.

TED: Oh . . . all right, I suppose so.

Ted stops the car. Mr. Gleason gets to his feet. He seems a bit groggy.

MR GLEASON: Get out of the car.

TED: Ah, hello again!

MR GLEASON: Get out of the car!

He tries the door but Ted has locked it. Mr. Gleason looks at them for a second and then spots something by the side of the road – a dirty old Coke bottle. He smashes the bottle. Dougal and Ted jump with fright. He then walks towards the car, ducks out of sight and we hear a hissing sound.

TED: Ah, now . . . (*Mr. Gleason goes to another tyre and punctures that as well.*) Now, come on there! There's absolutely no need for that

type of nonsense!

Mr. Gleason sticks the bottle into a third tyre.

DOUGAL: He's puncturing the tyres, Ted.

TED (*to Mr. Gleason*)**:** Well, I can tell you, you're not impressing anyone!

Mr. Gleason punctures the fourth tyre. He stands up and walks back in the direction they came from, still naked. Ted and Dougal sit there. The hissing continues as the car slowly sinks lower.

SCENE 24 EXT./DAY 2
SET: COUNTRY ROAD
Ted and Dougal walk along. They both look exhausted and cold.

DOUGAL: God, Ted, I'm so tired. Maybe we should go back.

TED: No, no, no, no, no . . . I'm not going anywhere near Noel Furlong again. God knows what they're getting up to by now.

SCENE 25 EXT./DAY 2
SET: CARAVAN PARK
We see the caravan rocking from side to side and up and down. We dimly hear music coming from within.

SCENE 26 EXT./DAY 2
SET: CARAVAN
All of Noel's gang are Irish dancing to the tune of 'Riverdance'. The music is very loud and they are all bunched so closely together that the scene is one of absolute madness.

SCENE 27 EXT./DAY 2
SET: CARAVAN PARK
The caravan topples over on its side with a loud bang. The music stops.

NOEL (*reprimanding in a jokey way*)**:** Oooooooohhhhh!!! Now who did that?

SCENE 28 EXT./DAY 2
SET: COUNTRY ROAD
Cut back to Ted and Dougal. Dougal hears something and turns round.

DOUGAL: Ted, Ted! It's a truck, Ted! It can give us a lift!

TED (*close to tears*): . . . Ohhhh!, thank Goddd . . .

They stick out their thumbs. We see that it's the articulated lorry that we saw at the start of the show. The truck pulls up. Tom sticks his head out of the window.

TOM: Hello, Fathers!

TED: Tommy! Thank God! Tom, we need a lift!

TOM: Fair enough, Fathers! Hold on there and I'll open the doors!

Ted turns to hug Dougal. Tom turns to look down at the buttons and frowns. He rubs his chin thoughtfully. Ted hears a noise from the bowels of the lorry. He looks up and sees a funnel jutting out of the truck and pointing directly at him and Dougal. The rumbling gets louder. Ted looks at Dougal, sighs, and looks back up at the funnel. Suddenly, we see gallons of sewage shooting out on to Dougal and Ted. This continues for a moment or two.

TOM: Sorry about that, Fathers.

He opens the passenger door. Dougal and Ted slowly, miserably, tramp round and climb in. The truck drives off, the three men staring ahead over the dashboard.

As the truck moves out of shot, we see a sign that it had been obscuring. It reads 'Pleasure World. Europe's most exciting adventure playground. 200 yards. Free entry to priests.'* An arrow points in the opposite direction. Roll closing credits.

POST-CREDIT SEQUENCE
SCENE 29 EXT./DAY 3
SET: LUXURY YACHT
Establish yacht.

SCENE 30 INT./DAY 3
SET: LUXURY YACHT
We see Jack asleep, seaweed in his hair. He suddenly wakes up.

JACK: Wha?! Arrrgh!

He stops shouting when he focuses on the sight before him. Three young women, all wearing swimming costumes, look at him with concern.

WOMAN 1: Father, you're awake! Thank God! It took us ages to pull you on board. Are you all right? (*The third woman stands beside a drinks cabinet. She opens it to reveal many, many bottles of different types of drink.*) Will you have something to drink?

Jack, coming out of his daze, looks at the camera.

THE END

---

* We really liked this final, cruel twist but it wasn't used because there was something confusing about it. It might have had to do with the arrow pointing in the opposite direction. Had they passed Pleasure World and ignored it, or what? Finally, we couldn't decide on whether it worked or not, so we erred on the side of caution.

think fast, father ted

ARTHUR: This was bumped into the second series from the first series. The dancing priest was inspired by a real priest in Northern Ireland who felt that dancing was the way forward. I remember a Unionist being very angry and feeling that he was being goaded by this priest – who was dancing just outside the man's front garden. We loved the whole idea and just elaborated on it, ending up with a priest who wakes up, starts dancing and doesn't stop until he goes to bed – and then drops dead.

GRAHAM : As you may or may not have already noticed, one way we had of creating characters was simply to put a word like 'monkey', 'dancing', 'laughing' or 'boring' in front of the word 'priest'. One of the great things about priests is that they all dress the same. So you can take a concept, impose it on a priest and it becomes funny almost automatically. Try it at home! The boring priest, Father Purcell, is about as basic an example of this as you could hope for.

The studio audience liked that, but they weren't so keen on the concertina car that Ted wrecks by giving it 'a little tap'. I thought it would get a real howl, but it didn't. In retrospect it's possibly because the joke lacks immediacy – there's a slight delay before you realise exactly how many times he must have had to give the car a little tap to achieve that result.

PART ONE

SCENE 1 INT./DAY 1*
SET: PAROCHIAL HOUSE
Credits. Music as normal. Everything as normal, in fact, except that the show is called 'Father Ben'. Before the helicopter crashes we cut to . . .

Dougal watching television. He seems excited.

DOUGAL: Ted! Ted! Quick! *Father Ben's* on!

Ted comes into the room. He's also excited.

TED: Oh, great! I love this!

SCENE 2 INT./DAY 1*
SET: FATHER BEN'S HOUSE
The set on the show looks very like the Parochial House, but with perhaps one or two subtle differences in taste. A priest, Father Ben, is reading a newspaper. Another priest, Father Brendan, comes in. He is wearing a pair of shorts on his head.

BRENDAN: God, Ben, I'm such an eejit that I've put the shorts on my head!

BEN: God almighty! You really are a big fool, Brendan!

SCENE 3 INT./DAY 1*
SET: PAROCHIAL HOUSE
Ted and Dougal are laughing mightily.

TED: God almighty! This really is top-notch stuff.

DOUGAL (*laughing his head off*): Brendan's such an eejit!

TED: God, I know someone *just* like Father Ben. Big thicko.

Cut to real credits.

SCENE 4 INT./DAY 1
SET: PAROCHIAL HOUSE
As we hear the closing music to 'Father Ben' we see Father Jack, asleep in his chair. His mouth is open and he is making his usual strange sleeping sounds. After a moment, a drip of water lands on his forehead, then another, then another. Cut to Ted and Dougal, who are chuckling away. Ted stands up and switches off the television.

---

*We moved scenes 1–3 to the beginning of Episode Six, The Plague, in the final version.

TED: Right, Dougal, come on. We can't sit around watching TV all day. It's a big waste. Chewing-gum for your eyes.

DOUGAL: No, thanks, Ted.

TED (*beat*): What do you want to do? (*He checks his watch.*) I tell you what . . . Will we break out the old crisps? We could spend half an hour eating crisps and have a break for ludo about ten.

DOUGAL: Then what?

TED: More crisps.

Cut back to Jack still asleep. A thin stream of water is now pouring on to his head. The water drips from his dangling hand into a glass beside his chair. Ted puts a big box full of packets of crisps on the table, punches a hole in the side and fishes out a pack, throws it to Dougal, then gets one for himself.

DOUGAL (*holding up a crisp*): This is what I do, Ted. I get a cheese-and-onion one *and* a salt-and-vinegar one, and I eat it in the same go!

He pops it into his mouth to demonstrate.

TED: No need to do that anymore, Dougal. Father Dunning gave me these. Cheese-and-onion *and* salt-and-vinegar flavour. In the same crisp!

He displays a bag, which has 'Cheese, salt, vinegar and onion flavour' written on it.

TED: Now *this* . . . is the life.

Suddenly, a torrent of water cascades on to Jack. Somehow, he manages to sleep through this. Cut to

Ted and Dougal.

TED: That leak is getting worse. Dougal, get . . . Dougal!

DOUGAL (*looking at a crisp*): What's that, Ted?

TED: Get that bucket. We'd better move himself and put the bucket under the leak.

DOUGAL: Fair enough!

Dougal brings the bucket over to Jack. He puts it down, then helps Ted lift the chair. Jack is still asleep. They have some difficulty lifting the chair while avoiding the water.

TED (*looking up at the roof*): God, that'll probably cost a fortune to fix. Where are we going to get the money? Think, Dougal . . . how will we raise some money . . . ?

DOUGAL: Hmnnnn . . .

TED: Ah, I think I know. Yes! Aha!

DOUGAL: Aha!

TED: Are you thinking what I'm thinking, Dougal?

DOUGAL: I think so, Ted!

TED: Yes!

DOUGAL: But . . . well, I don't know, Ted . . .

TED: What?

DOUGAL: I mean, Ted . . . it's a big step. And where are we going to get the guns . . .?

TED: What are you talking about?

DOUGAL: Well . . . Oh, wait now . . . actually . . . I might have been thinking about something different.

TED: You thought we were going to rob a bank, didn't you, Dougal?

DOUGAL: I did, yeah.

TED: This isn't a Bruce Willis film, Dougal. I was thinking more along the lines of a raffle. What'll we have as a prize, though?

DOUGAL: Oh, you've got me there, Ted.

TED (*thinks*): We should be able to get something . . . it's not as if we're asking for raffle prizes every day of the week. Under the rules of the diocese, I think we're allowed something every couple of years . . .

Jack has been moved out of shot. Dougal puts the bucket down. The leak stops.

DOUGAL: That's funny, Ted.

Cut to Jack, who has fallen asleep again in the background. Water starts cascading on to his head.

TED: God, we'll have to move him out of the room. Is the thing there? The thing for waking him up?

DOUGAL: Here it is.

Dougal hands Ted a steel, bar-like thingy. It is telescopic, and Ted extends it to its full length. He and Dougal go to the other side of the room and start poking Jack in the shoulder with it. There is no response for a moment. Then Jack wakes up with a roar and grabs the device.

TED (*from the other side of the room*): Father! Father! It's only us!

JACK: Get to feck!

TED: We're going to have to move you, Father!

JACK: Drink!

TED: Father! No! Don't drink that! It's —

Jack drinks, then spews it out immediately.

JACK: FECKIN' *WATER!*

SCENE 5 INT./DAY 1
SET: PAROCHIAL HOUSE
We see Ted on the telephone. Dougal is beside him, craning his head in order to listen.

TED: . . . And I was looking up the records, and the island hasn't been given anything to raffle since those two bags of coal in 1964 . . . I think we're entitled . . . under the rules of the diocese . . .

He suddenly gives Dougal the thumbs-up. Dougal doesn't react.

TED: . . . Oh, that'd be great . . . oh, that's wonderful! Yes, perfect! Thanks very much, Your Grace . . . yes . . . thanks again. All right, bye, Bishop Brennan! Bye!

Ted puts down the telephone. He claps his hands together happily.

DOUGAL: No luck then?

TED: Lots of luck, Dougal! They're giving us a car!

DOUGAL: A car! That's a brilliant prize! A car!

TED: Oh, it's not that unusual. Father Finnegan got a car last month. You know him, don't you, Dougal? The dancing priest? Dances for peace.

DOUGAL: Is he still going?

TED: He is indeed. He danced six thousand miles last year. New York to Los Angeles. He was mugged about once every fifteen miles.

DOUGAL: That's terrible! He's all right now, though . . . ?

TED: Oh, he's fine now, God bless him. (*He rubs his hands together.*) Great! We'll have the roof sorted out in no time! Hear that, Father? We'll have the roof back to normal before you know it!

Cut to a grumpy Jack in a showercap, giving them the finger.

SCENE 6 EXT./DAY 1
SET: PAROCHIAL HOUSE
We see Mrs Doyle standing outside the house, looking around expectantly. We hear an engine sound and then see Ted and Dougal appear in the driveway in a car. It is shiny and new, with 'For Reg' on the number plates. The car stops and Ted and Dougal get out looking very pleased.

MRS DOYLE: Cup of tea, Fathers?

TED: Eh, no thanks, Mrs Doyle. (*He nods at the car.*) What do you think of her?

MRS DOYLE (*distracted*): Yeah, great. Are you sure you won't have a cup?

TED (*ignoring the question*): It's not ours, Mrs Doyle, unfortunately.

DOUGAL: No. It's a prize in our big raffle.

MRS DOYLE: Oh, right. Will I pour it for you, then?

TED: Go on inside, Mrs Doyle. Let me take the tray.

MRS DOYLE: Oh . . . all right then, Father. I'll put the kettle on in case you want some more when you get in.

Mrs Doyle goes inside. Before Ted and Dougal can follow her, Dougal spots something.

DOUGAL: Ah, God, look at that, Ted, there's a dent in the car.

TED: What!?

He looks for somewhere to put down the tray and cups. He can't find anywhere so he throws them into a bush.

TED: Where's the dent, Dougal?

DOUGAL (*pointing at the front of the car*): Just there, Ted.

TED: God, how did that happen?

DOUGAL: It must have been when we hit that fella on the bike.

TED: Don't mention that to anyone, Dougal. He was all right, anyway. I saw him getting up . . . (*He examines the dent.*) Well . . . well, it's not too bad . . . Sure I can just straighten that out with a little tap. There should be a hammer there in that box.

DOUGAL: Good thinkin', Ted.

Dougal goes to a box beside the door and searches through it. He takes out a hammer. Ted takes it and taps at the dent. He pauses, then taps a little harder.

TED: Ooops! Didn't mean to do that. I'll just tap it the other way.

He continues tapping. Fade out. Fade back in again. It is early in the evening. We see Dougal, sucking his cheeks in and exhaling thoughtfully.

DOUGAL: It's no use, Ted. You'll never get it absolutely right.

Cut to Ted, still tapping away at the car. The car is now a total wreck. It looks as if it has been hit in the side by a train. Ted stands up.

TED (*very frustrated*): I thought I had it back there a while ago, you know? It was looking all right there for a while but like an eejit I had to keep bangin' away . . .

DOUGAL: You're a perfectionist, Ted, you know? It's not your fault. It's not too bad, though.

TED: Let me have another look at it.

Ted steps back to have a look. He muses for a second, but there's no way around the fact that it looks like

James Dean's car after his fatal accident. Ted is unnaturally calm. Pause.

TED: No . . . no, we can't give that away as a prize.

DOUGAL: Look, let's sleep on it, Ted. See how you feel in the morning.

TED: Maybe you're right. (*Pause.*) OK, then.

They enter the house.

SCENE 7 EXT./NIGHT 1
SET: PAROCHIAL HOUSE
It is very late at night. All the lights are off. It's very peaceful and quiet. Suddenly, we hear Ted's scream and a single light goes on. We hear Ted's voice.

TED: OH, JESUS! WE'RE DEAD! OH, GOD ALMIGHTY!

SCENE 8 INT./NIGHT 1
SET: TED AND DOUGAL'S BEDROOM
Ted is sitting up in bed, terrified. Dougal looks at him, worried.

DOUGAL: Ted, calm down, there! Come on!

TED: Calm down! Calm down? We've just destroyed a car that's worth seven grand! It looks like it's been bombed!

DOUGAL: Come on, Ted. It'll look better in the morning.

TED: Dougal, try and understand! WE'RE DEAD! The bishop'll kill us! We're dead! We're

dead! We're dead! We're DEAD!

Ted is totally hysterical. Dougal rushes over to him, unsure as to what to do. Finally, he slaps him in the face. Ted recovers after a moment.

TED: Thanks, Dougal . . . I probably needed that but . . . don't ever do it again.

DOUGAL: It was just you were getting a little hysterical there, Ted.

TED: Fair enough, but . . . don't ever do it again. Now, what are we going to do . . . ?

DOUGAL: We could run away.

TED: No . . . no, they'd just find us again. They always do.

DOUGAL: Oh . . . oh, you're right there, Ted . . . (*Pause.*) What about that other fella that has the car? The dancing priest . . .

TED: Finnegan! Yes! It'd be the same kind of car and everything!

DOUGAL: How could we get him to give it to us, Ted?

Pause.

TED: Maybe . . . maybe we could just get a lend of it . . .

DOUGAL: But when someone wins it in the raffle, Ted, they won't want to give it back.

TED: Well . . . now, this is going to sound very immoral, Dougal, but stay with me. What if . . . what if we rigged the draw so that we won it? Then we could bring it back?

DOUGAL: Oh . . . oh, that'd be terribly wrong, Ted. I don't think we should do that.

TED: It wouldn't even be cheating, really. It'd be just . . . structuring the raffle in such a way that the return comes to the benefactors rather than the beneficiaries.

DOUGAL: Hmmm . . .

TED: Dougal, seriously, listen . . . think of it this way . . . If Bishop Brennan finds out we wrecked the car, he *will* kill us, you know? And murder's a terrible, terrible sin, Dougal. So, by committing this *little* sin, we'll actually be *saving a Bishop's soul!*

Long pause. Dougal thinks.

DOUGAL: Fair enough, then, Ted.

SCENE 9 INT./DAY 2
SET: PAROCHIAL HOUSE
Ted and Dougal are finishing putting on their coats.

TED: Come on, Father.

Jack comes round the corner in his coat as Ted opens the door and they start to exit.

SCENE 10 EXT./DAY 2
SET: PAROCHIAL HOUSE
Ted, Dougal and Jack appear at the front door and run to the wrecked car, which is parked a short distance from the house. As they do so, they are attacked by thousands of squawking birds. Ted runs at the front, followed by Dougal who holds Jack by the arm. A huge crow pecks Jack on the cheek. Jack roars. When they get into the car, they behave as if they have experienced nothing more unusual than heavy rain.

TED: Right! Off we go!

SCENE 11 EXT./DAY 2
SET: FINNEGAN'S HOUSE
We see the wrecked car, still barely able to move, squeaking to a halt outside the house. It pulls up behind a new-looking car, also with 'For Reg' plates. Ted gets out.

SCENE 12 INT./DAY 2
SET: CAR OUTSIDE FINNEGAN'S HOUSE
We see Jack and Dougal in the back seat. Jack is sneezing loudly. Dougal is cowering away from him. There are thousands of crumpled tissues all over the back seat.

TED: God, look at it. It's the same colour and all. Dougal, you mind Jack here. I'll be as quick as I can.

DOUGAL: But, Ted —

Ted slams the door. Dougal is alone with Jack. Appalling sounds come from Jack's direction. Dougal looks nervous.

SCENE 13 INT./DAY 2
SET: FINNEGAN'S LIVING ROOM
We see Father Liam Finnegan dancing a twist in the manner so beloved of parents at school discos. Sixties-

type beat music plays. There is a light knock at the door of the room. It opens and Ted sticks his head around.

TED: Liam . . .

LIAM: Ted! Come on in! (*Ted enters.*) Will you join me?

TED: What, me? Dance? O'ho, no . . . I'm not much of a dancer, now.

LIAM: Come on, Ted. Prayer isn't the only way to praise God, you know. And it keeps you fit as well!

TED: Oh . . . all right, then . . .

Ted starts dancing in tiny, quick movements. He and Liam face each other, jiving away.

LIAM: You said something on the phone about taking a loan of the car.

TED: I did, yes. You'd be doin' me a great favour, Liam —

LIAM: Ah, don't be silly. Just look after it. Don't give it away in a raffle or something!

He laughs. Ted looks a little frightened, then he laughs, too. He laughs too loudly and a little too long.

TED: Someone said you were on television recently. In some documentary. You were dancing in Belfast or something?

LIAM (*coldly*)**:** That wasn't me. That's some other fella. Some young fella. Ripped off the idea. Don't like talking about him.

Uncomfortable pause.

LIAM: How is Dougal and old Father Jack?

TED: Fine. They're out in the car.

SCENE 14 EXT./DAY 2
SET: CAR
We see the car jolting wildly as Jack sneezes.

SCENE 15 INT./DAY 2
SET: FINNEGAN'S LIVING ROOM
Ted is jiving towards the door.

TED: All right, Liam! I'd better be heading off!

LIAM: Fair enough! Bye, Ted!

Ted dances out through the door. Liam dances a little

more, then suddenly clutches his heart and falls to
the ground.

SCENE 16 EXT./DAY 2
SET: FINNEGAN'S HOUSE
*Ted runs out of the house, shaking the car keys in
triumph. He runs towards the car, looking joyful. He
looks in at Dougal and knocks at the window.*

TED: Way-haaaaayyyyyy!!!!

DOUGAL (*winds down the window*)**:** No luck,
then?

Ted looks at him, deflated.

END OF PART ONE

* * *

PART TWO

SCENE 17 INT./NIGHT 2
SET: CAR
*Ted and Dougal are in the car. Dougal is drawing his
name in the condensation on the window.*

TED: Dougal, you'll leave a mark on the
window.

Dougal stops.

DOUGAL: Are we there yet?

TED: Dougal, it's a long drive. We won't be
there for a while. (*Pause.*) I must say, Father
Finnegan's looking well for a man of his age.
Dancin' away there . . . you should have seen
him. Ah, sure everything's fine now. Father
Ted Crilly saves the day once again! How are
you doing back there, Father?

He turns to check and Jack sneezes in his face.

TED: Aaaaaghhhh!!!

*Ted is momentarily blinded. The car swerves to the
other side of the road for an instant.*

TED (*wiping his eyes*)**:** My God! My God, what
have you been drinking, Father?! God, it's like
acid!

Ted finally gathers himself together.

TED: We really have to take care of this car.
We can't afford any accidents . . . this is the
only one we have now . . . dear God. Father,
try this. This'll clear you up.

*He hands Jack a nasal inhaler. Jack breaks the top
off and drinks the contents.*

DOUGAL: Aren't cars great, though, Ted?

TED (*not really listening*)**:** . . . Yes . . . they are,
all right . . .

Pause.

TED: Look . . . maybe you should have a rest,
Dougal. It's a long drive. You have a little sleep.

DOUGAL: Right so, Ted.

*Dougal puts his head back into the seat and closes his
eyes. Jack is asleep beside him. The car speeds into
the night.*

SCENE 18 INT./DAY 3
SET: CAR
*We see Dougal still asleep. The camera moves to show
Jack asleep beside him. Then Ted is revealed, also
asleep. The car travels on. We see the countryside
dwindling behind. Ted shifts to get more comfortable.*

SCENE 19 EXT./DAY 3
SET: ROAD
The car roars by.

SCENE 20 INT./DAY 3
SET: CAR
*Another shot of the three of them sleeping happily.
Ted slowly stirs himself. Then one eye opens. He
stretches and smacks his lips. Ted looks at the wheel
of the car, then at Dougal and Jack. He turns again
and looks out through the windscreen.*

TED: God, almost drifted off there . . . oh,
great, we're nearly home!

Jack and Dougal wake up.

SCENE 21 INT./DAY 3
SET: PAROCHIAL HOUSE
*Ted is looking at a notebook. He taps a pen against
his teeth. Dougal sits beside him. Jack is asleep
nearby, water still pouring on to his head.*

TED: Right, the raffle. Let's go through it
again. It's crucial we do it absolutely right . . .

DOUGAL: Fair enough, Ted . . .

TED (*produces a hat*)**:** OK . . . I'll fill the hat
with a load of tickets with the same number on

them. Say, eleven.

DOUGAL: Eleven . . . two ones. That's easy to remember, Ted . . .

TED: . . . Then when I'm doing the draw, we'll make sure that you have that number.

DOUGAL: Right. So we won't have to cheat at all?

TED: Well, that's actually how we're cheating . . .

DOUGAL: Oh, right. OK, so. Let me get this right . . . You'll be wearing the hat?

TED: No, no. I won't be wearing any hats. The *tickets* will be in the hat.

DOUGAL: Gotcha. But you'll put on the hat to give me the signal?

TED: I won't be giving you any signals, Dougal! I'll just pull out your ticket from the hat, you say 'That's my number', and then come up and collect the prize!

DOUGAL: There's a prize, Ted!? What is it!?

TED: THE CAR!!! (*Ted takes a breath.*) Dougal. Look. All you have to do is, when I call the number, you say 'Yes, that's my ticket', and come up on stage. Just remember that. Right?

DOUGAL: Right!

He gives Ted the thumbs-up. Ted returns to his notebook. Mrs Doyle enters, carrying a tray.

MRS DOYLE: Here's the sandwiches for tonight, Father. Ooops, wait. I forgot to do my test.

TED: What test is that, Mrs Doyle?

MRS DOYLE: I always take one sandwich at random and try it. If it doesn't meet my standards, the lot of them go in the bin.

She pulls out a sandwich and bites into it. Beat. Her face slowly screws up into a grimace. One eye flickers. She starts making gagging sounds. She starts to swallow it as if it's a piece of wood with nails sticking out of it. She thumps chest and makes unpleasant noises. Her head suddenly jerks back. Pause.

MRS DOYLE (*recovering immediately*): They're fine.

She leaves the room. Dougal approaches Ted.

TED: So! Are we all sorted?

DOUGAL: Rarin' to go, Ted! Oh, who's doing the disco?

TED: Father Billy O'Dwyer.

DOUGAL: 'The Spinmaster'! Great!

TED: Actually, I'm looking forward to this. Bet you I sell a load of tickets.

DOUGAL: Bet I sell more than you, Ted.

TED: Hmm . . .

Dougal pauses beside the open door.

DOUGAL: Do you know what it's a bit like, Ted? (*Acting cool.*) It's a bit like *The Sting* and I'm Robert Redford and you're Paul Newman.

He smiles and walks the wrong side of the open door, so that he's obscured by it. He emerges after a moment, looks sheepishly at Ted and walks out on the right side of the door.

SCENE 22 INT./NIGHT 3
SET: PAROCHIAL HALL
We see a priest, Father Billy O'Dwyer, setting up some DJ equipment. Ted approaches him.

TED: Ground control to the 'The Spinmaster'!

BILLY: O'ho! Ted, how are ya?!

Ted climbs up on stage to have a word with him.

TED: Fine, fine . . . God, it's like NASA. How do you keep track of it all?

BILLY (*proudly*): Oh, it's quite simple, really. Y'see here we have the two turn-tables, which I control from the mixing-desk here. Treble, bass . . . This switch helps you flip between the two records if you want to get a bit of a jam going. This is a new thing I got – Japanese thing that makes the sound a bit more tonal.

TED: Oh, I tell you, I can't wait. What records have you got for us?

Pause.

BILLY: Records.

TED: Bit of The Bee Gees, I suppose. Get them all jumping.

He sees that Billy has his head in his hands.

BILLY: Oh, God . . .

TED: Billy! What's up with you?

BILLY: I've forgotten the records, Ted.

TED: What?! Do you not have any at all!!?

BILLY: I knew there was something . . .

TED: Billy, what am I going to do? The whole island's coming to this thing!

BILLY: Hold on a sec, now . . . wait a sec . . . I might have one. I think I have one in the car.

He leaves the stage. Dougal and Mrs Doyle arrive. Mrs Doyle has a tray with teacups, etc . . .

MRS DOYLE: Tea, Father?

TED: Ah, Mrs Doyle! Would you like to be the first to buy a raffle ticket?

MRS DOYLE: Oh, I'd love to, Father! I haven't taken part in a raffle in donkey's years!

TED (*flips through the book of tickets*): How many will you have?

MRS DOYLE: Just the one, Father.

TED (*disappointed*): Just one? You should buy a couple, Mrs Doyle. You'll have better chance of winning.

DOUGAL: Well to be honest . . . (*He winks knowingly.*) . . . You won't have much chance of winning this one . . . no matter how many tickets you get!

TED: Dougal! Mrs Doyle has every chance of winning!

DOUGAL (*slyly*): Does she? I don't think so, Ted.

TED: Shut up, Dougal! Go on, Mrs Doyle. It's

for charity. Buy a few.

MRS DOYLE: No, I don't think I will. I'll just have the one.

TED (*sighs*): 50p.

MRS DOYLE: 50p! (*Reluctantly.*) Well . . . OK, then, Father.

She hands Ted the money.

TED: Grand.

MRS DOYLE: I only need the one ticket, anyway. My lucky number, never lets me down.

TED (*flips through book*): O'ho! I see! Which one is that?

MRS DOYLE: Eleven.

Dougal gasps.

TED: What?

MRS DOYLE: Eleven. It's always been lucky for me.

TED: Eh, we're out of elevens, Mrs Doyle.

MRS DOYLE: But I thought I was your first customer . . .

TED: Yes, but . . . I think this one came without elevens . . . Tell, you what, Mrs Doyle. I'll give you a number ten and a number one, and that'll add up to eleven. And you can have them both for 50p.

MRS DOYLE: No, I don't think so, Father. I'd better have the money back.

TED: Mrs Doyle, it's for charity. It's for the roof.

MRS DOYLE: Sorry, Father.

She holds her hand out, patiently. Ted sighs and gives her the money. She leaves. Ted looks at Dougal.

TED: Incredible woman . . . Now, where's Jack got to?

DOUGAL: He's with Father Purcell.

TED: Oh, God. I'd better rescue him. He'll be going mad!

DOUGAL: Oh, they're fine, Ted. They're having a chat.

TED: That'll be a one-sided chat if ever there

was one, Dougal. Purcell's the most boring priest in the world. He was working in Nigeria in some village a few years ago and he woke up one morning to find that everyone in the village had gone off. Oh, they'd had enough of him. Went off in a big boat that sank after about a mile and they were eaten by alligators, God love them. Anyway . . . just in case the same thing happens to Father Jack . . .

Ted moves off.

SCENE 23 INT./NIGHT 3
SET: CHANGING ROOM
Father Jack is being talked to by Father Austin Purcell, an extraordinarily dull man. Jack looks at Austin with absolute hatred, looking around for an escape route. Austin doesn't seem to notice. Ted sticks his head around the door, raffle tickets in hand.

AUSTIN: . . . So we run the gas off the electricity and the electricity off the gas and we save two hundred pounds a year. But a few weeks later, God, I'll never forget it . . . we got a new boiler.

Ted coughs lightly. Jack looks at Ted hopefully.

TED: Are you all right there, Fathers?

JACK: Help me.

AUSTIN: Hello, Ted! I was just telling Father Jack about the thing there last year. How did you fare with yours?

TED: Ah . . . I don't really know what —

AUSTIN: 'Cause if it's giving you any trouble at all they'll take it back. Oh, it's no trouble to them. Sure that's what they're paid for! They have *no* morals and *no* respect for human life. What they have, and no one can deny this, is the finest collection of boilers in the world. And I include Canada in that.

TED (*hasn't a clue what he's talking about*): Fine! Actually, Austin, if you don't mind, I need Father Jack for a moment.

JACK: Thank Christ!

Jack runs to the door and exits quickly.

TED: While I'm here, I don't suppose you'd like a few raffle tickets?

AUSTIN: Ah, God, I remember the first time I saw the boiler. Beautiful.

TED: A ticket, Father?

AUSTIN: . . . but you never know with these things – unless, of course, you get them wholesale and try to move them into the space that was occupied by, say, a wardrobe, or a big ceramic hob . . .

TED: Would you like a ticket, Austin?

AUSTIN (*pausing to look at the tickets*): Did you get them printed specially, Ted? 'Cause you know you can buy them in a shop. Any number you want . . . one . . . seven . . . twenty . . . three . . . nine . . . one hundred and twelve . . . anything you want up to . . . four hundred and nine, I think it is. If you want any more they can send off for them. They send them back in an envelope. Normal type of thing, rectangular, four corners . . .

Ted gives up. He smiles and backs out of the room, closing the door slowly behind him. Austin doesn't seem to notice and talks on regardless.

AUSTIN: . . . That's the way I like them, anyway, the old envelopes. No round envelopes for me! No way, José! Sid Vicious! That was a great name, wasn't it? He got into trouble with the drugs . . . .

SCENE 24 INT./NIGHT 3*
SET: PAROCHIAL HALL HALLWAY
Ted looks around.

TED: Father? Father? Oh, where's he gone . . . ?

SCENE 25 INT./NIGHT 3
SET: BACKSTAGE PAROCHIAL HALL
We see Jack wandering around, completely lost. He turns a corner and we see that the hallway is lined with crates of beer.

JACK: Oh, yessss!

SCENE 26 INT./NIGHT 3
SET: PAROCHIAL HALL
Ted is standing alone, no one is buying tickets from him. He sees Dougal, selling tickets hand over fist.

DOUGAL: There you go! Anyone else? All righty . . .

*We deleted this scene from the final version.

Ted looks at Dougal, annoyed. Cut to the stage. Ted comes up to the microphone.

TED: Sorry about the wait, folks. Bit of trouble with the old disco. Ah, luckily, though, I've got a few old pals to come up and do a few songs. Please welcome Father Tiernan, Father Cafferty, Father Rafter and Father Leonard!

Head-and-shoulder shots of four priests. We hear Kraftwerk music starting up and the camera pulls back to reveal that they are standing behind impressive synthesisers. They move only very, very slightly as they play, looking at the audience with no expression on their faces.

SCENE 27 INT./NIGHT 3
SET: SIDE OF STAGE
With the sound of German synthesiser pop in the background, Ted sees Father Billy and runs up to him.

TED: Billy! Where've you been?

BILLY: Sorry, Ted. I got the record!

TED: All right, all right. Listen, how about a ticket . . . 50p each, or four for a pound . . .

BILLY: Gambling, Ted. Ruined my father, and my grandfather. Both of them, Ted. Died without a penny to their name. That's not going to happen to me, Ted.

TED: Oh, come on, Billy. Have a few.

BILLY: No, Ted. It's like a disease. You don't want to get into that kind of thing.

TED (*a tad frustrated*): God, it's just for charity. It's not real gambling.

BILLY: Oh, go on, then.

TED: Great. How many tickets will you have?

BILLY: Give us two thousand.

Pause.

TED: Two thousand?

BILLY: Go on, there. I'll do you a cheque.

TED: That's a good lot of tickets, Billy.

BILLY: Ah, it's fine. Sure I'll have a much better chance of winning the car! There you go . . .

He rips out the cheque and hands it to Ted. Pause.

TED: No . . . no, I can't take this. It's too much.

BILLY: I can handle it, Ted. I've got a few friends who loan me cash from time to time.

TED: No, no, you keep this. You shouldn't be throwing this kind of money around.

He moves as if to rip up the cheque. Dougal comes up to him.

DOUGAL: Ted, I need another ticketbook. This one's run out.

TED: Already!! How could you have sold out already?!

DOUGAL: Don't ask me! I can hardly keep a straight face back there!

He grabs a ticketbook from Ted and moves off. Ted turns to Billy. Pause.

TED: What was it again, Billy, two thousand?

SCENE 28 INT./NIGHT 3
SET: BACKSTAGE PAROCHIAL HALL
Jack has just finished a can of beer. Cut to reveal that the hallway is covered with empty beercans. Jack tries to shake the can and looks inside it, then throws it on the ground.

JACK: Need more drink!

He stumbles towards a door and swings it open. We see the prize car just outside the door.

JACK: Ah, ha, haaaaaa!

SCENE 29 INT./NIGHT 3
SET: PAROCHIAL HALL
The disco is going full blast. Father Billy is playing 'Ghost Town' by The Specials at top volume. The hall is now quite full. The song ends, and Billy picks up the needle and returns it to the start of the record again. Cut to Ted and Dougal by the side of the stage.

TED: Right, here we go. You know what to do?

DOUGAL (*taps his head*): It's all in there, Ted.

TED: OK, let's go . . .

He moves on to the stage and motions for Billy to turn the music off. Billy does so. Ted moves towards the microphone.

TED: Thank you, Father Billy! And now . . . let's get on to the important stuff! The raffle!

The last raffle I was at was very interesting because the people who ran the raffle actually won the prize! So it's not unusual for that to happen every now and again. Right? OK . . .

Cut to Dougal in the audience. Cut back to Ted. He produces a hat, then pulls out a number.

TED: And the winning number is . . . number eleven!

Dougal looks at his ticket, disappointed.

TED (*worried*)**:** Number eleven!

Dougal looks around to see if anyone else has the ticket.

TED: Number eleven! If anyone has that number could they please come up on stage!

Pause.

TED: What's that, Father McGuire? You say you have the winning ticket?

DOUGAL: What?

TED: Well done! A big round of applause for our very own Father Dougal McGuire!

Dougal joins Ted on stage. Ted whispers to him.

TED: God almighty, Dougal! What were you doing?!!

DOUGAL: Sorry, Ted. I was looking at the ticket upside down.

TED: It was number *eleven*, Dougal! It looks the same both ways!

DOUGAL: Ah, now, it doesn't really, Ted. They've got the little standy-out things at the top.

Ted ignores him and turns to the crowd.

TED: Well, congratulations, Father Dougal! What a magical thing to happen, you living here and . . . winning the car . . (*He decides he'd better shut up.*) Anyway, wasn't that a fantastic evening? We've raised enough money to repair our roof and we had a great time as well. So thank you all for coming. And now, if I could ask you all to stand for our national anthem!

He gestures to Billy. Billy looks down at the turntable for a moment, then puts on 'Ghost Town' again. Everyone in the hall stands respectfully. Ted turns to Billy. Billy shrugs apologetically.

SCENE 30 INT./NIGHT 3
SET: PAROCHIAL HOUSE
We see Billy on the telephone.

BILLY: For God's sake! I'll have the money next week! Please! Please!!!!! One more chance, that's all I ask!!!!

Mrs Doyle comes up and offers tea. Father Billy puts his hand over the telephone.

BILLY: Thanks very much, Mrs Doyle. (*He returns to the telephone.*) Have some pity, for God's sake!!!!

Other guests chat away as Mrs Doyle mingles among them with her sandwiches. Cut to Dougal listening to Austin. Dougal looks across the room to see if he can see Ted anywhere. He can't manage to extract himself from Austin.

AUSTIN: Ah, they have you every way. I was in the AA there. The insurance is very expensive . . .

DOUGAL: Oh, right . . .

AUSTIN: . . . I ended up having to crash the car in the end, just to get the money back. But then they had witnesses, of course, who said that I steered it into the wall on purpose, so there was talk of me going to jail for a while . . .

Cut back to Ted. Mrs Doyle approaches him. She looks shocked. She taps him on the shoulder.

TED: Mrs Doyle, what can I do for you?

MRS DOYLE: Terrible news, Father.

TED (*concerned*)**:** What is it, Mrs Doyle?

He pulls up a chair and gets her to sit in it.

MRS DOYLE: It's Father Finnegan. He's had a heart attack.

TED: No!

MRS DOYLE: The doctor warned him to cut it down to twelve hours a day, but *he just couldn't stop dancing!!!*

TED: Oh, that's . . . that's terrible!

Dougal approaches.

DOUGAL: What's up, Ted?

TED: Father Finnegan had a heart attack.

DOUGAL: He hasn't! Are there any more chipsticks?

Ted and Mrs Doyle look disapprovingly at Dougal. Jack enters the room. No one notices him.

DOUGAL: Does that mean we can keep the car?

TED: Dougal! That's a terrible thing to say! The man has just – wait a second! You're right! We can keep the car!

Ted notices Jack. He has a crate of beer under one arm and an air-freshener tree-thing hanging from his face. He looks very drunk. Ted and Dougal look horrified. They walk over to Jack, who puts his hands over his crate of lager in a protective movement.

JACK: Feck off!

TED: Father . . . where did you get the air-freshener from?

JACK: Car . . .

TED: Oh, God.

JACK: Drived the car!

TED: Not the new car!

Pause.

JACK: Yeah!

TED: Tell me from the beginning, Father. Where'd you drive the car?

JACK: To shops! Drink!

TED: How fast were you driving? Were you driving fast?

JACK: Slow!

TED: You were driving slowly? Thank God.

JACK: Corner. Stopped the car. Got out. Fag! Turned around. TRUCK!

TED: A truck!

JACK: Two!

He brings his hands apart and smashes them together.

TED (*devastated*): All right . . . all right, where is it? Maybe we can salvage something from it.

SCENE 31 EXT./NIGHT 3
SET: PAROCHIAL HOUSE
We see the car from the front. It looks pristine,

although there is a slight dent over the front bumper. Dougal walks behind the car. Ted bends down and examines the dent.

DOUGAL: Ah, Ted. It's not that bad.

TED: Yes . . . God, I thought it'd be much worse than that . . .

He stands up and sees something. We get a side view of the car, which reveals that the back has been completely squashed into the front.

TED: Oh, bollocks. Dougal, how is this 'not that bad'?*

DOUGAL: Well, remember, Ted, when you tapped the other car and it ended up looking a bit like this one?*

TED: Yes . . . *

DOUGAL: Well, could you kind of do the opposite of that, and maybe, tap this one *back* so that it looks like a new one.*

TED: I *could* probably do that, Dougal. But probably by the time I've finished, we won't need cars 'cause we'll all be flying around in spaceships. Oh, well, at least we've still got the raffle money to fix the roof.*

SCENE 31A INT./NIGHT 3
SET: PAROCHIAL HOUSE
Billy is still on the telephone.

BILLY: Please! Just give me twenty-four hours! Please!

He hangs up, looking desperate. He sees a big bucket with 'Raffle Money' written on the side. He contemplates this.

SCENE 32 INT./NIGHT 3
SET: PAROCHIAL HOUSE
On television, we see a weather report.

WEATHERMAN: . . . So because of that low pressure, we'll probably be seeing a lot more rain, at least until July, or possibly until August . . .

Ted, Dougal and Jack sit around the room, watching the television. Each has an individual stream of water falling on to his head. They all wear showercaps. They look absolutely miserable.

TED: God almighty . . . how could someone be so *dishonest* as to steal raffle money from a priest.

DOUGAL: Well, it was a rigged raffle, though, Ted.

Ted tries to respond but can't think of any way to refute this. He looks enormously frustrated.

TED: Oh, well, I suppose it's not too bad. As long as a tree doesn't fall through the roof or something!

Outside we hear a thundercrack. The lights go off. There is a long, slow, creaking sound. They all watch the window, from where the noise is coming. The creaking sound gets louder, then stops.

TED: Ha. I thought there —

We hear a crash and the lights go out.

Roll closing credits.

POST-CREDIT SEQUENCE

SCENE 33 INT./NIGHT 3
SET: PAROCHIAL HOUSE
Father Austin Purcell is talking to camera.

AUSTIN: . . . Here's a piece of advice my Father gave to me, and this not only refers to lagging, but any form of insulation. He said, 'Don't ever . . .' No . . . it was 'Always . . . always make sure . . .' No, sorry, it was 'Never . . .' Ah. I've forgotten. Never mind. What's your favourite humming noise? Is it . . . hmmmmmmmm . . . or is it *hmmmmmmmmmmmmmmm* . . . I think hmmmmmmmm . . . is my favourite, but sometimes, if I'm in a bit of a funny mood, I prefer *hmmmmmmmmmmmmmm*. That would be the sound of a fridge. But the first one would be the sound of a man humming . . . you never hear women humming. I've often wondered what a more feminine hum would sound like . . . mmm . . . mmmm. I knew a woman once, but she died soon afterwards . . . What was Hitler on about? That's no way to run Europe. Great roads, but if you've got no car, you might as well have some kind of ski-lift. They go way up in the air . . .

THE END

*We deleted these lines from the final version.

tentacles of doom

ARTHUR: One of the things we liked best about the characters in *Ted* was that they didn't think too much about religion; they were frightened it would drive them mad and because they didn't have any theological knowledge, they were absolutely terrified of anyone mentioning the subject. So the arrival of three bishops was bound to throw them into a panic. I think I'm right in saying that upgrading the status of a relic – in this case the Holy Stone of Clonrichert, which gave Dougal 'a great buzz' in Series One – is something that doesn't happen. Upgrading happens with saints, when they go through stages before beatification, but I don't think it's the same with relics. I don't even think the Church is keen on relics any more.

Anyway, we needed three bishops to conduct the upgrading – one for each of our boys to destroy. Once we'd decided on that, the structure of this episode was fairly easy. Jack being taught to say, 'That would be an ecumenical matter' was the inspired suggestion of (by now ex) producer Geoffrey Perkins. We were just going to have him saying 'Yes' and 'No', but that phrase really lifted it. There was a third line, 'Temptation comes in many guises', but it didn't add anything so we dumped it in the end.

GRAHAM: I like Jack's spiffy look. Normally he was absolutely hideous – you don't really see on TV just how revolting he was. Frank Kelly was actually a very lonely man on filming days; he would have to eat lunch on his own because his make-up was so horrific that nobody could bear to sit opposite him. He was like the sun; you couldn't look directly at him for any amount of time. He had a river of wax coming out of his ear; dried chapped stuff around his mouth and a milky-white contact lens…Just in case you never noticed, take a look at the space behind Jack's chair. We asked the design people if they could make it look as if the area had been 'infected' by Jack sitting there for so long. The wall is going black, and there's all manner of matter stuck there.

There's a subplot in this draft involving Ted being asked to prepare a paper by one of the bishops. It made the show about five minutes overlong and really didn't go anywhere. When we took it out, it barely caused a ripple in the rest of the show. Really, if you can take out a plot strand without having to rewrite anything, then it probably shouldn't have been there in the first place.

PART ONE

SCENE 1 INT./DAY 1
SET: PAROCHIAL HOUSE BATHROOM
Ted is standing by the toilet, fixing something in the cistern. Dougal is standing beside him.

TED: That might do it. (*He presses the handle, but it doesn't flush.*) Ah, for pity's . . .

He goes round to the front of the bowl. He pushes the handle again, but still nothing happens. He puts his head into the bowl. He looks around inside for a moment. At this point, Dougal pushes the handle. The toilet flushes. Ted's head remains out of sight, in the toilet, until the flushing sound ceases. Pause. He finally takes his head out, soaking wet, and looks at Dougal.

DOUGAL: That's working now, Ted.

Ted turns slowly, takes a deep breath and tries again. This time it doesn't work.

DOUGAL: It's broken again . . .

TED (*still angry*): Maybe it only works when my head's in it.

DOUGAL: Ted, maybe we should call a plumber.

TED: No, no, there's no need to get them involved. It's just a tiny, simple thing. Anyway . . . I'd be a little embarrassed to tell them how I . . . broke it in the first place . . . you know . . . that I was trying to give it a more powerful flush.

DOUGAL: Well, Ted, I have to say, it was fine for me. It was a good powerful flush, I thought.

TED: Yes, but you know . . . I'm thinking

more about Jack. When he's involved you want to get that stuff away as (*He thrusts his arm forward.*) . . . as *fast* and as . . . as *hard* as possible. Best thing would be for us to flush here, and then have it pop out somewhere in Sierra Leone.

DOUGAL: You're right there, Ted.

TED: Oh, wait now . . . wait now . . . aha, aha, aha, aha, aha, aha . . .

He reaches into the cistern and fumbles about. He finally emerges with a bottle of Jack Daniels.

TED: I thought Jack might have stashed something in here.

He reaches down and pulls out another, and another.

TED: Right! Try it now.

Dougal flushes. It makes an incredibly loud flushing sound, so loud that Dougal and Ted would not be able to talk over it if they tried. They give each other a high five.

SCENE 2 EXT./DAY 1
SET: PAROCHIAL HOUSE GATE
We see a drain just outside the gate. A jet of water shoots out of it and goes about twenty feet into the air.

SCENE 3 INT./DAY 1
SET: PAROCHIAL HOUSE
Jack is reading a book. We see that it is called simply 'Girls'. There are a few pictures on the cover of girls circa 1960. They look like models who would adorn the cover of knitting magazines.

JACK (*to himself*): Girls . . .

Dougal comes in. Ted follows, a towel tied around his head like a turban. He is looking at a letter.

TED: Oh, God . . . Bloody hell . . . tsk . . .

DOUGAL: Good news, Ted?

TED: No, very, very bad news. It's The Holy Stone of Clonrichert. They're making it a Class Two relic.

DOUGAL: Oh, great!

TED: There's nothing great about it, Dougal. It means they'll be sending a few bishops over to do a ceremony. And you know what they're like. We'll have to be on our best behaviour. It must be even holier than we thought. It might have something to do with that fella from England last year. He touched it and he grew a beard.

DOUGAL: Wow, that's weird. That'd be nearly enough to upgrade it to a Class One.

TED: A Class One is rare enough, Dougal. That's bringing people back to life, and time travel and cloning dinosaurs. Very rare . . .

DOUGAL: But . . . there must be millions of relics all over the world. How do they know which ones to do?

TED: Oh, there's all these things they have to think about . . . The history of the relic, how the publicity will affect the Church. All sorts of considerations would go into making a decision like that.

SCENE 4 INT./DAY 2
SET: A ROOM SOMEWHERE
Cut to reveal a plush library-like room. Two priests are in the room. One is smoking a cigarette and reading a magazine. The other is at a computer. He hits a button and looks up.

PRIEST 1: How about . . . The Holy Stone of Clonrichert?

PRIEST 2 (*doesn't look up from the magazine*): Whatever.

SCENE 5 INT./DAY 2
SET: PAROCHIAL HOUSE
Ted looks glum.

DOUGAL: Ah, come on, Ted, cheer up. It may never happen.

TED: Well . . . it is happening. They're definitely coming.

DOUGAL: Oh, right. Ah, well, who cares anyway. They come in, they strip the wallpaper down, fumigate the place and they're gone. What's so bad about that?

TED: Dougal . . . they're *bishops*.

DOUGAL: . . . Ohhh, right . . . yes, yes.

TED: Dougal, what is this confusion you have with bishops? Are you *absolutely* sure you know what bishops actually do? *Nothing* to do with fumigating houses or anything like that. Have you got that?

DOUGAL: Got it! Come on, Ted, let's play a game and get your mind off it. (*He holds up two boxes.*) Chess or Buckaroo?

TED: Eh . . .

DOUGAL: Actually, I wouldn't mind a game of the old chess today.

TED: Really?

DOUGAL: No, only joking, Ted! Buckaroo of course. But only if you're ready for another thrashing!

TED: You've never actually beaten me, Dougal.

DOUGAL: Oh, right . . .

We see Jack on all fours, sticking his head into the

fire to get a light.

TED: Ah, Buckaroo! The Sport of Kings! I suppose it won't be so bad, really. The bishops will have a look around, see that we're just a normal, everyday parish and go away. Nothing to worry about at all.

Ted notices Jack, who turns from the fireplace with the now-lit cigarette in his mouth. Also, his hair is smoking and his face is reddened and blackened. He sits down and calmly continues smoking his fag. Ted absently puts a final object on to the toy donkey. It 'buckaroos', sending little plastic bits everywhere.

SCENE 6 INT./NIGHT 2
SET: TED AND DOUGAL'S BEDROOM
Dougal is in bed. He wears a T-shirt with 'It's a priest thing. You wouldn't understand' on it. Ted is in bed, reading an official-looking letter.

TED: So, the ceremony's on Thursday, and they'll be arriving tomorrow. (*He puts the letter away.*) Now, Dougal, this is crucial. Listen to me, all right?

DOUGAL: Right, Ted.

TED: These bishops are very important. I'll try and stay around you all the time, just in case. So I can stop you saying anything that you shouldn't say to them.

DOUGAL: Like what?

TED: Well, something like what you said to Bishop Linsey when he asked where I was when Kennedy was shot.

DOUGAL: Oh, yeah . . .

TED: I mean, you overreacted slightly there . . . That's just a question people *ask*. He wasn't accusing me of *anything*. And, of course, there's Jack.

DOUGAL: Couldn't we hide him somewhere for a couple of days?

TED: No. They'd hear him shoutin' 'girls'.

DOUGAL: Maybe we could train Jack to say something apart from 'drink' or 'feck' or 'girls'. Like, remember the dog on *That's Life* a few years back?

TED: Dougal, Father Jack may be bad, but he isn't a *dog* . . .

We hear a scratching from somewhere outside.

TED: There he is now. I think he wants to go outside.

Ted gets up and goes to the door. Then he pauses.

TED: Wait though . . . maybe we *could* . . . teach him to say one or two things, nothing too specific, some all-purpose sentences like . . . 'That would be an ecumenical matter.' Yes, . . . I can't think of any religious question that couldn't be answered by saying that. It's what I always say when people ask *me* questions. That's the great thing about Catholicism. It's very vague and no one really knows what it's about. I think this might work, Dougal. Yes, it will work! I know it will!

DOUGAL: It won't work, will it, Ted?

TED: It won't, no, but we've got to *try*!*

SCENE 7 INT./DAY 3
SET: PAROCHIAL HOUSE
Jack sits in his chair, looking his usual self. Ted goes over to the table, picks up a large card and returns, speaking to Jack as he does so.

TED: Right, Father . . . we're going to have a little elocution lesson.

JACK: Drink!

TED: Now, come on, Father. You can't be saying 'drink' all the time when the bishops are here.

JACK: Feck!

TED: No, you can't say that either, Father.

JACK: Girls!

TED: Look, Father, go back to 'drink' for the moment.

JACK: Drink!

TED: Right. I want you to have a look at this.

Ted holds up the large card. It has the following written on it in felt-tip ink:

1. That would be an ecumenical matter.

---

*In the final version we inserted a scene where a blind-folded knife-thrower who is throwing knives at Larry Duff is distracted by Larry's mobile phone ringing.

2. Yes.

He shows it to Jack and points at the first word of number 1.

TED: Right, Father, have a go at the first one here. 'That . . .'

JACK: Drink!

TED: No, no . . . *'That'* . . .

JACK: Drink!

TED: No, try and concentrate, Father. 'That . . .'

JACK: Drink!

TED: That . . .

JACK: Drink!

TED: That . . .

JACK: Drink!

TED: That . . .

JACK: Drink!

TED: That . . .

JACK: Drink!

TED: That . . .

JACK: Drink!

TED: That . . .

JACK: Drink!

TED: Father, now, come on, I know you can do it. There'll be a little drink in it for you if you can do it.

JACK: Drink?

TED: Yes, I promise, Father. So . . . try again. 'That . . .'

Jack moves his mouth as if to say 'That'. He puts his tongue to his top teeth and tries to get the sound out.

JACK: Th . . . th . . . thhhhhhhh . . . thhhhhhhdrink!

TED: Come on, Father! You almost got it there!

JACK: Thhhhhhhhh . . . thhhhhhhhhhh . . . thhhhhhhhhh . . . THAT!

TED: Great!

JACK: THAT!

TED: Brilliant, Father, well done! OK, let's keep going here . . . 'That would . . .'

JACK: That . . . drink!

Ted's look of happiness dissipates. He knocks over the easel.

SCENE 8 INT./DAY 3
SET: BATHROOM
Ted sticks his head around the door.

TED: Mrs Doyle, you've left the cooker on.

Cut to reveal Mrs Doyle giving Dougal a very soapy bath.

MRS DOYLE: Oh, right, Father, I'll be there in a second.

Ted leaves.

SCENE 9 INT./DAY 3
SET: PAROCHIAL HOUSE
We see a Clonrichert calendar on the wall. A date on it is circled in red, with 'Bishops!!!' scrawled beside it. Ted comes into the room. He walks over to the table and munches on a biscuit. Mrs Doyle comes into the room.

MRS DOYLE: Right, Father, everything's

ready. There's a big vat of tea steaming away, and I've got the Ferrero Rochers arranged in a big triangular pile. Oh, God, Father, I'm so excited! Taking on three bishops all at once! Oh, I can't wait!

Ted moves to another part of the room, but Mrs Doyle continues to talk to the space he last occupied.

MRS DOYLE: I think this is going to be the finest moment of my career, Father. It's almost as if my whole life was leading up—

TED: Mrs Doyle . . .

Mrs Doyle looks around in confusion.

TED: Mrs Doyle, I'm over here.

Mrs Doyle turns, but is still not looking in the right direction.

MRS DOYLE: Oh, so you are, Father.

Ted comes up close to her.

TED: Mrs Doyle—

MRS DOYLE: Aiiiee!!

TED: Mrs Doyle, have you your contacts in?

MRS DOYLE: Tsk, no. A dog ran off with them. I thought I'd get away with it but I suppose I'll have to wear the glasses. Ah, I don't like wearing them, Father. I always think they make me look like a frustrated old bag!

Mrs Doyle fumbles in her handbag for her glasses.

TED: Ha, ha, ha . . . aahhh . . . I can't imagine that, Mrs Doyle. I'd say they look fine on y. . . (*She puts them on and turns to Ted. They magnify her eyes hugely. She blinks and it looks like two trapdoors opening and shutting.*) Aaaaaaggghhhh!!!!!!

MRS DOYLE: God almighty! Are they that bad, Father?

TED (*recovering*): No . . . no, I was just thinking about a scary film I saw. They're fine, they really are.

Ted looks at her queasily.

TED: Great . . .

MRS DOYLE: Ah, that's much better. I'll just go and check on the tea.

She moves out of shot. Ted flicks some dust off his

shoulder. *We hear Mrs Doyle's voice from out of shot.*

MRS DOYLE: Father? I have absolutely no idea where the door is.

Cut to reveal that she has taken only one step away from Ted, and is facing the wrong way as she speaks.

SCENE 10. INT./DAY 3
SET: PAROCHIAL HOUSE
We see a clock on the wall that says three o'clock. Cut to the view of a windswept, barren road seen through a pair of binoculars. Cut to Dougal with binoculars looking through the window. He puts the binoculars down.

DOUGAL: No sign of them yet, Ted.

Cut to Ted.

TED (*confused*): Dougal . . . Dougal, they're here.

Cut to a wide shot of the room. We see three bishops. Two sit down but one, Bishop Facks, paces the room in a slightly threatening way. Ted is also in the room.

DOUGAL: Oh, right, yeah. Sorry about that.

The bishops are Bishop O'Neill, a serious, slightly boring bishop; Bishop Facks, an aggressive priest who emphasises every point by poking people in the chest and fidgeting with pens, etc; and Bishop Jordan, a nervous bishop with a severe heart condition.

TED: Sorry, Bishop O'Neill. You were saying . . .

O'NEILL: Yes. Very simple ceremony. We'll just need a little incense.

TED: Incense . . . oh . . . I don't think . . . I think we're out of it. Dougal, have we any incense, do you know?

DOUGAL (*slightly confused*): There was a spider in the bath last night.

TED: No, *incense, incense!*

DOUGAL: Oh, right. No, I don't think so. (*Laughing slightly.*) Ha, ha, remember, Ted, remember what happened last week when we ran out of incense and got the Windowlene and . . .

Ted coughs very loudly indeed until Dougal shuts up. Pause.

O'NEILL: Well . . . I'm sure we can find some.

TED: Have you done much upgrading around the country recently?

FACKS: We recently elevated a mushroom field in Cavan to a Class Three.

TED: Great.

O'NEILL: Our work takes us all over the country.

JORDAN: We're trying to organise a large meeting at the end of the year where all ranks of the clergy can discuss their views with representatives of the lay community . . .

We see Dougal and Ted, their attention drifting.

JORDAN: What do you think, Father Crilly?

Ted is looking around, not paying attention. He notices everyone looking at him.

TED: Sorry, what?

FACKS: Do you think a close relationship between the lay community on this particular matter is desirable? Or should a certain distance be maintained?

TED: Eh, yeah . . . good question. Well, you know, involve the lay community, but keep them at a distance.

FACKS: How much of a distance?

Pause.

TED: . . . Couple of miles?

Mrs Doyle enters the room, her head up, looking around in confusion. She carries a tray.

MRS DOYLE: Here we are, now, tea for everyone!

She walks straight through the room and out through the other door. Pause.*

O'NEILL: I'm interested in your views on this matter, Father Crilly . . . Do you think you could draw up a paper?*

TED: What?*

JORDAN: Maybe a ten-page summary of your ideas?*

Through the window we see Mrs Doyle. in the front garden with her tray, looking around in confusion.*

TED: Well, I eh . . .*

FACKS: Is there a problem?*

TED: Well, it's just that, you know, no one told me that I'd have to do any work.*

JORDAN: Ha, ha. But that would be splendid, if you could do that for us.*

TED (*very unhappy*): All right.*

JORDAN: Sorry?*

TED: I said, *yes.**

Facks touches the 'buckaroo' and it jumps up suddenly.

JORDAN (*jumps slightly*): Oooh!

TED (*confused*): Are you all right, Your Grace?

JORDAN: Yes, I . . . I had a minor heart attack last year so I have to take it easy. I got a bit of a fright there.

TED: Oh . . . right . . .

JORDAN: It's not a problem. Just . . . give us a bit of a warning if you're going to do anything sudden—

Dougal suddenly jumps in front of Jordan with his hands up.

DOUGAL: Aaaaaaaarrrggghhh!!!!

JORDAN: Aaahhh!!!

TED: Dougal! What are you doing?!

DOUGAL: Sorry, Ted. I just remembered *Aliens* is on after the News.

TED: For God's sake, Dougal! I'm terribly sorry, Bishop Jordan.

O'Neill tends to Jordan, who is trying to get his breath back. Ted leads Dougal away.

TED: Did you not hear what he was saying about his heart?

DOUGAL: It's just . . . it's the director's cut. (*To everyone.*) C'mon, everyone. Let's all have a big lads' night in!

---

*We deleted these lines from the final version.

TED: Dougal, just – just sit down. (*To Jordan.*) A *heart attack*. That's a rare enough thing, I'd say.

O'NEILL: There were certainly a lot of prayers said for Bishop Jordan around the country.

O'Neill prattles on. As he does so, Dougal leans over to Ted.

DOUGAL: I don't know why we can't look at *Aliens*.

TED (*fierce whisper*)**:** Dougal! Bishop O'Neill is speaking . . .

DOUGAL: But they'd love it, Ted!

TED: Dougal, we're not watching *Aliens*!!!

END OF PART ONE

* * *

PART TWO

SCENE 11 INT./DAY 3
SET: PAROCHIAL HOUSE
FACKS (*contemptuously regarding a magazine*)**:** I think our priority must be to fight back against the anti-clerical bias in the media. (*He pokes Ted.*) Do you know what I mean, Father? Do you see what I'm getting at?

TED: Yes, yes . . .

Mrs Doyle enters with her tray full of Ferrero Rochers.

TED: Ferrero Rocher?

O'NEILL: Aha! I think you are spoiling us, Father Ted!

Ted gives Mrs Doyle a signal but she doesn't see it.

TED (*sighs*): Mrs Doyle . . .

MRS DOYLE: Oh, right . . .

Mrs Doyle walks further into the room unsteadily. She holds the sweets just out of reach of Bishop Jordan. He reaches over with a grunt and takes one. She navigates her way around the rest of the room in much the same way, always holding the sweets out too far for anyone to reach.

TED: Sorry about that. You were saying . . .?

FACKS (*stabbing his shoulder with his index finger*): Ah, yes . . . I was saying we should fight back against the media. We have to make our voice heard!

JORDAN: Where is Father Hackett?

FACKS: Would that be Father Jack Hackett?

TED: Eh, yes . . .

FACKS: A friend of mine, Father Cave, was taught by him in Saint Colm's and still has very vivid memories of him.

SCENE 12. INT./DAY X*
SET: AN OFFICE
A priest is looking at himself in the mirror. We see there are loads of explosives tied to his chest. He closes his jacket over them, picks up a gun and walks out. We see loads of photographs of Jack all over the wall. After a moment, we hear an explosion.

SCENE 13. INT./DAY 3
SET: PAROCHIAL HOUSE
Ted stands up.

TED: Mrs Doyle, could you get Father Hackett for us, please?

MRS DOYLE: Certainly, Father.

JORDAN: I must say, Mrs Doyle, they keep you on your feet. My housekeeper isn't the best, I'm afraid. Sometimes I think that it's me

*We deleted this scene from the final version.

that should be making the tea for her!

Mrs Doyle laughs heartily. Everyone else laughs along. However, Mrs Doyle has now become hysterical.

MRS DOYLE: Ha . . . ha . . . ha . . . making the tea for her . . . ha, ha, ha, ha . . .

TED: Mrs Doyle . . .

MRS DOYLE: Ha . . . ha . . . ha . . . HA, HA, HA, HA . . .

TED: Ah, Mrs Doyle . . .

MRS DOYLE: HA, HA, HA . . . Making the tea for her . . .HA, HA, HA, HA, HA!!!

Ted nods at Dougal. They grab the still-laughing Mrs Doyle and carry her out of the room. Ted comes back in.

TED: Sorry about that! Ah, here's Father Hackett now . . .

After a second a completely transformed Jack enters; he is dressed relatively neatly – although his clothes seem 'off' somehow, perhaps a size too small? His hair is Brylcreemed so that it's very slick, and he smiles in a strange, forced way.

TED: He was very much looking forward to your visit, weren't you, Father?

JACK (*with a strange look at Ted*): Yes!

TED: Ah, ha. Well, this is Bishop O'Neill . . . (*The bishop makes a move forward.*) Don't get up, Bishop . . .

JACK: *Yes!*

TED: This is Bishop Jordan . . .

JACK: *Yes!*

TED: . . . and this is Bishop Facks . . .

JACK: *Yes!*

JORDAN: They're looking after you, then, Father?

Jack looks at Ted, who gives an imperceptible nod.

JACK: That would be an ecumenical m —

Ted interrupts him with a halting, coughing noise.

Pause.

JACK: *Yes!*

O'NEILL: I was just saying, Father, how I'm

looking forward to discussing the social effects of some of the Church's thinking as regarding issues of personal morality.

Jack steals a quick look at Ted.

TED (*under his breath*): Ecumenical . . .

JACK (*immediately*): That would be an ecumenical matter.

O'NEILL: Yes, I . . . I suppose it would. Good point, Father.

JACK: *Yes!*

FACKS: That's what we need, a more positive attitude like Father Hackett's.

TED: What?

O'NEILL: I agree. I can see Father Hackett making a valuable contribution over the next few days.

TED: Oh, God . . .

Ted gives a fake smile. Dougal seems happy. Jack looks uncertain, but still with his fixed smile.

JACK: *Yes!*

SCENE 14. INT./NIGHT 3*
SET: TED AND DOUGAL'S BEDROOM
Ted is sitting with a laptop computer. He is examining a bruise on his arm.

TED: God almighty! Bishop Facks is a big poking fan, isn't he?

DOUGAL (*examining a bruise of his own*): Oh, you're right there, Ted.

TED: What the hell am I going to write about, Dougal? What do I know about the relationship between the clergy and the lay community? And tomorrow . . . Oh, God . . . I don't know how long Jack can keep it up. I had to feed him another *gigantic* bottle of whiskey as a reward . . . Anyway . . . 'The lay people and the clergy' . . . Oh, God, this is turning into a nightmare.

DOUGAL: 'Lay people' . . . who are they again?

TED: People who aren't the clergy.

TED: Oh, right, yeah. Like Tom Hanks.

TED: He'd be one, yeah.

DOUGAL: Hitler . . . Ruby Wax, Denzel Washington . . .

TED: Yes . . .

DOUGAL: Bjork . . .

TED: . . . Yeah, the thing is, Dougal, he doesn't want me to *name* everyone who's not actually a member of the clergy.

DOUGAL: No?

TED: No. That'd take a hundred million years. No, I have to think of something of interest to say about them. God, this is so hard. And on top of all this we've got the Mrs Doyle problem.

DOUGAL: God, yeah. Where do you think she got to?

Ted shrugs.

SCENE 15. EXT./NIGHT 3*
SET: A FIELD
We see a cow and hear Mrs Doyle offscreen.

MRS DOYLE: Ah, go on, Father, have a cup. Will you not have a little cup? Just a drop?

We see Mrs Doyle standing beside the cow, the tea tray in her hands.

SCENE 16. INT./NIGHT 3*
SET: TED AND DOUGAL'S BEDROOM
Ted is still frowning at the computer. Suddenly, inspiration strikes.

TED: Yes. Yes. *Yes!* That's it! I'll start by describing how economic necessity has forced people to pay more attention to the day-to-day pressures of life at the expense of their spiritual health. If I cross reference that with the experiences of the clergy in the mid Fifties, I think gradually a coherent picture of where the Catholic religion is heading will emerge! Yes! It's so simple! And I tell you, Dougal, I'm not moving from this spot until I've finished it, even if it takes me all night.

He starts typing wildly. Dougal looks impressed.

---

*We deleted this scene from the final version.

SCENE 17. INT./DAY 4*
SET: PAROCHIAL HOUSE
Ted is talking to Bishop Jordan.

JORDAN: Yess . . . well, thanks very much for doing that report.

TED: Well, I enjoyed doing it.

JORDAN: There's just one thing, Father. You seem to have just done a big list of people who aren't priests.

TED: That's right, yes.

JORDAN: I was really hoping more for an examination of the relationship between lay people and the clergy.

TED: Were you? Oh, no! I thought you just wanted the list. Still, never mind. If you're ever compiling a list of people who aren't priests, it could come in very handy.

Jordan nods unenthusiastically and moves off. Dougal comes up to Ted.

DOUGAL: That other idea not work out, Ted?

TED: Nope.

*We deleted this scene from the final version.

SCENE 18. EXT./DAY 4
SET: FIELD
We hear O'Neill's voice.

O'NEILL: Heavenly Father, hear our prayer . . .

As we hear these words, we see a sign that reads 'The Holy Stone of Clonrichert – Admission £20.00. Students and O.A.P.'s £19.00'.

Cut to O'Neill blessing the rock. The other bishops stand beside him. Ted, Dougal and Jack are also present. Everyone wears ceremonial vestments, although Ted's, Dougal's and Jack's are very basic.

O'NEILL: . . . We pray that this rock be upgraded to a Class Two relic . . . (*Pull back to reveal the rock for the first time. It is tiny, about the size of a fist, but is at waist level on a plinth.*) . . . and by the grace of God bring healing to all who pass within a radius of two and a half to three feet of it, at Your discretion. And may all who are healed in such a way give glory to you, Our Lord, through your earthly form of the Class Two relic.

EVERYONE: Amen

DOUGAL: Eamon.

Silently O'Neill bows his head and steps back. He blesses himself.

O'NEILL: Right!

The priests relax and mingle.

TED: Great stuff. Right, will we head off?

FACKS: I'll stay here and have a little chat with Father Hackett.

Jack's eyes widen, the rest of his face still frozen.

TED: Oh. That's probably not a good idea. Father Hackett is very tired.

FACKS: Oh, nonsense. You'll stay and have a chat, won't you, Father?

JACK: *Yes!*

TED: No, Father. You're very tired, aren't you?

JACK: That would be an ecumenical matter!

Facks looks puzzled. Jordan butts in and takes Ted by the arm.

JORDAN: Come on, Father . . .

A nervous Ted is led away by Jordan. Facks and Jack are alone.

FACKS: Well, here it is. Fantastic, isn't it?

JACK: *Yes!*

FACKS: I suppose a lot of people would think it old-fashioned, this business of blessing relics . . . but we have to fight back against that kind of cynicism, Father. These days, you can't open a newspaper without seeing some trendy anti-clerical article written by some bearded Leftie.

JACK: *Yes!*

FACKS: What, Father?

JACK (*thinks*)**:** That would be an ecumenical matter.

FACKS: Of, course, Father. But we should act now, before it's too late.

He looks away from Jack, out to sea.

FACKS: All this materialism. People nowadays seem obsessed with earthly, unspiritual pleasures.

Jack notices that the bishop's back is turned away. He reaches into his sleeve and extracts a clear, plastic tube. He sucks at the tube and some whiskey shoots up into his mouth. His eyes cross as he drinks it. He quickly moves it back up his sleeve. The Bishop turns around.

JACK: Temptation . . . ecumenical matter . . . yes!!!

FACKS: How right you are, Father. How right you are . . .

As he says this, he taps Jack once on the shoulder with his index finger. Jack starts a little bit. He doesn't like that at all.

SCENE 19. EXT./DAY 4
SET: COUNTRY ROAD
Dougal and O'Neill are in front, Ted and Jordan about ten feet behind.

O'NEILL: So, Father, *do you* ever have any doubts about the religious life? Is your faith ever tested?

DOUGAL: Tested?

O'NEILL: Yes. Anything you've been worried about, any doubts you've been having about any aspects of faith, anything like that?

DOUGAL: Well, yes. You know the way God made us all, right? And he's looking at us from heaven and everything . . .

O'NEILL: Mmm, mmm . . .

DOUGAL: . . . And then his Son came down and saved everyone and all that . . .

O'NEILL: Yes.

DOUGAL: . . . And when we die we're all going to go to heaven?

O'NEILL: Yes, what about it?

DOUGAL: That's the bit I have trouble believing in.

Over to Ted and Jordan. They approach the driveway of the house. Ted looks nervously ahead of him at Dougal and O'Neill.

JORDAN: When you come face to face with death, it makes you think about things. I saw that film recently – *Apollo 13* – and it reminded me of my own brush with death. Do you know what I mean?

TED: You mean . . . you were in space when you had your heart attack? I didn't . . .

JORDAN: No. How could I be in space?

TED: I don't know . . . sorry. No, I suppose not.

JORDAN: No, I meant I know what it's like to be close to death.

TED: I'm sure you do. I've never been close to death myself, thank God, but a lot of my relatives are dead. Are you coming in?

JORDAN: I'll be in in a second. It is very bracing around here, isn't it?

TED: Bracing. Yes, actually I need to use the old W.C., so I'll go on . . .

JORDAN: Yes, you do that. I'll take the air. I feel very close to nature these days.

TED: Oh, yes, well you're in the right place if you want to be close to nature. It's all over the shop around here. Right, I'll see you soon . . .

Ted goes to the house. Jordan takes a deep breath and exhales.

SCENE 20. EXT./DAY 4
SET: DOOR OF THE HOUSE
Dougal unlocks the door.

DOUGAL: . . . So then, if God has existed forever, what did he do with all that time before he made the earth and everything? You know?

O'NEILL: Well, we all have doubts.

DOUGAL: And what about when you weren't allowed to eat meat on Fridays? How come that's all right now, but it wasn't then? Did people who ate meat on Friday then go to Hell or what? It's mad.

Cut to a very thoughtful bishop. Ted comes up.

TED: He's not bothering you, is he?

O'NEILL: No . . . no, it's . . . fascinating.

TED: Well, just call me if you need help. Now, I just need to . . . 'see a man about a dog'.

He flashes a look at Dougal and then goes up the stairs.

SCENE 21 EXT./DAY 4*
SET: COUNTRY ROAD
Facks is talking to Jack. He is leaning over him and poking him repeatedly in the shoulder. Jack looks from him to the poking finger, his expression a mixture of slight pain, irritation and anger.

FACKS: But do you see what I mean, Father? Do you see what I mean? Do you see what I'm getting at?

Jack's face is now red with anger. He clenches his teeth and raises his hand. Suddenly, Facks stops poking him. He turns around.

SCENE 22 INT./DAY 4*
SET: BATHROOM
We see Ted standing up, buttoning his trousers.

SCENE 23 EXT./DAY 4
SET: DRIVEWAY
We see Jordan walking outside. He stands over the grate that we saw the water shooting from earlier, covering it with his cassock. He looks around.

*We deleted this scene from the final version.

JORDAN (*deep breath*): Ahhhhh . . .

SCENE 24 INT./DAY 4
SET: BATHROOM
Ted finishes washing his hands. He goes to the door, remembers something, then goes back and flushes the toilet.

SCENE 25 EXT./DAY 4
SET: DRIVEWAY
There is a strange gurgling from below. Jordan's cassock starts to billow slightly. Suddenly, we hear a great rush of water shooting up. The cassock billows up around him as he tries to keep it down. The water roars in every direction. Close-up on his face.

JORDAN: Aaaaaaaarrrrrggggghhhhh!!!!!!

He clasps his chest and keels over. The water gradually eases down and out of sight.

SCENE 26 INT./DAY 4
SET: PAROCHIAL HOUSE
We see a Marilyn Monroe poster on the wall. It is the still from 'The Seven Year Itch' that shows her skirt billowing up. Cut to Dougal and O'Neill entering. They bump into Ted as he is about to go outside to join Jordan.

TED: Ah, there you are. I hope you had a nice chat.

DOUGAL: It was great.

O'NEILL: I think I reached some very interesting conclusions.

TED: Good. What exactly?

O'NEILL: Well, it's nonsense, isn't it?

TED: Sorry? What is?

O'NEILL: Religion.

TED: Eh . . .

O'NEILL: I've been struggling with my conscience for some time. But Father McGuire clarified the whole thing for me, really. God, Heaven and Hell . . . it's all a load of rubbish. Only a child could believe it, really. It's scarcely more credible than Santa Claus or the tooth fairy.

TED: Dougal! What have you been up to?

An innocent-looking Dougal shrugs. Suddenly,

there is a scream from outside. Mrs Doyle runs in and addresses the air beside the three men.

MRS DOYLE: Quick! It's Bishop Jordan! I think he's dead!

She runs outside, followed by the three men, feeling her way as she goes.

SCENE 27 EXT./DAY 4
SET: DRIVEWAY
Mrs Doyle turns the corner and points to the ground.

MRS DOYLE (pointing)**:** There! Oh, dear Lord, what's happened to him?

The three look to where she is pointing. Cut and we see what they are looking at. It is a dustbin on its side.

TED: Mrs Doyle . . .that's a dustbin.

MRS DOYLE: What? Oh, I mean . . . there!

She turns and points. We see the bishop on the ground behind them. Ted and Dougal turn and look at each other.

O'NEILL: God almighty! This is terrible! Where's Bishop Facks?

SCENE 28 EXT./DAY 4
SET: FIELD
Jack is calming down slightly.

FACKS: We have to straighten out the media. That's the important thing, Father. And we have to do it . . .

He turns around and raises his finger in the air. Close-up on the finger. Close-up of a primed, ready-for-action Jack. Facks brings his finger down and pokes Jack severely in the shoulder with it.

FACKS: Now!

Jack's eyes widen in pure rage.

JACK (Standing, arms raised to either side.)**:** Aaaaaaarrrrrrrrrrrggggggghhhhhhhhh!!!

Facks cowers on the ground. Jack grabs The Holy Stone in rage.

SCENE 29 EXT./DAY 4
SET: FRONT DOOR OF PAROCHIAL HOUSE
Ted and Dougal stand at the doorway. Out comes

O'Neill, in civvies. He also has a backpack slung over his shoulder. He grabs Dougal's hand and shakes it warmly.

O'NEILL: Dougal. Thank you.

DOUGAL (blank)**:** Ah, you're welcome, Bishop.

O'NEILL: No, no, Eddie.

TED: Are you sure you won't reconsider your decision—

O'NEILL: No. It's too late anyway. I'm off to India for two months with a few friends. Ah, there they are . . .

He runs off. Cut to see a brightly coloured van. The side door opens and three hippie-type girls wave him in. O'Neill steps inside, waves, and then slides the door closed. Next out is Facks. As he walks haltingly past them, we see that he is severely bow-legged.

TED: See you again, then! (Embarrassed.) Will it . . . will it still be a Class Two when they remove it?

Facks just looks at him. He walks off towards an ambulance.

DOUGAL: Bye!

A coffin is next. Ted and Dougal go quiet. It is wheeled out by two men.

TED (touches coffin)**:** Eh . . . God bless you . . .

The ambulance, the hearse and the van all drive away. Ted and Dougal close the door.

SCENE 30. INT./DAY 4
SET: PAROCHIAL HOUSE
Ted and Dougal walk into the room. They don't say anything. Ted looks at Dougal. Pause.

TED: Went pretty well, I thought.

THE END

the old grey whistle theft

ARTHUR: The original idea behind this episode was to give Dougal a friend. The second idea was to have law and order breaking down, and the two elements came together – not easily, but because they had to. It was tough to write and we felt that that might come across. Funnily enough, however, it turned out to be one of the best-loved episodes in this series.

It was nice to give Dougal a friend if only to get him out of the usual partnership with Ted, where he exists usually to misunderstand things, ask silly questions, come to mistaken conclusions and so on. This gave him an extra dimension, a bit of life outside Ted. We were glad to do this because it was sometimes easy to take Ardal for granted. He spent the first series feeling slightly insecure, I think, because people weren't giving him any acting notes. The truth was, we didn't need to. Whenever he widened his eyes and opened his mouth slightly, he simply became Dougal; everything he said sounded like Dougal and everything sounded funny. His line readings were invariably perfect, partly because of this quality but also because he shared our sense of humour. The character of Dougal was very delicate as he had the potential to be very annoying. As far as that goes, casting Ardal was the best decision we ever made.

GRAHAM: This was a big ol' son of a bitch to write. It went through about seven drafts and to us, never seemed to get any better. Somehow, despite our worries, a combination of elements – Joe Rooney as Damo, the illogical but funny ending, the image of Mrs Doyle standing in the darkness – made people forgive the plot, which was even more inconsequential than usual. (Although how this episode could be more inconsequential than anything that had gone before or after is probably only evident to Arthur and I.)

Mr Benson came in part from the penchant Irish parents have for using the phrase, 'The Man'. Whenever children are being loud or generally misbehaving in a restaurant or any other public place, you'll hear Irish parents scaring their children by pointing to the waiter/park keeper/whoever and saying, 'Here comes The Man! You've made The Man angry!' Mr Benson is the ultimate manifestation of 'The Man'.

PART ONE

SCENE 1 INT./DAY 1
SET: PAROCHIAL HOUSE

Ted and Dougal are standing beside a picnic basket, which is on the table. Ted is putting various snacks into the basket. Jack is asleep in another corner of the room.

TED: . . . So he was already having an affair with the sister, and this was when his wife was seriously ill in hospital . . .

DOUGAL: Wow.

TED: Incredible, isn't it? But then, of course, who does he get pregnant but the babysitter, so he doesn't know whether to stay with the wife, or the sister, or run off with the babysitter.

DOUGAL (*beat*)**:** When's his next confession?

TED: Tuesday. I'll keep you posted. (*Pause. Dougal goes to the basket. Ted looks at a list.*) Right! Let's see! Jam . . .

DOUGAL: Check . . .

TED: Pepperoni . . .

DOUGAL: Check . . .

TED: Mustard . . .

DOUGAL: Check . . .

TED: Bread . . .

DOUGAL: Check . . .

TED: Great. We're all packed then.

DOUGAL: No, no . . . (*He reaches into the*

basket and takes out a piece of paper.) They're all on this list.

TED: Right, so we both made lists . . . No problem. I'm sure I put them all in anyway. (*He smiles.*) I must say, I'm really looking forward to this.

DOUGAL: Ah, me too, Ted. It's good to take a day off every now and again. It shouldn't be just work, work, work, should it?

TED: Yes. It's not as if everyone's going to join some mad religious cult just because we go on a picnic for a few hours.

DOUGAL: God, Ted, I heard about those cults. Everyone dressing in black and saying that Our Lord's going to come back and judge us all.

TED: No . . . Dougal, that would be us, now. You're talking about Catholicism, there.

Mrs Doyle enters. She carries two heavy canvas shopping bags.

MRS DOYLE: Right. Here's the sandwiches, Father. The rest are in the hall.

TED: Great.

MRS DOYLE: I hope you like them, Father.

TED: Oh, I'm sure I will. I love an old sandwich from time to time. Doesn't matter what flavour it is as long as it's not egg. (*Mrs Doyle's smile freezes almost imperceptibly. She looks at Ted but her eyes glaze over slightly.*) . . . 'Cause you know how much I hate egg. Oh, God, even the smell of it brings me out in a terrible rash. I tell you I wouldn't eat an egg sandwich if you paid me – they're just horrible stinking things. As I've told you earlier, anything but egg, Mrs Doyle, and how I wanted anything at all except egg. They're egg, aren't they, Mrs Doyle?

MRS DOYLE: Yes.

TED: Great.

DOUGAL: I'll eat them, Mrs Doyle. I love egg. Sometimes I think I like egg so much that one day I'll turn into a big, giant egg.

TED: Oh, well, never mind. I'll just have a few Pepperoni. Right! Dougal! You ready?

DOUGAL: Ready as I'll ever be, Ted! I don't

think I've ever looked forward to something as much as I've looked forward to this picnic.

TED: OK, so!

DOUGAL: Oh, wait, I just remembered. I can't go.

TED: What? Why not? . . .

The doorbell rings. Dougal goes 'Oh!' and starts putting his coat on. Ted leaves the room.

SCENE 2 EXT./DAY 1
SET: PAROCHIAL HOUSE
Ted answers the door. Standing outside is a young priest of Dougal's age. He has a slightly sulky demeanour.

PRIEST: How'ya. Is Dougal in?

Dougal, carrying a football, rushes up behind Ted and runs past him. The young priest and Dougal immediately run off, Dougal bouncing the football along the ground. They chatter excitedly to each other as they disappear. Ted looks after them, puzzled. He is about to go back inside when he hears a voice.

VOICE: Hello, Father!

Ted turns to see the local policeman, Sergeant Hodgins, standing on the other side of the wall.

TED: Ah, hello, Sergeant.

HODGINS: Hello, Father. Just doing the rounds.

TED: On the trail of some crazed murderer, no doubt!

HODGINS: What was that?

TED: Sorry?

HODGINS: Something about a crazed murderer? Where? When did this happen?

TED: No, I was only joking.

Pause.

HODGINS: Oh, right. Well, if you ever hear anything about a crazed murderer on the loose, report it. That'd give me somethin' to do, you know.

TED: Yes.

HODGINS: Very quiet here, you know. Not much crime.

TED: It is very quiet, all right.

HODGINS: So, you know, if you hear anything . . . doesn't have to be a murder or a kidnapping, you know. Anything. A disappearance! That'd be great! Lord Lucan! Anyway . . . anything at all . . . a car wrongly parked, anything. Give me a call. By the way, that licence up to date on your car?

TED: Eh, it is yes.

HODGINS (*very disappointed*)**:** Yeah, thought it might be.

TED: Bye, Sergeant.

Ted closes the door. Hodgins sighs and looks round, totally bored.

SCENE 3 INT./DAY 1
SET: PAROCHIAL HOUSE
Ted walks back into the living room. Mrs Doyle comes in.

MRS DOYLE: Who was that young priest, Father?

TED: Hmmmm? Oh . . . I don't know . . .

MRS DOYLE: So Father McGuire's not going on the picnic.

TED: No. Never mind. I'm meeting Larry Duff and a few of the lads from Saint Colm's. I'd better give him a call, make sure they know where they're going.

SCENE 4 EXT./DAY 1
SET: ROADSIDE/ROADBLOCK
We see some soldiers and policemen with machine guns beside a car at a roadblock. They point the guns at four priests who have their hands in the air. One of them is Larry Duff. He slowly moves his hands down to a telephone, checking it's OK with a soldier who has a gun trained on him.

LARRY: Hello? Ah, hello, Ted!

TED: Larry. How are you?

LARRY: Ah, grand. Got a bit of a problem, though. We mightn't be able to make the picnic.

TED: Ah, God, Larry, why?

LARRY: You know Father Williams who was driving us over?

TED: Billy? What about him?

LARRY: Well, they found a big box of machine guns in his house.

TED: Really? God, I didn't think he'd be interested in that type of thing.

LARRY: Ah, yeah, you think you know someone. Anyway, there you go. Bye, Ted!

He puts the telephone down. In the background a priest runs out of shot. One of the soldiers sees this and lets loose with machine-gun fire. Larry looks at the scene with a blank expression.

SCENE 5 INT./DAY 1
SET: PAROCHIAL HOUSE
Back to Ted.

TED: Well. Just me, I suppose.

He spots something and looks back at Jack. Then very gingerly he bends down and brings two bottles of wine into shot. He very quietly puts the two bottles into the basket. Jack stirs, and Ted freezes. Then he lets go of the bottles and picks up a third. He very gingerly places it in the basket. We hear an almost inaudible clink as one of the bottles touches another.

JACK (*wakes suddenly*): Drink!!!

TED: Ah, it's not drink, Father. It's fizzy water.

Jack gives him a very suspicious look.

JACK (*thinks*): Jacobs Creek Chardonnay, 1991.

TED: No, I promise you, F— (*He looks at the bottle.*) My God – you can tell that just from the sound?

JACK: Drink!!! Drink!!! Drink!!!

TED: Well, I thought I might go on a little picnic, Father . . . on my own.

Jack stares at him. We stay on his face as Ted speaks.

TED: Outside. You wouldn't like it, Father. Honestly, you'd be happier here. You'd . . . there's . . . I . . . ah . . .

SCENE 6 EXT./DAY 1
SET: PICNIC AREA
We see a sign that reads 'Picnic Area'. The picnic area is a wind-blasted, rocky, awful-looking place. Ted and Jack are directly under the sign, which is bending dangerously and creaking loudly in the wind. Jack is sitting in his wheelchair, watching Ted with interest. Ted is holding up a large picnic rug. The wind is howling, wrapping the rug around Ted's body. Jack just looks at him. The sign suddenly spins and hits Ted on the back of the head. Ted falls over, still wrapped in the blanket.

TED: The flipping thing . . . Could you do something, Father?

Jack stands up, walks over to Ted, bends down and picks up a packet of cigarettes lying beside Ted. He then walks back to his seat, lighting a fag, sits down and calmly observes Ted's tribulations. Ted finally struggles over the blanket and holds it down. He gets some rocks and, with enormous effort, places them on each corner of the rug. Then he lies there, breathing deeply.

TED (*out of breath*): Right! There we go.

He kneels down and takes out the bottles of wine. He puts them beside him, some distance away from Jack. He turns to the picnic basket and takes out some bread. When he turns back, we see that the three bottles of wine are overturned and empty. Ted looks at Jack, who is twiddling his thumbs innocently.

SCENE 7 EXT./DAY 1
SET: FIELD
Dougal, and his friend Father Damo Lennon, are sitting on an old stone wall. A large house is some distance in the background. Father Damo Lennon is smoking. Dougal has his hands in his pockets and is kicking the wall in a lackadaisical manner.

DAMO (*offering Dougal a fag*)**:** Do you want one?

DOUGAL: Ah, no, thanks, Father Lennon. (*Pause.*) What time is your tea ready?

DAMO: Frosty usually has it about six.

DOUGAL: Who?

DAMO: Frosty. Father Frosty.

DOUGAL: Oh, wow . . . Frosty! Brilliant!

DAMO: What do you call your fella?

DOUGAL: Who, Ted? Ah, no . . . Just Ted, but . . . it's the way I say it, you know.

DAMO: He's an awful eejit, isn't he?

DOUGAL (*uncertain*)**:** Yeah . . . ha, ha . . .

DAMO: Who do you like better, Oasis or Blur?

DOUGAL: Eh, Blur.

DAMO: Wha?

DOUGAL: Oasis! I mean . . . Oasis.

We see a door open in the house behind the wall. A middle-aged priest steps outside. It is Father Frost.

FROST: Your tea's ready.

DAMO (*very rudely*)**:** I'll be in in a minute!

Dougal looks very impressed.

SCENE 8 EXT. DAY 1
SET: PICNIC AREA
Jack is now comatose. He snores loudly. Ted has finally managed to set everything up. He has a variety of flasks, a water purifier, bread, plates, etc.

TED (*rubbing his hands*)**:** Great! Here we go!

He takes out a book, 'The life of Mel Gibson', and settles back to read it. We hear an offscreen voice.

VOICE: What the fup are you doing here?

We see that a very nasty-looking middle-aged man

is standing over Ted. His equally horrible wife stands beside him. They are Mr. and Mrs Joyce.

MR JOYCE: This is my fuppin' spot. Get the fup off.

MRS JOYCE: Hit him, Frank.

TED: But there's lots of room. Could you not just go over there?

MR JOYCE: No fuppin' way!

MRS JOYCE: F.U.P.O.F.F.

MR JOYCE: Yeah fup off! We come here every fuppin' Sunday.

TED: But today's Saturday.

MR JOYCE: That doesn't fuppin' matter. The fact that we come here on Sunday means that this is our fuppin' spot. So fup off.

MRS JOYCE: Hit him Frank. I'll hit him.

MR JOYCE (*to Ted*)**:** She fuppin' would, too. And so would I, you fuppin' backstard.

TED: Why are you talking like that?

The man points to the picnic-spot sign. It has a list of rules and among them is 'No swearing'.

MR JOYCE: So fup off. You grasshole.

TED: I don't know why . . .

MR JOYCE: That's fuppin' it. I'm callin' the fuppin' man. (*He starts shouting.*) Hey! Hey! Hey! Hey! Hey! Hey!

We see a tiny hut about fifty or sixty yards away. A door suddenly opens and we see a man sitting in a chair. He leaps out of the chair and starts blowing his whistle furiously. He bolts the front door behind him and runs to a nearby bush. He goes behind the bush and raises a megaphone to his mouth.

MR JOYCE: Hey! Hey! Hey! Hey!

BENSON: I'm here, Mr. Joyce.

MR JOYCE: Listen, this backstard priest is in our spot.

BENSON: What's the problem there?

TED (*shouting*)**:** But we were just . . .

As he speaks, he raises his plastic fork to indicate something. Mr. Joyce jumps backwards.

MR JOYCE: Watch it!

TED: What? I wasn't going to—

BENSON: Put the fork down! Put the fork down!

The sound cuts out. Pause. Ted looks at the fork and drops it. It blows away, making a dwindling plink sound as it goes. Benson starts advancing slowly towards Ted.

BENSON: Now put your hands very slowly down to your sides – slowly! Keep them where I can see them.

Benson is close enough to speak to them normally.

BENSON: I'm putting the megaphone down, now, all right? Nice and easy . . .

He places the megaphone very deliberately on to the ground. He approaches Ted, palms held up.

BENSON: We don't want anyone getting excited. We're all friends here. Let's not do anything silly. All right? (*The atmosphere is very tense.*) I'm going to reach into my pocket now. All right? Everything's fine . . . (*He reaches into his pocket and takes out a packet of cigarettes. He offers one to Ted.*) Cigarette?

TED: Ah, no, thanks.

BENSON (*lighting up*)**:** I guess you're right. These things'll kill me someday. OK, Father . . . here's the story . . . I like to keep a quiet picnic area here. I want everyone who comes here to have fun – enjoy a few sandwiches, a bottle of lemonade, have a few laughs, and then go home.

TED: I think that's what I'll do now. I'll go home.

BENSON: You do that. Slowly.

TED: Right. Bye, then.

Ted turns around, secretly terrified. He starts to throw everything into the basket. Meanwhile Benson turns to the couple.

BENSON (*to the Joyces*)**:** All right, come on, get on with the picnic. Nothing to see here. Nothing to see here . . .

SCENE 9 INT./DAY 1
SET: PAROCHIAL HOUSE
Ted is unpacking the picnic basket, looking very annoyed. Dougal enters. He keeps his head to one

side so that we only see him in profile. Ted doesn't notice this at first.

TED: Ah, there you are. You wouldn't believe the day I had. You wouldn't – my *God.* That Mr Joyce is the *rudest* man . . . (*Dougal nods, still only showing Ted his profile. He sits down.*) And that Benson fella. Unbelievable . . . blowing that bloody whistle all the time. Someone should take it and . . . Where did you go off to, anyway?

DOUGAL: I just went off with Father Damo Lennon. He's over with Father Frost.

TED: Oh, yes. Father Frost said they might come over for a bit of a holiday.

DOUGAL: Father Damo's great.

TED: Maybe I'll . . . Why are you walking like that?

DOUGAL: Like what, Ted?

TED: Like what?

DOUGAL: Oh, right. Sorry, Ted.

Dougal turns quite sheepishly. We see that he is wearing a tiny earring.

TED (*turning*)**:** Right, I . . . Dougal, what's that?

DOUGAL: What? Oh, this . . . Nothing.

TED: Dougal, it's an earring.

DOUGAL: Oh, right, yeah. It is, all right.

TED: Dougal, what's got into you? You can't go round wearing an earring.

DOUGAL: Ah, Ted. All the young priests have them. Father Damo has one.

TED: What? Did he give you the idea?

DOUGAL: Yeah. He's great.

TED: Well, what next? I suppose he'll be giving you crack cocaine or something.

DOUGAL: Crack cocaine . . . ah come on, Ted.

Dougal looks disgusted, then his eyes light up.

TED: Well you'll have to take it out.

DOUGAL: Ah, Ted.

TED: Come on now, Dougal. You're helping with Mass later. I'm not having you looking like that. What'll your parents think when they get here?

DOUGAL: Ah Ted, you don't know what's going on with young people.

TED: I was young once, you know. God, when I think of the things we used to get up to in the seminary. Me and a bunch of the other lads there, once we mitched off to see a Dana concert.

DOUGAL: Dana? God, Ted, no one listens to Dana anymore. You'd want to be mad to listen to her!

TED: Father Bigley listens to Dana, and he's not mad.

DOUGAL: Why is he in that home then?

TED: He's in that home because . . . because of those fires. But that's nothing to do with Dana. Anyway, come on, take the earring out.

DOUGAL: Oh, all right. God, Ted, I should be able to do what I want. I am almost twenty-six. You still treat me like I was twenty-four.

TED: Well, Dougal, if you go round wearing earrings, then what do you expect? I'll start treating you like a twenty-six year old when you start acting like a twenty-six year old. Anyway, time for your bath.

DOUGAL: Is it? Oh, right. (*He gets up to leave.*) Just remember, Ted. Today's youth are the young people of tomorrow.

He leaves. Ted looks a bit puzzled.

SCENE 10 EXT./ NIGHT 1
SET: PICNIC AREA
We see the following from a mystery protagonist's

point of view. We are outside Benson's hut. It is very quiet. As 'we' approach, we hear Benson snoring. The door opens. We enter. The camera points down and closes in on the snoring Benson. We see Benson's whistle, attached to a row of keys, hanging on a nail behind him. Close in on the whistle. A hand comes into shot and tries to take it off the nail. It rattles noisily as it does so. We constantly turn to see if Benson has woken. But he has not, even though the noise is terrible. Finally, the hand takes it off the nail. The camera turns around and points out of the hut. We hear a panting sound as we run away at great speed from the hut. The camera shakes and judders as we run. This run lasts slightly longer than it perhaps should. Soon we pass by a man and his dog.*

MAN: Hello, Father!

VOICE (*completely out of breath*)**:** Ung!

'Our' hand comes into shot and waves at him. The camera shakes as we run on a little further.

END OF PART ONE

* * *

PART TWO

SCENE 11 EXT./DAY 2
SET: JOHN AND MARY'S SHOP
Ted is about to cross the road when he hears a noise from above. He looks up and squints into the sky. Cut to see a helicopter hovering about fifty feet in the air. Hodgins is sitting at the open side door.

HODGINS: Hello, Father!

TED: Ah, hello . . .

HODGINS: How are things?

TED: Fine . . . fine . . .

HODGINS: Good. (*There is a lull in the conversation.*) Well, I'll be off. See you later, Father! (*To the pilot.*) Go, go, go, go!!!!

The helicopter flies away. Ted stands there, confused.

SCENE 12 INT./DAY 2
SET: JOHN AND MARY'S SHOP
We see that Mary has John's head in a bucket of water.

MARY: You bastard!

She pulls John's head out of the bucket.

JOHN: Slag! Mmmmfbrrr. . .

Mary shoves his head back into the water again. Ted enters. Mary keeps John's head in the water.

MARY: Hello, Father!

TED: Hello, Mary . . . Ah . . .

Mary looks to where Ted is looking.

MARY: Oh.

She releases John. John stands up, gasping for air as he does so.

JOHN: . . . Haaaaaaaaaalllloooo, Father.

TED: Hello, John.

JOHN: Mary was just washing my hair. She has lovely soft hands.

TED: I was just looking for some firelighters.

JOHN: Oh yes. What type? Inflammable or non-inflammable?

TED: Eh, inflammable.

MARY: I'll get them. They're out the back.

Mary leaves.

TED: I didn't know Sergeant Hodgins had a helicopter.

JOHN: Oh, yes. He's had to get one in because of this whistle thing.

TED: Whistle thing . . . ?

JOHN: Yes. Look . . .

He hands Ted a copy of 'The Craggy Island Examiner' and Ted looks at it. The headline reads

'Mr Benson's whistle stolen. Full story pages 2, 3, 4, 7, 8, 11, 13, 14, 15, 20'.

MARY (*from back*): Isn't it terrible, Father?!

JOHN: The whole island's talking about it. Who would have thought law and order would break down here on Craggy Island?

MARY (*still out back*): God help us all, Father!

TED: Well, if it was just a whistle that was stolen . . .

JOHN (*not listening*): I've had to buy a shotgun and everything. (*He lifts the shotgun over the counter. As he speaks, he casually holds the shotgun so that it's pointing at Ted. Ted does a little nervous dance, trying to stay out of the line of fire.*) I wouldn't hesitate to use that, now. If that man comes in and tries to steal any of the whistles I have here, I'd blow his feckin' head off his shoulders. Ha, ha! (*Ted joins in the laughter uncertainly. Mary comes back in with the firelighters.*) Look Father. I've even got it cocked so I get a jump on him.

TED: Is it not dangerous to have it cocked like that, John?

JOHN: Not at all, Father. As long as you don't suddenly drop it or something.

He slams the gun, pointing at Ted, down on the counter. Ted jumps slightly.

MARY: There you are, Father. If they don't work, bring them back and we'll give you a refund.

TED: OK, so. Thanks very much.

He leaves. We see Mary grabbing the barrel of the gun and trying to wrest it away from John.

SCENE 13 EXT./DAY 2
SET: JOHN AND MARY'S SHOP
Ted closes the door behind him. An old woman, Mrs Glynn, approaches Ted.

MRS GLYNN: Father, did you hear about the whistle being stolen?

TED: Yes, I . . .

MRS GLYNN: I never thought I'd see such a thing. What next? Someone'll be murdered, I suppose. And then the porn kings and drug barons will move in. And then where'll we be? Drive-by shootings and the like. It'll be like *Boyz N the Hood*. And then they'll have all the hoors selling their wares on the street, and the pimps'll be using crack to keep the hoors under control.

We hear a muffled gunshot from inside the shop.

MRS GLYNN: I'm going home now, and I'm going to lock myself in the basement until they catch him. Goodbye, Father!

TED: Eh . . . goodbye . . .

SCENE 14 INT./DAY 2
SET: PAROCHIAL HOUSE
Dougal and Father Damo are sitting in front of the television, playing a computer game – 'Streetfighter 2'. Jack is asleep. Ted comes in. He carries the newspaper.

TED: Unbelievable . . . they really are making too big a deal about all this. Look! A pull-out supplement about whistles!

We see the supplement. It has a picture of a whistle on the cover and beneath it the word 'Whistles'.

TED: And there's even a crossword clue here that says 'Two across – Mr Benson had one stolen last night – seven letters'. I don't know—

Ted finally notices that no one is paying attention to him.

TED: Ah, Dougal. Aren't you going to introduce me to your friend?

DOUGAL: This is Father Damo.

DAMO (*without looking*): Howya?

TED: Hello, Father. Playing the old computer game there? (*Damo and Dougal stifle a laugh. Ted's a bit confused at this. The telephone rings. Ted picks it up.*) Hello, Father Ted Crilly speaking . . . Yes, ah, Father Frost. Yes, yes, I'll tell him. (*He puts his hand over the mouthpiece and addresses Damo.*) Eh, Father Damo, Father Frost says you're to go home. Your tea's ready.

DAMO: Tell him I'm not goin'. I'm havin' dinner here.

TED: Are you? Oh . . . (*To the telephone.*) Eh, hello, Father, eh . . . he says he's having dinner here. (*Pause.*) Father Damo, Father

Frost says you're to go home immediately.

DAMO: *Aw shite!* Didja tell him I'm having dinner here?

TED: Eh, yes . . .

DAMO: Well, tell him to feck off then.

Pause. Ted blinks for a moment, trying to think of how to relay this information to Frost.

TED: Father Damo's happy enough here for the moment. Right. OK. (*To Damo.*) Eh, Father Frost says if you don't come home for tea, he'll come down here and get you.

DAMO: Tell him that's fine. I don't care what he does. He's not my boss.

TED: Right. (*To the telephone.*) Eh . . .

DAMO: (*standing up*): Oh, all right, all right. I'm goin'. Tell him I'm goin'. Seeya Dougal.

He goes out through the door and gives Dougal a secretive signal to follow him. Dougal does so.

DAMO: Dougal, mind this for me.

DOUGAL: Oh, yeah, right.

Damo gives Dougal a packet of cigarettes.

DAMO: Give them back to me later. Frosty hates smokin'.

DOUGAL: OK, Damo. See ya!

Dougal puts the fags in the pocket of his jacket. To make more room, he takes something out. It is a set of rosary beads. He looks embarrassed.

DAMO (*sarcastically*): Prayin', yeah?

DOUGAL: What? Oh, no. They're eh, . . . they're Ted's.

DAMO: I'll see ya.

He leaves.

TED (*from inside*): Dougal!

DOUGAL: Oh, *God*. What does he want now?

Dougal 'tsks' theatrically and does an exaggerated 'cool' walk into the room.

SCENE 15 INT./NIGHT 2
SET: TED AND DOUGAL'S BEDROOM
We see Dougal, asleep. He starts mumbling.

DOUGAL: Consonant, vowel, consonant, vowel, consonant, vowel, consonant, vowel.

Cut to Ted, a pillow over his head. He takes it off and lies on it, facing away from Dougal. It's no use. He turns on the light, and starts to get dressed. He takes his jacket off the back of a chair and puts it over his arm as he walks out of the room.

DOUGAL: Consonant . . . put your clothes back on, Carol, I can't concentrate.

SCENE 16 INT./NIGHT 2
SET: PAROCHIAL HOUSE HALLWAY
Ted, in silhouette, opens the door to the room. He fumbles with the switch and finally manages to turn the light on. When he does so, we see Mrs Doyle standing right beside him, holding out a tea tray.

MRS DOYLE: Tea, Father?

TED: Good God almighty!!!

MRS DOYLE: Oh, sorry, Father, did I give you a fright?

TED: What are you doing up?

MRS DOYLE: Oh, I always stay up, Father. Just in case any of you need a cup of tea.

TED: Mrs Doyle, there's really no need. You should get some sleep. How long have you been doing this?

MRS DOYLE: Oh, about three years now.

TED: But we never get up at night.

MRS DOYLE: Well, you're up now, aren't

you, Father? Unless I'm hallucinating from lack of sleep. That's happened before, all right.

TED: Well, I was just going to go for a walk. So . . .

MRS DOYLE: OK, so, I'll stay here.

TED: There's really no need.

MRS DOYLE: Ah, go away with you. Have a nice walk, Father.

Ted thinks of saying something, then decides against it. He leaves the room, closing the door softly behind him. Mrs Doyle stands there, looking straight ahead, the tea tray in her hands. After a moment she looks at the light switch and turns it off. We see her standing there, in exactly the same position, in the darkness.

SCENE 17 INT./NIGHT 2
SET: PAROCHIAL HOUSE HALLWAY
Ted is at the hall door. He opens the door and puts on the jacket. It's far too small for him.

TED: Ah, God . . . (*He's about to take it off when he feels something in the pocket. It's Damo's packet of cigarettes.*) Oh, Dougal . . .

He opens it and examines the contents. He frowns, reaches in and pulls out Benson's whistle. Ted looks at it for a moment.

SCENE 18 INT./DAY 3
SET: PAROCHIAL HOUSE
Ted and Dougal are eating cornflakes at breakfast.

TED: Dougal . . . is there anything on your mind? (*Dougal looks at Ted, a blank look on his face.*) Let me rephrase that . . . You don't want to talk about anything? Something bothering you in some way?

DOUGAL: Like what, Ted?

TED: Well, let me put it this way. Have you done anything you might be a bit embarrassed about? (*Dougal looks vacant.*) Have you done anything bad, recently? Anything wrong?

DOUGAL: Wrong?

TED: Wrong, yes. Do you remember, Dougal: right and wrong? You know, the differences between the two. Page one of *How to be a Catholic.*

DOUGAL: Eh . . .

TED: Just think – 'Things that are wrong' . . . Anything happening there? What is 'wrong'?

DOUGAL: Eh . . .

TED: Honestly, Dougal, this is very basic stuff. What is wrong? Or is everything perfectly acceptable?

DOUGAL: Just give me a second, Ted. Eh . . .

TED: Arson. There's one. Murder. Infidelity. Swearing . . .

DOUGAL: Swearing, yeah . . .

TED: Anything else?

DOUGAL: Eh . . . (*He bites his lip.*) . . . Ummmmmmm . . . (*One eye twitches. Ted is holding his breath, silently urging Dougal on. Dougal opens his mouth and says with complete uncertainty.*) . . . lying?

TED: Yes! Well *done*, Dougal!

DOUGAL: Thanks, Ted. I —

Dougal looks a bit unsteady.

TED: Are you all right?

DOUGAL: I'm fine, Ted. I just need to sit down.

Ted takes Dougal by the arm and leads him to a chair.

TED: Sorry about that, Dougal. Probably pushed you a bit far there . . .

DOUGAL: No worries, Ted.

TED: But . . . another thing that's wrong is stealing. What I'm trying to say is . . . it's wrong to steal. It's just something you don't do.

DOUGAL: Right. Except you.

TED: Yes. What?

DOUGAL: You're allowed to steal.

TED: What are you talking about?

DOUGAL: The money from that Lourdes thing . . .

TED: Different thing, Dougal. First of all, the money was just resting in my account before I moved it on.

DOUGAL: It was resting for a long time, Ted.

TED: It was, yes, but —

DOUGAL: Good long rest.

TED: Dougal – let's forget about me. All right? This is about you. Is there anything you want to tell me? (*He takes out the whistle and gives it to Dougal.*) About this, for example.

Mrs Doyle enters. Ted instinctively grabs the whistle back from Dougal and puts it in his pocket.

MRS DOYLE: Father, Sergeant Hodgins and Mr Benson are here.

TED: Dougal, I heard a noise there. Could you go and get the . . . shears.

DOUGAL: Right y'are, Ted.

Dougal runs out of the room. Benson, in a wheelchair, is pushed into the room by Hodgins.

HODGINS: Hello, Father. Sorry to have to disturb you, but, ah . . . I felt we should meet, talk about this . . .

BENSON: You've heard about the whistle business, Father?

TED: God, yes. It's all a big load of fuss over . . . (*Benson and Hodgins glare at him.*) . . . what is obviously a very serious matter.

HODGINS: Yeah, a bit of excitement at last. This is the first bit of excitement since we thought the Boston Strangler might be a local man. Wow! We were *way* off there!

TED: What happened to you? The thief didn't break your legs or something?

BENSON: No, Father. When I woke up, and saw that my whistle had been stolen, I went into a state of shock and lost the use of my legs. Well, one of them. This one's fine. But the other one . . .completely lost all feeling. Look.

He takes Hodgins's baton and whacks himself on the leg with it, then immediately doubles up in pain.

BENSON: Oaaaaaaagghhhh, Sweet Jesus!

HODGINS: Yes. The shock also affected his

memory, Father. It's actually the other leg which doesn't have any feeling.

BENSON: Anyway, Father, come on. Have you heard anything?

TED: About what?

BENSON: About my whistle. Did you hear anything during Confession?

TED: No, no, now, come on. The Confessional is sacrosanct.

BENSON: So you have heard something, Father?

TED: No, I haven't heard anything.

BENSON: I've had that whistle for fifty years. It saved my grandfather's life.

TED: Did it really?

BENSON: Yes. He was being executed by the British. They had him up against a wall and they shot him. And the bullets all hit the whistle in his coat pocket and bounced off him.

TED: Really? The bullets bounced off him?

BENSON: Yes.

TED: God almighty! So he survived?

BENSON: No, no. They just reloaded and shot him again.

HODGINS: Listen, Father, I didn't want to say anything, but . . . Jim saw someone.

TED: Yes?

BENSON: He didn't get a good look, but did notice something . . . the collar. Jim says it was a priest. Who stole the whistle.

Dougal comes into the room with the shears.

DOUGAL: Oh, right. That'd be Ted.

TED: What!

DOUGAL: Do you remember, Ted? You were talking about stealing something, and then you showed me the whistle. You put it in your top pocket there.

(*Pause.*)

TED: Dougal, come on, now. Dougal sometimes gets confused . . . things get sort of mixed up in his mind and he . . .

DOUGAL: . . . Was the whistle sort of bent, with an inscription underneath that read 'To Billy from Padraig'?

BENSON: That's exactly right.

DOUGAL: Oh, right. That's the one Ted had.

TED: No, Dougal.

DOUGAL: It is, Ted. Try your top pocket. Go on, Ted, seriously. I bet you it's there. I'm sure it is. Give it a go.

Ted, defeated, reaches into his pocket and fumbles around.

DOUGAL: It's more to the right, there.

TED: *Yes, Dougal.* Thank you.

After a moment, he takes out the whistle. Hodgins and Benson stare at him.

TED: Hah! Yes! Right! Well there's an obvious explanation.

BENSON: Is there, Father?

TED: Oh, yes.

DOUGAL: What is it, Ted?

TED (*incredibly calm*): Well, I just have to go away for a couple of minutes. Then I shall return with a full and frank explanation.

BENSON: It better be a good one.

TED: It will be completely satisfactory. Just excuse me for a few moments.

Ted leaves the room.

SCENE 19 INT./DAY 3
SET: TED AND DOUGAL'S BEDROOM
Ted enters very slowly. He sits down on his bed and puts his head in his hands. He concentrates very hard.

SCENE 20 INT./DAY 3
SET: PAROCHIAL HOUSE
Benson and Hodgins seem a little uncomfortable. Dougal is not sure what to say.

DOUGAL (*to Hodgins*): So I hear your babysitter got pregnant . . .

Hodgins looks confused. He is about to say something when Mrs Doyle enters suddenly.

MRS DOYLE: More visitors, Father.

In come two priests, one of whom is Father Damo. He is being marched in by an older priest, Father Frost.

DAMO: Gerroff!!!

FROST: Right. Ah, I believe there's a Mr Benson who's had a whistle stolen?

BENSON: That's right. That'd be me.

FROST: Well, I have the culprit here.

BENSON: What?

DAMO: Yeah, yeah, I stole it. So what, it's only a whistle.

BENSON: But . . . why?

HODGINS: Yes. Why? Are you unhappy, Father Lennon?

Damo shrugs and says something under his breath.

FROST: I saw him with it on Tuesday morning. Then I heard Mr Benson's whistle had gone missing. I asked him about it and he said that he hadn't seen it, but he thought Father McGuire was the culprit. Sorry about that, Father McGuire.

DOUGAL: Well it was my fault for stealing it.

FROST: But you didn't steal it, Father.

DOUGAL: Oh, right.

FROST: He hid it in a packet of cigarettes, apparently.

DOUGAL: Oh, right. That must be how we

got a hold of it. 'Cause Father Damo gave me the cigarettes to mind.

The door bursts open. Ted comes in.

TED: Right! Right, I have a full explanation.

BENSON: Ah, Father, we were just . . .

TED: Hello, Father Damo, Father Frost. I was just about to tell everyone why I stole the whistle.

FROST: No, Father . . .

TED: No, no, I have to get it off my chest. It's been bothering me ever since I took it.

DOUGAL: Ted . . .

TED: Sh . . . Dougal. Fifteen years ago . . . I met a young boy, an orphan. His parents had been killed in some sort of bizarre accident involving trees . . . a tree fell on them, that's it. They were both crushed. This young boy has nothing, nothing to his name, except a dream.

DOUGAL: Ted. . .

TED: Shut up, Dougal. His dream was to own his own stable. With prizewinning horses in every . . . bit of the stable. But then, tragedy struck. A strange disease took hold of him, one that affected his speech so that he could only communicate by raising his eyebrows. Once for yes, twice for no. 'If only I had a whistle,' he thought. 'So that I could train my horses to win the Grand National and the Derby . . .This young, brave man wrote to me two weeks ago asking . . .

DOUGAL: Ted, Father Damo took the whistle . . .

TED (*immediately*): Did he? Oh, right. Well, that's that cleared up. See you all soon!

HODGINS: What's that about the horses?

TED: What? The horses . . . ah, nothing. I was going mad. Listen, you'd better go. I have to do another one of those Masses.

BENSON: Wait!

They all look at him. He is holding the whistle and gazing at it in wonder. He slowly puts his hands on the arms of the wheelchair. Slowly, he pushes himself up on to his feet, his eyes wide as if experiencing a miracle.

BENSON: Ah! I . . . I can walk! I can walk! I can waaalllkkk!!!!

He walks unsteadily out of the room with his hands in the air.

TED (*to Dougal*): Dougal, don't put too much faith in people who are 'cool'. Most of the time they're just on the fast track to a life of crime. Father Lennon will probably end up like that corrupt cardinal in *The Godfather III*.

DOUGAL: Oh, you're right there, Ted.

TED: So, have you learnt something from your experience?

Pause.

DOUGAL: No.

THE END

SONG FOR EUROPE

GRAHAM: While *Father Ted* was written very much with both an Irish and British audience in mind, we still had to be careful that we didn't alienate any of our British viewers by using plotlines that would only mean something to the Irish. Therefore, we had to use only those aspects of Irish life that were noteworthy enough to cross the Irish sea. For instance, the way Ireland kept winning the Eurovision Song Contest, and the oft-reported urban myth that stated we were going to pick a bad song in order to deliberately lose the contest and thereby avoid the expense of hosting it again.

We had two structures to fall back on here. The first was the rivalry with Dick Byrne, which had its own pattern, and the second was provided by the process of writing a song (writing the music and lyrics, going into a studio, doing a video and, finally, performing it live). It featured one of our all-time favourite characters, Jeep Hebrides.

Funnily enough, the scene when Ted and Dougal are wondering what the song should be about is a mirror image of Arthur and me doing the same thing when we were writing the episode. I said, 'What'll the song be about?' and Arthur replied, 'How about a lovely horse?' Five minutes later, when I was able to stand up again, we gave Dougal the line.

There's a little nod to *Seinfeld* in this episode: 'Not that there's anything wrong with that type of thing' is an 'Irishified' lift of a catchphrase from a brilliant episode called *The Outing*. (If you don't like *Seinfeld*, by the way, you get no muffins round at my house. I think it might be the best sitcom ever written.)

ARTHUR: The mumbling presenter was handed to us on a plate by Steve Coogan who used to do a fantastic impression of one of his relatives, who apparently mumbled like that. Our initial idea was that Steve might play the part himself, but we also wanted Jon Kenny in the show. He and his partner Pat Shortt (who plays the mad Tom) are the funniest comic actors in Ireland.

PART ONE

SCENE 1 INT./DAY 1
SET: PAROCHIAL HOUSE

Ted is humming softly to himself while reading a newspaper. Mrs Doyle has stopped her polishing and listens to him dreamily. Dougal sticks his head around the door.

DOUGAL: Ted, did you see my record collection?

TED: Your record collection?

DOUGAL: Yeah.

Ted picks up an old single that is beside him. He shows it to Dougal.

TED: Here it is. And Dougal, you have to have more than one record for it to be a 'collection'. What you have is a 'record'.

DOUGAL: Oh, right, yeah.

He goes to the record player and starts fiddling around with it. Ted starts humming again. Mrs Doyle stops what she's doing and looks up at Ted. She cocks her head and listens in a dreamy way.

MRS DOYLE: You know, you've a beautiful voice, Father.

TED: What? Ah, no I don't, really.

MRS DOYLE: No, you do. It's gorgeous.

TED: Well, thanks very much.

MRS DOYLE: Did you ever think of turning professional?

TED: Well, no, I'm a priest.

MRS DOYLE: You know, Father. I don't think I've heard anything more beautiful in my life. Sing something else there . . . Go on.

TED: Well, I don't normally do requests!

MRS DOYLE: Ah, sing something for me, Father.

TED (*enormously flattered*)**:** No . . .

MRS DOYLE: Do, Father, go on, please.

TED: Well, ha ha . . . (*He hums 'Wherever I Lay My Hat', drifting in and out of the lyrics.*) 'By the look in your eye, I can tell you're gonna cry . . . dum, dum, dum . . . I'm the type of guy . . . Wherever I lay my hat, that's my home.'

He finishes, then pauses.

MRS DOYLE: I didn't like that so much Father. I was a bit disappointed with that one, to be honest.

TED (*crestfallen*)**:** Well, yes, thank you, Mrs Doyle.

MRS DOYLE: God, I'm surprised at that . . . that wasn't very good at all.

TED: Yes . . .

MRS DOYLE: I used to love that song, but that version was *catastrophic* . . .

TED: Well, Mrs Doyle, I tell you what, I won't book Carnegie Hall just yet.

MRS DOYLE: I don't think they'd let you play Carnegie Hall with a voice like that.

She scurries out through the door. Dougal perks up.

DOUGAL: Carnegie Hall. Oh, Ted, here's one . . . How do you get to Carnegie Hall?

TED: Practise!

Pause.

DOUGAL: What?

TED: That's the old joke, isn't it? How do you get to Carnegie Hall? Practise.

DOUGAL: Huh?

TED: Oh, I see. Eh, you'd have to go to New York, Dougal.

DOUGAL: Oh, right. Do you mind if I put on my record?

TED: No, go ahead.

DOUGAL: I've got Eurosong fever, Ted.

TED: Oh yes?

DOUGAL: Oh, God, yeah. I love the Eurosong competition, Ted. I can't wait. I've got it all planned out. I'm going to keep the night free, get a big bag of popcorn and watch the whole thing.

TED: 'Keep the night free'. Right, so you'll have to reschedule . . . what exactly? Your annual address to the United Nations?

DOUGAL: What, Ted? (*Ted ignores him.*) God, Ted, I'm so excited. What time is it now?

TED: Half one.

DOUGAL: Half one. And the competition is on in . . . (*He looks at his watch.*) . . . May.

TED: That's eight months away, Dougal.

DOUGAL: I know! Isn't it incredible? It only seems like a couple of months back that the last one was on. God, Ted. Imagine winning the Eurosong! Wow! When you think of all the stars who've won it.

TED: Like who?

Dougal looks blank.

DOUGAL: Ted, you know they're looking for entries for this year's competition?

TED: Are they?

DOUGAL: Yeah.

TED: Yes, well . . .

DOUGAL: Why don't we . . .

TED: Dougal, don't say . . .

DOUGAL: I mean . . .

TED: Dougal . . .

DOUGAL: Come on . . .

TED: No.

DOUGAL: Imagine if we won, Ted. We'd be famous. Like Nelson Mandela and his mad wife.

TED: Dougal, we don't have the time to be entering Eurosong '96. Anyway, we'd have to write a song. That needs a certain type of person with a very special talent . . . Cole Porter, George and Irene Gershwin*, Chris de Burgh. Any old eeejit can't just take up the art of songwriting just like that. (*The telephone rings. Ted picks it up.*) Hello. Father Ted Crilly speaking.

We see who is on the end of the line. It is Father Dick Byrne.

DICK: Hello. Dick Byrne here.

TED (*darkens*): Ah, hello Dick.

DICK: Well, Ted, are you enterin' this year?

TED: What?

DICK: Eurosong '96. The young fella here has

---

*Ted obviously believes it was a husband and wife team.

me driven mad with it.

Cut to Father Cyril McDuff looking fondly at an album entitled 'The Best of the Eurosong Contest'.

DICK: Anyway, we thought we'd give it a go. Why don't you have a try as well, I'm sure you'd win . . .

TED: Well, thanks very much, but . . .

DICK: . . . If all the other contestants were killed! Ha, ha!

TED: Well, I'm sure we'd do just as well as you would, Dick.

DICK: No, you wouldn't.

TED: Yes, we would.

DICK: No, you wouldn't.

TED: Yes, we would.

DICK: No, you wouldn't.

TED: Yes, we would.

DICK: No, you wouldn't.

TED: Yes, we would.

DICK: No, you wouldn't.

TED: Yes, we would.

DICK: No, you wouldn't.

TED (*very annoyed*): Yes, we would, yes we would, yes we would.

DICK: No, you wouldn't times a thousand!

TED: Y—

DICK: Jinx! No comebacks!

An enraged Ted realises he's beaten and slams down the telephone.

TED: Dougal, get the guitar . . .

DOUGAL: But I thought you didn't . . .

TED (*roars*): I said get the guitar!!!!!!

Dougal hops slightly with the shock.

SCENE 2 INT./NIGHT 1
SET: TED AND DOUGAL'S BEDROOM
Ted and Dougal are in the bedroom. Dougal sits by a keyboard. Ted has a guitar. They sit on the edge of their beds.

TED: Right, what'll we write it about?

DOUGAL: How about a lovely horse?

TED: OK. We'll call it . . . 'My Lovely Horse'. (*He writes this down on a piece of paper.*) . . . My Lovely Horse . . . by . . . Father Ted Crilly.

DOUGAL: And Father Dougal McGuire . . .

TED (*a bit more reluctantly*): . . . And Father Dougal McGuire . . . right. Will we write the lyrics first? Or will we do the music?

DOUGAL: Eh . . . lyrics. Then we'll fit the tune around it.

TED: Right. Here we go!

Both of them just sit there, looking off into the middle distance. Pause.

DOUGAL: Maybe we should do the music first.

TED: Right! Here we go!

He strums one chord on his guitar. Pause.

DOUGAL: I liked that.

TED: Was that all right?

DOUGAL: Yeah, it was a bit sad.

TED: Good, good. I'll write it down. That was an 'A' I think. (*He writes it.*) OK, so . . .

Pause.

DOUGAL: I think . . . I think I have a line.

TED: Right! Lyrics! Go ahead, there, Dougal.

DOUGAL: What's it called again?

TED: 'My Lovely Horse'.

DOUGAL: All right, how about this . . . 'My lovely horse, I want to hold you so tight, I want to rub my fingers through your tail, and love you all night . . .'

TED: Dougal . . .

DOUGAL: 'I want to be with you all the time and kiss you on the head —'

TED: Dougal, Dougal, stop there. We want to keep out of the whole area of, you know, actually being in love with the horse.

DOUGAL: Oh, right.

TED: It's more that we're friends with the

horse. We want to jump around with it a little and, you know, just have a good laugh with it.

DOUGAL: Right. Chase rabbits.

TED: Yes, except I don't think horses actually chase rabbits. What does a horse do? That's a good start. Think about what horses actually do.

Pause.

DOUGAL: What about something like 'Take this lump of sugar, baby, you know you want it.' That'd be like something the rap fellas'd write.

TED: Forget about them, Dougal. Forget all about Icy Tea and Michael Jackson and those fellas. They won't help us. Anyway, come on . . . we're not moving from here until we finish the song. You ready?

DOUGAL: Ready, Ted! Let's do it!

TED: Now, Dougal, don't take it too seriously. It's only a bit of fun, all right?

We see a Pope-clock twisting to show the passage of time.

SCENE 2A INT./NIGHT 1
SET: TED AND DOUGAL'S BEDROOM
Fade up on Ted and Dougal. Ted is standing up with a cigarette in his mouth. Dougal is on the bed with the keyboard. There are cans and bits of paper on the floor, the room is filled with cigarette smoke and the atmosphere is much like the Rolling Stones' studio after fifteen hours of non-stop rehearsal.

Dashes indicate censorious bleeps.

TED: Just play the f—king note!

DOUGAL: The first one?

TED: No, not the f—king first one! The f—king first one's already f—king down. Play the f—king note you were f—king playing earlier! I've been f—king playing the f—king first one. We've got the f—king first one!

DOUGAL: So . . .

TED: Just play the f—king note you were just f—king playing there! The f—king thing you were just f—king doing! Play the f—king note!!!

The Pope-clock spins again.

SCENE 2B INT./NIGHT 1
SET: TED AND DOUGAL'S BEDROOM
Cut to reveal Ted and Dougal splayed out on their beds asleep. Dougal's keyboard is still on and is doing a slow samba rhythm. Ted is slumped over his guitar. Fade out.

SCENE 3 INT./DAY 2
SET: PAROCHIAL HOUSE
Ted is sitting on a stool with his guitar. Dougal stands beside him, behind the keyboard. An expectant Mrs Doyle and a grumpy Father Jack are on the sofa, watching them. Dougal presses one button and a drumbeat starts. He then stands back, not touching the keyboard for the rest of the song. Ted starts playing his guitar – the same note for each line.

TED: 'My lovely horse,
Running through the fields
Where are you going
With your fetlocks blowing in the wind.'

Shot of Jack and Mrs Doyle taking this in.

DOUGAL AND TED: (*chorus*)
'I want to shower you with sugar-lumps
And ride you over fences

Polish your hooves every day
And bring you to the horse dentist.
My lovely horse
You're a pony no more,
Running around with a man on your
back, like a train in the night.'

Ted does the one note again, and then moves his hand up the fretboard to do the final note. It goes wrong.

TED: Oh, wait, wait . . .

He tries again. It sounds off.

TED: Wait, I can do this.

He tries again. This time it sounds reasonably OK. The song ends. Ted puts the guitar upright and leans on it. Pause.

TED: It needs a bit of work here and there, but what do you think in general?

Ted and Dougal look expectantly at Jack and Mrs Doyle. Mrs Doyle cannot conceal her look of distaste. Jack looks at her, looks at them, reaches around the side of the sofa, picks up a shotgun and shoots the guitar.

TED (*looks at shattered guitar*): Right . . .

SCENE 4 INT./DAY 2
SET: PAROCHIAL HOUSE
Ted and Dougal are sitting on the sofa, looking glum.

TED: Father Jack's right. It's a terrible song. It really is. God almighty, what were we thinking?

DOUGAL: Ah, it's not that bad, Ted.

TED: Well, the lyrics are fine. There's no problem there. But there's no tune. It's just one note over and over again. Oh, God . . . and I went and booked time in that studio. I hope we can cancel.

DOUGAL: Ted. Can I put on my favourite Eurosong? Maybe that'll cheer us up.

TED: Yes. That might help. What is it?

Dougal goes to the stereo and puts on his record.

DOUGAL: Nin Huugen and the Huugen Notes. It came fifth in the 'Song for Norway' competition in 1976.

TED: Where on earth did you get that?

DOUGAL: Ah, you know me, Ted. I've always had an interest in rare, hard-to-find records.

TED: Dougal, can I remind you again, you've only got one record. That's not really an 'interest'. Maybe if you developed an interest in records that weren't hard to find, you might actually be able to find some records.

Dougal has put the record on, and it's quite tuneful.

TED: That's not too bad, actually.

DOUGAL: Oh, actually, that's the B side. I'll turn it over.

TED: No, leave it, leave it . . .

DOUGAL: It's nice enough, isn't it?

TED: Yes. If only we'd come up with something like that.

Pause. A strange sly look comes over Ted's face.

TED: I suppose not many people would have heard that song.

DOUGAL: Suppose not. First time I've heard it, anyway.

TED: A lot of people wouldn't really have much of an interest in the B side of songs that came fifth in 'A Song for Norway'. What are

the band doing now?

DOUGAL: Oh, God, Ted, it's a terrible story. They all died in a 'plane crash along with all the people who were involved in the song – the producer, the studio engineer, their manager . . .

TED: . . . The people who owned the publishing rights?

DOUGAL: Oh, yes.

TED: Tsk, that's terrible. (*Pause.*) Eh, Dougal . . .?

DOUGAL: Yeah?

TED: Wouldn't it be nice to commemorate all those talented people by keeping their music alive?

DOUGAL: What?

TED: Say, if we borrowed that tune for 'My Lovely Horse'. It'd help us out and commemorate their memory at the same time.

DOUGAL: So we wouldn't just be stealing the tune?

TED: Dougal, there's no way, just because we take their tune and put our lyrics over it, that we're stealing the tune.

DOUGAL: No?

TED: No. You'd have to be mad to jump to that conclusion. What we're doing is celebrating their memory. Secretly. Don't tell anyone, incidentally.

DOUGAL: Right. And I suppose, if the song wins and we make money out of it, we could give it to their relatives.

Pause.

TED: . . . Yyyyyyyyeah . . . we'll play it by ear.

SCENE 5 EXT./DAY 2*
SET: RECORDING STUDIO
We see Jeep Hebrides, engineer at Craggy Island Recording Studios. He is an old hippy with long hair – there seems to be something stuck in it – who seems to be a little dazed and confused, but he's a friendly type. He is staring intently at a dancing flower – one of those toys that moves whenever it 'hears' sound.

*We deleted this scene from the final version.

JEEP: What do you want with me? (*The flower dances and stops.*) Stop messin' with my head.

The door opens and Ted sticks his head around the door.

TED: Jeep, how are you?

Jeep looks at the flower.

JEEP (*to flower*): Oh, wow. I'm fine, man. (*He notices Ted.*) Huh!

TED: Father Ted Crilly. We booked the studio?

JEEP: Oh, yeah, it's just . . . I'm supposed to have some priests coming in.

TED: That's us, Jeep.

JEEP: Yeah? OK, come in, man . . .

They all enter the other half of the studio.

JACK (*as soon as he enters*): Drink!

Jack starts opening drawers, rummaging behind things etc in his search for drink. He continues to do this throughout the remainder of the scene. There are drums, speakers etc. littering the studio. Dougal looks at Jeep and notices, as we do, that there is a whole burger in his hair. Along the wall, we see photographs of Chris de Burgh, The Cranberries, U2, Enya, Bob Geldof and Van Morrison etc.

DOUGAL (*whispers*): Ted . . . Ted, he's got a burger in his hair.

TED: I know. Shh . . . (*To Jeep.*) Haven't seen you at mass recently, Jeep!

JEEP: Haven't been to mass in years, man. The whole Catholic thing is a joke.

TED: Ah, ha!

Dougal points out the photographs along the wall.

DOUGAL: Wow! Are these all the people who've recorded here?

JEEP: No. (*Beat.*) I go in there, man.

TED (*looking at photographs*): Oh, look! They're signed!

JEEP: No, man. I did that. Sometimes I have to see my name written down or I freak out.

He goes through a door and into the booth. There is a thick pane of glass between him and the priests.

TED: Where'll we set up, Jeep?

Jeep looks back at Ted. He can't hear what they're

saying, he looks puzzled.

TED (*louder*): Where do you want us to set up?

Jeep looks confused, he comes back out of the booth.

JEEP: What? Sorry, man. I couldn't hear you through the glass. It's soundproof.

TED: Should you not have headphones or something?

JEEP: Headphones? Oh, yeah!

He picks up a pair of earphones and puts them on.

TED: Should you not go in there, Jeep?

Jeep doesn't respond.

TED: Jeep, take the headphones off.

JEEP: What?

Ted signals for him to take the headphones off. Jeep does so.

JEEP: Ha, ha . . . sorry, man. I couldn't hear you with the headphones.

TED: I was just saying, maybe you should go in there.

JEEP: Oh, yeah.

He goes into the other part of the studio again.

TED: Got it now, Jeep?

Jeep looks at them blankly. He mouths, 'What?'

TED (*to Dougal*): Jeep hasn't missed a Glastonbury since it started.

SCENE 5A INT./DAY 2*
SET: RECORDING STUDIO
Jeep has headphones on and a huge joint hanging from his mouth. Hie eyes are closed. He smiles, opens his eyes, takes off the headphones and applauds.

JEEP: That was great, guys. You won't get it more perfect than that. I think we can call it a day.

Ted and Dougal look at him strangely. Dougal is fiddling with his keyboard. Ted has his guitar on and has one hand on a machine head.

TED: Eh, we're still setting up, Jeep. We haven't actually recorded anything yet. Maybe you should go back into the booth.

*We deleted this scene from the final version.

JEEP: Oh, yeah, OK, But, still, guys, well done. Seriously.

He leaves the room. We see him examining the ashtray, picking it up and looking puzzled.

SCENE 5B INT./DAY 2*
SET: RECORDING STUDIO
Back to Ted and Dougal.

TED: Right, Dougal, you ready?

DOUGAL: I think so. Which button do I press again?

TED: The one with 'Song' written on it. OK, let's go.

Ted strums the guitar, nods to Dougal who presses a key with 'Song' written on it. The instrumental Norwegian track starts playing. Ted starts singing and stops playing the guitar.

TED: 'My lovely horse,
Running through the fields'

SCENE 5C INT./DAY 2*
SET: ANOTHER ROOM/RECORDING STUDIO
We hear the song, muffled, nearby. We see Jack in another room, sitting on a plush red leather sofa. He uses a knife to rip the lining. He then pulls out some stuffing, searching frantically.

JACK: DRINK!

SCENE 5D INT./DAY 2*
SET: RECORDING STUDIO
Ted and Dougal are coming to the end of the song.

TED AND DOUGAL (*chorus*): 'Running around with a man on your back,
Like a train in the night'

Ted does the one note again, and then moves his hand up the fretboard to do the final note. It goes wrong.

TED: Oh, wait, wait . . . (*He tries again. It sounds off.*) . . . Wait. I can do this . . . (*He tries one more time. It sounds OK.*) . . . How was that?

Jack comes into shot with a trumpet. He points it right at Ted's head and blasts it incredibly loudly. Ted falls out of shot with the shock.

JACK: DRINK!

SCENE 5E INT./DAY 2*
SET: RECORDING STUDIO
From left to right, Ted, Dougal and Jack are standing at the door. Jack looks very impatient. We see this from over Jeep's shoulder as he says goodbye.

JEEP (*to each*): Bye, man. Bye, man. Bye, man.

He closes the door. They walk to Ted's car, get in and drive away. After a moment, another car, exactly the same make as Ted's, pulls up. Father Dick Byrne, Father Cyril McDuff and Father Jim Johnson get out and go up to the door. They knock, and after a second Jeep opens it. We see, over his shoulder, the three of them standing in the same positions as Ted, Dougal and Jack.

JEEP: Wuaaaaghhhh!

SCENE 6 INT./NIGHT 2
SET: TED AND DOUGAL'S BEDROOM
Ted and Dougal are in bed, staring happily at the ceiling.

TED: Well, I don't want to jump to any conclusions and get us all excited, but I think we're definitely going to win.

DOUGAL: Really? Great!

TED: There'll be a lot to think about . . . promotional gifts for journalists, the American tour dates . . . I think a big flyposter campaign . . . and of course, the obligatory video . . .

DOUGAL: A video! Wow! Are priests allowed to be rock stars, though, Ted?

TED: Oh, yes. I remember one lad at the seminary . . . Father Benny Cake. He recorded a song and it went to number one in England.

DOUGAL: Really?

TED: Yes. He didn't want people to know he was a priest, so he called himself . . . God, what did he call himself? . . . Anyway, I think the song was called 'Vienna'.

DOUGAL: Why didn't he want people to know he was a priest?

TED: Ah, people thought if you were a priest, you were a bit of a 'square'. You were 'uncool'.

DOUGAL: And then we came along!

*We deleted this scene from the final version.

TED: Right! Anyway, Dougal, you go to sleep. Sweet dreams.

He turns off the light. Close in on Dougal's face.

SCENE 7 EXT./NIGHT/DAY X
SET: VARIOUS
The following are the scenes from Dougal's ultimate rock video. This is a 'lifestyle' video with a dash of performance at the top. Each scene is shot in a very grey, dull kind of way, complete with the occasional zoom.

1. Ted and Dougal enter the shot from either side and start singing. They wear glittery jackets with very big lapels. The camera moves up and into a spotlight above the stage. Fade to . . .

2. Ted and Dougal playing table tennis in a grotty-looking youth-club-type place. Ted plays a really, really bad shot and the ball flies out of shot. They laugh happily.

3. Ted and Dougal on a horse, both wearing helmets.

4. Ted and Dougal in what looks like a yacht. The camera zooms back, in time to the music, to reveal that the yacht is absolutely tiny.

5. A horse looking around. Dougal looking around.

6. Ted and Dougal in a miserable-looking indoor swimming pool. A woman is in the pool, another woman is sitting at the edge. Ted's and Dougal's hair is completely dry. The four throw a ball to each other.

7. Ted and Dougal on a tandem.

8. Ted and Dougal looking at each other and singing as the camera circles them in a park.

9. Dougal and Ted standing beside the horse and laughing for no apparent reason.

10. Dougal (or Ted) hugging the horse.

11. The horse, Ted and Dougal all sitting down at a picnic.

12. For the instrumental part, we see a badly cut-out photograph of the horse's head – quite scary, in fact, with psychedelic colours radiating from it.

SCENE 8 INT./NIGHT 2
SET: TED AND DOUGAL'S BEDROOM
Cut back to Ted. Asleep. He frowns unhappily, then wakes up with a start. Dougal also bolts up at the same time. They look at each other.

TED: We'll have to lose that guitar solo.

END OF PART ONE

* * *

PART TWO

SCENE 9 EXT./NIGHT 3
SET: LARGE HALL
We see a banner outside the hall that reads 'A Song for Ireland '96'.

SCENE 10 INT./NIGHT 3
SET: DRESSING ROOM
Dougal and Ted are tuning up. They are very excited.

TED: Well, Dougal, are you nervous?*

DOUGAL: Oh, I never get nervous, Ted.*

TED: You've never been nervous? Never in your life?*

DOUGAL (*thinks*): I don't think so.*

TED: What about when you were doing your tests. At the seminary. You must have been nervous then . . .*

DOUGAL (*laughs silently*): God, no, Ted. They were just a laugh.*

TED: But your whole future depended on those tests.*

DOUGAL (*worried*): Did they? God almighty . . . *

There is a knock on the door. Two middle-aged men enter. One is the M.C., Fred Rickwood. The other is the show's producer, Charles Hedges. He looks at a clipboard while holding his other hand out to shake Ted's.

CHARLES: Hello, Father . . . Crilly. I'm Charles Hedges. I'll be producing the show. This is . . .

TED: Oh, you don't have to tell me. Mr Rickwood, it's great to meet you. I thought you did a brilliant job presenting last year's show.

Fred mumbles in a speedy, incomprehensible manner. Ted cocks his head as he hears this, looking puzzled.

---

* We cut this from the final version and replaced it with Mrs Doyle putting make-up on Dougal.

Pause.

TED: What?

Fred speaks again.

TED: Ha, ha. Yes.

Fred raises his voice, but speaks just as quickly. Ted smiles and nods.

TED: Mmmmmm . . .

Fred comes out with another stream of gibberish before walking to the door and giving them the thumbs-up before leaving.

TED: Ah, I have to say he sounded a lot better on last year's show.

CHARLES: Oh, once he gets on stage he's fine.

TED: Have you known each other long?

CHARLES: Well, he's been my partner for ten years.

TED: Oh, right. Do you run the production company together?

CHARLES: No, no, I mean, he's my lover.

Pause. They look at each other for a moment.

TED: He's . . . he's quite a catch. Ah, this is my partner, Father Dougal McGuire. Not my sexual partner! I mean, you know, my partner that I do the song with.

CHARLES: Yes. I guessed that.

TED: Right. Of course you did. Not that there's anything wrong with that type of thing!

CHARLES: I thought the Church thought that 'that type of thing' was inherently wrong.

TED: Ah, yes. It does. (*Pause.*) The whole gay thing. I suppose it's a bit of a puzzle to us all. (*Pause.*) I suppose it must be great fun, though . . . not the, eh, you know . . . but the nightclub scene and all that. The whole rough and tumble of . . . homosexual activity and . . . having boyfriends when you're a man. Like, with girlfriends, you couldn't bring them out to a match . . . but I'm sure with a man, he'd be dying to go. (*Pause.*) Anyway, don't worry about what the Church thinks. Sure they used to think the earth was flat. It's like . . . you know . . . sometimes the Pope says things he doesn't really mean. You know. We all get things wrong. Even the Pope!

CHARLES: What about Papal infallibility?

TED: Yes. I suppose so, but, ah . . . is that for everything, do you know? The infallibility?

CHARLES: I don't know!

TED: Right! Right! Of course, ah . . . anyway . . . (*Long, long pause.*) Nothing to do with me. (*Pause. Ted is mortified. He looks around.*) Look at Dougal! Bored out of his mind! (*Cut to a bamboozled Dougal.*) We could go on all night talking about gay issues, but, God . . . poor old Dougal! No interest in the subject whatsoever!

CHARLES: Anyway, I'm looking forward to your entry, Father.

Pause.

TED: Oh, right! The song! Yes, eh, me too.

DOUGAL: Do you think we'll win?

TED: It's not up to him, Dougal. It's the public who decide.

CHARLES: Not this year.

TED: No?

CHARLES: No. We've decided that this year I'll pick the winner. The old phone-in system wasn't really working out.

TED: Was it not? The song the public chose has won five years in a row.

CHARLES: Yes, but . . . ah . . . well, it's just . . . very complicated . . . and . . . eh . . . you're looking forward to the show then?

Pause.

TED: Oh, yes! It's a big thrill for us. A bit of a novelty, too, I suppose, seeing as we're priests.

CHARLES: Well, not really. There's another act tonight that's very like you. Father Dick Byrne and Father Cyril McDuff.

TED: God . . . I didn't think they'd make it this far . . .

DOUGAL: Flip! They'll win, Ted! We might as well give up now.

TED: That's a very defeatist attitude, Dougal.

DOUGAL: Actually it is. Sorry about that, Ted.

Dick bursts through the door. Dougal moves beside Ted. Cyril comes in as well, looking lost as usual.

DICK: But he's right, Ted!

TED: Dick!

DICK: You ready to be beaten, then?

TED: Hah! It's probably a terrible song altogether.

DICK: No, it's not! It'll be better than your one, Ted, you big fool.

TED: Take that back!

CHARLES: I'll, eh . . . get going.

TED (*turning into a priest again*): Oh, right. See you later, Charles. Thanks for everything so far. It really is a tremendous honour to be here.

DICK (*ditto*): Yes, I'm sure we'll all have a great time. (*There is a respectful silence for a moment as Charles leaves.*) I won't take it back! I bet we get a million points! And I bet you get minus seven thousand!

TED: Oh, yes? How much? How much do you bet?

DICK: Four pounds.

TED: You're on.

DICK: This is just on us winning, now. Obviously, that million points thing was an exaggeration.

TED: Oh, right, yeah.

A paper ball hits Dougal on the back of the head. Dougal looks around and sees Cyril looking innocent. Dougal looks around to see if anyone else is in the room. He is very confused.

DICK: All right, come on, Cyril! We're off to win the contest! Seriously, though, Ted, even if you don't win, I'm sure the song's very good.

TED: Do you really, Dick?

DICK: Nooooooooooo!

He and Cyril duck out through the door. Ted turns to the camera and pulls a hugely enraged face.

TED: Oooooh! I really hate Father Dick Byrne!

SCENE 11 INT./NIGHT 3
SET: SIDE OF STAGE
Ted and Dougal are beside our host, Fred Rickwood. He is in a slightly crouched position. His tie is loose, and his suit badly crumpled.

TED: Good luck tonight, Fred.

Fred mumbles something incoherently.

SCENE 12 INT./NIGHT 3
SET: STUDIO CONTROL
We see engineers, technicians, banks of television monitors, etc. Charles is sitting in his luxurious producer's chair.

CHARLES: Let's go!

We see very impressive television graphics, accompanied by a voiceover.

VOICEOVER: And now, live from the Theatre Royal, 'A Song for Ireland 1996', and here is your host, Fred Rickwood!!!!

SCENE 13 INT./NIGHT 3
SET: SIDE OF STAGE
Fred sucks on his cigarette one more time, steps on it and shuffles out of shot.

SCENE 14 INT./NIGHT 3
SET: STAGE
We see the television pictures of Fred striding on to the stage. He walks with an impressive stroll and his suit and tie are now immaculate. He waves to the audience, does a quick boxing shuffle and runs confidently to his microphone.

FRED: Helloooo and welcome to the thirty-fifth 'A Song for Ireland', the contest in which we select Ireland's entry for Eurosong '96. It's not often that priests appear on the show, but tonight we've got two acts comprised of clerical duos. We've also got some exciting new acts from all over the country, and a few names that will be very familiar to all of you out there in TV land. A word about the emergency exits – you'll find them on your left, and just behind the stalls. In the event of a fire, please make your way calmly to one of these.

SCENE 15 INT./NIGHT 3*
SET: CONTROL ROOM
We see Charles at the mixing desk.

CHARLES: What a pro.

*We deleted this scene from the final version.

SCENE 16 INT./NIGHT 3*
SET: THE AUDIENCE

We see Jack and Father Jim sitting beside each other in identical wheelchairs. The two identical Mrs Doyles adjust the blankets on the priests' laps. This irritates them and they wave their identical sticks in an identical manner at the two identical Mrs Doyles. The shot should be completely symmetrical.

SCENE 17 INT./NIGHT 3
SET: SIDE OF STAGE

Ted and Dougal are full of nervous tension. They can see Dick and Cyril at the opposite side of the stage waiting to go on. Dick is posing and looking very aloof. Between them and Dick, in the centre of the stage, Fred continues his introduction.

TED: Look at Dick Byrne there, showing off. He won't be too happy when we win and he comes last.

Ted catches Dick's eye. Dick gives him the two fingers. Ted returns it. They continue like this for a while.

SCENE 18 INT./NIGHT 3
SET: STAGE

Fred glances to the side just in time to see Ted's two-fingered gesture. Ted sees him and immediately turns his hand around to give him a friendly salute. Fred is doing his spiel.

FRED: . . . So . . . please welcome on stage the Euro-hopefuls from Rugged Island, Father Dick Byrne and Father Cyril McDuff.

SCENE 19 INT./NIGHT 3
SET: SIDE OF STAGE

Ted and Dougal, unimpressed.

SCENE 20 INT./NIGHT 3
SET: STAGE

Music starts. Dick and Cyril are revealed under single spotlights – Cyril slightly in the background on keyboard, Dick in the foreground, standing in a very dramatic way, his arms held apart, his head bowed low. The music swells slightly, and Dick raises his head and starts singing.

DICK: 'When I was young, I had a dream
And though the dream was very small
It wouldn't leave me.'

*We deleted this scene from the final version.

SCENE 21 INT./NIGHT 3
SET: SIDE OF STAGE

We see Ted and Dougal looking very superior.

TED: Dougal, Dougal . . .

He gets Dougal's attention and does a very childish impression of Dick Byrne.

SCENE 22 INT./NIGHT 3
SET: STAGE

Back to Dick. A single tear runs down his cheek.

DICK: 'To be a beggar or a king
To play the poet or the fool
And now you see me . . .'
(*Chorus*) 'And now the miracle is mine!!!!'

At this line, the rest of the stage is lit up and we see an entire backing band: a line of priests around a microphone singing along, violinists, etc. It all looks very impressive.

SCENE 23 INT./NIGHT 3
SET: SIDE OF STAGE

Ted is still doing his silly impression. He and Dougal see the impressive stage set-up and freeze, their mouths agape.

SCENE 24 INT./NIGHT 3
SET: STAGE

Back to Dick. He continues the chorus. As he does so, his actions are very dramatic and passionate.

DICK: 'The battle fought, the war begun!!!!!
And now I've nothing left but time!!!!! But still I reach out . . . to the sun!!!!!'

The song drops down again.

SCENE 25 INT./NIGHT 3
SET: SIDE OF STAGE
Ted has had enough.

TED: Hmrprh . . . I need a fag.

He walks off, leaving Dougal there.

SCENE 26 INT./NIGHT 3
SET: OUTSIDE A LIFT

Ted is standing outside the lift. The doors open and a technician comes out. He is whistling something. Ted looks at him, puzzled, then gets into the lift.

SCENE 27 INT./NIGHT 3
SET: A LIFT
Ted walks into the lift. He presses a button and the doors close. We hear lift muzak. Ted cocks his head, listening to it. He freezes, then goes into a panic. He starts hitting all the buttons frantically.

TED: . . . Oh, Ghoddddd . . .

SCENE 28 INT./NIGHT 3
SET: SIDE OF STAGE
Ted runs into shot and grabs Dougal.

TED: Dougal!!!! We can't do the song!

DOUGAL: What? Why not, Ted?

TED: I just heard it in the lift! They're piping it in in there! I heard someone *whistling* it!

DOUGAL: Well, that's good, isn't it? Shows what a great song it is.

TED: No, no no! They'll know we ripped it off!!! It must be more famous than we thought! We'll be found out! Oh God!

DOUGAL: Wh— what'll we do, Ted?

TED: Why did this have to happen to us? What did we ever do to deserve this? (*He thinks.*) Wait! Wait! I have an idea!

DOUGAL: What, Ted?

TED: Let's pray! We'll pray and ask God to help us.

DOUGAL: But Dick's probably thought of that! He probably prayed that we wouldn't win!

TED: God, yes! A pre-emptive pray! Maybe we can cancel out his pray with our one!

DOUGAL: Song's nearly over, Ted.

TED: Oh, no! We'll have to . . . Dougal . . . I think we'll have to resort to plan B.

Shot of a puzzled, then horrified Dougal.

SCENE 29 INT./NIGHT 3
SET: STAGE
Dick is now on his knees, coming to the end of the song. He repeats the chorus, bows his head and the lights go out with the sudden end of the song. The lights come on and Dick stands up to rapturous applause. He gestures to the rest of the band and

bows etc., etc., as he and Cyril move off. Dick shoots a smug look at Ted.

FRED: Well, how about that! Wonderful . . . (*He applauds.*) . . . OK, now to our next act, Father Ted Crilly and Father Dougal McGuire!

Ted and Dougal walk on to applause. They look very dispirited. Dougal goes up and stands beside Ted. They then proceed to do the original version of 'My Lovely Horse'. Ted plays the same note over and over. As they do the song we see various people listening . . .

*1. The two Jacks listening from the side of the stage, disgusted. Mrs Doyle has her head in her hands.**

*2. Fred, at the side of the stage, rumpled up once more, smoking a fag. He says something impenetrable and uncomplimentary.**

*3. Dick and Cyril rolling about on the floor, laughing their heads off.**

*4. Tom still in his 'I Shot JR' T-shirt, watching a television that's plugged into a lightbulb in his horrible, bare house.**

TOM: Brilliant! Mammy? Oh, she's dead.**

*5. The people in the producer's box, including Charles. They look at the screen with their mouths open, completely frozen.**

*Back to Ted and Dougal. They can hear Dick and Cyril laughing in the distance and look very uncomfortable. They come to the end of the song. Ted goes for that one different note on his guitar. It goes wrong.**

TED: Wait, wait . . . (*He tries again.*) I can do this. Wait . . . (*Last time. He does it. No applause.*) Ah . . . thank you.

They walk off to complete silence.

SCENE 30 INT./NIGHT 3
SET: DRESSING ROOM
We hear lots of laughter. Close-up on a champagne bottleneck. The cork pops off to a tremendous cheer. We gradually pull back to see that Ted is pouring the champagne into glasses belonging to Jack, Mrs Doyle, Dougal and Charles. Jack takes the bottle when Ted has stopped pouring.

---

*We deleted these lines from the final version and replaced them with the lyrics to 'My Lovely Horse'.

TED: Well, we did it Dougal! Don't ask me how, but we did it!

CHARLES: Well, the reason you won, Father, is quite simple. Yours was the best song.

TED: Well, I suppose so. Although I didn't really think the audience was going for it.

CHARLES: Audiences?! What do they know?!!!!

Fred mumbles something impenetrable and congratulatory.* Slight pause.

TED: Yes! (*He raises his glass. Everyone cheers.*) Ah, there's Dick Byrne! (*Dick and Cyril wander into shot.*) Well, Dick. Yet again, Rugged Island capitulates to sheer, raw talent.

DICK (*immediately to Charles*): What's going on? Our song was miles better than theirs!

CHARLES: Ah, well, we, ah, we thought . . .

DICK (*to Charles*): I mean, for God's sake! It was just one note over and over again!

CHARLES: Yes, we, ah . . . we admired its . . . *Fred mumbles something incomprehensible.*) Yes, exactly. Fred put it better than I ever could.

TED (*unconvincingly*): Hah! So there!

CHARLES: I mean, your song was good, but . . . a bit overblown. That can alienate people, you know . . .

DICK: But they were going mad for it . . .

CHARLES: Yes . . . but . . . ahem . . . oh . . . well, you know . . .

DICK: I mean, what's going on?! It's almost as if you wanted Ireland to lose the next Eurosong contest!

Charles and Fred exchange glances.

CHARLES (*long pause*): Ha. Ha. Nonsense. Why would we do that?

DICK: I don't know. Maybe because it was costing you so much to stage . . .

TED (*shakes his head sadly*): Dick, Dick, Dick, Dick . . . Now come on. Does that really sound plausible? I really think you should go and count your sour grapes before . . . they hatch.

*One of the things he mumbles is 'Shave a bullock'.

Dick goes to leave.

CYRIL (*to Dougal*): Better luck next time.

DICK: We lost, Cyril.

CYRIL: Really?

DICK: Come on . . .

Dick and Cyril leave.

CHARLES: Well done, again, Father. And I'm sure you'll do very well in the Eurosong contest.

He moves off.

TED: I think so! Next stop, Europe!

Charles goes over to Fred, who is standing beside the window. From the window beyond we can hear angry shouting.

CHARLES: We'd better sneak them out the back. That's a nasty crowd.

SCENE 31 INT./NIGHT 4
SET: BACKSTAGE AT EUROSONG
The following is shot as if we're watching it on television. We see Ted and Dougal sitting together on a yellow sofa. They have their spangle suits on and look quite excited. Jack is behind them, sprawled over a chair, completely out of it. Mrs Doyle is sitting behind looking very enthusiastic. Dougal and Ted smile and look at a monitor situated somewhere above and behind the camera – this is the classic Eurovision 'waiting for the points' pose.

VOICE: And now could we please have the points for Ireland?

We then hear, in a series of different accents and languages, each country give Ireland no points – 'Nil points, nada punten, keinen pune, no points, zero points'. Gradually the smiles die from their faces. The credits roll as Ted and Dougal examine their sleeves, look around, puff out their cheeks, scratch their heads, avoid each other's eyes, etc., etc. Mrs Doyle also looks very embarrassed.

THE END

the plague

ARTHUR: This was our *Fawlty Towers* episode. It's similar in that it relies on a great deal o physical comedy, with people running around and throwing themselves down stairs, and most o the action is set in real time. Not that we were ever in the *Fawlty Towers* league; we got better, bu we were never *that* good, and our plots were never that airtight. The surreal nature of *Father Tea* meant that our plots didn't have to make perfect sense. The plots may be more satisfying when they do make sense, but as long as they didn't test the audience's patience too much and kep delivering the jokes, we were usually forgiven. This plot is incredibly simple and it depends on a *complete* cheat: that the rabbits can get around the house without anyone noticing, and can breed in those kind of numbers from just one rabbit . . . overnight. Jim Norton (Bishop Brennan) had a terrible time with those rabbits. They did their business all over the place in the scene where he and Jack are in bed, and all the showers at the TV studios had broken down – Jim was not bes pleased . . .

GRAHAM: We had some incredibly stupid complaints about Jack calling the rabbits 'hairy Japanese bastards'. They bleeped it out in Canada because they thought it was racist, and in Britain someone phoned in and said it was an insult to his Japanese wife. I really don't understand that. First of all, Jack thinks they're rats – which shows how ludicrous the whole thing is – and the fact that he calls them 'hairy Japanese bastards' makes about as much sense as Dougal calling his rabbit Sampras because of the tennis/rabbit connection. It's just a senseless joke, a surrealisti silly jape – but you can never underestimate the desire some people have to be offended.

I dimly remember an old *Star Trek* episode called *The Trouble With Tribbles* which had a similar plot to this. Luckily, we didn't see it in the run-up to writing this show or we might have though it too similar.

PART ONE
SCENE 1 EXT./NIGHT 1*
SET: THE ISLAND

A particularly spooky part of the island. A man, woman and their daughter – posh, southside Dublin types – all in expensive hiking gear, are walking along a misty clifftop.

WOMAN: Come on. Nearly there. (*Pause.*) It's a bit creepy, isn't it?

MAN: Oh, come on, Jane. There's nothing out there that can—

A branch snaps behind them. They turn around and see, in the mist, the outline of a man. Close-up as the man's face comes out of the mist. It is Father Jack. We see, from Jack's point of view, a look of pure horror dawning on their faces.

THE FAMILY: Aaaaaaaarrrrgggghhhhhh!!!!!!!

SCENE 2 INT./DAY 2
SET: PAROCHIAL HOUSE

Dougal is looking at a cage on the table. Inside it we see a rabbit. Dougal looks at it lovingly, and then picks up a book with a big picture of a rabbit on it. The book is called 'My New Rabbit'. Jack is asleep in the background. Ted enters.

TED: Ah, there he is, anyway.

DOUGAL: He's great, isn't he?

Ted approaches the rabbit.

TED: He is all right. Does he have a name?

DOUGAL: I don't think so. Mrs Guthrie didn't mention one, anyway.† God, I dunno . . . how about 'Ted'? That's a good name for a rabbit.

TED: What? No, that's not a good idea, Dougal. Don't forget I'm called Ted as well.

Dougal thinks and then points at Ted in a 'you're right' gesture.

DOUGAL: Well, I could call you 'Father Ted'.

TED: No . . . seriously, Dougal . . . try and come up with something a bit more original.

Mrs Doyle comes in with a tea tray.

MRS DOYLE: Hello, Fathers.

TED AND DOUGAL: Hello, Mrs Doyle!

Mrs Doyle collects some cups and goes out again. Dougal looks after her for a few moments, a thoughtful look on his face.

DOUGAL: How about 'Mrs Doyle'?

TED: No, Mrs Doyle isn't a good name for a rabbit. You need something like 'Popsy' or 'Bruce'.

DOUGAL: Oh, right. (*Pause.*) Wait! I've got one!

TED: Yes?

DOUGAL: You know the way he's got big floppy ears flopping all about the place.

TED: Yes?

DOUGAL: Well, why don't we call him 'Father Jack Hackett'?

TED (*has had enough*): Perfect! Father Jack it is!

Jack wakes up.

JACK: What?

TED: Nothing, Father. Dougal's named his new rabbit after you.

JACK: What?

DOUGAL: Are you all right, Father Jack?

JACK (*confused*): What?

TED: He wasn't talking to you, Father. He was talking to the rabbit.

JACK: What?

DOUGAL: I think Father Jack wants a drink.

---

*Scenes 1-3 from *Think Fast, Father Ted* that featured the television show *Father Ben* were transferred to here in the final version.
† Mrs Guthrie the pet-shop owner was dropped from the final version and was referred to as 'the woman in the pet shop' instead.

JACK (*immediately happy*): Drink!

TED: Will we get him some water?

JACK: Water? Feck!

TED: No, Dougal, honestly. This will get very confusing.

DOUGAL: Ah, Ted. I've got used to calling him Father Jack. Could we not call Father Jack something else?

TED: Great idea! What'll we call him? Flipper? Flipper the priest. Flipper the priest it is!

JACK: What?

TED: No, Dougal, c'mon now, it won't work. Call him after someone you like.

DOUGAL: Someone I like?

Dougal muses. The telephone rings. Ted picks it up.

TED: Hello, Father Ted Crilly speaking.

SCENE 3 INT./DAY 2
SET: BISHOP'S HOUSE
We see Bishop Len Brennan in a large bath on a cordless telephone. His 'bishop stuff' is hanging neatly beside the bath. On the wall there is a massive painting of Len, kitted out to the nines, looking more like a Napoleonic figure than a religious one.

BRENNAN: Crilly, it's me.

TED: Oh, feck!

BRENNAN: What?

Ted freezes in horror.

TED: Ooo ees thees? Zere is no Creely heere.

BRENNAN: Crilly!

Ted slams down the telephone.

TED (*to Dougal*): God almighty! I just said 'feck' to Bishop Brennan!

DOUGAL: O'ho! He won't like that.

TED: It might be all right, though. I disguised my voice so he'd think he dialled the wrong number.

The telephone rings. Ted picks it up.

BRENNAN: Crilly!

TED: Ah, Bishop Brennan. I think you must have got the wrong number when you called there.

Ted looks at Dougal and crosses his fingers hopefully. Dougal does the same in a supportive way.

BRENNAN: What?! What are you on about now? When I was talking to you there, you swore at me, then put on a foreign accent and then hung up.

TED: Did I? I don't think so. You must have got the wrong number.

BRENNAN: No, I didn't. It was definitely you. God forbid there's more than one Ted Crilly in the world.

TED: O'ho, no! When God made me, he kept the mould and . . . didn't make anyone else with it . . .

BRENNAN: Shut up, Crilly! I'll make it quick. What would the words 'Jack', 'sleepwalking' and 'bollock naked' suggest to you?

TED: Oh, no . . .

BRENNAN: This is the third time in the last six months! You may have heard of Brian Noonan, a very important Junior Minister and a personal friend of mine. And I can tell you, the last thing he and his family needs is a vision of an elderly priest wearing only a pair of socks and a hat! I'll be over on Thursday to examine what kind of security you have – and Crilly?

TED: Yes?

BRENNAN: If you ever try to bullshit me like that again, I'll rip off your arms.

He clicks the telephone off and puts it to one side. As he does so, we get a very brief glimpse of a woman emerging from the water at the other end of the bath.

SCENE 4 INT./DAY 2
SET: PAROCHIAL HOUSE
Ted puts the telephone down.

TED: He's coming over.

DOUGAL: Oh, no. Why is he always bothering us? You'd think he'd have his hands full running that betting shop.*

TED: No, Dougal. Bishop Brennan is a bishop. There's a clue in his name – Bishop Brennan?*

DOUGAL: Oh, right. What was he calling about, anyway?

TED: Father Jack's been sleepwalking in the nude again.

JACK: What?

TED: Bishop Brennan is coming over to have a word with you, Father. About your nude sleepwalking.

JACK: Nudie Father Jack!

TED: That's right, Father. Can you think of any reason why you might be doing that?

Jack looks clueless.

TED: You're not having any doubts about your vocation, are you, Father?

JACK (*disgusted*): What?

DOUGAL: Maybe it's the Diet Whiskey, Ted . . .

Ted picks up a bottle with 'Diet Whiskey' written on the side.

TED: I don't think so. Anyway, he hasn't touched this. You don't like this, do you Father?

Jack grabs the bottle and throws it to the other side of the room, where it smashes.

TED: We really should talk about it, and remember you can always share your problems with us. Father Dougal and myself will always lend you a friendly ear. Isn't that right, Dougal?

DOUGAL (*beat*): Sorry, Ted?

TED: Don't forget, Father, we're your friends, and we're always here for you, no matter what you've done. Would you like to talk about it now?

DOUGAL: Well, Ted . . . *Byker Grove* . . .

TED: Oh, God, yes, after *Byker Grove*.

Ted and Dougal excitedly take their seats and hit the

*We deleted this from the final version.

remote control. *Jack watches them grumpily as the 'Byker Grove' music starts up.*

SCENE 5 INT./DAY 2
SET: PAROCHIAL HOUSE
Dougal is playing with the rabbit on the floor. He throws a little stick.

DOUGAL: Go on, boy. Go on! Get it, boy!

Ted walks in.

TED: C'mon, now, Dougal, get him in his cage. We don't want Bishop Brennan seeing him.

DOUGAL: Ah, Ted, he might like him.

TED: No, he won't, Dougal. Bishop Brennan doesn't like rabbits at all, now.

DOUGAL: Why not?

TED: It's a strange story. About ten years ago, he was in New York and he was trapped in a lift with about twenty rabbits for the whole night. They started nibbling his cape and everything.

DOUGAL: How did they get in?

TED: I suppose they must have burrowed in. You know rabbits. (*Ted sees the rabbit at his feet and picks it up.*) God almighty. They can move fast enough.

DOUGAL: Why do you say that, Ted?

TED: Well, he just shot across the room to me there. (*Ted notices that Dougal still has his rabbit as well.*) Wait now. That's your rabbit.

DOUGAL: Yeah.

TED: So where did this one come from?

DOUGAL: Eh, Ted . . .

Cut to Jack, asleep. There is another rabbit on his head.

TED: I don't like the look of this at all. Don't let your rabbit get mixed up with the other lads.

DOUGAL: All right. Come on, Sampras . . .

TED: Wh— what did you call him?

DOUGAL: Sampras. Like Pete Sampras.

TED: Why?

DOUGAL: Well, you know . . . rabbits, tennis . . . you know . . . that whole connection there.

Pause.

TED: Ah, right! (*Ted turns and pulls a 'what the hell was that all about?' face.*) Come on, we'd better round them up. We'll just release these spare ones into the wild. (*He picks up the two rabbits and puts them in a box. He looks at Sampras.*) Ah, look at him there. All alone with no other rabbits for company. He must feel like Brian Keenan when they took John McCarthy off to another cell. Anyway, he'll get used to it . . .

The camera closes in on the rabbit. Fade out.

SCENE 6 INT./DAY 2
SET: PAROCHIAL HOUSE
Fade back in on the rabbit. Time has passed. We pull back slowly from the close-up of the rabbit to reveal that the room is hugely populated by rabbits. They crawl all over the chairs and tables, and chew the carpets, etc. Jack is looking at them warily. Ted comes in, yawning, some letters in his hand.

TED: Morning, Father. (*He goes to the table and starts reading the letters.*) Bills, bills, bills . . .

Dougal enters.

DOUGAL: Morning, Ted!

TED: Morning, Dougal.

DOUGAL: What'll we do today, Ted?

TED (*walks to his armchair and sits*): Well, Bishop Brennan'll be here soon, so we'll have to get that rabbit of yours somewhere he won't see him. God, he'd go mad if he knew there was a rabbit around the place.

DOUGAL (*sits on sofa*): Fair enough, Ted!

TED: I hope he's in a good mood. Len can be a bit scary when . . . when, when . . . (*He looks around at all the rabbits.*) Aaaaggghhh!!!!

DOUGAL: Ted! What's wrong?

TED: Rabbits!

DOUGAL: Rabbits? Where – oh, wow!

TED: Where the hell did these ones come from?!

DOUGAL: It's like a big rabbit rock festival. Well, I suppose we'll just have to get used to it.

TED: Get used to it? Dougal, we have to get rid of these before Bishop Brennan arrives.

DOUGAL: Oh, right, yeah.*

TED: I'll call Mrs Guthrie. *

DOUGAL: She's gone on holiday, Ted.*

TED: Damn. What'll we do?*

DOUGAL (*frowns*): Well . . . if we . . . there's something we can do, if . . . wait a second, let me . . . I know . . . I know, I've got it, Ted!

TED: What?

DOUGAL: Well, the way I see it . . . if there's . . . ah . . . wait a second, what's the problem again?

TED: THE RABBITS!

DOUGAL: Oh, yeah, yeah! Sorry, Ted. Ah, why don't we try and give them to Father Duff? He's always going on about how he'd love a few rabbits running about the place.

TED: You're right! I used to think it was just a mad thing to say, but now— (*He picks up the telephone.*) Come on . . . come on . . . Larry?

SCENE 7 INT./DAY 2
SET: FATHER DUFF'S HOUSE
We see Father Larry Duff on the telephone.

LARRY: Ted! How's it hanging?

TED: Eh, it's hanging fine, Larry. Listen, we've

---

*As Mrs Guthrie was cut, in the final version Dougal said that he couldn't take the rabbit back because he bought it from a travelling pet shop that wouldn't return until spring.

got a bit of a problem here . . . Do you remember how you're always saying you'd love to have a few rabbits around the place?

LARRY: I do, Ted. That's one of my all-time fantasies. I'd love to have a few dozen rabbits all over the place.

TED: Well, today's your lucky day! We've got loads of the things!

LARRY: Sorry, Ted, won't be able to take them.

TED: Really? Oh, God, why not?

Cut from close-up to reveal that Larry is surrounded by Rottweilers.

LARRY: I sort of gave up on the rabbits idea – it just seemed too far-fetched – so I got twelve Rottweilers instead.

TED: Oh, right.

LARRY: I'd love to take the rabbits, but I'd be afraid the Rottweilers might maul them.

TED: Yes, yes, I understand. Bye, Larry.

Larry puts the telephone down. Cut to close-up again. We hear a dog growling.

LARRY: Bad dog . . . Don't you look at me like that . . . you're a very bad d—

The dog lunges and Larry disappears out of shot with a scream.

SCENE 8 INT./DAY 2
SET: PAROCHIAL HOUSE
Ted steps away from the telephone.

TED: He can't take the rabbits. He's got twelve Rottweilers.

JACK (*to Ted*): Hey! Hey! You!

TED: Yes, Father?

JACK (*pointing at the rabbits*): Wh— . . . rats . . . — . . . wh— . . .

TED: Oh, yes, Father, we can see them, too. You're not hallucinating.

Jack takes this in, then looks at the rabbits.

JACK (*to rabbits*): Hairy Japanese bastards . . .

Ted and Dougal exchange a look. Jack gets up and leaves. Cut back to Dougal and Ted.

TED: Do you know what this is like, Dougal? It's like a plague or something. A big rabbit plague. I wonder if God is punishing us for something. Maybe it's because I said feck to Bishop Brennan.

DOUGAL: God, if he sends down a plague of rabbits just because you said feck to Bishop Brennan, imagine what he'll do when he finds out about all the money you robbed from that charity!

TED: Dougal, that money was just resting in my account. I was keeping it there until I moved it on—

DOUGAL: Ted . . .

TED: . . . It was basically a non-profit-making subsidiary account . . .

DOUGAL: The rabbits have gone, Ted.

Cut to a wide view of the room. All the rabbits have gone.

TED: Where'd they go?

DOUGAL: They followed Father Jack out of the room.

TED: That's amazing. So it wasn't that the last rabbit was in heat at all. I've always thought Father Jack gave off a kind of furry smell. The rabbits must think he's some sort of rabbit God.

DOUGAL: Great! So if we just keep Father Jack out of the way . . .

TED: But Bishop Brennan's coming to see Jack. No, we'll have to get them out of here.

DOUGAL: Hey – Paddy Jordan!

TED: Paddy Jordan! Yes! He'd definitely take them for us! Definitely!

SCENE 9 EXT./DAY 2
SET: GREYHOUND TRACK
We see Paddy Jordan, a middle-aged fat man in a white coat and hat. Paddy, Ted and Dougal are at a small distance from the track and at a higher level, so we can see it clearly. There is a small, expectant crowd there, too. It is just grass, and a hundred metres long, like an athletics track. There are about seven lanes, with a box-like cage construction at the top of each one. We hear a buzzer. A badly constructed full-size cloth greyhound emerges on a rail running along the track. Then the trapdoor on each of the cages shoots up. The cloth greyhound hurtles along the side of the track as two or three rabbits emerge slowly from the cages. The other rabbits remain inside. We see the rabbits sniffing around. Cut back to the greyhound, which hits a bar at the end of the track and spins into the air before crashing to the ground. Ted, Dougal and Paddy stare as the rabbits slowly go about their business. Hold on this for just a moment too long.

PADDY: God, no, Father. They're even worse than the hares.

TED: Yes . . . they're not exactly 'going for it', are they? I tell you what – I'll go and give Tom a call. He might be able to help us.

Ted goes out of shot. Dougal and Paddy look at the rabbits.

PADDY: To be honest, Father, I think I'm going to have to close down the track.

DOUGAL: Why?

PADDY: It's just a really, really bad idea.*

SCENE 10 INT./DAY 2
SET: TOM'S HOUSE†
Tom opens the door – as usual, he wears his 'I Shot JR' T-shirt – and says into camera . . .

TOM: Hello, Father!!

---

*This didn't work because it was a joke on top of a joke. The idea was that Paddy has already been racing hares, and that the rabbits were much worse. Luckily, we changed this on location and the version that ended up on-screen (with Dougal's line about having some money on 'that little beauty') was much better.
† A new scene was inserted before this with Ted and Dougal waiting for Tom to answer the door.

Ted and Dougal enter the room. It is a bombsite. A big pile of rubble is in the centre of the room; there are plastic bags piled up in one corner, a faded poster of Farrah Fawcett Majors on the wall, a shredded mattress in one corner and the word 'Redrum' painted in red on the wall. The room is divided by a partition with a Perspex window, through which we can see shelves full of tools, and a doorway into this other smaller room.

TOM: Would you like something to eat, Father? I could do you a salad.

TED: Ah, no thanks, Tom. Some other time. Well, I have to say, you've done wonders with the place.

TOM: Right, Father, you said you had some rabbits for me?

TED: Yes, they're in the car.

TOM: Right! With you in a mo'.

Tom goes into the room with the shelves. Ted and Dougal talk in the foreground. Tom is in the background looking through the shelves.

DOUGAL: Ted, what's Tom going to do again?

TED: I don't know, really. He just said he'd take care of them.

Ted and Dougal don't notice, but in the background we can see Tom pick up a hammer and start swinging it around, testing it.

TED: I'd say he'll just collect them all together and put them somewhere safe.

Tom puts down the hammer, frowning, and picks up a baseball bat. He starts testing it, swinging it around wildly, knocking things off the shelves and stumbling around. Despite the noise, Ted and Dougal still don't notice.

DOUGAL: Ah, right. So he's just going to look after them.

TED: Yes. Basically, I think he'll just put them in a big pen where they can run around and have a bit of a play . . .

Tom puts down the baseball bat and picks up a huge chainsaw. He starts yanking the chain. It splutters once or twice.

TED: Ah, yeah, Tom's the man for a job like this. He'll try and keep the rabbits as comfortable as possible while they—

Ted's words are drowned out by the sound of the chainsaw. Tom raises it in the air as Ted keeps talking, Dougal nodding at what he's saying, voicing his agreement from time to time. We can't hear any of this, of course. After a moment or two, the chainsaw conks out and Tom looks disappointed.

TED: . . . so there's absolutely nothing to worry about.

Tom looks up and sees something out of shot. He disappears towards the door.

TED: He's taking his time, though. I wonder wh—. . . Ah, there he is . . .

Ted's voice trails off as he sees Tom walking slowly out of the room with a long Samurai sword poised for action.

TOM: All right, Father! Let's go for it!

TED: Ah, that's a very impressive sword, Tom. Eh, I just wonder . . . Where exactly are you going to put the rabbits?

TOM: In the vice, Father.

TED: In the vice?

TOM: Yeah . . . I'll show you . . . I've been practisin' with this toy one.

He takes out a toy rabbit from under his arm.

First you stun it . . .

He whacks its head off the side of the workbench.

Then you stick it in the vice . . .

He sticks the rabbit's head in the vice and tightens it with the handle.

You grab the legs there, Father . . .

Ted very reluctantly grabs the legs and pulls the rabbit out from the vice. We see Tom lifting the sword.

TED: Tom, you know the phrase 'to take care of something' . . .

TOM: Yes, Father . . .

TED: I realise now you meant that in a sort of Al Pacino way, whereas I was thinking more along the lines of Carla Lane.

TOM: Don't worry, Father. They won't know what's going on.

TED: No, Tom, I really don't think—

TOM: Come on, Father! Let's go! You can have a go if you want!

TED: No, honestly, Tom. It's a bit cruel.

TOM: I could run them down in me van!

TED: Dougal, I think we'd better be off . . .

DOUGAL: What's the problem, Ted?

TOM: Do you have nothing at all I can kill, Father?

TED: No, sorry about that, Tom.

TOM: Ah, feck! Feck it altogether!

Tom is breathing very heavily. He clenches the Samurai sword tightly and stares in a fixed way at Ted and Dougal. Pause.

TED (*somewhat nervous*): Well! We'll be off! Bye, Tom!

They open the door very slowly and, without making any sudden moves, back out, smiling and nodding at Tom. He watches them go, red-faced. Outside the door, Ted immediately speeds up.

TED: Run, Dougal. Run quite fast, quite fast.

They jog out of shot.

END OF PART ONE

* * *

PART TWO

SCENE 11 INT./DAY 3
SET: JACK'S BEDROOM
Ted leads Bishop Brennan into the room. We don't see any of the room's contents yet.

TED: . . . Well, I'm sure it won't happen again.

BRENNAN: It better not. Priests walking

around in the nude is the last thing we need.

TED: Yes, you're right. But as you can see, we've added a few modifications to Jack's bed.

We see Jack's bed. It looks more like a deranged cot, with bars around the sides that extend into downward and inward curving spikes. Barbed wire is around the top.

BRENNAN: Yes . . . (*He points at the barbed wire.*) That's new, isn't it?

TED (*nods*): Combined with the spikes, it'll make escape almost impossible. We've also got these new pyjamas . . . (*He holds up a one-piece pyjama suit.*) Very easy to put on, hard to get off, so that's the nudity sorted.

Brennan holds up a length of thick rope from inside the cot.

TED: Ah, yes, the rope. I'd like to see him chewing through that! . . .

Brennan makes a 'mmm' face and leaves the room. Ted looks at the rope. He speaks quietly, to himself.

TED: . . . again . . .

SCENE 12 INT./DAY 3
SET: PAROCHIAL HOUSE HALLWAY
Ted and Brennan have come downstairs.

TED: . . . plus, in the unlikely event of him getting out, this tracking device should give us a speedy recapture. That cost fifty pounds. Maybe we could get that back from the diocese . . .? (*He looks at Brennan hopefully. Brennan gives him a nasty look.*) Ha, ha . . . only joking . . .

They enter the living room. Dougal is there.

DOUGAL (*very cheery*): Ah, hello, Len!

BRENNAN: Don't call me Len. I'm a bishop.

TED: He's right, Dougal. Your Grace is more appropriate.

DOUGAL: Oh, Your Grace, right.

BRENNAN: Anyway, yet again, I am dragged away from my warm fireside to come and deal with the cast of *Police Academy*. Now, Jack, you behave yourself. (*To Jack.*) Are you listening to me, Jack?

JACK: No.

Jack pours himself a large drink from a bottle of whiskey.

TED: Oh, would you like a drink, Len? Your Grace! Your Grace!

BRENNAN: Yes . . . very well.

TED: I'll just . . .

Ted goes over to Jack. He attempts to take the bottle from him, but Jack grunts angrily and refuses to let go. There is a slightly embarrassing struggle. Brennan looks on.

DOUGAL (*to Brennan*): It must be fantastic being a bishop. Do you have any tips?*

BRENNAN: Tips?*

DOUGAL: Y'know. For the racing.*

Ted struggles a bit more, then quickly gives up and turns around.

TED: How about a cup of tea, Your Grace?

Mrs Doyle enters. She carries a saucer of water and some lettuce.

MRS DOYLE: Time for dinny-poos! Here's . . .

TED (*jumps*): Ah, yes! Thank you, Mrs Doyle.

Ted takes both and sits down in his chair. He starts drinking the water casually and munching the lettuce. Mrs Doyle and Brennan look at him strangely. Ted behaves as if nothing is wrong.

MRS DOYLE (*notices Brennan*): Ah, there you are, Bishop Brennan. I thought I should tell you – your car is parked outside.

BRENNAN: Yes, I know it is. I parked it there.

MRS DOYLE: The tyres look a bit flat. I'll give them a little blow up for you with the pump . . .

BRENNAN: No . . .

MRS DOYLE: What type of air would you normally put in them? We have ordinary and . . . well, that's all we have, actually. I don't think there's any other kind, really. Oh, and if you're looking for the wipers, I have them in the kitchen.

BRENNAN: What?

MRS DOYLE: They looked as if they needed a

*These lines were deleted from the final version.

wash. The only thing is, I'm afraid I broke the side window while I was snapping them off.

BRENNAN: Leave my car alone! Don't touch it again!

MRS DOYLE: Just one question, Your Grace . . . Eh, is your car diesel, or petrol?

BRENNAN: Just leave it, Mrs Doyle!

MRS DOYLE: No, this is just curiosity, Your Grace. Diesel or—

BRENNAN: Diesel! It's diesel!

MRS DOYLE: Right. So it's not petrol.

BRENNAN: No.

MRS DOYLE: Right, so it'd do a terrible

amount of damage if I put petrol in.

BRENNAN: Yes, it would. It would completely ruin the car's engine.

MRS DOYLE: Well, ha, ha! I certainly won't be doing that! Ha, ha!

She turns and we see her horrified expression as she scurries out of the room.

TED: I expect you must clock up a fair few miles during the year. Goin' round the old diocese . . .

BRENNAN (*interrupting*)**:** Crilly, where is my room?

TED (*finishing off the lettuce*)**:** Oh, it's the spare room, Your Grace. First on the right.

He gets up to leave. On the way, he passes the rabbit cage. There is a half-eaten leaf of lettuce.

BRENNAN: This lettuce . . .

TED (*sees the lettuce*)**:** Oh, no, I honestly couldn't. I just had some. You have it . . .

BRENNAN: No, I mean . . . what's it doing here? You don't keep rabbits, do you?

TED: No, no . . .

BRENNAN: It's just . . . I don't like them at all. I had an experience with some once. And it . . . it wasn't very nice . . . they got into a lift with me. They started nibbling my cloak . . . and everything.

TED: Well, you have absolutely no need to worry, Your Grace. That's just where we . . . grow the lettuce.

BRENNAN: You grow lettuce? Indoors? In a cage?

TED: That's right. It's safer and, ah, no one can steal it. As well as that, it, you know . . . brightens up the room.

Brennan looks at them for a second. He then walks towards the door. He looks down. There is a little mound of rabbit droppings just in front of it.

BRENNAN: What . . . is . . . this?

TED: That? Oh that's the eh . . . caviar.

BRENNAN: Caviar?

TED: Yes. Well, it's not every day we have a bishop staying with us, Your Grace. So we thought we'd get a bit of caviar out for you.

BRENNAN: So what's it doing lying in little piles on the floor?

TED: Oh, eh, eh . . . Japan.

BRENNAN: What?

TED: It's the Japanese tradition to eat off the floor. Great fun. And you don't need as many chairs.

BRENNAN: Right. So what you've done is you've spread some caviar down there so I can get down on my hands and knees and eat off the floor.

TED (*beat*)**:** Yes.

BRENNAN: What do you think I am, Crilly? A pony? I'm going to bed. (*To Jack.*) And you, keep in your room!

JACK: Feck off!

Brennan marches out of the room.

TED: Dougal, where'd you put them?

DOUGAL: The rabbits? Ah, ha, ha . . . somewhere really safe, Ted.

TED: Where?

DOUGAL: Guess. It's almost like the type of place you'd never even think of.

TED: God, where'd that be? That small room behind the kitchen?

Dougal shakes his head.

TED: The coal cellar?

Dougal shakes his head.

TED: Jack's room? Great idea!!!

DOUGAL: Nope, it's not Jack's room.

TED: God, I don't know . . .

DOUGAL: Think about it, Ted. Where'd be the last place you'd think I'd put them?

TED: The last place? God . . .

DOUGAL: Somewhere you wouldn't expect at all . . .

TED: Well, let's see . . . (*Ted thinks. Then his expression changes to one of horror. Hesitant, nervous.*) Well, now, I'd say the last place I'd think you'd put them would actually be Bishop Brennan's room.

DOUGAL: Bingo! Think about it, Ted. If you were trying to find some rabbits, where's the last place you'd look? I put them in the last place he'd ever expect them – in his own room! He'd never imagine there'd be a load of rabbits in there!

He steps back and moves his hands apart.

DOUGAL: Eh? Eh?

Ted raises his hand and grimaces. Dougal misunderstands this as a congratulatory gesture and waves him away humbly. Ted puts his hands up to his own head in horror, and again Dougal misunderstands, laughs and winks. This 'dance' goes on for a moment or two. Then Ted moves his hands up to Dougal's neck, thinks better of it and dashes out of the room.

SCENE 13 INT./NIGHT 3
SET: PAROCHIAL HOUSE LANDING
Brennan is just about to open the door. Ted appears over the top of the stairs.

TED: Your Grace! Your Grace!

Brennan stops and looks at Ted.

BRENNAN: Crilly. What is it?

TED (*slightly out of breath*): . . . Just wanted to say, the whole bishop thing, fair play to you.

Brennan doesn't say anything.

TED: I mean, you probably get a lot of this, but I just wanted to say, you know . . . Well done. Who would have thought that someone from Limerick would get this far? Ha . . . you know . . . all the ones you studied with in the seminary, the other priests . . . they must be feeling pretty sick at the moment! They'd be looking at the TV goin' 'How did that awful eejit get to be a Bishop?!' Ha, ha. But you know, that's no mystery to me. You have this sort of . . . bishopy air about you. Everything about you says 'I am a bishop.' You know, I think even if you were naked, like, you know, totally . . . naked . . . I think someone who didn't know you would still be able to go . . . 'That man's a bishop.' Even if you were naked. (*Pause.*) Can I just shake hands with you? (*He does so.*) Well done.

BRENNAN (*puts a hand on Ted's shoulder*): Crilly . . . I hate you. So all that means absolutely nothing to me.

He goes to enter the room. Ted quickly turns and intentionally falls down the stairs. He throws himself down them in one huge jump, going out of shot.

TED: Aggghhh! Oh, God, I've fallen down the stairs!

Brennan closes the door and goes over to look down the stairs.

BRENNAN: Crilly! What happened!

TED (*out of shot*): God, would you believe, I just fell down the stairs there.

BRENNAN: Well . . . are you injured?

TED: I'm not sure. There's a twinge all right. My arm! I can't move!

BRENNAN: Do you want someone to call an ambulance, Crilly?

TED: Ah, no. I'll just lie here for a while. Rest is probably the best thing for me now. Ah, yes . . . bit of a rest . . . Oh, did you see that documentary on Hiroshima last night? Who would have thought an atomic bomb could do so much damage?

BRENNAN: Crilly, I am going to bed.

Brennan turns towards the door again. Suddenly, Ted arrives back in shot. Brennan sighs and turns to face him.

TED: I'm all right! Bishop Brennan, I'm fine now. Thanks. Phew!

DOUGAL (*shouting, from downstairs*): Did Len find the rabbits, Ted?

Pause. Brennan and Ted look at each other. Ted's face is frozen in horror.

BRENNAN (*very angry*): What did he say?!

TED: Oh, God, look, I'd better tell you—

BRENNAN: Did he call me Len again!?! (*He shouts down.*) YOU ADDRESS ME BY MY PROPER TITLE, YOU LITTLE BOLLOCKS!

DOUGAL (*from downstairs*): Sorry . . . ah . . . Bishop Len Brennan . . .

BRENNAN (*calming somewhat*): What was he on about, anyway?

TED: Oh, God knows! (*He shouts down.*) Dougal, you big eejit! What are you on about now?! Ha, ha!

DOUGAL: I was just asking—

TED: Oh, shut up, Dougal, you big, mad fool!

Ted turns to see that Brennan is halfway into the room. He runs back.

TED: Bishop Brennan. Could I go in first?

BRENNAN: Why?

TED: I really need to go to the toilet. Eh, all the rest of the toilets in the house are broken. It's just number ones—

BRENNAN: I DON'T WANT TO KNOW!

Brennan moves out of the way and Ted goes in.

SCENE 14 INT./NIGHT 3
SET: BISHOP BRENNAN'S ROOM
Ted comes in and looks around, confused.

SCENE 15 INT./NIGHT 3
SET: PAROCHIAL HOUSE LANDING/BISHOP BRENNAN'S ROOM
Brennan looks at his watch and sighs. Finally, Ted comes out.

TED: Oh, God . . . I really needed that, I can tell you.

Brennan shoves Ted out of the way and goes into his room.

SCENE 16 INT./NIGHT 3
SET: BISHOP BRENNAN'S ROOM
Brennan comes in. He looks around, confused. Pause.

BRENNAN: But . . . there's no toilet in here.

He looks ever so slightly nervous.

SCENE 17 INT./NIGHT 3
SET: OUTSIDE BISHOP BRENNAN'S ROOM
Ted leans against the door, looking drained. Dougal appears up the stairs.

TED (*whispers*): Dougal, where are they? They're not in there.

DOUGAL (*whispers*): Are they not?

TED: No. It's a completely rabbit-free area. Are you sure you're not getting confused?

DOUGAL: No, I definitely put them in there, Ted.

TED: Then where are they? Where the hell are they? If Len runs into them, we're finished. And we'll be in a parish where it's a two-thousand-mile walk to the nearest newsagent.

DOUGAL: Wait! What about Jack's room? Maybe they smelled him, and they just had to see him one last time.

TED: That's possibly a slightly over-romantic way of putting it but . . . it's a good guess. Come on!

SCENE 18 INT./NIGHT 3
SET: JACK'S BEDROOM
They enter the room. It is dark, but we hear the scuffling sounds of rabbits crawling all over the place.

TED: God, Dougal, you're right! There's loads of them. How did they get in?

DOUGAL: They must have burrowed in. You know rabbits, Ted.

TED: We'll have to do it in shifts. Get them out of the house and as far away as possible. Try not to wake Father Jack, Dougal. He can be unusually violent when you wake him suddenly.

DOUGAL: Ted, why can't we just leave them in there?

TED: Because, Dougal, my nerves are shot. I won't be able to relax until the only rabbit left is the one sitting in your head working the controls.

Dougal goes into the small room adjoining Jack's.

DOUGAL (*offscreen*): There's more in here, Ted. Oh, look at this one. Doesn't he look like that fella, Harvey Keitel?

TED: Harvey Keitel? God, Dougal . . . (*He follows him out of shot.*) How could a rabbit look like Harv— . . . God almighty! . . .

Pause.

DOUGAL: Y'see?

TED: . . . He's the *image* of him. Amazing . . . Anyway, we haven't the time to think about things like that . . . Get that one there. Get that one before he . . .

We see, in silhouette, Jack standing up. He climbs out of his cot. We hear a lot of ripping and tearing.

SCENE 19 INT./NIGHT 3
SET: FRONT DOOR
We see Jack's hand coming into shot and trying the front door blindly for a moment or two in the dark. No luck. The hand retreats.

SCENE 20 INT./NIGHT 3
SET: JACK'S BEDROOM
Ted and Dougal come out of the adjoining room, holding rabbits. They stop in their tracks.

TED: Where've they gone?????!!!!

DOUGAL: Ted, where's Jack?

We see the cot. Jack's pyjamas are shredded and hanging from the barbed wire. Ted and Dougal put down the rabbits and run out.

SCENE 21 INT./NIGHT 3
SET: PAROCHIAL HOUSE HALLWAY
Ted comes to a sudden halt.

TED: Oh . . . my . . . God . . .

We see that the door to Brennan's room is ajar.

TED: We have to get them out! Oh, God, Dougal!

SCENE 22 INT./NIGHT 3
SET: BISHOP BRENNAN'S ROOM
The room is completely dark. Dougal's and Ted's silhouettes appear at the door. Then they close it gently.

TED (*whispers*): Dougal, get as many as you can! Come on!

DOUGAL: I am, Ted . . . c'mon, lads!

BRENNAN: Huh? . . . Who's . . .

The light suddenly comes on. Brennan is half-asleep, surveying the scene. We see Ted and Dougal, their arms filled with rabbits, frozen as they stare back at him. Also, there are dozens of rabbits crawling all over the bed and floor. This is held for one, awful moment. Then Brennan looks down and sees, in bed beside him, Jack, who is staring at him in confusion. Neither of them is wearing pyjamas. Again, we hold on this. Finally, after what seems an age . . .

TED: Ah, just a bad dream, Your Grace. It'll be over in a mo'.

Brennan blinks for a moment, then nods and puts his head back down on the pillow. Ted and Dougal look at each other. Then Brennan wakes up again, sits bolt upright and screams.

SCENE 22A EXT./NIGHT 3*
SET: PAROCHIAL HOUSE
Cut to an exit shot of the Parochial House as his scream fills the night.

POST-CREDIT SEQUENCE*
SCENE 23 INT.
SET: VARIOUS
Ted sitting down, reading. Loads of rabbits hop around the living room. Ted is oblivious to all this.

Jack trapped in his cot. He peers out from behind the bars like an overgrown baby.

Dougal throwing a tennis ball to a rabbit. Cut to a close-up of the rabbit. We see that it has a tiny tennis racket stuck to it and wears a headband and tennis gear.

Extreme close-up of Brennan. He may be in some kind of hospital. His face is locked in a grimace of absolute terror.

THE END

---

* We deleted this scene from the final version.

rock a hula ted

ARTHUR: There's really no point in pretending otherwise, is there? Niamh Connolly was inspired by Sinead O'Connor. Sinead's actually very friendly towards the show and came to the recording of the Christmas Special. And we must have had a great effect on her – she's become a priest. Archbishop Michael Cox, put a curse on our friend Paul Wonderful after he appeared on *The Late, Late Show* with a song called 'Bless Me, Father'. A week later he was ordaining Sinead O'Connor in a ceremony in a hotel room in Lourdes.

The Lovely Girls Competition is a low-budget version of The Rose of Tralee, a competition held annually in County Kerry, which used to be hosted by Gay Byrne. Girls, mainly of Irish extraction, come from all over the world and do a little turn, talk about world peace and so on. As with everything on Craggy Island, this is a low-budget version.

GRAHAM: We wanted to do a spoof of rock stars who saw themselves as preachers, and of the politically correct opinions being bandied about at the time. But it wasn't enough to satirise right-on opinions. We wanted to poke fun at the opposite viewpoint as well, which is how we arrived at the idea of a Lovely Girls Competition.

I love the 'take your bra off' stuff. Arthur and I love the word 'bra'; it's a brilliant word that just stops in mid-air. We just can't get enough of it. I'd love to have had a whole episode in which Ted and Dougal continually had to say the word 'bra': 'Maybe her bra's on too tight,' 'Dougal! Where did you put the bra?'. Oh, well . . .

Father Bigley's a character who didn't quite come off. We wanted to construct a character who would never appear on-screen because, from the way they described him, he'd be such a weird-looking Mister Potato Head that he couldn't possibly exist. We wanted to have him in every episode, adding an appalling physical attribute each time, but in the end, we couldn't find anymore than one or two occasions on which to do so.

PART ONE

SCENE 1 INT./DAY 1
SET: TELEVISION STUDIO

A television chat-show. Very like 'The Late Late Show'. A Gay Byrne type is interviewing a rock star, Niamh Connolly. She has short, black hair and wears a black T-shirt with blue jeans.

NIAMH: . . . and societies in Ancient India were ruled by women.

INTERVIEWER: Really?

NIAMH: And men weren't allowed around women without a licence, and they were put in a corner and were told off for being sexist.

INTERVIEWER: . . . Aaaaaanyway, you're going to do a song from your new album for us . . .

Cut to Ted and Dougal watching this. We see Mrs Doyle walking behind them. She is carrying a big hod full of bricks. She is bent under the weight of the load. Ted and Dougal don't see her, their attention held by Niamh. On one of the walls of the room, although our attention shouldn't be drawn to it at first, is a red fire-alarm bell.

TED: What an eejit. She's never happy unless she's giving out about something.

DOUGAL: You're right there, Ted.

Cut back to the television.

INTERVIEWER: I believe this new song is about the Catholic Church?

Cut back to Ted.

TED: Oh, here she goes!

NIAMH: That's right. It's about how the Church in Ireland secretly had lots of potatoes during the famine. And they hid the potatoes in pillows and sold them abroad at potato fairs.

INTERVIEWER: Really?

NIAMH: Yes. And then the Pope closed down a lot of factories that were making potatoes and turned them into prisons for children. And the nuns hid up trees and hit people unless they went to Mass . . .

Cut back to Ted.

TED: God almighty! She says that as if there's something *sinister* about it all. *What* is the problem with her?

DOUGAL: She seems to be taking the whole Catholic thing a bit seriously.

TED: Yes, Dougal.

DOUGAL: I mean, it's just a bit of a laugh . . .

TED: Stop talking, Dougal. I tell you what, though, it's this militant feminism lark that really gets my goat.

DOUGAL: Mad!

TED: This idea that the Church has some kind of negative attitude to women.

DOUGAL: Ted! She's doin' her song.

Cut back to the television. Niamh is at the microphone, singing.

NIAMH: 'Big men in frocks
telling us what to do
they can't get pregnant
like I do . . .'

TED: Mrs Doyle, you're a woman. What do you think of all this stuff? Do you think the Catholic Church is a bit sexist?

We see only a head-and-shoulders shot of Mrs Doyle as she answers this question. She doesn't look at Ted and Dougal as she answers, and they are unseen in this shot.

MRS DOYLE (*her face red from exertion*): God, no, Father. I always thought that the Church is extremely responsive to my views. I mean, I remember once I was having terrible problems at home, and the Church gave me great

support then. I mean, there's a lot of people who . . . (*Suddenly, we see Ted and Dougal, who have stood up while out of shot, walking past behind her. They pay absolutely no attention to her at all.*) . . . run the Church down. But they're just a load of old moaners. Moan. Moan. Moan. Anyway, thanks for asking, Father, but no . . . (*Ted and Dougal walk back into shot carrying bags of crisps, munching them and chatting to each other. They go back to their seats.*) . . . I really have no complaints at all.

She looks down at them. Ted and Dougal look up at her, as if they'd forgotten she was talking.

TED (*not interested at all*)**:** Yeah? Great.

Mrs Doyle staggers off. Cut to Niamh on television. A woman is 'translating' her lyrics into sign language as she sings.

NIAMH: 'You give us all your rules
But that's not the way it was,
When women ruled the land
of Tir Na Nog . . .'

The signing woman doesn't know the sign for Tir Na Nog, so she just shrugs. The fire-alarm thing

over Ted's head suddenly rings once.

TED: Oh, no!!!!

JACK: DRINK!!!!!

As Jack says this, a bottle hits Ted on the back of the head.

TED: Oooo, God . . . one second late and he goes mad. Here you go, Father. Your afternoon drink.

Ted gets a full bottle and carries it over to Jack. Jack puts down the magazine he has been looking at and we see him for the first time. His hair is very long and he has grown some type of goatee-and-sideburns affair.

TED: . . . You know you really should get a haircut. You're letting yourself go a bit, Father. You don't want to go too far down that Bob Geldof road.

DOUGAL: Oh, God, Ted, that's a bad road.

TED: It is indeed, Dougal, and there's no coming back once you're gone down it, as Bob himself would tell you. Ha, ha . . .

He nudges Jack playfully. In one quick move, Jack brings up his walking stick and whacks Ted in the face with it.

SCENE 2 INT./DAY 2
SET: PAROCHIAL HOUSE
A priest, Father Liam Deliverance, is looking up at Ted's bookshelves, in a contemplative stance.

LIAM: What'd ye pay for the shelves, Ted?

Cut to Ted pouring a cup of tea.

TED: God, Liam, I don't really remember . . .

LIAM: These won't last you. (*He points at one of the supports.*) Look at that. You could talk that into coming down.

TED: Well, they've lasted fine until now . . .

LIAM: Give us a go.

He reaches up and starts pulling as hard as he can on one of the higher shelves. At one point his feet come off the floor.

LIAM: I can feel it beginning to go, Ted.

TED: Don't . . . ah, Liam . . .

Liam lets go of the top shelf and starts slamming his foot down on to one of the lower ones. Bang! Bang! Bang! Bang! Bang! It breaks and all the books on that shelf tumble on to the floor.

LIAM: Ah, look at that, Ted. It's falling apart.

TED: Liam, how about a little cup of tea?

LIAM: Fair enough.

He walks over to Ted, who pours some tea from a teapot.

TED: So, what'd you want to talk about?

LIAM: You were planning on going to the Lovely Girls Festival this year, weren't you?

TED: Oh, I was, yes. Never miss a Lovely Girl Festival. My absolute favourite time of the year. How's Miss Lovely Girl 1995 doing?

LIAM: Oh, God, Ted, we had to strip her of her title.

TED: God almighty. Why? Oh, no, she didn't have a drink in public, did she?

LIAM: No, no. We found out she'd been in a film called *Stallion Farm*. I heard it's a bit rude. Anyway. I'm chairman of the organising committee this year, and I was wondering if you wanted to judge it.

TED: Judge it!!!! God, Liam, I'd love to! Oh! . . . and there's the dinner afterwards isn't there?

LIAM: Oh, yes. You have the honour of taking the winner out for a meal.

TED: And I think . . . who pays for it? It's not me is it? Did I hear that somewhere . . .?

LIAM: That's right. We had that idea a few years ago. *You* have the honour of taking her out to dinner and *she* has the honour of paying for it.

TED: Oh, lovely.

LIAM: How much did that stereo set you back?

He bends over the stereo.

TED: Oh, about a hundred pounds.

LIAM: I could have got you one for half price.

TED: Careful Liam . . . So, what were you saying?

LIAM: Ah, yes. When you take the lovely girl out to dinner, could you persuade her to wear one of me Mammy's dresses? She could use the publicity.

TED: Oh, right! How's the business going?

LIAM: Great! She sold one last week.

TED: Good. How many is that sold this year?

LIAM: That'd be one.

We hear a snap. Liam turns around and holds up the arm of the record player.

LIAM: Y'see? Now, that's no good at all. I can get you a great one from Father Clonkett. I could get you a few of them if you want.

TED (*slightly annoyed*): Don't worry about it, Liam.

LIAM: Basically, we thought it'd be a bit of a laugh getting a priest to judge it this year. Also, it eliminates any sexual aspect to the thing.

Ted doesn't know how to take this.

LIAM (*jokily*): Or am I wrong? I hope you won't be tempted by all those lovely girls!

TED: Oh, no chance of that, Liam! Ha! Ha!

LIAM: 'Cause we've had problems with that sort of thing before, you know!

TED: O'ho! Ha! Ha!

LIAM (*suddenly dead serious*): No, Ted, we really have had problems with that before.

TED (*serious*): Oh, right! No, you've nothing to worry about there, Liam.

LIAM: Anyway, I'll be off. (*He goes to the door.*)

TED: Bye, Liam.

LIAM: How much did this door cost you, Ted?

TED: Ah, I don't know, Liam. It came with the house.

Liam swings it open and closed a few times. Very roughly. He smiles back at Ted, then leaves, closing the door. Ted sighs and goes to sit down. Suddenly Liam's foot comes through the door. Liam looks through the hole he's made.

LIAM: Cowboys, Ted. They're a bunch of cowboys.

At last he leaves. Ted picks up a newspaper and browses through it. Dougal enters. He has a copy of a glossy magazine called 'Rock Cupboard'*. Ted puts down his paper. He notices a picture of Niamh on the front of Dougal's magazine. She is wearing boxing gloves and is staring angrily out from the cover. The headline reads 'I am still very angry – the Niamh Connolly interview'. One word is written on both gloves so that together they read 'Clit Power'.

---

*Rock Cupboard is an affectionate nod to Ireland's *Hot Press* magazine, for which Arthur worked as Arts Editor.

TED: Oh, God, look at her there. She's all over the place. (*Dougal sits down.*)

TED (*squints at the headline*): 'Clit Power'? What does that mean?

DOUGAL: Dunno.

TED: I used to know a Father Clint Power. Maybe she's having a go at him. What's the interview like? The same old nonsense, I suppose.

DOUGAL: Ah, I didn't read much of it. She's goin' around Ireland at the moment. She wants to buy a house on an island and live in it. She has her eye on some Godforsaken place off the west coast.

TED: Really? Did it mention what island she had her eye on, Dougal?

DOUGAL: It did, yeah, but I don't remember the name of it.

TED (*swallows, stands up*): Could you have a look there?

DOUGAL: 'Course I can, Ted.

Dougal flicks through the magazine.

DOUGAL: Ah, it's . . . ah . . . let me see . . . it's . . . Ahhhh . . .

SCENE 3 INT./DAY 2
SET: PAROCHIAL HOUSE
We see Niamh being interviewed on television by a wall in a street.

NIAMH: . . . Craggy Island. Yes. Craggy Island. Craggy Island is the place for me. (*Shot of Ted and Dougal looking miserable.*) I've always wanted somewhere peaceful to record my music and Craggy Island might just be the place. I see it as being a safe haven for those wishing to escape the hypocrisy of the mainland.

Cut to Ted and Dougal watching television, worried looks on their faces.

TED: Oh, God . . .

NIAMH: I want to create a world free of sexual and religious intolerance . . .

Ted and Dougal look at each other, worried.

TED: For f—

NIAMH: . . . Free of sexist patriarchal systems and hypocrisy.

TED: Oh, no, no, no! That's terrible news!

He marches over and turns off the television.

TED: Right. Basically, I think we'll just have to stand our ground. If she's on the island, I'm bound to bump into her somewhere. I'll just tell her that the people of Craggy Island will not stand for a world free of sexual and religious intolerance!

DOUGAL: No way, José.

Mrs Doyle comes in. She looks dirty and tired.

MRS DOYLE (*slightly out of breath*)**:** Father . . . , ah . . the roof should be all right now. I hoovered upstairs and I did the attic – top to bottom – and – ooooh, what else? . . . Oh yes, washed your car. Also, I built a little greenhouse near the garage. Would that be all for today?

Cut to Ted and Dougal. They obviously haven't heard a word of this. Ted turns and notices Mrs Doyle.

TED: Ah! Mrs Doyle! Any chance of a cup of tea for your two favourite priests?

Mrs Doyle takes this in, then nods, exhausted, and backs out of the room. Once there, she collapses.

SCENE 4 INT./MORNING 3
SET: TED AND DOUGAL'S BEDROOM
We see Dougal asleep in bed. Pull back to see Ted fully dressed beside him, busying himself. Dougal stirs.

DOUGAL: Uuuuhhhhh . . . Ted, . . . What time is it? (*He searches for his watch.*) God, Ted, it's only eleven. What are you doing up?

TED: I want to get away early to the Lovely Girls Competition.

DOUGAL: God, Ted. I wouldn't mind goin' but I don't think I'd know what to say to a lovely girl.

TED: God, there's no end of things you can talk about . . . What their father does for a living, if they have a boyfriend, dressmaking . . . anything to do with clothes or perfume, basically. Clothes is easiest to talk about because men wear

clothes but we don't wear perfume.

DOUGAL: Except Father Bigley.

TED: Except Father Bigley. Anyway, if y'ever meet a woman, I'm sure you'd be able to deal with it. Just be yourself, Dougal. Be yourself, make them feel at ease, and the golden rule, always let them have their way! It's easier in the long run. (*Dougal nods.*) Anyway, better be off. Don't want to keep those lovely girls waiting!

Ted leaves. Dougal picks up another notebook and starts writing . . .

DOUGAL: 'Be . . . yourself . . .'

SCENE 5 EXT./DAY 3
SET: MARQUEE
Establishing shot of marquee. We see a banner reading 'Lovely Girls Festival '96'.

SCENE 5A INT./DAY 3
SET: MARQUEE
In the foreground we see four men standing in a circle. They have pints of beer in their hands and white shirts over beerbellies. Lots of 'lovely girls' walk around smiling at everyone. The men look at them appreciatively and grunt at each other.

TERRY: Eh? Eh? She's comin' for you, Billy.

BILLY: Ha! Is she, yeah? O'ho, God . . .

DANNY: She's got her eye on Paddy . . .

PADDY: Ohhhh, ho . . . there we go now . . .

Ted comes into shot.

DANNY: Hello, Father.

TED: Hello, lads, how's it goin' there?

PADDY: O'ho, we're gettin' the eye from the girls, Father.

ALL: Oh, oh . . .

TED: Has Cupid been firing his arrows in the direction of the Casey brothers?

ALL: Oh, ho hooooooo!!!

TED: I hope you won't be getting into any mischief.

TERRY: Oh, you know us, Father.

TED: I do! And that's the trouble!

ALL: O'hooooooo!!!!!

Ted looks at his watch.

TED: Lads, lads, sorry, but I'd better run. The competition's starting any second.

Ted starts to move off, but he sees Jack nearby.

TED: Oh, no . . .

They all raise their beers as he dashes out of shot. One of the women comes up to the group.

WOMAN: Hello.

The men look down at the ground and don't say anything, mortified with embarrassment. After a moment, she shrugs and walks away; as she does so, they watch her go and say, almost simultaneously . . .

DANNY: O'ho . . .

TERRY: Oh, ho, ho, ho . . .

BILLY: Ooooohhhhh!!!!! . . .

PADDY: Oh, hooooo . . .

SCENE 5B EXT./DAY 3
SET: ANOTHER PART OF MARQUEE
We see Jack holding a tin with 'Live Aid' written on it. He looks very innocent. Someone puts money in it. Jack shakes the tin and runs to the bar. Ted approaches him.

TED: Now, Father, that's not on. Impersonating Sir Bob. And what would all those other Live Aid people think? Peter Gabriel and Queen and the other bands who were on earlier in the day. And Phil Collins flying all the way to Boston. (*Ted takes the box*

from him. Jack punches him in the stomach, takes the box back and walks out of shot. Ted is completely winded, but manages to glance at his watch.) Oh, God! (*He staggers off.*)

SCENE 6 INT./DAY 3
SET: BESIDE THE STAGE
Father Liam Deliverance is looking at his watch beside the makeshift stage. Ted comes into shot.

LIAM: Ted, for crying out loud. The girls won't stay lovely for ever, you know.

TED (*out of breath*): Sorry, Liam, Father Jack just punched me in the stomach . . . God . . .

LIAM: Come on, get up there!

Ted makes his way with difficulty to the stage, completely out of breath. We see four lovely girls in frocks with large sashes walking around on the stage and smiling. Ted can't speak. He doubles over, trying to get his breath back. He breathes very heavily. Liam puts the microphone in his hand. Ted climbs up on stage.

TED (*into microphone*): Hello . . . (*He takes a breath.*) . . . Lovely girls . . . Look at them there . . . walking around . . .

Ted stops talking and tries to get his breath back again. However, he does this into the microphone, and we pull back for a shot of the lovely girls walking around, with Ted's amplified heavy breathing on top of it. The girls look slightly worried by this.

SCENE 7 INT./DAY 3
SET: PAROCHIAL HOUSE HALLWAY
We hear the doorbell. Dougal comes into the hall. He is right beside the door but he looks up the stairs.

DOUGAL: Mrs Doyle? Someone at the door, Mrs Doyle! (*The doorbell rings again.*) Mrs Doyle!

SCENE 8 EXT./DAY 3
SET: PAROCHIAL HOUSE
We see the door open very slowly. Dougal peeks out.

SCENE 9 INT./DAY 3
SET: MARQUEE
Ted is talking to Imelda, one of the contestants.

TED: Well, Imelda, you're a lovely girl.

IMELDA: I will indeed, Father.

She looks at the notes. Pause. She turns the page and looks some more. Ted sighs.

SCENE 10 INT./DAY 3
SET: PAROCHIAL HOUSE
Dougal and Niamh are sitting down. Dougal looks terrified.

NIAMH: You haven't told me your name, Father.

DOUGAL: Mmmm . . . Be yourself . . . Father Dougal McGuire!

NIAMH: Oh, right. This is a beautiful house. I love the crude religious imagery.

DOUGAL: Uh . . . ah . . . uh . . . eh. Are you all right there? Is your bra all right?

NIAMH: What?

DOUGAL: Your bra? Is it comfortable? Do you have a bra?

Niamh gives him a look.

DOUGAL: It's not too tight? 'Cause you can loosen it if you want. Take it off, sure.

NIAMH: I . . .

DOUGAL: Or would you like some tea? I tell you what. I'll go and make some tea, and you take your bra off.

Dougal leaves the room. Niamh watches him go, flabbergasted.

SCENE 11 INT./DAY 3
SET: MARQUEE
Danny, Terry, Billy and Paddy are still standing in the same place.

ALL: O'ho . . .

BILLY: O'hooooo . . . Wh— Isn't that Bob Geldof there?

We see Jack sneaking into the marquee.

TERRY: No, it— Wait a second! It is, you know! He's lookin' a bit rough.

PADDY: Ah, he'd have lost all his money in that Live Aid thing.

BILLY: I'm not sure if it is Bob Geldof. Hang on there a second. (*He walks out of shot.*)

. . . lthough you had a bit of bad luck recently. I . . . ear your dog was knocked down by a car and . . . e was killed, is that right?

. . . MELDA: No, that was . . . that was my . . . ather.

. . . ed nods at this, and looks through his notes for . . . mething else.

. . . ED: And it says here you're twenty-two . . .

. . . MELDA: No, nineteen . . .

. . . ED: Oh, right. And you were born in Mayo. . . . hat's a lovely part of the world . . .

. . . MELDA: . . . Eh . . . eh, Dundalk . . .

. . . ED: I see. Ah well, it says here that you're a . . . lack belt in karate. So what would you do if I . . . ame at you like this . . . ?

. . . e rolls up the notes and holds them over his head, . . . s if to stab her with them. Imelda is terrified and . . . reams.

. . . ED: Imelda, Imelda! Sorry! Are you all right? . . . tell you what, could you have a look through . . . y notes and stop on any piece of information . . . hat's actually true . . .

BILLY (*offscreen*)**:** Excuse me, are you . . . ?

JACK (*offscreen*)**:** Feck off!

Billy comes back into shot.

BILLY: Ah, it's him all right.

SCENE 12 INT./DAY 3
SET: MARQUEE
Ted is at the microphone.

TED: And now . . . walking!

Cut to a wide shot of the girls in a line, walking between traffic cones.

TED: O'ho! Look at them there. Walking around. Look out there, Mary! Doesn't Mary have a lovely bottom!

Liam stands up from behind the table and beckons to Ted.

LIAM: Careful there, Ted. That might offend the girls.

TED: Right, Liam.

Ted turns back to face the crowd.

TED: Well, of course, they *all* have lovely bottoms!

Ted looks at Liam who nods and gives him the thumbs-up.

SCENE 13 INT./DAY 3
SET: PAROCHIAL HOUSE
Dougal leans over the kitchen door.

DOUGAL: Actually, Mrs Doyle is the one who makes the tea, and she's out . . .

SCENE 13A EXT./DAY 3
SET: PAROCHIAL HOUSE
We see a mound of earth beside a hole. A pick-axe appears briefly over the top of it and is then swung down again.

MRS DOYLE: Nyyaaaaaah!!!

SCENE 13B INT./DAY 3
SET: PAROCHIAL HOUSE
Back to Niamh and Dougal.

NIAMH: Wh— Why don't you just make the tea?

DOUGAL (*confused*)**:** But . . . Mrs Doyle makes the tea.

Pause. Niamh shakes her head.

NIAMH: Anyway, I'd better just tell you the reason I'm here. I'm looking for a house around this area, and I really, really like this one . . .

Pause. Dougal thinks very deeply about this, then looks at his notes.

SCENE 14 INT./DAY 3
SET: MARQUEE
Ted is examining a sandwich with a small measuring device. A lovely girl looks at him hopefully.

TED: I'm sorry, Jean, but your sandwich exceeds the required six centimetres in width. So that means it's between Imelda and Mary in . . . the Lovely Laugh Tiebreak. (*Applause.*) Right. In order to hear your lovely laugh, I'll have to tell you a joke! So, here we go! I'll have to do my Robin Williams impression now! OK, here we go. Here's the joke now. (*Ted's voice deepens as he reads from his notes*).

Secretary: 'Sir, the invisible man is waiting in reception.'

Got that?

Boss: 'Tell him I can't see him now!'

Ted holds the microphone up to Imelda and Mary to capture their laughter. They both do a 'tinkling' laugh for Ted.

TED: I think I have to say that Imelda's laugh was nicer. Sorry, Mary, but that leaves Imelda as the winner! (*Imelda goes mad. The other girls* *look disappointed. Ted puts a tacky crown on Imelda's head and gives her a rolled-up scroll.)* There's your Certificate of Loveliness, and of course you'll be going to dinner tomorrow at Craggy Island's top seafood restaurant, The Thai Cottage. And, Imelda, who'll you be inviting to dinner?

IMELDA: I'll be bringing my mother.

Pause.

TED: Just have another go at that, Imelda . . .

IMELDA: Oh! Sorry! Yes, I'll be inviting you, Father.

TED: Yes, you will. You know you're paying? It's not me. It's not me who pays.

IMELDA: Oh, right.

END OF PART ONE

* * *

PART TWO

SCENE 15 INT./EVENING 3
SET: PAROCHIAL HOUSE
Ted arrives, taking off his coat and scarf. Dougal comes down the stairs.

DOUGAL: Ah, there you are, Ted. How did the Lovely Girls Competition go?

TED: Brilliantly well, Dougal. And, as is the tradition, I get a free dinner tomorrow night!

DOUGAL: Great! Is Jack with you?

TED: Oh, God . . . Jack . . .

SCENE 15A INT./EVENING 3
SET: MARQUEE
We see Jack surrounded by lots of lovely girls. They seem very enamoured with him.

LOVELY GIRL: Wow! You really knocked Michael Hutchence* unconscious?

JACK: I *battered* him!

He demonstrates.

———————————————————

*Oops.

SCENE 15B INT./EVENING 3
SET: PAROCHIAL HOUSE
Ted and Dougal come into the living room.

TED: So! Anything happen while I was away?

DOUGAL: No, I can't think of anything. Oh, yer one. Niamh Connolly called.

TED (*panicking slightly*): What, Niamh Connolly? Oh, God. What did you say to her?

DOUGAL: Don't worry, Ted. It was fine. I just followed your advice about talking to girls and it was grand. She's upstairs now.

TED: She's still here!

DOUGAL: Yeah. I think she's in the toilet, actually. (*Niamh comes into the living room.*) Hello, again. I was just telling Ted you were in the toilet.

NIAMH: Hello.

TED (*slightly sniffy*): Hello, there. Father Ted Crilly. You must be Miss Connolly. Though I suppose that's sexist now! Calling a young lady 'Miss'! Well, I'm sorry but it's too late for me to change my ways now. You can't teach an old dog new tricks!

NIAMH: Yes. Well. It's getting a bit late.

TED: Oh, right, well, I won't keep you! Bye so!

NIAMH: Bye! (*Pause. They all look at each other.*) Goodbye, Father.

TED: Yes, goodbye.

Pause.

DOUGAL: Oh, that's the other thing, Ted. I sold Niamh the house.

TED: What?

Niamh exits to the kitchen.

DOUGAL: Well, actually, I gave it to her.

TED: You . . . wh— . . . No, wait a minute. You . . .

DOUGAL: Niamh's going to turn it into a studio! She says we can have all the recording time we want!

TED: Wait now, wait now. You *gave* her the house. How could . . . ?

DOUGAL: Oh, wait a second! Ted, where are we going to live?!

Ted bites his lip and makes a strangling gesture. Niamh re-enters the living room.

TED: Miss Connolly. Look, there's been a terrible mistake—

NIAMH (*not really listening*): Look, I have to record a duet with Peter Gabriel over the 'phone. Hope you don't mind if Alan and big Mike show you out.

TED: Well, Miss Connolly, I'm sorry, but we're not going anywhere.

Two large men in black tour jackets and baseball caps come into the room. They both advance ever so slightly.

TED: All right, I'm not sticking around to be insulted by you! Come on, Dougal, we're leaving. You can *have* the house. I wouldn't stay here if you gave me a million pounds!

SCENE 15C EXT./EVENING 3
SET: OUTSIDE THE DOOR
We see the door being slammed behind them.

TED: Wait a minute. What did I say there? I meant to say 'Please give us back the house.' What did I say? Why are we outside?

DOUGAL: Ted, where are we going to stay?

SCENE 16 EXT./NIGHT 3
SET: PAROCHIAL HOUSE/TENT
We see a tiny tent beside the house. A faint light glows inside.

SCENE 17 INT./NIGHT 3
SET: TENT

TED: God almighty, I go away for a few hours, and you've managed to make us homeless. Take me through it again. What exactly happened?

DOUGAL: I was just sticking to your rules, Ted. Number one, be yourself . . .

TED: No, no, no, no! 'Be yourself' is just something people *say*! Never be yourself with women! Never, never, never! What then?

DOUGAL: Well, I tried to make her more comfortable, like you said . . .

TED: Yes . . .

DOUGAL: So I asked her to take off her bra.

Long pause.

TED: We'll come back to that one. But how did you manage to give away our house? I mean, Dougal . . .

DOUGAL: What about the golden rule, Ted? Always give them what they want.

TED: No, that's the silver rule, Dougal. The golden rule is, if anyone ever says anything to you again, think about what you're saying, and then don't say it, and then run away somewhere. Right. All right. This is a long shot, but it's our only chance. I'm going to leave this pen and paper here, and hopefully in the morning God will have written down what we should do.

DOUGAL: That is a long shot.

TED: It's our only hope. (*He looks up to heaven*). C'mon God!

He puts the pen and paper down. Fade down.

SCENE 18 EXT./MORNING 4
SET: PAROCHIAL HOUSE
We see Ted and Dougal's tent. It is morning and we hear the birds singing.

SCENE 19 INT./DAY 4
SET: TENT
Ted wakes up and picks up the paper.

TED: Aaaaagggggghhhhhhh!!!!!!

Dougal wakes up with a start.

DOUGAL: TED! TED, WHAT IS IT? DID GOD WRITE BACK?!!!!

TED (*crumples up the paper*)**:** No, he didn't! Bollocks anyway! (*He looks up.*) All right, I'm going to have to take care of this myself. I'll persuade her that we're really hip priests who agree with her about absolutely everything. We'll show her that we're more of a forward-thinking parish than she thinks.*

DOUGAL: What do you mean by a 'forward-thinking parish' exactly?*

TED: I mean one that isn't too constrained by some of the more old-fashioned views of the Church.*

DOUGAL: But we'd still believe in God and all that?*

TED: Oh, I think so. The belief-in-God thing, that's very important to the Church. That'll be one of the last things to go. But on the whole, for now, I think we just have to stick with the New Testament. The Old Testament stuff won't go down well. That stuff about if your wife goes to the toilet, she has to be thrown down a big pit. To be honest, Dougal, I've always had a few doubts about that one myself. And all that stuff about pulling out your right eye if it offends you.*

DOUGAL: That's a strange one, isn't it, Ted? I mean, if you're seeing something with your right eye, surely you'd be seeing it with your left one as well.*

TED: Yeah. Your right eye would have to be nearly on the other side of your head.*

DOUGAL: Like Father Bigley.*

TED: Like Father Bigley. But still, I think if we stick to all the post-ripping-out-your-eyes stuff it'd be safer. Just think: this is the modern world – this is the modern Church. Right!*

They come out of the tent.

SCENE 20 INT./DAY 4
SET: PAROCHIAL HOUSE
Niamh, Ted and Dougal are in the living room.

TED: Basically . . . the thing is, the house. It really wasn't Dougal's to give away. So if you could give it back to us, it'd be great. I think you'd be interested in the kind of work we're doing here. We're a very progressive parish.

NIAMH: I hope it's not some kind of hideaway for paedophile priests. That whole thing disgusted me.

TED: Well, we're not all like that, Niamh. Say, if there's two hundred million priests in the world, and five per cent of them are paedophiles, that's still only ten million.

Niamh doesn't know what to say.

TED: No, Niamh, what we wanted to do here was create a world free of intolerance and hypocrisy.

NIAMH: Really, Father?

TED: Oh, yes. Niamh, if there's one thing I hate . . . (*Dramatic pause.*) it's hypocrisy.

Ted's attention is drawn to the window behind Niamh, where we see Father Liam Deliverance. He gives Ted the thumbs-up then holds up a newspaper, 'The Craggy Island Examiner'. The headline reads 'Father Ted gives thumbs-up to Lovely Girls' bottoms'.

NIAMH: I mean, the sexism that is rampant within the church . . . it's . . . appalling.

TED (*worried*)**:** Yes, yes . . .

---

*We deleted these lines from the final version.

NIAMH: It really distresses me. It really gets my goat.

Liam opens the newspaper to another page. We see a picture of Ted pulling a comical Kenneth Williams-type face as he's kissed on the cheeks by two lovely girls. Liam moves away from the window. Ted looks more worried.

TED: Anyway, we're very different on Craggy Island . . We don't like any of . . . that kind . . . of thing . . .

Liam arrives, holding the newspaper and carrying two evening dresses.

LIAM: Ah, Ted . . . (*He notices Niamh.*)

LIAM: Who's this lovely girl? Now, Ted you're only allowed to pick one!

NIAMH: Don't call me a lovely girl. I've sold twenty million records.

LIAM: What? Anyway, Ted. What do you think? (*He holds up the dresses.*) This one or this one? I like this one . . .

TED: That's a nice one, Liam.

LIAM: But I like the colour of this one. Oh, I just don't know . . .

TED: Liam, they're both great. I'm sure whichever one you'll pick, it'll look lovely.

LIAM (*touched*): Thanks, Ted.

He runs off, excited, Ted turns to Niamh.

TED: You see? All sorts of alternative lifestyles catered for. This is a refuge for priests like Liam. Where else could he give a sermon while he's dressed as Joan Crawford? Please don't take our house, Niamh! Please don't stop our good work here!

NIAMH: I had no idea. To be honest with you, Father, I've always had a bit of a blinkered view of priests.

Ted is standing beside the red bell.

TED: Well, you've probably got that old-fashioned perception of the drunken, old, lecherous priest. I promise you, Niamh, that stereotype is long gone.

Ted glances at his watch and immediately puts his hands up to the bell just as it goes off. He holds it so that it just makes a very faint 'clinkety-clinkety'

noise. It does so a few times and then stops. Pause. Ted looks up. We hear a bump. Then we hear footsteps from above. Ted and Niamh follow the footsteps as we hear their owner running around upstairs. Pause. We hear the footsteps coming down the stairs. Ted is still following where the noises are coming from with his eyes. Pause. Jack suddenly bursts through the door.

JACK: Drink! (*He sees Niamh.*) Woman!!!

TED: Hello there, Billy!!

Ted turns Jack around and leads him out into the hall.

TED: Won't be able to chat with you today, Billy. See you later.

JACK: Wha— . . .?

Ted pushes the front door open and pushes Jack out. He then walks back into the room.

TED: Father Billy would be more of an old-style priest. He sometimes comes over for a good old debate.

We see Jack looking through the window, puzzled.

NIAMH: But . . . he came from upstairs . . .

TED: Yes. He usually gets in through the upstairs window.

NIAMH: Why?

TED: Well, he sometimes likes hiding around the house, so he can spring a topic on me. Like . . . he might hide in the bathroom and I'd be going to the toilet and he'd jump out and say 'Women priests!' And I'd have to think really fast and say 'I'm in favour of them!'

Pause as Niamh takes this in.

TED: Anyway, the main thing I wanted to say is . . . we're all huge, huge fans here. I think we have every record you've ever made.

SCENE 21 EXT./DAY 4
SET: PAROCHIAL HOUSE
A. Ted bounds out of the door and runs at top speed out of shot.

B. Parochial house driveway. Ted running towards the gate.

C. Road. Ted running down the road.

D. John and Mary's shop. Ted running into shop. Pause. He runs out again, a number of records in his arms.

E. Road. Ted running up the road.

F. Parochial house driveway. Ted running through the gate and up the driveway.

G. Parochial house. Ted runs into the house.

SCENE 22 INT./DAY 4
SET: PAROCHIAL HOUSE
Ted runs in.

TED: Here . . . you . . . here . . . records here . . .

Ted is gasping for breath.

NIAMH: What would you like me to put on them?

TED (*still dying*): Don't care.

Niamh nods and sighs. Mrs Doyle comes in.

MRS DOYLE: Father, I've finished digging that drainage ditch.

TED (*still out of breath*): No . . . Mrs Doyle . . .

MRS DOYLE: But I have to say, I keep passing out, so I might go and have a little rest. I know you wanted me to clean the roof slates tonight but . . .

TED (*still gasping*): Mrs Doyle . . . No . . . don't.

MRS DOYLE: So I thought I might as well do them tomorrow when there's less chance of me falling off and being killed.

Niamh looks at Ted, outraged. Ted smiles in a sickly way.

SCENE 23 INT./NIGHT 4
SET: RESTAURANT
We see Mrs Doyle, Imelda and Niamh.

IMELDA: But . . . will Father Ted be coming later?

NIAMH: *No.* He has to stay home so Mrs

Doyle can come out. That's the only reason I let him have the house back. One night off every week for Mrs Doyle.

MRS DOYLE: Maybe I should just check on them . . .

NIAMH: Sit . . . down. (*She raises a glass*). Now come on, let's enjoy ourselves, sisters! No men around and we can do whatever we want! . . . (*Mrs Doyle starts eating.*) . . . Is that meat?

Mrs Doyle freezes. Imelda looks worried.

IMELDA: Do I still have to pay for this?

SCENE 24 INT./NIGHT 4
SET: KITCHEN
Ted and Dougal are in the kitchen. The kettle is boiling. Steam is billowing out. Pots rattle on the stove as their contents bubble dangerously. Ted and Dougal run around the kitchen in complete confusion and panic. Dougal has a pair of oven mittens on.

TED (*looking at the kettle*): There's no button! Where's the button!?

Dougal takes his hands, still in the mittens, out of the oven. They are on fire.

DOUGAL: Ted! Ted! I'm on fire!!!!!

Ted picks up the kettle and throws the water on Dougal's hands. The fire goes out and Dougal screams. The noise from all the different kitchen utensils is awful. Ted and Dougal huddle together in the centre of the room, clutching each other in fright.

TED: I just want my tea!!!!!!!

THE END

CIGARETTES AND ALCOHOL AND ROLLERBLADING

ARTHUR: Obviously Lent suggested the structure for this one. Finding a vice for each of them to give up was easy as far as Jack (alcohol) and Ted (cigarettes) were concerned, but Dougal was the wild card. We had no idea that rollerblading was one of his skills – it must have rubbed off on him from our visit to friends in New York, the rollerblading capital of the world. To make this episode work, we had to get Mrs Doyle out of the house, and she obliged by going on a Lenten pilgrimage to Croagh Patrick. It's a real hill, and people really do climb it in their bare feet.

As regards martyrs, we had a gift with a Dubliner called Matt Talbot, who became our Matty Hislop. Talbot was a terrible alcoholic who later renounced the booze and, as a penance for his wayward early life, went on to drape himself in chains and give himself a really terrible time. He loved tea, for example, so he'd brew himself a lovely hot pot and then wait until it was stone cold before drinking it. That was in the 1920s. Nowadays he'd be considered mad and given psychiatric help, but in Dublin there's a bridge and a street named after him.

GRAHAM: We thought it was funny that they should all fail immediately with their Lenten vows, but it meant that we didn't have anywhere for the plot to go. That's why we brought in Sister Assumpta (Rosemary Henderson) and her penances. When plotting an episode, we usually write a list of ten plot points before we write any dialogue, but this time . . . I have a feeling we started writing the script before we'd worked everything out, found ourselves in a corner and had to write our way out of it. . . but that sometimes works too.

PART ONE

SCENE 1 EXT./DAY 1
SET: PAROCHIAL HOUSE
Filmed from a distance, we see a silhouette of a figure bent low as he carries a large cross over the grounds of the Parochial House. Dramatic biblical music plays. Ted – for it is he – moves it into an upright position. The horizontal part of the cross suddenly slides down and conks Ted on the head. He drops out of shot. Slight pause. We hear a thunderbolt. It starts to rain very heavily.

SCENE 2 INT./DAY 1
SET: PAROCHIAL HOUSE
Mrs Doyle is cleaning up. Ted comes in rubbing his head; he is soaking wet.

MRS DOYLE: I see you put the old cross up, Father. What's that about?

TED: Oh, I thought people might have been sort of getting confused about where the Parochial House is. So I thought, I'll put a big cross up in the middle of the garden. I just hope people know it means that I'm a priest and not just some madman.

SCENE 2A EXT./DAY 1
SET: PAROCHIAL HOUSE
A couple walk by the house. They see the cross.

MAN: Look at that. Some madman's put up a cross.

SCENE 2B INT./DAY 1
SET: PAROCHIAL HOUSE
*Mrs Doyle gives the window a final wipe. When she's finished with it, it looks utterly filthy.**

MRS DOYLE: Lovely. Well, that's everything, Father. I'm heading off tomorrow.[†]

TED: Really? Where are you . . . oh, Croagh Fiachra![†]

MRS DOYLE: Oh, yes, Father, Croagh Fiachra. Every Lent I head off. It was wonderful last year. People from all over, giving up the simple pleasures to give thanks to the Lord. A lot of priests there, too.

---

* In the final version Mrs Doyle then fell off the windowsill.
† We deleted this from the final version.

Climbing up that mountain in their bare feet. Standing for hours in the cold and going without food for days and days. Have you ever been yourself, Father?[†]

TED (*begins to shake his head, then catches himself*): . . . Many, many times.[†]

Dougal walks in. He is dressed in rollerblading gear. He clanks along with some difficulty in the huge wheeled boots.

DOUGAL: Ted, I'm off rollerblading.

TED: Right so, Dougal.

Dougal trundles out through the door. The telephone rings. Ted goes to answer it.

TED: Hello. Craggy Island Parochial House. Father Ted Crilly speaking.

Cut to the other end of the line. It is Father Dick Byrne. He is in an uncharacteristically serious mood.

DICK: Hello, Ted. Dick Byrne here.

TED: . . . Dick . . .

DICK: I just wanted to call and wish you all the best for Lent this year.

TED: What? Oh, Lent, yeah. What are you giving up? Being the biggest eejit in the priesthood?!!!

DICK: No, seriously, Ted. If we can just put aside the joking for a moment, Lent is a solemn time of the year. I know we've had our disagreements in the past, but at the end of the day, we're both brothers in Christ.

TED (*mood changing*): Oh . . .

DICK: So, anyway, over here, we're making a special effort this year. I'm giving up cigarettes, Father Johnson is giving up alcohol, and Father McDuff is giving up skateboarding. And I have to say, the atmosphere of serenity and devotion to Our Lord in the Parochial House is very special this year.

TED (*a bit more serious*): Right.

DICK: So, would you like to do something similar? Why don't you give up the old cigarettes, and get the other two there to make an effort as well. Would you do that, Ted? Will you join us and go the extra mile this year?

TED: Well, Dick, I suppose you're right. Our chosen path is one of devotion to Our Lord. I suppose we should make a special effort, too.

DICK: Well, Ted, it'll be worth it. I'll see you soon. God bless you Ted.

TED: Goodbye, Dick. God bless *you*, Dick.

We cut back to Dick. He raises a cigarette to his lips, draws on it and chuckles. He then laughs more hysterically. It echoes in a sinister way.

SCENE 3 INT./DAY 1
SET: PAROCHIAL HOUSE
Dougal and Jack sit on the sofa, looking at Ted. Dougal looks glum. Jack is just trying to focus.

TED: . . . So that's it. I'm giving up the fags, Father Jack, I think, can lay off the old drink for a while, and no more rollerblading for you 'til Easter, Dougal.

DOUGAL: . . . Easter's miles away . . .

TED: It is, but it wouldn't be a sacrifice if it was too easy, would it? Don't forget why we're doing this.

DOUGAL: I know, I know . . . because of the sacrifice Our Lord made for us on . . .

TED: Yes, yes, but more importantly . . . I'm not havin' Dick Byrne beat me in a giving-things-up competition. And that's what this is, a giving-things-up competition. We've got to show him what we can do, especially after that Scrabble fiasco.

DOUGAL: You've never told us what happened there, Ted.

TED (*angry and embarrassed*): Oh . . . he . . . I don't know how he did it, he must have been cheating, he *must* have . . . but . . . he managed to get all his words to say, 'Useless Priest. Can't say Mass.' So, is that all right? No more drinking, rollerblading or smoking until Easter. Understood?

DOUGAL: But . . . I like rollerblading.

TED: Dougal, come on! What would Our Lord think of you if he knew you didn't want to give up rollerblading?

DOUGAL: Bet *he* didn't have to give up rollerblading.

TED: Dougal, which is worse? Being nailed to a cross or having to give up rollerblading?

DOUGAL: I'm not saying being nailed to a cross is easy. All I'm saying is at least he had the choice.

Mrs Doyle enters with a bottle of whiskey on a tray.

MRS DOYLE (*playfully*): Who wants their afternoon drink?

Jack wakes up suddenly. He looks delirious with delight.

JACK: DRINKKKKKK! O YES!!!!!!!!

TED: No Mrs Doyle. I'll have that.

Jack looks confused.

JACK: No?

TED: No, Father. It's Lent, remember. You said you'd give it up for a couple of days.

JACK: WHAT?!

TED: Do you not remember? You said you'd offer it up for Our Lord.

JACK: ARNOLD? WHO'S ARNOLD?

TED: No, no, 'Our Lord'. Well, I suppose I made your vow for you. Because I know that deep down you'd like to make a little sacrifice.

JACK: SACRIFICE? ARSE!

TED: Come on, Father. It's Lent, remember?

JACK: I DON'T CARE!

TED: Father, it's a very special time for us all . . .

JACK (*stumbles to the drinks cabinet*)**:** DRINK!

TED: You won't find any there, Father! I've put them in a very safe place.

JACK: WHERE?

SCENE 4 EXT./DAY 1
SET: CLIFF FACE
We see a remote-looking cliff face with a cave near some dangerous, choppy-looking waters and rocks below. It should look absolutely impossible to reach.

SCENE 5 INT./DAY 1
SET: CAVE
Inside the cave we see an absolutely mountainous pile of full whiskey bottles. Seagulls squawk outside.

SCENE 6 INT./DAY 1
SET: PAROCHIAL HOUSE
Jack has gone into a sulk.

TED: Now, Father, don't be like that. OK, here we go. No more cigarettes for me until Easter.

He holds up some fags, gets a pair of scissors and snips them at the filter. He throws them in the bin. Pause.

TED: Great. There's no problem with that at all. (*Longer pause.*) God, do you know what? I don't miss them at all. This is easy.

Pause.

TED: Ah, yes. I'm not even thinking about smoking. Not even *thinking* about it. (*Pause.*) Ha.

Fade to black. A caption comes up: 'Five minutes later'. We see Ted, sitting in his chair staring ahead in a fixed way, his hands gripping fiercely on to the armrests. He looks like someone experiencing massive G-force. Cut to Jack, who is in a similar state, and then to Dougal who is shaking slightly.

DOUGAL: It's beginning to kick in, Ted!

TED: I know! Me too! God, this is terrible! I don't like this at all.

DOUGAL: Maybe we can stick with it, Ted. I mean, we've come through worse together, and don't forget Dick Byrne . . .

Cut to Ted as he listens to Dougal. His eyes seem to glaze over. Cut to his point of view. We see that Dougal has been replaced by a giant cigarette with arms and legs. The arms are gesticulating, but all Ted can hear is . . .

DOUGAL/CIGARETTE: Blah, blah, blah, blah . . .

Cut back to Ted, who is now smiling gormlessly. Cut back to Dougal, who is again his normal self.

DOUGAL: Don't you think so, Ted?

TED (*rousing himself*)**:** I certainly do, Dougal. Absolutely. Anyway, how are you doing, Father Jack? You all right there? Do you want me to . . .

Cut to Jack. He is looking at Ted strangely. Cut to reveal that Ted looks like a giant pint of Guinness from his point of view. As the glass of Guinness gesticulates, white foamy bits splosh from the top.

TED/GUINNESS: Blah, blah, blah, blah . . .

Cut to Jack looking at Ted with an expression of delight. Cut back to the now-normal Ted, who is faltering slightly as he looks at Jack.

TED: Father? Father?

DOUGAL: Is he all right?

TED: Oh yes, I think he's just . . . circling the airport. (*The front doorbell rings.*) Better get that. You all right, Dougal?

DOUGAL: What? Oh, yeah . . .

Cut to Dougal looking at Ted. Then we see, from his point of view, that Ted has turned into a giant rollerblade skate; it slowly moves out of the room and turns towards the door. Dougal blinks dazedly.

SCENE 7 EXT./DAY 1
SET: PAROCHIAL HOUSE DOOR
We see John and Mary outside. Mary has a package.

JOHN: Now don't make a show of yourself in front of him: 'Yes, Father Crilly, No, Father Crilly. Oh, you're so great, Father Crilly.' Oh, it makes me sick.

MARY: I don't know what you're talking about. You're feckin' worse: 'Oh, Father, you're brilliant. Oh, Father, you should be Pope.' It doesn't impress him – it just sounds stupid. God, you are an awesome *divot*.

Ted opens the door.

JOHN AND MARY: Ah, Father . . .

TED: Hello, John, hello Mary.

JOHN: Father . . . you look wonderful. Is that a new outfit?

Ted, confused, looks down at his bog-standard shirt and collar.

TED: Eh . . .

MARY: My God, Father, you said a beautiful Mass on Tuesday. And the sermon! I think you'd be a brilliant writer. You should win awards for everything you've ever done ever in your life.

TED: I didn't do a Mass on Tuesday.

MARY: Did you not? Oh . . . (*Very embarrassed.*) Anyway, we just thought you might like some Easter eggs from the shop.

TED: Oh, that's terribly nice of you. Thank you very much indeed.

JOHN: I think it comes to about eight pounds.

Ted's smile disappears.

TED: Oh . . . right.

He hands over the money.

MARY: Yes, we thought we should get them to you. We're going on holiday, and we're not quite sure when we're getting back.

JOHN: Yes. We're going to Rome.

MARY: We're really looking forward to it. We might see your friend there.

TED: Who's that? Sophia Loren?!!!

They all laugh their heads off.

MARY: Ah, ha . . . No, Father. The Pope.

TED: He's no friend of mine!!!!

Ted laughs. John and Mary don't. There is an uncomfortable silence.

TED (*abashed*): Actually, that might have sounded a little disrespectful. sorry.

JOHN: No problem, Father.

John puts a cigarette in his mouth. Close-up of Ted's eyes widening. Cut back to John. He draws on the cigarette in slow motion, this is accompanied by an exaggerated furnace-like inhaling noise. Then he exhales. The exhalation goes on for far too long, smoke billowing out everywhere. Ted watches as the smoke curls and forms the words 'lovely fags'. Cut back to Ted in real time. He screams and slams the door on the couple. They look at each other.

SCENE 8 INT./NIGHT 1
SET: TED AND DOUGAL'S BEDROOM
We see Ted tossing and turning in his bed. He finally switches the bedside lamp on and sits up. He looks at Dougal, who is sound asleep, mouth agape. Ted gets up and walks to the door.

SCENE 9 INT./NIGHT 1
SET: JACK'S BEDROOM
Ted peeks in. He sees Jack in bed snoring in a fairly horrific way. Ted closes the door.

SCENE 10 INT./NIGHT 1
SET: PAROCHIAL HOUSE
Ted sits down at the table. He picks up a bin and rummages in it. He takes out a filter and the other half of a cigarette. He places them together. Cut to a shot from the back. He fiddles around with something. After a moment, he leans down on something and we hear the sound of a stapler, stapling.

SCENE 11 EXT./NIGHT 1
SET: PAROCHIAL HOUSE
We see Ted's silhouette running from the house. He runs towards a tiny shed nearby. Halfway there, he stops and looks around. Suddenly, the horizontal part of the cross slides into shot and conks him on the head, before sliding the rest of the way down. After a moment of groaning, he gets up and moves off.

SCENE 12 INT./NIGHT 1
SET: SHED
Ted comes into the shed. It is very dark.

TED: Ahhhh . . . here we go now.

He lights a match, which illuminates the interior of the shed. Ted freezes, the match not quite touching the stapled-together cigarette. Cut to what he's looking at: Jack, a bottle of carpet-cleaner almost to his lips, and Dougal, dressed in full rollerblading gear and frozen in the act of lacing up one of his boots. There is a 'moment'.

SCENE 13 INT./DAY 2
SET: PAROCHIAL HOUSE
Ted is on the telephone, waiting to be taken off hold. Dougal watches him, slightly abashed. Jack is gripping on to the armrests with an expression of horror.

TED (*to Dougal*): Well, I have to say, I'm very disappointed in us all. One day! You'd think we could go *one* day without giving in to temptation. God almighty, when I think of all the sacrifices Matty Hislop made.

DOUGAL: Who?

TED: Matty Hislop. He was a notorious drunkard who found God and then decided to punish himself for his sins. Oh, he did all kinds of things . . . like . . . he had a terrible allergic reaction to cats, so instead of avoiding them, he'd carry a kitten around in his pocket and sniff it from time to time. His head would just inflate like a balloon!

DOUGAL: God almighty!

TED: Also, they say he used to glue his hair to the ceiling in his kitchen and hang there for days and days. And he used to save money in a little cardboard box, and after he'd saved enough for a holiday, he'd throw the money into the Liffey and eat the box. I mean, Dougal, surely you can knock the old rollerblading on the head for a couple of weeks.

DOUGAL: I know, Ted, it's just . . . I used to be happy with the old bike, you know? I used to get a great buzz just goin' down to the shops. But after a while it just wasn't enough. I kept goin' for bigger and bigger thrills. But I can handle it, Ted. I could quit any time I want.

TED: But you tried to quit yesterday and you couldn't.

DOUGAL (*beat, then breaks down*): You're right, Ted! I admit it! I have a problem!

TED: Come on now, Dougal, there's no need for that. Not now that I'm getting outside help, anyway. (*He turns back to the telephone.*) Come on, come on, why do the nuns always have the most awful music when you're on hold . . . ? If I hear 'Ave Maria' one more time . . . Excuse me? Excuse me?

SCENE 14 INT./DAY 2
SET: CONVENT
We see a nun holding the telephone normally as she sings 'Ave Maria' into it. On the wall behind her there is a religious painting of a man with his hand in a toaster. This is Matty Hislop. He looks in great pain, but is being rewarded by a light from Heaven shining on his face.

NUN: Ave Mariaaaaaa . . .

TED: Excuse me?

NUN: Yes?

TED: How much longer am I going to be on hold?

NUN: She'll be with you in a second, Father. (*Continues singing.*) Ave Mariaaaaa . . .

A hand comes into shot and takes the telephone. It belongs to a nun who is sitting in front of a computer. We see many other nuns beside her, like a row of telephone operators, stretching into the distance.

NUN 2: Hello?

TED: Ah, hello there! Listen, my name is Father Ted Crilly. We were wondering if you

could send someone out? We're just having a very small problem keeping our Lenten vows. We need someone to keep us on the right path. We almost had a bit of a lapse last night, but . . .

Nun 2 starts rattling information into the computer.

NUN 2: . . . You just need someone to help you with your vows.

TED: Yes.

NUN 2: What is it you wish to give up, exactly?

TED: Cigarettes, and alcohol and . . . eh rollerblading.

NUN 2: Rollerblading. I don't really have a rate for rollerblading. I have skiing. How would you feel about giving up skiing?

TED: Eh . . .

NUN 2: Well, I'll put that down as a general Sports/Outdoor activity.

The nun types this into the computer.

NUN 2: All right, we have a special going this month . . . the Lenten package . . . That would be . . . (*She tots this up.*) one hundred and fifty . . . plus VAT . . . plus booking fee . . . two hundred pounds.

TED: Two hundred pounds! I'm not trying to buy cocaine!

NUN 2: All right, I suppose . . . (*Looking at the computer.*) We have a basic package for . . . fifty pounds.

TED: Oh, that'd be much better.

NUN 2: How do you wish to pay? We accept all major credit cards.

Another telephone rings.

NUN 2: Oh, can you hold on a moment, Father?

She hands the telephone back to the 'hold' nun.

NUN: Ave Maria . . .

SCENE 15 INT./DAY 2
SET: PAROCHIAL HOUSE
Jack jolts in his chair. He makes a slight, cut-off, strangled noise. Ted looks at him.

TED (*into the telephone*): Oh, listen, I'll have to call you back.

Dougal joins Ted as they walk over to examine Jack.

DOUGAL: What's up with him, Ted?

TED: Hmmmm . . . it looks like the last of the alcohol has left his system. I think he might actually be sober. (*To Jack.*) Is that it, Father? Seeing things as they really are, at last?

JACK: Oh . . . my . . . God.

TED: Yes, that's it all right. I suppose sobriety for Father Jack must be sort of like taking some mad hallucinogenic.

Jack looks up at them as if noticing them for the first time.

JACK: Where's the other two?

TED: The other two? Ah, I see . . . the old vision must be back to normal. No, Father, there's only two of us.

JACK: . . . Two? Oh, thank God.

TED: That's right. Two of us and one Mrs Doyle.

JACK: And what is it you do again?

TED: We're priests, Father.

JACK: What?! Priests? I'm not still on that feckin' island, am I?

TED: Well, yes . . . How do you feel, Father? It's good to sober up every now and again, isn't it? Or at least, every twelve years.

Jack goes to the telephone and examines it.

JACK: PHONE!

TED: Yes, that's right, Father.

Jack looks very pleased.

JACK (*pointing*): CURTAINS!

TED: Yes, well done.

JACK: FLOOR!

TED: All coming back to you is it, Father?

JACK (*points at Ted*): GOBSHITE!

Ted's smile disappears.

JACK: YES! I REMEMBER! I REMEMBER!

END OF PART ONE

* * *

PART TWO

SCENE 15A INT./DAY 3
SET: PAROCHIAL HOUSE
Mrs Doyle enters. She is dressed to go out and carries a small holdall. In the background we see Jack wandering around looking at things as if seeing them for the first time.

MRS DOYLE: I'll be off now, Fathers.

TED: Oh, right. Off to Croagh Fiachra.

DOUGAL: Where's that, Ted?

TED: It's a big mountain. You have to climb up it with no socks on, and then when you're up there, they chase you back down with big planks. Great fun.

MRS DOYLE: Oh, I don't want it to be any fun, Father. I want a good miserable time, keep me on the straight and narrow. I met a couple there last year, and it did them the world of good. They were a bit obsessed with the old S-E-X. Couldn't stop thinking about it. Then they went to Croagh Fiachra and that got it out of their system fast enough, I can tell you. God, I'm glad I never think of that type of thing, Father. That whole sexual world. God, when you think of it . . . it's a dirty, filthy thing, isn't it, Father? How does anyone ever do it? Can you imagine, Father, looking up at your husband with him standing over you with his chap in his hand wanting you to degrade yourself. God almighty . . . try and imagine that, Father.

Ted looks perturbed.

MRS DOYLE: Imagine that, Father. A naked man looking down on you with only one thing on his mind. Just think about that for a second, Father.

TED: N— . . . Well, no, I don't . . .

MRS DOYLE: Are you thinking about it, Father? It's disgusting, isn't it? Just picture it, there, Father. Get a good mental picture of it. Do you see what I mean? Can you see him there, ready to do the business?

We hear the doorbell ringing.

TED: DOORBELL! . . . I mean, doorbell, Mrs Doyle.

Mrs Doyle leaves.

JACK: Hey! Hey, you! YOU!!! (*He holds up a spoon.*) What the hell is this?

TED: Ah, that's a spoon, Father.

Jack nods, still confused, and puts it down.

TED: C'mon Dougal, this'll be her now. (*A nun enters.*) Hello, there. We . . . Sister Assumpta?

ASSUMPTA: Hello, Father.

TED: I didn't know you were doing this? How are you?

ASSUMPTA: Oh, I'm fine, Father.

TED: Dougal! Dougal, you remember Sister Assumpta . . .

DOUGAL: Ah, no . . .

TED: She was here last year, and then we stayed with her in the convent. In Kildare. Do you remember?

Dougal thinks, then shakes his head.

TED: Ah, you do. You were hit by the car when you went down to the shops. You must remember all that. And then you won a hundred pounds with the lottery card. You must remember.

Dougal bites his lip as he tries to remember.

ASSUMPTA: And weren't you accidentally arrested for shoplifting? I remember we went down to the police station to get you. And then the police station went on fire and you had to be rescued by helicopter.

TED: Do you remember?

Something seems to register in Dougal's face, but then it goes.

TED: You can't remember any of it? The helicopter? When you fell out of the helicopter over the zoo? The tigers? Do you not remember? (*Dougal slowly shakes his head.*) You were wearing your blue jumper.

DOUGAL: Ahhhh!!! Sister Assumpta, yes, hello there.

TED: And you remember Father Jack.

Assumpta steps back slightly.

ASSUMPTA: Oh yes.

JACK (*pointing*): NAN!

TED: No, no, it's 'nun', Father.

JACK: NUN!

TED: Father Hackett has just had a bit of a head-on collision with the real world. Anyway, I have to say I had no idea you were with the Matty Hislop crowd.

ASSUMPTA: Oh, yes. Ever since I read his pamphlets, abstinence has been both my keeper and my reward.

TED: Yeah? Great. Anyway, all we want is the basic fifty quid job. The bare essentials. Keep us all off the booze and fags. And rollerblading.

DOUGAL (*very grandly*): I'm afraid rollerblading is my own particular vice . . .

ASSUMPTA: Well, we'll do our best. I'm looking forward to it.

TED: You know . . . I sort of am myself. Do us a bit of good to exercise the old willpower. You looking forward to it, Father Jack?

JACK: I'm off for a wank!

Jack leaves the room. Pause.

ASSUMPTA: What did he s—

TED: Walk. He's off for a walk. He loves a good, long walk. I think, maybe, it'll just be me and old Dougal tomorrow. Father Jack's very old.

JACK (*from upstairs*): Nobody come upstairs while I'm having a wank! (*Really long pause. Everyone looks very thoughtful.*) All right?

TED: YES, ALL RIGHT!

SCENE 16 INT./MORNING 4
SET: TED AND DOUGAL'S BEDROOM
We see the alarm clock reads 5.00. Cut to reveal Assumpta standing beside the bed with a klaxon. She is dressed even more austerely than on the previous night. She presses a button and Ted and Dougal, frightened out of their minds, leap out of bed into a standing position in one quick movement.

TED: GOD ALMIGHTY!!!

ASSUMPTA (*stridently*): Good morning, Fathers. Breakfast in five minutes!

She leaves the room. Dougal and Ted stand panting, looking at each other in confusion. They look at the door, then at each other again.

TED: What . . . what was that thing? Is there a fire? Is there a fire in the house?

DOUGAL: I suppose it's just time to get up.

TED (*picking up the clock*): It's five a.m. Dougal! Look at this! Five a.m.!

Dougal comes over to look at the clock. They both stare at it for a moment too long.

DOUGAL: I've never see a clock at five a.m. before.

TED: Neither have I. God, there must be some mistake. She probably set her clock wrong. The flight from Dublin probably gave her very minor jetlag and she thinks it's twelve thirty midday.

DOUGAL: What'll we do?

TED: Well, she's obviously made a mistake. Let's just go back to bed.

DOUGAL: Fair enough. What are you doing?

We see Ted is writing something on a piece of paper.

TED: I'll just write her a note saying we usually don't get up 'til later.

DOUGAL: Good thinkin', Ted.

He opens the door and sticks the note on the other side. We see it. It says, 'You got the wrong time, Assumpta!!! See you at twelve p.m.' Ted comes back into the room. He walks to the bed and gets in. They both snuggle up under the blankets. Suddenly the klaxon sounds again, and we cut to reveal that Assumpta has somehow got into the room and is standing beside the bed again. Ted and Dougal leap out of bed in shock.

SCENE 17 INT./MORNING 4
SET: PAROCHIAL HOUSE
Dougal and Ted look shattered. They sit down at the table, looking at their table mats.

TED: I suppose a bit of breakfast and we'll be fine.

DOUGAL: Oh, God, I hope so, Ted.

We see Assumpta appearing in the background with two bowls.

TED: Sister Assumpta? You know, we really are only down for the fags, booze and rollerblading . . . deal. The getting-up-early thing, I mean, it's great but . . . (*He looks down at the bowl and stops talking. We see the contents of the bowl. It's water. Pause.*) . . . This is water.

ASSUMPTA: That's right, Father.

TED: All right, all right. Having a bit of a laugh with the big thickos from the island. Where's our real breakfast?

DOUGAL: I'd love a Pop Tart, Ted.

TED: That's right. Father Dougal loves his Pop Tarts first thing in the morning.

ASSUMPTA: I don't think Pop Tarts have any place in Our Lord's plan for the world.

TED: I think Pop Tarts have as much a place as anything else. Maybe Our Lord doesn't personally take an interest in them, but I'm sure he delegates it to someone almost as important.

DOUGAL: But he'd know about them?

TED: Oh yes, he'd know about everything. He wouldn't OK Pop Tarts unless they were part of his plan for the world.

DOUGAL: What about Coco Pops?

As Ted answers this, we cut to a shot that shows Assumpta with Ted and Dougal on either side of her in the foreground, listening to this nonsense, barely able to believe it.

TED: Again, the same thing. He mightn't have come up with the idea, but he'd be the one who'd give it the green light. No one would be able to sneak an idea like that past him. He'd know all about it.

DOUGAL: Oh, right. But if you look at something like, say, Sugar Puffs or Lucky Charms, it's hard to see how . . .

ASSUMPTA (*has had enough*)**:** FATHERS! COULD YOU PLEASE . . . could you please stop having this conversation. Finish your breakfast and come outside for your daily punishment.

TED: Oh, fair enough, I suppose. We'll just finish the . . . daily what? I'm sorry? Daily? . . . What did you just say there?

ASSUMPTA: Your daily punishment. Matty Hislop's ten-step programme to rid yourself of your pride. The single greatest obstacle to inner fulfilment.

TED (*unsure*)**:** Well, that sounds great . . .

SCENE 18 INT./DAY 4
SET: PAROCHIAL HOUSE
We see Assumpta looking down at something, the Parochial House in the background

ASSUMPTA: How are you two doing?

TED (*out of shot*)**:** F— f— fine, thanks.

ASSUMPTA: Fine? I hope it's good and cold.

Cut to Ted and Dougal in two baths filled with water. They are naked and freezing.

TED: No, no! When . . . w–when I say fine, I mean freezing cold. I mean fine in the sense of feeling really, really awful.

ASSUMPTA (*holds up a bucket*)**:** Are you sure you don't need more ice?

TED: NO! No, actually, to be honest with you, I might enjoy that too much. Very refreshing, the old ice.

ASSUMPTA: I'll go and get more, just in case . . . Soon we'll be able to begin the ten steps.

TED: What? Wait a second – this isn't the first one? There's still ten to go?!

ASSUMPTA (*laughs*)**:** Oh, Father, of course. This is just to cleanse you . . . it's a form of preparation.

TED: For what? Are we going into space? (*She moves off.*) I can't feel my legs!

An outraged Ted turns to Dougal. Dougal smiles at him, with not a care in the world. Ted takes this in. Cut to Jim passing by. He notices Ted and Dougal.

JIM: Ah, hello, Fathers.

TED: Hello, Jim.

DOUGAL: How's it goin' there, Jim?

JIM: Ah, fine. In the old bath, I see. (*Ted nods at this. Long pause.*) See you so.

Jim moves off. He sees something before he moves fully off. Cut to what he is looking at. It is the cross that Ted put up. Now, the horizontal part has slid almost to the very bottom of it, so that it looks like an inverted cross. Jim looks at it, worried, looks back at Ted, then gradually starts to run away. Pause.

TED: I'm beginning to think this might have a been a big, big mistake. Well, ten steps left. Hopefully, it'll just involve having a bit of a pray.

Dougal looks at him.

SCENE 19 EXT./DAY 4
SET: OUTSIDE HOUSE
We see Assumpta driving a tractor. Cut to an overhead shot of the same in which we see Ted and Dougal being dragged behind the tractor. Then we see the tractor going as fast as it can, pulling the lads into the distance.

SCENE 20 EXT./DAY 4
SET: OUTSIDE HOUSE
Assumpta is giving Ted a Chinese burn. Ted screams in pain.

We see Assumpta standing beside a wheelbarrow full of stones. She has one stone ready to throw. Cut to Ted and Dougal tensed. She wrongsteps them, and they duck and jerk to one side. Then she throws the stone and it hits Ted's shoulder. She looks very put out by this. She picks up another one. Ted and Dougal tense up again.

Assumpta giving Dougal a Chinese burn. He seems completely unperturbed. He looks at her, confused.

Assumpta sitting beside a table. There are some bowls of food on it. Ted and Dougal approach, looking like animals coming out of a forest, very nervous. They come close to the food on the table. Assumpta then takes out a gun and shoots at them. They run like crazy out of shot.

SCENE 21 INT./DAY 4
SET: TED AND DOUGAL'S BEDROOM
Dougal hops into the bedroom, completely contented. Ted follows, looking utterly exhausted and miserable.

TED: Ohhhhh . . . God, I'm looking forward to this . . .

He stiffens himself and makes a dramatic drop

backwards on to the bed. We hear a sickening 'clack' sound. Ted, now in incredible pain, opens his mouth in silent agony. Dougal pulls back the blanket on his own bed. We see that instead of the usual mattress, there is a large flat 'brick mattress'.*

DOUGAL: Ted, guess what she's replaced my mattress with.

Ted, his face frozen in the same expression of utter pain, manages a barely audible gurgling noise.

TED: Ohhhhh . . . That's it. That's it, she's obviously insane. Dougal, I've had enough. I don't care who she calls . . . If we have to go through this kind of misery one more day, God knows what'll happen. We might die! We're getting out of here.

DOUGAL (*dressing*): Where'll we go?

TED: No problem. We know loads of people.

DOUGAL: What about Mehwengwe? His parents are away for the week. He's got the whole place free *and* he's got satellite.

TED: Dougal, he lives in Addis Ababa.

Pause.

DOUGAL: What about Dick Byrne, Ted?

TED: Oh no, I'm not calling him . . . I know, Larry Duff. I'm sure he'll put us up for a while.

Ted reaches to the telephone beside him and dials.

SCENE 22 INT./NIGHT 4
SET: DARKENED ROOM
Close-up of a hand passing a ring around a circuitous line of copper wire. Pull back to reveal that the hand belongs to Larry, and he is just reaching the end of an incredibly long, twisty puzzle. A sign above it reads 'First Prize – £10,000'. Just before he reaches a sign that says 'End' his mobile phone rings and he starts slightly. The thing in his hand shudders and we hear a buzzer sound. Larry jumps with fright. We hear an audience going 'Awwwwwwwww'. Larry looks furious.

SCENE 23 INT./NIGHT 4
SET: TED AND DOUGAL'S BEDROOM
Ted puts the telephone down.

TED: Oh, wait a second, no. He told me not to call him tonight because he had this big

important thing on. Well, I suppose it'll have to be Dick Byrne. He'll hide us until she's gone. We'll leave a note saying that we've had to go to a funeral or something . . .

DOUGAL: What about an autopsy?! Could we say we had to go to an autopsy? That'd be more exciting.

TED (*writing note*): No, Dougal, a funeral would be more believable.

DOUGAL: Oh, right.

TED: OK, now, listen, we're going to have to do this as quietly as we can. Don't suddenly panic and make any noise. If we take it easy, we won't wake her.

They go through the open door.

DOUGAL: What was that?

TED: Run!!!!!

We stay on the open door as we hear them crash down the stairs like two out-of-control pianos. Their descent ends in a painful-sounding crunch. (N.B. The following sounds dwindle with distance but are still very loud.)

TED: AGH!

We hear the front door opening and closing with a slam, then footsteps crunching away. A car starts with a very loud and hesitant splutter. It then roars away. Then it roars back. The doorbell rings. It rings again. Then the door opens.

TED (*from downstairs*): Dougal!

DOUGAL: Sorry, Ted! I went the wrong way.

TED: Come on!

The door closes. Footsteps. Car splutter. Dwindling roar. Silence. Pause.

ASSUMPTA (*offscreen*): Who's up?

SCENE 24 INT./NIGHT 4
SET: TED AND DOUGAL'S BEDROOM
Assumpta comes into the room holding her klaxon. She presses it.

ASSUMPTA: Come on, Fathers, we have to get an early start or we'll miss the rain . . .

She notices that they have gone. She picks up a note on Ted's bed.

ASSUMPTA: Right!

She storms out of the room.

SCENE 25 INT./NIGHT 4
SET: CAR
We see Ted and Dougal pulling up outside the Rugged Island Parochial House.

TED: Right. They're probably asleep. I'll just knock very gently on the door.

DOUGAL: Oh, right. So you won't wake them up.

TED: Eh . . . no. I'll have to wake them up so they can let us in.

DOUGAL: Well then . . . shouldn't you just knock loudly?

TED: Oh, right. Yes, good point, Dougal.

They get out of the car.

SCENE 26 INT./NIGHT 4
SET: PAROCHIAL HOUSE
Assumpta comes into the living room and walks to the telephone. She picks it up and starts to dial, then looks up and sees the Easter eggs on top of the wardrobe. She pauses, then puts the telephone down, looking worried.

SCENE 27 EXT./NIGHT 4
SET: RUGGED ISLAND PAROCHIAL HOUSE
A corner of the house. We hear muffled laughing

and mucking about coming from somewhere.

TED (*coming around the corner*): . . . I knocked as hard as I could, Dougal. C'mon, we'll try round the back. (*They turn the corner and hear the muffled noises.*) What's that?

They see a window with light coming out of it. They creep up and look through. Inside they see Dick, Cyril, and Jim. Dick is smoking away happily. Jim is drinking from a bottle of whiskey and Cyril is in full skateboarding gear. Cyril does a little trick with the skateboard and Dick and Jim applaud happily. Ted and Dougal turn slowly to look at each other.

SCENE 28 INT./DAY 5
SET: PAROCHIAL HOUSE HALLWAY
Ted and Dougal come into the hallway. They look tired and defeated.

TED: I should have known. I should have seen it. You can't trust Dick Byrne. As priests go, he's a really bad priest.

DOUGAL: Ted, we've still got thirty-eight days of Lent to go.

TED: I know, I know . . . Still, maybe we should just stand up and take it like men.

They walk into the living room.

SCENE 29 INT./DAY 5
SET: PAROCHIAL HOUSE
Ted and Dougal come in then stop in their tracks. Cut to reveal Assumpta, Easter-egg wrappers shredded around her feet, chocolate smeared over her mouth, looking very guilty indeed. There is a 'moment'.

ASSUMPTA: This isn't what it looks like.

Ted looks at Dougal. He walks to the table and sits down. He touches his fingertips together and puts them to his mouth.

TED: Well . . . this certainly puts a new spin on things, doesn't it?

ASSUMPTA: You won't tell anyone? Will you? I couldn't help it! They're just so chocolatey . . . And I can't go back to the other nuns before Easter. Please don't tell them that I gave into temptation.

DOUGAL: She's been eating chocolate!

ASSUMPTA: Oh, God, please, Father. If there's anything I can do to make it up. You must be so disappointed in me!

TED: Well . . . ahem . . . *here's* a mad idea.

SCENE 30 INT./DAY 5
SET: RUGGED ISLAND PAROCHIAL HOUSE
A hallway. Music plays in the background. The doorbell rings and Dick Byrne comes into shot. He half-walks/half-dances to the door. He opens it. Assumpta is standing outside. Dick Byrne pulls on his fag, exhales . . .

DICK: Ah, Sister. How can I help you?

SCENE 31 INT./DAY 5
SET: PAROCHIAL HOUSE HALLWAY
Mrs Doyle enters. She is in a cheery mood. She calls inside to the living room.

MRS DOYLE: I'm back, Fathers.

We see that there is smoke oozing from under the door of the living room.

MRS DOYLE: Oh, my God!

SCENE 32 INT./DAY 5
SET: PAROCHIAL HOUSE
Mrs Doyle sticks her head round the door. She looks puzzled. We see that the living room is so filled with smoke that it's positively foggy. We see Ted with a line of about six cigarettes in his mouth. We see a row of bottles, all upside down and linked to intravenous tubes. They lead into Jack, who is looking delighted. Cut to window. We see a helmeted Dougal speeding by every now and again.

SCENE 33 EXT./DAY 5
SET: RUGGED ISLAND PAROCHIAL HOUSE
We see the Rugged Island priests all in their underpants, freezing. Assumpta walks among them as they sing Matins. Occasionally she whips them with a big branch. We segment the screen so we can see the different activities in both places. Credits.

THE END

new jack city

ARTHUR: Our idea here was to introduce someone even more unpleasant than Jack, but I think some people found Father Fintan Stack just *too* unpleasant. I don't mind him, and I like the way he does all these horrible pointless things like drilling holes in the walls. This is Graham's least favourite episode. It's not top of my list either, and I think the instance of Larry Duff (in the final, televised version) is the weakest. Yet the episode has its moments. I love the scene when they're driving back with Jack who actually throws himself out of the car because he simply can't wait to get his hands on a drink.

GRAHAM: I like the scene where Ted invites two other priests round to watch the Sports Day video, and they just end up gossiping about their fellow priests – this is when the several Father Windy Shepherd-Hendersons are mentioned. You can find them, and every other priest named in the series, on a website called the Craggy Island Examiner. It has nothing to do with us, but, interestingly, contains masses of information that we'd forgotten. I'd forgotten, for example, that there were at least four Windy Shepherd-Hendersons. But you really can't forget Fintan Stack, or the wonderful way Brendan Grace played the character. It was especially interesting how he interpreted his lines. We had written them as angry lines, but he played the part in a light, delicate, almost effeminate way, which makes the character far more threatening.

Apart from Brendan, I'm really not keen on this episode, but I think it's worth it for the title alone. I *love* that title. And I like Ted listening to the racing on the radio in the beginning, having placed his bet on a horse called Divorce Referendum. I wish we'd also had him put an accumulator on one called Abortion Referendum . . .

PART ONE
SCENE 1 INT./DAY 1
SET: PAROCHIAL HOUSE

Ted is sitting at the table listening to the radio, which is on the table. He seems very excited and has a rolled-up newspaper in his hand. We hear racing commentary coming from the set.

COMMENTATOR: . . . and it's Divorce Referendum in the lead followed by Glory Be to God . . . Glory Be to God nipping at Divorce Referendum's heels . . . Glory Be to God creeps ahead of Divorce Referendum!

TED: C'mon, Divorce Referendum! C'mon, Divorce Referendum!

COMMENTATOR: Divorce Referendum struggling to stay the pace as Glory Be to God increases its lead . . .

TED: Oh, no! C'mon, for pity's sake! C'mon!

COMMENTATOR: Divorce Referendum edges in front! Divorce Referendum is way in front!

TED: YES!! YES!! COME ON, DIVORCE REFERENDUM!

COMMENTATOR: The finishing line is in sight! Divorce Referendum is speeding towards victory!

TED: HA, HA!!!!!

COMMENTATOR: Oh no!

Ted freezes.

COMMENTATOR: Disaster for Divorce Referendum as he turns in the opposite direction and simply runs off the course! Glory Be to God takes advantage of the opening and steams home!

Ted's mouth is open. He stares at the radio in bewilderment.

TED: OHHHHH . . . FLIP!! YOU FLIPPING, FLIPPING . . . FLIPPPER! IT'S THE KNACKER'S YARD FOR YOU, PAL! OHHHHHHH, FFFFFFFLIP!!!!!

He hears the front door opening and quickly changes the channel, assuming a thoughtful expression at the table.

VOICE: . . . So what role do you see the Church assuming in coming months?

The door opens and Dougal pushes in an empty wheelchair.

DOUGAL: What you listening to there, Ted?

TED: Oh, it's a thing about, ah . . . the Church and . . . you know . . . God and . . . so on.

DOUGAL: Ah, right.

Ted turns off the radio. Dougal sits down and starts idly flicking through a copy of a magazine. Ted looks up. We see a shot of the empty wheelchair.

TED: Where's . . . eh . . . where's Father Jack, Dougal?

DOUGAL: Where's Father Jack?

TED: Yes. Father Jack. Where is he?

DOUGAL: He's in his . . . (*He looks at the empty chair.*) Ah . . .

TED: Yes . . . Where is he?

DOUGAL: He's, ah . . .

TED: He's supposed to be in the wheelchair, Dougal.

DOUGAL: Yes . . .

Dougal thinks for a second, looks at Ted, then looks at the wheelchair.

TED: You've lost him again, haven't you, Dougal?

DOUGAL: I have, Ted, yeah.

TED: So you took him out for his walk and you lost him. Again.

DOUGAL: That must have been what happened, all right.

TED: Well, what have you got to say for yourself?

DOUGAL: Well, like I said the last time, it won't happen again.

TED (*sighs*): Well, Dougal, I'll hold you to that. Try not to let it happen again.

Pause.

DOUGAL: What? . . .

Ted looks at him for a moment.

TED: Well?

DOUGAL: Yes, Ted?

TED: Are you not going to look for him?

DOUGAL: Ah, he'll come back on his own, Ted. Sure what's the worst can happen to him?

TED: Well, he could have an accident and be killed.

DOUGAL: Oh, right, yeah.

Dougal stands up and wraps his scarf around him

again. But then he sees something.

DOUGAL: Wait a second, Ted . . . Is that not Jack there?

We see Jack lying on the ground near his chair, breathing noisily. He is dressed to go out, in hat, scarf, etc.

TED: What? (*He stands up and goes over to where Jack is lying.*) Ah, Dougal, you didn't even get him out the door, did you?

DOUGAL: I thought the old wheelchair felt a bit lighter today, yeah.

TED: C'mon, let's get him up.

They lift him into his chair. Ted takes his hat off. H takes a handkerchief and wipes the inside of the brim. We see that there is a vast amount of brown grease on the hankie when Ted takes it away. He takes off Jack's scarf, then goes to put the hat and scarf away.

TED: Take off his gloves, there, Dougal.

DOUGAL: Right, so, Ted. (*He bends over Jack. Pause.*) Ted?

TED: Hm? . . .

DOUGAL: Ted . . . they're not gloves.

He holds up Jack's hands. They are exceptionally hairy. Ted walks over and examines them.

TED: God. They're very hairy hands altogether.

DOUGAL: Hairy is the word, Ted. Actually, Ted, I think the word is 'very hairy'.

TED: This is just typical. Father Dillon and Father Shanahan are coming up on Saturday. What are they going to think when they see the wolfman here?

DOUGAL: What do you think's wrong with him, Ted?

TED: I don't know.

DOUGAL: Do you remember the time his head went septic?

TED: Yes. I didn't think a whole head could go septic. Y'know, a *whole head*. But that's Jack for you. Anyway, I'd better look in the book . . . They really are exceptionally hairy.

Ted goes and takes a large, ancient-looking book

om the library. In the background we see Dougal ke out a comb. He gingerly combs Jack's hairy ands. Ted puts the book on the table and opens it.

ED: Right . . .

ed has opened the book at a page that shows a row f six photographs. The first is of a normal human and, the sixth one is of an ape's hand. The ones in etween show the various stages of progression.

ED: Hold up his hand there, Dougal.

ougal does so. Ted looks at the book.

ED: Hmmm . . . He got up to stage four after rinking that brake fluid . . . but this looks ke a stage six.

e slams the book shut. Mrs Doyle enters, carrying tray.

RS DOYLE: Hello to the lot of yous.

ED: Hello, Mrs Doyle.

RS DOYLE (looking at Jack): Ah, would ou look at him there with his hairy hands.

ED: . . . Yes . . . I think we'll have to call octor Sinnot.

RS DOYLE: He'll know what to do. I had go to him a couple of weeks ago.

ED: Really? I didn't know you were ill, Mrs oyle. What was wrong with you?

RS DOYLE: Oh, I'm afraid it was a bit of a oman's problem. I was having a bit of ouble with—

ED: Right! I'd better phone him now, ctually, before it gets too late.

e goes over to the table, leaving Mrs Doyle before e can say any more. There are two telephones on e table, one black and one red. Ted picks up the d one and presses a single button on the front of it.

CENE 2 INT./DAY 1
ET: OFFICE
e see a red telephone, exactly the same as Ted's, d hear it ringing. An ominous light starts ashing on it. In the background we see Doctor nnot examining a patient. He looks over at the lephone, a nervous expression on his face.

SCENE 3 INT./DAY 1
SET: PAROCHIAL HOUSE HALLWAY
We see Doctor Sinnot closing the front door behind him. He looks very tense, but businesslike. He carries a medical bag and a suitcase. Ted and Dougal are there to greet him.

SINNOT: Right, so it's the hairy hands?

TED: Yes.

SINNOT: Both of them?

TED: Yes.

SINNOT: And you say it looks like a stage six?

TED: It looks like it, yeah.

SINNOT: Hmmm . . . All right, I'll change upstairs.

Sinnot heads upstairs.

DOUGAL: Why's Jack so scared of doctors Ted?

TED: I think they just remind him of illness. He doesn't like thinking about his own mortality. That's why he always hated visiting the sick.

DOUGAL: Oh, God, yeah, he hates the sick, all right. And the poor, he hates them as well.

TED: Yes. The poor really get on his nerves.

DOUGAL: And the needy.

TED: Them as well. What was it he always used to say about the needy? He had a term he used for them . . .

DOUGAL: A shower of bastards.

TED: That's it. Anyway, listen, when we bring the doctor in, you're to act completely normal. Just pretend like he's a normal visitor. We can't let Jack suspect that anything's up.

Dougal nods. We hear a noise from the stairs. Ted looks up.

TED: Ah, doctor. Ready to go in? C'mon, Dougal. Remember, act perfectly normal.

The doctor comes into shot. He is dressed in protective gear that makes him look like Dustin Hoffman in 'Outbreak'. He follows Ted and Dougal inside.

SCENE 4 INT./DAY 1
SET: PAROCHIAL HOUSE
The doctor stands at the doorway, talking to Ted. We see there is a large crack in the visor of the helmet.

TED: So, it's off to Saint Clabbert's again, Doctor?

SINNOT: Yes. Well, the way I see it, it's more for your safety than for his. That hair thing can be very contagious.

TED: So . . . how long do you think you'll have him?

SINNOT: Hard to say. It could be a while . . . Actually, Father, you should be prepared . . . It might be better for him if . . . if he doesn't come back.

TED (*brightens*): Great! I mean, oh, no . . .

SINNOT: He is very old, and the nuns at Saint Clabbert's are trained to look after priests in their twilight years.

TED (*obviously delighted*): Yes, of course . . . Oh, well, just have to grin and bear it, I suppose. I'll break it to him gently. Thanks, Doctor.

He waves and closes the door.

SCENE 5 INT./DAY 1
SET: PAROCHIAL HOUSE
Jack is in his chair. Ted comes in and approaches.

TED: Father, do you remember that great time you had in Saint Clabbert's?

JACK (*suddenly shocked*): Huh?

TED: Do you remember the fun you had with all the nuns fussing over you?

Jack's face goes into a fixed, frozen look of absolute terror.

TED: Well, Doctor Sinnot thinks another little spell in there would do you the world of good . . .

Another shot of Jack wearing exactly the same expression.

TED: I know you might have to give up the odd glass of sherry for a while, but that'll be good for you.

Pause. Another shot of a frozen Jack.

TED: What do you say, Father? You ready to have just a great big laugh with all the nuns?

Another shot of Jack. Ted waits for an answer. He cocks his head slightly.

TED: Sorry, Father?

Jack is now beyond help. He stares ahead in that frozen way.

TED: Well . . . well, I'll just go and get you a packed.

Ted leaves the room, pausing one more time to look at the frozen Jack. When Ted leaves, Jack shakes himself out of his horrified trance and runs out, bumping into a confused Dougal at the doorway. Then he exits through the front door at top speed. Cut back to Dougal. Ted comes in.

TED: Right, if we— Dougal, where's Father Jack?

DOUGAL: I just saw him running out the door there.

TED: Oh, God. Where's he gone?

SCENE 6 EXT./DAY 1
SET: NEAR PAROCHIAL HOUSE
We see Jack driving away from the house in a one man tractor-mower that is far too small for him. A flurry of grass shoots out of the side of it as he drives. He bounces in his seat, urging it to go faster and looks behind him to see if Ted and Dougal are following. It makes a pathetic 'chucka-chucka' noise as it goes.

SCENE 7 INT./NIGHT 1
SET: TED AND DOUGAL'S BEDROOM
Ted and Dougal are in bed. It's very quiet.

DOUGAL: So, Jack's up there in Saint Clabbert's anyway.

TED: Indeed he is. And you know, despite the *Born to be Wild* act with the old Flymo there, I think secretly he's de-*lighted*.

DOUGAL: God, it's weird the way you get used to something, isn't it, Ted? It seems like only yesterday he was here, shouting at us and drinking his head off.

TED: Dougal, it *was* yesterday.

DOUGAL: Yeah, but, you know, that's why I said it seemed like yesterday.

TED: Oh, right, because it *was* yesterday.

Pause.

DOUGAL: What time are Father Dillon and Father Shanahan coming on Wednesday?

TED: Around six.

DOUGAL: Six o'clock?

TED (*sighs*): Yes.

DOUGAL: Right.

TED: It's just as well Jack won't be here, you know. He can get very irritable around strangers. That was the thing about Jack . . . always very bad around strangers.

DOUGAL: And people he knew.

TED: Yes. Very bad around strangers and people he knew. Oh, don't forget, the lads'll be bringing the video of the sports day, so don't be late.

DOUGAL: Oh, great! That was a brilliant day.

He turns off the light.

TED: Night, Dougal.

DOUGAL: Night, Ted.

Ted settles down. Pause.

TED: Oh . . . damn it . . .

He puts the light back on. He takes a notebook from his bedside table and starts flicking through the pages, grabbing a pen as he does so. Meanwhile, Dougal has got out of bed. He stretches and yawns and grabs a towel from the end of the bed. He undoes a few buttons on his pyjama top. He also turns on the radio and starts to whistle. Ted watches this quietly.

TED: Dougal, no. It's not morning yet. I just put the light back on.

Pause.

DOUGAL: Oh, right.

SCENE 8 INT./DAY 2
SET: PAROCHIAL HOUSE

Ted, wearing a dressing gown, walks into the room and stretches. He walks over to the table, where a bowl of breakfast cereal is waiting for him. He sits down and starts to eat. Just as he is about to put the first spoonful in his mouth, he looks up and freezes. Cut to an oldish priest, Father Fintan Stack, sitting where Jack usually sits. He is smoking a fag and observing Ted dispassionately.

TED: Ah . . . hello . . . ah, Father . . . Father, ah . . . who are you?

FINTAN (*gruffly*): Who are you?

TED: Father Ted Crilly. Pleased to meet you.

He stands up and walks over, holding his hand out. Rather than shaking it, Stack takes an envelope out and hands it to Ted.

TED: Oh . . . what's this?

He looks at Fintan uncertainly and wanders back to the table, opening the letter.

TED: Oh, it's from the Bishop . . . Oh, right . . . oh . . . so . . . so, you'll be taking Father Jack's place . . .

Fintan just looks at Ted, smoking his fag. Ted smiles and uncertainly resumes eating.

TED: Well, this is a bit of a surprise. Ah, has Mrs Doyle shown you round the house?

No response. Thinking Fintan might have said something . . .

TED: . . . Sorry?

No response.

TED: Anyway, well . . . ah . . . welcome to Craggy Island. Ah . . . meals are at eleven, one, half two, three, five, seven and nine. And if you ever want a quick snack, just ask Mrs Doyle. Ah, there's . . .

Fintan stands up and walks over to where Ted is. Without paying attention to anything Ted says, he takes the bowl Ted is eating from and pulls at it. Ted holds on to it for a moment and then lets go. Fintan takes the spoon, then walks back to his seat, calmly eating.

TED (*after a moment's hesitation*): Ah . . . that's actually mine . . . ah . . . Well, you go ahead there . . .

Dougal walks in.

TED: Ah, Dougal, this is Father Fintan Stack. He'll be staying with us now that Father Jack's gone.

DOUGAL: Oh, right, yeah.

Dougal nods a hello.

FINTAN: This the brains of the operation?

DOUGAL: Ah, no, that'd be Ted.

FINTAN: I want to listen to some music, all right?

TED: Yes, yes, go ahead there and—

FINTAN (*already up*): I wasn't asking for permission.

He takes a tape from his pocket and walks over to the stereo. He puts something on and presses 'play'. Incredibly loud Jungle blasts out of the speakers. Fintan goes back to his seat. Dougal and Ted look at each other as the music pumps out.

SCENE 9 INT./NIGHT 2
SET: TED AND DOUGAL'S BEDROOM
Ted and Dougal are in bed. We hear the repetitive beats of Jungle in the adjacent room.

TED: So . . . Dougal . . . What do you think of Father Stack?

DOUGAL: . . . Eh . . .

TED: In his note from the Bishop, it says that they've never been able to find a suitable parish for him . . . He's not a very nice man, is he?

DOUGAL: God, Ted, I've never met anyone like him, anyway. Who would he be like? Hitler or one of those mad fellas.

TED: He's nearly worse than Hitler. You wouldn't find Hitler playing Jungle music at three o'clock in the morning. . . . God, he nearly makes Jack seem normal.

DOUGAL: You know, he nearly does. You'd—

Dougal is interrupted by a massive roar. Ted holds his hand up and they listen for a moment, heads cocked. Pause.

TED: All right, carry on.

DOUGAL: I was just saying, you'd almost sort of miss Father Jack.

TED: I mean, he had his funny little ways. But, you know, whenever Jack'd hit us or whatever, he'd never do it out of spite. He'd only do it because, you know . . . he thought it was funny . . . or whatever.

DOUGAL (*laughs*): I suppose . . . thinking about it now, it was sort of funny, wasn't it?

TED: Yes, ha, ha! . . . Do you remember that time he . . . ha, ha! . . . gave you a big kick up the B-O-T-T-Y!?

DOUGAL: Ha, ha. And do you remember . . . do you remember when you were bending over him . . . !?

TED: . . . Yeah, ha, ha! . . . Yeah . . .

DOUGAL: . . . And he held your nose until you had to open your mouth, and then he put a big spider in it. Ha, ha, ha!

TED (*stops laughing*): No, that wasn't funny, Dougal. When he kicked you up the arse, that was funny. But it wasn't funny when he put the spider in my mouth.

DOUGAL: Ah, it was, Ted . . .

TED: No, it wasn't, Dougal.

DOUGAL: Ah, Ted.

TED: Dougal, did you have the spider in your mouth or was it me?

DOUGAL: It was definitely you, Ted. The look on your face!

Dougal does an impression of Ted's face.

TED: Dougal! Anyway, he's gone now . . . God, it's funny how you get used to someone's little ways . . .

SCENE 9A INT./EXT
SET: VARIOUS
Flashback. Beautiful, emotional music plays – perhaps 'Seasons in the Sun' – as we see a number of incidents involving Jack. All the scenes are shot in a very 'romantic', idealistic soft focus.

Ted and Jack putting up a sign that reads 'Home Sweet Home'. Ted holds the nail and Jack levels a hammer at it. He brings the hammer back and then whacks Ted on the head with it. He then goes to finish the job but Dougal and Mrs Doyle hold him back.

Ted in a bathroom. He walks towards the bath and suddenly Jack appears over the edge. He attaches a pair of clothes pegs to Ted's nipples. Ted turns to the camera and screams. The pegs are attached firmly. Jack laughs happily.

Ted lining up a moderately difficult putt on a very nice green. He aims, draws back the putter and hits the ball softly. It starts to roll towards the hole. Ted

makes a 'come on, come on' gesture. Then Jack drives a car into shot and knocks Ted down. Ted is splayed some feet away from the car. Jack, behind the wheel, laughs his head off.

Ted drifts back into reality and loses the faraway look on his face. We hear the noise from downstairs worsening.

TED (*getting out of bed*)**:** Ah, God, I've had enough. It sounds like he's drilling holes in the walls or something. I'm going to have a word.

DOUGAL: Careful, now!

SCENE 10 INT./NIGHT 2
SET: PAROCHIAL HOUSE
Ted walks into the living room. He turns to see Fintan drilling holes in the walls of the room, a fag hanging from his mouth. There are already many big, ugly holes dotting the walls. He turns to Ted and stops drilling.

FINTAN: What?

Ted can't think of anything to say. He leaves the room. Fintan continues drilling.

END OF PART ONE

* * *

PART TWO

SCENE 11 INT./DAY 3
SET: PAROCHIAL HOUSE HALLWAY
Ted opens the front door and sticks his head in.
There are two other priests behind him.

TED: Right . . . come on . . . I think he's gone out.

VOICE 1: What's up with you there, Ted?

VOICE 2: Ted's gone mad!

The two men laugh. Ted comes in and ushers them in. They are Father Ken Dillon and Father Rory Shanahan.

TED: All right, this way, lads.

RORY: Lead on, MacTed!

SCENE 12 INT./DAY 3
SET: PAROCHIAL HOUSE
Ted sticks his head in and we see that Fintan is nowhere to be seen.

TED: Right. Coast's clear.

The other two follow Ted.

KEN: Father Jack's not here?

TED: No, he has that hair thing again. He's up in Jurassic Park.

RORY: Oh, right. Saint Clabbert's. Father

Walton's up there, I hear.

TED: Sit down there . . . (*The other two sit down.*) Sherry all right . . . ?

RORY: Grand job.

KEN: Lovely.

Ted starts to pour some sherry.

RORY: Did you know Father Coogan, at all, Ted?

TED: Oh, God, yes. Tom Coogan. He was in Africa for a while, wasn't he?

RORY: He was. And he was with Father Shortall in Athlone.

KEN: And he was parish priest in Kenmare then.

RORY: And I think at one stage he was in Lucan.

KEN: And wasn't he in Boston for a while?

RORY: Yes. A great old pal of mine, Jim Doolan, was with him in Boston.

KEN: And he was back in Wicklow for about a year.

TED: I think Windy Shepherd-Henderson was parish priest while he was in Wicklow.

KEN: Is that Windy Shepherd-Henderson that was in Tralee with Larry Buckley?

TED: No, that was another Windy Shepherd-Henderson. There were about four of them.

KEN: Oh, at least. One of them was with Father Daley in Chicago.

RORY: Father Daley from Clones? Wasn't he the first man on the scene when Malcolm X was assassinated?

TED: No, that was Father Burke. Father Daley used to have the lump on the side of his head in the shape of Connaught.

KEN: Ah, yeah, like Father Carolan there. He lost the use of his ears in an accident.

RORY: He's deaf?

TED: No, no, he just lost the use of his ears. He used to be able to wiggle them. Now they're just completely paralysed.

KEN: Remember Father O'Reilly? Isn't he in

Clare now? They had to move him there after he owned up to that O.J. Simpson thing.

RORY: Father Costello in Athlone is related to that fella, the Japanese fella. Judge Ito. The little humpty fella with the fake beard. Father Merrigan from Ardee did his wedding, I think.

TED: Father Merrigan, isn't he dead now?

RORY: No, no, he always just looked dead.

KEN: Ted, did you say Larry Duff was coming to this thing?

TED: Actually I'll give him a call on his mobile. (*He picks up the telephone.*)

SCENE 12A INT./DAY 3*
SET: SMALL THEATRE
We see a blindfolded knife-thrower taking aim in a hushed theatre. We see Larry revolving on a circular board. The knife-thrower takes aim. We hear Larry's mobile phone ringing. We see the knife-thrower jump slightly as he is startled by the noise. He throws the knife and we hear a thunk. A woman screams in the audience.

SCENE 12B INT./DAY 3
SET: PAROCHIAL HOUSE
Cut back to Ted still on the telephone. After a while he puts the receiver down.

TED: He must have it turned off. (*He looks around.*) Where's Dougal got to?

RORY (*holding up a tape*): C'mon, Ted, you got the video player there?

TED: I do!

He puts in the video and presses 'play'. The priests settle down to enjoy themselves. They are very excited. All through the following scene, we hear the priests chattering excitedly among themselves.

Cut to the video. We see a line of priests, all in their usual uniform, running along in an egg-and-spoon

---

*In the final version this scene was moved to Episode Three, *Tentacles of Doom*. This scene was changed to show Larry making a house of cards. He is interrupted by the telephone ringing and when he picks up a stapler instead of the phone, he staples his ear to his head and then falls out of shot, knocking down the house of cards as he does so.

race. Ted is one of them.

ALL: Oh, look! O'ho! There y'are now!

We see another line of priests in a sack race. Dougal is one of them. In the background we see two priests throwing a frisbee to each other.

TED: God, where's Dougal at all?

Cut to a priest running around a real track. He carries a baton. He passes it to another priest, who runs on.

We see another priest running, then doing a long jump into a sandpit. He looks up, waiting for some scores, then punches the air triumphantly.

TED: Good old Father Smith. He broke the priest record with that one.

Fintan walks in from the kitchen, smoking a fag. He walks to his chair and sits looking at them. Ted's smile disappears. Rory and Ken remain 'up'. We see a priest doing a shot putt. He throws.

RORY: Rayyyyyyy!!!

He notices Fintan's glare and shuts up. The mood darkens considerably. A very long pause.

FINTAN: What are we watching?

Long pause. The three priests are very uncomfortable.

KEN: We're looking at the sports day.

FINTAN: Yeah? . . . Lots of young fellas runnin' around in shorts . . . (*Pointing at Rory.*) That's the kind of thing you like lookin' at, is it? Young fellas runnin' around a field in shorts.

Rory and Ken look very embarrassed. They are blushing wildly.

FINTAN (*pointing at Ken*): And I bet you like that, too. The only thing is, you're probably imaginin' what they'd look like without shorts. What do you think that'd look like? Young fellas runnin' around in the nude? (*Pause.*) You're sittin' there imaginin' that, aren't you? Thinkin' about it with a big smile on your face. You dirty fecker.

RORY: Well, I have to say . . . I think that you are a very rude man.

FINTAN: If you ever say that to me again, I'll put your head through the wall.

There is another long, uncomfortable pause.

TED: Father Stack, if you're trying to embarrass us, you're not succeeding.

FINTAN: Yes, I am.

Dougal walks in from the kitchen. He looks very disorientated. His hair is dishevelled and he doesn't look very well.

TED: Dougal, where were you?

DOUGAL (*very drunk*): TED! TED, HOW ARE YA!

He goes to hug Ted. Ted reels from Dougal's breath.

TED: Dougal, what the . . . ?!

DOUGAL: Guess what, Ted!

TED: What?

Pause.

DOUGAL: What?

TED: Have you been drinking, Dougal?

DOUGAL: Yeah, I have! I've been drinking like a mad eejit, Ted. Oh, wait!

He looks at Fintan and winks broadly. Very deliberately.

DOUGAL: No, I haven't.

TED: Dougal, I am ashamed of you!

DOUGAL: Ted, Ted. Ted. Ted. Ted, c'mere, Ted. (*He whispers.*) You're me best friend. God, I love being a priest! We're all going to heaven, Ted! Rayyy!

FINTAN: Perhaps I should explain. Your little friend and I were enjoying a bottle of whiskey which I found upstairs.

TED: Oh, well, that, that is the last straw!

DOUGAL (*holding up a bunch of keys*): I'm driving! I'm driving home! I'm perfectly capable!

Dougal falls over.

FINTAN: Oh, by the way, I got the keys of your car and I drove it into a big wall. If you don't like it, tough. I had my fun and that's all that matters.

DOUGAL (*from the floor*): Ted, Ted, I can see up your trousers, Ted.

TED: Well, frankly, I thought giving Dougal alcohol was the last straw. But it must just have been the second-last one, because this must definitely be the last bit . . . of . . . straw left in the . . . thing. There's *no* straw left, basically, is what I'm saying.

RORY: Ted, it's a little late . . .

KEN: Yes . . . I really think we should go.

TED: Oh . . . you don't have to.

RORY: I think we should.

FINTAN: Bye, girls . . .

The two men get up to leave. Fintan gets up and 'mock' chases them out through the door. Ted follows them. Ted walks back into the room. He seems very cross, but is trying not to show it.

FINTAN: Pair of wankers.

TED: Oh! I . . . Dougal, come on, I think we've had enough of Father Stack's company for this evening.

DOUGAL: To the pub, Ted!

Ted grabs Dougal, and they leave the room. After they go, Fintan takes out a knife and begins to rip one of the cushions.

SCENE 13 INT./NIGHT 3*
SET: PAROCHIAL HOUSE HALLWAY
Ted and Dougal come into the hall. Ted puts on his coat, then attempts to do the same for Dougal.

DOUGAL: Ted, Ted, what's going on?

TED: We're going to kidnap Jack from Saint Clabbert's.

DOUGAL: Kidnapping. Wow! How much will we get for him?

---

*In the final version we inserted a new scene, 12C, here which showed Mrs Doyle coming into the living room where Fintan is swaying to Jungle, smoking a fag and drinking some whiskey. Oblivious to all this, she holds up a sign reading, 'Will you have a cup of tea?' He shakes his head and carries on dancing so she holds up a second sign that says, 'Ah, go on.' He shakes his head. This continues for a while, with Fintan dancing and Mrs Doyle holding up the sign until she finally gives up and leaves.

TED: We're not doing this to make any kind of profit, Dougal. He's not the Lindbergh baby. We're just going to get him back so that we can jettison Father Stack. Are you with me?

DOUGAL: I'm with you, Ted!

TED: Then let's go!

Ted opens the door and walks out. Dougal closes the door after him and walks back down the hall. After a moment, we hear the doorbell ring. Dougal walks back to the door and opens it.

DOUGAL: Hello?

A hand comes into shot, grabs Dougal and pulls him out.

SCENE 13A EXT./NIGHT 3
SET: SAINT CLABBERT'S
We see a sign that reads 'Saint Clabbert's Old Priests Home'. Ted and Dougal are crouching under a window, whispering.

TED: Right. The best thing to do is find an open window, and creep in. The last time, he was in a room on the ground floor. That's where they keep the more 'difficult' ones.

DOUGAL: That's a bit mad, Ted. Why don't we just go to the nuns and say we want him back?

TED: Because Doctor Sinnot said he's sick and old, and moving him might be dangerous. But I got a second opinion.

DOUGAL: Ah, right. From who?

TED: Mrs Doyle.

DOUGAL: But, Ted, I'm not sure if this is a good idea, Ted. I mean . . . kidnapping . . .

TED: No, we're just bringing him back home to where he belongs. It's a bit like *Lassie Come Home* except with Father Jack as Lassie.

DOUGAL: Who are we, then?

TED: What? I don't know. The other people in the film. You're Roddy McDowell and I'm . . . Liz Taylor.

DOUGAL: Right. Well, that's fine. I just wanted to get all that straight in my mind.

The light turns off in the home.

TED: Right! Let's go!

SCENE 14 INT./NIGHT 3
SET: MAIN ROOM
The room is completely dark. A door opens and we see Ted and Dougal silhouetted for a moment.

TED (*whispering*): C'mon, Dougal. Get in, get in.

DOUGAL (*loudly*): I'm right behind you, T—

TED: Dougal! Shut up! We have to keep it quiet. Right. See if there's a light switch anywhere round there.

A moment's fumbling. Then the light suddenly comes on, revealing a frozen Ted and Dougal, Dougal's hand on the light switch, and about a dozen elderly priests in armchairs, all of whom wake up suddenly and start shouting at the top of their voices.

OLD PRIESTS: DRINK! FECK! ARSE!

They wave sticks, growl menacingly and bark out confused commands. Basically, it is Jack × 20. A lot of noise.

TED: Turn off the light! Turn off the light!

Dougal does so, and the noise immediately dies. Suddenly a woman's voice sounds from outside somewhere.

MONICA (*muffled*): What's all that noise?

TED: Dougal, quick, over here!

Pause. The door opens and the light comes on. Sister Monica stands there. All the priests immediately start shouting. We see that Ted and Dougal are sitting in two free seats, also shouting.

OLD PRIESTS: FECK! ARSE! DRINK! . . .

MONICA: Now, calm down, all of you! Some people are trying to get some sleep.

She turns off the light. All the priests stop shouting.

DOUGAL: Arse! Fe—

There is a 'thump' sound and Dougal shuts up. The nun pauses at the door, then finally closes it.

SCENE 15/NIGHT 3
SET: OUTSIDE SAINT CLABBERT'S
We see three figures stealing across the grounds towards a car. Ted and Dougal push the third figure into the car. Then we cut to Ted getting in on his side, Dougal getting into the passenger seat. They

both look around to the back seat and jump with shock. The priest in the back seat is not Father Jack, but Father Walton, another elderly priest almost completely covered in hair. He looks very like Lon Chaney in the early werewolf films, except that the hair covers his eyes.

TED: Dougal! That's not Father Jack! Hello, Father Walton.

He hears Ted's voice, but seems confused.

WALTON: Feck off . . .

DOUGAL: Will he not do, Ted?

TED (*ponders this for a few moments*): Emmm . . . no. I don't think so. No. Anyway, look at him. He's gone hair mad. It'd be very dangerous to move him around.

DOUGAL: OK, so.

TED (*in wonder*): God, a stage twelve. I never thought I'd see one. Right. Come on, let's get Father Jack!

SCENE 16 INT./NIGHT 3
SET: MAIN ROOM
A flashlight illuminates the face of a Jack-type.

BILLY: ARSE!

The flashlight switches off, then on. We see another Jack-type.

RONAN: FECK!

Off, on. Another Jack-type.

MICHAEL: DRINK!

Then a quick succession of Jack-types, illuminated by the torch, all of them saying either 'Drink', 'Feck', 'Arse' or 'Girls'. Soon they fly by in a blur of bad language. Then we see a slightly younger, clean-cut priest.

WILLIAM (*well spoken*): I really shouldn't be here.

Finally the light switches on to Father Jack.

JACK: DRINK! FECK! ARSE! GIRLS!

SCENE 17 EXT./DAY 4
SET: PAROCHIAL HOUSE
The car turns and starts up the driveway towards the house. We hear from within the sound of Father Jack.

JACK: DRINK! DRINK! DRINK!

Before the car stops, Jack opens the door and throws himself out of the car. He gets up immediately and runs towards the house.

JACK: DRINK! DRINK! DRINK! DRINK!

He runs towards the house at top speed. Then he gets to the front door and bashes into it. He starts banging at the door.

JACK (*with each blow*): DRINK! DRINK! DRINK! DRINK!

He runs back slightly to Ted and Dougal, excited out of his mind, pointing towards the house.

JACK: DRINK! DRIIIIINK!

Ted runs towards the house, pulling out some keys.

SCENE 18 INT./DAY 4
SET: PAROCHIAL HOUSE HALLWAY
Ted opens the door and Jack bursts in.

JACK: DRINK!!!!!!!!!!!!

Jack runs into the hall. He looks around in excitement.

JACK: DRINK!! DRIIIIINK!!!!!!!

TED (*recovering slightly*): Try upstairs, Father . . .

Jack runs upstairs.

SCENE 19 INT./DAY 4
SET: PAROCHIAL HOUSE
We see Fintan sticking the end of his cigarette into a lacy cushion. There are lots of cigarette holes all over it already. Ted comes into the room. Fintan keeps his back to him.*

TED: Ah, Father Stack, you burning holes in the cushions again?*

FINTAN: Yeah. Got a problem with that?

TED: None at all. You go ahead and enjoy yourself.

FINTAN: What was all that noise?

TED: Oh, that was Father Jack. He's the fella you replaced.

FINTAN: Yeah? Well, tell him to get lost, then. I'm here now.

TED: Oh, I thought you might like the pleasure of telling him that yourself. I thought you also might like to tell him what happened to his bottle of whiskey. Once he realises it's gone, I'm sure he'll—

JACK (*from upstairs*): Aaaaaaaaaaarrrrrrr rrrrggggggggghhhhhhhhhhhh!!!!!!!!!!!!!!!

TED: Ah, well, I'll let him fill in the rest.

FINTAN: Oh, I'm suppose to be scared, is that it?

Jack suddenly appears through the door, breathing heavily. Fintan turns around to face them. Jack, Ted and Dougal all stop talking and just stare at him. Cut to reveal that Father Stack is covered in hair. He is very hairy indeed. He looks at them.

FINTAN: What?

Ted, Dougal and Jack all look at each other.

SCENE 20 INT./DAY 4
SET: PAROCHIAL HOUSE
Ted and Dougal sit side by side on the sofa.

TED: Listen to that, Dougal.

---

*In the final version this scene was changed so that Fintan is jumping on a photo of Ted by Jack's chair when Ted comes into the room. Ted's first line was then changed as follows: 'Ah, Father Stack, you jumping on my picture again?'

DOUGAL (*puzzled*): I don't hear anything, Ted.

TED: That's what I mean. The sound of silence.

DOUGAL: No . . . I still don't hear anything. I was going to say, though, I'm really sorry I didn't disinfect Jack's chair like you told me. It's probably all my fault that lad got the hair thing.

TED: Oh, don't worry about it, Dougal. I'm sure he's fine up there in Jurassic Park. Best place for him, really. Keep him out of trouble. (*He looks over to Jack's chair. We don't see Jack.*) Do you remember him, Father? Father Stack? You didn't like him very much did you? Anyway, how are you getting on in there? It's a great little invention isn't it? And you won't have to go to Saint Clabbert's.

Cut to Jack in a bizarre large plastic bubble. We see his hands have gone hairy again.

JACK (*very muffled*): DRINK!

TED: Sorry, Father, can't hear you. Anyway, time for bed. C'mon, Dougal.

Ted and Dougal leave. We see Jack yelling from inside the bubble, but we can't hear him. Ted turns off the light.

SCENE 21 EXT./NIGHT 4
SET: SAINT CLABBERT'S
We see a silhouette of the house. The light of the ground-floor priests' room is on. We hear voices inside.

MONICA: Good night, Fathers.

PRIESTS: DRINK! ARSE! FECK! . . .

The light goes off and they stop. After a moment, incredibly loud Jungle starts up.

THE END

flight into terror

GRAHAM: This was our disaster-movie episode. Arthur was in Dublin, so we agreed that I leave London for a while and write an episode over there. I had recently developed a fear of flying that I believe came in part from the success of *Father Ted*. The better the show did, the more convinced I was that something terrible was going to happen. So I didn't enjoy the flight to Dublin. When I arrived, I talked about my ridiculous worries with Arthur and we both felt there was a plot to be taken from it.

The show seemed to write itself, as if we were listening to the characters and merely transcribing what they said. It also took just two days to write and nearly everything from the first draft ended up on screen. Structurally, it echoes episodes of *Dad's Army* as the characters are in a static situation which generates practically no action, a great deal of talk and a high joke density. There's really no ingenuity in the structure at all, but having all the priests trapped in the same place was perfect for developing really stupid ideas. I'm particularly proud of the essay competition. And we had to have the monkey priest back again because we loved the idea of a monkey let loose on a plane. I also managed not only to wangle myself a part, but also make sure that the final image of the second series was a long take of my huge face.

ARTHUR: Pauline McLynn is one of the paper-throwing nuns sitting behind Ted in the plane. Apart from a pre-recorded scene at the beginning, she wasn't in this episode at all, but she wanted to be a part of it because it was the final episode in Series Two, so here she is, really heavily disguised and throwing bits of paper at Ted.

PART ONE

SCENE 1 INT./DAY 1
SET: PLANE

A chartered plane. The seats are full of priests. Ted, Dougal and Jack walk down the aisle, Ted is checking the seat numbers.

TED: Twenty-two, twenty-three . . . Ah! This is us, Dougal.

DOUGAL: Great! You sure you don't want the window, Ted?

TED: No, to be honest, now, I'd be a bit nervous near the window.

DOUGAL: What's up with you, Ted?

TED: Never liked flying, Dougal. If God had meant us to fly, he wouldn't have put the airports so far from the towns.

They sit down with their duty free. Jack sits on an aisle across from them. Father O'Shea is sitting beside him. He looks rather snooty, and is certainly unhappy to have Jack sitting there. Jack sits, breathing noisily through his nose. O'Shea looks disgusted.

O'SHEA: Excuse me. Excuse me, you're sitting on my . . .

He yanks his coat from under Jack. Jack continues breathing through his nose.

O'SHEA: Could you . . . could you not breathe through your nose like that? You're making a noise.

Jack breathes more heavily, making a disgusting, rasping noise. He then reaches in his pocket and takes out a cigarette.

O'SHEA: Oh, now, I'm afraid this is a no-smoking—

Jack immediately delivers an almighty punch to the man's head, which snaps back immediately into a very deep unconscious state.

Across the way, Ted is talking to Dougal.

TED: Well, did you enjoy that, Dougal?

DOUGAL: I did, yeah. Kilnettle is great, isn't it? It must be the holiest shrine in the world.

TED: Top ten, anyway.

DOUGAL: Funny, isn't it, Ted? Our Lady appearing like that on a golf course. Where exactly did it happen again?

TED: Thirteenth hole. She appeared to a fella on the green there. Only about a yard from the pin. Apparently he was putting for a birdie and the ball hit her foot.

DOUGAL: God almighty. Then what happened?

TED: He just took a drop ball, put it down to experience.

A priest passes by. This is Father Joe Briefly.

JOE: Hello, Ted. On the old plane, I see!

TED: Ah, I am. Same as yourself!

They both laugh. Joe continues on his way.

DOUGAL: Who's that, Ted?

TED: Father Joe Briefly. An old pal of mine from Saint Colm's. We had a nickname for him there . . . what was it? Very funny . . . ha, ha . . . Oh, yes, we used to call him Himalaya Joe, because he had all this hair between his toes and it reminded us of the Abominable Snowman. Ha, ha! Oh, that was very funny. Ha, ha, ha, ha, ha . . .

DOUGAL: Ha, ha! Did you have a nickname, Ted?

TED (*immediately stops laughing*): No, I didn't.

Ted goes strangely quiet and serious.

DOUGAL: Ah, you must have had one, Ted.

TED: No.

DOUGAL (*standing*): Father Briefly!

TED: Dougal!

DOUGAL: Father Briefly! Do you remember at all what Ted's nickname was at Saint Colm's?

JOE: Well, let's see, what was it now . . . ?

All the priests are looking at Ted and Briefly.

TED: Don't worry about it, Joe! I'll tell him myself!

Briefly makes a 'fair enough' gesture and sits down. An angry Ted turns to Dougal.

TED: All right, shut up, Dougal. It was 'Father Fluffy Bottom'. The other priests caught a glance of my 'rear end' in the showers after a game of football once and, well, I had a bit of downy fluff around that whole area. (*Bitterly.*) 'Father Fluffy Bottom'. Oh, yes, hilarious stuff.

DOUGAL: Right. So, what did you do in the end, shave it off?

TED: Shave it off? Ha, ha . . . not at all . . .

DOUGAL: Ah, right. (*He stands up.*) Ah, Father Briefly? It was 'Father Fluffy Bottom'!

TED: Dougal!

JOE: Ah, yeah, right. 'Cause he had a big load of fluffy hair on his behind. What'd you do in the end, Ted? Shave it off?

All the priests in the plane laugh. Ted is mortified.

TED: No, I didn't! You can't get razors with a long-enough handle to go down . . . your back.

Everyone laughs again.

TED: Well, do you remember what we called you, Joe? Himalaya Joe! Because of all the big black hair in your toes. Do you remember? Ha, ha, ha, ha!!!

No one laughs. Very pregnant silence. We stay on Ted as we hear the following.

JOE: That was actually a medical condition, Ted.

There is a terrible silence. Ted has obviously brought up a taboo subject. Ted makes a jokey 'aha!' noise to ease the tension, but it doesn't work. He turns around and slinks into his seat.

SCENE 2 INT./DAY 1
SET: PLANE
Fade up on Ted and Dougal. Dougal is looking out of the window.

DOUGAL: God, Ted, you're missing this. Everything looks so small. All the cars look like ants.

TED: They *are* ants, Dougal. We haven't taken off yet.

DOUGAL: Ah, right . . .

Pause. Suddenly, a rolled-up piece of paper hits Ted on the back of the head.

TED: What— Who did that?

He turns and we see, from his point of view, a very small nun sitting beside a large nun, some young innocent-looking priests, and a shifty looking young priest wearing a pair of shades who is smiling sneakily. Ted, annoyed, turns back. Dougal is taking some stuff out of a bag.

TED: Someone's messing at the back there. What's that, Dougal?

DOUGAL: I got it at the gift shop back at the airport.

We see that it is a heavy, black sticky-tape dispenser that has 'Greetings from the Shrine at Kilnettle' written on it.

TED: God, Dougal, we've already got a tape dispenser back at the house. What do you want that one for?

DOUGAL: Ah. But it's not an ordinary one, Ted. Watch.

Dougal pulls out a bit of sticky tape and rips it off. A voice comes from the tape dispenser.

DISPENSER: You have used one inch of sticky tape. God bless you.

Ted regards Dougal for a moment.

TED: Dougal . . . That . . . is . . . brilliant. Already, I can see hundreds of uses for that. Did you get anything else?

DOUGAL: Oh, yeah. This.

He takes out a rubber mobile phone in a Cellophane bag. A piece of card is attached to the top with a drawing of a happy dog on it. Ted takes it and examines it.

TED: What does it do?

DOUGAL: Squeeze it there. It's a joke telephone.

Ted does so. It makes a squeaky noise. Ted squeaks it once or twice more.

TED: Dougal . . . this is a dog toy.

DOUGAL: What? No, it's not. It's a joke telephone.

TED: Dougal, it's a toy for dogs. This is something people give their dogs on their birthday.

DOUGAL (*a teeny bit annoyed*): Ted. Seriously, now. It's a *joke telephone*. Look, you give it someone and tell them it's a phone, and they'll try to make a phonecall on it.

TED: Dougal, who'd be fooled by this? Even dogs would know this isn't a phone. It's coloured yellow, for God's sake.

DOUGAL: Well, Ted, listen . . . we'll agree to differ, all right?

TED: No, we won't, Dougal, because you're very, very *wrong*. Did the picture of the dog on the packet not give you any sort of clue? Why do you think he's looking so happy? He's looking happy because someone got him a yellow rubber telephone that makes a noise.

DOUGAL: No, no, he's . . . he's laughing because someone's trying to make a phonecall on the telephone.

TED: No, Dougal . . . dogs don't have that kind of a sense of humour. They're not as advanced as us. I wish you'd spend your money sensibly. I mean, look at this, for example . . .

He takes out a bag and reveals what's inside. It is a little box with a model golfer on top. He is addressing a ball a couple of centimetres from a flag with '13' on it. It is incredibly garish.

TED: Put a coin in there, Dougal.

Dougal takes a coin from his pocket and puts it into a slot in the box. A little Virgin Mary pops up from a tiny flap in front of the hole.

DOUGAL: That is *fantastic!* What is it? A little money-box.

TED: Yes. God, it'd be easy to make something like this look cheap and tacky, but look at it there. Pure class.

DOUGAL: You're right there, Ted.

Ted tries to push the little Virgin Mary back into the flap and the whole thing falls apart in his hands.

DOUGAL: Thing broke there, Ted.

Ted stares at the thing in disbelief. Another rolled-up piece of paper hits him on the back of the head. He turns, and we see the same line-up as before – the innocent priests, the smiling priest with the shades and the two nuns.

TED: All right, now, come on! A joke's a joke!

The plane starts rumbling.

DOUGAL: Here we go!

TED: Oh, God!

DOUGAL: What's up with you, Ted?

TED: Ah, it's just the tension of taking off. I'll be OK in a minute.

He closes his eyes tight and grips the edge of his seat.

DOUGAL: It'd be terrible to be killed in a plane crash, wouldn't it, Ted?

TED: Yes.

DOUGAL: God, or if you just somehow fell out of a plane. Like if the floor just disappeared from under you and you just fell. I mean, you'd be falling for ages and ages and ages and ages and ages. And you'd be screaming your head off.

As Dougal is saying all the above, Ted bends down to take something out of his bag. He picks up the dog toy and squeezes it a couple of times so that it makes a squeaking noise. Dougal immediately shuts up and watches it intently, a dog-like expression on his face – in fact, it is an exact copy of the expression last seen on the dog's face on the packet. Fade out.

SCENE 3 INT./DAY 1
SET: PLANE
We see Dougal and Ted. Ted is reading the Michael Barrymore biography. Ted can't concentrate,

though. He shifts about, looking very nervous.

DOUGAL: Feeling a bit better, Ted?

TED: Not really, Dougal, no. I tell you what, maybe I'll give Larry Duff a call. He developed a fear of flying after all those crashes he was in, so he went to a hypnotherapist to cure it. Told me to give him a call whenever I'm feeling a bit nervous.

Ted picks up Dougal's dog toy and presses some 'buttons'. It squeaks noisily.

DOUGAL (*pointing*): Ahhhhhhhhhhh!!!!!!!!!! Ha, ha, ha!!!!!!

TED: Oh, for God's sake.

He reaches down and finds the real telephone, then starts dialling. Dougal continues laughing. The plane judders slightly.

TED: Ahhh!!!!! What was that?

DOUGAL: Just a bit of turbulence, Ted.

TED: Oh, right . . . right . . . God, I wish I wasn't so nervous. Larry told me once you have more chance of being trampled by a herd of stampeding donkeys than you do of being killed in a plane crash.

SCENE 4 EXT./DAY 1
SET: A FIELD
We see a sign that reads 'Glasrowan Donkey Derby'. We hear the 'bleep bleep' of a mobile phone. We also hear a diminishing rumbling sound. The camera slowly moves down and we see the mobile phone some distance away from a muddied hand. There are hoofprints all over the ground. Pull back to reveal that the hand belongs to Larry, groaning in pain, moving his hand uselessly towards the mobile phone. The rumbling sound gets louder again.

LARRY (*holding his head up to see*): Oh, God, no! Not again!

SCENE 5 INT./DAY 1
SET: PLANE
Ted turns off the telephone.

TED: Funny. He's not picking up.

Down the corridor come Father Noel Furlong and Father Fintan Fay. Noel looks his usual spritely

self and Fintan, as usual, holds on to his hand and walks like a monkey.*

NOEL: Ted!!!

TED: Ah, hello, Noel. Father Fay. How are you?

FINTAN (*pointing at Ted's book*): Oooh, ooh, ahh, eek, ooh . . . Ahhh . . .

TED: Ah, yes! It's very good, actually.

FINTAN: Oooh, ahh, eeh, eek, ook . . .

TED: Oh, yes, I'm a big fan, all right. Or should I say 'Awright!'?

FINTAN: Oook, eek, aaak, oowk, eek . . .

TED: No mention of it so far, no.

FINTAN: Ahh . . .

NOEL: Oh, God, Ted, he has me driven mad. He wants me to bring him up to see the cockpit.

FINTAN (*jumping up and down*): OOOOOH!!!!! OOOOOHHH!!!!

DOUGAL: The cockpit! Ted? Ted, can I have a look, too?

TED: Well, I'm not sure . . .

NOEL (*noticing something*): Oh, God, what's he up to now?! You're a mad priest!

We see Fintan. He has managed to locate a red uninflated life-jacket and is wearing it. It suddenly inflates and he falls over. He blows the whistle on the life-jacket loudly. Noel takes it off him.

NOEL: Oh, God, look, he's going mad with the excitement. I'd better go. Dougal, you might as well come with us.

DOUGAL: Great!

Ted stands up to let Dougal pass. Dougal moves out of shot with Fay and Noel. Ted shouts after them.

TED: Dougal, don't touch anything! We don't want an action replay of the Sealink incident.

DOUGAL (*calling back*): Fair enough, Ted!

SCENE 6 INT./DAY 1
SET: COCKPIT
Fintan, Noel and Dougal enter the cockpit. Inside

there is a pilot.

PILOT: Ah, there you are, Father. You wanted the official tour!

NOEL: Oh, God, yes. It's all he's been talking about all day.

FINTAN: Oooogh, aaggh, eeegghhh!!

NOEL: Y'see? Will you calm down, you little monkey-man!

PILOT: Well, basically, these are the main controls. Over here you have the meters for engines one, two and three . . .

Dougal turns to his side and sees a big red button. Over it are written the words 'Do Not Press'. Dougal's eyes widen. The camera gets closer and closer to the button as we keep cutting to Dougal's sweating face. The sound of his heartbeat fills the soundtrack. Finally, the camera is on top of the button. Dougal's heartbeat is deafening.

PILOT: Father?

DOUGAL: What?! What! I wasn't going to press it!

PILOT: Sorry? I was just asking, have you ever been in a cockpit before?

DOUGAL: No, but I was on the bridge of a Sealink ferry once. It's funny, but I was there and I—

Noel coughs ostentatiously, giving Dougal a meaningful look. Dougal seems to understand.

DOUGAL: It was very interesting.

SCENE 7 INT./DAY 1
SET: PLANE
Ted is trying to get to sleep. Another rolled-up piece of paper hits him on the back of the head.

TED: Right! That's it!

He stands up and walks to the back of the plane. He walks straight up to the priest with the oval shades, who's laughing his head off.

TED: What's so funny? What's so funny? Hey, come on now, the joke's over!

He pushes the priest slightly. The priest takes off a pair of earphones and looks up in Ted's general direction.

SHIFTY: Wh— who's there?

TED: What do you mean, who's there? Are you blind? I'm the man you've been pelting with rolled-up pieces of paper for the whole journey!

SHIFTY: But I haven't.

TED: What's so funny, then? What's the big laugh?

SHIFTY (*indicates his earphones*): I was listening to comedy on these. It's *Mr Bean.*

TED (*takes this in*): Oh, right.

SHIFTY: And, yes, I am blind, as a matter of fact.

TED: Is it since birth or a more recent thing?

SHIFTY: Since birth.

TED: Really? Oh, that's . . . very interesting . . . I suppose your other senses make up for it. I hear that sometimes, with blind people, their other senses become more alert. So to speak. I suppose you can smell things from up to ten miles away. And hear things before they happen.

SHIFTY: No.

TED: No sixth sense of any kind? Although with you I suppose it'd be a fifth sense, 'cause you've only got the four. Unless you've got another one missing I don't know about! How about sense of touch? That OK?

Ted playfully touches the by-now-quite-nervous man on the shoulder. The man doesn't respond.

TED: Ha! Ha!

He pats the man on the shoulder again and then

slaps his knee gently a few times. Pause.

SHIFTY: Could you please go away now?

TED: Yes, I'll . . . I'll do just that.

He starts to move off, looking mortified with embarrassment. Another piece of paper hits him on the back of the head. He turns around and we see the two nuns, who until now have been incredibly serene, laughing like two haggard old witches.

NUN: Ha, haaaa!!!!

Ted looks at them in horror.

SCENE 8 INT./DAY 1
SET: COCKPIT
Noel, Fintan and Dougal are still with the pilot. Dougal is staring intently at the 'Do Not Press' button.

NOEL: He's a great laugh, isn't he? Will you not calm down, you big ninny?

FAY: OOOOOH! EEEEEK!!!!

NOEL (*to Fintan*): Come on, now. We'll head back. Say thank you to Mr Pilot!

FAY: OOGH! AAAGGH! EEEGH!

He tries to lead Fintan out of the cabin. As Fintan is led out, he sees his reflection in one of the instrument panels. He goes mad and starts jumping around.

NOEL: Oh, God, he must have seen his reflection!!!!!

PILOT: What?

NOEL: He's not supposed to see his reflection! He doesn't know he's a priest!

Fintan goes mad. He storms around the cockpit, pressing buttons and shouting wildly.

PILOT: Come on now, Father. Settle down now!

Fintan finally grabs on to the pilot's head, putting his hands over the pilot's eyes.

PILOT: Get him off me! I can't see!

Noel tries to prise Fintan loose. Chaos. The pilot finally manages to shout . . .

PILOT: FATHER MCGUIRE! FATHER, PRESS THE EMERGENCY BUTTON!

Dougal, who has been staring at the 'Do Not Press' button in a reverie, finally notices the fracas.

DOUGAL: What?

PILOT: The emergency button! The emergency button!

We see a very clearly marked button with 'emergency' written above it. It is beside the button with 'Do Not Press' on it.

DOUGAL: What does it look like?

PILOT: The one with 'emergency' written over it!

Dougal looks at the buttons, puzzled.

END OF PART ONE

* * *

PART TWO

SCENE 9 INT./DAY 1
SET: PLANE
Ted is sitting down, his teeth gritted as another rolled-up paper ball hits him on the back of the head. Then another. Then another. Then another. Then another.

TED: Right!

He stands up and marches towards the two nuns, looking very determined indeed. When he reaches them, the big nun stands up. She is huge, unable even to stand up straight in the plane. Ted walks

straight past them and towards the toilets.

TED (*to himself*): Ahh, just go to the old toilet.

SCENE 10 INT./DAY 1
SET: TOILET
Close-up of the toilet door. A bolt slides, it opens in the usual folding way, and Ted steps in. He stops short, looking confused. Cut to reveal that the 'cubicle' is the size of, say, a small bedroom, with the toilet in the other corner. It is very clean and white. Beside the toilet stands an attendant, very well dressed.

TED: Ah . . . sorry, is this the toilet?

ATTENDANT: First-class toilet, Sir. Do you have a first-class ticket?

TED: Ah, no . . .

ATTENDANT: Then I'm afraid you have to go across the way.

Ted mouths an 'oh . . .' and starts to leave.

SCENE 11 INT./DAY 1
SET: PLANE
Dougal walks out of the cockpit. We see a brief glimpse of the chaos within as the door opens and closes. He walks to the seat, sees that Ted isn't there, and walks to the toilets. He sees two doors side by side. He knocks on one.

DOUGAL: Ah, Ted?

SCENE 12 INT./DAY 1
SET: ANOTHER TOILET
This toilet is so small that Ted has to assume a sort of question-mark shape in order to fit in it. He looks massively uncomfortable. He is trying to do up his belt.

TED (*generally annoyed*): What?

DOUGAL: Can I have a quick word, Ted?

TED: Oh, yes . . . yes . . .

He tries to wash his hands in the sink sticking into his back but only gets some water on his shoes. He gives up and tries to come out. It takes an age of pushing and pulling before he finally tumbles out.

TED: God almighty . . . What's wrong with you, Dougal?

DOUGAL: Slight problem, Ted.

TED: What?

DOUGAL: Well, apparently, someone, ah . . . someone pressed a button in the cockpit that, ah . . . It was something to do with the fuel, I think. I think the person might have emptied one of the fuel tanks by mistake. Anyway, it means that there's not enough fuel to make it to the airport.

TED: Right, so that would mean, what? An emergency landing or something?

DOUGAL: Yeah. An emergency landing.

TED: Right.

DOUGAL: But the thing is, we don't have enough fuel to get somewhere where we can make an emergency landing. Also, there's only two parachutes on board . . .

TED: Wait a second, before you go on. What did you say this film was called again?

DOUGAL: Eh, no, it's not a film.

TED: It's not a film?

DOUGAL: No.

TED: Right. So, this is actually happening.

DOUGAL: Yes.

TED: This is actually happening now. To us.

DOUGAL: Eh . . . it is, yeah.

TED: Right. This is just a mad guess out of the blue here, but did you press the button?

DOUGAL (*aghast*): Ah, now, Ted, come on!

TED: Did you, Dougal?

DOUGAL: Yes.

SCENE 13 INT./DAY 1
SET: COCKPIT
Ted bursts in, followed by Dougal. Fintan has been blindfolded, and stands quite calmly in one corner of the cockpit.

NOEL: Hello, Ted! Have you heard the news?

TED: Yes, Noel. (*To the pilot.*) Has anyone pressed this button?

Ted points at the 'emergency' button.

PILOT: No.

TED: Well, shouldn't someone give it a go?

DOUGAL: Careful, Ted. There might be a fine for improper use.

TED: Dougal, this is *definitely* an emergency!!! I think basically the most important thing is to keep the other priests calm. Not a word of this when we get back inside.

He presses the button.

SCENE 14 INT./DAY 1
SET: PLANE
At the front of the plane, a sign with 'emergency' written on it in red starts flashing on and off. An electronic voice says 'Emergency, Emergency, Emergency' accompanied by a repetitive buzzing noise. The priests look panicky.

SCENE 15 INT./DAY 1
SET: COCKPIT
Ted looks at the button.

TED: Nothing happened. What does it do, exactly?

PILOT (*shrugging*): Never needed it before. Father, who gets the parachutes?

TED: God, yes, it's a tough decision.

DOUGAL: Oh, you're right there, Ted. Maybe we should just not tell anyone about them. Throw them off the plane, pretend they never existed.

TED: No . . . I don't think we should do that. I've got a better idea . . .

The camera zooms slowly in on Ted, accompanied by music, as he smiles and nods. It zooms out again.

TED: Right . . . here's my idea . . . Basically, what we should do is this . . .

SCENE 16 INT./DAY 1
SET: PLANE
We see Ted at the top of the aisle. He has a pen and a piece of paper in his hand. Everyone else has a pen and a piece of paper as well.

TED: . . . So, no more than two hundred words on why you think you should get a parachute.

Father Joe Briefly puts his hand up.

JOE: So we should just write how great we are?

TED: Yes.

Father O'Shea puts his hand up.

O'SHEA: I got my housekeeper pregnant a couple of years ago and forced her to leave the country. Should I mention that?

TED: No, I wouldn't . . .

Joe puts his hand up again.

JOE: Are you going to take marks away for spelling mistakes?

TED: No. Only if we end up in a tie-break situation.

O'Shea raises his hand again.

O'SHEA: Who'll own the copyright on this?

TED: What?

O'SHEA: Say if I survived and I wanted to write a newspaper article or a book about this – could I use extracts from this thing I'm going to write or would you own the copyright on it?

TED: As far as I know, you own the copyright. But frankly, I think the chances of us surviving are very, very low.

O'SHEA: Oh, right.

GALLAGHER: Should we not just have a bit of an oul pray? Maybe God will help us in some way.

This results in a slightly uncomfortable silence as the priests look around in embarrassment.

TED: Aaaaanyway, we should start writing. Everyone has pens and everything?

O'SHEA: Can I use my laptop computer?

TED: Well, I don't think you're allowed to use them on planes. Aren't they dangerous or something? I think it might interfere with the radar . . .

O'SHEA: Yes, but we're going to crash anyway.

TED: Right, I see what you mean. Yes, go ahead and use it.

Ted resumes his seat. Everyone starts writing. There is a serious atmosphere, as in a schoolroom during an exam. While everyone is preoccupied with their essays, we see Jack calmly walking down the aisle with two parachutes. He goes out of shot.

DOUGAL: Ted, you're very calm about all this. Have you gone mad or something?

TED: It's just . . . I've always hated flying, but now we're in an emergency situation, the fear just seems to have transformed itself into affirmative action. You know what I mean?

DOUGAL: I do, Ted.

TED: Do you?

DOUGAL: No.

TED: Well, never mind. Right! (*Ted stops writing and stands up.*) Put your pens down, please.

The priests do so, except for O'Shea, who is still tapping away on his laptop.

TED: Father O'Shea? You didn't stop writing so I'm afraid you're disqualified.

O'SHEA: What? Awww . . .

He slams down the lid of his laptop and goes into a sulk.

TED: Father Cave, do you want to go first?

Father Cave stands up.

CAVE: I haven't written this down because . . . because it comes from the heart. (*He turns to the priest next to him.*) Father Gallagher. I've worked with you and been your friend for a long time, and now . . . I think it's important to say I love you. I love you like I've loved nobody else. (*Pause.*) I don't want the parachute! Give it to him!

He bursts into tears and sits down. Father Gallagher looks very embarrassed.

TED: Right . . . well done, Father Cave. Eh, Father Fay?

FINTAN (*looks at his paper*): OOK, EEK, OOOH, OOOH, AHK, AHK!!!!

Pause. Then everyone mumbles in an impressed way.

TED (*impressed*): Well, beat that . . . Joe?

JOE: I think I should get the parachute because I am great. In fact, I think I should get both the parachutes in case one of them doesn't work.

The other priests don't like this. They inhale disapprovingly.

TED: Not a popular one there, Joe. Father Flynn, what did you write?

FLYNN: I didn't write anything, because I'm not very good at that type of thing, but I did a drawing.

TED: Did you? Well, let's have a look.

Flynn stands up and shows a quite accomplished drawing of himself, completely naked with a dog on a lead. He has drawn it so that his back is to the viewer, so we can see his bottom in the drawing. He looks at the viewer with one hand over his mouth in an 'I'm being naughty' gesture.

FLYNN: What do you think?

TED: Well . . .

FLYNN: It's me in the nip! With a dog!

TED: How . . . how does that help you win the parachute?

FLYNN: What do you mean, parachute? I wasn't really listening at the start there. Why would I need a parachute?

TED: The plane's in trouble. This is a competition to see who gets a parachute.

FLYNN: Oh . . .

He looks at the drawing. He seems embarrassed. He folds the drawing away discreetly and sits down without saying another word.

TED: Okay, Father Jack, you next . . . Father Jack? Where's Father Jack?

O'SHEA: The parachutes!!! The parachutes have gone!!!

SCENE 17 INT./DAY 1
SET: DOORWAY
We see Jack standing by the open doorway. We hear the roar of the wind going by. Jack attaches one parachute to a drinks trolley and pushes it out through the doorway. Then he jumps out.

JACK: DRIIIIIIiiiiinnnnnkkkkkkk!!!!!!!!!!

SCENE 18 INT./DAY 1
SET: PLANE
Fade up. Everyone looks annoyed. Dougal wakes up from a nap, looking happy, then he frowns and 'tsks' loudly.

DOUGAL (*put out*): Awww . . . I just remembered that we're all going to die.

TED: Dougal, I just wanted to say . . . I know sometimes I'm a little short with you, sometimes I'm not as patient as I should be, but I just want you to know . . . in the end, we're the best of friends.

Pause.

DOUGAL: I don't understand.

TED: Well, I'm just saying that even though I might act like you get on my nerves, I suppose I secretly think it's quite funny.

DOUGAL: What is?

TED: You know . . . the way you mix things up sometimes and don't really get what's going on.

DOUGAL (*frowns*): Who are you talking about?

TED: You.

DOUGAL (*waits for more*): What about me?

TED: I'm just saying I like you, Dougal.

DOUGAL: Ah, but sometimes I get on your nerves.

TED: I know! I said that!

DOUGAL: Did you?

TED: Yes!

DOUGAL: Thanks very much. Who were you saying that to?

TED: YOU! I JUST SAID IT THERE!

Long pause.

DOUGAL (*looks around*): Hey! We're on a plane!

Ted has to rest his brain for a moment. The pilot rushes in and goes up to Ted.

PILOT: Father, do you know what a Section Tubing Stabilising Dart is?

TED: No.

PILOT: Do you know what a Shell Diversifier ER 20 is?

TED: No.

PILOT: Have you ever used a Jet Wrench Three-ply Shortstick?

TED: No.

PILOT: If you had a choice between two Oxygen Discharge Multi-enforcers – a 751 and a 98 Sten Magnet – which one would you choose?

TED: I don't know.

PILOT: Do you know who I am?

TED: You're the pilot.

PILOT: Great. I know what I did there, I started too big. Do you know what a fuel reserve is?

TED: Well, I imagine it's some sort of back-up to the main fuel tanks.

PILOT: That's exactly what it is. Well . . . we have a fuel reserve, but the line connecting it to the . . . ah, the thing at the front.

TED: The engine.

PILOT: The engine, yeah . . . that line is broken. The thing is . . . if we could somehow fix that line . . . we might have a chance. Even sticky tape would do, but I've asked around and there's none on the plane.

TED: That's where you're wrong! Dougal, give me that thing you bought. (*Dougal gives Ted the yellow telephone.*) This is the answer to all our problems.

PILOT: You shouldn't make any calls, Father. It interferes with radar—

TED (*throwing the telephone at Dougal*)**:** The sticky-tape dispenser!

Dougal hands it to him.

PILOT: Brilliant! So all you have to do is get out of the plane, climb out on to the wheel so that you're under the fuselage, and attach the line!

TED: And we'll be saved.

PILOT: Yes!

TED: Great! So all I have to do is climb out of the plane . . . hang on.

PILOT: What?

TED: I have to get out of the plane, then climb under it?

PILOT: Yes. There's really no one else I'd trust, Father. You've already proved you can keep a level head . . .

TED (*beat*): Then . . . I'll do it!!!

DOUGAL: But Ted—

TED: Dougal, I told you, this has brought out a new side of me. I love all this! When everything's going OK, I just keep imagining all the terrible things that can happen, but when one of those things actually happens, it's just a rush! I am fearless. Like that film with Jeff Bridges.

DOUGAL: I haven't seen that one.

TED: Not a lot of people have, Dougal, so it's probably a bad reference. Anyway, let's go, Captain!

PILOT: I'm not a captain.

TED: And I'm not a person who goes under planes to fix fuel lines! I think from now on, we're anything we want to be!

Big close-up of their hands as they shake them in a manly way. Dougal looks at them.

DOUGAL (*puzzled*): Can I still be a priest?

SCENE 19 INT./DAY 1
SET: DOORWAY
Ted is sitting with his legs dangling down a square hole in the floor. The pilot and Dougal look at him with admiration and concern.

PILOT: You're a very brave man, Father.

TED: I'm just doing a job. Dougal . . . hand me the sticky tape!

PILOT: I'd better get back to the cockpit. Good luck, Father Ted!

Dougal hands him the tape. Ted disappears down the hole. There is a pause. We hear tape being pulled out.

DISPENSER (*offscreen*): You have used three inches of tape. God bless you.

Another strip is pulled out.

DISPENSER: You have used four inches of tape. God bless you.

Another.

DISPENSER: You have used two and a half inches of tape. God bless you.

Another.

DISPENSER: You have used three and a half inches of tape. God bless you.

TED (*offscreen*): To be honest with you, Dougal, I can see how this might get a little annoying.

DISPENSER: You have used two inches of tape. God bless you.

TED: Ahh, shut up. Wait, I think . . . Yes! I've done it! Dougal, the line's sealed up! We're saved!

DOUGAL: Great!

TED: Everything's OK! We're going to live!

DOUGAL: Everything's completely back to normal, Ted! It's just a completely average, day-to-day, common-or-garden airplane journey.

Pause.

TED: Aaaaaaaaaaaaaggggggghhhhhhhhhhh!!!!!
WHAT AM I DOING ON THE FECKIN'
WHEEL? Aaaaaaaaaagggggggghhhhhhhh!!!!!!!!!!

Dougal looks worried.

SCENE 20 INT./DAY 1
SET: PAROCHIAL HOUSE
Dougal is on the telephone.

DOUGAL: Oh, right. Oh, right, thanks a lot.

He puts the telephone down. Mrs Doyle comes in.

DOUGAL: Still no sign of Father Jack, Mrs
Doyle.

MRS DOYLE: Oh, I hope he's all right. And
Father Crilly . . . I really hate seeing him like
this.

DOUGAL: Well, he's starting to loosen his
grip. I'd say he'd be down in about a week.

*Cut to reveal Ted, still gripping tightly on to the
shaft above a massive airplane wheel, which takes
up almost half of the room. He is gripping on to it
with all his might. His face is frozen in an
expression of pure horror. His hair is standing on
end.*

MRS DOYLE: Anyway, how would you like
a sandwich? I've cut it into the shape of an
airplane.

We see that she has indeed.

DOUGAL: No, thanks, Mrs Doyle. I think
Ted and I have had enough of planes to last

us a lifetime! Ha, ha, ha? Haven't we, Ted?

*Shot of an unresponsive Ted. Dougal shuts up and
eats his sandwich. Roll closing credits.*

POST-CREDIT SEQUENCE:
SCENE 21 EXT./DAY 1
SET: FIELD
*As the credits roll, we see Jack stuck up a tree,
entangled in his parachute. Nearby, just out of
reach, is the drinks trolley dangling from the other
parachute. There are no other trees for miles
around. Jack vainly struggles to reach out to the
drinks trolley.*

SCENE 22 INT./DAY 1
SET: PLANE
*Back on the plane, the pilot's voice comes over the
intercom.*

PILOT: This is your pilot speaking. The
emergency is over. We will be landing in
twenty minutes.

*Everyone cheers. We cut to Cave and Gallagher.
They cheer, but then something hits them. They sit
down, looking very embarrassed. One of them
starts whistling.*

THE END

a christmassy ted

GRAHAM: We wanted to put back the writing of Series Three for a while, so we suggested writing a Christmas Special as a stopgap, thinking it'd be easier. We were *waaaaaaaaay* off. This was infinitely harder to write than any other episode. It took forever to sort out and, to be perfectly honest, I think that comes across in the sprawling plot. Christmas Specials are dangerous anyway; by definition they have to revolve around Christmas, therefore losing an element of spontaneity, and they're invariably longer than normal episodes. That, I think, was the major problem here: we stretched the mad elastic of Craggy Island beyond sustainability. I even remember that it ran over time by four minutes and we begged Channel 4 to let us keep the extra time. Now I wish we hadn't.

However, it does have moments that, on reflection, are among the best in *Father Ted*. (I heard that a pregnant woman went into labour because she laughed so much at Mrs Doyle falling off the windowsill . . . at least, I assume she was pregnant.) But they're moments which would have been used better had they been peppered across a whole series, rather than packed willy-nilly into the one show.

ARTHUR: I think Graham's too hard on this one. I quite liked it at the time, and so did a lot of other people. Ratings-wise, it was a highly successful episode. Yet in hindsight there *is* a fairly fundamental flaw in the plot: to my mind it reads like two episodes strung together. We never made a proper, convincing connection between Christmas and the Golden Cleric Award that sends Ted into such a spin. The arrival of the mysterious Todd Unctuous, for instance, doesn't seem to belong in the same story as the priests in the lingerie section of the department store. No pun intended, but we *did* stretch the latter scene too far. Yet I liked the former, and especially Todd's *Mission:Impossible*-style attempts to steal Ted's Golden Cleric Award. When in doubt, use a film reference . . . (We should have put the *Mission Impossible* theme music to the scene.)

David Renwick, who writes *One Foot in the Grave*, really knows how to extend a show beyond the half-hour format – his Christmas Specials are tightly plotted and brilliantly sustained. I wonder if it's more possible to do that when the comedy is set within the real world . . . Perhaps Craggy Island is just too mad and too surreal to handle an hour of comedy.

PART ONE

SCENE 1 INT./DAY X
SET: BALLYKISSANGEL BAR
We see Ted sitting at a bar, flooded with sunlight. He finishes a drink.

TED: You know, I've been doing a lot of thinking recently and . . . well, I just don't think I'm cut out for the priesthood . . . I think it's time you and I faced facts.

Cut to reveal Assumpta – Dervla Kirwan – from 'Ballykissangel', sitting behind the bar.

ASSUMPTA: But Father, you're one of the best priests in the country, if not *the* best.

TED (*shakes his head*): Assumpta, Assumpta, Assumpta . . . why are we running from this? You know what I'm talking about, don't you?

ASSUMPTA: Yes, I . . . I suppose I do.

OFFSCREEN VOICE: I'll be off, then. (*Cut to reveal Father Clifford – Stephen Tompkinson – standing at the door with loads of bags.*) I said I'll . . .

TED: Yeah, yeah . . . bye.

ASSUMPTA: Bye.

He leaves, looking sad.

ASSUMPTA: C'mere you . . .

Ted leans forward. They are about to kiss when we cut to . . .

SCENE 2 INT./NIGHT 1
SET: BEDROOM
Ted, a smile on his face, is being shaken awake by Dougal.

DOUGAL: Ted, Ted . . .

TED: What? What is it?

DOUGAL: Would you like a peanut?

He is holding out an open bag of peanuts.

TED: A peanut? You woke me to offer me a peanut? God, Dougal!!

DOUGAL: Oh. Sorry, Ted.

TED: Go to bed! (*Dougal moves off.*) Now . . . where were we?

He falls asleep again with a smile.

SCENE 3 EXT./DAY X
SET: FIELD HILLTOP
Ted is running through a dark place, chased by three giant peanuts with legs. He is terrified.

SCENE 4 INT./NIGHT 2
SET: PAROCHIAL HOUSE
Dougal is standing beside a large Christmas tree. Ted is lying down underneath it, only his legs visible. Mrs Doyle is putting up Christmas decorations over the window. Jack is asleep in his chair.

TED: OK, here we go. One, two, three!

The tree lights come on.

DOUGAL: Yay!

TED: They on?

DOUGAL: They are, Ted. (*The lights go off.*) Oh, wait now.

TED: What?

DOUGAL: They've gone off again.

TED: Tsk . . . how about now?

DOUGAL: No – yes! They're on! Oh. No, Ted, they've gone aga— There you go! They're back, Ted! Keep doing whatever you're — Oh, wait, they're gone.

Ted is now standing beside Dougal; although Dougal hasn't noticed.

DOUGAL: That's it, Ted! Keep it like that for just a — Dohhh!!! Gone again! Back! Gone! Back! Gone! Back! Gone! Back! Gone!

TED: Dougal . . . you go and sit down. They're supposed to do that.

DOUGAL: Oh, right. Ah, can I open another

window on the Advent calendar first?

TED: All right, then. But remember, you're just allowed to open today's window.

DOUGAL: Great! (*He goes to the calendar and opens a window. It is a little shepherd.*) Brilliant! . . . A shepherd! Fantastic stuff! Oh, God, can I not open the other two?

TED: No, Dougal.

DOUGAL: God, I can't wait to find out what's behind tomorrow's one! I bet it's a donkey or something!

TED: So you've changed from your initial prediction. What was it? Ruud Gullit sitting on a shed.

DOUGAL: Heh . . . yeah . . .

TED: Where do you *get* these things? Do you know what, I'd say it's probably just a lovely angel. (*Turning to Jack, very friendly.*) What would you say is behind tomorrow's window, Father Jack?

JACK: A pair of feckin' women's knickers!

TED: Yes, well . . . who knows?

JACK: Knickers!

TED: Yes, father.

JACK: WOMEN'S KNICKERS!

TED: Yes, Father, yes, message understood. God almighty . . . Dougal, leave the calendar until tomorrow.

Dougal guiltily retreats from the calendar, picks up a 'Shoot' annual and starts reading. Cut to Mrs Doyle. She finishes putting the decorations over the window.

MRS DOYLE: There!

She turns around to step carefully down off the ledge, loses her balance and falls out of shot.

TED: Ah, dear. Another year gone – it's hard to believe, isn't it? (*He sighs.*) What's it all about, Dougal?

DOUGAL (*looks at the annual*): Well, it doesn't really have a story, Ted. It's just football and stuff.

TED: No, Dougal, I mean life. I mean, you slave away attending to the needs of your parishioners and what does it get you? A one-

way ticket to palookaville. (*He pauses and sighs.*) You know, I looked in the mirror this morning and I saw a middle-aged, grey-haired man staring back at me.

Long pause. Long, long pause. Stay on Dougal. Finally . . .

DOUGAL: Who was that, Ted?

TED: Me, Dougal.

DOUGAL: Oh, yes, of course.

TED: It's just, I had a postcard from Father Jez Flahavan yesterday. He's in Montana. He makes fifty thousand dollars a year and another two thousand in tips.

DOUGAL: Brilliant. How does he manage that?

TED: I don't know . . . lap dancing or something . . . And Father Buzz Dolan in Canada. He has his own show on cable. And I heard he's landed a bit part in the new Bond movie. It all started when he won that Golden Cleric award.

DOUGAL: Wow!!!

TED: God, it'd be great to be famous. Do you know what I'd love about being famous? People listen to you, they listen to what you have to say. And I've got a lot to say.

DOUGAL: What about when you're doing your sermons? People listen to you then, don't they?

TED: No, Dougal, I mean people I *respect*. I suppose the main thing I'd like . . .

DOUGAL (*talking over Ted's line*): God, I hope there's a good film on Christmas day.

TED (*simultaneous with Dougal's line*): . . . Would be to give a big speech . . . You just talked over me there. Even you don't listen to me.

DOUGAL: Ah, I do, Ted, that's not fair.

TED (*simultaneous*): Well, I don't know, it seemed to me that you just . . .

DOUGAL (*simultaneous with Ted*): Anyway, I suppose I should go and feed Sampras . . .

TED (*simultaneous*): . . . Completely ignored what I was saying there . . .

DOUGAL (*simultaneous*): . . . He's been looking

a bit sick recently, I suppose . . .

TED (*simultaneous*): . . . And just started on a completely unrelated topic . . .

DOUGAL (*simultaneous*): . . . He's just a bit homesick for the old warren.

Dougal walks away while Ted is in mid-sentence. Mrs Doyle has righted herself. She pats her hair into place.

MRS DOYLE: So, Father, you looking forward to Christmas?

TED: Oh, I am indeed, Mrs Doyle. A nice, quiet Christmas, that's what I want. A nice, quiet Christmas with no unusual incidents or strange people turning up. That would suit me down to the ground. A nice, quiet, everyday, normal Christmas.

Pause. Everyone just stands around, looking at each other. After a moment, the doorbell rings.

TED: Oh! There's the door.

Ted leaves the room.

SCENE 5 INT./NIGHT 2
SET: PAROCHIAL HOUSE HALLWAY
Ted opens the front door. On the ground, we see a baby in a little cot. There is wistful music. Ted gasps. He looks around and can't see anybody else. He bends down to pick the baby up, but a woman suddenly appears.

WOMAN: I'm sorry. Er, is this Mrs Reilly's house?

She picks up the baby.

TED: No. That's er, just down the road.

WOMAN: Oh. Thanks very much.

She walks away. Ted closes the door.

SCENE 6 INT./NIGHT 2
SET: PAROCHIAL HOUSE
Ted comes back into the living room.

DOUGAL: Who was that, Ted?

TED: Oh, someone looking for Reilly's. She had a baby. For a second I thought someone had just left it on the doorstep.

DOUGAL: God, Ted, can you imagine what would have happened if she'd left it with us?!

TED: Hah, yes, we'd have been trying to look after it and everything, and getting into all sorts of hilarious jams. The whole thing would have been very, very, funny.

DOUGAL: Well, it wouldn't have been that funny, Ted.

TED: Actually . . . no.

SCENE 7 INT./DAY 3
SET: DEPARTMENT STORE
Mrs Doyle is standing beside a salesman. The salesman is demonstrating some kind of moulinex-type thing with 'teamaster' written on the side. He is chirpy.

SALESMAN: . . . and the liquids just come out here. You've already punched in your selection for sugar and milk, so all the work is taken out of it, leaving the modern woman plenty of time for running a business or skiing. With a simple turn of the switch, she can access coffee, hot chocolate or Horlicks. Takes all the misery out of making tea. What do you say to *that*?

Dramatic close-up of Mrs Doyle, her face set in a very tough, Clint Eastwood-type way.

MRS DOYLE: Maybe I *like* the misery.

The salesman's smile disappears.

SCENE 8 INT./DAY 3
SET: DEPARTMENT STORE
Ted and Dougal are walking through the shop. Ted is looking at his shopping list.

TED: I thought I'd buy some perfume for Mrs Doyle.

DOUGAL: Good idea, Ted. Perfume is the ideal 'woman' present, isn't it?

TED: Yessss. Well, that's why God invented perfume, so you don't have to put any thought into it whatsoever. Oh, where'd you manage to stick Jack in the end?

DOUGAL: Oh, they've got this great place, Ted, where you can put people who don't want to go shopping. They can just stay there and have a laugh.

TED: Really? I've never heard of that. Were there other people there?

DOUGAL: Oh, loads of people, Ted. He'll be fine.

They move out of shot.

SCENE 9 INT./DAY 3
SET: DEPARTMENT STORE/CRECHE
We see Jack sitting against a wall. There are about a dozen children in with him, playing with blocks and messing about. Jack smokes a fag and looks quite happy.

SCENE 10 INT./DAY 3
SET: DEPARTMENT STORE/LINGERIE
Dougal and Ted are still walking.

TED: Perfume . . . perfume.

DOUGAL: You think you'd be able to smell it. Ted . . . where exactly are we now?

TED: Well, we're in the . . . in the . . . (*Ted looks around, suddenly terrified.*) . . . Oh, my God.

Cut wide, a blast of very dramatic music, and we reveal a sign over their heads that reads 'lingerie'. Frilly feminine fancies surround them. Ted looks around, panicking slightly.

TED: We're in lingerie. Dougal, we're in lingerie.

DOUGAL: What's the problem there, Ted?

TED (*as he ushers Dougal along*): Well, think about it Dougal. Two priests hanging around near women's secret things. It just doesn't look good.

They start walking quickly.

TED: Where's the exit? Oh, God, look, we're in bras! (*Dougal looks around, wide-eyed.*) This way . . . oh, no, that's . . . more underpants! Why in God's name do they need so many kinds of underpants! What, do they parade around in them, looking in mirrors all the time?

Dougal thinks about this, drifting off. They round a corner and see two other priests looking at lingerie.

TED: Billy? Terry?

BILLY: Ted? Ted Crilly?

BOTH: How's it going? Hello, there . . .

TED: Good to see you both. This is Father Dougal McGuire.

BILLY: Hello, Father Dougal.

DOUGAL: Hello, Father Dougal!? . . . What?

TED: No, that's you, Dougal, You're Father Dougal.

DOUGAL: Oh, right.

TED: We got lost a bit in the store. That's how we ended up here. We got lost. I suppose that's what happened to you as well.

Billy and Terry exchange a glance.

BILLY: Hmmmm . . . ? Lost? Yeaaaahhhh, that's it.

TERRY (*simultaneous with Billy*): We got lost, that's it.

TED: I don't suppose you'd know the way out of here?

BILLY: Eh . . . this way?

TED: No, we just came that way.

TERRY: It's Ireland's biggest lingerie section, I understand.

TED: Really?

TERRY: Yes . . . I read that . . . somewhere . . .

TED: Well, I just think it'd be a good idea to get out as quickly as possible. Four priests hanging around the frillies section . . .

BILLY: Yes, I . . . I see what you mean.

TED: Let's try this way . . .

To dramatic music, they start walking through the aisles.

SCENE 11 INT./DAY 3
SET: DEPARTMENT STORE/CRECHE
Jack is idly playing with building blocks, still surrounded by kids. We can see that he has spelt out the words 'Feck', 'Arse', 'Drink' and 'Girls' with the blocks.

SCENE 12 INT./DAY 3
SET: DEPARTMENT STORE/LINGERIE
Back to our heroes. Everywhere they look, though, they just see more lingerie.

TED: Ohhh, wait a second, we've been here . . . I remember those bras the first time round.

DOUGAL: God, they all look the same to me.

TED: No, no. These ones have double padding and the black lace outline with the little cotton supports and the extra strength straps. If we pass by any bras with a middle arch support and single padding, along with a white lace outline, we'll know we're on the right track.

BILLY: Someone's coming!

TED: Damn!

Before they can bolt away, they see another four priests coming around the corner.

TED: Oh my God.

They walk up to the priests and exchange greetings, shaking hands in a military, manlike way. The new priests are Father Deegan, Father Cleary, Father Reilly and Father Fitzgerald.

TED: What happened to you?

CLEARY: We were looking for the toilets and we wandered in here by mistake. How do you get out? It's huge!

TERRY: It's Ireland's biggest lingerie section, I understand.

TED: All right. This is the situation. Eight priests wandering around a lingerie section. If it was just one or two of us, well, that'd be embarrassing, but with the eight of us . . . I think we're talking national scandal.

DEEGAN: What are we going to do? All the aisles look the same.

TED: It's no use panicking. We're in this thing, let's try and get out of it. Billy, you go on point. Father Cleary, Father Deegan, I want you at the back. All right, let's go. And keep it quiet.

SCENE 13 INT./DAY 3
SET: DEPARTMENT STORE/LINGERIE
Our heroes are walking through the aisles in a line, like a platoon of soldiers. They walk slowly, clutching their shopping to their chests. Close-ups on the sweating, nervous faces of all the priests in turn. One of them wipes his face with a white cloth, realises it's a pair of frilly underpants, and throws it away with a yelp. A muzak version of 'The End' by the Doors is coming through the department store speakers. After a moment or two of this, Billy, walking at the front, a cigarette dangling from his mouth, raises his finger in warning. They all hunker down and wait. Ted passes along the line.

TED (*to priests as he passes*)**:** You all right? Shaping up? Hang in there . . .

He gets to Billy.

TED: What is it?

BILLY: I thought I heard something. Maybe I'm just going crazy. I've been in this damn lingerie section so long . . .

TED: No, wait . . .

We hear a rustling sound. All the priests stay low and quiet, keeping their eyes on where the sound is coming from – a neighbouring aisle that runs parallel to their one. Through the lingerie, we see glimpses of some people walking along.

TED: I don't think they've seen us. Take a rest, Father. Father Reilly, you're on point.

He passes by one priest who is breathing heavily.

TED: Father Deegan, you all right?

DEEGAN: There's no way out! There's just no way out! They're gonna get us! They're gonna get us!

Ted grabs Deegan around the head and puts a hand over his mouth, muffling him. He looks over at the shapes of the two girls, who stop talking for a moment. Everything is very still. Then the girls continue talking and walk away.

TED: Damn it, Father Deegan!

DEEGAN: Sorry. I . . . I . . .

TED: We've been in tighter corners than this and we've always gotten out. Haven't we? *Haven't* we?

DEEGAN: I only left the seminary two weeks ago! If they find out, I'll never get a decent parish! They'll send me off to some bloody kip! What are we going to do!!!

TED: Father Deegan. I'll make you a promise. One day, you and I, we're gonna be sitting in your lovely, new parish, drinking iced tea on the lawn, and all this will be a memory. I want you to hold on to that thought. Can you do that for me?

Deegan swallows his tears and nods.

TED: Good man. All right.

Ted raises his finger and gestures for everyone to move. At the back of the line, there's a scream, and Father Cleary falls to the ground. Ted rushes back to Father Cleary.

TED: Father Cleary, what happened?

CLEARY: I was messing about with one of those bras, and the strap flew back and hit me in the eye. I . . . AAAhhh!! I think I've twisted my ankle as wel . . .

TED: All right. Father Deegan, Father Reilly, give Father Cleary a hand here.

CLEARY: No, it was my stupid fault for

messing with the bras. Leave me here, I'll only slow you down.

TED: Dammit, man, we're a team. We're sticking together.

Deegan and Reilly grab him and help him to walk. They turn a corner but Ted stops them and ducks back. He peers around the corner and we see an exit with 'Exit 4' written over it. There are a good few people looking through the shelves nearby.*

TED: It's the exit. God, look at all those people.

BILLY: They'd definitely see us coming out. Maybe if we actually buy some underpants, it won't look so strange.

TED: They're women's underpants!

BILLY: Oh, yes, sorry . . .

A voice comes over the tannoy.

VOICE (*very boring monotone*): Please visit our restaurant on the first floor where we have a beautiful selection of Christmas-style food and beverages.

Ted sees something. He goes over to a metal box-like thing on the wall. An idea hits him.

TED: C'mere.

Everyone groups around.

TED: Who's got the most boring voice?

BILLY: What?

TED: Of the lot of us, who's got the most boring voice?

FITZGERALD (*incredibly boring voice*): That'd be me, Ted . . .

Murmurs of agreement.

TED: Father! Listen to me.

FITZGERALD: I have an awful, dreary, monotonous voice, God help me . . .

TED: Yeah, yeah, listen . . .

REILLY (*exciting, dramatic voice*): Ted, did you say you wanted a dramatic, exciting voice?

FITZGERALD: No, he said 'boring'. He wanted a boring voice.

REILLY: Then you must excuse me for my

*We moved scene 14 to here in the final version. The rest of this scene became scene 14A.

impetuous interruption!

TED: Right, this is what I want you to do . . .

Ted starts whispering to Father Fitzgerald. Nearby, Dougal turns to Billy.

DOUGAL: What's goin' on?

TERRY: I think Ted has a plan.

DOUGAL: No, I mean in general.

TERRY: We can't find our way out of the lingerie section.

DOUGAL: Oh, right.

Back to Ted and Fitzgerald. The latter approaches the steel box-thingy and presses a button. He speaks into a microphone sticking out of it and his voice is relayed around the store on a tannoy.

FITZGERALD (*incredibly boring voice*): Ladies and gentlemen, could you please bring your purchases to the checkout as the store is about to close. Hurry up! Come on there! Hurry up will you!

We see people looking nervous and annoyed as the tannoy badgers them. One person walks back in the opposite direction to everyone else.

TED: Not that way, for feck's sake! The other way!

The person turns and walks back. Ted looks around the corner. The area around 'Exit 4' is now completely cleared, not a soul in sight. The priests cheer and hug each other.

Ted runs across to the doors and opens them – a huge wind blows through. One by one he pushes the priests out and into the wind.

TED: Go! Go! Go! Go! Go! Go! Go!

Cut to outside where the priests cheer and hug each other.

SCENE 14 INT./DAY 3
SET: DEPARTMENT STORE/CRECHE
Jack stands up and walks shakily to the door. He waves to the kids and staggers out. Pause. Slowly, one by one but soon developing into a chorus, the kids start talking.

KIDS: . . . feck . . . arse . . . feck . . . feckity, feck, feck, feck . . . arse . . . feckin' arse . . . (*Louder.*) . . . Feck . . . .ARSE . . . FECK . . . FECKING FECKING FECK!

SCENE 15 INT./DAY 4
SET: PAROCHIAL HOUSE
Dougal is opening another window on the Advent calendar. He looks hugely expectant. It's the Three Wise Men pointing at a star.

DOUGAL: Oh . . .

He is obviously hugely disappointed.

TED (*reading a newspaper*)**:** What's wrong, Dougal?

DOUGAL: It's just . . . three lads pointing at a star. That's a bit disappointing.

TED: Why?

DOUGAL: Well . . . what's that got to do with Christmas?

Ted closes the paper. We see the headline: 'Pope denies claims'.

TED: Well, there's nothing in the Catholic scandal supplement about the lingerie episode. I think we got away with it.

The telephone rings. After a while, Ted answers.

TED: Hello. Craggy Island Parochial House. Father Ted Crilly speaking.

Cut to a very posh room with a bishop on the other end of the line. We see a caption that reads 'The Vatican' at the bottom of the screen. In the background we see more bishops having a laugh and drinking cans of lager and wine bottles from the neck. They all look rather dishevelled. Party music plays.

BISHOP: Hello, Ted! Tom McCaskell here!

TED: Tom, how are ya? And *where* are you? You left in an awful hurry.

BISHOP: Ah, I'm in Rome.

TED: When will you be back?

BISHOP: When things have died down a bit. I might have to head off to South America for a while. You know she's going to write a bloody book about it?!

TED: Ah, now that's not fair.

BISHOP: Did they ever catch up with you about that Lourdes thing? It looked a bit dodgy there for . . .

TED: Ah, ah, let me stop you there, Tom, that money was just resting in my account . . .

DOUGAL: Oh, ho!

TED: Shut up, Dougal!

BISHOP: Anyway, Ted . . . we owe you a big favour for getting the lads out of trouble the other day. We'd like you to have a Golden Cleric!

TED: A Golden Cleric? You're not serious?

BISHOP: I'm deadly serious.

TED: Ahaaa!!! What . . . what can I say? God, I don't feel worthy. When I think of all the other priests who've won it.

BISHOP: Well, you . . .

A bishop sitting behind a massive drum kit starts whacking it.

BISHOP: Alberto! Alberto, please.

The drummer stops with an 'oops, sorry' face.

BISHOP: You deserve it. You managed to avert a tricky situation and prevent another scandal in the Church. Father Billy and the rest of the lads will drop the award over to you tomorrow.

TED: . . . And is there, sorry about this, but is there any kind of cash prize with that?

BISHOP: No.

TED: Oh.

BISHOP: Actually, Ted, I'm a *wee bit* disappointed you asked that. Just a *wee bit* disappointed. Did I teach you nothing?

Tom puts down the telephone and turns to the chaos. One bishop is starting to drink a pint in one go. Tom joins in with the others in clapping and cheering him on. The drummer joins in on the high-hat. Cut back to the Parochial House.

TED: Dougal, fantastic news! . . .

DOUGAL: You're getting married?

TED: What? No, of course I'm . . . Was that a joke?

DOUGAL: Er . . . yes . . .

TED: No, I've just been awarded a Golden Cleric!

DOUGAL: Hurray!

TED: Oh, God, I'll have to write a speech! Oh, it'll have to be brilliant. It's not every day you win an award.

JACK: Award!!!!

TED: No, Father, you can't have one.

JACK: Why not?!! Award! Award! Award! Award! Award!

TED: All right, Father, all right . . .

He goes to the mantelpiece and takes a teacup from it. He goes to Jack and presents it to him.

TED: There you go, Father.

JACK: Yes! Photo! Photo!

TED (*sighs*): Dougal, take a photograph.

Dougal gets a camera and points it at Ted and Jack. Jack shakes hands with Ted, the other hand holding the trophy. They both look at the camera, like politicians, and Dougal presses the button. Flash and freeze on this image of Jack and Ted. When we go back to normal, Ted takes the trophy and puts it back on the mantelpiece.

DOUGAL: Oh, Ted, can I stay up tomorrow night to watch the scary film?

TED: What? Oh, no, no. The last time you watched a scary film, you had to sleep in my bed. I wouldn't mind, but it wasn't even *that* scary a film.

DOUGAL: Ah, come on, Ted. A Volkswagen with a mind of its own driving all around the place going mad! If that's not scary, I don't know what is!

TED: Dougal, that's a children's film! If you can't deal with that, how on earth would you be able to take a film about a burglar creeping into people's houses and killing everybody?

DOUGAL (*suddenly looks terrified*): Is that what this one's about?

TED: Yes.

Dougal looks terrified.

SCENE 16 INT./DAY 4
SET: PAROCHIAL HOUSE
We see a close-up of Dougal's hands. He holds a bottle of gum. He draws out a star shape on a piece of paper with the nozzle of the gum. He then spills out some gold sparkly stuff on the paper. It sticks to the gum and forms a star shape.

Cut to Dougal. The sparkly stuff is all over his face and shirt, along with bits of paper, etc. He is looking at the television as he works, the decorative materials on his lap.

SCENE 17 INT./DAY 4
SET: PAROCHIAL HOUSE
We see what Dougal is watching. We see a few shots of priests turning to the camera and smiling in front of cheap and cheerful backdrops.

VOICE: If you want to meet priests your own age . . . (*We see two priests, standing back to back, their jackets thrown over their shoulders, miming a gossipy conversation.*) . . . or just listen in on the latest gossip . . . (*The screen is divided into three separate shots. We see a priest listening to a Walkman, another pretending to take a photograph, another reading a magazine and pretending to look interested.*) . . . then call priest chatback, and speak to priests . . . you want to know.

SCENE 18 INT./DAY 4
SET: PAROCHIAL HOUSE
Cut to a wider view of the room. We see that there are now lots and lots of decorations all round, all over the walls. Mrs Doyle is on the window ledge again. She starts to step down from it, thinks better of it, then turns around and holds on to the side of the window. As she starts to lower herself when the side of the window comes off with a cracking noise and she falls backwards on to the floor. Everyone fails to notice this. Ted walks in with a glass case.

TED: Right. I got the presentation case for the award.

DOUGAL (*slightly bored with more award talk*): Great, Ted. Fantastic.

TED: I'll put my award here, over the creaky floorboard. (*As he puts it above the fireplace, the floorboard creaks loudly.*) If any burglars come in and try to rob my award, we'll hear them. Very few priests are given this award, you know. It'll mean that I'll be one of the top priests in the country when I get my award.

DOUGAL: Oh, right.

TED: Did you hear there what I was saying? I'm one of the top priests in the country. Did you hear that? . . . I said it there a second ago.

DOUGAL: Oh, I did, yeah.

Dougal has even more paper stuck to his hands and face. He's having trouble shaking it off.

MRS DOYLE (*righting herself*): Well, it's not before time, Father. I always thought you were one of the best priests in the country!

TED: Well, thanks very much, Mrs Doyle. (*Pause.*) One of the best? . . . (*Very jokily.*) Or maybe *the* best? Go on, Mrs Doyle, honestly, would you say I'm the best priest in the country at the moment?

MRS DOYLE: Wwwwwellll . . .

Mrs Doyle seems reluctant to answer.

TED: Well, what would you say? Honestly, if you don't think I'm the best priest in the country just say so!

Another shot of Mrs Doyle.

TED: I honestly won't mind!

MRS DOYLE (*still struggling*): I'd say, Father, you might be the . . . second best.

Ted nods. He doesn't say anything, he just nods.

MRS DOYLE: I mean . . .

TED: No, it's all right, Mrs Doyle. I'm not the best priest in the country, I'm only the second best. There's someone better than me, apparently.

MRS DOYLE: Well, I am thinking of those priests who work in very poor areas . . .

TED: Oh, yes, of course. *Those* fellas! Father Archbishop Desmond Tutu and the like.

MRS DOYLE: I think Archbishop Tutu is a Prostestant man.

TED: Oh, right, great, so a *Protestant* is better than me. Anyway, there's no need to continue this. I'm not the best, I'm only the *second* best.

Apparently, the Golden Cleric is a *runner-up* prize. Well, I'm *so* sorry. Obviously, I'm just an *idiot.*Obviously, I can't even say Mass properly.

MRS DOYLE: Father, I was just . . .

TED: No, don't take it back. That's what you said. You said I'm not the best priest in the country. That's fine. I just want to know where I stand. Obviously, I'm going to have to jack it in now.

MRS DOYLE: What?

TED: I'm leaving the priesthood.

MRS DOYLE: But, Father!

TED: No, that's it. I'm going to write a letter to Bishop Brennan and ask for early retirement. And maybe when I go, you can ask the other priest, Father Perfect Peter The Perfect Priest, to come here and you can work for him! Since he's obviously (*dripping sarcasm*) such a great priest.

He storms out of the room and slams the door. A piece of decoration falls down. Mrs Doyle looks at the decorations worryingly. Ted re-enters and collects his coat. He leaves and slams the door again. A paper bell falls off the back of the door. Mrs Doyle looks more worried. Ted enters again, embarrassed. He sheepishly collects his keys and painstakingly closes the door quietly. All the decorations fall to the floor with a series of jangles and pops. Mrs Doyle picks up one of the decorations, and gets back on the dangerous window. Dougal now has an entire square of paper affixed to his face.

SCENE 19 EXT./DAY X
SET: BEACH
We see Ted in silhouette, walking along the beach, looking out at the waves. A few similar shots, with Ted just walking along, with lots of fades and beautiful, melancholic sunset shots. Sad music plays. Close-up of Ted. He looks very sad. After a while, we hear Mrs Doyle's voice.

MRS DOYLE (*her voice, echoing, faraway*): . . . the second best priest in the country . . . the second best priest . . . second best . . . second best . . . second best . . .

Ted picks up a stone and skims it across the water with a loud whacking noise, it hits an old man in a rowboat, who until then was fishing peacefully.

TED: Sorry about that!

MAN: Ye feckin' eejit! Wait there, until I get *ye!*

The man starts rowing towards the shore. Ted runs away.

MAN: O'ho, wait'll I get you now. Ye little pup, ye.

Ted runs towards the camera.

SCENE 19A INT./DAY 4
SET: BLUE SCREEN
Mrs Doyle's disembodied face floats towards the screen.

MRS DOYLE: . . .the second best priest . . . second best priest . . . second best priest . . .

Then the old man in the boat's head joins her.

MAN: You feckin' eejit. O'ho, wait'll I get you now . . .

Jack's head floats by, laughing hysterically. Then Assumpta from Ballykissangel's head floats by followed by Father Clifford's.

ASSUMPTA: I'm not going out with you. You're just the *second* best priest in the country.

Then Clifford's ('Ballykissangel') head floats towards us, laughing in an evil mocking way.

CLIFFORD: Ahh, ha, ha, ha, ha!!!

Then, Dougal's head comes by, just looking confused. When it gets close to the camera, it doesn't know where to go, so it turns around and goes back again.

SCENE 20 INT./DAY 4
SET: PAROCHIAL HOUSE
Mrs Doyle is up on the dangerous windowsill, fixing the decorations. She turns and starts to get down off the window, remembers her usual trouble with it, and stops. She puts one hand on the window to steady herself and leans against it, starts to put her foot out to get down. The window swings open and she falls into the front garden.

SCENE 21 INT./DAY 4
SET: PAROCHIAL HOUSE
Ted goes into the living room. The television is on, and Ted looks over. We hear the end of the Priest Chatback advertisement. Ted looks at it, then at the telephone. Then he goes over and dials, half-singing the number to himself to remember it.

TED: Hello? Priest Chatback?

The screen splits. On one side we see a twin-reeled tape recorder clicking on in a dingy office. Beside it is an ashtray with a lit fag burning.

VOICE (*recorded voice*): Welcome to Priest Chatback. If you are under eighteen or not a priest, please hang up now. Calls cost forty-nine pence per minute and terminate in Sierra Leone. If you wish to speak about the Pope's visit to Mexico, say 'yes' now. (*Bleep.*) If you want to speak about the role of women within the church, say 'yes' now. (*Bleep.*)

At this last one, Ted raises his eyes to heaven.

VOICE: If you want to speak about being vaguely unhappy but not being able to figure out exactly why, say 'yes' now. (*Bleep.*) If you want to speak about your addiction to sherry, say 'yes' now . . .

TED: Oh, wait! Yes! YES! YES! Hello?

The screen splits into three. It now features two other priests as well as Ted. Both men are on the telephone and in different locations.

PRIEST 1: Hello? Is that someone else?

PRIEST 2: Hello? (*Ad lib extra 'Hello's'.*)

TED: Hello? (*Ad lib extra 'Hello's'.*)

PRIEST 1: Hello?

PRIEST 2: Hello, yes?

TED: Oh, yes, hello, there. Is this 'Being vaguely unhappy but not being able to figure out exactly why'?

PRIEST 1: No, this is 'How to break the news of a death'.

PRIEST 2: We were just talking about techniques. I say it's best to just get it over with quickly. 'Your husband's dead, and he's not coming back. Get used to it.'

PRIEST 1: Yes, but sometimes a few little hints help. Like, ah '. . . Do you remember how your husband *used* to love a good laugh?'

PRIEST 2: Hmmm, you have a point, but . . .

TED: Oh, well, you see. My problem is, I should be on top of the world because I'm about to be given an award, but, well . . .

VOICE: Duuhhh . . . stupid priests! Duhhhh!

Suddenly the screen is divided into four. In the new frame we see two teenagers in grungy-looking gear and with Oasis haircuts. Trying to suppress giggles, one talks while the other listens.

PRIEST 1: Hey! Who's that?

PRIEST 2: Have some respect!

TEENAGER: Duuuuhhhhhhh!!!

PRIEST 1: This is a priest-only line! Are you priests?

Ted sighs and hangs up. Mrs Doyle enters.

MRS DOYLE: Oh, by the way, Father, when you left for your walk, we got a phone call. I think you were supposed to do a funeral today?

Ted thinks for a moment, then puts on an 'oh my God' face.

TED: The funeral! I completely forgot about it!

MRS DOYLE: It's all right. Father McGuire said he'd do it.

TED: Oh, great. Well, that's th— DOUGAL'S DOING A FUNERAL?!!! YOU LET DOUGAL DO A FUNERAL???!!

SCENE 22 EXT./DAY 4
SET: GRAVEYARD
We see Dougal in his 'official' gear. Behind him, a hearse is on fire and halfway into an open grave. An ambulance is nearby, injured people limping into it. People lie around on the ground, being given assistance. A very angry man looks at Dougal.

DOUGAL: Sorry about that.

The hearse explodes.

SCENE 23 INT./NIGHT 4
SET: TED AND DOUGAL'S BEDROOM
Ted is sitting in bed, writing on a laptop computer. A single lamp illuminates his workplace. It looks as if the rest of the room is in darkness. We hear shuffling coming from Dougal's bed.

DOUGAL (offscreen): Oh . . . mmmm . . .

Shuffle, shuffle. Ted sighs, trying to concentrate.

DOUGAL: Hmmm mummprhh . . . Oh, it's no use, Ted! I'm so excited about Christmas. I can't sleep.

TED: Dougal, you'll never get to sleep like that. (Cut to Dougal on an exercise bike.) You'll have a better chance if you get off the bike.

DOUGAL: Oh, right. What are you up to yourself, Ted?

TED: I'm writing my speech for tomorrow. God, it's brilliant so far. This will be my Gettysburg Address. I might try and put it on the Internet and everything.

DOUGAL: What do you put in speeches? You normally thank everybody, don't you.

TED: Not in this case, Dougal. I got this award through my own initiative and hard graft. There's nobody else to thank but me. Actually, that's a good idea . . . I'll thank myself . . .

He taps at the keyboard. He takes some papers off the computer and tidies them into line. It looks like a fairly weighty tome.

DOUGAL: Wow. Is that the speech?

TED: What? No, these are just my notes. Here, for instance, here's a list of people who've really fecked me over down through the years. Father Jimmy Fennel . . . he needs taking down a peg or two . . . Father P.J. Clabbert . . . Wait . . . he's on the wrong list . . . He should be under 'Liars' rather than 'Twats' . . . Oh, at last. At *last* I get a chance to shine out, to stand out from the crowd. To be recognised.

DOUGAL: I recognise you. Look. It's Ted.

TED: No, Dougal . . .

DOUGAL: There you are there, now.

TED: Dougal, I mean recognition of my abilities, my achievements.

DOUGAL: Oh, right. What achievements are these?

Pause. Ted thinks. We hear the dripping of a tap from the kitchen. They both stand there for a long, silent moment.

TED: Shut up, Dougal. Oh, I hope Larry Duff's coming, catch my big moment. I'll give him a ring now, actually. I really hope he makes it. Larry's tremendous fun. He *loves* award ceremonies.

Ted dials.

SCENE 24 EXT./DAY 4
SET: SKI SLOPE/BLUE SCREEN
Cut to Larry happily skiing along. We hear his phone

ringing. Larry is distracted. Cut to stock footage of skier having horrific fall down slope. It should take a very long time. As he falls, he cries out in pain.

LARRY (*from afar*): Oh, dear God in Heaven . . . Ooof . . . agh! My leg! . . . Oh, Holy Mother of God . . . agh . . . Oh, Jesus, Mary and Joseph . . . all the Saints in Heaven, help me . . . God almighty . . .

SCENE 25 INT./NIGHT 4
SET: TED AND DOUGAL'S BEDROOM
Cut back to Ted.

TED: Oh, wait, no, I think he's on holiday. Well, I won't disturb him.

DOUGAL: All right, I'm going to try one more time to get to sleep. (*He closes his eyes, then opens them.*) Gaaaaahhhh!!! It's no use!

TED: Dougal, here's a good way to get to sleep. Just try and clear your head of all thoughts.

DOUGAL: Well, I'll give it a go, but I don't think . . . Zzzzzzzzzzzz . . .

Ted looks at him, then back at the computer. He starts writing.

TED: Heh, heh, heh . . .

END OF PART ONE

* * *

PART TWO

SCENE 26 INT./DAY 5
SET: PAROCHIAL HOUSE
We see another window of the Advent calendar being opened. It is a nativity scene.

DOUGAL: Aaaaggghhh!!! BRILLIANT! A LOAD OF PEOPLE IN A STABLE! The one thing I didn't expect!

TED: Dougal . . .

DOUGAL: Oh, wow! Unbelievable!

TED: Dougal, aren't you going to open your presents?

DOUGAL: Presents! Oh, wow! I completely forgot about the presents! First the calendar, now presents! It can't get any better than this!

He runs up to his presents. He is incredibly excited. He

rummages through them and he rips one open. We can't see what it is. He yells with delight.

DOUGAL: Aaaargh! BRILLIANT!

Ted hands Mrs Doyle a present.

TED: Happy Christmas, Mrs Doyle . . .

MRS DOYLE: Oh, Father, you shouldn't have. What is it? It's a . . .

She opens it. It is the tea-making machine we saw earlier. She stares at it without expression.

TED: I was racking my brains, thinking, 'What would Mrs Doyle really love?' So I thought . . . you know, something to take the misery out of making tea.

MRS DOYLE: Oh . . . thank you, Father, it's . . . it's just what I wanted.

TED: Yes, Mrs Doyle, the days of housekeepers making tea are over. We can't live in the Dark Ages any more. You've made your last cup of tea in this house.

Mrs Doyle takes this in.

MRS DOYLE (*recovering slightly*): I'll just put it in . . . in the kitchen, so . . .

TED: No need, Mrs Doyle. We can leave it in here and just get the tea ourselves.

MRS DOYLE: Oh. OK, so. I'll just go into the kitchen, then and . . . stand beside the cooker and . . . look out of the window for a while . . .

She turns so her back is to the camera, and walks slowly out of the room, as if she's walking in a funeral procession.

TED: If I know people the way I think I do, she really loves that present.

DOUGAL (*offscreen*): Ah, Ted, it's brilliant!

TED: You like it?

DOUGAL: Ah, yeah . . .

Cut to Dougal. He is dressed in full matador's gear.

DOUGAL: . . . I mean, how did you know?

TED: Don't think I hadn't noticed all those little hints you left lying about the place.

SCENE 27 EXT./DAY 5
SET: PAROCHIAL HOUSE
We see a finger coming into shot and pressing the

doorbell. The person who pressed the bell steps back and looks up - we see all this from behind. We see a huge banner across the front of the house that has on it the words, 'Ted, get me loads of matador stuff. Dougal.'

SCENE 28 EXT./DAY 5
SET: PAROCHIAL HOUSE
Jack approaches Ted, a fag hanging from his mouth.

JACK: Present. C'mon. C'MON, PRESENT! PRESENT!

Ted reaches down for Jack's present.

JACK (*snaps fingers*): C'mon, c'mon, c'mon.

Ted lifts up a bottle of whiskey. Jack grabs it.

TED: Happy Christ . . .

JACK (*walking off*): Yeah, yeah, yeah . . . feck off . . .

Ted is looking out of the window.

TED: Who could this be? The ceremony doesn't start until two.

The door opens. Mrs Doyle enters.

MRS DOYLE: Father, it's . . .

A priest barges past her.

TODD: Teeeeeeeeeedddddddd!!!

Ted obviously doesn't know who he is, but fakes it.

TED: Ahaaa!!! Ahhhh!! Helloooooo there!!!

Todd hugs Ted. We see by Ted's face that he doesn't know who he is.

TODD: You finally did it! You won the Golden Cleric. I haven't missed the ceremony, have I?

TED: What? Oh, right. No, not at all.

TODD: You haven't changed a bit, you rascal! Ha, ha!!

He attempts to engage Ted in some playful pretend boxing.

TED: Ha, ha! No, and you! Look at you! You haven't changed either!

TODD: What? Well, what about the hair?

TED: Oh, right, the hair . . . it's a different . . . shape . . .

TODD: Colour.

TED: Colour, yes. Of course, because it used to be . . . reeeed-black.

TODD: Blond.

TED: Blond! Blond, yes.

Todd sees Dougal.

TODD: Hello, there!

DOUGAL (*brightly*): Hello, there you back!

TODD (*to Dougal*): I suppose he's told you all about me!

DOUGAL: No. (*Beat.*) Who are you?

TODD: Who am I?

Todd looks at Ted and makes an 'introduce us' gesture. Pause. Ted begins to say something, then reaches for an address book and opens it.

TED: Actually, you might as well stick your name and address in the old book. Especially the name. It's very important that the name is very, very clear.

TODD: Ah, I'd love to, Ted, but I can't really write. One time last year I was running with scissors, and I fell. The nerve that controls handwriting was completely severed.

TED: There's a nerve that controls handwriting?

TODD: Apparently. And things like . . . you know . . . conducting.

He attempts to demonstrate by miming 'conducting', but grimaces in pain as soon as he starts. Ted nods. Pause.

MRS DOYLE: Father, aren't you going to introduce me to the new Father?

TED: Oh, right. This, as . . . this is . . . Actually

. . . (*Long pause.*) I tell you what. See if you can guess.

MRS DOYLE: Guess?

TED: Yes. Give it a go there.

MRS DOYLE: God, Father, it could be anything.

TED: Still, though. Give it a try.

MRS DOYLE: Father Andy Reilly.

TODD: No, ha, ha.

MRS DOYLE: Father Desmond Coyne. Father Kevin Cecil. (*Todd shakes his head.*) Father George Byrne. Father David Nicholson. Father Declan Lynch . . .

TODD (*enjoying this*): I'll give you a clue . . .

MRS DOYLE: NO CLUES! I'll get it in a second . . . Father Ken Sweeney . . . Father Neil Hannon . . . Father Keith Cullen, Father Kieran Donnelly, Father Mick McEvoy, Father Jack White . . .

Ted looks at Mrs Doyle and sighs. He sits down and covers his face with his hand. Fade down.

SCENE 29 INT./DAY 5
SET: PAROCHIAL HOUSE
Fade up. It is much later. Ted and Dougal are sitting down now, looking tired and bored.

MRS DOYLE: . . . Father Henry Big Bigeen. Father Hank Tree. Father Hiroshima Twinky. Father Stig Bubblecard. Father Johnny Hellsapoppin' . . . Father Luke Duke. Father Muhammad Stiff. Father Billy Furry. Father John Hoop. Father Hairycake Lynam. Father Chewy Louie. Father Rebulah Conundrum. Father Peewee Stairmaster. Father Tighthead Lips. Father Rick Cocksinger . . . Father Jemimah Racktool. Father Gerry Twigg. Father Spodo Comodo. Father Canabramalamar. Father Todd Unctious . . .

TODD: Yes! Well done!

TED: What? Really? Is that it? She's got it!

TODD: C'mon Ted! You knew already!

TED: Ha, ha, yes, I'm simply amazed that she got it right in . . . (*He checks his watch.*) Wow! Well under an hour! Well done, Mrs Doyle! So . . . Todd. Todd, Todd, Todd. Old Todd. There you are now. Todd. Good old Todd. Are you all right for tea, Todd? Would you like a hot toddy . . . Todd? Anything you want, Todd. Anything at all. Todd. (*He winks.*) Todd.

TODD: What time is the ceremony, Ted?

TED: Well, Todd, it's due to start around two. But it's not really a 'ceremony'. I'm sure it'll be a very quick, simple affair.

SCENE 30 EXT./DAY 5
SET: PAROCHIAL HOUSE
Lots of priests and nuns are milling around in a hive of activity. The following scenes are done in a series of quick montages, the style very naturalistic. There is a kind of 'roadie' priest at the microphone.

ROADIE PRIEST: ONE, TWO, ONE, TWO . . . (*To the sound priest.*) Sean, I'm getting feedback from the monitor. Can you? . . . One, two . . . Yeah, that's good.

A priest unwrapping a load of candles. Another priest watches.

WATCHING PRIEST: They're the wrong candles. These're feckin' christening candles. You want a number 12 candle for this.

The other priest looks annoyed. Cut to Dougal and Ted, sitting amongst all the chaos.

DOUGAL: Excited, Ted?

TED: Ah, yes.

DOUGAL: Something to tell the grandchildren about.

Ted gives Dougal a look. Cut to a priest, drinking casually from a styrofoam cup, looking at some cue cards that are being held up by another priest for him to check out.

PRIEST: Dominus albe turum . . . Change 'Dominus' to 'Cannus'. (*He motions for the priest to flip to the next card. The priest does so.*) I want you faster than this when we're on, Charlie. 'Teus Medras In Tumo Caneto'. God, who wrote this stuff?

Another priest raising a chalice. A priest behind him guides his elbow.

PRIEST BEHIND: You're going to have to bring it up quicker.

He shows him how to do it.

FRONT PRIEST: You're goin' to have to cue me. I'll be lookin' at Cyril, so I won't have to

see the audience.

PRIEST BEHIND: Uh-huh. That's no problem.

Back to Ted and Dougal. A priest wearing a pair of earphones approaches Dougal.

TED: Oh, God, I'm so nervous. I've never spoken in front of this many people before.

DOUGAL: Just imagine them naked, Ted. That's supposed to calm you down.

TED: I'm not imagining all these people naked! My brain might explode. Where's Todd, by the way? I thought he wanted to see this . . .

EARPHONES: Hi. Who's Ted and who's Dougal?

DOUGAL: Ah, I'm Ted, that's Dougal there.

TED: No, Dougal . . . sorry about that. I'm Dougal, he's Ted.

EARPHONES (*to Dougal*): We need you by the stage, Father . . .

TED (*to Dougal*): Why does he need you by the stage? He must mean me.

SCENE 31A INT./DAY 5
SET: PAROCHIAL HOUSE
Jack is asleep. Todd kicks open the door. He has a notebook and is writing notes. He looks at the display case for the award, and scribbles something down. A floorboard creaks. He takes out a very flash-looking hip flask from his jacket, unscrews the top and is about take a slug.

JACK (*through a sleepy haze, his eyes still closed*): Drink? Driiiink?

Todd looks at him, puzzled. He walks over and holds the flask near his head. He moves it towards Jack.

JACK: Drink? Driiink? Driiink?

As he moves it towards him, Jack's 'Drink?' becomes louder and he becomes more agitated in his sleep. When he draws it away, Jack gets quieter.

JACK: Drink! Driiink . . . driiink . . .

Todd puts the hip flask back in his coat pocket.

JACK (*sadly*): Drink? Drink? Driiiink!

He slumps back into sleep again. Todd continues taking notes.

SCENE 32 EXT./DAY 5
SET: SIDE OF STAGE
Ted is placed by the side of the stage. The earphones priest waits beside him. We see a wide view of the impressive set-up. On stage is a very handsome priest, Father Dick Mayo. Standing beside him is a co-presenter nun, Sister Helen Locklear.

DICK: Welcome to the fifth annual presentation of the Golden Cleric.

HELEN: Every year, the Catholic Church gives an award to a priest for outstanding achievement . . .

DICK: The award is presented to individuals who have helped advance the cause of the church through their actions . . .

HELEN: This year's winner is someone who has overcome controversy in the past. . .

TED: Nononononononono . . .

HELEN: . . . when rumours of financial irregularities . . . threatened his career in the Church.

TED: Shush, shush, nononononono . . .

DICK: But after a thorough investigation, no charges were brought . . .

TED (*offscreen, distant*): . . . *money was resting in my account.* . .

HELEN: Even though authorities were confused by what they saw as 'bizarre irregularities' in his accounts . . .

TED (*offscreen*): *Yes, they've had enough of that now . . .*

DICK: But he has overcome these personal setbacks to become this year's winner of the Golden Cleric! Father Ted Crilly!

Ted goes up and accepts the award. He walks to the microphone. Cut to Father Billy standing beside Father Terry.

BILLY: Oh, God, I hope he doesn't start going on about himself and settling old scores in public. He always used to do that in the debating society in Saint Colm's.

TED: Well. (*Pause.*) Well, well, well . . . (*He looks at the audience.*) I see a lot of familiar faces here today. Some more welcome than others. It looks as though I've had the last laugh on a lot of people who didn't really think I had it in me to be a brilliant priest. But what I would say to

those people is; look at me now. I am truly, as James Cagney said in that film about gangsters, 'on top of the world, Ma!'

Cut to Billy who has put his hand over his eyes in a sort of 'Ohhhh, God' gesture. Fade out. Fade back. A little bit later. Billy and Terry look irritated and bored. Cut back to Ted on the platform.

TED: . . . but I eventually escaped from his headlock. And now where are you, Father Eamonn Hunter? Working with some pygmies in the South Seas. And where am I? Accepting a Golden Cleric Award for being a top priest.

Fade out. Fade back. We notice there's less people in the seats. Ted natters away, oblivious.

TED: 'Yes, of course', he thought. 'It'd be a great idea to pour water on this young novice's mattress'. But of course, thirty years later, the smile has been very much wiped off Father Barry Kiernan's face. I believe he couldn't take the demands of the priesthood, and became a mandrax fiend.

Fade out. Fade back. There are only a few priests left – the ones from the lingerie section.

TED: . . . and now we move on to 'liars'. Ahem. Father Peter Sorton. Father Desmond Cairns . . .

SCENE 33 INT./EVENING 5
SET: PAROCHIAL HOUSE
Ted is examining the award. A few remaining priests – Fathers Terry, Billy, Reilly, Fitzgerald, Cleary, Deegan and an older priest – look on. There is a slightly embarrassed atmosphere.

BILLY (*unconvincingly*): Well . . . great speech, Ted.

TED: It went well, didn't it?

OLD PRIEST: You were wandering around in there for three hours?

TERRY: Yes. It's Ireland's biggest lingerie section, I understand.

Mrs Doyle comes in with a tray.

MRS DOYLE: Tea for everyone?

TED: Right . . . Oh, Mrs Doyle, put all that away and relax. We're going to try out the Teamaster.

BILLY: How's it work, Ted?

MRS DOYLE: But . . . b-b-b– . . . can I just put in the milk?

TED: Look, you just put the cup in there, slide in one of these cartridges and the tea just comes out here.

TERRY: God, that's fantastic.

TED: Yes, well, now that I've got an award, I can't be seen drinking tea that's just been made in a pot. Hah! The idea!

Everyone groups around the machine, leaving Mrs Doyle on her own. With her upper lip trembling madly, she leaves the room, unnoticed.

FITZGERALD (*boring voice*): It just seems just too good to be true. What's the catch?

TED: Sorry, Father? To be honest, your voice is just so boring, I couldn't concentrate on what you were saying.

FITZGERALD: Well, I do have an incredibly boring voice. I was just saying . . . what's the catch?

Pause.

TED: Sorry! I didn't get it there either.

REILLY (*very dynamic voice*): Ted, I was just thinking, the Tea-master thing . . . there must be some sort of catch.

TED: A catch? No, there's no catch. Watch this.

Ted slides a cartridge in. Immediately there is a massive grinding noise that goes on for ages, blocking all other noise out. It finishes and Ted takes out the cup.

TED: Y'see? Perfect. Now, perhaps you could all tell me what you thought of my speech.

Jack bursts in. The priests return to their chairs. The older priest is sitting on Jack's chair. Jack walks calmly to his chair and sits down on the old priest, crushing him against the chair. Jack doesn't seem to notice.

TED: Ah, Father Jack? Could you, ah . . . there's actually someone . . .

JACK: Wha—?

TED: There's someone . . . ah . . . you all right, Father?

PRIEST: Yes, I . . . it's actually quite hard to breathe . . .

Jack looks around in confusion, wondering where the voice is coming from.

TED: Father, could you just . . .

PRIEST (*red-faced and husky-voiced*): I really am finding it quite hard to breathe . . .

TED: Just stand up!

The priest wheezes unsettlingly.

JACK: What?

TED: Dougal, quick! Put on that music!

DOUGAL: What?

TED: Put on the music that makes Father Jack stand up!

Dougal bends over the record player. After a moment, 'La Marseillaise' starts up. Jack cocks his head, then slowly, uncertainly, stands up. Ted pulls the still-gasping priest away.

TED: Sorry about that. For some reason, that bit of music always makes Father Jack stand to attention.

JACK: Up! Up! Up!

TED: Yes. Father Jack likes us all to stand when that comes on.

JACK: Sing!

Cut to a wide shot of them all. Jack stands proudly to attention while the others sing along half-heartedly to the words. Fade down.

SCENE 34 INT./EVENING 5
SET: PAROCHIAL HOUSE
Fade up. The men are still standing up. They mumble the end of the song in a very unconvincing manner, trailing off and overlapping each other. Father Cleary walks over to Jack, holding a cracker.

JACK: Again, again, again.

CLEARY: Father, will you have a go of this with me?

Jack, slightly confused, reaches out for the cracker. Cleary grips it and pulls back. Jack looks confused and angry. He starts pulling hard.

JACK: Arrrch! GERRAWAY!!!

Jack stands up and leans backwards with the cracker. Cleary starts to look uncertain.

CLEARY: No, Father, it's just a bit of fun.

JACK: Aaarrrggghhh!!!

Jack punches Cleary and takes the cracker. He holds it up in the air with a victorious yell, then runs towards the window and tries to jump out. However, he simply whacks against it and falls back on to the floor.

TED: Ah, yes, we sort of thought Father Jack was jumping through that window a little too much, so we put in Plexiglass. Anyway! My speech! Tell me what you thought of it.

DOUGAL: Will we have a look at the Christmas film?

PRIESTS: Yaaaayyy!!!

Dougal switches on the television. All the priests flutter excitedly.

TV ANNOUNCER: That was *Indiana Jones and the Last Crusade*. And now, a special extended Latin Mass from Saint Martin's Cathedral in Dublin.

The mood descends a notch or two. Ted and Dougal look at each other.

TED: Oh . . . great . . . Mass.

We see that the other priests aren't terribly enthusiastic either. They ad lib fake keenness. Ted and Dougal sit, pretending to pay attention to the Mass. They occasionally shift their eyes to look at the other priests. Everyone is quite obviously bored out of their minds, sneaking guilty looks at each other.

TERRY: God, I've just remembered. I've got to do something terribly important . . . (*They all look at him.*) Actually what I have to do, I've, I've just remembered. I have to go and phone this fella on Death Row I befriended recently. He's being executed tomorrow for mass murder so I'd say he's very low at the moment.

TED: God almighty. And did he do it?

Terry wasn't expecting this question. He thinks about it.

TERRY: I don't know . . . yes.

BILLY: Do you need any help, talking to him?

TERRY: Ah . . .

BILLY: 'Cause, he might get hysterical and start crying, and then I could say, 'Pull yourself together, man!'

TERRY: All right.

Pause.

FITZGERALD: There's been a big accident. So I should go, too.

They all look at him.

FITZGERALD: I got a phonecall there when . . . you were all . . . somewhere else. So I should go.

BILLY: We're all off, so!

Todd enters.

BILLY: Father Unctious, are you coming? I could give you a lift.

TODD: Eh . . . no. I'll stay a while. Oh fantastic . . . Mass. Father Ultan Crosby is doing the Mass. (*He nods at the television.*) I'm a huge fan of his. He gives good Mass.

BILLY: He what?

TODD: He really knows how to work the altar. (*He watches the set in admiration.*) Look at that chalice work . . . effortless.

REILLY: Anyway, we'll be off. See you all again.

ALL PRIESTS: Bye, thanks, etc. . . .

TED: Bye! Thanks for coming to my awards ceremony where I won an award!

The priests leave. Ted and Dougal turn round and watch the television. Ted looks over at Todd, who smiles in an 'I'm really enjoying this' kind of way. Ted smiles, gives him a wink and sinks further in his seat. Fade down.

SCENE 35A INT./LATER THAT EVENING 5
SET: PAROCHIAL HOUSE
Fade up. Ted, Dougal and Todd are sound asleep. From behind the sofa, a groggy Jack stands up. He looks at the television, which is still showing the Mass. He looks at the three, goes over to the set and switches the channel.

ANNOUNCER: Now on BBC1, the director's cut of *Jurassic Park* with extra dinosaurs.

SCENE 36 INT./NIGHT 5
SET: TED AND DOUGAL'S BEDROOM
Ted and Dougal are in bed. Ted looks very grumpy.

TED: Well, that was a fantastic day.

DOUGAL: It was, Ted, wasn't it? What a brilliant day. Fantastic fun! That was one of the best Christmas Days ever!

TED: I was being sarcastic, Dougal.

DOUGAL: Oh, right. Ah, so was I.

TED: I don't think everyone was nice enough about my speech. Actually, I was glad when they left. You could *feel* the begrudgery and the jealousy leaving the room with them. (*He whispers slightly.*) And what's that fella doing, still here? I didn't invite him to stay. Did you?

DOUGAL: Huh?

TED: No, actually I barred you from inviting anyone after that tramp stayed for a week. Remember that? When I was away?

DOUGAL: He wasn't a tramp, Ted. He was the Prime Minister of France.

TED: No, he wasn't, Dougal. He just lied to you.

DOUGAL: Oh, actually, he did, yeah. And he stole the video.

TED: Todd Unctious, Todd Unctious . . . I don't remember him at all. Who the hell is he?

DOUGAL: Maybe he had a nickname. You know, like Terry Wogan.

TED: Terry Wogan? What's his nickname?

DOUGAL: What? (*Pause.*) Oh, you mean that's his *real* name!? Ah, well, don't let it worry you, Ted. He'll be gone tomorrow.

There is a knock on the door. Father Todd sticks his head round the door.

TODD: There y'are!

TED: Aha! Hello, there!

Todd comes in. He is wearing white Y-fronts and nothing else. Ted pulls the covers up slightly in an embarrassed, slightly guarded way. Dougal does the same.

TODD (*to Dougal*): Look at you, lyin' in there like a big eejit. Ha, ha!

Ted and Dougal make quiet, polite 'ha, ha', noises. Todd stands between the beds, hands on hips, legs apart.

TODD: Here we are now, anyway. All the lads.

TED: Yes . . . yes . . .

Todd sits at the end of the bed.

TODD: Just like the old days, eh? Do you remember all the fun we used to have in the showers?

He picks up a towel and flicks it at Ted playfully. Ted cowers.

TODD: Do you still have the big old hairy arse?

TED: Ah, fluff, Todd. It wasn't hair. It was a bit of downy fluff.

TODD: Ah, God . . . memories. Do you remember you all mitched off to that Dana concert? I couldn't go because I was recovering from a massive car accident. Did I ever show you the scar?

He walks over to Ted and points to a scar stretching down his leg from his boxer shorts. His leg is possibly a little too close to Ted's face for his liking. Ted pretends to take in the scar while looking at everything else in the room.

TODD: Y'see, there . . .

TED: God, yes . . .

TODD: See that little crescent shape . . .

TED: Phew. Yes.

TODD: . . . And this series of . . . Can you see them? . . . Tiny indentations along my inner thigh . . .

TED: That's . . . that's really . . .

TODD (*tracing it with his finger*): And they run all the way up there to my groin . . .

TED (*jumps out of bed*): Whoah! What do you say we all go to the pictures? I feel like going to see a good film.

TODD: Ted, it's half one in the morning.

TED: Oh, right.

TODD: No, you go off to sleep. I was just wandering around. Sometimes I can't sleep at night and I need a good walk to calm meself down. You don't mind, do you?

TED: No, no. You do that.

TODD: Good night, so. And . . . Happy

Christmas, Ted.

He holds his arms out. Ted realises that Todd wants a hug. Like a man condemned, he opens his arms and Todd embraces him. Ted's not having the greatest time of his life. Todd disengages. He does some pretend boxing and laughs. Then he leaves the room.

TED: Well, I'm not moving out of here until tomorrow. I don't want to bump into that weirdo walking around the house in his nudiness. Goodnight, Dougal.

SCENE 37 INT./NIGHT 5
SET: PAROCHIAL HOUSE
Jack comes into the living room, in his dirty, rotten pyjamas, and turns on the light. He walks over to the fireplace and picks up a massive bottle of whiskey and a funnel. As he walks back, he steps in front of the award and the floorboards creak. There's a bump from upstairs, we hear footsteps running down the stairs, and Ted bursts into the room wielding a tennis racket.

TED: Get away from that award!

JACK: Feck off!

TED: Oh, Father, it's you. Right. Eh, turn off the light before you go up, won't you? And please, don't slam the door.

Jack makes a grunting noise. Ted leaves the room and Jack follows him. He stops at the light, gives the unseen Ted the finger and goes out of the room, closing the door gently behind him. But before it closes, he thinks better of it, and slams the door.

SCENE 38 INT./NIGHT 5
SET: TED AND DOUGAL'S BEDROOM
Ted and Dougal hear the slam and jump with the shock.

SCENE 39 EXT./NIGHT 5
SET: PAROCHIAL HOUSE
The slam causes loads of birds to burst from the trees.

SCENE 40 INT./NIGHT 5
SET: CANADIAN SKI RESORT
We see Larry Duff, in a neck brace and lots of plaster. He hears the slam, and turns his neck slightly.

LARRY: Aaaaaowwww!

We hear a low rumble. Larry looks puzzled. He tries to turn and sees . . . an avalanche starting. The avalanche roars down and mingles with Larry's scream.

SCENE 41 INT./NIGHT 5
SET: PAROCHIAL HOUSE
Back to the living room. Pause. We hear a small shuffling noise. Cut to the grille in the ceiling over the award. It is moved to one side. Cut back to the living room. Pause. Suddenly, with a 'zzzzzz' noise, a figure descends into shot, suspended from wires, right in front of the award. He is dressed in cool 'Mission Impossible' cat-burglar gear. He is suspended directly in front of the award. He sticks a suction cup on to the glass and starts running a glass cutter around it. Suddenly there is a noise. He pulls on something and shoots back up with the same 'zzzzzz' noise. Mrs Doyle comes into the room, looking shifty. In one hand she holds a screwdriver. She goes up to the Tea-master, opens it and starts fiddling about inside it. We hear things breaking and snapping.

MRS DOYLE: Heh, heh, heh . . .

She finishes and walks out. The figure descends immediately with the 'zzzzzz' noise and gets back to work. He suddenly hears a noise and pulls the control for his wires; it brings him halfway up, but then something snaps with a 'ping' noise and he's stuck there, pointing slightly head-downwards.

Dougal enters the room, carrying a glass of milk, and turns on the light. The burglar waits for the worst. Dougal walks over to the television, completely oblivious of the figure hanging and turning slightly, right beside him – and switches it on. He sits down to watch. The burglar hangs there, silent and confused. We hear the dialogue from the television.

MAN 1 (*American accent*): . . . What's wrong, McKenzie?

MAN 2: I don't want you to panic . . . but there's a dangerous burglar in the house.

MAN 1: What?!

MAN 2: In fact, he may be in this very room. Hiding.

Dougal looks a bit spooked. He turns around, checking there's no one behind him.

MAN 2: A burglar. In the room, you say. My God.

MAN 1: Yes. In fact, I think it's safe to say that

the burglar is definitely in the room.

MAN 2: But where could he be?

MAN 1: There he is!

MAN 2: Where?

MAN 1: Right there, man! Use your eyes!

Dougal squints at the television, trying to see him.

MAN 1: THERE!

Dramatic music. Both Dougal and the burglar jump with the shock. Dougal squints again, looking at the screen.

SCENE 42 INT./NIGHT 5
SET: TED AND DOUGAL'S BEDROOM
Ted tosses and turns. He wakes up. He looks at Dougal's bed. Dougal isn't there. Ted shakes his head and gets out of bed.

TED: Dougal, Dougal, Dougal . . . you'll have nightmares . . .

SCENE 43 INT./NIGHT 5
SET: PAROCHIAL HOUSE
The burglar is still hanging from the wire. He stays perfectly still. Dougal hears Ted coming down, turns off the television and stands up. The burglar finally gets his harness thingy to work and whizzes up into the air, out of shot. Ted comes into the room.

TED: . . . Dougal, I thought I told you not to watch that film . . .

DOUGAL: No, Ted, I wasn't watching it. I just came down to . . . to . . . ah . . . (*He looks at his milk.*) . . . carry the milk . . . around.

TED: Go on. Up to bed with you.

Dougal skips out. Ted is about to follow him when he looks over at his award. He goes to it and takes it out of the case, poses with it, and then starts walking around the room in an extraordinarily poncy way, like a particularly vain king or Pope with his sceptre. He looks absolutely ridiculous.

In the background, Todd (the burglar), trying desperately to adjust his harness, starts slipping down into shot. Finally he hangs there, unable to do anything. He looks at Ted, who is now standing very close, with his back to him.

TED: Ah, Your Holiness, hello. Mr De Niro, Bob. I enjoyed you in *The Godfather II.* Ah,

President Robinson, well done on everything. (*He turns around so that his nose almost brushes Todd's.*) Ah, Todd. (*Beat*) Aaaaarrrrggghhh!!!

SCENE 44 INT./DAY 6
SET: PAROCHIAL HOUSE
Ted is talking to Sergeant Hodgins.

HODGINS: He won't be doing any more burglaries where he's going.

TED: Where's that?

HODGINS: Well . . . prison.

TED: Of course, of course, sorry . . . But Sergeant, how did he know so much about me?

Todd is being led out.

HODGINS: I'm curious about that myself . . . Unctious, if that is your real name.

TODD: I already told you it wasn't.

HODGINS: Did you? Oh, right, sorry. Forgot. Tell us how you knew so much about Father Crilly.

TODD: Is this off the record?

HODGINS: Of course.

TODD: I was in Cellbridge a few days ago, got to talking to this old priest in a bar . . .

SCENE 45 INT./NIGHT X
SET: AMERICAN BAR
We see Todd, listening to someone in a bar. We see a grizzled old priest like Tom Waits in another ten years - leaning on a bar in front of a bar sign for 'Miller' or another American brand. We hear country/honky tonk music in the background. Over this, Todd's narration continues, but we hear occasional snatches of the old priest's dialogue too - rising up through the gaps in Todd's spiel.

TODD: . . . he was cagey at first, but a few shots of J.D. and he was singing like a bird . . .

OLD PRIEST (*in hokey American accent*)**:** The Golden Cleric, they call it givin' it to an old pal of mine . . . Ted Crilly . . . met him on Dollymount Strand . . .

TODD: . . . as I listened, a plan formed in my head. We drank long into the night, me paying,

of course, him spilling his guts on the subject of a certain Father Ted Crilly . . .

OLD PRIEST (*drunker*): . . . got a mane of white hair kinda like you'd get on a mule . . . used to wet his bed in Saint Colm's . . . (*gestures with fingers*). . . big hairy ass . . .

TODD: The longer he talked, the better it got . . .

OLD PRIEST: . . . 'resting in his account', heh, heh . . . lives with a pig-ignorant old timer called Jack Hackett, and a poor, strange idyut-boy name of McGuire. . .

SCENE 46 INT./NIGHT X
SET: SLEAZY HOTEL BEDROOM
The old priest flops onto the bed. A pair of hands come into shot and starts to pull off his trousers.

TODD: After that, all I needed was the right costume . . .

OLD PRIEST (*almost unconscious*): . . . five-bedroomed house . . . Ted sleeps directly above living room . . . no alarm system . . .

We see Todd putting the trousers to one side. Fade down. Fade up, and Todd is putting on the last of the other priest's clothes in front of the mirror. He looks exactly the same as when he was in his own clothes. He sizes himself up.

TODD: Perfect.

SCENE 47 INT./DAY 6
SET: PAROCHIAL HOUSE
Back to Ted, Todd and Hodgins in the living room.

TED: But, you're a priest. I mean, why?

TODD: It's a long story. I used to be like you, a completely average, bog-standard, run-of-the-mill priest. But then I won first prize in the

County Westmeath Priest of the Year Competition. I guess it went to my head. Before I knew it, I was hitting the altar wine too much, going easy on people in Confession, getting backhanders for doing quicker Masses. All I wanted was trophies and prizes, and the one that really got me hard was the Golden Cleric . . .

TED: No, no, no, Todd. Sorry, what I was going to ask was . . . you're a priest. Why did you wear the other priest's clothes?

TODD: Oh. I'm not sure. It was just goin' that way.

HODGINS: Well, I've got bad news for you, so-called Todd Unctious. That wasn't off the record! I'm using that as evidence against you!

TODD: Oh! That's completely unfair!!

HODGINS: Take him away.

A policeman leads him out through the doorway. Dougal enters.

TED: Thank you, Sergeant!

HODGINS: There'll be a reward in this, Father! You both should be very proud of yourselves.

TED: A reward. Well. Not such a bad Christmas after all.

MRS DOYLE (*offscreen*): Well done, Father!

We see Mrs Doyle on the dangerous window ledge. She finishes adjusting something and then jumps off. Instead of falling, however, she just hangs there. We realise that she is using the burglar's wire contraption when she pulls something and lowers gently to the floor.

TED: That's a handy old thing, isn't it, Mrs Doyle? Modern technology is great, isn't it?

MRS DOYLE: Oh, yes, Father, thanks again. It's the best Christmas present ever!

TED: Well, what about the tea-making machine?

MRS DOYLE: Oh . . . yes . . .

TED: I'll go and crank it up now.

He walks over and slips in a cartridge. It makes its usual horrible noise. Mrs Doyle looks worried. Then it starts making another strange noise, exactly like someone hacking up a particularly horrible ball of phlegm and spitting it into a cup.

TED: Euuch. What was *that*? I didn't like that sound at all. Sorry, Mrs Doyle, we'll have to get it fixed.

MRS DOYLE: No, Father, don't! Please!

TED: What?

MRS DOYLE: Father, I *like* the whole tea-making thing. You know, the playful splash of the tea as it hits the bottom of the cup . . . the sheer unbridled excitement of adding the milk and seeing it settle for a brief moment on the surface, before it gently filters down through the rest of the cup, changing the colour from dark brown to . . . a kind of lighter brown. Perching an optional Jaffa Cake on the saucer . . . like a proud soldier standing to attention beside a giant . . . cup of tea . . . Just think, Father. Remember all the great times we've had, when I used to make the tea . . .

We see Ted's expression turn to one of nostalgia.

SCENE 48 INT./DAY X
SET: PAROCHIAL HOUSE
We see loads of flashbacks of Mrs Doyle offering teas to Ted. They're all exactly the same – Ted makes the same 'Ah, tea!' gesture in each one – but her aprons are a different colour. We hear accompanying nostalgic music.

SCENE 49 INT./DAY 6
SET: PAROCHIAL HOUSE
TED: Mrs Doyle, you're right. Tea out of a machine is like . . . milk from a baby's bottle. A baby doesn't want milk from a bottle, he wants it from his mother's . . . (*He realises he has made an analogy he doesn't want to continue.*) Anyway, Mrs Doyle, why don't you make us both a *normal* cup of tea?

MRS DOYLE: Right-O, Father. And don't worry, it'll be 'tea-riffic'.

Everyone laughs as in a Lassie film, heartily and for too long. Mrs Doyle leaves the room. They all stop laughing.

TED: 'Tea-riffic'. Bloody hell. You know, Dougal, being in the priesthood – it's not about awards and glamour. It's about hard graft. It's about applying yourself to the spiritual needs of your parishioners. You know, that Todd Unctious fella there . . . that could have been me.

DOUGAL: Really? Ahhh . . . that would explain a lot. *Pause.*

TED (*beat*): I don't think you quite picked up on what I meant there.

Dougal looks even more confused. The telephone rings. Dougal picks it up.

TED: I could have turned into a bad priest, like him. Selfish, arrogant, not giving a damn about my parishioners.

Dougal puts his hand over the mouthpiece.

DOUGAL: Ted, it's Mrs Gilcuddy. She wants you to do one of those remembrance Masses.

TED: I'm not in.

DOUGAL (*into the receiver*): Ah, he's not in at the moment. All right, so, bye.

He throws the receiver on to the table.

TED: Dougal, I'm sorry about my recent silliness. I think you deserve this award as much as me.

DOUGAL: Oh, well, Ted, thank you. That's brilliant. Thanks very much.

TED: So . . . will I put it back in the case?

DOUGAL: Better, I suppose.

TED: And my name on the plaque, we needn't bother changing that.

DOUGAL: No. I know the award's mine, and that's good enough for me.

TED: I think I'll run the bath. That'll calm me down after the day.

DOUGAL: OK, so.

Ted leaves the room. Dougal makes sure he's gone, then walks over to the trophy. He picks it up (there is a creaking noise) and starts walking around with it in a very poncy way. Dramatic close-up of Dougal. He starts laughing in a vaguely mad-scientist-type way.

DOUGAL: Heh, heh, heh . . . HEH, HEH, HEH . . . HAAA, HA, HAA, HAAA, HAAAAA!!!! . . .

He is cut short when he sees Ted standing at the doorway, looking puzzled.

TED: What are you doing, Dougal?

DOUGAL (*back to normal*): Oh, nothing. Just having a bit of a laugh.

THE END

are you right there, father ted?

GRAHAM: The great thing about an imaginary location such as Craggy Island is that it can expand and contract according to our needs. So in one episode we can say it's as small as four football fields, and in another it can be so big as to support a Chinatown that Ted has somehow never stumbled upon. The only constant is that it doesn't have a west side – that fell into the sea in Episode One.

The opening scene, which finds Ted in a delightful new parish, is actually an echo of the very first scene in Episode One, when Ted was asking Jack whether he could possibly say Mass at any time in the future. It's impossible to imagine Jack saying Mass, I know. We decided early on, in fact, that you would never see any of them saying Mass or doing any proper priestly business. It didn't feel right, somehow. I'd like to say we had some high-minded purpose in writing this one, but really we were just trying to be funny. If it does comment on racism at all, then fine. I'm really not sure what kind of comment we could possibly be making . . . racism is bad, perhaps? Pretty controversial stuff!

ARTHUR: This started with an idea, at that time unrelated to a theme, that Ted would pull a Chinese face without knowing that there were Chinese people watching. Then we realised this could tie in with one of our really old ideas – and possibly one of our first – that Craggy Island had been harbouring a Nazi for fifty years without anyone knowing. There *is* a connection between Nazism and Rome: after the war, there was some sort of Nazi escape route that led to the Vatican.

Another take on the racist theme, and a further embarrassment for Ted, is the way the Craggy Islanders react. They think they ought to become zealous racists – which is exactly the opposite of what Ted wants. It's the reverse of their reaction in *The Passion of Saint Tibulus*, when Ted actively wanted them to follow his example – which they spectacularly failed to do.

Someone asked why Jack keeps hiding in cupboards and clocks in the episode. It's this condition he developed. We called it claustrophilia: an addiction to small places.

PART ONE

SCENE 1 EXT./DAY 1
SET: ANOTHER PAROCHIAL HOUSE
We see a lovely Parochial House in beautiful surroundings. Trees, nice lawn, etc. Birds sing in the trees and it's a beautiful sunny day. We see a caption that reads 'Castlelawn Parochial House, Dublin'.

SCENE 2 INT./DAY 1
SET: ANOTHER PAROCHIAL HOUSE
A modern but cosy-looking Parochial House. Ted is sitting with a glass of port in one hand, looking at some notes on his lap. An older, kind-looking priest sits nearby, smoking a pipe. A man in a nice suit is poring over some ledgers on a table in the background.

TED: What about Tuesday? Can you do the eleven o'clock?

OLD (*posh, south Dublin accent*): Ted, I'll do the eleven and the twelve. You should have a rest after that weekend away.

TED: Well, Paris does tend to tire me out. Thanks, Father!

A younger priest bounds in. He has a white sweater tied around his shoulders.

YOUNG (*posh accent*): I'm off for a game. Ted, care to join me?

TED: No, thanks, Darren! What time are we off to the Curragh for the races?

DARREN: I suppose after lunch. Oh, and Mrs Dunne hopes you like pheasant!

TED: I love pheasant! (*Father Darren bounds off.*) Ah, yes, this is what it's all about. A fine port, beautiful surroundings and intelligent company.

OLD: Did you not have all that at your last parish?

TED (*darkly*): No.

OLD: Dublin seems to suit you, though. You've got a newfound gleam in your eye.

TED: Oh, yes, I'll be staying here for a good while . . . as long as I don't somehow mess it up for myself by doing something stupid!

The man at the table turns round. He peers over the top of half-spectacles.

MAN: Most of these accounts are in order, Father Smith, but I wonder if I could ask Father Crilly a thing or two about some of these things he's put down under 'expenses' . . .

SCENE 3 INT./NIGHT 1
SET: FRONT DOOR
The front door opens, revealing Dougal.

DOUGAL: TED!!!!!

We see Ted standing there in the rain, carrying two suitcases, dripping wet, miserable.

SCENE 4 INT./DAY 2
SET: PAROCHIAL HOUSE
Ted is sitting at the table, looking grumpy. The house seems to have become very grim since he's been away. We hear a constant squeaky, repetitive noise coming from somewhere in the room.

TED: What's that incredibly annoying noise?

DOUGAL: That's Renaldo. It was a bit lonely without you, Ted, so I got a hamster instead.

TED: Yes. Can I ask, though . . . does he ever stop running in that *fecking* wheel?

We see a hamster in a wheel. This is where the spinning, squeaky noise was coming from. Dougal is sitting at the table, mending a tiny bicycle.

DOUGAL: No. (*He holds up the bicycle.*) Ever since he rode this into his feedtray, he's had to use the wheel. But don't worry, I think there's just something wrong with the brakes.

Ted tries to take this in.

TED: Does he ever stop, though? You'd think Tommy Lee Jones was after him.

Dougal continues to work on the bicycle.

TED: How long has Jack been living in there?

DOUGAL: Ah, he started just a few days after you left.

Pause. Ted sits there, still in the same depressed slump. The wheel squeaks away relentlessly and in the background we can see the wheel spinning.

Suddenly Jack calmly gets out of a chest that was sitting in one corner of the room, walks over to the table and takes a sandwich from it. Then he goes back to the chest and climbs inside. Ted watches all this dispassionately.

TED: Maybe he's agoraphobic . . .

DOUGAL: Jack? Scared of fights? I don't think so, Ted.

Ted walks to the window and looks outside. Suddenly Mrs Doyle falls off the roof outside, passing by the window on her way. Ted stares out dispassionately. Pause.

TED (*almost to himself*): Mrs Doyle just fell off the roof. (*Pause.*) I think I might go out, Dougal – visit Father Fitzpatrick. I think he has a book belonging to me . . .

Ted puts on his coat. He is stopped halfway by the hamster's wheel suddenly speeding up, like a washing machine on spin-cycle. The hutch starts shaking. Ted watches, mesmerised.

SCENE 5 EXT./DAY 2
SET: SEAMUS FITZPATRICK'S PAROCHIAL
HOUSE
An old, grumpy-looking priest, Father Seamus Fitzpatrick, is looking through a shelf of books. In the background Wagner music plays on a stereo. There are two doors in the room, one leading out into the hall, the other closed and padlocked.

FITZPATRICK: . . . Let's see, let's see . . . (*We see Ted standing nearby. Fitzpatrick takes an old, dusty book from the shelf.*) . . . Ah, yes . . . Humanae Vitae . . . I sometimes leaf through it just to remind myself how far we've come . . . (*He puts it back on the shelf, then starts running his finger along the line.*) . . . The Celebration of the Christian Mystery . . . Daeus Canida . . . Ventra Mepolo . . . where is it, where is it . . . ah . . . Stephen King's *The Shining*. (*He takes it down and hands it to Ted.*) Here you are . . .

TED: Did you like it?

FITZPATRICK: . . . Well . . .

TED: Well, the one with the vampires is much better. But *Firestarter* is very good. It's about this psychic girl who can start fires on people just by looking at them. I'll get that one for you if you want.

FITZPATRICK: Ah . . . no. Thank you.

TED: OK, so . . . thanks for the tea! I'll see you next time we, ah . . we . . . Sorry about this, Father, but . . . if you don't mind me asking . . . what have you got a padlock on that door for? Is there something 'top secret' in there?!!

FITZPATRICK: Oh, my collection!

TED: Yes! I heard you have an interest in, ah, what was it? War memorabilia and all that.

FITZPATRICK: That's right, yes. Do you want to have a look?

TED: I'd love to!

Fitzpatrick starts unlocking the latch. He opens the door. We don't see the whole room all at once – just one 'exhibit' at a time. First of all, they stop in front of a shell-casing with a Nazi insignia on the side.

FITZPATRICK: This'd be from a German gun during the advance on Russia. See that? You see there's where the hammer strikes the shell-casing . . .

TED: Gosh, that's very interesting . . .

They move on to another 'display'. In it we see lots of helmets.

FITZPATRICK: These are helmets – infantry, mostly . . .

TED: These would be German as well, wouldn't they?

FITZPATRICK: That's right.

The next exhibit is a full S.S. uniform on a tailor's dummy.

TED: You don't have anything from the Allied side at all, do you?

FITZPATRICK: No, no, no. I wouldn't be interested in that type of thing, to be honest.

Cut wide to reveal the room in its entirety. Nazi banners and flags lie everywhere. There is a massive swastika hanging over the whole display. Ted looks ever so slightly worried.

TED: Right! Well, that's my curiosity satisfied . . .

Fitzpatrick puts an arm round Ted's shoulder, and shows him a photograph.

FITZPATRICK (*ignores him*): This man here, see him there beside the Führer? Sigmund Hoff. Did you know Sigmund would be the German equivalent of Seamus? That'd be *my* name if I'd been born in Germany . . . Stalingrad. God, we put up a great fight there.

TED: We? . . .

FITZPATRICK: We? Sorry, oh, no, I mean the Germans. Look. This is one of the last photographs taken of Herr Hitler. He's signing a few death warrants here.

TED: Yes, ha, ha . . . Funny how you get more right wing as you get older . . . anyway . . . It's great, all this stuff —

FITZPATRICK: A lot of people aren't too sure about it when they see it. But you seem genuinely interested.

TED: Oh, yes. I am genuinely interested.

Ted is backing away and he steps on something. We hear an old man screaming. Ted realises he has stepped on someone's foot. What Ted thought to be another display covered by a blanket is in reality an old man.

OLD MAN: Aaarrgh!!! Was ist das?

FITZPATRICK: What are you doing in here! I told you, no sleeping here!

The man says something in German. Fitzpatrick

responds in German. The man starts crying. He attempts a Nazi salute but Fitzpatrick grabs his arm and places it back by his side.

FITZPATRICK: This is just an old friend of mine, Ted. I'll see you again . . . (*The old man starts singing 'Deutschland über Alles'.*) Good luck Ted!

TED: Ah . . . yes . . . goodbye!

Ted leaves, the two men shouting behind him.

SCENE 6 INT./DAY 2
SET: HALL
Ted is passing by a grandfather clock. He notices that it is showing the wrong time. He looks at his own watch, then adjusts the hands on the clock. As he moves it to four, we hear a muffled clank of the bell inside, followed by 'feck!'. The muffled bell sounds again, and we hear 'arse!' It rings again, we hear 'drink!'. Ted opens the front of the clock. We see Jack, who looks at Ted for a moment or two, then slowly closes the door.

SCENE 7 INT./DAY 2
SET: PAROCHIAL HOUSE
Dougal is reading a book. Ted walks in. He goes to the mantelpiece, puts his finger on it, and notices a lot of dust. He then runs his finger more slowly along the shelf and we cut to reveal that a large pyramid of dust has formed where his finger has stopped.

TED: Right! That's it! I'm not living in filth any more! Dougal, we have to get this place cleaned. And look at you! Look at that hole in your tanktop. What if the parishioners saw that?

DOUGAL: Where, Ted— Ah, God, would you look at that—

He stands up to examine a tiny hole in his sweater. He turns around while still looking at it and there is a massive hole in the back, one that exposes everything from shoulders to waistline. Ted sees something else.

TED: And this here, look! A perfectly square bit of black dirt on the window. (*We see that it is a perfectly square bit of black dirt.*) How on earth can you get a perfectly square bit of black dirt on a window? Surely that's practically impossible!

DOUGAL: It's just, Mrs Doyle's back is very bad since she fell off the roof. She can't do any cleaning.*

TED: Well, then . . . damn it, I'm just going to come out and say it . . . We're going to have to clean the place ourselves!

DOUGAL (*gobsmacked*): What!!!!

TED: You heard me! Are you with me, Dougal?

DOUGAL: Well . . . yeah!

TED: Then let's go! Let's clean this mother!

DOUGAL: Yeah!

They look around, unsure of what to do. The energy level drops back to zero before our eyes. Ted picks up a can of beer, carries it over to the bin, and drops it in, but cautiously, as if he's not sure he's doing it right.

DOUGAL: What about that bit of the lamp that came off? I could pick that up.

TED: Good idea.

Dougal picks it up slowly. He seems delighted to have accomplished this difficult task.

DOUGAL: Wow.

TED: Well done, Dougal. (*Pause.*) I'm bored now.

DOUGAL: Yeah.

Ted takes the lamp off him.

TED: Dougal, look. (*He puts the lampshade on his head. He smiles and does a pathetic 'Chinaman' impression. Dougal doesn't laugh.*) I am Chinese, if you please . . . Come on, Dougal! Lighten up!

He turns around, still doing his impression, and freezes. Outside, looking through the window with hurt and disappointed looks on their faces, are three Chinese people: a man, a woman, and their son, who looks about seventeen.

TED: Uh . . . (*The Chinese people turn sadly and move away from the window. Ted's mouth drops open.*) Wha . . . wha . . . who . . . Dougal!! There were Chinese people there!

---

*In the final version, we inserted a scene here showing Mrs Doyle falling off the roof.

DOUGAL: Oh, right, yeah.

TED: They — I mean . . . what? What is . . . I mean . . .

DOUGAL: That's the Yin family. They live over there on the other side of the island.

TED: But . . . since when have Chinese people been living on the island?

DOUGAL: There's a load of them there in that Chinatown area.

TED: Chinatown area – there's a Chinatown on Craggy Island? But they . . . I wouldn't have . . . I wouldn't have done a Chinaman impression if I thought a Chinaman would actually see me doing a Chinaman impression!

DOUGAL: Why not, Ted?

TED: Because . . . because it's racist! They'll think I'm a racist! (*Putting on his coat.*) I've got to catch them and explain that I'm not a racist.

DOUGAL: You'd better be quick, Ted. They're getting into their car!

SCENE 8 EXT./DAY 2
SET: OUTSIDE PAROCHIAL HOUSE
Ted is in front of the car. The engine has started and the driver is revving aggressively. Ted is in front of it, his hands outstretched.

TED: . . . and basically, if I don't stretch my eyes like that from time to time, I get this thing the doctor calls 'fat eyes' . . . (*The driver starts beeping the horn furiously and revving towards Ted.*) . . . so I hope you wouldn't think that this'd be anything of a racial nature . . . (*He has to hop out of the way as the car goes past. He starts running alongside the car.*) . . . So I'm glad we cleared that up. Come again! See you, bye!!

The car has driven off.

SCENE 9 INT./DAY 2
SET: PAROCHIAL HOUSE
Later the same day. Ted comes into the living room.

DOUGAL: There you are, Ted. Where were you?

TED: I just went to order some stuff for the

house, get rid of this tat. Dougal, you don't think I upset those Chinese people earlier?

DOUGAL: I don't know, Ted. It's like the time when we had that variety show and you decided to do that impression of Stephen Hawking.

TED: Well, he's the last person you'd expect to turn up. That was a million-to-one chance. God, he can fairly move in that wheelchair when he's angry.

DOUGAL: Don't worry about it, Ted. (*He*

points at Ted's bag.) Ah, did you go to Habitat?

TED: No. Habit Hat. Like Habitat it sells soft furnishings, but also clothes for priests. It used to be called Habits and Hats, but when priests stopped wearing hats in 1965, they changed the name and started to sell soft furnishings instead. Instead of hats.

DOUGAL: Does it not get confused with Habitat, though?

TED: No, that's never happened. Except just there, when you did it.

DOUGAL: So, anyway, what stuff did you get?

TED: I got some priests' socks. Really black ones.

DOUGAL: I read somewhere – I think it was in an article about priests' socks – that priests' socks are blacker than any other type of socks.

TED: That's right. Sometimes you see lay people wearing what *look* like black socks, but if you look closely, you'll see that they're very, very, very, very, *very, very, very* . . . dark blue.

DOUGAL: Actually, that's true. I thought my Uncle Tommy was wearing black socks, but when I looked at them closely they were just very, very, very, very . . . *very, very, very, very* . . . dark blue.

TED: That's right. Don't ever get black socks from a normal shop, Dougal. They'll shaft you every time.

Ted leaves. Dougal looks worried at this final thought.

SCENE 10 EXT./DAY 2
SET: ROAD
Ted comes out of the house. He sees Colm Matthews, an old farmer, walking along the road. He is some distance away, so he has to shout.

COLM: Hello, there, Father!

TED: Ah, Colm, hello! Off on a stroll?

COLM: I am! Same as yourself!

TED: Good, good!

COLM: I hear you're a racist now, Father!

TED: What?!!

COLM: How'd you get interested in that type of thing?

TED: Who said I was a racist?

COLM: Everyone's saying it, Father. Should we all be racists now? What's the official line the Church is taking on this?

TED: No, no . . .

COLM: Only, the farm takes up most of the day, and at night I just like a cup of tea. I mightn't have the time to devote myself full time to the old racism. Who are we against, anyway?

An old woman, Mrs Carberry, comes on the scene. She also stops several yards away.

MRS CARBERRY: Good for you, Father!

TED: What? Oh, Mrs Carberry . . . what?

MRS CARBERRY: Good for you! Well, someone had the guts to stand up to them at last. Coming over here, taking our jobs and our women, and acting like they own the place. Well done, Father! Good for you! Good for you! I'd like to feckin' . . . (*She is apoplectic with rage. In an attack of physical inarticulacy, she punches the air suddenly as if attacking several people.*) FECKIN' GREEKS!!!!

COLM: It's not the Greeks, it's the Chinese he's after.

TED: I'm not after the Chinese!

MRS CARBERRY: I don't care who we get, as long as I can have a go at the Greeks. They invented gayness!

TED: Look, we're not having a go at

anybody! I'm not racist! All right? God!

Ted storms off. Colm and Mrs Carberry look at each other. Then Colm walks off. Mrs Carberry has another brief attack.

MRS CARBERRY: FECKIN' GREEKS!!!!

Pause. Mrs Carberry turns to Colm.

MRS CARBERRY: How's Mary?

COLM: Oh, she's fine. She got that job.

MRS CARBERRY: Great!

SCENE 11 EXT./NIGHT 2
SET: PUB
Ted looks very unhappy. He sees the pub and decides to go in.

SCENE 12 EXT./NIGHT 2
SET: PUB
Ted walks in. The pub is buzzing with activity. The noise suddenly stops. Ted freezes. The pub is filled with about thirty Chinese people, and they've all stopped to look at him: men holding pints of Guinness to their mouths, some old lads playing Mah-jong. Ted stands there and laughs uncertainly.

END OF PART ONE

* * *

PART TWO

SCENE 13 INT./DAY 3
SET: A HOUSE
The Yin family home. Father and son are having an argument.

FATHER: That is my final word.

SON: Father, be reasonable.

FATHER: I will not.

SON: Father, you must realise. The old ways are dying. This is a new world. The young have ideas of their own, roads they must travel—

FATHER: No. I am sorry, but there is nothing in gangster rap that appeals to me. It's just noise. Now maybe some of the West-Coast rappers, some of the lighter stuff like DJ Jazzy Jeff— (*The telephone rings.*) Hold on. (*He answers it.*) Hello? (*It is Ted on the line.*)

TED: Is that the Yin dynasty? Family! I mean family!

FATHER: Yes, this is Sean Yin.

TED: This is Father Ted Crilly.

FATHER: Oh . . .

TED: I just wanted to say how sorry I am about . . . I think there's been a *huge* misunderstanding.

FATHER: Father Crilly, I'm sure you meant nothing by it.

TED: Why not drop round to the Parochial House and we can have some tea or a few drinks and clear the whole thing up?

FATHER: Yes, yes. OK, Father. That would be nice.

TED: Right . . . I'll see you in a while, then. (*He puts the telephone down.*) Ah, ha, Dougal! That's everything cleared up. They're coming round this afternoon. I'll just be really nice to them, and people will stop saying I'm a racist. Great! Nothing can go wrong!

DOUGAL: Fantastic! So the story is, you're not a racist.

TED: Yes! What? No, it's not a 'story'. I'm not a racist!

DOUGAL: So if anyone asks me if you're a racist, I'm supposed to say . . . ?

TED: You're not supposed to say anything!

Mrs Doyle enters. She is still walking delicately, arms out from her sides, and she pushes a tea tray along the floor by giving it little kicks.

MRS DOYLE: Hello, everyone! Father Crilly, I hear you're a racist.

DOUGAL: No, Mrs Doyle. He's *not* a racist.

Dougal winks ostentatiously at her.

TED: I'm not! I'm not a racist! Mrs Doyle, we've got to do something for your back. You can't go on like this. (*He walks behind her.*) All right, I'm going to try something . . .

MRS DOYLE: No!

TED: Don't *worry*, Mrs Doyle.

Pause. Ted starts gingerly trying things.

MRS DOYLE: Ahhhhhhaaaaaahhhh!!!!!!! AHHHH!!!! OH, JESUS, MOTHER MARY AND JOSEPH! OH MY GOD! DEAR GOD, MAKE THE PAIN GO AWAY!

TED: All right! All right! OK, now, just relax . . . (*He takes her neck in a sort of choke hold. She starts whimpering.*) Don't worry . . .

MRS DOYLE (*tiny whimper*): Ohh, nooo, nooo, nooo . . .

TED: Mrs Doyle, just relax!

Ted wrenches her neck the other way with a single move and a cracking sound. Pause. Ted looks worried.

MRS DOYLE (*frozen in this final position*): Oh . . . oh, yes, that's much better.

TED: Are you sure? You look a bit . . .

She starts to move off, sideways, frozen in an absolutely horrendously painful-looking stance.

MRS DOYLE (*starts to move off, sideways*): No, no . . . this is great! I'll be fine now, Father . . .

TED: All right, maybe I should try . . .

MRS DOYLE: No! Seriously, Father, that's made all the difference. I feel twenty years younger . . .

She crabwalks from the room. Dougal is at the window.

DOUGAL: Ted, the Chinese people are coming.

TED: Oh, right . . . where are they? (*He throws a few cigarette packets, beer bottles and other bits of rubbish into the bin. He notices the black mark on the window.*) Oh, feck it, this big mark is still here. Never mind . . . (*He waves through the window to the Chinese people.*) Hello! Hello!

SCENE 14 EXT./DAY 3
SET: OUTSIDE HOUSE
The father and son are approaching.

SON: I don't know why we have to talk to this fascist.

FATHER: Now, come on, it may just have been . . .

They see Ted and start to wave, but stop short when

they notice something.

SCENE 15 EXT./DAY 3
SET: WINDOW
Cut to their point of view of Ted. From this position, the black mark on the window is directly below Ted's nose, and looks like a little Hitler moustache. Ted's waving resembles a Nazi salute.

SCENE 16 EXT./DAY 3
SET: OUTSIDE HOUSE
Father and son both frown. The son turns angrily and storms away. The father follows.

SCENE 17 INT./DAY 3
SET: PAROCHIAL HOUSE
Ted stops waving.

TED: Where are they going? (*Ranting.*) My God! I invite them up here, and then they won't even let me tell them my side of the story! . . .

Cut to a shot from the other side of the window. Ted's angry hand gestures make him look like a wildly gesticulating Führer.

SCENE 18 INT./NIGHT 3
SET: TED AND DOUGAL'S BEDROOM
We shouldn't be quite sure where we are at first. Jack is lying on the ground, in near-darkness, asleep with a smile on his face. The camera pulls back and rises to reveal that he is under Ted's bed. Ted and Dougal are in bed, Ted is sitting up and looking anxious.

TED: This is terrible. Everyone thinks I'm some kind of Nazi racist. But I'm not. You know, one of my favourite songs is 'Ebony and Ivory'. I almost bought that when it came out. Ohh, what can I do? . . .

DOUGAL: Ted, here's an idea right off the top of my head. I haven't thought it through, so it's probably not brilliant, but what the hell, I'll just talk and see what comes out. You ready?

TED: Hold on a second and I'll strap myself in.

DOUGAL: How about some kind of festival celebrating all the different cultures of Craggy Island? You could organise it, say a few

words, and then people will think you're a fantastic man, rather than a big racist.

Pause.

TED: My God.

DOUGAL: What?

TED: That's a good idea!

DOUGAL: No, it's not!

TED: It is, Dougal! It is!

DOUGAL: No, I'm sorry, Ted, I just can't accept that I had a good idea. You're just being nice.

TED: Dougal, you know me, I'd be honest with you. I mean, haven't I told you in the past when your ideas were crap? . . .

DOUGAL: Yes . . .

TED: . . . Because, frankly, you're not a hugely intelligent person.

DOUGAL: If anything, Ted, that's an understatement.

TED: Exactly. But this one, this is actually good.

DOUGAL: Ted, there's probably something wrong with it. You just haven't thought it through.

TED: Yes, but . . . usually your ideas . . . you immediately know that they're crap. I mean . . . (*He snaps his fingers.*) . . . like *that.*

DOUGAL (*rubbing his chin*): Yes . . .

TED: OK, you've had a brilliant idea. But just break it down for me a bit more. So what would an event celebrating all the different cultures of Craggy Island actually be like?

Pause. Dougal stares straight at Ted.

DOUGAL: What?

TED: What would the day involve? I mean, yes, a celebration. But what kind of celebration? What form could it take? (*Dougal looks a bit stressed.*) What would it—

DOUGAL: Ted, I want out.

TED: What do you mean?

DOUGAL: I went too far, too soon. I didn't know what I was getting into.

TED: Dougal, just relax.

DOUGAL (*stands up and picks up his duvet*): No, Ted. I didn't know you had to follow up a good idea with lots more little good ideas. I'm sorry. I'll sleep in the spare room.

TED: Dougal —

DOUGAL (*at the door*): I'm sorry.

He leaves. Ted sighs and turns out the light.

TED: GOODNIGHT, THEN, DOUGAL!

DOUGAL (*from outside*): GOODNIGHT!

Pause.

JACK: Goodnight.

TED: Goodnight, Father — Aaarghhh!*

Ted jumps out of bed, turns on the light and looks at his bed, terrified.

SCENE 19 INT./DAY 4
SET: SEAMUS FITZPATRICK'S PAROCHIAL HOUSE
This is the Parochial House we were in earlier. We are in the small room filled with Nazi memorabilia. Father Fitzpatrick is berating the old priest.

---

*This may be unclear – Jack's under the bed.

FITZPATRICK: You old fool. I've sheltered you for fifty years, and you've never once made me a cup of tea!

OLD MAN (*German accent*): You make the tea. I do the washing up!

FITZPATRICK (*gasps*): When have you ever done the washing up?

OLD MAN: I did it for all of 1947 and 1973.

FITZPATRICK (*gasps*): Oh! You liar! You kept dropping the plates and going (*Dreadful German impression.*) 'Ach, I am so tired. I never washed plates when I was with the Wehrmacht! Blah-di-blah-di-blah. . .' Oh! You're driving me insane! I'm going to take a valium.

OLD MAN: I want one, too!

FITZPATRICK: Why must you ape my every move? Oh, all right!

He takes out a bottle, empties two pills into his hand and gives one to the old man. They both down the pills with a glass of water.

FITZPATRICK (*splutters*): Wait! This isn't valium! These are the cyanide pills we kept for emergencies! You stupid fool! You put the cyanide pills beside the valium! That's just asking for trouble!

OLD MAN: Oh, shut up!

FITZPATRICK: You shut up! We're going to die in fifteen seconds!

OLD MAN: Well, that's just fine by me.

FITZPATRICK: Good. It's fine by me, too.

OLD MAN: I'm glad it is.

FITZPATRICK: Good. I'm glad, too.

OLD MAN: Good.

FITZPATRICK: Good.

They walk away from each other in a huff, then drop down dead.

SCENE 20 INT./DAY 4
SET: STAIRS
We see Mrs Doyle at the top of the stairs, her back still arched uncomfortably so that she's feeling her way down. We see her foot about to step on the tiny hamster bicycle. She steps on it and falls down the stairs.

MRS DOYLE: Oh, Mother of God! Oh, Jesus, Mary and Joseph! Oh, God help me!

She lands at the bottom of the stairs, going out of shot, and then jumps back up into shot.

MRS DOYLE: I'M CURED!!!!!

Ted and Dougal come into the hallway, putting on their coats.

TED: What happened, Mrs Doyle?

MRS DOYLE: I stepped on the hamster's bike and fell down the stairs, Father.

TED: Dougal, I told you to put that bike away safely!

DOUGAL: I did! I put it back in the cage!

MRS DOYLE: Don't worry, Father! I feel fantastic! This is great! I forgot my head could go right round like this!

TED: All right, well, listen, that delivery from Habit Hat is coming today, so when it arrives, give Father Jack . . . where is Father Jack?

MRS DOYLE: I think he's up the chimney.

TED: Right.

MRS DOYLE: Will I burn him out, Father?

TED: Good God, no. The smoke's back up and it'll be all over the house. No, leave him be – he's just going through a phase. Just leave his new clothes out when they come, or he'll be spreading dust all over the place like a big atomic cloud.

DOUGAL: God, yeah, it'd be like Hiroshima all over again.

TED: God, yes. But, Dougal, to be honest, we should never have brought him there in the first place. Anyway, Mrs Doyle, put all the stuff up . . . all the new . . . rugs and the . . . things for the . . . chairs . . . I don't know, that's your 'thing' really. I wouldn't know anything about all that sort of stuff, because I'm a man. Anyway, we're off to the celebration of Craggy Island's ethnic diversity.

SCENE 21 EXT./DAY 4*
SET: PAROCHIAL HALL
We see an exterior shot of the parochial hall. A banner outside reads 'Tonight – Special Event – a Celebration of Craggy Island's Ethnic Diversity'.

SCENE 22 INT./DAY 4
SET: PAROCHIAL HALL
We see a wide view of the hall. All the Chinese population are present, including the Yin family. The teenage Yin is wearing headphones. Rap music seeps out from them. Ted addresses the congregation. There is a white screen behind him.

TED: Welcome. Wilkommen. Bien venue. (*He says welcome in about six different languages.*) It's an honour and a privilege for me to present this celebration of the wide diversity of cultures that exists on Craggy Island today – namely, Chinese people, and people from Craggy Island . . . I have prepared a short slide presentation to reflect this multicultural mix, so without further ado, I shall start the show.

The lights go off. Ted presses a button. The first slide is projected on the wall behind him. It shows Ted with his arm around a black man. The man is normally dressed, wearing an Aran jumper and smiling.

TED: This man visited the island a few years ago. I forget his name, but I got on very well

*We deleted this scene from the final version.

with him. Just thought I'd throw that in at the start . . .

Cut to a shot of the unresponsive audience. Ted presses another button. Another slide, this time of a Maori.

TED: The Maori . . . (*Long pause.*) I'm sorry. Don't know how that got in there. Sorry about that, folks. Of course, there are no Maoris on Craggy Island.

MAORI (*insulted*): Hey!

Cut to a Chinese man in the audience.

CHINESE MAN: Will there be any free drink at this?

TED: Yes, there will be a limited supply of free drink afterwards.

CHINESE MAN: It's probably feckin' Harp.

Ted carries on, oblivious. Another slide, this time of Chairman Mao.

TED: Chairman Mao, Secretary of The Communist Party of China, one of the biggest Communist parties in the world, and in my view the best.

Another slide comes up. It is Mr Miyagi from 'The Karate Kid'.

TED: Mr Miyagi from *The Karate Kid*. One of my favourite films. Not because of the Karate Kid himself, but because of Mr Miyagi. Not a day goes by when I don't remember one of his words of wisdom. For instance, (*solemnly*) 'You look revenge, better start by digging two graves' and 'You make good fight, earn respect. Then nobody bother you.'

Next slide. It is Kato from the Pink Panther films, fighting with Peter Sellers.

TED: Kato! Where would he spring from next?

Next slide. David Carradine.

TED: Kung Fu. Named after his art. And played by the actor David Carradine.

Next slide. Ming the Merciless.

TED: Ming the Merciless.

The Maori and the Chinese man look at each other, confused. The next slide is of a big crowd of Chinese people.

TED: But best of all, the Chinese people themselves. Look at them there. They're great. Well done to you all! I applaud you for your great strength in times of adversity, such as the One Hundred Year's War, and the Cultural Revolution. A great bunch of lads. And lasses of course – mustn't forget the Chinese ladies. Right, I think I've addressed all aspects of Chinese culture . . .

A slide of Ted comes up, followed by a slide that reads 'Not a Racist'. This sequence of two slides repeats while Ted speaks.

TED: . . . And I'd like to thank you all for coming. It's been a great night . . . If anyone wants a word with me afterwards, feel free to come over and have a bit of an old chat . . .

He rambles on, the two slides repeating behind him.

SCENE 23 INT./DAY 4
SET: PAROCHIAL HALL
Everyone is standing around drinking. The father and son are still there.

FATHER: Well, the slide show was a big pile of crap . . .

DOUGAL: Ha! Told you, Ted!

FATHER: But the free drink is appreciated. Thank you, Father Crilly.

TED: I just wanted to clear things up. I'm not a fascist, I'm a pricst. Fascists go round dressing in black and telling people what to do. Whereas priests . . . (*Long pause. Ted has no idea what to say next.*) More drink!

EVERYONE: Hurray!

SCENE 24 INT./DAY 4
SET: PAROCHIAL HOUSE
Mrs Doyle is leading a young man into the living room. He has a huge box that he is dragging behind him.

MRS DOYLE: Anywhere around there. Would you like a cup of tea?

MAN: Oh, no, thanks. I have a kind of allergic reaction to it. It's very rare but pretty serious. If I drink tea there's a seventy per

cent chance that I'll die.

MRS DOYLE: Well, I'll make you a cup anyway, in case you change your mind.

MAN: Eh, thanks anyway.

He leaves. Mrs Doyle turns her attention to the large box that the delivery man left. She opens it up and takes a letter out of it. She looks at the letter, frowns, then looks into the box and frowns.

SCENE 25 INT./DAY 4
SET: PAROCHIAL HALL
A few of the Chinese men are playing traditional Irish music on bodhrans, tin whistles and fiddles. They're pretty good. Cut to Ted with the rest of the Chinese. Dougal looks on in confusion.

TED: To China!

EVERYONE: Hurray!

FATHER: To Craggy Island!

EVERYONE: Hurray!

TED: More drink!

BARMAN: I'm sorry, the bar is closed.

TED: Tsk. I tell you what, how about everyone comes back to my place?!

EVERYONE: Hurray!

DOUGAL: Wait! I need to go to the toilet first.

EVERYONE: Hurray!

SCENE 26 INT./DAY 4
SET: PAROCHIAL HOUSE
Mrs Doyle opens the door.

EVERYONE: Hurray!

TED: Mrs Doyle, we have guests! (*Aside.*) Did that stuff come?

MRS DOYLE: Oh, yes, Father. I felt so fantastic, I put it all up in less than an hour. And there was this letter . . .

Ted takes the letter, going towards the door of the living room. The excited Chinese people huddle behind him.

TED: Letter? (*He reads it.*) Dear Father Crilly, on the instructions of our recently deceased client, Father Seamus Fitzpatrick, here are some items which he specified you should have . . .

Ted absent-mindedly opens the door.

SCENE 27 INT./DAY 4
SET: PAROCHIAL HOUSE
Ted enters the room, followed by all the Chinese people. They all stop talking. Ted continues reading, oblivious to the fact that the entire room is covered in swastikas, Nazi memorabilia, etc.

TED: . . . In the event of his death . . .

He looks around at last. He doesn't do anything. There is a stunned silence. We then hear a 'ching-ching' noise. Ted moves one of the Chinese people to one side and the hamster, riding his little bicycle, cycles across the floor and past the group of men, into the hallway. It rings the bell again once it's in the hallway. Pause.

TED: I can explain everything. (*He looks into the hallway, into which the hamster has disappeared, then back into the room loaded with Nazi stuff.*) Actually . . . no, I can't.

POST-CREDIT SEQUENCE
SCENE 28 INT./DAY 4
SET: A HOUSE
Back in the Yin home, father and son are watching the television. The telephone rings. The father goes to answer it. The son eats a sandwich.

FATHER: Hello?

It is Ted on the line, looking hugely frantic.

TED: Ah, hello, have you opened that present yet?

FATHER: No. Looking forward to it, though. A year's supply of Whyte & Mackay whisky! How very generous of you!

We see a big box behind him, with 'Whyte & Mackay Whisky' written on the side. Cut back to Ted. We see there is a huge pile of empty whiskey bottles in one corner of the room.

TED: Yes, the problem there is, y'see . . . well, basically . . . Father Hackett's been having this rather unusual problem . . .

As Ted speaks, we see Jack, dressed in full S.S. gear, getting out of the box. The son's mouth hangs open, watching this. Jack drunkenly walks over to the table, grabs a bit of sandwich, then walks back and gets inside the box.

FATHER: All right, Father. Bye! (*He turns to the son.*) Apparently, we're not to open the box.

The son looks at him, a piece of meat hanging from his mouth.

THE END

chirpy Burpy cheap sheep

GRAHAM: This episode began life as something entirely different. The plot originally started with Ted and Dougal on an open-topped bus that was on a sightseeing tour of Craggy Island. The tour was terrible. They were exposed to the elements and it started raining, so they headed downstairs. But they were prevented from getting downstairs by a little dog barking like mad at them at the foot of the stairs. That's it. We thought we could make a plot out of that. We liked the idea for about a morning, but couldn't see where it would go (actually, I defy anyone to see where that could go). Finally we decided that the only thing we could keep was the title – which was at that stage *The Beast of Craggy Island* (a reference to the little dog) – and instead invent a *Hound of the Baskervilles*-type story, with Ted as Sherlock Holmes and Dougal as Dr Watson. So the original title had to go.

There's a nod to Stanley Kubrick in this episode. When Chris the sheep is looking at the two farmers and the camera pans from mouth to mouth, it's a straight copy from the scene where Hal lip-reads in *2001*. Also, the names of the farmers, 'Giant', Hud' and 'Fargo' come from three of our favourite wide-open-spaces movies.

ARTHUR: This doesn't exactly have an airtight plot, so don't look too closely. While we were happy with Ted and Dougal's story, we really didn't know what to do with Jack and Mrs Doyle. In the end, Jack being oddly affected by leap years gave us a chance to show him in a different guise – and one highly appropriate to Frank Kelly. Frank is actually very nimble, very light on his feet, so it was a pleasure to show him dancing. Mrs Doyle ended up doing the opposite – dragging her feet and making the most appalling din when walking. The theory is that she always makes that noise but they've only just noticed it.

Towards the end of this script, the Beck video reference (during Ted's denouement scene) is from Beck's video for their song *Devil's Haircut*. We wanted to copy the way the image freezes and zooms electronically into details you didn't notice before, but in our version, we put in ridiculous shots with fur coats, 'baa' sounds, party hats and crowns.

PART ONE

SCENE 1 EXT./DAY 1
SET: FIELD
We see a sign that reads . . . ' "King of the Sheep"
Weigh-in '98 – Officials and Competitors Entrance'.

SCENE 2 INT./DAY 1
SET: TENT
We see various shots of sheep being 'weighed in.' Cut
to a lone sheep standing in a sheep pen. Cut to a
farmer, Fargo Boyle, leaning over the gate of the pen
looking very fondly at the sheep. Another two
farmers, Giant Reid, and Hud Hastings, join him.

GIANT: Hello, Fargo.

FARGO: Ah, Giant, Hud, hello.

HUD (*looking at his sheep*)**:** You have Chris
looking great for the contest.

We see Ted turning up. He waves to Fargo.

FARGO: Thanks, lads. Father Crilly! Hello,
there!

He goes off towards Ted.

TED: Fargo, how's The Champ?

FARGO: Ah, he's great. Few quid on him this
year, Father?

TED: Oh, yes. Put the entire annual heating
allowance on him to win.

FARGO: But if he doesn't win, what does that
mean, Father?

TED: Oh, well, we won't have any heating for
the year. But if the rest of the year stays as
warm as the summer, we're laughing! But
come on, it's Chris! He's The Champ! Talk
about a safe bet! See you, Fargo!

Cut back to Hud and Giant.

HUD: Giant, have you heard about this
creature going around terrorising sheep on the
island?

As Hud continues to talk, the camera zooms slowly
between them, in on the sheep.

GIANT: No. Tell me more.

HUD: They say it's as big as a jaguar.

GIANT: The *car?!!*

HUD: No, the big cat thing. And its face is all

teeth – big sharp teeth as sharp as a knife. And
it makes a howling sound that seems to come
from the very gates of hell . . . And its favourite
food is mutton. Mutton from sheep.

GIANT: Has it killed yet?

HUD: No, but it's only a matter of time . . .

Fade out on close-up of a sheep's face.

SCENE 3 EXT./NIGHT 1
SET: SHEEP PEN
The sheep is asleep. It 'baas' uncomfortably in its
sleep. We hear the voices of Hud and Giant.

HUD'S AND GIANT'S VOICES: Mutton
from sheep . . . Has it killed yet? . . . Only a
matter of time . . . Its face is all teeth, all teeth,
all teeth . . .

The sheep wakes up with a start. We hear a distant,
unearthly howl . . .

SCENE 4 EXT./DAY 2
SET: PAROCHIAL HOUSE
Establishing shot of the Parochial House. We hear
various atmospheric sounds of birds and so on.

SCENE 5 INT./DAY 2
SET: PAROCHIAL HOUSE
Inside, the sound of birds, etc., is much, much louder.
Cut to Dougal sitting on the ground beside the record
player. He is looking at an album cover, 'BBC Sound
Effects Volume 4'. Ted is sitting down, reading a
newspaper. He turns the page, and instead of the
noise of the pages turning, we hear loads of pots and
pans rattling. He coughs, and we hear the sound of a

machine gun.

TED: Dougal, give the album a rest now.

DOUGAL: Ah, Ted, come on. It's brilliant! I think people will soon give up listening to pop music, and listen to this type of thing instead.

TED (*chuckles*): You know, when I hear some of the things in the charts today, I wonder if that's not happening already!

DOUGAL: What? This is so good, though, isn't it, Ted? They've got all kinds of things. As if by magic, I can create a big crowd of invisible ducks . . . (*He moves the stylus arm. We hear a steam engine.*) Or take you to darkest Africa . . . (*We hear an explosion.*) Or bring you into a spooky castle on a stormy night . . . (*We hear sounds of a car revving up.*) God, it's fantastic.

TED: Dougal, come on now, please!

We hear the telephone ringing.

TED: Is that the phone ringing or is it another sound effect?

DOUGAL: It's the phone. Unless someone else is playing a sound-effects record.

Ted picks up the telephone.

TED: Hello, Craggy Island Parochial House. Father Ted Crilly speaking.

SCENE 6 INT./DAY 2
SET: FARGO'S LIVING ROOM
We see Fargo the farmer.

FARGO: Father Crilly, Fargo Boyle here.

TED: Ah, Fargo. How's the prizewinner doing? We're all counting on you to come through for us again!

FARGO: Father, that's what I . . . Could you drop by later. I . . . need to speak to you urgently . . .

TED: Certainly, Fargo. What seems to—

We hear the dial tone. Fargo has hung up.

TED: Dougal, I have to go. Something's up with Fargo Boyle. I think there might be something wrong with The Champ.

Mrs Doyle enters the room. She looks a little jittery and a little tired.

TED: Mrs Doyle, are you all right? You look terrible. Doesn't she, Dougal?

DOUGAL: Awful, Ted.

MRS DOYLE: Ah, I didn't get much sleep, Father. I thought I kept hearing a terrible howling noise.

DOUGAL: Oh, that'd be the Beast.

TED: What's this now?

DOUGAL: God, Ted, have you not heard? Everyone's been talking about it . . . except you and me, obviously.

MRS DOYLE: There's something terrible on the moors, Father.

Dougal plays a brief burst of spooky, old-style, flying-saucer sounds. Ted gives him a look and Dougal stops.

TED: Moors? We don't have any moors.

MRS DOYLE: Well, then, there's something terrible roaming about the place where normally there would be moors. They say . . . it might . . . be a kind of giant fox!

Dramatic thunder sound.

TED: Dougal!!!

DOUGAL: Sorry!

TED: Well, I'm sorry, but I'm not going to be taken in by this type of nonsense. Do you remember that panic last year, when everyone was worried about The Small Man of Rochree?

MRS DOYLE: Well, he was a very small man, Father.

TED: That's not unusual in itself, Mrs Doyle. I myself have known many small men and they're just the same as the rest of us. Nothing to fear there at all.

DOUGAL: It couldn't be Jack, could it? You could see how someone would mistake him for a big mad cat.

TED: No, don't forget that during leap years Father Jack is very much affected by the changing of the seasons. For a short while, a marvellous serenity enters his life, and he is at one with nature.

SCENE 7 EXT./DAY 2
SET: FIELD
Cut to Jack, looking clean and rosy-cheeked, running through a field. He sniffs some flowers, pats a little girl on the head, and rolls around with some puppies.

SCENE 8 INT./DAY 2
SET: PAROCHIAL HOUSE
Cut back to Ted.

TED: Ah, yeah, he's great when he's in this mood. If only it lasted a bit longer.

SCENE 9 EXT./DAY 2
SET: FIELD
We see a load of cans of Special Brew on the ground. Jack is throwing up in a bush. He stands up and we see he is completely back to normal. He picks up a puppy and wipes his mouth with it.

SCENE 10 INT./DAY 2
SET: PAROCHIAL HOUSE
Mrs Doyle sees something on the table.

MRS DOYLE: Oh, look, there's my scissors . . .

She walks out of the room. As she walks, we hear a hideous slurping, popping and gurgling noise.

TED: Dougal, I said turn the record off!

DOUGAL: But . . . it is off . . .

Dougal is putting the disc back in its sleeve. They look at the door through which Mrs Doyle went. They look a tad horrified.

SCENE 11 INT./DAY 2
SET: FARGO'S HOUSE
Ted is talking to Fargo Boyle. Dougal stands nearby.

TED: What do you mean Chris won't be in the competition? He's The Champ. You *have* to enter him.

FARGO: All this talk of the Beast has got to him. His nerves are shot. I took a photo of him this morning . . .

He starts taking it out.

TED: His nerves? Fargo, it's a sheep.

FARGO: He always had a very artistic

temperament, Father.

TED: But, I mean, he's not a concert pianist. He's a sheep. I don't see how— (*Fargo shows him the photograph.*) Oh, my God . . . this is Chris?

Fargo hands Ted the photograph. We don't see it. Fargo nods gravely.

FARGO: I mean, when you compare it with what he looked like last year . . .

He hands Ted another photograph.

TED: It's like . . . it's like two completely different sheep!

We see the photographs. There is no discernible difference between the Chris of old and the new Chris.

FARGO: All this talk of the Beast has got to him. He's off his food, he's not sleeping, and he's started . . . burping.

TED: Burping? Can a sheep burp?

FARGO: They're not supposed to burp, I know that! And look at him . . . look at the rings around the eyes; the bored, unhappy turn of the mouth; the sad, dirty texture of his wool.

TED: What the hell happened to him?!

FARGO: Sheep can sense things, Father.

TED: That's very true. (*To Dougal.*) I read once they can feel evil vibrations in the air. In that respect they're very like plants or cars. My God, look at the old Chris . . . (*He smiles as he looks at the first photo.*) Those playful laughlines round the eyes . . . his fluffy coat of fur . . .

DOUGAL: Wool.

TED: Whatever . . . his confident black lips . . or whatever you call those things round their mouth. His cheeky grin. Yes, the whole feeling of 'sheep okayness' is there.

Fargo's composure cracks a bit.

FARGO: Oh, Father, what am I going to do? (*He holds up the second photograph.*) That *thing* out there, that's not Chris! I want Chris back!

TED: Don't say that, Fargo! He needs you now more than he's ever needed you! Come on! I want to see him!

FARGO: He doesn't want to see anybody.

TED: Fargo, that's an order! Take me to see Chris The Unhappy Sheep!

SCENE 12 EXT./DAY 2*
SET: SHEEP PEN
We see a very average-looking sheep standing in a pen. Ted, Dougal and Fargo are standing looking at him. The sheep burps loudly.

FARGO: Oh, God! . . .

Another shot of the sheep. Fargo spins round to Ted.

FARGO: Where is your kind, benevolent God now, Father?!! Where is he?! Tell me this, would a just God allow this to happen to Chris?!

The sheep burps.

TED: Ah, now, come on—

FARGO: It's all God's fault!

TED: Well, it's easy to blame God for everything, Fargo. Certainly he's let me down loads of times. (*Bitterly.*) I mean, *loads* . . . but you just have to presume that he knows what he's up to.

FARGO: I want to believe you, Father. But it's the eternal Catholic dilemma. I think it was Saint Thomas Aquinas who was tortured by doubts . . .

---

*We deleted this scene from the final version.

TED: Yeah? Great. Anyway, best not to think about any of that stuff at all, I find.

FARGO: But if God allows these terrible things to happen, how can we say he is benevolent?

The sheep burps. Ted looks very uncomfortable.

TED: Look, let's just concentrate on the job at hand—

FARGO: But how can there be a God if—

Dougal suddenly yells out and falls to the ground.

TED: Dougal! What's wrong!

DOUGAL: It's my stomach, Ted! I think I've been poisoned!

TED: Fargo, quick! Call Doctor Sinnot! Call Doctor Sinnot!

The sheep does one long, long burp.

SCENE 13 INT./NIGHT 2
SET: TED AND DOUGAL'S BEDROOM
Dougal is in bed, reading happily. Ted comes into the room and takes off his dressing gown.

TED: Well . . . good job, Dougal! That was a number three, though. I asked for number one.[†]

DOUGAL: Sorry about that, Ted.[†]

TED: Let's do a quick run-through now . . . Someone's asking me the difficult questions about religion . . . blah di blah di blah . . . and I give you the signal . . .†

Ted sticks out one finger.†

DOUGAL: Ted, I've just remembered! You have to go and do a big Mass!!†

TED: Very good. And . . .†

DOUGAL: Ah . . . the top half of the island's on fire and they need your help with the dead.†

TED: Great, and number three's the poison thing.†

DOUGAL: God, Ted, what do you think about this Beast affair? Are you scared?†

TED: No, I think it's just . . .†

DOUGAL: They say it's as big as four cats. And it's got one leg that it can retract into its body so it can leap up at you better. And it lights up at night. And it's got four ears and it uses two of them for listening and the other two are kind of backup ears. It's got claws the size of cups and you can't leave it by itself or it goes mad, and then if it goes near water it goes a kind of purple colour, and it's got a fear of stamps. And it can reproduce the smell of fifteen different types of cats . . . Oh, and it's got magnets on its tail so if you're made out of metal it can attach itself to you. And instead of a mouth it's got two faces . . .*

TED: It's only a legend, Dougal. It doesn't exist.

DOUGAL (*sarcastically*)**:** Right, Ted. The way the Phantom of the Opera doesn't exist.

TED: The Phantom of the Opera *doesn't* exist, Dougal. Look, I'm not going into this 'what does exist, what doesn't exist?' debate with you again. But I'm going to have to insist you add those last two examples to the chart.

---

† We deleted this from the final version and the scene began instead with Ted telling Dougal what a bad state Chris the sheep is in. To which Dougal replies that if he were a sheep, he'd be watching his back too.
*Ardal got bored saying this last line as written and changed it on the night without telling us he was going to do so, to, 'Instead of a mouth it's got four arses...', which was just fine by us.

DOUGAL: But, Ted! . . .

TED: Dougal!

Ted hands Dougal a marker. Dougal sulks a little and walks over to a big chart on the wall that reads:

THEY DON'T EXIST
Loch Ness Monster
Frankenstein
'Evil' Badgers
Magnum PI
Crocodile Dundee
Darth Vader

Dougal starts adding Phantom of the Opera to this list.

TED: I'm more worried about that bet I put on Chris being crowned King of the Sheep.

DOUGAL: You don't think he'll win, then?

TED: Come on, Dougal, you saw him. Damn. Ah, well, it's just the heating budget. I see this warm weather lasting a long, long time. (*He hears thunder outside.*) Oh, no, I forgot! Weather *changes*! I'll have to see if John and Mary will let me take my money back tomorrow.

DOUGAL: I might drop down with you and see if they've got Volume 5 of the *BBC Sound Effects* album.

TED: Fair enough. Good night, then, Dougal.

Ted turns off the light. We hear a low, distant howl. Ted turns on the light. Dougal is in bed beside him. They look at each other, scared.

SCENE 14 EXT./DAY 3
SET: JOHN AND MARY'S SHOP
Ted and Dougal approach the door.

DOUGAL: . . . and when it yawns it sounds like Liam Neeson chasing a load of hens round inside a barrel . .

TED (*nudges him*)**:** Hold on, Dougal. Hello, Fargo.

Fargo, who is coming out of the shop, looks at them sadly. He gives a slight wave and walks on, depressed. Ted sighs.

DOUGAL: . . . And it has no knuckles.

SCENE 15 INT./DAY 3
SET: JOHN AND MARY'S SHOP
We see John slamming the door of a broom cupboard.

JOHN: And you can stay in there until you learn some feckin' manners!

MARY: Let me out! You bastard!

Just as the door closes, we see Mary banging her head on the low ceiling of the cupboard.

MARY: Ow!!!!

He locks the door, opens the window and throws the key out.

JOHN: I've thrown the key away! How do you like that?! Eh?!

Ted and Dougal enter the shop.

TED: Hello, John! (*There is a banging from the cupboard.*) Ah . . .

JOHN: HELLO, FATHER CRILLY, HELLO, FATHER McGUIRE.

The banging stops. Ted and Dougal are a little shocked by the loudness of his greeting.

TED: Eh . . . Where's Mary?

JOHN: Oh, she's away at her mother's.

There's a bumping noise from the cupboard.

MARY: Ow!!!!

Pause.

TED: Is . . . is there someone in the cupboard?

Pause.

MARY (*from the cupboard*): Hello, Fathers!

TED: Mary?

JOHN: Ah, Mary, I forgot you were there! I thought you were at your mother's.

MARY (*from the cupboard*): Ah . . . no, I didn't go to my mother's after all. I'm in the cupboard.

TED: Mary . . . what are you doing in there?

JOHN: Eh . . . Oh, I know! It's because of this Beast of Craggy Island thing. I thought Mary would be safer in the cupboard.

MARY (*from the cupboard*): That's right. I'm better off in here.

Pause.

MARY: What can we do for you, Father?

TED: Ah, a pack of twenty Carrolls, please.

MARY (*from the cupboard*): Certainly, Father.

JOHN: I'll get them, love. You stay in the cupboard.

John goes to look for them.

TED (*to an offscreen John*): John . . . can I have a word? . . .

MARY (*from the cupboard*): Is Father McGuire there?

DOUGAL (*oblivious to anything unusual*): I am! Hello, Mary!

MARY (*from the cupboard*): It's a lovely day, isn't it, Father?

DOUGAL: Oh, yes . . .

MARY: You're looking great, anyway.

Over to Ted and John.

TED: I really need to get this money to the girl for this operation . . .

JOHN: Father, I'm sorry but . . . once a bet is put on, I can't cancel it.

TED: I wouldn't ask normally but . . . think about it, John. If you had no kidneys . . .

JOHN: So this woman has no kidneys at all?

TED: No. It's very sad.

JOHN: But if she has no kidneys, wouldn't

she be dead?

TED: Well, she has one kind of kidney the doctors threw together for her. It's made out of GoreTex, I think . . .

JOHN: I'm sorry, Father. A bet's a bet. It's a pity you didn't wait, Father. The odds have lengthened to twenty to one, due to his nervous troubles. Anyway, your cigarettes.

TED: Oh, right, thank you.

DOUGAL: Ted, they don't have the sound-effects album. Tschoh! We might as well just go.

MARY: Bye, Fathers!

They leave.

MARY: Well, I hope you're satisfied!

JOHN: Ah, shut up!

A fist smashes through the cupboard and smashes John in the head.

SCENE 16 EXT./DAY 3
SET: JOHN AND MARY'S SHOP
Ted and Dougal see Giant Reid cycling by on his tatty bike. He wears a big fur coat, like something Bud Flanagan might have worn.

TED: Look, there's Giant Reid. Hello, Giant!

Giant sees them and starts to cycle off hurriedly. The coat hampers this and the sight is oddly ridiculous as he shambles off. He also tries to hide his face with one of his hands.

SCENE 17 INT./DAY 3
SET: PAROCHIAL HOUSE
Ted and Dougal enter. They sit down. Ted is deep in thought.

DOUGAL: What are you thinking about there, Ted? You should see the big serious look on your face!

TED: Dougal, this changing weather business has got me worried. What if it does get cold in winter? All our heating budget is tied up in that load of quivering mutton.

DOUGAL: Well, Ted, I can't see anything we could do. It's pointless even thinking about it. You're only wasting your time. There's nothing we can do about the situation, and that's it. We

just have to accept it. There's nothing we can do. Accept the fact. That's it.

TED: How about we bring Chris here for a few days? The change might do him good.

DOUGAL: Oh, wow!!!! What a brilliant idea! Ted, you're a genius! Fantastic! I knew there'd be something we could do! Didn't I say it!? Didn't I say it to you there a second ago?

TED: No, you didn't. In fact, you said the exact opposite. That there was absolutely nothing we could do.

DOUGAL: Actually, Ted, you've done this to me before, so I took the liberty of taping the conversation. Let's have a listen . . .

He presses the 'play' button.

DOUGAL'S VOICE: . . . Anything we could do. It's pointless even thinking about it. You're only wasting your time. There's nothing we can do about the situation . . .

Pause.

DOUGAL: I stand corrected.

SCENE 18 INT./DAY 3
SET: PAROCHIAL HOUSE HALLWAY
We see Fargo leading Chris into the hall.

TED: There he is now, anyway!

Chris burps.

FARGO: I'm still not sure about this, Father.

TED: Don't worry, Fargo. By the next time you see him, he'll be a new sheep. If not, we'll make him into a jumper and a few chops! (*Fargo just looks at him.*) I'm terribly sorry. That was tasteless. I'm terribly, terribly sorry.

FARGO: I'll be off then, Father.

TED: OK, so, Fargo. And seriously, if there's one place he can be sure of a bit of peace and quiet —

There's a rumble and a roar as Jack falls down the stairs, causing as much noise as can be imagined. He demolishes all the railings as he descends. He finishes off by destroying a vase on a table with his foot. He stands up, looks dazedly at Ted and Fargo, and wanders off into another room in an exaggeratedly grand, vaguely pompous way.

TED: I think it would be an insult to you if I finished that sentence.

Fargo leaves.

DOUGAL: God, Ted. Poor old Chris. Do you think he'll ever be himself again?

TED: 'Course he will, Dougal. It could be a long process, though. We're just going to have to try very, very hard to cheer him up. And remember, not a word about B-E-A-S-T-S.

DOUGAL: Not a word about breasts?

TED: No. Not a word about . . . (*He does an impression of the Beast. He makes growling noises and shapes his hands like claws.*) . . . rowwr. The rowwwwr.

We see this from the sheep's point of view. Ted is going 'rowwwr' and pulling a face. The sheep looks up into the camera.

END OF PART ONE

* * *

PART TWO

SCENE 19 INT./DAY 4
SET: PAROCHIAL HOUSE
Ted is wearing a tracksuit. Mrs Doyle is serving tea.

MRS DOYLE: You're up early, Father.

TED: Well, we're off to try and get Chris into shape for the competition.

MRS DOYLE: Do you think that our new guest would like some tea, Father? The little sheep fella?

TED: I don't think they drink tea, Mrs Doyle. Unless you have some special Sheep Tea!!

MRS DOYLE: Yes.

TED: What?

MRS DOYLE: I do have some Sheep Tea in the kitchen.

TED: Really?

MRS DOYLE: Yes.

TED: Oh . . . oh, right. Well . . . give . . . give him some of that, then.

MRS DOYLE: OK, so!

She potters off. Dougal comes in, yawning and rubbing his eyes.

DOUGAL: God, Ted, do we have to get up this early?

TED: Has to be done, Dougal. Right. It's almost midday. That gives us half an hour before lunch.

DOUGAL: What are we going to do to cheer him up, Ted?

TED: Well, we'll try a few different things. And I'll keep a diary of how he progresses. Are you wearing a whistle? Oh, that won't do you any good, Dougal.

DOUGAL: Why not?

TED: Sheep can't hear high sounds such as whistles or women in hysterics. They can only hear very low sounds, like . . . (*he half-whispers*) farts. (*We hear a burp. Chris the sheep is in the room.*) Right, there he is. Now remember, Dougal, we've got to get him from looking like this . . . (*he throws down on to the table the photograph of the 'unhappy' Chris he was given by Fargo*) . . . to looking like this. (*He throws down a photograph of the 'happy' Chris. Fade this into . . .*)

SCENE 20 EXT./DAY 4
SET: LAKE
We see Chris the sheep, standing motionless in a boat in the middle of the water. Ted and Dougal look at him.

SCENE 21 INT./DAY 4
SET: TABLE
A Polaroid of Chris the sheep is thrown down on the table. Written underneath it is 'Day one'. Sad music accompanies this.

SCENE 22 INT./DAY 4
SET: PAROCHIAL HOUSE
We see loads of album covers on the living room floor – Brian Eno ambient records, Cocteau twins, The Orb, and so on – pan along these until we see the sheep wearing a pair of headphones. Ted and Dougal look on, expectant and hopeful.

SCENE 23 INT./DAY 4
SET: TABLE
A Polaroid is placed on top of what has now become a small pile of photographs. It has 'Day four' written on it. The sheep looks exactly the same, but the music is more hopeful.

SCENE 24 EXT./DAY 4
SET: ISOLATION TANK CENTRE
We see a sign reading 'Lonesome Float Ltd. Craggy Island's Premier Isolation Tank Centre'.

SCENE 25 INT./DAY 4
SET: ISOLATION TANK CENTRE
We see the sheep wearing an oxygen facemask and floating happily in one of the tanks. Ted and Dougal stand beside it. A lab technician in a white coat takes notes.

SCENE 26 INT./DAY 4
SET: TABLE
Another photograph, on which is written 'Day Seven'. The photograph of the sheep looks exactly the same, but the music does a kind of 'ta-daaaaa' thing, as if the difference is remarkable.

SCENE 27 INT./DAY 4
SET: PAROCHIAL HOUSE HALLWAY
Ted opens the door to a hopeful-looking Fargo.

FARGO: Hello, Father. Did you? . . . Is he? . . .

TED: I'm sorry. We tried everything.

FARGO: Ah, well . . . I suppose I'd better take him home.

Ted leads him into the living room, where Dougal is

waiting. The sheep is standing there. Fargo looks at him for a second, then gives an excited, joyous yelp.

FARGO: Ahhh!

TED: Ahhh-haaaa!!! Gotcha!

DOUGAL: Ahhh-haaaa!!!!!

FARGO (*delighted*)**:** What did you do?!!!! What did you do?!!!

TED: Oh, you know, just did my best . . .

FARGO: Oh, I don't know what to say! Father, can I buy you a drink to celebrate?

TED: Ah . . .

FARGO: Come on. I know you won't let me pay you anything . . .

TED: Well, actually, I've been meaning to talk to you . . .

FARGO: So at least let me buy you a drink in the pub.

TED: Yes. Interesting you brought up the issue of payment —

FARGO: One drink, Father! It's the least I can do!

TED: Yes, it may well be. The thing is, I am a bit low at the moment —

FARGO: That's settled then! You're coming for a drink!

TED: Oh, all right, then. Dougal, you mind Chris until we get back. And keep your eye on him. Don't let him wander off.

DOUGAL: Ah, come on, Ted. He's a fully grown sheep. How am I going to lose him? He's not going to fall through a crack in the floorboards!

TED: Sampras fell through a crack in the floorboards.

DOUGAL: Ah, Ted, Sampras was a rabbit . . . and it was a big crack.

TED: It was an ordinary crack until you widened it because you thought that Sampras had fallen down through the normal-sized crack.

DOUGAL: I didn't know where he was. I thought he . . .

TED: Shut up, Dougal. Just keep an eye on Chris. Keep that front door closed.

DOUGAL: OK, Ted.

Ted and Fargo leave. Dougal looks at Chris.

SCENE 28 INT./NIGHT 4
SET: PUB
Ted and Fargo are sitting at the bar. Fargo's a bit drunk.

FARGO: He's the best feckin' sheep ever. His little sheep face . . . and you have to say, great sense of humour . . . not a bad dancer, actually . . . Strangely enough . . .

TED (*not drunk, a little uncomfortable*)**:** Really . . . Great . . .

FARGO: He only cost twenty-three pounds! Twenty-three! There's some clause where I'll have to pay more if his image is ever used on stamps, but still . . . that's a great bargain for such a happy sheep.

Ted notices Hud Hastings, the second of the two farmers we saw earlier, sitting at a table a short distance away. There are two beautiful girls with him, and he wears a crown on his head.

TED: Is that Hud Hastings?

FARGO: Yeah . . .

TED: Isn't he . . . is he wearing a crown? (*He gets up and approaches Hud.*) Hello, there, Hud.

Hud immediately stops laughing and looks vaguely guilty.

HUD: Ah. Yes. Hello there, Father.

He indicates with a quick jerk of his head that the two women should leave. They click away on their high heels, looking sulkily at Ted.

TED: Hud . . . are you . . . are you wearing a crown?

HUD: Ah, yeah. I am. So what? That's not a sin is it? If I want to wear a crown?

TED: No, it's—

HUD: Then just mind your own business!

He storms off towards the girls. Ted looks at him, confused.

SCENE 29 EXT./NIGHT 4
SET: PAROCHIAL HOUSE
Fargo stops and waves. Very, very drunk by now.

FARGO: Yadaa . . . yaaa . . . blaaaa . . .

TED: Yes, yes! Bye, now!

Ted turns. He sees that the front door is wide open.

SCENE 30 INT./NIGHT 4
SET: PAROCHIAL HOUSE
Dougal is sitting in a chair, smiling happily, doing nothing. Ted enters the living room.

TED: I notice, Dougal, that the front door is wide open.

DOUGAL: Oh, it is, yes. Ted.

TED: Yes. And I see that we are currently without sheep.

DOUGAL: Oh . . . ah . . .

TED: I told you to keep that door closed! God, Dougal!!!

DOUGAL: Ah, now, Ted, just hold it there.

Dougal takes out his tape recorder, but is interrupted by a terrible howling noise.

TED: What was that?!

DOUGAL: The Beast!

TED: Come on!

They run out of the room.

SCENE 31 EXT./NIGHT 4
SET: PAROCHIAL HOUSE
They come out of the house.

DOUGAL: Ted, how will we know which way he went?

TED: Sheep, like all wool-bearing animals, instinctively travel north where it's colder and they won't be so stuffy. So we have to go north.

DOUGAL: Which way's north?

Long pause.

TED: I don't know. (*We hear another howl.*) Quick!

Ted and Dougal run in the direction of the howl.

SCENE 32 EXT./NIGHT 4
SET: WOODS
We hear howling. Ted and Dougal are behind a bunch of rocks.

TED: It seems to be coming from all around us. (*He looks up.*) The Sioux Indians in the Arizona desert used to be able to pinpoint the exact location of buffalo by looking at the position of the moon . . . and then putting their ears to the ground.

He puts his ear to the ground while closing one eye and pointing his thumb upwards to the moon. Pause.

DOUGAL: Actually, Ted, maybe the sound is coming from that stereo.

We see, in the tree right next to them, two speakers dangling from the branches of a small tree. Between the branches is a stereo system. Ted stands up. The side of his head is covered in muck. Ted and Dougal approach the record player. Ted lifts the needle off. The sound of the Beast stops. It's replaced by the sound of burping.

DOUGAL: Ted, it's Chris!

TED: Is he all right?

DOUGAL: He's fine. He must have realised it was just a big stereo hanging from a tree.

TED: Let's bring him home, Dougal. I think I'm beginning to figure out what's been going on . . .

SCENE 33 INT./DAY 5
SET: PRESENTATION AREA
A rather posh event, rather like the BAFTA Awards.

Everyone wears tuxedos, etc. We see Hud, Giant and Fargo, each standing with their respective sheep – Hud's and Giant's sheep are black. A sort of jury are talking among themselves. Then the head of the jury stands up.

JUDGE: Well, it's been an easy decision. There's one out-and-out winner and rather than waste time with a speech, I'll get on with the job of announcing the winner who today has come first in this competition to see who the winner is of the King of the Sheep competition . . . that we have all come to today with nerves jangling wondering who indeed will it be who wins the prize of King of the Sheep. The winner of this year's King of the Sheep is—

TED: STOP!

Everyone turns. Ted is standing at the back of the tent.

JUDGE: Good God! What is the meaning of this?

TED: This contest is a sham and a fraud and a sham!

JUDGE: What! How dare you!

TED: There has been a deliberate and scurrilous attempt to sabotage this high-profile sheep competition. And those responsible are in this very room . . . *Giant Reid and Hud Hastings!!!!*

General hubbub. One distant 'fucking hell'.

HUD: You'd better have something to back that up with, Father!

TED: Oh . . . I do. I do. You were the ones who constantly chatted nonchalantly of the so-called Beast of Craggy Island, always within hearing distance of Chris the sheep.

Flashback shows this:

(Note: The term 'Beck shot' in the following descriptions refers to the effect in the Beck video for the song 'Devil's Haircut' and the Nike advertisement of freezing on a wide shot and then zooming in on one particular frozen image.)

Beck shot: wide shot of earlier conversation between Hud and Giant; zoom in on Hud and Giant, then on to sheep.

TED: . . . And it was you who used a copy of *BBC Sound Effects Volume 5* to add weight to your fanciful claims. A naïve sheep could not help but be convinced by the late-night roarings of 'Terrible Monster Type A'.

Beck shot: a hand placing an album on a turntable. Zoom in on the words on the record label – 'Track 1: Terrible Monster Type A'.

JUDGE: Well. Well, well, well. What a pretty picture Father Crilly has painted. How dare you bring shame on this celebration of sheep!

TED: Don't be too hard on them . . . I'm sorry, I don't know your name—

JUDGE: Alan.

TED: Don't be too hard on them, Alan! They were simply pawns. The real villain of this piece I have yet to reveal. But I now will reveal him. It was . . . *(He spins and points.)* Fargo Boyle!

General hubbub. One 'fucking hell'.

FARGO: What? That's nonsense. I'll just go now and take my trophy . . .

TED *(the following over a montage of the events described)*: It was you who was disappointed at the poor odds Chris was receiving.

Beck shot: Fargo looks at a newspaper headline that reads 'Champion sheep odds-on favourite'. He looks worried.

TED: You who planned to manipulate those odds by sabotaging your own sheep, and then staging a miraculous recovery on the day of the competition.

Beck shot: Fargo slipping some money to a delighted Hud and Giant.

TED: You who paid Hud and Giant to talk about the Beast in front of Chris.

Beck shot: Fargo leaving John's and Mary's shop. Zoom in on guilty face and then on the sound-effects record under Fargo's arm.

TED: You who bought the BBC sound-effects record just before Dougal had a chance to.

Beck shot: wide shot of a field. Freeze and zoom in on Ted and Dougal and the sheep, all wearing party hats and laughing in a jolly manner.

TED: You who gave the sheep to me, knowing that as a priest with an intuitive understanding of sheep I could nurse him back to normal. You, Fargo! You! You! You! You!

Fargo begins to say something, but then turns and sees Chris standing around, no different from at any other time he's been standing around.

FARGO: Chris! It's not true! It's not true, I tell you! (*Chris just stands around.*) No, don't – DON'T LOOK AT ME!! DON'T LOOK AT ME!!!

Fargo slumps down on to the ground.

TED: You stood to make a fair profit, didn't you? But you didn't count on the vanity of your accomplices . . . using their newfound wealth to buy a fur coat, and a crown.

Fargo sobs.

JUDGE: Should I call the police, Father?

TED: No. He's lost the trust of his sheep. That's enough punishment for a farmer who deals primarily with sheep. Now, if you'll excuse me . . . there's a bit of a stench in here and I need some air.

He walks out, leaving the three farmers crestfallen and ashamed.

SCENE 34 EXT./DAY 5
SET: TENT
Ted comes out to where Dougal is waiting. He lights

a cigarette. Dougal sees Chris off to one side.

DOUGAL: What'll happen to Chris?

TED: I don't know, Dougal. It's a cold world out there and he's just been metaphorically shaved of his wool.

A young girl with her family sees Chris. She runs up to Chris and hugs him.

GIRL: Mammy, Daddy! It's a lovely sheep. Can I keep it?

FATHER (*with pipe*): 'Course!

They bundle it into a car and drive off. Chris looks out of the back of the window as it departs. Ted looks at this and gives a little wave.

TED: You know, Dougal . . . maybe it isn't such a cold world after all.

They walk off into the sunset.

DOUGAL: One thing, Ted . . . if Chris has been disqualified, doesn't that mean you've lost the heating allowance money on the bet?

Dougal walks off, leaving Ted alone.

SCENE 35 INT./DAY 5
SET: PAROCHIAL HOUSE
We see Ted in a woolly hat and mittens and warm-weather gear.

TED: It's a radical step, Dougal, but it is very, very cold.

DOUGAL: See you in three months, Ted.

Credits start over . . .

Ted gets into a cardboard box filled with straw. He packs the straw in around him and closes the box. Dougal gets into a similar box.

Credits end.

The box opens.

TED: Actually, better go to the toilet first.

THE END

speed 3

GRAHAM: We thought, 'How can we make a worse sequel than *Speed 2*?' and Dougal on an exploding milk float sounded promising. We worked backwards from that joke. What's Dougal doing on a milk float? He got a job working as a milkman. What happened to the last milkman? He was fired for fooling around with the local women while on the job. How was he found out? The babies have started growing facial hair. How does Ted know about the facial hair? He was judging a bonny baby competition. So we worked backwards until Ted walks into the room covered in baby sick.

The brick was inspired by my recent move into a new flat whose previous owner had left a brick on the floor, which he had been using to prop the front door open. I started thinking about what a strange thing it was, this brick on the floor. Take a brick out of its natural context and it becomes an ode to uselessness. Ah . . . I am aware how this story manages to be both insane and boring, by the way . . . so, that gave us the idea of this brick that keeps popping up and getting in the way. Until they find a use for it at a crucial moment. I'm telling you all this to illustrate how inspiration can come from the most boring places, and also to give you a small insight into the nightmare that is my life.

ARTHUR: The milkman who sleeps with housewives has all those 1970s connotations of Dick Emery, the *Confessions* . . . films and Benny Hill, which is possibly why we introduced some of the more risqué lines here – like the milkman wondering if he can put his giant tool in Mrs Doyle's box. That's really quite un-*Ted*. But what *is* very Ted (the character) is what he considers to be a practical solution to Dougal's plight. When all else fails, he turns to religion, and a Mass is conducted alongside the float (here's an instance of 'spot the writer' – I'm one of the priests saying Mass). That's so typical of Ted: when religion is the last thing that's needed, he suddenly finds his faith. And when that fails, they watch *The Poseidon Adventure* because Gene Hackman played a priest in it. This is supposed to be a *practical* solution, so they watch the entire film.

I'm very fond of this episode and, while it contains a lot of silliness, it provides one of the best illustrations of the dynamic within the Parochial House. They are, effectively, a family, with Ted as the father, Dougal as the son, Mrs Doyle as the mother and Jack as the grandfather. We thought we'd illustrate this by having Ted becoming emotional about Dougal striking out on his own to do his milk round.

PART ONE

SCENE 1 INT./DAY 1
SET: PAROCHIAL HOUSE
The living room is empty, except for Jack sleeping in one corner. We hear the front door opening and closing, then immediately Ted's and Dougal's voices.

TED (*from outside*): . . . even to talk to me! I don't want to hear it!

DOUGAL (*from outside*): Ted, I'm so sorry.

TED (*from outside*): You're judging a baby competition, you're not supposed to get them agitated! This happens every year and I'm sick of it!

Ted and Dougal come in. Ted is covered in a white, gooey, milky substance. It is in his hair, on his shoulders and down his front.

DOUGAL: I was just playing with them, Ted!

TED: Playing with them? You were doing this! (*He makes a vigorous shaking motion.*) You were agitating the babies! It was like Schumacher celebrating a win! Next time, when you're given a baby, just check that it doesn't have two heads, and hand it to me, and I will return it to its mother.

Ted dries himself off with a cloth. They both look exhausted. They flop down in chairs – Ted unbuttoning his collar so that it hangs off.

DOUGAL: I thought the standard this year was rubbish.

TED: It was awful all right. A lot of very sloppy babies who looked as though they really couldn't be bothered.

DOUGAL: I can't even remember who won. Who did win?

TED: Ah, just some baby. I can't even remember it's name now. They all looked the same. If they couldn't be bothered being a decent standard of babies, then why should I break my bottom judging it. And the hairiness of some of those babies. That was a very hairy baby parade.

DOUGAL: Exactly, Ted. If people aren't even going to shave their babies before they come out . . . I mean . . .

TED: Well, normally, you wouldn't have to shave a baby. It's like their hormones have gone mad.

Ted crosses over to the table but as he goes, trips over something.

TED: AAH!!! What the hell was— Mrs Doyle, did you put a brick in the middle of the floor?

Mrs Doyle enters. She is wearing a lot of make-up and a dress that is frillier than usual.

MRS DOYLE: I did, Father.

TED (*taking in the new look*): Eh . . . Well . . . Why?

MRS DOYLE: I thought it might be a good place for your paperclips. You can put them in that hollow there.

TED: But why in the middle of the floor? Why not on the desk?

MRS DOYLE: I got the idea in a magazine. Look.

She opens a glossy magazine called 'Design Today'. We see a photograph of a studio flat with a brick in the middle of the floor. A yuppie couple sit on a designer sofa in the background. The headline reads 'A new look for autumn – brick enlivens dull floor'.

TED: Yes, well, that may be all very well for Will Self or one of those fellas, but I like the traditional aspect of not putting bricks in the middle of the floor.

He puts it on the desk. Mrs Doyle is staring out of the window.

MRS DOYLE: EEP!

She has seen something out of the window. She jumps up with excitement and runs from the room.

TED: Mrs Doyle is looking very . . . different today.

DOUGAL: Was it definitely Mrs Doyle?

TED: Yeah . . . what's going on?

SCENE 2 EXT./DAY 1
SET: PAROCHIAL HOUSE
A milkfloat pulls up. We see two stickers on the back, which read 'World's Greatest Lover' and 'My Other Car is a Porsche'. We see a chain hanging around a hairy chest. The milkfloat stops. A cigarette falls on the ground beside it and is stubbed out by a leather boot/fashionable Italian shoe.

SCENE 3 INT./DAY 1
SET: KITCHEN
Mrs Doyle is in the kitchen. There's a knock on the door and she jumps. She checks herself in the mirror one more time and then opens the door.

Pat Mustard, the milkman, leans in. He is big, beefy, has his shirt open to reveal a hairy chest and a medallion, and sports big sideboards connecting to a handlebar moustache.

PAT: Oh, sorry, I was looking for Mrs Doyle.

MRS DOYLE: It is Mrs Doyle!

PAT: Wha'? I thought you were Marilyn Monroe!

Mrs Doyle giggles girlishly. Pat walks by her and puts two pints of milk on the table.

PAT: A few more pints for you.

MRS DOYLE: Oh, great! We're a bit low, actually.

PAT: There's more where that came from.

Mrs Doyle giggles girlishly.

PAT: I tell you, I shouldn't really be here. The police are after me.

MRS DOYLE: They're not!

PAT: Yeah. I'm so gorgeous, they want to put me under arrest. They think the women'll be after me, and there'll be no one to make the tea.

Mrs Doyle giggles girlishly. Pat pulls up his trousers

to reveal a massive bulge in his groinal area. Mrs Doyle steals one quick look.

PAT: Actually, Mrs Doyle, I'm a bit sad at the moment. I have to go to a funeral.

MRS DOYLE: Oh, no. Really?

PAT: Yeah, me last girlfriend. She died from exhaustion!

MRS DOYLE: Really? What was she doing?

PAT: Well . . . ah . . .

Ted sticks his head around the door.

TED: Hello.

MRS DOYLE: Oh, Father, this is Pat Mustard, the new milkman.

TED: Oh?

PAT: Yeah, just took over the south side of the island. Thought I'd spread meself around a bit . . .

TED: Mrs Doyle, you need to do a bit of dusting in Father Jack's room. And there's a huge cobweb in the shed that needs removing.

MRS DOYLE: Oh, right, Father.

PAT: I'll be on my way then, Padre . . .

Ted flinches a bit.

PAT: . . . Off on me rounds.

He leaves, whistling as he goes.

SCENE 4 INT./DAY 1
SET: PAROCHIAL HOUSE
Ted enters, holding a cup of tea. Dougal has a blackboard set up. As the following conversation takes place, he writes on it with a stick of chalk.

TED: We have a new milkman, Dougal.*

DOUGAL: Oh, yes. I saw him goin' on his milkfloat the other day. God, I wish priests could go round on things like that. You know, if milkmen can have those things, I don't know why priests can't.*

TED: Well, they use them to deliver milk, Dougal. Priests don't deliver milk in a professional capacity.*

DOUGAL: Well, we could use them to deliver things that priests deliver . . . What do you call those things? . . . Sacraments. We could deliver those. I don't know, Ted . . . as you get older, you start asking yourself if . . . you know, if you should start thinking about getting a job.*

TED: Dougal, you have a job. Being a priest is a job.*

DOUGAL: Ah, Ted . . . *

TED: It is! It's as much a job as being a milkman is – actually, it's more important than being a milkman. Much more important. Milkmen just deliver the milk. We deliver the milk . . . that comes from God.*

He sees that Dougal has written 'My name is Father Dougal McGuire' on the blackboard.

DOUGAL: Right, Ted. Watch this. Looks like an ordinary blackboard, doesn't it?

TED: Yes . . .

DOUGAL: That's what I thought. But watch this . . . (*He takes a duster and wipes off the letters.*) You see! You can rub off the letters!

TED: Well . . . you can do that with every blackboard, Dougal.

DOUGAL (*puzzled*): What?

Ted takes a sip of tea. We see that it is very milky. Mrs Doyle enters, carrying a can with 'Cobweb-Remover' written on it.

TED: That's very milky tea, Mrs Doyle.

MRS DOYLE: Well, yes, I thought you might like more milk . . . in your tea . . .

TED: This is almost an all-milk cup of tea, though. I mean . . . (*He tastes it.*) Is there actually any tea in here at all?

MRS DOYLE: Well . . . no.

TED: Anyone would think you were trying to use up more milk so that Pat Mustard can come here more often.

MRS DOYLE: Ha, ha, ha, ha! Actually, Father, Pat is very interesting. On the weekends he's a swimming instructor at the pool. And he fought in Vietnam, and he's a former Mr Universe and he taught Elvis Presley to play karate.

*We deleted these lines from the final version.

TED: Well, it sounds to me like he's telling you a few 'tall tales'.

DOUGAL: Well, Ted, I'm very cynical, as you know, but I do find all that a bit hard to believe. Especially that 'swimming instructor' business.

MRS DOYLE: Well, Father, it's not my place, I know, but it sounds to me like you're a little bit jealous.

TED: Jealous? Of Mr Milky Man? I very much think not.

He is.

SCENE 5 INT./NIGHT 1
SET: TED AND DOUGAL'S BEDROOM
Dougal has a little table in front of him as he sits in bed. Ted is sitting up in bed, reading something.

TED: What are you doing, Dougal?

DOUGAL: I was looking at some of the hairy babies from today. There's something about them . . .

TED: Let's see.

He crosses over for a look. We see the photos lined up. One baby has sideboards, another has long hair coming from the back of a bald head. The third has a very faint moustache.

TED: Well . . . oh, my God . . .

DOUGAL: What?

TED: Well . . . this is a terrible thing to say but . . . if you took this baby's moustache, this baby's head and this baby's sideboards and put them together . . . I think you'd get Pat Mustard!

DOUGAL: You're right, Ted! Do you think the babies are copying his style?

TED: No, Dougal. It's more likely that . . .

He looks at Dougal. Dougal has a very innocent face on.

TED: It's more likely that Pat Mustard has been . . . (*Dougal still looks innocent.*) . . . well . . . delivering more than dairy products . . .

DOUGAL: No! You mean he's been . . . (*Ted looks expectant.*) . . . he's been . . . I can't . . . oh! Ho-hoh! Of course . . . but . . . so he . . . no,

God . . . (*Pause.*) He's been what?

TED: I think we should do a little detective work, Dougal. Find out exactly what this Pat Mustard fella is up to.

SCENE 6 EXT./DAY 2*
SET: ROAD
Pat Mustard is coming down the road in his little milkfloat. Cut to a house in the road. Pat Mustard is knocking on the door. It opens and a tarty-looking woman appears in a negligée and pink slippers. 'Confessions of a Window Cleaner' type 1970s music plays.

SCENE 7 EXT./DAY 2*
SET: ROAD
We see Ted pulling up in a car. He wears shades.

SCENE 8 EXT./DAY 2*
SET: HOUSE
Pat Mustard is talking.

PAT: . . . Thought it was Marilyn Monroe . . .

SCENE 9 EXT./DAY 2*
SET: ROAD
Cut to reveal that Ted is actually right beside the pair. They turn to look at him. Ted looks away innocently, which is hard considering he's right beside them.

Pat walks up to Ted and raps on the window. Ted doesn't answer. He keeps looking the other way.

Pat raps again. Ted, still pretending not to notice Pat, turns the ignition in his car and drives slowly away, not looking at Pat once.

SCENE 10 EXT./DAY 2*
SET: HOUSE
From the point of view of the woman opening the door, we see a door opening to reveal Pat waiting.

PAT: . . . Marilyn Monroe!

In the background, Ted cycles by, from left to right, in and out of shot. Pat hands the woman some milk.

PAT: There's more where that came from.

Ted cycles back in the other direction.

PAT: Actually, I shouldn't be here because I'm

wanted by the police . . .

Ted cycles back in the other direction. A car is coming straight for him and beeps its horn. Ted swerves out of the way and heads straight for Pat. Pat is brushed to one side and Ted cycles up into the house and behind the camera.

PAT: Are you all right, Father?

Ted doesn't say anything. He just backs out in a pathetically slow way.

PAT: Do you want something? Father? Can I help you? Father?

Ted doesn't say anything. He just rights his bicycle and cycles off.

SCENE 11 INT./DAY 2†
SET: PAROCHIAL HOUSE
Dougal and Ted are in the living room. Ted is pacing up and down.

TED: That milkman is definitely up to no good with the women of the parish. Soon half the population will have been spawned by Pat Mustard. And they'll all be marrying each other in twenty years' time.

DOUGAL: Like Michael Jackson and Lisa Marie.

TED: They're not brother and sister . . .

DOUGAL: No. No, they're not, are they? Why did I think they were?

Jack enters. Ted walks behind him, trips over something, and goes headfirst into the wall.

TED: What's this bloody brick doing on the ground again?

Jack yanks a piece of string attached to the brick and it jumps out of Ted's hand, landing on his foot.

TED: Aaaah!!!

Jack continues pulling the brick after him on a piece of string. He sits down, picks up the brick, and puts it on his lap.

TED: What's going on there?

† We also deleted this scene from the final version but kept the theme of Jack being very fond of the brick, then suddenly tiring of it and throwing it at Ted and inserted it in scene 18.

*We deleted this scene from the final version.

DOUGAL: Jack's got very fond of that brick, Ted. They're great pals. He's a brilliant pet actually. Jack doesn't have to feed him or look after him or show him any affection like you'd have to with normal pets. It might catch on, actually, having bricks as pets.

JACK: I LOVE MY BRICK!

He hugs it affectionately.

TED: But it's fun showing pets affection. That's the whole point of them. I mean, what do you think pets are for?

DOUGAL: Eh . . . ah, just . . . someone to talk to when you're down. Someone to get advice from.

TED: You don't usually get advice from animals, Dougal. Anyway, I'm off. I won't rest until I've caught Pat Mustard 'on the job', so to speak. And I don't mean the job of being a milkman. I mean . . . the job of getting on top of women . . . which isn't really a job . . . but you know what I mean . . . (*He sees Jack hugging the brick with a blissful smile on his face.*) Oh, well . . . if Jack's found a new friend in a brick, then I suppose we should be happy for him.

JACK: AH, FECK IT! FED UP OF BRICK!

He throws the brick at Ted. It hits him with a loud 'conking' sound. Ted falls out of shot.

SCENE 12 EXT./DAY 2
SET: PAROCHIAL HOUSE
Ted comes out of the house and decisively throws the brick in the bin. He goes back into the house. Mrs Doyle comes out to put out some empty milk bottles. Coming back, she notices the brick in the bin. She takes it out.

MRS DOYLE: Tsk!

She wipes the brick and brings it back in.

END OF PART ONE

* * *

PART TWO

SCENE 13 INT./DAY 2
SET: KITCHEN
Mrs Doyle is sitting at the kitchen table with Pat. Ted comes in.

MRS DOYLE: Hello, Father. Pat was wondering if he could put his massive tool in my box.

TED: What!! How dare y—

PAT (*lifts up a giant wrench*): It's too big for the milkfloat. I'll pick it up tomorrow.

Mrs Doyle puts it away in a metal box.

TED: Mrs Doyle, could you leave us for a moment.

MRS DOYLE: Oh . . . yes, OK.

She does do. Ted spins on Pat.

TED: I know what you're up to, Pat Mustard. There's some hairy babies on Craggy Island, and I think you're the hairy babymaker.

PAT: Oh, yeah? I think you need proof for that kind of accusation, Father. And I'm a very careful man, Father. A very careful man.

TED: Except when it comes to taking precautions in the bedroom, Pat.

PAT: You wouldn't be advising the use of artificial contraception, would you Father?

TED: Yes, I . . no, I . . . If you're going to be . . . I . . . of course . . . you . . .

(*He goes quiet. There is an unnaturally long pause.*)
Just . . . feck off.

PAT: You can keep following me, Father. But you have to be up very early in the morning to catch me. Very early in the morning.

SCENE 14 EXT./DAY 3
SET: STREET
A caption comes up that reads 'Very early in the morning'. We see two houses next to each other. Pat comes out of one house and zips himself up. This turns into a frozen image and we hear a click. Cut to Ted taking the shot from his car with a camera with an amazingly long lens.

PAT: God, I really enjoyed riding Mrs O'Dowd.

Pat opens a milk carton and throws it back.

TED (*gasps*): Did you get that, Dougal?

We see Dougal with a pair of earphones on and a radar-type device pointing out of the window. Dougal gives the thumbs up.

PAT (*finishes milk*): Now to ride Mrs Reilly.

TED: God almighty. He really is quite reckless this early in the morning. (*Pat goes next door.*) Right. Now we wait.

DOUGAL: I'll put the volume up as loud as I can in case I can hear inside the house.

He does so, the radar still pointing out of the window. A truck passes by and sounds its incredibly loud horn. Dougal's eyes cross as the sound hits him. He faints. Ted, in the front seat, doesn't notice. Suddenly the door of the house opens.

TED: Oh my God!

Pat comes out, not wearing any trousers. He has very hairy legs. He gets in his milkfloat then, stops and bounds back to the house. The door opens.

PAT (*to woman*): . . . Forgot me feckin' trousers! . . .

SCENE 15 INT./DAY 3
SET: PAROCHIAL HOUSE
A well-dressed civil-servant type, Mr Fox, is looking as Ted puts a succession of photographs down in front of him. Mrs Doyle is nearby, listening in.

FOX: Right . . . yes . . . that's disgusting. I . . . shameful . . . I've never seen anything like this . . .

TED: These were all taken in the course of one morning . . .

FOX: Dear God . . . disgraceful . . .

TED: Look at him there, Mr Fox. Have you ever seen anything like that?

FOX: No, I have not. (*He stands up straight.*) All right, how will we do this? . . . How about . . . two pounds each for this, this and this, and a tenner for the rest.

TED: Eh . . . I wasn't trying to sell them to you. I just wanted to show you what one of your employees got up to on his round.

FOX: Oh! Oh, my God, yes!

TED: . . . Why? What did you think . . .?

FOX: I completely misread the situation! Please just . . . yes, this is *disgraceful* behaviour. This employee shall be removed from his job straight away. Thank you for bringing this to our attention, Father Crilly.

DOUGAL: Who's going to deliver the milk now?

As Mr Fox replies, Mrs Doyle calmly walks over to the table, slides one photograph off and quietly, calmly, leaves the room with it.

FOX: Actually, next week is a big week for us. We recently agreed to ease the milk-surplus problems of the newly liberated Eastern European republic of Krovtonova by buying seventeen thousand tons of milk from them. Pat's sacking couldn't have come at a worse time.

DOUGAL: It's terrible to think of all that lovely milk floating around and going sour, with no one dropping it off anywhere. I wish I could do it.

FOX: Well, Father, we could certainly trust you. You are, after all, a man of God.

DOUGAL: A what?

FOX: A priest.

DOUGAL: Well, yeah. (*Sulkily.*) Thanks for reminding me. (*He perks up.*) But I'd love to be a milkman for a while. That'd be fantastic. God knows, I do flip all around here.

FOX: Not a bad idea! You could certainly fill in for a while.

TED: I'm not sure. Father McGuire has other duties in the parish.

DOUGAL: Like what?

Very long pause.

TED: I'm not sure what the rules are on priests becoming milkmen. Let me look it up. (*He goes to the bookshelf, grabs an absolutely huge book from high up and flips through it very quickly.*) Hmm . . . apparently it's OK. Well . . . I really don't know, Dougal. God knows what sort of damage you could do on a milkfloat. How fast can those things go?

FOX: Pretty fast. Our new model can reach speeds of nearly ten miles an hour.

TED: Yeah, you see, that's pretty fast . . .

DOUGAL: But, Ted, I wouldn't be going that fast anyway! Unless there was an emergency! And what type of emergency could happen on a milkfloat! Oh, please let me, Ted. Please, please, please, please, please, please!

TED: Well . . . all right.

DOUGAL: Yes! I'm going to deliver bread!

TED: Milk.

DOUGAL: Milk! I'm going to deliver milk!

SCENE 16 INT./DAY 3
SET: PAROCHIAL HOUSE HALLWAY
Mr Fox stands at the door. Ted is adjusting Dougal's scarf.

TED: . . . And make sure you keep warm.

DOUGAL (*impatient whisper*): *Te-ed*, not in

front of Mr *Fox*.

TED: . . . And stay on the left side of the road.

DOUGAL: *Duu-uuh! I kno-ow!*

Ted licks a hankie and tries to wipe something off Dougal's face. Dougal wriggles uncomfortably. Cut to Mr Fox watching all this in complete wonderment.

DOUGAL: Stop it!

SCENE 17 EXT./DAY 3
SET: PAROCHIAL HOUSE
Dougal is sitting in the milkfloat. Mr Fox stands to one side.

FOX: All right, Father . . .

DOUGAL: Ah, no, today I'm not Father. I'm . . . ah, Milkman.

FOX: Right, ah, Milkman. I'd better take you through the workings of the old float here.

DOUGAL: Right.

FOX: That turns it on, that makes it go and that steers it.

DOUGAL: Rrrrrright.

FOX: OK! You're ready to be a milkman! You'd better get going, actually – milk gets sour, you know. Unless its UHT milk, but there's no demand for that because it's shite.

TED: Actually, I might as well be the first customer! Two pints please, Milkman!

DOUGAL: Oh. Right. OK. Right. Two pints. Right. Here we go. Right. Two pints.

He picks them up and hands them to Ted.

TED: Well! Thank you very much. (*Pause. Everyone just stands there.*) Actually, I just realised, we don't need any. Can I give this back?

Cut to Dougal driving out of the gate. He waves back at Fox and Ted. Ted looks worried.

FOX: He'll be fine, Father.

Ted wipes away a little tear, nods and goes into the house.

SCENE 18 INT./DAY 3
SET: PAROCHIAL HOUSE
Ted enters. He picks up the book he had earlier and

*puts it back, high on the shelf. Another book takes his interest. He starts to pull the book out and we see the brick on top of it. It falls and conks him on the head.**

TED (*intense pain*): OH, MY GOD!!!!!

The telephone rings. He picks it up.

TED (*still in pain*): Hello. Craggy Island Parochial House. Father Crilly speaking.

SCENE 19 INT./DAY 3
SET: TELEPHONE BOX
Pat is in the telephone box, telephone to his ear. He's not wearing his uniform any more, but a tracksuit. Cut back to Ted.

PAT: It's me, Father. Y'ignorant bastard . . .

TED: Who's that? Is that you, Pat?

PAT: It's me all right. I've got a score to settle with you, ye baldy fecker.

TED: Don't use that type of language. And I'm not bald. I've got a lovely head of hair.

PAT: You got me sacked, and now I'm having to yank meself off round the clock 'cause I'm not getting any proper sex with girls.

TED: Well! If you're going to use that kind of language! . . .

PAT: Wait! Don't hang up! I've got something to tell you. I've put a little present on that milkfloat your little friend took off me. Something to remember me by. A bomb.

TED: What?

PAT: That's right, Father. A very special bomb. When your little friends gets over four miles an hour, the bomb will be armed. But when he goes back under four miles an hour . . .

Pat makes a low, exploding sound. Ted moves the earpiece away in confusion.

TED: Pat, I lost you there. What'll happen if it goes under four miles an hour?

PAT: It'll blow up.

TED: Oh, no! Dougal!

He throws down the telephone. Pat doesn't notice.

*We deleted this and replaced it with Jack and the brick from scene 11.

PAT: Oh, yes. Your little friend is going to go boom . . .

SCENE 20 EXT./DAY 3
SET: ROAD
We see the speedometer of Dougal's float. It reads just under four miles an hour. Dougal stops the float and takes two pints from the back. He approaches the door of a customer.

DOUGAL: Mrs Millet . . . Two pints for her . . . two pints of milk . . .

It bursts open. We see a naked woman revealed.

WOMAN: Pat! FATHER! Oh, my God!

She covers her breasts up. Dougal, still concentrating on the order, hands over the two bottles. She covers her breasts with them.

DOUGAL: Two pints. Two pints. Two pints . . . there you go! Bye, then! (*The mortified woman closes the door.*) Hah! Right, who's next . . . ? Mrs Gleason.

SCENE 21 EXT./DAY 3
SET: ROAD
Ted's car is speeding along. Ted is inside.

TED: Come onnnnn . . . onnnnnnnnnn . . .

The car roars over a hill.

SCENE 22 EXT./DAY 3
SET: DOORWAY
The door opens. We see another naked woman. Dougal hands over the milk.

DOUGAL: Morning, Mrs Gleason!

The woman, totally shocked, slams the door.

DOUGAL: I'll leave it out here then!

He tootles away.

SCENE 23 EXT./DAY 3
SET: ROAD
Ted is driving along. We see, from his point of view, Dougal's milkfloat up ahead.

SCENE 24 EXT./DAY 3
SET: STREET
We see Dougal driving along. The speedometer is just about to reach four miles an hour. Ted drives the car up alongside Dougal.

TED: Dougal! Are you going over four miles an hour?

DOUGAL: Ah, Ted, I'm doing fine, leave me alone.

TED: Are you doing over four?

DOUGAL: Ah . . . not yet . . . now I am.

We see the speedometer hitting four.

SCENE 25 EXT./DAY 3
SET: UNDER MILKFLOAT
We see a device. A green light turns red. We see that the device is connected to explosives that run the entire length of the bottom of the milkfloat.

SCENE 26 EXT./DAY 3
SET: ROAD
Ted is driving along.

TED: Oh, no! Dougal, listen to me! There's a bomb on the milkfloat!

DOUGAL: A bomb? Right. Who's that for?

TED: No, you're not supposed to deliver it to anyone! It's going to go off and kill you!

DOUGAL: Ah, I'm sure there's nothing to worry about. It's probably there for a reason.

TED: Pat Mustard put it there because I got him sacked! When you go under four miles an hour it'll go off – the bomb will go off! Have you got that?!

DOUGAL (*hyperventilating*): Oh, God! Help! I don't want to be a milkman any more!

TED: You'll be safe as long as you don't slow down!

DOUGAL: Oh, no, Ted! (*He points out something ahead of him: pile of cardboard boxes in the middle of the road.*) It's a big bunch of boxes in the middle of the road!

TED: Just stay over four!

Ted drives up ahead and stops near the rubbish. In the background we see the milkfloat getting nearer. Ted jumps out of the car and starts moving the boxes away. Dougal's getting nearer.

Ted clears away more boxes, huffing and puffing. He moves them directly across the road in front of his car. *Dougal is getting nearer.*

Ted takes a break for a second to catch his breath. The milkfloat gets nearer.

Ted resumes picking up the boxes. He piles them up on the other side of the road. One drops off. He carefully replaces it. Dougal closes his eyes, ready for impact. Ted clears away the last box just in time and the milkfloat drives slowly past.

TED: Go! Go! Go!

Ted jumps into his car. Cut to the boxes. Ted rams his car through them.

Dougal is driving along. Ted drives up beside him.

TED: Just get to the roundabout and start circling it! I've got to have a think!

Ted pulls over to the side of the road.

DOUGAL: TED!!!!

SCENE 27 INT./DAY 3*
SET: PAROCHIAL HOUSE
Ted bursts into the living room and slides up to the telephone. He punches out some numbers. Mrs Doyle enters.

MRS DOYLE: What in the name of goodness gracious me is going on?

TED: I'm calling Father Darsoley. Dougal's in trouble and he might be the only person who can help.

MRS DOYLE: Oh yes, he helped the police with that hostage thing last year. I forget how it ended.

TED: He tried reverse psychology on the terrorists. He said something like, 'Oh, go ahead, kill them all! Who cares about them?!'

MRS DOYLE: Oh, dear God! Did it work?

Ted pauses. He hangs up the telephone.

TED: Actually, no, it didn't. I'll try Father Beeching. He did an evening course in counterterrorism when he was in Wicklow.

He starts dialling again.

*We deleted this scene from the final version.

SCENE 28 INT./DAY 3
SET: A PAROCHIAL HOUSE
A priest comes to the telephone. This is Father Beeching.

BEECHING: Hello, Barren Island Parochial House, Father Beeching here!

TED: Derek, I need your help. Dougal's got a job as a milkman and the previous milkman has put a bomb on the milkfloat that'll go off if the milkfloat goes under four miles an hour!

BEECHING: Yes. That is a problem. Well, don't panic, Ted. We'll find a way through this. But in the meantime, is there anything we can do to lift his spirits? Anything to keep his morale up?

TED: We have to do something practical. Something that will really help Dougal.

BEECHING: Wait! I've got it!

SCENE 29 EXT./DAY 3
SET: ROAD
Dougal is driving along. We see him from the side. Suddenly (albeit slowly) another milkfloat drives up alongside him, driven by a priest. The back of it has been taken off, so that it's sort of like a flatbed truck on the back of a truck. We see Ted, Father Beeching and another priest, Father Clarke, all dressed in vestments. A couple of altar boys are there as well. Father Beeching stands at the podium, Ted and Father Clarke sit down at the side of the altar.

BEECHING: The Lord be with you.

TED AND CLARKE: And also with you.

DOUGAL (*to himself*): Oh, no! Mass!

BEECHING: The Mass today is being offered for Father Dougal McGuire, who finds himself in a most trying and unfortunate situation. We pray that God will protect him from . . . (*The milkfloat jolts and Beeching falls over. He stands up again.*) . . . from harm at this time and deliver him to safety.

ALL: Amen.

He sits down. The other priest, Father Clarke, steps forward.

CLARKE: A reading from the letter of Saint Paul to the Corinthians: 'Verily do I say to you . . .'

Dougal, despite himself, pays attention.

SCENE 30 INT./DAY 3
SET: TELEPHONE BOX
Pat is still on the telephone.

PAT: . . . Oh, yeah . . . they'll be peeling him off the walls for weeks to come . . .

SCENE 31 EXT./DAY 3
SET: ROAD
Ted is now speaking.

TED: The Mass has ended. Go in peace to love and serve the Lord.

EVERYONE: Amen.

TED: DOUGAL! THERE'S THE ROUNDABOUT!

Dougal drives on. They stop.

TED: Dougal, keep driving round and round! Everything's going to be OK!

DOUGAL (*offscreen*): I'm getting dizzy, Ted!

TED: Don't get dizzy! (*To the other priests.*) All right, we've got to come up with a plan. Back to my house, and step on it!

The van drives off, incredibly slowly, Ted holding on to the side.

MONTAGE SEQUENCE
Ted drawing a complicated diagram on the board.

Dougal driving in circles.

Ted arguing with the other priests.

A battery level about to go into the red.

SCENE 32 INT./DAY 3
SET: PAROCHIAL HOUSE
Ted is looking at the other priests.

TED: That's the idea?

BEECHING: It's the best we've had, Ted!

TED: Another Mass? That's our best idea?

BEECHING: Well, I thought the other one went very well.

TED: He needs help, not Mass! He needs physical lifting off the milkfloat, not spiritual lifting of his . . . spirits. There's a time for Mass and a time for action. And this is a time for action!

BEECHING: Ted's right! Another Mass at this point would just waste time! We could sit here all night discussing the merits of saying Mass or not saying Mass, but we'd just be wasting precious time, and time is precious at the moment! It's the one thing we can't afford to waste! We can't afford to waste any more time sitting around here talking!

CLARKE: I agree with Father Beeching. We can't talk about this any longer. Father Dougal's out there, in trouble and we're the only ones who can help him. Sitting round here talking about whether another Mass would be wasting time is just wasting time! We've got to do something!

Pause.

BEECHING: Is there *anything* to be said for saying another Mass . . .? Just a small one. God, I love saying Mass.

CLARKE: Listen to him! Any excuse!

TED: For God's sake! Will you all just shut up and help me come up with a *practical* solution!

Mrs Doyle comes in.

MRS DOYLE: Tea for everyone! Father Beeching, biscuit or cake?

BEECHING: Biscuit or cake . . . biscuit or cake . . . let's see . . .

Pause.

TED: For God's sake, hurry up, man!

BEECHING (*flustered and panicky*): Don't rush me! Eh . . . eh . . . biscuit, no cake!

Cut to Jack in his chair listening to the telephone.

SCENE 33 INT./DAY 3
SET: TELEPHONE BOX
Pat is still on the other end.

PAT: I've seen the damage a bomb can do. It can blow your face on to the other side of a tree . . .

Jack looks intrigued. Cut back to the others.

BEECHING: . . . Well, it worked for them! And they saved *hundreds* of people. We just have to save one!

TED: It's not the same thing. That was a big building that caught fire. You can't apply the same criteria to rescuing a priest from an explosive milkfloat. And besides, they had Paul Newman and Steve McQueen.

CLARKE: God almighty. It's so long since I saw it, I forgot Steve McQueen was in it.

BEECHING: Yes, he plays the fire chief.

TED: WAIT A SECOND! I'VE GOT IT! *THE POSEIDON ADVENTURE*!

CLARKE: What?

TED: GENE HACKMAN PLAYS A PRIEST IN IT!

Ted goes to a cupboard and fishes out a video box. He takes the cassette out of the box and slams it into the

machine. *He turns out the lights. They sit down to watch the film. We hear the music beginning.*

SCENE 34 EXT./NIGHT 3
SET: ROUNDABOUT
Dougal is jerking himself back awake every now and again.

SCENE 35 INT./NIGHT 3
SET: PAROCHIAL HOUSE
The film ends. Ted stands up and turns on the light.

TED: That was no help at all.

Everyone mumbles agreement.

BEECHING: He didn't even say Mass.

TED: All right, let's go down to the roundabout. Maybe we'll think of something there.

They all stand up and head to the door. Ted trips over something and the rest go flying this way and that.

TED (*holding up brick*): This feckin brick! (*He runs out but then walks slowly back in.*) Wait a second . . . I've got an idea.

He looks back at the brick, then back at the blackboard, then at the brick again. During the following speech he starts drawing something on the blackboard in a passionate, assured manner, so the speech is punctuated by the clicking and scratching of the chalk.

TED: Yes! Gentlemen, Father McGuire is propelling the milkfloat by exerting a small amount of pressure on the accelerator. If we could replace his foot with an object that would exert the same pressure, we are in the position to safely remove Father McGuire from the vehicle. The pressure exerted can be effectively produced by a heavy object.

BEECHING: You mean . . .

TED: Yes! We put the brick on the accelerator.

Ted steps back from the blackboard. He has written, 'We put the brick on the accelerator.'

SCENE 36 EXT./NIGHT 3
SET: ROUNDABOUT
Dougal is nearly asleep at the wheel. Ted comes running up alongside him.

TED: Dougal!

DOUGAL (*snapping awake*)**:** Aaaaaahhhhh!!!!

TED: Sorry! Probably a bad idea to shout at you when you've . . . got all those explosives under you. Anyway! We've got an idea, but you've got to trust me! Take the milkfloat up to nine miles an hour!

DOUGAL: Ted, I want to be a priest again.

TED: And you will be, Dougal! It's not really for you, this type of thing, is it?

DOUGAL: No, I don't like it at *all*.

TED: All right, when I say step off the milkfloat, step off the milkfloat, all right?

DOUGAL: But what if it goes under four?

TED: I've got a plan. It's too complicated to explain to you at the moment so you'll have to trust me. Just brace yourself and keep saying, 'I want to be a priest again.'

DOUGAL: I want to be a priest again. I want to be a priest again. I want to be a priest again . . .

TED: Step off the milkfloat!

Ted waits until Dougal is well into the mantra, then guides him off the milkfloat. He quickly slams the brick on to the accelerator.

TED: Now, run, Dougal, run!

The milkfloat trundles away in a straight line off the roundabout and towards a telephone box.

SCENE 37 INT./NIGHT 3
SET: TELEPHONE BOX
Pat is still in the telephone box, talking, he thinks to Ted. We see the milkfloat trundling towards him.

PAT: Oh, yes, when that milkfloat goes off, you'll hear it all the way to . . .

SCENE 38 EXT./DAY 4
SET: NORTH POLE
An Eskimo standing beside a sign that reads 'The North Pole' hears a far-off explosion. He looks around, puzzled.

SCENE 39 INT./NIGHT 3
SET: PAROCHIAL HOUSE
We see the telephone receiver on the ground. The tone is making a static type of noise. Mrs Doyle sees it, then puts it back in its cradle.

SCENE 40 INT./NIGHT 3
SET: TED AND DOUGAL'S BEDROOM
Ted hands Dougal a cup of cocoa. Dougal is wrapped up cosily, sitting in bed and reading a pile of comics.

DOUGAL: Thanks, Ted.

TED: That's OK. Are you sure you don't want any milk in it?

DOUGAL: Oh, no, no. I'll stay off the milk for a while. God, thank— (*He takes a sip.*) Aaargh! . . . Thank God that's over. Why did I ever want to be a milkman? You should stick to what you're good at, and I'm good at being a priest.

TED: Eh, yes . . .

DOUGAL: It's scary out there, Ted. In the real non-priest world.

TED: Not every job is as dangerous as being a milkman, Dougal.

DOUGAL: No, Ted, I feel safer here.

TED: All right. Good night, Dougal!

Ted leaves the room. Dougal puts his cocoa and comics to one side, then lies down. He opens his eyes, and beside the lamp we see a tiny toy milkfloat. He looks at it for a second, sighs, and then turns out the light.

Almost immediately, the light comes on again. Dougal sits straight up in bed.

DOUGAL: THOSE WOMEN WERE IN THE NIP!

POST-CREDIT SEQUENCE
Ted takes big plastic bag of rubbish outside. He looks up at the moonlit sky. Everything is back to normal. He smiles. He sees what he thinks is a comet in the sky. It makes a descending whining sound. It gets louder. Ted suddenly looks alarmed.

TED: OH NO!!!

He is hit in the face by the brick and falls to the ground. The brick, slightly charred from the explosion, but still intact, lies beside him.

THE END

the mainland

GRAHAM: Richard Wilson unconsciously inspired this plot. Arthur and I were invited to see Le Cirque du Soleil at the Albert Hall and he was sitting right in front of us, watching acrobats performing extraordinary gymnastics and tricks. During the break, Arthur said that it would just be terrible – so tasteless and wrong – to lean forward every time one of the acrobats did something interesting and say, 'Eyyy don't *believe* it!' in the style of Victor Meldrew. Just imagining it made us curl up in embarrassment, and then we realised that Ted should do it. He would think it so amusing and original – it was perfect for him.

Directing Richard Wilson was terrifying, but he was terribly nice. At the end, when he appears at the door, we stood around for about five minutes talking about how he should say the famous line. We wanted the ultimate 'I Don't Believe It!' and we stood around the Parochial House location listening to him try out various versions. It was a very strange moment in my life . . .

ARTHUR: It made sense to base this episode on the mainland. Apart from the fact that it provides an adventure for the Craggy Islanders, it simply wouldn't have worked on the island itself. Everyone's so insane that we couldn't have had a proper AA meeting, and Mrs Doyle's tea-shop fight works because it's witnessed by normal people, as is Ted's fight with Richard Wilson. The mainland provides far greater scope for embarrassment: on the island Ted is the voice of sanity, but here he's as strange as the other Craggy Islanders.

He's not quite as strange as Jack however. I know we're not supposed to laugh at our own jokes, but we loved Jack on the mainland – when he reads the 'Feckarse Industries' chart at the optician's and also when (Graham's favourite scene, this) someone from the AA meeting tries to stop him having a drink in the pub and the camera cuts straight to the shot of an ambulance.

I'm slightly ashamed to say that the idea for the briefcase came from someone who approached us in a pub and asked us if we'd look after his briefcase for a minute. Graham turned to me and said, 'If someone came up and stole it I wouldn't do anything, would you?' I said, 'No'…We were trying to make each other laugh, I think, but we knew that Ted *definitely* wouldn't do anything.

PART ONE

SCENE 1 INT./DAY 1
SET: PAROCHIAL HOUSE
We hear the closing music to 'One Foot in The Grave'. Dougal is smiling away. Ted walks in with his coat on. He throws Dougal's coat over.

TED: Come on, Dougal, turn off the video.

DOUGAL: OK, so, Ted. That's a great show, though, isn't it? He's mad, isn't he, Ted? 'I don't believe it!' he says.

TED: Ha, ha. Which one were you watching?

DOUGAL: What?

TED: Which episode of *One Foot in The Grave* were you watching? Was it the one with the ventriloquist dummy? I love that one.

DOUGAL: Eh . . .

TED: Dougal, you've just finished watching it. Do you not remember anything from it?

Pause.

DOUGAL: I don't believe it! Ha, ha, ha! That's what he says.

TED: Right. Anyway, Dougal, hurry up, we're off to the mainland.

DOUGAL: Hurray! Why?

TED: We have to go the betting shop and collect my winnings. Four hundred quid on Father Liam Rice winning that limbo competition . . . Ha ha! What they didn't know is there's something wrong with his back! He always walks like that!

DOUGAL: I don't believe it!

TED: Ha, ha! I don't believe it! Ha, ha, ha!!!!

SCENE 2 INT./DAY 1
SET: PAROCHIAL HOUSE HALLWAY
Ted and Dougal emerge, and start putting on their coats.

TED: You'll have to get that mended, Dougal. There's a little hole in your tanktop, there.

DOUGAL: Really, Ted? (*Pause.*) I don't believe it!

They both laugh.

TED: Brilliant, Dougal.

DOUGAL: Can we go to the caves, then, Ted? After we go to the betting shop? I love the caves. They must be one of the great wonders of the world. Who do you think built them, Ted? The Egyptians? Or the Romans, or who?

TED: Well, it'd be the Irish if anyone, Dougal. Although I don't think anyone actually built them. They just kind of . . . became caves.

DOUGAL: Ah, Ted . . . you know I love the caves. Can we go, can we? Please, please, please, please, please, please!!!

TED: All right, Dougal, we'll go to the caves.

DOUGAL: Fantastic. Going to the caves. I don't believe it!

They both laugh.

TED: Stop, Dougal. Honestly . . .

They try to be serious.

TED: I don't believe it!

They both crack up again. Mrs Doyle emerges, pushing Jack in his wheelchair.

MRS DOYLE: Here we are now!

DOUGAL: I don't believe it!

Ted and Dougal laugh. Jack is confused.

JACK: Drink!

TED: Not now, Father. We're going to the opticians in Roundskin, remember? To get you a nice pair of glasses.

DOUGAL: I don't believe it!

They laugh again.

SCENE 3 EXT./DAY 1
SET: PAROCHIAL HOUSE
Ted, Dougal, Mrs Doyle and Jack come out of the house. Dougal is pushing Jack in his chair.

MRS DOYLE: We should all be very careful on the mainland. There's so much crime around. Arsonists and muggers everywhere. My friend Mrs O'Dwyer was robbed last week.

TED: Oh, no! How much did they get?

MRS DOYLE (*beat*): No, I don't think you understand, Father. She was robbed. They stole her.

TED: Oh . . . I see.

MRS DOYLE: It's a terrible thing when old people can't walk down the street for fear of being stolen.

TED: It is.

SCENE 4 INT./DAY 1
SET: CAR
Ted and Dougal are in the front. Dougal is sticking his head out of the window and letting his tongue hang out like a dog's. (Note: Could Dougal have a slightly longer tongue than is normal?) * *Mrs Doyle and Jack are in the back.*

TED: Come on, Dougal, I don't want any accidents.

MRS DOYLE: Oh, there's Mrs Dineen. You can drop me off here, Father.

TED: Right so . . .

Ted pulls up in his car beside a woman who looks very like Mrs Doyle standing outside a shop. The woman potters up to Ted's window. Ted rolls it down.

MRS DINEEN: Hello, Father Crilly!

TED: Hello, Mrs Dineen.

MRS DINEEN: What?

───────────────────────

*We tried this. Didn't work.

TED: Hello!

MRS DINEEN (*nods after a moment, smiling*): Yes.

MRS DOYLE (*through the window*): Will we go to the tea shop, Mrs Dineen? We can have a bit of a chat there.

Mrs Doyle opens the door and starts to get out.

TED: All right, goodbye, then!

Ted looks around for Mrs Dineen. No sign of her. Ted looks puzzled, then drives off.

SCENE 5 INT./DAY 1
SET: CAR
We see that Mrs Dineen is in the back of the car, where Mrs Doyle was sitting.

TED: God almighty, can you imagine spending any more time with those tw—

He sees Mrs Dineen in the rear-view mirror and slams on the brakes.

SCENE 6 EXT./DAY 1
SET: CAR
A few minutes later, the car screeches away again, leaving Mrs Dineen and Mrs Doyle by the side of the road.

SCENE 7 INT./DAY 1
SET: OPTICIAN'S
There are eye charts, spectacle frames, etc. The

optician, Thelma Fox, addresses Ted.

THELMA: So what happened to his last pair of glasses?

TED: No idea. He was just out of the house a few minutes, and when he came back, they were gone. He can't seem to hold on to a pair.

SCENE 8 EXT./DAY X
SET: PAROCHIAL HOUSE
Cut to a flashback. Jack, wearing glasses, is in his wheelchair outside the Parochial House. A bird sweeps down and takes the glasses off his nose, makes a loud squawking sound and flies off with them. Jack flails wildly with his arms.

Cut to the bird arriving back at its nest (complete with eggs, etc.) with the glasses in its beak. It drops the glasses into the nest. We see about ten other pairs there as well. The nest is completely constructed from pairs of glasses.

SCENE 9 INT./DAY 1
SET: OPTICIAN'S
Back in the optician's.

TED: Oh, it's a real pain. He's always bumping into furniture and knocking things over.

THELMA: Yes. And how's his eyesight?

TED: That's not great, either.

THELMA: All right. I'll give him another test and we'll see what we can do. Give me about an hour.

TED: OK, so . . . Come on Dougal, time to collect my winnings . . .

SCENE 10 INT./DAY 1
SET: TEA SHOP
Mrs Doyle and Mrs Dineen are sitting at a small table.

MRS DOYLE: . . . You remember Mrs Kiernan . . . ? She was walking to the shops the other day and a man came over to her and killed her and stole her pen.

MRS DINEEN: Killed her?

MRS DOYLE: Well, they think so – they're keeping her in for tests.

MRS DINEEN: Oh, dear.

MRS DOYLE: I was looking at the News there and they had this thing about how robbers outnumber normal people in Kildare. And murderers outnumber the robbers, so there's more murdered people there than people who aren't murdered.

MRS DINEEN: Well, you know what happened to old Mr Sweeney . . . These young fellas broke into his house and started messing with him . . . ruffling his hair and all types of nonsense. Calling him an ould fella . . . and they put a bra on him.

MRS DOYLE: Oh, poor Mr Sweeney, he wouldn't like that. I heard there were two hundred cases of forced transvestism involving Mr Sweeney last year.

MRS DINEEN: Oh, it's terrible. What's the world coming to?

The waiter comes to the table. Mrs Dineen and Mrs Doyle snatch up their bags protectively. They look very wary.

SCENE 11 INT./DAY 1*
SET: PUB
Dougal and Ted are sitting at a table in an alcove. Ted is counting his winnings from the betting shop.

TED: Ha! Ha! Ha!

The barman notices Ted laughing, frowns suspiciously, then goes back to his newspaper. Sitting near Ted is a city type, with a briefcase. We see a wide shot of the rest of the pub. There is only one other person present, sitting in a corner of the pub. Ted has a pint of Guinness in front of him. Dougal has a fizzy orange.

DOUGAL: God, Ted, I'm starving. I'm so hungry . . . (*He looks scared.*) There's no chance . . . I couldn't die? From the hunger?

TED (*sighs*): Not immediately, no. Not for a couple of hours, anyway. Have a look at the menu.

Dougal looks at the menu. The city gent leans over to them.

MAN: Excuse me, could you keep your eye on my briefcase for a minute?

TED: Yes, yes, of course. Secret documents?

---

*We deleted this scene from the final version.

MAN: Ha, ha, no.

DOUGAL: What's in the case, then?

TED: Dougal!

DOUGAL: What?

MAN: Well, I work in the bank over there, and—

TED: No, no, really. We don't need to know. We'll just keep an eye on it. (*The man gets up and goes into the Gents.*) God, Dougal . . .

A man sitting in the corner immediately stands up, walks over to the briefcase and picks it up. Cut to Ted and Dougal, glasses raised to their mouths. They're too stunned to react. The big man picks up the briefcase and walks out of the pub. Ted can't seem to take this in at all.

DOUGAL: Ted . . . the man just took the briefcase.

TED: Uh . . .

DOUGAL: The briefcase we were supposed to be looking after for that fella.

Ted seems to be still trying to assimilate all this information in his head. He starts to say something several times, but can't quite manage it. We hear the sound of the hand dryer from inside the toilet. Ted and Dougal look around at the door of the Gents.

TED: Dougal, let's run away.

DOUGAL: But what about our food?

TED: No, Dougal, we're running away. I've been weighing the various pros and cons and I think that running away is . . . the way to go here.

They both get up. Ted pulls Dougal out of shot after him.

SCENE 12 INT./DAY 1
SET: OPTICIAN'S
The optician comes over to Jack and takes away a metal contraption covering his eyes.

THELMA: Well, I'm very confused, Father. Your eyesight seems to be . . . better than ever before. You read right down to the very last line and even I can't see that one.

From another angle, we see the eyechart. It looks like this:

DRINK
DRINKDRINK
DRINKDRINKDRINK
DRINKDRINKDRINKDRINK
DRINKDRINKDRINKDRINKDRINK
DRINKDRINKDRINKDRINKDRINKDRINK

Ted enters the room.

TED: Are you finished with him yet?

THELMA: Well, I'm amazed. He seems to have perfect eyesight.

TED: Really? (*He sees the eye chart.*) Ah . . . well, I think I know what might have happened. You see, Father Jack has a great fondness for saying that particular word.

THELMA: Oh, I didn't know. It's the first time I've used this eyechart, actually. I got it free with a promotional crate of Carlsberg.

DOUGAL: Hey, do you have anything to eat? Like a plate of chips or a burger or a few chops? I'm out of me head with hunger.

THELMA: Ah . . . no. I'll just get another chart . . . Sorry about this, Fathers, this might take some time.

She leaves the room. Dougal stands up.

DOUGAL: Come on, Ted, let's go to the caves while we're waiting. Oh, no! I'm still starving! Maybe we should get something to eat first. God, I *really, really* want to go to the caves. But at the same time, I'm *really, really* hungry. God, I don't know what to do first! Oh, God, Ted!

TED: Well, they have a snack-bar place at the caves.

DOUGAL: Oh, really? Great. No need to worry. Sorry if I seemed a bit over-anxious there.

They leave. Thelma comes back in.

THELMA: This one was given to me by Slovakia's premier lens manufacturers – Feckarse Industries . . .

She turns it round. It's like the 'Drink' chart, except it has 'Feck' and 'Arse' written all over it. Ted and Dougal leave.

SCENE 13 INT./DAY 1
SET: TEA SHOP
Mrs Doyle is still chatting away to Mrs Dineen. There are a whole stack of cups on the table in front of them.

MRS DOYLE: Oh, God, no, don't ever try to be one of those have-a-go heroes . . .

MRS DINEEN: Well, I was surprised at my own strength. I heard this arm snap, and then it was just a case of lying on top of him until the filth arrived. (*She takes out her purse.*) We'd better go, Mrs Doyle. I'll get this.

Mrs Doyle takes out her purse as well.

MRS DOYLE: No, Mrs Dineen. Put that away. I'll get this one.

MRS DINEEN: No, you won't, don't be silly. I'll pay.

MRS DOYLE: No, no, no, no, no, you won't. Put that away.

MRS DINEEN: No, don't be stupid, Mrs Doyle.

MRS DOYLE: No, no, no, no, no, no, no, no, no . . .

MRS DINEEN: Now, just . . . put your money away . . .

MRS DOYLE: *You're mad!* No, no, no, no, no, no, no, no . . .

SCENE 14 EXT./DAY 1
SET: CAVES
We see a sign that reads:

'VERY DARK CAVES'

'IT'S ALMOST LIKE BEING BLIND!'

Tourists are milling about, taking photographs, and so on. Dougal is photographing Ted beside the sign for the toilets.

TED (*sees something*): God almighty . . .

DOUGAL: What?

TED: Look who it is! It's yer man!

Cut to reveal Richard Wilson, enjoying the scenery.

DOUGAL: Who?

TED: Yer man from *One Foot In The Grave*! The 'I don't believe it' man!

DOUGAL: Oh, wow!

TED: God, that's amazing. Look at him there. (*Pause.*) Ha, ha . . . Do you know what he'd love?

DOUGAL: What?

TED: He'd love it if someone came up to him and said his catchphrase.

DOUGAL: Oh, yeah, Ted, he'd love that! You should definitely do that!

TED: Should I?

DOUGAL: Oh, yeah, he'd *love* that! I'd say no one ever does that to him! He'll think you're hilarious!

TED: It would be good, wouldn't it?

DOUGAL: Seriously, Ted, that is a *fan-tastic* idea. This is one of those times when I'm absolutely one hundred million per cent sure that you'd be doing the right thing. I can safely say you definitely, *definitely* won't regret doing that.

TED: You know what? I'm going to do it!

DOUGAL: Brilliant, Ted!

TED: Will I?

DOUGAL: Yeaaaahhh!!! Go on!

Ted creeps away from Dougal and walks up to Richard Wilson, who is looking the other way. Ted looks back at Dougal one more time. Dougal gives him the thumbs-up. We see all this from Dougal's point of view, from a distance.

TED: Eyyyyyyyyyyy don't belieeeeeeve it!!!!!!!

Dougal sees Richard Wilson turn around and start to shout something at Ted, and then attack him. Ted protects himself. A few caves staff arrive on the scene and start holding Richard Wilson back. Ted cowers as Richard escapes, grabs Ted by the jacket and starts pulling it over his head. The staff are finally able to hold Richard back. Ted slinks back towards Dougal.

RICHARD (*in the distance*): . . . KICK YOUR ARSE! . . .

Ted arrives back with Dougal. He looks completely shellshocked.

DOUGAL: What'd he say? Did he laugh?

TED (*quietly*): No. Not really, no. No. No, he didn't. No. No. No, no, no. Ohhhhhhhh, no. No. No. I'm going to sit down now.

SCENE 15 INT./DAY 1
SET: OPTICIAN'S
Jack is wearing a new pair of glasses. He seems happy. The optician shakes hands with him.

SCENE 16 EXT./DAY 1
SET: OPTICIAN'S
Jack leaves the optician's. A bird swoops down and attacks him, knocking him over. It takes his glasses and flies away. Jack gets up. We see from his point of view that everything is a blur. He walks a short way, coming to a sign beside an open door,

JACK (*reading*): Dri . . . Drink? Drink!!! Drink!!!!

He goes into the building. We see now that the sign reads 'Had enough of drink? Join Alcoholics Anonymous. Meeting 4 p.m.'

SCENE 17 INT./DAY 1
SET: TEA SHOP
Mrs Doyle is on top of Mrs Dineen. She is holding out a tenner to a waiter.

MRS DOYLE: Take the money! TAKE THE MONEY!

MRS DINEEN: PUT YOUR MONEY AWAY!!!

She grabs it from Mrs Doyle. We see nearby a member of staff on the telephone.

MANAGER: Hello, police?

SCENE 18 INT./DAY 1
SET: ALCOHOLICS ANONYMOUS
About six people and Jack are sitting in a very bare room. One man, Peter, is standing.

PETER: . . . That was when I was drinking over a pint of vodka a day.

JACK: Yes!

PETER: Yes. All I could think about was where the next drink was coming from . . .

JACK: DRINK!

PETER: I didn't give a damn about my wife or kids.

JACK (*disgusted*): Nyaaahhhh!!!!

PETER: But now, with your help, I'm coming through it. I'm just taking it one day at a time.

He sits down. Everyone applauds. The chairman, Ronald, stands up.

RONALD: Thank you, Peter. Now, I notice we have a new member of the group today. Father? Do you want to tell us your story?

Jack stands up unsteadily.

JACK: DRINK! (*Everyone nods understandingly.*) DRINK! (*Jack is a little put out. No one seems to be giving him any drink.*) DRIIIIIIIINK!!!!

RONALD: We hear you, Father. Let it all out.

JACK: DRIIINK!!!! DRIIIIIIIIIINK!!!! (*He gets down on his hands and knees.*) DRIIIIIIIIIIIIIIIIIIIIIIIIIIIIIIIIIIIIIIIIIIIIIIIIIIIIIINK!!!!!

People are softly wiping away tears and nodding.

PETER: It's so true. So true . . .

SCENE 19 INT./DAY 1
SET: CAVES
The tour guide stops in front of some rocks.

TOUR GUIDE: And this rock here is actually granite.

TED: How long would that be there?

TOUR GUIDE: Many millions of years.

TED: Really? As long as that? That is fascinating.

DOUGAL: How come the rocks are all different sizes?

TOUR GUIDE: Well, you know . . . rocks are generally different sizes.

DOUGAL: Wow. I'm finding out all kinds of things I never knew about rocks.

The tour guide moves on. More people join in.

TOUR GUIDE: . . . Of course, at this time, most of the world would have been submerged under water.

DOUGAL: How did everyone breathe?

TED: They'd have some sort of apparatus . . .

DOUGAL: Oh, right. Wow! Look at that rock there!

He wanders off.

TOUR GUIDE: Anyway, the fossils were creatures that used to live at a depth of twenty thousand fathoms . . .

TED: Wow. I don't believe it.

A man in front of Ted turns around. We see that it is Richard Wilson.

WILSON: YOU AGAIN!

Cut to Dougal looking at a rock. He hears the fracas and turns to watch it. We see, from a distance, people holding Richard Wilson back. Ted and Dougal escape and run away. Richard Wilson looks flustered and angry. The tour guide comes over to him.

TOUR GUIDE: I'd better send someone after them. That part's not open to the public . . . Mr Wilson, can I just say how sorry I am about all the, all the, eh . . .

RICHARD: Oh, please. Just so long as I don't hear that bloody catchphrase again. Ha, ha.

Pause. Close-up of the tour guide. He is smiling inanely, as if suppressing something.

TOUR GUIDE (*his silent thoughts*): Oh, God. I really, really, want to say it. Eyyyyyyy don't believe it!

TOUR GUIDE (*guiding Richard Wilson away*): Anyway, there's lot of places around where you can get a bit of peace and quiet for the rest of your holiday . . .

SCENE 20 INT./DAY 1
SET: CAVES
Ted and Dougal come around a corner.

TED: I was sure we came in this way.

DOUGAL: God, Ted, I'm so hungry. I'm beginning to hallucinate.

TED: Dougal, don't exaggerate . . . (*We see Ted from Dougal's point of view. He is dressed as Abraham Lincoln.*) . . . and stop worrying. We'll be out of here in no time. Right, let's try over here . . .

SCENE 21 INT./DAY 1
SET: ANOTHER PART OF THE CAVES
They walk along a little further. Dougal hears something behind them. He keeps looking around.

DOUGAL: Ted . . . Ted, what's that?

TED: What's wh— (*They hear a low moaning noise.*) I don't . . . I don't know . . .

The noise grows louder. Ted's eyes widen as he sees something. Cut to his point of view. We see coming around the corner a classic 'sheet' ghost.

TED AND DOUGAL:
Aaaaaarrrrghhhhhhhhhh!!!!

The ghost stops, then whips off his pillowcase head. It is Noel Furlong. He has a beard. He looks delighted.

NOEL: TED!!!!!!!!

TED AND DOUGAL:
Aaaaaarrrrghhhhhhhhhh!!!!

END OF PART ONE

* * *

PART TWO

SCENE 22 INT./EVENING 1
SET: CAVES
We see Noel standing in the centre of a group of people. Ted, Dougal and the Saint Luke's Youth Group – Tony Lynch, Jerry Fields (both bearded) Janine Reilly and Nuala Ryan. Noel is singing. (Note: In the following, he acts out the words in a very theatrical way.)

NOEL: 'Bom, bom, bom, bom, bom, bom, bom, bom . . .
I see a little sillhouetto of a man
Scaramouche, Scaramouche will you do the fandango?
Thunderbolt and lightning, very very frightning!
ME! GALLILEO, GALLILEO, GALLILEO, GALLILEO, FIGARO, MAGNIFICO,
I'm just a poor boy, nobody loves me.
He's just a poor boy from a poor family,
Spare him his life from this monstrosity,
Easy come, easy go, will you let me go?
Basmillah! No! We will not let you go. Let me go!
Basmillah, will not let you go. Let me go!
Basmillah, will not let you go. Let me go!

No, no, no, no, no, no, no, no!
Oh, mama mia, mama mia, mama mia, let me
go.
Beelzebub has a devil put aside for me,
For me,
For meeeeeeeeeeeeeeeeeeeeeeeeeeeee!!!!!!!!'

He finishes. No response. Everyone looks very fed up.
Pause.

TED: . . . As I was saying. I think the thing to
do is try and find an exit before the caves close
for the evening.

TONY: Good idea, Father.

TED: How long have you been in here?

TONY: Two days now, Father. At least, I think
it's two days.

NOEL: We've been having a great laugh!

TED: It's just I wouldn't like to be here too long
. . .

NOEL: He wouldn't like to be here too long!
Would you listen to him! I suppose if he doesn't
get back to Craggy Island they'll all turn into
devil worshippers or something!

TED: No, it's just, I think everyone would
actually like to get out of here and get
something to eat and go home.

NOEL: Who can screech the loudest? Let's
have a screeching competition! I'll go first . . .
(*He emits a 'Jurassic Park' type screeching sound.*)

Ha, ha, ha! Gerry Fields, your go!

GERRY: I'd rather not, Father.

NOEL: Oh, go on. (*He screeches again.*) It's easy
peasy!

TED: Father, I really think we should think
about getting out.

NOEL: Oh, God, maybe you're right, Ted. If we
don't get out, we might have to eat each other!

Dougal sits up when he hears this and looks very
interested indeed.

NOEL: Like in that film *Alive*, where they get
into the plane crash and then they have to eat
all their friends. Look! Here's me eating Tony!

He starts miming, as if he's eating something, with a
jokey look on his face.

NOEL: Yum, yum, yum, yum, yum. And this'd
be Tony! 'Oh, no, get off me! I'm not dead yet!'
and I'd be like, 'But I'm hungry, Tony!' and
Tony'd be goin', 'No, no, go away!' Ha, ha, ha!
Wouldn't you, Tony? And this'd be Tony's
parents, hearing that I've eaten Tony. (*He mimes*
a boo-hoo crying action.) 'Oh, no, why'd you eat,
Tony? He was our only son!'

Tony looks very, very distressed at this.

NOEL: 'But Mr and Mrs Lynch, I was hungry!'
Ha, ha, ha! And then they'd be at the funeral,
and I'd be going, 'Best not show me head for
the m—'

TONY (*suddenly*): WILL YOU SHUT UP! WILL
YOU! WILL YOU PLEASE SHUT UP! WILL YOU
SHUT UP! SHUT UP! *SHUT UP!*

Pause.

NOEL: OOOOOOOOOOOooooooooooo!!!!!!
Someone got out of the wrong side of the bed
this morning! I wonder who that could be . . .
(*He points behind Tony's back.*) Come on, let's
have someone else for the screeching
competition . . . Janine Reilly, oh, she'd love a
go. Go on there, it's easy . . .

He screeches again. There is a slight rumbling in the
background.

TED: Eh, Noel . . . I wouldn't do that.

Noel ignores him. We see bits of rock falling from the
ceiling of the cave.

NOEL (*screeches again*): Ha, ha, ha!!!

TED: Seriously, Noel! . . .

He screeches again. Some rocks fall. Ted and Dougal jump out of the way. We hear a crash and everything goes black. Fade out.

Fade back. We see a pile of rocks and rubble. Noel's hand is sticking out of the rubble and gesticulating happily. We hear his voice from under the rubble.

NOEL: . . . So it was me, Father Collis and Father Duggan, and you'd think, wouldn't you, that someone like Chris Evans wouldn't want to hang around with the likes of us – especially when he's in that sort of condition. And you'd be right! He didn't want to hang around with us. He didn't want to hang around with us *at all*. What was that colourful phrase he used? Oh, that's right, 'If you don't get out of my house right now, I'll call the police.'

TED: Noel, sorry to interrupt, but are you not worried about being trapped under that big pile of rocks?

NOEL: Not at all, Ted. Sure aren't you here to keep me company? And the Youth Group will be back with help any moment. They said that they were just going to find the tour guide, tell them that I was buried under a pile of rocks, and come right back!

SCENE 23 INT./EVENING 1
SET: AIRPORT CHECK-IN DESK
An air hostess.

AIR HOSTESS: Right, that's four tickets to Paraguay. It leaves through Gate Three in an hour.

We see the Youth Group, looking anxious.

TONY: An hour? No! We have to leave now! NOW!

The rest of the Youth Group try to calm him.

SCENE 24 INT./EVENING 1
SET: CAVES
We hear Noel's voice from the rockpile.

NOEL: . . . but I *liked The English Patient*. Very confusing and far-fetched and very, very boring, but it was my kind of film. And now I suppose you could say I'm in that type of situation that Kristin Scott Thomas found herself in . . . (*We gradually pull back to see that Ted and Dougal have gone.*) . . . I liked *The Piano* as well. Did you see Harvey Keitel running around in the nip!? God! Did you see that, Ted? (*Pause.*) Ted?

SCENE 25 INT./EVENING 1
SET: ANOTHER PART OF THE CAVES
Ted is looking ahead. Dougal comes up behind him.

TED: I hate leaving Noel, but we're doing him no good sitting around listening to him screech.

DOUGAL: At least he'll be safe under that big pile of rocks.

TED: Let's just get out ourselves – then we can worry about Noel. God . . . where's this exit?

Dougal takes his coat off. His tanktop has unravelled, leaving only a sort of tanktop bra.

DOUGAL: Aahhh!! Ted, my tanktop has turned into some sort of woman's bra!

TED: What? It's after unravelling. Oh, my God, Dougal! We can find our way back with this! You obviously snagged this on something – if we follow it back, we can find our way out! Ha, ha!!!!

Ted stands still and starts winding the thread around his hands.

TED: Oh, thank God, Dougal! We'll be out in no time! Ha, ha!!!

DOUGAL: Ted, should you be winding it up like that? Or should we be following it?

TED (*still winding*): What?

DOUGAL: Well, what use will it be once you've finished winding it up?

Ted continues winding, looking at Dougal, looking at the thread, looking at Dougal, his smile slowly disappearing. After a few moments, he comes to the end of the thread. He looks at it.

TED (*beat*): I DON'T BELIEVE IT!!!!!!!!!!!!!!!!!!!!!!!

SCENE 26 INT./EVENING 1
SET: CAVES
Ted's words rebound off the walls of the caves in different locations. Ted and Dougal travel down various tunnels.

Finally we see Richard Wilson with the tour group.

TED'S WORDS: I DON'T BELIEVE IT! I DON'T BELIEVE IT! I DON'T BELIEVE IT!

Richard puts his hands over his ears and starts to scream.

SCENE 27 EXT./EVENING 1
SET: PUB
Jack is walking past the pub.

JACK: PUB! DRINK!!!!

He wanders in. A moment later, Ronald, from the AA meeting, walks past. He notices something. We see that he sees Jack through the window sitting at a table. Jack is pouring himself a large glass of whiskey. Ronald gasps and runs in to the pub.

RONALD: Don't do it, Father!

Jack is about to put the glass to his lips when Ronald reaches into shot and grabs Jack's arm.

JACK: ROWARRRREEEE?????

RONALD: I won't let you do it, Father. You can beat me, you can kick me, but I'm not going to—

SCENE 28 EXT./EVENING 1
SET: ROAD
Shot of an ambulance speeding past.

SCENE 29 EXT./EVENING 1
SET: CAVE EXIT
Ted and Dougal come into the open, looking very bedraggled. They see someone in a one-piece outfit very

like the ones all the tour guides wear. Ted grabs him.

TED: Listen, there's someone been buried in the caves. He's all right, but I really think you should get someone in there quickly. Thank you. Please hurry. Come on, Dougal. I want to get away before they rescue him.

They walk away. The man in the outfit shrugs and turns to pick up a large bin. He throws it into the back of a nearby bin-truck and jumps up on the back. He is driven away. Ted and Dougal don't notice this.

SCENE 30 INT./EVENING 1
SET: CAVES CAFE
Dougal and Ted are queuing up for food, sliding a tray along the rail. Dougal is piling things on to his plate, hopping with the excitement. Ted's mobile phone rings.

TED: Hello?

SCENE 31 INT./EVENING 1
SET: POLICE STATION
A policeman is on the telephone.

POLICEMAN: Hello. Is this Father Crilly?

TED: Yes. This is him. Or rather, this is me. This is . . . yes, this is Father Crilly. I *am* Father Crilly, is what I'm trying to say.

POLICEMAN: We've been trying to contact you all night. Do you know a Mrs Doyle? Full name. Mrs (*Telephone interference.*) . . . Doyle.

TED: Do I know a Mrs (*Telephone interference.*) . . . Doyle? Eh . . . (*Sensing trouble.*) I'm not . . . let me think . . .

DOUGAL: Ah, we do, Ted.

TED: OK, yes, yes. She's our housekeeper.

POLICEMAN: Well, I need you to come to the police station. She's been in a spot of trouble.

We see Mrs Doyle and Mrs Dineen in a cell in the background. They both look dishevelled and have scratch marks on their faces.

MRS DOYLE: Now, Mrs Dineen, if there's a fine or anything, I'll pay it.

MRS DINEEN: No, no, no, no, no . . .

Cut back to the policeman on the telephone.

POLICEMAN: OK, thank you, Father.

He puts down the telephone. Another policeman emerges, bundling Jack through the door.

MRS DOYLE: Father Hackett!

The policeman takes this in.

SCENE 32 INT./EVENING 1
SET: CAVES CAFE
Ted puts the mobile phone back in his jacket.

TED: Dougal, you're not going to be able to eat that. (*Dougal whimpers.*) We have to go and get Mrs Doyle and Mrs Dineen . . . (*Ted's phone rings again. He picks it up and nods.*) OK. (*He puts the mobile phone away.*) . . . and Father Jack out of prison. Come on.

He ushers Dougal away. Dougal picks up a fork and makes one final stab at a chip. We go into slow motion. The chip, in extreme close-up, seesaws on the fork, accompanied by a loud creaking sound. Dougal lifts the fork to his mouth and the chip, still in close-up, starts to fall off the fork. Dougal makes a lunge for it and misses it. He roars in slow motion.

DOUGAL: Nooooooooo!!!!!!!!!!!!!!

Back in normal speed, Ted grabs Dougal and pulls him out of shot.

SCENE 33 INT./EVENING 1
SET: POLICE STATION
Ted is at the front desk dealing with the policeman. Another policeman is looking at Dougal, slightly bemused.

TED (*To Policeman 1*)**:** I'm very, very sorry . . .

DOUGAL (*To Policeman 2*)**:** You wouldn't have a lasagne or some chicken curry or something?

POLICEMAN 2: No.

DOUGAL: OK. Well, maybe I'll just have a bag of chips. And could I have a Fanta orange as well?

POLICEMAN 2: I don't think you know where you are. This is a police station.

DOUGAL: Right . . . Hmnn . . . In that case I'll have the chicken satay and boiled rice.

Policeman 2 looks no less confused. Meanwhile, Policeman 1 has brought Mrs Doyle, Mrs Dineen and

Jack round to the other side of the desk and is handing them back into Ted's care. Ted is profoundly apologetic.

TED: . . . I hope you don't think this type of thing goes on all the time! We're not all criminals and troublemakers in the Church! I hope this won't stop you going to Mass!

POLICEMAN 1: I'm a Protestant actually, Father.

TED: Really? Oh . . . ah, sure . . . they're great . . .

POLICEMAN 1: We can overlook this bit of trouble, Father. Charges won't be pressed. But I'm afraid I'll need a sum of money as a guarantee against their future behaviour. Either that or they'll have to spend the night in the cell.

TED: A sum of money? Right . . . How . . . how much?

POLICEMAN 1: Two hundred pounds.

TED: Oh, well, I wouldn't have that money on me. Maybe a night in the cell would be the best option under the circumstances . . .

DOUGAL: Ted . . .

TED: Shut up, Dougal.

DOUGAL: Ted, you're not going to believe this, but I've got a brilliant idea! Why don't you use that two hundred pounds you won this morning? I mean, it's exactly the amount we need to get Mrs Doyle and Father Jack out! Ha, ha!!!! That bet you won! You have it there with you! Two hundred pounds. *Exactly!*

POLICEMAN 1: You do have it? Right, well then, we're all happy.

Ted reluctantly reaches into his coat and extracts the money from his wallet. The policeman nods a thank you and moves off.

DOUGAL: Never mind, Ted, you've still got two hundred pounds left.

TED (*to Dougal*)**:** Well, I must say . . . There was a time when the police in this country were *friends* of the Church. Drunk driving charges quashed; parking tickets torn up; even turning a blind eye to the odd murder. But now . . .

As he continues on his tirade the man who owns the briefcase comes up to the desk and begins talking to Policeman 2.*

BRIEFCASE MAN: Hello, I'd like to report a stolen briefcase . . .*

Cut back to Ted talking to Dougal.*

TED: . . . 'Oh, no, Father, I'm afraid you *were* doing ninety miles an hour.' I don't know . . . it's the criminals they should be after, not the clergy.*

Back to the briefcase man.*

BRIEFCASE MAN: . . . And I said to two *priests*, of all people, 'Could you keep an eye on this for me?' And they were the ones who ran off with it.*

POLICEMAN 2: Yes. This is just a hunch, but it wouldn't be those two men over there?*

He turns and looks amazed.*

TED: Believe me, this won't go unreported. I'll be writing a letter to . . . some bishop or something, telling him exactly how far we have fallen from those days of innocence when priests could get away with anything.*

He notices that the briefcase man and Policeman 2 are looking at him.*

TED: Ah . . . hello.*

SCENE 34 INT./NIGHT 1†
SET: POLICE CELL
Ted and Dougal sit in their cell, miserable. Mrs Doyle is outside.

MRS DOYLE: Don't worry, Father. We'll have you out in no time! All we have to do is raise another two hundred pounds. (*Ted, sadly, resignedly, hands over the other two hundred pounds to Mrs Doyle.*) Oh! Well . . . what did I tell you? Officer!

Food is slid in through the gap.

DOUGAL: PRISON FOOD!!!

Dougal is about to eat when the cell door opens.

POLICEMAN: All right, come on, you're free to go.

Dougal is about to chow down when Ted grabs him and pulls him out of the cell.

SCENE 35 EXT./DAY 2
SET: COUNTRY ROAD
Richard Wilson is walking along a country road. He inhales deeply, at peace at last. Despite this, he seems a bit lost. He consults a map, and when we cut we reveal the Parochial House nearby. The map doesn't help him, so he sets off towards the house.

SCENE 36 INT./DAY 2
SET: PAROCHIAL HOUSE
Jack, Dougal and Ted are present. Dougal is eating a plate of chips, Ted is reading a newspaper.

TED: What did I say, Dougal? God, there's always trouble when we go to the mainland. I must make a note of never, ever going there again. Unless it's completely unavoidable. Which it isn't. Unfortunately.

SCENE 37 EXT./DAY 2
SET: PAROCHIAL HOUSE
The front doorbell rings. Ted comes into shot and opens the door. We see Richard Wilson standing there. He turns around.

RICHARD: Hello, I'm terribly sorry, but— (*He takes in the fact that it's Ted.*)

I DON'T BELIEVE IT!!!!!!!!!!!!

POST-CREDIT SEQUENCE
SCENE 38 INT./NIGHT 2
SET: CAVES
The mound of rocks. Noel is still under it. We hear him singing.

NOEL: 'Fat-bottomed girls, they make the rocking world go round . . .'

THE END

---

*We deleted these lines from the final version.
† We deleted this scene from the final version.

escape from victory

GRAHAM: More film references. The title's an obvious one, and the opening, where Ted is stripped down to his vest, destroying his house and looking for bugs, is a straight lift of the end of *The Conversation*, a Coppola movie that Arthur and I love.

During the filming of the match, I spent most of the time shouting *'SLOWER!'* at the elderly footballers. We used four types of football; a normal one, one that was weighted so that it would move slowly, one that had water in it to make it wobble like a very, very old person and another that had a camera attached to it. Even with the wobbleball, the men sped about after it like excited puppies – I guess the instinct to run after a ball is hard to suppress. Mrs Doyle's friends were mostly extras, delightful well-mannered girls from Clare who were all willing to scream abuse at the players. There's a great half-time match discussion with Mrs Doyle and her two friends in this draft. We had to lose it due to length, sadly, but it's a neat little scene. Arthur and I have a very loose style of writing, which sometimes leads to shows being overlong. It suits us until we have to lose something like this from the final edit.

ARTHUR: This is probably one of the most insane plots in the series, and it's another example of a crazy situation being deliberately badly set up, as in the case of Ted saying that only a 'completely ludicrous' situation could demand a remote-control wheelchair and a pair of false arms – we love making our intentions clear in this way.

When we were plotting the episode we came up with the idea of forfeits rather than Dick and Ted's usual cash bet. We got a pleasant jolt when we realised that we could end the show with our first 'To Be Continued . . .' This was fortunate, not only because it cut a long story in half, but also because the words 'To Be Continued' seemed to lend the line, 'You have to kick Bishop Brennan up the arse!' a gravity it didn't deserve and gave us, I think, a solid, satisfying ending.

PART ONE

SCENE 1 INT./DAY 1
SET: PAROCHIAL HOUSE
*The living room looks pretty wrecked, with furniture
overturned and some wallpaper stripped off the wall.
Ted takes a picture off the wall and looks behind it.
He throws the picture on the floor. We see that he is
wearing a vest, looking very nervous and suspicious.
He grinds out a cigarette in a big pile of cigarettes.*

SCENE 2 INT./DAY 1
SET: PAROCHIAL HOUSE HALLWAY
*Dougal comes in through the front door. He has a
suitcase.*

SCENE 3 INT./DAY 1
SET: PAROCHIAL HOUSE
*Dougal comes into the living room. Ted is pulling up
a floorboard and looking underneath it.*

DOUGAL: Ted! How are ya?!

TED (*jumps up*): Dougal! Hello there! Did you
have a good time?

*Ted nods his head, indicating silently for Dougal to
say 'yes'.*

DOUGAL: What?

TED: Great! Great! (*He is furiously writing
something on a piece of card.*) I'm so glad to hear
that. Everything here has been fine. Nothing's
wrong at all. There's no problem here at all.

*He holds up the card, on which he has written, in
capital letters, 'WE'RE BEING BUGGED'. Dougal
takes it, frowns, looks up at Ted, then turns the card
around and writes something on the back. After a
moment, he holds it up. He has written, 'WHAT?'.*

*Ted takes the card back and writes something. His
side of the card now reads, 'I SAID WE'RE BEING
BUGGED'.*

TED: So, how was the school reunion? (*He
whispers.*) Keep talking.

*He sees a plug plugged into a socket, with a wire
leading off somewhere.*

DOUGAL: Ah . . . (*He clears his throat.*) . . . I
was at the old school reunion . . .

TED (*to himself*): Where does this go . . . ?

*He picks up the wire and follows it. It leads to the
door. He opens the door and follows it out.*

SCENE 4 INT./DAY 1
SET: PAROCHIAL HOUSE HALLWAY
*Ted follows the wire into the hallway and up the
stairs. He looks up the stairs.*

SCENE 5 INT./DAY 1
SET: PAROCHIAL HOUSE HALLWAY
Dougal shouts up after Ted, still very confused.

DOUGAL: Eh . . . well, it was all right. It was
weird, though. Everyone's changed so much, I
hardly recognised them . . .

*Dougal trails off. He looks confused. Mrs Doyle
enters, sticking her head around the door cautiously.*

MRS DOYLE: Father, do you think a cup of
tea might calm you down? . . .

*She sees that he's gone and then sees Dougal. She
runs up to him. She is worrying a succession of paper
handkerchiefs to pieces.*

MRS DOYLE: Father, Father, oh, you're back
at last, oh, thank God . . . Oh, dear, oh, dear,
oh, dear, oh, golly, oh golly . . .

DOUGAL (*oblivious*): Hello, Mrs Doyle!

MRS DOYLE: Oh, Father, you've got to do
something. He's gone mad. It's this football
thing.

DOUGAL: God almighty, is it that time of the
year again?

MRS DOYLE: Yes, and for some reason, he's
got it into his head . . . Well, he just thinks
Father Byrne is up to something . . . trying to
find out Father Crilly's tactics for the match. It's
only a stupid game of football, for goodness
sake!

DOUGAL: Mrs Doyle, I'm sorry, but no. I have to say no. I'm sorry, I don't want to be rude, but no. There's nothing stupid about football. And there's nothing at all stupid about the annual All Priests Five-a-Side Over Seventy-Fives Indoor Football Challenge match. (*Beat.*) Against Rugged Island.

SCENE 6 INT./DAY 1
SET: UPSTAIRS LANDING
Ted follows the lead to Jack's bedroom.

SCENE 7 INT./DAY 1
SET: JACK'S BEDROOM
Ted comes into the room. He lifts the lead and sees that it goes up to a tiny, white electric fan that Jack is fanning himself with in a rather fey way. He looks at Ted in confusion. Ted looks annoyed and closes the door.

SCENE 8 INT./DAY 1
SET: PAROCHIAL HOUSE
Mrs Doyle and Dougal are in the living room.

MRS DOYLE: Please, Father, please do something. I can't stand seeing him like this.

DOUGAL: Well . . .

Ted comes into the room.

TED: Anyway, Dougal, you were saying? About your school reunion?

DOUGAL: Oh, ah . . . Well, I didn't recognise many of them. And, do you know what? They all became firemen! I was the only one who wasn't a fireman! Can you believe that?

Ted stops.

TED: Em . . . you're sure you hadn't gone to a fire station or something by mistake?

Pause.

DOUGAL: Ahhhhhhhhhh . . .

Ted returns to his mad, paranoid business. He starts pulling up a floorboard.

DOUGAL: Ted, come on, you're going a bit mad, there.

Ted makes an urgent 'shut up' gesture.

TED: What? I'm sure I don't know what you're talking about. I'm absolutely fine!

There's nothing wrong with me at all.

He unscrews a lightbulb and looks in the socket.

DOUGAL: Ted, I'm going to have to do something, and you won't like it. But it's for your own good. Are you ready?

TED: Hmm . . . ?

DOUGAL: You won't like it, Ted, I just know it. Call it female intuition, or whatever the male equivalent of female intuition is, but this isn't going to go down well in the Ted camp at all.

TED (*not really paying attention*): I think—

Dougal slaps Ted in the face.

DOUGAL: Sorry, Ted. You were going a bit mad.

TED: What the— What are you— (*Pause. He looks around.*) Oh, my God. Oh, my God, look at this place! What have I done? What have I done? I've got to get a hold of myself. God almighty . . . I suppose I've never been able to get over last year. Do you remember? When Dick tried to find out about our tactics using the Internet? Remember? He printed all those details about us? And then someone in Holland accidentally sent us loads of hard-core pornography?

They drift off for a nostalgic moment.

DOUGAL: But Ted . . . being bugged by Dick Byrne! I don't think that's very likely now, do you? Come on, Ted, look at you! You look terrible.

TED: I've been having a lot of trouble getting any sleep. I'm going to try this stuff, 'Dreamy Sleepy Nightie Snoozy Snooze' . . .

DOUGAL: 'Dreamy Sleepy Nightie Snoozy Snooze'?

Ted produces it – a bottle of green fluid with its name on the label.

TED: Yes. It's a bran-based, alcoholic, chocolate sleeping-aid. It's banned in most European countries, so that means it's very good.

DOUGAL: In the meantime, Ted, I'll go and buy us an ice-cream. That'll calm us both down.

TED: Yes, that'd be nice. Where are you going to get an ice-cream, though?

DOUGAL: There's an ice-cream van outside . . .

TED: Is there?

He looks out of the window.

SCENE 9 EXT./DAY 1
SET: NEARBY FIELD
We see an ice-cream van.

TED: It'll never sell much out there . . .

SCENE 10 INT./DAY 1
SET: ICE-CREAM VAN
Cut to inside the van. Father Dick Byrne is crouched beside a large radar dish type thing in the back of the van. He is wearing headphones and is dressed in a white coat. Father Cyril McDuff is in the front seat. Dick takes off his earphones and slams them down.

DICK: They're on to us, Cyril! Let's go!!!

Cyril slams his foot down and the ice-cream van roars off, playing a slow nursery rhyme as it does so.

SCENE 11 EXT./DAY 1
SET: FOOTBALL FIELD
We see Ted and Dougal at the side of the pitch.

TED: Come on, Father Bigley! Get your arse in gear! Father Whelan, come on! You can move faster than that! Get into it! For missing the target from there you need shooting!

Cut to reveal three very old and frail-looking priests kicking balls very slowly at an equally frail-looking goalkeeper.

BIGLEY: Are we nearly finished? I'm very tired! I'm ninety-seven!

TED: Good God, that's an awful defeatist attitude, Father Bigley! I'm holding you back for extra training! You'll stay here till seven. Do fifteen laps of the pitch.

BIGLEY: But . . .

TED: Off you go . . .

Father Bigley reluctantly heads off at an incredibly slow pace around the pitch.

TED (*to Dougal*): God, I don't know. The

attitude of those lads. There was a time when the Over Seventy-Fives team put their hearts into it.

DOUGAL: I suppose these days they're too busy with their computer games and their Nike trainers.

TED (*not listening*): Yes, God, there's a distinct lack of pace in the team this year. And Dick Byrne's lot have a new fella that's supposed to be flip hot. An Italian fella.

DOUGAL: Ah, yes, the Italians know football all right. And, of course, the world of fashion! God, do you remember that fella who was so good at fashion they had to shoot him?

TED: Where's Nick Doorley? God almighty, our first training session and our star player can't be bothered to turn up. We're relying on his almost telepathic understanding with Father Jack to knock in a few goals. If anything happened to him, well, we'd be up to our necks in flip. And with this new fella on Dick's team, we need Nick at the very peak of his powers.

SCENE 12 INT./DAY 1
SET: A MORGUE
We see the body of an ancient priest laid out in a coffin. Pull back to reveal Ted beside a middle-aged priest. This is Father Niall Haverty. This morgue is very minimal, very white, with expensive, stylish fittings and track lighting.

TED: So, there's no way he'll be able to play?

NIALL: No. He's dead.

TED: Right. (*Pause.*) It's completely out of the question, then. (*Niall thinks this is rhetorical.*) Is it? It's completely out of the question?

NIALL: What? Oh, yes, yes, completely out of the question.

TED: Right. (*Pause.*) Wait . . . You . . . you don't hear breathing, do you?

NIALL: No, Ted, seriously, he's long gone.

TED: Right. Actually, Nick was a very dear friend of mine . . . Do you mind if I have a few minutes alone with him?

NIALL: Of course.

He leaves the room and closes the door behind him.

We go with him into a small reception area. After a second, we hear a thumping noise from inside the room. Niall frowns and re-enters the room. Ted is holding Father Nick beneath the arms, pulling his fists to his chest in a resuscitating movement. He sees Niall and stops.

TED: I thought I had something going there for a moment.

NIALL: Ah, come on, Ted, you're clutching at straws, man!

TED: Ah, you're right. Sorry, Father Nick.

NIALL: I told you, Father, he can't hear you, he's gone! C'mon, lads . . .

Some men in suits come in and take the coffin out. Ted watches this sadly.

NIALL: Ted, come on, cheer up. Look, have you seen my new watch? I got it from a catalogue. Look, if you press this button here, it tells you the time in Singapore. In Chinese! And then if you want to go back to normal time, you just press this here . . . (*He presses something a few times. This is accompanied by soft bleeping noises.*) . . . That's weird . . . it's supposed to . . . got the feckin' calculator now . . . come on . . . ah! And there you go, back to normal time. Half past ten.

TED: It's a quarter to two, Niall.

NIALL: Is it? Hold on a second and I'll set it to the right . . . to the right time . . . oh . . . God, the thing is fecked . . .

He starts pressing buttons again.

TED: That's an unusual-looking television.

NIALL: Ah, yeah, it's great, isn't it? It's voice activated. Tell it to come on, there.

TED: What?

NIALL: Say, 'I want to watch the television' or something.

TED: Ah, no, Niall, it's a bit mad.

NIALL: Go on!

Pause.

TED: I want to watch television!

Nothing happens.

NIALL: That's weird . . . it's supposed to . . .

come on there, now, television! COME ON! HE WANTS TO WATCH TELEVISION! COME ON!

TED: Niall, you've got to stop buying this catalogue stuff. It never works. The only thing you got that ever worked was that remote-controlled wheelchair.

NIALL: Yes, that worked perfectly, didn't it?

TED: But what use is it? You'd probably have more use for those joke fake arms you got!

NIALL: Oh, those things! They seemed funny at the time . . . Also, they reminded me of my own arms.

TED: Fake arms! Honestly, Niall! What the hell kind of situation could possibly require either a pair of fake arms or a radio-controlled wheelchair? Only, I would imagine, a completely ludicrous one.

NIALL: Yes. Anyway, Ted, do you think you can win the match without Father Nick?

TED: I don't know. He had a great partnership with Father Jack up front. God, if Dick Byrne won again . . .

The telephone rings. Ted picks it up.

TED: Hello?

We hear Father Dick Byrne's voice from the other end.

DICK: I *am* going to win again, Ted!

TED: Ha! I wouldn't be too sure of that, Dick! I think we've— Wait a second! How did you know I was here?!

We hear a click and a dial tone. Then, from outside, we hear the ice-cream van's bells dwindling again. Ted runs to the window and shakes his fist.

TED: Damn you, Father Dick Byrne!

SCENE 13 INT./DAY 1
SET: PAROCHIAL HOUSE
Dougal is wearing a tracksuit, kneeling down and going through the contents of a trainer's kit bag. Jack is asleep in his chair. He snores loudly. Ted is looking through 'The Over Seventy-Fives Priests Five-A-Side Rulebook'.

TED: Do you know what we need, Dougal? We need another Father Pinky Flood.

DOUGAL: Well, yeah . . . (*He looks nostalgic.*) Who is he, Ted?

TED: The greatest over seventy-fives player ever. He was to over seventy-fives football what George Best was to the world of players who were . . . average-age-type players. An absolute legend in the world of asthmatic, arthritic, hardly-able-to-move footballers with no teeth.

DOUGAL: There must be *someone*, Ted.

TED: I was just talking to Father Ned Fitzmaurice. He had a terrible stroke and fell from the roof of his house last week. He can hardly move. There's no way round it – I'll have to put him in goal.

DOUGAL: Oh God, Ted. I can't wait to get into the old physio's role again. Spraying things on to people's legs and running on to the pitch with the magic sponge. And doing all 'physio' type things.

TED: Yes. When they're injured, Dougal. (*Beat.*) Part of the skill of a physio is to wait until someone is injured before chasing after them with a sponge.

DOUGAL: Right.

TED: And while we're at it . . . Do you know exactly what the sponge does, Dougal?

Pause.

DOUGAL: . . . It . . . soaks up . . . germs . . .

TED: No, that's quite, quite wrong. Dougal, don't take this the wrong way, but . . . I don't want you to be a physio this year.

DOUGAL: Ted, if you don't want me to be physio this year, just come right out and say it.

TED: Ah . . . OK . . . Actually, Dougal, I was thinking of a new role for you, this year.

DOUGAL (*apprehensive*): Right . . .

TED: Yes. Very much a step-up in the whole off-the-field back-up-support team structure. An organisational change, you could call it.

DOUGAL (*apprehensively*): What is it, Ted?

TED: Eh . . . it's a very important job. One to which I'm sure you'll be able to bring all your qualities . . . ah . . . I want you to keep an eye on the corner flags. Make sure no one steals them.

Dougal looks at Ted very seriously, then breathes a massive sigh of relief.

DOUGAL: Oh, thank God for that! Phew! I thought you might be giving me something completely stupid to do, but wow! Watching the corner flags! Big responsibility!

Jack snores unusually loudly. Ted and Dougal look at him. Mrs Doyle enters with her tray of tea.

MRS DOYLE: Football! Football! Football! What you men see in it at all, I don't know! A load of men kicking a bit of leather around a field! Tscha! I don't know . . . you men. The things you think are great fun! Like going to the films. A load of men sitting around looking at films. And rollercoasters! A load of men in a big rollercoaster going up and down on a metal track. And fishing! A load of men fishing! And sailing. A load of men in a boat, floating about in the water! And shouting! A load of men going around shouting! And so forth.

TED: Hah, there's more to football than you think, Mrs Doyle. Here, I got you this book . . .

He hands her a book, 'Understanding Football for Women'. The cover features a drawing of a buxom lass in a clench with a Ryan Giggs type in a Manchester United strip, a blazing fire in the background, all drawn in a romantic-novel style.

MRS DOYLE: Ooh. All right, Father. I'll get on top of it right away.

Mrs Doyle goes out.

DOUGAL: God, Ted, he's been like that for a good long time. He wouldn't be dead again, would he?

TED: No, I don't think so. He's already died once, and it's very unlikely that he'd die again. God almighty . . .

DOUGAL: I hope he wakes up in time for the match, Ted. He looks like he's unconscious.

TED: Oh, I'm sure he's just dreaming of his old sporting days . . .

Cut to Jack. We fade into his dream.

SCENE 14 EXT./DAY 1
SET: TABLE
We see Jack at a table. He has 'Judge' written on a piece of card in front of him.

We pull wide to see him sitting beneath a banner with 'Wet T-Shirt Competition' written on it. Some women are in the foreground, their backs to us, being sprayed by another woman wielding a hose.

SCENE 15 INT./DAY 1*
SET: PAROCHIAL HOUSE
Ted sees something in one corner of the room. It is a video camera with a red light on, pointing at them and humming quietly.

TED: Dougal . . . how long has that video camera been there?

DOUGAL: What video cam— Oh . . . I don't know . . .

TED: Dick Byrne! Well, Dick, see how you like this!

He smashes the video camera to smithereens.

DOUGAL: Oh, wait, Ted, now I remember. That's actually your video camera. I thought I might do a fly-on-the-wall documentary about the match.

TED: What . . . It is my video camera!

The telephone rings. Dick Byrne is on the other end.

DICK: Hello, Ted!

TED: Oh, hello, Dick . . .

DICK: Ted, I was thinking . . . rather than a cash bet this year, how about some sort of forfeit?

TED: NO CASH BET! YOU BETCHA!!! I mean, yes, OK, if you're scared of losing . . . What kind of forfeit?

DICK: Oh, I've got a few ideas. But when you lose, you *have* to do it. No backing out, Crilly!

TED: Very well. One condition. Nothing illegal.

DICK: Agreed. And by the way, Ted, don't worry about the video camera. You can have a lend of *mine* if you want.

TED: Oh, thanks very much, Di— Wait a second! How did you know I smashed up my video camera?!

The line goes dead.

*We deleted this scene from the final version.

TED: Right . . .

DOUGAL: Ted! Where are you going?

TED: I'm going to find a way to shut Dick Byrne up once and for all!!

He leaves the room. We see this from the point of view of a black-and-white camera hidden in one corner of the room.

END OF PART ONE

* * *

PART TWO

SCENE 16 INT./DAY 2
SET: PAROCHIAL HOUSE
Dougal has a corner flag propped up in the middle of the room. He's staring at it intently. Ted comes in, rubbing his hands together.

TED: Well! Today's the day! (*Dougal doesn't say anything – he's concentrating too hard on the flag.*) Got the hang of it yet, Dougal?

DOUGAL: It's harder than you'd think, Ted. (*He turns to talk to Ted. Mrs Doyle enters, sees the flag, frowns, picks it up and carries it out of the room.*) The trick is to— (*He turns and sees that the flag has gone.*) Aaaaghh!

He starts to look around desperately for the flag. Mrs Doyle returns and approaches Ted.

MRS DOYLE: Well, Father, I have to say that book you gave me has got me really interested in football. It's brilliant! I even put a little bet on this season.

TED: Oh, great! Who'd you bet on?

MRS DOYLE: It's an accumulator bet. Arsenal to win the league, Inter Milan to win Serie A by four points from Fiorentina with Ronaldo not scoring less than thirty goals, Kevin Keegan resigning from Fulham before the end of the season, Wimbledon getting relegated, but not finishing last – I have Southampton to finish last – Jimmy Hill to grow back his beard to balance that moustache (that's just a bit of fun, that one), and how the final Premiership table will look. First, Arsenal; second, Manchester United; third, Liverpool; fourth, Chelsea; fifth, Newcastle . . .

Ted leaves the room as she continues speaking.

SCENE 17 INT./DAY 2
SET: PAROCHIAL HOUSE HALLWAY
Ted enters the hallway. Dougal is looking around desperately. He spots Ted and stands up.

DOUGAL: Ah, hello, Ted. I'm just . . . eating . . . my . . . breakfast.

TED (*admonishingly*)**:** Dougal . . . that's a fib. What are you really doing?

DOUGAL: I . . . I . . . I've lost the flag, Ted! I'm sorry! I just put it down for a second and the next thing it was gone! I'm so sorry! Ted, you've got to give me another job! I can't take this one! It's too much, too soon! Oh, God, Ted, I can't do it! I just can't do it.

TED: Dougal, there's no such word as can't.

DOUGAL: Yes, there is. It's short for cannot. I cannot do it, Ted! I simply cannot!

TED: Dougal! Eye of the tiger. Just remember that at all times! Eye of the tiger!

A beat, then Dougal nods bravely.

SCENE 18 INT./DAY 2*
SET: PAROCHIAL HOUSE
In the living room, Ted, Dougal and Mrs Doyle are looking very anxiously at a still-very-much-asleep Jack.

DOUGAL: God, Ted, do you think he'll wake up in time for the match? It starts in six hours. I'm getting worried.

TED: This is a bit unusual, all right. Let's try old faithful. (*He holds up a CD case.*) Ah, yes. Never fails.

Mrs Doyle, Dougal and Ted put on protective earwear. Mrs Doyle and Dougal hide behind the sofa, as if they're going to witness a nuclear explosion. Ted turns on the CD player, and then runs behind the sofa to join the other two.

SCENE 19 EXT./DAY 2*
SET: PAROCHIAL HOUSE
We hear from inside the house 'Smoke on the Water'. It is very, very, very loud.

SCENE 20 EXT./DAY 2*
SET: NORTH POLE
We see an Eskimo outside his igloo. We hear the

distant, faraway strains of 'Smoke on the Water'.

SCENE 21 INT./DAY 2†
SET: PAROCHIAL HOUSE
We see various objects in the room rattling with the noise. Ted turns off the music, and takes off his headphones. Dougal and Mrs Doyle emerge from behind the sofa.

TED: God, this is very serious. I wonder . . . (*He sees something on the ground behind Jack's chair.*) Wait a second . . . Oh, my God! (*He runs over and picks something up. It is an empty, oversized bottle with 'Dreamy Sleepy Nightie Snoozy Snooze'.*) He's drunk an entire bottle of 'Dreamy Sleepy Snoozy Nightie Snooze'!

DOUGAL: Yes, Ted. But why is he still asleep?!

SCENE 22 EXT./DAY 2
SET: SPORTS HALL
We see Dick Byrne's team. Everyone is very old, and can barely kick the ball, except for a player on the Rugged Island team, Father Romeo Sensini. He is very bronzed, with a thick mane of white hair; he looks super fit and wears a pair of cool shades. Dick watches as a mini-van pulls up. Ted and Dougal get out of it. Ted wears a massive Alex Ferguson-like manager's all-weather coat. Dougal wears a tracksuit. Dick and Cyril sidle up to Ted.

DICK: Well, there he is, Ted. Father Romeo Sensini.

We see Sensini being approached by two equally old women. He signs autographs for them in an offhand sort of way.

DICK: He has seventeen caps for the Vatican Over-Seventy-Fives. Very fit. Only drinks very, very fine wine. Can walk up two flights of stairs unassisted. Only needs one nun to help him get out of a chair. You won't have a chance.

TED: Hah! That's what you think, Dick. We've put Father Hackett through a rigorous training schedule and he's never been fitter.

---

*We deleted this scene from the final version.
† Following the deletion of scenes 18–20, the contents of this scene were incorporated into the previous scene.

Dick snorts and moves off. Cut to darkness. A door opens and we see that we're in the back of the van with the five players. The five men in the back gasp for air as soon as Ted opens the door.

TED: Sorry, Fathers! Probably a bit stuffy in there.

The men start to crawl out of the van. They reveal Jack, lying on the floor. Dick approaches Ted.

TED: Whatever you do, Dougal, don't let Dick—

Dick comes into shot.

DICK: Aha! Yes, Jack looks like a major threat, all right. Hmmmn, we may have counted our chickens too soon.

He turns round and laughs his head off. Cyril joins in and starts laughing, too, even though he has no idea what he's laughing at. His laughter dwindles as Dick looks at him with disdain.

CYRIL: Ha, ha . . . ahhhh . . . chickens . . .

He shuts up.

SCENE 23 INT./DAY 2
SET: VAN
Ted is looking at Jack.

TED: Father! Father! Please wake up! Oh, what are we going to do?! OH!!! I can't believe we're in this completely ludicrous situation! (*Ted stops short.*) Wait a second! That's it!

SCENE 24 INT./DAY 2
SET: SPORTS HALL
Cut to the pitch. The captains of each team are watching as the referee flips the coin.

REFEREE: What's that? Can anyone see that?

BIGLEY (*bends to look, then straightens*)**:** It's some kind of coin.

Cut to Mrs Doyle, who is joined by Mrs Norton.

MRS NORTON: God almighty, Mrs Doyle. How could you be interested in this type of thing?

MRS DOYLE: That's what I thought. But look at this.

She hands Mrs Norton 'Understanding Football for Women.' Cut to Ted on the sidelines. He is talking anxiously into his mobile phone.*

TED: Sorry to ring again, Niall, but I'm getting worried.†

Cut to Niall on the other end of the line.†

NIALL: No need to worry at all, Ted. Just look out for a white van. I'm amazed it hasn't got there already.†

TED: They're just about to kick off! Oh, no, wait!†

We see a white van pulling up outside. Ted sees it through the door. It has the following written on its side: 'NICK OF TIME DELIVERIES'.†

TED: Great!†

He hangs up. Cut back to the referee.†

REFEREE: Father McGuire, you're a man short. If he's not here by kick-off time, I'll have to award the match to Father Byrne's team. And where's your manager?†

DOUGAL: Ah. He had to go to the toilet. He's . . . ah, got diarrhoea.†

REFEREE (*cringes*)**:** I'm sorry, I'll have to give Father Byrne a walkover . . . Father Byrne?†

DOUGAL (*hears something*)**:** Wait!†

REFEREE: What's that noise?†

Cut to the doors of the stadium. There is a mechanical noise, growing louder. After a moment, to a burst of celebratory music, Jack speeds in, still asleep, in his mechanical wheelchair. Dick comes up to the referee.†

DICK: This can't be allowed, surely!†

Ted follows in through the door. He has fake arms.†

REFEREE: I'll look at the book . . . (*He consults his book, 'The Over Seventy-Fives Priests Five-A-Side Rulebook'.*) I can't see anything about wheelchairs . . .†

TED: Oh, they're definitely allowed. There's a precedent. Turn to page 166.†

The referee turns to page 166. We see an old picture, circa 1920s, showing an old-priests match. In an old bath chair is a fearsome old priest, wielding a stick.

---

*We deleted the previous two sentences from the final version.
†We deleted this from the final version.

Ted flips his fake hand on to the picture.†

TED: There. (*Ted realises he shouldn't be showing off his fake hand and flips it away.*) Father Pinky Flood.†

There is a reverent hush.†

TED: The greatest over seventy-fives priest footballer there ever was. This was his testimonial game against a Hungarian/Polish selection. He had a massive stroke during the pre-match warm-up, but he was still determined to play. He was held in such esteem that the referee let him play in a wheelchair.†

REFEREE: Well, I suppose, if there's a precedent . . .†

TED: Great!†

DICK: *Grrrr!* It's not fair!†

1. Kick-off†

2. One priest kicks the ball to another (Father Bigley). The ball moves terribly, terribly slowly. We see a moving-camera position from just behind the ball. As it rolls towards Bigley, we can see him looking afraid. It hits his foot and he falls over. We see that Ted is fiddling with a remote control under his jacket. His arms look very fake. We see Jack shifting around in his wheelchair, still unconscious, in a corner.

3. We see Father Romeo Sensini gain possession. He makes for the goal.

TED: Close him down! Close him down!

4. A priest very slowly starts to make towards Sensini. Sensini dribbles very slowly around him.

TED: He's running rings around you!

Sensini gets past the old man. He approaches the goal. Jack is blocking his way, asleep in his chair. Ted fiddles with the remote control under his coat and Jack makes towards Sensini. Without pausing, Jack goes right past Sensini and through the door by which he just came in. Meanwhile, Sensini is still moving slowly towards goal. Mrs Doyle approaches Ted.

MRS DOYLE: Sensini's got an open goal, Father. If you don't do something quick, he'll score in a matter of minutes.

We see Mrs Norton finishing 'Understanding Football for Women'.

MRS NORTON (*making managerial hand gestures*): Out! Out! Push out!

She hands the book distractedly to a cleaning woman, Mrs Cavanagh, who is mopping a floor nearby. She starts leafing through it. Sensini finally kicks the ball with a tremendous grunt. The ball travels incredibly slowly towards the line.

Very, very slowly it comes to a stop just on the line. We see the ball on the line. A very tense moment. Cut to Ted looking hugely anxious.

5. Father Whelan (from Ted's team) then very slowly moves from out of shot and kicks the ball away.

Cut back to Mrs Doyle and Mrs Norton. Mrs Cavanagh is still leafing through the book.

MRS DOYLE: Where did he come from?!

MRS NORTON: Great defending!

6. The ball goes to Father Bigley (Craggy Island).

TED: Get rid of it! Get rid of it!

Bigley looks around, confused.

BIGLEY: What?

TED: Don't look at me! Keep playing!

BIGLEY: I'm ninety-seven!

Bigley leaves the ball and takes a step or two towards Ted. Behind him, Sensini moves very slowly towards the ball.

TED: Turn around! Concentrate on the game!

BIGLEY: Is that Father Crilly? Hello, Father!

Cut to the spectators.

MRS DOYLE: Someone's going to have to get tighter on the Italian.

MRS NORTON: The tension is almost too much to bear. Tell me when he gets possession.

Mrs Norton turns around and hides her eyes. Mrs Doyle watches the match. We stay on this for about thirty seconds.

MRS DOYLE: Now.

Mrs Cavanagh finishes the book.

MRS CAVANAGH: Go wide! Go wide!

7. Sensini has possession of the ball and heads towards the goal. Cut to Ted. He looks alarmed. We see the wheelchair coming back through the door and heading straight for Sensini. A shot of Ted making an 'ouch' face as we hear a 'crump' sound. Cut to Sensini on the ground holding his leg. The referee blows his whistle.

TED: Penalty! Damn!

Sensini puts the ball on the penalty spot. He strikes coolly, and we see a shot from the ball's point of view. The ball very slowly goes one way while the goalkeeper goes the other.

MRS DOYLE: He's sent the keeper the wrong way!

The ball goes into the net. We see Dick Byrne, Cyril, etc., jumping up and down with excitement.

DICK: GOAL!

CYRIL: What's that, Dick?

DICK: We're going to win, Cyril. I think I'll want a souvenir of this day . . . Get me one of those corner flags.

CYRIL: Yes, Dick.

He walks out of shot. Ted looks downcast. He fiddles with the remote control.

TED: God, this remote control is tricky.

Dougal is standing near one of the flags. Cyril approaches. Dougal watches him warily. They do a little suspicious dance around the flag. The referee blows his whistle. It is half-time.

SCENE 25 INT./DAY 2
SET: DRESSING ROOM
The players sit around, exhausted.

TED: Right! I know you're tired. I know you want to go home. I know you're due back in the home by eight. But remember one thing – you're carrying the whole of Craggy Island on your shoulders.

Father Whelan puts up a finger.

WHELAN: Eh—

TED: Metaphor, Jim.

WHELAN: It's just, my back—

TED: Jim, metaphor, don't mean it literally. Try not to jump into the flow here.

SCENE 26 INT./DAY 2*
SET: CAFE-TYPE AREA
Mrs Doyle and Mrs Norton, with Mrs Cavanagh to their right, are sitting in what look strangely like half-time match-discussion positions.

MRS CAVANAGH: Mrs Doyle, an exciting first half. Any thoughts?

MRS DOYLE: Sensini's not getting picked up. The problem is he's got a free role in midfield. He's pulling the centre half all over the place.

MRS CAVANAGH: Lack of pace certainly a problem for Craggy Island.

MRS NORTON: It's not just lack of pace. Some of that marking from set pieces . . . you wouldn't see that in a school playground.

MRS DOYLE: That corner they had just before half-time—

MRS NORTON: The defending on that was a joke.

MRS DOYLE: You can't have the full backs staying on the post like that. You've got to have them push out, or they're leaving their front two onside. That's naïve defending. Do that too often and you'll get punished.

MRS CAVANAGH: Anyway, let's return to what should be a very exciting second half.

SCENE 27 INT./DAY 2
SET: CHANGING ROOM
Ted is still in spiel mode.

TED: All right, I want you all to go out there

*We deleted this scene from the final version.

and play the greatest game of what's left of your lives! I want you to take Dick Byrne's team and rip them to shreds!

WHELAN: Eh . . .

TED: Again, Jim, metaphor. Now, get out there and lick some arse! Kick! Kick some arse! Just go! Now!

SCENE 28 INT./DAY 2
SET: PLAYING FIELD
The referee blows his whistle. Father Whelan is standing around, not really knowing what's going on. The ball comes towards him and stops at his feet. Sensini comes into shot and tackles him roughly. Cut to Ted, as we hear Whelan scream and then a whistle blow. Ted stands up and runs to where some players have gathered around the fallen Whelan.

TED: This looks bad. It could be broken.

WHELAN: No, no, I don't think it's broken. I'll play on. Don't want to let the side down.

TED: Good man!

WHELAN: I might just have a little rest first.

He settles into a little snooze. Cut back to Dougal and Cyril. Cyril is trying to sneak up backwards on the flag. Dougal swoops in and discourages him at a vital moment.

Cut back to the match. One priest passes to another. Cut to Jack in his chair. We hear a kicking sound and the ball lands in Jack's lap.

TED: Go, Father Jack! Go!

We see Jack's chair accelerate through the players and steam through the Rugged Island goal.

TED: Yaaaayyy!!!

We see Mrs Doyle, Mrs Norton and Mrs Cavanagh clench their teeth and fists. They are surrounded by ten Mrs Doyle-alikes pointing and chanting.

MRS DOYLE AND HER COTERIE
(*chanting*): You're all very quiet over there, you're all very quiet over there . . .

8. Rugged Island kick off again and Jack steams through, gaining possession. He's heading straight for goal.

9. Sensini runs up and boots something on Jack's wheelchair. Smoke starts issuing from it and it goes round in a circle then heads towards the door again.

Jack goes through it for the last time.

TED: Foul, Ref, surely!

REFEREE (*making a gesture with his hands*): Play on!

10. The ball wanders into the path of Bigley.

TED: Open goal! Go on, Father Bigley!

BIGLEY: What?

TED: Don't look at me. You've only got the goalkeeper to beat!

11. We see this from behind the goal. Bigley kicks the ball. It slowly rolls under the keeper and into the goal. The final whistle is blown.

TED: Whhhhhhhaaaayyyy!!!!!!!

BIGLEY: Have I done something wrong?

Much joy. Ted and Mrs Doyle run out and celebrate. Cyril makes one more stab at stealing the flag. Dougal stops him again. Cyril walks off, defeated. Dougal beams happily, a job well done.

SCENE 29 INT./DAY 2*
SET: DRESSING ROOM
Ted and Dougal approach Dick and Cyril. The referee stands between them. Ted's fake hands hang uselessly by his side.

CYRIL: Six nil. God, we had it easy out there.

DICK: We lost two one, Cyril. Ted, I have to say, we've had our arguments down through the years but you played a good game.

During this speech, we cut to Dougal's, Niall's and the referee's admiring expressions.

DICK: Seeing your team out there, pulling together for the common good, well . . . it made me realise how much time we've wasted

---

* In the final version of this scene, Ted tells Dick his forfeit and Dick and Cyril go home, leaving Dougal and Ted to open champagne with the referee. It is he who notices something amiss when Dougal forces Ted to take a glass of champagne. A new scene was then added with Ted and Dougal back at the Parochial House. His ruse discovered, Ted must do Dick's forfeit, and in the final version the scene ends with a disbelieving Ted reading his forfeit out loud.

on our stupid rivalry. I accept my defeat, because it came at the hands of a better man. Put it there, Ted.

Ted stands there, his plastic hands hanging uselessly by his side. Long, long pause.

TED: No.

REFEREE: *No?*

TED: No.

DOUGAL: Ted, I didn't understand any of that speech, but even I know Dick's trying to make friends!

TED: Yes, but—

DICK: No, I understand. You think it's another trick. But listen to me, Ted. No more tricks. Take my hand and I will never, never let it go.

TED: Right . . . Ehh . . . Dick, I, too, wish to put our rivalry to one side. But I would rather do that . . . with a nod. Dick, please accept my nod of friendship.

He nods.

DICK: Ah, Ted, come on, shake hands. It'll make me feel better.

DOUGAL: Ted, I don't know what's wrong with you . . . (*Ted makes urgent facial expressions to remind Dougal of the hands.*) Shake his hand, Ted. What's wrong with you at all?

MRS DOYLE (*incredibly savagely*): DON'T DO IT, FATHER!!!!

Pause. Everyone is looking at Ted. He finally gives in and does a little jerk to swing his hand into Dick's. Dick catches it and shakes it, smiling warmly at Ted.

DICK: Now . . . let's hear it, what's the forfeit?

TED: Well, Dick, in the light of that lovely speech, what's say we go without the forfeit?

DICK: Oh, no, I don't think so. I believe the referee has the envelopes containing the forfeits?

Dick absent-mindedly scratches his face with Ted's now-detached fake hand. He notices it.

DICK: What the—

He looks down at Ted and sees where the hand is missing. He examines Ted's other hand. Fake. He pulls aside Ted's coat and sees Ted's hand holding the remote control. Pause. Dick's face gradually darkens.

DICK: You . . . you little cheating fibber!! I always knew you were a dirty little sneaky cheatbag! How *dare* you sully this holy football ground with cheating! You . . . cheating priest!

Ted hangs his head. Cyril approaches Dick.

CYRIL: Dick . . .

DICK: Just one second, Cyril. I want to get one last look at Crilly, just so the next time I think there's a cheat around, I'll know what to look for. (*He looks Ted up and down, shaking his head.*) There. I'm finished.

CYRIL: Great. I just wanted to know . . . even though we lost, do we still have to give all that money to their goalkeeper?

Dick just looks at Cyril while Ted's face lights up.

TED: Ahhhhhhhhhhhhhhhhhhhhhhhhh-hah! Well, well, well, well, well, well, well, well, well, well, well, well, well, well, well, well. Bribery, the most dishonest form of corruption there is. Even worse than swindling or fraud or prostitution rackets or skimming money off a parish account and putting it in a high-interest, special-needs savings account for a few years before moving it back . . .

DOUGAL: Oh, ho!

TED: Shut up, Dougal . . . Oh, much worse than that! I should have known. You . . . briber . . . or whatever the word is.

DOUGAL: Right.

REFEREE: Well. I think you're both a disgrace. And I think you should both do your forfeits.

TED: Fine by me.

DICK: Oh, me, too.

The referee opens one of the envelopes.

REFEREE: Father Byrne and Father McDuff first. Your forfeit is . . . oh, good God . . . Father Byrne has to kiss Father McDuff on the cheek.

Dick looks incredibly bored by this.

DOUGAL: Haaaaaaa!!!!! Ahghhghaaa!!!!!! WHAT A BRILLIANT IDEA TED!!!!! HA, HA, HA, HA!!!! Ted, you're a genius!!!!! I can't wait to see that!!!!

They both laugh in a very childish, superior way. Dick enters into shot.

DOUGAL: Oh, God, Ted, how did you think of that?! That's just the best —

DICK: . . . Did it.

TED (*beat*)**:** What?

DICK: I did it.

TED: But . . . but we didn't see it.

DICK: Well, they all saw it.

TED: Oh. (*To the crowd.*)**:** Was it funny?

Everyone shrugs half-heartedly. The referee opens the other envelope.

REFEREE: And now Father Crilly . . .

DOUGAL: Don't worry, Ted. It'll never be as good as your one.

REFEREE: You, Father Crilly . . . (*To Dick.*) Is this right? (*Dick nods, smiling. The referee looks concerned but reads on.*) You . . . Father Crilly, by this time next week . . . you have to . . .

Close-up on Ted. Dick steps forward and grabs the letter from the referee's hand.

DICK: Crilly . . . You have to . . . KICK BISHOP BRENNAN UP THE ARSE!!!!!!

Freeze on Ted's look of horror. Words come up on the screen: 'To Be Continued'.

POST-CREDIT SEQUENCE
We see a quiet road and hear a low mechanical noise. After a moment Jack passes by, still unconscious in his chair. Tilt up to reveal a sign that reads 'Pier'.

THE END

SERIES THREE ◈ EPISODE SIX

kicking Bishop Brennan up the arse

GRAHAM: Our idea of kicking someone up the arse and then pretending nothing had happened was influenced by a story told about the painter Magritte. Apparently, after he met a potential suitor for his sister, he brought him into the sitting room, kicked the suitor in the behind and then pretended that absolutely nothing had occurred – just to see what would happen. It's an intriguing concept. What would you do in that situation? And how long would it take you to become absolutely convinced that you had indeed been kicked? We thought it would work especially well here because of the relationship between Ted and Brennan. The latter knows Ted is *terrified* of him, so it would take him ages to make the intellectual leap of registering an attack.

That one idea drives the whole plot of this episode, so we had to expand it as much as possible. That's why we introduced Bishop Jessup, the sarcastic bishop. We needed a reason for the first attempt to fail. That sequence – Ted's run-up and subsequent leap out of the window – was originally supposed to be filmed in slow motion. Somehow it didn't work, so on a hunch someone suggested running it at the proper speed, and it was perfect. Jessup's fate – being locked in Jack's underpants' hamper – originally had the ending you'll see in this draft, but it was funnier on paper than in rehearsal. In the end, we decided to keep it simple and ended up with a nod to *The Vanishing*, which, if you haven't seen it, is one of the scariest films ever made.

ARTHUR: Len (Brennan) is extremely egotistical, so we used that as the reason for his arrival – Dick, knowing this, tells him that an apparition of his face has appeared on a skirting board. And that basic idea is not quite as ridiculous as it might seem. The Church is always investigating apparitions, many of which are totally bizarre and some of which are recounted in a book called *Beyond Belief* by Liam Fay, a friend of ours. Brennan's apparition was inspired by a passage in that book when an apparition of Jesus appears on a little girl's bedroom door and ten days later, the Virgin Mary follows suit by turning up on her built-in wardrobe . . . But other apparition stories really are beyond belief, like the sensation generated by an American advertisement for spaghetti. It was claimed in some quarters that the image of a forkful of spaghetti was, in fact, the face of Jesus. It *did* actually look like Jesus, but would he really appear in spaghetti?

So, getting Brennan to the Parochial House wasn't a problem, but we had to keep him there. Hence Mrs Doyle saying that he'll have to stay the night because they're 'taking in the roads' and storing them in a warehouse until the rain stops. It's another of those surreal aspects of Craggy Island, like the west side falling into the sea, that are best heard and not seen. They simply wouldn't work if we tried to show them, or went into them in any detail whatsoever . . .

PART ONE

SCENE 1 INT./DAY 1*
SET: SPORTS HALL
An American 'NYPD Blue' voice comes up over black.

VOICEOVER: Previously on *Father Ted*.

We then see cut-together scenes from 'Escape from Victory', but the scenes are filmed in the style of 'NYPD Blue' – the camera 'finding' the people who are speaking a near-documentary style. First of all, the referee scolding Ted and Dick.

REFEREE: Well. I think you're both a disgrace. And I think you should both do your forfeits.

TED: Fine by me.

DICK: Oh, me, too.

Then, the revelation of Ted's forfeit.

REFEREE: You, Father Crilly . . . (*To Dick.*) Is this right? (*Dick nods, smiling. The referee looks concerned but reads on.*) You . . . Father Crilly, by this time next week . . . you have to . . .

Close-up on Ted. Dick steps forward and grabs the letter from the referee's hand.

DICK: Crilly . . . you have to . . . KICK BISHOP BRENNAN UP THE ARSE!!!!!!

The camera finds Ted, looking shocked, then looks at his hand for no reason, then looks at Dougal, who is looking straight at the camera.

'NYPD Blue' style drums lead us into titles . . .

SCENE 2 EXT./DAY X
SET: EDGE OF A VOLCANO
We see a round volcano-hole. A little smoke comes up from the hole, with a flow of red lava around the rim. We see Ted – looking like a priest in a Graham Greene novel, unshaven, unwashed, etc. – being led up to the edge by two natives. We hear distant, menacing drums.

TED: Ah, now, lads, come on.

WARRIOR: Xatl, the Volcano God, is angry. We must appease his wrath.

TED: Volcano God! What kind of nonsense is that? Look, come on, I'll ask you one more time . . . Would you not give Catholicism a try?

WARRIOR: It'll never catch on here. We don't agree with the Pope's line on artificial contraception. It's the 1990s, for goodness sake.

They throw Ted in. He screams as he goes. A native woman (actually Mrs Doyle in a grass skirt and a bra made out of leaves) approaches the edge of the volcano.

MRS DOYLE (*looking down the volcano*): Cup of tea, Father?

Cut to Ted in the Parochial House. A startled look on his face. We hear Mrs Doyle's voice offscreen.

MRS DOYLE: Father? Cup of tea? God, Father, what's wrong with you? You're a million miles away.

TED: Hmm? Oh, I'm sorry, Mrs Doyle. I was just thinking about my next parish.

MRS DOYLE: You're not leaving us, Father?

TED: Well, Bishop Brennan is always threatening to send me somewhere unpleasant, and this time he just might go through with it. You see, I'm going to kick him up the arse.

MRS DOYLE: Ah, sure I'm sure he won't mind that, Father. He'll probably love a big hard kick up the arse.

TED: I'm not sure if he will, Mrs Doyle. And he certainly won't like *me* kicking him up the

---

* In the final version, this scene was altered to incorporate the changes to the final scene of *Escape from Victory*, footnoted on page 324.

arse. I'm on the horns of a dilemma. Very big horns sticking out of a giant dilemma cow.

Dougal rushes in with a newspaper.

DOUGAL: Ted, Ted, wait'll you hear this! You are not going to believe this! (*He reads aloud.*) Clint Eastwood has been arrested for a crime he didn't . . . oh, wait, no, it's a film.

Ted sighs.

TED: There was a time, Dougal, when that type of frankly . . . mental misunderstanding would have irritated me quite a lot, but now . . . (*He sighs deeply.*) To put it very bluntly, Dougal, the flip's hit the fan.

DOUGAL: Do you really have to kick him up the arse, Ted?

TED: I lost the bet, Dougal, and I have to do the forfeit. Do you remember last year, when Dick Byrne lost the darts tournament? He had to say 'bollocks' very loudly in front of President Mary Robinson. Well, he's not going to let me off this one.

DOUGAL: You're right, Ted. There's a code of honour involved. (*Pause.*) You could lie to him.

TED: No, he insisted you have to take a photograph as proof. (*Beat.*) Oh, God, Dougal! What am I going to do? I like this parish!

DOUGAL: Do you?!

TED: Well, no, but God, you should see some of the other parishes! Some of these places, you can only get three channels! And one of them's in Irish! And what if they send me abroad?

Jack snorts loudly.

TED: Father Jack. How can I leave Father Jack? Look at him there, drunk out of his mind, sleeping in his own filth, ready to lash out and whack someone if they get too close. I'll really miss him!

DOUGAL: But Ted, look at it this way. Bishop Brennan has only come to visit us twice in the last three years. He hates us, Ted. He thinks we're all a bunch of big eejits. Especially you, Ted. He thinks you're the biggest eejit of them all. Head honcho eejit number one. You never know. He may never come here again.

The telephone rings. Ted looks at it for a moment or two, then answers it.

TED: Hello? Yes. OK. (*He puts the phone down.*) That was Bishop Brennan. He's coming tomorrow.

DOUGAL: Oh, no, why?

TED: Well, what I gathered from that conversation is that Father Dick Byrne has told Bishop Brennan of a miraculous vision appearing in the skirting boards in the Parochial House here. He has told Bishop Brennan that within the woodgrain of the skirting boards you can clearly see what appears to be a perfect likeness . . . of Bishop Brennan.

DOUGAL: You found out all that just there?

TED: Yes, he's very excited about it.

DOUGAL: Wow . . . God, I must have a look. (*He goes over to the wall, throws himself on to the carpet and looks at the skirting board.*) Oh, God, I see it! It's him, Ted, it's him! It's just like Len! A big frown on him and all!*

TED: No, it isn't, Dougal. Firstly, it's in the spare bedroom not the living room, and secondly, Dick Byrne made up the whole

---

* We deleted these lines from the final version.

thing to lure Bishop Brennan here under false pretences.*

DOUGAL: What? Oh, right. (*He gets to his feet.*) That's one of those weird things, though, isn't it, Ted? The way Our Lord and Our Lady and all that crowd pop up on household furniture and in other mad places where you wouldn't expect them. Like the Turin Shroud. Or that time I saw God's face in that Weetabix. Do you remember I showed it to you?*

TED: It reminded me more of Leonard Nimoy. But people see anything they want in those things. (*He picks up a magazine. It has an advertisement for spaghetti.*) I mean, look at this . . . This to me looks like Elle Macpherson giving Kylie Minogue a piggy back.*

He tears out the picture and slips it in his pocket.

DOUGAL: . . . Maybe they just get fed up there in Heaven. They decide to go on a little tour of household appliances and sundry items. Do you remember that fella in Sligo? There was an image of Padre Pio in his wig. And Saint Martin De Porres appearing in those triangular teabags in Clare.*

TED: It's weird all right. It's one of those areas of Catholicism that's frankly . . . well, a bit mad.*

DOUGAL: Sure the whole Catholic thing is a bit of a puzzler, isn't it, Ted?*

TED: Careful, Dougal . . . But Len appearing on a skirting board . . . I bet he's just dying to see his big face on a bit of wood.*

DOUGAL: I'm a bit afraid of Len, Ted.*

TED: Hah! Join the club! But I'm not going to worry about it. The worst thing would be . . .*

SCENE 3 INT./NIGHT 1
SET: TED AND DOUGAL'S BEDROOM
Ted and Dougal sitting up in bed with the light on. We hear occasional thunder outside and heavy rain.

TED: . . . just to keep thinking about it, and becoming so anxious and obsessed that you can't sleep. I mean, that'd be just . . . Dougal? (*We see that Dougal is asleep.*) Dougal!

DOUGAL (*waking up suddenly*): What! God, that was weird. What happened there? The last thing I remember is . . . feeling very drowsy and tired . . . and then . . . God, I don't remember anything after that at all.

TED: Yes. It's called sleeping, Dougal. You do it every night. I don't know why you're finding it so easy to drop off. Tomorrow – today, in fact – you are going to be taking a photograph of me kicking Bishop Brennan up the arse. He won't like that either, you know. I mean, would you like someone taking a photograph of you being kicked up the arse? Put yourself in his place.

Dougal thinks. His face gradually darkens.

DOUGAL: I wouldn't like that at all!

TED: I thought you wouldn't!

DOUGAL: Who do they think they are? Taking photographs of me being kicked up the arse!

TED: Exactly! Now, imagine the 'they' you're talking about is me and you, Dougal. And imagine Bishop Brennan just said what you said there, and is as angry as you are now.

Dougal, still angry, thinks for a second. Then he looks scared.

DOUGAL: Oh, no!

TED: Exactly!

DOUGAL: Oh, God, Ted!

TED: It's a terrible situation, Dougal. But I'll just have to do it, and hope for the best.

DOUGAL: That's the spirit, Ted! I feel much better now. What were we worried about at all?!

TED: And his PA's coming. Father Jessup. The rudest priest in Ireland. He's bound to say something. I'd say one of the first duties of a personal assistant would be to point out when his boss has been kicked up the arse.

DOUGAL: Ted, when Len comes round—

TED: Dougal, stop right there. You've got to remember, don't call Brennan 'Len'. He's a bishop. What shouldn't you call him, Dougal? Let's get this right.

DOUGAL: Len.

TED: Very good. Now, just remember that.

DOUGAL: Len, Len, Len, Len, Len, Len, Len, Len, Len, Len . . .

TED: OK, now, let's just get a good night's sleep.

He thumps his pillow. He turns the light off and puts his head on the pillow. However, it's still as bright as it was when the light was on.

TED: Oh, God, it's morning! We must have talked all night! At least we'll still have a few hours before the— (*The alarm goes off.*) Oh, God! Well, I set it a bit early so we'd have plenty of time before Bishop Brennan— (*The doorbell rings.*) Oh, God!

SCENE 4 INT./DAY 2
SET: PAROCHIAL HOUSE HALLWAY
Mrs Doyle is walking to the door. Ted runs down the stairs, whispering fiercely.

TED: Mrs Doyle! Stall them for a few seconds! . . . Dougal, come on!

They run into the living room, yanking their clothes on. They are still a long way from being presentable. Ted throws his pyjama bottoms out of shot. Mrs Doyle opens the door. We see Bishop Brennan and Father Jessup. It is raining outside. They are very wet.

MRS DOYLE: Hello!

BRENNAN (*to Jessup*): This is the housekeeper.

JESSUP: Hmmm . . .

MRS DOYLE: Your Grace, is that a hat you're wearing?

BRENNAN: It's called a mitre.

MRS DOYLE: Is it?

BRENNAN: Yes.

Pause.

MRS DOYLE: Well, that's enough 'stalling'. Come on in!

SCENE 5 INT./DAY 2
SET: PAROCHIAL HOUSE
Mrs Doyle opens the door for Len and Jessup. They walk in and see Ted and Dougal, both wearing half-moon spectacles and both looking over a large book, 'The Catechism of the Catholic Church'. Ted is pointing at something over Dougal's shoulder.

TED: That's true, Dougal, and you can see the importance of the Eucharist in the Mass from what Saint Paul says here . . .

DOUGAL: The way I see it . . .

BRENNAN (*to Jessup*): Pretending to talk about religion. (*To Ted.*) Crilly.

TED: Ah!

DOUGAL: Len—

Len bristles.

DOUGAL: —d me a fiver, will you, Ted?

Ted catches on and does so.

TED: Certainly, Father McGuire. A fiver for you. Don't forget to pay me back! Ha, ha.

BRENNAN (*to Jessup*): This type of thing, twenty-four hours a day. (*To Ted.*) I'll make this short, Crilly. Show me the likeness and I'll be off. I have to go off to Rome tomorrow for an audience with the Pope.

DOUGAL: I love those programmes. Did you see the one with Elton John?

BRENNAN: You shut up. Aah! Damn! That car journey has played havoc with my . . . lower back . . .

TED: Sore around that whole area, yeah?

BRENNAN: Yes.

TED: Well. Better make sure no one . . . does anything to it. Hello, Father Jessup. Helping out Bishop Brennan, then?

JESSUP: No, I'm up in space doing important work for N.A.S.A.

He raises eyes to heaven.

BRENNAN: Show me this thing, Crilly.

TED: It looks very like you, Your Grace.

BRENNAN (*a bit flattered*): Does it?

TED (*jokily*): You're far better looking

though. I don't mean that . . . in an intimate way, of course . . . Nasty day, isn't it? . . . Did you come by the new road?

JESSUP: No. We went round by Southern Yemen.

He raises his eyes to heaven.

TED: Anyway . . . Oh, before you have a look at the skirting board, Your Grace . . . would you mind if Father McGuire took a few photographs? Dougal, get the camera there.

DOUGAL: Oh, right . . .

Dougal takes a camera from the table. Ted goes over to him. They start whispering to each other very conspiratorially. Cut to Jessup and Brennan looking at Ted and Dougal.

BRENNAN (*notices Jessup looking at him*): Oh, this is nothing. Nothing!

Dougal then wanders around the room trying to look casual, taking a few photographs.

TED (*terrified*): Right . . . I suppose . . . I suppose we'd better go . . .

Ted and Dougal let the other two go first. They look at each other. Dougal is terrified. They hug. Jessup and Brennan turn around and see this.

BRENNAN: This is a new one.

SCENE 6 INT./DAY 2
SET: SPARE ROOM
Brennan and Jessup enter. Ted and Dougal follow.

TED: Before we look at it, perhaps we should say a prayer.

Brennan sighs.

BRENNAN: No, Crilly, let's just . . . Oh, yes, very well.

They all bow their heads.

TED: Oh, Lord, at this time of great joy for Bishop Brennan, when you have seen fit to put his face in the skirting boards of our house, let us reflect on the gift of forgiveness. You are the most forgiving of all gods.

BRENNAN: Of all gods? What other gods are there, Crilly?

TED: Eh . . . false gods.

BRENNAN: All right, carry on.

TED: And who could not forget that wonderful scene at the end of *Jesus of Nazareth* when Robert Powell, playing you, forgave them for they knew not what they did. Do . . . do you remember that, Your Grace? How forgiving Our Lord was . . . What he said there . . .

BRENNAN: Get on with it, Crilly.

TED: Yes, of course . . . Oh, Lord, heap blessings upon wise Bishop Brennan, the best bishop in the world by miles. For he endureth without spite, Amen. There it is, Your Grace. Have a look at it. It's under the window there.

We see a piece of ordinary-looking skirting board. There are a few swirls in the grain that could, if stared at really, really hard, possibly resemble some sort of face. Brennan goes over and leans down to see it. Jessup bends over as well. Ted gets a view of his arse. His eyes widen.

BRENNAN: I don't see anything, Crilly . . .

Ted sees his chance. We see Ted, in a very dramatic slow motion, run up behind Brennan. Very dramatic music. Then we see Ted's expression turn from determination to terror; he turns in mid flight and heads towards the window. His momentum takes him through the frame and we hear a dwindling 'Aieeeee . . .' Cut back to normal speed. Brennan looks up.

BRENNAN: What happened there?

JESSUP: Crilly . . . just . . . he . . . jumped through the window.

Brennan goes over to the window and looks outside.

BRENNAN: Crilly? Crilly . . . are you out there? What's going on? Why did you jump through the window?

He looks at Dougal. Dougal can't think what to say.

DOUGAL: *An Audience with Lily Savage.* That was good as well. But the Pope . . . that'll be great.

Ted enters through the door, slightly out of breath.

BRENNAN: Crilly, there you are! Why did you jump through the window?

Long pause.

TED: Jump through the window? I didn't jump through the window, did I?

JESSUP: You did. You jumped through the window.

TED: Oh, right. Eh, it was because of shock. I saw your face! Did you not see it in the skirting board?

BRENNAN: No.

TED: God, did you not see it? I thought it smiled at me. Did you see it, Dougal?

DOUGAL: No.

TED: Did you not?

DOUGAL: Definitely, definitely not. I'm absolutely *positive*.

Ted winks furiously at Dougal. Dougal looks terribly confused.

TED: You must have seen it!

DOUGAL: Ahhhh . . . no. But I saw Ted winking . . .

TED (*quickly turns from Dougal*): God, it was extraordinary. And do you not notice the sort of holy smell in the room?

DOUGAL: Ted, that might just be Jack's underpants hamper. (*We see a horrible pile of*

dirty, horrible underpants overflowing from a hamper. We hear flies buzzing around it.*) I'll put it back in his room.

Dougal gingerly picks it up and exits with it. Ted goes over to the skirting board.

TED: Look at that. God, it really is uncanny. I'm surprised you're not appearing on more things, actually, since you're such a top-of-the-range bishop.

BRENNAN: It's just an indistinct squiggle, Crilly.

TED: Actually, the image usually is at it's best around twelve. It's *very* clear then. You can even pick out the laugh lines around your mouth! And a bit of stubble! The old image mustn't be using the old Gillette G2!

BRENNAN: I think this really is a waste of time.

He exits very quickly. Jessup accompanies him. Dougal and Ted follow quickly.

SCENE 7 INT./DAY 2
SET: PAROCHIAL HOUSE
The entourage enters the living room.

TED: . . . I think you should look at it again tomorrow.

BRENNAN: No, Crilly. Now, where's my coat . . .?

Mrs Doyle comes in.

MRS DOYLE: Your Grace, Father Crilly! I just heard on the News that they've taken the roads in.

BRENNAN: They take the roads in?

TED: Yes. When the rain is bad, they store the roads in a warehouse on the east of the island.

BRENNAN: Why do they take the roads in?

TED: Well . . . they get wet.

BRENNAN: What! I have to go to Rome tomorrow to see the Holy Father!

DOUGAL: Oh, they repeat those things all the time . . .

TED: Oh, they'll have built new roads by then. But you might have to stay the night.

BRENNAN: Bollocks!

MRS DOYLE: Will I make up the beds in the spare room?

JESSUP: No, we'll sleep outside in a ditch.

He rolls his eyes. Mrs Doyle looks confused.

MRS DOYLE: Eh . . . OK, so. Would you like a cup of tea, then?

JESSUP: No, I want to die of thirst.

MRS DOYLE: Really? OK, so . . .

TED: Mrs Doyle, I think Father Jessup was being . . . maybe a bit, ha, ha . . . sarcastic?

MRS DOYLE: What? Were you being sarcastic, Father Jessup?

JESSUP: No, I really do want to die of thirst.

MRS DOYLE: Ah, were you being sarcastic there?

JESSUP (*sarcastic*): No, I wasn't.

Ted brings Mrs Doyle aside.

TED: Mrs Doyle, I know it's confusing, but just do the opposite of what Father Jessup says.

MRS DOYLE: OK, so. (*To Jessup.*) So you *would* like a cup of tea.

JESSUP (*exasperated*): Oh, of course I want a cup of tea!

MRS DOYLE: Ah, go on.

JESSUP: Yes, I will.

MRS DOYLE: Ah, go on, have a cup.

JESSUP: Yes, I will! I want one!

MRS DOYLE: Are you sure? Have a little cup.

JESSUP: I want a cup of tea!

MRS DOYLE: You'll only want one later if you don't have one now.

JESSUP: But I want one now!

MRS DOYLE: One cup. Have one cup.

JESSUP: Oh, forget it! I don't want one now!

MRS DOYLE: Great!

She starts pouring him a cup. Jack wakes up and sees Brennan.

BRENNAN: Ah, the Kraken awakes. Did we disturb you, Father Hackett?

JACK: Arse biscuits.

JESSUP: What? How dare you talk to His Grace like that. Apologise immediately!

Jack does an impression of a timid little bunny.

JACK (*baby voice*): Awwwww . . . I'm so, *so* sorry.

Ted turns to Dougal.

TED: Now, *that's* sarcasm.

END OF PART ONE

* * *

PART TWO

SCENE 8 INT./NIGHT 2
SET: TED AND DOUGAL'S BEDROOM
Ted and Dougal are lying in bed. Ted has a newspaper.

TED: Dougal, there's no way I'm going to be able to kick Bishop Brennan up the arse. He's just too scary. I'd rather take my chances in another parish. (*He turns the page in his newspaper. A headline reads,* '200 priests fall to death in another parish'.) Oh, God!

DOUGAL: Ted, I might have a way you can kick Bishop Brennan up the arse and get away with it.

TED: If you did, Dougal, that would make you the most intelligent person in the world. Do you think that's likely?

DOUGAL: Ha, ha, I wouldn't go that far. I'm no Jeffrey Archer, I don't care what anyone says, but . . . well . . . Why don't you just kick him up the arse, and then act like nothing happened?

TED: What, and just hope he doesn't notice it?

DOUGAL: Ah, no, Ted, he will notice it. After all, you're giving him a kick up the arse.

TED: That's right. I'm giving him a big kick up the arse.

DOUGAL: But . . . I mean . . . well . . . look at it like this. How scared are you of Bishop Brennan?

TED: Very scared.

DOUGAL: Exactly. So how likely would it be for you to kick him up the arse?

TED (*thinks*): Well . . . not very likely at all.

DOUGAL: Exactly. So when you kick him up the arse, just carry on like nothing happened. He'd *never* believe that you'd be brave enough to kick him up the arse. He'd think he just imagined it.

Ted looks at Dougal, amazed.

TED: My God. It's so stupid it just might work! (*He gets out of bed.*) Dougal, I'm going to do it! I'm ready! As God is my witness, I will kick Bishop Brennan up the arse!

There is a banging on the wall.

BRENNAN: CRILLY! WILL YOU KEEP THE NOISE DOWN IN THERE!

Ted jumps into bed and pulls the covers up over himself. The bedclothes quiver.

SCENE 9 INT./DAY 3
SET. SPARE BEDROOM
Ted and Brennan enter the room. Jessup lingers at the door.

TED: . . . I just think it might be worth having one more look. You never know . . .

BRENNAN: I think I'll have to have a word with Dick Byrne for wasting my time.

TED: Well, things might pick up. You never know.

BRENNAN (*sighs*): Right. Let's see.

SCENE 10 INT./DAY 3
SET: CORRIDOR
Jessup sees Jack going towards his room, fag hanging from his mouth. He carries a bottle of Bailey's.

JESSUP: Hey! That's not yours. That belongs to His Grace! Give that back. (*Jack regards*

Jessup *coolly*.) Don't you look at me like that! You give that back or there'll be trouble.

Jack turns and goes into his room. Jessup follows.

JESSUP (*offscreen*): Come back here! What are you . . . No! No! Stop!! Aaaaargghhh!!!

Jack's door slams shut loudly.

SCENE 11 INT./DAY 3
SET: SPARE ROOM
Brennan is bending over. He hears the scream and turns.

BRENNAN: What was that?

TED: Hmm? Oh, probably mice or something. Do you see anything?

BRENNAN: No . . . I . . . Wait a second. There seems to be . . . I mean, it looks like some sort of crude watercolour painting of a man in a bishop's hat.

From Brennan's point of view, we see the drawing. It is very crude indeed.

TED: Really?

Ted kicks Brennan up the arse. Dougal pops up outside the window, takes a photograph – it flashes momentarily – and ducks down again. Brennan freezes, a look of frozen amazement on his face.

TED: Let me have a look. (*Ted bends down to look. Brennan looks at him in the same, frozen way.*) Ah, you're right. (*He stands up straight.*) I tell you what must have happened. Dougal probably didn't want you to be disappointed, so he must have drawn that himself. Ah, he meant well. (*He starts leading Brennan, who is walking like a zombie, to the door.*) Anyway, I suppose you'll want to be off, catch that ferry . . . We'll order you a taxi . . .

SCENE 12 INT./DAY 3
SET: PAROCHIAL HOUSE HALLWAY
Dougal comes through the front door, slightly out of breath, hiding his camera behind his back. He hears Brennan and Ted coming down and looks up.

TED: . . .so! Off to Rome to meet the Pope then. I bet you're really looking forward to that!

They come down the stairs. Brennan is still in shock.

DOUGAL: Did you see anything?

TED: No, nothing there at all, sadly. You were right, it was all a wild goose chase. I don't know what that Dick Byrne's up to at all. You really ought to have a word with him. Where's Father Jessup?

DOUGAL: Maybe he went on ahead? . . .

TED: Oh. OK, so, see you soon, Your Grace. Come back as soon as you can! (*They open the door and usher him out, Brennan still walking like a zombie.*) Bye!!

DOUGAL: Bye!!!

Pause. They peer through the letterbox. We hear a car starting up and moving off. Pause. Ted and Dougal look at each other.

TED (*hardly believes it*): I think we've done it.

SCENE 13 INT./DAY 3
SET: TAXI
The taxi driver looks at Brennan.

TAXI DRIVER: Your Grace! Your Grace, are you all right?

Brennan stares ahead. We see the car speeding into the distance.

SCENE 14 INT./DAY 3
SET: PAROCHIAL HOUSE
Ted is opening a bottle of champagne. Celebratory music blares from the hi-fi.

TED: You were right, Dougal. He didn't notice a thing! Ha, ha, ha!

DOUGAL: You gave him a really hard kick up the arse, and he didn't realise it at all!

TED: Maybe . . . maybe I didn't kick him up the arse . . .

DOUGAL: No, Ted, I took the photograph, remember.

TED: You're right! I did do it! Ha, ha! And I really went for it! I got a big rush of adrenalin just at the last moment and I gave him an even bigger kick up the arse than I meant to. God, I can't believe we got away with it . . . More champagne! I need more champagne!

Ha! Ha! Ha!

SCENE 15 INT./DAY 3
SET: AIRPORT
A woman at a check-in desk.

WOMAN: Did you pack these bags yourself, Your Grace? (*Beat. Cut to Brennan, still staring into the distance, open-mouthed.*) Your Grace?

BRENNAN: Whu . . . ?

WOMAN: Did you pack these bags yourself?

Cut back to Brennan. He is still staring into the middle distance.

SCENE 16 INT./DAY 3
SET: PAROCHIAL HOUSE HALLWAY
Jack leaves his room and goes down the stairs, passing by Mrs Doyle.

MRS DOYLE: Father . . .

JACK: Arse!

Mrs Doyle carries on, then hears something from Jack's room.

JESSUP (*from Jack's room*): Help!

Mrs Doyle frowns and opens the door.

SCENE 17 INT./DAY 3
SET: JACK'S BEDROOM
Mrs Doyle comes in.

JESSUP: Oh, thank God! Help me!

We see the underpants hamper, fastened up, with underpants coming out of the side and Jessup's face just visible through a slot at the front.

MRS DOYLE: Father Jessup, what are you doing in there?

JESSUP: Hackett locked me in here! The smell! Dear God!

MRS DOYLE: Are you not terribly uncomfortable in there?

JESSUP: Of course it's uncomfortable!

MRS DOYLE: Oh, right, you're being sarcastic.

JESSUP: I want to get out!!!

MRS DOYLE: Fair enough!

She starts to close the door.

JESSUP: Where are you going?! Help me!

The door closes.

SCENE 18 INT./DAY 3
SET: PAROCHIAL HOUSE
Ted is really, really, really drunk. He is standing in front of a chair. Dougal looks a little bored.

TED: This iss . . . dis isss what I did, Dougal . . .

He kicks the chair, then sticks out his tongue, makes a raspberry sound and gives the chair the V-sign with both hands. Ted stares at the photograph of him kicking Brennan.

TED: First thing tomorrow, Dougal . . . get this shot blown up. Arright? Ten by six. And I want two hundred copies for all me friends . . . feckin . . .

He makes the raspberry sound again. Jack enters the room.

TED: Feck off!!!!

Jack, terrified, backs out.

SCENE 19 INT./DAY 3
SET: PLANE
An air hostess approaches Brennan.

AIR HOSTESS: Have you finished your meal, Your Grace? (*Brennan is sitting in his chair, knife and fork held out at odd angles,*

staring into the middle distance.) Your Grace?

BRENNAN: Whu—?

AIR HOSTESS: Have you finished your meal?

BRENNAN: Whu . . . nuh . . .

The air hostess frowns and walks away. Brennan sticks his knife into some jam. He looks distracted again. We cut to see that he has smeared jam all over the palm of his hand. He looks down, takes this in vaguely, then resumes his staring position.

SCENE 20 INT./DAY 3*
SET: PAROCHIAL HOUSE
Ted is staring glassily at Dougal.

TED (*slurring his words terribly*): Put it on . . .

DOUGAL: Fair enough, Ted.

Dougal puts a little paper crown on Ted's head.

TED: I'm king o' thu wurld. I'm king o' thu wurld . . .

DOUGAL: I think it's time for bed, Ted.

TED (*like a ten year old*): 'Time for bed . . .'

SCENE 21 INT./DAY 3
SET: VATICAN
A line of bishops. Brennan is on the end, still staring into the middle distance. From behind, we

*We deleted this scene from the final version.

see the Pope moving along the line, his aide introducing him to the different bishops. Finally he gets to Brennan.

AIDE (*Italian accent*): . . . and from Ireland, this is Bishop Len Brennan.

The Pope holds out his ring for Brennan to kiss it. Beat. Brennan suddenly gasps.

BRENNAN: He *did* kick me up the arse!!!!!!!!

He pushes the Pope on to the ground and runs out of shot. He runs a little way, then stops and takes out a mobile phone. In the background we see people trying to help the Pope up.

BRENNAN: Get me on the first plane back to Ireland! Now, Goddamit!

He turns distractedly while waiting for the person on the other end of the line to continue talking. The other bishops are watching him in an admonishing way.

BRENNAN: What are you looking at?

SCENE 22 INT./MORNING 4
SET: TED AND DOUGAL'S BEDROOM
Ted wakes up. He looks very, very much the worse for wear. He sits up and rubs his head, stands up and walks to the window. He opens the window and takes a few deep breaths. Then his eyes widen.

SCENE 23 EXT./MORNING 4
SET: OUTSIDE PAROCHIAL HOUSE
From Ted's point of view, we see a car pulling up. Brennan gets out of the car and runs to the house like a bat out of hell, an unfeasibly long cloak extending behind him.

BRENNAN:
CRIIILLLLLLLLLLYYYYYYY!!!!!!!!!

SCENE 24 INT./MORNING 4
SET: TED'S AND DOUGAL'S BEDROOM
Ted looks mortified.

TED: Oh, no!

SCENE 25 INT./DAY 4
SET: FRONT DOOR
In a flash, Brennan charges through the door, knocking it off its hinges.

SCENE 26 INT./DAY 4
SET: TED AND DOUGAL'S BEDROOM
Ted bounces up and down on the balls of his feet, looking round the room, making noises like a frightened monkey and trying to spot a hiding place. Suddenly Brennan kicks in the door. We see him hold this 'kicking position' for a moment, then he marches in. Ted is nowhere to be seen.

BRENNAN: Crilly!!!!

Brennan opens the cupboard doors. There is no one there. He looks around, then sees a pair of feet sticking out from under the bed. He smiles and walks over.

BRENNAN: Crilly . . . (*No response.*) Crilly, I know you're under the bed. I can see you.

Pause.

TED: Bishop Brennan?! Hello! God almighty, what brings you back?

BRENNAN: Crilly, come out from there. Now.

Pause.

Ted: No.

BRENNAN: No? I'll give you ten seconds, Crilly.

TED: It's just . . . I think I see another vision of you, Bishop Brennan . . . These bits of fluff seem to be arranging themselves into a sort of 'Bishop' formation . . .

Brennan reaches down and starts to drag Ted out from under the bed. Ted tries to hang on with his fingernails.

TED: Ah! Hello! God, great to see you back. What brings you here?

BRENNAN: What brings me here? Well . . . the fresh air . . . the company . . . the view of the big pile of sludge from my room . . . but, number one on the list, I suppose, would be the matter of you kicking me up the arse. Yes, I think that would be the one I'd prioritise.

TED: Kicking . . . what? But . . . when did I kick—

BRENNAN: DON'T TRY MY PATIENCE, CRILLY!!!!! (*Ted cowers.*) YOU KICKED ME UP THE ARSE! TRY TO DENY IT AND I'LL HAVE YOU FED TO THE DOGS – if you have dogs.

TED: But why would I do that? You'd kill me!

BRENNAN: You're damn right I would!!!

TED: I would never, ever kick you up the arse. Sure I think you're great!

Brennan pauses.

BRENNAN: Well . . .

TED: Are you absolutely sure you're not making a terrible, terrible mistake? Do you think that could be possible?

BRENNAN: I don't . . . well, I admit it did seem unbelievable.

TED: It's unbelievable because it didn't actually *happen*. I swear, Bishop Brennan, on my life, on everything I hold dear, on my religion, on God and all the saints and angels in heaven . . . I did *not* kick you up the arse.

BRENNAN: Hmm . . . well . . . maybe I . . . maybe I need a holiday . . . Maybe I've been imagining things.

TED: You *have* been imagining things. Have a holiday! You *deserve* one!

BRENNAN: Shut up, Crilly.

TED: Okey dokey.

SCENE 27 INT./DAY 4
SET: PAROCHIAL HOUSE HALLWAY
Brennan is at the front door.

TED: Well, come back soon.

BRENNAN: No.

Brennan leaves the house. Dougal approaches Ted from behind. He has lots of photographs.

DOUGAL: Ah, Ted, I got those copies you wanted—

TED: Shut up, Dougal! Shut up! Bye, Bishop Brennan!

DOUGAL: But that one you wanted blown up, the six by ten, where do you want that?

TED: What do you mean, where do I want it? Bye, Bishop Brennan! We love you!

SCENE 28 INT./DAY 4
SET: PAROCHIAL HOUSE HALLWAY
Brennan is walking away from the house. He gets to his car and opens the door, then turns casually around. His face assumes his earlier, frozen look. He drops his keys. Cut to his point of view, so that we see a massive photograph, six foot by ten foot of the exact moment when Ted kicked Brennan up the arse, propped against the wall of the house beside where Ted is standing waving. Ted notices that Brennan is looking at something. He walks out from the house a little way, then turns to look at what Brennan's looking at. He sees the photograph. He whimpers slightly.

Brennan recovers and starts after him. Ted begins running. Brennan is gaining on Ted.

Ted falls over, and starts to get up. As he does so, Brennan catches up with him and kicks him. Cut to a low-angle shot, looking up. Ted flies about forty feet into the air, arcs, and crashes to the ground.

POST-CREDIT SEQUENCE
SCENE 29 INT./DAY 4
SET: HAMPER
We are inside the hamper. Jessup looks uncomfortable and afraid, hugging his knees. Underpants are bunched up around him. Suddenly the underpants are brushed to one side and a priest with a scraggly bear sticks his head out.

JESSUP: Aaaargh!

SCRAGGLY PRIEST 1: Calm yourself, my son. You need your wits about you if we're to escape.

Another priest sticks his head out.

SCRAGGLY PRIEST 2: Escape? Escape? You crazy old fool! We shall never escape from this place!

Another priest sticks his head out.

SCRAGGLY PRIEST 3: What news of the war? Is it true the Allies have taken France?

Jessup screams.

THE END

night of the nearly dead

GRAHAM: This arose from our desire to come up with a character for Patrick McDonnell, a plan which backfired on us somewhat. Writing it was like giving birth to a baby who needed extensive surgery to survive: constant rewrites were needed because we were never quite sure what the episode was about. In retrospect, we were perhaps too concerned with bending and shaping the plot around Patrick's character, Eoin McLove, until there was very little shape left.

I liked the sudden revelation in the final draft that part of Eoin's problem was that he didn't have a willy. That was Patrick's idea, but we really didn't do anything with it (or indeed without it). We just gave Patrick the go-ahead to say it, more or less on a whim. I think this is a good indication of the weakness of the episode. If it had been tightly plotted, or indeed, made any sense as a story at all, we probably wouldn't have had space for the line.

ARTHUR: This episode *is* flawed and in hindsight it might have been better to concentrate on Dougal's relationship with Eoin. Yet that would have had its own problems, as we'd already tackled the theme of Dougal and a friend by introducing Father Damo in *Old Grey Whistle Theft*.

I enjoyed Jack's out-of-character speech about beasts in the night, but it revealed one of the problems we were beginning to have with *Ted* and the reason we planned this to be the final series. Basically, the fact that all the characters (apart from Ted) were rather extreme caricatures was beginning to make it more and more difficult to come up with new things for them to say. This might explain Jack's outburst. But you can only play the out-of-character card once per series, and the fact that we were playing it at all pointed out the problem to us.

PART ONE
SCENE 1 INT./DAY 1
SET: PAROCHIAL HOUSE
On the television we see an Oliver Sacks-type psychologist on his hunkers beside a patient who sits in a rocking chair. A caption comes up that reads 'Doctor Oliver Sacks'. They are both outside on a porch in a sunny Caribbean-type location. The patient looks very like Jack.

SACKS (*to camera*): Strange, short emissions which the patient shouts out seemingly involuntarily . . .

PATIENT: FIRK!

Jack sits bolt upright in his chair, confused.

PATIENT: ARPSE!

JACK: ARSE!

PATIENT: GRALS!

JACK: GIRLS!

Dougal switches channels. Jack waits for a second, cocking his head to hear more, then, when nothing else comes, immediately slumps into sleep again. Ted comes in and sits down with a book.

TED: Dougal, there's nothing on. Why don't you read a book or something?

DOUGAL: Oh, all right.

Ted sits reading. After a moment, we pull back to reveal Dougal sitting beside and behind Ted reading the same book. Ted notices this.

TED: No . . . Dougal. Read a different book.

DOUGAL: Actually, Ted, it's been a few minutes. I'll see if there's anything good on now.

He goes back to the television.

TED: Honestly, Dougal, you've got to broaden your mind a little bit. Just for once you should try turning the TV off and reading a book. You're missing out on a whole world of thought and ideas and experience.

DOUGAL: What are you reading at the moment?

TED: I'm re-reading it, actually. (*He holds it up*) It's William Shatner's *Tek Wars*.

Dougal presses another button on the remote control. We see a country singer, Eoin McLove, in full flow, finishing a song. His name appears on a glittery backdrop behind him. Eoin is a fresh-faced man with the voice of a six year old.

EOIN: ' . . . My broookkken-hearted heart . . .'

DOUGAL: Oh, NO! This *eeeejit*!

EOIN: . . . 'is running around like a duck, it used to go "bibbety-bop", but now it goes "cluckety-cluck."'

Cut to a shot of the audience, which is made up of middle-aged or elderly women. Mrs Doyle bursts from the kitchen and slides a good six feet into the room.

MRS DOYLE: It's Eoin! Oh, Father, isn't he lovely!

DOUGAL: Tschoh! Ghod! Thscha!

As Mrs Doyle watches Eoin, she adjusts her clothes constantly in a nervous, compulsive way. Jack sees Eoin. He looks disgusted.

JACK: Uuugggghhhh!!!!

Cut back to Eoin. During the instrumental break in the song, he passes the microphone from hand to hand.

MRS DOYLE: He's a brilliant dancer as well!

The song comes to an end and the audience cheers wildly.

EOIN: Now, it's time to announce the winner of the fabulous poetry competition. You had to write a poem about me, and the prize is that I call round to the winner's house to have a lovely cup of tea.

DOUGAL: Ech! Ghod, can you imagine that? Oh, Ghod!

EOIN: So over I go to my Poetry Corner.

He moves out of shot. He arrives back in shot in what is obviously the same bit of set, but with 'Poetry Corner' written on a banner behind him. Mrs Doyle looks very expectant.

EOIN: OK, here it is. This is my favourite one. And the standard was very high indeed. This is the winner, anyway:

'Eoin Mclove is his name,
Singing songs is his game,

Some day I will say hello,
And for a cup of tea we will go."

The audience of old women goes 'Ahhhhh' and applauds gently.

And the winner is Mrs O'Neill from Kildare. And it says here she's a hundred and ten years old! She also asks me what my favourite things in the world are, and I'd have to say . . . jumpers . . . and cakes! Oh, no, look at this! (*He bends down out of shot and comes up with a puppy. The puppy has a little cast on its leg.*) It's a little puppy with a broken paw. I'd better go home and nurse it back to health. Goodbye, everybody!

Applause. Mrs Doyle sighs deeply.

TED: Hard luck, Mrs Doyle. Maybe next time.

MRS DOYLE (*to Ted*): Have you heard his latest album, Father? *Wispy Afternoons*? I'm going to go into the kitchen and stick it on the cassette recorder. Oh, God, I love him so much, I can't even wait to get into the kitchen.

She leaves the room.

TED: Women!

DOUGAL (*jumps up*): Where?!

TED: No, I mean (*With a chuckle and a shrug.*) 'Women!'.

DOUGAL: Oh, right, yeah. 'Women!'

TED: Tscha!

DOUGAL: Tscha!

TED: You can't live with them, and you can't live without them!

DOUGAL: Yeah! (*Pause.*) But there definitely aren't any women in here? . . .

TED: No, you're fine. You know what, I could write a poem and send it in to that show. After all, let's face it, the kind of poetry Mrs Doyle writes is bound to be *hopeless*.

DOUGAL: Oh, Ted! It'd be very unhip for a Parochial House if that fella came over here.*

TED: Dougal, it's not a priority for a priest to worry about how hip their parish is. I mean, 'The Man Himself' was probably regarded as being a bit of a square when he was alive.*

DOUGAL: Really, Ted?*

TED: Yes, Dougal. But after he was nailed to a cross, people began to think 'I see what he was on about.'*

DOUGAL: God almighty. Johnny Cash was nailed to a cross?*

TED: What? No – Jesus! The Man Himself is Jesus!*

DOUGAL: Oh, right . . . I was thinking of 'The Man in Black.'*

TED (*to himself*): I think I *will* write a poem for Mrs Doyle. It'd be great to hear something I wrote read out on television. Something with a little depth, not one of those birthday-card greetings you usually get on that show.*

DOUGAL: What are you going to write it about?*

TED: Ah, Dougal . . . inspiration can come from so many places . . .*

SCENE 2 INT./DAY 1
SET: MONTAGE
We see Ted, a pair of half-moon glasses on the end of his nose, a pen in his mouth, thinking. A thought strikes him, and he writes something down.

A drooping, dying flower. A petal falls off it. Ted looks at it, wipes a tear from his eye and writes

---

*We deleted these lines from the final version.

something down.

A little urchin begging for money. Ted sees him, looks sad, writes something down and then goes off without giving him any money.

Ted in the foreground, Mrs Doyle in the background doing something on the windowsill. She falls off and Ted laughs softly, shakes his head and writes something down.

A dog, crouching down to do a poo outside the Parochial House. Cut to Ted watching through the window. He writes something down.

Cut to a close-up of the letter. We see the words,

*'The Eoin McLove show
RTE, Dublin.'*

SCENE 3 INT./DAY 1*
SET: OFFICE
Start off on the same shot of envelope. Pull back to see a policeman and a woman – Patsy – looking at the letter. Posters of Eoin McLove cover the wall.

PATSY: But you understand why we called . . .

POLICEMAN: Yes, but I really wouldn't worry. Someone this simple-minded couldn't pose any real threat.

EOIN: I want extra security!

POLICEMAN: Really, I think this is just the work of a confused child, or someone who's quite seriously retarded.

SCENE 4 INT./DAY 2
SET: PAROCHIAL HOUSE
Ted and Dougal come into the living room in their dressing gowns, yawning.

MRS DOYLE: EOINMcLOVECMNGTOCR-AGGYISLAND!H'SCMNGTOCRAGGYISLAND!

TED: Mrs Doyle, calm down. What was that again?

MRS DOYLE (*deep breath*): EoinMcLOVE'S Cemming TOCRAGGYISLANDCRAGGY ISLANDCOMING! He read out my poem!

TED: Your poem? Well, Mrs Doyle, I wrote it as a sort of a surprise, but it was actually

* We deleted this scene from the final version.

my poem . . .

MRS DOYLE: No, it was mine.

TED: I'm . . . I'm sorry, Mrs Doyle but . . . I don't think so. What was the first line?

MRS DOYLE: 'Eoin McLove has a happy face.'

TED: That's not my poem!

MRS DOYLE: No, it's mine!

DOUGAL: I'm *hugely* confused, Ted. The only thing that I can think of that must have happened is that Mrs Doyle's poem was better than yours. But that couldn't be, could it, Ted? That your poem just wasn't as good as Mrs Doyle's. That just couldn't happen, could it?

Close-up of Ted. He looks very uncomfortable. An end-of-scene jingle sounds.

DOUGAL: Could it?

TED: Shut up, Dougal!

SCENE 5 INT./DAY 2
SET: SHOP
We see an absolutely huge box, about the size of a box that might contain a widescreen television, with 'Tower Teabags. The teabags shaped like a tower. Contents 40,000' written on it. It's on top of a shelf and Mrs Doyle is trying to pull it out. A little further down the aisle, we see two women gossiping and looking at Mrs Doyle. One of the women starts moving towards Mrs Doyle, sliding along as if on casters. She has her handbag held up in a prissy way and her mouth is pursed, also prissily. She silently glides up to Mrs Doyle. This is Mrs Boyle.

MRS BOYLE: When's he coming?!

MRS DOYLE (*jumps*): Aieeee!!!!

MRS BOYLE: When's he coming? Tell us!

MRS DOYLE (*recovering*): I can't say. It's a secret.

MRS BOYLE: Thursday? . . . (*Mrs Doyle remains stony-faced.*) Friday? (*Mrs Doyle remains stony-faced.*) Saturday? (*Mrs Doyle remains stony-faced.*) Sunday? (*Mrs Doyle's face, despite all her efforts, goes mental.*) Aha!!!

MRS DOYLE: Eoin wouldn't like anybody

to know. You won't tell anybody, will you?

MRS BOYLE: I swear I won't tell anyone. May I be struck down with every disease that it is possible for a middle-aged woman to suffer from. And you and I know, Mrs Doyle, that's a hell of a lot of diseases.

During this speech, she glides backwards.

SCENE 6 EXT./DAY 2
SET: ROAD
Mrs Boyle bursts out of the shop and walks along the road excitedly. She approaches a woman, Mrs Kierans, who is dressed like herself (scarf, coat, carrying a shopping bag) but is kicking a football up against a wall.

Cut to a long shot of the scene. We don't hear their conversation. Mrs Kierans listens to Mrs Boyle for a moment and then looks very interested. Mrs Boyle starts walking off again.

Cut to a red line on a map. As the red line travels all over the island, we see superimposed shots of Mrs Boyle's feet walking along at an amazingly fast rate. Also we see . . .

Mrs Boyle on the telephone, then another woman on the telephone, hearing the news she is relaying.

The red line travels to a location on the map. With 'Telegraph Office' superimposed, we see Mrs Boyle at one of those Morse-Code type things; she taps away, the same expression on her face. The red line travels to another location with 'Pigeon Sanctuary' superimposed; we see Mrs Boyle rolling

up a little note and putting it in to a tube on a pigeon's leg. We see loads of pigeons taking off.

The red line travels to a location with 'Internet Café' superimposed. Mrs Boyle is tapping away at a computer, the same demented expression on her face. (She doesn't look at the screen, or the keyboard – just types and maintains her expression.)

We see the words 'You have new E-Mail. Access?' coming up on a screen and flashing, an 'OK' information box is selected and the words 'Eoin McLove' travel across the screen, ending the montage.

SCENE 7 INT./DAY 3
SET: MIRROR
A mirror somewhere in the Parochial House. Mrs Doyle is putting on lipstick. She purses her lips in front of the mirror, seems satisfied and smiles. When she smiles, we see lipstick all over her teeth.

MRS DOYLE: Eeeek!

SCENE 8 INT./DAY 3
SET: PAROCHIAL HOUSE
Ted is sitting in a chair, looking grumpy. He and Dougal hear Mrs Doyle's 'Eek'. Ted looks up to where he imagines her to be.

DOUGAL (*goes to the window*): I think he's just pulled up, Ted. God – the good news is that he's only able to afford a crappy blue Ford Fiesta. Imagine going round in that thing.

TED: That's my car, Dougal.

DOUGAL: Oh, right. Still, you know what I mean.

SCENE 9 INT./DAY 3
SET: MIRROR
Mrs Doyle is still at the mirror.

TED: MRS DOYLE! HE'S HERE!

Mrs Doyle hears Ted and runs her lipstick halfway up her face.

SCENE 10 INT./DAY 3
SET: LIMOUSINE
Eoin and Patsy, his manager, are in the limo, which has stopped outside the Parochial House.

Patsy is in the driver's seat.

EOIN: Is this the place? What is it? A kind of a mental hospital?

PATSY: No, it's a Parochial House. This week's winner is the priests' housekeeper. Better go and prepare the ground.

Eoin, now sucking his thumb, nods his head.

EOIN: What's the story, then? Do I have to walk to the door?

PATSY: Yes.

EOIN: I have to walk to the door meself?

PATSY: Yes, Eoin, you have to walk to the door yourself.

Eoin looks very unhappy. He looks around for a moment, then, with quite a lot of effort, breaks off the headrest from the seat in front of him. Pause.

PATSY (*to herself*): Sheesus . . .

SCENE 11 INT./DAY 3
SET: PAROCHIAL HOUSE
Patsy is talking to Ted and Dougal. Jack is sitting in his chair in the background.

PATSY: Mr McLove will not allow any photographic record of the event, except one official picture for advertising purposes. Mr McLove will not sign autographs in ink. Mr McLove is not an equal-opportunities employer.

Patsy's mobile phone rings.

PATSY: Hello.

We hear Eoin's voice on the end.

EOINE: Hello. Is Patsy there?

PATSY: Yes, Eoin. This is Patsy.

Cut to Eoin outside the living-room door, standing in the hallway.

EOIN: This is Eoin here. I'm in the hall now. Is someone going to let me in or will I knock on the door, or what?

TED: Now, Dougal, he's our guest. Let's do this for Mrs Doyle . . .

DOUGAL: Yeah, I know, I know . . .

Patsy opens the door. Eoin steps in. Jack sees Eoin.

JACK: Feck!

EOIN: Hello. I'm Eoin McLove.

TED: Hello, Eoin. You're very welcome. (*Indicates Dougal.*) Father Dougal McGuire.

EOIN (*to Ted*): You're Father McGuire?

TED: No, I'm Father Ted Crilly.

DOUGAL: I'm Father Dougal McGuire.

EOIN: Hello. I'm Eoin McLove.

TED: That's Father Hackett.

EOIN (*to Dougal*): Father Hackett . . .

TED: No, Father McGuire.

EOIN: You're Father McGuire?

TED: No, I'm Father Crilly.

EOIN (*shakes hands with Ted*): Eoin McLove, hello.

TED: This is Father McGuire, here.

EOIN: I'm Eoin McLove. That's who I am, anyway.

Jack glares at Eoin.

EOIN (*to Jack*): Hello, I'm Eoin McLove.

He steps closer to Jack. We hear what is clearly the sound of a dog growling in a threatening way, coming from Jack. (Note: At various points in the show Eoin should pass near Jack, and we hear this growl building and subsiding.)

TED: Best, eh, step away there.

Pause.

EOIN: You're all priests, I see. Well done.

TED: Yes.

No attempt is made by Eoin to make the following conversation private in any way.

PATSY: I'll leave you alone, then . . .

EOIN: I'll talk to these two.

PATSY: Yes, Eoin.

EOIN (*indicating Ted*): What'll I do if the old one says something and I don't know what to say back to him?

PATSY: Just . . . I don't know . . .

EOIN: What about the thick-looking one.

He's looking at me weird.

PATSY: Eoin . . .

EOIN (*sniffs*): I smell wee. Where's that from? (*He's now beside Jack.*) It's this one. This one smells of wee.

Patsy gives Ted and Dougal an apologetic look and leaves.

EOIN: So where's the winner so I can go home and have me tea?

TED: Well, actually, you can have your tea here. Mrs Doyle!

The kitchen door opens and a terrified, heavily made-up Mrs Doyle enters slowly through it. She has a tray with loads of cups and a teapot on it. It vibrates slightly. She walks slowly towards Eoin and the tray vibrates even more. She tries to say something but can't seem to get the words out.

MRS DOYLE: Eghhh . . . eggghhh . . .

The tea things are rattling very noisily now as Mrs Doyle shakes violently. With each step nearer to Eoin, it gets worse.

EOIN: Hello. (*Mrs Doyle shakes all the tea things off the tray, wobbles around for a while and then collapses out of shot.*) I don't want tea off the carpet. I want proper tea. Where's my tea?

SCENE 12 EXT./DAY 3
SET: GATE OF PAROCHIAL HOUSE
The camera angle is very low. We see the house through the gate. Two middle-aged female legs move into shot. Then another pair. Dramatic music accompanies this.

END OF PART ONE

* * *

PART TWO

SCENE 13 INT./EVENING 3
SET: PAROCHIAL HOUSE
Mrs Doyle is sitting down in Ted's chair, still looking terrified. Eoin sits across from her on the sofa. Ted and Dougal are also present. Eoin is looking carefully at his watch, mouthing something to himself. Stay on this for a while.

EOIN: . . . Fifty-eight . . . fifty-nine . . . sixty! (*Stands up.*) Right, that's our twenty

minutes up. I'm off. Don't try to stop me.

Ted starts making 'hint-hint' motions towards Mrs Doyle with his head.

TED: Eh . . . did you like your tea, Eoin?

EOIN: What? Yeah, I don't know, whatever. I want to go home now. It's getting dark outside.

DOUGAL: You're not afraid of the dark, are you? It's only because the sun goes . . . Eh, it . . . there's this . . . eh . . . it . . . something to do with clouds?

TED: Our part of the earth is turned away from the sun.

DOUGAL: That's it, yeah. And, what was it? The clouds can't get through? . . .

Eoin gets up to leave.

EOIN (*struggling with the door*): How do you work this door handle? Is this a new kind of door handle? I'm used to the ones that go round.

Ted takes him gently aside.

TED: Before you go, Eoin . . . was there another poem that was very good this week?

EOIN: What? No.

TED: You sure?

EOIN: The only other letter I can remember was from this lunatic. We had to call the police because it was so demented. Anyway, I'm going to stop talking to you now, because I don't know what else to say to you.

Eoin opens up his mobile phone and dials.

EOIN: Hello, is Patsy there?

SCENE 14 INT./NIGHT 3
SET: PAROCHIAL HOUSE
Cut to Patsy waiting in the hallway. She answers her mobile phone.

PATSY: Yes, Eoin. This is Patsy.

EOIN (*as he comes into the hallway*): It's Eoin McLove here. Get the car and pull up right outside the door, so I don't have to walk far. (*Patsy starts going towards the door, followed by Eoin. Both are still on their mobiles. Ted follows* *behind.)* I want to be able to walk right into the car without touching the ground.

PATSY: Eh . . . I don't think that's going to be possible, Eoin.

EOIN: What? You're breaking up there. Why is not going to b— *(They are now standing next to each other talking on their mobile phones, both looking out of the window. Ted arrives on the scene.)* What? Why not? Oh, God.

SCENE 15 INT./NIGHT 3
SET: PAROCHIAL HOUSE
We see that there are fifty little old ladies outside the house. One, with big bottle-thick glasses, snaps her head up when she hears the door opening.

WOMEN: Hello, Eoin! Hello there, Eoin, etc.

Ted walks to one side of Eoin.

TED: Eh, hello, ladies . . . we'll be away now . . . Dougal, get around that side of Eoin.

They start walking slowly towards the car. The women start following at a distance. The men see the limo waiting ahead. Ted and Dougal stand on either side of Eoin and start walking quickly towards it. The women advance towards them.

TED: Better pick up the old pace a bit . . .

EOIN: Oh, God, here they come. What's on their mind at all?

They are easily able to outrun the women. They approach the limo. The door of the limo opens.

TED: Here we go . . .

Eoin gets in. We suddenly see that there are about seven old women in the car. The woman in the driver's seat turns around.

OLD WOMAN *(sinister)*: Hello, Eoin.

EOIN: Aarrgh!

Eoin jumps out of the car.

TED: OK, OK. We'd better get back inside.

The women in the car turn the headlights on. From above, we see the old women slowly approaching Ted, Dougal, Eoin and Patsy in a big, slow, horrible movement.

EOIN: I'm scared. It's like a big tide of jam

coming towards us. But jam made out of old women.

TED: There's a lot of them, but they're slow. Dodge between them!

Ted, Dougal and Eoin run towards the old women and then thread through them. The old women grab at Eoin but miss him. Ted reaches the door first.

TED: Come on!

Eoin falls over. The women start to advance towards him.

EOIN: Oh, God!

Ted runs back and grabs him. They run towards the door. The women start to advance towards them. They run through the door just before the women can catch up, and they slam it shut.

SCENE 16 INT./NIGHT 3
SET: PAROCHIAL HOUSE HALLWAY
Eoin relaxes against the door.

EOIN: Oh, thank God.

Suddenly a hand smashes through the window in the door and grabs Eoin around the neck. More hands follow and start grabbing madly in the air, some of them grabbing hold of Eoin.

EOIN: Help!

Ted grabs Eoin and tries to wrestle him away from the hands.

TED: Dougal!

Ted stretches his hand out to Dougal. Dougal smiles and waves at Ted.

DOUGAL *(cheerily)*: Hello!

TED: No, Dougal, I mean 'help', not 'hello'.

DOUGAL: Oh, right.

Dougal goes over and whacks some of the hands. Jack comes out and sees this. He goes back into the living room.

TED: Ow! That's actually *my* hand, Dougal. Try hitting some of the women's hands.

DOUGAL: OK, yes. Sorry, Ted.

Jack comes out of the living room with a chair and glass of whiskey. He sits on the chair and sips his whiskey, enjoying the scene.

SCENE 17 INT./NIGHT 3
SET: PAROCHIAL HOUSE
It is later on. The living room is gloomy. Ted sits by the window and lifts the curtain occasionally to look out. Patsy is talking on her mobile phone. A grandfather-clocky-type ticking noise is in the background.

PATSY: Battery's dead. Oh, God! What about your phone?

TED (*shakes his head*): I think they've cut the lines.

Pause.

JACK: 'They lie in wait, like wolves. the smell of blood in their nostrils, waiting, interminably waiting . . . and then . . .'

Ted looks at Jack, dumbfounded at this eloquence. Jack slumps back to sleep.

DOUGAL: He's right, Ted.

TED: Miss Bartley, we've got a problem. And you know what my motto is when I've got a problem? I'm going to solve that problem. (*Pause.*) Well, it's not really a motto, it's more a sentence. But anyway . . . here's the problem. We're surrounded by a bunch of thirty elderly women. (*Pause.*) Actually, when you put it that way, it doesn't sound so bad. Maybe we should just walk out.

PATSY: No, I don't think so. I've never seen someone mothered to death before, and it's not going to happen now, not on my watch.

TED: To be honest, he's got no one to blame but himself. When you've got album covers like this, you're just asking for trouble.

Ted holds an album cover up. It's called 'Eoin McLovenotes' and features Eoin dressed as a baby

with his arms outstretched.

SCENE 18 INT./NIGHT 3
SET: PAROCHIAL HOUSE
Meanwhile, Dougal and Eoin are in the kitchen.

EOIN: I'm hungry. Where's the jam?

DOUGAL (*gasps*): You're not supposed to eat before dinner.

EOIN: You shut up. I'm Eoin McLove. I can do what I like.

Eoin finds a pot of jam and gets a small spoon. Then he gets a bigger spoon and starts digging out spoonfuls and eating it. Dougal stares at him. Eoin stares back, eating the jam.

SCENE 19 INT./NIGHT 3*
SET: PAROCHIAL HOUSE
Ted is examining a pipe. The mood is calmer now. Patsy looks at him.

PATSY: You're a pipe man, Father.

TED: Ah, well . . . I thought I'd try it out. To be honest, I'm a bit disappointed by the amount of spit involved. You see, there's a build-up . . . sorry, that's disgusting. I don't know how you put up with your man. He'd drive me mad.

PATSY: Oh, he's all right. He's just so used to being taken care of he's going through some sort of second childhood.

SCENE 20 INT./NIGHT 3
SET: PAROCHIAL HOUSE KITCHEN
Eoin's face is now covered in jam. Dougal is still staring at him. Ted comes in. Dougal points at Eoin.

TED: Eoin!

EOIN: Wha'?

TED: Don't eat the jam from the jar. Get inside the other room there.

EOIN: You leave me alone. I can have you killed.

Ted pushes Eoin out. Dougal waits a moment, then goes over to the jam. He picks up a spoon and

*We deleted this scene from the final version.

starts licking it. Ted comes in and gives him a look. Dougal notices him and jumps with the fright.

DOUGAL: Just, eh . . . cleaning the spoon.

He licks it again and holds it up to the light.

SCENE 21 INT./NIGHT 3*
SET: PAROCHIAL HOUSE
Close-up of Ted smoking his pipe and reading a newspaper. We pull back to reveal Patsy on the sofa doing some knitting. Dougal and Eoin are also revealed, on the floor playing a game of draughts.

EOIN: I'm bored. Can I go home?

PATSY: We can't go anywhere, Eoin. Those women are still outside.

Dougal goes to the window and looks outside.

DOUGAL: Tsk . . . I'm no good at judging the size of crowds, but I'd say there's about a million of them out there.

TED: Well . . . more like forty, Dougal . . .

Eoin walks to the window and looks out.

EOIN: Still there. Why don't they leave me alone? Do you know what they send me as well? Big bras. Sure I have no need for them. I'd have to be very hard up for clothes to wear big bras. God almighty . . . This came in the post this morning. Look at the size of it. (*He reaches into his travel bag and pulls out a bra about the size of a widescreen-television screen.*) That'd fit two women.

Mrs Doyle walks in. Eoin jumps with the fright.

EOIN: Aaaah! Don't do that again! What's she doing in here, anyway? She should be out there with the rest of those eejits.

TED: Eoin! Don't be mean to Mrs Doyle! She's one of us!

EOIN: She's making me nervous. Tell her to get out.

TED: Mrs Doyle, maybe you should go and make some tea.

Mrs Doyle leaves, looking utterly crestfallen. Eoin goes over and prods Jack.

EOIN: Hey, wake up. (*He starts poking Jack.*) Wake up. Why are you asleep? Wake up and do something interesting.

PATSY: For God's sake, Eoin. Give it a rest.

TED: I really wouldn't do that, Eoin.

Eoin continues to push and poke Jack.

EOIN: Why not? I can do what I like. You're not the boss of me. (*He pokes Jack again a few times. Jack wakes up and stares at Eoin balefully.*) Hey, you, wake up. Do something interesting.

Cut to Ted as we hear the sound of a wild animal on the attack, mingled with Eoin's screams. Ted can't look, and he slowly turns and walks to the window. He looks out of the window for a moment or two, then turns around as the sounds subside.

Jack is asleep again. On the ground beside him is Eoin, tied up in his own jumper like a particularly gaudy Easter egg. All the jumper's 'orifices' have been tied together, so nothing can be seen of Eoin.

EOIN (*muffled*): What's going on? I'm bored again. Let me out.

DOUGAL; Ha, ha! He looks like a big Easter egg!

Ted, Dougal and Patsy laugh in an American film-type way. Ted puts his pipe in his mouth to complete the picture.

*We deleted this scene from the final version.

SCENE 22 INT./NIGHT 3
SET: PAROCHIAL HOUSE
Patsy is at the window. She starts shaking.

PATSY: I CAN'T STAND IT! THEY'RE SO QUIET. WHY ARE THEY SO QUIET?!

TED: Patsy, snap out of it!

A brick comes through the window. Everyone dives. Patsy screams. Ted recovers and picks up the brick. There is paper wrapped around it. He unfolds it and we see that it has 'Tell Eoin we think he's lovely' written on it. Mrs Doyle enters. She has a cake tin in her hand. She goes over to Ted, right up to his ear and whispers in it. We hear a very low murmur coming from her lips.

TED: What is it, Mrs Doyle?

Mrs Doyle whispers again. Ted gets up. She still whispers in his ear at an annoyingly close distance, as if she's glued to his ear. Ted frees Eoin from his jumper with difficulty.

TED: What? What? Yes . . . yes. Eoin, Mrs Doyle wants to know if you'd like a cake.

EOIN: Who?

TED: Mrs Doyle. This woman here.

EOIN: Oh, right.

Ted is now walking around, bent over, as Mrs Doyle continues to whisper in his ear.

TED: Eh, it's banana. She says she knows that's your favourite.

EOIN: Oh, God, yeah, I love that. I'll eat that. No one else is getting any. This is all for me. (*He digs into it with a knife. He pulls away a slice, but there is some resistance. There seems to be something baked in the middle of the cake.*) What's goin' on?

Mrs Doyle, with a pleased, excited yelp, whispers in Ted's ear.

TED: Oh, my God.

EOIN: What's happening? I'm scared.

TED: I'm not sure how to tell you this . . . (*Eoin is pulling something out of the cake with a horrified expression.*) Mrs Doyle has, in an unusual move . . . baked a jumper in the cake.

Eoin pulls it out with difficulty. It is indeed a jumper, with loads of cake bits sticking to it.

EOIN: I'm going to get sick. This is horrible. This is the worst thing that's ever happened to me. I'm not wearing a cake jumper. And I'm not eating a jumper cake. This is terrible. Oh, my God.

Mrs Doyle looks crestfallen.

TED: Right! I've had enough of this. You don't have to eat the cake, or wear the jumper, but you will stop acting like a baby right now and thank Mrs Doyle or I will personally throw you outside and let those women deal with you how they will. And believe me, if that happens, a jumper cake is the least of your problems. Got it?!*

Eoin is shocked by this. He sees Ted is serious. He turns and sees that Mrs Doyle is leaving the room sadly.

EOIN: Eh . . . you . . . (*Mrs Doyle stops.*) . . . Thanks for the . . . eh . . . cake-jumper thing.*

Mrs Doyle beams.

MRS DOYLE: Are you going to try it on?*

Eoin pauses, looks at Ted, then sighs and puts it on. He smiles.

EOIN: God, it's brilliant.*

He gives Mrs Doyle a kiss on the cheek. Mrs Doyle passes out. Eoin immediately starts scratching himself.

EOIN: There's bloody cake bits all over the place!*

---

* We deleted these lines from the final version.

SCENE 23 INT./NIGHT 3
SET: PAROCHIAL HOUSE

Ted is still thinking hard. We see Eoin in the corner of the room, asleep, sucking his thumb. Patsy is asleep, too. Ted and Dougal are conspiring together in another part of the room.

TED: We have to get him out of here. You know what we need? Some kind of distraction. Something to lead them away from him, and then he could escape. Some kind of misleading event. What could it be?

Pause.

DOUGAL: I know!

TED: What?

DOUGAL: A 'diversion'. That's what it's called. A 'diversion'.

Pause.

TED: I know it's called a diversion! I'm not asking you what it's called! I'm asking what the diversion should *be*! God almighty! Right, come on. Ideas, ideas.

Pause. Jack looks as if he's about to say something, then changes his mind, then leans forward, then changes his mind. Ted notices this movement, as does Dougal. They look at him and silently wait for him to speak. Finally, he leans forward and puts one finger in the air in a 'how about this?' type gesture.

JACK: Arse! Feck! Drink! Girls!

TED: Yes . . . thank you, Father Jack.

TED: We need more concrete ideas than that. What do older women like?

JACK: My cock in a burger bun.

Pause as they take this in.

DOUGAL: Do you know what they really, really love, Ted?

JACK: My cock in a burger bun!

DOUGAL: A great game of bingo. What about luring them into some kind of giant game of bingo?

TED: Right. How would we do that?

DOUGAL: Well. We could make up some bingo cards on our printing press, and then . . . Oh.

TED: Yes. It's the lack of a printing press that stops us there, Dougal. Plus we have no bingo balls. Or a big, glass, bingo-ball-dispenser thing that blows out the bingo balls. Or a microphone. Or, in fact, any bingo paraphernalia at all.

DOUGAL: Damn! So near and yet so far!

There is a noise from the window. Ted goes to it and lifts the curtain. About four old women are grouped together, looking in. They motion in a friendly way for Ted to open the window.

TED: No way. You just go home! Go on! Shoo!

WOMAN 1: Oh, Father, we just wanted to tell you what a brilliant Mass you did last week.

TED: Oh . . . oh, well, thanks very much. I was very happy with the sermon actually . . .

WOMAN 2: Oh, yes, how did it start again?

TED: Oh, what was it . . . 'I believe it was the actor Nick Berry who said . . .'

WOMAN 1: Sorry, Father? It's very hard to hear you through this window . . .

TED: Oh, right . . . (*He opens the window. They lean in.*) 'I believe it was the actor Nick Berry who said . . .' (*More women start filling the window.*) Actually . . . could you move back from the window there . . .

WOMAN 1: Where's Eoin?!

TED (*gasps*): You're not interested in my sermon at all!

WOMAN 2: We don't want any trouble, Father. Just send out the boy.

TED: I'm not sending out anyone. You lot should be ashamed of yourselves.

WOMAN 1: Ahh, look, there he is asleep.

WOMAN 2: Ahhhhh! He's lovely!

WOMAN 3: Aaaaahhhh!!!

WOMAN 4: Aaaaaahhhhhh!!!!

They start pushing their way through the window. Patsy wakes up.

PATSY: What are you doing? Why is the window open?!

The women are struggling through.

TED: I can't hold them back! Upstairs! Get upstairs!

They all run to the living-room door, except Jack, who is asleep. Cut to a map of the house, like a blueprint. We see a red line travelling through the hallway, then up the stairs, then into Ted and Dougal's bedroom.

SCENE 24 INT./NIGHT 3
SET: TED AND DOUGAL'S BEDROOM
Ted and Dougal come into the room. There are more women coming through the upstairs window.

TED: Back! Back!

The red line goes into a room labelled 'Bathroom'.

SCENE 25 INT./NIGHT 3
SET: PAROCHIAL HOUSE BATHROOM
Ted, Dougal, Patsy and Eoin come into the room. They lock the door.

TED: Oh, God, what do we do now?

SCENE 26 INT./NIGHT 3
SET: PAROCHIAL HOUSE
The living room is now full of middle-aged women, walking around like zombies, bumping into walls and furniture, and chanting 'Eoin, Eoin'. Jack wakes up and looks around, confused.

SCENE 27 INT./DAY 4
SET: PAROCHIAL HOUSE BATHROOM
The four are sitting around, looking anxious.

PATSY: Oh, God, what are we going to do? I'm not so worried for ourselves, Father. But the little ones. They have their whole lives ahead of them.

Dougal and Eoin sit on the side of the bath, looking sheepish. The door starts thudding, straining against the lock with each blow. Finally it bursts open. The women are revealed. Some of them move in. From somewhere outside, we hear a cock crow. Ted looks outside, through the window.

We see that it is dawn, and the light is getting brighter.

TED: Ladies, it's after seven. I think your husbands might be wondering where their breakfasts are? After all, I don't think you can expect a man to cook a few sausages and rashers for himself. (*The old ladies pause.*) Remember last year, Mrs Dunne? Your husband tried to make some toast and he burnt the house down. And Mrs Collins, when Mr Collins tried to make the bed on his own, didn't he lose a leg?

The old ladies very slowly reverse out through the doorway. Ted, Dougal, Eoin and Patsy breathe a huge sigh of relief.

SCENE 28 INT./DAY 4
SET: PAROCHIAL HOUSE
Eoin and Patsy are ready to leave. Eoin has a suitcase with him.

EOIN: Right, we're off.

TED: Eoin, did you have those suitcases with you when you came?

EOIN: No, they're yours. I just liked a lot of stuff here and I thought I'd pack it up and take it off with me.

DOUGAL: Oh, that's very cheeky.

EOIN: Patsy will pay for it. I'm just taking everything, and that's it. Come on, Patsy.

He goes out through the door with the cases.

PATSY: I'm sorry he was so much trouble, Father.*

TED: Oh, no . . . (*He looks at Dougal.*) I'm used to it . . .

PATSY: Bye, Father . . . (*She goes to leave. As she approaches the door, she turns.*) Father . . . you've been very kind to us. I wonder if you'd like to come to the show next week? Father McGuire tells me you're always trying to get on television.

TED (*coy*): Oh, no . . . that's not true.

DOUGAL: It is true, Ted. You're *always* trying to get on television. You told me that

_____

*Eoin's line 'I have no willy.' was inserted here in the final version.

it was your number-one ambition in the world.

TED: Did I? Oh, yes, I might have said that . . . jokingly, probably. I'm not really that bothered . . .

PATSY: There's a new part of the show where we get an audience member up on stage to take part in a quiz. There's a cash prize . . .

TED: I'll do it! Even though I'm not that interested. (*Pause.*) Do you know what the viewing figures are exactly?

PATSY: About two million.

DOUGAL: Not bad, Ted. When you were on that religious show there were only about thirty watching.

TED: Well, no one watches religious programmes. They're so dull. And it was up against the O.J. Simpson verdict. Can you imagine what those thirty people were like?

PATSY: If you do well, you could win five hundred pounds.

She leaves. Ted looks delighted with himself.

TED: Five hundred pounds . . . five hundred pounds.

SCENE 29 INT./DAY 5
SET: TELEVISION STUDIO
Ted is sitting in a chair, wearing a T-shirt. Eoin stands beside him with a question card in his hand.

EOIN: Well, Father, you've got four out of five right on your specialist subject, William Shatner's *Tek Wars*, so if you get the general-knowledge question, the five hundred pounds will be yours. All right . . . (*He reads the card.*) Oh! People will think this is rigged. What was the present Pope's original name before he took the name John Paul?

Ted freezes. Under his breath he mutters something like 'For fuck's sake'. We stay on Ted's tortured face. The end credits roll over this. Finally . . .

TED: Jim?

THE END

going to america

GRAHAM: I found out that Dermot had died the day after we filmed this, a show we had already decided would be the last *Father Ted*. The shock was indescribable. I had to call Arthur and tell him, and a few days later we had to go in and edit this episode, still reeling. Dermot was great in this episode, probably the best I've ever seen him, and I think on some unconscious level he was keeping himself going until the end of the series (in the same way that people often get sick at the end of a long location shoot). It's still unbelievable to Arthur and me that he's not here anymore.

Our original idea for the ending (published in this script) was to have Ted joining the suicidal priest on the window-ledge. Dermot's death wasn't the whole reason we decided not to use the scene. It just didn't work, and it would have been terrible to end the series on a joke that didn't work. Our alternative, to show a clip from every episode in reverse chronological order, seemed far more apposite. Even though Ted is stuck on Craggy Island forever, and he'll never have any of his wishes come true, there's something familiar and reassuring about a place that never changes.

ARTHUR: The idea of having a brash priest at the centre of an episode had been with us almost from the beginning. It ties in with a theme we liked, that of religion as a commercial activity, which brings us to Buzz Cagney. Buzz was based on someone I'd met a wedding; a desperately arrogant man who went to America and bought heavily into the 'work hard, play hard and reap rewards'ethic. We were originally going to take that idea even further and make a promotional video for Buzz's parish which featured American priests playing computer games and working out in a gym. Ted wouldn't have been able to resist the luxury of that.

PART ONE

SCENE 1 INT./DAY 1
SET: CONFERENCE ROOM

We see a banner that reads 'It's great being a priest! '98'. Below it, a group of priests are standing, facing a window. There is much worry and concern on their faces. Cut to outside, where we see a priest standing on a ledge, occasionally glancing down. From his point of view, we see cars far down below. A priest, Father Alan, steps forward.

ALAN: Father! Father, please come in!

KEVIN: Don't come near me! I'll jump!

TED: Let me through! (*The crowd parts and reveals Ted. He walks over to Alan.*) I'll take care of this, Alan. (*Alan moves back.*) Kevin? Kevin, what's going on for goodness' sake?

KEVIN: I can't go on!

TED: Don't be silly now, Kevin!

KEVIN: What's the point of living? We're all going to die anyway!

TED: Nonsense! We're not going to die!

ALAN: Yes, we are, Ted.

TED: Well, yes, but not for years.

KEVIN: It's pointless! What am I a priest for? What an utterly useless waste of time. I'd be more use sweeping up roads.

TED: Well, would you listen to him?!! It's fabulous being a priest! Think of all the comfort you bring to the sick and the dying, for instance! They love it! They can't get enough of it!

KEVIN: I've never heard one word of thanks from the sick or the dying. They're an ungrateful shower of bastards. I haven't got one friend in the world and I'd be better off dead.

TED: You have a room full of friends in here, Kevin! Father Alan here, for instance!

ALAN: I've never met him before.

TED: Well . . . (*He speaks to the priests.*) Who knows him? Anyone? No? All right. I'm your friend, Kevin!

KEVIN: Really?

TED: You better believe it! Now, come on,

stop this nonsense!

KEVIN: I suppose . . . yes . . . I'm coming in . . .

PRIESTS: HURRAY!

Kevin gets a shock and starts to fall off the ledge. Ted jumps forward and catches him. He starts to drag him up on to the ledge. Meanwhile, Alan is approached by a tanned, good-looking, well-to-do priest with an American accent. His name is Buzz Cagney.

BUZZ: That priest . . . what's his name?

ALAN: Why, that's Father Ted Crilly.

BUZZ: Crilly, eh? Thank you . . .

ALAN: And who are you? (*Alan turns around, but the priest has gone.*) What the . . .?

The priest suddenly appears again.

BUZZ: Sorry, I went over there. What did you say?

ALAN: I said, who are you?

BUZZ: My name's Cagney. Buzz Cagney. And I think I might have a proposition for this 'Father Ted Crilly'.

Ted has finally managed to pull Kevin up into the room.

TED: There you go.

ALAN: Is he all right?

TED: He's fine.

ALAN: Good.

All the priests immediately go back to talking, as if nothing had happened.

KEVIN: Thank you, Father. I . . . I don't know what came over me. I get a bit depressed.

TED: Oh, don't mention it. Eh . . . I hate to bring this up now, but that twenty quid you owe me . . . do you remember? . . . if you have it . . .

KEVIN (*reaching into his pocket*): Oh, of course!

TED: Sorry!

KEVIN: No problem. It . . . oh, wait, I might not have it on me. Could you wait until tomorrow?

TED: Yes, yes . . . as long as, eh . . . ha, ha . . . as long as you'll still be around!

KEVIN: Ha, ha!

Ted doesn't join in with Kevin's laughter. He was being serious.

SCENE 2 EXT./DAY 2
SET: CHURCH
Ted is talking to Dougal as the parishioners file past them out of church. He shakes hands with passing parishioners as he talks.

TED: . . . And then Harrison Ford jumps off the plane, and fires back up at the plane as he's falling!*

DOUGAL: Wow! It sounds great!

TED: I'd go again if you want to see it this weekend.

DOUGAL: Great!

Mrs Doyle is one of the parishioners.

TED: Oh, Mrs Doyle, when you go home, Father Kevin will be there. He's staying until this depression, or whatever it is, lifts.

MRS DOYLE: Oh, right. So I shouldn't say anything that might depress him?

TED: Yes, stay away from war and death and that whole *Mirror* pension-fund area.

---

*This same imaginary film is discussed in an episode of *Seinfeld*.

MRS DOYLE: All right. I'll stick to things like puppies and cushions.

TED: Puppies and cushions. I'm in a better mood already.

Mrs Doyle goes off. A parishioner, Eugene, stops to speak to Ted.

EUGENE: Father, that sermon today, frankly it bored the arse off me.

TED: Well, Eugene, I'm not here to entertain you. If you want that type of thing, go to see Jean-Michel Jarre or someone.

EUGENE: What the hell was it about, anyway?

TED: It was . . . (*He can't remember.*) What was the first line again?

Eugene, disgusted, moves off.

TED: God, I don't know why I bother . . . What was my sermon about today? Do you remember?

DOUGAL: Sorry, Ted, I was concentrating too hard on looking holy.

TED: Oh, well. To be honest, I don't give a toss.

Dougal is slightly shocked.

SCENE 3 INT./NIGHT 2
SET: PAROCHIAL HOUSE
Ted, Dougal and Kevin are playing Snakes and Ladders in the living room.

TED (*taking his go*): Ha! Well . . . this is much more fun than killing yourself, isn't it, Kevin?

KEVIN: S'pose . . .

TED: Oh, come on, Kevin, cheer up. That's me and Dougal's job now – we're in the Smile Brigade. Not the fire brigade – the Smile Brigade! We'll keep you happy and cheery until you can go to the bank.

KEVIN: Go to the bank?

TED: Go home. I meant go home. Now, come on, Kevin, things will get better. You wait and see!

Kevin throws a dice. He moves his counter.

TED: Nice move, Kev. Actually, Kevin . . .

You landed on a snake there. You . . . have to go down . . .

Kevin moves his counter down the snake. He starts weeping. Ted looks uncomfortable. Dougal thinks this is hilariously bizarre.

DOUGAL: What's wrong with you?

TED: Dougal, there's nothing wrong . . . Kevin, are you all right?

KEVIN (*cries a little*): . . . Yes, yes . . . I'm all right . . .

He is now weeping uncontrollably. Ted takes the dice and throws it. They continue playing, ignoring the weeping. It comes to Kevin's turn again.

TED: Your go again, Kevin.

Kevin wipes his face, blinks through the tears and throws the dice.

TED: That's a five . . . Oh . . . another snake.

Kevin moves his counter down the snake, weeping constantly throughout.

TED: Dougal, your go.

Dougal throws the dice.

DOUGAL: Hurrah!!!!! Ha, ha! If he keeps landing on snakes then I'll win for sure!

Ted glares at Dougal. Dougal moves his counter up a ladder. Play continues. It's Kevin's turn again.

TED: Oh, very near another snake, Kevin! As long as you don't get a one!

Kevin throws the dice. It rolls off the edge of the table and lands on the floor.

TED: Ah, you're all right there, Kevin. It's a six.

DOUGAL: No, it isn't, Ted. It's a one! Definitely!

TED (*intently*): I don't think it is, Dougal.

DOUGAL: It is, Ted! Look! It's a one! He's going to snaketown! (*Dougal moves Kevin's counter to the top of the snake and all the way down to a lower line.*) Weeeeeeeeeeee!!!!!

Kevin looks at this for a moment, then gets up from the table and runs off.

DOUGAL: Bye! . . . What's wrong with him, Ted?

TED: He's a panic depressive.

DOUGAL: A panic depressive?

TED: Yes. It's like a manic depressive, only you panic as well as getting depressed. It's a combination of Waaaaaghh!!! and . . . (*He makes childish 'depressed' noises.*)

DOUGAL: I think he just knew who the better player was.

Ted picks up an apple and leaves the room.

SCENE 4 INT./DAY 3
SET: PAROCHIAL HOUSE HALLWAY
Ted comes out of the room, idly eating an apple. Mrs Doyle is at the door, looking out at someone outside. She notices Ted.

MRS DOYLE: Ah, Father?

TED: Mmmmmm?

MRS DOYLE: A visitor, Father.

Mrs Doyle swings the door open slowly, revealing Buzz Cagney. He steps in and closes the door behind him.

BUZZ: Father Crilly, hello.

TED (*still eating his apple*): Oh, hello . . .

BUZZ: My name is Father Buzz Cagney. I was at the conference the other day. I was wondering if we could have a chat . . . *I think you might be interested in a little proposition.*

We stay on Buzz's mysterious expression and a mysterious-sounding sting plays. Beat.

TED (*chews, swallows*): Sorry about that . . . eating an apple. Yeah, all right! Come in, come in . . .

SCENE 5 INT./DAY 3
SET: PAROCHIAL HOUSE
Ted and Buzz are sipping sherry.

BUZZ: . . . and then I was in Utah for a few years. Osmond country. Not a good Catholic market. Mormons there got that polygamy thing going . . . big crowd puller. Guy in the street says to himself . . . 'I'm looking around for a religion to suit my lifestyle. With the Mormons, I can have five, ten wives if I want. That's a *lot* of action.'

TED (*not really getting it*): Action, yeah . . .

BUZZ: Hard to compete against that. Then I was in Reno . . .

TED: Reno. I hear that's very like Wexford. I did a mass in Wexford once. Very rough crowd. Very restless. You *have* to do a good sermon there or they'll hop all over you. Where are you at the moment?

BUZZ: I'm in Beverly Hills.

Ted's tongue literally hangs out with excitement.

TED: Bruberly Huls? Wa . . . Wow! You landed on your feet there. I suppose Gregory Peck drops in for an old chat about his grandchildren's first communion, and then you head off for a dip in his pool.

BUZZ: I do meet quite a lot of celebrities, yes.

TED: Yeah? Like who?

BUZZ: Kevin Spacey. He's a nice guy. He—

TED: Don't know him. What about Val Kilmer? I hear he's a complete bastard.

BUZZ: Did you ever think of going over yourself?

TED: Well, I usually go on holidays with my curate, Father McGuire . . . And he can't really take the sun too well . . .

Ted points out a row of pictures of Dougal on holiday. In every one of them his skin is a ludicrous colour of bright red. Dougal comes in.

DOUGAL (*notices Buzz*): Who are you? What are you talking about?

TED: Oh, this is Father Buzz Cagney. He's just on a quick visit. He's from America.

DOUGAL: America? We were just talking about that fella, Kurt Cobain from Nirvana, earlier on. He was from America. That was weird, wasn't it? Blowing his head off with a shotgun! God, how did he manage to survive that?!

TED: He . . . eh, he didn't, Dougal. He died.

DOUGAL: Oh . . . right.

TED: Anyway, you go to bed, I'll be up in a minute.

DOUGAL: All right, Ted. Goodnight!

Dougal leaves.

BUZZ: You'll be up in a minute?

TED: Yes, we sleep together. So who else do you know?

Mrs Doyle enters.

MRS DOYLE: Hello, everyone! Father, are you looking forward to dinner?

TED: Hmm? Oh . . . yes, I suppose so.

MRS DOYLE: I think you'll enjoy dinner tonight. You do like pheasant, don't you, Father?

TED: Pheasant? God, yes, I love pheasant!

MRS DOYLE: Well, that's a little clue as to what you'll be eating for dinner. The thing you'll be eating likes pheasant as well!

As Mrs Doyle talks, she puts on a protective visor and sits down on a chair in front of Jack. Buzz sees this and looks puzzled. Ted turns to Mrs Doyle.

TED: What are— Oh, Mrs Doyle, you're not doing his nails now, are you?

MRS DOYLE: I have to, Father. He's been worrying the armrests again.

We notice that there are two big piles of stuffing coming out of the armrests of his armchair.

TED: Oh, all right. Slip this on, Buzz.

He hands Buzz an old-style motorbike helmet. Buzz, puzzled, puts it on. Ted puts one on too.

TED: Anyway, Buzz, you were saying . . .

BUZZ: Eh . . . yes, I was curious . . . How much money did this parish bring in last year?

TED: How much money? God, I don't know. I suppose in an average month we'd take— (*Mrs Doyle clips a nail and the living-room window shatters as if a bullet has gone through it. Buzz jumps with the shock.*) Tsk. Another bloody window gone – I suppose we'd take in about a hundred and fifty pounds in collections. Maybe two hundred. (*Another nail is clipped and raps sharply against Ted's helmet.*) Mrs Doyle? Aim into the wall, *please*.

BUZZ: Two hundred pounds . . . what's that? Not even four hundred dollars. Do you know what I'd do with four hundred dollars? I'd wipe my ass with four hundred dollars.

TED: Good God. But . . . can that still be accepted as legal tender?

BUZZ (*not listening*)**:** My parish made two million dollars last year. That's a lot of sherry and steak dinners.

He raises his glass and salutes Ted briefly. Just as he's about to raise it to his mouth, another nail is clipped and the glass shatters.

TED: Mrs Doyle! Seriously, now, do it later!

MRS DOYLE: Oh, all right, Father.

Mrs Doyle leaves. Ted and Buzz take off their helmets.

BUZZ: I want to show you something. This is a brochure for Saint John's parish, Beverly Hills. This is the parish grounds.

Buzz picks up a brochure. He holds it in front of Ted, blocking his face. Ted starts leafing through it.

TED: Whoah! Is that the Hollywood sign in the background?

BUZZ: Uh-huh. All the usual features . . . (*He starts turning pages.*) . . . heated swimming pool in the basement . . . computer-games room . . . revolving restaurant giving you . . . I dunno, I suppose a pretty good view of the Hollywood Hills . . . it's really very nice.

He takes the brochure away. Cut to a two-shot of Ted and Jack. Ted is sitting with his head cocked to one side, mouth open and drooling slightly, just like Jack.

BUZZ: Ted . . . the other day I saw how you dealt with that suicide guy. You were the *Iceman.* Supercool. I liked what I saw, Ted. How would you like to work with me in L.A.? In a satellite parish to Saint John's?

TED: What? You mean? . . . *L.A.?* Dear God in . . . (*Dougal walks in, dressed in his pyjamas. Ted and Buzz stop talking. Dougal, a little confused, walks over to take a football annual off the table, then walks out again.*) . . . heaven! That'd be fantastic! Do you really think you could swing it?

BUZZ (*nods*)**:** It's a good parish, Ted, and if you work hard, the rewards are there.

TED (*disappointed*)**:** Yeah . . . spiritual rewards.

BUZZ: No! Real rewards!

TED: Really? Great!

BUZZ: It's the land of opportunity, Ted. You want something, you can get it.

TED: Well, I want it!

Buzz raises his hand in the air to move his hair back. Ted mistakes this as an invitation to give Buzz a 'high five' and starts to do so. But he misses and slaps Buzz in the face in a rather embarrassing way.

END OF PART ONE

* * *

PART TWO

SCENE 6 INT./MORNING 4
SET: PAROCHIAL HOUSE LIVING ROOM
Ted is on the telephone.

TED: Really? It's official? Yes! Yes, great news! OK! Thank you, Buzz, *thank* you!

He puts the telephone down and makes a 'yessssss' gesture. He is so excited that things keep occurring to him and the excitement is renewed. He sits down and then has to stand up again. He runs to the door, then stops.

TED: No . . . no . . . one step at a time. Get them all together . . . Dougal, Father Jack, Mrs Doyle . . . *I'm going to America!!!!!*

He jumps up and down with excitement. Kevin comes through the door.

KEVIN: Ted, could I speak with you a moment?

TED: Sure!

They sit down at the table.

KEVIN: Father, I'd like to thank you for talking me down off that ledge. It was very good of you. I can't pretend I'm any happier, I'm afraid. The world still looks to me a very dark, unpleasant place—

TED: YES!!!! (*Ted has jumped out of his chair. He walks around the room, talking to himself.*) I'll need to get all my stuff brought over somehow, but that won't be a problem. I'm sure the Washington parish can . . . Kevin! Hello! What can I do for you?

KEVIN: Eh, yes, I just felt I should tell someone where my thoughts have been leading me these last few weeks. Down some very dark and disturbing alleys . . . I think I'm experiencing what you might know as the dark night of the soul.

TED: Hold on a second, Kevin, do you mind if I put on some music?

KEVIN: What? Oh, no . . . go ahead. (*Ted goes to the record player.*) You see, I've begun to be plagued by doubts. Doubts about . . . oh, God! I mean . . . what if none of it's true? (*The music starts up. It is 'Shaft' by Isaac Hayes.*) What if there's nothing out there?

TED: 'Shaft'!

KEVIN: Sorry, Father?

TED: This is such a great song.

KEVIN: Yes . . . anyway . . . I just keep thinking about all the terrible, awful things that happen to people . . . War, famine, that whole *Mirror* pension-fund thing . . . (*Mrs Doyle comes into the room, hears the previous line, and turns and goes straight out again, an embarrassed look on her face.*) . . . and it just makes me despair—

TED: 'Who's the private dick who's a sex machine with all the chicks? Shaft!'

Ted starts grooving silently to the music, a million miles away. Kevin realises that Ted's not going to be much help, and sighs. After a moment, he starts to listen to the music. He starts slowly, gently grooving, his head bopping up and down.

TED: I love this bit . . . 'Daga, daga, daga, dang, daga, daga, dang.'

The music pours out. Ted looks at the album cover

and grooves slightly. Kevin stares at the record player. He smiles.

KEVIN: I do like this song, actually.

TED: Aw, it's great. Mrs Doyle got it at a car-boot sale.

They groove for a while.

BOTH: Shaft!

They groove for a while longer. The song ends.

TED: Sorry, Kevin. You were saying?

KEVIN (*smiling to himself*): Hmm? Actually . . . no, it doesn't matter. Thank you, Ted. I'd better be going home, actually. Do you want that twenty?

TED: Yea – actually, keep it.

KEVIN: Really? Oh. Thanks, Ted!

TED: No problem!

Kevin leaves. Ted jumps up and down with happiness.

SCENE 7 EXT./DAY 4
SET: PAROCHIAL HOUSE
Kevin walks away from the house, the theme of 'Shaft' still playing in his head. He smiles happily.

SCENE 8 INT./DAY 4
SET: PAROCHIAL HOUSE
Dougal comes in, dressed in his pyjamas.

DOUGAL: Yes, Dougal, I have some very good news. I've been asked to go and work in America!

DOUGAL: Really? As what?

TED: Well . . . as a priest . . .

DOUGAL: A priest, great. That's more or less the same as what you do here.

TED: Yes . . .

DOUGAL: God, America! Fantastic! When are we going?

TED: When are we – what?

DOUGAL: I am going, aren't I? You wouldn't . . . you wouldn't leave me behind, would you?

Ted looks at Dougal. From Ted's point of view, we

see that coming out of the collar, where Dougal's head should be, is a puppy. Cut back to Ted.

TED: Well . . . ah . . . yes.

DOUGAL: Brilliant, Ted!

Mrs Doyle comes in.

DOUGAL: Mrs Doyle! Wait'll you hear this! Ted's been offered a job in America and we're all going with him!!!!

MRS DOYLE (*makes squeaky noise*): We're geeng te Meerica? We're geeng te Meerica? We're geeng te Meerica? We're geeng te Meerica? (*By now she is holding on to Ted's collar.*) Are we? Are we really? Are we really, Father?

Ted looks at Mrs Doyle. We see her from his point of view. He sees a ruby-cheeked little girl dressed in frills, with a pathetically hopeful look on her face.

TED: Eh . . . yes . . . we . . . we're going to America . . .

DOUGAL: Tell Father Jack!

Father Jack is asleep. Ted looks at him. Mrs Doyle and Dougal look at Ted expectantly.

TED: Father Jack? Father Jack?

JACK (*wakes*): ARSE!

TED: Eh . . . Father Jack?

We see Jack from Ted's point of view. He is an old man in a Pringle jumper. He has the puppy we saw earlier in his lap, and the little girl has one hand on the back of the rocking chair he is sitting on. Music starts: 'I'll be seeing you in Apple Blossom time . . .' Cut back to Ted. He looks very confused.

TED: Actually, I think I'd better go and have a lie down . . .

He leaves the room unsteadily.

SCENE 9 INT./DAY 4*
SET: SACRISTY
We hear the murmur of a cheering mob outside the door. It opens. The cheering becomes louder and we see some jubilant islanders outside. Ted walks through them and they clap him on the back. He comes in, followed by Buzz and two altar boys. Buzz slams the door after Ted has entered. Ted turns to the altar boys.

TED: Yes! Woo-hoo! You guys! What a great mass! Buzz, what did you think?

BUZZ: Seeing you out there today, Ted, well . . . let me put it this way, I haven't been this excited about religion in thirty years. You really know how to work the room.

TED: Well, you inspired me, Buzz. (*He puts a towel around his neck, sits down and one of the altar boys starts giving him a neck massage.*) It was just one of those Masses when everything seemed to go right. I don't know what it was . . . I was just in the *zone*.

BUZZ: I liked the *Star Trek* joke.

TED: Yeah, I was trying to lighten the mood after the Offertory.

BUZZ: Well, people expect to be depressed after the Offertory, but nice idea. I like the way you're thinking. In the States you won't be in competition with Father Pat Shilleagh from Bally-Go-Assways anymore. You're up against Billy Graham and those Nation of Islam guys. Those mothers can put on a show like Judy Garland at Carnegie Hall. You have to grab the audience, Ted. And do you know where you have to grab them?

TED: Yeah. *By the balls!*

BUZZ: I was going to say by the shoulders.

TED: Oh, right, sorry. *God*, that was fantastic! I feel like going out and doing another Mass right away!

BUZZ: Pace yourself, Ted. I wouldn't do another Mass for a week.

Ted nods, thinking to himself, still very high.

TED: The way I feel now, I could convert gays.

SCENE 10 INT./DAY 5†
SET: PAROCHIAL HOUSE HALLWAY
A caption comes up that reads 'One month later'. Six teenagers in T-shirts with cool band names on them are getting Ted's autograph. Ted is signing for them happily.

---

* We moved scene 12 to here in the final version.
† We deleted this scene from the final version.

TED: There you go. See you at Mass on Sunday! You will be there, won't you?

TEENAGER 1: You bet, Father! Your Masses are the greatest!

TEENAGER 2: What's the sermon going to be about?

TED: Follow not false gods.

TEENAGER 1: Oh, right. Except you, Father!

TED: Ha, ha!

He closes the door and walks into the living room.

SCENE 11 INT./DAY 5
SET: PAROCHIAL HOUSE
Dougal is sitting, reading a big book called 'So you're a priest who is going to America'. Ted sees this and looks abashed.

DOUGAL: God, Ted! One week to go!

TED: Eh . . . yes.

DOUGAL: There were some fans outside looking for you. Did you see them?

TED: Yes, it looks as though I'll have to make this Sunday's Mass all-ticket.

DOUGAL: Actually, I just realised, I haven't seen the gloomy fella around lately. Where is he?

TED: He's gone home. I think he's all right now.

SCENE 12 EXT./DAY 5*
SET: BUS
Kevin is on a bus, smiling happily.

DRIVER: Father, do you mind if I turn on some music?

KEVIN: No, not at all!

He smiles happily. The driver turns a knob.

D.J. (*from the radio*): . . . From yesteryear, 'Alison' by Elvis Costello . . . Now . . . the new single from Radiohead: 'Asleep'.

The incredibly depressing song starts playing. Kevin listens to it, the smile slowly disappearing from his face. After a few moments, he looks totally miserable. The bus speeds off into the distance.

SCENE 12A INT./DAY 5
SET: PAROCHIAL HOUSE
Back to Ted and Dougal.

DOUGAL: Ted, how come you've got really good at saying Mass and you used to be crap?

TED: I wasn't crap at saying Mass. And don't say 'crap'. It's just Buzz has been a big inspiration to me. (*Pause.*) Dougal, about this whole America thing . . . I really have to talk . . .

Mrs Doyle enters.

MRS DOYLE: I'vc arranged for the phone and electricity to be cut off, Father, and someone's coming on Tuesday to take away all the furniture and burn it in a big fire.

TED: Mrs Doyle, Dougal, Father Jack . . . I have to tell you something. I have to be absolutely honest with you . . .

DOUGAL: The money was just resting in the account . . .

MRS DOYLE (*overlapping*): . . . just resting in the account . . . yes, we know that, Father . . .

TED: No, it's nothing to do with that . . . it's . . . (*He looks at them. They look really helpless.*)

* In the final version we inserted this scene after scene 8.

. . . well . . . (*He sees them again.*) . . . the thing is . . . (*He sees them again.*) . . . what I'm trying to say is . . . (*He sees them again.*) . . . you're not . . . you're not going to be . . . able to come with me . . . (*Mrs Doyle drops a cup. Dougal's face crumples.*) . . . when I go into space. I'm going to be the first priest in space! (*Long pause.*) Yes . . . I've been selected by N.A.S.A. to be the first priest in space. So . . . well, that's the news. Just thought I'd tell you that.

MRS DOYLE (*obviously relieved*)**:** Oh, great. Well, that's fine.

DOUGAL: But Ted, how will you breathe in space?

TED: Oh, I'm sure they'll . . . I'll have some sort of apparatus.

DOUGAL: God, Ted, first America, then space! What's next!? Mars or somewhere, I suppose.

TED: Well, who knows.

MRS DOYLE: Still, as long as we can all go with you to America, Father, that's the important thing. I think if I couldn't go for any reason, I would have to say it'd be the single most crushing thing of my entire life. A disappointment like that, well, I couldn't see how I'd live with it. I might even take the ultimate step and take my own life.

TED: Mrs Doyle! That's a terrible thing to say!

MRS DOYLE: Well, it doesn't matter anyway, because I *am* going to America! Ha, ha!

TED: Yes. Ha, ha.

She potters out. The telephone rings. Ted picks it up, still looking sheepish.

TED: Buzz, hello! Well, just one more Mass and I'm off!

SCENE 13 INT./DAY 5*
SET: HOTEL ROOM
Buzz is standing with a towel around his waist, just out of the shower. Room service comes in with a tray full of expensive goodies.

BUZZ (*to room service*)**:** Put it on the bed . . . Yeah . . . I've been meaning to talk to you about that . . . the people here . . . Well,

you're very popular here at the moment, Ted. They're going to find it hard to let you go . . .

TED: What? Oh, no, they'll be fine.

BUZZ: I don't know. Bishop Brennan received a petition the other day begging for you not to be sent away, signed by everyone on the island, including – and this is something I find a little bizarre – you.

TED: That's what that was? I assumed it was something to do with getting satellite TV. Don't worry about that. I'm out of here.

BUZZ: Hmm. This is the thing, Ted. It might be hard for me to get you to America if you keep doing these great Masses . . . I think something drastic is called for.

TED: I . . . you mean . . . *throw the Mass?!!!* You're not serious! No way, Buzz! I can't!

BUZZ: You want a shot at the big time, you've got to throw the Mass.

TED: No, Buzz, no! Please don't make me do it!

BUZZ: I'm sorry, Ted, but it's got to be like that.

Buzz gets up and leaves. Ted sits down, looking devastated.

SCENE 14 INT./DAY 5*
SET: SACRISTY
Buzz is waiting. The door leading out is opened. Outside, a group of people are looking at someone offscreen. They are very quiet. Ted passes through them. They part to let him through but they seem quietly angry.

TED: Ah . . . excuse me . . . thank you . . . yes . . . (*He comes in, followed by the two altar boys, and closes the door. The altar boys won't look at Ted.*) Ah, could you take my, ah? . . .

He holds out his stole for an altar boy to take. The boy does so, but without much enthusiasm. A man sticks his head through the door. He has an old-style hat with a card with 'Press' written on it stuck in the band.

PRESS: Father, can I ask you a few questions?

*We deleted this scene from the final version.

BUZZ: He ain't talkin' to no one! Get outta here!

PRESS: Lotta people sayin' you threw that Mass, Fadda. What you got to say to that?

TED: I don't throw Masses! You tell 'em Father Ted Crilly does not throw Masses!

Buzz goes to the door and forces the reporter out of it.

TED: I coulda had that crowd, Buzz. The way I felt . . .

BUZZ: I know how hard that was for you, Ted, going through the forty days Our Lord spent in the desert moment by moment. You were boring the ass off me. And that nasal, annoying voice . . .

TED: What nasal, annoying voice?

BUZZ: Hmm? Oh, I mean, ahm . . . you're going to America!

TED: Yay!!!!

SCENE 15 INT./DAY 6
SET: PAROCHIAL HOUSE
The living room has been cleared of all ornaments, pictures, etc. Ted walks in. Mrs Doyle is clearing stuff up.

TED: Wha—?!!!

MRS DOYLE: Come on, Father! We don't want to be late for our plane!

TED: Look, there's no easy way to tell you this but . . .

Dougal comes in carrying suitcases.

DOUGAL: Ha! God, Ted! I've just been looking at my passport photo! I look hilarious! Have a look. God, I've changed a lot . . .

He shows his passport photo to Ted. We see a photo of a baby.

TED: You haven't changed that much, Dougal. Anyway, listen carefully . . .

DOUGAL: Look at Jack, he's so excited about going to America he can barely keep still!

We see Jack in his chair, mouth open, asleep. We hear the clock ticking. Finally he rouses slightly in an involuntary way and makes a grunting noise.

DOUGAL: You see?!

TED: Yes, Dougal. Seriously, I need to say something . . .

DOUGAL: Oh, I can't wait to hear this! Every time Ted's talked to us over the last few days, it's just been more and more good news! Now you're going to tell us you're Santa, or something!

TED: No, Dougal, I'm not Santa. In fact, I'm the opposite to Santa.

DOUGAL (*afraid*): The anti-Santa?!

TED: I'm afraid . . . this is going to come as a terrible blow to you all . . . but I really can't put it off any longer. I have to tell you now.

We see Mrs Doyle, Jack and Dougal staring back at him.

SCENE 16 INT./DAY 6
SET: AIRPORT
Ted, Dougal, Jack and Mrs Doyle come through the door. We see a sign that reads 'Departures'.

DOUGAL: We'd better check in before we go to America.

TED: Yes, better. Ah, here's Buzz.

Buzz approaches. He notices Ted's mad, bush-wired hair.

BUZZ: Ted. What the hell's happened to your head?

TED: Wha—? . . . (*He remembers what he looks like.*) Oh. You don't like it? I'll put it back as it was.

He starts trying to smooth down his hair.

BUZZ: What are those guys doing here?

TED: Ah, they just came with me to the airport to say goodbye.

BUZZ: They don't think they're going as well, do they?

TED: Oh, God, no. I told them. I definitely made that very clear to them. I told them a million times.

BUZZ: Just say your goodbyes. Then you can check in and go to the executive lounge. Talk about your new parish.

Ted goes over to Dougal, Jack and Mrs Doyle. Buzz

sees them shaking hands, but can't hear them. Cut away from Buzz's point of view.*

TED: . . . So that's how to react when we meet people in America. Just shake hands, give them a firm greeting. Just as if they were normal Irish people. Mrs Doyle, I'll just show you as well . . . *

Cut to Buzz's point of view. Ted shakes hands with Mrs Doyle, then with Jack. Then he starts waving. Cut closer on Ted.*

TED: And it's basically the same, left-right movement for waving. Can you try that?*

From Buzz's point of view, we see a confused Mrs Doyle and Dougal waving back at Ted. Ted goes over to Buzz. Jack, Mrs Doyle and Dougal look at them.*

TED: Right. That's them dealt with.*

*We deleted these lines from the final version.

BUZZ: All right, I've checked in so I'll see you in the lounge. Get ready to rock!*

TED: Yes! (*Buzz walks off. Ted crumples.*) Oh, God!*

SCENE 17 INT./DAY 6
SET: CHECK-IN
Ted is waiting in the line with Mrs Doyle, Dougal and Jack. There are about four people ahead of them. Ted is a picture of horror.

DOUGAL: Oh, Ted, you know, all my life I've dreamed of something really special happening to me, and now it is. I think this is the greatest moment of my life.

MRS DOYLE: Me too.

JACK: Bras!

The line moves forward a little more, past a potted plant – a tall shrub.

TED: Oh, God!

There is one woman in front of them. Then it is Ted's turn. He checks in. The operator starts feeding information into her computer. Ted looks desperate.

TED: Dougal, Mrs Doyle, Father Jack, you go and wait in the restaurant. I'll check us in.

DOUGAL: Which restaurant, Ted?

TED: The one that isn't a Sock Shop, over there.

DOUGAL: OK, so.

They all move off. Ted watches them go. Ted sneaks off. He sees Buzz at the gate.

BUZZ: Ah, Ted! What's wrong?

TED (*doubled over*): Just a slight bit of guilt about leaving. Hold on a sec. (*He makes a horrible face, swallowing the guilt as if it were a lump of steak with nails in it.*) There it goes.

BUZZ: Right. Come on, Ted. There's a whole world out there to experience. Let's take the first step.

They walk through the gate.

SCENE 18 INT./DAY 6
SET: AIRPORT
Dougal, Mrs Doyle and Jack are sitting down.

DOUGAL: They're never going to serve us.

Cut wide to reveal that they are in a Sock Shop.

SCENE 19 INT./DAY 6
SET: A SCREEN
We see a 'Departures' display. Among those listed we see: 'AL 152 LOS ANGELES GATE 27. 17.30'

SCENE 20 INT./DAY 6
SET: AIRPORT
Dougal, Mrs Doyle and Jack are wandering through the emptying airport. They watch people going by, pushing their trolleys and smiling.

SCENE 21 INT./DAY 6
SET: A SCREEN
The same as earlier except that it now reads: 'AL 152 LOS ANGELES GATE 27. NOW BOARDING'.

SCENE 22 INT./DAY 6
SET: AIRPORT
Dougal, Mrs Doyle and Jack are hanging around in another location. They look ever so slightly forlorn, but still hopeful.

SCENE 23 INT./DAY 6
SET: PLANE
Ted is sitting beside Buzz.

TED: Sorry about that, Buzz. Anyway! Can't wait to get to America!

BUZZ: You'll like it, Ted. Going in at the deep end . . .

TED: Oh, great! The old swimming pool! Lovely. I packed my swimming trunks . . .

BUZZ: You won't have a swimming pool.

TED: No? OK . . .

BUZZ: You'll have a basketball court.

TED: Oh, good. That'll keep me fit, anyway.

BUZZ: One of the ways the parish has tried to cool tensions between the gangs in the past is through sports . . .

TED: Sorry, Buzz . . . stop you there for a moment . . . gangs? Did you use the word

'gangs' there? What does that mean exactly?

BUZZ: Well, L.A.'s gang problem is getting slightly better these days. Last year there were only five thousand, six hundred and twenty gang-related deaths.

TED: There's another use of the word 'gangs', which I asked about earlier. Also, I couldn't help noticing that it was closely followed by the word 'deaths'.

BUZZ: Yes. The good news is that drive-by shootings are down.

TED: Right, there I notice the word 'shootings'. *Pause.* Buzz?

BUZZ: Yes?

TED: I quit! I didn't know I was going out to America to umpire drive-by shooting tournaments. STOP THE PLANE!

BUZZ: It hasn't started yet, Ted.

TED: Well . . . even though . . . yes . . . Don't start the plane! . . . I'm getting off!

He runs to the exit.

SCENE 24 INT./DAY 6
SET: AIRPORT
Time has passed, and Dougal, Mrs Doyle and Jack are asleep in their uncomfortable chairs. Ted comes up and sits beside Dougal.

DOUGAL (*waking*): Ted? Is that you?

TED: Yes, it's me. Listen . . . I've been thinking about things . . . I really think it would be better if I didn't go to America. I think we'd all be happiest back where we belong. On Craggy Island.

DOUGAL: Fair enough, Ted. I didn't really want to go anyway.

Ted is taken aback. Mrs Doyle and Jack wake up.

MRS DOYLE: Oh, Father, you're back. What's going on?

DOUGAL: Ted's decided that it would be better if we didn't go to America.

TED: Huh?

MRS DOYLE: Really? Ah, he's probably right.

JACK: Drink!

MRS DOYLE: Come on, Father, we'll go home and get you a drink.

TED: I thought you really wanted to go.

MRS DOYLE: Yes, I thought I'd be a bit more disappointed, but now you've told us, I realise that I didn't really want to go at all. In fact, I don't think I *can* go. I haven't told my sister about it.

They get up.

DOUGAL: Come on, Ted. Let's go.

Dougal, Jack and Mrs Doyle get up. Ted slowly gets to his feet and follows them.

DOUGAL: Ah, yeah, Ted. You're here to stay! With me and Mrs Doyle and Father Jack for ever and ever and ever and ever . . .

Ted stops short.

SCENE 25 INT./DAY 6*
SET: CONFERENCE ROOM
We see a banner that reads 'It's still great being a priest!' Below it, a group of priests are standing, facing a window. There is much worry and concern on their faces. Cut to outside, where we see Kevin standing on a ledge, occasionally glancing down. From his point of view, we see cars far down below. The group of priests parts and Ted comes through them. He goes to the window and climbs out. He ushers Kevin along the ledge.

TED: Move up a bit.

THE END

_____

*In the final version we replaced this scene with a montage of clips from every previous episode of *Father Ted*.

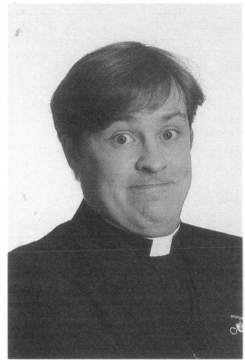
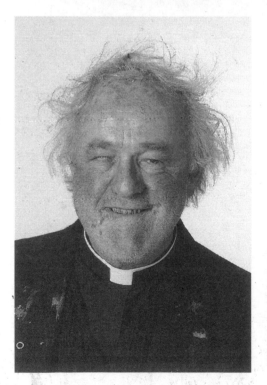

POLICY & POLITICS

POLITICS

in Nursing and Health Care

POLICY & POLITICS

in Nursing and Health Care

FOURTH EDITION

DIANA J. MASON, RN, PhD, FAAN
Editor-in-Chief
American Journal of Nursing
New York, New York

JUDITH K. LEAVITT, RN, MEd, FAAN
Associate Professor, School of Nursing
University of Mississippi Medical Center
Jackson, Mississippi

MARY W. CHAFFEE, MS, RN, CNAA, CHE, FAAN
Deputy Director, Navy Medicine Office of Homeland Security
Bureau of Medicine and Surgery
Washington, DC

SAUNDERS
An Imprint of Elsevier

SAUNDERS

An Imprint of Elsevier

11830 Westline Industrial Drive
St. Louis, MO 63146

NOTICE
Nursing is an ever-changing field. Standard safety precautions must be followed, but as new research and clinical experience broaden our knowledge, changes in treatment and drug therapy may become necessary or appropriate. Readers are advised to check the most current product information provided by the manufacturer of each drug to be administered to verify the recommended dose, the method and duration of administration, and contraindications. It is the responsibility of the licensed prescriber, relying on experience and knowledge of the patient, to determine dosages and the best treatment for each individual patient. Neither the publisher nor the editor assumes any liability for any injury and/or damage to persons or property arising from this publication.

Previous editions copyrighted 1998, 1993, and 1985.

ISBN-13: 978-0-7216-9534-1
ISBN-10: 0-7216-9534-5

Vice President, Nursing Editorial Director: Sally Schrefer
Executive Editor: Michael S. Ledbetter
Senior Developmental Editor: Lisa P. Newton
Publishing Services Manager: Catherine Jackson
Project Manager: Clay S. Broeker
Designer: Amy Buxton

CL / RDC

Printed in the United States of America.
Last digit is the print number: 9 8 7 6 5

About the Editors

Diana J. Mason, RN, PhD, FAAN, is Editor-in-Chief of the *American Journal of Nursing*. Since 1985, she has been a producer and moderator of *Healthstyles*, an award-winning weekly radio program on health and health policy on WBAI-FM in New York City. For 5 years, she served as project director for *Youth Pulse*, a project to train New York City youth in radio production on health and social issues. Part of a larger national initiative called *Sound Partners for Community Health*, the project was funded by the Benton Foundation and Robert Wood Johnson Foundation. She is a noted speaker and writer on policy and politics in nursing and health care for local, national, and international audiences. Following two research fellowships, she conducted and published research on managed care arrangements with nurse practitioners, as well as other policy-relevant topics. Her involvement in nursing and health care organizations is extensive, including leadership positions on local, state, and national levels. Dr. Mason has received numerous awards, including fellowship in the American Academy of Nursing and the New York Academy of Medicine, the Legislative Award from the New York State Nurses Association, and media awards from the Public Health Association of New York City, the National Association of Childbirthing Centers, and the American Academy of Nursing. She earned her BSN at West Virginia University, her MSN from St. Louis University (including graduate studies on medical care and public health in Norway at the University of Oslo), and her PhD from New York University.

Judith K. Leavitt, RN, MEd, FAAN, is Associate Professor at the University of Mississippi Medical Center, School of Nursing in Jackson, Mississippi. She serves as the Chair of the Advisory Committee for the Mississippi Office of Nursing Workforce. She was formerly Executive Director of Generations United, a national organization dedicated to intergenerational policies and programs. She served on the National Advisory Council on Education and Practice for the Division of Nursing, U.S. Department of Health and Human Services. Ms. Leavitt was selected by President Clinton to serve on the Health Professional Advisory Group to the White House Task Force on Health Care Reform. She served as the upstate coordinator for Geraldine Ferraro's 1992 New York campaign for the U.S. Senate, was chairperson of the American Nurses Association Political Action Committee, was chairperson of New York State Nurses for Political Action, and was instrumental in the founding of the New York State Nurses Association's Political Action Committee. She is a noted speaker and author of extensive writings on policy and politics. Her many awards include the Chancellor's Award for Teaching Excellence from the State of New York, the Health Policy Award from the Division of Nursing at New York University, the Legislative Award from the New York State Nurses Association, the 2000 Mississippi Nurses Association Nurse of the Year, and fellowship in the American Academy of Nursing. Ms. Leavitt earned her BSN from the University of Pennsylvania and her MEd from Teacher's College, Columbia University.

Mary W. Chaffee, MS, RN, CNAA, CHE, FAAN, is a U.S. Navy Nurse Corps officer serving as Deputy Director of the Navy Medicine Office of Homeland Security, Bureau of Medicine and Surgery, in Washington, DC. She previously served in the Office of the Assistant Secretary of Defense for Health Affairs in the TRICARE Management Activity where she was the liaison between multiple federal and civilian agencies involved in administering a multi-billion dollar Department of Defense managed care contract. She is Vice President of the Federal Nurses Association and served a 4-year term on the American Nurses Association Congress on Nursing Practice and Economics. She also serves on the Executive Board of the International Nursing Coalition on Mass Casualty Education. As an intern in the Office of Senator Daniel K. Inouye, she conducted a policy analysis of fraud in the Defense Health Program and crafted legislative language to address the problem. She lectures on a variety of topics and is managing editor of the journal *Policy, Politics & Nursing Practice*. A Fellow of the American Academy of Nursing, Ms. Chaffee was recognized as a Distinguished Alumni of the University of Massachusetts, the first nurse to receive this honor. The Maryland Organization of Nurse Executives selected her to receive the Helen King Scholarship for excellence in graduate Nursing Administration studies, and she has received awards from the University of Massachusetts School of Nursing and the American Association of Critical-Care Nurses. Her contributions to Navy Medicine and the Defense Health Program have been recognized with multiple individual awards. Ms. Chaffee is an honors graduate of the University of Massachusetts at Amherst where she received bachelor's degrees in Nursing and Public Health and completed an internship at the Welsh National School of Medicine. She received her MS degrees in Nursing Health Policy and Nursing Administration from the University of Maryland, Baltimore. She is currently a doctoral student in Nursing, with a focus on Health Care Administration, Ethics, and Policy, at George Mason University.

Contributors

Gwen Anderson, RN, PhD
Nurse Geneticist
Central Coast Genetic Resources
Watsonville, California

Jean Anselmo BSN, RN, HNC
BCIA Certified Senior Fellow in Biofeedback
Holistic Nurse Consultant
Private Practice
Bayside, New York

Allison Beard, MA
Communications and Public Relations Manager
American College of Nurse Practitioners
Washington, DC

Theresa L. Beck, RN, MPA
Director of Special Projects
Visiting Nurse Association of Central Jersey
Red Bank, New Jersey

Kaye Bender, RN, PhD, FAAN
Deputy State Health Officer
Mississippi State Department of Health
Jackson, Mississippi

Crystal Bennett, RN, DNSc
Research Scientist
Cedars-Sinai Health System
Los Angeles, California

Virginia Trotter Betts, MSN, JD, RN, FAAN
Director for Health Policy and Professor of
Nursing
University of Tennessee Health Science Center
Memphis, Tennessee

Linda Burnes Bolton, DrPH, RN, FAAN
Vice President and Chief Nursing Officer
Cedars-Sinai Health System
Los Angeles, California

Jeanne Bowden, PhD, RN
Associate Dean
Oregon Health and Science University School
of Nursing
La Grande, Oregon

Sharon A. Brigner, RN, MS
Senior Health Policy Analyst
Government Relations and Policy Department
National Committee to Preserve Social Security and Medicare
Washington, DC

Dorothy Brooten, PhD, RN, FAAN
Professor of Nursing
School of Nursing
Florida International University
Miami, Florida

Linda P. Brown, RN, PhD, FAAN
Miriam L. Stirl Professor in Nutrition
School of Nursing
University of Pennsylvania
Philadelphia, Pennsylvania

Amy O. Calvin, PhD, RN
Assistant Professor
School of Nursing
The University of Texas Health Science Center
at Houston
Houston, Texas

The Honorable Lois Capps, RN, MA
Member of Congress
22nd District of California
Washington, DC

Cecelia Capuzzi, PhD, RN
Professor in Community and Public Health
  Nursing
Chair of Population-Based Nursing Depart-
  ment
Oregon Health and Sciences University
Portland, Oregon

Toni G. Cesta, PhD, RN, FAAN
Director of Case Management
Saint Vincents Catholic Medical Centers
New York, New York
Partner
Case Manager Solutions, LLC
Tucson, Arizona

**Mary W. Chaffee, MS, RN, CNAA, CHE,
  FAAN**
Deputy Director
Navy Medicine Office of Homeland Security
Bureau of Medicine and Surgery
Washington, DC

Cyril Chang, PhD
Professor of Economics
Fogelman College of Business and Economics
University of Memphis
Memphis, Tennessee

Shirley S. Chater, RN, PhD, FAAN
Adjunct Professor
University of California San Francisco
Institute for Health and Aging
School of Nursing
San Francisco, California
President Emerita
Texas Woman's University
Dallas, Texas
Commissioner
Social Security Administration (1993-1997)
Washington, DC

Mary Ann Christopher, MSN, RNCS, FAAN
President and CEO
Visiting Nurse Association of Central Jersey
Red Bank, New Jersey

Pamela F. Cipriano, PhD, RN, FAAN
Chief Clinical Officer
University of Virginia Health System
Charlottesville, Virginia

Angela P. Clark, PhD, RN, CS, FAAN
Associate Professor of Nursing
The University of Texas at Austin
Austin, Texas

Sally S. Cohen, PhD, RN, FAAN
Associate Professor and Director
Center for Health Policy and Ethics
Yale School of Nursing
New Haven, Connecticut

Colleen Conway-Welch, PhD, CNM, FAAN
Nancy & Hilliard Travis Professor of Nursing
  and Dean
Vanderbilt University School of Nursing
Nashville, Tennessee

Phyllis Cunningham, RN, MS, EdD
Assistant Professor
Hunter-Bellevue School of Nursing
The Schools of the Health Professions
Hunter College, The City University of New
  York
New York, New York

Candy Dato, PhD, RN, CS, NPP
Associate Professor
Long Island University
Brooklyn Campus
School of Nursing
Brooklyn, New York

Karen A. Daley, MPS, RN
President, Massachusetts Association of Regis-
  tered Nurses
Past President, Massachusetts Nurses Associa-
  tion
Worcester, Massachusetts

Betty R. Dickson, BS
Executive Director
Mississippi Nurses Association
Madison, Mississippi

Donna Diers, PhD, RN, MSN, FAAN
Annie W. Goodrich Professor
Yale University School of Nursing
Lecturer, Department of Epidemiology and
  Public Health
Yale University School of Medicine
Clinical Coordinator, Finance
Yale–New Haven Hospital
New Haven, Connecticut

Joanne Disch, PhD, RN, FAAN
Professor and Director
Katharine J. Densford International Center for
  Nursing Leadership
Katherine R and C Walton Lillehei Chair in
  Nursing Leadership
School of Nursing
University of Minnesota
Minneapolis, Minnesota

Alma Yearwood Dixon, EdD, MPH, RN
Chair, Division of Nursing
Bethune-Cookman College
Daytona Beach, Florida

Catherine J. Dodd, RN, MS, FAAN
District Director, Congresswoman Nancy
  Pelosi
Former Region IX Director, U.S. Department
  of Health and Human Services
San Francisco, California

**Dorothy Doughty, MN, RN, FNP, FAAN,
CWOCN**
Wound Ostomy Continence Nursing Educa-
tion Center
Emory University
Atlanta, Georgia

Barbara Ehrenreich, PhD
Journalist and writer
Sugarloaf, Florida

**Dezra J. Eichhorn, MS, RN, ANP, CNS,
PMHNP**
Family Psychiatric Mental Health Nurse Prac-
tioner
North Arkansas Human Services System, Inc.
Mountain View, Arkansas

Diane Carlson Evans, RN
Founder and Chair
Vietnam Women's Memorial Project, Inc.
Washington, DC

Stephanie Ferguson, PhD, RN, FAAN
Associate Professor
Coordinator, PhD in Nursing Program
College of Nursing and Health Science
Coordinator, Washington Health Policy Insti-
  tute, Center for Health Policy, Research and
  Ethics
George Mason University
Fairfax, Virginia

Barbara A. Foley, RN, BS
Executive Director
Emergency Nurses CARE: Emergency Nurses
  Association Injury Prevention Institute
Alexandria, Virginia

Mary Foley, RN, MS
President
American Nurses Association
Washington, DC

Pat Ford-Roegner, RN, MSW, ACSW, FAAN
Executive Director
National Association of Addiction Profession-
als
Public Policy Consultant
Washington, DC

Eve Franklin, MSN, RN, CS
State Senator
Montana State Assembly
Assistant Professor of Nursing
Montana State University—Bozeman
School of Nursing
Great Falls, Montana

John Garde, CRNA, MS, FAAN
Executive Consultant
American Association of Nurse Anesthetists
Park Ridge, Illinois

Deborah B. Gardner, PhD, RN, CS
Chief of Strategic Planning and
  Organizational Development
Clinical Center, National Institutes of Health
Bethesda, Maryland

Kristine M. Gebbie, DrPH, RN
Elizabeth Standish Gill Associate Professor of
  Nursing
Director, Center for Health Policy
Columbia University School of Nursing
New York, New York

Beth W. Gering, MS, RN
Commander, Nurse Corps, United States Navy
National Naval Medical Center
Bethesda, Maryland

Barbara Glickstein, RN, MPH, MS
Director of Community Education and Out-
  reach
The Continuum Center for Health and Heal-
  ing
Producer and Moderator
Healthstyles, WBAI-FM Radio
New York, New York

Sharron E. Guillett, PhD, RN
Co-Chair, Associate Degree Program in Nurs-
  ing
School of Health Professions
Marymount University
Arlington, Virginia

Cathie E. Guzzetta, RN, PhD, HNC, FAAN
Director, Holistic Nursing Consultants
Nursing Research Consultant
Children's Medical Center of Dallas
Dallas, Texas

Barbara E. Hanley, PhD, RN
Consultant and Educator
Health Policy, Holistic Nursing and Comple-
  mentary/Alternative Health Care
Baltimore, Maryland

Charlene Hanson, EdD, RN,CS, FNP, FAAN
Professor Emerita, Georgia Southern Univer-
  sity
Statesboro, Georgia
Family Nurse Practitioner
Family Health and Birth Center
Rincon, Georgia

Pamela Haylock, RN, MA
Oncology Consultant
Doctoral Student
University of Texas Medical Branch
Galveston, Texas

Janet Heinrich, DrPH, RN, FAAN
Director, Health Care/Public Health Issues
U.S. General Accounting Office
Washington, DC

Peggy O'Neill Hewlett, PhD, RN
Professor and Associate Dean for Research
University of Mississippi Medical Center
  School of Nursing
Jackson, Mississippi

Martha Hill, PhD, RN, FAAN
Professor and Dean
School of Nursing
Johns Hopkins University
Baltimore, Maryland

Katie B. Horton, RN, MPS, JD
President
HealthPolicy R&D
Washington, DC

Carolyn Hutcherson, RN, MS
Executive Director
Center for Telemedicine Law
Washington, DC

Nadine M. Jacobson, MS, RN
Freelance health and health policy writer
Glen Burnie, Maryland

Catherine L. Jansto, RN, BSN, MS
Special Assistant
Office of Information Services
Centers for Medicare and Medicaid Services
U.S. Department of Health and Human Services
Baltimore, Maryland

Melinda Jenkins, PhD, CRNP
Assistant Professor of Primary Care
Director, Family Nurse Practitioner Program
School of Nursing
University of Pennsylvania
Philadelphia, Pennsylvania

Carole Jennings, PhD, RN
Assistant Professor and Coordinator of the
  Nursing Health Policy Graduate Program
University of Maryland School of Nursing
Editor-in-Chief, *Policy, Politics, & Nursing
  Practice*
Baltimore, Maryland

David Keepnews, PhD, JD, RN, FAAN
Assistant Professor
Department of Biobehavioral Nursing &
  Health Systems
School of Nursing
University of Washington
Seattle, Washington

Susan Kendig, RNC, MSN, WHCNP
Clinical Assistant Professor
Barnes College of Nursing and Health Studies
University of Missouri—St. Louis
St. Louis, Missouri

Mary Knudtson, MSN, FNP, PNP
Associate Clinical Professor/Director of FNP
  Program
Department of Family Medicine
University of California, Irvine
Irvine, California

Christine Tassone Kovner, RN, PhD, FAAN
Professor
Senior Fellow, John A Hartford Foundation
  Institute for Geriatric Nursing
Division of Nursing, Steinhardt School of Education
New York University
New York, New York

**Felissa Lashley, RN, PhD, ACRN, FACMG,
FAAN**
Dean and Professor
School of Nursing
Southern Illinois University—Edwardsville
Edwardsville, Illinois

Judith K. Leavitt, RN, MEd, FAAN
Associate Professor, School of Nursing
University of Mississippi Medical Center
Jackson, Mississippi

Patricia T. Leavitt, MS, FNP
Nurse Practitioner
Greater Portland Pediatric Associates
Gorham, Maine
Program Coordinator, Family Practice Nurse
Practitioner Program, Simmons College and
  the University of New England
Partnership in Primary Health Care
Portland, Maine

Elizabeth M. Lehr
Editorial Manager
Leesburg, Virginia

Sandra B. Lewenson, EdD, RN, FAAN
Professor and Associate Dean for Academic
  Affairs
Lienhard School of Nursing, Pace University
Pleasantville, New York

Kae Livsey, MPH, RN
Clinical Services Director
Good Samaritan Clinic
Morganton, North Carolina

Judith Lorette, MS, RN
Technical Advisor
Centers for Medicare and Medicaid Services
Center for Beneficiary Choice
Baltimore, Maryland

Beth Lyman, RN, MSN
Nutrition Support Nurse Coordinator
Children's Mercy Hospital
Kansas City, Missouri
Chair of the Nursing Practice Section
American Society of Parenteral and Enteral
  Nutrition
Silver Spring, Maryland

**Diane Feeney Mahoney, PhD, RN, CS, GNP,
  FGSA, APRN**
Director, Enhanced Family Caregiving
  Through Technology Program
Director of Nursing Research and Gerontech-
  nology Research and Development
Senior Research Scientist
Research and Training Institute
Hebrew Rehabilitation Center for the Aged
Boston, Massachusetts

Juanita V. Majewski, BSN, RN
School Nurse
Eden Central School District
Eden, New York

Diana J. Mason, RN, PhD, FAAN
Editor-in-Chief
American Journal of Nursing
New York, New York

Beverly Malone, PhD, RN, FAAN
General Secretary
Royal College of Nursing
London, England

Patrick S. Malone, PhD, FACHE
Lieutenant Commander, Medical Service
  Corps, United States Navy
Office of the Deputy Surgeon General, Bureau
  of Medicine and Surgery
Adjunct Faculty
School of Public Affairs, American University
Washingon, DC

Tracy A. Malone, MS, RN, CMCN
Captain, Nurse Corps, United States Navy
Office of the Assistant Secretary of Defense for
  Health Affairs
The Pentagon
Washington, DC

The Honorable Carolyn McCarthy, LPN
Member of Congress
4th District of New York
Washington, DC

Hollie Shaner McRae, RN, MSA, FAAN
President, CGH Environmental Strategies,
  Inc.
President, Nightingale Institute for Health and
  the Environment
Adjunct Faculty, University of Vermont
  School of Nursing
Visiting Scientist, Visiting Scholars Outreach
  Program, Harvard School of Public Health
Burlington, Vermont

Theresa Meyers, RN, BSN
Director, Emergency Services
Memorial Hospital
Colorado Springs, Colorado

Nancy Milio, PhD, RN, FAAN
Professor Emeritus of Health Policy and
  Nursing
University of North Carolina
Chapel Hill, North Carolina

Judith L. Miller, MS, RN
Clinical Assessment Associate
Peer Review Organization of New Jersey
East Brunswick, New Jersey

Doris Milton, PhD, RN
President, Pragmavisions
Faculty, University of Phoenix and Grand
  Canyon University
Phoenix, Arizona

Susan M. Miovech, PhD, RNC
Associate Professor of Nursing
Holy Family College
School of Nursing
Philadelphia, Pennsylvania

Lillian H. Mood, RN, MPH, FAAN
Community Liaison, Environmental Quality
  Control (retired)
South Carolina Department of Health and
  Environmental Control
Columbia, South Carolina

Linda Moore, PhD, RN, CNAA
Assistant Professor
Department of Public Health
Jackson State University
Jackson, Mississippi

Lynne Murphy, MSN, RN, CNSN
Chair, Public Policy Committee
American Society for Parenteral and Enteral
  Nutrition
Nutrition Support Clinical Specialist
Washington, DC

Susan R. Neary, PhD, RN, CS, GNP
Assistant Professor
Simmons College
Boston, Massachusetts

Marjory C. O'Brien, MS, RN
Legislative Analyst
New York State Assembly
Albany, New York

Jeffrey P. O'Donnell, DNSc, RN, FNP
Assistant Professor
Lienhard School of Nursing
Pace University
Pleasantville, New York

Judith A. Oulton, RN, BN, MEd, DS(hon)
Chief Executive Officer
International Council of Nurses
Geneva, Switzerland

Mickey L. Parsons, PhD, MHA, RN
Associate Professor and Coordinator
Graduate Administration Program
School of Nursing
University of Texas Health Science Center at
  San Antonio
San Antonio, Texas

Susan K. Pfoutz, PhD, RN
Professor
Eastern Michigan University
Ann Arbor, Michigan

Joyce A. Pulcini, PhD, RN, CS, PNP, FAAN
Associate Professor
Boston College School of Nursing
Chestnut Hill, Massachusetts

Sylvia Price, PhD, RN
Professor (retired)
College of Nursing
University of Tennessee
Memphis, Tennessee

Kay Randolph-Back, JD
Program Analyst, Health
W.K. Kellogg Foundation
Battle Creek, Michigan

Melinda Mercer Ray, MSN, RN
Director, Health Policy/Legislative Affairs
Association of Women's Health, Obstetric and
  Neonatal Nurses
Washington, DC

Susan C. Reinhard, RN, PhD, FAAN
Co-Director, Center for State Health Policy
Rutgers, The State University of New Jersey
New Brunswick, New Jersey

Rebecca Rice, RN, EdD, MPH
Deputy Director
Colleagues in Caring: Regional Collaboratives
  for Nursing Workforce Development
American Association of Colleges of Nursing
Washington, DC

**Paula Trahan Rieger, RN, MSN, CS,
  AOCN(R), FAAN**
President, Oncology Nursing Society (2000-
  2002)
Pittsburgh, Pennsylvania

Fatima Al Rifai, RN, MSN
Director of Nursing
Federal Department of Nursing, Ministry of
  Health
Abu Dhabi, United Arab Emirates

Darryl Roberts, BSN, RN
Graduate student
University of Maryland School of Nursing
Baltimore, Maryland

Shelagh Roberts, BA
Policy Analyst
Association of Women's Health, Obstetric and
  Neonatal Nurses
Washington, DC

Carol Robinson, RN, MPA, CNAA
Senior Associate Director of Hospitals and
  Clinics
Director of Patient Care Services
University of California Davis Health Systems
Sacramento, California

Judy Biros Robson, RN, BSN, MSN
State Senator–Wisconsin
Chair, Human Services and Aging
Majority Caucus Chair
Co-Chair Joint Committee on Administrative
  Rules
Madison, Wisconsin

Rita M. Rupp, RN, MA
Special Assistant
Office of the Executive Director
American Association of Nurse Anesthetists
Park Ridge, Illinois

Jo Ellen Rust, MSN, RN
President
National Association of Clinical Nurse Spe-
  cialists
Harrisburg, Pennsylvania

Barbara J. Sabol, RN, MA
Program Director, Health
W.K. Kellogg Foundation
Battle Creek, Michigan

Marla Salmon, ScD, RN, FAAN
Dean and Professor
Nell Hodgson Woodruff School of Nursing
Emory University
Atlanta, Georgia

Yvonne Santa Anna, RN, BSN, MSG
Deputy Director of Government Affairs
National Association for Home Care
Washington, DC

Nancy S. Schlossberg , BA, BSN, RN, CGRN
Immediate Past President
Society of Gastroenterology Nurses and Asso-
  ciates, Inc. (SGNA)
Norfolk, Virginia

Susan M. Schwartz, DBA, RN
Deputy Director, Government Relations for
  Health Affairs
The Retired Officers Association
Alexandria, Virginia

Nancy J. Sharp, MSN, RN, FAAN
Director of TeleHealth Policy
iTeleHealth, Inc.
Bethesda, Maryland

Linda J. Shinn, MBA, RN, CAE
Principal
Consensus Management Group
Indianapolis, Indiana

Allison Weber Shuren, RN, MSN, JD
Government Relations Counsel
Arent, Fox, Kinter, Plotkin, and Kahn
Washington, DC

Mary Cipriano Silva, RN, PhD, FAAN
Professor and Director of the Office of Health
 Care Ethics
College of Nursing and Health Sciences
George Mason University
Fairfax, Virginia

Gloria R. Smith, RN, PhD, MPH, FAAN
Vice President, Programs (retired)
W.K. Kellogg Foundation
Battle Creek, Michigan

Kathleen T. Smith, RN, BS, CNN
Vice President, Government Affairs
Fresenius Medical Care North America
Washington, DC

Shirley Smoyak, RN, PhD, FAAN
Professor II
Rutgers, The State University of New Jersey
Bloustein School of Planning and Public Policy
New Brunswick, New Jersey

Veronica Stephens, RN, MSN, ANP-C
Captain, U.S. Public Health Service
Senior Advisor for Public Health and Emer-
 gency Preparedness
Office of Public Health Preparedness
Washington, DC

Kathleen Taranto, RN, MA
Vice President, Patient and Family Services
Fairview University Medical Center
Minneapolis, Minnesota

Donna L. Thompson, MSN, CRNP, CCCN
Continence Specialist
Fair Acres Geriatric Center
Lima, Pennsylvania

Linda Thompson, DrPH, RN, FAAN
Associate Professor and Associate Dean, Policy
 and Planning
University of Maryland School of Nursing
Baltimore, Maryland

**Theresa M. Thompson, RN, MSN, MA,
 CCRN**
PhD Candidate, Health Policy & Manage-
ment,
Bloomberg School of Public Health
Johns Hopkins University
Baltimore, Maryland

Eileen H. Toughill, RN, APN, C, PhD
Director Community Health
Visiting Nurse Association of Central Jersey
Red Bank, New Jersey

Nancy Valentine, RN, PhD, MPH, FAAN
Vice President/National Nursing Executive
CIGNA Health Care
Hartford, Connecticut

Linda M. Valentino, RN, MSN
Healthcare Consultant
New York, New York

Connie Vance, EdD, RN, FAAN
Professor
The College of New Rochelle School of Nurs-
ing
New Rochelle, New York

Anita Serdyn van der Merwe, PhD, RN, RM
Advisor
Federal Department of Nursing, Ministry of
  Health
Abu Dhabi
United Arab Emirates

Mary B. Wachter, MS, RN
Chief of Staff
New Jersey Department of Health and Senior
  Services
Trenton, New Jersey

Mary K. Wakefield, RN, PhD, FAAN
Director, Center for Rural Health
School of Medicine and Health Sciences
University of North Dakota
Grand Forks, North Dakota

Joanne Rains Warner, DNS, RN
Dean of Nursing
Indiana University East
Richmond, Indiana

**Rev. Carmen Warner-Robbins, MSN, RN,
  MDiv, FAAN**
Coordinating Chaplain
San Diego County Correctional Facilities for
  Women
Director and Founder
Welcome Home Ministries
Publishing Consultant and Motivational
  Speaker
Editor, Topics in Emergency Medicine
San Diego, California

Kathleen White, PhD, RN, CNAA, CMAC
Associate Professor and Director for Faculty
  Practice
Johns Hopkins University School of Nursing
Baltimore, Maryland

Catherine A. Wilson
Captain, Nurse Corps, United States Navy
Deputy Director
TRICARE Mid-Atlantic Region 2
Norfolk, Virginia

Steven J. Wyrsch, RN, MHA, FAHM, CHE
Commander, Nurse Corps, United States Navy
Senior Health Program Analyst
Office of the Assistant Secretary of Defense for
  Health Affairs, TRICARE Management Ac-
  tivity
Falls Church, Virginia

JoAnne M. Youngblut, PhD, RN, FAAN
Professor of Nursing and Coordinator of Re-
  search
Florida International University
School of Nursing
Miami, Florida

Donna Zazworsky, MS, RN, CCM, FAAN
Managing Partner, Case Manager Solutions,
  LLC
Director of Home Health and Outreach, St.
  Elizabeth of Hungary Clinic
Adjunct Clinical Assistant Professor,
University of Arizona
College of Nursing
Tucson, Arizona

Dedication

To the contributors to this book

&

All nurses who make a difference

Contents

Foreword, *xxv*
Marla Salmon

Preface, *xxvii*

Introduction, *xxxii*
Barbara Ehrenreich

Unit I

INTRODUCTION TO POLICY AND POLITICS IN NURSING AND HEALTH CARE

1 Policy and Politics: A Framework for Action, *1*
Diana J. Mason, Judith K. Leavitt, & Mary W. Chaffee

2 Pride in Our Past: Nursing's Political Roots, *19*
Sandra B. Lewenson

3 Learning the Ropes of Policy and Politics, *31*
Judith K. Leavitt, Mary W. Chaffee, & Connie Vance

Vignette
The Nurse In Washington Internship, *44*
Sharon A. Brigner & Kathleen T. Smith

Vignette
The White House Fellowship, *46*
Stephanie L. Ferguson

Vignette
Learning the Ropes as a Congressional Staffer, *51*
Catherine A. Wilson

4 Policy Development and Analysis, *55*
Barbara E. Hanley

5 Political Analysis and Strategies, *71*
Judith K. Leavitt, Sally S. Cohen, & Diana J. Mason

Vignette
Abottsford Community Health Center and Pennsylvania Politics, *87*
Melinda Jenkins

6 Communication Skills for Political Success, *93*
Mary W. Chaffee

POLICYSPOTLIGHT
ACHIEVING HEALTH LITERACY, *107*
Carole P. Jennings, Linda Thompson, & Darryl Roberts

7 Conflict Management, *113*
Alma Yearwood Dixon

8 Coalitions: A Powerful Political Strategy, *121*
Rebecca Rice

POLICYSPOTLIGHT
SUCCESS THROUGH UNITY: A COALITION'S EFFORTS TO EXPAND THE U.S. MILITARY HEALTH PROGRAM, *130*
Susan M. Schwartz & Mary W. Chaffee

Vignette
The International Nursing Coalition on Mass Casualty Education, *135*
Colleen Conway-Welch & Veronica Stephens

9 Research as a Political and Policy Tool, *141*
Donna Diers

10 Role of Media in Influencing Policy: Getting the Message Across, *157*
Diana J. Mason, Catherine J. Dodd, & Barbara Glickstein

Vignette
Free Media Coverage: Using Letters (Messages) to the Editor and Calls to Radio Talk Shows, *171*
Catherine J. Dodd

Vignette
The Nurse on a TV News Team, *172*
Donna Zazworsky

11 Ethical Issues in Health Care, Public
Policy, and Politics, *177*
Mary Cipriano Silva

Case Study
**Transforming Vision Into Reality: The
Vietnam Women's Memorial,** *185*
Diane Carlson Evans

UNIT II
HEALTH CARE DELIVERY
AND FINANCING

12 Organization and Delivery of Health
Care in the United States: A Patchwork
System, *201*
Janet Heinrich & Theresa M. Thompson

POLICYSPOTLIGHT
COULD A NATIONAL HEALTH SYSTEM WORK IN
THE UNITED STATES?, *214*
Kristine M. Gebbie

POLICYSPOTLIGHT
MANAGED CARE AND MENTAL HEALTH: A
MIXTURE OF OPTIMISM AND CAUTION, *218*
Beverly Malone & Shirley Smoyak

POLICYSPOTLIGHT
RACIAL AND ETHNIC DISPARITIES IN HEALTH
AND HEALTH CARE, *222*
Phyllis Cunningham

13 Health Economics, *229*
Susan K. Pfoutz, Sylvia A. Price, & Cyril F. Chang

14 Health Care Financing, *241*
Joyce A. Pulcini, Susan R. Neary, & Diane Feeney
Maloney

Vignette
**Managing Managed Care: A Nurse
Practitioner Response to Barriers to
Direct Third-Party Reimbursement,** *265*
Susan Kendig

POLICYSPOTLIGHT
MEDICARE AT THE CROSSROADS, *272*
Mary K. Wakefield

POLICYSPOTLIGHT
MEDICARE PAYMENT AND REIMBURSEMENT
POLICIES FOR NURSE ANESTHESIA PRACTICE,
276
Rita M. Rupp & John Garde

POLICYSPOTLIGHT
SOCIAL SECURITY: KEY TO ECONOMIC
SECURITY, *287*
Shirley S. Chater

POLICYSPOTLIGHT
COMPLEMENTARY THERAPIES:
REIMBURSEMENT ISSUES, *293*
Doris Milton

Case Study
**Rationing Health Care: The Oregon
Story,** *299*
Cecelia Capuzzi & Jeanne Bowden

UNIT III
POLICY AND POLITICS IN THE
WORKPLACE

15 Contemporary Issues in the Health
Care Workplace, *311*
Pamela F. Cipriano

Vignette
The Politics of Case Management, *319*
Toni G. Cesta

POLICYSPOTLIGHT
THE ANCC MAGNET RECOGNITION PROGRAM
AND MAGNET HOSPITALS, *324*
Linda Burnes Bolton & Crystal Bennett

Vignette
**Achieving Excellence in Nursing
Practice,** *328*
Carol Robinson

16 Creating Change in the Workplace, *333*
Joanne Disch & Kathie Taranto

Vignette
Why Change Efforts Fail, *345*
Beth W. Gering

Vignette

Dancing with the Chaos: A Grassroots Approach to Transformation and Healing, *347*
Jeanne Anselmo

POLICYSPOTLIGHT

REALITIES OF IMPLEMENTING CHANGE IN A HEALTH CARE ORGANIZATION, *354*
Nancy M. Valentine

Vignette

Family Presence at the Bedside during Invasive Procedures and CPR: When Pigs Fly, *356*
Dezra J. Eichorn, Theresa A. Meyers, Cathie E. Guzzetta, Angela P. Clark, & Amy O. Calvin

17 Politics of the Nursing Workforce, *363*
Christine Tassone Kovner

18 Future of Advanced Practice Nursing, *371*
Charlene M. Hanson

Vignette

Managed Care Mandated Coverage in Maine: A Grassroots Success Story, *379*
Patricia ("Patsy") Leavitt

19 Collective Action in Health Care, *387*
Mary E. Foley

20 Politics of Nursing Research, *399*
Dorothy Brooten, Linda P. Brown, Susan M. Miovech, & JoAnne M. Youngblut

Case Study

Needlestick Injuries in the Workplace: Implications for Public Policy, *412*
Karen A. Daley

UNIT IV
POLICY AND POLITICS IN GOVERNMENT

21 Contemporary Issues in Government, *421*
Mary K. Wakefield, Deborah B. Gardner, & Sharon E. Guillett

POLICYSPOTLIGHT

THE EPIDEMIC IN HEALTH CARE ERRORS: ONE GOVERNMENT AGENCY'S RESPONSE, *437*
Linda E. Moore

POLICYSPOTLIGHT

GENETIC ISSUES: GOVERNMENT RESPONSES AND NURSING IMPLICATIONS, *443*
Gwen Anderson

22 Legislative and Regulatory Processes, *451*
Yvonne Santa Anna

Vignette

Maryland's Nurse Practitioners: Lessons Learned during the 2001 Legislative Session, *462*
Nancy J. Sharp

Vignette

How Regulations are Shaped: The Rules of the Game, *467*
Judith Lorette & Catherine L. Jansto

23 Nursing and the Courts, *471*
Virginia Trotter Betts & David Keepnews

24 Local Government, *479*
Juanita V. Majewski & Marjory C. O'Brien

25 State Government: 50 Paths to Policy, *491*
Susan C. Reinhard

Vignette

Journey to the Wisconsin Legislature, *498*
Judy Biros Robson

Vignette

Influence of the Nursing Community on Mississippi's Tobacco Settlement Allocation, *505*
Kaye Bender

POLICYSPOTLIGHT

ROLE OF STATE BOARDS OF NURSING IN POLICY, *510*
Carolyn Hutcherson

26 The Federal Government, *515*
Kathleen M. White

Vignette
The Nurse as Member of Congress, *533*
The Honorable Lois Capps

Vignette
I Believed I Could Make a Difference, *536*
The Honorable Carolyn McCarthy

Vignette
Zapping Asthma: Atlanta Leads a National Health and Environmental Initiative, *538*
Pat Ford-Roegner

27 Political Appointments, *543*
Betty R. Dickson, Steven J. Wyrsch, & Mary W. Chaffee

28 Lobbying Policymakers: Individual and Collective Strategies, *551*
Melinda Mercer Ray & Shelagh Roberts

Vignette
Lobbying: An Inside View, *561*
Katie B. Horton

29 The American Voter and Nursing's Leadership in Political Campaigns, *565*
Candy Dato

Vignette
Campaign Management: Policy's Primary Prevention Strategy, *579*
Joanne Rains Warner

POLICYSPOTLIGHT
POLITICAL ACTIVITY OF GOVERNMENT-EMPLOYED NURSES, *583*
Tracy A. Malone & Mary W. Chaffee

Case Study
Pilgrim in Politics, *588*
Eve Franklin

UNIT V
POLICY AND POLITICS IN PROFESSIONAL ORGANIZATIONS

30 Contemporary Issues in Professional Organizations, *601*
Linda J. Shinn

31 You and Your Professional Organization, *609*
Pamela J. Haylock

Vignette
Getting to the Top: Martha Hill, President of the American Heart Association, *621*
Martha N. Hill & Peggy O'Neill Hewlett

32 The Power and Influence of Special Interest Groups in Health Care, *627*
Patrick S. Malone, Mary W. Chaffee, & Mary B. Wachter

Case Study
Political Action Case Studies: Nursing Organizations in Action, *639*

Introduction, *639*
Linda M. Valentino

Ensuring Nurses Are at the Policy Table: American Association of Occupational Health Nurses, *640*
Kae Livsey

Interdisciplinary Advocacy: American Society for Parenteral and Enteral Nutrition, *643*
Lynne M. Murphy & Beth Lyman

Advocacy for Clinical Nurse Specialists: National Association of Clinical Nurse Specialists, *644*
Jo Ellen Rust & Angela P. Clark

Promoting Pain Management By Influencing Policy: Oncology Nursing Society, *646*
Paula Trahan Rieger

Shaping a State's Screening Policy: Society of Gastroenterology Nurses and Associates, 648
Nancy S. Schlossberg

Collaboration, Communication, and Persistence Make a Difference: Wound Ostomy Continence Nurses Society, 650
Donna L. Thompson & Dorothy Doughty

United We Stand: NP Response to the AMA's Citizen's Petition, 654
Allison Beard

UNIT VI
POLICY AND POLITICS IN THE COMMUNITY

33 Where Policy Hits the Pavement: Contemporary Issues in Communities, *659*
Nancy Milio

POLICYSPOTLIGHT
SPOTLIGHT ON CHILD CARE POLICY MAKING, *669*
Sally S. Cohen

Vignette
Emergency Nurses CARE: Where the Rubber Meets the Road, *676*
Barbara Foley

Vignette
Transition from Incarceration: An Innovative Community Faith-Based Program for Women, *682*
Carmen Warner-Robbins & Mickey L. Parsons

34 Working with the Community for Change, *687*
Mary Ann Christopher, Judith L. Miller, Theresa L. Beck, & Eileen H. Toughill

Vignette
Environmental Health Policy: Environmental Justice, *696*
Lillian H. Mood

POLICYSPOTLIGHT
TURNING POINT: COLLABORATING FOR A NEW CENTURY IN PUBLIC HEALTH, *701*
Gloria R. Smith, Barbara J. Sabol, & Kay Randolph-Back

35 Nursing in the International Community, *711*
Judith A. Oulton

POLICYSPOTLIGHT
EMERGING INFECTIOUS DISEASES, *722*
Felissa R. Lashley

POLICYSPOTLIGHT
LICENSING AND REGULATION OF NURSES IN THE UNITED ARAB EMIRATES, *728*
Fatima Al Rifai & Anita Serdyn van der Merwe

Case Study
Environmental Advocacy: A Nurse's Journey, *735*
Holly Shaner McRae

APPENDIXES

A Glossary of Health, Policy, and Political Terms and Acronyms, *745*
Elizabeth M. Lehr

B Internships and Fellowships, *755*
Jeffrey P. O'Donnell

C Health Care, Health Policy, Political, Government, and Media Resources, *765*
Mary W. Chaffee & Nadine Jacobson

Foreword Marla Salmon

As the financial cost of health care continues to rise in this country, so does the human cost. Health care today is in significant disarray, with the ultimate consequence being compromised care for those who have access to it, and inadequate care for those who do not. Despite great concern in virtually every sector of society, we continue to tolerate a "system" of health care that denies formal access to over 40 million people and does not meet reasonable standards of quality, access, and cost for most others in the United States.

Health professionals are in a particularly difficult position with respect to health services. Most, if not all, professional groups have experienced the increasing challenges of living up to their commitments in environments that have become more complex and frustrating. What is clear is that we health professionals have not uniformly understood or sought to shape one of the single most significant determinants of human health, which is *public policy* (and its absence). Most of us ignore this determinant or, at best, see it as falling outside of the responsibilities of our professional roles.

There are likely very good explanations for this "blindness" to policy as an important health determinant. Our educational programs, which are increasingly overwhelmed with the task of keeping up with advancements in health sciences, place policy in a relatively minor or invisible position. Faculty themselves may not understand the role of policy in health or their role in its development and execution. Professional organizations are challenged to act in the absence of action or support from their members. The overall decline of participation in civil society has created a broader sense of indifference to the political process. However, regardless of the origins of our blindness to the relationship between policy and our work, it is clear that we health professionals have too often operated on the assumption that it was someone else's responsibility to provide a context within which each of us could do the real work of caring and healing.

The days of comfort and complacency for health professionals are over. Almost every health professional organization is calling for major reform in health services delivery. Furthermore, for patients, families and communities, the sense of helplessness and frustration continues to grow. It is, in every way, an optimal time for nurses and other health professionals to assume responsibility—in partnership with those they serve—for aggressively managing policy as a determinant of health and creating a health system whose outcome is the effective and efficient provision of services to all in need.

The challenge, of course, is how does one proceed toward this goal? Where does the health professional turn when seeking to shape policy? Nursing is in an opportune position with respect to policy and politics. The presence of nurses as the single largest category of health professionals, the trust that people place in them, and their connections to people and communities all position nurses to play significant roles in shaping health through constructive policy. The profession of nursing and its members have only begun to tap their potential to not only shape but to lead in the enhancement of health through effective social and health policy. There is a great need for the development of skills that support policy development and political action.

Fortunately, for nursing and other health professionals, there are resources that can help develop the capacity to shape policy. Key among these is this book, *Policy & Politics in Nursing and Health Care*. It is a rich compendium that serves as resource, guide and even inspiration. Now in its fourth edition, this book reflects the exceptional vision and expertise of its editors and contributors, who are masters in the practice of health policy. Diana Mason, Judy Leavitt, and Mary Chaffee together provide a clear and actionable framework for nurses and other health professionals, regardless of career stage, and the more than 100 contributors in the book bring to life a rich array of exemplars, strategy, knowledge and wisdom only possible through great depth of expertise and experience. Together, the editors and contributors have produced an authentic book that is uniquely valuable and should be in the library of anyone who desires to improve health through policy.

In short, health professionals and their ability to enhance health through policy will be well served by tapping into the rich resources found in this book. I strongly recommend you begin reading and discover how you can make a difference.

Dr. Marla Salmon is Professor and Dean, Nell Hodgson Woodruff School of Nursing, and Professor, Rollins School of Public Health, Emory University. Formerly, she was Director of the Division of Nursing, U.S. Department of Health and Human Services.

Preface

"Never doubt that a small group of thoughtful, committed citizens can change the world. Indeed, it is the only thing that ever has."

MARGARET MEAD

This is the fourth edition of *Policy & Politics in Nursing and Health Care*. We would like to think that the previous editions have had an effect on nurses' political savvy and involvement in policy matters. However, this is "the winter of our discontent" as a worsening nursing shortage clouds many nurses' enthusiasm for their work and the profession. We have had to pause and reflect on, "Why a fourth edition?"

Certainly, we know many nurses who have developed and used their political and policy skills to transform practice and public policies, and some of them have contributed to this edition of the book. Consider the following examples:

- Theresa Meyers, Dezra Eichhorn, and Cathie Guzzetta have been changing hospital policies on the role of family members during codes and invasive procedures. These nurses bring vision, courage, a desire to take risks, and political skill to this challenge, and they *are* making a difference in the ways nurses practice, the care that patients and families receive, and helping hospitals to move beyond the rhetoric of family-centered care.
- Veronica Stephens played a significant leadership role in the aftermath of the September 2001 terrorist attacks on the United States, coordinating health and medical disaster response at the national level as a staff member of the Office of Emergency Preparedness. She was subsequently selected to serve in the newly created Office of Public Health Preparedness.
- As of 2002, three nurses are serving in Congress. Congresswomen Lois Capps, Carolyn McCarthy, and Eddie Bernice Johnson are championing policies to promote the health of the nation and ensure the future of nursing. Johnson is chair of the 107th Congressional Black Caucus.
- Marla Salmon serves on the Board of Trustees of the Robert Wood Johnson Foundation, the largest health care foundation in the world, which actively shapes health and health care through its funding priorities and projects.
- Once the chief of staff for former Senate Majority Leader and presidential candidate Robert Dole, Sheila Burke is a member of MedPac, an independent federal commission that advises the nation on Medicare policy.
- Mary Wakefield not only served on MedPac with Burke but is a member of the Institute of Medicine's Quality of Health Care in America Commission. She was instrumental in getting issues such as nurses staffing as priorities for future research into the Institute of Medicine's 1999 report, *To Err Is Human: Building a Safer Health System.*
- As the Director of Emergency Response for the International Rescue Committee, Gerald Martone works daily to define and deliver relief services to people around the world who have been devastated by war and other disasters.
- Rhetaugh Dumas was appointed to the President's Commission on Bioethics during a time when the nation is struggling with the myriad ethical issues arising in medicine and health care.
- Ruth Watson Lubic's work on developing childbirthing and family centers in underserved communities has received national recognition. She was awarded the prestigious Institute of Medicine's Gustav Leinhard Award and the so-called "genius award" from the John and Catherine T. MacArthur Foundation.
- Janet Heinrich frequently testifies before Congress as the Director for Healthcare–Public

Health Issues for the U.S. Government Accounting Office.
- Linda Aiken, Julie Sochalski, and Peter Buerhaus are some of the leading nurse researchers, providing data on the nursing workforce that is shaping professional, societal, and institutional responses to the shortage. Their research has been published in such influential journals as *Health Affairs* and the *Journal of the American Medical Association.*
- Clair Rosse recognized that 3% to 5% of all enrollees in health plans account for 60% of the plan's costs. She knew these enrollees needed intensive case management by nurses, and founded Future Health, a company that in 2000 improved the health of chronically ill patients, provided cost savings of 5% to 25% to health plans, employed 60 nurses, had $5.5 million in revenues, and demonstrated that nurses have the answers to our nation's ailing health care system.

These and so many other contemporary nurses are improving the lives of people, the places where nurses work, and the health of the nation through skillful political action and influencing the development and implementation of policy.

Why did it take the events of September 11, 2001 for the United States to realize nursing is an important national resource? Why must nursing continue to fight for a place at policy tables, whether in the workplace or government? While we can argue that nursing has long struggled to be an equal player in a world that continues to devalue women and the work that is done largely by women, the collective of nursing remains a "sleeping giant," or as Senator Edward Kennedy wrote in the first edition of this book, "an untapped resource."

One of the premises of each edition of this book is that collective action is almost always essential for truly transformational change. Certainly, each of us as individuals can and must use our political skills to make changes in our workplaces and communities. Patient care is a political endeavor, and failure to recognize it as such will relegate practicing nurses to playing the role of powerless discontents, a role we should not and must not accept. However, individual effort is rarely sufficient for moving the

profession forward and promoting the health of the nation. Even on an inpatient hospital unit, a cohesive, proactive group of staff nurses can provide the kind of savvy clinical leadership that will ensure job satisfaction, high-quality patient care, and collaborative practice arrangements with physicians and other providers.

Who is the collective? It is each of us, working together with vision and courage, ready to be creative and bold with ideas and strategies that will move mountains if need be. It is each of us when we feel vitalized and enriched by mutual support and learning from each other.

So, we bring you the fourth edition of this book, with the intention and hope that it will embolden readers as individuals and as members of a collective. We have no doubts about the value of nursing to this nation. We are driven to strategic action by a vision of professional nursing as a precious resource that is essential for the health of individuals, families and communities. We invite you to share our vision and join us in turning it into reality.

WHAT'S NEW

This book has evolved significantly since the first edition was published in 1985. While building on the vital foundational content of previous editions, this latest edition includes many exciting new topics, new contributors, and new sections. The fourth edition has been designed to reflect how the practice of nursing, health care in the United States, and society have changed, and what the policy and political implications of those changes are for nurses.

An important goal of this book always has been to provide nurses with the tools needed to be effective in political activity and policy making, especially as novices. We recognize that nurses who have made forays into the political world now need more than just the building blocks. This edition provides both content on the fundamentals *and* more content to encourage nurses to think analytically about the problems they face and how to develop strategies to resolve them.

Readers will find these changes in the fourth edition:

- The unit *Policy and Politics in the Workplace* is greatly expanded in recognition of the importance of nurses being proactive and politically astute in bringing about the much-needed changes in health care organizations. Either we transform these workplaces or we will continue to struggle with a nursing shortage and the issue of how to ensure that patients and families receive the care they need.
- There is more content on issues related to regulation and reimbursement of advanced practice nurses, an area that demands the most sophisticated political savvy as organized medicine continues to oppose further gains by advanced practice nurses and works to roll back what has been achieved in policy arenas.
- We heard from novice nurses, their teachers, and their mentors that we should bring back the chapter on *Learning the Ropes* that appeared in the second edition of the book. We have done so with a fresh new perspective and added a chapter on communication skills for political success.
- Over the past decade, nurses have been admonished that a lack of knowledge about health care financing and economics limits their potential to be leaders in various policy arenas. While the third edition of the book addressed this issue, we have revised the chapters on these topics and added policy discussions of the important health care financing issues of the times, such as Medicare, Social Security, and reimbursement of complementary therapies.
- In addition to *Vignettes* and *Case Studies,* we've added new sections called *Policy Spotlights* that explore contemporary health policy issues in depth, including patient and workplace safety, racial and ethnic disparities in health and health care, the rising use of alternative and complementary therapies, mental health parity, advances in genetics, child care, environmental issues, global policy on infectious diseases, and health literacy.
- To provide models of success, we've added more *Vignettes,* stories that illuminate the remarkable accomplishments of nurses who have faced obstacles, taken the path less traveled, developed politically astute strategies, and made powerful differences in the lives of others.
- To provide rapid access to the meaning of terms that may be new to some readers, we have included a glossary of policy and political terms as an appendix.
- The Internet has exploded since the previous edition of the book was published. To put our readers in touch with the rich pool of electronic information now available, we've added an extensive appendix of Internet resources on nursing, health policy, and politics.
- Recognizing the major role the U.S. military plays in the delivery of health care and as a major employer of nurses, we've added content about the military health system

American nurses are a diverse group. As with previous editions, we've invited contributors who reflect the profession's diversity in terms of geography, ethnicity, gender, political affiliation, practice setting, and position. We did not ask them to write with only one style or level in mind; instead, we wanted to provide a resource that students and nurses would enjoy reading while learning the basics of policy making and the political process. At the same time, we have included in-depth analyses of policy issues to meet the needs of those nurses with advanced knowledge and expertise. We wanted a book that speaks to nurses, in all practice settings, and at all educational and experiential levels.

USING THE BOOK

The book is organized to provide the reader with a framework for exploring policy and politics and the application of the content in the four spheres of nurses live: the workplace, government, professional organizations, and community. Unit 1, *Policy and Politics: A Nursing Perspective,* provides the context. The introductory chapter outlines the framework for the relationship of policy and politics. The subsequent chapters in Unit 1 explore the fundamentals of the policy process and political analysis and strategy development. These include how to "learn the ropes" and how to influence policy through communication, conflict management, coalitions, the media and research. The case study of the Vietnam Women's Memorial reflects how these fundamental concepts were used to make the vision of this monument a reality. As with the other units, it is interspersed with first person stories of nurses whose experiences illustrate the didactic content.

Unit 2, *Health Care Delivery and Financing,* explores the larger health care delivery system, the basics of financing that system, and the economics of health care. Policy issues like Medicare, Social Security, mental health, and the disparities in our system are explored. There are analyses of how our financing mechanisms do and do not support reimbursement of advanced practice nurses as well as the use of complementary therapies. The unit concludes with an updated version of the case study on nurses' involvement in shaping Oregon's health care system that has appeared in previous editions of the book. It is a fine example of how nurses can be key players in developing innovative models for health care delivery and financing.

Unit 3, *Policy and Politics in the Workplace,* begins the application of generic concepts to the specific spheres of policy and political influence. The workplace is the first sphere discussed to emphasize the importance of nurses' recognizing the political nature of patient care and their everyday work. Unit 4 applies the concepts to the sphere of government; Unit 5, to professional organizations; and Unit 6, to the community, including the global community. Each of these focused units begins with a discussion of contemporary issues and trends in the sphere, and a case study illustrating the concepts presented. The reader should note that although these units are separated according to sphere, the four spheres overlap. Indeed for nurses to be effective in one sphere, this interplay must be recognized and exploited.

There are three appendixes. The first is a glossary of terms to enhance learning about the language of policy. The second is an updated synopsis of internship and fellowship opportunities to assist nurses who want to continue to develop their knowledge and skills in policy and politics. The last is a comprehensive list of electronic resources to enhance the reader's opportunity for up-to-the-minute information about policy and political issues. We encourage all readers to take advantage of the Internet resource list in the appendices. Use these sites for the latest developments on the issues discussed in the book.

As noted above, this book is designed to be used by nurses anywhere on the continuum of novice to expert in political and policy matters. Of course, one could read the book from start to finish, but we know that how the book is used depends upon the reader and context of its use. For example, many nurses seek out the vignettes first, finding these personal stories of political struggles engaging and enlightening. Nurses who are interested in developing a strategy for change in the workplace might start with that unit, whereas nurses who are learning the ropes of governmental politics might start with the government unit.

As a textbook in undergraduate or graduate courses, the organization of the book can serve as an outline for a course on policy and politics. The book also can be used in courses on trends and issues, foundations of nursing, leadership and community health. Perhaps the best use of the book by schools of nursing is as a foundational text that stays with the student throughout the curriculum, with readings assigned even in clinical courses. Consider, for example, the unit *Policy and Politics in the Workplace.* Nursing students in their first medical-surgical nursing course could study select readings from this unit, then identify and analyze a clinical issue that nurses on their assigned clinical unit have been instrumental in changing. Once students are in the senior leadership course, they will be ready to expand their readings on politically astute change and use this information and their prior clinical experience to develop a change project in the clinical setting.

We encourage professional nursing organizations, including members of legislative committees and political action committees, to use the book as a guide for how to expand their influence. Furthermore, we challenge nurses working in a hospital or other health care organization to use the book to develop strategies to transform their immediate work environment for themselves and their patients.

ACKNOWLEDGMENTS

As with previous editions, one of the remarkable features of this book is the large number of contributors who have donated their time, energy, and expertise to further nurses' political development. Over 100 nurses participated in writing this edition. They are all extraordinarily busy people, yet they graciously responded to our pressures for meeting tight deadlines and collaborating with us to shape the book into a progressive contribution to the nursing literature. We're indebted to them for their commitment to this project. As with the previous two editions of the book, we and the publisher, Reed Elsevier, are sponsoring an annual scholarship on behalf of the contributors for a nurse to attend the Nurses In Washington Internship.

The book is also a reflection of the work of original coeditor Susan Talbott and the contributors to previous editions who helped establish the book's preeminence in the field. We continue to be grateful for their contributions.

Books require a team of people who often never appear in the table of contents but who are crucial to the production of a quality publication. First, you would not be reading this book right now if Beth Lehr, our phenomenal editorial manager, had not kept us on track. We continue to be indebted to our publisher Elsevier Science and our Executive Editor Michael Ledbetter for their support for educating nurses about policy development and political action not only through this book, but also through cosponsoring the NIWI scholarship. We are also indebted to the entire editorial and production team at Elsevier Science, especially our Project Manager Clay Broeker; Lisa Newton; and Lisa Neumann.

When we set out to produce this edition, Judy and Diana knew we needed a fresh perspective and lots of help, and Mary Chaffee provided these assets and more. The three of us embrace the perspective that the process is as important as the product and that the product will be better if the process is collaborative and creative. We are indebted to each other as good colleagues and friends who are committed to nursing and to a vision we believe can be prodded along through commitment, perseverance, creative thinking, laughter, good wine and food (and special thanks to Betty Dickson for that Southern Thanksgiving dinner), and mutual support. Our families and friends sustain us, and so we each have personal acknowledgments to add:

James Ware has been my partner, my daily support, and nurturer of both me and my work. I am grateful for his understanding of the special perspectives that nurses and women have on life and living. Also, my apologies to Billy for walks deferred and bones forgotten.

Diana J. Mason
New York, New York

As in previous editions, it has been my family and dear friends who have sustained me, nurtured me, and believed in the vision that this book conveys. My sons Noah and David, my newfound daughter Helen, my dear sister Joan Podkul and her family, my Dad who was my first mentor in policy and politics, and the memory of my husband of 31 years all showed me through their support and caring that this book is a legacy that must be shared if nurses are to become leaders in health policy. The Mississippi Posse, who are some of the smartest, most politically accomplished nurses I have ever met, kept me laughing by providing a perspective on what is most important in life—our relationships and the commitment we have to others. No one could have exemplified that more than my dear friend, Betty Dickson.

Judith K. Leavitt
Brandon, Mississippi

This book changed my life—twice; first as a graduate student discovering a challenging new professional path, and again when Diana and Judy invited me to join them in editing this edition. This has been a remarkable journey. Judy called this book a labor of love, and that is indeed an accurate assessment.

Many thanks to my family for their patience and support. My children, Thomas, Sandra and Christopher, generously shared their Mom with this book. For the support, comic relief, lunch therapy, and enthusiasm that kept me going during the gestation of this book, my gratitude goes to Joan Bold, Beth Gering, George Zangaro, Mike Donnelly, Dr. Warren Jones, Dr. Nancy Valentine, Dr. Don Arthur, Kathleen Smith, and Karolyn Klepacki Ryan.

I've learned critical leadership skills as a Navy Nurse—to take professional risks to improve patient care, to focus constantly on the development and growth of others, to build teams that can accomplish the impossible, to be persistent in the face of obstacles, and to be an advocate for others. These have served me well on this editorial odyssey.

Finally, thank you to Diana and Judy, my friends and mentors. My respect and admiration for you is immense! Your leadership and commitment to American nursing is indeed a powerful force, and I have truly been blessed to work with you.

Mary W. Chaffee
Washington, DC

Introduction Barbara Ehrenreich

The Emergence of Nursing as a Political Force

Fantasize for a moment about what it would be like if nursing were to emerge as a political force commensurate with its role in patient care. Can you imagine this headline? "White House Delays Medicare Reform to Meet with Key Nursing Leaders." Or a headline saying, "Nurses Denounce Pharmaceutical Company Profiteering—Stock Market Plunges." Or even the headline, "Nursing Organization Deprives Six Major Medical Schools of Accreditation—Inadequate Emphasis on Preventive Care Cited."

Of course, these are only fantasies. Nursing, 30 years after the revival of feminism in the 1970s and still a largely female profession, has not emerged as a political force. When it takes stands on major issues such as the need for expanded health insurance coverage, it is for the most part ignored by political leaders and the media. Sociologists still define nursing as a "semiprofession," and the public is apparently so unappreciative of nursing's role that some nurses have taken to displaying bumper stickers that say "Kiss a Nurse" or "Love a Nurse." Even feminists often have a low opinion of nursing. When the daughter of one of my feminist activist friends declared that she wanted to be a nurse when she grows up, my friend responded to her: "A nurse? Why not go all the way and be a doctor?" In part because of nursing's image as a subordinate—and largely silent—profession, fewer young people of either gender are opting for it as a career, and the result is a potentially calamitous national shortage of nurses.

The relatively powerless status of nursing should be alarming not only to nurses, but to anyone who is concerned about health policy. The low status of nursing in this country is, I will argue, one of the reasons why we have such a frantically profit-oriented, fragmented, deeply inequitable, two-class health care system. Consumer activists for better and more affordable health care need to under-stand that the problem of reforming the health care system is very much connected to the problem of changing the status of nursing and making it a more pivotal and influential profession. I think this becomes clear when we look at today's situation from an historical perspective.

From the point of view of nursing, we could divide the history of medicine in the last hundred or so years into two phases. The first could be called "Putting Nurses in Their Place," and the second, covering recent decades, could be called "Taking That Place Away." In both stages, the losers have been not only nurses and the nursing profession but women and health care consumers in general.

To sweep quickly through a little history of medicine and nursing, before there was a male medical profession in this country, and well into the nineteenth century, there was a long tradition of female lay healing, with roots in European and African cultures. In North America, the female lay healer was the prime health care giver for ordinary people until well into the nineteenth century. Typically, she was not formally educated person but learned her skills from other female healers, skills such as midwifery, the use of herbal remedies, even bone setting. In the female lay healing tradition, knowledge and skills were seen as a gift to be shared with other people, as part of one's responsibility as a community member. Well into the twentieth century, for example, African-American lay midwives in the rural south entered that occupation in response to receiving a call from God instructing them to serve their communities.

As forerunners of the nursing profession, two things stand out about early America's lay healers. First, they were autonomous healers, functioning independently of the few doctors and hospitals that existed. Second, their position as healers was sometimes connected to their leadership roles in the general community. Harriet Tubman, for example, who led so many slaves to freedom via the underground railroad, was also well known for her healing skills. Two centuries earlier, Anne Hutchinson, the religious dissident who fled Massachusetts to help found Rhode Island, was an accomplished midwife. In fact, her reputation as a midwife helped attract a female following for her unconventional view that women could communicate directly with the deity, without the mediation of a husband or male minister.

However, this proud tradition of female lay healing was crushed by the emergence of the almost entirely male medical profession in the late nineteenth and early twentieth centuries. In addition to gender, the big difference between the male medical profession and the female lay healers, was not, at that point, that doctors were more skilled or more scientific; this was an era when the very idea of scientific-based medicine was still considered revolutionary by many doctors. There was, however, a very profound economic difference between the lay healers and the emerging medical profession. The doctors saw healing as a commodity, something to be bought and sold, while the lay healers had tended to see it as a service intertwined with one's general obligations to the community (Ehrenreich & English, 1978). A traditional lay midwife, for example, often moved in with a family to help care for the new baby and other children while the mother recovered, and no one expected her to charge by the day or the hour. Doctors, in contrast, focused on dramatic interventions such as surgery—or, in the heroic days of old, bleeding and leeches—that could command a considerable fee; they did not have much interest in the mundane and time-consuming details of human care. In state after state, the doctors' lobbied to outlaw lay healers and midwives, whom they had come to see as competitors.

The emerging medical profession's emphasis on medicine as a commodity split the older conception of healing into two parts, which we could call, without judging the efficacy of either: *curing* and *caring*. The former, meaning at least the attempt to cure, was easier to measure and treat as a commodity, and easier, too, to construe as a bold and masculine undertaking, while the latter seemed to be something that women or servants had always done for their families. With its emphasis on dramatic interventions for payment, the medical profession also implicitly turned away from the many patients who could not pay their professional fees. Right from the start then, the male medical profession introduced two unfortunately persistent aspects of American medicine: its emphasis on sickness as opposed to health and prevention, and its unequal accessibility to people of different income levels.

Modern nursing arose as an effort on the part of women reformers to help clean up the mess the male doctors were making—and I mean this fairly literally. It was nurses, or rather some of the founders of nursing, who can take credit for introducing the first bar of soap to Bellevue Hospital. Strangely, the doctors, who had not yet accepted the germ theory of disease, had never noticed the absence of soap. However, instead of being grateful, the doctors were terrified that nursing might represent a new source of competition, the female lay healers reincarnate. Beginning in the late nineteenth century and continuing into the twentieth, the medical profession campaigned vigorously to put nursing in its place, or what they thought was its place. As an example of the mentality of the medical profession at that time, in 1901 the *Journal of the American Medical Association* reported with alarm that the nurse is "often conceited and too unconscious of the due subordination she owes to the medical profession of which she is a sort of useful parasite" (The unsentimental nurse, 1901). They opposed what they deemed "excessive" education for nurses, and carried on what Jo Ann Ashley described in *Hospitals, Paternalism, and the Role of the Nurse* (1976) as a concerted campaign to keep the status of nursing low, and against the introduction of higher education in nursing. In 1906 the *Journal of the American Medical Association* editorialized that, "Every attempt at initiative on the part of nurses should be reproved by the physician or the hospital administration" (Nurses' schools and illegal practice of medicine, 1906).

The campaign to keep nursing in "its place" fit in well with the medical profession's ideas about women in general. Well into the twentieth century the medical profession pretty much defined *female-*

ness as a disease; menarche was seen as a physiologic crisis, pregnancy as a disability, menstruation as an illness, menopause as a terminal disorder. Much of the medical view of women rested on the supposedly scientific theory that the human body contained only so much energy and if one body part was used too much, energy would drain from all the other parts. For men, this meant that they should not indulge in sex too much because it would drain energy away from their brains, energy which should be saved for achieving higher positions such as physician or general. For women, the opposite inference was drawn; if a woman used her brain too much, she would drain energy away from the reproductive organs on which she should be concentrating. In the late 1870s a Harvard medical professor wrote a book in which he used this "conservation of energy" theory to prove "scientifically" that higher education would cause women's' uteri to atrophy (Clarke, 1873).

Nursing, then, could not require education, only training. For the most part, doctors saw it as an instinctual activity, much as they saw women's appropriate passivity and docility as "natural" or instinctual traits. As femininity was being defined, not only by the doctors but in the larger culture, it could not coexist with things like intellect and initiative. Furthermore, because nursing was what the medical profession called an "essentially womanly task," nursing had to be especially passive, docile and obedient.

These theories about women and nurses in particular served the interests of the medical profession. Medical propaganda about women in general served to reinforce the idea that women as health care consumers should be passive, dependent, and unquestioning. At the same time, these theories discouraged women from seeking higher education, including medical education. They also had a more direct consequence for health care, effectively silencing for many decades the one voice from within the health care system that might have challenged the unrestrained commercialism and sexism of the medical profession—namely, the voice of nursing.

Moving on to phase two of this brief, historical perspective, after nursing was put in its place, that place was taken away. In this phase, which stretches roughly from the end of World War II to the present, we can no longer blame everything on the medical profession. Much larger corporate and bureaucratic forces have appeared on the scene to shake the health care system—or perhaps it should be referred to more narrowly as the *medical* system. First the medical schools and their affiliated teaching hospitals displaced the individual doctor as the center of the medical delivery system; then health maintenance organizations and insurance companies took center stage as the arbiters of who gets what sorts of care. To this picture we should add the pharmaceutical and medical equipment corporations that today increasingly define the nature of health care. About 200 years ago, health care was largely seen as a community service; today it is a multinational industry.

We have of course, seen tremendous advances in medical technology compared to the era of the female lay healer, but these have come at a considerable cost. For one thing, the medical system continually slights preventive care, which is neither commercially nor technologically interesting to many of the corporate interests that dominate medical care. Furthermore, not only the poor, but increasing numbers of middle class people, a total of almost 50 million Americans, are uninsured and hence often barred from medical care. Even insured people cannot easily keep up with skyrocketing medical costs, which do not reflect high salaries for the average health care worker, of course, but profiteering by those who dominate what has been called our "medical industrial complex." That domination has come at the expense of holistic health care for the individual patient whose medical contacts are increasingly restricted to machines and the technicians who operate them.

One example of this last point is a case of what seems like lunacy of the kind that is appearing in our corporate-dominated, machine-centered medical system. This is the introduction of fetal monitoring equipment as a routine part of obstetric care. Even obstetric leaders are willing to admit that they do not have the knowledge and experience to interpret every change that can be detected by fetal monitoring machines, and that the result of their use has been an alarming increase in cesarean sections. More to the point, this technology can do nothing to alleviate the major causes of infant mortality in this country, which are decidedly low-tech problems like poor maternal nutrition and the lack of prenatal care, especially in the wake of the Medicaid cuts that have come with welfare "reform." However, fetal monitoring as a multimillion-dollar business, is an example of what happens when corporations whose primary interest is profits define the nature of health care.

I am not just repeating the familiar line that professional nurses are "underutilized." In fact, I think that is a terrible expression because it implies that the solution is to "use" nurses more effectively, and as I look at it nurses have been used in various ways for long enough. The problem goes far deeper than anything the word "utilization" can encompass. To put it rather starkly, we have at this point a medical system that has become in some ways so distorted, so remote from human care, that the one potential generalist within it, the one person concerned with health caring in some sort of holistic sense—that is, the professional nurse—is an endangered species within it. Extinction is not imminent, but it has been the tendency over the last few decades. This is tragic, not just for nursing as a profession, but for the consumers of health care, because the only health system deserving of the name would be one oriented to health rather than sickness, one that is human centered rather than profit or machine centered, and this would have to be a health system in which nurses, as the last group of generalists, are not a subordinate or peripheral occupation but the central and leading one.

Conversely, the only kind of health care system in which nursing will have any possibility of achieving its full potential will be one in which health care is a right of all people, not a commodity for sale to those who can afford it. In a truly health-centered system, things like health education, prevention, and even environmental activism, which are now seen as peripheral to medicine, would be given top priority. However, to get to such a health system, nursing will have to emerge as a political force, and that will take much more than bumper stickers and an occasional conference on political activism in nursing. I think that if we comprehend the full horror of the situation that we now face—a medical system with no place for nursing and less and less place for human values—we can see that the solution involves nothing less than redefining in important ways what we mean by professional nursing.

We must include political activism and political commitment as part of the definition of nursing as a profession, and by political activism I mean something broader than lobbying alone. The professional activist nurse is not one who just happens to be concerned (a sort of bumper-sticker approach) and not one who happens to be a changed agent, but one who considers her or himself as a professional agent of change. This is the challenge I offer to the leaders of nursing—to assume a broader leadership role on behalf of the public as well as the nursing profession. If you accept that challenge, it will mean redefining the professional nurse as an activist, an advocate, and a risk taker, and this would have all kinds of implications for nursing education. For one thing, there would be more emphasis on recruiting people who are older than college age and already have experience with the health system (as parents, for example), community activists, and people who know what it is like to be at the bottom of the health care system whether as a health worker or a consumer. For another thing it means that professional nursing education must be cleared of the detritus of all the years in which the medical profession tried to put nursing in its place. Nursing students deserve a rigorous education not only in subjects like biochemistry and pharmacology, but also in subjects like the political economy of health systems, environmental hazards, women's studies, the history of social movements, and the techniques and strategies of political organizing.

If nursing is to take on a more visionary and activist role, nursing's professional organizations must be willing to back up and support activist nurses who are fired or get into trouble one way or another for their efforts, and there are many such activists in the rank and file. In addition, professional organizations should be willing to put themselves on the line on every issue that affects peoples' health and that goes beyond health issues as we narrowly define them—issues such as environmental degradation, occupational health and safety, welfare reform, even disarmament and peacekeeping. No issue is too large for the purview of organized nursing as the last group of generalists within our medical system.

Of course, those who profit from the current approach to health care will respond to such increased activism on the part of nurses by saying: "Well, that's not professional behavior, that's troublemaking." I hope that you'll have the determination to answer back: "Well, for the time being, troublemaking is our profession."

REFERENCES

Ashley, J.A. (1976). *Hospitals, paternalism, and the role of the nurse.* New York: Teachers College.

Clarke, E.H. (1873; reprint 1972). *Sex in education, or a fair chance for the girls.* Boston: James R. Osgood (reprint by Arno Press).

Ehrenreich, B. and English D. (1978). *For her own good—150 years of the experts' advice to women.* New York: Anchor Books.

Nurses' schools and illegal practice of medicine. (1906). *Journal of the American Medical Association, XLVII,* 1835.

The unsentimental nurse. (1901). *Journal of the American Medical Association, XXXVII,* 13.

ACKNOWLEDGMENT

This was originally published as "The Purview of Political Action" in *The Emergence of Nursing as a Political Force,* published by the National League for Nursing, 1978. Permission to reprint was granted by Jones & Bartlett Publishers, and it was updated for this book edition.

Dr. Barbara Ehrenreich is the author of 10 books, including Witches, Midwives, and Nurses: A History of Women Healers *(with Dierdre English) and* Nickled and Dimed—On (Not) Getting By in America. *She holds a PhD in biology, is the recipient of several prestigious writing awards, and is a frequent contributor to* Time, Harper's Magazine, The New Republic, The Nation, *and* The New York Times Magazine.

chapter 1

Policy and Politics: A Framework for Action

DIANA J. MASON

JUDITH K. LEAVITT

MARY W. CHAFFEE

"We must become the change we want to see."

GHANDI

On September 11, 2001, the health care and policy priorities for the United States changed abruptly. The terrorist attacks on the World Trade Center and the Pentagon, and the crash of another hijacked plane in Pennsylvania, led to one of the largest numbers of mass casualties in a single day in the history of the United States. Nurses provided emergency care at each site and continued to care for severely injured survivors and for the friends and families of those who died in the attacks.

However, an escalating shortage of professional nurses strained the capacity of health care centers in Washington and New York. At a major burn unit in New York City responsible for the highest caseload of patients with severe burns, the nursing staff was augmented by nurses from other parts of the country who were part of an emergency response program. It became apparent the country's ability to sustain an effective response to disaster or war would be reduced because of the shortage.

Before September 11, 2001, the media had been reporting on a national nursing shortage that was predicted to cripple the nation's health care system. Legislation to provide financial support for the education of new nurses and to improve workplace safety was introduced in Congress, but movement on these bills was glacial. It took a national disaster in the form of the September 11 events to move policymakers to action. A few weeks later, U.S. Department of Health and Human Services Secretary Tommy Thompson announced that $24.7 million would be allocated primarily to nursing education in recognition of the importance of nurses to the nation's preparedness.

Most nurses and other health providers feel the effect of the shortage of nurses. Nurses have protested large caseloads, mandatory overtime, replacement of nurses with poorly trained substitutes, and chaos in the workplace, but with only minimal progress. It took a national disaster to elicit real action.

The terror attacks caused a shift in American attitudes, including a recognition that perhaps our true heroes are police officers, firefighters, first responders, and health care providers (including nurses), rather than rock stars and basketball players. The attacks illuminated the vital work done by nurses when the nation was most in need. But without the impact of the terror attacks to focus policymakers' attention on the nursing shortage, where would nursing be today? Could the nursing community have influenced policymakers to achieve the same results? Are there enough nurses who recognize the importance of political activity in achieving a profession's goals?

Patient care is indeed a political endeavor—one that is influenced by policies developed at all levels of government and by the private sector, including

1

health care institutions. Yet far too few nurses view care through this lens. They therefore fail to see the vital role they can play in finding remedies to existing problems. If nurses recognize the benefits of understanding the political and policy-making processes, they can take action in an organized, strategic, and knowledgeable way. Lack of this perspective may jeopardize patient care, lead nurses to leave their jobs or, worse, lead nurses to remain in their jobs with little passion or commitment to improving their lives and the care of their patients.

As the United States quickly learned, there is too much at stake not to act. We cannot wait for another major disaster or terrorist attack to propel nursing's issues onto the public's agenda—issues such as improving nurses' work environments and establishing nurse/patient ratios that permit the humanistic care of people and adequate opportunity for patient teaching and prevention efforts.

As Dr. Barbara Ehrenreich writes in the introduction to this book, society and the nursing profession will benefit if nurses take on the roles of visionary activists and advocates. The number of nurses suggests that nurses have tremendous potential for shaping the health care values, policies, and politics of their communities and nation. What if:

- All nurses contacted their legislators during Nurses Week to encourage them to vote for legislation that would provide scholarships for anyone who wants to become a nurse and can't afford the cost of education?
- All nurses met in their workplaces to discuss leading the institution in recommitting to values of caring and changing policies to support these values?
- Nursing, rather than law, was the predominant professional background of members of Congress?
- The Secretary of the U.S. Department of Health and Human Services was a nurse?
- Every state legislature had a cadre of nurse-legislators?
- The media routinely covered major nurses' conferences and sought out nurses for expert commentary on health care issues?
- Nurses refused to work in hospitals that had not achieved magnet status or that were not

committed to creating the kind of professional work environment for nurses that is associated with magnet status?
- Every nurse was no longer an employee of a health care organization, but worked on contract through a nurse-run agency?
- Fifty percent of all children said they wanted to be nurses when they grow up?
- Nurses made up the majority of members of all health-related task forces and one physician was appointed as a token?
- The Surgeon General of the United States was a nurse?
- A course in policy and politics was required for every nursing student and included a clinical component or practicum for hands-on experience?
- Content on policy and politics was included on the state licensing exam?
- All nursing research included policy implications?
- Every community had a nurse to whom it turned for leadership and advice on health-related matters?

These are ideas that motivate many nurses to become advocates, activists, and risk-takers, no longer content to settle for the status quo. Are these outrageous fantasies or clear visions of a preferred future? Every major achievement begins as an idea—from sending an astronaut to the moon to eradicating smallpox. Now is the time for nurses to envision a better future and to turn their visions into reality.

This chapter provides a framework for nurses to consider how to shape policy in politically astute ways. It does so within the context of the failure of the "health care reform" movement of the 1990s that has contributed to the chaos in today's health care system. The chapter explores the values that underpin political and policy processes. It examines the relevance of these processes in each of the four spheres of a nurse's influence: government, workplace, organizations, and community. The framework assumes change is continuous and desirable and that the pace and direction of change can be shaped by nurses' deliberate efforts.

THE HEALTH CARE REFORM MOVEMENT

The tumultuous change in health care seen in the 1990s provides valuable lessons in how political forces shape health policy in the public and private sectors. Nursing itself is one of these forces. Whether nursing will remain a political force in the future depends on how well nurses understand the policy process and its political dynamics—and how engaged they are in the process.

NURSING AND THE HEALTH SECURITY ACT

In 1991 the American Nurses Association Political Action Committee (ANA-PAC) became the first health professional organization to endorse William Jefferson Clinton for President of the United States. His health platform was consistent with 1992's *Nursing's Agenda for Health Care Reform,* a consensus statement of the nursing profession describing the essential features of a reformed health care system. *Nursing's Agenda* reflects the centrality of a nursing perspective to quality health care. Both Clinton and nursing's leaders embraced a belief that government had a responsibility to guarantee access to quality health care for all. They also shared the belief that nurses had a significant role in providing that care. The word *nurses* appeared in Clinton's campaign speeches, organized rallies, interviews with the press, and policy statements. Nurses across the country campaigned energetically for his election. Nurses including Pat Ford-Roegner, a long-time political activist and former political director for the ANA and the Service Employees International Union, held leadership positions in the Clinton campaign. In November 1991 Bill Clinton was elected president, making him the first presidential candidate endorsed by organized nursing to win.

Nurses were excited about their newly achieved potential to influence national health policy. There was a great sense of accomplishment and collaboration within organized nursing. More than 70 national nursing organizations were signatories to *Nursing's Agenda for Health Care Reform.* The document defined the principles nursing believes should drive decision making in the U.S. health care system. It was timely and reflected the values of many progressive health groups, including the American Public Health Association, in relation to promoting access to care, ensuring universality of coverage through public and private financing, shifting resources to primary care, involving consumers in health care decision making, and emphasizing quality (Joel, 1993; Richardson, 1993). When health care reform took political center stage in the 1990 and 1991 elections, nursing was ready.

Nursing was ready because of a growing sophistication about the worlds of policy and politics. An increasing number of nurses understood they had to be players in shaping public and private policies that determine the nature of health care in this country and in their workplaces. They knew mobilizing community support for their issues was paramount. And they knew their efforts would in turn influence the level of health in the community. Nurses no longer questioned whether being professional included being political—it clearly did.

Health care reform was one of Bill Clinton's primary domestic policy agendas during his campaign. Once in office he involved nurses in the process of developing and reviewing his plan for health care reform, which became the Health Security Act (HSA). Nurses were appointed to task forces that worked on defining the elements of the HSA and participated in health care reform coalitions that included consumers, the business community, and other health care provider groups. Nursing was visible and influential. From 1992 to 1993, media coverage of nursing increased by 300%, and 95% of the coverage was positive (Trotter Betts, 1996). Advanced practice nurses (APNs) such as nurse practitioners (NPs) and nurse anesthetists were mentioned on the front pages of major newspapers and in more than 700 electronic and print news reports.

THE DEATH SPIRAL OF THE HSA

Congress never passed the HSA. Analyses of its demise indicate two primary reasons: The legislation was too complex, and Americans never fully understood it (Blumenthal, 1995; Fallows, 1996; Hacker, 1996; Yankelovich, 1995). The media covered the politics of health care reform more than the substantive reform issues. Major opponents to the plan developed effective counter-strategies, including the Health Insurance Association of America's "Harry and Louise" television advertisements (Annenberg Public Policy Center of the University of Pennsylvania, 1995), that undermined public support for the Act.

THE EFFECT OF THE DEMISE OF HSA

Was nursing's support for the Clinton campaign wasted? What were some of the outcomes of the rise and fall of the HSA? How did workplaces, communities, and nursing organizations respond? The demise of the HSA was itself a policy choice. The decision not to pass the Act was a statement in support of using market forces to design the health care system. The preeminence of market forces made cost containment the primary driving force moving health care organizations (e.g., hospitals and home health care agencies) to reorganize, reengineer, and redesign their own policies around employees and patient care. For-profit health care firms proliferated despite rising concern that, because of higher administrative costs and the need to deliver profits to shareholders, they dedicate fewer resources to the actual delivery of care than do non-profit entities (Woolhandler & Himmelstein, 1997). And in 1997 the federal government tackled the continued growth in costs of the Medicare program by passing the Balanced Budget Amendment (BBA), drastically reducing payment rates for hospitals and home health care agencies.

Comprising the largest and most visible part of a hospital budget, nurse labor costs began to be viewed as a financial liability by consultants that health care organizations hired to find ways to control costs. Many consultants saw they could achieve their contractual financial goals most easily by cutting registered nurse (RN) positions, sometimes replacing them with unlicensed assistive personnel (UAPs).

Staff nurses in particular began to express feelings of demoralization as the value of their caring appeared to be overshadowed by business values focused on financial goals. Patient-nurse ratios increased, as did the acuity of hospitalized patients. In too many health care organizations, it became nearly impossible to provide safe, humanistic care

to patients and their families. A study of the readership of the *American Journal of Nursing* (Shindul-Rothschild & Berry, 1997) announced the following findings among the more than 7500 nurses who responded:

- Sixty percent reported their institutions had reduced the number of RN positions.
- Forty-two percent reported that UAPs were being substituted for RNs.
- More than one third noted that their nurse executive had been dismissed and not replaced.

The health care workplace itself was becoming a barrier to high-quality patient care. Nurses were confronted with a choice: accepting situations that compromised their nursing values, becoming more militant in ways that included demonstrations and strikes, or leaving their jobs. Widespread discontent grew and received media attention, exacerbating a shortage that was inevitable given predictions of nationwide labor shortages from an aging workforce (Buerhaus, Staiger, & Auerbach, 2000). Another red flag was thrown up when Aiken et al (2001) reported that more than 20% of nurses in this country said they intended to leave their jobs within the coming year and 33% of nurses under age 30 planned to leave their jobs within a year.

NURSING'S BEST KEPT SECRET

An alternative existed that too few nurses were aware of or knew how to promote within their institutions. Since the 1980s research had accumulated that documented the characteristics and impact of hospitals that had excellent nursing care. These institutions, which came to be known as "magnet" hospitals, had relatively little difficulty recruiting and retaining highly qualified RNs. Magnet hospitals were shown to have lower mortality rates, higher patient and nurse satisfaction, lower nurse burnout rates, fewer nurse needlestick injuries, and shorter lengths of stay in hospitals and in intensive care units, all without higher costs (Aiken, Havens, & Sloane, 2000). Referred to as "nursing's best kept secret," the concept of magnet hospitals was slow to spread. By January 2002, only 43 institutions (hospitals and long-term care facilities) in the United States had achieved magnet status through a formal review program established by the American Nurses Credentialing Center (ANCC). However, a growing interest in the program may indicate more institutions will develop policies and practices that are supportive of a professional work environment for nurses. (See Chapter 15 for more information on magnet hospitals.)

OPPORTUNITIES FOR ADVANCED PRACTICE NURSES

With mounting threats to nursing practice, some have criticized nurses for turning toward self-protection rather than embracing broader health issues. On the other hand, nurses in states such as Oregon, Mississippi, Texas, and New York have been proactive in designing a preferred future for nursing and health care, developing strategies to move toward that future, and capitalizing on opportunities to develop innovative practice partnerships and opportunities to increase recruitment and retention. APNs in Mississippi created a for-profit arm of the state nurses' association to credential nurse practitioners (NPs); as a result NPs were included in provider panels for state employee health plans. Nurses in California pushed for a precedent-setting law that requires minimum nurse-patient staffing ratios in that state's institutions, and nurses in other states have began to follow suit (Kovner, 2000).

During the early years of the Clinton presidency, APNs gained visibility. Their potential value in a reformed health care system was recognized as nursing continued to push for long-standing policy goals, including reimbursement by third-party payors in all settings for all APNs at full levels of compensation. A major breakthrough occurred in the 1997 Balanced Budget Act, when Congress extended Medicare reimbursement to include all APNs regardless of geographic location (albeit at 85% of physicians' reimbursement rates). Nurses used the media and employed other strategies to garner public support for progressive state practice legislation as well as for other policy initiatives crafted to remove barriers to practice for all APNs and other nurses (Bifano, 1996; Sheridan-Gonzalez & Wade, 1998).

OPPOSITION TO NURSING'S PROGRESS

Many physicians changed their stance by not only embracing managed care but also learning how to benefit from it. There continued to be few practice networks composed of and developed by nurses, leaving nurses as an invisible provider in group medical practices (Mason, Cohen, O'Donnell, Baxter, & Chase, 1997; Cohen, Mason, Arsenie, Sargese, & Needham, 1998). Comparatively few nurses were positioned to be inside players in managed care systems.

Even after a decade of dominating the U.S. delivery system, most managed care organizations continue to develop policies reflecting medical and corporate models that, for example, fail to address credentialing and marketing of APNs as primary care providers. A highly publicized demonstration project between Columbia University and the Oxford Health Plan increased the visibility and inclusion of APNs in provider panels but also served to mobilize physician opposition (Grandinetti, 1997).

The continued gains by APNs attracted the attention of physicians, such that organized medicine launched major strategies to impede further progress in removing barriers to APNs' practice. A report of the American Medical Association (AMA) Council on Medical Service noted the AMA would "Pursue appropriate regulatory, legislative, and legal means to oppose any efforts to permit non-physician health care professionals to prescribe medication" (AMA takes umbrage, 2000). In a so-called "Citizen's Petition," the AMA put together a coalition of medical associations to challenge the federal government on the adequacy of its monitoring of the scope of practice of APNs being reimbursed under Medicare (see Unit 5 case study). Progress by nurse anesthetists to remove federal Medicare reimbursement requirements requiring direct supervision of their practice by anesthesiologists was stopped in 2001 when President George W. Bush supported anesthesiologists' objections and kept the supervision rule in place.

DEVOLUTION

Part of organized medicine's effectiveness in blocking progress by APNs has occurred because the medical associations recognized the value of working at the state level. They saw the locus of control in the public arena had shifted from the federal to state and local governments in a movement termed *devolution.* Devolution involves a shift of power from the federal to state and local governments. Fox-Piven and Cloward's classic 1971 work *Regulating the Poor: The Functions of Public Welfare* contends that throughout the history of the Western world, devolution has occurred in relation to economic prosperity and is accompanied by cutbacks in social welfare programs. When the economy is in a downturn, social upheaval increases and the cycle of increased federal control returns, as local communities become unable to meet the needs of their citizens. For organized medicine devolution has meant that states have become the primary battleground for skirmishes over the expansion of APNs' scope of practice. For nurses it has meant the same thing—and has reinforced the importance of being engaged on the state level to attain more-independent practice.

On the other hand, devolution has made the environment ripe for experimentation with new ideas for delivering health and social services. Nurses have responded through initiating innovative practices and involving themselves in local communities (Lamb, 1995; Leavitt et al, 1999). In the academic arena, financial pressures have led nursing faculty to develop community partnerships and to use a health framework that embraces other community sectors such as education and social welfare (U.S. Department of Health and Human Services, 1996). Some have received national recognition as models for promoting health and nursing and are acknowledged to be at the forefront of the community empowerment movement (Reinhard et al, 1996). Nevertheless, nurses should be mindful of societal trends that may indicate a shift back to central control.

Communities across the United States have been left without adequate health services as for-profit corporations have bought and then closed community hospitals. Those facilities that remain open struggle to balance budgets in the face of reductions in Medicare and Medicaid reimbursement rates. In November 1999 the Institute of Medicine (IOM) issued a report on errors in health care, noting that health care errors constitute the eighth leading cause of death in the nation (Institute of Medicine, 1999). Mounting public concern over hospital closings, a maldistribution of health care providers, with much specialty care available only in urban areas, and grave concerns about the safety of health care may be creating a public constituency that will increase pressure on the government to make health care "for people, not for profits" (Blumenthal, 1995). Even though the economic recovery between 1998 and 2000 created a citizenry that desired less governmental regulation and more individual control (e.g., Medical Savings Accounts and individual control of Social Security investments), the reality was the prosperity never touched the 41.5 million people (as of the end of 2001) who have no health insurance (FamiliesUSA, 2002). That number continued to rise by more than a million people per year, until it leveled off for a short time at the end of the country's economic boon in 2001. As the economy slows and state and local governments fear for their solvency, one could anticipate more federal control to safeguard the health and social welfare of the public.

This examination of the rise and fall of the HSA and the nursing community's involvement illustrates the complex interactive and cyclic nature of policy and politics. It reflects the values that drove the debate and public actions. Without a consensus that health care is a right for all, the values that emerged, and which ultimately undermined the HSA, reflected a belief in profits and market forces as the means to developing efficient, cost-effective health care. Americans have long been wary of governmental power and continue to prize individual freedoms. In the policy debate about health care, government was painted as an inflated bureaucracy that overregulates and interferes in people's lives. The primacy of health care for all was a value that lost out to the fear of big government.

This example of the HSA demonstrates both the impact that public and private policies have on nursing practice and the potential for nursing's effective use of power and influence. It serves as a lens through which to view the connections among the government, organizations, workplaces, and communities that shape public and private policies. It also suggests that, as a profession, nursing has grown in its influence but has not yet reached its full potential as a political force.

THE POLITICAL DEVELOPMENT OF NURSING

Where does nursing stand today with regard to its ability to influence policy? Cohen, Mason, Kovner, Leavitt, Pulcini, and Sochalski (1996) developed a conceptual model that describes the political development of the profession. The model's stages mirror the stages that individual nurses navigate to become key players in policy arenas. The stages are buy-in, self-interest, political sophistication, and leadership.

STAGE ONE: BUY-IN

Buy-in was a reactive stage when the profession began to promote the political sensitivity of nurses to injustices or changes needed in the policy arena. In the late 1970s and 1980s, nurses recognized they were excluded from power. Decisions were being made that influenced their practice but did not occur with their input. Leaders began to identify ways in which nurses could become politically active. Nursing's first PAC, Nurses Coalition for Action in Politics, was formed by a small group of savvy nurse leaders in New York. It later became the PAC for the ANA. Articles on political action began to appear with regularity in nursing journals and often called for enhanced efforts to educate nurses about policy and politics.

STAGE TWO: SELF-INTEREST

Self-interest occurred when the nursing profession began to develop its identity as a special interest and crystallized its uniqueness as a political voice. Nursing began to focus on issues around education and research and became involved in crafting legislation for expanded practice. Nursing coalitions began to garner political support for their issues in Congress and in state legislatures. The ANA-PAC became the third largest federal health care special interest group as individual nurses came to realize the collective power of their individual donations.

STAGE THREE: POLITICAL SOPHISTICATION

In the mid-1990s nurses began to be recognized by policymakers and health care leaders as having valuable perspectives and expertise in health policy. The ANA developed *Nursing's Agenda for Healthcare Re-*

form and brought together most national nursing organizations to speak with one voice about desired reforms in the health care system. Nurses were appointed to federal panels, agencies, and commissions. Increasing numbers of nurses campaigned for local, state, and national political offices and found support, not only among their peers, but also from the public.

STAGE FOUR: LEADERSHIP

Nursing developed a political identity exemplified by "setting the agenda" for change. This stage is the highest level of political involvement. Here nursing becomes the initiator of crucial policy change. Achieving appointments to positions outside of nursing, such as to university presidencies or as agency heads in federal and state government, characterizes stage four. Nurses are recognized for their unique expertise and perspective and are supported by multiple constituencies. In some instances in the last decade, the profession has been able to achieve this level; at other times the political status of nursing vacillates between stages three and four. The more nursing can function in stage four, the more the public will benefit from nurses' knowledge and leadership in solving issues related to the well-being of society.

THE CONTEXT OF POLICY AND POLITICS IN CLINICAL PRACTICE

Politics and policy continue to be remote, ethereal topics for too many nurses. To be seen as relevant, policy needs to be related to nurses' everyday practice in ways that will frame their personal and professional experiences as political ones. Policy and politics, that is, need to be explicitly related to clinical practice. For example, the nurse caring for a patient who has had cardiac bypass surgery needs to understand that this nurse-patient interaction is occurring within the context of a health care system that remains a disease-oriented system. Health care financing policies ensure the bypass surgery will be funded but won't guarantee payment for the nurse's time to teach the patient and family about posthospital care or to provide emotional support.

Some policies should raise concerns in the minds of nurses who are concerned about quality care. For example, when health care financing policies emphasize reduced hospital length of stay, the following practices may be reinforced:

- It is much quicker to feed an elderly patient by a nasogastric tube than to feed the patient slowly by mouth.
- It is quicker to catheterize an incontinent patient than to teach bladder control after a stroke.

Outside the hospital, public policies aimed at cost or professional control may have unintended consequences:

- A local community may try to save money by laying off the school health nurse, even though the preventive and supportive care provided by the nurse can save society money in tertiary care and lost potential of the child.
- When home health care nurses become pressured to care for more patients per day, they may leave the patient and family with the impression that the home health aide, not the nurse, is the one the family can really count on.
- An NP may be able prescribe controlled substances in one state but may be unable to do so in a neighboring state, resulting in added expense, confusion, and inconvenience for patients living near state borders.

These scenarios are driven by public and private policies. Politics shape these policies at every point in their development and execution: from which policies are considered to how an implemented policy is evaluated. Knowing the process enables nurses to identify where to focus their efforts so that policy can be implemented that supports their vision for health and health care.

THE DEFINITION OF POLICY

Policy has been defined as "the principles that govern action directed towards given ends" (Titmus, 1974, p. 23) and as "a consciously chosen course of action (or inaction) directed toward some end" (Kalisch and Kalisch, 1982, p. 61). Stimpson and Hanley (1991, p. 12) define it simply as "authoritative decision making." Policy encompasses the choices that a society, segment of society, or organization makes regarding its goals and priorities and the ways it will allocate its resources to attain those

goals. Policy choices reflect the values, beliefs, and attitudes of those designing the policy.

Consider the example of policies related to tobacco use. In the twentieth century, the federal government subsidized tobacco farming and the nation watched the Marlboro man riding across television screens. The Marlboro ads sent the implicit message that smoking was manly, "cool," good for social interaction, and sexy. To attract women to smoking, advertisements portrayed smoking as an attractive, independent choice, as in "You've come a long way, baby." But the 1990s brought a policy shift. By then, the Marlboro man himself had died of lung cancer, tobacco ads were banned from television and radio, states' attorneys general were carving up tobacco settlement funds to pay for health care services needed for the millions who spent their lifetimes smoking, and tobacco companies shifted their marketing plans to youth and Third World countries (Annas, 1997).

The tobacco example is also helpful in differentiating the various types of policy. *Public policy* is policy formed by governmental bodies—for example, legislation passed by Congress and the regulations written from that legislation. Public policy related to tobacco use includes laws that ban selling cigarettes near schools and that require health warning labels on cigarette packaging.

Social policy pertains to the policy decisions that promote the welfare of the public. For example, a local ordinance might set an age limit on the purchase of tobacco products. This policy would promote the welfare of children.

Health policy includes the decision made to promote the health of individual citizens. For example, the federal government could decide to pay for smoking prevention programs for all persons in the military and their families. A state government might require coverage for smoking cessation programs by Medicaid managed care plans.

Institutional policies are those governing workplaces: what the institution's goals are and how it will operate, how the institution will treat its employees, and how employees will work. For example, a hospital can institute a no-smoking policy that prohibits both patients and staff from smoking anywhere in the building.

Organizational policies are the positions taken by organizations, such as state nurses' associations or specialty nursing organizations. For example, a state nurses' association may develop policy banning smoking at its meetings, or a member might put forth a resolution calling on the association to offer free continuing education programs for nurses on smoking cessation.

THE DEFINITION OF POLITICS

Few words elicit the emotional response that the word *politics* does. Some people spit the word out like an epithet. It has come to be associated with negative images: smoke-filled rooms and shady deals made by power brokers, the corruption of Tammany Hall and Teapot Dome, bribes, unethical compromises, "pork barrel spending," payoffs, and vote buying, to name only a few. These images arise from media headlines of scandals and ethical breeches by elected officials.

Yet *politics* is actually a neutral term. It means simply the process of influencing the allocation of scarce resources. Examining this definition provides insight into what politics really is. *Influencing* implies opportunities exist to alter the outcome of a process. *Allocation* means decisions are being made about how to divide resources among competing groups or individuals. *Scarce* implies there are limits to the amount of resources available: that all parties cannot have everything they want. *Resources* are commonly thought of in financial terms but may also be time, staff, or other inputs in a process.

Nurses may say "She plays politics" with contempt to describe someone who achieved a goal. However, ask the same nurses if they want a nurse executive who is politically astute, and they will usually say "yes." *Politics* is thus a term associated with conflicting values. The perception of politics as negative or positive depends largely on these factors:

- An individual's own biases, experiences, and knowledge of politics
- How the "game" of politics is played—that is, the system in which politics is operating and the rules that have been established as acceptable within that system
- Whether the goals or ends are important
- Whether one is in a position to change the rules of the system

POLITICS, POLICY, AND VALUES

Making policy is a complex, multidimensional, dynamic process that reflects the values of those who are setting the policy agenda, determining policy goals and alternatives, formulating policy, and implementing and evaluating policy. When values are in conflict, as they often are in policy arenas with diverse constituencies, politics comes into play as participants attempt to influence the outcome of the policy process. Figure 1-1 illustrates the relationships among values, politics, and policy.

The values underlying policy-making activities related to tobacco and smoking illustrate this conflict. Should government be concerned about the economy of tobacco-growing states or the health of the public? Should the federal government support tobacco growers' businesses or should it discourage smoking through laws that limit the age for purchasing tobacco products and that restrict where one can smoke? Should state or federal governments, or both, engage in legal action against tobacco companies to recover the costs of health care of smokers whose care is paid for by Medicare or Medicaid, even if it means that the tobacco companies' viability and their workers' jobs are threatened? Should public funds be used to help people to stop smoking, or is smoking a private issue?

Although nurses are educated to understand the biomedical model of disease management, many recognize its limitations: Caring is not part of the biomedical model. When the biomedical model dominates policy development in and out of institutions, the health and well-being of individuals, families, and communities are limited by policies that fail to reflect nurses' values, concerns, and priorities. Support for nursing perspectives can be found in the work of those who value feminism and humanism.

HUMANISM, FEMINISM AND NURSING VALUES

American society is diverse, but policy-making bodies at local, state, and federal levels seldom reflect this diversity. The presence of sufficient num-

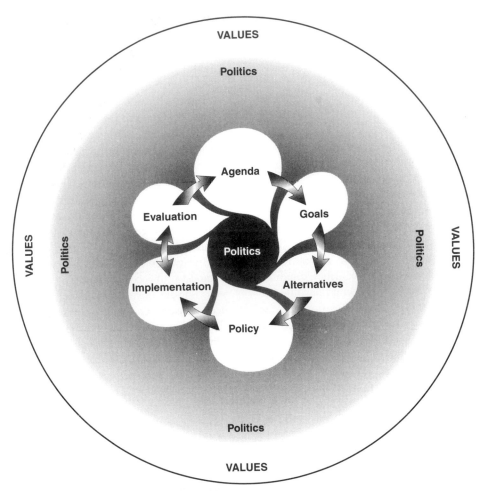

Figure 1-1   A values framework for politics and the policy process. The figure illustrates the steps in the policy process. Politics can influence the process at any step. Both the politics of policy development and the policy itself are grounded in and influenced by values.

bers of ethnic minorities, women, and nurses at policy tables often shifts the nature of policies that are developed. For example, analysis of the effect of women legislators on policy development has demonstrated that these policymakers are promoting agendas that were not a priority to their male counterparts, regardless of the women's political party affiliation (Ayres, 1997; Brenner, 1997). Women have been more likely to promote policies related to maternity leave, divorce, domestic violence, social safety nets, and family support (Dodson, 1997). In a qualitative study of nurses active in

health policy in government and organizations, Gebbie, Wakefield, and Kerfoot (2000, p. 309) found a similar theme of consistency in values that shaped their policy agendas: "Some participants said nurses' strong beliefs in the capacity and importance of people to care for themselves distinguishes nurses from other health professions that share many of the same skills. This belief becomes an orientation toward policy action to enable people to help themselves."

Caring is a concept that is central to nursing (Benner & Wrubel, 1989). But as a profession that continues to be composed primarily of women, nursing embraces this value in a society that refuses to value caring (Reverby, 1987). And yet, there are other groups that share the value of caring and can serve as partners to nurses—most notably, feminists and humanists. For these three groups, a caring model encompasses the values of wholeness, interconnectedness, equality, process, support, diversity, and collaboration (Gilligan, 1982; Mason, Backer, & Georges, 1991; Kurtz, 2000). It is not just women who hold these values. As some feminists and nurses are quick to point out (Gilligan, 1982; Pinch, 1996), caring is not gender based: Women do not "own" nurturing, compassion, and caring. To view caring as female trivializes the concept and precludes it from being integral to policy making.

Nursing's values of caring, collaboration, collectivity, and high-touch care often conflict with the dominant values of society: competition, individuality, high-tech care, and profit (MacPherson, 1987). Consider the following examples:

- Because access to prenatal care is not guaranteed in the United States, some women receive little or no prenatal care and deliver very-low–birth-weight infants who require immediate and prolonged care in neonatal intensive care units. Yet prenatal care in the United States costs relatively little compared with the high cost of neonatal intensive care, which is usually provided regardless of the family's wishes and financial situation. Once stabilized, the infant will be sent home without a guarantee that the mother will receive the support she needs to provide for the infant or that the infant will receive any developmental support and special education that may be needed.

- In a thorough review of research and demonstration projects aimed at improving the odds for high-risk children and families, Schorr (1989, p. xxii) noted that successful programs have repeatedly shown that risk can be reduced through comprehensive, intensive, and responsive services by "staffs with the time and skill to establish relationships based upon mutual respect and trust." Since Schorr's review, Olds et al (1997) have reported that home visits by nurses to low-income families reduced the

risk of child abuse and neglect when evaluated 15 years later. A replication of this study found nurses' home visits to low-income African-American women during pregnancy and the 2-year postpartum period resulted in a reduced rate of additional pregnancies and fewer childhood injuries, as well as other positive maternal-child health outcomes. Such humanistic approaches to health and social problems are too seldom embraced by policymakers. A disease-oriented value system is predominant in the public policy arena, rather than a holistic wellness model (Kitzman et al, 2000).

- Mandatory overtime is used by institutions to ensure adequate nurse staffing for patient care. Consider the potential impact of this policy on nurses who are parents and who could be forced to choose between commitment to their patients and commitment to their children.

- Many hospitals cite financial constraints in their argument against improving nurse-patient ratios. Yet Tenet Healthcare Corporation, a major for-profit hospital corporation, reported record earnings in the first quarter of 2001 while holding wages, salaries, and benefits constant (Tenet Healthcare Corporation, 2001). In 2000 and 2001, nurses at Tenet hospitals went on strike to protest staffing and mandatory overtime policies.

If nurses want institutions and government to develop policies that reflect nursing's values, then nurses must be a part of the decision-making process—the *political* process.

POLITICS AND POWER

The values that nursing shares with feminism and humanism can shape not just policies, but how these policies are developed. In the classic work *Toward a New Psychology for Women,* Miller (1976) noted that women and men often view power very differently. Whereas men tend to embrace hierarchic models of power embodied in the concept of "power grabbing" and inherent in terms such as *power over,* women tend to be more comfortable with power sharing, or *power with.* In the 1970s this view seemed both insightful and inspiring. In the years that followed, women's success in leading organizations, governments, workplaces, and communities was analyzed and found to be consistent with Miller's theory (Rosener, 1990). Transformational leadership became popular, and leaders of both sexes espoused it as a style that embraced collaboration, creativity, and empowerment.

EMPOWERMENT

The concept of empowerment extended the values associated with a model of caring to a wide range of arenas. Mason et al (1991) identified three components for the political empowerment of nurses:

- Consciousness raising about the sociopolitical realities of a nurse's life and work within society
- A sense of self-efficacy or self-esteem regarding nurses' ability to participate in the policy-making process
- Development of skills to influence the policy-making process: knowing how to use the traditional methods as well as new methods of relating to power and politics

Unfortunately, the word *empowerment* came to be used in nursing and throughout society in ways that belied its true meaning, trivializing both the concept and its application. For example, too many nurse managers spoke of "empowering staff" when what they really meant was getting staff to do what the manager wanted. Nonetheless, the idea of empowerment is one that remains important to nursing's political development, because it "requires a commitment to connection between self and others, enabling individuals or groups to recognize their own strengths, resources, and abilities to make changes in their personal and professional lives" (Mason et al, 1991, p. 73). Nurses will not be effective in politics and policy-making until they value their voices, develop policy agendas that embrace their core values, and learn the skills of policy making and influencing. Nurses who are involved in shaping health policy reinforce this perspective. Gebbie, Wakefield, and Kerfoot (2000, p. 310) found that nurses experienced in policy and politics used consensus-building skills that included "mobilizing and communicating with diverse groups," which the nurses saw as arising from their ability to "work with others, regardless of differences."

One can extend the concept of empowerment to societal approaches to problem solving. U.S. society functions primarily with a model of limited resources, whereby groups must compete to get their share. However, Smith (1997) has argued that it is possible to embrace a resource-sharing framework instead of a resource-limited one. A resource-sharing framework requires embracing values of empowerment, community collaboration, and partnerships. It assumes such partnerships can discover previously unknown resources and develop new ones to meet the needs of individuals, families, and communities. An example of this was seen after September 11, 2001, when the volume of blood donations exceeded all expectations: A new resource appeared as a response to a community need.

Such a framework also embraces the need for a global perspective on policy-making. Although most citizen action occurs on a local level, the decisions made there increasingly have a global impact. Promoting the health of local communities requires a focus on what is good for the world community, and vice versa. As a global perspective proliferates, the potential conflict in culture-bound values will need to be addressed. Nurses can be a leading voice in advocating for the values needed to integrate global perspectives on public policies and political action.

Public and private policies are a result of choices. These choices are based on values that come into play in the political dynamics of policy-making. When individuals and groups with disparate values enter into the policy-making process,

The International Council of Nurses (ICN) published a position statement, "Participation of Nurses in Health Services Decision Making and Policy Development" (2000). The statement identifies the role individual nurses can play in health services planning and public policy, as well as the responsibility professional nursing organizations have to promote and advocate for nursing participation in policy making. The ICN also published "Guidelines on Shaping Effective Health Policy" (2001) to encourage participation in policy and politics regardless of geographic setting.

consensus around policies can be difficult to attain unless values are clarified and agreement is reached on how to proceed despite any differences. Although groups with markedly different values sometimes agree to the same solution, they may do so because the solution manages to reflect their value sets. In addition, values around appropriate political behavior and strategies to highlight an issue and move an agenda should be clarified.

THE FOUR SPHERES OF POLITICAL ACTION IN NURSING

More than 25 years ago, a nurse and president of the National Organization for Women (NOW), Wilma Scott Heide (1973), called on nurses to become leaders in bringing about a humanistic society and health care system. Heide's vision remains relevant today in that she challenged nurses to embrace the profession's values and become leaders in all four spheres of political action.

Although political action and policy making are usually associated with the government, there are three other spheres in which nurses are politically active: the workplace, professional organizations, and the community. Figure 1-2 illustrates the spheres of the government, workplace, and organizations contained in the broader sphere of the community. These four spheres are interconnected and overlapping. The political effectiveness of nurses in one sphere will be influenced by nurses' involvement in the other spheres. Although this book is structured to address each of these spheres separately, the interaction and interdependence are evident throughout. Readers should look for this interaction and integrate it into their own plan for political activism.

THE FIRST SPHERE: WORKPLACE

The nursing workplace can be public or private. It can be a for-profit or a non-profit organization. The type of organization can influence who designs the policies and even the values that underlie the policies. For example, a for-profit home health care agency is more likely to terminate care for a chronically ill patient whose insurance has run out than is

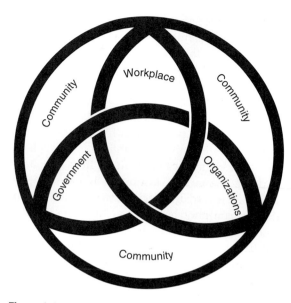

Figure 1-2   The four spheres of political influence in which nurses can effect change: workplace, government, professional organizations, and community (the encompassing sphere).

a charitable health care organization whose mission is to serve the poor.

Most nurses are familiar with "policies and procedures" manuals. These manuals list workplace policies, but other policies also exist that determine what kind of care is provided by whom—whether those policies are written or unwritten. Following are examples of policies found in many workplaces:

- Designation of no-smoking areas, or a ban on smoking in the entire facility
- Requirement for nurses to work overtime (mandatory overtime)
- Authority to delay a patient's discharge or refuse to admit a patient to the intensive care unit based on a nurse's professional assessment
- A clinical ladder program that rewards excellence in nursing practice with promotions and monetary incentives
- The referral process for a home health care agency that determines if a new patient can be referred by a nurse
- Substitution decisions concerning use of unlicensed personnel as substitutes for RNs to provide care in hospitals or homes

- The policy to permit family members to be present during emergency response or invasive procedure on their loved one (See the fourth Vignette in Chapter 16)

Because so much of a nurse's time is spent at work, the policies and political nuances of the workplace can have a profound impact on the quality of the nurse's professional life. Therefore, it is important to examine what influence nurses have over their organizations' policies. In fact, a hallmark of a "magnet" institution is the fact that nurses are involved in decision making at all levels of the organization and have an important voice in the development of its policies.

Workplace policies are also shaped by the policies of government, professional organizations, and the community. For example, occupational and health standards established by the federal government may drive a workplace to develop policies on the handling of hazardous wastes. A professional nurses' association may keep this issue visible and, through a resolution of its own, decide to pressure nurses' workplaces to use particular protective equipment in high-risk areas. A community may demand access to nurse midwifery services despite the opposition of an established hospital-based obstetrics and gynecology group practice.

In the late 1990s, there was growing concern within the nursing community regarding the continued presence of nursing executives at policy tables in many health care organizations. The elimination of nurse managers and nurse executives portended a lack of a nursing voice in workplace policies. Nurses at all levels in the workplace should work to ensure that a nursing perspective is provided, considered, and incorporated into policy decisions.

THE SECOND SPHERE: GOVERNMENT

Few parts of our lives are untouched by government. From laws requiring records documenting births to mandatory childhood immunizations, from the legal establishment of the age at which people may drink alcohol, cast a vote, or join the military to the laws determining what health services people are eligible for in old age and how assets are distributed upon a person's death, the actions of government touch nearly every part of

our lives. Government determines whether children receive services that contribute to health and education, what drugs may be used, how business relationships are conducted, and to what extent a country uses diplomacy and military approaches in managing world conflicts.

We live in a collective, organized society in which we are all connected, in which the welfare and safety of each one of us depends on the health and welfare of a cooperative and collective enterprise. Government has grown bigger and more centralized, not because we have become careless of our freedoms or less committed to individual values, but because the important tasks that need to be done in our nation today are beyond the reach of individuals. Making our society work—and civilization flourish—is everyone's business. It's what *we* do. Our individual freedom depends on our participating membership in democracy (Moyers, 1991).

Government plays an enormously important role in nursing and health care. It provides society with a legal definition of what nursing is, and it defines what a nurse may do. It influences reimbursement systems for health care and nursing services, and to a great extent, it determines who receives what type of health services.

Throughout the last part of the twentieth century, federal, state, and local governments made decisions about some major issues for our society:

- Whether women could receive full information about reproductive rights and who could provide that information
- Where smoking may take place, and where alcohol and tobacco products may be advertised
- The health services that are available in schools and whether schools may distribute condoms to prevent the spread of human immunodeficiency virus (HIV) and acquired immune deficiency syndrome (AIDS)
- Whether public funds can be used to distribute clean needles to intravenous-drug users to reduce the spread of HIV and AIDS
- The resources available to communities for low-income housing development and maintenance
- Whether violence is treated solely as a crime or as a public health issue, and whether the use of handguns is regulated

The sphere of government is extensive. The interplay between the public and private sectors means that public policy may become policy in the private sector as well. For example, a local ordinance banning smoking in public buildings would result in a ban on workplace smoking for many workers when their employers tried to comply or follow the trend. Government policy often drives the policies and programs in health care organizations. The government's actions are, in turn, shaped by the public and organizations, including nursing. The IOM (1988, p. 44) argues that although not all efforts to improve and promote the health of the public must be made by government, the government does have the responsibility for providing guidance in the policy process:

Policy formulation takes place as the result of interactions among a wide range of public and private organizations and individuals. . . . Although it joins with the private sector to arrive at decisions, government has a special obligation to ensure that the public interest is served by whatever measures are adopted."

In some cases government provides leadership in defining a problem for both public and private sectors to address. For example, the IOM's report on health care errors, *To Err is Human: Building a Safer Health System,* defined health care error, described the prevalence of error as a cause of death, identified the contributing factors, and recommended policy responses in both public and private sectors. The media featured the report with headlines such as "Nursing Mistakes Kill, Injure Thousands" (Berens, 2000). The issue was placed front and center on the public's agenda, by a quasi-governmental agency. The public and private sectors responded quickly and began to develop policies to prevent or reduce errors. (See the Chapter 21 Policy Spotlight The Epidemic in Health Care Errors: One Government Agency's Response.)

THE THIRD SPHERE: PROFESSIONAL ORGANIZATIONS

Professional organizations have been instrumental in shaping the practice of nursing—for example, in developing standards of practice, advocating for change in the scope of nursing practice, and playing a role in collective action in the workplace. Organizations are increasingly a significant force in the development of health policy.

Although powerful, nursing organizations could increase their influence if more nurses participated in them. The ANA represents the interests of all American nurses, yet less than 10% of the nurses in the United States are members. Some specialty nursing organizations include a greater percentage of members but rarely exceed 30%. Yet these organizations are essential for advocating for nurses and for values of caring and health promotion. A strong professional organization should be a visible force within its community: A national organization should have a national presence, and a local organization should be known in the local community. Organizations can and should identify issues of concern to nursing and health care, bring them to the attention of the public, and take a leadership role in calling for the development of policies that can improve the health of communities and ensure the provision of quality nursing care. To achieve this goal, organizations need the collective participation and support of nurses who will develop and use their political savvy to promote progressive policies.

THE FOURTH SPHERE: COMMUNITY

In years past, leaders such as Lillian Wald viewed the community as more than a practice site. It was seen as a social unit with a variety of special interest groups, community activities, health and social problems, and resources for solving those problems. A community can be one's neighborhood, or it can be the international online group with a common interest. The other three spheres of influence exist within the sphere of the community. As members of a community, nurses have a responsibility to promote the welfare of the community and its members. In turn, the community's resources can be invaluable assets for nurses' work in health promotion and health care delivery. Government officials, health care administrators, patients, corporate managers, presidents of private and public organizations—all players who can effect change in health policy—are affiliated with at least one community: the one in which they live. When nurses become visible in their communities, they represent the entire profession. Community networks can be called on to support nursing agendas.

Likewise, nursing should be called on to support the agendas of communities that are trying to develop a better place for citizens to live. Nurses can be and are involved in parent-teacher associations, senior citizens' councils, community planning boards, advocacy and civic organizations, and business groups. They can be instrumental in organizing and mobilizing communities on issues such as recycling, environmental cleanup, and safety. Although such activism may arise out of the private concerns of nurses for their own well-being and that of their families, it can also affect nurses' professional lives if, for example, they care for the victims of toxic waste disposal, pollution, or crime.

The interrelationships among nursing's four spheres of political activity become more distinct as nurses develop and use political skills. Ignoring one sphere can endanger one's effectiveness as a change agent. Developing one's influence in all four spheres, however, takes time and effort. While a nurse is developing such influence, networking and collaborating with colleagues who have already acquired significant influence is critical.

NURSING'S HISTORIC MANDATE

Many nurse heroines have established a mandate for political activism. Florence Nightingale was a consummate politician and visionary (Dossey, 2000). She transformed the British and Indian health care systems, and military health care as well. She knew the value of data in influencing policy and came to be recognized as the first statistician. Reflecting on her first administrative position in nursing, Nightingale wrote the following:

When I entered into service here, I determined that, happen what would, I never would intrigue among the Committee. Now I perceive that I do all my business by intrigue. I propose in private to A, B, or C the resolution I think A, B, or C most capable of carrying in Committee, and then leave it to them, and I always win. (Huxley, 1975, p. 53)

Nightingale oversaw the development of British health policy from her bed; she became frail after the Crimean War and took to her bed for much of the remainder of her life. Policymakers visited her. She sent flowers to new graduates of nursing schools, invited them to tea, and then sent them on difficult assignments they rarely protested. She was a leader who knew how to garner the support of her followers, colleagues, and policymakers and used her skills to change her environment.

Sojourner Truth was born into slavery and later provided nursing care to Union soldiers and civilians during the Civil War. She became an ardent and eloquent advocate for abolishing slavery and a supporter of women's rights. An accomplished orator, her words helped to transform the racist and sexist policies that limited the health and well-being of African-Americans and women. She worked to free slaves through the Underground Railroad, fought for human rights, and lobbied for federal funds to train nurses and physicians (Carnegie, 1986; Hine, 1989).

Lillian Wald's political activism and vision reflected feminist values. At the turn of the century, she recognized the connections between health and social conditions as she established the Henry Street Settlement House on the Lower East Side of New York City. The settlement house was a "safe place" where Wald and a group of nurse and non-nurse colleagues used consensus building to establish programs for the largely poor immigrant population living—and dying—in squalid conditions. She was a driving force behind the federal government's development of the Children's Bureau, arguing that it was shameful for a nation to have policies and departments protecting animals but not children. An ardent peace activist, she was called on by the White House on frequent occasions to participate in the development of national and international policy. A suffragette, she campaigned for presidents even when she herself could not vote (Coss, 1989; Daniels, 1989; Backer, 1993).

Finally, Margaret Sanger transformed a nation's attitudes and approaches to family planning, risking jail and her own life to do so. Having seen firsthand the health effects of multiple unplanned pregnancies, she distributed literature on birth control at a time when such distribution was illegal. She knew the power of information and civil disobedience (Chesler, 1992).

These nurse heroines had visions that reflected an understanding of the connections between health and the broader social issues of their times. Their vision was grounded in values that reflected caring for the well-being of individuals, families, and communities. They were not silenced when they realized policymakers did not share their values. Instead, they developed and used their political skills to transform neighborhoods, cities, states, nations, and the world. The work of these nurses can be used as exemplars for today's nurses who are embarking on challenging odysseys to improve the health of individuals, families, and communities. If we are successful, our actions will serve to ignite the efforts of nurses of tomorrow.

REFERENCES

Aiken, L.H., Havens, D.S., & Sloane, D.M. (2000). The magnet nursing services recognition program. *American Journal of Nursing, 100*(3), 26-35.

Aiken, L.H., et al. (2001). Nurses' reports on hospital care in five countries. *Health Affairs (Millwood), 20*(3), 43-53.

AMA takes umbrage. (2000). *American Journal of Nursing, 100*(12), 14.

Annas, G.J. (1997). Tobacco litigation as cancer prevention: Dealing with the devil. *New England Journal of Medicine, 336*(4), 304-308.

Annenberg Public Policy Center of the University of Pennsylvania. (1995). *Media in the middle: Fairness and accuracy in the 1994 health care reform debate.* Philadelphia: Annenberg Public Policy Center.

Ayres, B.D. (1997, April 14). Women in Washington statehouse lead U.S. tide. *New York Times,* A1.

Backer, B.A. (1993). Lillian Wald: Connecting caring with activism. *Nursing and Health Care, 114*(3), 122-129.

Benner, P. & Wrubel, J. (1989). *The primacy of caring: stress and coping in health and illness.* Menlo Park, CA: Addison-Wesley.

Berens, M.J. (2000, September 10). Nursing mistakes kill, injure thousands. *Chicago Tribune,* 1.

Bifano, L. (1996). Advanced practice politics and the Oregon nurses' trail. *Nursing Administration Quarterly, 20*(3), 54-62.

Blumenthal, D. (1995). Health care reform—past and future. *New England Journal of Medicine, 332*(7), 465-468.

Brenner, E. (1997, January 19). The power women share as lobbyists. *New York Times,* section 13, 1.

Buerhaus, P., Staiger, D.O., & Auerbach, D.I. (2000). Implications of an aging registered nurse workforce. *Journal of the American Medical Association, 283,* 2948.

Carnegie, E.M. (1986). *The path we tread: Blacks in nursing, 1854-1984.* Philadelphia: J.B. Lippincott.

Chesler, E. (1992). *Woman of valor: Margaret Sanger and the birth control movement in America.* New York: Simon & Schuster.

Cohen, S.S., Mason, J.M., Kovner, C., Leavitt, J.K., Pulcini, J., & Sochalski, J. (1996). Stages of nursing's political development: Where we've been and where we ought to go. *Nursing Outlook, 44*(6), 259-266.

Cohen, S., et al. (1998). Focus groups reveal perils and promises of managed care for nurse practitioners. *Nurse Practitioner, 23*(6), 48, 50, 57-60.

Coss, C. (Ed.). (1989). *Lillian Wald: Progressive activist.* New York: The Feminist Press.

Daniels, D.G. (1989). *Always a sister: The feminism of Lillian Wald.* New York: The Feminist Press.

Dodson, D.L.O. (1997). Women voters and the gender gap. In W. Crotty, J. Mileur (Eds.). *America's choice: The election of 1996.* New York: McGraw-Hill.

Dossey, B.M. (2000). *Florence Nightingale: Mystic, visionary, healer.* Springhouse, PA: Springhouse.

Fallows, J. (1996). *Breaking the news: How the media undermine American democracy.* New York: Vintage.

FamiliesUSA. (2002). *2 Million Americans lost their health insurance in 2001: Largest One-Year increase in nearly a decade.* Available online at www.familiesusa.org/media/press/2002/insurance_loss.htm.

Fox-Piven, F. & Cloward, R. (1971). *Regulating the poor: The functions of public welfare.* New York: Pantheon.

Gebbie, K.M., Wakefield, M., & Kerfoot, K. (2000). Nursing and health policy, *Journal of Nursing Scholarship, 32*(3), 307-315.

Gilligan, C. (1982). *In a different voice: Psychological theory and women's development.* Boston: Harvard University Press.

Grandinetti, D.A. (1997). Will patients choose NPs over doctors? *Medical Economics, 74*(14), 134-142.

Hacker, J. (1996). National health care reform: an idea whose time came and went. *Journal of Health Politics, Policy and Law, 21*(4), 647-696.

Heide, W.S. (1973). Nursing and women's liberation: a parallel, *American Journal of Nursing, 73,* 824-826.

Hine, D.C. (1989). *Black women in white.* Indianapolis: Indiana University Press.

Huxley, E. (1975). *Florence Nightingale.* New York: Putnam's Sons.

Institute of Medicine. (1988). *The future of public health.* Washington, DC: National Academy Press.

Institute of Medicine. (1999). *To err is human: Building a safer health system.* Washington DC: National Academy Press.

International Council of Nurses. (2000). *Position statement: Participation of nurses in health services decision making and policy development.* Available online at www.icn.ch/pspolicydev00. htm.

International Council of Nurses. (2001). *Guidelines on shaping effective health policy.* Geneva, Switzerland: International Council of Nurses.

Joel, L. (1993). Contemporary issues in nursing organizations. In D.J. Mason, S.W. Talbott, & J.K. Leavitt (Eds.). *Policy and politics for nurses: Action and change in the workplace, government, organizations and community* (2nd ed.). Philadelphia: W.B. Saunders.

Kalisch, B.J. & Kalisch, P.A. (1982). *Politics of nursing.* Philadelphia: J.B. Lippincott.

Kitzman, H., et al. (2000). Enduring effects of nurse home visitation on maternal life course: A 3-year follow-up of a randomized trial. *Journal of the American Medical Association, 283*(15), 1983-1989.

Kovner, C.T. (2000). Policy perspectives: state regulation of RN-to-patient ratios. *American Journal of Nursing, 100*(11), 61.

Kurtz, P. (2000). *Humanist manifesto: A call for new planetary humanism.* New York: Prometheus.

Lamb, G. (1995). Early lessons from a capitated community-based nursing model. *Nursing Administration Quarterly, 19*(3), 18-26.

Leavitt, J., et al. (1999). To have and have not, *American Journal of Nursing, 99*(11), 43-47.

MacPherson, K. (1987). Health care policy, values and nursing. *Advances in Nursing Science, 9,* 1-11.

Mason, D.J., Backer, C., & Georges, C.A. (1991). Toward a feminist model for the political empowerment of nurses. *Image: Journal of Nursing Scholarship, 23*(2), 72-77.

Mason, D.J., et al. (1997). Managed care organizations' arrangements with nurse practitioners. *Nursing Economic$, 15*(6), 306-314.

Miller, J.B. (1976). *Toward a new psychology for women.* Boston: Beacon.

Moyers, B. (1991). Yearning for democracy. *In Context, 30,* 14-17.

Nursing's agenda for health care reform. (1992). Washington, DC: American Nurses Publishing.

Olds, D., et al. (1997). Long-term effects of home visitation on maternal life course and child abuse and neglect: Fifteen-year follow-up of a randomized trial. *Journal of the American Medical Association, 278*(8), 637-844.

Pinch, W.J. (1996). Is caring a moral trap? *Nursing Outlook, 44*(22), 84-88.

Reinhard, S., et al. (1996). Promoting healthy communities through neighborhood nursing, *Nursing Outlook, 44*(5), 223-228.

Reverby, S. (1987). *Ordered to care: The dilemma of American nursing.* New York: Cambridge University Press.

Richardson, D. (1993). Federal government. In D.J. Mason, S.W. Talbott, & J.K. Leavitt (Eds.). *Policy and politics for nurses: Action and change in the workplace, government, organizations and community* (2nd ed.). Philadelphia: W.B. Saunders.

Rosener, J.B. (1990, November-December). The ways women lead. *Harvard Business Review,* 119-134.

Schorr, L. (1989). *Within our reach: Breaking the cycle of disadvantage.* Garden City, NY: Doubleday.

Sheridan-Gonzalez J. & Wade, M. (1998). Every patient deserves a nurse. In D. Mason & J. Leavitt (Eds.). *Policy and politics in nursing and health care* (3rd ed.). Philadelphia: W.B. Saunders.

Shindul-Rothschild, J. & Berry, D. (1997). Ten keys to quality care. *American Journal of Nursing, 97*(11), 35-43.

Smith, G. (1997, June 18). *Shaping the future health system through community-based approaches* (keynote address). Vancouver, British Columbia, Canada: International Council of Nurses' Congress.

Stimpson, M. & Hanley, B. (1991). Nurse policy analysts. *Nursing and Health Care, 12*(1), 10-15.

Tenet Healthcare Corporation. (2001). *Tenet reports first quarter EPS from operations up 40%.* Available online at www.tenethealth.com/InvestorRelations.

Titmus, R.M. (1974). *Social policy: An introduction.* New York: Pantheon.

Trotter Betts, V. (1996). Nursing's agenda for health care reform: Policy, politics and power through professional leadership, *Nursing Administration Quarterly, 20*(3), 1-9.

U.S. Department of Health and Human Services. (1996). *Models that work.* Washington, DC: U.S. Government Printing Office.

Woolhandler, S. & Himmelstein, D.U. (1997). Costs of care and administration at for-profit and other hospitals in the United States. *New England Journal of Medicine, 336*(11), 769-774.

Yankelovich, D. (1995, Spring). The debate that wasn't: the public and the Clinton plan. *Health Affairs (Millwood),* 7-23.

Pride in Our Past: Nursing's Political Roots

SANDRA B. LEWENSON

". . . what's past is prologue . . ."

WILLIAM SHAKESPEARE

The history of the modern nursing movement, which began in 1873, tells the story of a pioneering group of women who responded to the changing role of women in society. They advocated a new profession for women and better health care for the public. In forging the nursing profession in this modern period, nurses had to enter the political arena to gain legitimate authority over their education and practice. Over time, however, the history has blurred and often obscured from view the rich tapestry of nursing's political past. Nursing's political role and historical activism have been buried in the popular image of the nurse. When its political past is remembered at all, nursing has suffered accusations of conservatism and noninvolvement in the political arena and has been omitted from most women's histories. This can be explained in part by the fact that women are perceived by society to have historically played a small role in the political arena. Nursing, long considered women's work, shares with the overall women's movement the many negative, devalued perceptions of the worth of its role (Vance, Talbott, McBride, & Mason, 1985; Reverby, 1987). As a result of such a perception, nursing suffers from "nursism," which has been defined as "a form of sexism that specifically maligns the caring role in society" (Lewenson, 1996, p. 226).

Public perception of nursing often depicts nurses as handmaidens to physicians and as sub-servient members of the health care team. The notion that "nurses are born, not made" persists in the twenty-first century and provides the rationale for hiring less-educated workers to perform professional nursing roles. To cut costs, hospitals downsize by firing nurses with experience and advanced degrees and cross-train uneducated health care workers to do jobs once done by registered nurses. This acceptance of less-qualified nurses reflects the decreased value society continues to place on professional nursing care. Buresh and Gordon (2000) write about the invisibility of nurses' contribution to health care and the lack of recognition for their work. This invisibility and the assumption that women's work is somehow free and expected perpetuate the negative aspects of nursism.

The historical research of Rogge (1987) and others have begun to provide the needed evidence that shows how nursing's use of political power is neither new nor confined to the twentieth and twenty-first centuries. Pioneers in nursing honed their political expertise when they persuaded various members of the status quo (e.g., hospital administrators, physicians, members of community boards of health, state legislators, politicians) to open nurse-training schools, organize professional associations, and participate in social issues such as woman suffrage, public health, birth control, and integration. The history of the four national professional nursing groups, beginning in the United States in 1893, documents nursing's political activism. The creation of the American Society of Superintendents of Training Schools for Nurses in

1893 (forerunner of the National League for Nursing [LN], the Nurses' Associated Alumnae of the United States and Canada in 1896 (forerunner of the American Nurses Association [NA], the National Association of Colored Graduate Nurses (NACGN) in 1908, and the National Organization of Public Health Nursing (NOPHN) in 1912 provided a forum for nurses to be politically active. The history of these organizations illustrates nursing's efforts to control its own education and practice and its strong interest in the Woman Movement.[1]

These four nursing organizations embody nursing's passage through the stages of political development as defined by Cohen, Mason, Kovner, Leavitt, Pulcini, and Sochalski (1996). In the early years of each organization, nursing educators and practitioners joined forces to gain control and focus on professional development. Both the self-absorption with professional development and the beginning interest in the larger issues fit the "buy in" stage described by Cohen et al (1996). Nursing activists educated other nurses on the need for woman suffrage for personal and professional reasons (e.g., to obtain nurse registration laws). Once established as professional groups, these organizations formed strong coalitions with other nursing organizations (both in this country and abroad) to make their voices heard on social issues such as woman suffrage, public health, and women's rights. In this second stage, according to Cohen et al (1996, p. 261), nursing moves toward political activism and "develops its own sense of uniqueness." As these organizations matured, they showed interest in issues aside from those that solely affected the profession.

To address the misconceptions about nursing's active political past, this chapter provides examples where nurses have been politically active and have made a significant difference in health care. Examples include the influence of Florence Nightingale, the opening of nurse-training schools, the founding of professional nursing organizations, the support of woman suffrage, the work of Lillian Wald in

public health and Margaret Sanger in birth control, and the efforts of the NACGN, led by Mabel Staupers, to integrate African-American nurses into the U.S. armed forces. Because political activism in nursing parallels similar efforts of other women's groups in the same period, this overview examines the nursing profession's close ties with the Woman Movement of the nineteenth and early twentieth centuries, as well as its relationship with the more-recent women's movement of the mid-twentieth century.

BEGINNING WITH THE WOMAN MOVEMENT

The profession of nursing rose out of the political efforts of women during what is known as the Woman Movement of the middle nineteenth and early twentieth centuries (1848 to 1920). During this period, women sought political control of their personal lives. They looked to change the laws that regulated their families, their education, and their political freedom. Because of these efforts, women's work came under scrutiny both by those who wanted to preserve the status quo and by those who wanted reform.

During the middle of the nineteenth century, men represented the family to the outside world, and women remained in the home caring for the family. For some women the status quo sufficed, but for many the subordinate role they were expected to play did not, especially for women who did not marry and who did not accept the limitations of women's roles. By the 1830s schools for women opened, and women began to challenge their confined, set role in society. Society conceived women as the "natural born" caretakers for their families, responsible for the moral upbringing of its members. Some women, however, wanted to branch out of their allotted "separate sphere" and into the more "active sphere" of the world outside the home. For many women (especially middle-class women), this meant obtaining an education, finding a career, and financially supporting themselves. During the nineteenth century, these women sought opportunity for meaningful work, questioned the idea of marriage, and organized to bring

---

[1] *Woman Movement* is the term used for the movement in the late nineteenth and early twentieth centuries to change society's ideas about women. *Women's movement* is the term that describes women's efforts of the 1960s and 1970s.

about change in the social order (Cott, 1977; Lerner, 1977; Daniels, 1987).

POLITICAL AWAKENING AND THE MODERN NURSING MOVEMENT

The modern nursing movement began when Florence Nightingale opened the nurse-training program at St. Thomas Hospital in England in 1860. This landmark event signaled to the world that nurses required schooling for the work they did. It also provided one of the first opportunities for women to work outside the home and be self-supportive. In turn, the rise of modern nursing served as the catalyst for political activities of nurses.

Nursing was one of the first professions that women sought to control and organize. It is taken for granted that, because women provided care to their own families, they would automatically control the profession. However, historically this was not the case; nursing's roots in the church and military fostered patriarchal control. Nurses had to maneuver politically to control their professional education, work, and lives. Nightingale's writing supports a feminist stance on who should control the education and work of nurses (Lewenson, 1996). Nightingale believed that nursing should be controlled by nurses. A 1908 editorial comment published in the *American Journal of Nursing (AJN)* (Progress and reaction, 1908, pp. 333-334) acknowledged that her "brilliant essence lay in her taking from men's hands a power which did not logically or rightly belong to them, but which they had usurped, and seizing it firmly in her own, from whence she passed it on to her pupils and disciples." Like women's education, education for nurses was considered unnecessary. The general attitude held that women were natural-born nurses and therefore did not require an education. Yet, after the extraordinary success of Nightingale's ideas about sanitation and nurses' education, an "educated" nurse was sought to reform the deplorable conditions found in hospitals throughout the United States.

In an 1872 letter, Nightingale sent her ideas about separating nursing and medicine to the founders of the nurse-training school at Bellevue Hospital in New York City. Nightingale advised that "discipline and internal management" of nurses should be "entirely under a woman, a *trained* superintendent, whose whole business is to see that the nursing duties are performed according to this standard" (Florence Nightingale's letter of advice to Bellevue, 1911, p. 362). Bellevue and many other schools used Nightingale's concept as a model.

Nightingale, the reformer, emerges as a complex individual who often achieved her goals "by behind-the-scenes management of the committees and doctors" (Vicinus & Nergaard, 1989, p. 159). It was her letter-writing to influential people that helped Nightingale revolutionize health care and nursing education. Moreover, it was the acceptance, around the world, of her ideas about sanitation, education, and separation of nursing and medicine that contributed to her ability to facilitate change.

PROFESSIONAL EDUCATION AND THE OPENING OF NURSE-TRAINING SCHOOLS

Political activism of the early nursing pioneers took the form of creating the models for professional education. The year 1873 heralded the opening of Nightingale-influenced nurse-training schools and the beginning of the modern nursing movement in the United States. The first three schools credited with this distinction were at Bellevue Hospital in New York City; New Haven Hospital in New Haven, Connecticut; and Massachusetts General Hospital in Boston. Early nursing leaders implemented many of Nightingale's ideas about nursing. They skillfully demonstrated to hospital administrators that using nursing students improved sanitary conditions on wards and led to better patient outcomes. This success created a safer environment for the newly formed medical profession, consequently creating great financial incentives for hospitals to open such schools (Dock and Stewart, 1931). For 20 years (between 1873 and 1893), nurse-training schools proliferated in the United States, so that by 1910 the number of schools had risen to more than 1,129 schools (Burgess, 1928).

The schools opened between 1873 and 1893, but

they were not regulated by any professional group. Hospital administrators wanted these schools because it was cheaper to use student labor than to employ the graduates. Exploitation of students took on various forms. Education was secondary to work expected of the students. Often the students' education was limited by the size of the hospital. Many hospitals had too few beds to provide appropriate and sufficient learning opportunities.

Once a nurse's training was over, the school provided no support. Graduate nurses found themselves working in the only jobs they could find, such as private duty nursing or public health nursing. Physicians or pharmacists, as opposed to nurses, often controlled the private duty nursing directories, which distributed private duty work. This meant that the fee schedule rested outside the nurses' control, which often led to further exploitation of an already exploited group. The misuse of both the students and the graduate nurses contributed greatly to the strong political stance that early nursing leaders took when they formed professional nursing organizations.

POLITICAL ACTION AND THE RISE OF PROFESSIONAL ORGANIZATIONS

Professional nursing organizations began to form between 1893 and 1912. Their interest first revolved around the issues confronting the profession but later expanded to include social and political reforms affecting society. As each organization formed and matured, political power bases grew and expanded. They moved away from their initial purpose of "the protection and education of one class of women workers" (Palmer, 1909, p. 956) toward interest in more-global concerns affecting the health care of the public.

NATIONAL LEAGUE FOR NURSING

The first national nursing organization to form was the American Society of Superintendents for Training Schools, founded in 1893 and renamed the National League of Nursing Education in 1912 and the NLN in 1952. This organization originated at the nurses' congress that convened at the World's

Columbian Exposition in Chicago in 1893. Superintendents, chief administrators, and hospital nursing staff sought uniformity in nursing curricula and standards of nursing practice. Alone in their work, they felt isolated and powerless to go before the entrenched powers, such as the hospital boards and medical groups, that sought to control the developing profession. By joining together like other women's groups of the day, superintendents created an opportunity to work toward change. Leaders such as Isabel Hampton Robb, Lavinia Dock, and Sophia Palmer spoke out in favor of collective action. Their early speeches at the first few professional meetings reflected the political tone and progressive nature of the newly founded organization (Birnbach & Lewenson, 1993).

AMERICAN NURSES ASSOCIATION

Mindful of the needs of the majority of "trained" or "graduate" nurses, superintendents in the newly formed society urged training schools to form alumnae associations that would provide the basic structure for a second national nursing organization. In doing so, the superintendents spearheaded the founding of the Nurses' Associated Alumnae of the United States and Canada in 1896 (renamed the ANA in 1911). Sophia Palmer, first editor-in-chief of the *American Journal of Nursing*, called for a grassroots movement that would unite alumnae associations around the country for the purpose of political action and social reform. She urged small and large schools to form alumnae associations that would be able to come together in state associations and form a vital national professional organization. The state societies would form "for the definite and separate purpose of promoting legislation for state registration of nurses" (Palmer, 1909, p. 956). She recognized the inherent power that nurses would wield, given organization. Palmer said, "Organization is the power of the age. Without it nothing great is accomplished. All questions having ultimate advancement of the profession are dependent upon united action for success" (1897, p. 55). It was clear to the early pioneer leaders that organizing was the only way to remove the obstacles that nursing experienced on its way to becoming a recognized profession.

The state alumnae associations organized around the highly political issue of state registration. This issue galvanized the nursing membership and forced nurses to develop their political skills. Until 1903 anyone could call herself a nurse. It was not until 1903 that the first state nurse registration acts (in North Carolina, New York, New Jersey, and Virginia) were passed and the title *nurse* was protected by law. Although the early registration acts varied in their protection of the public from inadequate nursing education, they signified the political efforts of nurses and organized nursing. Nursing leaders in each of these states sought support for this legislation from legislators, politicians, other professionals, and the public through letter-writing campaigns, personal visits to the legislatures, use of the professional journals, and support of the public press (Birnbach, 1985).

Twenty-three nurse alumnae associations joined forces to form the Nurses' Associated Alumnae and met in New York in April 1898. At their first meeting, they learned firsthand how important it was for them to use their collective strength for political action. Just before the meeting, the United States entered the Spanish-American War. Isabel Hampton Robb, president of the new organization, led the group's effort to serve as gatekeeper for the nurses who served during the war. After a long battle on the home front against Anita Newcomb McGee, a physician and Washington socialite, on who should screen the applicants, organized nursing failed to reach its goal. McGee, as history shows, held on to this pivotal role. Robb believed that this outcome was due to the lack of professional organization. The ANA had organized too late to win this issue, but its leaders learned from this experience (Robb, 1900; Armeny, 1983). Robb and other nursing leaders recognized their potential political power as an organization and continued to lobby successfully in the years to come.

NATIONAL ASSOCIATION OF COLORED GRADUATE NURSES

Although the first two national organizations, the NLN and the ANA, addressed the needs of nurses, they primarily focused on issues within the mainstream culture. Discriminatory practices in parts of the United States barred many African-American nurses from membership in their state associations. This practice in turn prevented them from belonging to the ANA. Moreover, segregation and discriminatory practices throughout the country banned African-American nurses from attending most nurse-training schools and, in some states, prohibited them from taking state nurse registration examinations. In keeping with other women's organizations and the need for political activism, African-American nurses organized the NACGN in 1908. It was an organization created to overcome racial hostility and address professional issues. Along with issues of blatant racial discrimination, the NACGN focused on education, standards of practice, and the passage of state nurse registration acts (Johns, 1925; Staupers, 1937; Hine, 1989, 1990).

To determine the need for such an organization, Martha Franklin, nursing leader and founder of the NACGN, had undertaken a study on African-American nurses in 1906 and 1907. Franklin sent more than 1,500 surveys to African-American graduates of nurse-training schools, most of which had opened in historically African-American hospital settings (Thoms, 1929). From the survey results, Franklin learned that African-American nurses needed an organization to address issues pertaining to their particular needs. Here, too, Franklin recognized that only in the collective would they gain enough power to change discriminatory practices and affect conditions in nursing and in health care (Lewenson, 1996).

At the early meetings, the NACGN members sought to raise professional standards, provide a collegial atmosphere for the graduate nurse, discuss community health nursing, and address issues of racial discrimination. Its members constantly faced the double-edged sword of sexism and racism, which led to the political activism of the NACGN membership. A primary concern for the NACGN was the nurse registration acts that the profession as a whole sought. Not only did the organization support the passage of such acts, but its members also fought to ensure that nurses of color could sit for the state examination and be given the same examination as their white counterparts.

The collective action of the NACGN around the issue of racial discrimination toward African-American nurses in the military during World War II serves as another example of political activism in nursing. Not until after the armistice in World War I were African-American nurses accepted into the Army Nurse Corps. Furthermore, it wasn't until after a great political campaign waged by the NACGN during World War II that they were integrated into the armed services, albeit in limited numbers. Mabel Staupers, considered one of the people instrumental in the integration of African-American nurses into the military, prepared the NACGN to engage in the political effort needed to effect change (Hine, 1993). Staupers not only mobilized the NACGN but also sought the "allegiance of sympathetic white nurses within the profession" (Hine, 1989, p. 170). The NACGN used letter-writing campaigns, alliances with the other professional nursing organizations, membership in the newly established National Nursing Council for War Service, meetings with politically significant people, and collective action to change the course of events forever.

NATIONAL ORGANIZATION FOR PUBLIC HEALTH NURSING

At the beginning of the twentieth century the need for public health nurses increased as the United States experienced the outcomes of urbanization, industrialization, and immigration. Cities filled with people who wanted to find jobs in these growing industrialized centers. This change in demographics contributed to severely overcrowded housing, unsafe work conditions, inadequate sanitation, epidemics, and poor access to health care, causing progressive reformers to respond. The public health movement used trained nurses in public health departments and visiting nurse service agencies to bring their ideas about sanitation, immunization, and health care to the public. Between 1895 and 1905, 171 visiting nurse associations opened in more than 110 cities and towns. In 1902 there were only 200 public health nurses; by 1912 there were more than 3,000 (Fitzpatrick, 1975; Gardner, 1933). With this steady proliferation of visiting nurse associations came unscrupulous home health care agencies that offered substandard visiting nurse services. To overcome poor and inferior nursing practices, the ANA and the NLN exerted their political expertise and in 1912 formed the NOPHN. This organization's members joined with other civic-minded citizens to improve the health of the American public.

To create the NOPHN, in 1911 nursing leaders of the ANA and the NLN developed a plan to organize public health nurses. Letters sent to organizations that employed public health nurses requested that they send a representative to the annual nursing convention of the ANA and the NLN who could vote on the issue of starting a new organization. Most of the agencies responded favorably, and 1 year later, in 1912, the NOPHN organized. The NOPHN objectives were to "stimulate responsibility for the health of the community by the establishment and the extension of public health nursing" and "to develop standards and techniques in public health nursing service" (Gardner, 1933, p. 27). From the outset, the NOPHN recognized the political expediency of forming coalitions with other health professionals and lay people and included these other individuals as members. This provided strong affiliations with other groups and a broader political base on which to advocate change.

ORGANIZED NURSING AND WOMAN SUFFRAGE

While the four nursing organizations were forming, the campaign for suffrage was under way. Suffrage meant personal and political freedom and the means to control the laws that governed women. For nurses, suffrage meant gaining a political voice in the laws that regulated practice, education, and health. Professional nursing organizations provided the medium for nurses to share common experiences and thus find a collective voice. Once these organizations established themselves as viable associations, nurses expanded their horizons to include broader women's issues, including suffrage, in their political agenda (Lewenson, 1996). This period of political activism in nursing fits the description by Cohen and colleagues (1996) of the early stages of political development. Nursing, through the four organizations, had developed its identity, formed coalitions, built on its political base, and used the language needed for changing legislation. By advocating for patient rights, nurses began to shape policy. As nursing struggled to come to consensus over the issue of woman suffrage, they published a journal, formed coalitions among themselves and with non-nursing groups, and discussed the political ramifications of both sides of the suffrage question.

In 1900 the ANA and NLN used an important political strategy when they founded the publication *AJN* for the purpose of communicating and sharing ideas. So imperative was the need to find a public forum in which to exchange their views that members funded the journal. The nursing membership raised money to start the journal by buying shares in the journal company. They invested their money, time, and ideas in the professional journal and, in the process, formed a strong coalition from which to carry on their political activities.

The *AJN* provided a public forum for nurses to present ideas about nursing care interventions, public health, social issues, and other professional issues. Within the pages of the *AJN*, nurses had the opportunity to express their views on nursing's support of woman suffrage. Although many nurses wanted to maintain the status quo and sought to avoid confrontational political battles, a sufficient number of nurses ardently believed that the survival of the profession rested on gaining suffrage.

Organized nursing's efforts to support the political agenda of the international nursing community led to the formation of the American Federation of Nurses (AFN) between 1901 and 1912. This newly created federation, a coalition forged between the ANA and the NLN, enabled organized nurses in the United States to join the National Council of Women and thus become members of the International Council of Women and later the International Council of Nurses (ICN) (Lewenson, 1994). It is significant to note that by 1901, nursing in the United States was ready to form strong coali-

tions with other nursing groups both domestically and abroad. Nurse organizations gained a political voice in international health issues affecting women and were specifically interested in supporting suffrage.

Interest in suffrage and connections with women's groups first appeared in the *AJN* in 1906. The *AJN* published letters from the National American Woman Suffrage Association asking nurses to support the nineteenth amendment, giving women the right to vote (Gordon, Myers, & Kelley, 1906). Nursing's staunchest suffragist, Lavinia Dock (1907), argued for nursing's involvement in the suffrage movement and wrote that the national associations would fall short of their mission if they did not get politically involved. She warned against following "the narrow path of purely professional questions" (p. 895), and strongly advocated nursing's understanding and support of this movement.

The argument that nurses used to oppose participation in the political suffrage campaign centered on fear that it would harm political efforts to obtain state nursing registration legislation. In 1908, at the ANA's eleventh annual convention, held in San Francisco, the membership opposed a resolution in favor of the organization's support of woman suffrage. Although this event is often used as an example of nursing's conservatism and lack of political activism, this very defeat served as a catalyst for organized nursing to join forces with other women suffragists. Palmer (1908) noted that "the action in San Francisco has brought the matter of suffrage sharply before the nurses of the country" (p. 50). Within 4 years, nursing had responded to the efforts of nursing leaders to support the political franchise. By 1912 nursing organizations had voted to support women's right to vote (Christy, 1984; Chinn, 1985; Lewenson, 1996).

Proponents of nurses' support of woman suffrage linked health issues with the right to vote. Nurses could easily see the relationship between gaining the vote and improving the lives of their patients, families, and communities. Dock urged nurses to examine how the franchise would improve social conditions that led to illness. Using tuberculosis as an example, Dock (1908, p. 926) asked, ". . . take the present question of the underfed school children in New York. How many of them will have tuberculosis? If mothers and nurses had votes there might be school lunches for all those children."

The NACGN, although not invited to participate in the ANA and NLN resolution to support woman suffrage, did express grave concern for social issues that affected health. The NACGN became an invited member of the international nursing community through its membership in the International Council of Women. This affiliation reflects the NACGN's involvement in woman suffrage. Active discussions about woman suffrage, membership in the international women and nursing councils, and support for the ICN resolution to attain suffrage by 1912 indicated strong political activism among African-American nurses.

SHAPING HEALTH AND PUBLIC POLICY

Several visionary leaders emerged during this initial period of organization. Some worked with the support of organized nursing, and others did not. Each leader who championed ideas about health care, equal rights, and professional opportunity had to be politically astute to attain the goals. As nursing moved into the stage that Cohen et al (1996, p. 260) describe as "self-interest," many of the leaders were paving the way into the next two stages, characterized as "political sophistication" and "leading the way." Women such as Lillian Wald and Margaret Sanger learned to speak the political language that enabled them to succeed in their respective missions. They spoke to a large audience, served on various national boards and commissions, and built strong coalitions around broad health concerns that went well beyond nursing.

PUBLIC HEALTH: LILLIAN WALD

Before the formation of the NOPHN, trained nurses such as Lillian Wald and her friend from training school, Mary Brewster, understood the ramifications of economic, political, social, and cultural factors in regard to health. In 1893 Wald and Brewster opened the Henry Street Nurses' Settlement in New York City, providing nursing care, health education, social services, and cultural experiences to the residents of the Lower East Side (Fitzpatrick, 1975). Wald and the nurses at Henry Street lived within the community they served and became internationally noted for their success at addressing public health issues.

The work of the nurses at Henry Street reflected their ability to provide care in the home and to lobby for change in the body politic. Backer (1993, p. 128) noted that Wald "connected her caring with activism by initiating practice and policy changes via administrative and organizational skills, persuasiveness, coalitions, delivering testimony and political power." Wald promoted public health nursing education and the formation of the NOPHN. Moreover, Wald's astute political awareness led to many social changes affecting the health and well-being of the Lower East Side residents.

Children's health and well-being struck a chord with Wald. Concerned for the welfare of children, Wald turned the backyard at Henry Street into a playground. Recognizing that too many children played in the overcrowded streets of the Lower East Side, Wald argued for the opening of city parks and in 1898 successfully formed the Outdoor Recreation League. This group obtained land in New York City and turned it into municipal parks (Siegel, 1983).

Wald's nursing knowledge, social concern, and political savvy joined forces when she maneuvered the board of health into hiring a school nurse in 1902. Wald writes her account in her 1915 book, *The House on Henry Street,* about how she and Brewster recognized a community health problem and kept records on those children excluded from school because of medical problems. After collecting these data, Wald convinced the president of the department of health of the need for nursing services in the public schools. Although the department of health decided to use physicians to inspect the children at schools, when the time was right,

Wald encouraged the president to hire a public health nurse as well:

> The time had come when it seemed right to urge the addition of the nurse's service to that of the doctor. My colleagues and I offered to show that with her assistance few children would lose their valuable school time and that it would be possible to bring under treatment those who needed it. Reluctant lest the democracy of the school should be invaded by even the most socially minded philanthropy, I exacted a promise from several of the city officials that if the experiment were successful they would use their influence to have the nurse, like the doctor, paid from public funds. (Wald, 1915, p. 51)

To Wald's credit, the experiment was successful, and in October 1902 the city of New York paid for the services of a school nurse. The board of estimates had allotted more than $30,000 for the employment of trained nurses who were, in Wald's words, the "first municipalized school nurses in the world" (Wald, 1915, p. 53). New York City's Bureau of Child Hygiene was an outgrowth of this service (Wald, 1915; Siegel, 1983).

BIRTH CONTROL: MARGARET SANGER

At different points during the twentieth century, professional organizations and individuals engaged in political activism that attempted to address social ills. During the same period that organized nursing sought social change, Margaret Sanger, a nurse and noted political activist in the twentieth-century, led the struggle for birth control.

Sanger, like Wald and Dock, understood the importance of political activism for effecting social change but sought support outside of organized nursing. She formed coalitions with other women's groups, labor organizers, and philosophers of the period. Sanger's political strength emanated from her outrage over society's control of women's reproductive process and her belief in reproductive autonomy. This one political issue led Sanger to argue for legalizing family planning and making it accessible and acceptable in the United States (Cott, 1987; Chessler, 1992).

Sanger, a visiting nurse at the beginning of the twentieth century, politically challenged America's restrictive laws about birth control (and literature on the subject) and personally experienced the untoward effect of defying the government. For example, in 1912 Sanger wrote an article about syphilis for the socialist weekly *The Call*. The United States Post Office declared that issue unmailable because of the nature of the material, invoking the Comstock Act of 1873, which deliberately prohibited the distribution of information about contraception and abortion (Reed, 1980). Sanger's crusade to disseminate contraception began in 1914, when she traveled to Europe to seek out safe contraception measures. After returning to the United States, she claimed that women could separate procreation from the sexual act and published her ideas in *Woman Rebel*. Again the Comstock Act thwarted Sanger's efforts. Because of her writings, Sanger was indicted and fled the country in October of 1914. When she returned in 1915, after the death of her daughter, public sympathy led the government to drop the charges against her.

In 1916 Sanger, along with her sister, Ethel Byrne, opened the first birth control clinic in the Brownsville section of Brooklyn, New York. These two women provided mothers in Brooklyn with advice about birth control until the police closed the clinic's doors. Sanger again faced arrest, prosecution, and imprisonment. Sanger challenged the legal restriction to distribute information about contraception. Her strong belief and determination led to changes in interpretation of the law and eventually to the founding of the organization known today as Planned Parenthood of America.

ALLIANCE WITH THE WOMEN'S MOVEMENT, 1960-2000

Sanger's political action set the stage for nurses' activism half a century later. In the 1960s the latest women's movement spread throughout the United States. Interest in the rights of women had continued after women gained the right to vote in 1920. This second wave of activists could conceivably harness the vote and gain equal status for women in the law, at work, and in the home. Although nursing in the latter half of the twentieth century remained essentially a profession dominated by women and shared a similar heritage of sexism and oppression, it took time to develop an acceptance of the ideas of the feminism espoused in this movement. In the early 1960s, nursing's presence in the women's movement was "obscure" or "notably absent" (Chinn & Wheeler, 1985, p. 74). The political activism frequently associated with feminist groups was not reported to have carried over into nursing. An "uneasy" relationship existed between those in the traditional female profession of nursing and those engaged in feminist activities (Allen, 1985).

By the 1970s some nursing leaders had enumerated the value of developing ties with the women's movement. Wilma Scott Heide (1973), a nurse and leader in the feminist movement who served as president of the National Organization for Women (NOW) between 1970 and 1974, called for nurses to embrace the ideas of the feminist movement. Heide (1973) believed that nurses and all women shared the similar dilemma of being characterized as caring, nurturing, compassionate, tender, submissive, passive, subjective, and emotional. Whereas some of the traits enhanced the professional role, others served to suppress proactive, empowering behaviors. Heide believed that nursing needed to join with the feminist movement in addressing the inequalities that women faced in society.

Another nurse and feminist, JoAnn Ashley (1976), argued that nurses could no longer be pacifists in order to lead the health care changes that consumers needed. Ashley (1976, p. 133) recognized that "powerful, male-dominated groups, economically motivated, will not be reasonable with their interests and status threatened." Ashley challenged nurses to reflect on who they were and what their role was as nurses.

In the 1980s nursing became a metaphor for the "struggle of women for equality" (Diers, 1984, p. 23). Personal and professional empowerment served as essential qualities for gaining political power, and nurse leaders recognized that public policy would not change without advocates who could successfully use persuasive, political strategies. Feminism gave nurses "a world view that values women and that confronts systematic injustices based on gender" (Chinn and Wheeler, 1985). Nursing's acceptance of this definition of feminism

has assisted nursing's struggle for equality and can be traced to the early 1970s with the ANA's support of the Equal Rights Amendment; the formation of a group called Nurses-NOW; and the establishment of the Nurses Coalition for Action in Politics, nursing's first political action committee.

Changes in women's roles mirror society's perceptions of nursing roles. As women in the second half of the twentieth century challenged inequality and sought political power, nurses did so as well. Yet the political savvy of early pioneer leaders was lost to later generations of nurses. Too often nurses are not included in policy decisions, not involved in policymaking, or just not recognized at all (Gordon, 1997). Nurses have had to relearn political strategies and use them like Talbott and Vance (1981) even to be placed on the agenda of a women's conference on leadership. The nursism that exists within the broader society and at times within the women's movement has lessened, but nursing needs to be vigilant.

At the close of the twentieth century three nurses served in the United States House of Representatives, but as yet, no nurse serves or has served in the Senate. In 1998 32 states benefited from having nurses as legislators, either elected or appointed (Feldman & Lewenson, 2000). At the end of the century, just over 100 nurses could be found to hold a political office, or fewer than 0.005% of the more than two million registered nurses (Summers, 1996; Findings from the national sample survey of registered nurses, 1997). Mary Wakefield, Director of the Center for Health Policy and Ethics at George Mason University in Virginia, notes that "the profession has fielded a strong class of individuals who are influencing public policy through an array of positions and activities" (Wakefield, 1999, p. 205), but argues that still too few are taking advantage of the opportunities.

Lois Capps, a U.S. Congresswoman from California, commented in an interview that people trust nurses (Feldman & Lewenson, 2000). Trust is something that nurses can capitalize on and use when advocating for health care reforms such as gun control, Medicare reimbursement for medication, and other important consumer health care advocacy issues. Nurses know from their experience and education what constitutes quality health care and what a healthy society needs. But nurses must learn to recognize that their tremendous power lies in their knowledge of people, their ability to communicate, and their role to advocate for a healthier population. To do this, Wakefield (1999, p. 205) suggests that political advocacy become a larger part of the educational experience and that students be given "first-hand exposure to the links between health care and health policy." Slowly, as the profession builds on the political activism learned in Cohen and colleagues' third stage of political development (1996), it needs to move into stage four, which is characterized as "leading the way" (p. 262). Nursing will use the important strategic political skills such as coalition building, grassroots mobilization, issue-based collaboration, and media expertise to help set the future agenda for health care. Nurses will learn that its extensive knowledge base and experience lends itself to political activism. In preparation, nurses may benefit by reflecting on their past, understanding what the health care consumer needs, and politically activating their profession for change.

CONCLUSION

Nursing's legacy of political activism altered the course of events for the profession and for health care in this country. Forgetting this legacy has been detrimental to the profession because it denies the opportunity to learn from nursing's visionaries and leaders. Nursing leaders have used such strategies as persuasion, cultivation of political friendships, education, letter-writing campaigns, defiance of the law, and organization to harness the collective voice of nurses. In their quest to improve the standards and quality of health care in this country, nurses have had to participate in the political arena. Nurses must understand their past, share it with others outside of nursing, and use it to its best advantage. History lessons from the architects of the profession can provide a road map for political action today and help address the adverse affect of nursism. These lessons are essential for the health of the profession as well as the health and welfare of the community.

REFERENCES

Allen, M. (1985). Women, nursing and feminism: An interview with Alice J. Baumgart, RN, PhD. *The Canadian Nurse, 81*(1), 20-22.

Armeny, S. (1983). Organized nurses, women philanthropists, and the intellectual bases for cooperation among women, 1898-1920. In E. Condliffe Lagemann (Ed.). *Nursing history: New perspectives, new possibilities.* New York: Teachers College Press.

Ashley, J. (1976). *Hospitals, paternalism and the role of the nurse.* New York: Teachers College Press.

Backer, B. (1993). Lillian Wald: Connecting caring with actions. *Nursing and Health Care, 14*(3), 122-129.

Birnbach, N. (1985). Vignette: Political activism and the registration movement. In D. Mason & S.W. Talbott (Eds.). *Political action handbook for nurses: Changing the workplace, government, organizations, and community.* Menlo Park, CA: Addison-Wesley.

Birnbach, N. & Lewenson, S. B. (1993). *Legacy of leadership: Presidential addresses from the Superintendents' Society and the National League of Nursing Education, 1894-1952.* New York: NLN Press.

Buresh, B. & Gordon, S. (2000). *From silence to voice: What nurses know and must communicate to the public.* Ottawa: Canadian Nurses Association.

Burgess, M.A. (1928). *Nurses, patients, and pocketbooks.* New York: Committee on the Grading of Nursing Schools.

Chesler, E. (1992). *Woman of valor: Margaret Sanger and the birth control movement in America.* New York: Simon & Schuster.

Chinn, P. (1985). Historical roots: Female nurses and political action. *The Journal of the New York State Nurses Association, 16*(2), 29-37.

Chinn, P.L. & Wheeler, C.E. (1985). Feminism and nursing: Can nursing afford to remain aloof from the women's movement? *Nursing Outlook, 33*(2), 74-76.

Christy, T. (1984). Equal rights for women: Voice from the past. In *Pages from nursing history: A collection of original articles from the pages of* Nursing Outlook, The American Journal of Nursing and Nursing Research. New York: American Journal of Nursing.

Cohen, S.S., Mason, J.M., Kovner, C., Leavitt, J.K., Pulcini, J., & Sochalski, J. (1996). Stages of nursing's political development: Where we've been and where we ought to go. *Nursing Outlook, 44*(6), 259-266.

Cott, N. (1977). *The bonds of womanhood: "Woman's sphere" in New England, 1780-1930.* New Haven, CT: Yale University Press.

Cott, N.F. (1987). *The grounding of modern feminism.* New Haven, CT: Yale University Press.

Daniels, L. (1987). *American women in the 20th century: The festival of life.* San Diego: Harcourt Brace Jovanovich.

Diers, D. (1984). To profess—to be a professional. *The Journal of the New York State Nurses Association, 15*(4), 23.

Dock, L. (1907). Some urgent social claims. *The American Journal of Nursing, 7*(10), 895-901.

Dock, L. (1908). The suffrage question. *The American Journal of Nursing, 8*(11), 925-927.

Dock, L. & Stewart, I. (1931). *A short history of nursing* (3rd ed., revised). New York: Putnam's Sons.

Feldman, H.R. & Lewenson, S.B. (2000). *Nurses in the political arena: The public face of nursing.* New York: Springer.

Findings from the national sample survey of registered nurses, March 1996. (1997). United States Department of Health and Human Services Health Resources and Services Administration Bureau of Health Professions Division on Nursing. Available online at www.hhs.gov/aspe/minority/minhrsa2.htm.

Fitzpatrick, L. (1975). *The National Organization for Public Health Nursing, 1912-1952: Development of a practice field.* New York: NLN Press.

Florence Nightingale's letter of advice to Bellevue. (1911). *American Journal of Nursing, 11*(5), 361-364.

Gardner, M.S. (1933). *Public health nursing* (2nd ed., revised). New York: Macmillan.

Gordon, K.M., Myers, A.J., & Kelley, F. (1906). Equal suffrage movement. *American Journal of Nursing, 7*(1), 47-48.

Gordon, S. (1997). *Life support: Three nurses on the front lines.* Boston: Little, Brown.

Heide, W.S. (1973). Nursing and women's liberation a parallel. *American Journal of Nursing, 73*(5), 824-827.

Hine, D.C. (1989). *Black women in white: Racial conflict and co-operation in the nursing profession. 1890-1950.* Bloomington, IN: Indiana University Press.

Hine, D.C. (1990). The Ethel Johns Report: Black women in the nursing profession, 1925; From hospital to college: Black nurse leaders and the rise of collegiate nursing schools. In D.C. Hine (Ed.). *Black women in United States history: Vol. 2. Black women in American history: The twentieth century.* Brooklyn, NY: Carlson.

Hine, D.C. (1993). Staupers, Mabel Keaton (1890-1989). In D.C. Hine (Ed.). *Black women in America: An historical encyclopedia* (vol. 2). Brooklyn, NY: Carlson.

Johns, E. (1925). *A study of the present status of the Negro woman in nursing* (1.1, Series 200, Box 122, Folder 1507, pp. 1-43, Exhibits A-P, Appendixes I and II). New York: Rockefeller Archive Center.

Lerner, G. (1977). *The female experience: An American documentary.* Indianapolis: Bobbs-Merrill.

Lewenson, S. (1994). "Of logical necessity—they hang together": Nursing and the woman's movement, 1901-1912. *Nursing History Review, 2,* 99-117.

Lewenson, S.B. (1996). *Taking charge: Nursing, suffrage & feminism in America, 1873-1920.* New York: NLN Press.

Palmer, S. (1897). *First and second annual conventions of the American Society of Superintendents of Training Schools for Nurses,* Harrisburg, PA. (Also found in Birnbach, N., & Lewenson, S. (1991). *First words: Selected addresses from the National League for Nurses 1894-1933.* New York: NLN Press, and in Reverby, S. (1985). *Annual conventions 1893-1899: The American Society of Superintendents of Training Schools for Nurses.* New York: Garland.)

Palmer, S. (1908). Editorial policy explained. *American Journal of Nursing, 9*(1), 49-50.

Palmer, S. (1909). State societies: Their organization and place in nursing education. *American Journal of Nursing, 9*(12), 956-957.

Progress and reaction. (1908). *American Journal of Nursing, 8*(5), 334-335.

Reed, J. (1980). Sanger, Margaret. In B. Sicherman & C. Hurd Green (Eds.). *Notable American women: The modern period.* Cambridge, MA: The Belknap Press of Harvard University Press.

Reverby, S. (1987). *Ordered to care: The dilemma of American nursing, 1850-1945.* New York: Cambridge University Press.

Robb, I.H. (1900). Original communications [Address of the president]. *American Journal of Nursing, 1*(2).

Rogge, M.M. (1987). Nursing and politics: A forgotten legacy. *Nursing Research, 36*(1), 26-30.

Siegel, B. (1983). *Lillian Wald of Henry Street.* New York: Macmillan.

Staupers, M. (1937). The Negro nurse in America. *Opportunity: Journal of Negro Life, 15,* 339-341. Also reprinted in Hine, D.C. (1985). *Black women in the nursing profession: A documentary history.* New York: Garland.

Summers, B.J. (1996). Nurses and politics: What can we gain? *Tennessee Nurse, 59*(5), 36-37.

Talbott, S. W. & Vance, C. (1981). Involving nursing in a feminist group—NOW. *Nursing Outlook, 29*(10), 592-595.

Thoms, A. (1929). *Pathfinders: A history of progress of the colored graduate nurses.* New York: Kay Printing House.

Vance, C., Talbott, S. W., McBride, A., & Mason, D. J. (1985). Coming of age: The women's movement and nursing. In D. Mason & S. Talbott (Eds.). *Political action handbook for nurses.* Menlo Park, CA: Addison-Wesley.

Vicinus, M. & Nergaard, B. (Eds.). (1989). *Ever yours, Florence Nightingale: Selected letters.* London: Virago.

Wakefield, M. (1999). Public policy: Canaries in the mine. *Journal of Professional Nursing, 15*(4), 205.

Wald, L. (1915). *The house on Henry Street.* New York: Henry Holt.

3

Learning the Ropes of Policy and Politics

JUDITH K. LEAVITT

MARY W. CHAFFEE

CONNIE VANCE

"I am not afraid of storms for I am learning how to sail my ship."

LOUISA MAY ALCOTT

Every politically active person, from presidents of the United States to organizational leaders, *learned* the political and policy skills that catapulted them into positions of power and responsibility. Nurses are no different. Like others, nurses learn the skills of politics and policy through mentoring, role modeling, and trial and error. The most important catalyst is to find mentors—colleagues and friends who are politically involved—to teach us, to believe in and support us, and to celebrate our successes and build on our failures.

In this chapter, the reader will explore how to develop political skills through mentoring, education, and direct experience. Opportunities to apply this learning will be suggested. The student new to politics as well as the experienced nurse have unlimited ways to expand their knowledge and involvement. We never stop learning. We need only decide how much energy, time, and interest we have to stand up for an issue, advocate for our patients, or advance the profession. Success in the world of policy and politics demands the strengths and skills that nurses possess. Working in the policy arena will open doors to opportunities where nurses can be equal players and leaders. Stories of some of these nurses are the essence of this book.

POLITICAL CONSCIOUSNESS-RAISING AND AWARENESS: THE "AHA" MOMENT

How does one get started? Many find that there is a defining moment when the status quo is no longer acceptable. It might be the decision to speak up for patients when they are in need of care and have no advocate. It could be the urgent sense of concern when seeing small children riding in a car without a seatbelt or appropriate booster seat. It could be the frustration of the home health nurse who is unable to continue caring for her patient because Medicare payments ended. These are examples of "aha" moments. These are points when one's consciousness is raised because of an injustice, a danger, or a recognition that change is necessary. It is the adrenaline rush that urges, "Something must be done—and I can do it."

Until experiencing that defining moment, nurses may feel frustrated, angry, or hopeless. When the "aha" hits, we begin to see that it is some aspect of the *system* that is the problem, and that we must do something to change it. We understand that we can influence those who make the decisions to right the wrong, change the law, or create a new policy. We see that an injustice is no longer seen as someone else's problem. That is the meaning of the phrase "the personal is political." The problem in question requires political solutions, more than personal solutions, and it requires skills that can be learned.

Developing policies that promote the delivery of needed care means confronting the political nature of obstacles. When nurses accept that they are not at fault for the inadequacies of the health care system and instead believe that nursing can provide many of the solutions, the profession itself becomes political. Nurses then become proactive rather than reactive. The result is that the individual nurse, as well as the profession, becomes empowered.

GETTING STARTED

Through interviews with 27 American nurses involved in health policy at the national, state, and local levels, Gebbie, Wakefield, and Kerfoot (2000) set out to discover how and why these activist nurses became involved. Their results corroborated what we knew anecdotally:

- The majority of respondents had parents, most often fathers, who were active in policy and politics and who created a mentoring, supportive environment.
- Many were raised to be independent and to believe in their capacity to accomplish what they wanted.
- High school provided a training ground in political socialization.
- Nursing education provided role modeling and mentoring by faculty, deans, and alumni as well as the opportunity to increase political awareness through courses in policy, political science, and economics.
- Clinical practice often provided strong role models, and experiences in public health and community health provided a broad base of political insights.
- Graduate education opened doors for many, through such avenues as the study of law, health economics, and health policy.
- Some had their consciousness raised gradually through work experiences that exposed them to public policy and the need to understand how to influence the process.

The nurses who were interviewed confirmed that there are multiple points of entry into the policy arena. Whether this chapter, this book, a course in policy and politics, or a conversation with a colleague is your first exposure, you have already started.

The skills of politics—how to be persuasive, how to identify and use power effectively, how to analyze obstructions to goal attainment, and how to mobilize people to work collectively—are all learned. Nurses bring skills to the political arena that are learned through education and further refined in clinical practice. Politics requires the kind of communication skills that nurses use to persuade an unwilling patient to get out of bed after abdominal surgery or a child to swallow an unpleasant-tasting medication. All competent political experts possess effective communication skills. Nurses possess many of these skills. In addition, nurses, whether they realize it or not, are health care experts. Nurses can speak knowledgeably about what patients and communities need because they experience it firsthand.

THE POLITICAL DEVELOPMENT OF NURSING AND HOW IT RELATES TO THE INDIVIDUAL

Cohen, Mason, Kovner, Leavitt, Pulcini, and Sochalski (1996) developed a conceptual model describing the political development of the profession. Interestingly, it mirrors the stages that individual nurses go through to learn the ropes (see Chapter 1 for a fuller description of the model). The four stages are buy-in, self-interest, political sophistication, and leading the way.

STAGE ONE: BUY-IN

Buy-in is a reactive stage. For nursing it occurred when the profession began to promote the political awareness of nurses to injustices or changes needed in the policy arena. For the individual this is the "aha" moment. One begins to decide how to become involved.

STAGE TWO: SELF-INTEREST

At this stage the nursing profession began to develop its identity as a special interest and crystallized its uniqueness as a political voice. For the individual, this could be the time when one becomes most focused on specific issues related to one's practice, rather than the larger issues of health care and the profession. It is learning about the nuts and bolts of political activism. The individual might enlist the support and help of colleagues around the issues and together plan strategies to resolve the issues.

STAGE THREE: POLITICAL SOPHISTICATION

Political sophistication is the stage in which policymakers and health care leaders view nurses as having valuable expertise in health policy. For the individual this is the time when legislators and other policymakers turn to nurse experts to be on their health advisory committees, when nurses testify before state legislatures and local health-related boards and commissions, and when nurses get appointed to policy-making bodies.

STAGE FOUR: LEADING THE WAY

This stage is the highest level of political involvement, when nursing "sets the agenda" for change. Instead of just contributing knowledge, nursing becomes the initiator of crucial policy development. For the individual this is the point when individuals direct the dialogue and policy development of organizations and institutions whose mission is broader than health. This includes appointments to positions outside of nursing, to posts such as university president or department head in federal and state government. Nurses are recognized for their unique expertise and perspective and are seen by multiple constituencies as bringing solutions to issues related to the well-being of society as a whole.

Wherever one is in political development, there are higher stages to reach, if desired. Start somewhere. New graduates, pay attention to the work environment and let yourself be ready for the awakening, the "aha" moment. For experienced nurses, think of whether you are ready and how you want to share your expertise and knowledge with policymakers. You may even decide to become the policymaker.

THE ROLE OF MENTORING

At every stage of a nursing career—from student to novice to expert—mentor relationships are an essential element for professional success, socialization, and leadership development. This is particularly true in political and policy arenas in which nurses' involvement is relatively recent and the majority of nurses receive no formal training in their educational programs. In the traditional world of politics, the "old boys' network" consisted of strong mentoring components. Gaining entrée into the inner circle of policy and politics required the mentorship of political party leaders who served as sponsors, role models, and door-openers to aspiring "politicians." Nurses are discovering the necessity of receiving mentoring from a variety of leaders and peers at every career stage, particularly as they expand their influence from the bedside to wider spheres of policy and political involvement. Nurses' mentor connections will take them beyond traditional nursing boundaries, where they can influence decisions and policies that affect their patients and their professional practice.

A mentor or role model provides inspiration and encouragement to get involved, as well as coaching and tutoring in the nuts and bolts of political involvement. As with any other nursing skill, learning the political/policy process requires both theoretic and experiential knowledge. Political mentors can therefore be found in classrooms, clinical settings, professional associations, political parties, government, and community settings. Politically active nurses in one study (Winter & Lockhart, 1997) identified their nursing colleagues in various settings as important policy mentors. These mentors facilitated political involvement by modeling their expertise and inspiring those in their formative years. Nursing political leaders in another study stated that they had found traditional mentors or peer mentors who believed in their abilities, guided their learning, and nourished their self-worth (Leavitt & Barry, 1993). The nationwide "nurse-influentials" studied by Vance (1977) reported that their mentors were crucial "role models for change and risk-taking and for political and diplomatic action." These leaders claimed the mentoring support of nursing colleagues as well as those in administrative, political, and corporate circles.

Mentoring relationships among students, teachers, and colleagues are developmental and empowering. Mentors inspire, guide, advise, and model behavior as they interact with novices and peers

(Vance & Olson, 1998). In both formal and informal teaching situations, teacher and learner grow and mature together through a developmental process, and the same learning process occurs between mentor and protégé. There is also mutual empowerment as all persons in the relationship gain confidence, motivation, and strength (Cohen & Milone-Nuzzo, 2001).

In the nursing profession, the mentor model consists of both expert-novice and peer-peer mentor connections. The developmental and empowering aspects of mentoring relationships are necessary aspects of learning the policy and political ropes. One example of developmental mentoring is the modeling of political behavior at lobby days in Congress or in state legislatures that are sponsored by nursing associations. At these events, nurse lobbyists and nurse activists serve as mentor-guides and role models to nurses and students who are less experienced in the political process. They provide information and strategies and model effective behaviors while lobbying policymakers on specific legislation. These activists also provide the inspiration and vision of what can be done if nurses join together on behalf of shared goals. This is real-life experiential learning between mentor-experts and protégé-novices, and it is a highly effective and practical way of developing political awareness and know-how.

Mentors can empower others by drawing them into the process and inspiring them with their commitment to making change and a "can do" attitude that "we can indeed make a difference." Empowerment as a model for political action has been described as the development of three dimensions: consciousness raising about the sociopolitical realities of nursing; strong and positive self-esteem; and political skills for changing the system (Mason, Backer, & Georges, 1991). Political nurses demonstrate that there is power in numbers and in the collective strength of nursing. Association with optimistic mentors who are committed to their profession and who are not afraid to take risks on behalf of creating change through the political process is empowering to others, particularly those new to political activism. Nurses whose consciousness is raised by empowerment experiences with mentors often report that their professional pride,

confidence, and motivation are strengthened. They come to believe they, too, can improve nursing and health care by engaging in change activities.

Anecdotal and research data continue to demonstrate that mentoring activities and relationships are essential to the ongoing development of policy knowledge and expertise. This is a particular challenge in the formal education and professional socialization of most nurses. Studies continue to point to the lack of formal course work and the scarcity of formal mentors on policy and politics in nurses' education. In the political study by Gebbie et al (2000), nurse activists reported that they were not encouraged to seek mentoring or other developmental experiences and training. There still may not be adequate numbers of politically engaged nurses and faculty who can inspire and inform others as to the value of this involvement. One nurse in the Gebbie study noted that there are three "hooks" that pull nurses into health policy: personal experience, mentors, and dramatic interventions (p. 311). Clearly, mentors, whether they are experts, teachers, or peers, are a critical element in learning the ropes in political policy involvement. As greater numbers of nurses begin to value and engage in the political dimensions of their profession, they will mentor others in the how-tos of this crucial aspect of nursing.

FINDING A MENTOR

If you want to become involved in policy and politics, you can find a mentor, even if you don't know someone personally. Start with a list of what you would like to learn, who you would like to mentor you, people you know who might know the individual, and how to gain access to that person. You can contact the person directly, via e-mail, by phone, or with a note, or you can ask someone who knows the individual to make the first contact. One "mentee" known to the authors learned about the person she selected from others who knew her before she contacted the nurse leader directly. It helps to be able to state what you want to learn from the individual and why you selected that person. For instance, one author went to the campaign manager of the local congressman to learn how to organize nurses for his campaign. The campaign manager saw a motivated, committed volunteer in the author and was thrilled to be able to show her the "ins and outs" of organizing. That was the start of many such organizing campaigns that culminated in the author's achieving a major staff position with a U.S. Senate campaign. Remember the mentor need not be a nurse, and often the mentor is not. The important criteria for a mentor are knowledge and an interest in you. Sometimes the mentor need only get you started; in other situations a mentor becomes a lifelong friend and role model.

COLLECTIVE MENTORING

Because the majority of nurses are newcomers to political and policy activism, every nurse should possess the mentality of being both a mentor and a protégé in the political process. Learning politics is not a solitary activity. This means that nurses should be on the lookout for mentors who can serve as their teachers and guides as they hone political skills. Likewise, every nurse should assume responsibility for actively mentoring others as they refine their repertoire of skills and deepen their involvement. This reciprocal collective mentoring is extremely effective in expanding the political and power base of the profession and its members. Collective mentoring can occur in nursing schools, clinical agencies, and professional associations. This means that wherever we practice nursing, we can each refine our political skills by seeking mentors and serving as mentors to others.

Leavitt and Mason (1998) wrote a case study of the principles and activities associated with collective mentoring in a fledgling political action committee for nurses in New York. This small group of nurses used peer mentoring to develop their political knowledge and influence. They in turn reached out to coach novices in the skills of political organizing, fund raising, and public speaking.

Collective mentoring is a value about process and working together to extend nursing's solidarity of activists. It also is about recognizing that new, even inexperienced, voices can contribute to the development of the most seasoned mentors. Finally, collective mentoring is about moving a vision in creative ways and being committed to the development of people who can move that vision. (Leavitt and Mason, 1998, p. 162)

Joining with others to expand our political influence is a necessary strategy. Each nurse can learn with and from others, regardless of current level of knowledge.

Inherent in this form of mentoring is the development of networks of persons who are active in policy and who take responsibility for expanding these networks. The nurses in these networks should develop intentional strategies for mentoring political neophytes and for "claiming" nurses who may not be in traditional career paths (Gebbie et al, 2000). Organizational networks, including those in academic, clinical, and association settings, are a natural place to establish developmental mentoring activities. For example, politically active faculty members can network with political leaders in professional associations in order to provide undergraduate and graduate students with lobbying and leadership opportunities. Many state nursing associations are successfully reaching out to collectively mentor hundreds of nursing students through lobby days in national and state capitols. Nursing students and practicing nurses also have many opportunities to experience collective mentoring in learning the political ropes through relationships with leaders and peers in organizations such as the National Students Nurses Association, the American Nurses Association (ANA), specialty and state nursing associations, and volunteer health-related organizations. In addition, local political parties, community organizations, and the offices of elected officials offer nurses opportunities to learn through mentored experiences. These organizations can offer numerous mentoring opportunities for involvement in lobbying, policy development, media contacts, fundraising, and the political process in various venues.

HOW DO YOU LEARN THE ROPES OF POLICY AND POLITICS WITHOUT GETTING TANGLED AND STRANGLED?

There are many ways to develop the knowledge and skills that lead to effective action in health policy and politics. The tricky part is *finding* some of the wonderful educational opportunities, because they are scattered throughout a wide variety of places without standard labels. Whatever your educational appetite, there is something for everyone—from continuing education programs to graduate programs in political science and policy. With a little effort and some help getting started in the right direction, an exciting world of educational possibilities is available, leading down paths many nurses did not realize existed when they completed their initial nursing studies. Your specific interests will guide your choices.

PROGRAMS IN SCHOOLS OF NURSING

A few degree programs in policy have been established in schools of nursing. More commonly, nursing programs offer courses, either as core requirements or electives, related to health policy or with health policy content embedded (Box 3-1).

DEGREE PROGRAMS IN PUBLIC HEALTH, PUBLIC ADMINISTRATION, AND PUBLIC POLICY

Departments of public health, political science, policy science, and others are a rich source of policy content in academic programs. Programs in these areas take a little more effort to find because they reside under many different names in university and college departments (Box 3-2). Programs leading to degrees that include health policy content are widely available at the baccalaureate, master, and doctoral level. Numerous programs exist at all academic levels. Examples are listed in Box 3-3.

CONTINUING EDUCATION PROGRAMS

Annual programs are conducted by several academic institutions and professional associations (Box 3-4). Specialty nursing associations and state nursing associations often offer legislative workshops. Check websites and publications for the most current offerings.

EXPERIENTIAL LEARNING

There are various ways to obtain valuable practical experience, from internships to self-study programs.

Internships and Fellowships. Internships and fellowships provide outstanding learning op-

portunities. In addition to teaching nurses the ropes, these practical experiences offer valuable mentoring and networking opportunities and may lead to employment options. Internships may be arranged for credit in academic programs. Summer or year-long internships are available on Capitol Hill, in some federal agencies, and through professional associations. See Appendix B for a list of formal internships and fellowships.

Volunteer Service. A great way to learn politics is to volunteer to work on a political campaign. Volunteer time and energy is welcomed by candidates for elective office at all levels of government: local, state, and federal. First-time candidates with tight budgets are especially appreciative of volunteer assistance. Also consider contacting Democratic or Republican national party headquarters for training and information about volunteer activities.

Professional Association Activities. Many professional associations offer opportunities for volunteer service that lead to rich educational, mentoring, and networking experiences. Members of the ANA may participate in N-STAT, a national grassroots political activity program. N-STAT members are alerted about critical health care issues, encouraged to contact their members of Congress, and are even provided examples of how to write effective letters to legislators. Some N-STAT members serve as leaders: They interview and evaluate candidates for public office to determine whether to recommend that ANA's Political Action Committee (ANA-PAC) endorse a candidate's campaign. (See Chapter 29.)

Some specialty nursing associations and other health professional associations such as the American Public Health Association, the American Cancer Society, and the American Heart Association have strong advocacy and legislative programs. Opportunities to learn about policy exist through volunteer service in groups such as the Public Policy Work Group of the American Association of Critical-Care Nurses (AACN).

Opportunities for Nursing Students. Nursing students who are members of the National Student Nurses Association (NSNA) may learn the

BOX **3-1**   Degree Programs in Schools of Nursing

Graduate Program in Nursing/Health Policy, University of Maryland, Baltimore

School of Nursing
University of Maryland
615 West Lombard Street
Baltimore, MD 20214
Phone: (800) 328-8346 or (410) 706-7503, menu option #4
Website: nursing.umaryland.edu

The University of Maryland at Baltimore established the nation's first graduate program in nursing and health policy in 1980. The 37-credit curriculum prepares nurses to assume leadership positions in policy-making roles in both public and private sectors. The program, which can be completed on a full-time or part-time basis, includes courses in health care delivery systems, the political and social context of policy process, health economics, and nursing and health policy theory. Because of its proximity to the Maryland State House in Annapolis and Washington, DC, it offers many opportunities for practical experiences with leaders in state and federal policy-making roles. Students have completed internships in U.S. Senate and House offices, the Department of Health and Human Services, the U.S. Department of Justice, the American Nurses Association, the American Association of Health Plans, and others. Some University of Maryland students choose to pursue dual master's degrees, completing the Nursing/Health Policy Program in addition to a clinical master's degree. Students also have the opportunity to complete an advanced graduate certificate program in Health and Public Policy at the University of Maryland Baltimore County campus.

MSN in Nursing Management and Policy, Yale University School of Nursing Graduate Program in M.S. in Nursing Management and Policy, Yale University

Yale School of Nursing
100 Church Street South
New Haven, CT 06536-0740
Phone: (203) 785-2389
Website: info.med.yale.edu/nursing

The Nursing Management and Policy curriculum at Yale University prepares nurses for positions of leadership across all settings in the health system. Graduates are encouraged to explore and influence the environment and policies of the health system in acute care, long-term care, home care, and community-based institutions. The Nursing Management and Policy program combines class work, research, and practical experience and can be completed on a full-time or part-time basis.

PhD in Nursing (concentration in health care ethics, health care administration and health policy), George Mason University

George Mason University
College of Nursing and Health Science
4400 University Drive, MS 3C4
Fairfax, VA 22030-4444
Phone: (703) 993-1944
Website: www.gmu.edu/catalog/nursing.html

The PhD in Nursing program at George Mason University prepares nurses for executive roles in nursing and health care. Students learn to conduct and support research in nursing and health care ethics, health care administration, and health policy. Graduates will be prepared to influence the formation and implementation of public policy in health care through analysis of sociocultural, economic, fiscal, political, ethical, and government processes. The program builds on the master of science degree and requires 60 credits beyond the master's degree.

PhD in Nursing, University of Massachusetts, Boston (policy focus on the health of the urban family and elderly)

University of Massachusetts, Boston
100 Morrissey Boulevard
Boston, MA 02125-3393
Phone: (617) 287-5000
E-mail: enrollment.info@umb.edu
Website: www.umb.edu/academic_programs/graduate/cn/nursing/requirements.html

The PhD in Nursing program prepares nurses for careers as educators, policy analysts, and researchers in health policy. The 60-credit program can be completed on a full-time or part-time basis and includes a 6-credit policy internship. Courses include health economics, health care financing, integration of health policy and theory in dissertation research, and health policy I/II.

Continued

BOX **3-1**   Degree Programs in Schools of Nursing—cont'd

**DNSc in Nursing (Health Policy Track),
Columbia University**

Columbia University School of Nursing
Office of Student Services
630 West 168th Street, Box 6
New York, NY 10032
Phone: (800) 899-6728 or (212) 305-5756
E-mail: nursing@columbia.edu

Website: www.cpmcnet.columbia.edu/dept/nursing/
academics-programs/dnsp.html

The Doctor of Nursing Science program prepares clinical nurse scholars to examine, shape, and direct nursing practice. A health policy track may be selected. Core courses develop skill in research methodology and in health policy. Students develop a depth of knowledge through the creation of an individualized program of study.

BOX **3-2**   Searching for Policy, Health Policy, and Related Subjects

Search for policy-related subjects in the following college or university departments:
- Government
- Health Care Administration
- Health Policy
- Nursing
- Policy Science
- Political Science
- Public Administration
- Public Health
- Public Policy

ropes through NSNA's "Leadership U," the association's electronic education initiative. This virtual program encourages nursing students to develop leadership competencies, professional portfolios, and mentoring relationships. Leadership U online learning modules include the following:
- Legislation: why get involved?
- The legislative process: how the system works
- Working with legislators
- The power of public relations and political action committees

Nursing students have the opportunity to incorporate Leadership U activities into their nursing program curriculum for credit. Leadership U can be accessed at the NSNA website (www.nsna.org) through the Leadership U icon.

Self-Study. The value of reading and self-directed learning cannot be underestimated in learning about policy and politics. There is some-

thing for everyone—from scholarly peer-reviewed journals to *Politics for Dummies.*

Professional Journals. Many professional nursing and health care journals include updates on current political issues. The following journals are either wholly focused on policy and politics or include regular political content:
- *American Journal of Nursing,* the official journal of the ANA, a monthly publication that includes "Washington Watch," commentary on current political issues affecting nursing
- *Health Affairs,* a bimonthly journal published by Project HOPE that is known for thought-provoking articles that inform and influence discussion of health policy issues
- *Journal of the American Medical Association (JAMA),* the weekly publication of the American Medical Association, which covers health policy issues of interest to physicians
- *Journal of Health Politics, Policy and Law,* a bimonthly peer-reviewed publication of Duke University Press
- *Journal of Professional Nursing,* the official journal of the American Association of Colleges of Nursing, which includes a regular column on public policy
- *New England Journal of Medicine,* published weekly by the Massachusetts Medical Society, a journal that publishes innovative perspectives and background on health policy issues
- *Nursing Economic$:* a bimonthly publication that includes "Capitol Commentary," a regular feature that examines health care policy issues
- *Policy, Politics & Nursing Practice,* a peer-reviewed quarterly journal that publishes articles

BOX **3-3**   Sample of Degree Programs in Policy, Public Health, and Public Administration

Arizona State University School of Public Affairs Master of Public Administration

The Master of Public Administration program consists of 42 credits and prepares students for public service, public management, and policy analysis at the local, state, and national levels of government (spa.asu.edu/acadprog/mpa.htm).

Harvard School of Public Health Degree Programs in Health Policy and Management

The Department of Health Policy and Management is dedicated to addressing major management and health policy problems through research, advanced training, and dispute resolution. The department offers 80-credit and 40-credit master of science degrees, a doctor of science program, and a doctor of philosophy program in health policy (www.hsph.harvard.edu/academics/hpm).

Harvard University John F. Kennedy School of Government

The mission of the Kennedy School of Government is to prepare leaders for service to democratic societies and to contribute to the solution of public problems. A number of programs are available:

The Master in Public Policy program, through a rigorous 2-year sequence of studies, equips future leaders with the conceptual framework and the specific skills they will need to be successful in public service. The initial emphasis of the curriculum is on building a strong conceptual foundation for analysis, management, and advocacy.

The Master in Public Administration program is an intensive 2-year program designed to prepare its graduates for positions of significant responsibility in the public, nonprofit, and private sectors. The program's curriculum is flexible and lends itself to individual tailoring with guidance from faculty and administrators. Students are expected to have prior graduate-level training in a relevant field (such as economics, political science, or management), as well as at least 3 years of significant professional experience.

The PhD program in health policy is designed for students seeking teaching careers in institutions of higher learning or research careers in health policy. It is a collaborative program offered by the Kennedy School, the Faculty of Arts and Sciences, the Harvard School of Public Health, the Harvard Medical School, and the Harvard Business School.

The PhD program in political economy and government is intended for students interested in either academic or policy-making careers that require an advanced knowledge of both economics and political science. It is designed for the small number of students whose academic needs are not met by studies in economics, political science, or public policy taken alone.

The PhD program in public policy prepares qualified candidates to shape the direction of public policy research and to train the next generation of teachers for programs in public policy and the social sciences. It qualifies individuals to perform high-level policy analysis and to lead in the public sector (www.ksg.harvard.edu/).

Johns Hopkins University Department of Health Policy and Management Graduate, Doctoral, and Graduate Certificate Programs

The Department of Health Policy and Management, in the School of Public Health, offers master, doctoral, and graduate certificate programs (ww3.jhsph.edu/dept/hpm/degreeprograms/index.html).

Rockefeller College State University of New York (SUNY) at Albany Master of Arts in Public Administration and Policy

The 40-credit Master of Public Affairs and Policy program prepares students for careers as policy analysts and leaders in public service (www.albany.edu/rockefeller/pad/).

Ohio State University, School of Public Policy and Management Dual Master's Degree Program

The School of Public Policy and Management offers a dual master's degree in conjunction with the university's programs in health services management and policy, natural resources, law, and social work (www.ppm.ohio-state.edu/ppm).

The George Washington University Master of Political Management

The Graduate School of Political Management offers a master's degree program that prepares students for careers in professional campaign management. (www.gwu.edu/~gspm/academics/pm/index.htm)

Continued

BOX **3-3**   Sample of Degree Programs in Policy, Public Health, and Public
Administration—cont'd

The George Washington University
Master of Legislative Affairs

The Master of Legislative Affairs program prepares students for careers in government relations and to be lobbyists, legislative specialists, or policy analysts (www.gwu.edu/academics/mala/index.htm).

The University of Iowa College of Public Health
Doctoral Program in Health Management
and Policy

This program prepares students for careers in health services research, education, and policy leadership roles in universities, government, and health care organizations (www.pmeh.uiowa.edu/hmp/phddegree.html).

The University of Michigan School
of Public Health
Master's Degree and Doctoral Programs

The Department of Health Management and Policy offers a Master of Health Services Administration and a Master of Public Health program; both programs integrate health policy content (www.sph.umich.edu/hmp/).

The University of South Florida
Health Policy and Management Programs

Three Master's degree programs and the PhD are offered; all prepare professionals to assume leadership roles of multidisciplinary teams and to effectively develop, implement, and evaluate programs that affect the health of the public (www.publichealth.usf.edu/degprog.html).

---

on legislation affecting nursing practice, case studies in policy and political action, interviews with policymakers and policy experts, and articles on trends and issues

Books. Browse through the political science, government, or current events sections of your favorite bookstore. You can browse online bookseller sites such as Amazon.com or Barnesandnoble.com. Search for the words *politics, policy,* or *health policy* and see what piques your interest. Consider some of the following as good introductory guides:

- *The Dance of Legislation* by Eric Redman (Simon and Schuster, 1973). This book is a classic that traces the drafting and passage of a piece of health legislation, including the plots, maneuvering, failures, and successes.
- *Politics for Dummies* by Ann DeLaney (IDG Books Worldwide, 1995). We all have to start somewhere, and this is a good place for anyone who slept through civics class in high school.
- *The House and Senate Explained: The People's Guide to Congress* by Ellen Greenberg (W.W Norton, 1996). Greenberg provides an excellent guide to understanding what happens on Capitol Hill.

- *Tribes on the Hill: The U.S. Congress Ritual and Realities* by J. McIver Weatherford (Bergin and Garvey Publishers, 1985). This book provides a remarkable anthropologic exploration of how the "tribe" on Capital Hill behaves and why.
- *The Politics of Health Legislation: An Economic Perspective* (2nd ed.) by Paul Feldstein (Health Administration Press, 1996). An economist explores how individuals, groups, and legislators act in their own self-interest.
- *The Nurses' Directory of Capitol Connections* by Jan Bull, Nancy Sharp, and Mary Wakefield (available online from George Mason University, Center for Health Policy, Research and Ethics, at www.gmu.edu/departments/chp.). This directory, updated most recently in 2000, lists the names and contact information for nurses in the Washington, DC, area who are involved in a wide range of policy-making positions including bioethics, insurance, lobbying, policy analysis, quality, education, and reimbursement. It includes nurses who serve as federal and state legislators.

Newspapers. Most major metropolitan newspapers offer political analysis of national politics. Some that are recognized for their in-depth politi-

BOX **3-4**   Continuing Education Programs in Health Policy

Health Policy Institute, George Mason University
Fairfax, Virginia

The Center for Health Policy, Research and Ethics
George Mason University
4400 University Drive, MS 3C4
Fairfax, VA 22030-4444
Phone: (703) 993-1931
Website: www.gmu.edu/departments/chpre/
policyinstitute/

The Health Policy Institute is a 5-day program that provides individuals from various backgrounds the chance to study issues confronting health care providers, consumers, and policymakers. The institute provides an overview of how government systems work in developing policy, the players involved in crafting policy, and current health policy issues. Completion of the institute can earn three graduate credits. In addition to the institute, participants may elect to complete a Washington internship with a federal health agency, in a Capitol Hill office, or with a national policy organization. The internship offers 4-graduate credits. The Policy Leadership Training Program, which can be completed in addition to the Health Policy Institute, offers a third option for participants to develop leadership skills in linking health issues with policy development and strategies.

The Nurse in Washington Internship,
Washington, DC

National Federation for Specialty Nursing Organizations
East Holly Avenue, Box 56
Pitman, NJ 08071-0056
Phone: (609) 256-2333
E-mail: NFSNO@mail.ajj.com

The Nurse in Washington Internship (NIWI, pronounced "nee-wee") is a 4-day educational program that culminates in visits with members of Congress. Held each spring in Washington, DC, the program brings together nurses with diverse backgrounds from across the country to learn about the policy-making process, the development of the federal budget, ways to work with the media, and the legislative and regulatory processes. Two scholarships are available to nurses who are members of specialty associations that are members of the National Federation for Specialty Nursing Organizations (NFSNO).

A highlight of the program is the Nurses in Washington roundtable dinner. Hosted by the NIWI interns, the dinner brings together nurses involved in policy and politics in Washington, DC, for a night of networking and program by a guest speaker. Speakers have included former American Nurses Association President Virginia Trotter Betts, Congresswoman Lois Capps, and Sheila Burke, former Chief of Staff to Senator Robert Dole.

Johns Hopkins Summer Institute in Health Policy
and Management, Johns Hopkins University

Department of Health Policy and Management
Johns Hopkins School of Hygiene and Public Health
Johns Hopkins University
Baltimore, MD 21205
Phone: (410) 614-1580
E-mail: hpm-inst@jhsph.edu

This annual summer institute offers health professionals the opportunity to strengthen their public health and policy skills. The month-long institute includes content on managing and improving health services outcomes and costs, concepts and strategies in health education, promotion and communication; and health policy analysis.

cal reporting on health issues include the *Washington Post* (www.washingtonpost.com), the *New York Times* (www.nytimes.com), the *Los Angeles Times* (www.latimes.com), and *The Wall Street Journal* (www.wsj.com).

Television. All major news programs and television news-magazines address political issues and government activities. The ultimate viewing experience for true political voyeurs is C-SPAN. This channel is available as a public service created by the American cable television industry to provide access to the live gavel-to-gavel proceedings of the U.S. House of Representatives and the U.S. Senate and to other forums where public policy is discussed, debated, and decided. C-SPAN provides a wealth of information about the democratic process, without editing, commentary, or analysis. Its website is www.c-span.org.

Public Broadcasting. PBS is a private, nonprofit media enterprise owned and operated by the nation's 347 public television stations. PBS uses the power of noncommercial television, the Internet, and other media to broadcast quality programs and education services. Its website is www.pbs.org.

Radio

- National Public Radio. Founded in 1970, National Public Radio (NPR) serves an audience of more than 15 million Americans each week via 620 public radio stations and the Internet (www.npr.org). NPR provides carefully researched in-depth reporting.
- C-SPAN Radio. C-SPAN Radio offers public affairs commercial-free programming 24 hours a day. Listeners may listen through the radio or Internet. The broadcast schedule is available at www.c-span.org.

APPLICATION OF LEARNED SKILLS

Everyday, political decisions are made in hospitals, schools, legislatures, corporations, insurance companies, and professional associations that influence our professional practice. It is up to each nurse to determine how to be engaged. Nurses can opt to be engaged at any of three levels described by Trotter Betts and Leavitt (2001): the nurse-citizen, the nurse-activist, or the nurse-politician.

NURSE-CITIZEN

The *nurse-citizen* is a nurse who performs fundamental civic responsibilities (Box 3-5). The nurse-citizen brings the perspective of health care to the voting booth, to public forums, and to community activities. For example, at a school board meeting, nurses might speak about the vital role that school nurses provide in meeting the complex health needs of students. Nurses bring that same perspective to the voting booth when health issues are a particular concern in an election.

NURSE-ACTIVIST

The *nurse-activist* takes a more active role in the policy arena, often focusing on issues related to providing expert care to patients (Box 3-6). These may be practice issues related to working conditions that require legislation or collective action to bring about policy change. An example might be limits on practice, such as those challenged by advanced

---

BOX **3-5**   The Nurse-Citizen

- Registers to vote.
- Votes in every election.
- Keeps informed about health care issues.
- Speaks out when services or working conditions are inadequate.
- Participates in public forums.
- Knows local, state, and federal elected officials.
- Joins politically active nursing organizations.

Adapted from K. Chitty (Ed.). *Professional nursing: concepts and challenges* (3rd ed.). Philadelphia: W.B. Saunders.

BOX **3-6**   The Nurse-Activist

- Contacts public officials through letters, telegrams, or phone calls.
- Registers people to vote.
- Contributes money to a political campaign.
- Works on a political campaign.
- Lobbies decision-makers by providing pertinent statistical and anecdotal information.
- Forms or joins coalitions that support an issue of concern.
- Writes letters to the editors of local papers.
- Invites legislators to visit the workplace.
- Holds a media event to publicize an issue.
- Provides testimony.

Adapted from K. Chitty (Ed.). *Professional nursing: concepts and challenges* (3rd ed.). Philadelphia: W.B. Saunders.

---

practice nurses and nurse anesthetists, as well as issues such as mandatory overtime, which creates unsafe conditions for the nurse and patient. The nurse-activist applies political skills to challenge the stakeholders who attempt to restrict practice. Nurse-activists understand the necessity of collective political activity and collective political mentoring to advance the political skills of all nurses.

NURSE-POLITICIAN

The *nurse-politician* has experienced the power and satisfaction that comes from "making a difference" and seeks elective office or an appointment to a policy position (Box 3-7). Many examples are included in this book and are reflected in the contributor's stories. This activity reflects stage four of

BOX **3-7**   The Nurse-Politician

- Runs for elected office.
- Seeks appointment to a regulatory agency.
- Seeks appointment to a governing board in the public or private sector.
- Uses nursing expertise in the role of front-line policymaker to enhance health care and the profession.

Adapted from K. Chitty (Ed.). *Professional nursing: concepts and challenges* (3rd ed.). Philadelphia: W.B. Saunders.

nursing's political development, where nursing has attained the power and position to set the agenda and guide the process of policy development and implementation. Although it is often challenging and difficult, more and more nurses are willing to take this giant leap in political activism. In 2002, for example, there were about 100 state legislators who are nurses, along with three members of Congress and numerous local office holders. These nurses are making a difference. They are role models who are leading the way toward more enlightened health policies in the United States.

CONCLUSION

Nurses who have achieved success in influencing policy and politics usually start with little or no knowledge of the political process and little awareness of the contributions they could make. Although some came from families with political involvement, most of these nurses found that educational and practice experiences provided them with the basic skills to become involved in political action and policy development. Because they asked for help, they found mentors to provide inspiration, guidance, and support. They honed their skills through collective political networking and mentoring. Excellent communication skills, an understanding of the health care system, an ability to motivate others (including patients), a commitment to improve health, and a willingness to seek help are the skills needed in policy and politics. Nurses pos-

sess these skills and practice them daily in a variety of health care settings.

Once nurses experience an "aha" moment and realize that they need the political skills to drive change, they should seek mentors and educational opportunities to expand their knowledge about policy and politics. Through formal and informal educational programs, nurses can apply learning in the workplace, government, organizations, and the community.

As a nurse-citizen, nurse-activist, or nurse-politician, nurses use their skills and resources to improve the U.S. health system. Nursing's perspectives and values humanize the delivery of health services. With the right political skill and knowledge of policy-making, nurses can and will make a difference.

REFERENCES

Cohen, S., Mason, D., Kovner, C., Leavitt, J., Pulcini, J., & Sochalski, J. (1996). Stages of nursing's political development: Where we've been and where we ought to go. *Nursing Outlook, 44*(1), 20-23.

Cohen, S. & Milone-Nuzzo, P. (2001). Advancing health policy in nursing education through service learning. *Advances in Nursing Science, 23*(3), 28-40.

Gebbie, K.M., Wakefield, M., & Kerfoot, K. (2000). Nursing and health policy. *Journal of Nursing Scholarship, 32*(3), 307-315.

Leavitt, J.K. & Barry, C.T. (1993). Learning the ropes. In D.J. Mason, S.W. Talbott, & J.K. Leavitt (Eds.). *Policy and politics for nurses.* Philadelphia: W. B. Saunders.

Leavitt, J. K., & Mason, D. J. (1998). The good ol' girls and collective mentoring. In C. Vance & R.K. Olson (Eds.). *The mentor connection in nursing.* New York: Springer.

Mason, D.J., Backer, B.A., & Georges, C.A. (1991). Toward a feminist model for the political empowerment of nurses. *Image: Journal of Nursing Scholarship, 23*(2), 72-77.

Trotter Betts, V. & Leavitt, J.K. (2001). Nurses and political action. In K. Chitty (Ed.). *Professional nursing: concepts and challenges* (3rd ed.). Philadelphia: W.B. Saunders.

Vance, C. (1977). A group profile of contemporary influentials in American nursing (Doctoral dissertation, Teachers College, Columbia University, 1977). *Dissertation Abstracts International, 38,* 4734B.

Vance, C. & Olson, R.K. (Eds.) (1998). *The mentor connection in nursing.* New York: Springer.

Winter, M.K. & Lockhart, J.S. (1997). From motivation to action: Understanding nurses' political involvement. *Nursing and Health Care Perspectives, 18*(5), 244-250.

Vignette   *Sharon A. Brigner & Kathleen T. Smith*

The Nurse in Washington Internship

"Learning is the essential fuel for the leader, the source of high-octane energy that keeps up the momentum by continually sparking new understanding, new ideas, and new challenges."
WARREN BENNIS AND BURT NANUS

There are numerous ways for a nurse to learn about policy and politics, and the Nurse in Washington Internship (NIWI) is one of the best. NIWI (pronounced *nee-wee*) is a 4-day educational program conducted each spring in Washington, DC. The program broadens nurses' knowledge of the legislative and policy-making processes and promotes the involvement of nurses in the political process. For many years, nursing organizations have served as a primary vehicle for nurses to learn about policy and to advocate on issues. The National Federation for Specialty Nursing Organizations (the Federation), a coalition of 35 specialty nursing associations representing approximately 400,000 registered nurses, developed NIWI so its members could learn to be more effective. The Federation recognized that nurses could benefit from an educational program designed to prepare them to actively influence health policy issues, and in 1985 it conducted the first NIWI program. Since that time, more than 1,800 nurses have participated in the program. Beginning in 2002, the Nursing Organizations Alliance will be the NIWI sponsor.

THE NIWI PROGRAM

The 4-day NIWI program combines speaker presentations, networking, and the opportunity to apply newly learned skills during visits to Capitol Hill. The program includes presentations by nationally recognized speakers working in all branches of government, regulatory agencies, and advocacy groups. Speakers provide presentations on numerous topics, including the following:

- Linking practice, policy, and politics
- How to influence legislation
- The role of state boards of nursing
- Understanding the role of the Centers for Medicare and Medicaid Services (formerly the Health Care Financing Agency)
- The role of government commissions in influencing health policy
- The role of the media in influencing health policy
- Designing the federal budget in light of competing priorities
- The role of special interest groups in influencing health policy
- Using research findings to influence health policy

A briefing at the White House or Department of Health and Human Services is a highlight of the program. On the final day of NIWI, the interns head to Capitol Hill to meet with members of Congress or their legislative staff. Interns from the same state coordinate their visits and bring issues of mutual interest to the attention of legislators. Reading materials are provided to NIWI interns in advance, and guidance is given on how to set up appointments with legislators. No experience is required to attend NIWI—only a desire to learn.

NETWORKING

Networking is an important part of the NIWI experience. Each year the NIWI interns host the "Nurses in Washington Roundtable Dinner." The dinner offers the interns and NIWI alumni the opportunity to network with policymakers and nursing leaders from the greater Washington metropolitan area. The opportunity to network with fellow interns and speakers is highly valued by the participants. Interns are encouraged to network with other interns from their home states and with interns who share clinical and policy interests. NIWI alumni often continue to network long after their week in Washington is over. This has become easier in recent years through the use of e-mail.

NIWI SCHOLARSHIPS

A number of nursing specialty organizations provide scholarships to enable their members to attend NIWI. In addition, since 1995, the editors of *Policy and Politics in Nursing and Health Care* and the publisher, the W. B. Saunders Company, have offered a $1500 NIWI scholarship on behalf of all the book's contributors as a demonstration of their commitment to the education of nurses in health policy.

FOR YOUR INFORMATION

One NIWI Intern's Experience
Sharon Brigner, NIWI Intern, 1997

NIWI opened my eyes to numerous career opportunities in policy. Because I was exposed to these opportunities early in my career, I began to actively plan and strategize career choices so I could participate in the political process as a health professional. The networking opportunities at NIWI proved invaluable. When I attended in 1997, I was serving as President of the National Student Nurses Association and was graduating from nursing school within a few months. During NIWI I met one of the Chief Nurse Officers of the National Institutes of Health (NIH) in Bethesda, Maryland, who was serving as President of the American Association of Critical Care Nurses. In a casual conversation, I told her that I had been working for 2 years in a neurology intensive care unit as a student nurse and had planned to start my career in Texas. She told me about a neurology internship for graduate nurses at NIH and encouraged me to apply. Because of this discussion, I began to consider opportunities in the Washington, DC, area. I obtained several job offers in the area and decided to start my career at NIH. Had it not been for that networking opportunity, my career, and even my life, would not be as it is today. In fact, two of the speakers at NIWI became my employers and valuable mentors to me. As a direct result of my NIWI participation, I have obtained new jobs, found publishing opportunities and speaking engagements, and made new friends and colleagues.

NIWI opened new doors for me and solidified my interest and decision to pursue policy in graduate school and as a career. One highlight of my career was when the White House invited me to speak on Social Security and Medicare at the White House and to introduce President Clinton at a press conference! This experience was a direct result of my nursing association involvement and my networking activities, including NIWI.

I am currently employed as a senior health policy analyst and lobbyist at the National Committee to Preserve Social Security and Medicare. I am pursuing a joint JD/PhD degree and hope to continue using my health care background to influence public policy and the legislative process. NIWI played a critical role in my career. It was a truly empowering experience. I was very fortunate to meet nurses who have blazed a trail in policy and used their nursing knowledge as a catalyst for change. I hope to do the same!

Sharon Brigner, RN, introduced President Clinton at a press conference on Social Security and Medicare at the White House, February 1999. (L to R, Sharon Brigner, President Bill Clinton, First Lady Hillary Rodham Clinton.)

Vignette   *Stephanie L. Ferguson*

The White House Fellowship

"Opportunities multiply as they are seized."
                                        SUN TZU

Imagine waking up to answer the phone and hearing, "Hello, Dr. Ferguson? Congratulations, you have been selected by the President of the United States and the President's Commission on White House Fellowships to serve as a fellow in the Class of 1996-97. We will be sending you an official letter and expect to see you in Washington,

DC, in 2 weeks for placement week. Please fill out all the paper work for the fellowship and select the top six cabinet members you would like to work with. We will match your choices with the cabinet members interested in working with you. Congratulations!"

In shock, I simply said "Thank you." Instead of jumping up, screaming, and shouting for joy, I just exhaled, thanked God, and realized my life was going to change.

White House Fellow Stephanie Ferguson, RN, is welcomed to the program at a White House breakfast hosted by President George Bush.

The White House Fellows Program: Specific Selection Criteria

- Applicants must be U.S. citizens.
- Employees of the federal government are not eligible unless they are career military personnel.
- Applicants should be out of school and working in their chosen professions.
- Applicants are expected to have a record of remarkable achievement early in their careers; the skills required to serve at the highest levels of government; the potential to be leaders in their professions; and a proven commitment to public service.
- There are no formal age restrictions. However, the fellowship program was created to give selected Americans the experience of government service early in their careers.
- Fellowships are awarded on a strictly nonpartisan basis.
- The Commission encourages balance and diversity in all aspects of the program.

PURPOSE OF THE WHITE HOUSE FELLOWS PROGRAM

President Lyndon B. Johnson and John W. Gardner created the White House Fellows (WHF) Program in 1965. The purpose of the White House Fellows program is to provide talented and dynamic young Americans firsthand experience in the process of governing the United States and a sense of personal involvement in the leadership of society. Since its inception, more than 500 fellows have participated in the program and have gone on to become leaders in all disciplines, fulfilling the fellowship's mission to encourage active citizenship and service to the nation. Some notable alumnae include U.S. Secretary of State Colin Powell, Secretary of Labor Elaine Chao, CNN Chairman and Chief Executive Officer Tom Johnson, and General Wesley K. Clark, former Supreme Allied Commander, Europe.

Fellow Selection Process

The White House Fellows Program is strictly nonpartisan. The selection process is very competitive. Of about 500 to 800 applicants each year, 11 to 19 individuals are selected to serve as fellows. The application is rigorous and designed to capture remarkable achievements early in an applicant's career, demonstrated leadership qualities, a commitment to public service, and the skills necessary to serve as a special assistant to a cabinet officer or high-level government official. Once the applications are processed by the staff of the White House Fellows Program and screened by former fellows, 120 applicants are referred to regional panelists for interviews. The regional panelists select approximately 30 finalists to interview with the President's Commissioners on White House Fellowships in the Washington, DC, area.

Evidence of growth potential as a leader is a key criterion in the selection process. All national finalists are required to successfully complete background investigations to ensure the security clearance necessary to serve in high-level work assignments. The national finalists' interviews are intense, to say the least. Candidates are interviewed for three and a half days. The Commission then recommends to the president

The White House Fellows Application

The application includes writing several essays on your career, academic achievements, and community achievements; a creative and innovative policy memorandum to the president; an essay explaining why you want to be a fellow; and an essay on what you expect to do in your lifetime. The application also requests "candidate evaluations," or reference letters, from three to five individuals.

The White House Fellowship Application Process Timeline

February 1: Application deadline
Third week in March: Regional finalist selection
April: Regional finalist interviews
First week in May: Notification of national finalists
First weekend in June: National finalist interviews
Mid-June: Selection announcement by the President
Late June or July: Placement week, in which fellows interview with cabinet members and other high-level officials in various government agencies to determine their work assignments for the year
September 1: Beginning of fellowship

those individuals it finds most qualified for the fellowship.

Compensation for Fellows

Fellows are paid at a government level of Grade 14-Step 3, which is approximately $75,000 to $80,000 for the year. At the end of the fellowship year, fellows are encouraged to return to their former roles, with a new breath of knowledge and experience in public policy, well prepared to contribute to their professions, their communities, and the country.

MY WHITE HOUSE FELLOW EXPERIENCE
Interview and Selection

The White House fellowship selection process is very competitive and frustrating at times, yet I found it exhilarating. During the regional and final interviews, I met dynamic interview panelists. My regional finalist interview was held in Washington, DC, with community leaders from Washington, DC, Maryland, and Virginia. After being selected as a finalist in the selection process, I was interviewed at the Naval Academy in Annapolis, Maryland, for four and half days, with nine intensive interviews with commissioners appointed by President Clinton. I was then honored to be chosen as one of the select few fellows.

Placement Week

I arrived in Washington, DC, two weeks later to attend "Placement Week." During this time fellows interview with cabinet members and other high-level officials in various government agencies to determine their work assignments for the year. I selected the following people to interview with: Vice President Al Gore, Secretary of State Warren Christopher, and Secretary of Housing and Urban Development Henry Cisneros. I saw excellent opportunities with all of these leaders. With the Vice President, I could work on education policy and violence prevention. With Secretary Cisneros, I could use my research and volunteer work in housing developments with teen pregnancy prevention. With Secretary Christopher, I could explore national security issues.

When I received my schedule for interviews during placement week, I was surprised to find I had been selected to be interviewed by Vice President Al Gore; Dr. Kenneth Kiser, the Undersecretary of Health in the Department of Veterans' Affairs; Henry Cisneros, Secretary of the Department of Housing and Urban Development; and Dr. Donna Shalala, Secretary of the U.S. Department of Health and Human Service (DHHS). I was disappointed that I was not invited to meet with Secretary Warren Christopher.

I met with Dr. Shalala before going to my interview at the U.S. DHHS. She told me, "You have accomplished a great deal in your career and life. I want you to be with me and see what it is like to run one of the largest federal agencies in the nation. You will probably one day be where I am, so you need to understand how to run such an agency and work in policy now while you are young." At that point I was 33 years old (the average age of a White House fellow).

I met with Dr. Shalala for less than 10 minutes before she got up from her desk, and said, "Let's go meet the rest of the staff." I enjoyed meeting all of the staff in her immediate office: the deputy secretary, the executive assistants, the personal assistants, and others. I told her, "I have an interview at the Labor Department and I am already late." She said, "Don't worry. You are not going to work there any way. I will call them and I'll have a car take you over." I did make it to the Labor Department and finished the interview. I returned to the White House Fellows Office to meet with the Fellows Program Director, Jackie Blumenthal. Ms. Blumenthal said, "Donna Shalala called and *you will* be placed at the DHHS." There was no discussion: The whirlwind of interviews was over!

My Fellowship Begins

It was a privilege to serve as a fellow and special assistant to Secretary Donna E. Shalala. My first day on the job started out with protocol lessons, including which side of the car you sit in when accompanying the Secretary, where you sit with the Secretary at the Capitol or in DHHS meetings, and at official dinners. Thank goodness I am a quick study and have a sense of humor because indeed, I knew there would come a time when I was going to mess up protocol!

Formal Fellowship Training

In addition to my work assignments, approximately three to four times a week I attended the White House fellowship formal leadership training program. The White House fellowship's leadership development program included lectures by chief executive officers of Fortune 500 companies, Supreme Court justices, members of Congress, and others.

Fellowship Activities

I assisted the Secretary in the development and implementation of the national strategy to prevent teen pregnancy. I represented her on Capitol Hill advocating for health legislation, particularly legislation related to teen pregnancy prevention provisions, including the guidelines for abstinence education. I also worked on the national fatherhood initiative and the girl power initiative. I gave keynote addresses to various organizations for the Secretary, prepared reports, testimony, and briefings for the Secretary, and prepared correspon-

dence. I also represented the Secretary at a variety of federal agency meetings that pertained to welfare reform legislation, the president's child health initiatives, and nursing and nursing education initiatives. My hours were long: I worked about 18 hours a day.

Fellows travel throughout the United States to explore domestic policy issues and abroad to better understand global issues. During my tenure I worked with the United Nations and spent time in Panama learning about issues related to biodiversity and the Panamanian tropical rainforests, as well as working on the final negotiations for the return of the Panama Canal from the United States to Panama. I taught at the University of Panama and met with faculty in their graduate program in maternal and child health nursing. This was exciting for me because I am a perinatal and neonatal clinical nurse specialist and childbirth educator.

While in Panama, I learned the importance of packing light. My colleagues joked I had the biggest suitcase in the world! I had shoes and handbags for every suit and event. By the time I went on my next international trip to Africa, I impressed all of my fellow classmates with one backpack and one small piece of luggage for a three-week working trip to Africa! When in Africa, I represented the United States and the DHHS in South Africa and Mozambique. I learned about health, education, and human resources issues while also assisting in developing and evaluating programs. I worked with Gracia Michel, now the wife of Nelson Mandela, and Bishop Desmond Tutu. I learned about the struggles involved in sustaining democracy in post-Apartheid South Africa and post-Civil War Mozambique. While in South Africa, I organized the first post-Apartheid HIV/AIDS consortium meeting with nongovernmental organizations (NGOs) and governmental agencies in the eastern and western Capes of South Africa. I worked with several NGOs to decrease domestic violence and maternal-infant mortality in some of the townships in South Africa.

HOW THE FELLOWSHIP CHANGED MY LIFE

Becoming a White House fellow changed my life and catapulted my career in nursing. The fellowship is a priceless experience, and the networking opportunities along the way are invaluable. The program's leadership development component, work assignments, and domestic and international travel duties allowed me to meet some of the most notable people in the world. It was a privilege to be mentored by prestigious alumni of the program, and it broadened my vision and understanding of how Washington truly works.

The fellowship taught me how critical it is to be present "at the table" as a nurse, particularly when decisions and policies are crafted at the highest levels of government that affect the health care delivery system. If you want to get results in Washington, you must learn how to build and sustain alliances and relationships. I had to do this everyday when working on Capitol Hill and in the DHHS.

By shadowing Secretary Shalala, I learned valuable lessons in how to successfully lead and manage a large bureaucracy and the need to surround oneself with the best and the brightest, who also understand the value of being team players. Secretary Shalala is a no-nonsense person. She is very powerful, quite funny at times, caring, and sincere. Yet, she is also tough, demands results, and has high standards. The most valuable skill I learned from her is how to negotiate and then compromise with grace.

LIFE AFTER THE FELLOWSHIP

As a result of the White House fellowship experience, I have been appointed to serve as a leader, expert, and consultant on many prestigious commissions and task forces in the state of Virginia, at the federal level in the United States, and at the international level with the World Health Organization (WHO) and the Pan American Health Organization (PAHO). Dr. Shalala advised me to broaden my horizons, particularly in the international health arena. She assigned me as her assistant on projects related to international issues, particularly HIV/AIDS and children and women's health issues. The networks I established in the international health arena have truly made a difference in my career and my activities as a health policy analyst and clinician.

I have consulted extensively with the U.S. uniformed services in Germany and worked as a consultant representing PAHO at the WHO. The Secretary of the Air Force appointed me as a Civil Representative to the National Security Forum. I also served as a Visiting Scholar at the Judge School of Management Studies at Cambridge University in England. Additionally, I serve as a member of the International Task Force for Nursing for the American Red Cross. The fellowship provided me with the experience and connections needed to be appointed to several federal initiatives in the U.S. Office of Minority Health, where I served as an expert panel member on the Black Progress Review for Healthy People 2000 and as an expert panel member on the Ethnic and Cultural Diversity Workforce Task Force for the Division of Nursing.

I have had the opportunity to teach extensively, including courses in health policy, cultural diversity, administration, and leadership development at the graduate level at Howard University's Division of Nursing; international health policy and women's health courses at the undergraduate level at Stanford University in Washington, DC; and graduate courses in administration and health policy at George Mason University (GMU) College of Nursing and Health Science. I also serve at GMU as a faculty affiliate in the Center for Health Policy, Research and Ethics. Since the White House fellowship, I have been selected as a fellow in the American Academy of Nursing, Distinguished Practitioner in the National Academies of Practice, and International Scholar in Phi Beta Delta International Honor Society.

THE NEXT GENERATION OF FELLOWS

As an alumna of the White House Fellows Program, I now participate in making the first cut of individuals applying for the fellowship. I am in search of dynamic, innovative nurses interested in applying for membership in the nation's most presti-

Contact Information for the President's Commission on White House Fellowships

712 Jackson Place, NW
Washington, DC 20503
Telephone: (202) 395-4522
Fax: (202) 395-6179
Website: www.whitehousefellows.gov

gious fellowship for leadership development and public service.

Additional information about a White House fellowship can be found at the White House Fellows website at www.whitehousefellows.gov. If you want to learn the ropes in policy and politics in nursing and health care, consider applying for this prestigious, dynamic fellowship.

Vignette   *Catherine A. Wilson*

Learning the Ropes as a Congressional Staffer

"I was drenched in new knowledge. I felt shiny and new and very wise."

VENETA MASSON

For 15 months I had the privilege of serving on the staff of a U.S. Senator, Senator Daniel K. Inouye (D-HI), from December 1999 to April 2001. In 1989 Senator Inouye created a position for a mili-

Senator Daniel Inouye and Congressional Detailee Catherine Wilson, RN, in the Senator's office, 2001.

tary nurse to serve on Capitol Hill, usually for a year, as a full-time health policy advisor. The position, known as the Congressional Detail to the Committee on Appropriations Subcommittee on Defense, rotates among nurses in the U.S. Army, Navy, and Air Force. Each military service has its own selection process and, owing to the ever-evolving political climate and varied backgrounds of the individuals who serve, no two nurses have the same experience.

While in this role, I was actively involved in all aspects of the legislative process and functioned as a health legislative assistant (LA) responsible for health policy issues. Every member of Congress has a health LA, although many of the individuals serving in these positions do not have education or experience in health care. Nearly all health care lobbyists and advocacy groups who wanted the senator to support their cause met initially with me. Lobbyists frequently came to the senator's office with background materials on their issue and presented their agenda. Sometimes they wanted Senator Inouye to sponsor or cosponsor a bill that was either in committee or before Congress. At other times they were looking for appropriations or for specific legislative language to be inserted into a bill that would support their causes.

My nursing background enhanced discussions with lobbyists by affording them the opportunity to discuss complex issues without having to spend time defining basic concepts. My task was to assess their requests, conduct further research when warranted, and determine whether to forward the issue to the senator. If the request warranted the senator's attention, I would prepare a memorandum for him. These memoranda would thoroughly explore all facets of the issue and conclude with my recommendation for action. The document went directly from me to Senator Inouye and would subsequently be returned with his decision. I considered it a tremendous responsibility and opportunity.

For a new staffer, it is critical to learn "who's who" in congressional offices. I worked closely with and was guided by Senator Inouye's chief of staff, Patrick H. DeLeon, a psychologist and lawyer. He provided remarkable insight into political life on Capitol Hill and encouraged me to design and shape my own experience.

Learning to assess the political environment is vital in determining the potential for success of specific issues on the legislative agenda. During the second session of the 106th Congress, health care was a key issue and received intense attention in both the House and the Senate. Health issues on the federal agenda included prescription drug coverage, health care errors, the patient's bill of rights, Medicare reform and expansion of benefits, military health care for beneficiaries over the age of 65, privacy of medical records, stem cell research, and pain management during end-of-life care. Although this list is not inclusive, it provides a sense of the wide range of political issues in which a nursing perspective was beneficial.

I learned to draft legislative language to be inserted into various bills. I developed language for the appropriations bills for Defense, Veteran's Administration, Housing and Urban Development, and Labor, Health and Human Services, and Education. Language that is inserted into bills came from many sources: the senator himself, lobbyists from various groups and agencies, other senators, and, of course, the senator's chief of staff and other legislative personnel. At the conclusion of each legislative session, I was asked to prepare a report that summarized the legislative language that I submitted and saw enacted into law. One report was more than 80 pages long!

In addition to drafting legislative language, I learned to monitor the status of bills throughout the legislative process. That sometimes entailed attending committee staff meetings and hearings throughout bill mark-up and the conference process. One of the most exciting aspects of the experience was being on the floor of the Senate when bills were under debate.

Life on Capitol Hill is fast paced, and every day brings new issues and opportunities. To be effective one has to stay informed. Getting current information on "the Hill" is less of a challenge than finding the time to absorb it and pass it on. Effective reading and listening skills are therefore critical. I found it extremely valuable to attend briefings held for the House and Senate staff on the issues I was involved with. Lobbyists advocating for an issue tend to arrange these briefings and often provide excellent background information. These briefings also provide an opportunity for networking with other health LAs and others intimately involved with the subject matter. A similarly valuable activity is attending congressional committee hearings. During these hearings, individuals come before the members of the House and Senate to provide testimony relating to the issue at hand. This was an excellent way to learn from the experts and to get exposure to a variety of perspectives regarding pending legislative proposals.

On Capitol Hill, the opportunity to meet people and network is endless. Interacting with people from other disciplines, and learning about their professional challenges and accomplishments, expanded my viewpoint immensely. I saw firsthand the power of building coalitions—of coordinating efforts between various professions.

What are the skills that will help you be effective as you learn the ropes on Capitol Hill? Excellent communication skills are paramount. "People skills"—the ability to interact with a wide range of individuals with varied levels of education and experience—are essential. Political life is often about the "art of the deal," or the ability to persuade another person to see your point of view and to arrive at a compromise position. Although congressional staff may disagree on issues, disagreements are generally handled with courtesy and civility. No one "burns bridges" because they know that they could very well need that same staff member to help get their next bill or proposal approved.

There is no single path to prepare for a fellowship or internship on Capitol Hill. Understanding the legislative process and how a bill becomes law is foundational knowledge. The Senate provides an orientation program for new staffers. New staff usually find it helpful to research which members sit on committees and to learn what committees and subcommittees have oversight of issues in their portfolio.

Nurses possess many of the attributes that contribute to effective service on Capitol Hill and in other political environments. Nursing prepares us to deal with diversity. We know how to assess, plan, implement, and evaluate our actions. We are terrific advocates for our patients, and that translates well into the policy arena, where we advocate for the health and well-being of all our citizens. Nurses are great teachers and negotiators, and teaching and negotiating are critical skills in nearly every political endeavor. Nurses are skilled researchers and clinicians. Being able to interpret data and understand health and illness is an asset when designing health policy. Nurses are superb organizers and managers. My critical care nursing experience provided me with the ability to handle the hectic pace on Capitol Hill and gave me the time-management skills to manage the enormous workload.

Working on Senator Inouye's staff was an honor, and every day was ripe with opportunities to learn. My recommendations to other nurses who have the opportunity to serve on Capitol Hill are:

- Be confident that your nursing background has prepared you for most challenges.
- Find mentors who are available and willing to help you.
- Listen, listen, listen.
- Recognize that there is strength in numbers and that numbers are strengthened by building coalitions between groups with common goals.
- Keep your sense of humor.
- Rely on your instincts and people skills.
- Have fun: Enjoy every moment of the experience.
- Remember that compassion is important. Members of Congress are people like you and me—they work hard and enjoy being thanked for their efforts.

Policy Development and Analysis

BARBARA E. HANLEY

"A problem clearly stated is a problem half solved."
DOROTHEA BRANDE

Nursing's inroads in reaching full professional status, such as receiving direct insurance reimbursement, prescriptive authority, major funding for the National Center for Nursing Research, and higher levels of autonomy in practice, are due largely to nurses' active involvement in state and federal policy making. Escalation in the frequency of health system change continues to create power vacuums, offering new opportunities for nursing. Continued advancement and meaningful contribution to the debates on health care and Medicare reform necessitate nurses' understanding of how the policy making system works, analysis of proposals, and how to develop their own. Although nurses are increasingly employed or participating in policy-related positions, influence on institutional as well as governmental policy requires integration of policy-making knowledge and skills into all nursing roles.

Understanding the concepts, approaches, and strategies in policy making and having basic skills in policy analysis are essential to nurses' meaningful contribution to health policy development. This chapter clarifies the process through a theoretic and rational approach to the study of policy development, a process seemingly chaotic and impenetrable, and through a primer on identifying and analyzing policy issues.

Policy encompasses the authoritative guidelines that direct human behavior toward specific goals, in either the private or the public sector. It includes the broad range of activities through which authority figures make decisions directed toward a goal and levy sanctions that affect the conduct of affairs. Health care agencies or institutions make *private policy,* including directives governing conditions of employment and guidelines for service provision. *Public policy* refers to local, state, and federal legislation, regulation, and court rulings that affect individual and institutional behaviors under the respective government's jurisdiction, such as state licensure for professional practice and federal Medicare and Medicaid legislation. However, the two are closely linked because institutional policy frequently reflects implementation of or compliance with public policy. *Health policy* refers to public and private policies directly related to health care service delivery and reimbursement. *Policy analysis* is the systematic study of the background, purpose, content, and anticipated or actual effects of standing or proposed policies and the study of relevant social, economic, and political factors. The process of policy analysis is relevant to any setting.

PUBLIC POLICY MAKING

All public policy definitions refer to policy made on behalf of the public, developed or initiated by government, and interpreted and implemented by public and private bodies (Birkland, 2001). It applies to all members of society and prescribes sanctions for failure to comply. Although Anderson (1990) describes public policy as a purposive course of governmental action to deal with an issue of public concern, Dye's succinct definition (1992), "Whatever a government chooses to do or not to do," is directly to the point. The failure to take action is as important as a decision *for* action. For example, Congressional failure to enact some form of the Clinton Health Security Act in 1994 left a policy vacuum rapidly filled by the for-profit restructuring of the health care system into managed care models.

Processes to create public policy include the enactment of legislation and its accompanying rules and regulations that hold the weight of law; administrative decisions in interagency and intra-agency activities, including interpretative guidelines for rules and regulations; and judicial decisions that interpret the law. Schneider and Ingram (1997) extend this list to include more subtle indicators such as texts, practices, symbols, and discourses that define the value-laden delivery of goods and services.

POLICY SUBSYSTEMS AND STAKEHOLDERS

Policy subsystems include a network of elected or appointed officials, legislative subcommittees, and interest group representatives and individuals directly involved in shaping a policy. The term *stakeholders* is applied to actors that may be directly affected by its outcome. Stakeholders are also relevant in private sector policy making, although they may not be as highly visible. To address specific policy decisions over time, analysts must also consider the substantive input from researchers, specialist reporters, professional associations, and institutional policy specialists (Sabatier, 1991). The growing role of these policy subsystems underscores the importance of nursing research; nurse legislative and political action at local, state, and national levels; and the presence of nurse policymakers and analysts. Nurse practitioner coalitions and coalitions of nursing groups such as the Tri-Council for Nursing (American Nurses Association, National League for Nursing, American Association of Colleges of Nursing, and Association of Nurse Executives for general nursing issues ensure a unified nursing approach in key policy debates.

True, Baumgartner, and Jones (1999) observe that the American political system is designed to protect the status quo; change requires major mobilization efforts to destabilize the institutionalized gridlock created by policy subsystems. Cynicism of the system ignores the reality that citizens in a democracy hold the power and entrust authority for decision making to the three branches of government—the executive branch, the legislature, and the judiciary. Because the judicial process is usually reserved for resolution of dispute, in practice the basic policy loop includes the "Iron Triangle" of the executive branch, the legislature, and interest groups. Policy making thus has many points of access, enabling citizens, constituents, legislators, agency officials, interest groups, researchers and media representatives to exert influence at local, state, and federal levels. The input of substantive experts on behalf of these players is also increasing. Interest group activity is diversifying to include data gathering, mass marketing, and wholesale lobbying (Petracca, 1992). Finally, interaction between the public and private health policy-making sectors is increasing because of the complexity of policy implementation and the increasing role of corporate structures in health care finance and delivery.

Relationships between federal, state, and local governments are increasingly important (Sabatier, 1991). All three levels function interdependently, creating subgovernments to resolve complex policy issues such as the problem of the underinsured, the uninsured, and the medically indigent. *Federalism* refers to shared power between federal and state governments based on the Constitution. All powers not specifically granted to the federal government reside with the state. The federal role in health and social policy was greatly enhanced during the Great Depression, when states were unable to provide for the basic needs of citizens. The next spurt occurred in the 1960s with President Lyndon Johnson's "Great Society," including the enactment of Medicare and Medicaid to ensure health care for elderly and poor persons. As health care costs have consumed an increasingly greater proportion of the gross domestic product (GDP), federal policy increasingly focuses on limiting federal financial responsibility, thereby shifting the struggle among interest groups for increasingly scarce dollars back to state and local governments.

Changes in Medicaid policy over the past decade reflect this interrelationship, such as in the movement of Medicaid into managed care and the Child Health Insurance Program (CHIP). Medicaid is a federal program administered by the state with joint federal-state funding. State Medicaid costs rose sharply in 1991, fueled by an increase in federally mandated benefits under the program and by the loss of private health insurance as people lost jobs during the recession. Since 1994, encouraged by the Clinton administration and bolstered by an expanding economy, nearly all states have moved their Medicaid populations into managed care. Under CHIP, many states have developed programs to expand health insurance coverage of children under Medicaid or a special state program, thereby saving money and in some cases expanding the number of beneficiaries. However, the recession that began in 2001 is again escalating Medicaid costs as people lose their jobs, while the combination of tax cuts in 2000 and the cost of the war on terrorism have decreased the availability of federal funds to assist the states.

A recent example with far-reaching implications is implementation of the 1996 Kassebaum-Kennedy Health Insurance Portability and Accountability Act (HIPAA). Enacted as a major initiative for insurance reform to increase insurance availability and to ensure coverage when people change jobs ("portability"), HIPAA affects federal and state insurance provisions and allows for enforcement under both jurisdictions (Montgomery, 2001). Areas of particular concern include security of claims data, confidentiality of medical information, and patients' rights. Although many states have patient confidentiality statutes, HIPAA requirements may take precedence if there is discrepancy between them (Mills, 2001).

APPROACHES TO PUBLIC POLICY MAKING

Political scientists have established a number of conceptual models that provide varying perspectives on public policy making (Dye, 1992). Models such as the rational approach, incrementalism, the policy stream model, and the stage-sequential model enable one to organize one's thinking in relation to the policy process as applied to particular cases, and they offer explanations for its dynamics. Adherents to each model may therefore identify different variables or view the same variables differently in conceptualizing the way in which specific policy decisions are made. All models have merit, although each may have some limitation in its application depending on the policy in question (Sabatier, 1999).

THE RATIONAL APPROACH

The *rational* approach to policy decisions reflects the goals of an ideal world. Here, policymakers define the problem; identify and rank social values in policy goals; examine each policy alternative for positive and negative consequences, costs, and benefits; compare and contrast these factors among all options; and select the policy that most closely achieves the policy goals (Anderson, 1990; Dye, 1992). However, because the rational model holds the possibility of sweeping policy change, except for times of national crisis such as the Great Depression when major initiatives were essential, it is an unrealistic approach to general policy making. Its importance lies in its striving for the ideal solutions in the face of political pressures. The failed Clinton Health Security Act of 1994 provides a clear example. The Clinton plan proposed a total revision of the health care industry through a blend of market competition and regulation. However, the magnitude of the proposed change enabled those with a vested interest in the status quo to target numerous pieces, mobilize public fear, and ultimately defeat the proposal. Health care reform was relegated to the state level, where small changes have been made, primarily in insurance law, to increase citizens' access to private insurance. However, state experimentation with different models of health care reform may provide data for future national debate.

INCREMENTALISM

Policy changes in the United States are most often made *incrementally,* with small changes at the margins as opposed to radical restructuring of ineffective or dysfunctional systems. Proposals begin with the status quo, and the limited changes reflect the turf, goals, and politics of policy subsystems. The political dynamics among these subsystems are so important that policy options developed without addressing them would have little or no chance for success. Lindblom (1996) terms this approach "the science of muddling through." Consider the legislative success of the bipartisan HIPAA in 1996 in contrast to the rational and liberal Clinton Health Security Act. As an incremental step in increasing access to health insurance, HIPAA directly addresses the problem of "job lock," or the inability to leave a job because a preexisting health problem would prevent a person from accessing health insurance elsewhere. However, its effectiveness is limited by its failure to limit the amount individuals would have to pay for continued coverage. Further, its vague language left to regulators the problem of specifying the complex regulatory system necessary for its implementation. Resultant problems continue to plague both state and federal bodies.

Health care reform efforts continue at the state level, where experimentation is occurring with different models such as managed competition and universal access, and both private and public health care financing systems are being overhauled. *Nursing's Agenda for Health Care Reform* (1992), established during the Clinton initiative, provides criteria that are still useful for nurses to evaluate health care reform legislation. Power struggles over nurses' roles as primary care providers and network panel members, as well as disputes over prescriptive authority, will be fought in 52 venues. States are also struggling to develop strategies for resolution of the growing nursing shortage. Movement of state Medicaid populations into managed care and the CHIP program provided nurses a vital avenue to serve as patient advocates and to ensure key roles in primary care and health care management.

THE POLICY PROCESS

The *policy process* refers specifically to the steps through which a policy moves from problem to working program. Here we look at two models of how this has been conceptualized. A brief discussion of Kingdon's model (1995) will be followed by a detailed description of the stage-sequential model as described by Ripley (1996) and Anderson (1990). The stage-sequential model—the classic chronologic nuts-and-bolts approach—may be more helpful to neophytes.[1]

KINGDON'S POLICY STREAMS MODEL

Kingdon's model is based on Cohen, March, and Olsen's "garbage can" model (1972), which describes the process as a series of options floating around seeking a problem. Kingdon likens the situation instead to a "soup" that contains three streams of activities:

1. *Problem stream.* The problem stream describes with the complexities in getting policymakers to focus on one problem, such as the high out-of-pocket costs of prescription drugs for many elders, out of many problems facing constituents.
2. *Policy stream.* The policy stream describes policy goals and ideas of those in policy subsystems, such as researchers, congressional committee members and staff, agency officials, and interests groups. Ideas in the policy stream float around policy circles in search of problems.
3. *Political stream.* The political stream describes factors in the political environment that influence the policy agenda, such as an economic recession, special interest media campaigns, or a pivotal political power shift, such as the 2000 presidential election shift of power from Democrats to Republicans. Campaign platforms for both parties addressed health care policy, particularly Medicare reform and prescription drug benefit. An unprecedented second power shift, this time in the Senate and moving from Republican to Democratic power, early in the Bush administration increased the likelihood of bipartisan communication and congressional action on such issues.

[1]Sabatier's Advocacy Coalition Framework (1991, 1999) is another newer model that analyzes political development over at least 10 years. It addresses the dynamics of interaction within policy subsystems based on participants' values and beliefs and the role of policy learning over time. Readers who wish to delve more deeply into policy analysis may find this a very helpful approach.

Kingdon sees these streams as floating around and waiting for a "window of opportunity" to open through "couplings" of any two streams (particularly in the political stream), creating new opportunities for policy change. However, such opportunities are time-limited; if change does not occur while the window is open, the problems and options return to the soup and continue floating.

This approach can be seen in the evolution of the community nursing organization (CNO) model. CNOs provide capitated care to ambulatory elders to facilitate independent living, promote maximal wellness despite age-related health problems and chronic illness, and prevent or delay institutionalization. *Capitation* refers to a system whereby the CNO contracts with Medicare to provide health services for a panel of patients at a given sum of money per person. This practice model had long been advocated by nursing, but lack of appropriate reimbursement structures precluded the development of CNOs. The political debate over reducing prohibitive Medicare cost inflation created an opportunity for nurses to offer a cost-saving alternative for community care of elders. Legislation to authorize CNO demonstration projects was enacted in the Omnibus Budget Reconciliation Act of 1987; however, the Health Care Financing Agency (HCFA) (now called the Centers for Medicare and Medicaid Administration) did not issue its request for proposals for CNO demonstrations until 1991. The delay was because of administrative opposition to implementation, related to fear of added costs. Four demonstration projects were developed and operational by 1994, making it 7 years from legislation to a working program.

THE STAGE-SEQUENTIAL MODEL

This classic systems-based model views the policy process as a sequential series of stages in which a number of functional activities occur (Anderson, Brady, Bullock, & Stewart, 1984; Ripley, 1985, 1996; Anderson, 1990). In this model a policy problem is identified and placed on the policy agenda, and then a policy is developed, adopted, implemented, evaluated, and terminated. The process is dynamic and cyclical, with policy evaluation and oversight to identify either a well-functioning program or new problems, thereby restarting the cycle. However, in

reality, the stages are often not clear-cut, implementation and evaluation are often done in tandem, and proposals may move back and forth among the stages. Once established, programs are rarely terminated. Figure 4-1 provides Ripley's (1996) model, which includes stages, activities, and products.

Stage One: Policy Agenda Setting. The first step in setting a policy agenda is identification of a *policy problem,* a "situation that produces needs or dissatisfaction . . . for which relief is sought" (Anderson, 1990, p. 79). There are many public problems, but only those that gain policymakers' attention for action qualify as policy problems. Jones (1977) terms this the *problem to government phase;* for Anderson et al (1984), it's *getting the government to consider action on the problem.* Ripley (1985) cautions that there may be competition here among groups trying to attract governmental attention to their problems and competition over the definition of specific problems.

Next, the problem is refined to a *policy issue,* a problem with societal ramifications of concern to a number of people on which there are conflicting opinions for resolution. Values of the involved stakeholders play a large role here and determine the amount of political interest the issue will generate, the identification of policy options, and the analysis that should follow. Operationally, it is useful to frame the issue as a question: What could or should be done about this problem?

In practice, Wildavsky (1979) cautions, it is only through analysis that the true underlying issue is identified. For example, at the institutional level, hospitals have been developing policies for how to use unlicensed assistive personnel (UAPs). Comprehensive analysis of the problem reveals that the underlying issue is whether to delegate technical nursing functions. A critical component is identification of the short- and long-term implications of delegation to a new group of technical providers for patient care and professional practice, as well as the fiscal impact on the institution. But if the discussion is limited to *how* UAPs will be used, the importance of the underlying issue, and alternative strategies for its resolution that could be more beneficial in the long run, may be overlooked.

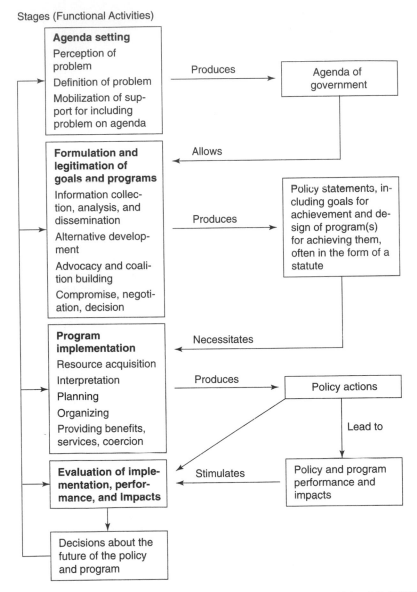

Figure 4-1   The flow of policy stages, functional activities, and products. (From Ripley, R.B. [1996]. Stages of the policy process. In D.D. McCool [Ed.]. *Public policy theories, models and concepts: An anthology.* Englewood Cliffs, NJ: Prentice-Hall.)

Problem and issue definition and mobilization of support move the issue to the governmental *policy agenda,* the list of issues being addressed by public policymakers. When seeking policy change, one must identify the policy-making body holding jurisdiction over the matter, as well as the individuals and groups who might support the position and be willing to work to achieve policy change. Policy agendas convey the notion of issue prioritization by policymakers, particularly in the first two stages (poli⋯ ⋯tting and policy formulation). The *discus⋯* ⋯ includes issues that merit policymakers ⋯ based on input from involved interest g⋯ ⋯umers, or policy elites in stage one. The ⋯ *⋯nda* designates those issues actively mo⋯ng through the formulation stage. Media coverage plays a major role in broadening public interest, enlisting group support, alerting policymakers to the issue, and it remains a vital force throughout the policy process. Finally, the *decision agenda* reflects policy issues in the last stages of legitimization by policymakers during the legislative or regulatory processes (Kingdon, 1995, Nelson, 1978). Political activity and negotiation are major forces in moving issues onto the decision agenda and through to final enactment.

The problem of excessive cost of prescription drugs for the elderly remains on the discussion agenda because supporters of Medicare reform, including the growing number of politically astute elders, continue to be active. However, failure to identify a proposal with enough support to ensure enactment has kept it moving between the discussion and action agendas during two administrations.

Stage 2: Policy Formulation. Here policymakers determine policy options to resolve questions such as, "What could or should be done to deal with *X?*" Formulation is a technical phase in which information on the issue is collected, analyzed, and disseminated, and legislative or regulatory language is drafted. Various interest groups and policymakers may develop alternative proposals, each of which must be evaluated in terms of its costs and benefits to the target group and the "spill over" effects on those external to it—the externalities (Gwartney & Stroup, 1987).

Policy proposals now move through the legislative or regulatory process, and the policy decision is made. A critical component here is the development of a program budget and the funding appropriation process. This phase is characterized by input from all those holding a stake in the issue: interest groups, policymakers, and target groups. However, the legitimate authority will make the final decision. Public pressure must be continued

or increased to move the issue forward on the action agenda until resolution is achieved in the form of a policy document such as a statute or regulation. Ripley (1985) stresses the importance of compromise and negotiation to reach a decision. As a result, policy and program design may be vague and sketchy; details for legislation will be defined in the less-contentious regulatory process. Jones (1977) describes this as the "action in government" stage.

Stage 3: Program Implementation. This stage reflects the government's formal response to the initial problem (Jones, 1977; Anderson et al, 1984). The executive or regulatory body charged with implementing the program develops the guidelines and regulations necessary for a functioning program. In effect, the implementing body translates the authorizing policy into a workable program. Although less contentious than the legislative process, implementation activities of legislative interpretation, planning, and organizing are still very political (Ripley, 1985). Anderson (1990) cautions that interest groups and those to be regulated frequently seek loopholes when implementation begins. Here, analysts identify criteria for program evaluation to determine whether it meets policy goals and objectives.

Nursing organizations should communicate with regulatory agency staff as soon as possible after enactment of policy affecting nursing practice to ensure that initial regulatory drafts reflect their position and legislative intent. Interested nursing groups must monitor the *Federal Register* and corresponding state publications for notices of proposed rule making and publication of rules, regulations, standards, and guidelines to ensure that these reflect the original intent of the legitimating body and to assess their impact on health care delivery and professional practice. Interest groups frequently use the regulatory process to include program elements they were unable to put into legislation, thereby undermining legislative intent. Further, interest groups often try to bypass legislative scrutiny by persuading regulatory bodies to initiate program changes favorable to their interest. Continuous monitoring of proposed state and federal regulations is a tedious but essential nursing organization responsibility.

Stage 4: Policy Evaluation. This "program to government" phase addresses the question "Did the policy work?" (Jones, 1977; Anderson et al, 1984). The program's implementation, performance, and impact are evaluated to determine how well the program has met its goals and objectives. Evaluation should identify whether a program has satisfactorily met the original concerns and should be continued, whether segments of the original policy goals remain unmet, and whether new issues have surfaced, thereby restarting the cycle. A program that has met its objectives or is superseded by a newer policy and is no longer necessary may be terminated. An example is the policy of deinstitutionalization of mentally ill persons and the subsequent closure of state mental institutions. The policy may have met its initial goal of reducing excessive institutionalization of the mentally ill; however, the problem of adequate community mental health services, especially for the homeless, remains unresolved.

Although the stages model offers a rational and systematic schema for policy making, it has many shortcomings. Dye (1992) argues that it fails to explicate who gets what and why in policy decisions, and Sabatier (1999) raises the concern that it fails to address the role of stakeholders' ideas and their underlying values during policy debate and evolution. Nevertheless, the stages model is useful in simplifying the "how" of a frequently confusing and complex process.

POLICY AND ISSUE ANALYSIS

Policy analysis is a systematic approach to describing and explaining the causes and consequences of government action and inaction. The consequences of inaction may be as important as those of action because they, too, constitute policy (Dye, 1992). Historically, many social science disciplines and professions have focused their research activities on government policies as system outputs. More recently the study of policy science theory and methodology has become an interdisciplinary subspecialty with programs in most major universities.

Formally, policy analysis is conducted in universities and policy research firms, which use principles and analytic tools from economics, probability theory, and statistics, as well as in legislatures, governmental agencies, or organizations. Based on the sponsoring organization's purpose and function, the analyst's role may vary from the academically oriented "objective technician," to the more politically oriented "issue advocate" who promotes societal welfare, to the "client advocate," whose role is to develop the best case for the employer (Jenkins-Smith, 1982). Nurses tend to function as issue advocates.

Nurses have a unique perspective for policy decision making because of their clinical knowledge and advocacy orientation. They are increasingly visible as stakeholders in health policy debates through policy positions in both legislative and executive branches of government and as members of special interest groups. The role of the nurse policy analyst is a distinct advanced-practice role because it includes components of research, leadership, and change agency (Stimpson & Hanley, 1991). Nurses now receive formal policy preparation in master's degree and doctoral programs; however, nurses in clinical practice roles also participate in policy debate and need a format to analyze policy decision making in either clinical or governmental settings.

ANALYST VALUES AND INHERENT BIAS

Any issue or policy analysis holds the inherent bias of the originating group based on the group's values, frame of reference, and ideology. Although the analyst strives for objectivity, the truth will be filtered through the stakeholder's values, ideology, perspective, and goals (Dunn, 1981). Consequently, the same data may be used to support opposing points of view; only the perspective in viewing the data changes. Nevertheless, analysts within the legislature and administrative agencies sometimes develop proposals not supported by data. Throgmorton (1991, p. 174) addresses the persuasive quality inherent in all policy analyses and suggests that "analysis should stimulate and maintain a conversation among scientist, politicians and lay advocates" to mediate rather than polarize their communication and perspectives.

CONTEXT (DEFINITION)	POLICY OPTIONS	EVALUATION OF OPTIONS	RECOMMENDED SOLUTION

Policy problem
Background
   Social
   Economic
   Ethical
   Political/Legal
Stakeholders
Issue Statement
	Identify policy goals/
	   objectives
	Specify policy options
	   (include "do nothing")
		Set criteria to meet
		   objectives
		Evaluate each option on
		   criteria
		Compare options (use
		   scorecard)	

Figure 4-2   Issue analysis for decision making.

ISSUE ANALYSIS

Policy analysis comprises a structured approach to problem solving and decision making that is useful in any setting. Stokey and Zeckhauser (1978) offer this useful five-point framework:

1. Establish the context, including definition of the problem and specific objectives.
2. Identify alternatives for resolving the issue.
3. Project consequences for the identified options.
4. Specify criteria for evaluating options' ability to meet objectives.
5. Recommend the optimal solution.

The policy issue paper format, the first step in the policy analysis process, serves as a valuable tool in these situations. Figure 4-2 outlines a model of the issue analysis process.

POLICY ISSUE PAPERS

Policy issue papers provide a mechanism to structure the problem at hand and identify the underlying issue. This step is essential in identifying stakeholders and specifying alternatives with their positive and negative consequences. It also identifies variables to be included in full analysis models such as cost-effectiveness or cost-benefit analyses (Hatry, Blair, Fisk, & Kimmel, 1976). Issue papers help one to clarify arguments in support of one's cause, to recognize the arguments of opposing stakeholders, and to develop strategies to advance the issue through the policy cycle.

POLICY ISSUE PAPER ORGANIZATION

The following list describes the sections of the policy issue paper. A sample paper on the Medicare

Prescription Drug Benefit is included at the end of this chapter.

1. *Problem identification.* Problem identification clarifies the underlying problem. It specifies problem causes, current and future effects on the community, those who raised the issue and those now interested in it, and how the problem moved to the public agenda (Hatry et al, 1976).
2. *Background.* Exploration of the background of the problem puts the problem in context and facilitates specification of the policy issue. It should include an examination of social, economic, ethical, legal, and political factors.
3. *Issue statement.* The issue statement, which is actually usually a question, should be phrased in a way that recognizes the underlying problem and conflicting values and seeks to identify options. Questions such as "How could or should *X* be addressed?" shift focus from a specific policy proposal to an objective analysis of the issue. The analyst maintains focus by keeping the issue statement in mind through each stage of the analysis.
4. *Stakeholders.* Stakeholders are the parties who have a stake in the outcome of the policy debate, such as policymakers with specific proposals related to the issue, those who would be potentially affected by the policy, special interest groups (who may or may not be included with the previous group), and those with a position on the issue.
5. *Policy objectives.* The policy goal should be stated succinctly. It is useful to keep the policy goal and objectives in mind when developing

Policy Issue Paper: Medicare Prescription Drug Benefit

Problem: Purchasing prescription drugs is a major problem for many elderly and disabled Medicare beneficiaries because it is not a Medicare program benefit. Medicare is an entitlement program, designed to provide primary and secondary health care services to those 65 years of age and over, as well as those eligible for Social Security Disability. Escalating prescription drug costs, the growth of the Medicare population, and that population's increasing use of prescription drugs to manage chronic illness are fueling debate on whether and how Medicare can be reformed to cover prescription drug costs. The move to cover prescription drugs reflects a substantive policy shift that is consistent with changing demographic, health status, and disease management patterns.

Prescription insurance coverage is a major factor in beneficiaries' obtaining needed drugs. Poisal and Murray (2001) found that in 1998, those not covered had 2.4% fewer prescriptions that the previous year, while those with prescription drug coverage had 9% more than the previous year. Because those who are not covered by a secondary insurance policy are more likely to have lower income and more health problems, this discrepancy points to an increasing lack of access to needed treatment. Medigap policies are designed to assist with the out-of-pocket Medicare costs associated with Part A, the hospital insurance plan, and Part B, supplemental medical insurance that pays for the costs of outpatient, diagnostic, and provider services, which are far outpacing inflation (Maxwell, Moon, & Segal, 2001). Although at least two thirds of beneficiaries have supplemental "Medigap" coverage through employer-based, state prescription drug programs or private plans, only three of the ten Medigap plans have prescription coverage. Further, this coverage is unstable, because less than 50% of beneficiaries had continuous coverage in 1995 and 1996. Medicare+Choice (Part C) allows beneficiaries to enroll in HMOs, most of which cover prescription drugs. Although Medigap coverage increased between 1992 and 1997, it began to decline in 1998 in all categories, when many HMOs withdrew from Medicare (Poisal & Murray, 2001).

Advances in medical technology and pharmacotherapeutics have created a healthier over-65 population that is increasingly faced with chronic disease requiring costly prescriptions. Although 70% of Medicare recipients have some prescription coverage through supplemental policies, the 30% without this coverage are often the "near-poor" with more health problems and significantly higher out-of-pocket health costs.

Clinton's Bipartisan Commission to Reform Medicare identified the issue in 1996 as one component of Medicare Reform. Although there was no consensus on the final report, the prescription drug benefit issue advanced to Congress' action agenda.

Background:

Social Factors: Improved health status has increased the life span for people worldwide. However, despite its wealth, the United States lags behind industrialized countries in the provision of health care, including prescription drugs, as an entitlement for elders. In a five-nation study, researchers found that Americans lacking drug coverage have problems both meeting living expenses and paying for needed medications (Donelan, Blendon, Schoen, Binns, Osburn, & Davis, 2000). This is particularly problematic for low-income women, who currently spend more than 50% of their income on—or forego—health care (Maxwell, Moon, & Storeygard, 2001). The brunt of the demographic shift in the United States with the aging of the post-World War II generation will occur between 2010 and 2030.

Beneficiaries without prescription coverage use fewer prescriptions, have greater out-of-pocket expenses, and spend less for drugs than those with coverage (Poisal & Chulis, 2000). Further, there is a 25% disparity in prescription usage by poor and near-poor eldersversus those with supplemental Medicare coverage. Because health status is related to income level, access to needed prescriptions for this population is a major nursing concern. There is also discrepancy in access to supplemental prescription insurance for minority groups and for beneficiaries living in rural areas (Stuart, Shea, & Briesacher, 2001).

Economic Factors: In FY 2000, Medicare spent over $200 billion. However, the emerging demographic shift will have a major impact on cost and increase the ratio of federal health spending to the GDP. Although 1999 health spending was 18.7% of GDP, it is expected to drop to 15% to 17% by 2010. However, without additional tax revenues, the percentage is expected to rise sharply to 53% by 2050.

Although a study of hospital utilization by Medicare beneficiaries who received prescription drug coverage revealed lower hospital costs, these savings may not occur for higher-income patients because of differences in disease patterns and the costs of needed drugs (Christensen and Wagner, 2000). Near-poor elders are less likely to have insurance coverage for prescriptions. The uninsured use fewer prescriptions, pay more per prescription, and spend less for health care services than those with insurance (Poisal & Chulis, 2000). One study of hypertensive

Policy Issue Paper: Medicare Prescription Drug Benefit—cont'd

elders reported that those with prescription coverage purchase more tablets than those without coverage, thereby improving their disease control and decreasing likelihood of dangerous complications. However, the very poor usually qualify for Medicaid and will have prescriptions covered.

The cost of a prescription drug benefit without overall Medicare reform will be substantial. The tradeoff will be how much of the financial burden will be assumed by beneficiaries through premiums and by taxpayers through general tax revenues.

Ethical Factors: The key principles in conflict here are justice as fairness (each receiving prescription drug therapy according to need) versus autonomy (payers' right to determine the amount they are willing to pay). A prescription drug benefit will provide all beneficiaries, particularly the near poor, with access to needed medication, thereby enhancing their health status and quality of life.

Taxpayers' autonomy in determining the amount they are willing to pay in tax to support social programs conflicts with beneficiaries' needs and the responsibility of a democratic government to provide services. Implementation of the 2001 tax cut has major implications for expansion of Medicare benefits, and even continuation of current benefits.

Political and Legal Factors: Allocation of scarce resources requires study of alternative uses for revenues. The debate over a prescription drug benefit under Medicare has been fueled by long-term budget concerns and program viability as the "baby boomers" age. Although both Democratic and Republican lawmakers recognize the need for a Medicare Prescription Benefit, they differ in their approach to program design. The Bipartisan Commission on Reform of Medicare recommended reform of Medicare to allow beneficiaries a choice among private health plans offering prescription drug coverage. The Clinton Administration rejected this approach in favor of an expansion of Medicare.

Before the Senate power shift, the Republican Bush administration obtained a major tax cut primarily benefiting the wealthy. Financing of the tax cut involves shifting and reducing tax revenues to Medicare. It has important implications for emerging Medicare policy because it limits the available general revenue source for development of the Medicare prescription drug benefit (MPDB). However, a congress with mixed-party control allows for more-balanced Republican/Democratic policy negotiations internally and with the executive branch.

Issue Statement: How should a Medicare prescription drug benefit be designed?

Stakeholders: The complexity and importance of this policy issue are reflected in the broad range of stakeholders: elders, the pharmaceutical industry, taxpayers, and the federal government. The near-poor among those age 65 and over and the aging baby boomers have much to gain from an MPDB, because they are least likely to be able to purchase prescription drugs now and in the future. Similarly, the pharmaceutical industry is a winner if an MPDB is enacted because more elders will be able to purchase increasingly costly drugs. On the negative side, taxpayers produce and contribute the revenues to support such a program. The benefit package will determine program costs and the need for tax support. The repeal of the 1988 Catastrophic Health Plan in 1989 because it required elders to pay more for expanded benefits precludes the likelihood of a surcharge for those who can afford it. Legislators, as representatives of constituents, have a need to demonstrate concern for voters, who put them in office and keep them in office. Physicians and nurses want to protect the health of their clients by ensuring that they have access to medications. The public also has a stake here because of the differing burdens faced by each age group: The young fear the increasing tax burden of paying for the growing body of elders; middle-aged people face the financial burden of caring for aging parents in need of costly medications; and elders want to preserve their health status and prevent disease progression thorough use of newer, more effective drugs. Finally, the federal government has a major stake in the design of an MPDB because of program and administrative costs.

Policy Objectives: The goal of an MPDB is to provide prescription medications to Medicare recipients while limiting out-of-pocket expenses to affordable levels. Policy objectives include the following:
1. Set premiums at an affordable level for all beneficiaries.
2. Prevent excessive out-of-pocket expenditures for needed prescription drugs, both common and specialized.
3. Design a program that will maintain Medicare's original goal of health care coverage for those 65 and over and the disabled.
4. Develop financing to ensure Medicare's future viability.

Continued

Policy Issue Paper: Medicare Prescription Drug Benefit—cont'd

Policy Alternatives: Policy options for the MPDB identified for this analysis include the following:

1. *Bush Proposal:* State subsidy ($12 billion) to provide full prescription drug coverage to elders with income up to $11,300, and partial coverage for those with incomes up to $14,600 for 4 years; stop-loss coverage for all elders with drug costs over $6,000/year.
2. *Restructure Medicare+Choice (RM+C):* Restructure Medicare, expanding Medicare+Choice so that beneficiaries can enroll in competing private plans including drug coverage (HMOs), in fee-for-service (FFS) plans with high deductibles, or in medical savings account (Bipartisan Commission).
3. *Prescription Drug Price Reduction for Medicare Beneficiaries (PDPR):* Allow pharmacies to purchase brand name prescription drugs from manufacturers, for Medicare beneficiaries, at the average price they are sold in other developed countries.
4. *Direct Medicare Prescription Drug Benefit (DMRxB):* Includes a $26 monthly premium, 50% coinsurance requirements, and a $2,500 cap on cost sharing; waives the premium for the near-poor up to 135% of the federal poverty level (FPL); subsidizes low-income elders whose incomes range from 135% to 150% of the FPL. (Maxwell, Moon, & Storeygard, 2001). This option would increase Medicare costs by $13.9 billion in the first year.

Evaluation of Options: *Criteria identified for analysis of the MPDB:*

1. Beneficiary coverage
2. Beneficiary cost sharing
3. Impact on Medicare program costs
4. Political feasibility

[Because this is a sample paper, only one option, the DMRxB, will be analyzed. In a full analysis, the following process below be repeated for each option. The final analysis and conclusion are therefore hypothetical.]

OPTION 1: Direct Medicare Prescription Drug Benefit (DMRxB)
This approach typifies several proposals that strive to preserve the integrity of the original Medicare program of entitlement to health care for elders and the disabled.

Beneficiary Coverage:
This criterion addresses whether the policy will cover all beneficiaries or only those at a given income level.
PRO: This option would expand access to prescription drugs for all beneficiaries, waiving premiums for the poor and subsidizing the near-poor. It would be consistent with preserving Medicare as an entitlement program for those 65 years of age and older and the disabled.
CON: Limiting definition of need to income excludes those without continuous, stable insurance coverage, with high out-of-pocket costs, and with multiple chronic problems (Commonwealth Fund, 2000).

Beneficiary Cost Sharing:
Out-of-pocket expenses faced by elders in purchasing prescription drugs are a major concern. These costs have risen more rapidly than inflation and beneficiary income, causing elders, on average, to spend 22% on their health care in contrast to 9% for the general population. But Medicare enrollees are already shouldering major costs. More than $50 billion of the projected 10-year budget surplus comes from a nearly 50% increase in Part B premiums mandated by the 1997 Balanced Budget Act (Commonwealth Fund, 2000).

policy options to ensure that they could resolve the underlying issue.

6. *Policy alternatives.* Wildavsky (1979) defines policy alternatives as hypotheses: If *x* is done, then *y* will be the result. Resources necessary for programs should be considered along with program objectives and criteria. Policy alternatives could include any current proposals, as well as one developed by the analysis sponsor. It is also useful to analyze the "do nothing" option because there may be strong pressure to preserve the status quo.

7. *Evaluation criteria.* Criteria must reflect the policy's potential to achieve policy goals and objectives, such as quality, access, fairness, cost, and administrative and political

Policy Issue Paper: Medicare Prescription Drug Benefit—cont'd

PRO: The DMRxB requires payment of a $26 monthly premium, but it waives payment for beneficiaries at incomes up to 135% of the FPL and would subsidize the payment for low-income beneficiaries at incomes from 135% to 150% of the FPL. It also caps the out-of-pocket expense incurred at $2,500.

CON: Given the prices of prescription drugs, and the rate of price escalation, even these levels may be high for low-income elders who are most likely to be in poorer health and in need of more medications. This approach does not address the price escalation in the most common prescription drugs.

Impact on Medicare Program Costs:
A Medicare benefit expansion will increase the government's financial risk, although estimates vary between executive and congressional experts. A key question is how much of the benefit cost should be paid by elders through premium increases and how much from society through tax revenues. Currently, Medicare Part B is financed 25% though premiums and 75% through general tax revenues.

PRO: Addition of the DMRxB within overall Medicare program restructuring would increase program costs by only 5.8% and it would increase Medicare's economic efficiency (Maxwell, Moon, & Storeygard, 2001).

CON: Without overall Medicare restructuring, addition of a benefit for all beneficiaries would produce a major increase in Medicare costs.

Political Feasibility:
Political will is essential in resolving policy debates. Negotiation will be needed for enactment of any major legislation, particularly when there is a narrow party split.

PRO: There is bipartisan consensus that this issue must be resolved. Both parties agree on need for decreased out of pocket expenses and stop-loss provisions. The major subissue is whether the benefit should be in the private sector or in the current Medicare structure.

CON: This is a Democratic Party approach; bipartisan support will be needed. Because more economically conservative legislators supportive of the pharmaceutical and insurance businesses have been elected in recent years, enactment of additional Medicare model mandates may not be politically feasible.

Results of Analysis: Analysis and comparison of the four options depicted in Figure 4-3 indicates that Option 4, the DMRxB, scores highest. It is weighted with at least one "+" on all four criteria, and highest on beneficiary coverage criterion, although it covers only on the basis of income, not need. The RM+C and PDPR options were tied with scores of three pluses and five minuses, although they differ on criterion strengths: RM+C scored negatively on beneficiary coverage because it does not assist the near-poor, and PDPR scored negatively on political feasibility because it is a Democratic plan and would be opposed by the pharmaceutical industry. Both scored equivocally on beneficiary cost sharing and Medicare financial risk. Finally, the Bush plan received two pluses and six minuses. It scored positively only on Medicare financial risk. Negative scores are based on the limited number of states having programs in place, the 4-year program limitation, and the lack of a stop-loss provision in beneficiary cost sharing. Based on this analysis, the Direct Medicare Prescription Benefit is the optimal policy option in providing elders access to prescription medications.

feasibility. Analysts may identify other criteria relevant for the policy or the sponsoring group (e.g., inclusion of reimbursement for nonphysician providers when analyzing proposals for health care and health insurance reform).

8. *Analysis of policy alternatives.* Alternatives are analyzed on each criterion, addressing both positive and negative potential.

9. *Comparison of alternatives/scorecard.* It is useful to summarize the analysis findings using a scorecard format. This is a two-dimensional grid, with the evaluation criteria on the vertical axis and the alternative policies on the horizontal. A summarizing notation is made for each alternative on the criteria, facilitating comparison of their strengths and weaknesses. Examples of scoring systems are the plus/minus system used in Figure 4-3 (an example of an alternatives matrix for Medicare drug benefit options), designation of "high, medium, and low," or brief verbal descriptions. In Figure 4-3, hypothetical scores are included for the other alternatives for illustrative purposes.

| | ALTERNATIVES | | | |
CRITERIA	BUSH PROPOSAL	RESTRUCTURE MEDICARE + CHOICE	PRESCRIPTION DRUG PRICE REDUCTION	DIRECT MEDICARE PRESCRIPTION BENEFIT
Beneficiary Coverage	− −	− −	+/−	+ +
Beneficiary Cost Sharing	− −	+/−	+/−	+/−
Medicare Financial Risk	+ +	+/−	+/−	+/−
Political Feasibility	− −	+/−	− −	+/−
	2+/6−	3+/5−	3+/5−	5+/3−

+ + Policy strongly meets criterion   − − Policy is strongly counter to criterion
+ Policy meets criterion   0 Policy neither meets nor counters criterion
− Policy does not meet criterion

Figure 4-3   Example of criteria/alternatives matrix (scorecard) for selected policies for Medicare drug benefit.

10. *Summary/recommended policy.* The closing section includes an analytic summary of the option comparison and identification of the most effective or feasible policy. Failure of one option to score significantly highly on most criteria, particularly political feasibility, indicates that tradeoffs among the costs and benefits of option components will have to be negotiated.

CONCLUSION

Nurses' participation in the policy process through their primary roles as analysts or their secondary roles as clinical professional advocates in institutions or organizations will ensure the inclusion of their unique perspective in private sector and governmental policy decisions. The definitions, sequential model of the policy cycle, and outline of a policy issue paper as described here offer tools to facilitate nurses' participation. This analytic approach is particularly valuable for nurses and nursing organizations because it highlights the arguments one will face when seeking or supporting policy change. Such information is essential in developing an effective political strategy. Nursing's participation in health care reform issues such as the Medicare prescription drug benefit enlightens the debate and en-

hances nurses' image as patient advocates. Finally, decision making in any professional situation requires clear, systematic thinking; the analytic approach described here is directly applicable.

REFERENCES

Anderson, J.E. (1990). *Public policymaking.* Boston: Houghton-Mifflin.

Anderson, J.E., Brady, D.W., Bullock III, C.S., & Stewart, Jr., J. (1984). *Public policy and politics in America.* Monterey, CA: Brooks/Cole.

Baumgartner, F. & Jones, B.D. (1993). *Agendas and instability in American politics.* Chicago: University of Chicago Press.

Birkland, A. (2001). *An introduction to the policy process: Theories, concepts and models of public policy making.* Armonk, NY: M.E. Sharpe.

Christensen, S. & Wagner, J. (2000). The cost of a Medicare prescription drug benefit. *Health Affairs, 19,*(2), 212-218.

Cohen, M.D., March, J.G., & Olsen, J.P. (1972, March). A garbage can model of organizational choice. *Administrative Science Quarterly, 17,* 1-25.

The Commonwealth Fund. (2000, November 17). Report: Designing a Medicare drug benefit. Available online at www.commonwealthfund.org/media/releases/stuart_designing_release11172000.asp.

Donelan, K., Blendon, R., Schoen, C., Binns, K., Osburn. R., & Davis, K. (2000). The elderly in five nations: The importance of universal coverage. *Health Affairs, 19*(3), 226-235.

Dunn, W.N. (1981). *Public policy analysis.* Englewood Cliffs, NJ: Prentice-Hall.

Dye, T.R. (1992). *Understanding public policy* (7th ed.). Englewood Cliffs, NJ: Prentice-Hall.

Gwartney, J.D. & Stroup, R.L. (1987). *Microeconomics: Private and public choice.* Orlando, FL: Harcourt Brace Jovanovich.

Hatry, H., Blair, L., Fisk, D., & Kimmel, W. (1976). *Program analysis for state and local governments.* Washington, DC: The Urban Institute.

Jenkins-Smith, S. (1982). Professional roles for policy analysts: A critical assessment. *Journal of Policy Analysis and Management, 2,* 88-93.

Jones, C.O. (1977). *An introduction to the study of public policy.* North Scituate, MA: Duxbury.

Kingdon, J.W. (1995). *Agendas, alternatives, and public policies.* Boston: Little, Brown.

Lindblom, C.E. (1996). The science of "muddling through." In D.C. McCool (Ed.), *Public policy theories, models and concepts: An anthology.* Englewood Cliffs, NJ: Prentice-Hall.

Maxwell, S., Moon, M., & Segal, M. (2001, January). *Growth in Medicare and out-of-pocket spending: Impact on vulnerable beneficiaries.* Washington, DC: The Commonwealth Fund.

Maxwell, S., Moon, M., & Storeygard, M. (2001, May). *Reforming Medicare's benefit package: Impact on beneficiary expenditures.* Washington, DC: The Commonwealth Fund.

Mills, M.E. (2001). Computer-based health care data and the Health Insurance Portability and Accountability Act: Implications for informatics. *Policy, Politics and Nursing Practice, 2*(3), 33-38.

Montgomery, K.L. (2001). Demystifying policy jargon. *Policy, Politics and Nursing Practice, 2*(3), 29-32.

Nelson, B.J. (1978). Setting the policy agenda. In J. May & A. Wildavsky (Eds.). *The policy cycle.* Beverly Hills, CA: Sage.

Nursing's Agenda for Health Care Reform. (1992). Washington, DC: American Nurses Publishing.

Petracca, M.P. (1992). The rediscovery of interest group politics. In M.P. Petracca (Ed.). *The politics of interests.* Boulder, CO: Westview.

Poisal, J.A. & Chulis, G.S. (2000). Medicare beneficiaries and drug coverage. *Health Affairs, 20*(3), 248-256.

Poisal, J.A. & Murray, L. (2001). Growing differences between Medicare beneficiaries with and without drug coverage. *Health Affairs, 20*(2), 74-85.

Ripley, R.B. (1985). *Policy analysis in political science.* Chicago: Nelson-Hall.

Ripley, R.B. (1996). Stages of the policy process. In D.C. McCool (Ed.). *Public policy theories, models and concepts: An anthology.* Englewood Cliffs, NJ: Prentice-Hall.

Sabatier, P.A. (1991). Toward better theories of the policy process. *PS: Political Science and Politics, 24*(2), 147-156.

Sabatier, P.A. (Ed.). (1999). *Theories of the policy process.* Boulder, CO: Westview.

Schneider, A.L. & Ingram, H. (1997). *Policy design for democracy.* Lawrence: University Press of Kansas.

Stimpson, M. & Hanley, B.E. (1991). Nurse policy analyst: Advanced practice role. *Nursing and Health Care, 12*(1), 10-15.

Stokey, E. & Zeckhauser, R. (1978). *A primer for policy analysis.* New York: W.W. Norton.

Stuart, B., Shea, D., & Briesacher, B. (2001). Dynamics in drug coverage of Medicare beneficiaries: Finders, losers, switchers. *Health Affairs, 20*(3), 86-99.

Throgmorton, J.A. (1991). The rhetoric of policy analysis. *Policy Sciences, 24* (2), 153-179.

True, J.L., Jones, B.D. & Baumgartner, F.R. (1999) punctuated equilibrium theory: Explaining stability and change in American policymaking. In P.A. Sabatier (Ed.). *Theories of the policy process.* Boulder, CO: Westview.

Wildavsky, A. (1979). *Speaking truth to power.* Boston: Little, Brown.

Resources

Families USA. (2001, January 29). *President's "helping hand" isn't* (press release). Available online at www.familiesusa.org.prpres.htm.

Families USA. (2001, June 12). *Prices of most-prescribed drugs for seniors rose more than twice the rate of inflation last year* (press release). Available online at www.familiesusa.org/press/releases/2001/enoughtomakeyousick.htm.

Hayes, M.T. (1992). *Incrementalism and public policy.* NY: Long-man.

Lindblom, C. E. (1987). Still muddling, not yet through. In D. L. Yarwood (Ed.), *Public administration politics and the people* (pp. 222-233). New York: Longman.

Stone, D. (1992). *The policy paradox: The art of political decision-making.* New York: W.W. Norton.

Vladeck, B.C. (1999). The political economy of Medicare. *Health Affairs, 18*(1), 22-36.

Williams, C.H. (1991). Doing critical thinking together: Applications to government, politics and public policy. *PS: Political Science & Politics, 24*(3), 510-516.

5

Political Analysis and Strategies

JUDITH K. LEAVITT

SALLY S. COHEN

DIANA J. MASON

"The difficult can be done immediately; the impossible takes a little longer."

U.S. ARMY CORPS OF ENGINEERS

Nursing and politics are a good match. First, nurses understand people. Success in any political situation depends on one's ability to establish and sustain strong interpersonal relationships. Second, nurses appreciate the importance of systematic assessments. Nurses engaged in the politics of the policy process will find that their efforts are most effective when they systematically analyze their issues and develop strategies for advancing their agendas. Finally, nurses bring to the deliberations of any health policy issue an appreciation of how policies affect clinical care and patient well-being. Few policymakers have such an ability. Thus nurses have much to offer public and private sector discussions and actions around health policy issues.

In its emphasis on the politics of government agencies and public policies, this chapter provides an organizing framework for political analyses and strategy development to enhance nurses' political leverage in any of the arenas in which policy is made. For example, nurses who want to improve working conditions in health care delivery systems, enhance community-based programs, or negotiate among professional organizations, will find the analyses and strategies discussed useful.

GENDER ISSUES AND CONFLICT

Nurses can enhance their political influence, individually and collectively, by acknowledging certain underlying assumptions about sex and conflict. Of particular importance is the notion that "gender politics" affects every political scenario that involves nurses. Working in a predominantly female profession means that nurses are accustomed to certain norms of social interactions (Tanner, 2001). They are most familiar with discourse among women and nursing colleagues. In contrast, the power and politics of public policy-making typically are male dominated, although women are steadily increasing their ranks as elected and appointed government officials (see Chapter 29 on campaigns and elections). Moreover, many male and female public officials have stereotypic images of nurses as women who lack political savvy. This may limit officials' ability to view nurses as potential political partners. Thus, nurses need to be sensitive to gender issues that may affect, but certainly not prevent, their political success. In fact, it is usually nurse legislators at the federal and state level who lead efforts to improve women's health and support work and family issues (see the Vignettes in Chapters 25 and 26 and the Unit Four Case Study).

Many nurses may find political work unsavory because of the inevitability of conflict. Conflicts between political parties, between those with different ideologic values, and between nurses and other stakeholders are inherent to the political process. Conflict is unavoidable, and it is also necessary for identifying the different viewpoints that will structure subsequent negotiations, compromises, and consensus building. Unlike other situations where conflict may be unwelcome, it is necessary in politics for establishing the parameters of discourse and the terms of compromise. This holds true for any setting in which nurses are involved with politics, whether it is the workplace, the community, or organizational or governmental arenas.

Conflict occurs whenever an individual's or group's ideas are opposed by another. Conflict also arises when there are limited resources or rewards, so that one individual or group gains at the expense of the other. Conflict is inevitable because in every society there is always a scarcity of goods or services. The ubiquitous nature of conflict should help nurses realize that, like power, conflict is unavoidable and something to be addressed rather than avoided. Nurses can learn how to deal positively with conflict as well as how to use power appropriately.

A renowned political scientist, E.E. Schattschneider (1960), developed a useful framework for understanding the role of conflict in political situations. He described how expanding the scope of a conflict, or what he called the "contagiousness of conflict," could affect the outcome of political deliberations. As he explained, "competitiveness is the mechanism for the expansion of the scope of conflict" (Schattschneider, 1960, pp. 17-18). The loser may call in outside groups to shift the balance of power. New scope and balance can make possible many things and can also make many things impossible. According to Schattschneider, every conflict has two parts: the individuals engaged and the audience attracted to the conflict. The audience is never neutral. Once people become involved, they take a side and influence the outcome. The larger the audience, the more likely there will be conflict. Therefore, the "most important strategy of politics is concerned with the scope of the conflict" (Schattschneider, 1960, p. 3).

Schattschneider also pointed out the importance of visibility. One can't expand scope without making issues visible to one's constituency and outside audiences. As he explained, "a democratic government lives by publicity" (p. 16). According to Schattschneider, "politics is the socialization of conflict." Moreover, as long as the conflict remains private, the political process is limited, if initiated at all. "Conflicts become political only when an attempt is made to involve the wider public" (Schattschneider, 1960, p. 39).

These words are significant to nurses looking to exert political influence: First, expanding the scope of conflict can be a strategy for achieving political change, used by one's friends and foes alike. Second, when the scope of conflict is expanded, it is important to engage the media and other avenues of publicity (see Chapter 10 on working with the media). Of course, this doesn't ensure that the outcome will be what one wants. The outcome depends on many other factors, including "which of a multitude of possible conflicts gains the dominant position" (Schattschneider, 1960, p. 62). Success in the political arena means knowing the environment, potential stakeholders, the misperceptions policymakers may have, recognizing the lack of sufficient information, and creating strategies to meet the challenges.

COMPONENTS OF POLITICAL ANALYSIS

The best approach to accomplish change must include a thoughtful analysis of the politics of the problem and proposed solutions. Although this chapter explores the *political* analysis of a problem and proposed solutions, Chapter 4 provides for an in-depth discussion of *policy* analysis. These two analytic processes should actually be done simultaneously. In fact, the impact of not doing so was exemplified in the demise of President Clinton's Health Security Act. Much attention and praise was given to the policy process of developing the president's plan for health care reform. Many small groups met to analyze the various dimensions of the problems in health care and possible solutions; however, a comparable process was not used for the political analysis of how to move the issue until the opposition had been mobilized.

A *political* analysis should include the following steps:

1. Identifying and analyzing the problem
2. Outlining and analyzing proposed solutions
3. Understanding the background of the issue: its history and previous attempts to address the problem
4. Locating the political setting and structures involved
5. Evaluating the stakeholders
6. Conducting a values assessment
7. Recognizing the resources, both financial and human, needed to reach the intended goals
8. Analyzing power bases

THE PROBLEM

The first step in conducting a political analysis is to identify the problem. Answering several questions is useful in framing the problem:

- What is its scope, duration, and history, and whom does it affect?
- What data are available to describe the issue and its ramifications?
- What are the gaps in existing data?
- What types of additional research might be useful?

Not all serious conditions are problems that warrant government attention. The challenge for those seeking to get public policymakers to address particular problems, such as poverty, the uninsured, or unacceptable working conditions, is to define the problem in ways that will prompt lawmakers to take action. This requires careful crafting of messages so that calls for public, as opposed to private sector solutions, are clearly justified. This is known as framing the issue. In the workplace, framing may entail linking the problem to one of the institution's priorities or to a potential threat to its reputation or financial standing. For example, inadequate nurse staffing could be linked to increases in rates of infection, morbidity, and morality—outcomes that can increase institutional costs and jeopardize an institution's reputation as a health care organization of excellence.

Sometimes what appears to be a problem is not. For example, proposed mandatory continuing education for nurses is not a problem. Rather, it is a possible solution to the challenge of ensuring competency of nurses. After an analysis of the issue of clinician competence, one might review the policy outcomes and establish a goal that includes legislating mandatory continuing education. The danger of framing solutions as problems is the possibility that it can limit creative thinking about the underlying issue and leave the best solutions uncovered.

PROPOSED SOLUTIONS

When asking public officials to devote resources to a particular problem, one must also provide possible solutions. Typically, there is more than one solution to an identified problem, and each option differs with regard to cost, practicality, and duration. By identifying and analyzing possible solutions, nurses will acquire further understanding of their issue and what is feasible for government to undertake. For example, if nurses want the federal government to provide substantial support for nursing education, they need to understand the constraints of federal budgets and the demands to invest in other programs, including those that benefit nurses. Moreover, support for nursing education can take the form of scholarships, loans, tax credits, aid to nursing schools, or incentives for building partnerships between nursing schools and health care delivery systems. Each option presents different types of support, and nurses would need to understand the implications of the alternatives before asking for federal intervention.

The amount of money and time needed to address a particular problem also needs to be taken into account. Are there short-term and long-term alternatives that nurses want to pursue simultaneously? How might one prioritize various solutions? What are the tradeoffs that nurses are willing to make to obtain stated political goals? Such questions need to be considered in developing the political strategy.

BACKGROUND

When striving to affect policy formation, one must know about previous attempts to move an issue. This will provide insight into the *feasibility* of a particular approach. For example, many child care advocates view federal child care standards as vital for protecting the health and safety of children in child care settings and for minimizing variation among states. However, a review of child care policy-making over the past few decades would reveal that federal child care standards were always contentious and that by 1990 most child care policymakers considered them politically impractical (Cohen, 2001).

Knowledge of past history will also provide insight into the *position of key public officials* so that communications with those individuals and strategies for advancing an issue can be developed accordingly. For example, if one knows that a particular legislator always questioned the ability of advanced practice nurses (APNs) to practice independently, then that individual would need special coaxing to support legislation allowing direct billing of APNs under Medicare.

Finally, *historical precedent* for one issue can affect the politics of another. For example, in the United States, one would not expect to be successful in moving social welfare legislation that was associated with high taxes because of our culture of individualism. Past attempts to raise taxes to cover the costs of government programs have led to the political demise of high-level leaders, most notably President George Bush in the early 1990s. Based on past experiences with requests for tax increases to subsidize budget shortfalls, new proposals to increase government support for health care, education, and other social issues through tax increases in the near future will likely fail.

POLITICAL SETTING

Once the problems and solutions have been clearly identified and described, the appropriate political arenas for influencing the issue need to be analyzed. Usually this begins by identifying the entities with jurisdiction over the problem. Is the issue primarily within the public domain or does it also entail the private sector? Many issues require a mix of public and private sector players, but responsibility for decision making will ultimately rest with one sector more than the other. For example, nurses interested in improving workplace conditions would first turn to their employers and other local stakeholders. It would not be prudent to turn to public officials until other efforts in the private sector had failed.

Nurses also need to clarify which level of government is responsible for a particular issue. For example, licensure and regulation of nursing practice falls under state jurisdiction; it generally would not involve federal lawmakers. On the other hand, reimbursement of nursing care under Medicare is under the purview of the federal government, not the states. Some issues, such as funding for nursing education, might entail a mix of federal, state, and local remedies. When communicating with legislators and developing strategies, it is critical to understand the distinct roles of federal, state, and local governments for a particular issue and how they may intersect.

In addition to the level of government, nurses need to know which branch of government (legislative, executive, or judicial) has primary jurisdiction over the issue at a given time. Legislatures are responsible for drafting bills and enacting laws. Executive branches of government are responsible for the implementation and regulation of programs after they have been enacted into law. And the courts, through the judicial branch, interpret laws and regulations. Although there is often overlap among these branches of government, nurses will find that a particular issue falls predominantly within one branch (see Chapter 22 on the legislative and regulatory processes).

If the issue is in the problem definition and policy formation stage, then nurses will focus on the legislative branch. They will want to know which party is in the majority for each chamber, names of key legislative leaders, major committees with jurisdiction over the issue, the chairs and ranking minority members of each committee, and previous bills that have been introduced. For each of these individuals, nurses need to identify and cultivate relationships with key staffers, especially at the federal level. The staff has the most in-depth understanding of issues and can influence legislators to take a certain position. It also would be useful to identify any nurse legislators and the feasibility of obtaining their support (see Chapter 28 on lobbying).

If an issue entails the implementation of a program, including promulgating regulations, then nurses will focus on the executive branch. They will want to know the organizational structure of the particular agencies involved and the key staff people responsible. Nurses will also want to know the process for writing rules and overseeing programs for that particular program.

Issues that are within the courts call for knowledge of the judicial system. In particular, nurses will want to know whether this is a civil or criminal case and whether the issue falls under state or federal purview. The opportunities for influencing the courts are different than those for the legislative and executive branches of government (see Chapter 23 on the courts).

Nurses can apply a political analysis to settings beyond government, in the workplace or community organization. Regardless of the setting, nurses will want to identify who has responsibility for decision making on a particular issue. They will want to know which committees, boards, or panels have addressed the issue in the past and who the key staff and appointed officials are for moving an issue. Nurses can seek committee appointments in their workplace and elsewhere to be part of the deliberations for important health policy concerns. They will want to understand the chain of command and organization structure to determine who has the formal power.

At an institutional level, once the relevant political arenas are identified, the formal and informal structures and functioning of that arena need to be analyzed. The formal dimensions of the entity can often be assessed through documents related to the organization's mission, goals, objectives, organization structure, constitution and bylaws, annual report (including financial statement), long-range plans, governing body, committees, departments, and individuals with jurisdiction.

Does the entity use parliamentary procedure? Parliamentary procedure provides a democratic process that carefully balances the rights of individuals, subgroups within an organization, and the membership of an assembly. The basic rules are outlined in *Robert's Rules of Order Newly Revised* (Robert, 2000). Whether in a legislative session or the policy-making body of large organizations, such as the American Nurses Association (ANA) House of Delegates, one must know parliamentary procedure as a political strategy to get an issue passed or rejected. Countless issues have failed or passed because of insufficient knowledge of rule making.

It is also vital to know the informal processes and methods of communication. A well-known example of the power of informal processes and communication is the case of the business lunch or the golf game, which in the past often excluded women. However, it is just as likely that informal communication occurs at cocktail parties, dinners, or other social situations in which personal connections are important.

STAKEHOLDERS

Once the political setting has been analyzed, the overt and potential stakeholders must be identified. Stakeholders are those parties who have influence over the issue or who could be mobilized to care about the issue. In some cases, stakeholders are obvious. These would be the overt stakeholders. For example, nurse practitioners are stakeholders in issues concerning reimbursement of primary care providers under Medicare. In other situations, one can develop potential stakeholders by helping them to see the connections between the issue and their interests. Many individuals and organizations can be considered stakeholders when it comes to Medicare reimbursement of APNs. Among them are payers (insurance companies), legislators, health policy analysts, employers, other professionals, and, of course, consumers.

Who could be turned into stakeholders by virtue of their interests and values? Nursing has increasingly realized the potential of consumer power in moving nursing and health care issues. For example, nurses have worked with AARP (formerly the American Association of Retired Persons) on long-term care, with the Children's Defense Fund in advocating for child health, and with the American Cancer Society on tobacco issues. Who has power in relation to the issue and other stakeholders? Who brings a powerful voice or presence to the issue? For example, before running for office, Congresswoman Carolyn McCarthy became a respected and powerful spokesperson around gun control through the media coverage of the fatal shooting of her husband (see her story in the second Vignette in Chapter 26). Certainly she was able to mobilize other stakeholders, such as victims of gun violence, during her campaigns for gun control and for election to Congress. But one of the most significant stakeholders she identified was the American Academy of Pediatrics, which brought significant clout and resources to the table.

What kind of relationships do you or others have with key stakeholders? Look at your connections with possible stakeholders through your schools, places of worship, or business. Which of these stakeholders are potential supporters or opponents? Can any of the opponents be converted to supporters? What are the values, priorities, and concerns of the stakeholders? How can these be tapped in planning political strategy? For example, as nurses determine how to increase recruitment and retention of nurses, it is obvious that some of the most important stakeholders will be other providers, such as hospitals and the home health and nursing home industries. In addition consumer groups, especially senior citizens, have a stake in whether nursing care will be available as they age. And when the nation considers the important role of nurses in its preparedness for a national disaster, federal policymakers become important stakeholders. Different stakeholders may have different stands on particular strategies for recruitment and retention of nurses.

Do the supportive stakeholders reflect the constituency that will be affected by the issue? For example, as states attempt to expand coverage of health services through each state's Children's Health Insurance Program (S-CHIP), it is vital to have parents of enrolled children lobby policymakers. These parents can share the personal stories of how the program has made a difference for their child. Yet stakeholders who are recipients of the services are too often not identified as vital for moving an issue. Nurses as direct caregivers have a pivotal role in ensuring that recipients of services are included as stakeholders.

VALUES ASSESSMENT

Every political issue, especially those entailing "morality policies," could prompt discussions about

values. Morality policies are those that primarily revolve around ideology and values, rather than costs and distribution of resources. Among the most well publicized morality issues are abortion, stem cell research, and the death penalty (Mooney, 2001). But even issues that are not classified as morality policies require that stakeholders assess their values and those of their opponents.

Values underlie the responsibility of public policymakers to be involved in the regulation of health care. In particular, calls for extending the reach of government in the regulation of health care facilities implies that one accepts this as a proper role for public officials, rather than as a role of market forces and the private sector. Thus, electoral politics affects the policies that may be implemented. An analysis that acknowledges the extent of congruence of nurses' values with the values of those in power can determine the success of policy implementation.

In an era of finite resources, calls for increasing federal funding for nursing education and research come at the expense of increasing government investments in other important areas, such as expanding health care coverage to the millions of uninsured Americans, spending on early childhood education, or improving the public health infrastructure. This analysis implies that nurses are placing a higher priority on the education and research related to their profession than other health or social policy endeavors. Although nurses may value a range of health and social programs, legislators will hear their calls for increased funding for nursing research and education within the context of demands from other constituencies. Any call for government support of health care programs implies a certain prioritization of values. Elected officials must always make choices among competing demands. And their choices reflect their values and the needs of their constituents. Similarly, nurses' choice of issues on the political agenda reflects the profession's values and political priorities.

One way of conceptualizing these decisions is through a framework that identifies four stages of nursing's political development (Cohen, Mason, Kovner, Leavitt, Pulcini, & Sochalski, 1996). In stage one, nurses become aware of the importance of political involvement. In stage two, nurses advocate for issues, such as funding for nursing education and research, that primarily are concerns of the profession. Although one could argue that patients, providers, and others may benefit from investments in nursing education and research, in the eyes of state and federal policymakers, they are primarily "nursing" issues. In the third stages, nurses participate in broad health policy discussions that extend beyond nursing's self-interest. And in the fourth and final stage, nurses lead the way and set the agenda for a host of health and other social policy issues (Table 5-1).

This framework can be useful in analyzing nursing's political strategies. According to the framework, nurses can be at more than one stage simultaneously, depending on the issue and a host of other factors. Moreover, nurses individually and collectively may move through these stages at different rates. Finally, the framework shows how certain themes, such as nursing education and research, are only one part of nursing's political development. When nurses focus on those issues to the exclusion of others, they are limiting their political potential and reflecting values that may be seen as more self-serving than when they advocate for broad health and social policy concerns.

RESOURCES

An effective political strategy must take into account the resources that will be needed to move an issue successfully. Resources include money, time, connections, and intangible resources, such as creative ideas. Analyzing the resources requires both short-term and long-term views.

The most obvious resource is money, which must be considered in relation to both the proposed solution or policy and the campaign to champion it. The proposed solution needs to include an analysis of the resources needed for the solution to be successful. Thus, before launching a campaign for a particular bill or program, campaign leaders must know how much the proposed solution will cost, who will be bearing those costs, and the source of the money. In addition, it is helpful to know how budgets are formulated for a given government agency or institution. What is the budget process? How much money is allocated to a

particular cost center or budget line? Who decides how the funds will be used? How is the use of funds evaluated? How might an individual or group influence the budget process?

The campaign to secure adoption of the solution requires a similar analysis, but it may be easier to substitute other resources for money. Sometimes many different individuals or organizations can share costs; however, this may require a mechanism for each entity to contribute a specific amount or to tally their in-kind contributions. In-kind contributions can include office space for meetings; use of a photocopier, telephone, or other equipment; or use of staff to assist with production of brochures and other communications. Other cost considerations include accessing the media or other publicity efforts; printing brochures and other educational materials; covering the costs of other office supports and supplies; paying for postage; and establishing access to electronic communications.

When nurses and other volunteers are recruited for a political issue, project, or campaign, a common response is lack of time for involvement. Nurses need to figure how to get volunteers while simultaneously protecting one of their most precious commodities, time. One must find creative ways to use available resources. For instance, an option for limited volunteer time might be contracting for specific services, such as writing testimony or other communications. In other cases, time and money may both be scarce. This requires delegating and sharing of responsibilities and setting realistic goals about what can be achieved in a given time. If not, creating a diversified coalition can enhance achievement of the goals (see Chapter 8 on coalitions).

Creativity is a precious resource that enables nurses and others to develop strategies that will be inspiring and captivating to one's audience. How much creativity is evident among the stakeholders? How can one stimulate and channel creativity? Allocating enough time for brainstorming and planning strategically will pay off in the end if well-designed and creative approaches emerge from such sessions.

POWER

In the workplace, government, professional organizations, and community, effective political strategy

TABLE **5-1** The Progress of Nursing: Four Stages of Political Development

	STAGE 1 (BUY-IN)	STAGE 2 (SELF-INTEREST)	STAGE 3 (POLITICAL SOPHISTICATION)	STAGE 4 (LEADING THE WAY)
Nature of action	Reactive, with a focus on nursing issues	Reactive to nursing issues (e.g., funding for nursing education) and broader issues (e.g., long-term care and immunizations)	Proactive on nursing and other health issues (e.g., *Nursing's Agenda for Health Care Reform* [1992])	Proactive on leadership and agenda setting for a broad range of health and social policy issues
Language	Learning of political language	Use of nurse jargon (e.g., *caring, nursing, diagnosis*)	Use of parlance and rhetoric common to health policy deliberations	Introduction of terms that reorder the debate
Coalition-building	Political awareness; occasional participation in coalitions	Coalition forming among nursing organizations	Coalition forming among nursing groups; active and significant participation in broader health care groups (e.g., Clinton's task force on health care reform)	Initiation of coalitions beyond nursing for broad health policy concerns
Nurses as policy shapers	Isolated cases of nurses being appointed to policy positions, primarily because of individual accomplishments	Use of professional associations to get nurses into nursing-related positions	Use of professional organizations to get nurses appointed to health-related policy positions (e.g., nurse position on ProPAC)	Outreach to many nurses to fill nursing and health policy positions because of value of nursing expertise and knowledge

Adapted from Cohen, S., Mason, D., Kovner, C., Leavitt, J., Pulcini, J., & Sochalski, J. (1996). Stages of nursing's political development: Where we've been and where we ought to go. *Nursing Outlook, 44*(1), 20-23.

requires an analysis of the power of proponents and opponents of a particular solution. Power is one of the most complex political and sociologic concepts to define and measure. It is also a term that politicians and policy analysts use freely, without necessarily giving thought to what it means.

Power can be a means to an end, or an end in itself. Power also can be actual or potential. The latter implies power as undeveloped but a "force to be reckoned with" (Joel & Kelly, 2002). Many in political circles depict the nursing profession as a potential political force given the millions of nurses in this country and the power we could wield if most nurses participated in politics and policy formation.

There are no absolute or definitive models of power, and at times, aspects of power can seem contradictory. That is, power may be considered a prerequisite for social or political action, or it may be an indicator of behavior or a result of a certain action. Sometimes power is asymmetric, as when one person or group has more control than another. In other circumstances, power is more symmetric, involving reciprocal influences between two parties, such as between leaders and followers (Duke, 1976). Power can also be considered a zero-sum entity in which one person's or group's possession of power precludes possession by another. In other cases, power is a less restricted and more "sharable commodity," with its benefits being distributed among many parties (Duke, 1976, p. 42). All these perspectives illustrate the dynamic nature of power and ways in which nurses can analyze and use power to their advantage. For example, when power bases among parties are determined to be asymmetric, consensus-building and shared decision making may be unlikely unless the dominant party values these methods of conflict resolution (see Chapter 7 on conflict management).

Any power analysis must include reflection on one's own power base. Power can be obtained through a variety of sources (French & Raven, 1959; Hersey, Blanchard, & Natemeyer, 1979; Mason, Backer, & Georges, 1991; Ferguson, 1993; Joel & Kelly, 2002):

1. *Coercive power* is rooted in real or perceived fear of one person by another. For example, the supervisor who threatens to fire those nurses who speak out is relying on coercive power, as is a state commissioner of health who threatens to develop regulations requiring physician supervision of nurse practitioners.

2. *Reward power* is based on the perception of the potential for rewards or favors as a result of honoring the wishes of a powerful person. A clear example is the supervisor who has the power to determine promotions and pay increases.

3. *Legitimate (or positional) power* is derived from an organizational position rather than personal qualities, whether from a person's role as the chief nurse officer or the state's governor.

4. *Expert power* is based on knowledge, special talents, or skills, in contrast to positional power. Benner (1984) argues that nurses can tap this power source as they move from novice to expert practitioner. It is a power source that nurses must recognize is available to them and tap. Policymakers are seldom experts in health care; rather, nurses are.

5. *Referent power* emanates from associating with a powerful person or organization. This power source is used when a nurse selects a mentor who is a powerful person, such as the chief nurse officer of the organization or the head of the state's dominant political party. It can also emerge when a nursing organization enlists a highly regarded public personality as an advocate for an issue it is championing.

6. *Information power* results when one individual has (or is perceived to have) special information that another individual desires. This power source underscores the need for nurses to stay abreast of information on a variety of levels: in one's personal and professional networks, immediate work situation, employing institution, community, and the public sector as well as in society and the world. Use of information power requires strategic consideration of how and with whom to share the information.

7. *Connection power* is granted to those perceived to have important and sometimes extensive connections with individuals or organizations.

For example, the nurse who attends the same church or synagogue as the president of the home health care agency, knows the appointments secretary for the mayor, or is a member of the hospital credentialing committee will be accorded power by those who want access to these individuals or groups.

8. *Empowerment arises* from shared power. This power source requires those who have power to recognize that they can build the power of colleagues or others by sharing authority and decision making. Empowerment can happen when the nurse manager on a unit uses consensus-building when possible instead of issuing authoritative directives to staff or when a coalition is formed and adopts consensus building and shared decision making to guide its process.

An analysis of the extent of one's power using these sources can also provide direction on how to enhance that power. This analysis can be done both for short-term and long-term purposes. For example, consider the nursing organization that finds itself unable to secure legislative support for a key piece of legislation. It can develop a short-term plan for enhancing its power by finding a highly regarded, high-profile individual to be its spokesperson with the media (referent power), by making it known to legislators that their vote on this issue will be a major consideration in the next election's endorsement decisions (reward/coercive power), or by getting nurses to tell the media their stories that highlight the problem the legislation addresses (expert power). Its long-term plan might include extending its connections with other organizations by signing onto coalitions that address broader health care issues and expanding connections with policymakers by attending fundraisers for key legislators (connection power); getting nurses into policymaking positions (legitimate power); hiring a government affairs director to help inform the group about the nuances of the legislature (information power); and using consensus-building within the organization to enhance nurses' participation and activities (empowerment).

There is ample evidence that nurses have succeeded in flexing their political muscles and have demonstrated the power behind their political effectiveness. Examples include direct Medicare reimbursement for APNs as part of the 1997 Balanced Budget Act; breakthrough enactment of legislation establishing the National Center for Nursing Research in 1985 and its subsequent legislated designation as the National Institute of Nursing Research in the early 1990s; and numerous collaborative efforts with other groups in areas such as advancing women's health and protecting patients' rights under managed care at state levels of government.

POLITICAL STRATEGIES

Once a political analysis is completed, it is necessary to develop a plan of action that identifies strategies for action. Political strategies are the methods and guidelines used in the formulation of a plan to achieve desired goals, including policy goals. They are the means to the goal. Well-planned and practiced strategies can make the difference between success or failure of a plan.

No single strategy works in all situations. However, an important guideline in selecting any strategy is to choose one that shows respect and consideration for policymakers. At no time should one threaten or be disrespectful. Sometimes that can happen in the "heat of battle." For women, particularly, it may be difficult to depersonalize the conflict in tense negotiations. Yet it is the successful advocate who understands that as passionate as one may feel about an issue, the opposition feels just as strongly. Remaining calm, showing respect, and listening well are qualities that make for success. "Do unto others as others would do unto you" is one of the most important principles for engaging in politics.

Politics, particularly to the novice, may have a negative connotation because of the long history of policymakers who used Machiavellian strategies in which political expediency takes precedence over morality (Machiavelli, 1984) to win issues. However, most policymakers who are effective are individuals with reputations for honesty, fair play, and commitment. Certainly, nurses have a trustworthy reputation in the public's eye and are seen as credible stakeholders. A Gallup poll done in November 2000 indicates that the public places nurses at the top of all other groups in honesty and ethical behavior (Carlson, 2000). This is where the ethics of politics becomes most critical. Will nurses be successful if they take the high road in politics? Should they sacrifice the public's trust and use Machiavellian tactics, reasoning that the ends are more important than the means? As more women enter politics, the approach for resolving conflicts through consensus building and principled negotiating has become much more common and provides nurses with options for political strategy development that can be both ethical and effective.

PERSISTENCE

Another consideration regarding the development of political strategies is the importance of persistence. Rarely does change happen overnight. Because of the conflict inherent in most policy initiatives, resolution often occurs after discussion, wrangling, delays, regrouping, and shifting of power bases. Securing changes in policy or establishing new public policies requires a commitment to a long-term process. But persistence can pay off. Consider the following nursing success story:

The story of the achievement of Medicare reimbursement for all APNs reflects the use of many political strategies. For more than 10 years, many nursing organizations, particularly the American Academy of Nurse Practitioners (AANP) and the ANA, worked with members of Congress to enact legislation that would allow for direct reimbursement of nurse practitioners and clinical nurse specialists under Medicare Part B. Under previous law, nurse practitioner reimbursement was limited to rural areas, long-term care facilities, and services deemed "incident to" physician care. (Policies for Medicaid reimbursement of nurse practitioners were different from those for Medicare because each state set its own payment rates, within Medicaid guidelines.)

Under the Balanced Budget Act (BBA) of 1997, Medicare law was changed to allow for direct reimbursement of nurse practitioners and clinical specialists regardless of site or geographic setting. The provisions, which went into effect January 1, 1998, set nurse practitioner reimbursement rates at 80% of the actual charge or 85% of the fee schedule amount for physicians, whichever is less.

Before 1997 medicare policies did not reflect the realities of practice because nurse practitioners and clinical nurse specialists were providing care to medicare beneficiaries without being recognized as the practitioner of record. However, it took years of lobbying and the orchestration of an effective grass roots campaign across the country to get congress to revise medicare law. Although most nurses would have preferred that the payment rates be set higher, nursing organizations recognized that compromises might be necessary to make these important first steps. In fact, earlier bills called for nurse practitioner reimbursement rates at 97% of the physician fee schedule, but it soon became clear that the legislators would not accept those terms.

There were many times before enactment of the BBA in 1997 when nursing organizations thought the battle had been won, only to find out that the provisions were not included in the final bill. Because nursing organizations never gave up, continued to work with the Health Care Financing Administration (HCFA; now the Centers for Medicare and Medicaid Services), lobbied legislators, and developed supporting testimony and fact sheets describing the value of APNs, they eventually had a fine-tuned and effective campaign. At the end of the 105th congressional session, when key congressional leaders negotiated behind closed doors, reimbursement for all APNs was included in the final BBA.

The nursing community was joyous. Why did this legislation finally pass? Certainly the cost savings to reimburse APN's at 85% of the rate for physicians had to be appealing at a time when Congress was determined to find ways to reduce expenditures for Medicare. The efforts of so many groups over a 10-year period had been heard and remembered by the conferees.

Legislation can take a long time to be passed. It took 10 years for all APNs to receive Medicare reimbursement. It took 18 years to pass the Family and Medical Leave Act that gave parents and family members 12 weeks of unpaid leave from their job for the birth, adoption, or care of a sick family member. During those intervening 18 years, much changed, except the continuing effort to lobby legislators. More women entered the workforce, and employers recognized that they could not lose critical workers because of the birth or adoption of children. By the time the bill was passed, the public and policymakers realized that act was necessary to maintain a stable workforce and enable workers to provide care for family members. In addition, a president was elected (Clinton) who supported the issue. Political work requires patience, perseverance, and an exquisite sense of timing.

Policy implementation almost always happens through incremental change. Incremental changes or actions may have a better chance of success than a change of major proportions. Resistance to change can often be overcome if a pilot or demonstration project is created to test an idea on a small scale. For example, some nurses have proposed pilot projects to study the impact of allowing family members to be present when a patient "codes" or undergoes an invasive procedures, knowing that once physicians and nurses experience "family presence," their support of an institutional family presence policy is almost guaranteed (see the Chapter 16 Vignette).

Many times we are confronted with situations in which we may not get all we want. One must be clear about what are acceptable solutions or alternatives and what are not. Identification of alternatives represents a good way to test one's convictions and to consider what the long- and short-term goals are. The initial failure to get reimbursement for all APNs had to be accepted in order to get reimbursement for some. The failure of President Clinton's health care reform legislation, which would have overhauled health care in the United States, was partly attributed to the fact that policy-making in this country is usually incremental rather than revolutionary. Though his package failed, Congress did pass the Health Insurance Portability and Accountability Act (HIPAA), an incremental policy to ensure that employees could maintain their health insurance when they leave or lose a job, so that individuals with "preexisting health conditions" could not be denied health insurance.

Failure to recognize the importance of timing and the primacy of incremental change can cause nurses to become discouraged and feel inadequate as political operatives. The following are helpful ways to minimize the frustrations that can accompany political work:

- Have a well-defined political plan with both long-term and short-term objectives.
- Evaluate one's progress, and modify the plan as needed.
- Seize opportunities that arise from unforeseen social changes.
- Identify how to turn seeming defeats into victories.
- Celebrate the small gains.
- Thank, keep informed, and actively support collaborating stakeholders.

Persistence and use of multiple political strategies are needed for a successful outcome to political action.

STRATEGIES FOR SUCCESS

LOOK AT THE BIG PICTURE

It is human nature to view the world from a personal standpoint, focusing on the people and events that influence one's daily life. However, this strategy requires that one step back and take stock of the larger environment. It can provide a more objective perspective and increase nurses' credibility as broad-minded visionaries, looking beyond personal needs. It also means that one should not get bogged down in details that may seem important at the time, but which in the larger schema may not be critical to the success of the issue. For example, solutions to address the discontent of nurses on a particular unit can get sidetracked by peripheral issues. Mandates that insist nurses not address physicians by first name lose sight of the real problem, which is to find ways to enhance communication between physicians and nurses. In government, legislation to address "patients' rights" under managed care plans became sidetracked by the amount of liability settlements patients could receive as a result of inadequate or improper care. The intent of the legislation was to give patients more choices for care under managed care plans. The original intent of the legislation became lost because certain stakeholders were more concerned with liability than patient rights.

In the heat of legislative battles and negotiations, it is easy to get distracted. However, the successful advocate is the one who does not lose sight of the big picture and is willing to compromise for the larger goal.

BE PREPARED

One often does not know beforehand when a particular policy will be acted on or have knowledge of every question that may arise about an issue. As a result, it is necessary that one not start advocating for an issue until one is adequately prepared. It is not sufficient to claim ignorance when confronted with questions that should be answered. It diminishes policymakers' respect of nurses. However, if one has done everything possible to prepare and is asked to supply information that is not anticipated, it is reasonable and preferable to indicate that one does not know the answer. It does mean that one must get the information as soon as possible and distribute it to the policymaker who requested it.

There are numerous ways to be adequately prepared:
- Clarify your position on the problem and possible solutions.
- Gather data, and search the clinical literature.
- Prepare documents to describe and support the issue.
- Assess the power dynamics of the players.
- Assess your own power base and ability to maneuver in the political arena.
- Plan a strategy, and assess its strengths and weaknesses.
- Prepare for the conflict.
- Line up support.
- Know the opposition and their rationale.

FRAME THE ISSUE ADEQUATELY

The content of an issue is important, but it may be secondary to the way the message is framed and conveyed to stakeholders. Know the context of the issue (as described earlier). Learn to use strong, affirmative language to describe nursing practice. Use the rhetoric that incorporates lawmakers' lingo and the "buzz words" of key proponents. This requires having a sense of the values of the target audiences,

be they policymakers, the public, hospital administrators, or community leaders.

Appealing to a variety of stakeholders often requires developing rhetoric or a message to frame your issue that is succinct and appealing to the values and concerns of those you want to mobilize or defeat. For example, "Cut Medicare" was an ineffective political message that the Republicans used in 1997 to try to gain public support for decreasing spending on Medicare. When the message was changed to "Preserve and Protect Medicare," the public was more supportive, even though the policy goals were the same. In the earlier example of reimbursement of APNs under the BBA, APNs framed their issue in terms of quality of care and cost savings. At a time when Congress was concerned about the amount of money spent on Medicare, the message of reducing costs without compromising quality resonated with the members. How you convey your message involves developing rhetoric or catchy phrases that the media might pick up and perpetuate (see Chapter 10 on the media). Nurses need to develop their effectiveness in accessing and using the media, an essential component of getting the issue on the public's agenda.

Often issues are not what they seem. It is just as important to be aware of the way one conveys information as it is to provide the facts. Communication theory notes that the overt message is not always the real message (Gerston, 1997). Some people say a lot by what they choose not to disclose. When legislators say they think your issue is important, it does not necessarily mean that they will vote to support it. The real question that needs to be asked is, "Will you vote in support of our bill?" What are the hidden agendas of the stakeholders concerned with the issue? What is not being said? When framing an issue, be aware of the covert messages. Be careful to make the issue as clear as possible and test it on others to be certain that reading between the lines conveys the same message as the overt rhetoric.

DEVELOP AND USE NETWORKS

Using the power that results from personal connections is often the most important strategy in moving a critical issue. Sometimes it comes down to one important personal connection. In the example of APN reimbursement, the original legislation that gave some APNs medicare reimbursement was greatly facilitated because the chief of staff for the senate majority leader was a nurse. Or consider the nurse who is the neighbor and friend of the secretary to the chief executive officer (CEO) in the medical center. This nurse is more likely to gain access to the CEO than will someone who is unknown to either the secretary or the CEO. Networking is an important long-term strategy for building influence; however, it can be a deliberate short-term strategy as well.

Developing networks involves keeping track of what one has done for you and not being afraid to ask a favor in return. Often known as *quid pro quo* (literally, "something for something"), it is the way political arenas work in both public and private sectors. Networking is an important skill for achieving personal and political goals. Leaders expect to be asked for help and know the favor will be returned. It makes the one doing the favor feel good to be asked. Because nurses interface with the public all the time, they are in excellent positions to assist, facilitate, or otherwise do favors for people. Too often, nurses forget to ask for help from those whom they have helped and who would be more than willing to return a favor. Consider the lobbyist for a state nurses association who knew that the chair of the Senate public health and welfare committee had a grandson who was critically injured in a car accident. She visited the child several times in the hospital, spoke with the nurses on the unit, and kept the legislator informed about his grandson's progress and assured him that the boy was well cared for. When the boy recovered, the legislator was grateful and asked the lobbyist what he could do to move her issue. Interchanges like this occur every day and create the basis for quid pro quo.

The successful networker collects business cards from anyone who may at some time be helpful. Record information about the individual on the business card: where you met or something unique about the person. When it is time to move on an issue about which one of those individuals can help, as a networker, you can make the connection and feel comfortable seeking assistance. At some point, the favor will likely be returned.

ASSESS THE TIMING

The timing of an issue is often the strategy that makes the difference in a successful outcome. A well-planned strategy may fail because the timing is off. An issue may languish for some period because of a mismatch in values, concerns, or resources. Yet suddenly, something can change to make an issue ripe for consideration. Before September 11, 2001, the issue of bioterrorism was of limited concern to the public and a low priority for most health care professionals. Yet warnings and preparations had actually begun. In response to the original bombing of the World Trade Center in 1993, President Clinton had convened a group of experts to develop a national strategy for responding to a bioterrorist attack. However, the effort received limited resources. After the attacks of September 11 on the World Trade Center and the Pentagon, the issue moved to the top of the congressional and presidential agenda. President Bush asked for and got billions of dollars to prevent and respond to bioterrorism.

Judging the right time to act is not always easy. Certainly, the timing was right for final passage of the BBA and the reimbursement of the APNs. One can deliberately strategize to "turn up the heat" on an issue when the environment seems favorable, and one way to do so is through the media (see the Unit I Case Study on the Vietnam Women's Memorial).

COLLABORATE

The successful achievement of policy goals can be accomplished only if supporters demonstrate a united front. Collective action is almost always more effective than individual action. Collaboration through coalitions (See Chapter 8 on coalitions) demonstrates broad support for the issue. The collaborative response of APNs to the AMA's Citizens Petition stopped the effort to discredit APNs (see the Unit Five Case Study). Besides having your own group organized and ready to be mobilized, what other networks do you have or can you develop?

Sometimes diverse groups can work together on an issue of mutual support, even though they are opponents on other issues. Public and private interest groups that identify with nursing's issues can be invaluable resources for nurses. They often have influential supporters or may have research information that can help nurses to move an issue. Rallies, letter-writing campaigns, and grass roots efforts by such groups can turn up the volume on nursing's issues and create the necessary groundswell of support to overcome opposition.

It is in nursing's best political interest to end the divisiveness among nurses and professional nursing organizations and to foster ways for nurses to become flexible and politically responsive. On the other hand, nurses are so diverse that perhaps we should not expect to agree on everything. Instead, we should look for opportunities to reach consensus or remain silent in the public arena on an issue that is not of paramount concern.

PREPARE TO TAKE RISKS

Nurses have always been risk takers. Margaret Sanger fled to England after she was sentenced to jail for providing women with information about birth control (Chesler, 1992). Clara Maas lost her life while participating in research on malaria (Kalisch & Kalisch, 1995). Harriet Tubman risked her life to transport and care for more than 300 slaves who sought freedom in the North before and during the Civil War (Carnegie, 1986). Such thoughtful risk takers weigh the costs and benefits of their actions. They consider possible outcomes in relation to the expenditure of available resources. For example, a nurse may decide to run for Congress, knowing that she has little chance of winning. She risks losing, but running will give her the opportunity to bring important health issues to the public's attention and will help her gain name recognition for her next race.

Risk taking requires analyzing both the risks and the benefits of an action. This can be much easier for an individual then for an organization, but nonetheless it warrants open and thoughtful discussion by those taking the risk. The strongest case for risk taking comes when the core values of an individual or organization are at stake.

UNDERSTAND THE OPPOSITION

A successful political strategy is one that tries to accommodate the concerns of the opposition. It requires disassociating the emotional context of working with opponents—the first step in principled negotiating. The person who is skillful at managing conflict will be successful in politics. The saying that "politics makes strange bedfellows" arose out of the recognition that long-standing opponents can sometimes come together around issues of mutual concern, but it often requires creative thinking and a commitment to fairness to develop an acceptable approach to resolving an issue.

One must also anticipate problems and areas for disagreement and be prepared to counter them: "A good offense is the best defense." When the opposition is gaining momentum and support, it can be helpful to develop a strategy that can distract attention from the opposition's issue or that can delay action. For example, one nurses association continually battled the state medical society's efforts to amend the nurse practice act in ways that would restrict nurses' practice and provide for physician supervision. Nurses became particularly concerned about the possibility of passage during a year when the medical society's influence with the legislature was high. Working with other non-physician provider organizations engaged in similar battles (e.g., optometrists, pharmacists), the nurses proposed a bill that would go after the medical practice act by removing all oversight authority. The physicians knew that there would be a large coalition supporting such a bill. As a result they agreed to drop efforts to amend the nurse practice act.

The other dimension of this axiom is creating opportunities for your opposition and power holders to gain firsthand experience with your issue. The many "walk a mile with a nurse" campaigns, when legislators or others spend time trailing a nurse, have provided hospital executives and public officials with the opportunity to understand the complexities of a nurse's daily work and the barriers that nurses confront (McEachen, Mason, & Jabara, 1992). Once they have seen issues through the nurse's lens, they may be more willing to find satisfactory policy solutions. Media coverage of your issue can also help to accomplish this end, particularly when personal stories are used to illustrate the conflicts or concerns raised by an issue.

CONCLUSION

The future of nursing and health care may well depend on nurses' skills in moving a vision. Without a vision, politics becomes an end in itself—a game that is often corrupt and empty. Instead, nurses can use the vision to define the goals. This chapter has presented how nurses can use a systematic analysis for delineating the political context of issues. Once that is achieved, a plan can be created that should incorporate issues such as gender politics, power dynamics, and the specific strategies that would be most appropriate to achieve the goals and the vision. Using the analysis and strategies discussed in this chapter will provide a way for nurses to achieve their policy goals, regardless of setting. It will ensure that nurses use their power, through their expertise and numbers, to protect and improve the health of all Americans.

REFERENCES

Benner, P. (1984). *From novice to expert.* Menlo Park, CA: Addison-Wesley.

Carlson, D.K. (2000). *Nurses remain at top of honesty and ethics poll.* Available online at www.gallup.com/poll/releases/pr001127.asp.

Carnegie, M.E. (1986). *The path we tread: Blacks in nursing, 1854-1984.* Philadelphia: J.B. Lippincott.

Chesler, E. (1992). *Woman of valor: Margaret Sanger and the birth control movement in America.* New York: Anchor Books.

Cohen, S., Mason, D., Kovner, C., Leavitt, J., Pulcini, J., & Sochalski, J. (1996). Stages of nursing's political development: Where we've been and where we ought to go. *Nursing Outlook, 44*(1), 20-23.

Cohen, S.S. (2001). *Championing child care.* New York: Columbia University Press.

Duke, J.T. (1976). *Conflict and power in social life.* Provo, UT: Brigham Young University Press.

Ferguson, V.D. (1993). Perspectives on power. In D.J. Mason, S.W. Talbott, & J.K. Leavitt (Eds.). *Policy and politics for nurses: Action and change in the workplace, government, organizations, and community* (2nd ed.). Philadelphia: W.B. Saunders.

French, J.R.P. & Raven, B. (1959). The basis of social power. In D. Cartwright (Ed.). *Studies in social power.* Ann Arbor: University of Michigan.

Gerston, L.N. (1997). *Public policy making: Process and principles.* Armonk, NY: M.E. Sharper.

Hersey, P., Blanchard, K., & Natemeyer, W. (1976). Situational leadership: Perception and impact of power. *Group Organizational Studies, 4,* 418-428.

Joel, L. & Kelly, L. (2002). *The nursing experience: Trends, challenges, and transitions* (4th ed.). New York: McGraw-Hill.

Kalisch, P.A. & Kalisch. B.J. (1995). *The advance of American nursing.* (3rd ed.). Philadelphia: J.B. Lippincott.

Machiavelli, N. (1984; originally published 1515). *The Prince.* New York: Bantam Classics.

Mason, D.J., Backer, B.A., & Georges, C.A. (1991). Towards a feminist model for the political empowerment of nurses. *Image: Journal of Nursing Scholarship, 23*(2), 72-77.

McEachen, I., Mason, D. J., & Jabara, I. (1992). Walk a mile with a nurse. *Nursing Spectrum, 4*(3), 5.

Mooney, C.Z. (Ed.). (2001). *The public clash of private values: The politics of morality policy.* New York: Chatham House Publishers.

Nursing's agenda for health care reform. (1992). Washington, DC: American Nurses Publishing.

Robert, H.M. (2000). *Robert's rules of order newly revised.* Reading, MA: Addison-Wesley.

Schattschneider, E.E. (1960). *The semi-sovereign people.* New York: Holt, Rhinehart & Winston.

Tanner, D. (2001). *Talking from 9 to 5: Women and men in the workplace: Language, sex, power.* New York: Quill.

Vignette   *Melinda Jenkins*

Abbottsford Community Health Center and Pennsylvania Politics

"It is time for us to stand and cheer for the doer, the achiever, the one who recognizes the challenge and does something about it."

Vince Lombardi

The recent expansion of nurse-managed health centers is due to nurses' energetic involvement in policy-making. Although the idea of direct access to nurses is more than 100 years old, recycled from Lillian Wald and Mary Breckinridge, the modern reality is quite sophisticated in terms of the conscious development of policies to initiate and sustain nurse-managed centers. In my experience, three policy changes were critical to keep our nurse-managed center alive: direct reimbursement through managed care, regulations supporting prescriptive authority, and an ongoing source of supplemental funding to provide for the care of uninsured patients.

AN URBAN NURSE-MANAGED COMMUNITY HEALTH CENTER

The story begins in 1991 with innovative thinking by Sue Heckrotte, a development grant writer at nonprofit Resources for Human Development. Sue responded to a federal call for proposals for "340A" public housing health centers. In contrast to most nurse-managed centers that were begun as teaching laboratories with funds from the Division of Nursing, Sue went for a funding stream dedicated to creating a number of community health centers within public housing developments. In writing the grant, Sue called upon Margaret Grey, DNSc, then a faculty member at the University of Pennsylvania School of Nursing, and Donna Torrisi, MSN, a University of Pennsylvania ("Penn") alumnus and family nurse practitioner (FNP) in the only local staff-model health maintenance organization (HMO). The

grant was written with a nurse practitioner (NP) at the center's helm rather than a medical director. Previously, only rural nurse-managed centers had been federally funded. This urban nursing center was funded, and Abbottsford Community Health Center, now renamed Abbottsford Family Practice & Counseling, opened in July 1992. It was the only "340A" with an NP director, Donna Torrisi, making it the first urban nurse-managed center with ongoing federal community health center funding. Supplemental private foundation money helped to renovate adjoining apartments into a health center.

In 1991 I was a PhD student at Penn; Margaret Grey was my advisor. Margaret encouraged me to apply for a joint clinical appointment at Abbottsford when I joined the faculty at Penn in September 1992. My interest in teaching and practice was fueled by my personal history. As a child, I lost my father to an accident on the job. My family was left without health insurance, greatly limiting the choices available for the mental health care that became necessary for my mother. Later in life, I saw many people without the financial means to pay for health care and trapped by few alternatives to standard medical customs. For example, customary care for the mentally ill during the 1960s was extended hospitalization in remote areas rather than the community-based treatment we use now. Customary care for childbirth in the 1970s was a hospital birth attended by a physician who performed a paracervical block and a routine episiotomy, rather than the current range of choices that include midwifery and home birth. I decided that teaching NPs would be the best way I could promote access to nursing's vision of primary health care for people with little money and few alternatives.

As I began to work at Abbottsford, we benefited from passage of the federal Omnibus Budget Reconciliation Act of 1989 (OBRA 1989), which authorized payment to NPs by Medicaid. Most of Abbottsford's patients were female-headed families living in public housing, so they received welfare and Medicaid. Although Medicaid fee-for-service payment was about half of the going rate for outpatient care, we were able to stay in business, with the federal grant funds making up the difference. Plus, our federal funds allowed for more comprehensive services, such as van service and outreach. We quickly built up a base of about 1600 active patients.

GETTING MANAGED CARE REIMBURSEMENT

In 1994, when Pennsylvania received a waiver to place Philadelphia's Medicaid recipients into managed care, our patients began showing up with Medicaid cards listing physicians as their primary care provider (PCP). Even though our patients claimed they had not intended to go elsewhere for care, the welfare office had assigned them another provider, who would then receive monthly capitation payments for them. When we applied for PCP status, we received it from one Medicaid HMO. We were denied at another, whose business office told us that the state HMO law would not allow them to contract with "nonphysicians." Quickly, Donna contacted the State Department of Health, Bureau of Quality Assurance, which has jurisdiction over PCP rules. The director visited our center to observe our care and review patient records, held a large meeting at the state Capitol to discuss the issue, and then, after several months had gone by, told us we could not be PCPs unless we were in a staff-model HMO.

Both then and now, there are very few staff-model HMOs (like Kaiser-Permanente) in our part of the country—most are independent practice associations. Based on what I had learned about HMOs in a health policy course in my PhD program at Penn, I responded right away that this decision was unworkable. We appealed the decision to the Deputy Secretary of Health and made it clear that a favorable ruling would increase access to care for vulnerable people served by several nursing centers that had sprung up in Philadelphia. Meanwhile, the Bureau of Quality Assurance director was

replaced, and the new director invited us to discuss the issue with the Bureau's attorney. We hired an attorney to go with us to the Department of Health, where we pointed out that under OBRA 1989 federal law, we were authorized to receive Medicaid payment and that a strict interpretation of the state HMO law jeopardized that payment. We helped write the language for "Technical Advisory 95-A," which allowed HMOs to contract with NPs, especially for care in underserved areas.

Subsequently, many developments in managed care payment have occurred in Pennsylvania. Abbottsford has obtained contracts with two more Medicaid HMOs and one private HMO. We have negotiated unsuccessfully to contract with the remaining Medicaid HMO and with Aetna/US Healthcare, the largest remaining private HMO, which refuses us a contract. Aetna/US Healthcare has told us that *PCP* stands for "primary care *physician*" and that to ensure quality of care, every patient in the Aetna system has a physician. Many other nurse-managed centers in Philadelphia that provide primary care have obtained HMO contracts, even though they have all experienced long delays in processing their applications and beginning to receive payment. When Medicaid managed care expanded to other areas of the state, nurse-managed centers run by Penn State and University of Pittsburgh Schools of Nursing and others could be paid as PCPs.

Vigilance Needed to Maintain Nurse Practitioner Reimbursement

In 1999 the Pennsylvania legislature passed Act 68, "patient protection" under managed care. In it, NPs and certified nurse midwives (CNMs) are listed as PCPs. After 2 years, final Department of Health regulations were published that maintained PCP status for NPs and CNMs. Though the statute is very clear, organized physician groups lobbied the regulators for 2 years to curtail the ability of NPs and CNMs to be paid directly under managed care. Advanced practice nurse (APN) groups have had to be very vigilant from 1994 to today, repeating testimonies and presenting letters to advocate for direct reimbursement for the care of our vulnerable patients. Even with legislation and regulation allowing PCP status for NPs and CNMs, existing paper-work within the Department of Health uses only the word *physician* with *PCP*, and initial credential-ing for NPs takes months longer than physician credentialing. Reimbursement by managed care and fee-for-service is crucial to our existence. As we have seen with changes in Medicaid and Medicare laws, when direct payment for nursing care is authorized, direct access to nurses will flourish.

GAINING PRESCRIPTIVE AUTHORITY

It seemed very strange to me that NPs would be designated and paid as PCPs but could not write a prescription for medication. Yet that was the reality in Pennsylvania, where NP regulations from 1977 were interpreted differently by the Board of Nursing (i.e., NP prescription of medication allowed) and the Board of Medicine (i.e., NP prescription barred). Joint regulation of NPs by both the Board of Medicine and the Board of Nursing had delayed and obstructed all attempts to clarify prescriptive authority for more than 20 years. (See www.panps.com for a detailed history.) Meanwhile, NPs were prescribing in roundabout ways: using scripts presigned by friendly physicians, asking a physician in the building to sign scripts just written, or phoning in prescriptions under a physician's name.

These methods were well known to the Board of Nursing; indeed, I testified to the Board myself in 1995 that they were used. The appearance of a physician's name on an NP's prescription resulted in confusion, particularly for pharmacies, emergency departments, and specialty physicians, when they assumed the physician named on the prescription bottle was directly involved in diagnosing and managing the patient. It also placed undue liability on a friendly physician. The fact that no one, in more than 20 years, had been prosecuted for illegal prescriptions of this sort denoted a tacit approval of NP prescribing. It was obvious that the more than 4000 NPs in Pennsylvania, all of whom were educated to select and prescribe medications appropriately, were doing it in underhanded ways. What was even more bizarre to me was the reality that any NP graduate from Penn, where I teach, could prescribe legally in nearby New Jersey, New York, Maryland, Washington, DC, and Delaware—and in a total of

47 states—but not in the state in which she or he was educated.

The Alliance of Advanced Practice Nurses

In 1995 Sister Teresita Hinnegan, a nurse-midwifery faculty member at Penn, recruited me to help plan a statewide summit meeting of 60 nursing leaders to discuss barriers to advanced practice. We developed a survey and a day-long meeting that was funded by the Independence Foundation and held at the Pennsylvania State Nurses Association headquarters. It was clear from survey respondents and meeting attendees that APNs should work closely together to push for prescriptive authority and full scope of practice for NPs, clinical nurse specialists (CNSs), CNMs, and certified registered nurse anesthetists (CRNAs) in Pennsylvania. Specialty groups designated representatives to attend regular planning meetings, and the Alliance of Advanced Practice Nurses was born. "Sister T" and I became the cochairs. It did not take long to examine our legal authority to realize that a major barrier preventing NP prescription of medications was joint regulation by the Board of Medicine and the Board of Nursing. CNSs and CRNAs wanted legal recognition as APNs. CNMs were regulated only by the Board of Medicine and decided to remain so, but they united with us in support of our efforts.

Active Lobbying for an Advanced Practice Nursing Statute

After much discussion between and among the APN groups, legislation was drafted and sponsors were solicited. Lobbyists employed by the four largest nursing groups (Pennsylvania State Nurses Association, Pennsylvania Coalition of NPs, Pennsylvania Association of Nurse Anesthetists, and Pennsylvania chapters of the American College of Nurse Midwives) were absolutely essential in this process.

In a big rally at the state Capitol, Representative Patricia Vance, a nurse from central Pennsylvania, introduced House Bill 50 in March 1998. Nearly half of the state Representatives signed on initially as cosponsors. The bill was to define advanced practice nursing to include NPs, CNSs, and CRNAs and to authorize these APNs to perform their full scope of practice, including prescription of medications. Three hearings were held on the bill. The hospital association supported the bill along with Abbottsford, the Regional Nursing Centers Consortium, and many other nursing organizations. The *only* opposition came from organized physician groups. Physician anesthesiologists were especially adamant that CRNAs were not advanced practitioners and could never prescribe medications on their own. Concurrently, there was a national debate regarding Medicare rules and payment for CRNAs and anesthesiologists. Physicians obviously believed their incomes and authority were threatened at several levels. An additional complication for us was the fact that the lobbyist for the physician anesthesiologists provided significant fundraising assistance to the chair of the committee in which the bill was introduced.

Nurse Practitioner Prescriptive Authority via Regulations, not Statute

While Representative Mario Civera (R-Upper Darby), the chair of the House Professional Licensure Committee, kept House Bill 50 in hearings, the Governor began to pressure the Boards of Medicine and Nursing to resurrect regulations for NP prescriptive authority. During this time, the Governor appointed a new chair of each Board. Representative Civera told us that he would not move the bill out of committee unless he thought it would pass. He also told us that he would not move the bill if the Boards could agree on regulations to provide NP prescriptive authority. Clearly, the Governor's office applied political pressure to trim down the demands of APNs and focus on the one issue of prescriptive authority for NPs. In short, the Governor won the first round. House Bill 50 died in committee without being brought to a vote. The more limited regulations for NP prescriptive authority were finalized by the Board of Nursing and the Board of Medicine in December 2000. Owing to the extensive "red tape" involved in applying for prescriptive privileges, as of September 2001, fewer than 500 NPs had been authorized to prescribe. However, nurses in Pennsylvania have seen what can be accomplished by speaking with one voice.

Ongoing Efforts

As cochair of the Alliance, I was intimately involved in every step along the way. Abbottsford, a nonprofit business with NP PCPs, had an obvious stake in the outcome of either House Bill 50 or NP regulations to prescribe. Additionally, many graduates of the University of Pennsylvania School of Nursing master's degree programs and the School-owned practices would be greatly affected by these legal maneuvers. Through the process, we were very successful in educating most state legislators and many state bureaucrats about advanced practice nursing—our education and roles. Many nurses across Pennsylvania got involved in talking with their legislators, writing letters, and requesting support letters from physicians and other allies. Alliance members developed a very useful e-mail listserv for advanced practice issues, which was supported by the University of Pennsylvania School of Nursing; we published an NP newsletter, created by an energetic NP and available at the website www.panps.com; and we strengthened the membership and involvement in several key nursing groups.

I have been elected to the Board of Directors of the Pennsylvania Nurses Association (www.psna.org), which has emerged as a leader to unify nurses across the state. The Alliance now has new cochairs in the ongoing struggle. In the fall of 2001, House Bill 2121 and Senate Bill 1208, identical companion legislation, were introduced to reestablish the State Board of Nursing as the sole regulatory authority for advanced NPs (ANPs). Abbottsford Family Practice & Counseling, with a sparkling, spacious, newly renovated sister center, is working to link with other nurse-managed public housing health centers in Philadelphia to share the advantage of federal funding. Several of the more than 30 nurse-managed centers in the National Nursing Centers Consortium (NNCC) plan to pool key data elements to assess the quality of the care we provide. Researchers from other like-minded groups at academic nursing centers around the country are also discussing common data collection. NNCC efforts to expand federally qualified health center funding also fits with President Bush's goal to create 1200 more access points for primary health care.

LESSONS LEARNED

We learned several important lessons in our efforts:

- *Capture the money!* Health care is one-seventh of the U.S. economy, and no nursing innovation will last without ongoing funding.
- *Stick together!* We are extremely powerful when we use our intellects and energies in common. Don't fight other nurses in public.
- *Pay our lobbyists!* It is essential to have continuous, active lobbies at state and national levels. Your state nurses association is definitely worth your investment.

- *Dreams do come true!* "Ask and you shall receive; seek and you shall find." Our goals will be met by united, persistent, assertive efforts.

Sustainable nurse-managed care depends upon direct reimbursement, full APN scope of practice, and ongoing funding to make up for the large numbers of uninsured patients. I was actively involved in expanding each of these avenues in Pennsylvania, and future national efforts will benefit us all.

6 Communication Skills for Political Success

MARY W. CHAFFEE

"Well, what we got here is a failure to communicate."
COOL HAND LUKE

In nursing school we find many professional skills can be learned in the classroom, in a learning lab, or by computer tutorial. We practice our skills on mannequins before being unleashed on an actual patient. As our careers advance, though, many of us find ourselves in situations that we were not prepared for in the safety of the classroom: participating in high-level board meetings; attending fund-raisers, receptions, and black tie social events; and being interviewed. We may find we are more comfortable responding to a cardiac arrest than making small talk with a stranger at a reception. It may be less terrifying to manage a sucking chest wound than to stand at a podium and address an audience. Scary or not, communicating effectively in a wide variety of environments and situations is critical to achieving professional, political, and policy objectives.

WHAT'S DIFFERENT ABOUT COMMUNICATION SKILLS FOR POLITICAL SUCCESS?

Politics is the process of influencing the allocation of scarce resources—literally influencing who gets a slice of the pie, how big it is, and whether they get ice cream too. The active word, *influencing,* occurs because people *communicate.* The process of influencing through communication can occur anywhere: in one-to-one conversations while scooping up shrimp from a buffet, in testimony provided to congressional committees, in e-mail, and in meetings. Daniel Goleman, author of *Emotional Intelligence* and *Working with Emotional Intelligence,* defines emotional intelligence as the skills that distinguish star performers in every field. He identifies the ability to communicate and influence as a critical emotional intelligence competency (1998). When nurses participate in political and policy-making activities, a whole range of communication and social skills become important in successfully achieving political and policy goals.

ENGAGING IN CONVERSATION

WHY CHAT?

Communication is the transfer of information. That sounds boring, but communication is anything but boring! Did you ever try to *not* communicate? To not screw up your face after biting into an excruciatingly sour pickle? To not leap up and whoop when the Red Sox score two runs to win the game in the bottom of the ninth? To not offer words of comfort when a friend's parent dies? Humans are designed to communicate with one another. As a species, we instinctively join together and form connections. Life is better when we share it with others—when we're adding new people and friends to our circle of colleagues. We link to each other in friendships, groups, and communities, and our link to one another is communication. It was the case when Neanderthals joined together to plan a mastodon hunt, and it is the same today when a group of nurses visits a policymaker to influence legislation being drafted.

We communicate for specific reasons: to gather information, to direct, to educate, to provide feedback, to question, and to understand. The tools we use are spoken words, eye contact, body position and movement, and written symbols. It sounds simple—but frequently it isn't. If it were, no one would hesitate when entering a reception full of strangers, no one would fear standing behind a podium to address 100 colleagues, no one would feel uncomfortable pulling a colleague aside in the hallway to discuss a problem, and no one would feel rejected when a hoped-for conversation fizzles into silence. Communicating is risky business.

An important aspect of communicating is that we can learn to do it better and we can learn new communications skills. Excellent communication skills set you apart as a polished and practiced professional (Sabath, 1993). In the world of politics and policy, where influencing others, making connections, and getting your views understood are absolutely critical to advancing issues, finely tuned communication skills are as necessary as oxygen. Becoming active in policy and politics can open up a whole new world of opportunities to influence health care. These opportunities may include new business and social activities. With practice, knowledge, and guidance from colleagues, you can develop all the skills you need to be effective in policy and politics.

ARRIVING AT AN EVENT

Michael just began a new job and is walking into his first meeting with organization executives. Caroline has just given her car keys to the hotel valet and is approaching an evening reception honoring a nursing leader. Sylvia is attending a political fundraiser at a museum. What do Michael, Caroline, and Sylvia have in common? They are all entering social situations where they must tackle those daunting tasks: mingling and making conversation. Many of us find the first few minutes of mingling to be most awkward. Walking into a roomful of strangers is the social equivalent of skiing down the Black Diamond

Trail (a ski run that is a challenge even to experts!). To ease your entry at an event, find something to do while you get your bearings.

- If the event is hosted, find the hosts and greet them. If they are worth their beans as a host, they will introduce you to others.
- If there is a registration table, register, pick up brochures, and chat with the staff working the event.
- Take a few minutes to survey the room. Are people talking in groups of twos? Larger groups? Who looks engaged? Who looks bored?
- Get a beverage or help yourself to offered food.
- If you're at a private party, offer to assist the host in food preparation.
- Really panicked? Visit the bathroom, take a deep breath, and head back in.

MEET AND GREET, GRIP AND GRIN

If you've run out of things to do on your own and no one has approached you, it's time to be brave: Introduce yourself to someone or commit a "B & E" (break and enter a conversation). The words you choose for a greeting will depend on the relationship and will vary if you have met the individual before. In a business setting or in meeting a senior colleague, you may need to be more formal ("Good morning, Senator Johnson, I'm Chris Winston. It's a pleasure to meet you.") If it's a social situation and you are greeting a stranger, less formal is fine ("Hi, I'm Gina Carroll. It's good to meet you.")

If you don't see anyone standing alone, you could wait for someone to find you and offer an introduction. Chances are, it won't happen, because approaching a stranger is as difficult for others as it is for you. Be brave and approach people who are already engaged in conversation. Look for a group of three or more who look like they are enjoying themselves (avoid groups of two who are leaning in toward each other and intently involved in conversation). Position yourself nearby the group. Most likely, members of the group will make eye contact and acknowledge you, thereby opening the group conversation to you. Feel free at this point to join the conversation. Be open to others who appear to want to join the group. When you see someone on the periphery, step back to make room and include the newcomer.

FIRST IMPRESSIONS

When we meet another person we instinctively assess, appraise, and form opinions within about 30 seconds (Boothman, 2000). It's important to recognize this instinct, especially if you are greeting someone that you need to connect with to advance an issue. To make a good first impression, remember that words and body language play a role in how you are perceived by others.

- Make your first words count. Introduce yourself clearly. Repeat the name of the person you are meeting (this will help you remember their name, and people like to hear their own names)
- Smile and make eye contact. Let your smile reflect that you are glad to be meeting the other person.
- Face the person you are meeting. If you are seated, stand up for the introduction.
- If you've made a name tag, make sure your name is written clearly

SHAKE IT UP

A handshake is the expected business greeting in the United States. Greet a stranger with an extended hand. How firm and how long should you shake? Grip the offered hand firmly—midway between wimpy and bone crushing. Shake hands only for as long as it takes to greet someone (Sabath, 1993). At social events and meetings where introductions are likely, keep you right hand free in order to greet others quickly. Make sure to stand up or come out from behind a desk when greeting someone.

FUELING THE CONVERSATIONAL FIRES

You've made it past the greeting; now what? If you have just met someone that you know something about, acknowledge that:

- "Dr. Connors, congratulations on the award you received from the Governor."
- "I read the article you published last month and was very impressed. How did you get involved in that project?"

- "I understand you are conducting research on back pain. I'm involved in a similar project."

With these comments, you've made it easy for someone to talk with you—you have offered several topics for discussion and made it clear the other person won't have to do all the conversational work. If you are speaking with a stranger, comment on any potentially shared experience:

- "Are you a member of the association?"
- "Have you heard the speaker before?"
- "What do you think of the proposed legislation?"
- "I got stuck in traffic on the way here." (This is a favorite line in Washington, DC!)

These are all lead-ins to *small talk,* a form of conversation that has really gotten a bad reputation. Small talk leads to developing rapport and can lead to the discovery of common interests. Rapport is the establishment of common ground, a comfort zone where two or more people can mentally join together (Boothman, 2000). Remember that with every important person in your life today, you had to start the relationship or friendship with small talk to get to know what you have in common.

To keep conversation going, respond to questions and add your own:

- "No, I'm not a member of the association, but I thought the meeting agenda looked great. What about you?"
- "I think this policy change offers a number of advantages to nurses. What do you think?"

Mandell (1996) points out the importance of being prepared for conversation by being familiar with the meeting agenda, organizational background, and leaders; by reading current journals and being conversant with current events; and by reading newspapers and other matter. Box 6-1 lists a few other tips for drawing people in. Although these tips will help, don't think you are a failure if you don't establish rapport. The person you're speaking with may just have learned disturbing news, you may resemble a former spouse, or the person may have a splitting headache. If conversation is not flowing, politely excuse yourself and chat with someone else.

BOX **6-1** Behaviors and Attitudes That Draw People In

- Sense of humor
- Good manners
- Confidence
- Nonthreatening appearance
- Smiling and eye contact
- Starting a conversation rather than waiting for someone else to do it
- Knowledge of the subjects at hand
- Not taking yourself too seriously
- Fearlessness
- Respect for cultural differences

From Mandell, T. (1996). *Power schmoozing: the new etiquette for social and business success.* New York: McGraw-Hill.

THE POWER OF LISTENING

Good conversationalists are not those who talk a lot. A good conversationalist does as much listening as speaking, and possibly more (Sabath, 1993). Active listening means *hearing* what people say, concentrating on their words, and responding appropriately. When listening, maintain eye contact; nod, smile, or laugh when appropriate; and make statements that reflect your interest.

Nurses tend to be very effective listeners. The skills that permit us to gather and process information from patients can be successfully applied in business and social situations too. Conversation can be a wonderful adventure when you listen carefully and encourage the individual you are speaking with to speak freely.

CONVERSATION STOPPERS

Just as there are ways to encourage comfortable conversation, there are many ways to bring it to a grinding halt. Avoid these errors if you want to keep things going:

- Being unprepared, or being unaware of topics of interest to the group you are with
- Complaining about the food, the room temperature, your tight shoes, the price of parking (you get the picture)
- Interrupting and not listening to others or competing and trying to "one-up" others (RoAne, 2000).

MORE COMMUNICATION SKILLS FOR SUCCESS

NETWORKING

Meeting new people and renewing relationships with previous acquaintances is the heart of networking. Networking can be defined as making contacts that may be valuable to you in some aspect of your professional activities. Networking is critical for nurses involved in policy and politics because most issues are advanced with the support and power of allies, colleagues, and those interested in attaining the same goal. Advocates of networking laud its benefits: information, feedback, referrals, and a sense of collegiality with others (Puetz & Shinn, 1998).

Sharing information is seen as a valuable benefit derived from developing a healthy network of professional contacts. Everyone needs information—to learn about employment opportunities, to track the status of a legislative issue, to identify colleagues who share a common interest, or to influence a policy. Effective networking is based on developing relationships with "contacts," or individuals from whom you may obtain information, advice, or business. Always carry business cards, and keep the ones you collect organized and accessible. Jot down notes about conversations on the back of a card to jog your memory.

Developing a wide range of contacts can be extremely enlightening. Puetz and Shinn (1998) recommend developing a network of colleagues who have less experience, equal experience, and more experience than you do. The social role of networking cannot be minimized. It is much more enjoyable to tackle a problem, write a press release, or plan a campaign working with a team of friends and colleagues than to do it alone.

WORKING A ROOM

Does that conjure up a mental picture of a cigar-smoking, overweight politician slapping backs and pressing the flesh at a fundraiser? That's not what it is now. RoAne (2000, p. xxviii) defines working a room today:

The ability to circulate comfortably and graciously through a gathering of people; meeting, greeting and talking with as many of them as you wish; creating communication that is warm and sincere; establishing an honest rapport on which you can build a professional or personal relationship; and knowing how to start, how to continue and how to end lively and interesting conversations.

Working a room isn't a cold, calculated process, but it does involve some thought and care. Before attending an event, think about what it is you'd like to accomplish. Do you want to learn about a Medicare funding proposal? Do you want to meet people in your professional association? Do you need to find colleagues to work on a grassroots campaign? Do you just want to have fun?

To survive mingling, and have fun, you should recognize the real benefits to working a room. Identifying these benefits gets easier with practice. As you make connections that turn into ongoing professional relationships, or even friendships, you'll feel better about tackling the next event or meeting on your schedule. Working a room is a new skill for many professionals. Learn from others who are experienced. Watch what they do to move effortlessly between conversations and what they do to make people feel comfortable.

Working a room is an exercise in strategic planning and an investment in the future. As you lose touch with some colleagues and develop new interests, it's one way to refresh your professional contacts. It can feel risky, though. But extending ourselves to others is almost always worth the risk, and it gets easier with practice. It can't hurt to try. RoAne points out that "no one ever died from eating spinach or from going to a charity fund-raiser" (2000, xxix).

ASKING FOR WHAT YOU WANT

Making things happen is what leaders do. And to make things happen—whether you are at a reception, a congressional hearing, or a meeting with your boss—you often have to ask for things. Whether you are asking for a budget increase for your unit, the support of a legislator, or a letter of reference, there are several key points to keep in mind. Your chances of success will increase if you:

- Say exactly what you want
- Say exactly when you want it
- Say exactly whom you want it from (Krisco, 1997)

The key word is *exactly.* The less precise you are in your request, the more chance there is for a less-than-desirable response. Another key is to make it as easy as possible for the person you are making a request of to comply with your request. If you are asking someone to provide a letter of reference, bring a draft that you have prepared. If you want your chief executive officer to meet with a group of nurse executives, offer to provide a briefing in advance. If you want policymakers to support specific legislative language in a pending bill, make sure they see what the benefits are. If you are asking someone to be the keynote speaker at a meeting, let him or her see that you will make the appearance effortless by providing all the meeting information in advance.

Making the request is only the beginning. Next, you need to discern what the response is. If you've made a distinct request, there are several replies possible from the person you have approached. They may:

- *Accept.* Your request is accepted as is.
- *Decline.* Your request is turned down; a reason may or may not be provided.
- *Make a counteroffer.* Some aspect of your request is modified.
- *Promise to reply later.* The response is on hold. If you are met with this delaying tactic, agree on when you can expect a decision.
- *Referral.* You may be referred to another individual for assistance.

Even when you make a clear request, you may receive a nonresponse. Nonresponses include "I'll think about it," "That's a great idea," "I'll see what my boss thinks," and "I'll look into it." These are all dodges or avoidance techniques. If you find yourself dealing with one, be respectfully persistent. "Does that mean you will do it?" or "I'd like to call you tomorrow to follow up on this issue." These comments send a message that you want an answer one way or another.

GETTING PHYSICAL: BODY LANGUAGE

Body language—the wide range of conscious and unconscious physical movements we make—can either strengthen your verbal messages or sabotage you. Because of the range of movements and subtlety, body language can sometimes be tough to interpret—and to control (Heller, 1998). But in a business or social situation, it's extremely important to monitor your own body language and to monitor the nonverbal cues you receive from those who are speaking with you. Pay attention to:

- *Your signals.* You signal interest in others by maintaining eye contact, by holding a comfortable body position, and by not doing anything that signals your mind is wandering. If you want to continue a conversation, try to avoid fidgeting with jewelry, checking your watch, scanning the room, or constantly shifting position—these all indicate you are trying to break contact.
- *Reading body language in others.* Be alert to physical cues that are being sent to you while you are engaged in conversation. If the person you are speaking with is maintaining eye contact and remains facing you, she is probably comfortably engaged and interested in continuing to speak with you. If you are speaking with someone who is looking behind you, checking the food table, picking lint off his sleeve or backing up, you're being told that he is ready to move on and speak with someone else.
- *Sexual messages.* Sexual body language excludes others from conversation. Nonsexual body language keeps conversation open and keeps you a part of the group rather than in a private, exclusive huddle. In business and professional situations, sexual body language is inappropriate. It can include the following:
  - Leaning in closely to the person you're speaking with, which excludes others from conversation
  - Speaking in soft, intimate tones that discourage others from joining the conversation
  - Touching the other person or touching your own body, hair, or clothes (Mandell, 1996).

ESCAPING UNWANTED CONVERSATION

There are few social situations as tricky—or as uncomfortable—as being trapped in conversation that you desire to end. If you are seated at a dinner,

you are probably stuck, so try to make the best of the situation. If you are at a meeting or "stand-up" social event and find yourself in an extended conversation that you would like to politely wrap-up, there are several strategies you may employ. Mandell encourages telling the truth as the first choice, as should be the case with all communicating (1996). After making a comment, extend your hand and say, "It was nice to speak with you." You may want to add a concluding comment like, "It was nice to see the pictures of your family" or "I'm glad you told me about your work with the association." If you say you are going to get another drink or food as a segue to escape, you risk finding yourself with company. If you are having a conversation that is unpleasant, merely say as you shake hands, "I hope you enjoy the rest of the meeting/party/conference." When you extricate yourself from a conversation, move at least one quarter of the room away (RoAne, 2000).

If you are attending an event with a friend or partner, you may want to plan a subtle "help" signal that will alert your friend to assist you. The person responding to a signal for help could join your conversation by saying, "Excuse me, could I borrow Diane? There is someone I wanted to introduce her to."

CULTURAL DIFFERENCES

Recognizing cultural differences is vital in communicating effectively. In today's "global village," there is one universally recognized gesture: the smile. From that point on, things get a little more complex (Sabath, 1993). When you interact with others from cultural backgrounds different from your own, whether you are in the United States or traveling internationally, the key to success is respecting differences.

Physical gestures and language that are acceptable in one culture may be vague or even offensive in another. Not recognizing or respecting cultural differences can lead to disaster in business and social communications. The Ford Motor Company was puzzled by poor sales of the Ford Pinto in Brazil. Ford had not recognized that in Portuguese—spoken in Brazil—the word *pinto* means "small penis." Few Brazilian men wanted to be associated with a Ford Pinto (Morrison, Conaway, & Borden, 1994).

These general caveats may be helpful in navigating the slippery slope of intercultural communications:

- *Gestures.* Recognize that gestures and other nonverbal language mean different things in different cultures. The traditional North American thumb and forefinger symbol for "okay" may be offensive to someone from Denmark. Pointing a finger is considered rude by the Chinese, hugging in public is not acceptable in Singapore, and shaking your head "no" may mean "yes" in some cultures (Heller, 1998). Take time to learn about the etiquette and behavior codes of other cultures if you will be working with or socializing with people from a background unfamiliar to you.
- *Handshakes.* In some cultures, touching is a sensitive issue. In Europe and North America, the handshake is a welcome gesture, but that may not be the case in the Mid-East, especially if you are a woman greeting a man. If you are traveling in unfamiliar territory, find out in advance what is acceptable and what is considered rude.
- *Personal space.* The British and North Americans tend to require more personal space and are more likely to move away from others if their space is "invaded."
- *Jokes.* Be judicious in using jokes to communicate with people from other cultures, especially if you dealing with a language barrier. Jokes may not translate well and could be embarrassing.

A MILLION THANKS! EXPRESSING GRATITUDE

One simple act can set you apart from others and demonstrate your exceptional social expertise: saying thank you. As you advocate for action on issues, request help from others, and lead others, it is vital to recognize the contributions and support you receive. Never pass up an opportunity to show your appreciation. When people extend themselves, they always appreciate knowing that their efforts were recognized, whether the person is a U.S. Senator or one of your neighbors who helped stuff envelopes for a candidate. When you receive any type of significant assistance, send a brief thank-you note. A phone call or e-mail note will suffice for other efforts to assist you or help you advance a project. When you are writing a note to express gratitude, describe in some detail exactly what you are grateful for. Comment on why you are appreciative, and close with one or two sentences unrelated to the thank-you. Try to avoid general remarks such as "thanks for your help" (Maggio, 1990).

DEMANDING SITUATIONS AND HOW TO SURVIVE THEM

PUBLIC SPEAKING

Polls suggest that some people are more frightened of public speaking than of dying. Speaking publicly may be frightening (at first), but it can be a powerful tool in advocating for a specific issue or moving a project forward. You may not recall the first steps you took as a toddler, but odds are, you fell down. After some practice, walking becomes effortless. Public speaking may never be effortless, but with practice you can become comfortable and effective. You may not recognize it, but you have been speaking publicly all your life—from reading a paragraph aloud in your sixth grade class to talking about the work schedule at a staff meeting. Public speaking, in a broad sense, is making a presentation to three or more people who are sitting still to listen to what you have to say (Figler, 1999).

To develop comfort and skill in speaking to audiences, start with some "low-risk" groups, such as speaking at your place of worship, presenting to a small group of colleagues in your workplace, or teaching a class in your community. Hone your skills every chance you get, and then take advantage of speaking to more-challenging groups. Some suggestions for success:

- *Practice.* Plan your comments to fit the allotted time and practice, whether it's in front of your mirror or with a tape recorder. Ask for feedback from a trusted friend. Consider learning the ropes with a group like Toastmasters International.

- *Keep focused.* Be clear about your objective and why you are speaking to a specific group.
- *Know your audience.* What is the background of the people in the audience, and what do they expect from you? How many will be present? If you are speaking to an organized group, do your homework. Learn about them through their website or by talking to members.
- *Meet and greet your audience.* If you have the chance to speak with members of your audience in advance, it will be less frightening to merely continue your conversation with them from the podium.
- *Observe the experts.* Watch expert public speakers and note what they do that works.

BRIEFINGS

Providing a briefing can be a powerful method of influencing how someone views an issue or course of action. You may have the opportunity to brief a leader in your organization, a policymaker, or a community leader about a health care topic. These factors that will contribute to successful briefings:

- Know your topic.
- Present it in a concise and logical manner. (It is called a *brief* for a reason.)
- Be prepared for questions, but able to say "I don't know."
- Make yourself available for follow-up.

Your organization may use a standard briefing format. It might be referred to as a position paper, a decision brief, or simply a "one-pager." You may want to prepare a one-page paper if you are meeting with a policymaker or the policymaker's staff. It will reinforce your verbal comments and leave them with a document to refer to. A standard briefing paper usually includes the following:

- Summary of the issue
- Background information
- Analysis of alternatives
- Your recommendation for action
- Your contact information

Box 6-2 gives an example of a briefing paper.

WORKING WITH JOURNALISTS AND THE MEDIA

The media offer diverse opportunities to get your message out. You may have the opportunity to influence an issue's progress through writing a press release, by writing a letter to the editor, or by participating in an interview. (See Chapter 10, The Role of the Media in Influencing Health Policy: Getting the Message Across.) The American Nurses Association (ANA) has developed tools to help nurses build skills so they may serve as experts in media interviews. A tool kit of information and other resources are available at the ANA website (www.nursingworld.org). Click on "RN = Real News," then click on "Nurses' Toolkit." ANA and some nursing specialty associations offer training for nurses to develop media skills. ANA also offers a guidebook and video titled "ANA Media Relations & You" that provides guidance on effective communication and how to participate in print, radio, and television interviews and related activities (American Nurses Association, 1999).

ENCOUNTERING FAMOUS PEOPLE AND CELEBRITIES

The world of politics swirls with well-known policymakers and officials, famous journalists who cover politics, and internationally recognized business leaders. Politically active celebrities ranging from Mohammed Ali to Christopher Reeve to Mary Tyler Moore provide testimony and make appearances to draw attention to causes. You may find yourself at an event where a celebrity is present. Mingling with a "star" can be intimidating and can bring out strange behavior. If you feel you *must* meet a celebrity, make a brief introduction, compliment the star's most-recent film, book, or show, and make a graceful exit. Martinet (1996) advises the following when meeting celebrities:

- Take a deep breath and stay relaxed.
- Be respectful and admiring, but not worshipful and gushing.
- Project an attitude of not wanting anything from the celebrity.

If you do have a specific reason for wanting to meet someone famous, be careful about making a pitch. Recognize that your request for an interview, sup-

BOX **6-2**   Example of a Briefing Paper

DECISION BRIEF

To: Chief of Staff, Senator Catherine Smith

From: Mary Chaffee, Health Policy Analyst, 202-555-1234, Mary.Chaffee@abc.xyz

Re: **HEALTH CARE FRAUD IN THE MILITARY HEALTH SYSTEM**

ISSUE

Health care fraud burdens the Department of Defense (DoD) with enormous financial losses while threatening the quality of health care. Assuming that between 10% and 20% of claims paid are fraudulent, the annual loss to DoD is $600 million to $1.2 billion.

BACKGROUND

- The U.S. Attorney General has identified health care fraud as the second priority for law enforcement, following only violent crime.
- Because health care fraud perpetrators target DoD, Medicare, Medicaid, and private health insurers simultaneously, the Defense Criminal Investigative Service (DCIS) cooperates extensively with many federal agencies in joint health care fraud investigations.
- Because of the support of the President and Congress, federal agencies fighting health care fraud, except DoD, have received additional resources to enhance their efforts.
- Despite successfully contributing to the recovery of over $600 million in FY 1997, DCIS is undergoing a 37% budget reduction from its 1995 level.
- The CHAMPUS/TRICARE Program Integrity Office currently has a staff of 10, and a caseload of 1000 active cases.
- The 1996 Kennedy-Kassebaum legislation provided for 80 additional U.S. Attorneys to be hired specifically to prosecute health care fraud and abuse.

ALTERNATIVES

1. **ENHANCE PROSECUTION.** Provide state attorneys general with an incentive to participate in the prosecution of DoD health care fraud by offering a portion of recovered funds from successfully prosecuted cases.

   Advantages: Could increase the total number and speed with which DoD health care fraud cases are prosecuted.

   Disadvantages: Does not address the problem of inadequate resources dedicated to detecting and investigating DoD health care fraud cases.

2. **ENHANCE DETECTION AND INVESTIGATION.** Provide a portion of recovered funds (5% to a maximum cap of $15 million annually) to the federal agencies charged with detection and investigation of DoD health care fraud to enhance their efforts.

   Advantages: The bottleneck in government efforts to control military health care fraud is at the first two steps, detection and investigation. Returning a portion of recovered funds would serve both as an incentive for superior performance, as well as permitting increased efforts in the anti-fraud fight. Current budget restrictions have precluded significant deterrent efforts; additional resources would be used to develop computer applications that detect and deter health care fraud more effectively.

   Disadvantages: Funds previously recovered and returned to the DoD would be returned specifically to detection/investigation agencies.

3. **CONTINUE WITH CURRENT EFFORTS.** No change in current detection, investigation, and prosecution efforts.

   Advantages: Current efforts will uncover a certain level of health care fraud and will continue to recover a portion of fraudulent claims to the government.

   Disadvantages: Fraud perpetrators will become increasingly sophisticated in their activities and will be able to outwit overburdened government investigators.

4. **DEVELOP ADDITIONAL DATA.** Direct the General Accounting Office to conduct a study on the feasibility of alternatives.

RECOMMENDATION

Direct the Controller General of the United States to undertake a study and provide a report to Senator Smith on the feasibility of above alternatives. Because of the magnitude of federal expenditures on health care, and the loss from health care fraud, it is incumbent to discern the best alternative based on data.

port for your cause, or other activity is probably one of dozens the celebrity receives each day. You may be referred to one of the celebrity's staff member. Make a connection with that person and obtain a business card for follow-up.

Celebrity presence can help you draw attention to a political cause or health care issue. If you are hosting an event where a celebrity will appear, make careful preparations with the person's staff. Be prepared to handle security, to provide a private space, and to handle excitable fans. Baldridge (1993) recommends not permitting autograph signing unless it is agreed to in advance. Make arrangements for photographs as the celebrity's staff directs. Find out the celebrity's preferences for meeting fans, signing books, and dining (for example, any special food requirements). If you make the celebrity comfortable, you'll begin what could be a long-lasting relationship.

PROTOCOL

If you have the opportunity to attend an event at the White House or another venue with high-level government representatives in attendance, you will be faced with the rules of protocol. Good manners are the rules that guide behavior in everyday contacts, but protocol is the set of rules prescribing good manners in official life and ceremonies involving governments, nations, and their representatives. Protocol includes the observance of the order of precedence at all functions where officials of a government are present. Precedence drives seating of individuals at public or private events. Failure to recognize proper rank and precedence is considered an insult (McCaffree & Innes, 1997).

The order of precedence begins with the President of the United States and winds down through cabinet secretaries, ministers of foreign powers, Supreme Court justices, senators, governors, members of the House of Representatives, directors of federal agencies, undersecretaries of executive departments, flag and general officers of the military, and many others. Protocol also includes rules for using the correct titles and forms of address for all officials, extending and responding to invitations, arranging table seating, and parading the U.S. flag.

COMMUNICATION DISASTERS

Have you ever asked a woman with a roundly protruding belly when her baby is due only to receive a cool look as she informs you she's not pregnant? Have you ever greeted a well-known senator by the wrong name? Have you ever introduced a keynote speaker and used the wrong title? Even the most socially adept among us have

made faux pas that defy understanding. Sooner or later, you may join the ranks of those who have survived "foot in mouth disease." When a communication disaster happens to you, what is the best way to handle it? We can learn from those who have been down the "path of disaster" before us. One health care professional who was attending a small meeting of very senior officials in his organization spilled a 32-ounce drink into the center of the table as the meeting began. As he mopped up the lake of iced tea spreading out before him, he apologized and smiled at all of the participants. "People have trouble being annoyed at you when you are smiling at them," he reports.

A nurse, newly elected as a leader in a specialty association, tripped as she approached the podium to address the association members. Recovering her footing, she greeted the group and said "I guess you all will remember me!" She revisited the event 3 years later when she addressed the meeting again. In her opening comments, she talked about her growth as a professional, saying "Three years ago I tripped on my way up here; last year, I shook the whole time I spoke; this year, I stand in front of you full of confidence." Her words were very well received, and she used her ability to not take herself too seriously to make the best of the situation.

If you find something has slipped out of your mouth inadvertently, acknowledge your error. Don't pretend it didn't happen. If you can use humor to defuse the situation, humor can make people comfortable again quickly. A self-deprecating comment can go a long way to get a conversation back on track.

ELECTRONIC COMMUNICATION: BEEP, BUZZ, RING, VIBRATE

The wonders of technology have transformed how, when, and where we communicate with one another. Just as with face-to-face communication, there are steps you can take that demonstrate how professional and thoughtful you are, and they will help you be as effective as possible.

SMART MESSAGES BY PHONE

The telephone can be a vital communication tool or an instrument of torture. Remember those phone manners mom drilled into you when you were a child? They still work today. A few phone basics will make you a telephonic success:

- Answer your business line with a cheerful greeting and your full name ("Good morning. This is Brad Hill."). If you answer calls directly (without first being referred by another staff member), greet callers with both your name and organization ("Good afternoon, West Side Health Center, this is Mr. Austin.").
- When you place a call, identify yourself and the purpose for your call ("Hello, Mr. Thompson. This is Hannah Davis. I'm calling about the organ donation legislation you are sponsoring.")
- Return every phone call—quickly. Returning calls promptly demonstrates your respect for the caller and is always appreciated.
- If you find yourself in a game of "telephone tag," leave very specific information about where and when you may be reached.
- If you must put a caller on hold, ask permission ("Excuse me, may I put you on hold for a moment?"). Use this feature only when it is absolutely essential. Don't leave a caller on hold for more than 30 to 60 seconds. When you return, thank the person that you put on hold.

SMART MESSAGES BY VOICEMAIL

If you use voicemail to greet callers and record messages when you are not available, record a clear and coherent outgoing message that lets callers know when they can expect to hear from you. You may want to write out your outgoing message to callers and practice it before recording. The words you use and your inflection project an image to callers. Your outgoing message should include your name, title, and location as well as a brief message to inform the caller when they may receive a call back from you: "Hello, you've reached Ann Ryan, Legislative Director for Congressman Owens. I'll be out of the office on August 12 but will return calls on August 13. Please leave a message and I'll contact you when I return." Change your outgoing message whenever your circumstances change.

When you leave a voicemail message for someone, summarize the reason for your call in a few sentences. Be brief. A lengthy message can be tedious, and the recipient may hit the delete button before getting to the most important part. Make it easy for someone to return your call by speaking clearly when you leave your name and phone number. If you are a first-time caller, consider repeating your name and number.

JUST THE FAX

The key to success with sending a fax is to ensure that you use a cover sheet that provides your contact information so the recipient may reach you. Make sure you include your name, title, phone and fax numbers, and e-mail addresses. When you send faxes, check the transmission record to determine if the fax was sent successfully. A phone call made to a wrong number will usually give you immediate feedback that you misdialed, but the same is not so with a fax. A fax sent to the wrong number will end up in fax never-never land. Make sure you send your fax to the correct number. If you are faxing to an individual who shares a fax machine in a workplace, you may want to send a courtesy e-mail to let the person know that a fax has been sent to them.

CELL PHONES AND PAGERS

The jury is in on the use of cell phones and pagers in meetings and conferences: No one wants to hear your phone ring or your pager go off. When you are in a meeting, at a restaurant, or at an event, keep you pager or phone set to silently vibrate so as not to intrude on conversation or interrupt activities, or turn off electronic devices completely.

NETIQUETTE—GETTING THE MOST OUT OF THE INTERNET

Electronic mail (e-mail) is a quick, easy, and direct means of communication that has proven to be a social phenomenon as well as a technologic one. The Internet is a major thoroughfare for communications, carrying millions of messages a day. It is viewed by some as the most politically potent technology ever invented (Carr, 1998). Like other means, it can be used with finesse or employed in a manner that is annoying and frustrating to others. "Netiquette" is an informal code for behavior in "cyberspace." It lets you communicate effectively and avoid gaffes. Etiquette permits you to display good manners at the dinner table; netiquette lets you do the same at your computer terminal. Keep these suggestions in mind so you can be a good "netizen" (Internet citizen):

- Keep it short and spell it right. Many Internet users are inundated with e-mail, so keep your messages concise and use appropriate spelling and grammar.
- Use a signature line. Set up your e-mail account so that each e-mail message contains your contact information including your address, phone, and fax numbers and alternate e-mail addresses. This will be extremely helpful to those who need to contact you and don't have your business card. Keep the e-mail signature about four lines long.
- Avoid fatal errors. If you are writing an emotional message, pause and carefully review what you are writing and exactly who you are sending it to before hitting the send button. You can't take your words back, and once they are sent, they can be forwarded to others. Don't assume any e-mail will remain completely private.
- DON'T SCREAM IN ALL CAPS! Words typed in all upper case are "heard" by most Internet users as shouting.
- Always reply. If someone contacts you asking for something, let the person know you received the message even if you don't have an answer yet. No response leaves the writer unsure if the message got to the right place.
- Cool your enthusiastic forwarding. Don't assume everyone in your e-mail address book wants to read all the jokes, urban myths, sermons, poems, virus alerts, and other junk mail that someone sent to you. Be selective in forwarding mass e-mail: not everyone appreciates it.
- Don't be a bandwidth hog. Be considerate in forwarding attachments that take up huge amounts of bandwidth and may severely tax the hard drive of the computer receiving the message. Bandwidth hogs include graphics and audio files as well as executable files (files that end with .exe). Besides taking up bandwidth, executables could transfer a virus, so delete any that you receive (The Essayist, 1999).
- Hide the addresses. If you are sending an e-mail to many recipients, consider using the BCC (blind copy) feature to hide all of the recipients' names and e-mail addresses. Your colleagues may greatly appreciate your discretion.
- Clean up e-mails that have been forwarded multiple times. When forwarding e-mail (if you must), remove headers from previous mailing, including the e-mail addresses, and delete the >>>> symbols on the left margin that indicate a message has been forwarded.

COMMUNICATION ACCESSORIES

BRIEF BIOGRAPHY

Do yourself a favor and prepare a one-page brief biography that summarizes your career, professional activities, and accomplishments. Box 6-3 is an example. It can serve as a quick introduction to you and your activities, and you will probably find multiple uses for it. Begin with your current position and then provide a brief summary of your career, specific professional highlights, and educational background. Consider embedding a current photo and your business or organization logo for a professional look. By maintaining your biography in an electronic file, you can update it frequently and e-mail it whenever it is needed.

CURRICULUM VITAE AND RESUME

As with a brief biography, you will probably find multiple professional uses for your curriculum vitae and resume outside of the traditional use in employment searches. A curriculum vitae (CV) is a document that contains extensive detail of your professional life: education, employment, publications, presentations, association contributions, academic activities, research activities, honors, and

BOX **6-3**   Example of a Brief Biography

Mary W. Chaffee, RN, MS, CNAA, CHE, FAAN
Brief Biography

Business
Navy Medicine Office of Homeland Security,
Bureau of Medicine and Surgery
2300 E Street NW, Washington, DC 20372
(202) 123-4567   Mary.Chaffee@abc.def

Home
123 Park Place, Small Town, Maryland 20886
(301) 123-4567   Mwchaffee@abc.com

Mary Chaffee is a registered nurse with 18 years of military and civilian nursing and health care experience. Currently assigned as Deputy Director of the Navy Medicine Office of Homeland Security, she leads Navy Medicine's efforts to prevent, protect against, and respond to threats or attacks. An active duty Navy Nurse Corps Officer, she has served in a variety of roles including staff nurse in critical care and emergency nursing, nurse manager, staff educator, computer systems administrator, and health policy analyst.

Ms. Chaffee is the Vice President of the Federal Nurses Association, a constituent member of the American Nurses Association. She lectures nationally on a variety of topics; is the managing editor of the nursing journal, *Policy, Politics & Nursing Practice;* and is the co-editor of *Policy and Politics in Nursing and Health Care.* She represents Navy Medicine on the International Nursing Coalition on Mass Casualty Education.

Ms. Chaffee is an honors graduate of the University of Massachusetts where she received two Bachelor's degrees. In 1998 she received Master of Science degrees in Nursing Health Policy and Nursing Administration, as well as an Advanced Certificate in Health and Public Policy, from the University of Maryland.

Ms. Chaffee was recognized in 2001 as a Distinguished Alumni of the University of Massachusetts—the first nurse to receive that honor. She is a Fellow of the American Academy of Nursing. The Maryland Organization of Nurse Executives selected her to receive the Helen King Scholarship for excellence in graduate Nursing Administration studies, and she received a Distinguished Alumni Award from the University of Massachusetts School of Nursing in 1998. She was honored in 1996 with the Excellence in Caring Practices Award presented by the American Association of Critical-Care Nurses. Her contributions to Navy Medicine have been recognized with the Navy Meritorious Service Medal, the Navy Commendation Medal, and the Navy Achievement Medal. She is a member of Sigma Theta Tau Nursing Honor Society and Phi Kappa Phi Honor Society.

Updated April 2002

awards. A CV can be quite long and provides the reader with global view of your professional contributions. A resume, on the other hand, is a shorter version of the CV. It should be no more than two pages in length and should summarize your work and educational history and other professional activities. There are many resources available that offer guidance and examples of both effective CVs and resumes. The critical factor in successfully managing both is to update them frequently to keep them current.

BUSINESS CARDS

Your card is a vital networking tool: Don't leave home without it! Business cards can be your link to important new professional relationships. You won't dazzle anybody by tearing a napkin in half and writing your name and number on it. As you collect business cards from colleagues, you may want to jot notes about the acquaintance on the card so you don't forget an important connection. Keep the cards you collect in a file so you can access a needed card quickly.

WEBSITES

Your organization may post information about you on the company website (another use for that brief biography you wrote), or you may choose to create your own website. If you do, accuracy of information is critical. Review it carefully or have a colleague with a sharp eye review it for you to catch mistakes. Make sure you periodically review website content to ensure that it is current and accurate.

CONCLUSION

ETIQUETTE—YES, I SAID ETIQUETTE

Etiquette has taken on a whole new life as professionals and leaders recognize the immense impact of personal relationships on the outcomes of business and political initiatives. If you bite off a carrot and dip it back into the ranch dip at a reception, pick broccoli out of your teeth with a toothpick at a formal dinner, or blow your nose into someone's expensive white linen napkins, even if you are the most brilliant thinker in the Western hemisphere, your manners will probably limit your success.

Business etiquette means using good manners in interacting with people and putting them at ease (Andrica, 1999). Purchasing a book on manners and etiquette will serve you well, such as the *New Complete Guide to Executive Manners* by Letitia Baldridge. Etiquette has become so important that consultants, resources, and training programs abound (Box 6-4). Personal coaches can be hired to provide one-on-one etiquette coaching. Courses are available on how to outclass the competition, effective business entertaining, the art of working a room, and basic manners and office politics.

ATTIRE

Are you any less knowledgeable or committed if you wear comfortable old jeans and sandals to a meeting with a policymaker? No. Will you be taken as seriously as if you had on a business suit? Probably not. In contemporary society, a professional image is important. Take care with your attire and how you present yourself, just as you do with your language and nonverbal communication. Whether we like it or not, opinions are formed about us initially based on our appearance. When you are attending a social event, check the invitation or speak with the host to confirm appropriate attire.

COMMUNICATION AND LEADERSHIP

Communication is the heart of leadership (Tappen, 2001). Leaders lead by *communicating* a vision so that others may move toward it. Without clear, effective communication, leadership crumbles, and goals can't be achieved. But look what leaders can do with effective communication:

- Take positions
- Present evidence to back up their position
- Speak simply
- Propose a course of action
- Address objections before they are raised
- Press their case with conviction (Toogood, 1996)

Exceptional communication skills enhance all leadership actions, including those in the arenas of policy and politics. Taking risks, learning new skills, and fine-tuning those skills you possess will make you more effective and will ultimately benefit the people you are advocating for.

REFERENCES

American Nurses Association (1999). *ANA Media Relations & You.* Washington DC: American Nurses Association.

Andrica, D.C. (1999). Business etiquette. *Nursing Economic$, 17*(1), 63.

Baldridge, L. (1993). *Letitia Baldridge's new complete guide to executive manners.* New York: Rawson Associates.

Boothman, N. (2000). *How to make people like you in 90 seconds or less.* New York: Workman Publishing.

Carr, N. (1998, March-April). The politics of e-mail. *Harvard Business Review,* 12-13.

The Essayist. (1999). *Spam is not the worst of it: Email etiquette and related gripes.* Available online at unquietmind.com.

Figler, H. (1999). *The complete job search handbook.* New York: Henry Holt and Company.

Goleman, D. (1998). *Working with emotional intelligence.* New York: Bantam Books.

Heller, R. (1998). *Communicate clearly.* New York: DK Publishing.

Krisco, K.H. (1997). *Leadership and the art of conversation.* Rocklin, CA: Prima Publishing.

Maggio, R. (1990). *How to say it: Choice words, phrases, sentences and paragraphs for every situation.* Paramus, NJ: Prentice-Hall.

BOX **6-4** Examples of Business Etiquette Resources

The Protocol School of Palm Beach
Protocol and Etiquette Seminars for Today's Business Leaders
www.etiquetteexpert.com
Etiquette International
Corporate services, business and international etiquette, one-on-one personal coaching
www.etiquetteintl.com
AllEtiquette.com
A how-to guide that cultivates image, manners, and business and international etiquette
www.alletiquette.com

Mandell, T. (1996). *Power schmoozing: The new etiquette for social and business success.* New York: McGraw-Hill.

Martinet, J. (1996). *Getting beyond "hello".* New York: Citadel Press.

McCaffree, M. J., & Innis, P. (1997). *Protocol: The complete handbook of diplomatic, official and social usage.* Washington, DC: Devon Publishing Company, Inc.

Morrison, T., Conaway, W.A., & Borden, G.A. (1994). *Kiss, bow or shake hands: How to do business in sixty countries.* Holbrook, MA: Adams Media Corporation.

Puetz, B.E. & Shinn, L.J. (1998). Networking. In D.J. Mason & J.K. Leavitt (Eds.). *Policy and politics in nursing and health care* (4th ed.). Philadelphia: W.B. Saunders.

Roane, S. (2000). *How to work a room.* New York: HarperCollins.

Sabath, A.M. (1993). *Business etiquette in brief.* Holbrook, MA: Bob Adams, Inc.

Tappen, R.M. (2001). *Nursing leadership and management: Concepts and practice.* Philadelphia: F.A. Davis.

Toogood, G.N. (1996). *The articulate executive—Learn to look, act, and sound like a leader.* New York: McGraw-Hill.

POLICYSPOTLIGHT

ACHIEVING HEALTH LITERACY

Carole P. Jennings, Linda Thompson, & Darryl Roberts

"Words have a magical power . . . Words are capable of arousing the strongest emotions and prompting all men's actions."

SIGMUND FREUD

DEFINITION OF THE PROBLEM

Being able to access and understand information about one's medical treatment, medication regime, and advice related to managing illness or staying healthy is increasingly as important as carrying a health insurance card. Today, more than 90 million Americans, or 46% of the adult population, have limited literacy skills, a burden that profoundly affects the quality of their health care. The American Medical Association reports that the problem of patients being unable to understand, interpret, and act on basic health information, such as instructions on prescriptions, appointment slips, informed consent documents, discharge instructions, insurance forms, and other health educational materials, results in $73 billion in unnecessary health expenses nationwide (Lovern, 2001).

Alarmingly, one in three seniors does not have a sufficient level of health literacy to understand instructions for prescriptions, complete medical forms, and follow providers' directions for self-care activities. The relationship between age and health literacy is rather remarkable, with the prevalence of inadequate health literacy steadily increasing from 15.6% of individuals age 65 to 69 years to 58% of those age 85 years or older (Eng, Maxfield, Patrick, Deering, Ratzan, & Gustafson, 1998). Recent research also shows that persons with low health literacy who have a chronic disease, such as diabetes, asthma, or hypertension, have less knowledge of their disease and its treatment and fewer correct self-management skills than literate patients. These factors help to explain why patients with inadequate functional health literacy are more likely to be hospitalized than those with adequate health literacy (Gazmararian, 1999).

Compounding this already-acute problem among English-speaking adults is rising multilingual diversity. Persons with English as a second language are often in low-paying jobs without health insurance. They are unable to advocate for themselves and their families or use existing health information networks to their benefit. In such situations, the capacity for self-help strategies is greatly reduced. The challenge to all health care providers in each of these instances is great.

A hallmark of nursing practice is patient advocacy and patient education. Nurses are the frontline practitioners and are often the first contact for individuals with low health literacy. Nurses can help by recognizing problems of low health literacy, simplifying written and oral communications, and verifying that patients have received and understood the message. Nurses need to focus on health literacy in every patient assessment, including a patient's reading aptitude, mental status, physical limitations, comprehension level, and ability to speak effectively (Cole, 2000). Health literacy can be assessed using the Short Test of Functional Health Literacy in Adults (S-TOFHLA), which takes about 12 minutes to administer and is available in both English and Spanish versions. An advantage to using the S-TOFHLA is that it uses actual materials that patients might encounter in a health care setting, such as hospital forms and labeled prescription bottles (Gazmararian, 1999). Persons with low health literacy are most able to benefit from a multidisciplinary treatment approach. Collaboration with other health and social service providers is essential for producing desirable patient outcomes.

Health literacy is defined as "a collection of proficiencies, including a functional level of reading and math, that allow the individual to adequately read, understand, and act on health care information" (Gazmararian, 1999, p.545). This cluster of skills increasingly determines a person's level of health competence or his or her ability to negotiate the health care system on one's own behalf and on behalf of one's family and community. The World Health Organization (WHO) cites that functional levels of health literacy are needed for active participation in sustainable health promotion efforts within communities. The technology gap is slowing efforts by low-income communities to help themselves. A growing number of global civic activists believe that modern communications networks are an increasingly important tool for fostering civic engagement. Ability to participate in health care decisions means empowerment for many groups such as, women, elderly people, children and indigenous peoples who have been excluded, in the past, from playing a full role in creating health-supporting environments. Achieving acceptable levels of health literacy is essential for maximizing the full potential for health worldwide and moving toward health and social equity (World Health Organization, 1998).

Information technology is key to enhancing literacy levels, and there is little doubt that knowledge and information play a substantial role in achieving optimal states of health literacy. They have emerged as powerful tools capable of transforming the U.S. health care delivery system from one where authority and control rest with an elite group of policymakers, health professionals, health care administrators, and insurance executives to one that acknowledges the power of the everyday health care consumer.

POLICY CHALLENGE

Increased professional and public attention is being focused on the problem of low health literacy and its correlates with an individual's health status, self-care strategies, access to current scientific information, and emotional and peer support. Evidence is mounting that low levels of health literacy substantially affect cost and quality of services, and they affect consumer empowerment in technologic and political spheres as well. The policy challenge is great and can be framed with the following question: "How does a nation or society achieve health and social equity and reduce the gap between the health information 'haves' and 'have-nots'?" (Eng et al, 1998, p. 1371). The major policy goal or response has been to increase efforts to achieve universal access to health information and support.

Information technology has become an essential part of the policy solution to low health literacy because of its proven track record in reducing health disparities resulting from low literacy. Two primary policy objectives are to eliminate barriers to accessing information technology and to ensure the quality of health information.

Eliminating Barriers to Access to Information Technology

Eng et al (1998, p. 1371) write that, "Although American society seems to tolerate unequal access to health care, we now have a window of opportunity to avert a similar inequity in access to health information and support." They cite three arguments for viewing universal access to health information and support as a social, public good: public information, public health, and cost savings. They argue that public information, the great volume of health knowledge generated by public funds either directly or indirectly, should be freely available to all; that making health information available is an essential public health function because enhancing access to information and support improves the quality of individual health-related decisions and supports public health goals; and that improved access to information and support resources may lead to better clinical decisions and more-responsible and efficient use of limited health care resources, thereby reducing the strain on current financial "safety nets" and lowering health care costs.

Individual barriers to access to information technologies include cost (socioeconomic status), geographic location, illiteracy, and disability. Information technology can potentially augment existing proposals related to personal health and public health initiatives in communities. As health services are increasingly shifted from institutional health care settings to the home and community, the ability to obtain and use the tools of information technology become a prerequisite to obtaining health services.

The Internet and other types of information technologies hold the promise for interactive health communication, allowing for the tailoring of information based on an individual's level of literacy, method and point of access, health status, and psychosocial variables. The Internet, in particular, has tremendous ability to support people in making informed health decisions and in demanding more appropriate, cost-effective, high-quality health care. The Internet can also bridge differences in socioeconomic status and geographic location.

Since the first web browser was developed in 1993, the Internet has grown from the humble government and university ARPAnet to the World Wide Web (www, or "the Web"). The web currently boasts 163.4 million users in the United States. Currently, the most common platform for accessing on-line health information is the personal computer. However, just 26% of households earning less than $35,000 a year have on-line access at home, whereas 60% to 70% of families with an income of $75,000 or more have access to Internet sites on home computers. Today nearly every public library and many community centers, senior centers, and schools provide ready, and often free, access to on-line resources (Health on the Net Foundation, 1999). One example, Libraries On-line!, a joint project of Microsoft Corporation, the American Library Association, and the Center for Technology in the Public Library, was created to increase Internet access to underserved communities through local libraries. Library systems that receive support offer training and support to small businesses, families, and students who are unlikely to have access to the Internet at home (Benton Foundation, 1999).

The costs of providing universal access to health information and support are significant barriers, and lack of access to infrastructure and hardware is a problem for many communities. Infrastructure costs include the costs of communication lines, routers, servers, modems, and interfaces with users such as computers, kiosks, television-based Internet, and personal communication devices. Other costs include training fees for information intermediaries such as health professionals, librarians, and educators. However, the cost of providing universal access to health-related resources may be lower than expected because the infrastructure costs for such access can be shared among social, educational, and community service organizations (Eng et al, 1998). Additionally, the costs associated with personal computers and communication services are rapidly declining, and the promise of converging information appliances may make home access more affordable.

An important policy consideration is the fact that the replication of health information on the Internet has little or no variable cost. Once information or an application is developed and published on the Internet, there is little to no marginal cost for additional persons to use them. In contrast with the high cost of providing access to health care, providing access to information through Internet-accessible resources is virtually free of cost.

Ensuring Quality of Health Care Information

The quality of health information available on the Internet is critically important because it could potentially affect health outcomes for millions of people. Developing objective, reproducible, widely accepted criteria that can be used to evaluate the quality of information available on the Internet is an essential component of the policy solution to ensure universal access to health information and support. Ultimately, the best protection against inaccurate, misleading, and self-serving sources may be in teaching users how to judge information for themselves. To this end, librarians at Widener University have developed useful criteria for evaluating health information on the Internet (Alexander & Tate, 1999):

- *Accuracy.* How reliable and free from error is the information? What editorial review process was used?
- *Authority.* What are the author's credentials and qualifications for writing on the subject? How reputable is the publisher?
- *Objectivity.* Is the information presented with a minimum of bias? To what extent is the information trying to sway the opinion of the audience?
- *Currency.* Is the content of the information up to date? Is the publication date clearly stated? Is the date the information was last revised indicated?
- *Coverage.* What topics are included in the work? To what depth are the topics explored?

Numerous formal efforts are underway to help Internet users find health information that is reliable and to help them avoid information that is misleading or deceptive. Some of the efforts include the creation of trusted gateways to information on the Internet. The U.S. Department of Health and Human Services (DHHS) sponsors *healthfinder,* a website that gathers links to government health agencies, public health and professional groups, universities, medical journals, support groups, and new sites. The Health on the Net Foundation (HON), a Switzerland-based nonprofit organiza-

tion sponsored by Sun Microsystems, the Swiss Institute of Bioinformatics, and the State Bank of Geneva, seeks to raise standards for website developers. Its HON code commits developers to certain requirements (Benton Foundation, 1999):

- To state the qualifications of people giving advice on their sites
- To pledge to avoid disrupting existing relationships visitors to the site have with their current health care provider
- To maintain confidentiality
- To cite source material
- To support any claim with evidence
- To provide contact addresses for people seeking further information
- To disclose how the sites are financed
- To clearly distinguish between advertising and original materials created by site developers

Sites that adhere to the code can display the HON logo (Benton Foundation, 1999).

CONCLUSION

Advances in information technology offer our citizens an unparalleled opportunity to achieve equity in health information access and to build acceptable levels of health literacy for the twenty-first century. Harnessing technology to combat low levels of health literacy can help people increase their knowledge of health, enhance their ability to negotiate the health care system, understand and modify their health risk behaviors, and acquire coping skills and social support (Eng et al, 1998). Nationally and globally, information technology can reduce the information divide and bring all societies closer to health and social equity.

The issue of low health literacy is a wake-up call for nurses in all settings. If effective communication is the cornerstone of nursing intervention, then the goal of patient education must be the empowerment of consumers in a market-driven, and increasingly information-driven, health care system. Nurses will have to dramatically change their practice orientation by partnering with patients to create an atmosphere of shared decision making. This means that all patient care providers would need to clarify and amplify the information patients retrieve on the Internet, help them determine the risks and tradeoffs associated with different treatment options, and then support them in their choice of an approach based on personal priorities and attitudes about risk.

Additionally, nurses can help achieve policy goals by focusing research efforts on literacy screening, on methods of health education for patients with low levels of health literacy, and on health outcomes and economic consequences associated with low literacy and by understanding the causal pathway of how health literacy influences health (Ad Hoc Committee on Health Literacy for the Council on Scientific Affairs, 1999).

Increasingly, health is seen as a byproduct of culture, income, education, the environment, spiritual orientation, and social cohesion. Health care professionals, policymakers, individuals, and communities must take a fresh look at what creates and sustains health. Information technology is creating a new synergy with health care delivery systems. Kendall and Levine (1997) write that the burgeoning use of information technology in health care is creating the opportunity for a smarter and more cost-effective health care system. They propose building a "health information network" in which each person would have a "health management account" containing an electronic patient record and insurance coverage information, performance information on choice of health care providers, and a plan for automated notification of new studies that could help with individual medical problems. In the information age of today, information and knowledge are powerful determinants of who has ready and equal access to high-quality, affordable health care.

REFERENCES

Ad Hoc Committee on Health Literacy for the Council on Scientific Affairs, American Medical Association. (1999). Health literacy: Report of the Council on Scientific Affairs. *Journal of the American Medical Association, 281*(6), 552-557.

Alexander, J. & M.A. Tate. (1999). *Web wisdom: How to evaluate and create information quality on the web.* Lawrence Erlbaum Associates. Available online at www.muse.widener.edu/Wolfgram-Memorial-Library/webevaluation/webeval.htm.

Benton Foundation. (1999). *Report: Networking for better care: Health care in the information age.* Available online at www.benton.org/Library/health/.

Cole, M.R. (2000). The high risk of low literacy. *Nursing Spectrum, 10*(20), 10-11.

Eng, T.R., Maxfield, A., Patrick K., Deering, M.J., Ratzan, S.C., & Gustafson, D.H. (1998). Access to health information and support: A public highway or private road? *Journal of the American Medical Association, 280*(15), 1371-1375.

Gazmararian, J.A. (1999). Health literacy among Medicare enrollees in a managed care organization. *Journal of the American Medical Association, 281*(6), 545-551.

Health on the Net Foundation. (1999). *Fifth HON survey on the evolution of Internet use for health purposes.* Available at www.hon.ch.

Kendall, D.B. & Levine, S. R. (1997). *Creating a health information network: Stage two of the health care revolution.* Washington, DC: Progressive Policy Institute.

Lovern, E. (2001). Patients blamed for medical errors. *Modern Healthcare, 31*(2), 4.

World Health Organization. (1998). Promoting health locally, nationally and globally. *World Health 51*(2), 3-5.

Conflict Management

ALMA YEARWOOD DIXON

"Be a good listener. Your ears will never get you into trouble."

FRANK TYGER

She knew that his care would be difficult. A teenage gang member with gunshot wounds to his abdomen and leg would pose several challenges because of his medical condition and behavior. He refused to follow the diet suggested and instead ate food brought in by his friends, some of whom were gang members too. When his friends visited they played loud music and showed little regard for other patients or staff members. Whenever security was called, they treated the officers with disdain and called them "wannabe cops."

Whenever she cared for the teenager, his behavior was dismissive and his language insulting. It was one thing to have a sullen teenager at home and quite another to care for a rude one at work. It was apparent that he did not share or appreciate any of her values and concern for his health and well-being. Each day he seemed to challenge all of the reasons she chose nursing as a career.

Whenever two people interact, the potential for conflict exists because of the unique way that each person perceives the situation, processes information, and forms an opinion. Conflict within the work setting is a natural occurrence as people define and work toward common goals. The need to work for a "common good" facilitates conflict resolution. However, the current environment in health care has resulted in increased discord among staff, who are being engulfed by changes dictated by socioeconomic forces outside the profession. These changes are driving nursing education and practice in profoundly different ways. Consensus building

and teamwork are more difficult because the players and the playing field are unfamiliar. Therefore, nurses need to acquire new skills in conflict resolution and the art of negotiation.

TYPES OF CONFLICT

Conflict can be defined as the internal discord that occurs as a result of incongruity or incompatibility in ideas, values, or beliefs of two or more people. As opposed to a misunderstanding, conflict is more than a failure in interpretation; it usually represents some combination of a perceived threat to power or social position, scarcity of resources, and differing value systems. Conflict induces incompatible or antagonistic actions between two people or among groups (Ury, 2000).

Conflict can take many forms. It can occur in a concentric fashion, beginning with incompatible personal thoughts, values, perceptions, or actions (intrapersonal conflict). It can then radiate to differences in relationships between individuals (interpersonal conflict) or groups of people (intergroup conflict) and to incompatibility with organizational demands, policies, or procedures (organizational conflict).

INTRAPERSONAL CONFLICT

Intrapersonal conflict occurs within the individual nurse and represents an internal struggle to clarify values, perceptions, or needs. Nurses hold many responsibilities, including responsibility to the organization, to superiors, to peers, and ultimately to patients as well as to their individual families. These responsibilities may conflict, and that conflict may be internalized. It is imperative that the nurse practice self-awareness and gain the skill in taking a personal inventory to resolve intrapersonal conflict as soon as it is felt in order to avoid impairments in physical or emotional health. This type of conflict can occur when a nurse is challenged to behave in ways that are not consistent with felt beliefs about professional ethics and practice, although the action may achieve organizational goals. For example, no matter where they practice, nurses are constantly challenged to question what they personally believe about health care and the practice of nursing with questions such as the following:

- Is quality care sacrificed with shortened hospital stays?
- Am I sacrificing quality care when I am forced to work overtime? If I say no, will I have a job?
- Does a person's right to die influence my practice?
- What do I do when I cannot compromise what I believe in?

Intrapersonal conflict can serve as the impetus for personal growth and change. According to Kritek (1994), conflicts are teaching experiences that call forth a commitment to courage, self-honesty, and learning. Recognizing that conflict resolution requires an exploration of alternatives, "one is divested of the illusion of a belief in 'the one right way,' [and] the doors open to a myriad of ways, each with some truth and some distortion" (Kritek, 1994, p. 21).

INTERPERSONAL CONFLICT

Conflict between individuals can be manifested by angry, hostile, or passive behaviors. These behaviors may be verbal, nonverbal, or physical. According to Brinkman and Kirschner (1994), interpersonal conflict occurs when the emphasis is placed on differences between people, and as a result, "united we stand, divided we can't stand each other" (p. 38).

Interpersonal conflict can impair working relationships, hinder productivity, and damage morale. Brinkman and Kirschner (1994) suggest strategies of blending and redirecting to resolve conflict in a timely and efficient manner. Blending involves reducing differences by finding common ground and mutual understanding, and redirecting is a process of using the rapport to change the trajectory of the communication toward a positive outcome.

To accomplish these strategies, one must be able to communicate and to listen until the issue is understood. The following steps are suggested:

1. Demonstrate listening and understanding by posture, voice volume, and action.
2. Backtrack or repeat some of the words used.
3. Clarify meaning and intent.
4. Summarize what was heard.
5. Confirm to find out whether understanding was reached.

These steps to careful listening and understanding facilitate conflict resolution by enabling the participants to define the problem clearly and by setting a climate for cooperation.

INTERGROUP CONFLICT

As a nurse manager, she had definite beliefs about the nature of conflict; she firmly believed that conflict has clearly differentiated borders of rightness and wrongness, people who wear the white hat of fairness versus those who wear the black hat of injustice. She assumed that there is one way to solve a problem or approach a situation. Therefore, she expected that nurses on the units would welcome the newly hired graduates of a baccalaureate program because these new hires would provide relief to the often-overworked staff. In fact, as far as she was concerned, the sign-on bonus, used as a recruitment tool, was money well spent to alleviate the constant complaints of long shifts and overtime.

She was completely surprised when a new graduate tearfully came into her office to complain that the more-experienced graduate of an associate degree program embarrassed her when she asked for help. In fact, the older nurses often asked her and her fellow graduates, "Didn't they teach you anything in nursing school?" The nurses also complained that their workload was actually harder because they needed to take time to explain things to the new recruits.

Intergroup conflict occurs between two or more groups of people, departments, or organizations. When intergroup conflict occurs, the participants form cohesive teams that "circle the wagons" against the other teams, who are perceived as the enemy with opposing views. Each team tends to recognize only the positives within its membership and only the negatives within the other teams. Typical behaviors include "we/they" language, gossip and blaming, back stabbing, and sabotage.

The resolution of intergroup conflict involves a process of identifying shared goals, focusing on the benefits of differences and diversity, valuing the input of all team members, and clarifying misperceptions.

ORGANIZATIONAL CONFLICT

On an outpatient unit the nurses were up in arms. One of the staff nurses, deemed a know-it-all who was often avoided by her colleagues, was given the responsibility to audit everyone's charts to make sure that all medications and treatments were recorded. Senior hospital administration ordered the audit because it was suspected that charges were not being implemented in a cost-effective manner because the nursing staff was not making the appropriate chart notations. The nurse selected for the audit was chosen because of her thoroughness and attention to detail.

Her colleagues felt betrayed and acted as if there were a spy in their midst. The audit revealed several areas of misunderstanding that could be simply addressed by clarifying charting procedures. A directive was issued for the nurses to attend a workshop on the relationship of charting to patient fees. The astute nursing staff development person charged with the responsibility to "fix the nurses" knew she was walking into a landmine zone.

Organizational conflict can reflect intrapersonal, interpersonal, and intergroup conflict. This form of conflict may occur between superiors and their subordinates or between staff and management. It usually concerns policy, power, and status. In contrast, horizontal conflict involves individuals with similar power and status in the organization. It usually occurs over discord related to authority, expertise, or practice issues.

Organizations are large, complex social systems with interacting forces that exert influence on nursing in all practice and education settings. These influences include the constant pressures of shrinking resources and financial constraints, the expanding needs and expectations of clients, the increasing militancy of nurses and students, and the persistent problems of interprofessional competition. These influences add to the prevalence of organizational conflict.

Nurses are required to function with political astuteness and prudent skill in identifying the subtle forces that have an impact on practice. They are required to make a realistic assessment of the circumstances, discern the obvious, and grasp and comprehend the obscure. Effective nurses have a grasp of the situation, with a logical shrewdness. However, when faced with conflict, too many nurses resort to a spontaneous emotional response without thinking of circumstances or consequences.

Effective organizations are composed of competent individuals who are able to practice in environments where differences are both valued and used as the impetus for constructive change. Organizational conflict that is not resolved can result in warring factions, reduced productivity, and disruption of teamwork.

CONFLICT RESOLUTION

Conflict resolution involves a process of negotiation toward a mutually acceptable agreement. Methods for resolving conflict may result in win-lose solutions or, ideally, in win-win solutions.

WIN-LOSE SOLUTIONS

According to Roe (1995), win-lose solutions can be categorized in the following manner:

1. *Denial,* or *withdrawal,* involves attempts to get rid of the conflict by denying that it exists or by refusing to acknowledge it. If an issue is not important, or if it is raised at an inopportune time, denial may be an appropriate strategy. However, if the issue is important, it will not go away and may grow to a point where it becomes unmanageable and builds to a greater complexity.

2. *Suppression,* or *smoothing over,* plays down the differences in the conflict, and the focus is placed on areas of agreement rather than on differences. Smoothing over may be appropriate for minor disagreements or to preserve a relationship. It is especially inappropriate when the involved parties are ready and willing to deal with the issue. It is important to note that the source of the conflict rarely goes away and may surface later in a more virulent form.

3. *Power* or *dominance* methods to resolve conflict allow authority, position, majority rule, or a vocal minority to settle the conflict. Power strategies result in winners and losers, and the losers do not support the final decision in the same way that the winners do. Although this strategy may be appropriate when the group has agreed on this method of resolution, future meetings may be marred by renewal of the struggle.

4. *Compromise* is considered a mutual win-lose method of conflict resolution that involves each party's giving up something (losing) to gain and meet midway (winning). In our culture, compromise is viewed as a virtue. However, bargaining has serious drawbacks. For example, both sides often assume an inflated position because they are aware that they are going to have to "give a little," and they want to buffer the loss. The compromise solution may be watered down to the point of being ineffective, and there is often little real commitment to the solution. Further, compromise may result in antagonistic cooperation because either or both parties perceive that they have given up more than the other. Despite these drawbacks, compromise can be useful when resources are limited, when both sides have enough leeway to give, and when it is necessary to forestall a total win-lose stance.

WIN-WIN SOLUTIONS

The goal of win-win solutions is to manage discord so that the conflict is a constructive impetus for growth, innovation, and productivity. Two win-win strategies are collaboration and principled negotiation.

Collaboration. The goal of collaboration is for everyone to win: No one has to give up anything. According to Marquis and Hurston (1994), "In collaboration, both parties set aside their original goals and work together to establish a supraordinate goal or common goal. Because both parties have identified the joint goal, each believes they have achieved their goal and an acceptable solution.

The focus throughout collaboration remains on problem solving, and not on defeating the other party" (p. 290).

This approach to conflict resolution requires that all parties to the conflict recognize the expertise of the others. Each individual's position is valid, but the group emphasis is on solving the problem rather than on defending a particular position. All involved expect to modify original perceptions as the work of the group unfolds. The belief is that ultimately the best of the group's collective thinking will emerge because the problem is viewed from varied vantage points rather than one limited view.

Collaboration takes time and commitment to the problem-solving process. It requires mutual respect, listening skills, and an environment in which facts, assumptions, and feelings are verbalized and heard.

Principled Negotiation. Principled negotiation is a method of conflict resolution that is used as an alternative to positional bargaining. It was developed at the Harvard Negotiation Project and can be summarized in four basic steps, as identified by Fisher, Ury, and Patton (1992):

1. *Separate the people from the problem.* This step recognizes that all players in the negotiation are human beings with emotions, felt needs, deeply held values, and different backgrounds, experiences, and perceptions. Therefore, each person views the world from a selective vantage point, and perceptions are frequently confused with reality.

Because conflict is a dynamic process that begins on an intrapersonal level and expands to include relationships between people, it is easy to understand that negotiations are often clouded by the problem and the relationships. Therefore, conflict resolution that results in a battle over wills and positions fosters identification of the positions with personal egos. Those positions are defended against attack and become nonnegotiable. Saving face becomes necessary to reconcile future decisions with past positions. Moreover, arguing over positions endangers ongoing relationships and entangles the relationship with the problem.

In separating the people from the problem, one must pay careful attention to perception, emotion, and communication. Attempts are made to see the situation from the other person's viewpoint and to have an empathetic understanding of the other point of view. This includes suspending judgment and actively listening. The parties each work to avoid blaming the other for the problem or putting the worst interpretation on each action and instead discuss each perception. Emotions are valued, and creative ways are sought for their expression.

2. *Focus on interests, not on positions.* Interests define the problem, and the conflict in positions is usually a conflict between needs, desires, concerns, and fears. Interests are the motivators behind positions, and identifying them allows for alternative positions that satisfy mutual interests. Dirschel (1993, p. 164) explains:

Identify the facts and feelings behind each side's desires and concerns. Behind opposing positions often lie shared and compatible interests. If the focus is on positions rather than interests, the parties will have difficulty brainstorming other options, because they will be intent on keeping their bottom-line positions.

3. *Invent options for mutual gain.* Having only one answer to a dispute is counterproductive and leads to negotiations along a single dimension. Wiser decision making involves a process of selection from a large number of possible solutions. The more options identified, the more chances there are for creative, productive solutions for all parties concerned.

Successful negotiations that result in several options are often impeded by seeking the single answer because it is believed that resolution to discord requires narrowing the gap between positions rather than broadening the options available. Negotiations that are bound by a "fixed-pie" approach also dictate win-lose battles because there are only a few good options to go around. (The fixed-pie approach is based on the assumption that options for resolution of a conflict are limited, as opposed to believing that creative thinking can lead to more and better options.)

The process of brainstorming is one method to invent options without judging them. Participants in the exercise are encouraged to identify as many ideas as possible without judgment or criticism. Attempts should be made to invent ideas that meet shared interests. These interests need to be explicit and stated as goals.

4. *Insist on using objective criteria.* To ensure a wise agreement between opposing wills involves negotiation on some basis of objective criteria. These criteria need to be based on a fair standard and, ideally, be prepared in advance of the agreement. Discussion of the criteria, rather than of positions to be gained or lost, allows for deferment to a fair solution instead of bruised egos and hurt relationships.

Fisher et al (1992, p. 14) conclude that, "In contrast to positional bargaining, the principled negotiation method of focusing on basic interests, mutually satisfying options, and fair standards typically results in a wise agreement. The method permits you to reach a gradual consensus on a joint decision efficiently without all the transactional costs of digging in to positions only to have to dig yourself out of them."

The settings in which nurses practice and teach will continue to require expertise in conflict resolution as the challenges of transforming health care continue. According to Kritek (1994), negotiating often occurs at an "uneven table," at which some participants are at a disadvantage that others do not acknowledge. Uneven tables represent situations in which the assurance of justice, equity, or fairness is uncertain or unlikely. The nurse is challenged to recognize conflict as an impetus to change that requires personal growth, while choosing a method of conflict resolution depends on personal style and the situation. The recommendations outlined in Box 7-1 are useful no matter what method you use to resolve the conflict.

According to Rhode (1996), the steps to reaching a positive solution begin with identifying the parties involved in the conflict. It is important to get all parties to list, in writing, their positions (what is wanted) and their interests (why it is wanted). This fosters understanding of positions taken because of vested interests and hidden agendas. Shared interests can serve as common denominators in the resolution process. A climate of trust can be established by open communication, with parties using "I" statements as personal ownership of positions and problems. Rules that prohibit zapping, backstabbing, and sarcasm enhance trust. Yelling and aggressive body language violate that trust.

BOX **7-1**   Steps to Conflict Resolution

1. Determine whose conflict it is.
2. Identify a common denominator.
3. Set a climate of trust.
4. Separate the people from the problem.
5. Stay in the present and the future.
6. Stick to the topic at hand.
7. Brainstorm options.
8. Develop objective criteria for evaluating options.
9. Look for consensus.

Separating the person from the problem allows for addressing the problem without attacking the person involved. Personal attacks impede communication and conflict resolution. Past injustices and hurt feelings have no place in resolving present conflicts; therefore, stay in the present and focus only on the problem at hand. Use the process to identify ways to make sure the problem does not reoccur in the future.

The temptation may be to tackle more than one problem at a time. However, success depends on the ability to stick to the topic at hand and handle only one conflict at a time. Finally, in looking for consensus, it is useful to remember that if 75% of the parties involved agree, and a maximum of 25% dissent but agree to support the solution, a resolution can be reached.

A Tool Kit for Survival in Times of Conflict

As discussed in this chapter, conflict may occur in a concentric fashion, beginning with intrapersonal conflict that radiates to interpersonal conflict, intergroup conflict, and the overarching conflict that encompasses organizational discord. Regardless of the source of the conflict, a nurse will be facilitated in his or her response if a set of skills are identified and practiced as tools for survival in the face of conflict. The identified steps to conflict resolution focus on managing or resolving the conflict; the tools identified here are broader life-enhancing skills that are illustrated through the scenarios used in the chapter.

ANOTHER PERSON'S REALITY DOES NOT DICTATE MY RESPONSE

The nurse who was challenged in her role of competent caregiver was in fact dealing with the internal thoughts and feelings of a nurse caring for a teenager both in the workplace and at home. In this situation, the reality of adolescence is one of tumultuous emotions, testing behaviors, and skewed values. All adults who interact with teenagers need to communicate clearly in as few words as possible. This leaves little room for miscommunication and recognizes the often-short attention span that accompanies adolescence. Positive behavior should be acknowledged and the consequences for poor choices clearly identified. Then, the nurse or adult must let go. Everyone has the right to learn from experience.

SIMPLE SOLUTIONS ARE OFTEN JUST THAT—SIMPLE

The nurse manager who was operating on the linear path of "right and wrong" and "fairness and injustice" was seeking a single solution to a complex problem. In fact, nurses often, in the interest of time and preservation of energy, address what seems to be the problem at hand when in fact the problem is symptomatic of several more complicated issues. Inevitably these issues will surface in many forms and demand attention. It is important to remember that there are few, if any, simple fixes, and an effective nurse has the skill to recognize that people and problems exist in many realms, often all at once. Therefore he or she can "apply a Band-Aid while recognizing that surgery is needed."

I CAN LEARN FROM PEOPLE I DON'T LIKE

The nursing staff development person astutely recognized the untenable situation that senior hospital administration helped to create. A "know-it-all" may be unpleasant to work with, but this does not mean that his or her work contributions are not valuable, nor does it mean that the task at hand does not have to be accomplished. Therefore the staff development person is not charged with the responsibility of forming a cohesive, loving group. Instead, he or she is responsible for setting the ground rules of identifying shared goals, valuing everyone's input, and clarifying misperceptions. People have to be reminded that they can learn from someone they don't like and that they don't have to "invite that person home for dinner."

CONCLUSION

This chapter was not meant to suggest one method of conflict resolution. Instead, varied strategies were presented to assist nurses in coping with intrapersonal, interpersonal, intergroup, and organizational conflict. The nurse will need to be able to reduce disharmony within an internal set of values, needs, and perceptions as they are called into question by an increasingly complex, differentiated system of health care delivery. Competence in managing interpersonal and organizational discord will be essential as work groups become more diverse and the chance for differing viewpoints increases. Nurses can play a pivotal role in facilitating an environment in which conflict is used to enhance the exploration of new approaches and alternatives to problems.

REFERENCES

Brinkman, R. & Kirschner, R. (1994). *Dealing with people you can't stand.* New York: McGraw-Hill.

Dirschel, K. (1993). Dynamics of conflict, and conflict management. In D.J. Mason, S.W. Talbott, & J.K. Leavitt (Eds.). *Policy and politics for nurses* (2nd ed.). Philadelphia: W.B. Saunders.

Fisher, R., Ury, W., & Patton, B. (1992). *Getting to yes: Negotiating agreement without giving in* (2nd ed.). New York: Penguin.

Kritek, P.B. (1994). *Negotiating at an uneven table.* San Francisco: Jossey-Bass.

Marquis, B. & Hurston, C. (1994). *Management decision-making for nurses* (2nd ed). New York: J. B. Lippincott.

Rhode, H. (1996). *Conflict resolution and confrontation skills.* Boulder, CO: CareerTrack.

Roe, S. (1995). Managing your work setting: Positive work relationships, conflict management, and negotiations. In K.W. Vestal (Ed.). *Nursing management: Concepts and issues* (2nd ed.). Philadelphia: J.B. Lippincott.

Ury, W. (2000). *The third side: Why we fight and how we can stop.* New York: Penguin.

Coalitions: A Powerful Political Strategy

REBECCA RICE

"When spider webs unite, they can tie up a lion."
ETHIOPIAN PROVERB

In the mid-1990s certified nurse midwives (CNMs) in Virginia failed in their first attempt to achieve third-party reimbursement for their services through the state legislature. There were several reasons for their failure. Of 75,000 licensed nurses in Virginia, fewer than 300 are CNMs. Acting alone, these CNMs worked their bill through the legislative process but were blocked by powerful physician groups. And when asked how the nurses' professional association stood on the bill, Virginia Nurses Association spokespersons took no stand, because they were unaware of the bill's existence.

Upon failure of the bill, Virginia nursing leaders took note of what they had done. They had not worked together to deliver a united front to the legislators, and they had failed to support one another. From this experience emerged the Legislative Coalition of Virginia Nurses, which brings together nurses from all specialty areas, nurse educators, nurse administrators, and the professional association to develop a common legislative agenda and strategies for influencing the enactment of legislation favorable to nurses and nursing. Within the first year of the coalition's existence, nurses joined in a collaborative effort with the nurse midwives to gain third-party reimbursement.

This example illustrates the power of coalitions in the political process—bringing people together from diverse perspectives around a single purpose to achieve a common goal. Strength lies in numbers: in working together and in strategizing for success.

BIRTH AND LIFE CYCLE OF COALITIONS

Coalitions almost always arise out of a challenge or opportunity. For example, in 1995 the Robert Wood Johnson Foundation (RWJF) issued a call for proposals for a new national program called *Colleagues in Caring: Regional Collaboratives for Nursing Work Force Development (Colleagues)*. The challenge was to build a nursing workforce with the capacity to adapt to the changes in the nation's health care system and the ability to perform in ways that are at once cost efficient and which continue to protect and improve the health of the public (The Robert J. Wood Foundation, 1995). Applicants for funds had to indicate their commitment to using a collaborative approach through a coalition to achieve the program's goals. The Colleagues experience illustrates many of the attributes and processes associated with coalitions. These include the coalition life cycle; essential ingredients for coalition building and maintenance; and the actual work of the coalition in policy development, implementation, and evaluation.

Coalitions can be short-lived or last many years. Short-lived coalitions form around a single purpose, such as to advocate for a community health center. Once their aim is achieved, they disband. Long-lasting coalitions usually begin around one challenge and then stay together as other challenges emerge. The original 20 Colleagues coalitions have been in existence since 1995, although several had been working for years prior to joining the Colleagues network. For example, the Minnesota Colleagues coalition was formed at the time of the call for proposals. Bringing together nursing leaders representing various constituencies in Minnesota, the drafters of the proposal obtained written commitment from the leaders to forge the coalition that would work on Colleagues goals. On the other hand, the California Strategic Planning Committee for Nursing had been in existence for 3 years before the call for proposals to work on collecting and analyzing data on the nursing workforce. The California coalition members used their existing coalition to form the basis of the Colleagues work in that state.

BUILDING AND MAINTAINING A COALITION: THE PRIMER

ESSENTIAL INGREDIENTS

To build and maintain an effective coalition, three ingredients stand out. They are leadership, membership, and serendipity. First and foremost is *leadership.* Coalitions cannot exist without outstanding leadership. Leaders may exist a priori or may emerge early from coalition membership, but without leaders, coalitions will falter and fade away.

Two types of leaders are critical to coalition work, and rarely are the two types found within one person. No coalition can exist without an inspiring or passionate leader—one who possesses the inner qualities critical to coalition success, such as passion for the coalition's mission and energy to achieve coalition goals. This leader motivates others to participate and meet their obligations. The inspiring leader balances a personal inner drive to move forward while assisting coalition members to solve problems and make decisions, knowing when to steer forward, when to idle, and when to back up if necessary. The leader intuits the sense of the coalition members while continually urging them to remain on target. The leader also works to build leadership capacity in other coalition members. Finally, the leader has a sense of humor and knows when to use it, to defuse situations and help put weighty issues into perspective.

The second type of coalition leader is the organizational leader. This person possesses the skills to keep members on track between meetings, ensures that the communication methods are in place, and follows through on coalition assignments. Depending on the fiscal resources of the coalition, this leader may be compensated for his or her work, whereas other leaders and members may be volunteers (Berkowitz & Wolff, 2000; U.S. Department of Transportation, 2001).

As important as leaders are, they are no more important than the coalition *members,* without whom the coalition would not exist. Members increase the productivity of the coalition: the more members, the more the potential for getting work accomplished (as well as the potential for more conflict). They also increase the visibility of the coalition, because they each represent diverse constituencies and networks. Members learn new skills as part of their membership roles, and these skills can be transferred to their constituent organization. Thus, membership is mutually beneficial for the coalition and the individual (American Association of University Women, 1996; Berkowitz & Wolff, 2000).

Finally, an essential ingredient for coalition success is *serendipity*—the happy occurrence of an opportunity not specifically sought—so long as coalition members take advantage of the serendipitous event or opportunity. Successful coalitions use resources at hand, devise innovative ways to sustain their work, seize opportunities that come along unexpectedly, and are willing to take risks. In order to effectively use serendipity, leaders and members must obligate themselves to conduct continual environmental scans, such as tracking current events, connecting with many different kinds of people, and spending time thinking creatively.

These three ingredients have assisted successful Colleagues sites to take wing. The very successful Colleagues sites have incredible leaders and members. Leadership is not vested within one person in these coalitions, but in a combination of individuals whose skills complement one another's to create vision, strength, and organization. For example, the

New Jersey Colleagues project is led by Geri Dickson, PhD, RN, and several others who have combined their skills to create and sustain the coalition. The coalition members each contribute time toward the coalition work. Since the inception of the Colleagues program, they have successfully advocated for enhanced supply data collection from the NJ Board of Nursing. With funds awarded by the Helene Fuld Trust, they are enhancing educational mobility in the state. They have cultivated a relationship with a state senator to sponsor a bill that would create a nursing workforce center in New Jersey. The coalition members participate in project work groups that have been successful in achieving additional project outcomes such as the development of an integrated competency model for the nursing workforce.

Successful Colleagues projects have also seized on serendipitous opportunities. The Kansas City (KC) Colleagues have created an entrepreneurial nonprofit enterprise known as Health Resource Partners, a web-based workforce development center that provides an on-line job search platform, educational and career guidance resources, and on-line registration for health care community events. Most of the start-up funding for Health Resource Partners and other KC Colleagues work has been provided by a fund trustee in KC who has developed a special bond with the KC nurses. Another example of serendipity involves the North Central West Virginia Nursing Network. When the U.S. Veterans Administration (VA) health system moved to require a baccalaureate degree for RNs, the West Virginia Colleagues coalition seized the opportunity to develop a multi-entry, multiple-exit, regional educational mobility system to assist the nurses employed at the Clarksburg Veterans Administration Medical Center. Thus, VA nurses can select from a variety of educational programming leading to the baccalaureate or master's degrees. In reality, this program is helping all RNs in the region to meet their educational needs.

COALITION STRUCTURE

Structure refers to the organization of the coalition, and it defines the procedures by which the coalition operates. The structure serves the members, not the other way around. It also includes how members are accepted, how leadership is chosen, how decisions are made, and how differences are mediated (Berkowitz & Wolff, 2000, National Network for Health, 2000). Coalitions operate using group process, meaning that they go through a life cycle that involves "norming and storming" (creating group behavioral norms and settling disagreements) before working together. Having a structure helps to provide a framework for the processing that must take place in order for the coalition to be active and successful.

Coalition structure, while necessary, is difficult to determine. Some structures will be tight, with formal committees, task forces, or work groups and communication mechanisms; others will be more loosely structured, with shared leadership and work done by ad hoc groups. Moreover, the structure changes with time. For example, at the outset of the Colleagues program, most sites structured their activities around the five major goals of the program: data, prediction modeling, practice/education issues, consortium building, and sustainability. The more-structured projects subdivided each of these goals into other work groups, so that the data group might have two or three different subgroups—one for demand, one for supply, and one for need. Over time, however, many of these work groups found they were duplicating efforts and collapsed their work into more streamlined entities. On the other hand, some work groups may decide that the scope of their charge is too broad for one group, and they subdivide to achieve better results. The New Jersey Colleagues project has a work group on recruitment, retention, and leadership. To become more productive, this group divided into three separate working areas.

Coalition structure should make provisions for a governance group. This is especially true if the size exceeds approximately 15 people. Beyond this number, the group becomes too large for effective, efficient decision making. The governance structure should, at the very least, include all committee and work group chairs to facilitate communication among the various parts of the coalition. The governing committee should represent the diversity of the coalition members (Proteous, 1995; Berkowitz & Wolff, 2000). In the Colleagues program, there is a constant requirement that leadership be shared between practice and education. All work groups must be cochaired by a nursing service leader and an educator. This is a deliberate strategy to keep education and service together to resolve nursing workforce issues.

No matter what the groups call themselves or how they structure themselves to accomplish their work, the important factor to achievement is to have appropriate support systems. Someone must agree to do a task, and that someone should have the means to get the task done. The work may be done by volunteers, as it is in many coalitions. However, there may be consequences to all-volunteer efforts. The compensation is always zero, and that, unfortunately, may also be the outcome. On the other hand, a paid support system can deliver on the tasks and move the coalition along more effectively.

DECISION MAKING

Decision making is a source of great concern, usually in the beginning of a coalition's life. Because people joining a coalition represent different constituencies, there is a natural lack of trust among members. Everyone wants to protect his or her own turf. As the coalition decides on its mission and goals, it also has to figure out how it will make its decisions. Almost always within coalitions, decisions are made without votes (Berkowitz & Wolff, 2000). It is more common for the members to simply agree or disagree. Voting connotes a formal rigid structure that rarely exists in coalitions.

Most of the Colleagues coalitions chose early in their work to make decisions by consensus. The South Dakota Colleagues project developed a set of group norms that indicated the majority of decisions would be made in this manner. "Each member must be able to live with the decision, even though the desired outcome may not be achieved exactly as intended" (South Dakota Colleagues in Caring, 1996). What has evolved among the Colleagues sites is a process that involves discussion, outlining of diverse points of view, evaluation of the pros and cons of actions, and then a decision by a nodding of heads on the next course of action. There is usually the sense that "we'll give it a try, and if it doesn't work, we'll go back to the drawing board."

MEETINGS

Coalitions have to meet. Otherwise, the work doesn't get done. People come to coalition meetings for at least two reasons—to get work done and to make social connections. The meetings must combine both, in just the right combination, to keep people coming back.

From the work angle, the leaders should create an agenda and circulate it before the meeting. Agenda items should be assigned time slots, and the leader should stick to the schedule. The leader should also make certain that all members know about the disposition of decisions made: what they were, who is in charge of accomplishing them, the timeframe for accomplishment, and the expected outcome.

From the social side, leaders should build in time for mingling either before or after the meeting. Having food is good. Leaders should greet members enthusiastically and allow opportunities for laughing and sharing.

Timing is very important. The time interval between meetings should be long enough that work can be accomplished between meetings with reports on accomplishments made at the meetings. If the interval is too long between meetings, little work will get done, as the human response is to wait until right before a meeting to get one's work done.

The content of the meeting should be focused on problem solving and decision making. A good meeting has energy. If the meeting is primarily conducted to exchange information, some members will see this as a waste of their time, and they may choose to drop out. Alternatives such as e-mail exist for disseminating information. Consequently, coalition leaders and members should regularly assess the content of the meetings to see what works and what doesn't work and to make necessary adjustments.

PROMOTING THE COALITION

What good is a coalition if no one knows it exists? Coalitions are formed to advance a common agenda, and communication is the vehicle with which that agenda is advanced. Early on in the coalition's life, members must develop and implement a communications plan aimed at getting the coalition's message out to the broader community of interest.

The advantages of publicizing the work of the coalition are twofold, both internal and external to the coalition. Internally, publicity attracts members. When others hear about the work that the coalition is doing, they may join because they want to be associated with an active group. Publicity also attracts resources, such as financial support. Further, publicity is needed for growth. Without others knowing what it is doing, the coalition will die.

Externally, publicity achieves its most vital purpose, and that is to reach the people that the coalition needs to reach in order to get its work done. For example, one of the goals of the Colleagues program relates to sustaining the work when Foundation funding ceases. Several Colleagues sites have been able to get bills introduced in their state legislatures to fund a nursing workforce center. This achievement would have been impossible without adequate publicity of their accomplishments. The Mississippi Colleagues site, through the lobbying efforts of the Mississippi Nurses Association, was successful in obtaining $150,000 to support an office of nursing workforce development. This too would have failed if the coalition had not promoted the work that had already been done—expanding and improving nursing workforce data collection and analysis, developing a career counseling system for nurses in transition, and developing and implementing a competency model for nurses at all levels of education.

FUNDING

Coalition work takes money. Some coalitions run on little or no money, using the time and talent of their members. These coalitions may be unable to sustain their work over the long haul because of lack of resources. Most coalitions require funds to pay for staff and buy the necessary resources to achieve coalition goals. Where does the money come from?

Membership dues help to fund the coalition. Dues may be modest and on a sliding scale, depending on the resources of the representative constituencies. Requiring dues helps to get buy-in from the members: "If I'm paying for it, I'd better be there."

Generally speaking, however, coalitions may need to look for additional sources of funds to stay solvent and accomplish their work. How much money is needed depends on several factors. First are the mission and aims of the coalition. A strategic plan will point to the resources needed, and then members can decide on how to best obtain the funds they need. Accompanying the strategic plan, the members must develop a fundraising plan that would include tailoring the message to prospective funding sources, assigning people to make the contacts, communicating the mission and aims of the coalition, and seeking funding.

Where are the sources of funds for coalition work? If the coalition or a member organization has charitable tax exempt status, foundations and individuals will more likely be encouraged to contribute. Coalition members may also look for grant opportunities, either through the public or private sector. This means that resources must be freed up to write proposals for grants. It takes money to get money.

The Colleagues coalitions that received RWJF funding had to provide matching funding from the outset to receive Foundation money. Some of that match has always come from in-kind support of members, including time, copying expenses, payment for telephone calls, development and maintenance of websites, hosting of meetings, and so on. Other sources of funds have come from membership contributions to the coalition. Still others have come from other grantors, such as the Helene Fuld Trust and the Murdock Trust, which fund selected portions of the coalitions' work.

EVALUATING COALITION EFFECTIVENESS

Evaluation should be both formative and summative and should occur at regular intervals. The coalition is created to bring diverse groups of people together around a common cause. From a formative perspective, the coalition should assess whether the right members are at the table. Who is missing? Are all equal players? Why or why not? Members should look at the work of the coalition. How is it being accomplished? Is there a better way? What is it? How would we know? Where are the barriers and facilitators?

From a summative perspective, annually the coalition should evaluate whether it has achieved its goals set out for the year. Which have been achieved? Why? Why not? Are the goals still relevant to the mission of the coalition? What needs to be changed?

When the Colleagues program first started, the major emphasis of the first two goals was assessing and predicting the capacity of the nursing workforce to meet the population's health care needs. For most coalitions these goals took priority: How could one propose changes in practice and education if one did not know about the supply, demand, and need for nursing in one's region? In some states, adequate systems were in place for data analysis, and these coalitions moved rapidly to make sets of recommendations for education and practice. This was the case in South Carolina and South Dakota, which have rich data on the nursing workforce. However, this was not the case in most of the Colleagues sites, where little or no supply and demand data were available. Since the inception of the program, however, the balance of supply and demand has changed, and the demand for nursing has risen tremendously at the same time that the supply is decreasing. Hence, the coalitions have been more successful in advancing the need for data than they were in the earlier years of the program. Some have been able to advocate for legislative changes that will require state boards of nursing to expand their data collection activities.

In most cases, their data work is still not totally complete; however, the Colleagues coalitions are now moving forward on other components of their mission and goals. This includes work in educa-tional mobility and work environment issues. Hence, the coalitions use an evaluative process to reformulate priorities for action.

PITFALLS AND CHALLENGES

Coalitions usually start out with a flurry of excitement and activity. Leadership plays a critical role in sustaining the excitement and guiding the activity. Nevertheless, coalition work is difficult and complex, with lots of challenges. Here are some common pitfalls and challenges, with suggestions for overcoming them.

FAILURE TO GET THE RIGHT PEOPLE TO PARTICIPATE

Coalitions attract those who are most interested in seeing that the work gets done, and these members will commit to participating in the coalition. There may be a broad array of other stakeholders who may be interested in the coalition's mission but will not become members. These may include constituencies related to nursing such as insurers, hospital executive officers, consumers, and business leaders. These people want nursing to be the best it can be because the health of the population depends on good nursing care. To engage these stakeholders, the coalition must develop a plan that includes regular communication with these individuals. The coalition should also assign members to present the coalition's work face-to-face with the broad community.

PERSISTENT DISTRUST AMONG COALITION MEMBERS

Distrust is perhaps one of the thorniest challenges that coalition leaders face, because much of the success of coalitions comes from the ongoing interaction among members that allays misperceptions and builds trust. Two examples of sources of distrust include member disengagement and perceived member inequality or unworthiness. When members become disengaged from coalition work, their absence can derail progress, especially if they fail to keep their own constituencies informed. Another source of distrust emanates from long-standing perceived inequalities among members, such as active membership of licensed practical nurses or certified nursing assistants in a nursing coalition. To overcome distrust, leaders and members must work diligently on including these potentially disenfranchised members. To achieve inclusion, leaders may meet individually with these individuals, seeking their advice and asking for their assistance in the mission of the coalition. In the end, people must feel valued or treasured for all their participation and contributions to the enterprise.

BEING CONTROL FREAKS AND PROTECTING TURF

The tendency to hold control and "turf" can happen at the individual member level and at the coalition level. At the individual level, there are those in whom coalition success breeds a new brand of person—one who knows "the truth" and is always willing to share it. These individuals need to be gathered back into the fold and made to feel that their ideas are worthy, but at the same time, they must understand that they do not possess all the answers to the work at hand.

The same holds true at the coalition level, when coalitions become successful and an upstart coalition or other group appears to be invading the coalition's territory. This is a time for reflection among coalition members. Are the coalitions competing? Why is another group forming? What does this all mean? Are there opportunities for collaboration among the coalitions? Or a joining of forces?

Colleagues coalitions have had many opportunities to evaluate the work of other groups related to nursing workforce issues, and with the nurse shortage, these opportunities are increasing. For example, the Connecticut Colleagues project emerged at a time when several other groups were involved in workforce initiatives. Over the past few years, the Colleagues coalition has carved out its work to be more discrete from other initiatives in the state, while increasing its share of expertise in the areas that it does well. The Colleagues coalition is seen as the repository for supply and demand data on the nursing workforce. In addition, the coalition has established a systematic method for analyzing these data and making recommendations

from them. Other Colleagues work, such as that related to educational mobility, is vested with the Connecticut League for Nursing's committee on educational articulation, which reports its activities to the coalition.

POOR HANDLING OF DIFFERENT PERSPECTIVES

By their very nature, coalitions consist of individuals representing constituencies with differing perspectives on issues. For example, hospital associations are concerned with maintaining an adequate nursing workforce to preserve patient safety and quality of care, but at the same time, they must be pragmatic about the economic viability of their member hospitals. Also concerned with safety and quality patient care, nurses' associations advocate to safeguard the practice of individual nurses. Sometimes the two organizational perspectives conflict, as in cases of the use of mandatory overtime or staffing ratios. These two organizations are representative of only two perspectives of nursing coalitions, yet both are vested in safe, quality patient care.

If coalition goals are meaningful and relevant, all members have a vested interest in keeping the coalition together. Therefore, all have a responsibility to see that they stay focused on the mission and goals, while appreciating differences in their perspectives. Sometimes staying focused is easier when coalitions are grassroots phenomena, with local or regional interests. In these coalitions, many members may in fact be bona fide members of several constituent groups. For example, in the Colleagues coalitions, it is not uncommon for an individual coalition member to be a member of the nurses' association as well as the nurse executive organization, a specialty nursing organization, and perhaps one other group. Consequently, maintaining a strict position representing one association becomes a difficult task.

The task of appreciating differences while moving forward on meeting coalition goals is easier if members commit to attend meetings and join in the work of the coalition. That said, coalition leaders have a responsibility for seeking diversity of opinions at meetings and working toward achieving decisions with which members can live. It may be that some strategies have to be abandoned because the coalition cannot achieve consensus on issues. Or there may be situations in which members will agree to disagree and conduct their disagreements in the open without rancor. This latter situation can happen when members respect one another, having worked together over time in the coalition.

FAILURE TO ACT

Coalitions begin with fire in their bellies. Unfortunately, going from words to action is sometimes more difficult than members had originally thought. Some coalitions formulate and reformulate action plans ad infinitum without getting to the action piece. However, action is the coalition's currency. Without action, there will be no funds to support the work. The failure to move forward most probably resides with weak leadership, and the resolution may need to be a coup d'etat to replace that leadership. At some point members will have to determine that they are not moving forward. Then they leave, they arrange a takeover, or they assist the leaders to moving toward action.

LOSING BALANCE

Coalition leaders and members wear out. Managing, leading, and working in a coalition drain energy. All members are entitled to personal lives and must know that they do not have to keep their coalition jobs for life. Each person must assess his or her readiness to step aside and support the leadership and membership activities of new incumbents. Thus, coalitions should set in place a means for distributing the leadership at regular intervals.

POLITICAL WORK OF COALITIONS

Should coalitions speak out on issues that matter to them? Should nursing coalitions speak out for nursing? Of course. But advocacy work has its up sides and down sides.

REASONS TO ADVOCATE

If policy is enacted into law or other goals are achieved, the reason for the coalition may cease to exist. In other words, the coalition may have done its job. Many of the Colleagues coalitions are seeking to have state-legislated centers for nursing workforce development. These centers would analyze data about supply and demand, make recommendations for nursing education and practice, and broker arrangements that would facilitate the implementation of these recommendations. The public would be well served by a nursing workforce that is adequately prepared to care for it, in whatever format that preparation should take. If the centers are successfully put in place while offering a forum for diverse opinions and perspectives, the need for the Colleagues coalition will cease.

REASONS NOT TO ADVOCATE

When coalitions advocate for a certain position, they anger those who are opposed to that position. The further coalitions go out on the limb, the more people line up to saw off the limb. In fact, coalitions stand to lose their financial support if they go too far. In addition, there are legal restrictions on advocacy by tax-exempt groups in lobbying, so coalitions may be forced to pull back if they become too forcefully active.

HOW TO ADVOCATE WITH GRACE

The solution, of course, is to proceed with care. Advocacy, by its very nature, involves risk. Coalition members should work out their differences and carefully select the words they will use when advocating for positions. The coalition members should agree in advance the advocacy approaches they will take that will not jeopardize their legal status as well as disenfranchise funders and members. Here are some effective approaches, using the five Rs (derived from Berkowitz & Wolff, 2000).

- *The right preparation.* Advocating spokespersons should know their facts by researching the issue and doing their homework. When presenting, members should know what they want to say and how to say it.

- *The right communicator.* The coalition should select the right persons to deliver the message. These individuals should be media savvy, knowledgeable on the issues, and able to communicate with the intended audiences. Building relationships with the audiences in the community is very important.
- *The right message.* The coalition should agree on the message that will be given. The messengers should state clearly why decision makers should adopt their point of view, show why those reasons are in the decision makers' own best interests, back up their reasons with facts, and give successful examples of similar decisions made.
- *The right request.* The coalition should decide itself on which requests will be made to whom and when. At the time of request delivery, the requests should be feasible for the decision maker to act on. These requests may be for legislative initiatives, support for a community-based program, or any other aim of the coalition.
- *Repetition.* The coalition should start back at the beginning and repeat as necessary. This means that each coalition initiative will most likely need an iterative process while working on its goals. For example, in 2001, the Hawaii Colleagues project supported the Hawaii Nurses Association's lobby for a nursing workforce center in Hawaii. The bill failed in its first submission; however, the constituencies are working on strategies to advocate for the center in the next legislative session.

CONCLUSION

Coalition work can be extremely exciting and fulfilling. In bringing together individuals who represent varying perspectives, coalitions can achieve their goals through active involvement of these diverse members and their constituencies. Leaders must emerge or be selected who are passionate about the cause and who can simultaneously attend to detail and create an organized structure for the coalition work. Coalitions must meet regularly and take action on their decisions. In the end, coalitions must advocate for their mission. Nursing coalitions must advocate for nursing, knowing that nursing is critical to the public's health care needs. Coalitions must continually reinvigorate and reinvent themselves if they are to sustain their work.

Resources

American Association of Colleges of Nursing. (1998). *A guide to grassroots activism: Moving nursing education's public policy agenda* (2nd ed.). Washington, DC: Author.

Glotzbach, P.A. (2001, May-June). Conditions of collaboration. *Academe,* 16-21.

Gray, J.E. (1996). *Systems change, coalition building, and collaboration.* Available online at www.usc.edu/dept/gero/hmap/ libarary/blueprint.html.

University of South Florida. (1999). *Barriers to coalition building & strategies to overcome them.* Available online at hsc.usf.edu/ ~kmbrown/ Barriers_to_Coalition_Building/htm.

White, J.A. & Wehlage, G. (1995). Community collaboration: If it is such a good idea, why is it so hard to do? *Educational Evaluation and Policy Analysis, 17*(1), 23-38.

REFERENCES

American Association of University Women. (1996). *Coalition tips.* Available online at www.aauw.org/1000/tipsbd.html.

Berkowitz, B. & Wolff, T. (2000). *The spirit of the coalition.* Washington, DC: American Public Health Association.

National Network for Health. (2000). *Building a coalition.* Available online at www.nnh.org/immunization/immun79.htm.

Proteous, S. (1995). *Coalition building* [On-line]. Available online at protest.net/activistshandbook/coalition.html.

The Robert J. Wood Foundation. (1995). *Colleagues in Caring: Regional collaboratives for nursing* (application instructions). Princeton, NJ: The Robert J. Wood Foundation.

South Dakota Colleagues in Caring. (1996, September). Consortium meeting minutes. Unpublished manuscript.

U.S. Department of Transportation. (2001). *Community how-to guide on coalition building.* Available online at www.nhtsa.dot.gov/people/outreach.

Success Through Unity: A Coalition's Efforts to Expand the U.S. Military Health Program

Susan M. Schwartz & Mary W. Chaffee

"Let us endeavor to preserve the health of those who bravely enter the field of battle or expose themselves on the boisterous ocean in defense of their country."

Surgeon Edward Cutbush

In October 2000 when the budgets of most health care organizations were being tightly controlled, the U.S. Congress approved sweeping changes that expanded the Department of Defense (DoD) health program. Clearly, powerful forces were involved to drive through such extensive policy change. In this case, one of the most effective forces was a politically skillful coalition: The Military Coalition. This coalition successfully shepherded legislative language through the 106th Congress that has been referred to as a "tsunami of change" by Vice Admiral Michael Cowan, Surgeon General of the U.S. Navy.

Policy change such as this occurs when a problem reaches the agenda of policymakers and a window of opportunity for change opens. In this case, the unified voices of many U.S. military retirees brought a highly charged, emotional issue to the attention of elected representatives. Additionally, the political environment was ripe for change to occur.

THE POLICY PROBLEM

Members of the U.S. uniformed services and their families are eligible to receive generous health benefits while serving on active duty and upon retirement from uniformed service. However, before 2001, military retirees, their spouses, and their survivors "aged out" of some military health care benefits at age 65. On reaching the age of Medicare eligibility, these individuals lost eligibility for the health benefits through the military health system that they had received for most of a lifetime.

Many inequities in the U.S. health care system do not receive attention. Military retirees drew attention to their cause by tapping into well-developed political skills, effective teamwork, and savvy grass roots political organizing, all coordinated through an experienced coalition. Nothing less could have convinced Congress to expand health care coverage so generously.

U.S. DEPARTMENT OF DEFENSE HEALTH PROGRAM

To appreciate the scope of this health policy change requires an understanding of the U.S. Department of Defense health program. The U.S. Air Force, Army, and Navy jointly operate an integrated, worldwide health system with two missions:

1. To provide *peacetime* health care to approximately 8 million active duty service members, their families, military retirees, spouses and survivors
2. To be ready to respond to *wartime* health care demands anytime, anywhere

The Army, Navy, and Air Force operated medical centers, hospitals, clinics, and other health care delivery sites around the world. When military medical facilities did not have the capacity to provide care or did not have necessary specialty care available before 1995, military patients received civilian services through the Civilian Health and Medical Program for the Uniformed Services (CHAMPUS). CHAMPUS provided traditional fee-for-service health insurance benefits for family members and retired military members and their families until they reached the age of 65 (or became entitled to Medicare Part A).

In the 1980s and 1990s, the military health system suffered the same problem that plagued the civilian health system: rapidly escalating costs. But it also was troubled by problems unknown in the civilian sector: military base closures ordered by Congress (and the closure of their health facilities) and a mandate to shrink the size of the staffs of the military medical departments without comprising the quality of care.

In response to the challenge of maintaining medical combat readiness while providing high-quality peacetime health care for all eligible personnel, TRICARE (Figure 8-1), a regionally managed health care program integrating the Air Force, Army, and Navy health systems, was introduced in 1995 (*An introduction to TRICARE,* 2001). TRICARE transformed the Defense Health Program into a contracted partnership between the military medical system and a civilian network of providers and facilities. This partnership was created to ensure access to quality health services in a managed care environment that would control cost (Chaffee & Mills, 2001).

The vital link that ensures the military readiness of the United States, TRICARE now:

* Provides health care for more than 8 million active duty military personnel, retirees, family members, and survivors who are eligible for military health care
* Has more than 4 million people enrolled in an HMO-like benefit, TRICARE Prime
* Has more than 160,000 military health system personnel who operate 80 military hospitals and 513 clinics worldwide
* Has more than 161,000 providers, 2,000 facilities, and 28,000 pharmacies in the TRICARE civilian network (*TRICARE stakeholders' report,* 2001).

TRICARE, designed to improve access, maintain high quality standards, and control cost, was not congressionally mandated to provide services for one age group, though: military retirees, their spouses, and their survivors who had reached their 65th birthday or were otherwise entitled to Medicare Part A. This was a source of great discontent, frustration, and anger for individuals who had served their country, spent most of their lifetime receiving health services through a single system,

and felt they had been promised "health care for life" by the U.S. military.

This festering dissatisfaction drove the efforts of a coalition that would achieve a seemingly impossible legislative goal: the expansion of the military health system to provide health care and pharmacy services for an additional 1.4 million retirees and their families who had previously lost their eligibility for some benefits.

Political Considerations

Congress enacts no program of this magnitude without great pressure. What were the political factors involved that would compel Congress to spend billions of dollars to expand health care benefits to a relatively small group of citizens?

The Broken Promise

Until the early 1990s, the government recruited service members with a promise of free lifetime health care benefits for them and their family members in return for their service of 20 or more years in uniform. Military retirees argued that the government had violated its promise of free lifetime health care by requiring them to use Medicare on reaching age 65. This loss of benefits was construed as unfair because all other federal retirees kept their right to access employer-sponsored health care on reaching age 65. Military service members were the only federal employees to lose this benefit owing to "aging out." Thus, the debate arose in the second session of the 106th Congress (a group facing the pressure of an approaching election) around the question of equity and keeping faith with military retirees. Expansion of retiree health benefits, proponents argued, was critical to demonstrate that the military does indeed keep its word and to assist recruiters in persuading young men and women to join the uniformed services.

2001 NATIONAL DEFENSE AUTHORIZATION ACT

Congress passed the 2001 National Defense Authorization Act (NDAA-01) in October 2000, and President Clinton signed it into law (P.L. 106-398). To remedy the "broken promise," the bill includes provisions to significantly expand health benefits for

Figure 8-1   The TRICARE logo.

Medicare-eligible military retirees. This historic achievement, the single greatest legislative victory for military retirees in 50 years, was brought about by years of effort by military and veterans' service organizations, congressional sponsors, grass roots networks, and individual activists as well as the skillful efforts of The Military Coalition.

THE MILITARY COALITION

The Military Coalition is a politically powerful advocacy organization composed of 31 organizations representing more than 5.5 million members of the uniformed services—active, reserve, and retired members plus survivors and veterans (and their families). Through the Military Coalition, each member organization, with its own program and purposes, unites with others to provide advocacy and representation for the collective memberships on Capitol Hill and within the Department of Defense.

The Military Coalition's Genesis

In 1985 several uniformed services organizations joined forces to oppose the Gramm-Rudman-Hollings deficit reduction law, which would have reduced military retiree pay by 22.5%. The group's success in getting the law repealed encouraged them to form a permanent advocacy group. The Military Coalition was thus formed to work for quality-of-life issues for active, retired, Reserve, and National Guard service members, veterans, their families, and their survivors.

During its 15-year history, the Military Coalition has advocated for issues that have had a profound effect on members of the uniformed services community. The Military Coalition's philosophy holds that by working together on issues of mutual agreement, the participating organizations can harness the grass roots support of more than 5.5 million members plus their families and accomplish far more than the individual groups could by working on these initiatives separately. Passage of NDAA-01 culminated the coalition's long-standing lobbying campaign to rectify inequitable treatment of Medicare-eligible uniformed service retirees and their families.

Members of the Military Coalition

Air Force Association (AFA)
Air Force Sergeants Association (AFSA)
Army Aviation Association of America (AAAA)
Association of Military Surgeons of the United States (AMSUS)
Association of the United States Army (AUSA)
Chief Warrant Officer and Warrant Officer Association of the United States Coast Guard (CWO & WOA)
Commissioned Officers Association of the United States Public Health Service, Inc. (COA)
Enlisted Association of the National Guard of the United States (EANGUS)
Fleet Reserve Association (FRA)
Gold Star Wives of America (GSW)
Jewish War Veterans of the United States of America (JWV)
Marine Corps League (MCL)
Marine Corps Reserve Officers Association (MCROA)
Military Chaplains Association of the United States of America (MCA)
Military Order of the Purple Heart
National Guard Association of the United States (NGAUS)
National Military Family Association (NMFA)
National Order of Battlefield Commissions (NOBC)
Naval Enlisted Reserve Association (NERA)
Naval Reserve Association (NRA)
Navy League of the United States (NLUS)
Non Commissioned Officers Association (NCOA)
Reserve Officers Association (ROA)
The Retired Enlisted Association (TREA)
The Retired Officers Association (TROA)
Society of Medical Consultants to the Armed Forces (SMCAF)
United Armed Forces Association (UAFA)
United States Army Warrant Officers Association (USAWOA)
USCG Chief Petty Officers Association (CPOA)
Veterans of Foreign Wars (VFW)
Veterans' Widows International Network

THE POWER OF AN EFFECTIVE COALITION

To achieve success, a coalition's strategies and energies must be carefully focused. In this case, the Military Coalition functioned like a symphony orchestra. Specific political strategies that contributed to

The Military Coalition's Philosophy

By working together on issues of mutual agreement, the participating organizations in the Military Coalition can harness the grass roots support of more than 5.5 million members (and their families) and accomplish far more than one organization can when working on these initiatives separately.

The Military Coalition's Goals

- Maintain a strong national defense by recruiting and retaining skilled and highly capable personnel in the seven uniformed services.
- Maintain uniformed services compensation and benefits at levels sufficient to attract and retain professional uniformed service members for careers in service to the nation.
- Represent the interest of the entire uniformed services community, including members' families and survivors.
- Educate the public on the extraordinary demands and sacrifices associated with a career in the uniformed services and the need to maintain a unique system of compensation and benefits.

its success in expanding the military health benefit in 2000 included the following:

- *Unified strategy.* The Military Coalition developed a unified legislative strategy and message to achieve passage of health care legislation and other issues of importance to the uniformed services community.
- *Power in numbers.* Using the strength of the 31 member organizations, the Military Coalition was able to generate a tremendous groundswell of grass roots clout, focusing the attention of the 106th Congress on the need to restore uniformed services retirees' health care benefits. Elderly Americans are recognized as a powerful voting block. Pressure was on legislators to listen—and act—in the best interest of this vocal and politically active constituency.
- *Grass roots action.* The unity of the Military Coalition members and their ability to generate

tremendous grass roots activity played a major role in NDAA-01 passage. The Military Coalition kept its members informed and educated through publications, Internet contacts, and local chapter meetings. The coalition assisted its 5.5 million members in writing letters, sending e-mails, making phone calls, and making personal contacts with their elected officials. Congress paid attention. These efforts to keep the pressure on Congress, especially in an election year, were essential to the successful passage of NDAA-01.

- *Collaboration.* The Military Coalition organization members publicized one another's initiatives. In addition, a representative of the coalition was frequently on Capitol Hill, meeting with key legislators and committee staff to present the concerns of the uniformed services community.
- *Joint congressional testimony.* In the spring of 2000, the Military Coalition was invited to testify before the House and Senate Armed Services Committees Personnel Subcommittees in hearings regarding retiree health care issues. Testimony presented on behalf of the entire coalition lent greater weight and unanimity to the testimony than if an individual association had presented it.
- *A single message.* Members of the Military Coalition, as well as individual military retirees, lobbied Members of Congress with a plea to "keep the promise." The promise referred to the promise of health care for life that veterans believed had been made to them when they were recruited to military service. This message became the rallying point for the campaign to expand military retirees' health benefits. It was used in testimony, lobbying efforts, and news articles. In an era of sound-bites and short attention spans, it crystallized this campaign into three words.
- *"Don't turn us away from the trough when it is overflowing."* A critical practice in lobbying for a specific policy is being prepared for arguments critical of the policy proposal. A common congressional response to proposals for new

spending is, "Something else would have to be cut to pay for this." The Military Coalition leveraged the federal budget surplus in their efforts to expand TRICARE. In testimony to the House Armed Service Committee's Subcommittee on Military Personnel, the Military Coalition testified, "With a burgeoning budget surplus, our older uniformed services beneficiaries cannot accept lack of funding as a valid reason for Congress' failure to meet it obligation to them" (*Improving access to TRICARE,* 2000).

- *Capitalizing on all sources of support.* Many individuals supported the Military Coalition's efforts to make military retiree health care a major legislative initiative, including the Chairman of the Joint Chiefs of Staff. House and Senate Armed Services committees' staff members worked tirelessly to get the bill through the arduous conference process. Senate Armed Services Committee Chair John Warner (R-VA) and Personnel Subcommittee chair Tim Hutchinson (R-AK) proposed TRICARE for Life (TFL), an expanded health benefit, and guided it through the Senate, even fighting off a point of order challenge by Robert Kerry (D-NB). Congressman Steve Buyer (R-IN) won support for overcoming mandatory spending obstacles by enlisting the support of House Speaker J. Dennis Hastert (R-IL) and Senate Majority Leader Trent Lott (R-MS) by creating the retiree health care trust fund, making "TRICARE for Life" a permanent entitlement funded from the U.S. Treasury.

- *Displaying gratitude.* The Military Coalition displayed its appreciation for the support of Congressional subcommittees and individual Members of Congress by recognizing them in testimony provided before a variety of groups.

THE FRUIT OF THE MILITARY COALITION'S EFFORTS

TRICARE for Life

The health benefit known as TFL permits eligible beneficiaries *permanent* access to TRICARE, as well as a substantial prescription drug benefit through the TRICARE Senior Pharmacy Program (TSRx). Through TFL, TRICARE serves as second-payer to Medicare, which is similar to a "Medigap" supplement covering out-of-pocket expenses. Congress established TFL as a permanent fully funded entitlement and established a retiree health care trust fund funded out of the U.S. Treasury beginning October 1, 2002. Therefore, retiree health care will no longer have to compete with discretionary funding items within the defense budget.

The cost of TFL is expected to range from $4 billion to $6 billion dollars annually. If this retiree health care program were launched as a stand-alone enterprise, it would be comparable in size to a Fortune 500 Company. This initiative means huge savings for military retiree beneficiaries by eliminating the need for them to purchase expensive Medicare supplemental policies. What does this policy change mean for a Medicare-eligible military retiree? The average Medicare-eligible military retiree or spouse will save about $3,000 per year on medical insurance premiums through TFL (The Retired Officers Association, 2001).

TRICARE Senior Pharmacy Benefit Expansion

The Military Coalition lobbied for and attained expanded pharmacy benefits, in addition to the expanded health care services for Medicare-eligible military retirees provided in NDAA-01. On April 1, 2001, the TRICARE Senior Pharmacy program was implemented. This new program limits out-of-pocket cost and provides expanded access to Department of Defense pharmacy programs, to include retail pharmacies and a national mail order service. Dr. J. Jarrett Clinton, Acting Assistant Secretary of Defense for Health Affairs, stated, "Drug therapy for many of our retired service members is one of their greatest and most costly medical needs. This is a comprehensive drug benefit that makes pharmacy care accessible and affordable" (U.S. Department of Defense, 2000).

Significant savings are now available to Medicare-eligible military retirees and families. Prescription medications attained through a military medical pharmacy are available at no cost to the user. The National Mail Order Pharmacy

(NMOP) program offers eligible users the option of mailing in a prescription and obtaining up to a 90-day supply of most medications for $3 for a generic medication or $9 for a brand-name drug. Although there are some quantity and formulary limits, this is an effective way to obtain maintenance drugs. Prescriptions for immediate need can be obtained through a TRICARE network pharmacy (a civilian partner) for a copayment of $3 for generic medications or $9 for brand-name medications for up to a 30-day supply (The Retired Officers Association, 2001).

THE WORK DOESN'T END WHEN THE BILL IS PASSED

The Military Coalition's effort to influence legislation was the first step in the strategy to restore health care benefits to uniformed services retirees. The second step is interpretation of the law and policy implementation. Representatives of the Military Coalition are working closely with TRICARE Management Activity (TMA) and the Office of the Secretary of Defense for Health Affairs (OSD/HA) to develop implementation policies for TRICARE for Life. A challenge the Military Coalition faces is communicating the health benefit changes to its collective members. The Coalition has served as the conduit that the Defense Department used to educate beneficiaries following passage of NDAA-01 in October 2000.

The Military Coalition remains united in its unwavering resolve to ensure that America's commitment to its service members is honored. As the Coalition looks to the future, it will use the lessons learned during the work to expand benefits for Medicare-eligible retirees to guide its next efforts.

REFERENCES

Chaffee, M.W. & Mills, M.E. (2001). Navy medicine: A health care leadership blueprint for the future. *Military Medicine, 166*(3), 240-247.

Improving access to TRICARE and other priority actions necessary to provide equitable health care to the uniformed services community. (2000, March 115). Hearings of the 106th Congress, 2nd Session (testimony of Virginia Torsch and Susan Schwartz).

An introduction to TRICARE. (2001). Available online at www.tricare.osd.mil.

The Retired Officers Association. (2001). *TRICARE for Life— The road to honoring health care commitments.* Available online at www.troa.org.

TRICARE stakeholders' report. (2001). Available online at www.tricare.osd.mil.

U.S. Department of Defense. (2000, December 8). *TRICARE senior pharmacy benefit details announced.* Available online at www.defenslink.mil/news/Dec2000.

Vignette   *Colleen Conway-Welch & Veronica Stephens*

The International Nursing Coalition on Mass Casualty Education

"These are the times that try men's souls."

THOMAS PAINE

A diverse group of nursing leaders joined forces in 2000 to achieve an audacious goal: crafting standard education competencies to prepare *all* nurses to respond effectively to mass casualty situations. The International Nursing Coalition on Mass Casualty Education (INC-MCE, pronounced *ink-mick*), even in its early stages, was remarkably focused on its mission and possessed a sense of urgency that drove the coalition's work. Notably absent in this coalition-building process were some of the demons that often complicate coalition work: power struggles, turf-protection battles, and the advancement of personal agendas. Multiple factors contributed to the rapid growth of this coalition, including a conducive environment, powerful leadership, government direction, adequate funding, and a uniform recognition of the critical need to achieve the coalition's objectives.

THE PROBLEM

A mass casualty event caused by either a natural disaster or an intentional attack is recognized as a significant threat in the United States (Chaffee, Conway-Welch, & Stephens, 2000). In an event with extensive casualties, nurses in all practice settings would likely be called upon to respond. The complexities of responding to a biologic, chemical, or other mass casualty event would demand nursing care and decision making that few nurses are prepared to provide. In the 1960s, when it was recognized that cardiac rhythm could be restored with cardiopulmonary resuscitation, all health care providers began to be trained in how to respond to cardiac arrest. We have now recognized the need to train health care providers to respond effectively to another situation—mass casualty events—and the International Nursing Coalition of Mass Casualty Education is making this vision a reality.

A RIPE ENVIRONMENT

Natural disasters such as earthquakes and hurricanes have challenged the United States in the past to provide emergency care to hundreds or thousands of victims under difficult circumstances. A new threat has emerged: the threat of a mass casualty incident caused by the intentional use of a chemical, biologic, radiologic, nuclear, or high-yield explosive (CBRNE) weapon. CBRNE weapons pose a threat to health, safety, food, property, and the environment.

In the past some have attempted to minimize the potential of a terrorist attack in the United States because of failed past attempts and hoaxes. Actual attacks have indeed occurred, such as the inoculation of some restaurant salad bars in Oregon in 1984, the New York World Trade Center bombing in 1993, the release of Sarin gas in a Japan subway in 1994 and again in 1995, the Oklahoma City bombing in 1996, and the U.S. Embassy bombings in Kenya and Tanzania in 1998 (American College of Emergency Physicians, 2000). The September 11, 2001, terrorist attacks in New York City and at the Pentagon in Virginia should remove any doubt that the United States is at risk of sustaining a large-scale intentional disaster. Although these events were tragic, if a biologic or chemical weapon had also been employed, the effects would have been far worse. The *Washington Post*, in a September 2000 editorial on the threat of bioterrorism, asserted that "a serious attack would likely overwhelm the medical system" (Taking bio-warfare seriously, 2000). Preparing health care providers for the unique demands encountered in mass casualty events is a critical step in ensuring that the health system is not overwhelmed and that the health and safety of the public are protected and maintained.

STEPS IN THE CREATION OF THE COALITION

Government Directives

The first government directive that empowered federal agencies to plan for and react to CBRNE events was crafted in response to the Oklahoma City bombing. This directive, Presidential Decision Directive 39 (PDD-39), was issued in June 1995. PDD-39 defines policies regarding the federal response to threats or acts of terrorism involving nuclear, biologic, and chemical (NBC) material or weapons of mass destruction (WMDs) (Presidential Decision Directive-39, 1995).

Building on PDD-39, President Clinton signed Presidential Decision Directive-62 (PDD-62) in May 1998, adding definitive directions to the federal partners who support the Federal Emergency Management Agency (FEMA) in the Federal Response Plan. The U.S. Department of Health and Human Services (DHHS) was designated the lead agency to plan and to prepare for a national response to medical emergencies arising from terrorist use of WMD. DHHS, with support from other federal agencies, was directed to do the following (Presidential Decision Directive-62, 1998):

- Provide enhanced local response capabilities through the development of Metropolitan Medical Response Systems.
- Develop and maintain the National Disaster Medical System (NDMS), including the National Medical Response Teams.

The Federal Response Plan

The Federal Response Plan outlines how the federal government implements the Robert T. Stafford Disaster Relief and Emergency Assistance Act, which assists state and local governments when a major disaster overwhelms their ability to respond effectively. The Federal Response Plan delineates the responsibilities of 27 federal agencies and the American Red Cross when the President declares a major disaster or emergency. The purpose of the plan is to save lives; protect public health, safety, and property; alleviate damage and hardship; and reduce future vulnerability (Federal Emergency Management Agency, 1999).

- Work with the Department of Defense to ensure deployability of NDMS response teams, supplies, and equipment.
- Ensure that adequate stockpiles of antidotes and other necessary pharmaceuticals nationwide would be available by working with the Department of Veterans Affairs.

The Government Directive to Educate Health Care Personnel

PDD-62 also contains language that identified the need for the development of INC-MCE. This directive gives DHHS the responsibility to ensure that health care personnel are educated and trained to work within the NDMS system. Because the U.S. military, a significant source of CBRNE management expertise, was experiencing significant downsizing, the DHHS was called upon to broaden its scope of training and education to include all emergency responders.

There is no dispute among experts that the primary consequence of a CBRNE event will be the effect on human health, requiring an unprecedented health system response. It is on this premise that the U.S. DHHS, through the Office of Emergency Preparedness (OEP), builds the nation's contingency plans for dealing with the health consequences of a terrorist attack with a CBRNE weapon.

In response to the directive to train and educate emergency personnel, OEP (as the action agent for the DHHS) enlisted the aid of the American Col-

lege of Emergency Physicians (ACEP) to create a taskforce compiled of representatives from emergency medicine, emergency nursing, and the first responder communities. The taskforce:
- Examined the present educational preparation of these providers
- Identified barriers to new educational programs in the area of WMD and mass casualty care
- Developed standards particular to each profession in the areas of awareness, proficiency, and the sustaining of skills necessary for mass casualty care

Action is Spurred

ACEP, within the scope of it mission assignment, and in completion of its task, indicated that emergency personnel need training in mass casualty response. During the 2 years from task assignment to release of the ACEP report, world events drew attention to the increased risk of a terrorist attack. As a result of this awakening, OEP questioned whether the ACEP assessment that only emergency personnel needed training to respond to an event went far enough. For example, in a biologic attack, victims would develop symptoms over a period of time and visit a health care professional for care mainly in primary care settings, initially. Clearly, more than just emergency nurses, physicians, and paramedics needed to be prepared to respond to mass casualty situations. The end result was an attempt by OEP staff to identify key players from within the respective targeted professions who could become the catalyst or champion to represent their profession in a bold new approach to influencing education and training for CBRNE events.

SPARKING A REVOLUTION IN NURSING EDUCATION
Coalition Leadership

To accomplish the goal of altering the basic education and training of every nurse in the United States to include preparation in response to mass casualty situations is a daunting undertaking. It was clear that powerful leadership would be a critical factor in the project's success. Captain Veronica Stephens, on the staff of the OEP in Rockville, Maryland, was asked to lead the agency's efforts. She identified Dr. Colleen Conway-Welch, Dean of the Vanderbilt University School of Nursing, as one who could champion the cause and enlist the support of nurse educators, professional organizations, and licensing and credentialing bodies. Captain Stephens and Dr. Conway-Welch had worked together previously on a successful project, so Captain Stephens contacted Dr. Conway-Welch and asked her to host a meeting of nursing leaders. A skilled health care leader with much expertise in how Washington DC works, Dr. Conway-Welch had the political savvy and interpersonal skills that would be powerful drivers in developing the coalition.

Coalition Membership

Representatives from all nursing arenas were invited to participate in the development of INC-MCE. Because of the scope of the coalition's goal, it was vital to access the knowledge and leadership of nurses in academia, agencies involved in emergency response, professional associations, the military services, the U.S. Public Health Service, regulatory bodies, and others.

To move forward as expeditiously as possible, it was essential to build on work that had already been done. Coalition members learned that the University of Ulster in Northern Ireland offers a masters degree in disaster relief nursing. Captain Stephens visited the program in December 2000.

The University of Ulster program involves six universities in the United Kingdom, Spain, and Finland. It is research based and leads to a master's degree in disaster relief nursing in planning and management. Although it is a fledgling program, it has the backing of some of the most prestigious relief and aid organizations in the world. This was just the international link that INC-MCE needed to begin the coalition building process.

THE COALITION MEETS FOR THE FIRST TIME

The first meeting of the International Nursing Coalition for Mass Casualty Education was held at Vanderbilt University School of Nursing in Nashville, Tennessee, in March 2001. It was a high-energy consensus-building, strategic-planning, and brainstorming event that served to crystallize and focus the work of the group. OEP staff provided briefings on mass casualty threats and the structure of Federal Response Plan, including the National Disaster Medical System. The need to design competencies and develop training programs was unequivocal, and moving ahead quickly was a goal voiced by members. Barriers and facilitators to the group's work were identified. Strategies for influencing nursing curricula were delineated. The work of the group was "divided and conquered" when the coalition formed workgroups to manage specific tasks.

The Coalition's Mission

INC-MCE's mission was designed at the first meeting of coalition members. The mission is to lead the preparation of all nurses to respond to mass casualty events, to design competencies for integration into basic nursing education at every level, to design continuing education modules for practicing nurses that would be available on the Internet, and to recommend a curriculum of advanced content for master's degree-prepared nurses, who would play a strategic or leadership role in the management of the response to weapons of mass destruction. A clearinghouse for information and web links is being maintained by the School of Nursing at Vanderbilt University. The intent of INC-MCE is to infuse into community health nursing curriculum the competencies that allow nurses to provide leadership effectively in the community to control panic and protect the health and safety of citizens.

INC-MCE Makes Its Public Debut

The OEP invited Dr. Conway-Welch, along with representatives from the University of Ulster, to participate in a presentation in Dallas, Texas, at the National Disaster Medical System Conference in April 2001. She presented an overview of INC-MCE and the coalition's goals. Feedback on the coalition's initial activities was invited and considered.

Media Efforts

The coalition members recognized the importance of informing nurses that this project was underway and understood the need for nurses' support. A press release was crafted and an article about the coalition was published in *The American Nurse* in July/August 2001 (Chaffee, Conway-Welch, & Sabatier, 2001). A second article, focusing on the real threat of a biologic weapon attack, appeared in the *American Journal of Nursing* and highlighted the leadership that nurses were providing through INC-MCE (Chaffee, Conway-Welch, & Stephens, 2001).

The Coalition's Second Meeting

A second meeting of INC-MCE was held at the U.S. Public Health Service Noble Training Center in Fort McClellan, Alabama, in June 2001. Noble Training Center serves as a federal training facility to prepare responders for multiple types of casualty situations. The coalition's membership became more defined at this time. This was critical in order to leverage each group's communication tools such as newsletters, websites, journals, and workshops to get the word out about the INC-MCE. The coalition's own awareness was increased with briefings on terrorism and a tour of the Noble Training Center. Workgroups continued to focus on media efforts and competency development. The group finalized its mission statement and developed a purpose statement to guide its activities.

POLITICAL SUPPORT

It has been said that a vision without funding is a hallucination. An important step in achieving the coalition's goals was to attain funding to support the group's work. Coalition members contacted key political leaders to gauge the type of support that might be available. Initial funding to begin work was provided through OEP in September 2001.

THE COALITION JOINS A COLLABORATIVE EFFORT

INC-MCE was invited to join a consortium for health care provider education organized in 2001 by Louisiana State University, Division of Continuing Education, Academy of Counter-Terrorist Edu-

Organizational Members of the International Nursing Coalition on Mass Casualty Education

American Academy of Nurse Practitioners
American Association of Colleges of Nursing
American Nurses Association
American Social Health Association
Centennial Hospital, Nashville, Tennessee
Columbia University School of Nursing
Federal Bureau of Investigation (FBI) National Domestic Preparedness Office
George Mason University School of Nursing
Georgia Southern University School of Nursing
Institute for Johns Hopkins Nursing
Jacksonville State University College of Nursing and Health Sciences
National League for Nursing Accrediting Commission
Navy Medicine Office of Homeland Security
Office of the Air Force Surgeon General, Medical Readiness and Nursing
Tennessee Department of Health
U.S. Department of Health and Human Services, Office of Emergency Preparedness
U.S. Department of Veterans Affairs
U.S. Health Resources and Services Administration
U.S. Public Health Service
University of Kentucky School of Nursing
University of Massachusetts at Amherst
University of Texas at Austin School of Nursing
University of Ulster, Northern Ireland
University of Washington School of Nursing
Vanderbilt University Department of Preventive Medicine and Infectious Disease
Vanderbilt University School of Nursing

cation. This moved INC-MCE into a collaborative effort to broaden the curriculum core competencies project for nurses into a broader curriculum project and into development of core competencies for all health disciplines.

CONCLUSION

The work of this coalition became even more critical after the events of September 11, 2001, when the United States was attacked and emergency response was seriously tested. On September 11, many nurses and other health care providers found themselves first responders at the scene of horrific mass casualty. Nursing has the opportunity to play a powerful role in preparing the health system of the future to respond effectively to situations that nurses may have never expected to confront. INC-MCE, despite being a coalition of diverse members, got off to a strong start through excellent leadership, careful identification of key stakeholders, assessment of avenues for political support, and a firmly maintained focus on the important purpose of the group's work.

International Nursing Coalition for Mass Casualty Education website: www.mc.vanderbilt.edu/nursing/coalitons/INCMCE
Office of Emergency Preparedness website: www.ndms.oep.gov

REFERENCES

American College of Emergency Physicians. (2000). *Developing objectives, content, and competencies for the training of emergency medical technicians, emergency physicians, and emergency nurses to care for casualties resulting from nuclear, biological, or chemical (NBC) incidents.* Dallas: ACEP Reports.

Chaffee, M.W., Conway-Welch, C., & Stephens, V. (2001, July-August). Nursing leaders plan to educate nurses about response to mass-casualty events. *The American Nurse.*

Chaffee, M.W., Conway-Welch, C., & Stephens, V. (2001, November). Bioterrorism in the United States: It's Inevitable. *American Journal of Nursing, 101*(11), 59, 61.

Federal Emergency Management Agency. (1999). *Federal response plan.* Washington, DC: Federal Emergency Management Agency.

Presidential Decision Directive-39. (1995). Washington, DC: Library of Congress.

Presidential Decision Directive-62. (1998). Washington, DC: Library of Congress.

Taking bio-warfare seriously. (2000, September 23). *The Washington Post,* B6.

Research as a Political and Policy Tool

DONNA DIERS

"We are drowning in information but starved for knowledge."

JOHN NAISBITT

Personal Values Get in Way of Bridging Science, Policy

By Abram Katz, *New Haven Register*

Translating science into effective public policy would be simple if everyone agreed on the best ways to stop AIDS.

But they don't. No amount of science can convince some politicians to support controversial programs; nor will many scientists defer to emotional or moral persuasion.

A federal panel of scientists has concluded that needle exchange programs and safe-sex education are effective in preventing the spread of AIDS. The panel also is critical of policy-makers who it says ignore the scientific evidence while people are dying from the disease.

State Sen. Thomas F. Upson said he's not sure why policy-makers should heed scientists.

And he doesn't see the logic in trying to prevent the spread of HIV through needles by giving away needles.

Upson, a Waterbury Republican and deputy minority leader, sponsored bills this year to repeal the state's needle exchange programs.

One bill stalled in the judiciary committee; the other is before the public health committee.

"Taking of drugs is illegal in Connecticut. We're providing something illegal," Upson said.

"We don't provide set-ups for alcoholics or masks for bank robbers. It's a slippery slope," he said.

Injection drug users should be offered drug counseling. "If they can afford drugs, they can afford to buy their own needles," he said.

That attitude greatly disturbs public health officials.

"We have really been far too slow in implementing prevention programs," said Dr. Michael H. Merson, chairman of epidemiology and public health at Yale University School of Medicine.

Merson, an internationally known expert on AIDS, was one of 15 scientists who addressed the federal panel in February.

"First and foremost, this is a public health problem. While we must respect each other's morals and culture, we're dealing with a serious public health risk. AIDS is the leading cause of death in people between 25 and 44," Merson said.

"We need to set policy first and foremost on science . . . not just what we think," he said. "We have a Victorian heritage. We stigmatize people with HIV. It's disgusting, it's sexual, it happens in marginalized groups," Merson said.

There's no way Jane Salce, executive director of the Christian Coalition of Connecticut, will be convinced by scientists that needle exchange programs or explicit sex education are the right way to prevent HIV-infections.

Salce said teaching the general biology of reproduction is appropriate. Sexual relationships should be discussed at home, she said.

"Now we're getting explicit in school under the guise that teenagers will bumble into sex. Abstinence is the way. We're sending them a mixed message. 'You shouldn't do this, but here's a condom in case you do,'" she said.

"That's like saying, 'We don't do drugs, but here's a clean needle.'"

Salce said no amount of scientific evidence would change her mind. "Some might say I'm living in a fantasy world. If you teach children right from wrong at an early age, we'll see a lot of problems lessened by a major degree."

When science slams into skepticism, where does that leave officials responsible for protecting public health?

"I don't have an answer to that question," said Beth Weinstein, director of AIDS programs in the state Department of Public Health. "It has to do with how we set public policy. I can't begin to figure out what to do," she said.

"We've danced around preventive issues in this country since the beginning," she said.

"In the end there's no substitute for political courage. There's going to be resistance to these programs. We need to educate the public and policy-makers on the facts," Merson said. [From the *New Haven Register,* April 8, 1997]

This story shows the complicated relationship between research and policy-making and how data do not necessarily have the same meaning for different people.

The National Institutes of Health (NIH) Consensus Conference actually held that "needle exchange programs 'should be implemented at once,'" which provoked a moderated response by Donna Shalala, then Secretary of Health and Human Services, saying that needle exchange programs "can be an effective component of a comprehensive strategy to prevent HIV [human immunodeficiency virus] and other blood-borne infections" (Editor's note, 1997). The NIH report followed (by 2 years) a well-distributed report by the National Academy of Sciences (Normand, Vlahov, & Moses, 1995), which had found that "well-

implemented needle exchange programs can be effective in preventing the spread of HIV and do not increase the use of illegal drugs." But a congressional ban on funding needle exchange programs remains in effect.

From the point of view of the quality of the science, the peer review, and the consensus of the scientific community, the policy action to be taken in Connecticut is clear. However, the political consensus is not. In fact, on January 20, 2001, the same newspaper reported that despite the fact that needle exchange programs were legal in the state, police in one town were arresting participants, testing their now-legal syringes for heroin residue, and then arresting them for possession of a controlled substance. The science and policy consensus run up against countervailing agendas of stakeholders other than the public health community.

"Health services researchers must not imagine that research findings are sufficient to determine the course of health policy," Tanenbaum (1996, p. 517) whinges.[1] She had studied the Canadian and U.S. policy response to studies of medical ineffectiveness and found very different responses based on the *same data.* Therefore, she says, the data must be ambiguous because they do not seem to lead to the same implications for action.

As Tanenbaum recognizes, research all by itself does not make policy. Politics intervene. The research doesn't get to the right people. Policy agendas shift. In Tanenbaum's study an equally viable conclusion is that the U.S. and Canadian medical systems are so different that it is not surprising that different responses follow from the same data. Whether the research is really any good is not the question.

Research may be a tool to help carve policy, if it is in the right hands and is carefully sharpened and skillfully applied. But because research design is never perfect, probabilistic reasoning does

---

[1] *Whinge* is a peculiarly appropriate verb often used in political commentary in Australia, Canada, and the United Kingdom. It means to whine with a petulant, needy edge, something beyond *complain* but short of *snivel.* It is not in U.S. dictionaries; more is the pity.

not satisfy legislators who want a quick and simple "does it work?" answer. The role of research in policy-making is more complicated than it looks.

What makes policy decision making such a fertile field for analysis is the fact that it is so difficult to shape and even more difficult to control. That is exactly what makes it frustrating to action-oriented disciplines such as nursing and so tiresome to analysts like Tanenbaum, who believe the action that should follow from the data is obvious. The making of *public* policy is even more involved because, by definition, it includes the acts of government or governmental agencies shaped by the will of the people, whether by formal vote, lobbying, or contributions to political campaigns. Finally, public policy-making, at least in the United States, is *public* to some degree, inviting the participation of all who wish a piece of the action, no matter how ignorant or biased those participants may be.

SHAPING AGENDAS

The first step in policy-making is shaping the agenda. John Kingdon (1995) is the master of analysis of agenda setting. He answers the question "Why do some problems come to occupy the attention of governmental officials more than other problems?" And the answer, he says, lies in how policymakers learn about issues and how the issues come to be defined as problems. Much of this work occurs behind the scenes, made public strategically by involved parties or accidentally by the media, especially when there is what Kingdon (1995) calls a *focusing event,* a disaster, crisis, personal experience, or powerful symbol. The work of the American Medical Association (AMA) in shaping the agenda for gun control and tobacco regulation on the basis of research is instructive in the following examples.

GUN CONTROL AS PUBLIC HEALTH

The leadership in advocating unrestricted access to purchasing and using guns is the National Rifle Association (NRA). The NRA's agenda combines an interpretation of the "freedom to bear arms" clause of the Bill of Rights with the interests of people who hunt for sport or food and with an as-yet-small but highly visible set of militarists, separatists, and paramilitary groups not necessarily united on their own policy agendas.[2] The NRA website (NRA.org) is forthright on the Constitutional claim.

The federal Centers for Disease Control and Prevention (CDC) has a small unit that tracks statistics on causes of injuries, including product failures, car crashes, and injuries from guns. CDC data come from hospital data, in which reasons for hospitalization and emergency treatment from injuries are coded for computer use (E codes in the *International Classification of Diseases* [ICD-9-CM]) and transmitted as reportable to CDC, much as infectious disease is reported. Research, some funded by CDC, began to link the availability of handguns to homicide, suicide, crime, and accident epidemiology (Sloan et al, 1988; Sloan, Rivara, Reay, Ferris, & Kellerman, 1990). The NRA demanded that the researchers be investigated for lapses of scientific integrity (Kellerman, 1993), the most serious allegation possible in academic circles. The complaint was dismissed after internal review at CDC. As more studies were done, with similar findings, the politics escalated, and CDC's injury control program was threatened with loss of funds (Kellerman, 1993).

The AMA put a toe in the water when its executive director signaled a gun control position in a letter to Congress on one piece of legislation, the Brady bill, which simply proposed a waiting period for gun purchase (Todd, 1991). Later the AMA Council on Scientific Affairs (1992) took a formal position on assault weapons as a public health hazard, reflecting, perhaps, then-Surgeon General C. Everett Koop's use of the "bully pulpit" of the office and the forum of the *Journal of the American Medical Association (JAMA)* and its then editor, George

---

[2]In spring 1997 the actor Charlton Heston won a seat on the NRA board on a platform the media reported as his wish to bring the organization back to center, away from the "right," separatist end of the spectrum. Contemporary NRA advertisements feature him and other public figures in a reframing of NRA's agenda away from the right to bear arms and toward gun safety.

Lundberg, to speak out for a national gun policy (Koop & Lundberg, 1992).[3]

Throwing the clout of organized medicine behind gun control, if only assault weapon control and a waiting period, as a *public health* issue changed the political field (Blendon, Young, & Hemenway, 1996). The public health and health care perspectives shifted the agenda from NRA's definition of the issue as possession of guns to their use, which is much more subtle and complicated and less easy to regulate. Death and injury from gun use are irrefutable—and impossible to put to a public test through referendum or vote. The school shootings, especially Columbine High School in Colorado, provoked a rash of state legislative initiatives to require trigger locks, to restrict access to gun purchase, and so on. The shooting of President Reagan, the injury to Jim Brady at the time of Reagan's shooting, and the school shootings are examples of crises that create a policy agenda.[4]

---

[3]In the previous iteration of this chapter, I wrote, "*JAMA* and *NEJM* [*New England Journal of Medicine*] are remarkably editorially free from their respective sponsoring organizations— AMA and the Massachusetts Medical Society. How free any journal is depends on its relationship with its sponsor and on its editor. Lundberg at *JAMA* and Franz Inglefinger, then Arnold Relman, and then Jerome Kassirir at *NEJM* have all taken positions and used their editorial resources to espouse points of view not necessarily subscribed to by their sponsor . . ." (Diers & Potter, 1997). Hardly a year after that appeared, both journals had fired their editors. Lundberg was fired because he allegedly rushed into print a polling study that showed that Americans sampled did not equate oral sex with intercourse, just at the time of the Clinton impeachment hearings (Goldsmith, 1999). Kassirer tangled with the Massachusetts Medical Society over the Society's wish to use NEJM's considerable name recognition for product endorsement (The departure of Jerome P. Kassirer, 1999). The timing, coincidental as it was, illustrates the new pressures on science and publication. Because both journals have such huge international circulation, are so important to advertisers, and so significant in fields other than medicine, they have enormous weight in the policy community. *JAMA* and *NEJM* also make available news of cutting-edge scientific advances to the media before publication, which makes the media happy. The public interest in accurate perception of science may be left out of this equation.
[4]In April, 2001, National Public Radio reported that gun sales in the United States were down 53% in the previous 3 years, owing not so much to restrictive regulation but to the public's increasing reservations about gun possession and ownership.

SMOKING AND POLICY

The health effects of tobacco smoking have long been debated as a matter of the quality of the research, with the questioning led by the tobacco industry itself but joined by researchers who disputed methods and statistics. The link between smoking and lung cancer in humans was and still is a correlation, not a randomized, controlled clinical trial, which would require prescribing smoking randomly to one group and not to another, followed out 25 years or so. The tobacco industry took advantage of the methodologic problems to hold off health warnings for years.

In July 1995 *JAMA* published an analysis of previously secret tobacco industry documents in which the addictive properties of nicotine and the carcinogenic effects of smoking were revealed to have been known to the industry for 30 years (see Glantz, Fox, & Lightwood [1997] for review). Behind the scenes, David Kessler, then Commissioner of the Federal Drug Administration, and his staff had already been working to assert jurisdiction over cigarettes and smokeless tobacco, which FDA did on August 28, 1996 (Kessler, Barnett, Witt, Zeller, Mande, & Schultz, 1997). This story is so dramatic that a part of it became the Oscar-nominated film *The Insider*. Kessler's personal account of this struggle reads like a detective story, and there are plenty of villains (Kessler, 2001). With the acknowledgment that the effects of smoking were known to industry researchers as a result of their own studies, their credibility has been seriously compromised. Here the science was at first suppressed, then turned against the very industry that had produced the research. Then the research was used to force financial settlements to victims of smoking, as well as to cause new legislation to prohibit cigarette advertising that targets young people, among other efforts.[5]

---

[5]Julius Richmond, a child psychiatrist, was the Surgeon General who implemented the warnings on cigarette packages. I served on a committee with him once and he would graciously autograph cigarette packages where they said, The Surgeon General has determined . . ." He always wore a tie with the no-smoking logo.

GETTING ON THE AGENDA

Much of the work—and the success—of nursing in policy-making to date has been less in shaping the agendas than in casting nursing issues to match existing policy agendas. Nursing has just begun to participate in setting the agenda for health policy "beyond issues that would be more traditionally defined as relevant to nursing" (Cohen, Mason, Kovner, Leavitt, Pulcini, & Sochalski, 1996, p. 263).

Kingdon (1995) observes that not all "conditions" are "problems" and that an issue does not hit the agenda until it is defined as a problem. Even then, not all problems achieve high agenda prominence. Cobb, Ross, and Ross (1976) distinguish among three models for agenda building: the outside initiative model, the mobilization model, and the inside initiative model. In the first, the idea first reaches the public agenda, and only then does it make the formal, or governmental, agenda. This is the "hit 'em on the head to get their attention" model, and it depends on media coverage. Because the public media are more often hooked by anecdote than data, the most-effective information for shaping the formal agenda in this model is the sound bite.[6] If data exist to address the policy/political agenda, this is the time to get them in. Legislators do not wish to be taken for fools and need to position themselves to respond to something that is engaging the attention of their constituents, as reflected in the newspapers and on television. "Drive-through deliveries" advocated by insurance companies, for example, came to public attention largely through media reports (Deliver, then depart, 1995; Maternity leave, 1996).

Several states have considered and usually passed legislation to curtail drive-through deliver-

ies, and the federal government has also passed legislation. But the decision was not made on the basis of data. There actually aren't any data on the best postpartum length of hospital stay for the (normal) mother and (normal) baby, which is why insurers originally got by with the 1-day stay provision. But the accounts of new mothers were so embarrassing to a civilized society, including insurers, that they could not defend the insurance practice.

In the second model, the mobilization model, the policymakers have already decided on an agenda and a course of action and now need to sell it. Here, the trick is to figure out what the agenda really is and, if possible, associate nursing's interest with it. Bringing along media attention reinforces nursing's contribution when possible.

The work of nursing in Tennessee to insert nurse practitioners (NPs) into TennCare, the state's managed Medicaid system, is instructive. The governor had already decided on a managed Medicaid plan, but it depended on having an adequate supply of primary care providers. The Tennessee Medical Association (TMA) tried to stonewall: TMA members would not accept Medicaid patients under Tenn Care. Tennessee NPs seized the opportunity to insert themselves and their own agenda—changing a very restrictive practice act and prescribing language—and appear to be the good guys. They did, and it worked (a much longer story, of course) (Mirvis, Chang, Hall, Zaar, & Applegate, 1995; Bonneyman, 1996; Gold, 1997). The Tennessee nurses received a lot of good publicity for being ahead of nurses in many other states in moving into the managed Medicaid primary care arena. In fact, however, only one small restrictive provision—site-specific prescribing authority—was changed. Still, in the smoke and mirrors of advanced practice, the law and legislation count less than the public perception. In Tennessee, NPs were portrayed as out there where doctors feared to tread. The Governor used NP eagerness to serve to hold TMA's feet to the fire.

The inside model proposes that there are some issues that never go "outside" the internal governmental sphere because they are too arcane, controversial, or complex. Many of these issues deal with regulatory change rather than legislation. Here, re-

---

[6]One of the leading health policy journals, *Health Affairs,* has recognized the value of the anecdote or narrative in policy making by creating a regular section called "Narrative Matters." An early entry in this section is a contribution from a former state legislator, John E. McDonough, writing about the power of anecdote in convincing legislators to support the financing of bone marrow transplant for advanced breast cancer. There still is no evidence that bone marrow transplant works for this condition. Barbara Sharf follows this article with an elaboration of the breast cancer story in the same issue of this journal. (See McDonough, 2001 and Sharf, 2001.)

search and other forms of lobbying information go straight to the legislators or federal agencies without necessarily playing to the public media.

The recent success of organized nursing to change the way in which Medicare will pay for services of nurse practitioners is an example of the inside model. There is no huge public interest in the rules Medicare uses for paying practitioners; this is not an intriguing problem to AARP, for example, which ordinarily cares a lot about Medicare.

Under Medicare, the services of nurse practitioners could be billed only as "incident to" the provision of medical care by a physician. Nursing organizations banded together to convince the Health Care Financing Administration that it would be in their financial interests to let NPs bill in their own names, albeit at a lower rate (85% of allowable physician charge) (Price & Minarik, 1998, 1999). Nursing's issue was identity and autonomy as well as recognition for services rendered. If NPs cannot bill in their own names, with their own Medicare provider numbers, there will never be any data about their safety or effectiveness.

Organized medicine saw this and other recent changes in regulation for nurse-midwives and nurse anesthetists as a challenge to its hegemony. Some 49 physician organizations petitioned HCFA, but as a "Citizens Petition" (AMA "Citizens Petition" sent to HCFA, 2000) to restrict billing to physicians. Some 250 nursing organizations responded (Nursing's response to AMA "Citizen's Petition" sent to HCFA, 2000). None of this activity hit the major public media. The issue is simply too technical. Even the usual attention AMA gets in the public media did not happen this time. Kingdon (1995) notes that there are numerous examples of legislation passed over the opposition of powerful and well-funded groups such as AMA. New actors, including consumers and, one would argue, nursing, are blunting the so-called "iron triangle" of power elites: physicians, hospitals, and legislators or regulators.

NURSING ON THE AGENDA

Where nursing has made progress on issues that have to do with our parochial interests, such as li-

censure, scope of practice, third-party reimbursement, and prescriptive authority, the progress has generally been made by sophisticated political minuet rather than data-based argument. On these issues we have not had sufficient data and still do not. For example, there is very little literature on the effect of granting advanced practice nurses (APNs) prescriptive authority. If nurses can prescribe, do we do it? Do we do it right? How often do we consult a physician, even with full-scope prescribing authority? Yet prescribing authority in one form or another exists in most states (Pearson, 2001) over the opposition of physicians and pharmacists and essentially without data.

An important exception to the lack-of-data rule is in nurse-midwifery, where data collected now for more than 50 years on the safety and effectiveness of nurse-midwifery practice has been used to enact legal authority for practice in all 50 states, Guam, and Puerto Rico (Diers, 1992b; Varney, 1996).

Nurse-midwifery made important progress when it attached its interests in legal authorization to the existing public agenda in implementation of Medicaid. Because much of the research showed the effects of nurse-midwifery in underserved populations, and because the Medicaid program targets women and children, that strategy made sense. It also built on a carefully crafted strategy that began at the federal level when Senator Daniel Inouye caused legislation to be passed to allow direct payment to nurse-midwives under Medicaid in jurisdictions with legal authorization for practice.[7] The literature on effectiveness was used to demonstrate the willingness of nurse-midwives to care for poor women and babies and to counter the allegations of lack of safety made by organized medicine (Diers, 1992b).

Contemporary nursing's political strategy in many states involves hooking the APN's concerns to expand scope of practice and prescribing authority to the "managed care" agenda, which is

---

[7]Senator Inouye is proud to announce that he was assisted into the world by a midwife. He also credits nurses who cared for him when he lost an arm in World War II.

about money, not practice. Although the research on the cost-effectiveness of advanced practice nursing is still slim, it has been cleverly analyzed and combined with regulatory options by Barbara Safriet, an attorney and Associate Dean of the Yale Law School, in a monograph that is often made part of public testimony (Safriet, 1992). Having this information compiled by an attorney who is not a nurse has the effect of making the data even more powerful because it does not seem self-serving.

CREATING THE AGENDA: A MINI CASE STUDY

The American Nurses Association (ANA) took a very unpopular stance to support Medicare very early on (Lewis, 1961; Marmor, 1973) because Medicare would bring access to care, which meant more nursing jobs. The implementation of the prospective payment system and diagnosis-related groups (DRGs) under Medicare in 1983 had been resisted by organized nursing in public testimony on the basis of predictions of nursing jobs lost (Cole, 1982; Curtis, 1983; Diers, 1992a). By 1986 or so, the effect of the payment system was being felt in hospitals that had cut registered nurse (RN) positions because decreased admissions were anticipated. RN vacancy rates (not jobs lost) rose. The American Hospital Association (AHA), stimulated by the American Organization of Nurse Executives (AONE), did several "quick and dirty" surveys. The average community hospital RN vacancy rate rose from 4.4% in 1983 to 11.3% in December 1987 (American Hospital Association, 1988).

At the same time, the Division of Nursing of the Bureau of Health Manpower of the Health Services and Resources Administration in the U.S. Department of Health and Human Services, which collects data on nursing numbers and employment rates, was reporting that there was no shortage of nurses (Division of Nursing, 1984).

Using U.S. Department of Commerce statistics under a model that estimated population trends and requirements for nursing personnel across settings, the National League for Nursing (NLN) concluded that the supply of associate degree graduates would exceed demand in 2000 and that the supply of baccalaureate and master's prepared nurses would be under demand by about 0.5 million each (Maraldo & Solomon, 1987).

So already there are already four different nursing agendas, producing four different sets of numbers. The ANA's agenda is jobs: more nurses. AONE's is recruitment and manpower: more nurses. NLN's is education and the health of schools of nursing in the supply pipeline: more nurses. The agenda of the Division of Nursing, as part of the executive branch of government, is to decrease federal expenses: Less funding is needed because there are enough nurses.

To make a long and now old story short, the Secretary's Commission on the Nursing Shortage (1988) took testimony from all the aforementioned players and from others who had done other kinds of analyses of requirements for nursing. Aiken and Mullinix (1987) showed that when nursing salaries began to approximate salaries of other women workers, nursing vacancies declined. They also showed that the salary compression in nursing—meaning that nurses employed for a long time did not make a compensatory amount greater than that of newly hired nurses—was another factor. "Oligopsony," an economic term meaning that where there are only a few large employers (hospitals) and an adequate supply of nurses, the employers effectively have a monopoly in the nursing market and can conspire, deliberately or not, to constrain nursing wages and salaries, was revealed. Other testimony nailed down the problem: It wasn't the *supply* of nurses, it was the *demand*. The payment system changed and the incentives for hospitals were to admit fewer "easy" patients and try to discharge the "harder" patients earlier. This meant that nurses were confronted with caring for patients whose stay in the hospital could consist entirely of "acute" days, which require more nursing care (Thompson, 1988).

The conversion of the agenda from supply to demand is still not well understood by committees and special commissions, who do not take into consideration the changing nature of patients and care requirements in hospitals, outpatient settings, nursing homes, and home care spawned by changes in funding.[8]

The nursing shortage data, flawed as they were, pushed hospitals even in rate-regulated states to raise salaries so that nursing staff could be hired and retained. But within 5 years, something happened, and now conventional "wisdom" held that highly paid nurses were part of the cause of escalating health care costs and should be reengineered and downsized out in favor of lower-paid, unlicensed personnel. California was engulfed by managed care.

Buresh and Gordon (2000) report the fight for "safe hospital staffing" legislation in California. It is a remarkable story of political sophistication and coalition building between unions and nursing to eventually pass the first state law that mandates nurse/patient staffing ratios. The effort involved changing the political landscape to help elect a Democrat as governor and a sophisticated media campaign. About 5 years passed between the first, unsuccessful bill and the one signed by Governor Gray Davis in 1999. The story illustrates many of the facets of politics and policy reflected throughout this book, including using the media to advantage, framing the issues correctly, and building coalitions. That California had been the first state to embrace managed care made this effort all the more important as a signal to the industry, "enough already!" This success is not without controversy. Some worry that mandated staffing levels will become the maximum rather than the minimum (Buerhaus, 1997).

---

[8]The most-recent nursing shortage report issued in July 2001 by the General Accounting Office (GAO) is considerably richer than most such governmental reports are, due, no doubt, to the fact that it was produced under the direction of a nurse, Janet Heinrich, who is now Director of Health Care—Public Health Issues at GAO (Nursing workforce: Emerging nurse shortages due to multiple factors, 2001). Heinrich has wide experience in Washington public policy and nursing circles.

AGENDA SETTING: THE CONTINUING STORY OF NURSING SHORTAGES

In the previous nursing shortage, Shindul-Rothschild, Berry, and Long-Middleton (1996) conducted a study for the *American Journal of Nursing* that highlighted the effects of downsizing and other corporate restructuring efforts on nursing practice through a national survey of the opinions of nurses. The study received considerable media play because it feeds into both the media's interest in juicy health care error stories and the national concerns for layoffs and job losses in a recovering economy. These are "people" stories, which make for easy sound bites and quick public testimony.

In summer 2001 a worldwide nursing shortage was beginning to receive media attention (Shortage of nurses hits hardest where they are needed the most, 2001). Experts seem to agree that this shortage is not like the shortage caused by the prospective payment system in 1988 (Buerhaus & Staiger, 1999). Now the "condition"—there aren't enough nurses—turned into a "problem" in Kingdon's (1995) model. Nursing is getting on the agenda, and it will be our challenge to play this agenda out. Claire Fagin (2001) has made her usual unique contribution in a monograph for the Milbank Memorial Fund (www.milbank.org). While she collects and reports the research, the most interesting contribution is to reframe the nursing shortage as *diminishing access to adequate nursing,* which turns the issue from a parochial nursing concern about job availability to an issue of the public's right to nursing care. This will open the potential for new coalitions with the public, and thus with publicly elected officials.

The Institute of Medicine's study, *Nursing Staff in Hospitals and Nursing Homes: Is It Adequate?* (Wunderlich, Sloan, & Davis, 1996) expressed "shock" at the lack of available data on hospital quality and called for stepped-up research on quality outcomes and their link to nurse staffing. A number of studies have been funded and are just beginning to be reported at this writing (Needleman, Buerhaus, Mattke, Stewart, & Zelevinsky, 2001). Nursing has suffered from lack of data to attribute the effects not only of nursing interventions on patient outcomes, but also of nursing as a resource. Large administrative data sets, whether they are claims files, national collections, or single hospital data sets, have not often been mined for data on effects of nursing as resource. Linda Aiken's study of magnet hospitals—good places for nurses to work—opened a door for health services research (Aiken, Smith, & Lake, 1994). Others (Blegen & Vaughn, 1998; Kovner & Gergen, 1998) have now established that nursing matters. The agenda that is being shaped, however, is not about nursing resources as the number of warm bodies. It is about the working conditions for nursing (Aiken et al, 2001). In the long run, that will be a more effective strategy for the profession, although how that translates into public policy or regulation is a much more subtle question. It is not at all clear that the proper fix to nursing working conditions could or should be a matter of public policy. It might be a matter for accreditation, for example. Hospitals must retain their accreditation status to be able to collect reimbursement from Medicare, even though accreditation is a private function in the United States.

RESEARCH AS POLITICAL: PRACTICE GUIDELINES AND AHCPR

The Agency for Healthcare Research and Quality (AHRQ, formerly the Agency for Health Care Policy and Research [AHCPR]) is funded in part by a 1% "tax" on NIH research grants to support evaluation of the use of public money for medical scientific research. The story of how this unusual provision came to be is itself an interesting commentary on policy-making[9] (Gray, 1992). AHCPR's portfolio evolved over the years to include evaluation of health services, outcome studies, and the important work to pull together the existing science to support clinical practice guidelines under programs called *practice outcome research teams* (PORTs)

[9]The original name for the agency was Agency for Health Care Research and Policy, which produced an unfortunate acronym (see Gray, 1992).

(*Medical Care,* 1994, 1995). Multidisciplinary committees, which regularly included nurses in highly visible roles, reviewed literature related to their assignment (e.g., pain, incontinence, depression in primary care, cataract treatment) and developed publicly available guidelines in two forms, one for the consumer reader and one for health professionals. The proposed documents were peer reviewed and then published and widely distributed by the government. The process is rather straightforward, essentially nonpolitical, and grinding hard academic work, but then it goes public.

One of the topics AHCPR picked was low back pain. The expert panel generated its report and subsequent guidelines, which said that 8 of 10 patients with acute back pain will recover in a month or so without therapy, that studies showed surgery benefits in only 1 in 100 patients, and that much diagnostic imaging was futile and unnecessary. Were the practice guidelines based on these findings to be implemented, there would be billions of dollars of savings, and patients would be protected from unnecessary tests and ineffective treatment. The American Academy of Orthopaedic Surgeons endorsed the guidelines.

However, the North American Spine Society, a group of surgeons, opposed the finding and got the attention of two Texas Republican representatives to Congress, who agitated to cut off AHCPR's funding entirely (A spineless attack on the AHCPR, 1996). A concerted lobbying effort by the Association for Health Services Research (AHSR) (now the Academy for Health Services Research and Health Policy; www.academyhealth.org), which welcomes nurse members, eventually produced a compromise that took AHCPR out of the guideline business and into being "science partners" so that users can "develop their own high-quality, evidence-based guidelines" (AHCPR drops guideline development, 1996). There was, of course, no requirement that anybody ever use the AHCPR guidelines, but clearly it would have been in the interest of payers, including Medicare and managed care insurers, to monitor the extent to which they were paying for evidence-based practices. AHCPR came close to losing its entire funding over this issue.

MENACING THE MESSENGER

Research isn't completed until it is peer reviewed and made available for public information and criticism. Recent reports have exposed the lengths to which special-interest groups or others who do not like the results of certain studies will go to prevent publication or use of the science. Deyo, Psaty, Simon, Wagner, and Omenn (1997) have collected their own and others' experiences. They show that the ox gored by the spine studies was the manufacturer of a pedicle screw sometimes used in spinal fusion. The manufacturer was being sued by patients alleging poor results from use of the device. Attorneys for the defendant subpoenaed documents from the original investigators, tying up their work for some time. Another pedicle screw manufacturer unsuccessfully sought a court injunction to prevent AHCPR from publishing its guidelines (Deyo, Patsy, Simon, Wagner, & Omenn, 1997).

Simon, one of the authors working with Deyo et al, was caught in another controversy when research from his team questioned the value of immunodiagnostic tests often used to support disability and liability claims for chemical sensitivity (Deyo et al, 1997). The science was attacked by "parties whose financial interests depended on [the] testing: plaintiffs' attorneys, advocacy organizations for people with chemical sensitivity, . . . testing laboratories" (Deyo et al, 1997, p. 1177), and allegations of scientific misconduct were made to the federal Office of Research Integrity and the medical board in Washington State. Individual patients at Group Health Cooperative, where Dr. Simon worked, were "contacted and encouraged to attack his credibility."

The April 16, 1997, issue of *JAMA* contains a fascinating report (Rennie, 1997) of a study that took 9 years to reach publication because it called into question the superior efficacy of Synthroid, a synthetic thyroid preparation (Dong, Hauck, Gambertoglio, Gee, White, Bubp, & Greenspan, 1997). The study had been funded by the manufacturer of Synthroid, and several preparations other than this company's were tested. The investigators had submitted the manuscript to *JAMA*, with a cover letter to the effect that the sponsor of the research disagreed with the conclusions. While the results, which showed that all the preparations were essen-

tially bioequivalent, were under review for possible publication, the manufacturer suddenly remembered that the agreement to fund the research held a provision that the manufacturer had the right to approve any potential publications. The university counsel's office had not caught this provision, which is the type of restriction that universities typically do not tolerate.

The manuscript was peer reviewed and eventually approved for publication, but it was abruptly withdrawn by the investigators when the manufacturer brought legal action against the university. At this time the company was being considered for acquisition by another pharmaceutical firm, and the comparative efficacy of its most important product was at issue. The company did its own reanalysis of data, reaching conclusions opposite to those of the original study, and published its findings in a new journal for which the company's investigator was an associate editor. The situation reached the notice of the *Wall Street Journal*. Suddenly an "inside" model situation converted to "outside."

The issue became a matter of public policy when the U.S. Food and Drug Administration entered (David Kessler appears again) and alleged that the company had mislabeled its product's efficacy, using the results of its own reanalysis, a violation of law. That apparently brought the company to negotiations with the university, and eventually the company agreed not to challenge publication of the original manuscript, which *JAMA* did finally publish (Dong et al., 1997). Several letters, including correspondence from the new owners and the original investigators, were also published in the same issue. "Thyroid Storm," *JAMA* called this sorry story (Rennie, 1997).[10]

---

[10]The curious reader might note that the Deyo article and the Rennie/Dong sequence were published by two different journals one day apart, April 16 and 17, 1997. Yet another example appears in the same issue of NEJM. Suzanne Fletcher (1997) describes her experience as part of the NIH Consensus Conference on breast-cancer screening, which had concluded that "the data available do not warrant a universal recommendation for mammography for all women in their forties" (p. 1181) and set off a firestorm of protest. Readers are urged to follow these arguments for themselves; they are very intricate as science, politics, and policy.

NURSING'S RESEARCH QUESTIONED

In nursing we have not had to contend with this level of intimidation, but we have had our own experience with having research called into question or rejected when the conclusions offended conventional political wisdom.

The most recent example is Mary Mundinger's randomized controlled clinical trial (RCCT) of the effectiveness of nurse practitioners and physicians in primary care in clinics run by Columbia University in New York City (Mundinger et al, 2000) published in the first issue of *JAMA* under a new editor.[11]

There is a long, boring history of how research on nurse practitioners has been criticized on political grounds, summarized in the previous iteration of this chapter (Diers, 1997). Mundinger and her colleagues took on the task of designing the best possible, perfect RCCT. It is interesting that the report of the methods for this study is a whole lot longer than the report of the findings in the published article. In general, there were no differences between NP and MD care. *JAMA* asked Dr. Harold Sox, a longtime commentator on NP research, to generate his analysis (Sox, 2000). He applauds the study design as the "gold standard" but still suggests that patients were not followed long enough to detect the awful consequences of being cared for by NPs.[12]

However, simply declaring that the right study hasn't been done ignores more than 1000 research articles that have been summarized in federal documents (Office of Technology Assessment, 1988), analyzed in reviews (Safriet, 1992; Brown & Grimes, 1995), and used to argue for more federal funding to train NPs. Medicine's agenda has been to change the definition of the issue from freedom of choice of practitioner to safety, which has always been code for economic opposition to advanced practice nursing and incursion into physician independence. Organized medicine does not worry about advanced practice nursing so long as the physician's own control and independence are preserved.

RESEARCH DESIGN FOR POLICY

A new analysis of "morality policy" (Mooney, 2001) asserts that some public and private policy issues profit less from research than from interest group influence and polling. Morality policy issues include abortion, clinician-assisted suicide, perhaps needle exchange as HIV care, anything having to do with sex, or "sins" such as gambling, smoking, or drug use. Mooney's work is useful to distinguish potential policy issues that might require different modes of attack.

It should be obvious by now that the quality of research may have little to do with its impact on policy. There are, however, some ways in which research can be made more useful and usable in policy decision making.

In the first place, research can be used to help *define a problem,* particularly to determine how big it is. The new research about nursing staffing and working conditions may be an example of that. Aiken et al (2001) have an international study that suggests that the working condition issues in the United States are similar to those in Canada and Scotland, and to a lesser extent, Germany. They suggest that working conditions predict nurses' intentions to stay or leave their present positions and that work is bringing nursing into the political and health policy environment in totally new ways. The public policy implications are clearer in countries with a nationalized health care system than they are in the United States.

Changing agendas have now put studies of out-

[11]The new editor is Catherine DeAngelis, who is proud to call herself a nurse and a pediatric nurse practitioner and a physician. After the embarrassing debacle of changing editorial leadership at *JAMA,* Dr. DeAngelis is a calming influence. Readers who worry about journals might examine how *JAMA* has turned more gentle, but hardly less rigorous, under DeAngelis' hand.

[12]The worst comment on the quality of NP practice was generated by Dr. Walter Spitzer (who, oddly enough, had invented NP practice in Canada) in a famous set of articles, collectively known as the "Burlington Trials [sic] of the Nurse Practitioner" (Spitzer, Sackett, Sibley, Roberts, Gent, Kergin, Hackett, & Olynich, 1974). In one comment on someone else's publication about NP practice, he alleged that over time, nurse practitioners would turn out to be Thalidomide, a tranquilizer used in Great Britain that caused birth defects in children, which was put into distribution without enough testing (Spitzer, 1984).

comes and "evidence based practice" in the spotlight. The present attention to "errors" in hospital care could give nursing a way to cast research on this agenda. Surely there can be no resistance to the notion that errors ought to be decreased. That is why the data released by the Institute of Medicine in 2000 (Kohn, Corrigan & Donaldson, 2000) grabbed public attention and resulted, among other things, in a sensational series in the *Chicago Tribune* on nursing errors (Berens, 2000a, 2000b, 2000c). That series again highlighted nursing shortages as reasons for some kinds of errors. It also exposed the problems with state regulatory responsibility, without resources, for tracking nurses with substance abuse history.

Aggregating studies in the form of literature reviews or metanalyses is becoming an important research strategy. Metanalyses and similar techniques are now embedded in web-based resources, especially the Cochrane Library (www.cochranelibrary.com). The intricacies of metanalysis are beyond the scope of this chapter, but the advantage of metanalysis or carefully constructed literature reviews is clear: Small-sample but important studies can be made additive.

Pickiness about research design is not always relevant when the goal is to boil down a collection of disparate studies or other data to make a policy point. This is not at all the same as fudging the numbers. Politicians and policymakers are generally not entranced by arcane academic standards for methodologic technicalities. The 1998 gathering of NP literature by the Office of Technology Assessment (OTA), as well as Safriet's (1992) use of OTA and other studies, read, to the academic eye, as insufficiently critical of the studies cited. The Shindul-Rothschild (1996) study sample consisted of readers of the *American Journal of Nursing* who chose to send in a tear-out questionnaire—not a representative sample. But to do an academic critique on either piece of work is surely beside the point of having this information gathered together by an unbiased critic, on the one hand, and an adroit use of a survey of nurses' experience on the other. Using a tight methodologic critique would be shooting ourselves in the foot.

Policy is often about money. Cost analysis or *cost/benefit analysis* are new tools for nursing research. Cost/benefit analysis is covered elsewhere in this book.

Linda Aiken has provided many good examples of *large data set research* for policy, including her linking of magnet hospitals to lower mortality rates, which conceptualized the nursing magnet in a way that made sense outside the field (Aiken et al, 1994; Aiken et al, 1997). For nursing, the trick is to conceptualize the variables in large data sets as *nursing* so that the results can be attributable to nursing (Buerhaus & Needleman, 2001. Length of stay and mortality are powerful variables from a policy point of view, and they can be linked to nursing given appropriate conceptualization and study design. There are many variables, especially in standard, computerized hospital information systems, that can be taken as evidence of the effect of nursing.

Research aside, it is now clear that there is a role in policy-making for the cleverly selected and carefully placed anecdote. Nurses might see ourselves as having a very deep pit of narratives and anecdotes that can be brought to public attention. No other profession is in possession of the stories of patient experiences with the health care delivery system, which is what health policy is all about.

CONCLUSION

For research to be useful in policy, the policy agenda ought first to be clear either to the researchers as a possibility or in an existing policy agenda. Elizabeth Hadley (1996) writes from her experience as an assistant attorney general, a lobbyist, and federal agency staffer about how the internal divisions within nursing compromise our policy strivings and make using data difficult. We must simply get over this.

Kingdon (1995) notes that academic research influences policy to the extent that the researcher makes it available, including targeting congressional staffers regularly. The official publication of nursing's largest professional organization, the *American Journal of Nursing* for ANA, under new leadership, is increasingly becoming a forum for policy debate. The *American Journal of Nursing's*

ANA and paid subscription circulation is larger than *NEJM's* and larger than *JAMA's* paid subscription circulation. The largest circulation scholarly journal in nursing, *Image,* for Sigma Theta Tau, does not take policy positions, but it publishes important discussion of policy issues, much as *NEJM* and *JAMA* do.

Research is not something to be plugged in when a policy or political crisis rears up. Timing is everything. Nurses, as politicians, policymakers, and researchers, need to keep (or have access to those who keep) such close touch with what is happening in the policy and political environment that we can anticipate trends and design studies to address them. We need to have networks of information, which is simpler now with Internet web pages such as www.nursingworld.org, MEDLINE, Nexus, Lexus, and all the other computer tools. We need to learn when anecdote is more powerful than statistical significance and how to present our research to make a difference. We need to keep data on our own practices, especially advanced practice, because there will—trust me—come a time when those data will turn a challenge around.

These, then, are the multiple and simultaneous strategies:

- Keep or find nursing data. Find and use the computerized information systems in the practice or the institution. Don't worry about whether the data are labeled as nursing. If you do the work, you own the information.
- Understand the agenda. Things are not always what they seem. Ask "What is the problem here?" Or "To what problem is this (reengineering, downsizing, policy change) a solution?" And follow up with "How do you know? What are the data?"
- Shape the agenda. Believe (because it is true) that others do not necessarily know more than you do about the work, even if they are administrators or doctors. Know the players, teams, and organizations. What do *you* think ought to happen, and how can you get there? What's *right*? What's simple, cost-effective, or important? Data are powerful, often more powerful than they deserve to be. But she or he who hath the data hath it all.

- Do good research. Nobody wants to do bad research, so what this is meant to signal is only that carefully designed and conducted research can stand on its own even in the face of methodologic criticism, which will always come. If the research can have a policy hook—money, quality, equity—so much the better.
- Ride in on others' research. Read the research literature, mine it, distill it, use it to advantage even when it's not perfect.
- Recognize when anecdote is more powerful than large samples and multiple regression statistics. Learn how to write evocatively. Back up anecdote with numbers when you can. True stories from real people can move mountains that no amount of data can. Don't be afraid to tell those stories. Nurses have millions of them.
- If you're a researcher and want to get your findings published, think about using the public relations (PR) people in your institution. Sorry about this, but researchers are often boring. PR people know how to convert boring information into powerful stories. Use them.
- Partner with nurses doing policy work. Every nurse who manages anything, including case management, is doing policy-related work.

Finally, recognize that no amount of research will save us. Because research runs by the rules of science, it is rational, perhaps suprarational, according to those who would wish a less quantitative and more qualitative, human, and respectful notion of science. Politics, political science, and even policy-making have their own rules that are equally rational (Paltiel & Stinnett, 1996). Making research serve policy and political ends means learning the rules when research or science collide with political or other entrenched values.

Acknowledgment: The author thanks Sally Cohen, RN, PhD for colleagueship, especially in supplying new resources.

REFERENCES

AHCPR drops guideline development. (1996, June). *HSR Reports,* 4. Association for Health Services Research, 1130 Connecticut Ave. NW, Washington, DC 20036.

Aiken, L.H., et al. (2001). Nurses' reports of hospital quality of care and working conditions in five countries. *Health Affairs, 20*(3), 43-53.

Aiken, L.H. & Mullinix, C. (1987). The nurse shortage: Myth or reality? *New England Journal of Medicine, 317,* 641-646.

Aiken, L.H., Smith, H.L., & Lake, E.T. (1994). Lower Medicare mortality among a set of hospitals known for good nursing care. *Medical Care, 32*(8), 771-778.

Aiken, L.H., Sochalski, J., & Lake, E.T. (1997). Studying outcomes of organizational change in health services. *Medical Care, 35*(Suppl), NS6-NS18.

AMA "Citizens' petition" sent to HCFA. (2000, June 27). Nursing World/Legislative Branch. Available online at www.nursingworld.org/gova/federal/agencies/hcfa/hcfaama.htm.

American Hospital Association. (1988). *Draft report of the 1987 Hospital Nursing Demand Survey.* Chicago: Author.

American Medical Association, Council on Scientific Affairs. (1992). Assault weapons as a public health hazard in the United States. *Journal of the American Medical Association, 267,* 3067-3070.

Berens, M.J. (2000a, September 10). Nursing mistakes kill, injure thousands. *Chicago Tribune,* 20.

Berens, M.J. (2000b, September 11). Training often takes a back seat. *Chicago Tribune,* 7.

Berens, M.J. (2000c, September 12). Problem nurses escape punishment. *Chicago Tribune,* 1.

Blegen, M.A. & Vaughn, T. (1998). A multisite study of nursing staffing and patient outcomes. *Nursing Economic$, 16*(4), 196-203

Blendon, R.J., Young, J.T., & Hemenway, D. (1996). The American public and the gun control debate. *Journal of the American Medical Association, 275*(22), 1719-1722.

Bonneyman, G. (1996). Stealth reform: Market-based Medicaid in Tennessee. *Health Affairs, 15*(2), 307-314.

Brown, S.A. & Grimes, D.E. (1995). A meta-analysis of nurse practitioners and nurse-midwives in primary care. *Nursing Research, 44*(6), 332-339.

Buerhaus, P.I. (1997). What is the harm in imposing mandatory hospital nursing staffing regulations? *Nursing Economic$, 15,* 66-72.

Buerhaus, P.I. & Needleman, J. (2001). Policy implications of research on nurse staffing and quality of care. *Policy, Politics & Nursing Practice, 1,* 5-15.

Buerhaus, P.I. & Staiger, D.O. (1999). Trouble in the nurse labor market? Recent trends and future outlook. *Health Affairs, 18*(1), 214-222.

Buresh, B. & Gordon, S. (2000). *From silence to voice: What nurses know and must communicate to the public.* Ottawa: Canadian Nurses Association.

Cobb, R., Ross, J.K., & Ross, J.H. (1976). Agenda building as a comparative political process. *The American Political Science Review, 70,* 125-138.

Cohen, S.S., Mason, D.J., Kovner, C., Leavitt, J.K., Pulcini, J., & Sochalski, J. (1996). Stages of nursing's political development: Where we've been and where we ought to go. *Nursing Outlook, 44*(12), 259-266.

Cole, E. (1982, November 22). *Testimony before the House Subcommittee on Health and Environment of the Committee on Energy and Commerce* (Serial 97-183). Washington, DC: U.S. Government Printing Office.

Curtis, B. (1983, February 14). *Testimony before the Subcommittee on Health of the House Ways and Means Committee (Serial 98-6).* Washington, DC: U.S. Government Printing Office.

Deliver, then depart. (1995, July 10). *Newsweek, 126*(2), 62.

The departure of Jerome P. Kassirir. (1999). *New England Journal of Medicine, 341*(17), 1310-1313.

Deyo, R. A., Psaty, B. M., Simon, G., Wagner, E. H., & Omenn, G.S. (1997). The messenger under attack: Intimidation of researchers by special-interest groups. *New England Journal of Medicine, 336*(16), 1176-1179.

Diers, D. (1992a). Diagnosis-related groups and the measurement of nursing. In L.H. Aiken (Ed.). *Charting nursing's future.* Philadelphia: J.B. Lippincott.

Diers, D. (1992b). Nurse-midwives and nurse anesthetists: The cutting edge in specialist practice. In L.H. Aiken (Ed.), *Charting nursing's future.* Philadelphia: J.B. Lippincott.

Diers, D. (1998). Research as a policy/political tool. In D. Mason & J. Leavitt (Eds.). *Policy and politics in nursing and health care.* Philadelphia: W.B. Saunders.

Diers, D & Potter, J. (1997). Understanding the unmanageable nursing unit with case-mix data. *Journal of Nursing Administration, 27*(11), 27-32.

Division of Nursing, Bureau of Health Manpower, Health Research Services Administration, U.S. Department of Health and Human Services. (1984). *The registered nurse population, findings from the national sample survey of registered nurses, November 1984.* Washington, DC: Author.

Dong, B.J., Hauck, W.W., Gambertoglio, J.G., Gee, L., White, J.R., Bubp, J.L., & Greenspan, F.S. (1997). Bioequivalence of generic and brand-name levothyroxine products in the treatment of hypothyroidism. *Journal of the American Medical Association, 277*(15), 1205-1213.

Editor's note. (1997). *New England Journal of Medicine, 336*(14), 1034-1035.

Fagin, C.M. (2001) *When care becomes a burden: Diminishing access to adequate nursing.* New York: Milbank Memorial Fund.

Fletcher, S. (1997). Whither scientific deliberation in health policy recommendations? Alice in the wonderland of breast-cancer screening. *New England Journal of Medicine, 336*(16), 1180-1183.

Glantz, S.A., Fox, B.J., & Lightwood, J.M. (1997). Tobacco litigation: Issues for public health and public policy. *Journal of the American Medical Association, 277*(9), 751-753.

Gold, M. (1997). Markets and public programs: Insights from Oregon and Tennessee. *Journal of Health Politics, Policy and Law, 22*(2), 633-666.

Goldsmith, M.F. (1999). George D. Lundberg ousted as JAMA editor. *Journal of the American Medical Association, 281*(5), 403.

Gray, B.H. (1992). The legislative battle over health services research. *Health Affairs, 11*(4), 38-66.

Hadley, E.H. (1996). Nursing in the political and economic marketplace: Challenges for the 21st century. *Nursing Outlook, 44*(1), 6-10.

Katz, A. (1997, April 8). Personal values get in way of bridging science, policy. *New Haven Register*, A6.

Kellerman, A.L. (1993). Obstacles to firearm and violence research. *Health Affairs, 12*(4), 142-153.

Kessler, D.A. (2001). *A question of intent: A great American battle with a deadly industry.* New York: PublicAffairs.

Kessler, D.A., Barnett, P.S., Witt, A., Zeller, M.R., Mande, J.R., & Schultz, W.B. (1997). The legal and scientific basis for FDA's assertion of jurisdiction over cigarettes and smokeless tobacco. *Journal of the American Medical Association*, 405-418.

Kingdon, J.W. (1995). *Agendas, alternatives, and public policies* (2nd ed.). New York: HarperCollins.

Kohn, L.T., Corrigan, J.M., & Donaldson, M.S. (Eds.). (2000). *To err is human: Building a safer health system.* Washington, DC: National Academy Press.

Koop, C.E. & Lundberg, G.B. (1992). Violence in America: A public health emergency—time to bite the bullet back. *Journal of the American Medical Association, 267*, 3075-3076.

Kovner, C. & Gergen, P.J. (1998). Nurse staffing levels and adverse events following surgery in US hospitals. *Image: Journal of Nursing Scholarship, 30*(4), 315-321.

Lewis, E.P. (1961). Pressure points. *American Journal of Nursing, 61*(6), 41.

Maraldo, P. & Solomon, S. (1987). Nursing's window of opportunity. *Image: Journal of Nursing Scholarship, 19*(2), 83-86.

Marmor, T. (1973). *The politics of Medicare.* Chicago: Aldine.

Maternity leave. (1996, February). *Harper's Magazine, 292* (1749), 14.

McDonough, J.E. (2001). Using and misusing anecdote in policy making. *Health Affairs, 20*(1), 207-212.

Medical Care. (1994, Annual supplement). *32*(7).

Medical Care. (1995, Annual supplement). *33*(4).

Mirvis, D.M., Chang, C.F., Hall, C.J., Zaar, G.T., & Applegate, W.B. (1995). TennCare: Health system reform for Tennessee. *Journal of the American Medical Association, 274*(15), 1235-1241.

Mooney, C.Z. (2001) *The public clash of private values: The politics of morality policy.* New York: Chatham House.

Mundinger, M., et al. (2000). Primary care outcomes in patients treated by nurse prctitioners or physicians: A randomized trial. *Journal of the American Medical Association, 283*, 59-68.

Needleman, J., Buerhaus, P.I., Mattke, S., Stewart, M., & Zelevinsky, K. (2001, February 28). *Nurse staffing and patient outcomes in hospitals* (final report). U.S. Department of Health and Human Services, HRSA Contract 230-99-0021.

Normand, J., Vlahov, D., & Moses, L. (Eds.). (1995). *Preventing HIV transmission: The role of sterile needles and bleach.* Washington, DC: National Academy Press.

Nursing's response to AMA "Citizens' Petition" sent to HCFA. (2000, August 17). Nursing World/Legislative Branch. Available online at www.nursingworld.org/gova/federal/agencies/hcfa/ama.htm.

Nursing workforce: Emerging nurse shortages due to multiple factors (report to the Chairman, Subcommittee on Health, Committee on Ways and Means, U.S. House of Representatives). U.S. General Accounting Office GAO-010944, July 2001. Available online at www.gao.gov.

Office of Technology Assessment. (1988). *Nurse practitioners, physician assistants and certified nurse-midwives: A policy analysis.* Washington, DC: U.S. Government Printing Office.

Paltiel, A.D. & Stinnett, A. A. (1996). Making health policy decisions: Is human instinct rational? Is rational choice human? *Change, 9*(2), 34-39.

Pearson, L. (2001). Annual update on how each state stands on legislative issues affecting advanced nursing practice: A survey of legal authority, reimbursement status and prescriptive authority. *The Nurse Practitioner, 26*(1), 7-15.

Price, L. & Minarik, P. (1998). More on Medicare reimbursement: Clarification of direct billing and "incident to" billing. *Clinical Nurse Specialist, 12*, 246-249.

Price, L. & Minarik, P. (1999). Update on federal Medicare rules affecting advanced practice nurses. *Clinical Nurse Specialist, 13*, 90-91.

Rennie, D. (1997). Thyroid storm. *Journal of the American Medical Association, 277*(15), 1238-1243.

Safriet, B. (1992). Health care dollars and regulatory sense. *Yale Journal on Regulation, 9*(2), 417-488.

Secretary's Commission on the Nursing Shortage, U.S. Department of Health and Human Services. (1988, December). *Final report* (Vol. 1). Washington, DC: U.S. Department of Health and Human Services.

Sharf, B.F. (2001). Out of the closet and into the legislature: Breast cancer stories. *Health Affairs, 20*(1), 213-218.

Shindul-Rothschild, J., Berry, D., & Long-Middleton, E. (1996). Where have all the nurses gone? Final results of our patient care survey. *American Journal of Nursing, 96*(11), 25-39.

Shortage of nurses hits hardest where they are needed the most. (2001, January 24). *Wall Street Journal*, A1, A12.

Sloan, J.H., et al. (1988). Handgun regulations, crime, assault and homicide: A tale of two cities. *New England Journal of Medicine, 319*(19), 1256-1262.

Sloan, J.H., Rivara, F.P., Reay, D.T., Ferris, J.A., & Kellerman, A.L. (1990). Firearm regulations and rates of suicide: A comparison of two metropolitan areas. *New England Journal of Medicine, 322*(6), 369-373.

Sox, H.C. (2000). Independent primary care practice by nurse practitioners. *Journal of the American Medical Association, 283*, 106-107.

A spineless attack on the AHCPR. (1996). *Geriatrics, 51*(4), 9-10.

Spitzer, W.O. (1984). The nurse practitioner revisited: Slow death of a good idea. *New England Journal of Medicine, 310*, 1049-1051.

Spitzer, W.O., Sackett, D.L., Sibley, J.C., Roberts, R.S., Gent, M., Kergin, D.J., Hackett, B.C., & Olynich, A. (1974). The Burlington randomized trial of the nurse practitioner. *New England Journal of Medicine, 290*, 251-256.

Tanenbaum, S.J. (1996). Medical effectiveness in Canadian and U.S. health policy: The comparative politics of inferential ambiguity. *Health Services Research, 31*(5), 517-532.

Thompson, J.D. (1988). DRG prepayment: Its purpose and performance. *Bulletin of the New York Academy of Medicine, 64*(1), 25-51.

Todd, J.S. (1991, May 3). *Support for H.R. 7, the "Brady Handgun Violence Prevention Act"* (letter to members of the U.S. House of Representatives). Chicago: American Medical Association.

Varney, H. (1996). *Varney's midwifery* (3rd ed.). Boston: Jones & Bartlett.

Wunderlich, G.S., Sloan, F.A., & Davis, C.K. (Eds.). (1996). *Nursing staff in hospitals and nursing homes: Is it adequate?* Washington, DC: National Academy Press.

Role of the Media in Influencing Policy: Getting the Message Across

DIANA J. MASON

CATHERINE J. DODD

BARBARA GLICKSTEIN

"Congress shall make no law . . . abridging the freedom of speech, or of the press, or the right of the people peaceably to assemble, and to petition the Government for redress of grievances."

U.S. CONSTITUTION, FIRST AMENDMENT

"Whoever controls the media—the images—controls the culture."

ALLEN GINSBERG

The first amendment of the U. S. Constitution gives the "press" constitutional protection not afforded any other enterprise in the country. Many would argue that this protection is essential because the press plays a crucial watchdog role in our system of government. Indeed, a true free press, one not wholly owned by a handful of corporate interests as is becoming the case today, should serve to monitor and report on the unchecked power of the president and Congress (Kalb, 1997).

The last decade of the century was considered "the information age," and now we are in the "telecommunication age." Information is crowded into "sound bites" and visual images that communicate instant messages and shape public opinion.

Although some argue that sound bites represent superficial communications, Jamieson (2000, i) counters that they can be substantive: "Substantive soundbites are the stuff of which the best news stories are made."

Certainly, instant messaging is changing the role of the individual in our government. Today, political leaders and well-financed special interests use the wonders of modern technology—television, telephone, satellite, cable, and personal computers—to send scientifically tested and well-crafted messages in an instant and, almost as quickly, to receive feedback from members of the public who have access to these media. In fact, telecommunication systems have provided people with direct access to policymakers. It is transforming our democracy from representational government to a direct democracy. Our constitution, the doctrine that protects freedom of the press, was designed to separate the rulers from the ruled. Every citizen can participate in electing representatives who conduct the business of government. The founders of our country created a representational republic (Grossman, 1997). But that is changing.

Representatives today are listening to the instant feedback from their constituents who have the means and motivation to communicate and are modifying their positions based on these public opinions. Lawrence Grossman (1997), former president of NBC News and Public Broadcasting Service, questions whether this new "electronic republic" will make government more responsive to the people or whether it will be manipulated by individuals pursuing their own ends at the expense of those without access to telecommunications or motivation to participate.

In addition, media profoundly influences who gets elected to public office. An effective media strategy can shift voters' decisions late in the campaign. In fact, no candidate for national or state office can expect to capture voters' commitment on election day without a well-designed media campaign. Indeed, such media strategies have become the prime stimulus for escalating costs of running a campaign. Candidates either have to bring their personal wealth to their campaigns, or they have to be willing to spend the majority of their time in fundraising. Will this distort who can run for public office and whether our public officials are representative of the constituency they serve?

In the 1990s nurses became increasingly concerned about their invisibility in the media (Buresh, Gordon, & Bell, 1991; Sigma Theta Tau International, 1998). Although gains have been made, this invisibility limits nursing's ability to advocate for health policy (Chaffee, 2000). Nurses are viewed by the public and by policymakers as credible, moral, and trustworthy, and they must participate in the new "electronic republic." This chapter discusses the role of media in policy and politics and provides nurses with strategies to access and use the media to promote healthy public policies.

POWER OF THE MEDIA

A classic example of the power of media in shaping health policy arose during the first months of William Jefferson Clinton's presidency. When President Clinton took office in 1992, one of his primary domestic policy priorities was the guarantee of comprehensive health care coverage for every American. In September 1993 he proposed the Health Security Act to Congress and the public with the hope and anticipation that this would become landmark legislation. The nursing community was particularly supportive of this legislation because it recognized advanced practice nurses as important providers of primary care. Clinton's proposal initially had substantial public support, because many believed the country had a moral imperative to extend health care coverage to all who lived here. However, two curious characters, Harry and Louise, had a tremendous impact on shifting the public's sentiments, dashing the hopes of President Clinton and nurses, who saw the legislation as an important remedy for an ailing health care system.

Harry and Louise were characters in a series of television advertisements sponsored by the Health Insurance Association of America, which adamantly opposed the president's plan. Actors portrayed this couple voicing grave concerns about the bill. They said, "Under the President's bill, we'll lose our right to choose our own physician," and "What happens if the plan runs out of money?" Although the advertisements were not the only reason for the demise of the Health Security Act, Harry and Louise effectively planted fear and negativity in the hearts and minds of many citizens within the span of 60 seconds (Annenberg Public Policy Center of the University of Pennsylvania, 1995). Suddenly, many of those Americans who had been concerned about the growing numbers of uninsured became more concerned about how the bill would affect their own health care options and withdrew their support from the Act.

What many do not realize about the Harry and Louise commercials is the fact that the target audience was not the public, directly. Rather, it was policymakers and those who could influence how the public perceived the issue: journalists. The ads originally aired in Washington, DC, Los Angeles, New York City, and Atlanta and were subsequently seen and reported on by journalists. In fact, the ads got more air time by becoming part of the journalists' news stories. Many people who saw the ads did so through viewing them as part of the evening news (Annenberg Public Policy Center of the University of Pennsylvania, 1995), not as a paid advertisement.

The Harry and Louise commercials are an example of a deliberate media strategy to mobilize a public constituency around a public policy issue. It is one illustration of the power of media in policy and politics. The media saturate this nation and much of the world with images that change people's opinions, shape their attitudes and beliefs, and transform their behavior (McAlister, 1991).

INDIVIDUAL VERSUS AGGREGATE FOCUS

Schmid, Pratt, and Howze (1995) argue that individual-focused interventions for changing health behaviors are limited in long-term effectiveness; rather, they maintain that community or aggregate-focused interventions hold the greatest promise for improving the health of communities. An example of aggregate-focused interventions is public policy such as U.S. sanitation laws, which had a dramatic effect on the health and quality of life for many people. The media provide a potentially powerful aggregate approach to influencing public policies that can promote health. Certainly, media can be viewed as a political tool. Turow (1996, p. 1240) notes, "Journalists now recognize that public discussions of medicine are necessarily political—i.e., they are ultimately about the exercise of social power."

The media's power arises from its ability to get a message to large numbers of people, or to key people instantly. Talk radio, which has proliferated in the past decade and has become more popular because of long commuting times and cellular phones, is a volatile medium. The loudest and most provocative radio voices often produce higher ratings and command higher prices for advertising. Information presented by talk show hosts and their callers is not screened by editors for accuracy and objectivity. Talk show hosts are often chosen for their provocative style rather than their broadcast skills (Rehm, 1997). Nurses can play an important role in providing fair and factual information on health issues and concerns when talk radio is misrepresenting issues.

For example, during a single payor health care campaign several talk shows hosted guests to discuss the pros and cons of a single payor system. Nurses and other advocates of a single-payor system served as "radio response squads" to shape the debate. When the American Nurses Association (ANA) president is on a talk show, state nurses associations in the area are asked to get their members ready to call in. Hundreds of thousands of people are listening to these calls. (Box 10-1 provides more information on calling in to talk radio.)

The Internet is increasingly taking center stage as a vehicle for sharing information and shaping public opinion. It provides uncensored access, speed, and a snow-balling effect in which the message can take on a life of its own. Former Speaker of the House of Representatives Tom Foley (D-WA) found that his reelection defeat in 1994 was brought about by an Internet campaign against him launched by a few dissatisfied citizens. It quickly became an initiative to test the power of the Internet in defeating a political candidate.

Paid advertising also influences the public's perceptions and knowledge about health issues. Each of us is now confronted with thousands of paid messages per day. Advertising is found on cereal boxes, on milk cartons, in journals, in magazines, in

BOX **10-1**   Calling in to Talk Radio

When you want to call a talk radio show, listen to the host a few times before calling. Does he cut off callers or let them respond to feedback? If he cuts them off, it is important to get factual data in during your first "sound bite."

Practice your message. If you can, write it down, and say it slowly.

Hosts are sometimes nicer to "first-time callers," so if you are a novice, say so when you identify yourself. (If you end up being a regular caller that won't work, but once a month it will.)

Popular talk shows are difficult to get into, so use the redial function on your phone. If the producer asks, "Do you agree or disagree with what is being said?" be prepared to say you have a question (and have one). Then, when you get on the air, state your credentials and make your point: "I am an oncology nurse and I care for people with HIV and I know firsthand that the state must provide higher reimbursement rates for home care services." Following a point such as this with a story from your practice can be powerful.

Do not just hang up after you've finished. The host or guest might respond to your opinion, and you can attempt to respond.

newspapers, at bus stops, on billboards, even on the sides of buses. Television ads often include text on the screen because many people use a "mute" button during the commercials.

In 1997 the Food and Drug Administration (FDA) changed the rules and regulations governing pharmaceutical advertising to consumers. Direct-to-consumer advertising can now be seen in news magazines, in train stations, on television, on the radio, and everywhere the public travels. Consumers in turn ask their providers for these advertised drugs, which are often more costly than generic forms. This advertising has contributed to increases in health care spending that began during the late 1990s and has put prescription drug coverage on the agenda of state and federal policymakers.

Although FDA regulations require that the ads not misrepresent the product, pharmaceutical companies carefully select images that send messages beyond the stated or printed word. For example, the FDA sent letters to the manufacturers of drugs used to treat HIV, cautioning them about their advertising. Many of these ads showed strong and healthy-looking individuals engaged in strenuous physical activity. In San Francisco, the director of sexually transmitted disease prevention and control services at the city's department of health said the ads were false portrayals of HIV-infected clients. He also suggested that the ads contributed to risky behavior because the impression from the ads is that HIV is easily manageable with medication.

NURSING AND THE MEDIA

Two studies during the 1990s documented nursing's invisibility in the media (Buresh et al, 1991; Sigma Theta Tau International, 1998). The most recent of these is the *Woodhull Study on Nursing and the Media*, which found that nurses were included in health stories in major print media (newspapers and news magazines) less than 4% of the time, even when they would have been germane to the story. An even more disturbing finding was the fact that nurses were represented in health care industry publications less than 1% of the time. Buresh and Gordon (2000a) suggest that findings such as these could be systematic journalistic bias against nurs-

ing. But they also note that nurses are not proactive in accessing the media. (See Buresh and Gordon's book *From Silence to Voice: What Nurses Know and Must Communicate to the Public*, 2000b).

Nurses are often keenly aware of how the media misrepresent them and their work. In many news articles, nurses may appear in the text and story without being identified. In the mid-1990s, organized nursing mounted a strategic campaign to shape public opinion about the importance of what nurses contribute to health care. During this decade the cost-focused reengineering, restructuring, and downsizing of health care organizations led many organizations to eliminate nursing positions and substitute nurses with unlicensed assistive personnel. In response to the ANA campaign slogan "Every Patient Deserves a Nurse," the New York State Nurses Association invested several million dollars to launch a media campaign with the message "Every Patient Deserves an RN—a Real Nurse" (Sheridan-Gonzalez, & Wade, 1998). Television, radio, and print ads appeared in targeted areas throughout the state, including the capital city of Albany, where policymakers and their staff would see the ads. The campaign offered a "hospital evaluation kit" that people could use to evaluate the adequacy of nursing in their hospital, and the association distributed 75,000 kits. Policymakers talked about the campaign, as did nurses' neighbors, friends, and family. It put nursing on the public's agenda and created support for nursing's legislative agenda.

Nurse researchers need to be more proactive in communicating their work to journalists. In many cases, researchers can and should be turning to their institutional public relations department for expertise and support in developing press releases and pitching the story to journalists. But the public relations people will need the researcher's help in describing the relevance of the research to journalists. Most journalists are not interested in conceptual frameworks and details beyond descriptive and summary statistics. They want to know why the research would be of interest to the public, what the primary findings were, and how these findings can be used. Some doctoral programs now require that their students define both the policy and public relevance of their research. A more aggressive approach to public dissemination of nursing research would enhance the public's perception of nursing as a science while promoting research utilization, including by policymakers.

GETTING ISSUES ON THE PUBLIC'S AGENDA

What the media do or do not cover is equally powerful in determining what issues are considered by policymakers. Here are a few examples:

- The epidemic of human immunodeficiency virus/acquired immune deficiency syndrome (HIV/AIDS) is recognized as having been exacerbated by a lack of coverage by the media and journalists who saw it as a problem limited to promiscuous gay men and drug abusers (Shilts, 1987).
- When the front page of an influential newspaper carries a headline and story about the use of nurse practitioners as primary care providers, the issue is "on the agenda" of policymakers and the public.
- In 2000 the front page of *USA Today* reported on a study of family presence during resuscitation and invasive procedures published in the *American Journal of Nursing.* This and other widespread television, radio, print, and Internet coverage prompted debates on the issue and pressure on health care institutions to examine and change their policies.
- Walt Bogdanich and his colleagues at *The Wall Street Journal* published a front-page article in February 1987 on the misreading of Pap smears by laboratory technicians that left some women with a misdiagnosis. One year later, Congress passed the Clinical Laboratory Improvement Amendments, requiring minimum standards for laboratory operations and technician training (Otten, 1992).
- When the *Washington Post, Wall Street Journal,* and *The New York Times* publish articles on the nursing shortage, local media pick up the issue and cover it with a local perspective. President George W. Bush's first budget was rumored to slash spending for the education of health professionals. Instead, he proposed continuing the 2001 allocation for nursing education, most

likely as a result of the enormous media attention that the shortage was receiving at the time the budget was being finalized.

Milio (2000) points out that policymakers are increasingly relying on "information brokers" to be informed about policy matters. Public officials often first learn about an issue through the press. In fact, a bill can be wallowing in the mire of legislative bureaucracy with no hope of passage until media highlight the issue that the bill addresses. For instance, many states and local communities had considered policies to restrict teenagers' access to cigarettes, but it took a media exposé on the deliberate targeting of adolescents by a cigarette manufacturer through the "Joe Camel" ads to get some of the legislation passed.

Although the news media are instrumental in getting issues onto the agenda of policymakers, non-news entertainment television programs can mobilize public constituencies around an issue. Turow (1996, p. 1249) points out that non-news television entertainment is particularly loaded with rhetoric that often stereotypes power relationships and may be more successful than the news in shaping people's images of the world:

Highly viewed TV presentations of medicine hold political significance that should be assessed alongside news. Like the rhetorical struggles in news about medicine, series such as *ER, Dr. Quinn, Medicine Woman, Diagnosis: Murder,* and *Chicago Hope* are ultimately about power. Every week, they act out ideas about the medical system's authority to define, prevent and treat illness.

Such programming can shape people's expectations, beliefs, and opinions of medicine, nursing, and health care (Brodie, Foehr, Rideout, Baer, Miller, Flournoy, & Altman, 2001). The television show "ER" has had episodes with seniors needing emergency care because the husband took the wife's medications when they could not afford to buy the drugs prescribed for each of them. Another episode showed the plight of a poor minority patient who did not receive the same treatment referral as a white, well-insured patient. The popular White House-inspired "West Wing" series has covered ergonomic regulations for workplace injuries, abortion, the death penalty, homophobia and hate crimes, homelessness, clean air, Cuban refugees, and tax cuts.

EVALUATING PUBLIC POLICY

Media can also highlight the outcomes of a public policy. In 1989 New York decided to try to reduce the mortality rate after cardiac bypass surgery by requiring all hospitals to report on the case mix, risk factors, and outcomes of this surgery. The state analyzed these data, developed a method of ranking hospitals on their mortality rates, and released these rankings to the public. The media responded with feature stories highlighting "the best" and "the worst," or which hospital outranked another in the same community. In addition, one newspaper won a court case requiring the state to release the ranked data by individual surgeon. Unfortunately, not all journalists knew statistics well enough to realize that some of the differences in rankings that they were highlighting were not statistically significant or clinically meaningful. As a result of such misinterpretations of the data, the state decided to educate journalists about the outcome initiative, interpretations of the data, and the need to emphasize what hospitals and surgeons were doing to improve the quality of care. Subsequent media coverage has highlighted the quality improvements that were made. Although the state once feared that the media coverage could undermine the effort to push for public reporting of medical outcomes, the program is now considered a model that has been replicated in other states and for other conditions or procedures (Chassin, Hannan, & DeBuono, 1996), and public reporting of outcome data is expected of health plans and institutions.

CAMPAIGNING AND ELECTION OUTCOMES

Media can also determine who gets elected to public office. When a candidate running for public office wakes up to a news report on his or her own questionable financial dealings, the candidate worries, even if the story is unfounded. The image of the candidate in the minds of many can be tarnished forever. Similarly, the candidate's campaign manager and staff will read the letters to the editor of the newspaper to see which issues and positions are of concern to a community. They will also stage *media events.* These are a type of on-site press conference at a place that provides the visual images (for television and press photos) representative of an attention-getting problem that the candidate commits to resolve through policy initiatives. For example, the ANA announced its endorsement of the Clinton-Gore ticket in 1991 at a hospital in California in which patients, staff, and nurses from all over the state gathered to show support for the nomination. This event highlighted Clinton's commitment to health care and the support of nurses, a group that the public trusts.

The presidential election in 2000 was controversial, not just because of chads and other balloting problems, but because the news media called the outcome of the Bush-Gore race before the votes were tallied sufficiently to accurately predict who would be the next president. When one television news anchor said that Bush had won, then later retracted the statement, both Republicans and Democrats cried foul, recognizing that a premature call on the outcome of a race can actually change what those who have not yet voted decide to do (including whether to even go to the polls and bother to vote in a race that that has already been called). In fact, media coverage of elections has become quite controversial and a focal point for discussions of ethics in journalism.

WHO CONTROLS THE MEDIA

With all this power vested in the media, concern exists about who controls the media. This is becoming increasingly important as large corporations buy up networks of television or radio stations (Naureckas, 1995). Federal funding of public media, such as National Public Radio and the television's Corporation for Public Broadcasting, has been reduced in recent years, raising concerns about whether there will be any media in the United States that are not privately controlled. In recent years, public radio and television stations began providing more visible and lengthy acknowledgments of corporate contributions. Although the style of these notices usually differs from that of ads on commercial stations, their impact is noticeable and raises concerns about the corporations' influence on programming and bias. For example, when the local community hospital begins significant underwriting of a radio station's programming, will that station hesitate to report on the hospital's nurses' strike, or on a recent citation from the state for unsafe care?

As health care has become more corporate, so has the media. A few wealthy corporations have bought newspapers, television, radio, and cable networks. It is essential that the public view the media with the understanding that "he who owns the network controls the message." Protecting public broadcasting service is imperative to maintaining balanced reporting.

FOCUS ON REPORTING

One can also argue that individual journalists are equally responsible for their choice of issues to cover and how they cover them. Getting to know the nature and quality of particular journalists' work can help you to decide how much trust to place in their work.

- Do they frequently misrepresent issues?
- Are their stories sensationalized, overplayed, or exaggerated?
- Do they present all sides of an issue with accuracy, fairness, and depth?

Journalists rarely have the same depth of knowledge about a topic as insiders. Fallows (1996) provides an informative critique of and challenge to the media in his book *Breaking the News*. He argues that the media have contributed to a public cynicism of politics and policymakers that has resulted in a largely uninvolved citizenry. This is due partially to journalists' having limited expertise on particular issues; as a result, they often cover only the political dimensions of an issue rather than the details of the policy options (see also Turow, 1996).

In addition to the Harry and Louise commercials, the media influenced the demise of President Clinton's Health Security Act in other ways that demonstrate this point. Dorfman, Schauffler, Wilkerson, and Feinson (1996) reported that in-depth analysis and explanation of the issues and the legislation were scarce in local news coverage; the focus tended to be superficial coverage of the risks and costs of the legislation to specific stakeholders. In

fact, Milio (2000) notes that full debate of approaches to remedying an ailing health care system was not available to most citizens, because the single-payor alternative was rarely covered by the press. In an analysis of media coverage of the issue, the Annenberg Public Policy Center (1995, p. iv) found that the press concentrated on only a few of the alternative proposals for health care reform, focused reporting on strategy rather than on the pros and cons of proposals, magnified the impact of negative fear-based advertisements by focusing on them, and "had a tendency to filter both elections and policy debates through a set of cynical assumptions, including the notion that politicians act out of self-interest rather than a commitment to the public good."

ANALYZING THE MEDIA

Although this chapter advocates that nurses more frequently and effectively use the media as a political tool, the first obligation that all nurses have is to be knowledgeable consumers of media messages. Each nurse needs to be able to critically evaluate media messages. Box 10-2 provides an exercise to analyze newspaper reporting critically.

WHAT IS THE MEDIUM?

The first step is to ask yourself where you get your information and news.

- What television and radio news-related programming do you regularly tune in to? Do you read a daily newspaper?
- What is the station's, program's, or paper's reputation? Is it known for balanced coverage of health-related issues? Is it partisan?
- Does it cover national as well as state and local issues?
- Is it a credible source of information about health issues and policies?

These questions provide a basis for you to judge whether the information and news that you are getting is credible and representative of a broad sector of public opinion. On any particular issue of concern, you will want to sample various media presentations of the issue and evaluate their messages and effectiveness.

BOX **10-2** How to Analyze Newspaper Reporting

The following exercise on how to analyze a newspaper expands one that was developed by Douglas (1991) for Fairness and Accuracy in the Media (FAIR), a national media watch group that critically analyzes news reports to raise consciousness about, and to correct, bias and imbalance.

- Get a recent copy of two or more national newspapers. Find an issue of concern and compare the papers on their coverage of the issue.
- First, note where the article is placed. Is it on the front page? Is it buried amid advertisements in a small portion of one column in the last section of the paper? Why do you think it received front, or last, page coverage?
- Second, note who wrote the article. The reputation of journalists can give you a sense of what bias might appear in the reporting, whether the coverage is likely to be balanced, and whether this journalist is someone who is known for in-depth investigative reporting.
- Third, what are the sources of information that are reported in the article? Every time a government official (e.g., president, other administration official, congressional representative, or staff) says something, highlight the passage with a yellow marker. This includes "anonymous high-placed

public officials" whose names and formal titles are not included. Every time the source is nongovernmental, highlight the passage with a pink marker. With a blue marker, note every time a woman or a person of color is mentioned or quoted. Now compare these passages. The ratio of yellow to pink to blue suggests what and who are routinely considered most important.

- For health reporting, note how often journalists quote or refer to nurses as opposed to physicians. How might the article be different if nurses were a primary source of information on the topic?
- What is the focus of the article? Does it present all sides of an issue? Is the coverage confined to the politics of an issue, rather than the content of the issue itself? (Fallows, 1996)
- Do any photographs included in the article reflect the issue and the people involved in it? If it is a story on some aspect of patient care, for example, does the photograph include and name nurses who are providing the care? Or are only the physicians shown and named?
- Who sits on the board of directors of a newspaper, and what interests do they represent? What is or is not being said in the editorials that might be directly or indirectly critical of these interests?

WHO IS SENDING THE MESSAGE?

Who is sponsoring the message and why? Part of understanding what the real message is about comes from knowing who is behind the message. You could interpret the real message behind the Harry and Louise commercials against President Clinton's health care reform legislation once you knew they were sponsored by the Health Insurance Association of America (HIAA). If the legislation had passed, the majority of insurance companies would have been locked out of the health care market. Instead, their media success left them in control of health care in the United States.

WHAT IS THE MESSAGE AND WHAT RHETORIC IS USED?

What is the ostensible message that is being delivered, and what is the real message? What rhetoric is used to get the real message across? The debate

over keeping Medicare solvent illustrates the importance of rhetoric. As projections emerged in the 1990s that Medicare would be bankrupted if changes in the program were not made before the baby boomers retired, policy options were framed as "saving Medicare" or "preserving Medicare" when one supported the policy option. But opposition to the same policy option spoke of "cutting" or "killing" Medicare. This same rhetoric was used to support (or oppose) a variety of Medicare proposals.

Images also convey important messages. Health insurance companies advertise to employed individuals and families using pictures of healthy active adults and bright-eyed children. Health insurers have never used images of obese individuals or people disabled by arthritis to attract new members to their insurance products. These are examples of targeted media messages.

IS THE MESSAGE EFFECTIVE?

Does the message attract your attention? Does it appeal to your logic and to your emotions? Does it undermine the opposition's position?

IS THE MESSAGE ACCURATE?

Who is the reporter, and what reputation does the reporter have? Is the reporter credible, with a reputation for accuracy and balanced coverage of an issue? What viewpoints are missing? Whose voice is represented in the message or article?

RESPONDING TO THE MEDIA

One of the most important ways to influence public opinion is to respond to what is read or seen or heard in the media. The vignette at the end of this chapter describes the power and use of letters to the editor and of listener call-ins to talk radio programs. There are several other ways to respond to the media: writing an opinion editorial, mobilizing grassroots efforts to boycott sponsors and call producers, being proactive, and saying thanks.

WRITING AN OPINION EDITORIAL

Opinion editorials (Op eds) allow more in-depth response to current issues and provide a way to get an issue on the public's agenda. Although they are often solicited by a newspaper or magazine, particularly in large cities, local community papers are often eager to receive editorials that describe an important issue or problem, include a story that illustrates the impact of the problem, and suggest possible solutions.

MOBILIZING GRASSROOTS EFFORTS TO BOYCOTT SPONSORS AND CALL PRODUCERS

For commercial media, disturbing programs and stories can be suppressed by threatening to boycott the sponsors who bought advertising time or space attached to the program or by expressing concerns to the producers, editors, or station managers. A successful grassroots effort by nurses arose in response to the airing of *Nightingales,* a prime-time television program that portrayed nurses as mindless sex objects. Nursing organizations contacted their members and asked them to write to the producers and sponsors of the program, noting that they would not buy the sponsor's products. When a sponsor knows that a group of more than 2 million people (with family, friends, and professional colleagues) doesn't like the program their ads are paying for, they'll think twice about continuing to sponsor such programs. *Nightingales* was canceled by the network before the first season was over.

BEING PROACTIVE

Contacting producers can also be done proactively to ensure appropriate representation of nurses or an issue. A powerful example came in the 1960s with the airing of *Dr. Kildare* and *Ben Casey,* two television programs featuring smart, caring, "nice guy" physicians. The American Medical Association (AMA) actively encouraged the producers to present these images.

In return for showing their organization's seal of approval at the end of each program, AMA physicians demanded the right to read every script and make changes in the name of accuracy. To them, however, accuracy also meant a proper doctor's image. During the height of its power in the 1960s, the AMA Advisory Committee for Television and Motion Pictures tried to make sure that with few exceptions the physicians who moved through doctor shows were incarnations of intelligent, upright, all-caring experts. AMA physicians were even insistent about the cars their TV counterparts drove (not too expensive), the way they spoke to patients (a doctor could never sit on even the edge of a female patient's bed), and the mistakes they made (which had to be extremely rare). . . . [Later] Doctors' organizations expressed anger that the programs were holding nurses and psychologists to the same status as MDs. (Turow, 1996, p. 1241)

Although the AMA's influence over television programming waned in the 1970s, physicians are frequently consulted on health-related entertainment programs. Nurses have also served as consultants, and sometimes they have volunteered their services to a producer.

SAYING THANKS

One of the most important strategies that nurses can use to influence the media is to thank the journalist who did a fine job in covering an issue of importance on nursing and health care. This can be done in person or in writing. It goes a long way toward developing a relationship with the journalist that can be of help later when you have a story or an issue you would like covered.

GETTING THE MESSAGE ACROSS

Getting your message to the appropriate target audience requires careful analysis and planning. For example, you might want to target a message to local homeowners, many of whom watch a particular TV station's evening news. To get television coverage, you must have a visual attraction. California nurses staged a media event on a senior health issue by staging a "rock around the clock" marathon, with seniors in rocking chairs outside an insurance company. They received press coverage of the event, which elicited some supportive letters to the editor as well as some negative press from seniors who said that they were stereotyping elderly persons.

The following guidelines will help you shape your message and get it delivered to the right media:
1. *The issue*
   a. What is the nature of the issue?
   b. What is the context of the issue (e.g., timing, history, and current political environment)?
   c. Who is or could be interested in this issue?
2. *The message*
   a. What's the angle? What is news?
   b. Is there a sound bite that represents the issue in a catchy, memorable way?
   c. Can you craft rhetoric that will represent core values of the target audience?
   d. How can you frame nursing's interests as the public's interests (e.g., as consumers, mothers, fathers, women, taxpayers, health professionals)?
3. *The target audience*
   a. Who is the target audience? Is it the public, policymakers, or journalists?
   b. If the public is the target audience, which segments of the public?
   c. What medium is appropriate for the target audience? Does this audience watch television? If so, are the members of this

audience likely to watch a talk show or a news magazine show? Or do they read newspapers, listen to radio, or surf the Internet? Or are they likely to do all of these?
4. *Access to the media*
   a. What relationships do you have with reporters and producers? Have you called or written letters or thank-you notes to particular journalists? Have you requested a meeting with the editorial board of the local community newspaper to discuss your issue and how the members of the board might think about reporting on it?
   b. How can you get the media's attention? Is there a "hot" issue you can connect your issue to? Is there a compelling human interest story? Do you have a press release that describes your issue in a succinct, compelling way? (Box 10-3 provides a sample press release.) Do you have other printed materials that will attract journalists' attention within the first 3 seconds of viewing it? Are there photographs you can take in advance and then send out with your press release? Can you digitalize the images and make them available on a website for downloading onto a newspaper?
   c. Whom should you contact in the medium or media of choice?
   d. Have you been getting prepared all along? Are you news conscious? Do you watch, listen, clip, and track who covers what and how they cover it? What is the format of the program, and who is the journalist? What is the style of the program or journalist?
   e. Who are your spokespersons? Do they have the requisite expertise on the issue? Do they have a visual or voice presence appropriate for the medium? What is their personal connection to the issue, and do they have stories to tell? Have they been trained or rehearsed for the interview?
5. *The interviews*
   a. Prepare for the interview. Get information on your interviewer and the program by reviewing the interviewer's work or talking

BOX **10-3**   Sample Press Release

Date press can release a story *and* whom to contact for more information, including phone number and e-mail address	For Immediate Release: April 5, 2001 Contact: Stacie Paxton 272-226-7747 spaxton@netnet.com

Focused header to get journalist's attention

REP. CAPPS INTRODUCES BIPARTISAN BILL TO ADDRESS NATION'S NURSING SHORTAGE CRISIS

Former Nurse Fights to Ensure More RN's Enter and Remain in the Workforce

Place of release *and* primary focus of release

Washington, DC—Representatives Lois Capps (D-CA), Sue Kelly (R-NY), Rosa DeLauro (D-CT) and 25 other members yesterday introduced landmark, bipartisan legislation to address the nursing shortage crisis facing our nation's hospitals, nursing homes, and other health institutions. Similar legislation was introduced in the Senate today by Sens. John Kerry (D-MA) and James Jeffords (R-VT).

Quote

"As a registered nurse, I know that patient care will be compromised if we don't address this crisis immediately," said Rep. Capps. "My bill will encourage more people to enter the nursing profession by providing incentives that other service careers already provide."

Explanation of release's focus, making it self-explanatory

The Nurse Reinvestment Act establishes a National Nurse Service Corps to provide educational scholarships to nurses who commit to serve in a health facility determined to have a critical shortage of nurses. Grants would also be available to help individuals at any level of the nursing profession—from a nursing aide to an individual pursuing a doctoral degree—obtain more education. The bill also provides funding for public service announcements and supports nursing recruitment grants for educational facilities. In addition, it would expand Medicare and Medicaid funding for clinical nursing education and reimburses some home health agencies, hospices and nursing homes for nurse training.

Quote on impact

"Nurses are a critical part of our health care system," said Capps. "Fewer people are entering the nursing profession and the current RN workforce is aging. If Congress doesn't act now to attract more individuals into this profession, this shortage will turn into a major crisis that will be felt by every American needing medical attention."

Background, with enough detail that a journalist can write story without additional information

According to the National League of Nursing, the number of individuals graduating from nursing programs has declined 13% between 1995 and 1999 and this decline is expected to continue. Today, the average registered nurse (RN) is 45 years old and by 2010, 40% of the RN workforce will be over 50. Capps worked closely with the American Nurses Association, American Organization of Nurse Executives, American Association of Colleges of Nursing and other groups to develop legislation to address the documented shortage of individuals entering the nursing profession.

Description of person or organization issuing release

Capps—an RN for 41 years—earned her nursing degree at the Pacific Lutheran University in Tacoma, Washington. She has worked as a nursing instructor in Oregon, as head nurse at Yale New Haven Hospital and as a school nurse in Santa Barbara County for more than 20 years.

Hash marks indicating end of release

###

with public relations experts in your area. Select the one, two, or three major points that you want to get across in the interview. Identify potential controversies and how you would respond to them. And rehearse the interview with a colleague.

b. During the interview, listen attentively to the interviewer. Recognize opportunities to control the interview and get your primary point across more than once. What is your sound bite? Even if the interviewer asks a question that does not address *your* agenda, return the focus of the interview to *your* agenda and to *your* sound bite with finesse and persistence.

c. Try to be an interesting guest. Come ready with rich, illustrative stories. Avoid yes or no answers to questions.

d. Know that you do not have to answer all questions and should avoid providing comments that would embarrass you if they were headlines. If you don't know the answer to a question, say so and offer to get back to the interviewer with the information.

e. Avoid being disrespectful or arguing with the interviewer.

f. Remember that being interviewed can be an anxiety-producing experience for many people. It's a normal reaction. Do some slow deep-breathing or relaxation exercise before the interview, but know that some nervousness can be energizing.

6. *Follow-up*

a. Write a letter of thanks to the producer or journalist afterward.

b. Provide feedback to the producer or journalist on the response that you have received to the interview or the program or coverage.

c. Continue to offer other ideas for stories on the same or related topics.

BEING PROACTIVE

MEDIA ADVOCACY

Harnessing the media for your own purposes is an important strategy if you are seeking public support for health-promoting policies. Media advo-cacy is the strategic use of mass media to apply pressure to advance a social or public policy initiative (Jernigan & Wright, 1996; Wallack & Dorfman, 1996). It is a tool for policy change—a way of mobilizing constituencies and stake holders to support or oppose specific policy changes. It is a means of political action (DeJong, 1996).

Often, well-financed lobbies will develop public marketing messages and air them in only the districts where there are "swing votes" in Congress. Those constituents see the ads, and call their member of Congress. The ads usually portray only part of the information. One of Republican President George W. Bush's earliest actions was to propose a $1.6 trillion tax cut. Television and radio ads were aired using the voice of former Democratic President John F. Kennedy explaining why a tax cut would be good for the economy. The ads were aired in states with Democratic U.S. senators who were considered "swing" votes, meaning that they might be persuaded to vote for the tax cut with the Republicans if they heard from their constituents.

Media advocacy differs from social marketing and public education approaches to public health. Table 10-1 delineates some of these differences. Media advocacy defines the primary problem as a power gap, as opposed to an information gap, and thus, mobilization of groups of stakeholders is

TABLE **10-1**   Media Advocacy Versus Social Marketing/Public Education Approaches to Public Health

MEDIA ADVOCACY	SOCIAL MARKETING/ PUBLIC EDUCATION
Individual as advocate	Individual as audience
Advances healthy public policies	Develops health messages
Changes the environment	Changes the individual
Target is person with power to make change	Target is person with problem or at risk
Addresses the power gap	Addresses the information gap

Adapted from Wallack, L. & Dorfman, L. (1996). Media advocacy: A strategy for advancing policy and promoting health. *Health Education Quarterly, 23*(3), 297, Copyright 1996 by Sage Publications. Reprinted by permission of Sage Publications.

needed to be able to influence the process of developing public policies. Wallack and Dorfman (1996) use the example of tobacco control to illustrate the focus of media advocacy. The dangers of smoking were well known, albeit not admitted by tobacco companies until 1997. During the past 25 years, public policies that attempted to limit smoking created "a shift in the acceptability of smoking" (Wallack & Dorfman, 1996, p. 298). More recently, advocates have focused on the tobacco producers instead of the users. As Wallack and Dorfman (1996, p. 298) summarized, "In tobacco control, as in other public health issues, the challenge we face is to change the environment, and media advocacy provides a tool to help us meet that challenge." Since the tobacco settlements enriched state budgets, some states have used the money to reframe the public's thinking about tobacco and gain public support for stricter anti-smoking policies. Fichtenberg and Glantz (2000) report that such a campaign launched by California was associated with a reduction in deaths from heart disease.

The success of Mothers Against Drunk Driving (MADD) is another illustration of the power of media advocacy. Over the past 2 decades, MADD developed a policy agenda aimed at preventing drunk driving. They developed a "Rating the States" program to bring public attention to what state governments were and were not doing to fight alcohol-impaired driving. Then, after a national press conference just after Thanksgiving, the beginning of a period of high numbers of alcohol-related traffic accidents, MADD representatives held local press conferences with their state's officials and members of other advocacy groups to announce the state's rating. Local and national broadcast and print press coverage resulted in the exposure of an estimated 62.5 million people to the story. Subsequently, action was taken in at least eight states to begin to address the problem of drunk driving (Russell, Voas, DeJong, & Chaloupka, 1995).

Getting on the news media agenda is one of the functions of media advocacy (Wallack, 1994). With numerous competing potential stories, media advocacy employs strategies to frame an issue in a way that will attract media coverage. But *how* the message is presented is as important as simply getting the attention of the news media. The demise of the Health Se-

curity Act demonstrates this point. It got on the media's agenda, but the important messages were lost in the discussion of managed competition and the strategic use of the Harry and Louise commercials.

FRAMING

Getting on the agenda and then controlling the message require *framing*. Framing "defines the boundaries of public discussion about an issue" (Wallack & Dorfman, 1996, p. 299). *Framing for access* entails shaping the issue in a way that will attract media attention. It requires some element of controversy (albeit not over the accuracy of advocates' facts), conflict, injustice, or irony. The targeted medium or media will shape how the story is presented. For example, television requires compelling visual images. If a broad audience is to be reached, several media need to be targeted. It also helps to attach the issue to a local concern or event, anniversaries, or celebrities or to "make news" by holding events that will attract the press, such as releasing research or in some other way being "newsworthy" (Jernigan & Wright, 1996).

Framing for content is more difficult than framing for access. Although a compelling individual story may gain access to the media, there is no guarantee that the reporter will focus on the public policy changes that are needed to address problems illustrated by the individual. Wallack and Dorfman (1996) note that this framing "involves the difficult process of 'reframing' away from the usual news formula" (p. 300). The authors suggest that this reframing can be accomplished by the following:

- Emphasizing the social dimensions of the problem and translating an individual's personal story into a public issue
- Shifting the responsibility for the problem from the individual to the corporate executive or public official whose decisions can address the problem
- Presenting solutions as policy alternatives
- Making a practical appeal to support the solution
- Using compelling images
- Using authentic voices—people who have experience with the problem
- Using symbols that "resonate with the basic values of the audience" (Wallack & Dorfman, 1996, p. 300)

- Anticipating the opposition and knowing all sides of the issue.

Jernigan and Wright (1996, p. 314) argue that media advocacy is most effective when it is "linked to a strong organizing base and a long-term strategic vision." In addition, it is enhanced by a long-term strategy that incorporates continually setting up future efforts. For example, highlighting the way that one group in a community is negatively affected by an issue can lead to that group's lending its support to the next media advocacy strategy around the issue. Training and designating spokespersons are important to controlling the message.

Increasingly, computer-based electronic communication systems, including specific networks (e.g., SCARNet, an electronic communication network that has been used by advocates in the alcohol control movement to plan strategy jointly and rapidly) and the Internet, are being used by media advocates.

CONCLUSION

The media in our society are tremendously powerful and may be the single most influential force shaping public policy. The media are diverse—including everything from network television and Hollywood movies to your local *Pennysaver* and your hospital newsletter. They may contain information and points of view that strive to be fair and balanced, as well as opinions with the singular goal to change your mind or get your money. Nurses, like all members of our society, have a big stake in what gets reported and how an issue is treated. Nurses, both individuals and groups, can influence public policy by supporting candidates that support nurses, by writing letters to journalists and congresspersons, and by simply responding to media messages, from whatever source, both positively and negatively.

REFERENCES

Annenberg Public Policy Center of the University of Pennsylvania. (1995). *Media in the middle: Fairness and accuracy in the 1994 health care reform debate.* Philadelphia: Author.

Brodie, M., Foehr, U., Rideout, V., Baer, N., Miller, C., Flournoy, R., & Altman, D. (2001). Communicating health information through the entertainment media. *Health Affairs, 20*(1), 192-199.

Buresh, B. & Gordon, S. (2000a). From silence to voice. *Journal of Nursing Scholarship, 32*(4), 330-331.

Buresh, B. & Gordon, S. (2000b). *From silence to voice: What nurses know and must communicate to the public.* Ottawa, Canada: Canadian Nurses Association.

Buresh, B., Gordon, S., & Bell, N. (1991). Who counts in news coverage of health care? *Nursing Outlook, 39*(5), 204-208.

Chaffee, M.W. (2000). Health communications: Nursing education for increased visibility and effectiveness. *Journal of Professional Nursing, 16*(1), 31-38.

Chassin, M.R., Hannan, E.L., & DeBuono, B.A. (1996). Benefits and hazards of reporting medical outcomes publicly. *New England Journal of Medicine, 334*(6), 394-398.

DeJong, W. (1996). MADD Massachusetts versus Senator Burke: A media advocacy case study. *Health Education Quarterly, 23*(3), 318-329.

Dorfman, L., Schauffler, H.H., Wilkerson, J., & Feinson, J. (1996). Local television news coverage of President Clinton's introduction of the Health Security Act. *Journal of the American Medical Association, 275*(15), 1201-1205.

Douglas, S.J. (1991). Reading the news in more than black and white. *EXTRA!, 4*(7), 1, 6.

Fallows, J. (1996). *Breaking the news: How the media undermine American society.* New York: Vintage Books.

Fichtenberg, C.M. & Glantz, S.A. (2000). Association of the California tobacco control program with declines in cigarette consumption and mortality from heart disease. *The New England Journal of Medicine, 343*(24), 1772-1777.

Grossman, L.K. (1997). The electronic republic. In T. Walker & C. Sass (Eds.). *Perspectives, readings on contemporary American government.* Alexandria, VA: Close Up Foundation.

Jamieson, K.H. (2000). *Everything you think you know about politics . . . and why you're wrong.* New York: Basic Books.

Jernigan, D.H. & Wright, P.A. (1996). Media advocacy: Lessons from community experiences. *Journal of Public Health Policy, 18*, 306-329.

Kalb, M. (1997). The Value of a Free Press. In T. Walker & C. Sass (Eds.). *Perspectives: Readings on contemporary American government.* Alexandria, VA: Close Up Foundation.

McAlister, A.L. (1991). Population behavior change: A theory-based approach. *Journal of Public Health Policy, 12*, 345-361.

Milio, N. (2000). *Public health in the market: Facing managed care, lean government and health disparities.* Ann Arbor, MI: University of Michigan Press.

Naureckas, J. (1995, November-December). Corporate ownership matters: The case of NBC. *EXTRA!, 13.*

Otten, A.L. (1992, Winter). The influence of the mass media on health policy. *Health Affairs,* 111-118.

Rehm, D. (1997). Talk radio and the public dialogue. In T. Walker & C. Sass (Eds.). *Perspectives, readings on contemporary American government.* Alexandria, VA: Close Up Foundation.

Russell, A., Voas, R.B., DeJong, W., & Chaloupka, M. (1995). MADD rates the states: Advocacy event to advance the agenda against alcohol-impaired driving. *Public Health Reports,* *110*(3), 240-245.

Schmid, T.L., Pratt, M., & Howze, E. (1995). Policy as intervention: Environmental and policy approaches to the prevention of cardiovascular disease. *American Journal of Public Health,* *85*(9), 1207-1211.

Sheridan-Gonzalez, J. & Wade, M. (1998). Every patient deserves a nurse. In D.J. Mason & J.K. Leavitt (Eds.). *Policy and politics in nursing and health care* (3rd ed.). Philadelphia: W.B. Saunders.

Shilts, R. (1987). *And the band played on.* New York: St. Martin's Press.

Sigma Theta Tau International. (1998). *The Woodhull study on nursing and the media: Health care's invisible partner.* Indianapolis: Sigma Theta Tau Center Nursing Press.

Turow, J. (1996). Television entertainment and the U.S. health care debate. *Lancet, 347,* 1240-1243.

Wallack, L. (1994). Media advocacy: A strategy for empowering people and communities. *Journal of Public Health Policy, 15,* 420-436.

Wallack, L. & Dorfman, L. (1996). Media advocacy: A strategy for advancing policy and promoting health. *Health Education Quarterly, 23*(3), 293-317.

Vignette   *Catherine J. Dodd*

Free Media Coverage: Using Letters (Messages) to the Editor and Calls to Radio Talk Shows

"The need for a powerful nursing voice has never been greater."

SUZANNE GORDON

In 1987 after Congresswoman Nancy Pelosi was elected to the U.S. House of Representatives, I was asked to join her staff because of the effective role I played in coordinating a "Nurses for Pelosi" effort within her campaign. I quickly learned many lessons in working for a member of Congress. One of my first assignments was to rotate through the early morning "letter to the editor" clipping and faxing job in the office. This meant leaving the house by 5 AM to purchase the first issue of the morning paper at an all-night newsstand and arrive at the San Francisco Congressional Office by 5:30 AM to read, clip, and fax back to Washington, DC, the editorial page with the letters to the editor so that they would be on Congresswoman Pelosi's desk by 9 AM. Why? Because newspaper subscribers tend to be homeowners, and homeowners vote in every election.

Letters to the editor reflect what voters are thinking about local issues. The editor of the editorial page usually does not publish a letter until more than one letter on the same issue has been received, so published letters reflect the views of lots of voters. A catchy, well-written letter to the editor that is published has much more political weight than a personal lobbying letter on an issue. (So if you are going to write just one letter, write the letter to the editor; better, though, is to write your lobbying letter, as well!)

This in no way means that Congresswoman Pelosi concerned herself only with homeowners and newspaper subscribers. She represented a district that is overwhelmingly Democrat, so her re-election was certain. She is an advocate for voters and those unable to vote—children and the many noncitizens who live in San Francisco. She still listens to and is concerned about what the voters think.

Today, in campaigns for ballot initiatives as well as candidates, press staff are orchestrating letters-to-the-editor campaigns to show "voter support" of candidates and issues. For statewide issues and candidates, only six different letters are needed. Six basic letters are drafted and faxed to six volunteer letter submitters in the geographic area of every major daily in the state. The letter submitters put the text of the letter on their personal letterhead and fax the same letter to the same paper to which five other people are faxing their letters. The same plan works on local issues as well. Major papers like to demonstrate the breadth of their circulation, so they frequently publish letters received from nearby cities and suburbs. Editors of the editorial page want to be viewed as fair, so they will attempt to balance the number of letters written by women and men. This gives women an excellent chance of being published, because women do not write as much or as often as men.

In a graduate class on health policy and politics at San Francisco State University, I offered nursing students extra credit for every letter to the editor they write. In 1994 California voters passed Proposition 187, a mean-spirited, anti-immigrant initiative that, among other things, denied prenatal and emergency care to undocumented persons. After the election and just before Thanksgiving, a student who had immigrated from Russia with her family wrote a letter to the editor about how our country's first immigrants would not be celebrating Thanksgiving. They would be hiding from immigration officials had Proposition 187 been the law of the land at that time. It was published with headlines on Thanksgiving day and was the subject of several days' worth of subsequent letters supporting the provision of prenatal care and education to undocumented people. Those extra credit points had a lasting effect. Other students report the therapeutic effect of writing a letter on something you feel angry or passionate about and knowing that, if published, it will reach the eyes of tens of thousands of readers.

A similar strategy can be used for radio talk shows, which reach hundreds of thousands of people at one time. (General commercial radio audiences, as opposed to public radio listeners, cannot be categorized as perennial "always" voters.) Radio talk shows can be used to educate the public about new treatment modalities, changes in the quality of care, dangerous patient care situations, or any number of issues that nurses are concerned about. Having a group or "radio response squad" of well-prepared registered nurses listening to a talk show and prepared to call in on an issue or during an "open" session can be an effective advertising tool. Callers should be cautioned to write down the three points they want to make and practice them on a friend. If they get to the producer and are asked what their position is, they should be neutral and have a question they want to pose. (If there has just been an on-air caller who expressed your position, the producer will not air another caller with the same position.) Once on the air, callers should make their point and say, "I will stay on the air for your response," being prepared to defend their statements. "Taking a response off the air" allows the host or talk show guest to have the last word.

Regardless of the medium, if you are advocating for the public (as opposed to advocating for nursing's professional interests), always identify yourself as a registered nurse. The public trusts and values nurses, and your message will carry more clout.

Vignette   Donna Zazworsky

The Nurse on a TV News Team

"News is a business, but it is also a public trust."
    DAN RATHER

"How did you get on television?" This is the most frequently asked question I get. The answer is simple: I made myself known and available to the public relations (PR) department in the hospital by giving them story ideas and interesting people who would portray a positive image on TV. When they asked if I would give flu shots to the morning team on TV, I said, "Of course. When?" So when the local TV station approached the PR people and asked them to recommend a physician for their new team of medical experts, the PR team's immediate response was, "You don't need another doctor, you need a nurse . . . and we've got just the one for you." I started the following month.

Being the only nurse teamed with three physicians for the Four on 4 Medical Team of Experts on the NBC affiliate in Tucson, Arizona, I am in a wonderful position to teach people about the many dimensions of nursing and health care. Nurses influence the community's health and their healthcare delivery systems. We teach people about their health, provide care for people and populations, and evaluate our impact on health, day in and day out, in our professional and personal lives. Therefore, I see my role as the nurse on the team as a prime opportunity to promote healthy public policies and public image and influence nursing through positive stories, messages, and action items.

NURSES AND THE MEDIA

Most people still associate nurses with a jaded view portrayed in the entertainment media. Everyone remembers the wicked Nurse Ratched from "One Flew over the Cuckoo's Nest" or the righteous Audrey in "General Hospital." Unfortunately, nurses are almost invisible in the news media. What does this say about nursing? What is the real image that people have of nurses? Why aren't there more nurses in the news media? Perhaps it's an issue of comfort, preparation, or accessibility. Whatever it is, we must increase the public's awareness of the following:

- The role nurses play in influencing the health of local and global communities
- The impact of public policies on the health and wellbeing of communities
- The unique perspective nurses bring to discussions of health policy and health
- What a wonderfully rewarding and diverse career nursing offers individuals

What better way to accomplish this but through the media?

Nurses can influence the public with media through a variety of story themes, such as the following:

1. Influencing the community's perception of what nursing is about through stories that

depict nurses as clinicians, teachers, and researchers
2. Influencing public health through health education on hot topics and community needs
3. Influencing public policy and action through stories on political issues related to health

The following sections discuss some tips on how to work with the media and paint a positive picture of nurses from my own experience as a health expert for a television news program.

MEDIA TIPS

Get Started, but Be Ready!

As my father would say, I've always had the "gift of gab." I was in plays in junior and senior high school, took a drama class in college, and dabbled in video education in graduate school. Taking piano lessons for 10 years and performing yearly helped, too. My piano teacher taught her students how to perform in public. Through successes and mistakes, she taught professionalism, grace, and public respect. She was an incredible mentor and gave me those gifts for life.

I enjoy being in front of an audience and have developed a natural and comfortable style. This style was put to the test when I began my first management job in the late 1970s as the program manager for the lifestyle, evaluation, awareness, and planning program—the LEAP Program, a health promotion program for employees.

After a brief start-up of hiring and training a staff of nurses to do health screenings and education, the hospital's PR Department arranged a TV interview for me to kick-off a new wellness program at Carondelet St. Joseph's Hospital in Tucson. I was interviewed about the program for a 60-second segment on the 5 PM and 10 PM news, highlighting nurses doing blood pressures, measuring body fat, and reviewing results of healthy individuals. I had to get my message across quickly. So I challenged the public by asking, "How healthy are you? We can help you find out."

I was quickly schooled on the power of media. The next day was havoc! Within the first hour of opening, over 150 phone calls tied up the hospital lines. Excitement and terror filled our office. I called in several nurses to help with the phone calls and scheduling. Obviously, the public was ready for this program and took my challenge seriously. We filled up the schedule book for the next few months, and in order to accommodate the demand, I had to re-open a building the hospital had previously closed. This was my first lesson in the power of the media: *Choose your message and be ready!*

Messaging and Call to Action

Developing a clear message and call to action are critical steps for a successful TV story. I teach a class for nursing students at the University of Arizona College of Nursing, where the major focus of the class is on messaging and call to action. Using media education materials provided at a Sigma Theta Tau International (STTI) biennial convention (Hill Howes, 1993), I have the students formulate topics that they would like me to pitch to the TV station.

In small groups the students prepare a story with three key messages and a call to action. One person from each group presents the group's story ideas. We have fun dissecting the story line and discussing whether their ideas are news worthy and have the right messages.

For example, one student group wanted to address the dangers of the scooter craze and promote safety issues. They presented a story line that would take place in an emergency room and would high-light a child who had had an accident on a scooter. Here were their three messages:

• The number of emergency room visits and types of accidents
• Prevention equipment (helmets)
• Safety tips for parents

The call to action was how and where people can get free helmets.

Finally, the students came up with a second possible scene for the safety tips piece. They proposed going to a local toy store that had a display of one scooter with an "out of stock" sign perched on it, and next to it was a huge pile of helmets: a real scene witnessed by one of the students.

This was an excellent story—great story line, people, messages, and call to action. Unfortunately, the timing was not appropriate. The TV station had just done a story on scooters and bicycles, so there was not an interest at this time. However, it remains a very good story, worth pitching again in a few months or perhaps when school is out.

Timing

Timing is another key issue for stories to successfully get picked up by the media. I see timing in two perspectives. First, you must know when to pitch a story based on what is happening in the local, state, and national scenes. Second, you must be available when the media comes to you for your insights in a breaking story.

Let's take the first perspective of timing: Know when to pitch a story. I keep an eye on what is going on in the news, in TV, radio, and newspaper coverage. For example, I was involved on a community coalition to build an adaptive aquatic center for the disabled community. We had gotten the mayor and city council to bring the bond to a general election along with the other bonds being brought forth. Our coalition met to build a strategy on how to get the information out to our groups on the voting options. We also gave input about the general public vote strategy being handled by a local PR firm.

As I watched the different news venues unfold the bond issues, the local newspaper had numerous stories and regular letters to the editor. One letter raised an issue from an opposing group claiming that the land designated for the building would take up more park space. Knowing that this information was inaccurate, I saw an opportunity to educate the public on the center and correct the misinformation.

I built my TV story on the water exercise classes that I lead for people with multiple sclerosis and arthritis at the parks and recreation pools. I talked about the benefits and need for an adaptive aquatic center for all disabilities. I then obtained the architect's drawing that illustrated where the center was proposed and clarified the misconception of city property. This story aired three days before the vote on the evening news and then again on the morning news shows, reaching over 150,000 people. The bond passed.

The second perspective on timing is availability. If you want to be recognized as an expert, you must be seen regularly. This means that you must be ready to respond to issues when the media or PR department contact you. I am always ready to provide information, but I am very careful to frame my message depending on the topic.

For example, I was called on a Sunday afternoon to do a short segment on childhood sleep apnea. The news crew wanted a local face to a national clip that they had received on this topic. So, I quickly called a local hospital and received permission from the nursing supervisor to do the story at the hospital for the setting. Next, I went to the web and downloaded some information. In an hour, I was at the hospital with the TV crew shooting the story. I provided general information about normal childhood sleep problems, how to keep a diary of your child's eating and sleeping habits, and the importance of having a good relationship with your child's provider, so that the provider really knows your child's normal patterns.

One final message in timing: If you want the media to work with you regularly and do stories, you need to be available and flexible to their timeframes. I always tell students and nursing audiences that when the media asks you to do a story, your response is, "Yes. When?"

Choosing Your Talent

When doing a media story, the reporter will usually want someone (a patient) to give a personal testimony related to the story line. Knowing this, I ask people (patients) who will project a message and an image I hope to achieve with the story. For example, I invited the health reporter to a class I was doing on vitamin use in the elderly. This story focused on the need for and potential overdose of common vitamins. The TV reporter wanted to talk to a participant after the program. Because I do monthly classes at this particular senior site, I know the people. I asked a Hispanic woman who often helps me by interpreting to other Hispanics attending the class. She is a very colorful and upbeat senior citizen in both clothing and personality. She was delighted to talk about her vitamin habits and tell the

reporter what she learned at the program. She even joked with the reporter saying, "I'm just an old chicken, but I can still learn new things."

Giving Recognition

The nursing profession needs to increase the number of stories told and honored through the public news media. But what about the reverse? Do we honor public media celebrities in our nursing arenas? Some nursing organizations recognize nursing stories in the public media. But in many cases, it's still the nurses receiving the award. I think it's important to acknowledge the media personalities for their work in promoting nursing.

I submitted a local medical reporter, Stacey Adams, for a regional public media award through STTI. Stacey and I usually do two health stories a month. She has gained a new appreciation on the wealth of story angles a nurse can bring to her segments. Our segments received the award, and Stacey attended the regional meeting to accept the award. She was so excited about receiving this award that she wanted to get started on more health stories.

Donna Zazworsky, RN (left), is the only nurse on the Four on 4 Medical Team of Experts on KVOA, Channel 4, in Tucson, Arizona. She collaborates with news anchor and medical reporter Stacey Adams (right).

Getting and Giving Public Recognition

Getting the public to recognize the station and giving positive remarks on the stories are critical elements for a successful station. I have many people who come up to me in a restaurant and thank me for a particular story or tell me about the impact of the story. I encourage then to write or e-mail the station and tell the station what they liked or learned from our segments. The station wants feedback, and it will only enhance the likelihood that the station will seek out nurses for future stories.

Giving public recognition is just as important for the station and the anchors. Recently, Stacey and I did a story on her award from STTI. We were able to talk about this prestigious organization and its commitment to nursing excellence in practice, education, and research. These images build a public legitimacy of the nursing profession.

Building Relationships and Being Responsive

Relationship, relationships, relationships! Need I say more? Build strong and friendly relationships with PR, newspaper, radio, and TV people. I let them know that if I can't do the story, I will find someone who can. I also make sure that their job (be it the job of the camera person, the anchor, or the producer) will be easy and quick. I put the stories, people, and settings together, and I make it happen with very little effort on their part. Finally, I am easily accessible. In other words, I take and return calls immediately, and I check my e-mail regularly.

REFERENCES

Hill Howes, D. (1993, November 29-December 3). *Radio and television presentation skills.* Presentation at STTI 32nd Biennial Convention.

Ethical Issues in Health Care, Public Policy, and Politics

MARY CIPRIANO SILVA

"Ethics and politics are not oxymorons!"

LEAH CURTIN

Both health care ethics and public policy have the ability to stir passions in American politics. Why? Both disciplines are in a constant state of flux. What was "state of the art" thinking about these disciplines a decade ago is considered outdated or in need of revision today. Both disciplines are also concerned about the public good. But what is the public good in either health care ethics or public policy is difficult to discern in an increasingly culturally diverse and politically divided country such as ours. To compound the preceding matters, the restructuring of health care and the technologic and genetic revolutions have precipitated new ethical political issues, value conflicts, and uncertainty about the roles of health care providers and policymakers.

One area of deep concern in both ethics and public policy is access and right to health care (Boylan, 2000; Hein, 2001; Hinderer & Hinderer, 2001). According to Hinderer and Hinderer (2001), about 40 million people in the United States lack health insurance, and the number is increasing rapidly. Suppose as a nurse expert in health care reform, you are now serving on an interdisciplinary advisory board that is to make recommendations to the president about how to best meet the needs of Americans who have little or no health insur-

ance. Discussion among the board members is contentious, and this contentiousness has polarized and immobilized the group. There is lack of agreement on both the ethical and policy issues surrounding access and right to health care, and each board member appears to have a personal agenda. What could you do to help end the stalemate?

To help address this question, this chapter will focus on four things: (1) definitions and contexts that help clarify the links between health care ethics and health care public policy; (2) conceptual considerations; (3) values and political ethical conflicts; and (4) nurses, ethics, and policy making. These four areas are interrelated and provide only a glimpse into the complexities of these topics.

DEFINITIONS AND CONTEXTS

HEALTH CARE ETHICS

Health care ethics is that branch of philosophy that focuses on right and wrong or good and evil in human conduct or character related to matters of health and health care. As such, its focus is on what one morally ought to do or be. Although many definitions of ethics exist, there are commonalities. These commonalities center around content and process. *Content* addresses foundational topics such as the nature of morality; ethical codes, theories, and principles; virtue ethics; and feminist ethics

(Silva & Kroeger-Mappes, 1998; Veatch, 2000; Beauchamp & Childress, 2001), as well as applied topics such as ethical issues related to privacy and confidentiality, health care reform, euthanasia, and genetic technology (Boylan, 2000; Hein, 2001, Hinderer & Hinderer, 2001). *Process* addresses problem-solving skills or states of being that lead to moral justification of actions or to character development. Health care ethics, then, is a systematic process of mindful reflection related to the moral life and matters of health and health care that culminates in a morally justified course of action based on ethical tenets and on a virtuous character. The courses of action taken or the virtues that dominate may differ among persons. These potential differences lead us to the relationships between health care ethics and values.

The relationships between health care ethics and values provide the contexts for ethical decision making. Values include those enduring beliefs shaped by life experiences, including the belief that some ethical positions taken and acted on are preferable to other ethical positions taken and acted on. Personal values, cultural values, and professional values also help guide one's behaviors and the development of one's character. These notions are included in the 2001 American Nurses Association (ANA) *Code of Ethics for Nurses with Interpretive Statements* and the 1995 ANA *Nursing's Social Policy Statement*. Both documents stress that nurses must act to safeguard the public trust and that there is a reciprocal social contract between nursing and society, including not only the ethics but also the public policies of a society.

LINKS BETWEEN HEALTH CARE ETHICS AND HEALTH CARE PUBLIC POLICY

According to Shapiro (1999), ethical values underlie many public policies but too often go unnoticed or unarticulated. The task before us, then, is to make explicit the links between ethics and public policy so that professionals do not think of one without the other. Examples of these links include:

- One important goal of both ethics and public policy is achieving the public good.
- Achieving the public good for both ethics and

public policy is dependent on a cultural value of service to others over self.
- Underlying public policy issues are many potential and real ethical issues.
- Underlying ethical issues are many potential and real public policy issues.
- What is ethical is ultimately good policy and good health care public policy.

CONCEPTUAL CONSIDERATIONS

In analyzing the preceding links between ethics and public policy, three current conceptual considerations are helpful: (1) serve rather than steer, (2) community rather than individuals, and (3) one code rather than separate codes.

SERVE RATHER THAN STEER

Denhardt and Denhardt (2000) have developed a new conceptual approach to traditional public administration and management that they have labeled the *New Public Service*. They have based their approach on "theories of democratic citizenship" (p. 552); "models of community and civil society" (p. 552); and "organizational humanism and discourse theory" (p. 553).

Regarding democratic citizenship, Denhardt and Denhardt (2000) are in agreement with those scholars who believe that citizens should look beyond self-interests and become involved with the good of the greater community. Regarding community and civility, Denhardt and Denhardt agree with scholars who believe that a sense of community and civility has deteriorated in America and that good government can play an important role in bridging the links between communities and citizens. Regarding organizational humanism and discourse theory, Denhardt and Denhardt agree with scholars who believe that the focus should be more on needs of people and less on issues and control. In addition, these authors believe that open discourse among all groups in a society should enhance public dialogue and a sense of community, which in turn leads to a "corresponding increase in citizen trust" (p. 552).

Based on the preceding beliefs, Denhardt and

Denhardt (2000) identified seven principles on which the New Public Service is based:

1. *Serve, rather than steer.* "An increasingly important role of the public servant is to help citizens articulate and meet their shared interests, rather than to attempt to control or steer society in new directions" (p. 553).

2. *The public interest is the aim, not the by-product.* "Public . . . [servants] must contribute to building a collective, shared notion of the public interest. The goal is not to find quick solutions driven by individual choices. Rather, it is the creation of shared interests and shared responsibility" (p. 554).

3. *Think strategically; act democratically.* "Policies and programs meeting public needs can be most effectively and responsibly achieved through collective efforts and collaborative processes" (p. 555).

4. *Serve citizens, not customers.* "The public interest results from a dialogue about shared values, rather than the aggregation of individual self-interests. Therefore, public servants do not merely respond to the demands of "customers," but focus on building relationships of trust and collaboration with and among citizens" (p. 555).

5. *Accountability isn't simple.* "Public servants should be attentive to more than the market; they should also attend to statutory and constitutional law, community values [ethics], political norms, professional standards, and citizen interests" (p. 555).

6. *Value people, not just productivity.* "Public organizations and the networks in which they participate are more likely to succeed in the long run if they are operated through processes of collaboration and shared leadership based on respect for all people" (p. 556).

7. *Value citizenship and public service above entrepreneurship.* "The public interest is better advanced by public servants and citizens committed to making meaningful contributions to society than by entrepreneurial managers acting as if public money were their own" (p. 556).

The preceding seven principles provide fertile terri-tory for conversations about the interrelationships among public policy, ethics, and a person's charac-ter. According to Dobel (1998):

> Virtues [good character traits] do not replace laws, norms, or duties in political life, but they give life to these moral imperatives. When situations grow complicated or no self-evident moral answers emerge, virtues provide the stability of judgment and endurance to pursue moral commitment across time and obstacles. (p. 75)

When reflecting on virtues and the seven princi-ples on which the New Public Service is based, one can see that virtue traits are embedded in the princi-ples. Regarding public policy, then, a person's char-acter matters and should be perhaps the most impor-tant attribute in selecting persons for public office.

COMMUNITY RATHER THAN INDIVIDUALS

Our country was founded on rugged individualism and individual rights, and these concepts, until re-cently, also dominated health care ethics. According to Morone (1997), "In the past two decades, critics have attacked liberalism for sanctioning rampant individualism and neglecting the common good" (p. 996).

Morone (1997) also builds the link between community and morality. He notes that our forefa-thers survived by helping one another within the context of community. This tradition, grounded in culture, is envisioned today as a way "for invigorat-ing public life and initiating political reforms" (p. 996). He cautions, however, that how community and public policy engage can either unite or divide; what makes the difference between the two is morality, and in particular, morality in politics. Ac-cording to Morone, morality in politics is centered around the boundaries of moral images (i.e., im-ages of who is deserving and undeserving of health care and health care benefits). Thus, "moral images powerfully shape public policy. They frame the po-litical agenda" (Morone, 1997, p. 999).

The import of Morone's message (1997) is the belief that from the time of our forefathers to the present, cultural values have played an important role in shaping moral images, and it is these moral images that drive policy. At present, the emphasis is on community and community values (Aroskar,

1998; Ubel, 1999; Davis, 2000), and, thus, public policy and politics are focused on this particular agenda.

ONE CODE RATHER THAN SEPARATE CODES

In 2001 the ANA published the revised *Code of Ethics for Nurses with Interpretive Statements.* This revision was an outgrowth of the restructuring of health care, the need to update outdated concepts in previous *Codes,* and the effect of globalization on our professional and personal lives. But we are not alone. Many other health-care-related professions also have their own codes of ethics, including the American Medical Association, the American Hospital Association, the American College of Health Care Administrators, and the American College of Health Care Executives.

In contrast, a diverse group of health care and other professionals who named themselves the Tavistock group believes that a simple shared code of ethics would better serve the public and persons involved in health care and health care public policy (Berwick, Hiatt, Janeway, & Smith, 1997). The 15 members initially met in London but continued their efforts afterward and developed a draft entitled *A Shared Statement of Ethical Principles for Those Who Shape and Give Health Care* (Smith, Hiatt, & Berwick, 1999). This draft contained a preamble, five ethical principles, and interpretive commentary for each principle.

The Tavistock group, with feedback from other professionals, has since revised its principles. According to Davidoff (2000), the revised ethical principles are as follow:

1. *Rights.* People have a right to health and health care.
2. *Balance.* Care of individual patients is central, but the health of populations is also our concern.
3. *Comprehensiveness.* In addition to treating illness, we have an obligation to ease suffering, minimize disability, prevent disease, and promote health.
4. *Cooperation.* Health care succeeds only if we cooperate with those we serve, each another, and those in other sectors.
5. *Improvement.* Improving health care is a serious and continuing responsibility.

6. *Safety.* Do not harm.
7. *Openness.* Being open, honest, and trustworthy is vital in health care.

Davidoff (2000) also noted that in April of 2000, in Cambridge, Massachusetts, the Tavistock group convened a group of 150 persons—from nursing, medicine, labor unions, hospitals, industry, and health policy, among others—to dialogue about the principles. Several issues related to ethics and health policy emerged. Is health care a right and, if so, who bears the responsibility to ensure that right? How can a balance between caring for populations and individuals occur in any health care system that is inherently unjust? What kind of politics and public policies are needed to implement these principles?

In addition to Davidoff's preceding comments, cooperation in formulating public policy is sometimes hard to attain. The cultural diversity of America compounds this situation; often common values are hard to discern, leading to value conflicts and political ethical conflicts. According to Brosnan and Roper (1997), "A political ethical conflict occurs when what one is told to do (either covertly or overtly) by those having more power in the organization or what one feels compelled to do by the organization is in conflict with one's ethical belief structure" (p. 42).

VALUES AND POLITICAL ETHICAL CONFLICTS

What can nurses as public servants engaged in health care public policy do when faced with political ethical conflicts? There is no easy answer. One approach for conflict resolution consists of the following three principles (Silva, 1990):

1. Values that support ethical professional practice and patient [community] well-being should take priority over those that do not.
2. Stronger values that support ethical professional practice and patient [community] well-being should generally take precedence over weaker values that support ethical professional practice and patient [community] well-being.
3. All things considered, values of persons [communities] who will be most affected by the

decision should take precedence over values of persons [communities] who will be less affected by the decision.

Although these principles are broad, they provide an organizing framework for assisting in the resolution of values and political ethical conflicts. It is the framework and the thinking process inherent in the framework, as well as knowledge of ethical and political theories and principles, that help public servants to arrive at health care public policy that is ethical.

Weston (1997) offers several valuable perspectives on the issue of conflicting ethical values. First, he believes that individuals tend to polarize ethical values into only two possibilities—that is, for or against a position. Second, he believes that individuals tend to think their ethical position is the only right one. He then raises the question, "Can both sides be right?" (p. 51). His response is as follows: "In nearly every serious ethical issue, the truth is that both sides have a point. Or rather, all sides have a point, since there are usually more than two. All sides speak for something worth considering" (Weston, 1997, p. 52). The challenge is to consider those points worthy of moral consideration and justification—that is, "what *each* side is right *about*" (Weston, 1997, p. 54). Weston calls this "right versus right" (p. 54), which is in sharp contrast to the polarizing positions of right versus wrong, whether addressing ethics or policy.

The key to conflicting ethical values for Weston (1977) is integration and compromise. In integration, the common ground among positions and not the points of contention are sought and respected. Through finding the common ground of what is right about each position, Weston believes that ethical value conflicts are elevated to a higher level of creativity and respect for persons.

If right versus right turns out to be incompatible, Weston then recommends ethical compromise. Although he did not define compromise, the word suggests that each or all sides concede something in order to reach a mutual agreement. He does describe the result of compromise:

It is left to us now to insist that this position is not somehow disgraceful or weak-willed or politically second-best, but instead a clear headed (and long overdue) acknowledgment of the diversity of values at stake and an attempt to answer at least partly to both (all) of them. (Weston, 1997, p. 59)

The preceding quote makes sense both ethically and politically in order to avoid gridlock that immobilizes dialogue about, plans for, and implementation of health care public policy. Health care professionals, especially those in policy positions, cannot without good cause consider refusing to compromise because they may unwittingly belie the public trust and harm the public good.

NURSES, ETHICS, AND POLICY MAKING

INTERDISCIPLINARY ADVISORY BOARD AND CONCEPTUAL CONSIDERATIONS

Let us now return to the beginning scenario with the interdisciplinary advisory board that is in gridlock over the ethical and policy issues related to access and right to health care. As a nurse expert in health care reform, you have considerable knowledge about health care ethics, public policy, and conflict resolution. You know that honest disagreements can occur among honorable persons regarding what ethical theories can best resolve an ethical issue. For example, you know that those advisory board members who believe in "the greatest good for the greatest number" and that "the end justifies the means" are using utilitarian or consequence-based thinking. They most likely would not accept the argument that every American citizen has a right to health care or to its access because of the consequences of such a decision (e.g., too much money would be spent on health care and other areas of need would suffer). Other advisory board members may believe that "the means justify the end." In order for such a stance to be ethical, the means used to justify the end must also be ethical; unethical means can never justify the end, even if such means end in a good outcome. Still other advisory board members may believe that factors other than means, ends, or consequences determine what is right or good. One such factor is duty. Certain duties must always be done unless superceded by competing stronger duties. This type of deontologic thinking has come to be translated as "do unto others as you would have them do unto you." These duty-focused advisory board members most likely would accept the argument that every American citizen has a right to health care or to its access because our government has a duty to provide it.

In addition to the preceding notions, the fact that each advisory board member appears to place her or his own personal agenda before service to others is troubling. This stance violates both the ethical and public policy tenet that the public good supercedes self interests. We are reminded here of Denhardt and Denhardt's (2000) New Public Service, where public servants "serve, rather than steer" (p. 553). A part of this concept is that the role of public servants is not to steer society in the directions they want but rather to help citizens seek their common interests, directions, and destinies. In addition, as previously noted by Morone (1997), it is time to think about community rather than individualism because in the United States the common good has been too often neglected.

Another possible source of contention within the advisory board is its interdisciplinary nature. Although there are often commonalities among disciplines, it is the differences that usually breed misunderstandings and conflicts. Misunderstandings occur because each discipline has its unique language, code of ethics, methods of communication, and ways of using power. Conflicts occur because of turf battles and an unwillingness to keep an open mind. The work of the Tavistock group in attempting to craft one code of ethics across the health care professions calls for open-mindedness (Smith, Hiatt, & Berwick, 1999). Perhaps a discussion of each profession's code would encourage genuine communication among advisory board members.

POLITICAL ETHICAL DECISION MAKING

What could you, as the nurse expert in health care reform, do to help end the stalemate occurring within the interdisciplinary advisory board? First, you must recognize that most health care decisions, especially difficult ethical and political ones, are negotiated by groups; thus, understanding of group dynamics is imperative. Second, you must understand why it is difficult to achieve ethical integrity in institutions or bureaucracies. Hinderer and Hinderer (2001, pp. 53–56) offer four reasons, which are paraphrased and reflected on here:

1. Moral values often do not receive a high priority in bureaucratic settings. These values are frequently trumped by institutional, political, legal, and economic considerations because these considerations are seemingly less abstract and more urgent than ethical considerations.

2. Institutional structures or bureaucracies are prone to "hierarchical diffusion of responsibility" (p. 54). Whether talking about a major medical center or the government of the United States, this phrase boils down to passing the buck so that the person responsible for poor judgment or wrongdoing cannot be clearly identified and, thus, cannot be made accountable.

3. Health care providers and politicians frequently work in fast-paced and stressful environments. As a result, they may find ethical issues too divisive; that is, they have the potential to undermine relationships with colleagues.

4. Many health care providers and politicians view ethical issues as intractable and, thus, incapable of resolution. In reality, this may not be the case, but sometimes it appears to be so because sensational ethical dilemmas make the headlines, whereas more mundane but often important and resolvable ones do not.

In light of the preceding four factors, the nurse expert in health care reform on the interdisciplinary advisory board might feel challenged. However, she knows that responsible problem-solving processes for ethical and political decision making may help turn the board's tide. The following political ethical decision-making process may be useful to the board or to policymakers in general.

1. *Gather information related to the political ethical problem or goal (in this case, access and right to health care for the under- or uninsured).*

2. *Identify the political ethical problem or goal.* Keep in mind that ethical problems or goals may not necessarily be ethical dilemmas, which

tend to dichotomize issues and limit problem solving (Weston, 1997, p. 30).

3. *Prioritize the key players related to the political ethical problem or goal and determine their values.* Important values, for example, may include beliefs related to religion, ethics, role of government, and perspectives on health. The person most affected by the decision to be made should receive the highest priority.

4. *Discuss the most viable ethical solutions to the political ethical problem or goal.* By discussing the *most viable* ethical solutions and not *all* possible ethical solutions, the problem-solving process is simplified and made more efficient. Ethical solutions are based on ethical theories, principles, facts, values, and so forth. However, an ethical solution that has little or no chance of being implemented owing to political or other constraints remains only an intellectual exercise.

5. *Resolve or minimize value conflicts that interfere with discussion or selection of a viable ethical solution to the political ethical problem or goal.* Some ideas on how to accomplish this process were discussed previously under Values and Political Ethical Conflicts.

6. *Select the most viable ethical solution and evaluate its effectiveness in decreasing the political ethical problem or attaining the political ethical goal.* Although this step is important, another aspect to this step should not be overlooked. That is, in reaching step 6, compromise and majority opinion may have ruled. Thus, some of the key players may feel their voices were diminished. Thus, sensitivity to those key players whose values and opinions are different than our own is important ethically and for future collaborations.

CONCLUSION

This chapter has focused on health care ethics and its links to health care public policy; conceptual considerations related to serving rather than steering, community rather than individuals, and one code versus many codes; values and political ethical conflicts; and nurses, ethics, and policy making. But

to what end does all this information serve? One crucial question that must be asked and addressed is this: Do nurses have an ethical responsibility to be involved in public policy? The answer is an unequivocal yes! All nurses should be familiar with

---

FOR YOUR INFORMATION

ANA's Revised Code of Ethics for Nurses: Changes with Implications for Nurses Working in Policy and Politics

Mary Cipriano Silva

The following are highlights from the 2001 *Code of Ethics for Nurses with Interpretive Statements* that have implications for nurses who are active in health policy and politics:

- "Nurses act to change those aspects of social structures that detract from health and well-being" (p. 5).
- "The complexity of health care delivery systems requires a multi-disciplinary approach to the delivery of services that has the strong support and active participation of all the health professions" (p. 10).
- "Nurses have a duty to remain consistent with both their personal and professional values and to accept compromise only to the degree that it remains an integrity-preserving compromise" (p. 19).
- "Nurses can . . . advance the profession through participation in civic activities related to health care or through local, state, national, or international initiatives" (p. 22).
- "The nurse has a responsibility to be aware not only of specific health needs of individual patients but also of broader health concerns such as world hunger, environmental pollution, lack of access to health care, violation of human rights, and inequitable distribution of nursing and health care resources" (p. 23).
- "Nurses can work individually as citizens or collectively through political action to bring about social change. It is the responsibility of a professional nursing association to speak for nurses collectively in shaping and reshaping health care within our nation, specifically in areas of health care policy and legislation that affect accessibility, quality, and the cost of health care" (p. 25).

The revised *Code of Ethics for Nurses with Interpretive Statements* can be ordered from the American Nurses Association (www.nursingworld.org).

how their codes of ethics relate to public policy, and all nurses should vote on issues related to public policy. Some nurses must also be actively involved at the highest levels of community, state, national, and international politics so that nursing's voice in health care public policy is heard and implemented. As Curtin (2001, p. 6) noted, "Ethics and politics are *not* oxymorons!"

REFERENCES

American Nurses Association. (2001). *Code of ethics for nurses with interpretive statements.* Washington, DC: Author.

American Nurses Association. (1995). *Nursing's social policy statement.* Washington, DC: American Nurses Publishing.

Aroskar, M.A. (1998, December 31). Administrative ethics: Perspectives on patients and community-based care. *Online Journal of Issues in Nursing.* Available online at www.nursingworld.org/ojin/topic8/topic8_4.htm

Beauchamp, T.L. & Childress, J.F. (2001). *Principles of biomedical ethics* (5th ed.). New York: Oxford University Press.

Berwick, D., Hiatt, H., Janeway, P., & Smith, R. (1997). An ethical code for everybody in health care. *British Medical Journal, 315,* 1633-1634.

Boylan, M. (2000). *Medical ethics: Basic ethics in action.* Upper Saddle River, NJ: Prentice Hall.

Brosnan, J. & Roper, J.M. (1997). The reality of political ethical conflicts: Nurse manager dilemmas. *Journal of Nursing Administration, 27*(9), 42-46.

Curtin, L. (2001). Ethics and politics are *not* oxymorons! *Policy, Politics, & Nursing Practice, 2*(1), 6-8.

Davidoff, F. (2000). Changing the subject: Ethical principles for everyone in health care. *Annuals of Internal Medicine, 133,* 386-389.

Davis, R. (2000). Holographic community: Reconceptualizing the meaning of community in an era of health care reform. *Nursing Outlook, 48,* 294-301.

Denhardt, R.B. & Denhardt, J.V. (2000). The new public service: Serving rather than steering. *Public Administration Review, 60,* 549-559.

Dobel, J.P. (1998). Political prudence and the ethics of leadership. *Public Administration Review, 58,* 74-81.

Hein, E.C. (Ed.). (2001). *Nursing issues in the 21st century: Perspectives from the literature.* Philadelphia: J.B. Lippincott.

Hinderer, D.E. & Hinderer, S.R. (2001). *A multidisciplinary approach to health care ethics.* Mountain View, CA: Mayfield.

Morone, J.A. (1997). Enemies of the people: The moral dimension to public health. *Journal of Health Politics, Policy and Law, 22,* 993-1020.

Shapiro, H.T. (1999). Reflections on the interface of bioethics, public policy, and science. *Kennedy Institute of Ethics Journal, 9*(3), 209-224.

Silva, M.C. (1990). *Ethical decision making in nursing administration.* Norwalk, CT: Appleton & Lange.

Silva, M.C., & Kroeger-Mappes, J. (1998). Ethical frameworks into the 21st century. In J. Dienemann (Ed.). *Nursing administration: Managing patient care* (2nd ed.). Stamford, CT: Appleton & Lange.

Smith, R., Hiatt, H., & Berwick, D. (1999). A shared statement of ethical principles for those who shape and give health care: A working draft from the Tavistock group. *Annuals of Internal Medicine, 130,* 143-147.

Ubel, P.A. (1999). The challenge of measuring community values in ways appropriate for setting health care priorities. *Kennedy Institute of Ethics Journal, 9*(3), 263-284.

Veatch, R.M. (2000). *The basics of bioethics.* Upper Saddle River, NJ: Prentice Hall.

Weston, A. (1997). *A practical companion to ethics.* New York: Oxford University Press.

Transforming Vision into Reality: The Vietnam Women's Memorial

Diane Carlson Evans

"I may be compelled to face danger, but never fear it, and while our soldiers can stand and fight I can stand and feed and nurse them."

Clara Barton

The Vietnam Women's Memorial was dedicated on the National Mall just yards from the Vietnam Veterans Memorial, "The Wall," on November 11, 1993, in Washington, DC. One may think that the approval, placement, and financing of a statue for such a just cause would be a relatively simple process; after all, this was the first memorial on the Mall of our nation's capital to honor the military service of women. However, to the contrary, the process was long and arduous and included two separate pieces of Congressional legislation and the approval of three federal commissions. The dedication of the Vietnam Women's Memorial represented the culmination of a 10-year struggle by thousands of volunteers who overcame controversy, rejection, and challenge by those who thought that a women's memorial was not needed. This case study is about the passion, the process, and the politics of turning a vision into reality and how one former Army nurse made a profound difference in women's history (Vietnam Women's Memorial Project, Inc., 1993).

I am grateful for the unstinting help from so many who gave their time, expertise, and talents to make the Vietnam Women's Memorial a reality. Special thanks to Colonel A. Jane Carlson, United States, Retired (Army Nurse Corps), and Diana Hellinger, whose wisdom, inspiration, and encouragement helped make this case study possible.

MOVING A VISION

When this monument is finished, it will be for all time a testament to a group of American women who made an extraordinary sacrifice at an extraordinary time in our nation's history: the women who went to war in Vietnam . . . You went. You served. You suffered . . . And yet your service and your sacrifice have been mostly invisible for all these intervening years. When you finished what you had to do, you came quietly home. You stepped back into the background from which you had modestly come. You melted away into a society which, for too long now, has ignored the vital and endless work that falls to women and is not appreciated as it should be. (Powell, 1993)

General Colin Powell's words rang with passion and purpose on the day of groundbreaking for the Vietnam Women's Memorial, July 29, 1993. After listening to his every word on that historic day, one couldn't help but drift and digress to many years before. Thousands of women left the comforts of America to find themselves in the midst of guerilla warfare. Having volunteered, they served in helmets and flak jackets, spending long hours easing the pain and suffering of wounded soldiers.

On July 1, 1980, President Jimmy Carter signed legislation granting the Vietnam Veterans Memorial Fund (VVMF) authorization to construct a memorial on a site of two acres in Constitution Gardens near the Lincoln Memorial in Washington, DC. The legislation read that the memorial would honor men and women of the armed forces of the United States who served in Vietnam. Two years after authorization was received, the design and plans were approved and construction was under way. The Vietnam Veterans Memorial, designed by Maya

Lin and commonly referred to as "the Wall," was formally dedicated on November 13, 1982.

Just as the Vietnam War had divided our nation, the veterans themselves were divided on the design of their memorial. Some argued that the V-shaped wall was inadequate and demanded something more heroic. Some called it a big black scar, a black gash of shame, a hole in the ground. A compromise was struck to settle the dispute. Former Secretary of the Interior James Watt had refused to authorize construction of the Wall unless a statue of an American soldier was added to it. The directors of the VVMF agreed to commission the highest-ranking sculptor in the design competition, Frederick Hart, of Washington, DC. He would design a bronze sculpture of three infantrymen to accommodate concern that the Wall lacked specific symbols of the veterans and their patriotism. Hart described his design as follows:

The portrayal of the figures is consistent with history. They wear the uniform and carry the equipment of war; they are young. The contrast between the innocence of their youth and weapons of war underscores the poignancy of their sacrifice. There is about them the physical contact and sense of unit that bespeaks the bonds of love and sacrifice that is the nature of men at war. And yet they are each alone. Their strength and their vulnerability are both evident. Their true heroism lies in these bonds of loyalty in the face of their aloneness and their vulnerability. (Vietnam Veterans Memorial Fund, 1982)

In 1983 a photograph of a bronze statue portraying three military men appeared in national newspapers, raising painful personal awareness that our country did not and might not ever know the women who served alongside those depicted. "Consistent with history." These words crystallized for me the need to change that consistency, that image. In 1983 when I saw the design commissioned by Hart, I was moved by what I did not see. His account that the "portrayal of figures was consistent with history" reflected the belief that only men serve and therefore are portrayed.

The names of eight women nurses who died in Vietnam are etched on the granite wall. The Wall, in its minimalistic concept and simplicity, was complete, as Maya Lin had described it. The names of men and women who died in Vietnam were etched together in granite for eternity. With the dedication, Americans began to learn about the lives and losses of the male and female soldiers. They were able to begin their healing journey. I was struck by a belief that the addition of the Hart statue honoring the living implored another point of view, and another healing element. Although people would see men in bronze, a whole and true portrait of the women who served during the Vietnam War, a portrait depicting their professionalism, dedication, service, and sacrifice, had yet to be seen, and their stories yet to be heard. Women, too, needed a healing place and a healing process. Historically, women who have served humanity during America's struggles and wars have not been included in the artistic portrayals. They slip into history unrecognized and forgotten, compounding the myth that either they did not serve or their service was not noteworthy. Furthermore, as before, they had disappeared off the landscape of the Vietnam era.

Although many thought that the addition of the statue portraying three servicemen completed the Vietnam Veterans Memorial, it is paradoxical that it rendered an incompleteness. A piece of history remained missing. By all public accounts, the profound legacy of women's service in Vietnam was sealed, closed from view, and dispensable. However, the time had in fact come. The norm of leaving women out of the historical account of war had to change.

Believing that people would support a memorial honoring women if given the information and the opportunity, I gave my first speech in 1983 at a Lions Club. My anxiety grew as I looked out on the room and thought about the public, which had once been hostile toward and unappreciative of those who served in Vietnam. Reexperiencing the feelings I had when I stepped off the plane on my return from Vietnam and was greeted by angry war protesters, my knees went limp and I started to shake. I was reluctant to speak experientially, to open myself up to strangers. I talked about the other women and said that more often than not it was an American nurse who a soldier looked to during the last moments of his life. I talked about the Vietnam Veterans Memorial, about how beautiful and fitting it is, but also about how women needed to be honored and remembered as well. There were many questions about my own service. The speech ended with a standing ovation. I was stunned and realized I would have to overcome fear and personal anxieties and share some of my own stories. I remembered what Eleanor Roosevelt said: "You gain strength, courage, and confidence by every experience in which you really stop to look fear in the face . . . You must do the thing you think you cannot do."

Perhaps it was fate that year when I attended my first veterans reunion in my home state of Minnesota. It included an exhibition of war art by veterans, but no images of women were depicted. There I saw a work of sculptor Rodger Brodin entitled *The Squad,* a realistic depiction in bronze of 13 "grunts" on patrol. I was instantly taken back to Vietnam. I felt compelled to call and ask the artist whether he had ever thought of sculpting a woman soldier. We met, and over the course of 5 months Brodin listened to my stories of the women who had served in the war, of the deaths, and of the weariness and frustration of seeing young Americans and Vietnamese mutilated. Using a 21-year-old model, he created a 33-inch bronze composite of a military nurse. She was to become the galvanizing force and symbol affectionately named "the Lady" by former soldiers. To Brodin she was *The Nurse.*

Having never been involved in political action, raised funds, or spoken to the media or the public, and with a suspicious view of government and the press because of my personal experience in the Vietnam War, I now had to find the courage to work toward justice. Hard work did not frighten me. Failure to achieve rightful honor for women did. I had an unsettling feeling of powerlessness reminiscent of wading into uncharted territory—not unlike stepping off a helicopter in Vietnam, entering a field hospital, and asking, "Where do I start?"

The anxiety was justified. Little did I know that this vision would require a full-time, 10-year campaign convincing government agencies, Congress, journalists, and the public about the need for a memorial. Some engaged in vilifying our service and

undermined our intent to honor women, and it took time for them to understand us, a core of nurses, veterans, and others who had profound stories to share and a firm belief in a common cause. We would be misjudged and our motives challenged, questioned, and discounted. It would be our role to teach, move the mission forward, and create a national consensus while overcoming ignorance and denial. We would not be rebuked, censured, or deterred, because as Thomas Jefferson said, "When things get so far wrong, we can always rely on the people, when well informed, to set things right."

DEVELOPING STRATEGIES

Our first core meeting was held in February 1984 with sculptor Rodger Brodin and four people, all veterans. Soon thereafter I made telephone calls, wrote letters, and extended invitations to other veterans, lawyers, and a representative from the Minnesota Nurses Association. Nine people attended the second meeting. In the words of Margaret Mead, "Never doubt that a small group of thoughtful, committed citizens can change the world; indeed, it's the only thing that ever has." Together we decided to organize a national nonprofit organization for the purpose of fund raising and moving the vision forward. Officers and a board of directors were elected, and the organization was named the Vietnam Nurses Memorial Project. Later we changed the name to the Vietnam Women's Memorial Project, Inc. (VWMP) to embrace all the military and civilian women who had served during the Vietnam era in our education and recognition efforts. We laid the groundwork, developed a mission statement that included objectives, wrote bylaws, filed articles of corporation, applied for Internal Revenue Service (IRS) nonprofit tax status, and wrote a policy and procedures manual filled with guidelines for meeting our objectives.

We began building the team and the coalitions that could help meet our three objectives: (1) to identify the women who served during the Vietnam era and facilitate research, (2) to educate the public about the contributions of these women, and (3) to erect a monument on the grounds of the Vietnam Veterans Memorial in Washington, DC, thus ensuring a place in recorded history for women Vietnam veterans. We recruited advisory members to serve on the corporate advisory board, the education council, and the monument council. We looked for individuals who would lend their name and those who could do the work. We were all volunteers.

About 3 months after our first meeting, we organized a special event to unveil Rodger Brodin's statue *The Nurse.* We invited the press and made our first official public announcement that we wanted to place this statue honoring female veterans at the Vietnam Veterans Memorial in Washington, DC. We were an intrepid group! We had yet to feel the heat of the backlash or experience the entanglements inevitable in government bureaucracy. Furthermore, unknown to us, a new law was in the making—the Commemorative Works Act, enacted in 1986 after the Project's signed agreement with Rodger Brodin. This law made it necessary for the VWMP to meet the requirements of federal regulatory review and approval.

A Minneapolis corporation donated a small office space to be used by the core group of volunteers and later by staff. We created management and organizational systems for daily operations, including mail and phone logs, form letters for "thank you" notes, general information responses, an annual budget, and financial accountability systems. We set up a regional infrastructure of volunteer coordinators who would assist in publicizing the mission of the VWMP, solicit funds, amass additional volunteers, and seek endorsements from politicians and organizations. The American Nurses Association donated a small space in its Washington, DC, office for the use of our national volunteer coordinator.

Still with some stage fright, I found on the speakers' circuit that I was influencing people simply by sharing the stories of women's service and placing the tangible symbol, *The Nurse,* in front of them. Many were moved and wanted more information. They wanted to know names of books on the subject. They wanted to know whether women had been affected by Agent Orange and suffered from posttraumatic stress disorder, as did their male counterparts. I began to learn the enormous scope and responsibility of our undertaking, and I realized how much I needed to learn so that I could adequately answer questions and better represent the service of women. I became acutely aware of the non-nurse veterans, such as physical therapists, dietitians, administrators, air traffic controllers, Red Cross workers, USAID workers, and others who asked to be equally honored and remembered.

I was not ignorant of strong foes. At times I was described as a radical feminist. One person who so described me said I was using the Vietnam dead to further my cause. With increased public awareness of the vision, there were those who insisted on changing it or opposing it altogether. Our vision triggered hate mail, threats, and angry phone calls. Some said women had not been in combat, did not suffer, and were too few in number to be honored. Many people were comfortable with the popular stereotype of the all-male American military.

In February 1985 a meeting was held in the Old Executive Office Building of the White House. We met with the associate director of the Office of Public Liaison to discuss the subject of recognizing the contributions of women in service to our country. Here we met women from the Pentagon and the Veterans Administration, representatives of the military services and other overseas civilian services (e.g., the Red Cross), and the woman who served as campaign director for the building of the Vietnam Veterans Memorial and as an independent fundraising consultant. People brought their divergent views of how to go about recognizing women. Some left with an interest in a presidential proclamation honoring all women veterans and others with an interest in building a memorial to all women who served throughout America's history, in war and peace. It was an important meeting. For us it led to funding connections, volunteers, and visibility. For others, it led to an all-encompassing memorial to military women. Subsequently, in March 1985, legislation was authorized to build a memorial to all women who had served since the time of the American Revolution. It would be called the Women in Military Service for America (WIMSA) Memorial and would be built at the entrance to Arlington Cemetery.

We sent testimony from VWMP to Congress, supporting the legislative effort. Later a federal commission would use the WIMSA Memorial as an argument against the efforts of the VWMP. However, we continued with our mission to complete the Vietnam Veterans Memorial with the addition of a sculpture portraying women.

By Fall 1985 we had four 33-inch bronze replica statues of *The Nurse* traveling across the country and being exhibited in California, Connecticut, Delaware, the District of Columbia, Florida, Illinois, Indiana, Iowa, Kentucky, Louisiana, Maryland, Minnesota, Missouri, New York, Oregon, Texas, Washington, and Wisconsin. Accompanying the statue were VWMP press releases, photographs of *The Nurse*, brochures, and information packets with requests for donations. The statue became the primary focus and vehicle through which women veterans came out of hiding. At war's end, many had gone their separate ways, getting on with their lives and careers. Unknown within their communities and even among each other, they joined with their sister veterans—many for the first time—and with their male counterparts. A decade after the war's end, the cathartic process of healing began. The outpouring of interest and the offers to volunteer were phenomenal. Our office was flooded with letters of inquiry and letters from veterans and families expressing appreciation. Still, there were those who doubted that the effort was worth fighting. One letter from a former military nurse asked, "Do you think anyone will give a damn?"

At the Project's small Minneapolis headquarters, we developed short- and long-range plans of action for grassroots and national support, fund raising, education, and public relation activities. We wrote fact sheets, position papers, media advisories, and press releases, and we designed brochures. Our plan included action steps, a checklist, timelines, and plans for who would do what, when, and where. At the outset, garnering national support seemed like an overwhelming and formidable task. We broke it down into manageable lists. We targeted the audiences we wanted and developed the message that would motivate them to respond. For example, we designed a flyer with the slogan "A Small Donation Makes a Monumental Difference" and sent copies to volunteers to distribute at civic organizations. We began with small action steps focused on veterans and nurses.

For the short-range plan, I determined to start at the grassroots level and visit the local posts of veterans service organizations: Veterans of Foreign Wars, the American Legion, Disabled American Veterans, Paralyzed Veterans of America, and the Vietnam Veterans of America. I was also "testing the water." There were a lot of unknowns regarding interest or potential support within this community, but, if moved, male veterans could take ownership and meet the many challenges ahead with us. Galvanizing them now would ignite their energy and unleash the collective strength needed for a nationwide campaign.

With local support and a formal resolution in hand, I went to the district and state conventions. The language of the resolutions was fine tuned in committees, voted on, and forwarded to national offices. As hoped, some veterans and their auxiliary members were excited and proud to be a part of the process. They lobbied long and hard within their groups to defend what they had supported. After researching each of their unique procedures and parliamentary rules, I requested time to speak from the floor of their national conventions in 1985. Lines of individuals behind the "con" microphones were much longer than those behind the "pro." Comments were heated, and some questions were laced with barbed cynicism. Miraculously, having engaged strong and powerful support early on, the pros won. By the end of that year, we had the support of the five major veterans' organizations and their 6 million members.

I became active in these veterans' organizations and remained highly visible during the 10-year effort. It was important for the VWMP to establish a reputation of trust and credibility. Using the strategy model of the veterans' organizations, we asked nurses who were politically active in their organizations to represent the project and employ their influence. More than 100 did so with pride and enormous success.

In the long-range plan, we targeted a variety of civic and humanitarian groups with a clear intent to co-opt both genders and the age groups before and after the Vietnam era. We worked toward that end because numbers would count. The grassroots appeal gained national momentum.

Our first highly visible major fundraiser was held in September 1986 in Washington, DC, near the Lincoln Memorial. It was cosponsored by Senator Edward Kennedy (D-MA) and the William Joiner Center of the University of Massachusetts. About 300 people gathered in a tent. Senator Kennedy took the podium, commending those "gallant and courageous women who served our country in Vietnam" and stressing the need to "recognize those women who served under the colors of our flag and who lost their lives." Senator John Kerry (D-MA) followed, saying, "Any of the names on the Wall could be any of us that are here. Our mission is to remember, and no one can remember in the way we ought to remember until there's a statue that reflects the service of women in Vietnam." A year later we would need the help of these senators in asking their fellow members to put these words into action.

We were on our way. Our media plan went into action, heightening awareness across America. Volunteers received official status to represent the VWMP and spoke at local and national association conferences, conventions, and civic organizations. Radio, television, and newspapers called asking for interviews. After a while, I found that the most predictable statement was, "I didn't know there were women who served in Vietnam." The most predictable question was, "Were you ever rocketed or attacked?" We would negate the myth and defy the stereotype on both counts. Yes, women were there, and, yes, they were wounded and killed. After what seemed a long media blackout, journalists were finally interested in the real-life stories of women veterans.

Simultaneously, we appealed for contributions of goods and services from businesses and organizations. Two major corporations printed thousands of brochures for the project pro bono, and another prepared a short documentary for fund-raising purposes. We asked supporters to help us identify and approach corporate sponsors and private foundations. Northwest Airlines agreed to provide air cargo free of charge for the 150-pound *Nurse* as it made stops around the United States. We sought professional counsel from an advertising agency. The slogan "A Small Donation Makes a Monumen-

tal Difference" made a poignant appeal in fundraising materials and advertisements. By July 1987, $250,000 had already been raised from corporate gifts, individual donations, appeals at veterans' meetings and conventions, and special fundraisers. More than $100,000 worth of in-kind services (e.g., management consultant services, legal fees, rent) had also been received. A pharmaceutical company approached us for a market tie with a surgical scrub used by medical personnel that subsequently netted the project another $500,000.

Armed with a clear vision, a tangible symbol, public support, and preliminary funding, and grounded with a legitimate nonprofit corporation, we were ready to ask for the endorsement of the VVMF, the organization that built the Wall and placed the bronze statue of three servicemen. VVMF founders Jack Wheeler, the chairman, and Jan Scruggs, the president, offered an official endorsement, as required by the Memorandum of Conveyance, in the spring of 1986.

The ensuing months were filled with fund raising, education, public relations, sister search activities, and plotting of strategies for seeking formal approval from federal agencies. However, in 1986, in view of the rapidly diminishing outdoor sites in the nation's capital suitable for the erection of commemorative works, Congress enacted the Commemorative Works Act (CWA). We read it with trepidation. The regulations were new and very complicated. We saw loopholes, language that was left up to the interpretation of the reader. We believed that our proposal was simply an addition to an existing memorial and therefore not subject to the CWA, which did not address additions. CWA governed new memorials intended as a commemoration of an individual, group, or event, requiring them to be authorized by an Act of Congress. We sought legal counsel and asked a lot of questions. Unanimous formal approval for a commemorative work, including additions to existing memorials, was needed from the Secretary of the Interior, the Commission of Fine Arts, the National Capital Planning Commission, and the National Capital Memorial Commission. Subsequently, we spent inordinate hours researching the role and authority of each. This knowledge alone should have been enough to deter even the most hearty and committed of souls. Indeed, that was the Act's intent, to stop the proliferation of memorials in Washington, DC.

With the endorsement of the VVMF in hand, we proceeded as planned and took our first major step. In September 1987 the Secretary of the Interior approved our proposal to add a statue representing women at the Vietnam Veterans Memorial. This permission was based on his conclusion that our proposal was an addition to an existing memorial and thus not subject to the CWA. The Secretary forwarded the proposal, bearing the Department of Interior's official approval, to the Commission of Fine Arts. Elated, we requested a hearing with the Commission of Fine Arts. As the "gatekeeper" to memorials in Washington, the Commission's purpose is to supply artistic advice related to the aesthetic appearance of Washington, DC, and to review the plans for all public buildings, parks, and other architectural elements in the capital (Kohler, 1985). While waiting for the hearing date, we prepared testimony and informed our supporters and the public at large of the upcoming hearing.

On October 22, 1987, we went before the Commission of Fine Arts. We listened to impassioned testimony from the opposition, letters of dissent from members of the public, and discussion and comments from the six presidentially appointed commissioners. We were thunderstruck that some minds and powerful pens in Washington, DC, had already been made up before we had an opportunity to testify before the prestigious and powerful Commission. Minutes before we entered the hearing room, someone handed us a copy of the *Washington Post* containing an article by Benjamin Forgey entitled "Women and the Wall Memorial Proposal: Honor without Integrity":

It has the lofty ring of a just cause, but the proposed Vietnam Women's Memorial, which has been approved by the Secretary of the Interior and which will be considered today by the Commission of Fine Arts, is not a very good idea. To be precise, it's a bad one. This is not to say that the women who served in the U.S. armed forces in Vietnam were not brave, did not perform essential duties, do not deserve our respect. It is simply to point out that if our female veterans deserve more conspicuous honor

than they already have received at the Vietnam Veterans Memorial in Constitution Gardens, where the names of the eight female dead are inscribed along with those of their male counterparts, then they should be given such honor elsewhere. To add a statue of a nurse to that extraordinary memorial—the central feature of this misguided proposal—would create a serious symbolic imbalance in one of the nation's preeminent commemorative places.

As I took my seat I thought: "So! Nurses and women aren't good enough for this sacred ground!" I knew we were in trouble before we entered the door, and soon the words out of the commissioners' mouths would echo those of Mr. Forgey. Backroom discussions had unmistakably taken place.

Our testimony included commentary on the lack of other memorials to women in our nation's capital. Of the 110 memorials in Washington, DC, at that time, only three were to women, and none of these honored military women. We addressed the history of women's service and issues of compatibility, dignity, need, simplicity, completeness, honor, and healing for all veterans, as well as the merits of a statue. Members of a prestigious Washington, DC, landscape architectural firm testified in support of our site and design.

Opponents to the concept insisted that an addition would encourage other groups and ethnic minorities to claim statues as well. One antagonist said that the Wall was complete "as is" and that attempts to depict everyone literally can only diffuse its symbolic power and weaken the memorial. Maya Lin, artist of the original design, protested further, concerned about "individual concessions" to special interest groups. "I am as opposed to this new addition as I was to [Hart's sculpture]" Lin concluded. "I cannot see where it will all end" (Minutes of the Commission of Fine Arts, 1987).

There were derisive and heated remarks by commissioners. Frederick Hart, sculptor of *Three Fighting Men* (who disqualified himself from casting a vote), argued against the addition by insisting that the statue of three men stood for the whole veteran population regardless of sex. He held that his work had created a "fragile balance" with the Wall, a balance likely to be disturbed by the intrusion of added elements. Another commissioner called it an "unneeded clarification." J. Carter Brown, Chairman of the Commission, delivered the coup de grace. He declared that the three male figures by Hart were already "symbolic of humankind and everyone who served." He asserted that a proliferation of statues would be uncontrollable, saying, "The Park Service has even heard from Scout Dog associations." He referred to the VWMP statue as "an afterthought, sort of a putdown, almost a ghettoization." Mention was made of a statue already dedicated to nurses—the Nurse's Monument, which overlooks the graves from the top of a hill in Arlington National Cemetery. We were urged to believe that this was enough for nurses. I knew from my research that this monument had been placed in honor of Army and Navy nurses in 1938. It was rededicated by the chiefs of the Army, Navy, and Air Force in 1971.

The Commission voted four to one to reject our proposal. The commissioners' comments seemed to mirror those in the *Washington Post* column, which had branded the project a "bad precedent," saying, "*The Nurse* in answer to Hart's statue has no psychological or physical relationship with the memorial as a whole" (Forgey, 1987).

Minutes after the vote, some of us talked to waiting members of the press. When asked about the hearing, I stated matter-of-factly that the Commission ignored the support of thousands of Americans and treated women veterans with arrogance and insensitivity, and I said that we would be back. One journalist asked me what it would take to place a statue of a woman at the Wall. Quite spontaneously, I said, "An act of God and an Act of Congress." Chairman Brown also talked to the press: "It could be a work of art done by Michelangelo, which it isn't, and it would still detract from the enormous power of the memorial" (*Washington Times,* 1987).

Balance with the existing memorials was a focus of debate. "What Brown neglects to specify, however, is precisely how much *The Nurse* might dilute the power of the Wall as compared to how much the existing statue on the site—*Three Fighting Men*—already compromises the Wall's inclusive embrace by its omission of women" (Marling & Wetenhall, 1989).

I knew we were in for a long, tough fight. We would need legislation in our hands to challenge a hostile Commission of Fine Arts again. Navigating a twisted bureaucratic path would require researching the laws and using them to our advantage, activating even more of Americans to use their voices and power, cultivating relationships with federal agencies and legislative staff, finding more money, compromising, and plotting a good map. Hours after the Commission hearing, we regrouped and started charting the map. We would use our nursing skills to practice patience, diplomacy, and advocacy, and we would exercise the art of grace. Above all, we would need perseverance and a good sense of humor to keep ourselves balanced amid an endless barrage of what we considered irrational opposition. We viewed the roadblocks and setbacks as detours.

Before us loomed our tremendous responsibility to the people of America who shared our fervent hope that a memorial would find the way to its appropriate place of honor. We could not let Americans down, and we were soon to learn that they would not let us down. Morley Safer of the television program *60 Minutes* learned of the Commission of Fine Arts hearing. Featuring our efforts on one of the programs, Safer interviewed five military nurses who had served during the Vietnam War. He placed their extraordinary and compelling stories of service and our mission to build a memorial in front of several million households for 14 minutes. This was to be a major turning point.

NEW STRATEGIES

Our first new strategy was to win the support of more Americans by building coalitions of various interests and groups. We had a strong infrastructure of dependable, reliable, and enthusiastic volunteers, and we accomplished our long-range goal of achieving the endorsement of 40 national organizations. Because we did not believe that this was a special interest "nurses'" or "women's" movement, we appealed to people of all ages, both sexes, veterans of all wars, and peacetime soldiers—in other words, to all citizens of America. Through efforts such as the *60 Minutes* program and numerous interviews with the electronic and newsprint media, we built a large audience of American citizens who became a strong and effective constituency of loyal supporters, and we had evidence of this support. A clipping service we used sent us copies of hundreds of heart-rending, supportive letters to the editor, editorials, opinion pieces, and stories from newspapers around the country. Many of them were in response to negative pieces written about our efforts. More evidence arrived in the form of donations: thousands of dollars in small amounts poured in, many with a note attached saying that the giver wished it could be more.

These constituencies were integral in the success of our second strategy—lobbying Congress. In November 1987, just 1 month after the rejection by the Commission of Fine Arts, Senator Dave Durenberger (R-MN) introduced SJ 215 in the Senate. Representative Sam Gejdenson (D-CT) introduced companion bill HR 3628 in the House, authorizing the building of a Vietnam Women's Memorial at the Vietnam Veterans Memorial. Furthermore, consultation with a Washington insider and former lobbyist helped to familiarize us with the political process and prepare us for future hearings. (The VWMP office was moved from Minnesota to Washington, DC, facilitating our national and legislative efforts.)

In February 1988, we testified at hearings on the bill (changed to SJ 2042) before the Senate Subcommittee on Public Lands, National Parks, and Forests. The bill was received favorably and marked up to the full committee, and in June 1988 the Senate passed SJ 2042 by a vote of 96 to 1. Also in June 1988, we testified at a hearing held before the House Subcommittee on Libraries and Memorials. Management and financial questions were posed. Preparation equals performance, and we were prepared. We answered questions honestly, clarifying and identifying the actions that met the committee's concerns. However, having our day in court brought out a myriad of contentious old conflicts, including those of a woman's place, tensions left over from the Vietnam war, and flare-ups of the original controversy regarding the design of the Vietnam Veterans Memorial. We were dealing with more than just a memorial proposal. Our project had political and sociologic undercurrents.

After extensive debate between the House and the Senate over the language of SJ 2042, the House rejected Senate language and on September 23, 1988, passed another version of the bill. On October 12, 1998 the Senate passed an amended version of SJ 2042 as passed by the House. A week later the House rejected the Senate's amendment. The Senate then conceded to the House position.

We unhappily settled for a watered-down version of the original specific language regarding site and design. At the eleventh hour, as Congress adjourned on November 14, 1988, Public Law 100-660 authorized "the Vietnam Women's Memorial Project to establish a memorial on federal land in the District of Columbia or its environs to honor women of the Armed Forces of the United States who served in the Republic of Vietnam during the Vietnam era." *This was important for what it did not say.* It was not specific regarding placement of the memorial on the Mall. Although Congress stipulated that it would be most fitting and appropriate to place the memorial within the 2.2 acre site of the Vietnam Veterans Memorial in the District of Columbia, it was *our* sense that, because of the standards of the CWA, the three federal governing agencies would yet have the last say, having the leverage to place our memorial anywhere in the *environs* to the exclusion of the Vietnam Veterans Memorial. We had yet to face the hostile Commission of Fine Arts, whose members had made it clear that they did not wish to see anything added within the 2.2 acre site of the Vietnam Veterans Memorial. Moreover, although the Senate bill penned the word *statue,* the House of Representatives bill would not. It would not dictate design by specifying *statue* but opted for the more generic term *memorial.* We determined to go back to Congress during the next session and start the legislative process over to get the bill we needed that would firmly secure the site at the Vietnam Veterans Memorial. However, the word *memorial* would remain.

Within a month of the passage of the first bill, we initiated a second and more powerful legislative campaign to put our strategies into play. We hired a public relations consultant who helped us generate thousands of stories across America from the women who served, asking them to share in their own words their personal experiences—the veritable substance behind the quest for a Vietnam

Women's Memorial—with the public. The response was phenomenal.

Throughout 1989, members of our board and staff met frequently with congressional members and the staff of legislative committees. We adopted a policy always to go in groups of two or more, depending on the circumstances. This allowed us to debrief, compare notes about what was said, discuss any conflicting messages, and subsequently write a summary for later reference (our own as well as that of the full board of directors). When deemed necessary, we set the record straight by sending a memorandum of understanding to legislative staff. Together we formulated a new slate for the 101st Congress and worked to identify panels of witnesses representing different organizations and interests for the hearings. In addition, I again spoke before committees and testified at four congressional hearings in the House and Senate.

Throughout the duration of the legislative process, we successfully employed the "Seven Rules for Testifying before Congress," even before Thomas E. Harvey's work of the same name was published in the fall of 1989! We used common sense, respect, and assorted advice from experienced sages in the veterans' and nurses' organizations and from trusted legislative staffers. Furthermore, we used a plan.

A third strategy was to activate our supporters. Using the volunteer network, we initiated a massive campaign asking supporters to contact congressional members by telephone, mail, or personal visit. As the bills progressed through the political process, these efforts were targeted to specific legislators. One by one, the legislators signed on. We accomplished this strategy by the dissemination of information through the national newsletters of endorsing organizations, through local newsletters whose mailing lists we were fortunate to have obtained, through highly active telephone trees designed by the volunteers, and through appeals to the public through media relations activities. We sent press releases and fielded questions at press conferences.

It was critical for our supporters to know the goal, the progress of lobbying with Congress, and our expectations of them. With updates and the dissemination of information, we kept the vision of the VWMP before them and provided a guiding force. Information is powerful. We found that our weakest links in the networking chain were those groups that had not been given the information. They did not act, and some lost faith because they felt overlooked or abandoned. At every national convention of the veterans' organizations, I gave briefings and asked specific actions of the members. VWMP board members and more than 150 official volunteers performed these same duties at the meetings of nurses' associations, women's organizations, social clubs, patriotic and civic organizations, schools, universities, and other groups. Mobilizing them and hundreds of unofficial volunteers toward action required articulating expectations through consistent distribution of information. Giving them something tangible to work with proved enormously successful.

With the help of an advertising agency, we designed a promotional poster for the legislative effort that read, "Not all women wore love beads in the '60s." It depicted a female soldier's name imprinted on dog tags connected to stainless steel beads. On the reverse side, hundreds of signatures petitioned lawmakers to appeal on behalf of Vietnam's forgotten veterans. Thousands of these petitions and pallets of cardboard mailing tubes were sent to volunteers and supportive coalitions across America. At shopping malls, veterans' clubs, nurses' meetings, and street corners, Americans were asked to sign the petitions and forward them to their senators and representatives. More than 25,000 posters and tubes were sent to the national veterans' conventions alone in one summer. Legislators became so tired of receiving the tubes they said, "No more!" They had gotten the message. Later, we learned that many posters never made it to their appropriate destinations because the unique design was so well liked they ended up in frames on office walls.

BACKLASH

When our prolific and unrelenting lobbying efforts were covered by newspapers, the backlash was often fascinating:

Congress should resist efforts to tinker with one of the most effective and powerful memorials built in this country—the Vietnam Veterans Memorial in Washington's Constitutional Garden...It's hard to vote against the flag or Army nurses. But, in this instance, congressmen should. The Vietnam Veterans Memorial is as close to perfection as it can be. To add anything to it would only be to detract from the powerful memorial it has become. (Indianapolis News, 1988)

We pressed on, and our legislative strategy won. On November 28, 1989, President George Bush signed legislation authorizing Area 1, the Mall, the central monumental core of the Capital City, as the site for the Vietnam Women's Memorial. However, the explicit criteria of the CWA had still to be met. We had yet to win the approval of the federal authorizing agencies to place the memorial near the Vietnam Veterans Memorial or prove that the "subject of the memorial is of pre-eminent historical and lasting significance to the Nation" (National Capital Memorials ETC, 1986).

When speaking before these agencies, I asked:

Is not the selfless service of 265,000 women, all volunteers, who served during the Vietnam era around the world, 10,000 of them—the majority of whom were nurses—in Vietnam under grave and life-threatening conditions, saving the lives of 350,000 American soldiers, of the greatest historical significance and worthy of this nation's eternal gratitude?

Supported by drawings, sketches, mockups, and reports from engineers, planners, and landscape architects, in a 5-month process of informal and formal hearings, we finally gained the approval of regulatory agencies for our preferred site within Area 1. Site review ensured that the site selected was relevant to the subject and did not interfere with or encroach on existing memorials or features. In April 1990 the Commission of Fine Arts voted to accept a recommendation to locate the Vietnam Women's Memorial on the Mall near the Vietnam Veterans Memorial. We had held fast to the vision, and our determination was vindicated. We now had a site worthy of the women who had served.

Because our first design, *The Nurse,* had been rejected in 1987, we launched a nationwide, open one-stage design competition to solicit a new design for the Vietnam Women's' Memorial. The competition would provide us with the opportunity to discover the most creative and appropriate work of art. It was an exciting way for Americans to participate in designing a national memorial that honors forever the heroic spirit of more than 265,000 American women. We were confident that a jury of eminent architects, renowned members of the arts community, and highly regarded Vietnam veterans would select a design worthy of the women who served. Ultimately, however, the VWMP board would make the final decision. With the guidance of a professional competition adviser, site feasibility consultants, technical advisers, and legal counsel, we developed the design standards, rules, and procedures to be used by the design competition applicants. We put out the call for the memorial design entries and required that they be received between August 1990 and the end of October 1990.

The design phase was arduous and demanding, and required hundreds of hours of work by committed individuals from August 1990 through March 1993. In the weeks and months that followed the design competition results, we worked with the artists who won first place to develop their designs further. Ultimately the board of directors of the VWMP decided to move forward with the design offered by Glenna Goodacre of Santa Fe, New Mexico, who had won an honorable mention in the design competition. We did not schedule meetings with the federal agencies to review her design until we had solicited the opinions of representatives of several of the project's endorsing organizations: the American Legion, Veterans of Foreign Wars, Vietnam Veterans of America, Paralyzed Veterans of America, and Disabled American Veterans. Again, this was a part of our overall philosophy and strategy to be inclusive and inform our supporters, to seek their input, and to ask their counsel. In quiet celebration while meeting together in Washington, DC, they unanimously embraced the design placed before them as fitting, appropriate, and worthy of the women who served. With their positive consensus on the Goodacre design, we were ready for the last phase.

During 1991 we met with the National Capital Memorial Commission, the Commission of Fine Arts, and the National Capital Planning Commission to present and review Goodacre's bronze model of a multi-figure sculpture-in-the-round depicting three Vietnam era women, one of whom is tending to a wounded male soldier. By Fall 1991, after many staff meetings, hearings, and unsuccessful bureaucratic attempts to alter the concept, the design was approved by all three commissions. In Santa Fe, Goodacre proceeded to build the life-size monument in clay for its final review. On March 11, 1993, the clay sculpture-in-the-round was approved by all the regulatory agencies. The monument would now be cast in bronze.

By this time, the news media neither helped nor hindered the approval efforts. Opinions continued to be voiced by well-known syndicated columnists and small-town journalists, but there was no turning back. "Monumentitis is making the Mall in Washington a monument to Mars and to irritable factions" (Will, 1991). However, most of the media were now on the side of building the memorial. They would be the chief catalyst for informing America (and foreign countries) of the upcoming dedication.

Finally, on November 11, 1993, female veterans were thanked by a grateful nation during the dedication ceremony entitled "A Celebration of Patriotism and Courage." The Vietnam Women's Memorial statue was unveiled on the grounds of the Vietnam Veterans Memorial 300 feet southeast of the statue of three servicemen near the Wall. Many in attendance shed tears and shared thoughts and sentiments. Former Chairman of the Joint Chiefs of Staff Admiral William Crowe noted, "This moving monument finally completes the Vietnam circle by honoring the spirit and achievements of the women who participated in that effort. But more impor-

Vietnam Women's Memorial. Glenna Goodacre, sculptor. Gregory Staley, photographer. (Copyright 1993 by Vietnam Women's Memorial Project, Inc.)

tant, it will serve as a shining beacon for future generations of American women." A wounded Marine said, "I would not be alive today without the super professional service of the American women the memorial honors." Gail Hager, a woman who served in Vietnam, said in a letter to the project's office, "I'm so grateful for your perseverance, commitment, and passion to make the women's statue become a reality . . . My heart is still overflowing with feelings from my experiences in DC. You have given each of us women a priceless gift—the gift of hope and healing. For us to be recognized, honored, appreciated, and united was unbelievable." For the VWMP's commemorative book, *A Celebration of Patriotism and Courage* (1993), Charles T. Hagel said, "The dedication of the Vietnam Women's Memorial will complete the long march toward universal recognition of all who served their country in Vietnam. This memorial honors the commitment and inspiration of the American women whose service during this turbulent and difficult time cannot be overstated."

Vision, that picture of desired results, is just that—a vision. Although I provided the vision and leadership, accomplishment was achieved with the help of many who provided the complex combination of necessary abilities. Keeping the vision clearly out in front of the American people, having a board and staff committed to written policies and speaking with one voice, and maintaining commitment to strategic planning and results—these helped realize the victory. Moving the vision of the VWMP forward is truly a testament to the will of the people. It took a creative team of diverse talents and personalities. Many came and went at critical junctures, offering expertise and guidance, and all made a difference. It was important to listen. Ultimately, it was collective persistence and determination in using political action that moved a nation. Eleanor Roosevelt said: "It is deeply important that you develop the quality of stamina. Without it, you are beaten. With it, you may wring victory out of countless defeats." Her words rang true more than once.

It is easy to be intimidated by the mysteries of politics, politicians, and the political process. Yet this is where action, driven by our personal aspirations, values, and beliefs, can force change—and even alter the way people view the world. The secret to the process isn't all that mysterious after all. Demystifying it is analogous to breaking the intricacies of nature down into understandable parts. "By viewing Nature, Nature's handmaid Art, Makes mighty things from small beginnings grow" (Dryden, 1995).

A small group grew to the thousands of veterans, other Americans, and people from around the world who went to Washington, DC, on Veterans Day 1993 to dedicate the Vietnam Women's Memorial and say "thank you" to women who served our nation. Vice President Al Gore, a Vietnam veteran, praised his sister veterans during the dedication ceremony, stating, "Let's all resolve that this memorial serve as a vehicle for healing our nation's wounds. Let's never again take so long in honoring a debt" (Gore, 1993).

One of the four figures of the Vietnam Women's Memorial. Glenna Goodacre, sculptor. Gregory Staley, photographer. (Copyright 1993 by Vietnam Women's Memorial Project, Inc.)

REFLECTIONS

The original target date for dedication of the Vietnam Women's Memorial was 1988, 4 years after the founding of the organization. Ultimate success would require 5 more years. During those wakeful nights and stress-filled days, it was difficult not to become discouraged and wonder whether the struggle was worth it. We had received many offers of pared-down memorial concepts and different sites. We could have accepted them and gone on with our lives. We lost volunteers, we lost some support, and some of us lost friends. The personal price and the price to the organization had to be weighed. Our particular crusade required waiting, working harder and longer, and taking new risks. Externalizing the destructive criticism and skepticism, which became part of the norm, was critical to maintaining harmony amid the balancing act of family and project responsibilities.

It became clear that to succeed the achievement of the vision before us would require some compromise, but giving up was not an option. When it became necessary, we found a new design, but we would not concede on the choice of a site. I often had to remind myself of my own words before the national veterans' service organizations in 1988 when requesting their legislative support:

> We wish to stand near the Wall of names of those we cared for in death and the bronze statue portraying the men we helped come home. We were with them in the war and we want to be with them now. I want the women who served to know that they are not forgotten, that there is a special place for them, too, on honored ground.

The nature of a nation's memory of war can be contentious and emotionally charged. Commemoration does not simply encourage people to reflect on war and remember the veterans and their contributions to society; it also affects how that war is viewed. Do memorials and commemoration shape the memory of war, or does memory shape the memorials? It took the political process to create an inclusive remembrance for the thousand of nurses and other women who served their country during the Vietnam war. The debates surrounding the need for such commemoration offer Americans enlight-

ening vision of how people think about the past, the present and the future in response to a tumultuous time in our history—and the role of women in it.

CONCLUSION

Commemoration of the women who served during the Vietnam War has begun a healing process for that silent contingent of military personnel while changing the imagery of those who serve during wartime. The Vietnam Women's Memorial is a place to remember and heal. War buddies, families, and mourners are consoled by the strength and compassion represented by the women caring for the wounded. Many leave with a greater sense of peace. The Memorial provides a glimpse into a historical experience previously unrecorded and unheralded. Beyond the intention of honoring women veteran's service, the monument prompts thought and questions. Hundreds of students, ranging from fourth graders to doctoral candidates, request the VWMP's assistance in research projects. Colleges and universities have become more inclusive and invite women veterans—along with the men—to speak to students and participate in educational forums and workshops. Several times a year, the VWMP sponsors oral history storytelling at the site of the memorial entitled "Vietnam: In Their Own Words." The stories of the women cast in bronze come to life as veterans tell "in their own voices" about their experiences. The symbolic figures of the Vietnam Women's Memorial not only offer insight into the war but also create a gathering place for stories that serve as living history.

POSTSCRIPT

Many women veterans who volunteered to go to Vietnam to help save lives and who experienced the carnage of war came home to the same hostile treatment as the returning combat soldiers. The women suffered posttraumatic stress disorder with all the accompanying problems, as well as pancreatic and uterine cancer and other diseases related to combat. However, only recently have major studies been initiated and appropriate health services provided. More than a decade of research and numerous publications looked at the psychobiologic consequences of combat on male theater veterans, but

Profile of Those who Served

POPULATION

More than 265,000 women served in the military during the Vietnam War. Although an accurate number of the women who were actually stationed or performed military duty in Vietnam is not available, it is estimated that 10,000 to 11,000 served "in country." Within the total population of military women, 85% were enlisted. However, 90% of the women stationed in Vietnam and the adjacent waters were officers. The majority (87%) were military nurses.

SERVICE SPECIALTIES

In addition to being nurses, women served in a variety of military positions, including intelligence, public affairs, supply, air traffic control, special services, administration, finance, occupational therapy, physical therapy, and dietetics.

Although it is difficult to determine the exact number of civilian women who served in Vietnam, their contributions are no less important. These women served as news correspondents and workers for the Red Cross,

the USO, the American Friends Service Committee, Catholic Relief Services, USAID, and other humanitarian organizations.

CASUALTIES

Eight military women (seven Army nurses and one Air Force nurse) lost their lives in Vietnam. Their names are engraved on the Vietnam Veterans Memorial along with those of 58,209 other military personnel who made the ultimate sacrifice for their country. More than 50 civilian women died in Vietnam.

Fewer then 2% of the casualties treated in Vietnam died. However, more than 350,000 casualties were treated, and 75,000 of these people were permanently disabled.

Other facts about the women who served in Vietnam:
- About 5.8% were wounded in Vietnam.
- About 1.3% were wounded in combat situations.
- Approximately 1.2% received the Purple Heart.
- More than 20% have service-connected disabilities.

The major source for the following information is the tables from the *National Vietnam Veterans Readjustment Study* (Department of Veterans Affairs, 1988).

no biologic trials with female Vietnam veterans in the theater of operations have been published. Research has provided some basic information, but much more is needed to understand the complex issues surrounding combat theater assignment of female military personnel (Department of Veterans Affairs, 1998). In 1996 the first major female veterans study with a national outreach was commissioned by the Department of Defense and the Veterans Affairs Department. In 2000 a Congressionally mandated study of Vietnam veterans, including women, was conducted by Columbia University in New York. The study examined aspects of exposure to combat, trauma, and herbicides in Vietnam, and the VWMP worked with the scientists in facilitating this research. (Additional information can be obtained through the *Newsletter of the Vietnam Veterans Health Study,* 600 West 168th Street, 6th floor, New York, NY 10032.)

Further information about the Vietnam Women's Memorial and the storytelling project may be obtained from www.vietnamwomensmemorial.org.

REFERENCES

Commemorative Works Act. Public Law 99-652-H.R. 4378 40 U.S.C. 1001.

Department of Veterans Affairs. (1988). *National Vietnam Veterans Readjustment Study.* Washington, DC.

Department of Veterans Affairs. (1996). *Vietnam nurse veterans psychophysiology study information sheet.* Washington, DC: Author.

Dryden, J. (1995). *Songs of the earth.* Philadelphia: Running Press.

Forgey, B. (1987, October 22). Women and the wall memorial proposal: Honor without integrity. *Washington Post,* E1, E11.

Gore, A. (1993). Dedication speech at the Vietnam Women's Memorial. Washington, DC.

Harvey, T. (1989, September). Bearing witness: A practical guide to testifying on Capitol Hill. *Government Executive,* 29.

Indianapolis News. (1988, February 19). *Additions that detract.*

Kohler, S. (1985). *The Commission of Fine Arts: A brief history, 1910–1984.* Washington, DC: US Government Printing Office.

Marling, K.A. & Wetenhall, J. (1989). The sexual politics of memory: The Vietnam Women's Memorial Project and "The Wall." In *Prospects: An annual of American cultural studies.* New York: Cambridge University Press.

Minutes of the Commission of Fine Arts. (1987, October 22). Washington, DC.

National Capital Memorials, ETC. (1986). National capital memorials and commemorative works. Washington, DC: US Government Printing Office.

Powell, General C. (1993, July 29). Groundbreaking ceremony remarks. Washington, DC.

Scruggs, J.C. (1985). *To heal a nation: The Vietnam veterans memorial.* New York: Harper and Row.

Senate Joint Resolution 2042, 100th Congress, November 15, 1988.

Senate Joint Resolution 207, 101st Congress, November 28, 1989.

Vietnam Veterans Memorial Fund (1982). *National salute to veterans* (program souvenir of events of November 10-14, 1982). Washington, DC: Author.

Vietnam Women's Memorial Project, Inc. (1990). *Vietnam Women's Memorial National One-Stage Open Design Competition Program: Design standards, rules, and procedures.* Washington, DC: Author.

Vietnam Women's Memorial Project, Inc. (1993). *Celebration of patriotism and courage.* Washington, DC: Author.

Washington Times (1987, November 11). Vietnam women veterans' statue now going the legislative route.

Will, G.F. (1991, August 26). Monumentitis is making the mall in Washington a monument to Mars and irritable factions. *Newsweek.*

Resources

Annual Report of the Commonwealth Fund. (1993) *Innovators: The President's essay.* New York: Margaret E. Mahoney.

Flikke, J.O. (1996). Nurses in action: Wars of the twentieth century In P.M. Donohue (Ed.). *Nursing, the finest art* (2nd ed.). St. Louis: Mosby.

Naythons, M. (1993). *The face of mercy: A photographic history of medicine at war.* New York: Random House.

Ratzloff, T. (1993). Return from the front. *Minnesota Nurse, 1*(14), 6.

Organization and Delivery of Health Care in the United States: A Patchwork System

JANET HEINRICH

THERESA M. THOMPSON

"We are not just one good Health Affairs article away from solving the problems of the U.S. health care system."

IAN MORRISON

CORE VALUES

As a nation we embrace diversity and pluralistic approaches to problem solving. We have a historical distrust of "big government" and centralized control, part of our Jeffersonian inheritance, and at the same time we demand government regulations that will "level the playing field" because we value fairness and equal access to opportunity. We pride ourselves on being fiercely independent, yet we also expect that neighbors and communities will help one another in times of need. These basic values have been at the heart of the health care delivery system in the United States. Even in the mid-1800s, in spite of the ever-present danger of death from smallpox, malaria, and other infectious diseases, Americans resisted the implementation of basic state government-initiated public health laws that incorporated new science and technology into the control of these deadly epidemics (Shattuck, 1850).

HISTORICAL DEVELOPMENT

Social insurance and national systems of compulsory sickness insurance became the norm in Europe, starting with Germany in 1883 (Starr, 1982). In the United States, government was highly decentralized, leaving any actions related to health to private and voluntary action at the state and local levels. Trade unions, cooperatives, and social reformers argued for sickness funds and compulsory insurance against sickness, but there was very little political support for any form of national insurance through the 1920s in the United States.

In 1921 Congress passed the Shepherd-Towner Act, which provided matching funds to the states for prenatal and child health centers. Lillian Wald, the founder of the Henry Street Settlement and public health nursing in the United States, aggressively supported this legislation. These centers, staffed mainly by public health nurses, sought to reduce rates of maternal and infant mortality by teaching women how to care for themselves and their families. By following the rules of basic hygiene, the program resulted in the prevention of many common diseases. This highly successful program was discontinued in 1927 at the urging of the

American Medical Association (AMA), whose members considered it to result in excessive federal interference in local health concerns (Starr, 1982).

During the 1930s concern grew about the costs and distribution of medical care. Harry Moore, staff director of the Committee on the Costs of Medical Care (CCMC), described medical services as maldistributed and badly organized, with no coordination beyond the walls of any particular hospital or clinic (Starr, 1982). The final report of the committee endorsed group practice and group payment for medical care but opposed compulsory health insurance. Instead, voluntary plans were the preferred next step. In spite of the efforts of the CCMC to include leaders from the AMA in the study and in the development of recommendations, the report was denounced as "socialized medicine" by the AMA and failed in its efforts to achieve consensus even on recommending voluntary health insurance.

Reformers made several more attempts at articulating the health care needs of the American people throughout the Roosevelt New Deal period. Most of the recommendations, however, called for state subsidies to expand public health and maternal and child health services, to expand hospital facilities, and to increase aid for medical care for special populations. Public opinion polls during this time reflected public support for government funds to help pay for needed medical care, but not if this meant higher Social Security taxes to pay for health insurance (Starr, 1982). A clear public mandate for public national health insurance did not exist. A bill introduced in 1943 by Senator Wagner (D-NY), Senator Murray (D-MA), and Representative Dingell (D-MI) to create a comprehensive and universal national health insurance system met with strong opposition from the AMA. Even when President Truman made national health insurance a campaign issue and won the election, his proposal succumbed to charges of socialism from the AMA. Only the first recommendation of Truman's plan, the Hospital Survey and Construction Act (the Hill-Burton Act), passed with support from the AMA and the growing hospital industry.

With the federal government pouring money into construction, the development of powerful new antibiotics and other wonder drugs, and the rise of private hospital insurance, hospitals evolved into meccas of biomedical science. Medical specialization increased dramatically with new scientific breakthroughs after World War II, resulting in the fragmentation of medical practice and the segmentation of patient ailments into specific disease categories affecting different body parts. Policy options after the war and into the 1960s recommended more and better-trained general practitioners, training in "comprehensive care" (e.g., the promotion of health, prevention of disease, diagnosis and treatment, and rehabilitation), and the development of multispecialty group practices. A small and controversial subgroup advocated for group practices linked either with the prepayment of fees or with health insurance (Somers & Somers, 1962).

The progressive groups that had once supported a national health insurance system were completely splintered by the 1950s. The middle class could buy private insurance, labor unions used collective bargaining to gain health insurance benefits for workers, and American veterans had their own system of hospitals and clinics. Instead of a universal system, American society provided health insurance for the wealthy, the well organized, and those with political influence. The poor remained uninsured. Many cities and counties tried to provide indigent care by building or expanding public hospitals and clinics, forming the origins of our current and crumbling "safety net."

The 1965 twin Great Society insurance programs, Medicare and Medicaid, gave hospitals and physicians new streams of income for treating elderly, poor, and disabled persons and created new subsidies for academic medical centers. These programs did not offer the comprehensive coverage of services at reasonable costs or the more-efficient use of scarce resources through a rational organization of services for which many advocates had worked. They are nonetheless public programs and, in the case of Medicare, are linked with private insurance carriers to provide payment for acute medical care services to people 65 years of age and older. Medicare, an insurance program that covers acute episodes of illness, is operated by the federal government and supported primarily with tax dollars. Medicaid, with matching state and federal funds, was established to provide health services for poor persons as defined by the individual states. State Medicaid programs provide for many of the long-term care services needed by families with elders, as well as for the essential health care service needs of mothers and children.

THE TIGHTENING VISE OF THE MEDICAL-INDUSTRIAL COMPLEX

The 1970s and 1980s were decades of continued but unsuccessful efforts to curtail the growth of total dollars spent on health care. There were efforts to limit increases in the number of beds and the use of new technologies in communities through comprehensive health planning. National legislation made it possible for states to establish health-planning agencies that had the authority to control the expansion of health facilities and the building of new ones. Efforts were made to coordinate, through regional health planning, health facilities and the health programs offered in a geographic area for specific conditions such as heart disease and cancer. In spite of these efforts, hospitals continued to expand, so that by 1999 there were an estimated 5,890 community hospitals in the United States (American Hospital Association, 2001). These facilities varied by size, type (generalized or specialized), and ownership (public, private, nonprofit voluntary, or for-profit investor owned). Teaching hospitals associated with universities and medical schools, nursing schools, and other training programs also expanded their capacity, providing an environment for education and research. These teaching institutions received higher Medicare and Medicaid payments for services because of their teaching responsibilities and their provision of services to indigent populations. As new procedures, technologies, and treatments were developed and tested, these teaching hospitals evolved into high-technology tertiary centers, treating patients with the most complex conditions. The research institutions were closely linked with pharmaceutical companies and with the manufacturers of drugs, biologics, and devices. The medical-industrial complex arrived, with a focus on new biomedical breakthroughs to prolong life at any cost.

The late 1980s and the 1990s were turbulent times in the hospital industry. In a frenzy of merger, acquisition, and consolidation activity, organizations attempted to position themselves to respond to an increasingly competitive market. Across the United States, many hospitals converted from nonprofit, religion-sponsored organizations to for-profit conglomerates and changed from individually managed and controlled hospitals into systems of jointly managed organizations (Claxton, Feder, Shactman, & Altman, 1997). This "horizontal integration" was expected to bring about efficiencies and cost reductions. There was also a surge of "vertical integration," whereby hospital systems bought outpatient clinics, nursing homes, and home care agencies in an effort to better coordinate and manage services across the spectrum of care. Many hospital administrators also bought into the concepts of reengineering, or restructuring, as a way of improving productivity and decreasing costs. Common strategies included the use of new treatment technologies, new information systems, and computerized patient records, the reduction of staff and the substitution of less highly trained staff for more highly trained staff, the closure of acute care beds coupled with the opening of "subacute" beds that are less costly to staff, and a decrease in length of hospital stays with the early discharge of patients to the home (Steinwachs, 1992). The success of vertically integrated delivery systems in achieving such goals as improved coordination of services, reduced excess capacity, and improved cost-effectiveness and quality is yet to be well established (Newhouse & Mills, 1999). As large health employers become increasingly wary of entering the risky insurance business and large provider groups that sponsor health maintenance organizations (HMOs) face more direct and intense competition from national health insurance plans, evidence of vertical disintegration in the health care marketplace is emerging, with a shift from ownership arrangements to contractual agreements between health plans and providers (Robinson, 1999).

Spending for health care reached $1.2 trillion, or 13.0% of the gross domestic product (GDP), in 1999 (Health Care Financing Administration [HCFA], 2001). Although this was slightly less than the 13.4% GDP spent in 1993, a recent increase in the annual growth rate for health care spending sparked predictions of higher future spending on health care (Heffler, Levit, Smith, Smith, Cowan, Lazenby, & Freeland., 2001). Factors driving the higher spending include a recent relaxation of utilization controls by health plans in response to consumer demands for greater choice of providers and increased prescription drug use driven in part by the proliferation of insurance plans with low copayments for drug coverage, improved treatment regimes calling for the use of higher-cost brand name drugs, and more aggressive direct-to-consumer marketing efforts. As well as paying more for health insurance premiums, consumers are increasingly paying a greater share of total health care costs. In 1999 consumers paid "out-of-pocket" for 5.9% of total costs, up from a low of 2.7% in 1997 (HCFA, Office of the Actuary, 2001). Many health plan arrangements that require consumers to bear a greater share of the cost of certain benefits and services do so in an effort to contain costs by making consumers more cost conscious (Medicine & Health Perspectives, 2001). One of the most successful of such strategies is a tiered payment scheme for prescription drug benefits, a tactic that incorporates different cost-sharing formulas for the coverage of "off-formulary" and brand name drugs. As a nation, we have yet to find an acceptable way to limit patient access to expensive services, control physician preferences to use newer and more expensive treatments and technologies, or to generate new sources of revenue—namely, taxes!

GROWTH IN NURSING HOMES

The passage of Medicare and Medicaid legislation in 1965 prompted rapid growth in the number and size of nursing home facilities. Despite the minimal standards of care established by this legislation, nursing homes were essentially unregulated in most states and were governed almost entirely by market forces. The rapid growth of nursing home facilities coupled with inadequate regulation resulted in the provision of substandard care for the most vulnerable older population (Institute of Medicine, 1986). In the 1970s, the nursing home industry came under increased scrutiny as a number of corruption and abuse cases were exposed (Sultz & Young, 1997).

More than half of nursing home revenues come from state and federal funds, making states and the federal government accountable for the care provided. In an effort to control their budgets, states began to develop mechanisms to control the number of nursing home beds and to develop alternative community-based services for people who require long-term care. States also attempted to improve the quality of care by putting in place a number of regulations focused on staffing mix, physical facility characteristics, and the level of need based on various characteristics of nursing home residents. At the same time, there were strong efforts in Congress to totally deregulate the nursing home industry. As a result of national legislation passed in 1987, nursing homes are now required to do individual resident assessments and to develop care plans that maximize each resident's health and functional status. There is strong evidence, however, that these laws are not enough to improve quality without ensuring adequate nursing staff to provide the necessary services (Wunderlich, Sloan, & Davis, 1996). Complicated by growing nursing workforce shortages, the concern for quality of care in nursing homes continues today and is a volatile issue for health care providers and policymakers at all levels of government (Wunderlich, Sloan, & Davis, 1996; Institute of Medicine, 2001b). For the first time in decades, there has been a slight decrease in the number of certified nursing homes in the United States, a 3.7% decline from 1997 to 1999 (Harrington, Carrillo, Thollaug, Summers, & Wellin, 2000). This change is in part attributed to the fact that more people are receiving needed long-term care in their homes.

GROWTH OF HOME CARE SERVICES

Home care services were first organized under visiting nursing services as philanthropy in many communities. During the 1950s and 1960s, home care programs were often coordinated with general public health nursing services, with an emphasis on generalized services to families. Categorical public health funding changed this broad community approach, as did higher payments for medically focused home care services under Medicare (Gebbie, 1995). With increased financial pressure to shorten the number of days that patients stay in the hospital, there is now a new focus on providing a variety of high-technology health care services in the home.

Home care services are one of the fastest growing components of the health care industry, with many types of for-profit and nonprofit organizations providing a range of services, from skilled nursing care to social or homemaker services. The voluntary, nonprofit visiting nurse service organizations have not grown over the past several decades, but there has been exponential growth in the number of hospital-based home care programs and for-profit proprietary agencies. Nationally, there are an estimated 20,000 home care providers, with state requirements for licensure of home care providers varying tremendously. Fewer than half (7747 in 1999) of these providers meet the requirements for Medicare participation (National Association for Home Care, 2000). Although many home care agencies are certified by national organizations, the decentralized nature of monitoring the quality of services delivered in people's homes is of mounting concern. Growing charges of fraud and abuse have many consumer groups seeking increased state-level regulation to ensure patient safety.

Concerns about quality and cost-effectiveness also make home care a target for budget cuts, even though patients and families may prefer home care. The HCFA funded four demonstrations in the mid 1980s, the Community Nursing Centers, to begin to identify methods for providing needed nursing care to a defined population for a set fee. To curb the growth in Medicare payments for home care services, the Balanced Budget Act (BBA) of 1997 replaced Medicare's cost-based payment system for home care with a prospective payment system (PPS). Since October 2000 home health agencies have received an all-inclusive payment for services provided in a 60-day episode of care. With poor oversight systems for home care services, however, there is a concern that a fixed payment per episode of care may control spending but also

inadvertently provide a financial incentive for home care providers to limit services or to provide a less-appropriate mix of services (General Accounting Office, 2000).

SHRINKING "SAFETY NET"

Beginning in the 1970s, many communities experimented with neighborhood health centers in an effort to provide comprehensive community health services that were closely linked to the needs of the community. These centers expanded into medically underserved communities, such as isolated rural areas and economically depressed inner-city communities, reaching out to provide access to care for more than 10 million medically underserved people (National Association of Community Health Centers, 2001). Today, nearly 700 community and migrant health centers provide comprehensive, case-managed primary and preventive care in the United States. There are approximately 3500 federally designated rural health clinics, with the majority of the funding for these clinics coming from Medicare and Medicaid (General Accounting Office, 2001c). With few physicians available to provide needed services, these centers are often staffed with nurse practitioners and physician assistants. Neighborhood health centers are seen as successful in providing for the care of indigent populations. Recent increases in federal support for such programs should enable community health centers to expand delivery sites in order to improve access to services for medically underserved populations.

Some freestanding clinics have developed to serve specific needs, such as community mental health centers, drug and alcohol treatment centers, family planning clinics, abortion clinics, clinics for treatment of persons with acquired immunodeficiency syndrome, and free clinics to serve homeless populations. The number of freestanding clinics is unknown. These clinics may be staffed with lay people, volunteers, and paid physicians and nurses and may be funded by private donations, foundation support, or local, state, or federal government. They may charge patients on a sliding fee schedule based on the individual's ability to pay.

Other important components of the safety net of services available to individuals without some form of medical insurance include the care provided by about 1200 public hospitals financed by state and local governments. Another aspect is the emergency care that all Medicare-participating hospitals must provide to any person with an emergency medical condition regardless of that person's ability to pay. Enacted in 1986 because some emergency departments refused to treat indigent patients or inappropriately transferred uninsured patients to other facilities, the Emergency Medical Treatment and Active Labor Act (EMTALA) has increased access to care for uninsured persons (General Accounting Office, 2001b). EMTALA does not, however, ensure that care is provided in the most appropriate and cost-effective setting, nor that care is coordinated. Some hospital and physician providers of this uncompensated care argue that mandating the provision of emergency care has actually had a negative impact on the availability of emergency care in many communities. They argue, for example, that EMTALA has contributed to emergency room overcrowding and to the more frequent diversion of emergency response vehicles to other hospitals.

Health care has also been made more available to low-income adults and children by the recent expansion of public health insurance programs. Nearly 41 million people received Medicaid in 1998 and 3.3 million low income children were enrolled in the State Children's Health Insurance Program (SCHIP) in 2000, up from 1.96 million in 1999 (HCFA, 2001).

A robust economy and the incremental expansion efforts of public health insurance programs are credited with reducing the number of uninsured persons. In 1999 the number of persons without health insurance declined slightly for the first time in 12 years to 42.5 million people, or 15.5% of the population (Census Bureau, 2000). Yet limited resources at the local level and a downturn in the economy hinder the further extension of safety net services to indigent persons. A recent Kaiser Family Foundation survey (2000) found that there is little public will to pay for broader health care coverage for indigent persons. Although 53% of Americans surveyed were willing to pay more than $30 per month to cover the uninsured, 46% were willing only to pay $5 per month.

PUBLIC HEALTH SERVICES: SEAMLESS OR SEPARATE?

Many of the major improvements in the health of our communities can be attributed to the success of public health measures and our public health infrastructure. Every state and territory and many counties and cities have a public health department. Each state and local government is different, however, and the health departments operate under unique public health laws and regulations. They may be organized as freestanding entities or combined with environmental, mental health, or social service agencies. The diversity of combinations of agencies and legal mandates reflects the fact that the majority of their support comes from local tax dollars, with limited support from other sources. Many suggest that the systems in place guarantee that the health of the public is in "disarray" (Institute of Medicine, 1988). Federal, state, and local public health agencies have traditionally been responsible for the control of epidemics, for ensuring safe food and water, and for providing personal and preventive health services to vulnerable and indigent populations such as mothers and children. There is growing recognition of the role of public health as the first line of defense against bioterrorism.

How services and programs are organized at the local level often depends on outside funding sources. As a means of survival, public health agencies became dependent on Medicaid fee-for-service payments for personal care services and "categorical funding" for tuberculosis, family planning, and crippled children's programs. Categorical funding "disease specific funding" for public health clinics supports part of the safety net of services available to medically indigent persons. Funds for personal services, however, are not used for community assessments or assurance activities, critical core elements in ensuring the public's health (Conley, 1995). Many organizations now advocate for a return to the basic public health core functions of assessment, policy development, and assurance, as articulated by the Institute of Medicine's (1988) study *The Future of Public Health,* and they call for a renewed focus on essential public health services. However, many state and local agencies lack the necessary funding to provide these essential services at a time when managed care organizations (MCOs) are competing with them for the Medicaid dollars that cover personal care services.

Some state and local health departments are developing strategies to collaborate with MCOs so that health promotion and disease prevention services—such as prenatal programs for high-risk women, immunization programs, and tuberculosis and other infection control programs—are well coordinated in a community. For example, MCOs can provide care to patients with tuberculosis and supervise their medication use, but the local health department remains responsible for overseeing contact tracing to find other people in the community with the disease. Everyone in the community benefits when the focus is not only on the health of individuals and families, but also on the health of the total community. The roles and responsibilities of state and local health departments are still evolving to hold MCOs and other types of organizations linked with insurance products accountable for clinical outcomes and for the health status of the populations served (Lipson, 1997).

LARGE FEDERAL SYSTEM OF CARE

The Department of Defense (DoD) health program, TRICARE, provides medical care for about 8.3 million active duty service members and retired beneficiaries and their respective dependents and survivors. Health care is managed on a regional basis at military hospitals and clinics and may be supplemented by contracted civilian services. TRICARE has undergone dramatic changes in the last decade. There are now five managed care support contractors that administer the TRICARE health benefit in 11 regions in the contiguous United States through provider networks. It has become a triple-option benefit program designed to give beneficiaries a choice among a health maintenance organization, a preferred provider organization, and a

fee-for-service benefit. Cost sharing varies among the three options from a low per-service cost for active-duty families to a percentage of allowable charges for others. Recent legislative changes will have an impact on these copayments for active duty beneficiaries and also for Medicare-eligible uniformed services retirees (General Accounting Office, 2001d).

The Department of Veterans Affairs' (VA) health care system provides services to approximately 3.65 million veterans. The VA uses hundreds of delivery locations to provide services such as primary care, specialized medical care, mental health care, geriatric services, and extended care. The VA system also provides medical backup to the DoD and other federal, state, or local agencies during national emergencies. In a recent reorganization, the VA system created 22 regional offices to manage 150 hospitals. Congress passed the Veterans Health Care Eligibility Reform Act of 1996, which provided tools for the VA to develop new eligibility rules that allow the VA to treat veterans in the most appropriate setting; introduce managed care principles including a continuum of services within a uniform benefits package; and expand the ability to purchase services from private providers and to generate revenue by selling excess services to nonveterans. The VA system has made significant progress in moving toward a primary care case management system and shifting care to outpatient settings. These changes have produced excess inpatient capacity at most VA hospitals. As the VA's transformation continues, the system will face the challenges of determining whether to close hospitals, and where (General Accounting Office, 1999).

The Indian Health Service (IHS) is an agency of the U.S. Public Health Service, Department of Health and Human Services and operates as a comprehensive health service delivery system for approximately 1.5 million of the nation's 2 million American Indians and Alaska Natives. Its annual appropriation is approximately $2.2 billion. Federally recognized Indian tribes and Alaska Native corporations have a government-to-government relationship with the United States of America. The IHS provides for maximum tribal involvement in developing and managing programs to meet their health needs. The goal is to raise the health status of American Indian and Alaska native people to the highest possible level.

IHS services are provided directly and also through tribally contracted and operated health programs. Health services also include health care purchased from more than 2000 private providers. As of October 1998, the federal system consisted of 37 hospitals, 59 health centers, 44 health stations, and 4 school health centers. Of 151 service units, 85 were operated by tribes. In addition, 36 urban Indian health projects provide a variety of health and referral services. The IHS clinical staff consists of approximately 840 physicians, 380 dentists, 100 physician assistants, and 2580 nurses and allied health professionals, such as nutritionists, health administrators, engineers, and health records administrators (www.ihs.gov).

The U.S. Department of Justice Federal Bureau of Prisons was established in 1930 to provide more progressive and humane care for Federal inmates. Today, the Bureau consists of 100 institutions, 6 regional offices, a central office, 3 staff training centers, and 28 community corrections offices. The Bureau is responsible for the custody and care of approximately 154,000 federal offenders, 130,000 of whom are confined in Bureau-operated correctional institutions or detention centers. The remainder are confined through agreements with state and local governments and through contracts with privately-operated community corrections centers, detention centers, prisons, and juvenile facilities. The Health Programs Section coordinates the Bureau of Prisons' medical, dental, and mental health services to Federal inmates. A full range of health services is enhanced through the use of telehealth and electronic health records (www.bop.gov).

EVOLUTION OF MANAGED CARE

The vast majority of insured Americans are covered by one of a growing variety of managed care arrangements. Managed care arrangements entail some connection between the financing and delivery of care, usually with cost management as a prime goal. They range from tightly controlled staff-model health maintenance organizations (HMOs) to preferred provider organizations (PPOs) and point-of-service (POS) contracts (which allow consumers to choose providers not affiliated with the HMO), to managed indemnity plans and other hybrids that incorporate some aspects of traditional managed care such as utilization review.

Although staff models of MCOs were developed in the early 1930s, the AMA fought the idea of physicians becoming employees of corporations, as opposed to independent providers reimbursed on a fee-for-service basis as they had been for more than half a century (Starr, 1982). There was renewed federal government encouragement of the managed care concept and physician group practice arrangements in the 1960s, and again in the 1990s, as a way to contain spiraling health care costs.

In the early 1990s, about 40 million Americans were enrolled in health maintenance organizations and 50 million more were enrolled in more loosely organized preferred provider organizations (PPOs). By 1995 the number of HMO enrollees jumped to 60 million, and the number of individuals covered by PPOs nearly doubled to 91 million (American Association of Health Plans, 1996). Today HMOs and PPOs remain the predominant health insurance plans, with 76% of all covered employees enrolled in such plans. The Managed Care On-Line resource company reports that 80.9 million persons were enrolled in HMOs in 2000 and 84.5 million more were covered by PPO plans (www.mcareol.com). PPO enrollment is, however, growing at a more accelerated rate than HMO enrollment as consumers become less satisfied with the restrictive managed care plans that limit their choice of providers and their access to certain services. Although more restrictive health plans have had greater success with containing health care costs, consumers and providers alike question whether these plans involve a trade-off between cost and quality (Reschovsky, Kemper, Tu, Lake, & Wong, 2000). Public health insurance plans are also trying to rein in costs by encouraging beneficiaries to enroll in some type of managed care plan. By 2001 states had succeeded in moving 56.8% of Medicaid beneficiaries into managed care plans (www.mcareol.com). The Centers for Medicare and

Medicaid (CMS, formerly HCFA) continues to encourage its 40 million Medicare beneficiaries to enroll in Medicare+Choice managed care plans versus the traditional Medicare fee-for-service plan.

MCOs use a variety of methods to control utilization and costs. These include using market power to negotiate discounts from physicians, hospitals, and other provider groups and providing financial incentives to "gatekeepers," usually primary care physicians, to reduce the utilization of hospitals, specialists, and laboratory tests. The gatekeeper role has become less prominent in recent years as growing consumer dissatisfaction with restricted access to care providers has sparked a backlash against managed care. Other cost control methods used by MCOs involve paying provider groups a fixed payment per patient, or a capitated rate, that is independent of amount of services used. MCOs may also seek out the most efficient providers, based on data collected via medical claims histories or provider profiles (American Academy of Nursing, 1993).

Although managed care eliminates perverse incentives for inappropriate overutilization, it also provides an incentive to reduce costs by potentially undertreating patients who need care. Critics of MCOs have voiced concern about the denial of services to individuals and families as a way of rationing services (Eddy, 1997). Individuals with special health care needs, such as those with severe mental illness, chronic conditions such as cystic fibrosis, or complex conditions that involve multiple comorbidities, often complain that they do not have access to necessary specialists or special technologies. Others appreciate the lower cost of premiums of MCOs and access to preventive services. MCOs provide incentives to initiate cost-effective programs to keep individuals, families, and communities healthy. There is a growing interest in promoting self-care and in teaching families what they can do to enhance their own personal health outcomes.

Methods of systematically monitoring and evaluating the quality of care provided by MCOs are still being developed, and there is keen interest at the state and federal levels in the concerns voiced by patients and health care providers alike. In 1996 a special Presidential Advisory Commission on Consumer Protection and Quality in the Health Care Industry was named to address concerns over the quality of care. The commission's final report, issued in 1998, noted that several types of quality problems existed, including avoidable errors, underutilization of services, overuse of services, and variations in service use. The report advanced more than 50 recommendations centered around six core purposes (Advisory Commission on Consumer Protection and Quality in the Health Care Industry, 1998). The recommendations included disseminating evidence-based practice guidelines, developing error reporting and investigation systems, standardizing the reporting of quality measures by each health industry sector, giving consumers greater access to quality information on providers to enable them to compare providers, and holding all industry participants accountable for improving quality. To date, consumers and other purchasers of health care are not incorporating available data on quality performance measures into purchasing decisions or provider selection. State and federal governments have taken measures to hold insurers financially accountable for inappropriately denying care and are evaluating how well programs comply with the Consumer Bill of Rights and Responsibilities proposed by the advisory commission. A quality report released in 2001 by the Institute of Medicine's Committee on the Quality of Health Care in America underscores that enormous changes need to be made to America's current health care system if substantive and substantial improvements in the quality of care are to be realized (Institute of Medicine, 2001a).

The managed care backlash is a national phenomenon, prompting introduction of remarkably similar patient protection legislation in state legislatures despite differences in local communities experiences. The Medicare program, Medicare+Choice, is shrinking. In employment-based insurance there is a clear trend toward more loosely managed products, away from the more restrictive "true" managed care programs. Patients in HMOs report less satisfaction, less trust in physicians, and lower ratings of physician visits than patients in other plans (Center for Studying Health System Change, 2000).

FUTURE POSSIBILITIES

Since the decisive defeat of the comprehensive national health care reform proposals that were presented to the 103rd Congress in 1994, more-incremental health care initiatives have been pursued to contain health care costs and to provide all Americans with more-equitable access to health care. Our health insurance system has evolved on the basis of private coverage linked to an individual's job, with job loss meaning the loss of insurance and access to usual health services. Individuals older than 65 years are covered by Medicare, and individuals and families who meet varying state definitions of poverty are covered by Medicaid. Insurance plans each have different services that are paid for, and each plan requires different levels of copayments. Insurance premiums are also based on the health status of the individual, as opposed to charging everyone the same rate (community rating). The Health Insurance Portability and Accountability Act of 1996 has improved access to health insurance for employed people and prohibits exclusion from insurance coverage when an individual has an existing illness.

In 1997 Congress identified a new revenue stream to provide states the option of extending insurance coverage to children in families with incomes above the poverty line. There have been few efforts, however, to address the problem of the increasing number of uninsured adults in the United States, many of whom are working but lack access to ongoing health care services from the private sector insurance market (Hacker & Skocpol, 1997). Recently, some communities have begun pilot programs that use a managed care approach to provide health care to low-income adults who are ineligible for public insurance programs. These initiatives are not entitlement programs and do not guarantee benefits. Instead, they use existing charity care funding to provide preventive and primary care services to targeted groups of uninsured adults with the goal of reducing the use of more-costly inpatient and emergency care services (Felland & Lesser, 2000). Incremental measures have also been taken in response to the concern about growing health care costs, but sufficient policies are not in place to restrain price increases, to reduce the volume of services used, or to limit access to new technologies and new drugs. Consequently, spending for many health care sectors, such as inpatient hospital services, outpatient services, home care, and prescription drugs, is projected to grow unabated.

While the rapid growth of managed care and the recent merger and consolidation frenzy among hospitals and other health care institutions has dramatically changed the U.S. health care delivery system, managed care is predicted to have only a marginal effect on limiting health care cost increases in the future (Ginzberg, 1997). Shifts in ownership from traditional nonprofit institutions to national and international corporate conglomerates that answer to stockholders and capital markets are nonetheless challenging our basic beliefs and values that health care is a basic human right, not a commodity. Today the terms *change* and *chaos* are used interchangeably to describe the current state of the U.S. health care system. No one seems to have a clear vision of how health care services will be organized and delivered in the future. Employers continue to encroach on the role previously played by health plans and providers, providers continue to venture into the domain of insurers, pharmaceutical companies and suppliers are becoming disease state managers, hospitals are now seen as cost centers and are either closing beds or going out of business, and health care education and delivery are moving to the Internet, where consumers can find their own information on how best to manage their health problems.

Some people predict that the future U.S. health care delivery system will be a three-tiered system that is based on an individual and family's ability to pay for insurance, with more rationing of services occurring at the lower two tiers (Reinhardt, 1996). Managed care will be used as a strategy for rationing care for the population in the middle tier, and rationing in the bottom tier will occur by limiting public expenditures for public hospitals and clinics. Well-to-do Americans in the top tier will continue to have open-ended access to health care services and providers of their choice (Weil, 2000). The potential of capitated managed care, which was only recently being advocated by corporate leaders as a less costly method of providing health insurance coverage to workers and by politicians for Medicare and Medicaid populations, is already being questioned. Some insurers have even retreated from capitated reimbursement payments because of the great strife, conflicts of interest, and financial problems it has created in provider communities (Medicine & Health Perspectives, 2001). In 1996 Shortell and Hull predicted the evolution of new highly integrated organized delivery systems with varying forms of ownership and diverse alliances among hospitals, physicians, and insurers that would be designed to capture market share and provide cost-effective care to a defined population (Shortell & Hull, 1996). It was also suggested at that time that these integrated systems could develop structures of political accountability in their communities and develop new governance structures that encouraged true coordination and tough allocation decisions at the local level (Emanuel & Emanuel, 1997). Key characteristics of integrated delivery systems (IDSs) include the provision of a seamless continuum of primary, short-term, and long-term care; the transfer of financial risk to hospitals and physician providers; the improved tracking and use of clinical and financial outcome data; the horizontal and vertical integration of services, including physician services; and the integration of an array of clinical services in a local market.

Recent consolidation activity in the health care industry has contributed to the formation of politically and fiscally powerful organized care delivery networks, but Weil (2000) argues that these networks have a limited interest in reshaping America's health system. They tend not to proactively implement initiatives that focus on providing more comprehensive and coordinated care, but rather tend to be more reactive in their actions to cut costs when faced with reduced reimbursement from managed care plans or federal and state health insurance payers. Kindig (2000) argues that even though Americans are reluctant to embrace comprehensive policy reforms, as a nation we must better define and measure the health outcomes and quality standards that we desire and use these standards to purchase health care at the community or population level. The World Health Organization (WHO) (2000), which ranked 191 countries on the basis of the

organization and performance of their health care systems, supports the concept of strategic purchasing of health system inputs as well as outputs. Furthermore, the WHO emphasizes that although public and private health sectors must work together to improve the health of a nation, the ultimate responsibility for stewardship and for the performance of a country's health system lies with the government. The United States ranked first on health system responsiveness and first in the level of health expenditure per capita. On other measures, however, such as the fairness of financial contributions across population groups and the level of health achieved in relation to the resources consumed, the United States ranked considerably lower than some other developed and developing nations. An overall health system performance ranking of 37 indicates that performance improvement is possible and greater stewardship is necessary.

Most advocates continue to support taking an incremental approach to health system reform. They support modest insurance reforms, the targeting of services to specific populations, such as children, and the expansion of coverage to include such specific services as breast cancer screening (Hacker & Skocpol, 1997). Others are hopeful that the current chaos will nuture support for moving toward a single-payer system with significant government regulation to ensure equitable care for all Americans. Advocates for this approach do not view markets as working well in the provision of health care services and view health care as a right that should be provided along the lines of any other public service. These advocates point to models in other developed countries, such as Canada and the United Kingdom, for the achievements of such "international standards" for health care systems as: (1) universal coverage of the population, (2) comprehensive coverage of principal benefits, (3) financial contributions based on income through a progressive tax system rather than through individual insurance purchases, (4) cost control through administrative mechanisms such as binding fee schedules, global budgets, and limitations on system capacity (Evans, 1997).

What is clear today is that economic incentives and concerns will continue to drive future health system changes, and that business and corporate America will increasingly have more of a say in how the future health care delivery system will be organized. Perhaps the next wave of change will be influenced even more by informed consumers, who will exert their power over corporate and government payers, insurers and health care providers, and politicians. If this is to occur, the basic information about health plans and coverage, patient satisfaction ratings, access, cost, and quality needs to be better conveyed to consumers (Isaacs, 1996). We also need to develop better strategies for promoting public accountability and informed purchasing by the American public.

The U.S. health care system remains a patchwork of diverse systems that several experts predict will continue to be in crisis. Many see the conflicts inherent in the trends of declining private insurance and reduced capacity to provide uncompensated care (Smith, 1997). Findlay and Miller (1999) outline the factors such as the increasing cost of premiums that are contributing to a decline in employer-based coverage, and several independent surveys also show a gradual erosion of employer-sponsored health insurance for early and Medicare-eligible retirees (General Accounting Office, 2001c). Some employers are beginning to limit their exposure to rising health care costs by moving toward defining a fixed contribution that the employer will give to each employee to purchase any of the health insurance plans available.

The patchwork of systems that has evolved for health care delivery in America has not solved the problems of access, cost, or quality. In fact, while lacking health insurance is a major barrier to accessing health services, even individuals who have insurance report problems accessing needed health care services (Kaiser Family Foundation, 2000). Health care costs continue to escalate in spite of efforts to use market forces to control costs through competition. Managed care companies, which once were holding down premiums on insurance policies, are now raising premiums. Finally, quality remains a growing concern for health care consumers. Many providers and consumers voice fears of decreasing safety and quality at the same time that we are trying to decrease costs and capacity in health care.

The existing system is still oriented toward acute care and episodes of illness rather than toward health promotion and comprehensive care. We have learned that it is difficult to control costs piecemeal and that there are limits to expanding access using an incremental approach. Partial remedies just don't work and often have negative and unintended side effects. Yet we have not been able to mobilize our political system around a solution that will ensure a rational health care system for all of us.

REFERENCES

Advisory Commission on Consumer Protection and Quality in the Health Care Industry. (1998). *Quality first: Better health care for all Americans.* Retrieved online, August 12, 2001, from www.hcqualitycommission.gov/final.

American Academy of Nursing. (1993). *Managed care and national health care reform: Nurses can make it work.* Washington, DC: Author.

American Association of Health Plans. (1996). *HMO and PPO trends report.* Washington, DC: Author.

American Hospital Association. (2001). *Hospital statistics, 2001 edition.* Chicago: Author.

Census Bureau. (2000). *Health insurance coverage: 1999.* Retrieved online, August 11, 2001, from www.census.gov/hhes/www/hlthin99.html.

Center for Studying Health System Change. (2000). *Issue brief: Do HMOs make a difference?* (number 28). Available online at www.hschange.com.

Claxton, G., Feder, J., Shactman, D., & Altman, S. (1997). Public policy issues in nonprofit conversions: An overview. *Health Affairs, 16*(2), 13.

Conley, E. (1995). Public health nursing within core public health functions: "Back to the future." *Journal of Public Health Management and Practice, 1*(3), 1.

Eddy, D.M. (1997). Balancing cost and quality in fee-for-service versus managed care. *Health Affairs, 16*(3), 169.

Emanuel, E.J. & Emanuel, L.L. (1997). Preserving community in health care. *Journal of Health Politics, Policy and Law, 22*(1), 179.

Evans R.G. (1997). Going for the gold: The redistributive agenda behind market-based health care reform. *Journal of Health Politics, Policy and Law, 22*(2), 433.

Felland, L.E. & Lesser, C.S. (2000). *Local innovations provide managed care for the uninsured* (issue brief no. 25). Washington, DC: Center for Studying Health System Change.

Findlay, S., & Miller, J. (1999). Down a dangerous path: The erosion of health insurance coverage in the United States. Washington, DC: National Coalition on Health Care. Retrieved online, March 2001, from www.nchc.org/1999PolicyStudies/DownADangerousPath.html.

General Accounting Office. (1999). *Veterans' affairs: Progress and challenges in transforming health Care* (GAO/T-HEHS-99-109). Washington, DC: Author.

General Accounting Office. (2000). *Medicare home health care: Prospective payment system will need refinement as data become available* (GAO/HEHS-00-9). Washington, DC: Author.

General Accounting Office. (2001a). *Defense health care: Disability programs need improvement and face challenges* (GAO-2-73). Washington, DC: Author.

General Accounting Office (2001b) *Emergency Care: EMTALA implementation and enforcement issues* (GAO-01-747). Washington, DC: Author.

General Accounting Office. (2001c). *Health centers and rural clinics: Payments likely to be constrained under Medicaid's new system* (GAO/HEHS-01-577). Washington, DC: Author.

General Accounting Office. (2001d). *Retiree health benefits: Employer-sponsored benefits may be vulnerable to further erosion* (GAO-01-374). Washington, DC: Author.

Gebbie, K.M. (1995). Follow the money: Funding streams and public health nursing. *Journal of Public Health Management and Practice, 1*(3), 23.

Ginzberg, E. (1997). Managed care and the competitive market in health care: What they can and cannot do. *Journal of the American Medical Association, 277* (22), 1813.

Hacker, J.S. & Skocpol, T. (1997). The new politics of U.S. health policy. *Journal of Health Politics, Policy and Law, 22*(2), 333.

Harrington, C., Carrillo, H., Thollaug, S.C., Summers, P.R., & Wellin, V. (2000). *Nursing facilities, staffing, residents, and facility deficiencies, 1993 through 1999.* Retrieved online, August 5, 2001, from www.hcfa.gov.

Health Care Financing Administration. (2001). *Aggregate enrollment statistics for federal fiscal years 1999 and 2000.* Retrieved online, August 11, 2001, from www.hcfa.gov/init/children.htm.

Health Care Financing Administration, Office of the Actuary. (2001). National health expenditure projections 2000-2010. Retrieved online, August 5, 2001, from www.hcfa.gov/stats/nhe-proj/.

Heffler, S., Levit, K., Smith, S., Smith, C., Cowan, C., Lazenby, H., & Freeland, M. (2001). Health spending growth up in 1999; faster growth expected in the future. *Health Affairs, 20*(2), 193-203.

Institute of Medicine. (1986). *Improving the quality of care in nursing homes.* Washington, DC: National Academy Press.

Institute of Medicine. (1988). *The future of public health.* Washington, DC: National Academy Press.

Institute of Medicine. (2001a). *Crossing the quality chasm: A new health system for the 21st century care.* Washington, DC: National Academy Press.

Institute of Medicine. (2001b). *Improving the quality of long-term care.* Washington, DC: National Academy Press.

Isaacs, S. L. (1996). Consumers' information needs: Results of a national survey. *Health Affairs, 15*(4), 33.

Kaiser Family Foundation. (2000). *NewsHour/Kaiser survey spotlights misconceptions about the medically uninsured: Survey examines difficulties faced by those without health coverage.* Retrieved online, August 11, 2001, from www.pbs.org/newshour.

Kindig, D.A. (2000). *Purchasing population health: Paying for results.* Ann Arbor: University of Michigan Press.

Lipson, D.J. (1997). Medicaid, managed care, and community providers: New partnerships. *Health Affairs, 16*(4), 91.

Managed Care Online (MCOL). *Managed care fact sheets: National statistics.* Retrieved online, February 16, 2002, from www.mcareol.com/factshts/mco/fact.htm.

Medicine & Health Perspectives. (2001). *No end in sight to rising premiums, Wall Streeters say. 55*(29). Washington, DC: Healthcare Information Center.

National Association of Community Health Centers. (2001). Community Health Center Facts. Retrieved online, August 11, 2001, from www.nachc.com/top_nav/frame/map.htm.

National Association for Home Care. (2000). Basic statistics about home care. Retrieved online, August 11, 2001, from www.nahc.org/NAHC/Research/research.html.

Newhouse, R., & Mills, M.E. (1999). Vertical system integration. *Journal of Nursing Administration, 29*(10), 22–29.

Reinhardt, U.E. (1996). Rationing health care: What it is, what it is not, and why we cannot afford it. In S. Altman & U. Reinhardt (Eds.). *Strategic choices for a changing health care system.* Chicago: Health Administration Press.

Reschovsky, J.D., Kemper, P., Tu, H.T., Lake, T., & Wong, H.J. (2000). *Do HMOs make a difference?: Comparing access, service use and satisfaction between consumers in HMOs and non-HMOs* (issue brief No. 28). Washington, DC: Center for Studying Health System Change.

Robinson, J.C. (1999). The future of managed care organization. *Health Affairs, 18*(2), 7–25.

Shattuck, L. (1850; reprinted 1948). *Report of the Sanitary Commission of Massachusetts, 1850.* Cambridge, MA: Harvard University Press.

Shortell, S.M. & Hull, K.E. (1996). The new organization of the health care delivery system. In S. Altman & U. Reinhardt (Eds.). *Strategic choices for a changing health care system.* Chicago: Health Administration Press.

Smith, B.M. (1997). Trends in health care coverage and financing and their implications for policy. *New England Journal of Medicine, 337*(14), 1000–1003.

Somers, H.M. & Somers, A.R. (1962). *Doctors, patients, and health insurance.* Garden City, NY: Doubleday Anchor Book.

Starr, P. (1982). *The social transformation of American medicine.* New York: Basic Books.

Steinwachs, D.M. (1992). Redesign of delivery systems to enhance productivity. In S. Shortell & U. Reinhardt (Eds.). *Improving health policy and management.* Chicago: Health Administration Press.

Sultz, H.A. & Young, K.M. (1997). *Health care USA: Understanding its organization and delivery.* Gaithersburg, MD: Aspen.

Weil, T.P. (2000). Management of integrated delivery systems in the next decade. *Health Care Management Review, 25*(3), 9–23.

World Health Organization. (2000). *Health systems: Improving performance.* Geneva, Switzerland: Author.

Wunderlich, G.S., Sloan, F.A., & Davis, C.K. (1996). *Nursing staff in hospitals and nursing homes: Is it adequate?* Washington, DC: National Academy Press.

COULD A NATIONAL HEALTH SYSTEM WORK IN THE UNITED STATES?

Kristine M. Gebbie

"What a time to be a part of the American health care system. There is a revolution afoot. . .and American nurses have the chance to be American health care revolutionaries."

JOSEPH CALIFANO

The United States is often singled out as the only economically developed country on the globe that does not ensure universal access to health services for its population. Such a guarantee is provide elsewhere through a variety of arrangements that include government-operated care systems, government-managed finance systems, or government-mandated financing. Moves toward a universal system were made at several points during the twentieth century, most recently in the 1993-1994 proposal by President Clinton that died without coming to a vote in Congress. The issue is a real one in a country that spends more per capita on health (by about 40%) than any other nation yet is far from leading the planet on measures of health such as years of healthy life lived or proportion of infants living to their first birthday. Exploring the potential for a national health system can reveal strengths and weaknesses and begin to answer whether such a system is possible in the United States.

POSSIBLE APPROACHES TO A NATIONAL SYSTEM

The two major approaches to a national system are based on some form of financing that is all-encompassing or some form of service system that is universally available. For each of these forms, there are at least two structural options, and each will be briefly discussed.

Universal Payment

Universal payment as a route to a national health system assumes that if funds were available, the services would follow. This discussion of payment will not take up the problematic reality of such an assumption. It is notable, however, that today some people who have financing for care are unable to get access because practitioners are not available for reasons such as geographic maldistribution, professional workforce shortages, or some form of social discrimination (e.g., denial of Medicaid to some immigrants).

National tax. The conceptually simplest form of universal payment would be a national program in which tax funds are used to pay providers for care rendered as needed. The tax could be a special one (such as that currently used to support Medicare for those over 65) or some portion of general revenues. The payment from this single national payor could go directly to those providing care (parallel to the province-based single payor system of Canada) or could be managed by fiscal intermediaries (as is now the case for Medicare). If truly universal, there would be little or no administrative burden for enrollment, because everyone would automatically be eligible. There would be a need to negotiate with providers of care for fee levels and methods of reimbursement; a single payor controlling all health dollars would be a formidable bargaining agent for hospitals and clinicians to confront.

Multiple payors. Alternately, a universal payment system could be constructed with multiple payors. For example, all employers, no matter how small or large, could be required to provide a certain level of health insurance for all employees and their families, with Medicare continuing for those over 65 or disabled and a form of Medicaid used for the unemployed and their families. This less monolithic system is the heart of the rejected Clinton plan and shares features with that in place, for example, in Germany. It allows for a range of payment mechanisms, with more room for bargaining and less sense of the government as the overwhelming controller of the purse strings. For a system such as this to work successfully, there would have to be rules governing the components of coverage and dual coverage in families with more than one worker. The employment-based coverage would be financed as it is now, with funds that would otherwise be available for wages or other benefits. The other components would require taxation, as they do now. Although this setup might be more palatable to practitioners or institutions, many employers, especially those with few employees, would find the mandate objectionable.

Universal Care

A more radical approach to a national health system would be to make the actual provision of care universal.

National health system. This system is the National Health Service approach begun after World War II in Great Britain. National tax dollars (general or special taxes) are used to pay primary care providers throughout the country for basic health services and to pay specialists and hospitals for their share of needed services. This system essentially makes the provision of care a government service, whether the caregivers and hospital staff are put directly on a government payroll or are employed by contract. The managers of the system would be obligated to find sources of care for everyone throughout the country. To do so, they might need some flexibility, such as making differential fees available to recruit providers to serve remote areas. This approach would also lend itself to careful investment in only as many hospital beds and specialized services as population size and health statistics suggested were needed, with a clear disincentive for continuing the expensive practice of having large numbers of excess beds or competing diagnostic services. There are many fears that such a system would have too many incentives to control cost and not enough incentives to be user-friendly or maintain high quality.

State-based system. Universality could be achieved with similar results but greater flexibility by placing the requirement for access on the states

through some combination of funding incentives and penalties. Expecting each state to use its tax authority and funds provided through national tax resources to ensure access for everyone would allow each state to employ and deploy its own preferred mix of generalists and specialists and community-based and hospital-based services. Within a national minimum expectation, states with more income could choose a richer mix of services, but no one would be without access to care.

For providers of care, either a national or a state-based universal care system presents a radical change from the current realities. Such centralized control of purse strings makes it far less likely that individual entrepreneurs or entrepreneurial systems would survive. And it is not clear that the current infusion of private capital into development of pharmaceuticals or equipment would continue. As evidence, it is worth noting that prescription drug manufacturers have opposed adding a prescription drug benefit to Medicare on the grounds that it makes this large government purchaser more likely to pursue some form of price controls.

BARRIERS TO RESOLVING THE LACK OF UNIVERSALITY

Describing ways that universality could be achieved does not deal with the reality that universality of access to care or funding for care has not been popular in the United States. The history of care and payment has been a blend of entreprenurialism, private charity, and public charity.

American Enterprise

Entrepreneurs have been free to develop care or care products and sell them, subject for nearly 100 years only to the strictures of federal or state safety regulation and professional licensing laws. Private groups, particularly religious ones, have offered hospitals, clinics, home care, and other services to those unable to purchase care for themselves, although this charity role has diminished in the face of rising costs and a greater number of reimbursement programs. Governments have offered public hospitals, various clinics, and a few finance systems to ensure that the neediest citizens have access to at least the rudiments of care. There is a often a personal cost to these "free" services, paid in extended waiting time for care and loss of personal dignity.

Incrementalism

Over the latter half of the twentieth century, the United States edged toward universality with the convergence of specialized programs such as Medicare, community and migrant health centers, expanded Medicaid, state insurance purchasing initiatives, and the Child Health Insurance Program. However, these positive moves were offset by the growing number of jobs that do not offer a health insurance benefit, either for workers or for workers' families, or offer a benefit at a cost that is not affordable. There has been no indication that this trend will be reversed any time soon.

Political History

It is also important to remember that the political history of the United States includes suspicion about government and a reluctance to use government as the solution to a problem. The election of 2000 returned to office a party that has consistently run against "big government," proposes tax cuts in part so that the funds will not be there to tempt Congress to spend, and that touts private solutions to social concerns. Polling by a number of groups continues to show that although people agree that lack of access to care is a problem, they are divided on solutions and reluctant to either spend more money or give up some current services to make better access possible. Given the abrupt reversal of public policy on catastrophic coverage for seniors in the 1980s, the disastrous 1993–1994 health reform debate, and the conflicting views of the public, it seems highly unlikely that any major effort to achieve universality would be attempted in the near future. Even on the most popular of issues, extending a Medicare prescription drug benefit, there is strong push to limit the benefit to include only low-income senior citizens, rather than making drug coverage a regular benefit of the program.

POTENTIAL POSITIVE FORCES

Despite the negative forces, there are some forces that might push the country in the direction of universality.

A Balancing Act

The major factor is the conundrum of balancing cost and quality without leaving an even larger number of individuals without care. A number of states attempting health reform and universal coverage in the 1980s and 1990s dealt with this problem extensively. The problem can be described as similar to trying to get complete control of a large, slightly underfilled balloon: When you grab it in one place, it simply bulges out in another. The expectation that the care system will achieve a higher quality of error-free care may require additional staff, different staff, or new information systems, all of which entail cost. Under the existing system, adding any staff or capital equipment without jeopardizing quality or raising cost can be accomplished by reducing the number of individuals cared for. If, however, it is very clear that no one can be moved outside—that is, left without care—we will be forced to have the dialogue needed to make a collective agreement on all three points: how much care, of what quality, and at what cost. No state has the legal authority to require participation in any state-specific universal plan, by the Medicare program or companies that choose to self-insure and are thus exempt from state regulation by ERISA,[1] so state efforts have at best been only partially successful.

The Public's Role

Public awareness and concern may be, in the end, what makes the change possible. A policy change such as that needed in the United States to develop a national health system can only happen when there is a confluence of a perceived problem, a potential solution, and the political will to act. The potential solutions are many and have been in circulation for many years. The exact combination of funding and

---

[1] The Employee Retirement Income Security Act (ERISA) exempts self-insured health benefits plans from regulation by the states, meaning that self-insured companies may limit benefits, arbitrarily change coverage, or exempt certain conditions in ways that would otherwise be limited by state law if offered through ordinary insurance companies. When enacted in 1974, ERISA was focused primarily on eliminating duplicate oversight of pension plans for companies operating in many states. Hawaii had a mandate for universal employment-based insurance predating ERISA and is the only exemption to the law.

organization that would achieve universality in the United States may be unknown, but its component parts are most likely already within the policy menu. It is the perception that we have a real problem, and the political will to solve it, that are missing.

Economics Matter

The sense that there is a problem has dissipated since the wave of support for health reform in 1992 and 1993. The perception could be rekindled if the economy were to take a serious downturn, bringing home to many more individuals the reality that under the present "nonsystem," many people are only one paycheck or one layoff away from being unable to finance needed health care for themselves and their families. Because those who are uninsured come disproportionately from often-disenfranchised groups, the concerns of the uninsured have not been heard. Emergence of a larger group more representative of the economic and ethnic mix of the nation would make the problem real. This public awareness that can then be used to stimulate the political will to make the needed changes.

The use of an awakened public to make such a major change as national health a reality in the United States is unlikely, however, because it would require a sustained lobbying effort that lasts longer than one election cycle and is loud enough to be heard over the voices of the currently enfranchised nonsystem. The fears of clinicians, hospitals, suppliers, employers, and insurance companies that they will lose autonomy, face tough regulation, and face even tougher price negotiations means that they will argue loud and long to avoid creation of any single national voice about health. And there is no way to achieve true universality, or a truly national system, without that single national voice.

Related Association Websites

Information about current debates on improved coverage and on movements toward universal coverage can be followed through the websites of major professional associations such as the following:
- www.ana.org/
- www.americanmedicalassociation.org/
- www.apha.org/
- www.aha.org/

Information is also available through the websites of these foundations with a particular interest in health reform:
- www.commonwealthfund.org/
- www.kff.org/
- www.milbank.org/
- www.rwjf.org/

MANAGED CARE AND MENTAL HEALTH: A MIXTURE OF OPTIMISM AND CAUTION

Beverly Malone & Shirley Smoyak

"It is the mind that makes the body."
                                        SOJOURNER TRUTH

Although managed care is a relatively new financial strategy in general health care, the public sector in the United States has always had a de facto version of managed care. For more than a century states and counties have generated yearly budgets that have included the costs of maintaining public psychiatric hospitals and, more recently, community mental health centers and units within general hospitals. Administrators have had to live within these budgets or pay the consequences of failing to meet the demand for psychiatric services by their citizens. If expenditures exceed the allocations, the shortfall has often resulted in poor service or no services provided.

AN "AS IF" SYSTEM

The fragmented, rather independent, and loosely connected public/private mental health facilities and services have been referred to by analysts and critics as a "nonsystem." Regier, Goldberg, and Taube (1978) and Regier, Narrow, Rae, Manderscheid, Locke, and Goodwin (1993) have described the current state of affairs as a de facto mental health service system or an "as if" system. Ordinary citizens are frustrated and overwhelmed by the lack of coherence they encounter by the gatekeepers and rule makers. For people struggling with serious mental illnesses, the associated stigma adds still more barriers to accessing the needed care. Services that should be available and accessible turn out to be largely illusory, or "as if."

Mental disorders account for more than 15% of the burden of disease around the world, ranking second only to cardiovascular disease. Almost 25%

of all adults and 21% of U.S. children gain access to some element of the system each year. There are four major sectors of this elusive system:

- The *specialty mental health* sector is composed of mental health professionals such as psychiatric nurses, psychologists, psychiatrists, and psychiatric social workers. These providers are specialists in the area of mental health and provide treatment largely in outpatient settings such as office-based practices, public/private clinics, schools, and criminal justice settings. Special psychiatric units or beds located within general hospitals provide the preponderance of acute care. Small numbers of private psychiatric hospitals and residential treatment centers for children provide intensive care in the private sector. Other services available include state/county mental hospitals and multiservice mental health facilities, which include inpatient care and intensive care management as well as partial hospitalization.

- The *general primary care* sector consists of health care professionals such as nurse practitioners, family medical practitioners, general internists, and pediatricians, who practice in offices, clinics, acute medical/surgical hospitals, and nursing homes. The general primary care sector has been identified as the initial point of contact for many adults and children with mental health disorders. Unfortunately, mental health may not be viewed as an integral part of overall health, especially in the primary care sector. More than 6% of adults and 3% of children use this sector for mental health services.

- The *human services* sector includes social services, school-based counseling, residential rehabilitation services, vocational rehabilitation, criminal justice/prison-based services, and religious professional counseling. Approximately 5% of adults and 16% of children use this sector for mental health services. For children, it is a major entry point into the de facto mental health system.

- The fourth sector can be described as the *voluntary support network*. It is composed of self-help groups, such as 12-step programs and peer counselors. It is a growing enterprise within the mental and addictive disorder treatment system, almost doubling in use over a 10-year period.

TRADITIONAL FUNDING: PUBLIC/PRIVATE PAYORS

The public payors are government agencies at the federal, state, county, and local levels. These payors include Medicaid, a federal and state program for individuals who are poor or disabled, and Medicare, a federal health insurance program primarily for older Americans and those who retire early owing to disability. Mandatory managed care for Medicaid beneficiaries who require mental health services has been implemented (or is in the planning process) in every state. The conversion from the traditional fee-for-service model to managed care models is well underway (Department of Health and Human Services, 2000a; 2000b).

Public payors may finance a program in the private sector. Historically, state and local governments have been major payors for mental health services. These services include community mental health block grants and community support programs. The public sector provides payment for individuals without health insurance, those with health insurance but no mental health coverage, and those who have exhausted limited mental health benefits in their health insurance. These public sector–funded programs serve as a "safety net," or catastrophic insurer, for those with the least resources and the most critical problems.

COSTS ASSOCIATED WITH MENTAL ILLNESS

The types of cost imposed by mental disorders include emotional and financial burden on ill individuals, their families, and their communities; indirect costs measured in reduced or lost productivity to the nation; and direct costs determined by medical resources used for care, treatment, and rehabilitation.

In 1990 indirect costs of all mental illness represented almost a $79 billion loss to the U.S. economy (Rice & Miller, 1996). Morbidity costs ($63 billion) were the highest proportion of this loss. Mortality costs account for nearly $12 billion, and productivity losses were almost $4 billion (costs for incarcerated persons and individuals providing family care). A hallmark of the cost associated with mental illness is the morbidity cost, a glaring 80% of the indirect costs. This fact correlates with the early onset of mental disorders and the resultant loss or reduced productivity at the workplace, school, and home (Rupp, Gause, & Regier, 1998).

The World Bank and the World Health Organization reported on a study that identified indirect costs of mental disorders related to years lived with a disability, with and without years of life lost owing to premature death. The Disability Adjusted Life Years (DALYs) are being used as a global measure to describe the burden of disability and premature death resulting from the full range of mental and physical disorders. Of the estimated $943 billion spent on health care, 7% was spent for mental health services in 1996. Yet spending for mental health care has declined as a percentage of overall health spending in the past decade. The decrease in spending may be due to increased access to innovative prescription drugs and an increase in outpatient treatment with a decreased number of costly hospitalizations. Other possibilities are increased reliance on non-mental health services and increased difficulty in circumventing the barriers to service access. These findings may reflect the optimism and caution of managed care and mental health.

The economic burden of mental illness in the United States, when both productivity and health care costs are combined, is estimate to be more than $170 billion per year. However, only one in four adults and one in five children needing mental health services actually receive appropriate care. The federal government, through the Medicare and Medicaid programs, spends more than $17 billion each year on beneficiaries' mental health services. Beyond these direct services, the Department of Health and Human Services (DHHS) spent about $1.9 billion in 2001 on other mental health activities under the Center for Mental Health Services in the Substance Abuse and Mental Health Services Administration (SAMHSA) and the research unit, the National Institute for Mental Health (NIMH) (Department of Health and Human Services, 2001).

MANAGED CARE

The underlying forces shaping the financing of mental health through managed care include the drive to deliver more highly individualized, cost-effective care, a greater emphasis on health promotion and disease prevention, and a commitment to cost containment to control moral hazard (the payors' fear that users of insurance who no longer have to pay full cost will overuse the services).

An additional financial concern that managed care attempts to address is adverse selection, which is the fear that plans that provide the most generous coverage will attract individuals with the greatest need for care, elevating the costs for the insurer. The insurers' responses to the economic forces of moral hazard and adverse selection have tended to be overexaggerated. For example, some insurers assign higher cost sharing for mental health services, such as placing a 50% copayment on outpatient psychotherapy. These cost containment efforts that restrict mental health coverage leave people to bear catastrophic costs themselves. These strategies go beyond the boundaries of managed care and include, for example, even fee-for-service insurance systems.

Types of Managed Care Plans

Health maintenance organizations (HMOs) were the first type of managed care. The first HMO was originally developed by the Kaiser Foundation to provide health services to employees on a pre-paid, per capita (capitated) basis. Medical staff were salaried. More recently, however, HMOs have developed networks of physicians, or independent practice associations (IPAs), and have paid IPA physicians on a fee-for-service basis under common management guidelines. In the beginning HMOs funded treatment for only those mental disorders responsive to short-term therapy. They relied on public mental health systems for any catastrophic coverage, chronic disorders, or severe mental disorders.

Preferred provider organizations (PPOs) and point of service plans (POSs) are managed care plans that contract with network providers to supply service. PPOs and POSs both allow the enrollees to use out-of-network providers (providers not named as participants in the plan) for additional costs. POS plans combine the strategies of prepaid, capitated, and fee-for-service insurance.

The *carve-out managed behavioral health care plan* is popular. It segments insurance risk according to service or disease, thereby isolating mental health coverage from the overall insurance risk. With carve-outs, either the enrollee chooses the separate carve-out vendor for mental health care or the health plan subcontracts with a carve-out vendor. Owing primarily to the cost reduction benefit of managed care, there is wide use of this type of funding for mental health services. In fact, in 1999 almost 177 million Americans with health insurance were enrolled in managed behavioral health organizations, which represented a growth of 9% from the previous year (OPEN MINDS, 1999). This cost reduction is achieved primarily case by case through shifting treatment from inpatient to outpatient settings, using utilization management techniques to limit unnecessary services, and negotiating discounted hospital and professional fees. This strategy may involve financial incentives for providers.

There is concern that these cost management strategies are strongly associated with poorer quality of services, undertreatment, and less accessibility. Existing research suggests that when management and financial incentives limit access to mental health care, including access to specialists, or encourage a shift to general health care services for mental health care, disability may increase and work performance may decline (Salkever, 1998; Rosencheck, Cramer, Allen, Frisman, Xu, Thomas, Allen, Henderson, & Charney, 1999). On the other hand, the use of case management, utilization review, and implementation of standardized criteria may improve the quality of care by encouraging adherence to professional treatment guidelines. However, current practices often provide little incentive to improve quality (Department of Health and Human Services, 1999). The President's Advisory Commission on Consumer Protection and Quality in the Health Care Industry strongly recommended additional research to determine the effects of industry competition on costs, access, and quality (Department of Health and Human Services and Department of Labor, President's Advisory Commission on Consumer Protection and Quality in the Health Care Industry, 1997).

Parity: Hope for Managed Care

One solution to managing mental health care to improve quality and access is the concept of parity. Parity refers to an initiative that results in treating mental health financing on the same basis as financing for general health services. With calls for managed care to control costs without limiting benefits, a parity mandate becomes affordable to the nation. However, the gap in insurance coverage between mental health and other health services has been increasing. Interestingly, while health care costs per employee grew from 1989 to 1995, behavioral health care cost decreased (Department of Health and Human Services, 1999). This decrease probably reflects the multiple limits on benefits that ultimately restrict access. These extensive limits create catastrophic financial burdens for patients and their families.

The need for parity can clearly be seen in the following example. For a family with mental health expenses of $35,000 a year, the average out-of-pocket burden is $12,000, whereas out-of-pocket spending for medical/surgical treatment is $1500 (Department of Health and Human Services, 1999).

One major step toward parity began with the Federal Mental Health Parity Act of 1996, which stated that group health plans providing mental health benefits could not impose a lower lifetime or annual dollar limit on mental health benefits than exists for medical/surgical benefits. There is evidence that the implementation of this law has resulted in minimal increase in expense for mental health services (less than 1%). Following this law, President Clinton used an executive order to mandate that all Federal Employee Health Benefit Plans (FEHBP) provide parity for mental health services beginning January 2000.

A new bill, the Mental Health Equitable Treatment Act (S 543), a significant improvement on the 1996 parity law, is modeled after the FEHBP parity requirements. The bill prohibits health plans from limiting the scope and duration of mental health treatment more than they do medical treatment,

and it opposes discriminatory copays, deductibles, and coinsurance caps on mental health benefits (Lehmann, 2001). The bill includes all categories of mental illnesses listed in the DSM IV.

Congress was unwilling to pass this new legislation in 2001, although 63 Senators sponsored the bill. The 1996 sunset provision of the Mental Health Parity Act expired on October 21, 2001. Senators Pete Domenici (R-NM) and Paul Wellstone (D-MN) continue to attempt to raise awareness about this bill.

Insurers' fears that such legislation would put health insurance out of reach for some Americans has been countered by Darrel Regier, executive director of the American Psychiatric Institute for Research and Education (APIRE). In July 2001, testimony before the Senate Health, Education and Labor, and Pensions committee, he stated that parity insurance coverage for mental disorders is affordable, addresses a specific market failure, and can support cost-effective treatment to reduce disability. (Regier's testimony, which included many examples with financial data, is posted on American Psychiatric Association's website at www. psych.org/pub_pol_adv/drregiertestimony71301. cfm.)

CONCLUSION

The marriage of managed care and mental health brings both optimism and caution. The cost reduction strategies are appealing to employers and other payors. However, the abuse of these strategies can result in undertreatment, poorer quality of care, and limited access. As David Mechanic points out, "Managed care significantly changes the decision calculus and requires provider organizations and clinicians to think much more carefully about how to organize services. It encourages much more dependence on research evidence and considerations of the cost-effectiveness of alternative treatment strategies" (Mechanic, 1999, p. 164).

Only when parity is introduced does optimism rise. Psychiatric nurses have always been advocates for their patients and families, using their clinical and administrative skills to make things better. Now there is the opportunity for nurses to be advocates in the policy and political arenas, speaking out and using strategies to gain parity for mental health services. Expanding nursing practice in this way will provide the added benefit of enhancing personal mental health and well being.

REFERENCES

Department of Health and Human Services. (1999). *Mental health: A report of the Surgeon General.* Washington, DC: Author.

Department of Health and Human Services. (2000a). *Mandatory managed care: Early lessons learned by Medicaid mental health programs.* Washington, DC: Author.

Department of Health and Human Services. (2000b). *Mandatory managed care: Changes in Medicaid mental health services.* Washington, DC: Author.

Department of Health and Human Services and Department of Labor, President's Advisory Commission on Consumer Protection and Quality in the Health Care Industry. (1997). *Quality first: Better health care for all.* Washington, DC: Author.

Lehmann, C. (2001). Parity is cost-effective and affordable, APA tells senators. *Psychiatric News, 36*(15), 1, 27.

Mechanic, D. (1999). *Mental health and social policy: The emergence of managed care.* Boston: Allyn and Bacon.

OPEN MINDS. (1999). *Behavioral Health and Social Services Industry Analyst,* 11, 9.

Regier, D. (2001). *Parity for mental health services.* Available online at www.psych.org/pub_pol_adv/drregiertestimony71301.cfm.

Regier, D., Goldberg, I., & Taube, C. (1978). The de facto U.S. mental health services system: A public health perspective. *Archives of General Psychiatry, 35,* 685-693.

Regier, D., Narrow, W., Rae, D., Manderscheid, R., Locke, B., & Goodwin, F. (1993). The de facto U.S. mental and addictive disorders service system. Epidemiologic catchment area prospective 1 year prevalence rates of disorders and services. *Archives of General Psychiatry, 50,* 85-94.

Rice, D. & Miller, L. (1996). The economic burden of schizophrenia. Conceptual and methodological issues and cost estimates. In M. Moscarelli, A. Rupp, & N. Sartorious (Eds.). *Handbook of mental health economics and health policy. Vol. 4: Schizophrenia.* New York: John Wiley & Sons.

Rosencheck, R., Cramer, J., Allen, E., Frisman, L., Xu, W., Thomas, J., Allen, E., Henderson, W., & Charney, D. (1999). Cost effectiveness of clozapine in patients with high and low levels of hospital use: Department of Veteran Affairs cooperative study group on clozapine in refractory schizophrenia. *Archives of General Psychiatry, 56,* 565-572.

Rupp, A., Gause, E., & Regier, D. (1998). Research policy implications of cost-of-illness studies for mental disorders. *British Journal of Psychiatry Supplement, 173*(36), 19-25.

Salkever, D. (1998). Psychiatric disability in the workplace. *Insight,* 5.

POLICYSPOTLIGHT

RACIAL AND ETHNIC DISPARITIES IN HEALTH AND HEALTH CARE

Phyllis Cunningham

"Injustice anywhere is a threat to justice everywhere."
MARTIN LUTHER KING, JR.

THE PROBLEM

In the past decade, numerous reports have emerged in the scientific literature and the public media concerning disparities in the health status of racial and ethnic populations in the United States. These populations experience higher incidence, prevalence, mortality, and disability from an overwhelming number of diseases and other adverse health conditions. These inequities in health status are attributed to biologic, socioeconomic (including poverty, income, and education level), cultural, familial, occupational, and environmental factors, as well as to discrimination and lack of access to health care (Northridge & Shepard, 1997; Davis & Curley, 1999; National Institutes of Health, 2000). The biologic, ethnic, and cultural factors have been disputed. For example, Graves (2001, p. 176), a molecular biologist who disputes the biologic basis for racial disparities in health, argues that the African-American population is hybridized, having heterozygote advantage: "African Americans would have the lowest disease rates if genetics were the key."

There is a growing body of scientific evidence indicating that racism is significant in determining income, education, housing, environmental status, and access to care and that it is the root cause for disparities in health and health care of racial and ethnic minorities (Cohen & Northridge, 2000; Thomas, 2001). Manifestations of racism, such as prejudice, discrimination or bias, and segregation, determine many socioeconomic aspects of daily living for ethnic and minority populations (Collins, 1999; Williams, 1999; LaVeist, 2000).

Access to health care has been correlated with disparities. Lack of financial resource, including the ability to afford health insurance, is a primary factor in lack of access. A mammography promotion program sponsored by the Health Insurance Plan of Greater New York was successful in eliminating racial differences in breast cancer survival (Fiscella, Franks, Gold, & Clancy, 2000). A publicly funded health center for an uninsured population in the Midwest reduced the number of emergency department visits and provided access to health care to satisfied consumers (Smith-Campbell, 2000). However, even when access to care is adequate, the type and quality of care have been reported to be inferior for members of minority populations (Fiscella et al, 2000; Allen, 2001; Geiger, 2001; Jauhar, 2001).

Historical Context

The Report on Black and Minority Health, released in 1985 by the U.S. Department of Health and Human Services' (DHHS) Task Force on Black and Minority Health, called attention to minority health (DHHS, Task Force on Black and Minority Health, 1985). The 3000-page report focused on the health status of Asians and Asian Pacific Islanders, Native Americans, black persons, and Hispanic persons. The report identified race, ethnicity, and social class as predictors of health-related outcomes, although persons of higher income within groups had better health (Nickens, 1996). As a result of the

report, the Office of Minority Health (OMH) was established by DHHS. "The mission of OMH is to improve the health of racial and ethnic populations through the development of effective health policies and programs that help to eliminate disparities in health" (Office of Minority Health, 2001). In carrying out its mission, OMH's many roles include promoting and monitoring efforts on federal, state, and local levels to achieve the goals of Healthy People 2010, the nation's comprehensive public health agenda for promoting health and preventing illness, disability, and premature death (DHHS, 2000).

In 1990, with the encouragement of Congress, the director of the National Institutes of Health (NIH) created the Office of Research on Minority Health (ORMH). During its 10-year existence, the ORMH, through its Minority Health Initiative, engaged in biomedical and behavioral research and research training programs addressing specific minority health disparities.

In 1997 President William Jefferson Clinton announced a national campaign called *One America in the Twenty-First Century: The President's Initiative on Race.* He challenged members of his cabinet to respond within the context of their agencies. In 1998 he set 2010 as the goal for the elimination of disparities. The sixteenth U. S. Surgeon General, Dr. David Satcher, spearheaded the initiative. DHHS Secretary Donna E. Shalala responded to the President's challenge in December 2000 with the report *Closing the Gap: Eliminating Racial and Ethnic Disparities.*

This work in the 1990s set the stage for the 106th Congress' passage of Minority Health and Health Disparities Research and Education Act of 2000 (Public Law 106-525), an amendment to the Public Health Service Act to improve the health of minority individuals. Title I of the Minority Health and Health Disparities Research and Education Act (2000) called for the establishment of National Center on Minority Health and Health Disparities (NCMHD) within the NIH. The general purpose of the NCMHD is the conduct and support of research, training, dissemination of information, and promotion of other programs with respect to minority health conditions and other populations with health disparities. The center, working with other NIH institutes and centers to address elimination of disparities, focuses on three major areas: research; research infrastructure; and public information and community outreach (NIH, 2000). In its strategic research plan, the NIH identified the following six focus areas in which racial and ethnic minorities experience serious disparities in health and health care access: infant mortality, cancer screening and management, cardiovascular disease, diabetes, human immunodeficiency virus (HIV) infection and acquired immune deficiency syndrome (AIDS), and immunizations.

Since 1979 the U.S. government has developed goals and objectives for improving the health of the nation's people through the Healthy People programs. While Healthy People 2000 aimed at *reducing* health disparities, Healthy People 2010 seeks to *eliminate* health disparities. The disparities being addressed include those differentials that occur because of sex, race and ethnicity, education, income, disability, geographic location, or sexual orientation. The other overarching goal of the 2010 initiative is to increase quality and years of healthy life (DHHS, 2000).

Despite the efforts expended at federal, state, and local levels over the past decade, disparities have not decreased significantly. Consider the following information on disparities in health, as reported in the *NIH Strategic Research Plan to Reduce and Ultimately Eliminate Health Disparities* (NIH, 2000):

- *Infant mortality.* "Infant mortality is an important measure of a nation's health and a worldwide indicator of health status. Despite a 16% overall decline in the rate of infant mortality in the U.S. over the last decade, the infant mortality rate remains twice as high among African Americans as compared to Caucasians, even when controlling for socioeconomic factors. Native American and Alaskan Native infants also have a death rate almost double that of Caucasians."
- *Cancer.* "Cancer is the second most common cause of mortality in the U.S. In the year 2000 about 1.2 million cases [were] expected to be diagnosed, with 552,200 Americans dying from the disease. Many minority groups suffer disproportionately from cancer, and disparities exist in both mortality and incidence rates. For example, African Americans have both a higher overall incidence and death rate than any other racial and ethnic group. The death rate from stomach cancer is substantially higher among Asians and Pacific Islanders, including Native Hawaiians, than among other populations. Vietnamese women in the U.S. have a cervical cancer incidence rate that is five times greater than Caucasian women, and African-American and Hispanic women have higher cervical cancer death rates than the overall U.S. population."
- *Heart disease and stroke.* "Despite impressive progress in reducing cardiovascular mortality over the past several decades, there still exists a disproportionate burden of death and disability from cardiovascular diseases in minority and lower-income populations. For example, the prevalence of coronary health disease in African Americans has increased steadily since the early 1970s, with coronary health disease mortality 40% higher for African Americans than Caucasians. Similarly, fewer African Americans survive severe cardiomyopathy as compared to Caucasians—a difference which is attributed to both biological and socioeconomic factors. Stroke is the third leading cause of death in the U.S., killing approximately 150,000 Americans every year. The incidence of stroke is disproportionately high in African Americans, where the mortality rate is nearly 80%."
- *Type 2 diabetes.* "Diabetes affects nearly 16 million Americans and leads to more than 300,000 deaths annually. It is also the leading cause of end stage kidney disease, peripheral neuropathy, adult blindness, and amputation. More than 90% of those affected have type 2 diabetes, which is disproportionately manifested in minority groups. The prevalence of diabetes in African Americans is nearly 70% higher than in Caucasians. Native Americans, Hispanics, African Americans, and some Asian Americans and Pacific Islanders, including Japanese Americans, Samoans, and Native Hawaiians, are at particularly high risk for development of type

2 diabetes. Most strikingly, diabetes prevalence rates among American Indians are two to five times those of Caucasians, with the Pima tribe of Arizona experiencing one of the highest rates of diabetes in the world."

- *HIV and AIDS.* "HIV and AIDS continue to affect minorities disproportionately. Of all U.S. cases reported to the Centers for Disease Control and Prevention (CDC) in 1998, 45% were among African Americans, 33% among Caucasians, 20% among Hispanics, and less than 1% among Asians and Pacific Islanders and Native Americans and Alaska Americans. The rate of new AIDS cases reported in 1998 per 100,000 population was 81.9 among African Americans, 34.7 among Hispanics, 8.4 among Caucasians, 9.4 among Native Americans and Alaska natives, and 4.1 among Asians and Pacific Islanders. HIV incidence is growing at a greater rate in women than in men, particularly among minority women. The proportion of new AIDS cases among women more than tripled from 1985 to 1998, from 7% to 23%. In the U.S., by the end of 1998, more than 77% of women infected with the AIDS virus were from minority groups, with 57% of these being African American and 20% being Hispanic."

In the coming decades minority populations are projected to increase from 28% of the population in 1998 to approximately 40% in 2030 (National Institutes of Health, 2000). It thus becomes incumbent on the nation to continue our commitment to understanding the dynamics of disparities, minimizing them by addressing root causes, and making needed changes in access to care and quality of services to benefit racial and ethnic minorities, and thus the health of the nation.

IMPLICATIONS FOR NURSING

Nurses, as the largest component of professional health care workers, can affect the elimination of racial and ethnic disparities in health and health care. Policy can be generated and implemented in all four spheres of nurses' political action, on many levels of nursing practice, and in various other arenas, such as nursing education and nursing research. In the role of advocate, nurses are commit-

ted to protecting the health, sa
clients whether individual, fan
community. In many instances
required. "A determined desire
in health makes obvious the ne
tion to effect fundamental social change (Cohen & Northridge, 2000, p. 842).

Diversity of the Nursing Workforce

The lack of diversity within the nursing profession has been cited as contributing to cultural incompetency. In 1999 Buerhaus and Auerbach published their analysis of trends in the education, employment, and earnings of minority registered nurses (RNs) from 1977 to 1997. Attempts to increase the number of minorities in nursing have produced minimal results. These efforts involved nursing education programs, professional nursing organizations, employers, and major foundations such as W. K. Kellogg and Robert Wood Johnson. The number of minority RNs grew from 6.3% in 1977 to only 9.7% in 1997. Buerhaus and Auerbach (1999, p. 183) attribute the slow growth to a combination of several reasons:

Data are needed to determine how and to what extent racism, discrimination, and other barriers within nursing education programs and health care organizations cause minorities to not choose nursing as a career. Similarly, investigators should assess the extent to which discrimination and acts of racism exist both among minority groups and between minority and majority RNs. Such researchers should also assess whether majority and minority RNs perceive that the quality of care is different for minorities.

Noting that it is crucial for the profession to address this issue, Buerhaus and Auerbach continue (1999, p. 183):

The perspective of the minority RN is needed to help educators, employers, policymakers, and interested philanthropic leaders understand the changes needed to lower the barriers confronting minorities who desire—or could be induced—to attain a nursing education and remain in the profession.

Indeed, nursing needs to reflect the population it serves, not only for promotion of cultural compecy in nursing but also because it is neither right nor just that persons from minority groups be dissuaded or excluded from pursuing a career in nursing. The nursing literature is rich with content on recruitment and retention related to nursing education but lacks information on retention in nursing practice.

PROFESSIONAL ORGANIZATIONS

Advocacy demands action in order to effect change. Dollinger (2000) speaks about the duty, responsibility, and privilege of nurses participating in professional associations to influence development of an accessible, equitable, and high-quality health care system. In addressing inequities, nurses should actively be involved in shaping and implementing standards, such as the code of ethics and position statements of the American Nurses Association (ANA). The ANA's code for nurses (2001), its position statement on ethics and human rights (1994), and the position statement on discrimination and racism in health care (1998) all address the need for nursing to initiate, implement, and support policies that redress racial and ethnic inequities in health and health care in the United States. The ANA's 1998 position statement, Discrimination and Racism in Health Care, is a directive to the profession. In its summary it says the following (ANA, 1998, p.1):

> Discrimination and racism continue to be a part of the fabric and tradition of American society and have adversely affected minority populations, the health care system in general, and the profession of nursing. Discrimination may be based on differences due to age, ability, gender, race, ethnicity, religion, sexual orientation, or any other characteristic by which people differ. The American Nurses Association is committed to working toward the eradication of discrimination and racism in the profession of nursing, in the education of nurses, in the practice of nursing, as well as in the organizations in which nurses work. The ANA is further committed to working to egalitarianism and the promotion of justice in access and delivery of health care to all people.

The ANA has been engaged over the years in many efforts to address diversity and racism in the profession and in health care. It was the only nursing group represented on the Steering Committee to Eliminate Racial and Ethnic Disparities in Health. The Steering Committee is a diverse group of national leaders representing government agencies, major health care organizations, philanthropic foundations, faith-based groups, and the labor community. The formation of the committee, cosponsored by the American Public Health Association and the U.S. DHHS, was announced at a Washington news conference in August 2000. It subsequently issued a call to the nation to form a national coalition to focus on strategies for eliminating the disparities.

WORKPLACE POLICIES AND SERVICES

As health care providers, nurses collectively have immense knowledge and understanding of factors and conditions that contribute to the development of health and illness. Lack of access to health care including promotion and prevention services, inadequate and inappropriate health care including denial of services, and cultural incompetence are within realm of nursing's focus and mission.

By becoming aware of manifestations of racism and discriminatory practices—unintentional and intentional—nurses can act to ameliorate them. Personal and collective behavior and practices of nurses and other health care workers may need to be addressed, not only by personal introspection but by staff development efforts and conferences or workshops regarding cultural competency and sensitivity that include discussions of racism, its manifestations, and, particularly, covert bias.

Awareness of discriminatory policies and practices on units and in health care institutions should be confronted and corrected. In view of the lack of awareness of the extent of discrimination and the erosion of affirmative action, attention to the areas where discriminatory practices are likely to exist is warranted. Institutional regulations and policies should be carefully examined for covert bias. Changes in these policies should be initiated and supported by nurses and nurse administrators, made public, and enforced. Nurses should also advocate for services that provide care where there are inequities.

Nursing must ensure that there are stipulations in health care agencies' quality assurance mechanisms to guarantee appropriate care to racial and ethnic minority individuals. Accrediting bodies for health care organizations should include criteria for accreditation that specifically address disparities in health care. This would require standardized methods for collecting data that would elucidate any existing patterns of inequality in health care.

PUBLIC POLICIES

Understanding the dynamics of disparity in health or in health care prepares nurses and nursing organizations to act politically. DeMott (1995, p.35) warns us not to ignore the need for political action that focuses on the development of public policies, because justice will not occur simply from "acts of private piety which substitute for public policy while the possibility of political action disappears into a sentimental haze."

Barriers to equity in health care documented in the literature include lack of access (owing to financial resources, absence of providers and services, especially in underserved areas of the population, and discriminatory policies and practices), inequity in treatment and quality of service, lack of cultural competency including language services such interpreters, and inadequate inclusion of minorities in research. Social determinants of disparities in health include socioeconomic factors (including poverty, income, employment, education level, and housing) and environmental factors (including workplace, living, and social environments). These barriers and determinants are all issues that can be addressed through public policies. Issues such as minimum wage, welfare reform, unemployment, affordable housing, and environmental racism are appropriate targets for political action by nurses. To effectively advocate for health, nurses and the profession must view health broadly, understanding and addressing the social determinants of health.

EDUCATION

Nursing education has the responsibility to include content on racial and ethnic disparities in health and health care, as well as to prepare nurses with the political skills to move this issue forward. Healthy People 2010, the road map for improving the nation's health, should be integrated into curriculum. Besides political competency, students need to be prepared for cultural competency.

Knowledge and understanding of oppression and racism are significant elements in the delivery of culturally competent nursing care. Core course content focusing on culture, ethnicity, and oppression, including racism and its manifestations, should be required in all nursing curricula.

Access to nursing education by minorities can be a strategy for addressing disparities. Nursing education must examine practices, procedures, and policies for discrimination and remedy those found. One has to look only at the number of RNs from minority groups to surmise that nursing education needs to address recruitment and retention issues.

It is imperative that nursing education, beginning with educators themselves, probe the intricacies of racism. This is possible through faculty development conferences and workshops focusing on oppression and including racism. Practices, procedures, and policies related to curriculum content; clinical placement; and faculty recruitment and retention from minority groups should be examined. In addition, educational accrediting bodies need to develop, for all nursing programs, specific criteria that address issues of racial and ethnic disparities.

RESEARCH

There have been implications for nursing research concerning disparities throughout this policy spotlight. Understanding the link between racial and ethnic backgrounds can elucidate innovative ways to prevent and eliminate racial and ethnic disparities in health. Freeman (2001, p. 3) noted the following:

We need to understand our . . . cultural populations, much better than we do. . . . So this requires, in my opinion, something we call social marketing. In other words, to study the populations you want to reach, find out how they communicate, how they receive messages and try to communicate to them in the way they will receive the message, just as the tobacco industry does when it sells cigarettes.

Funds have been made available by various federal agencies, such as the Agency for Healthcare Research and Quality, for research initiatives to eliminate racial and ethnic disparities in health and health care. Such research will give direction to policy development.

CONCLUSION

Nursing, more than any other profession, has the knowledge and skills to address racial and ethnic health and health care disparities in a variety of arenas and ways. Nursing is mandated to be involved in political action and policy formation in its advocacy role to advance and protect the health of populations. In 1999 the Quad Council of Public Health Nursing Organizations addressed political activism in their standards for practice to advocate "for health and social policy, and delivery of public health programs to promote and preserve the health of the population" (pp. 18–19). It's time for nurses as individuals and groups to use this activism to eliminate ethnic and racial disparities in health and health care.

REFERENCES

Allen, C.E. (2001). 2000 presidential address: Eliminating health disparities. *American Journal of Public Health, 91*(7), 1142-1143.

American Nurses Association. (1994). *Position statement on ethics and human rights.* Kansas City, MO: Author.

American Nurses Association. (1998). *Position statement on discrimination and racism in health care.* Retrieved online, July 20, 2000, from www.nursingworld.org/readroom/position/ethics/etdisrac.htm.

American Nurses Association. (2001). *Code for nurses with interpretive statements.* Washington, DC: Author.

Buerhaus, P. & Auerbach, D. (1999). Slow growth in the United States of the number of minorities in the RN workforce. *Image: Journal of Nursing Scholarship, 31*(2), 179-183.

Cohen, H. & Northridge, M.E. (2000). Getting political: Racism and urban health [editorial]. *American Journal of Public Health, 90*(6), 841-842.

Collins, C.A. (1999). Racism and health: Segregation and causes of death amenable to medical intervention in major U.S. cities. *Annals of the New York Academy of Sciences, 896*, 396-398.

Davis, C.M. & Curley, C.M. (1999). Disparities of health in African Americans. *Nursing Clinics of North America, 34*(2), 345-357.

DeMott, B. (1995, September). Put on a happy face: Masking the difference between blacks and whites. *Harper's Magazine,* 31-38.

Department of Health and Human Services (2000). *Healthy people 2010: Understanding and improving health* (2nd ed.). Washington, DC: U.S. Government Printing Office.

Department of Health and Human Services, Task Force on Black and Minority Health. (1985). *Report of Secretary's Task Force on on Black and minority health.* Washington, DC: Author.

Dollinger, M.L. (2000). Professional associations: Ethics, duty, and power. *Journal of the New York State Nurses Association, 31*(2), 28-30.

Fiscella, K., Franks, P., Gold, M.R., & Clancy, C.M. (2000). Inequality in quality: Addressing socioeconomic, racial and ethnic disparities in health care. *Journal of the American Medical Association, 283*(19), 2579-2584.

Freeman, H.P. (2001, November 14). *Race and health: In genes or injustice?* New York: Gene Media Forum, New York Academy of Science.

Geiger, H.J. (2001). Racial stereotyping and medicine: The need for cultural competence. *Comedian Medical Association Journal, 164*(12), 1699-1700.

Graves, J.L. (2001). *The emperor's new clothes: Biological theories of race at the millennium.* New Brunswick, NJ: Rutgers University Press.

Jauhar, S. (2001, June 19). Hidden in the world of medicine, discrimination and stereotypes. *New York Times,* F6.

LaVeist, T.A. (2000). On the study of race, racism, and health: A shift from description to explanation. *International Journal of Health Services, 30*(1), 217-219.

Minority Health and Health Disparities Research and Education Act. (2000). Public Law No. 106-525. 42 USC 202 note.

National Institutes of Health. (2000). *Addressing health disparities: The NIH program of Action.* Retrieved online, September 28, 2001, at healthdisparities.nih.gov/whatare.html.

National Institutes of Health (2000, October 6). *Strategic research plan to reduce and ultimately eliminate health disparities: Fiscal years 2002-2006* (draft). Available online at www.nih.gov/about/hd/strategicplan.pdf.

Nickens, H.W., 1996. A compelling research agenda. *Annals of Internal Medicine, 125,* 237-239.

Northridge, M.E. & Shepard, P. (1997). Environmental racism and public health. *American Journal of Public Health, 87*(5), 730-732.

Office of Minority Health. (2001). *About OMH.* Retrieved online, September 27, 2001, from www.omhrc.gov/OMH/sidebar/aboutOMH.htm

Quad Council of Public Health Nursing Organizations. (1999). *Scope and standards of public health nursing practice.* Washington, DC: American Nurses Association.

Smith-Campbell, B. (2000). Access to health care: Effects of public funding on the uninsured. *Journal of Nursing Scholarship, 32*(3), 295-300.

Thomas, S. B. (2001). The color line: Race matters in the elimination of health disparities. *American Journal of Public Health, 91*(7), 1046-1048.

Williams, D.R. (1999). Race, socioeconomic status, and health: The added effects of racism and discrimination. *Annals of New York Academy of Sciences, 896,* 173-188.

Health Economics

SUSAN K. PFOUTZ

SYLVIA A. PRICE

CYRIL F. CHANG

"Money is like a sixth sense, and you can't make use of the other five without it."

W. SOMERSET MAUGHAM

Nurses, as the largest group of health care professionals, have a long history of caring for individuals, families, and communities in a variety of settings. The focus of this caring is the improvement of health and well-being of the clients in our care. In the current health care environment, providing effective services in a cost-conscious manner is an increasing concern. Although the economic consequences of health care have not been a primary focus of attention for clinicians, current circumstances require increasing attention to this aspect of the delivery of health care. Economic tools assist policymakers at all levels of decision making.

As previous chapters in this book have elaborated, the organization of health services continues to undergo many changes to improve access and quality and reduce cost. These changes include the decrease in the length of hospital stay, the need for preauthorization for many services, and shift of health care delivery to alternative settings. These changes dramatically affect the practice of nursing and the career opportunities available to nurses. Therefore, an understanding of the economic perspective on decision making is critical to function successfully in the current health care delivery system.

ECONOMIC PERSPECTIVE

Economics is the science that studies how consumers, firms, governmental bodies, and other organizations make choices to overcome the problem of scarcity. *Scarcity* exists when there are not enough resources to satisfy all wants or desires.

With the massive expenditures on health and health care, it may be difficult to perceive a scarcity of health care resources. The health care system includes the resources required to provide the facilities, equipment, and health care professionals required to provide health and illness services. The United States expends more than any other country to provide health care services:

- More than $1.3 trillion per year
- Approximately 13.2% of the gross domestic product (GDP)
- Some level of public spending for almost half of U.S. expenses (Health Care Financing Administration, 2001)

Along with massive health care expenditures, policymakers at the local, state, and federal levels are analyzing the evidence of unmet health care needs. Approximately 43 million people, representing 16% of the population, have no health insurance (Bureau of the Census, 1998). Many individuals and families who do have insurance find that their insurance provides limited coverage of services. Services that are not covered, as well as substantial deductibles and copayments, result in substantial out-of-pocket expenses. An example is Medicare coverage for those over 65 years of age (Health Care Financing Administration, 2001). During the 2000 presidential election, a major focus was placed on providing prescription drug assistance to seniors because this cost is not covered by Medicare. These examples demonstrate scarcity in the midst of plenty.

MARKET SYSTEM

In the United States economic activity is based on a market economy. This is an economic system based on private ownership of resources with allocation of resources through the interactions of individuals and businesses. The following questions must be addressed by an economic system:

- *What goods and services shall be produced?* In a market system, goods are produced for consumers who choose to buy them. As the population becomes more health conscious, products such as healthier food and exercise equipment become more available.
- *How will services be provided?* Producers of goods and services strive to produce their product at a minimum cost. In recent years, hospitals have sought to reduce costs by decreasing length of stay and reorganizing with the goal of decreasing their personnel costs.
- *For whom are the services provided?* Typically goods and services are provided for those who are able and willing to pay for them. In the case of health care, consumers are able to purchase health care through insurance coverage. Those who have no insurance must pay for the services themselves. The society must then decide how to provide for people without resources for care through government programs or charities (Chang, Price, & Pfoutz, 2001).

DEMAND

Demand reflects the quantity of a good or service that consumers are willing to purchase at a variety of prices. For most goods, the quantity of a good or service that is demanded increases as the price decreases. A demand schedule refers to a table or graph that illustrates the amount demanded for a given price. Table 13-1 and Figure 13-1 provide an example of the demand for aspirin. Table 13-1 shows the relationship between the price of aspirin per bottle and the number of thousands of bottles demanded per month. Figure 13-1 demonstrates the same relationship graphically. The demand curve slopes down to the right to illustrate that more aspirin is demanded when the price decreases. This relationship of increased demand with decreased price pertains for most goods.

TABLE **13-1** Market Demand Schedule for Aspirin

PRICE PER 100-TABLET BOTTLE ($)	QUANTITY DEMANDED PER MONTH IN BOTTLES
5.00	40
4.50	50
4.00	60
3.50	70
3.00	80

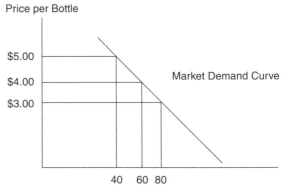

Figure 13-1 The market demand for aspirin.

Although price is a major determinant of demand, other factors also affect demand. Income is another factor. Usually demand for a good or services increases as income increases. This increase in income shifts the entire demand curve to the right, reflecting the demand for more of the good or services at each level of price. Another factor that affects demand is taste or preferences. Some people value health more than other people do and are more likely to consume more health care goods and services as a whole. Within health care goods and services, consumers choose from a wide variety of products. An example of this is maternity care. Women can receive care from a family practice physician, an obstetrician, a nurse midwife, or a lay midwife or may not see any health care provider. The choice of provider is related to the perception of how well the care provided meets the needs and preferences. If a woman chooses a nurse-midwife, she must determine not only the absolute cost of

TABLE **13-2** Market Supply Curve for Aspirin

PRICE PER 100-TABLET BOTTLE ($)	QUANTITY SUPPLIED PER MONTH IN BOTTLES
5.00	80
4.50	70
4.00	60
3.50	50
3.00	40

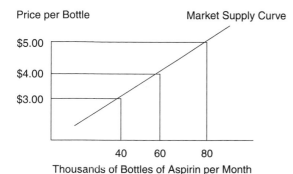

Figure 13-2 The market supply schedule for aspirin.

the service, but also whether insurance provides reimbursement for this choice of health care provider.

A *substitute* is a good or service that can be used in place of another good or service. In the maternity care example, women will consider the quality and price of all the health care providers who may substitute for one another. When the price of one provider increases, the consumer may consider purchasing a substitute product. Advance practice nurses, such as nurse midwives, are promoted because they provide a quality service at a lower cost.

SUPPLY

Supply refers to the quantity of a service or product that producers are willing to sell at various prices. Unlike demand, supply increases as the price increases. This results in a supply curve that rises with increases in price. Using the same example from Table 13-1 and Figure 13-1 for bottles of aspirin, Table 13-2 and Figure 13-2 illustrate how the numbers of bottles of aspirin supplied increase as the price increases.

In health care there are a variety of examples. As Medicare and Medicaid restrict the amount that can be charged for services, physicians and other health care providers become less willing to provide services. Typically, more nurses have been willing to work less desirable schedules as the pay increases. That is the principle behind shift pay differentials.

Although price is a major determinant of supply, there are also other factors. The prices of inputs to produce a good or service also affect supply. When the price of inputs decreases, the supplier is willing to supply more of the product. Conversely, when the price of inputs increases, the supply will decrease. These changes in input prices cause a shift in the supply curve.

Technology is another factor. Although the cost of technology may initially be large, technology may allow the production of a larger quantity in a shorter period of time at a lower unit cost. For example, disposable medical products allow a health care facility to have immediate access to products without hiring people and equipment to sterilize the products for reuse.

Another factor in supply is the number of suppliers. The supply curve shifts to the right, increasing supply, when there are new suppliers or shifts to the left, with decreases in supply, when there are fewer suppliers. In the current health care environment, many health care agencies are merging to form larger systems. Mergers often result in the closure of some of the original facilities, resulting in lower overall supply of some services.

PRICE DETERMINATION

Because both supply and demand are fundamentally influenced by price, an important question is how price is determined and how price is maintained. There are basically three types of pricing conditions. A stable, or equilibrium, price exists when the quantity demanded equals the quantity supplied. In such a situation there is no pressure for the price to change. A surplus exists when the quantity supplied exceeds the quantity demanded. Then pressure exists for the price to decrease. A shortage exists when the quantity demanded exceeds the quantity supplied. Then there is pressure for the price to increase.

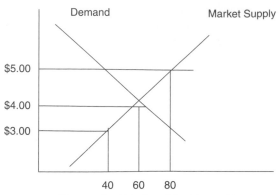

Figure 13-3 The market price for aspirin.

How do these concepts apply to the aspirin example? As shown in Figure 13-3, if the price of the components of aspirin decreases and the manufacturers increase their supply, they may be producing more aspirin than consumers are willing to purchase. When there is an excess of aspirin, there is an incentive to decrease the price so consumers will purchase the excess. If there were a shortage of aspirin, suppliers would increase the price.

COST OF HEALTH CARE

THEORIES OF HEALTH CARE COST

Pricing concepts can be applied to the cost of health care. There are two major theories concerning the rising cost of health care, or health care inflation. One is the *demand-pull theory* of inflation; the other is the *cost-push theory* of inflation. A discussion of these theories demonstrates that both affect the rising cost of health care.

Demand-Pull Theory. The demand-pull theory of inflation suggests that increases in the cost of health care occur from excess demand and spending on health care with an insufficient supply of goods and services to accommodate the demand. Income of most people has risen since World War II. With this rise in income, people are demanding more services, such as health care. The population distribution has also changed, with a larger propor-

tion of older people. The population of people over 65 years of age has grown from 4.1% of the population in 1900 to 8.1% in 1950 and subsequently to 12.8% of the population in 2000. The percentage of elders is projected to grow to 20.4% of the population by 2050 (Department of Health and Human Services, 2001). Because older people have more chronic conditions and greater health care needs, they require more health care expenditures.

Another factor in the increased demand for health services is the increased use of insurance coverage. Insurance is called third party payment because health care consumers (the first party) receive care from health care providers (the second party). However, most expenses are paid by an insurance company or government agency, which is considered to be a third party. Because consumers do not pay the bills directly, they are protected from the actual cost of health care. This distance from the actual cost of care may cause consumers to use more services than if they were paying the entire cost of care.

Health care costs have also been treated favorably by the tax system. Employees usually receive health insurance through their place of work. The health insurance benefits provided through work and the out-of-pocket health care expenses receive favorable tax treatment under federal laws. This encourages the growth of tax-free insurance benefits. Greater insurance benefits create the incentive for greater use of health care services.

The following are examples of the effect of greater insurance coverage:
1. Many people now have coverage for comprehensive health services such as dental care and eye care.
2. Expensive health prevention services, such as mammography and sigmoidoscopy may be postponed or foregone when there is no insurance coverage or until insurance will cover the service.
3. Various levels of government provide programs to decrease the financial barriers to services deemed beneficial not only to the individual but also to the society. Examples of these services are immunizations, communicable disease treatment, and prenatal care.

4. People with higher levels of income may choose elective procedures that will not be covered by insurance such as cosmetic surgery, laser eye surgery, or alternative therapies.

Cost-Push Theory. The cost-push theory of health care inflation suggests that higher prices result from the rising costs within the health care business. In health care a large proportion of cost comes from personnel expenses. As wages rise, the cost of health care also rises. In addition, new technologies that either advance the process of care or provide new products for health care delivery can increase the cost of care. These costs include facilities, equipment, supplies, treatments, and pharmaceuticals.

Another cost of doing health care business is concern with malpractice. Fear of lawsuits increases the cost of health care through malpractice insurance. Health care providers may also prescribe more tests and treatments to defend themselves against potential lawsuits. This is frequently called defensive medicine (Chang et al, 2001). Once could also argue that in an increasingly competitive health care market, advertising for new clients and recruiting staff create other costs that increase health care expenses. These examples demonstrate that both increased demand and rising cost of providing health care services affect the cost of health care.

COST CONTAINMENT EFFORTS

Frequently, attempts to control costs in health care are categorized as regulatory or market based. Regulatory strategies are actions of some level of government to control costs. Some of these strategies have had a broad focus; others have been more narrowly targeted.

There have been two major broad-based cost containment strategies of the federal government. Under President Richard Nixon in 1971, the Economic Stabilization Program was created to provide wage and price controls. Prices remained low while the controls were in effect, but they rose sharply after the controls were lifted. In 1977 President Jimmy Carter enacted the Voluntary Effort in which hospitals were urged to reduce inflation by 2% to 3% below the levels of the previous year.

The proposal was defeated in 1979 owing to lobbying efforts of the hospital industry and apparent slowing down of health spending. Economists who studied these efforts determined that both these strategies were largely ineffective because price controls were relaxed and health care providers found new ways of increasing their revenues (Getzen, 1997; Phelps, 1997).

Another regulatory strategy was *Certificate of Need* legislation developed by states to control health care costs (Sloan, 1983; Dranove & Cone, 1985). Such state-level legislation required hospitals to gain approval from state health-planning agencies for capital expenditures that exceeded a specified amount. The goal was to avoid duplication of expensive facilities and equipment in communities where additional capacity was not needed. Again, health economists found the Certificate of Need approach to be ineffective because it did not provide sufficient incentives for agencies to participate in regional level planning (Feldstein, 1999). Health care agencies that desired particular equipment or facilities to attract patients often found alternative funding.

In 1983 the federal government changed the system for reimbursement for hospital services under Medicare. Until this time, hospitals were reimbursed for each service they provided. The incentive was to provide as many services as possible in such a fee-for-service system. A *prospective payment system* (PPS) was created in which hospitals were reimbursed a set amount according to the patient's diagnosis. This was called *prospective* because the amount to be reimbursed was determined before the care was given. Under this system diagnosis-related groups (DRGs) were developed according to the patient's diagnosis. These diagnostic groups form the basis for Medicare reimbursement. The reimbursement rates for these groups are reviewed annually to reflect changes in costs. There are approximately 495 DRGs that can vary in reimbursement according to the region of the country. Teaching hospitals have also been allowed higher rates. With this system health care providers now shared the risk of health care costs. When the cost of care to a given patient exceeded the DRG rate, the hospital has to absorb the cost above the DRG-specified rate. Conversely, if the cost of care was less than the DRG rate, the health care provider could keep the excess (Chang et al, 2001).

What has been the impact of the DRG prospective payment system? Since hospitals, on average, receive approximately half of their income from Medicare, changes in Medicare have a great effect on their revenue. Frequently, other insurance providers follow the systems established by Medicare. The Prospective Payment Assessment Commission (1996) estimated that hospitals held their costs well below the historical growth trend in the first year of prospective payment. However, the cost of each Medicare case rose sharply in the following years. The annual cost per case again slowed in 1993 to 1.2%, which was the smallest increase in Medicare history (Health Care Financing Administration, 1997).

Another approach to cost containment is to use market strategies to decrease the costs of health care. Such an approach would use the concepts of supply, demand, and pricing to control the price of health care.

Managed care refers to a health care system that combines the financing with the delivery of health services in a single organization. Historically, health insurers have not provided services, but have paid for services delivered by external health care providers. By combining these functions, managed care organizations have grown as a proportion of the health care market. It was estimated in 1997 that 75% of the private sector, 32% of the Medicaid population, and 12% of the Medicare population were insured through some form of managed care (Health Care Financing Administration, 1997). By the end of the twentieth century, 56.7% of Medicaid recipients were enrolled in managed care organizations (Health Care Financing Administration, 2001).

Strategies used by managed care organizations to control costs include:

- *Provider networks and selective provider contracting at a favorable reimbursement rate.* This strategy restricts consumers' choice of providers. Practices vary from paying only for providers in the system to newer *point of service (POS) plans* that pay a substantially greater proportion of the costs for in-plan providers.
- *Payment methods with risk sharing.* Reimbursement includes an incentive for providers to limit the cost of care. One such arrangement is *capitation,* in which providers receive a set amount of money per month per subscriber to provide all health services required. If the cost of services remain under that level, providers make money. Conversely, providers lose money if costs exceed the predetermined amount.
- *Gatekeeping.* This mechanism requires approval by primary care providers for specialty services. The goal of this practice is to prevent unnecessary resource utilization.
- *Utilization review.* This refers to a variety of practices that require appropriate use of resources by clinicians. *Preauthorization* is the requirement that specified services, such as hospitalization or emergency room care, be approved before they are provided. *Case management* refers to a process of care in which consumers are guided through the health care system as quickly as possible using the minimum required resources. *Practice guidelines* are used to provide research-based best practices for given health conditions.
- *Favorable selection of clients.* One criticism of managed care organizations is that many seek to enroll younger and healthier individuals who will require fewer resources (Chang et al, 2001).

While this chapter describes a variety of mechanisms to contain health care costs, many people fear the effect of these actions on the quality of care and resulting health outcomes. The question is how to compare one means of providing care with other approaches. Economic analysis provides one possible approach to choosing among competing options.

USING ECONOMIC ANALYSIS AS A STRATEGY

STRATEGY FOR PRACTICE POLICIES

Health care organizations are faced with many decisions about what projects to implement, knowing that funding all would be impossible. Clinicians frequently evaluate their actions by the clinical outcomes or implications. In addition, all health care decisions involve the use of resources. By definition, economics reflects decision making in the presence of scarcity. Limited resources require that choices be made from a variety of options.

There are many examples of research that has been conducted to examine the health outcomes and financial implications of various interventions or programs. Brooten et al (1986) have been pioneers in conducting nursing research that includes financial outcomes for low-birth-weight infants and nurse practitioner follow-up of elders discharged from the hospital (Naylor et al, 1999). Wikblad and Anderson (1995) compared various dressings used after cardiac surgery for differences in healing, required frequency of change, skin integrity, ability to observe the wound, rate of infection, and cost. A meta-analysis was conducted to synthesize knowledge of the impact of using normal saline versus heparin in flushes of peripheral heparin locks (Goode, Titler, Rakel, Ones, Kleiber, Small, & Triolo, 1991). Heparin and saline were shown to be comparable in patency of the port and freedom from phlebitis, but saline costs considerably less.

Other research has examined the effect of larger changes in practice on the outcomes of nursing care. Disease management programs are promoted to save health care dollars as well as improve consumer quality of life. These programs are aimed at addressing the health care needs of the most costly patients. The goal is to manage care by implementing preventive measures and by attending promptly to problems in order to minimize crises that will result in hospitalization. One example of a disease management program is the asthma management model system that is continuously updated to provide clinicians with current information related to asthma treatment. This model also uses an information system tool to analyze clinical problems and their long-term effects for asthma patients. The system allows science-based decision making using evidence-based medicine in asthma management. This program maintains continuously updated information through its website (nhlbisupport.com/asthma/index.html).

STRATEGY FOR WORKPLACE POLICIES

Hendrix and Foreman (2001) investigated the optimal long-term care nurse-staffing levels. Using the prevalence of decubiti ulcers as an indicator of quality care, they developed a model to determine staffing levels that would maximize quality while minimizing cost. Results demonstrated a negative relationship between a facility's annual cost for decubitus care and both the annual nursing cost per patient and the annual cost for nurse aides. In other words, as nursing hours increase, the cost of decubitus care decreases. These data support staffing with more RNs for supervision and nurse aides for direct care.

These examples demonstrate how research can be used to influence policy choices at the agency level as well as to support the implementation of evidence-based practice guidelines.

STRATEGY FOR GOVERNMENT POLICIES

Economic analyses can be a strategy to support policy or legislation at the state or national level. Issues in which economic analyses have been used include the following:

- Determining the required length of stay after delivery or surgery
- Establishing requirements for safer equipment to prevent health care worker injury, such as needlesticks
- Supporting increased use of advanced practice nurses
- Supporting sufficient staffing patterns to achieve desired patient health outcomes

When selecting among various options for a particular health care intervention or program, the value of alternative solutions not chosen is also important. A specific cost that economists consider is the *opportunity cost.* Opportunity cost is the value of the alternative use of resources that was not chosen.

Example of Opportunity Cost. Infant mortality is a national health concern. Although infant mortality has declined since 1900, the infant mortality rate in the United States remains higher than that of other industrialized countries. A variety of approaches could be used to address the infant mortality rate:

- Support family planning clinics to decrease the number of unplanned pregnancies
- Increase the availability of prenatal care
- Increase preparation of nurse midwives to practice in underserved and poor areas

- Expand the Women, Infants, and Children (WIC) program that provides food supplementation to pregnant and lactating women as well as to young children who meet the economic criteria
- Expand research into neonatal health conditions
- Expand neonatal intensive care services

All of these approaches address the reduction of infant mortality rates. However, there are insufficient resources to implement all of them. At the point of choosing the desired solution or solutions, it is important to consider the options *not chosen* by examining the value of the forgone option or options, which is the opportunity cost. Building an expensive neonatal unit will limit the funds available for the preventive services, such as family planning or the WIC nutrition program.

CLINICAL ECONOMICS: A TYPE OF ECONOMIC ANALYSIS

Clinical economics is a specific type of economic analysis that assists the user in choosing between various health care actions or interventions that compete for the same resources. Building on the foundation of the opportunity cost concept, such an evaluation asks whether a procedure, service, or program is worth implementing, knowing that the resources used will be unavailable for other worthwhile options. When applied properly, techniques of clinical economics assist in the allocation of scarce resources to maximize the health outcomes for the relevant population. The following discussion describes three commonly used methods of economic analysis: cost-identification, cost-benefit, and cost-effectiveness analyses.

COST IDENTIFICATION ANALYSIS

This technique focuses on the question of how much a health care service costs. This question is answered by a thorough identification of all costs related to a health good service. Once costs are specified, alternative approaches to delivery of the same service can be compared by their cost. Frequently, the results of such an analysis compare the costs of competing approaches to service delivery. *Direct costs* include the personnel, equipment, and supplies necessary to the provision of a service. The *indirect costs* include the supervision, utilities, facility, and other expenses that are necessary for the support of service delivery (Chang et al, 2001). One example of measuring costs is the publication of a model by the participants in the Iowa Intervention Project (2001). This model presents a method for assigning direct and indirect costs to the nursing interventions included in the nursing intervention classification.

One example of this technique is the implementation of home-based total parenteral nutrition (TPN). Because of the complex nature of this service, TPN has been traditionally provided only in the hospital setting. Curtas, Hariri, & Steiger (1996) used cost-identification analysis to describe the cost of providing TPN in the home. The direct personnel cost of personnel was $1982 per patient per year. Indirect costs including other personnel, space, and furnishings were included, and the cost was $2070 per patient per year. Since these costs have been identified, a comparison can be performed to compare the two approaches to this health concern, hospital and home-based TPN service.

Another example of cost identification analysis examined the cost of providing nursing care to a homeless population through a nurse-managed clinic. After detailed examination of the costs, it was determined that the average cost of providing care for one patient was $63 at the center, $61.82 at the county-operated clinic, and $213.27 at the emergency room (Hunter, Ventura, & Kearns, 1999). Such analysis provides policymakers with information to choose among options for providing health care to the homeless population.

Even the small practice change of using saline rather than heparin to flush peripheral heparin ports can lead to significant cost savings for a health care organization. Goode et al (1991) reported cost savings estimated by different hospitals in their meta-analysis that ranged from $19,000 to $40,000 per year.

COST BENEFIT ANALYSIS

Cost-benefit analysis is a technique that allows the analysis of different programs or services according to the amount of estimated benefits and costs. This method requires that both the outputs of the service, or benefits, and inputs, which are the people, materials, and equipment used in producing the service, be measured in dollars. The advantage of this process is the fact that interventions for different purposes can be analyzed using the results.

Results of cost benefit analysis can be reported as *net benefits.* Net benefits represent the total benefits of the program or intervention minus the total costs. However, interpretations of these results can be misleading. A large number of interventions may result in greater net benefits, while a smaller number may affect more people. For example, the early discharge of a small number of premature infants may result in greater net benefits than the implementation of a much greater number of saline flushes. Another limitation of this method is the difficulty of measuring benefits in dollars. Particular outcomes, such as quality of life and satisfaction, are challenging to quantify (Chang et al, 2001).

A cost-benefit ratio can also be calculated as the result of dividing total benefits by the total cost of the intervention. All programs with a ratio greater than 1 have benefits greater than their costs. This ratio is expressed as *cost-benefit ratio,* or *B/C.* The main advantage of using the cost-benefit ratio to evaluate competing projects is the fact that projects that are smaller in scale can be compared objectively with larger ones without being overwhelmed by the total dollars of net benefits typically associated with the scale of the larger projects.

Bridges et al (2000) conducted a cost-benefit analysis to examine the effectiveness and cost-benefit of influenza vaccination in well adults. Approximately 600 adults received influenza vaccine, and a similar number received a placebo in Winter 1997–1998 and Winter 1998–1999. In 1997–1998 the vaccine did not match the circulating virus, so there was no decrease in rate of influenza-like illness, frequency of physician visits, or number of lost work days for those who received the vaccine. There was not a net benefit, but there was a net social cost of $65.59 per person. In 1998–1999 when the vaccine did match the prevalent virus, there was a significant decrease in all three measures. However, a net social cost remained, at $11.17. Even

with a larger number of cases, this study does not support the universal influenza immunization of healthy adults.

COST-EFFECTIVENESS ANALYSIS

Cost-effectiveness analysis is designed to examine competing interventions or programs that address the same health concern. A ratio is computed by dividing the total cost in dollars per unit of outcomes. The numerator consists of the costs, and the denominator includes the units of outcome.

A cost-effectiveness analysis was conducted at the University of Minnesota (Chen, Kane, & Finch, 2000). Subjects were compared on their functional status as measured by activities of daily living at 6 weeks, 6 months, and 12 months following hospitalization. Costs were measured using Medicare claims data for the year before hospitalization to 1 year after hospitalization. Post-acute care expenditures were determined by actual Medicare data or calculations of resource consumption. An incremental cost-effectiveness ratio (CER) was calculated to represent the cost in dollars paid for a 1% functional improvement in a specific post-acute care setting. At 6 weeks, stroke patients discharged to home health care showed the greatest functional improvement in activities of daily living, followed by those released to rehabilitation facilities, those sent home without home care, and, finally, those moved to skilled nursing facilities. A similar pattern was demonstrated for patients with chronic obstructive pulmonary disease (COPD), patients with congestive heart failure (CHF), and hip procedure patients who were discharged with home care. These groups had improved functional status over those who were discharged with no home care. Costs differed by setting, with higher costs for institutional placements in skilled nursing facilities and rehabilitation centers than for community placement with home care. With stroke patients, the CER for each 1% improvement in functional status was $31 for home health care and $893 for rehabilitation facilities. Further analysis demonstrated a similar pattern with other diagnoses. This cost-effectiveness analysis allows comparison of cost per 1% improvement in functional status among the available post-acute care treatment options.

For comparative analysis, the cost analysis techniques should be consistently performed. The perspective of the analysis determines which costs and benefits should be included. The perspective can be the individual and the family, the insurer, or society. The individual/family perspective would include only the costs and benefits experienced by the person and the family. The insurer perspective would focus on only the costs and benefits relevant to the insurer. Both of these perspectives address a somewhat narrow focus. Only a societal perspective includes all the costs and benefits that pertain to the individual, the family, and the insurer as well as members of society.

A panel of experts was convened in 1993 to standardize the process of cost-effectiveness analysis. The largest perspective, and the one most useful for policy development, is that of society. The expert panel examined the approaches to analyzing costs and benefits with a reference case to guide the process of analysis. The costs recommended to be considered are ones associated with health services, experienced by patients and their families, and borne by society (Robinson, 1993a; 1993b; Gold, Siegel, Russell, & Weinstein, 1996; Russell, Gold, Siegel, Daniels, & Weinstein, 1996; Siegel, Weinstein, Russell, & Gold, 1996; Weinstein, Siegel, Gold, Kamlet, & Russell, 1996). Others have specifically applied these principles to nursing (Chang & Henry, 1999; Brosnan & Swint, 2001).

CONCLUSION

This chapter focuses on the relevance and application of the basic economic concepts of supply, demand, and price determination for the development and evaluation of health policy. To compete effectively in the health care market, nurses must understand the economic and financial realities affecting health care delivery such as the determination of the cost of health care and cost containment efforts. Market strategies are another approach used to reduce the costs of health care using the concepts of supply, demand, and pricing to control the price of health care.

Managed care is a health care system that relies on financial incentives and consumer choice to deliver quality services at a reasonable cost. Market strategies used by managed care organizations to control costs emphasize provider networks and selective provider contracting at a favorable reimbursement rate, payment methods with risk sharing such as capitation, gatekeeping to prevent unnecessary resource utilization, and utilization review.

Health care organizations are concerned with decisions regarding what projects to implement. All of these health care decisions involve the use of resources from an economic perspective. Limited resources require that choices be made from a variety of options considering the opportunity cost, the value of the alternative use of resources that was not chosen. Clinical economics refers to several methods of economic analysis that assist in choosing between various health care actions or interventions. Three commonly used approaches to the economic evaluation of clinical decisions are cost-identification, cost-benefit, and cost-effectiveness analysis. All three of these approaches can help nurses make rational decisions regarding cost effectiveness of health care and can assist policymakers in selecting wise and beneficial policies.

REFERENCES

Bridges, C. Thompson, W., Meltzer, M., Reeve, G., Talamonti, W., Cox, N., Lilac, H., Hall, H., Klimov, A. & Fukunda, K. (2000). Effectiveness of and cost-benefit of influenza vaccination of healthy working adults. *Journal of the American Medical Association, 284*(13), 1655-1663.

Brooten, D., et al. (1986). A randomized clinical trial of early hospital discharge and home follow-up of very-low-birth-weight infants. *New England Journal of Medicine, 315*, 934-939.

Brosnan, C.A. & Swint, J.M. (2001). Cost analysis: Concepts and application. *Public Health Nursing, 18*(1), 13-18.

Bureau of the Census. (1998). *Health insurance coverage: 1997.* Available online at www.census.gov/80hhes/hlthins/hlthin97/asc.html.

Chang, C.F., Price, S.A., & Pfoutz, S.K. (2001). *Economics and nursing: Critical professional issues.* Philadelphia: F.A. Davis.

Chang, W.Y. & Henry, B.M. (1999). Methodologic principles of cost analysis in the nursing, medical, and health services literature, 1990-1996. *Nursing Research, 48*(2), 94-104.

Chen, Q., Kane, R.L., & Finch, M.D. (2000). The cost effectiveness of post-acute care for elderly Medicare beneficiaries. *Inquiry, 37*(4), 359-375.

Curtas, S., Hariri, R., & Steiger, E. (1996). Case management in home total parenteral nutrition: A cost-identification analysis. *Journal of Parenteral and Enteral Nutrition, 20*(2), 113-119.

Department of Health and Human Services (2001). Available at www.aoa.dhhs.gov/aoa/stats/Agepop2050.html.

Dranove, D. & Cone, K. (1985). Do state rate-setting regulations really lower hospital expense? *Journal of Health Economics, 4*(2), 159-165.

Feldstein, P. (1999). *Health economics* (5th ed.). Albany, NY: Delmar Publishers.

Getzen, T.E. (1997). *Health economics.* New York: John Wiley & Sons.

Gold, M.R., Siegel, J.E., Russell, L.G., & Weinstein, M.S. (1996). *Cost effectiveness in health and medicine.* New York: Oxford University Press.

Goode, C.J., Titler, M., Rakel, B., Ones, D.S., Kleiber, C., Small, S., & Triolo, P.K. (1991). A meta-analysis of effects of heparin flush and saline flush: Quality and cost implications. *Nursing Research, 20*(9), 54-58.

Health Care Financing Administration. (1997). *Managed care in Medicare and Medicaid: Fact sheet.* Available online at www.hcfa.gov/stats/nhe-oact/nhe.htm.

Health Care Financing Administration. (1998). Available online at www.hcfa.gov/stats/nheoact/nhe.htm.

Health Care Financing Administration. (2001). *Publications and forms.* Available online at www.hcfa.gov/pubforms/mhbkc02.htm.

Hendrix, T.J. & Foreman, S.E. (2001). Optimal long-term care nurse-staffing levels. *Nursing Economics, 19*(4), 164-175.

Hunter, J.K., Ventura, M.R., & Kearns, P.A. (1999). Cost analysis of a nursing center for the homeless. *Nursing Economics, 17*(1), 20-28.

Iowa Intervention Project. (2001). Determining cost of nursing interventions: A beginning. *Nursing Economics, 19*(4), 146-160.

Naylor, M.D., Brooten, D., Campbell, R., Jacobsen, M.S., Mezey, M., Pauly, M., & Schwartz, S. (1999). Comprehensive discharge planning and home follow-up of hospitalized elders: A randomized clinical trial. *Journal of the American Medical Association, 281*(7), 613-620.

Phelps, C.E. (1997). *Health economics* (2nd ed.). Reading, MA: Addison-Wesley.

Prospective Payment Assessment Commission (1996). *Medicare and the American health care system.* Washington, DC: Author.

Robinson, R. (1993a). Cost-effectiveness analysis. *British Medical Journal, 307*(6907), 793-795.

Robinson, R. (1993b). Costs and cost-minimization analysis. *British Medical Journal, 307*(6906), 726-728.

Russell, L.B., Gold, M.R., Siegel, J.E., Daniels, N., & Weinstein, M.C. (1996). The role of cost-effectiveness analysis in health and medicine. *Journal of the American Medical Association, 276*(14), 1172-1177.

Siegel, J.E., Weinstein, M.C., Russell, L.B., & Gold, M.R. (1996). Recommendations for reporting cost-effectiveness analyses in health and medicine. *Journal of the American Medical Association, 276*(16), 1339-1341.

Sloan, F.A. (1983). Rate regulation as a strategy for hospital cost control: Evidence from the last decade. *Milbank Memorial Fund Quarterly/Health and Society, 61*(2), 196-221.

Weinstein, M.D., Siegel, J.E., Gold, M.R., Kamlet, M.S., & Russell, L.B. (1996). Recommendation of the Panel on Cost-Effectiveness in Health and Medicine. *Journal of the American Medical Association, 276*(15), 1253-1258.

Wikblad, K. & Anderson, B. (1995). A comparison of three wound dressings in patients undergoing heart surgery. *Nursing Research, 44*(4), 312-316.

chapter 14

Health Care Financing

JOYCE A. PULCINI

SUSAN R. NEARY

DIANE FEENEY MAHONEY

"Can anyone remember when the times were not hard and money was not scarce?"

RALPH WALDO EMERSON

An elderly woman living in an urban metropolitan center is hospitalized after suffering a cerebral vascular accident and is sent home with multiple medications and the need for home health services, speech therapy, and physical therapy. The Visiting Nurse Association is called, but this person has enrolled in a Medicare+Choice program and has limited home health benefits and prescription drug coverage. Family members live 500 miles away and cannot assist with her care. What are the prospects that this patient will have adequate care at home and be spared a lengthy nursing home stay if her condition deteriorates? Will the available health care resources adequately meet this person's needs now and throughout the remainder of her life?

This chapter describes and analyzes the features of the health care financing system in the United States. It first presents a historical perspective to provide a basis for understanding the current system. The chapter then explores the financial and economic forces that drive the health care system and describes measures to contain costs. The health care financing system is described, including the public and private sectors. A major focus is financing of long-term care as well as acute and primary care. Finally, implications for nursing are discussed.

HISTORICAL PERSPECTIVES

History reveals some dominant values underpinning the U.S. political and economic systems. From its origins, the United States has had a long history of individualism, an emphasis on freedom to choose among alternative options, and an aversion as a nation to large-scale government intervention into the private realm (Kingdon, 1999). Social programs have been the exception rather than the rule and have arisen primarily during times of great need, such as in the 1930s and 1960s. Health care in the United States had its origins in the private sector, and as a result, strong resistance has been raised to government intervention in health care, particularly by physician and hospital groups.

The Great Depression of the 1930s saw the creation of Blue Cross, an insurance plan to cover hospital care, and then Blue Shield, to cover physician care. Starr (1982) describes the initial reluctance of the American Hospital Association and of the American Medical Association to adopt any form of prepaid hospital or medical expenses. But hospitals in 1933 and physicians in 1938 experienced enough bad debt to motivate them to endorse plans that laid the foundation for what is now Blue Cross and Blue Shield. The belief that persons should pay for their medical care before they actually got sick, thus ensuring some security for both providers and consumers of medical services in time of need, was the rationale behind instituting such private insurance plans. Starr (1982) points out that the development of these plans effectively diffused a strong political movement toward legislating a compulsory health insurance plan. The Social Security Act of 1935, a comprehensive piece of social legislation, is striking for its failure to include health care. A national health program did not reach the national agenda again until the 1960s.

Blue Cross and Blue Shield continued to dominate the health insurance industry until the 1950s, when commercial insurance companies entered the market. These insurance companies had been discouraged from entry partially because of discounted room rates negotiated with hospitals by Blue Cross. Moreover, state regulations required Blue Cross/Blue Shield to use *community rating,* or rates based on the total utilization of health care services across a whole population or community. Commercial insurance companies were able to compete with Blue Cross and Blue Shield by using *experience rating,* targeted to a select, low-risk population or community. Experience rating decreases the price of health insurance because high-risk individuals are more likely to be excluded from the plan. The distinction between Blue Cross/Blue Shield and commercial insurance companies has become increasingly blurred, and many Blue Cross/Blue Shield plans have converted to for-profit status and established companion nonprofit foundations. Blue Cross/Blue Shield now offers the same range of managed care products as commercial insurance companies as it competes in the current health care marketplace (Kovner & Jonas, 1999).

The United States in the 1960s enjoyed relative prosperity along with a burgeoning social conscience that led to a heightened concern for poor and elderly people in this country. Another issue at this time was the failure of health insurance to protect persons who had catastrophic illness. The catalyst for a governmental solution to the lack of health care for these populations was the framing of these issues as a series of "crises" that garnered public support and created an atmosphere for change (Alford, 1975). As a result of these forces, Medicaid and Medicare, two separate but related programs, were created in 1965 by amendments to the Social Security Act. Medicare, or Title XVIII, is a federal program for the aged and disabled, and Medicaid, or Title XIX, is a program jointly funded by both federal and state governments, with eligibility determined by income and resources (Health Care Financing Administration [HCFA], 2000a).

Within a few years of the passage of Medicare and Medicaid, it became clear that these programs were contributing greatly to escalating costs of health care. The government and society's inability to react to the escalation of health care costs is one of the root causes of our current fiscal crisis in health care. In fact, it was within a decade after the passage of Medicare and Medicaid that cost began increasingly to dominate all policy decisions in health care.

The health care field has evolved from rather small and disorganized private and public enterprises to a large, multifaceted business affected by interrelated forces. The role of third-party payors in the financing of the health care industry has grown tremendously in the past 40 to 50 years. Historically, the majority of payments for health services came from first- or second-party payors (from the patients or their families, respectively). In 1940 81.3% of health care was paid for by the individual or family and 18.7% was financed by third-party, or intermediary, payors. By 1980 these figures had reversed themselves, with 32.9% of costs borne by the patient or family and 67.1% of these costs by third-party or public payors (Gibson & Waldo, 1982). Figure 14-1 shows the change in payors in 1940 versus 1980.

Currently, the majority of people in the United States are covered by employer-based health insurance. In 1998 86% of these individuals were enrolled in a managed care plan (Gabel, 1999). Yet many full-time jobs with benefits have been replaced with part-time positions without benefits. This phenomenon is occurring particularly in lower-paid positions in the service sectors of the economy. Others who do not have health insurance available through the workplace must attempt to obtain private insurance if they can afford it or qualify for governmental supported care through Medicare or Medicaid. Most employers require some portion of the monthly premiums to be paid by the individual. Generally, about 80% of the premium is paid by the employer and 20% by the individual. Two decades ago, most employers offered

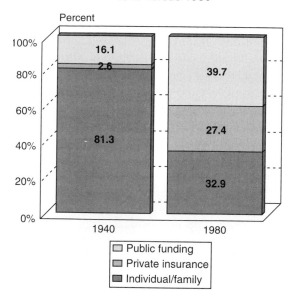

Figure 14-1   Changes in payors over time.

100% payment as a fringe benefit; however, the sharp escalation of health care costs has brought a drive to share these costs with employees.

Another vulnerable group is the 55- to 65-year-old individuals who either have taken an early retirement or have been laid off from their jobs. In recent years several proposals have been introduced to allow people ages 62 to 65 and displaced workers ages 55 to 65 to buy into Medicare (HCFA, 2000b). At the same time, health care costs are projected to rise incrementally as the average life expectancy is extended and the current "baby boomers" age, leading to proposals for a delay in the time when Medicare Part A benefits can be accessed.

Cost escalation in health care has created a powerful incentive to alter the system. Table 14-1 provides a graphic picture of the costs of health care from 1960 to 1999. As costs rose in the 1970s and 1980s, the balance of power changed in the health care field. More and more groups outside the health field became involved in attempts to contain costs. Leaders from business, large corporations, and labor offered solutions to the problems because they were purchasing or negotiating for health care ben-

efits. Patients also became disillusioned, initially with the quality of health care that they were receiving and later with the high cost of this care. Physicians who had traditionally managed hospitals and health care facilities were increasingly replaced with business executives who focus on cost-containment efforts. By the 1990s health care had undergone radical changes that ultimately revolutionized the financing and delivery of health care to include a deep penetration of managed care plans.

COST CONTAINMENT IN HEALTH CARE

Efforts toward cost containment have taken on many faces as providers, insurers, employers, unions, and individuals have become alarmed about the current and long-term economic consequences of the escalating costs of health care. A range of strategies have been used to curb these costs over the last 35 years.

REGULATION VERSUS COMPETITION

In the 1970s the preferred solution to the escalating cost of health care was government regulation. Regulation took the form of health planning at all levels of government and included Certificate of Need programs, which were administered by health systems agencies (HSAs) at the federal, state, and local levels. These programs were intended to avoid duplication of new technologies and certain health care services, limit capital expansion, and ultimately cut unnecessary costs. Professional groups, such as physicians, responded to cost containment through self-regulation mechanisms such as professional standards review organizations (PSROs). PSROs were created by the 1972 Medicare amendments to monitor the quality of federally funded care and to ensure its delivery in the most efficient and economic manner (Davis, Anderson, Rowland, & Steinberg, 1990). In 1983, peer review organizations were created and placed under contract to the HCFA for utilization review and quality-of-care assessments of hospitals, health maintenance organizations (HMOs), and some office practices.

Many of the regulatory efforts of the 1970s and 1980s went by the wayside because they did not

TABLE **14-1** National Health Expenditures: Aggregate and Per Capita Amounts and Percent Distribution,* by Source of Funds (Selected Years 1960-1999)

ITEM	1960	1970	1980	1990	1995	1999
U.S. population[†] (number in millions)	186.2	210.2	254.2	254.2	267.8	277.8
Gross domestic product[‡]	$527	$1040	$2796	$5803	$7400	$9299
National health expenditures (percent of GDP)	5.1%	7.0%	8.8%	12.0%	13.3%	13.0%
National health expenditures (amount in billions of dollars)	$26.7	$73.1	$245.8	$695.6	$987.0	$1210.7
Private	$ 20.1	$ 45.5	$ 141.0	$ 413.2	$ 528.8	$ 662.1
Public	$ 6.6	$ 27.6	$ 104.8	$ 282.4	$ 458.2	$ 548.5
Federal	$ 2.8	$ 17.6	$ 71.3	$ 192.6	$ 323.9	$ 384.7
State and local	$ 3.8	$ 10.0	$ 33.5	$ 89.8	$ 128.6	$ 163.9
National health expenditures (per capita amount)	$143	$348	$1067	$2737	$3686	$4358
Private	$108	$216	$612	$1626	$1975	$2384
Public	$ 35	$131	$455	$1111	$1711	$1975
Federal	$ 15	$ 84	$309	$ 758	$1210	$1385
State and local	$ 20	$ 48	$146	$ 353	$ 502	$ 590
National health expenditures (percent distribution)						
Private	75.2%	62.3%	57.4%	59.4%	53.6%	54.7%
Public	24.8%	37.7%	42.6%	40.6%	46.4%	45.3%
Federal	10.6%	24.0%	29.0%	27.7%	32.8%	31.8%
State and local	14.2%	13.7%	13.6%	12.9%	13.6%	13.5%

From Health Care Financing Administration, Office of the Actuary: National Health Statistics Group; U.S. Department of Commerce, Bureau of Economic Analysis; and U.S. Bureau of the Census.

*Numbers and percents may not add to totals because of rounding.

[†]July 1 Census, resident-based population.

[‡]U.S. Department of Commerce, Bureau of Economic Analysis.

significantly reduce costs. Although regulation did involve consumers and community agencies in the process of thinking about cost containment, the solution to the problem was beyond its grasp. Local health planning agencies were often controlled by provider groups or consumers with vested interests, who were unwilling or unable to curb expanding health care costs. Professional groups, while discussing cost reduction, continued to respond to the overwhelming economic incentives inherent in the health care system, and as a result HSAs disappeared or lost much of their influence during the 1980s.

The 1980s saw an emphasis on competition as a mechanism to cut costs. Competition is based on the premise that the health care system has enough similarities to the free market that cost would be controlled by the entry of a large number of competing elements. The problem is the fact that, at least at the level of the patient, the health care system does not act like a free market system and, indeed, has few similarities to a fully competitive market in economic terms (Pulcini, 1984). Chapter 13, which focuses on economics, more fully describes the mechanisms underlying the market system.

Although it is not a perfect solution, competition is based on the economic assumption of scarcity—that is, health care is not an unlimited resource, so choices must be made as to how it will be allocated. Competition forced the public to more directly experience the effect of market forces in health care. The 1980s saw attempts to change the existing incentives in health care so that providers and patients could begin to understand the financial effects of high-cost care. Competition has been used effectively at the health plan level, especially with the entry of many new managed care organizations that do compete vigorously with each other. In this realm the purchasers of health insurance tend to be large corporations, businesses, or unions that buy health benefits for their employees or members. The major impetus for cost containment in the 1980s came from these groups, which are indeed the ultimate buyers of health insurance.

Other examples of cost-containment mechanisms are copayments, deductibles, and coinsurance, which not only discourage unnecessary use but also may increase pressures on low wage earners who cannot afford these extra direct costs. Some argue that although these efforts have had some effect, they have tended to discourage early identification of health problems. One can question whether these efforts have, in effect, decreased access to primary prevention and increased the overall cost of care initiated at later stages in an illness episode. By the end of the 1980s, there was a realization that neither pure competition nor regulation would be effective as a solution but that some combination would be needed. Managed competition, as put forth by President Clinton's Health Security Act, was an example of this concept. At the level of the individual patient, care received is dependent to a great extent on what will be reimbursed by insurance companies and covered by managed care plans.

PROSPECTIVE PAYMENT VERSUS FEE-FOR-SERVICE FINANCING

Pressure on the government from corporations and business groups to change financing from fee-for-service, or retrospective, reimbursement to prospective modalities increased in the 1980s. Because the federal government has direct control only of its own programs, it targeted Medicare Part A by developing in 1983 a prospective payment system (PPS) for hospital care, establishing payment based on as diagnosis-related groups (DRGs). DRGs set a payment level for each of 503 diagnostic categories typically used in inpatient care. The goal was to place a cap on escalating hospital costs. Prospective payment measures have helped to slow the rate of growth of hospital expenditures and had a major impact on length of stay (Fuchs, 1988; Heffler, Levit, Smith, Smith, Cowan, Lazenby, & Freeland, 2001). Initially, DRG rates were allowed to increase each year, and payment rates were also adjusted for geographic differences in wage levels. Certain services (such as outpatient and long-term care services) and certain hospitals (such as children's hospitals, psychiatric facilities, and rehabilitation hospitals) were originally excluded from the PPS. Capital and training expenses were reimbursed at cost. Since its initial passage, PPS has undergone some changes, but generally the payment received per hospital discharge is based on what is called the DRG relative weight and a national average cost per discharge.

The PPS contributed to significantly increased patient acuity in inpatient settings, and resulting gaps and problems still exist. Decreased length of hospital stay caused a ripple effect in the home care industry, which has had to care for more acutely ill persons in the home. Between 1967 and 1998, Medicare spending for inpatient hospital services declined from 70% to 49%. Costs for skilled nursing facilities (SNFs) and home care increased rapidly, especially for the most elderly (Lubitz, Greenbery, Gorina, Wartzman, & Gibson, 2001).

BALANCED BUDGET ACT OF 1997

The Balanced Budget Act (BBA) of 1997 was signed into law on August 5, 1997, as PL 105-33. This legislation made major changes in the Medicare program, including a $116.4 billion reduction in net spending over the following 5 years until 2002 and a $393.5 billion cut over 10 years. As a result of this legislation, the exhaustion of the Medicare Part A trust fund was delayed from 2001 to 2007. Savings came first from reductions in payments to hospitals and then will come from private plan payment reductions as well as increases in Medicare Part B premiums to a projected $105 per month in 2007. Payment methods were restructured for rehabilitation hospitals, home health agencies, SNFs, and outpatient services (HCFA, 1997b).

This law also contains the largest spending reductions for Medicaid since 1981 with a saving of $17 billion over 5 years and $61.4 billion over 10 years by greatly expanding the substantial discretion that states have in administering their Medicaid programs, by eliminating minimum payment standards, and by allowing states to require most beneficiaries to enroll in managed care organizations. Although it left most of the critical elements of the Medicaid program intact, it did limit Medicaid eligibility for persons who had legally immigrated since August 1996. This act also established the State Child Health Insurance Program (SCHIP) (HCFA, 1997a).

Prospective payment schemes and particularly the Balanced Budget Act of 1997 and its amendments had a significant effect in decreasing inpatient costs in the 1990s. Although hospital spending increased slightly both in 1998 and 1999, it continued to fall as a share of personal health care spending. Medicare spending for inpatient care also fell in the 2 years since the passage of the Balanced Budget Act of 1997, with relative declines in inpatient case mix intensity. This change may be attributed to Balanced Budget Act provisions affecting home care, shifts to ambulatory care, and changes in hospitals' coding of admissions (Heffler et al., 2001).

Before the mid-1990s, the enormous federal budget deficit led to political pressure to decrease outlays by cost-saving measures aimed at Medicare Part B, which primarily covers outpatient care. In March 1992 physician payment reform was initiated by means of the resource-based relative value scale (RBRVS). Its goal was not only cost savings but also a redistribution of physician services to increase primary care services and decrease the use of highly specialized physician care. The RBRVS was developed by William Hsiao and his colleagues (1988) to establish comparable fees for medical services based on time and intensity of effort, with consideration of typical overhead and malpractice costs. Other Medicare Part B cost-saving measures are limitation of home health care services and institution of fixed payments for outpatient care.

Medicaid and more recently Medicare are increasingly using managed care arrangements to contain costs. These will be discussed further in the federal programs sections on Medicare and Medicaid in this chapter.

HEALTH CARE EXPENDITURES

From 1995 to 2001 the United States experienced a booming economy and an unprecedented budget surplus after years of budget deficits. This surplus was projected to be $5.6 trillion over the first decade of the twenty-first century. Of that amount, just under $2.5 trillion would come from excess Social Security revenue, which the Congressional delegations from both the Republican and Democratic parties pledged would be used to reduce the $3.1 trillion national debt or to strengthen the retirement system (Stevenson, 2001a; 2001b). In May 2001 the Congress passed a $1.35 trillion tax cut to be implemented over the next decade (Stevenson, 2001a; 2001b).

Health care expenditures as a percentage of the gross domestic product (GDP) had been increasing steadily since the passage of Medicare and Medicaid in 1965 to 1993, when it was 13.4%. By 2000 health care expenditures had declined slightly to 13.1% as a percentage of the GDP (HCFA, Office of the Actuary [OA], 2001). This was the slowest growth rate in health care spending in more than three decades. This growth stabilization was due in part to some of the aforementioned cost-containment measures but also may be accounted for by major upward revisions of the GDP owing to a booming U.S. economy (Heffler et al, 2001). One important factor in this equation is the fact that the private share of health care spending grew rapidly between 1997 and 1999, caused in part by rapid increases in spending on prescription drugs, which are generally not covered by Medicare. Also, cost-containment strategies of managed care plans may have produced a one-time cost-cutting effect in the 1990s, but this effect is not expected to continue (Heffler et al, 2001). As a result, real health care spending is again projected to grow 4.3% per year on average until 2010, when it is projected to be 15.9% of the GDP (HCFA, OA, 2001; Heffler et al, 2001).

Expenditure on prescription drugs is an important area to single out. The total spending on prescription drugs rose 16.9% in 1999 alone to a high of $100 billion (Heffler et al, 2001). Much of this growth, though, was in private health insurance payments for prescription benefits because the Medicare benefits are at this time limited. There is no prescription drug coverage under original fee-for-service Medicare, and benefits under Medicare+Choice plans are subject to varying deductibles and coverage limits (HCFA, 2000b). Although prescription benefits from private health plans increased, the out-of-pocket share of this spending decreased to 35% of all prescription drug purchases in 1999 from more than 50% in 1993. Prescription drug spending is expected to rise by 14.6% per year between 2000 and 2004. After 2004 drug price increases are expected to slow because a large percentage of brand name drugs will lose patent protection at that time, and generic alternatives will most likely be developed and be affected by price competition (Heffler et al, 2001).

With this change, Berk and Monheit (2001) report that from 1977 to 1996, a very stable 5% of the population has accounted for 55% of the health care expenditures. This has occurred in spite of major changes in financing, including prospective payment systems, managed care predominance, and use of other cost-cutting mechanisms. Those in the lower 50% in health care expenditures spent 3% of the resources. Those in the top 1% in health care expenditures spent an average of $56,459 per year, and those in the bottom 50% used an average of $122 per year in medical costs. They also show that a majority of those in the high-expenditure group were not elderly and that costs were unaffected by enrollment in a managed care plans. Although much health services research is being conducted in this area of high-cost care, more studies are needed using nursing models of care delivery and their effect on cost outcomes.

MANAGED CARE

By 2000 managed care became the dominant health care financing and delivery system in the United States. As of 2000, 165.4 million persons were enrolled in a managed care plan, which is more than triple the 51.1 million persons who were enrolled in an HMO in 1994 and a 600% increase from enrollments in 1988 (Bodenheimer, 1996; Kongstvedt, 2001; Managed Care On Line, 2001). As of June 2000, 55.8% of the total Medicaid population, or 18.8 million persons, were enrolled in managed care plans. This figure represents a 40.1% increase from 1996 to 2000 (HCFA, OA, 2001). As of 2000, 6.9 million Medicare beneficiaries, or 17.2% of the total, were enrolled in managed care plans (Managed Care on Line, 2001).

Managed care had its origins in the early prepaid health plans that have been in existence in the United States from at least the 1920s. A managed care system shifts the emphasis of the provision of health care away from the fee-for-service mode toward a system in which the provider is a "gatekeeper," or manager, of the client's health care. In a managed care system, the provider or insurance company assumes some degree of financial responsibility for the care that is given. According to Curtiss (1989), managed care implies not only that spending will be controlled but also that other aspects of care will be controlled and managed, such as price, quality, and accessibility.

In managed care systems, the primary care provider has traditionally been the gatekeeper, deciding what specialty services are appropriate and where these services can be obtained at the lowest cost. More recently, though, insurance companies themselves are becoming involved in patient care decisions in their attempts to authorize payment for less-expensive procedures. Many providers are questioning this type of intervention in direct patient care and have started their own plans that leave more of the decisions to the providers themselves.

Many types of managed health care plans exist. They range from models that have increased control, accountability, and operating complexity to plans that incorporate some aspects of managed care but not all. Kongstvedt (2001) places these on a continuum from closed-panel HMOs to managed indemnity plans (Figure 14-2). HMOs assume responsibility for organizing and providing compre-

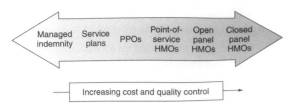

Figure 14-2   Continuum of managed care. (From Kongstvedt, P. [2001]. *Essentials of managed care* [4th ed.]. Gaithersburg, MD: Aspen.)

hensive health care services for members in return for a monthly set payment. HMOs incorporate four key concepts:

- An enrolled population
- A prepayment of premiums
- Coverage of comprehensive medical services
- Centralization of medical and hospital services

Closed-panel HMOs include staff model HMOs, in which physicians/providers are salaried employees, and group model HMOs, which contract with multispecialty physician group practices to provide all physician services to its members.

Open-panel HMOs include network HMOs, which contract with more than one group practice, and the individual practice association (IPA) type of HMOs, which contract with an association of physicians to provide services to members.

In *point-of-service* (POS) plans and in *preferred provider organizations* (PPOs) patients are allowed to self-refer to a specialist but must pay higher premiums if they do so. The POS plan is distinguished from the PPO in that the enrollee belongs to an HMO and must have a designated primary care provider, or gatekeeper, but can opt to see a provider outside of the HMO at a greater cost to the enrollee. PPOs are entities through which employer health plans and insurers contract to purchase health care services for covered beneficiaries from a selected group of participating providers. In PPOs the insurance company generally accepts the financial risk rather than the PPO itself, whereas in POS HMOs, the provider accepts the risk.

The managed indemnity plan is the most traditional model and uses only some managed care mechanisms, such as precertification of elective admissions and case management of catastrophic cases. The service plan may, in addition, have minimal contractual relationships with providers regarding allowable fees (Kongstvedt, 2001).

Provider groups or managed care plans also can incorporate elements of managed care through quality control, utilization review, or bundling of services into units for the purpose of establishing prospective prices (Curtiss, 1989). Many plans attempt to manage quality by providing incentives to increase behaviors that promote a healthy lifestyle, such as smoking cessation or exercise programs. Yet capitation—establishing a monthly payment "per capita," or per enrollee that is independent of actual usage of services—seems to be a key element in containing cost. Although HMOs using capitation have clearly cut the number of hospital admissions and reduced lengths of stay, other forms of managed care have not yet been proved to have a major cost-cutting effect. One reason may be that fee-for-service systems have taught our consumers to shop around for medical care, and the consumer movement has increased the power of the recipients of health care. Managed care systems have clearly moved in the direction of cost containment but have grown in recent years to a predominance of the less-restrictive plans, which limit the gatekeeper function and give consumers more freedom of choice to choose providers. In addition, there has been a proliferation of health plans with low copayments for coverage of drugs. This phenomenon has occurred partially because of a tight labor market, leading employers to offer broader employee benefits in their attempt to attract and retain more workers (Heffler et al, 2001).

The quality of care in managed care organizations has also become a major issue. Many states and the U.S. Congress have passed regulatory legislation in the form of health plan accountability laws to further regulate managed care plans (Kongstvedt, 2001). These laws encompass a variety of areas such as grievance procedures, confidentiality of health information, requirements that patients are fully informed of the benefits they will receive under a managed care plan, antidiscrimination clauses, and assurances that various quality assurance mechanisms are in place so that patient satisfaction is measured and efforts to control costs do not curtail needed care. At least 39 states have adopted policies giving health plan enrollees a right to appeal plan determinations involving a denial of coverage to an independent medical review entity, which is often a private organization approved by the state (American Association of Health Plans, 2001).

THE HEALTH CARE FINANCING SYSTEM IN THE PUBLIC REALM

FEDERAL LEVEL

The health care financing system is composed of many interrelated parts at the federal, state, and local levels. Both government and private sectors play a role at each level. No single entity oversees or controls the entire system. At the federal level, Medicare, Medicaid, and now SCHIP are financed at least in part through the Centers for Medicare and Medicaid Services (CMS, formerly HCFA), an agency of the U.S. Department of Health and Human Services. Federal health expenditures totaled $384.7 billion in 1999, and the federal government financed 31.8% of all health care expenditures in that year (HCFA, OA, 2001). Medicare outlays were $213.6 billion in 1999, and 39.1 million aged and disabled persons were served. Medicaid outlays in 1999 were $108.2 billion, including expenditures for SCHIP expansion, with 31.9 million people receiving care through this program (HCFA, OA, 2001). This represents a decrease in enrollments in the Medicaid program from 33.2 million in 1996, before the Personal Responsibility and Work Opportunities Act came into effect with greater employment of this population and a delinking of Medicaid eligibility and welfarer with the passage of Temporary Assistance for Needy Families (TANF) (HCFA, OA, 2001; Heffler et al, 2001).

Federal Programs. Federal health care programs other than Medicare, Medicaid, and SCHIP exist to provide services for specific segments of the population and are funded from general tax revenues.

Programs for Veterans. Eligible military veterans are covered through the U.S. Department of Veterans Affairs (VA). These veterans can access a wide range of general health and medical services called Civilian Health and Medical Program of the Veterans Administration (CHAMPVA) plus services that are specifically geared to veterans, such as the Agent Orange Health Effects and Vietnam Veterans Programs. The VA funds several notable research initiatives such as the Centers of Excellence in Hepatitis C Research and Education. Elderly veterans are afforded the full range of long-term care programs, hospice programs, home-based primary care, geriatric evaluation and management programs, adult day health care, and respite care. The Foreign Medical Program is a health care benefits program for U.S. veterans with VA-rated service-connected conditions who are residing or traveling abroad. More information is available at www.va.gov.

Military Programs. Active duty service members in the Army, Navy, Air Force, Marine Corps, and Coast Guard and their dependent families are covered through TRICARE, formerly the Civilian Health and Medical Program of the Uniformed Services (CHAMPUS), a program within the Defense Department. This program offers three options to TRICARE-eligible beneficiaries ranging from TRICARE Standard, a benefit similar to the original CHAMPUS program, TRICARE Extra, a network of civilian preferred providers, and TRICARE Prime, which is an HMO-like program. The annual budget expenditure in the Department of Defense (DoD) Health Program is about $21 billion. The CHAMPUS program is notable because it was one of the first federal programs to reimburse nurses for their services (DoD, 2001). An evaluation of this program is available at www.tricare.osd.mil.

Federal Employee Program. The Federal Employees Health Benefits Program (FEHBP) is another federally administered plan that has required direct payment to nurse practitioners (NPs) and physician assistants authorized to practice in their respective states. It is important to remember that just because care is reimbursed through federal policy, it doesn't mean that nurses, as providers of that care, can be covered if state laws interfere. An example is a state with nurse practice acts that limit nurses' scope of practice. For further information, see www.opm.gov/insure/01/index.html.

Native American Program. The Indian Health Service (IHS) is an agency within the U.S. Department of Health and Human Services and provides direct health services to Native American populations throughout the country. The IHS is the principal federal health care provider and health advocate for Indian people, and its goal is to ensure that comprehensive, culturally acceptable personal and public health services are available and accessible to American Indian and Alaska Native people. The IHS currently provides health services to approximately 1.5 million American Indians and Alaska Natives who belong to more than 550 federally recognized tribes in 35 states. For further information see www.ihs.gov.

Programs for Rural Populations. The U.S. Public Health Service provides a wide range of services for rural health. One key program is the National Health Service Corps (www.bphc.hrsa. gov/nhsc) and other initiatives that provide services in rural health areas and which fund rural health clinics.

Medicaid. Medicaid is a jointly funded program of both federal and state governments, and until 1997, eligibility was determined by income and resources. Those eligible included persons receiving Aid to Families with Dependent Children (AFDC); persons older than 65 years of age who are income eligible; blind and totally disabled persons who received cash assistance under the Supplemental Security Income (SSI) program; pregnant women; and children born after September 1983 in families with incomes at or below the poverty line. To qualify for federal Medicaid matching grants, a state must provide a minimum set of benefits, including hospitalization, physician care, laboratory services, x-ray studies, prenatal care, and preventive services; nursing home and home health care; and medically necessary transportation. Medicaid programs are also required to pay the Medicare premiums, deductibles, and copayments for certain low-income persons (Bodenheimer & Grumbach, 1998).

Eligibility and Populations Covered. In 1997 major changes began to occur in Medicaid, particularly in eligibility requirements. Public law (PL) 104-193, the Personal Responsibility and Work Opportunities Act of 1996, eliminated the AFDC cash assistance program and replaced it with a block grant program called Temporary Assistance to Needy Families (TANF). Under this welfare law, Medicaid was delinked from AFDC and SSI so that automatic coverage is not guaranteed. By September 1997 states were required to redetermine the Medicaid eligibility of many individuals, including children currently eligible for SSI and many individuals who are not U.S. citizens or who had been receiving disability cash assistance (SSI) based on alcoholism and drug addiction. Under PL 104-193, states are permitted to deny Medicaid benefits to adults and heads of household who lose TANF benefits because of refusal to work. However, this law exempts poor pregnant women and children from this provision and mandates their continued Medicaid eligibility (HCFA, 1997a).

As an optional service, states may continue to cover the "medically needy." These individuals are often poor or have spent enough on medical bills to bring them to poverty level after a catastrophic illness. However, they earn too much money to qualify for TANF or SSI and would be eligible for one of these programs only by virtue of being in a family with dependent children, more than 65 years of age, blind, or totally and permanently disabled. It is under this medically needy category that many elderly individuals or persons with life-threatening chronic illnesses such as acquired immune deficiency syndrome (AIDS) may qualify for Medicaid (Bodenheimer & Grumbach, 1998).

Medicaid is increasingly becoming a long-term care program of last resort for elderly persons in nursing homes. Many of them had to "spend down" their life savings to become eligible for Medicaid. In 1998 67% of those receiving Medicaid were low-income adults or children, but they accounted for 26% of Medicaid's total expenditures, whereas 26% of those receiving Medicaid were elderly or disabled persons living in nursing homes or long-term care facilities, and this group accounted for 71% of Medicaid's expenditures (HCFA, OA, 2001).

Family NPs, pediatric NPs, geriatric NPs, and certified nurse midwives must also be reimbursed under Medicaid if, in accordance with state regulations, they are legally authorized to provide Medicaid-covered services. NPs are working to promote the passage of legislation that mandates Medicaid managed care plans to recognize all NPs as primary care providers within provider panels (American College of Nurse Practitioners, 2001).

Current Financing. Medicaid is funded partially by a general fund allocation of the federal budget but is a matching government program with state revenue budget allocations. It was originally intended as a dollar-for-dollar match between state and federal governments. However, the federal matching formula is calculated on a per capita income base, so many of the poorer states actually pay less than half and do not match dollar for dollar. In 2000, Medicaid served the needs of 33.7 million of the nation's poor, and roughly 25% of enrollees live below the federal poverty level (HCFA, OA, 2001).

As stated earlier, Medicaid programs in the states are increasingly using managed care organizations to provide care for recipients. In many states, waivers afford the state flexibility to: (1) develop and implement creative alternatives to placing Medicaid-eligible individuals in medical facilities such as nursing- or community-based facilities (home- and community-based waivers), or (2) waive the requirement that beneficiaries may select their own Medicaid providers (freedom of choice waivers). States may also apply for research and demonstration waivers that test new policy ideas related to Medicaid. Because of the waivers, the TANF block granting process, and SCHIP, many are concerned that state Medicaid programs are so diverse that we have, in essence, 50 different Medicaid programs nationwide.

Child Health Provision of the 1997 Balanced Budget Act. As was discussed earlier, an important development in the BBA of 1997 was the inclusion of $24 billion in child health block grants over 5 years for the SCHIP. SCHIP funds can be used to expand Medicaid, to create a new state program for children's health insurance, or to do both. Up to 10% of a state's allocation can be spent on a combination of administrative costs, outreach, direct health services for children, and other health initiatives. Depending on the state, children with family incomes at or below 200% of the federal poverty level may be covered. A state running a child health insurance program must provide, at a minimum, the benefits covered by certain specified, commercial health insurance plans. To receive federal funds, a state must pay matching amounts. The state's matching percentage is 70% of its matching rate under Medicaid (Children's Defense Fund, 2001).

In 1998 $4.2 billion was allocated to states, which had 3 years to spend the money to enroll uninsured or underinsured children in this program. By September 30, 2000, which marked the end of the third year of SCHIP, all 50 states had chosen to participate in this grant program, but only 3.3 million of the over 9 million uninsured children had enrolled, and $2 billion remained unspent. At this point only 12 states had used all of their CHIP monies. In December 2000 Congress passed the "Medicare, Medicaid and SCHIP Benefits Improvement and Protection Act of 2000," which adjusted the funding formula for how the unspent 1998 monies would be reallocated to states (Children's Defense Fund, 2001).

Medicare. Medicare legislation was passed in 1965 as an amendment (Title 18) to the Social Security Act of 1935, to enable older people pay for their health care in retirement. Before enactment of Medicare, elders were more likely to be uninsured and more likely to be impoverished by excessive health care costs. This was particularly true for the "oldest old." According to the National Center for Health Statistics (cited in Lubitz et al., 2001), in 1962 and 1963, 61% of persons between ages 65 and 74 and only 41% of persons aged 75 and older had hospital insurance. Before the enactment of Medicare, half of older Americans had no health insurance; today 96% of seniors have health care coverage through Medicare (Federal Interagency Forum on Age-Related Statistics, 2000). As evidence of Medicare's beneficial economic effect, the percentage of persons over age 65 living below the poverty line decreased from 35% in 1959, when elders had the highest poverty rate of the population, to 11% in 1998 (Federal Interagency Forum on Age-Related Statistics, 2000). Medicare has also had a beneficial effect on the health of the elderly, facilitating access to care and to medical technology (Lubitz et al, 2001).

Eligibility and Populations Covered. Medicare coverage includes Part A, hospital insurance (HI), and Part B, supplementary medical insurance (SMI). Individuals are eligible for Medicare Part A at age 65, the age for Social Security eligibility. Part A is financed through payroll deduction to the Hospital Insurance Trust Fund at the current payroll tax rate of 1.45% (Social Security and Medicare Boards of Trustees, 2001). All Americans (and their spouses) who have worked for at least 10 years and have paid Medicare taxes are automatically enrolled in Part A. Disabled persons younger than 65 who are receiving Social Security disability benefits (Supplemental Security Income), may also enroll in Part A after a 24-month waiting period. This waiting period was waived, under the Consolidated Appropriations Act of 2001, for persons with amyotrophic lateral sclerosis (ALS). Persons with permanent renal disease who are undergoing dialysis or who have had a renal transplant are also eligible for Part A, regardless of age. Part A offers partial coverage for 150 days of inpatient hospital treatment per benefit period and up to 100 days of posthospital care in a SNF. Medicare reimbursement for hospital costs is subject to a $792 deductible per benefit period for the first 60 days of hospitalization, followed by a daily deductible of $198 per day for days 61 through 90, and $396 per day for days 91 through 150 (HCFA, 2001a). Part A also pays for "medically necessary" part-time skilled home care services and for 20% of the costs of durable medical equipment. Hospice benefits, through a Medicare-certified hospice program, are provided under Part A for individuals who have a life expectancy of less than 6 months. Under the Medicare hospice program, traditional Medicare benefits are expanded to include partial prescription drug coverage for analgesics, 95% of respite care costs, skilled care from nurses and therapists, and medical equipment and supplies (HCFA, 2000b).

Current Financing. Persons enrolled in Medicare Part A may choose to sign up for Part B, which partially covers outpatient services. Part B is funded through the SMI Trust Fund, which is supported by enrollee contributions and a share of general revenues. Enrollee contributions generally contribute approximately 25% ($21 billion in 2000) of Part B costs, with the remaining 75% ($66 billion in 2000) coming from general revenues (Social Security and Medicare Boards of Trustees, 2001). Under the provisions of the Balanced Budget Act of 1997, a prospective payment system was established for some services covered under Part B. These include outpatient services such as immunizations, casting, partial hospitalization for mental health disorders, and other services traditionally covered under Part B. Under PPS Medicare reimburses the provider a set amount for these services. The consumer may be responsible for a copayment (Social Security Administration, 2000a).

Individuals must apply for Part B during a 7-month enrollment period that starts 3 months before their 65th birthday. For those who delay enrollment, the cost of Part B goes up by 10% for each year that Part B could have been in place, resulting in increased consumer lifetime costs (HCFA, 2001b). Part B requires a yearly $100 deductible and a monthly copayment by enrollees ($50 in 2001). Covered services include 80% of the fees for physician services, outpatient medical services and supplies, home care, durable medical equipment, laboratory services, physical and occupational therapy, and outpatient mental health services (Social Security Administration, 2000a; HCFA, 2001a).

Gaps in Medicare Coverage. Despite its success in facilitating the provision of basic health care to elders, significant gaps in Medicare coverage remain. Medicare has maintained an acute care focus that has led to inadequate coverage for preventive services, case management, prescription drugs, vision and hearing services, and, most significantly, long-term care and catastrophic illness coverage (Cassel, Besdine, & Siegel, 1999). *Custodial* long-term care is not covered under Part B, an omission that shifts provision of care for the approximately 12 million Americans who need long-term care to families and to the Medicaid program (Feder, Komisar, & Niefeld, 2000). Another gap in Part B coverage is reimbursement for certain preventive services. Although Medicare has expanded Part B reimbursement for preventive care to cover mammogram screening, Pap smears, prostate and colorectal cancer screening, diabetes monitoring, and immunizations, important preventive services such as vision care, dental care and dentures, routine foot care, and routine annual physical exams are not covered (Cassel et al, 1999; Social Security Administration 2000a).

Fee-for-Service Versus Managed Care Medicare. At its inception in 1965, Medicare was modeled after private employer-provided fee-for-service insurance plans (Atherly, 2001). With passage of the 1997 BBA, Medicare enrollees, under the Medicare+Choice program, were given a choice of three Medicare plans. These include the original Medicare fee-for-service coverage, Medicare managed care, and privately insured fee-for-service Medicare. Medicare+Choice was designed to involve the private sector in the provision of care to Medicare patients. A second goal was to increase competition among Medicare providers and thus lower costs (Neuman & Langwell, 1999). The original Medicare fee-for-service plan, which covered 83% of Medicare beneficiaries in 2000 (Oberlander, 2000), offers the beneficiary a choice of hospital and provider. It requires, however, the payment of an annual deductible, a fee each time the service is used, and the payment of the difference between the Medicare-approved amount for the covered service and the Medicare payment (i.e., "balance billing"). Under this plan consumers pay considerable out-of-pocket charges for health care, including charges for "Medigap" insurance to supplement services not covered under Medicare. Over the past 10 years, out-of-pocket expenses for health care have increased for elders across all income groups, with the poor paying a larger portion of their income for health care. In 1998, according to the Federal Interagency Forum on Age-Related Statistics (2000, p. 42), persons in the bottom fifth of the income distribution spent 13% of their resources on health care, whereas those in the top fifth spent 9%.

Unlike the original Medicare fee-for-service plan, private fee-for-service Medicare pays fixed monthly payments to certain plans, from which beneficiaries purchase private indemnity health insurance policies. The consumer maintains choice of provider and health care setting and receives extra services such as partial prescription drug coverage, but the individual must pay deductibles and premium fees that may exceed those charged by the original Medicare. The plan, not the provider, determines the rate of provider reimbursement, and providers may be allowed to balance-bill Medicare patients 15% above the payment level set by the plan. Medicare private fee-for-service is not available in all areas. Patients with end stage renal disease, covered under original Medicare, are not covered under private fee-for-service (HCFA, 1999).

Although the majority of Medicare recipients remain in the fee-for-service sector (Federal Interagency Forum on Age-Related Statistics, 2000), Medicare managed care has received increased attention as a strategy to control costs. In 1983, Congress, under the Tax Equity and Fiscal Responsibility Act (TEFRA), authorized Medicare payments to qualified "risk-contract" HMOs (Social Security Administration, 2000a). In risk plans, now called "coordinated care plans," the beneficiary is required to receive all services from within the organization's network of providers. Medicare beneficiaries can also enroll in "cost plans." Under cost plans, care may be received outside of the provider network or service area. Under Medicare+Choice, several managed care options, including PPOs and PSOs, were added to the risk HMO option. All Medicare+Choice plans are required to institute a quality assurance program to monitor and report quality indicators and health outcome measures (Jencks et al, 2000).

Subscribers to Medicare HMO plans must be enrolled in Medicare Part B and are required to pay a copayment for services. Costs not covered under fee-for-service Medicare, including preventive care and prescription drugs, may be covered under Medicare managed care plans (Social Security Administration, 2000a). Participation in a managed care plan may offer additional consumer savings by negating the need for supplemental Medigap insurance.

There was steady growth in enrollment in managed care plans in the early 1990s, with doubling of enrollment between 1993 and 1997. This early growth was fueled by the prospect of low premiums and extended benefits, including prescription drug coverage (Oberlander, 2000). In the last 2 years, however, there has been a decline in Medicare HMO enrollments and a return of some beneficiaries to the fee-for-service sector. According to Oberlander (2000), enrollment in Medicare HMOs reached a peak of 6.4 million in 1999 and has since steadily declined. This decline is related to both patient disenrollment and to HMO withdrawal from the market.

Several explanations have been offered to explain patient disenrollment from Medicare managed care, including restriction in choice of providers, restrained access to care, and caps on prescription drug benefits (Baker & Weisbrot, 1999). Rector (2000), in a large study of Medicare beneficiaries in four network-model health plans, found that exhaustion of prescription drug benefits, as a result of caps on drug coverage, was associated with a twofold increase in the likelihood of voluntary disenrollment by beneficiaries.

According to Ahl and Wergin (2000), more than 1.5 million elders had disenrolled from a Medicare risk HMO by January 1, 2000, primarily as a result of the HMO's leaving the Medicare market or reducing service area coverage. Medicare+Choice plans dropped coverage for more than 750,000 enrollees in 1998 and 1999 and dropped another 930,000 in 2000 (Etheredge, 2000). Attempts to reduce Medicare costs by increasing HMO enrollment have not resulted in financial benefits for the HMO provider organizations. It has been proposed that the sickest Medicare patients, who account for the majority of Medicare costs, enrolled in Medicare managed care programs in order to obtain prescription drug coverage. If prescription drug use is a proxy for overall health status, these patients use more health services as well (Baker & Weisbrot, 1999; Rector, 2000). In order to remain financially viable, managed care organizations must either cap services or raise premiums. With reimbursement rates set by Medicare, there is little opportunity for the latter. In addition, there is variation in Medicare reimbursement by region, conferring additional financial strain on managed care programs in low reimbursement areas (Neuman & Langwell, 1999; Cooper & Vladeck, 2000; Dowd, Coulam & Feldman, 2000; Healthcare Financial Management Association, 2000).

Medicare Reform. According to the Social Security and Medicare Boards of Trustees (2001), the HI Trust Fund, which is financed through payroll taxes, will remain solvent until 2029 but is at risk for insolvency because of a growing gap between income and costs. The SMI Trust Fund is at less risk because the majority of costs are funded through general revenues and anticipated costs are budgeted each year. Costs for both HI and SMI are projected to grow from 2.3% of GDP in 2001 to 4.5% in 2030 and 8.5% in 2075. Revenues, particularly from payroll contributions to HI, will not keep up with costs, however, and are projected to increase from 2.4% of GDP in 2001 to 5.3% in 2075.

Because the shift by some beneficiaries to Medicare managed care in the 1990s did not produce intended savings, there have been numerous proposals for insuring the solvency of Medicare. Proposals for Medicare reform include delaying the age of retirement; increasing payroll taxes for higher income taxpayers; offering so-called premium support (where Medicare pre-funds premiums for individuals) to Medicare enrollees to encourage them to join HMOs; and improved risk-sharing between Medicare and HMOs (Burman, Penner, Steuerle, Toder, Moon, Thompson, Weisner, & Carasso, 1998; Etheredge, 1999; 2000; Dowd, Coulam & Feldman, 2000; Gorin, 2000; Oberlander, 2000; Seidman, 2000). The 1997 Balanced Budget Act attempted to modernize Medicare financing and created the National Bipartisan Commission on the Future of Medicare, with the aim of long-term structural reform. The BBA mandated demonstration projects to test the hypothesis that applying market principles could cut Medicare costs (Nichols & Reischauer, 2000). The Medicare Medical Savings Account Plan, for example, was proposed as one premium-support model with potential cost-savings to both consumers and to Medicare.

Medical savings account (MSA) plans have two components: a tax-sheltered Medicare-funded savings account for health care expenses and a private catastrophic health insurance plan with a high deductible (not more than $6000) (HCFA, 1998; Kendix & Lubitz, 1999). Recipients receive a capitated (capped) amount from Medicare, equal to

95% of the traditional costs of fee-for-service Medicare. From the capitated amount, Medicare pays the premium for the catastrophic insurance and deposits money into the individual's MSA. Money in the savings account is used to pay the deductible on the insurance policy, if needed. Beneficiaries who have insufficient money in the savings account must pay the balance of the deductible out of private funds. If the beneficiary does not use the money in the savings account in a given year, the money accumulates in the savings account for use in another year. MSAs could potentially cut Medicare costs, because Medicare saves 5% on the capitated amount. Consumers would also be motivated to save health care dollars, because they would be responsible for costs incurred over the amount in the MSA up to the deductible. MSAs would also eliminate the need for supplemental, or Medigap, coverage, again resulting in consumer savings (Kendix & Lubitz, 1999).

MSAs and other attempts at premium support have been criticized for moving the healthiest and wealthiest persons from traditional fee-for-service Medicare to the private insurance sector. This results in overall increased costs to the Medicare system (Baker & Weisbrot, 1999; Kendix & Lubitz, 1999; Oberlander, 2000). According to Oberlander (2000), premium-support plans actually reduce choice for many Medicare recipients, who are already overwhelmed by the options available under Medicare+Choice. These elders, many of whom will be chronically ill, frail, and financially challenged, will choose a plan according to what they can afford, rather than according to what they need. The issues facing this group, particularly coverage for prescription drugs and long-term care, must be addressed by proponents of Medicare reform.

Prescription Drug Coverage. An increased proportion of personal health care spending is attributable to growing expenditures on prescription drugs. Owing to more intense direct advertising by drug companies, augmented in insurance copayments for prescriptions, and the increase in numbers of persons with chronic illnesses, the percentage of personal income spent on prescription drug coverage is anticipated to reach 16% by 2010 (Heffler et al, 2001). Seventy-three percent of Medicare

beneficiaries had some prescription drug coverage in 1998 (Poisal & Murray, 2001), either through Medigap policies, HMO enrollment, or coinsurance by Medicaid. Continuity of coverage over time is problematic, however. Stuart, Shea and Briesacher (2001) noted that fewer than half of noninstitutionalized Medicare beneficiaries had continuous coverage over a 2-year period in 1995 and 1996. Lack of prescription coverage has implications for both health and financial well-being because elders who do not have prescription coverage use fewer medications and pay more for medications out-of-pocket than do those with prescription coverage (Frank, 2001).

Prescription drugs are not covered under original Medicare fee-for-service, and a growing number of Medicare+Choice plans are either capping prescription coverage or increasing out-of-pocket costs to consumers. To date, efforts to expand prescription drug coverage have been unsuccessful. In 1999, for example, the Clinton administration proposed an expansion of Medicare, Part D, envisioned as a voluntary program similar to Medicare Part B, under which 50% of prescription costs would be reimbursed up to a specified cap. Part D would be financed partly through premiums and partly through the general revenues, adding approximately $136 billion to federal Medicare costs (Christensen & Wagner, 2000). This proposal was unsuccessful, however, and concerns about the need for additional federal revenues, consumer worries about additional Medicare premium costs, and pharmaceutical industry concerns about price control have stalled progress on prescription drug coverage (Christensen & Wagner, 2000; Iglehart, 2000).

Home Care. Trends in Medicare spending reflect a decrease in inpatient hospital costs and an increase in Medicare payments to both home care and skilled nursing facilities. Expenses for hospital care declined as a percentage of the Medicare budget from 70% in 1967 to 49% in 1998 (Lubitz et al, 2001). Spending on home care, however, grew dramatically in the 1980s and early 1990s, increasing an average of 31% per year from 1988 to 1996. Proliferation of home care programs was encouraged by a payment system that reimbursed agencies on a per-visit basis. The 1997 BBA, however, dramatically revised the payment system, shifting first to an Interim Payment System (IPS) and in October 2000 to a PPS for home care. Since the implementation of IPS, the number of home care visits dropped dramatically. From the implementation of IPS in 1997 to the fourth quarter of 1999, total Medicare spending per quarter declined from $4 billion to $1.8 billion (McCall, Komisar, Petersons, & Moore, 2001). Savings to Medicare, however, resulted in a cost shift to Medicaid and to private funding by consumers: A decline of $6.1 billion in Medicare spending since 1996 has been partially offset by an increase in Medicaid spending by $1.1 billion and by an increase of $4.4 billion in total private spending (Heffler et al., 2001).

The Medicare home care benefit is based on "medical necessity," with the provision of visits tied to an episode of care related to recovery from an acute illness. This model, however, fails to consider the need for ongoing custodial care that would provide compensation for the functional limitations that impede frail elders' abilities to stay in their own homes, avoiding nursing home placement (Cassel et al, 1999). Since the implementation of IPS, this medical model of care has been reinforced. The number of home health aide visits per quarter has declined by half, and the number of skilled visits (nursing and therapies) has increased. These visit trends reflect, according to McCall and colleagues (2001), the BBA's goal of controlling and limiting personal care costs.

Long-Term Care. Despite the widespread consumer belief that Medicare covers long-term care, only limited benefits are provided for SNF care, with no coverage for chronic custodial care. As the proportion of the oldest and frailest elders has increased, Medicare spending on skilled nursing facility care has grown dramatically. Two factors influencing the growth of SNFs were implementation of the hospital prospective payment system in 1983, which shifted care of elders from acute care to subacute SNFs, and the 1988 Catastrophic Coverage Act (repealed in 1989), which reduced restrictions on reimbursement for skilled nursing facility care (Lubitz et al, 2001). Provisions of the 1997 BBA limited SNF benefits and resulted in a decline in

Medicare SNF spending growth from 15.4% in 1997 to 6.5% in 1998, with a further 9.6% drop in 1999 (Heffler et al, 2001). The 1999 Balanced Budget Refinement Act (BBRA) increased nursing home reimbursement for the sickest elderly; consequently, Medicare spending for nursing home care is expected to increase 10.8% on average between 2000 and 2001 (Heffler et al, 2001).

Because Medicare does not cover most long-term care costs, particularly costs for chronic custodial care, long-term care expenses account for a considerable portion of elders' out-of-pocket health care expenditures. Out-of-pocket expenses represent 14% of medical care expenditures for elders, but they account for 28% of their long-term care costs (Cohen, Miller, & Weinrobe, 2001).

Medicaid is a significant payor for long-term care (accounting for 40% of long-term care financing in 1998 [Feder, Komisar, & Niefeld, 2000]), but it requires that elders spend down their assets before becoming eligible for reimbursement. This requirement has created a financial incentive for beneficiaries to spend down and transfer their assets in order to become Medicaid-eligible. The Health Insurance Portability and Accountability Act of 1996 included a provision that makes it a federal crime to purposefully transfer assets within 3 years of applying for Medicaid. The BBA clarified this provision to include estate planners and lawyers who knowingly assist consumers in transferring or hiding assets in order to qualify for Medicaid (Kaiser Commission on Medicaid Facts, 2001).

Because Medicare does not cover most long-term care costs, private insurers have entered the market. Long-term care insurance generally includes some combination of home care benefits and coverage for nursing home care. Although there was an annual average growth rate of 21% in sales of long-term insurance from 1987 to 1997, consumers have been reluctant to purchase long-term care insurance because of high premium costs and because of the general belief that such coverage is unnecessary (Temkin-Greener, Mukamel, & Meiners, 2000/2001). There have been several legislative initiatives, including proposed tax credits, to encourage purchase of this insurance. Beginning in 1997, for example, persons with long-term care policies can exempt from taxable income the first $68,875 in annual long-term care insurance benefits. Newer initiatives, such as Senate bill 627, proposed by Senators Grassley (R-IA) and Graham (D-FL), would issue tax credits for both the provision of long-term care and the purchase of long-term care insurance. In addition, employers would be encouraged to offer long-term care insurance, as well as flexible spending accounts, as employee benefits. Other incentives include "public-private partnerships," state programs that would allow persons with private long-term care insurance asset protection if nursing home costs exceed their insurance coverage (Mellor, 2000).

Nurse Practitioner Reimbursement and Medicare. The Omnibus Budget and Reconciliation Act (OBRA) of 1997 extended Medicare Part B coverage of NP and clinical nurse specialist (CNS) services. Earlier legislation (OBRA, 1990) provided reimbursement for NPs and CNSs in rural areas. OBRA 1997 extended coverage of nurse-provided services, removing geographic and setting restrictions. Under this legislation, all NPs and CNSs are able to obtain a Medicare provider number and directly bill Medicare for reimbursement at 85% of the Medicare physician fee schedule for services that they are legally authorized to perform under their state practice acts. NPs or CNSs may bill for services that they provide directly or that they provide "incident to" services provided by a physician. The new regulations do not require a physician to be on-site when an NP is delivering care in order for NP services to be reimbursed. Neither does the law require that physicians make an independent evaluation of all NP or CNS patients. There is a requirement, however, for physician "collaboration," loosely defined as a relationship with a physician that enables consultation on cases outside the nurse's scope of practice (Abood & Keepnews, 2000).

Social Security. Although America has always valued individualism, the Great Depression of the 1930s taught U.S. workers that they were financially vulnerable because of factors beyond their control. The Social Security Act of 1935 provided a base of economic security that allowed older Americans to live with dignity and independence. The act was carefully crafted to distinguish the program from welfare programs and to promote its acceptance as social insurance.

Principles of Social Security. Social Security was established based on the following principles (Kingson & Schulz, 1997; Schulz, 2001; Steuerle & Bakija, 2000):

Individual equity or fairness. This principle means that the amount a worker pays into the system determines how much he or she will earn in benefits.

Social adequacy (horizontal equity). According to this principle, benefits are calculated by means of a weighted formula that ensures a minimum floor of protection for workers with lower lifetime earnings. Benefits are also adjusted for inflation, which offsets financial erosion with time. The concept of social insurance and protection of individual dignity evolved from this principle. The social insurance aspect includes three important tenets. First, insurance protection is provided not only to workers, but also to their dependents. Second, all eligible workers participate; individuals cannot opt out of the system. Exceptions to eligibility include most federal employees hired before 1984, railroad employees with more than 10 years of service, some state and local employees, and children under age 21 who work for a parent (Social Security Administration, 2001b). Third, contributors are protected against destitution by pooling risk of lost income among all contributors.

Economic efficiency. This principle dictates that the highest possible benefits be provided to retirees with minimum administrative costs both to the beneficiary and to the nation.

Individual dignity. A belief in individual dignity dictates that there be no means test for a person to qualify for benefits and that benefits be considered a statutory right.

Eligibility and Populations Covered. To be eligible for Social Security, one must earn 40 credits—one credit for each $830 of earnings (Social Security Administration, 2001b)—by working and paying taxes into Social Security for approximately 10 years. The amount of Social Security benefits received is based on a formula that takes into consideration earnings, wage inflation, and, until 2003, intended retirement date (whether the beneficiary is planning to retire early, with reduced benefits, starting at age 62 or to wait for full benefits at age 65). After 2003 the retirement age will gradually increase to age 66 for persons born in 1950 and beyond and up to age 67 for those born in 1960 or later (Social Security Administration, 2000b).

Approximately 45 million Americans (9 of every 10 retirees) collect some type of Social Security benefit (Social Security Administration, 2000a). The majority (approximately 66%) do so because of retirement, but others collect because they are disabled, a dependent of someone who receives Social Security, or a spouse or a child of a Social Security beneficiary who has died. Social Security is the major source of income for two-thirds of the elderly and the sole source of income for one third of elders. Social Security provides approximately 40% of the average worker's preretirement earnings (Social Security Administration, 2000a).

Current Financing. Social Security is financed through the Federal Insurance Contributions Act (FICA), which authorizes payroll deductions for Social Security. In 2001 the Social Security part of the tax was 7.65% of gross wages, up to $80,400 in wages (Social Security and Medicare Boards of Trustees, 2001). Employers match the workers' tax payment. Self-employed persons pay taxes equal to the combined employer-employee tax, but half of this payment is deductible as a business expense. These taxes are deposited in the Social Security Trust Funds, financial accounts in the U.S. Treasury from which Social Security and Medicare benefits are paid. There are four Social Security trust funds:

- Old Age and Survivors Insurance (OASI)
- Disability Insurance (DI)
- Hospital Insurance Trust Fund (HI, or Medicare Part A)
- Supplementary Medical Insurance (SMI, or Medicare Part B)

The 7.65% Social Security tax deduction is allocated as follows: 5.30% to the OASI, 0.9% to the DI (combined 6.20% to OASDI) and 1.45% to the HI (Social Security and Medicare Boards of Trustees, 2001). Persons who make more than $80,400, the

ceiling for OASDI deductions, continue to pay Hospital Insurance (HI) taxes (1.45%) on all earnings. Currently, the Social Security Trust Funds take in more per month than they pay out: In 2000, income to OASDI was $568.4 billion, with outflow of $438.7 billion. The surplus is deposited daily in U.S. Treasury Bonds, which are the safest, but also one of the lowest-paying, financial investments. In 2001, total tax contributions to OASI are projected to be $604 billion, with expenditures to beneficiaries of $439 billion (Social Security and Medicare Boards of Trustees, 2001).

The "social insurance" aspect of Social Security makes the program more than just a retirement plan. The Social Security Administration refers to Social Security as "America's Family Protection Plan" (Social Security Administration, 2000b). In addition to retirement benefits, Social Security pays survivor benefits to spouses age 60 or older (50 or older if disabled) and to spouses of any age if the spouse is caring for one child under age 16, for multiple children under age 18, or for a parent if the earner had provided more than one half of the parent's support. In addition, Social Security pays a one-time $255 lump sum death benefit to a spouse or minor children (Schulz, 2001; Social Security Administration, 2000a).

Social Security was never designed to be the only source of retirement income. Retirement income is seen as a *three-legged stool,* with one leg as Social Security benefits, the second as pension income, and the third as personal savings and investments. Social Security is seen as replacing 40% of a worker's salary after retirement; it thus provides a "safety net," but not the entire amount (approximately 70% of preretirement income) necessary to support a comfortable retirement (Social Security Administration, 2000b).

Solvency: "Social Insecurity." Current projections by the Social Security and Medicare Boards of Trustees (2001) show the Social Security Trust Funds will be adequately funded until 2038. OASI funds will be able to pay full benefits until 2040 and DI until 2026. Starting in 2016, however, expenditures will exceed revenues, owing to enhanced longevity, increased numbers of retirees, and proportionately fewer younger workers paying into the system (Social Security and Medicare Boards of Trustees, 2001). The Social Security Administration estimates that 76 million baby boomers will begin retiring in 2010 and that the number of workers paying into Social Security will drop from 3.4 to 2.1 (Social Security Administration, 2000b). There is widespread apprehension, among the public and among legislators and policy analysts, that Social Security will be unable to provide the promised safety net for future generations of retirees. The actual extent of the crisis is hotly disputed, with both liberals and conservatives weighing in on reform proposals. These proposals include privatizing Social Security, changing eligibility requirements, decreasing cost of living adjustments (COLAs), and raising payroll taxes.

Privatization of Social Security. Advocates for privatization of Social Security argue that the current system of investing Social Security revenues in U.S. Treasury bonds will not provide a rate of return sufficient to meet the retirement needs of today's younger workers. Rather than a pay-as-you-go system, "privatizers" argue, Social Security needs to be an individually controlled savings plan, with some funds invested in private securities. Under pay-as-you-go, workers pay into the system with the promise that they will be entitled to funds when they retire. There is currently no guarantee that funds will be available to future generations, especially with the anticipated decline in the proportion of workers to retirees. Proponents of privatization contend that the current rate of return on private investments exceeds the achievable rate of return on Social Security funds (2.2% for persons born in 1950 [Schulz, 2001]) and that an enhanced rate of return will compensate for future shortfalls in contributions to the system (Cordes & Steuerle, 1999). Opponents of privatization assert that the rate of return from private investment is overestimated, claiming that these returns are subject to the vagaries of the stock market and that over time, the rate of return would not exceed the current rate for Treasury bonds (Baker & Weisbrot, 1999; Williamson, 2001).

Eligibility Requirements. The age of retirement at which persons receive Social Security benefits was adjusted by the 1983 Social Security

Amendments on the assumption that future generations of retirees would be healthier and would live an increasingly long period of time after retirement. Beginning in 2000, for workers born in 1938 or later, the retirement age increases gradually from age 65 to age 67 by the year 2022 (Social Security Administration, 2001b). Some would delay the age of retirement still further. Opponents of this proposal note that both life expectancy and health status differ among economic and racial groups and that increasing the retirement age would place undue burden on minority and lower-income individuals (Baker & Weisbrot, 1999). Delaying retirement age also goes against the current trend toward earlier retirement. In 1950 the typical man retired at age 69; in 1994 the average male retiree was under 64 years old (Burman et al, 1998). Potential retirees' desire for more leisure time, as well as the impetus by employers to make way for younger workers, may constrain efforts to postpone retirement age. Proposed incentives include eliminating the Social Security tax after age 65, allowing Medicare to take effect before Social Security eligibility, and creating wage subsidies (Earned Income Tax Credit) for persons over 65 (Burman et al, 1998).

Means testing. One of the basic principles of Social Security was its universality. The program has received wide political support because all workers are eligible for Social Security, regardless of income. Social Security is more than a welfare program that benefits only the poor. Some Social Security reform proposals have included the concept of "means testing," which would restrict Social Security benefits to persons who meet an income standard and who demonstrate financial need. Advocates of means testing propose that allocating Social Security benefits to wealthier elders is costly and actually takes benefits away from recipients who are in greater financial need (Baker & Weisbrot, 1999). Opponents of means testing cite its incompatibility with the basic principles of Social Security. Critics note that adoption of means testing would turn Social Security into a welfare program, incur enhanced administrative costs, serve as a disincentive to retirement saving, and weaken political support for the program (Kingson & Schulz, 1997;

Baker & Weisbrot, 1999; Blahous, 2000; Steuerle & Bakija, 2000; Schulz, 2001).

Decreasing cost of living adjustments. Social Security recipients currently receive an annual cost of living adjustment (COLA), based on the Consumer Price Index (CPI). In 2002, based on the increase in the CPI from the third quarter of 2000 through the third quarter of 2001, Social Security and SSI beneficiaries will receive a 2.6% COLA (Social Security Administration, 2002). Conservatives have proposed less-generous COLAs as a means of saving Social Security. Liberals criticize this proposal, saying that decreasing COLAs would have a regressive effect on lower-income workers and women. According to Weisbrot (Baker & Weisbrot, 1999), if COLAs had been decreased 10 years ago, over 600,000 more seniors would be living in poverty now.

Raising payroll taxes. According to Steuerle and Bakija (2000), from the inception of Social Security it was apparent that the aging population would continue to grow, that taxes would be unable to keep up with expenditures, and that eventually, a political limit on more taxation would be reached. The Trustees of Social Security now estimate that over the next 75 years, actuarial balance could be achieved by a 13% reduction in benefits, a 15% increase in payroll taxes, or some combination of the two (Social Security and Medicare Boards of Trustees, 2001). Payroll taxes have risen steadily since the start of Social Security, to a current combined (employer and employee) rate of 15.3% (Social Security Administration, 2001a). The 1983 Social Security Amendment, by including federal employees and other previously noncovered workers under Social Security, increased the potential tax base. This legislation also imposed an income tax on Social Security earnings above a defined minimum ($32,000 for married couples and $25,000 for singles in 2000 [Social Security Administration, 2000a]). The issue of raising taxes even more is hotly debated. Proponents of increasing the payroll tax cite the possible bankruptcy of Social Security after 2020 when the majority of the Baby Boomers are retired (Schulz, 2001). Opponents note that increasing payroll taxes places an undue burden on lower-income workers, for whom the tax is *regressive,* representing an increased percent-

age of total income compared with the rate for higher-income workers. Tax increases also impose a greater burden on later birth cohorts (born in 1970 or later), for whom the rate of return on payroll taxes will be proportionately less. There is also a level at which raising payroll tax rates becomes intolerable to taxpayers and politically unacceptable (Kingson & Schulz, 1997; Baker & Weisbrot, 1999; Blahous, 2000; Schulz, 2001).

STATE LEVEL

Some federal health programs such as Medicaid and the SCHIP are administered at the state level. Another example of state administration of a federal program is the Title V Maternal-Child Block Grant Program, which has as its objective the improvement of maternal, infant, and adolescent health and the development of service systems for children at risk of chronic and disabling conditions.

States also have an important role in designing health policy through health planning efforts and in regulating health care costs and insurance carriers through rate-setting efforts. States take on responsibility for ensuring quality health services through oversight of health care providers and facilities. Local government health services are also authorized at the state level.

In addition, the state insurance regulation agency has a major role in regulating insurance companies through the insurance laws. It is in this capacity that states are increasingly becoming involved in regulating the quality of care provided in health insurance plans or managed care programs.

Individual state decisions around financing for Medicaid are being driven by the overwhelming demands on health care budgets and by the continued pressure on states to decrease taxes. States are often using managed care plans to provide services for Medicaid recipients and are seeking cost-effective solutions to what has continued to be a crisis in health care at the state level as state legislators become more cost conscious. Currently 48 states offer some form of Medicaid managed care (HCFA, OA, 2001).

A major issue for states is the fact that the Medicaid program has specific requirements for uniformity across the state program and a freedom-of-choice clause, which mandates that to receive matching Medicaid grants, states may not restrict the choice of providers for Medicaid enrollees. The BBA eliminated the need for states to apply for waivers to implement mandatory managed care. Before the BBA of 1997, states were required to apply for waivers from the restriction of choice or uniformity requirements that exist in federal Medicaid regulations so that a mandatory managed care initiative could be instituted for their Medicaid programs. Thus, many states applied for waivers so that they could alter their Medicaid programs and cut costs. The federal government grants two kinds of Medicaid managed care waivers. Section 1915(b) waivers, or freedom-of-choice waivers, permit states to waive beneficiaries' rights to select their own Medicaid providers and require beneficiaries to enroll, for example, in managed care plans. Under this waiver program, states may also apply to waive the requirement that services must be comparable statewide in order to adjust the program to needs in different parts of states. Section 1915(c) waivers, or home- and community-based services waivers, afford states the flexibility to develop and implement creative alternatives to placing Medicaid-eligible individuals in medical facilities such as nursing homes and allow alternatives in home-based or community-based programs. Under this kind of waiver, services may allow the person to stay at home and avoid institutionalization. States may also target these waiver programs to individuals with a specific illness or condition such as persons with AIDS, physical and developmental disability, mental illness, or mental retardation. States applying for these waivers must demonstrate that the new approaches are budget neutral and do not add costs to the Medicaid program (HCFA, 2001d). Section 1115 research and demonstration waivers allow states to test new approaches to benefits, services, eligibility, program payments, and service delivery.

LOCAL LEVEL

Local governments, along with state government, have the ultimate responsibility for protecting the public health. Local governments also may decide to fulfill a responsibility for indigent care by funding public hospitals and clinics. New York City's Health and Hospitals Corporation and Chicago's Cook County Hospital are good examples of this type of control. Even these hospitals, while receiving a subsidy from their local government, tend to get large amounts of operating money from Medicaid and Medicare, so public hospital care is indeed dependent on the decisions made within these two programs. In the early 1990s in many areas of the country, public hospitals were in danger of being sold or privatized or were otherwise in jeopardy because of mergers or acquisitions by larger hospitals or networks. As the costs of care have increased and more care has been performed in the home and in the community, competition between hospitals has intensified. Another problem for hospitals has been the increased supply of medical specialists and a decreased supply of primary care providers. The 1997 BBA included a nationwide expansion of a program that began in New York City and that offers financial incentives to hospitals that train fewer doctors, especially in the medical specialties, with the idea that savings would occur with a reduction of the physician supply (One Thousand Hospitals, 1997). Since that time many public hospitals such as the New York Health and Hospitals Corporation hospitals have successfully begun to reduce costs and operate with decreased subsidies. Only recently has that trend reversed, with increased deficits in large public hospital systems resulting in increased pressure on insurers to increase their reimbursement rates (Freudenheim, 2001; Steinhauer, 2001).

With the cost-constraint strategies of the 1980s and 1990s and the misconception that infectious diseases were no longer a major threat, population-based health services such as those originating from state and local health departments received proportionately less and less funding (Institute of Medicine, 1988). Traditional public health nursing functions to provide surveillance in this important area were minimized or eliminated in this period because they were viewed as having a lower priority than individual health (morbidity) services, which were also being cut back. The crises in the control of infectious diseases such as measles and tuberculosis have taught us important lessons on the need for strong local public health agencies (Brudney & Dobkin, 1991). The onset of AIDS greatly escalated the problem and has reinforced the need for primary prevention and basic public health strategies. When public health strategies are superseded by an emphasis on the individual, major health problems can "fall through the cracks" of the system, and the whole of society will suffer. The 1990s brought a resurgence of interest in integrating these public health strategies and reemphasizing community-based approaches.

PRIVATE HEALTH CARE SYSTEM

The private component of the health care system consists of all nongovernmental sources and, in fact, is the largest component because most health care facilities in this country are run by private for-profit or nonprofit corporations. The entire health insurance industry is also within the private system. Included as part of what has been called the "medical-industrial complex" are the pharmaceutical companies, suppliers of health care technology, and the various service industries that support the health care system (Meyers, 1970; Relman, 1980). Because so much of the industry is controlled by private sources, it is difficult for cost controls to reach all segments of the health care industry equally. The for-profit health care system is growing in this country, as well as internationally, as public sector health care costs rise and more of the responsibility to deliver health care is relegated to private organizations (Smith & Lipsky, 1992). The greatest growth in this country has come from the for-profit sector, with for-profit firms' purchase of or consolidation with private nonprofit hospitals (Lutz & Gee, 1995). In 1997 Columbia/HCA Health Care was the nation's largest for-profit hospital system, owning 350 hospitals in 38 states while maintaining a 20% gross profit target (Herman, 1997). The health care industry has been transformed in the past 10 years by a business philosophy that has and will continue to have far-reaching effects on the overall health care system. Although this chapter has largely described the public sector in health care, one must also recog-

nize the large role the private sector plays in today's health care system.

INNOVATIVE FINANCING AND IMPLICATIONS FOR NURSING

Nursing has a major role in creating cost-effective but viable options for patients who are in need, particularly the chronically ill and elderly who need care as well as cure. Consider the community nursing organizations that care for patients with human immunodeficiency virus infection and chronic illness at home. Nursing organizations such as visiting nurse services are providing innovative solutions for patients who need care across a full continuum of services but with a reconsideration of patient needs and costs of care. Technology itself has been harnessed with the use of computers and "telehealth" services to reach patients at home without an actual home visit each time the patient needs a contact. Computerization supplements nursing care in a way that can actually increase the number of contacts that can be made with patients, thus increasing the chances that they will remain stable at home (Mahoney, Tarlow, & Sandaire, 1998; Mahoney, Tennstedt, Friedman, & Heeren, 1999; Mahoney, 2000).

CONCLUSION

Since 1970 the health care system in the United States has grown to almost unmanageable proportions and complexity. The medical-industrial complex pervades all sectors of our economic system and employs a vast number of citizens. It consumes more than 13% of our gross national product and only recently has begun to level off in any significant way. Although currently costs have come under control, the large-scale retirement of the baby boomers in 2010 and growing prescription costs will stress the system to the point that another crisis is inevitable. Also, the financing system has had a reprieve with the booming U.S. economy and large returns on investments. In a recession more pressure for further cutbacks in health care services occurs. But we need to remember the classic Friedland quote (1995, p. 16), "If unmet needs are not financed collectively, then they must be financed individually, or not at all."

Perhaps nursing will find the creative solution of integrating the uncoordinated long-term care and acute care services, creating a continuum of services that everyone is eligible for regardless of setting. Providers need the ability to track a patient's status and to integrate services across hospital, adult day care, home care, and institutional care settings. The present system blocks this integrated care approach. Nurses as providers must decide what the ultimate health product should be and give that message to policymakers. Nurses need not be passive participants in the policy debate about the reshaping of health care and its financing. Rather, they can shape health care policy and the resulting decisions that are made.

REFERENCES

Abood, S. & Keepnews, D. (2000). *Understanding payment for advanced practice nursing services. Volume 1: Medicare reimbursement.* Washington, DC: American Nurses Publishing.

Ahl, D. & Wergin, K. (2000, October). Fee-for-service joins the Medicare+Choice product line. *Healthcare Financial Management, 54*(10), 41-43.

Alford, R. (1975). *Health care politics: Ideological and interest group barriers to reform.* Chicago: University of Chicago Press.

American Association of Health Plans. (2001). *Independent medical review of health plan coverage decisions: Empowering consumers with solutions.* Washington, DC: Author.

American College of Nurse Practitioners. (2001). *2001 public policy agenda.* Available online at www.nurse.org/acnp.

Atherly, A. (2001). Supplemental insurance: Medicare's accidental stepchild. *Medical Care Research and Review, 58*(2), 131-161.

Baker, D. & Weisbrot, M. (1999). *Social Security: The phony crisis.* Chicago: The University of Chicago Press.

Berk, M.L. & Monheit, A.C. (2001). The concentration of health care expenditures, revisited. *Health Affairs, 20*(2), 9-18.

Blahous, C.P. (2000). *Reforming Social Security: For ourselves and our posterity.* Westport, CT: Praeger.

Bodenheimer, T. (1996). The HMO backlash: Righteous or reactionary? *New England Journal of Medicine, 335*, 1601-1604.

Bodenheimer, T. & Grumbach, K. (1998). *Understanding health policy: A clinical approach* (2nd ed.). Boston: Jones & Bartlett.

Brudney, K. & Dobkin, J. (1991). Resurgent tuberculosis in N.Y.C.: Human immunodeficiency virus, homelessness and the decline of tuberculosis control programs. *American Review of Respiratory Disease, 144*(4), 745-749.

Burman, L., Penner, R., Steuerle, G., Toder, E., Moon, M., Thompson, L., Weisner, M., & Carasso, A. (1998). *Policy challenges posed by the aging of America: A discussion briefing pre-* pared for the Urban Institute Board of Trustees Meeting, May, 20, 1998. Washington, DC: Urban Institute Press.

Cassel, C.K., Besdine, R.W., & Siegel, L.C. (1999). Restructuring Medicare for the next century: What will beneficiaries really need? *Health Affairs, 18*(1), 118-131.

Children's Defense Fund. (2001). What's CHIP? An introduction to the Children's Health Insurance Program. Available online at www.childrensdefense.org.

Christensen, S. & Wagner, J. W. (2000). The costs of a Medicare prescription drug benefit. *Health Affairs, 19*(2), 212-218.

Cohen, M.A., Miller, J., & Weinrobe, M. (2001). Patterns of informal and formal caregiving among elders with private long-term care insurance. *The Gerontologist, 41*(2), 180-187.

Cooper, B.S., & Vladeck, B.C. (2000). Bringing competitive pricing to Medicare. *Health Affairs, 19*(5), 49-54.

Cordes, J.J. & Steuerle, C.E. (1999). A primer on privatization. Washington, DC: Urban Institute Press. Available online at www.urban.org/retirement/reports/3/retire_3.html.

Curtiss, F.R. (1989). Managed health care. *American Journal of Hospital Pharmacy, 46*, 742-763.

Davis, K., Anderson, G., Rowland, D., & Steinberg, E. (1990). *Health care cost containment.* Baltimore: Johns Hopkins University Press.

Department of Defense. (2001). *Tricare.* Available online at www.Tricare.OSD.mil.

Dowd, B., Coulam, R., & Feldman, R. (2000). A tale of four cities: Medicare reform and competitive pricing. *Health Affairs, 19*(5), 9-29.

Etheredge, L. (1999). Three streams, one river: A coordinated approach to financing retirement. *Health Affairs, 18*(1), 80-91.

Etheredge, L. (2000). Medicare's governance and structure: A proposal. *Health Affairs, 19*(5), 60-71.

Feder, J., Komisar, H.L., & Niefeld, M. (2000). Long-term care in the United States: An overview. *Health Affairs, 19*(3), 40-56.

Federal Interagency Forum on Age-related Statistics. (2000). *Older Americans 2000: Key indicators of well-being.* Hyattsville, MD: Author.

Frank, R.G. (2001). Prescription drug prices: Why some pay more than others do. *Health Affairs, 20*(2), 115-128.

Freudenheim, M. (2001, May 25). Medical costs surge as hospitals force insurers to raise payments. *New York Times.* Available online at www.nytimes.com.

Friedland, R.B. (1995). Medicare, Medicaid, and the budget. *The Public Policy and Aging Report, 7*(1), 1, 2, 14-16.

Fuchs, V. (1988). The "competition revolution" in health care. *Health Affairs, 7*(3), 5-24.

Gabel, J.R. (1999). Job-based health insurance, 1977-1998: The accidental system under scrutiny. *Health Affairs, 18*(6), 62-74.

Gibson, R.M. & Waldo, D.R. (1982). National health expenditures, 1981. *Health Care Financing Review, 4*(1), 1-35.

Gorin, S. (2000). A "society for all ages": Saving Social Security and Medicare. *Health & Social Work, 25*(1), 69-73.

Health Care Financing Administration. (1997a). *Medicaid: Professional/technical information.* Washington, DC: Author. Available online at www.hcfa.gov/medicaid.

Health Care Financing Administration. (1997b). *Medicare: Professional/technical information.* Washington, DC: Author. Available at www.hcfa.gov/medicare.

Health Care Financing Administration. (1998). *Your guide to Medicare medical savings accounts* (publication no. HCFA-02137). Baltimore, MD: Author.

Health Care Financing Administration. (1999). *Your guide to private fee-for-services plans: A new type of Medicare health plan* (pub. no. HCFA-10144). Available online at www.medicare.gov.

Health Care Financing Administration. (2000a). *Medicare 2000: 35 years of improving Americans' health and security.* Hyattsville: MD: Author.

Health Care Financing Administration. (2000b). *Your Medicare benefits* (pub. no. HCFA-10116). Baltimore, MD: U.S. Department of Health and Human Services.

Health Care Financing Administration. (2001a). *Medicare basics: Medicare premium amounts for 2001.* Available online at www.medicare.gov/Basics/Amounts2001.asp.

Health Care Financing Administration. (2001b). *Medicare basics: What is Medicare?* Available online at www.medicare.gov/Basics/WhatIs.asp.

Health Care Financing Administration. (2001c). *Medicare plan choices: Medicare health plan choices/choices in 2001.* Available online at www.medicare.gov/choices/choices.asp.

Health Care Financing Administration. (2001d). 1915(b). *Freedom of choice waivers.* Available online at hcfa.gov/medicaid/hpg3.htm.

Health Care Financing Administration, Office of the Actuary. (2001). *HCFA Data and Statistics.* Hyattsville, MD: Author. Available online at www.hcfa.gov/stats/nhe.oact

Healthcare Financial Management Association. (2000). Medicare HMOs hurt by payment formula. *Journal of the Healthcare Financial Management Association, 54*(6), 22.

Heffler, S., Levit, K., Smith, S., Smith, C., Cowan, C., Lazenby H., & Freeland, M. (2001). Health care spending growth up in 1999: Faster growth expected in the future. *Health Affairs, 20*(2), 193-203.

Herman, E. (1997). Downsizing government for principle and profit. *Dollars and Sense, 210,* 10-13.

Hsiao, E., Braun, P., Dunn, D., & Becker, E. (1988). Results and policy implications of the resource-based relative value scale. *New England Journal of Medicine, 319,* 881-888.

Iglehart, J. K. (2000). Medicare and drugs: The elusive prize revisited. *Health Affairs, 19*(2), 6-7.

Institute of Medicine. (1988). *The future of public health.* Washington, DC: National Academy Press.

Jencks, S.F., et al. (2000). Quality of medical care delivered to Medicare beneficiaries: A profile at state and national levels. *Journal of the American Medical Association, 284*(13), 1670-1676.

Kaiser Commission on Medicaid Facts. (2001, March). *Medicaid's role in long-term care.* Available online at www.kff.org/content/2001/2186.

Kendix, M. & Lubitz, J. D. (1999). The impact of medical savings accounts on Medicare program costs. *Inquiry, 36*(3), 280-290.

Kingdon, J. (1999). *America the Unusual.* New York: Worth Publishers.

Kingson, E.R. & Schulz, J.H. (1997). *Social Security in the 21st century.* New York: Oxford University Press.

Kongstvedt, P. (2001). *The managed health care handbook* (4th ed.). Gaithersburg, MD: Aspen.

Kovner, A. & Jonas, S. (1999). *Jonas and Kovner's Health Care Delivery in the United States* (6th ed.). New York: Springer.

Lubitz, J., Greenbery, L.G., Gorina, Y., Wartzman, L., & Gibson, D. (2001). Three decades of health care use by the elderly, 1965–1998. *Health Affairs, 20*(2), 19-32.

Lutz, S. & Gee, P. (1995). *The for-profit health care revolution: The growth of investor-owned health systems in America.* Chicago: Irwin Professional.

Mahoney, D. (2000). Developing technology applications for intervention research. *Computers in Nursing, 18*(6), 260-264.

Mahoney, D., Tarlow, B., & Sandaire, J. (1998). A computer-based program for Alzheimer's caregivers. *Computers in Nursing, 16*(4), 208-216.

Mahoney, D., Tennstedt, S., Friedman, R., & Heeren, T. (1999). An automated telephone system for monitoring the functional status of community-residing elders. *The Gerontologist, 39*(2), 229-234.

Managed Care on Line. (2001). *Managed care national statistics.* Available online at healthplan.about.com/industry/healthplan/GI/dynamic/offside.htm.

McCall, N., Komisar, H.L., Petersons, A., & Moore, S. (2001). Medicare home care before and after the BBA. *Health Affairs, 20*(3), 189-198.

Mellor, J.M. (2000). Private long-term care insurance and the asset protection motive. *The Gerontologist, 40*(5), 596-604.

Meyers, H. (1970, January). The medical-industrial complex. *Fortune,* 90-91, 126.

Neuman, P. & Langwell, K.M. (1999). Medicare's choice explosion: Implications for beneficiaries. *Health Affairs, 18*(1), 150-160.

Nichols, L.M. & Reischauer, R.D. (2000). Who really wants price competition in Medicare managed care? *Health Affairs, 19*(5), 30-43.

Oberlander, J. (2000). Is premium support the right medicine for Medicare? A challenge to the emergent conventional wisdom. *Health Affairs, 19*(5), 84-99.

One thousand hospitals will be paid to reduce supply of doctors. (1997, August 25). *New York Times,* A16.

Poisal, J.A. & Murray, L. (2001). Growing differences between Medicare beneficiaries with and without drug coverage. *Health Affairs, 20*(2), 74-85.

Pulcini, J. (1984). Perspectives on level of reimbursement for nursing services. *Nursing Economics, 2,* 118-123.

Rector, T.S. (2000). Exhaustion of drug benefits and disenrollment of Medicare beneficiaries from managed care organizations. *Journal of the American Medical Association, 283*(16), 2163-2167.

Relman, A. (1980). The new medical-industrial complex. *New England Journal of Medicine, 303,* 963-970.

Schulz, J.H. (2001). *The economics of aging* (7th ed.). Westport, CT: Auburn House.

Seidman, L.S. (2000). Prefunding Medicare without individual accounts. *Health Affairs, 19*(5), 72-83.

Smith, S.R. & Lipsky, M. (1992). Privatization in health and human services: A critique. *Journal of Health Politics, Policy and Law, 17*(2), 233-253.

Social Security Administration. (2000a). *Annual statistical supplement, 2000 to the Social Security Bulletin.* Washington, DC: Author. Available online at www.ssa.gov/statistics/supplement/2000.

Social Security Administration. (2000b). *The future of Social Security* (publication no. 05-10055). Available online at www.ssa.gov/pubs/10055.html.

Social Security Administration. (2001a). *Fast facts & figures about Social Security* (publication no. 13-11785). Washington, DC: Author.

Social Security Administration. (2001b). *How you earn credits* (publication no. 05-10072). Available online at www.ssa.gov/pubs/10072.html.

Social Security Administration. (2002). *Social Security online: Cost of living adjustments.* Available online at www.ssa.gov/cola.

Social Security and Medicare Boards of Trustees. (2001). *Status of the Social Security and Medicare programs: A summary of the 2001 annual reports.* Washington, DC: Author. Available online at www.ssa.gov/OACT/TRSUM/trsummary.html.

Starr, P. (1982). *The social transformation of American medicine.* New York: Basic Books.

Steinhauer, J. (2001, May 23). New York public hospital system faces $210 million deficit. *New York Times,* A25.

Steuerle, C.E. & Bakija, J.M. (2000). *Retooling Social Security for the 21st century.* Washington, DC: Urban Institute Press. Available online at www.urban.org/pubs/retooling/chapter2.html.

Stevenson, R.W. (2001a, May 27). Congress passes tax cut, with rebates this summer. *New York Times,* A1.

Stevenson, R.W. (2001b, May 27). Still uncertain, budget surplus is gobbled up. *New York Times.* Available online at www.nytimes.com.

Stuart, B., Shea, D., & Briesacher, B. (2001). Dynamics in drug coverage of Medicare beneficiaries: Finders, losers, switchers. *Health Affairs, 20*(2), 86-99.

Temkin-Greener, H., Mukamel, D.B., & Meiners, M.R. (2000/2001). Long-term care insurance underwriting: Understanding eventual claims experience. *Inquiry, 37*(4), 348-358.

Williamson, J.B. (2001). Social Security reform, privatization, and political ideology. *The Gerontologist, 41*(2), 280-284.

Vignette   *Susan Kendig*

Managing Managed Care: A Nurse Practitioner Response to Barriers to Direct Third-Party Reimbursement

"And don't think you have to win immediately, or even at all, to make a difference. Sometimes it's important to lose for things that matter. Don't think you have to be a big dog to make a difference. You just need to be a persistent flea."

SOJOURNER TRUTH

Disease prevention and health promotion are a major focus of public policy discussions. Research demonstrates increasing evidence that emotional health is intimately related to physical health and that lifestyle and behavioral factors influence at least 80% of overall health. Recommendations abound regarding nonmedical interventions to enhance health and prevent disease. As a nurse practitioner, I am an expert in health promotion and disease prevention. It would seem that the latest research and health-related marketing set the stage for limitless opportunities for nurse practitioner practice. Naively, I believed that recognition as an advanced practice nurse (APN) would open the door to true independent practice with third-party reimbursement.

In 1995 I joined with a women's health psychologist to found Women's Healthcare Partnership, Inc. Women's Healthcare Partnership (WHCP) offers comprehensive, integrated health care by providing clinical and consulting services that incorporate a population-based approach and cover the full spectrum of women's health care. Services include health promotion, early intervention, and disease state management. This approach to women's health care is based on a comprehensive, integrated model that blends behavioral health and women's health nursing to provide education, risk management, and lifestyle modification assistance. Our team includes behavioral health specialists, a women's health nurse practitioner, nurse educators, a nutritionist, and other allied health specialists. Clinical services include collaboration with women's health care providers around complex women's health diagnoses (i.e., high-risk pregnancy, postpartum adjustment, pelvic pain, sexual dysfunction, menopause problems) to improve health outcomes, reduce medical costs, and increase satisfaction. Our consulting services include development and implementation of innovative women's health programs designed to conserve health care costs while maintaining and improving client services.

Within this practice I provide assessment, health education, and counseling services to women individually and through psychoeducational group classes. Clients with physical symptoms or health education needs are referred to an APN for evaluation. Clients may self-refer or be referred by their primary care/women's health care provider or behavioral health specialist. The typical client accessing nursing services has multiple physical symptoms and requires time-intensive assessment to determine the physical and emotional factors affecting health. Services include case management to ensure appropriate use of resources, follow-up to ensure access to services, and communication with the health care provider. Because WHCP works in collaboration with the existing health care provider, services fall within the scope of nursing practice as defined by the nurse practice act in the state of Missouri. Diagnosis, treatment, and prescriptions are made by the woman's primary health care provider in collaboration with WHCP's APN.

The merits of this comprehensive, collaborative approach to women's health care have been recognized by area health care providers, as evidenced by consistent referrals for services. However, barriers to direct reimbursement for the APN component remain, thereby limiting access to services.

REIMBURSEMENT CHALLENGES

Lack of direct third-party reimbursement is one of the three most frequently cited barriers to inde-

pendent nurse practitioner practice. Third-party payors' decisions regarding direct reimbursement for APNs are influenced by a number of factors, including state rules and regulations governing nursing practice, payor billing policies, and understanding of APN scope of practice. Policy regarding third-party reimbursement of APNs differs from state to state and among the different nongovernmental companies in the insurance industry.

One of the first steps we took in initiating the WHCP model of care was to begin gathering information regarding third-party reimbursement. Our model was different in that it was an integrated model that blends behavioral health and nursing. A collaborative practice agreement with a physician is not required for this type of practice. Although such a collaborative practice agreement could make third-party reimbursement a little easier, we chose not to identify a collaborating physician for three reasons. First, approximately 45 area physicians refer patients for behavioral health services. Linking the practice with one physician had the potential to limit referrals, particularly when third-party payors encourage billing under the physician, rather than the APN. Second, I do not diagnose, treat, or prescribe in this practice, as an APN (I evaluate patients and provide recommendations, but diagnosis and treatment are done by the referring provider). In Missouri these are considered "medically designated acts" requiring a collaborative practice agreement. Therefore, my practice falls within the scope of the Missouri Nurse Practice Act and a collaborative practice agreement is unnecessary. Third, this is a nursing model of care, and we believed it was important to make the case for independent reimbursement of nursing services.

As I contacted various third-party payors, I was told:
1. To bill under my physician's name
2. To apply for provider status (but no application information was forwarded)
3. To send credentialing information, which received no response

I also began contacting insurers directly when physicians referred clients, in order to obtain payment information before the visit. I was told that my services (preventive/risk-reduction counseling) were not reimbursable as an independent nurse practitioner. However, I was told that if I saw the woman in my collaborating physician's office, he would be reimbursed for the services and pay me. This would of course require the patient to leave Dr. A (the referring physician) and become a patient of Dr. B (my collaborating physician in another practice).

In the meantime, other companies were approaching us to help them develop an integrated approach to a variety of wellness-oriented, population-based programs for women. Consistently, behavioral health and medical care were reimbursable under traditional models, but the nursing component, which would provide the prevention-focused case management and the bridge between the disciplines, was not reimbursable. The reason? We were ahead of our time.

Early in our practice, I attended a women's health conference. Approximately 90% of the attendees were physicians, and the rest were APNs. Most of the topics were new research, presented primarily by physicians. One speaker, a physician and professor at one of the country's most prestigious medical schools, gave a particularly compelling presentation regarding the role of health education and prevention as keys to improved health outcomes for perimenopausal women. Following her presentation, the audience responded with a heated debate about how much physician time this would take and the lack of reimbursement for such services. The speaker assured them that she was participating in a Health Plan Employer Data and Information Set (HEDIS) task force addressing the issue of appropriate physician reimbursement for counseling services. At that point, I stated that in my experience, many members of the health care team were responsible for the preventive counseling provided to this population and asked how the issue of reimbursement for other team members, such as APNs, behavioral health specialists, nutritionists, and so on, was being addressed by the HEDIS group. The speaker's response? "You are doing God's work. Whenever we choose our career, we know that some people will be doing work that they will be paid for, or be paid

more for, and others will not." This was my call to action.

It became increasingly clear to me that the current system was not going to change to include direct reimbursement for APN services or nursing services unless nursing was able to effectively articulate the critical role nurses play in positive health outcomes. At that point, I decided that I would work to affect policy that reflected the true value of nursing.

Since that day, I have had many opportunities to "sit at the managed care table." I was hired to write integrated protocols for one large private company's successful proposal for Medicaid managed care funding. In another instance, I was asked to develop a managed care guide for working with APNs. This manual describes the scope of practice, educational requirements, and credentialing requirements for nurse practitioners generally, and for adult, family, pediatric, and women's health nurse practitioners, specifically. In addition, it provides information about key APN rules and regulations in Missouri, application of National Committee for Quality Assurance (NCQA) credentialing elements to APN practice, and a credentialing flow sheet delineating APN activities requiring a collaborative practice agreement versus those that do not. After review by appropriate APN organizations' personnel and practice counsel, the managed care organization's (MCO's) quality improvement and credentialing committee adopted the manual. These activities have led to my appointment to the physician advisory committee (quality improvement) of a local managed care organization and have given me opportunities to make numerous presentations regarding the advantages of APN practice to MCO committees and physician groups. I was also appointed to the managed care task force at the Missouri Department of Health. These activities have placed me in a critical position to influence policies affecting APN practice at the organizational and state level. In addition, I have gained valuable insight into how to address the reimbursement issue. In working toward equitable reimbursement policies for APNs, I learned it is necessary to address the issue within the MCOs, through legislation and the regulatory process. It is not an overnight process, but rather a series of small, incremental steps.

LESSONS FROM THE FRONT LINE

My practice as an APN encompasses both a traditional model, working in an OB/GYN practice within a collaborative practice agreement; and the WHCP model, which supports an independent, nursing-based practice model for APNs. Despite legislation at the federal and state level that appears to support direct third-party reimbursement of APNs, the barriers that I have experienced in these practices are twofold:

1. APNs working in a traditional practice still have difficulty securing empanelment (inclusion in the authorized provider lists of MCOs); as a result, mechanisms to track APN productivity and profit are difficult to put in place.
2. Nursing activities within the WHCP model are reimbursable when performed in a traditional practice. Third-party reimbursement is a challenge when the activities are not tied to a physician practice, although they are within the scope of independent nursing practice.

As I have tried to better understand third-party reimbursement and explore strategies to increase APN reimbursement, I have gained valuable insights into how to approach managed care executives, physicians, legislators, and other decision makers. The following are some comments to consider in the effort to remove barriers to third-party reimbursement for a wide range of APN practice models.

Lack of Understanding

In working with managed care companies, it is important to remember who wrote the rules. Physicians make up most of the committees governing the managed care companies, and a medical director chairs most departments. Credentialing elements set forth by NCQA are based on a medical education model. Empanelment applications also reflect a medical education model. Even the descriptions for the reimbursement structure—CPT codes and ICD-9 codes—are based on a medical model. APN practice has been forced to fit this medical model, rather than the unique nursing skill set that is more inclusive.

The following are some of the key concerns identified by the MCOs, physician groups, and even nurses that impede full recognition:

- A variety of requirements exist for entry to practice, ranging from certification programs to graduate programs.
- There are a variety of certifying bodies with different requirements. Master's degree-level preparation is not required by all certifying bodies.
- State rules and regulations governing practice are confusing and cumbersome.
- The definition of APN scope of practice set at the national level is inconsistent with some state rules and regulations.
- Certification by a nationally recognized credentialing body is not required by all states.
- Certification by a nationally recognized body is not required or even available for all specialties.
- Scope of practice is not clearly understood by physician groups and MCO personnel.
- Skill acquisition and evidence of competency in performing special procedures, such as colposcopy, is not understood.
- Didactic and clinical practicum requirements are not fully understood.

Learning to speak the MCO language helped me to explain how the NCQA credentialing elements applied to a nursing model. It increased their understanding of our scope of practice and expertise and enabled me to avoid trying to justify it within a medical framework.

The Challenge of Empanelment

Missouri legislation passed in 1998 (376.407 RSMo) stated that "any health insurer, as defined in section 376.806 RSMo, nonprofit health service plan or health maintenance organization shall reimburse a claim for services provided by an advanced practice nurse, if such services are within the scope of such nurse." Because this is a state law, only those MCOs not covered by Employee Retirement Income and Security Act (ERISA) are affected. This mandate would seem to open the door to direct reimbursement of APNs. However, barriers still remain. Although reimbursement is mandated, empanelment is not, so many APNs remain out-of-network providers. Although the Department of Insurance now requires a consistent application for provider status, which also recognizes APNs, many APNs report difficulty getting empanelment information from MCOs. Others report denial of legitimate claims. The Missouri Nurses Association is tracking this problem.

Rules and Regulations

In her landmark 1992 article, Safriet (1992) identified four statute recommendations necessary for true independent nurse practitioner (NP) practice (also see Pearson, 2001):

- Eliminate references to mixed regulator entities and vest regulatory authority solely with the Board of Nursing.
- Amend the Nurse Practice Act to specifically acknowledge advanced practice nursing and include a basic definition of APNs.
- Amend the Nurse Practice Act definition of nursing to include APNs regulated by the Board of Nursing with empowerment to the Board of Nursing to promulgate all regulations for APNs.
- Eliminate statutory requirements for any APN/MD collaboration, practice agreements, supervision, or direction.

In Missouri APNs were defined in statute in 1993. The Board of Nursing and the Board of Healing Arts then jointly promulgated rules with input from the Board of Pharmacy. Three areas of focus within the rules and regulations place restrictions on full independent scope of practice: geographic restrictions, methods of treatment to be covered in the collaborative practice agreement, and requirements for physician review of services. Although national APN standards support diagnosis, treatment, and prescriptive authority as functions of APN practice, Missouri rules and regulations define diagnosis, treatment, and prescription as delegated medical acts requiring a collaborative practice agreement. Because coding for direct reimbursement requires a medical diagnosis, this definition may place an undue barrier to direct reimbursement for APNs practicing within the scope of the Missouri Nurse Practice Act, whose practice does not require a collaborative practice agreement. In other states, language that does not include "diagnosis, treatment, and prescriptive authority" within the scope of APN practice may also limit access to direct third-party reimbursement.

Supervision

Collaboration means true partnership, in which the power on both sides is valued by both, with recognition and acceptance of separate and combined spheres of activity and responsibility, mutual safeguarding of the legitimate interest of each party, and a commonality of goals that is recognized by both parties. This is a relationship based upon recognition that each is richer and more truly real because of the strength and uniqueness of the other. (American Nurses Association [ANA], 1981, p. 7)

Ideally, collaboration occurs between the client and professionals from many disciplines to affect optimal health outcomes. Legislative and regulatory language requiring collaboration, consultation, or supervision opens the door to the implication that collaboration still requires supervision, or that collaboration is a "team effort" with the physician as head of the team. Research clearly shows that APNs practicing within a fully independent scope of practice have at least the same health outcomes, often with greater client satisfaction, than do their physician counterparts (American College of Physicians, 1994; Mundinger, Kane, Lenz, Totten, Tsai, Cleary, Friedewald, Siu, & Shelanski, 2000). Critics claim that many of the studies are flawed because they do not examine the quality of services without physician involvement. However, studies of physician effectiveness involve nursing. No health care professional practices in isolation. Physicians often discuss their cases with physician colleagues, nurses, and other health care providers to provide the best possible care for their patients. APNs have the same professional intelligence to determine when this is necessary in their practice. The difference is that physicians are not mandated to have a written collaborative agreement with their "consultants." Activities that require a collaborative practice agreement versus those that do not are often misunderstood by third-party payors. In my experience, third-party payors have interpreted the rules and regulations requiring a collaborative practice agreement in Missouri to mean that any APN activity requires a collaborative practice agreement. In trying to obtain credentialing information from one large MCO, I was told that I could not practice without a doctor: "You must be new to our state and just don't understand our rules." Actually, my preceptor in graduate school was one of the members of the rule-making team, and I had attended several of the meetings.

Fragmentation of the Profession

APNs are certified and practice within a variety of specialties. Some specialties have established nationally recognized certification procedures; others have not. At the national level, NPs have a minimum of two generalist organizations, and clinical nurse specialists (CNSs), certified nurse midwives (CNMs), and certified registered nurse anesthetists (CRNAs) all have their own organizations. The NP specialties each have their own organizations. Although the individual organizations play a valuable role in speaking for APNs and specialty interests, the result is considerable fragmentation.

A Different Language

In the legislative arena, it is important to recognize that the effort to influence APN practice and reimbursement policy is not only tied to nursing legislation. Each health care bill has the potential to affect APN practice, just as each nursing or health professions bill has the potential to affect patient outcomes. A bill that supports reimbursement for a number of prevention services would be considered good and garner support from most health care providers. However, if the access language identifies only physicians as providers, access to APN care and reimbursement for APN services could be limited. Conversely, a bill that supports access to "health care providers and APNs," but limits payment for prevention services to only 25% of the cost, would be a deterrent to access, although seemingly supportive of APN services.

Several points are important in efforts to ensure inclusion of APN practice in legislative and regulatory language:

- Know how your state defines the term *health care provider*. Are APNs included in the definition, or

should each type of APN (i.e., NP, CNS, CNM, CRNA) be identified in the legislation? The legislative documentation office at your state capital will provide this information.
- Work with your state nurses association, APN groups, or both to ensure the most-supportive language in legislation or regulation. It is important to give legislators consistent messages.
- Educate legislators about the appropriate language to support APN practice that should be included in any health or health professions-related legislation. It is much easier to proceed if legislators get it right the first time than if you have to try and change the language once the legislative process has begun.

Use of Data to Craft the Message

Certainly direct reimbursement for APN practice is important for access to APN services and validates the value of our profession. However, a lobbying or educational approach that focuses only on getting paid, and getting paid because we are so important, will fail. Rather, know why access to APN services is important in your particular area. Is there a health care professional shortage? Are there problems with access to care for a certain population? Are patients requesting your services but finding access limited because of reimbursement? How can APN services improve the current system? Be ready to show the numbers!

Managed care organizations and health systems are data driven. Although there is much in the literature that supports WHCP's proposed approach to practice, we are continually asked to provide information regarding our outcomes. We evaluate our integrated postpartum adjustment program using the SF 36, the Edinburgh Depression scale, and qualitative measures. Although the data are limited at this point, our results consistently show evidence of improvement. Anecdotally, women who access the nursing services report high satisfaction and improved outcomes. Although we have not worked out all the difficulties with reimbursement for nursing services, women are referred and choose to pay fees for our service. Additional data linking our services to reduction in the use of medical services, a decrease in the number of emergency room visits, improvements in compliance with the prescribed medical regimen, reduction in the frequency of hospitalizations, and so on can also show improved health, cost effectiveness, and the value of preventive services.

In short, payors, be they individuals or MCOs, don't pay APNs just because we are deserving. They pay because we have something valuable to provide and have positive outcomes. Know your value and your data, and be able to articulate them in 30 seconds or less any time you're given the chance.

Relationships

As I have become more involved in reimbursement issues, I have found that cultivating a network of nursing colleagues and other professionals with expertise has been invaluable. For instance, when I wrote the APN manual for the managed care company, I sent the initial draft of information regarding the specialties to the specialty organizations. The Missouri Nurses Association was instrumental in reviewing the information and had it reviewed by ANA and Missouri practice attorneys. All of these people provided helpful input to ensure the accuracy and credibility of the document. I could not have completed the work without them. in addition, liaison with a local business coalition to gain entrée to MCOs has helped me with information about coding and reimbursement practices.

Building relationships with key organization leaders, attorneys who specialize in APN issues, consumers, key legislators, and other colleagues is key in moving APN policy forward within MCOs, the health care community, and the legislature. Recognize the avenues to cultivating mentors:

- Do not just pay dues to a professional organization. Get involved. This provides valuable and quick information when needed.
- Know who the nursing leaders are, and talk with them. There is a wealth of knowledge, energy, and experience within our profession. In my experience, our leaders are excellent and nurturing role models.
- Find mentors outside of nursing. We have much to learn from our colleagues in business, law,

education, and other areas. Some of my most valuable information and opportunities have come from working with these groups.

GAINING RECOGNITION FROM MANAGED CARE ORGANIZATIONS

Empanelment, recognition of primary care or specialty status, and inclusion in the provider manual are keys to direct access to APN services and direct reimbursement for such services. The following strategies have enabled me to gain recognition with MCOs:

- Show up, join committees, and be involved in your professional association. Those who show up make 90% of decisions.
- Maintain your nursing identity. I always try to focus on my unique skill set as an advanced practice *nurse,* rather than demonstrating how my practice is similar to physician practice.
- Remember that true collaboration is key. My practice has its own place in the health care system. I do not enhance, extend, or substitute for any other profession. Rather, I am an essential, integral part of the team. Learn to articulate why this is true in your own practice.
- Keep in mind that nothing can replace credibility.

Although the United States has the best health care technology in the world, many of our public health indicators are more like those of developing countries. What is missing? Our system is based on a medical model. Too often nursing has accepted, rather than challenged, this approach. Nursing is grounded in a holistic approach, with expertise in health promotion and disease prevention. This is not a "value added" service. This is a reimbursable service. Nurses marry policy to the realities of patient's lives. It is time that we begin to marry policy to the realities of our profession.

REFERENCES

American College of Physicians. (1994). Physicians assistants and nurse practitioners. *Annals of Internal Medicine, 121*(9), 714-716.

American Nurses Association. (1981). *Nursing: A social policy statement.* Kansas City, MO: Author.

Mundinger, M.O., Kane, R.L., Lenz, E.R., Totten, A.M., Tsai, W.Y., Cleary, P.D., Friedewald, W., Siu, A.L., & Shelanski, M.L. (2000). Primary care outcomes in patients treated by nurse practitioners or physicians: A randomized trial. *Journal of the American Medical Association, 283*(1), 59-68.

Pearson, L. (2001). Annual legislative update. *Nurse Practitioner, 26*(1), 7-57.

Safriet, B.J. (1992). Health dollars and regulatory sense. *Yale Journal of Regulation, 9*, 478-486.

POLICYSPOTLIGHT

MEDICARE AT THE CROSSROADS

Mary K. Wakefield

"What's great about America is that although we have a mess of problems, we have a great capacity—intellect and resources—to do something about them."

HENRY FORD II

The federal government established the Medicare program in 1965. This national insurance program was designed to ensure that Americans over the age of 65 would have improved access to health care by decreasing the financial burden the elderly (and later the disabled) faced in obtaining medically necessary acute care services. Driving this landmark legislation was concern about the significant proportion of elderly who were without health insurance coverage or the means to purchase health care. The overarching goal of the Medicare program then, and now, is to ensure that beneficiaries have access to medically necessary acute care of high quality in the most appropriate clinical setting. The

Reprinted from *Policy, Politics, & Nursing Practice.* (2001, May). 2(2), 98-102. Copyright by Sage Publications, Inc.

Mary K. Wakefield, PhD, RN, FAAN, is director, Center for Rural Health, University of North Dakota School of Medicine. She is the only nurse serving as a commissioner on the Medicare Payment Advisory Commission. The commission is responsible for advising the U.S. Congress on Medicare policy.

efficient provision of services is a program priority to avoid undue financial burden borne by either beneficiaries or taxpayers (Medicare Payment Advisory Commission [MedPAC], 2001). When it was established, Medicare directly reimbursed (i.e., fee-for-service) health care facilities and clinicians for certain health care services. The federal agency charged with responsibility for administering the Medicare program, as both payer and purchaser, was the Health Care Financing Administration (HCFA, now the Centers for Medicare and Medicaid Services [CMS]).

Because Medicare Part A primarily pays for inpatient care and as such is not a comprehensive coverage program, most beneficiaries choose to pay for government-subsidized Part B coverage, which covers some costs associated with home health physician services and outpatient care. To a lesser extent, beneficiaries also purchase supplemental insurance which provides beneficiaries with a choice of insurance products, although not all are available in all parts of the country and premiums vary both by product and by geography. The three types of Medigap policies that offer prescription drug coverage for example, have high premiums and require significant out-of-pocket spending. In both the original fee-for-service program and Medicare+

FOR YOUR INFORMATION

The 107th Congress will be faced with the task of Medicare reform. It may only take the form of a limited prescription drug benefit or it may involve comprehensive structural reform. For nearly 36 years, the Medicare program and its structural components, entitlement status, financing methodology, and basic benefit package have remained fairly stable. The Medicare Catastrophic Coverage Act passed in the late 1980s and repealed a year later would have achieved substantial reform, especially in the area of prescription drug coverage. Concern about the solvency of the Medicare trust fund after the year 2030 provides an even more urgent call for reform.

Choice (a more recent addition to expanded managed care options), beneficiaries have liability for some health care costs, although that liability varies and is limited. Financial liability is often expressed in required copayments and deductibles as well as payment for health services not covered by the Medicare benefit package. To limit their liability, as previously indicated, most Medicare beneficiaries enroll in Part B and many others obtain other supplemental coverage. In spite of obtaining supplemental coverage, in 1999, noninstitutionalized beneficiaries spent an average of $2370 (18% of their income) on out-of-pocket health care costs (Caplan & Foley, 2000).

In general, the intent of the Medicare program was to treat elderly persons uniformly in terms of the services covered, entitling them to a set of health care benefits that was consistent regardless of their economic, geographic, or health status. Since 1965, almost all older Americans have joined the ranks of the insured, leaving behind, as of 2000, approximately 42 million nonelderly Americans without such coverage.

Medicare, a program that entitles by law the elderly and disabled to an established set of benefits, is now, 35 years later, being revisited. Since the 1980s, policymakers and advocacy groups have been concerned with unsustainable increases in Medicare program expenditures, currently reaching about $200 billion annually. To address spending, a hospital inpatient prospective payment system (PPS) was established to replace the poorly controlled cost-based payment method and increase the efficient provision of necessary services. Shortly thereafter, a new payment system was also established for physicians. While these payment systems enhanced efficiency and extended program solvency, they also had unintended consequences. For example, the PPS jeopardized geographic access for some beneficiaries as hundreds of rural hospitals closed as a result of their inability to extract the same efficiencies from their systems as urban hospitals.

The next significant modification to the Medicare program came in the Balanced Budget Act (BBA) of 1997, when wider managed care coverage was introduced as well as provider payment changes that were designed to contain costs by holding down the rate of growth in spending. Prospective payment was extended to an array of outpatient services, including skilled nursing care, home health care, and ambulance services based in part on evidence of overpayment for some services (MedPAC, 2000a). And, managed care options, through the establishment of the Medicare+Choice program (Medicare Part C), were added to provide beneficiaries with choices among different health care delivery systems and benefit packages (using the fee-for-service benefit package as a minimum benefit set). In exchange for their ability to choose among plans that provided additional benefits, limits were placed on beneficiaries' choice of providers. This alternative then, stood in contrast to the traditional fee-for-service program, which allowed beneficiary choice of providers but provided coverage only for those services included in the defined benefit package. Interestingly, although beneficiaries in areas of the country rich with participating managed care plans had access to a wide array of previously uncovered benefits, often including prescription drugs and physical exams, many of their counterparts, especially in rural communities had few or no managed care options available to choose from. This disparity constitutes a serious breach of the comparability or equity of benefits accessible to beneficiaries.

By 2000, it was clear that the BBA was more successful than expected at reducing spending on health care facilities and providers, with a decrease in all inpatient hospital margins (MedPAC, 2000b). However, the extent of this decrease varied by hospital type, leaving some hospitals with razor-thin Medicare margins, and some, particularly rural hospitals, with negative margins. What was also clear was the anemic rate of managed care participation in the Medicare+Choice program, with plans exiting the Medicare program and leaving thousands of beneficiaries to pursue other options. In response, the Benefits Improvement and Protection Act (BIPA) of 2000 was enacted, primarily to ameliorate the unexpected adverse financial impact of the BBA. The provisions included in BIPA are expected to infuse approximately $35 billion over 5 years into healthcare-related services for Medicare beneficiaries. A significant portion of this funding was made available to shore up Medicare+Choice participation by managed care plans to continue the availability of private insurance choices for Medicare beneficiaries.

Today, significant program restructuring is being contemplated, driven in part by concerns regarding the future solvency of the program. By 2025, a 70% increase in the number of elderly is expected to be drawing on Medicare program resources. Also contributing to rapid growth in program expenditures is the increased use of costly technology (Fuchs, 2000). Although technology and prescription drugs have generally contributed to both quantity and quality of life, they have come with a significant financial cost. For example, between 1995 and 1998, pharmaceutical spending grew faster than any other personal health category of spending, accounting for 20% of the total increase in health spending in 1998 (Levit, Cowan, Lazenby, Sensenig, McDonnell, Stiller, & Martin, 2000). Concern about the future solvency of the Medicare program is not unique to policy makers. In fact, in one survey, more than half of individuals age 50 to 70 expressed fear that they will not be able to afford the health care they need (Schoen, Simantov, Duchon, & Davis, 2000).

Redesign is also being discussed, given that the benefits to which Medicare beneficiaries are currently entitled reflect an appropriate mix of health care services as they existed in the mid-1960s, not as they do in the 21st century. For example, although Medicare was designed to primarily support inpatient acute care, 63% of the current Medicare beneficiary population of 40 million people have at least two chronic illnesses that account for 95% of the program spending (Medicare Reform, 2001). Clearly, much of the care for the chronically ill can and should occur in outpatient settings and might best be provided through disease management programs that are supported in only a very limited way by Medicare. Furthermore, accompanying shorter average lengths of stay and decreasing hospital patient census, nonhospital care options are now dotting the health care landscape, ranging from outpatient surgical centers to care provided in some assisted living facilities. Where many services are provided, the mix of clinicians providing them has clearly changed since the inception of the Medicare program. Nevertheless, given the significant policy and political ramifications of substantially altering this program, and the fact that there are no easy solutions available to address the myriad issues, major Medicare redesign is not likely to unfold smoothly. Furthermore, as changes are proposed and implemented, the need for ongoing evaluation of their impact on access to quality health care will be in order to avoid adversely affecting the health of Medicare beneficiaries. Evidence of access and quality problems could indicate inadequate or inappropriate policies or program efforts.

To hold down spending and ensure program solvency through retirement of the baby boom generation, current and foreseeable policy discussions revolve around very different strategic approaches that employ different philosophies. For example, many Republicans believe that the Medicare program should further capitalize on market-driven approaches that incorporate private sector competition and less regulation. In its extreme, the role of government could be to finance the program through a fixed subsidy and let beneficiaries use the premium, and any other purchasing power they may personally have at their disposal, to purchase their preferred benefit package from the private sector. Some role would likely continue for government to ensure payment for services where market competition is nonexistent. Alternatively, the government could prescribe a minimum level of benefits that all participating private plans would be required to offer and an established premium would be supported through a government contribution. The government could also subsidize the full cost of premiums for low-income beneficiaries. This strategy tends to fall into a category referred to as managed competition with managed care plans competing for beneficiaries. An alternative view, held by many Democrats, asserts the need for continued significant government involvement, including government financing and program administration, to protect beneficiary access to health care.

In addition to policy dialogue about whether to strengthen a strong government role or further introduce the private market's role in the Medicare program, discussion is revolving around upgrading and expanding program benefits to cover therapeutic interventions now commonly used. Most important in this debate is inclusion of a prescription drug benefit that, although extremely important to a significant portion of Medicare beneficiaries, is likely to be accompanied by tremendous cost burdens to the Medicare program. Although some Medicare beneficiaries have drug coverage through Medicare+Choice, Medigap, or employer-sponsored health benefit plans, the extent of coverage varies considerably. Currently, about 32% of beneficiaries have annual drug expenses of over $1000 and 6% have expenses exceeding $3000 (Gluck, 1999).

Simple to state but highly complex to consider are issues around designing a drug benefit, including whether the benefit should be mandatory or voluntary for beneficiaries and whether coverage should be obtained through private insurance plans or through direct government subsidies. Even the population for which the benefit is targeted is in dispute. The Bush administration, for example, supports targeting a drug benefit only to low-income, Medicare beneficiaries through state block grants, whereas Democrats in Congress tend to support making this benefit available to all beneficiaries. One area of agreement in the thicket of contentious drug coverage issues seems to be around the need for catastrophic drug coverage. Far more difficult to solve will be how best to restrain growth in costs driven by

a multitude of factors, not the least of which are: (a) direct to consumer advertising, (b) the flow of new technology, and (c) intellectual property protection that includes special treatment granted to the pharmaceutical industry (Hunt, 2000).

In addition to ensuring the affordability of prescription drugs for the elderly, another costly item for this population is nursing home care. A minimal amount of this care is currently being covered through long-term care insurance purchased by beneficiaries. The rest of this care is paid for primarily out-of-pocket by beneficiaries or their families, or through the Medicaid program that reimburses the care of individuals unable to afford nursing home care. Consequently, the federal government shares the financial liability for much of the costs of nursing home care with the states. However, in times of economic downturns, state budgets are stretched to meet an array of obligations, and nursing home care can quickly become a very high-cost item. With economic pressure, states generally turn to the federal government for financial assistance and policy changes that can dissipate financial burden. Couple state concerns with increasing numbers of elderly likely to use nursing home care and pressure may build to consider some type of Medicare benefit to offset costs incurred by individuals and states.

Should the Medicare program move further toward embracing a competitive, market-based approach to health care for beneficiaries? Applying this orientation from public sector control to a market-based approach will constitute a tectonic shift. Clearly, some policy makers view incorporating market approaches as a means to ensure long-term program viability that occurs as a result of competition among private plans and providers—competition that theoretically can increase efficiency and improve quality. On the other hand, other policy makers are concerned that Medicare beneficiaries are entitled to the continuation of this program as social insurance that encompasses a public commitment operationalized through government regulation and purchasing power.

Before the country are two very different approaches to reconfiguring one of the most important health care programs in the nation. Recent proposals offered by Democrats and Republicans, do not by themselves assure program solvency for the next generation of retirees. The crossroads at which this program finds itself offers no definitive path to sustainability, access, and quality. Policy makers, joined by other stakeholders, are just beginning to wrestle with choosing their way among paths littered with rhetoric and ill-defined outcomes. In spite of clear signs that maintaining program solvency will require more change than any one proposal currently offers, policy decisions will be made. Regardless of the path chosen and whether we move incrementally or in leaps down it, ongoing vigilance and research effort absolutely must be directed toward ascertaining the impact of programmatic changes.

REFERENCES

Caplan, C. & Foley, L. (2000, May): *Structuring health care benefits: A comparison of Medicare and FEHBP* (no. 2000-05). Washington, DC: AARP Public Policy Institute.

Fuchs, V. (2000, Spring): Medicare reform: The larger picture. *Journal of Economic Perspectives, 14*(2), 57-70.

Gluck, M. (1999, April): A Medicare prescription drug benefit. (Medicare brief no: 1). National Academy of Social Insurance. Available online at www.nasi.org/Medicare/Briefs/medbr1. htm.

Hunt, M. (2000, September): *Prescription drug costs: Federal regulation of the industry.* Blue Cross and Blue Shield Association. Available online at BCBSHealthIssues.com.

Levit, K., Cowan, C., Lazenby, H. Sensenig, A., McDonnell, P., Stiller, J., & Martin, A. (2000, January-February). Health spending in 1998: Signals of charge. *Health Affairs, 19*(1), 124-132.

Medicare Payment Advisory Commission. (2000a, March). *Report to the Congress: Medicare payment policy.* Washington, DC: Author.

Medicare Payment Advisory Commission. (2000b, June). *Report to the Congress: Medicare payment policy.* Washington, DC: Author.

Medicare Payment Advisory Commission. (2001, March). *Report to the Congress.* Washington, DC: Author.

Medicare reform needs to address chronically ill in addition to drug benefits. (2001, January 26). Available online at www. medscape.com/reuters/prof/2001/01/01.26/20010125manc 002.html.

Schoen, C., Simantov, E., Duchon, L., & Davis, K. (2000, July). *Counting on Medicare: Perspectives and concerns of Americans ages 50-70.* New York: Commonwealth Fund.

POLICY SPOTLIGHT

MEDICARE PAYMENT AND REIMBURSEMENT POLICIES FOR NURSE ANESTHESIA PRACTICE

Rita M. Rupp & John Garde

"I was taught that the way of progress is neither swift nor easy."

MARIE CURIE

A number of federal initiatives in the last two decades have had a significant impact on the nurse anesthesia profession. Three federal reimbursement policies significantly affected the American Association of Nurse Anesthetists (AANA) and its 27,000 members. Three case studies related to federal reimbursement and payment policy are presented here to demonstrate the degree to which federal policy can affect the economics of a profession, the ability of federal rules to create barriers to practice, and the ability of federal regulations to cause inefficiencies in the delivery of anesthesia services. The cases demonstrate the politics that are generated when the interests of overlapping professions—nurse anesthesia and physician anesthesia—have high stakes in the outcome.

THE NURSE ANESTHESIA PROFESSION

Certified registered nurse anesthetists (CRNAs) are educated in the specialty of anesthesia at the graduate level in an integrated program of academic and clinical study. CRNAs are licensed and certified to practice anesthesia. In addition, they must meet the requirement of recertification every 2 years. CRNAs are eligible to receive reimbursement for their services directly from Medicare, from nearly half of all Medicaid programs, from TRICARE (formerly the Civilian Health and Medical Program of the Uniformed Services [CHAMPUS]), and from a multitude of private insurers and managed care organizations.

Today CRNAs working with anesthesiologists, physicians such as surgeons, and, where authorized, podiatrists, dentists, and other health care providers, administer approximately 65% of all anesthetics given each year in the United States. CRNAs provide anesthesia for every age and type of patient using the full scope of anesthesia techniques, drugs, and technology that characterize contemporary anesthesia practice. They work in every setting in which anesthesia is delivered: tertiary care centers, community hospitals, labor and delivery rooms, ambulatory surgical centers, diagnostic suites, and physician offices. CRNAs are the sole anesthesia providers in more than 70% of rural hospitals, affording anesthesia and resuscitative services to these medical facilities for surgical, obstetrical, and trauma care.

Historical Perspective

Nurses were the first professional group to provide anesthesia services in the United States. Established in the late 1800s, nurse anesthesia has since become recognized as the first clinical nursing specialty. The discipline of nurse anesthesia developed in response to surgeon requests for a solution to the high morbidity and mortality attributed to anesthesia at that time. Surgeons saw nurses as a cadre of professionals who could give their undivided attention to patient care during surgical procedures. Serving as pioneers in anesthesia, nurse anesthetists became involved in the full range of specialty surgical procedures, as well as in the refinement of anesthesia techniques and equipment.

The earliest existing records documenting the anesthetic care of patients by nurses were those of Sister Mary Bernard, a Catholic nun who worked at St. Vincent's Hospital in Erie, Pennsylvania, in 1887. The most famous nurse anesthetist of the nineteenth century, Alice Magaw, worked at St. Mary's Hospital (1889), in Rochester, Minnesota. That hospital, established by the Sisters of St. Francis and operated by Dr. William Worrell Mayo, later became internationally recognized as the Mayo Clinic. Dr. Charles Mayo conferred on Alice Magaw the title of "mother of anesthesia" for her many achievements in the field of anesthesiology, particularly her mastery of the open-drop inhalation technique of anesthesia using ether and chloroform and her subsequent publication of her findings. Together, Dr. Mayo and Ms. Magaw were instrumental in establishing a showcase of professional excellence in anesthesia and surgery. Hundreds of physicians and nurses from the United States and throughout the world came to observe and learn their anesthesia techniques. Alice Magaw documented the anesthesia practice outcomes at St. Mary's Hospital and reported them in various medical journals between 1899 and 1906. In 1906 one article documented more than 14,000 anesthetics being administered without a single complication attributable to anesthesia (Surgery, Gynecology, and Obstetrics, 1906).

In 1909 the first formal educational programs preparing nurse anesthetists were established. In 1914 Dr. George Crile and his nurse anesthetist, Agatha Hodgins, who became the founder of the AANA, went to France with the American Ambulance group to assist in planning for the establishment of hospitals that would provide for the care of the sick and wounded members of the Allied Forces. While there, Hodgins taught both physicians and nurses from England and France how to administer anesthesia.

Since World War I, nurse anesthetists have been the principal anesthesia providers in combat areas of every war in which the United States has been engaged. Although nurse anesthesia educational programs existed before World War I, the war sharply increased the demand for nurse anesthetists and, consequently, the need for more educational programs. Founded in 1931, the AANA is the professional association representing more than 27,000 nurse anesthetists nationwide. The AANA promulgates education and practice standards and serves as a resource to both private and governmental entities regarding nurse anesthetists and their practice. The accreditation of nurse anesthesia educational programs and the certification and recertification of nurse anesthetists is a function of the AANA autonomous multidisciplinary councils.

NURSE ANESTHESIA REIMBURSEMENT

Nurse anesthetists gained Medicare direct reimbursement in 1986. To fully understand the history leading to this achievement, a beginning understanding of the structure of the Medicare program is important. Medicare Part A establishes the regulations by which hospitals and ambulatory care facilities are reimbursed for services, supplies, drugs, and equipment used in the care of Medicare patients. Medicare Part B sets forth the payment regulations for health care professionals who are eligible to receive direct reimbursement through the Medicare program. The requirements that must be met to receive direct reimbursement from Medicare Part B are distinct and separate from those in Medicare Part A.

With the advent of the Medicare program in 1965, payment for the anesthesia services provided by nurse anesthetists was provided through both Part A and Part B of the Medicare program. For the services provided by CRNAs who were hospital-employed, the hospitals were reimbursed under Part A for "reasonable costs" of anesthesia services. For the services provided by CRNAs who were employed by anesthesiologists, the anesthesiologists who employed and supervised CRNAs could bill under Part B as if they personally performed the anesthesia case. These forms of payment were workable until 1983, when the Prospective Payment System (PPS) legislation was passed by Congress in an effort to control hospital costs to the Medicare program. The law provided that all services by providers, other than those reimbursed through Medicare Part B, would be bundled into a hospital diagnosis-related group (DRG) payment. The legislation created serious problems relative to the payment for nurse anesthesia services: (1) hospitals would have been required to pay for their CRNA employees from the fixed DRG payment, jeopardizing their ability to recoup actual costs and creating a disincentive for hospitals to employ CRNAs; and (2) because PPS precluded the unbundling of services, anesthesiologists who employed CRNAs would have been forced to contract with hospitals to get the CRNA portion of the DRG. Simply put, CRNA services were effectively nonreimbursable.

In addition, it was the hospitals that had accrued Medicare cost savings by using the services of CRNAs that stood to be hurt the most by the move to a DRG payment system. Hospitals using more physicians for such services did not need to take the costs from the DRG payment because physician services were reimbursed from Medicare Part B and were not part of the services to be paid through the DRG. This offered the prospect for hospitals to reap a so-called "windfall profit" for using more-costly providers and a strong incentive for hospitals using CRNA services to shift such services to physicians. For every $1 paid to CRNAs, anesthesiologists were being paid $3 to $4. If the substitution of anesthesiologists for CRNAs were to increase, the cost of anesthesia care to Medicare beneficiaries could be expected to escalate (Garde, 1988).

ADVOCACY ISSUES

Because of the potential negative effect of the PPS legislation on nurse anesthetists, AANA advocated the following legislative changes:

1. A provision should be established to allow a temporary pass-through of hospitals' CRNA costs for a 3-year period, which would assure hospitals of no financial loss on CRNA services.
2. A single exception to the unbundling provisions of the law should be allowed for anesthesiologist-employed CRNAs, because it was questionable if anesthesiologists could bill for CRNA services under the new provision.

3. The Omnibus Budget Reconciliation Act (OBRA) of 1986 should include direct reimbursement for CRNAs to become effective January 1, 1989, with extension of the two temporary provisions to the effective date of the legislation.

The mission of the AANA was to convince Congress and the Health Care Financing Administration (HCFA, renamed the Centers for Medicare and Medicaid Services [CMS] in 2001) that CRNAs were concerned about health care costs as well as equitable reimbursement for their services. Even though the American Society of Anesthesiologists opposed the direct reimbursement legislation, AANA's message was understood because it made financial sense. Use of CRNAs in the provision of anesthesia services represents substantial cost savings from several standpoints. On average, the income of CRNAs is one third that of anesthesiologists. Also, the educational cost of preparing CRNAs is significantly less than that needed to prepare anesthesiologists. The anesthesiologists knew these numbers, and those within their ranks that opposed direct reimbursement for nurse anesthetists had to have been concerned about the potential for increased competition that could come about if the nurse anesthetists were to have equity in the market for anesthesia services.

A convincing case was made before Congress, and legislation was passed granting CRNAs direct Medicare reimbursement. Two payment schedules were incorporated in the law: one for CRNAs not medically directed by anesthesiologists and the other for CRNAs working under anesthesiologists' medical direction (Gunn, 1997).

As a result of this legislation, all CRNAs, regardless of whether they are employed or are in independent practice, have the ability to receive reimbursement from Medicare directly or to sign over their billing rights to their employer. In addition to Medicare direct reimbursement, CRNA are reimbursed through many health plans. Although CRNAs still face a variety of practice barriers in some facilities and health plans, they can and do serve as an exclusive provider for the full range of anesthesia services at hospitals and ambulatory surgical facilities.

TAX EQUITY AND FISCAL RESPONSIBILITY ACT OF 1982

The Tax Equity and Fiscal Responsibility Act of 1982 (TEFRA) was enacted into federal law as a means to control escalating Medicare costs for hospital-based services including anesthesiology, pathology, and radiology. Among the many cost concerns that TEFRA addressed was a need to ensure that an anesthesiologist provided specified services when billing Medicare for medical direction when a CRNA was administering the anesthesia. Before enactment of TEFRA, anesthesiologists could bill for their services in conjunction with supervision of hospital-employed CRNAs without demonstrating that he or she provided specific services to qualify for such payment. The 1976 Medicare manual (4-76, 2050.2, Rev. 3-512, 2.21) did require that the "physician be close by and available to provide immediate and personal assistance and direction." The Medicare manual stated that availability by telephone did not constitute direct, personal, and continuous service. In the next years, private payers began refusing to reimburse anesthesiologists for more than two concurrent procedures owing to the fact that many anesthesiologists were being paid for supervision of nurse anesthetist-administered cases in which the anesthesiologists were unavailable. At the same time that these physician payment practices were coming under increased scrutiny, AANA had been preparing its case for Congress in pursuit of direct reimbursement for CRNAs. Part of the reimbursement argument that AANA advanced related to the issue of the lack of equitable reimbursement between substitutible providers, in this case, CRNAs and anesthesiologists. As previously discussed, there were numerable instances across the country where anesthesiologists were being paid for participation in cases in which CRNAs were the sole provider administering the anesthesia. The anesthesiologists were unavailable, yet they were billing for the case as if they were involved.

In 1983 HCFA published the final rules implementing TEFRA relative to payment for anesthesiology physician services. In instituting the rules, HCFA chose a 1:4 ratio for medical direction, limiting payment to an anesthesiologist to no more than four concurrent procedures administered by

Department of Health and Human Services Health Care Financing Administration Medicare Program: Provisions to Payment under the Physician Fee Schedule

405.552 Conditions for payment of charges: Concurrent anesthesiology service	415.110 Conditions for payment: Medically directed anesthesia services (proposed language)	415.110 Conditions for payment: Medically directed anesthesia services (final language)
Performs a preanesthetic examination and evaluation.	Performs a preanesthetic examination and evaluation, or reviews one performed by another qualified individual permitted by the State to administer anesthetics.	(a) General payment rule. Medicare pays for the physician's medical direction of anesthesia services for one service or two through four concurrent anesthesia services furnished after December 31, 1998, only if each of the services meets the conditions in Section 415.102(a) and the following additional conditions:
		(1) For each patient, the physician:
Prescribes the anesthesia plan.	Participates in the development of the anesthesia plan and gives final approval of the proposed plan.	(i) Performs a preanesthetic examination and evaluation.
Personally participates in the most demanding procedures in the anesthesia plan, including induction and emergence.	Personally participates in the most demanding procedures of the anesthesia plan.	(ii) Prescribes the anesthesia plan.
Ensures that any procedures in the anesthesia plan that he or she does not perform are performed by a qualified individual as defined in program operating instructions.	Ensures that any aspect of the anesthesia plan not performed by the anesthesiologist is performed by a qualified individual as specified in operating instructions.	(iii) Personally participates in the most demanding aspects of the anesthesia plan including, if applicable, induction and emergence.
Monitors the course of anesthesia at frequent intervals.	Monitors the course of anesthesia at intervals medically indicated by the nature of the procedure and the patient's condition.	(iv) Ensures that any procedures in the anesthesia plan that he or she does not perform are performed by a qualified individual as defined in operating instructions.

CRNAs. The rules implemented seven conditions that an anesthesiologist must satisfy to obtain reimbursement for the medical direction of CRNAs (U.S. Department of Health and Human Service, 1983). The original TEFRA conditions are listed in the accompanying table (48 FR March 2, 1983).

Over time, it has been found that the TEFRA regulations that stipulate the role of anesthesiologists in anesthesia care have served to create disruptions in the overall delivery and flow of services in the operating room settings, causing needless and costly delays. The AANA believes that changes favoring less-restrictive conditions would allow more flexibility in allocation of anesthesia personnel and effect a more expedient service provided to patients. For example, if CRNAs could initiate the induction of the patient rather than waiting for the anesthesiologist to be physically present in the room as required by TEFRA, the surgical case flow and use of personnel could be more efficiently and effectively managed.

In the early 1990s, in the course of the Physician Payment Review Commission's study of anesthesia payments (which was intended to examine ways to reduce anesthesia team payments in cases involving both anesthesiologists and CRNAs), government-related study groups and individual research studies were reporting the need for changes in TEFRA. The 1992 Center for Health Economics

Department of Health and Human Services Health Care Financing Administration Medicare Program: Provisions to Payment under the Physician Fee Schedule—cont'd

Remains physically present and available for immediate diagnosis and treatment of emergencies. Provides indicated postanesthesia care.	Remains physically present in the facility and immediately available for diagnostic and therapeutic emergencies. Provides indicated postanesthesia care or ensures that it is done by a qualified individuals	(v) Monitors the course of anesthesia administration at frequent intervals. (vi) Remains physically present and available for immediate diagnosis and treatment of emergencies. (viii) Provides indicated postanesthesia care. (2) The physician directs no more than four anesthesia services concurrently and does not perform any other services while he or she is directing the single or concurrent services so that one or more of the conditions in paragraph (a) (1) of this section are not violated. (3) If the physician personally performs the anesthesia service, the payment rule in Section 414.46 (c) of this chapter applies (physician personally performs the anesthesia procedure).
Source: As adopted as 48 FR 8938 (March 2, 1983, effective October 1, 1983)	Source: As proposed as 63 FR 30884 (June 5, 1998)	Source: As adopted as 63 FR 58912 (November 2, 1998; effective January 1, 1999)

From the Federal Register (1998, November). 211.

In addition to these regulatory changes, new proposed language on documentation was put forth as follows: "Medical documentation. The physician personally and inclusively documents in the patient's medical record that the conditions set forth in paragraph (a) (1) of this section have been satisfied, specifically documenting personal participation in the most demanding aspects of the anesthesia plan."

Research (CHER) report to the Physician Payment Review Commission (PPRC) recommended the following: "Refinements to the TEFRA provisions should be considered in view of the reductions in payments to the anesthesia care team. In particular, opportunities for increasing the flexibility of role functions should be reviewed. Considerations should also be given to the appropriateness of promulgating specific practice standards within a payment policy" (PPRC Report to Congress, 1993). The CHER report went on to say that "with the implication of a capped payment, the HCFA should consider whether to review the TEFRA requirements to see if modifications of the TEFRA

rules would permit greater efficiencies without decreasing the quality of care" (PPRC Report to Congress, 1993). Even though the federal government did not initiate efforts to revise the TEFRA conditions, PPRC's report did acknowledge that there was merit to study the issue. More importantly, these PPRC policy deliberations on payment for the anesthesia team led the PPRC to conclude that "the use of the anesthesia care team seems to be determined by individual preferences for that practice arrangement. There appears to be no demonstrated quality of care differences between the care provided by the solo anesthesiologist, solo CRNA, and the team." No longer could anesthesiologists argue that medical direction of CRNAs by anesthesiologists and the TEFRA conditions under which medical direction is provided represent any safer or higher standard of care than the care provided by a CRNA practicing alone or an anesthesiologist practicing alone. The final conclusion reached by PPRC on anesthesia payment represented a milestone in the recognition of anesthesia services provided by nurse anesthetists. A single payment methodology for anesthesia services was recommended by PPRC and adopted by Congress, which resulted in a policy that the payment for anesthesia services—whether provided by a CRNA-anesthesiologist team or by a solo anesthesiologist or solo CRNA—would be the same. The payment to the team would be split so that each practitioner receives 50% (PPRC Report to Congress, 1993).

In 1997, as part of its legislative agenda, the AANA initiated a congressional lobbying effort to revise the TEFRA conditions of payment for medical direction by anesthesiologists of CRNAs. In 1998 the AANA shifted its focus from legislative strategies for revision of TEFRA to revision through the regulatory process. In a joint meeting in 1998 with the American Society of Anesthesiologists (ASA), AANA, and HCFA, proposals were advanced by both AANA and ASA for revisions in the seven conditions of payment for physician medical direction. The ASA and the AANA reached consensus on a revised recommended set of medical direction requirements that are listed as proposed revisions in the preceding table (63 FR June 5, 1998). However, it came to AANA's attention in a publication titled *Anesthesia Answer Book—Action Alert* (1998) that ASA had second thoughts about the agreed-on revisions and indicated that it disagreed that the groups had reached a consensus on this issue. HCFA's response to the concerns posed by the ASA membership and several state anesthesiologist societies was to retain the current requirements established in 1983 (63 FR, November 2, 1998). HCFA did decide that the medically directing physician must be present at induction and emergence for general anesthesia and present as indicated in anesthesia cases not involving general

anesthesia (63 FR, November 2, 1998). HCFA announced plans to study the medical direction issue further, welcomed comments, and suggested it might propose changes in the future (63 F. R. November 2, 1998).

AANA continues to monitor the impact that the TEFRA rules for physician reimbursement for medical direction of CRNAs have on operating room efficiency, patient care, and CRNA practice through anecdotal reporting from CRNA anesthesia department managers and clinical practitioners. Because it is difficult for a health care provider organization to advocate and succeed in changing another provider's mechanism of payment, changes in the TEFRA conditions for payment have to come about incrementally as more evidence supports the problematic impact these conditions have on operating room efficiency and cost.

AANA has been able to influence certain changes in the formulation of the TEFRA conditions for physician medical direction payment and reimbursement for CRNA services in the following ways:

1. The adoption of a 1:4 medical direction ratio rather than a 1:2 ratio, which ASA actively proposed and lobbied for in the formulation of the physician payment schedule in 1983 and 1984
2. A published statement by HCFA that the criterion for medical direction should not be considered quality-related standards, but payment criterion
3. Adoption of 1998 revisions that facilitate some degree of increased flexibility in practice
4. A published requirement that the physician document personal and inclusive involvement in satisfying the conditions for medical direction payment
5. Adoption of a 50% split in payment by the anesthesiologist and CRNA for a case as long as the ratio of medical direction does not exceed 1:4
6. Adoption of a 50% split in payment between the anesthesiologist and CRNA when the medical direction is 1:1. (Before this change, the physician received 100% of the payment.)

PHYSICIAN SUPERVISION OF CRNAs: MEDICARE CONDITIONS OF PARTICIPATION

The current Medicare regulations require physician supervision of CRNAs as a condition for hospitals, ambulatory surgical centers (ASCs), and critical access hospitals (CAHs) to receive Medicare payment. These regulations do not require that a CRNA be supervised by an anesthesiologist.

During the 1990s, AANA pursued a revision of these Medicare conditions of participation that would remove the physician supervision requirement for CRNAs. As of February 2002, 31 states have no physician supervision or direction requirement of CRNAs in nurse practice acts, board of nursing rules, regulations, medical practice acts, board of medicine rules, or their general equivalents. Clearly this is an indication that many states, as a matter of public policy, believe it is unnecessary to require physician supervision of CRNAs.

In December 1997 HCFA released for comment the proposed revisions in the Medicare Conditions of Participation for Hospitals, ASCs and CAHs, which would eliminate the requirement for physician supervision of CRNAs, deferring instead to state law. HCFA's proposal to remove the physician supervision requirement was opposed by the ASA, which expressed its opposition through lobbying the administration, conducting media campaigns, soliciting its members and the public to write to the administration and Congress, and pushing for a legislatively mandated study that, if enacted, would preempt HCFA from publishing the final rule. The ASA's main message has been that patients will die if the rule is implemented. Another frequently used argument claimed that a change in this rule would be detrimental to Medicare beneficiaries. In support of their claim, ASA conducted a survey of seniors that reportedly indicated that they were not in favor of HCFA's proposed rule change. To counter the claims, the AANA commissioned a survey of Medicare patients conducted in October 1999 by an independent research firm, Wirthlin Worldwide. The survey revealed the following: (1) 88% of Medicare beneficiaries surveyed would be comfortable if their surgeon chose a nurse anesthetist to provide their anesthesia care; (2) 81% surveyed prefer a nurse anesthetist or have no preference between a nurse anesthetist or physician anesthesiologist when it comes to their anesthesia care; and (3) 62% of those surveyed find it acceptable for the nurse anesthetist to not be supervised by their surgeon, but to work collaboratively with the surgeon who would be present throughout the surgery ("Nine out of 10 Medicare patients," 2000).

From the time that the proposed rule was announced, the AANA implemented a number of key activities to advocate its position on this supervision issue. These included but were not limited to the following:

1. AANA representatives met with many key government personnel to advocate on behalf of CRNAs on the issue of supervision. Meetings were held with HCFA analysts, the Administrator of HCFA (Nancy-Ann Min DeParle), members of Congress and their staff, the Secretary of Health and Human Services (HHS) (Donna Shalala), staff members of the White House, the staff of the Office of Management and Budget, and others.

2. As ASA's opposition to the proposed rule increased, together with the delay in HCFA's announcement of the final rule, AANA called upon Senator Kent Conrad (D-ND) and Representative Jim Nussle (R-IA) to introduce legislation requiring HCFA to implement the proposed regulation related to deleting physician supervision of CRNAs in the hospital, ASC, and CAH as conditions for receiving Medicare payment.

3. AANA retained outside legislative consultants to assist in the promotion of its legislative initiatives.

4. AANA's public relations endeavors focused on increasing the public's awareness of the issues and advocating the position of the vital role that CRNAs play in anesthesia delivery in the country. Efforts included advertising in many news publications, including Capitol Hill newspapers and *USA Today*; assisting with media training for AANA officers and staff to

increase their effectiveness on radio programs and in interviews; and developing radio advertisements in Washington, DC to garner support for AANA's position.

5. AANA retained grass roots political action consultants to assist in gaining letters of support for the new proposed regulations from key members of Congress.

6. AANA solicited a broad base of support from the nursing organization community, national hospital associations, related health professional associations, civic organizations, individual nurses, physicians, and the general public.

These advocacy efforts yielded an extensive base of support from all sectors. AANA gained support for the proposed rule ranged from the American Hospital Association; VHA, Inc.; Premier, Inc.; National Rural Health Association; Federation of American Health Systems; St. Paul Fire and Marine Insurance Company; Kaiser Permenante Central Office; California and Oregon Kaiser System; and numerous rural hospitals across the country. The list of national and health professional associations, individual nurses and physicians, and the public at large that have written letters to HCFA on this issue is extensive.

On March 9, 2000, after deliberating for more than 2 years, HCFA informed ASA and AANA that the proposed rule removing the physician-supervision requirement for nurse anesthetists from the Medicare conditions of payment for hospitals, ASCs, and CAHs would be forthcoming. HCFA further indicated that the final rule would be published in the *Federal Register* in June 2000. However, it was not until January 18, 2001, that HCFA published the final rule in the *Federal Register*, removing the federal physician supervision requirement for nurse anesthetists and deferring to state law on the issue. On January 20, 2001, the incoming Bush administration announced that it was placing a 60-day blanket moratorium on all regulations published in the final days of the Clinton administration. In accordance with the moratorium, the final rule was scheduled to take effect March 18, 2001. This action was not unexpected. Every new administration takes the opportunity to review pending regulations that are not yet in effect. However, this is a bipartisan issue with members of Congress from both parties on either side of the issue. The AANA continued to work with the Bush administration and urged supporters on Capitol Hill to communicate with administration officials to ask that the scheduled implementation of this rule be allowed.

In reviewing HCFA's final rule and the rationale for its decision, it is evident that all of the major arguments advanced by the ASA opposition were thoroughly refuted. Examples of several of HCFA's conclusions reached in its study of the supervision issue are as follows:

- States have constitutionally and traditionally acted in matters of licensure and scope-of-practice and have not been found to be negligent in their exercise of this authority.

- There is no research in the past 10 years that conclusively demonstrates a need for this federal requirement nor demonstrates that physician or anesthesiologist supervision makes a difference in anesthesia outcomes. HCFA stated in the final rule that studies purported by the American Society of Anesthesiologists (ASA) to demonstrate such findings had serious limitations and did not in fact support such conclusions. Further, HCFA stated that it cannot agree with ASA's belief that anesthesia administration is the practice of medicine and therefore can be done only after medical school training.

- HCFA's rule noted the safety of anesthesia today as reported in a study published by the Institute of Medicine (IOM) (Institute of Medicine Committee on Quality of Health Care in America, 2000). HCFA stated that the improvements in anesthesia safety reported by IOM confirm the soundness of the approach taken in the final rule, which broadens the flexibility of states and providers to make decisions about the best way to improve standards and implement best practices.

- The flexibility resulting from the rule change would provide increased access to services in some areas and broaden the opportunity for providers to implement professional standards of practice that improve quality of care and promote more efficacious models of care delivery for anesthesia services.

This decision by HCFA supports AANA's position that CRNAs provide safe, high-quality anesthesia care and advocates states' rights over federal government regulation, which is generally the norm in health care matters. The decision is also a giant step in enabling hospitals and ambulatory surgical centers to exercise more latitude in the use of anesthesia providers and improve operating room efficiency without affecting quality.

The AANA took its case on supervision to Health and Human Services Secretary Tommy Thompson in February 2001 and continued to urge the 107th Congress to leave the final regulation published by HCFA on January 18, 2001, in place. Although ASA reintroduced legislation calling for continuation of the supervision requirements pending a study on supervision, AANA continued to oppose ASA legislation and urged the Bush administration to do so as well.

On July 5, 2001, CMS (formerly HCFA) published in the *Federal Register* its new proposed rule (66 FR 35395-35399), which, if implemented, would replace the January 18 rule. The AANA identified two main issues of concern with the rule:

1. *State exemption from federal supervision requirements.* The proposed rule enables states to "opt-out" of (or seek an exemption from) the federal supervision requirement for CRNAs. Hospitals, ambulatory surgical centers, and critical access hospitals in a particular state would be exempted from the requirement if the governor submitted a letter to CMS requesting the exemption. The letter would need to attest that the governor:
   - Consulted with the boards of medicine and nursing about issues related to access and the quality of anesthesia services in the state.
   - Concluded that it is in the best interests of the state's citizens to opt-out of the physician supervision requirement.
   - Determined that opting out was consistent with state law.
2. *Prospective anesthesia outcome study.* The proposal would have the Agency for Health Research and Quality (AHRQ) design and conduct a prospective study to assess *only* CRNA practices with input from CMS,

anesthesiologists, and CRNAs or, alternatively, establish a registry to monitor *only* CRNA practice.

The proposed rule was considered by AANA to be a potential political nightmare that, without appropriate modifications, would allow state medical boards to dictate how nurse anesthetists would be regulated on a state-by-state basis. In addition, the governors would be the targets of intense lobbying by organized medicine, and any exemption from supervision could be removed at any time because of this political pressure, creating a constant state of legal and professional limbo for CRNAs and the facilities they serve.in communicating with other national nursing organizations, AANA noted the negative effect this rule, as written, would have for the nursing profession. In essence, it would allow organized medicine to control the practice of nursing and foster the creation of barriers to patients' access to care provided by advanced practice nurses. In AANA's view, the end result would be limiting competition in health care markets and restricting the public's right to quality care provided by nursing specialists.

AANA's response to CMS in response to the July 5 proposed rule presented the following arguments:

1. Revert to the January 18, 2001, final rule and defer to state law concerning anesthesia services regarding the issue of physician supervision of CRNAs. This was the correct approach that was also reflected in HCFA's December 19, 1997, proposed rule.
2. If CMS reverts to the January 18 rule, it should consider either a scientifically valid study comparing anesthesia outcomes of patients receiving anesthesia from unsupervised CRNAs with those receiving anesthesia from anesthesiologists personally providing the service or a monitoring effort comparing anesthesia outcomes of CRNAs before and after the removal of physician supervision requirements. If outcomes are similar, then CMS should take appropriate action to eliminate entirely the federal CRNA supervision requirement.

The AANA recommended to CMS that if it did not revert to the January 18, 2001, final rule, a number of amendments to the July 5 proposed rule should be made, which included implementing automatic waivers for all states that do not require physician supervision of CRNAs and considering either a scientifically valid study or a monitoring effort to involve both nurse anesthetists and anesthesiologists, as described in the second item in the response to CMS.

Many organizations and individuals wrote to CMS in response to the July 5 rule, requesting that it revert to the January 18, 2001, rule. As one example, in August 2001 the American Hospital Association issued to its members a regulatory advisory noting that it will continue to advocate that the administration return to the HCFA standard published in the January 18, 2001 rule.

Whatever the outcome of the July 5 proposed rule, the AANA has taken the position that, based on HCFA's decision with the January 18 final rule and the strong arguments made by HCFA in support of this rule, this in and of itself represents a victory. It is not only a victory for the nurse anesthesia profession, but a victory as well for the public who rightfully deserve to have full access to quality anesthesia services wherever they may need or choose to seek it.

LESSONS LEARNED

The primary impetus for seeking direct reimbursement legislation was the problem created by a new Medicare payment system that had the potential of threatening the viability of the nurse anesthesia profession. However, AANA saw a clear opportunity to seek this legislation not only as a means of correcting bad legislation but also as a means of obtaining equity in payment for the services provided by nurse anesthetists, thus creating a more equitable market in which to promote their services as fully qualified anesthesia providers.

The AANA has learned from its experience in the political and legislative arena that politics is the use of power for change. Although politics may not always be nice or fair, it is critical that health care professionals engage in the political process. As has been illustrated in the federal policy initiatives discussed in this chapter, there are generally other forces at work to attempt to influence policy decisions that can have a detrimental impact on one's profession. Therefore, the choice of whether to engage should be a simple one. The achievements won in the federal policy arena by AANA could not have been possible without the commitment and dedication of its members, who provide grass roots support; participate in local and national campaigns of elected members of Congress; provide congressional testimony; participate in public relations campaigns; write letters; make phone calls; organize communications systems; meet personally with leaders of business, industry, and government agencies; and provide donations to the political action committee, CRNA-PAC. One illustration of the strength of the AANA members' support is the fact that in December 1999, AANA was ranked for the first time on the *Fortune* magazine list of Washington's most powerful lobbying organizations. AANA was the only nursing organization and the only non-physician health care group association to make the list of 114 associations, labor unions, and interest groups. AANA registered at 101 out of 114 on the list of influential entities (Fortune, 1999).

However, it is very rare for a single group to be able to promote legislation or to effect major policy change. In the case of the federal supervision requirement for nurse anesthetists, networking with other groups, especially with nursing organizations, has been critical to achieving support on Capitol Hill and in communications with the executive branch. When nursing speaks with one voice, it is a formidable force. In the case of the nurse anesthetists and their supervision, many have rallied and provided support. The message to legislators has been loud and clear: Remove restrictive barriers to practice when it is in the public's interest and is sound health care policy.

REFERENCES

Fortune. (1999, December 6). *The Fortune Magazine power list.*

Garde, J.F. (1988). A case study involving prospective payment legislation, DRGs, and certified registered nurse anesthetists. *Nursing Clinics of North America, 23*(3), 521-530.

Gunn, I.P. (1997). Nurse anesthesia. In J.J. Nagelhout & K.L. Zaglaniczny (Eds.). *Nurse anesthesia.* Philadelphia: W.B. Saunders.

Institute of Medicine Committee on Quality of Health Care in America. (2000). *To err is human: Building a safer health system.* Kohn, L.T., Corrigan, J., & Donaldson, M.S. (Eds.). Washington, DC: National Academy Press.

Magaw, A. (2000, March 9). A review of our fourteen thousand surgical anesthesias (AANA press release). Park Ridge, IL: American Association of Nurse Anesthetists.

Nine out of 10 Medicare patients are comfortable with nurse anesthesia care. (2000, January 24). *Roll Call.*

PPRC Report to Congress. (1993). *Payments for the anesthesia care team.* Washington, DC: Physician Payment Reviews Commission.

Providing anesthesia into the next century. (1997, January). Park Ridge, IL: American Association of Nurse Anesthetists.

Surgery, Gynecology and Obstetrics. (1906, December). *3*, 795-799.

U.S. Department of Health and Human Service. (1983). 48 FR, March 2, 1983.

U.S. Department of Health and Human Service. (2001). 66 FR, January 18, 2001.

U.S. Department of Health and Human Service. (2001). 66 FR, July 5, 2001.

POLICYSPOTLIGHT

SOCIAL SECURITY: KEY TO ECONOMIC SECURITY

Shirley S. Chater

"There is one thing stronger than all the armies in the world: an idea whose time has come."

VICTOR HUGO

Popular stories suggest that older Americans frequently choose between buying food and medications. It is well known that poverty contributes to illness and poor health. Without some degree of economic security, there can be no health security. The Social Security Act, signed into law in 1935 by President Franklin Delano Roosevelt, provides a minimum "floor of protection" for retired workers. Later Social Security was broadened to provide benefits for workers and their families who face a loss of income due to disability or the death of a family wage earner. Social Security, covering more than 150 million workers and paying benefits to more than 45 million people, is recognized as the most successful domestic federal program.

During the last few years, the program has come under attack from some policymakers, selected members of Congress, and the press, with allegations that the program will be "bankrupt": that benefits paid will exceed tax revenues and that Social Security will not be there when it is needed. This argument has some merit, but the situation is not catastrophic, and the financial instability has not reached a crisis level, despite what some would have us believe. It is true that fewer workers are paying into the system now than before and that benefits are being paid for longer periods of time as longevity increases. In 2000 there were 3.4 workers for each retiree; by 2044 that number will be reduced to about 2 workers for each retiree. Today there are more than 35 million Americans over the age of 65, but by 2030 there will be twice as many. Americans over the age of 85 represent the fastest-growing population group. The persuasive facts regarding the future financial status of the program come annually from the report of the trustees of the program. Therefore, although there is no "crisis," there are compelling reasons why the Social Security program should be reexamined to see what solutions will guarantee fiscal stability for the future.

SOCIAL SECURITY PROGRAM

Social Security is a family program, providing monthly benefits to retirees, to survivors, and to persons who are disabled. The program is based on the simple concept that if you work, you pay taxes into the system, and when you retire or become disabled, you, your spouse and your dependent children receive monthly benefits that are based on your earnings. Your survivors collect benefits when you die. Most people think of social security as a retirement program. Of all beneficiaries, 61% *are* retirees, but others are survivors of those who died— a widow, widower, or child. Still others are persons with disabilities who have worked, paid into the system, and qualify under the definition of disability used by the Social Security program. Of the 45 million people receiving benefits from Social Security in the year 2000, 31 million are retired workers and family members, 7 million are survivors, and 6.7 million are disabled persons. It is interesting to note that owing to retirement, survivor, and disability benefits earmarked for children of American workers, more children, a total of 3.8 million, are covered by benefits from Social Security than by any other government program (Social Security Administration, 2000a).

The Social Security program is financed by a "pay as you go" system with present day workers paying for present day beneficiaries. Each worker pays Social Security taxes of 7.65% (6.2% for social security and 1.45% for Medicare) of gross salary. The employer also pays an equal amount. For the self-employed, both parts of the payroll tax are paid by the individual, but one-half is tax-deductible as a business expense. In 2001 Social Security taxes are paid on gross salary up to $80,400. There is no maximum limit for taxes paid for Medicare. The taxes are paid into the Social Security Trust Fund. According to the law, excess funds not needed for immediate payment to beneficiaries or for administrative expenses are invested with interest in U.S. government bonds. Funds are returned for Social Security purposes as needed.

Eligibility for coverage of Social Security is acquired by earning "credits" for working and paying into the system. People who are dependents or survivors may receive benefits based on another's work record. The worker earns one "credit" for each $830 earned, up to four credits per year. Many people still refer to credits as *quarters* or *quarters of coverage*. The dollar amount required to be earned per credit is established every year. Most workers need 40 quarters to qualify for benefits, although younger people need fewer credits to qualify for disability or

> The specific rules and regulations for calculating the benefit formula and implementing the program are complex. Readers are advised to visit Social Security's website at www.ssa.gov for easy-to-use on-line benefit calculators or seek consultation from a local Social Security office.

for family members to be eligible for survivor benefits if the worker dies. How much workers pay into the system helps to determine how much they will receive in benefits. High-wage earners get higher benefits than low-wage earners. However, the benefit formula is weighted in favor of the low-wage earner by providing 53% of preretirement earnings compared with the replacement of 40% of an average wage earner's preretirement earnings.

Retirement

For people retiring today, the usual retirement age is 65, and the average monthly benefit is $844. Some, however, choose to retire as early as age 62 with a benefit amount that is 20% less than the full retirement amount. In 1981 Congress passed a law that changed the retirement age to 67 for those born in 1938 and later. The change gradually increases from 65 to 67 beginning in 2003, so that by 2027, the retirement age is 67. For those whose full retirement age is 67, retirement at age 62 is still an option, but with a reduction in benefits of 30%. Generally speaking, early retirement is calculated to give you about the same total Social Security benefits over a lifetime but in smaller amounts. This takes into account the longer period the early retiree receives benefits. On the other hand, delaying retirement and continuing to work adds earnings to the worker's record, increasing the eventual benefit amount. The dual result of retiring later than the usual retirement age is an increased benefit when Social Security benefits are finally paid.

During the time a worker receives retirement benefits, a spouse can also receive benefits on the worker's record if the spouse is 62 years or older. (The spouse can also receive benefits at retirement age on his or her own work record, and Social Security pays whichever benefit is higher.) At full retire-

Age to Receive Full Social Security Benefits

YEAR OF BIRTH	FULL RETIREMENT AGE
1937 or earlier	65
1938	65 and 2 months
1939	65 and 4 months
1940	65 and 6 months
1941	65 and 8 months
1942	65 and 10 months
1943-1954	66
1955	66 and 2 months
1956	66 and 4 months
1957	66 and 6 months
1958	66 and 8 months
1959	66 and 10 months
1960 and later	67

From the Social Security Administration. Available online at www.ssa.gov/retirement.

ment age, the spouse receives one-half of the retired worker's full benefit.

When the worker retires, other benefits are paid to family members who meet the requirements (Social Security Administration, 2000b):

- A spouse under age 62, if caring for the worker's child who is under age 16 or disabled
- A former wife or husband age 62 or older
- Children up to age 18
- Children ages 18 or 19 if they are full-time students through grade 12
- Children over age 18 if they are disabled

There are certain limits on how much money a family may receive. First, the full amount of the worker's benefit is provided. Then, if the benefits of all other family members exceed the limit, they are adjusted proportionately, keeping the total equal to the limit set by law.

Several factors affect the amount of Social Security benefits paid monthly. First, if the worker chooses to receive benefits at age 62 and decides to work as well, there is a penalty in which $1 in benefits will be deducted for each $2 in earnings above an annual limit. The limit for 2001 is $10,680. In other words, the worker, age 62, can earn $10,680 without reducing his Social Security benefits. During the months of the year the worker becomes 65, he is penalized $1 for every $3 earned over the limit of $25,000 for the year 2001. Limits are established every year. After reaching full retirement age, the worker can work as much as he likes without penalty.

Survivors Benefits

When a family member who has worked and paid into Social Security dies, his survivors may qualify for benefits. Survivors include widows, widowers (as well as divorced widows and widowers), children, and dependent parents. This life insurance benefit helps to keep families together after the breadwinner dies. Widows or widowers receive full benefits at full retirement age or reduced benefits as early as age 60. Widows or widowers who are raising children under age 16 or who are disabled can get full benefits at any age. Children under age 18 are also eligible for benefits, and if they are still in school at age 19, they too qualify for survivor benefits. Dependent parents who are 62 or older also qualify.

Disability

Social Security also provides benefits to persons who become disabled. According to the Social Security administration, studies show that a 20-year-old worker has a 33% chance of becoming disabled before reaching retirement age. Social Security pays benefits to those who are unable to work for a year or more because of a disability. Social Security uses a definition of disability different from other programs. For example, it does not pay for partial disability. Disability, as defined by Social Security, exists if workers cannot do the work they did before, if workers cannot adjust to other work, and if the disability is expected to last at least a year or to result in death. Certain family members may also qualify for benefits while the worker is disabled. After age 65 (or full retirement age), disability benefits cease, and retirement benefits begin.

Supplemental Security Income Program

Many people confuse the Social Security program with the Supplemental Security Income (SSI) program because the Social Security Administration manages both. Social Security, as previously noted, is based on the philosophy that if one works and pays taxes for the program, one will qualify for retirement, survivor, and disability benefits. The program allows older Americans and family members to remain independent and to have a degree of economic security. The SSI program is a federal/state welfare program, providing benefits to the most needy. It pays benefits to people who are 65 and older, blind, or disabled and to children who are blind or disabled. To qualify, recipients must have little income and own very little as well. Many SSI beneficiaries also receive food stamps and Medicaid. SSI is funded from general revenue. *Money from the Social Security program is never used to pay for the SSI program.*

SOCIAL SECURITY: A PROGRAM FOR WOMEN

Social Security is a gender-neutral program. But because women live so much longer than men, spend down their savings, and live on pensions (if they have them) that are not usually adjusted for inflation, women depend heavily on their cost-of-living adjusted annual Social Security income. Age differences between women and men tell the story (Annual Statistical Supplement, 2000):

- Total beneficiaries over age 65: 32,711,640
  Women: 19,189,200
  Men: 13,522,440
- Total beneficiaries over age 85: 4,033,170
  Women: 2,878,750
  Men: 1,154,420
- Total beneficiaries over age 100: 39,480
  Women: 33,890
  Men: 5,590

When the Social Security program was signed into law in 1935, few women worked outside the home and the law reflected this. Women were covered under their husbands' work record. Now that more than 60% of women work outside the home, some of the regulations of the program are considered to be antiquated and unrelated to present circumstances. On the other hand, some of the rules of the program are especially helpful to women and need to be retained. Important policy decisions will be made during the next few years as the financial security of the program is debated. Women, women's groups, nurses, and nursing organizations need to follow the debate to ensure that women's benefits are not unnecessarily reduced.

Coverage for widows and divorced women may be targets for future changes. At present widows receive about 71% of the deceased husband's benefit amount if they take benefits at age 60, or 100% if they are age 65. Consistent with the increase in retirement age to age 67, and depending on the year of birth, this rule will change beginning in 2005 and will gradually increase to age 67 by 2029. Divorced women may receive benefits based on an ex-husband's record if he is receiving benefits (or is deceased) if she had been married for 10 years or longer, assuming she is unmarried and at least 62 years of age. If women qualify for benefits on their own work record *and* on their husbands' or former husbands' record, Social Security pays whichever benefit is higher, but not both. Personnel from the Social Security Administration will always study the individual record of each inquiry and suggest the best option, guaranteeing the highest benefit under the circumstances.

FINDING FINANCIAL STABILITY FOR SOCIAL SECURITY

The Board of Trustees of the Social Security Administration reports annually to Congress about the financial stability of the program. In the 2001 report, the trustees estimated that the program would be solvent until 2038, when there would only be enough money to pay approximately 73% of expected benefits (2001 OASDI Trustees Report, 2001). In order to "fix" the program, many policy options have been and will continue to be suggested. These options fall either into categories of increasing revenues through taxation or reducing benefits. Neither option is easy: It seems unlikely that Congress will favor increased payroll taxes, nor will the American people readily accept major benefit reductions. Future policies will certainly be controversial. Many believe that the best solution to the financial problem is a combination of new policies that would slightly reduce benefits, while also increasing revenue to the Social Security trust fund. These thoughtful suggestions for creating a "package" of minor changes in the program assume that the present structure of the program would be retained. Further, the program's shortfall over 75 years (the period for creating estimates) is 1.86% of payroll, an amount that could be made up with small changes in the program.

The following policy changes are the most frequently suggested remedies for the solvency of the Social Security program:

- *Add all new employees of state and local governments.* At present about 5% of state and local government employees do not pay into the Social Security program. Adding them or adding all new state and local employees to the program would help to increase revenues.
- *Reduce the cost-of-living adjustment (COLA).* Social Security is one of the few programs adjusted annually for the cost of living. Some believe that the COLA, determined by the federal Bureau of Labor Statistics, is too high. If research determines that the COLA should be reduced, it would cut the monthly amount of the Social Security check.
- *Increase the retirement age.* Some suggest that the retirement age should be extended to age 68 or 70 because people are living and working longer. Others suggest that the retirement age, which is scheduled to rise to 67 from 65 by 2027, be accelerated so that it would be in effect for people who turn 67 in 2016. Increasing the retirement age could adversely affect laborers and others who can no longer work at hard manual labor. Ethnic considerations need to be considered also, because some minority groups have shorter life spans.
- *Change the formula for calculating benefits from 35 years to 38 years of highest earnings.* At present, benefits are calculated by using the worker's highest 35 years of earnings. It was presumed that the average time a worker spends in the workplace is 35 years. As people live and work longer, there is rationale to increase the number of years to 38. If this were changed, however, women would be adversely affected because they tend to spend less time than men in the workforce. Using 38 years to calculate the formula gives a minor reduction in benefits but saves money for the system.
- *Change the formula for calculating benefits across the board.* The formula by which benefits are calculated is complex. It uses highest number of years worked and highest earnings earned. By modifying the formula across the board, benefits would be cut depending on the modifications in the formula.

- *Means test to reduce benefits.* It is frequently suggested that high earners should not receive benefits, even though they have paid into the system. This is the extreme case. Others suggest that benefits should be lower for those who earn more than a certain amount. The fear regarding means testing is that eventually those who pay into the system and get little or nothing from the system in return will want to "opt out" of what is now a universal system. Means testing is seen by some to undermine the system and its philosophy.
- *Raise the amount of earnings on which payroll taxes are paid.* As of 2001 Social Security (payroll taxes) were paid on earnings up to $80,400 but not on dollars earned over that amount. This cap differentiates it from Medicare taxes, which are paid on total earnings. The amount of earnings on which taxes are paid is adjusted annually. Some favor removing the cap altogether; others recommend that a higher cap be established. Currently about 85% of workers earn less than the 2001 cap of $80,4000.
- *Increase income tax paid on Social Security benefits.* Social Security benefits are taxable if income exceeds certain amounts. If one is single and earning between $25,000 and $34,000, 50% of benefits are subject to income tax. If earning over $34,000, 85% of benefits are taxed. For married couples filing jointly, and earning between $32,000 and $44.000, 50% of benefits are taxed. If earning over $44,000, 85% of benefits are taxed. Interestingly, revenue generated from the 50% tax goes to the Social Security trust fund, whereas the proceeds from the difference between 50% and 85% tax go into the Medicare trust fund. To increase revenue, the tax received from benefits could be increased, or the portion that goes to Medicare could instead be deposited in the Social Security trust fund.
- *Invest Social Security funds in the stock market.* Present law requires that trust funds be invested in Treasury bonds, which generate about 3% interest and provide the maximum safety for investments. When the stock market is doing well, suggestions abound that Social Security funds should be invested in the stock market. This raises questions about the role of the federal

government and its potential influence on the economy. When the stock market is down, less enthusiasm emerges about the risks involved. One can expect to see the private sector promoting privatization, and the organizations concerned with the aging population denouncing it.

These suggestions maintain the current structure of the Social Security program as it was designed in the 1930s. Many espouse the philosophy that if it isn't broken, don't fix it. But others believe that the system is outmoded and that it *is* broken. They suggest that one way to change the structure is to add to it an opportunity for workers to manage a personal, private account in addition to the regular benefit payment program that we have today. Private accounts would be established by individuals who would be allowed to invest 2% to 5% of payroll taxes in the stock market or bonds. Those who favor this idea point especially to members of the younger generation who don't believe that Social Security will be there when they retire. Private accounts provide tangible evidence of savings for retirement. Opponents point to the cost involved, because the 2% to 5% allowed for personal investment would be money withheld from the government trust fund, making the overall solvency problem even more severe than it is. Some worry that many Americans have no or little experience with investments or the high price of investing in the stock market. Many questions remain unanswered, including what will happen to the worker who chooses to retire during a downturn in the stock market with little or no equity.

ATTEMPTS TO CHANGE POLICY

A total of nine commissions and advisory panels have been formed over the past 2 decades, charged with finding solutions to the perceived financial crisis of Social Security. Most of the commissions' and panels' recommendations were never enacted into law, illustrating how difficult it is to change one of America's most popular domestic programs.

The most successful attempt to make changes in the program was the National Commission on Social Security Reform created by executive order, which met from 1981 through 1983. Its recommendations included a proposal to freeze the cost-of-living adjustment, increase the payroll tax, and raise the retirement age from 65 to 67. These recommendations were enacted into law.

In 1994 President Clinton appointed 32 members to the Bipartisan Commission on Entitlement and Tax Reform. That commission proposed an increase in the retirement age for full benefits to age 70, a reduction in the cost-of-living adjustments, and the creation of mandatory private supplemental retirement accounts. No legislation was enacted. Then from 1994 to 1996, the Advisory Council on Social Security, with members named by the Secretary of Health and Human Services, met to discuss long-term remedies for the program. The Council advocated three alternative solutions, each a combination of reducing benefits and investing part of the trust funds in the stock market or in private accounts. None of the three plans was enacted into law.

In 1997 the National Commission on Retirement Policy, a private commission , proposed the creation of private accounts using part of the payroll tax paid by workers. Some benefit cuts were also recommended. Again, no legislation was enacted.

The newest Social Security Commission appointed by President George W. Bush in May 2001 was different from past commissions because it was given a specific charge to develop a plan whereby individual personal accounts would become part of Social Security. The 16-member commission presented its report to the President in December 2001. Rather than presenting a single plan that could easily be considered for legislation, it produced three plans, each one complicated and controversial from the start. Each would allow individuals to divert a certain percentage of their payroll taxes to private accounts to be individually invested. Each plan also recommended selected benefit reductions from Social Security.

Because 2002 is an election year, the chances of policy changes to implement Commission's report appear slim. Politically, the objectivity of the membership of the Commission was questioned from the beginning because all members favor private accounts. In addition, the long-term cost to the Social Security program would be substantial as funds are diverted from payroll taxes to private accounts, even with benefit reductions. The status of the stock market will also surely influence whether it is timely to suggest individual accounts.

CONCLUSION

It is likely that Social Security's long-term fiscal problems can be solved with a combination of some of the aforementioned policy changes. Each has advantages and disadvantages. Each solution must be studied to see how various population groups would be affected. Women must be especially attentive to potential changes in the program that would adversely affect them. Social Security is an anti-poverty program, lowering the poverty rate among the elderly from approximately 50% in 1935 to 11% today. Nurses appreciate the relationship of economic security to health security and must serve as advocates for maintaining the protective elements of the program while supporting minor changes to ensure long-term financial solvency. Nurses should become informed about the program and participate in policy discussions and proposed changes, letting Congress know what effects these changes will have on the elderly, the disabled, and children.

Social Security is one of the most successful programs of the United States government, helping millions of retirees and their families retain their independence and their dignity as they age. The problem is that we are living healthier and longer lives, and as a result, more retirees are using the program. In addition, families are having fewer children who will eventually work and pay payroll taxes; thus, there will be less money in the program. Whether the problems related to the fiscal solvency of the program are solved with a package of small legislative policy changes or an overhaul of the program's structure, it is certain that Congress will have heated debates over the next few years. As professional nurses and good citizens, we have a role to play in that debate.

Resources

Social Security Administration. (1999a). *Supplemental Security Income* (SSA publication no. 05-11000).
Social Security Administration. (1999b). *Understanding the benefits* (SSA publication no. 05-10024).
Social Security Administration. (1999c). *What every woman should know* (SSA publication no. 05-10127).
Social Security Administration. (2000a). *Disability benefits* (SSA publication no. 05-10029).
Social Security Administration. (2000b). *Survivors benefits* (SSA publication no. 05-10084).
Social Security Administration (2001). *Basic facts* (SSA publication no. 05-10080).

REFERENCES

2001 OASDI trustees report. (2001, March 19). Baltimore, MD: Social Security Administration, Office of the Chief Actuary.
Annual statistical supplement. (2000). Washington, DC: Social Security Administration, Division of Publications.
Social Security Administration. (2000a). *Fast facts and figures about Social Security* (SSA publication no. 13-11785).
Social Security Administration. (2000b). *Retirement benefits* (SSA publication no. 05-10035).

POLICYSPOTLIGHT

COMPLEMENTARY THERAPIES: REIMBURSEMENT ISSUES

Doris Milton

"If you find a path with no obstacles, it probably doesn't lead anywhere."

FRANK A. CLARK

Many terms are used, sometimes interchangeably, for healing therapies that are not yet integrated into conventional health care. *Alternative therapies* is the most common term used for nonmainstream healing modalities, yet it should be reserved for those that are substitutes, or those used instead of conventional medical care. *Complementary therapies* are those that are helpful adjuncts to

Definitions

Alternative therapies are ones that are used instead of a conventional treatment.

Complementary therapies are ones that are used in addition to conventional treatment.

Integrative health care is a synthesis of conventional, alternative, and complementary care options.

Allopathic medicine is conventional, biomedical medicine that uses treatments such as surgery and medications to work in opposition to the factor believed to cause the disease or condition.

Holistic health care is based on the integration of mind, body, and spirit; treatment is geared to the whole person, rather than just the disease or condition.

Homeopathy is a healing system that uses a much-diluted preparation of a substance that caused symptoms in a healthy person to treat symptoms in a sick person.

Naturopathy is a healing system that uses natural methods to relieve symptoms or disease.

conventional medical care. The term *complementary* is often used as a synonym for *alternative* because it is perceived as a less emotionally charged word. Recently the term *integrative* has been used to describe a blend or synthesis of alternative and complementary therapies and conventional medical care.

The emphasis in the definitions on *medical,* not *nursing,* care is intentional because many of these therapies are part of nursing, but not medical, practice. For example, music therapy, use of imagery, other relaxation techniques, therapeutic touch, massage therapies, and spirituality have long been components of nursing education and practice. However, other therapies, such as acupuncture, homeopathy, use of herbal products, nutritional supplements, and reflexology are still not included in most nursing or medical education programs or considered mainstream practice.

Many of these therapies evolved from other healing traditions or systems. For example, although acute care homeopathic remedies are safe and readily available, homeopathy is actually a different healing system. Homeopathy is based upon the "law of similars," that like cures like, whereas the allopathic healing system is based upon the "law of

opposites." And acupuncture is not an isolated healing therapy, but one that evolved from traditional Chinese or oriental medicine with its own view of health and illness, as well as diagnostic and treatment methods.

INCREASING USE OF ALTERNATIVE AND COMPLEMENTARY THERAPIES

The use of these therapies implies a paradigm of care that has essential values that differ from the conventional one. Integrative health care is viewed as a partnership between provider and patient; providers believe that people are entitled to an array of health care options. The therapies that are the least invasive and least risky should be used initially. Valid healing therapies can evolve from cultures and traditions other than conventional American medicine.

Use of alternative and complementary therapies has risen substantially in recent years, mainly from an influx of new users rather than from more-intensive use by those who were already using them (Eisenberg, Davis, Ettner, Appel, Von Rompay, & Kessler, 1998). This increased use is happening at the same time that society in general is interested in a greater array of health care options and people want more control over their health care. The aging of the population is thought to have an effect on usage as well. Many use these therapies for chronic health conditions that do not respond to conventional care, or because they do not like the side effects of conventional treatment. Also, many people presume that alternative and complementary therapies have fewer side effects and cost less than conventional care, although this is not always the case.

Use of alternative and complementary therapies has increased also because of their increased visibility since the establishment of the National Center for Complementary and Alternative Medicine (NCCAM) at the National Institutes of Health (NIH). The mission of NCCAM is to provide information about the safety and effectiveness of complementary and alternative medicine. NCCAM was established in 1992 as the Office of Alternative Medicine (OAM) within the office of the director of the NIH. Its name and status were changed when it became a center within NIH in 1998. This change led to greater visibility within NIH and an increased ability to initiate and fund research and research training projects. For example, funding for research projects sponsored by NIH rose from $2 million in 1993 to $68.7 million in 2000 (ncam.nih.gov/an/general). The Omnibus appropriations bill that raised the OAM to a center also established the White House Commission on Alternative Medicine, which will determine future directions for practice, education, and research.

Those who integrate alternative and complementary therapies are pleased that there is a federal center whose focus is on evaluating their clinical efficacy and disseminating information about these therapies. There is concern, however, with the label *medicine* in the title. Physicians often see all health care therapies falling under the category of medicine, rather than health care in general. This view often allows physicians, rather than a multidisciplinary group, to decide the appropriate use of therapy and qualifications of valid practitioners. Another important concern with the use of the term *medicine* in the center's title is the fact that many of the therapies evolved from other healing systems and cultures, and practitioners often adopt the therapies without recognition of the other system or culture. For example, conventional practitioners include the use of therapies such as acupuncture, herbal preparations, and homeopathic remedies in their practice, without acknowledging their base healing system.

STATUS OF CURRENT REIMBURSEMENT FOR ALTERNATIVE AND COMPLEMENTARY THERAPIES

A majority of managed care organizations and insurance providers offer some coverage for acupuncture, biofeedback, chiropractic care, nutrition counseling, and osteopathy (Pelletier & Astin, 2002). Often insurers will not reimburse the full amount of alternative therapies, but will arrange with a network of providers to offer discounted services.

The two types of providers most likely to be reimbursed for alternative therapies are physicians who expand their practice to include alternative options and providers of specific alternative therapies only. If there is a formal practice act that gives providers other than physicians specific rights to practice particular therapies, the supply of those providers and the use of those therapies is likely to increase (Sturm & Unutzer, 2000-2001).

A factor that strongly influences insurer coverage is the state mandate for that coverage. The most common therapies that are authorized for coverage are acupuncture, massage therapy, and naturopathy. More than 40 states and the Department of Defense have mandates for chiropractic care, a healing system can no longer be considered alternative. Washington is the most stringent; it requires every health plan to cover treatments by all categories of providers regulated by the Department of Health (Sturm & Unutzer, 2000-2001).

FACTORS INFLUENCING COVERAGE (REIMBURSEMENT OR DISCOUNTED SERVICES)

Several factors determine whether an insurer or health plan covers a complementary or alternative therapy.

Clinical Efficacy

The major concern of insurers is a therapy's demonstrated clinical efficacy, with few complications or side effects. An example of such a therapy is one that includes a low-fat diet, moderate exercise, yoga, and participation in support groups. Numerous study replications have demonstrated reversal of atherosclerosis through such a program (Ornish, Brown, Scherwitz, Billings, Armstrong, Ports, McLanahan, Kirkeeide, Brand, & Gould, 1990; Ornish, Scherwitz, Billings, Gould, Merritt, Sparler, Armstrong, Ports, Kirkeeide, Hogeboom, & Brand, 1998). That program has the additional benefit of perceived cost-effectiveness: The formal program is not extensive, but the potential savings are high. Also, therapies (such as acupuncture, which uses needles and breaks the skin barrier) that have little perceived difference from allopathic care are more easily accepted (Pelletier & Astin, 2002).

Competency

Insurers want providers of healing therapies to be knowledgeable about their strengths and limitations. Most alternative and complementary therapies do not have nationally accepted training and practices, and their acceptance varies. If practitioner competence cannot be easily established, it becomes more challenging to obtain malpractice insurance to cover nonconventional therapies.

Market Differentiation

Insurers are more interested in providing reimbursement of complementary and alternative therapies if coverage would help their ability to attract new enrollees or retain their existing enrollee base. Many people who are using these therapies want to be able to continue their use if hospitalized. Health care systems, too, may increase their appeal to those in a particular culture by providing therapies they often use.

STRATEGIES TO INFLUENCE HEALTH CARE POLICY

Knowledge of these factors can help nurses to develop strategies for shaping public and private reimbursement policies. Consider the following strategies.

Research and Research Utilization

Because perceived clinical efficacy and positive outcomes are significant to insurers, more research is needed. Longitudinal studies or meta-analyses that explore potential cost savings are especially valuable. Demonstration projects and integrative research reviews that synthesize the results of individual, related studies so that the findings have more validity are needed as well. Outcomes models such as those used to examine conventional care are essential for future studies and utilization projects. Models that include combinations of therapies, conventional and alternative, would provide support for those therapies that work best for specific symptoms or conditions. Surveys of practitioners and the public to determine the perceived value of different therapies would be helpful as well.

Provider Credentialing

Nursing leadership and involvement are needed to participate in the development of the educational and experiential qualifications for many therapies. Insurer coverage is more difficult to attain without established standards because provision of care by qualified practitioners cannot be guaranteed. Credentialing is a less-complex process if there is a model curriculum for practitioner training and established policies, procedures, and standards of practice. For example, Nurse Healers—Professional Associates International, the official organization of therapeutic touch, has those components in place, making it easier to identify competent practitioners.

Integration of Content into Formal and Informal Education

Credentialing would be simpler if content about alternative/complementary therapies was integrated into the formal curriculum of health care professionals, including nurses. Nurses and other professionals need a strong foundation for practice and must to be able to answer questions from patients and families. In addition, alternative therapy content could be integrated into existing continuing education, such as pain management programs. That would allow integration of therapies into conventional care that is already reimbursed by insurers. Nurses can help the public by becoming more knowledgeable about therapies, such as herbal products and nutritional supplements, that can have risks if used inappropriately.

Education of Legislators and Industry Leaders

Changes in health policy to increase reimbursement for a greater number of valid alternative and complementary therapies requires knowledgeable legislators. Legislators rely on health care professionals and representatives of professional associations to educate them. For example, instead of state-by-state mandates or other legislation, nurses can encourage our representatives to support legislation such as the federal Access to Medical Treatment Act, which would require that all options be available to patients. Legislators, too, are key to research support, especially for funding levels for NCCAM at the NIH.

Business leaders, as the largest purchasers of health care insurance in the United States, can negotiate for coverage of alternative and complementary therapies for their employees. Nurses can help provide knowledge about which therapies are valid, as well as the strengths and limitations of particular therapies. Also, we can encourage employees to request that coverage of alternative and complementary therapies be included in their health care benefits.

Need for Common Terminology

One of the factors inhibiting reimbursement for alternative and complementary therapies is the lack of common terms and procedures. What one provider terms *guided imagery,* another may call a form of *hypnotherapy.* Fifteen minutes is considered an adequate imagery session by some providers; others believe that nothing of value can be accomplished in that brief interval. Many insurers do not even have a billing code for imagery or other commonly used therapies. Nurses can help to address this concern by participating in developing common procedure terminology (CPT) codes, such as the insurance billing codes developed for nursing and other disciplines by reputable companies such as Alternative Link in Las Cruces, New Mexico (www.alternativelink.com).

Involvement in Professional Associations

Nurses can influence reimbursement policy for alternative and complementary therapies by working with professional nursing associations, including their specialty organizations. Many professional associations sponsor research and research utilization projects, as well as providing fact sheets and other information to legislators and industry leaders. Through this mechanism, nurses can request conference sessions and workshops at annual, regional or local meetings on alternative and complementary therapies and ways of integrating them into conventional care. Objective articles are needed for journals and newsletters sponsored by professional associations and groups.

CONCLUSION

People are using alternative and complementary therapies and expect nurses to be knowledgeable about them and ways that these therapies can interact with conventional care. Nurses have responsibility as well for influencing health care policy so that studies are funded to examine the outcomes, positive or negative, of alternative and complementary therapies. We need this information so therapies with demonstrated clinical efficacy can be reimbursed by insurers. People need to have access to all valid health care options.

REFERENCES

Eisenberg, D.M., Davis, R.B., Ettner, S.L., Appel, S., Von Rompay, M., & Kessler, R.C. (1998). Trends in alternative medicine uses in the United States, 1990-1997: Results of a follow-up national survey. *Journal of the American Medical Association, 280,* 1569-1575.

Ornish, D., Brown, S.E., Scherwitz, L.W., Billings, J.H., Armstrong, W.T., Ports, T.A., McLanahan, S.M., Kirkeeide, R.L., Brand, R.J., & Gould, K.L. (1990). Can lifestyle changes reverse coronary disease? The lifestyle heart trial. *Lancet, 336,* 129-133.

Ornish, D., Scherwitz, L.W., Billings, J.H., Gould, K.L., Merritt, T.A., Sparler, S., Armstrong, W.T., Ports, T.A., Kirkeeide, R.L., Hogeboom, C., & Brand, R.J. (1998). Intensive lifestyle changes for reversal of coronary heart disease. *Journal of the American Medical Association, 280,* 2001-2007.

Pelletier, K.R. & Astin, J.A. (2002). Integration and reimbursement of complementary and alternative medicine by managed care and insurance providers: 2000 update and cohort analysis. *Alternative Therapies in Health and Medicine, 8,* 38-48.

Sturm, R. & Unutzer, J. (2000-2001). State legislation and the use of complementary and alternative medicine. *Inquiry, 37,* 423-429.

UNIT **TWO**

Case Study

Rationing Health Care: The Oregon Story

Cecelia Capuzzi & Jeanne Bowden

"A journey of a thousand miles begins with a single step."

CHINESE PROVERB

In 1805 Lewis and Clark blazed across the country and reached the Pacific Ocean, traveling through the territory that is now Oregon. They have since been followed by hundreds of thousands of people who have migrated to the Northwest, bringing with them a culture of progressiveness and independence. This pioneering spirit is reflected in the state's political system. Oregonians pride themselves on having a legislature composed of ordinary citizens who meet every 2 years to enact the will of the people; often it is referred to as a "user friendly" legislature. State legislators are accessible to the public, and citizens frequently testify at legislative hearings on bills of interest. In this political climate, the Oregon Health Plan (OHP) was created in 1989 to improve the health of people in the state.

RATIONING OF HEALTH CARE: AN IMPLICIT POLICY

Before the enactment of the Oregon Health Plan, the Oregon legislature made its funding decisions biennially, trying to match available dollars with citizen needs. Frequently decisions about the funding of health care resulted in some citizens' becoming uninsured; health care rationing occurred implicitly. There were no explicit rules to determine how this allocation process would occur, nor were the consequences of these actions openly acknowledged as "rationing" (Capuzzi, 1994).

Several events that occurred in the 1980s caused the issue of access to health care to reach the political agenda. In the mid-1980s, the state's economy

was improving and Oregon increased its spending on health care, but 350,000 Oregonians (16%) less than 65 years of age still did not have health insurance (Oregon Health Services Commission, 1991). In addition, certain health indicators were worsening; for example, for the first time in 10 years, the state's "inadequate prenatal care rate" (the number of births to women who had fewer than five prenatal care visits or had no prenatal care until the last trimester of pregnancy) was increasing (Oregon Health Division, 1987).

Not all of the uninsured were jobless. In fact, 65% of those without health insurance were employed either part-time or full-time or were dependents of employed individuals (Joint Legislative Committee on Health Care, 1990). As health care costs in the United States continued to escalate, employers' insurance costs increased 18% to 30% (Governor's Commission on Health Care, 1988), and many small companies dropped health insurance benefits for their employees. Additionally, an increasing number of individuals were unable to obtain affordable health insurance because they had a preexisting health condition that raised their health insurance rates.

In 1987 the issue came to a head. The state's Medicaid program was experiencing financial problems, and the Oregon legislature was considering more than $48 million in social program needs but had only $21 million in the budget (Kitzhaber, 1991). The policy solution was to discontinue funding for 30 organ transplants, totaling approximately $800,000, and to use the monies to extend health care to approximately 3,000 other Oregonians who lacked health insurance (Kitzhaber, 1990). This policy was attacked by the media, which featured a young boy with leukemia who died when his family was unable to pay for a bone marrow transplant. Rationing had become a reality.

During the next 12 years, both authors became involved in the Oregon Health Plan. In 1989 Cecelia had a legislative internship and represented a non-profit advocacy group at the sixty-fifth session of the Oregon legislature, where the beginnings of the Oregon Health Plan were introduced. Her subsequent involvement during the legislative session and afterward during the initial implementation has been described in previous publications of this case study (Capuzzi, 1993; 1998). Cecelia also had a research analyst position at the Oregon Office of Health Policy (now the Office for Oregon Health Plan Policy and Research) during her sabbatical in 1994 in which she conducted research analyses on managed care, cost containment strategies, and quality of care as part of a Robert Wood Johnson grant and staffed two Oregon Health Council subcommittees.

Jeanne became involved when asked to serve on the nine-member Oregon Health Council (OHC) in 1996. This chapter updates the progress of the Oregon Health Plan illustrating continued involvement by nurses.

RATIONING OF HEALTH CARE: AN EXPLICIT POLICY
Issue Adoption

Cecelia began the legislative internship in January 1989 and spent the first 6 weeks familiarizing herself with the political and legislative processes while attempting to keep abreast of current events. Six weeks later, she sat in a large room on the Willamette University campus adjacent to the state capitol, listening to a presentation of a pilot project report on prioritizing health services. After the presentation, Senate President John Kitzhaber unveiled his plan for decreasing the number of uninsured Oregonians before an audience that included key state leaders, as well as health lobbyists and the media. We knew that the issue of access to health care had been adopted by this legislature and that this legislation would be a major priority during the 1989 session.

Senator Kitzhaber's plan to increase access to health care consisted of three pieces of legislation. The first bill, Senate Bill (SB) 27, expanded Medicaid to include all individuals whose income was below

the federal poverty level. The second bill, SB 935, created a health insurance pool and offered tax credits to small-business employers so that they would provide health insurance to their employees and their dependents. The third bill, SB 534, created a high-risk insurance pool for those who were unable to obtain affordable health insurance because they had preexisting conditions (Capuzzi & Garland, 1991).

SB 27, the most controversial of the three bills, proposed the development of a list of health service priorities by an 11-member commission. Critics called this "rationing health care." After it was determined which services would be offered, this package would constitute the basic health care package offered by Medicaid, the small business insurance pool, and the high-risk insurance pool. Moreover, leaders envisioned that this package would eventually govern the required insured health services offered by all insurance plans in the state. SB 27 required that the basic health services be provided by managed care systems when feasible. Making decisions about spending for health care became explicit.

Policy Implementation

By the end of the 1989 session, these three bills were enacted into law. Now began the process of implementation. The implementation of SB 27 had three stages: priority setting, budget setting, and implementation (Capuzzi & Garland, 1991). Each stage involved a different set of actors. The table on page 301 summarizes the activities of each stage, identifies the actors, and gives the dates of involvement. Implementation of the other two bills that made up the Oregon Health Plan, SB 534 and SB 935, occurred within Oregon's insurance division. The implementation of the OHP occurred over the next 4 years, and the directives of SB 27 began after Oregon received the Health Care Financing Administration (HCFA) waiver in 1994.

Issues of Concern to Nurses

During the first 4 years of the issue adoption and policy implementation stages, there were several issues of concern to nurses. A core group of nurses was particularly interested in this legislation: staff and members of the state nurses association, nurses involved with other advocacy groups, and faculty

Implementation Stages of SB 27

STAGE	DESCRIPTION	ACTORS	YEARS
Priority setting	Developed the ranked list of paired condition/treatment health services using input from the public, communities, advocates, and health care providers Ranked the list to include provider services, supplies, inpatient and outpatient services, health promotion, and disease prevention services	Health Services Commission (HSC)	1989-1991
	Included values of Oregonians	Oregon Health Decisions	
	Attached actuarial costs to each	HSC	
Budget setting	Determined how many of the ranked condition/treatment pairs could be funded*	Oregon Legislature	1991
Implementation	Sought waiver from Health Care Financing Administration (HCFA, now the Centers for Medicare and Medicaid Services [CMS]) to implement the plan.[†] Established criteria for providers and insurance companies to offer health care to groups of Medicaid clients under managed care contracts[‡]	Oregon Medical Assistance Program (OMAP)	Began 1994

*By law, the legislature could not change the order of the list. If legislators wanted to fund more conditions or treatments, the legislature had to allocate additional monies.

[†]Oregon needed to seek a waiver because the Medicaid funding portion of the OHP was at variance with that allowed by HCFA rules. The first area of variance was the list of services provided. By using the ranked list of conditions/treatments, Oregon Medicaid was not providing some services mandated by federal guidelines. The other area of variance concerned the populations to be served. Medicaid would include all individuals who fell below the federal poverty level; this group included single adults who were excluded in the federal regulations.

[‡]Before OHP, individual health care providers treated Medicaid patients and then billed directly for reimbursement on the basis of a fee-for-service model; now health providers had to be part of a managed care plan and payment was based on a capitated system.

from the Oregon Health Sciences University School of Nursing. After study and discussion of the proposed legislation, we concluded that although the plan benefited the majority of citizens in the state, we still had several concerns.

One major concern was ensuring that nurses had adequate representation and a voice in the policy as well as in the practice setting. A second concern was broadening the focus from medical care to health care. Although the language of the bill and accompanying speeches by Senator Kitzhaber and his aides discussed the changes needed in the health care system, most of their examples related to the delivery of medical care. A related issue was the desire to broaden the focus from acute medical care to health promotion and prevention. A final issue was to ensure that implementation of this legislation did not limit consumer access to a broad range of health care services and that quality care was maintained. Part

of this issue was to ensure that there were sufficient monies to fund what we considered the minimum needed services. Earlier versions of this case study elaborate on these issues (Capuzzi, 1993; 1998).

Political Strategies Used by Oregon Nurses

A number of political strategies were used to ensure that nurses' input and concerns were heard before and after implementation of the legislation.

• *Gain access.* The first strategy was to gain access to the political arenas where the policy was being formulated: the senate president's office, committee hearings, work sessions, and interest group meetings. After the Oregon Health Plan was enacted, we continued to access the political and policy arenas where implementation occurred (e.g., the Health Services Commission [HSC] and the Oregon Health Decisions' [OHD] community values project).

- *Present testimony.* Before the legislation was enacted, we testified at the legislative hearings and presented our concerns, provided expert knowledge about the difficulties our patients had in gaining access to health care services, and advocated for a package of comprehensive health services. We presented data about the effectiveness of having nurses provide certain types of health care services and asked that the language of the bills not be limited to physician providers. We continued presenting testimony during the implementation of the OHP at the HSC meetings, at the public hearings, and at the OHD community values meetings. For example, we advocated to the HSC that case management be included in the list of provided services.
- *Market nursing.* These activities were often the same as those involved in gaining access and presenting testimony. For example, during the legislative session, we met with key policymakers and provided information about the nursing profession, nurses' roles in the health care system, and the cost-effectiveness of health and nursing care delivered by nurses. We invited key players to meetings such as the state nurses association's annual conference, where the senate president was invited to speak on SB 27 and answer questions. During the implementation stages, the marketing strategy was continued in order to make the commissioners aware of our expertise and value as a resource.
- *Network.* We were members of our professional organizations but also of other advocacy groups. An advantage of belonging to such groups was the opportunity to interact with other health professionals who shared our interest in the legislation. We explained our concerns, and our fellow health professionals became our advocates; we in turn listened to their concerns and often supported issues of importance to them. At times, coalitions were formed. The networks we developed also provided us with a means to obtain pertinent information before it appeared in the media, thus giving us extra time to plan and respond, as well as to squelch rumors. We continued this strategy during the implementation stages.

- *Mobilize other nurses.* Through our informal networks, we identified other nurses who could monitor the legislation, testify at hearings, and speak to their local legislators. At times we provided nursing colleagues with the tools necessary to participate: one-page summaries of the key issues, guidelines for the preparation of testimony, information about upcoming hearing dates and times, and names of legislators to lobby on various issues. This strategy also was continued during the implementation stages.

These political strategies helped Oregon nurses to be successful in alleviating our major concerns: having adequate representation and voice and broadening the foci to health care and health promotion and prevention. The language in SB 27 was amended to use the term *health care* rather than *medical care,* and language was added that prohibited managed care systems from excluding the services offered by nurses or other health care providers. The issues of consumer access and quality of care continued to need monitoring and nurses' input as additional legislation was added or modified the original intent of the OHP in subsequent years.

AFTER ENACTMENT: POLICY REALITIES

The opportunity for nurses' involvement in health policy can come when least expected. One summer day in 1996, Jeanne received a call from the office of now-Governor Kitzhaber, asking if she would be interested in serving on the nine-member OHC. Living in a rural town located more than 300 miles from the state capital of Salem, she first thought, "why me?" In answer, she was told that the governor wanted a woman from eastern Oregon to represent rural Oregon. After discussing the Oregon Health Plan (OHP), philosophy of access, and duties of participation, the governor's aide set up an interview with Jeanne. Before she knew it, Jeanne's role in state policy had begun.

The OHC serves by legislative mandate as the primary health policy advisory body to the governor, the legislature, and the health plan administrator. The OHC advises on health care-related components of the state budget, sets broad priorities for strengthening and expanding the OHP, and recommends strategies for building community partnerships. The council considers far-reaching policy to ensure that lower-income Oregonians who do not presently have health care will have the opportunity to gain access to care in the future. The OHC mission reads as follows:

As the State's primary health care advisory body, the Council will examine public policy issues and make recommendations for improving the health and health care of Oregonians through universal access to health coverage. The objective of the Council is to increase the availability of and access to quality, affordable health care. In pursuing this objective, the Council will provide a forum for the development of consensus-based policy recommendations (Oregon Health Council Meeting Minutes, 1998).

The OHC has a history of providing advice on specific health issues at the discretion of the governor. Some governors appointed members to the OHC and issued specific directives; usually the members' terms ended with the end of the governor's term in office. Some governors did not use this body. During the 1995 Oregon legislative session, SB 1079 reorganized Oregon's health-related agencies, and one change was to transfer oversight of the OHC to the Office for Oregon Health Plan Policy and Research (Oregon Legislative Administration Committee, 1995). Additional membership guidelines and functions were codified (About OHC, no date).

To fulfill the goals of the mission, the OHC makes recommendations regarding state health planning, collaborates with all health policy advisory bodies, provides a forum for health care issues, takes public stands on major issues, recommends changes in state law and regulation, and participates in the development of legislative concepts and in the drafting of legislation. Because of Jeanne's role with the School of Nursing, she considered her participation on the OHC an opportunity to educate and strengthen nurse and nurse practitioner practices across the state and widen health care access for underserved populations, especially those living in rural areas.

As the associate dean on the OHSU School of Nursing campus serving eastern Oregon, Jeanne oversees the education program, the Eastern Oregon University student health service, a public school health system network serving six school districts (Health Network for Rural Schools), and two rural primary care nurse practitioner clinics where a disproportionate share of the uninsured and Oregon Health Plan participants in a geographically isolated region of the state receive health care. Broad health policy decisions affecting these programs gave Jeanne the motivation to accept her charge to serve on the OHC.

Access to Health Care: An Ongoing Challenge

Increasing assess to health care is a main objective of the OHC, which recognizes that barriers to health care access are unique to each community. Access affects both those eligible for the OHP and those who are ineligible. In the rural towns of eastern Oregon, nurse practitioners discovered that barriers of eligible families to sign up for the OHP included simple problems, such as lost Social Security cards. Individuals who lose their cards find that applying for new cards is a lengthy and daunting process. Some rural clients do not have the means to travel to the Social Security office and consider it risky to send documents through the mail. Yet having a Social Security card is a necessary part of applying for the OHP. In addition, some clients found it difficult to obtain documents for employment verification and to gain access to copy machines. Another barrier is limited understanding of health needs and benefits of comprehensive insurance. Many rural families believe that savings will be adequate for emergencies and provider visits. Many rural dwellers lack education concerning preventive medicine and how having insurance can keep children and families healthy. Yet another barrier is insufficient resources. Some clients do not have phones and, in rural communities, residents are isolated by a lack of public transportation. For some individuals health insurance is not a priority, and for others, distrust of government keeps them from pursuing health insurance. When one of the outreach workers asked a patient if he would like information on how to sign up for the OHP, the individual stated, "Does this mean I'll have to go find a real job?" Concerns about government agencies getting involved in people's private lives is a deterrent to health coverage.

Barriers exist for access to health care for ineligible families as well. If a client has had insurance within 6 months of applying for the OHP (including such limited policies as catastrophic or school sports insurance), application to the OHP is prohibited. Often self-employed farmers will include children in their catastrophic medical coverage, thereby making their children ineligible for OHP or S-CHIP (State Children's Health Insurance Program) insurance. Or the client may exceed the $2000 liquid assets limitation. This is a serious disadvantage for families who are receiving divorce or death benefits and who would like to use these benefits to further their own education, save for their children's education, put money aside for emergencies, or save for other future expenses. Spending this money on private insurance, as one widowed parent told our clinic staff, "is like throwing money to the wind." Many of our clients are minimum wage earners who work one or more jobs and make just a little too much for eligibility. Paying for private insurance is not an option for these families.

Alien resident status also affects eligibility. For example, one migrant family from Mexico decided to stay on as residents and make a life for themselves in the United States. The parents had green cards but the children did not. The children were enrolled in school but were ineligible for the OHP because of their nonresident status, even though their parents pay federal employment taxes. We find that rural dwellers lack awareness of health insurance or OHP information. Isolation means that people are often unaware of resources available to them. Service and small business employers often do not offer health benefits.

A national survey on the uninsured conducted by the NewsHour with Jim Lehrër and the Kaiser Family Foundation (2000) found that 8 in 10 uninsured individuals are workers or their dependents. The majority of these uninsured persons have been without insurance for an average of 2 years, and most report they cannot afford health insurance. Understandably, the profile described the uninsured as having less access to care and being seven times more likely not to receive care for a serious illness in the previous year. The OHC organized solutions to give uninsured workers and children access to insurance coverage, and in 1998, two programs, the Family Health Insurance Assistance Program (FHIAP) and the State Children's Health Insurance Program (S-CHIP), were developed to improve and expand access to health coverage. The OHC spent several months advising the governor's office on policy issues regarding both programs.

FHIAP is an innovative program that subsidizes private insurance premiums for families with incomes between 100% 170% of the federal poverty level, to help these families purchase coverage. By July 1999 FHIAP had enrolled more than 6000 of the estimated 30,000 low-income working people who met the eligibility criteria and lacked health coverage. These family wage earners can use the subsidy to help cover the employer-sponsored health plans or enroll in individual health insurance plans offered by private sector health plans approved by the state. During the 1999-2000 legislative session, owing to a cut in the Office of Medical Assistance Programs (OMAP) budget, decreased funding for the state-funded FHIAP prevented the program from enrolling additional members until the current membership had been reduced by attrition. In February 2001, 4804 individuals were enrolled in FHIAP, with 15,654 persons on the reservation list (Oregon Family Health Insurance Assistance Program, 2001).

S-CHIP, under Title XXI, is a Medicaid look-alike program that covers children up to 19 years of age in families with incomes up to 170% of the federal poverty level. Of the approximately 30,000 S-CHIP–eligible children, 17,571 were enrolled as of February, 2001 (T. Gilmore, personal communication, February 20, 2001). The CHIP program has the same application process as Medicaid, requiring families to reapply every 6 months.

The goal of these two major programs was to increase the availability of and access to health care. The OHC realized that marketing and outreach efforts would be important in letting the public know about the eligibility requirements and the programs in general. About the time these two programs were being launched, the state received a Robert Wood Johnson Foundation (RWJF) "Covering Kids" grant, a national health access initiative for low-income, uninsured children to help states and local communities increase enrollment of eligible children who might benefit from health insurance programs. For instance, in eastern Oregon, the grant allowed our Health Network for Rural Schools to hire two outreach workers whose sole mission was to sign families up for the OHP, FHIAP, CHIP, and other health insurance products. The RWJF funded Oregon's project for 3 years, beginning in 1998.

Some leaders at the state level did not want to continue this generous grant from RWJF for fear that marketing and outreach would heighten awareness of the Oregon Health Plan and the increased numbers in the OHP caseload would overwhelm the program's funding. Given the high numbers of the uninsured in various pockets around the state and the access mission of the OHC, Jeanne was able to get the issue on the November 4, 1999, meeting agenda, where the OHC unanimously passed a motion to support outreach to children and families. Word was spread to our nursing partners that the RWJF grant was being considered for termination, and support for its continuation began pouring in to legislators and state leaders. Jeanne and a colleague met with our rural senator and representative, attended the December 9 Emergency Board of the Legislature and witnessed whole-hearted support of the Health and Human Services Subcommittee to continue with the Covering Kids grant. Efforts from Covering Kids have shown significant improvements in the number of children covered by S-CHIP and the OHP. For instance, one school in eastern Oregon went from a 29% uninsured rate of kindergarten to twelfth grade children to 8% in 3 years (Linker, 2001).

Financing Health Care: A Balancing Act

Having provided primary care in rural towns for most of her career, Jeanne was well acquainted with the issues affecting rural health clinics. Most often, these clinics are the sole providers of primary care within a 30-mile radius. When the OHP debuted in 1994, Oregon became the first state to request and receive a waiver from the federal government to discontinue cost-based Medicaid reimbursement to rural health clinics (RHCs). Oregon's Medicaid agency, OMAP, preferred uniformity in all payment methods and was determined to bring capitated managed care—with a fixed monthly payment per person in the plan, regardless of services provided—to the entire state, including the most rural areas.

In theory, the concept of managed care would extend coverage to greater numbers of uninsured. However, the across-the-board plan did not take into consideration the low population density of rural counties and the fragile financial state of RHCs. The loss of cost-based Medicaid reimbursement for Oregon's RHCs has had severe consequences. At a time when the numbers of clinics nationwide increased by 41% (between 1995 and 1997), Oregon's net growth was only 9%, and several clinics actually closed their doors. Several others have had to reduce access to care for the uninsured, the elderly, the poor, and those without reliable transportation. An Office of Rural Health survey shows that Oregon's 23 RHCs lose an average of $75,000 each per year and recover only 70% of their operating costs through patient revenues. For the RHCs in eastern Oregon, the waiver meant that each OHP visit would be reimbursed at about $20 per visit rather than the approximately $60 that it costs to see a typical patient. RHCs are a vital part of our nation's health safety net. Because RHCs are often the only provider in the community, they are particularly dependent on Medicaid as a source of payment. Consequently, underpayment by Medicaid threatens the availability of health care for all individuals who live in rural underserved communities, not just the Medicaid population.

Financing health care is a two-way street: Providers are asked to be socially responsible and care for those who are uninsured or on the OHP; at the same time, providers need to be compensated at a reasonable rate for caring for this vulnerable population. The OHC grappled with this "hydraulic relationship" and decided to go the citizens of the state for input.

The OHC, congruent with Oregon's participatory culture, embarked on two rounds of statewide community meetings, one in 1998 and the other in 2000. The first round, "Searching for Fairness: Citizen's Values about Financing Health Care," was conducted for the OHC and the Office for Oregon Health Plan Policy and Research (OHPPR) by

Oregon Health Decisions, an organization dedicated to promoting public participation in health care issues. Five categories were distilled from the 1998 community meetings, which engaged more than 2200 people in the statewide conversation regarding values about fairness. The first three categories related to the theme of sharing costs. The value of equality emerged as a concept to make the burden equal across socioeconomic lines. The participants stressed the importance of assisting households with low incomes, but, at the same time, they did not want to penalize financial success. *Responsibility* appeared consistently throughout the state as a value that endorses healthy lifestyles, encouraging individuals and corporations to contribute to society and to foster awareness of health care costs. Sharing health care costs prompted Oregonians to focus on participation as a way to attain this goal by undertaking such activities as having the healthy aid the sick and contributing to the system through volunteer service. The remaining two categories focused on the elements that made sharing the cost worthwhile: (1) efficiency in the structure of the health care delivery system through the control of costs and sharing resources, and (2) access for everyone, especially children (Oregon Health Decisions, 1998). Knowing what the citizens of Oregon value in terms of financing health care continues to guide OHC members in shaping health policy.

The second round of meetings, "Making Health Policy 2000," was sponsored by the OHC, the Health Services Commission, OHPPR, and the Oregon Medicaid Advisory Committee. Once again, these meetings were organized by Oregon Health Decisions. This particular round of town meetings was held to gather ideas from the public about shaping Oregon's health care system to better serve all Oregonians. Sixteen community meetings were held in eight Oregon cities, with about 600 participants.

A statewide random sample telephone survey and three focus groups were conducted with 900 individual Oregonians, targeted to increase minority participation. Findings from this set of meetings concluded that cost and affordability were concerns calling for effective cost containment (including a growing concern about the price of prescription drugs) so that more Oregonians could be covered.

The second major finding was the problem with access to health care, particularly to minority populations, rural citizens of the state, children, and uninsured workers. Participants brought up a third issue: the belief that all Oregonians should share a basic package of service benefits within the limits of financial resources. Fourth, participants said the delivery system is inefficient, and bureaucratic processes need to be simplified and become more responsive to cultural differences (Oregon Health Decisions, 2000).

Citizen participation in town hall meetings and public opinion surveys is a strategy that health leaders have adopted as a means to achieve "public buy-in" (Jacobs, Marmor, & Oberlander, 1999). Since 1982 activities promoting public participation in health care issues have given all Oregonians the opportunity to give candid opinions, offer solutions to perceived problems, and assist in the work of leadership across the state. These local outreach efforts from government also give nurses ample opportunity to volunteer with community organizing, serve as round table facilitators, or simply show up at the town hall meetings. Nurses have expert knowledge of the health care delivery system and need to be visible if they are to have a voice in policy.

Even though the community meetings gave policymakers a good deal of information on public desires, values, and expectations, taking action on any of these major reform ideas presents significant challenges. Michael Garland (2000), cofounder of Oregon Health Decisions, discovered four similar strategies in the "Making Health Policy 2000" report and Governor Kitzhaber's (2000) "Summit on the Oregon Health Plan" address: (1) basic benefits based on priorities; (2) social responsibility to care for the poor; (3) the goal of universal coverage; and (4) effective cost control. The governor realistically pointed out the barriers to these goals—including federal policy constraints, medical inflation, and the failure to share risk—which make universal coverage an ideal, that policymakers view as a long-term goal at best.

Issues of Concern to Nurses

One issue of concern to nurses is the invitation to sit on the OHC or other influential boards and councils, locally, statewide, and nationally. Two individuals were considered for Jeanne's OHC seat, and it was only chance that a nurse was chosen for the position. The majority of the members are required to not be providers of health care. It will be important for the OHC body to continue to recruit at least one nurse to the membership in order to continue the discussion of nursing issues. When nurses volunteer their time to these boards, the word gets out, and often they are invited to additional positions of policy influence.

Nurses who work with underserved populations are acutely aware of access problems in their communities. Many children and low-income adults lack access to primary and preventive health care. Many Oregon "safety-net" clinics are operated by nurse practitioners. These clinics are financially fragile, with two Oregon rural health clinics closed in 2002. The Committee on the Changing Market, Managed Care, and the Future Viability of Safety Net Providers found that safety net providers across the nation are at greater financial risk today than ever before owing to several factors: "(1) the rising number of uninsured individuals; (2) the full effect of mandated Medicaid managed care in a more competitive health care marketplace; and (3) the erosion and uncertainty of major direct and indirect subsidies that have helped support safety net functions" (Institute of Medicine, 2000, p. 8). Every day nurses experience the effects of lack of access to health care.

Expanding coverage to Oregonians through FHIAP and S-CHIP helped to close the gap in access to care for uninsured individuals. Attending the community forums and using data pointing to problems of access has helped nurses demonstrate the relevance of access as a statewide problem, not just a local aberration.

THE OREGON HEALTH PLAN TODAY

The Oregon Health Plan is succeeding in expanding access to health insurance. In the early 1990s, approximately 18% of Oregonians were uninsured; by 1998 the rate was between 10% and 16% (OHPPR, 2000; Vaidya, 2001). The number of children less than age 18 years without health insurance has dropped from 18% in 1990 to 8% in 1999. Additionally, more than 15,000 Oregonians who were unable to obtain health insurance because of a pre-

existing condition now have coverage through the high-risk insurance pool, and more than 21,000 employers now offer insurance through the Insurance Pool Governing Board. The amount of hospital charity care has declined by more than 30% since the OHP was created and emergency room use has declined almost 10%. The percentage of expectant mothers receiving adequate prenatal care has risen to 81%, and the infant mortality rate has dropped to 5.8 per 1000 live births in 1997 (Kitzhaber, 2000).

This progress, however, has not been uniform across socioeconomic, racial, or geographic boundaries. Higher rates of uninsured individuals were found in households with moderate incomes, among racial and ethnic minorities, and in rural areas of the state.

Although the majority of persons participating in the Medicaid program in 1996 indicated satisfaction with access (88%) and health care services (84%) and considered their health to be good to excellent (76%) (Oregon Health Plan Administrator's Office, 1997), this proportion dropped in 2000. When Oregonians were asked whether they believe Oregon is doing a good job in the provision of health care, the perception dropped from 75% to 66% from 1998 to 2000. Oregon Population Survey staff indicated that the high and rapidly increasing costs played a significant part in the public perception (Vaidya, 2001).

Health care costs continue to be a concern. When the program began, it was to cost about $350 million per year; today, it costs $800 million annually (Health Plan Growing Beyond Good Reason, 2001). On the other hand, the rise in Oregon's costs is lower than the national rate (OHPPR, 2000).

The work ahead for the OHC will include policy guidance for additional federal waivers in order to increase access for uninsured Oregonians with income up to 185% of federal poverty guidelines, a 2001 mandate from the legislature to insure more Oregonians. The primary goal of this legislative act is to "increase access by Oregon's low-income, uninsured children and families to affordable health care coverage" (Oregon Legislative Assembly, 2001, p. 1). This bipartisan approach to whittling down the number of uninsured creates increased access while simultaneously helping small health care practices, such as those in eastern Oregon, re-cover the costs in providing care.

LESSONS LEARNED

Many of the nurses who were involved in the development and implementation of the Oregon Health Plan had expertise in policy. They had previous experience in dealing with other issues and were knowledgeable about the use of effective political strategies and the creation of health policy. Although the Oregon story reinforces what is written in the literature, this experience produced some additional lessons.

- *Get involved early.* Involvement in the policy process begins early in the game and continues after legislation is enacted. Most authors discuss the implementation of policy (e.g., lobbying, testifying) but do not emphasize the importance of being involved during the issue recognition and adoption stages. Early involvement allowed us a voice in shaping the issue and setting the agenda; entry at a later point allows only for working on what already has been created. We were able to shape the Oregon plan so that it included prevention, case management, and a broad array of services that are often ignored. Moreover, being involved early facilitated our entry into other policy arenas as the project proceeded. Volunteering to do some of the tedious work and attending all meetings had a payoff. In several instances, we were able to ensure that key points were preserved in the plan because we had taken notes and had attended all the meetings. Enactment of the legislation was just the beginning of change: The process of implementation needs to be monitored to ensure the desired outcomes. Additionally, as new related legislation in health care reform is proposed and enacted, these policies need to be critically evaluated and monitored.
- *Use expertise as a source of power.* Nurses' expert knowledge is a valuable source of power to shape health care reform. Furthermore, when nurses are willing to contribute their expert knowledge, they are seen as a priceless resource. For example, after we had offered to provide information in one area, the Health Services Commission came back for

assistance with other problems. Health care reform must be dealt with in all states—and the need for many to lend their expertise is great. Nurses' expert power is gained largely through critical knowledge, professional skills, and experience. Nurses' constant presence in the health care delivery system, at every level, gives them pervasive insight into the system's strengths and those barriers that compromise access to care. When we determined that sending the RWJF grant back to the funding organization would seriously hamper children's and families' access to care, we gathered stories from nurses attesting to clients' barriers to health insurance and health care.

- *Link with advocacy groups and coalitions.* Involvement in both advocacy groups and coalitions of health professionals is vital. The nursing profession stresses the importance of nurses' involvement with their own organizations, and this approach has merit, but nurses must also collaborate with other health professionals and with public advocacy groups if they are to influence the development of creative and effective policies needed to respond to the health care crises that face our country.
- *Seize opportunities.* An opportunity for influence in access came to Jeanne with another phone call. This time a representative of the Oregon Health Action Campaign called to invite her to sit on the Safety Net Committee. She had been referred because of her reputation of "thinking outside of the box" and joined several others statewide to find a means to help fund Oregon's safety net clinics. Two nurse leaders have been involved in this work since June 2000, working with a cross-section of individuals on solutions to fund health access in both rural and urban areas of Oregon. These safety net providers include a broad range of local nonprofit organizations, government agencies, and individual providers who share the common mission of delivering health care to persons who experience barriers to accessing the health care they need, such as lack of insurance, geographic isolation, or inability to pay. The group was been active during the 2001 legislative session in educating house and senate members about their plan to help fund these clinics and

ultimately close the gap in access to primary care. Again, this work was taken to the OHC and a safety net clinic resolution, demonstrating commitment to ensure adequate funding for a safety net system, was passed unanimously at the April 19, 2001, meeting.

• *Participate for the long term.* Political and policy involvement is a long-term endeavor. Again, most other books on politics and policy omit this fact, even though common sense leads to this conclusion. Books discuss the policy process, implying that there is an end point. We have learned that this is inaccurate. Although one aspect of the issue may be solved, new, related issues emerge; new twists and turns occur. Policymaking is truly incremental and ongoing. Nurses need to be prepared to be involved for the long term, especially if significant changes are to occur. But long-term involvement does produce effective results, and that is rewarding. Serving on the OHC has been an opportunity to advocate for access to quality and affordable health care. Council service has opened doors to other levels of participation such as membership on statewide committees to address issues of basic-benefit packages and efforts to sustain safety net clinics. Participation by nurses at the local level offers visibility and voice, demonstrating to the public that nurses hold expert knowledge of what citizens expect in the areas of quality, cost, and access. Nurses' voices are held in high esteem and are listened to with respect. The lesson of this experience is to become active, be seen and heard, and do one's part in expressing thoughts and feelings from the expert vantage point of nursing.

• *Differentiate universal coverage and universal access.* Even though the original goal of the OHP was to close the gap between the insured and uninsured, there are more than 363,000 uninsured Oregonians and uncounted others with access problems (Castanares, 2000). Experience has shown that the insurance model of health coverage has not worked. Even though families and individuals may be eligible for the OHP, about 30% of eligible individuals do not enroll. This phenomenon is not unusual.

Historically, about 70% of those eligible for Medicaid nationally are enrolled at any given time. Even when Oregon expanded Medicaid eligibility to all persons below 100% of the federal poverty level, approximately 30% of the "new eligibles" remained unenrolled (OHPPR, 2001, p. 2).

CONCLUSION

Over the last decade, many nurses have shaped health care delivery in Oregon. Some of the actions of the original OHP have resulted in positive outcomes; other issues, such as lack of insurance and rising health care costs, continue to be prominent. Much of the national debate triggered by this legislation has abated, although health policy experts continue to monitor what is happening in Oregon. Because health care reform at the national level has stalled, it continues to be at the state level that experiments in improving health care are occurring (Capuzzi, 1997). It is at this level that nurses need to continue to be actively involved.

References on the Critique of the Oregon Health Plan

Budette, P.P. (1991). Medicaid rationing in Oregon: Political wolf in a philosopher's sheepskin. *Health Matrix, 1,* 205-225.

Callahan, D. (1991a). Commentary, ethics and priority setting in Oregon. *Health Affairs, 10*(2), 78-87.

Callahan, D. (1991b). The Oregon initiative: Ethics and priority setting. *Health Matrix, 1,* 157-170.

Daniels, N. (1991). Is the Oregon rationing plan fair? *Journal of American Medical Association, 265*(17), 2232-2235.

Fox, D. (1991). Rationing care in Oregon: The new accountability. *Health Affairs, 10*(2), 7-27.

Strosberg, M.A., Wiener, J.M., Baker, R., & Fein, I.A. (1992). *Rationing America's medical care: The Oregon plan and beyond.* Washington, DC: The Brookings Institution.

REFERENCES

About OHC. (No date). Retrieved online, April 6, 2001, at www.ohppr.state.or.us/health/leg_context_health.htm.

Capuzzi, C. (1993). Rationing health care: The Oregon story. In D.J. Mason, S.W. Talbott, & J.K. Leavitt (Eds.). *Policy and poli-*

tics for nurses: Action and change in the workplace, government, organizations and community (2nd ed.). Philadelphia: W.B. Saunders.

Capuzzi, C. (1994). The Oregon model of decision-making and its implications for nursing practice. In J. McCloskey & H.K. Grace (Eds.). *Current issues in nursing* (4th ed.). St. Louis: Mosby.

Capuzzi, C. (1997). Toward a comprehensive health care system: Example of a statewide system. In J. McCloskey & H.K. Grace (Eds.). *Current issues in nursing* (5th ed.). St. Louis: Mosby.

Capuzzi, C. (1998). Rationing health care: The Oregon story. In D.J. Mason & J.K. Leavitt (Eds.). *Policy and politics in nursing and health care* (3rd ed.). Philadelphia: W. B. Saunders.

Capuzzi, C. & Garland, M. (1991). The Oregon plan: Increasing access to health care. *Nursing Outlook, 38*(6), 260-263, 286.

Castanares, T. (2000, September). *The safety net*. Paper presented at the meeting of the Governor's Summit Oregon Health Plan: Consolidating Gains, Moving Forward. Eugene, OR.

Garland, M. (2000, October). *Review of "Making health policy 2000"*. Paper presented at the Oregon Health Council Meeting, Wilsonville, OR.

Governor's Commission on Health Care. (1988). *Report to Governor Neil Goldschmidt on improving access to health care to all Oregonians*. Salem, OR: Oregon Office of Health Policy.

Health plan growing beyond good reason. (2001, January 20). *[La Grande] Observer*, 16.

Institute of Medicine. (2000). *America's health care safety net: Intact but endangered*. Washington, DC: National Academy Press.

Jacobs, L., Marmor, T., & Oberlander, J. (1999). The Oregon health plan and the political paradox of rationing: What advocates and critics have claimed and what Oregon did. *Journal of Health Politics, Policy and Law, 24*(1), 161-179.

Joint Legislative Committee on Health Care. (1990). *The Oregon health standard*. Salem, OR: Oregon Legislature.

Kitzhaber, J. (1990, June 12). *Presentation to the Catholic Health Association*. Paper presented at the meeting of the Catholic Health Association, Washington, DC.

Kitzhaber, J. (1991). A healthier approach to health care. *Issues in Science and Technology, 7*(2), 59-65.

Kitzhaber, J. (2000, September 13). Summit on the Oregon Health Plan. Paper presented at the Governor's Summit Oregon Health Plan: Consolidating gains, moving forward. Eugene, OR.

Linker, A. (2001, April 26). Children first. *[La Grande] Observer*, 3A.

NewsHour with Jim Lehrer & Kaiser Family Foundation. (2000). *National survey on the uninsured*. Available online at www.kff.org/.

Office for Oregon Health Plan Policy and Research. (2000, August). *Varying rates of uninsurance among Oregonians: A critical comparison of two household surveys*. Available online at www.ohppr.state.or.us/.

Office for Oregon Health Plan Policy and Research. (2001). *CHIP TOO: A strategy for expanding access to more uninsured children* (unpublished manuscript).

Oregon Family Health Insurance Assistance Program. (2001). *FHIAP snapshot of program activity, 2/5/2001*. Available online at www.IPGB.state.or.us/.

Oregon Health Council Meeting Minutes. (1998, May 7). Wilsonville, Oregon.

Oregon Health Decisions. (1998). *Searching for fairness: Citizens' values about financing health care*. Portland, OR: Author.

Oregon Health Decisions (2000). *Making health policy 2000*. Portland, OR: Author.

Oregon Health Division. (1987). *Oregon vital statistics, 1986*. Salem, OR: Oregon Department of Human Resources.

Oregon Health Plan Administrator's Office. (1997, March). *Health, health insurance and children in Oregon: A summary of findings from the 1996 Oregon population survey*. Salem, OR: Author.

Oregon Health Services Commission. (1991). *Prioritization of services: A report to the governor and legislature*. Salem, OR: Author.

Oregon Legislative Administration Committee. (1995, October). *1995 summary of major legislation, Oregon Legislative Assembly*. Salem, OR: Author.

Oregon Legislative Assembly. (2001). House Bill 2519, seventy-first Oregon Legislative Assembly.

Vaidya, K. L. (2001). *2000 Oregon population survey summary of findings*. Available online at www.econ.state.or.us/opb/.

Chapter 15

Contemporary Issues in the Health Care Workplace

PAMELA F. CIPRIANO

"To achieve the impossible, it is precisely the unthinkable that must be thought."

TOM ROBBINS

The famous introduction to Charles Dickens' *A Tale of Two Cities,* "It was the best of times, it was the worst of times," is appropriate to today's health care workplace. Although there are unrelenting demands on nurses, these times also present unique opportunities for nurses to demonstrate their value to the public.

The issues in the health care workplace are diverse. Most pressing are concerns about quality of care, safety, and error prevention; recruitment and retention of health professionals; regulatory requirements; financial viability; and the use of expensive technology. Nurses are affected greatly by these issues and must play a leadership role in crafting workplace policies to address them.

QUALITY, SAFETY, AND ERRORS

Without question, the attention of the public and the federal government is on quality as the driving force in determining appropriate health care. Nurses are well positioned to use this information to promote wholesale change in our health care system, influence health care policy, and affirm the values nurses bring to health care. Likewise, nurses play an important role in the prevention of errors and promotion of patient safety.

HEALTH CARE ERRORS

Headlines about health care errors grabbed the attention of the American people in recent years. The public appears less confident about the quality of health care now than at any time in the past. Nurses, too, report concerns about decline in quality because they have less time to provide needed nursing care (American Nurses Association, 2001).

In 1999 the Institute of Medicine released the report *To Err is Human: Building a Safer Health System,* and in 2001 it issued the follow-up report, *Crossing the Quality Chasm: A New Health System for the 21st Century.* The initial report sounded an alarm about the loss of life and livelihood as well as the monumental costs of health care errors. It was the first public acknowledgment of what was deemed a national epidemic (Committee on Quality of Health Care in America, 1999). President Clinton charged the Quality Interagency Coordination Task Force (QuIC) to evaluate the report and develop strategies to prevent mistakes in the health care delivery system (Quality Interagency Coordination Task Force, 2000). The task force suggested a variety of approaches from greater recognition of errors to public-consumer-private partnerships to establish safer systems. The report released in March 2001 proposes a major redesign of the health care system that would be safe, effective, patient centered, timely, efficient, and equitable (Committee on Quality of Health Care in America, 2001).

PATIENTS' RIGHTS AND SAFETY

The nursing community has advocated for the rights of patients by working to enact federal patient safety legislation. The Patient Safety Act, reintroduced in a new version in 2001, aims to publicize information on staffing levels and mix, as well as patient outcomes measurement. The American Nurses Association lobbied members of Congress for several years to have this legislation adopted. Other legislative efforts in the 107th Congress (2001-2002) focus on a "patient's bill of rights" to provide consumer protection under managed care.

In all work settings, ensuring patient safety has assumed paramount importance. Not only is it important to the professionals who care for and safeguard patients, but also it is an expectation of accrediting bodies. The Joint Commission on the Accreditation of Healthcare Organizations (JCAHO) includes specific safety measures in its environment of care, patient rights, and treatment standards. Significant focus has been placed on ensuring safer systems such as those for medication dispensing and administration, identification of the surgical site, prevention of falls, prevention of violence and abuse, and appropriate use of seclusion and restraints.

REPORTING OF DATA

In the course of ensuring safety in the health care environment, as well as providing quality monitoring and improvement, the need for voluntary reporting of undesirable outcomes is essential. Internal mechanisms for reporting and identifying opportunities for improvement should capture serious events as well as routine system failures. More importantly, institutions must have mechanisms in place for a systematic process of investigation, plans to correct deficiencies, implementation of corrective action, and evaluation of the results of the action. In July 2001, JCAHO implemented revised patient safety standards. The revised standards require patients to be notified of the outcomes of their care, including adverse outcomes. It must be focused on the populations served, especially for high-risk, high-volume problem-prone situations. JCAHO also has a formal but voluntary process of reporting serious undesirable outcomes, called sentinel events.

GROWING DEMAND FOR CARE

Shifts in social patterns have resulted in increased demand for health care services. As social programs providing safety net services for children, families, and patients requiring mental health services have become inadequate or absent, people seek care through emergency departments. Social problems such as drug use and violent crime, including domestic violence, are major health care problems. Schools are microcommunities where social challenges manifest themselves as health care needs. These may include issues such as sexually transmitted diseases, violence, adolescent pregnancy, drug use, emotional problems, and chronic medication management for disorders such as attention deficit hyperactivity disorder. Today, nurses in these settings are dealing with problems never imagined years ago. Metal detectors, bulletproof glass, and round-the-clock security guards are the norm in many schools. Inadequate budgets in health departments and schools and restrictive local policies may restrain a nurse's ability to inform young adults about contraception and the health risks of unprotected sex and drug use. Lack of referral sources for mental health care and coverage of medication costs for indigent patients may result in exacerbations of illness and serious morbidity. Too often these are the patients who end up in emergency departments.

As nurses struggle to provide adequate services, the lack of integration of care across systems becomes apparent. Although "integrated delivery systems" were the desired organizational model of the 1990s, they were an economic failure. It may have been because the concept was derived as an economic model, rather than a coordinated system of health care delivery to specific populations. Organizational leaders thought that mergers to create a continuum of services would yield higher payments and market share. To the contrary, consumers wanted to preserve provider choice and reacted with a backlash against health care conglomerates that limited choice of providers (Goldsmith, 2000). The backlash also targeted managed care firms through attempts to secure the right to sue an insurance plan for denial of services. Because integrated delivery systems did not decrease costs or stem inflation, especially for supplies and medications, the greater good of continuity of care was never realized. Communities abandoned their publicly funded hospitals, retaining only basic public health services, and shrinking those as well or "privatizing" to save money.

The aging of the population in the United States is expected to continue to increase the demand for health care services and, in particular, nursing care. The size of the population over age 65 is expected to grow about 53% by the year 2020 (U.S. Department of Health and Human Services, Health Care Financing Administration and Office of Inspector General, National Center for Health Workforce Information and Analysis, 2000). Typically this population consumes a great deal of health care services, particularly at the end of life.

NURSING WORKFORCE

The public is greatly concerned about an adequate supply of registered nurses (RNs) now and in the future. National media and trade journals are filled with horror stories related to lack of nurses. Health care organizations are using a wide array of enticements to attract nurses, such as sign-on bonuses and premium pay, abandoned during the retrenchment of the 1990s when organizations trimmed costs. There continues to be debate about whether there is a true shortage as defined by economists, but health organization reports and Congressional action indicate the increased need for nurses in many settings. No obvious quick-fix solutions are on the horizon (United States General Accounting Office, 2001).

The ability of institutions to hire nurses is based on budget. As nursing salaries rise in acute care facilities, settings not affiliated with hospitals often struggle to compete for RNs. As a result, there are fewer professional nurses in settings where their expertise could benefit populations at risk, such as elders in nursing homes and disadvantaged groups who seek care in community-based systems. Home health agencies, whose reimbursement was severely curtailed with the implementation of the Balanced Budget Act of 1997, have reduced the number of RNs in favor of licensed practical nurses.

SUPPLY OF NURSES

The aging nurse population and declining school enrollments are affecting the supply of nurses. The full impact is expected to be felt by 2010 when the baby boomers become eligible for Medicare and the nursing workforce is inadequate to meet demands (Buerhaus, Staiger, & Auerbach, 2000). Furthermore, the replenishment of the work force is occurring at a slower rate than the pace at which demand is rising. Nursing school enrollments have been reported to be lower in the aggregate, particularly in baccalaureate programs.

The aging of society is affecting other health care workers. Shortages of professionals and other personnel are predicted in fields such as pharmacy, laboratory, and imaging. Every professional nursing association is tackling the nursing shortage. The Robert Wood Johnson sponsored project "Colleagues in Caring" has funded 20 sites to implement programs that take into account educational, practice, and community issues in resolving the work force issues. The first phase of the project, instituted between 1996 and 1999, created 20 coalitions, collected and analyzed nursing supply and demand data, built models for predicting work force requirements, refined definitions of "differentiated practice," and outlined strategies to enhance educational mobility. The projects funded through 2002 are creating permanent systems of nursing work force planning (American Association of Colleges of Nursing, 2001). (See Chapter 8 for more on coalitions.)

SHORTAGES OF NURSES

The current shortfall in numbers of RNs appears to be most acute in hospitals with rotating shifts and uncertainty about overtime, safety, and workload. The aging nurse may seek a less-demanding physical work environment such as a clinic, physician's office, or outpatient surgery center where on-call time and evening, night, and weekend time commitments are not required. Nursing homes traditionally have difficulty attracting RNs because of lower pay scales. Nurses working in settings where there are shortages often experience pressure for higher productivity. This may lead to frustration and eventually a reduction in work force participation, thereby exacerbating the shortage (Brewer & Kovner, 2001).

Recruitment and Retention. As attention has focused on recruiting individuals into nursing, employers find themselves participating in health career fairs and offering to support more nursing student experiences. An increasing portion of expense budgets is shifting to support recruitment incentives and competitive wages and benefits. Incentives range from signing bonuses to relocation assistance, subsidized housing, guaranteed educational support, and shortened work hours. There has been a resurgence of the use of short-term contract (travel) nurses and other temporary help.

Employers are scrambling to compete for the experienced work force by trying to improve the workplace. Initiatives are aimed at retaining the current work force while trying to attract more recruits as well.

Compensation and Other Rewards. Compensation often ranks as one of the top factors in nurse satisfaction and has the quickest results in terms of recruitment and retention of staff (H-Works, 2000). Nurses want a safe and supportive work environment and greater recognition in the workplace. Although staff appreciate and deserve economic rewards, nurses also place high value on recognition from peers, supervisors, and other professionals.

Clinical Advancement. The opportunity to advance clinically is important to the RN. Unlike other settings, hospitals are often the only places to offer a formal advancement program such as a clinical ladder. However, any employer can reward nurses for additional education, certification, and exemplary performance. The American Nurses Association (ANA) advises nurses to be well informed about "pay-for-performance" systems, which are designed to reward better performers and represent a change from the traditional cost of living adjustment. These systems may also be cost-effective for employers.

Control over Work Hours. Predictability of work hours and adequate time off are emerging as critical factors in the satisfaction and retention of nurses. Quality of life is important, and time away from the workplace to alleviate stress and provide for self renewal is essential.

Mandatory Overtime. The issue of mandatory overtime has incited nurses nationally. Mandatory overtime has fueled aggressive organizing as well as strike activity in recent years. Nurses are torn professionally between employer demands for adequate coverage and their personal need to balance their lives. Many believe the propensity for errors is increased with loss of sleep from frequent overtime assignments. As of February 2002 (Whittaker, 2002), 17 states had introduced legislation to prohibit mandatory overtime for nurses, and the legislation has passed in three states: Maine, New Jersey, and Oregon. The move to ban overtime has striking similarities to age-old practices in the airline industry where the prevention of error is deemed necessary to protect lives.

Generational Issues. Employers are realizing that the work force consists of multiple generations of workers who have different needs and desire different incentives and rewards. To retain a diverse workforce culturally as well as generationally, institutions must create programs and incentives that meet the different expectations. Four generations are recognized to exist in the current workforce: the mature generation (born between 1909 and 1945), baby boomers (born between 1946 and 1964), generation X (born between 1965 and 1981), and generation Y (born in or after 1982). Younger generations are interested in clear career paths and meeting personal career aspirations. Generation X workers, who are often the most challenging, are accused of lacking a work ethic. Conversely, "Xers" are also characterized as pragmatic, independent, and resourceful (Kupperschmidt, 1998). Both generation X and Y workers seek mentoring, coaching, and feedback. This is consistent with the desire of younger workers to be rewarded adequately for performance rather than for length of service (Santos & Cox, 2000). Organizations can address these differences by aligning benefits and compensation incentives with employee suggestions and providing an environment that responds to changing expectations for career advancement (Lovern, 2001).

PROFESSIONAL PRACTICE ENVIRONMENTS

Nurses believe that the environment in which they practice should support professionalism. This includes involvement in decision making, support and trust in co-workers, competency and commitment to quality care, management support, effective internal communication, and the presence of resources sufficient to provide appropriate care.

Magnet Recognition. The only program that recognizes excellence in nursing services is the American Nurses Credentialing Center's Magnet Recognition program (Aiken, Havens, & Sloane, 2000). The program recognizes "excellence in nursing services, development of a professional milieu, and growth and development of nursing staff" (American Nurses Credentialing Center, 2000, p. 13). As of May 2002, 50 hospitals across the country have received this prestigious review. Magnet recognition demonstrates a commitment to a professional practice environment and public recognition of an organization with excellent nursing care. Given the competition for nurses in the current labor shortage, the designation is also being used as a recruitment tool to entice nurses to work at an institution that can retain nurses and demonstrate job satisfaction.

Workplace Advocacy. Disagreements between staff nurses and management are a reality of the workplace. The concept of workplace advocacy has been promulgated as a comprehensive program to promote the rights of nurses and provide a process of communication, collaboration, and inclusion of RNs in decisions about their practice. The most strictly defined type of workplace advocacy is unionization, which requires formal contracts and enforcement of mutually agreed upon provisions. Nurses often prefer less formal means of defining working relationships between staff and management. Examples include professional practice organizations (PPOs), bylaws, joint governance structures, and staff-management committees.

Interdisciplinary Relationships. Equally important as relationships with management are relationships with other professionals. Whether interactions occur routinely with physicians, pharmacists, therapists, physicians' assistants, or others, the ability to work as colleagues and experience mutual respect is a major source of satisfaction for nurses. It is essential that organizational leaders ensure healthy working relationships by establishing structures that bring professionals together, make expectations for behavior clear, and support teamwork. Well-established collegial relationships are important when conflicts arise among different disciplines.

Education. Educational opportunities play a key role in promoting retention. Nurses find personal satisfaction in enrolling in baccalaureate and higher-degree programs and recognize the importance for their professional development and marketability to higher-level positions. Continuing education is a backbone to most nursing employment. With the shortage of staff, it is important to provide more on-site offerings or permit staff to take advantage of programs outside of an institution. Employers are increasingly offering tuition reimbursement options as well as scholarships for degree programs.

The majority of nurses remain employed in hospitals, and these workplaces can provide numerous opportunities. Nurses, known to have diverse talent and skill sets, are deployed to programs such as quality improvement, utilization management, occupational safety and health, education, employee health, infection control, and risk management. Although these roles and programs are valuable to organizations, some employers question the removal of scarce nursing resources from direct patient care. A challenge for the future will be achieving a balance between a sufficient number of nurses at the bedside and opportunities for practicing in new roles.

WORKPLACE SAFETY

VIOLENCE PREVENTION

In recent years protection of the nursing workforce from unsafe conditions and work-related injuries has become a priority. Employers have provided security to employees by ensuring that weapons are not brought into the workplace and by providing assistance to deal with unruly patients or visitors who might use force. Organizations protect workers from violence by requiring identification badges, arranging for security officers to be present for potentially volatile staff or patient/family interactions, and having an emergency response system to muster additional assistance. In areas with a higher probability of violence, more extreme measures such as bulletproof materials, metal detectors, and mechanically secured entrances protect staff from unknown public threats.

INJURY PREVENTION

Prevention of needlestick injuries, falls, back injuries, anaphylactic reactions from latex allergy, electrical shocks from equipment, and mishandling of blood and body fluids are all part of an employer's responsibilities to safeguard staff. The Needlestick Safety and Prevention Act went into effect in April 2001 (see the Unit III Case Study Case Study). The law requires use of safer devices to prevent needlesticks from contaminated needles. Wearing protective devices to prevent airborne or tactile transmission of harmful bacteria is essential. Instruction in safe moving and lifting techniques helps prevent back injuries. More organizations are instituting the use of "lift teams" as well as assistive devices to help move and lift heavy patients, especially in response to the aging of the workforce. Organizations must follow recommended governmental guidelines by the Centers for Disease Control and the Occupational Safety and Health Administration to provide current protection for staff.

REGULATORY REQUIREMENTS

Increasing economic and regulatory pressures place enormous stress on organizations and providers of health care. Throughout the last decade, the federal regulatory agencies have tightened their grip on health care organizations to force compliance with laws governing the conduct of billing practices. To receive reimbursement from federal sources, organizations have had to adopt practices in concert with federal requirements deemed to improve health care services to consumers.

MEDICARE FUNDING

Most organizations depend on the federal government to pay for services, particularly for Medicare recipients. The policies and conditions governing Medicare reimbursement, promulgated by the Centers for Medicare and Medicaid Services (CMS, formerly the Health Care Financing Administration [HCFA]), have become the benchmark for most third-party payors. The method of reimbursing inpatient charges by diagnosis-related groups (DRGs) for Medicare was implemented in 1983. In 2000 the use of ambulatory payment classifications (APCs) was created as part of the outpatient prospective payment system (U.S. Department of Health and Human Services, Health Care Financing Administration and Office of Inspector General, 2000). A similar plan was implemented in January 2002 for rehabilitation using case mix groups (CMGs). Routine analysis of the costs, charges, and reimbursements for the Medicare population is made possible through large public domain data sets.

ACCREDITATION

To comply with CMS rules, hospitals must comply with a lengthy, complex set of guidelines called "Conditions of Participation." These conditions prescribe such requirements as providing for patients' rights, ensuring systems for measuring outcomes and resource utilization, and using appropriate business practices. The federal government requires that organizations be accredited by an approved (deemed) organization to receive Medicare reimbursement. For hospitals and home care agencies, that organization is JCAHO. Hundreds of requirements must be met and measured on an ongoing basis to maintain current accreditation status. The cost for the survey visit to a medium-sized to large hospital is about $100,000, which is minimal in relation to the amount of federal dollars received for treating Medicare patients, but it is still a significant cost of doing business.

ANTI-FRAUD COMPLIANCE

In recent years, additional scrutiny has been directed toward analyzing appropriate billing practices, particularly for physician and ancillary services. The federal government has had several programs to expose fraudulent billing and seek repayments, including hefty fines and penalties associated with unsound business practices. The U.S. Office of the Inspector General (OIG) has investigated teaching hospitals through its PATH (Physician at Teaching Hospital) audits as well as random audits of organizations that receive reimbursement from CMS. Despite a lack of intent to violate the law, organizations found to be in violation are not only paying large settlements but are also instituting expensive programs to ensure compliance with federal billing rules. Organizations must demonstrate remedial and ongoing education for all staff and providers who, in any way, participate in the process of billing for services. Nurse providers who bill for their services need to be knowledgeable about compliance requirements of billing in addition to general corporate compliance policies.

CHANGING LANDSCAPE OF MEDICARE ECONOMICS

Legislation that changes the financing of Medicare has an impact on health care organizations. One such example was the Balanced Budget Act (BBA) of 1997. One of the aims was to preserve the Medicare Trust Fund. As such, more than $115 billion dollars of cuts came from Medicare, but after a careful analysis the cuts were expected to be closer to $190 billion. Reductions affected most hospital-based services such as inpatient acute care, outpatient care, home health care, skilled nursing care, medical education, and indigent care (Lewin Group, 2000).

The Balanced Budget Refinement Act, passed in 1999, restored approximately $15 billion of the Medicare funding cut in the BBA. Additional adjustments made in 2001, in the Benefits Improvement and Protection Act of 2000 (BIPA), restored some of the cuts supporting graduate medical education. Payments were increased slightly to facilities not reimbursed by DRGs such as psychiatric, rehabilitation, dialysis, and long-term care facilities.

It is important to recognize that dramatic shifts in financing of health care organizations can have severe effects on the services delivered, and in particular on the workforce. As a result of some of the BBA changes, home health agencies closed or laid off RNs. Nursing home beds for Medicare and Medicaid recipients were curtailed, and hospitals already under siege from shrinking third-party reimbursements and managed care restrictions had to tighten their belts an additional notch to brace for the decrease in Medicare funds. The answer for the future is for the health care industry to move to a more integrated care system. The piecemeal system that is so dependent on reimbursement for subsets of services makes providers vulnerable to the vagaries of governmental and insurance industry actions.

PRIVACY AND CONFIDENTIALITY

Privacy of health information is a significant concern. To promote systems to ensure data security and integrity, Congress passed the Health Insurance Portability and Accountability Act (HIPAA) in 1996. The aim of the legislation was to provide standards in three areas: transactions, privacy, and security. After much debate, delays, and failure of an anticipated moratorium on implementation, the law went into effect April 14, 2001, with a full compliance deadline of 2003. The requirements are specific to Medicare and Medicaid providers, but in reality, they will affect how an organization handles all its data and transactions. The ultimate goal is to encourage the development of a health information system that uses established standards for uniform and secure transmission of electronic health information. The law applies primarily to health plans, providers, and health information clearinghouses. Although no one can refute the need for privacy, confidentiality, and data integrity, serious concerns have been raised about the onerous expenses involved in meeting the compliance deadlines. Others are pursing legal challenges because they believe the U.S. Department of Health and Human Services, charged with implementing the regulations, has exceeded its authority by imposing these rules on the private sector. ANA has been an avid supporter of this legislation because of the need to protect patient confidentiality and a belief in the cost saving and other benefits from the standardization (Tieman, 2001).

TECHNOLOGY

Health care organizations, like individuals, have become dependent on instantaneous communication through the use of electronic mail, online databases, and automated transactions to conduct business. The quest for a paperless documentation system continues to drive most health care organizations to improve its information technology. Computerized reporting and data repositories are not sufficient to manage patients as effectively as possible. The need for integration of all information—clinical data, images, financial data, demographic information, and outcome data—plagues many providers. Great strides have been made to automate data. These may include provider notes after a patient visit or bar coding of patient medication and administration.

Multiple systems of patient and staff data as well as tracking systems for equipment, specimens, and records have helped automate and organize work. In some settings cost and a reluctance to change patterns of work have delayed the use of technology. Robots can be used to pick up and deliver blood products, laboratory specimens, supplies, and drugs or intravenous bags. Robots can also be used to fill carts with routine medications or assist in surgery.

Manual documentation systems prevail in most care settings despite knowledge that greater use of information technology can enhance safety and be more efficient. The cost of human capital will soon outpace the cost-benefit ratio for implementing technology solutions. Health care technology companies are selling off-the-shelf systems with artificial intelligence, wireless devices that transmit orders, and barcode systems to avoid medication errors (see Chapter 21).

FUTURE OPPORTUNITIES

Despite these challenges, the future holds significant opportunity. Through intense research and systems reengineering, we will dramatically reduce errors in health care. Financial incentives to implement technology solutions will help expedite results. A breakthrough in the advent of fully integrated information systems will occur soon so that patients, providers, and payors can have ready access to appropriate data. Explosion in the use of technology will free workers from burdensome menial tasks, preserving their time for interventions requiring human interaction. Broader use of the Internet will replace most routine communication we know today. Patients will receive instructions and education from care providers, transmit clinical data, order medications, and seek other useful information via the Internet.

An appropriate balance in government oversight and regulations will evolve as the health care industry reaffirms its commitment to protect the public. Striking this balance requires a heightened level of trust between providers, employers, workers, and payors, one of the greatest challenges we face.

We will reinvent the acute care workplace. We will promote and preserve RNs for care roles and bring them back from the diffusion of their expertise in areas where individuals with other degrees and expertise can fill the gaps. Although the locus of care will continue to move into the community and home, aging baby boomers will still depend primarily on hospitals for care. To attract and keep an adequate nursing work force in hospitals, organizations will need to implement patient-centered care initiatives designed by nurses. Nurses must welcome and engage families in care across the life span. The practice environment must facilitate interdisciplinary collaboration among nurses and other professionals.

REFERENCES

Aiken, L.H., Havens, D.S., & Sloane, D.M. (2000). The magnet nursing services recognition program. *American Journal of Nursing, 100*(3), 26-35.

American Association of Colleges of Nursing. (2001). Colleagues in Caring project. Retrieved online, July 21, 2001, at www.aacn.nche.edu/caringproject/about.htm.

American Nurses Association. (2001). ANA poll: RNs say poor working conditions affect care. *The American Nurse, 33*(2), 1-2.

American Nurses Credentialing Center. (2000). *The magnet nursing services recognition program.* Washington, DC: Author.

Brewer, C. & Kovner, C.T. (2001). Is there another nursing shortage? What the data tell us. *Nursing Outlook, 49*(1), 20-29.

Buerhaus, P.I., Staiger, D.O., & Auerbach, D.I. (2000). Implications of a rapidly aging registered nurse workforce. *The Journal of the American Medical Association, 283*(22), 2948-2954.

Committee on Quality of Health Care in America, Institute of Medicine. (1999). *To err is human: Building a safer health system.* Washington, DC: National Academy Press.

Committee on Quality of Health Care in America, Institute of Medicine. (2001). *Crossing the quality chasm: A new system for the 21st century.* Washington, DC: National Academy Press.

Goldsmith, J. (2000). The virtual IDN and beyond. In *Cerner report: Health care under siege.* Kansas City, MO: Cerner Corporation.

H-Works. (2000). *Attracting and retaining nursing talent.* Washington, DC: Advisory Board.

Kupperschmidt, B. R. (1998). Understanding generation X. *Journal of Nursing Administration, 28*(12), 36-43.

Lewin Group. (2000). *The impact of the Medicare Balanced Budget Refinement Act on Medicare payments to hospitals.* Retrieved online, March 16, 2000, at www.aha.org/bba/lewinreport.html.

Lovern, E. (2001). New kids on the block. *Modern Healthcare, 31*(5), 28-32.

Quality Interagency Coordination Task Force. (2000). *Doing what counts for patient safety: federal actions to reduce medical errors and their impact.* Washington, DC: Author.

Santos, S.R. & Cox, K. (2000). Workplace adjustment and intergenerational differences between matures, boomers, and Xers. *Nursing Economics, 18*(1), 7-13.

Tieman, J. (2001). Praise HIPAA. *Modern Healthcare, 13*(3), 36-40.

U.S. Department of Health and Human Services, Health Resources and Services Administration, Bureau of Health Professions, Division of Nursing. (2001). *The registered nurse population, national sample survey of registered nurses—March 2000, preliminary findings, February 2001.* Rockville, MD: Health Resources and Services Administration.

U.S. Department of Health and Human Services, Health Care Financing Administration and Office of Inspector General, National Center for Health Workforce Information and Analysis. (2000). *HRSA state health workforce profiles.* Rockville, MD: Author.

United States General Accounting Office. (2001). *Nursing workforce emerging nurse shortages due to multiple factors: Report to the chairman, Subcommittee on Health, Committee on Ways and Means, House of Representatives.* Washington, DC: Author.

Whittaker, S. (2002). The nationwide state legislative agenda. *American Journal of Nursing, 102*(2), 24.

Vignette   Toni G. Cesta

The Politics of Case Management

"There is nothing more difficult to take in hand, more perilous to conduct, or more uncertain in its success, than to take the lead in the introduction of a new order of things."

MACHIAVELLI

My career in case management began in 1988, when I became involved in the first study funded by the United Hospital Fund of New York (UHF) to look at nursing care delivery and its relationship to length of hospital stay. The UHF is a philanthropic organization in New York City that supports health care research in various forms. This project, called "The Nursing Initiatives Program," was the first nursing research that the UHF had funded. Five New York City hospitals were selected as research sites. I was hired by Long Island Jewish Medical Center to direct its study.

The study had several goals, including reduction in length of stay and improvement in nursing and staff satisfaction through the introduction of new and different ways of delivering care. As I began to implement the study on the first pilot units, little did I know that I was designing and implementing a case management model. In essence, this meant that specified nurses, whom we were then calling patient care managers, were removed from direct patient care to coordinate the care process for their patients, with an eye to speeding up the care process and reducing length of stay. Satisfaction scores for patients and staff were also tracked for the 2 years of the study (Ake, Bowar-Ferres, Cesta, Gould, Greenfield, Hayes, Maislin, & Mezey, 1990).

In New York City in 1988, this was radical thinking. With very little managed care penetration in the area and barely an understanding of the prospective payment system, the notion of length-of-stay reductions was revolutionary. Yet there were some physicians who believed that practice guidelines (critical paths) were the right way to go and were interested in supporting the study. We were able to get several clinical groups together, with physician participants, and develop these radical new tools for cost and length-of-stay management.

Unfortunately, the resistance to change in the organization came not so much from the physicians as it did from the administration. One administrator told me that the critical paths would increase length of stay. He believed this to be true because if the path called for a 5-day length of stay and the patient was ready to go home after 4 days, then the nurse would keep the patient the extra day. During these years, it was hard to get length-of-stay data because these numbers were considered confidential. Case management had not yet taken the firm foothold it would take during the next few years.

The study was a success. The length of stay went down, and patient and staff satisfaction scores improved on most of the units. This type of successful pilot study of case management is needed to propel the model. Each successful research study, demonstration project, or pilot gives additional data that support the need for case management and demonstrate that it truly does work. Since 1988 I have directed the implementation of case management in four hospitals in New York City and consulted with many others across the country. I have seen the power of this model when implemented correctly. I have made mistakes and learned from them. And I have influenced others in their thoughts regarding case management, a care delivery model that I believe is essential for our present and future health care systems.

HISTORICAL DEVELOPMENT OF CASE MANAGEMENT

Case management, despite its popularity today, is not new to health care. It has been around for more than 75 years and began as a community model within the fields of psychiatry and social work. In the 1930s case management was adopted and used by public health nurses. Case management was first introduced into acute care settings in 1985 in response to the prospective payment system. Today, case management is defined as a care delivery system that supports cost-effective, patient outcome-oriented care (Cesta, Tahan, & Fink, 1997).

In the 1970s several demonstration projects funded by the federal government studied the effects of case management on long-term patient populations. These initial demonstration projects offered comprehensive case management services to Medicare, Medicaid, and some patients under private reimbursement. Populations such as the mentally ill and the elderly were targeted for case management that provided services across the continuum and included nursing, social work, medical care, physical and occupational therapy, and nutrition services (Cohen & Cesta, 1994).

It became clear in the late 1970s and early 1980s that these case management approaches were effective in coordinating services for complex groups of patients. In the 1980s the federal government began its first significant attempt at controlling health care costs. It was apparent that health care costs were out of control and that much of this cost was associated with misuse or overuse of resources. It was further recognized that much of this waste was occurring in hospital settings (Cohen & Cesta, 2001). The demonstration projects of the 1970s had shown that patients could be effectively managed in alternative care settings outside the acute care environment, and that they could do very well.

Prospective Payment

During several years in the early 1980s, a prospective payment system for hospital care reimbursement was developed to control the cost of health care and the use of resources. The diagnosis-related groups (DRGs) were created to categorize "like-type" patients into groupings that would determine hospital reimbursement. The industry abruptly moved from a fee-for-service reimbursement to a fixed-sum reimbursement. Health care providers could no longer bill and be paid for each and every thing they did, or for each service they provided, essentially without question. DRGs meant fixed sums of reimbursement based on the category into which the patient was placed after discharge. This wake-up call to health care providers meant that they had to control their own expenditures because the dollars flowing in were now finite and fixed.

Managed Care

It was during this period that the managed care organizations began to take a firmer foothold in the industry, negotiating extremely competitive insurance rates. And although the prospective payment system had little impact on physician income, a managed care system meant heavy income cuts, either in the form of negotiated discounted rates or capitated risk contracts. To survive, physicians formed alliances such as physician groups and independent practice associations (IPAs), with the goal of pooling resources, managing costs, and maintaining profits.

Hospital-Based Case Management

In 1985 case management was introduced into hospitals as a care delivery system for controlling cost and length of stay under both the prospective payment and the managed care reimbursement systems (Cohen & Cesta, 2001). It became apparent that the means of delivering care in acute care settings had to change dramatically if organizations were going to survive. Though case management was initially slow to gain popularity, a direct relationship can be seen between the amount of managed care penetration in a geographic area and the degree to which case management is being used as a delivery system. The initial case management models were introduced in direct response to prospective payment, but it quickly became evident that there was a relationship between case management and managed care. Today, organizations are more likely to view case management as a system to respond to managed care; thus, the perceived need for this type of delivery system has grown.

Community-Based Case Management

As case management began as a community-based model, in 2001 we saw its return to community-based settings. As the saying goes, "What goes around, comes around." Many community-based organizations are recognizing the need for case management, whether in hospital-based clinics, free-standing community-based organizations (CBOs), or dialysis centers. Nurses, particularly advanced practice nurses, are staffing many of these programs. Professional nurses find themselves in a unique place and time in which their mere presence can have a profound affect on how and when patients receive care, as well as how nurses are perceived by the general public.

CHANGE IS STILL A DIRTY WORD

I am often asked where I find the greatest difficulties and barriers in implementing case management in hospitals and community organizations. The greatest resistance to change comes from two factions. The first are the staff nurses. Many staff nurses continue to function in a political void. They may have a limited understanding of what is going on in health care in the broad sense, and they therefore are incapable of translating these broader issues to their daily experience where they work. If they have not stayed abreast of current events and the professional literature, "selling them" on case management takes months and years. This resistance comes from a failure to understand the reasons that changes need to take place and what they will mean to our profession with time. Some nurses do not understand that the ability to demonstrate skills that no other profession has, such as those of the nurse case manager, makes us marketable and indispensable. I conduct on-site educational programs that include topics such as health care reimbursement systems, the role of the case manager, and outcomes management. The more educated the nurses are, *and the more educated all the disciplines are,* the more supportive they will be.

The other highly resistant group is the physicians. Although a few accept case management because they see it as a means to an end, a greater number almost seem to blame the very vehicle that can help them. I believe that this resistance is completely driven by financial considerations. In markets such as New York, where managed care penetration is around 30%, physicians still believe that tremendous financial gains can be made by inappropriately admitting patients, extending the length of stay, and using vast amounts of resources. They choose not to acknowledge that these are the very behaviors and attitudes that have brought managed care to our doorstep. Not until the financial rewards have completely dissipated will the majority of physicians support case management as a strategy for survival.

The value and success of the case management staff and department must be demonstrated every day. The leadership of the case management department holds the responsibility and accountability for making this happen. Unlike other departments whose value and importance in the organization may be more obvious, the case management department's impact and successes may be less tangible and less well understood. Our political influences as leaders will be just as important as our day-to-day running of the department. So we must "walk the talk" each day and be astute to the changing needs of our organizations.

A CASE MANAGER IS A CASE MANAGER IS A CASE MANAGER

Confusion continues to surround case management and the role of the case manager. In managed care organizations, the utilization functions of the insurance company are conducted by an employee of the managed care organization, using the title of case manager. This role is typically one of utilization review conducted by the insurer. Length of stay, resource utilization, and discharge planning benefits are distributed or denied on the basis of these reviews. Because this function is a financial one, some physicians and administrators are confused when case management is introduced into a care delivery setting outside the insurance company. Many have had experience with the case manager in the insurance company and are not familiar with the clinical functions of a case manager in a care delivery setting, where the role is more clinical and less financial.

Time and resources are needed to educate the physicians and other care providers to clinical case management and the various types of case managers, and to assist them in understanding that in the care delivery setting, the case manager has functions beyond those of utilization review. Today's case managers are found in all care delivery settings across the continuum, including acute care, community care, and sub-acute, long-term, and home care. They perform clinical functions including assessment, planning, monitoring of outcomes, negotiation of benefits with third-party payors, discharge planning, and patient education, to name a few.

DESIGNING CASE MANAGEMENT MODELS

In the hospital setting, case management can be designed in a number of different ways. When an organization decides to implement a case management model, design issues must be agreed on. These include some fundamental and basic questions:

- Who will be the case manager?
- What role functions will the case manager assume?
- How will other departments be affected by the creation of a new role?
- Will a case management department be necessary?
- What other jobs or positions in the organization can be eliminated with the introduction of this new role?
- To whom will the case managers report?

Clearly, these design questions may represent serious restructuring issues for an organization considering development of a comprehensive case management model.

Although it seems logical to assume that a care delivery system would be designed to meet the needs of the patients and the organization in the most effective way, this has not always been the case. Internal political battles rage around case management's place in the organization and its functions and scope of responsibility.

Case management departments have been restructured under many different departments, including operations, nursing, quality assurance, medicine, social work, and finance. Typically, once an organization has decided to implement case management, many departments may vie for case management to come under their jurisdiction. Although these decisions should clearly be based on the case management department's design, goals, and staffing, in reality there may be other driving forces. These are generally political.

Implementation of a comprehensive case management model will result in the integration of previously disconnected departments. This may cause tremendous *turf battles* for the administrative incumbents who are trying to protect their departments. Ultimately the decisions driving design and accountability may be based on the political strength of an administrator or department.

For example, it may be more appropriate to place the case managers under operations or under nursing. The vice president of operations may have less political strength than the physician leadership, and the case managers may ultimately find themselves reporting to a physician, although this design may not be the best for the organization.

SUCCESSFUL CASE MANAGEMENT

The key to a successful case management model lies in the organization's ability to put aside politics and, as objectively as possible, create a design that meets the organization's current and future needs. The ability to put logic ahead of politics may be so subjective that outside consultants may be necessary. External consultants can be directed by the organization in a particular way, or they can be given free reign to design the model. If given free reign, they will have no political allegiance or agendas and may be best prepared to make the most objective decisions for the organization. If the model is designed solely around political intentions, it may not be designed for success.

In the final analysis, effective case management models must incorporate design elements that meet the goals of the organization. The case managers must be clinically competent and must assume enough role functions to be effective. If their function is redundant, the model will be too expensive to operate, and the outcomes and goals will not be achieved. In other words, clear delineation of the case manager's job functions and responsibilities must be teased out from those of others already in the organization. These others may include social workers, utilization review nurses, and discharge planners. Education must be an emphasized step in the implementation process. Educational programs should be geared toward physicians, nurses, social workers, administrators, and all support departments. A lack of education will make the change process much more difficult and potentially less successful.

CONCLUSION

We have finally begun to see case management move toward being viewed as a specialty area with a unique set of skills and a specialized knowledge base. This recognition is taking place in professional organizations such as the American Nurses Association and in academia. Universities and colleges are acknowledging the need to introduce case management concepts and related issues into undergraduate and graduate programs. Topics such as health care reimbursement systems, quality care measures, and continuous quality improvement are being added to curricula. This formalization of case management as a specialty will fully legitimize it and, it is hoped, help it finally be fully accepted by our profession. After all, how can we expect other disciplines to accept case management when our own profession still struggles to define and recognize it?

If politics is indeed defined as "influencing the allocation of scarce resources," then the role of the case manager may be considered first and foremost a political one. Case managers balance health care resources with the clinical needs of their patients—resources that are generally dictated by a third-party payor. Case managers must balance dwindling health care dollars against the patient's needs, the physician's plan, and the available resources, and they make these kinds of decisions every day.

Developing and implementing a new case management delivery system takes courage and commitment on the part of the organization, the leadership, and the care providers. In today's increasingly complex health care system, how can we expect anything less?

REFERENCES

Ake, J. M., Bowar-Ferres, S., Cesta, T., Gould, D., Greenfield, J., Hayes, P., Maislin, G., & Mezey, M. (1990). The nursing initiative program: Practice-based models for care in hospitals. In I.E. Goertzen (Ed.). *Differentiating nursing practice into the twenty-first century.* Kansas City, MO: American Academy of Nursing.

Cesta, T.G., Tahan, H., & Fink, L. (1997). *The case manager's survival guide: Winning strategies for clinical practice.* St. Louis: Mosby.

Cohen, E. & Cesta, T. (1994). Case management in the acute care setting: A model for health care reform. *Journal of Case Management,* 3(3), 110-116, 128.

Cohen, E., & Cesta, T. (2001). *Nursing case management: From essentials to advanced practice applications* (3rd ed.). St. Louis: Mosby.

POLICYSPOTLIGHT

The ANCC Magnet Recognition Program and Magnet Hospitals

Linda Burnes Bolton & Crystal Bennett

"To create this new health care system, nurses need to be far less humble and far more assertive in promoting their profession and its achievements."
                                                    SUZANNE GORDON

The American Nurses Credentialing Center (ANCC) is the largest and most prestigious nursing accrediting and credentialing organization in the United States. The Magnet Recognition Program for Excellence in Nursing Services, developed by ANCC in 1994, provides national recognition to facilities that provide the very best in nursing care.

The program was developed to recognize facilities that provide excellent nursing care and uphold the tradition within nursing that supports professional practice. The program also provides a vehicle for the dissemination of successful practices and strategies among hospital nursing systems. As of March 2002, 47 acute care organizations and 1 long-term care organization had received magnet designation.

The Magnet Recognition Program focuses on recruitment, retention, quality indicators, and standards of nursing practice as defined in the American Nurses Association (ANA) *Scope and Standards for Nurse Administrators* (1996). Both qualitative and quantitative factors of nursing services are measured. Recognizing the link between quality patient care and nursing excellence, the program recognizes, at a national level, nursing services in acute and long-term care facilities, and it provides consumers with an additional benchmark by which to measure the quality of care they can expect to receive. The program seeks to promote the reputation and high standards of the nursing profession.

OBJECTIVES OF THE MAGNET RECOGNITION PROGRAM

The following are the objectives of the Magnet Program:

- To recognize nursing services that use the *Scope and Standards for Nurse Administrators* (ANA, 1996) to build programs of nursing excellence in the delivery of nursing care to patients
- To promote quality in a milieu that supports professional nursing practice
- To provide a vehicle for the dissemination of successful nursing practices and strategies among institutions using the services of registered professional nurses
- To promote positive patient outcomes.

The benefits of magnet designation include enhanced recruitment and retention of highly qualified professional nurses, thus facilitating consistent delivery of quality patient care. Since this recognition award indicates excellence in nursing services, the recipient is a model for other nursing service systems. Staff nurses within the recognized agnet nursing service system may also be contacted by other nurses for consultation services. Further benefits of the magnet designation include enhanced recognition of the nursing services within the community; increased use of the facility by consumers and health care networks; and increased stability in patient care systems across the organization.

According to ANCC, in today's competitive health care environment, facilities often focus too much attention on financial concerns and not enough on the quality of care provided to patients. ANCC magnet designation allows the facility to validate its excellence in nursing services and nursing care. Designation as a magnet facility is made for a period of 4 years. The 4-year designation promotes increased staff commitment, the opportunity to influence a variety of stakeholders in the marketplace, as well as the ability to attract and retain quality staff who have the knowledge and ability to uphold this superior reputation. Ultimately, magnet designation has a positive effect on the financial situation of the facility (Aiken, Havens, & Sloane, 2000).

MAGNET RECOGNITION BACKGROUND

As the early 1980s brought on a severe nursing shortage, studies were conducted to identify nurses' feelings about nursing as a career and to determine what nurses found dissatisfying about their job. These studies were conducted in an effort to make nursing a more appealing career choice (Havens & Aiken, 1999). Research findings indicated that nurses want more autonomy in the decision-making process about patient care, working conditions, and hospital governance (Institute of Medicine, 1983; National Commission on Nursing, 1983).

Concurrently, the American Academy of Nursing (AAN) conducted research aimed at identifying and describing variables that created an environment that attracted and retained well-qualified nurses who were dedicated to delivering quality patient care. The AAN studied the characteristics of hospitals nationwide that had high rates of recruit-

ment and retention and that were delivering high-quality nursing care, despite the national nursing shortage. Ultimately, 41 of 165 nominated hospitals were designated as magnet hospitals because of their success in recruiting and retaining nurses. These magnet hospitals were characterized by having high nurse satisfaction, low job turnover, and low nurse vacancy rates (McClure, Poulin, Sovie, & Wandelt, 1983).

These 41 hospitals shared the following five core organizational attributes:
- The nurse executive was a member of the highest decision-making body in the hospital.
- Nursing services were organized in a flat organizational structure.
- Decision making was decentralized to the unit level.
- Administrative structures supported the nurses' decisions about patient care.
- Good communication existed between nurses and physicians.

RELATIONSHIP OF MAGNET RECOGNITION STATUS TO PATIENT CARE OUTCOMES

Research has documented that magnet hospitals achieve better patient outcomes, shorter lengths of stay, and higher nurse and patient satisfaction than comparable nonmagnet hospitals (Havens & Aiken, 1999). Aiken, Smith and Lake (1994) suggest that nurse autonomy, control, and positive relationships with physicians may be intervening variables that help explain the relationship between magnet hospitals and positive patient outcomes, such as a 4.6% lower mortality rate ($p = 0.026$), such that 0.9 to 9.4 fewer deaths occur per 1000 discharges (95% confidence interval).

Aiken et al (2000) documented the validity of the ANCC magnet program by comparing data on ANCC magnet hospitals with the original magnet hospitals. They found that nurses at ANCC-recognized magnet hospitals experienced lower burnout rates and higher levels of job satisfaction and rated the quality of care provided at their hospitals higher than did nurses at the original magnet hospitals.

Gleason, Sochalski, and Aiken (1999) discuss magnet hospital research that describes and evaluates the professional practice of nurses within these organizations. They suggest that visionary, responsive, and effective leadership of the nurse administrator is key to the establishment of a cohesive and efficient work team and ultimately to the success of the service. Attributes of the professional nursing staff include the ability of the nurse to establish and maintain therapeutic nurse-patient relationships, nurse autonomy and control, and presence of collaborative nurse-physician relationships.

Magnet Nursing Services Recognition Program Eligibility Criteria

Applicants to the Magnet Nursing Services Recognition Program must meet the following five eligibility criteria:

- The applicant nursing service system exists within a health care organization.
- The health care organization nursing service includes one or more nursing settings with a single governing authority and one individual serving as the nurse administrator.
- *Scope and Standards for Nurse Administrators* (ANA, 1996) are currently implemented by the nursing system.
- In the 5 years preceding the application, the applicant nursing service must not have committed an unfair labor practice as determined in a fully and finally adjudicated proceeding before the National Labor Relations Board (NLRB) or other grievance resolution body, and/or a reviewing federal, state, or international court. If an unfair labor charge or grievance is pending before the NLRB or other appropriate governing body at the time an application is being processed, no action will be taken on the application until the NLRB or an appropriate governing body finally resolves the dispute.
- Applicants are required to participate in ANA's National Database of Nursing Quality Indicators (NDNQI), which addresses issues of patient safety and quality of care arising from changes in health care delivery. The NDNQI has been piloted in several states, and preliminary findings indicate that when there are more registered nurses, patients experience fewer complications,

shorter lengths of stay, decreased mortality rates, and lower overall costs.

MAGNET NURSING SERVICES RECOGNITION PROGRAM APPRAISAL PROCESS

The Magnet Nursing Services Recognition Program appraisal process consists of the following four phases: the application phase, the submission of written documentation and evaluation phase, the site visit phase, and the magnet decision phase.

Application Phase

Applicants must demonstrate their compliance with the standards of the Magnet Nursing Services Recognition Program, which include six standards of care and eight standards of professional performance. The standards are those of the ANA *Scope and Standards for Nurse Administrators* (1996).

Submission of Written Documentation and Evaluation Phase

Preparation of written documentation to be submitted for appraiser review is a critical part of the application process, which includes selection of evidence that best reflects compliance with the measurement criteria for each of the 14 standards.

The six standards of care address assessment, diagnosis, identification of outcomes, planning, implementation, and evaluation. The eight standards of professional performance address quality of care and administration practice, performance appraisal, education, collegiality, ethics, collaboration, research, and resources utilization.

Core measurement criteria are essential for maintenance of applicant status. For example, Standard I under standards of care is assessment. A measurement criterion under assessment is 1.1: "Identifies assessment elements including nursing-sensitive indicators appropriate to a given organizational context." Once all of the core measurement criteria have been implemented, the appraisers review any remaining measurement criteria.

Each measurement criterion is evaluated and scored on a 0-5 Likert scale:

0 = No evidence of compliance

1 = Very little evidence of compliance; substantial evidence is missing

2 = Some evidence of compliance is provided; however, additional evidence is needed to substantiate compliance

3 = Substantial evidence of compliance; minimal additional evidence is needed to substantiate compliance

4 = Evidence suggests that compliance has been achieved

5 = Evidence suggests that compliance has been exceeded

Site Visit Phase

After the written documentation has been reviewed and compliance with the standards and measurement criteria is established, a site visit will be scheduled. The purpose of the site visit is to verify, clarify, and amplify the content of the written evidence and to evaluate the organizational environment in which nursing is practiced.

Magnet Decision Phase

Once the appraisers determine that both core and other measurement criteria are consistent with Magnet Nursing Services Recognition Program requirements, a final report is submitted to the Commission on Magnet (COM). The COM then determines if the applicant is to be awarded the 4-year magnet status. Throughout the 4-year period, the Magnet Health Care Organization is required to notify the Magnet Nursing Services Recognition Program office in writing of organizational changes that might affect the ability to meet program standards.

CONCLUSION

According to Aiken et al (2000), ANCC magnet hospital designation is a valid marker of good nursing care. Magnet recognition ensures that patients will get the very best in nursing care available at a facility that is recognized as among the best in the nation. For more information on the designation, contact the American Nurses Credentialing Center.

Contact Information on the ANCC Magnet Recognition Program for Excellence in Nursing Services

American Nurses Credentialing Center (ANCC)
600 Maryland Avenue SW
Suite 100 West
Washington, DC 20024-2571
(202) 651-7264

REFERENCES

Aiken, L., Havens, D., & Sloane, D. (2000). Magnet nursing services recognition program. *American Journal of Nursing, 100*(3), 26-35.

Aiken, L., Smith, H., & Lake, E. (1994). Lower Medicare mortality among a set of hospitals known for good nursing care. *Medical Care, 32*(8), 771-787.

American Nurses Association. (1996). *Scope and standards for nurse administrators.* Washington, DC: Author.

Gleason, J., Sochalski, J., & Aiken, L. (1999). Review of magnet hospital research. Findings and implications for professional nursing practice. *Journal of Nursing Administration, 29*(1), 9-19.

Havens, D. & Aiken, L. (1999). Shaping systems to promote desired outcomes. The magnet hospital model. *Journal of Nursing Administration, 29*(2), 14-20.

Institute of Medicine. (1983). *Nurses and nursing education: Public policies and private actions.* Washington, DC: National Academy Press.

McClure, M., Poulin, M., Sovie, M., & Wandelt, M. (1983). *Magnet hospitals: Attraction retention of professional nurses.* Kansas City, MO: American Academy of Nursing.

National Commission on Nursing. (1983). *Summary report and recommendations.* Chicago: The Hospital Research and Education Trust.

Vignette   *Carol Robinson*

Achieving Excellence in Nursing Practice

"If you really want something, you can figure out how to make it happen."

Cher

A s the director of nursing in a magnet hospital, I am frequently asked to describe the effects of magnet hospital designation on the nursing organization: Does it promote recruitment and retention of staff? How has it changed the nursing staff? The question might as well be, "Which came first, the chicken or the egg?"

THE CHICKEN

In our experience, the "magnet culture" of the organization existed before our application for the magnet hospital designation. This is the chicken part of the story. For my hospital the process of becoming a magnet hospital was not about preparing to meet standards or criteria as one would for a Joint Commission on Accreditation of Healthcare Organization (JCAHO) visit. We did not set out to achieve this designation with the idea that it would help us recruit or retain nurses. Our efforts began 4 years before our magnet application when we decided to create a culture conducive to the professional practice of nursing. We applied for magnet designation because we sought recognition for the work our staff members had done to actualize their dreams in the practice setting. We wanted the designation to reaffirm the reasons we chose to be nurses.

For us, the process began when we wrote our philosophy of nursing. Staff nurses identified their values and visions for a professional practice environment. Six months later we had a document that was value driven, poetic, and inspiring and which articulated our core beliefs about our purpose as a nursing organization.

We knew from our review of Aiken, Haven, and Sloane's (2000) work comparing two groups of magnet hospitals that excellence in nursing care positively affects patient and institutional outcomes. Our vision was to be the best professional nurses we could be despite the economic and political turmoil in health care.

Our vision is evidenced in everything we do or try to do. It underpins all decisions about the organization. We protect professional nursing practice when policies or financial budgets are devel-

Nursing Philosophy

We, The Nurses of UCDMC:

Believe that our mission is to provide science-based, technologically precise, compassionately delivered nursing care;

Define nursing as a scientific discipline that takes a holistic approach to the diagnosis and treatment of potential and actual responses to illness with a goal of lessening the effects of illness, promoting comfort and healing, and assisting patients to achieve an optimal level of self care;

Practice in a dynamic university medical center that promotes ongoing learning for all health professionals;

Strengthen our practice through a commitment to innovation and nursing research based on nursing theories;

Accept professional accountability to patients, families and the community;

Recognize the uniqueness of each person, and respect, protect and advocate for the individual's right to self-determination, self-expression, confidentiality and dignity;

Believe that we best serve through collaboration with other health care professionals who join with us in treating and advocating for those who need our nursing care;

Believe that the relationships we build have an inherent capacity to promote health, healing, and wholeness; and

Commit ourselves to support, acknowledge and nurture one another, thereby creating an environment of mutual respect and caring.

oped. Our nurses have been represented by a collective bargaining union, the California Nurses Association (CNA), for the past 19 years. CNA representatives actively support professional nursing practice despite expected clashes over union priorities and business necessities. CNA representatives enthusiastically participate in magnet hospital designation activities. The union presence has been incorporated into our culture.

The overall organizational culture evolved in such a way that very few changes were needed to complete the magnet application. Activities to elicit buy-in from the other departments and disciplines within the hospital were not required because a climate of collegiality and mutual respect existed and was expected by our nurses. Our physicians are quietly supportive. We don't expect or need continuous praise, but we revel in the fact that they listen and act on our observations about patients and patient care issues. Two academic physician chairs mentioned recently that nurses at our institution are "without parallel excellent, but because there are few problems, the nurses don't generate the kind of attention that other departments usually receive."

Cultural expectations seem to engender self-respect and empowerment. We want nurses to feel powerful and not develop a victim mentality. Our patients expect a powerful nurse to advocate for them, and we work to keep this expectation a reality. I always introduce discussion in the orientation sessions for new employees about the responsibility of the nurse to "rescue the patient" through timely observation and reporting of changes in patient condition. At the same time I emphasize that there is support for the nurse when making difficult or controversial clinical decisions about a patient's care regardless of the time of day or night and that the chain of command can be used up to and including myself.

THE EGG

Now comes the egg part of the story, the revelation of outcomes achieved before, during, and after magnet designation. A senior student nurse called me because she had read a paper I'd written about the transformation of a nursing service and the process required to earn the Magnet Nursing Service Recognition award to become a magnet hospital. This student was about to graduate from a program more than 1000 miles from my institution. She told me that if we were as good as I indicated in my paper, then we were her first choice. She then asked me very tough questions about the practice environment, the collective bargaining climate, and the degree of support available for a new graduate. This nurse already had an idea about the institution from my paper, and her questions were very sophisticated, probing, and direct. Her intent was to find out if we were a suitable match for her talents and ambitions and to review the evidence for herself. I hoped we were good enough for this nurse. She made the decision to join our staff and is a fine addition to the nursing profession.

The outcomes attributed to magnet hospitals now become important evidence for recruiting and retaining nurses such as this one. Our turnover rate last year was under 6%, which compares favorably with a reported national average turnover rate of between 15% and 20%. Our turnover rate in the early 1990s before our magnet designation approached 14%. We do not use any travel or registry nurses. Our vacancy rate varies monthly between 6% and 7%, and again, this compares favorably with national and regional vacancy rates that are reported to be as high as 22% and as low as 10% (Advancing Health in America, 2001). We do not pay sign-on bonuses to attract nurses to our institution. The reputation of our staff is our sharpest recruitment instrument.

Anecdotal comments from nurses in magnet hospitals indicate that nurses in these hospitals display the same characteristics and enjoy working in very similar environments. They are well respected by their peers, by physicians, and by the other medical professionals they work with. Their opinions about patient care are valued and sought. In our institution the former chief of surgery was overheard telling his new residents that they would learn more from the nurses than from him. Nurses in magnet hospitals are rarely subjected to verbal or physical abuse from physicians, nor do they verbally or physically abuse the physicians. In fact, there are mechanisms in place to promote a nonviolent environment and to report such abuses immediately.

Multiple research articles describe indicators of job satisfaction, which usually include collegiality and respect as significant factors for nurses (Kreitzer, Wright, Hamlin, Towey, Marko, & Disch, 1997; Dracup & Bryan-Brown, 1999). Blegen (1993) used meta-analysis to describe the relationships between job satisfaction and many variables such as group cohesion and social integration. Fleeger (1993) found evidence of mutual respect and cooperation in hospital environments with cultures that encourage team players and common goals.

In environments with patients and workers from a variety of cultures, differences in culture create an element of dissonance that must be addressed. We support a multicultural environment that stresses tolerance for differences and embraces diversity. Celebrations of diversity are held annually, which include ethnic food festivals, entertainment, and art displays. Our cafeteria serves different ethnic foods and changes decorations to recognize different countries monthly. We provide numerous professional educational opportunities to learn and practice within a culturally diverse setting and several of our research projects have added a focus on diverse populations. These are just a few of the relationship-building aspects of our profession that are nurtured in the workplace to maintain a healthy practice environment for our nurses.

RELATIONSHIPS

Relationship-based environments promote relationship-based practice. Magnet nurses are strong patient advocates. They do not focus on mechanical behaviors or tasks. They refuse to be victims of their environment, and they recognize the power they have to make clinical decisions affecting their patients. They also recognize that they must incorporate research into their practice to advance the profession and build respect as science-based practitioners.

Nurses throughout our institution implemented a practice called Five-Minute Therapeutic Time at the bedside after learning about the project from Cedars-Sinai Medical Center in Los Angeles. There was some doubt about the effectiveness of the process when it was first initiated. Nurses determined through an experimental study that they could understand their patients' fears, anxieties, and needs by spending 5 minutes of uninterrupted time listening to the patient at the beginning of each shift. Therapeutic time refers to the nurse's full presence of mind, body, and spirit when listening to patient or family needs and concerns. It was hypothesized that patients would feel more comfortable and secure knowing that their nurse was aware of their need and consequently reduce the use of the call lights. The number of call lights used per shift was reduced by 16% on one of the test units and 39% on the second test unit. Patient satisfaction scores improved significantly during the pilot period, as shown in the figure. The enthusiasm of the staff members became infectious when they realized that they could create time to establish a relationship with the patient.

FINAL THOUGHTS ON OUTCOMES AND PROCESSES

Preventing hospital-acquired infections, medication errors, and patient falls; improving survival after cardiac or respiratory arrests; and reducing the prevalence of pressure ulcers are a few of the outcomes being measured and benchmarked to provide evidence of nursing value. We have measures by unit and by month of nurse-sensitive infection rates. For example, in the burn unit, the pooled mean rate for Foley catheter-associated urinary tract infection rates was 3.93 for the 6 months between July 1999 and December 1999. The National Nosocomial Infections Study conducted by the Centers for Disease Control (CDC) (2000) reported a pooled mean of 9.8 for the same time period in burn units. We collect patient fall data for the entire inpatient area, and our rate for 1999 and 2000 was 1.7 falls per 1000 patient days. The reported national median is 2.54 falls per 1000 patient days (University Health Center Consortium, 1998). There are few national research studies documenting survival rates after resuscitation of cardiac or respiratory arrests. Our immediate survival rate after resuscitation for cardiac or respiratory arrests was 70.62% in 2000, compared with a 5-year-old benchmark of 46%. Failure to rescue results in poor patient survival rates. In this case, success in rescuing the patient is one of our relatively new in-

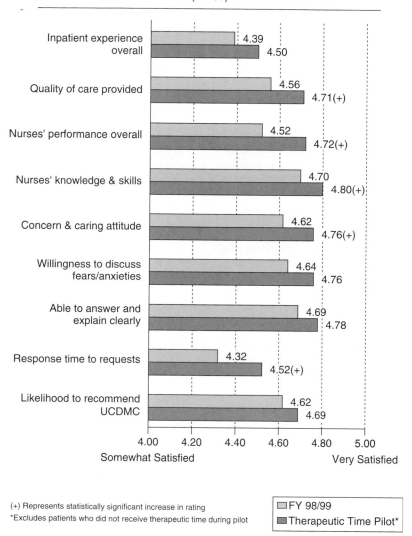

UCDMC "Therapeutic Time" Pilot
Mean Patient Satisfaction Ratings
(n=157)

(+) Represents statistically significant increase in rating
*Excludes patients who did not receive therapeutic time during pilot

FY 98/99
Therapeutic Time Pilot*

dicators of effective nursing intervention. We have always believed that the registered nurse is far more effective when the patient assignment is manageable and there are few supervisor responsibilities added to the patient assignment. That is why we maintain the all registered nurse nursing staff on the inpatient units. We do not use team nursing, licensed practical nurses, or unlicensed assistive personnel in the inpatient care units. Primary nursing is our chosen model of nursing care.

Nurses working in magnet hospitals describe opportunities for professional development as indicators of a professional practice environment. Many hospitals provide tuition reimbursement and free educational programs. We go beyond that by helping the nurse build a resume while working for us. Staff members are encouraged to share their knowledge with others. We reward nurses for participating in in-services, lecturing in courses, presenting poster sessions, or writing abstracts about research projects or ideas. The most popular way of rewarding staff members who submit and have abstracts, posters, or presentations accepted by their specialty organizations is to pay all their expenses to the conference. Exceptionally innovative staff nurses have figured out that acceptance at an international conference in England or Italy is particularly fun and rewarding. Since 1996 we have paid for 882 nurses to participate in conferences at a total cost of $123,360. This is a small price to pay for supporting the career development of staff and igniting the interest in research.

The benefits of achieving magnet hospital designation are many. Nurses at our facility have been inspired to greatness by the actions of their colleagues. During the magnet site visit, many staff members had the opportunity to hear colleagues on other units describe their research projects or their patient care improvement projects during the lunches held with the surveyors. We did not prepare any staff nurses to answer the questions of the site reviewers because we didn't know what to expect. Management was excluded from these lunches. We surmised that the staff must have been sniffing helium from the welcome balloons because they were floating near the ceiling when they came out. We were amazed at their enthusiasm and pride. There is no other way to describe the euphoria other than joy in the professional practice of nursing. While that initial euphoria high does not last for the duration of the magnet designation, I can safely say that nurses continue to practice with quiet competence, confidence, and pride. I have seen their posters and displays developed for the redesignation process. Just underneath the surface there is a playful and joyful mood. Although we are not perfect, I believe we are actively fulfilling our dreams and living our vision of being the best professional nurses we can be.

REFERENCES

Aiken, L.H., Havens, D.S., & Sloane, D.M. (2000). The Magnet Nursing Services Recognition program: A comparison of two groups of magnet hospitals. *American Journal of Nursing, 100,* 26-35.

Advancing Health in America. (2001). *The hospital workforce shortage: Immediate and future.* Available online at www.ahapolicyforum.org/trendwatch/twjune2001.asp.

Blegen, M.A. (1993). Nurses' job satisfaction: A meta-analysis of related variables. *Nursing Research, 42,* 36-40.

Centers for Disease Control and Prevention. (2000). *National nosocomial infections surveillance report.* Available online at www.cdc.gov/ncidod/hip/nnis/dec2000sar.pdf.

Dracup, K. & Bryan-Brown, C. (1999). Searching for satisfaction. *American Journal of Critical Care, 8,* 356-358.

Fleeger, M.E. (1993). Assessing organizational culture: A planning strategy. *Nursing Management, 24,* 39-41.

Kreitzer, M.J., Wright, D., Hamlin, C., Towey, S., Marko, M., & Disch, J. (1997). Creating a healthy work environment in the midst of organizational changes and transition. *Journal of Nursing Administration, 27,* 35-41.

University Health Consortium. (1998, August). *Patient fall prevention survey.* Oak Brook, IL: Author.

Creating Change in the Workplace

JOANNE DISCH

KATHIE TARANTO

"People tend to want to follow the beaten path. The difficulty is that the beaten path doesn't seem to be leading anywhere."

CHARLES M. MATHIAS, JR.

In her landmark book, *Leadership and the New Science*, Margaret Wheatley (1992, p. 13) put words to the hope of many health care workers regarding their workplace environments:

> Our concept of organizations is moving away from the mechanistic creations that flourished in the age of bureaucracy. We have begun to speak in earnest of more fluid, organic structures, even of boundary-less organizations. We are refocusing on the deep longings we have for community, meaning and dignity in our organizational lives.

Leigh (1997, p. 26) adds, "People come to work with more than their bodies and minds; they bring their individual talents and unique spirits."

Yet the environments within many health care organizations have become spirit breaking. A combination of financial pressures, staffing shortages, interpersonal conflicts, higher census levels, dysfunctional operating systems, and overwhelmed and underequipped managers have resulted in stressed and unhappy health care providers in many settings.

"A healthy work environment is a work setting in which policies, procedures, and systems are designed so that employees are able to meet organizational objectives and achieve personal satisfaction in their work" (Disch, 2001, p. 741). Several things must be in place for this to occur: commitment by senior administration; ongoing communication that is "regular, open and candid" (Petry, Mujica, & Vickery, 1996, p. 31); employee involvement; training and education; systems and processes that support a healthy work environment; and consequences when individuals deviate from the expectations.

This chapter explores the concepts of change and transition, particularly as they relate to altering the culture of a work environment. Because the culture of an environment provides the context within which everything occurs and all goals are pursued, culture change is often the most daunting and crucial.

CHANGE THEORY

Change has been a part of the American personality since the country's founding. More than 150 years ago, DeTocqueville noted:

> Born often under another sky, placed in the middle of an always moving scene, himself driven by the irresistible torrent which draws all about him, the American has no time to tie himself to anything. He grows accustomed only to change, and ends by regarding it as the natural state of man. He feels the need of it, more, he loves it; for the instability, instead of meaning disaster to him, seems to give birth only to miracles all about him. (Bridges, 1993, p. 10)

Since DeTocqueville's time this zest for change has been studied extensively, and a number of theories and "microtheories" have been developed to help explain change. In *Planned Change Theories for Nursing*, Tiffany & Lutjens (1998) highlight three theories as being particularly well used by nurses to examine change.

Lewin's (1951) very familiar theory on "unfreeze, move, re(freeze)" is well known to nurses and non-nurses and, actually, because of its familiarity, is often overused and underappreciated for its sophistication. This theory describes the processes required in first helping individuals "unlearn" something, incorporate the new content or skill, and then integrate it into existing paradigms and context. Considered microtheories, his ideas actually reflect a set of small, specific, tightly interwoven subtheories.

From 1961 through 1985, Bennis, Benne, and Chin were responsible for several editions of *The Planning of Change,* in which they and others shared observations and insights on planned change. Rather than developing a specific theory on change, they invited authors to address issues related to change, including problem diagnosis, the choice or development of innovations and strategies for dealing with change, ethical concerns, and evaluation. For many nurses during these decades, these authors were considered to be the experts on change.

The Rogers (1995) diffusion model offers many implications for planning, implementing, and, of special assistance, evaluating the effects of change. Based on research done in the 1940s on the diffusion of hybrid seed corn in Iowa, the model provides a framework for tracing and fostering the diffusion of an innovation throughout a social unit. Emphasizing the importance of communication and cooperation in facilitating change, the model is well-used today by researchers, clinicians, managers, and quality improvement leaders.

Although each of the aforementioned models has been helpful in certain times and for certain types of issues, in the 1990s a new view of change evolved, one that challenged our ability to "manage" change as we had in the past. First, the *pace* of change continued to accelerate. This pace was not new, but with the increasing impact of technology on innovation and dissemination, the rapidity of the changes were being felt in new ways. Furthermore, competitive advantage was fueling this pace. Second, there was the sense that *everything* was changing: the nature of organizations, the role of work, the employee/employer compact, large things, small things. Third, the *idea that change is a discrete process* that can be planned for and managed was being questioned. The linear process of unfreezing, moving, and refreezing had less utility in the 1990s when incalculable numbers of changes were occurring simultaneously. Fourth, changes embodied more of an *all-or-nothing quality* because there was rarely time to sufficiently pilot, test, revise, and improve. Finally, writers such as Wheatley (1992) were reminding us that change—and chaos—are *normal parts of a healthy system* and not something to be avoided or controlled, but rather fostered and celebrated. This thinking resonated with many health care workers who had been struggling to get on top of their workloads and responsibilities. The new challenge, true in the 1990s and today, is not to manage change, but to anticipate it, recognize it, take advantage of it, and learn from it. A new flexibility and resilience is needed.

Change occurs "when something new starts or something old stops, and it takes place at a particular point in time" (Bridges, 1993, p.17). Bridges suggests that change is different from transition. "It isn't the changes that do you in, it's the transitions . . . Change is situational: the new site, the new boss, the new team roles, the new policy. Transition is the psychological process people go through to come to terms with the new situation. Change is external, transition is internal." (Personnel Decisions International, 2000, p. 281). It is the transition, rather than the change or impetus, that calls forth the energy, time, and effort to resolve.

Individuals vary in their ability to tolerate change. Yet in today's frenetic workplace environment, a tolerance—if not an appetite—for change is needed. Previously, employees could acknowledge that they had a difficult time with change, and co-workers or managers would accept that fact. Today it needs to be an acquired skill. In at least one institution, nursing leaders made "managing change" a required competency of all registered nurses. The feeling was that competency in change was as essential to nurses as a competency in reading electrocardiographic monitors was to intensive care unit nurses. It's essential for basic practice.

Organizations, too, differ in their ability to tolerate change. Questions that can reflect your organization's "change hardiness" include the following:

- How often does major organizational change occur in my organization?
- How many changes are made within a month in my patient care unit?
- For how many of these changes were we alerted beforehand?
- How readily do people in my organization accept change?
- Who decides on what changes are going to take place?
- How many people must approve an idea?
- Do people view change as an opportunity or necessary evil?
- How are people who think differently viewed in my organization?
- If I had an interesting new way to change some aspect of patient care, what would the response of my colleagues be? My supervisor?
- Are the following phrases often heard?

"When we get done with all of these changes . . ."
"Why can't we leave well enough alone?"
"What's wrong with how we've always done it?"

CHANGES IN ORGANIZATIONAL CULTURE

One of the most difficult changes or transitions for an organization to make is creating a new culture. This is a predictable requirement given the large numbers of mergers, acquisitions, alliances, and integrations that have occurred within health care. In addition, a number of leaders have realized that the organizational culture within their health care institutions is not necessarily healthy for their workers. Thus, changes in organizational culture are being sought for that reason as well.

A working definition of culture is "it's the way we do things around here." Culture is the collection of mental models, beliefs, and values that have developed over time to: (1) provide inner cohesiveness to the group and (2) enable it to survive and thrive in its environment (M. Kenfield, personal communication, January 17, 1997).

Organizations have multiple cultures, and when two organizations come together, the complexity rises exponentially. With a merger, one of four outcomes is possible (M. Kenfield, personal communication, January 17, 1997):

- *Separation.* The groups do not come together, but bounce off each other. Unless an external force pushes them together, they will not mix.
- *Coexistence.* Members of the two groups work together side by side, yet they never lose their identity and association with their original groups.
- *Integration.* The cultures of the two groups influence each other and together create a new "third way," incorporating the best of both cultures.
- *Absorption.* One group with its culture overtakes the other, thus eliminating the culture of the second group.

Obviously, the preferred outcome is integration, yet understandably this is the most difficult outcome to achieve. Many individuals who have provided leadership during mergers say that coexistence is a more feasible first level to achieve.

The following case study describes efforts to create a new culture within an organization, and then the application of the same principles when a merger occurred and yet another new culture had to be created with physicians actively engaged as key partners in the process.

THE HEALTHY WORK ENVIRONMENT INITIATIVE

In the late 1980s a work group of staff nurses and nursing leaders at the University of Minnesota Hospital and Clinic (UMHC) came together to explore ways in which to address the burgeoning issue of abuse in the workplace. A survey within UMHC at the time indicated that more than 60% of the nursing staff stated that they had experienced verbal or physical abuse within the workplace.

An ad hoc group of interested nursing staff began to address the issue. Four principles formed the underlying foundation for this initiative (Kreitzer, Wright, Hamlin, Towey, Marko, & Disch, 1997):

1. Abuse, neglect, and violence are learned behaviors with rewards.

2. These behaviors can be unlearned.
3. The patterns are cyclical and reinforcing; they are passed from generation to generation.
4. We can control ourselves, not others. Thus, we can change only ourselves, not others.

From discussions among staff and leadership, an expansion of the original focus emerged. Although the initial goal was eliminating abuse and violence from the workplace, it became apparent that this goal was insufficient. Eliminating abuse and violence would not, of itself, result in a work environment that fostered positive growth and performance. Thus, the work group refocused the discussion and described the characteristics of a desirable work environment. The group developed the document "Characteristics of a Healthy Work Environment," which served as the focal point for work within nursing for the next 10 years (Figure 16-1). A companion document was developed to describe concretely the desired behaviors within the environment (Figure 16-2).

What these nurses were reporting was consistent with what researchers were finding. Cox (1991a, 1991b) found that almost 98% of nurses reported that they had been victims of verbal abuse, and Felton (1997) found that 59% of nurses reported that they had been victims of physical abuse. Nurses in some clinical areas—long-term care (Felton, 1997; Gates, 1998), critical care (Drury, 1997; Williams & Robertson, 1997), emergency rooms (Barlow & Rizzo, 1997; Robinson 1998), and psychiatric facilities (Warshaw & Messite, 1996)—seemed to be at particular risk. Studies have shown that abuse and violence are escalating (Felton, 1997; Williams & Robertson, 1997; Gates, 1998; Robinson, 1998).

In 1992 the staff of UMHC embarked on a journey to position the institution for survival within the aggressive managed care market of Minneapolis and St. Paul. This journey, with its lessons learned, has been described elsewhere (Disch, 1996; Kreitzer et al, 1997). Numerous changes were made in all facets of the organization's structure, processes, and practices. A prevailing commitment for the leadership team in nursing was to adhere to the principles of the healthy work environment. Nursing staff would often ask nurse managers and the directors of nursing, "How can you talk about a healthy work environment when we're having to go through such painful change?" The response was consistently, "Isn't that when we *most* need to adhere to the principles?"

In 1996 it became apparent that in spite of major reductions in cost and improvements in service, UMHC would need another organization as a partner to obtain the needed primary care base and to survive. On January 1, 1997, the Fairview Health System of Minneapolis bought the UMHC facilities and merged UMHC and Fairview Riverside Medical Center (FRMC), creating Fairview-University Medical Center (FUMC). FUMC is one entity consisting of two campuses, the university campus and the Riverside campus, facing each other across the Mississippi River. Reorganization and integration at an even greater magnitude ensued. Nursing leaders began the work of bringing the nursing staffs together (Disch & Towey, 1998).

INTERDISCIPLINARY COLLABORATION

For the new organization to successfully evolve and address its tripartite mission of service, education, and research, more than nurses had to effectively work together. Physicians, nurses, social workers, respiratory therapists, and individuals from all professions and job classes had to come together and create a new culture, hopefully blending the best of the two former cultures, FRMC and UMHC. Application of the characteristics of the healthy work environment was extended to this effort as well.

Collaboration is the "process of joint decision making among interdependent parties, involving joint ownership of decisions and collective responsibility for outcomes. The essence of collaboration involves working across professional boundaries" (Liedtka & Whitten, 1998, p. 186). A related concept is trust: "the willingness to rely on others under conditions of risk and the expectation that others' behavior is predictable and beneficial" (Succi, Lee, & Alexander, 1998, p. 399). Researchers have found that trust in the context of a collaborative effort influences attachment to the group, commitment to the group's goals, and final support of the decisions made by the group (Korsgaard, Schweiger, & Sapienza, 1995).

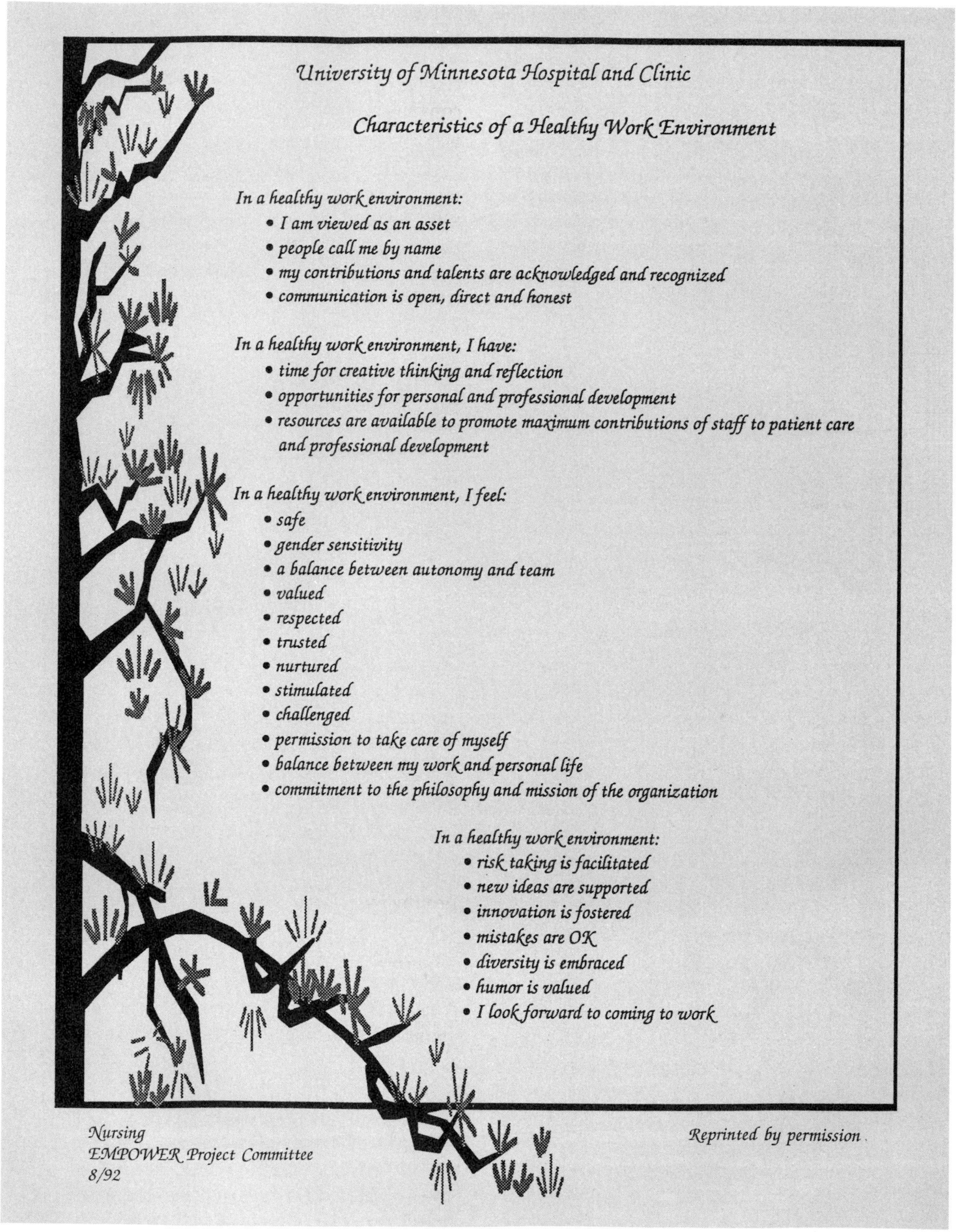

University of Minnesota Hospital and Clinic

Characteristics of a Healthy Work Environment

In a healthy work environment:
- I am viewed as an asset
- people call me by name
- my contributions and talents are acknowledged and recognized
- communication is open, direct and honest

In a healthy work environment, I have:
- time for creative thinking and reflection
- opportunities for personal and professional development
- resources are available to promote maximum contributions of staff to patient care and professional development

In a healthy work environment, I feel:
- safe
- gender sensitivity
- a balance between autonomy and team
- valued
- respected
- trusted
- nurtured
- stimulated
- challenged
- permission to take care of myself
- balance between my work and personal life
- commitment to the philosophy and mission of the organization

In a healthy work environment:
- risk taking is facilitated
- new ideas are supported
- innovation is fostered
- mistakes are OK
- diversity is embraced
- humor is valued
- I look forward to coming to work

Nursing
EMPOWER Project Committee
8/92

Reprinted by permission

Figure 16-1 Characteristics of a healthy work environment. (Reprinted with permission of the Nursing EMPOWER Project Committee, August, 1992.)

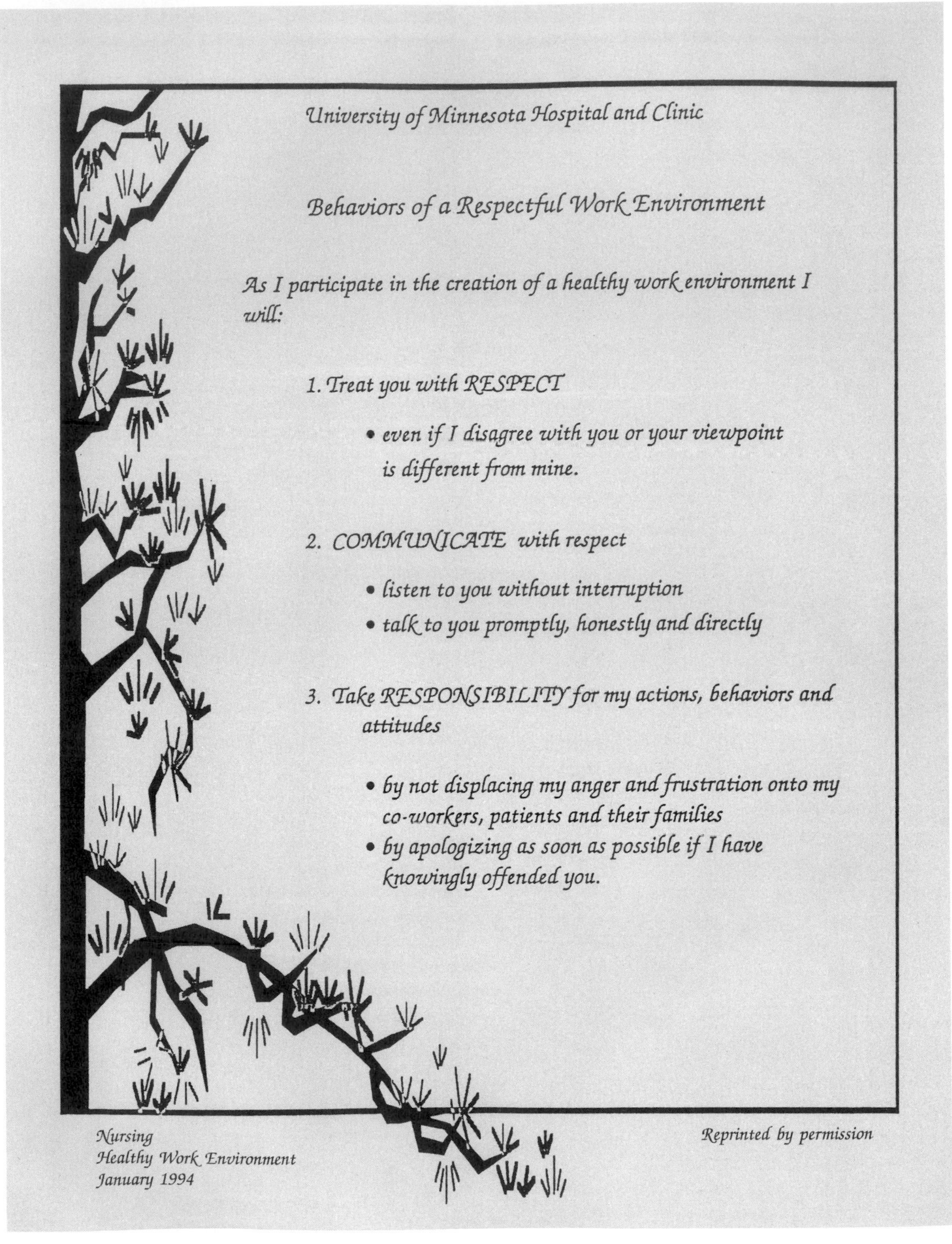

University of Minnesota Hospital and Clinic

Behaviors of a Respectful Work Environment

As I participate in the creation of a healthy work environment I will:

1. Treat you with RESPECT

   • even if I disagree with you or your viewpoint is different from mine.

2. COMMUNICATE with respect

   • listen to you without interruption
   • talk to you promptly, honestly and directly

3. Take RESPONSIBILITY for my actions, behaviors and attitudes

   • by not displacing my anger and frustration onto my co-workers, patients and their families
   • by apologizing as soon as possible if I have knowingly offended you.

Nursing
Healthy Work Environment
January 1994

Reprinted by permission

Figure 16-2 Behaviors of a respectful work environment. (Reprinted with permission of Nursing Healthy Work Environment, January, 1994.)

A growing body of literature demonstrates that collaboration also affects patient outcomes (Knaus, Draper, Wagner, & Zimmerman, 1986; Zimmerman, Shortell, Rousseau, Duffy, Gillies, Knaus, Devers, Wagner, & Draper, 1993; Lassen, Fosbinder, Minton, & Robins, 1997; Curley, McEachern, Speroff, 1998; Baggs, Schmitt, Mushlin, Mitchell, Eldredge, Oakes, & Hutson, 1999; Sommers, Marton, Barbaccia, & Randolph, 2000). This makes sense. Caregivers who demonstrate mutual respect, exchange information, work well together, and help one another will be better able to communicate and function as members of a team with quality patient care as a common goal.

Our merger brought together physicians and nurses from two very different cultures. Differences arose from merging a community hospital with a university hospital associated with an academic health center; a public and private organization; a nursing staff, half of whom were covered by union contract (the former FRMC nurses) and half of whom were not (the former UMHC nurses); and community physicians and academic physicians. The differences were evident in almost every aspect of patient care, such as caregiver roles and responsibilities, practices, priorities, and systems. One simple example serves to illustrate this: How would physicians be contacted? In the teaching hospital, accessing a physician usually involved a chain of command, starting with the resident and ending with the attending physician. On the other hand, community physicians were more accustomed to having a nurse contact them directly. Understanding the different practices and the nuances inherent in the purpose and structure of teaching hospitals and community hospitals was very important and tremendously complex.

A MODEL FOR ENGAGING PHYSICIANS IN THE CHANGE PROCESS

Silversin (1997) has developed an excellent model for helping organizational leaders collaborate more effectively with physicians in advancing change. It has applicability for nursing leaders working with physicians within the organization. The following are the key components.

ALIGNED LEADERS

These are the individuals who step forward, make others uncomfortable with the status quo, occasionally initiate changes themselves so that others become supportive of the process, and hold others accountable. Key roles for those involved in change include acting as *sponsors* (who have the power to sanction change), *agents* (who are responsible for making the change happen), *advocates* or *champions* (who are important opinion leaders), and *those expected to change.*

CULTURE/COMPACT

A compact is an arrangement, which can be explicit or implicit, between individuals or between individuals and an organization, and it strongly influences the culture. It reflects the expected commitment and reciprocal responsibilities among the parties involved. When individuals and leaders in organizations are clear about and agree on the terms of the relationship, change can occur. But often there are misunderstandings about the nature of the compact, which, if unaddressed, can create resistance and dysfunctional relationships.

TENSION AND REMEDY

Change requires reason to change and an option, or remedy, that is seen as feasible, helpful, and attractive. The reason to change can stem from a desire to move toward a better situation or a desire to move away from a negative one. This latter situation is often characterized by the "burning platform" metaphor, which symbolizes choosing the lesser of two unpleasant options: staying on a burning platform or leaping off it.

HUMAN DYNAMICS OF CHANGE

These factors incorporate the individual's willingness and capacity to change and the predicable steps in the human process of change and transition (Bridges, 1993). Dealing with resistance is a major skill that leaders must develop. Silversin (1997) recommends avoiding what he calls the "make-wrong cycle," or shaming others when they resist change. He recommends four steps in working through resistance:

1. Bring the resistance to the surface.
2. Honor the resistance.
3. Go deeper; explore the resistance.
4. Check out your understanding of what you've heard.

MEASUREMENT, FEEDBACK, AND INCENTIVES

For behavioral change, some level of evidence is necessary to build the case. This can take the form of performance statistics, research data, patient feedback, quality improvement results, and so on. But some form of measurement of the extent of the problem is necessary as a start. A second necessary element is some form of feedback loop so that as individuals make the change, they can see results and consequences. Finally, incentives for making the change are important and may have to be of several types, such as money, resources, pride, commendation, access to resources, and affiliation. These incentives need to be aligned between the individuals' motivations and the organization's priorities.

All five of these elements require attention, and change will stall when any of these elements are not present. For example, change will be difficult when leaders aren't on board with change, when there's lack of clarity about the new compact, when there is insufficient urgency about the need for change, when inadequate attention has been paid to the human nature of change and transition, or when the tools for measuring the need for change and progress toward change are absent or ineffective.

With this model in mind, planning for cultural integration at FUMC proceeded with four major *objectives:*

1. Gain understanding of others' ways of doing things.
2. Create an open environment for moving to a new way of doing things.
3. Provide opportunities for problem solving and joint decision making.
4. Deliver quality patient care through a variety of different practice patterns, yet with sufficient consistency in key principles.

Several *strategies* were recommended by those of us assigned to lead the integration:
- Ensure definitional clarity of what integration looks like.
- Enlist collaborative support as caregivers learn one another's practice patterns.
- Offer learning opportunities for understanding cultural differences.
- Begin meetings with relevant groups of physicians to discuss patient care needs.
- Institute a common clinical information system.
- Create rituals for people to "let go" and move to a new way of doing things.
- Celebrate accomplishments achieved by the new organization.
- Establish "merger rounds," regularly scheduled interdisciplinary meetings during which care delivery communication incidents can be reviewed and resolved.
- Create a joint practice committee for review and resolution of issues related to care delivery spanning multiple service lines and departments.

THE JOINT PRACTICE COMMITTEE

The FUMC senior management team and medical staff executive committee (MSEC) supported the establishment of a joint practice committee (JPC) in 1998. Its purpose was "to provide an interdisciplinary forum to discuss patient care issues, barriers to change and to recommend policy changes related to those issues which cross departmental and disciplinary lines at FUMC" (Fairview-University Medical Center, 1999b). Its scope of authority was defined as follows:
- To address quality improvement issues as charged by the lead quality committee, MSEC, and FUMC senior management.
- To make recommendations and endorse changes in interdisciplinary practice.
- To provide oversight and direction to the development of the FUMC care delivery model.
- To promote the establishment of consistent patterns of practice at FUMC.
- To charter groups to examine specific practice issues.

The 20 members of the committee were carefully selected and represented a wide array of disciplines and departments, with equivalent representation from the two former institutions, FRMC and UMHC. The co-chairs were the vice president for family/patient services and a well-respected community surgeon who was an opinion leader among the entire medical staff, which had been integrated earlier in the merger process. The committee met monthly and provided an excellent forum for joint problem solving and decision making.

CASE EXAMPLE

At one meeting of the JPC, a nursing leader from the perioperative services area shared an experience that had troubled the nursing and anesthesia staff in the operating room. A situation had occurred in which the nursing staff believed that a planned surgical intervention would pose a potential problem to the patient and that the possibility for patient harm was imminent. Nurses thought that someone should intervene and give the surgeon some important information. No one stepped forward, and an unfortunate patient situation almost occurred. The nurse leader asked what the committee could do to prevent such situations in the future and provide support to staff for speaking up in the interests of patient care.

The committee thought that this was an appropriate issue to address for several reasons:

- The issue involved concern for patient safety, and how to support staff in speaking up when an incident might result.
- Several disciplines and departments were involved.
- This kind of situation could occur in several clinical areas.
- Strong leadership and advocacy would be needed to create change.

During discussions within the committee over many months, a number of issues were raised:

- Individuals in situations such as this question their perception of the situation.
- Individuals feel powerless or afraid to intervene or even to raise a question.
- How receptive are physicians to being questioned about their practice?

- It wasn't clear who would be the appropriate person to intervene.
- What support would there be if someone intervened and the individual was wrong in the assessment of the situation?
- What impact would intervening have on patient care? Could it delay an appropriate procedure or affect interpersonal relationships among caregivers?
- How can a process be developed that embodies the principles of mutual trust, respect, and open communication found in the healthy work environment documents?

These questions would be challenging ones to answer in any organization. However, given the merger and the status of integration, they were particularly difficult and sensitive. It was already well known that the two nursing and medical staffs had approached care very differently over the years and developed a number of practices that were unfamiliar to caregivers from the other campus. Determining what is different from what is dangerous occupied a great deal of attention in routine discussions about care delivery practices and about selecting or creating the best practices. Adding a time-sensitive situation such as occurs in the operating room considerably raised the stakes and complexity of the issue.

Using Silversin's model, the committee tackled the issue. Over many meetings, the group developed a draft proposal for a process for intervening in emergent situations when there is disagreement about the plan of care (Fairview-University Medical Center, 1999a).

1. *Aligned leaders.* Many committee members eagerly supported the draft, sensing that it would be of great assistance to them. The physician members of the group had more reservations. Being equally concerned about quality of patient care, they weren't sure how well surgeons might respond if someone intervened. They were concerned that intervention would delay needed treatment and perhaps be used indiscriminately throughout the organization when there was a disagreement about care. Since the merger, there had been countless disagreements and "learnings," as is to

be expected. How would this policy help or hinder patient care and interpersonal relationships?

It was essential that this issue be resolved. A proposal such as this one could not go forward without full committee support, and particularly strong leadership by the physician members who would have to encourage its adoption by the medical staff executive committee. Silversin's four steps in understanding resistance and taking the time to fully examine the issue helped immensely. The physician members were fully committed to quality patient care; they just needed some time to examine the issue and to have opportunities to have their concerns heard and incorporated into the document.

2. *Culture/compact.* Silversin (1997) notes that a compact with professionals incorporates a number of elements about which there can be a great deal of disagreement. Consequently, it is important to discuss these elements and the impact of change on them. Some of the elements and possible thoughts about them are presented here:
   - Autonomy: "I'm a professional; leave me alone."
   - Accountability: "There are consequences to actions."
   - Alignment around decisions: "If I'm not involved, it can't move forward."
   - Hierarchy: "Is it okay to treat staff disrespectfully? If I bring in the most money, don't I get special privileges?"
   - Risk avoidance: "We can't make changes without perfect data."
   - Physician-administrator relationships: "They're against us."
   - Strength of governance: "I'll go along as long as it helps us out."
   - Expectations of leaders: "I want them to do what we think is needed."

   In this particular situation, a number of these issues had to be discussed. For example, this proposal would modify the autonomy of physicians in some situations, but most committee members thought that problem would be far outweighed by the potential benefits to the patient. The issue of hierarchy and being able to be disrespectful to one another, or "to pull rank," was another topic that received much attention. The principles of the healthy work environment initiative had been adopted by this group and provided a foundational document for the discussions and decisions. Framing the desired change to clarify and strengthen the compact with the physicians was the objective.

3. *Tension and remedy.* All of the committee members agreed that preventing a serious patient incident was a critical priority. Becoming comfortable with the remedy, and how that could be brought forward to the medical staff, however, occupied much time in committee meetings. Fortunately, once the proposal addressed their two major concerns, the physicians became more supportive and believed the policy did need to move forward. First, they could see that there were mechanisms in place so that it could be done expediently; and second, it was only for emergent situations. Everyone could agree that the intent was to foster smooth delivery of care and also to provide support to staff or physicians in those very exceptional situations when a concern for patient safety arose.

4. *Human dynamics of change.* Attention was then paid to how to best move this forward through the organization, gaining the necessary approval of the key stakeholders. In this instance, this meant the FUMC senior management team and the executive committee of the medical staff. Both groups needed to support this recommendation because it had implications for the hospital staff and physician practice.

Approval by the senior management team was fairly straightforward. These executives had been kept informed on this process, and some of them actually looked forward to putting the policy being in place because some of the vice presidents had had to deal with situations that arose under the current rules, or lack thereof.

The executive committee of the medical staff was a different matter, and in retrospect, some aspects of it could have been handled better. The original plan of the committee was to have the two co-chairs bring forward the proposal and to have the surgeon co-chair provide most of the presentation. Some members of the joint practice committee also sat on the executive committee, and the proposal had been discussed before the meeting with other executive committee members. Additionally, several members of the senior management team also sat on the executive committee, including the vice president of patient/family services (co-chair of the JPC). Therefore many people who would be at the meeting were familiar with—and supportive of—the proposal.

On the morning of the presentation, the surgeon co-chair was called to perform emergency surgery. A decision was made that the vice president for patient/family services would continue with the presentation, which was the wrong decision. The physicians on the medical staff responded as the JPC physicians initially had. There was dismay, anger, and disbelief by some that any physician would be in a situation that could warrant such disruption. Furthermore, given that a proposal with such potential for affecting physician autonomy was being brought forward, even with strong physician support from the JPC, the executive committee began to question its earlier decision to sponsor a JPC. Most likely, when the proposal for a joint practice committee was originally brought forward, it seemed benign. Now, the JPC was fulfilling its charge, and significant change was being recommended. Finally, no comments were made by the members of the senior management team. The unfortunate outcome of the discussion was to place the proposal on hold until the executive committee could review the JPC's charge, responsibilities, and membership. However, after several months of review, the policy was passed by the medical staff executive committee with minor revisions. The JPC continues today.

5. *Measurements, feedback, and incentives.* The proposal identified the steps that should be taken, accountabilities of individuals in the situation, and feedback and monitoring loops that would be instituted to track both the number of occurrences and their outcomes.

The incentive for the change was an improvement in patient care, and standardizing (and depersonalizing) a process could actually improve interpersonal relationships. Since the institution of the policy, it has served as a source of pride within the organization that FUMC has a policy that proactively addresses this situation, which occurs across the country in every health care facility.

LESSONS LEARNED

The following lessons were learned related to the specifics of the case study:

1. With a sensitive proposal such as this, the physician leader was crucial in gaining support, and the presentation should have been deferred until he could be present. The team had assumed that enough people were supportive and would speak up. That did not happen.

2. Perhaps of greater importance was the reminder that individuals need time to go through change or transition in fairly predictable patterns. Although the physician members of the JPC had made this transition, the members of the Medical Staff Executive Committee had not. They deserved time to digest the implications, examine the issue, and work through it just as the other physicians had done. The time needed is proportional to the perceived enormity of the change, and this one could have been anticipated as huge.

3. When discussing a major change with stakeholders, expectations of what is expected of them should be clearly stated. Before the presentation, the members of the executive committee of the medical board should have been specifically asked to speak up at the meeting and indicate their support. It was disappointing that statements weren't forthcoming, but in retrospect, that should perhaps have been predicted. When powerful individuals stay silent to avoid conflict or support their colleagues, they can significantly undermine support for change.

Some other broader lessons have been learned as the work with cultural integration and collaboration has progressed:

1. "Either/or" thinking must be eliminated. Few options are right or wrong, good or bad, black or white. Collins and Porras (1994, p. 44) discuss the "tyranny of the *or* and the genius of the *and*." Their point is that visionary companies operate with a mindset that challenges their employees to practice in a way that seems paradoxical and yet is highly effective—namely, a "both/and" philosophy. For example, this means, preserving a cherished ideology and stimulating change; promoting quality while being efficient; and practicing ethically while being sound financially. Individuals also perform better when able to look for alternatives. In this situation, with two very different cultures merging, this philosophy was necessary yet very difficult. In times of stress and change, humans typically revert to familiar ways. In this situation, they must be supported to move into the unknown. Also, nursing leaders must tackle the seemingly paradoxic task of fostering a strong nursing identity while advancing a pervasive interdisciplinary spirit.

2. Information is power, but relationships are the key. Networks, linkages, connections, and relationships form the basis for support during turbulent times. Max DePree (1989, p. 23) comments that "we would like a work process and relationships that meet our personal needs for belonging, for contributing, for meaningful work, for the opportunity to make a commitment, for the opportunity to grow and be at least reasonably in control of our destinies." Again, there may be little in a situation that can be guaranteed. However, the way in which individuals work together and provide support to one another *is* within the group's control.

CONCLUSION

In times of turbulent change, people often resort to policies or mandates to drive change in a certain direction, believing that time is of the essence and any movement is preferable to none. However, policies developed without participation or support for their implementation will not advance an organization. For successful change, a combination of *policy, politics,* and *power* is necessary. Policies provide specific guidelines and expectations of action, yet the process of developing the policies and ensuring their adoption requires the application of power and politics, along with time and much effort. The challenge here was to create, disseminate, and gain support for a policy that would improve patient care and interpersonal relationships. The principles of the healthy work environment initiative served as a framework for advancing interdisciplinary collaboration and decision making. A participative approach makes the entire experience richer and more satisfying, and it significantly increases the likelihood that the environment supports patients, families, and all caregivers.

REFERENCES

Baggs, J.G., Schmitt, M.H., Mushlin, A., Mitchell, P.H., Eldredge, D.H., Oakes, D., & Hutson, A.D. (1999). Association between nurse-physician collaboration and patient outcomes in three intensive care units. *Critical Care Medicine, 27*(9), 1991-1998.

Barlow, C.B. & Rizzo, A.G. (1997). Violence against surgical residents. *Western Journal of Medicine, 167*(2), 74-78.

Bennis, W.G., Benne, K.D., & Chin, R. (Eds.). (1985). *The planning of change* (4th ed.). New York: Holt, Rinehart & Winston.

Bridges, W. (1993). *Surviving corporate transition.* Mill Valley, CA: William Bridges.

Collins, J.C. & Porras, J.I. (1994). *Built to last: Successful habits of visionary companies.* New York: Harper Business.

Cox, H. (1991a). Verbal abuse nationwide. Part 1. *Nursing Management, 22*(2), 32-35.

Cox, H. (1991b). Verbal abuse nationwide. Part 2. *Nursing Management, 22*(3), 66-69.

Curley, C., McEachern, J. F., & Speroff, T. (1998). A firm trial of interdisciplinary rounds on the inpatient medical wards. *Medical Care, 36*(8; suppl), AS4-AS12.

DePree, M. (1989). *Leadership is an art.* New York: Dell.

Disch, J. (1996). Building strategic linkages for nursing. In J. Disch (Ed.). *The managed care challenge for nurse executives.* Chicago: American Organization of Nurse Executives/American Hospital Association.

Disch, J. (2001). Creating healthy work environments for nursing practice. In N. Chaska (Ed.). *The nursing profession: Tomorrow and beyond.* Thousand Oaks, CA: Sage.

Disch, J. & Towey, S. (1998). The healthy work environment as core to an organization's success. In D.J. Mason & J.K. Leavitt (Eds.). *Policy and politics in nursing and health care* (3rd ed.). Philadelphia: W.B. Saunders.

Drury, T. (1997). Recognizing the potential for violence in the ICU. *Dimensions of Critical Care Nursing, 16*(6), 314-323.

Fairview-University Medical Center. (1999a). *Disagreement over plan of care in an emergent and non-emergent situation: Resolution & follow-up.* Minneapolis, MN: Author.

Fairview-University Medical Center. (1999b). *Joint practice committee.* Minneapolis, MN: Author.

Felton, J.S. (1997). Violence prevention at the health care site. *Occupational Medicine, 12*(4), 701-715.

Gates, D.M. (1998). Preventing violence in health care settings. *Journal of Healthcare Safety Compliance and Infection Control,* 259-265.

Knaus, W.A., Draper, E.A., Wagner, D.P., & Zimmerman, J.E. (1986). An evaluation of outcomes from intensive care in major medical centers. *Annals of Internal Medicine, 104,* 410-418.

Korsgaard, A.M., Schweiger, D.M., & Sapienza, H.J. (1995). Building commitment, attachment and trust in strategic decision making teams: The role of procedural justice. *Academy of Management Journal, 38*(1), 60-84.

Kreitzer, M.J., Wright, D., Hamlin, C., Towey, S., Marko, M., & Disch, J. (1997). Creating a healthy work environment in the midst of organizational change and transition. *Journal of Nursing Administration, 27*(6), 35-41.

Lassen, A.A., Fosbinder, D.M., Minton, S., & Robins, M.M. (1997). Nurse/physician collaborative practice: Improving health care quality while decreasing cost. *Nursing Economics, 15*(2), 87-91.

Leigh, P. (1997). The new spirit at work. *Training and Development, 51*(3), 26-33.

Lewin, K. (1951). *Field theory in social science.* New York: Harper

Liedtka, J.M. & Whitten, E. (1998). Enhancing care delivery through cross-disciplinary collaboration: A case study. *Journal of Healthcare Management, 43*(2), 185-205.

Personnel Decisions International. (2000). *Successful manager's handbook.* North America, Europe, Asia and Australia: Author.

Petry, E.S., Mujica, A.E., & Vickery, D.M. (1996). Sources and consequences of workplace pressure: Increasing risk of unethical and illegal business practices. *Business and Society Review,* 25-30.

Robinson, K.S. (1998). Nurses caught in the crossfire: Assisting patients outside. *Journal of Emergency Nursing, 24*(5), 380-381.

Rogers, E.M. (1995). *Diffusion of innovations.* (4th ed). New York: Free Press.

Silversin, J. (1997, March 13). Presentation at the Fairview Health System Quality Leadership Conference.

Sommers, L.S., Marton, K.E., Barbaccia, J.C., & Randolph, J. (2000). Physician, nurse and social worker collaboration in primary care for chronically ill seniors. *Archives of Internal Medicine, 160*(12), 1825-1833.

Succi, M.J., Lee, S.D., & Alexander, J.A. (1998). Trust between managers and physicians in community hospitals: The effects of power over hospital decisions. *Journal of Healthcare Management, 43*(5), 397-414.

Tiffany, C.R. & Lutjens, L.J. (1998). *Planned change theories for nursing.* Thousand Oaks, CA: Sage.

Warshaw, L.J. & Messite, J. (1996). Workplace violence: Preventive and interventive strategies. *Journal of Occupational and Environmental Medicine, 38*(10), 993-1006.

Wheatley, M. (1992). *Leadership and the new science.* San Francisco: Berrett-Koehler.

Williams, M.L. & Robertson, K. (1997). Workplace violence: Prevalence, prevention, and first-line interventions. *Critical Care Nursing Clinics of North America, 9*(2), 221-229.

Zimmerman, J.E., Shortell, S.M., Rousseau, D.M., Duffy, J., Gillies, R.R., Knaus, W.A., Devers, K., Wagner, D.P., & Draper, E.A. (1993). Improving intensive care: Observations based on organizational case studies in nine intensive care units: A prospective, multicenter study. *Critical Care Medicine, 21*(10), 1443-1451.

Vignette   *Beth W. Gering*

Why Change Efforts Fail

"You don't become a good sailor by sailing calm seas."

JOHN MAXWELL

Some change efforts produce history-changing successes, such as the mission to land a person on the moon. Other efforts are dismal failures, such as the Bay of Pigs invasion and the effort to institute a standard educational entry level in nursing. We are told frequently that the only constant in society today is change, but change doesn't just happen. Much careful planning and effort is involved in every change effort, whether the proposed change is in a workplace process or a major policy change in government.

When one thinks of change, two words come to mind: *opportunity* and *uncertainty*. Initially, one may romanticize the tremendous benefits change can have, but during the planning and implementation phases, a sense of uncertainty is often present. Nearly every organization conducting business today is undergoing some type of transformation, but not all organizations succeed in their quest to transform. Why do some organizations fail in their efforts while others succeed? John P. Kotter, a Harvard Business School professor and expert on change, identified in his book *Leading Change* (1996) the most common reasons why change efforts fail. Kotter's insights are vital to all who attempt to initiate change.

Kotter suggests accepting complacency is the most significant error made when attempting to implement change. Complacency is often a result of past success or of a lack of visible crisis, which leaves people content with the status quo because it appears to be working. Leaders may have a complete understanding of the need for change, yet they may fail to effectively communicate this need and create a sufficient sense of urgency in the early stages of the change process.

Failing to create a powerful guiding coalition can severely handicap change efforts. Many underestimate the difficulties in producing change. One person alone cannot assemble sufficient energy to effect change. Instead, most successful transformations are crafted by a team or coalition of individuals who are committed and focused.

Leaders of change may underestimate the power of vision, which is a critical error. According to Kotter (1996, p. 7), "Vision plays a key role in producing useful change by helping to align and inspire actions on the part of large numbers of people." Leaders should be able to describe the vision driving the change in 5 minutes or less and get a reaction that demonstrates understanding as well as interest.

According to Kotter, it is essential for leaders to provide a clear vision, and they need to ensure it is communicated by disseminating it to all levels in a variety of formats. Often, in failed transformation, vision is greatly undercommunicated. The vision of the goal must be repeated and continually reinforced. Belief in the vision needs to be modeled by leaders, or change efforts can become undermined.

Because change takes time, leaders must keep momentum going. Kotter (1996, p. 11) states, "Complex efforts to change or restructure risk losing momentum if there are no short-term goals to meet and celebrate." In order for transformation to succeed, leaders must focus on meeting objectives and rewarding individuals who support the success. Producing short-term wins can reduce complacency as well as inspire critical thinking, which can be used to tailor the transformation process.

Another obstacle to success occurs when organizations undergoing change declare victory too soon. This premature conclusion can result in a retreat to previously established traditions. Kotter notes (1996, p. 13), "Until change sinks down deeply into the culture, which for an entire company can take 3 to 10 years, new approaches are fragile and subject to regression." He recommends that change be anchored into the culture. He adds, "Until new behaviors are rooted in social norms and shared values, they are always subject to degradation as soon as pressures associated with change are removed" (p. 14). To anchor the changes, leaders must specifically demonstrate how individual behaviors and attitudes have assisted in making an improvement work.

Kotter (1996, p. 15) concludes that committing any of the aforementioned errors can result in "slowing down the new initiatives, creating unnecessary resistance, frustrating employees, and sometimes completely stifling needed change." Many resources are available to guide the implementation of change. As important as it is to know the steps to implement change, it is equally important to recognize common errors that contribute to failure so measures can be taken to avoid them.

REFERENCES

Kotter, J. P. (1996). *Leading change.* Boston, MA: Harvard Business School Press.

Vignette Jeanne Anselmo

Dancing with the Chaos: A Grassroots Approach to Transformation and Healing in Nursing

"You really can change the world if you care enough."
MARION WRIGHT EDELMAN

CHAOS THEORY, NURSING, AND POLICY MAKING

Researchers and physicists tell us that underlying what looks like random, unceasing disorder is the beauty of pattern and organization. Within the chaos of our times, from downsizing and reengineering to the nursing shortage, old paradigms are being dismantled, leaving opportunity for our profession to transform itself and the health care system. This chaos offers an opportunity to realign with the true essence and values of nursing, emphasizing the quality of life and quality care for ourselves and the communities we serve. We become aware of the importance of protecting value-based practice, including creating a healing environment for ourselves to work and in which our clients can heal.

Nursing, like life, is ever changing. Dancing with this chaos allows us to create new opportunities, to transform and heal our personal and professional wounds, and to learn to be partners with our colleagues in a new way. Transforming ourselves and understanding the ways we live and work together may also lead us to understand how to influence larger systems. This act of conscious awareness in the face of chaos is vital to our personal, professional, and collective health, well-being, and wholeness. In turn, creating a process that supports our values reawakens our commitment to value-based national health policy making in a time when financial outcomes have overshadowed quality and safety of human life and care.

According to American anthropologist Margaret Mead, "Never doubt that a small group of thought-ful committed citizens can change the world—indeed, it is the only thing that ever has." Mead's inspirational statement is grounded in physics: the butterfly effect. Chaos theory teaches us that the beating of a butterfly's wings can create a breeze that, joined by unpredictable forces, can culminate in the development of a tornado in another part of the world. Our choices amidst chaos have larger implications and can have a cumulative impact far greater than we can ever imagine. Greg Bradon, a physicist and author of the *Issaah Effect* (2001), says it this way: "Quantum science suggests the existence of many possible futures for each moment of our lives. Each future lies in a state of rest until it is awakened by choices made in the present."

Using Bradon's work, Dr. Barbara Joyce, RN, former president of the New York State Nurses Association, wants nurses to wake up to this awareness of "co-creation" and "co-participation." "We are in that moment in time between death and rebirth. It takes knowledge and inner wisdom to move into the higher dimensions. The old ways are not going to be there anymore" (B. Joyce, personal communication, September, 2001).

Many nurses believe there is another way, an unfolding process, that reflects this truth of quantum physics: *that we can co-create our possible future, through the choices we make and the way that we make them.* These nurses have learned that our choices are important, but that the process and values reflected in those choices are even more essential. The ways they have chosen to awaken a new future is through co-creating and participating in *process:* various forms of grassroots dialogue, nursing healing circles, nursing town meetings, and nursing vision summits. These nurses have found that value-based *process* and practice are more important than outcomes or finances. This does not

Tips for Nursing Circles (and Potential Ground Rules)

1. *Begin with creating a safe, nurturing space.* Place chairs in a circle with flowers in the center; play peaceful music before the circle begins; offer herbal tea and snacks; and most importantly, develop group ground rules. Maintain confidentiality with such reminders as "Keep it in the circle. Save it and bring it back to the circle." Don't let circles deteriorate into socializing. Respect the value of the process.
2. *Begin and end with a meditation.* Meditation can center, calm, and relax participants and is an element of self-care. Some facilitators are flexible about starting or ending on time; others believe it is important to start and end promptly, especially when incorporating student learning experiences. Turn pagers and cell phones to vibrate. Forget titles and credentials. Invite each person to share from the heart. Remember that everyone needs time to share, so be brief, listen, and be open to what each person is saying. Sometimes using a "talking stick" (a Native American tool that invites members to listen to the holder of the talking stick, which is passed around the circle) helps maintain ritual, and it prevents cross-talk and promotes listening.
3. *Speak for yourself, rather than telling people what they should be thinking or doing.* Learn the principles of conflict resolution and negotiation (see Chapter 7). Invite your group to study conflict resolution and diversity skills together. When facing a difficult situation in the circle, practice nonjudgmental approaches and try what Sandy O'Brien suggests: "I do my best to greet it gently, and to try to understand what they are feeling."
4. *Use seed questions to begin dialog.* Alternatively, invite issues from the group.
5. *Don't be afraid to ask for help.* If problems arise beyond the scope of skills of the group, call in resource people from human resources, nursing education, social work, or psychology departments. Before a problem arises, contact members of other departments and get to know them. Explore whether their philosophy and style match the needs of your group. Build relationships; ask whether they could provide support if necessary. If the circle is in the community, call local colleagues in institutions or private practice for support and information. Build relationships.
6. *Enjoy.* Enjoy being together, sharing, supporting one another, building alliances, and creatively solving problems.

have to preclude a financially solvent health care system.

One of the process oriented approaches is the *nursing circle.* Nursing circles are created when two or more nurses come together either formally or informally with the understanding that every nurse is a leader: that in every nurse resides wisdom and a necessary part of the story and solution to the problem. Circle members focus on support, creative problem solving, self-care, and leadership development, and they choose to follow the process and values explored in the nursing circle tips described in the box.

Nursing town meetings expand the concept of a nursing circle to include input from nurses of a particular region or area. They are held at a public venue offering circle process and values in addition to the input, inspiration, and guidance of two to four nurses with expertise in various areas of interest or relevance to the major topic under discussion at the town meeting.

Tips for Town Meetings

1. *Find a local space or organization interested in partnership with your group.* Follow the tips for nursing circles to create the process, ground rules, and atmosphere.
2. *Keep your meetings simple.* Invite two to four resource persons to act as catalysts for discussion, information, and support. The resource nurses might be people with experience in professional organizations, innovation, political activism, or community involvement. The purpose of the meeting is to stimulate the spontaneous sharing of those attending and to learn from each other. If possible, try to offer resource persons an opportunity to meet and socialize before the town meeting, so that they can get to know one another and learn their areas of interest. Mix various philosophies, ideas, and backgrounds to give depth, variety, and breadth to the meetings. Include all views.

Grassroots nursing summits focus on a theme. Ours have focused on leadership and visioning, on diversity and community wisdom, and on creating a healing environment at work and on the planet. At grassroots nursing summits, nurses come from across the country and engage in educational offerings prepared by nurses from different backgrounds, offer rituals and ceremony, and participate in small circle dialogue and whole group dialogue.

Global nursing peacemaking (GNP) began as an international offering at the 1999 International Congress of Nursing in London, inviting international dialogue around various nursing values and process initiatives focusing on transformation, leadership, creation of a healthy work environment, and healing. GNP has a website, www.nursingvision.org, offering practical tips on beginning a value-based process initiative, with the hope that other nurses will create their own circles and continue to benefit from this process.

BEGINNING THE PROCESS

In the early 1990s, New York City began its turn experiencing what other parts of the country (and world) had already encountered or were soon to encounter: managed care, downsizing, "right sizing," and reengineering. Nurses were being "out placed" or "pink slipped" in droves. Today, short-staffed nursing units know why they are struggling, but in 1995, the unknown presented the greatest source of negative stress. We needed to create vehicles of support, strategy, and information.

In the spring of 1995, a diverse group of nurse friends and colleagues gathered to pool our diverse backgrounds of practice in order to access information, strategies, and experience that nourished us on many levels. Together, we came up with creative approaches to issues and problems that none of us would have been able to come up with or accomplish alone. We were able to encourage one another's efforts and support self-care, and we felt a renewal from our connection and commitment to nurses and nursing. Our group is an informal nursing circle. We realized that most nurses during this crisis were becoming more isolated and did not have the opportunity to reconnect with one an-

other, with themselves, or with the inner source that moved them to become a nurse.

Around the same time, I was offering self-care and healing circles for nurses at various hospitals and clinics. Some groups consisted of the entire staff, from housekeepers to the medical director, but most focused on self-care for nurses only, otherwise known as nursing circles. The multidisciplinary groups offered an opportunity for improving communications, breaking down barriers and stereotypes, and improving conflict resolution and departmental problem solving. Some deep work emerged from these groups, but the deep work around nurses' issues of wounding and experiences of an oppressive system were unable to be explored as deeply in the interdisciplinary groups as they were in the nursing circles.

Nursing circles provide a safe place for nurses to support one another and share their experiences and feelings about the changing health care system. The nursing circles format was simple. After an opening relaxation exercise, the next step was to go around the circle and "check in." The nurses shared how they were doing and what was happening in their work and lives. This was all voluntary. The facilitator cultivated an atmosphere of support, encouraging nurses to share ideas, feelings, and needs. It was amazing how readily nurses accepted a safe forum in which to share their pains, worries, concerns, and interests. Whether on a unit or in a department-based nursing circle, nurses in nursing circles were sharing their deep concerns with colleagues they worked with each day. The level of need was great, and the fear and the pressures that the nurses were under required a safe, nurturing environment.

IMPORTANT ROLE OF THE FACILITATOR

The job of the facilitator is crucial. The role of facilitator is to help each member feel safe, feel vital to the group, and feel appreciative of each group member's role and contribution. The group needs to develop understanding, collaboration, and synergy, even while working through problems. Therefore, developing ground rules or group guidelines is essential. Leaderless groups can also be extremely nurturing, creative, and effective, although having a facilitator for unit-based groups when the unit or organization is in crisis can be a more effective strategy. Sometimes I began as the facilitator, but as the group progressed, other group members took on the facilitator role. It is often difficult for the charge nurse to be the facilitator. It can be hard for charge nurses to be heard as fully participating members of the group because they are still in a role of responsibility, especially since one ground rule is to forget all credentials and titles at group meetings. An outside facilitator can help by working with all members of the group, including the charge nurse. Creating a safe environment, encouraging participation, and establishing a process orientation take time. Those embarking on this path need to build on an understanding for themselves and the group that "trust grows." It does not arrive fully formed just because we need it or want it. Each experience the circle encounters, even if difficult, is another opportunity to nourish trust.

Seed Questions for Use at Healing Circles, Town Meetings, and the Nursing Summit

1. What is your vision for your practice of nursing? How would you like to improve your practice? What skills, personal and professional, would you need to develop? What are your strengths?
2. Why did you become a nurse? Has that reason changed over time?
3. What ways do you stop or undermine your own efforts to move toward your vision? What would help you to change that pattern? What supports do you already have to help you? What supports do you need to cultivate? What resources have you learned about in this forum that could help you think, be, and act differently in your vision?
4. What do you want nursing to become? What do you want nursing practice to be in 10 years? 20 years? 50 years? Why do you want youth and adults to become nurses? What do you see as nursing's commitment and contribution to society? What should it be? What could it be?
5. What is the true essence of nursing practice? Does your practice today reflect that essence? How would you want to change your practice? What resources can you access personally and professionally to do so?

TOWN MEETINGS

During the nursing circles, I would share with the unit nurses some of the insights and information that my colleagues had shared with me from work on state, national, and international levels; hence, the seed for the nursing round table (now called nursing town meetings) was planted. The New York Open Center, an urban holistic education center, offered our group a date and space in its catalog to advertise and a room to hold a forum for dialogue. In the fall of 1995, the first nursing open round table was held. Approximately 40 nurses attended, and my three nurse colleagues and I served as resource people or catalysts for the discussions. We decided that we needed to maintain the circle format, seeing and hearing each other on equal ground. This event and subsequent meetings provided opportunities to expand on the nursing circle process by bringing together nurses from different places to network, share experiences and feelings, and identify other avenues for shifting their own practice and influencing the changing health care system. After the initial period of meditation, the four resource people and 40 additional nurses introduced themselves, briefly sharing why they had come and what interests they wanted addressed.

At the first forum, we discussed many important and controversial issues: replacement of nurses with unlicensed technicians, managed care, political issues in nursing, holistic practices, entrepreneurship, and expanded roles. Nurses in the group participated by voicing their opinions, asking questions, making comments, and listening to one another's ideas. Subsequent town meetings have brought together three or four different nursing resource people who shared their vision and experience with approximately 30 to 50 nurses. Mixing together resource nurses of diverse backgrounds, such as nurses from holistic nursing with nurses from state political action committees, weaves together a variety of ideas and reflects the wholeness of our profession.

A NURSING SUMMIT TO DANCE WITH THE CHAOS

The need to expand on the town meetings became apparent during the summer and fall of 1996, when the rate of downsizing in hospitals began to escalate. Nurses were despairing as they lost jobs, were transferred to clinical areas outside their expertise, saw nursing management jobs eliminated, and tried to cope with the financial concerns that were outweighing the value of caring and quality patient services in their facilities. The nursing community was stunned, shocked, and grieving. Most attendees and presenters at local nursing conferences seemed to have few answers or ideas, as they grappled with the chaos and the unknown. We realized we needed to draw on a larger source, our collective knowledge and experience in order to offer hope, possibility, experience, and wisdom available in nursing and other disciplines. Hence, the grassroots nursing summit called on nurses from across the country to create a gathering to explore the issues we were confronting, support each other, grieve our losses together, and create a possible vision. In Fall of 1997, at the Omega Institute for Holistic Studies in Rhinebeck, New York, the first of our nursing summits was held. A self-formed grassroots steering committee titled it "Dancing With the Chaos."

We began with a plan that came from our well-worn thinking patterns: to gather for 4 days at Omega to strategize and create an action plan for our vision for nursing's possible future. We ended up developing a process-oriented healing and vision summit including the following:

Tips for a Nursing Summit

1. *Expect the unexpected.* In a volunteer, grassroots group, things change and people come and go. Resources may or may not be available. Be flexible! Have a support team. Stay open to what is emerging; it may be better than your original plan. Don't be attached to outcomes. Even if the event does not unfold, remember we are building a long-term vision and reality.
2. *Choose a theme or vision to build the summit.* Invite your steering committee to develop a vision, philosophy, and infrastructure for the summit that reflects committee members' shared values and philosophy. Do what you say. Do the process work and train your facilitators and committee. Invest in your members.
3. *Learn about new paradigm leadership.*

1. *A pre-summit educational day.* This day was designed to help support and develop another generation of nurse facilitators and leaders focusing on diversity, international nursing, environmental nursing, the future, organizational partnering, creation of a healthy work environment, and self-care.
2. *Resource faculty sharing their experiences and innovations.* More than 30 faculty and resource people, from universities and institutions from Florida to Maine and from Minnesota to Maryland, donated their skills and energy.
3. *Time for connecting with others who share a common ground.* The summit allowed time for nurses to share their concerns and grief, with rituals to help them acknowledge and then move beyond their losses.
4. *Small-group and large-group meetings,* offering time for nurses to think about and write out their vision for nursing and health care, which was then placed in a time capsule in the archives of the New York State Nurses Association to be opened in the year 2020.
5. *Exploration of new possibilities* for nurses and the health care system.
6. *Time to enjoy* one another as nurses and as human beings.

WHAT CAME NEXT

After the first summit, we continued our town meetings and offered summit reunions locally at the New York Open Center. District 14 of New York State Nurses Association (NYSNA) offered a "mini summit" for Long Island nurses. New nurses attended local events after hearing about the summit from colleagues who had attended and came eager to connect with the passion and enthusiasm their colleagues had on their return. The board of directors of NYSNA held a summit for their board members to vision the future of the organization. Under the leadership of Barbara Joyce, PhD, RN, the board decided to work to create "healthing circles" (another name for healing circles) in hospitals throughout the state, which would be led by NYSNA-trained facilitators.

The grassroots nursing visioning summit steering committee from the first summit decided to

Suggested Summit Ground Rules and Guidelines

1. *Forget titles.* Create common ground and an equal playing field for all. Check out your beliefs, expectations, assumptions, and approaches with a variety of nurses from different backgrounds to determine whether you are being inclusive. Don't try to explore and resolve all issues; remember, this is an open-ended process that started before the event and will continue afterward in another form. What will be most helpful to explore in this moment?

2. *Remember that diversity brings richness, joy, depth, and deep nurturing.* We are all blessed to have a diversity of races, ethnicities, cultures, specializations, education, and ages represented in nursing. Encourage diversity, inclusiveness, and safety. Consciously invite nurses of diverse backgrounds, ethnicities, races, and specializations and education. Don't try to please everyone; some attendees will want to spring ahead faster, and others will choose not to participate.

3. *Support one another and ourselves.* We will need more time to integrate what is offered. Learning and support are ongoing processes that begin before the event and continue after it. We need to learn to be supportive of one another as nurses. (This learning—that nurses were heard, respected, and supported and that they cared about one another—was one of the most highly praised dimensions of the summit.)

4. *Bring your spirit and deep intention into this work.* What touched us was that, regardless of our tradition, we all wove spirit into our work. Bringing spirit out in ritual, candle-lighting ceremonies, bereavement rituals, dancing, and celebration nourished us deeply, inspired us for the journey ahead, and supported our true intention. Take a risk. Tell your story. Open-hearted sharing and creativity in a safe and respectful space is very simple and very transformational. Nurses reported that standing together under the stars in a circle, with candles lit, being part of a close-knit group in ceremony, has helped to sustain them since the summit.

5. *Take care of yourself and have fun.* Again, "never doubt that a small group of thoughtful, committed people can change the world—after all, it is the only thing that ever has."

proceed with plans for a second nursing summit and met regularly at various institutions around the metropolitan area. Out-of-state steering committee members kept in touch by attending these meetings via conference call. The focus of the second summit was "Celebrating our wisdom, our diversity, and our community." We worked "to walk our talk" and invited representatives of as many of the ethnic, racial, religious, and cultural nursing organizations as were able to attend. Gender and sexual preference concerns were also represented on the steering committee and at summit. We were determined to address our diversity of education, professional practice, and personal backgrounds, which represented both nursing's strengths and greatest source of inner professional conflict.

We prepared steering committee members by inviting two facilitators skilled in conflict resolution and diversity training to do a retreat with us and attend our planning meetings to: (1) monitor our process, (2) help us to explore our own conflicts, and (3) prepare us to act as supports, and group facilitators, during the summit. The power, connection, and commitment of the steering committee meetings continued at the summit, which was attended by a diverse group of 100 nurses from all over the country in the fall of 1998. The attendees were deeply moved by the process, wisdom, and stories shared. Nurses were amazed that we clearly invited safe exploration of our diversity issues of race, ethnicity, age, sexual preference, and gender. It was hard for any stereotypes to be at play after sitting face to face and heart to heart with one another for 3 days, sharing our stories. Fascinatingly enough, although most would have expected these issues to be the most challenging, the small and whole group process demonstrated openness, spaciousness, support, and inclusion. We laughed and cried with one another as we explored our common ground and our uniqueness. The only time the group encountered an impasse was when the issue of diversity of education became the focus. The process exploded into long-held beliefs and attitudes about what constituted professional education. Within minutes the community of nurses who had "left their credentials at the door" and been sharing heart to heart, nurse to nurse, started *talking at* one another rather than *listening to* one another. The strongly held beliefs and attitudes left little room for dialogue or exploration. Although this explosion did surprise us, it illustrated what often happens in our daily work. As such, it did not undermine the well-being, community, harmony, and connection of the summit. It did alert us to an area nursing needs to heal if we are to be able to understand one another.

ENERGY, UNPREDICTABLE FORCES, AND OUTCOMES

The process requires us to let go of outcomes and trust the energy and the process. In short, we can hope for a continuation or outcome, but all we can *do* is to continue to do our best in this moment and see what happens. Sandy O'Brien, RN, MSN, the nurse manager of a methadone center, gave us one example of an unplanned outcome. Sandy came back after the first nursing summit and began a self-care healing circle in the fall of 1997, which meets once a month, and continues today. "We didn't want to lose the momentum, so we found a way to keep it going."

Other examples are Janet Hand, MA, RN, founder and director of Pathways to Wellness in Glen Head, NY, and Margo Governo, EdD, CNPP, FNP, a professor at Wagner College, who ran NYSNA healthing circles in the community and at local hospitals, respectively. They found that consistency, patience, and ground rules were very important. Margo also suggested that when facilitating a circle in a facility other than your own, "you need someone respected and trusted, who believes in what you are doing" at the facility to help remind colleagues and support participation and help to encourage attendance in the early stages.

In 1999 Margaret Flatt, PhD, RN, and Susan Vorce, MSN, RN, of Michigan's Saginaw Valley State University, used the tips and guidelines found in this vignette (third edition) to create a nursing circle and summit process for their Michigan Nursing Association Leadership Planning Retreat. Margaret used the process with the Michigan Student Nurses Association (MSNA), as well. Both Michigan groups enjoyed the process. MSNA students used their discussions about the nursing shortage to articulate ideas for addressing nursing shortage issues. Using the process of small group and large group dialogue, they created an action report to bring to the MSNA House of Delegates, which was presented at a meeting of the National Student Nurses Association. They also shared the action report with Michigan Nursing Association, which brought it to the state's Board of Nursing as a future nurses' perspective against mandatory overtime and its danger to patient safety.

UNDERSTANDING PROCESS OUTCOMES

Nurses committed to process and self-care initiatives know that we are not looking for short-term outcomes. Even though an initiative may end and resurrect in another form or under another name, that is just part of the process. The energy is never lost; it just may take a different form or name and reappear in or at another facility. Not every specific effort will bear fruit, and yet we know that no effort is ever lost. Eleanore Schuster, RN, who created many successful retreats and environmental summits in Florida, worked on projects for 2 years with wonderful local and international committee members only to find that there was not enough energy or money, or the timing was off. And yet nurses, like builders of cathedrals, know that although we may not always see the results of our efforts, we are committed to a larger vision that touches the spirit, heart, mind, and body—the essence of what it is to be truly human and humane. Our circle work reflects our commitment to a human and humane movement based on process and values; our dedication to bringing out the best in ourselves and our profession; and our goal of improving our quality of life and the quality of care in our country and on our planet.

REFERENCES

Bradon, G. (2001). *The Isaiah effect: Decoding the lost science of prayer and prophecy.* New York: Crown Publishing.

Bohm, D. (1996). *On dialogue.* London: Routledge.

Chinn, P. (1999). *Peace and power: Building communities for the future* (4th ed.). New York and Sudbury, MA: National League for Nursing; Jones and Bartlett.

Serge, P. (1994). *The fifth discipline fieldbook.* New York: Doubleday.

Wheatley, M. (1994). *Leadership and the new science.* San Francisco: Berrett-Koehler.

Wheatley, M., & Rogers, M. (1996). *A simpler way.* San Francisco: Berrett-Koehler.

REALITIES OF IMPLEMENTING CHANGE IN A HEALTH CARE ORGANIZATION

Nancy M. Valentine

"In spite of illness, in spite even of the archenemy sorrow, one can remain alive long past the usual date of disintegration if one is unafraid of change, insatiable in intellectual curiosity, interested in big things, and happy in small ways."

EDITH WHARTON

Given the impact of the information explosion, coupled with pressure to contain costs in the production of all goods and services, there is a revolution in how every aspect of health care is delivered, financed, measured in terms of quality and outcomes, and accessed by consumers. Change is a reality that influences nearly every aspect of the health care industry, whether one looks at clinical care, education, research, delivery systems, or financing. On a macro level, federally-driven change in health care financing is part of the daily dialogue among health care executives. At the unit level, technology and pharmaceutical development constantly change clinical practice.

NURSING'S CRITICAL ROLE IN CHANGING THE HEALTH CARE WORKPLACE

As the single largest group of health care professionals, nurses can create systems of care that work and environments that are satisfying to work in as change is occurring. But nurses have to balance many competing demands. As a result of the associated stress, they may get caught up in the inability to resolve and move beyond conflicts in interpersonal relationships. Often, conflict resulting from change is handled by methods that do not maximize resolution, such as avoidance, appeasement, compliance, or change of employment. Dysfunctional reactions to change can result in "workplace blues." Workplace blues result from a combination of difficult workload and unsatisfying interpersonal relationships in the workplace.

Promoting nurses as pivotal change agents must be supported with education and expertise in topics critical to success: leadership, communication, personnel management, collective bargaining, team development, conflict resolution, and change management. Today's nurse needs to be a manager, group dynamics expert, business-minded contributor, patient advocate and ethical decision-maker (Kersbergen, 2000).

To move from where we are today to a new vision, in which nurses more adeptly manage change, is largely a matter of getting nurses themselves to choose to give up what is not working and move on with fresh ideas to get the job done. This requires a renewed focus on career self-development, for nurses at every career stage. The process of managing change begins with managing the fears, frustrations, and uncertainties that occur when one's organization is evolving and the comfortable old ways are disappearing.

Keeping the organizational vision in view while developing change management skills needs to become the norm for all nurses. Organizational leaders must verbally paint a picture for all staff of where the organization is going, and they must repeat it frequently in times of intense change. It is incumbent on nurses to develop their own abilities to successfully deal with change in the workplace. Nurses must conduct a self-assessment of their learning needs and plan a personalized strategy for assuming increased responsibility for the success of their enterprise. Self-assessment should lead to a plan of how to develop needed skills.

THE DANGER OF RESISTANCE

The role that nurses can play in the swirl of change is potentially enormous and exciting. Unfortunately, a barrier to moving nurses to the forefront of championing change in health care is the perception among some colleagues that nurses can be difficult to work with. Some see nurses as resistant and reactive when faced with meeting the challenges involved in organizational change. As part of establishing a healthier workplace, a central challenge is how nurses as individuals and a group can work with others to effectively change such perceptions and work through the problems to move organizational change ahead.

Given the opportunity, nurses can turn around a negative image to one where the nurse is perceived to be a natural change agent and partner in the change process. Nurses have many of the critical-thinking skills that can be applied to developing health care solutions. Applying these problem-solving skills to challenges in every arena in which nurses practice will produce results. With vision and purpose, nurses can move to a new level of comfort with making and implementing important changes.

OUTCRY FOR INNOVATION

Innovators rarely see the world in negative terms. Such individuals are neither personally angry nor professionally disenfranchised. They see each problem as a challenge: as something that needs to be fixed or as a situation begging for someone to design a creative solution. For innovative nurses, much of this approach is driven by a combination of personal attitude and the nursing environment. Fortunately, with so much change occurring in so many different arenas, old hierarchies and bureaucratic approaches are being abandoned and fresh ideas are being considered. Opportunities abound in many settings for those who are willing to take the risks, step forward, and march ahead on new paths. Ferreting out these opportunities requires looking for new approaches to old problems and being willing to expend the energy necessary to take a leadership role.

The potential positive outcomes are limitless. When nurses find change a challenge rather than something to be avoided, they begin to take an active leadership role, whether they are staff nurses or executives, and they embrace change rather than shun it. Nurses, who so often see themselves in subordinate positions of reacting to change rather than leading it, should place themselves in situations where they are driving change. This will increase the quality of care as well as improve the level of satisfaction among nurses.

Nurses need to leverage their interest in breaking down the intraprofessional, interprofessional, and external barriers that currently exist in some settings. The challenges are many, but one central question must be raised: What is it going to take to move nurses from feeling complacent where we are now to transforming the workplace? In reframing the vision, nurses are proactive, risk-taking, effective team players who have the skills and knowledge to optimally function as both problem solvers and catalysts involved in revitalizing health services delivery.

COURAGE TO CHANGE

A well-known saying by Reinhold Niebuhr encourages us to "accept the things we cannot change, have courage to change the things we can and have wisdom to know the difference." Niebuhr's philosophy is readily applicable to the health care workplace. Change management in the health care workplace is one of the greatest challenges a nurse will encounter. Consider the following as you navigate the constant change in today's health care workplace:

- Recognize that there are always barriers to be overcome in making change or adapting to change in the workplace.
- Do not shun change. Take a job that requires you to stretch yourself. Deliberately seek out positions in environments that are changing because they are always more interesting and challenging.
- In making a commitment to an organization, inventory your strengths and weaknesses. Develop a strategy for taking a leadership role whenever possible in the change process.
- Where there are people, there are problems. Dealing with difficult people is part of managing change.
- Develop and maintain a positive attitude. Do not personalize conflicts with managers and co-workers. Remember that every experience is an opportunity for learning and growth.
- Strive to be a partner. Administrators and staff share many of the same challenges. Work to decrease the barriers that exist between the groups and eliminate the *us* and *them* divisions.

- Recognize that communication is key and most problems in managing change are related to miscommunications that lead to misunderstandings.
- Treat everyone you contact with dignity and respect. Work toward establishing a truthful and trustworthy atmosphere. Do not let conflicts fester.
- Know yourself. Evaluate your style in managing and dealing with change. Seek opportunities to get feedback and mentoring in how to do the most effective job.
- Commit to be a life-long learner. Develop your own career goals and structure a personalized continuing education curriculum that will assist you in meeting these goals. Be consistent in meeting your education goals.
- Seek out involvement in local, state, or national political issues that are of interest to you. Network with others who have similar interests and are involved in special interest groups and coalitions. Take this information back into the workplace and share with co-workers.
- Read at least three professional journals each month: one in the area of general nursing issues, one in your area of specialty interest, and a third in the general health field. Note issues and trends as these relate to the challenges and changes you are facing in the workplace.
- Develop a professional peer network that extends beyond co-workers. Such a group can function as an important support during times of change and is a resource bank for testing out new ideas or learning how problems were solved in similar or different arenas.
- Join a professional association and volunteer for a committee. Bring new perspectives into your workplace.
- Innovate. Try new approaches, experiment with alternatives, pilot new programs. Keep track of findings and evaluate the results.
- Take risks. Do something you never thought you would be capable of doing.
- Expect a high level of job satisfaction and you are more likely to get it.

REFERENCES

Kersbergen, A.L. (2000, March-April). Managed care shifts from an altruistic model to a business framework. *Nursing and Health Care Perspectives, 21*(2), 81-83.

Vignette

Dezra J. Eichhorn, Theresa A. Myers, Cathie E. Guzzetta, Angela P. Clark, & Amy O. Calvin

Family Presence at the Bedside during Invasive Procedures and CPR: When Pigs Fly

"Here in America we are descended in blood and spirit from revolutionists and rebels—men and women who dared to dissent from accepted doctrine."

DWIGHT D. EISENHOWER

Nurses who are committed to meeting the needs of their patients and families inevitably will be confronted with difficult clinical problems and decisions. Such a situation confronted Theresa, a trauma case manager, the day that she encountered a critically ill 14-year-old trauma patient and his family. The patient had sustained a grade IV liver laceration after falling from a tree. After surgery, he had been in and out of cardiopulmonary arrest. The staff caring for the patient notified Theresa and the family that it was "okay to come in now." When they reached his room, however, the door opened and they were told "it's not a good time." As the door shut in their face, Theresa knew the patient had arrested again. The patient's mother looked at Theresa and said she understood what was going on and wanted to be with her son. Theresa explained what was happening, but the mother was insistent that she needed to be at her son's side. Instead of escorting them back to the waiting room, Theresa went into the trauma room. She explained the situation to the team and asked whether she could bring the parents in. Although reluctant, the physician in charge agreed, and the parents were escorted to the bedside. Here they had the opportunity to talk to their son, coach him in the fight to keep going, and tell him how much they loved him before he died.

After this incident, some members of the health care team criticized Theresa's actions. There was talk that she might lose her job. One physician told her "pigs would fly" before family members would be allowed at the bedside during a resuscitation. Theresa defended her actions in subsequent "on-the-carpet" meetings by stating that the family had made their needs perfectly clear and that in this situation, the right thing had been done. They wanted to be at their son's bedside during his last moments of life.

In the days that followed, Theresa agonized about the incident. Such reflection caused her to move from an analysis of the incident to a more general examination of the rationale directing traditional practice. Then the clinical problem emerged. Theresa asked a simple question: Why do we do that? Why do we ban all family members from the bedside during cardiopulmonary resuscitation (CPR)? Convinced that some families had a strong need to be with their loved ones during resuscitative efforts, Theresa set out on a path to change practice.

STRATEGIES USED TO CHANGE PRACTICE

Resolving a clinical problem often can be accomplished using one of several strategies: changing a policy or procedure; using administrative decision making; taking educational approaches; or conducting scientific research (Granger & Chulay, 1999). Theresa set out on her path believing that

the unwritten hospital policy of banning all families from CPR could be resolved using the first strategy or by creating a new policy that permitted families at the bedside in the emergency department (ED) during CPR.

Theresa teamed with her trauma department director and the trauma psychosocial clinical nurse specialist to begin the change. They met with nurses and physicians in management positions to discuss creating a written family presence policy. It became apparent from the many personal issues and legitimate concerns voiced that the environment was not ready for an immediate change by instituting a written family presence policy. Many health care practitioners understood the desires of family members to be at the bedside but felt that the potential risks for the medical team outweighed the benefits for the patient and their family.

As the family presence team gathered the data from opponents who cited their reasons why family presence should not be permitted, it became clear that most of the arguments against family presence were based on opinions and beliefs not supported by research. For example, colleagues stated several problems they thought could happen if families were brought to the bedside during CPR:

- Family members might lose control or faint.
- Family members might disrupt or interfere with patient care.
- The team did not have time to take care of anxious family members because patient care came first.
- The event would be too traumatic for family.
- The risk of liability might increase.

Although opposition to family presence was great and attempts to create a family presence policy were unsuccessful at this stage, the discussion provided a forum by which nurses and physicians could voice their concerns. These discussions were important in the process of change and also were productive in gathering the data about the issues and fears involved. Considering the strong opposition encountered, the family presence team consulted the hospital's nursing research consultant, who recommended seeking administrative support and educating the health care provider about the existing research on family presence.

Believing that practice might be changed by an administrative decision, the family presence team then set out to gain the support of key administrative players. They met with the president and chief executive officer of the hospital and with the senior vice president of nursing. They discussed the issues regarding the first family presence case, the problems that confronted them, and their intent to change practice, and they asked for support. Although receiving unanimous support from these key individuals, they learned that any administrative decision to change the existing policy banning families from the bedside needed to be initiated by the ED.

Over time the team became aware that educational efforts would be ineffective in changing practice because there was little clinical or research documentation on family presence. However, team members distributed the clinical and research articles that did exist (Doyle, Post, Burney, Maino, Keefe, & Rhee, 1987; Hanson & Strawser, 1992) to their colleagues. These educational efforts were assisted when the Emergency Nurses Association (ENA) published an 84-page guideline on implementing family presence programs during invasive procedures and CPR (ENA, 1995).

CHANGING PRACTICE THROUGH RESEARCH INVESTIGATION

Because the family presence team was unable to change practice by developing a family presence policy, by achieving administrative decision making, or by conducting staff development, and because little research had been conducted on family presence, the group determined that the best strategy for changing practice was to scientifically investigate the issue. In doing so, the issue of family presence was made scientific instead of emotional, allowing agreement among even some of the strongest opponents that scientific investigation was warranted.

In earlier discussions, opponents told the family presence team that the family members of patients admitted to their county, regional, level-I trauma center probably would not want to be present at the bedside with their loved one during CPR. To determine the validity of this belief, the family presence team worked closely with the hospital's nursing research consultant to conduct a retrospective survey of family members of patients who had died in the ED in the prior year to determine whether they would have wanted to be present during their loved one's CPR. With her direction, the team developed a retrospective survey on family presence and collected data from 25 family members within a few months.

The findings supported what the team surmised from clinical experience: 80% of families said they would have wanted to be in the room during CPR had they been given the opportunity and believed it would have been helpful to them and to the patient if they had been at the bedside (Meyers, Eichhorn, & Guzzetta, 1998). In fact, these findings were later found to be consistent with the cumulative results from national and local surveys and polls, which have revealed that between 60% and 70% of families would want to be present in the ED with a loved one who is undergoing emergency procedures (Redley & Hood, 1996; Klein, Taliaferro, Meyers, Eichhorn, Guzzetta, Clark, & Calvin, 1998; Boie, Moore, Brommett, & Nelson, 1999; USA Today, 2000).

After determining that the majority of the families wanted to be at the bedside, the team developed another research proposal that used both qualitative and quantitative approaches to identify the problems and benefits of family presence during invasive procedures and CPR. Additional nurse researchers were added to the team, blending the resources of academic and clinical expertise. The family presence protocol used in this study was adapted from the ENA's guidelines on family presence (ENA, 1995). In this protocol, a nurse or chaplain was designated as the family facilitator who determined whether family members were suitable family presence candidates by assessing individuals for appropriate levels of coping and the absence of combative behaviors, extreme emotional instability, or behaviors consistent with an altered mental state. Agreement to bring a family member to the bedside was sought from conscious patients and the attending physician. Appropriate family members were then offered the family presence option and prepared for the visit with an explanation of the patient's appearance, what they would see and hear in room, and the importance of their supportive role. The family facilitator brought the family members to bedside, stayed with them, and guided them through the experience.

Surveys were developed to identify the problems and benefits of family presence from the perspectives of the patient, family member, and health care provider (i.e., nurses, physicians). During the proposal development phase of the research study, the family presence team also consulted with the chief of emergency medicine, chief of surgery, trauma surgeons, the hospital and medical school attorneys, and individuals in risk management, infection control, and psychiatry to garner advice and incorporate their recommendations into the research study. The study was approved by the hospital and Institutional Review Board and was funded by a grant from the national Emergency Medicine Foundation and Emergency Nurses Foundation.

The study, completed in the ED over a 16-month period, included 43 cases of family presence (24 invasive procedures, 19 CPRs). The overall patient mortality was 56%. A total of 39 family members, 9 patients, 60 nurses, and 36 physicians were surveyed. Complete findings of this study have been published previously (Meyers, Eichhorn, Guzzetta, Clark, Klein, Taliaferro, & Calvinal., 2000; Eichhorn, Meyers, Guzzetta, Clark, Klein, Taliaferro, & Calvin, 2001). For families, family presence was perceived as a right, as a family obligation, and as a natural event that they described as a positive experience. All family members said it was helpful to them to see and hear what was going on and said it helped them to understand the seriousness of the situation and to understand that everything possible had been done to help their loved one. While at the bedside, family members had a job and a meaningful role. They were emotional supporters who provided comfort and prevented aloneness. They touched, kissed, calmed, and prayed with the patient. They were staff helpers who provided information about the patient. Their presence also served as a reminder that the patient was a person and part of a family. For dying patients, family presence gave family members a chance to say goodbye and come to closure on a shared life. All families

said that given a similar situation, they would do it again (Meyers et al, 2000).

The patient experiences with family presence were also positive. Patients related that family members provided them comfort and help and were a reminder of "personhood" to the healthcare providers. The following are a few examples of patients' comments about having a family member at the bedside (Eichhorn et al, 2001, p.30):

- "It makes the stress easier on the patient."
- "You know somebody is there that cares about you."
- "They could help me communicate because it was a little difficult for me to do that . . . in that much pain."
- "I think there is a lot more compassion from the doctors and nurses if a family member is standing there."

Most (85%) of the nurses and physicians surveyed felt comfortable with families at bedside during the emergency. Likewise, most supported family presence during CPR (76%) and invasive procedures (73%) and wanted the family presence program continued at the institution (88%). The majority thought the experience helped meet the family's (78%) and patient's (73%) emotional and spiritual needs. Many nurses and physicians thought family presence made them more mindful of the patient's dignity, emphasized the need for privacy and pain management, and encouraged more professional behavior and conversations at the bedside (Meyers, et al., 2000).

CHANGING CLINICAL PRACTICE BASED ON EVIDENCE

Resolving a clinical problem can be accomplished by research investigation. Often the results of an isolated study, however, provide insufficient evidence to change clinical practice. Thus, when changing clinical practice, nurses will need to arm themselves with the data from published investigations.

After completion of the study, for example, the family presence team revisited the literature and found additional outcome studies on family presence that consistently documented the multiple benefits of this practice. For the families, these benefits include knowing that everything possible was done and removing the family's doubt about what was happening to the patient (Anderson et al, 1994; Doyle et al, 1987; Hanson & Strawser, 1992; Timmermans, 1997; Robinson, Mackenzie-Ross, Campbell-Hewson, Egleston, & Prevost, 1998), reducing their own anxiety and fear (Shapira & Tamir, 1996; Robinson et al, 1998; Powers & Rubenstein, 1999), feeling they had supported and helped the patient (Doyle et al, 1987; Hanson & Strawser, 1992; Sacchetti, Carraccio, Leva, & Harris, 1996; Shapira & Tamir, 1996; Powers & Rubenstein, 1999), coming to closure on a life shared together (Hanson & Strawser, 1992), and facilitating their grieving (Anderson et al, 1994; Doyle et al, 1987; Hanson & Strawser, 1992; Sacchetti et al, 1996; Belanger & Reed, 1997; Timmermans, 1997; Robinson et al, 1998).

In addition, research findings reveal that given a similar event, nearly all family members would do it again (Belanger & Reed, 1997; Doyle et al, 1987; Powers & Rubenstein, 1999). Investigators also have found no disruptions in the operations of the medical team during family presence events (Anderson et al, 1994; Doyle et al, 1987; Hanson & Strawser, 1992; Sacchetti et al, 1996; Belanger & Reed, 1997; Robinson et al, 1998) and no adverse psychologic effects among family members who participated in bedside visitation (Belanger & Reed, 1997; Robinson et al, 1998).

After completion of our study, the family presence team presented the results to the staff. Because of the positive experience with family presence over a 16-month period and the findings that emerged not only from our study but also from others, a family presence policy was developed using the ENA guidelines and later approved by the hospital's policy and procedure committee for hospitalwide use (Parkland Health & Hospital System, 1999).

The practice of family presence has changed in our institution, and it is changing nationwide. For example, family presence has recently been incorporated into the trauma nursing core course (Trauma Nursing Core Course, 2000) and the emergency nursing pediatric course (Emergency Nursing Pediatric Course, 1998). Moreover, the American Heart Association began recommending for the first time in its new *Guidelines 2000 for Cardiopulmonary Resuscitation and Emergency Cardiovascular Care*

that whenever possible, health care providers should offer family members the option to remain with their loved ones during resuscitation efforts (American Heart Association & International Liason Committee on Resuscitation, 2000). The arguments for implementing a family presence program can become even more powerful when the need to comply with such guidelines is included in the dialogue.

LESSONS LEARNED

Many individuals from other hospitals have contacted us about their plans to start a family presence program. In personal communication, colleagues report fewer obstacles to overcome than we encountered. They attribute their success to having research findings available. They have said that instituting a family presence protocol in their hospitals has been a fairly simple process involving educating staff and implementing a policy. Theresa Meyers experienced this simplified process when she became the ED nurse manager in a private hospital a few years after she had the initial family presence case. When she presented a packet of the research findings to the health care provider team, they readily agreed to offer the option of family presence to their patients and patients' families. The team agreed that their core philosophy of care was to provide care that addresses the emotional needs as well as the physical needs of their patients.

When we encountered opposition to our ideas, we learned that a project needs a champion. A champion is an effective leader who creates a new vision, articulates it to others, and then moves to institutionalize that vision (Ulschak & SnowAntle, 1995). Moreover, a team effort is needed to accomplish the task. Both a physician advocate and administrative support are imperative. Allowing colleagues to voice their opinions and discuss potential barriers is essential in the change process. Providing staff with research-based articles and current documentation supporting family presence not only raises awareness but also provides the solid evidence by which to counter emotional, fact-free arguments. Preparing a draft family presence policy using ENA guidelines and adapting it to meet the needs of the institution can lay the foundation for discussing and resolving conflicts and incorporating essential recommendations from the hospital community. Consultation with colleagues in nursing, medicine, surgery, trauma, risk management, psychiatry, social work, pastoral care, law, and infection control will ensure that various legal, ethical, and biopsychosocial concerns have been addressed in the policy. Piloting the policy as a demonstration project allows staff and administration to learn the issues, gain experience with the practice, and embrace the concept. Our research findings and those of others have demonstrated that health care providers who initially oppose family presence often become advocates for the practice after experiencing its many benefits for patients and families (Meyers et al, 2000; Robinson et al, 1998; Sacchetti, Carraccio, Leva, Harris, & Lichenstein, 2000).

We strongly believe that the successful results we achieved were solely possible through our joint effort because of the varied resources and talents each team member contributed to the project. For all the multiple times we were ready to give up, we have been rewarded repeatedly as families continue to share their powerful stories about family presence and the impact the event has had on their lives.

REFERENCES

American Heart Association & International Liaison Committee on Resuscitation. (2000). Guidelines 2000 for cardiopulmonary resuscitation and emergency cardiovascular care. *Circulation, 102*(suppl), 1-19.

Anderson, B., McCall, E., Leversha, A., & Webster, T. (1994). A review of children's dying in a paediatric intensive care unit. *New Zealand Medical Journal, 107*(985), 345-347.

Belanger, M.A. & Reed, S. (1997). A rural community hospital's experience with family-witnessed resuscitation. *Journal of Emergency Nursing, 23*(3), 238-239.

Boie, E.T., Moore, G.P., Brommett, C., & Nelson, D.R. (1999). Do parents want to be present during invasive procedures performed on their children in the emergency department? A survey of 400 parents. *Annals of Emergency Medicine, 34*(1), 70-74.

Doyle, C.J., Post, H., Burney, R.E., Maino, J., Keefe, M., & Rhee, K.J. (1987). Family participation during resuscitation: An option. *Annals of Emergency Medicine, 16*(6), 673-675.

Eichhorn, D.J., Meyers, T.A., Guzzetta, C.E., Clark, A.P., Klein, J.D., Taliaferro, E., & Calvin, A.O. (2001). Family presence during invasive procedures and resuscitation: Hearing the voice of the patient. *American Journal of Nursing, 101*(5), 26-33.

Emergency Nurses Association. (1995). *Presenting the option for family presence* (program educational booklet) (2nd ed.). Park Ridge, IL: Author. Available by calling (800) 2-GETENA.

Emergency nursing pediatric course (2nd ed.). (1998). Park Ridge, IL: The Emergency Nurses Association.

Granger, B.B. & Chulay, M. (1999). *Research strategies for clinicians.* Stamford, CT: Appleton & Lange.

Hanson, C. & Strawser, D. (1992). Family presence during cardiopulmonary resuscitation: Foote hospital emergency department's nine-year perspective. *Journal of Emergency Nursing, 18*(2), 104-106.

Klein, J.D., Taliaferro, E., Meyers, T.A., Eichhorn, D.J., Guzzetta, C.E., Clark, A.P., & Calvin, A.O. (1998). *Family presence during invasive procedures/resuscitation: Final report submitted to the Emergency Medicine Foundation and the Emergency Nursing Foundation* (unpublished). Irving, TX.

Meyers, T.A., Eichhorn, D.J., & Guzzetta, C.E. (1998). Do families want to be present during CPR? A retrospective survey. *Journal of Emergency Nursing, 24,* 400-405.

Meyers, T.A., Eichhorn, D.J., Guzzetta, C.E., Clark, A.P., Klein, J.D., Taliaferro, E., & Calvin A. (2000). Family presence during invasive procedures and resuscitation. *American Journal of Nursing, 100*(2), 32-42.

Parkland Health & Hospital System. (1999). *Protocol for family presence during invasive procedure and resuscitation.* Available online at www.PMH.org.

Powers, K.S. & Rubenstein, J.S. (1999). Family presence during invasive procedures in the pediatric intensive care unit. *Archives of Pediatrics & Adolescent Medicine, 153,* 955-958.

Redley, B. & Hood, K. (1996). Staff attitudes towards family presence during resuscitation. *Accident and Emergency Nursing, 4*(3),145-151.

Robinson, S.M., Mackenzie-Ross, S., Campbell-Hewson, G.L., Egleston, C.V., & Prevost, A.T. (1998). Psychological effect of witnessed resuscitation on bereaved relatives. *Lancet, 352,* 614-617.

Sacchetti, A., Carraccio, C., Leva, E., Harris, R.H., and Lichenstein, R. (2000). Acceptance of family member presence during pediatric resuscitation in the emergency department: Effects of personal experience. *Pediatric Emergency Care, 16* (2), 85-87.

Sacchetti, A., Lichenstein, R., Carraccio, C.A., & Harris, R.H. (l996). Family member presence during pediatric emergency department procedures. *Pediatric Emergency Care, 12*(4), 268-271.

Shapira, M. & Tamir, A. (1996). Presence of family member during upper endoscopy. *Journal of Clinical Gastroenterology, 22,* 272-274.

Timmermans, S. (1997). High touch in high tech: The presence of relatives and friends during resuscitation efforts. *Scholarly Inquiry for Nursing Practice, 11*(2), 153-168.

Trauma nursing core course (5th ed.). (2000). Park Ridge, IL: Emergency Nurses Association.

Ulschak, F.L., & SnowAntle, S.M. (1995). *Team architecture: The manager's guide to designing effective work teams.* Ann Arbor, MI: Health Administration Press.

USA Today. (2000, March 7). *Would you want to be in the ED while doctors worked on a family member?* Available online at www.USATODAY.com.

Politics of the Nursing Workforce

CHRISTINE TASSONE KOVNER

"The measure of success is not whether you have a tough problem to deal with, but whether it's the same problem you had last year."

JOHN FOSTER DULLES

THE NURSING WORKFORCE

There were almost 2.7 million registered nurses (RNs) in the United States in 2000. What we know about the RN workforce comes primarily from the National Sample Survey of Registered Nurses (Health Resources and Services Administration [HRSA], 2001). A typical RN is Caucasian, more than 45 years old, had her basic RN education at the associate degree level, and worked full time. Almost 60% of RNs work in hospitals. The actual average annual salary for full-time RNs was $46,782 in 2000. When adjusted for inflation, this average salary was essentially the same as it had been in 1996.

FUTURE OF THE NURSING WORKFORCE

The 2.2 million RNs who are employed in nursing are a vital force in the U.S. health care system. Ensuring that there is an adequate supply of RNs is of great concern to government, employers, consumers, and the nurses themselves. Estimating the future supply and demand for RNs, however, is at best an educated guess.

APPROACHES TO ESTIMATING THE FUTURE SUPPLY AND DEMAND FOR REGISTERED NURSES

Government agencies and private groups collect some data and use existing data to estimate the fu-

ture supply and demand for RNs. These groups put together supply data such as the number of licensed RNs and their demographic characteristics, applications, enrollments, and graduations from nursing programs and track trends in NCLEX-RN examination passage rates. To estimate future demand, they also guess at the future configuration of the health care system and include factors about the future U.S. or local population data, such as age and illness incidence to estimate the demand.

Groups count either people (bodies) or positions (jobs), which explains in part why data from different sources do not agree. The Bureau of Labor Statistics (BLS) within the Department of Labors (DOL) is the federal agency that keeps track of the U.S. labor market and projects what is likely to happen in the future. BLS primarily tracks positions and includes broad economic trends when it estimates the future demand for RNs.

The Health Resources and Services Administration (HRSA) also monitors the health labor force and intervenes in various supply and demand issues. Within HRSA the Division of Nursing (DON) conducts a sample survey of all U.S. RNs every 4 years. These data describe people at a particular time. HRSA has also developed models to estimate future demand. For example, HRSA developed the integrated demand model to estimate further demand for nurse practitioners (NPs) under a variety of scenarios of managed care penetration. This is a computer software program that can be used to estimate the future demand for NPs in a geographic area.

Academic researchers either individually or as part of a center or institute also estimate supply and demand. Their studies or estimates are sometimes undertaken at the request of a funding agency such as a foundation or as an initiative of the researcher who seeks money from a non-university source. An example of an academic center is the Center for the Health Profession at the University of California, San Francisco. Researchers at this center conduct a variety of studies on the health workforce, including RNs. Several years ago with funding from the Pew Charitable Trusts, this group forecast that there would be a dramatic decrease in the demand for RNs by the early twenty-first century and that the U.S. would have an excess of almost 300,000 RNs. This is an example of how difficult it is to predict demand. This group was wrong by hundreds of thousands of RNs.

On some occasions interest groups such as professional associations or unions hire consultants to conduct studies. For example, a union may hire a polling or survey company to find out RNs' perceptions of the need for RNs in the hospitals in which they work. For those who use these data, it is important to recognize the source of the data, the source of the funds for the project, and the definitions used. Some organizations may use biased definitions or phrase questions in the survey to ensure that the data will support their position.

DATA ON THE REGISTERED NURSE WORKFORCE

Workforce issues include the quality and quantity of data available, research priorities, the role of government in intervening in the supply and demand for RNs, and the broad area of staffing issues.

One of the major problems confronting people who study the health workforce and those who depend on workforce data is the lack of good, uniform data. Among the problems are a lack of data in general, lack of uniformly defined and collected data, and long delays in access to data.

LACK OF DATA

Accurate numbers as simple as how many licensed RNs there are in the United States are unavailable. To practice as an RN, the nurse must register in the particular state in which he or she wants to practice (except for RNs working for a federal facility, who must hold a license from only one state). Many RNs are registered in more than one state for a number of reasons: Perhaps they have moved, live near the border of another state and want to maintain licenses in both states, or simply remember from graduation the dictum, "Once you have a license in a state, don't give it up." Thus, each state maintains a list of every RN licensed in the state. However, if one adds up the number of RNs in all of the states and territories, the number vastly exceeds the number of RNs that likely exist. RNs can be licensed in as many states as they want. No federal agency or private organization combines these state lists, looks for duplicates, and develops a list of RNs from which one could obtain a count.

LACK OF UNIFORMITY IN DATA COLLECTION

In some cases data exist but have not been uniformly collected. Despite the effort of the Interagency Task for on Nursing Definitions, there is still no uniform approach to definitions of terms about the nursing work force, even within the various departments of the federal government. Each agency or group that collects data about the nursing workforces uses its own definitions. Of particular concern is the definition of a "full-time equivalent" (FTE) and how it is calculated. There is no standard answer to how many hours an RN must work to be considered part-time. Most labor economists count anyone who works fewer than 35 hours per week as part-time; others use 30 hours. Of course, someone who works 10 or 20 hours is almost always considered part-time. To obtain an estimate of FTEs, some sources add up the number of hours each part-timer works and equates every 35, 37.5, or 40 work hours to one FTE. Other sources, such as the American Hospital Association (AHA), use a formula that calculates as one FTE every two part-time workers. Using the AHA approach, a hospital that had four RNs each working 10 hours per week would have two FTEs, whereas another hospital that had two rns each working 20 hours would have one FTE. Yet each hospital would have the same number of paid hours.

LACK OF TIMELY DATA

Even if data measurement were consistent, the problem of timeliness would remain. For example, the primary source of current data about RNs is the National Sample Survey (NSS) completed by HRSA's DON. Because the DON conducts a sample survey of all RNs in the United States only once every 4 years, these data are quickly outdated. Data are not usually available until at least 1 year after the survey. The most recent survey was conducted in March 2000. Preliminary findings were available in February 2001. Thus, by the time that the first few pieces of data (e.g., age, workplace) were available, they were already a year old. Data that can be used for state analyses are not generally available for 18 months to 2 years after the survey.

Another important source of data that is used to estimate the future supply of RNs is information about applications and enrollments in schools of nursing. At one time the National League for Nursing (NLN) was the primary source for such data, although the data were often 1 to 2 years old by the time they became available. Now there are two primary sources of data about enrollments, the NLN for all nursing programs and the American Association of Colleges of Nursing (AACN) for baccalaureate and higher-degree programs. Although the AACN data are available within 1 year of data collection, the NLN data are not available for somewhat longer. In addition, the AACN data do not include all baccalaureate and master's degree programs, so the absolute number of enrolled students and trends over time are difficult to estimate.

There are two other major sources of employment data: the Department of Labor's BLS, which actually collects data on jobs or positions, and the Bureau of the Census, which collects data about people. BLS data are available within 6 months of collection. Two types of data about people are available from the Bureau of the Census. They are data from the decennial census, which are available as soon as 1 year following collection but quickly go out of date, and data from the Current Population Survey (CPS), a monthly sample survey of people living in the United States. Although the CPS data are quickly available, because the data come from a

sample, the number of participants is too small to use for small geographic areas. Buerhaus, Staiger, and Auerbach (2000) used CPS data to describe the U.S. RN population. In some cases data from 1 year or more can be combined to find out about RNs from an area as small as a city. For example, Berliner, Kovner, and Reimers (in press) use 3 years of CPS data to describe the RN workforce in Los Angeles.

RESEARCH ON THE REGISTERED NURSE WORKFORCE

RN workforce research focuses on the supply and demand for RNs and factors that affect the balance between supply and demand. Particularly when there is a shortage of RNs, research in this area becomes more important to policymakers. Examples of research include descriptive studies about RNs who work in hospitals such as studies by Aiken and colleagues (Aiken, 1997; Aiken, Clarke, & Sloane, 2000; Aiken, Sochalski, & Anderson, 1996) and by Kovner, Jones, and Gergen (2000) and studies about the impact of managed care on RNs such as those by Buerhaus, Staiger, and Auerbach (2000), Buerhaus and Douglas (1999), and Mason, Alexander, Huffaker, Reilly, Sigmund, & Cohen (1999). It also includes more-theoretic work such as Brewer's (2000) work on RN workforce participation (why RNs do or do not work).

There is neither a federal agency nor a foundation whose focus is RN workforce research. The DON has responsibility for conducting the NSS, but the DON has no funds for research. A small percentage of its budget is allocated to the Bureau of Health Professions' research and evaluation branch, which funds studies almost exclusively by contract (in some cases competitive, but in many cases noncompetitive), and which rarely studies RNs. Even though the National Institute for Nursing Research (NINR) funds nursing studies, it funds studies about patients or people who could benefit from nursing care, not about nurses themselves (i.e., studies about nurses' demographic characteristics). Some funds from other agencies are occasionally available. For example, Brewer's (2000) study was funded by the Agency for Healthcare Research and Quality. The Berliner et al (in press) study of Los Angeles nurses was funded by the Department of Labor through Los Angeles County. The National Institute for Occupational Health and Safety funds could fund a study of RN occupational injuries. Thus, compared with other areas of nursing, there is little money for workforce studies.

GOVERNMENT INTERVENTION IN THE SUPPLY AND DEMAND FOR REGISTERED NURSES

Both the federal government and state governments have a long history of intervening in the supply and demand for RNs.

INTERVENTION IN SUPPLY

In terms of supply, government intervention has primarily been directed at increasing the overall supply of RNs, particular types of RNs such as NPs, or in affecting the racial and ethnic composition of the RN labor force. The general approaches are scholarships to individuals or subsidies to programs either for program development or for scholarships for these programs to distribute to students. The DON's primary focus is to influence the supply of RNs through a variety of funding mechanisms. In 2000 the DON spent about $56 million on programs to increase the preparation of advanced practice nurses and to increase the racial and ethnic mix of RN students who were in programs to prepare them to be eligible to take the RN licensure examination.

Activities of the DON are the best known. The DON has a variety of programs to give nursing programs some program development funds for advanced nurse education to increase the supply of nurses such as nurse anesthetists. In addition the DON provides funds to nursing programs to increase the number of graduates from underrepresented racial or ethnic groups. Less well known is the substantial funding that the Centers for Medicare and Medicaid Services (CMS, formerly the Health Care Financing Administration [HCFA]), provides to hospital-based nursing programs under the Medicare program funding (Aiken & Gwyther, 1995).

Medicare payments to hospitals include funding for nurse education at hospitals. Most of this funding goes to hospitals that operate diploma nursing programs.

The federal government can also intervene in the supply of RNs by changing immigration regulations. Increasing the number of RNs who can immigrate to the United States will increase the supply of RNs. For example, if the immigration laws were changed so that nurses from other countries could enter the United States more easily, it is likely that more nurses who were educated in other countries would come to the United States to work.

At the state level, states have or have had programs similar to those of the DON. For example, New York has had scholarship programs through its hospital reimbursement system. The most important impact on the supply for RNs is each state's licensing regulations. These regulations restrict who can perform nursing care in a state. Licensing requirements such as the type of educational program that is required or definitions of who can perform certain activities such intravenous drug administration serve to limit the available supply of RNs.

INTERVENTION IN DEMAND

The federal government and state governments have also been involved in efforts that change the demand for RNs. At the federal level HCFA implemented regulations in 1987 that mandated minimum staffing regulations in nursing homes that receive Medicare or Medicaid funding. In some cases this resulted in an increased demand as nursing homes hired additional RNs to meet the staffing requirements.

State government can also increase the demand for RNs by requiring facilities in the state to employ a certain number of RNs. New York and New Jersey require hospitals to have a particular level of RN-to-patient ratios in certain intensive-care units. California recently passed legislation that sets RN-to-patient ratios in all hospitals in the state.

State board of nursing regulations about nursing practice also can decrease demand. For example, New York permits psychiatric technicians to administer medications in state mental health facilities. Without such a ruling, the demand for RNs and licensed practical nurses would be higher in New York.

State governments have also been involved in more-general efforts to decrease the demand for RNs, through time-limited special programs. For example, in 1992 New Jersey implemented the Nursing Incentives Reimbursement Program (Kovner, Hendrickson, Knickman, & Finkler, 1993; Finkler, Kovner, Knickman, & Hendrickson, 1994). This program provided funds to hospitals in the state to implement a variety of approaches thought to decrease demand, such implementing computer use in nursing units, which could save nurses time. For example, if a physician directly entered an order into a computer, the nurse would not have to spend time deciphering the handwriting and copying the order onto other forms.

The appropriate role for government to assume in influencing the supply and demand for RNs is controversial. On the one hand, government has a responsibility for the health and safety of its population and therefore must intervene when there are shortages of health workers such as nurses. On the other hand, market economists argue that labor markets should be free to adjust to supply and demand without government intervention.

Often government intervention can get the market to respond more quickly. The usual approach to a shortage of workers in any industry is for employers to substitute other workers or increase wages to draw workers into the workforce. The health care labor market is not a free market, because government already affects the supply by state regulation of who can and cannot practice nursing. In addition, government can intervene to increase supply quickly by approaches such as scholarships to encourage more students to attend nursing school.

REGISTERED NURSE STAFFING ISSUES

The current controversial workforce issue is RN staffing. In a free market, firms decide the conditions of employment including wages, overtime requirements, and the number and type of workers that they need to produce the good or service that they produce. In that situation, a restaurant can decide the

number of cooks and wait people that they require to produce and deliver the food. Cooks and wait people are free to accept the conditions of employment or not work at the firm. Similarly, in a free market, hospitals would decide the types of people to employ to produce health care services. However, in almost all cases, issues around employment are subject to collective bargaining decisions. Thus, in most industries workers can organize and sign a contract that sets working conditions in addition to wages.

Some RNs participate in collective bargaining units that negotiate with employers such as hospitals to establish working conditions and wages. These collective bargaining units are sometimes part of professional associations, such as state nurse associations, and in other cases part of traditional trade unions, such as the Service Employees International Union. Over the last 10 years it has been increasingly common for staffing ratios to be negotiated as part of collective bargaining. These agreements have ranged from forming employer-employee committees that will establish ratios to actually having ratios as part of the agreement. Registered nurses who do not work in nursing homes (which have federally set RN levels) can participate in discussions about staffing levels in their workplaces through other means. For example, they could bring up staffing levels in committee discussions such as quality of care committee meetings. Many organizations have staff councils or other committees in which this issue could be discussed.

NURSE-TO-PATIENT-DAY STAFFING RATIOS

Because the government has decided that health is an important public good, government also has established staffing ratios. As previously discussed, the federal government mandates staffing levels in nursing homes for homes that receive federal funding. Some argue that these ratios are inadequate and that the federal government should establish higher ratios (Harrington, Kovner, Mezey, Kayser-Jones, Berger, Muhler, Reilly, Burice, & Zimmerman, 2000). However, the federal government has not mandated RN staffing levels in hospitals.

Some state governments have set RN-to-patient-day staffing ratios. In 1999 California adopted a law requiring its State Department of Health Services to establish minimum, specific, and numeric licensed nurse-to-patient ratios by hospital unit in hospitals (see the California Nurses Association's press release for more information, as well as the full text of the bill, at www.calnurse.org). In addition to setting the ratios, California's health department will implement regulations to ensure compliance with the ratios. The legislation has been very controversial. Some argue that the minimum will become standard; others say staffing ratios should be set according to patient needs, not government prescription.

Despite research efforts on the relationship between staffing and patient outcomes in hospitals, there is no research that supports a specific level of nurse staffing, either defined as number of RNs or RNs as a percentage of nursing staff, as safe, good, or ideal in hospitals. Average RN staffing levels for various groups of hospitals are available (Kovner & Gergen, 1998; Health Forum, 1999; Kovner, Jones, & Gergen, 2000). In some cases, using these average numbers, hospital managers make decisions about staffing levels based on research, their experience, consultants' reports, and literature. These decisions take into consideration both a manager's experience at a particular facility and cost constraints.

Government regulation of RN staffing levels in hospitals is very controversial. It is a divisive issue within nursing that has tended to split staff nurses from nurse managers. The hospital leadership usually opposes such regulation. Many staff nurses, on the other hand, see such regulation as helping their working conditions as well as helping their patients. Lobbyists will continue to pressure state legislatures to institute minimum staffing levels. Evaluation of states' actions or the federal government's response or proactive stance about staffing levels is a major health policy issue.

There is disagreement about which aspects of hospital practice should be regulated by the government to protect the public's health and which aspects are best left to voluntary accreditation or to each hospital to manage on its own. On the pro side, regulation protects the public's health, but on the con side, a market free of regulation will respond to consumer demands and permit institutional flexibility.

Staffing ratios in nursing homes seem less controversial. To receive Medicare or Medicaid funding, nursing homes must meet the HCFA/CMS requirement that there be an RN director of nursing and an RN on site 8 hours per day and that a licensed nurse be on duty evenings and nights. In addition, some state governments have established staffing ratios in intensive care units (Official Compilation of Codes, Rules, and Regulation of the State of New York, 2000).

MANDATORY OVERTIME AND USE OF AGENCY PERSONNEL

Other staffing issues include mandatory overtime and use of agency personnel. These issues are also subject to collective bargaining agreements. Most managers in health organizations think that mandatory overtime and use of agency personnel are managerial decisions that are sometimes necessary to maintain quality of patient care. Many RNs, on the other hand, think that both of these "solutions" can actually decrease the quality of care. Unfortunately, research is not available to support either position. There is some movement to subject mandatory overtime to government regulation. California has implemented a law regulating mandatory overtime, and other states are following suit.

CONCLUSION

Government policies affect numerous nursing workforce issues. These include the supply and demand for RNs, RN staffing ratios, and overtime work. If, how, and when the government should intervene remains controversial. These government decisions should be made with the full input of the RNs who are affected by them. Getting involved in health workforce policy offers nurses an opportunity to become involved in an issue that directly affects the way nurse practice nursing.

REFERENCES

Aiken, L.H. (1997). Studying outcomes of organizational change in health services. *Medical Care, 35*(11), ns6-ns18.

Aiken, L. H., Clarke, S. P., & Sloane, D. M. (2000). Hospital restructuring: Does it adversely affect care and outcomes? *Journal of Nursing Administration, 30*(10), 457-465.

Aiken, L., & Gwyther, M. (1995). Medicare funding of nurse education. *Journal of the American Medical Association, 273*(19), 1528-1532.

Aiken, L., Sochalski, J., & Anderson, G. (1996). Downsizing the hospital nursing workforce. *Health Affairs, 15*(4), 88-92.

Berliner, H., Kovner, C., & Reimers, C. (In press). The health care workforce in Los Angeles and New York City: A comparison and analysis. *International Journal of Health Services.*

Brewer, C. (2000). Work attitudes and future intentions of Western New York nurses. Unpublished manuscript.

Buerhaus, P. & Douglas O. (1999). Trouble in the nurse labor market? Recent trends and future outlook. *Health Affairs, 18*(1), 214-222.

Buerhaus, P., Staiger, D., & Auerbach, D. (2000). Implications of an aging registered nurse workforce. *Journal of the American Medical Association, 283*(22), 2948-2954.

Finkler, S., Kovner, C., Knickman, J., & Hendrickson, G. (1994). Innovation in nursing: A benefit/cost analysis. *Nursing Economics, 12*(1), 25-29.

Harrington, C., Kovner, C., Mezey, M., Kayser-Jones, J., Berger, S., Muhler, M., Reilly, K., Burice, R., & Zimmerman, D. (2000). Experts recommend minimum nurse staffing standards for nursing facilities in the United States. *Gerontologist 40*(1), 5-16.

Health Forum. (1999). *Hospital statistics.* Chicago: Health Forum and American Hospital Association Company.

Health Resources and Services Administration. (2001). *The registered nurse population: National sample survey of registered nurses—March 2000: Preliminary findings, February 2001.* Rockville, MD.

Kovner, C. & Gergen, P. (1998). Nurse staffing levels and adverse events following surgery in U.S. hospitals. *Image: Journal of Nursing Scholarship, 30*(4), 315-321.

Kovner, C., Hendrickson, G., Knickman, J., & Finkler, S. (1993). Changing the delivery of nursing care: Implementation issues and qualitative findings. *Journal of Nursing Administration, 23*(11), 24-34.

Kovner, C., Jones, C., & Gergen, P. (2000). Nurse staffing in acute care hospitals, 1990-1996. *Policy, Politics, and Nursing Practice, 1*(3), 194-204.

Mason, D., Alexander, J., Huffaker, J., Reilly, P., Sigmund, E., & Cohen, S. (1999). Nurse practitioners' experiences with managed organizations in New York and Connecticut. *Nursing Outlook, 47*(5), 201-208.

Official compilation of codes, rules, and regulations of the state of New York. Title 10 (Health), Section 405.22, 2000.

18

Future of Advanced Practice Nursing

CHARLENE M. HANSON

"In the middle of difficulty lies opportunity."

ALBERT EINSTEIN

The hypothesis of Malcolm Gladwell's best-selling book, *The Tipping Point* (2000), should be well received by advanced practice nurses (APNs). His notion that a few people can cause big change to happen, much the same way as an epidemic spreads, can be compared to the way that advanced nursing practice affected the health care system and patient care in the last half of the twentieth century. Gladwell (2000) contends that only a few people, by their example, can bring about change in large complex systems, such as the health care industry. APNs have made great strides over the years in accomplishing this task in order to bring nurse-based health care to patients. The future will depend on the ability of APNs to continue the progress in a highly competitive and unstable environment. The focus of this chapter is to examine the past and present challenges that confront APNs from a health policy, regulatory, and political perspective and to identify issues that will take precedence in the next decade.

The future of advanced practice nursing depends upon four major factors. First and foremost, APNs must identify and maintain the niche within health care that we have created as bona fide health care providers. It will be essential for APNs to embrace and implement the nurturing, care-giving, nurse-based provider role that we have crafted over time. Second, it will be critically important for APNs to maintain recognition as health care providers through adequate and equitable reimbursement

mechanisms in a variety of venues. Third, and equally important, there must be a way for APN nurse educators to ensure the quality and competence of APN graduates who are practicing in the difficult milieu that is heath care in the United States today. Last and vitally importantly, APNs will need to continue to work toward organizing ourselves toward a cohesive whole that allows us to speak as a single voice. Accomplishment of these important components and many others will require a serious commitment on the part of all APNs in the areas of clinical and interpersonal competence, leadership, mentoring, and collaborative relationships.

ADVANCED PRACTICE NURSING: LEARNING FROM PAST EXPERIENCE

Several factors have influenced the success of advanced practice nurses since the early 1960s when Loretta Ford and Henry Silver first coined the term *nurse practitioner* based on the Colorado experience preparing pediatric nurse practitioners (NPs) to provide well-child care. Even before then, nurse midwives had offered birth care to women in rural Kentucky. From the beginning, the nursing component of the advanced practice role has remained dominant and has provided APNs with the strong foundation needed to withstand adversity. It is important for APNs to consider these early roots and decisions that paved the way for current APN practice in order to know how to move forward.

The world wars of the twentieth century played a major role in the introduction of nurses as direct health care providers. A shortage of physicians in the 1950s, much the same as the nursing shortage we are now experiencing, was pivotal to the creation of nurse providers who could diagnose and treat patient care problems, deliver babies, offer postnatal care, and administer anesthesia. The concepts of primary care and preventive care were important adjuncts as well. Physicians in the United States have consistently chosen specialty and subspecialty practice over primary care practice upon graduation, and APNs have recognized and accepted the need for community-based primary health care. The early nurse practitioners made their niche by offering primary care services to rural and underserved populations. Data from this era (1970-1990) continue to present strong support for NP quality of care (Office of Technology Assessment, 1986). The success of the early NPs, certified nurse midwives (CNMs), and certified registered nurse anesthetists (CRNAs) provided a strong foundation for the APNs who followed.

It is instructive to remember some of the barriers that APNs struggled to overcome. Barriers such as restrictions on scope of practice, limits to prescriptive authority, restrictions on reimbursement, and difficulties in obtaining admitting privileges have all limited the ability of APNs to practice fully to the limit of our abilities. During the decades of the 1960s through 1980s, APNs fully or partially overcame many of these impediments to practice and set in place policy and regulatory statutes at both federal and state levels that promulgated changes in nurse practice acts, state rules and regulations, and federal mandates to support independent and collaborative advanced nursing practice and APN prescriptive authority. State by state, policymakers changed nurse practice acts and rules and regulations to accommodate APN scope of practice. At the same time, federal and state laws regarding prescriptive privilege were being sought and won. At the federal level, APN leaders and policymakers worked tirelessly with the Health Care Financing Administration (HCFA, now the Centers for Medicare and Medicaid Services [CMS]) and congressional committees to include APNs in reimbursement schemas that would ensure that APNs were directly reimbursed for their services through Medicare and Medicaid and federal employee health plans. At the same time, APNs at the state level were pressing insurance commissioners for approval for state-controlled Medicaid and private insurance reimbursement. As Medicare and Medicaid policies changed, allowing reimbursement for APNs, private insurers slowly followed suit. Since 1989, federal laws had required state Medicaid regulations to reimburse only certified family and pediatric NPs. However, in 1997 Congress passed legislation, the Balanced Budget Amendment of 1997, to provide Medicare coverage of NP and clinical nurse specialist (CNS) services in all geographic settings (Malone & Keepnews, 1998).

It is important to consider the response that APNs made in 2000 to a threat to our autonomy from the American Medical Association (AMA). The AMA Citizens Petition to HCFA requested physician supervision of APNs and restrictions to APN reimbursement. The APNs' political response was to offer APN practice sites for HCFA's review rather than reacting negatively to the AMA language is a fine example of the strides that APNs have made in how we respond to threats to our practice (see the Unit V Case Study). The ongoing work toward full reimbursement is very difficult, but it is critical to the success of APNs as direct providers of care for patients.

In the mid-1980s NPs and nurse midwives lost their liability insurance coverage and mounted a national campaign to have this important coverage reinstated. It was clear that liability insurance companies had little understanding about APN education and practice. This regulatory emergency brought APNs together in a common fight for survival that did much to solidify the APN movement. Advanced practice nurses joined together in solidarity to overcome this barrier to practice. The outcome of this emergency was an improved liability insurance market and coverage and, more importantly, the inclusion of APNs on high-ranking insurance boards and risk management committees.

During this time, APNs in a myriad of settings successfully navigated the policy world and built a strong unified base from which to enhance APN education and practice. Although considerable strides have been made to improve the ability of APNs to function as full health care partners, many barriers continue to exist, and new ones continue to arise. APNs are not yet established by CMS as primary care providers (PCPs) of record. (*PCP of record* refers to a term used by Medicare and Medicaid to establish the PCP designed for each patient). The mix of the health care workforce is continually changing. For example, the need for APNs is affected by the numbers and types of medical specialists. Changes in reimbursement for health care providers have taken a toll on all providers.

During the early evolution of the NP movement, APNs, and NPs in particular, have had difficulty working together and organizing into a cohesive whole. Separate national NP organizations continue to exist predicated on specific specialty, mission, and purpose. This diversity, at times, has placed the policy agenda for APNs at risk. The different goals have inhibited good decision making and lessened the effectiveness of APNs' political power. Recently, positive strides have been made in working together that have strengthened the position of APNs nationally.

ADVANCED PRACTICE NURSES: THE PRESENT

APNs are well positioned to work through the many challenges that are present in the health care system today. Nurses in the last century crafted and defined advanced nursing practice into an institution of care (preventive, episodic, and long-term) that well serves patients in a wide variety of settings. The broad base of nursing education and clinical experience positions APNs in a positive role; however, several challenges currently face APNs. It is important for APNs to consider the complex elements that make up the advanced practice environment in which we practice. Factors such as the organizational structure and culture, regulatory and credentialing requirements, business aspects, reimbursement and payment mechanisms, outcome evaluation and performance improvement, marketing, and contracting are all important considerations for APNs. Figure 18-1 illustrates how environmental factors encompass APN practice.

CHALLENGES: THE DATA DILEMMA

One of the major problems that has plagued APNs since the early days and is a serious problem in the current marketplace has been the consistent lack of useful, high-quality data about APNs and our contributions to health care. Demographic and outcomes data are sorely lacking on APN numbers, mix, geographic location, scope of practice, practice population, appropriate decision making, and patient satisfaction. APNs cannot be successful in policy-making and legislative venues without concrete data that withstand serious scrutiny. Data collection is a responsibility of all APNs, whether they provide care locally or are in high-power policy positions.

The lack of data is a serious current challenge that will affect any future considerations about APNs. However, the collection, analysis, and publication of authentic data continue to be difficult for APNs to achieve. Len Nichols (2001), a policy analyst from the Urban Institute, and others have been adamant in reminding APNs that we must define and measure productivity, process, and outcomes in a very serious way to be competitive in the marketplace. Speaking at the 2001 National Organization of Nurse Practitioner Faculties Annual Meeting in San Antonio, Nichols recommended that APNs do three things:

1. Fight the "old guard" with data proof.
2. Focus on evidence of the positive outcomes of APN-provided care.
3. Reach out to public policy boards, especially Medicare boards, with data that show APN competence and patient satisfaction (Nichols, 2001).

Data proof will be required to carve out and sustain a major role in health care policy, to maintain and pursue new reimbursement mechanisms, and to be responsive to consumers. APNs must participate in policy-making with well-respected data about how we fit into the provider workforce. We must define productivity, measure it in every setting, and show why we should be considered in health care policy decisions that affect our education and practice. Every APN must accept the challenge to respond to requests for demographic information about our education and practice and to

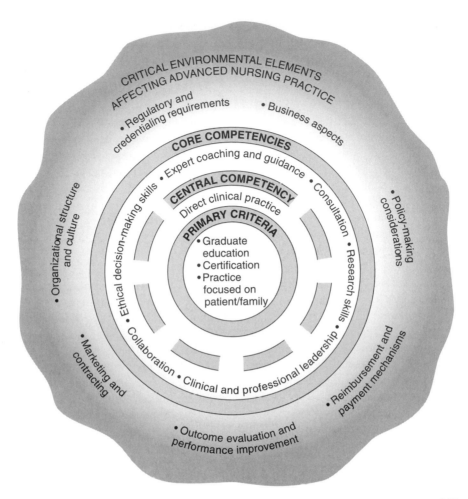

Figure 18-1   Critical elements in APN environments. (From Hamric, A.B., Spross, J.A., & Hanson, C.M. [2001]. *Advanced nursing practice: An integrative approach* [2nd ed.]. Philadelphia: W.B. Saunders.)

implement innovative studies about the professional nursing role and practice.

INDEPENDENCE AND COLLEGIALITY

One of the most-difficult responsibilities facing APNs today and in the future is maintaining the balance between autonomy and collaboration. For many years, APNs have worked conscientiously to achieve the autonomy and independent licensure needed to care for our patients. Unprecedented strides have been made in guaranteeing a place for APNs as bona fide health care providers who are respected and paid for services rendered. Several difficult hurdles have been overcome based on supervision and delegated practice. However, nursing is

virtually the only profession that has "collaboration" as a legal mandate, and APNs have fought hard to move to independent licensure (Buppert, 1999).

First and foremost, APNs view independent practice as the ability to practice and be governed by nursing license alone. This fact is one of the major differentiations between APNs and our physician assistant colleagues, for example, who work "under the supervision" of the MD license. From a regulatory standpoint, *independent* is the appropriate language. At the same time, it is clear that in health care, no provider, including physicians, can function without collaboration with others. This puts APNs in a difficult position, politically. How do APNs protect independent licensure and at the same time participate as collaborators? The semantics of independence—autonomy versus supervision versus collaboration—is extremely volatile. This dilemma is embedded in how APNs are able to interface with physician colleagues and others and how APNs view themselves as players in a health care system. Through careful political strategies, coalition building, and careful placement of APN leaders on key boards and policy-making bodies, regulatory language has changed from *supervisory* to *collaborative*. Although this is an important step, collaboration as a legal requirement will restrict practice now and in the future. For APNs to view collegiality as a step beyond independence is a challenge and will require serious deliberation.

For this reason, the steps for APNs from autonomy to independence and on to collegiality have been difficult. Currently, the approach in health care is clearly for all providers to be collaborative and to work as a team to integrate care. All providers rely on their peers and colleagues for support and consultation. This is a fine line, and it is important for APNs to see this reality. However, from a practice standpoint, few health care providers, physicians included, see themselves as practicing in an independent milieu. From a political standpoint, APNs may be viewed as elitist in policy circles if we demand independent language at all cost.

Covey (1989) helps us to see this view when he places interdependence on a higher hierarchic plane than independence. Independence must be achieved first and is based on competence. Once competence has been achieved, then interdependence and collegiality with peer groups is the next level to achieve. This will be one of the most significant struggles in the next few years. The true test will be how well APNs can walk the line for legally unrestricted practice in statute while collaborating in clinical practice.

The ability to practice collaboratively is critical to the survival of all health care providers. Some perceive it as a moral and ethical imperative: Good patient care requires it (Gianakos, 1997). The medical and nursing literature is replete with success stories of better outcomes with team approaches to care (Lassen, Fosbinder, Minton, & Robins, 1997; Well, Johnson, & Salyer, 1997; Hamric, Spross, & Hanson,

2000). The success of APNs over the next decade will require careful attention to how we fit into a multifaceted and volatile system of health care as providers. It will be incumbent on national APN organizations to come together to position the best APN leaders on interdisciplinary boards at CMS (formerly HCFA) and on other prestigious policy-making committees and groups where guidelines and policy are promulgated. The key is to portray the unique niche that APNs provide and how well we are able to achieve quality care outcomes. Clinical competence is inherent in this process. In order to be considered members of an interdisciplinary patient care provider team, APNs need exemplary clinical and interpersonal skills. Placing APNs as full partners on this team as PCPs will require an APN workforce that is highly educated, independently regulated, and able to function collaboratively in clinical practice and in the policy arena.

REIMBURSEMENT ISSUES FOR ADVANCED PRACTICE NURSES

Significant strides have been made in the ability of APNs to be appropriately reimbursed for care. Several major categories of public and private payment mechanisms affect APNs, including Medicare, Medicaid, private indemnity insurance companies, a myriad of managed care organizations, and public and private contracts. The complexity of understanding and working within Medicare and Medicaid and other reimbursement schemes is a major requirement for APN education and practice. CMS is currently seeking input from providers to enhance positive change strategies. APNs need to be an active part of this process. For example, a key to the solution for reimbursement issues is the need for APNs to be able to submit claims in our own right. In order to do this it will be necessary for us to be listed on managed care panels as the PCP of record. Accomplishing this task within the present environment will be difficult. Complying with regulations that vary from state to state, from specialty to specialty, and from setting to setting is a challenge. Billing and coding language is often complex and confusing. As health care providers assume more financial risk, we need detailed knowledge and practical skills to be successfully reimbursed. The presence of APN leaders on key policy-making boards and committees will be integral to fair and equitable reimbursement. APN leaders will need input from those practicing in the field to make important decisions. The right for patients to choose their PCP and for the provider to be reimbursed is a major issue facing APNs.

PCP status as the provider of record will take a significant component of APN time and commitment in the near future. In terms of Medicare, the language of billing "incident to physician care" is also under scrutiny by CMS. "Incident to" service billing is defined by CMS as "service furnished as an integral, although incidental, part of the physicians' personal professional services in the course of diagnosis and treatment of an injury or illness." Nonphysicians such as APNs can qualify for reimbursement under Medicare as long as the physician supervises such care and is directly on site (Buppert, 1999). This Medicare language continues to cause confusion for Medicare billing by physicians who employ APNs and will be another issue of prominence for APN policy considerations. The key to reimbursement of the future will be acceptance by patients.

ANTITRUST ISSUES THAT HINDER PRACTICE

From the early days of APN practice, it has been necessary for nurses to carefully monitor and influence antitrust issues that affect our education and practice in terms of ability to care for patients and to be reimbursed for services. The role of the Federal Trade Commission (FTC) is to investigate anticompetitive practices of an institution. There are many examples of events that fall under the jurisdiction of right to practice and are subject to antitrust protection, such as practice arrangements that limit the ability of APN practice or impinge on APN scope of practice, denial of staff privileges, restrictions of prescriptive authority in authorized states, arbitrary insurance reimbursement policies, and imposition of insurer limits for APNs (Sheehey & McCarthy, 1998). It can be an antitrust issue if a hospital denies admission to a CNM's patient who has given birth in a free-standing birth center but needs hospitalization owing to unforeseen complications. Refusal of physician-owned insurance companies to pay for APN services may also

have antitrust components. The current issues surrounding the right of APNs to be granted primary care provider status also falls into this category as competition for patient reimbursement persists. APNs collectively and independently need to work toward achieving policy decisions that allow us to exist in a competitive marketplace.

FUTURE CHALLENGES

Several important trends challenge new NPs entering the APN workforce. First, the health care system in the United States is unstable. Economic realities are forcing change to occur; service drives the system (Wilson & Porter-O'Grady, 1999). The struggles with technology and cost cannot be underestimated. Computerization and Internet access play a major role. Quality of care is undergoing careful scrutiny. Many believe that patient satisfaction will drive health care and the choice of providers for the future. APNs have much to offer patients, families, and communities with our unique blend of nursing, medical, and interpersonal skills. It will be important for APNs to maintain our strong nursing attributes that include caring, nurturing, education, support, and family-focused care. Although the future looks bright for APN nursing, there are many challenges on the forefront of APN education and practice.

APN EDUCATION

The development, continuation, and quality of APN education are important considerations now and for the future. The role that the federal government and the profession plays in supporting educational initiatives will drive how NPs are prepared and how we fit into the marketplace. It will be incumbent on APNs and APN faculty to carefully monitor federal, state, and professional policy decisions about graduate nursing education. Specifically, APNs need to be appointed or elected to key positions on nursing education policy-making boards and commissions.

Clinical competence is inherent in this process. In order to be considered members of interdisciplinary patient care provider teams, APNs will need exemplary clinical and interpersonal skills. This puts the onus on educators to prepare APNs who are able to compete in the health care arena. Choice of program and an appropriate curriculum will be important considerations because APNs will need to prepare for a variety of workplace settings and positions both in the community and in hospitals and long-term care facilities. Careful advisement by experienced nurse faculty will be vital to the success of future APNs. The use of interactive television and web-based learning will be the norm for future education. Careful considerations about the quality of clinical experiences and evaluation of outcomes will be needed to ensure that graduates are qualified and competent. Experienced faculty and high-level APN preceptors will be required to accomplish this task and to evaluate outcomes. APN education will continue to change over time as the role of APNs evolves to meet changes and needs in health care. Quality APN education is integral to the future success of nurses in APN roles.

TELEPRACTICE: EXPANDING THE BOUNDARIES OF PRACTICE ELECTRONICALLY

A key challenge for the future will be how the nation resolves the issues surrounding telepractice. Virtual technologies such as the Internet and other telehealth modalities offer unlimited ways to improve access to care, reduce costs, and offer new innovations for quality care. However, the potential for telepractice modalities to enhance health care is being hindered by the dysfunctional aspects of the regulatory regime for health care providers (Safriet, 1998).

Mutual recognition offers a regulatory solution for dealing with the challenges of technologic advances and the need to make state boundaries more permeable to allow for access to nursing and APN care. The mutual recognition model in nursing states that the nurse is held accountable for the nursing practice laws and regulations of the state where the nurse provides care while holding licensure in the home state (Williamson & Hutcherson, 1998). The work by the American Nurses Association, the National Council of State Boards of Nursing, the American Association of Colleges of Nursing, and other specialty nursing associations to create policy language by which APNs and other health care providers can practice virtually across state lines is underway and will require careful monitoring and input by APNs before it can be implemented. Grassroots APNs who care for patients at local levels will be important to ensure that policy fits for those providing the care in remote areas. Regulation that supports virtual telepractice configurations, although still in the early stages, will be important work for APNs in the next decade.

USE OF TECHNOLOGY FOR APN POLICY AND PROFESSIONAL DECISION MAKING

One of the most exciting components of moving into the new millennium is the overwhelming access to information and communication through electronic means. The use of computer technologies that allow APNs, no matter how remote geographically, how overworked, or how isolated, to monitor cutting-edge legislative and policy directives and to take an active part in policy interventions is unsurpassed. Staying abreast of current changes in policy and regulation through the myriad available websites, staying connected to professional groups, and accepting ownership of professional tasks to further APN education and practice is a responsibility of all APNs. The quality of website information and the accessibility of web-based links have improved markedly over the past 2 years. Congressional and state hearings on issues around Medicare, Medicaid, nurse practice acts, and rules and regulation are easily available. It is incumbent on individual APNs to master the intricacies of computer interaction and to maintain this competency over time.

PROFESSIONAL IMAGE

It is often difficult for APNs who are working every day caring for patients to think about how the public, the press, the medical community, and others view the overall image that is perceived as APN practice. Misinformation and miscommunication are difficult to change. The image that APNs portray to the public will set the tone for the future.

The 2001 NP marketing campaign "Nurse Practitioners: Rx for America's Health," was a cooperative venture between multiple APN professional groups and individuals. It is an excellent example of how APNs need to collaborate to provide visibility and positive images to promote the use of APNs as caregivers. The theme of the campaign was to inform policymakers, insurers, and the public that NPs make a significant difference in the delivery of health care every day and are qualified and acceptable health care providers.

As time goes on, patients will be asked to make choices about who will provide their health care, and it will be critical that they have a clear and positive understanding of the role and scope of practice of APNs. First, every APN must continually educate the public, the press, and our professional and business colleagues about our role. This difficult task is never-ending and is a priority for success in the future. The NP marketing campaign is providing the needed infrastructure to assist APN leaders to gain the skills needed to positively interact with the media. APNs are raising the money necessary to place themselves strategically in high-visibility situations. As part of this effort, the marketing campaign is providing workshops and skills training to groom APNs in the art of presenting themselves cogently in a variety of media venues.

SOUND BUSINESS PRACTICE

Business acumen will be a basic requirement for all APNs who practice. The federal and state regulatory bodies that provide oversight for community-based practice for physicians, advanced practice nurses, and other persons providing care to patients will require higher levels of responsibility and accountability. Sound business practices including practice guidelines, safety regulations, proper billing and coding systems, and guidelines for appropriate documentation will be the norm for practice that is financially stable and professionally rewarding.

EXEMPLARY LEADERSHIP

Several leadership challenges based on the current dynamic environment in health care confront APNs. This dynamic environment is driven by several important factors: the aging of the population, increasing cultural diversification, unprecedented

changes in technology, increasing demands by consumers for adequate provider performance, and a movement toward integrated systems of health care. These factors present a serious challenge to APNs and will require increased attention to quality APN leadership, collaboration, collegial relationships, and a more in-depth understanding and movement toward integrated systems of care (O'Neill, 2001). This will be hard work that will test the mettle of APNs both in the workplace and in the local and national policy arena. The development of excellent leadership and interpersonal communication skills will be basic to the future success of APNs in all settings. Shaver (2001) suggests that vision, the ability to think broadly and adjust to change, to take risks, and to empower others will be the key to finding the niche for APNs of the future. It is interesting to note that these same attributes are routinely cited as the foundation for the early success of the APN movement in the 1960s before APN practice was deemed essential to ensure the health and well-being of all.

The evolution of advanced nursing practice has had far-reaching effects on both the nursing profession and on the members of society for whom APNs care. Regulatory issues will lead the list of issues confronting APNs of the future. Overarching standards and competency measures will be the norm not only for APNs but also for other health care providers (Hanson, 1998). It will be important to direct regulatory policy from an interdisciplinary level and not as a way to keep barriers in place within the disciplines. This will be difficult work and will require a higher level of interprofession cohesiveness than APNs thus far have been able to achieve.

APNs are core constituents in identifying and providing solutions to the pressing problems in health care delivery though competent practice and astute policy and political involvement. "Change never asks for permission. Opportunity never waits for readiness" (Wilson & Porter-O'Grady, 1999). APNs of the future will need to build on the past and use whatever opportunities arise to forge new roles and opportunities for APN education and practice.

REFERENCES

Buppert, C. (1999). *Nurse practitioner's business practice and legal guide.* Gaithersburg, MD: Aspen.

Covey, S.R. (1989). *The seven habits of highly effective people. Powerful lessons in personal change.* New York: Simon & Schuster.

Gianakos, D. (1997). Physicians, nurses, and collegiality. *Nursing Outlook, 45*(2), 57-58.

Gladwell, M. (2000). *The tipping point.* Boston: Little Brown.

Hamric, A.B., Spross, J.A., & Hanson, C.M. (2000). *Advanced nursing practice: An integrative approach* (2nd ed.). Philadelphia: W.B. Saunders.

Hanson, C.M. (1998). Regulatory issues will lead advanced practice nursing challenges into the new millennium. *Advanced Practice Nursing Quarterly, 4*(3), v-vi.

Lassen, A., Fosbinder, D., Minton, S., & Robins, M. (1997). Nurse/physician collaborative practice: Improving health care quality while decreasing cost. *Nursing Economics, 15*(2), 87-91.

Malone, B. & Keepnews, D. (1998). Ensuring the future of nurses in clinical practice: Issues and strategies for staff nurses and advanced practice nurses. In D.J. Mason & J.K. Leavitt (Eds.). *Policy and politics in nursing and health care* (3rd ed.). Philadelphia: W.B. Saunders.

Nichols, L. M. (2001, April 6). *What role should nurse practitioners play in the 21st century American health care system?* (presented at the National Organization of Nurse Practitioner Faculties annual meeting). San Antonio, TX.

Office of Technology Assessment. (1986). *Nurse practitioners, physician assistants and certified nurse midwives: A policy analysis.* Washington, DC: U.S. Congress, HCS 37.

O'Neill, E. (2001, April 5). *Health care leadership for the future* (presented at the National Organization of Nurse Practitioner Faculties annual meeting). San Antonio, TX.

Safriet, B.J. (1998). Still spending dollars, still searching for sense: Advanced practice nursing in an era of regulatory and economic turmoil. *Advanced Practice Nursing Quarterly, 4*(3), 24-33.

Shaver, J. (2001, April 5). *Generating the power of influence through leadership* (presented at the National Organization of Nurse Practitioner Faculties annual meeting). San Antonio, TX.

Sheehey, C.M. & McCarthy, M.C. (1998). Advanced practice nursing: Emphasizing common roles. Philadelphia: F.A. Davis.

Well, N., Johnson, R., & Salyer, S. (1997). Interdisciplinary collaboration. *Clinical Nurse Specialist, 12*(4), 161-168.

Williamson, S.H. & Hutcherson, C. (1998). Mutual recognition: Response to the regulatory implications of a changing health care environment. *Advanced Practice Nursing Quarterly, 4*(3), 86-93.

Wilson, C. K., & Porter-O'Grady, T. (1999). *Leading the revolution in health care. advancing systems, igniting performance.* Gaithersburg, MD: Aspen.

Vignette   *Patricia ("Patsy") Leavitt*

Managed Care Mandated Coverage in Maine: A Grassroots Success Story

"One never notices what has been done; one can only see what remains to be done."

MARIE CURIE

On a steamy summer day in June, 1999, I was driving the 50 miles home after witnessing Governor King of Maine sign public law (PL) 396, "An Act to Increase Access to Primary Health Care Services." Alone in my vehicle, I suddenly realized that a small piece of history had been made, and I let out a whoop. Amused by the thought of passing truckers scratching their heads at this crazy lady, I chuckled to myself, relishing the moment. For weeks afterward, I would catch myself saying, "I just can't believe we did it." The sense of accomplishment left me with a high feeling not unlike the one I got the time I bicycled 100 miles in one day, or skied a snow bowl in the White Mountains after a 3-hour hike.

In a personal sense, this effort was a natural outgrowth of my family and nursing background. Brought up in a family whose values of heeding the voice of the people combined with a Yankee work ethic made for a nurse who was comfortable with consensus-building and willing to work for it. In my role as a nurse administrator, I learned to value and depend on grassroots support from nurses, physicians, technicians, maintenance workers, and house-

Governor Angus King signing PL 396, an act to increase access to primary health care, June 1999. He is surrounded by nurse practitioners, nurse midwives, sponsoring legislators, and lobbyists from the Maine Nurse Practitioner Association. Patsy Leavitt is fourth from the right, behind the infant.

keepers in order to move the nursing agenda forward. By participating in the Medicare reform grassroots campaign spearheaded by Margie Koehler (A/GNP) in 1995, I learned firsthand the power of a grassroots strategy.

Maine's political conditions had a major part in contributing to our successful effort. Maine is a predominantly rural state with a population of just over 1.2 million people. Our state legislature has one of the lowest citizen-to-representative ratios in the nation. In practical terms this means that every Senator or Representative is likely to know of one of the state's approximately 550 nurse practitioners (NPs). The Maine state legislature also has a long-standing reputation of distrust for big business (such as insurance) and an affinity for solving constituent's problems. Like all Americans, our legisla-

tors hold nurses in high regard and perceive us as trusted professionals.

Nurses have a long history of using a grassroots approach to brokering change. The values of teamwork, consensus building, and willingness to accept a task are natural to nurses and critical to the success of a grassroots campaign. What brought the daunting task of changing reimbursement policy to fruition was the collective effort of NPs and certified nurse midwives (CNMs) all over Maine, who conducted a true grassroots effort. The same NPs and CNMs who take care of thousands of Maine citizens took their case to those very citizens. The Maine legislature had been impressed with the solidarity of advanced practice nurses during a hard-fought, 3-year battle ending in 1996 that won a revision of the Nurse Practice Act, moving advanced practice oversight from the Board of Medicine to the Board of Nursing. The celebration of this victory for independent practice was tainted only by the parting words of the lobbyist for the Maine Medical Association (MMA) as the final vote was taken: "You'll never get paid." These words were to haunt Maine's NP pioneers for the next two years.

The physician-dominated boards of the managed care companies did, in fact, enforce policies which excluded NPs and CNMs from participation in managed care organizations (MCOs) as participating providers or, in the case of NPs, as primary care providers (PCPs). In addition, NPs and CNMs working with collaborating physicians were consistently denied the opportunity to be individually credentialed or listed in patient information booklets. While for most NPs and CNMs this was not a barrier to providing services, all of Maine's NPs and CNMs found themselves in the ethically questionable place of billing for their services under a physician's provider identification number (PIN). NP and CNM practice patterns relative to utilization and quality were therefore invisible to the insurance carrier and consequently the public.

Motivated by the major barriers imposed by such policies, individual NPs in independent practices and Maine Nurse Practitioner Association (MNPA) board members met with representatives of major payer groups in the state. They all heard the same message: "Our board will not approve the credentialing of nurse practitioners." Given the divisive nature of prior experiences fighting the MMA in the halls of the State House, the MNPA was reluctant to reopen old wounds; however, after 18 months of unsuccessful attempts to negotiate with carriers, the leadership of MNPA opted to pursue a policy change, whether legislative or regulatory. Our External Affairs Committee, cochaired by Persis Hope (NP) and myself, was asked to develop and implement a strategy to address the policy issues and find a solution to these practice barriers. We knew that if any efforts in the legislative arena were to succeed, we would need the undivided support of our membership and at least a tacit agreement on strategy. We were cognizant of the fact that, as in most groups, a few MNPA members would be activists in the effort and the majority

would not have time or energy to devote to the process. We also knew, from past experience, that members are very willing to perform single tasks (e.g., "call or e-mail your legislator in the next 48 hours to support legislative document [LD] 321"), provided the tasks are time-specific and that specific instructions are given. We therefore published a statement from our chairperson outlining the issue and our plan to seek a legislative solution. We invited dissent but noted that if we heard none by a target date, we would proceed as planned. Further, we advised members of specific tasks that they might be asked to perform as the issue gained momentum. Using a strategy pioneered by Margie Koehler (A/GNP) in the Medicare Grassroots effort, we set up an Internet listserv to coordinate and streamline communication and used it to issue updates as the process moved forward.

The first action by our committee and by the leadership of MNPA was to reconvene the ad hoc working group for the independent practice legislation, the Coalition of Nurses in Advanced Practice. The working group members, representing NPs, CNMs, nurse anesthetists, and nurse clinical specialists, were wholeheartedly in support of legislation to provide third-party reimbursement to NPs and CNMs and PCP status to NPs. When the original members of the coalition were invited to be included in the legislative language, only the nurse midwives opted to participate. We continued to enjoy the support of other advanced nursing providers throughout the process, but as these providers did not find existing insurance reimbursement practices to be a barrier to practice, they opted not to be included in the legislation.

The next critical step was to engage the assistance of an experienced and competent lobbyist, Bob Howe, a former state representative. He had led us in the independent practice battle, so he was a natural fit. It was fortuitous that his wife is an NP in independent practice! He immediately put us to work surveying states that had enacted similar legislation, to garner as many legislative ideas as we could find.

After a review of options we found that as an organization we had a critical decision to make. In order to achieve the goals we desired, we could either look for strengthening regulatory language to allow the credentialing of NPs and CNMs and the designation of NPs as PCPs (so-called "any willing provider" language), or ask for a legislative mandate to this effect. Howe led us through a critical evaluation of each approach after we had looked at what other states had done and got a feel for the climate of the Maine insurance commission. Our advisors inside the commission staff indicated that a legislative mandate would be the best option in terms of enforceability.

Mr. Howe then suggested a multipronged approach. His proposal was to write four separate pieces of legislation to address our main issues. His rationale was that such an approach would accomplish the following:

1. Broaden our base of legislators who could be listed as "sponsors."
2. Separate and clearly delineate the issues for legislators.
3. Give legislators the opportunity to decide which components might be combined into a comprehensive piece of legislation.
4. Give legislators at the committee level the opportunity to "kill" one component without endangering the others.

The four pieces of legislation were as follows:

1. *An act to establish parity for patients of certified nurse practitioners and certified nurse midwives.* This bill requires reimbursement of NPs and CNMs in independent practice for services that are subject to reimbursement when the NP or CNM is *not* in independent practice.
2. *An act to require coverage for services performed by certified nurse practitioners and certified nurse midwives to patients referred by primary care providers.* This bill requires reimbursement to any NP or CNM if the patient is referred by a PCP.
3. *An act concerning certified nurse practitioners as primary care providers.* This bill would require managed care plans to allow certified NPs to serve as PCPs within their scope of practice.
4. *An act to facilitate the collection of data concerning the health care services provided by certified nurse practitioners and certified nurse midwives.* This bill requires managed care

companies to assign personal identification numbers (PINs) to NPs and CNMs for purposes of tracking their services performed.

With this "multiple choice" approach we were offering the legislators some control up front with the thought that they might be less likely to make substantive changes to our proposed language. In addition, with one or two major sponsors per bill we had legislative champions for each key ingredient, thus reducing the likelihood of the sponsor's language getting eliminated out of hand.

The next strategy advised by Bob Howe was to regroup with our legislative supporters, specifically the seven nurse legislators who had shown us support in the past. We invited those legislators to a "Maine suppah" meeting a few weeks in advance of cloture (the date by which a bill's language must be submitted for consideration) to ask for their advice and thoughts. Far from having merely made a polite gesture, we came away from this meeting with a number of new ideas for our strategy. In true nurse fashion, the legislators had made the meeting a working session. They agreed that despite the universal dislike of mandates among legislators and in the administration, we really had no choice but to ask for a mandate. They confirmed that the strategy of putting forth multiple bills was an excellent option for our complex issue, and several members "signed up" on the spot for sponsorships. They advised, however, that we seek cosponsors who were from both "sides of the aisle," perceived as business-friendly, and not from the nursing community. Furthermore, they assisted us in a careful review of the membership of the committee that would hear our legislation and advised us of possible opposition. They confirmed that the PCP component—the third bill in the list above—would be the most likely to garner opposition, since the PCP concept was traditionally thought to be exclusively under physician purview and any change to it would likely draw active opposition from organized medicine.

The process of "writing the language" deserves some discussion. As with any strategy, it is well to see the endpoint and visualize the outcome. At the advice of our lobbyist we looked carefully at the regulatory language already in place and determined how we wanted that language to read when all was said and done. As a critical part of that process our lobbyist firmed up some relationships with people on the insurance commission staff and offered to assist in the writing of the final regulations, should our legislation pass. In this way, our lobbyist was keeping a hand in the process and maintaining some control over the all-important language.

Once sponsors were identified and final language agreed upon for each of the four bills, we set about preparing for a hearing of the bills before the joint legislative committee on banking and insurance. While we had some firm support as NPs and CNMs who were experiencing restraint of trade, we knew that access to care would be the more pertinent and compelling issue for legislators. To that end, we invited the testimony of patients who had been denied access to NP services due to the standing policies of the MCOs. We also solicited testimony from physician colleagues and patients who used NP services within physician practices, but who could not name their NPs as PCPs because of MCO policies. We prepared statements by the MNPA leadership that focused on access to care and confirmation of the quality and cost-effectiveness of NPs and CNMs.

Our behind-the-scenes strategies were just as important as our preparations for the hearing. We continued negotiations with insurance companies, stressing our wish to resolve the issue without a mandate while assuring them that we would be seeking the mandate. Interestingly enough, just two days before our bills were to be heard the largest carrier in the state, Blue Cross/Blue Shield of Maine, agreed to write a contract with two NPs in independent practice. This was after almost two years of negotiations. Needless to say, we did not withdraw our proposed legislation. At Mr. Howe's urging we contacted the two medical associations in the state, the MMA and the Maine Osteopathic Medical Association (MOA). Mr. Howe had done some consulting for the MOA, but had contacted them to confirm there was no conflict of interest. We met with the MOA, stressing that this legislation had no impact on existing NP-physician relationships. We pointed out that the provision for independent practice was already state law and that reimbursement was a separate issue. They agreed to stand mute on the subject. For reasons that still remain unclear, the MMA's executive director indicated they would stand mute too, though they did not take up an offer to meet with our leadership.

Meanwhile, we kept a high profile with our own MNPA membership, updating them via listserv and newsletter. As the hearing date approached, we called NPs and CNMs in key districts (i.e., those of joint committee members who had not committed support to the legislation) and asked them to call their legislators to ask for their support. We tracked the number of people we asked to make calls, realizing that the legislators, though responsive to constituent concern, could become annoyed by excessive calls. We asked NPs and CNMs to attend the hearing, hoping to fill the room, and while we did not prevent any individuals from testifying we did request that all testimony be coordinated. Again, the membership was cooperative with a team approach. We also made efforts to create a presence in the State House throughout the session. Armed with weekly e-mail updates of upcoming legislative hearings on a variety of health care issues, MNPA members provided welcome testimony in support of a number of public health initiatives. Enthusiastic nurses from all of the advanced practice nursing groups gathered to host our first "Advanced Practice Nurse Day" at the State House, complete with free health screenings (blood pressure, cholesterol, blood-sugar checks), information booths on lifestyle modifications, and information about NPs, CNMs, and the legislation we were promoting. We provided a catered lunch ("fish chowdah") and made many new friends.

On the day of the hearing, the committee was scheduled to hear another mandate bill prior to ours. Far from being a disadvantage, this turned out to be fortunate. The bill involved mandating payment for surgical first assistants. A representative of the MMA provided testimony in support of the first-assistant legislation and extolled the virtues of nurses. Such testimony left the MMA lobbyist hard-pressed to then turn and oppose legislation supporting nurses. Because of the time of day and the length of the prior testimony and questions, we were forced to rearrange the order of our presenters to afford one of our patients, a brittle diabetic, to testify early so she might be excused to eat.

This woman gave the most compelling testimony of the day. A young mental health worker earning little more than the minimum wage at the state mental hospital, she told the story of her battle with juvenile onset diabetes. She shared how she had been referred to an NP diabetes specialist by her PCP to help her control her disease, and convincingly testified that the NP had "saved her life" through intense teaching about and monitoring of her disease. The patient had not however, been able to obtain reimbursement for those services from her employer-provided health plan (a health maintenance organization). She had to pay for the visits out of her own pocket.

She was followed by NPs and CNMs telling stories of their clients, and by our MNPA leadership's testimony to the facts and statistics of NPs' quality and cost-effectiveness as PCPs. Opposition came primarily from the insurance industry. One insurance company representative (whose employer had the contract for state employees) claimed that NPs are more costly providers because of the greater referral rates of NPs compared to physicians. This assertion drew much interest from the committee members. The company representative was unable to produce any data to support his claim, but maintained his stand. He also asserted that the implementation of credentialing systems for NPs and CNMs would be excessively costly and that this cost would be passed on to the state.

As is usual, the bills went to a series of work sessions where, as anticipated, the legislators combined the bills into one (LD 857) incorporating all of the key concepts. At the work sessions the MNPA leadership was able to quickly counter the insurer's claims regarding referral rates by producing factual data from several practices, representing together over 6,000 patients throughout the state. This date proved that NP referral rates were comparable to physicians (7% vs. 6%). This showing up of the insurance carrier's false claims may have influenced committee members greatly.

The issue of the cost to implement credentialing was of much concern to our group. Any bill with fiscal impact suffers the possibility of incurring a "fiscal note," which effectively kills the bill. A study of the proposed mandate and its cost implications was requested by the banking and insurance committee, part of the normal process for any mandate. Again, our lobbyist had ongoing contact with staff members, who indicated that any and all information and data that we could provide would help make the study process move along more efficiently.

A document that would summarize our position and outline all the current research on the subject was needed, but would have been a tall order even if a reasonable time frame was given. In fact, the document needed to be prepared in two weeks. In one of several weekly sessions held by our legislative committee, we frantically started the search for a person who could write such a document. While many of the committee members were capable of such a work, the amount of time needed to do the task well was not available to them. We approached one of our members, Lisa Parent, who had been in touch by e-mail and listserv and who was studying for her NP degree while doing course work toward a PhD in public health policy. Ms. Parent, a CNM who lived in the far northern corner of the state on the Canadian border, was "volunteered" for the project. She promptly hired a babysitter to watch her three youngsters and set to work, pulling several all-nighters before the document was done. In her paper she addressed the 19 points outlined by the state insurance commission as being considered when a mandate is proposed. In general, these points cover benefit to the public, access to care, and cost impact of the mandate.

When the insurance commission staff reported back to the legislative committee their report was favorable. Their actuary had calculated a cost of $0.12 per plan member for those in the state health insurance plan, or a $75,000 one-time cost to credential Maine's NPs and CNMs. The staff noted that the cost would probably be significantly less, as they been convinced by MNPA Chair Evelyn Kieltyka (MSN, MS, FNP) that the number of NPs eligible to seek PCP status was only 63% of the total. She had also been able to convince the director of the health insurance office that NP and CNM care was cost effective.

With a positive staff report, the committee saw no difficulty in voting the bill out of committee as a unanimous "ought to pass." Our attention as an organization then turned to our membership. We needed to make the final push for a grassroots campaign as the bill made its way to the floors of both chambers. Members of the MNPA External Affairs Committee telephoned and e-mailed more than 250 NPs and CNMs and asked them to contact their legislators. Many responded. Though the bill never saw any debate on either floor, we could rest assured that our legislature had heard from the NPs and CNMs of Maine. The bill was voted unanimously in both chambers and then went on to the final challenge, the Governor's signature.

Our lobbyist, through well placed sources in the administration, learned at the last minute of a possible veto from the Governor. He was known to oppose mandates, and there were several pending. Several eleventh-hour discussions ensued. A nurse senator who had the Governor's ear was able to convince him that this bill was a logical outgrowth of current Maine statute and would have minimal fiscal impact.

Governor King did sign the bill, and the rest is NP history. A small group of MNPA leadership and External Affairs Committee members (those who could free up their work schedules) attended the signing of the bill. Ms. Parent, so committed to the cause, drove four hours each way, toting her 18-month old daughter, to be present.

One by one, after some initial foot-dragging and whining, the MCOs in the state have initiated the credentialing process for NPs and CNMs. We still run Nurse Day in the legislature every year (with "chowdah"), and continue to put forth and support legislation to improve the health of Maine citizens and access to advanced practice nursing.

Chapter 19

Collective Action in the Workplace

MARY E. FOLEY

"That is what political and economic power is all about: having a voice, being able to shape the future."

MADELEINE KUNIN

The health care climate of the early 2000s is one in which care is delivered—or withheld—in an atmosphere dominated by financial high stakes and mergers of health care facilities into large corporations. Hospital mergers, closures, and acquisitions have transpired at dizzying rates. Serious staffing cuts have occurred nationally, and quality nursing care is jeopardized. Retaining adequate staffing, quality of care, health and safety in the workplace, job security, and an effective voice in the changing systems demand collective action. It is imperative in this climate that nurses be aware of the tools available to initiate collective action in the workplace.

Hospitals and other health care organizations do not want nurses to organize. Just as in other industries, managers do not want nonmanagerial personnel overseeing and participating in management issues. If collective bargaining is seen as a power struggle between union and management—and in many cases that *is* how it is defined and played out—the opposing parties are seen as rivals, manipulating each other in an effort to improve and advance their respective positions. One definition of collective bargaining in the health care sector describes these broadly defined bargaining objectives (Stern, 1982, p. 11):

1. To protect the economic position and personal welfare of the worker.

2. To protect the union's integrity as an ongoing institution.
3. To recognize the limits imposed on collective bargaining outcomes by the economic conditions of the industry and of the employer, and by the climate of opinion.

Collective action strategies can range from shared governance to union representation, and many variations exist. This chapter is not meant to be a primer on achieving or administering any specific strategy; it is meant to serve as an overview and to stimulate an interest in further exploration. Each setting will be different, depending in part on the administrative structure and more so on the beliefs and style of the chief administrative staff. These factors can change with time, and strategies should be evaluated on a regular basis.

This chapter will also discuss collective bargaining for nurses from a policy perspective. Collective bargaining is a highly political and complicated legal process, and many guidelines govern the conduct of bargaining. Further, laws vary between the public and private sectors. In the public sector, laws may differ among states, and the federal system has its own regulations. Please refer to the wide range of other resources available for specific details (see References).

CONTROL OF PRACTICE

Specific objectives identified by professional nurses as essential for control of their practice include the following:

- To improve the practice of professional nurses and all nursing personnel.

- To recommend ways and means to improve care.
- To make recommendations to the hospital management: for example, to advise when a critical nurse staffing shortage exists.
- To identify and recommend elimination of hazards in the workplace.

Mechanisms to address practice issues within the institution derive from the nurse councils, practice committees, and other practice bodies that are established and empowered by either a governance model or a contract. At the heart of each governance model is the interaction between the group and the leadership. Group problem-solving is possible in any structure that encourages participation and has a leadership that accepts the outcome of that participation. Committees are an example of group participation. Committees can be given a specific task, such as to collect data, analyze it, and make recommendations. A committee can be representative (nonspecialist membership), comprised of individuals with specialized knowledge and direct interest in the issue at hand, or both at once. The downside of this may be a prolonged process, and a compromise that fails to address the problem at hand may not really satisfy any of the participants.

NURSE COMMITTEES

Nurse committees, assisted by experts in nursing, can advocate against dangerous nurse reductions. New patient-care models must undergo careful analysis. When the nurse committee and management collaboratively design and implement a practice model, both nurses and the public will be better served. When layoffs are necessary, as in true downsizing, every effort should be made to ensure safe care. The talents and expertise of nurses affected by the changes should be addressed by facilitating nurses' transitions to new areas of practice. The nurse practice committee can assist in enforcing standards and competencies in the new arenas and can participate in designing and overseeing transitional learning opportunities for displaced nurses.

MAGNET HOSPITALS

In the 1980s the American Academy of Nursing developed the concept of "magnet hospitals" (American Academy of Nursing, 1983). A magnet hospital is one that has a reputation of recruiting and retaining nurses and that welcomes staff involvement in unit and hospital decision-making in a way that positively influences practice. In 1994, the American Nurses Credentialing Center, a subsidiary of the American Nurses Association (ANA), developed the Magnet Nursing Services Recognition Program for Excellence in Nursing Services (ANA, 1998). Based on quality indicators and standards defined in ANA's *Scope and Standards for Nurse Administrators* (ANA, 1996), the program measures qualitative and quantitative aspects of nursing services. Since 1994, almost 40 hospitals and one long-term care facility have been awarded a magnet credential, and almost 20% of the facilities awarded this recognition have a collective bargaining agreement with the nurses.

The significance of this program is its recognition that an organization that has nursing as one of its highest priorities, professionally and clinically, will succeed on many planes. The resulting "forces of magnetism" have been shown to result in lower nurse turnover, higher patient satisfaction, higher nursing satisfaction, and even fewer needlestick injuries of the nursing staff (Aiken, 1994).

SHARED GOVERNANCE

Shared governance is a professional practice model defined as an arrangement of nursing staff and management that attempts to emphasize principles of participatory management in areas related to the governance and practice of nursing. Also labeled variously as *self-governance, participatory decision-making, staff bylaws,* and *decentralized nursing services,* shared governance attempts to involve practitioners in the control of their practice. Shared governance is an accountability-based governance system for professional workers (Porter-O'Grady, 1987). This model works when nursing managers and practitioners create an atmosphere of joint ownership that is based on trust and not limited by structures that restrict true professional involvement. Although shared governance requires *some* structure, it requires structure that is decision based and is constructed from the center of the workplace rather than hierarchical. Authority rests in specified processes, not in identified individuals. For this model to succeed, every nurse in the organization must believe in it. Nursing staff participants should be elected, not hand-picked favorites. Leadership of the committees may be rotated between managers and staff to be more equitable. It is not recommended that individual nursing units attempt to initiate the model unless the entire setting is committed, because this can lead to unit elitism and lack of interface within nursing. In some settings, once the nursing department adopts the rules or bylaws that govern them, these rules are approved by the hospital trustees. The model can also include a management decision-making forum for issues that concern support of practice, such as financial and interdepartmental conflicts.

There are some serious limitations to shared-governance models in practice. Some shared-governance models make no effort to conceal the fact that, in spite of the appearance of participation, a unilateral, managerial, decision-making authority remains in the institution. Such a practice negates the intent of *shared* governance and only further distances management from nurses. Other problems arise when the shared-governance model is used to bypass or conflicts with an already existing structure that has participation as a component, such as a collective bargaining agreement. Shared governance *can* exist in a unionized or nonunionized setting, but care must be taken to delineate clearly those topics to be handled by the shared-governance mechanisms and those subject to collective bargaining. For example, members of the shared-governance committee could be identified by the union, much as it selects a practice committee representing all units. Another caution with collective bargaining is the legal precedent set in the academic setting, in which faculty members became so involved in the governance structure offered by the shared-governance model that their roles became indistinguishable from those of managers. This made them ineligible for representation by collective bargaining (*Yeshiva,* 1980). And perhaps the greatest risk is lack of sustained commitment. The wisdom, courage, and patience of the managers and the staff may not survive the ups and downs of implementation.

WORK ASSIGNMENTS

Registering an objection to an inappropriate work assignment is an important professional obligation of nurses. Institutions provide staff with an internal mechanism, known as an *incident report* or *notification report,* to communicate unexpected events or to document problems; however, these forms are protected as proprietary property of the institution, and access to this data is restricted. Nurses have also filed a form called an *assignment despite objection* or *assignment under protest* while completing an objectionable assignment. If a nurse does not object to an inappropriate assignment, she or he risks charges of abandonment (see state practice laws for details). These forms are usually filed because of concerns over inadequate staff, poorly prepared staff, high patient acuity, and unsafe practice situations. The practice committee and nursing administration can then review the circumstances leading to the protest. If there is a pattern of such protests, a long-term solution can be developed. This strategy is not unique to the unionized setting, and could be successful in any setting in which the channels of communication are supportive of joint problem identification and resolution. The union environment, however, ensures a more formal follow-up.

WHISTLEBLOWER PROTECTION

Professionals who speak out about working conditions, especially about issues of patient care, may not be protected from action by their employer. Holding a professional license may necessitate that you act as an advocate, but it will not ensure employment protection if what you say is unpopular with your employer. Such protection, known as *whistleblower* protection, is not adequately in place to protect registered nurses (RNs) who are using their professional judgement and decide to speak publicly when all other steps fail. The ANA supported the inclusion of whistleblower-protection language in the Patient Safety Act and in the ANA-endorsed version of the Patient Bill of Rights, pending in Congress in late 2001. Many states have addressed this issue in health reform, patient protection, and nurse supportive legislation, and as of late 2001, 16 states have introduced or enacted whistleblower protection laws.

NEW MODELS OF LABOR–MANAGEMENT RELATIONS

There is some optimism that new models of labor-management relations will evolve in the coming century. Studies have been made under the auspices of the U.S. Department of Labor, and in 1994 a report was issued by the Commission on the Future of Worker-Management Relations (U.S. Department of Labor, 1994). Underlying the report was a theme of employee participation and problem solving that could enhance workplace productivity.

A nurse-specific example of new relationships is the work being done under the U.S. Department of Labor Transitional Workforce Stability Provisions. More than $200 million was appropriated for retraining and other worker adjustments to assist health care workers affected by the transition to a restructured health care delivery system. The Michigan Nurses Association, a member of the ANA, participated in a 3-year grant-funded project paid for by the Department of Labor to assist acute-care nurses in making transitions to other settings.

CONTROL OF PRACTICE THROUGH COLLECTIVE BARGAINING

Collective bargaining agreements for nurses have traditionally been used as a means to equalize the power between management and nurses. Nurses have used contracts as a form of collective action to improve working conditions, hence care. Generally, unions in the health care setting stimulate better hospital management by fostering formal, central, and consistent personnel policies with better lines of communication, and lead to improvements in the workplace so that recruitment and retention become easier (Juris & Maxey, 1981).

SHOULD NURSES ORGANIZE?

In most definitions, the members of a "profession" are said to have attained expertise after a specialized education. Society grants the professional a measure of autonomy in her or his work in recognition of their expertise and of the value of their service to the larger community. Autonomy permits professionals to make independent judgments and deci-

sions and to have special client-provider relationships, such those traditional in law and medicine. Nursing has struggled with a modified definition of *profession*. Nurses have traditionally worked as *employed* professionals—employed first by hospitals, nursing homes, and other health agencies, and now by health systems. Even though nursing meets many of the other criteria of a profession (e.g., education, expertise, a value recognized by society, some autonomy in judgment), the role of nurses as employees has compromised the client-provider relationship. Hospitals have been organized as bureaucratic structures and have relied on hierarchical boundaries that are not congruent with the notion of a professional practice. Conflict arises when professionals believe that their professional autonomy and clinical judgment are challenged and care compromised as a result. Medicine is now facing similar conflicts, with fewer physicians in private practice and managed care plans forcing clinical decisions that erode professional autonomy. Cost containment, productivity measurements, and issues of resource utilization are the stressors that stimulate interest by health professionals in collective action. Physicians are beginning to use collective action, including collective bargaining, to reestablish professional authority, a remedy sanctioned by the American Medical Association (Jaklevic, 1997).

Nursing has also used collective bargaining to its benefit, achieving professional goals and protecting and promoting the public interest through lobbying efforts and political action. other forms of collective action have a serious limitation: they work only when all parties agree that they should. When no oversight exists to force compliance, the relationship can fail. Disappointed expectations of benevolence from an industry that wasn't and isn't benevolent may explain why nurses have been willing to organize for collective bargaining. Nurses who support collective bargaining view it as a way to control practice by a redistribution of power within the structure of a health care organization.

A Kansas City employee and labor relations consulting firm set out to ascertain why hospital employees and nurses join unions and how union organizers garner their support (Stickler & Velghe, 1980). The study was intended for use by hospital managers seeking to define strategies to avoid outside representation for professional nurses. Their conclusion: Hospital management widely subscribes to the myth that big powerful unions organize professional nurses, but in fact, outside unions do not organize nurses: nurses organize themselves. They do this because administrators and nursing supervisors fail to recognize and address nurses' individual and collective needs.

Another study—this one from the University of California, Berkeley (Parlette, O'Reilly, & Bloom, 1980)—found that nurses who engage in collective bargaining do so because they believe it is the only solution to a management-employee power struggle. The authors concluded that nurses decide to unionize out of their "inability to communicate with management and their perception of authoritarian behavior on the part of management" (Parlette, O'Reilly, & Bloom, 1980, p. 16). The age of this study by no means diminishes its importance or accuracy, because nurses of the 2000s who are selecting collective bargaining representatives are doing so in the face of great struggles over patient-care issues with managers who appear to have lost sight of the purpose of health services.

Nursing has been unable to come to closure on the debate about whether professional nurses should organize for collective bargaining. On one side of the debate are those who want nursing to be a profession that relies on its prestige to ensure recognition. On the other side are those who view nursing as a professional or occupational group that can and should use collective action, specifically collective bargaining, to secure recognition. Virginia Cleland (1981), a legendary professor of nursing administration, is an exponent of the former view. "The power bestowed upon the nursing profession," she states, "should derive not from the hospital administrator's benevolence, but rather from the public's view of the value of services provided by the practitioner" (p. 17). Ada Jacox (1980), another esteemed nursing professor, criticizes nursing departments that fail to acknowledge nurses as professionals and suggests that collective bargaining may be a way for nurses to achieve collective professional responsibility.

Hospitals have undergone extensive organizational restructuring in the 1990s and beyond, in part to survive changes in reimbursement brought by growth in managed care and by reductions in federal funding pursuant to a balanced budget. In a 1994 survey, 38% of 700 hospitals surveyed planned to reduce their work force. Nursing personnel were one of the targets of those cuts. In a survey released in 1995, more than 53% of the respondents stated that RNs were taking care of more patients than before (Himali, 1995a). Unfortunately, cost reductions took precedence, and the RN role in enhancing care was overlooked (Buerhaus, 1995).

The difficulties faced by RNs have remained acute through the turn of the century, and bode poorly for the working environment for nurses who still wish to practice in the hospital environment. Multiple surveys and publications document the stress and perceived deterioration of nurse satisfaction, and potentially, the quality of patient care.

The results of an online survey conducted by the ANA conducted an in 2000 reflect the depth of despair nurses are feeling (ANA, 2001b). One of the most discouraging findings was that 52% of nurses stated they would not recommend nursing to a relative or friend.

As the twenty-first century dawned, nurses were trying to balance an increasingly acute patient population, increasing numbers of patients per nurse, and a new stressor—mandatory overtime. Mandatory overtime first began to be reported in late 1999, and by 2000 was an epidemic. Three major strikes by state nurses associations occurred in 2000 (Worcester, Massachusetts; Nyack, New York; and Washington, DC) and one in 2001 (Youngstown, Ohio). Mandatory overtime was the primary reason for these strikes by RN collective bargaining units. RNs reject mandatory overtime for a number of reasons. It diminishes the sense of control nurses have over their work life. Nurses with family or other personal obligations found that inability to plan their work schedule added to their stress and their dissatisfaction with their work life (ANA, 2001b). From a professional practice perspective, mandatory overtime and short staffing may be contributing to the rate of medical errors documented in the Institute of Medicine report on health care errors, *To Err is Human—Building a Safer Health System* (Institute of Medicine, 1999). The ANA is the lone voice recognizing these potential contributing factors and has led the way in pushing research agendas that quantify safe hours of work and how patient safety can be assured. As with the whistleblower issue, the ANA and the state nurses associations are in the lead in influencing federal and state legislative efforts to address overtime and staffing in the context of safe patient care.

A comprehensive and accurate compendium of recent changes in nursing and patient care is found in a *When Care Becomes a Burden: Diminishing Access to Adequate Nursing* (Fagin, 2001), a publication funded by the Milbank Memorial Fund and edited by an esteemed nursing leader, Claire Fagin. This document, like numerous other written and spoken sources of testimony, predicts that the present hospital work environment will seriously jeopardize both recruitment and retention efforts. Attention to work environment quality will be critical to counteracting the downturn in interest in nursing as a professional choice and in retention of nurses as many members of the current workforce age into their early and mid 50s.

Nurse health and safety have been directly affected by the restructured workplace. The combination of reduced staff, higher patient acuity, and pressure for increased productivity has led to an increase in nurse and other health worker injuries. These findings have been documented by an analysis by the Minnesota Nurses Association of employer-provided data from 97 health care facilities for the years 1990 through 1994 (Himali, 1995b). The first phase of this study confirms what had previously been only anecdotal: The rise in patient acuity and the concurrent staffing changes has caused a near doubling of RN workplace injuries.

It is important for nursing representatives to point out the connection between practice trends and health and safety issues. Health and safety issues are potential organizing issues and appropriate subjects of bargaining.

HISTORY OF COLLECTIVE BARGAINING IN NURSING

Nurses in the early 1900s were frustrated by their working conditions. Receiving little support from the established nursing organizations, a few thousand joined trade unions for assistance. In the 1940s, nurses in California, Ohio, and Pennsylvania were assisted in their workplaces by the ANA constituent member associations (CMAs) formerly known as state nurses associations. In 1946, after considerable urging by the leaders of the state associations representing nurses, the ANA unanimously adopted a national economic security program. It was the ANA's intent to encourage the CMAs to act as the exclusive agents for nurses in the important fields of economic security and collective bargaining.

Other unions subsequently organized nurses, with more than 20 expressing an intent to solicit nurses in 1974. The competition has become more intense over the years as the stakes have gotten higher. Unions such as the Meatpackers, Paperhangers, United Food and Commercial Workers, Longshoremen, Teamsters, American Federation of Teachers, United Mine Workers, Service Employees International Union (SEIU), and Association of Federal, State, County and Municipal Employees (all members of the American Federation of Labor-Congress of Industrial Organizations [AFL-CIO]) have competed for nurse membership among themselves and with the CMAs.

Some nurses have chosen to be organized in independent unions, unaffiliated with either an AFL-CIO union or a CMA. One well-known independent union is the Committee for the Recognition of Nursing Achievement at Stanford University in Palo Alto, California. Formed in 1964, this union has had a successful history of working closely with nursing administration to advance nursing standards and nurse recognition. Independent unions are at risk of raiding by other unions because of the difficulty and cost of providing the complex and expensive services of representation.

In the United States, the fraction of all workers represented by a labor organization is declining. According to the 1999 Current Population Survey, approximately 13% of all employees are unionized. This is down from 14.5% in 1996 and almost 25% in the 1970s. The RN workforce reports approximately 18.5% coverage by collective bargaining agreement, with 16.1% holding union membership (United American Nurses/American Nurses Association, 2001).

WHO REPRESENTS NURSES (AND DOES IT MATTER)?

Who the bargaining representative is *does* matter to nurses. First, it is certainly going to have an effect on the public's perception of the profession. It can also determine who has the political clout in issues of legislation and regulation.

Nurses who are considering a collective bargaining agent must do some values clarification. The underlying question that must be addressed is: Do nurses have identity *primarily* as nurses or as workers? CMA collective bargaining agreements have been historically nursing-practice oriented, and their contracts are replete with references to the professional standards, codes of ethics, and professional practice committees that give nurses a voice in patient care concerns. Unions, on the other hand, are worker-oriented; their expertise has been in attaining wage and benefit packages and, in some cases, advocating for health and safety issues. Yet in a paper prepared for the Albert Shanker Institute, Richard Hurd (2000) has observed that while professional associations are struggling to respond to their members' needs more like unions, many unions are attending to professional workers' needs more like professional associations.

The October, 1995 election of John Sweeney (previously head of the SEIU) as president of the AFL-CIO has ensured that competition for nurses by the trade unions will increase. The SEIU represents more health care workers than any other union and, under Sweeney's leadership was the only major union to grow in size during nationwide union membership losses.

In 1998, the ANA started to work on a two-track strategy: to explore the possibility of an affiliation with the AFL-CIO while creating a defined labor arm of the ANA. In 1999 this arm—the United American Nurses—was created by an overwhelming vote of the delegates attending the ANA House of Delegates meeting. In 2001 the United American Nurses became an affiliate of the AFL-CIO. The full potential of the new structure and of the new relationship with AFL-CIO has yet to be realized. One immediate implication is a mutually respectful working relationship that will essentially end a neg-ative type of competition that has existed between the AFL-CIO unions and the CMAs: namely, raids (see Raids and Decertifications).

However, nurses will still have to decide whether to join the United American Nurses or more traditional trade unions as new bargaining units are organized, since many trade unions still intend to recruit nurses, just as the United American Nurses intends to bring more nurses into its membership.

COLLECTIVE BARGAINING PROCESS

ELECTING THE AGENT

When nurses decide to elect a collective bargaining representative, they are guaranteed legal protection, as all workers in the private sector are, by the National Labor Relations Act (NLRA). The employer is also ensured some protection, especially protection against disruption of the workplace during the organizing or election process. Once the nurses (or other employees) start a campaign for representation and 30% of the eligible nurses have signed cards signaling their interest in electing a representative, the employer is prohibited from engaging in certain activities defined as unfair labor practices:

- It may not fire the organizers for their union activity.
- It is prohibited from interfering with, restraining, or coercing employees who choose to organize, form, join, or assist a labor organization.
- It cannot refuse to allow dissemination of union information in the workplace.
- It cannot ignore a request for a vote of the workers for representation by the union as a collective bargaining agent.

After the campaign, a vote is conducted under the guidance of the National Labor Relations Board (NLRB). Other unions may enter the race at this time. A vote of 50% of those voting plus one (i.e., a simple majority) is required to select the agent.

RAIDS AND DECERTIFICATIONS

Nurses represented by a bargaining agent have the right to drop or change (decertify) that agent by a similar campaign of signatures (30%) of the affected members, followed by a vote, again, of 50% plus one. This is an increasingly common event, particularly given the competition between trade unions and nursing unions and among trade unions themselves. When a union tries to decertify an existing union, the campaign is called a *raid*. Raids are one of the easiest ways to recruit new members, making this practice more and more attractive. It is easier and cheaper to recruit a bargaining unit that is already organized than to recruit unorganized nurses (remember, nurses generally do not get organized from the outside; they organize themselves!). Competing unions often make exaggerated promises, and the larger trade unions have resources to use on raids. Critical questions must be asked: Has the union delivered on such promises in the past? Would the services of the new bargaining agent in fact be better? Would the nurses actually be better represented?

RECOGNITION APPEALS

An employer may choose to bargain in good faith on matters concerning employee working conditions by voluntarily recognizing the bargaining agent in lieu of awaiting the outcome of an election. This may occur if the support for one union is evident and a strong majority exists. More commonly, however, the employer will appeal employee requests for representation to the NLRB. The appeal may be based on a technical distinction or definition, but the purpose behind the appeal is the desire of the employer to prevent union representation in the workplace.

During such an appeal, arguments about why, by whom, or how nurses will be represented are made before the NLRB. The net effect of the appeal may not change the outcome of the process, but it does come at a high price to the union and the nurses in staff time, resources, and often loss of focus and momentum.

INSULATION

Early challenges to nursing unions arose when the hospitals challenged whether a state nurses association was properly structured to be a labor union. In question was the membership of the SNAs; all RNs could belong to the association. Because RN managers could belong to the SNA, it was necessary to provide a real and substantial "insulation" of the collective bargaining program of the SNA from any potential managerial influence. This protection is required by the NLRB and prevents employers from interfering in, dominating, or discriminating in an employee's pursuit of a representative for collective bargaining. In spite of a precedent-setting case in 1979, some hospitals appealed the SNA structure, and a series of cases in the 1980s ensued. Eventually the issue was resolved successfully for the SNAs and the nurses.

UNIT DETERMINATION

Another class of challenges to nursing unions are the appeals on the issue of unit determination. When the NLRA and the subsequent 1974 amendments covering health care employees were adopted, Congress intended simultaneously to limit the number of individual bargaining units that an employer or industry would have to recognize and bargain with while allowing for distinctions among employees that may have unique issues or circumstances. Nurses have historically been organized into all-RN bargaining units because RNs were believed to have a unique "community of interest" in the way they worked within the health care system.

In 1984 a dramatic change in nurse unit determination occurred when the NLRB ruled in a case involving St. Francis Hospital (in St. Paul, Minnesota) that the nurses were no longer eligible for a distinct, all-RN bargaining unit and, instead, would have to be included in what was called an *all-professional unit.* An all-professional unit could include respiratory therapists, social workers, physical therapists, librarians, pharmacists, medical clergy, the architect, and the business officer. This determination wreaked havoc with organizing, and it coincided with the beginning of the last great national nursing shortage in the late 1980s. That shortage led to serious nurse staffing problems and working conditions that were deplorable and unsafe. As conditions worsened in hospitals, nurses all over the country were requesting organizing assistance. Despite the demand, there were very few successful elections from 1984 to 1991, mostly because of the NLRB ruling on all-professional units. First, it was difficult to organize and achieve a satisfactory election outcome among such a diverse group of health care employees. Second, though it might be possible to stimulate enough interest among employees to warrant representation, election of a single bargaining agent to represent the diverse needs of so many work classifications would be almost impossible.

The ANA and the unions representing nurses for collective bargaining decided to challenge the NLRB's decision. The major opponent in the challenge was the American Hospital Association, which worked strenuously to keep the determination in favor of the all-professional unit. After a ruling by the NLRB affirming the rights of RNs to be organized in all-RN units, the American Hospital Association challenged that ruling in a federal court and an injunction was issued. Realizing that this issue stood in the way of nurses' being represented for collective bargaining as they tried to improve working conditions and protect patient care, the ANA and the NLRB appealed the case to the Supreme Court. In May, 1991 the Supreme Court confirmed that the NLRB had ruled properly and reinstated all-RN bargaining units.

THE REGISTERED NURSE AS SUPERVISOR

Soon another employer-initiated legal strategy challenged the nursing profession and the future protection of nurses by the NLRA. In a shocking decision in May, 1994, the Supreme Court ruled that any nurse who "directs other employees" is to be classified as a supervisor and can be fired for protesting job conditions or questioning management decisions that the nurse sees as putting the quality of patient care at risk (*NLRB v. Health Care & Retirement Corp. of America,* 1994). Nurses inevitably supervise a wide range of ancillary personnel, such as assistants, clerks, and, in the case of RNs, licensed practical/vocational nurses; it had been a 20-year policy of the NLRB that nurses' direction or assignment of others is exercised in the interest of the patient, not of the employee. The 1994 ruling overturned this policy and was a staggering setback for all nurses as they advocate for patient safety and quality in a climate of downsizing and restructur-

ing. It is threatening to all unions, who strongly protest the "supervisory" label for nurses because it makes nurses ineligible for collective bargaining. Because of the 1994 decision and the subsequent confusion it has created, the Supreme Court instructed the NLRB to reconsider its definition of "supervisory" as it pertains to nurses and to be consistent in the use of that term throughout all industries, not treating nurses or the health care industry with any distinction. Employers have used this legal discrepancy and unsettled issue to delay or avoid bargaining with nurses. Circuit court decisions following the 1994 Supreme Court decision continued to be split on the question of RN status as employees or supervisors, so the Supreme Court considered another case in late 2000 (*NLRB v. Kentucky River Community Care Inc. et al,* 2000). The ANA submitted an amicus curiae brief in support of the NLRB, in coordination with the four other AFL unions who represent large numbers of nurses.

The critical issue, again, revolved around the following question: When an RN exerts professional judgement in assigning and directing junior colleagues and nonprofessional assistants, are they are doing so as a licensed professional or as a manager? To nurses' great disappointment, in May, 2001 the Supreme Court voted five to four to strike the NLRB interpretation of what constitutes supervisory independent judgement (ANA, 2001a). While this may further complicate which nurses will be eligible for collective bargaining, the court did note that it might be possible to distinguish employees who direct the manner of others' performance of discrete tasks from employees who direct other employees.

JOB SECURITY OR PROFESSIONAL AND CAREER SECURITY?

The economic environment in the health care industry, coupled with rapidly advancing technological breakthroughs and a renewed interest in primary and preventive care, has dramatically shifted health care away from the inpatient hospital setting. Many nurses who previously practiced in the acute-care setting have chosen to move to settings that offer a more satisfactory environment and recognize the value of the RN. In the 2000 Division of Nursing Sample Survey, the total number of nurses involved in care was found to have risen to 2.7 million RNs from 2.6 million in 1996 (Bureau of Health Professionals, 2001). About 2.2 million nurses are still reported as working in nursing. Where are the 500,000 who do not report working? About 59% of nurses are now employed by acute care institutions. More acute care positions are vacant, and remain vacant longer, and this trend is intensifying. Hiring incentives are commonplace, and nurses are being offered sign-on bonuses and relocation packages never seen before. Efforts to retain RNs have not had the same attention, and that is why the concept of "magnetism" and attention to the work environment are critical to keep the current expert-knowledge worker, the experienced RN, in the system. As this country's senior population grows in size and scope of health needs, inpatient censuses will remain high, and hospitals will struggle with fewer staff, busier schedules, emergency department diversions, and surgical delays.

New organizing will be difficult in light of smaller acute care settings and widely dispersed outpatient and home-care employee groups. The new conditions present an organizing dilemma to all representatives as resources and needs are spread further, the interests of nurses become more diverse, and the numbers who can be organized in each campaign grow smaller. Another formidable barrier to new organizing is the size and financial power of large, nationwide corporate systems, some of which have deep-seated and well-funded opposition to union activity.

These new paradigms have challenged nurses and their representatives to modify bargaining strategies and turn attention to maintaining the essential role of the RN in the acute care setting through bargaining agreements and workplace advocacy while simultaneously helping nurses prepare for changing settings and roles. Will nursing care be improved if we adopt fixed ratios of nurses to patients? These are professional-practice issues that continue to deserve debate and study, and which may distinguish the unions who can advocate for a profession from a traditional union. The struggle to simultaneously address current staffing shortages and safe standards of care as defined by patient load and hours of work, and to prepare to address the future nursing shortage, is a challenge for all representatives and advocates for nursing.

REFERENCES

Aiken, L. (1994). Lower Medicare mortality among a set of hospitals known for good nursing care. *Medical Care, 32,* 771-787.

American Academy of Nursing. (1983). *Magnet hospitals: Attraction and retention of professional nurses.* Washington, DC: American Nurses Association.

American Nurses Association. (1996). *Scope and standards for nurse administrators.* Washington, DC: Author.

American Nurses Association. (1998). Looking for quality patient outcomes: The American Nurses Credentialing Center's Magnet Program recognizes excellence. *Nursing Trends and Issues, 3*(4), 1-6.

American Nurses Association (2001a). ANA not dissuaded by Supreme Court decision on "supervisors." *The American Nurse, 33*(4), 1-2.

American Nurses Association. (2001b). ANA poll: RNs say poor working conditions affect care. *The American Nurse, 33*(2), 1-2.

Buerhaus, P. (1995). Economics and reform: Forces affecting nurse staffing. *Nursing Policy Forum, 1*(2), 8-14.

Bureau of Health Professions. (2001). *The registered nurse population* (preliminary findings, March 2000, National Sample Survey of Registered Nurses). Washington, DC: Health Resources and Services Administration.

Cleland, V. (1981). Taft-Hartley amended: Implications for nursing—the professional model. *Journal of Nursing Administration, 11,* 17.

Fagin, C. (2001). *When care becomes a burden: Diminishing access to adequate nursing.* New York: Milbank Memorial Fund.

Himali, U. (1995a). ANA sounds alarm about unsafe staffing levels. *American Nurse, 27,* 2.

Himali, U. (1995b). An unsafe equation: Fewer RNs—more workplace injuries. *American Nurse, 27,* 5.

Hurd, R. (2000). Professional workers, unions, and associations: Affinities and antipathies. In *Seminar on unions organizing professionals.* New York: Albert Shanker Institute.

Institute of Medicine. (1999). *To err is human—Building a safer health system.* Washington, DC: National Academy Press.

Jacox, A. (1980). Collective action: The basis for professionalism. *Supervisor Nurse, 11,* 22.

Jaklevic, M. (1997). Doctors and unions. *Modern Healthcare, 27*(40), 99-106.

Juris, K. & Maxey, C. (1981). The impact of hospital unionism. *Modern Healthcare, 11,* 36.

Lutz, S. (1994). Let's make a deal: Health care mergers, acquisitions take place at a dizzying pace. *Modern Healthcare, 24,* 47-50.

NLRB v. Health Care & Retirement Corp. of America, 114 U.S. 1778 (1994).

NLRB v. Kentucky River Community Care Inc. et al., 121 U.S. 1861 (2001).

Olson, M. (1977). *The logic of collective action.* Cambridge, MA: Harvard University Press.

Parlette, G.N., O'Reilly, C.A., & Bloom, J.R. (1980). The nurse and the union. *Hospital Forum, 23,* 14.

Porter-O'Grady, T. (1987). Shared governance and new organizational models. *Nursing Economic$, 5*(6), 281-287.

Providence Hospital, 320 NLRB No. 49 (1996).

Stern, E. (1982). Collective bargaining: A means of conflict resolution. *Nursing Administration, 6,* 9.

Stickler, F.B. & Velghe, J.C. (1980). Why nurses join unions. *Hospital Forum, 23,* 14.

Sullivan, E. & Decker, P. (1988). *Effective management in nursing.* Menlo Park, CA: Addison-Wesley.

United American Nurses/American Nurses Association. (2001). *Trends in the registered nurse workforce.* Washington, DC: American Nurses Association.

U.S. Department of Labor. (1994, May). *Health care workforce transition.* Washington, DC: Author.

Yeshiva, supra, 103 LRRM at 2553 (1980).

20 Politics of Nursing Research

DOROTHY BROOTEN

LINDA P. BROWN

SUSAN M. MIOVECH

JOANNE M. YOUNGBLUT

"Research is removed from politics—it is pure and almost holy."

DOROTHY BROOTEN (1984)

"Not hardly!!"

THE AUTHORS (2002)

For the naive, or for perhaps a very few basic scientists who are able to isolate themselves from the outside world, research may appear to be immune to political influence. For other researchers, however, especially those whose work involves patients, providers, health care delivery systems, and academia, politics is an ever-present part of the work. It influences all aspects of research, from the very definition of what constitutes nursing research to the choice of a topic and the dissemination of results.

WHAT CONSTITUTES NURSING RESEARCH?

While debate on what constitutes nursing research has been going on for some time, the recent exponential growth of doctoral programs in nursing, with corresponding need for faculty research to undergird these programs, has renewed and enlivened the debate. For decades, proponents of nursing history have argued for inclusion of historical research in the definition of nursing research and in the

funding mechanisms of the National Institutes of Health (NIH), especially of the National Institute of Nursing Research (NINR). In the past 5 years, proponents of educational research—research into the most effective teaching methods, how students best learn, and so on—have begun to argue forcefully for placing such research under the rubric of nursing science. Opponents, who view nursing as a practice discipline, argue that nursing research must build nursing knowledge for the improvement of care to patients. And indeed, the NINR's mission statement notes that it:

Supports clinical and basic research to establish a scientific basis for the care of individuals across the life span—from management of patients during illness and recovery to the reduction of risks for disease and disability, the promotion of healthy lifestyles, promoting quality of life in those with chronic illness, and care for individuals at the end of life. (NINR, 2001)

As debate continues over what constitutes nursing research, political issues and associated benefits and dangers of choices made throughout the research process grow as well.

CHOICE OF RESEARCH TOPIC

Most researchers consider a number of factors when choosing a research topic: importance or significance, scope, cost, and potential yield. The political gain or loss associated with choosing a certain topic is also considered. The choice of topic has potential political ramifications for the researcher's professional career, the institution in which the researcher works, the researcher's professional group, and the availability of funding for the research, in addition to broader societal implications.

PROFESSIONAL CAREER

In some ways, the selection of a topic is a personal statement. The choice may express the researcher's personality characteristics and style. Some conservative individuals consistently choose relatively safe studies over which they have maximum control. Risk-takers and renegades choose topics that challenge the status quo and conventional wisdom, thus placing them in the spotlight or isolating them from the mainstream of colleagues and support. Certain individuals focus on the abstractions of philosophical inquiry (Fawcett, Watson, Neuman, Hinton Walker, & Fitzpatrick, 2001). Some researchers prefer to study a narrow area in depth, whereas others superficially study the globe. In each case, the choice of topic reflects the researcher's values and societal context and, to some extent, collegial and professional associations.

Obviously, your choice of research topic will have political consequences. You should try to envision the influence of your topic choice. Will it increase your personal and professional contacts, improve professional or personal networking with key individuals or groups, or lead to further studies? When starting a program of research, especially in a time of scarce resources, ask yourself the following questions:

- Why is this topic important to me, to my organization, and to society?
- What will be the potential yield for me as an individual and researcher?
- Is this work a potential career enhancer?
- Is this the best research area I can choose to study?
- Who else is interested in this topic, and why?
- Is it timely, and will it still be important when completed?

INSTITUTIONAL INFLUENCE

The choice of a research topic can be a fit or a misfit within your work setting. Sometimes, whether a topic is a fit or a misfit may be a result of informal and evolutionary influences. Increasingly, for example, individual schools of nursing are becoming known for their lead in specific research areas (e.g., elder care, chronic illness, women's health, cardiac risk reduction in children, health outcomes research). Faculty recruitment for these areas and informal pressure on current faculty to fit their research within them can be substantial and can have benefits for or negative consequences on faculty promotion and retention. A school's research focus also changes as groups of investigators move to other institutions or progress to other areas of research, and what research is needed for the discipline also changes over time. In general, progression from development of grand theories of nursing to middle-range theories with more tangible application to nursing practice has occurred over several decades. We have also seen what appeared to be a singular focus on physiologic research in many institutions progress to recognition of the need for behavioral research.

If your research is in keeping with the stated mission and goals of your organization, it can promote the institution's image, improve the delivery of its services, or reduce the costs of providing those services. Research in these directions is likely to be supported in some way or at least not blocked. On the other hand, research topics at odds with institutional philosophy, mission, or informal priorities are not likely to be facilitated and may even be stymied because of institutional disapproval.

For example, you cannot expect a Catholic institution to provide support for work on abortifacients. Other examples may be less obvious. For instance, a study of the feasibility of earlier discharge of low-birth-weight infants may be received differently, depending on the institution. If the payor mix for the care of low-birth-weight infants is such that longer hospitalization is revenue-generating for a particular institution, the proposed research is not likely to receive much support from that institution. Alternatively, if the hospital's costs of providing care to this group exceed the charges for which it can be reimbursed, the institution is likely to support the work.

In considering potential institutional influence on a research topic, determine how the topic might improve care or teaching, and for how many patients or students it might do so. How might it decrease costs or solve major nursing or health care problems within the organization? Perhaps the study will improve the institution's image or improve relationships among disciplines or between institutional and community groups.

INFLUENCE ON THE PROFESSIONAL GROUP

The choice of a research topic also has potential import for your professional group. Ask if your study will accomplish the following:

- Improve health care.
- Improve the profession's image with the public or with policymakers.
- Add to nursing's knowledge base.
- Provide data on the cost-effectiveness of nursing services.
- Help increase future funding for nursing.
- Fit with regional or national funding or health care priorities.

Alternatively, the choice of a research topic can have a divisive effect on a professional group. For example, studies that pit one sub-discipline or level of nursing against another usually waste much energy that might be better spent on ways to improve patient care.

FUNDING

Securing funding for research raises a host of political issues:

- Will you need funding to conduct the study?
- Given the topic you have chosen to pursue, what is a likely funding source, and what are the politics involved in securing funding from that organization?
- If you receive funding, what will be the political fallout in the institution in which you work and with other staff?
- What are the political ramifications of receiving one level or another of indirect cost recovery (i.e., overhead, or the costs above those incurred to directly conduct the study) on the grant?
- Will you, the investigator, or perhaps your division or department, receive any of the indirect cost recovery?

Even if your study can be conducted without funding, you may experience pressure to have it funded anyway. The motive may be to secure extra money for the institution or division, to use the funded research to improve the organization's image or ranking, or to establish your funding track record (Meleis, 2001). Conducting funded pilot work also may be necessary to establish credibility to receive full-scale funding. In settings where senior faculty have not received funding for research, there may be pressure to *not* pursue funding, or disincentives when funding is received.

Where to apply for funding is also a political issue. Federal funding, such as that from the NIH, carries substantially greater indirect cost recovery (now called Facilities and Administration by federal agencies) than do most private sources. Federal indirect cost recovery ranges from 40% to 65% of the money needed to actually do the work (i.e., direct costs) and is additional to it. Thus, a grant of $100,000 granted to an institution that has negotiated an indirect cost recovery rate of 55% actually costs the funding agency $155,000. This $55,000 indirect cost recovery is for the institution's maintenance of its libraries, research space and research facilities, and so forth. Although the indirect cost recovery on federal grants is continuously under review, federally funded research grants still carry much higher indirect cost recovery than do privately funded research grants or training grants, for which the rate is generally around 10%.

Some institutions and schools are reluctant to allow investigators to seek private research funding because of the small indirect cost recovery. They claim that the cost of providing the research space and support that investigators need far exceeds the indirect cost recovery provided by such grants. If private funding is needed, the next step may be to investigate the unpublished priorities and politics of the funding agency. This is usually done through informal networking and contacts, a political exercise of its own. Furthermore, a given research topic may not be fundable from a political standpoint; this has been true in nursing for decades. The work of Dr. Ann Burgess and Dr. Lynda Holmstrom during the 1970s is illustrative. In 1972, little scholarly research existed on the problems of rape victims and on the provision of counseling services to them. However, none of the agencies to which Burgess and Holmstrom submitted grant proposals stepped forward with funding. One agency, a foundation supporting research in women's studies, told them that their proposal was very well-written but the agency could not become involved in their topic. Burgess and Holmstrom went ahead with the project without funding, fitting their research activities around full teaching loads. Within a year, they interviewed 146 rape victims at all hours of the day, conducted weekly followup interviews, and attended the rapists' trials. The study was completed and published widely. Today Dr. Burgess is an acknowledged national leader in the area of research on rape, violence, and victimization, and continues to conduct research in these areas. Obtaining funding for this line of investigation is much easier now than it was in 1972.

More recently, the dean of social sciences at the University of Chicago was notified that researchers at his institution had been awarded more than $1 million in federal funding to study the social patterns that govern the choice of sexual partners among adults. Several weeks later, he was informed that the funding had been delayed indefinitely because NIH grant officials were unwilling to submit the proposal request for review to the parent agency, the U.S. Department of Health and Human Services. A few years previously the same team of researchers, at the request of the federal government, had designed a major national survey of sexual behavior to provide data needed by public health officials to understand the spread of acquired immunodeficiency syndrome (AIDS) and other sexually transmitted diseases. The House Appropriations Committee killed funding for that program some months later, citing its controversial aspects (Suplee, 1991). Congressional interests and influence thus have a clear and direct effect on the direction of and financial support for research.

Special interest group also have a direct effect. Currently, debate on the use of fetal tissue in research is ongoing between antiabortion activists, legislators who support them, and researchers at the University of Nebraska. The University of Nebraska's fetal-tissue research, led by an award-winning neuro-scientist, has potential to greatly help victims of Alzheimer's, Parkinson's, and other diseases. Anti-abortion activists, however, liken researchers who work with fetal tissue to the doctors who performed medical experiments in Nazi concentration camps (Schmidt, 2001). Their lobbying efforts are aimed at promoting a Nebraska bill that would ban the University of Nebraska Medical Center and other state institutions from using tissue obtained from elective abortions. Antiabortion lawmakers and activists in other states and in the nation's capital have already begun looking to the Nebraska bill as a model. A ban on fetal tissue research is seen as a forerunner of bans on human embryo research and any other type of research opposed by antiabortion activists (Schmidt, 2001). Such activity can affect funding, careers, and the direction of institutional research.

Managed care also has affected research funding, especially for clinical research. Academic medical centers for many years supported clinical research with the income generated by medical faculty practices. In addition, some clinical research costs (e.g., for tests and medications) were underwritten as patient care costs. However, managed care organizations have refused to pay such research-related costs and have forced academic medical centers to compete in the marketplace by lowering their costs for providing patient care. This has reduced both revenue for medical clinical research and the time physicians have to conduct clinical research, as physicians are forced to increase clinical practice time to maintain the same income level as before the incursion of managed care (Mechanic & Dobson, 1996).

Yet managed care may favor nursing research, and for several reasons. First, far less research conducted by nurses has been subsidized through clinical practice and patient care costs. Second, managed care organizations are interested in and supportive of research whose findings can be applied immediately to patient care. They are far less interested in basic research with findings that will benefit patients in future decades. Because patients remain in managed care plans for an average of 2 years, managed care executives are interested in findings that provide a market edge and can be used before enrollees change plans. Third, administrators of managed care plans are interested in research that prevents illness and minimizes disability, a strength of nursing research (Brooten, 1997).

The funding of research also involves personality factors. Not all researchers approach the issue of funding in the same way; several character types are discernible. "Research purists" are heavily invested in a line of research—so invested that they will not change areas, no matter what, including unavailability of funds to conduct the work. The work may thus never really flourish. "Research prostitutes," on the other hand, have no particular line of research but will conduct any type of research, so long as the funding is available, and in the long run do not develop a program of research or a body of knowledge. "Research realists" are invested in a program of research but are also cognizant of the reality of needing funds to conduct the work. Realists generally seek several potential funding sources and can slant a proposal to coincide with the organization's funding priorities, providing that the integrity of the research can be maintained. Some organizations that support research even have the equivalent of "research pimps." Unlike a developmental model, in which a senior researcher gathers junior colleagues and works with them to develop their research skills and thus their independence, research pimps create a dependence model. The research pimp writes proposals *for* junior colleagues rather than *with* them. The end result, if the proposals are funded, is a short-term increase in the organization's research funding; unfortunately, the junior colleagues are not taught by this process to conduct research or to prepare the subsequent followup study proposal. They become increasingly dependent on research pimps for the next proposal and for maintaining the status that often accompanies funded research. Ultimately the organization will suffer, as will science, because research pimps can oversee only a limited number of people unprepared to conduct what should be their own independent work. Unfortunately, the organization may reward its research pimps well, and those who become ever more dependent on them will do the same. This method may come to be viewed, often by non-research-intensive institutions, as the only viable solution for producing grant applications,

but is shortsighted in regard to the long-term development of the organization.

CONDUCT OF RESEARCH

There are as many political considerations associated with the actual conduct of a research project as there are with selection of a research topic. They begin with development of a research team, choice of research team members and the role each plays in the project, and selection of the site of data collection. The politics of the home institution are a significant potential source of conflict.

SELECTION OF THE RESEARCH TEAM

While some in nursing may still argue for research conducted by "only nurses," research to improve patient care necessitates involvement of interdisciplinary health care teams and a recognition that nursing alone does not control patient outcomes. However, who is included on the research team and who is excluded can be a political hot potato. Careful selection of members of the research team—co-investigators, project directors, specialty personnel (e.g., economists, statisticians, clinical specialists), and research assistants—is critical. In some institutions, the chief executive officer or department head may not support an individual's being included on a research team. This may be due to a personal dislike or fear of the person or a wish to dismiss him in the future. Success on a study, even as a team member, might make future termination more difficult, so the individual's participation is opposed.

A major concern of principal investigators is putting together a team that can work effectively as a collective. This can be problematic from the start. In one study examining caffeine intake during pregnancy, a physician refused to participate as a coinvestigator if the obstetrical nursing clinical director was a member of the research team. Apparently, these two individuals had a longstanding history of problems. Avoid such problems by investigating relationships among potential team members ahead of time.

Choose research team members not only for compatibility but for essential knowledge and skills, resources, and influence. For example, in clinical studies, access to patient populations is essential. Physicians often act as gatekeepers, sometimes blocking access to the patient group under investigation unless they are involved in the project. In one of our studies, which examined the most effective nonpharmacologic methods for treating breast engorgement in nonlactating women, a key physician in the obstetrical department would not grant access to inpatient postpartum women because "there is a pill to treat this problem." On further investigation it became clear that he felt bypassed because he had not been consulted on the research proposal before it was funded. Ego problems of this sort are not uncommon.

When physicians serve as coinvestigators, there are often benefits: added expertise and different views, access to subjects, increased subject safety, and opportunities for nurse-physician collaboration. Additionally, collaborative relationships with members of other disciplines promote a positive image of nurses as rigorous researchers and valued colleagues. Benefits to physicians and members of other disciplines from involvement in nurse-led research include money, involvement in funded research, publication, and presentations. For new physicians, this involvement often provides needed research training, research courses not being part of the required medical school curricula (Clinical Research Summit, 1999).

Research that requires nursing staff participation can be facilitated if key members of the staff are involved as coinvestigators, project directors, or research assistants. If the staff members are not compensated or do not see the value of their involvement, the result can be devastating. Feelings of frustration and outright resistance can occur when staff members believe that their time is being consumed by research tasks not clearly linked with patient care or their job responsibilities. They may also resent the fact that patients' available time is being used to meet research requirements rather than for needed care.

Staff nurses who are involved in developing research protocols generally have a clearer understanding of why a certain protocol is necessary and provide extremely valuable information concerning practical day-to-day aspects of conducting the research within their institutions. The specific role that staff nurses play as members of the research team is determined by a variety of factors, among which are available time, job requirements, interest, research preparation, and institutional support for these activities. Benefits can accrue to individuals involved in the project, too: tuition subsidy, coauthor status on publications, the opportunity to present the research, participation in additional research, and participation in a mentoring relationship with senior researchers. The potential career advantages for staff members are apparent in one example involving a funded pilot study on factors affecting milk volume in mothers delivering low-birth-weight infants (Brown, Hollingsworth, & Armstrong, 1990-1991). A staff nurse was the study research assistant at the data collection site. She was able to document her participation in the study in her application to a doctoral program, receive a small stipend plus tuition reimbursement for two doctoral courses, present one paper and two posters on the study, be listed as second author on one publication (Brown, Spatz, Hollingsworth, & Armstrong, 1992), and gain research skills that were helpful to her during her doctoral program. On completion of her terminal degree, she became a coinvestigator on a study funded by the NINR (Brown, Meier, Spitzer, Finkler, Jacobsen, & Spatz, 1995-2000).

SELECTION OF SITE FOR DATA COLLECTION

Numerous factors affect selection of the site for data collection: the number of available subjects, the number of other studies being conducted at the site, pragmatic concerns such as travel to and from the site, established connections at the potential site, and the feeling of cooperation (or lack thereof) with key people. Political considerations are significant, as the following example shows.

Several years ago, a nursing colleague who had received major NIH funding for a study on elderly persons found herself embroiled in a fight for access to adequate numbers of subjects. A physician (who had a smaller amount of funding) wanted to begin his study with the same subject population and informed the nurse researcher that she could "have" the subjects he would not be using. However, the nursing research review committee for the hospital had reviewed and approved her study several months previously, while the physician had never bothered to submit his study to the committee. Citing overlap with an ongoing study previously approved, the committee denied the physician access to subjects at the site. Though this was a "gutsy call" by the group, they were backed up by longstanding procedures at the institution. Situations such as this demonstrate the need to follow established institutional review guidelines, monitor the site continually for potential difficulties, and maintain lines of communications and good relationships with key individuals at the data collection site. Ongoing communication is particularly important in today's climate of institutional reorganization, restructuring, and partnering.

The political game at the site may be a matter of raw power—or, at the opposite extreme, only of naiveté. In a study involving children with AIDS, a nurse researcher was denied access to a data collection site (one of two in the city) unless she turned the study and its data over to a physician as principal investigator. The study was her idea, and she had already developed the proposal. She chose to seek access to the other site and was successful; however, her subject numbers would have been doubled if she had been permitted entry into both institutions.

In another example, a nurse researcher had been conducting a pilot study on caffeine and pregnancy for more than a year. She invited a toxicologist to be a coinvestigator after the study had been developed and funded. His laboratory ran the analyses of serum and salivary caffeine. His was the only laboratory doing these analyses in the city, but there was no reduction in the price of the analyses, even though he was named as a coinvestigator. When the head of his department wanted to know what studies would be submitted for major funding within the next year in the department, the toxicologist telephoned the nurse principal investigator. He indicated what information was needed by his department head and said that if a major study were to be submitted based on the pilot, it would have to come from his department, not from the nursing school, because his department, as he informed her, needed the indirect cost recovery. Not sure whether

he was naive or attempting a power move, the nurse researcher was firm: if major funding was sought as a result of the pilot, the application would originate from the nursing school. She pointed out that she had come to him with a study already developed and funded and had asked him to join the work, that he was providing no reduction in the cost of the analyses, and that the nursing school also needed indirect cost recovery from its researchers. She concluded by saying that she hoped that her position was clear and that she had addressed his concerns, because although she would prefer not to end their work together she would send her samples to a laboratory in another city if necessary. He not only grasped the message but gained a new perspective on nurses.

It is unfortunate that competitive nursing colleagues often play similar games. In another study, a nursing clinical director stopped progress on a nurse's study for months to demonstrate her own power and expertise. The clinical director, who served on the hospital nursing research review committee, would not approve this study, citing "lack of scientific merit." She claimed that the investigators were not attempting anything new and that their methods were flawed. The investigators received from her a two-page, single-spaced list of questions to be answered before the committee. Not one member of the committee had directed a funded research study, and most had never been involved in research. As a result, the principal investigator had to educate the committee about research, as well as respond to their questions, many of them tangential at best. Although the study was ultimately approved, the delay of 3 months (during the summer, a time of high productivity for investigators in academia), put the study significantly behind schedule. The nursing clinical director who created such serious roadblocks had been a project manager and research assistant on a federally funded study; however, the study under review by the hospital nursing research review committee had already been approved and funded by four national organizations (a fact overlooked by and perhaps not important to her).

Similar issues can occur with large parent organizations' institutional review boards. It is important to determine the actual functioning of an institution's research review board. The board is formally charged with assessing the protection of human subjects but often reviews the scientific merit of studies, though this is not its primary responsibility. It is important to know the committee members, their research knowledge and experience, and their review biases and practices. It is also important to contact or court a committee member who can champion your study.

In selecting a site for data collection you can go through the proper channels and maintain relationships and communication, but often you cannot counteract the behaviors of individuals who view themselves as research or practice experts in competition with you. Situations like the examples cited are not uncommon. Other commonly experienced problems involve physicians who cannot comprehend why a nurse is investigating a certain problem they view as a "medical" one.

HOME SITE POLITICAL ISSUES

Researchers always contend with political issues in their home institutions, the recipients of the money for their research. Some such issues result from politics inherent in the parent organization (e.g., university), while others arise from school or unit politics. At the university or parent-organizational level, there are many political issues. Because nursing was the one of the last disciplines to join academia and because most nursing schools are among the smallest schools in their universities, nursing often lacks power in the university. In addition, members of the university community may not know that nurses conduct their own research and may not understand or respect the type of research that nurses conduct.

In many institutions, nursing is thus seen as a minor player (or no player at all) in the research arena. As a result, nurses are often excluded from forums where research issues are decided. At one university, when the search committee for a high-level institutional research official did not include a representative from nursing, the nurse administrator was told that this was because the university was looking for committee members who "knew something about research." When a meeting of the schools' research deans was scheduled for a time when the nurse representative was out of town, she was told that the time was selected based on the availability of "the important people."

When a funder's request for proposals specifies that only one grant can be submitted from an institution, the nursing school may not be invited to even submit a proposal for the internal competition, and if invited, the nursing proposal is often are not selected because of concern on the university's selection committee's part that nursing proposals will not fare well in the external funder's competition. Selection of a nurse principal investigator for an across-school collaborative grant often requires considerable lobbying behind the scenes.

Political issues at the school or department level are numerous, including conflict about the value of research, the type and focus of research, and allocation of scarce resources. At one time there was a considerable divide between nurse educators and nurses in practice. Educators often chided practicing nurses for not delivering "state of the art" care, while practicing nurses accused nurse educators of not being clinically relevant; "If you can't do, teach" was a refrain commonly heard from practicing nurses. Much of this divide has closed as educators practice, clinicians seek further education, and positions for clinician-educators increase in schools of nursing.

Currently, however, a similar divide exists between education and research in many schools of nursing. Faculty members are often divided into camps over which part of the school's mission—education or research—should get priority. Arguments are frequently heard that there is too little emphasis on teaching and students, too much on research. Other disputes center on what is the operational definition of nursing research and whether faculty research need be funded when the faculty member is being considered for promotion and tenure. Each issue is loaded with political ramifications.

In reality, research can bring substantial financial support to a school. Indeed, in fiscal year 2000, the five schools with the highest amount of NIH funding in the U.S. received between $3.7 million and $12.4 million for research (NIH, 2001). Proponents of funded research argue that in addition to the funds that directly support the research study, funded research provides indirect cost recovery, substantial financial support for students, enhanced educational experiences for students, and improvements in nursing practice and subsequently in patient outcomes. In many research-intensive schools of nursing, dollars for student financial support realized through funded faculty research exceed those from all other sources of student scholarship aid combined. This is also true for schools with very large endowments. Students also benefit by participating in the faculty's research by publishing and presenting with faculty. One undergraduate group, for example, presented at the 1999 American Academy of Nursing meeting in Acapulco (Brooten, Youngblut, Donnelly, & Brown, 1998; Brooten, Youngblut, Roberts, Montgomery, Standing, Hemstrom, Suresky, & Polis, 1999). Proponents also note that research brings indirect cost recovery dollars to the school or unit, freeing other money for new initiatives or additional faculty or as a hedge against years with decreased student enrollment. This is an especially important factor for schools of nursing in private institutions. The research dollars for direct costs pay a portion of the faculty salary of the investigator and coinvestigators as well as of the costs of conducting the research and of support for students employed on the project as research assistants, data entraps, project directors, and so on. And knowledge gained to improve nursing practice is essential to teaching "state of the art" nursing care.

An essential point often missing from these debates is critical to nursing education: Faculty research is necessary in teaching doctoral students, just as faculty practice is in teaching Master's degree students. It is as sterile for doctoral students to be taught to conduct and publish research by faculty who do not conduct and publish research as it is for nurse practitioner students to be taught by faculty who do not practice. Faculty research is to doctoral education what faculty practice is to nurse practitioner education.

Apart from these political issues, pragmatic issues regarding allocation of scare resources (especially space, release time, and support services) are very real for all investigators and fraught with poli-

tics. The need for space to do the research and the need for support services, such as secretarial services, are often some of the first issues to be resolved in any newly funded study (Youngblut & Brooten, in press).

Securing the space needed to conduct the research often requires education of the administration, money to underwrite the cost of the space, and political pull. If the conduct of funded research is a relatively new activity for the institution, the administration may not understand your need for space. One investigator was informed that because she did not have an animal colony, she did not need research space. She was expected to store her equipment, supplies, and data forms in her existing— and already overcrowded—office and to carry data forms back and forth from her home to her office in a suitcase. The situation was eventually resolved through several discussions with the chief executive officer of the organization.

Because institutional space costs money, you will be far better able to negotiate space needs if your research is funded. If the institution receives indirect cost recovery from the study, the indirect costs should cover your space needs. But indirect cost recovery may be inadequate to pay for the space needs, or there may not be any available space. Sometimes this problem can be addressed in the proposal and additional money secured for space rental for the duration of the study, and sometimes the space issue is political. An analysis of organizations often reveals individuals who have no funding but have ample research space, whereas other, well-funded investigators have little, even inadequate space. Sometimes this has to do with the timing of space allocation—who needed it first—and sometimes it is a statement of value and control by the head of the organization. Allocation of space sends a powerful message. In some instances, being an organization player or a confidante to the chief or to those in control of resource allocation will count far more than one's merit as a nurse researcher.

Another political issue often encountered at the home site involves the negotiation of release time to conduct the study. If the study has received major funding, a proportion of the principal investigator's salary has been included in that funding to pay for their release to conduct the study. In theory, the organization uses this money to pay someone else to conduct that portion of the investigator's regular work from which they are released. Sometimes it actually works this way, but some investigators ignore this expectation and are funded through a combination of grants for 100% or more of their salary. Obviously, the funding sources do not know that the investigator is committed for more than 100% of salaried time. This approach brings more money, resources, or power to the investigator or their department. Some organizations set up disincentives to such behavior. In these situations, the investigator may be funded for only 30% of the time that is to be allocated to the study. Rather than assisting the investigator by relieving their workload, the organization simply assumes that the individual will conduct the study in addition to the current workload—and uses the 30% salary support for other purposes. The investigator, concerned with maintaining the success of the investigation, is compelled to assume an extra-heavy workload. This is an intolerable situation, even in the short run.

POLITICS IN DISSEMINATION OF RESEARCH FINDINGS

Just as politics affects the choice of research topic and the conduct of work, so it colors the dissemination of research findings. Here the issues generally center on three questions:

1. Where should the findings be disseminated?
2. Whose names should appear on the publications and in what order?
3. Who should participate in the research presentations?

The actual study findings should influence decisions on where to publish and present the results. It seems clear that study results with broad public-policy implications should be disseminated to the broadest possible audience, but even these situations may be fraught with political overtones. One nursing study demonstrated a reduction of 27% in hospital charges and a reduction of 22% in physician charges when low-birth-weight infants were discharged from the hospital early and received home followup by nurse specialists (Brooten, Kumar, Brown, Butts, Finkler, Bakewell-Sachs, Gibbons, & Delivoria-Papadopoulos, 1986). The nurse researchers submitted the study results to the *New England Journal of Medicine* because they knew that papers published in this respected journal tend to receive broad attention in the lay professional press. Although the research was published and received national and international media coverage, this did not stop nursing colleagues, including some in rather powerful positions, from criticizing the investigators for publishing their findings in a medical rather than a nursing journal. Other nurse researchers have reported that responses to their requests to the national nurses' professional association for help in further disseminating their research findings have been negative on the ground that the researchers' findings were reported in a medical rather than a nursing journal. Such a myopic view does not help to highlight nursing's contribution to improving health care with multiple audiences.

The politics involved in deciding whose names should appear on publications and in what order, and who should make presentations, is common to all studies. The principal investigator of a study has the responsibility for oversight of the rigor, integrity, and successful conduct of the study, and this includes dissemination of the study findings. Though the principal investigator is therefore first author on the main findings, coinvestigators may be first authors on secondary findings from the study. Inclusion of additional coauthors generally depends on their contributions to the manuscript. A general rule is that a coauthor must have made a significant contribution to the manuscript's development and submission. Currently, many journals (e.g., *Journal of the American Medical Association, Journal of the American Public Health Association*) now require statements indicating the role of each author in the development of the manuscript. Principal investigators should be listed as authors of all manuscripts resulting from studies they have conducted. Their authorship demonstrates oversight and agreement regarding the validity of the data presented and any conclusions drawn from work they headed.

Each research team or each principal investigator ultimately has to decide how to handle these issues.

ISSUES	GREAT/FINE					PROBLEM
1. Topic—Importance and Potential Yield to:						
a. Me—my career, program of research	5	4	3	2	1	0
b. My organization	5	4	3	2	1	0
c. Profession	5	4	3	2	1	0
d. Society	5	4	3	2	1	0
2. Funding Possibilities						
a. Federal	5	4	3	2	1	0
b. Private	5	4	3	2	1	0
c. Level of indirects	5	4	3	2	1	0
3. Research Team—Who, Why, Compatibility						
a. Specific skill people						
1. _____	5	4	3	2	1	0
2. _____	5	4	3	2	1	0
3. _____	5	4	3	2	1	0
b. Access people						
1. _____	5	4	3	2	1	0
2. _____	5	4	3	2	1	0
c. Students/staff						
1. _____	5	4	3	2	1	0
2. _____	5	4	3	2	1	0
4. Site for Data Collection						
a. Established connections/key people	5	4	3	2	1	0
b. Available subjects	5	4	3	2	1	0
c. Ongoing studies with same population	5	4	3	2	1	0
d. Research review committee—facilitative?	5	4	3	2	1	0
e. Travel to site	5	4	3	2	1	0
5. Home Site						
a. Space needs	5	4	3	2	1	0
b. Release time	5	4	3	2	1	0
c. Research support services	5	4	3	2	1	0

Figure 20-1   Politics of research: A checklist from the trenches.

Continued

ISSUES	GREAT/FINE					PROBLEM
6. Dissemination—Where, By Whom						
a. Main findings						
1. Interdisciplinary	5	4	3	2	1	0
2. Intradisciplinary	5	4	3	2	1	0
3. First author	5	4	3	2	1	0
4. Coauthors—who, why						
a. _____	5	4	3	2	1	0
b. _____	5	4	3	2	1	0
b. Secondary findings						
1. Interdisciplinary	5	4	3	2	1	0
2. Intradisciplinary	5	4	3	2	1	0
3. First author	5	4	3	2	1	0
4. Coauthors—who, why						
a. _____	5	4	3	2	1	0
b. _____	5	4	3	2	1	0

Figure 20-1, cont'd Politics of research: A checklist from the trenches.

With a team approach, the work usually receives broader dissemination, and more people can gain from the effort. The cost of inclusion is generally minimal; the cost of exclusion is generally much greater. One guiding rule for principal investigators, however, is to control their own data. It is not uncommon for associates to publish or present study results as their own, without attribution to the team or the principal investigator or the funding agency. These situations can be minimized if the rules regarding publication and presentation are established at the start of the study, agreed to, recorded, and reviewed periodically during the course of the study. Problems can also be minimized if the principal investigator is the only one with access to the most current study results. This point became clear in one situation in which a physician coinvestigator planned to present at a research conference, as his own work, the preliminary findings of a study headed by nurses. He was stymied because the principal investigator was the only member of the team with the most current findings and would share them only during the routinely held meetings of the team.

Politics is an ever-present part of research, from the definition of what constitutes nursing research to choice of the research topic, conduct of the work, and dissemination of the findings. Refer to Figure 20-1 to evaluate the political health of your research and areas needing attention.

On behalf of all those who ever saw research as apolitical, pure, and holy, we now say: *Were we naïve, or what?!*

REFERENCES

Brooten, D. (1984). Making it in paradise. *Nursing Research, 33,* 318.

Brooten, D. (1997, February). *Nursing research in a managed care environment* (presentation to the National Institutes of Health). Washington, DC.

Brooten, D., Kumar, S., Brown, L., Butts, P., Finkler, S., Bakewell-Sachs, S., Gibbons, A., & Delivoria-Papadopoulos, M. (1986).

A randomized clinical trial of early hospital discharge and home follow-up of very low-birth weight infants. *New England Journal of Medicine, 315,* 934-939.

Brooten, D., Youngblut, J. M., Donnelly, S., & Brown, C. (1998, October). *Disseminating our breakthroughs: Enacting a strategic framework* (paper presented at the annual conference of the American Academy of Nursing). Acapulco, Mexico.

Brooten, D., Youngblut, J. M., Roberts, B. L., Montgomery, K., Standing, T. S., Hemstrom, M., Suresky, J., & Polis, N. (1999). Disseminating our breakthroughs: Enacting a strategic framework. *Nursing Outlook, 47,* 133-137.

Brown, L., Hollingsworth, A., & Armstrong, C. (1990-1991). *Factors affecting milk volume in mothers of VLBW infants.* Funded by grants from the Nutrition Center, Children's Hospital of Philadelphia, and Sigma Theta Tau International.

Brown, L., Meier, P., Spitzer, A., Finkler, S., Jacobsen, B., & Spatz, D. (1995-2000). *Breastfeeding services for LBW infants: Outcomes and cost.* Funded by a grant from the National Institute of Nursing Research (Grant No. R01-NR03881), National Institutes of Health, Washington, DC.

Brown, L., Spatz, D., Hollingsworth, A., & Armstrong, C. (1992). Promoting successful breastfeeding of mothers of LBW infants. *Journal of Perinatal Education, 1,* 20-24.

Clinical Research Summit. (1999). *Breaking the scientific bottleneck. Clinical research: A national call to action.* Washington, DC: Association of American Medical Colleges & American Medical Association.

Fawcett, J., Watson, J., Neuman, B., Hinton Walker, P., & Fitzpatrick, J. J. (2001). On nursing theories and evidence. *Journal of Nursing Scholarship, 33,* 115-119.

Mechanic, R. & Dobson, A. (1996). The impact of managed care on clinical research: A preliminary investigation. *Health Affairs, 15,* 72-89.

Meleis, A. (2001). Scholarship and the R01. *Journal of Nursing Scholarship, 33,* 104-105.

National Institutes of Health. (2001, March 19). *NIH support to US nursing schools, fiscal year 2000* Available online at silk.nih.gov/public/cbz2zoz.@www.nur.fy2000.dsncc.

National Institute of Nursing Research. (2001, June 17). *Mission statement.* Available online at www.nih.gov/ninr/a_mission. html.

Schmidt, P.S. (2001). A clash of values in the heartland. *The Chronicle of Higher Education, 47*(30), 25-28.

Suplee, C. (1991). Sex study is scrapped due to political concerns. *Philadelphia Inquirer, 324*(88), 14A.

Youngblut, J. M., & Brooten, D. (In press). Institutional research responsibilities and needed infrastructure. *Journal of Nursing Scholarship.*

Needlestick Injuries in the Workplace: Implications for Public Policy

Karen A. Daley

"Never doubt that a small group of thoughtful, committed citizens can change the world; indeed it is the only thing that ever has."

MARGARET MEAD

By July 1998, my clinical nursing career had spanned more than 25 years. For 22 of those years, emergency nursing was my chosen specialty. My entire nursing career had been spent in the same large Boston-area teaching hospital where, over many years, my professional practice and growth had been nurtured. I always felt fortunate and proud to be a nurse there. It was also the place where, in a split second, I was thrust into an unknown world—a world for which nothing in my previous experience could have prepared me.

In this world, I have been forced to deal with uncertainties that threatened every aspect of my life—my health, my career, my financial security, my self-image, and my relationships with others. Now, almost 3 years later, as I think back to my injury and its life-altering consequences, I see how easily it could have been prevented. Like so many injuries in the workplace, it did not have to happen.

MY INJURY

There was nothing unusual about that shift in July 1998. Like many others, it was busy. That particular day, I was assigned to perform triage. With a little more than an hour left in my 12-hour shift, a colleague asked if I would try to draw blood from one of her patients. I had someone cover triage and I went to see the patient—a frail, elderly man with dementia. I drew the blood and while holding pressure on the puncture site, I turned to dispose of the needle I had used. As I introduced the needle into

the sharps container on the wall behind me, I felt a sudden, sharp sting. A second needle wedged inside the needle box had stuck my index finger.

I have often been asked since then how I felt at that moment. I remember my first reaction was anger—the needle box had been a source of complaints in our unit. The second reaction was a strong impulse to ignore what had just happened. I remember thinking that I didn't want to deal with what would follow once I reported my exposure: staying beyond the end of my scheduled shift to be evaluated, coming in on my days off for follow-up lab tests, and the anxiety of thinking about what I might have been exposed to while waiting for results. I simply wanted to return to triage, finish what was left of my shift, and pretend it had never happened.

Fortunately, the nurse who had asked me to draw the blood was there when my injury occurred and must have sensed what I was thinking, because she insisted I sign in to be seen as a patient. As required by policy, 2 days later I returned to the hospital's occupational health clinic for baseline lab work and counseling. In the weeks and months that followed, I worked hard to put my injury out of my mind. I was largely successful in that effort—in fact, too successful.

Within 6 to 8 weeks, I began to experience a number of vague symptoms that I couldn't account for: weight loss, fatigue, insomnia, episodic nausea, and abdominal pain, among others. I just didn't feel well. Initially, I related my symptoms to the first anniversary of my closest brother's sudden death in a car crash. His death had been one of the most profound losses I had ever suffered, and it seemed a logical explanation for my symptoms.

However, my symptoms persisted, and by the time I finally scheduled an appointment with my primary care physician, I had lost about 12 pounds. An unremarkable examination and negative lab results failed to identify the underlying problem. Because it never occurred to me that my needlestick injury could in any way be related to my symptoms, I never thought to mention it.

After one more visit to my primary care physician, almost 5 months after my exposure, blood tests performed as part of routine occupational health clinic follow-up revealed incomprehensible news: my needlestick had infected me with both the human immunodeficiency virus (HIV) and hepatitis C virus (HCV).

NEEDLESTICK INJURIES AND WORKPLACE SAFETY

It is estimated that 400,000 to 600,000 needlestick injuries occur each year in the United States. There is also evidence to suggest that more than 80% of those injuries could be prevented through the use of safe needle technology available for more than 3 decades. Based on existing data at the time of my injury, and despite widespread and long-standing accessibility, it also appeared that less than 15% of employers were providing their employees with one or more types of these safer devices within their practice setting (American Nurses Association [ANA], 2000c).

As soon as it happened, I knew my injury could easily have been prevented, either by a safer disposal box or by some type of protective needle design. Such is the case for a large majority of needlestick injuries that occur every year in the United States. In the weeks that followed my injury, I learned more about the scope of the problem and the preventable nature and emotional toll of these injuries—before I ever knew the personal toll of my needlestick—and I asked legislative staff at the Massachusetts Nurses Association (MNA) to encourage introduction of a needlestick prevention bill. It would be the first such bill introduced in Massachusetts.

THE PERSONAL BECOMES PUBLIC

After the initial shock of learning that I was infected with two potentially life-threatening viruses, I kept the news largely to myself. I learned pretty quickly how emotionally draining it was for me to share the news with others. I also knew I needed to conserve emotional energy to deal with what had happened to me. For the first few weeks, I told only my closest friends and family. I also asked the occupational health staff not to disclose my identity to anyone else in the hospital. They respected my request.

It soon became apparent there were a number of decisions I would need to make, but initially I felt so overwhelmed that I focused only on those I actually had to make at that time, such as choosing a new primary care physician, one whose practice was not based in the setting where I had practiced for more than 25 years. I was referred to an infectious disease physician who specialized in the care of HIV-infected patients.

Almost immediately after learning about the infections that resulted from my needlestick, I decided not to return to clinical nursing in the emergency department where I had practiced since 1977, an emotional and extremely difficult loss for me. I left behind a practice that I loved and many close friends and colleagues, but within just a few weeks of beginning treatment, the debilitating effects of the drugs to combat the HIV and HCV would make it a physical impossibility for me to return to such a demanding setting.

A short time later, after returning from a trip to North Carolina to tell my younger sister the devastating news in person, I began to see my new primary care physician. For the first couple of months, I made almost weekly visits to see him because of the difficulty in stabilizing my care and treatment regimen. At the same time, I was learning about both viruses and focused on coming to terms with what had happened to me. Absolutely nothing in my world was the same as it had been just a few months before.

I then began a slow, deliberate process of disclosing my illnesses. First, I met face to face with several key hospital executives and shared with them the profound personal and physical effects of my injury: how preventable I realized it was; the uncertainties I was now facing as a result; and the importance of doing what they could to prevent similar injuries. I left that meeting with the assurance that they were committed to doing what was possible to prevent this from happening to others within the institution. To this day, they continue to meet that commitment. Safety sharps devices were introduced in a pilot program in the year after my injury and are now in use throughout the institution.

Once I had met with the hospital administration, I knew it wouldn't take long for the news to reach other hospital and MNA staff, so I decided to meet with my colleagues from the emergency department. Many were beginning to ask why I had been out of work so long. That meeting, although difficult, allowed me to tell them in person what had happened while reassuring them by my presence that I was doing well. I also asked the MNA's executive director to read a letter on my behalf that I had written to the staff sharing with them what had happened.

In the months that followed, I underwent aggressive medical therapy to reduce my viral loads and prevent further damage to my immune system and liver. It's impossible for me to describe what this ordeal has been like for me: the physical toll of the drugs; the energy they stole, leaving me with numbing fatigue; the fear and uncertainty I experienced at times; and the moments when it actually seemed to me that the effects and toxicities associated with the treatments might be worse than to simply allow damage from the viruses to progress unchallenged over time. Looking back over these past 2½ years, sometimes I'm amazed I was able to get through it. The support of friends and family helped so much. Today I feel extremely grateful, more than anything else.

PUTTING A FACE ON THE ISSUE

I struggled for some time to come to terms with the anger I felt and to understand why this had happened to me. But I've also always believed that things happen for a reason, regardless of whether it appears to make sense at the time. Once I moved beyond the anger, I was able to see more clearly that although I couldn't do anything to change what had happened to me, I could perhaps use my experience and position within the nursing community to prevent an injury like mine from happening to others.

Beyond my work setting, the first real opportunity I had to put a face on this issue was at a legislative hearing before the Massachusetts Joint Health Care Committee in April 1999. At that hearing, I spoke publicly for the first time about my injury and the infections I suffered as a result, and I offered testimony on the needlestick prevention bill MNA had endorsed the previous November. Following my testimony and that of other health care community representatives, the committee voted unanimously that same afternoon to report the bill favorably. As a result of the hearing testimony and the attention paid to it by statewide print and television media, the commissioner of public health also called for the immediate formation of a Needlestick Prevention Advisory Committee under the Department of Public Health (DPH). He charged the committee with examining regulatory approaches to reduce needlestick injuries to health care workers across the state.

By April 1999, there was evidence of a burgeoning movement around the United States to prevent needlestick injuries among health care workers. The previous July, California had become the first state to enact legislation mandating use of safer devices. Tennessee followed in early 1999, becoming the second state to pass such a bill, one that called for state health officials to review available safer technologies and make further recommendations. In 1999, needlestick prevention legislation was introduced in a total of 22 states; by the end of the year, 5 had enacted it (ANA, 2000a).

Since 1982, the ANA had been at the forefront of the issue, advocating federal legislation to mandate the use of safer devices through amendment of the Occupational Safety and Health Administration (OSHA) Bloodborne Pathogen Standard. Senator Harry Reid (D-NV) was the first to champion the cause in Congress, sponsoring a needlestick prevention bill in every session since 1997, but with little success despite the consistent support of the ANA and other health care worker unions.

Following my testimony on the MNA bill, I attended the spring 1999 ANA Constituent Assembly, a 2-day meeting of state association presidents and executive directors held in Washington, DC. I expected some colleagues at the meeting would have heard about my situation. With the permission of the ANA president and Constituent Assembly chair, I addressed the assembly shortly after the meeting opened. I shared with them what had happened to me as a result of a needlestick and my willingness to do whatever I could to raise awareness among nurses and help move legislation within their individual states. That moment became the catalyst for a whirlwind of activism on local, state, and national levels, and I began to speak around the country. Over the next 2 years, I traveled to more than 15 states to assist in an ongoing campaign to educate nurses and legislators on the importance of needlestick injury prevention.

A COMING TOGETHER OF INTERVENING FACTORS

The time was right for serious reform to occur for several reasons. Safer needle systems and technologies had evolved to the point where many products were clearly demonstrating their effectiveness in the settings where they were in use. The pioneering spirit and courage of a Pennsylvania nurse named Lynda Arnold, who had contracted HIV several years before from a needlestick, laid important groundwork and brought attention to the issue as she waged a campaign to encourage hospitals to voluntarily commit to using safer devices. In the spring of 1999, OSHA was also engaged in a process of collecting data from hospitals to assess the overall effectiveness of engineered sharps protection devices in preventing needlesticks (OSHA, U.S. Department of Labor, 1999). That request for information would subsequently provide unequivocal evidence of the effectiveness of safer needle devices. Every one of the more than 300 responding hospitals using safer devices in their work settings reported a reduction in the number of needlestick injuries.

Several other factors brought about a shift in the political environment. An expanded coalition of powerful stakeholders, including the ANA, the American Hospital Association (AHA), specialty nursing organizations, other health care worker unions, and manufacturers were working together

to educate employers and workers as well as to put pressure on legislators.

Hepatitis C, now considered the greatest health risk faced by health care workers resulting from needlesticks, and the primary reason for liver transplants in the United States, was gaining widespread attention in the media. Finally—and most unfortunately—stories like Lynda Arnold's and mine were becoming all too familiar and were viewed as a serious wake-up call for the health care industry and policymakers who had the power to bring about needed reform.

REGULATORY AND LEGISLATIVE ACTIVITY

In May 1999, Representatives Pete Stark (D-CA) and Marge Roukema (R-NJ) co-sponsored House Resolution (HR) 1899, also known as the Health Care Worker Needlestick Prevention Act of 1999, to amend OSHA's Bloodborne Pathogens Standard by requiring health care facilities to use safer sharps devices and systems. An identical bill sponsored by Senators Barbara Boxer (D-CA) and Harry Reid (D-NV) was introduced into the Senate 6 days later. At a press conference held at the U.S. Capitol before the National Press Corps to announce the introduction of the House bill, I offered a statement on behalf of the ANA, along with Representative Stark, the vice president of Kaiser Permanente in California, and the president of the Service Employees International Union (SEIU).

In June of the same year, the ANA launched a new "Safe Needles Save Lives" campaign in an effort to coordinate all the needlestick injury prevention professional advocacy activities—including federal and state regulatory, workplace, and collective bargaining strategies—within ANA and its constituent member state associations (ANA, 1999a). As part of the campaign over the next year, the ANA co-sponsored educational conferences in a number of states to train nurses in the evaluation, selection, and implementation of safer devices in the workplace.

In September, I traveled on two separate occasions to Washington, DC, again at the invitation of the ANA. The first event was an educational briefing hosted by the Congressional Women's Caucus, where I shared my story to educate congressional staff who wanted to learn more about needlestick injuries. By the time the briefing was held, HR 1899 had gained the bipartisan support of 120 sponsors in the House as well as the support of more than 30 organizations representing a coalition of health care workers, nurses, physicians, public health associations, consumer advocacy groups, and manufacturers (ANA, 1999b). It had been hoped beforehand that the briefing would attract additional House sponsors; afterward, the entire Caucus membership signed on in support of the bill.

I returned to Washington for the second time in September on a 2-day visit. My mission this time was a bit more challenging. The Senate bill, although identical to the House version, was not garnering as much support—and little, if any, support from Senate Republican members, who controlled the majority vote at the time. It was clear that without bipartisan support in both the Senate and the House, the bill was unlikely to pass.

My goal was to meet with the staff of key Senate Republican leaders to solicit additional sponsors for the bill. Over those 2 days, an ANA legislative staff member and I met with top-level staff of 11 Republican leaders, among them Representative Cass Ballenger (R-NC), who would later play a pivotal role in moving the federal legislation forward.

Resistance to bill sponsorship related to several areas of concern expressed by the Republican leadership of the time: the increased cost of safer devices; the widespread perception that employer investment in safer needle systems was not cost-effective and that it would add an undue financial burden, particularly in rural settings; lack of willingness to support any legislation that created new OSHA mandates for constituents; and finally, a clear reluctance to offer support for the legislation if it meant standing alone or apart from other Republican senators.

During those meetings, the most common questions I heard from legislative staff, often even before they requested any background or information on the bill, were "What will this bill cost?" and "Who else is supporting it?" Staff resistance seemed to lessen, however, as I shared my own personal experience and provided evidence that these devices were demonstrating effectiveness in preventing needlestick injuries, thereby reducing follow-up costs. Most legislative staff members were also initially unaware of the fact that, once safer devices became the norm within the industry, market costs would approach the amount currently being spent on conventional devices.

In October, Senate floor debate began on the bill. Co-sponsors included Senators Reid (D-NV), Kennedy (D-MA), Boxer (D-CA), and Jeffords (R-VT), chairman of the powerful Health, Education, Labor, and Pension Committee.

REGULATORY AND LEGISLATIVE VICTORIES

In November, two major victories occurred. First, OSHA released a new Bloodborne Pathogens Standard Compliance Directive that, based on the experience reported by over 300 hospitals, recognized safer devices as the primary line of defense against needlestick injuries. The directive instructed OSHA compliance officers who inspect health care facilities to fine employers for failing to use engineering and work practice controls to reduce needlestick injuries. Second, the National Institute of Occupational Safety and Health (NIOSH) published an alert called *Preventing Needlestick Injuries in Health Care Settings,* which focused additional media attention on the importance of health care worker involvement in needlestick injury prevention efforts (National Institute of Occupational Safety and Health, 2000).

While a welcome step forward, the compliance directive fell short of providing assurance that employers under federal jurisdiction would comply with new OSHA recommendations requiring the use of safer devices for several reasons. First, enforcement required a site visit by an OSHA compliance officer to a facility, which was triggered only by an employee complaint. Second, despite its new directive, OSHA had been provided no additional resources for enforcement and at its current funding level was budgeted to make a spontaneous inspection visit to any facility only about once every 75 years. Finally, amendment of the actual Bloodborne Pathogens Standard (originally adopted in 1991) through normal channels and processes could reasonably be expected to take up to 10 years. In the meantime, many more hundreds of thousands of preventable needlestick injuries to health care workers could be expected to occur.

By May 2000, HR 1899 had 177 sponsors in the House. While the number of Democratic sponsors on the Senate side had grown considerably, Republican sponsorship had not. In states across the country, however, the issue was gaining visibility and legislative support. Since California first enacted legislation in 1998, 10 more states, including New Jersey, Tennessee, Texas, West Virginia, Maine, Hawaii, Maryland, Georgia, Indiana, and Minnesota, had enacted legislation of one kind or another. Legislation had been introduced for consideration in the 2000 session in another 20 states (ANA, 2000b). The message to Congress should have been clear at that point—that the need for such health and safety legislation crossed all geographic, regional, and political boundaries. Instead, it appeared the groundswell of state activity was having little effect on the Republican leadership in Congress.

Less than a month later, in June, a congressional hearing was convened before the Subcommittee on Workforce Protections of the House Committee on Education and the Workforce. Scheduled by Representative Ballenger's chief legal counsel, the purpose of the hearing was to receive testimony on the adequacy of the OSHA compliance directive in addressing health and safety needs of providers with respect to needlestick injury prevention.

Once again I had the opportunity to provide testimony on behalf of the ANA, along with the four others invited to speak by the committee chair, among them OSHA Secretary Charles Jeffress. In my testimony, I shared the ANA's position on why it was so important for Congress to take action beyond the OSHA directive and amend the Bloodborne Pathogens Standard through federal statute.

By the time the 2-hour hearing concluded, subcommittee chair Ballenger and ranking member Major Owens (D-NY) voiced a new appreciation for the serious and preventable nature of health risks from needlesticks and a clearer understanding of the limitations of the OSHA compliance directive. Most important, both expressed interest in moving needlestick prevention legislation through their subcommittee and Congress before the session was due to adjourn in October.

In the weeks following the hearing, under Representative Ballenger's leadership, meetings were convened with the major stakeholders involved in the issue, including the ANA and AHA, device manufacturers, key legislative leadership, and other health care worker unions. On October 4, a new bill, entitled the Needlestick Prevention and Safety Act, built upon changes reflected in the November 1999 OSHA compliance directive, was introduced on the House floor by Representative Ballenger. In the absence of any dissenting debate, the bill passed the same day by unanimous consent. On October 24 an identical Senate version also passed by unanimous consent. Senator Kennedy was kind enough to call me shortly after its passage to inform me personally that the bill was now on its way to President Clinton's desk.

On November 6, 2000, I was honored to be among about 20 individuals invited to the Oval Office to witness President Clinton sign the Needlestick Safety Prevention Act into law. That moment represented the culmination of years of effort by individuals across the country, many of them nurses, who worked tirelessly to educate policymakers and build coalitions in order to bring about needed reform.

The new law amends the OSHA Bloodborne Pathogens Standard to require the use of safer devices "where appropriate." Exceptions to the mandate are granted only in cases where the technology is shown to be not yet advanced enough to meet a specialized need, as in the case of small children or certain medical procedures. Also mandated by the new law is the collection of device-specific information on all injuries, including manufacturer. Most important, the new federal law requires that employers involve front-line health care workers in the selection and evaluation of these devices (OSHA, U.S. Department of Labor, 2001).

A few months earlier, in August 2000, Massachusetts became the eighteenth state to enact needlestick prevention. The Act Relative to Needlestick Injury Prevention extends the requirement for use of safer devices to all hospitals licensed by the Massachusetts DPH. Compliance with the provisions contained in the new state law is tied to hospital licensure in Massachusetts, creating an exceptionally

Karen A. Daley, RN, MPH, was a leader in the development and passage of legislation to protect nurses from needlestick injuries. Her instrumental role was recognized when she was invited to the White House Oval Office to witness President Bill Clinton sign the Needlestick Safety and Prevention Act into law on November 6, 2000. The signing represented the culmination of years of effort by individuals across the country, many of them nurses, who worked tirelessly to educate policymakers and build coalitions to bring about needed reform.

strong incentive for employers. In addition, hospitals in Massachusetts—as well as ambulatory centers covered under any such license—are now required to develop and update an exposure control plan and to report sharps injury log data annually to the DPH. The law also established a Needlestick Injury Prevention Advisory Committee that advises and assists the DPH and hospital employers as the newly promulgated regulations are implemented.

CHALLENGES AHEAD

The political strategies illustrated by the regulatory and legislative successes related to needlestick injury prevention are ones used successfully throughout public policy arenas to influence change. Whether working for change in the workplace, the community, or the government, effective strategies are likely to include coalition building, identification of obstacles and solutions, seeking out those who have the power to influence and create change, and active participation in the political process.

I wish it were possible to say that the reform necessary to prevent the majority of future needlestick injuries occurred with recent passage of state and federal legislation. While there is no question that those reforms represent important progress, the changes health care workers will experience as a result—most notably improved access to safer devices—are simply initial steps toward creating a safer environment for health care workers.

Challenges remain with regard to every aspect of health and safety in the workplace. For employers, it means making a firm commitment to create a culture of safety. Injury prevention, not treatment, should be the true priority. Occupational health systems must be designed to both support and facilitate care of employees. Routine sharing of best practices needs to become the norm in all health care organizations.

For health care workers, the challenge means knowing your rights and no longer tolerating unacceptable health and safety risks in the workplace. It means observing health and safety precautions, reporting injuries when they occur, and getting actively involved on safety committees. As opportunities arise to offer input into the selection and evaluation of safer needle devices in a nursing unit, it means being willing to perform a pilot study and provide feedback on device effectiveness. It also means identifying existing obstacles to safety, and working with colleagues and management to identify and implement strategies to overcome them. Collective action is one of the most valuable tools for addressing health and safety issues in the workplace.

Perhaps one of the most important things to remember is that when it comes to creating needed change in your workplace or practice, you are the expert. Legislators and policymakers depend on shared personal experience and professional expertise to make informed decisions and formulate sound public policy.

It is time for the health care industry and nurses across the country to adopt a culture in which the health and safety of those who provide the care should be at least as important as that of the patients we provide care for—a radical but timely concept, and one necessary for the health and survival of our profession.

REFERENCES

American Nurses Association. (1999a, June 11). Needlestick prevention bill introduced in the Senate: ANA announces "Safe Needles Save Lives" campaign. *Capitol Update, 17*(10), 1.

American Nurses Association. (1999b, September 17). Congressional briefing on needlestick protections. *Capitol Update, 17*(15), 3.

American Nurses Association. (2000a, January 5). *Needlestick injury prevention legislation: Department of Government Relations chart.* Washington, DC: Author.

American Nurses Association. (2000b, May 4). *Needlestick injury prevention legislation: Department of Government Relations chart.* Washington, DC: Author.

American Nurses Association. (2000, July 21). ANA testifies on needlestick prevention legislation. *Capitol Update, 18*(11), 2.

National Institute of Occupational Safety & Health, Department of Health and Human Services. (2000). *Preventing needlestick injuries in health care settings* (publication no. 2000-108). Available online at www.cdc.gov/niosh/2000-108.html.

Occupational Safety and Health Administration, U.S. Department of Labor. (1999, May 20). *OSHA report: Record summary of the request for information on occupational exposure to bloodborne pathogens due to percutaneous injury.* Available online at www.osha-slc.gov/sltc/needlestick.

Occupational Safety and Health Administration, U.S. Department of Labor. (2001). *Revision to OSHA's bloodborne pathogens standard: Technical background and Summary.* Available online at www.osha-sic.gov/needlesticks/needlefact.html.

Chapter 21

Contemporary Issues in Government

MARY K. WAKEFIELD

DEBORAH B. GARDNER

SHARON E. GUILLETT

"Double—no, triple—our troubles and we'd still be better off than any other people on earth."

RONALD REAGAN

HISTORICAL PERSPECTIVE

Throughout the 1980s the relationships among local, state, and federal governments underwent significant change. With an expanding federal deficit and a struggling economy, more demands were placed on shrinking resources. Even while fiscal remedies were sought, the rhetoric of the 1980s—including "read my lips, no new taxes"—fueled voter resistance to tax increases. Federal officials were sensitive to voter sentiment, so instead of raising taxes to meet growing needs, the federal government withheld dollars and pushed more of the fiscal burden onto state and local governments. In response, state governments initially helped to fill the funding void faced by local governments. By the end of the decade, however, many states were experiencing budget shortfalls of their own and consequently reduced support to local governments.

In this environment, surging health care costs became particularly burdensome. By the end of the 1980s, the federal government was still long on rhetoric and short on action when it came to devising a plan that would contain rising health care costs and increase access to care. Under tremendous fiscal pressure, states were left to their own devices. By 1990, the United States spent 13% of its gross domestic product on health care while 15% of the population (37 million people) was without insurance for regular health care. In the same year, opinion polls found that 90% of the American public believed that fundamental change or a complete rebuilding of the health care system was needed (Pew Health Professions Commission, 1995). These circumstances led President Bill Clinton, in 1993, to propose major health care reform through the introduction of the Health Care Security Act. Caught up in a maelstrom of political and policy battles, the legislation was ultimately rejected.

Two opposed yet valid concerns made health care reform in the early 1990s more complex: (1) inadequate access (manifested primarily through uninsured status), and (2) rising health care costs. The strategies fashioned to address these policy challenges were viewed by powerful stakeholders, such as the business and insurance industries, as unpalatable. Reluctant to embrace sweeping reforms after the political backlash against the Clinton Health Care Security Plan, Congress preferred smaller, politically acceptable changes, including enactment of the Health Insurance Portability and Accountability Act and the State Children's Health Insurance Plan (S-CHIP). Meanwhile, in the vacuum left by the failure of comprehensive national reform, all states enacted legislation that incrementally improved access while containing costs.

Also in the early 1990s, the budget deficit had accrued to a grand total of around $3.6 trillion, and bipartisan consensus developed around the need to produce a balanced federal budget and eliminate the deficit. The deficit was problematic for policy-makers because money had to be continually borrowed to pay interest on the deficit, which meant that less money was available for other federal programs, including health care. Viewing the substantial and ever-increasing debt burden as unsustainable, the Administration and Congress coalesced around the need to eliminate the deficit and balance the federal budget. However, deficit reduction occurs through spending cuts and revenue generation (i.e., raising taxes), with few exceptions, and the latter is generally politically unpalatable. Consequently, proposals to create new federal programs and to renew or increase spending for old ones were examined for their effect on the federal budget. Interestingly (and quite unexpectedly), by the end of 1997 balancing the federal budget appeared to be an easier task because of consistent strong and unexpected economic growth and low inflation. However, by this time major changes in federal spending had been enacted, including serious cuts in the rate of growth in spending on the Medicare program.

By the end of the twentieth century, thanks to a strong economy and low rates of unemployment, discussion of the deficit disappeared from policy dialogues and was replaced by discussion of how to use the *surplus*. In the first few months of 2001, the Republican-controlled White House and Congress prioritized three options for using the budget surplus: (1) pay down the federal debt, (2) enhance federal programs, and (3) pass tax relief legislation. By Memorial Day 2001, Congress had enacted legislation to reduce taxes, a move that would consume over $1.2 trillion. Advocates from health, education, and other arenas predicted that, over time, pressure would be placed on important federal spending programs to accommodate the new tax cuts. Meanwhile, the number and types of strategies for developing an efficient health care system have increased as states "experiment." Given the interdependency of the state and federal governments, successful efforts to achieve increased efficiency and effectiveness in the health care system will be collaborative.

EMERGING HEALTH POLICY ISSUES: BALANCING COMPETING CONCERNS

For the foreseeable future, health policy concerns will continue to be highly visible in state and federal public policy arenas. An array of factors, including changing demographics, increasing prevalence of chronic illness, and technology breakthroughs, and many others, will continue to compete for the attention of policymakers.

MEDICARE

With support building throughout the 1990s to balance the federal budget, large federal programs experiencing significant growth captured the attention of policymakers. Social Security, defense spending, interest on the national debt, and Medicare were the largest components of the federal budget. Spending on other federal programs, such as education, foreign aid, and welfare, paled in comparison Compounding these circumstances were rapidly increasing health care costs. Annual health care costs exceeded $1 trillion in 1995 (Health Spending Projections, 1996) and are projected to reach $2.3 trillion by 2008 (www.hcfa.gov/stats/NHE-proj2000). Given the predicted bankruptcy of the Medicare Trust Fund in 2025 (www.ssa.gov/policy/pubs/SSB/v63n1y2000/631ss1.pdf), policymakers are turning their attention to the nation's most costly health care programs, Medicare and Medicaid.

Contributing to a projected increase in Medicare spending are demographic trends indicating that whereas 9% of the population was 65 or older in 1960, this number will be increased to 20% in 2030 by the retirement of the baby boom generation beginning in about 2010. In addition to pending demographic changes, utilization patterns of various health services have already changed markedly in the last 10 years. For example, the home health benefit became the fastest-growing part of the Medicare program, rising from $3.7 billion in 1990 to $12.7 billion in 1995 (Leon, Neuman, & Paremte, 1997). This increase amounted to an average annual growth rate of 38%, reflecting a surge in volume of services. It came as no surprise, then, that costs associated with the home health benefit received considerable attention and that plans to move it and other benefits, such as outpatient and skilled nursing facility care, to a prospective payment system were adopted in 1997. These payment changes, while putting palpable strain on health care systems, clearly helped to reign in Medicare spending and helped put off the projected bankruptcy of the Medicare program until the second decade of the twenty-first century.

With pressure both to keep Medicare solvent and to provide adequate payment coverage for its enrollees, a number of policy options continue to be considered. Debate surrounds how much money needs to be saved by Medicare and how those savings should be achieved, how to extend a needed prescription-drug benefit, and how to pay for long term care for Medicare beneficiaries. Comprehensive solutions to both challenges remain elusive.

Prescription Drug Benefits. It is not uncommon to hear anecdotal accounts from health care providers of elderly individuals on fixed incomes being forced to choose each month between paying for medications or for basic necessities such as clothing, rent, and food. While senior citizens rely more heavily on prescription drugs than other age cohorts, the problem of drug affordability is not unique to them. For example, it is estimated that 10 million children are uninsured, making their families vulnerable to high pharmaceutical costs (Cauchi, 2001).

Prices of prescription drugs can vary dramatically according to one's insurance coverage, place of purchase (e.g., pharmacy vs. mail order), identity of purchaser, drug country of origin, and other factors. For example, in 1999, Vermont women who traveled to Canada were able to purchase the widely prescribed breast cancer drug Tamoxifen at one tenth the U.S. price (Sanders, 2001). One source reported that U.S. consumers pay drug prices 72% to 102% higher than those paid by their counterparts in Canada and Mexico (Allen, 2000). These disparities prompted the organization of bus trips to Canada for senior citizens in search of less expensive drugs. Such trips were often referenced in the campaign rhetoric associated with more than one congressional race in 2000.

The fact that sick elderly persons without prescription drug coverage pay far more for drugs than do people with supplemental private insurance or coverage through Medicare managed-care plans has launched heated policy and political debates. In fact, the lack of affordable drug therapy for individuals and the cost of coverage through public programs such as Medicaid have prompted state actions, including price control legislation and antitrust cases (Frank, 2001). Nurses see the frustration and cynicism created among health care consumers by this situation; health care providers also question what is driving rapidly increasing drug costs.

Policymakers have concluded that health care costs are rising largely because of advances in medical technology and pharmaceuticals (Swartz, 2000). Prescription drugs are a vital tool for treatment of both chronic and acute medical conditions. Spending for prescription drugs in the United States was $91 billion in 1998, more than double that in 1990 (Poisal & Murray, 2001). According to the Center for Medicare and Medicaid Service (CMS), since 1995 the rate of increase in drug expenditures has been approximately twice that of total health care expenditures (Iglehart, 2001). In 1999, prescription drug spending increased by 18.4%, to $100 billion, while total health care spending increased 5.3% (Cauchi, 2001). The rapid growth of drug prices, enhancing their unavailability to vulnerable populations such as the poor elderly, has provided much of the political passion driving Congress to consider adding outpatient prescription drug coverage to Medicare benefits.

Prescription Drug Coverage and Supplemental Insurance Coverage. Prescription drug coverage is provided for a vast number of persons enrolled in private health insurance, government employee plans, or Medicaid. Currently, however, many of the 40 million elderly and disabled persons enrolled in Medicare have significant need for "affordable" access to prescription drugs. With few exceptions, Medicare provides drug coverage only to beneficiaries who are hospitalized or in skilled nursing facilities. Medicare beneficiaries are also responsible for covering some other health care services. In fact, the Medicare benefit package leaves beneficiaries liable for nearly half the costs of acute care services. In addition, beneficiaries pay 20% of physicians' fees with no annual cap on the amount. Thus, for Medicare beneficiaries prescription drugs are only one of a significant number of cost items. Currently, the average Medicare beneficiary pays more than $3000 out of pocket each year for health care, excluding long-term care (Moon, 2001).

To protect themselves from high out-of-pocket costs, in the 1990s many Medicare beneficiaries began to purchase supplemental coverage; approximately 85% of Medicare beneficiaries have some type of supplemental insurance coverage. However, only about 65% have some form of prescription drug coverage. Medicaid (which supplements 15% of low-income Medicare beneficiaries) and employer-sponsored retirement benefits (available to about 46% of Medicare beneficiaries) fill some of the gaps. Unfortunately, there are still approximately 13.5 million beneficiaries without drug coverage (Gross & Brangan, 1999).

An important trend to note is that employer-sponsored plans, used by about a third of beneficiaries, are becoming less available as retiree health coverage declines. Private supplemental (Medigap) plans—which are used by about 25% of beneficiaries—are becoming unaffordable for those with an average income (Moon, 2001). Prescription drug coverage is also available under the 1997 Medicare+ Choice (M+C) program, which allows managed care plans to participate in the Medicare program and offer a range of benefits that exceed those available through traditional fee-for-service plans. These plans have been particularly attractive to Medicare beneficiaries (about 15% enrolled in 1998) because of the drug benefits provided. However, a number of managed care plans have left the M+C program or have withdrawn from certain geographic areas because of concern that Medicare's payments were inadequate. (Several major studies offer a different perspective, concluding that in fact Medicare has *overpaid* managed care plans [e.g., Iglehart, 2001].) Whatever the catalyst for a decline in plan participation, limited or nonexistent plan offerings in large geographic areas and, more broadly, an uncertain financial future for the M+C program suggest that this vehicle is questionable at best for ensuring drug coverage for beneficiaries.

Out-of-Pocket Spending on Prescription Drugs. The highest out-of-pocket expenses are incurred by individuals without health insurance. Ironically, people who have no coverage and who consequently must pay cash for prescriptions also face the highest prices. Often these people are the least privileged in the country. Some analysts claim that the discounts obtained for some Americans through large purchasing agreements by insurance companies or federal government programs shift costs to others. Those who lack coverage, many of whom are poor and sick, pay the highest prices (Frank, 2001).

Because of limitations in the Medicare benefit package, beneficiaries who use many drugs spend much more than the average beneficiary. In 1998, 42% of beneficiaries had expenditures of $1000 or more and 7% had drug costs that exceeded $4000. The 7% with the highest expenditures accounted, in fact, for an estimated 32% of total drug expenditures (Iglehart, 2001).

Although beneficiaries with supplemental drug coverage spend substantially less out of pocket on drugs than those without such coverage ($325 per year vs. $590, on average), having coverage does not necessarily protect beneficiaries from out-of-pocket costs. Those beneficiaries whose primary source of supplemental coverage is from individually purchased policies incur annual out-of-pocket drug costs that are among the highest of any group ($570 on average [Gross & Brangan, 1999]). One recent study assessed the impact of a policy that increased prescription drug cost-sharing for elderly and welfare recipients (Tamblyn, 2001). The health outcome results were disturbing. After the policy was introduced, both essential and less-essential drug use decreased and the incidence of serious adverse events and emergency room visits increased. Thus, the policy had the intended effect of reducing the use of less-essential drugs (a principal method of fiscal control), but had the unintended effect of reducing the use of drugs essential for disease management and prevention. Finally, Medicare beneficiaries without coverage who consider themselves to be in poor health spend even more out of pocket, an average of $820 annually (Poisal & Murray, 2001).

Policymakers have identified the instability of drug coverage as another factor related to out-of-pocket spending. In a recent study, the sources and stability of prescription coverage maintained by Medicare beneficiaries over a 2-year period were analyzed (Stuart, Shea, & Breisacher, 2001). The results showed that fewer than half of all beneficiaries had continuous drug coverage, while almost a third were without coverage for some part of the study interval. It was also found that public plans offer more stable prescription benefits than do private plans. The findings bolster the argument that Medicare should include drug coverage because of the instability of currently available drug prescription plans.

Characteristics of Beneficiaries with and without Drug Coverage. Income level is the most distinct difference between beneficiaries with and without prescription drug coverage. Almost 45% of beneficiaries without drug coverage have incomes at or below 200% of the federal poverty level.[1] Age is also notably correlated to lack of drug coverage, beneficiaries without drug coverage being more likely to be age 75 and over. In terms of gender, limitations in activities of daily living (ADLs), and health status (fair/poor), those with and without drug coverage are similar (Gross & Brangan, 1999).

Drug Prices. Drug prices are rising twice as fast as inflation. At the same time, the number of Americans with health insurance covering prescription drugs is declining by a million people per year (Berndt, 2001). The Health Care Financing Administration (HCFA) has predicted that pharmaceutical costs, which accounted for 9.4% of personal health care expenditures in 1999, will account on average for 12.6% of personal health care expenditures yearly over the next decade, reaching 16% in 2010 (Heffler et al., 2001).

[1]In 1999, the projected federal poverty levels for persons under age 65 are $8760 per year for individuals and $11,334 for couples. For persons age 65 and over, the projected levels are $8075 for individuals and $10,185 for couples.

It appears paradoxical that although managed care and cost containment efforts flourished during the 1990s, and only one fifth of the increase in drug expenditures between 1995 and 2000 could be attributed to higher prices, the U.S. pharmaceutical industry continued to be the most profitable sector of the economy because of rising drug expenditures (Berndt, 2001). Berndt explains the rapid growth of drug expenditures as the result of four key factors.

First, there has been an increase in the demand for existing drugs. Spending for outpatient prescription drugs is the third largest component of health care costs (8%) after hospital costs (34%) and physician services (20%). Although 8% may not seem critical, it is important to remember that in 1999 alone prescription drug spending increased 18.4% while all other health spending increased only 5.3% (Cauchi, 2001).

A second factor contributing to growth in drug expenditures is product innovation. This supply-side phenomenon is driven by the successful introduction of new pharmaceutical products. Facilitating the annual introduction of new drugs is the fact that the mean approval time for drugs at the Food and Drug Administration (FDA) has fallen by almost 50% since 1994. While the importance of new pharmaceutical products as drivers of increased spending has been debated, it is estimated that 46% of drug spending growth since 1997 is directly tied to new products (Berndt, 2001).

The third factor leading to increased drug expenditures is the expansion of coverage provided by third-party insurance. In 1965, private insurance plans covered about 3.5% of prescription drug spending; in 1998 they covered almost 70% (Berndt, 2001). Health plans that traditionally absorbed most enrollee drug costs, leaving enrollees with low copayments, have also increased drug expenditures (Poisal & Murray, 2001).

The fourth factor thought to drive expenditures is aggressive technology transfer and marketing. In 1999, drug companies spent $13.9 billion on marketing, including journal advertising, physician detailing, product samples, and direct-to-consumer (DTC) marketing. There is increasing concern that DTC marketing may contribute to inappropriate use. The FDA relaxed restrictions on prescription drug advertising in 1997, and DTC marketing has risen sharply since that time.

DTC-marketed drugs are usually products that deal with chronic or episodic rather than with acute conditions. The conditions these drugs impact are thus generally not life-threatening, but are widespread. In 1999, total DTC advertising of pharmaceuticals was $1.8 billion, a 40% increase from 1998. About 58% of DTC marketing dollars involved television, 40% magazines, and 2% newspapers. The effects of DTC marketing on health status, provider/patient relationships, and pharmaceutical use have not been well researched, and deserve high investigative priority (Berndt, 2001).

Reform Proposals. Medicare was designed in the 1960s to focus primarily on coverage for acute health care needs. When Medicare was enacted, drugs did not have the same health care role they do today. Currently, 63% of Medicare beneficiaries have at least two chronic illnesses and 95% of program spending is tied to care for these beneficiaries. Beneficiaries' needs are now more chronic in nature, and Medicare should broaden its benefits to incorporate prescription drugs and long-term care (Poisal & Murray, 2001).

During the 35 years since Medicare was first implemented, several unsuccessful attempts have been made to add outpatient drug coverage to the benefit package (Iglehart, 2001). The most recent federal legislative effort was in late 2000, when Congress passed a bill allowing pharmacists to reimport prescription drugs manufactured domestically but sold in other countries at reduced prices. However, upon review by President Clinton, the bill was deemed "unworkable." Controversy centered around the legislation's enforceability; drug manufacturers were not required to cooperate with the reimportation process, thus endangering drug safety and potential costs savings (United Press International, 2001). The 107th Congress continued the debate.

The present Bush administration and Congress recognize that enactment of a national drug benefit will require an expansion of coverage through both Medicare traditional fee-for-service coverage and Medicare Plus Choice managed care plans. Both parties have proposed substantial coverage of drug costs for beneficiaries with low incomes and protection against catastrophic drug expenses (Iglehart, 2001). However, whether to deliver of these benefits as part of Medicare (as preferred by Democrats) or through private insurance companies (as preferred by Republicans) is contentious. President Bush has proposed a two-part strategy to expand benefits. Phase One would make federal funds available for a state-based approach to providing prescription drug coverage for low-income Medicare beneficiaries. Phase Two would create a White House task force that would develop a plan for a comprehensive reform of Medicare. Under this restructuring, Medicare beneficiaries could choose to enroll in a private health plan or remain in Medicare's traditional fee-for-service plan. Prescription-drug coverage would be included as a Medicare benefit. Which drugs would be covered, and what Medicare recipients' cost-sharing responsibilities would be, are not clear (Public Citizen, 2001). Democrats have opposed the proposal, arguing that it will take too long to be operationalized and that many Medicare recipients will be left out. The Democratic alternative would add a standardized drug benefit to the traditional Medicare program starting in 2002. The Democratic strategy would provide partial coverage for routine drug costs and greater coverage for large, unexpected drug costs such as those incurred by a small proportion of beneficiaries (Iglehart, 2001).

The critical question policymakers will have to grapple with is how much money to allocate for prescription drug coverage and the needs of specific populations. A Medicare drug benefit will likely stimulate greater demands for medications and may impose a financial burden that taxpayers could find untenable.

State Proposals. While the question of a prescription drug benefit has remained unresolved at the national level, health care devolution has motivated many states to limit rising pharmaceutical costs. In 1999 and 2000, more than 35 state legislatures struggled with this issue. Prescription drug discounts, rebates, price controls, and bulk purchasing were the primary policy strategies to emerge. Proposals affecting the prices paid by individuals were put forward in 25 states. Over the past two decades, a growing number of states have created special pharmaceutical assistance programs for seniors and people with disabilities; as of January 1, 2001, 22 states had passed some type of pharmaceutical assistance law. Some states have adjusted eligibility for Medicaid, with its prescription benefit, to cover more people. Another strategy focuses on statewide programs aimed at substantially lowering pharmaceutical prices for broader categories of consumers. This type of legislation seeks to use Medicaid-style rebates, other discount rates, or "current lowest available price" as bases for retail prices, instead of providing a direct state-funded subsidy. A new law in Maine and proposals in several other states also call for state price controls that would apply to public consumer purchases (Cauchi, 2001).

GENETICS AND HEALTH CARE POLICY

"Genetic testing" is a broad term. In relation to health care it refers to testing to screen for inherited diseases or for early diagnosis of certain conditions, some of which are treatable and others are not. Complex ethical and policy issues include cost of treatments, chances of success for new treatments, and adverse selection for employment and insurance purposes. Legal concern over discrimination and privacy protection issues has now extended to encompass cloning, xenotransplantation, gene therapy, genetically modified organisms, and genetic testing.

At last count, 10,000 distinct genetic disorders were listed in the National Institutes of Health database (Jones, 2000). To complete the map of deoxyribonucleic acid (DNA) was a triumph of genetics as science. Its success as a technology, however, has yet to be established. According to a published report (Jones, 2000), public expectations are far too high concerning the impact of genetic research. Jones (2000) argues that genetic screening and diagnosis (which are effectively done only on a few rare diseases) will not quickly translate to dramatic changes in medical practice and or to treatments for common diseases: "DNA is simple, but illness is complicated." However, due to its po-

tential power, many new social policy issues have erupted around genetic technology.

Current Policies. In the mid-1990s the findings and recommendations of the National Institutes of Health/Department of Energy (NIH/DOE) Ethical, Legal and Social Implications (ELSI) Working Group and the National Action Plan on Breast Cancer (NAPBC) served as the foundation for federal oversight practices and for much proposed or enacted legislation at the federal and state levels. The Health Insurance Portability and Accountability Act of 1996 (HIPAA) was the first step in implementation of the NIH/DOE ELSI working Group and NAPBC recommendations on health insurance and protection from discrimination. HIPAA prohibits exclusion of an individual from group coverage because of past or present health problems or genetic information. Group-market health insurance is prohibited from charging a higher premium to any individual than to others in the group and limits exclusions for preexisting conditions to 12 months. If the condition was previously covered, then no exclusion is allowed. However, gaps remain. HIPAA does not (1) limit the collection of genetic information by insurers or prohibit insurers from requiring an individual to take a genetic test, (2) limit the disclosure of genetic information by insurers, or (3) prohibit the use of genetic information as a basis for charging more for health insurance.

New HIPAA regulations have increased the protection of personal medical records. Mandated by Congress in December, 2000, the new standards limit the nonconsensual use and release of private information. They also give patients new rights of access to their medical records and to information about who else has accessed them. Protection of information is accomplished through a number of strategies, including restriction of health information to the minimum needed and criminal and civil sanctions for improper use. These sweeping regulations govern all personal health information (www. ornl.gov/hgmis).

Currently, certain federal antidiscrimination laws apply to genetics. The Americans with Disabilities Act of 1990 is one of the most important sources of protection against genetic discrimination in the workplace. For example, it states that genetic information cannot be obtained by federal government agencies from employees or job applicants and cannot be used in hiring and promotion decisions. This standard was set in February 2000 through the Executive Order to Prohibit Discrimination in Federal Government Based on Genetic Information.

Although several bills have been introduced during the past decade, there is still no legislation protecting against genetic discrimination in the workplace. For example, four such bills were defeated in the 106th Congress (1999-2000).

A primary concern influencing future legislation is the fact that DNA samples can be held indefinitely, creating the added threat that samples could be used for purposes other than originally intended (www.ornl.gov/hgmis). One House bill and three Senate bills focusing on the gaps in HIPAA were introduced in the 107th Congress. All were focused on genetic nondiscrimination in health insurance and/or employment.

Emerging Issues. In September, 2000, shock waves were felt through the scientific research community after the death of 18-year-old volunteer Jesse Gelsinger. Gelsinger's death was hastened by a gene therapy experiment. This event triggered Congressional inquiries and actions. Since 1974, gene therapy research has been regulated by the FDA and overseen by NIH's Recombinant DNA Advisory Committee. Inquiry into the incident uncovered failure to report adverse events such as injuries and deaths. Over 650 adverse events were discovered that had never been reported to oversight agencies. Additionally, no database had been established by the FDA to track gene-therapy clinical trials, despite instructions to do so from a House Appropriations subcommittee in 1995 (Waxman, 2000).

The recent tremendous progress in genetic research has been due to the coordinated efforts of innovative scientists, private industry, and flexible public policy. While genetic research has made progress, investigations into underlying problems with the oversight mechanisms automatically triggered by federal funding raise serious issues. Federal regulatory and professional-control mechanisms,

innovative research ideas, and financial support from commercial enterprise form a complex web. Government has the social and ethical responsibility to enforce public accountability of researchers and corporations.

Gene patenting refers to the patenting of a process that involves isolation of DNA and an associated chemical substance. "Working" human genes make up 4% of the total human genome; the remainder of our genetic information is made up of sequences that do not presently have known functions. However, uses for these genes will probably be discovered. The desire to own these future uses has triggered a barrage of patent requests from the biotechnology industry (American Medical Association, 2001a). Equally strong are the attacks from academic researchers, medical ethicists, and patient groups arguing that ownership of the basic building blocks of life is a barrier to genetic research and testing (Gillis, 2000). The problem with widespread gene patents is that they could make genetic testing of patients prohibitively expensive, impeding access to care. If a license fee were attached to each test, with different firms owning different tests, testing of many genes simultaneously could not be effectively used to help patients. The converse may also be true; if companies do not have some protection for their discoveries, then research costs may not be recouped and less incentive might exist for investment (American Medical Association, 2001a). Again, federal actions must balance research innovation and private investment with public expectations, protection of the public, and management of increasing health care costs.

Another highly visible issue at the nexus of policy, research, and ethics is *stem cell* legislation. Stem cells techniques have the potential to solve complex problems such as regeneration of nerve tissue (American Medical Association, 2001b). Diseases such as Parkinson's and Alzheimer's might be treatable by such techniques. Policy debate revolves around whether the government should provide federal funds to researchers who use stem cells (precursor cells that give rise to multiple tissue types). Research in human developmental biology has led to the discovery of several kinds of human stem cell, including embryonic stem (ES) cells, embryonic germ (EG) cells, and adult stem cells. Techniques have been developed for the in vitro culture of stem cells, enhancing our ability to study human embryology (Chapman, Frankel, & Garfinkel, 1999).

ES cells come from early human embryos and EG and fetal stem cells from aborted fetal tissue. Consequently, the possible use of stem cells for generating human tissues is subject to ongoing public debate that encompasses ethical, legal, religious, and policy questions. President Bush has declared his opposition to stem cell research that would require destruction or discarding of live human embryos. Consistent with this position, his administration has reviewed all relevant rules and executive orders implemented by the Clinton administration, including those addressing abortion-related research (Fournier, 2001).

Complex Policy Challenges. Jones (2000) offers several ideas and questions for clinicians and policy makers who partner in the development of health care policy. He suggests that health policymakers need to ask what a technology offers, what it costs, and how its worth is measured. For genetics, however, both costs and benefits may be ambiguous. For example, under what circumstances should genetic screening be offered? Many individual single-gene diseases are so rare that it is economically infeasible to test for them. Advocacy groups for specific diseases exert significant pressure in the public policy arena, but the fact that many conditions have an incidence on the order of one in 10,000 makes it dubious whether federal funds should be used to support related research.

In the final analysis, science does not exist in isolation from the larger community. Broad human values should direct the work of both science and health care policy. Where highly controversial matters are involved, development of health care policy must take all stakeholders into account. Significant policy challenges such as maintaining health benefits already offered to the aged population, increasing benefits to address chronic illness needs, and improving access to healthcare for the uninsured are inextricably linked with emerging considerations tied to genetics.

LONG-TERM CARE

Because of the aging of the U.S. population, another emerging policy challenge is the financing of accessible long-term care of high quality. Demand for long-term care occurs when physical or mental disabilities interfere with an individual's ability to perform ADLs. Long-term care services support basic ADLs such as eating, dressing, bathing, and toileting, as well as instrumental ADLs such as cooking, shopping, housekeeping, and transportation.

More than 13 million Americans are in need of long-term care services, and this number is expected to explode over the next three decades (Alliance for Health Reform, 2000). Contributing to the need for long-term care are advances in medical science, technology, and trauma care that have extended lives. In fact, the prevalence of disability among children and adults under 65 has increased, so that about 6 million people in this age group are in need of long-term care. This number is predicted to increase further. Additionally, as baby boomers age, the number of individuals over 85 is expected to triple by 2030 (Congressional Budget Office, 1999). While there is hope that future elderly populations will live longer, healthier lives, the number of elderly with long-term care needs is expected to increase from 8.8 million in 2000 to 12.1 million in 2040. The combined growth in these populations will create an unprecedented demand for long-term care services, ultimately raising the costs of providing this care (Niefield, Obrien, & Feder, 1999).

In 1996, 1.7 million persons were living in nursing homes (Alliance for Health Reform, 2000), almost half of whom were 85 or older. Contrary to current perceptions, most long-term care (88%) is provided to persons living at home or in the community, not in nursing homes (Niefield, Obrien, & Feder, 1999). Of these, two thirds receive informal, unpaid care from friends and family and 5% receive total formal care. The remainder receive some combination of formal and informal care.

The policy issues related to long-term care fall into the same broad categories as those related to health care in general (i.e., *access, quality, cost*). Embedded in these broad categories are specific issues such as enforcement, staffing, and resident's rights

(Administration on Aging, 1998; Institute of Medicine, 2000).

Access. Access to long-term care is more than the ability to obtain needed service; it is the ability to obtain needed service in an appropriate form. Yet current reimbursement policies drive persons who might be well cared for in community settings to be placed in nursing homes. For example, in many states, residential care facilities are not certified to receive Medicaid funds. This requires individuals to first exhaust personal funds, then move to nursing homes. Additionally, several state ombudsmen report that individuals are often not allowed to enter the nursing homes of their choice because nursing home administrators prefer residents with higher reimbursement rates linked to Medicare or private-pay systems. This practice, referred to as "cherry picking," has been identified as a problem in 20 states (Administration on Aging, 1998). Nursing homes in several states have also been found to deny admission to individuals requiring certain levels of care, such as those with dementia or behavioral problems, those who are obese, and those on ventilators. In some states, residents of nursing facilities and board-and-care homes who have behavioral problems are moved inappropriately to psychiatric centers. Several states have also reported problems with involuntary transfer and discharge actions driven by reimbursement.

Issues around long-term care emerge not only in the legislative and executive branches of government but in the judiciary. For example, in the state of New York the right of a nursing home resident to a full due-process hearing before being involuntarily removed from the facility was successfully litigated, resulting in a judicial order that the state's Department of Health revise its procedures to afford all persons full due-process protections.

Other issues related to access involve the lack of specialized equipment and assistive devices in nursing homes, of appropriate facilities available for younger persons with disabilities, and of affordable alternatives to nursing home care. According to the Institute of Medicine (IOM; 2000), access to home-based and community-based services and personal-assistance services for people with disabilities is a largely unmet need. Persons with disabilities have argued against Medicaid's "institutional bias" as a violation of their rights under the Americans with Disabilities Act, which provides for care in the "least restrictive setting." A recent Supreme Court case, *Olmstead v. L.C.,* upheld this right and may spur states to action (Rosenbaum, 1999).

The IOM's recommendations on access (IOM, 2000) also call for the Department of Health and Human Services (DHHS) to develop and fund a research agenda to investigate the effect of access on quality and to explore limitations of differing models of long-term care.

Quality. Quality in long-term care, particularly in nursing homes, has been a longstanding concern (Alliance for Health Reform, 2001; IOM, 1987, 2000; Niefield, Obrien, & Feder, 1999). Public initiatives date back to the passage of the Older Americans Act in 1965. This act was amended and reauthorized in 2000 (Administration on Aging, 1998). A 1987 IOM study led to regulatory changes in the Omnibus Budget Reconciliation Act of 1987 that have served to improve some aspects of nursing home care, such as limitations placed on the use of physical and chemical restraints. However, according to a more recent IOM study (2000), "serious quality of care problems persist, including pain management, pressure sores, incontinence, and malnutrition." A report on nutrition among nursing home residents indicates that between 35% and 85% of residents are malnourished (Kayser-Jones, 2001). More than a quarter of all nursing homes are cited annually for violations that cause harm to patients (Niefield, Obrien, & Feder, 1999). Even more disturbing is lack of enforcement that allows homes to continue operating without correcting violations so that repeat offenders appear in subsequent surveys (Administration on Aging, 1998).

In any health care setting, quality of care is inextricably linked to the abilities of those providing that care. According to the IOM (2000), "long-term care services are labor intensive and therefore the quality of care depends largely on the performance of care-giving personnel." Most research related to staffing and quality of care is focused on nursing homes. This research clearly demonstrates not only the importance of *adequate* staffing but of *appropriate* staffing. According to the IOM:

Abundant research evidence indicates that both nursing to resident-staffing levels and the ratio of professional nurses to other personnel are important indicators of high quality care . . . [P]articipation of registered nurses in direct care giving and . . . hands-on guidance to nurse assistants is positively associated with quality of care. (Wunderlich & Kohler, 2001, p. 190)

The American Health Care Association (AHCA; 2001) has projected that the need for registered nurses will increase 66.1% by 2020, with similar growth in the need for licensed practical nurses and home health aides. Various staff-to-patient ratios and their attendant costs are discussed in the AHCA's report. Depending on the ratio proposed, increasing staffing to meet need would increase costs anywhere from $3 billion to $15 billion. Cost, however, is not the only deterrent to adequate staffing; the nation faces an unprecedented shortage of nurses.

Measuring quality in long-term care is a complex issue because of the variety of services, providers, and locations employed to deliver these services. Standards may be set at local, state, or federal levels, and each governing body has different reporting requirements and methods. For example, since all nursing homes are required to meet certification standards as well as federal regulations for reimbursement, much data has been collected on the quality of care provided in these facilities. However, evidence related to the quality of home care is more limited in both amount and scope. Data collected on home care is generally focused on satisfaction with services rather than on outcomes of those services. The CMS is seeking, through a new quality-improvement initiative, to determine Medicare reimbursement for home care.

The IOM (2000) recommendations on quality are as follows:
- The DHHS should fund scientifically sound research toward the development of assessment instruments.
- The HCFA's monitoring of state survey processes should be improved, and whether the HCFA will need additional funding to accomplish the task should be determined.

- States should develop programs to (1) disseminate information to consumers about various long-term care settings and (2) establish oversight mechanisms for all settings.
- Both federal and state agencies should develop and fund consumer advocacy programs.

The IOM recommendations on staffing are as follows:
- HCFA should enforce the 1996 recommendation to require registered-nurse presence 24 hours per day and develop minimum staffing levels.
- Reimbursement rates should be adjusted to account for increases in staffing requirements based on case mix.
- Work environments should be improved to attract qualified staff.
- Education and training of staff should be provided.
- Legislation should be enacted requiring background checks before the hiring of any long-term care personnel.

Cost. According to the Alliance for Health Reform (2000), the main barrier to improving long-term care is cost, with the average annual per-person cost of nursing home care in 1998 being $56,000 and the annual per-person cost of a half-time home health aide being $10,000.

Currently, the breakdown of nursing facility residents by payor source is as follows: Medicaid 68%, Medicare 9%, private payor 23% (AHCA, 2001). The Congressional Budget Office projects that annual inflation-adjusted spending on the long-term care needs of the elderly will triple by 2040, to almost $350 billion. Public programs will continue to be liable for most of these costs. While out-of-pocket spending will also remain high, it is hoped that increased coverage by long-term care insurance will offset some personal spending.

Congress will continue to carefully watch federal spending on long-term care. For example, in 1997 Medicare's payment policies were changed by the Balanced Budget Act in an attempt to slow down spending growth in home health care. Members of Congress have also begun to introduce legislation that would make long-term-care insurance more affordable. In 2000, recognizing that the majority of individuals receive care at home as long as they are financially able, the National Caregiver Support Program was added as an amendment to the Older Americans Act. This program authorized $125 million for state grants to provide caregiver support and to support other home-based and community-based services.

Insurance is viewed as the best approach to meeting the financial demand for long-term care in the future (Niefield, Obrien, & Feder, 1999). A public sector approach would provide tax incentives that encourage people to purchase long-term care insurance. However, given the public financial burden for long-term care, private sector approaches are unlikely to resolve the problem alone. Public sector approaches are also needed, such as expansion of long-term care insurance through already existing programs. The IOM (2000) recommends that states carefully assess impact on access and quality before changing Medicaid reimbursement policies. The Bush administration's plan is to provide tax relief by making the full cost of long-term care insurance tax-deductible and providing a substantial tax credit to long-term caregivers.

THE UNINSURED

We will not nationalize our health care system. We will promote individual choice. We will rely on private insurance. But make no mistake. In my administration, low income Americans will have access to high quality health care. (George W. Bush, 2000)

In spite of a strong economy and the fact that unemployment rates were at a 30-year low, approximately 43 million Americans (one-sixth of the population) were without health insurance in 1999 (Census Bureau, 2000). Uninsured persons are less likely to seek preventive health care, more likely to delay needed treatment should they become ill, and less likely to have prescriptions filled (Dalen, 2000; Glied, 2001). According to the Alliance for Health Reform (2000), uninsured persons are also more likely to experience avoidable hospitalizations and more likely to die while hospitalized. These facts combine to make the problem of the uninsured a public policy priority.

The number of uninsured Americans has increased at a rate of about 1 million per year over the last 8 years despite measures taken by the federal government to expand coverage to children and protect adults from losing coverage when changing jobs (Alliance for Health Reform, 2000). A number of factors have contributed to this growth, including welfare reforms that have decreased Medicaid enrollment, limited eligibility for public programs (especially for adults without children), decreasing numbers of employers who provide health insurance, and insurance premiums beyond the reach of the working poor (Glied, 2001; Holahan & Kim, 2000).

The most important safety net for the uninsured is the Medicaid program, financed by both state and federal governments. Federal Medicaid spending was projected to be $115 billion in 2000 (Alliance for Health Reform, 2000). Medicaid expansion is the most common means of providing health care coverage to the uninsured. However, resolving the problem of the uninsured is complex from a policy perspective for a variety of reasons, not the least of which is the diverse composition of the uninsured population. Among working people, uninsurance rates are highest for the poor or near poor, those employed in small firms, and those between the ages of 25 and 44. However, uninsurance rates are also high among persons nearing retirement, those with poor health, and immigrants (Glied, 2001). In addition, 11 million children are uninsured, as are most non-citizens, the homeless, and unemployed persons not eligible for Medicare. Added to the problem of diversity is the fact that the uninsured pool is constantly changing as people move in and out of coverage based on income, employment status, and changes in personal situation. The transitoriness of coverage is significant. According to the Survey of Income and Program Participation, as many as 55 million Americans were without insurance for some portion of each year (Schoen & DesRoches, 2000).

Given the complexity of the issue and the inability of the previous administration to accomplish comprehensive health reform, the policy options selected are likely to be incremental.

Working Poor. In the United States, private health insurance has been linked to employment since the 1940s. However, 84% of the uninsured are employed or members of working families. The majority of these individuals work in small private-sector businesses that employ 25 or fewer people. Such businesses, unable to absorb rising costs associated with providing health care benefits, are either cutting back on health coverage options offered or requiring employees to pay a portion of the premiums. Three states have attempted to make employer-based health care mandatory, but only Hawaii has been successful in obtaining a federal exemption from ERISA. Acs and Blumberg (2001) predict that a decline in employee-sponsored health insurance is likely to continue until 2008.

A number of policy options addressing these concerns have been advanced. These options include automatic enrollment (Davis, Schoen, & Schoenbaum, 2000), expansion of federal programs such as Medicaid, Medicare, and S-CHIP (Short, Shea, & Powell, 2000; Weil, 2000), individual premium assistance through tax relief or vouchers (Weil, 2000; Zelenak, 2000); purchasing pools (Curtis, Neuschler, & Forland, 2000), employer incentives (Merlis, 2000; Meyer & Wicks, 2000; Rosenbaum, Borzi, & Smith, 2000), extending the Federal Employee Benefit Program (Fuchs, 2000) and reinsurance plans (Davis, Schoen, & Schoenbaum, 2000).

All of these options have advantages and disadvantages. For example, premium assistance may make non-group insurance more affordable to people, but it may be difficult for individuals to navigate selection decisions (Glied, 2001). Automatic enrollment increases access to insurance but is difficult to administer, and while pools may reduce insurance costs and make administration easier, there is a risk for adverse selection if people at low risk find the non-group insurance more attractive or decide to remain uninsured.

President Bush has proposed to address the insurance needs of individuals not eligible for S-CHIP or Medicaid by using some of these policy options. He has supported tax relief for individuals and such small business incentives as tax credits and allowing businesses to form coalitions across state lines to purchase insurance. According to some experts, however, these measures would provide insurance to less than 25% of those in need.

Children. Despite the enactment of S-CHIP by Congress in 1997, 11 million children were uninsured in 1999. S-CHIP is a federal program administered through the CMS that allocates $24 billion over 5 years (starting in 1999) to states to expand health care coverage to uninsured children. This program enables states to provide insurance to children from working families whose incomes make them ineligible for Medicaid yet are unable to afford private health insurance. Each state is required to submit a plan that either expands existing Medicaid coverage, develops a separate state program, or combines the two. Once the plan has been approved, the state receives matching funds up to a specific amount determined by a population-based formula. As of July, 2000 all 50 states, the District of Columbia, and five U.S. territories had approved plans in place. In January, 2001 the Secretary of Health and Human Services announced that the final regulations regarding S-CHIP had been published and that S-CHIP enrollment had reached 3.3 million in fiscal year 2000 (HCFA, 2001a; 2001b).

The high number of children who remain unenrolled is a major concern for policymakers. It is estimated that 80% of these children are eligible for services and are in fact receiving some aid through other federal programs such as the school lunch program and the Women Infants and Children Nutrition program (Davis, Schoen, & Schoenbaum, 2000). Increasing outreach efforts, streamlining of enrollment processes, and automatic enrollment are some of the approaches being considered to enroll these children.

The DHHS took a step in this direction when it issued guidance to states regarding S-CHIP waivers that would extend coverage to low-income parents. In January, 2001 the CMS announced that the first of these waivers had been approved. The first three states to have waivers approved were New Jersey, Rhode Island, and Wisconsin. New Jersey's plan enrolls parents of children eligible for Medicaid and S-CHIP with incomes up to 200% of the federal poverty level (FPL) and pregnant women with incomes between 185% and 200% of the FPL. Rhode Island enrolls parents between 100% and 185% of the FPL and pregnant women with incomes between 185 and 250% of the FPL. Wisconsin's plan covers parents between 100% and 185% of the FPL. Given that Republicans control the White House and the House of Representatives in 2002, and given the Republican philosophy that federal government should respect the traditional authority of states to regulate health insurance (Republican National Committee, 2000), policies that encourage and support such state innovation and flexibility have lately been the preferred method for addressing these issues. The following statement, made by the Republican National Committee (2000), underscores this position:

Republicans want to ensure . . . that states have the flexibility to innovate [and to] expand family coverage without interference from HCFA . . . [T]he first order of business at the DHHS will be to eliminate regulations that are stymieing the effectiveness of the S-CHIP program and to stop imposing unwarranted mandates.

Protecting Insured Workers from Disenrollment. Millions of Americans have medical histories or preexisting conditions that make it difficult to get comprehensive insurance coverage. Additionally, small businesses often have difficulty getting group insurance policies for their employees when even one employee has a medical problem. The Health Insurance Portability and Accountability Act (HIPAA; Public Law 104-191) was designed to help millions of families by making it easier to get and keep comprehensive health insurance. HIPAA first took effect on July 1, 1997 and was fully implemented starting in 2000. The law's group-market reforms apply not only to traditional insurance companies but also to health plans operated by employers who self-insure. This policy primarily helps people who have access to group insurance coverage through employers or unions. Since plans operated by self-insured employers are beyond the reach of state insurance laws, federal regulation in this area is particularly critical.

In addition, there are some provisions that have the potential to help people who leave a group plan and seek individual policies for themselves or their families. According to the HCFA (2001), HIPAA may have the following effects:

- Increase an individual's ability to get health coverage for themselves and their dependents when starting a new job.
- Lower the chance of losing existing coverage.
- Help maintain continuous coverage when changing jobs.
- Help individuals buy insurance on their own if coverage is lost under an employer's group health plan.

HIPAA also offers several protections. It limits the use of preexisting condition exclusions and prohibits discrimination in the form of denying coverage or charging extra for coverage for individuals based on poor health (past or present).

One shortcoming that needs to be addressed is the fact that HIPAA does not limit how much insurers can charge for coverage, so there is no guarantee that individuals can afford to purchase it. Nor does HIPAA require employers to offer or pay for health coverage. However, it does offer millions of Americans protections against the loss of health care coverage. This law is particularly significant for women who are now protected from denial of or loss of coverage related to pregnancy.

HEALTH CARE QUALITY

Historically, policy actions to ensure health care quality have been far less frequent or significant than actions designed to increase access to care or decrease health care costs. Quality has long been the least visible part of the cost-access-quality triad, and media accounts of consumer backlash against managed care and fiscal pressures on health care systems have fueled concern that quality of care was is being eroded and patient safety jeopardized. Consequently, on September, 1996 President Clinton signed an executive order creating the Presidential Advisory Commission on Consumer Protection and Quality in the Health Care Industry. The President directed the 32-member Commission to make recommendations to him on how to preserve and improve quality in the health care system. The

Commission charted needed strategies for addressing quality, some of which were immediately acted on, others of which have, to date, been ignored.

In 1999, the IOM Committee on Quality of Health Care in America released a damning report titled *To Err is Human—Building a Safer Health System,* which suggested that between 44,000 and 98,000 people die annually in American hospitals as a result of health care errors. Congress and the White House immediately responded, prompted no doubt in part by nationwide front-page stories reporting this startling assertion. The Congress held five committee hearings between the end of 1999 and mid-2000, and a number of bills were introduced to address some of the IOM's recommendations. By the beginning of fiscal year 2001, $50 million had been appropriated to the federal Agency for Health Care Research and Quality to study patient safety. Other legislation was subsequently introduced to address issues around reporting of medical errors.

In spring 2001, the same IOM committee released its final report, titled "Crossing the Quality Chasm." This made recommendations for achieving threshold quality improvement in health care. Many of the IOM's recommendations and much of the subsequent discussion speak directly to issues ranging from licensure and scope of practice to changing reimbursement patterns for health care services. This heightening of interest in health policies that protect consumers and promote quality is likely to continue. As long as change characterizes the health care delivery system, ongoing assessment and related interventions will be part of the policy equation. Policy initiatives may take many forms, including changing accreditation and licensure requirements, prohibiting payment schemes shown to put quality of care at risk, and ensuring that consumers are informed about provider performance and able to exercise choice among plans and providers. Clearly, nurses have tremendous expertise to bring to this critically important policy discussion.

CONCLUSION

The state of the nation's health results from a confluence of factors, including policies implemented years earlier. Achieving significant improvement of the public's health is thus a formidable task, in no small part because of various levels of government activity (local, state, federal), multiple players, and pervasive underlying social problems. As Henry Kissinger notes, "A frustrating paradox is faced by policymakers: when their scope for action is widest, their knowledge is often minimal, and when their knowledge is greatest, their scope for action has frequently disappeared" (Kissinger, 1988, p. 15).

The scope of action for health care is extensive. However, what knowledge exists regarding how to solve problems in health care is often rejected because of political ideology, fiscal constraints, and power struggles. The lesson for nurses intent on forging solutions to our health care problems is not that the task is insurmountable; it is that a myriad of patterns, threads, and colors are woven into the health care tapestry. Nurses, in addition to understanding nursing's position within the health care system, must acquire a macro view of health care and health policy.

REFERENCES

Acs, G., & Blumberg, J. (2001). How a changing workforce affects employer-sponsored health insurance. *Health Affairs, 20*(1), 178-183.

Administration on Aging. (1998). *Long-term care ombudsmen report—FY 1998.* Available online at www.aoa.gov/ltcombudsman/98.

Allen, T. (2000, February 21). Policy briefing: How can Congress reform Medicare to include prescription drug benefits? *Roll Call.* Available online at www.rollcall.com/pages/pb/00/02/pb21h.html.

American Heath Care Association. (2001). *Today's nursing facilities and the people they serve.* Available online at www.acha.org/who/profile3.htm.

American Medical Association. (2001a). *Gene patenting.* Available online at www.ama-assn.org/ama/pub/category/2314.html.

American Medical Association. (2001b). *Stem cell legislation: Position statement.* Available online at www.ama-assn.org/ama/pub/article/2318-3763.html.

Berndt, E.R. (2001). The U.S. pharmaceutical industry: Why major growth in times of cost containment? *Health Affairs, 20*(2), 100-114.

Cauchi, R. (2001). *Prescription drug discount, rebate, price control and bulk purchasing legislation, 1999-2000.* National Conference of State Legislatures. Available online at www.ncsl.org/programs/health/drugsdisc.htm.

Census Bureau. (2000). *Population reports.* Available online at www.gov.

Chapman, A.R., Frankel, M.S., & Garfinkel, M.S. (1999). *Stem cell research and applications: Monitoring the frontiers of biomedical research*. American Association for the Advancement of Science and Institute for Civil Society. Available online at www.aaas.org/spp/dspp/sfrl/projects/stem/report.pdf.

Congressional Budget Office. (1996). *Health spending projections*. Washington, DC: U.S. Government Printing Office.

Congressional Budget Office. (1999). *An analysis of the President's budgetary proposals for fiscal year 2000*. Available online at www.cbo.gov.

Curtis, R., Neuschler, E., & Forland, R. (2000). Private purchasing pools to harness individual tax credits for consumers. *Inquiry, 38*(2).

Dalen, J. (2000). Health care in America. *Archives of Internal Medicine, 160*(17). Available online at archinte.ama-assn.org/issuesv160.

Davis, K., Schoen, C., & Schoenbaum, S. (2000). A 2020 vision for American health care. *Archives of Internal Medicine, 160*(22). Available online at archinte.ama-assn.org/issues/v160n22/ffull/isa00017.html.

Fournier, R. (2001, January 26). Bush opposes stem cell research funding. *Health and Science*.

Frank, R.G. (2001). Prescription drug prices: Why do some pay more than others? *Health Affairs, 20*(2), 115-128.

Fuchs. B. (2001). Increasing health insurance coverage through an extended federal employees health benefits program. *Inquiry, 38*(2).

Gillis, J.G. (2000, December 30). Research success spurs profit debate. *The Washington Post*.

Glied, S. (2001). Challenges and options for increasing the number of Americans with health insurance. *Inquiry, 38*(2).

Gross, D. & Brangan, D. (1999). *Medicare beneficiaries and prescription drug coverage: Gaps and barriers*. American Association of Retired Persons. Available online at research.aarp.org/health/ib39.html.

Health Care Financing Administration. (2001a). *What is HIPAA?* Available online at www.hcfa.gov/Medicaid/hipaa/content/more.asp.

Health Care Financing Administration. (2001b). *HHS Approves first SCHIP waivers*. Available online at www/hcfa.gov/init/20010118.htm.

Heffler, S., Levit, K., Smith, S., et al. (2001). Health spending growth up in 1999, faster growth, expected in the future. *Health Affairs, 20*(2), 193-203.

Holahan, J., Kim, J. (2000). Why does the number of uninsured continue to grow? *Health Affairs, 19*(4), 185-196.

Iglehart, J.K. (2001). Medicare and prescription drugs. *The New England Journal of Medicine, 344*(13), 1010-1015.

Institute of Medicine. (1999). *To err is human: Building a safer health system*. Washington, OC: National Academy of Science.

Institute of Medicine. (2000). *Improving the quality of long-term care*. Available online at www.nas.edu.

Jones, S. (2000). Genetics in medicine: Real promises, unreal expectations. Milbank Report

Kayser-Jones, J. (2001). Starved for attention. *Reflections in Nursing Leadership, 27*(1), 10-45.

Kissinger, H. (1998). *Knowledge and power: Occasional paper of the Council of Scholars* (report no. 6). Washington DC.

Leon, J., Neuman, P., & Paremte, S. (1997). *Understanding the growth in Medicare's home health expenditures: Kaiser Medicare policy report*. Washington, DC:

Merlis, M. (2001). Public subsidies for required employee contributions toward employer-sponsored insurance. *Inquiry, 38*(2).

Meyer, J. & Wicks, E. (2001). A federal tax credit to encourage employers to offer health coverage. *Inquiry, 38*(2).

Moon, M. (2001). Medicare. *The New England Journal of Medicine, 344*(12), 928-931.

Niefield, M., Obrien, E., & Feder, J. (1999). *Long-term care: Medicaid's role and challenges* (policy brief #2172). Washington, DC: Kaiser Foundation.

Pew Health Professions Commission. (1995). *Critical challenges: Revitalizing the health professions for the twenty-first century*. San Francisco. UCSF Center for the Health Professions.

Poisal, P.A. & Murray, L. (2001). Growing differences between Medicare beneficiaries with and without drug coverage. *Health Affairs, 20*(2), 74-85.

Public Citizen. (2000). *Position statement: Congressional Democratic prescription drug plan proposal is inadequate, bill is "half a pill."* Available online at www.citizen.org/.

Public Citizen. (2001). *Position statement: Critique of the Bush prescription drug proposal*. Available online at www.citizen.org/congress/drugs/bushstateplan.html/report.html.

Republican National Committee. (2000). *Retirement security and quality health care: Our pledge to America*. Available online at www.rnc.org/2000/2000platform5.

Rosenbaum, S. (1999). *Olmstead v. L.C.: Implications for older persons with mental and physical disabilities*. Washington, DC: American Association of Retired Persons.

Rosenbaum, S., Borzi, P., & Smith, V. (2001). Allowing small businesses and the self-employed to buy health care coverage through public programs. *Inquiry, 38*(2).

Sanders, B. (2001). *Position on prescription drug pricing-reform*. Available online at bernie.house.gov/prescriptions/index.asp.

Schoen, C. & DesRoches, C. (2000). The role of insurance in providing access to care. *Health Services Research, 35*(1), 187-207.

Short, P., Shea, D., & Powell, M. (2001). A workable solution for the pre-Medicare population. *Inquiry, 38*(2).

Stuart, B., Shea, D., & Briesacher, B. (2001). Dynamics in drug coverage of Medicare beneficiaries: Finders, losers, switchers. *Health Affairs, 20*(2), 86-99.

Swartz, K. (2000). Health insurance problems are not going away. *The Journal of Health Care Organizations, Provisions, and Financing, 37*(3). Available online at www.inquiryjournal.org/viewFall2000.html.

Tamblyn, R., et al. (2001). Adverse events associated with prescription drug cost-sharing among poor and elderly persons. *Journal of the American Medical Association, 285*, 421-429.

United Press International. (2000, December 27). Prescription drug challenge shifts back to Congress. Available online at bernie.house.gov.

Waxman, H. (2000, June 5). Policy briefing: How best can Congress provide oversight of gene therapy? *Roll Call.* Available online at www.rollcall.com/pages/pb/00/06/pb05f.html.

Weil, A. (2000). Buying into public coverage: expanding access by permitting families to use tax credits to buy into Medicaid or CHIP programs. *Inquiry, 38*(2).

Wunderlich, G.S. & Kohler, P.O. (Eds.). (2001). *Improving the quality of long term care.* Institute of Medicine. Available online at www.nas.edu.

Zelenak, L. (2001). A health insurance tax credit for uninsured workers. *Inquiry, 38*(2).

POLICYSPOTLIGHT

THE EPIDEMIC IN HEALTH CARE ERRORS: ONE GOVERNMENT AGENCY'S RESPONSE

Linda E. Moore

"First, do no harm."

HIPPOCRATES

In December, 1999 the Institute of Medicine (IOM) of the National Academy of Sciences published a major report, *To Err Is Human: Building a Safer Health System* (1999). The report was commissioned by the U.S. Congress in response to the increasing number of adverse events in health care facilities being reported in the medical literature and the media almost daily. The IOM's major finding—that 44,000 to 98,000 Americans die every year because of health care errors—shocked the nation. The report stated that "no single action represents a complete answer, nor can any single group or sector offer a complete fix to the problem. However, different groups can, and should, make significant contributions to the solution" (IOM, 1999, p. 6). The report suggested that the best approach to error reduction is to focus on improvement of systems and processes rather than on performance of individuals. The IOM challenged all health care organizations and professionals to evaluate their commitment to patient safety and identified the following goals:

1. A 50% reduction in medical errors by 2005.
2. The creation of a Center for Patient Safety.
3. A mandatory error-reporting system.
4. A law to keep patient safety data secret.
5. The development of a patient safety curriculum for healthcare workers and students.
6. Examination and renewal of licensure for physicians, nurses, and key providers based on competence and knowledge of safety practices.
7. Collaboration among health care organizations and professionals to identify unsafe practices.

The Department of Veterans Affairs (VA) was referenced as a model organization that was well on the way to achieving most of these goals. How did a mammoth organization like VA institute system-wide change while leaving other private and public sector health care organizations lagging far behind?

The Veterans Health Administration (VHA) is the health care arm of the VA. It is the largest integrated health care system in the world, serving over

4.1 million patients at over 1000 sites (including 172 medical centers, 135 nursing homes, 43 domiciliaries, and 781 outpatient clinics) located in 50 states plus the District of Columbia, Puerto Rico, the Virgin Islands, and the Philippines (U.S. Department of Veterans Affairs, 2000). Despite the tremendous size of the VHA, it has responded rapidly to the epidemic of health care errors.

Fundamental to the VHA's response is the belief that a culture of safety must be created which moves away from the traditional "name-blame-shame-and-train" approach toward a systems-thinking approach. This approach is necessary because providers of health care can be overwhelmed by health care's "capacity to create far more information than anyone can absorb, to foster far greater interdependency than anyone can manage, and to accelerate change far faster than anyone's ability to keep pace" (Senge, 1990, p. 69).

Systems thinking creates a mindset for seeing wholes rather than individual isolated parts, patterns of activity rather than snapshots. Basic to systems thinking is the concept of *feedback*. Feedback is an outcome originating from the interaction of two or more actions or states. Senge (1990) describes it as a "reciprocal flow of influence . . . where every influence is both cause and effect" (p. 75). A basic principle of the systems perspective is that structure influences behavior; that is, when placed in the same system, people, however different, tend to behave similarly. A second principle is "there is no blame"(Senge, 1990, p. 67). There is no blame because the causes of problems are multi-dimensional, involving relationships among people, processes, and structures or things. Therefore, solutions to problems involve fixing these relationships.

To create a culture of safety, the VHA redesigned its *systems,* beginning with the creation or revision of a number of major policies. These included guidelines for which errors to evaluate and report and how to do so, how preventive measures would be disseminated, the integration and coordination of patient safety activities, and what relationships the VHA would have with other organizations or committees concerned with patient safety. One such committee, the Quality Interagency Coordination (QuIC) Task Force, was established by President Clinton to identify patient safety programs already in place and to set a patient safety agenda for the nation. Its membership includes all federal agencies that provide or fund health care.

STRATEGIES TO REDUCE HEALTH CARE ERRORS
National Patient Safety Partnership

In 1997, the VHA intensified its efforts to improve patient safety by initiating the National Patient Safety Partnership (NPSP). The NPSP is a VHA-initiated partnership of 13 public and private health care organizations. Its purpose is to address patient safety concerns on a national level. Typically, this group formulates positions on a variety of high impact issues and disseminates this information to health care organizations and providers and the public. The membership of the partnership is given in the box below.

One example of actions that this group has taken thus far is a campaign to call public attention to "preventable adverse drug events," describing actions that could be taken to minimize the public's chances of being victims of adverse drug events (Bagian, 2000). The NPSP was instrumental in identifying potential malfunctions of medical equipment and computers related to the Y2K software bug.

Membership of the National Patient Safety Partnership

Department of Veterans Affairs*
American Medical Association*
American Hospital Association*
American Nurses Association*
Joint Commission on Accreditation of Healthcare
    Organizations*
Association of American Medical Colleges*
Institute for Healthcare Improvement*
National Patient Safety Foundation at the American
    Medical Association*
Department of Defense
National Institute for Occupational Safety and
    Health Administration
Food and Drug Administration
Agency for Healthcare Quality and Research
Health Care Financing Administration

*Charter member

National Patient Safety Registry

In 1997, the VHA also initiated the National Patient Safety Registry, a database for information on adverse patient events, their root causes, and systematic improvements to prevent future occurrences. This database is available to all VHA health care facilities. The VHA is of the firm belief that employees can learn from the mistakes of others and thus avoid repetition of the same type of adverse events at different facilities within the organization. Due to extensive use of the Internet, safety alerts can be publicized immediately.

VHA Handbook on Patient Safety Improvements

In January, 1998, the VHA formalized its policy on patient safety with the publication of *VHA Handbook 1051/1: Patient Safety Improvement* (U.S. Department of Veterans Affairs, 1998). This handbook outlines the VHA's policy on patient safety, identifying the following five goals:

1. Analyze service delivery systems before adverse events occur to identify system redesigns that will reduce the likelihood of error.
2. Expedite identification and reporting of all adverse events.
3. Review adverse events to identify both root causes of errors and system changes needed to reduce the likelihood of recurrence.
4. Disseminate information about effective systems modification throughout the VHA.
5. Inform patients and their families about injuries resulting from adverse events and about the options available to them.

This handbook is available online at www.va.gov/vhadir.htm.

National Center for Patient Safety

In 1998, the National Center for Patient Safety (NCPS) was created by the VHA. The purpose of this center is to lead and integrate patient safety efforts for the entire organization. One of the center's first tasks was to develop a method to identify, analyze, and correct weaknesses in the system affecting patient safety. This method, the *root cause analysis* process, has been invaluable in identifying systems issues that impede safe practices and is a fundamental tool for evaluating adverse events. Root cause analysis is a process for identifying as many causes of and contributing factors to adverse events as possible. A series of "Triage Questions" and a "Root Cause/Contributing Factor Interview Tool" are used to uncover the facts pertaining to and possible explanations for the adverse event being investigated. The investigation culminates with an action plan designed to correct the problems that contributed to the adverse event. The NCPS designed reporting systems that would capture not only actual adverse patient events but potential adverse patient events, so-called "close calls." VHA believes that "close calls" provide the best opportunity to learn about and implement preventive strategies because they reveal system weaknesses *before* a patient is injured. Patient safety is a VHA priority, and to reinforce this the Director of NCPS has a direct reporting relationship to the Under Secretary for Health.

Bar Code Medication Administration

A number of interventions have been implemented to prevent medication errors. The most significant is the Bar Code Medication Administration (BCMA) system. This system, coupled with physician order entry, practically eliminates medication errors in VHA facilities caused by administration of the wrong medication or wrong dose to the wrong patient. This system works in the following manner:

- Medication orders are entered into the computer by the physician.
- The orders are automatically transmitted to the pharmacy, where the medication ordered is labeled with the patient's name, identification number, and a bar code.
- The labeled medications are delivered to the unit.
- When the nurse is ready to administer a medication, she or he scans the bar code on the patient's identification arm bracelet and the bar code on the medication.
- The computer verifies that the medication has been ordered for the patient. If the patient or medication is incorrect, the computer will immediately display a message which warns the that the nurse has the wrong patient or the wrong medication.

This system was implemented in all VA facilities in 1999 following a pilot study which demonstrated a 67% reduction in medication errors (Bagian, 2000a).

Elimination of High-Risk Drugs

Another strategy to reduce medication errors is the elimination of high-risk drugs from ward stock. All medication errors are reported nationally, and when a serious medication error occurs that is caused by a systems problem, all VHA facilities immediately receive a patient alert via the Internet. The alert describes the adverse event, its causes, and corrective actions. The same type of error is thus avoided at different facilities, based on lessons learned and disseminated by the facility making the first error. For example, when a number of patients across the nation received overdoses of potassium chloride, notification was immediately made via computer to all VHA facilities using the patient safety alert system, and access to this drug was restricted.

Mandatory Safety Education

The VHA also believes that one of the causes of health care errors is a lack of knowledge among health care providers about patient safety. To correct this problem, VHA has mandated that all employees complete 20 hours of training annually on patient safety. Topics vary from one medical center to another depending on the identified need. Typical topics are identified in the box below.

Compliance with this mandate is monitored through the performance measurement system, which evaluates outcomes quarterly. In addition, the VHA is involved in the development of a pa-

tient safety curriculum, which will be used at affiliated medical, nursing, and health professional schools. The VHA is in an excellent position to lead this effort because of its role in training health care professional in the United States. The VHA is affiliated with 105 medical schools and many more nursing and other health professional schools. If VHA is unable to convince academic programs to include safety training as part of their curriculum, it will be included as part of the medical center orientation of all affiliating students who use VHA for their clinical practicum.

Collaborative Breakthrough Series Model

The Collaborative Breakthrough Series Model was developed by the Institute for Healthcare Improvement (IHI) to rapidly achieve significant quality improvement changes in health care systems. This model creates interdisciplinary teams whose task is to achieve specific outcomes within a limited timeframe. The model relies on the dissemination and adaptation of existing knowledge in multiple settings to accomplish a common aim. The Patient Safety Center of Inquiry in White River Junction, Vermont collaborated with the IHI in 1999 to conduct a 7-month series of educational programs on the reduction of adverse drug effects. Participating in this project were 27 VA Medical Centers. Each team focused on a specific area related to adverse drug events involving heparin, intravenous therapy, chemotherapy, warfarin, insulin, or drug allergies. The teams met for three 2-day educational and planning sessions conducted by IHI faculty and content experts. Between each session, teams implemented changes they had agreed upon during the session. Teams reported their progress monthly to the larger group on a website designed for information sharing. During the formal project and the immediate 6-month followup period, 3699 medication errors were averted (Weeks, Mills, Dittus, Aron, & Batalden, 2001).

Virtual Learning Center

The Virtual Learning Center (VLC) is a national web site that describes successful practices to all VHA employees (www.va.gov/vlc). It enables individuals to post their innovations and lessons

---

Selected Mandatory Patient Safety Education Topics

Missing patients
Bar code medication administration
Patient identification
Blood transfusions
Fire safety
Hazardous wastes
Medical equipment
Patient restraints
Management of suicidal behavior

learned online for others to see. This permits individuals across the country to save time and resources by learning for others' experiences rather than starting from scratch. As of June 15, 2001, over 1300 lessons were described in the VLC. Of that number, 143 were about patient safety. Some examples of patient safety lessons are listed in the box below.

Research on Patient Safety

The VHA believes that research is an important component of its patient safety program. In 1998, the VA issued a call for research proposals on patient safety and prevention of adverse events. This call will remain open as long as funding is available to support it. Between 1997 and 2000, the VHA has invested over $2 million in patient safety research. In 1999, the VA established four Patient Safety Centers of Inquiry. These centers conduct research on critical patient safety challenges. Their research is on implementation of patient safety devices or systems, not basic research. Research topics range from fall prevention to how poor communication contributes to adverse patient events. The centers are located in Florida, California, Ohio, and Vermont. Each center has identified a number of projects designed to improve patient safety. For example, the key objective for the center in Tampa, Florida is to:

Deploy comprehensive patient safety and fall prevention programs across the continuum of care. To that end, we have initiated/expanded the following applied research projects and programs: gait and mobility clinics to prevent patient falls and injuries; use of consistent clinical

protocols to prevent injuries due to falls; telemonitoring program to minimize patient falls and self-medication errors in persons with Parkinson's disease; and a planning team to test alternatives to bed rail use in long-term care facilities. (Quigley, 2000, p. 62)

The Gait and Mobility Clinic is conducting research that compares the fall rate for patients in one of three gait and balance training groups: (1) strength training, (2) T'ai Chi, or (3) a combination of the two.

The center in Palo Alto, California is using a simulated operating room to permit surgeons and anesthesiologists to practice responses to common variations without endangering patients. This center has developed a checklist to be used as a safeguard against errors during surgery.

The center in White River Junction, Vermont is focusing on adverse drug events.

Patient Safety Improvement Awards Program

The VHA has also instituted an awards program to focus interest on and reward innovations in identifying and fixing system weaknesses. Since the inception of the program a number of awards, ranging from $100 to $5000 each, have been made to VHA employees.

CONCLUSION

Four basic factors have contributed to the VHA's success in making system-wide changes to improve patient safety. Most significant is the presence of strong leadership that is committed to improve the quality of patient care delivered. When the IOM report was released in 1999, President Clinton made a number of public statements making reduction of health care errors a priority for the nation. VHA leaders set the standard of making the VHA the best health care system in the nation and provided employees with a road map (*Patient Safety Improvement*) describing exactly what the goals were.

Second, VHA leadership demonstrated its commitment to patient safety by allocating funds to support new technology such as the BCMA program, the VLC, and automatic infusion pumps. Other resources, such as staff to support patient safety programs and education, were also provided.

A third factor that has contributed to the VHA's success is the extensive use of the Internet to

---

Examples of Patient Safety Lessons

1. A Multidisciplinary Program to Reduce Patient Fall Rate
2. Avoiding Wrong Site Surgery
3. A Team Approach to Bar Coded Medication Administration
4. Bedrails as Hazards
5. Eliminating Potential Problems with Prescription Data Entry
6. Preventing Blood Transfusion Errors in the Operating Room

communicate safety concerns to all facilities. The Internet is used to alert providers to errors and potential errors, and the VLC provides VHA employees with a way to learn from previous mistakes.

Fourth, VHA health care providers are held accountable for implementation of safety practices. Safety standards have been incorporated into annual performance-measure and evaluation systems. Monitors to track adverse events are in place so that leadership is always aware of the VHA's track record on patient safety.

Dr. Thomas Garthwaite, the former VA Under Secretary for Health, summarized the VHA's commitment to patient safety before the House Veterans Affairs Subcommittee on Health. He said, "We believe that patient safety can only be achieved by working towards a 'culture of safety'. Patient safety improvements require a new mindset that recognizes that real solutions require an understanding of the 'hidden' opportunities behind the obvious errors" (Garthwaite, 2000, p. 5). Weeks and Bagian (2000) summarized the VHA's commitment to patient safety very succinctly, stating "the VHA's leadership has taken steps to promote a culture of safety by making public commitments to improving patient safety, allocating resources toward establishment of special centers, enhancing employee education on patient safety, and providing incentives to promote safety" (p. 270).

The IOM report *To Err Is Human* served as a validation of the VHA's commitment to improving patient safety, as all of the IOM recommendations applicable to the VHA were in place or in the process of being implemented before its release. The VHA's efforts can serve as an example for other health care organizations as they engineer a culture of safety in the workplace.

REFERENCES

Bagian, J. (2000a, January). *VA's patient safety initiative: Status update* (paper presented at the meeting of the South Central Veterans Health Care Network's Health Care Advisory Committee). Jackson, MS.

Bagian, J. (2000b, February). *Statement of James Bagian, Director of the National Center for Patient Safety on VA Patient Safety Program, before the Committee on Ways and Means Subcommittee on Health.* Washington, DC: Department of Veterans Affairs, Office of Congressional Affairs. Available online at www.va.gov/oca/testimony.

Garthwaite, T. (2000, February) *Statement of Thomas L. Garthwaite, M.D., Deputy Under Secretary for Health, Department of Veterans Affairs, on VA Safety Program, before the House Veterans Affairs Subcommittee on Health and House Commerce Subcommittees on Health and Environment and Oversight and Investigations.* Washington, DC: Department of Veterans Affairs, Office of Congressional Affairs. Available online at www.va.gov/oca/testimony.

Institute of Medicine. (1999). *To Err Is Human: Building a Safer Health System.* Washington, DC: National Academy of Sciences.

Quigley, P.A. (2000). Patient safety center of inquiry makes clinical care innovations a priority. *Veterans Health System Journal, 5*(4), 61-62.

Senge, P.M. (1990). *The fifth discipline: The art and practice of the learning organization.* New York: Doubleday/Currency.

U.S. Department of Veterans Affairs. (1998). *VHA handbook 1051/1: Patient Safety Improvement.* Washington, DC: Veterans Health Administration.

U.S. Department of Veterans Affairs. (2000). *Departmental performance plan FY 2002.* Washington, DC: Office of Budget.

Weeks, W.B. & Bagian, J.P. (2000). Developing a culture of safety in the Veterans Health Administration. *Effective Clinical Practice, 3*(6), 270-276.

Weeks, W.B., Mills, P.D., Dittus, R.S., Aron, D.C., & Batalden, P.B. (2001). Using an improvement model to reduce adverse drug events in VA facilities. *Journal of Quality Improvement, 27*(5), 243-254.

GENETIC ISSUES: GOVERNMENT RESPONSES AND NURSING IMPLICATIONS

Gwen Anderson

"Ultimately, politics in a democracy reflects values much more than makes them."

ARNOLD A. ROGOW

Existing law has failed to ease the public's sinking feeling that its genetic privacy is not secure and that human dignity may not be respected in this era of genomic medicine. Members of the public are wary of how insurance companies and employers will use genetic information; they anticipate ever-widening racial, ethnic, and disability exclusions; they are fearful of discriminatory policies and practices, and question whether health care professionals are knowledgeable about hereditary forms of common diseases. Further, the public requires reassurance that the professionals who provide genetic services are qualified. These and a wide range of other issues raised by genetic science, genetic testing, and the disclosure of genetic information have captured the attention of policy makers and legislators in the United States.

This essay will explore the key issues arising from genetics that are fueling national debate, raising questions of policy and law, and drawing forth legislative responses. Five key issues are identified and outlined that frame current legislative priorities and activities at the federal and state levels. The legislative response to each of these issues is then discussed, and some implications of these genetic issues and legislative responses for nursing are summarized.

GENETIC TESTING AND PRIVACY

Americans are suspicious about undergoing genetic testing because they know that their genetic material might be stored and used in the future for some purpose for which they never gave consent. People realize that it might be possible for a third party such as a computer hacker, government employee, or criminal to access their genetic information, which involves both their private identity and that of their family or ethnic group. Merely giving blood or tissue samples in the context of health care services or medical research might open a breach in privacy could that could harm them, their children, or their grandchildren (Slaughter, 1998).

Americans are concerned about the potential use of their genetic information by employers who make decisions about hiring or firing and about possible violations of privacy or consent by genetic researchers:

In 1998 the National Center for Genome Resources surveyed 1000 American adults, and found that the majority (85%) believed that employers should not have access to patients' genetic information, and 63% indicated that they "probably" or "definitely" would not undergo genetic testing if they knew that insurers or employers could discover the results. (Jeffords & Daschle, 2001, p. 1250)

Concern about privacy was evident again in a Gallup poll conducted in 2000 for the Institute for Health Freedom, in which 93% of American adults 18 years or older said they believe that researchers should obtain their permission before using their genetic information (Jeffords & Daschle, 2001).

The idea that one family member could ask another to undergo genetic testing also might be daunting for individuals who treasure and want to protect their genetic information, perhaps even from themselves. Some people believe that it could be harmful to them to know their "genetic destiny."

GENETIC TESTING AND INSURANCE DISCRIMINATION

There is a widely accepted belief that health and life insurance companies can and will discriminate against people who seek genetic testing for diagnosis of a disease or for assessment of genetic predisposition to disease (Slaughter, 1998). That is, the public is concerned that insurance companies will use genetic information to increase some persons' insurance premiums beyond what is fair and affordable, or that a current insurance policy might be cancelled or coverage of an essential benefit might be denied, or that persons might be blacklisted and not be able to obtain a new policy if they need one in the future. Many people believe that if an individual or a family member is tested, an insurance company may somehow access that information without a person's knowledge or consent. In fact, such fears are not entirely unrealistic. If a person tests positive for a deleterious genetic mutation, then whether or not they are ill, certain benefits could be denied on the ground that the mutation is a preexisting condition (Jeffrey, 1999).

Without consistency or public input, genetic counselors have focused on the topic of genetic discrimination in their discussions with patients (Hall & Rich, 2000b). They have encouraged some people to pay out-of-pocket for predisposition testing so that they can withhold their genetic information from insurance companies and employers, and dis-couraged other people from obtaining genetic testing until nondiscrimination laws are in place (Slaughter, 1998). To protect people's privacy, some genetic professionals have purposefully avoided maintaining complete medical records related to genetic information. While these practices are intended to protect the public, they have encouraged sweeping suspicion and avoidance of genetic services by many people who could benefit from this information (Jeffrey, 1999). In fact, some genetic professionals claim that concern over genetic discrimination is greatly exaggerated (Hall & Rich, 2000a; Reilly, 1998).

The questions at hand are as follows: Can federal and state legislation protect and reassure a skeptical public? Can legislators shift public concern about discrimination toward maximum utilization of fair access to genetic services for all patients and families?

GENETIC TESTING AND RACIAL, ETHNIC, AND DISABILITY GROUP STIGMA

The BRCA1 and BRCA2 gene mutations are often referred to together as the "Jewish gene" or the "Jewish panel" in education materials for the public and professionals. People who are Jewish may fear this becoming the basis of yet one more way of discriminating against them. The Commission for

Women's Equality of the American Jewish Congress demonstrated its sensitivity to this issue by deciding in 1997 to support legislation that bars genetic discrimination by insurance companies (American Jewish Congress Conference, 1996).

Further, some people who live with a genetic condition may take offense to being labeled by medical and nursing professionals as mentally or physically "handicapped" when they do not feel that way. They resent any experience of oppression caused by such a label (Newell, 2000). And historical memories of the eugenics movement in North America and abroad, as well as of sickle-cell carrier testing in African American populations in the 1970s in the United States, still strike a cord of distrust with certain ethnic groups that fear stigmatization by government policies. Some researchers and opinion leaders believe that genetics proves that there is biologic evidence for racial differences, further solidifying classifications of human superiority. Influenced by such thinking, some children who are challenged mentally or physically due to genetic conditions might question their worth or even whether they ever should have been born, or might wish that genetic enhancements could be developed to make them "normal."

GENETICALLY-MEDIATED DISEASES, THE LAW, AND A PROVIDER'S DUTY TO WARN

There have been only two civil cases heard in the United States pertaining to a physician's duty to convey genetic-risk information. Both of these cases point to the inevitable need to fully address the issues of genetic privacy and confidentiality while upholding a duty to warn at-risk relatives of the patient who may be able to avoid harm.

In July, 1995, the Supreme Court of Florida (661 So.2d 278) dismissed allegations of medical malpractice despite the fact that prevailing standards of medical care require health care providers to warn patients to test their children when a genetically transmittable disease is known to exist in the family. In this case, Marianne New was diagnosed with medullary thyroid carcinoma (a feature of a hereditary disease). When Hedi Pate, her daughter, was diagnosed with the same disease 3 years later, she claimed that had she known of the genetic nature of the condition she would have been genetically tested, taken precautions to reduce her risk, and undergone surveillance for early diagnosis. She claimed that the physician was negligent in failing to tell her mother that the disease was inheritable and that her children should be tested for the mutation. The court decided that the daughter did not have a physician-patient relationship, and that consequently the physician had no duty to warn her. However, the court's dismissal precluded answering the question of whether the physician was negligent in failing to warn the patient about the inheritable nature of her disease and implications for her at-risk family members.

In July 1996, the Superior Court of New Jersey (291 N.J. Super.619, 677 A.2d 1188) heard a case where a plaintiff claimed that her father's physician had failed to warn her of the hereditary nature of her father's multiple polyps, which the physician had diagnosed and treated in the 1950s and 1960s. After obtaining her father's medical records and learning that he had died from the same cancer she now suffered from, the plaintiff alleged that her father's physician had been negligent in not warning her of the hereditary nature of the disease (which was known to be hereditary at the time). In dismissing the case, the court held that a physician had no "legal duty to warn a child of a patient of a genetic risk" (p. 4). Again the rationale offered was that there was no physician-patient relationship between the plaintiff and the physician. However, in both this and the Florida case it was recognized that a physician does have "a duty to warn those known to be at risk of avoidable harm from a genetically transmissible condition" (p. 5). In the Florida case, it was decided that it is the patient rather than the physician who is obliged to warn family members. In the New Jersey case, the court decided that this duty is owed by the physician not only to the patient but also to members of the immediate family who may be adversely affected by not being informed. Given these contradictory legal judgments, this issue remains unresolved.

Nurses need to be acutely aware of their duty to obtain complete and accurate family history information, and to assess, discuss, and rule out all possible disease risks associated with familial patterns of disease and known hereditary disease patterns.

Nurses must inform the patient about the potential for increased risk in other family members, offer a referral to a clinical geneticist (for family members too), provide appropriate information regarding surveillance, and follow up according to screening guidelines. Nurses need to document this aspect of their practice, including the patient's and family's responses to genetic information, in their professional notes and/or final consultation letters.

PUBLIC DEMAND FOR QUALIFIED GENETIC PROFESSIONALS

There is concern that health care professionals lack basic knowledge and skills required for providing genetic services. Consequently, there is a need to establish a means to ensure that those who are providing these services are qualified to do so. Furthermore, genetic counselors are pursuing licensure so that they can bill insurance companies directly, without the oversight of a physician (which is now required for every patient). Nurses who are involved in genetic services are strongly motivated to retain and expand their role in the field; consequently, this push for legislation and certification is forcing them to develop formal mechanisms for demonstrating their qualifications (Anderson, Monsen, Prows, Tinley, & Jenkins, 2000; Smolenski & Kolb, 2001). Otherwise, they face exclusion from roles in delivery of genetic services.

LEGISLATIVE RESPONSES
Federal Policy Responses

At the federal level, lawmakers have been slow to respond to scientific breakthroughs for fear of enacting premature regulations (Bettelheim, 2001). Despite the introduction of numerous new bills and amendments to existing bills since 1991, the Health Insurance Portability and Accountability Act (HIPAA) of 1996 is the only federal law that directly addresses the issue of protecting people's genetic privacy and prohibiting genetic discrimination. This legislation, like other attempts at the national and state level, is based on key elements of the Genetic Privacy Act (Annas, Glantz, & Roche, 1995), a model piece of genetic privacy legislation drafted in response to the Human Genome Project.

One of the aims of the HIPAA is to ensure that employees can change jobs without risking the loss of insurance coverage. To this end the HIPAA prohibits group health plans from using a genetic diagnosis as the basis of a preexisting condition exclusion when the person tested is asymptomatic, presymptomatic, or an unaffected carrier of a recessive disorder. This prevents insurers from denying, canceling, or refusing to renew insurance as long as enrollees are asymptomatic and receive no medical treatment for the condition diagnosed. (White, 1999, p. 341)

In 1994, President Clinton and Congress banned federal support of all human embryo research (Marshal, 1994). This ban became federal law in 1997; however, it is revisited each year. President Bush supports this ban despite lobbying efforts by scientists who laud the benefits of embryo research and the use of human embryos to facilitate stem cell research (Vogel, 2001a). The ban now in place appears to be prudent, given new knowledge that embryo research using animal models or human placentas may be as effective as research using stem cells from human embryos (Vogel, 2001b). Current policy and legislative discussions related to stem cell research are linked to defining and regulating human cloning and ethically permissible human genetic enhancements (Scully Leach & Rehmann-Sutter, 2001).

July 11, 2001 marked the first-ever Congressional hearing on genetic discrimination in the United States. The hearing, titled "The Potential for Discrimination in Health Insurance Based on Predictive Genetic Testing," was held by the Senate Commerce Subcommittee on Commerce, Trade, and Consumer Protection. Federal bills aimed at improving access to genetic information and prohibiting genetic discrimination by insurers and employers are introduced with each new Congress; see, for example, the bills introduced in the 106th Congress (www.nci.nih.gov/legis/sept99/genetic.html) and the bills introduced in the 107th Congress (www.1pa.org/1papublic/policy/status/statusof.htm); one of these bills have been approved as yet. Experts at the Human Genome Research Institute anticipate that genetic discrimination cases will become more frequent in the future and that legislation will not arrive soon enough nor be extensive enough to protect people from disputes and litigation.

Despite progress to date, many issues surrounding genetics have yet to be addressed by legislation. For instance, there are no laws governing stem cell research, human cloning, deoxyribonucleic acid (DNA) data banking, or availability of and access to genetic services and genetic tests. For information about genetics related legislation in the 50 states, contact the National Conference of State Legislatures at 1560 Broadway, Suite 700, Denver, CO 80202; phone (303) 830-2200; fax (303) 863-8003; website www.ncsl.org.

The myriad social, health, public policy, and legislative implications of these topics are being explored by the National Bioethics Advisory Commission and the Department of Health and Human Services Secretary's Advisory Committee on Genetic Testing.

State Policy Responses

In the United States, 39 states have some legislation in place or in process to address issues of genetic privacy, confidentiality, and discrimination. Some of the regulatory bills are comprehensive and broad in scope, while others are narrowly focused or outdated. According to government officials, individual "states have a patchwork of genetic-information nondiscrimination laws, none of them comprehensive" (www.ornl.gov/hgmis/elsi/legislat.html, p. 2). However, each of the states, in varying degrees, recognizes that genetic health care data and genetic research data should be kept private and confidential. In a review of proposed or enacted legislation, the following themes emerged:

- Health insurers should not require an individual to obtain a genetic test or disclose genetic information about a family member to determine insurability or premium rates.
- Insurers and employers should not ask whether a person has undergone genetic testing or ask the results of such testing.
- Insurers should be prohibited from canceling, denying, limiting, or establishing differential premium rates based on a genetic test.
- Insurers should be prohibited from making or permitting any unfair discrimination. Insurers

Proposed Legislation Regarding Genetic Information in the 107th Congress

CONGRESSIONAL SPONSOR	PROPOSED FEDERAL LEGISLATION
Snowe (R-ME)	S 328: *Genetic Information Nondiscrimination in Health Insurance Act* Focuses on insurance discrimination and would bar insurers from using genetic information to deny coverage or raise premiums.
Hutchinson (R-AR)	HR 583: *Privacy Commission Act* Calls for a commission to consider privacy issues.
Daschle (D-SD), Slaughter (D-NY)	HR 602, S 318: *Genetic Nondiscrimination in Health Insurance and Employment Act* Would prohibit health insurance and employment discrimination against individuals and their families on the basis of predictive genetic information or genetic services.
Greenwood (R-PA)	HR 1215: *Medical Information Protection and Research Enhancement Act* Would enact the medical privacy laws called for by the Health Insurance Portability and Accountability Act (HIPAA) of 1996 and repeal medical privacy regulations issued under HIPAA.

From www.lpa.org/lpapublic/policy/status/statusof.htm.

should be prohibited from releasing any genetic information to a third party without written prior authorization.

• Insurers should not be liable for inadvertently receiving genetic test results or family history information.

• Life, disability income, or long-term care insurers should be allowed to use genetic information or genetic propensity in underwriting policies if these are based on sound actuarial principles.

• An insurer should use genetic testing information if the results are favorable to the applicant and voluntarily submitted.

• Health care professionals are obliged to obtain written informed consent prior to performing a genetic test. They are prohibited from disclosing genetic information unless preauthorized by written informed consent for each disclosure.

• State laws should enforce penalties for unlawful disclosure of genetic information.

Licensure of Genetic Professionals

There is an emerging national trend toward enacting state laws that regulate the practice of genetic counseling. For example, in September, 2000 the Genetic Test Disclosure and Genetic Licensure Bill, introduced by Senator Patricia Johnston (D-CA), became law in the state of California. This paves the way for other states to enact similar legislation, as in the state of Utah, where the Genetic Counselors Licensing Act mandated licensure for the practice of genetic counseling starting on January 1, 2002. New York, North Carolina, and other states are engaged in this same legislative process.

Nurses must already be licensed to practice their profession, and genetic counseling is a communication skill, which falls within the scope of nursing practice. However, nurses will need a credential to verify their competence to deliver genetic counseling services. The International Society of Nurses in Genetics began offering the first Advanced Practice Nurse in Genetics credential, the APNGc, in December, 2001 (Monsen, 2001). An international agenda for advancing policy for genetic nursing education (Anderson, Read, & Monsen, 2000), an international call for a declaration on human rights, nursing, genetics, and public health (Anderson & Rorty, 2001), and an International Council of Nurses monograph promoting international genetic nursing (Feetham, in press) all seek to facilitate nursing education, credentialing, and eventually certification in genetics.

GENETIC PRIVACY, PERSONAL FREEDOM, AND HUMAN DIGNITY

The tension between the right to privacy and the threat of unauthorized access to personal information has raised national attention regarding genetic testing and genetic information. Legislators have drafted bills that would restrict access of genetic information to prevent violations of privacy. The notion of *genetic privacy* stems from a broad definition of privacy that is based on the human right to be left alone, which implies a right to either grant or withhold access to your personal information. The right to privacy is linked to the right to informed consent and the constitutional right to personal freedom. Amendments to the Patient Bill of Rights and the Medical Information Act have been proposed in an effort to protect a person's right to decide whether to *receive* genetic information about him or herself. Of major concern is the circumstance under which a person shares information with family members, health care professionals, employers, insurers, or others who may have a financial interest in knowing about a person's current or future health. To protect the public from employment discrimination and the damaging use of genetic health information, Rothstein (2001) and others also propose reinterpretation of the American Disabilities Act to include anti-genetic-discrimination language.

IMPLICATIONS FOR NURSING

Nurses, like other professionals, are incorporating genetics practice into existing professional roles. Because the public is so concerned about issues surrounding genetics, nurses must be prepared to address patients' and families' questions and concerns. Whether or not patients and families use genetic services or participate in genetic research depends on their values and beliefs about the benefits and harms of genetic technology—and these often mirror the values and beliefs held and promoted by health care professionals. Nurses must avoid promulgating unrealistic fears of genetic discrimination while always protecting patients' privacy (Woogara, 2001). Equally important, nurses need to participate in policy and legislative discussions and publications. Two websites are particularly useful for achieving this goal: (1) *Thomas: Legislative Information on the Internet* (thomas. loc.gov/) and (2) the George Mason University Center for Health Policy website (www.gmu.edu/ departments/chpre/policyinstitute/).

As patient advocates, nurses are privileged to bring the voices of patients and families into public forums and policy setting arenas such as task forces, advisory boards, university councils, and hospital leadership circles. Updating our knowledge about genetics, policy, legislation, and precedent-setting legal cases must be part of ongoing continuing education for genetic nurses in practice, education, and research.

REFERENCES

American Jewish Congress Conference. (1996). *Understanding the genetics of breast cancer.* Available online at www.ajcongress. org/health/genetics.htm.

Anderson, G., Monsen, R., Prows, C., Tinley, S., & Jenkins, J. (2000). Preparing the nursing profession for participation in a genetic paradigm in health care. *Nursing Outlook, 48*(1), 23-27.

Anderson, G., Read, C., & Monsen, R. (2000). Genetics, nursing, and public policy: Setting an international agenda. *Policy, Politics, & Nursing Practice, 1*(4), 245-255.

Anderson, G. & Rorty, V.M. (2001). Key points for developing an international declaration on nursing, human rights, human genetics, and public health policy. *Nursing Ethics, 8*(3), 259-271.

Annas, G., Glantz, L., & Roche, P. (1995). *The Genetic Privacy Act and Commentary.* Boston, MA: Boston University School of Public Health.

Bettelheim, A. (2001, June 23). Cures may arise from genome mapping, but congress anticipates headaches. *CQ Weekly,* 1505-1506.

Esserman, L., Aubry, W., Ziegler, J., & Crawford, B. (2001, January-February). Insurance issues in genetic testing for cancer: Summary of a workshop. *Managed Care & Cancer,* 12-16.

Feetham, S. (In press). *Nursing and Genetics—Leadership for Global Health.* Geneva, Switzerland: International Council of Nurses.

Hall, M. & Rich, S. (2000a). Laws restricting health insurers' use of genetic information: Impact on genetic discrimination. *American Journal of Human Genetics, 66,* 293-307.

Hall, M. & Rich, S. (2000b). Patients' fear of genetic discrimination by health insurers: The impact of legal protections. *Genetics in Medicine, 2*(4), 214-221.

Jeffery, N. (1999, October 18). A change in policy: Genetic testing threatens to fundamentally alter the whole notion of insurance. *The Wall Street Journal,* p. R1.

Jeffords, J. & Daschle, T. (2001). Political issues in the genome era. *Science, 291*(5507), 1249.

Marshal, E. (1994). Human embryo research: Clinton rules out some studies. *Science, 266*(5193), 1634-1635.

McCall Smith, A. & Revel, M. (2001, April). Rappators for the United Nations Educational, Scientific and Cultural Organization: Division of Human Sciences, Philosophy and the Ethics of Sciences and Technology. *The use of embryonic stem cells in therapeutic research: Report of the International Bioethics Committee on the ethical aspects of human embryonic stem cell research* (paper presented at the Seventh Session of the International Bioethics Committee). Paris, France.

Monsen, B.R. (2001). Credentialing committee report. *ISONG Newsletter, 12*(1), 2.

Newell, C. (2000). Biomedicine, genetics and disability: Reflections on nursing and a philosophy of holism. *Nursing Ethics, 7*(3), 227-236.

Reilly, P. (1998). Genetic risk assessment and insurance. *Genetic Testing, 2*(1), 1-2.

Rothstein, M. (2001). Genetic Privacy and confidentiality: Why they are so hard to protect. In B. Longest (Ed.). *Contemporary health policy.* Chicago: Health Administration Press.

Scully Leach, J. & Rehmann-Sutter, C. (2001). When norms normalize: The case of genetic "enhancement." *Human Gene Therapy, 12,* 87-95.

Slaughter, L. (1998). Genetic Information must remain private to prevent discrimination, spur research. *Genetic Testing, 2,* 1.

Smolenski, M. & Kolb, S. (2001). The road to nursing certification. *ISONG Newsletter, 12*(1), 5-6.

Vogel, G. (2001a). Bush grapples with stem cells, cloning. *Science, 292*(5526), 2409-2411.

Vogel, G. (2001b). Can adult stem cells suffice? *Science, 292* (5523), 1820-1822.

White, M. (1999). Underlying ambiguities in genetic privacy legislation. *Genetic Testing, 3*(4), 341-345.

Woogara, J. (2001). Human rights and patients' privacy in UK hospitals. *Nursing Ethics, 8*(3), 234-246.

22 Legislative and Regulatory Processes

YVONNE SANTA ANNA

"Passage of a bill requires that at critical points in the policy-making process "a problem is recognized, a solution is available, the political climate makes the time right for a change, and the constraints do not prohibit action."

JOHN KINGDON

INFLUENCING THE LEGISLATIVE PROCESS

Public policy formation in the United States often appears to be indecisive and slow, and it can be difficult for the casual observer to distinguish the subtleties of the process. These nuances require that the observer select a conceptual model of policy-making to assist in understanding the specifics of the policy-making process—that is, why a particular proposal is enacted or defeated. In Chapter 4, Hanley sets forth several models for policy analysis. These can clarify how an issue is placed on the formal agenda for authoritative decision-making. Nurses who understand this process can better influence the system toward the development of sound health policies for their patients, their patients' families, and the profession of nursing.

This chapter will describe the path by which a bill becomes a federal or state law in the United States. To illustrate the state-level process, we have utilized political scientist John Kingdon's adaptation of Cohen, March, and Olsen's "Garbage Can Model of Organizational Choice" (1984), which describes the dynamics of the policy-making process and the progression of one bill through the Maryland legislature. The legislative path differs only slightly between the federal and state levels and from state to state.

INTRODUCTION OF A BILL

Only a member of the U.S. Congress (or of a state legislature) can introduce bills, though the idea for a bill can come from anyone, including constituents. A legislator can introduce any one of several types of bills and resolutions by simply giving their bill to the clerk of the house or, in Congress, placing the bill in a box called the *hopper* (Congressional Quarterly, 2000). In the U.S. Senate, a senator can postpone the introduction of another senator's bill by one day by voicing an objection. Legislation is often introduced simultaneously in the Senate and the House of Representatives as a pair of companion bills.

A member of Congress or state legislator who understands the legislative process in depth can contribute more to either the passage or defeat of a bill than one who is an expert only on its substance. However, the numerous players involved (the executive branch, the legislature, constituents, and special interest groups) and the complexity of the legislative process make it far easier to defeat a bill than to pass one.

Of the thousands of bills introduced annually, relatively few rise to the formal decision-making agenda. For example, during the 106th Session of Congress (1999-2000), the House and Senate saw a total of 8968 bills introduced (5681 and 3287, respectively). Of this number, 1976 were health-care-related bills (1259 in the House and 717 in the Senate). Of the 8968 bills introduced, the President signed 580 bills into public law (Library of Congress, 2001).

Every bill introduced in Congress faces a 2-year deadline; it must pass into law by then or die by default. Box 22-1 provides an overview of the various types of bills that can be introduced by members of Congress. Legislators introduce bills for a variety of reasons: to declare a position on an issue, as a favor to a constituent or a special interest group, to obtain publicity, for political self-preservation. Some legislators, having introduced a bill, claim that they have acted to solve the problem that motivated it but do not continue to work toward enactment of the measure, blaming a committee or other members of the legislature if no further action is taken. Passage of a bill requires that at critical points in the policy-making process "a problem is recognized, a solution is available, the political climate makes the time right for a change, and the constraints do not prohibit action" (Kingdon, 1984, p. 93). Although meeting these conditions helps a bill to rise on the decision agenda, nothing can guarantee enactment.

INFLUENCING THE INTRODUCTION OF A BILL

Nurses can influence the introduction of bills as constituents and as members of professional associations that lobby Congress. They can call attention to problems in funding health care, such as the need for expanded services for uninsured children, the need for prescription drug coverage under Medicare, or the need to increase reimbursement for nursing services. Legislators like to work with organized groups that have strong positions on a bill, such as the American Nurses Association, American Association of Colleges of Nursing, American Association of Nurse Anesthetists, American Nephrology Nurses' Association, or the state nurses associations.

Frequently associations are asked to assist in drafting legislation and in lobbying members of the legislature. Coalitions of interested organizations are created to present a united front, a clear message, and a strong constituency to persuade legislators to support a particular bill (see Chapter 8). Enactment, if achieved at all, may take several legislative sessions.

BOX **22-1** Types of Bills in the U.S. Congress

Bill: This is used for most legislation, whether general, public, or private (i.e., initiated by non-Congressional sources). The bill number is prefixed with HR in the House, S in the Senate.

Joint resolution: This is subject to the same procedures as bills, with the exception of any joint resolution proposing an amendment to the Constitution. The latter must be approved by two thirds of both chambers, whereupon it is sent directly to the Administrator of General Services for submission to the states for ratification, rather than to the President. The bill number is prefixed with HJ Res in the House and SJ Res in the Senate.

Concurrent resolution: This is used for matters affecting the operations of both houses. The bill number is prefixed with H Con Res in the House, S Con Res in the Senate.

Resolution: This is used when a matter concerns the operation of either chamber alone; adopted only by the chamber in which it originates. The bill number is prefixed with H Res in the House and S Res in the Senate.

From Congressional Quarterly (2000). *Guide to current American government.* Washington, DC: Congressional Quarterly.

Identifying the appropriate sponsor to introduce a bill is critical to its success. In selecting a primary bill sponsor, it is best to ask a member of a committee that has jurisdiction over the program or issue you wish to have addressed. For example, in the U.S. Senate, the Finance Committee has jurisdiction over the Medicare program and decides which Medicare-related legislation gets sent to the full Senate for a vote. Legislation that would address changes in direct reimbursement of nurse practitioners (NPs) or nurse anesthetists under Medicare would be less likely to be tabled (i.e., never acted upon) if a member of the Senate Finance Committee was a primary sponsor of the measure.

COMMITTEE ACTION

Committees are centers of policy making at both the federal and state levels. It is in committee that conflicting points of view are discussed and legislation is often refined and amended. Successful committee consideration of bills requires organization, consensus building, and time; only about 15% of all bills referred to committees are reported out for House and Senate consideration.

The Senate and House have separate committees with distinct rules and procedures. Committee procedure provides the means for members of the legislature to sift through an otherwise overwhelming number of bills, proposals, and complex issues. Within the respective guidelines of each chamber, committees adopt their own rules to address their organizational and procedural issues. Generally, committees operate independently of each other and of their respective parent chambers (Schneider, 2001).

There are three types of committees at the federal level: *standing; select;* and *joint.* A *standing* committee has permanent jurisdiction over bills and issues in its content area. Some standing committees set *authorizing* funding levels and others set *appropriating* funding levels for proposed laws. This two-step authorizing-appropriating process is designed to concentrate the policy-making decisions within the authorizing committee and decisions about precise funding levels within the appropriations committees.

A *select* committee cannot report out a bill and is often created by the leadership to address a special problem or concern. A *joint* committee consists of members of both the House and Senate. One type of a joint committee is the *conference* committee, in which members of each chamber and party work together to address differences in their respective bills.

In Congressional committees, leadership and authority is centered in the chair of the committee. The chair, always a member of the majority party, decides the committee's agenda, conducts its meetings, and controls the funds distributed by the chamber to the committee (Schneider, 2001). The senior minority party member of the committee is called the *ranking minority member* (or *ranking member*). The committee's subcommittees also have chairs and ranking members. Often, but not always, the ranking member assists the chair with some of the responsibilities of the committee or subcommittee. The committee chair usually refers a bill to the subcommittees for initial consideration, but only the full committee can report out a bill to

the floor (Schneider, 2001). For example, the House Ways and Means Committee refers most Medicare bills to the House Ways and Means Subcommittee on Health. If the subcommittee wishes to take action on the bill, it usually will schedule at least one hearing to discuss the substance of the proposed legislation.

In very unusual circumstances, a few bills will bypass the committee process. This can only happen if the leadership of the majority consents. For example, according to a U.S. House Select Committee on Aging fact sheet, "Since the Roosevelt era, major pieces of social legislation, including civil rights reforms and labor reforms, such as the wage and hours bill, were forced to bypass committees of jurisdiction because the committees refused or delayed in allowing the House to consider them" (Pepper & Roybal, 1988, p.1). In the end, however, committees and subcommittees usually select the bills they want to consider and ignore the rest. Committees thus perform a gatekeeping function by selecting from the thousands of measures introduced in each session those that meet their party's leadership priorities and that they consider to merit floor debate.

Consideration of bills whose content overlaps the jurisdictions of different committees falls to the leader of the chamber to decide. Health care issues, for example, can cut across the jurisdiction of more than one committee. When this occurs in the House, upon advice from the Parliamentarian, the Speaker of the House will base his or her referral decision on the chamber's rules and precedents for subject matter jurisdiction and identify the appropriate *primary* committee and other committees for the bill's referral (Schneider, 2001). The Parliamentarians in both chambers have a key role in advising the member of Congress presiding over a bill on the floor. While a member is free to take or ignore the Parliamentarian's advice, few have the knowledge of the chamber's procedures to preside on their own. The primary committee has primary responsibility for guiding the referred measure to final passage. Referrals to more than one committee can have a positive effect by providing opportunities for greater public discussion of the issue and multiple points of access for special interest groups, but this can also greatly slow down the legislative process (Davidson & Oleszek, 1996).

A committee can handle a bill in any of the following ways (Congressional Quarterly, 1993):
• Approve a bill with or without amendments.
• Rewrite or revise the bill and report it out to the full House or Senate.
• Report it unfavorably (i.e., allow it to be considered by the full House or Senate, but with a recommendation that the bill be rejected).
• Take no action, which kills the bill.

AUTHORIZATION AND APPROPRIATION PROCESS

To understand the legislative process and to analyze individual pieces of legislation, it is important to know the distinction between *authorizing* legislation and *appropriating* legislation. Because a considerable amount of Congressional activity is concerned with decisions related to spending money and because much of this activity has a direct effect on health care and nursing programs, it is especially important for nurses to be familiar with the authorization–appropriation process. Programs and agencies such as the Nurse Education Act, Scholarships for Disadvantaged Students, the National Health Service Corps, the National Institute of Nursing Research, the National Institutes of Health, and the Agency for Health Care Policy and Research are all subject to the authorization–appropriation process.

Before any of these programs can receive or spend money from the U.S. Treasury, a two-step process usually must occur. First, an *authorization* bill allowing an agency or program to come into being or to continue to exist must be passed. The authorization bill is the substantive bill that establishes the purpose of and guidelines for the program and usually sets limits on the amount that can be spent. It gives a federal agency or program the legal authority to operate. Authorizing legislation does not, however, provide the actual dollars for a program or enable an agency to spend funds in the future. Renewal or modification of existing authorization is called *reauthorization.*

Second, an *appropriation* bill must be passed. The appropriation bill enables an agency or program to make spending commitments and to actually spend money. In almost all cases an appropriation bill for an activity is not supposed to be passed until the authorization for that activity is enacted. That is, no money can be spent on a program unless it first has been authorized to exist. Conversely, if a program has been authorized but no money is provided (appropriated) for its implementation, that program cannot be carried out (Collender, 1991).

The authorization–appropriation process is determined by Congressional rules that, like most Congressional rules, can be waived, circumvented, or ignored on occasion. For example, failure to enact an authorization does not necessarily prevent the appropriations committee from acting. If an expired program—such as, the Nursing Education Act—for example, is deemed likely to be reauthorized, it may receive funds. These must be spent in accordance with the expired authorizing language.

Today, much of the federal government is funded through the annual enactment of 13 general appropriations bills. Whether agencies receive all the money they request depends, in part, on the recommendations of the authorizing and appropriating committees. Each chamber has authorizing and appropriating committees, and these have differing responsibilities. For federal nursing education and research activities, the authorizing committees are the Senate Labor and Human Resources Committee and the House Commerce Committee. The appropriating committee for federal nursing education and research programs are the Senate and House appropriations committees and their subcommittees on Labor, Health and Human Services, and Education.

COMMITTEE PROCEDURES

Committee consideration of a measure usually consists of three standard steps: hearings, markups, and reports.

Hearings. *Hearings* can be legislative, oversight, or investigative; each of these types of hearing may be either public or closed (Schneider, 2001). When the committee leadership decides to proceed with a measure, it will usually conduct hearings to receive testimony in support of a measure. From

HOW A BILL BECOMES A LAW

The Federal Level

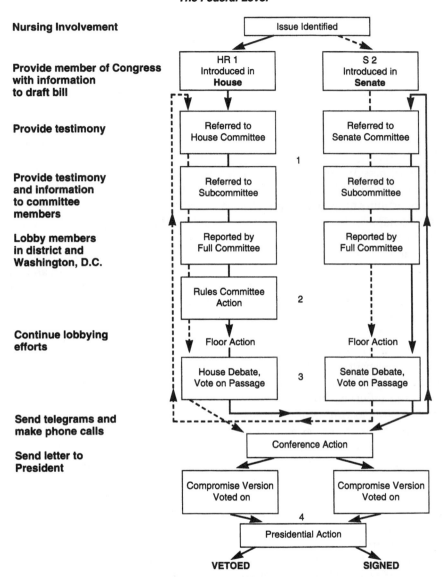

Nursing Involvement

**Provide member of Congress
with information
to draft bill**

Provide testimony

**Provide testimony
and information
to committee
members**

**Lobby members
in district and
Washington, D.C.**

**Continue lobbying
efforts**

**Send telegrams and
make phone calls**

**Send letter to
President**

Issue Identified

HR 1
Introduced in
House

S 2
Introduced in
Senate

Referred to
House Committee

Referred to
Senate Committee

1

Referred to
Subcommittee

Referred to
Subcommittee

Reported by
Full Committee

Reported by
Full Committee

Rules Committee
Action

2

Floor Action

Floor Action

House Debate,
Vote on Passage

3

Senate Debate,
Vote on Passage

Conference Action

Compromise Version
Voted on

Compromise Version
Voted on

4

Presidential Action

VETOED   **SIGNED**

[1] A bill goes to full committee first, then to special subcommittees for hearings, debate, revisions, and approval. The same process occurs when it goes to full committee. It either dies in committee or proceeds to the next step.
[2] Only the House has a Rules Committee to set the "rule" for floor action and conditions for debate and amendments. In the Senate, the leadership schedules action.
[3] The bill is debated, amended, and passed or defeated. If passed, it goes to other chamber and follows the same path. If each chamber passes a similar bill, both versions go to conference.
[4] The President may sign the bill into law, allow it to become law without his signature, or veto it and return it to Congress. To override the veto, both houses must approve the bill by a $2/3$ majority vote.

these hearings the committee will gather information and views, identify problems, gauge support for and opposition to the bill, and build a public record of committee action that addresses the measure (Schneider, 2001). Although most hearings are held in Washington, DC, field hearings in the members' respective states are also held.

Most witnesses are invited to testify before the committee by the chair, who is a member of the majority party and who sets the agenda for the hearing proceedings. The ranking minority member may have an opportunity to request a witness, but it is up to the discretion of the chair to agree to the selection of the witness. Written testimony can also be submitted to the committee by persons who do not have the opportunity to speak their position on a measure in person.

Nurses can influence the policy-making process by testifying at bill hearings. Frequently committees prefer to deal with large, organized groups that have a position on an issue rather than with private individuals. Professional nursing organizations testify on behalf of their members. Congressional hearings are listed in the official House and Senate web sites at www.house.gov and www.senate.gov. The C-SPAN website (www.c-span.org) provides live and recorded coverage of hearings.

Constituents can influence the committee process by meeting with and writing to the members of the committee. Concerns expressed by constituents are given serious consideration.

Lobbyists often meet with all members of the committee to express their client's position on a measure. Professional associations often activate a grassroots network of members, asking them to contact the committee members to request cosponsorship of or opposition to the measure.

The hearing process at the state level is similar, as is the importance of an organized approach to presenting testimony. When several representatives of nursing plan to testify on a bill, it is more efficient and effective for them to coordinate their testimony, raising different aspects of an issue rather than repeating the same points. It is also important for various nursing representatives to emphasize those issues where there is agreement; a unified message can strengthen the impression of a powerful coalition. And a hearing room packed with a supportive audience makes a powerful statement to legislators about support for an issue.

Markups. When legislative hearings are concluded, a subcommittee decides whether to attempt to report a measure. If the chair decides to proceed with the measure, she or he will generally choose to continue with the legislative process to "mark up" the bill. A *markup* is the committee meeting where a measure is modified through amendments to clean up problems or errors within the measure (Schneider, 2001). A quorum of one third of the committee is required in both chambers to hold a markup session (Schneider, 2001). A markup session can weaken or strengthen a measure. Pressure from outside interest groups is often intense at this stage. Under Congressional "sunshine rules," markups are conducted in public, except on national-security or related issues.

After conducting hearings and markups, a subcommittee sends its recommendation to the full committee, which may conduct its own hearings and markups, ratify the subcommittee's decision, take no action, or return the bill to the subcommittee for further study.

Reports. The rules of both the Senate and House dictate that a committee *report* accompany each bill to the floor. The report, written by committee staff, describes the intent of legislation (i.e., its purpose and scope). It explains any amendments to the bill, and any changes made to current law by the bill, estimates the cost of the bill to the government, sets out documentation for the bill's legislative intent, and often contains dissenting views on the measure from the minority-party committee members.

A committee's description of the legislative intent of the bill is extremely important, especially for the government agency that will implement and enforce the law. Sometimes the report contains explicit instructions on how the agency should interpret the law in regulations, or the report may be written without great detail. Sometimes an agency will interpret the law narrowly, particularly if it is written vaguely. For example, when certified nurse midwives received reimbursement authority under the Medicare program, the agency chose to reimburse them only for gynecologic services, not for all the services covered by Medicare, which they are legally able to provide. This was a narrow interpretation of the law and was not the intent of Congress.

The committee report is also important because it offers those interested in the bill an opportunity to promote or protect their interests. Committee staff frequently include the report language suggested by special interest groups if it is congruent with the bill.

FLOOR ACTION IN THE HOUSE AND SENATE

After a bill is reported out of committee, it can be placed on a calendar of chamber business and scheduled for floor action by the leadership of the majority party (Schneider, 2001). If the bill is not controversial, it may be dealt with expeditiously. Otherwise it is placed on the chamber's calendar for future consideration. Both the rules governing the calendar on which a bill is placed and subsequent floor procedures differ between the House and Senate and among state chambers. Box 22-2 compares the House and Senate procedures for scheduling and raising measures.

The influence of the committee chair and ranking member of the committee that reports out a measure is maintained throughout the floor proceedings. They continue to manage the measure by "planning parliamentary strategy, controlling time for debate, responding to questions from colleagues, warding off unwanted amendments, and building coalitions in favor of their positions" (Schneider, 2001, p. 6). Box 22-3 compares House and Senate rules for floor consideration of a measure. In the House, the Committee on Rules governs proceedings on the floor; there is no such committee in the Senate.

When a bill moves to the floor, special interest groups continue to lobby its opponents, its proponents, and particularly undecided legislators, attempting to influence the outcome of the vote. This process is usually begun after the introduction of the bill, when lobbyists meet with the members of the referring committee to gather support for the measure, and continues until the bill is signed into law. When a bill moves to the floor, constituents are activated to contact the members of the legislature from their own districts. Members listen attentively to their constituents, and so lobbying should continue until the moment of the vote, especially lobbying of undecided members. Lobbyists are known to wait outside the cloakroom in the "lobby" to catch the attention of members as they move in and out of the chambers.

A vote on the bill is taken after the debate and amendment process is completed. There are three methods of voting: (1) *voice vote,* which calls for members to answer yea or nay (victory is judged by ear); (2) *division vote,* which requires a head count of those favoring and those opposing an amendment; and (3) *recorded teller vote,* which records each legislator's name and position taken on the vote.

Recorded votes are the most valuable to lobbyists and constituents because they document how the member voted—helpful information in determining whether to continue support for a legislator and as a predictor of a legislator's future stands on issues.

CONFERENCE ACTION

Before a bill can be sent to the executive branch for consideration, identical bills must be passed in both chambers. Frequently the bills originally considered by the House and Senate chambers are not identical, so members of each chamber must meet to resolve the differences. This is often where much of the hard bargaining and compromising takes place in the passage of legislation. The leaders of each chamber appoint *conferees,* usually senior members of the committees with jurisdiction over the bill, to meet with the conferees of the other chamber.

A joint conference offers another opportunity for groups and individuals to persuade members to support various positions on controversial aspects of the bill. Frequently there is controversy over the amount of money allocated to a federal program. For example, House and Senate funding authorizations for nursing education programs can differ by tens of millions of dollars. Generally, supporters of a program would lobby for the version of the bill authorizing the largest amount of funding for it.

When agreement is reached on the controversial provisions of the measure, a conference report is written explaining the differences considered in resolving the issue. Both chambers must then

BOX **22-2**   Scheduling and Raising Measures in the U.S. House and U.S. Senate

House	Senate
Five calendars (Union, House, Corrections, Private, Discharge)	Two calendars (Legislative and Executive)
Special days for raising measures*	No special days
Scheduling by speaker and majority party leadership in consultation with selected Representatives	Scheduling by majority party leadership in broad consultation with minority party leaders and interested Senators
No practice of "holds"	Individual Senators can place "holds" on the raising measure, within limits
Powerful role for Rules Committee	No committee with role equivalent to that of House Rules Committee
Special rules (approved b majority vote) govern floor consideration of most major legislation	*Complex unanimous consent agreements* (approved by unanimous consent) govern floor consideration of major measures
Noncontroversial measures usually approved under *suspension of the rules* procedure	Noncontroversial measures approved by *unanimous consent* procedure
Difficult to circumvent committee consideration of measures	Easier to circumvent committee consideration of measures

*Adapted from Schneider, J. (2001). *House and Senate rules of procedures: A comparison* (Congressional research service order code RL30945, CRS-6).

BOX **22-3**   Floor Procedures of U.S. House and the U.S. Senate

House	Senate
Presiding officer has considerable discretion in recognizing Members	Presiding officer has little discretion in recognizing Senators
Rulings of presiding officer seldom challenged	Rulings of presiding officer frequently challenged
Debate time always restricted	Unlimited debate;* individual Senators can filibuster
Debate ends by majority vote in the House and in the Committee of the Whole (i.e., the membership of the House)	Super-majority vote required to invoke cloture; up to 30 hours of post-cloture debate allowed[†]
Most major measures considered in Committee of the Whole	No Committee of the Whole
Number and type of amendments often limited by special rule; bills amended by section or title	Unlimited amendments; bills generally open to amendment at any point
Germaneness of amendments required (unless requirement is waived by special rule)	Germaneness of amendments not generally required
Quorum calls usually permitted only in connection with record votes	Quorum calls in order almost any time; often used for purposes of deliberate delay
Votes recorded by electronic device; electronic vote can be requested only after voice or division vote is completed	No electronic voting system; roll call votes can be requested almost any time
House routinely adjourns at end of each legislative day	Senate often recesses instead of adjourning; legislative days can continue for several calendar days

Adapted from Schneider, J. (2001). *House and Senate rules of procedures: A comparison* (Congressional research service order code RL30945, CRS-6).
*Except when complex unanimous consent agreements or rule-making provisions in statues impose time restrictions.
[†]Adoption of the motion to table by majority vote also ends Senate debate. Use of this motion, however, is generally reserved for cases when the Senate is prepared to reject the pending bill.

approve the conference version of the bill for the bill to become law.

EXECUTIVE ACTION

After both chambers have passed identical versions of a bill, it is ready to go to the executive branch. The executive (President or Governor) has the power to sign a bill into law, veto it, or return it to the legislature with no signature and a message stating his or her objections. If no further action is taken, the bill dies; or, the legislature may decide to call for another floor vote to overturn the executive's veto. A two-thirds vote is required to override an executive veto in Congress and in many states. Under the U.S. Constitution, a bill becomes law if the President does not sign it within 10 days of the time she or he receives it, provided Congress is in session. Presidents occasionally permit enactment of legislation in this manner when they want to make a political statement of disapproval of the legislation but do not believe that their objections warrant a veto. If Congress adjourns before the 10-day period expires, the unsigned bill does not become law. In this case the bill has been defeated by the *pocket veto* (Congressional Quarterly, 1993).

REGULATORY PROCESS

As important as it is to become skilled at influencing the legislative process, it is equally important to influence the regulatory process (see p. 460). Regulations have a direct impact on a nurse's work and professional life. As changes in health care financing and delivery structures are driving changes in the current health-care-provider licensing system, many states are considering changes in the regulation of nursing, from amending the Nurse Practice Act to accomplishing a major overhaul of the entire licensing system. Many of these changes will take place in the regulatory arena within a nurse's state.

Though some regulations may be developed or amended without legislation, other regulations are created by the details of new or amended laws. The development of such regulations takes months and sometimes years. It is this important step—the development of regulations—that may be overlooked by organized groups and individuals working to influence policy and the political process.

In 2001, during the first session of the 107th Congress, a flurry of activity surrounding health care providers' regulatory burdens occurred in the executive and legislative branches of government. On June 8, 2001, the Secretary of the Department of Health and Human Services (HHS), Tommy G. Thompson, announced a department-wide initiative to reduce regulatory burdens in health care and respond faster to the concerns of health providers, state and local governments, and individual Americans affected by HHS rules and regulations. In his statement to the press, Secretary Thompson said that:

Over-regulation undermines quality of care and health care delivery by using scarce resources unproductively. We can help improve patient care by bringing more common sense into the regulatory process. . . . We need to act quickly when there are problems with our regulations. That means listening more closely to the people who are affected by our rules. It also includes going back to Congress to change individual provisions of the law, when that may be necessary. (Thompson, 2001, p. 1)

HHS has 11 major operating divisions with over 300 programs. Nurses interested in participating in the process of streamlining federal regulation of a specific program should first visit the HHS website (www.hhs.gov) to review that program's specifications, rules, and regulations. They will then be in a position to provide informed feedback to regulators. For example, nurses knowledgeable about Medicare can share their experience with policymakers as well as HHS's regulatory reform work groups. They have much to contribute about the regulatory burdens and programmatic problems that impede efficient and quality patient care.

Secretary Thompson established three regulatory-reform work groups, including a local health care providers' group, a Washington, DC, health care lobbyists' group, and an in-house expert group from the Medicare program. These groups have been established to discuss regulations that prevent hospitals, physicians, NPs, Medicare-certified home health agencies, and other health care providers from effectively helping Medicare beneficiaries.

THE REGULATORY PROCESS

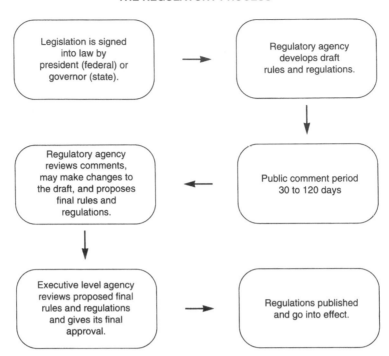

They will help HHS determine what rules need to be better explained, what rules need to be streamlined, and what rules need to be deleted—all without increasing costs or compromising quality (Scully, 2001).

The Centers for Medicare and Medicaid Services (CMS, formerly the Health Care Financing Administration [HCFA]), is also working with providers and Congress to streamline the regulatory process. According to CMS Administrator Thomas Scully, proposed CMS activities, such as developing a quarterly compendium of all changes to Medicare, initiating electronic rule-making processes through the CMS website, and exploring the use of new information technologies, will go a long way toward relieving providers' fears and decreasing their paperwork burden (Scully, 2001).

A major role of government regulation is to interpret the laws. As Congress and state legislatures pass laws, they rarely contain enough explicit language to closely guide their own implementation. It is the responsibility of the administrative agencies

to promulgate the rules and regulations that fill in the details of those laws. The health policy positions of the executive or legislative branch of government will determine the laws that are passed, but once enacted, laws and their accompanying regulations will shape the way health policy is translated into programs and services.

Regulations specify definitions, authority, eligibility, benefits, and standards. Their development is shaped not only by the law but by the ongoing involvement and input of professional associations, providers, third-party payers, consumers, and other special interest groups (Box 22-4).

The administrative agencies, usually part of the executive branch of government, may enact, enforce, and adjudicate their own rules and regulations, thus assuming (in this context) the functions of all three branches of government (legislative, executive, and judicial). For example, some administrative agencies can sit in judgment of previously enforced agency regulations that are now in dispute and judge whether to uphold or overturn them.

BOX **22-4**   How to Influence Legislative and Regulatory Processes

- Become informed about the public policy and health policy issues that are currently under consideration at the local, state, and federal levels of government.
- Become acquainted with the elected officials that represent you at the local, state, and federal levels of government. Communicate with them regularly to share your expertise and perspective on health care and nursing issues.
- Call, write, or send a fax or e-mail message to your legislator, stating briefly the position you wish him or her to take on a particular issue. Always remember to mention that you are a registered nurse and that you live and vote in the legislator's district.
- Request that legislation be introduced or a regulatory change made. Offer your expertise to assist in developing new legislation or in modifying existing legislation and rules.
- Become active in your professional association and work to activate a strong grassroots network of

- members who are prepared to contact their elected representatives on key health care issues.
- Attend a public hearing on a bill or regulation to show support for an issue, or actually testify yourself.
- Build your own political resume by becoming active in local politics in your area.
- Volunteer to work on the campaigns of candidates who are knowledgeable and supportive of nursing's perspective on health care issues.
- Seek appointment to a government task force or commission to have the opportunity to make legislative, regulatory, and public policy changes.
- Seek election to public office or employment in an administrative or executive agency.
- Explore opportunities to be involved with the policy and legislative process through internships, fellowships, and volunteer experiences at the local, state, and federal levels.

Agencies are created through legislation that broadly defines their structure and function. They must develop their own regulations that set policy to govern the behavior of agency officials and regulated parties; spell out their procedural requirements, such as rules governing notices of intent, comment periods, and hearings; and develop enforcement procedures. For example, the Food and Drug Administration sets and monitors standards for foods and tests drugs for purity, safety, and effectiveness, while the Environmental Protection Agency, among other activities, controls health risks from water-borne microbes in drinking water through the development and implementation of regulations.

The promulgation of regulations is guided by certain rules. Key among these, at the federal level, is the requirement that the agency responsible for implementing a law publish a draft of any proposed regulation or set of regulations in the *Federal Register*. The publication of proposed regulations offers an opportunity for interested parties to react to the draft before it becomes final. Commenting on draft regulations is one of the most important points of involvement in the entire legislative process (Longest, 1997). States follow similar procedures.

CONCLUSION

By participating in the legislative and regulatory processes of government, nurses can improve access to and the delivery of health care services. They can also affect the practice of their profession in both state and federal programs. Understanding these processes is an important first step toward influencing them.

REFERENCES

Cohen, M., March, J., & Olsen, J. (1972). A Garbage Can Model of Organizational Choice. *Administrative Science Quarterly 17,* 1-25.

Collender, S. E. (1991). *The Guide to the Federal Budget.* Washington, DC: Urban Institute Press.

Congressional Quarterly. (1993). *Congress and the legislative process.* (1993). Washington, DC: Congressional Quarterly.

Congressional Quarterly (2000). *Guide to current American government.* Washington, DC: Congressional Quarterly.

Davidson, R.H. & Oleszek, W.J. (1996). *Congress and its members* (5th ed.). Washington, DC: Congressional Quarterly.

Department of Legislative Services, Maryland General Assembly. (2001, March). *Fiscal note on HB 473.* Available online at mlis.state.md.us/2001rs/billfile/hb0473.htm.

Johnson, C. (2000). *How our laws are made* (U.S. House of Representatives document 1-6-197). Washington, DC: U.S. Government Printing Office.

Kingdon, J. (1984). *Agendas, alternatives, and public policy.* Boston: Little, Brown.

Library of Congress. (2001). *Thomas: Legislative information on the Internet.* Available online at www.thomas.loc.gov.

Longest, B.B., Jr. (1997). *Seeking strategic advantage through health policy analysis.* Chicago: Health Administration Press.

Pepper, C. & Roybal, E. (1988). *H.R. 3436 fact sheet: Financing and cost controls.* Washington, DC: U.S. House of Representatives Select Committee on Aging.

Schneider, J. (2001). *The committee system in the U.S. Congress* (report no. RS 20794). Washington, DC: Congressional Research Service.

Scully, T. (2001). *Testimony of the Administrator for Medicare & Medicaid Services on educating providers and reducing burden before the House Committee on Small Business.* Washington, DC: U.S. Government Printing Office.

Thompson, T. (2001, June 8). HHS launches initiative to reduce regulatory burden. *U.S. Department of Health and Human Services News.*

Vignette Nancy J. Sharp

Maryland's Nurse Practitioners: Lessons Learned during the 2001 Legislative Session

"The job of a citizen is to keep his mouth open."
GUNTER GRASS

OVERVIEW OF THE LEGISLATIVE ISSUE

Maryland House Bill (HB) 473, "Health Maintenance Organizations [HMOs]—Patient Access to Choice of Provider" (HB 473), was originally introduced in 1998 by several Maryland State Delegates, including Marilyn Goldwater, RN. The provisions of the bill included: (1) altering the standards of care for HMOs to make them apply to services of nurse practitioners (NPs) in addition to those of physicians; (2) requiring HMOs to allow the designation by a member or subscriber of a NP as a primary care provider; (3) limiting the number of NPs on an HMO's panel of providers to 50% of the total number of providers on the panel; and (4) requiring the State Board of Nursing to create and maintain an individual profile on each NP certified by the Board.

HB 473 was considered in each of the following years but did not move through the legislative process until the 2001 legislation session. With the assistance of NPs and registered nurses (RNs) from all around the state, both the House of Delegates and the Senate passed HB 473, granting Maryland NPs primary care provider (PCP) status in HMOs in Maryland. The final votes on HB 473 were 73 to 49 (with 72 needed to pass) in the House, on March 21, 2001, and 24 to 23 in the Senate, on April 5, 2001. Having squeaked through by one vote in both chambers, the bill was sent to the Governor, only to be vetoed by him.

Back in 1998, the bill was hardly on the legislative agenda. In each of the following 3 years, however, the NP community worked very hard to increase political support, obtain more cosponsors, and achieve broader visibility among Maryland's legislators. The bill finally passed both chambers in 2001. Each year, the bill was referred to both the House Environmental Matters Committee and the Senate Finance Committee. After 4 years of very intense lobbying by nurses working with the members of the legislature and the general nursing and health care community at large, the measure rose higher and higher on the legislative agenda, until it achieved passage. It was then, however, that Governor Parris N. Glendening vetoed the bill, though both committees of jurisdiction had voted out the bill favorably and both chambers had passed it.

Although NPs and other stakeholders were completely surprised by the governor's final veto action, they celebrated "the process" as a significant victory because they had worked so diligently and pushed their issue to the top of the state's legislative agenda (Edmunds, 2001).

THREE-STREAM PROCESS

John Kingdon's adaptation of Cohen, March, and Olsen's "Garbage Can Model of Organizational Choice" (Kingdon, 1984) supplies a descriptive framework in which to understand the legislative process in the State of Maryland's policy-making environment. It includes three "streams": problem, policy, and political.

Problem Stream

According to Kingdon (1984), conditions become defined as problems when policymakers believe that something should be done about them. Further, a problem is defined according to a combination of indicators, focusing events, and feedback. The components of the problem stream are presented below to describe how the NP issue became defined as a problem for those persons inside and outside of government. Several factors influenced members of the Maryland General Assembly to perceive patients' lack of access to NPs as PCPs in Maryland HMOs as a problem:

- Patient constituents were telling legislators that access to provider of choice was not available in HMOs in Maryland.
- NPs had a long history as PCPs in other programs; e.g. school-based clinics, indemnity insurance plans, Medicaid, Medicare, TRICARE, Veterans Administration (VA) programs, and the Federal Employees Health Benefits Program.
- Recognition of the value of NPs by one powerful insurance company that advocated for modification of the state's insurance law so that the language in commercial HMO law would be in compliance with the language for every other payer system in the state (Scudder, 2001).

Certain *focusing events* heightened participants' recognition of the problem. In 1996, as part of the strategic planning process for having NPs named as PCPs by HMOs, an NP who was also an attorney began a series of meetings with the presidents of five major HMOs in the state. In those meetings the NP–attorney laid out the statistics, benefits, and financial gains for HMOs that would hire NPs as PCPs.

About 1 year later, in the fall of 1997, Prudential Insurance Company, wishing to credential NPs as PCPs within their HMO system, asked the Maryland Insurance Administrator for an opinion on the legality of this designation under Maryland code. After a careful examination of the language, the state's Insurance Administrator concluded that under current law only physicians could be designated as PCPs in commercial HMOs in Maryland. The Insurance Administrator was careful to add that this decision was not a commentary on the qualifications of NPs, but rather was an interpretation of current code (Scudder, 2001). Following this disclosure, the Nurse Practitioner Association of Maryland (NPAM) became even more focused on intensifying its lobbying efforts and sharpening its political strategies toward the ultimate goal of passing into law HB 473.

NPAM is an extremely active organization in Maryland, with its own office, its own association management staff, its own lobbyist, and a toll-free telephone number. Its website is www.npamonline.org/. The website is used extensively to keep NPAM members updated on legislative news, continuing education events, and inform NPs need concerning the profession, and as a communication vehicle for action alerts and rapid responses to issues.

As part of NPAM's lobbying efforts, a positive communication campaign was initiated. Three fact sheets were developed and distributed to legislators and the professional staff members of the Environmental Matters and Senate Finance Committees. On February 15, 2001, NPAM dispensed a fact sheet to policymakers titled *Physicians versus Non-Physicians as Primary Care Providers—Myths that NPAM Needs to Address Up Front with Environmental Matters.* The fact sheet detailed the following points:

- HB 473 is not a scope-of-practice measure, because NPs already have the authority to prescribe medications, refer patients to specialists, and receive reimbursement.
- NPs are not attempting to gain independent practice; they will continue to work in collaboration with physicians.

- HB 473 is not a mandate on either the HMOs or enrollees, because HMOs would retain the choice of whether or not to have NPs as PCPs and enrollees would still have the ability to select either a physician or NP.
- The fear that HMOs will move to employ more NPs than physicians is groundless because there are only 1500 NPs in Maryland and 10,000 physicians.
- HB 473 is a consumer choice bill (NPAM, 2001).

A second fact sheet detailed more specifically why HB 473 should not be classified as a scope-of-practice bill. A third, titled *How Do Other States Address NPs As Primary Care Providers?*, made the following points:

- NPs have been provided PCP status in the commercial HMO or insurance statute in 8 states, the latest being the State of Maine, which passed such legislation in May 1999. (See the Vignette in Chapter 18.)
- Furthermore, 15 states allow NPs to be recognized as PCPs in some form: Alaska, California, Delaware, Idaho, Kentucky, Maine, Minnesota, Missouri, Montana, New Jersey, New Mexico, Oregon, Texas, Washington, and West Virginia.
- A number of other states have statutory or regulatory language that requires health plans to provide enrollees or subscribers with a list of participating PCPs, as well as of other health care providers, including NPs. These are Hawaii, Kansas, Kentucky, Michigan, Minnesota, New Hampshire and Wisconsin.
- In Maryland, NPs are recognized as PCPs by Maryland's HealthChoice Program (Medicaid), Medicare, VA Hospitals, TRICARE (military health care), and the Federal Employee Health Benefit Program, and in other practice settings.
- Under current Maryland law, NPs are authorized to deliver primary care (Maryland Code [COMAR] 10.27.07.02). Under the Insurance Article, indemnity health insurers are specifically mandated to reimburse NPs for health care services rendered by NPs (Insurance Article 15-703; NPAM, 2001).

Policymakers also learned more about the issue through feedback from a growing coalition of NPs and others in the health care community. Phone calls, constituent visits, letters and NPAM fact sheets from policymakers' constituents presented a clear, strong message that lack of choice of provider in the HMOs of Maryland was indeed a problem. Additional constituent feedback urged state legislators to correct this deficiency by cosponsoring and passing needed legislation. The feedback supported NP-rendered patient care. Constituents expressed their belief that NPs practices were of high quality and that they were very satisfied with this class of provider. Constituent feedback heightened awareness in the offices of Maryland's state legislators.

Policy Stream

According to Kingdon (1984), certain criteria determine a bill's viability. These include: (1) technical feasibility, (2) value acceptability within the policy community, (3) tolerable cost in view of budgetary constraints, (4) anticipated public acquiescence, and (5) political receptivity among decision-makers (Kingdon, 1984, p. 138). There needs to be a agreement among participants inside government and experts outside of government who advise policymakers that a measure is technically feasible to enable the measure to reach higher agenda status.

Did Maryland's policymakers and legislators, including the governor, committee staffers, policy experts, and other state health care departments, view HB 473 as technically feasible? Several indicators reveal that the measure was deemed to be of value and not only technically feasible, but cost-effective and appealing to public and policymakers alike. HB 473 was known to be technically feasible since the infrastructure was in place in the state HMOs to implement the law and NPs were available to take the positions. The State Insurance Administrator had not spoken out against the measure (he remained neutral), and this lukewarm support helped define the bill's value to policymakers and staff. The measure made it through the committee processes, where it had been reported favorably out of both the House Environmental Matters Committee and the Senate Finance Committee. This helped cultivate a broader awareness of the measure's receptivity among decision-makers and to raise the bill's value among policymakers who had not yet given their complete support. The bill was also considered a viable solution because it would allow wider choice of provider in Maryland's HMOs. According to a fiscal summary by the Department of Legislative Services of the Maryland General Assembly, HB 473 would have no fiscal effect on local and state business. Furthermore, the measure's cost effectiveness was never questioned, since it had already been established for many years in Maryland that NPs were cost-effective in the state Medicaid program as well as in other state programs. There was public acceptance about the issue within the patient, health professional, and legislator communities. The measure was also fairly well accepted among decision-makers in the state government.

Political Stream

The third process stream involves the political stream. The components of the political stream are "swings of national (or state) mood, vagaries of public opinion, election results, changes of administration, shifts in partisan or ideological distributions, and interest group pressure campaigns" (Kingdon, 1984, p. 93). In this stream, participants inside and outside of government judge whether the balance of political forces within the political stream are inhibiting or promoting the issue to higher agenda status.

In 2001, the mood regarding NPs as PCPs was one of increased acceptance among consumer groups, employers, some physicians, the media, and legislators. Despite this degree of acceptance by a broad constituency, the state physician association, the Maryland Medical Chirurgical Society, or "MedChi," launched fierce opposition and lobbied legislators and the governor to defeat HB 473.

The final days during the 2001 legislative session were very painful. NPs and NP lobbyists as well as Med-Chi's opposition lobbyists were at the Maryland General Assembly day and night. On April 21, 2001, the House passed the measure by one vote after its third reading. A few days later, the Senate convened and the measure was defeated by one vote, also after the bill's third reading. The NP lobbyist was distressed and quickly notified the NPAM president by telephone. The president immediately sent word out to the nursing community via e-mail

that the bill had lost in the Senate by one vote. However, two hours after the first e-mail had been broadcast to the nursing community, the Maryland NP lobbyist telephoned the president of NPAM to say that the Senate had just voted to "reconsider the third reading" of HB 473. Mounting pressure from the nursing community had moved the Senate to vote once more on the bill. The final vote was cast and the results were 24 for and 23 against: a win of one vote. Another e-mail went out to all NPs updating them on this good news. NPs throughout the state were elated that *their* bill, HB 473, had finally passed both chambers.

But HB 473 had one more step to take as it moved along the legislative path to enactment. The final step was for the governor to sign the bill into law. After several weeks of waiting, the NP lobbyist reported to the NP community that Governor Glendening had vetoed the bill. The governor with one quick signature vetoed this bill for which the NP community had organized and worked so long and hard, and which had passed both houses of the legislature. The nursing community and NPs were understandably devastated.

The NP community had been supportive of Governor Glendening during his term in office, and the community and governor had maintained a mutually respectful relationship. Nurses had worked on Glendening's campaign when he was running for governor. In retrospect, the NP community wonders if it did not focus enough attention on the executive branch and perhaps too much on the legislative branch.

In the defeat of this important bill, one of the key lessons learned is that a group should not let it's vigilance falter and must remain on high alert to all activities in all branches of government during the entire campaign. Special interest groups keep their eyes and ears open constantly to catch the drift of what's happening "on the street," listening for any leads on "inside" information.

HB 473 did not appear to be a "win or lose my seat" issue for any legislator, because the measure involved a small portion of the state population— members of the commercial HMOs in the State of Maryland and approximately 1500 NPs. Rumors were heard, however, that some physicians had threatened to withhold financial support from those legislators who voted in favor of the bill. The supportive legislators were dismayed and saddened at the governor's veto, which they said was based only on personal political reasons. The governor was finishing his second term in office, so he did not have to remain solicitous to any particular group of people; on the other hand, he could have been paying back campaign support from organized physician groups, who had given generously to his election campaign. Perhaps the governor needed future powerful allies and sought the physicians' support for other measures on his personal political agenda, measures that have not yet appeared on the state's legislative agenda. Although these are only suppositions, they nevertheless present some reasonable plausible reasons as to why the governor vetoed HB 473.

Other reasons for the governor's veto are presented in his veto message address to the speaker. In this message the governor praised the nursing profession as a "valued part of the health care delivery system" but stated that he believed that the measure raised significant questions regarding the delivery of health care services by HMOs (Glendening, 2001). Specifically, the governor's public justifications for vetoing HB 473 were as follows:

I am concerned that HMOs will undermine the intent of this law and restrict access to physicians. While I understand that House Bill 473 contains provisions to address this concern, I do not believe that these provisions go far enough. Under these provisions, the number of nurse practitioners that an HMO may include on a primary care provider panel may not exceed 50% of the total number of providers on the panel. However, this provision does not address whether an HMO will terminate a physician from a panel to replace that physician with a nurse practitioner. This situation could be very troubling to members who have established a relationship with that physician. Equally troubling could be the situation where the limited number of physicians requires a member to

either choose a nurse practitioner as his/her primary care provider or switch HMOs. Moreover, it is unclear whether HMOs could use incentives to encourage members to choose nurse practitioners as their primary care providers. This bill, designed to improve consumer choice, could have the undesired effect of using economic measures to unduly influence consumer choice. I believe that this issue needs to be clarified to ensure that the intent of this legislation is not misinterpreted . . . I urge both sides of this issue to work together to reach consensus on this issue in time for the 2002 Session. (Glendening, 2001, pp. 1-2)

Clearly, the political climate within the governor's office impeded HB 473 from being enacted. The NP community will need to assess its chances for victory in 2002. New alliances will need to be made, especially with the next governor and her or his policy staff. Existing relationships with other political elites within both chambers and on the committee staffs will need to be continued. To launch another legislative effort like the 2001 campaign will require more capital funds, more NP members for NPAM, more lobbying staff, and more time, energy, and resources from the organization.

The NPs of Maryland will ultimately have to decide if this battle is worth the effort. They came very close to victory in 2001.

REFERENCES

Edmunds, M.W. (2001). The physiology of primary care provider legislation. Part 1. *Nurse Practitioner Journal, 26*(7), 55-57.

Glendening, P. (2001, May 17). *House Bill 473: Governor's veto message.* Available online at mlis.state.md.us/2001rs/veto_letters/hb0473.htm.

Kingdon, J. (1984). *Agendas, alternatives, and public policy.* Boston: Little, Brown.

Nurse Practitioner Association of Maryland. (2001). *H.B. 473.* Available online at www.npamonline.org/legislative_report.htm.

Scudder, L. (2001). Lessons learned in Maryland. *Advance for Nurse Practitioners, 9*(9), 16.

Vignette Judith Lorette & Catherine L. Jansto

How Regulations are Shaped: The Rules of the Game

"The stakes . . . are too high for government to be a spectator sport."

BARBARA JORDAN

The successful passage of a piece of legislation is almost always a cause for celebration among those responsible for its development and implementation. A bill becoming law represents the culmination of many months, sometimes years, of intense research, lobbying, fundraising, and grassroots efforts to obtain support for the bill's underlying concept. However, successful passage is only another beginning, as the time after passage provides critical opportunities for those nurse-analysts or clinicians who wish to impact the implementation of the law by participating in the regulatory development process.

Ultimately, it is laws that regulate; however, the exact regulatory provisions composed by those agencies charged with oversight and operationalizing of laws clarify and define how the laws will be implemented. In many respects, therefore, regulations are "where the rubber meets the road." As a result, nurses interested in the realization of health care legislation would be well advised to plan, far in advance of a bill becoming law, to be at the starting gate as the subsequent regulatory provisions begin to be crafted. If nursing's goals are to be advanced, more nurses need to be actively involved in the entire continuum of producing health care legislation, including the next step after passage: the making of regulations.

REGULATORY PROCESS

Often the language in laws is vague, suggesting a desired outcome without delineating the steps that should be taken to bring it about. Therefore, in ac-

The authors acknowledge the assistance of Raemalee Loen, Melissa Fannin, Vivian M. Lindsay, and J. Edgie Russell in the preparation of this Vignette.

cordance with the Administrative Procedures Act, regulations are composed to translate enacted legislation into specific requirements. With federal laws, it falls to the Department of Health and Human Services, the Department of Justice, or other executive-branch entities to flesh out an implementation approach and create a roadmap for those who must comply with the law.

During the regulation formation process, stakeholders may find opportunities to expand favorable aspects or minimize perceived losses in the law through skillful maneuvering. To be involved in the process at the right time is crucial. Also, nurses must be familiar with the language of regulations, how and where the task of developing them is assigned, the precise timeline to be followed, and the rules surrounding how one communicates a policy position on a particular subject. There are rather narrow windows of opportunity to comment on a regulation, so, as the saying goes, "If you snooze, you lose." One has to understand the process to play . . . and win!

FEDERAL REGISTER

The *Federal Register* is published each business day, providing notice to the public of pending regulations and other governmental actions. All changes to federal regulations are published in the *Federal Register* (available online at www.access.gpo.gov/nara). Documents are arranged under headings such as Presidential Documents, Rules and Regulations, Proposed Rules, and Notices (e.g., Notices of Intent).

The *Federal Register* is required reading for health care providers interested in following or impacting legislation. Nurses serving as lobbyists for organizations such as the American Nurses Association or the American Academy of Nurse Practitioners keep a watchful eye on the *Federal Register*, as it will alert them to opportunities to submit position papers and targeted comments on proposed rules or regulations that will affect nursing issues.

TYPES OF REGULATORY DOCUMENTS

A few key types of documents play a role in the implementation of statutes. First, there are *rules* and *regulations.* Essentially, these have the same meaning in the *Federal Register*'s system of terminology. *Proposed rules* are an agency's notice of its intent to establish a new policy or to change or suspend a policy previously published or understood. When a proposed rule is published, anyone is permitted to submit written comments for consideration by agency policymakers. The "comment period," during which these comments must be received to be given consideration, is generally 60 days long, although it can vary under certain circumstances. For example, when the Centers for Medicare and Medicaid Services (CMS; formerly the Health Care Financing Administration) was preparing to implement the Medicare+Choice managed care program, it published a proposed rule, providing the public and advocacy and professional organizations an opportunity to write to the agency. Agencies have a responsibility to carefully consider all comments and respond to comments if they proceed with a *final rule* (the actual, enforceable rule).

The importance of public comments cannot be overstated. Depending on the level of specificity of a statute, there can be significant latitude in exactly how its provisions are interpreted in regulations—and the exact wording of a regulation can affect whether or not a statute is implemented as its makers expected.

ROLE OF NURSES AS POLICY ANALYSTS

At the CMS headquarters in Baltimore, Maryland, many nurses fill positions with policy-making implications. Over the last 5 years, CMS nurses have been a part of implementing major new legislation such as the Health Insurance Portability and Accountability Act of 1996, Balanced Budget Act of 1997, Balanced Budget Refinement Act of 1999, and Benefits Improvement and Protection Act of 2000. They have seen the importance of timing, persistence, well-articulated opinions, and strong lobbying, as well as the damage caused by silence and late arrivals on the scene.

No single value can provide an adequate basis for public decision-making, and rarely does the position of one profession or industry represent the best interests of all persons. For nurses to be effective analysts—that is, effective patient advocates—objective technical analyses of the policy alternatives must therefore be crafted. Nurses are in a position to give proper emphasis to nursing's position in these analyses, but must receive timely evidence through appropriate channels so it is on hand when policy discussions occur. Nursing's ability to advocate for nurses' and patients' interests is enhanced when it is backed up throughout the legislative and regulatory process with unbiased, methodologically sound data. It is also important for nurses to present well-articulated policy options in a framework understandable to nonclinicians.

The need to push hard for a health policy goal does not end when a law is passed. It is precisely at this time that federal agency regulators are most in need of consistent and reliable nursing expertise.

STYLES OF OTHER STAKEHOLDERS

There is no denying the very powerful role of the health care industry's government-relations representatives, paid to be strong and ever-present communicators, doggedly working to be sure that regulations advantageous to their members will win the day. Much of their ability to be heard by regulators depends upon their being recognized as influential stakeholders (i.e., players). This status is not easy to attain for those new to the policy arena; the playing field is typically highly charged and quite intense. One must not be afraid to speak up at associations meetings and policy forums, particularly those attended by regulatory agency leadership. However, any position presented must be well-supported, and the speaker must be prepared to defend his or her position against those of well-financed national organizations. In addition, persistent write-in campaigns can help develop name recognition within an agency.

One must know other rules of the game, too. Knowing how to get pro-association public surveys published in newspapers at precisely the moment an agency is crafting a proposed rule can be an effective tool. Effective players know how and when to strike while there is still time for agency "policy wonks" to hear their concerns and take action. They also maintain a presence on Capitol Hill, visiting with the committees (e.g., Senate Finance, Appropriations, or Ways and Means) charged with oversight of the agency that is writing the regulations or the piece of legislation at the heart of the matter. Their message is consistent and relentlessly presented—and they know to speak with one voice.

TIMING IS EVERYTHING

In recent years, some nursing organizations have entered the picture at CMS long after other (presumably better resourced) associations have entered the scene, after agency decisions have been made, and after regulation comment periods have closed. Late arrivals frustrate all parties. After the public comment period, agency officials are precluded from discussing regulation decision-making with the public. They can listen to the positions of concerned parties but are not allowed to respond or to provide information on the contents of pending final regulations. Once final regulations are published, they can be revised, but it is a difficult, tedious and time-consuming process. Trying to insert new language into an existing regulation (e.g., adding nurses to the definition of *providers,* allowing for changes in reimbursement rates for home nursing care) is extremely difficult. If an interest group desires specific regulatory language, it should:

- Speak up early.
- Be persistent and articulate.
- Use well-prepared arguments and supporting statistics that illustrate how its particular position supports the statutory intent.
- Address the needs of hundreds of thousands of citizens (patients and nurses) around the country.
- Identify how the interest of the legislators sponsoring the bill is served.

Providing specific target language to the regulatory agency and, where feasible, a chart "crosswalking" the proposed language and outcomes to the relevant parts of the statute are often effective

measures. This approach can be effective in getting an agency to consider modifications of existing regulations. However, even convincing arguments for change may not rise to the top of an agency's priorities. Being in the game when initial regulations are being composed for a new legislative mandate is the best way for stakeholders to influence the outcome.

THE MEDICARE+CHOICE FINAL RULE

In the case of the Medicare+Choice regulation process, CMS published interim final regulations in the *Federal Register* on June 26, 1998. Representatives of the managed-care industry, advocacy organizations, professional associations, and the public then had a chance to review CMS's proposed regulations for operationalizing the Medicare managed care sections of the Balanced Budget Act. Because of potential significant impacts on the managed care industry, many organizations were tracking the rulemaking process, staying in touch with CMS staff, waiting for the opportunity to submit comments on the issues most likely to affect their respective organizations. Nursing, physician, and other provider associations submitted official written-comment letters and met with CMS policy makers to offer their support for or to present their concerns about the direction the agency was planning to take with the Medicare+Choice program.

Under the interim final rule, the agency signaled its intention to interpret the Medicare+Choice rule very broadly, including a wide range of health care professionals. However, by the time of publication of the final Medicare+Choice rule in June, 2000, there had been a critical change that impacted nursing reimbursement and participation opportunities: As a result of interpretation of statutory intent and over the objections of nursing organizations, a political decision was made to limit certain provider participation requirements to physicians, thus excluding registered professional nurses from independent reimbursement eligibility in certain settings. A number of professional nursing organizations saw this change as a lost opportunity to expand the realm of nursing practice in managed care settings. Unfortunately, many nursing organizations representing registered nurses potentially impacted by the regulations did not submit comment on the regulations when they had an opportunity to do so.

QUALITY IMPROVEMENT SYSTEM FOR MANAGED CARE

The Quality Improvement System for Managed Care (QISMC) is a set of quality standards and guidelines published in September, 1998 for the purpose of implementing the quality provisions of the Medicare and Medicaid managed care provisions of the Balanced Budget Act. It addresses quality and performance improvement, appeals and grievances, health services delivery, and delegation of services. Although in 1998 the QISMC guidelines were not published as mandatory regulations because they essentially mirrored and had roots in the quality provisions of the Balanced Budget Act and many of the quality-related portions of the Medicare+Choice regulations, compliance by managed care organizations with QISMC became a contractual requirement for participation in Medicare program. Modeled after the recommendations of President Clinton's Advisory Commission on Quality for Health Care Consumers and consistent with the language and objectives of a proposed "Patient Bill of Rights," the QISMC document became a key compliance tool, particularly with respect to quality assessment and performance improvement, health services management, and delegation of services.

Nurses on Capitol Hill and within CMS, the managed-care industry, various advocacy organizations, and state public health departments were key authors of the document. As it came down to its final form, two out of three of the CMS staff charged with making revisions and arguing the fine points of the document had master's degrees in nursing. Interesting conflicts arose; professional nurses faced conflict between the professional ideal of promoting the common good of patients and the practical necessity of serving their immediate client (employer). As they endeavored to maintain the perspective of patient advocate, they also had to face the political realities of a never-ending balancing act between scientific and ethical appropriateness and political expediency. Were quality standards to be effectually implemented, or was the opportunity to raise the quality bar going to fall under the weight of swirling stakeholders' arguments, all soft evidence? The nurses concerned learned to be patient, persistent, good negotiators, and to recognize when one small step had to suffice. Thanks to a lot of hard work, a clinically sound document was born. To this day the QISMC Standards and Guidelines represent a giant step forward for patients' rights as a whole.

NOT JUST A FEDERAL ISSUE

Nurses in a variety of practice settings can impact regulations by participating in developing organizational standards and regulation formation at the state and local levels. According to Vivian Lindsay, Vice President of Customer Relations and Government Programs at the Neighborhood Health Partnership in Florida, nurses—including those in the managed care arena—can impact the regulatory process by identifying the health concerns of members on a "real-time" basis, then sharing these with regulators charged with overseeing quality of care issues.

Nursing and the Courts

VIRGINIA TROTTER BETTS

DAVID KEEPNEWS

"The illegal we do immediately. The unconstitutional takes a little longer."

HENRY KISSINGER

The courts are an important forum for nurses to advocate for themselves and their patients. The legal and judicial system is a major arena in which the American people have traditionally sought vindication of their rights. Legislative initiatives and administrative regulations are often tested, affirmed, or invalidated through the courts. The circumstances under which employees can bargain collectively have often been matters of court rulings. Professional licensing laws, scope of practice, and antitrust laws are statutes that reflect existing rights that are enforceable through the courts.

Nurses, like most nonlawyers, often think of legal and judicial processes as arcane, mystical, frightening, or highly technical and better left to legal experts to address and understand. However, just as nurses have learned that they can and must shape legislation and regulations that affect the profession, they need to understand how judicial decisions also affect nursing practice and roles and how, especially through their professional associations, nurses can positively impact legal decisions. Nurses should not regard the legal system as the exclusive domain of lawyers and judges any more than they regard the legislative process as the exclusive domain of legislators and lobbyists.

As activists interested in achieving particular policy outcomes, nurses always need to consider their broadest set of alternatives in developing a plan for success in policy development and implementation. Policy analysts, social activists, and legal scholars have differing opinions as to the effectiveness of using the judicial branch of government and its action instrument, the courts, to bring about social change. Nevertheless, the courts can be an important arena for policy action by organized nursing and should be more widely and proactively utilized.

This chapter provides an overview of the legal and judicial system and the role of the courts in shaping policy by drawing on relevant examples from nursing and health policy. It is not a comprehensive overview of this important area. Rather, it aims to provide the reader with a general understanding of this area and its critical importance for nursing.

ROLE OF THE COURTS IN SHAPING POLICY

THE JUDICIAL SYSTEM: A BRIEF OVERVIEW

The United States has two major, parallel court systems: federal and state. The federal courts have jurisdiction over matters that involve the U.S. Constitution, federal legislation and regulation, and rights conferred under federal law. Federal courts can also hear complaints that arise between parties in different states if a minimum monetary amount (currently $75,000) is in dispute. The trial courts for the federal system, the entry point for most federal cases, are district courts; there are 94 federal judicial courts located throughout the United States and its territories. Federal courts of appeals are organized into 11 geographic circuits plus the District of Columbia Circuit Court and the Federal Circuit Court (Want, 1997). The U.S. Supreme Court is the court of last resort for federal cases.

Each state has its own court system, which generally interprets the laws of its state and the state constitution. State courts also hear some claims that arise under federal law or the U.S. Constitution. Generally, the state court system includes trial-level and appellate courts, with a high court (usually the state supreme court) as the court of last resort. Often, trial courts are further subdivided on the basis of subject matter, an amount or a remedy in dispute, or another specific legal issue. (For instance, various states may have family court, probate court, municipal court, drug court, etc.) On certain matters, decisions of a state supreme court may be appealed directly to the U.S. Supreme Court, whose decisions become the law of the land.

EVOLUTION OF THE COURTS

As the U.S. court system has evolved, there have been varied periods of judicial activism in shaping social policy for the nation. The first era of judicial activity (from 1776 through the 1930s) established the very principles that gave form to judicial influence. In the 1803 case of *Marbury v. Madison,* the U.S. Supreme Court established the most important of these principles by asserting its power to declare an act of the legislative or executive branch null and void if the act exceeded, by the Court's own interpretation, the powers granted to that branch by the Constitution. This fundamental concept of "judicial review" has evolved into one of the most important powers belonging to the courts because it grants courts the power to make law by striking down other laws, thus enabling courts to exert tremendous influence over governmental activities. Another doctrine that has increased the prominence of the courts as a force in social policy is the legal maxim of *stare decisis. Stare decisis,* or "let the decision stand," sets the course for judicial precedents by adhering to previous findings in cases with substantially comparable facts and situations (Filippatos, 1991). Prior decisions bind not only because they make good sense, but also because they embody rules of law that make expectations of life and law predictable. Armed with these two weapons of influence, courts have shaped the law rather than merely interpreting it, thus establishing a true third branch of government.

As the legislative and executive branches of government slowly responded to public debate on and demand for social reform, the U.S. Supreme Courts of 1953 to 1968 and 1969 to 1986 extended the concept of individual liberties and civil rights. Their decisions found expanded rights in the Constitution and the Bill of Rights, including the right to enforce contractual relationships free from discrimination and the right to privacy in making health decisions.

The current Supreme Court (1987 to the present), seen as more conservative in its ideology than the prior two Courts, has disregarded some precedents and, in some ways, has narrowed the scope of the Bill of Rights (Chermerinsky, 1991). This translates into a narrowing of individual rights, giving rise to an increased necessity for activists to turn to legislators for protection of those rights or to develop new strategies for action outcomes.

IMPACT LITIGATION: ESTABLISHING RIGHTS

A strong tradition, particularly in the past several decades, has been for advocates to utilize the courts to establish, affirm, or clarify rights under the Constitution or a particular statute. Litigation that seeks to have a broad social impact in this manner is often referred to as "impact" litigation, the goal of which has been described as "win[ning] cases to establish good precedent for future cases" (Johnson, 1999; Parmet, 1999). A particularly prominent example of impact litigation is *Brown v. Board of Education,* a 1954 case in which the U.S. Supreme Court struck down school segregation and mandated that states begin a process of desegregating their public schools. The Court found that segregated public school education constituted a state policy of inferior education for African-American children, and that it thus violated the Equal Protection Clause of the Fourteenth Amendment to the U.S. Constitution.

Another example of utilizing the courts to establish social policy is *Roe v. Wade,* in which the U.S. Supreme Court in 1973 found that women had a right to the medical procedure of abortion during the first two trimesters of pregnancy. The Court made this ruling on the basis of its interpretation of various amendments to the Constitution that, it found, conferred a right of self-determination in seeking a medical procedure to terminate pregnancy. Though *Roe v. Wade* has been modified and narrowed in some respects by subsequent Supreme Court decisions, the basic right to choose abortion established by the Court in 1973 has remained intact and continues to be current (although frequently challenged) reproductive health policy.

In more recent years, a series of cases has focused on establishing rights in another area—the right to die. In *Cruzan v. Missouri Dept. of Health* (1986), the U.S. Supreme Court established the right of individuals to refuse life-sustaining treatment. This right is now codified in measures such as the Patient Self-Determination Act (PSDA) (P.L. 101-508, 1990). Critics question the effectiveness of the PSDA in clinical practice as, after a decade, most Americans still do not have advanced directives for health care (Collins, 1999).

More recently, some groups have sought to establish physician-assisted suicide for terminally ill patients as a legal right. These advocates have challenged existing state enforcement actions against physician-assisted suicide or pushed state-level initiatives to establish such a right, as in Oregon. In 1997 the U.S. Supreme Court ruled for the first time on the issue of physician-assisted suicide. It rendered a unanimous decision, finding that there is no constitutional right to assisted suicide. However, the justices offered three different opinions, signaling a recognition that both the specific issue of assisted suicide, and the broader issues of end-of-life decisions and care of the terminally ill, will continue to be the subject of debate and reflection throughout American society (*Vacco v. Quill, 1997; Washington v. Glucksberg,* 1997). The Court basically returned the issue to the states to determine policy on assisted suicide and reaffirmed the distinction between withdrawing life-sustaining treatment and providing active assistance in committing suicide. Justice Stephen Breyer, in his concurring opinion, suggested an approach to the question of assisted suicide that "would use words roughly like 'a right to die with dignity.' [A]t its core would lie personal control over the manner of death, pro-

fessional medical assistance, and the avoidance of severe physical suffering—combined" (*Vacco v. Quill,* 1997).

COURTS AS ENFORCERS OF EXISTING LEGISLATION

The courts are commonly used as a means to enforce existing legislative and regulatory requirements and processes. For nurses, this means that the courts can be a source through which nurse practice acts or other relevant laws are enforced.

For example, in 1992, the Alabama State Nurses Association and the Alabama Board of Nursing, with the support of the American Nurses Association (ANA) and the Emergency Nurses Association, sued local hospitals that sought to place emergency medical technicians in the emergency department to provide nursing care. The nurses alleged that such assignment violated the Alabama Nurse Practice Act by allowing individuals to practice nursing without being appropriately educated and licensed. The nurse plaintiffs prevailed in the suit, and the hospitals were forced to end this practice.

In Oklahoma the state board of nursing, supported by the Oklahoma Nurses Association, sued St. John's Hospital over its practice of using unlicensed assistive personnel (UAPs) to provide some technical aspects of nursing care. This private hospital had sought to utilize an exception to the state's nurse practice act that permitted UAPs, under some circumstances, to provide care within public health programs. The hospital argued that because it served indigent patients, including Medicaid recipients, it should fall within this exception. The Board of Nursing challenged the hospital. The board lost at trial, and the case went to appeal. The ANA submitted an *amicus curiae* brief in support of the Board of Nursing's position. The appellate court judge concluded that the hospital was skirting the mandates of the Nurse Practice Act and remanded the case back to the lower court for further review. At that point the matter was settled before going to trial again. Thus, though this out-of-court-settled case produced a less definitive and less generalizable legal result than the Alabama case discussed previously, it does represent an example of the use of the courts to seek enforcement of the state nurse practice act. It is an effective method to protect the professional nurse's scope of practice.

ANTITRUST LAWS

Federal and state antitrust laws are designed to protect consumers by prohibiting anticompetitive business practices. These laws have their roots in the turn of the century, when large and powerful businesses combined into alliances and agreed on prices, distribution, and other market-sensitive areas, effectively eliminating competition between them and eliminating newer companies from entering the market, to the detriment of the consumer. Antitrust protections have been an area to which nurses and others have looked for relief from practices that block their full participation in the health care marketplace. Federal antitrust laws are enforced through two federal agencies, the Federal Trade Commission (FTC) and the Antitrust Division of the Department of Justice (DoJ). Individuals can also bring antitrust suit in federal court, although the cost of a private antitrust action can be extremely high. Several states have parallel antitrust laws, which are generally enforced through the offices of the state attorney general and through private lawsuits in state court.

Traditionally, health professionals were essentially free from antitrust scrutiny under an exemption for "learned professions." The U.S. Supreme Court in a 1975 case, *Goldfarb v. Virginia State Bar,* essentially eliminated that exemption. The past 25 years have seen significant interest in antitrust laws as they apply to the health care industry. Courts have invalidated such practices as agreement by a county medical society to set fees for medical procedures (*Arizona v. Maricopa County Medical Society,* 1982). Merger activity among hospitals, insurance companies, and health systems has brought attention from antitrust enforcement agencies. In recent years, the DoJ and FTC have issued joint guidelines for antitrust enforcement in the health care industry, intended to offer general guidance on which practices are and are not likely to trigger action by these enforcement agencies (U.S. DoJ and Federal Trade Commission Statement of Antitrust Enforcement Policy in Healthcare, 1996).

One case in which nurses brought an antitrust action to confront anticompetitive business practices involved a group of certified nurse midwives in Tennessee. In 1980 these nurse midwives were forced to close their newly opened family-centered nursing practice and midwifery services after meeting the concerted resistance of several Tennessee physicians, hospitals, and a prominent physician insurance company. The nurse midwives were barred from receiving hospital privileges, physician supervision, and an opportunity for collaborative practice. About 9 years after closure of their practice, and extensive litigation, the nurse midwives won settlements against some of the defendants (*Nurse Midwifery Associates v. Hibbett et al,* 1990). In the end, the Court found that several of the defendants had indeed violated antitrust laws.

Some physician groups have made "reform" of antitrust laws a policy priority and have sought at least a limited exemption for some activities by physicians that would otherwise violate antitrust laws. For instance, the American Medical Association (AMA), which has long championed antitrust exemptions for physicians, has more recently supported congressional proposals to allow for joint negotiations by physicians with managed care organizations and other payors. The AMA has characterized "antitrust relief for self-employed physicians" as one of its "top priorities" (American Medical Association, 2001). Such proposals pose significant concerns for nurses and other nonphysician health care providers, since they would remove an important means through which such providers can challenge anticompetitive activities by physicians.

LIABILITY (TORTS, PRODUCT LIABILITY) AS A MEANS TO EFFECT SOCIAL CHANGE

Another area of the law that presents nurses with a means to effect change is the tort system. Tort law (laws through which individuals and corporations are held financially accountable for acts or omissions that cause injury to others) is often what nurses think of first when the subject of "legal issues in nursing" is raised. Indeed, one aspect of tort law includes professional malpractice issues. Recent reviews indicate that nurses are held accountable for their professional care and judgment (Smith-

Pittman, 1998). However, this area is broad, and nurses can often use tort law to address problems and issues that affect them and their practice.

Health care workers have, at times, successfully sued their employers for failure to take reasonable measures to protect employee health and safety. Some such suits have been for failure to provide reasonable security measures, which resulted in injury to health care workers, or failure to switch to needleless systems, resulting in nurses becoming infected with human immunodeficiency virus or hepatitis B virus from needlesticks. The impact of such legal actions has implications beyond any individual plaintiff because other employers may be influenced to take measures to provide protection for employees to avoid potential future liability (General Accounting Office, 2000). The experiences of nurses and other health care workers infected with bloodborne pathogens as a result of needlesticks has also led to federal legislation addressing the issue, the Needlestick Safety and Prevention Act of 2000 (see the Unit III Case Study).

Antitobacco advocates have also made much use of tort and product liability law. Through both individual lawsuits and class actions (discussed next), advocates have sought to hold that industry accountable for illnesses and deaths caused by tobacco use. These legal efforts have also helped publicize important, previously undisclosed information about the industry and its practices and about the health outcomes of tobacco use, adding ammunition to both legal and political efforts to limit access to and use of tobacco. After years of important but generally unsuccessful litigation, 46 states settled a lawsuit against U.S. tobacco manufacturers, agreeing on payments to states of over $200 billion, as well as restrictions on advertising and marketing of tobacco products (Levin & Weinstein, 1998). (See also the second Vignette in Chapter 25.)

CLASS ACTION SUITS

Class action suits have been another means through which advocates have sought to make an impact on health, safety, and social justice issues. Such suits seek to vindicate the rights of an entire class of individuals who share a common interest that gives rise to the suit and who seek a common outcome.

Generally, such suits are brought on behalf of a large group by a smaller number of class representatives. Class action suits have been brought on behalf of recipients of silicone breast implants, of citizens of a geographic area who have suffered ill effects from the dumping of toxic wastes, of female employees of a public university system who have suffered wage discrimination, and of airline flight attendants who have been injured by second-hand smoke.

CHALLENGING INAPPROPRIATE GOVERNMENT ACTION

The U.S. Constitution and state constitutions offer citizens and residents a number of protections, including protection from unreasonable government action in a number of areas. For instance, the government cannot take an individual's property or liberty without due process. Individuals are free from unreasonable searches and seizures. All individuals are guaranteed equal protection under the law. These guarantees have been made more specific as they apply to the actions of government agencies through a federal Administrative Procedures Act and similar acts at the state level that define the processes for and restrictions on administrative action. In addition, administrative agencies are generally limited to acting within the parameters set for them by legislation. A license to practice a profession such as nursing, once granted by the state board of nursing, is considered a property right of that individual and cannot be taken away without due process following established legal procedures. Disciplinary actions that result in licensure revocation are serious matters that reflect seriously flawed professional behavior (Carruth & Booth, 1999).

Together, these constitutional and legislative protections provide a basis for challenging inappropriate or unreasonable government action—or, perhaps more accurately, action by a government agency that an individual or group believes or alleges to be inappropriate or unreasonable. For instance, in 1988 a coalition of providers challenged rules by the U.S. Department of Health and Human Services that would have prohibited providers in federally funded family planning clinics from discussing abortion as an option for pregnant clients or from offering such clients referral to an agency that performs abortions (Regulations on Title X-Funded Family Planning Projects Issued to Regional Health Administrators of the U.S. Department of Health and Human Services, 1988). Although the challenge to these rules continued, the issue was resolved on the second day of President Clinton's first term in 1993, when the president signed an executive order removing these gag rules. Under the Bush administration, attempts to place similar restrictions on health professionals may resurface.

ACTING "DEFENSIVELY"

Though court decisions can have a positive effect on issues that concern nurses and other health care advocates, they can also have an adverse impact. Nursing is sometimes faced with trying to react to, address, and mitigate the impact of a negative court decision. A recent example of this is action by the U.S. Supreme Court regarding the applicability of the National Labor Relations Act to nurses. That act provides employees, including nurses, with a number of protections, including the right to engage in concerted action regarding wages and working conditions, to organize unions, and to bargain collectively with their employers. Some employers have argued that nurses, because they direct the work of other employees, are "supervisors," who are not covered by the act. In *NLRB v. Health Care and Retirement Corp.* (1994), the Supreme Court invalidated the rationale that the National Labor Relations Board (NLRB) had been using to find that nurses were not "supervisors" simply because they directed the work of others. (The NLRB had argued that nurses direct the work of other staff, such as licensed practical nurses and nursing assistants, in the interests of patient care, and not "in the interests of the employer.")

The decision understandably caused a great deal of concern among nurses because it eliminated the reasoning by which the NLRB had found most nurses to be eligible for collective bargaining. Because supervisors (as defined by the National Labor Relations Act) do not have the right to bargain collectively, the potential implications of the decision

jeopardized the collective bargaining rights of many, if not most, registered nurses (RNs).

Since the time of the decision, however, the ANA has worked to mitigate its impact. It challenged employers' efforts to claim that large numbers of nurses are ineligible for collective bargaining and has supported the NLRB in its decision to find alternative approaches to ruling that directing the work of others in providing patient care does not make RNs ineligible for collective bargaining. Recently, the U.S. Supreme Court revisited the issue of nurses as supervisors as presented in *NLRB v. Kentucky River Community Care* (No. 99-1815, 2001). This decision—a 5-4 decision, like that in *Health Care and Retirement Corp.*—rejected the NLRB's argument that, in directing the work of others, nurses do not exercise "independent judgment" as used in the National Labor Relations Act to (in part) define "supervisors" (see Chapter 19). The long-range implications of this decision, which was issued in 2001, are not yet clear.

ROLE OF *AMICUS CURIAE*

Amicus curiae, or "friend of the court," briefs provide an important tool for advocacy groups to make their views known on a case with broad implications even when they are not parties to that case. An *amicus curiae* brief is filed (with the court's permission) by a group with an interest in the case in order to advise the court on how it should rule. Generally, the brief offers the court a group's unique knowledge of and perspective on the issue brought before it.

Nursing has used this avenue to make its policy preferences and professional viewpoints known in appellate-level federal and state cases throughout the country. In *NLRB v. Health and Retirement Corp.* and *Kentucky River,* discussed previously, the ANA filed amici briefs with the U.S. Supreme Court in order to offer its unique perspective as the nation's largest professional and labor organization for RNs in explaining why direction and oversight of ancillary personnel is an integral aspect of nursing practice and not a "supervisory" function. The ANA joined with the American Medical Association and other nursing and physician groups to offer the perspective of health care providers regarding physician-assisted suicide by filing a joint *amicus curiae* brief in *Washington v. Glucksberg* and *Vacco v. Quill.* The ANA has also made its voice heard in cases regarding appropriate bargaining units for hospital employees; the right of publicly employed nurses to speak out on the job regarding safe patient care; and the right of Medicare recipients enrolled in HMOs to receive adequate services and procedural protections (*Grijalva et al v. Shalala,* 966 F. Supp. 747; D. Ariz. 1996). The ANA has also addressed criminal prosecution of pregnant women for drug or alcohol abuse (*Whitner v. South Carolina,* 22 Fam. L. Rep 1427; S.C. 1996) and the issue of what constitutes a "serious health condition" under the Family and Medical Leave Act (*Victorelli v. Shadyside Hospital,* decision pending). The *amicus curiae* brief is a particularly useful and attractive option for nurses to use in speaking out on important legal issues that affect the profession or on those for which the profession has important substantive concerns, but where nurses are not party to the action itself.

ADVOCATING EXPANSION OF LEGAL RIGHTS THROUGH LEGISLATION

Because Congress and the state legislatures are sources of federal and state law, respectively, legislative authority provides the foundation for future legal action. In other words, laws passed at the federal or state level create legally enforceable rights or remedies that can be actionable through the courts for implementation or clarification. For instance, the Americans with Disabilities Act (ADA) provides for equal treatment for disabled Americans and bars discrimination in a number of areas, including employment and public accommodations. For example, a person with a disability who is able to perform the essential aspects of a job with reasonable accommodation cannot be fired or denied a promotion on the basis of her or his disability. Though many would argue that the ADA merely applies principles of equality and fair play that are basic to American law and public life, it also creates specific actionable rights through a specific statutory scheme. Simi-

larly, the Family and Medical Leave Act (FMLA) grants specific rights for employees to take unpaid leave under certain circumstances in order to receive or provide care to a family member. The FMLA, signed into law by President Clinton after being vetoed by former President Bush, was strongly supported by the ANA. The act defines a number of new and important parameters for families' rights.

Another example of legislation granting a right is the Boren Amendment. Through the Boren Amendment, Congress gave providers of Medicaid services a right to receive payment at a level comparable to that paid by private insurers. As a result of the Boren Amendment, many health care institutions had sued their state Medicaid programs to force them to pay higher rates. Many state governments objected to the obligation imposed on them by this law, and repeal of the Boren Amendment— an objective of the National Governors Association and others who seek to turn greater control of the Medicaid program over to the states—was achieved with the enactment of P.L. 105-33, the 1997 Balanced Budget Act (BBA). Without an enforceable "right" to protect reimbursement rates, some providers may experience serious consequences from implementation of the BBA.

Using a similar strategy in 1996, New York nurses developed and supported state legislation to grant professional licensing boards the power to seek judicial interventions to prevent the unauthorized practice of a profession. For instance, under rights granted by this proposed legislation, the board of nursing would have been able to seek to stop the use of UAP, who would then be practicing nursing without a license. This legislation would have given nurses a significant tool to use in preventing the dangerous, inappropriate use of UAP by health care institutions. Unfortunately, New York governor George Pataki vetoed the bill passed by the state legislature.

PROMOTING NURSING'S POLICY AGENDA

Health care is experiencing rapid and chaotic change in which the rules of the game are being developed more in closed corporate board rooms than in the halls and auditoriums of public policy assemblies. Thus nursing needs a greater range of effective strategies to achieve its preferred outcomes. Organized nursing must become comfortable, proficient, and well prepared to be successful in all policy arenas and at all levels of government.

Understanding litigation as a winning strategy, enhanced risk-taking skills, and sufficient resource building for expensive litigation must be developed by organized nursing on a proactive basis. Nowhere may this become more important than at the state and local levels, where here-and-now issues of material interest ripe for litigation and judicial decision will arise that may affect the whole of nursing or all health care consumers. In addition to many of the current nursing and litigation issues mentioned, nurses must prepare to address effectively a variety of evolving professional concerns, such as managed care panel development, private insurer reimbursement, enforcement of the Nurse Practice Act in ways that expand and protect nursing practice, and establishing the right of nurses to form professional corporations. Using the courts and the judicial process may be the action of choice for addressing each of these concerns with a "nurse-friendly" solution.

Organized nursing, at the national, state, and local levels, must prepare nurses to evaluate issues and opportunities to promote health and social policy though the judicial system. When achieving nursing's policy objectives is likely to be best accomplished through the courts, nursing must be ready, willing, and able to play and win in that arena of government.

REFERENCES

Alabama Nurses Association, Alabama State Board of Nursing, et al, v. Samuelson and the Alabama State Department of Public Health. (1992). Case Nos. CV-92-2275 and CV-92-2477.

American Medical Association. (2001, February 23). Antitrust relief needed for physicians. Available online at www.ama-assn.org/ama/pub/article/4030-3979.html.

Arizona v. Maricopa County Medical Society. (1982). 457 U.S. 332.

Breyer, S. (1997). Concurring opinion in *Washington v. Glucksberg,* 521 U.S. 793.

Brown v. Board of Education. (1954). 347 U.S. 483.

Carruth, A. & Booth, D. (1999, November). Disciplinary actions against nurses: Who is at risk?. *Journal of Nursing Law,* 6(3), 55-62.

Chermerinsky, E. (1991, June 16). Rehnquist's court: Activism from the right, *Courier Journal,* D1-D4.

Collins, Susan. (1999, November). Rethinking the Patient Self Determination Act: Implementation without effectiveness. *Journal of Nursing Law,* 6(3), 29-46.

Cruzan v. Mo. Dept. of Health. (1990). 497 U.S. 261.

Filippatos, P. (1991). Doctrine of *stare decisis* and the protection of civil rights and liberties in the Rehnquist court. *Boston College Third World Journal,* 335-377.

General Accounting Office. (2000). Occupational safety: Selected cost and benefit implications of needlestick devices for hospitals. GAO-01-60R

Johnson, K.R. (1999). Lawyering for social change: What's a lawyer to do? *Michigan Journal of Race and Law, 5,* 201.

Levin, M. & Weinstein, H. (1998, November 28) Last of 46 state officials sign tobacco accord. *Los Angeles Times,* A-1.

Marbury v. Madison. (1803). I Cranch 137.

NLRB v. Health Care and Retirement Corp. (1994). 114 S. Ct. 1778.

Nurse Midwifery Associates v. Hibbett et al (1990). 918 F. 2d 605 (6th Cir.).

Parmet, W. (1999). Tobacco, HIV and the courts: The role of affirmative litigation in the formation of health policy. *Houston Law Review, 36,* 1663.

Patient Self-Determination Act of 1990. Public Law 101-508. Sections 4206, 4751 of Omnibus Budget Reconciliation Act. 42 USC 1395 et seq.

Roe v. Wade. (1973). 410 U.S. 113.

Smith-Pitmann, M. (1998) Nurses and litigation: 1990-1997. *Journal of Nursing Law,* 5(2), 7-20.

Vacco v. Quill. (1997). 521 U.S. 702.

Want, R. (Ed.). (1997). *Federal-state court directory.* New York: Want Publishing.

Washington v. Glucksberg. (1997). 521 U.S. 793.

24 Local Government

JUANITA V. MAJEWSKI

MARJORY C. O'BRIEN

"Think globally; act locally."

ACTIVIST SLOGAN

Los Angeles, California: L.A. may snuff out smoking in city parks

WASHINGTON POST, OCTOBER 28, 2001

Poughkeepsie, New York: Whooping cough hits Red Hook

POUGHKEEPSIE JOURNAL, JANUARY 13, 2001

New York City: Fewer children are hospitalized for asthma since 1997 city effort

NEW YORK TIMES, AUGUST 6, 2001

Syracuse, New York: County program has sharply reduced lead poisoning

SYRACUSE HERALD JOURNAL, JULY 29, 2001

Sleepy Hollow, New York: Poison control center decertified

SCHENECTADY GAZETTE, JULY 4, 2001

Staten Island, New York: Residents tie health problems to city's mosquito spraying

STATEN ISLAND ADVANCE, MAY 31, 2001

Middletown, New York: Deceased Nevele worker had tuberculosis

MIDDLETOWN TIMES HERALD, MARCH 23, 2001

Spring Valley, New York: County promotes TB education for immigrants

ROCKLAND JOURNAL NEWS, MARCH 9, 2001

Syracuse, New York: County is ahead of new SIDS guidelines

SYRACUSE HERALD JOURNAL, FEBRUARY 6, 2001

Commonly filed under health issues, these headlines represent a growing concern for local governments. How are local governments structured, and what are their responsibilities for health care?

Increasing media attention on national and state governments and their relationships with big business and special interests has heightened public interest in and understanding of these levels of government. Because we take local governments largely for granted, we tend to know less about them—the counties, cities, towns, villages, and school districts in which we reside—than about higher levels such as the state or federal governments. Localities, however, have great authority over many aspects of our daily lives. Nurses who understand the structure and function of local governments can influence decisions that affect not only their immediate community but also the society at large.

IMPORTANCE OF LOCAL GOVERNMENT

Local government is the vital link between citizens and the state or the nation. Providing services and carrying out policies prescribed by state and federal governments, local governments distribute billions of local, state, and federal dollars to community agencies. In their role as administrative agents, cities and counties often have the authority to modify the application of centrally determined policies because of locally different social, economic, and cultural patterns.

The obligations of local government grow continually in scope and importance. Public education,

479

public health, a potable water supply, sewage disposal, police protection, solid waste management, and recreation are among the resources and services provided principally by local governments. The quality of life in a community is directly affected by decisions about such resources and services.

Localities, those government units closest to popular control, are profoundly influenced by their constituency. Citizen pressure often results in changes in local policy and may ultimately affect state or national policy. Issues that are common to many municipalities become increasingly significant and pass from local to higher-level governments for action. They become state or national concerns not because they are statewide or national in nature, but because growing local concerns demand response on state and national levels.

Local government, particularly at the state and county levels, is also responsible for other health-related services such as those provided by the county coroner or medical examiner, state and county laboratories, offices for the aging, and long-term health care facilities. Perhaps most important is the local government's provision of physical and mental health services through public hospitals and clinics.

Providing health care services is often overlooked in an examination of the responsibilities of local government. The federal government is recognized as the entity responsible for setting broad health policies and for funding research into disease prevention and protection from environmental hazards. State government provides many of the same health functions as the federal government and also acts to implement state and federal policies.

The effect of the devolution of responsibility from the federal government to state governments and ultimately to local governments can be seen in the growing concern over the loss of federal and state funds for uncompensated care provided by community-supported public hospitals. Although many public hospitals started as poorhouses, they evolved through the years into a system of safety nets funded largely through federal and state governments, and from private-pay and third-party reimbursement, for what in 1997 amounted to $18.5 billion in uncompensated care costs (Mann, Zuckerman, Bazzoli, Davidoff, & LoSasso, 2001). As

this financing of care for the uninsured has waned, public hospitals have struggled to provide care for people seeking both routine and emergency health care. Today, some of these hospitals continue to represent the safety nets that local governments count on to deliver care to the uninsured, but others have closed or privatized (Offner, 2001). In 2001, the Center for the Study of Health System Change reported that physicians were providing less charity care, contributing to a strain on hospital emergency departments and academic medical centers to meet community health care needs (Reed, Cunningham, & Stoddard, 2001).

But public hospitals do more than just care for the uninsured. They also protect community health overall, offering important but unprofitable services such as trauma centers and burn units, treating public health threats such as acquired immune deficiency syndrome (AIDS) or drug-resistant tuberculosis, and creating outreach programs for high-risk pregnancies, violence prevention, or immigrant health (Lewin, 1997).

The terrorist attacks on the United States in 2001 highlighted the importance of public health efforts for prevention, early diagnosis, and treatment of illness from biologic, chemical, nuclear, and other attacks. They drew attention to the inadequacies in the public health infrastructure to handle this challenge. Public health services, which began in response to epidemics and the need to control the spread of disease through quarantine and later sanitation, were well established as state responsibilities by the end of the nineteenth century. Funding for local health departments was reduced during the latter part of the twentieth century, as policymakers and much of the public began to view public health as services for the poor, when in fact local governments must rely on public health departments for surveillance of diseases and other health problems, early detection, health policy development, and other activities to protect the entire community (Institute of Medicine, Division of Health Care Services, Committee for the Study of the Future of Public Health, 1988; Lee & Estes, 2001).

Despite this withering support for an adequate public health infrastructure in many communities, county public health offices worked to keep pace with the expansion of knowledge about disease transmission and the impact of the environment on the health of individuals and society. Sanitation and immunization responsibilities expanded into health education and even clinical care, although the latter area is one that many local health departments are shedding as they try to ensure adequate resources for their core mission. Contemporary public health issues such as AIDS, access to health care for the indigent, injuries, teen pregnancy, control of high blood pressure, smoking, substance abuse, toxic substances, and Alzheimer's disease are debated at the national and state levels, but it is most often at the local government level that policies are implemented and action occurs.

Another challenge facing many localities is related to the 1996 federal welfare reform bill, the Personal Responsibility and Work Opportunity Reconciliation Act, which eliminated the link between cash assistance under the Aid for Dependent Children program and Medicaid eligibility, making it more difficult for this segment of the population to gain access to needed services. Before this bill, welfare recipients automatically qualified for Medicaid. Garrett and Holahan (2000) documented that 49% of women and 30% of their children were uninsured a year or more after leaving welfare. Today, localities have the option of making it easier or harder to enroll in Medicaid, depending on their budgets and ideology (Brown & Sparer, 2001). Another 2001 report, from the Center for the Study of Health Systems Change, noted that local community outreach efforts are essential for increasing the enrollment of children in Medicaid (Felland & Benoit, 2001). For many localities, the commitment to ensuring health care for those who are disadvantaged may be undermined by a national or local economic downturn. This picture is further complicated by the fact that an increase in the number of unemployed and uninsured usually accompanies a national or local recession. Thus, many local governments are working with businesses, their communities, and state and federal officials to spur community economic development.

School districts are a form of local government with the power, as noted earlier, to tax, borrow, and spend public funds to provide a community service. They are also policy-making institutions and are subject to requirements of both state and federal governments. Most states require schools to provide periodic health examinations, specific screening services, health assessments, health referrals, and immunization compliance. Federal government requirements for school health services is included in the Individuals with Disabilities Act, originally the Education for All Handicapped Children Act of 1975 (PL 94-142), which requires schools to guarantee a free and appropriate public education in the least restrictive environment to all students, regardless of their disability. This has often been judged to include provision of health and social services limited only by the needs of the student. But the cost of such services is beyond the means of many localities. In rural areas, in particular, some needed services may simply not be available.

School-based health centers operate under a variety of models, from limited in-house services provided by the school nurse to affiliation with a university hospital or a health maintenance organization. These school-based clinics rely on the knowledge and priorities of the local community, which may indicate a need to provide other services, from health education to mental health screening and prenatal services to pregnant teenagers (Morone, Kilbreth, & Langwell, 2001).

Nurses remain the primary caregivers in all school-based programs. In many cases, they are also the initiators of expanded services through their interaction with students and their awareness of community problems. Nurses serve as community health educators, as coordinators of health and social services, and as advocates for the needs of the community. They serve as the early warning system for environmental hazards such as lead poisoning and as statisticians alert to the ever-changing patterns of youth behavior and their effects on a healthy society.

TRENDS IN LOCAL GOVERNMENT

The many forms of local government are, or should be, engaging in self-scrutiny and strategic planning. Duplication and overlapping of services by different levels of government that are contiguous or geographically inclusive create fiscal burdens for localities and become increasingly difficult to sustain (O'Toole, 2000). Economic recessions hit local communities particularly hard, as there is usually a concomitant decline in federal and state assistance and revenue sharing, which contributes to local budget shortfalls for many jurisdictions. In addition, some governors believe that restricting state aid can force local solutions paid for with local resources.

During the 1980s and 1990s, many regions of the country experienced unprecedented economic growth while some large cities were faced with loss of viable economic bases. Some of those localities have been on the cutting edge of developing strategies to address the impact of business or industry relocation and major population shifts. At the turn of the twenty-first century, an economic downturn challenged many local as well as state governments.

Changes already taking place in our society require reevaluation of the scale, mix, and financing of services. Various solutions and concepts are being promoted by elected and appointed officials, planners, government analysts, economists, and other experts. Based in large part on economies of scale, these proposals are introduced under a variety of names and designs—consolidation of services, regionalism, metropolitan government, city-states, and government mergers being among the most common. All plans have a common goal: to make governments more efficient and cost-effective and to promote economic revitalization. Resistance to such proposals is not uncommon; neither citizens nor officials want to lose local autonomy.

Some plans are fairly simple, such as a regional planning agency to forge consensus among communities to provide maintenance of roads and highways that pass through many different localities. Other plans are emotionally volatile, as in mergers of city police precincts or of sheriff and local departments, where one jurisdiction lies within another. Residents fear losing protection, and departmental personnel fear losing jobs. Mergers of public hospitals generate similar fears, especially when the loss of small local hospitals limits access by underserved populations.

At the other extreme is the vision of collaborative networks of local governments such as those configured in Indianapolis, Indiana; Baltimore, Maryland; Minneapolis/St. Paul, Minnesota; Charlotte/Mecklenburg, North Carolina; and Dallas/Fort Worth, Texas. Common themes in these metropolitan regions include strategies to address education reform, poor and underserved populations, environmentally sensitive land use, and the health and housing needs of our aging population. For example, in Charlotte-Mecklenburg during the 1980s, many firms began to relocate to the area, creating an expanding regional economy. Growth provided many opportunities but began to threaten those very qualities that attracted growth: livability of the area and economic vitality. Eight critical issues—growth assumptions, environment, public services and facilities, development, neighborhoods, citizen involvement, urban design, and local government—were identified in strategic planning that involved businesses, neighborhood leaders, developers, and civic leaders. The resulting "2005 Plan" is a long-range land use plan that incorporates the vision of providing opportunity for economic mobility for all segments of the population (Kemp, 1993, 1999).

In the 1980s, civic and political leaders in Indianapolis, Indiana, determined to make Indianapolis a "city of distinction," and today that city is a strong, united community that operates under its "uni government" system. Most of Indianapolis and Marion County government functions were consolidated and managed by a local legislative body responsible for policy and budgeting for all city and county units. The mayor administered through a strong relationship with his cabinet and literally spoke for the community in all competitive relationships. Under this system cost savings were not significant, but this was not a primary goal. It was agreed, however, that the intent to operate efficiently and effectively was realized (Pierce, 1993).

Today, as in the past, restructuring local government might be the answer to ensuring basic needs. Some experts who believe there are too many local government units have long advocated such action. Public officials, economists, and planners are promoting new organizational forces and greater interdependence among the various levels of government. The various models of consolidated governments or shared services that exist in such metropolitan areas as Dallas/Fort Worth, Texas, which incorporates two cities, and Charlotte/Mecklenburg, a city-county planning approach, remain of interest to local communities and to the nation (Katz, 2000).

INFLUENCING LOCAL GOVERNMENT

As the largest group of health care providers, we nurses recognize our responsibility to speak out and act on behalf of those to whom we deliver care. We have developed skills and organized our numbers to achieve lobbying successes at the state and federal levels of government. Like the public in general, however, we have not always recognized the power of local government and the important role it has in shaping public policy.

The growing number of services provided by local governments and the changes taking place in federal-state-local relationships require that we turn our attention to working with and within local governments. The opportunity to have an impact on local government decisions is, in fact, much greater than in the state and federal governments (which tend to be more complex and distant). Access to officials is easier simply by virtue of geography, and more important, these officials may well be neighbors, members of our religious communities or clubs, professional colleagues, or co-workers in a volunteer school or community project (Rubin, 2000).

GATHERING INFORMATION

To be effective in influencing local government, one must first have a good understanding of how local systems operate. The form of government determines in large part who wields power and in what context that power is exercised.

Attending meetings of the city council, town or village board, or county legislature is one way to learn not only how that governmental body works but also what the current issues are. Meetings of local planning, zoning, and school boards are open. Minutes of these meetings are public record and are available at the municipal hall; public libraries often have a copy of the community boards' proceedings.

Knowledge of the political climate and the power brokers is important. Because of perceived stability or benign neglect, some localities see little competition for elected office and have long-term incumbents. This occurs most in small, long-established communities with little change in population. In newer areas, there is a wider cross section of people, significant grass roots activity, and more individuals who vie for elected and appointed positions. In either case, some basic information is essential:

- Which members of the elected body have the most power, both formal and informal?
- Who outside the government unit has influence and should be considered in devising strategy—a former public official, members of a powerful family, an influential business leader?
- Is there a political dynasty controlled by a family or a powerful interest group?
- What strategies have resulted in successful grass-roots initiatives?
- Is there evidence of a spoils system in which appointments to powerful boards or committees are granted on the basis of political connections rather than on merit?

This kind of information is more difficult to gather. The extent to which any of these conditions exist in different communities varies, but an understanding of these dynamics increases the possibility of achieving policy goals.

FORMULATING A PLAN

The form of government and the nature of the specific issue will determine which tactics are best for achieving change in local policy. For example, if you want to protest a budget that freezes the hiring of nurses, you must know where to lodge the protest. In a hospital operated by a small city in which the government is a weak-mayor-council form, you must organize to lobby the council members. In a health department run by a county with an elected executive and council, there is shared power and strong checks and balances. Both the county executive and the council must be targeted.

Enlist support of those who share the same or similar positions on the issue. If the issue is one of widespread concern or has a negative effect on a large segment of the community, numbers alone can be most effective. Officials therefore often do not respond to persistent or impassioned pleas until large numbers support the cause. Elected officials who have not identified and addressed a concern are put on notice by large-scale citizen efforts. Their reelection is threatened when they fail to serve their constituencies.

Movements typical of this kind of activity often fall into the "not in my backyard" (NIMBY) category. Projects such as landfills, construction of 200- to 300-foot cellular transmission towers, and group homes for drug or alcohol recovery or for mentally impaired persons are examples. In the case of group homes, nurses can play a valuable role in mustering support for the project by educating the public and helping to allay their fears, which are generally grounded in a lack of understanding.

Numbers are not and should not be the sole approach. In many instances, expert support is extremely valuable in persuading local decision makers. For example, rural landfill operations can be a source of revenue for a community, and despite many objectors, officials may decide that a company with a record of well-maintained sites may be a compatible enterprise. Possible contamination of groundwater supplies by effluent and runoff can be documented by hydrologists, environmental conservation officers, or soil and water conservation experts. Nurses can seek out such experts and act as facilitators to educate their local board about the possible health hazards (see the Vignette on environmental justice in Chapter 34).

Legislation and policy development are incremental, growing and changing during the course of many information-sharing and negotiating sessions. Rarely is a proposal adopted in its totality, but small successes do make a difference. Laying the foundation for further change and developing a support base for future initiatives are necessary and valid short-term goals.

GETTING INVOLVED

Nurses can influence government in a variety of ways, individually or collectively, with professional colleagues or private citizens, in small groups or large. There are a number of paths from which to choose:

- Serving on volunteer committees of community, school, or church groups results in developing new skills and fine-tuning others. This also creates a local network that can provide informal information or become part of an issue advocacy group.
- County and city hospitals, community health and elder services, and emergency treatment centers are often major employers in a community. Nurses in these facilities can participate in the resolution of problems confronting them or the populations they serve.
- Testifying at public hearings and speaking out on issues at meetings of local government bodies are opportunities for nurses to become recognized as experts.
- Coalitions and citizen movements are increasing. There is strength in numbers, but you must choose carefully which efforts to support, because some groups employ tactics of emotion and misinformation. Well-intentioned, informed groups are good places for nurses to develop competency in influencing policy decisions.
- Nurses can take the initiative to form committees to study a problem and make recommendations to local officials.
- Advocacy and expertise can be demonstrated by responding to health concerns with letters to the editor or to the officials who have jurisdiction over the matter. Video editorial comments are part of the growing information system available on some television networks and provide an opportunity to reach even wider audiences.
- The local electoral process provides several ways to influence who will make policy. Nurses can join local party committees to have a voice in the candidate selection process. They can work on the campaigns of candidates who share their values and goals.
- A local nursing association's political action committee (PAC) is an effective way to create a stronger presence by endorsing candidates and organizing nurses to work for them. Monitoring voting records is also an important function of a PAC.

As nurses become more involved and more visible in a wide range of community activities, they become more proficient and will often be sought for their expert opinion and to serve on boards or commissions.

Nurses should actively seek appointment to local boards and committees and become part of the decision-making teams. Health facilities and hospitals are units where nurses can logically become members of the board of directors. Planning, zoning, and conservation boards are also powerful authorities, as are school boards. Remember, too, that the many special districts discussed earlier are units of government and are managed by elected or appointed members. There will be much specific information to learn in such positions, but nurses should be confident that they have many skills and talents that will benefit their local governments and communities.

Becoming a decision maker as a member of a community board can be the first step to running for office. A network of supporters is established, new skills in management and communication are developed, and knowledge of broad issues can be used as preparation for higher office.

We are accustomed to hearing about the exorbitant levels of spending needed to win elections at the federal and state levels. Candidates for office in large cities or counties may also have to spend large sums to be viable. The smaller cities, towns, and villages do not require such vast financial resources. Candidates rely on extensive networks of family, coworkers, and neighbors to spread their message. The candidate's achievements may already be well known. Leaflet distribution, ads in local papers or trade publications, and door-to-door campaigning by the candidate and spokespersons are the tools to use effectively in races at this level. These activities often become opportunities to invigorate neighborhoods and generate cooperation and camaraderie.

It is not uncommon for local government officers to run for higher office. In fact, many regard local government as the training ground for state and national office. Public officials often attain their first positions in local office by accident rather than by design; that is, they move from community activism to elected office because of their involvement in issues. Others, particularly those from families with extensive involvement in political activity or public office, decide early on to follow that course.

Service on a local school board allowed one nurse to use her background and influence to convince other board members of the importance of seat belts on school buses and the need for monitoring environmental hazards in school buildings. It is hoped that more and more nurses will be convinced that holding public office is the way to influence public policy and will make early decisions to do so.

CASE EXAMPLE: MAKING A DIFFERENCE IN LOCAL GOVERNMENT

Elementary and secondary schools are faced with growing populations of at-risk students who fail to fulfill their physical and mental promise. Emotional and behavioral deficits are barriers to learning that have consequences for society as well as for the individual, but communities too often have no comprehensive approach to addressing these issues.

When a small rural school district established its federally funded Safe and Drug-Free Schools Committee, the elementary school nurse volunteered to serve. The nurse advocated early intervention and prevention programs for the primary grades. For the first 3 years, however, all the initiatives supported by the committee targeted the high school population. This was due to the proportionately higher representation of high school staff, highly visible and pressing problems at that level, and lack of understanding of the effectiveness and value of early intervention versus crisis intervention in later years. Goals in serving the high school were to provide support to students at risk of academic failure or dropping out of school. The approach was fragmented, with a variety of programs but with no long-term evaluation or follow-up.

The nurse continued to educate committee members as a body and individually about the need for a long-range plan for all students, kindergarten through twelfth grade, with a focus on early intervention. Information about a particular primary-level program with documented success for 25 years was strongly recommended by the nurse. Support was built formally and informally, and the committee eventually funded the recommended program as a 2-year pilot project. The program has been positively evaluated by elementary-level teachers whose students had fewer school adjustment problems and who were helped.

A broad-based holiday celebration, also initiated by the school nurse, was planned and carried out by a subcommittee of the Safe and Drug-Free School Committee. Business, government, churches, and the school district cooperated in providing both in-kind service and financial support for a family-oriented, intergenerational drug- and alcohol-free New Year's Eve event. Attendance was double the number the steering committee had planned for. Postevent evaluations completed by attendees, vendors, and performers revealed strong support for the event to be held annually.

Though it is sometimes possible to accomplish sweeping change, this is not usually the case. Nurses acting as change agents must understand that achieving change requires patience, persistence, and an understanding of the incremental nature of policy development.

Establishing a support network will strengthen the chances of accomplishing a goal. This network should include both formal and informal power brokers. The school nurse targeted two committee members likely to be supportive of the need for comprehensive early intervention—one a highly respected elementary teacher who was also a school board member in a neighboring district; and the other an active parent of elementary students who had served several terms on the local parent-teacher association's board of directors. They in turn generated additional support. The principal of one of the elementary schools lent early support after reading program material provided by the nurse.

A knowledge of government structure, as well as of the history of the informal power system and decision-making process, helped this nurse and members of the celebration subcommittee to get their effort off the ground. The most common form of town government, similar to the weak-mayor-council form, was in place. Commitment to the event was secured informally by lobbying individual council members and then sending a project proposal to be acted on at an official meeting of the town board. The strong appeal of the program content provided momentum and generated community support.

CONCLUSION

Providing assistance and services to local residents, once the responsibility of local governments, was gradually assumed by the federal government through such programs as Social Security, Medicare, grants for higher education, Housing and Urban Development funds, and the so-called war on poverty. During the 1990s, however, funding for health and human services, as well as support for state and local government operations, came under attack.

Cutting services or raising property taxes is the choice with which many localities must grapple, because local taxing and borrowing limits are capped by the states. Economic factors dictate that governments become more efficient in their operations. Despite shrinking revenues, citizens often expect the same level of services or even demand additional amenities.

Both nurses and local governments have long histories of intervening in social problems. Nurses should continue to expand their efforts to participate in policy development, both as grass roots lobbyists and as elected or appointed officials. The nursing profession recognizes the importance of these endeavors, and nursing associations at the national, state, and district levels support nurses involved in such activities through political action and candidate training workshops. As always, nursing looks to the future, and we should determine now what our role will be in the governments of the future and position our profession to shape that role. Understanding and participating in local government is a critical foundation for those activities.

As the largest group of providers in the health care system, our responsibility as nurses in caring for and about people requires our skills, resources, and power to improve the socioeconomic and political climate for all. The more we understand local government, the better equipped we will be to make sound decisions about how and toward whom we should direct our activities.

FOR YOUR INFORMATION

Forms of Local Government

There is wide variation in the number, size, and type of local governments throughout the nation, but a fairly common format does exist (Kemp, 1999). The structures and responsibilities have undergone continual growth and change, but present-day forms of government essentially reflect colonial models established by the original settlers. Counties and townships, created by the states to administer basic state functions within geographic subdivisions, are often described as *involuntary units*. As counties grew, additional duties and powers were delegated. In contrast, cities and villages are described as *voluntary units,* created by the state at the request of the residents to meet particular needs.

Our system of local government is complex, not only because of the varied models that evolved, but also because of enormous differences in population, wealth, geography, climate, and culture. The local patterns and functions are further complicated by overlapping authority of units, particularly in large urban centers. There is no commonly accepted definition of a local government; in practical use, the term simply refers to a particular local community. The U.S. Census Bureau, however, has developed detailed criteria that a unit must meet to qualify as a local government body. These criteria are divided into four major categories: counties, municipalities, towns and townships, and special districts.

COUNTY GOVERNMENT

Generally, counties are the largest local governments in most states, although these units are called *parishes* in Louisiana and *boroughs* in Alaska. The number of counties varies widely among states; however, there is no relationship between the number of counties and the population or size of the state.

Early duties of the counties were few and practical: to provide citizen protection and to maintain law and order. To ensure reliable travel to county jails and courthouses, counties additionally became responsible for the construction and maintenance of roads. Today, counties administer a vast array of additional services: health and social services, election law, sanitation, and parks and recreation. Services outside the jurisdiction of the county's governing body are administered by row officers, who are separately elected. These may include sheriffs, prosecuting attorneys, county clerks, trea-surers, coroners, and judges. Various forms of county government include the elected board or commis-

sion, the board of supervisors, the county executive or county manager, and the mixed county board.

Elected Board or Commission

The most prevalent form of county government, the elected board or commission performs both executive and legislative duties. Members might oversee services jointly or separately as heads of departments. Some boards focus strictly on policy development and appoint managers to run departments. In some states, members are elected from geographic districts apportioned according to population, whereas in other states all members are elected at large.

Board of Supervisors

The board of supervisors is the oldest form of county government and, despite functional disadvantages, continues to be fairly prevalent. The supervisors are elected as town officers in town elections and serve collectively to manage the county's executive and legislative functions.

County Executive or County Manager

Most often found in urban areas, the county executive or county manager form of government has an elected board that is responsible for policy and legislation. In addition, there is either an elected executive with broad executive power or a board-appointed manager with no independent authority, who is responsible for administrative functions and accountable to the board.

Mixed County Board

Mixed county boards are most common in southern states. Elected judges and county representatives perform executive and legislative duties. The judges officiate in judicial capacities in addition to their normal governing roles.

MUNICIPALITIES

Municipalities exist in all 50 states and are called by many names, including *cities, boroughs,* and *villages.* Functionally, municipalities carry out some functions as instruments of the state and perform some operations to benefit primarily their own residents. Although they are less inclusive of territory than counties, many municipalities exercise more power and provide more services than do county governments. Their powers are defined by state charters and statutes that spell out the differences between villages and

Continued

FOR YOUR INFORMATION—cont'd

cities. Four basic forms of municipal government have evolved: mayor-council, commission, council-manager, and mayor-manager.

Mayor-Council

The mayor-council form of municipal government is the most common and can exist in either of two forms: weak-mayor–council or strong-mayor–council. The weak-mayor system is the oldest form of local government, and nearly every municipality functioned under this plan into the nineteenth century. The council, elected either by district or at large, has both executive and legislative powers. The mayor, also a member of the council, may be elected directly by the voters or selected by fellow council members. Under this form, power is fragmented. Authority over administrative and appointive decisions is held by the council, and the mayor has limited or no veto power. This form remains in many municipalities today, especially in villages and smaller cities.

Rapid urban expansion in the nineteenth century frequently paralyzed the decision-making process of the weak-mayor-council system as disputes arose over priorities. Failure of councils to act and the power void in the office of mayor gave rise to the political machine and its boss, willing to provide a variety of needed services in return for votes. Reforms led to the development of the strong-mayor plan, in which the mayor, elected by the voters, is the chief executive and administrative head and the council is the policy-making body. Most contemporary large cities and some medium-sized cities employ this form.

Commission

The commission model gained wide popularity after its adoption by Galveston, Texas, in 1901. The corrupt incumbent government, unable to handle the crisis that followed a destructive tidal wave, was suspended by the state legislature and replaced by a five-member commission. All executive and legislative authority was vested in the commission, with each member responsible for administering a different department; one member was designated as mayor but had little additional power. Several variations of the commission plan evolved, but, like the weak-mayor-council model, the absence of checks and balances hampers decision making and action when serious disputes arise among commission members. Many cities subsequently reverted to strong-mayor-council government or the newer council-manager

plan. Despite the drawbacks, some small to medium-sized cities still use some form of commission government, such as Miami, Florida.

Council-Manager

Another solution to inefficient government, the council-manager form, models private business and relies on an appointed professional manager for administrative control. The elected council sets broad policy, and the position of mayor, if it exists, may be filled by one of the council members or be elected by the people. In most cases the mayor is relegated to a minor role and functions in a ceremonial capacity.

This form gained great momentum after it was adopted in Dayton, Ohio, after a destructive flood in 1912. It is prevalent in municipalities with populations of 10,000 to 200,000 people but also occurs in larger cities, including Dallas, Phoenix, and San Diego. The arrangement is attractive to those who seek to eliminate the politics of city administration by vesting authority in qualified professionals. However, managers may be subject to pressures from current or potential council members, on whom continued employment depends.

Mayor-Manager

The newest improvement in city government, the mayor-manager form provides a strong system of checks and balances. The elected mayor appoints a chief administrator and concentrates on executive duties of budget preparation, appointments, and certain veto powers over council actions. The council retains policy-making power.

TOWNS AND TOWNSHIPS

The term *town* is used informally to refer to communities large or small in rural or suburban areas. In a formal application of the term, however, town government is that which originated and still exists in some New England states. In the colonial period, New England settlements refused to be governed by royal charters, as were other, urbanized areas of the colonies. Fiercely independent, the settlements established town meetings, at which all in attendance voted to enact laws, levy taxes, appoint officials, and make other administrative decisions. The number and kinds of issues directly voted on at modern town meetings have been greatly reduced, but towns tend to have a larger number of elective offices. Rural areas, known as *plantations* in Maine and *lo-*

FOR YOUR INFORMATION—cont'd

cations in New Hampshire, are included in the use of this term.

Townships may be rural in nature and function, being simply organized and supplying few services. Urban townships are adjacent to highly urbanized areas and may have populations greater than those of some small cities. They are granted more self-governance and are increasingly becoming units of urban government.

Towns and townships, like villages and counties, have a variety of elected officials with specific administrative responsibilities: clerk, receiver of taxes, assessor, judge, and superintendent of highways. Except for the level of participation, townships operate like municipalities, providing similar types of services and retaining revenue-raising authority. In general, there is no separate executive branch. The town board or council is composed of a supervisor and members elected at large, and its structure is similar to that of the weak-mayor-council system. As administrator and chief financial officer, the supervisor is responsible for day-to-day operations but has no veto power or independent authority for policy.

SPECIAL DISTRICTS

Special districts, which provide a variety of single or limited services, are the most numerous of local governments and exist in all states but Alaska. School districts whose budgets are not part of a municipal budget are the most predominant and familiar of the special districts. They are properly regarded as governmental units with the power to tax, borrow, and spend public funds for a specific service. Budgets, policy, programs, and appointments are the responsibility of an elected board of local citizens who serve without salary. The superintendent of schools attends meetings and works with the board. In some communities, positions on the school board are viewed as prestigious or powerful, and races for a seat on the board generate a good deal of competition, controversy, or both. In addition, greater interest has been shown in these positions in recent years because of the desire of parents or other interest groups to control policy, curriculum development, and budget expenditures.

Other major types of special service districts are fire protection, water supply, and soil conservation. They, too, have power to tax, borrow, and spend public funds and are governed by boards whose elected or appointed members are called commissioners. Citizens do not always recognize these districts as units of government, however, and people may take note of them only when the assessment appears on their tax notices.

Demand for a greater number and variety of services continues as new suburban areas develop and special districts proliferate to meet the needs and wishes of a community. Only those who reside within the boundaries of a specific district can be taxed for that service. Districts can be very parochial, serving very few, or so broad that portions of—or even entire—local governments may be involved. For example, citizens in heavily populated subdivisions within a rural area may request sidewalks or street lighting. If the majority of property owners agree, these amenities are installed, and only those who derive the benefit are taxed. Sewer districts are an example of more expansive special districts, which may require the cooperation and participation of towns, villages, and counties. A public hospital district often serves at least one city and the surrounding rural area.

REFERENCES

Brown, L.D. & Sparer, M.S. (2001). Window shopping: State health reform politics in the 1990s. *Health Affairs, 20*(1), 50-67.

Felland, L.E. & Benoit, A.M. (2001, October). *Communities play key role in extending public health insurance to children* (issue brief no. 44). Washington, DC: Center for the Study of Health System Change. Available online at www.hschange. org/content/377.

Garrett, B. & Holahan, J. (2000). Health insurance coverage after welfare. *Health Affairs, 19*(1), 175-184.

Institute of Medicine, Division of Health Care Services, Committee for the Study of the Future of Public Health. (1988). *The future of public health.* Washington, DC: Government Printing Office.

Katz, B. (Ed.). (2000). *Reflections on regionalism.* Washington, DC: Brookings Institution Press.

Kemp, R.L. (Ed.). (1993). *Strategic planning for local government.* Jefferson, NC: McFarland & Co.

Kemp, R.L. (Ed.). (1999). *Forms of local government: A handbook on city, county and regional options.* Jefferson, NC: McFarland & Co.

Lee, P.R. & Estes, C.L. (2001). *The nation's health.* Boston: Jones and Bartlett.

Lewin, T. (1997, September 3). Hospitals serving the poor struggle to retain patients. *New York Times,* A1, A20.

Morone, J.A., Kilbreth, E.H., & Langwell, K.M. (2001). Back to school: A health care strategy for youth. *Health Affairs, 20*(1), 122-136.

Offner, P. (2001). Politics and the public hospital in our capital. *Health Affairs, 20*(4), 176-181.

O'Toole, L.J., Jr. (Ed.). (2000). *American intergovernmental relations.* Washington, DC: CQ Press.

Pierce, N.R. (1993). *Citi-states: How urban America can prosper in a competitive world.* Washington, DC: Seven Locks Press.

Reed, M.C., Cunningham, P.J., & Stoddard, J. (2001, August). *Physicians pulling back from charity care* (issue brief no. 42).

Washington, DC: Center for the Study of Health System Change. Available online at www.hschange.org/content/356/?words=safety+net+hospital.

Rubin, B.R. (2000). *A citizen's guide to politics in America: How the system works and how to work the system.* Armonk, NY: M.E. Sharpe.

Zuckerman, S. Bazzoli, G., Davidoff, A., & LoSasso, A. (2001). How did safety-net hospitals cope in the 1990s? *Health Affairs, 20*(4), 159-168.

25 State Government: 50 Paths to Policy

SUSAN C. REINHARD

"Doing what's right isn't the problem. It is knowing what's right."

LYNDON B. JOHNSON

State governments allow nurses to practice. Charged with constitutional mandates to protect the public, states develop laws and regulations that define and limit the scope of nursing practice, which varies across states and time. The 50 different governments that compose the United States are often not united in their approaches to permitting advanced practices nurses to prescribe medications, providing insurance coverage to the poor, or paying for home care services for frail older adults and persons with disabilities. Nurses who are concerned about their practice—and the health of the people they serve—need to understand what state governments control, how that jurisdictional control is growing, and how to influence the state health policy agenda and decisions.

TRENDS IN STATE GOVERNMENT

Since the early days of the country, there has been a fundamental tension between the power of the federal government and the power of the states. There is no dispute that the federal government is charged with protecting all of us from foreign invasion. There is also no dispute that each state is responsible for determining which of us can drive a car and under what circumstances that privilege can be revoked. However, there are many areas that fall between these two power points, and the pendulum

can swing either way depending on the political forces of any given time.

For most of U.S. history, states have had the main responsibility for developing and implementing health care policy, particularly in public health (Patel & Rushefsky, 1999). The role of the federal government in social and health policy was expanded during the New Deal era of President Franklin D. Roosevelt, who led the country out of an economic depression and state poorhouses and into a broad national policy of social security programs. Federal financing of the Medicare and Medicaid programs in the 1960s Great Society period considerably expanded this role. However, since the 1970s the prevailing climate has been "state's rights," with ever-increasing power accorded to states, particularly in health care policy (Sparer, 1998). Passing responsibility from federal to state governments, known as "devolution of power" to the states, has been an evolutionary process accelerated by the failure to gain a national consensus on health care reform legislation in the 1990s (Lipson, 1997).

The rationale for devolution is to move policy development and program management, or decision making, closer to the people, thereby limiting the role of the federal government. The notion is that reducing federal micromanagement and increasing state flexibility allows the states to become "laboratories of reform." Those who support devolution purport that the policy instruments of the federal government are too blunt to develop creative solutions to complex issues—the states are closer to the front lines and can do a better job. Those who are concerned about devolution say it promotes disparities among the states in reaching the underserved and it is just a way for the federal government to cut programs and shift the blame to the states (Lipson, 1997).

There is no doubt that devolution has put the spotlight on states, notably in health care and social policy reform. The State Children's Health Insurance Program (S-CHIP) is a key example of the devolution concept (Rosenbaum, Johnson, Sonosky, Markus, & DeGraw, 1998). Title XXI of the federal Social Security Act created S-CHIP as a block grant to the states and gave states much discretion in the design of their programs, eligibility criteria, and avenues for reaching eligible children (Riley & Pernice, 1999; Flowers & Riley, 2000). The different ways that states have chosen to administer these block grants and their variable success to date in enrolling eligible children will affect public support for future devolution of major health and social programs to the states (Schulte, Pernice, & Rosenthal, 2000).

Given the current expanding role of state government, nurses should be more involved in state policy than ever before. For example, although the president and Congress can put a spotlight on public education reform and alter some funding and federal regulations to help steer the course, the states (and local governments) provide the bulk of school funding, set and enforce teacher certification requirements, determine curriculum mandates, and have the power to raise minimum teacher salary levels. The states determine whether or not there will be a death penalty, for which state crimes it applies, and by what means it will be effected. They decide speed limits for state roads, whether or not you have to put your young child in a car seat or wear a helmet when riding a motorcycle, and the amount citizens will pay in state taxes.

In the health policy arena, states are considering ways they might prohibit mandatory overtime for nurses, strategies to promote the recruitment and retention of nurses and other health care workers, and establish multistate licensure to make it easier for nurses to practice across state lines, especially over the telephone and on the Internet. States control about one third of all public expenditures for health care (Brecher, 1999), about $238 billion in 1999 (National Association of State Budget Officers and the Reforming States Group, 2001). Most states are considering ways to help older adults get the prescriptions they need. Some are considering ways to deal with the growing issue of people who cannot obtain health care because they are uninsured or underinsured. Some are leading the way in developing more home- and community-based alternatives for long-term care, respite services for family caregivers, school-based health services for children, and strategies for preventing life-threatening errors in hospitals and other health care settings.

These examples reflect the many areas in which one or a few states can lead the way for other states and the federal government. Regardless of the prevailing political climate, states have a distinguished history in promoting progressive health and social policy. For example, Tennessee was the first state to require drivers to use infant car seats for small children in the 1970s. Washington was the first to permit nurses to prescribe medications independently. Maryland and New Jersey were leaders in mandating insurance coverage for a minimum 48-hour hospital stay for newborns and their mothers. State governments are worthy focal points for nurse activism.

STRUCTURE OF STATE GOVERNMENTS

The structure of any given state government affects how a nurse is able to influence health and social policy in that state. There are some similarities between state governments, but there is also considerable variation, particularly in the legislative and executive branches (for specifics, see your state's website). Nurses should be aware that states have a judicial branch of government. State courts can set precedents that influence policy nationwide, such as the Karen Anne Quinlan case, which addressed the fundamental right to make end-of-life decisions. However, the emphasis here is on state structures and processes that nurses can more directly influence.

STATE LEGISLATURES

Every state has a legislature that enacts laws, confirms the governor's appointments to critical departments and other agencies that govern health care and nursing practice, and approves state budgets. All but one of these legislatures (Nebraska) has two houses. Beyond these consistencies, individual differences abound (Chi, 2001). Most legislatures meet every year, and some (seven) meet only every other year. Most state legislators serve part-time and have other job responsibilities in addition to their legislative duties. Few are health care professionals or have expertise in the field, which means that the 97 nurses who held legislative office in 38 states in 2001 have an enormous challenge and opportunity (Farmer, Henderson, & Ladenheim, 2001).

Although state legislatures have different rules and procedures, they have a common leadership structure that nurses should be familiar with. Each house has a legislative leader who is elected by the political party that holds the majority of seats (Rosenthal, 1998). That leader usually appoints the chairs of the various committees that first consider bills that have been introduced. The chairs wield a great deal of power in determining which bills will be heard, sponsoring some of the most important bills and often blocking bills they do not want to see passed. In many states, those leaders have many years of seniority. However, with more states (18 at present) enacting term limits restricting the number of times that a legislator can run for reelection, this classic power structure is shifting (Chi, 2001). There are many more new legislators with fresh perspectives, and less control is placed in the hands of a few. Of course, these new legislators often have little information about the critical issues that concern nurses, which means there is a continuing need to meet new representatives to educate them about important issues. Reapportionment after the national census every 10 years also changes the political dynamics. Whoever is in control of the legislature determines new districts, and the process is done within the first 2 years after the census. It is a contentious, highly politicized process. A given state may alter state legislative district borders, making it more or less easy to elect people from a particular political party, minority group, or key interest area.

The main activity of state legislatures is introducing, hearing, and passing bills that become law once signed by the governor. The process is similar to the federal legislative process. The most impor-tant thing for nurses to know is that when you take a problem to legislators, they will want to know the relevance to their constituents, what bill is related to that issue, or if there is a need for a new law. They are rarely interested in a conceptual discussion. They are concrete lawmakers who will run for office on the strength of their records on sponsoring or co-sponsoring laws that matter to the constituents who vote for them.

EXECUTIVE BRANCH

Each state has a governor, who presides over the executive branch. More than half of the states also have a lieutenant governor, who may or may not work closely with the governor depending on the election politics of that state. Although devolution has expanded their roles, governors' powers vary widely. All governors are responsible for proposing a state budget to legislators for approval, and for managing that budget throughout the prescribed budget cycle. However, most governors do not have the power to selectively reduce the amount of appropriations allocated to particular budget items that legislators add to the "wish list" of things they want to please their constituents. Governors have to persistently negotiate with individual legislators and the legislative branch as a whole to get their budgets approved. They can introduce policy ideas and work with legislative colleagues and leaders to sponsor legislation (if needed) to implement those ideas. They can sign legislation into law or they can veto a bill outright or provide a conditional veto, either of which requires further legislative action to overcome.

One of the most important powers a governor has is to appoint people to powerful positions that influence policy. Some states elect an attorney general who interprets laws and issues opinions that affect major social and health policies, though some governors have the power to appoint this individual. Governors also appoint members of boards that regulate the practice of health professionals and other occupational groups (state boards of nursing, medicine, dentistry, pharmacy, acupuncturists, beauticians, tattoo artists, and many more), and oversee public health, hospitals, casinos, transportation, and many other significant areas.

Perhaps most important is the gubernatorial appointment of the heads of state agencies that affect health and human services, aging and disability policy, insurance regulation, and education. These agency heads oversee the development and implementation of policy for their particular jurisdictional area. They develop detailed rules and regulations to implement the laws that legislators pass and governors sign. Regulations can affect the daily work of nurses: staffing ratios, hospital admitting privileges, Medicaid payment formulas, nursing delegation, and an almost endless list of other practice concerns. Although they are often confirmed by the state legislature, these state agency heads serve at the will of their governors. They appoint (or recommend) people to critical rule-making bodies, task forces, commissions, and other forums that consider ideas, make policy recommendations, and vote on actions that affect nurses. Clearly these agency heads are key people for nurses to know.

The power of state agencies to influence health and social policy varies across and within states, and across time. For example, the state department of health may be a stand-alone agency with a department head that reports directly to the governor, or a division within a larger umbrella agency. Some commissioners and deputy commissioners of health have had enormous influence in shaping managed care regulations, services for people with HIV infection, senior services, and the distribution of tobacco settlement funds to support public health and community-based care. State Medicaid directors, responsible for administering one of the largest components of any state budget, may have the primary role in designing the S-CHIP program or they may be subject to the authority of the governor's policy office that makes most of the decisions. It is important to know who is running the show and their scope of authority.

Regardless of the power that agency heads might have, they all interact with the governor's staff— typically the chief of staff, the policy chief, the chief counsel, the lead budget person (often the treasurer), and the director of communications. These are the people who help the governor develop the priority policy agenda, advance or block policy initiatives, and secure their governor's "legacy."

WHO'S WHO

To some extent, the 50 states demonstrate 50 ways of governing. This variation means that nurses in each state need to understand how their state works—its legislature, its executive branch, and its political culture and trends. Yet there are enough commonalities to recommend the major kinds of state policymakers that nurses should get to know:

- The leadership of the state legislature, including the leaders in each house and the committee chairs for important areas such as health, human services, senior services, children's issues, women's health, and education (however they are structured)
- Your own legislator, who may be willing to sponsor legislation for you, an important constituent with many nursing colleagues, patients, friends, and relatives
- The governor and the governors' core staff, which changes even during a given governor's tenure
- State agency heads and their chief staff, including the Medicaid director and top officials for public health, children's health, adult health, senior services, disability services, insurance regulation, and regulation of facilities (hospitals, nursing homes, assisted living, home care, outpatient care, and the like)
- Heads of professional regulatory boards, especially the state boards of nursing, medicine, and pharmacy

POTENTIAL ACTION

Nurses can and should influence the development of sound and creative health policy. They have expert knowledge of how the health care system works and its weaknesses. Nurses have insightful and practical ideas for change based on clinical experience, research, and a fervent desire to ensure better care for the people they serve. They are respected and trusted by the public and by policymakers at all levels of government.

To exert this considerable influence effectively, nurses need to know potential leverage points for advancing (or stopping) any given policy. They need to focus their energies on those who can assist them to achieve specific objectives. For example, if a nurse wants to advocate changes in prescriptive authority, it will do little good to call a member of Congress, such as a federal senator, because it is not a federal issue. Prescriptive authority is a state nurse practice act policy issue that requires action by state policymakers; indeed 30 bills to change some aspect of state nurse practice acts were introduced in 17 states in 2000 (details on these policy initiatives are available online at www.ana.org/gova/state/pracacts.htm). To implement a change, it is helpful if the state board of nursing supports the legislative change in the practice act and is prepared to develop rules and regulations to implement the new law once enacted. Nurses need to find persuasive state legislators (especially those in leadership positions) to sponsor the legislation and get it passed in

the committees and on the floors of both houses. The governor's legal team (who attends to the constitutional and legal details) and the chief of staff (and other core advisors who steer the governor's political course) will advise the governor whether or not to sign it into law. Nurses must exert influence at all of these leverage points, and perhaps others depending on the structure and political dynamics of that state.

The state's political calendar and budget cycle will determine the timing of political action. Nurses in states that hold year-round legislative sessions and have an annual state budget that begins every July have different patterns of activity than nurses in states with legislatures that meet less frequently and have a 2-year budget cycle that begins every other January. In the former situation, the case for

Susan Reinhard (middle), RN, PhD, FAAN, joins former Governor Christine Todd Whitman and husband Tom Reinhard to celebrate the new Department of Health and Senior Services in New Jersey. As Deputy Commissioner for the department, Reinhard was instrumental in its conceptualization and creation.

retaining more nurses in nursing homes by raising salaries through a Medicaid "pass-through" of state budget dollars to nursing staff must be made in the fall to the state agencies developing budget recommendations to the governor. For legislators and the governor's staff, the case must be made during the winter and spring as they negotiate the final state budget voted in during June. That is a 9-month window of opportunity. If nurses are not successful during this period, they have about 3 months to develop another budget proposal (that could be quite similar) and start again in September for the following June budget vote. For nurses residing in a state that has a 2-year cycle, advocacy is more focused during a shorter time frame as the state budget is shaped. The pace may be even more frenetic at that time, and the chance to "get another bite at the apple" occurs less frequently.

Election cycles should also be considered. Some of the best "teachable moments" for gubernatorial and legislative candidates occur during the 6-month period preceding both the primary and general elections. These are perfect times to meet with those who may soon have the power to advance or block policies of concern to nurses. This is the time to support nurse candidates and others who will help advance nursing's policy solutions. It is also a good time to get to know these future policymakers' core staff members, provide helpful information, and position nurses for critical appointments to gubernatorial and agency transition teams. These teams will begin to shape the ideas and governmental processes to initiate change for the next several years. It is also a good time to position nurses for appointment to the highest levels of state government.

CONCLUSION

With so much at stake and so many ways to influence the policies and financing that affect their daily practice and personal lives, how can nurses navigate the complex world of state government? The easiest way is to join the state nurses association or other group expert in the state's particular nuances in policy structures, calendars, leaders, and political climate. These organizations have their

BOX **25-1** State Government Resources

For information and trends related to policy issues that are engaging nurses in specific states, see the website for the American Nurses Association, particularly the state government relations (www.ana.org/gova/state.htm). Each state nurses association offers more specific information on health policy in that state on its website. Membership in these organizations offers newsletters with details on policy proposals and specific actions that nurses can take, such as "Call Senator Smith at (888) 888-8888 to ask for her support on Assembly bill 1302 when it comes to the Senate floor for a vote later this Fall. This article provides the reasons to support this bill. If you have any questions, call our lobbyist Samantha at (111) 111-1111."

For broad insights into what issues are concerning the states' governors and their positions on various policies, contact the National Governors Association (www.nga.org). The address is National Governors Association, Hall of States, 444 North Capital Street, Washington, DC 20001 (phone [202] 624-5300).

The National Conference of State Legislatures (NCSL) can provide links to state legislative websites, session calendars, election results, and forecasts of state budget actions and major issues likely to be debated in state legislatures (www.ncsl.org). NCSL is located at 444 North Capital Street, NW, Suite 515, Washington, DC 20001 (phone [202] 624-5400).

Several websites provide useful information about health policies that states are considering, research and statistical data related to state health policy, and links to other resources. For an example, see the website for Rutgers' Center for State Health Policy (www.cshp.rutgers.edu).

own newsletters, websites, meetings, and many other ways to help nurses know what is going on in their particular state—and who to contact about specific issues. Members can "plug in" wherever and whenever they choose and find many colleagues interested in the same issues. Nurses can also find many details on their states' websites, and other helpful resources are listed in Box 25-1. The most important thing to remember is that nurses have the respect and power to advocate for the kinds of policies they want for the future.

For Your Information

Promoting Policy to Prevent Medication Errors

As the Deputy Commissioner for the New Jersey Department of Health and Senior Services, I was responsible for the policy, budget, and administration of $1.6 billion in programs, including the Pharmaceutical Assistance for the Aged and Disabled (PAAD) program. As a community health nurse, I wanted to use this opportunity to make the reduction of polypharmacy and medication errors a major policy goal for the PAAD program. I began by convening a policy summit on state pharmaceutical programs that included the other two large programs (Pennsylvania and New York) and other states, and two smaller meetings on the subject of preventing medication errors. Based on ideas gathered from these meetings, a review of research, and consultation from experts in information systems, my staff and I developed a proposal for an automated prospective drug utilization review (PRO-DUR) program that could work in New Jersey. Simply described, the older adult with a PAAD card would go into a pharmacy with a prescription, and the pharmacist would enter that prescription into a database. Based on clinical edits developed by an advisory board of scientists, prescribers, and pharmacists, the prescription might be rejected, perhaps because the dose was too high for an older adult. To make sure the clinician who prescribed the medication had an opportunity to discuss the situation, we advanced a way to allow "medical exceptions" that brought the clinician into an evidence-based dialogue with peers about why the older adult might need a higher dose of medications than research would support. The same process would be followed for possible drug-drug interactions and other potentially serious medication errors for older adults.

Knowing that this policy might engender opposition, I began the policy process by reaching out to stakeholders who might resist "bureaucratic interference" from the state in prescribing medications, but should support rational efforts to significantly reduce medication errors. I enlisted the support of the New Jersey State Nurses Association, the New Jersey Medical Society, state boards of nursing and medicine, all pharmacy groups, the drug manufacturers, and the AARP. I also brought the governor's deputy chief of policy into the discussions and talked with legislative leaders on the health, senior services, and appropriation committees in both the general assembly and senate; and I kept my own staff (especially Kathleen Mason, who directs the PAAD program, and her chief pharmacist, Carl Tepper) fully engaged in this effort. After the successful passage of authorizing legislation, I made strategic recommendations for the governor's appointees to the advisory board, and pushed for procurement of a capable group of professionals who could handle the medical exceptions part of this new system. Knowing that the press and legislators would react strongly the first time an older adult walked out of a pharmacy without a prescription filled, my staff and I prepared press releases and sent letters to all legislators to explain how the state was going to implement a new way to protect seniors—and noting that New Jersey's AARP leaders were in strong support of it.

New Jersey's automated PRO-DUR went into effect in 2000. In less than a year, it saved 200 lives and an estimated $500,000 a month in unnecessary and harmful prescriptions.

REFERENCES

Brecher, C. (1999). The government's role in health care. In A.R. Kovner & S. Jonas (Eds.). *Health care delivery in the United States* (6th ed.). New York: Springer.

Chi, K. (2001). State government, management, and policies: Trends and issues. In D. Sprague (Ed.). *The book of states, 2000-01 edition.* Lexington, KY: Council of State Governments.

Farmer, C., Henderson, T., & Ladenheim, K. (2001). Nurses in state legislatures: Gaining an inside edge on vital health policy issues. *State Health Notes, 22*(341), 1, 5-6.

Flowers, L. & Riley, T. (2000). *An analysis of policy issues in SCHIP and Medicaid implementation.* Portland, ME: National Academy for State Health Policy.

Lipson, D.J. (1997). State roles in health care policy: Past as prologue? In T.J. Litman & L.S. Robins (Eds.). *Health politics and policy* (3rd ed.). Boston: Delmar.

National Association of State Budget Officers and the Reforming States Group. (2001). *1998-1999 state health expenditures report.* New York: Milbank Memorial Fund.

Patel, K. & Rushefsky, K. (1999). *Health care politics and policy in America* (2nd ed.). New York: M.E. Sharp.

Riley, T. & Pernice, C. (1999). *If you build it, will they come? Case studies on CHIP implementation.* Portland, ME: National Academy for State Health Policy.

Rosenbaum, S., Johnson, K., Sonosky, C., Markus, A., & DeGraw, C. (1998). The children's hour: The State Children's Health Insurance Program. *Health Affairs, 17*(1), 75-89.

Rosenthal, A. (1998). *The decline of representative democracy: Process, participation, and power in the state legislatures.* Washington, DC: Congressional Quarterly Press.

Schulte, S., Pernice, C., & Rosenthal, J. (2000). *Progress and innovations in implementing CHIP: A report of four state site visits.* Portland, ME. National Academy for State Health Policy.

Sparer, M. (1998). Devolution of power: An interim report card. *Health Affairs, 17*(3), 7-16.

Vignette Judy Biros Robson

Journey to the Wisconsin Legislature

"A life is not important except in the impact it has on other lives."

JACKIE ROBINSON

I am the first—and, for the time being, the only—nurse to serve in the Wisconsin Senate. I was elected in 1998 after serving 11 years in the state assembly.

All new legislators bring their own perspectives and biases to the legislature based on their upbringing; the type of community from which they come; their age, race, sex, and education; and their work and life experiences. We all bring our own baggage, which influences our legislative priorities. My bag is obvious. It is black canvas with the words "nurse legislator" embossed in large letters on the side. When I sling the bag over my shoulder, I say to all, "I am a lawmaker and a nurse." I am proud to be both.

I am proud to have helped forge a new field in nursing: legislative nursing. This new field combines political skills with the job skills all nurses use. Getting elected to the state legislature does not require substantial political experience. My philosophy is, "If you want to do it, go for it!"

STARTING THE JOURNEY

The roots of my political activism began in the 1960s. As a young Kennedy idealist, I accepted the president's challenge to find out what I could do for my country. I was attracted to political activism for the same reasons I was drawn to nursing. I viewed each as a way to help the powerless and vulnerable and to make a difference in people's lives.

My prior experience in political campaigns was limited to volunteer work, such as addressing envelopes and door-to-door campaign literature drops. I served as president of the district nurses' association, congressional district coordinator for the American Nurses Association (ANA), and board member for the League of Women Voters. I served as a nurse intern in a state legislator's office to fulfill a requirement for a graduate nursing course. It was a big leap, however, to leave the security of a faculty position in college to embark on the uncertainty of a high-profile political campaign—but it was worth it.

Professionally, I was ready to run. Though I had worked contentedly for 9 years as a nursing instructor, I frequently challenged students in a trends course to become politically involved. "The political stakes are too high for a nurse to be a passive observer," I rallied. The tables were turned when a legislative seat was unexpectedly vacated; maybe I should practice what I preach and run for the seat.

At the same time the health care system, where I practiced for more than 25 years, was "morphing" into an industry. Emerging terms such as *market shares* and financial *bottom lines* reflected new values that were sharply challenging professional standards and nursing practice. It was becoming obvious that nurses needed to sit at the policy table during this time of upheaval in health care.

Equally important were previous negative experiences that frequently undermined my role as a geriatric nurse practitioner in collaborative practice:

- As part of my practice I would visit the homes of elderly patients after their hospital discharge. I would assess a bedridden client in her home, create and coordinate a plan of care, and be her advocate. For Hattie, my visit prevented an expensive, uncomfortable ambulance ride to the clinic for the same assessment. However, these less costly services were not reimbursable. Insurance would only cover the more expensive alternative: the ambulance ride and physician office visit.
- Vera was a lonely woman, with a chronic illness. She often feigned acute attacks and called for an ambulance to take her to the hospital. In a single month she was transported eight times to the emergency department. Again, insurance paid

for the expensive, unnecessary trips to the emergency department but not for my home interventions, which virtually eliminated these costly trips. In the office, I would be the provider who examined and counseled elderly patients, but the physician had to "pop in," sign my prescription pad, and leave—ceremonial steps, required by federal regulation, in order for costs to be reimbursed.

My collaborating physician and I lobbied state, federal, and private insurance companies about the cost-effectiveness and unique contribution of nurse practitioners and the value of preventive care. We submitted an article to a state medical journal on our unique practice and the value of geriatric nurse practitioners. Our voices fell on deaf ears. I felt powerless, and it seemed we had few advocates.

I wanted change, but how could it be accomplished? An opportunity arose when an open seat became available in the Wisconsin Assembly. Men outnumbered women in the legislature 4 to 1, and no woman had ever served my assembly district. An open seat is a golden opportunity to counter the advantage of incumbency. With no incumbent candidate, the two newcomers start out on a more level playing field.

RUNNING FOR OFFICE

Running for the Assembly felt like working in the emergency department on Friday night after a tornado has devastated a trailer park. Initially I tried doing everything—responding to the constant phone calls, incessant press inquiries, friendly advice on winning strategies (most of it conflicting)—while I continued teaching full-time in a difficult clinical rotation. I was naive and unprepared to handle the press or understand partisan politics. The stakes were high and the pressure intense.

The governor called a special election within 6 weeks of the incumbent's resignation, one of the shortest election spans in Wisconsin history. This short time frame put me at a distinct disadvantage, which was the intended strategy. My opponent already had great momentum from high name recognition. My time for campaigning was limited by a full-time teaching load. I was clearly the underdog, so much so that my own party fielded a candidate

against me in the primary: a well-liked county supervisor and farmer.

CAMPAIGN STRATEGY

To overcome the odds, I had to work harder and smarter. My campaign strategy was logical, a bit unorthodox, and hard work! The strategy was to identify those most likely to vote in a special election in the middle of June and visit as many of them as possible. After work and on weekends, I donned my white nursing shoes and knocked on the doors of regular, faithful voters. I complemented each home visit with friendly postcards, both before and after my personal visits.

I believe nurses are natural campaigners. We are people oriented and problem solvers, and we know how to listen. As a result, people trust us. Strangers invited me into their kitchen and easily shared conversations. I often found myself listening to detailed health problems instead of discussing political issues. I listened, I cared, and people responded positively. To this day, they still remember my visits.

This campaign strategy was not without its skeptics. Many friends urged me to abandon this unconventional door-to-door canvassing and to follow a more traditional campaign like my opponent's—visit downtown merchants and bankers, and attend ice cream socials and church picnics. Their goal was to have me attend as many group activities as possible and be highly visible. Because I was a novice in uncharted waters, it was hard to resist this well-meaning advice. Others argued that I should stay focused on the fact that special elections turn out few voters, and the voters who do show are dedicated. However, I stuck to my original plan to maintain the door-to-door effort and visit committed, faithful voters.

My opponent from the other political party was a formidable candidate. He was the executive director of the chamber of commerce, a former police captain, a school board member, and a legendary auctioneer. From these public perches, he was able to garner visibility and press attention. As a nursing instructor, I had no such public platform. I was practically invisible to the media; whereas he, as director of the chamber, was often seen cutting ribbons for new offices or giving speeches at large community events. One afternoon he even showed up on the stage at my son's high school graduation. I sat in the audience, steaming and demoralized. However, his front-runner status and glad-handing style began to work in my favor. Convinced he was a sure winner, his political party diverted resources earmarked against me to another, seemingly needier special election. This decision leveled the playing field for me. A cardinal rule in politics was violated by the opposition—never underestimate your opponent!

My own county political party was equally unimpressed with my potential to win. However, they became enthusiastic after I trounced the farmer, their anointed candidate, in the primary. The most enthusiastic volunteers were the nurses. I relied heavily on them—faculty members, Wisconsin Nurses Association members, and students willing to do literature drops, campaign mailings, and phone banks. To bolster esprit de corps, we called ourselves the "White-Shoe Army" and looked more formidable than we felt. We reasoned, it's tough to beat a nurse. A nurse running for political office is more than a curiosity (not many run) because nurses have an intrinsically positive image. Nurses project a natural aura of trustworthiness, honesty, and caring, qualities not often associated with politicians. This message sparked interest and ignited the campaign.

ELECTION DAY

As election day approached, I began to feel the momentum of grassroots support. The tide was turning, despite apathetic coverage from the only newspaper in town. The paper regularly featured photos of my opponent at community events, and the editor, a friend of my opponent, also regularly printed his supportive letters to the editor and withheld mine. Friends sent us copies of the letters they sent that were never published, and a whistleblower at the paper "snitched" about the backlog of letters. An attorney friend made a personal visit to the editor, challenging the newspaper for its bias. Soon afterward, an avalanche of supportive letters for me were published.

To sustain this momentum and capitalize on the door-to-door effort, we organized a phone bank for a "get out the vote" (GOTV) strategy. It's one thing to identify likely supporters, and another to be sure they actually get out to vote on a hot June day. They called likely voters on the night before the election. On the afternoon of election day, volunteers cross-checked the precinct poll list with our supporter lists and called again to remind voters to get to the polls. Voter turnout was heavier than expected because of our GOTV efforts. Enthusiasm for my outsider status helped, as did nurses who spontaneously called health care facilities to remind nurses to vote after work.

On election night, nervous supporters, friends, and family huddled around the radio, waiting for news. The polls closed at 8 pm, and by 8:30 we knew that I had won. What satisfaction to see television and radio crews who were sitting at my opponent's campaign headquarters suddenly pack up their equipment and race over to my election-night headquarters! Three special elections were held in the state, but I was the only Democrat in decades to win a special election. I was an instant celebrity in political circles. The headlines in the paper the next day read, *Robson Wins an Upset,* and there were my husband and I, grinning like Cheshire cats.

EARLY TRANSITION

Eager to start and overwhelmed with the reality of representing 50,000 people, my first day to work in the capitol was unforgettable. I was stopped by the highway patrol for speeding! Would this be a symbolic foreshadowing of coming events? The bumpy transition from nurse to legislator was perhaps not as rapid as my driving, but was hastened by my immediate immersion into the hectic budgetary process. Many seasoned capitol observers told me that this was the worst time to be elected. With 25 years of solid nursing skills behind me, I thought I was prepared for anything. Well, not exactly.

The transition from nurse to legislator was made more difficult by partisan egos. Though I nominally had an office in the state capitol, the opposing party, still upset over my victory, refused to vacate it. I felt parachuted into the middle of alien territory with little support—no office, no desk, no staff, and worst of all, no phone. Because of the work on the budget, orientation for new legislators was nonexistent. For several weeks I shared an office with a colleague, awkwardly working at his conference table. I naively thought that partisan politics ended with the campaign. In fact, partisanship colors every decision: office assignments, furniture, chairmanships, bill priorities, and fund raising. I had a lot more to learn.

BUDGET WARS

The situation in the capitol during budget deliberations is like war games. Budget building is the most time-consuming, intensive component of the 2-year legislative calendar. Everyone presses for advantage, scores points, collects personal favors, or outmaneuvers others or the opposing party. Lobbyists swarm like locusts, legislators scurry for amendments, and leadership maneuvers for key votes to pass the budget bill.

I thought the worst was behind me when I left the operating rooms of temperamental surgeons who threw instruments and publicly belittled nurses. However, the worst moments in surgery did not prepare me for the budget caucus, a partisan meeting set up so that members could discuss the budget bill, pending legislation, or strategies for partisan advantage.

Any resemblance to group process is purely coincidental. The budget caucus is chaotic. Members represent a variety of constituencies and interests ranging from fishermen and dairy farmers to inner-city youth. They all vie for attention and advantage. Their comments are sometimes pure theater, sometimes eloquent, and sometimes just plain nutty. Often an angry legislator stalks off, shouting, "I'm off the budget." (the translation being "I'm taking my bat and ball home until you play the game my way"). Another might whine, "I never get my amendments in the budget. Leadership always sticks it to me," and another may tearfully shout, "When are we going to take care of our dairy farmers?" A cry rises: "What do Democrats stand for, anyway?" So it goes for days and weeks.

Our caucus met in a hot, windowless, sticky hearing room. The capitol building in Madison is made of beautiful marble that heats summer hearing rooms to oven temperatures. As the hours dragged from day to night and into morning, tempers flared. We were tired and sweaty and needed fresh clothes and healthier food. My nursing diagnosis: "Inadequate decision making related to stress, sleep deprivation, and junk food."

After another late, hot evening, I finally bellowed, "Why don't we move across the street to the air-conditioned hotel? It's healthier." Cold stares from leadership locked me into frozen silence. A buddy came up later and whispered that leadership preferred this hot room to speed up the budget process. Afterward I was labeled the "nurse-legislator."

This early baptism by fire, the biannual budgetary process, was great training for subsequent floor periods. I had to learn fast and hit the ground running during the next session, working on an ambitious agenda of health care in the district's interest. Bills signed into law included a loan forgiveness program for nursing students, an insurance mandate for screening mammograms, immunization law changes to improve compliance, a primary health grant program for public health departments, academic credit transfer for associate-degree registered nurses (RNs), a task force on cocaine-addicted babies, grants for health care workers for assessment and treatment of cocaine-addicted babies, statute revisions to strengthen public health, emergency medical services legislation to improve the health care delivery system, and independent prescriptive authority for advanced practice nurses (APNs).

This bill-passing process is challenging but fun. Winning is everything, and when you win, it feels terrific. The pomp and ceremony surrounding the governor's bill signing underlines this achievement. A variety of skills are required: tenacity, negotiation, people pleasing, and balancing on political tightropes. We depend on the same skills as nurses, whether negotiating with doctors about discharge plans, motivating difficult patients regarding a major lifestyle change, or soothing a hassled nursing team to maintain quality of care with fewer staff.

PRESCRIPTIVE AUTHORITY BILL

Often I am asked to reflect on my legislative accomplishments. There are two pieces of legislation that were particularly difficult to pass, and of which I am most proud. One bill gave prescriptive authority to APNs. The other created a tobacco control board and dedicated a substantial portion of the state's tobacco settlement to antismoking programs.

Passage of an independent prescriptive authority bill for nurses was a textbook example of how a bill becomes a law. The legislative road to passage of bills is strewn with obstacles both formal and informal; this bill had a hefty share of both. Legislative rules may dictate the process, but politics can dictate success or failure because of detours or personal intrigue. For example, a committee chair may hold up a bill not on merit, but for leverage or revenge. Legislators, in turn, may vote for or against a bill because of a partisan label attached to the author. Striking a balance and keeping bills out of partisan potholes requires agility.

Forging alliances was the first skill I honed on the road to passage of prescriptive authority. Before introducing a bill, I built coalitions and developed consensus outside the legislature. I wanted to avoid a repeat of the divisive "Entry into Nursing Practice" bill. At that time, legislators heard nurses fight and criticize each other harshly during public hearings. Legislators hate being caught in the crossfire, especially with nurses. Nurses took a credibility hit by not having their act together and by attacking each other in public. Legislators accused nurses of "turf guarding" and "elitism." Nurses defeated themselves and defeated the bill, which died in committee.

This time would be different; nurses would be unified and focused. Before the introduction of the bill, I met with representatives from nursing organizations to flush out problems and reach consensus. Months dragged on as we perfected the draft. One of the major sticking points was certification and Master's degree educational requirements for an APN. We often discussed side issues: the changing role of nurses in primary care, definitions of scope of practice, and other legal issues. Although frustrated by the pace and tedium of this process, I remained committed to developing a consensus before I took the bill to the legislature.

In retrospect, this decision was wise. During the public hearings on the bill, nurses were focused and unified. We knew the process, stuck together, and supported each other. This unified front was essential to withstanding the criticism and strong lobbying that would surely come later from physicians and pharmacists.

The bill, now law in Wisconsin, certifies APNs (nurse practitioners and clinical nurse specialists) to prescribe medications according to their educational specialty, independent of physicians or protocols.

The introduction of prescriptive authority landed in the middle of the enthusiastic debate on health care reform initiated by President Clinton. Changing the health care system at the state level was at the top of the legislative agenda. The practical message that nurses improve access to primary care and provide cost-effective services was backed up with years of nursing research describing patient satisfaction, professional outcomes, and cost-effectiveness. Prescriptive authority was viewed as a necessary and noncontroversial component of health care reform by legislators. In addition, the bill landed on politically friendly territory: the speaker of the state assembly was a baccalaureate-prepared nurse. He liked the bill and referred the bill to a friendly committee, which I chaired.

A CALL FOR NURSING ACTION

The bill needed co-sponsors. The more legislators who sign up as co-sponsors, the stronger the bill becomes. Nurses rallied and contacted legislators to explain the need for the bill and to ask for their support. Legislators' responses were positive. Nurses, through their professional organizations or unions, had built an effective political network over many years. Nurses worked on campaigns, invited legislators to special events, and endorsed them in the latest election. The bill listed an impressive array of co-sponsors from both parties, including a senator whose husband was a doctor. The Wisconsin Nurses Association (WNA) had endorsed her in a tough reelection bid, and she remembered.

The next step was the public hearing. I was concerned about stiff opposition by the state medical society, a powerful legislative force. The medical society employs several lobbyists, and if an issue is a priority to them, additional contract lobbyists are hired. In contrast, the WNA had one part-time lobbyist.

We waited anxiously for testimony from physicians asserting that this step by advanced practice nurses would doom Western medicine, or that patients would be in harm's way if nurses were allowed to prescribe medications. Such testimony did not materialize. At the public hearing, the state medical society registered "neutral," neither for nor

Senator Judy Robson rallies for nurses on the steps of the Wisconsin legislature with Assemblyman DuWayne Johnsrud (in the background). They authorized a bill to prohibit mandatory overtime. The shoes symbolize the need for nurses in understaffed hospitals and other health care settings.

against the bill. We were surprised and pleased with this position and met with the physicians later to work out some of their objections raised during the public hearing. The physicians' main concern focused on the need for additional pharmacology credits and the jurisdiction and composition of the committee designated to write the administrative rules for implementing the new law.

The bill passed the Assembly unanimously and was promptly sent to the Senate for its own public hearings, debate, and vote. When the Assembly passed the bill unanimously, we expected smooth sailing in the Senate. It was not quite as smooth as we wanted; the hospital association lobbyist suddenly emerged with a "harmless" amendment that would make the hospitals "more comfortable." This

harmless amendment translated into institutional licensure, which would destroy the intent of the bill. Individual hospitals would have authority to certify nurses, rather than the Wisconsin Department of Regulation and Licensure and nursing organizations. We again rallied the nurses, via the Wisconsin Organization of Nurse Executives, the WNA, and our statewide newsletter, *Nursingmatters,* which is sent to all RNs in the state. Protests from nurses bombarded the Senate, and the "harmless" amendment was deep-sixed. The bill passed the Senate.

The last hurdle was the governor. How could we get him to sign this bill? The WNA executive director and I decided to invite the governor, who was up for reelection, to sign the bill at a WNA workshop day at the capitol. He agreed! Several weeks later, with 1000 enthusiastic nurses as background, the governor signed our bill into law.

NURSE AS LEGISLATOR

When giving speeches to nursing organizations, I am often asked, "Do you miss nursing?" At first I was startled by the question, but now I reply, "I *am* practicing nursing!" I'm at the policy table instead of the bedside. I write and rewrite laws affecting nursing. I find ways to improve access to health care for children and the uninsurable. I monitor policy that affects nurses, their patients, and public health. Nursing skills easily transfer to practice in the legislature. We are problem solvers. We have great people skills. We are team players. We are organized and have lots of stamina.

Of course, the capitol is not the hospital. Being a "political nurse" requires new skills and attitudes. You have to grow thick skin to withstand the rough-and-tumble of political life. Politics is a tough game for anyone to play, and it is a game where winning is everything. A winner is toasted; a loser is ignored.

Anyone moving into the public arena must be prepared to live in a fishbowl. Eyes will peer at you from all sides; your personal life will be scrutinized, and your public life will be criticized. The hometown newspaper will print nasty attacks in letters to the editor and snooty, condescending editorials. You cannot take the criticism personally. It is not about you, but about the issue. More often than not, it is a partisan potshot. People need to vent frustration, and elected officials are easy targets.

Nurses may be on call part of the time, but legislators are on call all the time. Whether you are rushing to the supermarket to buy groceries, going to church, or biking with your family, someone wants to give you their two cents' worth about this issue or that problem. There are no days off. Protecting personal time, ensuring family privacy, and coping with the lifestyle change require major adjustments.

An important aspect of the transition from nurse to legislator is the change in power you wield. All of a sudden, you can make things happen. You confront the rich and mingle with the famous. You talk to the governor and have calls returned personally by your congressmen. When the president of the United States comes to town, you are given VIP status: a seat behind him, a conversation, and a photo opportunity. You are called *representative* and your mail is addressed to *the honorable . . .*

Some people let the privilege of office go to their heads, but good legislators balance the advantage of privileges without abusing them. Part of the balance is to remember that it is the office to which the titles belong, not you. Committee chairmanships, prized seats on the legislative floor, office assignments, nice office furniture, and special parking stalls are marks of seniority. Seniority at its best reflects tenacity and stability, and at its worst simply longevity in office.

Among other things, tenacity means that you reflect an identifiable set of values that you represent to your electorate and to legislative colleagues. Any legislator who starts to feel like a big shot, giving orders instead of taking them, soon remembers the thousands of "bosses" out there who have the power to fire you every 2 years at the ballot box.

In striving to represent your electorate, you have to remember that you cannot please all the voters all the time. As a legislator, you have to make tough choices on polarizing issues, such as abortion and gun control. On hot-button issues, you are bound to disappoint many voters. This hot seat may be tough for women legislators, and for nurses, who are oriented to the business of people pleasing. We come to nursing because it is a helping profession. As an elected official, it can be painful to realize that some people have a mindset *not to like* you or your job performance purely because of party affiliation or a single vote.

NURSES USE THEIR POLITICAL CLOUT

I believe nursing has found its political groove. Nurse activists have matured into sophisticated political players. The long, lean years of grass roots lobbying and cultivating friends in legislatures have paid off.

In my early years as *the* nurse legislator, I enjoyed being the chief author of all nursing-related bills. In those days, I had to educate my colleagues to gain their support. Recently I noticed a change. Now my colleagues want to be chief author of the nursing bills. Other legislators are authoring bills to create whistleblower protection for health care workers, to help alleviate the nursing shortage, and to expand the scope of practice for nurse midwives.

At first, I must admit, I was somewhat miffed that my colleagues were treading on my turf. After all, I am *the* nurse legislator. Then it dawned on me: this is a good thing. They realize nurses have political clout. They realize people like and respect nurses. We have a lot of credibility in the eyes of the public. Advancing pro-nurse legislation is a win-win proposition for legislators and nurses.

Another reason for nurses' considerable political clout is that we are geographically apportioned for political power. Sizable numbers of nurses live in each and every Assembly and Senate district. In Wisconsin there are over 44,000 RNs. We vote. We have yards for yard signs. We make great campaign volunteers. Unions, trial lawyers, doctors, bankers, and realtors are significant players in legislative races because of the amount of money they contribute to campaigns. However, on election day they can only deliver votes in the legislative districts where they live. Aside from teachers, nurses are the only professional group who live in every candidate's district.

Nurses are exercising their political clout through candidate endorsements. In Wisconsin, the WNA mails every legislative candidate a questionnaire. WNA members in each candidate's district interview the candidates and make recommendations for WNA endorsement. The endorsements are printed in statewide newspapers prior to the election, and candidates quickly add the prestigious endorsement to their campaign literature. In addition, the Wisconsin Federation of Nurses, associated with the AFL-CIO, bring considerable union clout to the endorsement and election process. Envy the candidate who gets their endorsement and help.

When the questionnaires go out to candidates, my colleagues in the legislature ask me, "What do the nurses want?" I am happy to oblige in these teachable moments. I know the nurses' endorsement is important to legislators because I hear from my unhappy colleagues who do not receive the endorsement.

Nurses also show their political clout through their fund-raising prowess. It is impossible these days to get elected without raising a substantial amount of campaign cash. A candidate can go door to door until her shoes wear out, but she still needs to spend money on mass media to help get her message out. Even with the discounts given to candidates, media buys are expensive. That's why money is called the "mother's milk of politics." Even if we took out the influence of big-money special interests, candidates who are not wealthy enough to finance their campaigns would still have to do grass roots fundraising. Nurses have paychecks, and that helps them elect one of their own to political office.

In my first race for state Senate, nurses organized two fund raisers for me. These events not only raised money for my campaign, but raised the profile of organized nursing in the inner circle of polit-ical consultants and observers. The fund raisers were well attended and included such notables as the mayor of Milwaukee. If political clout is compared to baseball, the nurses hit a home run. The politically astute white-shoe brigade scored for their candidate.

CONCLUSION

Nurses have moved successfully into the sometimes harsh world of politics. We have won elections against the odds, shepherded bills through legislatures, and shaped policy at the local, state, and federal levels. However, our full impact has not been realized. Think what influence we could wield with a more united front. The sheer number of nurses working together makes a powerful advocacy group to lobby for prenatal care, child abuse prevention programs, and well-funded tobacco control programs.

At nearly 2.7 million, nurses are the largest group of health care providers in the nation. Imagine a million-nurse march up to the Washington Monument or 3000 nurses parading to their state capitol. The white-shoe brigade could be a tsunami wave. Nurses make a significant difference. We light candles instead of cursing the darkness. We create hope when others despair. I am grateful to be one of you.

Vignette   *Kaye Bender*

Influence of the Nursing Community on Mississippi's Tobacco Settlement Allocation

"The essential ingredient of politics is timing."
PIERRE ELLIOTT TRUDEAU

The story of the influence of the nursing community on Mississippi's tobacco settlement allocation actually began with a nursing project to reduce teenage pregnancy in 1983. Mississippi had one of the highest teen birth rates in the country. Pregnancy was one of the primary reasons that adolescents dropped out of school, and children born to these adolescents were continuing the cy-cle of poverty. An opportunity to pilot a school-based approach to teen pregnancy reduction developed, and a partnership between the state public health agency and a few local schools ensued. As the Director of Public Health Nursing at that time, I became involved in the development of a school nurse program whose goal was to reduce teen pregnancy. In a few short months, there were 42 new school nurses working in a dozen Mississippi middle schools. It was an exciting project, and those of us who were involved saw an opportunity to promote nursing in a role that was vitally needed.

The project funding lasted from 1984 to 1987. During that time, the statistics in the schools demonstrated exactly what we had hoped for. Teen pregnancy rates went down; sexually transmitted disease reports went down; daily attendance was up; and nurses were satisfactorily working in a high-profile, somewhat autonomous role. We were on our way toward the passage of legislation that would require school districts to add a school nurse to their staff. The progress was significant, but the story only begins here.

In the state public health agency's zeal to advocate for the role of the nurse, and in the school nurses' enthusiasm from their accomplishments, we went too far too fast for a conservative state on a socially controversial matter. The government's role in providing family planning services in a school setting without parental consent was more than some parents and advocacy groups could take. What started out as an exciting, productive project turned out to be the most controversial matter that the state legislature dealt with in 1987. I was not sure that school nursing would ever recover. We not only lost the program, but many of us felt that nursing had lost credibility in the public policy arena.

LESSONS LEARNED—FIRST TIME AROUND

We met to lick our wounds and to assess the damage. What had we done wrong? That reflection led us to the conceptual underpinnings of the current movement in our state to effect the allocation of the tobacco settlement dollars. These are the lessons we learned from what we did wrong:

1. The state public health agency (with nurses in the lead) attempted to secure legislation to authorize the school nurse program statewide. In advocating for statewide expansion for a program that had been accepted by only a few schools, we moved too fast. There was not enough grassroots involvement.
2. The school nurses were employees of the state public health agency, not of the local school district. Although this was comfortable to the schools involved in the pilot, it was scary for other schools that nurses who were not their

employees would be taking up precious space in their buildings. They also feared that their activities would take time from an already crowded curriculum.

3. The job descriptions of the school nurses were very standardized. We left no room for local flexibility and control, either at the school level or with the individual nurse.
4. We waited until the legislative session started to begin the discussions with the legislators about the benefits of the program. With their already crowded agenda, there was not enough one-on-one time to allow legislators to get to know the nurses and the details of the jobs they were doing with the school children.
5. The state public health agency attempted to advance legislation with minimal support requested from other organizations, including the Mississippi State Nurses Association. This left us advocating for a nursing program without support from major partners.

In our defeat, we failed to recognize that a small seed had been planted with key legislative leadership. That seed would be watered over time through a series of related activities. The state nurses association adopted school health nursing as a policy priority that permeated many related activities over the course of several years. Eventually, a statewide school health coalition was organized, developing a plan for the state that was ultimately endorsed by the state's boards of health and education. Through that effort, a unified approach to public policy development aimed at improving the health of our school children emerged. We garnered support from the same legislators who had supported the previous school health nurse effort.

RENEWED OPPORTUNITY

A window of opportunity opened. In 1996, Mississippi Attorney General Mike Moore negotiated a settlement with the tobacco industry for $62 million to prevent and reduce youth tobacco use over a 2-year period. Because Mississippi had been the first state to file a lawsuit to recover Medicaid costs related to tobacco use, our state was able to negotiate this settlement based on a "most favored nation" clause in a similar Florida settlement.

In October 1997, the court approved the amount to be placed in escrow for the state to develop a pilot program unique to Mississippi to reduce tobacco use. This was the beginning of discussions about improving the health of youth in our state. The state established a nonprofit organization called the Partnership for a Healthy Mississippi, which brought together many local and statewide organizations to administer the tobacco funds. The project covered several targeted areas: law enforcement, community (e.g., coalitions, ordinances), advertising and media, medical and research (including smoking cessation), and school health.

REEMERGENCE OF SCHOOL HEALTH NURSING

During the 1998 Mississippi legislative session, public health leadership in the legislature, working with the Mississippi Nurses Association, requested that the state public health agency oversee the implementation of a pilot project, which would utilize school health nurses to reduce or prevent youth tobacco use. Approximately $2.5 million of the youth tobacco settlement was allocated to the agency for the purposes of setting up these projects. A request for proposals was developed, and 50 grants were awarded to the schools with the most successful grant applications. At my invitation, several nurses served on the review panel. The state department of health provided the training, the protocols, and the general oversight for the project. The schools employed the nurses and supervised them. As long as the requirements of the grant were met, the school and the nurse could negotiate added job responsibilities. The lessons we learned from the 1980s school health programs were critical to our effectiveness with the tobacco nurse projects.

An Independent Evaluation

The school health nurse tobacco prevention program was designed to be a 2-year pilot. An evaluation of its impact was completed in 2000 and indicated that, although specific reductions in teen tobacco use could not be measured in such a short period of time, the activities conducted by the school health nurses were appropriate. If those research-based activities continue over time, the evaluation stated, the ultimate goal of reducing teen tobacco use should be realized. We also learned that all of the tobacco prevention program components working together had changed the social environment in which teens function.

MISSISSIPPI'S LARGER TOBACCO SETTLEMENT

On July 2, 1997, Mississippi settled its larger tobacco lawsuit so that it would receive a lump-sum initial payment of $170 million from the tobacco industry This would be followed by annual payments beginning at $68 million in state fiscal year (FY) 1999 and increasing annually over 5 years before "leveling off" with annual payments of $135 million continuing in perpetuity. These annual payments are subject to two adjustments: an annual increase of 3% or the Consumer Price Index, whichever is greater, and an annual increase or decrease based on the volume of domestic tobacco sales. Subsequently, an additional $500 million, payable during the first 5 years, has been added to the total. The state now had a financial opportunity to address some of its health status problems. Though some elected officials had doubts about the strategy of suing the tobacco industry, we experienced an unprecedented bipartisan effort in planning for the most effective use of the state's tobacco settlement dollars. In a small state where the health needs are great and, historically, the state dollars have been few, effective policymakers not only considered an accountable means by which to allocate the resources, but also availability for future generations.

Health Care Trust Fund

On March 25, 1999, the Mississippi legislature took the lead in establishing the Health Care Trust Fund. The bill protects the principal of the tobacco settlement funds and allows investments similar to those already in place in the state's retirement system. The anticipated annual payments from the combination of revenue and interest provides $50 million in the year 2000, with payment increasing by approximately 10% annually until 2004. At that point, and in subsequent years, health care will receive payments totaling the average earnings of the lifetime of the trust fund. Mississippi State Treasurer

Marshall Bennett stated in a press release on the day the legislation was passed, "This is a phenomenal accomplishment for the state. By 2007 annual payments will exceed $100 million for health care to benefit generations to come." As Deputy State Health Officer, I was called by then Lieutenant Governor Musgrove (now Governor) to be part of the press conference and the celebration of the signing of the bill. It was an accomplishment of which we could all be proud. However, the work had really just begun.

Policy Development Using Tobacco Settlement Dollars

The annual allocation of the funds would be the next major policy matter. I worked with the Mississippi Board of Health to develop a concept paper on the importance of using the money for preventive services. I knew this would be a hard lesson to sell, given the major health care problems in our state. The benefits of prevention take a long time to measure, whereas the immediate effects of purchasing "illness-related" services are evident. We soon learned that a combination of the two approaches would be necessary to achieve consensus on the funds allocation.

The following reflects a list of how the tobacco settlement funds were used and how nurses were involved:

- *State Children's Health Insurance Program (S-CHIP) match.* A nurse practitioner serves on the S-CHIP medical advisory committee, a former pediatric public health nurse serves as the policy coordinator for the S-CHIP commercial insurance program, and a nurse serves as the policy coordinator for the Medicaid component. I continue to serve as a policy advisor to the statewide board of health on these matters. All of these nurses keep in close contact to ensure continuity in policy decisions and legislative proposals.
- *Expansion of services under Medicaid.* Mississippi's match rate for drawing down potential federal Medicaid dollars is one of the best in the country. Utilization of some of the tobacco settlement funds to enhance coverage for services such as eyeglasses, dental care,

home- and community-based nursing services, and other, similar programs has been a priority for all of the nurses who work with these patients and their families. The tobacco settlement has been the primary source of matching funds for these enhanced services.

- *Creation of a statewide trauma network.* Because Mississippi is a rural state, trauma services have been fragmented. The tobacco settlement funds have allowed a statewide network to be created and sustained, with reimbursement allocated for indigent trauma care. Nurses are involved in the Trauma Care Task Force and in the ongoing management of the network, as well as serving as care providers to this population.
- *Enhanced rehabilitation services.* A little over $2 million was all that was needed to enhance rehabilitation programs for the deaf and hard of hearing, for vocational rehabilitation, and for independent living programs. Nurses provided testimony about the effectiveness of these programs following inpatient rehabilitation services.
- *Expanded mental health services.* Approximately $7.5 million has been allocated for the enhancement of mental health services for Alzheimer's patients, for crisis centers, for substance abuse programs, and for community-based mental health services. Nurses have provided much of the testimony for these enhanced services as well.
- *Increased nursing scholarships.* Through the Mississippi Institutions of Higher Learning, student financial aid for nursing scholarships now total $500,000. This is an increase over previous years. After July 1, 2001, funds became available for medical loan repayment for primary care physicians who agree to serve in rural areas of the state.

RECENT DEVELOPMENTS IN SCHOOL HEALTH NURSING IN MISSISSIPPI

Progress continues to be made to prevent and reduce youth tobacco use. In 2000, the Mississippi Board of Health sponsored a blue ribbon panel to develop a statewide tobacco prevention and cessation plan. The plan was endorsed by all of the partner organizations and contains the components of such a program as recommended by the Centers for Disease Control and Prevention (CDC). In April 2001, the plan became a separate chapter in the Mississippi State Health Plan. Nurses were involved in the development of the plan and in its ultimate adoption as official state public policy. A nurse member of the state's board of health chaired the blue ribbon panel.

Another step was made when Mississippi Attorney General Mike Moore negotiated with the courts for $20 million of the larger tobacco settlement funds to be earmarked for statewide tobacco prevention and cessation efforts. The money was allocated directly to the Partnership for a Healthy Mississippi. The CDC recommends a range of $8 million to $40 million for a state the size of Mississippi to spend to conduct effective tobacco prevention and control programs. No state has yet reached the recommended spending level, but Mississippi has one of the highest allocations for tobacco prevention in the country.

The 2001 Mississippi legislature approved the continuation of the school nurse program using funds from the larger tobacco settlement. There is a waiting list of schools applying for these grants. The biggest advocates for the program have come from outside the nursing community this time: from school principals, from the state's attorney general, from the governor, and from those legislators who remained supportive of school health nursing in previous years. Nurses were recognized as leaders in implementing policy to improve the public's health.

CONCLUSION

The Mississippi experience with nurses influencing the allocation of the tobacco settlement funds has taught me a lot about advocacy. I offer the following guidelines for nurses who want to be involved in advocating public policy change:

- Talk with your peers often. A history of communication and working relationships among nursing leaders, and between nursing leaders and other health-related policymakers can be the most helpful ingredient in changing public policy.
- Support your elected officials. As they become allies for nursing's role in improving health, they will create a platform for discussions with nurses that influence policy outcomes.
- Find the leaders and get them on your side. The most difficult moments occurred when leaders struggled to keep their eyes on the agreed-upon outcome, often at the risk of losing one of their individual issues.
- Learn how to compromise. Active participation in an emerging, somewhat controversial policy issue will require compromise.
- Just get in there and do it! You may have to figure out some of the strategy as you go.

ROLE OF STATE BOARDS OF NURSING IN POLICY

Carolyn Hutcherson

"The price of freedom is eternal vigilance."

THOMAS JEFFERSON

HISTORICAL FOUNDATIONS

The purpose of any governmental regulation of professional practice, including nursing, is the protection of the public health, safety, and welfare. The regulatory mandate for this protection is consistent with the nursing imperative of providing safe and effective nursing care. Criteria for regulation should reflect minimum requirements for safe and competent practice and should be the least burdensome criteria consistent with public protection.

Based on the Tenth Amendment to the U.S. Constitution, each state is empowered to establish laws to protect its citizens. A component of this "public protection" mandate is the responsibility for establishing standards for health care professionals who provide services for citizens of that state. In the late 1800s, individual states began to license physicians who met established criteria. Nursing followed suit in the early twentieth century, with North Carolina being the first state to adopt a nursing "registration" law in 1904. By 1910, 20 states had established registration laws, and by 1930, all 48 states had laws regulating nursing.

The early laws authorized an examination for training school graduates and protected the title "registered nurse," but did not provide a legal definition of nursing or limit practice to those who were qualified. In 1938, New York was the first state to establish a scope of nursing practice and make licensure compulsory. However, it was not until the mid-1960s that all states incorporated legal definitions of nursing and established mandatory licensure laws.

WHY NURSING IS REGULATED

The decision to license a profession results from a combination of social, political, and professional policy considerations. In the United States, the government has adopted a substantial role in requiring that health care providers meet specified standards. Considerations about whether a profession or occupation should be regulated include the potential risk of harm to the consumer, whether or not specialized education is required, the complexity of skills and abilities required for professional practice, and the level of autonomy required of the provider. The paramount consideration is establishment of a regulatory process that ensures public safety through safe and effective practice of the profession. Licensure is the necessary regulatory approach when professional activities are complex, specialized knowledge and skill are required, and independent decision making is essential. Additionally, licensure laws stipulate that a specific scope of practice may be performed only by legally licensed individuals, with those individuals being subject to disciplinary authority for violation of the laws.

HOW NURSING IS REGULATED

Each state legislature authorizes creation of an entity with the express purpose of regulating nursing. In most states, this entity is the board of nursing. The governor typically appoints members to the board of nursing, although some states have other mechanisms for selection. The number of board members ranges from 7 to 25, with each state law determining the composition of the board of nursing. Typically the board comprises of a mix of registered nurses, licensed practical or vocational nurses, advanced practice registered nurses, and consumers; some have physicians. All 50 states, the District of Columbia, and the five U.S. territories (Guam, Virgin Islands, Puerto Rico, American Samoa, and the Northern Mariana Islands) have boards of nursing. California, Georgia, Louisiana, Texas, and West Virginia have two boards of nursing—one for registered nurses and one for licensed practical or vocational nurses.

Professional organizations establish a variety of standards for clinical practice, standards for specialty certification, or other forms of voluntary recognition. However, only boards of nursing are empowered to issue nursing credentials that grant legal authority to practice nursing within a specified scope of practice. Licensure is the essential foundation for nursing practice. Certification for expertise or specialty practice granted by professional organizations is voluntary and is never an alternative to licensure.

ELEMENTS OF REGULATION

In this first century of nursing regulation, the roles and responsibilities of boards of nursing have evolved to include the specification of safe and effective nursing practice in the respective states. Each state authorizes the powers and duties of the board of nursing. The powers and duties include, but are not limited to, the following:

- Overall enforcement of the provisions of the nurse practice act
- Establishment of administrative rules to implement the act
- Development and enforcement of qualifications for licensure
- Development and enforcement of standards for nursing practice and nursing education
- Licensure of qualified applicants by examination or endorsement, and renewal and reinstatement of the license
- Development of standards for maintaining the competence of licensees continuing in or returning to practice
- Discipline of licensees as needed

Recent scrutiny about the efficacy of the current regulatory scheme has prompted boards of nursing to engage in a process of analysis about whether these elements of regulation indeed yield public protection. Early response indicates that the public has come to see as important the regulatory role that boards of nursing play in monitoring and enforcing standards for nursing practice.

NATIONAL COUNCIL OF STATE BOARDS OF NURSING

The National Council of State Boards of Nursing (NCSBN) is a not-for-profit organization whose membership is composed of all the boards of nursing in the states and territories. The mission of the NCSBN is to lead in nursing regulation by assisting member boards, collectively and individually, to promote safe and effective nursing practice in the interest of protecting public health and welfare.

The purpose of the NCSBN is to provide an organization through which boards of nursing act and counsel together on matters of common interest and concern affecting public health, safety, and welfare, including the development of licensing examinations in nursing. The major functions of the NCSBN include developing the NCLEX-RN and the NCLEX-PN examinations, performing policy analysis, promoting uniformity in relation to the regulation of nursing practice, disseminating data related to the licensure of nurses, and conducting research pertinent to the NCSBN's purpose. It is important to note that the NCSBN has no direct authority over boards of nursing but affords a mechanism for the boards to counsel together about issues of common interest.

CRITICAL ISSUES IN NURSING REGULATION
Licensure Examinations

To ensure public protection, each jurisdiction requires a candidate for licensure to pass an examination that measures the competencies needed to perform safely and effectively as a newly licensed, entry-level registered nurse. The NCSBN develops a licensure examination, the NCLEX, which is used by state and territorial boards of nursing to assist in making licensure decisions. The test plan reflects entry-level practice based on a job analysis of newly licensed registered nurses. The content and scope of the licensing examination incorporates specific needs, concepts, and processes fundamental to the practice of nursing. The examination content falls into four categories:

- Safe, effective care environment
- Health promotion and maintenance
- Psychosocial integrity
- Physiologic integrity

Computerized adaptive testing (CAT) is a method of administering tests that uses computer technology and measurement theory. The NCLEX examination administered via CAT uses standard NCLEX examination multiple-choice questions. With CAT, each candidate's test is unique. It is assembled interactively as the individual is tested. Boards of nursing face ongoing pressure to ensure that licensing examinations effectively provide the critical determinant ensuring that a candidate is capable of safe and effective nursing practice.

With intense focus on safety and quality in health care, the licensing process affords a vital baseline to ensure that nurses meet defined criteria to practice nursing. Clinical practice is being made more complex by the torrent of new scientific information. This poses a great challenge to create a psychometrically sound and legally defensible examination capable of determining each potential nurse's ability to practice. Concerns have been voiced that new graduates are not being prepared or qualified to practice in today's clinical environment. Boards must ensure that each candidate for licensure meets established standards and demonstrates mastery of the knowledge, skills, and abilities necessary to engage in safe nursing practice.

Nursing Shortage

Boards of nursing have no direct role in recruiting nurses into the profession or ensuring an adequate supply of qualified nurses. They are, however, expected to establish standards that are safe—not so high as to limit entry into the profession or so low as to allow unqualified persons to enter nursing practice. During times of a critical shortage of nurses, some states have been pressured to establish lower standards in order to facilitate entry of greater numbers of providers into the workforce. The January 2001 NCSBN Response to the Nursing Shortage states that, "The need for public protection through regulation has never been greater, due in large part to the nursing shortage. Failure to maintain standards of practice could lead to an increase in errors, increased risk for patient harm, and a lack of public confidence. During shortages of health care professionals, one potential and predictable policy direction is to deregulate thereby reducing practice standards . . . [However], any trend of deregulation is assumed to increase the risk of harms to patients."

Advanced Practice Nursing

Nurses in advanced practice roles must have clear authority for their practice. Without this clear authority for the advanced level at which they func-

tion, nurses in advanced roles may be practicing beyond the jurisdictional scope of nursing practice, or could be held accountable for practicing medicine without a license. Federal regulations defer to state authority regarding credentialing for advanced practice nurses. However, the wide disparity of credentialing mechanisms has proven to be a substantial impediment to the mobility of advanced practice nurses. The absence of a uniform national standard for advanced practice nurses has resulted in confusion for the public, legislators, nurses, and other health care providers about the role and authority of advanced practice nurses. During the 2001 National Council Delegate Assembly, Uniform APRN Licensure/Authority to Practice Requirements were adopted as guidelines for boards of nursing. Each state must evaluate its own political environment and determine the appropriate timing and climate for adoption of these standards.

Disciplinary Oversight

Since the inception of boards of nursing, the integral role has been enforcing the laws governing nursing. One aspect of this enforcement is ensuring that nurses who violate the law or fail to meet the legal standards of practice are subject to appropriate disciplinary action. Each state law ensures that full due process is afforded any nurse charged with violating the nurse practice act. Potential actions for violation of the nurse practice act range from a reprimand to limitations imposed on the license or actual loss of the license. Most states publish a listing of disciplinary actions with the basis on which the action was taken.

At the direction of Congress, two federal data banks have been created to serve as repositories of information about health care providers in the United States. The National Practitioner Data Bank (NPDB) was created for tracking information primarily about physicians and dentists. In 1987, legislation expanded the NPDB to include nurses, but the legislation has not yet been implemented. Another databank was created through the 1996 Health Insurance Portability and Accountability Act (HIPAA). The purpose of the Health Information Portability Data Base (HIPD) is to combat fraud and abuse in health care insurance and health delivery. Boards of nursing were required to submit reports of disciplinary action from August 21, 1996, as well as any new actions taken from November 22, 2000, forward.

Multistate Practice and Licensure

As the health care delivery system undergoes rapid transformation, advances in use of technology have been made to provide care through telehealth services. In recognition of the dilemmas inherent in the established state-based licensure system and the challenges of ensuring authority for nursing practice, the NCSBN has proposed a new model for nursing regulation called *mutual recognition.* This system, in which nursing boards adopt an interstate compact, allows the boards to legally accept the licensure of a nurse licensed in another "compact" state. The nurse obtains a license in the home state (state of residence), and that license is recognized in other compact states without the requirement for duplicate licensure. This mutual recognition does not apply to nurses practicing in states that have not adopted the interstate compact (available online at www.ncsbn.org).

Patient Safety and Medication Errors

Because nursing regulation is designed with the express purpose of protecting the public health, safety, and welfare, any compromise in patient safety is cause for serious concern. Boards of nursing regularly investigate reported failure to provide safe care, including reported medication errors. Collectively, many boards of nursing maintain data about medication errors and are attuned to factors that contribute to errors. Boards have a range of options for responding to reports of errors as well as promoting efforts to reduce the likelihood of future errors. Although boards of nursing recognize the impact of the practice environment (system) on the ability of a nurse to practice safely and effectively, state nurse practice acts empower the boards to grant licenses to individual nurses who meet established criteria. The law establishes individual accountability for practice. Thus, although boards readily acknowledge that system weaknesses impact nursing practice, individual nurses are licensed and must practice in accordance with legal standards of practice. In evaluating complaints brought before the board, consideration is given to all circumstances, including problems in the "system" that fulfill their mandate of regulating individual nursing practice. Other organizations are charged with holding other components of the system accountable for practice.

CONCLUSION

State laws charge boards of nursing with ultimate accountability for protecting the health, safety, and welfare of state citizens related to nursing practice. Licensure standards must ensure that only qualified nurses are awarded a license and that unsafe practitioners are prohibited from practicing. Consumers must have confidence in the legally established mechanism that exists to address their concerns and issues about nursing practice. The ultimate policy role of boards of nursing is to ensure that legally defined safe nursing practice is a reality.

26 The Federal Government

KATHLEEN M. WHITE

"All politics is local."

THOMAS P. "TIP" O'NEILL, FORMER SPEAKER
OF THE U.S. HOUSE OF REPRESENTATIVES

The United States Constitution gives the federal branch of the government broad responsibility for the health care of the nation with the phrase "promote the general welfare." The federal government is therefore involved in many decisions and actions that affect nursing and health care in this country, specifically the organization, financing, and delivery of health care services. It is involved in the allocation of funds for nursing education and nursing research, the delineation of practice rules and reimbursement for services provided by advanced-practice nurses, the passage and interpretation of labor laws, and many judicial decisions affecting health care and the quality and safety of the workplace.

Federal policy decisions are influenced by legislative and regulatory processes, elected and appointed officials, the political and economic climate, individuals, and special-interest groups. Nurses, as the largest group of health care providers, must have an active voice in nursing and health care legislation and policies. To do so, however, they must first understand the workings of the federal government. Knowledge is power; nurses can play a key role in the federal legislative and regulatory arenas *if* they are informed and visible.

This chapter will focus on how each of the three branches of the U.S. federal government is involved in the government of this country, the processes that each branch follows, and the issues it face. The three branches of the U.S. government are the executive, legislative, and judicial branches.

EXECUTIVE BRANCH

The executive branch of the federal government is made up of the Executive Office of the President; the Executive Agencies or Cabinet Departments; and many independent agencies, boards, commissions, and committees, such as the Central Intelligence Agency, the Federal Communications Commission, the Federal Trade Commission, the Environmental Protection Agency (EPA), and the Nuclear Regulatory Commission, to name a few. Boards, commissions, and committees are created to advise the President and Congress on specific topics (Box 26-1). For example, the EPA, established in 1970 as an agency of the executive branch, provides leadership in environmental science, research, and education. The EPA's mission is to protect human health and safeguard the natural environment. It works closely with local, state, and other federal agencies to develop and enforce regulations, set national standards, and issue sanctions when necessary.

The Federal Emergency Management Agency (FEMA), founded in 1979, is an independent agency of the federal government reporting directly to the President. Its mission is to protect life, property, and our nation's critical infrastructure from disasters through a comprehensive, risk-based, emergency management program of preparedness, mitigation, response, and recovery. The FEMA is a 2,500-person agency with over 5,000 standby disaster reservists. Through its Project Impact, the

BOX **26-1**   Organization of the Executive Branch

1. EXECUTIVE OFFICE OF THE PRESIDENT

White House
Cabinet
Council of Economic Advisers
Council on Environmental Quality
Domestic Policy Council
National Economic Council
National Security Council
Office of Administration
Office of Faith-Based and Community Initiatives
Office of Homeland Security
Office of Management and Budget
Office of National AIDS Policy
Office of National Drug Control Policy
Office of Science and Technology Policy
President's Foreign Intelligence Advisory Board
Office of the United States Trade Representative

2. EXECUTIVE AGENCIES (CABINET AGENCIES)

Department of Agriculture
Department of Commerce
Department of Defense
Department of Education
Department of Energy
Department of Health and Human Services
Department of Housing and Urban Development
Department of the Interior
Department of Justice
Department of Labor
Department of State
Department of Transportation
Department of the Treasury
Department of Veterans Affairs

3. INDEPENDENT ESTABLISHMENTS AND GOVERNMENT CORPORATIONS

Broadcasting Board of Governors
Central Intelligence Agency
Commission on Civil Rights
Commodity Futures Trading Commission
Consumer Product Safety Commission
Corporation for National and Community Service
Defense Nuclear Facilities Safety Board
Environmental Protection Agency
Equal Employment Opportunity Commission
Export-Import Bank of the United States
Farm Credit Administration
Federal Communications Commission
Federal Deposit Insurance Corporation
Federal Election Commission
Federal Emergency Management Agency
Federal Housing Finance Board
Federal Labor Relations Authority

Federal Maritime Commission
Federal Mediation and Conciliation Service
Federal Mine Safety and Health Review Commission
Federal Reserve System
Federal Retirement Thrift Investment Board
Federal Trade Commission
General Services Administration
Institute of Museum and Library Services
Inter-American Foundation
International Broadcasting Bureau
Merit Systems Protection Board
National Aeronautics and Space Administration
National Archives and Records Administration
National Capital Planning Commission
National Credit Union Administration
National Education Goals Panel
National Endowment for the Arts
National Endowment for the Humanities
National Labor Relations Board
National Mediation Board
National Railroad Passenger Corporation
National Science Foundation
National Transportation Safety Board
Nuclear Regulatory Commission
Occupational Safety and Health Review Commission
Office of Compliance
Office of Government Ethics
Office of Personnel Management
Office of Special Counsel
Overseas Private Investment Corporation
Panama Canal Commission
Peace Corps
Pension Benefit Guaranty Corporation
Postal Rate Commission
Railroad Retirement Board
Securities and Exchange Commission
Selective Service System
Small Business Administration
Social Security Administration
Tennessee Valley Authority
Trade and Development Agency
United States Commission on Civil Rights
United States Agency for International Development
United States International Information Program
United States International Trade Commission
United States Postal Service

4. BOARDS, COMMISSIONS, AND COMMITTEES

Dozens of boards, commissions, and committees, including many with implications for health care

5. QUASI-OFFICIAL AGENCIES

Dozens of agencies

From www.firstgov.gov/us_gov/executive_branch.html.

FEMA works with states, local communities, and organizations that are part of the nation's emergency management system (e.g., the American Red Cross) to reduce risk *before* disaster strikes (www.fema.gov).

EXECUTIVE OFFICE OF THE PRESIDENT

The Executive Office of the President consists of the President and Vice President, the Office of Management and Budget (OMB), the National Security Council, the United States Trade Representative, the Office of National Drug Control Policy, and the newly created Office of Homeland Security.

The President is the highest-ranking elected federal official and the head of the executive branch. The power of the executive branch is limited; the powers granted to the President in the Constitution are actually few. The Constitution says that the President is the Commander in Chief of the armed forces and has the power to grant pardons and to make treaties with the consent of the Senate. The President also has the power to appoint, with the advice and consent of the Senate, cabinet secretaries, U.S. attorneys and marshals, ambassadors, justices of the Supreme Court, federal judges, and federal officers of the military, the Foreign Service, and other independent agencies. Approximately 4000 civilian and 65,000 military nominations are submitted by the President to the Senate during each congressional cycle (www.senate.gov/learning/brief_3.html). The President also has the power to recommend to Congress for its consideration any measures that he shall judge necessary. The President must report regularly on the "state of the union" and can convene either or both houses of Congress in extraordinary circumstances. Finally, the President has the power to veto acts of Congress. The veto is an effective means of preventing passage of legislation not supported by the President, and the constant threat of its exercise brings about many changes and compromises in legislation before passage. There are two types of veto available to the President. The first is the direct veto of a piece of legislation that the President does not support. A two-thirds majority in both the House and the Senate is necessary to override a direct veto. The other type is called the "pocket" veto. Once

Congress has passed a bill the President has 10 days (not counting Sundays) to sign or veto the bill. If Congress adjourns during this ten-day period and the President has not yet acted, the bill automatically dies (www.firstgov.gov/us_gov/executive_branch.html).

Office of Management and Budget. The mission of the OMB is to assist the President in overseeing the preparation of the federal budget and to supervise the administration of the agencies of the executive branch. The OMB assists the President in the development and execution of presidential policies and programs, and has four divisions organized by program area: the Resource Management Office, the Budget Review Office, the Legislative Program Office, and the Statutory Office. The Resource Management Office develops and supports the President's management and budget agenda; the Budget Review Office analyzes trends and consequences of budget policy; the Legislative Program Office coordinates the review of legislative proposals and statement on bills going through the Congress, often requiring resolution of competing views or priorities; and the Statutory Office develops policies and procedures for management of federal resources (www.whitehouse.gov/omb).

EXECUTIVE AGENCIES AND CABINET DEPARTMENTS

There are 14 executive agencies and cabinet departments that are charged with the enforcement and administration of federal laws:
- Department of Agriculture
- Department of Commerce
- Department of Defense
- Department of Education
- Department of Energy
- Department of Health and Human Services
- Department of Housing and Urban Development
- Department of the Interior
- Department of Justice
- Department of Labor
- Department of State
- Department of Transportation

- Department of the Treasury
- Department of Veterans Affairs

Five of these are of special interest to nurses because of their mission, activities, and policymaking role: the Department of Health and Human Services (DHHS), Department of Defense (DoD), Department of Education (DoE), Department of Veterans Affairs (DVA), and Department of Labor (DoL).

Department of Health and Human Services.

The DHHS is the U.S. government's principal agency for protecting the health of all Americans and providing essential human services, especially for those who are least able to help themselves. Through over 300 programs, the DHHS seeks to promote medical and social-science research, prevent outbreaks of infectious disease, assure food and drug safety, provide financial assistance for low-income families, offer substance abuse prevention and treatment, provide health care services for Native Americans, and improve maternal and infant care. Medicaid, Medicare, and Head Start are among its programs. The DHHS is the largest grant-making agency in the federal government, giving 60,000 grants per year, and its budget is second only to that of the DoD. Its programs are administered by the 11 "operating divisions" of the DHHS itself, eight agencies of the U.S. Public Health Service, and three Human Service Agencies (Figure 26-1).

In a press conference held on September 28, 2001, DHHS Secretary Tommy Thompson announced a series of grants and contracts to increase both the number of qualified nurses and the quality of nursing services across the U.S. The available monies, totaling more than $27.4 million, include grants for basic and advanced nursing education programs, practice grants, workforce diversity grants, and public health leadership grants (www.hhs.gov/news/press/2001pres/20010928c.html).

DHHS Human Services Operating Divisions. The Centers for Medicare and Medicaid Services (CMS, formerly the Health Care Financing Administration [HCFA]), was created on July 1, 2001. Its new name reflects its increased emphasis on improving quality and on responsiveness to beneficiaries and providers. The CMS provides health insurance to 75 million Americans through Medicare, Medicaid, and the State Children's Health Insurance Program (SCHIP). Additionally, CMS performs several quality-focused activities, including regulation of laboratory testing, development of coverage policies, surveying and certification of nursing homes and continuing care providers, and quality-of-care improvement. CMS provides health care to about one in every four Americans, including 38 million elderly and disabled individuals, 34 million low-income persons, and 2.2 million children. The newly reorganized CMS has three centers to support its functions. First, the Center for Medicare Management manages the traditional fee-for-service Medicare program, including development of payment policies and management of the Medicare fee-for-service contractors. Second, the Center for Beneficiary Choices provides beneficiaries with information on Medicare, Medicare+Choice, and Medigap options. It also manages the Medicare+Choice plans and grievance and appeals functions. Third, the Center for Medicaid and State Operations focuses on the programs administered by the states, including Medicaid, SCHIP, insurance regulation, and the Clinical Laboratory Improvements Act (CLIA) (www.cms.gov).

The Administration for Children and Families (ACF) is responsible for promoting the economic and social well-being of families, children, and communities through programs aimed at welfare recipients, children and youth, and communities. The ACF administers the new state-federal welfare program (the Welfare to Work Challenge) and the Temporary Assistance for Needy Families (TANF) program. The ACF also administers the national child-support enforcement system, foster care and adoption assistance, child abuse and neglect programs, family preservation and family support services, child welfare services, Head Start, community support services, social-service block grants, low-income home energy assistance, and the Administration for Native Americans (www.acf.dhhs.gov).

The Administration on Aging (AoA) is the federal advocacy agency administering programs mandated by the Older Americans Act. Some AoA programs help older Americans to keep living in their own homes by providing supportive services, including

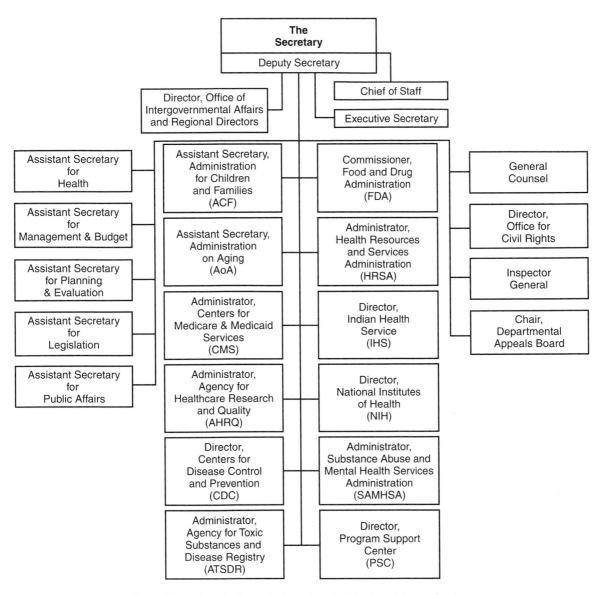

Figure 26-1 Organization of the Department of Health and Human Services.

Meals on Wheels; others allow older Americans to enhance their health and contribute actively to their families and communities (www.aoa.dhhs.gov).

DHHS Public Health Service Operating Divisions. The U.S. Public Health Service includes agencies that are charged with protecting and improving the nation's health, supporting and conducting research, preventing and controlling dis-

ease, and enforcing the laws in these areas. The Office of the Surgeon General oversees the 6000-member Commissioned Corps of the U.S. Public Health Service and is part of the Office of Public Health and Science and the larger DHHS (www.os.dhhs.gov/phs).

The Agency for Health Care Research and Quality (AHRQ) is charged with conducting research to help improve the quality and outcomes of health care, reduce the costs of health care, address patient safety issues and health care errors, and broaden access to effective medical services. The AHRQ was first created in 1989 as the Agency for Health Care Policy and Research and reauthorized as the AHRQ in 1999. AHRQ coordinates several major ongoing quality-improvement projects. Under its medical effectiveness research effort (1992-1996), it produced clinical practice guidelines for 19 diseases or medical conditions. These guidelines describe consumer, payer, and provider practices that are associated with better health outcomes. The Healthcare Cost and Utilization Project, sponsored by the AHRQ, is a federal/state/industrial partnership designed to develop a multi-state health care data base for research, policy analysis, and quality improvement. The National Guideline Clearinghouse, developed in partnership by the AHRQ, the American Medical Association, and the American Association of Health Plans, provides online access to evidence-based clinical practice guidelines. The U.S. Preventive Services Task Force, sponsored by the AHRQ, is a panel of preventive-health experts charged with evaluating scientific evidence for the effectiveness of clinical preventive services and with producing age-specific and risk-specific recommendations for preventive services (www.ahrq.gov).

The Agency for Toxic Substances and Disease Registry (ATSDR) is the principal federal public health agency charged with evaluating human health effects of exposure to hazardous substances from waste sites, unplanned releases, and other sources of environmental pollution. The ATSDR works with the states and with other federal agencies, especially the Centers for Disease Control and Prevention, to prevent exposure to hazardous substances from waste sites. These collaborating groups conduct public health assessments and health studies and do surveillance activities for the EPA's national priority list. The Administrator of the ATSDR also serves as Director of the Centers for Disease Control and Prevention (www.atsdr.cdc.gov).

The Centers for Disease Control and Prevention (CDC), with a $4.2 billion annual budget, is the leading federal agency for protecting the health and safety of the people. The CDC's mission is to promote health and quality of life by preventing and controlling disease, injury, and disability. It serves as the national focus for disease prevention and control, environmental health, and health promotion and education activities to improve the health of the people of the United States. The CDC monitors and seeks to prevent health and injury risks and outbreaks of disease. Its mission includes fighting infectious diseases, with particular emphasis on emerging and antimicrobial-resistant infectious diseases and reemergent infectious diseases. The CDC also plays a significant role in strengthening the local, state, and national capacity to respond to growing threats from biological and chemical terrorism (www.cdc.gov).

The Food and Drug Administration (FDA) is a science-based enforcement agency mandated by law to ensure the safety and effectiveness of products under its jurisdiction. The FDA, with a $1.3 billion annual budget (fiscal year [FY] 2002), seeks to ensure that foods are safe, sanitary, and properly labeled; that human and veterinary drugs are safe and effective; that medical devices are safe and effective for their intended use; and that cosmetics are safe and properly labeled. The FDA's Center for Drug Evaluation and Research oversees the research, development, manufacture, and marketing of prescription, nonprescription, and generic drugs and reviews clinical-trial evidence of their safety and effectiveness before approving them for use by the general public (www.fda.gov).

The Health Resources and Services Administration (HRSA) directs programs that improve the national health by assuring quality health care for underserved, vulnerable, and special-need populations and by promoting appropriate workforce capacity and practice in the health care professions, particularly in the primary care and public health arenas. Its goals are to eliminate barriers to care and to eliminate health disparities. The HRSA has four bureaus to accomplish its mission: the Bureau of Primary Health Care, the Bureau of Health Professions, the Maternal and Child Health Bureau, and the HIV/AIDS Bureau (Figure 26-2). Health centers funded by the HRSA provide comprehensive primary and preventive health care to over 9 million persons at over 3,000 sites. In FY 2002, the HRSA's budget was $6.2 billion, including $1.4 billion to

DEPARTMENT OF HEALTH & HUMAN SERVICES
Health Resources and Services Administration

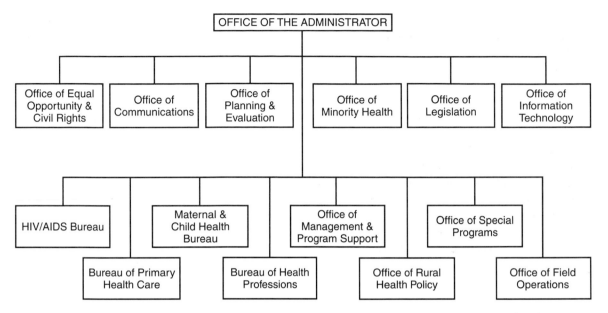

Figure 26-2 Organization of the Health Resources and Services Administration.

provide primary health care in underserved areas, $1.9 billion through the Ryan White Care Act to care for people with human immunodeficiency virus/acquired immunodeficiency syndrome (HIV/AIDS), $942 million to improve maternal and child health, and $533 million for health-professions training and quality assurance (www.hrsa.gov).

The Bureau of Health Professions, an agency of the HRSA, provides national leadership in coordinating, evaluating, and supporting the development of the nation's health personnel. This Bureau is charged with assessing health care workforce requirements, forecasting workforce demand, and administering federal programs for targeted healthcare personnel development and utilization, such as the National Health Service Corps Program, the Nursing Education Loan Repayment Program, and the Public Health Service Scholarship Training Program and Loan Repayment Program. The Bureau of Health Professions has recently undergone a major reorganization to enhance its effectiveness. The

Division of Nursing, an agency within the Bureau of Health Professions, is the key federal agency for nursing education and practice, seeking to assure a supply and distribution of qualified nursing personnel adequate to the health needs of the nation. The strategic goals of the Division of Nursing are as follows:

• Enhance nursing's contribution to primary health care and public health.
• Develop and promote innovative practice models for improved and expanded nursing services.
• Enhance racial and ethnic diversity and cultural competency in the nursing workforce.
• Promote improved and expanded linkages between education and practice.
• Improve and expand nursing services to high-risk and underserved populations.
• Enhance nursing's contributions to achieving the Healthy People 2000 and Healthy People 2010 objectives and health systems change.

• Build capacity for meeting the nursing-service needs of the nation.

The Division of Nursing has four main branches: Nursing Data and Analysis, Nursing Education and Practice, Nursing Special Initiatives and Program Systems, and a National Advisory Council on Nurse Education and Practice. Every four years the Division of Nursing surveys the nation's registered nurses (RNs) to determine nursing workforce trends. The latest National Sample Survey of Registered Nurses was released in 2001 and shows an aging nursing workforce and a continued need for cultural diversity in the profession. This report can be downloaded from the Bureau's website (www.hrsa. dhhs.gov/bhpr). A study commissioned by the AHRQ and undertaken by nurse-researcher Dr. Peter Buerhaus and staff members from the CMS, AHRQ, NINR, and HRSA, *Nurse Staffing and Patient Outcomes in Hospitals,* can also be found on this website. This study, released April 20, 2001, looked at the relationships between nurse staffing variables and patient outcomes in acute care hospital units.

The Division of Nursing also has a series of grant programs. Basic Nurse Education and Practice grants strengthen basic nursing education programs that improve access to care in medically underserved communities, improve cultural competence, and provide education in informatics. Advanced Education Nursing grants support nurses enrolled in advanced degree programs, such as nurse practitioners, clinical nurse specialists, nurse-midwives, nurse anesthetists, nurse educators, nurse administrators, and public health nurses. Increasing Nursing Workforce Diversity grants are designed to increase opportunities for students from racial and ethnic minorities who want to pursue a nursing career (bhpr.hrsa.gov/dn/dn.htm).

The Indian Health Service (IHS), with an annual budget of $3 billion (FY 2002), serves 1.5 million American Indians and Alaska Natives. The IHS directly operates 37 hospitals, 60 health centers, three school health centers, and 46 health stations, and transfers IHS services to an additional 13 hospitals, 160 health centers, 76 health stations, and 160 village clinics in Alaska (www.ihs.gov).

The National Institutes of Health (NIH) is the federal agency overseeing health care research in the United States. The NIH works to uncover new knowledge by conducting research in its own laboratories; supporting research by non-federal scientists in universities, medical schools, hospitals, and other research institutions; helping train research investigators; and fostering the communication of medical information. There are 27 separate Institutes and Centers comprising the NIH (www.nih. gov and Box 26-2).

The National Institute of Nursing Research (NINR) began as the NIH Center for Nursing Re-

---

BOX **26-2** National Institutes and Centers of Health

National Cancer Institute
National Eye Institute
National Heart. Lung and Blood Institute
National Human Genome Research Institute
National Institute on Aging
National Institute on Alcohol Abuse and Alcoholism
National Institute of Allergy and Infectious Diseases
National Institute of Arthritis and Musculoskeletal and Skin Diseases
National Institute of Child Health and Human Development
National Institute on Deafness and Other Communication Disorders
National Institute of Dental and Craniofacial Research
National Institute of Diabetes and Digestive and Kidney Diseases
National Institute on Drug Abuse
National Institute of Environmental Health Sciences
National Institute of General Medical Sciences
National Institute of Mental Health
National Institute of Neurological Disorders and Stroke
National Institute of Nursing Research
National Library of Medicine
National Institute of Biomedical Imaging and Bioengineering
Warren Grant Magnuson Clinical Center
Center for Information Technology
National Center for Complementary and Alternative Medicine
National Center for Research Resources
National Center on Minority Health and Health Disparities
John E. Fogarty International Center
Center for Scientific Review

search in 1986 and became a separate institute on June 10, 1993. The NINR administers grants to support the work of nurse researchers both inside and outside the NIH. NINR program priorities include promoting health and preventing disease, managing the symptoms of and disabilities resulting from illness, improving the environments in which care is delivered, and the integration of biological and behavioral research. To these ends, the research agenda of the NINR covers seven broad areas: (1) chronic illness and long term care, (2) health promotion and risk behaviors, (3) cardiopulmonary health care and critical care, (4) neurofunction and sensory disorders, (5) immune responses and oncology, (6) reproductive and infant health, and (7) end-of-life and palliative care. The NINR has a National Advisory Council for Nursing Research with six ex-officio members and 15 appointed members. This council provides the second level of review of grant applications and recommends to the Director which applications should be considered for funding. The Advisory Council also reviews the NINR's extramural programs and makes recommendations on its intramural research activities (www.nih.gov/ninr).

The Substance Abuse and Mental Health Services Administration (SAMHSA) was established in 1992 to strengthen the nation's capacity to provide prevention, diagnosis, and treatment services for substance abuse and mental illnesses. With an annual budget of $3 billion (FY 2002), SAMHSA works with states, local communities, and private organizations to address community needs and risk factors that contribute to substance abuse and mental illness. Through its Knowledge Development and Application grants, SAMHSA funds hundreds of programs nationwide to improve prevention and treatment methods shown to be effective and to promote their use. SAMHSA's programs also include the Center for Mental Health Services, the Center for Substance Abuse Prevention, and the Center for Substance Abuse Treatment (www.samhsa.gov).

Department of Defense. The DoD provides health services to approximately eight million active-duty service members and their families around the world. The Army, Navy, and Air Force each have a corps of nurses, and there are about 35,000 RNs on active, reserve, or National Guard duty. The Assistant Secretary of Defense for Health Affairs heads the Office of Health Affairs; this office is charged with creating policy that enables the military health system to sustain the health of members of the armed forces, their families, and others under the full range of military deployment conditions. Health services are provided through TRICARE, the military health system. TRICARE, a partnership of military health care facilities and civilian contractors, expanded its health benefit on October 1, 2001 with its "TRICARE for Life" program, making an additional 1.5 million uniformed-services retirees, their family members, and survivors age 65 and older eligible for benefits (tricare.osd.mil).

Department of Education. The DoE operates programs that touch every area and level of education to promote its mission, educational excellence for all Americans. The DoE provides billions of dollars for grants, loans, and work-study programs to more than 8 million postsecondary students, including nursing students. In FY 2001, a record $42 billion in federal grants, loans, and campus-based programs helped students continue their education, including $9 billion in Pell Grants, which serve the neediest students. The FY 2002 request dropped significantly to $19.2 billion. The DoE also administers the Federal Education Loan program, including Federal Direct Stafford/Ford loans, Federal Direct Unsubsidized Stafford/Ford loans, Federal Direct PLUS loans, and Federal Direct Consolidation loans. Through vocational education and special populations programs, the DoE provides money to nursing programs located in community colleges (www.ed.gov).

Department of Veterans Affairs. The DVA serves America's veterans and administers programs that provide benefits and other services to veterans and their dependents and beneficiaries. These programs include the Veterans Health Administration (VHA), the Veterans Benefits Administration, the Center for Minority Veterans, the Center for Women Veterans, and the National Cemetery Administration. The VHA provides medical, surgical, and rehabilitative services to eligible veterans. It operates 173 Veterans Administration (VA) Medical Centers nationwide and in Puerto Rico and is the largest health care system in the United States. It is a major employer of nurses, with 34,000 RNs and 26,000 LPNs and nursing assistants. The Under Secretary for Health serves as the chief executive officer for the VHA and as a chief consultant of the Nursing Strategic Healthcare Group (NSHG), the center for nursing leadership within the VHA. The NSHG provides innovation and caring across the nursing service delivery within the VHA system. It works in collaboration with other disciplines to identify incentives for and eliminate barriers to interdisciplinary teamwork for quality patient-centered care (www.va.gov).

Department of Labor. The DoL is charged with preparing the American workforce for new and better jobs and ensuring the adequacy of America's workplaces. It administers over 180 federal laws created to protect employees' wages and rights to a healthy and safe work environment. It monitors employment and pension rights; promotes equal employment opportunities; administers unemployment insurance and workers' compensation programs; collects, analyzes, and publishes labor and economic statistics; and strengthens free collective bargaining. All nurses are affected by the activities of the DoL. The American Nurses Association (ANA), through its State Nurses Associations and its official collective bargaining arm, the United American Nurses, has represented nurses in collective bargaining for over 55 years. These programs are governed by federal labor laws enforced by the DoL. The DoL has many subdivisions, including the Bureau of Labor Statistics and the Occupational Safety and Health Administration (www.dol.gov).

The Bureau of Labor Statistics is the principal fact-finding agency of the federal government for labor statistics and economic information. The Bureau collects, processes, analyzes, and disseminates essential statistical data to federal agencies, Congress, state and local governments, business, labor, and the public. The Bureau of Labor Statistics estimates that 331,000 RNs, 15% of the current workforce, will retire between 1998 and 2008, even while the aging U.S. population is expected to increase its demand for nursing services (www.bls.gov). The large number of practicing RNs who are nearing retirement is of great concern because it has been reported that less than 10% of RNs are under 30 years of age. This means there are fewer nurses coming into the profession at a time of increased need.

The mission of the *Occupational Safety and Health Administration* (OSHA) is to ensure safe and healthful workplaces in America. According to OSHA (www.osha.gov/as/opa/oshafacts.html), workplace fatalities have been cut in half and occupational injury and illness rates have decreased by 40% since the agency was created in 1971, even while U.S. employment has nearly doubled. OSHA conducts thousands of federal and state inspections, promulgates new rules for the workplace, and provides training and partnership development for employer and employee compliance programs. OSHA estimates that 5.6 million workers in the health care industry and related occupations are at risk of occupational exposure to bloodborne pathogens, including human immunodeficiency virus (HIV), hepatitis B virus, hepatitis C virus, and others. According to *NIOSH Alert* (March 1999), 600,000 to 800,000 needlestick injuries and other percutaneous injuries occur annually among health care workers, and the majority reported by nurses were related to the disposal process. In response, Congress passed the Needlestick Safety and Prevention Act in 2000 (see the Unit Three Case Study). OSHA has revised its Bloodborne Pathogen Standard to conform to the requirements of the new act (Final Rule, January 18, 2001 Federal Register #66:5317-5325). Also in early 2001, after many months of preparation and hearings, OSHA released its long-awaited Ergonomics Standard, written to protect nurses from disabling back injuries and musculoskeletal disorders. The ANA testified at several hearings that as much as 38% of nurses suffer from back injuries and stressed the importance of the Ergonomics Standard, which includes work restriction protections and "action triggers" to aid in the identification of hazards. Additionally, OSHA has been quick to respond to the hazards of our present-day work environment and has published on its website (www.osha.gov) a "Fact Sheet and Reference on Worker Health and Safety for Anthrax Exposure" and "OSHA Recommendations for Handling Suspicious Letters or Packages."

Other Independent Government Agencies. The National Academy of Sciences is a private, nonprofit society of scholars engaged in scientific and engineering research. It received its charter from Congress in 1863 with a mandate to advise the federal government on scientific and technical matters. The services of the National Academy of Sciences have proven so essential that Congress and the White House have issued legislation and executive orders over the years to affirm its unique role. Members of the Academy are elected in recognition of their distinguished and continuing achievements in original research. It has an active membership of about 1,900 members. The Academy is governed by a council of 12 members and by five officers elected from the membership. The Academy also includes the National Academy of Engineering, the National Research Council, and the Institute of Medicine. The Institute of Medicine provides objective, timely, and authoritative information and advice concerning health and science policy to the government, the corporate sector, the professions, and the public. It has recently focused its efforts on the safety and quality of the U.S. health care system. Several of its recent reports are available for download or ordering at the National Academy of Sciences website (www.nationalacademies.org): *Informing the Future: Critical Issues in Health* (2001), *Crossing the Quality Chasm: A New Health System for the 21st Century* (2001), *The Right Thing to Do, The Smart Thing to Do: Enhancing Diversity in Health Professions* (2001), and *To Err Is Human: Building a Safer Health System* (1999). These reports have resulted in national, state, and local organizational efforts to reduce medical errors and improve safety in our health care institutions. In *Crossing the Quality Chasm*, all health care professionals are challenged to participate in crossing the "quality chasm" in our health care system. The report identifies six aims for twenty-first century health care: safety, effectiveness, patient-centeredness, timeliness, efficiency, and equity (www4.nas.edu/iom/iomhome.nsf).

LEGISLATIVE BRANCH

The legislative branch of the U.S. government is the bicameral Congress, made up of the Senate and the House of Representatives. The chief function of the Congress is to make laws. The Congress also approves treaties and nominations made by the President. The Senate is made up of two senators from each state, who are elected for six-year terms. Every two years, one third of the Senate is up for re-election. The members of the House of Representatives are elected for two-year terms. The number of representatives from a state depends on its population. There are presently 435 members of the House. Every ten years, based on the results of the census, the House membership is reapportioned.

At the beginning of each Congressional session, which lasts for 2 years (e.g., the session of 2001-2002 is the 107th Congress), the members of the House and Senate choose their leaders and make committee assignments. The Constitution requires a Speaker of the House and a president and president pro tempore of the Senate. The Senate and House also elect majority and minority leaders and majority and minority whips (assistants to the majority and minority leaders). The offices of majority and minority leader and whip are not Constitutionally defined; they are party positions, and the Constitution does not mention political parties or define a two-party system.

The Speaker of the House is the presiding officer of the House of Representatives and is second in line of succession for the presidency if both the President and the Vice President should die or be removed from office. The Speaker is nominated by the majority party in the House and voted on by the full House membership. The Speaker has tremendous influence over committee assignments, the scheduling of bills to be heard in the House, and other procedural maneuvering that occurs on the House floor.

The majority leader is elected by vote of the majority party at the beginning of each session of Congress. The majority leader works closely with the Speaker and is the party's chief strategist and spokesperson for the promotion of the party position on key legislation. The minority leader heads the opposition party's efforts against the majority party. The majority and minority whips serve as assistants to the majority and minority leaders and have the responsibility to lobby members of the party for votes and keep the party membership in line.

BOX **26-3** Senate Standing Committees

Agriculture, Nutrition, and Forestry
Appropriations
Armed Services
Banking, Housing and Urban Affairs
Budget
Commerce, Science, and Transportation
Energy and Natural Resources
Environment and Public Works
Finance
Foreign Relations
Governmental Affairs
Health, Education, Labor, and Pensions
Rules and Administration
Small Business
Veterans' Affairs

BOX **26-4** House of Representatives Standing Committees

Committee on Agriculture
Committee on Appropriations
Committee on Armed Services
Committee on the Budget
Committee on Education and the Workforce
Committee on Energy and Commerce
Committee on Financial Services
Committee on Government Reform
Committee on House Administration
Committee on International Relations
Committee on the Judiciary
Committee on Resources
Committee on Rules
Committee on Science
Committee on Small Business
Committee on Standards of Official Conduct
Committee on Transportation and Infrastructure
Committee on Veterans' Affairs
Committee on Ways and Means
Joint Economic Committee
Joint Committee on Printing
Joint Committee on Taxation

The Vice President serves as the president of the Senate. The president of the senate has little power, but does vote to break ties. The president pro tempore is elected by the members of the Senate from the majority party and is third in succession to the presidency. The positions and duties of majority and minority leaders and whips in the Senate are similar to those in the House of Representatives.

The duties of the U.S. Congress are to conduct hearings on topics that may generate legislation; draft legislation; determine the impact of proposed legislation; enact or defeat legislation; review the success or failure of legislated programs; levy taxes; determine budget levels for programs; appropriate funds for federal operations; confirm or reject presidential nominations for certain federal positions, including the Supreme Court; and, on occasion, override presidential vetoes.

Because of the volume and complexity of its work, Congress has organized itself into a committee system to accomplish its tasks. There are close to 250 committees and subcommittees in Congress (Boxes 26-3 and 26-4). Each committee has a specific legislative jurisdiction and is governed by a set of rules. The committees are the heart of the legislative process; they hold hearings, study issues, initiate and write bills, report the bills out to the floor for a full House or Senate vote. Legislation may be defeated in committee (i.e., never presented for a full House or Senate vote). Party membership ratios on congressional committees are determined at the beginning of each session of Congress, mirroring the membership ratio in each chamber. The chairman of each committee and the majority of the committee members come from the majority party.

The committee system exerts significant influence over the legislative agenda for the Congress. The chairman of each committee establishes the priorities for the committee, controls the committee's business, and has significant influence over the enactment of legislation. The committee determines what measures will be heard; that is, whether a measure will pass out of the committee so that the full House or Senate can deliberate on it.

There are four types of congressional committee. The first is the standing committee. These committees are the permanent and well-known committees of the Senate and the House, and they have broad responsibilities in particular areas, as specified by the title of the committee. The House and Senate have approximately parallel structures of standing committees. Each standing committee has a system of subcommittees. The second type of committee is the Select or Special Committee. These are temporary, and are formed to address a particular issue for a period of time. The third type, the Joint Committee, is made up of members of both the House and the Senate and is formed to study and report on a specific issue. The fourth type, the Conference Committee, is formed to resolve differences between House and Senate versions of the same legislation.

COMMITTEES AND SUBCOMMITTEES OF INTEREST TO NURSES

The Subcommittee on Research, Nutrition, and General Legislation of the Senate Committee on Agriculture, Nutrition, and Forestry has jurisdiction over legislation relating to food, nutrition, and hunger; food stamps; the school breakfast and lunch programs; the national summer food program for children; the special milk program for children; special supplemental nutrition program for women, infants, and children; and nutritional programs for the elderly.

One of the most important committees is the Senate Committee on Appropriations. Its role is defined by the Constitution, which states that "appropriations made by law" must occur prior to any money being spent by the government. The Committee on Appropriations annually allocates federal funds to many government agencies, departments, and organizations for their programs. The Subcommittee on Labor, Health and Human Services, and Education of the Senate Appropriations Committee drafts legislation to allocate funds to agencies under their jurisdiction, including some involved with nursing and health care: the Administration on Aging, the Bureau of Labor Statistics, Child Welfare Services, Community Health Centers, the CMS, the HRSA, the AHRQ, the NIH, the NINR, Nursing Workforce Development, the National Health Services Corps, the Nurse Education Act, Health Services Research, the Public Health Service, and the Social Security Administration.

The Senate Budget Committee and House Budget Committee together draft Congress's annual budget plan and monitor action on the budget. The Senate Finance Committee (similar to the House Ways and Means Committee), in contrast, has legislative jurisdiction over taxes, Social Security, Medicare, Medicaid, and other entitlements. The Committee on Appropriations provides the funding for government programs.

The committees charged with budgetary responsibilities have overlapping and sometimes confusing functions. This shared jurisdiction can complicate and sometimes slow the passage of legislation.

The Senate Finance Committee's Subcommittee on Health Care has responsibility for general revenue spending, tax reform, Social Security, unemployment insurance, Medicaid, and the Medicare, including support of diploma nursing schools and money for graduate nursing education, including reimbursement for nurse practitioners and clinical nurse specialists.

The Senate Committee on Health, Education, Labor, and Pensions (sometimes referred to as *HELP*) has jurisdiction over all measures relating to education, labor, health, and pensions. This includes measures relating to agricultural colleges; the arts and humanities; biomedical research and development; child labor; convict labor; domestic activities of the American Red Cross; equal-opportunity employment; Gallaudet College, Howard University, and Saint Elizabeth's Hospital; handicapped individuals; labor standards and labor statistics; mediation and arbitration of labor statistics; occupational safety and health; private pension plans; public health; railway labor and retirement; regulation of foreign laborers; student loans; and wages and hours of labor. HELP has four subcommittees: the Subcommittee on Aging; the Subcommittee on Children and Families; the Subcommittee on Employment, Safety, and Training; and the Subcommittee on Public Health. In November 2001, while still reeling from the World Trade Center disasters, this Committee approved two bills aimed at easing the nursing shortage in the United States. These bills, the Nurse Re-Investment Act and the Nurse Employment and Education Development (NEED) Act, create new programs to offer scholarships for nurses in exchange for service in public health hospitals, Indian Health Service facilities, and other shortage areas. The future of the health care workforce depends on this powerful committee to move this and other similar legislation forward.

The Senate Committee on Veterans' Affairs has legislative and oversight responsibility for veterans' benefits and services, assures adequate funding levels for VA health care, and creates programs to enable the VA to recruit and retain top quality physicians and nurses.

The House Committee on Appropriations Subcommittee on Health and Human Services, and Education has legislative jurisdiction over the NIH, NINR, National Health Service Corps, CDC, FDA, DoL, OSHA, National Labor Relations Board, DoE, DHHS, and any money appropriated specifically for nursing education and research, health services research, and the Nurse Education Act.

The House Committee on Education and the Workforce has two subcommittees that are important to nurses. The Subcommittee on Workforce Protections has responsibility for legislation regarding workers health and safety, OSHA, wages and hours (including overtime), the Fair Labor Standards Act (including child labor laws and laws regarding worker's compensation), and the Family and Medical Leave Act. The Subcommittee on Employer–Employee Relations deals with pensions, health and other employee benefits, the Employee Retirement Income and Security Act (ERISA), the National Labor Relations Act, and the Bureau of Labor Statistics.

The House Committee on Energy and Commerce Subcommittee on Health has jurisdiction over public health; hospital construction; mental health and research; biomedical programs and health protection in general, including Medicaid and national health insurance; food and drugs; and drug abuse.

The House Committee on Veterans' Affairs Subcommittee on Health oversees the VA's effectiveness in providing timely benefits and quality health care and has legislative jurisdiction for the Departments of Veterans' Affairs health care programs and the VA's health care system.

Finally, the House Ways and Means Committee's Subcommittee on Health has responsibilities similar to those of the Senate Finance Committee's Subcommittee on Health. It has jurisdiction over programs providing payments for health care, such as Medicaid, Medicare (including money for diploma nursing schools and graduate nursing education),

and reimbursement for nurse practitioners and clinical nurse specialists. It also has responsibility for telehealth programs.

LEGISLATIVE PROCESS

Any Senator or Representative can introduce a piece of legislation. The legislation is referred to a committee specialized to deal with the subject matter (see Chapter 22).

The *Congressional Record* is published daily by the Government Printing Office when either the House or the Senate or both are in session. This is the main source of information on what happened on the floors of the House and Senate. The *Record* reports an edited account of the floor debate and any action that was taken during the session; any extended remarks by Senators or Representatives that were not given orally but were entered into the record; a summary of committee, subcommittee, and conference committee meetings; bills reported; and conference reports given. Finally, the *Record* also publishes an index twice a month.

BUDGETARY PROCESS

The federal budget has two purposes. The first purpose is to collect revenue and allocate resources to meet national objectives, and the second is to provide for a measure of the country's expenditures and debts to promote economic stability and growth.

There are three main processes in each budget cycle: authorization, appropriations, and budget resolution. Authorization laws have two purposes: (1) to establish, continue, or modify a federal program as a prerequisite under House and Senate rules for the Congress to appropriate budget authority for programs, and (2) to provide for direct, or mandatory, spending from an authorization law (Box 26-5).

The authorization laws that provide for direct, or mandatory, spending cover either permanent spending programs (e.g., IHS) or programs that require periodic renewal, such as the Food Stamp program. Over half of all federal spending now comes from authorizing legislation that creates budget authority for itself.

Mandatory spending is often referred to as *entitlement spending*. However, entitlement spending is

BOX **26-5** Budget Glossary

Appropriations act: A statute that provides authority for the federal agencies to incur expenses and make payments for specified purposes.

Authorization act: A statute that establishes or continues the operation of a federal agency or program for a period of time. Also specifies or authorizes a funding level for the agency or program to function.

Budget authority: The authority Congress gives to government agencies to spend money now and in the future.

Budget resolution: The process that allows Congress to develop revenue and spending proposals within the framework of its own budget plan (i.e., to develop, revise, or reaffirm the Congressional budget). Allows for a fast-track legislative procedure and has to be agreed upon by both Houses.

Continuing resolution: An appropriations resolution that allows for temporary budget authority for the federal agencies to continue their operations until a budget can be passed.

Deferrals: Proposal contained in a special message from the President that temporarily withhold or delay the obligation or expenditure of budget authority.

Direct spending or mandatory spending: Language that was set forth in the Budget Enforcement Act of 1990 and that refers to programs that are authorized by permanent law and have their budget authority provided for in some other way than by appropriations (as do several entitlement programs, such as the Food Stamp program and Social Security).

Discretionary spending: Spending subject to the annual appropriations process, such as that for housing, education, defense, and foreign aid.

Emergency spending: Language that was set forth in the Budget Enforcement Act of 1990 and refers to legislation for expenditures that is deemed an emergency by both the President and Congress.

Mark-up: A meeting of Congress where the committees work on the language of the bills or resolutions.

Omnibus bill: A bill that contains several related legislative proposals.

Pay-as-you-go: Language that was set forth in the Budget Enforcement Act of 1990 and requires Congress to pay for any changes to programs or creation of new programs that result in an increase in direct spending. Payments can be made through cuts in other entitlements or an increase in taxes. This may result in an omnibus reconciliation act

Reconciliation: Expedited legislative procedures for the enactment of changes in direct or mandatory spending (usually reductions) to achieve changes in revenues.

Rescissions: Proposal contained in a special message from the President canceling in whole or in part previously appropriated budget authority.

Sequestration: Executive branch action.

---

actually only a subset of mandatory spending. The laws providing for entitlement spending contain criteria that specify who is eligible for the program. For example, the Social Security Act sets the criteria under which retired workers receive benefits based on length of time worked and their earnings.

The authorization laws that provide for discretionary spending, which is about one third of all federal expenditures, specify the basis for operating a program and the level of funding for the program, either as a specific dollar amount or as "sums as necessary." Examples of discretionary spending include funding for the DoD, the Internal Revenue Service, and the EPA.

Authorizations may be permanent or may cover only specified time periods. The authorizations that are for specific time periods may be annual or multiyear. When the authorization expires and Congress wants to extend the program, reauthorization legislation is passed.

Most of the authorization work for health programs in Congress occurs in the House Ways and Means Committee, the House Energy and Commerce Committee, the Senate Finance Committee, and the Senate Health, Education, Labor and Pensions Committee.

The appropriations process sets the amount of funding that each program is allocated for the specified time period. If a program receives all of the money that was requested for operations, then the program has full authorization. The House and Senate Appropriations Committees have the responsibility for appropriations. The appropriations work is distributed among many subcommittees.

The Concurrent Budget Resolution is passed each spring and limits the amount of funds that can be appropriated by setting a ceiling on total federal funding.

In 1974 Congress passed the Budget and Impoundment Control Act to establish procedures for the development of the annual budget and created the congressional standing budget committees, the House and Senate Budget Committees. These budget committees have the responsibility to set economic priorities, draft Congress's annual budget plan, and monitor action on the budget for the government. The Act also created the Congressional Budget Office (CBO), which is responsible for producing annual economic forecasts, providing Congress with data on revenues and expenditures, and reviewing the President's annual budget submission. In 1985 Congress enacted the Balanced Budget and Emergency Deficit Control Act, also known as the Gramm-Rudman-Hollings Act. This Act established maximum deficit amounts and stated that if the deficit exceeds these statutory limits, the President is required to issue an order to reduce all nonexempt spending by a uniform percentage. This was amended in 1987 to give this responsibility to the OMB of the executive branch. In 1990 Congress passed the Budget Enforcement Act to replace the Gramm-Rudman-Hollings Act with two independent budget deficit enforcements: caps on discretionary spending and a "pay-as-you-go" requirement for direct spending and revenue legislation. The size of the federal budget has increased over the years due to a larger economy, inflation, and the increase in our population, and its proportions have changed dramatically (Figure 26-3).

The budget process begins each February. (For a summary of the budget timetable, refer to Box 26-6). The President is required to submit the Administration's budget to the upcoming to Congress by the first Monday in February. Prior to this submission, the President must begin preparing the budget at the end of the previous summer by working with the federal agencies to gather their budget requests for the next fiscal year, which begins October 1. This proposed budget includes work by all of the executive agency officials and their staff, who channel budget requests through the Cabinets to the OMB. The OMB reconciles the requests with the President's programs.

BOX **26-6** Summary of Budget Timetable

Summer and Fall	President works with federal agencies to develop budget; Office of Management and Budget reviews budget
1st Monday in February	President submits budget to Congress
February 15	Congressional Budget Office sends budget report to Congress
March	Budget committees of each House receive input
April 1	Senate Budget Committee reports budget resolution
April 15	Congress completes budget resolution or, they do not, pay-as-you-go measures are put in place
May and June	Appropriations legislation is heard in the House
June 30	House completes appropriations bills
October 1	New fiscal year begins

After receiving the President's budget request, the Senate and House Budget Committees hold hearings on the budget in February. During these hearings, Congress receives testimony from Administration officials, experts from the academic and business communities, representatives from national organizations and special interest groups such as the American Nurses Association, members of the Congress, and the general public. While the hearings are going on, other committees of Congress review the budget and determine its impact on their committee and on the functioning of programs it oversees. In February the CBO also sends both Budget Committees their report on the budget and the economic outlook.

In March, the Budget Committee of each House drafts a congressional budget plan based on the President's budget request, the public hearings, and the CBO's reports. This is done publicly, unlike the President's formulation, in a series of public committee hearings called "mark-ups." When the mark-ups are complete, the House and Senate Budget Committees report to the full House and Senate a

Three decades ago, nearly two-thirds of the federal budget was available for discretionary programs:

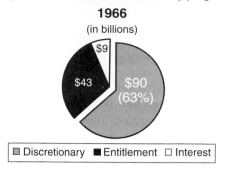

1966

(in billions)

$9
$43
$90 (63%)

☐ Discretionary ■ Entitlement ☐ Interest

In the 1970s, entitlement spending jumped, placing a crimp on discretionary spending:

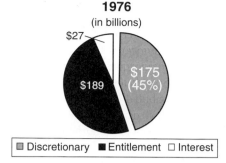

1976

(in billions)

$27
$189
$175 (45%)

☐ Discretionary ■ Entitlement ☐ Interest

By the mid-1980s, interest payments on the national debt began to rise:

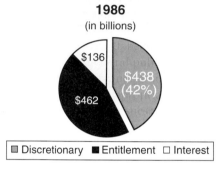

1986

(in billions)

$136
$462
$438 (42%)

☐ Discretionary ■ Entitlement ☐ Interest

By 1996, entitlement spending took half of the budget pie. In just 30 years, the amount left over for roads, police, defense, and most other government services shrunk to a third of the budget:

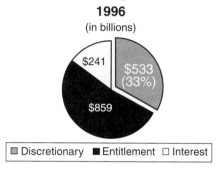

1996

(in billions)

$241
$859
$533 (33%)

☐ Discretionary ■ Entitlement ☐ Interest

Current budget projections show the same trend. By 2006, entitlement spending will demand the majority of the federal budget. Interest payments will continue to be a major drain on the Treasury, and the remaining amount will be divided among discretionary programs:

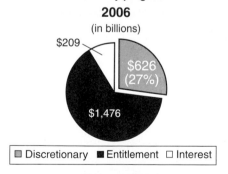

2006

(in billions)

$209
$1,476
$626 (27%)

☐ Discretionary ■ Entitlement ☐ Interest

Where Does the Money Go?

While the size of the annual federal budget has increased in dollar terms (reflecting inflation, increased population, and economy) over the years, the *proportion* available for common government services has shrunk dramatically. Competition among federal agencies for funding is heating up.

Over the last three decades, discretionary spending has been cut significantly to accommodate rapid growths in other expenses. Discretionary spending covers everything from road building to police protection to medical research to our national defense — most of the government services with which Americans are familiar. All other spending is mandatory — required by law regardless of what is left over for discretionary spending. Mandatory spending includes entitlements such as Social Security and Medicare, and the enormous interest the U.S. must pay every year to finance the national debt.

Figure 26-3 Where does the federal money go?

Concurrent Budget Resolution setting forth the budget totals, spending by function, reconciliation instructions, budget enforcement mechanisms, and statements of budget policy for the upcoming year. Once the Concurrent Budget Resolution is presented, all members of the House and Senate have an opportunity to offer amendments and to debate the pros and cons of the budget. When the Senate and House have passed their respective versions of the budget resolution, they appoint a conference committee to resolve the differences in the two budgets. The Budget Act requires that Congress complete all of this action on the budget by April 15; however, it often fails to meet the deadline.

JUDICIAL BRANCH

The judicial branch of the federal government is composed of the U.S. federal court system. The Constitution provides for one Supreme Court and "inferior courts," as Congress shall establish. The Supreme Court is the highest court and is composed of the Chief Justice of the United States and, currently, eight Associate Justices (this number has varied over the years). Each year, the Supreme Court hears a limited number of cases that have usually originated in the local or state courts and involve some important question about the Constitution and federal law. The Supreme Court also has original jurisdiction over treaties made and over all cases affecting ambassadors to the United States, other public ministers and consuls, and those in which a state is party. Additionally, the Supreme Court is authorized to review decisions of the lower federal courts and the highest courts of the states.

The court system is divided into two parts: the federal courts and the state courts. The federal court system includes district courts and twelve circuit courts of appeal. There are 12 circuit courts of appeal that are created to cover specific geographic areas (Figure 26-4), with each state assigned to a circuit court. The circuit courts hear appeals of cases originally decided by the federal trial courts. They are also empowered to review and enforce orders of many federal administrative agencies, resolving (among other issues) those relating to federal regulations and policies that affect nursing and

health care. The decisions of these courts of appeal are subject to appeal only to the Supreme Court.

There are 94 district courts that are the trial courts of the federal judicial system. Each state has at least one district court. These district courts have jurisdiction over nearly all categories of federal cases, including both civil and criminal matters. Opportunities for influence within the judiciary are limited. An amicus curiae (Latin for "friend of the court") is a party who assists the court by furnishing information or advice regarding questions of law or fact. This "friend of the court," such as the American Nurses Association or other interested body, is not a party to a particular lawsuit but nevertheless has a strong interest in it, and is allowed or invited by the court to file an amicus curiae brief. This is a statement of a particular view on the subject matter of the lawsuit. Such briefs are often filed in cases involving public-interest matters (e.g., entitlement programs, consumer protection, civil rights). This can often be the only way to have influence when the court is hearing a particular case. (See Chapter 23 for further discussion of the judicial branch.)

CONCLUSION

Understanding the organization and processes of the federal government is the first step toward effective involvement. The next step is to recognize one's opportunities to influence the process. The federal government plays an important role in the everyday life of the nurse at work, whether in a hospital, nursing home, or community health center. Policies that have originated at the federal level govern the quality and safety of our work settings, what we do for our patients, and how we are paid. Nurses have a unique and comprehensive understanding of the health care of this nation and their input is needed. Nurses can influence the future not only of their own profession but that of the health care delivery system in general. Nurses are needed at every level of government for their expertise and influence, not just at the local and state levels. Ask questions, get comfortable with speaking out, contact your nursing organizations and get involved. Nursing must be visible and seen as influential and speaking with one strong voice.

- 1st Circuit
- 2nd Circuit
- 3rd Circuit
- 4th Circuit
- 5th Circuit
- 6th Circuit
- 7th Circuit
- 8th Circuit
- 9th Circuit
- 10th Circuit
- 11th Circuit
- DC Circuit
- Federal Circuit

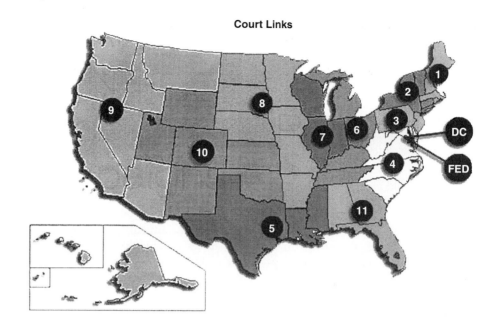

Court Links

Figure 26-4   Map of the federal circuit court.

REFERENCES

Agel, J. & Gerberg, M. (2001). *The U.S. Constitution for everyone.* New York: Perigee.

Delaney, A. (1995). *Politics for dummies.* New York: Hungry Minds, Inc.

Heineman, R.A. (1995). *Political science: An introduction.* New York: McGraw-Hill.

Heineman, R.A., Peterson, S.A., & Rasmussen, T.H. (1995). *American government.* New York: McGraw-Hill.

United States Senate Budget Committee (1998). *The Congressional budget process.* Washington, DC: U.S. Government Printing Office.

Vignette   The Honorable Lois Capps

The Nurse as a Member of Congress

"Experience is not what happens to you; it's what you do with what happens to you."

ALDOUS HUXLEY

If someone had told me on the day I earned my nursing degree from Pacific Lutheran University that I would become a member of Congress, I never would have believed it. But here I am today—a nurse, a mother, and a member of Congress. I didn't come to Congress under normal circumstances. My husband, Walter Capps, was elected to the U.S. House of Representatives in 1996 and I went with him to Washington, DC, where we were both excited about making a difference. Tragically, our time together there was cut short when he died suddenly of a heart attack on October 28, 1997. Of course my life changed forever. While grieving for the loss of my husband, I was also faced with questions about who would take his place in Congress. In the midst of the numbness and shock, I was approached about running to fill his seat. I was filled with so many questions. How could I run? What could I offer to the community? Was I qualified to be a member of Congress? To be true to myself, I had to be able to translate my life experiences into a tangible vision for how to improve the quality of life in California's Central Coast, the area I would represent. Although the campaign was hard, the answers to my questions were easy—I was and would always be a nurse.

While I never imagined running for office, I now know how relevant my nursing background is in my work in Congress. I spent most of my career as a public health nurse in schools, where among other things I helped teen mothers and fathers complete their education and learn to care for their children. Most of a school nurse's time is spent working for and with families whose children lack adequate resources for health care. Perhaps it is the child who fails a vision or hearing screening with no money for glasses or insurance for follow-up care. It may be the many children in our schools with gaping holes in their teeth who have never been to see a dentist. It may be those who experience abuse at home, who are depressed or even suicidal. Meeting these children and countless other experiences during my nursing career have given me a unique perspective on the health care issues before Congress. Whether we're debating how to keep Medicare or Medicaid solvent or the need to expand health care coverage to the uninsured, my years of training and experience give me firsthand knowledge not available to many of my colleagues. As I prepare to vote or speak on the floor of the U.S. House of Representatives, I often recall a particular student, young mom, or encounter that inspires me to work to improve the lives of people back at home.

Nurses have a particular interest in how health care is delivered, how patients are cared for, and the continued advancement of health care delivery and services. We are advocates for our patients and we aren't afraid to get our hands dirty. But we need to make sure our voices are heard. Special interests are everywhere, fighting for what's in their best interests, not in patients' best interests. And at no time has this been more glaringly apparent than during the discussions on managed care reform—the debate over the so-called "Patients' Bill of Rights."

Practicing nursing for 30 years prepared me for service in Congress in many ways. First, legislators and nurses must both be good listeners. I believe that quality representation means taking the time to understand the views and problems of one's constituents. As a nurse, I was an advocate for my patients. Today as a Congresswoman, I'm an advocate for my constituents. Nurses learn to withhold premature judgment, to work as a team, to set goals and priorities, and to meet them. Also, nurses are taught to put the common good before their personal ambition and ahead of political interests. I developed these important skills during my nursing career and they have served me well as a member of Congress.

Many of my legislative priorities come out of my experiences as a nurse. I worked hard to be appointed to the powerful House Committee on Energy and Commerce, which has jurisdiction over health issues. From this position, I have been able to play an active role in shaping health care policy in Congress. I'm proud of many of the things we have accomplished, including passing the Breast and Cervical Cancer Treatment Act, increasing funding for the National Institutes of Health, modernizing the Food and Drug Administration, and improving children's health benefits. I've introduced my own legislation to help amyotrophic lateral sclerosis patients gain immediate Medicare coverage, to improve mental health care services, to recognize and help educate new mothers about postpartum depression, to eliminate youth drinking, and to teach cardiopulmonary resuscitation in schools—all of which were enacted.

But there are still so many challenges before us, and we need your help. As I write these words, I'm still working to pass a strong Patients' Bill of Rights (to include a prescription drug benefit in Medicare), to pass campaign finance reform, and to expand health care coverage to the uninsured. Another issue directly affects our profession: We are currently experiencing a shortage of nurses of crisis proportions and we need to encourage more people to enter the nursing workforce. And who better to introduce and lobby for legislation addressing the shortage than a nurse? I've authored the Nurse Reinvestment Act to establish a National Nurse Service Corps that would help pay for a nurse's education in exchange for a commitment to work for a period of time in a facility with a shortage of nurses. The bill would help current nurses afford more training and education so they can advance to the next level of nursing. The bill also provides funding for public service announcements to help change the public's perception of nursing and for facilitating relationships between schools and health care facilities to help educate young people about the rewards of a nursing career.

In drafting this legislation, I called on my own experiences and sought the expertise of the people who know what needs to be done to fix the crisis—nurses. And nurses around the country have been flexing their political muscle to help pass this important bill. Members of the American Nurses Association, the American Organization of Nurse Executives, the American Association of College Nurses, and many other nursing organizations have lobbied members of Congress across the country—and the political spectrum—to support the bill. Because of this intense lobbying effort by nurses, I'm confident that we can pass this legislation. This is only one example of how nurses can significantly affect public policy.

Nurses can also become part of the political process by volunteering on a campaign. Nurses in my district came out in droves to support my campaign.

They organized phone banks, walked precincts, and made phone calls to support my candidacy. Having their support has been invaluable. I would not be in Congress today if it were not for the dedication and hard work of these nurses and other citizen groups, as well as the endorsement and support of the American Nurses Association's Political Action Committee.

Don't be afraid to put your own name on the ballot. As I've already pointed out, my nursing experience made me uniquely qualified to serve in Congress. The same is true for most nurses. Get out there and do it. Start serving on a local committee or run for city council or for the school board. Or if you're someone who feels less comfortable in the spotlight, volunteer on campaigns of candidates who share your ideals. It's never too late to get involved. I was 60 when I was first elected to Congress.

Nurses have credibility and respect. People trust us. Our professional knowledge enables us to advocate for safe, quality health care; promote education for children, and address other issues on patients' behalf. I am one of only three nurses in Congress. We need more nurses to become involved. When I first ran for office, my critics attacked me by saying, "What does a nurse know about politics or public policy?" But politics is everywhere—whether you're in a hospital, a school district or in the halls of Congress. Nurses have unique experiences that distinguish us from traditional politicians. We have an important voice in the legislative process and when we use it there is no limit to what we can accomplish. As you move forward in your nursing career, I hope that you will consider becoming part of the political process as well. We need you—and your community will thank you.

Vignette   The Honorable Carolyn McCarthy

I Believed I Could Make a Difference

"You gain strength, courage and confidence by every experience in which you really stop to look fear in the face. You are able to say to yourself, 'I lived through this horror. I can take the next thing that comes along.' You must do the thing you think you cannot do."

ELEANOR ROOSEVELT

There are many routes to becoming a member of Congress. Few members' journeys to Capitol Hill, though, have gained the attention of the public—and the media—as Carolyn McCarthy's has. McCarthy was a suburban Long Island homemaker and licensed practical nurse most of her adult life. However, since 1996, she has had a movie of her life produced by Barbra Streisand, addressed the Democratic National Convention, appeared on Oprah, and had her story chronicled in a Lifetime Television "Intimate Portrait."

McCarthy's path to Congress has received great attention because it is like few others. She was thrust into the national media spotlight when the fabric of her family life was torn apart by violence.

In 1993, McCarthy lived with her family in the same Long Island home that she was raised in. McCarthy's husband Dennis, a 56-year-old stockbroker, and her only child Kevin, then a 26-year-old employee of the same firm his father worked for, commuted together to and from New York City. On the evening of December 7, 1993, they were sitting together on a train on the Long Island Rail Road coming home. A lone gunman with a 9-mm semiautomatic pistol walked through two cars and shot 25 people. McCarthy's husband, Dennis, was one of six killed, and her son, Kevin, was one of 19 wounded. Kevin, shot in the head, was paralyzed and in a coma. He was given little chance of recovery. McCarthy devoted herself to his recovery and asked the question "Could this have been prevented?" (Wilson Biographies, 2001).

Was it the tragic shooting itself that motivated McCarthy to seek a seat in Congress? No—it was the action of her Congressional Representative on gun violence. A little over 2 years after the Long Island Rail Road shootings, Representative Daniel Frisa, the Republican Congressman representing her district, voted in March 1996 to repeal a ban on some types of assault weapons. McCarthy was outraged and sensed—correctly—that other citizens in her district were too.

After deciding to run against Frisa, she met many obstacles. Although she had been a lifelong Republican, the local Republican party would not back her and *she became a Democrat. Her opponent, incumbent Frisa, painted her as a "one-issue candidate" (Shapiro, 1996). She rejected that charge and demonstrated her commitment to many political issues. However, her gun control advocacy made her a target of the National Rifle Association. This served to harden her resolve.*

Despite obstacles, McCarthy won a resounding victory and became the first woman to represent any part of Long Island in the House of Representatives. On the night of her election, the Nassau County Republican Party Chairman applauded McCarthy, saying, "Mrs. McCarthy has shown great courage, grit and determination" (Wilson Biographies, 2001). She was sworn in on January 1, 1997, a few days before her 53rd birthday, and has been reelected twice. In May 2000, EMILY's List, the nation's largest funding resource for federal candidates, honored McCarthy for her leadership in Congress on gun-safety issues. EMILY's List President Ellen Malcolm presented an award to McCarthy and said, "It's not easy to be booed on the floor or threatened with political defeat but . . . Carolyn McCarthy chose not to take the easy course" (EMILY's List, 2000).[1]

My mother always said, "You can't go forward until you know where you've been." In that spirit, I have analyzed how my nursing background and other events in my life shaped my journey to Congress. When I was a teenager, I took care of a friend of mine who had been in a car accident. He and I were very close, and it hurt quite a bit to see him in pain, but I realized I could help, and I wanted to do that for the rest of my life. I find it ironic that the biggest challenge I faced as a young adult—losing someone—was the reason I became a nurse. The same event became the reason for my decision to enter politics.

December 7, 1993, is the date when havoc was wreaked in my family's life. Anticipation of the holiday season quickly turned to dread when my husband Dennis was killed and my son Kevin seriously injured as a result of the Long Island Rail Road incident. My family life changed dramatically in a span of mere minutes. Suddenly I was a wife without a husband, had a son without a father, and our extended family was without a brother, uncle, and

nephew. Thankfully—but even more tragically—Dennis and Kevin had recently become closer than ever commuting into the city together on the very train that tore them apart.

After Dennis' death and Kevin's recovery, I became committed to taking action on easy access to guns in our country. I asked my Congressman in Washington, DC, to vote against repealing the ban on assault weapons—but he voted to repeal the ban! I thought he was out of touch with his constituents on Long Island. A reporter caught me shortly after and asked if I was angry enough at my Congressman's vote to run against him. I said, "Sure, I'm Irish and I'm mad enough!" Well, the next day, the papers all said "McCarthy to run against Frisa!" The phone started ringing, people started backing me, and the rest is history.

There are many days I wake up and still can't believe I serve in Congress. Since I've been here, I've used my nursing experience. I've worked to educate the American people—and my colleagues—on gun violence and the costs of gun violence on our health care system. No one talks about those who survive gun violence and struggle for years to regain what they've lost, but I've lived that with my son Kevin and know the struggle all too well.

One of my top priorities in Congress is the protection of all health care workers. I'm happy to report that in 2001 we passed the Needlestick Safety Prevention Act. This Act requires hospitals to use safer needles and find money for safe training. Another very important policy issue is the Whistleblower Protection Act. Nurses shouldn't have to worry about losing their jobs when they report problems and threats to patient safety. The Whistleblower Act protects nurses from threats of firing, discrimination, or demotion.

Nursing is confronting a major workforce crisis. I want to see sweeping legislation passed that would provide scholarships, loan forgiveness, and new ways to attract and keep more people in nursing. After the Michigan school shooting when one 6-year-old killed another, I began looking into ways schools could use federal funding to pay for school nurses. Currently, only 14 states mandate a nurse in every school. I want to change that—there should be a nurse in every school.

---

[1] Introduction by Mary W. Chaffee.

We know that 10 children are killed every day by gun violence. In 1997, 4223 children and adolescents were killed by firearms according to the Centers for Disease Control and Prevention. If we are going to expel students from school for having guns, then we should educate children and parents about the importance of using child safety locks. We should print brochures to send home to parents and guardians, and educate children and adults about child safety locks. Only then will American school children have a fighting chance to learn their school lessons, rather than the lesson that life is too short.

On the grassroots level, nurses must face their legislators and ask them: "What are you doing to help me keep this country healthy?" You have to ask the questions because most politicians today are hoping nobody does. Demand an answer, and if you don't like the answer, tell them what you think and what you want them to do.

I often tell groups that one person can make a difference. However, even more can be done when one person is joined by two and three and four and then thousands. That's when a real difference is made! After 30 years of nursing, I learned to pray for patience and faith. I drew on that strength before I came to Congress. I often think being a member of Congress is not so different than the years I was a working in a hospital. Back then I had a floor of patients to take care of; today, I have 435 patients! Nursing is a practice built on patience and education, and so is service in Congress.

REFERENCES

EMILY's List. (2000). *EMILY's List honors Rep. Carolyn McCarthy and Sen. Dianne Feinstein for their leadership on gun-safety issues.* Available online at www.emilylist.org.

Shapiro, B. (1996, November). Running against the gun: McCarthy on Long Island. *The Nation.*

Wilson biographies plus illustrated. (2001). Available online at www.hwwilson.com.

Vignette   *Pat Ford-Roegner*

Zapping Asthma: Atlanta Leads a National Health and Environmental Initiative

*"As long as you're going to be thinking,
THINK BIG."*

DONALD TRUMP

LAYING THE GROUNDWORK

I served President William Jefferson Clinton and the American people as regional director of the U.S. Department of Health and Human Services (DHHS) from 1993 until 1999. It was both an honor and a privilege. My region was the largest and the poorest of the ten regions established by the DHHS. It spread from North Carolina to Mississippi, up to Kentucky and down to the Florida Keys, and comprised 22% of the HHS budget.

The regional director position, under a very activist presidential administration, was at times both exhilarating and frustrating. The needs were great, but the resources were limited. Competing and complementary presidential initiatives flew like flocks of geese out of the White House. Initiatives soon followed from the Secretary of the DHHS. The challenge for my office was to keep the White House outreach office in touch with the realities of the grassroots efforts while being responsive to good ideas with positive outcomes. Tempered by limits on resources, I found ways to target our efforts with the support of career managers and staff.

I wanted to consolidate the health and human services initiatives for building a healthy community in a few manageable geographic areas of the region. I wanted to offer our combined federal power to support communities in their efforts to redress inequities and create healthy places to live, play, and work. One of the first areas in need was in my own backyard of Atlanta, Georgia.

Two events occurred that helped pave the way for a number of community-based initiatives in the area of Atlanta.

ADDRESSING ENVIRONMENTAL AND HEALTH ISSUES IN ATLANTA

On February 11, 1994, President Clinton issued an executive order on environmental justice. He called upon each federal agency to make this action part of its mission and defined the action to be taken as follows:

Whenever practicable and appropriate, each agency shall collect, maintain and appropriate information on the race, national origin, income level, and other readily accessible and appropriate information for areas surrounding facilities or sites expected to have a substantial environmental, human health or economic effect on the surrounding populations . . . Such information shall be made available to the public, unless prohibited by law. (Clinton, 1994)

The lead agency on this initiative would be the Environmental Protection Agency (EPA), but the DHHS, especially through the Centers for Disease Control and Prevention (CDC), would play a major role.

About the same time, then Vice President Al Gore was asked by the President to head up the Administration's major effort to build sustainable and livable communities in the most economically depressed sections of inner cities and rural areas. Communities were required as part of the initiative to develop a strategic plan through a collaborative process and to compete for a significant influx of federal dollars and business tax incentives. If they met certain criteria and were successful in the competition process, communities would be officially designated as either empowerment zones or enterprise communities. The big prize was the empowerment zone designation, which meant $100 million dollars, in a one-time block grant, to be drawn down over a 10-year period. The federal agencies making the selections were the DHHS, Housing and Urban Development (HUD), and the Department of Agriculture. Regional appointees, like myself, were asked to lead both the environmental justice and the sustainable community initiatives, since we were closest to the people whose lives would be affected.

In 1995, Atlanta was the site of a regional conference on environmental justice issues. The meeting was held at Clark University, a historically black university, and featured faculty and students from the University's new Center on Environmental Issues. Community organizers from around the region were on hand for testimony regarding the disproportionate placement of environmental polluters in poor communities. Federal officials from the CDC, EPA, Justice Department, and other federal agencies listened and learned. It was here that I met key major players in what was to become the Atlanta Zap Asthma Project.

Next I participated in several intensive community-based meetings held at the Carter Center. This collaboration was part of the outreach and inclusion process required for Atlanta's application to HUD and the DHHS to become an empowerment zone. Atlanta's plan included a major health and human services component to coincide with the economic development in the poorest sections of the city. The city that hosted the 1996 Olympics would learn in the months ahead that it was one of the small number of areas selected as empowerment zones, with a $100 million grant from the DHHS. The same health leadership involved with environmental health issues was engaged in these community sessions, working with local residents to identify the health needs of their communities.

COALITION FORMS TO TACKLE CHILDHOOD ASTHMA

Dr. Joyce Essien of the CDC and of the Rollins School of Public Health at Emory University; James Monroe, a community organizer and staff at the CDC's National Center for Environmental Health; Joe Reid, from Mayor Campbell's office; and Valena Henderson, community matriarch and Empowerment Community Board member, were four powerful individuals I met at Clark University. We became allies through our desire to help community members take control of their lives. We were determined that better health outcomes would be part of the legacy of the empowerment zone.

To lend the DHHS Secretary's support to the initiative, I attended a series of community empowerment zone meetings at the CDC with CDC Director Dr. David Satcher and the Mayor of Atlanta, Bill Campbell. At one of these community meetings I met Sharon Williams, RN, BSN, a school nurse who had developed, with very limited resources, a prevention-based high school program to assist students and their families with asthma. Sharon shared her program with community leaders such as the aforementioned Essien, Monroe, and Henderson. The work of these leaders led to the formation of the coalition which created the Atlanta Zap Asthma Project. Zap Asthma, Inc. became a community-based model for coordination and collaboration among public, private, nonprofit, and community sectors to improve the quality of life and health of children in Atlanta's empowerment zone neighborhoods. Sharon was later honored with an award by the Zap Asthma, Inc. Partnership for her work in improving health outcomes for children and adolescents coping with asthma.

Partners in the Zap Asthma, Inc. Coalition

American Association of Health Plans
American Lung Association of Georgia
Atlanta Empowerment Zone Corporation
Blue Cross/Blue Shield of Georgia
Centers for Disease Control
Cigna Health Care of Georgia
Clark Atlanta University Center for Environmental Justice
Community Empowerment Advisory Committee
Department of Health and Human Services Regional Office
Emory University Center for Public Health Practice
Fulton County Health Department
Grady Health Systems
Kaiser Permanente
Office of the Mayor of Atlanta
Southwest Community Hospital
United Health Care of Georgia
Visiting Nurses Association of Atlanta

ZAP ASTHMA, INC.: A PARTNERSHIP THAT WORKS

Each year over 2000 emergency room visits and 300 hospitalizations were reported at Grady's Hughes Spalding Children's Hospital, located in the Atlanta Empowerment Zone (AEZ). The team that designed Zap Asthma included nursing and physician faculty from Emory University's public health programs, Clark University's Environmental Resource Center, physicians and nurses from the local health department, and key staff—primarily nurses—from several managed care organizations. Funding for the initial work came from the CDC and the Foundation of the American Association of Health Plans.

The project's goal was to enroll over 400 children with asthma, ages 5 to 12, who lived in the AEZ. It consisted of a 3-year study to determine if changing known triggers in the home and providing health education would decrease asthma attacks and reduce the cost of treatment and management of the disease. The research model that was developed is called "participatory research," which actively engages residents in design and implementation.

I played a major role in convincing CDC Director Dr. David Satcher and others that the health workers hired to do health education should be residents of the AEZ. At a series of strategy meetings, I presented case histories of previous federal initiatives. I voiced my concern that we not repeat what had too often happened: community organizers would become involved and then lose their employment once a program ended. I didn't want their valuable training and experience to be lost. The 12 community health workers (CHWs) would be employees of the Southwest Hospital, with the potential for continued employment in the health field after the project's end. They would assist families in learning how to change the environmental conditions that trigger asthma attacks though home visits and relationship building. Health workers would receive intensive training in understanding the causes, treatment, and management of asthma; obtain a certification; and be supervised through a contract with the Visiting Nurses Association. Soon these CHWs became the center of the project. They taught healthy lifestyle choices, educated families about how to prevent and manage diseases, and facilitated access to formal and informal health systems and related services.

DHHS REGIONAL DIRECTORS: FAST LEARNERS

Because I was the liaison for the Secretary of the DHHS in the region, I organized a regional directors meeting for a full day of briefings on CDC initiatives. Dr. Essien presented our work on Zap Asthma to the regional directors. Since our meeting was held at CDC headquarters in Atlanta, Dr. Satcher and Dr. Dick Jackson, Director of the CDC's Environmental Center, joined the meeting. The regional directors soon spread the word that here was a practical application of how to address a chronic health issue in the community. The Atlanta Zap Asthma Project was a true partnership that addressed a burgeoning health and environmental justice issue, created meaningful positions for community residents, and helped families access their health care systems.

DHHS SECRETARY GETS THE MESSAGE: ACTION AGAINST ASTHMA IS LAUNCHED

Later that summer, the office of the First Lady, Hillary Clinton, called my office for information on a project they had heard about regarding children and asthma. It seemed a report was being pulled together on this topic for her to review. Because the Deputy Secretary of the DHHS, Kevin Thurm, attended our meeting in Atlanta, he briefed the Secretary of the DHHS, Donna Shalala, on the issue. The regional directors always let their voices be heard. Donna Shalala, hearing about children and asthma from many venues, was quick to focus on the issue.

In Fall of 1997, the DHHS convened a high-level workgroup to assess the most urgent needs and opportunities for tackling the growing problem of asthma. An Interagency Task Force on Environmental Health and Safety Risks to Children, co-chaired by Secretary Shalala and EPA Administrator Carol Browner, decided to take immediate government action to address environmental aspects of childhood asthma. A strategic plan, "Action Against Asthma" was finalized in 1999. The Atlanta Zap Asthma Pro-

ject is highlighted in the report in this way: "The unique features of this project are the prominence of public and private partnerships in implementing this project and the hiring of community residents as community health workers" (Department of Health and Human Services, 1999).

On February 5, 2001, the CDC's National Center for Environmental Health announced grants to 23 other sites to improve the health of inner city children with asthma. These intervention projects support the DHHS strategic plan "Action Asthma" and are based on the model of Zap Asthma. They will assess the effectiveness of asthma programs to reduce asthma especially on minority populations and those living in poverty. (See www.cdc.gov/phtn/asthma for further information.)

OUTCOMES AND LESSONS LEARNED

The Atlanta Zap Asthma Project demonstrates what can happen when a few individuals, sensitive to the needs of various communities, work together with the government and enlightened private partners, to build a healthier community.

One of the greatest challenges of maintaining a project like this is sustaining participation of the CHWs and project leaders once a crisis passes and other issues take precedence in the lives of the participants. It is difficult, for example, to keep families involved in the program monitoring their children when the crisis of an asthma attack is over. Time became a major limitation for follow-up health visits, education programs, and prevention strategies.

Another issue was related to changes in availability of families for home visits. Once mothers became involved in Temporary Assistance to Needy Families work requirements, it was difficult to find a time when parents were home for teaching and follow-up.

Keeping local elected leadership engaged is always a challenge. The CHWs and the leaders of this project have developed a series of innovative strategies to address these issues, from work with local churches to incentives for keeping health visits. Once the program was up and running, these leaders lost interest and so to did the media. It was hard to keep the momentum alive.

A positive outcome of the project was the formation of a larger collaboration with leaders from the Atlanta Zap Asthma Project. The Healthy Atlanta Forum was such a project, created to address the current and future community health needs of the citizens of the larger metro-Atlanta area. Because of the positive work done through Zap Asthma, these leaders were ready to tackle larger and more challenging projects.

Wherever one lives, there are numerous opportunities to improve the health of one's community. Nurses know the unmet health needs; we only need to take the first step to bring community leaders, health professionals, and interested citizens together to create projects like Zap Asthma. I have already started exploring something similar in my new backyard in Silver Spring, Maryland, as a private citizen.

REFERENCES

Clinton, W.J. (1994, February 11). *Federal actions to address environmental justice in minority populations and low-income populations* (executive order EO 12898). The White House.

Department of Health and Human Services. (1999, March 22). *Action Against Asthma: A strategic plan for the Department of Health and Human Services.*

Zap Asthma, Inc. (1997, March 22). Zap Asthma Connections. Atlanta: Zap Asthma, Inc.

Chapter 27 Political Appointments

BETTY R. DICKSON
STEVEN J. WYRSCH
MARY W. CHAFFEE

"Ask not what your country can do for you. Ask what you can do for your country."

JOHN F. KENNEDY

When Lil Peters, ARNP, a psychiatric-mental health nurse, got the call from the Kansas State Nurses Association inviting her to consider an appointment to the state's Hospital Closure Commission, she accepted the challenge because she thought her patients should have a voice through her. Lil Peters was convinced that registered nurses should be involved in developing health policy and accepted the appointment. She said, "I wanted to influence the decisions that were made and to protect patients and their families. Nurses are often hesitant to get involved but, having served, I realize we need to participate in the decision-making process." Shaping policy through a political appointment constitutes a journey that runs through America's smallest towns, increases in scope at the state level, and reaches its pinnacle in federal appointments.

WHY SEEK AN APPOINTMENT?

Although the political firestorm associated with the John Ashcroft and Linda Chavez nominations is not the norm in the screening process, situations such as these beg the question "Why should nurses seek political appointments and expose themselves to such public display?" A member of the House Committee on Veterans Affairs commented about nurses, "Collectively, your voice is very strong. If you don't use your voice, your voice will not be heard." This emphasizes the value of participation in the political process and the enormous implications for nurses. This serves as a reminder of how important it is for nurses to take an active role in defining the national health agenda by entering the political arena.

WHAT MOTIVATES APPOINTEES?

Another consideration for nurses contemplating political appointment is their motivation. What motivates someone to seek a political appointment? Money, power, or personal gain might be a logical answer. However, nurses and politicians both have a simple answer: *to make a difference* (Lieberman, 2001; S.M. Roit, personal communication, March 1, 2001).

A political appointment places the appointee in the public spotlight. In his book *In Praise of Public Life,* Senator Joseph I. Lieberman (D-CT) provides a sound perspective about entering public life for anyone wishing to pursue a political career. He states, "I assume that everything I do in my life— *everything*—could possibly become public and therefore I should not do anything privately that I could not justify publicly" (Lieberman, 2000, p. 51). In today's politically charged environment, it is essential that anyone seeking a politically appointed position examine his or her past closely, applying the "front page rule" to every experience that could draw public attention. The "front page rule" is a critical thinking tool. Ask yourself the question "How would this look on the front page of the *Washington Post* or *New York Times?*" Only this level of honest personal reflection will prevent embarrassing situations.

NOMINEE SCRUTINY

The review and examination of a candidate's past is called the "vetting" process. Political vetting involves the review of financial records, personal records and relationships, tax records, business transactions and ventures, family history, and other personal credentials. Vetting can also involve the process of preparing a candidate for the nomination hearing process. Scrutiny reveals that recent federal nominations are replete with examples of defeats, withdrawals, and controversies caused by the incomplete review and examination of nominees' past experiences. Consider the circumstances surrounding the 2001 confirmation hearings for the nominee for Secretary of Labor, Linda Chavez. Chavez was forced to withdraw her nomination following the revelation that she had paid an illegal immigrant to clean her house. At the state level, scrutiny will be much less intense.

POLITICAL PARTY AFFILIATION

Political party affiliation is essential in securing support for a political appointment. Most appointments are made as rewards for loyal support. The support could be as simple as volunteering in a local or state party office, organizing a fund-raising event for your party, or writing letters. Virginia Trotter Betts identified her political affiliation as key to her appointment as a senior-level political appointee serving the Surgeon General of the United States. She cited a long-standing relationship with the Clinton-Gore administration after the American Nurses Association (ANA) became the first heath care group to endorse the candidates in 1992. She also noted the work done on health care reform through a coalition of nursing organizations as being a major factor in her appointment. Betts was a Robert Woods Johnson fellow in the office of then Senator Al Gore. When he ran for the position of Vice President, she worked on his campaign.

So you've decided that you are interested in a political appointment. How do you get started? Determine where your interests and experience lie. Is there something you wish to change or a service you desire in your community? Is the local school board spending a disproportionate amount of money on administrators' salaries instead of teachers' salaries? Is there no school nurse available to your child? Are nurse practitioners allowed to give physical exams to student athletes? Could your presence on the school board effect change? Is your ultimate goal to seek political office? Will serving in a political or public role enhance future advancement in your career?

IDENTIFY OPPORTUNITIES

How does a nurse determine where the opportunities are? The types of political appointments run the gamut. For instance, a position on the state board of health affords an opportunity to develop policy, whereas an appointment to an election commission is a mechanism for carrying out state law.

Most state nurses associations, specialty organizations, and other professional organizations outside of nursing offer appointment information. The ANA developed the document *Seeking Federal Appointment—A 2001 Guide for Nurses* and an application form to guide the nurse through the process. The ANA has recognized the opportunity to promote the collective voice of the nurses through key political appointments. The ANA provides guidance to nurses in obtaining political appointments as well as support for nurses running for elective office. Their goal is to place 30 nurses either into appointed positions, or on advisory committees or councils each year. To date, the ANA has averaged about eight successful placements every year (S.M. Roit, personal communication, March 1, 2001). State nurses associations (now referred to as *constituent member associations* by the ANA) can offer guidance in exploring appointments at the state level.

Other sources might be nonpartisan organizations such as the League of Women Voters. There may be coalitions, such as National Women's Political Caucus or Women in Government, to appoint specific persons to positions. Political parties may be responsible for some appointments.

Nurses can contribute at many levels, and the appointment doesn't necessarily have to be in health care. Beginning at the community level, nurses could serve on county health boards, task forces on redevelopment, or even a local recreation committee to address policies to prevent children from getting hurt on the playing field. Community and county appointments could include the zoning commission, planning commission, hospital boards, boards of education, councils on aging or economic development—the list is endless, and all these positions affect the quality of life where you live.

INFORMATION SOURCES ON POLITICAL APPOINTMENTS

STATE GOVERNMENT RESOURCES

Contact the offices of individual secretaries of state or check their websites for appointment opportunities at the state level. For example, search online for "California Secretary of State."

FEDERAL GOVERNMENT RESOURCES

The federal government provides many public resources. Visit the U.S. Senate home page for the Government Affairs Committee at www.senate. gov/~gov_affairs/. Under the "Special Reports" link on the home page, there are helpful links to information about the federal appointment process, including a link to the official "Plum Book." Every 4 years, just after the presidential election, Congress publishes *United States Government Policy and Supporting Positions,* more commonly known as the Plum Book. (The Plum Book is so called because of the color of the book.) The Senate Committee on Governmental Affairs and the House Committee on Government Reform alternate the task of review, validation, and publication of this massive document. At the end of the 106th Congress in November 2000, the Plum Book catalogued over 7000 federal civil service positions in the legislative and executive branches of the U.S. government that are potentially available for noncompetitive appointment. The electronic version of the Plum Book is actually located at the Government Printing Office's website at www.gpo.gov/plumbook/2000/ index.html. However, because the congressional committees oversee the publication of the document, the supporting information is located at the committee sites (www.senate.gov/~gov_affairs).

OTHER VALUABLE RESOURCES

There are many political sites and grass roots lobbying sites that can help provide information and assistance in seeking a nomination. Some of the most useful are:

- *The National Women's Political Caucus* (NWPC) (www.nwpc.org). The NWPC is a grassroots membership organization that assists in the identification, recruiting, training, and support of women for elected and appointed office at all levels of the government. The NWPC is also the chair of the Coalition for Women's Appointment, a 60-member organization that assists women who seek presidential and gubernatorial appointments.
- *The National Council of Women's Organizations* (NCWO) (www.womensorganizations.org). The NCWO is an organizing council of over 100 women's organizations representing more than 6 million members. Their goal is to advocate change on many issues of importance to women, including equal employment opportunity, economic equity, media equality, education, job training, women's health, and reproductive health, as well as the specific concerns of mid-life and older women, girls and young women, women of color, business and professional women, homemakers, and retired women.
- *The Women's Appointment Project* (www.appointwomen.com). The Women's Appointment Project is an organized effort by the NWPC, NCWO, and 60 other partner sponsors that seeks to ensure that qualified women are appointed to posts at all levels and in each agency of the new presidential administration. The project has advised every administration on potential women appointees since its inception in 1976. The site provides information on successfully appointed women, information on the partner sponsors, and helpful links to sites that provide additional information.
- *Brookings Institute.* The Brookings Institute provides information for those interested in pursuing a presidential nomination. *The Survivor's Guide for Presidential Nominees,*

BOX **27-1** Finding Opportunities to Serve

Although health and health care services appointments may be attractive to nurses, there are many types of appointments, not directly related to health, where nursing expertise can benefit constituents. These include the following:

Licensure and regulatory boards. State boards of health determine policy regarding the health of the public, including drinking water, restaurant inspections, and health care provider licensure. State boards of nursing regulate the practice of nursing and offer the opportunity to nurses to serve on their governing boards. Some state boards of medicine make decisions regarding the practice of nurse practitioners and may have seats available for a nurse appointee.

Commerce and economic development. Tourism and industrial development appointments could benefit from nursing expertise. A nurse's knowledge of the health care system could provide industries considering relocation with valuable information about what they can expect for their employees' health care. In many states, health care is one of the top three industries.

Conservation. Environmental issues affect the health care of every community. For example, a nurse could provide expertise regarding hazardous waste, the value of clean water systems, or preserving green space.

Corrections. Nurses' expert health care knowledge could play a valuable role in policy decisions regarding the health care and education of incarcerated persons. Nurse practitioners provide much of the health care in many of today's correctional facilities, public and private.

Education. Nurses could offer valuable insight on policy decisions regarding school-based health care services and health curriculum. A nurse's knowledge of budgeting and cost-effective management could assist in the budget process.

Higher education. Policy decisions are made by state agencies and boards that have authority over colleges and universities.

Health and human services. A wide variety of appointments exist at the local, state, and federal levels.

Public safety. Nurses can bring important perspectives to agencies and boards involved in public safety related to domestic violence, gun laws, and motor vehicle safety.

Transportation. Nurses have seen firsthand the effect of motor vehicle accidents and can be valuable partners in improving safety through political appointments on transportation and highway safety organizations.

published as a component of the Presidential Appointee Initiative, provides a comprehensive summary and guide for anyone who has been asked to serve in an appointed position (available online at www.appointee.brookings. org/survivorsguide.htm) (Box 27-1).

MAKING A DECISION

Seeking a political appointment, at any level, is not a decision to be taken lightly. Consider some of the following questions to gain perspective on whether this path is right for you. Some questions will be more important if you are considering a full-time federal assignment rather than a part-time community role.

- Can you take time away from your job or your family to meet the demands of the position?
- How often will meetings be held? What will your time obligation be? Is this a full-time position or a group that meets occasionally?

- Will your employer support you? Will you have family support?
- Will your employer provide the time for you to serve, or will you be required to take vacation time?
- Why do you want to serve in this position? Can you articulate why you are qualified?
- What are the strengths and weaknesses you would bring to the position?
- What is your connection to your community? Do you know your neighbors? Have you served in volunteer organizations? Having a solid base of support from your neighbors, your friends, and your fellow volunteers in local organizations will enhance your chances of success.
- Where do you fit in the political spectrum? Are you registered to vote as a Democrat, Republican, or Independent? Party affiliation provides important linkages to support from individuals and groups.

- How will your education, background, and experience serve you in the desired appointment? Candidates should be able to identify aspects of each that will qualify them for the position.
- How are your health and your family's financial situation? Careful analysis should be given to each.
- Who makes the appointment? Is it the governor, the lieutenant governor, Speaker of the House of Representatives?
- Are there educational or geographic requirements? In Mississippi the nurse practice act requires a baccalaureate degree as the basic qualification for one board of nursing position and an associate degree as the basic qualification for another. One position is designated for an advanced practice nurse, and another for a nurse educator. Some appointments require certain credentials (e.g., being a physician or a nurse).
- Which stakeholders care about who gets this position? Do you have influence with them? Are there other nominees under consideration?
- Is there is a match between your qualifications and the requirements of the position? Carefully review local, state, or federal laws applicable to the appointment.
- Do you have a chance of getting the position? What connections do you have with individuals and organizations that will make the decision?

PLAN YOUR STRATEGY

GETTING NOMINATED

When you've identified the appointment you are interested in, the next step is getting nominated. Determine the process used for nomination and identify who will make the appointment. Having the support of more than one organization strengthens your chance for nomination.

MAKE IT EASY FOR PEOPLE TO HELP YOU

Dr. Mary Wakefield, Director of the Center for Health Policy and Ethics at George Mason University, has served as a chief of staff to a U.S. Senator and has been appointed to several federal health care commissions. She states, "Expertise alone might get you a position, but frequently it won't." She emphasizes the need to have the support of nursing organizations and influential individuals that can advocate for you. Wakefield says that to successfully obtain an appointment you must have a two-pronged approach: You need to have the expertise required by the position and a network of relationships built over time with policymakers. Wakefield highlights the importance of making it easy for people to help you. She recommends that nurses not just ask someone to write a letter of support, but that the potential nominee write the letter and provide it to the person providing the recommendation or that person's staff. If you desire, a phone call be made on your behalf. Provide the person making the call with a brief memo about your qualifications and why you would make a great candidate (2000, p. 55).

THE POWER OF NETWORKS

Patricia Montoya, another federal political appointee, echoes many of Wakefield's comments. Montoya served as a political appointee in the U.S. Department of Health and Human Services from 1998 to 2000. Following Senate confirmation, she was appointed as commissioner to the Administration on Children, Youth and Families by President Clinton. Montoya reports that she was appointed to her position because she had both the expertise and a well-developed political network. Several influential individuals who were familiar with her qualifications advanced her name as a nominee. Montoya says that she has always mixed practice and politics in her career, and she credits her activities in the ANA for advancing her political education (Thompson, 2000).

CONFIRMATION OR INTERVIEW

Depending on the position you aspire to, you may need to participate in confirmation hearings or interviews. It is vital to be familiar with the position and the organizational hierarchy in which it falls as well as current issues facing the agency.

When preparing for either a hearing or interview, consider the following questions:
- What do I need to bring?
- Who will be conducting the hearing or interview?

- What questions will I be asked?
- Will I have the opportunity to ask questions?
- Should I have representation or sponsorship at the confirmation hearing?

AFTER THE APPOINTMENT

RELATIONSHIPS WITH YOUR SUPPORTERS

Congratulations! You've passed the background checks, survived interviews, and have been appointed to a challenging position! There is nothing more important than thanking all those who supported your appointment. Send letters of appreciation to recognize the efforts of others in helping you attain your appointment.

Once you are appointed, consider whom it is your duty to serve. If yours is a public appointment, your allegiance must be to your constituents. If it is to a health care organization's board of directors, your responsibility is to the patients and community. It is important that you retain your autonomy if the appointment is of a regulatory nature. If an association or other group was instrumental in your nomination and subsequent appointment, maintain open communication to keep them informed and to listen to their concerns. If your assignment is to represent a specific group on a task force where input from the organization was requested as a part of the appointment, close communication is necessary to convey the viewpoints of those you represent.

EXPERIENCES OF NURSE APPOINTEES

FEDERAL APPOINTEE: PATRICIA FORD-ROEGNER, U.S. DEPARTMENT OF HEALTH AND HUMAN SERVICES REGIONAL DIRECTOR

Patricia Ford-Roegner was appointed as regional director in the U.S. Department of Health and Human Services (DHHS) by President Clinton in 1994. Because the position was a senior executive, noncareer appointment, Ford-Roegner had launched an intense lobbying effort to obtain the nomination. Her activities in the Democratic Party, her volunteer efforts on the Health Professionals Review Group, and her outstanding reputation as a clinician and entrepreneur allowed her to develop a strong network of supporters who assisted her in securing the nomination. She served in the post until 1999.

Upon her appointment, she faced immediate challenges. Although the budget for the region comprised nearly 22% of the total DHHS budget and covered eight states and nearly 50 million people, the region had not taken any significant steps to improve or coordinate health care. Also, because her appointment occurred with the transition from a Republican to a Democratic White House, she was afforded virtually no turnover or orientation.

At first, it appeared to be a job of enormous proportion and insurmountable complexity. However, Ford-Roegner considered her appointment an excellent opportunity to develop, implement, and sustain outreach and social programs. By creating public and private partnerships throughout the region, she was able to organize collaborative efforts leading to the development of prevention and treatment programs for asthma, teen pregnancy, women's health, and children's health. Her efforts led to the first regional public dialogue on women's health and senior care-giver issues in the nation. During her tenure, the Southeast region became the first in the country to implement a Medicare Beneficiaries Advisory Committee and a multiagency coalition to prevent Medicare fraud (P.A. Ford-Roegner, personal communication, March 9, 2001). Ms. Ford-Roegner had a significant impact on the health care system in the southeastern United States—nearly all of the programs she initiated remain in place today.

STATE APPOINTEE: BARBARA NICHOLS, WISCONSIN SECRETARY OF REGULATION AND LICENSING

Barbara Nichols served as the President of the ANA from 1978 to 1982. Because of her visibility in ANA and her work as a loyal supporter of the Democratic Party, her name appeared on several lists of potential candidates for political appointments in the state of Wisconsin. When the call came from Wisconsin's governor asking if she was interested in a state political appointment, Ms. Nichols was skeptical but intrigued. She believes she was a "politically attractive" candidate for the nomination due to her reputation within the nursing community, her loyal support to the political party of the governor, and her work with minority groups. Although she was not in the governor's "inner circle" of possible political appointees, she would embody several "firsts" if nominated: the first woman, the first African American, the first health care professional, and the first nurse. This increased her attractiveness from a political perspective. By selecting Nichols, it would appear that the governor was expanding his cabinet with cultural, gender, and professional diversity as operative goals.

To prepare for a successful interview with the governor, Nichols knew she must be fully primed to discuss nursing and health issues with policy implications in the state. She prepared by talking with numerous state officials such as the district attorney, political party representatives, members of the governor's staff, and other "political insiders." She met with the American Medical Association to gain their support. The position she was to be nominated for carried the state's authority for licensing and regulation of physicians, nurses, 17 professional boards, and 57 other professions. She went into the interview confident that she could address almost any of the issues that could affect health care regulation and licensing in Wisconsin. Interestingly, there were no substantial clinical, nursing, or even health care issues brought up during the interview with the governor. About 10 days after the interview, Nichols was offered the appointment.

Because the Secretary of Regulation and Licensing required state senate confirmation, Ms. Nichols needed additional preparation for the nomination hearings. As the date approached, she employed the same strategy she used to prepare for the interview with the governor. She called local and state officials, contacted health care organizations to keep abreast of current issues, researched the questions posed to former nominees for the post, and worked with the political party to be informed of political trends. As the final measure, the Wisconsin Nurses Association sponsored a reception in her honor. She was confirmed.

Once appointed, Nichols seized the opportunity to create a level of trust within the state government that surprised even the governor. She built a reputation for honesty and sincerity in dealing with the intricacies of licensing, regulation, and policy development. Because of her excellent interpersonal skills and ability to articulate the issues, Nichols was able to create new standards for the health disciplines licensed in the state, implement regulatory standards for child boxing, and permanently put an end to the controversial "Toughman" competition in the state. She made significant strides to increase communication throughout the state on matters of licensing, regulation, and reform by publishing newsletters, distributing information to the state legislature, and reaching out to build a strong trust throughout the executive and legislative branches of the Wisconsin government (B.L. Nichols, personal communication, March 16, 2001).

COMMISSION APPOINTEE: KAYE BENDER, INSTITUTE OF MEDICINE COMMISSION MEMBER

Another nurse who was ready to serve was Kaye Bender, RN, PhD, FAAN, deputy state health officer, Mississippi State Department of Health. When the committee Assuring the Health of the Public in the 21st Century was convened by the Institute of Medicine (IOM), the American nursing community saw there was no nurse appointed to the committee. Nursing represents the single largest workforce in public health. ANA sent Dr. Rita Gallagher to the first IOM committee meeting to formally inquire as to why a nurse had not been selected to the committee. The IOM was apologetic about the oversight and gave the ANA a few days to submit nominees' names and credentials. Because Bender had received the Pearl McIver Public Health Nurse award from the ANA the previous summer, her name was placed into consideration. The nursing community mobilized to support Bender's appointment, and she was selected to serve.

Bender credits her active participation in public health nursing organizations and work with the ANA and her state nurses association. Her selection for the McIver award and 24 years experience in public health helped considerably in her attaining this appointment. Bender says the quick mobilization by the nursing community was key to this appointment.

CONCLUSION

When Catherine Dodd, a nurse from California, was interviewed by former Secretary of the DHHS Donna Shalala for an appointment as a regional director, Shalala commented that she had appointed three nurses to federal positions. Shalala's respect for nurses was clear in her appraisal, according to Dodd. Shalala stated, "Nurses understand health care issues, they can talk to anybody and they come prepared to work—they can hit the ground running."

Entering public life is a noble endeavor that every nurse who wishes "to make a difference" should seriously consider. Senator Lieberman provides the best insight into this motivation: "American democracy and self-government are endangered today by the American people's retreat from their government and politics. Our country's future requires that they reengage—at least to vote, at best to serve" (Lieberman, 2001, p. 161).

REFERENCES

Lieberman, Joseph I. (2000). *In praise of public life.* New York: Simon & Schuster.

Thompson, L. (2000). In the health policy spotlight: An interview with Commissioner Patricia Montoya. *Policy, Politics & Nursing Practice 1*(3), 189-193.

Resources

American Nurses Association. (2001). *Seeking federal appointment: A guide for nurses.* Washington, DC: American Nurses Publishing.

Chaffee, M.W. (2000). In the health policy spotlight: An interview with Dr. Mary Wakefield. *Policy, Politics & Nursing Practice, 1*(1), 53-59.

Coalition for Women's Appointments. (2001). *A project convened by the National Women's Political Caucus.* Washington, DC: Author.

National Women's Political Caucus. (1997). *A guide to running a winning campaign.* Washington, DC: Author.

A survivor's guide to presidential appointees. (2000, November). Washington, DC: Brookings Institution. Available online at www.appointee. brookings.org/survivorsguide.htm.

United States government policy and supporting positions. (2000, November 8). Washington, DC: Committee on Governmental Affairs, United States Senate. Available online at www.senate. gov/~gov_affairs/issues.htm.

Chapter 28

Lobbying Policymakers: Individual and Collective Strategies

MELINDA MERCER RAY

SHELAGH ROBERTS

"The greater the obstacle, the more glory in overcoming it."

MOLIÈRE

What does the word *lobbying* mean to you? To some, it suggests a mysterious world where inside-the-beltway power brokers are paid mighty retainers to arrange secret deals with members of Congress behind closed doors. The word has the effect of intimidating many people, who assume that lobbyists wield power and influence that regular citizens don't enjoy. Actually, the way the term came into usage was very simple and practical.

The word *lobbyist* comes from the early days of the United States government when constituents with interests in legislation or policy would wait outside the doors of the House or Senate chambers—in the lobby—to approach their legislators as they entered or exited. The idea of a citizen government may seem far removed from today's hectic political environment, where politicians enjoy star status; certainly, members of Congress are better flanked and protected from the citizenry than they used to be. Still, with the right combination of dedication, strategy, and persistence, the U.S. electorate can experience a high degree of access to and accountability from its elected officials—and you don't have to be a professional lobbyist to make a difference.

The number of professional lobbyists has increased over the last hundred years as the financing and power of the states has shifted to the federal government. Since 1920, we have seen the development of special interest groups and the relocation of many national headquarters to Washington, DC—power central. If an association does not have its headquarters in Washington, DC, it will often establish a satellite office there. Professional lobbyists must file with the Federal Election Commission (FEC) and comply with the regulations and guidelines set forth by the FEC in pursuing their lobbying efforts. What hasn't changed is that regular people—people like you—have the most important power: the power of the constituent. And you have even more power on your side: the power of the nurse.

Nearly everyone knows a nurse. Nurses are recognized as the most trusted group of professionals, ranking number one for trustworthiness in the Gallup Organization's most recent poll on honesty and ethics in professions (2000). Nursing is 2.7 million individuals strong, comprising the largest group of health care professionals in the United States. The combination of reputation and presence is important to legislators. Think of the number of times people have said to you, "I could never do what you do." It is this profound respect that will assist you with your lobbying efforts.

Have you ever written a letter to a local, state, or federal legislator to express your opinion on a current issue? Have you ever come face to face with an elected official and asked why funding is being cut for a program you support? Have you ever presented administrators in your workplace information or resources to support or oppose a certain internal policy? If you answered yes to any of these questions, congratulations, you are already a lobbyist!

This chapter contains information to help you develop specific strategies to make the most of your expert knowledge and to communicate with legislators in ways most likely to bring success.

WHY LOBBY?

The most common reason people get involved with lobbying is because they see something that needs to be fixed. As a nurse, you may see circumstances on a daily basis in your practice that inspire passionate feelings about the way things should be. Perhaps you see sick patients struggling with insurance companies to get approval for medically necessary procedures. Maybe this has made you an advocate for a strong patients' bill of rights. Once you start focusing on an issue that has sparked your interest, you may notice newspaper articles and television news coverage that deals with the issue. You may find legislation related to the issue being debated in your state legislature.

Maybe a particular news report will grab your attention and make you think about policy in a new way. You may be looking through your local newspaper and come upon a story that profiles a local student who is desperately looking for a bone marrow donor. A story like this can touch you in a way that causes you to ask yourself, "What can I do to help? Why are the obstacles to recruiting people to become bone marrow donors? Could the government offer incentives to encourage more donations?" It is often the search for solutions to a specific problem that spurs the citizen or nurse lobbyist.

Unless you represent your professional association as a so-called hired gun or you serve as an appointed or elected representative in local or state politics, you will take on the task of lobbying most likely for the sake of your personal and professional convictions. You will become a lobbyist because you feel strongly that certain policies should be en-

acted, and your motivation will be strong enough to translate your concern into action.

ARM YOURSELF WITH KNOWLEDGE

The first step in the lobbying process is to find out as much as you can about your area of interest or the issue that concerns you. Aside from paying attention to what you see in your workplace, in the newspaper, or on television, you should become a kind of detective, trying to discover the legislative history, dynamics of power, and policy particulars of bills related to your issue of interest. Your job is to learn as much as you can about the issue so that you can decide what your best lobbying approach will be.

Many professional nursing or other health care associations and think tanks regularly post position statements on controversial issues on their websites. The American Nurses Association (ANA) and the Association of Women's Health, Obstetric and Neonatal Nurses (AWHONN) are two examples. Many such websites have legislative affairs sections that display sample letters or issue briefs to help you frame your arguments in favor of or in opposition to a particular bill.

If you are a member of a professional organization, you may want to contact someone in the federal government affairs department who has expertise on the issue and might be able to provide you with related issue briefs, reference articles, government reports, or testimony. Additionally, as a result of such communication you may get support from your association and your employer to coordinate your lobbying efforts with an overall strategy or lobbying plan at the federal level.

Now that most government agencies and legislative branches make detailed documents, including bill texts and summaries, federal agency reports and studies, and countless sources of federal data available online, the Internet is a great place to search for information. The Library of Congress's website, www.thomas.loc.gov, offers complete listings of bills that can be searched by subject, key word, co-sponsor, date of introduction, and bill title or number. In addition, every state has its own web page with detailed information regarding elected officials and legislative activity. While the states' websites vary in the degree of detail they provide, almost every state website includes the names of and contact information for state senators and representatives, as well as a search function to identify your legislator according to zip code or city name. These searches will identify bills that allow you to review proposed legislation on your issue of interest in great detail and can help you gain thorough knowledge of the legislative histories behind a given subject. Obtain a copy of past voting charts and a list of bills introduced or co-sponsored by a legislator. Knowing the legislative history of an issue is vital if you are to make suggestions consistent with possible legislative remedies, to identify allies who support your issue, and to present yourself as a credible representative on the issue.

Such a search can also help you identify members of Congress or state legislatures who have been leaders on the particular issue. For example, if you search a legislative site using the key word *breastfeeding,* you can identify several legislators with a long history of introducing or co-sponsoring breastfeeding legislation. When approaching the legislator for support, you will be able to build on his or her previous initiatives or pending legislation to craft a workable legislative strategy.

Once you identify the issue that you want to lobby on, and you have educated yourself as to its legislative history and the current status of bills related to it, the next step is to determine: (1) whom you need to contact to bring about change and (2) the best mode of communication to accomplish that change.

WHO TO LOBBY

At the federal level, your primary contacts are the Congressional staff people who work with other offices and outside interest groups to create and iron out detailed provisions in legislation. Your first step in building relationships at the federal level is to identify the person in a legislator's office who is responsible for your issue; for many nursing issues, this will be the staff liaison who works on health care policy. Sometimes, though, responsibility for health care issues can be divided among several staff people, particularly if the member of Congress serves on a committee that has jurisdiction over such issues; therefore, it is best to obtain specific information about who covers your particular issue of interest, not just who covers health care issues. Usually, the easiest way to identify the correct person on your issue is to telephone the member's Capitol Hill office and simply ask the person who answers the phone for the name of the individual who handles that issue Once you have identified the proper staff member, you should address all correspondence or requests for meetings to that person.

Capitol Hill is known for high turnover rates; the average staff member has been serving in his or her current position for less than 2 years, is in his or her 20s, and has some type of liberal arts degree. The high turnover of the staff means that you should always double-check that the contact information you have is current, particularly if you are relying on a published directory. Because many Hill staffers are relatively young, they are often open to relying on experts in the field to help them understand the background of certain legislative issues. For example, the impending nursing shortage is gaining a great deal of attention, especially with the most recent release of Health Resources and Services Administration (HRSA) data quantifying the decrease in the number of nurses graduating from entry-into-practice programs and revealing that the average age of nurses continues to increase. A staff member would need input from experts who actually work in nursing in order to get a firm grasp on what might account for the decline in interest in nursing as a profession. Only a registered nurse would have the credibility to paint an accurate picture that would capture some of the problems, such as mandatory overtime requirements or harried work environments. Even though many of the staff are well read and quick studies, they still rely on the firsthand professionals to help demonstrate why certain policies or practices are working or why they need to be changed.

At the federal level, there are two types of staff: those in the members' personal offices and those who work at the committee level. Some members of Congress are leaders on an issue because they have a personal or constituent-related connection to it, whereas others serve on committees that have jurisdiction over significant health care matters, such as the committees that oversee federal health programs or appropriations. Although there are also regional offices for both representatives and senators in the members' home states, these offices generally handle constituent services rather than policy-making responsibilities, and they are not usually the place to turn to for policy issues except for those related to a specific constituent.

Opportunities to build personal relationships are often more common at the local and state levels than at the federal level, for the simple reason that there are more occasions for networking and building informal personal relationships with policymakers. In your own town, you can invite an official to meetings of your professional organization or provide him or her an invitation to address the group at a meeting or luncheon. You can also frequent local and state meetings or committee hearings on issues of interest to you, volunteer to serve on a task force in your community, take part in a political campaign, or run for office yourself. Through the informal exchanges with legislators and policymakers these activities provide, you can build the foundations for lasting relationships.

Staff members also enjoy tremendous responsibility and influence at the state and local levels. As at the federal level, it is important to identify the appropriate staff contact at the state level and to work with that individual to exert some influence on developing legislation. Staff reliance on outside experts' information, research, and experience remains significant at the state level, with a few added benefits for you as a constituent. The chances are higher at the state or local level that a staffer or legislator will have some direct knowledge either of your place of work or of the specific issues you face in your town or city. Officials and staff at the state or local level will also likely be more concerned with more provincial issues or issues that are particular to your geographic location than federal officials, simply because they have a smaller jurisdiction and constituency to serve. At both state and federal levels, it is very important to recognize the critical role that the staffer plays in crafting legislation and helping to determine legislative priorities for the member of Congress he or she works for. You should always treat a personal office or committee staff representative with the same respect you reserve for the legislator. With the broad range of issues that members of Congress must address, they frequently rely on staff to brief them on issues that are assigned to them, and they also look to staff to craft legislation and make recommendations about what issues to champion. It is unrealistic to expect a meeting with a member of Congress in most circumstances. Although it may be more feasible to meet with a local or state representative, it takes careful planning and advanced notice to arrange meetings with all elected officials because of the demands on their time. Exceptions to the rule are if you have a personal relationship or connection with the member, although you should be careful not to exaggerate the relationship in order to get a meeting, or if you are part of a coalition or group that has broad appeal to the member.

Kealy, Kendig, Ray, Nolan, Percy-McDaniel, and Roberts (2000) encapsulate the simple power of the nurse in legislative affairs:

Nurses who have something to say about an issue, a bill or a problem that requires legislative action have several ways to voice their concerns. The methods are tried and true: writing a letter, telephoning or meeting your legislator, testifying before committees and sending personalized or legislative action e-mails are some of the ways to express your viewpoint. Even nurses with little time can write letters or make phone calls to elected officials. A few simple sentences are all that are needed to begin, and such steps can create a big impact. The legislative process is open to everyone. (p. 7)

COMMUNICATING WITH POLICYMAKERS AND STAFF

COMMUNICATING BY PHONE

Some pitfalls of communicating by phone are that there is no written record of a phone call, and you have no visual proof that you actually made the call. Additionally, when you communicate with staff via telephone, you have no way of guaranteeing that either your message or your personal information, such as your name, telephone number, or address, is recorded correctly. And even if they are recorded correctly, you have no assurance that they will be forwarded to the correct person. A telephone call may be worthwhile simply to express your support for or opposition to a legislative issue that is currently on the floor of the House or Senate for debate and will be coming up for a vote. For instance, if debate is occurring on a specific patients' bill of rights, you may want to take the time to call the office and register your wish that the member of Congress vote for the bill. Most congressional offices do keep a running tally of yes or no votes from constituents who call the office during a contentious debate. Telephone calls can also be a good means of obtaining brief information or following up with someone with whom you have already established a relationship.

In general, telephone calls are not ideal for introducing yourself to a legislative assistant. Most people find it annoying to hear a stranger start in on a diatribe about who they are, what their issue is, and what needs to be done, constituent or not. In general, it is better to write a letter or make a personal introduction at an appropriate forum, such as a legislative briefing, to make the initial point of contact. After a letter has been received, it is perfectly acceptable to call the legislative assistant to whom you have written in order to confirm that the letter was received or to ask if he or she would like any further information. Telephone calls are, of course, expected if you are actively working with a legislative assistant or other staff member on a particular piece of legislation or you have an ongoing relationship with that person. Placing numerous telephone calls to someone with whom you have no established relationship, however, can identify you as a nuisance. With written communication or e-mail, the person can respond according to his or her own timetable, whereas a phone call is sometimes an unwelcome interruption.

WRITING A LETTER

Most, if not all, members of Congress consider constituent mail services as absolutely essential elements in their constituents' perceptions of them. Members of Congress have been known to say that their constituents place a far greater value on their personal responses and experiences with their congressional offices than on familiarity with their voting records when it comes time for reelection. The two-way communication between legislator and constituent relies on the correct "mix of elected officials motivated to respond and capable citizens motivated to make demands, with an active two-way communications network between the two" (Frantzich, 1986, p. 116).

Public opinion polls throughout the 1990s consistently reveal that people rate their own local or statewide representatives' job performance higher than they do Congress's job performance as a whole. This disparity can, to some degree, be accounted for by an individual's personal experience with a legislator's office; most commonly by mail. Some members of Congress have been known to emphasize constituent mail with an ever-watchful eye toward reelection, crediting their success to an excellent constituent services record (Frantzich, 1986).

When you write a letter to a member of Congress or a state or local official, there are some general guidelines to follow. First, target your letter according to the legislator's responsibility. Do not write a letter regarding problems with your state's practice act to a federal legislator, who has no authority on that issue. At the federal level, you are most likely to have an impact and have your correspondence taken seriously if you deal with the member of Congress who represents the geographic area in which you live. If you have developed a national reputation as an expert, however, or you can demonstrate another reason your expertise is more far-reaching, you may successfully meet with other national legislators from different states who are working on the same issue. Keep in mind that personal letters convey far more sincerity and carry more weight than form letters, telegrams, or phone calls. When possible, you should time your letter to give the staff or member plenty of time to address and work with you on the issue before any pressing legislation goes to the floor. Last-minute attempts to influence policy are rarely successful, and when they are it is usually because a trusted colleague or expert, not a first-time constituent, has convinced the member to listen to his or her concerns (Frantzich, 1986).

In crafting the message of your letter, be sure and identify yourself as a nurse, particularly if the legislation has anything to do with health care. Identifying yourself as a nurse means identifying yourself as an expert. Include information about how proposed legislation would influence your personal experiences, or provide personal anecdotes that demonstrate your firsthand knowledge of and experience with a certain issue. Your letter should include a specific request from the representative or senator about an action that you request him or her to take. Where appropriate, include relevant committee or hearing information and bill numbers in your correspondence, in discussing federal and state legislation. Vague or general requests are not particularly useful to your member of Congress and usually result in a "so what?" response when the staff is finished reading the letter. Finally, keep your letter relatively brief (no more than two pages) and to the point. Include hospital or other practice setting information as well as professional credentials, and make sure to include a return address, telephone number, and e-mail address if appropriate.

PERSONAL VISITS

Face-to-face lobbying is generally perceived by both staff and members of Congress as the most effective lobbying strategy. If you have arranged a personal visit with a legislative assistant or other staff member, or with a member of Congress or state or local official, you can apply many of the same guidelines for crafting your message that you would employ in letter writing on the issue. Other useful strategies include knowing the current status of legislation; keeping the visit brief, as time is usually short; keeping your points succinct and germane to the topic; illustrating your expertise or concern with personal, firsthand examples; and identifying your practice setting, particularly if you think the person you are meeting with is familiar with it. Finally, don't forget to ask for a specific action or request to close the meeting—for example, "We hope we can count on you to vote against Amendment XXIII on Wednesday."

Other helpful strategies include providing a one- or two-page fact sheet, or *leave-behind,* that illustrates your examples in a different way. For exam-

ple, if you are demonstrating the need for increased funding for nursing scholarships, you could provide a graphic representation—a chart or table—that illustrates the low rate of increase for nursing scholarships since they were initiated, particularly compared with grants or scholarships for other medical professions. Any resource that provides data or illustrates points in the form of easily digestible tidbits, or *talking points,* can be a useful resource to the staff member when he or she is briefing the senator, writing speeches, or drafting a press release. For a personal meeting, you should always bring several copies of your business card, as it may turn out that other people will be invited to sit in.

If the person you are scheduled to meet with is unavailable for some reason, it is best to politely and enthusiastically accept an offer to meet with another staff member, even if the person is in a lower position of authority. You should then follow up with the person you met with as well as with the person you were originally scheduled to meet with.

In general, always follow up a personal meeting with a note thanking the person for his or her time, and if you indicated that you would provide additional information or find an answer to a question, by all means do so in a timely manner.

E-MAIL CORRESPONDENCE

E-mail correspondence has become, for many members of Congress and their staffs, the preferred mode of communication. E-mail correspondence has many advantages:

- *Directness.* The information is sent directly to the person you identify.
- *Timeliness.* Correspondence is immediate, in most cases.
- *Flexibility.* Legislative aides can open e-mail in their own time frame, unlike phone calls, which are often interruptions.
- *Attachments.* Important articles, reports, or other information that support your ideas can be attached with e-mail. (Note that if you do not have an established relationship with the person you are e-mailing, he or she will most likely not open attachments for fear of computer viruses).

When sending e-mail, always remember to include your name, address, phone number, and e-mail address so that your correspondence can be responded to or you can be contacted for further information. Observe the usual rules for written correspondence, as well as issue tips listed in the previous section on letter writing.

E-mail is also a valuable tool if you are actively working with other organizations or with congressional staff on documents that need to be shared, such as when you are drafting legislation.

There are a few disadvantages of e-mail to keep in mind. Just as with telephone calls, people may get literally hundreds of e-mails each week, so you may want to follow up e-mail with a telephone call. You can also use an e-mail as a follow-up device to confirm that someone received your letter. Another, more intangible disadvantage is that e-mail is now sometimes seen as impersonal as well; there is neither a voice nor a handwritten signature attached with it. E-mail is probably most useful as a lobbying tool when it is used in conjunction with other lobbying strategies.

THE INTERNET'S ROLE IN LOBBYING

We have heard that the Internet will replace the television and telephone, just as e-mail has already replaced traditional letter writing, and will also be the only lobbying tool that will make it into the year 2000. Well, the year 2000 has come and gone, and though the Internet has undeniably revolutionized both the content and delivery information, the Internet and its partner, e-mail, have come out of the 1990s as equal and complementary partners to more traditional modes of communication.

In terms of revolutionizing politics and lobbying, the most influential change has been an increase in the quantity and depth of information related to legislative affairs that is now accessible to all Americans, instantaneously. The Freedom of Information Act, coupled with the instant access of information from the Internet, has allowed Americans to view in great detail full bill texts, voting records, texts of committee hearings, government agency reports and recommendations, and campaign contributions as reported to the FEC. Many predicted that public interest groups such as trade associations, membership organizations, and other traditional centers for like-minded people to come

together would be replaced by countless individuals who could find out everything and communicate to Congress instantaneously—during a speech on the floor of the House or Senate—and assume control of lobbying at the grassroots level. After all, the Internet provides a low-cost mode of communication that could be a great equalizer and enable individuals to compete with organized groups in ways they couldn't have imagined in the past.

What has happened, though, is that the large, traditional interest groups that have helped shape and generate grassroots interest in the past have utilized the Internet to expand membership, increase their public presence, and utilize their websites to provide enhanced information and value-added services for their members. They are using their websites to communicate with their respective constituencies and are "adapting their communication strategies to the presence of the Internet, rather than being left behind" (Davis, 1999, pp. 63-64). In addition to being the great equalizer, the Internet allows the opportunity for traditional groups to communicate with an interested general public as well as with its membership. Organizations fill their websites with information that highlights their accomplishments and instructions on how to become a member. They post position and policy statements, overall mission and goals of the organization, news releases, resource or publication information, and details about meetings or conventions (Davis, 1999).

With the development of e-mail lists from websites, many organizations now have the capability to generate an immediate call to action for groups who share a common interest. Many organizations, associations, and interest groups keep legislative alert lists in house so they will have a list of parties who are interested in legislative affairs at their fingertips, but, just as with letter writing, it is important to personalize your e-mail. Some staff and members of Congress have indicated that group or "spam" e-mails have acquired the same status as other bulk postal mailings. One congressional staffer commented that, "The e-mail address for the Congressman has to be one of the biggest wastes of taxpayers' dollars—the whole thing is a real headache for staff and of no value to the actual constituents" (Davis, 1999, p. 81). Simply signing onto a host website, selecting a draft letter provided, and filling in your name will not have a significant effect; letters should be personalized whenever possible.

At the end of the first presidential debate with Bill Clinton, Republican candidate Bob Dole was the first presidential candidate to announce his World Wide Web homepage. Many people forecast the Internet as the future of all communication, as well as political campaigning, but the drawback is that people must be interested enough to *choose* to visit a website and find out more (Davis, 1999). With the Internet, you are really attracting only the motivated constituent anyway, rather than reaching the sought-after demographic not already engaged in political issues.

TESTIMONY

Providing testimony for a political hearing is a prominent and common method used to go on record on an issue on behalf of an organization or as a constituent. As an individual or on behalf of an association, you may request to testify on a particular issue, or you may receive a call from a legislative office requesting that you testify. Testimony is accepted in two forms for most committees: as oral remarks (those who are asked to testify) and written testimony. Written testimony can be provided to the committee by the witness as a supplement to the oral remarks, or it can be provided by any association or individual choosing to submit it for the record. This testimony, including the transcript of the hearing, will eventually be compiled and published as a permanent record of the hearing.

Being asked to testify as a witness by far more exciting, providing the highest degree of visibility and often the greatest amount of personal satisfaction. You should be as prepared as possible if you find yourself in this situation. There are some things to keep in mind that will help make the experience positive for you:

Know the Rules. All committees and their subcommittees have a format they use to conduct the hearing; formats differ not only from state to federal committees, but from one committee to the next. These rules cover the conduct of the hearing, the order of witnesses, the time provided for each witness

to provide his or her remarks, and the manner in which the questions and answers are provided. If you are not familiar with these details, ask the association representative who invited you to be a witness on behalf of the association, or the committee staff member what these details are. It is a rare occasion when a House or Senate committee pays the travel expenses of a witness, so you should budget for these expenses when determining whether you can participate in the hearing. If you are asked to testify and you agree, it is assumed that you will shoulder these costs. In the case of an association inviting an individual to testify on its behalf, the association frequently will pay for all expenses and provide substantive and logistic support for the testimony.

Generally, there is a time limit placed on the length of an individual's remarks. As a guideline, the time limit usually falls between 3 and 10 minutes. You will use this time to present your position on the legislation or issue in an interesting and informative way. Some committees use a green-yellow-red light system to keep the witnesses on track. It is important that you follow the rules and conclude your comments when the red light comes on or your time has elapsed. Frequently, this is not your last word on the subject, as the committee will often engage in a question-and-answer period with a witness following the presentation of testimony.

A senior legislator chairs the committee hearing. The hearing is called to order, and the chair often begins with remarks. Following the chair's remarks, any other legislators on the committee that choose to provide opening remarks will be given the opportunity to do so. The hearing then turns to the panel(s) of witnesses for their comments on the legislation or issue being considered at the hearing.

In many ways, the question-and-answer period is the most informative and dynamic part of the hearing. It is during the dialogue between the legislators and the witnesses that you can begin to appreciate the position and concerns that legislators have on a particular issue. As a witness, it is important to be briefed by your association representative or the legislative office requesting you to testify, especially as it can often provide insight into the expected dynamics of the committee hearing. Being well prepared for the question-and-answer period of the testimony is vitally important to your perception as a credible witness. The question-and-answer period can be used by opponents to try to poke holes in your testimony, so it is important to anticipate opposition and be prepared with appropriate responses for maximum effectiveness.

Know the Issue. You do not need to be *the* expert on an issue to present coherent, strong testimony, but it is essential that you know the issue well enough to represent it to the committee and be able to answer questions. Witnesses are often selected based on their constituency and not necessarily on their expertise, though the best witness is a constituent who has expertise in the subject matter of the hearing.

If you are asked to testify, it is important that you learn all you can about the politics and the issue before your testimony. This is where association representatives are invaluable. Typically, they will be the ones who call and ask you if you would be willing to provide testimony. If you receive the call from them, rely on them for the drafting of remarks, briefing on the issue and the politics, the rules of the hearing, and other matters. Request that they attend the hearing with you and support you through the process. If you receive a request directly from a legislator's office, you may choose to call your association representative to see if he or she is willing to provide you support for your testimony. Frequently, associations are very willing to provide this support.

Be Familiar with your Prepared Remarks. Very few of us are expert public speakers who can give a cogent speech under the scrutiny of a House or Senate panel. Therefore, unless you are one of these talented folks, take the time to prepare and practice your remarks before the hearing. Some tips that might help:

- Have your remarks printed in large, bold font. Everyone has a different preference for style, but the format may make a difference in your comfort level in giving your testimony.
- Practice, practice, practice. Review your remarks; practice them before friends, family, and colleagues—even your bathroom mirror. Make sure you personalize your testimony and use phrases that are comfortable for you. If you practice, you will be able to appear much more conversational when you give your remarks. Although there is nothing wrong with directly reading your prepared remarks, a good, interesting witness will provide the committee with eye contact in order to develop a rapport.
- Make sure you are not the only one with a copy of your remarks. Okay, you think it will never happen to you, but it could. Your remarks could be left on the plane or at the hotel. Give a backup copy to the association representative or a friend. Such a precaution will definitely decrease your anxiety level.
- Identify some of the questions you might be asked and think through your responses. That way you won't be caught off guard or become discomfited by the questions.
- Prepare an appropriate response for occasions when you do not know the answer to the question. If you do not know the answer, do *not* make something up. Instead, state that you are not able to respond to that question but will try to find the answer and communicate it to the committee. Of course, if you commit to this kind of response, it is important that you follow up.

Use the Opportunity to Promote Yourself. When you come to town to be a witness for a hearing, it is important to make contact with your state senator and representative. It is polite to call them a few days or weeks in advance and let them know that you will be a witness on a particular issue. If you have your remarks complete, you may want to send them a copy. If you have the time, stop by their offices before or after the hearing for an informal visit. It is not unusual that, if their schedule allows, they may briefly attend the hearing and recognize you as a constituent.

In the same manner, you may want to let your local press know about your testimony. If you are asked to testify by your professional association, your association representative may arrange for local press releases to be sent to news sources in your area. If the issue of media does not come up in discussion, feel free to ask if it is a possibility.

Providing testimony is a critical part of health policy formation process. If you are asked to testify, consider it an exciting challenge and accept! There are many resources available to make it a successful adventure for you.

POWER IN NUMBERS

Although the power of the individual nurse-constituent is great, the power base multiplies when nurses come together with a unified voice to advocate for change. There are a number of ways to add your voice to the collective voice for nursing leaders. Public interest, professional, or networking groups can begin at the local, or grassroots, level. Joining a local nursing organization or networking group is often a first step toward lending your voice to nursing concerns. Many local groups provide excellent resources for sharing information about public policy, networking with colleagues to discuss the state of nursing practice, or providing opportunities to advocate for women's health, such as a sign-on letter.

Nursing groups or organizations at the local level can be influential with policymakers at all levels of government—from a local board of supervisors to the U.S. Representative for their district. Elected officials often welcome opportunities to address the core constituencies in their districts to show that they care about the issues back home, and the possibility of good coverage in local newspapers can also be an incentive to those representatives with an eye toward reelection.

Local nursing groups can sponsor legislative luncheons or celebrate National Nursing Week by inviting a policymaker to join them at a meeting or to address the group, or by sharing the group's recommendations with an elected official. Such grassroots activities are excellent ways to increase awareness of nursing issues and to make sure that nurses are represented when health care policy is being developed at any level.

The other model for grassroots action works in a reverse organizational pattern. Many national nursing organizations have local or statewide chapters. The headquarters of an association might be in Washington, DC, while the local chapters, sections, or branches can be spread out nationwide. This model is effective because the local or regional branch of the organization has the name recognition, resources, and prestige of the national association on their side as they pursue activities at the local level. In this way, local chapters enjoy the added strategic benefit of integrating their grassroots activities with the overall strategic lobbying goals of the national organization. The local group can then look to the national organization for position papers, copies of testimony, briefing documents, or other data on a given issue for use at the local level. Coordination of activities at the local and national levels of the same organizations is critical to ensure that all representatives of the umbrella organizations are spreading consistent messages and positions with policymakers and to avoid any conflicts that might undermine the overall lobbying strategy.

In terms of collective lobbying strategies, one of the most common, and increasingly most effective, options to bring about change is to create or join a coalition. As the number of interest groups has increased, with almost every niche group having its own association or group, it has become more important to reach consensus and refine priorities with groups that share your interests before approaching federal policymakers with priorities or legislative remedies. Coalitions simplify the workload of legislators and their staff by allowing them to spend less time meeting with one coalition that represents 25 groups than they would if they had to arrange 25 separate meetings with individual representatives from each group. In fact, coalition expert Kevin Hula (1995) states that because of increasing demands on time, "Groups are pressured to work out their differences before approaching Congress, rather than requiring Congress to sort out a seemingly infinite number of differences among groups" (p. 243).

Coalitions provide excellent public stature or cover so that lawmakers can boast of widespread support for an initiative from a wide, diverse pool of organizations on any measure—an important benefit, particularly if the issue is controversial. In the past, if legislators worked too closely with any one public interest group, they ran the risk of being accused of "being in the pocket" of that group or industry. Broad-based support provides public credibility and prominence to any initiative (Hula, 1995).

In addition to the their popularity among policymakers, coalitions can provide unique benefits to their members. The main goal of any coalition usually amounts to maximizing influence by providing strength in numbers in order to pursue strategic policy goals, but there are other advantages, which Hula refers to as "selective benefits . . . such as information or timely intelligence about the policy process . . . as a symbolic gesture . . . to convince their own members that they are working on an issue, or to demonstrate solidarity with another organization" (1995, p. 241).

CONCLUSION

You have the ability to make a difference. Whether you exercise your power as the power of one—the power of the nurse—or as part of the voice of nursing with collective lobbying strategies, you can make a difference. Nurses are experts in health care and enjoy the respect and trust of the American people, as well as the respect of policymakers who recognize that nurses are highly skilled professionals who work in stressful and life-threatening situations every day. The hardest part is getting started, and there are countless ways to begin to get involved at every level of decision making to make a difference in the policies that affect the nursing profession and the health of all Americans.

REFERENCES

Davis, R. (1999). *The web of politics: The Internet's impact on the American political system.* New York: Oxford University Press.

Frantzich, S.E. (1986). *Write your congressman: Constituent communications and representation.* New York: Praeger.

Gallup Organization. (2000). Annual honesty and ethics poll. Princeton, NJ: Author.

Hula, K. (1995). Rounding up the usual suspects: Forging interest group coalitions in Washington. In A.J. Cigler & B.A. Loomis (Eds.). *Interest group politics* (4th ed.). Washington, DC: Congressional Quarterly, Inc.

Kealy, M., Kendig, S., Ray, M., Nolan, L., Percy-McDaniel, H., & Roberts, S. (2000). *AWHONN legislative handbook: How to get started.* Washington, DC: Association of Women's Health, Obstetric and Neonatal Nurses.

Vignette   *Katie B. Horton*

Lobbying: An Inside View

"Good ideas are not adopted automatically. They must be driven into practice with courageous patience."

ADMIRAL HYMAN RICKOVER

When I graduated from Georgetown University School of Nursing in 1985, I was headed for professional experiences I couldn't have imagined. I practiced critical care nursing in a traditional hospital setting, delivered patient care to indigent children in developing countries, and obtained a master's degree in public health and later a law degree. I then took my skills to Capitol Hill, where I served in professional health staff positions. Finally, I started and currently operate my own health policy firm in Washington, DC. I've had an intimate view of the lobbying process—from both sides of the fence. I have found that the skills I used in my clinical practice—effective advocacy, communication, leadership, basic clinical knowledge, and a sense of community and responsibility to that community—play an important role in my effectiveness in advocating for health issues in the political arena.

CAPITOL HILL: A GREAT LEARNING LABORATORY

Being a "staffer" on Capitol Hill is a great learning experience. In 1993, in the midst of President Clinton's health care reform efforts, I was introduced to

Congressman Fortney Pete Stark, a Democrat from California, and was invited to join his staff. At the time, Congressman Stark was chairman of the Health Subcommittee of the House Committee on Ways and Means. This is one of the key subcommittees in Congress responsible for health reform efforts as well as federal health programs such as Medicare. Congressman Stark and his staff director, Bill Vaughan, were the first to teach me about federal health policy and the skills needed by a good "staffer."

Lessons Learned on a Representative's Personal Staff

The most valuable lessons learned in my work as Congressman Stark's legislative director included:

- *The patient comes first.* Every health policy option and decision should be assessed for its impact on the patient—not on the future fundraising capabilities of a member of Congress.
- *Being a "government servant" is an honor and a privilege that should never be abused.* If you find yourself less than excited about being on Capitol Hill, it is time to find something else to do, at least for a little while.
- *Treat every person you meet with respect and kindness.* Most important, do so because one should behave this way—but also because individuals in Washington rotate through many jobs in a lifetime. The person who lobbies you today could be your boss tomorrow! You may not agree with his or her opinion, but you have the duty to listen carefully, to learn about the person's point of view, and to consider it when making a recommendation to the member of Congress.

Lessons Learned on a Committee Staff

I also served on the staff of the Senate Finance Committee handling Medicare issues for the committee's members, specifically, Senator Daniel Patrick Moynihan (D-NY). In this role, I was on the receiving end of hundreds—perhaps thousands—of lobbying efforts to influence Medicare policy. I had the opportunity to observe effective lobbying strategies—and some less-than-effective lobbying strategies.

Calling them advocates. Washington, DC, is full of lobbyists. Some are employed full-time by one of the many trade associations and health organizations. Others are employed by large law firms or "lobbying shops" or work as independent contractors serving many different clients. A comment about the term *lobbyist:* just as the term *stewardess* has been replaced with *purser* or *flight attendant,* so has the term *lobbyist* been replaced with a more politically correct term. Lobbyists are now commonly referred to as *advocates.*

Characteristics of successful advocates. Despite differences in purpose among the organizations and the positions they represent, successful advocates conduct their business with a common set of principles. In my experience, the most successful advocates closely adhere to the following principles:

Prioritization of advocacy issues. Successful advocates recognize the importance of prioritizing issues in their advocacy agenda. They know that the universe of issues before policymakers and the demands on public resources are tremendous. Effective advocates encourage consideration of one or two priority issues that have been selected by their clients or organizations. It is critical that each priority be carefully defined.

Advocating effectively. Effective advocacy encompasses more than just letter writing and visits to the U.S. Congress. Many governmental and nongovernmental bodies exercise authority over various aspects of the study, prevention, treatment, and management of disease. Payment for services and accreditation of facilities are also major considerations for health care advocates. Successful advocates maintain contacts with the Department of Health and Human Services (HHS), including the Centers for Medicare and Medicaid Services (CMS, formerly the Health Care Financing Administration [HCFA]), the National Institutes of Health (NIH), the Centers for Disease Control and Prevention (CDC), and the Health Resources and Services Administration (HRSA). Outreach to other organizations includes, but is not limited to, the Joint Commission on Accreditation of Healthcare Organizations (JCAHO), the Medicare Payment Advisory Commission (MedPAC), and the Institute of Medicine (IOM). Broad advocacy outreach and carefully nurtured connections ensure that the organization's message is understood not only on Capitol Hill, but also in organizations that advise, implement and influence policy.

Recognition of the role and importance of media and public relations. Successful advocates put a face on the issue for which they are advocating. They weave science and real-life experiences to create a compelling advocacy message. They use patients and their stories to communicate their message to members of Congress or their staffs. Along with sending a scientist or provider to testify before Congress, successful advocates often send patients.

Successful advocates also acknowledge the inherent link between advocacy and public relations. Advocacy priorities should be communicated to policymakers and the general public in a proactive manner. Efforts should include strategies for enlisting media coverage where appropriate and for shaping the media's portrayal of issues to the greatest extent possible. In addition, the organizations and their grassroots counterparts take an active role in public relations by preparing targeted opinions and editorials, radio commentary, and television spots.

The press plays an important role in translating what is often a complicated legislative provision into a simple but powerful story about everyday lives. It is these stories of constituents that often catch the attention of a member of Congress. Effective advocates and organizations invest heavily in the combination of science, data, and experience. These investments pay off in the form of a persuasive message, grounded in science and data but told with a "human touch" through anecdote. This strategy forces policymakers to consider the person living with the disease, rather than merely the science of the disease.

Wise use of data. One prominent strategy adopted by successful advocates is the use of data to influence policy. Many effective advocates and organizations invest in specialized "policy/data studies" to help articulate their priorities. Policy studies are used extensively in an advocacy campaign to support and provide credibility to an organization's advocacy request. The typical policy study used by a successful advocacy organization is targeted to test a very specific premise that furthers the organization's advocacy priorities. These studies often address the impact of the policy on the federal budget or federal health insurance program in which a legislative change is sought. Such studies are used to influence the Congressional Budget Office, which ultimately must assign a "score" or cost of the policy advocated to the federal government. Successful advocates utilize sophisticated policy staff and also budget for policy studies conducted by consultants or outside experts from a variety of sources, including academic institutions.

Participation in coalitions. Successful advocates participate in coalitions of organizations with common policy interests. Working collectively, coalition members are able to pool resources and share contacts that enable them to deliver their advocacy message to a larger audience. They are also able to share access to members of Congress and their staffs.

Creation of advocacy champions among policy leaders. Successful health care advocates identify legislators or leaders in senior policy positions (or their family members) who are directly affected by the disease or condition of interest to the organization. Because these leaders identify directly with the organization's mission, they often work vigorously on the organization's behalf. Such champions can also give high-profile support in public information and prevention campaigns.

Engagement and effective use of grassroots activities. For maximum impact, successful advocates effectively communicate to policymakers through extensive grassroots efforts. Involvement of grassroots members is vital to effective advocacy. Members of regional and local chapters of national organizations may be in the best position to tell the organization's real story.

Not being an occasional advocate. Monitoring legislative and administrative activities is meaningless if key issues are not identified and an action plan implemented to achieve the identified priorities. Monitoring legislative and regulatory activity is important but should not be considered an end in itself. Effective advocates get actively involved in all phases of policy making for their expressed priority issues, including the preparation of model legislation. They advocate year round by using a multidimensional advocacy strategy.

Teamwork. Successful advocates make activists out of their members or volunteers. Organizational activists reach out to policymakers on a different level, reminding them that they, their family members, and their constituents are also vulnerable to disease. The overall focus of an effective advocacy campaign should be to gain multiple opportunities for advancing the organization's advocacy priorities. Successful advocates establish benchmarks of success and intermediary goals as stepping stones to achieving the advocacy priority. These successes motivate volunteers and show progress in reaching the advocacy priority.

Investment in advocacy. Most organizations define *advocacy staff* broadly to include staff with expertise in lobbying, policy, data analysis, and public relations. Successful advocacy organizations invest significantly in the quality of their advocacy staff. This investment includes recruiting, training, and retaining an adequate number of staff have significant experience with federal and state policy making. Key qualities sought in staff include diverse contacts, education, previous experience both in government and in the private sector, and the ability to network effectively. Equally important, the staff should have a deep understanding of the policy issues that the organization considers important, or the ability to develop such expertise.

Nurses are trained to be advocates for their patients. Those same advocacy skills can be used to benefit larger groups of patients when nurses become involved in political advocacy. I encourage all nurses to follow their interests, learn more about the advocacy process, and find a place to make a difference.

29 The American Voter and Nursing's Leadership in Political Campaigns

CANDY DATO

"The ballot is stronger than the bullet."

ABRAHAM LINCOLN

The electoral college; butterfly ballots; dimpled, pregnant, and hanging chads. American voters dusted off their memories of high school civics class and sprinkled their conversation with previously unfamiliar terms following the disputed 2000 presidential election. The media made critical errors in their declarations of winners on election night, and American voters—indeed the whole world—waited 5 weeks for a definitive answer to the question of who had won the presidential election. The impact of this hotly contested election on the American voter will not be fully known for several years.

A recent survey (Gallup Poll, 2000) shows that Americans continue to support a constitutional amendment to abolish the electoral college, which would allow for direct election of the president. There is widespread support for the federal government to standardize ballots and voting procedures across the country. This might include different ways of voting, such as the use of mail balloting in Oregon, optical scanning, or uniform electronic voting systems. However, there are concerns about the possibilities and implications of late-breaking news for western states whose polling sites remain open after eastern states have closed theirs. Internet voting offers promise, but it raises the question of the digital divide. Changing election day to Sunday is another option. The disputed election also raised other issues concerning voter registration, absentee ballots, faulty equipment, ballot design, training of election officials, voter education, and unclear election laws.

American voters have been courted relentlessly by a stream of media, e-mail, and old-fashioned paper messages throughout what often feels like an endless campaign season. Americans are not voting as they have in the past, and the degree of cynicism has risen. Yet the process continues—and nurses continue to be involved in political campaigns.

Nurses affect the political process through their individual and collective support of candidates. Nurses and other health care workers can have considerable influence on those with whom they come into contact by explaining the importance of voting and its effect on their daily lives. Health care issues are tied to public policy and are thus dependent on the votes of elected officials. Pushing for the passage of health care legislation is one way nurses can show the public that patient advocacy does not stop at the health facility door. Imagine 2.2 million nurses with buttons saying "I am a nurse. I vote—do you?"

Nurses must take part in the discussion of the complex issues surrounding campaigning and electioneering. We must understand the issues related to electioneering and campaigning in addition to developing the knowledge and skills to participate effectively in these processes.

CURRENT ISSUES AND TRENDS

VOTING PATTERNS

The most political act every nurse—indeed every citizen—can perform is to vote. Nurses can also make certain that family, close friends, colleagues, and students vote.

For many years, government relations professionals and political scientists have sounded the alarm about national trends of declining participation in electoral politics in the United States. The highest level of participation was in the 1960 presidential election, when 63% of the voting-age population actually voted. Between 1976 and 1988 the levels did not exceed 54% in any presidential election year. There was an increase during the 1992 election, when numbers reached 55% and caused many to question whether this was a sign of a shift in behavior. The 1996 elections demonstrated that there had been no such shift: The 49% turnout represented a decline in both the percentage and the actual number of voters from 1992, and the turnout in 2000 went up only slightly, to 51% (Federal Election Commission, personal communication, 2001). The 1996 election witnessed the lowest voter turnout for a presidential election since 1924, when women were first enfranchised and still unfamiliar with voting, and when laws discriminated against the registration of immigrants. The U.S. government gives legitimacy to countries that have elected governments, but the United States itself rates low, number 17, in comparison with other Western industrialized nations in voter turnout figures (Solop & Wonders, 1995). Midterm elections fare worse, with one third of the electorate, and local elections may only draw one fourth.

Another cause for concern are the demographics of those who do vote. Nonvoting is disproportionately more common among those of lower socioeconomic status and people of color. Table 29-1

TABLE **29-1** Percentage of Voter Turnout in Federal Elections by Race/Ethnicity

RACE	1986	1988	1990	1992	1994	1996
White	47	59	47	64	47	56
Black	43	52	39	54	37	51
Hispanic	24	29	21	29	20	27

From Federal Election Commission. (No date). *Voter registration and turnout in federal elections by race/ethnicity 1972-1996.* Retrieved online, August 19, 2001, at www.fec.gov/pages/Raceto.htm.

shows differential rates of voter turnout in federal elections according to race or ethnicity. The entire electorate is older, with only 38% of the 18- to 20-year-olds voting in 1992, compared with 46% of the 21- to 24-year-olds and 70% of those over 45. "The data are unambiguous in portraying an electoral system in which older, affluent, majority-culture citizens are much more likely to participate in electoral politics than younger, less affluent individuals and people of color" (Solop & Wonders, 1995, p. 70).

The reasons for this phenomenon among all groups have been attributed to both personal reactions (e.g., cynicism, alienation, social disconnection, boredom, satisfaction with the status quo, lack of a sense of political responsibility) and structural problems in the voting process (e.g., political action committees, negative campaigns, lackluster candidates, political media, television, the educational system, the "me generation"). The League of Women Voters (1996) found in a survey that nonvoters are less likely to grasp the impact of elections on issues that concern them, discuss political issues less often than voters, believe that they lack sufficient information on which to base their votes, and find the voting process difficult and cumbersome. In addition, they are less likely to be contacted by organizations that encourage voting, and they attach less importance to voting than to other, daily activities. The researchers also found that forms of personal contact such as encouragement by family and friends were instrumental in changing voting behavior.

It has been posited that a knowledge gap affects Americans' views on politics and their voting behavior. "Whether uninterested, uninformed or simply ignorant, millions of Americans cannot answer even basic questions about American politics, according to a survey by the *Washington Post,* the Kaiser Family Foundation and Harvard University" (Morin, 1996, p. A1). Theories as to why Americans don't know more about government include insufficient basic education about it, less time to keep informed about current events; and the use of television as the primary source of information. In a random sample of 1514 adults, those with more knowledge were compared with those with less. The adults with more knowledge were more mistrustful of government but also had more faith in the political system. They saw their vote as a remedy and were twice as likely to have voted (Morin, 1996). "The information gap is affecting how politics is practiced, dumbing down democracy and making political campaigns increasingly negative and character-based" (Morin, 1996, p. A7).

One group of Americans—African Americans—has shown some contrary patterns. A U.S. Census Bureau study showed that voter turnout was down from 1994 to 1998 for Caucasians and Asian/Pacific Islanders, as well as all ages and genders; turnout among Hispanics remained the same. However, African-American turnout percentages increased during this time. On the other hand, African Americans felt more strongly about the contested presidential election of 2000, which divided the country along both party and racial lines. African Americans felt more "cheated," "bitter," and "angry" than white Americans about the election. This negative perception extends beyond the election, with 76% of African Americans saying that the election system in the United States is discriminatory, versus 62% of Caucasian Americans (Simmons, 2000).

Contributing to the problem of low voter turnout are immigrants who maintain allegiance to and interest in their country of origin, which serves as a major reason for their not becoming citizens and not voting. In the nineteenth century, political clubs were the moving force behind immigrants becoming citizens and voting. The clubs helped immigrants through the process in return for their loyalty. With more restrictions on patronage and election law changes such as the secret ballot, incentives for political parties to encourage immigrant voting have greatly diminished (Barnes, 2000).

Piven and Cloward (2000) suggest that politicians not only lack interest in finding new voters, they correctly assess that they are better off with a small number of loyal voters for primary elections.

Another gap in voting, the gender gap, reached its peak in the 1996 elections, causing one author to refer to 1996 as the "Year of Women Voters" (Dodson, 1997). Men were evenly divided in voting for Clinton (44%) and Dole (43%), whereas women voters' support for Clinton was considerable (54% versus 38%) (Dodson, 1997). This large gender gap grew out of a full-scale effort to win women's votes by "connect[ing] private concerns of home and family to the political as never before" (Dodson, 1997, p. 27). Women have been found to differ from men in their views on government, with women viewing government as being able to help solve problems and men more likely to see government as the problem. Women are also less likely to support spending cuts on social programs because women are more supportive of the social safety net and the human impact of public policy in general. Furthermore, women are more tolerant of gay rights, are more concerned about the environment, and place a higher value on the notion of community (Dodson, 1997).

As the American electorate ages, the importance of issues of concern to senior citizens, such as Social Security and Medicare, will increase. In the 2000 election, 22% of the electorate were over the age of 60 (Berke, 2001). These senior voters are not a cohesive group, and they are less reliably Democratic than in the past. On the other end of the age spectrum, the percentage of young people aged 18 to 24 who vote is declining, despite the fact that an increasing percentage of them are engaged in community volunteerism (Ponomareff, 2001).

NATIONAL VOTER REGISTRATION ACT

Another view of low voter turnout is that it is reflective of a structural problem—access to the voting process. Starting in the 1980s, several national groups (e.g., Project VOTE, Human SERVE, National Coalition of Black Voter Registration) were mobilizing local groups to change the power structure. Grassroots efforts for inclusion were begun to challenge the prevailing political system, which was seen as victimizing the poor and disadvantaged. Past social movements had successfully led to legalization of the right to vote for many people. Later, voting rights were extended to women (1920) and youth (1971). However, barriers to voting persisted for a while; poll taxes were not eliminated until 1964 and literacy tests until 1965.

Local barriers were initially targeted, until it became evident that it was more efficient to join together to work on the problem nationally in order to bring sweeping reforms of voter registration to the struggle for the disenfranchised. The League of Women Voters was a major leader in the coalition to support the passage of legislation designed to reform the current system and encourage voter participation by making it easier to register.

In the late 1980s, voter registration reform was seen as a partisan issue that the Democrats supported and the Republicans did not. President Clinton came into office with the expansion of voter registration as part of his platform. The goal was to empower those without money to have access to government. He signed the National Voter Registration Act (NVRA) into law on May 20, 1993, and it went into effect January 1, 1995. Clinton's success is the success of a broad and influential political struggle and social movement and an appealing attempt to engage the masses. It was hoped that through the expansion of the population registered to vote, the NVRA would destabilize the status quo and lead to a reconstitution of power relations (Solop & Wonders, 1995).

The NVRA provides for the establishment of several mechanisms to increase voter registration, the key one being "motor voter" registration. Any application, renewal, or change of address for a driver's license or nondriver's identification card triggers an application for voter registration. Agency registration established distribution of voter registration application forms and assistance at a variety of governmental and nongovernmental agencies, including unemployment, public assistance, vocational rehabilitation, and Social Security agencies as well as libraries. Mail-in registration was also established in those states where it did not already exist. The NVRA also eliminated the purging of nonvoting registrants from voter registration lists and required election officials to send all applicants a notice informing them of their voter registration status.

Human SERVE (1996) and the League of Women Voters (Duskin, 1997a) reported that the NVRA brought about the largest expansion of voter registration in a 2-year period in the history of the United States, an estimated 12 million new voters. Some states such as Georgia had phenomenal increases (from 85,000 registering in 1994 to 181,000 in the first 3 months of 1995). Although it had been projected that nearly half of the added registrants would actually vote, the numbers were much lower in the 1996 presidential election, suggesting that structural issues are not the only reasons for low voter turnout. The trend toward increased voter registration continued in the second 2 years after the NVRA; however, the number of Americans actually voting declined from 1994 to 1998 (Federal Election Commission, no date).

CANDIDATES

Women as Candidates. Elected officials at all levels of government do not reflect the gender composition of the United States. Women have largely been restricted in their journey to the heart of political power in this country. In 1992, the "Year of the Woman," that pattern was altered somewhat when women moved into national and statewide elected offices in greater numbers than ever before. The number of female candidates for Congress, statewide elective executive offices, and state legislatures has been climbing steadily for the past 20 years. In 1976 there was 1 woman candidate for the U.S. Senate, 54 for the House of Representatives, 2 for governorships, and 1258 for state legislatures. Records were set in 1992, with 11 for the U.S. Senate; in 1994, with 10 for governorships and 2285 for state legislatures; and in 2000, with 122 for the House of Representatives. The number of female candidates declined for some offices in 1996, with 9 candidates for the Senate, 6 for governorships, and 2273 for state legislatures (Center for the American Woman and Politics, 1996, 2000).

Record numbers of women were serving in the Senate (13) and the House (59) in 2001 (Center for the American Woman and Politics, 2001). The number of women in statewide elective executive posts, such as governor or comptroller, dropped from the 1995 record of 85 to 81 in 1997, representing 25.1% of available positions. In 1997 women legislators held 21.4% of the 1588 available seats. This represents an increase of five times the 4% held in 1969 (Center for the American Woman and Politics, 1997). The number of women of color remains a particular concern; for example, only 21 have ever served in Congress (Duskin, 1997b).

Increasing the numbers of elected and appointed women is more than an issue of justice and equality. The Center for the American Woman and Politics studied the impact of women in state legislatures and found that female elected officials differed from their male counterparts in terms of their attitudes and their top-priority bills. Women were more likely to emphasize women's rights and bills dealing with "women's traditional areas of interest—health care, the welfare of children, the family and the elderly, housing, the environment and education—that stem from women's roles as caregivers in the family and in society more generally" (Carroll, Dodson, & Mandel, 1991, p. 7). Women legislators from both parties were more likely to support feminist and liberal policy positions than their male colleagues. The study found "compelling evidence that women are having a distinctive impact on public policy and the political process" (Carroll et al, 1991, p. 3). It also found that the commitment to represent the interests and issues of women does not diminish as women legislators move into leadership positions.

Women legislators differ from men in their leadership styles and are changing political processes and institutions as well as influencing public policy. Women legislators involve citizens more, finding their input helpful. They are more likely to bring government into the public view. They are more responsive to the economically disadvantaged, working to bring them greater access (Carroll et al, 1991).

Congresswoman Carolyn McCarthy (D-NY), a nurse, embodies many of the characteristics of a female candidate coming up against a male incumbent. She overcame numerous obstacles and is viewed as a hero to many. Like many other women, she was not considered to be a serious contender and was thought of as a one-issue candidate because of her strong stance on gun control following her husband's death in the much-publicized Long Island Railroad Massacre. What mobilized people to support her was her media exposure and her commonsense approach to a variety of issues.

The well-publicized and well-financed 2000 race for the Senate seat from New York tells another story. Hillary Clinton (D-NY) ought to have had a natural base among women voters; however, her campaign staff was concerned about the very mixed reactions of women to candidate Clinton. These concerns proved unfounded, and she won the election with a unexpectedly strong 12-point lead. Exit polls found that 60% of women voters supported her (Bumiller & Murphy, 2000), and she became the first female U.S. senator from New York—and what's more, the first First Lady to hold national office.

The ratio of male to female candidates still remains 2 to 1 (Duskin, 1997b). Many women candidates belong to or receive formal and informal campaign support from women's organizations, women's political action committees (PACs), and professional associations such as the American Nurses Association (ANA), whose members are mostly women (Carroll et al, 1991). Women continue to juggle their home and work responsibilities, and they are concerned about the tenor of political races (Duskin, 1997b). Incumbents, who are largely men, win elections 95% of the time (Duskin, 1997b). The current campaign finance laws favor incumbents. Women candidates have the same problems as challengers in general: they are lacking in money, name recognition, and the built-in advantages that incumbency offers. For example, incumbents receive seven times more PAC money than challengers (Duskin, 1997b), and expensive campaigns rely on media coverage. Women challengers do, however, win as often as male challengers. The dual, and often related, concerns about the power of the media and the exorbitant cost of campaigns geared to short television spots without substantive discussions of issues plague American voters.

The 107th Congress has more women than any other. A December 2000 Gallup poll (Simmons, 2001) reports that 57% of Americans say the United States would be governed better if more women were in office (only 28% thought so in 1984). Further optimism for women in U.S. politics can be found in the Gallup report that 92% of Americans would vote for a woman for president.

Diversity and Redistricting. Nurses have been concerned about the lack of balanced ethnic representation by candidates for public office. The power of incumbency is a major obstacle to increasing diversity—ethnically and racially, as well as by gender. Ethnicity, race, or gender alone is not sufficient for a candidate to win. Candidates must have a broad understanding of the issues and must form alliances with groups other than their own.

In 1965, the Voting Rights Act required equality of opportunity for racial minorities to vote. That major piece of civil rights legislation gave the U.S. Department of Justice authority to ensure that redistricting plans reflected racial balance. Redistricting is designed to equalize the population among congressional and state legislative districts, and it is a highly political process. On the one hand, it has enabled more minority candidates to seek elected office (Duskin, 1997b). However, it is a limited strategy for increasing minority representation in state legislatures and in Congress. It has often been used to protect incumbents through gerrymandering (manipulation of district boundaries to favor one party over another). Legislators thought that the creation of *majority/minority districts* (in which a minority group represents the majority in the district) through redistricting would increase voter turnout in those areas. Preliminary studies have not upheld this belief. "Empowerment, in the sense of having a much greater chance of electing a legislative candidate of one's choice (frequently equated with of one's own group), does not invariably lead to greater participation" (Brace, Handley, Niemi, & Stanley, 1995, p. 201).

The 2000 census could have a major impact on the composition of Congress and state legislatures. The U.S. Constitution requires that every state's representatives must be elected from districts of equal population. The total number of congressional districts must be 435. Each state is entitled to at least one representative, and the remaining members are apportioned among the states by population. It is primarily the responsibility of state legislatures to redraw congressional districts, after the decennial census, with the majority party clearly having an opportunity to redraw districts to its own advantage. In the 2000 census, some states lost members while others increased their representation. The congressional elections in 2002 will reflect redrawn districts.

The major requirement of federal law is that race may not be used as the "predominant motive" of redistricting. It remains to be seen whether the increase in the number of minorities, especially Latinos, will significantly change the composition of the House of Representatives and state legislative bodies. In almost every state in the country, battles are being waged over power shifts created by redistricting (Rosenbaum, 2001).

Pennsylvania and New York are protecting incumbents through restrictive measures that require candidates to get thousands of signatures within a short period in order to have their name placed on the ballot. In one election district in Brooklyn, New York, 21.3% of registered voters in 1996 and only 13.3% in 1998 voted. This particular district had been redrawn in the last round of redistricting. It seems to have no sense of community, a lack of cohesiveness, and a sense of alienation (Barnes, 2000).

Term limits were implemented in many states and localities as a reform measure against incumbency. In state legislatures there has been an increase in attempts to reverse the term-limit legislation from the late 1980s. Lawmakers mourn the loss of experience, but voters' responses are harder to predict with regard to repealing term limits (Verhovek, 2001). The future of federal term limits will require action by Congress. Many believe that its members will refuse to support term limits out of self-interest.

ROLE OF POLITICAL PARTIES IN CAMPAIGNING AND ELECTIONEERING

Political parties, activists, and interest groups recruit candidates to run for office. Incumbents leaving political life often endorse a successor. The political parties promote candidates from within their ranks, support them, and get them elected.

There has been increasing interest in "third parties" by those Americans who do not feel well represented by our predominantly two-party system. Information is readily available online about both the two major parties and the myriad of "third parties" (Chaffee, 2000). The basic difficulty lies in the inability of third parties to deliver enough resources and votes to get their candidates elected. Some wind up aligning themselves with one of the major parties in the end, whereas others are viewed as losing the election for one of the major parties. In the 2000 presidential elections, Ralph Nader and the Green Party failed to garner the minimum of 5% of the popular vote to qualify the party for public campaign financing in the 2004 elections (Daniel, 2001); but the closeness of the Bush-Gore race suggests that, had Nader withdrawn from the race and supported the Gore ticket, Gore would likely have won.

ELECTRONIC DEMOCRACY

There has been an overnight explosion of "electronic democracy" through the use of computer-mediated political communication, the systematic use of the Internet to reach large numbers of citizens with a potentially interactive approach to communication. In the political arena the Internet has been used to inform constituents, to raise money, and to gather support via petitions and requests for e-mail messages. There has also been an exponential increase in electronic access to federal, state, and local elected officials. Political scientists and communication specialists are examining whether the expanded use of these systems will actually enhance democracy or possibly actualize concerns about oppression and control (Tedesco, Miller, & Spiker, 1999). There has been an expansion of the number of computers available to citizens in their own homes, schools, libraries, commercial sites, and government offices. Concerns still exist about the digital divide in terms of those citizens for whom access to computers is limited, even in this time of generally expanded access. The Internet also provides a means of communication for all candidates, regardless of their relative campaign budgets, thus giving more access to candidates of all political parties. The question that will take several more election cycles to answer is whether the use of computer-mediated communication will increase

the level of citizen involvement in politics, specifically voter participation.

INVOLVEMENT IN CAMPAIGNS

Today, political campaigns are often paradoxical scenes of chaos and organization. Nurses are highly sought as campaign volunteers or as staff because of their experience in creating order out of chaos.

NURSES AND CAMPAIGNS

Nurses have been expanding their collective experience in political campaigns since the early 1980s. Nurses were encouraged to take advantage of a variety of political training workshops offered by the National Women's Political Caucus, the Women's Campaign Fund, the political parties, the ANA, and others. Nurse campaigners are now a part of the cadre of experienced volunteers and paid staff available to candidates and campaigns of both political parties. Elected officials regularly recommend nurse campaigners to their colleagues.

Campaign experiences have provided nurses with the knowledge and skills needed to become candidates themselves. An ever-increasing number of nurse candidates are running for and winning state legislative and county races. In 1997, approximately 80 nurses held seats in state legislatures.

In 1992, Eddie Bernice Johnson of Texas became the first nurse elected to Congress, followed by Carolyn McCarthy in 1996 and Lois Capps from California in 1998. Voters are looking for candidates who offer a credible and fresh approach to problem solving. Nurse candidates fill that vacuum.

Nurses must make sure that the campaign staff know they are nurses. Being a nurse is a professional identity and can add to political identity. Nurses have numerous skills that are invaluable in a campaign, so they should make their talents known. As volunteers, nurses must take the initiative to make sure their worth is recognized. Nurses considering volunteering for a political campaign should assess campaign needs and their own availability, interests, talents, and experiences. After identifying the leadership of a campaign nurses can introduce themselves, explain how much their time is worth, and tell about what they are doing or would like to do in the campaign. To get what they want, nurses have to use their communication and negotiation skills to make a place for themselves in areas of responsibility, such as scheduling and coordinating other volunteers or even running the overall campaign. High visibility in a campaign can earn nurses enormous political credit.

RECRUITING CANDIDATES

Politically active nurses are recruiting candidates. These candidates include both nurses and non-nurses who support important issues in nursing. There are responsibilities associated with the recruitment of candidates. Some candidates will need education and support as they run for office at various levels. Nurses have taken advantage of political training programs for women candidates.

Campaigns need time, money, and volunteers. Nurses encouraging someone to run for office must deliver each of these commodities. If the recruited candidate wins, nurses will have influence with this new member of a particular political body. They may also have accomplished the additional goal of delivering a clear message to the opposition, who may, in fact, have been one of nursing's opponents. If nurses can affect just one election, they will already have political power, and for politicians whose main goal is getting elected and reelected, the political power of nurses will be not only acknowledged but sought after.

Nurses have developed long-range plans for grooming nurse leaders who will take on increasingly advanced leadership roles in electoral politics, including running for office. This type of visionary planning will ensure nursing's rightful place at the policy-making levels of health care. It will also help increase the number of women and minority-group members in public office. Nurses are challenged by the power of incumbency and the barriers it presents to diversity.

Voter registration drives provide an excellent opportunity for nursing students or nurses new to political action to get involved. In university settings, it is an opportunity to reach the younger population who are eligible to vote but may not have been exercising that right. Such drives can also provide a public relations opportunity by enabling nurses to become visible in large educational, health care, and other facilities, thereby gaining credit for promoting community involvement. Increasingly, nursing has built stronger ties with consumers in order to generate support for its health care agenda. Nurses can get specific details about organizing and conducting a voter registration drive from organizations such as the National Women's Political Caucus, the Women's Campaign Fund, and the League of Women Voters.

Voter registration efforts have been targeted both at the general public and more specifically at nurses. The ANA and state nurses associations (SNAs) increased efforts to register nurses in 1996 in their "Registered Nurse/Registered Voter" campaign, launched during the ANA's centennial, which reached almost 200,000 nurses. The ANA and SNAs sent out colorful posters featuring a photo of Isabel Hampton Robb, with the caption "This nurse couldn't vote" (ANA, 1996).

Think of the effect on an election if the more than 2 million nurses in this nation voted! As the 2000 presidential elections illustrated, every vote does count.

CHOOSING A CANDIDATE TO SUPPORT

Nurses often work on campaigns through their affiliation with organized nursing efforts such as ANA-PAC, the political action committee of the ANA. Through PACs, nurses are able to pool their financial resources for a candidate endorsed by their nursing organization. (Although either the organization or its PAC can endorse a candidate, only the PAC can make a financial contribution to the candidate's campaign fund.) Endorsement decisions are made based upon knowledge of the candidate, the organization's priorities, and the political landscape. The organization or PAC usually conducts interviews with candidates or sends them questionnaires to complete, to ascertain their positions on nursing and health issues. Sometimes organizations will decide to make endorsements based upon a single issue. At other times there is a broad agenda to consider, and other political factors become important. For example, an organization may be displeased with an incumbent who has not been fully supportive of its legislative priorities, but the incumbent is the chair of the health committee and is unlikely to be unseated by the challenger.

Nurses also join local groups working with a particular candidate or groups of nurse colleagues. Many work on campaigns of candidates they support as individual citizens, nurses, or members of other organizations. Whatever the situation, choosing the right candidate is important, because nurses have a positive public image to uphold and want to use their time wisely and effectively.

Nurses choose candidates whose values, beliefs, and priorities are closely aligned with their own and those of the profession. Candidates may be evaluated based on their previous legislative work. Nurses may know candidates as a result of their political party activities, their participation in community organizations, or from the neighborhood. Candidates are evaluated on their position on issues, voting records, qualification, and electability. Many factors that have an impact on a candidate are taken into account (Box 29-1).

EXPLORATORY COMMITTEES

Exploratory committees enable candidates to test the political waters. Before a campaign begins, they must determine which of the people encouraging them to run for office are ready to commit time and money. It is a time for candidates to assess their relationship with the political party and gauge the amount of support, financial and otherwise, available for a campaign. Candidates use this period to determine what segments of the registered voter population will be in their corner and how to reach those who are swing voters or independents. It is a

---

BOX **29-1** Questions to Ask When Considering Support of a Candidate

CANDIDATE

- What kinds of experiences would the candidate bring to the office?
- Is the candidate's political knowledge and skill respected by his or her peers?
- What is the candidate's voting record in the office for which he or she is running or in a previous office?
- In what committees and positions of leadership has the candidate served while in office?

CAMPAIGN STAFF AND PLAN

- Does the campaign have an overall plan and component parts?
- Has the staff researched the political unit and obtained an up-to-date profile of the district where the candidate is running?
- Is the campaign plan realistic?
- What is the budget, and are the plans for raising funds realistic?
- Is the campaign managed in a professional manner?
- Are schedules adhered to and tasks completed on time?
- Do the candidate and campaign manager work well together?
- Do they recognize that in areas such as polling, public relations, and fund raising, hiring political professionals may be well worth the cost?
- Are there creative plans to combine professional and volunteer help?
- Is the volunteer coordinator personable and capable of planning and staffing key events?
- How well will the candidate and the team work together?

ELECTABILITY

- What is the likelihood of the candidate's being elected?
- Do polls show a high positive or negative rating for the incumbent?
- Does the voting public recognize the challenger's name?
- Does the candidate have the party's backing? If not, why not?
- Is the candidate a good public speaker and does he or she appear to enjoy campaigning?
- How much does the candidate want to win?
- What are some of the factors that will influence electability, including the political, economic, and ethnic makeup of the district?
- What is the percentage of voters who voted in the last election? Is this a presidential election year, in which one can expect a higher voter turnout?
- Is this candidate challenging an incumbent? What was the incumbent's margin of victory in the previous election? Is this an open seat because of the incumbent's retirement, or is it a new seat created as a result of redistricting?
- What are the major media sources?

OVERALL ASSESSMENT

- What is the risk/benefit ratio?
- What is the potential damage to the nursing organization supporting a candidate if the candidate loses?
- Does this potential damage outweigh the benefits of supporting the candidate?

time to develop relationships with both individuals and groups and is invaluable to a campaign.

Exploratory committees may be formal, with a long list of prominent names on a raised letterhead, or informal and small. Seats on these committees are often prestigious, with membership a sign of having "arrived" as a valued political participant. The significance of these committees increases with the level of office sought. The legalities surrounding the formation of exploratory committees for fund-raising purposes are regulated by the Federal Election Commission or by state election commissions.

CAMPAIGN MANAGERS

An important early step for candidates is choosing a campaign manager. This critical decision may be influenced by the political party, as well as by the candidate and those working closely with him or her. The political network of former candidates and current activists will supply a candidate with suggestions for a manager. Politics involves finding out who knows what and whom and keeping in touch with them.

Experience, especially in successful campaigns, is important. Campaigns for higher public office often require an experienced campaign manager. Nevertheless, enthusiastic, energetic, and talented organizers can manage their first campaigns successfully.

From the beginning, the candidate and the manager must understand each other's roles. A campaign can begin to fall apart if the candidate is managing the campaign instead of the person hired to do so. A trusting relationship is essential.

CAMPAIGN CALENDAR

A campaign calendar is a critical part of campaign planning. It is a tool used to divide the numerous campaign activities into manageable pieces. A good campaign will have carefully thought-out goals, priorities, and phases that are meticulously scheduled throughout the campaign period.

The calendar outlines a schedule for the campaign, supports the staff's focus on details, and helps to prevent internal crises. For example, planning "get out the vote" telephone banking before election day involves knowing that the telephone company needs 3 weeks' notice to install additional lines, and that a friendly union will be scheduling its phones for several candidates. Building this requirement into the plan ensures that the telephones will be in place on schedule. Without such planning, the campaign might have no telephones, but it would have many angry and frustrated volunteers as well as additional expenses as a result of the effort to obtain telephones on short notice.

CAMPAIGN VOLUNTEERS

Volunteers are the core of any political campaign. In a low-budget campaign, they can be the campaign themselves. First, volunteers must be recruited. Active, enthusiastic nurses can be drawn from all health-related areas: hospitals, clinics, doctors' offices, temporary agencies, community health agencies, schools of nursing, and others. If enough volunteers are recruited, no one will be overburdened.

One way to recruit volunteers is through a "candidates' night," to which all candidates for a particular office are invited by a nursing organization. Once the slate of candidates is determined, ask all of the candidates for their schedules (well in advance) and select a date when all will be available. Advertise the event as a special reception for nurses. Work backward from the date of the event, and plan every detail. Create a flyer and distribute copies to area nurses; arrange other publicity; contract for a meeting place; order refreshments; and decide who will introduce the candidates and determine the format, including how long each is to speak and whether there is to be a question-and-answer period. Then delegate the tasks to get the job done. At the event itself, have an attendance sheet at the entrance, requesting name, address, and telephone number. If it is feasible, spend time with each guest and ask if he or she is interested in volunteering for upcoming political activities. Take notes (name, address, and telephone number), and follow up later with a telephone call to confirm the volunteer's commitment. For larger crowds, distribute volunteer cards and make a strong pitch for volunteers (Box 29-2).

Local community issue groups can provide additional information on volunteer recruitment. Handbooks are developed on a regular basis by a broad range of organizations such as the American

BOX **29-2**   Recruiting Volunteers

- Schedule an event that will involve one or more candidates—perhaps a coffee in someone's home or at a public meeting place. Candidates should make opening remarks, respond to questions, and ask for the support of nurses.
- Host a social event with a political theme for area nurses. Make it festive and fun. Invite several local political personalities to attend.
- Co-sponsor an all-day political skills seminar in conjunction with local political parties. At the conclusion, sign people up for jobs that appeal to them.
- Call a meeting to discuss upcoming political projects. Encourage each member of the core group to bring two friends. Then involve the guests in the conversation, planning, and strategy. By evening's end, they will be ready to help.
- Organize informal get-togethers ("brown bag lunches") at or near nurses' workplaces. Invite a local campaign manager or politically active nurse to speak, and then sign up volunteers.

BOX **29-3**   Effective Use of Volunteers

- Plan work for volunteers in advance of their scheduled time to volunteer.
- Give volunteers information about the type of work they will be involved in ahead of time.
- Keep to a realistic and accurate work schedule.
- Have the work ready for the volunteer's arrival, including any necessary equipment and supplies.
- Provide clear, detailed instructions.
- Have an experienced staff member or volunteer available for questions.
- Enlist the volunteers' help in making the most appropriate assignments, based on their strengths and weaknesses and the campaign needs.
- Maintain a comfortable and pleasant work atmosphere.
- Arrange for volunteers to work with friends or colleagues when possible.
- Provide appropriate snacks and cold drinks.
- Keep records of jobs that volunteers have done so that they may be called on again.
- Ask volunteers for feedback on the work assignments.
- Invite all volunteers to the election night celebration.
- Remember that not enough can be said about voicing appreciation. Whether the campaign is successful or not, people who gave their time to the campaign should be recognized and appropriately thanked.

Association of Retired Persons and the League of Women Voters.

Volunteers should be carefully cultivated, cared for, trained, appreciated, and treated with respect; their time should be well used, accounted for, and recognized. Volunteers can enjoy the time they spend working together. The team of volunteers in a campaign should feel as though they are an integral part of that effort, and they should be thanked and thanked—and thanked again (Box 29-3).

FUND RAISING

Candidates' war chests and their ability to raise money demonstrate their seriousness. One must raise money to get money. Major contributors who give large donations to a campaign want to know how much money a candidate has raised before they will contribute. It is also the first question asked by PAC directors. A volunteer or group that successfully raises money will definitely be appreciated.

Fund raising is both an art and a skill. Most organizations recognize the value of contracting with professional fund raisers and find that it is worth the initial outlay. The manner in which a fundraising appeal is conducted is vital. An error-free, attractive, and creative appeal for donations is worth the effort. An expert fund raiser knows how to do it and how to get the best price.

Candidates or volunteer fund raisers should start with family, friends, and colleagues. If time and money permit, messages should be targeted at specific groups in order to get the most from the appeal.

Much can and should be explored with respect to fund raising. Additional tips are provided in Box 29-4.

INDIVIDUAL VOTER CONTACT

Everyone involved in a campaign—the candidate, staff, and volunteers—is in the campaign to win, which means garnering more support than the

BOX **29-4** Fund-Raising Tips

- Determine the amount of money the campaign wants to raise and state it publicly.
- Remember that the most effective method of fund raising is one-to-one through direct, personal contact with a potential donor. (It is much harder for people to say no face-to-face.)
- Know that the most effective fund raiser is often the candidate. The candidate's time should be used wisely for the expected high-level donors.)
- Remember that people expect to be asked to give money, and most people don't give unless asked. Fund raisers cannot be shy. If you believe in your cause and organization, you should be asking for support and contributions of money.
- Always ask individual donors for more than they might be expected to contribute. (People never give more than what is asked of them.)
- When planning a fund-raising event, keep in mind that expenses should not exceed one third of the price of the ticket; otherwise the effort cannot be justified.
- Remember that people like raffles and 50/50 drawings, which produce many small individual contributions. They can be included in any fund-raising event, meeting, or gathering.
- Keep asking. The techniques of fund raising (mail solicitation, phone calls, personal contact) can be varied, but ask repeatedly.
- Keep records of those who contribute. Never give the list of donors away; lists are power. (If some other group asks for money, the people on your list may give to them and not to you the next time.)
- Thank people in person if possible. Send a thank-you note immediately. If the fund raiser is for a candidate, the campaign staff should send a thank-you note from the candidate.

opponent does. This is accomplished with a plan that is based on knowledge of the district voters—that is, who will support the candidate, who will not support the candidate, and who is undecided. Once voters have been identified, they must be contacted personally. One important fact here that often surprises those new to politics is that campaigners do not want to contact all voters—just those who will or might vote for their candidate.

An effective campaign gets the voters' attention. Voters are bombarded by information during a campaign. The goal is to get voters to notice the candidate, think about his or her commercial, and open mailed advertising pieces. Candidates are noticed when their messages are presented clearly and creatively and repeated over and over. Repetitive contact and following up that contact are essential to persuading voters.

The three most traditional ways to contact individual voters are through telephone banks, canvassing, and direct mail. Telephone banks and door-to-door canvassing are labor intensive, so a large number of volunteers must be recruited. They will also be needed to make follow-up contacts. Telephone banks, if well organized, can reach more voters in a shorter amount of time than canvassing. For telephone banks, a well-prepared script for volunteers is necessary. The numerous details involved in these efforts necessitate good planning. For example, 2 or 3 hours of telephoning per night is all a volunteer can usually do, so you must consider a number of variables when planning a telephone bank project: the hours, the number of telephones, the number of calls to be made, and so on. Telephone lists must be obtained, or numbers will have to be looked up before the telephoning can be done. In some areas, electronic dialing is available, utilizing names or numbers of members of political parties or organizations. Nurses and other volunteers new to phone banking may prefer coming in as a small group. Organizing groups of nurses from a particular hospital may be a way to bring in new volunteers.

A campaign kit is essential for canvassing. This kit can include information about the candidate, his or her position on issues of interest to the target group, volunteer cards for interested individuals to complete, campaign buttons, maps of the area, and sample outlines of what to say to the voters. It is necessary to avoid planning telephone or canvassing events that conflict with popular events such as the World Series.

Direct mail should be well designed, attractive, and personalized. If possible, a specific message should be directed to the concerns of particular voters, such as nurses, senior citizens, parents, or teachers. Such targeted messages are known to be among the most effective. Many campaign managers believe it is worth the expense to obtain professional help in writing direct-mail pieces.

New approaches to voter contact include organized efforts through churches and social organizations. Technology is expanding the horizon as well, with Internet pages and e-mail messages abounding.

MEDIA

Successful campaigns combine a well-funded and strategic media plan with a well-funded and carefully targeted voter contact program and field operation. The media plan should complement efforts to contact the individuals. Next to personal contact, television and radio are the most persuasive methods. Advertisements or articles that appear in local newspapers are often useful in local races, especially when money is tight. Television time is expensive, although creative campaigners can get free coverage through innovative campaign techniques. For example, a candidate can schedule "work days," such as spending a day in a clinic with a nurse or in an elementary school with a teacher, and obtain coverage for the experience. (See Chapter 10 for a discussion of gaining access to and using media.)

GETTING OUT THE VOTE ON ELECTION DAY

The final campaign step is getting people to vote on election day. Volunteers will be needed to telephone people, reminding them to vote. The intensity of the campaign heightens in the last few days. Voters may need babysitters or a ride to the polls. It is important to assist voters in many ways. Besides poll watchers, volunteers are needed to circulate near the voting place to persuade voters who are as yet undecided.

AFTER YOUR CANDIDATE WINS

After the glow of the victory celebration has worn off, it is important to build on one's relationship with the candidate, who is now an elected official. Most elected officials take their role in representing their constituencies seriously and need to hear from a broad range of voters. Nurses can continue to offer these officials a wealth of information about issues affecting the health and welfare of the community. Nurses interested in paid or appointed positions can then campaign for themselves, using the same skills that were successful in electing their candidate. Nurses frequently take on volunteer advisory roles on health issues. Those seeking staff positions may have assumed considerable responsibility during the campaign. They may continue to do so by, for example, creating events that help the newly elected official have access to a greater number of constituents. They may ask other supporters to recommend them to the elected official.

CONCLUSION

Nurses have a potentially important voice and role in all aspects of the political and electoral process. They have proven themselves to be capable campaigners, organizers, candidates, and voters. As nurses continue to work within campaigns at all levels of government, they can have an effect on the health and welfare of the citizenry. Simultaneously, they can contribute to the positive image of nursing.

REFERENCES

American Nurses Association. (1996). *Help make nursing count in Election '96*. Available from www.nursingworld.org/gova/voteintr.htm.

Barnes, J.E. (2000, October 1). The empty booth. *New York Times*, pp. CY1, 15.

Berke, R. (2001, March 21). An older electorate, potent and unpredictable. *New York Times*, special retirement section, 8.

Brace, K., Handley, L., Niemi, R.G., & Stanley, H.W. (1995). Minority turnout and the creation of majority-minority distrcts. *American Politics Quarterly, 23*(2), 190-202.

Bumiller, E. & Murphy, D. (2000, November 9). First Lady emerges from shadow and is beginning to cast her own. *New York Times*, A1, B18.

Carroll, S.J., Dodson, D.L., & Mandel, R.B. (1991). *The impact of women in public office: An overview*, New Brunswick, NJ: Center for the American Woman and Politics, Eagleton Institute of Politics, Rutgers—The State University of New Jersey.

Center for the American Woman and Politics. (1996). *Fact sheet: Summary of women candidates for selected offices, 1968-1996*. New Brunswick, NJ: National Information Bank on Women in Public Office, Eagleton Institute of Politics, Rutgers—The State University of New Jersey.

Center for the American Woman and Politics. (1997). *Fact sheet: Women in elective office 1997*. New Brunswick, NJ: National Information Bank on Women in Public Office, Eagleton Institute of Politics, Rutgers—The State University of New Jersey.

Center for the American Woman and Politics. (2000). *Fact sheet: Summary of women candidates for selected offices, 1970-2000*. New Brunswick, NJ: National Information Bank on Women in Public Office, Eagleton Institute of Politics, Rutgers—The State University of New Jersey.

Center for the American Woman and Politics. (2001). *Election 2000: Summary of results for women*. New Brunswick, NJ: National Information Bank on Women in Public Office, Eagleton Institute of Politics, Rutgers—The State University of New Jersey.

Chaffee, M. (2000). Policy web sites: Election information. *Policy, Politics, and Nursing Practice, 1*(2), 146-147.

Daniel, E. (2001, June/July). Making it work. *National Voter.* Available online at new.lwv.org/elibrary/nv/2001/voter_0601_1.html.

Dodson, D. (1997). Women voters and the gender gap. *Center for the American Woman and Politics: News and Notes, 2*(2). New Brunswick, NJ: Center for the American Woman and Politics, Eagleton Institute of Politics, Rutgers—The State University of New Jersey.

Duskin, M.S. (1997a). League reaches out to push participation. *National Voter, 46*(2), 4-7.

Duskin, M.S. (1997b). Number of women officeholders edges upward. *National Voter, 46*(2), 11-12.

Federal Election Commission (No date). The impact of the National Voter Registration Act on the administration of elections for federal office 1997-1998. Retrieved online, August 19, 2001, at www.fec.gov/pages/9798NVRAexec.htm.

Gallup Poll. (2000). The Florida recount controversy from the public's perspective: 25 insights.. Available online at www.gallup.com/poll/releases/pr001222b.asp.

Human SERVE (1996). *The impact of the National Voter Registration Act (NVRA) January 1995-June 1996: The first eighteen months.* New York: National Motor Voter Coalition.

League of Women Voters. (1996). *League of Women Voters.* Available online at www.lwv.org.

Morin, R. (1996, January 29). Who's in control? Many don't know or care. *Washington Post,* A1, A6, A7.

Piven, F. & Cloward, R. (2000). *Why Americans still don't vote: And why politicians want it that way.* Boston: Beacon Press.

Ponomareff, S. (2001). The first time shouldn't be the last time. *League of Women Voters—The National Voter.* Available online at www.lwv.org/elibrary/nv/voter_0301_4.html.

Rosenbaum, D.E. (2001, August 13). As redistricting unfolds, power is used to get more of it. *New York Times.* Retrieved online, August 19, 2001, at www.nytimes.com.

Simmons, W. (2000). Black Americans feel "cheated" by election 2000. *Gallup News Service.* Available online at www.gallup.com/poll/releases/pr001220.asp.

Simmons, W. (2001). Majority of Americans say more women in political office would be positive for the country. *Gallup News Service.* Available online at www.gallup.com/poll/releases/pr010104.asp.

Solop, F.I. & Wonders, N.A. (1995). The politics of inclusion: Private voting rights under the Clinton Administration. *Social Justice, 22*(2), 67-87.

Tedesco, J.C., Miller, J.L., & Spiker, J.A. (1999). Presidential campaigning on the information superhighway: An exploration of content and form. In L.L. Kaid & D.G. Bystrom (Eds.). *The electronic election: Perspectives on the 1996 campaign communication.* Mahwah, NJ: Lawrence Erlbaum Associates.

Verhovek, S.H. (2001, May 21). In state legislatures, 2nd thoughts on term limits. *New York Times.* Retrieved online, August 23, 2001, from www.nytimes.com.

Vignette   Joanne Rains Warner

Campaign Management: Policy's Primary Prevention Strategy

"Bad officials are elected by good citizens who do not vote."

GEORGE JEAN NATHAN

Policy work for nurses is important, but campaigns and elections are the "primary prevention" of this work. By this I mean that campaigns are the activities that precede policy making. Just as efforts in primary prevention in medicine seek to eliminate causes of disease or to create the conditions for health, campaigns can create optimal environments for good policy work. Campaigns determine who is at the policy table, deliberating over potential policy and making significant decisions. They determine whether elected officials understand the health implications of policies or nursing's contribution to societal health and well-being. With this in mind, I have managed or consulted with nine campaigns in the last 13 years, ranging from state representative to national professional organization presidency to local school board races. This vignette chronicles a school board election in which I simultaneously managed two separate but complementary campaigns. The local nature of the race belies the scope, drama, and significance of this election. The following story describes how 7 months of campaigning and $12,000 won two seats from a field of six candidates and positioned our community for a preferred educational future. The vignette recounts the background, planning, implementation, and implications of this process.

BACKGROUND OF THE BOWER AND SCHIESSWOHL CAMPAIGNS

About 30 years had passed since a major renovation of the New Castle Chrysler High School, located in a quiet, rural Indiana community. School administrators and the school board recruited a broad-based citizen group to study the building needs and locally viable options. Noting here that I served as cochair of that group reveals my bias. A $30 million project was proposed, accepted by the school board, and moved forward through proper channels. During this process, another citizen group formed, the self-named "Taxpayer Team" (TPT). The TPT opposed the renovation, criticizing cost and claiming administrative negligence in building maintenance. The TPT then succeeded in securing two seats on the five-member school board, positions they used to question the renovation and most other administrative actions. In an upcoming campaign cycle, two members would be elected: one who lived inside the city and one outside the city. The TPT sought to fill at least one of those positions to secure a board majority, halt the renovation, and reverse some other practices. Those who supported the construction proposal identified the renovation as adding critical technology, science and media lab improvement, disability access, and other features that supported student success and community viability to the existing facility. This group needed victory in both seats to advance their agenda.

The context was a community hotly divided in a new way. The division was not partisan, socioeconomic, or generational, but rather ideological: it was along lines of perspective on tax money management, community priorities, and the future of education. The conflict played out on editorial pages and at school board meetings in fervent exchanges. This highly visible election would settle the stakes and serve as a watershed moment for our community.

CREATING THE CAMPAIGN PLAN

After conversations with several community leaders, I agreed to build a short-term infrastructure to support two pro-construction candidates. Unlike other campaigns, there were no party or professional organizations to use as resources or even to validate my role as campaign manager. I knew my first strategic step involved fielding only one excellent candidate for each seat; this matched the TPT approach and reduced the likelihood of dividing votes among like-minded candidates and delivering victory to the TPT.

Securing only two electable candidates would involve a grass roots process and, ultimately, some finesse. A memo invited 52 community activists to "join a few good people to strategically prepare for the successful election of two positive advocates for education." The invitation paraphrased Edmund Burke, an eighteenth-century British statesman, who said, "The world becomes a worse place not by people doing bad things, but by a few good people failing to do something." I structured the meetings so that the group could interview candidates who were considering running and then give the weight of its endorsement to the strongest candidate. We emerged after several meeting with a board incumbent, Dr. Lynn Bowers, willing to serve another term in the outside-the-city seat, and a relative newcomer to the community, Cynthia Schiesswohl, to run for the inside-the-city seat. Unfortunately, two other candidates persisted, one in each race. With interpersonal finesse and respect for democratic freedom, I had private conversations with each, explaining the vision of advancing education and the significance of not dividing the vote. Each expressed a continued desire to run, and by the deadline to file a declaration of candidacy, each seat had three candidates. The drama intensified.

The next step involved recruiting a marketing expert to assist in theme development and media layout. When Sandy Broadstone agreed, I knew our past campaign partnership successes would be a predictor of future victories. Collaborating with reliable and energetic partners is key to electoral success, as well as preserving one's own sanity and enjoyment.

Theme development was our next challenge. What do you want to say to voters that answers the question, Why me now? (and by implication, Why not my opponent?). This one overarching theme must be reflected in all media and all statements. It was here that we realized we needed to run two separate campaigns. The incumbent board president brought the strength of experience and continuity but the baggage of supporting the school renovation. Cynthia Schiesswohl was an electoral unknown whose challenge was name and identity recognition. Together they carried the collective baggage; separately they were stronger. This decision to separate the campaigns increased our work, but it provided the opportunity for clearer messages from each candidate.

Developing the theme was a creative process of distilling knowledge of the voters, candidate, and context into something compelling, relevant, and succinct. "Putting Our Children First" emerged as Lynn Bowers' theme, an apt phrase for a pediatrician and experienced school board president. Messages credited Dr. Bowers with the recent school accomplishments, and highlighted his understanding of the issues. Presenting Cynthia Schiesswohl was more challenging; her personal and professional credentials were assets but not a ready match with the local preferences. In this conservative, rural setting, it was not an asset to be an educated woman, a lawyer who worked an hour away at an institution of higher education, a certified conflict mediator, and a minister's wife whose family could be transferred unpredictably. Add to that list an unfamiliar last name! Cynthia became "Cindy"—a mom who was skilled at "Taking Responsibility for Our Children." The visual was a chalkboard bordered with an elementary-style alphabet and "Cindy" scrolled across it. Her ads and image were warm and homey. Her local newspaper ads, billboards, and yard signs all conveyed this theme.

We believed that each of these themes would strike a responsive chord in the hearts of voters. The emphasis on theme development here reflects its importance in the campaign. A theme and the resulting message strategy form the foundation of all voter communication. Together our team (the candidate, his/her spouse, marketing consultant, and me) worked to demonstrate that the candidate is the message: an integration of biography, image, character, and issues. We worked to manage that message in every instance, repeating our theme, controlling agendas, and presenting the compelling answer to the question, "Why me now?"

Planning also involved targeting and research. This was more difficult than in a partisan race because in the latter, you can analyze prior election data and predict voter behavior. Our only data was one previous school board election when two TPT representatives were elected. Studying the information gave assurance that we could win, but no real guidance as to where to target effort, mailing, or media. We sensed that the momentum belonged to the TPT (due to their last election victories)—and that we were in for an uphill climb.

We planned our media activities to accomplish several objectives: name recognition, image promotion, and to a lesser extent, issue presentation. All media efforts remained in concert with the theme. The logistics of this process started with the creativity of our marketing consultant, timely reactions from the candidates and manager, and compliance with an overall calendar of media buys. We focused on print media (one local newspaper, billboards, and yard signs). Television was not affordable, and we believed the radio would not reach the people who would vote for Lynn and Cindy.

Funding plays a significant role in campaign infrastructures, and communicating that information with respect to a school board race was new to this community. Some prior elections had been won by candidates who had merely filed their candidacy, appeared at one candidate forum, and responded to one newspaper survey. I privately sought some significant funding to begin our process and planned several other strategies.

The last planning component is to ensure that leadership and management are adequate. Although I trusted my abilities, I was anxious about the most precious resource in a campaign: time. The demands of managing two campaigns while providing full-time administrative leadership for both an associate and baccalaureate nursing program would extract its toll. My belief in the significance of this election and the fervor of like-minded colleagues sustained me when sleep and relaxation were lacking. I trusted our plan and set out to implement it in ways that built community and healed rifts.

IMPLEMENTING THE PLAN

The campaign calendar was booked solid from February through the May 5 election. Many items were internal deadlines and reminders such as "Get approval for letter," "File campaign reports at court-house," or "Order yard signs." The following section, however, describes various external events and efforts designed to spark interest and promote voter turnout. Because an ideological division characterized the context, our goal was not to change people's minds and persuade the persuadable, but rather to get our like-minded colleagues to the polls on election day. Those efforts included the kickoff event, targeted mailings, door-to-door canvassing, yard signs, absentee ballots, a community debate, and paid media.

We held one kickoff event for both candidates, in part to clarify that there were two separate campaigns. I coordinated the evening by introducing speakers and inspiring the crowd to action. My remarks were framed around a "frequently asked questions" (FAQs) format, beginning with "Are Lynn and Cindy the *other* team? Are they running together?" FAQs allowed me to dispel rumors and plant positive perspectives on the work ahead. One FAQ named an emotion felt by the community at large, which was related to the future of our schools: "I'm afraid. Ain't it awful?" I responded that fear does very little that is positive, and the only awful thing that could happen is failure to take every opportunity to say to registered voters that this crucial election was winnable. I asked that we move with a sense of positive momentum in the context of civility and professionalism. The enthusiasm was high; we had begun the public phase of the campaign.

From this point to election day, we promoted the visibility of the two candidates through voter contact. Targeted mailings went to groups that we determined were invested in the sound economic development of our community and forward direction of education. These included active as well as retired teachers, the medical community, and church groups.

Door-to-door canvassing was an important strategy, especially for Cindy, as she worked to improve name recognition and identity. Candidates worked tirelessly, with volunteers and family members accompanying them. Though this was Lynn's third election, he had never before been required to run such a comprehensive campaign. Canvassing was augmented with small teas and club gatherings. Throughout the campaign, we kept emphasizing the themes and reinforcing the images.

Communities differ on their preference for yard signs; ours requires them. We designed them to be consistent with the theme and ensured that they were readable for people passing by at 50 miles per hour. Additionally, we arranged strategic locations for them (alongside the two main arteries of the city) and put them all up one Friday evening. We wanted to produce the effect "Wow, everyone must be voting for Lynn (or Cindy)!"

Absentee ballots can provide the winning edge, and this was accounted for in our strategy. We used the e-mail network of recent high school graduates to inform alumnae of this crucial election. Having a recent graduate son and being familiar with this group of young activists, I sent an e-mail saying, "Hi, college folks! I'm David Rains' mom, writing you an SOS. This isn't the usual Save-Our-Ship-SOS, but a crucial Save-Our-School-SOS." I explained about the election, referred them to the candidates' informative websites, and urged their involvement. I gave them important deadlines for absentee voting, offered to assist them, and encouraged them in their college studies. Many people responded; I counted it as a positive effort in these campaigns and part of the ongoing socialization of tomorrow's generation of citizens.

The only other joint appearance besides the kickoff was the debate that included all six candidates. Prepared remarks were written by the candidates, rehearsed, and critiqued the previous evening in my living room. I was grateful for coachable candidates and knew their responsiveness to feedback was a mark of success. I planned a robust attendance of supporters at the debate to continue the sense of dynamic momentum and to communicate to the candidates they were not in this alone.

The last public implementation strategy involved paid media. Media design, printing, and placement consumed 85% of our budget. We ran the first ad for four weeks, familiarizing voters with themes and reinforcing names. Our second and third ads ran for one week each, and we concluded with a compelling ad on the night before the election. We placed 26 ads for Cindy and 12 for Lynn, whose name recognition required less media reinforcement. The expertise of our media consultant and her familiarity with local markets were the keys to our media effectiveness.

Candidate websites were new to this community's election repertoire and were well received. The distinctiveness of each campaign was communicated in our media, and the general public had little idea that one manager was coordinating both.

We chose to not spend resources on polling and consequently went into election day with no data on predicted outcome. Election day activities were therefore thorough and vigorous. Volunteers worked at each polling area, the candidates made appearances at high-volume sites, phone banks were operational, and offers of rides to the polls were made. An inherent anxiety propelled the campaign through the 12 hours of voting, and when the polls closed at 6 PM, we gathered at one home to await the precinct-by-precinct announcements.

Cheers accompanied most announcements, with Cindy winning 18 of the 25 precincts and Lynn winning 21 out of 25. In three-way races, Cindy and Lynn each garnered 53% of the vote. The newspaper called the wins "convincing." The winners declared the outcome a message to move ahead with school renovation and requested healing in a community splintered by the controversial building project and other issues.

IMPLICATIONS OF THE PROCESS

The decisive victories affirmed our strategic map and message. I credit the victories to our well-developed themes, which resonated with voters, and the opponents' failure to develop images and themes that could cut through communication chaos. Experience has taught me that theme development and early planning make or break a campaign.

I often reflect on the purposes of campaigns and elections. The obvious purpose involves securing the preferred perspective and voice at the policy table. As mentioned earlier, this form of "primary prevention" eliminates the possibility of some problems and establishes channels of communication with decision makers. The implication is that an election is only one step in influencing policy and public processes. This primary purpose doesn't dim the significance of two other campaign outcomes: community building and engaged citizenry.

My campaign modus operandi emphasizes the potential of community building. Especially at the local level, I remember that on the day after the election, when I will meet opponents in the grocery or at church, I want to be proud of all my words and actions. What keeps this possible is a focus on what I'm working for, not against, as well as the integrity of fact and intent. My community-health nursing background nourishes these beliefs and grounds me in my environment.

An engaged citizenry is also a part of the process of community building. I consider it a privilege to help my neighbors and friends believe in democracy and act as if their action matters. Campaigns present significant opportunities to model my own civic involvement and belief in the effectiveness of one engaged citizen. Nursing is both the origin of these beliefs and the avenue to express them, as I pursue with others a healthier, vibrant community.

Nursing has provided me with great preparation for my campaign management experiences. It taught me multitasking on a limited budget under serious time constraints. It prepared me to reconcile competing demands and accommodate contentious personalities with professional grace (usually while under public scrutiny). I also credit nursing with my belief in the power of one engaged citizen and the potency of an organized collective. Therefore, campaign management is for me the practice of nursing, that is, the application of my nursing skills and values in pursuit of a better world.

POLICYSPOTLIGHT

POLITICAL ACTIVITY OF GOVERNMENT-EMPLOYED NURSES

Tracy A. Malone & Mary W. Chaffee

"Government of the people, by the people, for the people, shall not perish from the Earth."

ABRAHAM LINCOLN

Citizens of the United States revel in their many freedoms—celebrating Independence Day, speaking out on radio call-in shows, and conducting public demonstrations when a political issue lights a personal fire. It seems to be a paradox, then, that the U.S. government restricts the type of political activity in which government-employed nurses, as well as other employees, may participate. This policy may appear to be a restriction of political freedom and the right to free speech, but the limits serve as a means of protecting the employee from coercion. Nearly 60,000 nurses nationwide are subject to these restrictions.

Two major regulations affect the political behavior of government-employed nurses. First, the Hatch Act limits the political activity of civilian nurses serving in a variety of government agencies, including the Veterans Administration, the Department of State, the U.S. Public Health Service, and the civil service system. Second, a Department of Defense regulation limits the political activity of nurses who serve on active duty in the Army, Navy, and Air Force.

THE HATCH ACT

The Act to Prevent Pernicious Political Activities, more commonly known as the Hatch Act, was passed in 1939. The Hatch Act restricts the political activity of executive branch employees of the federal government, the District of Columbia government, and certain state and local agencies. Because the original Hatch Act was extremely restrictive, multiple attempts have been made to amend the legislation and loosen restrictions. In 1993, Congress passed legislation that substantially amended the Hatch Act, allowing most federal and DC employees to engage in many types of political activity. While these amendments did not change the provisions applying to state and local employees, they do allow most federal and DC government employees to take an active part in political management or in political campaigns. The Office of Personnel Management (OPM) published the translation of the amendment into specific regulations in the July 5, 1996, *Federal Register.*

Nurses employed by the federal government in any status (i.e., full-time, part-time, permanent, temporary) are subject to restrictions on political activity. Nurses covered by the Hatch Act include the following:

1. Federal employees
2. District of Columbia employees
3. Employees of state or local agencies in programs funded by the federal government
4. Commissioned officers in the U.S. Public Health Service

The political activity of government employees is restricted to protect employees from coercion by corrupt politicians and political organizations. In the 1930s a Senate panel discovered that certain federal employees had been coerced to support specific political candidates in order to keep their jobs. Senator Carl Hatch of New Mexico introduced legislation that was enacted in 1939 to end this practice. Senator Hatch also feared the development of a national political machine made up of federal employees following the directions of their employers. Additionally, the Hatch Act maintains the political neutrality of government offices.

Political activity is defined as any activity that is directed toward the success or failure of a political party, candidate for partisan political office, or partisan political group. A general overview of political activity and all federal employees is provided in a presentation on the U.S. Office of the Special Counsel website at www.osc.gov/hatch.

For nurses covered by the Hatch Act, a wider range of political activities is now possible because of Hatch Act reform, with some specific restrictions.

Nurses covered by the Hatch Act *may:*
- Register and vote as they choose.
- Assist in voter registration drives.
- Express opinions about candidates and issues.
- Participate in campaigns where none of the candidates represent a political party.
- Contribute money to political organizations.
- Attend political fund-raising functions.
- Attend and be active at political rallies and meetings.
- Join and be active members of a political party or club.
- Sign nominating petitions.
- Campaign for or against referendum questions, constitutional amendments, or municipal ordinances.
- Campaign for or against candidates in partisan (political party—affiliated) elections.
- Be candidates for public office in nonpartisan elections.
- Make campaign speeches for candidates in partisan elections, as long as the speech does not contain an appeal for political contributions.
- Distribute campaign literature in partisan elections.
- Help organize a fund-raising event, as long as they do not solicit or accept political contributions.
- Display a partisan bumper sticker on a private automobile used occasionally for official business.
- Contribute to a political action committee through a payroll deduction plan.

Nurses covered by the Hatch Act *may not:*
- Solicit or receive political contributions from the general public.
- Coerce other employees into making a political contribution.
- Become personally identified with a fund-raising activity.
- Participate, even anonymously, in phone-bank solicitations for political contributions.
- Solicit political contributions in campaign speeches.
- Display partisan buttons, posters, or similar items on federal premises, on duty, or in uniform.

- Participate in partisan political activity while:
    On duty
    Wearing an official uniform
    Using a government vehicle
    In a government office
- Sign a campaign letter that solicits political contributions.
- Use official authority or influence to interfere with an election.
- Solicit or discourage political activity of anyone with business before their agency.
- Be candidates for public office in a partisan election.
- Wear political buttons on duty.

Although Hatch Act reform has resulted in greater opportunity for political participation, handling political contributions remains off limits. Personally accepting, soliciting, or receiving political contributions is not permitted under current regulations.

Enforcement of the Hatch Act

The U.S. Office of Special Counsel (OSC) is an independent federal agency charged with enforcing the Hatch Act and several other federal laws. Headquartered in Washington, DC, the OSC investigates and, when warranted, prosecutes violations before the Merit Systems Protection Board. The OSC serves a dual role under the Hatch Act. Its mission includes preventing Hatch Act violations through the use of advisory opinions, and enforcing and prosecuting violations of the act when they do occur. Each year the OSC issues approximately 2000 advisory opinions, enabling individuals to determine whether and how they are covered by the act, and whether their contemplated activities are permitted under the act. The OSC also enforces compliance with the act, receiving and investigating complaints alleging Hatch Act violations.

The OSC is currently looking into over 100 allegations of Hatch Act violations from the 2000 presidential election. Although the OSC is still in the process of investigating these cases, the majority involve situations where federal and state government employees have engaged in political activity while at work in government offices. Specifically, some of these violations include posting campaign materials in government work space and using government e-mail to solicit support for political candidates. Most of the state government employee violations involve members who were unclear as to their ability to run for public office while serving in state government.

With the wave of new political appointees about to enter government service as a result of the 2000 presidential election, the OSC has stepped up efforts to get the message out that federal employees, political and career, must use the many opportunities available to them to learn about the Hatch Act's requirements. Although the OSC will prosecute violations of the Hatch Act, it views its primary role as helping federal employees avoid such violations in the first place.

The OSC provides advisory opinions to anyone seeking advice about political activity and the Hatch Act. Advice may be requested in writing or by calling the OSC using the following contact information: Hatch Act Unit, U.S. Office of Special Counsel, 1730 M Street, NW, Suite 300, Washington, DC 20036-4505; phone: (800) 854-2824 or (202) 653-7143; website: www.access.gpo.gov/osc.

Penalties for Violating the Hatch Act

Federal employees who violate the Hatch Act may be punished by removal or by a minimum 30-day suspension without pay. Violations of the Hatch Act applicable to state and local employees are punishable by removal or by forfeiture, by the employer, of an amount equal to up to 2 years of the charged employee's salary. In matters not sufficiently serious to warrant prosecution, the OSC will issue a warning letter to the employee.

Case Study

Violations of the Hatch Act often become publicized when they involve Senate-confirmed presidential appointees. In December 2000, the acting administrator of the Health Care Financing Administration (HCFA), an office of the Department of Health and Human Services (DHHS), resigned from his post rather than face disciplinary action for violating the Hatch Act's prohibition on soliciting funds for a partisan political purpose. The employee hosted a fund raiser for a congressional candidate in his home in May 2000. This particular federal employee began working for the federal government in 1998, when he was appointed as the HCFA deputy administrator. Although the employee advised the OSC that he had received an orientation package of materials including educational publications from both the OSC and HHS regarding the Hatch Act and its prohibitions at that time, he admitted that he had not reviewed the material.

Approximately a week and a half after the fund raiser, the employee received a request from the DHHS to respond to a letter from the Senate Governmental Affairs Committee regarding campaign activities by the DHHS political appointees. The Senate committee's request prompted the employee to consult with the HCFA's Designated Ethics Officer (DEO). After consulting with the DEO, the employee voluntarily reported his violation to the OSC. The employee fully cooperated with the OSC throughout its investigation. In light of his cooperation, the OSC agreed to settle this case without seeking further action.

DEPARTMENT OF DEFENSE REGULATIONS

Restrictions similar to those in the Hatch Act regulate the political behavior of the 11,520 nurses on active duty in the Army, Navy, and Air Force. The "spirit and intent" of Department of Defense Directive 1344.10prohibits any activity that may be viewed as associating the DefenseDepartment with a partisan political cause or candidate.

Nurses in the Army, Navy, or Air Force *may:*

- Register, vote, and express their personal opinions on political candidates and issues, but not as representatives of the uniformed services.
- Encourage other military members to vote, without attempting to influence or interfere with the outcome of an election.
- Contribute money to political organizations, parties, or committees favoring a particular candidate.
- Attend partisan and nonpartisan political meetings or rallies as spectators when not in uniform or on duty.
- Join a political club and attend meetings when not in uniform.

- Serve as nonpartisan election officials, if:
  They are not in uniform.
  It does not interfere with military duties.
  Approval is provided by the commanding officer.
- Sign a petition for legislative action or for placing a candidate's name on a ballot, but in the service member's personal capacity.
- Make personal visits to legislators, but not in uniform or as official representatives of their branch of service.
- Write a letter to the editor of a newspaper or other periodical expressing personal views on public issues or political candidates.
- Display a political bumper sticker on a private vehicle.
- If an officer, seek and hold nonpartisan civil office on an independent school board that is located on a military reservation.

Nurses in the Army, Navy, or Air Force *may not:*
- Use their official authority to influence or interfere with an election.
- Solicit votes for a particular candidate or issue.
- Require or solicit political contributions from others.
- Participate in partisan political management, campaigns, or conventions.
- Write or publish partisan articles that solicit votes for or against a party or candidate.
- Participate in partisan radio or television shows.
- Distribute partisan political literature.
- Participate in partisan political parades.
- Display large political signs, banners, or posters on a private vehicle.
- Use contemptuous words against the president; the vice president; Congress; the secretaries of defense, transportation, or the military departments; or the governors or legislators of any state or territory where the service member is on duty.
- Engage in fund-raising activities for partisan political causes on military property or in federal offices.
- Attend partisan political events as official representatives of the uniformed services.
- Campaign for or hold elective civil office in the federal government, or the government of a

state, territory, the District of Columbia, or any political division in those areas.

Nurses serving in the military are encouraged to obtain an official opinion from a military lawyer if they are unsure about participating in a specific political activity.

American nurses have created new horizons in policy and politics by becoming increasingly sophisticated in their political knowledge and by becoming actively involved in influencing health care in many environments. Many have translated professional nursing skills into effective political skills. Government-employed nurses should have their voices heard, as all other nurses have the opportunity to do, and participate actively in the political process. However, it is critical that they be aware of and abide by the laws and regulations designed to offer them a nonpartisan workplace and protection from coercion. Although the availability of information and educational materials on political ac-

tivity and government employment is abundant, it is the nurse's responsibility to review and understand the provisions of the Hatch Act and Department of Defense regulations to avoid any unnecessary violations or misuse of their key positions in the U. S. government.

Resources

American Nurses Association. (1992). The political nurse: Your rights under the Hatch Act. *Capital Update, 10*(1), 4-5.

Hatch Act Reform Amendments of 1993, 5 U.S.C., 7321-7326.

Head of HCFA is forced to quit for Hatch Act violation. (2000, December 16). *Washington Post,* A17.

Political activities by members of the armed forces on active duty (Department of Defense Directive 1344.10). (1990, June 15) (with Change 2, dated February 17, 1994).

Shafritz, J.M. (1993). *American government and politics.* New York: HarperCollins.

U.S. Office of Special Counsel reaches disciplinary action settlement in Hatch Act Case involving acting HCFA administrator (U.S. Office of Special Counsel press release). (2000, December 15).

Pilgrim in Politics

Eve Franklin

"I don't know what your destiny will be, but one thing I do know. The only ones among you who will be really happy are those who have sought and found how to serve."

ALBERT SCHWEITZER

HOME ON THE RANGE—AGAIN

The Missouri River was running just below flood stage as the early June warmth melted the unusually heavy snowpack high in the Rocky Mountains. The snowmelt combined with the heavy spring rains put much of north-central Montana at risk of serious flooding. The Sun River—the waters the Blackfeet called the Medicine River, originating from springs at the continental divide—was rising over its banks. Trotting along the river trail with a few other early-morning joggers, on such a clear and promising day, it was difficult to perceive the danger in the water spilling over Black Eagle Dam. But the thunderous pounding of 30,000 cubic feet of water per second crashing over the concrete dam structure and the uncharacteristic whitecaps on the Missouri were unmistakable signs of a river system poised to create chaos along its banks.

I was home from the state capital, Helena, at the close of the 1997 legislative session. In budget language, I was a "vacancy savings" during my 90-day stint as a full-time legislator in the Montana State Senate. In layman's terms, I was taking a leave of absence without pay from my "day job" on the faculty of Montana State University College of Nursing. While the college cobbled together a jigsaw arrangement of faculty assignments during my absence, I relinquished my faculty salary and instead collected the grand sum of $58.60 per day for my legislative service. Montana is a rural state with a strong agricultural economy, and we meet on a biennial schedule stretching from January to April. During the

period between full-time sessions, we have responsibilities to serve on interim legislative committees and a moral obligation to engage in necessary constituent service.

The service may include such varied activities as following up on delinquent child support, assisting an individual to understand the state contract bidding process, advocating a small business loan, unearthing the details of a bungled pension application or workers' compensation claim, and perhaps, though no particular grievance may be identified, meeting a generally dissatisfied constituent for coffee. This service is an expected portion of our role, and the legislator receives no remuneration for the hours of essentially volunteer work accomplished without the luxury of staff or material resources.

I am always struck with what a good background nursing is for the role of a citizen legislator—we learn to accomplish a great deal without the benefit of very much institutional support.

The 4-month January-to-April schedule was originally designed to make it possible for legislators who were primarily engaged in farming and ranching to attend to the details of state government during the slack times on the ranch. In 1997, we still had more farmers and ranchers serving in the legislature than representatives of any other single vocation. We certainly had more ranchers than lawyers, which probably set us apart from the majority of other state legislatures.

As I worked my way along the trail, the tumultuous waters are a curious contrast to the peace I felt at being at home on the high plains of Montana. This peace of mind had been a long time coming—years, in fact. It had a great deal to do with a grateful entry into my middle years, in which I have achieved a more grace-filled relationship with my family, my friends, my professional life, and myself. I almost didn't recognize it for what it is at first. It can be easier to cling to the more familiar anxiety, the tension of a pressured existence, than to learn the skills of living a more integrated life. I have often described myself as a relatively low-key person functioning in a "type-A" life.

A solid 6 years of service in the state senate, two campaigns of my own, multiple campaigning for others, a full-time job teaching nursing, multiple board responsibilities, community involvements, and marriage have challenged my basically slow-paced personality to perform at a level I never would have imagined possible even 10 years ago.

"I don't remember how to relax," I confessed to a friend during my first week back in Great Falls. On the ninetieth day, the president of the State Senate dropped the gavel, announcing in Latin, *"Sine die"* to mark the end of the fifty-fifth session of the Montana legislature. I had made a decision shortly after that moment to take a summer hiatus, which meant making an effort to act like a normal person by: (1) working in the garden, (2) reading mystery novels, (3) not accepting a summer job to make up for my lost salary during the legislature, and (4) putting a few limits on my legislative activity to enjoy the brief Montana summer. Yet I felt like I was in some sort of purgatory between work and play, not wanting to do the first and not knowing how to do the second.

"Run," advised my friend Barbara. "Every morning, get up and do some vigorous exercise." Not surprising advice from a woman who, at 57, regularly ranked at the top of her age class in competitive runs. I did, however, follow her guidance, not out of any particular commitment to physical fitness, but rather out of desperation. I had to find a way to join the rest of the world. The chafing of role demands and personal need has a good deal to do with the reality of being a state senator in a rural state, in a close-knit community that expects a very personal relationship with the legislators, whose home telephone numbers are in the directory and who assume they will be contacted—and we are. We would be considered irresponsible if we did not make ourselves readily available to several thousand constituents (or anyone else in the state, for that matter) that might have something to say. In a state whose political history is deeply rooted in the concept of an accessible citizen legislature, where your state senator or representative might also be your son's math teacher or work the neighboring farm, there is a strong connection to the individual elected to serve in state government. There is an instant intimacy that is very much a parallel of the relationship that nurses have with patients. Both nurses and legislators come in contact with individuals at times of crisis and share an intensity of thought and feeling, listening to their most precious concerns and needs and trying to solve their problems.

I was first elected to the Montana State Senate in 1990 after having lived in Great Falls for less than 3 years. At 32 years of age, I came to make a life different from what I'd known as a "genetic" New Yorker. Despite the style differences, I found life there to be oddly familiar to my soul and a profoundly good fit for the adult I had become and the person I still hoped to be. A geographic transplant, I came west to Montana a few years before the wave of "nouveau Montanans" flooded the western part of the state. These refugees from southern California, New York, and Oregon who had escaped to purchase a 20-acre Montana "ranchette" generally arrived with little regard for Montana history, culture, or community.

One of the sweetest comments I heard during my first years in Montana was made to me by a friend who had grown up in Anaconda, Montana, in the 1950s (pronounced *Anda*-conda by the local folk, though no one seems to know why). Anaconda, then a bustling company town, was dominated by the Anaconda Copper Company. It was a rough-and-tumble society, the legacy of the copper kings and the railroad barons, with fiercely close-knit ethnic populations of Irish, Slavs, and Italians. Along with Butte, it has been the beating heart of the Montana labor movement.

"A lot of people move to Montana, and they don't *get* it, Eve," confided my Anaconda friend. "You get it." This was a balm to the soul of a "new girl" who wanted very much to belong in her new home. But exactly what was it that I seemed to "get"? Through the years, as I developed a deeper sense of the social and political context of Montana society, this passing comment assumed importance to me on different levels. A comment made in a casual conversation became more than a compliment about my ability to get along. It was a trigger for thoughts about community, class, and political context. Why did this eastern urbanite feel so much at home in rural Montana?

What has become clear to me is that what we define as *community* has a great deal to do with a transcendent appreciation that grows from the mutual need of neighbors, be they rural or urban. Montana homesteaders knew they could not get through a harsh winter without their neighbors; growing up in a working-class neighborhood in New York City, I knew that neighbors counted on neighbors to help them through a multitude of situational crises of daily living. This often involved borrowing a needed household item, a small loan for a quart of milk, and of course, sound advice on the trials and tribulations of life that was passed down through generations of Sicilian and Jewish women. What I shared with my Montana neighbors was a traditional sense of community not based on the unique idiosyncrasies of rural or urban lifestyle, but instead grounded in an economic reality that was fertile soil for a real connection between neighbors: interdependence, necessity, and ultimately friendship.

The "nouveau Montanans," who identified strongly with right-wing political thought, came to Montana with a romantic notion of the "independent West" based on John Wayne movies and Merle Haggard songs. "Take your retirement and take your so-called social security," Merle sang in the 1980s. "Set me free somewhere in the middle of Montana."

I'm not sure how Merle planned for these folks to take care of themselves in their old age. We in public policy suspect that it would have had something to do with tax dollars contributed by other citizens—neighbors—who did not entertain the luxury of feeling quite so "free" of the constraints of civic responsibility.

The "nouveau Montanans" brought with them a desire for 20 acres of land designated "agricultural" for tax purposes, a Rottweiler, and a no-trespassing sign. These folks were a part of the electorate that begrudged funding for public schools and public services and rejected the use of federal funds (except

for road construction, money that is miraculously cleansed, unlike the "tainted" federal money that would be channeled for Head Start, Educational Goals 2010, or health care). This self-involved attitude is actually the antithesis of historic Montana attitudes. Although Montana culture has always valued independence and self-sufficiency, these qualities are seen in the context of community.

This morality play is not unique to Montana. We are a microcosm of the political and social struggles for community throughout the country. We all have a stake in the collective fate of our community, whether it's New York, California, Wisconsin, Indiana, or Montana. A no trespassing sign does not release us from our shared destiny.

THE LADY WITH THE LAMP—AND THE GAVEL

Most of us who enrolled in nursing school were affected by an altruistic notion of ministering to a pained world, healing bodies and spirits one at a time. I recall drinking in the stories about visionary nursing pioneers: Mary Breckenridge, founder of the Frontier Nursing Service, who traveled on horseback "from holler to holler" in rural Kentucky; Lillian Wald, who climbed tenement steps and negotiated rooftops on the lower east side of Manhattan to reach her patients; Dorothea Dix, who made great strides in humanizing mental health care; Margaret Sanger, who educated poor women about their ability to control their reproductive lives, ultimately enduring prison and exile for violating the Comstock Laws; and, of course. Florence Nightingale, who revolutionized modern hospital care. Many of my classmates in 1974 came from a traditional model of nursing, religion, and womanhood. When St. Ursula's School in the Bronx released its senior class of girls, an overwhelming percentage of this high school graduating class ran across the Grand Concourse, a wide boulevard lined with prewar brick apartment buildings, and registered for the nursing curriculum at Lehman College. Not being a member of that comfortable enclave of parochial-school girls who had been putting bandages on their cats since childhood, I came to the nursing program with a still-unformed jumble of ideas about nursing and my relationship to it. I knew it had something to do with implementing social justice and good works, about choosing meaningful work in a superficial world. I also knew it was how I could make sense of personal and familial history and my integration with the larger world: pioneering Zionism meets rural Kentucky, the labor union activist meets Mother Teresa, the action of the young anti-Nazi partisan Chana Senesh meets the abstraction of feminist historian Barbara Ehrenreich. Nursing provided a way for me to give personal voice to social action and form to feminism. It seemed that there was nothing more radical, more challenging, more "womanly," than to be a strong woman in traditional woman's work. We novice nurses did not have the luxury of assuming the male vestments of power used by women who entered traditionally male fields of law, medicine, and business. Feminist nurses would meet the challenge of health care with the inspiration of our foremothers, our wits, and a darned good baccalaureate education.

Adult developmental theory suggests that both personal and professional growth follows a path that has recognizable patterns and dynamics. The making of a nurse legislator includes a personal journey as well as professional growth. To become an effective nurse and advocate, one must not allow the idealism of youth to be lost; rather, the idealism becomes strengthened by the intimate knowledge of work that has to be done and the wisdom of having been around the block a few times, as the saying goes. In the 1980s, a social observer described the *impostor complex.* This syndrome particularly hounded young professional women in their 30s who found themselves acknowledged as experts on the job and as functioning well in roles with significant responsibility, and yet who lived with the dirty little secret that they felt somehow they were play acting, as though they were impostors. A wonderful epiphany occurs when we are able to shed the fears of being a professional play actor, a big kid in grownup's clothes, and accept on a visceral level that we do indeed have expertise to offer patients and colleagues. We have learned our trade through intellectual inquiry, curiosity, and perseverance.

I recall being asked in 1991, at the start of my first legislative session, "Who do you work for?" The assumption was that a woman in her 30s with a relatively unpretentious style and in tailored clothing was likely someone's secretary (and lucky to have her, I might add). Or someone would ask me who my husband was, assuming I was a legislator's spouse. Since I had not yet married—nor could I word-process very well—I was bemused by these assumptions and corrected them: "I'm Senator Franklin." My delight was the embarrassment of lobbyists who knew they would have to redeem themselves after this faux pas. However, the identity errors made because of my newness to the political scene in the first few weeks of my first legislative session soon evaporated. My impostor struggles were dissipating as I reached new levels of confidence.

Despite having spent all my adult professional life tending to the feelings and needs of others, I was not at all confused about where the desire to care needed to change to a commitment to battle and, in the political context, an absolute requirement to fight. In politics as in nursing, caring means little if you can't deliver; compassion is limited if you don't have the gumption to fight for good outcomes; and kindness is as vacuous as being "nice" if it doesn't mean beneficent action and advocacy.

Our foremothers knew this: Florence, Dorothea, Mary, Margaret, Lillian, and so many others who effected change. They were nurses and expert politicians. They worked the system to create change, and they changed the system when it didn't serve human needs. They tapped into power, influence, and money when it helped the cause. They knew that without connecting to powerful forces in our culture—either the power of the elite or the power of the "masses"—their work simply could not be done.

By the end of the 1991 session, I had gained a reputation as a nurse legislator who had passion for and knowledge about health care issues. I had sponsored a bill requiring insurance companies to cover the cost of mammography on a preventive model. This was a contentious requirement, known in insurance lingo as a *mandated benefit.* It was a public policy demand that private and public insurers make mammography as an early screening tool available to their customers without their having been diagnosed with breast disease.

Senator Eve Franklin (right), Vice-Chair of the Senate Finance Committee, holding budget hearings.

The health care and consumer advocates argued for the bill, using the adage "An ounce of prevention is worth a pound of cure." Wouldn't we be saving great sums of money and oceans of human misery if we could spend a little money up front for preventive measures instead of paying such a high price at the other end? The insurance companies bared their fangs and fought back relentlessly. Of course, we have sympathy for the poor victims of breast cancer, they intoned when testifying at committee hearings, but we can't possibly cover mammograms—it will raise rates for all our customers. They could report to the penny how much it would raise monthly premiums to cover the cost of this screening tool, but they simply could not grasp the concept that prevention is less costly than tertiary care. Those of us who had been around this block before knew the dark reality that the acute-care paradigm drives the system. Whether or not the insurance people could get this concept was not the real issue. They didn't want to get it because a paradigm based on prevention would irrevocably alter life and business as they knew it.

Finally, the bill passed—not necessarily because of my fine legislative prowess, but because several legislators on the health committee who were generally most sympathetic to insurance industry posi-

tions had been touched by great personal sadness in their own lives, having lost a wife or another beloved relative to breast cancer. These were the humanizing moments, when even the most hardcore apologists for the insurance industry's position blushed with embarrassment while they held tenaciously to the "bottom line" theory of financing for the delivery of health care services.

MODERN HEALTH CARE REFORM, OR THE RED MENACE IN WHITE SHOES

In the interim period between legislative sessions, I was asked by our senior U.S. senator, Max Baucus, to participate in a citizens' effort to explore options and recommend changes in the health care system at the state level. Max (Montana citizens like the familiarity of being on a first-name basis with their legislative delegation, except in the most formal settings) had the vision and savvy to see that, although the Clintons were beginning to examine health care reform at the federal level, the action had been at the state level throughout the early 1990s. Minnesota, Vermont, Oregon, and North Dakota, to name a few, had undertaken serious reform efforts spurred on largely by the escalating cost of health care and the explosive effect on state Medicaid budgets. Max wanted to ensure that Montana was not left behind in the rapidly changing health care scene. He and his staff assembled a variety of people, representing business, labor, agriculture, seniors, Indian nations, and consumers, as well as the dean of the Montana State University College of Nursing—and one nurse legislator. The senator supported this exciting effort with staff and resources from his Montana office. With breakneck speed and intensity, the committee met to develop what we hoped would be the basis for legislation that would address the unique health care needs of Montana.

The vast geography of Montana defines many of our important policy issues and has determined the history of settlement, economic development, and health care beliefs. Rural health care theory is accepted throughout academia as a legitimate theoretical framework in which to view the health needs of rural people and to find relevant responses. No one anecdote summarizes classic rural stoicism, which has been documented by theorists, as succinctly as the conversation I had with a family during a 3-day telephone outage during the first month after my arrival in Montana. Opal's husband had chronic heart disease and had experienced episodic acute symptoms that required medical attention. They were both in their mid-70s and lived on a small ranch about 35 miles from town.

"Are you concerned about being without your telephone?" I asked sincerely.

Opal gazed at me a bit quizzically. "Well, now," she responded rather matter-of-factly, "I just load 'im in the pickup and drive to town." Silly me, but of course, I'd just come from a health care environment where some of my patients would call 911 for a hangnail. Seriously.

Health as a concept in rural theory has been defined as the ability to do one's work. Tom T. Hall, a popular country music singer in the 1970s, recorded a song with a poetic title: "Who's Gonna Feed Them Hogs?" This 4-minute song describes an incident in which the narrator is briefly hospitalized and finds himself sharing a hospital room with a very ill hog farmer. The clever ditty goes on to say that, in his delirium, worrying desperately about his farm chores, the old farmer calls out repeatedly, "Who's gonna feed them hogs?" Finally, in the last bar of music, the farmer shakes off his delirium, puts on his overalls, and leaves the hospital to slop his livestock. Congruent with perceptions of health described in rural health theory, this fictional character had recovered his health. Where there's work, there's health. I use this song as a teaching tool in the classroom with nursing students to illustrate the very poignant and real aspects of health care beliefs and behaviors.

The vastness and isolation of Montana have also led to a health care system with huge gaps in service, resulting in innovative and sometimes quirky practices designed to respond to community need. There are many anecdotal examples that highlight the realities of health care and the challenges to reforming health care delivery in a rural state. One afternoon a legislator from Wibaux (pronounced *Wee-bow*), a community so far to the eastern part of the state that it is 700 miles from the western border, stopped me in the senate cloakroom for a little

consult. The cloakroom is a narrow vestibule that is a pivotal part of legislative culture, a place out of the public eye where for a few moments, legislators can shed the armor, chuckle over events of the day, share a cigarette in the "smoking corner" (not me, of course), or do a little insider horse trading.

"What do you know about pharmacy law?" she asked, showing real concern. It had come to her attention that a common custom in the health care delivery system of that community could potentially be a violation of state law. Wibaux does not have a pharmacy. For the citizens of Wibaux to have prescriptions filled, the bus driver for InterMountain Bus Line would pick up a prescription in a larger community 70 miles away and would transfer the needed medication to the interested party at the crossroads of Highway 94 and Highway 7. A question apparently came up as to the legality of this practice—the dispensing of medication not by a licensed pharmacist but by a bus driver. This legislator was feeling considerable consternation that an integral part of the health care delivery system in that isolated community was threatened.

The parking lot at the local Great Falls hospital center has electrical outlets for recreational vehicles. It is not unusual for families to camp out in their RVs when traveling with an ill family member seeking care. As a mental health nurse, I became particularly aware that many people who needed mental health services received it only in the form of a trip to a general practitioner's office, and they may have had to travel a considerable distance at that.

The size of the region has also been a deterrent to recruiting and retaining health care providers in rural areas. Health care professionals may have been drawn to the beauty of the place but often succumb to the strain of professional isolation and the rigors of being the only provider in a vast area, having no one with whom to share calls or to consult with on a regular basis over a cup of coffee. I have a professional acquaintance, a psychiatric nurse who was for many years the only mental health resource in a small city in eastern Montana. The only way she could take a vacation was to leave town because everyone knew where she was and when to reach her in the most informal of ways: "Oh, you need to talk to Marge? I just saw her at the grocery store, and she should be home in a few minutes."

As we moved into an era of serious discussion of health care reform at the federal level, these rural characteristics only highlighted for me the need for a state-driven effort to examine our health care needs and define the kind of delivery system best suited to respond to those needs. If even our own state's regulatory practice, as in the case of the pharmacy issue, did not always acknowledge the realities of health care delivery in a rural context, then we had reason to be concerned about the implementation of aspects of a system designed at the federal level or by private industry headquartered in another part of the country. With a heightened awareness of issues affecting rural health care delivery, our Montana Citizen's Health Care Advisory Group worked with a great sense of purpose.

In 1993, Hillary Clinton visited Great Falls, Montana, at the invitation of Senator Baucus after we had passed our health care reform bill. Participating with Mrs. Clinton on a panel before 500 local people was an exciting experience indeed. She charmed us all with her warmth and straightforward manner, but I watched her win the hearts of the audience when she said, "I've traveled all over this country, exploring health care. I've seen rural in Tennessee, I've seen rural in North Carolina and Georgia—but this, this is mega-rural." Hillary was right on target, and any changes in our health care delivery system had to be sensitive to our "mega-rural" nature.

As our citizens' committee evolved, our lively discussion and research made some things clear. We agreed on certain principles of improved access, quality, and attempts at cost containment. We also agreed on solid support for advanced-practice nurses as a way to improve access and quality. However, the disagreement between the activists who wished to formally recommend a single-payor system and those who wished to follow a more familiar, regulated multipayor model could not be resolved. In October 1992, the committee completed a document that we described as a "principled framework" that could act as a model for either payment system.

Major provisions of the framework included a commitment to guarantee health benefits for all Montana citizens, a data collection process to serve as a tool for future policy research, insurance reform that would deal with the onerous practice of establishing the preexisting-condition exclusion and provide for guaranteed cost control mechanisms, and a network of regional planning boards that would focus on community involvement and planning. A high-level, "blue-ribbon" panel was created—the Montana Health Care Authority, whose mission would be to study and steer the health care reform efforts of the state. Appointed by the governor with bipartisan input, the five members of the authority would become our policy experts and sages on the matter of reform. One of the most exciting aspects of the model was an ambitious plan for public input in the form of town meetings and public hearings to be conducted all over the state.

We expected the document would become a bill that, if passed in the 1993 session, would empower this panel of trusted Montana citizens to put the full resources of the state behind a deliberate legislative process of reform spelled out in our recommendations. It was a time of great enthusiasm and hope for nurses and other consumer advocates who had devoted themselves to improving health care. I was proud that our document and our eventual bill would so closely parallel many aspects of the American Nurses Association's policy statement, Nursing's Agenda for Health Care Reform.

During the 1993 session I ate, drank, and dreamed health care reform legislation. I was the chief sponsor of the bill, and we glibly tried to dub it HealthMontana. However, the pedestrian practice of referring to bills by number prevailed, and no one, including me, could use that catchy name. We all referred to the legislation by its computer tracking number, Senate Bill 285. Taking on sponsorship of a weighty bill means that you are head shepherd, facilitator, negotiator, cajoler, counselor, conniver, compromiser, peacemaker, and sometimes, when you simply have to be, capitulator. It was a tough but exhilarating time. I stretched every muscle and fired every synapse that I could muster in my sophomore legislative session. I was playing with the big kids, and it was a very serious sandbox with real-world implications for our health care future. This bill was the embodiment of everything I held dear in nursing.

The bill had the backing of our Republican governor, obtained logistic assistance from our Democratic insurance commissioner, and received enthusiastic support from groups as varied as the Montana Cattlewomen's Association and the AFL–CIO. The bill passed the Senate 49 to 0 and sailed through the House. I had done everything in my power to keep from politicizing the effort or exploiting it as a divisive partisan issue. I argued that this issue was bigger than all of us and that if we stayed true to our task, partisan politics could not destroy our sincere desire to improve health care delivery. Exhausted but driven, I returned home after the session, ready to face the challenge of reforming health care through Senate Bill 285—Lillian Wald, Florence Nightingale, and me.

Admittedly, the legislative approach in Senate Bill 285 represented a big change in thinking in relation to health care. However, the progressive 6-year process of benchmarked activities set forth in the bill allowed for much intellectual and philosophical freedom. I felt secure in the knowledge that we were embarking on the first 2-year phase of health care reform—that reason and sincere concern for the welfare of our citizenry would win against resistance born of narrow industry interests.

By the summer of 1993, the Montana Health Care Authority members were appointed, and a brilliant, nationally recognized health policy consultant was engaged to facilitate the education of authority members—as well as the public—regarding the options available to us in the structuring, organizing, and financing of health care services. The Montana Health Care Authority, made up of some of the state's most illustrious citizens, set out on the road in a dizzying schedule of work sessions open to the public, engaging citizen groups from Libby in the northwest corner to Miles City in the southeast in this public conversation. As they began this larger-than-life task, detractors emerging from the shadows were sowing the seeds of fear and distrust. Some detractors, resistant to any change, called it a million-dollar study bill, and other naysayers found no comfort in the deliberate data-gathering and study aspects of the legislation, calling it much too radical.

Ah, but it was a brief moment in the garden. An alliance of right-wing ideologues, fringe insurance peddlers, and, sadly, a large number of Montana physicians were formed to discredit the effort before it had really begun. Within 9 months of the governor's putting his signature on Senate Bill 285, and after the hope-filled inauguration of the Montana Health Care Authority, the threads were beginning to unravel. In January 1994, a leader of a right-wing tax protest group held a press conference in conjunction with half a dozen other professional obstructionists, including the Christian Coalition, Montana Right to Life, and Montana's junior U.S. senator, a Republican, to announce their vigorous opposition to the direction of the Montana Health Care Authority. Their agenda included an effort to wholly discredit the health care reform effort and to embarrass our moderate Republican governor, whose presence was requested at the press conference.

They called the plan "perverted," essentially insisting that our true intent was to deny health care to old people, euthanize the terminally ill, and promote "abortion on demand." It was labeled a plan that undermined everything good, true, and American. It was almost laughable to make such accusations, but they were deadly serious, and I was having a little trouble maintaining a sense of humor.

Thus the assault on health care reform began in earnest, and it did not stop until the demonization of Montana health care reform was complete. Although largely quiet during the legislative discussion, the Republican right wing, pivotal supporters of the governor's party, became wild-eyed in their accusations about the unwholesome nature of the provisions of Senate Bill 285 upon its implementation. The popular governor who had so vocally supported health care reform—he even included it in his State of the State Address in 1993—distanced himself from the Montana Health Care Authority. His withdrawal of active support paralleled the rise of the radical and religious right in our state's political power dynamic. Though the Montana Health Care Authority continued its phase-one mandate, which included 18 months of planning and study and the implementation of small-group insurance reform, an effective alliance of the industry status quo operatives and the religious right continued to detract successfully from the reform plan.

Later, in the spring of 1994, a nurse colleague of mine in another city reported to me with some distress a comment that had been made during public testimony at a Montana Health Care Authority town meeting. A physician vehemently opposed to the health care reform effort had alerted the assembled citizens to the potential dangers ahead: "Remember what happened the last time we listened to someone named Eve!" he warned. My, my—state health care reform and my championing of it had reached biblical proportions deserving of Old Testament wrath. Eve in the garden had eaten of the apple of health care equity. Could she ever again be an innocent, or had she been changed forever by the no-holds-barred rules of health care politics? Answer—she would be forever changed.

Part of my tenacity in fighting the fight that lay ahead was fueled by my recognition that the dynamics of this struggle paralleled every struggle nurses have ever had with physicians at the bedside over patient care. It was archetypal that some of the state's most visible champions of health care and some of the most publicly vocal opponents were physicians.

I had completed my first 4-year term in the State Senate and stood for reelection. A statewide militantly antireform group based in Great Falls, made up largely of obstructionist physicians and a few of their disciples, made my involvement in health care reform a major rallying point in their efforts to defeat my bid for a second term. Their one issue was the establishment of a health care system based solely on medical savings accounts (MSAs). No deviation from the dogma of total devotion to MSAs would be tolerated. They backed my opponent, footing the bill for a fund-raising letter mailed widely in conjunction with the local chapter of a nationally organized right-wing religious extremist group. Never was the adage "Politics makes strange bedfellows" more apt. To torture myself, I would multiply the membership of the physician group—approximately 75—by $500, the maximum legal contribution for one physician and one spouse. My arithmetic told me they had the potential to raise $37,500 to defeat me, three times the budget for a typical Montana legislative race. That was a war chest so stocked that it made me break into a

metaphorical fund-raising sweat. In retrospect, this was just the motivation I needed. My competitive urges were in overdrive, and I'd be damned if I'd allow an honest desire to improve health care to be distorted into something unrecognizable. The antireformers' extreme and one-dimensional focus on "patient responsibility" left me furious. It mimicked the sociologic concept of "blaming the victim." When in this whole process did it become the patient's fault that the health care system wasn't working? I raised more money, knocked on more doors, built more yard signs, talked to more voters, and smiled beatifically. I chose to think that the credibility of nursing's commitment to health care was vindicated when I won the reelection campaign with 61% of my district's vote.

PEGGY LEE HEALTH CARE REFORM PLAN: IS THAT ALL THERE IS?

What I came to understand was, though I had survived politically, the work of the Montana Health Care Authority had been irreparably damaged by campaigns of innuendo and policy bashing. The authority had generated a huge body of work but, because of unbearable political pressure, was not permitted to continue past the first phase set forth in the provisions of Senate Bill 285.

As a member of the Montana Health Care Authority would say to me later, "I was afforded a million-dollar education in health care that I am not being permitted to use." The governor withdrew his support, feeling, I can only assume, that he had spent just about all the political capital he wished to spend on this whole affair. After the failure of the Clinton health care plan, most were in a duck-and-cover mode when it came to health care. The 1995 legislative session, with a new Republican majority that owed much to the right wing, passed a bill nullifying Senate Bill 285 and putting in its place an ineffectual poor cousin of a committee with little stature and minimal resources. The legislature passed a few bills touted as moderate health care reform. In fact, they were in large part a codification of insurance custom, with the modification of a few of the more onerous measures related to preexisting conditions. Tweaking of insurance law passed for "incremental reform," and I couldn't get an honest hearing for a retooling of the Montana Health Care Authority in the Republican-controlled committee. Moderate Republicans were on the run from the right wing of their party and wouldn't touch health care with a 10-foot pole. The die had been cast in the world of power politics, and I would be persona non grata in the legislative health care scene for one session. I became a Leadership Circle contributor, pledging $250 to the American Nurses Association's political action committee, and prepared for the next round.

Occasionally people would ask, "Are you discouraged that the work of the Montana Health Care Authority wasn't followed through?" My answer was always the same: "I'm a nurse. I've worked with chronically ill patients for years. I don't get discouraged in the face of chronicity." You take pleasure in the small triumphs and the increments of progress and acknowledge that you're in it for the long haul.

Though the Republican majority played bait-and-switch with public opinion, and the Montana Health Care Authority was being discarded in the legislative scrap heap, Montana was being alerted to the new reality of the health care industry. In 1993, when Senate Bill 285 was passed, the rest of the big markets in the country were becoming battlegrounds for big managed care companies. At that time we had one fledgling health maintenance organization (HMO) network operated by Blue Cross-Blue Shield of Montana. However, Montana's attitude toward health care reform was about to come of age. In the period between 1995 and 1997, our insurance commissioner and the Montana Department of Public Health and Human Services went to work to create a body of state law that would provide oversight for the managed care industry, which was knocking on the regulatory doors of our state. The big managed care companies had eaten California, and rumor had it that they were heading our way.

"You thought government involvement in health care was bad?" I'd say to anyone who would listen. "Wait until private industry takes the market share. Everything you worried about in relation to government—bureaucracy, lack of choice of provider, and even high cost—will occur under the auspices of private industry. But industry control will be a lot less benign than government control."

Ironically, though I was perceived by the health care foes as being some kind of Nurse Ratchet of big government, I've never been a proponent of a so-called government-sponsored system. Nevertheless, I have the deepest reservation about the concept of the free market at work in health care. There is big money to be made from the vulnerability of others, but I suspect it has more to do with the strict application of the corporate bottom line than with healthy competition. Who said it was acceptable for corporations to get rich from the misery of others? Certainly not Lillian, and certainly not I.

YEAR OF THE BLACK HELICOPTERS

In 1997, in a surprise move during a Democratic Party caucus, I was drafted to be minority whip for our merry band of partisans. This position is second in command to that of the minority leader, who is the chosen leader of the Senate Democrats. I was honored, pleased, and a little horrified. At 42 years of age, I had mercifully been released from an impostor complex. Now, instead of saying, "Who, me?" my insides started saying, "Why not me?" Once again, my belief that a good nurse is prepared to meet any challenge was confirmed by events. The whip role was curiously familiar, reminding me of a combination of my days as a hospital administrator and the hours worked in a psychiatric emergency room.

The 1997 session came on the heels of the infamous Jordan, Montana, standoff, in which members of the Montana militia movement holed up on a remote ranch kept both local law enforcement and the Federal Bureau of Investigation (FBI) at bay. This was the atmosphere that preceded our return to Helena to tend to the business of the state.

My beloved citizen legislature, that of the state that sent great humanists like Mike Mansfield and Pat Williams to Congress, was undergoing a seizure that gripped other parts of our nation as well. The 1997 legislature was heavily influenced by right-wing thought. We debated and in some cases passed bills that dealt with these issues: public bare-butt paddling, reintroduction of corporal punishment in the public schools, and new censorship laws that included libraries and schools, to name a few. We passed a resolution or two condemning the United Nations and the federal government. My colleague and seatmate, in an attempt at satire, drew up an amendment to one of these resolutions, condemning the use of black helicopters to monitor citizen activity. Black helicopter surveillance is a favorite paranoid fantasy of militia sympathizers. If he had actually followed through and presented it on the Senate floor, it might have passed.

In this environment, the Senate dealt with health care issues by passing a managed care regulatory bill and state codification of the Kennedy-Kassebaum insurance reform bill. In an atmosphere where insurance interests ruled supreme, I was publicly accused by another legislator (with whom I regularly battled over ideologic health care) of being a member of a dark, unnamed "special interest group." I took great pleasure in owning up to that membership in a letter to the editor of a major daily newspaper. "Yes," I declared, "I belong to the Montana Nurses Association, a group of 1400 nurses dedicated to improving health care. Our special interests are quality health care, consumers, and supporting the professionalism of nursing."

WHERE DO THEY SEND OLD LEGISLATORS?

A political event at the ballot box in 1992 changed the face of Montana politics for the foreseeable future. A public opinion campaign, focused on bringing the concept of term limits to the Montana legislature, was waged. This notion played on the frustrations of the average voter, pounding home the idea that those "old dogs" just wouldn't get out of the way for new thought. Montana maintains a part-time citizen legislature. Remuneration is modest, with (as mentioned previously) a salary of approximately $58.60 a day while in session (90 days every other year), with per diem and salary for the committee meetings attended in the interim. No showy perks to speak of; you pay for your own stationary, your own business cards, and your own telephone calls to the state capitol when performing constituent work. No interim office, no interim personal staff, and of course, no interim compensation. Those of us who thought that imposing term limits was a flawed idea pointed out that in this

part-time structure it took years to become truly sophisticated about complex issues of budget and policy, and interestingly, the legislature turned over by approximately one third each session due to voluntary retirements and changes at the ballot box. We argued that that pattern provided the right combination of "new blood" and necessary stability. However, cynicism prevailed as the term limit measure passed in 1992. Legislators such as myself were "grandmothered" in—or *out,* as the case may be, and allowed to serve (if elected) two additional terms. My term is up in December 2002. It is with both sadness and relief that I anticipate the transition to civilian life. In so many ways, I have always had a love-hate relationship with the legislative role. I am essentially an introvert in an extrovert's life, a somewhat slow, drifting individual functioning in a type-A mode. I can do it, chameleon that I am, but it takes its toll, even on a changeling of a lizard like me. The relief comes from a knowledge that I will in fact gain greater control over my time and be in a place where my life is more my own. The sadness is that I know how absolutely critical it is to have a nurse in a decision-making role in state government.

A FEW THOUGHTS ON WHAT I HAVE LEARNED

I have often extolled the virtues of nursing education and practice as fine preparation for a legislative position. We are well grounded in the use of assessment skills at every level, we know how to construct an action plan, we are outcome oriented, and we possess the skills to evaluate our actions. We practice "stick-to-it-iveness" and feel a commitment to follow through, and we are in touch with many of the existential issues of the human condition. There are, however, some inherent dichotomies in being both a nurse and a legislator. So much of our professional socialization in nursing prepares us to support the needs of others, deflect attention from ourselves, and avoid conflict. One seldom thinks of political animals deferring to others, smoothing troubled waters, or taking a back seat in a public arena.

For nurse activists to be successful, we must develop a set of skills that have not been reinforced through nursing education, a comfort with our own skills, and an understanding of how to use the power of our personalities. We must shed the albatross of nursing, the need to be "liked." It is in learning these new dimensions of our role—in fact, of our personhood—that we become effective in more than one style of advocacy.

Blending conventional political skills with nursing consciousness creates a synergistic power cell. We are living out a new model of political action, transforming in the process both the political arena and ourselves. The behaviors that are traditionally associated with altruism are powerful medicine in a society that needs social, political, and economic healing. The ethic of professional nursing has provided the way to meet the challenge of meaningful social involvement and political action.

The nuances of policy making are arcane, subtle, and powerful in terms of how nursing care and health care are affected. So many of the outcomes that have been positive for health care depended on years of work to understand the process. Outcomes have often depended on the relationships that I have forged with other legislators, industry executives who have come to know my work and appreciate or at least acknowledge my perspective, department heads in state agencies who have come to view me as an individual with knowledge of health care issues and the ability to shape the budget and the policy that affects their work. Legislative work has been a calling, not unlike one that draws an individual to nursing school or the religious life. My mission over the next year is to recruit another nurse, one who is "nurse identified" to run for a legislative seat. It is absolutely essential to have nurses not only in lobbying positions, but to have one on the inside. As for myself, I occasionally ask where life and activism will take me. Where does a nurse legislator with an esoteric body of knowledge go when she is put out to pasture? Then I grin and say, "I never planned before. Why start now?"

30 Contemporary Issues in Professional Organizations

LINDA J. SHINN

"Alone we can do so little; together we can do so much."

HELEN KELLER

The United States has moved from a product-driven to a customer-driven society. The impact of this fact for professional organizations is huge. Most have yet to respond to this basic truth, even though they may be intellectually aware of it. They have yet to re-create themselves into a radically new model that can attract and retain customers and members into the next decade.

The contemporary challenges that membership organizations face are as follows:

- Competition in the marketplace
- Demands for improved service
- Need for more efficient and effective operation
- Members who want an immediate, tangible return for their investment of dues dollars

The programs or products that the organization thinks are good for their members will no longer suffice. Rather, members or customers will drive what an organization is and does, and technology is driving what they expect.

This chapter will explore the changing environment faced by all associations and the implications of these changes for nursing organizations.

MEMBERSHIP

About 7% of the nation's nurses belong to the American Nurses Association. It is estimated that another 13% belong to specialty nursing organizations (Foley, 2001). Nursing organizations, however, are not offering something of value to the remaining 80% of the nation's nurses.

The days of joining an organization for altruistic reasons are over. The association that will fare the best in the future is the one that focuses on the question "What tangible value can we give to the member?" rather than "What we can take from the member?" People today are asking, "How will membership help me? How will membership 'put money in my pocket?" Members and prospects will gravitate to associations that can answer these questions—and it likely will not matter whether the organizations are nursing organizations.

While there is some competition for membership between nursing organizations, the major competition is coming from the Internet. People in every walk of life give the same two reasons for joining an association: networking and information. The Internet is a treasure trove of information that can be downloaded at the click of a button. Chat rooms, buddy groups, and listservs all provide opportunities for instantaneous networking. These information and networking opportunities are often free or cost only a few dollars a month.

GENERATIONAL CONSIDERATIONS

Generational differences are also important considerations for membership recruitment. Those in Generations X and Y:

- Have little interest in politics and voting

- Believe skills are more important than credentials
- Expect greater balance between work and personal life
- Want to focus more on family and friends
- Learn from sound bites and find information on the Internet

These attitudes make it harder for organizations to sell memberships and certification credentials or to solicit political contributions from members of these generations.

Baby boomers present a different challenge for nursing organizations. Organizations such as AARP are gearing up to woo aging boomers by focusing their publications and products on the boomers' changing interests and lifestyles. Since the majority of nursing organizations' memberships are boomers, attention to their changing interests is critical.

MEMBER BENEFITS

Associations have historically provided members with a generic, "one size fits all" set of benefits, programs, and services. Information and advocacy have been the mainstay of the programs offered by most associations, including nursing associations.

Information.   The raison d'etre of most associations has been the information business. The association has often been the best source of information for the trade or profession it represents, delivering information through scholarly journals, newsletters, or educational programs. The World Wide Web, however, enables every member to search for information (in many instances, free information), making it increasingly difficult for the association to serve as a single source of information for a profession. Technology is also driving members to expect more information, products, and services from their associations and to want them faster. The success of the Cable News Network demonstrates that people want information both quickly and on demand.

At the same time, consumers (association members are consummate consumers) want products and services customized to fit their unique needs and wants. For example, the Levi Strauss Company makes it possible for the customer to buy a custom-fit pair of jeans for only $10 more than the usual re-tail price. Nurses want programs and products that help them with their practice, work setting, and families. In other words, nurses want services customized to their individual situations.

The emerging role of associations is to help members figure out how to sort, interpret, and use the information coming their way to add value to their businesses or professions. Associations might become the "middlemen" between information producers and information users, helping members decide what information is relevant, useful, and meaningful. This information will have to be customized to member needs, and it will have to be delivered in a print or electronic format when the members want it, not when the association wants to provide it. Large tomes of information will have to be synthesized by the association and provided to members in "bites." The desire for information in bite-sized, easily digested chunks provides a great challenge for nursing associations that have long published scholarly journals and treatises on professional issues.

Education programs have been the prevalent strategy for delivering information to members. The increased necessity for lifelong learning for members to be able to survive in today's job market could be a boon for continuing education programs. However, the number of "e-learning" groups and organizations that offer distance learning makes it easy for a nurse to access education from a computer or television without having to belong to an association or attend its educational events. In addition, colleges, universities, and private entrepreneurs are inundating nursing organizations with requests to sponsor programs or provide endorsements. These groups find association partnerships and endorsements attractive, as they provide access to member information and add legitimacy to their educational offerings.

Speed is also of the essence. Organizations can no longer take 12 months to plan an educational offering and another 6 months to market it. The pace of change, the advent of new information, and the dispatch with which people want new knowledge necessitates offering educational opportunities at lightning speed. The American Society of Association Executives developed and offered a technology conference for association executives in 3 months (Schweitzer, 2001).

Advocacy

Legislative and Regulatory Work. Influencing legislation and regulation is a key program for many associations in fulfilling their missions. There are a number of trends that influence association legislative and regulatory work. Trends and related implications include the following:

- Mistrust and cynicism about government at all levels may manifest itself in increased mistrust or lack of support for association governmental affairs programs.
- Concerns over political fund raising may result in increasing difficulties for fund raising by nurses' political action committees (PACs).
- The shift of federal responsibilities to state and local levels of government will necessitate a shift of national resources, including personnel and money, to state and local levels of an association.
- The interest in reinventing government at all levels, including greater public-private partnerships in doing work traditionally performed by the government, requires associations to remain vigilant of "reinvention" schemes and to partner with government in the association's area of expertise.

Policymakers at all levels of government are now tapped into the Internet and are urging their constituents to provide immediate opinions or views through e-mail or chat rooms. The role of the association as the intermediary between member and policymaker may shift toward helping members learn how to be influential with legislators, regulators, and other policymakers on the Internet.

The increasing shift of federal responsibilities to the state governments will also impact how nurses influence public policy. Nurses have built a formidable national mechanism to influence health policy in three major ways: (1) through the development of grass roots networks that can be relied on to relay nursing's views to Congress, (2) through building a well-funded PAC to help elect members of Congress who are favorable to nursing, and (3) through grooming nurses to be spokespersons, lobbyists, and office holders. Though it is important to fortify national mechanisms to influence public policy, focusing more attention on influencing the views of state and local office holders on health matters, con-

tributing to state and local candidate coffers, and supporting nurse candidates for office will increase nursing's strength and influence in public policy. Strengthening state and local resources necessitates more collaboration and alliances among nursing associations at state, chapter, district, and local levels.

Nurses have historically partnered with government to improve the nation's health. Immunization programs, acquired immunodeficiency syndrome (AIDS) awareness activities, and health screening initiatives are good examples. In this age of greater interest in public-private partnerships, nursing has an opportunity to get even more done through local government than it has in the past. Jarrat, Coates, Mahaffie, and Hines (1994) suggest that associations might:

- Offer training programs for local elected officials
- Channel issues, ideas, and know-how into the process of reinventing government
- Set up voluntary teams to help state and local governments develop public policy

Nursing is well suited to each of these roles. For example, a district nurses association might conduct a seminar for a county council on Medicaid cost savings achieved by publicly supported prenatal care programs, an organization of nurse executives might provide expertise on organizational restructuring, or a chapter of occupational health nurses might offer policy consultation on workplace safety standards.

The media have become the most significant influencers in shaping public policy. "At the same time, government shapes public opinion by using more showmanship, such as televised town meetings" (Jarrat et al, 1994, p. 122). Nursing's focus on state and local initiatives is important, but more attention must also be given to grooming and supporting a cadre of media-savvy nursing representatives to help shape public opinion in every community (see Chapter 10).

Historically, the American Nurses Association took the lead on legislative and regulatory initiatives at the federal level. Today, specialty nursing organizations are playing an increasing role in shaping public policy. Organizations such as the American Society of Pain Management Nurses (ASPMN) are creating public policy programs. ASPMN, for example, has joined the Coalition for

Pain Management and other interested groups to influence the Pain Relief Promotion Act. ASPMN has testified before Congress and has appointed a past president to act as a liaison to legislative and regulatory bodies. (See the Unit Five Case Study.)

Collective Bargaining and Workplace Advocacy. Other important advocacy programs for nurses come through collective bargaining and workplace advocacy activities. The American Nurses Association and its constituent member associations have been the leaders in addressing the workplace concerns of nurses. It is estimated that about 350,000 of the nation's 2.2 million nurses are union members today (Freudenheim & Villarosa, 2001). Roughly one third of these nurses are represented by United American Nurses (UAN), the union arm of the American Nurses Association (ANA). Some 20 other unions represent nurses for collective bargaining, and a number of these unions are vying with the UAN to represent nurses. In an effort to strengthen the UAN, they voted to affiliate with the ALF-CIO in 2001 (see Chapter 19).

The following issues are the subjects of bargaining unit work:
- Staff restructuring
- Mandatory overtime
- Health and safety
- Job security
- Professional practice (e.g., needlestick injuries, quality of care)
- Professional development
- Wages and benefits

In recent years, ANA and its constituent member associations have worked hard to develop additional tools for nurses to use to address workplace concerns. These "workplace advocacy" tools range from consultation on health and safety issues, advice on ethical dilemmas, securing whistleblower protection, and advocacy before boards of nursing to coalitions focused on prevention of violence and mandatory overtime. In addition, rights that were previously restricted to unionized employees are now found in the non-union workplace. For example, the National Labor Relations Board, in a July 2000 decision entitled *Epilepsy Foundation of Northeast Ohio,* reversed a long-standing precedent by determining that employees not represented by a union have a right to have a coworker present at an investigation interview that the employee believes could result in disciplinary action. In this case, two employees of the Epilepsy Foundation had problems with a supervisor and told the foundation executive director that they no longer needed the supervisor's oversight and criticized the supervisor's work. The supervisor and executive director requested a meeting with one of the employees, who asked that the other employee be present for the meeting. The request was denied, the employee expressed opposition to meeting alone with the supervisor and executive director, and he was fired for gross insubordination. Subsequently, the second employee was fired (Carson & Franklin, 2001).

Multipurpose Organization. As noted earlier, organizations will become more and more customer driven. The ANA is struggling with this phenomenon at the moment. While the organization has tried valiantly to be a multipurpose association serving the educational, practice, and workplace needs of its members, there has been a constant push and pull related to priorities and resources. The major struggles have been related to the amount of money devoted to the labor relations program and to the philosophical underpinnings of the program. Three of the ANA's constituent member associations voted to leave the association, believing that they could use the ANA's dues more effectively "at home" to support their labor programs. One of the associations has affiliated with another labor union. Several other constituent member associations have divested themselves of their collective bargaining programs. In several of these states the ANA and its loyalists are working to rebuild a state-based association, but progress is slow. This loss of membership puts the future of the ANA at risk.

Dues. While associations are faced with the demand for customized products and services, members will also want their association payments tailored to their usage. For example, a member of the Oncology Nurses Association (ONS) may want the ONS Career Resource Kit and 12 issues of the *ONS News* but not the *Oncology Nursing Forum,* which is also part of the member benefits. Nursing associations will be faced with developing both a core package of member benefits for all members and a menu of services from which members can select additional programs or products that meet their specific needs. This will necessitate constant attention to member needs and discarding some programs that have served altruistic purposes in the past but have had few tangible advantages for members. Some associations are moving away from traditional memberships and toward "customerships." Customers can pay a premium for a package of special services, as the traditional member once did, or pick and pay for only what they want.

STRUCTURE AND GOVERNANCE

LEADERS

Almost all associations are "graying," particularly at the leadership table. The majority of associations are filled with baby boomers who may give up leadership responsibilities during the next 20 years or want to contribute smaller chunks of time and effort than they do at the present. On the other hand, there are predictions that the boomers will work longer and many will prefer part-time work. This inclination has implications for managing multiple generations of members and volunteers in one organization.

Associations will be challenged to develop and implement plans to groom and train future leaders, plans that provide for a mix of seasoned and fresh leaders for the association. Long leadership ladders in associations, that is, moving from committee member to committee chair to board member to officer to president, are no longer acceptable. People will not commit this amount of time to an organization.

Some organizations report that academics are assuming the bulk of leadership roles in nursing associations. This is being done to meet the community service requirement for promotion and tenure. Practitioners do not have the same demand for community service in their employment setting or the same time to give to associations. Care will have to be taken to ensure a balance of nursing interests and employment settings at the association leadership table.

Association nominating committees must begin to serve as search committees and work year round to identify and develop talent for the association. The limited human resources available to lead professional nursing organizations necessitate profession-wide attention to grooming leaders for the future, not just organization-by-organization planning.

In addition, nursing leaders must sharpen their capacity to forecast the future, including changes in the marketplace that will demand differing numbers of nurses with differing skill sets for different practice sites. Nursing leaders are also going to have to sharpen their ability to learn from events, mistakes, and miscalculations. For example, the profession missed the mark in not anticipating the restructuring that would take place in health care institutions and the subsequent consequences for nurses. At this time, nursing's leaders should be anticipating what will happen after "managed care" and should be readying the profession to meet the next wave of change and challenge. Nursing's leaders must also strive to unite the profession around a common agenda. Too often, nursing's professional organizations have been successful only in uniting the profession around a common enemy—for example, the registered care technologist.

DECISION MAKING

Few associations are structured in terms of their mission and goals. Perlov (1995) notes that associations are trying to operate in a twenty-first-century milieu with a nineteenth-century structure. Many association structures were fashioned around the hierarchical industrial model. In addition, history, personalities, and politics drive the structure and governance of most associations, rather than the mission, goals, or plan of work.

Many associations are saddled with decision-making structures that make it almost impossible to arrive at a policy stance or take advantage of any opportunity without engaging a large decision tree, such as consulting a myriad of committees or chapters, or waiting for a house of delegates to meet. Such modes of doing business must give way to a cadre of leaders who have an eye on the mission, a finger on the member pulse, an ear to the ground, and the confidence, trust, and backing of those who elected or appointed them to make the necessary decisions. Members are also going to have to permit leaders to take risks and make mistakes. The consequences will have to be seen as learning opportunities and forward movement, rather than letting the organization remain trapped in the stasis of ever more layers of decision-making, cross-checking, and second-guessing leaders.

Trends in structure and governance include smaller boards, fewer committees, and an ad hoc approach to getting business done. For example, some associations select a committee structure once the association's strategic plan is in place. A committee is created on the basis of the work identified in the plan, is given an assignment to carry out and the tools and resources necessary to complete the job, and is disbanded when the job is done.

Technology has done away with the need for an association executive committee, traditionally created to act on behalf of a board of directors between meetings. Today, all board members can be convened to act on behalf of an association at almost any time. Increased use of technology, such as audio and video conferencing, requires that association leaders be trained in the use of these tools for decision making. Technology also permits convening special interest groups, task forces, or committees for one-shot assignments or one-time input.

Every nursing organization must ensure that decision-making mechanisms are built for action. Each organization must guarantee that it is mission driven, that it is sensitive to its members and market in its work, and also that its structure and governance evolve from its strategic plan.

CHAPTERS

Members and prospective members initially identify with an organization based near the area where they live and work. In fact, a national association's identity (what it is and does) and image (the *perception* of what it is and does) are shaped at the local level. Chapters are the heart of many nursing organizations and the point of attachment for most members.

Trend spotters report that members increasingly look for an association that can provide customized programs and products to them when they want

them and is located close to home or in their homes (i.e., through the Internet, audio conferencing, videotapes).

In most organizations the well-being of the local level organization is leader dependent. Local leaders report that it is hard to get people to fill leadership roles and to get people to attend meetings. Some organizations also report that the same people are recycled through leadership roles year after year.

In some groups state and national organizations compete with each other for members and funds. In other groups the local association duplicates the programs and services of the national association. Most national nursing associations are struggling with how best to relate to the local level of the organization.

There should be clearly delineated responsibilities for each level of an organization. Technology makes it possible to experiment with different ways of delivering services to members at the local level. For example, in those locales where creating and sustaining a chapter is not feasible, an online chapter might be created to connect members to each other and to the national association. National organizations can also partner with local organizations to use technology to deliver products to the member at home. New ways of doing business locally are a must.

TOO MANY NURSING ORGANIZATIONS

Another issue facing many organizations is the fact that there are many membership societies performing the same services as the organization. Many of these groups vie for the same member market whereas others have a distinctive membership niche.

It is estimated that there are about 100 nursing organizations in the United States. Many of these organizations do similar things, such as standard setting, certification, education, and lobbying. Even vendors, suppliers, and grant-making agencies report that they are often asked by different nursing organizations for funds to do the same or similar things. Most striking is the fact that even with 100 nursing organizations, 80% of the nation's nurses belong to no organization at all. This raises the following questions: "Do we need this many groups?" "Is this the best use of nursing's fiscal and human resources?" "Are these organizations relevant given the needs of today's nurses?"

COLLABORATION

Collaboration among the many nursing groups occurs most frequently when there is a mutual external threat to the profession, such as the registered care technologist. It is often hard for some of these groups to see eye to eye on internal matters of policy such as interstate regulation or licensure.

The most significant challenges for nursing organizations are to figure out how to come together to maximize what each is good at, and to share resources and expertise in order to strengthen the profession and strengthen the bonds among nursing's organizations at the national and local levels. At the time of printing, the National Federation of Nursing Specialty Organizations and the Nursing Organization Liaison Forum have agreed to join together as the Nursing Organization Alliance (or The Alliance).

The level of customization and attention to individualized needs demanded by consumers in all marketplaces is becoming increasingly prevalent in nursing organizations. Nurses may demand a much greater partnership between nursing organizations so that an array of customized products and services can be provided. The nursing consumer market may call for a kind of "nursing association mall," where nurses can stop once and shop for all their needs. In other words, associations might better serve their members and the profession by joining together to provide a centralized access point where nurses can view and order the full array of products and services available from nursing organizations. For example, information about standards, continuing education offerings, certification,

position statements, and practice guidelines could all be included in a nursing association "mall." Today's technology makes this possible.

Each of these nursing groups will have to continuously work to be unique. Failure to build a distinguishing brand will result in a failure to compete with other organizations and with the Internet. Even the American Medical Association (AMA) is dealing with the issue of multiple organizations representing physicians' interests. The AMA is giving serious consideration to the idea of becoming a federation of medical organizations.

CONCLUSION

The trends that influence contemporary nursing organizations are many, and the possibilities for today's nursing organizations to reinvent themselves are endless. The abilities to focus on what makes a nursing organization unique and to eliminate obsolescent programs and products are required. Superb customer/member service and timely response to needs and wants are required. Valuable and valued member benefits are a must. Increasing the risk tolerance level of the organization, the use of pilot programs, and strategic partnerships with competitors as well as allies is key to survival.

REFERENCES

Carson, W. & Franklin, P. (2001, February). Workplace advocacy: How can it help you? *American Journal of Nursing, 101*(2), 55.

Foley, M. (2001, March/April). ANA: Preserving the core while preparing for the future. *American Nurse, 33*(2), 5.

Frudenheim, M. & Villarosa, L. (2001, April 8). Nursing shortage is raising worries on patients' care. *New York Times,* 1.

Jarrat, J., Coates, J.F., Mahaffie, J.B., & Hines, A. (1994). *Managing your future as an association.* Washington, DC: Foundation of the American Society of Association Executives.

Perlov, D. (1995). *Personal papers* (unpublished). New York.

Schweitzer, C. (2001, April). Professional development forums fast. *Association Management, 53*(4), 77.

Chapter 31
You and Your Professional Organization

PAMELA J. HAYLOCK

"The ultimate measure of a person is not where one stands in moments of comfort and convenience but where one stands in times of challenge and controversy."

MARTIN LUTHER KING JR.

It is said that organizations are "alive and screaming political arenas that host a complex web of individual and group interests" (Bolman & Deal, 1997). This perspective, reflecting the underlying assumptions for the information presented in this chapter, is summarized in five central propositions:

1. Organizations are coalitions of individuals and interest groups.
2. Enduring differences in values, beliefs, information, interests, and perceptions of reality exist among members.
3. Most important decisions involve the allocation of the organization's resources.
4. Scarce resources and enduring differences make conflict a central feature in organizational dynamics, and power the most important resource.
5. Organizational goals and decisions emerge from bargaining, negotiation, and jockeying for position among different stakeholders.

The internal politics of organizations provide a training ground—a practice arena—in which nurses can observe, learn, prepare, and perfect the skills needed to be influential within and outside the professional nursing organization. This experience can be parlayed into added influence in work set-tings, community-based activities, and the broader policy arena. The ways in which organizational politics are played out, and the mechanics through which members can be actively and successfully involved, are the foci for this chapter.

JOINING A PROFESSIONAL ORGANIZATION

Most nurses join organizations for continuing education to be updated on professional issues and for networking opportunities. When a nurse joins an organization, it is with the expectation that there will be a reasonable return on the member's investment of dues and commitment of time and energy. Tangible membership benefits include such things as professional journals, newsletters, discounted purchases of the organization's publications and subsequent access to state-of-the-art information, discounted conference and certification fees, and other forms of professional education. Perhaps more significant are the intangible benefits of membership, including the ability to network with colleagues in similar work settings, the chance to contribute to the development of standards and materials useful in nursing practice, and opportunities to mentor and to be mentored. Finally, and perhaps most important, professional organizations generally provide members opportunities to develop and fine-tune leadership skills that are critical for nurses who aspire to any level of influence within and outside their professional organization.

Being a member of a professional nursing organization is a voluntary endeavor. One's voluntary membership can be compared to the evolution of a long-term relationship—one in which the individual member *and* the organization benefit from the affiliation. For the relationship to work for both parties, short-term and long-term goals must be complementary. The prospective member's and the organization's major priorities should match. For example, a member who seeks involvement in health policy should assess the organization's commitment to health policy, its political action in general, and its likelihood of addressing the prospective member's health-related concerns.

Nurses who aspire to influential roles within the organization should get a complete understanding of the organization's mission, goals, priorities, and political agenda, as well as an individual's potential to be heard within the organization. After joining, a member can work toward achieving his or her desired level of influence. Choosing carefully and wisely among the many nursing organizations can make the difference between an exercise in frustration and a truly enriching volunteer experience.

WHICH ORGANIZATION TO JOIN?

There are many nursing organizations, each with a unique mission or reason for existence and varying degrees of compatibility between the interests of potential members and the organization's purpose. Some organizations outside of the United States focus on international issues of relevance to American nurses. The American Nurses Association (ANA) is the professional organization that advocates positions of relevance to all professional nurses. There are also more than 70 other national specialty or ethnic nursing organizations that offer members specific educational opportunities and collegial support through which members can address shared professional practice issues.

ASSESSING COMPATIBILITY: MEMBER NEEDS AND THE ORGANIZATION

It is unlikely that any one organization will address each member's array of professional needs and interests. Nurses often find it valuable to join more than one professional organization and one or more social organizations. Nurses are encouraged to join the ANA, through which generic professional issues are addressed. Specialty organizations are likely to focus resources on issues within that arena. Organizations whose members represent the various disciplines connected to a specialty area—for example, organizations that include nurses, physicians, social workers, and administrators—expand the context of the issues being considered. The missions of many social organizations, such as "gender equality in education and health," promoted by the American Association of University Women, may provide additional support and resources in addressing particular policy-related concerns.

ORGANIZATIONAL STRUCTURE AND PROCESSES

If a member hopes to find a rewarding professional experience through influence and power within an organization, it is important to have a thorough understanding of the organization's formal structure and processes—why it exists, what it purports to do, how it runs, and who runs it—as well as informal norms and expectations. Formal structure is determined by the organization's mission statement and bylaws. Governing policies and processes operationalize the mission statement and bylaws. The mission statement, bylaws, and policies are published, public documents that are easily accessible to potential and current members. Processes, including step-by-step procedural directions, are generally made available to members upon request. The subtler, implied norms and expectations are discernible through formal and informal networking, collegial discussion, and astute observation.

MISSION STATEMENT

The mission statement defines what the organization has been established to accomplish (Nanus, 1992). For example, the mission of the ANA is "to work for the improvement of health standards and availability of health care services for all people, foster high standards for nursing, stimulate and promote the professional development of nurses, and advance their economic and general welfare." Priorities being addressed by the ANA include labor, wages and benefits, workplace safety, and nurse staffing. The missions of the following organizations allow them the flexibility to address issues of concern to the majority of members through appropriate means: American Academy of Ambulatory Care Nursing, to advance the art and science of ambulatory care nursing; the Oncology Nursing Society, to promote excellence in oncology nursing practice and quality cancer care; and the American Nephrology Nurses' Association, to advance the professional development of registered nurses practicing in nephrology, transplantation, and related therapies, and to promote the highest standards of patient care.

BYLAWS

Bylaws, the organizational "rule book," govern internal affairs and identify who has power and how that power works. They outline the purpose of the organization; membership criteria; financial and legal procedures; the number of board meetings; how the governing board operates; and the size, number, selection, and tenure of board members (Hummel, 1996). Most important, bylaws outline provisions for changes—amendments to the bylaws—defining who can bring suggested changes forward, and how the amendment process works. The significance of bylaw changes is reflected in the formality of the process. Most organizations require that proposed changes come forward in a specific format and within a designated time frame. It is often important that proposed bylaw changes be reviewed by legal counsel and a parliamentarian prior to being submitted to the governing board. The board then reviews proposed changes and sometimes offers an opinion as to the value and consequence of the changes. Rationale and arguments for and against the proposed changes are often required components of the proposal, and sponsors are usually identified when the change is submitted to the organization's voting body.

A look at just a few bylaw changes approved by nursing organizations demonstrates how profoundly these member-generated changes can affect an organization. In the early 1980s, a change in the organizational bylaws of the (then) International Association of Enterostomal Therapy (IAET) meant that non-nurses were no longer eligible for "active" membership status. A 1992 bylaw amendment allowed the IAET to change its name to the Wound, Ostomy, and Continence Nurses Society, reflecting recognition of the expanded focus of the specialty and the organization. A bylaw change proposed by members of the Oncology Nursing Society (ONS), voted down several times but finally approved in 1997, established provisions for "associate membership" that offers non-nurse health care professionals limited membership benefits. Another ONS bylaw change approved by members in 1997 changed its mission statement from one that focused primarily on nursing education to a broader quality cancer care agenda. An ONS bylaw change in 1998 increased the presidential term from 1 to 2 years. Clearly, changes in an organization's bylaws can have a lasting effect on leadership roles and the focus of the organization.

GOVERNANCE POLICIES

The organization's values and perspectives are blended into policy that codifies what staff can or cannot do, and the governing board's process and relationships (Carver, 1997). John Carver, a theorist and consultant on governance design, suggests that organizational effectiveness is supported by board policies that fall into four groups: (1) the desired "ends"—the reason the organization exists; (2) the principles of prudence and ethics that guide staff; (3) the relationship between the governing board and the staff executive(s); and (4) the manner in which the governing board provides strategic leadership to the organization.

PROCESSES AND PROCEDURES

Step-by-step "how-to" directions are offered in organizational policy and procedure manuals. The most common processes available to general members who wish to influence organizational direction or agendas, aside from bylaw amendments, include:

- The drafting and presentation of organizational resolutions and position statements
- Suggestions for organizationally branded projects, products, and services

- Introduction of issues for consideration by the governing board
- Presenting issues for discussion in forums offered during general business meeting agendas

Resolutions are statements that reflect the organizational mission and goals, and are proposed to the organization for endorsement and action by members. Resolutions are used to inform members or other designated constituencies about an issue, and to show support (or lack of support) for programs or a legislative initiative. Many organizations use commemorative resolutions to recognize contributions of members, individuals, or organizations. Members who submit resolutions are, again, asked to follow a formalized process that initially includes meeting established deadlines and using the accepted format. The procedure likely requires submission of the resolution itself, supporting data and information, recommendations for how the intent of the resolution is to be carried out, review of the potential financial impact of acting upon the resolution, and identification of members who support it. Resolutions that meet established criteria are then put before the organization's voting body. The actual procedure varies from one organization to another; meeting established and organization-specific criteria is essential for members to give thoughtful consideration to the implications of resolutions, and their acceptance by voting members.

Position statements are documents issued under the auspices of the governing board that articulate the organization's official stance on issues relevant to its mission. The need for an organizational stance may be identified and suggested by general members as well as members in formal leadership roles. General members would communicate this need via normal member-leadership channels: face-to-face discussion, telephone or other electronic communications, or a written request for consideration by the governing board. The board may choose to craft the position statement on its own or may elect to appoint members with acknowledged expertise to the task. Either way, position statements are released only after the governing board gives its final approval. Many nursing organizations now post position statements on their websites so that their perspective is accessible to a broad audience.

Projects, products, and *services* that are consistent with an organizational mission offer important and exciting opportunities for involvement and participation of members. Quite often, this is where the "Wow!" factor—described by Tom Peters (1994) as the excitement members get from being part of something important and meaningful—comes into play. Shepherding an idea from conception to completion and successful dissemination is probably one of the most rewarding aspects of organizational membership. Projects, products, and services come to be because they are identified as things that members need and are therefore critical benefits of membership. When they are perceived as valuable, these things reflect well on the organization. This level of work is generally assigned to committees, working groups, and task forces composed of appointed expert members. Through such involvement, nurses get to exercise creativity while being part of a collaborative effort that also affords opportunities to be mentored or to mentor others, to be exposed to new ideas and new ways of doing things, and to achieve success in a potentially complex process. Volunteering to be part of a working group whose charge reflects a member's interests and expertise is a common route to gaining exposure and the credibility necessary to be influential enough to effect change. Most projects, products, and services mirror the creators, thus providing members with the ability to influence policy in subtler ways. For example, work on a patient education tool provides the nurse member with the opportunity to convey ideas she or he believes are important directly to the patient population and ultimately, to effect changes in nursing practice. Organizational publications, generally an important benefit of membership, provide numerous ways to affect organizational direction. Serving as a manuscript reviewer, a contributing editor, or as an editorial board member allows a member to influence what is published under the auspices of the organization, another avenue for influence within and outside of the organization.

Application and selection processes for these working groups vary widely among nursing organizations, but this procedural information should be easy to find. Authored submissions, "letters to the editor" in organizational publications, and other organizational endeavors provide ways to attract the attention of those responsible for making appointments. Performing successfully in these groups once an appointment occurs is essential. Group members need to understand group norms that will help establish a new member's standing as a valued colleague. By way of introduction to a new group, it is helpful to briefly identify the basis of one's interest in this group's work and describe the attributes one brings as a group member. It is helpful to talk with the team leader or committee chairperson, describing one's areas of interest and expertise, existing skills—public speaking and writing skills are especially valued—and areas in which one would welcome mentoring or would be able to serve as a mentor.

Board agendas outline the work of the governing board. Most organizations offer members the chance to have issues placed on the board's meeting agenda. Bylaws usually stipulate how and when board meetings occur and identify the means through which general members can contribute to board deliberations. Most often, informal communications with board members are enough to have an issue of concern placed on an agenda, but informal mechanisms will not guarantee that the issue is discussed. Formal communication, written letters and/or electronic mail, generally assure the member that a response of some sort will be forthcoming from the board. Of course, the response may not be the one the member hopes to receive, and as a result the member may seek alternative means—a resolution, a bylaw change, a position statement, or a discussion forum—to have the issue addressed.

General business meeting agendas offer another way members can bring issues and concerns to the attention of the governing board as well as other members and colleagues. General business meetings are usually conducted according to some form of parliamentary procedure, often a variant of the tried and true *Robert's Rules of Order* (Robert, Evans, Honemann, Balch, & Robert, 2000). Members who wish to use the business meeting as a mechanism for addressing issues need to be fully informed about the recognized procedure that will allow this to occur. One or maybe two procedural blunders might be tolerated, but a number of them cast the member in a negative light that can be difficult to shed. Being knowledgeable of parliamentary

procedure ensures that a member's concerns cannot be dismissed because of violations of that procedure. Proficiency with the rules of order conveys the member's commitment to effectively presenting an issue to colleagues who may share the concern.

TAX-EXEMPT STATUS

Tax-exempt status is allocated based on the mission, bylaws, and governance of the organization, and it is essential to understanding the degree to which advocacy efforts are allowed. Most voluntary nursing organizations are established as nonprofit organizations. Nonprofit status can lead to confusion because some board members, staff members, and general members view political action as unseemly, irrelevant to an organization's mission, illegal, or having the potential to alienate existing and prospective members (Sparks, 1997). In fact, nonprofit advocacy and lobbying are both legal and necessary to promote organizations' missions (Sparks, 1997). Most nursing organizations are established around a variety of advocacy issues such as improved nurse wages and work conditions, patients' needs for access to care, and evolution of a nursing specialty. Nonprofit status is granted under individual states' jurisdiction, but the classification for federal tax law directly affects what the organization can and cannot do (Yale, 1997). For example, organizations granted nonprofit status under Section 501(c)(3) of the Internal Revenue Code can accept tax-deductible contributions but are subject to severe restrictions on lobbying activities. Those classified as social welfare organizations under Section 501(c)(4) or as business leagues under Section 501(c)(6) may lobby (Hummel, 1996). Most nursing organizations operate under Section 501(c)(6) nonprofit status, in which there is no limit on lobbying. Support of specific candidates and any direct financial support to candidates, however, must be managed through separate political action committees (Yale, personal communication).

NURSING ORGANIZATION LIFE CYCLE

Organizations go through life cycle stages from "conception" and "infancy" to "adulthood" and finally "old age" (Tecker & Fidler, 1993). For an organization to flourish and succeed in achieving goals, its leaders must adjust to changes in its environment and the resulting needs of members. An organization that is in its conception or infancy stage, characterized by struggles to survive, is unlikely to have either the resources or expertise to affect issues beyond its own immediate survival. In the "young adulthood" stage, organizations formalize policies, and internal politics become evident. By "adulthood," an organization and its management are peaking, have mastered the environment, and serve members' needs. In "late adulthood" and "old age," organizations experience diminished excitement, member complacency, and lack of zeal and sense of urgency, and they finally lose the ability to serve members' needs. Organizations need not follow this cyclical decline. To avoid it, organization leaders must apply appropriate strategies to maintain vitality and members' commitment. The vital, successful, and exciting organization is more likely to experience success, thereby providing members with a variety of opportunities to contribute to meaningful projects and services, mentor others, learn and practice new skills, and ultimately have the positive experience that only active participation in a vital organization can offer.

ORGANIZATIONAL LEADERSHIP AND POWER

There are many routes to achieving power and influence in contemporary nursing organizations. Certainly, members who have attained leadership roles in the organization have achieved some level of power and influence, as have highly placed staff members. General members can attain equally influential positions. Regardless of one's membership status, achieving power and influence requires knowledge and understanding, not only of the organization's structure, processes, and policies, but also of the personalities and priorities of key organizational staff and leaders.

Power is the ability to get things done through the attainment and mobilization of resources (Kantor, 1977). There are nurses who use coercion or fear to rule other nurses, but this situation typifies powerless organizations in which oppression and deceit

are used to meet goals (Carlson-Catalano, 1994) and typifies an organization in "old age" and on a path toward its demise (Tecker & Fidler, 1993). Clearly, an organization that evidences these traits is to be avoided if a prospective member hopes to be part of a respected, successful, and influential organization.

It can be useful to assess sources of power within the organization. The political interests of the organization's chief staff executive (executive director, chief executive officer), chief elected officer (e.g., president, board chairperson), and leaders in elected board roles will be mirrored in the organization's priorities. Do printed or spoken messages reflect an interest or priority in pertinent issues, or do the messages simply reflect a fleeting focus? These seemingly innocuous communiqués can be revealing with regard to the import leaders attach to a particular issue.

ELECTED AND APPOINTED LEADERS

The possibilities for professional and personal growth that accompany service in leadership capacities are infinite. Organizations' elected leaders are offered unique experiences: opportunities to meet colleagues from a variety of settings at local, national, and international levels; the chance to explore concerns and goals and to work toward solutions to shared problems; and the capacity to interact with a host of leaders representing other disciplines who hold different, interesting, and challenging notions about addressing common concerns.

Many nurse leaders have parlayed organizational leadership skills into public policy roles, including election to national and state congressional seats, jobs as critical staff to elected leaders and policy-related agencies, and appointments to policy-making commissions (Feldman & Lewenson, 2000). Sheila Burke credits her active participation in the National Student Nurses Association as the catalyst that led to her policy-related achievements, including serving as Senator Robert Dole's (R-KS) highly respected chief of staff. Virginia Trotter Betts was elected president of the Tennessee State Nurses Association and was president of the American Nurses Association during the Clinton administration's attempts to reform the U.S. health care system. From there, Betts went on to become Senior Advisor on Nursing and Policy to the Secretary and Assistant

Secretary of Health, U.S. Department of Health and Human Services. U.S. Representative Lois Capps (D-CA), a former school nurse, uses her professional experience to advocate for her priority issues, education and health care. It is worth noting that it was less than a decade ago that the first nurse, Eddie Bernice Johnson (D-TX), was elected to the House of Representatives (after being the first nurse elected to the Texas Senate) and that, as of 2001, there has yet to be a nurse elected to the U.S. Senate.

Elected members affect organizational direction and development of policy. A governing board or board of directors is accountable for the organization and exists on behalf of the larger group of members, who, in the case of nonprofit organizations, morally own the organization (Carver, 1997). This board is responsible for achieving what it should and avoiding the unacceptable. The board, acting as a body, defines, delegates, and monitors, but usually does not carry out, organizational work. Each governing board member holds a position that confers different responsibilities and expectations, and requires mastery of a specific skill set in order to perform well in that role.

Organizations may differ in the use of titles, but generally, governing boards identify key officers—sometimes referred to as the "executive committee." Specific officers may be mandated by laws of the state where the organization is incorporated but usually consist of, at a minimum, the chief elected officer (e.g., president, board chairperson), a treasurer, and a secretary. The specific duties and powers of each officer are outlined in organizational bylaws. Depending upon organizational bylaw and policy provisions, key officers or the executive committee may be conferred with additional responsibilities not expected of other board members. For example, the executive committee might be called upon to make decisions in lieu of a full board action. The executive committee may be expected to play active roles in evaluation of key staff members, or lead important committees and task force efforts. Finally, members of the executive committee could be in the direct line of leadership succession should another leader be unable to fulfill an elected role.

Additional governing roles are devised to meet the unique needs of the organization and are usu-

ally outlined in bylaws. Roles such as "director at large" might serve organizational needs for geographic and constituency representation. Organizations that have an international focus might incorporate the international perspective within its board structure by allocating a board role specific to these interests. Some nursing organizations include laypersons who bring the consumer or patient perspective into governing structures. As leaders recognize a specific need not being met by members, board members with expertise in highly specialized areas such as fund raising, health policy, international affairs, and organizational change are appointed to governing boards.

Although not explicit in legal or even organizational bylaws and policies, it is essential that organizational leaders convey commitment and passion, expressing that they care deeply about what the organization does (Bolman & Deal, 1997). Beyond this, and regardless of the elected or appointed position, governing board members have three general duties owed to the organization while serving in these roles: the duty of care; the duty of loyalty; and the duty of obedience (Yale, 1997). The duty of care implies that the responsibilities inherent in the role are taken on in good faith, with the care expected of a prudent person in a similar role, and in a manner that is in the best interests of the organization. The duty of loyalty suggests that the board member conducts himself or herself for the good of the organization and does not receive direct or indirect improper financial gain. Violation of this duty is sometimes referred to as a "conflict of interest." Elected and appointed organizational leaders are usually expected to sign agreements that identify potential conflicts of interest. Conflicts of interest might occur when a company or institution that in some way competes with or is in conflict with the organization employs a board member. Distribution of funding may pose dilemmas when a board member's employing agency, or a colleague in the same facility, has applied for project funding granted on the basis of a board vote. In these situations, board members might be asked to refrain from voting. The duty of obedience alludes to one's obligation to follow organizational documents and applicable laws.

ORGANIZATIONAL ELECTIONS

Organizational elections, operating under a variety of more or less democratic principles, determine which members will be officially accountable for the organization's operation and direction. Organizations differ to some extent in the processes used to elect members to official leadership roles. Members who aspire to these roles, as well as general members who interact with elected leaders, should be fully informed about which positions are open on a given electoral slate; the qualifications, expectations, and time commitments of the various elected roles; the nomination and slating processes; campaign expectations and guidelines; and the voting process.

Some organizations elect leaders through a popular vote in which general members vote for candidates placed on ballot through nomination and slating processes. Some might employ a system in which delegates are elected or appointed and, in turn, are charged with the responsibilities of voting. Other organizations select designated members of the governing board through a popular election, while the chief elected officer might be elected by a vote of those serving on the board. Organizations, according to their bylaws, may hold elections in which each voting member must cast a ballot in person, whereas other organizations might allow voting to be done by postal mail. Video teleconferencing offers the means for more members to actively participate in formal meetings and other processes, and voting is increasingly being done electronically via the Internet and e-mail.

A decision to pursue an elected leadership role in an organization should be made after very thoughtful consideration. Elected roles require a great deal of work. Nominees and candidates must make truly informed decisions about seeking elected office. The existence and level of staff support in the organization is an important factor in the time commitment and expectations of volunteer leaders. Family members might be involved in a prospective candidate's decision to run for election, as normal family roles and routines are likely to be disrupted at least occasionally. Elected roles consume ever-increasing amounts of time, work, and energy of volunteer members—time that may require absences

from one's primary work role. Time away from a job can be a source of conflict for elected leaders and employers. Some organizations offer stipends to partially compensate elected leaders. A stipend may be offered to an employer in compensation for the elected employee's time away from the job or may be offered directly to the elected leader. Some organizations mandate evidence of commitment and support from employers.

Important prenomination considerations include the efforts, and costs, of mounting an election campaign. Knowledge of organizational policies and expectations with regard to campaigning is essential. Reflecting the debate surrounding national campaign finance reform, many organizations closely monitor candidates' campaign efforts with regard to truth and fairness. If organizational norms call for targeted member mailing, printing and postage costs can be substantial—so substantial in fact, that qualified potential candidates may forgo the process. Candidates from less populous constituencies may lack the collegial and financial resources of candidates from urban or tertiary care settings. It was these considerations that led the Oncology Nursing Society, for one, to forbid formal campaigning for organizational elections.

Most nurses lack high-level organizational experience and are unprepared and naive as they enter association leadership roles. Most newly elected board members are shocked by the complexity of debate and decision making that occurs at these governing levels. Few new board members are prepared to question or challenge the authority of highly placed staff members—the chief staff officer, for example (Ernstthal, 2001)—leaving the governing board somewhat weakened until new members gain confidence in their work. Annual turnover as a result of organizational elections, in at least a portion of the board, results in some level of instability and inconsistency within the board. Most organizations attempt to compensate for this constant personnel change by staggering board vacancies, which leaves a majority of experienced members who can effectively welcome and orient newly elected members.

It is increasingly recognized that talent, experience, and leadership style—not tenure within the

BOX **31-1**   Critical Skills for Organizational Leaders

- Embrace and create chaos and change that stimulates creativity and innovation (Cufaude, 2001).
- Offer members exciting opportunities and projects that create personal connection, challenge, and professional development and provide members with a return on their investment of dues and commitment (Peters, 1994).
- Use facilitation behaviors to encourage others to bridge differences and focus on essentials.
- Collaborate with internal and external stakeholders.
- Act as talent scouts who recognize and nourish the development of members who bring valuable interests, skills, and talents.
- Work toward building a "hierarchy of imagination," where an individual's imagination and passion, rather than position and political power, are the determinants of his or her voice in organizational strategy making and innovation (Hamel, 2000).
- Speculate *not* on what might happen, but on what they can actually *make* happen (Hamel, 2000).
- Are prepared to champion the association's core values and ensure the preservation of the organization in an ever-changing environment (Collins & Porras, 1994).
- Are passionate about their role and contributions to the organization, and to learning about the passions of other members.

organization—matters most (Cufaude, 2001). A strong organization and wise, confident leaders will create and support processes that help members attain the talent, experience, and leadership needed to ensure the vitality and success of the organization. Box 31-1 identifies these basic talents and skills.

CHIEF EXECUTIVE

A nursing organization's elected leaders come and go. The chief staff executive—chief executive officer (CEO), chief staff officer (CSO), or executive director (ED)—is the one constant advocate for the mission and values of the organization. The chief executive reports to and receives executive authority from the governing board (Carver, 1997). The chief staff executive reflects and is the primary agent in shaping and sustaining the culture of the organization—the values, beliefs, rituals, and rules that are the unspoken assumptions about what matters and how things are done in the organization. Organizational leaders invest a great deal of trust in the chief executive, and consequently, this person assumes power that extends beyond administrative and program arenas (Albert, 1993). Organizations' governing boards hold the responsibility for monitoring the work, effectiveness, and outcomes of the chief staff executive (Tecker & Fidler, 1993).

LEADERSHIP

Active participation in organizational work that comes to the attention of organizational leaders is a simple way to begin the process of developing influence and power in that organization—in short, to become an organizational leader. Here again, it is important to know and understand organizational norms, protocols, and expectations. Most organizations operate general member and governance board meetings according to bylaws provisions—under some version of *Robert's Rules of Order,* guidelines based on parliamentary practice. *Robert's Rules,* now in its tenth edition, was first published in 1876 by Army engineer Henry Martyn Robert as an attempt to bring order to the chaos of presiding over meetings (www.robertsrules.com). *Robert's Rules* still afford order to leaders who are experienced in their use or have the wherewithal to use professional parliamentarians. Even in the absence of a handy copy of *Robert's Rules,* or when an organization uses alternative guidelines, "rules of order" are generally printed and stipulated as a first agenda item in any business meeting.

Other common group norms, some that might seem innocuous, can affect one's organizational standing. Such conventions as arriving on time for meetings, arriving at meetings well prepared for discussion and debate, paying attention to implied or explicit dress codes, meeting the commitments inherent in the designated role, and going above and beyond role expectations are important to gaining the recognition and respect of organizational colleagues.

BARGAINING AND NEGOTIATION: COPING WITH ORGANIZATIONAL CONFLICTS

Large groups of people rarely achieve unanimous agreement on important issues. There is usually disagreement among members on which issues are considered important to an organization or how these issues ought to be addressed. Given the differences in values, beliefs, information, interests, and perceptions that exist among an organizational membership, disagreement and conflict should be accepted as the norm rather than the exception. In truth, conflict has costs and benefits (Bolman & Deal, 1997). Too much conflict or conflict that is poorly managed produces infighting and destructive power struggles. Alternatively, lack of conflict is symptomatic of an organization in which members and leaders are apathetic, uncreative, stagnant, and unresponsive. Conflict challenges the status quo and can stimulate new ideas and approaches to problems. It is key that leaders handle conflict well and achieve a balance that stimulates creativity and innovation.

Conflicts that emerge within an organization usually revolve around allocation of limited resources and prioritization of goals (Bolman & Deal, 1997), but issues that arise between volunteer members and the staff are another common source of conflict (Kincaide, 2001). A group of members may prefer that resources be used, for example, to influence a particular legislative issue, while another group desires the creation of an internal leadership development project. Staff and volunteer members, each group with its unique perspective, may differ on approaches to organizational concerns. How these differences of opinion play out can be the source of considerable conflict, or of innovative strategies that accommodate both sides.

Fisher, Ury, and Patten (1991), in their bestseller *Getting to Yes,* recommend what they call "principled negotiation" to arrive at mutually acceptable agreements: issues are decided on merits alone, as opposed to the personalities of those who raise the issues, and options are devised that satisfy groups on both "sides" of an issue. Strategies that "mine the talents" of member constituencies can be used to guide resolution of differences (Kincaide, 2001). A critical step in conflict resolution involves helping all parties agree on a philosophical framework. Gail Kincaide, executive director of the Association of Women's Health, Obstetric and Neonatal Nurses (AWHONN), credits a philosophical framework that focuses on commitment, trust, and consistency with the success of AWHONN's reorganization, a process that for many organizations is fraught with conflict.

Leaders must be sure that organizational policies and processes support the bargaining and negotiation processes that are the critical elements of conflict resolution. Each member is obligated to use organizational processes that are in place, or find ways to change processes through bylaw amendments, policy and procedural changes, position statements, and resolutions. Members acting in collaboration with other members are more likely to be viewed as having valid concerns than a member acting alone. Attempts to address an issue via an existing segment of the membership is generally a good starting place. For example, a clinical issue might be discussed among members of a clinical practice committee or relevant interest group. A policy issue might be discussed among members of a government relations committee or legislative task force. Shared concerns and suggestions are then brought forward to organizational leaders. Any member, leader or not, must have good supportive data at hand in order to influence change. Passion for an issue is important, but passion without solid information and effective communication is unlikely to change opinions or effect change. Relevant data include the scope of the problem, its relevance to the organization's mission and goals, the anticipated outcomes of nonaction versus the proposed action, a synopsis of proposed ways by which the issue could be addressed (including organizational costs), and the number of members who share this concern.

Box 31-2 identifies elements that are essential to managing organizational conflict.

PROMOTING HEALTH POLICY FROM AN ORGANIZATIONAL PERSPECTIVE

In the foreseeable future, most, if not all, professional nursing organizations will be increasingly involved in attempts to influence public and private policies that affect nursing and health care. Con-

BOX **31-2** Resolving Organizational Conflict

- Examine and identify shared core values.
- Frame the issue within the organization's mission, goals, and priorities.
- Build and reinforce a shared philosophy of commitment, trust, and consistency among those on both sides of the conflict.
- Use existing processes to address the issue.
- Pick your battles and do not argue about everything; instead, take on only issues that are meaningful.
- Be informed about the pros and cons of an issue or strategy to the extent possible.
- Anticipate and be prepared to address opposing perspectives.
- Act in collaboration. Look for and enlist like-minded colleagues, and find ways to get the attention and support of elected and appointed leaders.
- Make sure every communication surrounding the issue is clear.
- Look for the "win-win" scenario that characterizes a mutually acceptable agreement.

flicts may arise, however, concerning *which* issues and *which* policies organizational resources should be used to address, the level of resources to be expended on particular causes, and determination of the acceptable end points. Nurses have only occasionally united in collaborative political efforts. A notable exception is the 1993 effort to reform the American health care system. The ANA and a majority of specialty nursing organizations agreed on three defining principles for a new health care system—access, quality, and cost-containment—and united in efforts to see that these principles were apparent in any proposed change to health care policy (Keepnews & Marullo, 1996). Since then, the nursing profession has not formed a strong and united approach to any single issue. Instead, individual nurses and professional nursing organizations have differed on critical and basic issues such as the health care delivery system and universal insurance, Medicare and welfare reform, assisted suicide, a woman's right to abortion, and the nursing profession's entry-level educational requirements. Specialty nursing organizations use their resources to address issues that are more narrowly defined within their specialty arena, diminishing nurses'

potential for a cohesive approach to broader health policy and professional issues.

REFOCUSING ORGANIZATIONAL PRIORITIES

Use of the organization's resources reflects the priority given to political and policy-related efforts within the organization. Appointment of identified staff roles—including the credentials, qualifications, and number of staff—that support political and policy efforts within the organization is evidence of support for policy-related work. Rather than hiring staff members whose roles are completely dedicated to policy work, many nursing organizations, especially those with smaller membership bases and limited fiscal and personnel resources, become associated with business entities that provide "health policy" consultants on a contractual basis. In this situation, the health policy consultant, sometimes referred to as a "lobbyist," may be contracted to work with several nursing organizations, providing expertise in the policy-making process. Legal firms with established bases in state capitals and Washington, DC, also offer health policy lobbying services on a contractual basis. Because this contractual person or team of persons may or may not have specialty expertise, it is critical that the organizations' leaders and other experts provide solid direction in setting the organizations' policy-related priorities. Being among these recognized experts is a way in which an individual member can influence an organization's health policy priorities and efforts.

Organizational policies and processes offer the mechanisms through which any member or group of members can be a catalyst to changing the organization's focus, goals, and priorities. Usually, governing boards create a health policy agenda or governmental relations strategy, an established plan that is available to members in which policy priorities are clearly identified. These priorities are influenced in the same way that other organizational priorities are: by members who communicate with leaders about issues that are relevant to the profession, the organization, or its mission. Bylaw or mission statement changes, generated by members, can profoundly affect organizational direction. Resolutions and position statements, generated by members, can redirect organizational focus and allocation of resources. For example, an organization that creates a position on pain management is obligated to affecting change according to action statements included in the position. Resolutions are equally binding. Many nursing organizations, for example, have passed resolutions that establish antitobacco activities among their priority issues.

CONCLUSION

Basic nursing education focuses on meeting individual patient needs. It is, however, increasingly clear that planning, provision, and evaluation of care is grounded in population-based approaches, formulated from policy, which in turn evolve from political processes. The Woodhull Study on Nursing and the Media advises, "when the nursing perspective is overlooked, there is a distinct gap in reported information" (Sigma Theta Tau International, 1997). Nurses must be included, with parity to other health care disciplines, in political processes and subsequent development of health policy. Being included in the policy arena comes to the nursing profession as a result of its achieving and maintaining influence and power. Professional nursing organizations offer one avenue through which individual nurses, professional nursing organizations, and the profession as a whole can, in fact, achieve influence and power.

REFERENCES

Albert, S. (1993). *Hiring the chief executive: A practical guide to the search and selection process.* Washington, DC: National Center for Nonprofit Boards.

Bolman, L.G. & Deal, T.E. (1997). *Reframing organizations: Artistry, choice, and leadership* (2nd ed.). San Francisco: Jossey-Bass.

Carlson-Catalano, J. (1994). Invest in yourself: Cultivating personal power. *Nursing Forum, 29*(2), 22-28.

Carver, J. (1997). *Boards that make a difference* (2nd ed.). San Francisco: Jossey-Bass.

Collins, J. & Porras, J. (1994). *Built to last.* New York: HarperCollins.

Cufaude, J.B. (2001). Telling a new leadership story. *Association Management, 53*(1), 43-50.

Ernstthal, H.L. (2001). Provocative questions for volunteer leaders. *Association Management, 53*(1), 60-62, 64.

Feldman, H.R. & Lewenson, S.B. (2000). *Nurses in the political arena: The public face of nursing.* New York: Springer.

Fisher, R., Ury, W., & Patton, B. (1991). *Getting to yes: Negotiating agreement without giving in* (2nd ed.). New York: Penguin.

Hamel, G. (2000). *Leading the revolution.* Boston: Harvard Business School Press.

Hummel, J.M. (1996). *Starting and running a nonprofit organization* (2nd ed.). Minneapolis: University of Minnesota Press.

Kantor, R.M. (1977). *Men and women of the corporation.* New York: Basic Books.

Keepnews, D. & Marullo, G. (1996). Policy imperatives for nursing in an era of health care restructuring. *Nursing Administration Quarterly, 20,* 19-31.

Kincaide, G.G. (2001). Planned partnership. *Association Management, 53*(1), 52-54, 56, 58-59.

Nanus, B. (1992). *Visionary leadership: Creating a compelling sense of direction for your organization.* San Francisco: Jossey-Bass.

Peters, T. (1994). *The pursuit of Wow!* New York: Vintage.

Robert, H.M., Evans, W.J., Honemann, D.H., Balch, T.J., & Robert, H.M. (Eds.) (2000). *Robert's rules of order newly revised.* Cambridge, MA: Perseus.

Sigma Theta Tau International. (1997). *The Woodhull Study on Nursing and the Media.* Indianapolis: Sigma Theta Tau International Honor Society of Nursing.

Sparks, J.D. (1997). *Lobbying, advocacy and nonprofit boards.* Washington, DC: National Center for Nonprofit Boards.

Tecker, G. & Fidler, M. (1993). *Successful association leadership: Dimensions of 21st century competency for the CEO.* Washington, DC: Foundation of the American Society of Association Executives.

Yale, G.A. (1997). *Responsibilities and liabilities of Texas nonprofit organization directors.* San Antonio: Nonprofit Resource Center of Texas.

Vignette   Martha N. Hill & Peggy O'Neill Hewlett

Getting to the Top: Martha Hill, President of the American Heart Association

"If it were easy, it would have been done before."
JEANNE YEAGER

A glass ceiling shattered in 1996 when Dr. Martha Hill was selected as the president-elect of the American Heart Association (AHA). In the 74 years of the association's existence, Dr. Hill was the first nonphysician, the first behavioral scientist, the first community and public health professional, and the first nurse to serve as the president.

The AHA, an internationally recognized voluntary nonprofit organization, began when groups of cardiologists across the United States became interested in improving the quality of patients' lives. These physicians promoted cardiovascular research and continuing medical education for cardiologists. By 1997 the organization had grown to 53 affiliates, approximately 4.3 million volunteers, and 2400 staff members with headquarters in Dallas, Texas.

It was never Dr. Hill's goal to become the president of the AHA. She began by serving as an AHA volunteer but soon "progressed through the ranks" to assume more responsible volunteer positions. Enjoying her work with other volunteers and staff, she participated in conferences and spent many weekends in retreats and long-range planning sessions. Her nursing career enabled her to understand many strategies used by the AHA to meet its mission. These included understanding the importance of evidence-based practice and scientific discovery, the excitement of clinical trials, the challenges of continuing education, and the need to disseminate research findings and develop strategies to implement these findings into practice and organizational and public policies.

In a series of interviews, Dr. Hill shared her experiences and insight into how she was able to move into one of the most prestigious organizational leadership positions in the United States. She shares the following lessons.

LESSON 1: GET FOCUSED

Dr. Hill experienced several turning points in her career. While working on a master's degree at the University of Pennsylvania, she was seated beside the noted nursing theorist Martha Rogers at a luncheon. Between bites of lunch and small talk, Rogers leaned over and asked Hill when she planned to begin doctoral studies. Martha replied, "I have not even gotten my master's yet!" But Rogers was relentless, asking her no less than three times during the meal when she was going on for the PhD. This chance interaction left a lasting impression.

Soon after the lunch, Dr. Hill became involved in clinical drug trials. In one trial, the pharmaceutical company sponsoring the research needed case report forms quicker than the research team was able to produce them. The delay was not because the work was not completed on time, but because the principal investigator (PI) had to physically sign each form before releasing it to the company. This was when Hill learned that the title "PI" sometimes stands for "practically invisible!" Since Hill processed every form, a suggestion was made to the pharmaceutical company that Martha be given signature authority, enabling the release of case reports every night. A physician in charge of the study would not approve her as a co-investigator because, he said, "you do not have the right initials after your name." She was seen as being very competent, but her role was limited because she was not appropriately credentialed to be a co-investigator. This was a defining moment for Dr. Hill. She felt the problem could be fixed by going back to school to get a PhD.

While at the University of Pennsylvania, Hill began to lay the groundwork for her doctoral studies. After moving to Baltimore, she took the leap and entered the School of Hygiene and Public Health at Johns Hopkins University and graduated with a PhD. It enabled her to augment her strong clinical background with the scientific rigor necessary to develop a multidisciplinary research program focused on hypertension care and control in underserved urban African-American communities. Her belief that nursing needed practitioners grounded in human behavior and related research was put into practice.

When getting focused, remember:

- No one is proficient in everything, so find a niche.
- Plan a career trajectory around an area of interest.
- Become an expert and share that expertise with others.

LESSON 2: COLLABORATE

The AHA was Dr. Hill's first experience with professional organizations. It was when she was enrolled in the MSN program and employed as a nurse practitioner at the University of Pennsylvania Division of Hypertension and Clinical Pharmacology that she got her first nudge into volunteering for the AHA. She was actually volunteered by someone else. Dr. Karl Engleman, a physician for whom she worked, served on Pennsylvania's Heart Association Hypertension Committee. He took the liberty of volunteering Hill to help with educating physicians in the treatment and control of hypertension, insisting that she be invited to speak at every program because of her expertise in patient education. At the time, he advised her that volunteering for the AHA "may be the most important thing you ever do!" She took his advice and spoke whenever and wherever she was invited. Others saw her skill and expertise emerge.

The AHA began a project with the American Nurses Association (ANA) in which each state affiliate of the heart association and nursing association sent one member to a training program in Dallas, Texas. The idea was for teams to go back to their home states and replicate the study through professional education. Through this experience

Dr. Hill met Cheryl Boyer. They set up multidisciplinary "road shows" with a smorgasbord of content. Boyer represented the Pennsylvania Heart Association as the staff educator, and Hill shared her expertise in hypertension treatment and control. The locals set the agenda while the Hill-Boyer team designed the training programs. It was during this time that Dr. Hill became passionately involved in work with the AHA.

Forging working relationships with physicians has been a critical part of Dr. Hill's work. Physicians often take the lead in advocating for public policy issues related to health and health care. If nurses are to contribute to this process, they must learn the art of collaborative professional work. Through the years, Hill worked closely with physicians and pharmacists. Dr. Hill's philosophy was that patients need good nurses as well as good doctors. She asked, "If nurses practice with them, why do they not do research with them?"

Hill found the physicians' weekly hypertension clinic presented opportunities for nurses to forge collaborative relationships. Five to eight physicians staffed the clinic, each having 30 to 40 years in practice. The physicians were older, with well-established private practices, where patients had come for decades. They did not know what to think about nurse practitioners. Hill realized early on that it was the little things that mattered in building professional relationships and gaining acceptance. For instance, she would volunteer to take patients' blood pressures while the physicians were on vacation. Dr. Hill met the patients and wrote pertinent notes on their charts. When the physicians returned, they were pleased that their patients had been handled so well. Acceptance for the new role was slowly emerging; advanced practice nurses were beginning to be appreciated.

When collaborating, remember:

- Collaborate with other disciplines to ensure success.
- Bring your own expertise to the forefront.
- Look for opportunities to participate in interdisciplinary work.

LESSON 3: COMMIT TO VOLUNTEERING

Dr. Hill is often asked why she puts so much effort into her work with the AHA. First, she is passionate about the mission: to reduce death and disability due to heart disease and stroke. Second, her ongoing learning as an AHA volunteer has greatly enhanced her professional life. More than the scientific learning about cardiovascular disease and stroke, she values the leadership development, professional networking, and the opportunities for collaborations with professional colleagues. She has received far more than she has given. Hill appreciates the staff and volunteers she works with; many of whom have become her personal friends. Volunteering makes her feel valued.

The AHA and other health organizations need nurse volunteers—people who "get" the mission and are good at organizing and motivating people to complete a task. Their clinical and interpersonal skills and their breadth of understanding about cardiovascular disease from the perspectives of the patient, family, and community make them invaluable contributors to the work of organizations.

The synergy that comes from the right "match" between a volunteer or member and an organization can lead to a productive long-term relationship. Without commitment to and passion for the mission of the organization, a nurse cannot be credible. Using one's professional expertise as a volunteer lends integrity and value to all other aspects of one's life.

Almost 25 years ago, Martha's first committee assignment at the AHA was on the Annual Scientific Sessions Program Committee of the Council on Cardiovascular Nursing. She learned the value of staff and the importance of creating a working relationship with the other members. Volunteers arrived for meetings not always prepared. The staff were always prepared. After the meeting volunteers left; the staff remained. Almost as important as what happens in meetings is what occurs between meetings. Staff can be highly influential in this regard. Being a volunteer requires being a team player.

When volunteering, remember:
- Show mutual respect for peers and colleagues.
- Recognize the need for interdependent roles within an organization.
- Learn to manage diverse personalities and egos.
- Recognize the potential and limitations of the other members.
- Partner effectively with staff.

- Demonstrate willingness to do whatever work needs doing, and then do it well.

LESSON 4: OPEN THE DOOR WHEN OPPORTUNITY KNOCKS

Successful professionals recognize unique opportunities that present themselves. If one stays the course and seeks only safe options, chances for making an impact will likely be equally safe and limited.

Dr. Hill agrees that it is difficult to quantify how much of a successful career can be attributed to the "luck of the draw," or being in the right place at the right time. She stresses the need to recognize and seize unique opportunities. She shared the story of a visit from a graduate student who sought advice about starting doctoral studies. The young woman was newly married and concerned that having a family and conducting research might not be compatible. Dr. Hill encouraged this student to talk about priorities in her personal and professional life. She assured the student that doctoral studies would limit her time with her husband and that perhaps the time was not right for the commitment required. Would the opportunity for pursuing a PhD come again? Probably so, but all the pros and cons need to be weighed in taking on a new challenge.

Even beyond recognizing and taking advantage of good opportunities, Hill believes most accomplishments relate directly to how hard one is willing to work. You have to be willing to put the time in. You get to be a professor at Johns Hopkins University or the president of the AHA by working hard—over a long period of time. It is essential to recognize and appreciate those working with you. Their efforts make you shine.

When taking advantage of opportunities, remember:
- Try to set goals in 5- or 10-year blocks of time.
- Getting to the top may require sacrifice of personal time.
- Timing is everything, so set priorities accordingly.
- Work longer and harder than anyone else.
- Credit those who contribute to your success.

LESSON 5: FIND A MENTOR

Dr. Hill strongly believes that mentors are essential to one's career development. She has retained some of the same ones over the years but now finds herself spending more time serving in the mentoring role.

Dr. Karl Engleman, her early colleague at the University of Pennsylvania, insisted that she move forward with hypertension research. He once needed an abstract for a paper and handed it to Hill with the instructions for her to write it. He told her to critically examine abstracts in the journals, telling her they were all based on "formula writing." With his support she wrote the abstract and submitted it on behalf of their study. Upon receiving notice that they had been chosen to present the paper, he decided not to go to the meeting and sent her in his stead. Dr. Hill admits to having more apprehension about making the presentation than writing the abstract. Dr. Engleman had her rehearse in journal club every Thursday, and within a month deemed her "ready." The presentation went well, and Dr. Hill was always cheered by the idea that he thought her a worthy representative. Most important, she learned the true value of a mentor, one who believes and invests time in you.

Another mentor Dr. Hill credits with having tremendous influence on her career is Dr. Robert Levy. They met when he was director of the National Heart, Lung and Blood Institute (NHLBI) and she was the ANA representative on a National Institutes of Health (NIH) committee affiliated with the NHLBI. She had published two articles on her hypertension research in the *American Journal of Nursing,* and the NHLBI staff picked them up for wide national distribution. Dr. Hill became one of only four registered nurses whose publications were included in the NHLBI hypertension program bibliography. Levy chaired the NIH committee during a time when it was still intimidating for a nurse to sit at the table with the research experts. Dr. Hill claims she was the "token nurse," a role she came to excel in and perform frequently. She clearly understood the need to be invited "to the table" in order to bring the nursing research agenda forward. Conversely, Dr. Levy saw the value that she, as a nurse, brought to the arena. Dr. Hill thinks that perhaps this relationship developed because she was an independent thinker who could justify her position and find ways to work with people from different backgrounds. Her participation on the committee

enabled her to gain respect and have access to people she respected.

One other person who profoundly affected Dr. Hill's career was Dr. Claire Fagin, then dean at the University of Pennsylvania School of Nursing. Dr. Fagin arrived at Penn when Hill was a master's student and, through the introduction of doctoral education, effectively ended the master's as the terminal nursing degree. Dr. Fagin was a visionary with a clear idea of what changes needed to occur within the profession. Dr. Fagin not only endorsed Dr. Hill's "out-of-the-box" thinking, but encouraged it.

Dr. Hill has a group of professional women friends who call themselves a "kitchen cabinet." Only one of them is a nurse; the others are well-known leaders from other disciplines. They frequently meet informally at each other's homes over a cup of coffee or for dinner and a swim. This type of support is critical for high-profile women who need a private and safe outlet for friendship and good advice.

When finding a mentor, remember:
- You need more than one mentor.
- Look for people you admire.
- Be assertive and introduce yourself.
- Search for mentors who have the skills you need.
- Be open to feedback and be willing to change.

LESSON 6: KNOW THYSELF

Having insight into oneself is a real strength. Dr. Hill describes her leadership style as democratic, although she can be both laissez-faire and autocratic depending on the situation and need. She surrounds herself with the most talented people she can find and builds teams that are mutually respectful and cross trained, and who enjoy working together. She is able to delegate and let people carry out their responsibilities, informing her as needed. To maximize the effectiveness of her team and minimize the likelihood of being surprised with bad news, she is available, approachable, respectful, and responsive to others. She admits to having to a lingering tendency to overreact or micromanage at times. When she is anxious about something going wrong, she gets the necessary information to determine the extent of a problem or the potential for one. If and when a corrective plan is needed, she feels confident about instituting one.

Dr. Hill knows her strengths and limitations. She is honest with her staff about her idiosyncrasies and work patterns and uses humor to point out that even though she is inconsistently inconsistent, there is a pattern of clear priorities, strong organization, and high energy.

When examining oneself, remember:
- Seek critical analysis of your leadership style.
- Utilize the talents of others to increase your effectiveness.
- Work to shore up your weaknesses.
- Capitalize on your strengths.

LESSON 7: FILL IN THE LEARNING GAPS

When elected president of the AHA, Dr. Hill knew that some of the other leaders might take exception to a nurse serving in this capacity. Most people believed that a highly qualified person had been chosen. Hill admits that she had to call on all her skills to learn to work with a new group of people, but thinks she rose to the challenge.

Dr. Hill found it necessary to reflect on her long-term understanding of the AHA with its own culture and set of issues. The decision was made during her year as president to change the organizational structure from 50 to 15 affiliates. She had to prepare herself to work with the stress and egos of many, while assuring constituents that the AHA would continue to take the lead in cardiovascular research and policy.

During her tenure, Dr. Hill claims that her success was directly related to some of the graduate school courses she had taken. Classes in organizational and human behavior, abnormal psychology, and change theory, along with research design and methods including epidemiology and advanced biostatistics, helped her to be an effective AHA president.

Many of the problems that confront leaders are due to differences in perspective and value rather than differences in substantive content. Dr. Hill was able to analyze situations clearly, reframe issues at a conceptual level in terms of mutual goals and concerns, recognize fact from speculation, bring people together, and, by consensus, develop a common vision and strategies for achieving shared goals.

When finding out what you need to know, remember:

- Inventory your skill set.
- Develop success strategies based on past education and experiences.
- Know your group and work to bring out their best.

LESSON 8: MAINTAIN YOUR SENSE OF HUMOR

Dr. Hill relies on her sense of humor to keep her perspective and diffuse tension. When conflict seems inevitable, she is often heard to say, "The differences we have identified seem to be about political science, not biomedical science." The use of humor and recognition of how people were behaving helped diffuse the need for people to argue that their science was more important than someone else's, and allowed them to refocus on how they were going to work together to meet common goals.

When maintaining a sense of humor, remember:
- Do not take yourself too seriously.
- Work hard and play hard.
- Try to excel at doing nothing as one way to relax.

FINAL THOUGHTS

Reflecting on her professional journey, Dr. Hill says, "I was probably born thinking outside of the box. At least that's the way it seemed very early in my life. I was always able to look at things differently and see possibilities in a set of variables that others just didn't seem to see. Somewhere along the way people have to be allowed and encouraged to move at different paces and along different pathways." It is undoubtedly this ability to see the world from another view that has served her well through the years. "If I had it to do all over again, I'd still be a nurse. I have never regretted my move into the profession and have never felt the need to leave it. There are no 'former nurses.' It's like being a nun . . . for life! You are imprinted in some way when you are a nurse. I always found nursing to be an extraordinary platform for a career and for volunteer work. I brought my nursing with me and have never hidden it. I am grateful for what nurses have taught me and helped me to become. Those who leave traditional nursing take their nursing with them and can sometimes represent the profession in a much broader venue."

32 The Power and Influence of Special Interest Groups in Health Care

PATRICK S. MALONE

MARY W. CHAFFEE

MARY B. WACHTER

"Eat here or we both starve."
SIGN OUTSIDE THE TAYLOR GROCERY AND RESTAURANT, 7 MILES SOUTH OF OXFORD, MISSISSIPPI

In his earliest writings on life in the United States, Alexis de Tocqueville presented a thought-provoking opinion as to the explanation for America's successful democratic system. One reason for success, he wrote, was the propensity for Americans to participate in voluntary associations or interest groups. Today, de Tocqueville would be proud. Interest groups number in the thousands, covering almost every conceivable interest from agriculture to health care to veterans. Are interest groups good or bad? No one answer would be accurate. Indeed, interest groups represent everything good about our system: organizations looking after their constituents and advocating for preferred policy choices. But interest groups can also wield untoward power. Regardless, through their use of professional expertise, lobbying tactics, and political action committees (PACs), there is little argument that interest groups exert significant influence on policy, politics, and, ultimately, our society.

In this chapter, we take a comprehensive look at interest groups, their origins and development, their strategies, and their impact on the world of nursing and health care.

BRIEF HISTORY OF INTEREST GROUPS

Interest groups find their genesis mostly in occupational and professional organizations. Early development was influenced by the rapidly budding industrial era in the late nineteenth century. The subsequent expansion and professionalization of the economy led to the growth of many types of organizations, where the development of one group would often lead to the appearance of an opposing body. Nonprofit associations such as the American Cancer Society would be countered by profit-based associations such as the Tobacco Research Council. Large corporations tended to sponsor for-profit-sector interest groups while the government and nonprofit organizations would support nonprofit groups.

IRON TRIANGLES

By the 1940s and 1950s, "iron triangles" were solidly in place. These were networks of private interests, bureaucrats, and government officials linked in mutually beneficial relationships, and they are powerful fixtures in American politics even today. In typical cases, an iron triangle would be composed of a congressional committee or subcommittee, interest groups (trade or industry associations), and a federal agency. For instance, in the timber industry, an iron triangle may include the Agriculture Committee's Subcommittee on Forests, the U.S. Forest Service as the federal agency, and an interest group representing the timber industry. These groups all support and benefit from one another.

LIBERAL FOUNDATIONS

In the 1960s, interest groups with more ideological and liberal foundations sprang up. Fueled by the tumultuous social climate of the Vietnam era and the fight for civil rights, Americans began questioning their democratic system of government and raising their voices about race relations, economic policy, and foreign involvement. Sit-ins, boycotts and protests punctuated the decade.

RIGHT-WING INFLUENCE

In the 1970s and 1980s, the United States witnessed a rebound response to the liberal 1960s. There was a proliferation of right-wing conservative interest groups such as the New Christian Right. Interest groups also began to take center stage in American politics. As a result of the Federal Election Campaign Act amendments of 1974, revisions in campaign finance laws led to a more prominent role for interest groups in the electoral process. This legislation laid the foundation for future debates about interest groups, their influence, and public confidence in the integrity of the political process (Berry, 1997).

A DOMINANT ROLE

In the last 10 years, interest groups have come under increasing scrutiny for their powerful political influence. This comes as no surprise, given the expansion of the funds, staff, and expertise of interest groups. Furthermore, the changing demographic and religious makeup of the country has introduced many groups, some previously disenfranchised, to the political scene, and many minorities find themselves better represented than ever be-

fore. As more players arrive on the political stage, the mix of power, influence, and policy alternatives grows more enigmatic—and outcomes more difficult to predict.

WHY DO INTEREST GROUPS EXIST?

Interest groups have long been a part of the American political landscape. Although they have not always met with favor, they tend to be an accepted fact of political reality. James Madison considered interest groups to be simply an extension of human desire, based on the propensity of the citizenry to have different opinions concerning religion and government. He also believed the causes of factions to be "sown in the nature of man" (*Federalist Papers*, 1961, p. 79).

With Madison's views as background, it is important to note that interest groups have not always been met with open arms. Some question their value as agents of mobilization. Indeed, one of the more interesting dilemmas regarding interest groups centers on their role in political mobilization, versus that of political parties. Political scientists have traditionally taken the position that parties were more beneficial than interest groups as mechanisms for mobilization (Walker, 1997). In truth, there is room for both. By serving as a check on majoritarianism, interest groups ensure there is a political voice for special, often minority, interests. Parties, conversely, fight for the majority interest (Dye, 1998). Still, others argue that interest groups are elitist and nonrepresentative in nature. Schattschneider's (1960) description of the flaw in the pluralist heaven is often quoted: "The heavenly chorus sings with a strong upper class accent."

This leads to a crucial distinction between interests and interest groups. Though it may seem trite, the distinction is an important one. To borrow an example from Berry (1997), farmers are not interest groups, but the American Farm Bureau Federation (AFBF) is. The difference lies in one thing—organization. Although not all farmers belong to the AFBF, the AFBF represents the interests of all farmers. Therein lies an indicator of the political power of the interest group. Their influence lies not only in their membership, but also in their ability to represent the interests of a much larger body.

FORMING AND JOINING

Political scientists have long struggled with the reasons that make people join interest groups and why interest groups form. Truman (1951) considered interest groups to be a group of people with shared values who join together to influence other groups in society. In essence, he felt that their creation is a result of natural interaction and societal disturbances. Mancur Olson (1965) argued that people join groups for selective benefits or as a result of coercion. In his view, group development Is problematic. Salisbury's (1969) answer to the formation problem lay in the role of the entrepreneur. As part of his Exchange Theory, Salisbury argued it takes the work of individual catalysts to ensure group formation. These entrepreneurs seek to assume the early organizational costs in return for a staff job with the group. Scholars since Salisbury have suggested that politics may play a greater role in that there may be more incentive involved in contributing to the collective political benefits than originally thought.

Quite simply, people join interest groups to realize one of three types of benefits: material, solidary, and purposive (Clark & Wilson, 1961).

- Material benefits involve tangible rewards.
- Solidary benefits designate social rewards that occur from association with the group.
- Purposive benefits tend to be ideologically based or issue-oriented goals, not tangible in nature.

Olson (1965) later added selective benefits (benefits available only to members of the organization) and collective benefits (those that accrue to both members and nonmembers) to this list.

CLASSIFICATION OF INTEREST GROUPS

Interest groups take a number of forms, structures, missions, and types (Dye, 1998). Some of the more common differentiations follow:

- *Organizational structure.* Interest groups may be national, regional, state, or local. They may have centralized or decentralized structures. They

may cater to groups or individual members, organizations (e.g., trade associations), or even governments (e.g., National League of Cities). Finally, they may have large or small staffs, be mail based, or even be Internet based.

- *Economic focus.* Economic interest groups, such as the Business Roundtable, base their mission in the economic interests of their members. People for the American Way and other non-economic interest groups have goals that are more ideological in nature. Interest groups may even bridge the gap between economic and non-economic goals depending on their ideological, informational, and instrumental functions.

- *Type of benefit.* Interest groups vary widely in the types of benefits they seek to obtain for their members (Box 32-1). Groups such as Greenpeace and the Christian Coalition offer mainly ideological benefits that are more purposive in nature. Members of the United Auto Workers enjoy material benefits from their membership such as higher pay and health benefits. Members of the National Organization for Women gain a feeling of solidarity in their relationship with others in the organization. Finally, some organizations, such as the American Association of Retired Persons, offer a combination of all these types of rewards for their members.

- *Goals and mission.* Interest groups pursue unique goals. Business groups and trade associations seek to influence lawmakers to enhance their business interests. Professional associations and labor groups attempt to further the specialized status and interests of their fields. The goals of groups may be public interest in nature, seeking a collective good on behalf of the general public, or they may exist to pursue a single agenda, focusing their energy on one cause. An example of a single-issue group is the National Rifle Association.

INTEREST GROUP ACTIVITY

Lobbying legislators is considered the primary tool of interest groups to further their causes. This is not surprising. Indeed, interest groups are expert at

BOX **32-1** Select Examples of Interest Groups (by Type)

BUSINESS

Business Roundtable
National Small Business Association
U.S. Chamber of Commerce

TRADE

American Petroleum Institute
Home Builders Association
Motion Picture Association of America

PROFESSIONAL

American Medical Association
American Nurses Association
National Education Association

UNION

American Federation of Labor–Congress of Industrial
   Organizations
American Federation of Teachers
United Steel Workers

AGRICULTURAL

National Cattleman's Association
National Grange
Tobacco Institute

WOMEN

League of Women Voters
National Organization for Women

PUBLIC INTEREST

Common Cause
Public Citizen

IDEOLOGICAL

American Conservative Union
Americans for Democratic Action
People for the American Way

SINGLE ISSUE

National Rifle Association
National Right to Life Committee
National Taxpayers Union

ENVIRONMENTAL

Environmental Defense Fund
Nature Conservancy
Sierra Club

RELIGIOUS

American-Israeli Public Affairs Committee
Catholics for Choice

CIVIL RIGHTS

American Indian Movement
National Urban League
Rainbow Coalition

AGE RELATED

American Association of Retired Persons
Children's Defense Fund

VETERANS

American Legion
Veterans of Foreign Wars
The Retired Officers Organization

DEFENSE

Air Force Association
American Security Council

GOVERNMENT

National Association of Counties
National Conference of State Legislators
National League of Cities

using lobbying to influence agendas, legislation, and policymaker actions. The way that interest groups exert influence, however, is more complex than lobbying alone. The strength—indeed, the currency—of the interest group is information. The data and expertise of the staff and membership of interest groups represent a tremendous force. Because information is power, this places interest groups in an excellent position to be creative in determining strategic approaches to electoral influence or political mobilization.

INTEREST GROUP STRATEGY

Interest groups use a variety of tactics to persuade lawmakers or sway public opinion. Most can be defined as one of two types: inside strategies or outside strategies (Walker, 1997). *Inside strategies* are direct and focused in nature. These include tactics such as direct lobbying or political action committee (PAC) contributions. Interest groups using inside strategies often depend on the use of financial resources and subject matter expertise to influence public officials. Conversely, *outside strategies* are more broadly focused. Although they may be used in concert with inside schemes, outside strategies are generally used to influence the general public, or a segment of the population. Outside strategies may simply plant the seed for future political support—months or even years down the road.

Aside from direct and more informal contacts with legislators and government officials, interest groups may exert their influence on legislation in the form of lawsuits or the filing of amicus curiae (friend of the court) briefs. They may organize coalitions or protests to pressure legislative decision makers. Interest groups will often target constituents directly through letter writing, telegrams, e-mail, or telephone calls to mobilize support. They may enlist the media to mobilize the public around a specific policy issue, a strategy known as media advocacy. Groups may also attempt to influence elections through campaign contributions, candidate endorsements, or volunteer campaign work. Finally, using their subject matter expertise, interest groups play an important role in drafting legislation and regulations. By assisting congressional staffs through this type of inside strategy, interest groups wield tremendous power in shaping policy and law.

Which strategy is the best? Given the number of approaches available to interest groups, one may wonder when an interest group will choose a particular tactic. Unfortunately, interest group scholars find themselves at a loss to explain the strategy choices interest groups make. Baumgartner and Leech (1998) note that interest group behavior is unpredictable. First, most groups use a variety of strategies as opposed to a single tactic. Second, the choice of strategy depends on the contextual nature of the situation as well as the unique characteristics of the group.

POLITICAL ACTION COMMITTEES

PACs are the campaign funding arm of special interest groups. They are money-making machines that raise funds to contribute to candidates' legislative, gubernatorial, congressional, and presidential campaigns. Political incumbents receive the majority of PAC contributions. PAC contributions, however, do not buy votes. In fact, there is very little evidence that PAC funding directly affects a legislator's vote on a given bill (Weissert & Weissert, 1996). What PAC contributions buy is *access.*

FUNCTION

The PACs are one part of a three-pronged approach—direct lobbying, grass roots lobbying, and PAC contributions—used by special interest groups to influence policy decisions (Weissert & Weissert, 1996). The influence exerted by PACs is directly related to the amount and timing of contributions made to candidates. Candidates who receive PAC dollars, particularly when this support is rendered early (e.g., before primary elections), are more likely to meet with those groups and listen to their positions on issues. Thus PAC contributions gain access to decision makers at critical times (Heineman, Peterson, & Rasmussen, 1995).

There are other functions of PACs that can influence policymakers besides direct monetary contributions. Organizations with large memberships are impressive voting blocks that candidates and elected officials pay close attention to—especially if their race is hotly contested. The endorsement of a candidate by the PAC of a large group can be leveraged into votes. Endorsements by PACs are publicized to the membership of the interest group. The endorsement is the group's seal of approval and indicates that the candidate being endorsed has met a number of criteria. Possible reasons for endorsement include: (1) alignment of the candidate's position on issues with that of the group, (2) sponsorship of legislation supported by the group, and (3) the electability of the candidate (Heineman et al, 1995). In the case of incumbents, a voting record that is favorable to the group and the candidate's holding a key leadership position may also be conditions for endorsement (Weissert & Weissert, 1996).

Decisions about contributions and candidate endorsements are generally made by the governing body of the PAC. This usually consists of members of the interest group who are either appointed or elected by the membership.

REGULATION OF THE CAMPAIGN MONEY TRAIL

There are ethical implications of a political process where interest groups give money to elected officials who are then supposed to make unbiased policy decisions in the best interests of their constituents. For this reason, PACs are heavily regulated political entities. There are federal, state, and local PACs, and each is subject to specific designated regulations. State and local PAC regulations vary widely throughout the United States. For the purposes of this discussion, the regulations set forth by the Federal Election Commission (FEC), the government agency with regulatory oversight of federal PACs, will be discussed.

The PACs raise money primarily through contributions by special interest group members. Individuals may contribute up to $5000 per calendar year to a PAC. There are limits on the amount that a PAC can contribute to a candidate's campaign. This amount may range from $1000 to $5000 per candidate per election depending on whether the PAC has been approved by the FEC as a one-candidate or multicandidate PAC. Candidates use PAC money to pay the ever-increasing costs of running a campaign—especially the cost of advertising. In the 2000 campaign cycle, candidates, parties, and interest groups spent $3 billion to secure elected positions. This represents a 50% increase in expenditures from the 1996 election cycle (Dwyer, 2000).

Historically, PACs are well-known for their contributions to political parties, especially the National Democratic and Republican Committees. The parties then spend this money on activities that benefit the candidates. The FEC limit on contributions from a PAC to a political party is $20,000 per calendar year. All contributions must be reported quarterly to the FEC and represent public information that can be reviewed at the FEC website (www.fec.gov) (FEC, 2001).

ANA-PAC

The American Nurses Association Political Action Committee (ANA-PAC) is the campaign funding arm of the ANA, the most prominent nursing special interest group, which speaks for all 2.7 million registered nurses in the United States. ANA-PAC was established in 1974 to strengthen ANA's voice in the nation's capitol. Since that time ANA-PAC has grown to become one of the top health care PACs in the United States. For the third consecutive election cycle, ANA-PAC has raised more than $1 million from nurses throughout the country. There are many nurses who are high donors, but the average contribution is about $42 per year per nurse.

The purpose of ANA-PAC is to assist candidates who are friends of nursing win elections for federal office, thus increasing the number of federally elected officials who understand and support the ANA's policy agenda. ANA-PAC is committed to increasing the number of registered nurses (RNs) in public office at every level of government. During the 2000 election cycle, ANA-PAC was successful in helping to reelect three nurses to the U.S. House of Representatives. ANA-PAC also endorses candidates for office (ANA, 2001).

FOLLOW THE MONEY

MONEY AS INFLUENCE

Money plays a prominent role in the ability of interest groups to achieve their goals. Money reflects the power of the group, buys access to policymakers, and ensures the visibility of the interest group. Money is important to incumbents, and even more important to challengers (Jacobsen, 1990; Berry, 1997). Along with information, it is the lifeblood of interest groups.

HARD AND SOFT MONEY

Political contributions are described as *hard* or *soft*. Hard money donations are those made directly to candidates. Soft money donations are earmarked for party-building activities (e.g., registration voting drives) but have often been used for advertising candidates, an activity now regulated by new campaign finance laws. In the 1999-2000 election cycle, Republicans raised $447 million in hard money and $244 million in soft money. Democrats raised $270 million in hard money and $243 million in soft money (Dwyer, Cohn, McNamee, & Palmer, 2001).

Let there be no mistake: Interest groups do not hesitate to use money to influence elections. Interest groups spent tens of millions of dollars in the U.S. House and Senate races in Fall of 2000. One study by the Center for the Study of Elections and Democracy at Brigham Young University (BYU) suggests that some of the closest races of the recent election cycle may have been strongly influenced by interest groups (Allen, 2001). The study found that interest groups spent over $95 million for radio and television advertisements alone. Other interest group-funded activities included phone calls, direct mailings, and billboard advertisements.

CAMPAIGN FINANCE REFORM

Campaign finance reform has threatened to curb the influence of money on the political system. The 1974 campaign finance reforms, well intended as they were, provided legitimacy to fund raising. Post-Watergate efforts to reform campaign finance laws have proven relatively ineffectual due to the fund-raising prowess of clever campaign managers. Indeed, campaign officials have historically met with great success in securing large donations to political parties that subsequently end up in the hands of the candidates.

By far the most significant attempt at reform has been the McCain-Feingold Bill, sponsored by Senator John McCain (R-AZ.) and Senator Russ Feingold (D-WI). The final version of the bill, sponsored by Representative Christopher Shays (R-CT) and Representative Martin T. Meehan (D-MA) passed in March of 2002. The bill bans corporations, individuals, and unions from giving unregulated soft money to national parties, an amount that totaled nearly $500 million in 2000. It also limits soft-money contributions to state and local parties, capping them at $10,000 and barring their use in federal campaigns. The campaign finance reform also increases contribution limits for candidates running against wealthy candidates who finance their own campaigns; creates stricter disclosure requirements; and prohibits fundraising on federal property and from foreign sources (Brookings Institution, 2002; Center for Responsive Politics, 2002).

The bill also raises hard money contribution limits by individuals to $2000 for House, Senate, and presidential candidates, and $25,000 for parties. Most significantly for interest groups, the McCain-Feingold Bill limits the ability of unions, nonprofits, and corporations to broadcast political advertisements (issue advertisements) targeting specific federal candidates 60 days before a general election and 30 days before a primary election (Dewar, 2002).

The debate on campaign finance reform has not been silenced. Deliberations on both sides of the issue continue. Some interest groups have raised concern that the portions of the bill restricting issue advertisements in the final phases of a campaign may tread upon rights of free speech. Others believe reform efforts are imperative in rescuing a political system controlled by big money and large corporations.

Campaign finance reform is expected to remain of the agenda, but how reform may eventually be enacted is unclear. Democrats and organized labor groups have concerns about the fairness of the legislation. Republicans, meanwhile, appear poised to benefit early from reform efforts as a result of their prowess at securing hard money donations. Representative Albert Wynn (D-MD) stated, "A Republican passing a hat in a country club can make a lot more hard money than a Democrat talking to regular people" (Squitirei, 2001). Whatever the ultimate outcome, the implications of reform are significant. Kutner (2001) writes, "How societies' richest and most powerful interests are permitted to undermine democracy by substituting a large check for a democratic mobilization of voters has its most profound implications for substantive politics" (p. 4).

EVOLVING ROLE OF POLITICAL PARTIES

Political scientists have come to question the viability of the American political party in the face of the growing power of interest groups. Are the two alike? Do they serve similar functions? Are they compatible, or in conflict with each other?

Early political party structure was heavily influenced by religious, geographic, and ethnic loyalties.

Immigrants to the United States found connections and jobs through the patronage system by affiliating with a local political boss. The resulting strength and allegiance of these relationships were solid. As the U.S. political system matured, other mechanisms evolved to mobilize the public. Foremost among these were interest groups.

Political scientists have debated the compatibility of the interest group and the political party system. Some contend that the rise in interest groups splinters party influence, and when parties have control of the national agenda, the influence of interest groups is lessened (Schattschneider, 1960). Others suggest that parties and interest groups have unique roles in different circumstances (Walker, 1997). As noted earlier, interest groups ensure that there is a political voice for special, often minority, interests, whereas parties fight for the majority interest (Dye, 1998). During election cycles, political parties tend to be more active. Between cycles, interest groups are extremely active.

HEALTH CARE INTEREST GROUPS

INTEREST GROUP POWER

Health care interest groups compete no differently than others in their quest for influence on the political stage. In the 1960s, the American Medical Association (AMA) reigned as the powerhouse of health care lobbies. By 1994, the year of President Clinton's intense efforts at health care reform, the AMA's preeminent status had changed. The AMA was still a force to be reckoned with, but it was competing with many other groups that had emerged or strengthened their political footing—including nurses. Broder (1994) writes that more than 1100 interest groups weighed in on the 1994 health care reform initiative.

Today, health care interest groups wield tremendous influence. The BYU research makes specific note of the influence of Citizens for Better Medicare (underwritten by the pharmaceutical industry) on the fall 2000 federal elections. Indeed, spending by health care interest groups has doubled since 1992.

Health care interest groups were a potent force in the 2000 election cycle (Center for Responsive Poli-

tics, 2001). Health care interest groups contributed almost $54 million, 62% of which went to incumbents (Box 32-2). Republicans garnered the most financial support, with 58% of the money, or just over $31 million. Democrats received 41%, or almost $23 million. Presidential candidate George W. Bush topped all candidates, with $4.1 million in donations from health care interest groups. Rounding out the top five recipients of health care largesse were presidential candidate Al Gore ($1.3 million), presidential candidate Bill Bradley ($1.2 million), Senate candidate Rick Lazio ($1.1 million), and Senate candidate Hillary Rodham Clinton ($752,000).

Physicians, nurses, and other health professional associations are generally the largest campaign contributors in the health care industry, but the pharmaceutical industry has rapidly become a major player (Center for Responsive Politics, 2001). In fact, the political donations made by pharmaceutical companies have been doubling about every four years. This is primarily due to the current focus on expanding Medicare coverage for prescription medications. The threat of legislated controls on drug prices is not desirable to pharmaceutical manufacturers and has mobilized great activity on their part. Thus, pharmaceutical groups are expected to overtake health care provider and health care organizations as the most generous health interest groups.

BOX **32-2** Top Ten Health Care Contributors: 2000 Election Cycle

1. Bristol-Myers Squibb ($2,371,669)
2. Pfizer Inc. ($2,339,881)
3. American Medical Association ($2,083,819)
4. Eli Lilly & Co. ($1,636,995)
5. American Hospital Association ($1,629,769)
6. Slim Fast Foods/Thompson Medical ($1,568,200)
7. Glaxco Welcome Inc. ($1,516,503)
8. American Dental Association ($1,366,617)
9. Shering-Plough Corp. ($1,212,297)
10. American Society of Anesthesiologists ($1,116,002)

From Center for Responsive Politics. (2001). *Who's giving.* Washington, DC.

INTEREST GROUPS AND THE FAILURE OF HEALTH CARE REFORM

To see evidence of the power of health care interest groups, one need look no farther than the health care reform attempts of the first Clinton administration. The historic role of interest group activity in health care reform is nothing new. Blue Cross successfully stopped post-World War II reform efforts by developing extraordinary advertising campaigns asserting that private mechanisms were superior to government programs in meeting the health care needs of the citizenry. In 1948, the AMA mobilized physicians in grass roots efforts to defeat President Truman's plan for a national health insurance program. The AMA also played a critical role in the passage of the 1966 law creating Medicare and Medicaid. In the most recent health reform attempt, the role of interest groups was prominent as well.

The attempt toward reform of the U.S. health system in the early 1990s was a significant one. In fact, the Center for Public Integrity found that the 1993-1994 health care reform effort was the most heavily lobbied initiative in U.S. history, with expenditures exceeding $100 million. Although President Clinton's initial proposal was strong, symbolic, and persuasive, neither he nor his staff were prepared for the opposition that would follow, opposition orchestrated largely by interest groups.

President Clinton's inability to effectively communicate his vision caused problems from the beginning, and the lack of support from major interest groups was a fatal blow. In his attempt to build a cadre of experts to guide national health care reform, President Clinton depended on alliances of hospitals, physicians, labor, and the elderly (Morone, 1994; Skocpol, 1994, 1996; Waldman, Cohn, & Clift, 1994; Yankelovich, 1995). Although these parties agreed on the need for universal coverage, they differed significantly on how to finance it. One of the most serious blows to the Clinton plan was the lack of supportive major business groups and trade associations (though some initially supported it). The Business Roundtable, the Chamber of Commerce, the National Association of Manufacturers, and the AMA all refused to support the Clinton proposal (Shick, 1995).

Many groups played a role in the opposition effort. The AMA led all PACs by spending $1.3 million to lobby physicians to fight a reform plan that could limit physicians' personal earnings (Birenbaum, 1995; Laham, 1996; Glied, 1997). The American Hospital Association (AHA) sent information packets to each of its 4900 member hospitals containing advice on how to mobilize 4 million health care employees and thousands of volunteers (Center for Public Integrity, 1994). The Federation of American Health Systems, representing a membership of 1400 for-profit hospitals, formed the Health Leadership Council, composed of the chief executives of the 50 largest health care companies. Their efforts included convincing politicians, journalists, and citizens of the dangers of Clinton's reform proposal. Meanwhile, the National Association of Health Underwriters embarked on a campaign to support their interests.

Opponents of the Clinton plan capitalized on the fear of the unknown, convincing Americans to mistrust changes to the health care system they did not understand (Birenbaum, 1995). An effective combination of advertising, mailings, television ads, lobbying, and grassroots activity was enough to destroy any hope of significant health care reform.

Particularly noteworthy were the efforts of the Health Insurance Association of America (HIAA), a coalition of mid-sized and small insurance companies that would have been negatively impacted by the success of Clinton's proposal (Jacobs, 1994; Skocpol, 1994; Jacobs & Shapiro, 1995; Laham, 1996). The HIAA, using its established infrastructure, utilized print and television advertisements in their "Campaign to Insure All Americans." Directing their message at insurance company employees, small business, veteran's organizations, and the elderly, the HIAA and its members contended that the Clinton plan would "cost jobs and would mean bureaucratic controls" (Kosterlitz, 1992). In addition to hiring former Ohio Republican Congressman Willis Gradison as its chief strategist, the HIAA spent almost $15 million on the infamous "Harry and Louise" advertisements, featuring a middle-class couple who bemoaned the risks of the Clinton plan (Kosterlitz, 1994).

The Clinton plan for health reform was doomed. Opposition by interest groups and multiple stakeholders, coupled with a divide in the Democratic party over the best method for achieving reform, dealt the Clinton reform effort its fatal blow (Gergen, 1996; Laham, 1996; Patel & Rushefsky, 1995).

NURSING AS A SPECIAL INTEREST GROUP

EARLY SUCCESS AS AN INTEREST GROUP

One of nursing's greatest successes as an interest group working to influence public policy occurred in the early years of the twentieth century. Nurses sought to control their profession by developing standards of practice and educational requirements, but the profession had no means to do so because it was unregulated. Not only was nursing unregulated, but nurses were women. Women had no political voice—because they had no vote—in the United States at the turn of twentieth century.

The key to obtaining professional control lay in passing state practice acts, but a profession without the right to vote was at a huge disadvantage. Acquiring the vote would increase the chance of success in passing state laws regulating nursing. Nursing therefore actively supported the women's suffrage movement. In another act of collaboration that would contribute to success, the four active nursing organizations built a strong coalition. These organizations included the Nurses Associated Alumnae of the United States and Canada (later the ANA), the American Society of Superintendents of Training Schools for Nurses (later the National League for Nursing [NLN]), the National Association of Colored Graduate Nurses (later absorbed into the American Nurses Association), and the National Organization for Public Health Nursing (which later joined the NLN) (Lewenson, 1996).

The collaborative work toward a common goal paid off. The first nurse practice acts were passed by state legislatures in 1903, 17 long years before women would achieve the right to vote. This was an extraordinary political achievement that set the standard for what nurses could achieve through focused political efforts.

BARRIERS TO NURSING'S POLITICAL INFLUENCE

Despite a three-pronged strategy, nursing's success as an interest group has not been steady. Legislative victories have occurred, such as the passage of the Needlestick Safety and Prevention Act in October 2000, a federal law designed to protect nurses and other health care workers from needlesticks in the workplace. Nursing's influence as an interest group has often suffered because of two weaknesses, a lack of focus on core issues and the "free rider" problem.

Lack of Focus on Core Issues. Feldstein (1996) writes that when members of a group have similar interests, the costs of organizing are less. Large differences in position may be viewed as political weakness and may cause members to defect. Feldstein further notes that legislators may be confused about who speaks for members' interests if there are multiple voices supporting different positions. Another reason for the lack of focus on core issues is the great range of levels of nursing education, practice settings, and specialties. The ongoing specialization of nursing has led to the growth of over 100 nursing specialty groups, each with its own agenda and political goals. Although membership in a specialty association may meet the educational and networking needs of nurses, it also may be contributing to the overall fragmentation of nursing's image, message, and political influence.

"Free Rider" Problem. When individuals with a common interest organize to achieve favorable legislation, all individuals with that common interest gain, whether or not they are a member of the organization (Feldstein, 1996). The individuals who do not participate as members yet still benefit from the activities of the group get a "free ride." Every nurse in the United States benefits from the political activity that the American Nurses Association conducts on behalf of all 2.7 million American nurses—yet less than 10% of American nurses are members of state nurses associations and the ANA. Feldstein (1996) points out a critical issue for nurses: Unless a group overcomes the "free rider" problem, they may be unable to raise sufficient funds to lobby for desirable policies.

To overcome these two barriers to political influence, as well as to maintain the organization's viability, the ANA created the Futures Task Force in 2000 to define its future direction and organizational focus. Five core issues have been identified that will drive the ANA's work in the future: appropriate staffing, workplace health and safety, workplace rights, patient safety and advocacy, and continued competency (Foley, 2000).

Interest groups competing with others may attempt to carve out a political niche or policy domain that is recognized as theirs alone (Weissert & Weissert, 1996). A group does this by defining specific issues for itself. The ANA's identification of five core issues that will define their policy agenda clearly stakes out the organization's territory.

CONCLUSION

From their earliest days, interest groups have met with equal amounts of disdain and admiration. Some view them with skepticism as elite influences on the political system, restricting the access of average citizens to legislators. Others perceive interest groups to be of great value, providing expertise to legislators and a political voice to millions of Americans. Whatever one's view, the place of interest groups is firmly woven into the fabric of American political life. Furthermore, despite recent reform efforts, it is unlikely that their influence will unravel anytime soon.

REFERENCES

Allen, M. (2001, February 5). Interest groups a force in congressional elections. *Washington Post*, A5.

American Nurses Association. (2001). *American Nurses Association Political Action Committee (ANA-PAC)*. Available online at www.nursingworld.org/gova/federal/anapac.

Baumgartner, F.R. & Leech, B.L. (1998). *The importance of groups in politics and political science*. Princeton, NJ: Princeton University Press.

Berry, J.M. (1997). *The interest group society*. New York: Longman.

Birenbaum, A. (1995). *Putting health care on the national agenda*. Westport, CT: Praeger.

Broder, D. (1994, January 31-February 6). Can we govern? *Washington Post National Weekly Edition*, 23.

Brookings Institution. (2002). *Governmental studies*. Washington, DC. Available online at www.brook.edu.

Center for Public Integrity (1994). *Well-healed: Inside lobbying for health care reform*. Washington, DC: Author.

Center for Responsive Politics. (2001). *Who's giving*. Washington, DC.

Center for Responsive Politics. (2002). *Elections: Campaign finance reform*. Washington, DC. Available online at www.opensecrets.org.

Clark, P., & Wilson, J. (1961, September). Incentive systems: A theory of organizations. *Administrative Science Quarterly, 6*, 129-166.

Dewar, Helen. (2002, March 21). Campaign reform wins final approval: Senate votes 60-40; Bush says he will sign "flawed" bill. *Washington Post*, A01.

Dwyer, P. (2000, December 4). The candidate as a campaign spectator. *Business Week*, 38.

Dwyer, P., Cohn, L. McNamee, M., & Palmer, A. (2001, April 16). Campaign reform: Where do we go from here? *Business Week*, 42.

Dye, T.R. (1998). *Politics in America*. Upper Saddle River, NJ: Simon & Schuster.

Federal Election Commission. (2001). *Contributions*. Available online at www.fec.gov.

Federalist papers. (1961; original 1788). New York: New American Library, 77-84.

Feldstein, P. (1996). *The politics of health legislation: An economic perspective* (2nd ed.). Chicago: Health Administration Press.

Foley, M. (2000). *Opening session of the 2000 ANA convention*. Available online at www.nursingworld.org.

Gergen, D. (1996). And now, the fifth estate? *U.S. News and World Report, 120*(17), 84.

Glied, S. (1997). *Chronic condition: Why health reform fails*. Cambridge, MA: Harvard University Press.

Heineman, R.A., Peterson, S.A., & Rasmussen, T.H. (1995). *American government* (2nd ed.). New York: McGraw-Hill.

Jacobs, L.R. (1994). The politics of American ambivalence toward government. In J.A. Morone & G.S. Belkin (Eds.). *The politics of health care reform: Lessons from the past, prospects for the future*. Durham, NC: Duke University Press.

Jacobs, L.R. & Shapiro, R.Y. (1995). Don't blame the public for failed health care reform. *Journal of Health Policy Politics and Law, 20*(2), 411-423.

Jacobson, G.C. (1990, May). The effects of campaign spending in House elections: New evidence for old arguments. *American Journal of Political Science, 34*, 334-362.

Kosterlitz, J. (1992, March 25). Insurers are gearing up. *National Journal*, 706-707.

Kosterlitz, J. (1994, June 25). Harry, Louise, and doublespeak. *National Journal*, 1542.

Kuttner, R., (2001). The McCain mutiny. *American Prospect, 12*(7), 4.

Laham, N. (1996). *A lost cause: Bill Clinton's campaign for national health insurance*. Westport, CT: Praeger.

Lewenson, S.B. (1996). *Taking charge: Nursing, suffrage, and feminism in America, 1873-1920*. New York: National League for Nursing Press.

Morone, J.A. (1994). Introduction. In J.A. Morone & G.S. Belkin (Eds.). *The politics of health care reform: Lessons from the past, prospects for the future.* Durham, NC: Duke University Press.

Olson, Jr., M. (1965). *The logic of collective action.* New York: Schocken.

Patel, K. & Rushefsky, M.E. (1995). *Health care politics and policy in America.* New York: M.E. Sharpe.

Salisbury, R.H. (1969). An exchange theory of interest groups. *Midwest Journal of Political Science, 13*(1), 1-32.

Schattschneider, E.E. (1960). *The semi-sovereign people.* New York: Holt, Rhinehart and Winston.

Shick, A. (1995). How a bill did not become law. In T.E. Mann & N.J. Ornstein (Eds.). *Intensive care: How Congress shapes health policy.* Washington, DC: Brookings.

Skocpol, T. (1994). Is the time finally ripe? In J.A. Morone & G.S. Belkin (Eds.). *The politics of health care reform: Lessons from the past, prospects for the future.* Durham, NC: Duke University Press.

Skocpol, T. (1996). *Boomerang: Clinton's health security effort and the turn against government in U.S. politics.* New York: W.W. Norton.

Squitieri, T. (2001, May 8). Campaign reform in jeopardy: Congressional Black Caucus may oppose finance overhaul. *USA Today,* A-1.

Truman, D.B. (1951). *The governmental process: Political interests and public opinion.* New York: Knopf.

Waldman, S., Cohn, B., & Clift, E. (1994). How Clinton blew it. *Newsweek, 123*(26), 28.

Walker, J.L. (1997). *Mobilizing interest groups in America.* Ann Arbor, MI: University of Michigan Press.

Weissert, C.S. & Weissert, W.G. (1996). *Governing health: The politics of health policy.* Baltimore: Johns Hopkins University Press.

Yankelovich, D. (1995). The debate that wasn't: The public and the Clinton health care plan. *Brookings Review, 13*(3), 6.

Political Action Case Studies: Nursing Organizations in Action

"Action is the antidote to despair."

JOAN BAEZ

INTRODUCTION

Linda M. Valentino

The public policy-making process is influenced by societal pressures to apply accumulated knowledge (Sabatier, 1991), and professional organizations can be considered centers of accumulated knowledge. Shinn (1998) describes information as the "raison d'etre" of most associations. The organization's role is to sort, analyze, utilize, and disseminate information to advance its policy agenda, meet its mission, and satisfy its members.

The seven vignettes that follow represent efforts by national nursing organizations to influence public policy development. They highlight various approaches to shaping health policies, including communicating to and mobilizing members; actively lobbying policymakers; conducting and disseminating research; and educating members, policymakers, and the public. Policy agenda setting can be activated by external factors, such as the introduction of specific legislation to which an association needs to respond, or by the core mission of the association, such as the prevention of colon cancer or the safety of employees in the workplace.

Collection and dissemination of information are a vital part of an association's accomplishment of its policy goals. Many of the vignettes describe deliberate structures set up to use and to disseminate information. The vignette by the American Association of Occupational Health Nurses (AAOHN) describes a structure created at the local level to feed information in a timely way back to the national association, and vice versa. Lobbying is one method used by these associations to disseminate information about a specific issue and is included in most of the vignettes as a strategy to educate stakeholders.

One theme that emerges throughout the seven vignettes is that the organizations use collaborative efforts to influence policy using their collective power. The American Society for Parenteral and Enteral Nutrition is an interdisciplinary association, and its vignette highlights the value of "speaking with one voice." Gathering support for a particular issue from an interdisciplinary group was extremely effective in changing health policy. The Oncology Nurses Society, along with the American Nurses Association and other associations, effectively lobbied to halt legislation that would have undermined effective pain management. These collective efforts speak on behalf of 28,000 registered oncology nurses, as well as other nurses, physicians, and lay people concerned about the quality of pain management—and they are impressive.

The section contributed by the National Association of Clinical Nurse Specialists shows the importance of an association's mission and core purposes to shaping a policy agenda. Theirs defines a "complementary" relationship with other professional nursing organizations and, thus, embraces in its core mission an important political strategy.

The external forces driving health care policy are represented in these vignettes. Health care cost and quality issues related to patient care are of primary concern to nursing organizations. Their role in advocacy for the profession of nursing and high-quality patient care has brought associations together on many issues.

The final vignette focuses on a coalition of nursing organizations united to oppose physicians' efforts to restrict the practices of advanced practice nurses. It illustrates that interorganizational collaboration is essential for nursing's success in policy arenas.

One clear message throughout all of the vignettes is *be persistent*. Influencing policy making can be a long process. The vignette by the AAOHN illustrates the small steps that build over decades to shape public policy and meet the mission of the organization. Even if policy can be changed quickly, this is a process that almost always requires persistence and tenacity. The following vignettes demonstrate that a commitment to a common goal, deliberate political strategizing, and a willingness to create partnerships and alliances with other organizations to achieve success are key to effective policy making.

ENSURING NURSES ARE AT THE POLICY TABLE: AMERICAN ASSOCIATION OF OCCUPATIONAL HEALTH NURSES

Kae Livsey

Occupational health nurses are key to the success of workplace health and safety programs. They are largest group of occupational health care providers, and often the only providers at the workplace. Occupational health nurses develop and manage programs to promote and protect the health and safety of workers in many different work settings, including health care organizations. The occupational health nurse's field experience, coupled with business expertise, brings practical perspectives and cost-effective solutions for the prevention of workplace illness and injury. The AAOHN is the professional association for nurses working in this specialty.

The AAOHN began to understand the need to be involved in shaping health policy when the Occupational Safety and Health Administration (OSHA) issued a highly controversial standard that excluded occupational health nurses from the definition of "health professional." In the executive branch, OSHA is the primary federal agency that deals with matters affecting occupational health nursing practice. OSHA failed to recognize the contributions that occupational health nurses make in educating employees about health and safety issues. This event was a wake-up call to get the membership organized and involved, and to launch the governmental affairs program for the association. The AAOHN recognized that occupational health nurses must be included in policy-making bodies, legislation and regulation development, and judicial challenges at the federal and state levels.

Changing the Definition

Initially the AAOHN established three specific goals: (1) to get occupational health nurses on key health and safety policy committees, such as the National Advisory Committee on Occupational Safety and Health; (2) to get occupational health nurses on the management staff at OSHA; and (3) ultimately, to establish an independent Office of Occupational Health Nursing at OSHA. Accomplishing these goals took more than 10 years, involving work with both the legislative and executive branches of the federal government.

Goal One: Nurses in OSHA

The association's first goal was to get OSHA to hire an occupational health nurse. After OSHA continued to ignore the House and Senate Appropriations Committees' recommendations to hire an occupational health nurse, the AAOHN embarked on an intensive legislative strategy. The strategies included communicating and meeting with numerous congressional offices, and testifying before congressional committees to document the contributions that occupational health nurses make to worker health and safety. Eventually specific language was included in the Senate Appropriations Subcommittee Report (1989) *directing* OSHA to hire an occupational health nurse. The strategy worked so well that the AAOHN continued to lobby through the appropriations process to get language into the 1993 Senate Appropriations Subcommittee report supporting establishment of a separate Office of Occupational Health Nursing. The office, with four full-time positions, is now well established and has proven to be one of the most productive departments within the federal regulatory agency.

Nurses in Other Policy Venues

Getting occupational health nursing expertise within OSHA is not the only association strategy for getting nursing input into policy making. The AAOHN participates in stakeholder meetings to influence regulatory proposals by other federal agencies and routinely responds to regulatory proposals by submitting comments developed from member input.

Many OSHA standards with medical and health surveillance requirements specified that a physician must oversee or perform these functions, even though many of these functions are within the scope of nursing practice. The AAOHN worked with OSHA for many years to use language in health standards that broadly defines "health care professional" to ensure that occupational health nurses can fulfill these functions. Strategies included meeting with standards development teams, providing written comments and documentation, speaking at hearings, and conducting research about occupational health nurses' participation in surveillance and providing the data to OSHA. In its most recent health standards, such as the Bloodborne Pathogens Standard, the Methylene Chloride Standard, and the revised Respiratory Protection Standard, OSHA has acknowledged that licensed health care professionals other than physicians are fully capable of fulfilling surveillance requirements included in the standards. Previous standards included language to require physician oversight for all medical and health surveillance activities.

Advocacy

Maintaining confidentiality of personal health information collected at the work site is a major issue for occupational health nurses. In fact, it is the primary issue for which members seek assistance and counsel from the association. The vast majority of this information is unrelated to employees' abilities to perform their jobs. However, only a patchwork of state laws currently regulates release of this information to employers and others, leading to many disparities and complexities both for individuals and for multistate employers.

For occupational health nurses, the lack of legal protection of this information presents difficult ethical dilemmas. A number of occupational health nurses have lost their jobs for refusing to disclose personal medical or health information and attempting to protect an individual's privacy. Even more distressing, the courts have ruled that there is no policy to support nurses' attempts to protect an employee's health information from improper disclosure.

For more than 8 years, the AAOHN has worked with Congress, presenting documentation of the need for federal regulation to protect personal health information held in the work environment. The AAOHN members have testified at congressional hearings and contacted their congressional representatives about the issue. One member presented research documenting the numerous ethical dilemmas faced by occupational health professionals. The AAOHN has documented members' loss of jobs over this issue in congressional hearings and in the general media.

In lieu of a specific bill addressing the issue, the AAOHN has attempted to get language added to several health care bills and has actively participated in the development of the health information privacy regulations recently issued by the Department of Health and Human Services, as required by the Health Insurance Portability and Accountability Act of 1996. However, the new regulations fail to protect occupational health nurses (OHNs) from disclosing employee health information to employers. The AAOHN continues to build on years of work in Washington to promote the passage of federal legislation and regulations to provide legal protection for health information. This remains the association's top legislative priority.

Court Action

Influencing policy sometimes requires action in the judicial branch. The American College of Occupational and Environmental Medicine (ACOEM) filed suit over the new OSHA Respiratory Protection Standard, which no longer requires physician oversight to fulfill the medical and health surveillance requirements of the standard.

Partnering with the American Nurses Association (ANA), the AAOHN became an intervening party in this legal challenge. As a result, the Eleventh Circuit U.S. Court of Appeals upheld the broad language in the standard that allows licensed health care professionals other than physicians, acting within their licensed scope of practice, to fulfill the health and medical surveillance requirements.

This ruling was a tremendous victory for the entire nursing community, especially for occupational health nursing. However, there is still work to be done. The language in the standard defers to state law to determine scope of practice issues surrounding the required surveillance activities. Therefore, members in *each state* must contact their board of nursing to obtain a determination about whether the surveillance requirements of the standard fall within the scope of their nursing practice. The AAOHN has prepared and distributed information packets and talking points to state chapters, and staff are available for telephone consultation to assist them in this effort.

Grassroots Action

This outcome and other trends toward more nursing regulatory issues, such as multistate licensure, being addressed at the state level pushed us to recognize that the AAOHN must be more politically active at the *state* level. However, this can only be accomplished by "growing" grassroots activists in the organization.

For several years the AAOHN sponsored conferences in Washington, DC, for chapter leaders to motivate their participation in shaping policy. They learned about lobbying strategies and current issues, and how to directly influence members of Congress. The AAOHN also encourages members to become grass roots activists by sponsoring four scholarships to the Nurses In Washington Internship, sponsored by the National Federation of Specialty Nursing Organizations (NFSNO), of which the AAOHN is a member.

During this time, the AAOHN developed a Key Contact program for members who are fully committed to being congressional contacts for the association. Key Contacts play a valuable role in the AAOHN's governmental affairs grass roots activities. They commit to establishing an ongoing personal relationship with their legislators to ensure that occupational health nurses are represented in health policy decisions. Key Contact program participants automatically receive specific information on how to contact their legislators, special training opportunities, and a quarterly update on issues pertinent to the AAOHN. Members participating in the program are requested to contact their elected officials at least four times a year, and to respond rapidly to AAOHN action alerts.

The AAOHN Governmental Affairs Program has been effective for a relatively small association,

and is highly valued as an important member service. To continue to strengthen the program and our influence, we are developing new methods for communicating and disseminating information to members and formulating a new structure for mobilizing grass roots activity.

The AAOHN has a new communications and training model to develop appointed State Legislative Coordinators (SLCs) in each state who will be a point of contact and coordinate state-level governmental affairs activities. SLCs will compose a national network of trained members who are constituents of elected officeholders important to the AAOHN, and who will build relationships and communicate the association's stand on issues. This program will help leverage the association's resources to increase its political influence at both the state and national levels.

Partnerships

The AAOHN also realizes it can be more effective by partnering with other groups with similar concerns. In 1993, the AAOHN participated in the Worksite Health Promotion Alliance to ensure that language in health care reform proposals did not discourage employers from having work site health promotion programs, the lack of which could have resulted in loss of occupational health nursing positions within companies.

The AAOHN also has been participating in a task force with the Association of Peri-Operative Nurses (AORN) to encourage additional research and potential regulation of smoke generated from electrocautery and lasers during surgical procedures.

Small Fish with Influence

Despite being "small fish in a big pond," these years of effort are beginning to pay off. Members of Congress are finally beginning to recognize that personal health information at the work site is an issue that needs to be addressed. They are just not sure how to fix the problem, because of the myriad competing interests present when legislation is crafted to address health information privacy. It took us 10 years to get visibility at OSHA, and it may take at least 10 years to get the right confidentiality legislation passed. Regardless of how long it takes, nothing can be accomplished without the dedication and commitment of nurses involved in the process of developing and influencing health policy.

INTERDISCIPLINARY ADVOCACY: AMERICAN SOCIETY FOR PARENTERAL AND ENTERAL NUTRITION

Lynne M. Murphy & Beth Lyman

The American Society for Parenteral and Enteral Nutrition (ASPEN) is an interdisciplinary, research-based, patient-centered clinical nutrition society. The mission of the society is to ensure that every patient receives optimal nutrition care. Membership in the organization consists primarily of nurses, dietitians, physicians, and pharmacists. The interdisciplinary nature of our society distinguishes us from traditional, nurse-only organizations. The provision of specialized nutritional therapies requires a team approach with input from all the disciplines. Successful patient outcomes can be achieved when we work together and speak with one voice. A recent small, but potentially serious, problem related to the reimbursement methodology for Medicare beneficiaries receiving enteral alimentation (tube feeding) highlights our interdisciplinary "one voice for patient care" philosophy.

Patient Advocacy First

The Health Care Financing Administration (HCFA) (now the Centers for Medicare and Medicaid Services [CMS]), the agency that administers Medicare, uses contractors referred to as Durable Medical Equipment Regional Carriers (DMERCs) to process claims for medical equipment and supplies. In an effort to contain spending on equipment and supplies, the DMERCs can propose price changes up to 15% in a new, streamlined process called *inherent reasonableness*. In an effort to control the costs of enteral nutrition (tube feeding), the DMERCs surveyed the costs of oral nutritional supplements for comparison. Parenteral and enteral nutrition, sometimes referred to as parenteral and enteral nutrition (PEN) services, are covered under Medicare as prosthetic devices. This means that for the costs of these services to be reimbursed, there must be a test of "permanence." The HCFA defines permanence as a minimum of 3 months. Dyspha-

gia, malabsorption, and upper gastrointestinal obstruction (e.g., cancer) are conditions that the HCFA regards as permanent. If these conditions are met, then patients are reimbursed for enteral (or parenteral) nutrition at home. They also receive supervision and other professional services as needed, which are built into the overall pricing structure.

The rule change for reimbursement under the new inherent reasonableness provision means that our patients would get inappropriate formulas without education or supervision by nutrition support professionals. Research has demonstrated improved patient outcomes when a team of experts provides nutrition support. The members of ASPEN realized that nutrition support using inappropriate formulas and without patient education or supervision would be certain disaster for many of our patients. Colleagues in the home care community joined ASPEN's efforts to question this decision.

Interdisciplinary Action

ASPEN and other groups involved with the many changes proposed by the DMERCs contacted staff of the Subcommittee on Health of the Ways and Means Committee of the House of Representatives to outline our concerns. The subcommittee staff agreed that our concerns were valid. The chairman of the committee was asked to request comments from the General Accounting Office (GAO) regarding the survey methods used by the DMERCs to set the inherently reasonable price changes and the ways in which this might affect patient access to the named medical products.

ASPEN's executive director helped organize a conference call with the staff at the GAO tasked with examining the changes in the provision of medical products used for our patients. The conference calls included clinical experts in tube feeding who also were familiar with the workings of the GAO and public policy issues in general. The geographically diverse group from ASPEN included two physicians, two nurses, one pharmacist, and two dietitians. All are experts in enteral nutrition as well as members of ASPEN's Public Policy Committee or Board of Directors. The investigators from the GAO are not experts in nutrition support, nor do they profess to be. The GAO staff members are professionals in business and public administration, economy, social science, engineering, information management, and accounting. Their reports are considered accurate, thorough, and objective, and they are staples at congressional hearings and in news reports of government activities.

The GAO staff asked key questions regarding preparation of both the formulas for tube feeding and the patients who would receive them. ASPEN's expert panel explained that oral nutrition supplements, sold over the counter, are rarely used for tube feeding. We were able to explain the concept of osmolarity and its role in the digestion and absorption of nutrients. We explained the role of fiber in tube feeding formulas and the differences between polymeric and monomeric nutrients. We offered to send copies of our *Guidelines and Standards of Practice for Nutrition Support.* We invited the GAO staff to visit our clinics and other care settings (they declined). Finally, we explained the need for professional services, especially education and supervision, in the care of these Medicare beneficiaries.

It became clear from our discussions that the DMERCs had not completed an informed review of the use of tube feeding by Medicare beneficiaries. The sessions with the GAO staff were mutually beneficial regarding the use of enteral nutrition in the Medicare population.

The GAO reviewers explained the survey methods they would use to evaluate the inherent reasonableness provision as it applied to tube feeding. Each member of the clinical expert panel sent a copy of the formularies of enteral formulas used in our respective facilities. ASPEN members who participated in the exchange thought the discussions were helpful.

Interdisciplinary Success

The results of our interdisciplinary interaction with the GAO reviewers were a success for our patients. The inherent reasonableness rule did not stand up to careful scrutiny in this particular case. The GAO published a written report (GAO/HEHS-00-79) outlining the problems we had discussed with them. They found that while the inherent reasonableness rule could be applied in many cases, the DMERCs did not "follow rigorous methodology to ensure that the payment amounts set for these items were

appropriate" in this case. For now, there will be no reduction in reimbursement under this rule for our patients.

It was rewarding to hear an interdisciplinary team speak with one voice for the benefit of our patients, even though the matter of cost containment was not solved. We do know that when we speak with one voice as patient care experts, we can provide federal decision makers with the best possible information to do their jobs to the best of their ability as well. In this case, everybody won!

ADVOCACY FOR CLINICAL NURSE SPECIALISTS: NATIONAL ASSOCIATION OF CLINICAL NURSE SPECIALISTS
Jo Ellen Rust & Angela P. Clark

In the late 1980s, the Indiana University School of Nursing Program sponsored a 3-day national conference titled *Strategies for Cost Effective Patient Care through Clinical Nurse Specialists.* The conference became a biannual event and continued the theme of clinical nurse specialist (CNS) care from 1990 to 1996, attracting clinical nurse specialists, nurse educators, and nurse administrators both nationally and internationally.

CNSs constitute over one third of the advanced practice nurse population. Unlike certified registered nurse anesthetists (CRNAs), certified nurse midwives (CNMs), and nurse practitioners (NPs), CNSs had no national organization to provide leadership and development. The National Association of Clinical Nurse Specialists (NACNS) was an outgrowth of the spirit and commitment of the regular attendees of this conference over a 6-year period. In the fall of 1995, the official launch meeting was held in Indianapolis during an off year for the educational conference. Forty percent of the regular attendees committed to participating in this meeting to establish the bylaws and to appoint the first board of directors. In 18 months, the membership of this organization grew from the original 67 to 530. By the first quarter of 2001, the membership exceeded 1000.

Mission and Purpose

The NACNS exists to enhance and promote the unique, high-value contribution of the clinical nurse specialist to the health and well-being of individuals, families, groups, and communities, and to promote and advance the practice of nursing.

The purposes of the NACNS are complementary to the purposes of existing organizations in working to meet society's need for the full complement of nursing service. They guide the association in setting a policy agenda. The purposes of the NACNS include:

- Provide educational, networking, and mentoring opportunities for the continuing professional development of the CNS
- Promote the visibility of CNSs' impact on cost, quality, and access to nursing care and to health care systems or organizations
- Provide education to communities, health care organizations, and the public regarding the unique contributions of CNSs to the well-being of individuals and groups
- Provide a forum for the identification and discussion of issues and trends that affect and shape the evolution of CNS practice
- Promote the unification of CNSs in their advanced practice roles regarding competencies, spheres of influence, standards of performance, and educational preparation
- Provide for the development and dissemination of position statements regarding health care policy issues pertinent to quality of, cost of, and access to nursing care; strategies to improve the appropriate use of health care resources; and the need for and preparation of CNSs
- Serve as a clearinghouse for information pertinent to CNSs and CNS practice
- Collaborate with other groups (particularly specialty nursing organizations) in addressing issues of common concern to advanced practice nurses
- Contribute to the body of knowledge regarding CNS practice and patient care

Defining CNS Practice and Competencies

The primary work of this organization over the first 18 months was the development and publication of the Statement on Clinical Nurse Specialist Practice and Education (by its Research and Practice Committee, led by Dr. Sue Davidson). The document articulates the nature of CNS contributions to society and describes CNS competencies with implications for CNS education. A total of 70 CNS position descriptions from 22 states were used to assist in the development of this document and to validate the conceptual framework used for the competency statements. A second draft was reviewed by the membership from all specialty areas and yielded a 15-state response. The NACNS developed this document as a generic description of CNS practice competencies. The NACNS sees itself not in competition with any specialty practice competencies required for the individual CNS's scope of practice (e.g., neuroscience, critical care, oncology) but adjunctive to articulating CNS practice. The organization continues to refine this document. The NACNS also embarked on an extensive survey of educational programs that prepare Clinical Nurse Specialists. The statement is viewed as an initial effort to help standardize CNS curricula and is being used as such by some schools of nursing (Division of Nursing, Bureau of Health Professions, Health Resources and Services Administration, U.S. Department of Health and Human Services, 2001).

Legislative and Regulatory Agenda

The Legislative and Regulatory Committee of the NACNS, with the leadership and expertise of Dr. Brenda Lyon, reviewed the language in all but two state nurse practice acts. Two states did not make their practice acts available. The purpose of the review was to ascertain the current regulatory language regarding advanced nursing practice, particularly the language recognizing or governing the practice of CNSs. This review led to a comprehensive assessment of the legislative or regulatory barriers to CNS practice and preceded the NACNS's development of model regulatory language for CNS practice. This language was published in *Clinical Nurse Specialist: The Journal for Advanced Nursing Practice* in 2001 (Lyon & Minarik, 2001).

Advanced Practice Certification

The NACNS recognizes that existing certifications for nursing are frequently focused on specialty-based knowledge. The availability for certification is not always at the advanced practice nursing level and does not always meet the specialty competencies of clinical nurse specialists. This creates additional barriers for CNS practice. The organization continues to collaborate and explore with professional nursing organizations and certification bodies strategies to remove these barriers.

Clinical Nurse Specialists at the Policy Table

The NACNS is committed to representing the needs of its membership. As noted in the state practice act review, there are state and regional issues impacting CNS practice. To better understand and address these issues, the NACNS adopted an affiliate model in 1999 to promote the communication and dissemination of information regarding CNS issues between local, state, or regional groups of CNSs. By 2001, there were 10 national affiliates. The NACNS also completed a Census 2000 survey of its membership to more accurately ascertain demographics on practicing CNSs. The NACNS participates in the Nursing Organization Liaison Forum (the ANA's coalition of national nursing organizations) and seeks to work collaboratively with specialty nursing organizations, especially those that have a constituent group of CNSs. The *Statement on Clinical Nurse Specialist Practice and Education* has been used as a position paper in a variety of national and state arenas to shape policy by clarifying the scope of CNS practice for nursing and health care leaders. For the past 3 years, dissemination of the statement to administrators, educators, national nursing organizations, state boards of nursing, and other decision makers has defined and shaped thinking about CNS roles in health care. In addition, NACNS is represented in many advanced practice leadership groups working collaboratively on federal policy issues of concern to nursing and advanced practice.

The NACNS is fulfilling its mission and purposes. It is committed to promoting the unique, high-value contribution of the CNS to the health and well-being of individuals, families, groups, and communities, and to promote and advance the practice of nursing. As nursing is core to the title of CNS, the NACNS is committed to collaborative relationships with all who represent nursing at policy tables today and in the future.

PROMOTING PAIN MANAGEMENT BY INFLUENCING POLICY: ONCOLOGY NURSING SOCIETY

Paula Trahan Rieger

The Oncology Nursing Society (ONS), with more than 28,000 registered nurses and other members of the health care profession, is the largest cancer-related specialty organization in the world. Its vision is to "lead the transformation of cancer care" through its mission of promoting excellence in oncology nursing and quality cancer care. Inherent in the ability to meet these goals is attention to health policy in matters impacting nursing and cancer care. Although members have historically been intimately connected to the patient-care aspects of cancer treatment, they have not always been comfortable in the "how-to" of shaping public policy. To be successful in the public policy arena, the ONS must not only be aware of current issues at both the state and national levels that will affect cancer care, but also must give consideration to teaching its members the skills needed to speak out about these issues. The failed Pain Relief Promotion Act of the 106th Congress provides an excellent example of how ONS resources were mobilized to oppose the bill.

Legislation Red Flagged

During the 106th Congress, Congressman Henry Hyde (R-IL) and Senator Don Nickles (R-OK) introduced a bill called the Pain Relief Promotion Act. Although on the surface the bill appeared to promote pain relief, many organizations with an interest in adequate pain control felt the bill would have the opposite effect. In essence, the bill would have given Drug Enforcement Administration (DEA) agents explicit authority to investigate and second-guess the medical judgment of a physician, pharmacist, nurse, or other practitioner who dispensed a controlled substance (e.g., morphine) to relieve the pain of a dying patient. If the patient died and the DEA somehow thought the practitioner's "intent" or "purpose" was to hasten death rather than control pain, the practitioner could face criminal charges punishable by a minimum 20-year prison sentence. To make the bill appear more acceptable, it was given a positive-sounding name, and a token, poorly designed grant program was included to support training in pain control.

More than 40 other national health organizations opposed this legislation. The bill contained a dangerous precedent—that of empowering federal law enforcement officers to oversee health care professionals in their practice of pain management. Even the DEA publicly admitted that it did not have the expertise or resources to determine with any certainty what was in the mind of a health care provider and his or her patient when a powerful pain drug was administered. As a result, the DEA would have to probe medical records and interview staff and grieving family members after their loved one had died. Significant concern existed that the impact of a public accusation by a powerful law enforcement agency—together with the legal cost, time, and disruption of fighting the DEA—would deter many physicians, nurses, pharmacists, and other practitioners from aggressively treating pain with powerful narcotics. As a result, patients would suffer needlessly.

ONS Policy Tool Kit

To focus its efforts in health policy, the ONS uses its *Health Policy Agenda.* This agenda is drafted for each new congressional session by a task force that includes leaders, members, and the ONS health policy associate, who is a member of the law firm in Washington, DC, that the ONS retains to represent it on the Hill. The ONS Board of Directors then approves the final draft, and the agenda is printed with a preamble that speaks to the ONS's beliefs and values, which guide decisions on policy positions and actions. This Health Policy Agenda is available to members and external audiences and serves to guide ONS leadership and members as they advocate on behalf of patients and for the profession on issues related to cancer care. The ONS Health Policy Agenda is part of the ONS Health Policy Tool Kit, which members can obtain for free by contacting ONS customer service at (412) 921-7373, or by e-mail at customerservice@ons.org. This kit provides information about the legislative process and how to contact one's representatives. Pain and end-of-life legislation was included in the ONS 106th Congress Health Policy Agenda.

The ONS, as an organization, also uses position statements to articulate its beliefs on issues. At the time this bill was under debate, the ONS had positions on pain, the use of placebos in the management of pain, and assisted suicide. The issue of assisted suicide was of special concern during the debates on this bill, as the bill's real aim was to stop physician-assisted suicide in Oregon, the only state in which it is currently legal. The society's position on assisted suicide spoke to the nurse's adherence to the American Nurses Association code of ethics and the fact that untreated or undertreated pain is often a determining factor in the patient's decision to take such life-ending action. Nurses must proactively promote quality pain care and symptom management for all people living with cancer. Studies of the use of physician-assisted suicide in Oregon found that 46% of patients requesting physician-assisted suicide since November 1997 decided not to end their lives once they had received adequate pain and symptom management (Oregon Nurses Association, 2001). This demonstrates the deterrent effect of proactively addressing pain and symptom management.

Timing and Strategy

The ONS used a variety of strategies on Capitol Hill. The bill had passed in the House; thus efforts were focused on defeating passage in the Senate. The ONS worked in collaboration with other groups opposed to the bill. The ONS health policy associate made numerous trips to the Hill to speak with senators who also were opposed to the bill and to gain their support in voting against its passage. The ONS members made Hill visits to speak to their legislators about the importance of adequate pain control and the impact this bill would have on it. The society used its website to educate members about the current status of the bill, provided examples of letters that could be used to write congressional representatives, and mobilized its network of state health policy liaisons (SHPLs) to spread the word to other nurses in their states. Thousands upon thousands of letters were sent at crucial times to voice opposition to the bill. The ONS and other groups worked diligently to keep the Pain Relief Promotion Act off the Senate floor or from being attached to any other legislation.

As closing of the legislative session for the year neared, Senator Nickles attempted to attach the bill as an amendment to a variety of must-pass bills. At this juncture, ONS members began to call the offices of senators to voice opposition to this tactic, and it was ultimately defeated. Members were encouraged to call the aide of then Senate Minority Leader Senator Tom Daschle (D-SD) so he would hear from the leaders of each health, medical, and patient organization that letting this bill go to a vote was a terrible idea, and why it would be detrimental to patient care. The calls came in such volume that members were requested to stop, as they had begun to shut down the phone lines. Toward the end of the legislative session, calls were even placed to the White House to voice opposition to the bill and its attachment to spending bills.

The society also provided sample op-ed pieces for members to write and send to their local newspapers, and response was fairly brisk. The ONS health policy associate put out a call for stories on pain care management, or the lack of it, and associated problems. These stories were given to one of the bill's opponents, Senator Ron Wyden (D-OR), who planned to use these stories on the Senate floor, if necessary. This is a striking example of the true power that nurses hold: the knowledge of how potential legislation will impact patients and health care professionals in the clinical setting. (Every nurse has a story to tell!) Several congressional briefings were held, at which ONS members with expertise in pain management testified and educated congressional members and staffers about pain management and barriers to effective pain control in this country.

Eleventh-Hour Victory

Opposition of the bill required months of work. Ultimately, late on Friday night, December 15, 2001, the U.S. Senate adjourned for the year without taking up or voting on the misnamed Pain Relief Promotion Act. As a result, the bill was dead for the year and the 106th Congress. Last-minute, behind-the-scenes efforts by the bill's proponents to attach the legislation to a massive end-of-year budget bill were rebuffed by the White House after objections and concerns were voiced by many members of Congress, led by Senator Wyden, and after months of intense public opposition.

Literally thousands of patients experiencing pain, along with their families, joined forces with nurses, physicians, pharmacists, pain experts, hospice workers, cancer professionals, and many others

from around the country to educate Congress and the administration not only about the harm this bill would cause, but also about the pain crisis in America, about how pain is grossly undertreated. It was only through these combined forces that success was achieved. Thousands of e-mails, phone calls, and letters to Capitol Hill reinforced the dozens of personal visits made to members of Congress and the White House. More than 35 newspapers from across the United States wrote editorials in opposition. Many also published letters to the editor or op-eds from citizens. For the first time, members of Congress were alerted to the hidden pain epidemic in our nation and learned about the tremendous need to do more to fight the undertreatment of pain. Thus, a real opportunity now exists to work with Congress on genuine solutions to the pain crisis.

As an organization, the ONS gained several things from this effort. It established the presence and recognition of oncology nurses on the Hill. Nurses were viewed as credible sources of information, and the power of our numbers was felt. We collaborated successfully with other organizations to defeat this bill. We used the resources we had in place to their fullest measure to provide members with the information and skills needed to fight passage of this bill. As the ONS president, I tried to communicate to members the effectiveness of our efforts through channels of communication open to me (e.g., our monthly newsletter). At the annual convention in May 2001, the presidential address noted the success of this effort. It is vital that leaders share such information with members when we ask them to respond quickly to pending legislation. Positive reinforcement will foster a willingness to participate in such efforts on an ongoing basis. In this instance, the ONS, as an organization, and oncology nurses in particular, made a difference. This sets the stage for future successes.

SHAPING A STATE'S SCREENING POLICY: SOCIETY OF GASTROENTEROLOGY NURSES AND ASSOCIATES

Nancy S. Schlossberg

Gastroenterology nurses frequently witness the benefits of colorectal cancer screening. Nurse members of the Old Dominion Society of Gastroenterology Nurses and Associates (SGNA), a regional chapter of the national SGNA, initiated a policy process to introduce legislation in the state of Virginia in 1998 to promote this screening. The president of the Old Dominion SGNA wrote to Virginia State Senator Emily Couric,[1] Democrat from Charlottesville, asking her to develop a legislative mandate based on national guidelines for Virginians not otherwise covered by Medicare. Enacting such legislation would save many lives in this state and hopefully set a standard for the rest of the country to follow.

In July 2000, Virginia became the first state in the United States to mandate insurance coverage for colon cancer screening through the use of colonoscopy to all individuals, including those covered by indemnity plans and Medicaid. The following story describes how the Old Dominion SGNA was instrumental in this historic achievement.

Need

Colorectal cancer is the second leading cause of cancer death in the United States. Available screening methods include digital rectal exam, fecal occult blood test, flexible sigmoidoscopy, barium enema, and colonoscopy. Each option carries different risks, benefits, and initial costs. However, evidence suggests that colonoscopy every 10 years is the most effective colorectal cancer prevention test currently available. The American College of Gastroenterology guidelines recommend colonoscopy every 10 years as the preferred screening strategy for average risk screening, beginning at age 50 (American College of Gastroenterology, 2000). As of January 1, 1998, Medicare entitled all beneficiaries to regular colorectal cancer (CRC) screening at intervals based on risk stratification. As of July 2001, Medicare coverage included colonoscopy every 10 years for average-risk individuals; however, the majority of individuals covered by Medicare are ages 65 and above.

The Virginia legislation offered a perfect call for involvement of gastroenterology nurses in the state of Virginia already unified under the national SGNA umbrella. SGNA membership consists of

6700 professional nurses and associates dedicated to the safe and effective practice of gastroenterology and endoscopy nursing. Rallying around colorectal cancer screening, a familiar area to GI nurses, helped to demystify the legislative process, which is often overwhelming to nurses. Working with colleagues from the American College of Gastroenterology, the Virginia Gastroenterological Society, the American Cancer Society, the Virginia Legislative Nursing Coalition, and professional patient organizations enabled us to speak as one voice on behalf of "the right thing to do!"

Strategy and Process

Throughout 1999, a core team testified and lobbied before various General Assembly committees. This team was made up of a nurse from the Old Dominion SGNA as the regional representative of the national SGNA, a physician member of the American College of Gastroenterology, a well-spoken patient with a compelling story, lobbyists from the Virginia chapter of the American Cancer Society, and our champion, Senator Couric. Several key team members lived at least 1½ hours from the state capitol. Therefore, we designated a back-up team, available on a moment's notice in the capitol.

The core team developed a unified approach. Our successful plan relied on selecting a credible reference for standards of the screening tests, anticipating the routing of the bill, developing a game plan for committee presentation, and, finally, presenting to committees.

We adopted the 2000 American College of Gastroenterology (ACG) guideline as a reference for standards of testing. The language of the legislation, "in accordance with the most recently published recommendations established by the American College of Gastroenterology, in consultation with the American Cancer Society, for all ages, family histories, and frequencies referenced in such recommendations," ensures that Virginia does not tie itself to outdated testing methods. In other words, if colonoscopy becomes obsolete for colon cancer screening, the law will not have to be rewritten.

Our game plan consisted of presenting a brief, concise set of slides outlining etiology, incidence, prevalence, risk factors, and pros and cons of each colon cancer screening method, and the economics

---

[1]Senator Couric was the sister of *Today Show* co-host Katie Couric, whose husband died of colon cancer in 1998. The senator died of pancreatic cancer on October 19, 2001.

of screening and prevention in terms of cost and quality of lives saved. The physician, the nurse, and the patient followed with brief presentations outlining how colon cancer screening and prevention affected each of them. (I emphasize that these were short, concise, well-articulated presentations that spoke from the heart as well as the wallet.) We left legislators with copies of the slide presentation and reference material backing up our economic data on the use of screening colonoscopy. In fact, the economic data were instrumental in making sure that the insurance companies did not openly oppose the legislation. We disseminated data showing that screening for colon cancer using risk-based strategies saves lives and is cost-effective. Overall, our verbal and printed take-home messages underlined that endorsing this bill in this election year was endorsing the standard of care.

A number of days before each meeting, legislators received fact sheets and personal communications specifically geared toward their committee's charge. Letters were sent from physician, nurse, and patient constituents previously identified by core team members. For example, the Special Advisory Commission on Mandated Health Benefits and the Budget and Finance Committee information and testimony related to dollars and cents. Senator Couric's concurrent success working behind the scenes derived from physician, nurse, and patient expertise of the core team.

The Virginia General Assembly passed S.B. 26: 38.2-3418.71, Coverage for Colorectal Cancer Screening:

Effective July 1, 2000: Coverage for colorectal cancer screening, specifically screening with an annual occult blood test, flexible sigmoidoscopy or colonoscopy, in appropriate circumstances radiologic imaging, shall be provided in accordance with the most recently published recommendations established by the American College of Gastroenterology, in consultation with the American Cancer Society, for all ages, family histories, and frequencies referenced in such recommendations. (An Act to Amend and Reenact §§ 2.1-20.1 and 32.1-32.5, Code of Virginia, 2000).

The passage of this legislation will save lives. Our hope is that other gastroenterology nurses will proactively pursue this effort and follow Virginia's lead. It is gratifying to know that nurses can make a difference simply by initiating a phone call or writing a letter. Nurses can help create a demand for this type of benefit at the local, regional, state level. Nurses can and should volunteer their expertise in their communities as media contacts. The public listens to and respects nurses. Local papers print editorials penned by nurses. Nurses can appropriately direct change by taking the extra step to educate and promote screening and prevention strategies to their patients, friends, family, and community. Nurses need to encourage their patients to demand coverage for screening and preventive tests that save lives and the quality of lives.

COLLABORATION, COMMUNICATION, AND PERSISTENCE MAKE A DIFFERENCE: WOUND OSTOMY CONTINENCE NURSES SOCIETY

Donna L. Thompson & Dorothy Doughty

The patient advocate hat is one of the most critical that we as nurses wear, and one of the most difficult, since it frequently puts us in challenging and potentially confrontational situations. However, advocacy is the heart of nursing—whether we are fighting for a patient's right to informed consent, better pain control, or access to products and services—because, as advocates, we are truly providing health care.

The Wound Ostomy Continence Nurses Society has a history of advocacy. We began as ostomy care nurses, and in this role we worked with the United Ostomy Association to improve reimbursement for ostomy supplies. Our scope of practice later expanded to include wound care and continence care, and again we became involved in regulatory and reimbursement issues, as well as clinical issues. We collaborated with a number of professional organizations, vendor groups, and consumers to expand coverage for surgical dressings to include chronic wound care products; we also played a key role in the development of clinically sound utilization parameters. These parameters are used by the four DMERCs to govern coverage and reimbursement for wound supplies, support surfaces, ostomy products, and urological supplies.

Most recently we have played a key role in obtaining a national Medicare coverage decision for the use of biofeedback and electrical stimulation in the management of incontinence. In this vignette we will briefly outline the steps we took and the sequence of events leading to this coverage decision, highlighting the factors that we see as key to our success: collaboration, communication, and persistence.

The Power of One

Our road to success began with just one visionary and determined nurse specialist. In 1997, Marta Krissovich, RN, MSN, CCCN, recognized a trend toward restricted payment or nonpayment for conservative continence services such as biofeedback and pelvic floor electrical stimulation. At that time, the decision regarding coverage of these services was made at the local level, by the individual Medicare carrier (insurance company with a contract to handle the Medicare claims for a particular region).

As a member of both the Society for Urologic Nurses and Associates (SUNA) and the Wound Ostomy Continence Nurses (WOCN) Society, Marta conceived and sold to both boards of directors the concept of a joint task force to address regulatory and reimbursement issues related to continence care. That vision resulted in the formation of the Continence Coalition, a task force of four nurses dedicated to preserving access to conservative continence services.

First Steps

The coalition began by developing a position statement on conservative therapy for incontinence; key points were as follows:
- Urinary incontinence is a common and costly health care problem.
- Conservative therapies such as biofeedback-assisted pelvic muscle reeducation are effective treatment strategies and should be considered first-line therapy for many patients, a position promulgated by the Agency for Health Care Policy and Research—now the Agency for Healthcare Research and Quality—in *Guidelines for Management of Urinary Incontinence in Adults* in 1996 (Fantl et al, 1996).
- Patients have a right to reimbursement for these services (Continence Coalition, 1997).

The position statement was approved by both organizations' boards of directors. The Coalition members then disseminated the document to other professional organizations with a request for endorsement (or for development of a position statement of their own).

The coalition had begun work at a critical time. In response to increasing questions and requests to consider a national payment policy on biofeedback for the treatment of incontinence, the HCFA (now CMS) had commissioned a Technology Assessment by the Blue Cross/Blue Shield Technical Evaluation Center (TEC) (1997). Although that report was not widely disseminated, the coalition members were able to obtain a summary report, which was clearly not favorable to conservative therapies. The consensus of opinion among continence care clinicians and manufacturers of biofeedback equipment was that the trend toward nonpayment for such services was likely to continue.

Data Gathering

In March 1998, we were invited to send a representative to a meeting between one of HCFA's medical directors and a vendor to discuss reimbursement for biofeedback services. Upon the advice of our legislative consultant, we accepted the invitation and sent incontinence specialist Diane Smith, RN, MSN, CRNP, to be our "eyes and ears" during that meeting. As our legislative consultant pointed out, so long as we made it clear that we were attending the meeting on an informational basis only and not in support of the vendor, we had a lot of information to gain and nothing to lose.

He was correct; the information we gained in that meeting was invaluable. First of all, we learned that HCFA was reluctant to consider a national coverage policy for these therapies, in part due to concerns that such a policy would result in abusive use of such services. Secondly, we learned that the push for a national coverage decision carried significant risk. Should the decision be negative (remember the Blue Cross/Blue Shield technology assessment), there would be no reimbursement for biofeedback or electrical stimulation and no short-term recourse. Finally, we heard clearly that we needed broad-based multidisciplinary support for the use of conservative therapies if we hoped to counteract the negative impact of the TEC report.

An additional benefit of our participation in that meeting was the opportunity to articulate our position and to establish a personal relationship with a key HCFA official. He told us he was impressed with the cohesion demonstrated by our position statement and encouraged us to continue our efforts to unify and activate involved clinicians.

One Message, One Voice

Throughout 1998, the coalition focused on unifying clinicians, consumers, and manufacturers in support of conservative therapies using a variety of strategies, including continued dissemination of the position statement, personal communication, and formation of an e-mail distribution group known as Friends of Biofeedback. One potential problem was the fact that the clinicians who were most supportive of biofeedback were not always supportive of electrical stimulation. Our approach was to try to keep everyone focused on the big picture, to keep all interested individuals informed of any new developments via e-mail, and to enlist the support of potential challengers by involving them personally in our ongoing initiative. Our goal was to create one unified voice, one consistent message in support of conservative continence management. We also maintained contact with HCFA officials, following up on our initial meeting and providing them with updated materials.

The coalition also developed a Plan B. We realized that we would need to pursue legislative mandates for coverage should we fail to effect change via the regulatory process. We compiled a list of key legislators (members of the Senate Finance Committee and the House Ways and Means Committee) with their contact information, and identified individuals who knew them personally and could enlist their support should it be needed. We also involved our legislative consultant in identifying powerful legislators whose support would be critical should legislative action be required.

New Approach to Decision Making

While we were busy enlisting support and building a unified front, HCFA was equally busy revising the process for making national Medicare coverage decisions. In the past, such decisions had been made behind closed doors; the new process was designed to incorporate clinician and consumer input and to be "transparent" (HCFA, 1999). The revised approach began with the formation of the Medicare Coverage Advisory Committee (MCAC), which was charged with providing advice to HCFA on clinical issues related to Medicare coverage. The MCAC was structured to include six medical specialty panels (corresponding with the six major benefit categories) and an Executive Committee. The revised process for determining coverage for any specific therapy included three major steps:

1. The specific therapy and evidence regarding its safety and efficacy would be reviewed by the appropriate medical specialty panel in an open forum; interested individuals would be allowed to submit materials and to provide testimony. The panel would then be asked to vote on specific questions, and their findings would be submitted to the MCAC Executive Committee for ratification.

2. The MCAC Executive Committee would review the evidence and the panel's findings and would vote either to ratify their findings, to reverse their findings, or to send the issue back to the panel.

3. The Executive Committee's recommendations would be forwarded to HCFA, where the decision regarding coverage would be made.

Presenting Our Case

In 1999, the coalition was informed that conservative continence therapies had been selected for a national coverage decision using the new process. Diane Smith was invited to participate on the clinical panel as a nonvoting member; she was the only nurse on the panel. In addition, the coalition obtained slots on the presentation list, and our chosen representatives prepared dynamic evidence-based presentations targeting the posted questions for each of the therapies. The coalition also posted a notice to Friends of Biofeedback; by this time, multiple organizations had either endorsed our position statement or drafted one of their own, and a number of these organizations also requested presentation time. Finally, the coalition coordinated a campaign to obtain patient testimonials and provided the panel's consumer representative with a large but well-organized packet of letters from patients. The panel hearing was scheduled for April 2000, and we were ready!

The panel hearing was very disappointing and very frustrating. On the day of the hearing, the MCAC modified the posted questions to limit evidence to controlled studies comparing pelvic floor reeducation without biofeedback or electrical stimulation to pelvic floor reeducation incorporating these therapies. Although there is strong clinical evidence that many patients require biofeedback or electrical stimulation to rehabilitate their pelvic floor muscles, there are essentially no controlled studies that target the questions posed by the MCAC.

In addition, it soon became evident that the panel had not been given the advance material submitted by the coalition and other clinicians, and in fact had not even been given the Agency for Health Care Policy and Research (AHCPR; now the Agency for Health Care Research and Quality) *Guidelines on Urinary Incontinence in Adults.* (The person responsible for disseminating materials to the panel members stated that materials were sent upon request.) However, panel members *had* received the technical assessment compiled by Blue Cross/Blue Shield, which did not support conservative therapies. Despite strong and unified testimony from a number of clinicians and consumers, the panel voted that there was insufficient evidence to state that pelvic muscle reeducation using biofeedback or electrical stimulation was more effective than pelvic muscle exercises alone. Several of the panel members stated openly that they were frustrated with the very restrictive process, and that the very narrow questions forced them to vote negatively despite the fact that they would use or recommend these therapies for their patients.

Never Say Die

The coalition was saddened and angered by the process, but we were not ready to give up. We believed strongly that the panel's recommendations resulted from a seriously flawed process that failed to weigh any evidence other than randomized control trials focused on very narrow questions. Barbara Woolner, RN, CRNA, BCIA-C, CCCN, Chair

of the Continence Coalition, called for a meeting at the SUNA Conference in May, and at that time mobilized the group to rally in protest. We initiated letter-writing campaigns targeted to key HCFA officials, all members of the MCAC, and members of relevant Health and Human Services committees. We sent formal letters of protest regarding the flawed process and refusal to consider all relevant evidence; two of the panel members also wrote official letters of protest. We mobilized our members and the members of other organizations, who joined our letter-writing and e-mail campaigns. Even the American Medical Association (AMA) lodged a protest regarding the process. HCFA received a strong and unified message that the "new and improved" process for making coverage decisions was seriously flawed; in addition, they continued to hear all clinicians and consumers speaking with one voice in support of conservative therapies.

Another Setback—Then Success!

At the MCAC meeting, we again presented testimony refuting the process and the decision; although the MCAC agreed that the process should be reviewed, they voted to ratify the panel's findings. It was now up to HCFA. The coalition and Friends of Biofeedback continued to write letters to all involved legislators and HCFA officials, and the coalition chair was invited to attend a face-to-face meeting with then HCFA Administrator Nancy Ann Min-de-Parle, along with other selected individuals. During that meeting, the problems with the review process were again addressed, as was the value of conservative therapies in the management of incontinence and our willingness to assist with the development of responsible utilization parameters to prevent abuse.

When HCFA finally issued its decision regarding coverage of biofeedback and pelvic floor electrical stimulation, it was positive and appropriate; these therapies would be covered for patients who met certain diagnostic criteria and who had failed primary pelvic muscle reeducation (Health Care Financing Administration, 2000a, 2000b).

Keys to Success

In reviewing this process, we believe our success can be attributed to three major components of our approach: collaboration, communication, and persistence. We worked with all involved clinicians, vendors, and consumers to ensure that HCFA consistently heard *one message, one voice.* We involved our best communicators and we made sure we were *listening* as well as talking; for example, we heard HCFA's concerns and advice during our first meeting and responded appropriately. Finally, we were persistent; even when we encountered obstacles and setbacks, we continued to send the same message and we did *not* go away.

Collaboration, communication, and persistence are vital nursing skills. Use them to make a difference!

UNITED WE STAND: NP RESPONSE TO THE AMA'S CITIZEN'S PETITION[2]

Allison Beard, Allison Weber Shuren, and Mary Knudtson

The NP specialty has had more than 30 years of turbulence to defend its existence. Over those years, there have been few examples of cohesive efforts by different nursing organizations representing NPs to further their cause. One of the most effective efforts NPs have made in presenting their stance was recently spearheaded by a coalition of 11 nursing organizations in response to the American Medical Association's Citizen's Petition (see the box on this page for a list of the members of the coalition).

Cause for Unity

In the summer of 2000, the AMA urged the HCFA (now CMS), to issue guidelines to ensure that APNs, including NPs and CNSs, were not practicing outside their scope of practice. In the past, when faced with such attacks on the credibility of NPs, various NP organizations responded separately, which decreased their effectiveness and the power of their voices. The unification of these NP and other nursing organizations in response to the Citizen's Petition proved an effective way to set up a strong counterattack to the AMA's efforts, one that

---

[2]This case example has been prepared by Ms. Beard of the ACNP on behalf of the coalition of nursing organizations involved in responding to the AMA's Citizen's Petition. The ACNP is located at 1111 19th Street, NW, Suite 404, Washington, DC 20036; phone: (202) 659-2190; e-mail: acnp@acnpweb.org; website: www.nurse.org/acnp.

Members of the Nursing Organization Coalition

American College of Nurse Practitioners (ACNP)
American Nurses Association (ANA)
American Academy of Nurse Practitioners (AANP)
American Association of Critical-Care Nurses (AACN)
American College of Nurse Midwives (ACNM)
American Organization of Nurse Executives (AONE)
American Psychiatric Nurses Association (APNA)
Association of Women's Health Obstetric and Neonatal Nurses (AWHONN)
Nurse Practitioners in Women's Health (NPWH)
National Association of Pediatric Nurse Practitioners (NAPNAP)
National Organization of Nurse Practitioner Faculties (NONPF)

elicited a response from the HCFA, impressed by the number and scope of co-signers in the coalition.

Though it is unclear whether the final battle has been fought over the AMA's Citizen's Petition, a valuable lesson was learned by NPs: when such organizations as the American College of Nurse Practitioners (ACNP), the ANA, and the American Academy of Nurse Practitioners (AANP) come together, more can be done than could be accomplished by the groups separately.

In May 2000, the AMA circulated a Citizen's Petition to national medical societies and physician groups that addressed the issue of physician-nurse collaboration under Medicare (see the box on p. 655). The AMA sought endorsements and signatories from other organizations prior to filing the petition with the HCFA.

In basic terms, the AMA wanted the federal government to "promulgate regulations that were unduly burdensome on non-physician's scope of practice." One of the issues specifically addressed by the petition was the Medicare policy on physician-nurse collaboration. The 1997 Balanced Budget Act (BBA) expanded the circumstances under which nurses could directly bill Medicare while still requiring that NPs' services be provided in collaboration with physicians in order to be separately payable by Medicare. The AMA urged the HCFA to issue a guideline or instruction to Medicare carriers or intermediaries to ensure that collaborative

Citizens' Petition

The American Medical Association (AMA) and the undersigned organizations represent this country's physicians. On behalf of the AMA's and the undersigned organizations' physician members and their patients, the AMA and the undersigned organizations hereby petition the Health Care Financing Administration (HCFA), under 5 U.S.C. Section 553(e) and the Petition Clause of the First Amendment, to:

- Implement a system to ensure that Medicare payments to nurse practitioners (NPs) and clinical nurse specialists (CNSs) are made only in connection with those services furnished in collaboration with a physician and within their state law's scope of practice requirements, as the Social Security Act requires.
- Limit distribution and renewal of Medicare billing numbers only to those NPs and CNSs who comply with the collaboration and state law scope of practice requirements.
- Issue detailed instructions to Medicare carriers on implementation of a system to ensure compliance with the collaboration and state law scope of practice requirements.
- Conduct an immediate "baseline" audit, followed by future periodic audits, to ensure that Medicare payments to NPs and CNSs are limited to services furnished in collaboration with a physician and within their state law scope of practice requirements.

Failure to take these actions will perpetuate HCFA's neglect of an important requirement of the Medicare program. This nonfeasance allows unchecked possible abuse and misuse of Medicare, as well as possible substandard quality of medical services provided to the nation's elderly, disabled, and end-stage renal disease patients. HCFA unquestionably owes Medicare beneficiaries and taxpayers a duty to ensure that Medicare, through its payment policies, requires NPs and CNSs to work in collaboration with a physician and within their scope of practice. To our knowledge, HCFA has not made any serious effort to assure compliance with these collaboration and scope of practice requirements.

The AMA and the undersigned organizations stand by to work with other interested organizations and to assist HCFA address these important issues.

Respectfully submitted,

American Medical Association
American Academy of Child and Adolescent Psychiatry
American Academy of Family Physicians
American Academy of Facial Plastic & Reconstructive Surgery

American Academy of Neurology
American Academy of Ophthalmology
American Academy of Otolaryngology-Head and Neck Surgery
American Academy of Pain Medicine
American Academy of Pediatrics
American Academy of Sleep Medicine
American Association of Clinical Endocrinologists
American Association of Electrodiagnostic Medicine
American Association of Neurological Surgeons
American Association of Orthopaedic Surgeons
American College of Emergency Physicians
American College of Obstetricians and Gynecologists
American College of Osteopathic Emergency Physicians
American College of Osteopathic Family Medicine
American College of Osteopathic Surgeons
American College of Physicians-American Society of Internal Medicine
American College of Radiology
American Osteopathic Association
American Psychiatric Association
American Society for Gastrointestinal Endoscopy
American Society for Therapeutic Radiology and Oncology
American Society of Cataract and Refractive Surgery
American Society of General Surgeons
American Society of Plastic Surgeons
American Urological Association
Arkansas Medical Society
California Medical Association
Congress of Neurological Surgeons
Illinois State Medical Society
Massachusetts Medical Society
Medical Association of Georgia
Medical Association of the State of Alabama
Medical Society of New Jersey
Medical Society of the State of New York
Medical Society of Virginia
Michigan State Medical Society
Mississippi State Medical Association
National Medical Association
New Hampshire Medical Society
North American Spine Society
Pennsylvania Medical Society
Renal Physicians Association
Society of Cardiovascular and Interventional Radiology
Society of Medical Consultants to the Armed Forces
Tennessee Medical Association
Washington State Medical Association

agreements were in place and that NPs were not billing Medicare for services beyond those permitted by state law.

The AMA sought to use the petition as a tool to "correct the shortcoming of the [executive branch's] regulations and guidance." On July 14, the AMA filed its "Citizen's Petition on Physician-Nurse Collaboration" with the HCFA, containing the names of 49 signatory organizations. In addition to the national physician organizations, the AMA's signatories included several state medical associations.

The 17-page petition urged the HCFA to ensure that NPs and CNSs were not practicing outside their standards of practice. The document did not, however, urge the HCFA to include or even mention physician assistants (PAs) or other nonphysician providers, even though physician's assistants also received Medicare reimbursement in the BBA of 1997.

Specific points of the petition included a statement that the HCFA's noncompliance on this matter could spark Medicare fraud and abuse by APNs, as well as the delivery of substandard health care. The AMA's suggested interpretation of the definition of collaboration was that APN services "must be provided with medical direction and appropriate supervision."

The Citizen's Petition urged several actions by the HCFA. First, it suggested that the HCFA develop a system to ensure that payment is made only to those APNs who adhere to state laws. This would have included regular audits of Medicare carrier verification and documents as well as "clear education" for APNs and Medicare carriers. The petition also suggested terms of collaboration for states whose nurse practice acts did not include such language. The petition continued by saying that those terms were necessary so that APNs are not encouraged to work outside state law.

The AMA also suggested that Medicare billing numbers be distributed and renewed only for APNs complying with collaborative agreements and state scope of practice laws, in addition to filling out a form to guarantee they are working in a collaborative relationship and adhering to scope of practice laws.

United Response

This attempt by the AMA and the other signatories to the petition to create overbearing and unnecessary obstacles to practice was met with strong feelings in the NP community. After NP leaders became aware of the existence of the petition, the use of the Internet made the speed and effectiveness of the response possible in the following weeks. Several motivated NPs regularly monitored the AMA's website, watching for any issues that effected NPs.

Understandably, NPs and their professional organizations were concerned with the news of the petition. One of the early decisions made was to attempt to control a response, to prevent any rash actions and to respond in a unified voice, something that NPs failed to do previously. One of the initial decisions made was to discourage individual responses to the HCFA, to resist bombarding the agency with complaints.

It was at this time that the AANP and the ACNP began a coalition to discuss a united NP response. Eventually 11 groups in all would join the coalition, and more than 200 nursing organizations would ultimately sign on to the coalition's letter.

To begin the initial response, this group had to decide what would be the most effective response— a proactive or reactive response. Both responses had their merits. Since time was of the essence, the decision had to be made quickly, but also carefully. The ultimate decision made by the coalition was to promote a multifaceted response.

After analyzing the AMA's claims, this initial group of NP organizations planned a response in four steps:

1. Respond directly to the AMA's letter.
2. Attempt proactive work on Capitol Hill to make the NP position known.
3. Develop materials to guide the collaborative relationship between NPs and physicians.
4. Meet with HCFA officials.

This approach was very effective; it showed that the nursing community was capable of responding in a very methodical way to issues. One of the initial decisions the coalition made was for these national nursing organizations to urge their individual members not to take any action on their own.

By early August 2000, all of the 11 nursing groups had signed on and come together to draft a letter to the HCFA. With representatives from all the organizations, a letter was drafted to then HCFA Administrator Nancy Min DeParle. Through the quick mobilization of the coalition's members via phone, fax, e-mail, and the Internet, more than 200 national nursing groups had endorsed the effort within one week.

The final letter to the HCFA, submitted on August 17, 2000, was a well-crafted and succinct response to the Citizen's Petition. In it, the coalition of nursing groups defined their multilevel response by examining the AMA's charges one by one, claiming that they were ungrounded allegations. The letter also made efforts to suggest that the nursing groups shared the same goals as the HCFA and were "committed to working cooperatively with the HCFA to meet these goals in a sound and justifiable manner."

The coalition's letter broke the AMA's arguments down further, saying that there was no sound rationale to support additional federal regulation of NPs or CNS practices for the following reasons:

1. Federal rules already provide clear guidelines for collaboration.
2. Scope of practice policies and requirements for collaboration are a matter of state law.
3. Mechanisms already exist for easing compliance with Medicare requirements.
4. The AMA's petition suggests only theoretical problems.
5. Actual problems can be evaluated cooperatively.

The letter ended with a request to meet with HCFA Administrator DeParle to discuss the issue further.

It was because of this measured, well-planned response and the more than 200 cosigners of the document that the nursing coalition was able to get a response from the HCFA. In the autumn of 2000, representatives from the 11 coalition members met with representatives from the HCFA. The HCFA's response to the coalition's request for a meeting was a good indication of their willingness to respond to such an organized response. Most of the coalition's representatives found the discourse with the HCFA useful and left the meeting confident that the nursing groups' views would be seriously considered.

In the latter part of 2000, the HCFA's decision-making process slowed considerably. As of October 2001, no word had been received from the agency about changes to be made to the existing ruling, and this lack of "noise" can be taken as some degree of success, since the points made by the AMA were not immediately approved.

In the case of NPs and their response to the AMA's Citizen's Petition, it was a significant achievement for NPs and CNSs to respond as a unified group, and resulted in significant attention by the HCFA. The actions of the nursing coalition can now serve as a blueprint for future action; the means are there, and the vast network of APNs is ready for future action.

REFERENCES

American Cancer Society. (2000). Guidelines for the early detection of cancer: Update of early detection guidelines for prostate, colorectal, and endometrial Cancers. *CA Cancer Journal Clinics, 51,* 38-75.

American College of Gastroenterology. (2000). Colorectal cancer prevention 2000: Screening recommendations of the American College of Gastroenterology. *American Journal of Gastroenterology, 95,* 868-877.

Blue Cross/Blue Shield Technology Evaluation Center. (1997). *Biofeedback in the treatment of adult urinary incontinence: Executive summary.* Washington, DC: Author.

Continence Coalition. (1997). *Position statement: Coverage for pelvic floor biofeedback.* Laguna Beach, CA: Wound Ostomy Continence Nurses.

Division of Nursing, Bureau of Health Professions, Health Resources and Services Administration, U.S. Department of Health and Human Services. (2001, February). *The Registered nurse population: National sample survey of registered nurses—March 2000.* Available online at bhpr.hrsa.gov/dn/survey.htm.

Fantl J.A., Newman D.K., Colling J., DeLancey, J., Keeys, C., Loughery, R., McDowell, B., Norton, P., Ouslander, J., Schnelle, J., Staskin, D., Tries, J., Urich, V., Vitousek, S., Weiss, B., & Whitmore, K. (1996). *Urinary incontinence in adults: Acute and chronic management* (clinical practice guideline no. 2, 1996 update. AHCPR publication no. 96-0682.) Rockville, MD: U.S. Department of Health and Human Services, Public Health Service, Agency for Health Care Policy and Research.

Health Care Financing Administration. (1999). Medicare Program: Procedures for making national coverage decisions. *Federal Register, 64*(80) 22619-22625.

Health Care Financing Administration. (2000a). *Quality of care coverage process: Biofeedback for treatment of urinary incontinence tracking sheet.* Available online at www.hcfa.gov/coverage/8b3-x.htm

Health Care Financing Administration. (2000b). *Quality of care coverage process: Pelvic floor electrical stimulation for treatment of urinary incontinence tracking sheet.* Available online at www.hcfa.gov/coverage/8b3-w.htm.

Johnson, D.A. (1999, July). Colon cancer screening prevention (handout provided to Virginia Mandated Benefits Commission). Norfolk, VA: Author.

Lyon, B.L. & Minarik, P.A. (2001). National Association of Clinical Nurse Specialists model statutory and regulatory language governing clinical nurse specialist practice. *Clinical Nurse Specialist, 15*(3), 115-118.

National Association of Clinical Nurse Specialists. (1998). *Statement on clinical nurse specialist practice and education.* Harrisburg, PA: Author.

Oregon Nurses Association. (2001, January 1). *ONA provides guidance on nurses' dilemma.* Available online at www.oregonrn.org/services-whitepaper-0001.php.

Provenzale, D., Homan, R.K., and Oddone, E.Z. (1999). Screening colonoscopy in average risk individuals is cost effective compared with other practices (abstract). *American Journal of Gastroenterology, 94,* 2682.

Sabatier, P.A. (1991). Political science and public policy. *Political Science & Politics, 24*(2), 144-147.

Shinn, L.J. (1998). Contemporary issues in professional organizations. In D.J. Mason & J.K. Leavitt (Eds.). *Policy and politics in nursing and healthcare* (3rd ed.). Philadelphia: W.B. Saunders.

33 Where Policy Hits the Pavement: Contemporary Issues in Communities

NANCY MILIO

"I am of the opinion that life belongs to the community . . . and as long as I live . . . it is my privilege to do for it whatever I can."

GEORGE BERNARD SHAW

Communities are places where policy hits the pavement, where most people experience the effects of public policy making and where they may best learn the importance of public policy in their lives and how to raise their voices in praise or challenge. Here, too, nurses and other health professionals see the effects of policies and have their most immediate opportunities to promote necessary changes.

This chapter will explore the nature of community environments and the policies that shape them and people's prospects for health. It will suggest how nurses, as they increasingly move outside institutional walls, can use their limited time and resources to support improvements in policies affecting health.

WHAT IS A COMMUNITY?

A community is a bounded space in which an identifiable population lives, works, learns, plays, and shares in public life.

These activities, all essential to the public health, are housed in institutions—homes, schools, recreation and entertainment centers, businesses, and governmental and voluntary organizations, including faith groups. These assets, along with streams of communications and transportation, form a community's infrastructure. Their quality, availability, and accessibility to all its members (e.g., how clean and pure its water, air, and food are; how adequate its housing, health, education, police, and fire services are; how open its media, civic, and social life are; how dense its neighborhood, community, and labor groups are; how strong its safety net is) make the difference in the health prospects of the people. All of this depends on publicly led policy, planning, and financing to promote and complement private efforts.

These community spaces in the United States are officially bounded by the lines of over 3000 counties and 500 Native American and Alaskan entities, which contain about 16,000 school districts, over 400 urbanized areas, and 28,000 neighborhoods (U.S. Bureau of the Census, 2000). Nurses work in all of them.

Whereas entrepreneurs define the boundaries of their interest as a market—where the greatest likely buying power is available—health professionals must be concerned about entire populations in a given area regardless of people's economic potential, knowing that where that potential is lower, health risks are higher (Geronimus, 2000).

Together, all elements of a community—its environment, organizations, and population—evoke a social climate. This composite is the foundation for building changes to improve people's health. Some refer to this potential as social capital. Recent nursing literature has tended to emphasize the psychologic nature of community, including such as factors as consciousness and interpersonal connectedness (Davis, 2000).

A more politically practical and empirically useful view of community—and the one used here—is that of a bounded space with a defined population and the resource and infrastructure aspects described above, identified by its policy jurisdiction (e.g., a school district, a city, or a county). This bounded-space view seems to be the most workable approach to addressing the policy issues of a community because governmental units are ultimately accountable for the welfare of the population and have access to reliable funding and authority (Harris, 1999). The Centers for Disease Control and Prevention (CDC) has a simple, printable set of demographic, health, and economic information for every county in the country, available for the first time in 2000, which is usable by public officials and as an aid to nurses and community groups (www.communityhealth.hrsa.gov).

However they are identified, communities require collective action to move toward sustainable health improvement for their populations. Local groups tend to look after their own. Although many voice a willingness to do more with other entities, most have few surplus resources. Half of all faith communities, for example, have fewer than 100 attendees and budgets less than $100,000 (Kretzman, McKnight, & Turner, 2000; Hartford Institute for Religious Research, 2001).

ISSUES IN CONTEXT

In short, a community is not, for purposes of health improvement, an amorphous thing; nor is it an idealized image of action as a whole. It is, rather, a place with some level of infrastructure, including groups that work together sufficiently—though not always amicably—to decide about getting and using resources for chosen purposes. Whatever the extent or quality of community life, all that it is and does is affected by decisions that occur outside it. Decisions about the local economy and community infrastructure may be made by distant, sometimes multinational industries, communications giants, and higher levels of government that invest and disinvest in, and arrange international agreements on, trade, environment, and public health. These choices are made according to priorities that are not necessarily those of community members. Local players must be aware of this larger context.

A new dimension adding to the complexity of community work emerged with the 1996 welfare reform and other legislation and a presidential executive order providing for "charitable choice" in eligibility of religious groups for many federal social program funds. The new distinction, compared with previous decades of funding to such agencies as Jewish Social Services, is that "pervasively religious" organizations, such as churches and temples, can receive federal dollars. In the past, religious *motives* for service were acceptable; today religious *practice* is legally acceptable. For example, religions can receive funds but retain their right to discriminate in hiring according to employees' beliefs. They are not required to tell clients of their right to refuse service or to go to alternative agencies. Proponents, complaining that only 13 of 50 states have implemented charitable choice, argue that it is mandatory. Collaboration, they say, is not enough; affirmative action to draw in churches to apply for grant awards is necessary. Opponents say the policy infringes on free speech rights and the prohibition of state-favored religion under the First Amendment, and it will further deprive current safety net programs, since no new monies are planned for religious groups. This issue is likely to provoke heated discussion and perhaps court action in some communities (Center for Public Justice, 2000; Friends Committee on National Legislation, 2001).

Thus the concerns of community groups over issues affecting their health directly (e.g., environmental, workplace, or personal health care) or through their capacity for sustainable incomes (e.g., access to living wage jobs, training, education, child care, affordable housing) often are beyond the resources and control of the community itself. It is only governmental authorities whom citizens have a right to petition and be heard by, and if necessary citizens must pursue change in political arenas or in the courts (Harris, 1999). It behooves community leaders—of which nurses and their institutions are one set—to learn how to travel the paths of policy making in the interests of public health, to track and report the development and impacts of policies on public health to interested groups, and to support community health action (Milio, 1980).

Despite the breadth and complexity of local communities briefly sketched here, it is nonetheless possible to work with them to make progress in the hard task of improving health for everyone at the policy level. Nurses, as professionals and citizens, can share in—and sometimes lead—the efforts.

POLICY AND POLICY MAKING

Public policy is simply a guide to government action intended to prevent what would occur without its intervention. It is, more concretely, a decision about the amount and allocation of public resources committed to priority issues. The overall amount, most visible in government budgets, tells us just how much the nation or a community recognizes its responsibility for the general welfare of its people. The allocation of those resources shows which priorities are most important—how much goes for prisons, schools, housing, health care, highways, and public transit.

The ways in which these choices are made are *policy-making processes,* one side of which is *designing* a policy—such as fiscal policy (taxation and spending), provision of child care, or enforcement of lead paint regulations. The other side of policy making is *politics*—the equally essential work of moving and modifying the design through the decision making that occurs both inside and outside the formal policy arenas (whether legislatures or councils, governors' or mayors' offices, regulatory agencies or local boards) and, in alliance or contention with other players, in the stakeholder groups whose interests are affected by particular public policies.

POLICY ISSUES AND EFFECTS: DOWNSIDE AND UPSIDE

Virtually every community faces some if not all of the major issues that shape the health of Americans—disparities in health care; lack of affordable housing, child care, livable wages, and health insurance; budget constraints on public institutions; privatization and profitization of government services; related deregulation; and decentralization of many decisions and much financing (Milio, 2000a). Together, these trends, mounting over the last 20 years, may vary in each community but are at least present. They suggest an agenda for policy work to improve the health of the local population and present a challenge for those whose profession calls on them to do just that.

Even a brief review of recent federal and state policies reveals their health impact on communities:

- Welfare reform (the Temporary Assistance to Needy Families program of 1996) is partly responsible for the drop in the welfare caseload across the country by almost 50% between 1993 and 1998, but 60% of postwelfare working single mothers were either poorer or gained a net of $50 per year, thus remaining in poverty (Primus, 1999).
- Almost 700,000 of those leaving welfare lost Medicaid and continued to be uninsured, including 40% of single working mothers (Families USA, 1999).
- Child poverty, at 22%, compares poorly with other rich countries: 2.6% in Sweden, 12.2% in Japan, and 15.5% in Canada. The difference results from comparatively limited U.S. family policies, such as child care, minimum wage and unemployment benefits, affordable housing, health care, education, transportation, and regressive taxation (UNICEF Innocenti Center for Research, 2000). The American Public Health Association has recently called for monitoring the prevalence of low incomes as a health indicator, and making its reduction a public health objective (2001).
- The single largest factor slowing the increase in child poverty in the United States in the 1990s was the Earned Income Tax Credit (EITC) (Center on Budget and Policy Priorities, 1998).

- Large increases in funding for tuberculosis programs for health departments in the early 1990s, after large cuts in the 1980s, brought dramatic declines in TB rates within a year (General Accounting Office, 2000).
- Federal funds for payments to private doctors, schools, and health departments produced a large increase in measles immunization rates and closed the gap in rates between white and minority children (Milio, 2000b).
- State-funded abortions for poor women led to reductions in late prenatal care, births to teens, and premature births, compared with states that did not finance this service, where these rates increased (Milio, 2000b).
- Local control and enforcement over the use of lead-based paint, such as requiring certification of landlords to qualify for receiving tenants' housing subsidies, greatly reduce children's risks of dangerous blood levels compared with communities where regulation or enforcement is weak (Sargent, 1999).
- Mandatory seat belt and bike helmet laws lowered rates of injuries and accidents in communities where they were enforced not only through education and monitoring, but also by penalties that were publicized (Frost, 1997).
- Pricing policies for healthy food vending machines in school and in the workplace encouraged increased consumption of low-fat snacks without loss of revenues to the vendor (French, Jeffrey, Story, Breitlow, Baxter, Hannan, & Snyder 2001).
- Tobacco taxation reduced smoking initiation and use of cigarettes, especially by young people, and restrictions on smoking in public spaces helped all smokers to cut down on their habit (CDC, 2000).

Other timely issues in communities include gun control; implementation of the states' legal settlement with the tobacco industry to improve health; comprehensive school health programs, currently available in only 5% of schools; community-wide provision of clinical preventive and early treatment services; and ending discrimination against minorities, beginning with health care delivery systems (CDC, 2000; Slifkin, 2000; Zuvekas & Cohen, 2000).

PRESSURES ON THE SAFETY NET

Because most states have shifted Medicaid dollars mainly into for-profit managed care organizations (MCOs), safety net organizations—public and voluntary hospitals, health centers, and health departments—have generally been deprived of those funds, which formerly accounted for up to one third or one half of their revenues (Milio, 2000a). There has been little collaboration between health departments, which have a mandate for maintaining population health, and for-profit systems (Felt-Lisk, Silberman, Hoag, & Slifkin, 1999).

As one strategy to sustain themselves, over a quarter of safety net facilities have attempted to profitize, most without much success (Gray & Rowe, 2000; Thorpe, 2000). As incentives for Medicare clients to join health maintenance organizations (HMOs) increased, more public funds were shifted to for-profit systems. But when prospects for HMO profits dimmed with congressional efforts at cost containment, over 300 HMOs closed their doors to Medicare enrollees at the end of the century, leaving over a million enrollees to seek others; about 300,000 had no other HMO options (Cunningham, 1999). In some communities, this meant that the safety net providers had to attempt to fill the gap quickly. Sometimes this was impossible because of the extreme difficulty, for example, of re-creating home care programs once they have been shut down (Milio, 2000a). The fragility of the safety net (Institute of Medicine, 2000) leaves little strength in many community facilities for broader community health initiatives. These rapid and continuing changes have posed virtually unprecedented challenges to community health workers, most of whom are nurses.

THE CHALLENGE

Virtually all nurses work and live in communities that face policy-related challenges that alter people's prospects for health. Nurses cannot help but be aware of many of them through anecdotal or statistical information and the mass media. At any particular time, one or more groups are speaking out on local issues, attempting to shape the community agenda. One obvious route for nurses to fulfill their responsibilities as professionals or as citizens is to bring knowledge, skills, and commitment to one or more of these groups.

HEALTH PROFESSIONAL AND CITIZEN

For example, impoverished areas of communities often have poor access to healthy foods, correlating with unhealthy nutrition and high chronic disease rates. Measurable improvements in these factors occur when people, especially low-income families, have a local supermarket with wider food choices and lower prices (Morland, 2000). A nurse might engage faith groups, housing shelters, soup kitchens, minority groups, and health organizations in developing and advocating new options to expand the capacity and variety of local foods. These could include Small Business Administration grants, local community development incentives, improvements in public transit, establishment of a local farmers' market, and developing ethnic eating places. These would not only increase access to affordable healthy foods but also bring public and private investment and jobs into the area.

Alternatively, and sometimes more appropriately, a nurse may expose less obvious, critical problems and take the lead toward a solution, such as access to affordable housing. This could mean running for local office or serving on a local housing board. Today, the first step toward such options is easy, as many local public authorities and other groups have websites that announce and allow online application for such activities.

In one well-to-do community of 45,000, for example, a nurse, long aware of the close links between adequate housing and health, volunteered for the county's Affordable Housing Task Force and led the development of its report defining the extent of this increasingly severe problem. There had been more than a 250% increase in immigrant Hispanics, yet most of the new housing being built cost above a half million dollars, and the average price of all old and new houses was $300,000. She advocated the necessity for an assured, large source of funds for rental units that would be maintained at an affordable price, among several other measures. Although there was some success in obtaining a local bond referendum for affordable housing construction, it would meet less than 5% of estimated need. Prospects for further movement in the political arena would be slow. A few other individuals sharing the same view, including the head of a nonprofit housing development group and a local councilor, then formed a revolving load fund to provide low-interest loans to nonprofit housing development organizations to create and sustain affordable rental housing. The fund is capitalized by lenders, donors, and grantors, including foundations, governments, corporations, religious organizations, banks, civic and education entities, and individuals, within terms negotiated with the fund. Conditions apply to the size, term, and rate of interest on loans, set below market rate.

This fund would allow groups such as Habitat for Humanity to borrow construction and rehabilitation funds to create and manage rental housing at an affordable level (30% or less of income, including utility costs). The media reporter for the local press had "never thought about" all of the ways the nurse described how housing adequacy affects health, such as injury from accidents due to poor wiring, gas leaks, plumbing, infestations, and weather extremes; how high costs limit other family health necessities such as food and health insurance; and how insecurity of tenure makes family and work life more difficult and hopeful planning seem futile. This lack of media awareness is a signal that much education of the public, the media, and policymakers must accompany advocacy of measures to improve community conditions to the point that people can be healthy.

Such ventures may or may not be part of a nurse's workday. In any case, they are likely to require many evening hours. At the same time, the immediate rewards include the excitement of working with committed people from diverse backgrounds and entering worlds that otherwise might be unknown.

THE WORLD OF WORK

In the traditional work world, changes in policy have brought changes both in the settings where nurses work and in the type of work they perform. This has meant that they are moving not only outside institutional walls but also increasingly into managerial and administrative positions, the venues through which policy changes can more readily be addressed—in health departments and health centers, occupational settings, home care, and elsewhere. More nurses are in leadership positions in sites outside of institutions than inside (Bureau of Health Professions, 1998). Many feel ill prepared for the work at a time when they are urged to do more with less—and faster (Center for Health Workforce Studies, 2000; Gebbie, Wakefield, & Kerfoot, 2000). As health departments downsize and reduce nursing staff, many public health nurses (PHNs) are understandably reluctant to see or to respond to the new opportunities for policy as their clinical work is shifted to private delivery systems (Public Health Foundation, 1997).

Yet nurses could have a lot to do with change. PHNs represent 25% of public health professionals and more than 8 in 10 are in local health departments, although most nurses in the community work in home health or for primary care agencies (Bureau of Health Professions, 2000). Because 2 out of 3 health departments serve small populations and have few resources, PHNs are formal or de facto leaders at the local level (Milio, 2000b). This affords them a degree of discretion in allocating time and agency resources for community purposes (e.g., space, communications, electronic technologies, contacts, information) and offers them new opportunities to lead and make a difference.

STRATEGIES AND TOOLS FOR THE TWENTY-FIRST CENTURY

The most important step in policy development is to address the problem. Recommendations deriving from assessments of problems and research-derived evidence often require policy changes in governments or organizations. These changes involve the allocation of funds (or other resources) and a reprioritization of the importance of certain groups, and they are thus inevitably political in nature. No group wants to lose resources or power.

Policy change is harder in today's climate. In the past, the public believed they could trust the government to do what is right. In the 1960s, three out of four Americans had this confidence, compared with only 29% in the early 1990s (Judis, 2000). A careful study of the federal government's "50 greatest policy endeavors" since World War II concluded that bipartisanship, adequate spending, effective

regulation, and universal benefits are needed for success, which in turn require organized endurance, building of consensus, and patience rooted in a coherent policy strategy (Light, 2001). The case for health support must be strongly argued before governments will intervene where the private sector has failed to provide a population-wide basis for health. Today's political leaders tend to avoid risky policies in favor of safe rewards; the voting public demands quick success, and the media tends to punish necessary trial and error in favor of a good "another government failure" story.

NEW METHODS BY ADVOCATES AND OPPONENTS

Until the 1960s, advocacy groups worked behind the scenes, and relatively few traditional interest groups in the professions and industry dominated the process. Pro-health advocacy groups have begun to multiply in recent decades. Drawing from a familiar list of strategies, they act to reach the public (through education, media announcements, demonstrations, and rallies) and influence legislators (through lobbying, joining task forces, proposing drafts, and testifying). In the last decade, the list has become more sophisticated and expanded, as advocates responded to new opposition tactics, such as campaign financing, litigation, counter-suits, and "stealth" tactics (Dearlove & Glantz, 2000; Mangurian & Bero, 2000).

Some opposition industries, seeing health advocacy groups as a threat to their markets, are using more aggressive and costly tactics to counter health-related policies. These include *front groups*—a type of stealth organization—such as smokers' rights groups, which fight for their cause by centralizing weak state preemption legislation to override strong local measures; using misleading anti-smoking control advertising; feeding news articles that, for example, portray a positive image of cigar smoking; and funding glossy publications targeted at so-called upscale males, spurring a dramatic increase in cigar sales in upper-income men (MacDonald, Aguinaga, & Glantz, 1997; Burns, 1998).

When faced with the possibility of new tobacco control legislation, the industry conducted allegedly bogus cost studies purporting to show economic damage if restrictions were made on places where smoking is allowed. Other dubious tactics include filing suit against health officials in four states, charging them with illegal political lobbying when they visited legislators to support tobacco tax increases. Although such charges were dismissed in the courts, they have cost officials time and money and produced self-censorship and caution in other states' health officials. Elsewhere, public health leaders worked behind the scenes with their state tobacco-control coalitions (Bialous, Fox, & Glantz, 2001).

As health advocacy groups attempted to engage in policy change in local, state, and national arenas, they also used a more diverse strategic menu in seeming David-and-Goliath encounters with large opposing interests, such as the tobacco, gun, alcohol, and fossil fuel industries. These methods, once rarely used by health advocates, include class action lawsuits, media campaign contracts with ad agencies, public opinion formation, and polling. They also use public exposure of stealth tactics to create controversy and public debate to help "unfreeze" previously held opinions as well as initiate voter referenda and voter election education campaigns (MacDonald et al, 1997). Gun control advocates in Maryland, for example, asked political candidates to pledge support for gun legislation and then distributed lists of endorsers without actually endorsing candidates or making campaign contributions. This strategy met with success when supportive legislative candidates, as well as the gubernatorial candidate, were elected to office and passed the desired legislation, which produced a 25% drop in gun sales within a year. This approach was also used for legislation on tobacco control and child health insurance expansion (DeMarco & Schneider, 2000).

NEW INFORMATION AND COMMUNICATIONS TECHNOLOGIES

To find new ways to deal with more aggressive tactics from their opponents, health advocates are taking advantage of the new information and communications technologies. Using the Internet, they access population databases to develop and support health constituencies, form and mobilize alliances, produce and disseminate sophisticated print and video materials, and reach otherwise inaccessible decision makers through the press and cable networks. Yet high-speed Internet access remains a problem for many safety net organizations, including health departments (Humphreys, Ruffin, Cahn, & Rambo, 1999), disadvantaged groups, and communities (National Telecommunication and Information Administration, 2000; General Accounting Office, 2001).

In the health advocacy arena, strategic information (or "political intelligence" in contrast with scientific data) is intended to persuade as well as to educate, to mobilize support, and to demonstrate the political, social, and economic feasibility of a proposed policy. This means developing supportive public and media opinion, obtaining organizational endorsements, designing model policy language, and formulating key points and examples of solutions, among other activities. Strategic information is shaped to the interests of specific audiences. Most media personalize health problems and the responsibility for addressing them. This tends to sidetrack discussions about policies for addressing community health issues (Frost, 1997; Moynihan, Bero, Ross-Degnan, Henry, Lee, Watkins, Mah, & Soumerai, 2000).

NEW ADVOCACY CONFIGURATIONS

Recently, new advocacy groupings are emerging, in part because of the ease of identifying otherwise unknown kindred groups on the Web (Schultz, 2000). The new configurations are a necessity, because some of the traditional health advocacy organizations in medicine, nursing, and public health have stepped back from the fray in some state tobacco control, gun control, and health care delivery issues. Some medical societies, for example, may have other priorities for their political efforts, such as payment issues. Nationally they are losing membership, as are some nursing organizations (Jacobsen, Wasserman, & Raube, 1993; Milio, 1996; Zakocs, 1999; Reichard, 2000). They therefore have problems forging a coherent legislative agenda, which weakens their influence. Other traditional public health entities may be intimidated by opposing groups or are fearful of taxpayer disapproval. Whatever the reasons, older organizations have been less willing to take up-front positions and so might simply sign on to efforts led and funded by others, spurring advocacy groups to search for new coalitions and strategies with more active partners.

Traditional coalition formation is not a self-evident path to effective health policy action. There is little evidence that community coalitions for general health promotion, even those with some resource commitments, have done much more than share information, make assessments of problems, and write reports with recommendations. It is either questionable or unknown whether follow-up action, if any, has produced changes in the public health (Schauffler, 1997; Kegler, 1995). Even in the tightly monitored and evaluated community heart health and smoking-control trials, which require close and well-funded local collaboration, the results in the United States have been disappointing (Koepsall, Diehr, Cheadle, & Cristal, 1995; CDC, 2000).

COALITIONS THAT LAST

Where coalitions are effective, groups come together around an issue they already recognize as a problem and operate more like an action task force. Their question is not so much, "What do we know?" but rather, "What is to be done?" Their activities include seeking wider endorsements of an actual plan of action, such as raising the tobacco tax or funding local public schools. But to be sufficiently pursued, the action plan must be supported by a paid staff, however small, to coordinate volunteer work and joint group efforts, communicate, follow up, and monitor events closely. All partners should share in some benefits, such as greater recognition and legitimacy and new resources, while protecting their core missions. All this is essential to enabling sustained and timely action (Rhein, 2001).

CONCLUSION

What these overall realities may mean in any state or locality requires an on-site assessment. Awareness of general trends helps inform local organizational and political analysis. For nurses and others who want to promote a health-supporting measure, it is important to assess the political situation and forge links with particular, perhaps already ac-

tive, groups involved in seeking to change policy on a widely recognized community problem. Almost invariably, such an issue will have a direct or indirect connection to public health, whether it is access to housing, child care, primary care, or reducing poverty. Any are worthy of nurse-agency commitment and involvement of nurses as professionals and as citizens. Any of the issues could benefit from the liaison, voice, and access to data and expert sources that nurses could provide. The benefits to nurse agencies are also many, including first-hand understanding of community perceptions, expansion of contacts with groups otherwise inaccessible, building of mutual trust and support, and new awareness of those who are committed to community building (Rhein, 2001).

In addition to a willingness to seek new allies beyond the conventional set for improving community health, involvement in serious changemaking may mean trying some of the newer, controversial strategies noted earlier. As a convener, liaison, or participant in an advocacy group or coalition, appropriate activities for a nurse agency or nurse-run program might include developing so-called talking points for media use by group leaders; gathering information on the organization and funding of any potential front groups and streams of outside opposition funding; accessing data and transforming it into viewer-friendly formats and graphics through either agency or university expertise; helping shape a simple media message by framing the issue from a health perspective; helping write op-ed pieces; and planning letter-writing campaigns.

Nurses are also in a position to seek additional supportive information, such as analyses of any dubious studies that may be used by opposing stakeholders or the legislative or administrative history of the issue in question. They can also identify potential supporters and opponents among officials and meet with appropriate legislative aides to offer health-informed assistance in policy assessment and development (Givel & Glantz, 2000).

A final important contribution that a nurse agency or nurse might make—one that is often forgotten or neglected after an apparent policy success—is to monitor persistently and report on implementation of any policy of interest. Too often this neglect has meant losing the war after winning the policy battle, as public funds and program organization erode and shift behind the scenes. This assessment of the policy making experience can be fed back into community groups—and nurse organizations—to add to organizational memory and create more adept policy work in the future. Models for guiding such information gathering are now available (Heiser & Begay, 1997; Campaign for Tobacco-Free Kids, 2000).

Many local issues are beyond communities' capacity to address them. Solutions may require the state to enable legislation or funding. They may need federal funds and other resources, such as technical assistance. Nurse agencies can assist in this kind of access, too.

What nurses do in communities will depend on how significant numbers of nurses and nurse organizations—service providers and educational, research, publishing, and professional member organizations—see the changes in health care and the persistent gaps in health. These issues could be an opportunity to change and relearn, as well as to become collaborators with organizations that seek healthy community living conditions, which can be embodied in the economic and political aspects of public health, including assured personal health services.

The underlying question for all health professionals is whether people are merely customers in a market industry or citizens of the planet, with equal rights to the basic conditions for good health, regardless of their standing in the market. The mission of public health commits us to the latter view.

REFERENCES

American Public Health Association (2001). Resolution 200020: Raising income to protect health. *American Journal of Public Health, 91*(3), 504-505.

Bialous, S, Fox, B., & Glantz, S. (2001). Tobacco industry allegations of "illegal lobbying" and state tobacco control. *American Journal of Public Health, 91*(1), 62-67.

Bureau of Health Professions (2000). *National Center for Health workforce information and analysis.* Washington, DC: U.S. Department of Health and Human Services, Health Resources and Services Administration.

Burns, D. (1998). *Cigars: Consumption and health effects.* Washington, DC: U.S. Department of Health and Human Services, National Institutes of Health.

Campaign for Tobacco-Free Kids. (2000). *1998 46-state tobacco settlement allocations for tobacco control.* Washington, DC: Author.

Center for Health Workforce Studies. (2000). *Meeting the nursing needs of New Yorkers.* Albany: State University of New York.

Center for Public Justice. (2000). *Report card of compliance on charitable choice.* Washington, DC: Author.

Center on Budget and Policy Priorities. (1998). *Strengths of the safety net.* Washington, DC: Author.

Centers for Disease Control and Prevention. (2000, December 22). Reducing tobacco use: A report of the surgeon general. *Morbidity and Mortality Weekly Report, 49,* RR-16.

Cunningham, R. (1999, November). Budgetary impact of the BBRA of 1999. *Medicine and Health Perspectives, 22,* 1-4.

Davis, R. (2000). Holographic community: Reconceptualizing the meaning of community in an era of health care reform. *Nursing Outlook, 48*(6), 289-301.

Dearlove, J. & Glantz, S. (2000). *Tobacco industry political influence and tobacco policy making in New York, 1983–99.* San Francisco: University of California, Institute for Health Policy Studies.

DeMarco, V. & Schneider, G. (2000). Elections and public health. *American Journal of Public Health, 90*(10), 1513-1514.

Families USA. (1999). *Loss of health insurance for welfare leavers.* Washington, DC: Author.

Felt-Lisk, S., Silberman, P., Hoag, S., & Slifkin, R. (1999). Medicaid managed care in rural areas: Lessons from 10 states' experiences. *Health Affairs, 18*(2), 238-245.

Friends Committee on National Legislation. (2001, February). *An act of faith.* Washington, DC: Author.

French, S., Jeffrey, R.W., Story, M., Breitlow, K.K., Baxter, J.S., Hannan, P., & Snyder, M.P. (2001). Pricing and promotion effects on low-fat vending snack purchases: The CHIPS study. *American Journal of Public Health, 91*(1), 112-117.

Frost, K. (1997). Relative risk in the news media: A quantification of misrepresentation. *American Journal of Public Health, 87,* 842-845.

General Accounting Office. (2000, October). *Trends in tuberculosis in the U.S.* Washington, DC: U.S. Congress.

General Accounting Office. (2001, February). *Survey of Internet users.* Washington, DC: U.S. Congress.

Gebbie, K., Wakefield, M., & Kerfoot, K. (2000). Nursing and health policy. *Journal of Nursing Scholarship, 32,* 307-314.

Geronimus, A. (2000). To mitigate, resist, or undo: Addressing structural influences on the health of urban populations. *American Journal of Public Health, 90*(6), 867-872.

Givel, M. & Glantz, S. (2000). Failure to defend a successful state tobacco control program: Policy lessons from Florida. *American Journal of Public Health, 90*(5), 762-767.

Gray, B. & Rowe, D. (2000). Safety net health plans. *Health Affairs, 19*(1), 185-195.

Harris, D. (1999). *Health care law and ethics.* Chicago: Health Administration Press.

Hartford Institute for Religious Research. (2001, March). *Faith communities today.* Hartford, IL: Hartford Seminary.

Heiser, P. & Begay, R. (1997). Campaign to raise the tobacco tax in Massachusetts. *American Journal of Public Health, 87,* 968-973.

Humphreys, B., Ruffin, A.B., Cahn, M.A., & Rambo, N. (1999). Powerful connections for public health: The National Library of Medicine and the National Network of Libraries of Medicine. *American Journal of Public Health, 89,* 1633-1665.

Institute of Medicine (IOM). (2000). *American's health care safety net: Intact but endangered.* Washington, DC: National Academy Press.

Jacobson, P., Wasserman, J., & Raube, K. (1993). Politics of antismoking legislation. *Journal of Health Politics, Policy & Law, 18,* 787-818.

Judis, J. (2000). *Paradox of American democracy: Elites, special interests, and the betrayal of public trust.* New York: Pantheon Books.

Kegler, M. (1995). *Community coalitions for tobacco control: Factors influencing implementation* (unpublished doctoral dissertation). Chapel Hill, NC: University of North Carolina School of Public Health.

Koepsall, T. Diehr, P.H., Cheadle, A., & Kristal, A. (1995). Invited commentary: Symposium on community intervention trials. *American Journal of Epidemiology, 142*(6), 594-599.

Kretzman, J., McKnight, J., & Turner, N. (2000). *Voluntary associations in low-income neighborhoods: An unexplored community resource.* Evanston, IL: Northwestern University, Institute for Policy Research.

Light, P. (2001). *The government's greatest achievements of the past half century.* Washington, DC: Brookings Institute.

Macdonald, H., Aguinaga, S., & Glantz, S.A. (1997). Defeat of Philip Morris' "California Uniform Tobacco Control Act." *American Journal of Public Health, 87,* 1989-1996.

Mangurian, C. & Bero, L. (2000). Lessons learned from the tobacco industry's efforts to prevent the passage of a workplace smoking regulation. *American Journal of Public Health, 90*(12), 1926-1930.

Milio, N. (1980). *Promoting health through public policy.* Philadelphia: F.A. Davis.

Milio, N. (1996). U.S. policy support for telehealth: Organizational response to a new policy environment. *Journal of Telemedicine and Telecare, 2,* 87-92.

Milio, N. (2000a). Impact of recent changes in public health insurance on community-based health care in the USA. *Nursing Inquiry, 7*(4), 266-273.

Milio, N. (2000b). *Public health in the market: Facing managed care, lean government, and health disparities.* Ann Arbor: University of Michigan Press.

Morland, K. (2000). *Contextual effects of local food environments on residents' diets* (unpublished doctoral dissertation). Chapel Hill, NC: University of North Carolina School of Public Health, Department of Epidemiology.

Moynihan, R., Bero, L., Ross-Degnan, D., Henry, D., Lee, K., Watkins, J., Mah, C., & Soumerai, S.B. (2000). Coverage by the news media of the benefits and risks of medications. *New England Journal of Medicine, 342*(22), 1645-1650.

National Telecommunication and Information Administration. (2000). *Falling through the net: Toward digital inclusion.* Washington, DC: Author.

Primus, A. (1999). *Initial impacts of welfare reform.* Washington, DC: Center on Budget and Policy Priorities.

Public Health Foundation. (1997). *Privatization and public health: A study of initiative and early lessons learned.* Washington, DC: Author.

Reichard, J. (2000). AMA trims operating losses. *Medicine and Health, 54*(48), 1.

Rhein, M. (2001). *Turning Point: Advancing community public health systems.* Washington, DC: National Association of City and County Health Officials.

Sargent, D. (1999). Child exposure to lead paint in two counties. *American Journal of Public Health, 89*(11), 1778-1783.

Schauffler, H. (1997). *Health promotion and managed care: An assessment of collaboration by state directors of health promotion.* Berkeley: University of California School of Public Health.

Schultz, J. (2000). The community tool box: Using the Internet to support the work of community health and development. *Journal of Technology in Human Services, 17*(2/3), 193-215.

Slifkin, R. (2000). *Race and place: Urban-rural differences in health for racial and ethnic minorities.* Chapel Hill, NC: Rural Health Research and Policy Analysis Program, University of North Carolina at Chapel Hill.

Thorpe, K. (2000). Hospital conversion, margins, and the provision of uncompensated care. *Health Affairs, 19*(8), 187-197.

UNICEF Innocenti Center for Research. (2000). *Child poverty in rich countries.* Milan: Author.

U.S. Bureau of the Census. (2000). *Maps and more: Your guide to Census Bureau geography.* Washington, DC: Government Printing Office.

Zakocs, R. (1999). *Correlates of local organizations' gun control advocacy efforts at the local level* (unpublished doctoral dissertation). Chapel Hill, NC: University of North Carolina School of Public Health, Department of Health Behavior and Health Education.

Zuvekas, S. & Cohen, J. (2000). Racial and ethnic differences in access to and use of health care services, 1977–1996. *Medical Care Research and Review, 57*(suppl 1), 36-54.

CHILD CARE POLICY MAKING

Sally S. Cohen

"The greatest natural resource that any country can have is its children."

DANNY KAYE

In recent years, child care has emerged as one of the most important issues facing federal, state, and local policymakers (Cohen, 2001). Between the 1997 and 2002 fiscal years, the federal government will provide states with $20 billion to subsidize child care for welfare and nonwelfare families (General Accounting Office [GAO], 2001). This formidable investment is due to policymakers' acknowledgment of several key demographic, political, social, and economic trends. Yet despite the large rise in public funds spent on child care, millions of children lack affordable and high-quality care. Nursing organizations have yet to take their place among the hundreds of organizations that have been advocates for child care. This spotlight describes the variables that shape child-care policy making and identifies opportunities it presents for nurses to assume leadership roles.

DEFINING CHILD CARE AS A POLICY ISSUE

A recent report issued by the National Research Council and the Institute of Medicine stated, "Second only to the immediate family, child care is the context in which early development unfolds . . . for the vast majority of young children in the United States" (National Research Council & Institute of Medicine, 2000, p. 297). In its broadest sense, child care includes care of infants, toddlers, preschoolers and school-age children. Children receive care from an array of providers, often depending on the child's age, providers' availability, parents' work schedules, and family preferences. In 1997, 54% of infants and toddlers with employed mothers received care from parents or relatives. The rest received care in child-care centers (22%), in family child-care settings (17%), or from babysitters (7%). (Family child care is given by an individual in that person's home.) In contrast, approximately 35% of 3- and 4-year-olds with employed mothers were cared for by parents or relatives, 45% by child-care centers, 14% by family child-care providers, and 6% by babysitters (Shonkoff & Phillips, 2000). Child-care centers operate under various auspices, including religious organizations, public schools, private entities, proprietary chains, and community-based agencies.

Nuances of Child-Care Policy Making

The growth in public spending on child care is partly a result of the successful lobbying activities of state and national child advocacy organizations. This includes groups representing children, child health professionals, social service agencies, educators, public health administrators, state and local officials, labor unions, and women. These organizations have formed coalitions, testified before legislative committees, worked with government officials, collected and disseminated data on child care and child development, and brought to the media's and public's attention the importance of child care for America's families. They have also argued that enhancing the availability of quality child care can help employers reduce employee absenteeism and improve productivity.

Despite the surge of interest in child-care policies, some public officials remain reluctant to support child care, in particular for infants and toddlers. These individuals often have stereotypical images of child care as warehousing of children or think that working mothers of very young children have rejected their roles as maternal caregivers. Some of these same public officials find it easier to support programs for 3- and 4-year-olds, framed as preschool or school-readiness initiatives, than to support child-care proposals encompassing care of very young children.

But such views contradict the realities of family life for many Americans. Specifically, labor force participation rates of mothers with young children have steadily increased over the past 5 decades. For example, employment rates for women with children under the age of 6 soared from 25.3% in 1965 to 62.3% in 1996. Moreover, employment rates for women with children aged 6 years or older have been well above 70% for years (U.S. House Committee on Ways and Means, 1998). Furthermore, the nuclear family (married parents raising children) that flourished in the 1950s has faded. Instead, children are being raised in a variety of family configurations, including single-parent families, typically headed by women. The number of such families rose 25% in the 1990s (Schmitt, 2001). Single-parent families often lack the financial resources and social supports of two-parent families. Although men have stepped up to the plate in assuming household responsibilities, the decisions about child rearing and housework in most families still fall to women. Thus child care plays a critical role in enabling women, including nurses, to pursue their career goals and provide for their families.

Head Start

Contrary to popular belief, Head Start is not a child-care program, strictly speaking. It is a compensatory program that offers comprehensive services to disadvantaged children. Grants are made from the federal government to local entities. Although Head Start offers many benefits to children from poor families, it cannot meet the child-care needs of most low-income working families. This is because Head Start programs typically are half-day, operate only during the school year, target very poor families, and enroll mostly 3- and 4-year-olds. Thus, it leaves gaps in care for parents who work full-time, have infants and toddlers, or have incomes too high to qualify for the program.

Recent federal, state, and local initiatives aim to link Head Start with other early-education programs, such as school readiness initiatives and child care, so as to enhance the availability of seamless, comprehensive services for young children. Each state has a Head Start collaboration grant from the federal government to promote such efforts. Early Start, an expansion of Head Start launched in the mid-1990s, extends Head Start services to infants and toddlers from eligible families.

Many aspects of Head Start serve as models for child-care providers. In particular, Head Start's requirement to provide comprehensive services, including health care, social services, and nutrition counseling, are exemplars for child-care providers. Head Start's requirements for parental participation are another aspect of the program that many child-care providers have emulated. Finally, legislation enacted in 1994 required the Department of Health and Human Services (DHHS) to develop specific performance measures for Head Start to assess its ability to achieve desired outcomes (General Accounting Office, 1998). Many early education experts are following the implementation of these standards with interest because of their potential to be applied to other early-childhood programs.

Care for School-Age Children

Although most child-care policies focus on children below age 6, public and private leaders have recently taken a strong interest in before- and after-school programs for older children. Some of this interest was spurred by the rise in teen violence and other harmful behavior. The thinking is that structured programs for school-age children can prevent risk-taking behaviors such as substance abuse, teen pregnancy, and crime. As a result, the federal government spent nearly $850 million in the 2001 fiscal year on school-age programs under the 21st Century Community Learning Centers initiative. Private foundations, especially the Charles Stewart Mott Foundation, have also invested handsomely in school-age care. Some legislators find it easier to support care for older children than for infants and toddlers, because school-age care does not carry the stigma of mothers leaving very young children in the care of others.

ENSURING ACCESS TO AFFORDABLE AND HIGH-QUALITY CHILD CARE

Access to Child Care

Child-care policy experts identify access, affordability, and quality as the three main components of child-care policy making. In many ways, these three concepts are interrelated. For example, good quality care is often hard to find and costs more than substandard care. By understanding the dynamics of these three aspects of child-care policy making, nurses will be well positioned to work with public policy officials and other organized interests to advance child care as a public policy concern.

The availability of child care is affected by many factors. Shortages are most noticeable in rural areas, which typically lack community resources to support such programs. Furthermore, regardless of locale, transporting children to and from child care can be a problem, especially when providers are located far from home or work and parents must rely on public transportation.

Access to child care can also be shaped by economic factors. In a strong economy, child-care workers, many of whom are women, can find work in more lucrative industries, which reduces the child-care workforce. Similarly, as families are forced to rely on two incomes to make ends meet, the availability of family members who might otherwise be available to help care for children has dwindled.

Finally, many low-income families work minimum-wage jobs on evening or night shifts, during which child care is typically unavailable. This is accentuated by welfare reform, which has led many women into service sector jobs that require shift work (Carton, 2001). When evening or night care is available, it is too expensive for many families. The need for child care during off hours is also a concern for nurses who provide 24-hour care for patients in a variety of settings.

Affordable Child Care Is Elusive for Many Families

Quality child care is expensive, with costs varying by location, child's age, and the extent to which government subsidies are available to a particular family. Among families paying for care for children under age 13, the average monthly expense was $286 per month, or 9% of earnings, in 1997 (Giannarelli & Barsimantov, 2000). But these figures obscure significant differences. For example, "in 1995, poor families who paid for care spent 35% of their income on child care, compared with 7% spent by nonpoor families" (Smith, 2000, p. 2).

Geographic factors also are at play. In parts of the country, child-care costs run between $4000 and $6000 per year, with some families spending over $10,000 annually per child. In many urban areas the average annual cost of child care for a 4-year-old in a child-care center is nearly twice the average annual cost of public college tuition in the same state. Families in rural areas also face high child-care costs, although rates are usually lower than in urban areas (Children's Defense Fund [CDF], 2000).

Infant care is typically more expensive than care of older children because of the high staff-to-child ratio that infant care requires. According to a CDF survey, the average cost of center care for a 12-month-old is above $5750 per year in almost 66% of cities surveyed (CDF, 2000).

One of the major federal subsidies for child care is the dependent care tax credit (DCTC), which allows taxpayers to claim a credit against income tax liability for a limited amount of employment-related dependent care expenses. (A qualifying dependent is a child under the age of 13 or a physically or mentally incapacitated dependent or spouse.) However, the DCTC is not refundable, making it of no value to families without any tax liability. It also has not been indexed to keep pace with inflation. As of 2001, the maximum amount of employment-related expenses allowed under the DCTC was $2400 for one child and $4800 for more than one child. In 1998, the average credit claimed per return was $452, hardly enough to cover child-care expenses that exceed thousands of dollars per year. Recent legislative proposals in Congress include making the credit refundable, extending it to families with stay-at-home parents, and adjusting it to reach more low-income families.

Employers have several options for helping employees afford and arrange for child care. However, generally such efforts fall short of the need. According to a 1997 study, 13% of respondents had an employer that offered direct financial assistance for child care, and 29% had employers that put pretax dollars into an account to pay for child or other dependent care. Less than 3% of employers offered on-site child care (Bond, Galinsky, & Swanberg, 1998). Ford Motor Company recently set a new precedent with its ambitious plans to create employee benefits such as child-care centers, summer camps, and activities for teens in towns across the country (Greenhouse, 2001).

Quality of Care

Quality of care is a growing concern; policymakers acknowledge that good, quality care can enhance a child's development, whereas poor care can impede it. One way of protecting the well-being of children in child-care settings is state regulation of child-care providers. Child-care centers and family child-care providers are usually required to be licensed or registered in order to operate legally. But in most states, child-care regulations are insufficient for ensuring adequate child-care quality, especially in terms of curriculum, staff-to-child ratio, and provider qualifications. As a result, many providers apply for accreditation by private entities, such as the National Association for the Education of Young Children (NAEYC). Accreditation assures that programs have met standards beyond basic competency and offer high-quality care. It complements, not replaces, licensing.

One of the most important factors affecting quality is staff preparation and retention. Compensation for child-care staff remains woefully inadequate. In 1997, teachers in the lowest levels earned an average of $6.00 per hour or $10,500 per year, while those in the higher levels earned only $12,500 per year. Furthermore, turnover among staff is very high (Center for the Child Care Workforce, 1998). These high turnover rates make it difficult for centers to ensure good quality of care, since having a consistent provider is important for children's sense of security, attachment, and other aspects of development.

Finally, in the last decade, research has revealed concerns for the quality of child care, especially for poor children (Cost, Quality and Child Outcomes Study Team, 1995). Poor quality of care, as evidenced by low staff-to-child ratios, lack of developmentally appropriate curricula and resources, and staff that do not nurture children's physical and emotional development, can be detrimental to children (National Research Council & Institute of Medicine, 2000). Inconsistencies in quality of care have prompted state and federal legislators to introduce bills that provide financial incentives for providers to be accredited. Recently, the media have highlighted results of national studies that pose questions about the effect of child care on child development. However, the findings of these studies are often not properly reported and do not account for care quality. In general, there are no conclusive studies demonstrating that child care per se is harmful to children.

PUBLIC POLICIES TO PROMOTE CHILD CARE

The major source of federal and state child-care funding is the Child Care and Development Block Grant (CCDBG). The 1996 welfare reform law, the Personal Responsibility and Work Opportunity Reconciliation Act (PROWRA) (Public Law [PL] 106-193), authorized the CCDBG for 7 years. Both welfare reform and the CCDBG are due to be reauthorized in 2002. Much of the recent debate about child-care policy making focuses on the importance of child care for welfare reform and the need to ensure that low-income families not on welfare also receive support.

Child Care and Development Block Grant

The CCDBG is a block grant to states that subsidizes child care for eligible low-income families with children under 13 years of age. The CCDBG also supports state efforts to enhance the supply and quality of child care. The federal government spent approximately $4 billion on the CCDBG for the 2001 fiscal year. States must spend at least 4% of their total expenditures on activities to improve the quality and availability of child care.

States may set income eligibility no higher than 85% of the state's median income. However, fewer than 10 states have set their CCDBG income eligibility levels that high (U.S. GAO, 2001). As a result, millions of children are eligible for but not receiving child-care subsidies.

The CCDBG has three funding streams—discretionary, mandatory, and matching—each with its own requirements and formulas. Each year, Congress determines the exact amount of CCDBG *discretionary* funds that will be appropriated. Under *mandatory* funding, states are guaranteed to receive a fixed amount each year. States must spend at least 70% of their mandatory funding on welfare recipients. To receive federal *matching* funds, states must maintain child-care program spending at a specified level, referred to as a state's maintenance of effort. In addition, states must match the federal grant with some of their own funds.

Several provisions of the 1996 law are aimed at giving parents flexibility in their child-care options. For example, the 1996 law prohibits states from withholding or decreasing assistance to mothers who cannot obtain child care within a reasonable distance from their home or job and have children under age 6. Also, families who receive child-care subsidies under the CCDBG have the option of using a *voucher,* "which is a certificate assuring a provider that the state will pay a portion of the child care fee" (GAO, 2001, p. 9). Parents may also use a provider who has a contract with the state to render care for subsidized families. Most of the CCDBG care is delivered in centers and funded with vouchers (GAO, 2001). Interestingly, the use of child-care vouchers, although somewhat controversial, has not been subject to the same criticism as school vouchers. This is partly because child-care vouchers have existed for decades under other federal programs and also because many policymakers consider child care a social service not under the rubric of education. The CCDBG also subsidizes care offered by relatives and religious agencies, so that parents can choose the caregiver that best meets their needs and values. (For an overview of the CCDBG, see Box 33-1.)

The Child Care Bureau of the DHHS is the agency responsible for implementing the CCDBG and coordinating federal child-care programs. One of the bureau's most important programs is Healthy Child Care America (HCCA). Its "Blueprint for Action" identifies 10 steps for communities to take to improve the health and safety of child care (U.S. DHHS, Child Care Bureau and Maternal and Child Health Bureau, 1996). The American Academy of Pediatrics, with support from the Child Care Bureau and the federal Maternal and Child Health Bureau, has been coordinating the HCCA campaign since 1996. Many nurses have been leaders of state and national activities under HCCA. Extensive information about this program,

---

BOX **33-1**   Overview of the Child Care and Development Block Grant

Purpose: Block grant to states for direct subsidizing of child care and improving the quality and availability of child care; due to be reauthorized in 2002.

Funding streams:
1. Discretionary (requires annual appropriations).
2. Mandatory/entitlement (granted to all states according to a formula; capped annually; 70% must be spent on Temporary Assistance to Needy Families [TANF] recipients).
3. Matching (requires state maintenance of effort).

Eligibility: States may set income eligibility as high as 85% of state median income for eligible families with children under age 13.

Quality set-aside: States must set aside at least 4% of funding for activities to improve the quality and availability of child care.

Transfers: States may transfer up to 30% of TANF block grant funds to the Child Care and Development Block Grant (CCDBG) and may finance child care directly out of TANF. States may not transfer CCDBG funds to TANF.

Eligible providers: Organized child-care facilities, family child-care providers, informal caregivers, religious agencies, and certain relatives.

Federal agency: Child Care Bureau, within the Department of Health and Human Services.

---

including details about the program in each state, can be found at www.aap.org/advocacy/hcca.

Linking Welfare Reform and Child Care Poses Policy Challenges

The 1996 welfare law revamped the welfare system with Temporary Assistance to Needy Families (TANF). The law ended the federal guarantee of cash assistance to all eligible low-income mothers and children and replaced it with TANF block grants that gave states broad authority in administering their welfare programs. Under the 1996 reform, families are eligible to receive TANF benefits only for a limited amount of time. In particular, recipients are required to work within 2 years of receiving benefits and may receive TANF assistance only for a total of 5 years.

Several aspects of the 1996 law have implications for child care. For example, under the 1996 law, states may exempt mothers with children under age 1 from TANF work requirements. The CCDBG allows states to transfer up to 30% of their TANF block grant funds to the CCDBG, but funds used that way must adhere to CCDBG rules. In the 1999 fiscal year states transferred a total of $1.7 billion from their TANF block grants to the CCDBG (GAO, 2001). States may also finance child care directly out of their TANF grants and not be subject to CCDBG guidelines. They may not transfer funds from the CCDBG to TANF.

The need for publicly subsidized child care has increased under the mandatory work participation requirements of the 1996 welfare reform law. The PRWORA requires that parents enrolled in the TANF program work or risk losing cash assistance. By 2002, states must have 50% of their TANF caseload engaged in work activities or else lose federal funds. Subsidized child care is seen as a critical factor in enabling states to sustain their work participation rates, and thereby receive federal funds. Research has shown that child-care subsidies can increase the likelihood that welfare recipients will achieve self-sufficiency.

In implementing the CCDBG, states need to balance the competing needs of TANF recipients, families transitioning off TANF, teen mothers, parents of children with special needs, low-income working families whose incomes are too high to qualify for TANF but who struggle to make ends meet, and middle-class families who also have difficulty arranging child care. Most states have given priority to TANF recipients and those transitioning off TANF. But state officials are unclear on their ability to sustain support for these families, given the uncertainty of future federal funding levels. Furthermore, most states have not been able to meet the child-care needs of low-income families, many of whom have incomes not much higher than families on welfare (GAO, 2001). Thus many child-care advocates have called for greater attention to low-income families. Ironically, failure to help these families could result in many of them landing on welfare because of their inability to sustain work and afford child care.

CHILD CARE AS AN IMPORTANT POLICY ISSUE FOR NURSES

The interaction among federal, state, and local governments in administering and funding child care makes it an issue that offers many opportunities for nurses to become involved (Cohen & Misuraca, 2001). The first step in doing so is to learn about the CCDBG and how it is implemented in one's own state. The federal Child Care Bureau and other agencies also have websites with extensive information on the subject (Box 33-2). The CDF issues reports on the status of child care and on early-education policies in each state. It also offers legislative updates.

At the state level, nurses can connect with several important child-care organizations. Among them are the state child-care resource and referral agencies that are responsible for providing parents with information about how to locate care in their

---

BOX **33-2** Selected Websites on Child Care and Early Childhood Education Policies

Each site has publications available online or for purchase and links to other websites and resources:

American Academy of Pediatrics: www.aap.org
Children's Defense Fund: www.childrensdefense.org
Families and Work Institute: www.familiesandwork.org
Fight Crime Invest in Kids: www.fightcrime.org
National Association for the Education of Young Children: www.naeyc.org
National Child Care Information Center: www.nccic.org
National Conference of State Legislators: www.ncsl.org
National Governors Association: www.nga.org
National Institute on Out-of-School Time: www.niost.org
National Resource Center for Health and Safety in Child Care: www.nrc.uchsc.edu
National Women's Law Center: www.nwlc.org
U.S. Child Care Bureau: www.acf.dhhs.gov/programs/ccb
U.S. Head Start Bureau: www.acf.dhhs.gov/programs/hsb

From Cohen, S.S. & Misuraca, B. (2001). PNPs as catalysts in child care policymaking. *Journal of Pediatric Health Care, 15*(2), 56.

vicinity. Child-care resource and referral agencies also monitor state developments, including the relationship between child care and child health. State affiliates of the NAEYC are open to any interested individual and offer ways for nurses to be involved. To understand how child care is regulated, check with the agency responsible for such activities in your state. It is usually part of the department of public health or social services. Nurses might want to consider inviting representatives of these organizations as guest speakers at state and local nursing functions.

At the local level, nurses can check with their board of education, mayor's office, interfaith groups such as councils of churches and synagogues, and other community agencies to learn who runs child care, Head Start, or other early-education programs. The administrators of those programs will often welcome nurses as paid or unpaid consultants who address health and safety issues.

Finally, nurses can communicate with federal, state, and local government officials about the role of child care in building safe communities. In recent years, public officials have come to accept the role of government in improving child care. The challenge is to ensure that the funding is adequate to reach all eligible children and that the quality of care will promote child development. These are issues well suited for nurses who work with families, young children, public health issues, and a host of community-based concerns. With knowledge of child-care policy making and clinical insight into health systems and communities, nurses are well poised to assume leadership roles in child-care policy making.

REFERENCES

Bond, J.T., Galinsky, E., & Swanberg, J.E. (1998). *The 1997 national study of the changing workforce.* New York: Families and Work Institute.

Carton, B. (2001, July 6). In 24-hour economy, day care is moving to the night shift. *Wall Street Journal,* A1, A4.

Center for the Child Care Workforce (1998). *Worthy work, unlivable wages: The national child care staffing study, 1988-1997.* Washington, DC: Author.

Children's Defense Fund (2000). *The high cost of child care puts quality care out of reach for many families.* Washington, DC: Author.

Cohen, S.S. (2001). *Championing child care.* New York: Columbia University Press.

Cohen, S.S. & Misuraca, B. (2001). PNPs as catalysts in child care policymaking. *Journal of Pediatric Health Care, 15,* 49-57.

Cost, Quality and Child Outcomes Study Team (1995). *Cost, quality and child outcomes in child care centers: Executive summary* (2nd ed.). Denver: Economics Department, University of Colorado at Denver.

General Accounting Office. (2001). *Child care: States increased spending on low-income families* (GAO Publication No. 01-293). Washington, DC: Author.

General Accounting Office. (1998). *Head Start: Challenges in monitoring program quality and demonstrating results* (GAO/HEHS Publication No. 98-186). Washington, DC: Author.

Giannarelli, L. & Barsimantov, J. (2000). *Child care expenses of America's families* (Assessing the New Federalism occasional paper no. 40). Washington, DC: Urban Institute.

Greenhouse, S. (2001, May 13). Child care, the perk of tomorrow? *New York Times,* 14.

Shonkoff, J.P. & Phillips, D.A. (2000). *From neurons to neighborhoods: The science of early childhood development.* Committee on Integrating the Science of Early Childhood Development, Board on Children, Youth, and Families, Commission on Behavioral and Social Sciences and Education. Washington, DC: National Academy Press.

Schmitt, E. (2001, May 15). For the first time, nuclear families drop below 25% of households. *New York Times,* A1, A20.

Smith, K. (2000). Who's minding the kids? Child care arrangements. *Current Population Reports, 70-70.* Washington, DC: U.S. Census Bureau.

U.S. Department of Health and Human Services, Child Care Bureau and Maternal and Child Health Bureau. (1996). *Healthy Child Care America: Blueprint for action.* Washington, DC: U.S. Government Printing Office.

U.S. House Committee on Ways and Means. (1998). *1998 Greenbook.* Washington, DC: U.S. Government Printing Office.

Vignette — *Barbara A. Foley*

Emergency Nurses CARE: Where the Rubber Meets the Road

"Do not go where the path may lead. Go instead where there is no path and leave a trail."

RALPH WALDO EMERSON

When I saw the results of alcohol-related traffic crashes firsthand as an emergency nurse (EN), I couldn't ignore it. Other concerned ENs and I began a journey to make a difference—and it turned out to be quite a roller coaster ride. We were able to make a difference: With persistence, the political support of key players, patience, and sometimes luck, I used my skills as a nurse to develop a small community-based education program that became a nationwide success. It has been quite a journey!

In November 1981, the weekend before Thanksgiving, I was working as a staff nurse at the University of Massachusetts Medical Center in Worcester—a level-one trauma center with a medical helicopter service. On Saturday morning, a 17-year-old male was admitted to the trauma room, paralyzed from a car crash after drinking and driving. The next morning when I came to work, there was a 19-year-old young man in the same bed, paralyzed from the neck down due to a car crash after drinking and driving. His mother was stroking his arm and his girlfriend was holding his hand, but I was the only one in the room to know that he could not feel anything. He had broken his neck, had a breathing tube in place, and was on a respirator. He was trying to mouth some words, and his mom asked if I could help them understand what he was trying to tell them. He said, "Thank God I'm alive!" I left the room with tears in my eyes because I knew what was ahead for this young man and how difficult life can be from a wheelchair—one of my uncles is a paraplegic.

WHEN IS THIS GOING TO STOP?

On Thanksgiving Day, I was the charge nurse on duty when LifeFlight landed with an 18-year-old male with multiple traumas from a car crash where alcohol was involved. His family did not come to the emergency department, which was very unusual. This young man was going to surgery with a 50/50 chance of survival. When I called his family, they said the patient's brother and cousin where killed in the crash. Another nurse, Pam Bell, and I discussed our dismay at alcohol-related driving injuries. I said, "When is this going to stop? If people could see what we see on a daily basis due to drinking and driving, maybe they would think twice." With that thought in mind, we decided to show them. The following week, Pam and I wrote 15 letters to Worcester area high schools, asking if we could visit their students and discuss what we see in the emergency department when teens drink and drive. We received seven responses.

OUR FIRST INVITATION

Our first invitation was to a health fair at a local community college. We didn't have a slide presentation ready yet, but we couldn't turn down our first invitation. We loaded a Striker frame in the back of a station wagon and displayed one slide in our exhibit space that read, "Use common sense when driving." We demonstrated what it is like to be a multiple-trauma patient and to need a Striker bed. We were a hit! Students stood in line waiting to see our demonstration of the Striker frame and to ask us questions. We were overwhelmed and overjoyed!

THE PRESENTATION

We created a 45-minute slide presentation that addressed the consequences of underage alcohol use, drinking and driving, and safety belt noncompliance—and how these behaviors can impact families and friends. It was accompanied by a short video showing what happens to a crash victim, including an emergency airlift to a trauma facility. The video included a coroner telling a mother and father that their child was dead.

Once our slide presentation was prepared, we visited the other six schools that had invited us in the spring of 1982. One was a high school that asked us to show the program to the school committee before we were allowed to address the students. We often had to show our program to Parent-Teacher Associations or a group of teachers to gain support. Our biggest advocates and supporters were always the students—especially when the teachers or principal asserted, "We don't have a drinking problem in our school." The students knew the real extent of teen drinking and driving.

U-MASS WANTS TO KEEP YOU ALIVE

We called our fledgling program "U-Mass Wants to Keep You Alive, Don't Drink and Drive." We never wrote another letter asking if we could present our program! For the next two years, we received many phone calls in the emergency department asking if the "drinking and driving nurses" could do a presentation. This was great until 1984, when the volume of calls became overwhelming. Pam and I installed an answering machine at her house and used that as our base of operations. The emergency department secretary referred callers to our answering machine.

BARRIERS TO PROGRESS

During the first 2 years, we had a lot of ups and downs, and money was a big problem. Pam and I were frustrated, because despite starting the program in a Worcester hospital, we were unable to gain access to the Worcester school system. One day we presented the program to the Worcester Rotary Club, and the group asked what schools in Worcester we had been invited to visit. When we answered, "none," one Rotarian said, "You will be." We finally obtained approval from the Worcester Superintendent of Schools. During the next year we presented to all Worcester middle schools and most high schools and continued to visit these schools annually. During the tough times it was always the kids themselves who kept us going. Their thanks were important—as well as their feedback. After we presented the program to one school before their prom, we were told that it was the first time in four years they had an alcohol-free prom.

EMERGENCY NURSES CARE IS BORN!

We conducted over 100 programs during the 1984-1985 school year! We presented the programs on our day off—sometimes doing as many as six programs morning to night. There were many times we considered quitting because of the time and expense. Pam and I were paying for all of our expenses: copying materials, mailings, travel, and phone calls. We decided to ask for help from the Massachusetts Governor's Highway Safety Bureau (MGHSB), but before we did we wanted to change our name. We considered lots of suggestions, but finally selected "Emergency Nurses CARE" (CARE standing for *Cancel Alcohol Related Emergencies*).

MEDIA ATTENTION

We presented the program to the Governor's Highway Safety Representative, Mr. Terrance Schiavone, and his staff. They thought it was great that ENs were reaching out to the community but felt the program was too graphic. They also told us that although there was no money available that year, we could try for funding the next year. We were discouraged, but what happened next lifted our spirits. We received a letter from Massachusetts Governor Michael Dukakis informing us that Pam and I would be receiving the highest award in the state for public service, and we were invited to be featured on a Boston-based television magazine, *Chronicle*. We were so excited! We received the award and appeared on television in December of 1984.

In January 1985, we were invited to a reception with Governor Dukakis before being his guests at his State of the State Address. He told the audience about our education program to prevent alcohol-related injuries and introduced us on television. It was an unforgettable evening! That media attention resulted in many phone calls: from nurses who wanted to join our organization, from schools that wanted our program presented to them, and the most important phone call, from Mr. Schiavone of the Governor's Highway Safety Office, telling us he had found $5000 for us!

THE TEAM GROWS

We had presented our safety program to 30,000 students in 3 years and had learned a lot. Pam and I

Nurses who developed the Emergency Nurses CARE program receive the Manuel Carballo Governor's Award for Excellence in Public Service, December 1984. From left to right, Johanna Canfield, RN, Pam Bell, RN, Massachusetts Governor Michael Dukakis, and Barbara Foley, RN.

knew that the two of us alone could not keep up with the demand for the program, so we began to train other nurses to present it. We found out that nurses are not taught much in nursing school about alcohol use or other drugs. We prepared a training manual with information on alcohol, drugs, and safety belts as well as guidance on how nurses could make the program a success in their communities. We included form letters to schools to introduce the program, presentation tips, evaluation forms for students, and much more. Most important, we put together an 8-hour training program for nurses who wanted to implement the program along with continuing education credit. We taught them how to use audiovisual equipment and shared all the blunders we had made over the

first 3 years (such as failing to number the slides and dropping the carousel just before a presentation). Each hospital or group of nurses who chose to participate in the program received a set of slides and a script.

We incorporated Emergency Nurses CARE in April 1985 as a nonprofit organization and applied for 501(c)(3) tax-exempt status. We held our first training session for other nurses that month. Attending the first training session were 50 nurses from Massachusetts, New Hampshire, and Connecticut. Then we were off to the races: Have projector, will travel! We traveled to six states that year, training over 200 nurses. We charged for the training sessions only to cover our expenses. We never did and still do not charge for our programs.

Remember Mr. Schiavone, who at first thought the program was too graphic? He called to tell us he saw it in a school where you could have heard a pin drop during the program. He wanted to make sure his daughter saw the program before she graduated from high school and wanted to know how he could arrange it. We made that happen, and he was very grateful.

A POT OF GOLD

In the spring of 1986, a state legislator, Representative Angelo Scaccio, called us after seeing the Emergency Nurses CARE program at a school and asked what he could do for us. We asked if there was any funding available, not expecting a great deal. Pam and I were still working full-time and wanted to cut our hours in the emergency department to permit more time to work on Emergency Nurses CARE. Our political naiveté was apparent: Representative Scaccio was on the Massachusetts legislature's Ways and Means Committee, and he wrote a 3-year, $75,000-per-year line item in the budget for Emergency Nurses CARE.

GROWING PAINS

The program's success meant we needed more space, so in September 1986 we opened an office in Westboro, Massachusetts. Pam had family obligations that made it impossible for her to work with Emergency Nurses CARE any longer. Janet Lassman, RN, who was in the first training class, came to work for Emergency Nurses CARE in our new office, and we hired a secretary. I became the full-time executive director and Janet was the director of volunteers.

After moving into our new office, we really had a cash flow problem, because state grants usually work on a reimbursement schedule. Just before Thanksgiving 1986, just 2 months after moving into the office, I did not have enough to pay December's rent. I was in a panic. I had an appointment at Hanover Insurance to ask for funding. I brought my slide projector and program and showed the program to two vice presidents and the president. I told them that our program helped students make informed choices about getting behind the wheel when someone has been drinking. We

would be decreasing injuries and deaths due to drinking and driving and therefore would contribute to decreasing their insurance claims payments. I also told them about our cash flow problem and that I did not have enough to pay our office's December rent. I left feeling like they would probably send $100 and say it was a good program. I spent Thanksgiving with my family and returned to the office on Friday, upset and not knowing what to do about the rent. The mail came at noon, and there was a check for $5000 from Hanover Insurance!

CONNECTION TO THE NATIONAL HIGHWAY TRAFFIC SAFETY ADMINISTRATION

I was invited to speak at the National Association of Governor's Highway Safety Representatives Conference by Massachusetts's own representative to the group, Mr. Schiavone. I was nervous—the room was full and it was scary speaking in front of so many state and national government representatives. The room was silent throughout my presentation, and afterward they gave me a standing ovation. I was invited to Washington, DC, by the administrator of the National Highway Traffic Safety Administration (NHTSA), Diane Steed, who was in the audience.

In December 1986, I flew to Washington to present the Emergency Nurses CARE program to 10 staff members at the NHTSA. I arrived to greet a roomful of 50 people, and everything went wrong, of course. The slide projector bulb didn't work, I was a nervous wreck, and I didn't have enough handouts—but I made it through and began a lasting relationship with this federal agency! I later met with four NHTSA staff members, who asked what I needed from them. I said we could use money for materials, and they asked how much. I said $25,000 and they said okay. I couldn't believe it—I should have said $50,000!

In 1987, with funding from the NHTSA, the MGHSB, Hanover Insurance, and the training sessions, our budget grew to over $100,000. After reading about a nonprofit organization whose executive director took off with some money, I became concerned. I did not want anyone to think that I wasn't honest in running this organization, so I put together a board of directors. Mr. William O'Brien, president of Hanover Insurance, was our first chairman. I continued to run Emergency Nurses CARE's daily operations, and the board met twice a year and advised me on major decisions.

RUNNING A NONPROFIT ORGANIZATION

There were many challenges in running a nonprofit organization. I needed feedback from all the nurses conducting the program around the county to document how many people we were reaching, so we could obtain more funding, which proved difficult. I established a toll-free telephone number for our nurse-trainers to call, we started a yearly conference in 1990 for all our members in order to encourage networking, and we gave out awards to those nurses who contributed the most to traffic safety education. These actions met with success, and I was able to gather the information needed. I hired two more staff members, an accountant and a fund raiser. Cash flow remained an issue, sometimes to the point that our checking account balance got down to $50.

FROM COMMUNITY EDUCATION TO ADVOCACY

I became involved in safety belt and impaired driving legislation in Massachusetts because of Emergency Nurses CARE. I found that when I told students to buckle up because it decreases injuries and saves lives, their response was, "Then why isn't it a law?" I testified on this issue before Massachusetts legislators. I brought the co-chair of the safety committee, Senator James Jajuga, to a head injury facility to show him what taxpayers are paying for following preventable tragedies. In 1988 Janet and I became involved in forming the Massachusetts Advocates for Traffic Safety, a coalition of 60 organizations that began working on getting a safety belt law in Massachusetts as its first order of business. It wasn't easy, but we were successful.

In 1990 I wrote a letter to the editor of the *Worcester* (Mass.) *Telegram and Gazette* about the seemingly inconsistent requirement for emergency personnel to report dog bites, gunshot victims, child abuse, elder abuse, and communicable diseases, but not impaired drivers. Because of the letter I was asked by a Massachusetts legislator to testify about a bill introduced in the state legislature that would decrease the legal limit for driving impaired from a blood alcohol concentration of .10% to .08%

Emergency Nurses CARE Continues to Grow

We continued traveling all over the country doing "train the trainer" sessions—to train nurses to teach other nurses to present the community education programs. Nurses were presenting our program to teens, college students, and parents. In 1992 we worked with Marion Merrill Dow (MMD) Pharmaceuticals to develop a program for older Americans about alcohol, the interaction of alcohol and medications, safe medication use, and highway safety issues. We added a program for elementary students. We designed an interactive slide presentation for third- through fifth-graders that addresses the use of alcohol, helpful and harmful drugs, decision making, and peer pressure.

AFFILIATION WITH THE EMERGENCY NURSES ASSOCIATION

NHTSA continued to provide funding for Emergency Nurses CARE, and we received grants from UPS, Mitsubishi Motors, Kemper Insurance, and area banks and car dealers—but it was just never enough. I came to believe that if Emergency Nurses CARE were affiliated with a large national organization, we could be even more successful. In 1994 I approached Sue Sheehy, president-elect of the Emergency Nurses Association (ENA), about the possibility of the ENA sponsoring Emergency Nurses CARE. The ENA is the largest emergency nursing organization in the world but did not have any real community outreach focus at the time. Sue Sheehy and I presented the Emergency Nurses CARE. program to the ENA executive director and board of directors, and they supported sponsorship. Emergency Nurses CARE. became an affiliate of the ENA on September 1, 1995. At the same time, NHTSA, with a new administrator, Dr. Ricardo Martinez (an emergency physician), invited me to serve in the Washington, DC, office as a contractor for a year. I would be one of the first nurses to serve on the staff of this federal agency!

NEW FRONTIERS

We closed the Emergency Nurses CARE office in Massachusetts but continued our work: Janet from her home in Massachusetts and I in the NHTSA office in Washington 3 days a week—and 2 days a week for Emergency Nurses CARE. My job at the NHTSA was in the Office of Outreach and Communication, National Organization Division. I worked with 15 nursing organizations to coordinate their efforts to improve highway safety. My 1-year contract with the NHTSA turned into 4 years, beginning in 1995 and ending in 1999. During that time, I opened the ENA's satellite office in Alexandria, Virginia, in February 1997, which houses Emergency Nurses CARE and the ENA's Government Affairs office. Emergency Nurses CARE expanded its program area from just alcohol education programs to include child passenger safety and gun safety. Because of this expansion of our scope, our name evolved from "Emergency Nurses Cancel Alcohol Related Emergencies" to "Emergency Nurses CARE." In 1999, Emergency Nurses CARE became the ENA's Injury Prevention Institute.

Working for the NHTSA was a great experience, and I met wonderful people. I had great learning experiences and was able to observe the federal budget process in action. I was constantly impressed with the dedicated staff at the NHTSA, whose work saves thousands of lives every year.

INVITATION TO THE WHITE HOUSE

I was invited to the White House on March 3, 1998, when President Clinton directed the Secretary of Transportation to work with Congress, several federal agencies, the states, and concerned safety groups to develop a plan to promote the adoption of a legal limit of .08% blood alcohol concentration. I met the president and had my picture taken with him, but I could barely speak. I was overwhelmed to think how far things had come from two nurses talking in an emergency department about a safety problem.

ONE PERSON CAN MAKE A DIFFERENCE

In 2000, Emergency Nurses CARE continued its growth by expanding the institute to include bike helmet safety and domestic violence prevention. Emergency Nurses CARE now has over 6000 nurses presenting injury prevention programs that reach thousands of people annually. Emergency Nurses CARE supports the activities of many safety advocacy groups, including Mothers Against Drunk Driving (MADD), Students Against Drunk Driving (SADD), and National Organizations for Youth Safety (NOYS).

The starfish is Emergency Nurses CARE's mascot—this story explains why. Once upon a time, there was a little girl standing on the beach. As

EN CARE Contact Information

Emergency Nurses CARE
205 South Whiting Street, Suite 403
Alexandria, VA 22304
(703) 370-4050

E-mail: ENCARE@aol.com

Website
www.ena.org
Click on EN CARE link

EMERGENCY NURSES
CARE
Emergency Nurses Association
INJURY PREVENTION INSTITUTE

EN CARE (Emergency Nurses CARE) is a not-for-profit organization with more than 5000 trained emergency health care professionals who volunteer their time in their local communities in 47 states. Its mission is to reduce preventable injuries and deaths by educating the public to increase awareness and promote healthy lifestyles.

EN CARE's Philosophy: As emergency health care professionals, we have an obligation to educate the public on health and safe lifestyles.

EN CARE's Mission: The mission of Emergency Nurses CARE is to reduce preventable injuries and deaths by educating the public in order to raise awareness and promote healthy lifestyles.

she stood on the shore, waves threw starfish onto the sand. The little girl began to throw them back, one after another. A man walked by and watched the little girl throwing the starfish into the water, one at a time. After watching her for a few minutes, he said, "You know, what you're doing makes no sense. You can't possibly keep up with the waves. What you're doing makes no difference at all." The girl looked at the man as another wave threw more starfish onto the beach. She picked one up and

threw it back into the water. Then she looked back at the man and said, "It made a difference to *that* one."

One person can make a difference. The work we did wasn't easy, but what we have done is extremely important. For my work with traffic safety education, I recently was honored with the ENA's Lifetime Achievement Award and was inducted into the ENA Hall of Fame. I cherish these honors but take more pride in what a couple of nurses concerned about a problem were able to accomplish.

Vignette   *Carmen Warner-Robbins & Mickey L. Parsons*

Transition from Incarceration: An Innovative Faith-Based Program for Women

"Few will have the greatness to bend history itself, but each of us can work to change a small portion of events."

Robert F. Kennedy

- "I've been in jail now for 3 months, and no one has come to visit me or even write to me. I feel so alone."
- "I know I'm getting out next week, but I have no one to pick me up or even care for me. I am afraid of what might happen."
- "I hate my life and what I've done. I can't seem to do anything right. Most of all, I hate being in jail, receiving this punishment."
- "I can't imagine that I will ever amount to anything. I am such a failure. I feel so worthless."
- "When I get out, I really want to find a job and become independent. I want employers to trust me."
- "I have no confidence and do not believe I can ever face people again."
- "I feel I have no purpose, no meaning to my life. I am such a failure."
- "I miss my children so much. It seems hopeless, and I may never get my children back in my life."

- "Where will I stay when I am released? There is no one who wants me or believes in me. I can't bear to sleep on the ground again."

REALITY OF JAIL LIFE

The feelings and emotions just described are commonplace with women who are presently incarcerated in our county's correctional institutions. As they contemplate release, these women will enter into the community, and their situations of homelessness, joblessness, hopelessness, and abandonment present a real community health issue and challenge. It is crucial for nurses who work in our community to seek various options, opportunities, and solutions for these women, so that they will not reenter the jail system again and again. The potential for success in our community concerning the well-being of these women is exciting, realistic, and workable.

A study of women in prison found that the majority committed nonviolent crimes—primarily drug-related offenses—and had two or fewer prior convictions. Substance abuse was a common problem, with daily use reported by over 40% of all convicted female jail inmates; furthermore, 43% of state inmates and 22% of federal prisoners reported a history of physical and sexual abuse. The majority (76%) were between 25 and 44 years of age, and 80% were mothers.

Before incarceration, the mothers had had custody of their children and had been their primary source of support (Jinnah, 1994). These findings were confirmed by Philips and Harm (1997, p. 1), who found that "as a consequence of 'the war on drugs' and 'take a bite out of crime' policies, the number of women incarcerated was growing rapidly."

A COMMUNITY FAITH-BASED PROGRAM

The volunteer supervising chaplain for women in the San Diego County jail system, Carmen Warner-Robbins (an ordained minister and registered nurse), recognized that understanding the circumstances that led to incarceration and the needs of women upon release was essential for effective community program planning. Working with women in transition, who were forced to reflect upon the reality of their past, the pain of their present, and the uncertainty of their future, presented great challenges. However, in attempting to understand the multiple and complex factors that might lead to incarceration, the chaplain, together with the incarcerated women, began to soften and change jail policy and instituted the prototype of the Welcome Home incarceration model.

Incarceration Model

The incarceration model, developed with the inmates' input, tells a composite story of being born into poverty—often of an ethnic minority—obtaining inadequate education, and suffering child abuse, abandonment, and rejection. In attempting to deal with abuse and neglect, many of the women became involved with gangs and drugs. These women were running away from the pain of life, seeking money and acceptance from the wrong people. The experience was described as "a cycle with no backing out or exit," and "feeling helpless, hopeless, and trapped," which led to incarceration; for too many, it led to multiple incarcerations (Parsons & Warner-Robbins, 2002a)

The design of this model and the development and issuance of a questionnaire that incorporated input from incarcerated women reflecting needs prior to and upon release was directed by the chaplain herself. The deputies, however, under the authority of the county sheriff, supported and encouraged the women's role in the process by changing the jail's policy that women were able to interact with the chaplain only for one-on-one counseling and prayer. This change reduced the women's feelings of loneliness, which helped to break the bonds of pain and punishment.

Needs Assessment

The next step after development of the incarceration model was to assess the women's needs prior to release. The same 16 women designed a questionnaire with the support of the facility's social worker and the nurse-chaplain. Following distribution and completion of the form (29 of 31 completed the questionnaire), a demographic summary was completed.

The most frequently mentioned factor that would make a difference in preventing reincarceration was to be able to return to a drug-free environment. Get-

---

FOR YOUR INFORMATION

Statistics

- In 1998, there were 84,427 women under State or Federal Corrections.
- From 1990 to 1998, there was a 92% increase in female prisoners, compared with an increase of 67% for male inmates.

From Beck, A. & Mumola, C. (1999, August). Bureau of Justice statistics. NCJ, 175687.

FOR YOUR INFORMATION

Demographic Questionnaire Summary (n = 29)

- Ages ranged from 24 to 47 years.
- About 83% of the women were mothers.
- All but four of the women had multiple arrests.
- Substance abuse was the most common cause of repeat offenses.
- About 38% of the women had other family members in jail.

From Welcome Home Ministries Needs Assessment.

ting a job and participating in a rehabilitation program were the most frequently mentioned needs upon release from jail.

Often the pressure of reentry, the lack of support resources, and the influence of previous contacts may become not only overwhelming but frightening as well. When the environment places demands on a person that are greater than the resources and opportunities available to her, she faces considerable stress (Lazarus & Cohen, 1977). For example, if a woman is released at 5:30 AM with no available transportation, no place to stay, no job, and no clothing or food, the chance that she will contact those individuals who contributed to her incarceration is quite strong. This contact, though not initially planned, may be the only resource she has to help her meet basic human needs.

Contact upon Release

As a result of the women's input, policies and procedures were changed within the jail itself. Before the Welcome Home program, the policy stated that the chaplain would not have contact with inmates upon their release. Based on successful intervention within the jail and integration into the community, policy was changed to facilitate this continually developing reentry model. As a result of this change, the women did not experience the loneliness that had been previously common. The fear experienced prior to release was significantly diminished by the support and community building present during incarceration.

On the day of release, women would be introduced into their new Welcome Home family in the following manner:

Release: A warm 5:30 AM Welcome Home greeting at the time of release (by the chaplain and former inmates)

Breakfast: An early morning breakfast

Basic needs: A special love basket of basic health, sanitary, and comfort items

Transportation: A ride to a prearranged place of housing, rehabilitation program, or residence

Reentry appointment: An interview with a local reentry program

Support group: A weekly gathering for counseling, prayer, encouragement, and networking

New community: An opportunity to build a new community through a positive network of caring, goal-oriented women who themselves are making a difference in their own lives as well as the lives of others (Parsons, 1999; Parsons & Warner-Robbins, 1999; Parsons & Warner-Robbins, 2002b)

At periodic intervals after their release, women would seek audience with the sheriff to relate personal successes and to share ideas about jail policy and health care. Following only two such meetings, certain aspects of jail health sanitation policy were modified. Seeing that their voices were being heard and answered, the women's previous feelings of low self-worth were improved. As the success of Welcome Home spread and community interest heightened, the women themselves were interviewed on radio and television; were asked to speak at community gatherings, Sigma Theta Tau meetings, and service organizations; and even participated in a documentary video.

HEALTH-PROMOTING ORGANIZATION

A comprehensive mind-body-spirit framework to develop Welcome Home Ministries as a health-promoting organization was defined, and intervention for health and wellness occurred at each of the five levels (organizational leadership, interpersonal, individual, municipal community, and public policy) (Parsons, 1999).

Low Recidivism

The confidence previously lacking in these women was restored as they shared their stories and their successes. Consistent with the cost savings to the taxpayer and the successful program results evidenced by a 6% recidivism rate (compared with a national rate of 75%), the sheriff agreed to the establishment of a county-wide commission addressing the health needs, general well-being issues, and the status of deputy-inmate cooperation and interaction. To our knowledge, this is the only such commission in the country.

Employment

As women began to achieve success by attending college and securing a quality living environment, employers began to open their doors to women with felony records. Historically, women with felony convictions were immediately excluded from most quality positions. The leadership of the Welcome Home women established a task force to contact and educate employers on the credibility of women in the program. Consequently, eight employers from large companies and production firms have changed their policies to offer equal employment opportunities to women with felony records. This change resulted in a decreased jobless rate and increased self-esteem and motivation. With many Welcome Home women enjoying successful employment, three who had previously experienced difficulty with job security wrote and submitted a solicitation for proposal (SFP) through California's Faith-Based Initiative Program. Of 231 proposals submitted, Welcome Home was selected as 1 of 20 programs to receive funding for training the difficult to employ (i.e., post-incarceration women). The allocation of funds was deemed a milestone for the recognition of and belief in the women. Officials from the governor's office personally acknowledged the proposal's quality and publicly stated their support for the well-being of these women. These women experienced great joy from the fact that even people from the governor's office had heard their voices and acknowledged their worth and potential.

Housing

As the wave of support and belief in the welfare and well-being of these women continues, Habitat for Humanity has agreed to build a transition home for women needing a safe place to reside following incarceration. Again, the women are taking an active role in the planning and implementation of the project, proving their enthusiasm for achievement and growth and opening the lines of communication for continued partnership between Habitat for Humanity and other reentry programs.

Collaboration

Although Welcome Home Ministries was started as a practical response to the problems women experienced upon release from jail, it was soon evident that the problem was systemic and had to be addressed both within the institution and in the community. The collaborative work with the Sheriff's Department has brought about several small but significant changes in jail policy that have greatly affected the quality of that environment. Possibly the most enduring change in the jail has been the adjustment in the attitudes and cooperation of both the inmates and the deputies.

CONCLUSION

Welcome Home Ministries has become a vehicle to heighten awareness to the community health and social problems posed by the lack of resources and intervention strategies for this population of women. Even though small steps have been taken to address public policy issues, as in the case of the faith-based initiative, a broad-based, more comprehensive and holistic approach must be considered. Welcome Home Ministries has provided another glimpse of a larger picture, one in which women are being incarcerated in ever-increasing numbers. At the same time, it is recognized that women are the stabilizers and the guiding force for families, and that the family is the cornerstone upon which the society is built. This may present one of the more significant challenges not just for community- and institutionally based nurses to build on the momentum initiated by Welcome Home Ministries, but for our society at large.

REFERENCES

Beck, A. & Mumola, C. (1999, August). Bureau of Justice statistics. *NCJ*, 175687.

Jinnah, D. (1994, October). *Research and development: Women in prison.* Washington, DC: Prison Fellowship Ministries.

Lazarus, R.S. & Cohen, J.B. (1977). Environmental stress. In I. Altman & J.F. Wohlman (Eds.). *Human behavior and the environment: Current theory and research.* New York: Plenum.

Parsons, M.L. (1999). Health promoting organizations: A systems model for advanced practice. *Holistic Nursing Practice, 13*(4), 80-89.

Parsons, M.L. & Warner-Robbins, C. (1999, April 23). *Health promoting organizations and an operational example—Welcome Home Ministries* (paper presented at the Seventh International Conference on Health Promoting Hospitals). Swansea, Wales.

Parsons, M.L. & Warner-Robbins, C. (2002a). Factors that support women's successful transition to the community following jail/prison. *Health Care for Women International, 23,* 6-18.

Parsons, M.L. & Warner-Robbins, C. (2002b). Nursing on the front lines: Community program helps women's transition from jail to society. *American Journal of Nursing, 102.*

Phillips, S., & Harm, N. (1997). Women prisoners: A contextual framework. *Women & Therapy, 20*(4), 1-7.

34 Working with the Community for Change

MARY ANN CHRISTOPHER

JUDITH L. MILLER

THERESA L. BECK

EILEEN H. TOUGHILL

"We are all faced with a series of opportunities brilliantly disguised as impossible situations."

CHUCK SWINDOLL

School-based comprehensive family service institutes, neighborhood school-based health centers, nurse-managed community health centers, senior center wellness programs, development of community water systems, community-conducted health fairs, and revitalization of an urban school—such have been the community collaborations facilitated by registered nurses (May, Mendelson, & Ferketich, 1995; Courtney, Ballard, Fauver, Gariota, & Holland, 1996; Glick, 1999; Campbell & Aday, 2001; Faulk, Coker, & Farley, 2001). In the current climate there are several imperatives that make the ability of nurses to collaborate with communities a particularly relevant and marketable skill. Shrinking revenues for acute care hospitalization, third-party payers concerned with meeting the needs of populations, and reduced reimbursement for services are the variables driving the health care industry to redefine itself. Compounding the issue is a global nursing shortage (Armstrong, 2001; Boyle, 2001; Caro & Kaffenberger, 2001; Smith, Inoue, Ushikubo, & Amano, 2001). The nursing shortage heralds the need to relook at the health care delivery system and underscores the need to work with communities if societal health is to be realized.

An emphasis on population-based and community-based prevention of disease, injury, disability, and premature death will force a realignment of the role and responsibility of the public health sector. Indeed, states have already begun to redefine the role of the public health sector, placing increased emphasis on effective community collaboration. The only way that total health care system costs will be controlled is to focus significantly on the prevention of illness conditions, which will improve the collective state of health (Gebbie, 1999). Nursing is at the core of this shift to community collaboration.

Implementation of the *Healthy People 2010* health objectives is tied to effective community collaboration at the local level (*Healthy People 2010: Understanding and improving health*, 2000). Any risk reduction program or health care service must reflect a community-based response that incorporates the behavioral norms within groups (Rawlings-Anderson, 2001).

FRAMEWORK FOR WORKING WITH COMMUNITIES

What framework should nurses use to build on their strong tradition of community-based leadership? The ability to work effectively with communities is tied to the mastery of three basic concepts: (1) the differentiation between community and population, (2) a broad conceptualization of health, and (3) a methodology that fosters participation.

COMMUNITY AND POPULATION

Understanding the differential concepts of community and population is critical to effective community collaboration. Population refers to a collective of individuals with common properties, whereas community exists when individuals share a locale and engage in patterns of social interactions, share a common identity and participate in interdependent activities, and work toward shared goals and collective activities. It is this concept of community, grounded in locality development, that has been the hallmark of effective community collaboration. This model has its emphasis on problem solving by a cross section of community members in a geographical area (Kang, 1995). The failure of managed care to have an impact on the immunization rates of children is due in part to managed care organizations' focus on population rather than community. In other words, within a given geographical area, a managed care organization would focus on the needs of its beneficiaries only; uninsured or underinsured children within that community would not have the benefit of outreach. This has become such a critical issue among the Hispanic population in three neighborhoods in New Jersey (two urban, one suburban) that networking among religious organizations, local health officers, and the Visiting Nurse Association of Central Jersey (VNACJ) resulted in the establishment of child health conferences for immunizations and well-child visits.

At the VNACJ, an effort to establish a neighborhood advisory council linked to every regional office for the visiting nurses required modification based on the population-versus-community concept. The councils included members from various neighborhoods served by a regional office, with their selection based on a specific population represented by the member. Because of the diversity of socioeconomic, ethnic, and cultural needs of the populations served from individual regional offices, a reduction in participation rates in the councils indicated that people identify with neighborhood-specific issues rather than regional ones. As a result, a strategy has been developed to establish several neighborhood advisory councils in a community, rather than just one council. Even though this approach is labor intensive, it is the only strategy deemed to be effective.

CONCEPTUALIZATION OF HEALTH

Another critical skill in working with communities successfully is to conceptualize and define health broadly. Nurses who are the most effective with community collaboration are those who have a comfort level with program designs that define roles in nontraditional ways. A broad conceptualization of health is based on a definition that encompasses physical, emotional, social, and spiritual dimensions of well-being. A healthy community is defined as more than merely the absence of disease; it includes those elements that help people live productive lives (*Health People 2010*, 2000).

Environmental Health. An example of this focus on social and living conditions in the community is an activity that the VNACJ engaged in under funding from the Robert Wood Johnson Foundation. Titled the Supportive Services Program for Older Adults, this project centered around a needs assessment conducted on elderly persons in our service area. Whereas staff identified programs such as geriatric case management, medical adult day care, and respite care as the critical products to be offered through the program, seniors themselves overwhelmingly identified chore and home repair services as their critical need. As a result, the program Your Senior Connection took on a home repair focus rather than a traditional professional health care focus. The outcome of this initiative was that in maintaining the physical structures of their homes, seniors' overall health status was affected positively through reduced falls, less frequent relocation, and lower reported emotional stress.

Another example, the Rural Elderly Enhancement Project, was a nurse-initiated grant funded by the W.K. Kellogg Foundation (Faulk et al, 2001). The major purpose was to develop a model of community participation and empowerment. Leadership development of citizens increased their capacity to organize volunteer coalitions, secure funding, implement projects, and affect public policy. Accomplishments included volunteer coalitions to assist the elderly with housekeeping and structural repairs, and development of two water systems serving over 500 families.

Psychosocial and Mental Health. Since 1984, the VNACJ's Mobile Outreach Clinic Program (MOCP) nurses have delivered on-site health assessment and case management to more than 2000 deinstitutionalized mentally ill residents living in single-room occupancies and boarding homes. Understanding that meaningful work is a vital health component for all adults, the MOCP has undertaken a collaborative initiative with the county division of social services to help identify clients in the community that are appropriate for work rehabilitation. Based on a complete biopsychosocial and skills assessment, these nurses are linking clients to necessary health services, which will facilitate improvement in overall functioning and entry into the workforce.

When communities indicated that the needs of the community were better met by relocating selected numbers of deinstitutionalized mentally ill persons to other counties, the nurses' role again changed from a traditional health focus. A nurse actually accompanied the residents on a van throughout the state as they sought new housing, easing the anxiety that accompanied their relocation and assisting them in the process of selecting a new home. The nurses' presence fostered the residents' ability to make an informed choice. In addition, it demonstrated to communities at large and to policymakers that anticipatory planning must accompany any major policy shift.

The conceptualization of health as encompassing hope is never more evident than with children who have experienced severe loss through the death of a parent, sibling, or friend. The VNACJ Hospice Program began a bereavement program, Children Adjusting to New Situations (CANS) (Aldrich, 1989), for children of the agency's Hospice Program patients. Groups meet weekly for 6 consecutive weeks to discuss the effect of death and loss, and to reinforce with participants that they are not the only ones experiencing sadness. This message of hope was brought to the larger community by a

VNACJ nurse practitioner working in a school-based program at a local high school. Understanding that loss can have many precipitous effects, she introduced CANS into the high school to enable the children to cope with the anger that comes from the loss of income, health, family stability, and housing.

Family-Centered Health. Yet another project was the "rural elderly project" in Alabama, funded initially to maintain the independence of elderly persons. The project developed an intergenerational focus in response to community demand. Outcomes of the project included the development of volunteer coalitions to address the activities-of-daily-living needs of elderly persons, creation of after-school and summer tutoring programs for children, development of a referral system to link communities to provider agencies, and establishment of a school-based community health center. These outcomes have facilitated the attainment of the project's initial goal, which was to develop a rural health and human services delivery system that was family centered, coordinated, and accessible (Farley, 1995).

Holistic Health. Literacy is a critical component of health. The nurses of the VNACJ's Mobile Outreach Clinic Program identified this need while addressing the complex needs of homeless families living in motels in various communities. After years of moving from motel to motel to escape a battering father, a 7-year-old child was illiterate and starting her third year of kindergarten. Alarmed at the social and psychologic implications of this, the nurses initiated a reading program at the motel. The goal was to demonstrate to mothers, overwhelmed by life demands, how to use reading as a tool to help their children learn, and as a tool to reinforce bonding between parent, child, and siblings.

Not long after this project began, the primary care providers at the VNACJ Primary Care Centers became involved in the national Reach Out and Read program (ROAR). Under the ROAR program, the primary care centers receive grants to purchase children's books. When a child comes for a well visit, the advanced practice nurse writes a special "prescription" for an age-appropriate book, and the child is allowed to choose a book to take home. ROAR has the double effect of promoting literacy and rewarding well-child follow-up visits.

PARTICIPATION METHODS

The third competency that has implications for effective community collaboration is the development of the collective mindset. The two dimensions of that changed mind-set are the focus on aggregate needs and participative interventions. It is often in ministering to individuals that nurses have the ability to mobilize and facilitate community involvement that contributes to the health of the aggregate (Drevadhl, 1995). The goal of building community collaboration is achieved because barriers are reduced, trust is increased, and common goals are identified.

The VNACJ spent several years developing a neighborhood nursing philosophy of care, which is built on exactly this premise of community collaboration (Reinhard, Christopher, Mason, McConnell, Toughill, & Rusca, 1996). As an example, one nurse found that, in her caseload, significant numbers of elderly persons were malnourished, which resulted in frequent hospital readmissions. This observation, based on her care of individual patients, led her to work with the community and local churches to develop an extensive program of home-delivered meals for patients who did not meet the eligibility requirements of the federal entitlement program for senior citizens. Staff working with individuals in communities have the opportunity and responsibility to act on trends that are individually manifested but geographically significant. For example, a community health nurse, having witnessed the social isolation and depression of seniors living in the only unlocked housing facility in a high-crime area, petitioned the town council and the county to secure the building.

The second dimension of the collective mind-set is a true belief in the power of partnerships and participation. Participatory approaches are most effective because they increase interpersonal relationships and feelings of personal and political confidence. For example, in addition to attending traditional health-related community events such as health fairs, neighborhood nurses at VNACJ participate in town parades, Parent-Teacher Association (PTA) meetings, and city celebration days, often in the evening, on weekends and holidays. These activities further validate for the community that the organization is a partner and that the nurse is engaged in the fabric of community.

Partnership is defined as the negotiated sharing of power between health professionals and community members (Courtney et al, 1996). The basic condition of partnership is trust, whereby members become confident that other participants will uphold formal and informal agreements. The mutuality in contributions to the partnership means that the professional does not take on all the responsibility, accountability, or authority. Partners play a mutual role in determining goals and actions, with the ultimate goal being to enhance the capacity of communities to act more effectively on their own behalf (Kang, 1995).

Issues that must be resolved for community collaboration to work are power and control, protection of turf, competition among partners, and challenges of sustainability (Gauthier & Metteson, 1995). A critical action step is to identify what each partner wants from the relationship. Participation and collaboration are a transformative process in which the community ceases to view itself as a victim and learns ways to identify and solve problems. Such a process considers cultural relevance not as a barrier, but as a matrix through which problems are solved. The feelings of community members are changed from helplessness to efficaciousness (May et al, 1995).

This movement away from victimization was evidenced recently during strategic planning in a blighted urban municipality. Community members insisted on the inclusion of strengths—not just on the traditional problem list and negative statistics. Programs flowing from these assessments must build on strengths rather than be focused solely on need.

Another example occurred as the result of a phone call from an inmate at the Monmouth County Correctional Facility to the VNACJ's acquired immunodeficiency syndrome (AIDS) "Warmline." His call for assistance led to 7 years of letters and correspondence with the judicial system, culminating in the establishment of the Life Improving Network to the Community (LINC) program. This innovative program, staffed by professionals and peer educators, targets incarcerated human immunodeficiency virus (HIV)-infected men and women. LINC helps inmates remain compliant with HIV treatment and make the successful transition back to life in the community.

It is critical that nurses involved in effective community collaboration guard against the trap of falling into the rhetoric of empowerment. This rhetoric just reinforces the power of the professional and strengthens the view that the professional knows best. The rhetoric of empowerment has caused competent communities to be invaded, captured, and weakened by mottoes that speak of collaboration and empowerment but actually reinforce feelings of powerlessness (Courtney et al, 1996). In these cases, needs of organizations are met, rather than the needs of communities.

An example of the power of collaborative mutuality was demonstrated in a project conducted by community health nurses in a local Hispanic community. As part of an annual festival, a committee of community leaders and health care professionals developed a health fair based on their assessment of need. Although satisfaction rates were positive, overall participation was low. In the second year a committee of peer outreach workers, nurses, and community members determined through an extensive focus group process the thrust that the fair should take. More community members actually participated in presenting the fair, with the result that participation increased by 400% (May et al, 1995).

Yet another example of transforming the professional role into a partnership role occurred in a Hispanic urban center when school officials approached nurse practitioners to conduct a school-based health fair. Aware that an overall objective in the community was to increase parental involvement in the school, the nurse practitioners formed a planning committee of parents, invited parents to administer health surveys at the fair, and guided the health club students to run the first-aid booth. The results of this project were so positive that the health fair was replicated in other elementary schools (Courtney et al, 1996).

This mutuality among partners and patients was highlighted when the VNACJ and five other service providers were approached by a regional funder to identify a community project. Sensitive to the community's spoken concern that funded activities should be "of the people," the service providers engaged the community in the development of a community leadership program. Applications were distributed throughout the city of Asbury Park, New Jersey, inviting residents to be leaders with an idea to benefit the community. Enthusiasm abounded and many applied, with 10 leaders being selected. After a weekend retreat, the leaders met weekly for 12 weeks to learn about the history and resources of the city, community development, and leadership skills. The provider agencies, which serve as repositories of the funding, provide a project site and mentorship for the leaders. Among the community projects that the leaders have launched are the following: senior citizen women working with young, school-aged girls in a program called "Be Yourself, Support Yourself"; a creative cultural arts program for elementary school children; a "fun to fitness" group of girls aged 5 to 14 years to learn about their bodies and minds; a Haitian program for children aged 14 to 18 years to encourage them in the development of greater cultural understanding and to teach them how to interact within the community; an entrepreneurial training course for older youth, aged 18 to 21 years, to teach them how to set up their own vendor business; a read-aloud group for children aged 6 to 12 years; a performance art program; and an environmental program titled "We Sea," in which children aged 7 to 12 years are exposed to hands-on activities along the beach. The outcomes of this project were threefold: resolution of community need, development of community pride and well-being, and development of future community leaders.

COMMUNITY ORGANIZING

A community organizing approach, rather than a traditional medical or health-planning model, supports community collaboration and participation. In the medical model, community participation is minimal and the health professional maintains control. Community participation is greater in the health-planning model; however, the intent is to maximize the resources of the professionally defined program, not those of the community itself. In contrast, in the community organizing approach, the community is mobilized through community participation and control, and the professional is the resource and catalyst for change. The program and direction come from the community itself.

An example of the community organizing approach is a community health center launched in a medically underserved area by the VNACJ. The center is a freestanding organization with a board of trustees derived from local community-based organizations and the community itself, and the role of the nurse practitioners in the center has taken on a form much different from that in other community health centers in similar geographical locales. For instance, one of the nurse practitioners spends time weekly at the boys' club, the girls' club, and a middle school to provide education on relevant topics such as health and sexuality. In yet another example, a nurse practitioner provides outreach to senior citizens on the issues of substance abuse, medication compliance, and social isolation. This center has truly taken the form of the community it serves because of a board structure that provides the community a forum for input and control.

As an outgrowth of her experience at the middle school, the nurse practitioner recognized the lack of attention being paid to the emergent issue of neglected adolescent health. Collaboration between the Community Health Center and the local school district enabled the VNACJ to secure a three-year demonstration grant from the Robert Wood Johnson Foundation to augment traditional school nurse services with nurse practitioner services at the middle school. Additionally, the VNACJ's grant writer worked with the district's high school and other community providers to secure funding for the School-Based Youth Services Program from the New Jersey Department of Human Services.

Another method of ensuring that program and direction come from the community itself is to hire from the community in which an organization operates. This is the basic reason for the success of the peer worker programs that have been so effective with hard-to-reach groups such as youth (Sanders, 2001).

The 125 Flower Estate health project in Sheffield, England, has worked to improve the health of people under age 18 since 1998. After identifying that young adults were not utilizing available health services, the group initiated education workshops in which teenagers explore a variety of health topics (e.g., smoking, substance abuse, sex, relationships). The involvement of peer educators using young people with a lot of street credibility proved to be an effective way to discuss risk-taking behaviors and explore ways for youth to resist pressure from peers (Sanders, 2001).

Community organizing and participation require three phases of development: locality development, social planning, and social action. In the locality development phase, the outcome is the cultivation of community capacity to provide self-help, with the professional assuming the role of coordinator and enabler. Social planning involves data collection, with the professional assuming the role of fact gatherer and facilitator. During the social action component, there is a shift in the relationship in an attempt to address social injustices and to create institutional change, with the health care professional assuming the role of activist. Community collaboration thus becomes a self-perpetuating process in which residents initiate future activity after the organization's formal role has been completed (Drevdahl, 1995).

Throughout this process, several action steps must be initiated. It is critical that an exploration of environmental conditions that contribute to illness or interfere with wellness be undertaken. Coalitions must be formed to engage the community in the process. Critical dialogue must be facilitated with community members, and conditions that interfere with full participation must be changed. Finally, because of the interrelationships among local issues and national and international trends, the global environment must be evaluated relative to the grass roots problem that has been identified. Critical discussions focusing on methods available to change larger sociopolitical structures must be conducted (Drevdahl, 1995).

For instance, the economic situation in a locality, state, or nation has a significant impact on how people live and feel. Changing demographics in the community heightened the need for community organization and action in a community served by the VNACJ nurses. Concurrent gentrification and immigration of non-English-speaking residents had taxed health care providers, schools, and churches. Initiated by the School-Based Youth Services Program at the high school, a "unity day" brought the community together.

Another example of the relationship among issues is the Welfare to Work initiative occurring nationally. In New Jersey the process for rolling out the Welfare to Work initiative is overseen on a local level by workforce investment boards comprising welfare beneficiaries and the private and public sectors. A critical issue now being raised is how the initiative will be sustained in the face of large corporate and similar employer downsizing in the area.

These are the kinds of discussions in which nurses must meaningfully participate.

VISIONARY LEADERSHIP

Visionary leadership is imperative in effective community collaboration. The visionary leader is one who remains simultaneously tenacious and decisive, as well as caring and flexible. The group is best served when the leader helps the followers to develop their own initiative. Visionary leadership strengthens individuals in the use of their own judgment and allows them to grow and become better contributors. The shift must be from the health care providers to the community for visionary direction (*Healthy People 2010: Understanding and improving health,* 2000).

An example at the VNACJ involved a collaborative venture with a local Hispanic church. Church leaders and a local physician had identified the need for an on-site primary care center to be situated in a trailer in the church's parking lot. Inquiries by the VNACJ about the possibility of collaboration resulted in the organization's management being sought for a consultation role. Initially the VNACJ manager assumed the role of directing the group, designing a nurse practitioner-physician collaborative model, and preparing proposals to foundations. What quickly became apparent was that the physician and the church leaders felt threatened by what they perceived to be a control issue by the manager.

In a meeting between church leaders and the VNACJ administration, the administration asked a simple question: "What would you like us to do?" That simple question, aimed at returning the locus of control to church leaders, resulted in the VNACJ's role being defined by the group. The VNACJ will continue as a participant, providing on-site nursing, immunization services, and community-based outreach.

Increasingly, the leader is a gatherer of people and a facilitator of processes to help reach agreement (Porter-O'Grady, 1997). Success demands that attention be paid to the external environment. Bennis (1991) identified four basic dimensions as contributing to visionary leadership: management of attention, of meaning, of trust, and of self.

Management of attention is defined as the ability to focus on the vision, even in times of uncertainty and chaos. The critical vision that must underlie any community partnership is the fact that professional-citizen mutuality can be sustained even during the transition process. In fact, professional-citizen mutuality must be maintained not only to sustain partnership but also to achieve the ultimate vision. The VNACJ, in response to community need, developed and began to implement plans for a nurse-managed, community-based primary care center in a high-risk, isolated urban municipality. Stresses within the community were such that political uncertainty existed: controversy among agencies, residents, and city government was the norm. Fourteen city and school elections and re-elections had taken place in less than 4 years. In response to the challenge, the VNACJ leadership met frequently with both elected officials and city management. However, the players and the agenda often changed from meeting to meeting. Management focused on repeating the same message of our vision and mission. In addition, management joined with residents and colleagues at meetings to state the vision and mission. Foremost in those statements were family and community needs as the core reason for the proposal. The vision prevailed, and the center was awarded a certificate of occupancy by the city and a designation as a Federally Qualified Health Center Look-Alike by the federal government. Keeping mission and community partnership foremost, the VNACJ then invited the local health department and the area hospital into partnership, a significant gesture because both had been opponents during the competitive process.

Management of meaning has to do with the ability to communicate. Continuous communication is critical so that professional and citizen participants understand and have input into the direction of the program. Since 1987 a VNACJ manager had served on the boards and committees of three counties, as well as at the state level. Recognized as an expert in the management of services for persons and families with HIV/AIDS, she achieved success in creating partnerships among fiercely competitive organizations as a direct result of her communication style. Through discussion, negotiation, caring, and understanding, the VNACJ manager exhibited active listening, which created a constant feedback loop for participants. She also extended her communication outreach to the grass roots county- and state-level constituencies. As a result of her management of meaning, this regional HIV/AIDS consortium is recognized as a model in the state.

Management of trust is facilitated by ensuring that all stakeholders have a place at the table, and that these collaborators stay involved over time. On December 11, 1992, the importance of management of trust to the promotion of positive community health outcomes was elucidated as a northeaster ravaged the coast of central New Jersey. The VNACJ staff was mobilized to action. Outreach to the American Red Cross, area police departments, and emergency management services resulted in the VNACJ nurses staffing multiple shelters throughout the area. Because of the decade-long relationships in the communities, staff were able to mobilize local merchants and pharmacists to donate and deliver infant formula, clothing, pharmaceuticals, food, and water to the facilities. Many of these efforts necessitated that these persons be transported by means of police department vehicles from their homes to their places of business. On an infrastructure level, the VNACJ brought stakeholders together after the disaster to plan procedures for the future. Issues that were addressed included the temporary placement of frail elderly persons in county long-term care facilities, the emergency release of medications and supplies from area hospitals, and a for-

malized relationship between the VNACJ and the American Red Cross.

This trust was repeated and strengthened after the World Trade Center disaster on September 11, 2001. Building on the relationships developed over the years, VHACJ quickly networked with local chapters of the United Way and the Red Cross to provide emergency relief for victims and families. Staff were mobilized to provide in-home nursing care for victims and respite for mothers with young children. VHACJ also worked with the local mental health board to establish necessary bereavement programs. Long-standing relationships with local health departments also brought community nursing to the forefront as health departments and hospitals developed a countywide disaster plan.

Management of self revolves around the leader's understanding of and sensitivity to her own strengths and weaknesses. If the nurse leader is particularly adept at managing and responding to the global environment, but is less adept at managing operational details, she must pair her own abilities with the abilities of the group. The leader must always be sensitive to enhancing the visibility and accomplishments of the entire group. Successful organizers are those able to enjoy the reflective glow of others' successes.

A program launched by a VNACJ pediatric nurse practitioner (PNP) provides intensive home visiting to vulnerable new patients. Although the PNP brought extensive clinical, managerial, and public health experience to the program, she was not a layperson living in a low-income, blighted urban area. She recruited community members, training them to provide ongoing support and anticipatory guidance. At state and county meetings, the PNP described the success of the program in terms of the peer worker and family accomplishments.

NURSING'S ROLE IN THE COMMUNITY

Working with communities provides the most fertile opportunity for the nursing profession in the new millennium. Key competencies that health care professionals will need in the future include expertise in healthy lifestyles, preventive and primary care, improved communication skills, and enhanced community health and partnership abilities involving complex negotiations. According to Gebbie (1999), public health focuses on populations, communities, and building coalitions. It is key to the community infrastructure and must continually ensure that essential services are available when needed.

Cognizant of the changing expectations of the competencies of registered nurses, the Northeastern University College of Nursing, in collaboration with the Boston University School of Medicine (Gauthier & Metteson, 1995), established four community health centers with the city department of health and hospitals to revamp nursing education. A center for community health, education, research, and science was created, enabling students participating in this project to spend half of their total clinical time in one neighborhood.

Increasingly it is being urged that the concepts of poverty, caring, and activism be included as building blocks of nursing curricula, with home visits and health strategies the teaching tools employed to reinforce these core competencies (Erickson, 1996). The Rural Alabama Health Professional Training Consortium provided interdisciplinary training for nurses and other health professionals from 1990 to 1996 in impoverished rural areas (Leeper, Hullett, & Wang, 2001). There was a significant increase in clinical practice, with over 80% of students considering employment in a rural area after graduation. The VNACJ, with funding from the W.K. Kellogg Foundation, developed a competency-based practice model based on the novice-to-expert continuum. Among the skills required for the expert community health nurse are networking, critical thinking, community development, assessment (of individual, family, and community), care planning, leadership, caseload management, clinical and intervention skills, teaching, case finding, and screening.

At the foundation of effective community collaboration is clinical competence. The role of mentorship will become increasingly critical as society expects nurses not only to master the art of nursing but also to establish networks and foster collaboration. Mentors provide career guidance, role modeling, intellectual stimulation, inspiration, advice, and emotional support. Mentoring is reciprocal; thus it strengthens the profession and enhances leadership role preparation (Vance, 2001; Vance & Olson, 1998).

CONCLUSION

Because of the changing imperatives in the health care delivery system, nurses are uniquely positioned to build on their strong tradition of community-based partnerships. Three concepts that require mastery in this role are a keen understanding of the differentiation between community and population, a broad conceptualization of health, and the development of a collective mind-set. Nurses must seek and understand aggregate data and the community organizing approach. A sensitivity to the larger sociopolitical environment is critical.

Strategies that are essential to succeeding in this role include drawing partners from the grass roots community itself, addressing the needs of the community (not for the community), facilitating community members' ability to be advocates for themselves, and maintaining relationships with stakeholders through time. As a society, we must be committed to maintaining the well-being of communities—the infrastructure of our culture.

REFERENCES

Aldrich, L. (1989). *Children adjusting to new situations.* Moorestown, NJ: Samaritan Hospice.

Armstrong, F. (2001). Addressing workforce issues. *Australian Nursing Journal, 9*(1), 28-30.

Bennis, W. (1991, Winter). Learning some basic truisms about leadership. *Phi Kappa Phi Journal,* 13.

Boyle, A. (2001, August 13). Wanted: More than a few good nurses. *New York Times,* 14CN-3.

Campbell, J. & Aday, R.H. (2001). Benefits of a nurse-managed wellness program: A senior center model. *Journal of Gerontological Nursing, 27*(3), 34-45.

Caro, F.G. & Kaffenberger, K.R. (2001). The impact of financing on workforce recruitment and retention. *Generation, 25*(1), 17-22.

Courtney, R., Ballard, E., Fauver, S., Gariota, M., & Holland, L. (1996, June). The partnership model: working with individuals, families, and communities toward a new vision of health. *Public Health Nursing, 13*(3), 177-186.

Drevadhl, D. (1995, December). Coming to voice: The power of emancipatory community interventions. *Advances in Nursing Science, 18*(2), 13-24.

Erickson, G.P. (1996, June). To pauperize or empower: Public health nursing at the turn of the 20th and 21st centuries. *Public Health Nursing, 13*(3), 163-169.

Farley, S.S. (1995, June). Leadership for developing citizen-professional partnerships: Perspectives on community. *Nursing & Health Care, 16*(4), 226-228.

Faulk, D., Coker, R., & Farley, S. (2001). After the funding is gone. *Nursing and Health Care Perspectives, 22*(4), 184-186.

Gauthier, M.A. & Metteson, P. (1995, November). The role of empowerment in neighborhood-based nursing education. *Journal of Nursing Education, 34*(8), 390-395.

Gebbie, K.M. (1999). The public health workforce: Key to public health infrastructure. *American Journal of Public Health, 89*(5), 660-661.

Glick, D.F. (1999). Advanced practice community health nursing in community nursing centers: A holistic approach to the community as client. *Holistic Nursing Practice, 13*(4), 19-27.

Healthy People 2010: Understanding and improving health (2nd ed.). (2000). Washington, DC: U.S. Department of Health and Human Services.

Leeper, J., Hullett, S., & Wang, L. (2001). Rural Alabama health professional training consortium: Six-year evaluation results. *Family and Community Health. 24*(2), 28-26.

May, K.M., Mendelson, C., & Ferketich, S. (1995, February). Community empowerment in rural health care. *Public Health Nursing, 12*(1), 25-30.

Porter-O'Grady, T. (1997). Quantum mechanics and the future of healthcare leadership. *Journal of Nursing Administration, 27*(10), 15-20.

Rawlings-Anderson, K. (2001). Working with older people from minority ethnic groups. *Nursing Older People. 13*(5), 21-25.

Reinhard, S., Christopher, M.A., Mason, D.J., McConnell, K., Toughill, E., & Rusca, P. (1996). Promoting healthy communities through neighborhood nursing. *Nursing Outlook, 44*(5), 223-228.

Sanders, K. (2001). Three of the best. *Community Practitioner, 74*(7), 253-255.

Smith, R.D., Inoue, T., Ushikubo, M., & Amano, S. (2001). Nursing in Japan. *Australian Nursing Journal, 9*(1), 39-40.

Vance, C. (2001, February-March). The value of mentoring. *Imprint, 38-41.*

Vance, C. & Olson, R.K. (1998). *The mentor connection in nursing.* New York: Springer.

Vignette   Lillian H. Mood

Environmental Health Policy: Environmental Justice

"Only within the moment of time represented by the present century has one species—man—acquired significant power to alter the nature of his world."
RACHEL CARSON

A LANDFILL APPLICATION

In late December 1995 the South Carolina Department of Health and Environmental Control (DHEC) received an application from SERR, Inc., for a permit to construct and operate a landfill. The landfill was proposed to receive debris, including asbestos, from construction and demolition projects. By the time the application was received, two important steps had already been taken. First, the applicant had bought a tract of land just outside the city limits of the county seat, in a rural county, and adjacent to a neighborhood known as the Helena community. Second, the applicant had applied to the county council and had received a *letter of consistency,* stating that this project was consistent with the county's solid waste management plan, a prerequisite in state statute for DHEC consideration of the permit application.

CITIZEN INVOLVEMENT

Other actions had also been taken. A group of citizens from the nearby neighborhood, the Involved Citizens of Helena, had appeared before the county council, asking the council not to approve the project and asking the applicant to choose a different site for his business. The council's response was to send a second letter to DHEC, expressing "unanimous opposition to the location." The applicant's response, as reported in the local newspaper, was that he "would not come into a community where he was not wanted."

The citizens left the council meeting feeling relieved, thinking they had averted what they saw as a damaging addition to their neighborhood, only to learn afterward that the application had been submitted and the county administrator had informed DHEC that the second letter did not rescind the required letter of consistency. I had been alerted to the brewing situation by one of our field staff, who sent me the news account of the council meeting, but my active involvement began with a call from the permitting staff in our state office, asking for help with a citizen request for a "public hearing" on the permit application.

THE NURSE'S ROLE

My job title is Director of Risk Communication and Community Liaison. I work in the deputy area of Environmental Quality Control (EQC) in the state agency charged with responsibility for public health and environmental protection, which includes responsibilities delegated by the United States Environmental Protection Agency (USEPA). After 22 years in public health nursing, in home health services, and on the commissioner's staff, I transferred to EQC because, in the deputy commissioner's words, the environmental programs "needed a nurse." He was speaking of an increased requirement and demand for public participation in regulatory decision making. Through the years his staff of engineers and other environmental scientists had experienced the recurring nightmare of public meetings where they were battered by anger, accusations, and criticism. The messages were: You are not doing enough, you are not acting quickly enough, you are not letting people know enough, and we do not trust you!

Why a nurse? My position is not discipline specific, but my background means that I am comfortable in communities and with citizens in settings where many of our environmental experts feel least comfortable. Calls to my office may come from citizens, from our field or state program staff, from legislators, or from agency management. I am a safe person to call and ask for information or help, or to report a problem. Callers may identify themselves or not, though I always ask if there is a way that I can get back in touch with them. Part of the job is responding to specific concerns. A call may involve a complaint, an inquiry, or the need to get information out to the public on a permit, a spill, or a cleanup plan.

ASSESSING THE SITUATION AND PLANNING FOR PUBLIC PARTICIPATION

When a call relates to a specific site or situation, I put great importance on *being there,* and so it was with the call about the Helena landfill. After getting a little background information from my coworker, I asked who had requested the public hearing and was given the name and telephone number of a retired schoolteacher and administrator. I called him (hereafter referred to as *Mr. R*) and asked whether I could visit him to hear and understand his concerns.

I went to Mr. R's home, armed with the knowledge that our staff was willing to have a meeting even before we reached a point in the process where the law calls for a "public hearing." The date, place, and format were up to me to coordinate. As I sat at Mr. R's dining room table and looked at and listened to the evidence of the citizens' effort, I was impressed with the energy, insight, and commitment of this community to preserve the character of a place they were trying to maintain and improve. I got an even more vivid picture as we drove through the neighborhood and around the site. The Helena community traces its history to the mid-1800s; it was once a township. It has always been a predominantly African-American community (99%), and many residents have a low income. A number of community members who have achieved greater prosperity have chosen to build homes and remain in the community. They are proud of the three churches in the neighborhood and of the plans to build a new middle school nearby. The sense of place, of belonging, and of community spirit is strong. Also strong is the belief that we can accomplish much if we work together, within the community and with institutions such as elected bodies and state agencies. Quiet dignity and persistence were strengths evident on my first contact and were consistent throughout my work with my citizen colleagues in Helena.

We did hold a public meeting on an evening convenient for the residents and in their preferred meeting place (the county courthouse). Those attending included more than 100 citizens, our staff, the applicant, the county administrator, members of the county council, the state senator, a candidate for the state house of representatives (formerly an attorney for DHEC), and the local news media. Citizen attendance was boosted by Mr. R's assistance in distributing flyers that were prepared by our media relations staff. I served as the moderator for the lively and sometimes heated exchange of issues and information.

PUBLIC POLICY ISSUES

When the evening ended, we had a clear map of the issues, which fell into three major policy areas: land use, technical requirements of environmental law and regulations that are designed to protect the public health, and environmental justice.

Land use policy is primarily and predominantly a responsibility of local government. Restrictions on use of land and planning for orderly growth are the products of local ordinances, both city and county. The county council determines where the boundaries lie between commercial, industrial, and residential areas in an unincorporated area. In this county, and in a number of others in South Carolina, councils have been silent on this policy issue. In these counties, there are no land use ordinances to guide development, restrict how an individual may use his property, or protect his neighbors from an undesirable use.

Environmental law and regulations are administered by a combination of state and federal jurisdictions. The waste management laws are state statutes, and DHEC is delegated the authority by the USEPA to enforce the applicable federal requirements. Issues such as protection of wetlands and groundwater, management of storm-water runoff, and protection of air quality are addressed in this policy arena. Permits issued by DHEC to landfill owners and operators specify requirements for construction and operation to protect public safety and environmental quality. DHEC field staff monitor compliance with the requirements of the permits and for any evidence of environmental damage. Enforcement action for violations can be civil action, through the process defined by the State Administrative Procedures Act, or criminal prosecution, if the permit holder "willfully and knowingly" violates the law. Every permit requirement and every enforcement action must withstand the scrutiny and challenge of legal appeals by the

applicant or any person or group with legal standing to appeal. The appeals go through staff review, to DHEC's citizen board, which is appointed by the governor and approved by the state senate to govern the agency, and on to the court(s) with jurisdiction.

Environmental justice is a concept that invokes the protection of the federal Civil Rights Act to ensure that low-income and minority communities do not bear a disproportionate burden of environmental pollution or degradation. In 1994 President Clinton added substantial weight to this principle in Executive Order 12898 by requiring every federal agency to make "environmental justice part of its mission by identifying and addressing, as appropriate, disproportionately high and adverse human health or environmental effects of its programs, policies, and activities on minority populations and low-income populations." (See the third Vignette in Chapter 26.) There is not yet a body of case law clarifying what conditions and what criteria are sufficient to support a decision based on ensuring environmental justice.

POTENTIAL SOLUTIONS

Two unexpected possible solutions also emerged from that early public meeting. A county councilman said that DHEC should have communicated directly with the council rather than the administrator on the apparent contradiction in the letters we received. We said we would revisit that issue with the council. Citizens began to hope that the council would rescind the letter of consistency, which would stop the DHEC permitting process but would likely lead to the applicant's filing suit against the council. The second possible solution came as an offer by another councilman to meet with the applicant to discuss a possible "land swap" for a more suitable site. Again, hopes rose that an amicable solution could be found. When parties with disparate agendas are willing to meet and have civil discussions, win-win outcomes are possible that are unavailable if only adversarial methods are employed to resolve issues. Encouraging, advocating, arranging for, and facilitating such discussions are major features of my practice.

An expected question from the citizens in the public meeting was directed to us as regulators: "Do you have or would you want a landfill in your neighborhood?" We responded that we would not want to share our neighborhoods with a landfill. This acknowledgment of common ground on the undesirability of landfills in residential areas was important because it not only affirmed the reasonableness of the citizens' objective but also has kept the focus on what we have the legal authority to do, not on what we might *want* to do. It has also freed me to state openly and candidly, in my conversations with citizens and elected officials and in staff policy discussions, that my agenda is to find a legally defensible way to "do the right thing."

At this point, we did confirm with the county council members their decision that the proposed landfill was consistent with their plan for waste management. We recognized that they saw benefits in avoiding litigation, in gaining the 50-cent-per-ton revenue for the county from the landfill's operation, and in attracting additional industrial development by having the infrastructure for industrial waste disposal.

ENVIRONMENTAL JUSTICE

The environmental justice questions were addressed in several ways. Our staff prepared maps, using Geographic Information Systems (GIS) technology, to examine patterns of landfill locations and the demographics of the population across the state. We did not find a pattern of siting in minority communities. One of our senior managers and I took the maps to Mr. R and a minister from the citizen group and went over what we had done, so they would have this information before the formal public hearing. The issue of whether census block data are specific enough to make judgments about nearest-neighbor populations was raised in the hearing, and the citizens' attorney signaled an intent to make environmental justice an issue. The citizens, however, put their initial focus on unfair treatment, treatment that discriminates on the basis of race, on the county council's actions. They filed a complaint with the U.S. Justice Department, citing Title VI of the Civil Rights Act. The complaint was disallowed, however, because the county government did not receive federal funds and so did not fall within the Justice Department's jurisdiction.

ADMINISTRATIVE PROCEDURES PROCESS

Our staff completed its review of the technical issues and issued public notice of a draft permit, with a prescribed comment period and a public hearing. Again with the assistance of Mr. R, flyers were distributed and a notice was published in the newspaper. This time there were about 200 citizens who spoke "on the record," citing the reasons for their opposition to the landfill. My role was to work with the citizens to get the speakers in the order they wished, to welcome people, to honor one citizen's request that he begin by offering a prayer, and then to explain how the procedure for a formal hearing would be different from our earlier meeting. Then I listened. A hearing officer and a court reporter took responsibility for managing the hearing. I felt admiration for the thoroughness with which the citizens got every relevant point into the formal proceedings. It was also gratifying to see the support they had assembled: the leader of a statewide environmental advocacy organization, a competent and articulate attorney to serve as their legal counsel, and the newly elected state representative, who became their effective advocate. In addition, we responded to inquiries on the community's behalf from a U.S. senator and from legal counsel in the governor's office.

The staff's work after the hearing was to consider each of the issues raised, prepare a written response, and reach a final decision on whether the permit should be issued. In that process, two new laws affected the application: one was a more restrictive limit on the area of wetlands that could be affected, and the second was a provision that the landfill area (the "footprint") could not be within 1000 feet of the nearest residence. The combined effect of these two factors resulted in a decrease by nearly one third in the area available for landfill use. Despite these limitations, the applicant revised his plans accordingly and continued his pursuit of a permit.

KEEPING THE COMMUNITY INFORMED

When the staff completed their review and their response to all the issues noted at the hearing, the permit engineer, two senior management staff, and I met with representatives of the Involved Citizens group to go over the changes in the application and the staff conclusion that all the permit requirements had been satisfied. In addition to four members of the citizens' group, we were joined by the state representative and one of the Caucasian owners of the adjacent land. The representative requested that we delay a decision until we obtained a court opinion on the status of a regulation cited at the hearing. The adjacent land owner asked that we allow him additional time to negotiate a different site with the applicant, and the Helena citizens expressed despair that their community's concerns would not affect the outcome.

When we displayed two maps showing the effect of the two new laws on the landfill area, the landowner said, "Wait a minute! My father just put a mobile home on the shore of the pond at the corner of the property. I know it is within 1000 feet of the landfill!" On inspection, and after verification that the mobile home met the definition of a "residence" (i.e., a well, a waste disposal system permit, and a county seal), the applicant was notified that the permit could not be issued because the plans as presented violated the 1000-foot buffer. Within hours the applicant submitted a revised application that met the requirement and further decreased the area of the footprint by 20%.

POSSIBLE OUTCOMES

The staff called me on vacation to tell me that the permit had been issued, and when I returned, I learned that the citizens had filed an appeal. Any of several outcomes could be envisioned at this point in the process:

1. *The applicant could withdraw his application or find a different site.* The owner of the adjacent land met with the applicant to propose alternative locations. The applicant's attorney (also a former DHEC attorney) told me that he would advise his client to take that option if a reasonable alternative were available. Another suggestion was that the citizens offer to help defray the applicant's environmental investigation costs for a new site with resources they would otherwise invest in litigation. The applicant was unwilling to consider an alternative site.

2. *The county council could decide to rescind its letter of consistency.* There was renewed energy among some of the citizens at the hearing to approach the council once again.

3. *The administrative law judge hearing the appeal could find that the regulation cited by the citizens' attorney and their representative was grounds for denial of the permit.* The regulation cited has not previously been applied in similar applications. The DHEC legal staff examined the implications of its application in this case. The finding and recommendation of the administrative law judge would have to be upheld by the DHEC governing board.

As unlikely as it seemed to many who were closely watching the process, the county council did submit a letter to DHEC rescinding their letter of consistency. The letter was received after all evidence had been presented to the administrative law judge, and it was unclear how the new letter should be incorporated into the process. The letter was submitted by DHEC to the judge, asking that it be considered in the decision. The judge ruled in favor of the community and against the permit on the basis of that letter. The DHEC governing board upheld the judge's ruling, and the landfill was not built.

COMMUNITY ORGANIZATION AND STRENGTHS

How do we account for the success of this citizen group, in the face of what must have seemed to them overwhelming odds? They were a small community, inexperienced in regulatory procedures and with limited financial resources. But more important were the following features:

- They had a clear message and they delivered it firmly and consistently: "A landfill should not be built so close to where people live."
- They had a vision for their community: "A landfill in our neighborhood will kill people's dreams. When you kill dreams, you kill people. What child can hope and aspire to achieving when his daily view is a 'dump'?"
- They pulled together and organized their effort.
- They were present, visible, and persistent at every step of the process.

- They pooled their resources to acquire the legal help they needed.
- They made allies, not enemies.

CRITERIA FOR WORKING WITH COMMUNITIES

In reviewing my own and my professional colleagues' participation in this project, I hear five recurring themes of public expectations, and I use them as my personal quality indicators. Repeatedly, in many different ways, citizens tell me they expect us to

- Listen
- Take them seriously
- Treat them with respect
- Give them straight information
- Do what we say we will do

My assessment is that we were true to these standards with the Helena community.

Our staff often feel the stress of the legal limits of their regulatory authority to address community priorities. They do their work for environmental protection in the context of a political climate that is sensitive to "government interference" in individual property rights, and where great value is placed on economic development. An ongoing part of my job will be explaining the process as it unfolds and interpreting the reasoning behind decisions to a variety of people, who may or may not be happy with the outcome.

DOING THE RIGHT THING WITHIN THE RULES

In this case, the county council, the regulatory agency, the judicial process, the DHEC board, and, most of all, the community found a way within the regulations to "do the right thing." This experience gave me renewed determination to continue to give the community a voice in decisions that affect them, to articulate citizens' perspectives in policy discussions, and to be an advocate for aggressively using whatever tools we have to prevent environmental problems. Perhaps most important, all of us will continue to search for ways to ensure that a broad definition of healthy communities, like the one envisioned and modeled by the Involved Citizens of Helena, is supported in public policy.

POLICYSPOTLIGHT

TURNING POINT: COLLABORATING FOR A NEW CENTURY IN PUBLIC HEALTH

Gloria R. Smith, Barbara J. Sabol, & Kay Randolph-Back

"You see things, and you say, 'Why?' But I see things that never were, and I say, 'Why not?'"
                                    GEORGE BERNARD SHAW

A current initiative of the W.K. Kellogg Foundation has much to teach nurses about informing policy change. *Turning Point: Collaborating for a New Century in Public Health* (1996 to 2002) has supported partnerships in 41 communities in 14 states. Nurses are active members and leaders in a number of these broad-based partnerships. Indeed, the reader may quickly gain a feel for the work of Turning Point overall from a concrete story about the involvement of nurses in the initiative.

The W.K. Kellogg Foundation

The W.K. Kellogg Foundation (www.wkkf.org) has made significant contributions to the practice and discipline of nursing in the course of its 72 years of philanthropy. A strong alignment exists between nursing and the foundation's values. *To help people help themselves,* the visionary and timeless mission W.K. Kellogg gave to the foundation he formed, is good for all seasons. A few simple words express a profound belief in people—in their intrinsic worth and their capacities—and conviction about their abilities to face challenges and solve problems. During the time he was determining how he would deploy the great wealth he had accumulated since beginning in business selling brooms at the age of 14, Mr. Kellogg was invited to the 1930 White House Conference on Child Health and Protection, which deeply influenced him (W.K. Kellogg Foundation, 1991). To carry out his decision to invest his money in people (Powell, 1956), Mr. Kellogg established a foundation in 1930.

TURNING POINT PREVIEW AND NURSES' INVOLVEMENT

One of the Turning Point partnerships in a southwestern state represents two quite distinct minority groups. One is a reservation-based Native American community. Another is an African-American faith-based partnership in a city where off-reservation, urban Native Americans also reside. With the leadership of women—a Native American nurse who heads the reservation health department and an African-American urban pastor—the two partnerships are now working together, sharing resources, and collaborating on a diabetes control plan to serve both off-reservation Native Americans and African Americans, as well as Hispanic, Asian-American, and other community members. Urban residents are being mobilized through Neighborhood Healing Circles, and the members of a local nurses' organization are volunteering their time for conducting workshops, health fairs, and one-on-one counseling on diabetes. The educational materials are provided by the state.

In this introductory illustration we can see several important things happening. Under its nurse executive's leadership, the reservation's health de-partment has gained an urban ally and partner in serving the needs of off-reservation Indians. The urban faith-based organization (FBO) has gained a public health partner. The ability of an FBO to mobilize neighborhood residents has been combined with the professional expertise of the public health partner and the nurse volunteers. The work of these volunteers, who use public health materials from the state to serve community members mobilized by the FBO, has the effect of expanding the public health workforce available for diabetes control in underserved communities.

Changing Awareness of Public Health

Let us look at this illustration from another perspective. We see community members, community organizations, public agencies, and volunteering professionals becoming actively engaged together in a process that is awakening people from many walks of life to the awareness that they can participate in improving the public's health. Thus, this story illustrates not only the "how to" in Turning Point, but also the initiative's premise that *everyone has a stake in public health.* Turning Point is demonstrating the ability of broad-based partnerships to awaken and engage communities around "ownership" and action on public health. Community awakening and engagement can bring new resources, energy, ideas, and promise to the renewal of public health. In addition, the promise for renewal through partnership brings nurses new opportunities to make contributions that are both uniquely theirs and essential to healing and health in communities. What nurses can offer is so special that it really gives rise to a duty—a moral obligation, if you will—to work with communities. We will attempt to show why we believe nurses are uniquely qualified to be community change agents by examining Turning Point and its implications from three perspectives:

- The viewpoint "on the ground"—how Turning Point is being implemented and how nurses are involved
- The conceptual viewpoint—why informing policy change *is* nursing
- The grant maker's viewpoint—where Turning Point fits strategically

VIEWPOINT ON THE GROUND: CASE STUDY OF TURNING POINT'S IMPLEMENTATION AND NURSES' INVOLVEMENT

Public health has a long tradition of lengthening life span and improving quality of life, but new threats demand new approaches to public health. Violence, for example, is now a public health problem because it ranks high among causes of death and disability. Community health statistics also show consequences from risk taking by youth that older public health approaches are hard-pressed to deal with (e.g., human immune deficiency virus [HIV], acquired immune deficiency syndrome [AIDS]), pregnancies among increasingly younger children, and drug-related deaths. Finally, the shift from infectious diseases to chronic diseases as the nation's major killers calls for new approaches. Vaccines and quarantine will not prevent or control heart disease that develops throughout a lifetime. Community norms, community health education, and opportunities the community offers for healthful choices and lifestyles contribute significantly to the prevention of chronic diseases. To address the new challenges, public health must innovate and mobilize new partners and resources. Unfortunately, because its infrastructure of organizations and professionals has weakened over the years, the U.S. system of protecting public health is poorly equipped for innovation and mobilization.

Renewal and transformation of public health are the purpose of Turning Point: Collaborating for a New Century in Public Health. At the local level, it provides public health systems with practical opportunities for results-oriented innovation and mobilization. A joint initiative of two foundations, Turning Point also provides support at the state level. In this joint effort, started in 1996, the Kellogg Foundation funded partnerships in 41 communities located in 14 states in which the Robert Wood Johnson Foundation funded state health departments. Since local and state public health functions are complementary, the two foundations created Turning Point as a joint initiative in which complementary grants would be made to the two levels in the same states. (The Robert Wood Johnson Foundation later added to the initiative 7 states that have no local funding component.)

The multisector partnerships in 41 communities were funded to organize around what they defined as priority community health issues. Community engagement in solving community health problems was intended to make public health—in a broad sense, not as a governmental department—visible and meaningful across diverse sectors. The theory was that, by bringing new resources, strategies, commitment, and purpose to public health, the local partners would increase the ability of the whole community, including its public health agency, to meet twenty-first-century challenges. The Turning Point experience has borne out the theory. As people and organizations came to recognize their own stake in public health, they brought their energy and resources to creating new solutions to community health problems. Turning Point demonstrates how communities can change to a model of broad-based partnership and community engagement for carrying out local public health responsibilities.

The National Association of County and City Health Officials (NACCHO) is the Kellogg Foundation's intermediary for the initiative. It has been funded to regrant money to the communities and to provide various types of technical assistance for the communities and the foundation. Initially, through NACCHO, the foundation awarded each community partnership $20,000 a year for 3 years along with an opportunity to apply after 2 years for a supplementary grant for implementing a system improvement plan developed during those 2 years. During the design of Turning Point the premise was established that readiness exists in the field, and providing modest incentives and the occasion for action would activate the readiness and catalyze transformation.

The partnerships are very broad based. They include community-based organizations, churches, hospitals, police and fire departments, schools, parent organizations, youth groups, tribal governments, county commissions, civic groups, and businesses. Local health departments participate but do not run the show.

The partnerships designed and implemented unique projects. Working together on projects served to develop trust among the partners and capacity within their partnerships to take their work to the next stage of development through which they would continue to take action. They used their relationships and their experience and accomplishments with projects to develop and submit the longer-range plans for improving the systems that the initiative's premise called for. Projects and planning were both supported by processes for assessing community health and for engaging the community in setting priorities. In December 2000 NACCHO funded 17 of the 41 communities for 1 year of plan implementation.

Involvement of Nurses in Turning Point

Many nurses are involved in the Turning Point partnerships, as members and leaders. The significant contributions of nurses will be illustrated by stories from three partnerships in urban, rural, and reservation settings.

Nurturing community decision making and leadership in an urban setting. One leader is a nurse who is employed as the senior executive of the city-county health department in a mid-sized city in the southern United States. Her work for Turning Point began because of that position. Although her position with the health department has remained the same, her role in Turning Point has evolved. It is a sign of the high quality of her leadership that her role in Turning Point is no longer that of leader but of consultant. Her position allows her to place Turning Point partnership issues on the health department's agenda and to support the partnership's plans with resources. She still has formal authority in the partnership, but she has handed off functional leadership. The second-round funding this partnership has received to implement its system improvement plan will strengthen the leadership capacity she has nurtured in the community. The partnership is establishing the Center for Empowered Decisionmaking in the city to enhance the opportunities for residents to continue to work together on public health. The center will foster the development of community leadership, collaborative planning, community-based research, neighborhood-level data collection, and policy development. What the nurse leader who formally heads this partnership has done to help people help themselves may be inherent in how nurses practice. It may manifest the inherent ethos in nursing.

Nurturing nontraditional leaders in a rural setting. In a quite different Turning Point setting, another nurse leader is demonstrating the power of treating others as leaders to produce positive results. The setting is a remote town in a sparsely populated southwestern state. A nurse leader in the area's Turning Point partnership has put special emphasis on recognizing the leadership capacity of people who are seen negatively—because of their criminal records—by the power structure within the community. She has created a place and a space at the table for them where they are now able to say to the mayor, the judge, and the city council members at the meeting, as well as to her, "This is what we need you to do." Again, the recognition and nurturing of nontraditional leaders involves not only sharing and transferring power, but also sharing and transferring resources through which the emerging nontraditional leaders can "make positive things happen."

Fostering cooperation on a reservation. A nurse heads a tribal health department in another southwestern state. Even in the comparatively homogeneous and cohesive environment of a reservation, the service agencies and the hospital were compartmentalized in their own silos. Organizations that should have been connected around common interests in public health and disease prevention were not. There were no links with non-Native American public health, and there was no Native American voice in public health broadly, although the factors that affect health do not themselves honor reservation and departmental boundaries. With her leadership, agreements were reached for common disease reporting within the reservation boundaries and data sharing across the reservation boundaries between the tribal council and the state. Another boundary-crossing development spearheaded by this Turning Point partnership was the decision by NACCHO to include representation of tribal health authorities on its board.

Policy Work of the Turning Point Partnerships

This case study views policy very broadly as decisions in both the public and private sectors that potentially affect the health of the people in a community. Employing this broad definition, the case study offers the reader information about the policy work in Turning Point at three levels: (1) the bird's-eye view, (2) examples to illustrate the range of strategies, and (3) the actual work of two partnerships. The bird's-eye view is of the themes of system improvement strategies. These are six areas in which, according to Turning Point experience, action is essential if public health in communities is to be transformed. The case study then moves in closer to the concrete work by using examples to illustrate the wide range of the particular strategies for action pursued by Turning Point partnerships. Finally, the case study drills down on the work of two partnerships.

Themes of system improvement strategies. The thought and work of many parties at the local and national levels have gone into Turning Point. The intermediary, NACCHO, brings this thought and work together in a recent publication, *Advancing Community Public Health Systems in the 21st Century: Emerging Strategies and Innovations from the Turning Point Experience* (Rhein, Lafronza, Bhandari, Hawes, & Hofrichter, 2001). This book captures the essence of the complement of policy and systems changes necessary to transform public health in the following six themes of system improvement strategies (p. 33):

- Creating and sustaining organizational structures that support collaborative decision making and action
- Expansion of the scope of public health to address social, economic, and environmental determinants of health and quality of life
- Building capacity for assessing, monitoring, and reporting community health and well-being
- Aligning policy environments and policy development processes with the new public health vision
- Fostering public awareness and engagement in the work of public health
- Strengthening the human resources of public health: transforming workforce and community leadership

Range of policy targets. Partnerships defined their own work to improve health in the community. Neither the foundation nor the intermediary gave the partnerships preset targets for work in policy; indeed, it would have contradicted the principle of community ownership to have done so. As a result Turning Point has a wide spectrum of diverse policy targets. As one would expect, community-defined priorities for public health action differed widely and reflected local issues, capacities, and characteristics. The range of policy targets mirrors the uniqueness of communities. For example, one partnership chose a sewer system as its target for policy change, while another chose to restructure governance for rural public health in 12 towns in order to create new authority and oversight for community health improvement. A third partnership gave priority to a rural transportation system, and a fourth focused on water fluoridation. In another community the partnership actively backed a millage tax increase that created extra funds for public health and worked with a business group and speakers' bureau to win the support of the local community, private businesses, and public organizations. Laws for seat belt use and graduated drivers' licenses were one partnership's targets. In another area, a collaborative effort that coalesced through the Turning Point partnership brought together federal grant dollars with volunteered labor, engineering expertise, and landscaping and construction equipment to create a bike trail.

In 1997 the national media covered Chautauqua, New York, because an alarming rise in HIV-positive tests was traced to one young male drug dealer. Shaken, the community sought a Turning Point grant to initiate a new public health approach to adolescent risk taking: developing members of the youth population—the population *at* risk and *taking* risks—to provide leadership for changing behaviors and reducing risks. Today, youth who are called "kidsultants" work with public health professionals, host youth summits, participate in public health decision making, and guide the growth of a youth alliance for behavioral change initiatives. Young people also apply for grants to promote youth well-being. Through reframing leadership, redeploying resources, and recognizing youth as the solution, not the problem, the partnership has created an environment in which youth have chosen to become active stakeholders in public health.

Asthma was one focus of the partnership effort in Decatur, Illinois. People were mobilized by a desire to reduce the burden of asthma, which falls especially heavily on low-income minority children. The intermediary's new publication reports the following:

> Until recently, Decatur was the only community with a population over 75,000 in Illinois that still allowed leaf burning. Turning Point partners took advantage of the momentum established by a leaf-raking project involving more than 1000 youths to build pressure for policy change. The city council passed an ordinance for a burn ban that began in October 2000. The partnership has also influenced city-funded programming. Overall, the Decatur Community Partnership has fostered a new relationship with the city's decision-makers, and members are recognized as legitimate and valued community spokespeople. (Rhein et al, 2001, p. 44)

The evolution of the partnership's work on asthma is very instructive for understanding how to work with communities for change. So far, we can see progression from reducing leaf burning by mobilizing youth to volunteer to help seniors by raking leaves for removal, to securing city council adoption of an ordinance to ban leaf burning. To see the next stage in this progression, we should now add another aspect of the partnership to the picture: Decatur has developed two related lines of community health improvement in parallel. It has coordinated projects at the same time that it has facilitated multifaceted community engagement and action planning to strengthen policies and systems that undergird those projects. This planning work resulted in the third stage of asthma-related work: organizing ongoing work among partners on improving air quality.

Here is how the third stage came into being. While the partnership conducted and capitalized on the leaf-raking project, it also engaged in long-range planning. The partnership used a comprehensive community engagement process to learn the community's priorities and drafted action plans on the five top priorities for the community to review. One priority for continued work is the environment. Decatur is one of the 17 (out of the original 41) Turning Point communities to receive a supplementary grant to implement a system improvement plan. The planned work on improving air and water quality includes development of a relationship-building model involving business. The Decatur Turning Point Partnership is taking work that began with

youth's raking leaves to improve the lives of kids with asthma, to work in the corporate sector to address air quality for all the community.

This concrete project exemplifies Turning Point, as it addresses the problem of asthma by starting a line of progressive development arising from both components of partnership work—projects and planning. The strategic design of the initiative allows participants to build relationships of trust by working together on concrete projects and to gain momentum from early, concrete results. The longer-range planning places those results within the context of systems change and creates the possibility of sustaining and building on the results.

CONCEPTUAL VIEWPOINT: INFORMING POLICY CHANGE IS NURSING

Having discussed what the partnerships have done and how nurses have been involved, we now offer a concept the reader may use as a novel lens to bring into focus the implications of the Turning Point experience for the practice and discipline of nursing.

Helping people help themselves is both the mission of the Kellogg Foundation and the essence of nursing. The vision held by the National League for Nursing of a health care system centered on the patient (National League for Nursing, 1993, p. 6) embodies belief in the worth and innate authority of the individual as a human being *and* the gifts and powers the patient has to contribute to health and healing.

Nurses' Experience with Helping Communities

Nurses are highly skilled in helping individuals and families solve problems and help themselves. But what is the experience of nurses that is relevant to helping people solve their communities' problems that affect the health of many individuals and families? The experience may be greater than nurses generally recognize. The historical tradition of public health nursing in neighborhoods laid the foundations of professionalism and impact for a discipline that later became more institution centered, in the hospital and the university. That tradition began a resurgence in the last decade with developments in health professions education and practice that have been characterized as bringing nurses "out of the tower and onto the streets" (Meservey & Zungolo, 1995, p. 1). Developing in the 1980s, the parish nurse movement is also noteworthy because it deploys nurses as sources of primary care and referral for congregations and brings nursing care into community places of worship. Another point to recognize is that, as caring and active people, nurses become involved with their communities, but perhaps do not see themselves as wearing their nursing "hats" when doing so. Rather, many may see themselves as nurses only at the bedside, the nursing station, the nursing administrator's desk, the clinic, or the physician's office. Finally, nurses are repositories of knowledge about the social determinants of health that they have learned from practical experience. Recent research is building a body of scientific evidence about these determinants (Kawachi & Kennedy, 1999; Kawachi, Kennedy, & Wilkinson, 1999), but nurses have practical working knowledge, based on their daily practice, of the impact of determinants such as poverty and racial and class discrimination.

Nurses, then, are beginning to expand their vision of the whole person they care for. Nurses are increasing their understanding that this vision encompasses not only the family but also the community and even the society to which the person belongs. When we look at this larger sphere of relevance to health, we see that the policies within this sphere are the result of collective decision making. We are moving from the sphere of individual choice that affects the individual's health and is made by a patient we are working with, to the sphere of collective choice that affects the health of individuals, including patients we are working with. As nurses, we need to see the whole person within the context of choices made by others, collectively, that can have a more pronounced effect on the person's health than the microbe for which a prescription has been written.

Role of Policy in Helping Communities

Policies of different kinds can have an effect on the health of the individual. At the Kellogg Foundation we speak of public, institutional, and marketplace policies as relevant to health. They certainly do not all involve law or regulation. They are all contained, of course, within the larger realm of social policy. An illustration of marketplace policy is the coalition of large health care purchasers (e.g., General Motors) known as the Leapfrog Group that selects health care suppliers (i.e., providers) based on the suppliers' documented performance on measures of patient safety (Milstein, Galvin, Delbanco, Salber, & Buck, 2000). The Leapfrog Group's is a private-sector response to reports on patient safety, such as *To Err Is Human* (Institute of Medicine, Committee on Quality of Health Care in America, 2000). It deploys power in the marketplace to promote positive change. This is in contrast to governmental power to license health care organizations, authority that is not infrequently codified in public health codes and vested in public health departments. As we think about the implications of Turning Point for nursing and policy, we should keep in mind that decisions affecting population health can be made in many places and that, as a result, many people are already acting as stakeholders and influential forces in the public's health without necessarily seeing themselves as such.

Role of Nurses in Helping Communities through Policy Change

In working with individuals and families, nurses focus on people who are helping themselves through making individual and family decisions and choices directed toward improving and assuring health and preventing harm to health. When nurses are prompted by their vision of the whole person to work on the community context for their patients, the essence of what they do does not change, but the level within the social structure at which they do it does. *Nursing practice in and with communities keeps the focus on people who are helping themselves but moves the locus for making decisions and choices to the collective.* We have defined policy as the result of collective decision making. The inherent nature of nursing practice—to help people help themselves—undergoes a developmental unfolding when nurses widen their scope of practice to include the communities of the individuals and families they serve. The move to the collective venue might be said to transform patient education into policy education. The fundamental thrust of the nursing discipline does not change when the venue changes, but the potential impact of that thrust does. Sound collective community decision making is essential to the health of individuals and families because the decisions shape the social determinants of health. Change in policy can affect many individuals and families, more than a single practitioner can serve with personal services.

Policy making, of course, has levels too. State and national policies are determined by elected or appointed officials. At the local and community levels, people can participate actively and *directly* in the policy setting done by public and private local authorities. Collective decisions and choices have as much potency, if not more, as individual and family decisions and choices in improving and assuring health and preventing harm to health. Helping people in communities help themselves by bringing about policy and systems change is central to Kellogg Foundation programming. Since the foundation and the nursing profession share the goal of helping people help themselves, is there an implication for nursing in the foundation's practice of supporting work on policy change and systems change as a way of helping people help themselves? We suggest that the answer to that question is yes and offer for consideration the concept that *informing policy is a central role and responsibility in nursing practice at the community level.*

GRANT MAKER'S VIEWPOINT: WHERE TURNING POINT FITS STRATEGICALLY

Strategic Action to Achieve Lasting Change

The Turning Point Initiative belongs to a strategic plan for achieving lasting social change that improves health status and health care. The foundation's strategic plan is directed toward achieving an overall health goal of *improving the health of people in communities through increased access to integrated, comprehensive health care systems that are organized around primary health care, public health, and prevention and that are led, managed, and staffed by a broad range of appropriately prepared personnel.* The premise of the plan is that improving the health of people requires action on four fronts:

* *Access:* Access to care must be increased.
* *Service delivery:* The system to which people have access must be stronger and be able to promote and maintain health at affordable cost while also treating the very sick.

* *Health workforce and leadership development:* The people who work in and lead the health system must be educated for the stronger focus on primary care, prevention, and public health in meeting the health needs of an increasingly diverse population.
* *Policy education and change:* These are necessary for *enabling* and *sustaining* improvements in access, services, and preparation of caregivers and leaders.

Foundation grantees build models of primary care and public health, develop leaders and caregivers in health services and researchers in health policy and evaluation, build the pipeline for increased participation by minorities in the health professions, and strengthen the ability of communities to inform health policy.

Programming addresses access and cost issues by supporting a shift in focus from tertiary care to primary care. For example, in a number of projects nurse-managed primary care is creating access to high-quality, cost-effective, affordable care for underserved people. The strategic approach goes further, however, placing individual health within the context of family and community and incorporating public health and prevention into the definition of the health system. The Turning Point experience demonstrates that nurses are key leaders in building new partnership models for protection of community health.

A Tradition of Public Health Programming

The foundation has a strong tradition of public health programming. From 1931 to 1951, it provided $6.3 million to the Michigan Community Health Project in seven rural Michigan counties, directly employing more than two dozen nurses who worked with communities. New health departments were established and subsidized, and models of rural public health were created to inform the nation. The project became a field-training center for students in health professions from all geographic areas and disciplines. Other centers were established in universities.

Following World War II, the foundation's health focus shifted away from public health. In the 1980s, as it worked in new ways with community-based organizations, the foundation again gave attention to public health and funded the Institute of Medicine study, *The Future of Public Health,* which reported that America's system of providing public health services was weakened and in disarray (Institute of Medicine, Committee for the Study of the Future of Public Health, 1988).

The Community-Based Public Health Initiative (1991 to 1996) connected communities to the academic preparation and actual practice of public health professionals. Consortia in seven sites brought local public health and community-based organizations together with schools of public health and other health professions schools, including schools of nursing in some sites. The Turning Point Initiative builds on learning from the Community-Based Public Health Initiative about strengthening practice through community involvement in improving the public's health.

CONCLUSION

Nurses infuse the power of relationships into the processes of healing and creating health. Relationships are resources for health. In patient-centered care, nurses create new resources for health and healing by forming relationships with patients. Nurses also activate, enrich, and maintain resources for health and healing by bolstering relationships between patients and their family members or other caregivers. The caregiving that is given by or supported by nurses is more than giving care; it is also giving caring. It moves beyond transactions between people to human relationships, which are life-transforming forces. Nurses nurture relationships. The Turning Point Initiative nurtures community partnerships, that is, relationships among organizations, groups, and residents. Productively participating in partnerships like those in Turning Point is, therefore, natural for nurses. Partnership, like relationship in general, creates resources. The relationship itself is a resource, and the act of working in relationship uncovers and mobilizes *untapped* resources and may even create *new* resources. Turning Point can even be seen as an application of the principles, premises, and practices of nursing to *community* health and healing, rather than to health and healing of the individual patient.

Nurses are acculturated into the principles, premises, and practices of nursing and their application to patient-centered care. Nurses can develop skills that enable them to apply the principles, premises, and practices to the collective level. The work of nurses in Turning Point offers models; but innovation involves creating models, not just following them. Thus, Turning Point offers an inspiring lesson more important than any given model: by working *with* communities, *you* can nurture, awaken, create, and deploy forces and resources for the health and healing of the collective by the collective—health and healing that are of, by, and for the community.

REFERENCES

Institute of Medicine, Committee for the Study of the Future of Public Health. (1988). *The future of public health.* Washington, DC: National Academy Press.

Institute of Medicine, Committee on Quality of Health Care in America. (2000). *To err is human: Building a safer health system.* Kohn, L.T., Corrigan, J., & Donaldson M.S. (Eds.). Washington, DC: National Academy Press.

Kawachi, I. & Kennedy, B.P. (1999). Income inequality and health: Pathways and mechanisms. *Health Services Research* 34(1), 215-227.

Kawachi, I., Kennedy, B.P., & Wilkinson, R.G. (Eds.). (1999). *The society and population health reader: Vol. 1: Income inequality and health.* New York: New Press.

Meservey, P.M. & Zungolo, E. (1995). Out of the tower and onto the streets: One college of nursing's partnership with communities. In P.S. Matteson (Ed.). *Teaching nursing in the neighborhoods: The Northeastern University model.* New York: Springer.

Milstein, A., Galvin, R.S., Delbanco, S.F., Salber, P., & Buck, C.R. (2000, November/December). Improving the safety of health care: The leapfrog initiative. *Effective Clinical Practice.* Retrieved online, August 10, 2001, from www.acponline.org/journals/ecp/novdec00/milstein.htm.

National League for Nursing. (1993). *A vision for nursing education.* New York: Author.

Powell, H.B. (1956). *The original has this signature—W.K. Kellogg.* Englewood Cliffs, NJ: Prentice-Hall.

Rhein, M., Lafronza, V., Bhandari, E., Hawes, J., & Hofrichter, R. (2001). *Advancing community public health systems in the 21st century: Emerging strategies and innovations from the Turning Point experience.* Washington, DC: National Association of County and City Health Officials.

W.K. Kellogg Foundation. (1991). *I'll invest my money in people* (6th ed.). Battle Creek, MI: Author.

35 Nursing in the International Community

JUDITH A. OULTON

"We cannot live for ourselves alone. Our lives are connected by a thousand invisible threads . . . our actions run as causes and return to us as results."

HERMAN MELVILLE

In the late 1960s Marshall McLuhan coined the term *global village*. McLuhan was referring to the fact that through advances in communications, time and space have vanished. Not only was there a new, multisensory view of the world in 1967, but people from around the world could communicate as if they lived in the same village. Yet when McLuhan outlined his vision nearly 35 years ago, the Internet did not exist, nor did the World Trade Organization and its Global Agreement on Trade in Services. Acquired immune deficiency syndrome (AIDS) was a little-known wasting disease in Africa, and the world was celebrating its first heart transplant and bypass operations.

During the past 30-odd years we have witnessed the increased globalization of commerce, travel, information, trade, and disease. In 1967, the United States recorded 13.4 million international passengers on U.S. scheduled airlines. In 1999, Air Transport Association records showed 53.1 million international passengers (Air Transport Association, 2001). In 2002, people, images, and messages move about the world with ease, and we truly have a sense of being a global village. Today we have a professional obligation to understand the village/world in its broader context and to base our decision making on a broader understanding of ourselves, our clients, and our circumstances. By having a global view, we are capable of synthesizing a broad range of information to make informed decisions. It begins with understanding the policies and politics of globalization and of other key international health and nursing issues.

GLOBALIZATION

Globalization is the growing interdependence of the world's people, integrating economy, culture, technology, and governance. Globalization changes the way nations and communities work; shrinking time, space, and borders. It means that national policy and action are increasingly shaped by international forces.

Globalization creates new economic and cultural zones, such as Silicon Valley, and it brings new people to our countries and communities. The increase in international travel means the ready spread of disease as people move freely across borders and continents. Today, both countries and health professionals must learn to care for new illnesses and to deal with the added risks of exposure (United Nations [UN] Development Programme, 1999). The easing of trade restrictions has made mobility and migration easier.

MIGRATION: A CASE IN POINT

It is estimated that more than a million people daily are migrating from place to place (De Leon Siantz, 1997). People move about for many reasons: work;

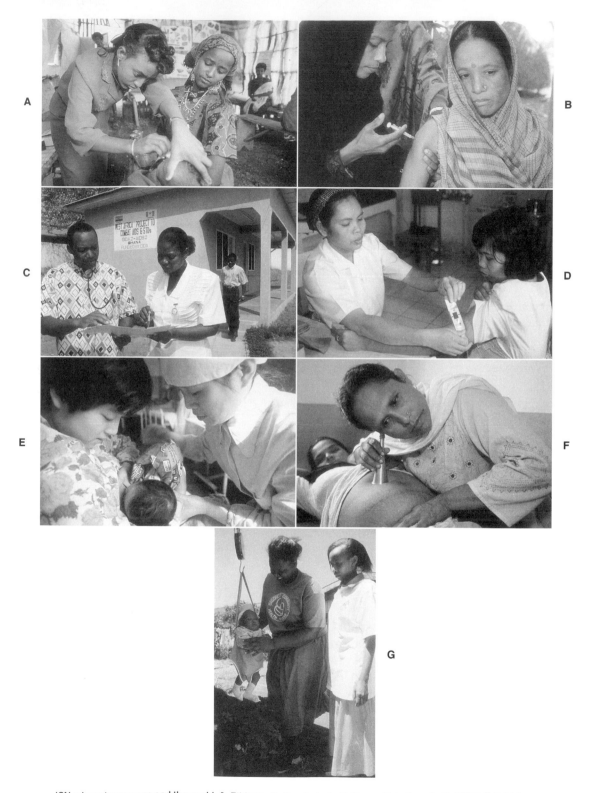

ICN advocates: nurses and the world. **A,** Ethiopia; **B,** Bangladesh; **C,** Ghana; **D,** Indonesia; **E,** China; **F,** Pakistan; and **G,** Kenya. (Courtesy of David Barbour **(A),** Nancy Durrell McKenna **(B, D,** and **F),** Pierre St. Jacques **(C),** Roger Lemoyne **(E),** and Stephanie Colvey **(G),** as well as ACDI/CIDA.)

study; pleasure; to receive health care; or to escape violence, poverty, and famine in their native countries. This movement brings with it the problems of unemployment, discrimination, racial tensions, and harmful cultural practices, such as female genital mutilation. Today's nurses must understand health, illness, and coping mechanisms from the perspectives of many cultures. Equally important is the need for the profession to be an advocate for sound health and nursing policy that considers the well-being of the client along with that of the profession and its practitioners.

Governments—bilaterally, regionally, or through the World Trade Organization—negotiate terms for the movement of goods and people for economic gain. With the growing shortage of health professionals, particularly nurses, in many parts of the world, individuals and institutions at all levels—governments, employers, policymakers, the public, the professions, and professionals—are interested in the movement of nurses.

Substantial numbers of nurses are on the move. Nurses from the Caribbean are moving to North America and the United Kingdom, as are nurses from the Philippines. A significant number of Indian nurses and doctors are migrating to the Gulf states. There is also considerable movement in Africa as nurses leave Zimbabwe, Ghana, and other countries to work in South Africa, and as South African nurses migrate to the United Kingdom, the United States, Canada, Australia, and New Zealand.

Migration enables nurses to earn a living, continue their education, experience other cultures, or expand their professional experience. Most nurses searching for work abroad do so because of poor salaries and working conditions in their home countries. In many countries, employers have failed to address long-standing deficiencies related to hours of work, salary, continuing education, staffing levels, security, housing, and day care facilities. For example, a nurse in Trinidad and Tobago recently told the International Council of Nurses (ICN) that she works alone at night caring for 50 patients. In Botswana, nurses told the ICN they are leaving, even though salaries and living conditions are good. Nurses are exhausted from working short-handed,

World Trade Organization

The World Trade Organization (WTO), to which more than 130 countries belong, has a mandate to ensure that trade in goods and services flows as smoothly, predictably, and freely as possible. It does so by:
- Administering trade agreements
- Acting as a forum for trade negotiations
- Settling trade disputes and reviewing national trade policies
- Assisting developing countries in trade policy issues, through technical assistance and training programs
- Cooperating with other international organizations

Multilateral trade agreements are the legal ground rules for international commerce that countries trade rights to and bind governments to keep their trade policies within agreed limits. The General Agreement on Trade in Services (GATS) is a multilateral agreement to reduce barriers to international trade in services. It seeks to improve trade in services and investment conditions through a set of mutually agreed upon rules, including a dispute settlement system (World Trade Organization, 2001).

and frustrated that they can give only symptomatic relief to the AIDS patients crowding their wards.

Nurses also choose to migrate as a means to learn new knowledge and skills, or to practice more autonomously in innovative environments. Others move for new cultural experiences, to be with families, or for personal safety and political reasons (Oulton, 1998).

In 1999, the ICN, together with the World Medical Association (WMA) and the World Health Organization (WHO), undertook a collaborative project to determine the migration patterns of nurses and physicians. The nursing data showed that pay, learning opportunities, career opportunities, working conditions, job security, and opportunities for family members were all strong incentives for migration, while differences in language and culture were strong disincentives (International Council of Nurses, 1999).

The nursing community has been vocal both nationally and internationally in addressing migration policy and practice.

World Health Organization

The World Health Organization (WHO), established in 1948, has more than 190 countries in its membership. Its objective is the attainment by all peoples of the highest possible level of health. Through six regional offices, a Geneva-based secretariat, and offices in many countries, the organization promotes technical cooperation for health among nations, carries out programs to control and eradicate disease, and strives to improve the quality of human life.

WHO has four main functions:

- To give worldwide guidance in the field of health
- To set global standards for health
- To cooperate with governments in strengthening national health programs
- To develop and transfer appropriate health technology, information, and standards

WHO defines *health* as "a state of complete physical, mental and social well-being and not merely the absence of disease or infirmity" (World Health Organization, 2001a).

International Council of Nurses

The International Council of Nurses is a federation of national nurses associations (NNAs) representing nurses in more than 120 countries. Founded in 1899, the ICN is the world's first and widest-reaching international organization for health professionals. Operated by nurses for nurses, the ICN works to ensure quality nursing care for all, sound health policies globally, the advancement of nursing knowledge, and the presence worldwide of a respected nursing profession and a competent and satisfied nursing workforce.

The ICN advances nursing, nurses, and health through its policies, partnerships, advocacy, leadership development, networks, congresses, special projects, and its work in the arenas of professional practice, regulation, and socioeconomic welfare. The ICN is particularly active in ethics, AIDS, advanced practice, research, leadership development, the international classification of nursing practice, women's health, credentialing, human resources development, occupational health and safety, conditions of work, career development, and human rights.

The ICN works closely with agencies of the United Nations (UN) system, such as WHO, UNAIDS, UNICEF, UNESCO, and ILO, and international, regional, and national nongovernmental organizations (International Council of Nursed, 2001).

- The nursing brain drain from South Africa to the United Kingdom prompted the South African government to protest in late 1999 against aggressive recruitment. Nurses were in critical short supply in South Africa, and the national nurses association, DENOSA, lobbied government and employers for better working conditions and sound workforce planning. However, they lobbied at the same time to oppose any restrictions on nurses' right to emigrate.
- Many national nurses associations have actively lobbied their governments for ethical recruitment of nurses. In line with the ICN position on nurse retention, transfer, and migration, nurses have condemned the practice of recruiting offshore rather than effectively addressing human resource planning (including the problems that cause nurses to leave the profession and discourage them from returning to nursing) (International Council of Nurses, 1999).
- National nurses associations are monitoring employers to ensure that the rights of the new nurses are upheld, and are helping to ensure that immigrating nurses have adequate support systems in place.
- Some governments (such as those of the United Kingdom, the Netherlands, New Zealand, and Canada) are responding to pressure from the nursing profession by issuing recruitment guidelines for employers, launching studies of working conditions, and reviewing nursing resource plans.
- The ICN has embarked on a joint project with the WHO and the Royal College of Nursing, UK, to study nurse migration patterns, with specific focus on the flow within economic free-trade blocs. Migration incentives and disincentives will be identified and a national forecasting model developed.

THINK GLOBALLY, ACT LOCALLY

This slogan, coined in the 1990s as part of the environmental movement, has been adopted by many other sectors as globalization, advances in biotechnology and communications, and rising public activism impact the roles of individuals, groups, and nations on a global scale. Initially a call to consider the global impact of pollution and to take local action, it is also used to address issues such as poverty, access to health care, AIDS, gender issues, and other global trends affecting the health and nursing communities.

POVERTY

Today poverty is the world's most devastating scourge. The World Bank estimates that there are about 1.3 billion extremely poor people in the world, with women representing 70% of the absolute poor (UN Development Programme, 1997). One third of the world's children are hungry and undernourished, and about 2.5 million annually die of malnutrition (WHO, 1998). More than 80 countries have lower income per capita than they did 10 years ago. To put it in context, the assets of the world's top three billionaires in 1999 was greater than the combined gross national product of the 49 least-developed countries and their 600 million people (UN Development Programme, 1999). Unequal distribution of wealth and of health services has dire consequences for the poor, whether in developing countries or in the United States. The poor have a greater burden of ill health and disability, attributable in large part to infectious diseases, malnutrition, and the complications of childbirth. Children living in absolute poverty are five times more likely to die before the age of 5 than children who are not poor (WHO, 1999).

Poor countries have few public services, and these are of poor quality. This means longer travel and waiting times for care, fewer drugs, shared beds, and more corruption and graft. Often it means user fees and out-of-pocket payments at a time when people are ill and most in need of care. Although user fees may bring in money to buy more supplies, they often create unanticipated problems.

World Bank

The World Bank, established in 1944, is composed of the International Bank for Reconstruction and Development, the International Development Association, the International Finance Corporation, the Multilateral Investment Guaranty Agency, and the International Centre for Settlement of Investment Disputes. The World Bank is owned by its 183 member countries and staffed by 8168 employees in Washington, DC, and 2545 people overseas.

The World Bank's mission is summarized as follows:
- To fight poverty with passion and professionalism for lasting results
- To help people help themselves and their environment by providing resources, sharing knowledge, building capacity, and forging partnerships in the public and private sectors
- To be an excellent institution able to attract, excite, and nurture diverse and committed staff with exceptional skills who know how to listen and learn

The World Bank is the world's largest source of development assistance, providing nearly $16 billion in loans annually to its client countries. It works with governments, nongovernmental organizations, and the private sector and within more than 100 developing economies, bringing a mix of finance and ideas to improve living standards and eliminate the worst forms of poverty.

To become a member of the World Bank a country must first join the International Monetary Fund (IMF) (World Bank Group, 2001).

For example, they may keep the working poor from seeking care, leading to enhanced chronicity and disability. A 1997 survey in Nigeria showed that user fees deterred at-risk women from seeking antenatal care, thus increasing the number of emergency admissions and accounting for 70% of maternal mortality (Kelsey, 1997). And in places where crime and hunger are rampant, user fees leave the nurse, who handles the money, vulnerable to attack.

Health care has deteriorated in numerous countries, and previous gains are being lost as decision makers reduce resources for health, education, and social services. However, our increasing ability to demonstrate the economic advantage of good health is beginning to be heard. Though the conclusions remain suggestive rather than definitive, studies show that healthier people are more productive. Preliminary results from a study in Latin America and the Caribbean show that growth in gross domestic product (GDP) is statistically associated with increased life expectancy. Mexican data suggest that every added year of male life expectancy means an added 1% increase in GDP 15 years later (WHO, 1999).

This growing body of evidence has added weight to calls by the UN organizations and nongovernmental groups (NGOs) such as ICN for a concerted attack on poverty. As a result the G8 countries (Canada, France, Germany, Japan, Italy, Russia, the United Kingdom, and the United States) have committed billions of dollars to a massive effort to fight the diseases of poverty. These diseases—primarily tuberculosis, human immune deficiency virus (HIV) and AIDS, malaria, childhood diseases (such as measles and diarrheal conditions), and the complications associated with pregnancy and delivery—inflict a terrible and disproportionate toll of death and disability among the world's poorest people. Yet a number of effective health interventions that drastically reduce mortality from these main killers already exist. The new Global Health Fund is dedicated to scaling up the global effort and pooling resources to fight these diseases and reduce poverty. The ICN was among the 200 experts on health, advocacy, and public relations present at the October 2000 meeting called to mount the initiative.

In Spring 2001, the European Forum of National Nursing and Midwifery Associations and WHO released a public statement calling on nurses and midwives to: (1) accept their responsibility in addressing the issue of poverty; (2) recognize the important role they can play in protecting and promoting the health of poor people; (3) commit knowledge, skills, and experience in practice and research; and (4) support and initiate multisectoral participatory approaches to tackling poverty. These actions were seen as imperative to ensure that health systems effectively address the needs of poor people, including policy development and partnerships that meaningfully involve poor people in analysis and decisions. The statement also calls on European governments to recognize that nurses and midwives

International Monetary Fund

The International Monetary Fund (IMF) is an international organization of 183 member countries, established in 1946 to promote international monetary cooperation; to facilitate the expansion and balanced growth of international trade; to promote exchange stability; to assist in the establishment of a multilateral system of payments; to make its general resources temporarily available to its members experiencing balance of payments difficulties under adequate safeguards; and to shorten the duration and lessen the degree of disequilibrium in the international balances of payments of members.

Its operations involve surveillance, financial assistance, and technical assistance. Financial assistance includes credits and loans extended by the IMF to member countries with balance of payments problems to support policies of adjustment and reform. As of January 31, 2001, the IMF had credit and loans outstanding to 91 countries for an amount of about $65.3 billion (U.S. dollars).

The bulk of the IMF's resources derives from members' subscriptions (called *quotas*) that are broadly based on each member's relative size in the world economy (International Monetary Fund, 2001).

can contribute significantly to poverty reduction in addition to providing accessible, comprehensive, and coordinated health care services and continuing care (European Forum of National Nursing and Midwifery Associations & WHO, 2001).

HIV AND AIDS

If poverty is the world's greatest scourge, then AIDS is surely second. AIDS has penetrated every nation of the world. Globally there are 36 million people living with HIV/AIDS, and the United States has an estimated 422,000 infected adults and children as of mid-2000 (Centers for Disease Control and Prevention, 2000). Reports from 2001 show the virus surging through black communities; AIDS is the leading cause of death among African Americans between the ages of 25 and 44 years (Herbert, 2001). In the year 2000 the Russian Federation reported more new HIV infections than in all previous years combined. In sub-Saharan Africa, an estimated 3.8 million adults and children became infected with HIV during 2000, bringing the total number of sub-Saharans with HIV and AIDS to 25.3 million. In India, roughly 3.7 million people have been infected with HIV (UNAIDS, 2000; UNAIDS & WHO, 2000).

More than 16,000 individuals become infected daily, 95% of them in developing countries (UN Development Programme, 1999). The disease is devastating communities and nations, and creating a generation of AIDS orphans. It is also taking its toll among the nurses who care for the ill, and who may be infected themselves. In the nursing satellite meeting during the 2000 World AIDS Conference in Durban, a student nurse brought the audience to tears speaking of the impact of this dreadful disease. She noted that the young people in her community don't talk about which party or film they want to attend, but which funeral of a friend or relative they will be attending.

Nursing has played a key role in the fight against AIDS. Nurses have been at the forefront of care, management, research, education, and politics. In more than 30 countries, nurses have formed special interest groups to advance their knowledge of the disease and of care, to support nurses in their roles as provider and persons living with HIV/AIDS, and to lobby governments for increased funding for research, education, treatment, and care. Nurses form the core of care in most countries, particularly in the developing world, where money and drugs are scarce, beds are full, and myths flourish. Nurses, working alone or in collaboration with other sectors, continue to develop and deliver education programs and to counsel individuals, families, and groups worldwide. In addition to convincing adolescents of their vulnerability, the biggest problem for nurses in African countries is changing the social attitudes toward sex, including the myth that having intercourse with a virgin can rid a man of HIV. Nurses in Africa are also advocating for better home care and self-care, and are carrying out research in these areas. A study led by the University of California, San Francisco, in partnership with Botswana, Lesotho, South Africa, and Swaziland, is looking into self-care and family symptom management for HIV disease.

Care has been the missing piece in much of the UN's work, and nurses have yet to be utilized to their full potential within the UN system. As recently as 2000, WHO appointed a physician to head its HIV/AIDS Care Services, over the objections of nurses, and UNAIDS eliminated its nursing position and appointed a physician to head care and prevention services. This example illustrates the policy and personnel imbalance within the UN and many national health systems, where nurses play a minor role in health policy development. It also illustrates the prevalent UN notion that "care" is equivalent to "medical care."

NURSING'S POLICY VOICE

Achieving nursing's policy potential is perhaps the greatest challenge facing the profession in the twenty-first century. Nursing's success in shaping policy is variable, depending on the country, the issue, and the group under consideration. On the other hand, the limiting factors are fairly universal and include nursing's image, perceived value and social status, educational requirements, gender issues, and numbers. The ratio of nurses to other health workers, the scope of practice, and legislation and cultural norms affect the influence of nurses, as does the presence of strong national nursing associations. Equally important is the extent to which nurses are perceived to be interested in improving health for all, versus being interested in only personal and professional gains.

There is no doubt that policy influence is an uphill battle for many. In some newly independent countries, nurses are engaged in learning about nursing autonomy and lobbying for the right to chart their own actions. Nursing groups are lobbying in several countries to create a government Chief Nurse, to maintain the position, or to reinstate it. Nursing too often lacks a single senior nurse, let alone a cadre of influential nurses, within the health department.

Without nurses in key positions in international health departments, there is little or no focus on nursing or the effects of decisions on nursing. For example, new technologies and programs may be introduced without any assessment of their impact on the current deployment of nurses. This problem is compounded when there is no strong national nursing organization to monitor the quality of care or human resource issues.

NURSING WITHIN GOVERNMENTS AND THE WORLD HEALTH ORGANIZATION

The lack of influential nurses within governments has handicapped nursing, particularly compared with the influence of physicians. The same is true within the WHO. Of the number of WHO professional posts in the category that includes dental, medical, nursing, and veterinary staff, 90.8% are medical specialists and 2.9% are nurses (WHO, 2001b).

WHO has one nurse scientist within its Geneva-based secretariat, and the same secretariat is unable to state the numbers of nurses in other positions, despite repeated requests by the ICN. Only five of the six WHO regional offices have designated Regional Nurse Advisors. The Pan-American Health Organization (PAHO), the regional office of the Americas, has none.

Physicians are the most numerous professional personnel within WHO. Mostly from the "old school" of health care, WHO physicians are inclined to overlook the potential roles nurses could play. Most of them see the general practitioner as the pivotal professional in health care and do not see the need to address nursing issues.

The current nursing shortage and the global health care reform movement offer an opportunity to change the influence of nurses within WHO and nationally. Most countries have a growing disease burden along with shrinking health resources, including personnel. Strengthening nursing is seen as a means to address health care problems, and the World Health Assembly, made up of representatives of ministries of health from nearly 200 countries, has resolved to address nursing issues. The resolution, passed by the assembly in May 2001, acknowledges the nursing shortage; recognizes that nurses/midwives play a crucial and cost-effective role in promoting healthy lifestyles and reducing excess mortality, morbidity, and disability; and concludes that further action is needed to maximize the contribution of nurses and midwives. Among a series of actions, the resolution urges governments to do the following: (1) involve nurses and midwives in health policy development, planning, and implementation at all levels; (2) establish comprehensive human resource development programs that support the recruitment and retention of a skilled and motivated nursing and midwifery workforce within health services; (3) develop and implement policies and programs that ensure healthy workplaces and quality work environments for nurses and midwives; and (4) develop/enhance nursing's evidence base (WHO, 2001c).

Nursing has been on the WHO agenda periodically for more than 40 years, placed there through the lobbying of groups such as the ICN and interested governments. Sceptics might say that this resolution represents more of the same. However, there is a difference this time as a result of the pervasiveness of the nursing shortage, the bleakness of nursing recruitment, the new challenges of an aging population, the double burden of chronic and infectious diseases that most nations face, and the rising costs of health care.

Governments now have increasing evidence of the impact nurses can have. This is evident in the new Family Health Nurse initiative under way in WHO's European region. For Europe, the Family Health Nurse concept is based on a professional nurse whose work focuses on prevention and providing care. The nurse is trained to detect early signs of emerging problems, make appropriate referrals to other health professionals and other services within the system, and give family members advice suited to their age, lifestyle, and gender. The Family Health Nurse is also an active member of local community health programs. Nurses are skilled in community development and are able to translate experience with families into programs for the community. The nurse is, in other words, an effective agent for community-based care. Today there are 18 pilot sites throughout Europe, several of them in countries where nursing traditionally has enjoyed no autonomy or recognition of the profession's potential.

At the national level, policymakers in many nations are seeing nursing as part of the solution. There is increased interest in the nurse practitioner movement in several countries, and eight countries are experimenting with added nurse autonomy in prescribing[1]. The UK has introduced the consultant nurse, and in the United States there is growing acceptance that nurse anesthetists need not work directly under the supervision of an anesthesiologist.

Telecommunications is offering new alternatives, and countries such as the United States, the UK, Japan, Portugal, Australia, and Norway are using telecommunications for education, consultation, and treatment. Telenursing, particularly telephone triage by nurses, is the fastest-growing new nursing-related initiative by governments in many years.

The number of government chief nurses is growing in Europe and in Central and Eastern Europe and the former Soviet Union. Lobbying for positions in South America continues, while the Caribbean and some African countries seem to be losing posts as part of health care reform. There is little activity in the French-speaking states in Africa or Europe, where there is no history of the position and little call for it. The lack of a strong united nongovernmental nursing voice in many of these countries means that nursing continues to be disadvantaged in the policy arena.

In South America a growing number of strong national and regional nursing groups have had some success, particularly in raising the level of nursing education. In English-speaking Africa, as in most other Anglophone countries, nursing has a long tradition of influence. In many African countries nurses hold high nonnursing positions in government and remain staunch supporters of the profession. Nursing has a growing policy and political voice in Asia through both the nurses associations and nurses in parliament. Finally, the Middle East and South Pacific are also seeing the rise of a stronger nursing voice, particularly through the professional association.

The number of nurses in elected and appointed houses of governments is also growing. Iceland, Canada, the United States, the UK, Aruba, Australia, New Zealand, Thailand, Korea, and Norway have elected or appointed nurses to parliament (or other national legislature) in the past two years. Nursing's policy influence in this century will require more nurse politicians, more unity of voice, and more strategic alliances, along with leadership development and added political and policy skills for all new graduates.

Currently a real danger in many countries is the potential split in the external nursing voice as more specialty organizations develop, particularly outside the umbrella of the national nurses association. The United States has felt the impact of divided nursing interests for many years and has developed mechanisms, such as forums and issue-specific lobbies, to bring the nursing voice together on key issues. Such strategic alliances are part of today's socioeconomic and political fabric. Touted first by management gurus and then applied to industry, strategic alliances have come to the fore in international health.

PARTNERSHIPS AND STRATEGIC ALLIANCES: A WAY FORWARD

There has been a long tradition of partnership between NGOs and the UN agencies, such as WHO. The ICN was the first health professional group to attain official relations status with WHO in 1948. Since then, about 60 UN and intergovernmental agencies have been created, and more of them have begun to address health care issues. Many regional intergovernmental groups and regional NGOs have been created, including regional nursing groups such as the Northern Nurses Federation, the Caribbean Nurses Organization, the European Union Permanent Committee on Nursing, and the Commonwealth Nurses Federation. Today there is more collaboration among intergovernmental agencies themselves, among NGOs, and between UN agencies and NGOs. In 1996, the European Region of WHO created the European Forum of National Nursing and Midwifery Associations and WHO in order to accomplish the following (WHO, 1996):

- Inform the debate of improving health and quality of care in Europe
- Promote the exchange of information, ideas, and policies between nursing/midwifery and WHO

- Support the integration of appropriate policies for health-for-all into nursing practice as well as education
- Formulate consensus/policy statements and recommendations on health and nursing/midwifery-related issue.

The ICN works with the European Forum and with other regional and international groups, including the WMA and the International Pharmaceutical Federation (FIP), representing pharmacists. In 1999, the ICN, WMA, and FIP created the World Health Professions Alliance, launched publicly during the World Health Assembly. Through pooled resources, the alliance not only strengthens collaboration among the three professions but also addresses key health issues, such as health resources planning, human rights, tobacco addiction, antimicrobial resistance, AIDS, and medical ethics.

The ICN is party to a number of other strategic alliances. Some involve nursing groups only and really are joint ventures to deliver services. Examples of these include a joint venture with the East, Central, and Southern African College of Nurses to deliver the ICN's Leadership for Change program to nurses in 14 African countries. Others involve UN agencies, donors, and NGOs.

A new twist to strategic alliances within the UN system has been the addition of the corporate sector as partner. Recently, several new initiatives have involved key UN agencies, the World Bank, foundations, transnational corporations, and NGOs. Operating under the direction of one of the agencies or through creation of a new third-party vehicle, such as a management board, these new issue-specific entities address key public health issues. The Global Alliance for Vaccines and Immunization (GAVI) is a case in point, as is the WHO's attack on tobacco.

GAVI represents a historic alliance of public- and private-sector partners assembled into a worldwide network. The partners are the Bill and Melinda Gates Children's Vaccine Program, the International Federation of Pharmaceutical Manufacturers Associations (IFPMA), public health and research institutions, national governments, the Rockefeller Foundation, UNICEF, the World Bank Group, and WHO. GAVI's mission is to protect children of all nations and of all socioeconomic levels against vaccine-preventable diseases. The alliance addresses its objectives by working to secure adequate funds, improve donor collaboration, strengthen national immunization services, enhance coordination among governments and development partners, and to enhance collaboration with global vaccine industry partners to provide the highest-quality vaccines at the lowest appropriate pricing (GAVI, 2001).

GETTING INVOLVED

Shared goals, vision, and values are key ingredients to policy and program initiatives such as GAVI. The same is true for nursing. Any significant advancement toward realizing nursing's policy potential nationally, regionally, and internationally will require multiple strategies and joint efforts on many fronts. Ultimately it means the commitment of individual nurses who share a vision and values, and believe that nurses can make a difference for themselves and, most of all, for the people they serve. There are many ways to participate:

1. Begin at home—get involved. Know the issues and values. Support organized nursing initiatives. This may mean working on issues and policy papers, engaging in lobbying activities, or running for public or nursing office.
2. Think globally, act locally. Cultivate a worldview when addressing local nursing and health issues. Be sensitive to the cultural aspects of policy and practice.
3. Commit to learning more about trade agreements and how they affect your practice and your potential. Though some aspects are positive, there are pitfalls too. Health services will be part of the WTO agenda in the next 3 years. Ministries of trade and foreign affairs have already consulted nursing representatives in some countries. Make sure yours is one of them.
4. Through the association or your workplace, help colleagues in other countries as they work to strengthen nursing and health care. Nurses in many countries are working against

incredible odds and would welcome help at work and in their associations. Remember, the developing world carries 90% of the disease burden, yet enjoys only 10% of health resources.

5. Undertake research to build evidence of nursing effectiveness in areas key to nursing's progress. Pilot new nursing roles, such as the Family Nurse.

6. Advocate, initiate, and document nursing's role in policy.

7. Know where your government stands on key international health and nursing matters and lobby them to support the initiative. Lobby them to pay their UN dues if they are lagging behind. Without funds, it is impossible to accomplish much.

8. Join others in ensuring national and local structures are in place so that nursing's voice is heard in policy and practice.

9. Ensure that new graduates know about policy and politics, how to analyze the environment, how to develop strategy, and how to work together.

10. Get involved in international issues and team up with like-minded groups and individuals at home and internationally.

11. Know the stance taken by regional and international organizations, such as the ICN, on key nursing and health issues.

12. Share your ideas and achievements through publications and the Internet, and papers presented at international conferences.

CONCLUSION

Nursing remains the backbone of health systems worldwide. If we are to achieve better health for all people, it will be through evidence that we are a strong profession, committed to sound nursing and health policies and practices, and skilled in policy, politics, and care. One of the key tenets of primary health care is that communities should participate in decisions affecting them. It follows, then, that nursing, as a community and as part of the global society, needs to be engaged in all aspects of health policy.

REFERENCES

Air Transport Association. (2001). *Traffic summary 1960-1999: U.S. scheduled airlines.* Retrieved online, March 18, 2000, from www.air-transport.org/public/industry/24.asp.

Centers for Disease Control and Prevention. (2001). *HIV/AIDS surveillance report 2000, 12*(1), Table 1. Retrieved online, June 26, 2001, from www.cdc.gov/hiv/stats/hasr1201/table1.htm.

De Leon Siantz, M.L. (1997). A global profile of the immigrant/migrant child. In *Global migration: The health care implications of immigration and population movements.* Washington, DC: American Academy of Nursing.

European Forum of National Nursing and Midwifery Associations & World Health Organization. (2001). *Statement on the role of nurses and midwives in poverty reduction.* Copenhagen: Author.

Global Alliance for Vaccines and Immunization. (2001). *More about GAVI.* Retrieved online, March 18, 2001, from www.vaccinealliance.com/reference/moreabout.html.

Herbert, B. (2001, January 11). In America: The quiet scourge. *New York Times.* Retrieved online, April 15, 2001, from www.nytimes.com/pages/opinion/index.html.

International Council of Nurses. (1999, October). *Nurse retention, transfer and migration* (ICN position statement). Geneva: Author.

International Council of Nurses. (2000). *ICN/WMA/WHO mobility survey* (internal correspondence). Geneva: Author.

International Council of Nurses. (2001). *About the International Council of Nurses.* Retrieved online, March 25, 2001, from www.icn.ch/abouticn.htm.

International Monetary Fund. (2001). *About the IMF.* Retrieved online, June 21, 2001, from www.imf.org/external/about.htm.

Kelsey, H. (1997, March). Maternal mortality in Nigeria: The real issue. *African Journal of Reproductive Health, 8.*

Oulton, J.A. (1998). International trade and the nursing profession. In *International trade in health services: A development perspective.* Geneva: United Nations Conference on Trade and Development.

UNAIDS. (2000, December). *AIDS epidemic update 2000.* Retrieved online, March 18, 2001, from www.unaids.org/wac/2000/wad00/files/WAD_epidemic_report.htm.

UNAIDS & World Health Organization. (2000). *India: Epidemiological fact sheet on HIV/AIDS and sexually transmitted infections: 2000 update.* Retrieved online, June 26, 2001, from www.unaids.org/hivaidsinfo/statistics/june00/fact_sheets/pdfs/india.pdf.

United Nations Development Programme. (1997). *Human development to eradicate poverty: The human development report 1997.* New York: Oxford University Press.

United Nations Development Programme. (1999). *Globalization with a human face: The human development report 1999.* New York: Oxford University Press.

World Bank Group. (2001). *About us.* Retrieved online, June 21, 2001, from www.worldbank.org/html/extdr/about/.

World Health Organization. (1996, November). *European Forum of Nursing and Midwifery Associations and WHO established "a formidable force for change."* (Press Release EURO/07/96. Copenhagen: WHO Regional Office for Europe.

World Health Organization. (1998). Life in the 21st century: A vision for all. *The World Health Report 1998* (p. 140). Geneva: Author.

World Health Organization. (1999). Making a difference. *The World Health Report 1999* (p. 9). Geneva: Author.

World Health Organization. (2001a). *About WHO.* Retrieved online, March 15, 2001, from www.who.int/aboutwho/en/mission.htm.

World Health Organization. (2001b). *Human resources: Annual report, 2000. Report by the Secretariat* (107th Executive Board. Doc EB107/14, 11 January 2001). Geneva: Author.

World Health Organization. (2001c). *Strengthening nursing and midwifery.* 54th World Health Assembly. Doc WHA 54.12. 21 May 2001. Geneva: Author.

World Trade Organization. (2001). *The WTO.* Retrieved online, March 25, 2001, from www.wto.org/english/thewto_e/thewto_e.htm.

POLICYSPOTLIGHT

EMERGING INFECTIOUS DISEASES

Felissa R. Lashley

"I skate to where the puck is going to be, not to where it has been."

WAYNE GRETZKY

As we enter the twenty-first century, the problem of infectious diseases, especially those considered to be emerging, demands new attention and resources. Throughout history, various authors and historians have documented the relationship between infectious disease and political, economic, and social instability. These events serve dual roles as both causative factors and outcomes.

BACKGROUND

In the mid-twentieth century, it was widely believed that infectious diseases could be controlled by hygienic and sanitary practices, antibiotics, and immunizations, and therefore did not present a meaningful threat to the public health. The well-known immunologist and Nobel laureate Sir MacFarlane Burnet wrote in 1962 that "one can think of the middle of the twentieth century as the end of one of the most important social revolutions in history, the virtual elimination of infectious disease as a significant factor in social life" (Burnet, 1962, p. 3). Indeed, the number of deaths resulting from infectious diseases in the United States had decreased significantly for a number of reasons. These included the discovery and use of antibiotics, widespread immunization programs, and strong public health infrastructure and surveillance systems.

Between 1980 and 1992, this changed and the death rate from infectious diseases increased 58% (Centers for Disease Control and Prevention [CDC], 1999). The most famous emerging infectious disease contributing to significant morbidity and mortality worldwide was, and still is, the human immunodeficiency virus (HIV) disease and acquired immunodeficiency syndrome (AIDS), along with associated sequelae such as multidrug-resistant tuberculosis. Among the reasons for the increased emergence of certain infectious agents and drug-resistant organisms has been a prevalent complacency that infectious diseases are no longer a threat, particularly to developed countries.

Another trend that eventually shaped policies in a negative way for public health (although in a positive way for patient rights) is the emphasis of individual rights over the needs and "greater good" of the community and population (Richards, 2001).

In this light, Nobel laureate Joshua Lederberg noted that today "restraining the rights and freedoms of individuals is a far greater sin than allowing the infection of others," and went on to say that "the restraints placed on Typhoid Mary might not be acceptable today, when some would prefer to give her unlimited rein to infect others, with litigation their only recourse" (Lederberg, 1997, p. 422). Typhoid Mary (Mary Mallon) was a cook who was an asymptomatic typhoid carrier. She infected numerous families for whom she worked in New York with typhoid during the period of 1906 to 1915. She was isolated twice—an early isolation period, from which she was released, only to infect more people, and a second, permanent confinement to North Brother Island from 1915 till her death in 1938.

In 1992, a report was released by the Institute of Medicine (IOM) that called attention to the global problem of emerging infectious diseases (Lederberg, Shope, & Oaks, 1992). This was followed by two reports from the CDC (1994, 1998). *Emerging infectious diseases* were defined as new, reemerging, or drug-resistant infections whose incidence in humans has increased within the past two decades or whose incidence threatens to increase in the near future. *Reemerging diseases* refers to the reappearance of a known disease after a decline in incidence (Lederberg et al, 1992). This has been elaborated upon to include not only newly recognized organisms and new diseases caused by known organisms, but also an extension of the geographic range of an organism or one causing infection in a new host, such as a disease that has moved from animals to humans (Lashley & Durham, 2002). The emergence or reemergence of infectious diseases may be due to a variety of factors, alone or in combination. These factors include the following:

- Social and behavioral changes, including increased use of child care
- Increased use of antimicrobial agents, including those used in animal feed
- Globalization of travel and trade, and demands for exotic and imported foodstuffs
- Increased eating in restaurants and fast-food establishments, combined with greater popularity of buffets

- Widespread travel and recreational pursuits bringing animals and people into closer contact
- Demographic factors such as population growth, migration, population demographics, and housing density
- Environmental alterations, such as land use development, irrigation, deforestation, and natural disasters
- Climatic and weather changes such as global warming and increased rainfall
- Disasters such as earthquakes, and wars and conflicts resulting in stress, crowding, and declines in disease control
- Decline in the public health infrastructure resulting in deficiencies in communication and information, fewer and less-prepared staff, and limited public health laboratory capacity
- Microbial evolution such as mutation, new tissue specificities, and cross-species transmission
- Health care and technology advances such as iatrogenic immunosuppression, increases in organ transplantation, and use of medical devices (Cohen & Larson, 1996; Lashley & Durham, 2002; Lederberg et al, 1992)

The actual and potential role of emerging infectious diseases in the national security of the United States and of other countries is well recognized (National Intelligence Council, 2000). Certain microorganisms remain potential agents for bioterrorist activities, especially those causing anthrax, smallpox, plague, and botulism, as well as more sophisticated approaches such as genetically altered influenza viruses. A troubling recent example is the deliberate dissemination of anthrax in parts of the United States beginning in September 2001. In late 2000, additional provisions for public health emergencies were signed into law as part of the Public Health Improvement Act (Public Law [PL] 106-505). This allowed an immediate response to public health emergencies, including infectious disease outbreaks or bioterrorist attacks.

Today, emerging infectious diseases are truly global, as one can travel around the world in only 30 hours, and cannot be considered as only internal or domestic. For example, the West Nile virus was recognized in the Western hemisphere only in 1999, yet it was recognized earlier as a cause of encephalitis in Africa, the Middle East, and parts of Europe (Hughes, 2001). Thus, international cooperation for surveillance, prevention, epidemiological investigation, rapid diagnosis, and research across disciplines (including among those who focus on animals and insects and those who focus on humans) will be essential in the future.

The major policies associated with emerging and reemerging infectious diseases are communicable disease surveillance and reporting, immunization, quarantine, travel and immigration restrictions, the use of antimicrobial agents, sanitation, vector control, clean drinking water and food, and restrictions related to import and export of goods and animals. This policy spotlight concentrates on the first five of these.

SURVEILLANCE AND REPORTING POLICY

For the most part, policies that address emerging infectious disease threats take place on the national, state, or local level, rather than the international arena. There is, however, a legal treaty known as the International Health Regulations, the most recent version of which has been in force since 1971 and amended in the 1980s, long before epidemics of the viral hemorrhagic diseases such as Ebola were known. Under the treaty provisions, signature countries agree to report certain diseases to the World Health Organization (WHO), and three quarantinable diseases—yellow fever, plague, and cholera—are specified. In the recommended revision due to be submitted to the World Health Assembly in 2004, instead of three diseases that must be reported to WHO, any event of urgent international public health importance will be specified. Coordination with other groups such as the World Trade Organization and the Food and Agriculture Organization will be important because of measures related to food safety and standards (WHO, 2001).

Surveillance and reporting relies on both formal and informal systems. Examples of these systems include the following:

- In the United States, the CDC has mandated reporting from the states for certain diseases such as AIDS.
- The CDC also has other surveillance activities, such as the National Electronic Disease

Surveillance System and the Health Alert Network.
- An example of an international regional system is the Binational Infectious Disease Surveillance (BIDS) project, which has been developed along the United States/Mexico border with the cooperation of Mexico, the United States, the Pan-American Health Organization (PAHO), and local and state health departments. BIDS focuses on surveillance in sister cities, such as Nuevo Laredo, Mexico, and Laredo, Texas. An example of the fruits of these efforts in detecting emerging infectious diseases has been the detection of dengue fever at the United States/Mexico border.
- As mentioned before, WHO has the Global Outbreak Alert and Response Network. WHO also has specific outbreak verification lists and surveillance networks such as the WHO Influenza Surveillance Network.
- ProMED (www.promedmail.org) is an online information system and discussion forum for infectious disease professionals worldwide.
- The Global Public Health Intelligence Network and the Global Public Health Information Network are electronic search and retrieval systems of Health Canada for early detection of global outbreaks of infectious diseases. They are unavailable to the public.
- PulseNet is a surveillance system for infectious diseases in a partnership with the CDC, the Food and Drug Administration (FDA), the U.S. Department of Agriculture (USDA), the Association of Public Health Laboratories, and others (Hughes, 2001).
- Surveillance for nosocomial infections has been part of CDC activities through the National Nosocomial Infections Surveillance.

Despite these networks, many of the laws governing the reporting of communicable diseases became somewhat weakened in the period of time when the public health infrastructure was not well funded and began to deteriorate (Richards, 2001).

An interagency task force on antimicrobial resistance was created in 1999 to formulate a public health action plan to combat antimicrobial resistance. These agencies included the CDC, FDA, National Institutes of Health, Agency for Healthcare Research and Quality, Health Care Financing Administration, Health Resources and Services Administration, Department of Agriculture, Department of Defense, Department of Veterans Affairs, and the Environmental Protection Agency. The first part of the plan, unveiled in January 2001, deals with domestic issues and the second part, which is under development, will focus on international issues. Among the highlights of the plan are a coordinated national surveillance plan for monitoring antimicrobial resistance, monitoring patterns of antimicrobial drug use, and improving surveillance for antimicrobial resistance in agricultural and veterinary settings. It includes both prevention and control activities, including appropriate drug use policies, improved diagnostic practices, addressing rates of infection transmission, research, and product development (U.S. Department of Health and Human Services, 2001).

IMMIGRATION POLICY

Immunization laws are specific for school entry, children, and immigrants. They spell out the types of vaccinations that are needed in various circumstances as well as the information on the risks and benefits of vaccination that must be given to parents and guardians before their child is immunized. School immunization laws are state mandated and exemptions, such as for religious reasons, are specified. At this time immunizations for travel and for adults are recommended but not mandated. As of July 1997, all individuals seeking permanent entry to the United States must prove that they have been inoculated against all vaccine-preventable diseases (CDC, National Vaccine Program Office, 2001). Among the recommendations from an Institute of Medicine report on immunization practices and policies were calls for strengthening federal and state immunization partnerships, developing a strategy for increasing financial support, and ensuring that immunization policy be national in scope (Guyer, Smith, & Chalk, 2000). In the United States in 2002, whether or not to engage in preemptive mass vaccination against small pox is being debated. Arguments for it include protection against the release of small pox by terrorists; arguments

against it include possible vaccine-related illness and the possible deaths of immunosuppressed persons (Fauci, 2002).

QUARANTINE POLICY

Quarantine is a major tool to contain contagious diseases. The United States maintains a Division of Global Migration and Quarantine within the CDC's National Center for Infectious Diseases. In 1967, when it moved from the Department of Health, Education, and Welfare, it had more than 500 staff members and 55 quarantine stations at every port, international airport, and major border crossing. Today, the staff numbers about 80, and quarantine stations with responsibilities for all ports in assigned regions of the United States are located in Atlanta, New York, Miami, Chicago, Los Angeles, San Francisco, Seattle, and Honolulu, as well as overseas posts in Frankfort and Bangkok. They have delegated authority to detain, medically examine, and conditionally release individuals and wildlife suspected of carrying a communicable disease. The Division of Global Migration and Quarantine works in cooperation with other agencies, such as state and local health departments, the U.S. Customs Service, the Immigration and Naturalization Service, the U.S. Fish and Wildlife Service, and the U.S. Department of Agriculture. A list of quarantinable diseases is found in an Executive Order of the President. It includes such diseases as cholera, plague, infectious tuberculosis, yellow fever, and viral hemorrhagic fevers (CDC, National Center for Infectious Diseases, Division of Global Migration and Quarantine, 2000). Special quarantine policies may apply in wartime.

TRAVEL AND IMMIGRATION POLICY

The movement of people for travel or migration has had effects on communicable diseases, both for the travelers and for natives of the recipient nation. As the pandemic of HIV and AIDS grew, a movement began in the mid-1980s to "secure national boundaries" against travelers, migrants, refugees, and immigrants with AIDS (Gellert, 1993). Immigration laws in the United States have excluded aliens (defined as any person not a citizen or national) for health-related reasons since 1879, when such legislation was first enacted. Distinction may be made between immigrants, long-term and short-term travelers, temporary residents, and refugees seeking political asylum. Since then, modifications have been added and several U.S. agencies have become involved with immigration laws. One of these is the Public Health Service, a branch of the Department of Health and Human Services; another is the aforementioned Division of Global Migration and Quarantine. Among the health-related criteria for exclusion of aliens is "affected with any dangerous contagious disease." Quarantine and exclusion had rarely been used in the United States in recent years. In 1994, however, an outbreak of plague was reported from a region in India, and several countries closed their borders to travelers from India and discontinued air flights to and from India. Some countries behaved irrationally, banning such items as Indian postage stamps (Garrett, 2000). Under the International Health Regulations described earlier, plague is quarantinable, and vehicles and passengers may be detained or inspected. The CDC worked with airline employees, representatives of the INS and U.S. Customs in recognizing symptoms of plague. Heightened surveillance in place in the United States detected 13 persons with suspected plague—6 identified in airports, and 7 who had reached private physicians. None actually had the plague (Fritz, Dennis, Tipple, Campbell, McCance, & Gubler, 1996). However, Garrett (2000) points out that the majority had already left their planes. Thus, if they had been ill with plague, they would have allowed exposure to many more contacts, including their fellow passengers.

In the late 1980s and early 1990s, amidst a political storm, more than 50 countries instituted mandatory HIV testing for aliens despite appeals of various organizations, including the World Health Organization. An HIV test may be an entry requirement even for travelers staying in a given country for as little as 2 weeks. Some countries accept certification from the person's health care provider in their own country while others do not. A major impetus behind this type of testing was supposedly to prevent HIV-infected persons from becoming an economic burden to the country they were entering, yet many viewed this as discrimination.

Another recent example of the widespread effects of an infectious disease outbreak is the foot-and-mouth disease outbreak that began in England in February 2001. Early responses were not forthcoming from the European Union, and countries responded individually to the threat. Responses have included the banning of the importation of livestock, milk, and other bovine products first from Britain and then, as disease spread, from other countries affected. Other responses included the incineration of nearly 3 million farm animals in Great Britain, mass immunization, compensation to farmers whose animals were destroyed, and increased restriction of access of tourists and travelers to agricultural areas in affected countries. In some cases, returning travelers were not only questioned about whether they had visited farms, but had their shoes sprayed with disinfectants. The tires of vehicles returning from the United Kingdom were disinfected. There were severe economic consequences that extended to tourism and other seemingly unrelated industries, such as the scarcity of meat for zoo animals (BBC News, 2001). This outbreak points out the need for quick and cooperative global response to emerging infectious disease threats in order to provide effective containment. For the United States it has pointed out another vulnerable area for a bioterrorist attack.

CONCLUSION

In the last few decades, health care and medicine have focused on cures. As we move further into the new millennium, preventive health, along with appropriate policies, must receive new attention, not only from the government and health professionals, but with public enthusiasm for a full partnership in this essential endeavor. Research, education, and funding must be directed to shape policies that will rebuild the public health infrastructure and ensure readiness to deal with future public health emergencies in the area of emerging infectious diseases.

The current climate in the United States, and indeed in the entire world, has been molded by the terrorist attacks of September 11, 2001, and the aftermath may result in shifts in public policy initiatives related to emerging infectious diseases. These shifts may result in stronger legislation to protect the greater public, with a lessening of emphasis on individual rights and considerations. There may also be increased funding to support additional surveillance and protective initiatives, including such things as mass immunization for smallpox if necessary. It is hoped that the financial resources long sought by the public health community not only to maintain programs but to recruit needed experts will be forthcoming. Greater speed and efficiency of reporting unusual symptoms or circumstances to central points (such as the CDC) by electronic surveillance means will be the norm across the country after the inadequacy of the present systems became apparent during the anthrax episodes of October 2001. Greater restrictions in regard to travel and immigration can also be expected. Thus nurses will be involved not only in their professional roles but also in their roles as citizens.

REFERENCES

BBC News. (2001, June 4). Foot-and-mouth in Europe. Accessed online, August 5, 2001, at news.bbc.co.uk/hi/english/world/europenewsid_1191000/1191046.stm.

Burnet, F.M. (1962). *Natural history of infectious disease* (3rd. ed.). Cambridge, England: Cambridge University Press.

Centers for Disease Control and Prevention. (1994). *Addressing emerging infectious disease threats: A prevention strategy for the United States.* Atlanta: U.S. Department of Health and Human Services, Public Health Service.

Centers for Disease Control and Prevention. (1998). *Preventing emerging infectious diseases: A strategy for the 21st century.* Atlanta: U.S. Department of Health and Human Services.

Centers for Disease Control and Prevention. (1999). Control of infectious diseases. *Morbidity and Mortality Weekly Report, 48,* 621-628.

Centers for Disease Control and Prevention, National Center for Infectious Diseases, Division of Global Migration and Quarantine. (2000, May). *History of quarantine.* Accessed online, July 5, 2001, at www.cdc.gov/ncidod/dq/history.htm.

Centers for Disease Control and Prevention, National Vaccine Program Office. (2001, July 14). *Immunization laws.* Accessed online, August 1, 2001, at www.cdc.gov/od/nipo/law.htm.

Cohen, F.L. & Larson, E. (1996). Emerging infectious diseases: Nursing responses. *Nursing Outlook, 44,* 164-168.

Fauci, A.S. (2002). Smallpox vaccination policy: The need for dialogue. *New England Journal of Medicine, 346*(17), 1319-1390.

Fritz, C.L., Dennis, D.T., Tipple, M.A., Campbell, G.L., McCance, C.R., & Gubler, D.J. (1996). Surveillance for pneumonic plague in the United States during an international emergency: A model for control of imported emerging diseases. *Emerging Infectious Diseases, 2,* 30-36.

Garrett, L. (2000). *Betrayal of trust: The collapse of global public health.* New York: Hyperion.

Gellert, G.A. (1993). International migration and control of communicable disease. *Social Science & Medicine, 37,* 1489-1499.

Guyer, B., Smith, D.R., & Chalk, R. (2000). Calling the shots: Immunization finance policies and practices. Executive summary of the report of the Institute of Medicine. *American Journal of Preventive Medicine, 19*(3S), 4-12.

Hughes, J.M. (2001). Emerging infectious diseases: A CDC perspective. *Emerging Infectious Diseases, 7*(suppl 3), 494-496.

Lashley, F.R. & Durham, J.D. (2002). *Emerging infectious diseases: Trends and issues.* New York: Springer.

Lederberg, J. (1997). Infectious disease as an evolutionary paradigm. *Emerging Infectious Diseases, 3,* 417-423.

Lederberg, J., Shope, R.E., & Oaks, S.C., Jr. (Eds.). (1992). *Emerging infections: Microbial threats to health in the United States.* Washington, DC: National Academy Press.

National Intelligence Council. (2000, January). *The global infectious disease threat and its implications for the United States* (National Intelligence Estimate 99-17D). Washington, DC: Author.

Richards, E.P. (2001). Emerging infectious diseases and the law. *Emerging Infectious Diseases, 7*(suppl 3), 543.

U.S. Department of Health and Human Services. (2001, January 18). HHS releases action plan to combat antimicrobial resistance. *HHS News.*

World Health Organization. (2001). Renewing the international health regulations. *Global Health Security Epidemic Alert and Response.* Geneva: Author.

Vignette   Fatima Al Rifai & Anita Serdyn van der Merwe

Licensing and Regulation of Nurses in the United Arab Emirates

"Conquering, holding, daring, venturing as we go the unknown ways. Pioneers! O pioneers!"

WALT WHITMAN

THE VISION

In 1987, I had to write a so-called vision paper as part of course requirements for my graduate studies at Case Western Reserve University in Cleveland, Ohio. This paper provided me with the opportunity to actively reflect on my experience and role as an Emirati nurse in the Middle East. It is a place where major changes are influencing, as well as creating, new Ministry of Health structures, mechanisms, and directions.

Thinking back now, I realize that I was deeply concerned with the concept of visibility. At that time, all of the health systems within the Ministry of Health (MOH) were affected by ideas and influences from various cultures and health systems. Nursing as a service and profession was just emerging. The entire health care system, including nursing, was challenged to envision meaningful and beneficial strategic options. For the MOH, the options were numerous.

For my "vision," there was one core option to make nursing and nurses visible. I chose to call it "The Professionalization of Nursing in UAE." There were three goals that would need to be met to make the vision a reality. The first was the establishment of a Department of Nursing at the MOH, the second was the establishment of a nursing association, and the third was the formation of a nursing council in the United Arab Emirates (UAE). At the time my paper was written, all of these were probably well developed in many countries, but they were still only a vision for nursing in the UAE.

ABOUT THE UNITED ARAB EMIRATES

The UAE has come a long way since the early beginnings of pearling, fishing, simple agriculture, and nomadic life. The financial profits of marketing oil since the 1960s were used to develop a strong infrastructure in our country. Established in December 1971, the UAE is a successful federation of seven emirates, the largest being Abu Dhabi. Abu Dhabi the city is also the capital of the federation. The emirate of Dubai is world-famous for its business enterprises and shopping festivals. Sharjah, on the other hand, is well known for its unique cultural and artistic festivals. The emirate is proud of its many museums, souqs (local markets or bazaars) that reflect traditional Islamic designs, theaters, and educational institutions.

A traveler in the UAE will be fascinated with the beauty of contrasts—the constant interplay of classic and contemporary, traditional and modern in architecture, customs, and practices. The values in the UAE are derived from the Islamic religion and the Arabic heritage. The country and its visionary leaders have supported tolerance toward different religions and cultural backgrounds. As a result the country has attracted many skilled and unskilled workers

Seven Emirates of the United Arab Emirates

1. Abu Dhabi
2. Dubai
3. Sharjah
4. Fujeirah
5. Ajman
6. Ras Al Kaimah
7. Umm Al Quwain

to be engaged in business enterprises, construction, agriculture, health, and educational services.

The population of the UAE as of 1999 is estimated at 2,938,000 people. There is a large expatriate community seeking job opportunities. The ratio of males to females is 2 to 1. The population growth during the last 5 years ranged between 4.2% and 6.6% per year.

Health Services

The health status of the UAE population has improved significantly over the past decade and compares favorably with other Gulf Cooperation Council (GCC) states. For example, the infant mortality rate (IMR) in 1999 was 6.57 per 1000 live births, compared with 11.4 in 1990. The maternal mortality rate (MMR) was 0.003 per 100,000 live births compared with 0.3 in 1990, and the life expectancy at birth was 74 years for females and 72 for males in 1999 (Planning Department, Statistics Section, 1999).

The considerable growth in population and the improved health statistics necessitated major changes in the health care infrastructure. The Ministry of Health is the country's largest health care provider, operating approximately 30 hospitals with a total capacity of about 4473 beds. The MOH is also responsible for 105 primary health care centers, 72 dental facilities, 11 school health centers and 546 schools, 169 pharmacies, and 102 maternal and child health facilities. The MOH employs a workforce of more than 17,000 people, 78% of whom are expatriates (Planning Department, Statistics Section, 1999).

Abbreviations

> *EMRO:* Eastern Mediterranean Regional Office of the World Health Organization
> *GCC:* Gulf Cooperative Council (which includes UAE, Bahrain, Saudi Arabia, Kuwait, Qatar and Oman)
> *ICN:* International Council of Nurses
> *MOH:* Ministry of Health
> *UKCC:* United Kingdom Central Council
> *UAE:* United Arab Emirates
> *WHO:* World Health Organization

There are approximately 10,000 nurses working in the country, 6000 of whom are working in MOH facilities. The remaining 4000 are employed in the private sector, the Dubai Government Department of Health, Defense Forces health facilities, and other government institutions. The majority of these nurses are expatriates from more than 103 different countries. Emirati nurses currently constitute only 3% of the total number of nurses working at MOH facilities.

Formal Nursing Education

There are five MOH-funded schools of nursing. The first was created when formal education began in 1973. At that time it was a 1.5-year training program. It was later upgraded to a 3-year technical program. The 3-year program was changed to require secondary-school graduates. In 1998 the program focused on primary health care and case-based learning. Other institutions, such as the Dubai government and the federal government, fund programs—one of which serves the UAE Defense Forces in Abu Dhabi. This program admits both male and female UAE nationals after completion of secondary education. The Higher Colleges of Technology were responsible for upgrading this curriculum to a Higher Diploma in 1998 under an agreement with the regulatory Ministry of Higher Education and Research. In September 2000, the University of Sharjah launched a bridging baccalaureate degree in addition to a direct-entry baccalaureate program for nurses. This is the first baccalaureate program in the country.

THE JOURNEY BEGINS: ESTABLISHING A DEPARTMENT OF NURSING

The journey toward the visibility and professionalization of nursing started in 1992, when the Federal Department of Nursing was established. In 1989, I had returned from graduate school in the United States with new knowledge, skills, and experiences related to community health, organizational theories, and leadership. Most important, I had a profound concern about nursing's visibility in our health system. Until 1992, I worked at the School of Nursing in Abu Dhabi as an administrator and teacher. During the last 2 years I became more involved in MOH committees and activities. The MOH was going through important organizational changes, and I was ready to take on new challenges and responsibilities. In 1992, it was the opportune moment to integrate my "vision" of the MOH to establish a Department of Nursing. I accepted the position as the first director of nursing, and the MOH agreed to recognize nursing's unique identity within the health system structure.

Regulation of Nurses

In those early days I personally recruited professional nurses and administrative assistants to form a core team at the department. This team worked closely with the directors of nursing and of Ministry of Health facilities (hospitals, community health-based facilities, and schools of nursing) and soon gained the respect and status both as a representative of nursing in the MOH and as a representative of the nursing profession in the UAE.

The department team agreed to address the issue of regulation as one of our main activities. We identified two areas of concern: there was an absence of a centralized nursing database, and there was fragmentation of processes related to the evaluation, selection, and credentialing of nurses to be recruited for MOH facilities.

We found that nurses in the UAE are regulated under a variety of authorities:

- Nurses and nurse auxiliaries working in MOH facilities are regulated through various rules and systems. Two cabinet resolutions are involved. One resolution specifies minimum criteria to recruit all "technicians," including nurses. It deals with technicians "not obtaining higher qualification" and specifies an intermediate general education and three years of nursing education as the minimum criteria for qualified technician/staff nurse. The second resolution deals with medical technicians, including nurses with "high qualifications." The entry qualification is secondary-school general education followed by a 4-year bachelor's degree. Both resolutions contain grading and salary scales.

- The Private Medical Licensing Department of the MOH regulates nurses working in the private sector. A 1984 law gives it authority to organize the practice of "medical" professions excluding physicians and pharmacists. This law regulates the practice of all technicians, including nursing staff working in the private sector.
- The UAE Defense Ministry defines and regulates those in their employment. Dubai has an internal system of selection and regulation of those nurses working in the facilities of the government of Dubai and in the private sector of Dubai.
- The non-MOH government funded oil and gas companies' health facilities are self-regulated.

POLICY AND POLITICS OF REGULATION IN THE UNITED ARAB EMIRATES: POLICY FORMULATION

Defining the Problem

There was no unified nursing regulatory mechanism, and as a result there were many different definitions of the roles and responsibilities of nurses. The categories of nursing professional levels were unclear, there were different criteria for the evaluation of nurses within government and the private sector, doctors and other health professionals were the ones evaluating nursing credentials, and nursing was invisible within the health system.

In 1993 the department team engaged in strategic planning activities under the guidance of a World Health Organization (WHO) consultant, Ms. Catherine Hawkins. We developed a 10-year strategic plan. A major goal of this plan was to create a mechanism for regulating the various types of nurses. It was not easy for such a young department to launch a project of this scale when there were so many other administrative and service issues to be addressed. Our first task was to establish a nursing registration system and build a database of MOH Registered and Practical Nurses.

Collection of Information

We spent most of 1993 collecting information about the needs and perceptions of MOH officials and nurses concerning registration and regulation issues. We conducted interviews with top management and senior nurses, visited MOH health facilities, and talked to as many nurses as we could.

Top MOH management welcomed the idea of having an organized procedure for credentialing and evaluating nurses for recruitment. Senior nurses expressed their concerns regarding the process of evaluating nurses' certificates and experiences by other health professionals. They thought that a nursing registration system would allow them to have more authority over the evaluation of nurses for recruitment. Nurses, on the other hand, were happy to have their own registration system but were worried that the new requirements could adversely affect them.

We also studied the situation in the neighboring GCC countries and were inspired by the Bahrain experience. They were pioneers in nursing regulation in this region. In addition, we reviewed International Council of Nurses (ICN) and WHO publications that detailed the regulatory experiences of other countries.

POLITICAL STRATEGIES
Using the Media

It was very important for us to make top management, health professionals, other government institutions, the private sector, and most important, the public aware of our intention to set up a registration system as a step toward nursing regulation. Reporters from the major newspapers and a number of magazines interviewed us. We also arranged to participate in a number of TV and radio shows.

Being Prepared

We conducted several meetings with and presented the Nursing Registration System proposal to MOH officials. I still remember a very important meeting in 1993 with the MOH Assistant Undersecretary for Finance and Administration and his team. We presented our proposal using colored overhead projector slides and involved him in the discussion of analyzing the benefits of implementing such a system for MOH. The Assistant Undersecretary was impressed by our logical approach. He later approved our requests for more office space, for hiring more staff, and for buying the hardware equipment to de-

velop a computerized database for all nurses registering with the department.

Coalition Building

From the beginning we elicited the support of directors of nursing and involved them in the process. We included the issue of registration on the agenda of almost every meeting during 1993 and 1994. The support of other directors helped to resolve many issues related to implementation. Also, it made us aware of the concerns related to clinical practice and the definition of registration criteria.

Repetition of the Issue

We wanted to ensure that our Minister of Health and other health officials were aware of and supported the registration and regulation of nurses. We included the issue on every agenda, wherever they went:

1. MOH Nursing Strategy, 1994-2004
2. GCC Nursing Strategy, 1992-1996 and 1997-2000
3. GCC Health Ministers' resolution on nursing regulation and registration
4. Arab Health Ministers Council meeting and resolutions
5. Eastern Mediterranean Regional Office of the WHO (EMRO) Health Ministers meetings

POLICY IMPLEMENTATION

Due to the federal department's establishment within the MOH, the department had the authority to establish the registration system. It was also charged with forming the Committee to Organize the Nursing Profession, which directly guides and supports the registration process. The registration system was implemented by

- Recruiting four full-time personnel to staff the Registration Section.
- Developing a computerized database that recorded all nurses registering with the department. The original database system was expanded to include a nursing management information system capable of supporting administrative and decision-making functions of the Department of Nursing. This has enabled us to track the recruitment of MOH nurses, to

record their ongoing training and education, and to register nurses from both the public and private sectors.

Other achievements included the following:

- Drafting a Nurse Practice Act by bringing together nurse leaders representing Dubai Department of Health, Defense Forces, Higher Colleges of Technology, and the private sector.
- Creating stronger links between the evaluation, selection, and recruitment of nursing candidates and the registration criteria and standards.
- The establishment and refinement of registration criteria to focus on the requirements of academic achievement and experience of foreign national applicants.
- The formation of a Nursing Registration Examination Committee to review examinations for registration.

The committee developed recommendations to improve the system.

- The establishment of a Midwifery Task Force under the direction and supervision of the Department of Nursing, with a mandate to study and make recommendations to the Minister of Health for the regulation and practice of midwifery in the UAE.

United Arab Emirates Nursing Practice Act

Nurses in the UAE are regulated by more than one authority. The Department of Nursing believed that the credentialing of nurses should be done by nurses and that a national database needed to be developed. We realized that implementing a Nursing Practice Act would take a longer time and require substantial negotiations, but the registration process and the database could be done more quickly. In 1996, we decided the time was right within the Department, the Ministry, and other health institutions for nursing regulation. In addition, the topic was widely discussed and promoted at regional (GCC) and international (WHO, ICN) meetings.

The Department of Nursing formed a committee to organize the practice of the nursing and to support the development of standards and criteria for registration. In November 1996, the Department invited Ms. Fadwa Affara, an ICN consultant and WHO advisor on nursing regulation, to facilitate a workshop and an awareness seminar on developing a regulatory framework. The aim of this joint activity included raising awareness of the need for a national regulatory mechanism for nursing and opening a dialogue between the senior nursing staff representatives of various federal, local, and government institutions, as well as private health care facilities.

At the end of the consultation project the regulatory mechanisms were reviewed, the skeleton of the Nursing Practice Act was developed, and a plan of action for finalizing the act was outlined. In 1997, the Regulation Committee was enlarged to include nursing representatives from the Ministry of Health, the Higher Colleges of Technology, the UAE Defense Forces, the Dubai Department of Health and Medical Services, and the private health care sector. The committee worked intensively through 1997 and 1998 to develop a draft version of the UAE Nursing Practice Act.

The draft was widely circulated with directors of nursing in the MOH, the Dubai Department of Health and Medical Services, the UAE Defense Forces, and some private hospitals for review and feedback. The Regulation Committee and the Department of Nursing met with the MOH officials and legal advisors to review the feedback and to revise the draft to ensure closer compliance with existing UAE legislation. Review, input, and support were received from Dr. Enam Abu Yousif, the previous WHO nursing advisor (from EMRO), and Ms. Fadwa Affara. To enhance the influence of nurses, the Federal Department of Nursing also prepared a proposal for the establishment of a Nursing Advisory Committee at the MOH level to advise MOH executives on nursing practice and related issues.

The draft of the UAE Nursing Practice Act is currently under further legal review within the Ministry of Health.

POLICY EVALUATION

Timing was critical in evaluating how effective we were in making our vision a reality but the most important factor was the will, dedication, and concerted effort of an inspired team.

This photograph was taken after the opening of the seminar on "Nursing Regulation in UAE," which was held in Abu Dhabi, UAE, on November 10, 1996. Dignitaries in the photograph are, from left to right: Dr. Mahmood Fikry, Assistant Undersecretary for Preventive Medicine, MOH; Mr. Hassan Al Keem, Undersecretary for Finance and Administration, MOH; Ms. Fadwa Affara, ICN consultant; His Excellency Mr. Hamad Al Madfaa, Minister of Health; author Fatima Al Rifai, Director of Federal Department of Nursing, MOH; and Mr. Mohammad Saeed, nursing representative from the Armed Forces.

Supportive Factors

The establishment of the Department of Nursing and of the Nursing Registration System within the MOH is considered a major step toward nursing regulation in the UAE. Supportive factors included the following:

- GCC Nursing Committee and the EMRO/WHO Nursing Groups addressed the importance of regulation of the nursing profession at GCC.

- There were well-documented and supportive groups who created strategic plans, guidelines, and resolutions needed to get the process approved.
- Technical support was available from EMRO and the United Kingdom Central Council (UKCC).
- Other international and regulatory bodies provided support and impetus, and the availability of senior nurses with knowledge to

regulate systems within their own countries provided further support.

- MOH authorities were willing to sponsor and support activities related to nursing regulation.

Barriers

As with any policy process there are always barriers to face. It was no different for us. Barriers included the following:

- There were difficulties in securing an adequate budget and human resources to support the work of the Federal Department of Nursing and its committee related to the regulation and registration of nurses.
- The process of drafting and implementing a Nursing Practice Act took longer than anticipated.
- There was a delay in forming two groups to establish nursing standards for education and practice as recommended by the WHO Temporary Advisor.
- There was difficulty maintaining continuous contact with nursing representatives from non-MOH authorities who participated in drafting the act.
- The task of evaluating the qualifications and credentials of nurses applying for registration from more than 103 foreign countries was massive.
- There were four different systems to regulate nurses in the country.
- The establishment of an autonomous nursing council is not a familiar and practiced concept in GCC countries.

CHALLENGES

As we look to the future, nurses in the UAE are challenged to address the following issues:

- National expertise in the area of registration and regulation must be developed.
- The number and leadership capacity of Emirati nurses must be enhanced.
- All nursing leaders of different sectors in the country must continue to work together to support the proposed Nursing Act approval and implementation.
- We must determine how to find creative ways to work within the confines of original mandates

that categorize nurses as technicians. They are not congruent with proposed requirements of the Nursing Practice Act.

- We must secure adequate financial and human resources to support the implementation of the act as well as the expansion of activities for registration and regulation.
- Committees must be formed to establish nursing standards for education and practice.
- We must continue to raise the level of awareness of and support for the various aspects of regulation among nurses, relevant authorities, and the public.
- We must establish the Registration Information Network for GCC countries, and expand it in the future to the EMRO region.

CONCLUSION

If one remembers that substantial initiatives for the regulation of nursing started only in 1993, then the achievements are enormous. Many countries are proud of a long history of nursing regulation. UAE nurses are proud that we have achieved so much in such a short time, especially in a unique region of the world.

The major challenge within the next few years is the strengthening of emirati nurses, both individually and collectively. The first steps have already been taken to establish an Emirati Nursing Association, which should further enhance the image and strength of the nursing profession in the UAE.

The ideals created in my vision paper of 1987 are becoming a reality because of the ongoing efforts of the Department of Nursing staff, the strong collegial support of all directors of nursing of MOH facilities, the encouragement and backing of Ministry of Health top management, and our other health professionals colleagues. We have progressed on the long journey to achieve nursing regulation to protect public safety and enhance professional visibility. As Napoleon Hill said, "Effort only releases its reward after a person refuses to quit."

REFERENCES

Planning Department, Statistics Section. (1999). *Annual statistics* (Arabic document). Abu Dhabi, United Arab Emirates: Ministry of Health.

Case Study

Environmental Advocacy: A Nurse's Journey

Hollie Shaner McRae

"We won't have a society if we destroy the environment."

Margaret Mead

My tenth-grade ecology teacher asked me to read poetry to my class as part of an Earth Day program in 1970. When I finished reading the poem, I had tears in my eyes, and my audience were teary-eyed as well. I can't recall the poem, but it spoke of the sacredness of the earth and of our responsibility to make choices that would protect the environment. Little did I know that environmental advocacy would become my consuming professional passion.

I RECYCLE AT HOME—WHY NOT AT WORK?

High school and college flew by, and before I knew it, I was a registered nurse. I practiced in a variety of clinical settings, including critical care, hemodialysis, pediatrics, medical-surgical, cardiac care, school nursing, flight nursing, legal nurse consulting, and alcoholic detoxification. It was while working in a post-anesthesia care unit (PACU) in the late 1980s that I became aware of the great quantity of waste generated in my workplace largely as a result of direct nursing care. At home I had modified my lifestyle to include environmentally friendly purchasing, trash recycling, and composting. I paid attention to the choices I made about products I used and the waste by-products I created in the process. It troubled me that those practices were foreign to the hospital setting. "Caring and healing" were producing vast amounts of waste and toxic chemicals, but there was little awareness of the problems associated with disposing of health care waste. I implemented recycling programs for my nursing unit but quickly realized that for the program to be truly effective, many hospital departments needed to be involved.

A Problem is Uncovered

I learned that my state, Vermont, had passed a waste reduction law that mandated a 40% reduction in solid waste and the closure of all unlined landfills. I was curious what my employer was doing to comply with the new regulations and was surprised to find out the answer was "nothing"—and they were unaware of the new regulation. So I took it upon myself to learn about just how much waste the hospital was generating on a regular basis, and what a 40% reduction would mean. I found that my hospital produced between 2 and 3 tons of solid waste per day. A 40% reduction would mean we would have to reduce our waste output by more than 1 ton per day—a huge task. I talked with the hospital's housekeeping director to explore how this goal could be accomplished. We discovered we could achieve the mandated decrease in part by diverting paper and cardboard for recycling. I volunteered my time and was assisted by a facilities management environmental specialist to research recycling companies, select and distribute recycling bins, and identify waste vendors that could meet the hospital's needs.

Hospital-Wide Recycling Begins

In May 1990, we distributed several hundred recycling bins throughout the hospital and obtained a compactor for corrugated cardboard. I again volunteered my time to help the hospital find companies to haul away the collected recyclable materials. The results were dramatic: within a few months, the staff of nearly 4000 people were participating in recycling. The key to success was making it convenient.

Cost Savings and Other Successes

The hospital housekeeping staff was very support-ive, even though their workload changed. The housekeepers now had to make separate trips to dispose of trash, since the wastes were being segre-gated into solid waste (trash) and recyclable paper and cardboard. These recycling efforts saved $67 for every ton of material diverted from the landfill to recycling markets and $89 for each hauling trip to the landfill that was eliminated by reducing trash volumes. All in all, recycling saved the hospital about $15,000 the first year. The recycling program was extremely popular with the hospital staff and leadership. It fit well into the total quality manage-ment philosophy that the hospital had embraced. It was seen as a cross-disciplinary project with many benefits—including empowering individuals to create change in the workplace, saving the organi-zation money, protecting the environment, and complying with city and state regulations.

Critical Support

After working as a volunteer to set up the basic re-cycling programs and conduct the operating room (OR) MedCycle research study, I was given the op-portunity to write my own ticket and create a job description that would shift my responsibilities from nursing care to environmental management. I took a chance and wrote a new job description for myself and had the position approved through the human resources department. I was now applying my nursing knowledge of health care systems with an environmental twist. My new patient was our environment, and the care plan included modifying systems within the hospital to take better care of the environment or at least lessen the adverse environ-mental impact resulting from day-to-day health care delivery processes.

HEALTH CARE PRODUCT PACKAGING—GIFT WRAP WITH A HIGH PRICE TAG

One particularly busy night shift in the PACU, I was frantically caring for the maximum number of pa-tients our unit could accommodate. Many patients were trauma victims, and several were unstable. The staff was constantly ripping open more sup-plies to do venous cutdowns, insert chest tubes, and start arterial lines. At one point during the shift, the unit was in complete disarray. Every waste con-tainer was overflowing with packaging materials and remnants from procedures. The countertops were cluttered with trash from patient care. I thought my kids would be shocked to see their mom working in such a messy place—and not tak-ing time to sort and recycle. Much of this waste was clean and, in some cases, sterile packaging wrap, but we had no process for managing this waste. I recognized another problem that needed attention.

An Important Personal Connection

It wasn't long before I heard about an upcoming recycling conference in Burlington, Vermont. I contacted the conference organizers and offered my services as a volunteer in exchange for confer-ence registration. When 1100 people registered, my offer of help was gladly accepted. I attended a workshop given by Connie Leach of The Restore. Connie described how The Restore collects clean industrial scrap from area businesses and sells it for reuse in other settings. Following her inspiring talk, I introduced myself and invited her to visit the hospital to see all the health care waste that could be reused in other settings. I told her how nurses reuse blue surgical wrap for packing when moving, and how some surgical packaging makes great pots for plants, boot trays, dog dishes, and more. She was interested and agreed to come to the hospital.

Connie visited the hospital in early 1990 and we watched the operating room set up for an open-heart surgery case and another for a joint replace-ment case. I showed her how much of the waste from surgery is generated before the patient ever enters the room. I pointed out that this extremely clean and interesting packaging material is what many people consider "medical waste." She was fas-cinated by all the packaging and containers and asked if she could have some. The operating room (OR) staff was more than happy to part with their trash and honored her request by handing over bags of the preoperative packaging wastes. Connie brought the bags of wastes back to her store and shared the items with her board members at their next meeting.

We Need to Better Understand the Nature of Waste

Connie and I decided to do a research project to better understand the composition of health care waste. We applied for a grant from the Vermont Agency of Natural Resources (ANR) to study hospital waste minimization. In the grant application, we included a videotape of me dumping a 30-gallon plastic bag of OR waste on the floor and providing a nurse's perspective on a guided tour through the packaging materials from an open-heart surgery procedure. The grant was awarded to our hospital, and Connie and I were designated as the primary researchers. We designed a timeline and met with staff to see what how we could best design the study given the constraints of a real-world clinical setting. We formed a steering committee with members of the housekeeping staff, infection control staff, OR nurses, and the hospital's environmental specialist. We designed a convenient system to capture all the preoperative waste in blue bags in blue bins in each OR suite. The project was named *MedCycle,* a word I later trademarked.

MedCycle Starts!

The research project was based in the surgical services division of the hospital. The staff members were instructed to place all waste materials generated prior to the beginning of each surgical procedure in the blue bags. At the end of a surgical case, the blue bags were taken to three designated bins labeled "MedCycle Depot." The bins were then taken to a designated location in the hospital basement, where the bags were unloaded and weighed. Then the bins were returned to their location adjacent to the surgical suites. I transported most of the waste—before, during, and after work. I felt like I was living at the hospital during the research project. In all, we collected 3565 pounds of waste materials from 982 surgical procedures during a 1-month period. Each bag was labeled and methodically sorted, piece by piece, into 23 waste categories.

What Is all this Stuff Made of?

Once we sorted the wastes, we needed to identify the materials they were composed of. We needed to know so we could seek out recycling markets for those items that couldn't be safely reused in other settings, as art supplies or goods sold at Connie's nonprofit organization, The Restore. Some products and packaging were labeled with the recycling logo, so material identification was easy. Most, however, were not labeled according to their material contents. We sent letters to product manufacturers—after getting their names and addresses from the packaging items we were sorting. We informed them of our project and asked for their help in identifying packaging materials. In many cases, we got no response. In a few cases, we were told the information was proprietary and couldn't be released. As we sorted materials by type, we placed them into bags. At the end of the sort, we had hundreds of bags of solution bottles (made of polypropylene plastic), Tyvek, wrappers, plastic films, rigid trays of all shapes and sizes, blue wrap (Kimguard), white wrap, surgical glove packaging, unused tubing, unused plastic suction tubing connectors, colorful end caps from bypass tubing, and other surgical product packaging items.

Lessons Learned from Examining Trash

The hospital's purchasing director was quite interested in the project going on in the basement beneath his office. He was chagrined to see the many little yellow tickets (charge tickets) that we had been collecting—we actually had several sheets filled with them. These were noncaptured hospital charges representing tens of thousands of dollars of products. We found that expensive pacemakers and joint replacement parts had been opened and not used—representing thousands of dollars of wasted health care resources.

MEDIA ATTENTION

News of the MedCycle project appeared in the Associated Press wire service, and we found out our story was national news. Photos of Connie and me sorting waste in the hospital basement were featured in newspapers throughout the United States. Shortly after this occurred, it was time for my performance evaluation at work. My new head nurse in the PACU told me I had to make a choice: Either I was a recycler or a nurse, but I couldn't do both while working in her unit. She said she was worried patients wouldn't understand if my colleagues joked, "You have the trash nurse taking care of you today." She was not happy with the numerous phone calls I was receiving from housekeepers and other managers seeking guidance about recycling. She actually starting tracking how many calls I was getting. I had to decide what to do. I wanted to continue nursing, but I was committed to change in the workplace.

When One Door Closes . . .

I was still working in the PACU when the MedCycle research project ended. The hospital's chief operating officer asked me about the MedCycle program. I told him it was a pilot and that it had ended. He asked why I couldn't keep doing it. I told him about the conflict that had developed with my supervisor. He suggested I create a job description for a new position, if it was what I wanted to do—since it was saving the hospital a significant amount of money. I sought guidance from the hospital's human resources department, developed a job description, and asked if I could transfer to the housekeeping department as the "clinical waste reduction coordinator." My request was approved! I contacted the Vermont Board of Nursing to find out if my new job would be considered nursing. The board determined it was—and I began working in that capacity part-time. I had been able to combine my two passions: nursing and waste reduction.

KITCHEN GREASE, BATTERIES, AND LIGHT TUBES

In my new position, it seemed every day I discovered another form of waste in the hospital that was being neglected or could be better managed. I implemented programs to collect and recycle kitchen grease from the fryers. The company that collected the used grease recycled it into dog food, soap, and cosmetics. This program kept over a ton of grease out of the landfill or the sewers each month. Then I focused on all the batteries in the hospital. There were thousands of them: alkaline, nickel-cadmium, lead acid, zinc air, lithium, and others. Most of these were going in the trash, or worse yet, into sharps containers, despite the fact that many batteries are considered hazardous waste. I set up programs to

collect batteries throughout the entire facility. Fluorescent light tubes were the next waste form I conquered. I worked with members of the hospital's electrical shop staff who changed bulbs and set up a recycling program for them. I had a lot to learn about each waste form that I encountered. There are federal, state, and local regulations that define and govern different types of waste materials.

Plastics were the most difficult to figure out, but with the help of area plastics experts I was able to identify recycling markets for plastics that the local recycling effort could not handle. Plastics are bulky and have many different chemical compositions. Health care plastics in particular are not as common as those used in households. One observer of the programs I set up described the plastic recycling program as a "boutique plastics recycling effort." I coordinated collection, densification, transport, and documentation of recycling plastic types 1 to 7 with a regional recycler who was willing to accept small quantities of diverse materials. I also designed a food-waste composting program in partnership with a local organic farm. After the farm site acquired proper permits, we were able to compost the hospital's food preparation waste there for a lower cost than dumping it in the landfill. We negotiated an agreement with the farm to grow organic produce for the hospital kitchens. This project was featured on ABC's *World News Tonight* and in the *New York Times* garden section as a "waste to table circuit."

MANAGING MERCURY

During my tenure as waste coordinator at the hospital, I worked on phasing out mercury products. I co-authored four publications for the American Hospital Association on waste minimization, pollution prevention, and becoming a mercury-free facility. I served as the preceptor for four students enrolled in a hazardous waste course at the University of Vermont. Their project was to conduct a mercury audit to see how well our committee had done in eliminating mercury from the hospital. Much to my chagrin, the students found many mercury thermometers in the first weeks of the project. Word of the mercury project got around, and I was invited to serve on the Vermont governor's Advisory Committee on Mercury Pollution (www.

mercvt.org). Vermont is one of very few states to have adopted product-labeling laws for mercury and to ban products containing mercury from landfills. I was also invited to serve as an advisor on a project involving 800 dental practices that circle Lake Champlain in New York and Vermont. The dental project was a yearlong effort to develop a guidebook for dentists to improve their waste disposal practices and reduce mercury pollution in Lake Champlain. The booklet teaches dentists how to modify their practice to ensure that mercury from amalgams is properly disposed of and doesn't end up polluting the lake via wastewater discharges or incineration.

MOVING EFFORTS TO THE FRONT END

I joined the hospital's product standards committee, the group that evaluates products for use in the hospital. I volunteered to serve on the committee because it seemed that if more careful purchasing decisions could be made at the front end, we might not have so much waste at the back end. My role on the committee was somewhat awkward at times. Staff members would come before the group, present their request for a new or different product, and tout its attributes. I would ask the odd but necessary questions: What is it made of? How does it come packaged? Can it be recycled? Do we have to buy it as a disposable item, or does it come in a reusable form? Some staff wondered why they were subject to this scrutiny. I pointed out that in addition to the purchase cost, they needed to evaluate the disposal cost of the product and the packaging.

SOMEBODY OUGHT TO WRITE A BOOK ABOUT THIS!

I found my phone was ringing all the time with people asking questions about recycling. I found myself telling the same story over and over again. I said, "Somebody ought to write a book about this!" My future husband, Glenn McRae (whom I met through recycling work), was the director of the Association of Vermont Recyclers. Glenn, Connie, and I decided to write a book about what we had collectively learned and to publish it ourselves. We developed an outline and divided up the work. We were approached by the American Hospital Association to write a book on hospital waste reduction

and recycling. Our first book, *An Ounce of Prevention,* was published in 1993 (Shaner, McRae, & Leach-Bisson, 1993).

FLORENCE NIGHTINGALE LIVES ON

I got lots of support from colleagues who enjoyed watching my evolution from clinical nurse to environmental advocate. One called me a "modern-day Florence Nightingale," and I wasn't really sure what that meant, so I picked up a copy of *Notes on Nursing* by Florence Nightingale and read her original notes. I was amazed to read of her concerns about clean air, clean water, and waste management! She wrote that it is the nurse's role to manage the environment to promote positive life processes. That is what I was doing! I learned all I could about this visionary nursing leader.

"GREENER" PASTURES

In 1991, Glenn, Connie, and I formed a company, CGH Environmental Strategies, Inc., so we could assist other facilities and "green up" health care. I read about many pollution issues and became extremely concerned about dioxin. I learned dioxin is one of the most toxic compounds on earth and that in every animal species studied, it causes cancer. How ironic, I thought, that the waste from hospitals could create a toxic substance that would cause cancer.

I was perplexed by the avid support of incineration as the best way to manage hospital waste. I learned about federal and state laws that govern waste oversight and management. I found that many published articles use the term *medical waste* but are really referring to *biohazard waste.* I found that there was much confusion about Occupational Safety and Health Administration (OSHA) and medical waste regulations. Glenn and I saw the need to write another book to address these issues. It was published in 1995 as *The Hospital Guidebook for Waste Reduction Program Planning and Implementation* (Shaner & McRae, 1995).

HEALTH AND THE ENVIRONMENT

I became interested in the links between the environment and human health. I decided to pioneer dioxin-free medical waste management and set up a program at the hospital where I worked to have all medical waste autoclaved except for body parts (pathologic wastes) and chemotherapy wastes, which were designated for incineration. I discussed my work with Ellen Ceppetelli, who had taught community health nursing for more than 20 years. She was a visiting scholar at the Harvard School of Public Health and was very aware of the connections between human health and the environment. We met several times, and she suggested that I should consider becoming a visiting scholar to further my work on dioxin-free health care waste management. Thanks to Ellen's encouragement, I applied for and was accepted into the Harvard School of Public Health's visiting scholars program. I took additional courses in industrial hygiene, indoor air quality, and occupational health.

HEALTH CARE WITHOUT HARM

In 1996 I was invited to a meeting in Bolinas, California, that launched the national campaign called Health Care Without Harm. At this initial meeting, I found I was not the only person concerned about the waste and pollution from hospitals and health care settings. I met dozens of people from environmental, religious, labor, community, and other groups who were similarly concerned. Twenty-eight organizations gathered to address the irony that medical waste incinerators had been cited as among the top sources of dioxin pollution. Health Care Without Harm has now grown to over 330 member organizations in 27 countries.

Health Care Without Harm is a coalition that promotes pollution prevention, supports the use of environmentally safe materials, and educates health care institutions, providers, workers, and consumers about the environmental and public health impact of the health care industry. This includes advocating policies to eliminate indiscriminate incineration of medical waste, suggesting safer waste disposal alternatives, and building a broader environmental health movement (Health Care Without Harm, 2001).

THE ELECTRIC CAR AND OUTREACH ON THE BEACH

After building and managing a hospital waste program for 6 years, I handed the torch to a colleague for daily oversight. A position was created for me in the hospital's department of community health

Health Care Without Harm

Health Care Without Harm
The Campaign for Environmentally Responsible Health Care
c/o The Center for Health, Environment and Justice
PO Box 6806
Falls Church, VA 22040
Phone: (703) 237-2249
E-mail: hcwh@chej.org
Website: www.noharm.org

Health Care Without Harm's mission is to transform the health care industry worldwide, without compromising patient safety or care, so that it is ecologically sustainable and no longer a source of harm to public health and the environment. The campaign's goals are:

1. To work with a wide range of constituencies for an ecologically sustainable health care system.
2. To promote policies, practices, and laws that eliminate incineration of medical waste, minimize the amount and toxicity of all waste generated, and promote the use of safer materials and treatment practices.
3. To phase out the use of polyvinyl chloride (PVC) plastics and persistent toxic chemicals in health care and to build momentum for a broader PVC phase-out campaign.
4. To phase out the use of mercury in all aspects of the health care industry.
5. To develop health-based standards for medical waste management and to recognize and implement the public's right to know about chemical use in the health care industry.
6. To develop just (i.e., fair) site and transportation guidelines that conform to the principles of environmental justice. No communities should be poisoned by medical waste treatment and disposal.
7. To develop an effective collaboration and communication structure among campaign allies.

Health Care Without Harm is an international coalition representing more than 350 groups in 38 countries. For more information or to get involved in the campaign, please visit www.noharm.org.

improvement, and I began exploring ways to work in the community on the issue of environmental health and children. I was interested in air quality issues, having had asthma for many years, and I found vehicle emissions were the biggest source of air pollution in our community. I also learned that

Vermont had an electric car program. I convinced the hospital to lease an electric car for a year so that I could use it as a teaching tool in the community. Any hospital employee with a valid driver's license could borrow the car under the condition that they learned how to drive it and participated in a presentation on the relationship between air pollution, transportation, and respiratory health. The program was a success! Many employees signed up to use the electric car. I loaned the car to the dean of a medical school, and she really liked it! She wanted to integrate an experience with the electric car into the medical school curriculum, so we launched a pilot program. Medical students were offered an opportunity to use the car as part of one of their elective courses, so that- they could learn about the relationship between respiratory disease, air pollution, and transportation and teach their peers at their clinical site about it. About a dozen students made use of the car during the semester, logging hundreds of miles.

Another use of the car was the Outreach on the Beach project. I used the electric car to visit area swimming pools teaching sun safety and distributing sunblock and sunglasses to children and their families. Another creative use of the car was for an "Elderfest" community program. Senior citizens attending the event were offered rides in the car. Tacking on radon education to the adventure created an additional learning opportunity. The health department provided free radon testing kits and information, which were stored in the car's trunk. The electric car activities led to an invitation for me to serve on the board of the Evermont project. Through this project, I had repeated opportunities to meet with the governor of Vermont and encourage public policy that would promote the protection and improvement of respiratory health.

NEW HORIZONS

In 1999, I was invited to become an adjunct faculty member at the University of Vermont School of Nursing. I had been giving guest lectures for years in the schools of nursing, engineering, and business, telling my story about environmental projects that saved money and promoted sustainability. In July 2000, I resigned from my part-time position at the hospital to dedicate my time to working solely on pollution prevention in health care. I divide my time now between working for CGH Environmental Strategies, Inc. (the firm my husband, Connie, and I created), and consulting for hospitals, health care suppliers, and government agencies. I serve as president of the Nightingale Institute for Health and the Environment—an institute I founded to promote greater awareness among health professionals of environmental issues related to health care.

ADVOCATING FOR POLLUTION PREVENTION IN HEALTH CARE

I love being a nurse. It allows me not only to care for individuals and populations but also to be at the table when important decisions are made. Since I combined my nursing practice and interest in environmental protection and pollution prevention, I have been invited to participate in meetings of the U.S. Environmental Protection Agency, the North American Free Trade Association Commission for Environmental Cooperation, and state and local governments. I have worked with health care supply companies, the World Bank, and international agencies to share what I have learned about health care and pollution prevention.

In 1995, I proposed a resolution to the Vermont State Nurses Association (VSNA) to promote environmentally responsible clinical practice. It stated that nurses have the right to be advocates for environmentally responsible actions in their workplace, -such as recycling, using of recycled-content paper products, advocating the elimination of products and devices containing mercury, and eliminating toxic chemicals from the workplace. VSNA passed the resolution. In 1997, Betty Carney, the president of VSNA, proposed a similar resolution to the American Nurses Association (ANA) House of Delegates. Her resolution included eliminating all nonessential incineration of health care waste, managing mercury, and other initiatives. The ANA House of Delegates approved the measure overwhelmingly, and the ANA joined the Health Care Without Harm campaign. I served as a consultant to the ANA to develop the Nurse's Pollution Prevention Kit (ANA, 1998).

I was asked to provide a presentation at the International Council of Nurses (ICN) conference in 1998. Participants from more than a dozen countries were startled and concerned by what they learned about health care's environmental impact. The ICN developed and passed an environmental resolution calling for nurses worldwide to work on this issue.

LESSONS LEARNED

What have I learned from these varied but related experiences in promoting the health of our environment?

1. The Nursing Perspective Is Important to Policy Development

It makes a difference when nurses are at the table wherever policy is set and evaluation criteria developed and reviewed. In fact, the "nursing lens" is often a valuable contribution when working in groups and a perspective that many others are unable to define. Nurses tend to be systems thinkers. We understand how complex systems can interact. Many of us have this skill as a result of our understanding of human anatomy and human health systems. We are all too familiar with the interrelatedness of human organ systems. That systems thinking and the appreciation for the essential connectedness of all things (within as well as beyond human anatomy) are important in public policy arenas.

2. Seize Opportunities to Sit at the Policy Table

How do you get to the table? Sometimes you are asked; sometimes it pays to just show up. Sometimes your presence may be welcome, sometimes you may be viewed as a nuisance or unwelcome advocate. Nonetheless, in most cases it is very important that the nursing perspective be shared.

3. Prevention Really Is Central to Promoting the Public Health

After many years of caring for sick people and witnessing much pain and suffering, most nurses readily appreciate the full value of prevention. If we can prevent one child from getting burned, one elder from falling and fracturing a hip, or one person from being the victim of random violence, we tend to appreciate the full meaning of that capacity in a way that nonclinical persons cannot. Whether it's being an advocate for safe and healthy schools, the elimination of products containing mercury from our hospitals, or helping to provide safe and affordable public transportation—nurses make convincing witnesses for prevention programs. Keeping people well and safe are important functions of any society. Prevention is difficult to measure. When a nurse helps everyday citizens make the connection between miles driven in a car, air pollution in their local community, and asthma, suddenly the need for electric vehicles or other less polluting means of transportation (e.g., mass transit) and creating no-idling zones near schools takes on a new importance.

4. Know When and How to Make the Economic Argument

It's important to know how to measure the value of your services and understand the cost of resources around you for delivering care. Any suggestions you make to improve care that lead to the use of fewer products or decreased length of stay have value. Learn some basic finance principles to be able to make the case for ideas you have and measure the benefits. I obtained my Master's degree in business to better understand what was happening in the clinical setting. Before that, I didn't appreciate the value of the resources I used to care for people ("How much is that chemotherapy drug? That x-ray? Those supplies?") or the cost of services.

It's bizarre that most of us work in environments where we have no idea of the cost of running things, supplies, or our time. In most facilities, nursing is part of the room charge—we are invisible. I think I first realized this when I noticed that at nighttime, when I'd do a 12-lead electrocardiogram (ECG) on someone who was having symptoms, and I'd call in the findings to the resident on call, there would be no charge to the patient. However, when a 12-lead was done on the day shift or evenings by an ECG technician, the patient would be charged for the ECG itself and for reading it. In addition, the patient would have the inconvenience of waiting for the results, and yet another stranger would be doing something to them. It is vitally important for a nurse to learn to measure his actions and their benefits, as well as to convert that information to numeric values. If we don't measure our actions and document them, it's as if they never happened.

When I first began my work in health care waste management, I realized how important it was to record and measure the benefits of the programs. The administration understood and resonated with graphic images of financial data. Sure, recycling was morally the right thing to do, but the economic benefits, measured in avoided landfill and hauling costs for trash, made it a viable project. Additionally, since everyone was making more thoughtful disposal decisions overall, the added benefit of biohazard waste reduction was worth measuring, resulting in tens of thousands of dollars per years in savings.

If you are good enough at math to calculate medication doses and titrate drips, you are good enough to begin measuring the value of what you do. It's just using a different set of formulas. If you haven't taken accounting or statistics, give them a whirl—you may find out just how fun it is to have the skill to identify improvements, implement them, and take credit for saving your organization thousands of dollars. Most nurses are very creative. If you have figured out a way to do something more effectively or efficiently, you should perform a case study and calculate just how much that brilliant idea saved your hospital. One nurse in a cardiac catheterization lab requested that additional packaging materials be eliminated from the custom kit to create less waste. That simple change alone reduced the cost of the kit by over a dollar, and there were additional savings on waste not created—the simple change having resulted in 10,000 fewer pieces of plastic packaging in the waste stream.

Another example comes from a nurse on a product standards committee. Her facility was considering switching to a new syringe that was packaged in plastic instead of paper but cost the same as the other type. The nurse calculated that changing syringes, based on usage rate and the additional weight of the plastic packaging would increase waste by more than 10 tons per year. If that waste were discarded in the biohazard waste stream, it would cost the facility an additional $6000 per year. If it were discarded in the solid waste, it would cost the facility an additional $700 per year. The bottom line was that having a product with packaging that weighed more was going to cost more to dispose of.

5. Be Professional

Keep current; belong to your professional organization. During the years when my children were young, work was not the primary focus in my life; they were. All the while, I subscribed to professional journals and read them on my breaks and at home. I felt it was important to keep current. It is also important to read the literature of nursing and related fields. After all, would you want someone caring for you who was not up to date? I continue to be amazed by how many of my respected colleagues do not belong to any professional nursing organization or read any of the nursing journals or other professional journals. They rely on their employers to provide them with relevant in-service workshops and rely on the national television news shows for their knowledge. I learned that it is vitally important to stay current in knowledge and research in fields related to nursing. Currently I subscribe to a variety of journals focused on nursing, infection control, and waste management. I also read several daily, weekly, and monthly lay publications that focus on current affairs.

CONCLUSION

Many nurses and other health care providers are focused on care delivery, and we collectively neglect to examine our ecological footprints and resource consumption. There are many ways to make a difference in the workplace, the community, and the government. Find out how medical waste is managed in your organization and your community—and question if it can be done better. Find out whether environmental impact is being considered when health care product purchasing decisions are made. If not, request that such consideration be integrated into product selection. Nurses must begin to take on more responsibility for the products we use in delivering care and how those products are disposed of. A hundred years from now, when future nurses look back on our practices and learn of the pollution and exorbitant resource consumption we have been responsible for, they may wonder how we could have been so careless. Every purchasing and disposal decision made by nurses makes a difference.

REFERENCES

American Nurses Association (ANA). (1998). *Pollution prevention kit for nurses.* Washington, DC: Author.

Health Care Without Harm (2001). *About Health Care Without Harm.* Available online at www.noharm.org.

Shaner, S. & McRae, G. (1995). *Guidebook for hospital waste reduction planning and program implementation.* Chicago: American Hospital Association.

Shaner, S., McRae, G., & Leach-Bisson, C. (1993). *An ounce of prevention: Waste reduction strategies for health care facilities.* Chicago: American Hospital Association.

Glossary of Health, Policy, and Political Terms and Acronyms

COMPILED BY ELIZABETH M. LEHR

"The illiterate of the twenty-first century will not be those who cannot read and write, but those who cannot learn, unlearn, and relearn."

ALVIN TOFFLER

TERMS

Access: A patient's ability to obtain health care determined by factors such as the availability of services, their acceptability to the patient, the location of health care facilities, transportation, hours of operation, and cost of care.

Accreditation: An official authorization or approval to an organization against a set of industry-derived standards.

Allowable charge: The maximum fee that a third-party payor will reimburse a provider for a given service.

All-payor system: A system under which the government and private insurance plans ("all payors") pay the same amount for the same service.

Amendment: A request to change the wording or essence of a bill by adding, substituting, or subtracting material.

Appropriation bill: A bill to provide funding for a particular piece of legislation. It grants money already approved by an authorization bill and allows government agencies to take on obligations and to make payments for specific purposes.

Authorization: As it applies to managed care, authorization is the approval of care (e.g., hospitalization). Preauthorization may be required before admission takes place or care is given by non-health maintenance organization (HMO) providers.

Authorization bill: A bill that sanctions (authorizes) specific programs. It defines a program's aims and the way it will be run. Unless open-ended, the authorization bill puts a ceiling on the amount of money to be spent on the program.

Balanced Budget Amendment: An amendment to the Constitution that would require the federal budget to be balanced in a designated number of years. This would mean that the government could no longer spend more than it took in.

Ballot initiative: Some states provide for ballot initiatives whereby if enough signatures get into petitions, a legislative proposal will be brought before the people of the state for a referendum.

Beneficiary: A person who is eligible to receive insurance benefits.

Bill: A proposed law. Bills can be either public bills (those that deal with general matters) or private bills (those that deal with matters concerning an individual; e.g., specific immigration and naturalization cases). At the federal level, when passed by both House and Senate and signed by the President, a bill becomes either a public law or a private law. A bill that does not go on to become a law dies with the Congress in which it was introduced and must be reintroduced in the next Congress. In the House, bills are designated "HR" followed by a number; in the Senate, "S" followed by a number.

Bipartisanship: The idea that Republicans and Democrat should put aside partisan differences.

Block grants: Lump sums given to the states by the federal government for loosely defined purposes, such as child care or maternal child health.

Blue Cross/Blue Shield Association: Blue Cross/Blue Shield is a system of independent corporations that are collectively the nation's oldest and largest private health insurer and the largest third-party administrator of Medicare benefits. Each plan is an independent corporation.

Blue Dog Democrats: Fiscally conservative U.S. House democrats who tend to vote together as a coalition on budgetary and economic issues.

Budget: A financial report estimating federal government revenue and expenditures for the year beginning October 1 and ending September 30. Submitted to Congress by the president, it forms the basis for congressional action. States have a similar process.

Budget authority: Legal provision for a government agency to take on obligations that require immediate or future payment of money. The basic forms it takes are appropriations, contract authority, and borrowing authority.

Capitation: A per-member, monthly payment to a provider that covers contracted services and is paid in advance of its delivery. In essence, a provider agrees to provide specified services to plan members for a fixed, predetermined payment for specified length of time (usually a year), regardless of how many times the member uses the service. The rate can be fixed for all members or it can be adjusted for the age and sex of the member based on actuarial projections of medical utilization.

Case management: The process whereby a health care professional supervises the administration of health services to a patient. Case managers

reduce the costs associated with the care of such patients while providing high-quality services.

Case mix: The number and frequency of hospital admissions or managed care services utilized, reflecting the assorted needs and uses of a hospital's or managed care organization's (MCO's) resources.

Catastrophic health insurance: Insurance beyond basic and major medical coverage for severe and prolonged illness, which poses the threat of financial ruin.

Caucus: A group of like-minded people. Party caucuses are formal organizations of Democrats and Republicans that usually decide such matters as procedures, rules, and assignments. Alliances may also be formed across party lines to develop policies on issues important to a member or to his constituents (e.g., the Legislative Black Caucus).

Centers for Medicare and Medicaid Services (CMS): Formerly the Health Care Financing Administration (HCFA), the renamed organization was created on July 1, 2001. CMS provides health insurance to 75 million Americans through Medicare, Medicaid and the State Children's Health Insurance Program (S-CHIP).

Certificate of need (CON): A document provided by a state governing body to a health care institution at the institution's request, which allows the institution to build additional physical facilities to handle more customers/patients.

Civilian Health and Medical Program of the Uniformed Services (CHAMPUS): A federal program formerly providing health care coverage to families of military personnel, military retirees, and certain spouses and dependents of such personnel. It has been absorbed into the TRICARE program.

Coinsurance: The percentage of the costs of medical services paid by the patient. This is a characteristic of indemnity insurance, point of service (POS), and preferred provider organization (PPO) plans. The coinsurance is usually about 20% of the cost of medical services after the deductible is paid.

Collective bargaining: A process in which an organization's management and a labor union representing the employee population negotiate aspects of the union contract and other details of the employees' work life.

Community rating: A method to determine the cost of health insurance premiums, the yearly amount that individuals must pay for an insurance policy. The community rating premium is based on the average medical cost for all covered people in a geographic area. It does not consider any one person's medical condition.

Companion bill: A bill introduced in one chamber that is almost identical to one introduced in the other.

Conference committee: A committee made up of House and Senate members (called managers) whose job it is to settle matters of disagreement. Because the President or a governor can only be sent a bill that has passed both House and Senate in identical form, when neither chamber is willing to accept the other's amendments, a conference is requested. Each of the bill's provisions must then be agreed to by a majority of the House managers and a majority of the Senate managers. If they fail to agree, they may return to their chambers for instruction or simply report their failure and allow the House and Senate to proceed as they wish (e.g., call for another conference, make changes in the bill).

Conference report: The compromise bill fashioned by a conference committee and signed by a majority of conferees from each chamber. Both the House and Senate vote on the report without any further amendments. If one or the other rejects the report, a new conference may be called or another bill introduced.

Congressional Budget Office (CBO): A support agency that provides Congress with basic budget data, this is the legislative counterpart of the President's Office of Management and Budget and the Council of Economic Advisers. Among other things, the CBO prepares 5-year cost estimates of proposed legislation, assesses the inflationary impact of bills, analyzes and forecasts economic trends, and examines the president's annual budget. Through it all the CBO is meant to remain impartial, siding with neither political party.

Congressional Research Service (CRS): A support agency located in the Library of Congress that serves all members, committees, and staff aides. Among other things, it researches specific requests, publishes digests of bills and briefs on topics of general legislative interest, translates members' official correspondence from or into a foreign language as needed, provides charts for presentation of statistics, and has telephone hot lines from the House and Senate floors to answer questions during debates.

Consolidated Omnibus Budget Reconciliation Act (COBRA): A law that requires employers to offer continued health insurance coverage to employees who have had their health insurance coverage terminated.

Continuum of care: A range of services and care settings that a patient may require at different stages of his or her illness.

Copayment: A nominal fee charged to enrollees in insurance plans to offset costs of paperwork and administration for each office visit or pharmacy prescription filled.

Cost-based reimbursement: A method of paying hospitals for actual costs incurred by the patient. Those costs must conform to explicit principles defined by third-party payors.

Cost containment: A strategy that aims to reduce health care costs and encourages cost-effective use of services.

Cost of living adjustment (COLA): Through the use of a COLA, additional budget authority is given to such entitlement programs as Social Security.

Cost sharing: A health insurance provision that requires individuals to cover some part of their medical expenses. Examples include co-insurance, co-payments and deductibles.

Cost shifting: The redistribution of payment sources. Typically, cost shifting occurs when a discount on provider services is obtained by one payer and the providers increase costs to another payer to make up the difference.

Credentialing: Examination of a health care provider's credentials to determine whether he or she should be entitled to clinical privileges at a hospital or to a contract with a managed care organization (MCO).

Dear colleague letter: A mass-produced letter of Congress sent by one member of Congress to all fellow members, usually to ask for a member's vote on an issue.

Deductible: A fixed amount of health care dollars that a person must pay all of before his or her health benefits begin.

Diagnosis-related group (DRG): A program in which hospital procedures are rated in terms of cost and intensity of services delivered. A standard rate per procedure is derived from this scale, which is paid by Medicare for their beneficiaries, regardless of the cost to the hospital to provide that service.

Earmarked: Funds dedicated for a specific program or purpose.

Employee Retirement Income Security Act (ERISA): A 1974 federal law (PL 93-406) that set the standards of disclosure for employee benefit plans to ensure workers the right to at least part of their pension. The law governs most private pensions and other employee benefits, and overrides all state laws that concern employee benefits, including health benefits.

Employer mandate: A regulation, rather than a tax, directed at employers. One such mandate would be to require that all employers offer and pay for a portion of their workers' health coverage.

Entitlements: Government benefits, including health care benefits, that go automatically to all qualified individuals. They are part of mandatory spending programs. Examples are Social Security, Medicare, Medicaid, and food stamps.

Experience rating: A method used to determine the cost of health insurance premiums. The cost is based on the previous amount a certain group, such as the employees of a business, paid for medical services. Indemnity insurance companies most often use experience rating when determining rates for businesses.

Federal Employees Health Benefits Program (FEHBP): The health benefits program for federal employees, administered through the U.S. Office of Personnel Management.

Federalism: A political system in which two levels of government control the same territory and citizens. It is typical of the United States, where federal political systems divide power and resources between central and regional governments.

Fee for service: Traditional provider reimbursement in which the provider is paid according to the service performed. This is the reimbursement system used by conventional indemnity insurers.

Fee schedule: A comprehensive listing of fees used by either a health care plan or the government to reimburse physicians or other health care providers on a fee-for-service basis.

Fiscal intermediary: An entity, usually an insurance company, that has a contract with the Centers for Medicare and Medicaid Services (CMS) to determine and make Medicare payments for Part A and certain Part B benefits to hospitals and other providers of services and to perform related functions.

Fiscal policy: A policy of adjusting federal government taxing and spending levels to stimulate a sluggish economy or to reduce inflationary pressure.

Fiscal year: The year between one reckoning of accounts and another. The fiscal year of the U.S. government runs from October 1 through September 30 and carries the date of the calendar year in which it ends. States and private entities vary in the designation of their fiscal year.

Formulary: The panel of drugs chosen by a hospital, managed care organization (MCO), or other health plan that is used to treat patients. Drugs outside of the formulary are only used in rare, specific circumstances.

Gatekeeper: Most health maintenance organizations (HMOs) rely on the primary care physician, or "gatekeeper," to screen patients seeking medical care and effectively eliminate costly and sometimes needless referral to specialists for diagnosis and management. The gatekeeper is responsible for the administration of the patient's treatment, and this person must coordinate and authorize all medical services, laboratory studies, specialty referrals, and hospitalizations. In most HMOs, if an enrollee visits a specialist without previous authorization from his or her designated primary care physician, the medical services delivered by the specialist will have to be paid in full by the patient.

General Accounting Office (GAO): A support agency that acts as Congress's watchdog over government spending. Its chief functions are to: (1) initiate audits and review agencies and programs; (2) set up accounting standards; (3) provide legal opinions, usually regarding an agency's authority to spend public funds; (4) settle claims by or against the government; and (5) fulfill congressional requests for special investigative reports. The GAO is headed by the Comptroller General of the United States.

Gerrymandering: Deliberate rearrangement of the boundaries of congressional districts to influence the outcome of elections.

Health Care Financing Administration (HCFA): The organization now called the Centers for Medicare and Medicaid Research (CMS). HCFA was part of the Department of Health and Human Services and administered Medicare and Medicaid.

Health Employer Data and Information Set (HEDIS): A set of performance measures designed to help health care purchasers understand the value of health care purchases and measure health plan performance.

Health maintenance organization (HMO): A form of health insurance in which its members prepay a premium for health services, which generally includes inpatient and ambulatory care. For the patient, it means reduced out-of-pocket costs (i.e., no deductible), no paperwork (i.e., insurance forms), and only a small copayment for each office visit to cover the paperwork handled by the HMO.

Health plans: The benefits offered by health insurance providers to individuals and companies. The term sometimes refers to methods of paying for health care.

Hearing: A committee session in which witnesses are called. Hearings are generally held first by a subcommittee to decide whether a bill is worth taking up in the full committee. Later the full committee may itself decide to hold hearings.

Indemnity insurance: Traditional fee-for-service coverage in which providers are paid according to the service performed.

Individual practice association (IPA) model: The IPA contracts with independent physicians who work in their own private practices, and see fee-for-service patients as well as health maintenance organization (HMO) enrollees. They are paid by capitation for the HMO patients and by conventional means for their fee-for-service patients. Physicians belonging to the IPA guarantee that the care needed by each patient for which they are responsible will cost less than a certain amount of money.

Integrated health care systems: Health care financing and delivery organizations created to provide a "continuum of care," ensuring that patients get the right care at the right time from the right provider. This continuum of care from primary care provider to specialist and ancillary provider under one corporate roof assumes that patients will be cared for appropriately, thus saving money and increasing the quality of care.

Joint Commission on Accreditation of Healthcare Organizations (JCAHO): A private, nonprofit organization that evaluates and accredits health care organizations that provide mental health care, ambulatory care, home care, and long-term services.

Joint venture: A business endeavor in which two or more health care entities enter into an agreement to provide centralized health care services or a particular service by combining expertise and resources.

Lame ducks: Elected officials who will not return to office but who are finishing out their current term.

Legislative assistant (LA): See *Personal staff.*

Legislative history: The trail left as a newly introduced bill follows the path toward becoming a law. It includes such material as the original measure and its amendments, the committee report, the conference report, and references to it in the *Congressional Record.* A law's legislative history is used to determine what Congress had in mind and is especially helpful to agencies that must operate under the law.

Length of stay: The number of consecutive days a patient is hospitalized.

Logrolling: An informal pact between members to vote for the other's priorities.

Majority leader: The floor leader and chief strategist of the party holding more than half the seats in the chamber.

Majority whip: The assistant majority leader, elected by the party's caucus. The whip helps marshal majority forces in support of party strategy, encourages party discipline, and makes sure members show up for votes and quorum calls.

Managed care organization (MCO): A type of health-care delivery that aims to control costs by using "gatekeepers" to coordinate patients' use of health services. Managed care networks usually are organized by insurance companies, employers or hospitals. One such network is the type run by health maintenance organizations (HMOs), in which a patient sees one physician who determines the medical care—both general and specialized—that the patient will receive. A patient's access to medical services is controlled in this system.

Managed competition: A brainchild of the Jackson Hole group, managed competition is a health-care system in which insurance companies and health care providers would create health plans that would compete with other health plans for large groups of consumers. Under managed competition, individuals would be organized into large health purchasing groups to buy insurance. Health care providers, organized in a network, would vie for their business. A purchasing group would bargain with a network to obtain the best cost per individual. The concept is popular on Capitol Hill because it promises to provide universal coverage with low costs.

Mandatory spending: Spending (budget authority and outlays) controlled by laws other than annual appropriations acts. This covers such entitlements as Social Security and Medicare.

Medicaid: Publicly financed health "insurance" for the poor. Cofinanced by the federal government and the states, it has different eligibility criteria in different states.

Medical savings account: An account similar to an individual retirement account into which an employer and employee can make tax-deferred contribution and from which the employee may withdraw funds to pay covered health care expenses.

Medicare: A federal program that provides health "insurance" for all persons 65 years or older, regardless of income or assets. It also covers blind and permanently disabled people and persons with end-stage renal disease, regardless of their age. It pays for acute care (e.g., hospitals, doctors) but not for long-term care.

Medicare Part A: The universal part of Medicare that pays for hospital care. The hospital insurance program covers inpatient care after beneficiaries meet a deductible. The program also provides short-term nursing care.

Medicare Part B: The voluntary part of Medicare, known as Supplementary Medical Insurance, that helps pay providers' bills. Medicare Part B works by covering 80% of certain medical and nonhospital services after beneficiaries meet a deductible. It is financed by patient premiums and general federal revenues.

Medigap: Insurance provided by carriers to supplement the money reimbursed by Medicare for medical services. Because Medicare pays physicians for services according to their own fee schedule, regardless of what the physician charges, the individual may be required to pay the difference between Medicare's reimbursable charge and the provider's fee. Medigap insurance is meant to fill this gap in reimbursement so that the Medicare beneficiary is not at risk for the difference.

Minority leader: The titular head of the loyal opposition and floor leader of the party holding fewer than half the seats in each chamber.

Minority whip: The assistant to the minority leader, elected by the party's caucus. The whip's role is similar to that of the majority whip.

Muckraking: Searching or exposing real or alleged political corruption and scandal.

National health care: A health care insurance system that covers all citizens and various other residents. It often refers to a single-payor system in which the federal government is the payor. Under many such plans, the government sets all fees for hospitals, physicians and other providers.

N-STAT: A national grassroots political activity program for members of the American Nurses Association (ANA). N-STAT members are alerted about critical health care issues, encouraged to contact their members of Congress, and even provided examples of how to write effective letters to legislators. Some N-STAT members serve as leaders, interviewing and evaluating candidates for public office to determine whether to recommend that ANA's Political Action Committee (ANA-PAC) endorse a candidate's campaign.

Office of Management and Budget (OMB): A support agency to the president, OMB acts as a central clearinghouse, coordinating and sifting through the recommendations made to the president by party platforms, Congress, and pressure groups. It helps the President develop a legislative program by deciding how and where federal funds should be spent.

Omnibus bill: A piece of legislation made up of several bills. In both chambers one objection to a particular bill is enough to eliminate it from the package. When passed, the omnibus bill reverts back to the many bills of which it is composed, and each is engrossed and sent to the other chamber as if it had been individually passed.

Open shop: A health care organization in which the workplace is open for union workers and nonunion workers alike. This also generally indicates a working environment in which employee participation is encouraged.

Outcomes analysis: An evaluation system associated with managed competition that rates medical treatments according to outcomes or success rates. For a health care plan to qualify to offer its services to consumers, the providers in the plan must show results that are average or better. Analysts disagree, however, on whether reliable data to assess outcomes exist.

Out-of-pocket expenses: Costs of health care that people pay out of their own pockets (i.e., with cash, check, or a credit card), as opposed to costs covered by insurance.

Oversight committee: A committee or subcommittee of the House or Senate that keeps tabs on how the executive branch, through its agencies, is administering the laws Congress has passed.

Personal staff: Aides to members of Congress. Personal staffs may handle constituent services, correspondence, and public relations and give clerical, legal, and legislative help. In general, administrative assistants (AAs) run the office, and legislative assistants (LAs) work on current legislation and keep the member up to date on it.

Petition: A request by a citizens' group or organization for support on a particular piece of legislation or for favorable consideration of a matter not yet on the legislative agenda. In both chambers, petitions are sent to the appropriate committees for disposition.

Play or pay: A universal coverage plan in which employers either provide their workers with a basic health benefits package or pay into a government insurance pool. It is a combination of employer mandate ("play") and the single payer system ("pay").

Pocket veto: A way for the President to kill a piece of legislation by taking no action. If the President does not sign a bill within the 10 days allowed, and if during those 10 days Congress adjourns without setting a time for reconvening, the bill does not become law even though the President has exercised no formal veto. Similar rules exist for the states.

Point-of-service (POS) plan model: A health insurance plan in which patients are encouraged to use a select group of providers but are permitted to see out-of-network care providers. An individual who selects a POS plan may have to pay higher premiums, coinsurance, or deductibles than with a standard health maintenance organization (HMO). This feature enables an HMO to provide more flexibility.

Political action committee (PAC): Supply campaign funds to candidates with whom they are compatible. They represent such groups as labor unions, corporations, and trade and professional societies. They are regulated by campaign financing laws.

Pork barrel legislation: Legislation loaded with special projects for members of Congress to distribute to their constituents as an act of largesse courtesy of the federal taxpayer.

Preferred provider organization (PPO): Under this contract system of a health maintenance organization (HMO), providers (usually organized by "networks" or panels) give care for a set fee. Various benefits such as lower coinsurance and better coverage create incentives for patients to see "preferred" physicians.

Privatization: Transferring responsibility for providing services (e.g., prison operation, building maintenance) from government agencies to private firms.

Prospective payment system: A pay scale, adopted in 1983, to compensate hospitals and home care for Medicare services. The scale is based on the complexity of services a patient requires and uses the diagnosis-related groups (DRGs), a classification system that sets standard Medicare reimbursement rates

Provider: Anyone providing medical services. In fact, it may be used to refer to anything that provides medical services, such as a hospital.

Quality indicators: Any measure in the health care workplace that can be reviewed in the interest of ascertaining relative quality of service, such as patient satisfaction and delivery statistics.

Ranking member: The member of the majority party on a standing committee, next in seniority to the chair.

Ranking minority member: The chief member of the minority party on a standing committee, usually the person with the most seniority. The ranking minority member appoints and supervises the committee's minority staff and in general looks out for party interests.

Rate setting: System the government uses to reimburse doctors and hospitals for services. It implies strict control of costs. Under Medicare, the government has a complicated reimbursement formula that takes into account the procedure and the provider's cost.

Reconciliation bill: A bill that makes changes in legislation already enacted or enrolled to ensure that the expenditures laid down in the concurrent budget resolution will be met. Like all bills, it must be passed by both chambers and signed by the President.

Referendum: Special elections in which the people vote to approve or disapprove a legislative proposal. In a sense, the people become citizen legislators, taking over some legislative functions.

Relative value scale (RVS): Medicare put the RVS in place in 1992 pursuant to a 1989 law in an effort to shift Medicare funding toward primary care and away from specialists. The scale assigns a value to each medical procedure in the new Medicare Fee Schedule, based on the complexity of the procedure. A simple Medicare office visit may have a value of 1, while complex surgery may have a value of 3. The RVS uses a conversion factor that translates the number into a dollar amount.

Report card on health care: A tool used by employers, the government, employer coalitions, and consumers to compare and understand the actual performance of health plans. Report cards provide health plan performance data on topics such as health care quality and utilization, consumer satisfaction, administrative efficiencies, financial stability, and cost control.

Resource-based relative value scale (RBRVS): Effective in January 1992, RBVRS is a financing mechanism that reimburses health care providers on a classification system that measures training and skill required to perform a given health care service.

Rider: A non-germane amendment, one that has nothing to do with the subject of a bill. When a bill is blocked in committee, the Senate may add it as a non-germane floor amendment to another bill. Non-germane amendments may sometimes be the result either of logrolling or of courtesy extended to a member who strongly favors the measure. Riders are sometimes approved simply because they are popular, with full knowledge that they will be dropped in conference.

Risk: The possibility that the revenues of an insurer will not be sufficient to cover expenditures incurred in the delivery of contractual services.

Risk adjustment: Increases or reductions in the amount of a payment made to a health plan on behalf of a group of enrollees to compensate for health care expenditures that are expected to be higher or lower than average.

Risk pool: A group of people seeking insurance. This can refer to people who can afford insurance but cannot obtain it for medical reasons.

Risk selection: Enrollment choices made by health plans or enrollees on the basis of perceived risk relative to the premium to be paid.

Roll call vote: A recorded method of taking the yeas and nays. Members are usually given 15 minutes in which to vote.

Second party: A caregiver or provider. See *Third-party payor.*

Self-insurance: A form of private coverage in which an employer, rather than an insurance company, assumes the risk. Third-party administrators or insurers, however, may administer the plan.

Single-payor system: A universal coverage plan under which the government collects insurance premiums and administers health care benefits for everyone in the state or country, cutting out the role of insurance companies. Proponents argue that this is the best way to dramatically cut national health care costs.

Skilled nursing facility (SNF): An institution that has a transfer agreement with one or more hospitals, provides primarily inpatient skilled nursing care and rehabilitative services, and meets other specific certification requirements.

Social insurance: A government program in which everyone is entitled to benefits, regardless of income, but only if they have paid into a fund (e.g., required through employment).

Subcommittee: A division of a committee. Subcommittees hold hearings, mark up a bill, and then report in back to their full committees for further action.

Third-party payor: Anyone paying for health care who is not the patient (the first party) or the caregiver (the second party). This includes public and private insurance providers such as Medicaid, Medicare, Blue Cross/Blue Shield, and most commercial health insurance companies.

TRICARE: The Department of Defense's worldwide managed health care program. TRICARE was initiated in 1995, integrating health care services provided in the direct care system of military hospitals and clinics with services purchased under the Civilian Health and Medical Program of the Uniformed Services (CHAMPUS).

Underinsured: The number of people with inadequate health insurance for reasons including: high deductibles that discourage people from seeking preventive care; policies that do not cover needs such as substance abuse rehabilitation or mental health care; and policies that impose a waiting period before coverage kicks in. Also underinsured are people covered by Medicaid who are unable to find a provider willing to treat Medicaid clients.

Uninsured: An individual with no third-party coverage (private or public). This is sometimes called self-pay.

Universal coverage: A plan designed to give everyone in a country or state access to health insurance. Ways to do that include employer mandates, single-payer systems, and "play or pay" systems.

Veto: The President or governor's method of saying no to a bill or joint resolution (other than one proposing an amendment to the Constitution).

ACRONYMS

AAPCC: Adjusted average per capita cost
AARP: American Association of Retired Persons
AMA: American Medical Association
ANA: American Nurses Association

BC/BS: Blue Cross/Blue Shield

CBO: Congressional Budget Office

CMS: Center for Medicare and Medicaid Services

COBRA: Consolidated Omnibus Budget Reconciliation Act

COLA: Cost of living adjustment

CON: Certificate of need

CRS: Congressional Research Service

DHHS: Department of Health and Human Services

DRG: Diagnosis-related groups

ERISA: Employee Retirement Income Security Act (of 1974)

FDA: Food and Drug Administration

FEHBP: Federal Employees Health Benefits Program

GAO: General Accounting Office

HCFA: Health Care Financing Administration

HEDIS: Health Employer Data and Information Set

HHS: Health and Human Services

HMO: Health maintenance organization

JCAHO: Joint Commission on Accreditation of Healthcare Organizations

LOS: Length of stay

MHS: Military health system

OMB: Office of Management and Budget

PMPM: Per member per month

POS: Point of service

RBRVS: Resource-based relative value scale

RVS: Relative value scale

SNF: Skilled nursing facility

Resources

Harrington, C. & Estes, C. (1997). *Health policy and nursing: Crisis and reform in the U.S. health care delivery system* (2nd ed.). Sudbury, MA: Jones and Bartlett.

Heineman, R., Peterson, S., & Rasmussen, T. (1995). *American government* (2nd ed.). New York: McGraw-Hill.

Lombardi, D. (2001). *Handbook for the new health care manager.* San Francisco: Jossey-Bass/AHA Press Series.

Kongstvedt, P. (2001). *The managed health care handbook.* Gaithersburg, MD: Aspen.

Greenberg, E. (1996). *The House and Senate explained.* New York: W.W. Norton & Company.

Internships and Fellowships

JEFFREY P. O'DONNELL

"Life is meant to be a never-ending education, and when this is fully appreciated, we are no longer survivors, but adventurers."

DAVID MCNALLY

For those interested in pursuing interests in the area of health policy, presented here is a list of public policy internships and fellowships offering a variety of financial assistance and time commitments. Included is information on the type, pur-pose, eligibility criteria, and duration for each program. Financial data have been provided based on the best available information at the time of printing. Address, telephone number, and uniform resource locator (URL) to access the program's Internet site have been provided wherever possible. Additionally, many associations, think tanks, and government agencies offer paid and unpaid internships, so check the websites of organizations of interest.

NAME OF PROGRAM	TYPE	PURPOSE	ELIGIBILITY	FINANCIAL DATA	DURATION	APPLICATION REQUESTS
American Association of University Women's American Fellowships	Support for women doctoral candidates writing their dissertations and scholars seeking postdoctoral/ research leaves or funds.	To offset a scholar's living expenses while she completes her dissertation. Education is the key to achieving equity for women of all ages, races, creeds, and nationalities.	1-year postdoctoral research leave fellowships for women who will have earned a doctorate by Nov. 15. Dissertation fellowships for women who will complete their dissertations between July 1 and June 30.	1-year postdoctoral/ research leave fellowship stipend of $30,000; dissertation fellowship stipend of $20,000.	July 1 to June 30.	AAUW Educational Foundation Department 60 2201 N. Dodge St. Iowa City, IA 52243-4030 (319) 337-1716, ext. 60. www.aauw.org/ 3000/fdnfelgra. html
Brookings Institution Fellowships in Economic Studies, Foreign Policy Studies, and Governmental Studies	Resident fellowships for policy-oriented predoctoral research in economic, foreign policy, and governmental studies during the coming academic year.	Fellowships are designed for doctoral candidates whose dissertation topics are directly related to public policy issues and thus to the major interests of the Institution.	A graduate department must nominate candidates; sponsorship by individual faculty members cannot substitute for the formal designation of the department.	Fellowships carry a stipend of $19,500, payable on a 12-month basis. Supplementary assistance will be provided for copying and other essential research requirements in an amount not to exceed $750; reimbursement for transportation, up to $750; for research-related travel; and some access to computer facilities.	11 months of research in residence at Brookings and 1 month of vacation from September 1 to August 31.	The Brookings Institution 1775 Massachusetts Ave., NW Washington, DC 20036-2188 (202) 797-6000 www.brook.edu/ admin/ fellowships.htm
Carter Center Internship Program	Internship program designed for those who wish to combine academic study	Offers unique and diverse opportunities for undergraduate, graduate, and	Offered throughout the year to students who have demonstrated superior academic ability and who have	Financial support is not provided for internships. Offers a limited	Most interns commit a minimum of 15 hours per week for at	Director, Educational Programs The Carter Center One Copenhill

Program	Description	Eligibility	Stipend	Duration	Contact
	with practical application and experience. Interns participate in Center projects and conduct research under the guidance of academic fellows and project staff.	professional students who are interested in contemporary international and domestic issues. course work, professional or personal experience, and career interests related to Carter Center programs.	number of stipends to currently enrolled graduate and professional students who have completed at least 1 year of graduate study.	least one semester. Many interns are encouraged to extend their internship.	453 Freedom Parkway Atlanta, GA 30307 (404) 420-5151 www.cartercenter.org/internships.html
Congressional Black Caucus Foundation (CBCF) Congressional Fellows Program	Provides students with financial resources; create opportunities for minority students to obtain a college education; and enhances their political education and exposure to the legislative process. Assists in the development of legislative and public policy initiatives while fellows working as congressional staff. Educational enrichment is a major element of the program	Open to individuals who are students just completing graduate coursework, professionals with 5 or more years of experience pursuing graduate studies, or college faculty members who have an interest in the legislative policy-making process and who show evidence of an understanding of and commitment to Black political empowerment.	CBCF Fellows receive compensation in the amount of $25,000. Fellows are responsible for their own travel arrangements, expenses and housing.	All fellows must serve for the 9 months of the academic year.	Congressional Black Caucus Foundation 1004 Pennsylvania Ave., SE Washington, DC 20003 (202) 675-6730 www.cbcfonline.org/fellows/index.html
Congressional Hispanic Caucus Institute Fellowships and Edward R. Roybal Fellowship	Open to candidates pursuing careers in any field of public policy. The Edward Roybal Health Fellowship is offered specifically to individuals pursuing a degree in a nonclinical, nonhospital, Through in-depth discussions of public policy, presentations by members of Congress and policy experts, and professional and leadership skills workshops, the meetings offer participants concrete	Recent college graduates (within 1 year of graduation) and currently enrolled graduate students. Applicants must demonstrate active community involvement and participation through public service, superior communication and	Round-trip transportation to and from Washington, DC within the United States, health insurance coverage, and a monthly stipend of $2061.	Program runs from September to May.	Congressional Hispanic Caucus Institute 504 C St., NE Washington, DC 20002 (202) 543-1771 (800) EXCEL-DC www.chci.org/programs/fellow.htm

Continued

NAME OF PROGRAM	TYPE	PURPOSE	ELIGIBILITY	FINANCIAL DATA	DURATION	APPLICATION REQUESTS
	health-related field	opportunities to find their own niche and strategies to accomplish their personal goals.	analytical skills, and U.S. citizenship.			American Association for the Advancement of Science (AAAS) 1200 New York Ave., NW Washington, DC 20005 (202) 326-6600 www.aaas.org/spp/dspp/stg/cover.htm Note: AAAS selects and funds two of its own fellows, and runs an umbrella program for the fellows selected and funded by other national scientific and engineering societies.
Congressional Science and Engineering Fellows Program	Fellows spend 1 year working as special assistants in legislative areas requiring scientific and technical input on the staffs of members of Congress or congressional committees. Fellows are integrated into the staff and often must apply their science broadly. Committee assignments may provide an opportunity to focus more specifically on a scientific or technical legislative area of interest.	Fellowships are designed to provide a unique public policy learning experience, to demonstrate the value of science-government interaction, and to make practical contributions to the more effective use of scientific and technical knowledge in government.	Applicants must have a PhD or equivalent doctoral level degree at the time of application (January), but persons with a Master's degree in engineering and at least 3 years of post-degree work experience may apply. All applicants must be U.S. citizens. Applications for the fellowships are invited from candidates in any physical, biologic, or social science, or any field of engineering. It is acceptable to apply to more than one society. Stipends, application procedures, timetable, and deadlines vary.	$55,000, with allowances for health insurance and relocation.	Fellowship year begins in September.	
Coro Fellows Program in Public Affairs	Programs immerse participants in the many facets of society to study the intricate relationships among organizations and	To strengthen the democratic process by preparing individuals for effective and ethical leadership in the public arena.	Seeks bright, self-motivated men and women who are committed to public service. The strongest applicants are those who have demonstrated	Tuition for the program is $3500. Deferred payment plans are available. Financial stipends are available,	9-month program.	Coro Centers www.coro.org/programs/fellows_program/fellows_program.html 44 Wall St., 21st Floor

Program	Purpose	Description	Eligibility	Award	Contact
		social systems. Participants experience firsthand the breadth, complexity and pressures of public affairs, developing tools to become tomorrow's leaders.	leadership ability, integrity, and a commitment to public service. A Bachelor's degree of equivalent experience is required, and postgraduate academic study and/or work experience is desirable. Successful candidates have been active in civic or campus activities.	based on financial need, to assist with living expenses. Financial assistance is intended to assist with living and program-related expenses.	New York, NY 10005 (212) 248-2935 425 6th Ave., 17th Floor Pittsburgh, PA 15219 (412) 201-5772 1730 S. 11th St., Suite 102 St. Louis, MO 63104 (314) 621-3040 811 Wilshire Blvd., Suite 1025 Los Angeles, CA 90017-2624 (213) 623-1234 690 Market St., Suite 1100 San Francisco, CA 94104 (415) 986-0521
Employee Benefit Research Institute Fellows	Designed to aid the Institute in carrying out its mission of research and education. It allows individuals from the government, private sector, academia, and media to undertake projects on health, retirement, and other economic security issues.	To build a closer alliance between academics interested in employee benefits and economic security policy and the researchers at EBRI, its sponsors, and its wider constituency in the government, the media, and the private sector.	Must have a demonstrated knowledge and expertise in the employee benefits field based on an accomplished career in academia, government, the media, or the private sector. Applicants must be able to apply quantitative or practical skills to relevant public policy questions.	Varies based on type of fellow.	Employee Benefit Research Institute Fellows Program 2121 K St., NW Suite 600 Washington, DC 20037-1896 (202) 659-0670 www.ebri.org/fell/ebrifell.htm

Continued

NAME OF PROGRAM	TYPE	PURPOSE	ELIGIBILITY	FINANCIAL DATA	DURATION	APPLICATION REQUESTS
Helene Fuld Health Policy Leadership Fellows Program	Intensive fellowship to develop leadership and health policy skills.	Promotes the development of leadership skills and effective participation in health policymaking.	Post-baccalaureate nurses.	Only available through scholarships awarded by the program.	6 days, including attendance at the Washington Health Policy Institute.	Center for Health Policy, Research and Ethics George Mason University 4400 University Dr., MS 3C4 Fairfax, VA 22030-4444 (703) 993-1959 hpi.gmu.edu
John Heinz Senate Fellowship Program	Fellow will be in a position to be active in developing legislative proposals, attend hearings, participate in conferences' and brief legislators for committee sessions and floor debates.	To develop the knowledge and leadership capabilities of applicants by providing professional firsthand experience in issues that affect the aging. Children's issues will be the focus in odd-numbered years, and seniors, issues in even-numbered years.	Must be already active in the appropriate interest area and display the potential for future contributions to that area following a year of hands-on experience as a fellow.	Fellows will be paid annual stipends not to exceed $53,300 plus standard federal government benefits options.	Duties commence each September and end the following August.	Heinz Family Foundation 3200 CNG Tower Pittsburgh, PA 15222 (412) 497-5775 www.hfp.heinz.org/senate/
Kaiser Media Fellowships Program	Fellows are encouraged to do reporting based on their fellowship research and to experiment with different media or forms of writing. Each fellow pursues their own individual	To provide journalists with a highly flexible range of opportunities to pursue individual projects combined with group briefings and site visits on	Applicants must be U.S. citizens or must work for an accredited U.S. media organization, with at least 5 years experience as a journalist. Must be interested in health policy, health financing, and public health.	Annual stipend of $55,000 (prorated for length of actual fellowship). Travel for research purposes is also available.	Annual.	Executive Director Kaiser Media Fellowships Program Kaiser Family Foundation 2400 Sand Hill Rd. Menlo Park, CA 94025

Program	Aim / Description	Eligibility / Criteria	Funding	Timing	Contact
Kellogg National Fellowship Program	projects, so their fellowship experience varies widely. Basic aim is to assist future leaders in developing skills and competencies that transcend traditional disciplinary and professional methods of addressing problems. 3-year program designed for individuals in the early years of their professional careers. Fellows spend 25% of their time on fellowship-related activities, including a self-designed learning plan for personal and professional development.	U.S. citizens able to take part in all program activities and able to schedule 25% release time to complete individual inter-disciplinary learning activities.	a wide range of health and social policy issues. Fellows may receive a stipend of up to $32,000 over the 3 years according to the type and tax status of their employer.	3 years.	Kellogg National Fellowship Program W.K. Kellogg Foundation PO Box 5196 Battle Creek, MI 49016 (800) 819-9997
Morris K. Udall Scholarship Program	To preserve and protect the national heritage by the recruitment and preparation of individuals skilled in effective environmental public policy conflict resolution. Awards dissertation fellowships to doctoral candidates whose dissertation is in the area of environmental public policy and environmental conflict resolution.	Primary criterion for fellowship awards is scholarly excellence. Dissertation fellowship applicants must be a U.S. citizen or permanent resident and are open to scholars in the area of environmental public policy and conflict resolution.	Two dissertation fellowships are intended to cover both academic and living expenses. Fellowships carry a stipend maximum of $24,000.	Fellowship year beginning July 1.	Morris K. Udall Scholarship and Excellence in National Environmental Policy Program 2201 North Dodge St. PO Box 4030 Iowa City, IA 52243 www.udal.gov/p_fellowships.asp
National Center for Health Statistics (NCHS)/Academy Health Policy Fellowship	To promote the study of issues of concern to policymakers and the health services research community through the use of the NCHS data systems. On-site fellowship at NCHS	Education or experience in health services research, reflecting disciplines such as health care administration and the health professions, including nursing. Doctoral students in their dissertation	Full-time fellowship for 12 months, or part-time for 2 years. Stipend ranges from $36,000 to $97,000.	Two fellowships awarded annually.	Academy for Health Services Research and Health Policy 1801 K. St., NW Suite 701 Tech L Washington, DC 20006 (202) 292-6700 Email: nchs@ahsrhp.org

Continued

NAME OF PROGRAM	TYPE	PURPOSE	ELIGIBILITY	FINANCIAL DATA	DURATION	APPLICATION REQUESTS
Nurse in Washington Internship (NIWI)*	4-day intensive learning experience that culminates in a trip to Capitol Hill for visits with senators and representatives.	To provide nurses the opportunity to learn how to influence health care through the legislative process. Participants learn from health care policy experts and government officials, network with other nurses, and visit members of Congress.	Registered nurses and student nurses interested in better understanding health policy and the legislative/regulatory process.	Complimentary registration and recipient must assume responsibility for any travel, hotel, and incidental. Some specialty nursing organizations fund attendance for their officers and boards.*	4 days in early Spring.	www.academyhealth.org/nchs/brochure.pdf National Federation for Specialty Nursing Organizations East Holly Ave. PO Box 56 Pitman, NJ 08071 (856) 256-2333 www.nfsno.org/activity/default.htm
Open Society Institute Community Fellowships	Supports individuals (e.g., scholars, writers, artists, activists, advocates, practitioners) who have new ideas and innovative ways of approaching the myriad problems of an open society.	To promote the just inclusion of all community members to access adequate social resources to full participate in society.	Seeks applicants from diverse backgrounds and communities who wish to employ their skills in creating innovative public interest projects and demonstrate a solid background of working with the community (New York City and Baltimore) they wish to serve	Stipend award in the amount of $48,750. Project support grant in the amount of $2000, and an additional $1000 travel grant	Awarded for a term of up to 18 months.	Open Society Institute 400 West 59th St. New York, NY 10019 (212) 887-0187 www.soros.org/fellow/community.html
President's Commission on White House Fellowships	Each Fellow works full time as a special assistant to a Cabinet member or senior presidential advisor and also participates in an	Offers outstanding young Americans the opportunity to participate in the day to day business of	U.S. citizens only, to be judged on their professional, academic and other accomplishments, their current leadership skills and evidence of growth	Salary and benefits like other government employees. Salary is paid uniformly at the federal pay grade GS-14, step 3	Fellowship year from September 1 to August 31.	President's Commission on White House Fellowships 712 Jackson Place, NW Washington, DC 20503 (202) 395-4522

phase, recent graduates of doctoral programs, and junior faculty are eligible.

Continued

Program	Description	Eligibility	Cost/Stipend	Duration	Contact
	education program designed to nurture his or her development as a leader.	potential in those skills.	(approximately $74,000).		www.whitehouse fellows.gov
Public Policy and International Affairs (PPIA) Summer Institutes	To provide intensive exposure to topics in economic analysis, quantitative methods, public policy and international affairs. Summer institutes at Princeton University, University of California—Berkeley, University of Maryland, and University of Michigan.	Must demonstrate an interest in and a commitment to a career in public or international affairs. Applicants must be from historically underrepresented minority backgrounds.	Stipend, travel support, and room and board for the 7 weeks of the program.	7-week program.	Public Policy and International Affairs PO Box 18766 Washington, DC 20036-8766 (202) 261-5788 www.ppiaprogram.org
Robert Wood Johnson Health Policy Fellows	Designed to develop the capacity of outstanding mid-career health professionals in academic and community-based settings to assume leadership roles in health policy and management. Fellows have an extensive orientation that brings them into contact with key policy leaders in the nation's capital and prepares them for their 9 month work assignments with members of Congress or the executive branch.	Faculty member at an academic health center of a college or university with a medical school. Candidates for the program must be nominated by the chief executive officer of their home institution.	Annual stipend equal to salary prior to entering the program up to $75,000.	1 year.	Robert Wood Johnson Health Policy Fellows Institute of Medicine National Academy of Sciences 2101 Constitution Ave. Washington, DC 20418 (202) 334-1506 www.rwjf.org/app/health/fellowse.htm
Washington Health Policy Institute	Provides an opportunity for individuals to study current issues confronting health care consumers, providers and policymakers. Graduate or continuing education course on health policy making.	Health care professionals, journalists, government employees, faculty and graduate students interested in health policy.	$625 for three graduate credits or $550 for four CEUs. Housing not included.	5-day program in the summer with the option of an additional 5-day health policy internship.	Washington Health Policy Institute George Mason University 4400 University Dr., MS 3C4 Fairfax, VA 22030-4444 (703) 993-1959 hpi.gmu.edu

*The editors, contributors, and publisher of this book sponsor a NIWI "Policy and Politics Scholarship" annually.

NAME OF PROGRAM	TYPE	PURPOSE	ELIGIBILITY	FINANCIAL DATA	DURATION	APPLICATION REQUESTS
Women's Law and Public Policy Fellowship Program	Fellows are supervised by attorneys at different organizations, including women's rights groups, civil rights groups, Congressional offices, government agencies, and the Georgetown University Law Center Sex Discrimination Clinic. They are required to work exclusively on women's rights issues.	To enable law graduates with a special interest in women's rights to work in the nation's capital on legal and policy issues affecting women.	Law graduates interested in spending 1 year working on women's rights issues in the Washington, DC area.	$35,000 stipend and standard fringe benefits.	1 year.	Women's Law and Public Policy Fellowship Program 600 New Jersey Ave., NW, Suite 334 Washington, DC 20001 (202) 662-9650 www.wlppfp.org
Women's Research & Education Institute— Congressional Fellowships On Women And Public Policy	A fellow works 30 hours per week as a legislative aide on policy issues affecting women.	Places graduate students in Congressional offices and on strategic committee staffs with an eye to encouraging more effective partici-pation by women in the formation of public policy at all levels, to examining how policies affect women and men differently, and to encouraging the formulation of policy options that recognize the needs of all people.	Available to scholars who are currently enrolled in a graduate school or professional degree program at an accredited institution in the United States.	Stipend of $1150 per month for the 9-month academic year, $500 for the purchase of health insurance, and up to $1500 for tuition remission	September to May.	Congressional Fellowship Program Women's Research and Education Institute 1750 New York Ave., NW, Suite 350 Washington, DC 20006 (202) 628-0444 www.wrei.org/fellowships

Health Care, Health Policy, Political, Government, and Media Resources

MARY W. CHAFFEE

NADINE JACOBSON

"Sufficiently advanced technology is indistinguishable from magic."

ARTHUR C. CLARKE

Like the printing press and the telephone, the Internet has revolutionized how many of us communicate and access information. The Internet provides rapid, easy access to vast amounts and diverse types of information to anyone who can use a personal computer and computer network. The Internet revolution has been especially powerful in the fields of health care and politics. In health care, huge databases across the country can be tapped into, digitized images can be sent between health care facilities, and meetings can be conducted between health professionals at different sites using webcams and computer monitors. In politics, citizens can contact their elected officials directly through e-mail, grassroots political activity can be planned in chat rooms, political leader's voting records can be scrutinized, and voters can make campaign contributions through cyberspace.

To assist health professionals to tap into the extensive resources available on the Internet, this appendix provides a brief description and web address (uniform resource locator [URL]) for significant health care, health policy, government and related websites. This appendix is extensive but not exhaustive, as continuous growth is a characteristic of the Internet. Readers are encouraged to use search engines to seek out new websites and sources of information. It is also recognized that websites do not last forever. Every effort has been made to include websites that are expected to be active for a substantial amount of time, but there can be no guarantee that any particular website will remain in existence in perpetuity.

Health Care, Health Policy, Political, Government and Media Websites

AGENCY, ORGANIZATION, OR FIRM	WEB ADDRESS	DESCRIPTION
ABC	abcnews.go.com	Is a public news outlet.
Academy for Health Services Research and Health Policy	www.academyhealth.org	Seeks to stimulate the development, understanding, and use of the best available health services research and health policy
Advance for Nurses	www.advancefornurses.com	Provides general nursing news and information.
Agency for Health Care Research and Quality (formerly Agency for Health Care Policy and Research)	www.ahrq.gov	Provides evidence-based information on health care outcomes; quality; and cost, use, and access.
Alan Guttmacher Institute	www.agi-usa.org	Is a nonprofit organization focused on sexual and reproductive health research, policy analysis, and public education.
American Accreditation Healthcare Commission	www.urac.org	Is a nonprofit charitable organization founded in 1990 to establish standards for the managed care industry.
American Association of Colleges of Nursing	www.aacn.nche.edu	Contains government affairs link with bulletins, issue summaries, and briefings.
American Association of Retired Persons	www.aarp.org	Advocacy group representing needs of individuals over 50 years of age.
American Heart Association	www.amhrt.org	Provides program information, news, legislation, and research.
American Health Line	www.americanhealthline.com	Provides extensive health care news, policy changes, market dynamics and inside industry information (by subscription).
American Hospital Association	www.aha.org	Is a trade association website.
American Journal of Nursing	www.ajn.org	Acts as the official journal of the American Nurses Association.
American Nurses Association	www.nursingworld.org	Contains information on political news, N-STAT, and links to government and specialty nursing association websites. Contains policy and political information.
American Organization of Nurse Executives	www.aone.org	Provides legislative information and advocacy.
American Public Health Association	www.apha.org	Acts as an advocacy organization working to stop sexually transmitted diseases and their harmful consequences to individuals, families, and communities.
American Social Health Association	www.ashastd.org	Provides news from the Associated Press.
Associated Press Wire	wire.ap.org/public_pages/ WireWelcome.pcgi	Acts as a trade association for independently operated health insurance plans.
Blue Cross/Blue Shield Association	www.bluecares.com	

Health Care, Health Policy, Political, Government and Media Websites—cont'd

AGENCY, ORGANIZATION, OR FIRM	WEB ADDRESS	DESCRIPTION
Brief Guide to State Facts	www.phoenix.ans.se/freeweb.holly/state.htm	Provides statistics and facts on the states.
British Medical Journal	www.bmj.com	Often carries full-text articles of interest to U.S. health providers and policymakers.
Brookings Institution	www.brook.edu	Includes policy papers and publications on health care issues.
Bureau of National Affairs	www.bna.com	Provides news on health policy, business, labor, law and other topics.
Capitol Source	www.politicsusa.com/politicsusa/capsousrce/source-1.html.cgi	Contains a guide to 7000 officials, groups and organizations in Washington, DC.
CapitolHearings.org	www.capitolhearings.org	Carries a service from C-SPAN to provide audio of hearings.
CBS	www.cbs.com/news	Is a public news outlet.
Center for Health System Change	www.hschange.org	Focuses on activity in the dynamic health care environment.
Center for Mental Health Policy and Services Research	www.uphs.upenn.edu/~cmhpsr	Researches the organization, financing, and management structure of mental health care systems and the delivery of mental health services.
Center on Budget and Policy Priorities	www.cbpp.org	Is a nonpartisan research organization and policy institute with an emphasis on policies affecting low- and moderate-income people.
Centers for Disease Control and Prevention	www.cdc.gov	Provides information on disease control and occupational hazards.
Centers for Medicare and Medicaid Services (formerly Health Care Financing Administration)	cms.hhs.gov	Provides Medicare and Medicaid information.
Children's Defense Fund	www.childrensdefense.org	Provides a voice for the children of America who cannot vote, lobby, or speak for themselves.
CNN	www.cnn.com	Is a cable news outlet.
Commission on Graduates of Foreign Nursing Schools	www.cgfns.org	Protects the public in relation to evolving health-care policies and standards of professional practice for migrating health-care professionals.
Congressional Budget Office	www.cbo.gov	Provides everything one ever wanted to know about the federal budget.
Congressional Digest	www.congressionaldigest.com	Offers pro and con arguments on political issues.
Congressional E-Mail Directory	www.webslingerz.com/jhoffman/congress-email.html	Contains a directory of e-mail addresses for members of Congress.
Children's Defense Fund	www.childrensdefense.org	Provides a voice for all the children of America who cannot vote, lobby, or speak for themselves.

Continued

Health Care, Health Policy, Political, Government and Media Websites—cont'd

AGENCY, ORGANIZATION, OR FIRM	WEB ADDRESS	DESCRIPTION
Congressional Quarterly	www.cq.com	Provides Capitol Hill news, analysis and bill tracking.
Congressional Record Text	thomas.loc.gov/home/r104query.html	Provides the full text of the *Congressional Record*.
Consumer Law Page	www.consumerlawpage.com	Includes information of product liability and consumer protection.
C-SPAN	www.c-span.org	Is a cable television industry public service providing public access to the political process.
Democratic National Committee	www.democrats.org	Acts as a Partisan site with the latest news from the Democratic Party.
Department of Veterans Affairs	www.va.gov	Acts as the Veterans Health Administration website.
Division of Nursing, Bureau of Health Professions, Health Resources and Services Administration	bhpr.hrsa.gov/dn/dn.htm	Provides national leadership to ensure an adequate supply and distribution of qualified nursing personnel to meet the health needs of the Nation.
drkoop.com	www.drkoop.com	Includes health policy news.
The Economist	www.economist.com	Provides economic news and analysis.
Electronic Activist	www.epn.org	Provides national policy information and health policy links.
Environmental Protection Agency	www.epa.gov	Contains information on the agency's press releases, publications, initiatives, and regulations.
Families USA	www.familiesusa.org	Is a national nonprofit, nonpartisan organization dedicated to the achievement of high-quality, affordable health and long-term care for all Americans.
Federal Election Commission	www.fec.gov	Describes the rules and regulations of campaign finance.
Federal Emergency Management Administration	www.fema.gov	Provides federal disaster response information.
Federal Government Legislative Resources	www.lib.umich.edu/libhome/documents.center/fedlegis.html	Offers extensive legislative information.
Federal Register	www.access.gpo.gov	Acts as the official site for publication of federal documents.
Federal Statistics	www.fedstats.gov	Provides statistics from over 70 U.S. agencies.
Federal Web Locator	www.law.vill.edu/fed-agency/fedwebloc.html	Contains links to government agencies.
Find Law	lp.findlaw.com	Acts as an online legal research resource.
FirstGov	www.firstgov.gov	Acts as a portal to all U.S. government information and resources.
Florence Project	www.florenceproject.org	Effects political change by increasing public awareness of health issues.

Health Care, Health Policy, Political, Government and Media Websites—cont'd

AGENCY, ORGANIZATION, OR FIRM	WEB ADDRESS	DESCRIPTION
Food and Drug Administration	www.fda.gov	Contains policy and regulatory information.
Fox News	www.foxnews.iguide.com	Is a public news outlet.
Gallup Organization	www.gallup.com	Carries out and publishes public opinion polls.
Gay and Lesbian Medical Association	www.glma.org/home.html	Provides content on maximizing the quality of health and health services for lesbian, gay, bisexual, and transgender people.
General Accounting Office	www.gao.gov	Acts as the official site of the investigative arm of Congress.
Georgetown University Institute for Health Care Research and Policy	www.cfm.georgetown.edu/ihcrp.html	Provides research, health policy analysis and educational programs.
GoverNet	www.governet.com	Provides legislator voting records.
Government Printing Office	www.access.gpo.gov/su_docs	Contains congressional bills since 1993, a Congressional directory, economic indicators, and the U.S. Code.
Guide to U.S. Government Documents	www.wcs-online.com/usgovdoc	Contains a complete list of federal documents.
Harvard School of Public Health	www.hsph.harvard.edu/grhf	Acts as a research library, with discussion forums and links on health issues, gender issues, politics, population policy, and other topics.
Health Affairs	www.healthaffairs.org	Is a journal dedicated to the exploration of domestic and international health issues.
Health Care Quality Commission	Hcqualitycommission.gov	Acts as the website of the President's Advisory Commission on Consumer Protection and Quality in the Health Care Industry.
Health Insurance Association of America	www.hiaa.org	Is a trade association representing the private health care system.
Health Law Hippo	hippo.findlaw.com	Provides policy and regulatory information.
Health Policy Coach	www.healtlhpolicycoach.org	Equips one with the tools, strategies and information needed to create policy change in the local community.
Health Policy Tracking Service	www.stateserv.hpts.org	Provides state legislation summaries, issue briefs, and other information from the National Conference on State Legislatures.
Healthcare Leadership Council	www.hlc.org	Provides public policy and legislative information.
HealthCast	www.kaisernetwork.org/health_cast/hcast_index.cfm	Acts as the webcasting service of kaisernetwork.org, streaming health policy events including seminars, conferences, press briefings, and congressional hearings.

Continued

Health Care, Health Policy, Political, Government and Media Websites—cont'd

AGENCY, ORGANIZATION, OR FIRM	WEB ADDRESS	DESCRIPTION
HealthLeaders.com	www.healthleaders.com	Is a media company that encompasses three entities: HealthLeaders News, HealthLeaders Research and HealthLeaders Magazine.
Healthy People 2010	www.health.gov/healthypeople	Is a national health promotion and disease prevention initiative.
Henry J. Kaiser Family Foundation	www.kff.org	Is an independent philanthropic organization focusing on the major health care issues facing the nation.
Heritage Foundation	www.heritage.org	Acts as a research and educational institute (a think tank) whose mission is to formulate and promote conservative public policies.
The Hill	www.hillnews.com	Provides daily news from Capitol Hill.
House Democratic Caucus	www.house.gov/demcaucus/welcome.html	Provides details on Democratic caucus activities.
House Home Page	www.house.gov	Acts as the website of the U.S. House of Representatives.
House Republican Conference	www.hillsource.house.gov	Provides House Republican information.
Institute for Children's Health Policy	www.ichp.edu	Provides content on health policies, programs, and systems that promote the health and well-being of children.
Institute of Medicine	www.iom.edu	Strives to advance and disseminate scientific knowledge to improve human health.
International Council of Nurses	www.icn.org	Includes policy statements on international issues.
Internet Healthcare Coalition	www.ihc.net	Acts as an organization devoted to better heath care resources on the Internet.
INurse	www.iNurse.com	Acts as the website for multiple specialty nursing associations.
JAMA	jama.ama-assn.org	Acts as the official journal of the American Medical Association.
Journal of Health, Politics, Policy and Law	www.jhppl.org	Is a multidisciplinary publication of Duke University Press.
Journal of Public Health Policy	members.aol.com/jphpterris/jphp.htm	Provides editorials, articles and book reviews on epidemiology and public health policy.
Kennedy School Online Political Information Network	www.hjarvard.edu/-ksgpress/opinhome.htm	Provides a wide variety of political information.
League of Women Voters	www.lwv.org	Acts as a nonpartisan political organization encouraging active participation of citizens and working to increase understanding of major public policy issues.

Health Care, Health Policy, Political, Government and Media Websites—cont'd

AGENCY, ORGANIZATION, OR FIRM	WEB ADDRESS	DESCRIPTION
LegiState	www.legistate.com	Provides news from every state capitol.
Library of Congress	www.lcweb.loc.gov	Contains the most comprehensive resource library in the world.
Maternal Child Health Policy Research Center	www.mchpolicy.org	Specializes in health care issues affecting children, including those with special health care needs and those from low-income families.
Medicare	www.medicare.gov	Acts as the official government website for people with Medicare.
Medicare Payment Advisory Commission	www.medpac.gov	Is an independent federal body that advises Congress on the Medicare program.
MSNBC	www.msnbc.com	Is a public news outlet.
The Nation	www.TheNation.com	Provides discussion of political and social questions.
National Academy of Press	www.nap.edu	Publishes reports of a number of national academies, institutes, and councils on topics in science, engineering, and health and health policy, and includes books that can be purchased or read online.
National Academy for State Health Policy	www.nashp.org	Acts as a nonprofit, nonpartisan public policy think tank.
National Center for Policy Analysis	www.ncpa.org	Provides multiple policy resources.
National Clearinghouse for Alcohol and Drug Information	www.health.org	Is a primary site for information on alcohol and drug topics.
National Coalition on Healthcare	www.americashealth.org	Is a coalition committed to health care quality.
National Committee for Quality Assurance	www.ncqa.org	Is a private not-for-profit organization dedicated to improving health care.
National Conference of State Legislatures	www.ncsl.org	Acts as a forum for advancing ideas.
National Council against Health Fraud	www.ncahf.org	Is a private nonprofit, voluntary health agency that focuses upon health misinformation, fraud, and quackery as public health problems.
National Council of State Boards of Nursing, Inc.	www.ncsbn.org	Includes policy and regulations.
National Governor's Association	www.nga.org	Acts as the collective voice of the nation's governors.
National Health Policy Forum	www.nhpf.org	Is a nonpartisan education and information exchange program primarily serving federal legislative and executive agency staff working in health care and related areas.
National Institute of Nursing Research	www.nih.gov/ninr	Acts as the National Institute of Health's research branch for nursing.

Continued

Health Care, Health Policy, Political, Government and Media Websites—cont'd

AGENCY, ORGANIZATION, OR FIRM	WEB ADDRESS	DESCRIPTION
National Institute for Occupational Safety and Health	www.cdc.gov/diseases/niosh.html	Includes information on violence in the workplace, air quality, and other safety issues.
National Institutes of Health	www.nih.gov	Provides an organizational overview, a calendar, and special reports.
National Journal	www.nationaljournal.com	Provides news and analysis (by subscription).
National League for Nursing	www.nln.org	Provides education and workforce information.
National Library of Medicine	www.nlm.nih.gov	Contains extensive health care resources
National Republican Congressional Committee	www.nrcc.org	Contains Republican information.
National Review	www.nationalreview.com	Provides conservative news and commentary.
Nation's Health	www.apha.org/journal/nation/tnhhome.htm	Is the online newspaper of the American Public Health Association.
New England Journal of Medicine	www.nejm.org	Contains abstracts as well as full text of some features.
New York Times	www.nytimes.com	Provides daily news.
Newsday	www.newsday.com	Provides daily news.
NPR	www.npr.org	Acts as the website of National Public Radio.
Nurse Advocate	www.nurseadvocate.org	Provides workplace safety information.
NurseWeek	www.nurseweek.com	Is a weekly publication that includes legislative updates.
NursingCenter.com	www.nursingcenter.com	Acts as an interactive web portal, providing access to reference materials; products and services; and information on social, ethical and political topics.
NursingNet	www.nursingnet.org	Acts as a nursing "megasite."
Occupational Health and Safety Administration	www.osha.com	Includes information on occupational health and current issues.
Office of Management and Budget	www.whitehouse.gov/omb	Acts as the official website for the organization that assists the President in the development and execution of policies and programs, and has a hand in the development and resolution of all budget, policy, legislative, regulatory, procurement, and management issues on behalf of the President.
Pan American Health Organization	www.paho.org	Acts as the regional office for the Americas for the World Health Organization.
Partnership for Organ Donation	www.transweb.org/partnership	Is a nonprofit organization dedicated to organ donation.
PBS	www.pbs.org	Is a public news outlet.

Health Care, Health Policy, Political, Government and Media Websites—cont'd

AGENCY, ORGANIZATION, OR FIRM	WEB ADDRESS	DESCRIPTION
Pew Health Commission	futurehealth.ucsf.edu/pewcomm.html	Assists educational institutions and workforce policy makers produce health care workers who meet the changing needs of the American health care system.
Policy, Politics & Nursing Practice	www.sagepub.com	Is a nursing journal focused on policy and politics.
Politics1	www.politics1.com	Contains extensive information on dozens of political parties in the United States.
Project Hope	www.projhope.org	Provides international health education, policy research, and humanitarian assistance.
Rand Institute	www.rand.org	Is a nonprofit institution that supports policy analysis and improved decision making; includes health topics.
Reuters Health Information Services	www.reutershealth.com	Provides the top health news stories.
Robert Wood Johnson Foundation	rwjf.org	Is the largest U.S. foundation devoted to improving the health and health care of all Americans.
Roll Call	www.rollcall.com	Provides Capitol Hill news and analysis.
Senate Home Page	www.senate.gov	Acts as the U.S. Senate home page
Sigma Theta Tau	www.nursingsociety.org	Acts as the international honor society of nursing.
Sigma Theta Tau International	www.nursingsociety.org	Contains information on research grant opportunities.
Slate	www.slate.com	Is an online political magazine.
SpeakOut.com	www.speakout.com	Acts as a political activity forum.
Thomas: Legislative Information on the Net	www.thomas.loc.gov	Provides information on legislation, voting records, committees, and historical documents.
TRICARE	tricare.osd.mil	Provides information on the U.S. military health system.
The 2Minute Activist	www.ccnet.com/zen7/zen7.html	Provides a way for busy people to get involved in the political process.
U.S. Census Bureau	www.census.gov	Provides U.S. social, demographic, and economic information.
U.S. Constitution	www.constitutionfacts.com	Provides the text of the most important document in U.S. history.
U.S. Department of Health and Human Services	www.dhhs.gov	Provides mission statements, publications, and press releases.
U.S. House of Representatives	www.house.gov	Providers information on bills, members, schedules, and being a visitor.
U.S. House of Representatives Internet Law Library	law.house.gov	Contains links to sources of federal law, state law, the U.S. Code, and the Code of Federal Regulations
U.S. Senate	www.senate.gov	Provides information on bills, members, schedules, and being a visitor.

Continued

Health Care, Health Policy, Political, Government and Media Websites—cont'd

AGENCY, ORGANIZATION, OR FIRM	WEB ADDRESS	DESCRIPTION
U.S. Treasury	www.ustreas.gov	Contains detailed information on the federal budget.
UCLA Center for Health Policy Research	www.healthpolicy.ucla.edu	Conducts research on national, state, and local health policy issues; provides public service to policy makers and community leaders; and offers educational opportunities for graduate students and postdoctoral fellows.
Urban Institute	www.urban.org	Is a nonpartisan economic and social policy research organization.
USA CityLink Project	www.usacitylink.com	Provides access to sites featuring U.S. states and cities.
USA Today	www.usatoday.com	Is a public news outlet.
VoteNet Solutions	www.capweb.net	Is a nonpartisan, non-ideologic technology solutions firm for the public policy and politics market that helps political organizations to use the Internet to achieve their strategic goals and objectives.
Wall Street Journal	www.wsj.com	Is a daily nationwide newspaper.
Washington Post	www.washingtonpost.com	Is a daily Washington, DC newspaper.
WebMD	www.webmd.com	Provides online articles for consumers and practitioners.
The White House	www.whitehouse.gov	Contains a virtual library, citizens handbook, and tour.
Whole Nurse	www.wholenurse.com	Provides varied nursing information.
Women's Internet Page	www.aauw.org	Acts as a website, maintained by American Association of University Women, to encourage political involvement.
World Health Organization	www.who.ch/welcome.html	Provides services and hyperlinks.

Search Engines

To locate a website when you do not know the web address, use a search engine or metasearch engine to locate it. Metasearch engines do not search themselves; they send search requests to multiple search engines and compile the results on one Internet page.

SEARCH ENGINE	WEB ADDRESS	DESCRIPTION
Achoo!	www.achoo.com	Health-related topics search engine
Alta Vista	www.altavista.digital.com	General interest search engine
Dogpile	www.dogpile.com	Meta-search engine
Excite	www.excite.com	General interest search engine
Google	www.google.com	General search engine
Health A to Z	www.healthatoz.com	Health topics search engine
Hotbot	www.hotbot.com	General interest search engine
InfoSeek	www.infoseek.com	General interest search engine
Lycos	www.lycos.com	General interest search engine
Magellen	www.mckinley.com	General interest search engine
Metacrawler	www.metacrawler.com	Meta-search engine
Yahoo	www.yahoo.com	General interest search engine

Index

A

AAAA. *See* Army Aviation Association of America
AACN. *See* American Association of Colleges of Nursing; American Association of Critical-Care Nurses
AANA. *See* American Association of Nurse Anesthetists
AANP. *See* American Academy of Nurse Practitioners
AAP. *See* American Academy of Pediatrics
AARP. *See* American Association of Retired Persons
Abbottsford Community Health Center, 87-91
Abbottsford Family Practice & Counseling, 87, 90
Abortion, 662
Absorption, 335
Access, framing for, 169
Access to child care, 670-671
Access to health care, 301, 303-305, 708
    "An Act to Increase Access to Primary Health Care Services" (PL 296) (Maine), 379, *380*
    universal, 309
Access to information technology, 108-110
Access to long-term care, 430
Access to Medical Treatment Act, 296
Accountability, 179, 341
Accreditation
    of child-care centers, 672
    of health care organizations, 316
Accuracy, 110
ACEP. *See* American College of Emergency Physicians
ACF. *See* Administration for Children and Families
ACNP. *See* American College of Nurse Practitioners
ACOEM. *See* American College of Occupational and Environmental Medicine

Acquired immunodeficiency syndrome (AIDS). *See* HIV/AIDS
Act to Prevent Pernicious Political Activities (Hatch Act), 583-586
"Action Against Asthma" plan, 541
Action agenda, 61
Activist nurses, 32
Adams, Stacey, *175*
Administration
    PhD in Nursing (concentration in health care ethics, health care administration and health policy), George Mason University, *37b*
    physician-administrator relationships, 341
    procedures process, 699
Administration for Children and Families (ACF), 518
Administration for Native Americans, 518
Administration on Aging (AoA), 518-519, 527
Administrative Procedures Act, 475
Advanced Education Nursing grants, 522
Advanced Practice Nurse Day, 383
Advanced Practice Nurse in Genetics credential (APNGc), 447
Advanced practice nurses (APNs), 5-6
    Alliance of Advanced Practice Nurses, 89
    antitrust issues for, 376
    business practice, 378
    certification of, 645-646
    collaboration with AMA, 84
    critical environmental elements for, 373, 374f
    data dilemma, 373-374
    education of, 376-377
    fragmentation of, 270
    future of, 371-385
    lobbying for, 89-90
    managed care agenda, 146-147
    media coverage of, 3

Advanced practice nurses (APNs)—cont'd
past experience, 371-373
prescriptive authority of, 146, 502
present situation, 373-376
professional image, 377-378
recommendations for, 373
regulation of, 512
reimbursement for, 375-376
managed care, 88-89
Medicare, 81
third-party, 265-272
supervision of, 269-270
technology for policy and professional decision-
making, 377
Uniform APRN Licensure/Authority to Practice
Requirements for, 512
Adverse drug events, preventable, 438
Advertisements
"Harry and Louise" commercials, 4, 158-159, 635
for tobacco use, 8, 161
Advisory Committee on Genetic Testing, 446
Advisory Committee on Mercury Pollution, 738
Advisory Council on Social Security, 292
Advocacy. *See also* Lobbying
by AAOHN, 641
activities for, 283-284
for clinical nurse specialists, case study, 644-646
from community education to, 680
continuous, 563
effective approaches for, 128-129, 562-563
environmental, case study, 735-744
for expansion of legal rights through legislation, 477
with grace, 128-129
guidelines for, 509
interdisciplinary, case study, 643-644
investment in, 564
media, 168-169
as member benefit, 603-604
new configurations, 665-666
new methods for, 664-665
nurse anesthesia issues, 278-279
patient, case study, 643
policy leader champions, 563
for pollution prevention in health care, 741-742
prioritization of issues, 562
reasons for, 128
suggestions for associations, 603
workplace, 315, 604
Advocacy groups, 308
Advocacy staff, 564
Advocates, 339, 562, *712*

Aetna/US Healthcare, 88
AFA. *See* Air Force Association
AFBF. *See* American Farm Bureau Federation
AFDC. *See* Aid to Families with Dependent Children
Affara, Fadwa, 732, *733*
Affordable child care, 671
AFL-CIO. *See* American Federation of Labor-Congress
of Industrial Organizations
AFN. *See* American Federation of Nurses
African Americans
genetic testing of, 444
health status of, 223, 224, 225
voter turnout in federal elections, 566, 566*t*, 567
African-American nurses, 23, 24
AFSA. *See* Air Force Sergeants Association
Agency for Health Care Policy and Research (AHCPR),
149, 150, 454
Agency for Healthcare Research and Quality (AHRQ),
149, 227-228, 435, 519-520, 527
Agency for Toxic Substances and Disease Registry
(ATSDR), 520
Agency personnel, 368
Agenda(s), 146-147
board, 613
general business meeting, 613
getting issues on, 161-162
getting on, 145-146
mini case study, 147-148
models for building, 145
setting, 33, 148-149
shaping, 143-144
Agent Orange Health Effects Program, 249
Agents, 339
Aggregate focus, 159-160
AHA. *See* American Heart Association; American
Hospital Association
"Aha" moment, 31-32
AHCA. *See* American Health Care Association
AHCPR. *See* Agency for Health Care Policy and Research
AHRQ. *See* Agency for Healthcare Research and Quality
AHSR. *See* Association for Health Services Research
Aid to Families with Dependent Children (AFDC), 250,
481
AIDS. *See* HIV/AIDS
Aiken, Linda, 149, 152
Air Force Association (AFA), 132*b*
Air Force Sergeants Association (AFSA), 132*b*
AJN. See American Journal of Nursing
Al Keem, Hassan, *733*
Al Madfaa, Hamad, *733*
Al Rifai, Fatima, 728-734, *733*

Alabama: rural elderly projects in, 689
Alabama Board of Nursing, 473
Alabama Nurse Practice Act, 473
Alabama State Nurses Association, 473
Alaska: nurse practitioners in, 464
Alaska Natives
    health care for, 207-208, 250
    health status of, 224, 225
Alcohol blood levels, 680, 681
Aligned leaders, 339
Alignment around decisions, 341
Alliance of Advanced Practice Nurses, 89
Allocation, 9
Allopathic medicine, 294*b*
All-professional units, 394
Alternative Link, 297
Alternative therapies, 293
    definition of, 294*b*
    increasing use of, 294-295
    reimbursement for, 295
    values underlying, 294-297
Ambulatory payment classifications (APCs), 316
American Academy of Nurse Practitioners (AANP), 81,
    139*b*
American Academy of Nursing, 50, 325
American Academy of Orthopaedic Surgeons, 149
American Academy of Pediatrics (AAP), 673
American Association of Colleges of Nursing (AACN),
    56, 139*b*, 365, 452
American Association of Critical-Care Nurses (AACN),
    36
American Association of Nurse Anesthetists (AANA),
    276, 278
    advocacy, 278-279, 282, 283-284, 285, 286, 452
American Association of Occupational Health Nurses
    (AAOHN), 639, 640-643
American Association of Retired Persons (AARP), 75
American Cancer Society, 36, 75, 649
American College of Emergency Physicians (ACEP), 137
American College of Gastroenterology, 649
American College of Health Care Administrators, 180
American College of Health Care Executives, 180
American College of Nurse Midwives, 89
American College of Nurse Practitioners (ACNP),
    654*n*
American College of Occupational and Environmental
    Medicine (ACOEM), 641
American Dental Association, 634*b*
American Farm Bureau Federation (AFBF), 628-629
American Federation of Labor-Congress of Industrial
    Organizations (AFL-CIO), 392, 393, 504

American Federation of Nurses (AFN), 25
American Federation of State, County, & Municipal
    Employees (AFSCME), 392
American Federation of Teachers, 392
American Health Care Association (AHCA), 431
American Heart Association (AHA), 36, 360, 621-625
American Hospital Association (AHA), 147
    and all-RN bargaining units, 395
    code of ethics, 180
    data collection, 364
    and health care reform failure, 635
    historical perspectives on, 241
    political contributions from, 634*b*
    support for AANA, 284
    website, 217*b*
American Indians
    diabetes among, 225
    health care for, 207-208, 250
American Jewish Congress, 444
American Journal of Nursing (AJN), 21, 25, 38, 139, 148,
    152, 161, 624
American Legion, 195
American Library Association, 109
American Medical Association (AMA), 202, 372, 634,
    635
    Advisory Committee for Television and Motion
        Pictures, 165
    amicus curiae briefs, 476-477
    antitrust relief, 474
    Citizens Petition, 5, 84, 146, 372, 654-657, 655*b*
    code of ethics, 180
    Council on Medical Service, 5
    Council on Scientific Affairs, 143
    gun control, 143-144
    historical perspectives on, 241
    JAMA, 144*n*
    political contributions from, 634*b*
    website, 217*b*
American Nephrology Nurses' Association, 452
The American Nurse, 139
American Nurses Association (ANA), 15, 20, 22-23, 35,
    81, 139*b*, 152-153, 159, 189
    advocacy, 452, 603, 604
    agenda, 147
    Alabama nurses, 473
    all-RN bargaining units, 394-395
    amicus curiae briefs, 476-477
    "ANA Media Relations & You," 100
    Code of Ethics for Nurses with Interpretive Statements,
        178, 180, 183*b*
    constituent member associations (CMAs), 392, 544

American Nurses Association (ANA)—cont'd
    Discrimination and Racism in Health Care position
        statement, 226
    endorsement of Clinton-Gore ticket (1991), 162
    "Every Patient Deserves a Nurse" slogan, 160
    "free rider" problem, 636
    Health Care Without Harm campaign, 741
    Leadership Circle, 597
    membership, 601
    mission statement, 610-611
    "Nurses' Toolkit," 100
    Nursing's Agenda for Health Care Reform, 7, 594
    Nursing's Social Policy Statement, 178
    professional activities, 36
    purpose of, 604
    "Registered Nurse/Registered Voter" campaign, 572
    Safe Needles Save Lives campaign, 415
    *Seeking Federal Appointment—A 2001 Guide for
        Nurses,* 544-545
    state government relations, 496*b*
    state policy initiatives, 495
    statements on controversial issues, 552
    support for Equal Rights Amendment, 28
    support for Medicare, 147
    Tri-Council for Nursing, 56
    website, 183*b*, 217*b*
    and woman suffrage, 25
American Nurses Association Political Action
    Committee (ANA-PAC), 3, 7, 36, 569, 632
American Nurses Credentialing Center (ANCC), 5
    Magnet Recognition Program for Excellence in
        Nursing Services, 315, 324-327, 388
American Organization of Nurse Executives (AONE),
    147
American Psychiatric Association, 221
American Public Health Association (APHA), 3, 36,
    217*b*, 661
American Red Cross, 50
American Samoa: boards of nursing, 510
American Social Health Association, 139*b*
American Society for Parenteral and Enteral Nutrition
    (ASPEN), 639, 643-644
American Society of Anesthesiologists (ASA), 279, 282,
    634*b*
American Society of Pain Management Nurses
    (ASPMN), 603-604
American Society of Superintendents of Training
    Schools for Nurses, 19-20, 22, 636
Americans with Disabilities Act (ADA) of 1990 (PL 101-
    336), 427-428, 430, 448, 477
America's Family Protection Plan, 258. *See also* Social
    Security

Amicus curiae briefs, 473, 476-477, 532
AMSUS. *See* Association of Military Surgeons of the
    United States
"An Act to Increase Access to Primary Health Care
    Services" (PL 296) (Maine), 379, *380*
"ANA Media Relations & You," 100
Analysis
    issue, 63
    policy, 55, 62-63
    political, 71-91
Analyst values, 62
ANCC. *See* American Nurses Credentialing Center
Anecdotes, power of, 145*n*
Anesthesia. *See* Nurse anesthesia
Anti-fraud compliance, 316-317
Antitrust issues, 376, 474
"Any willing provider" language, 382
AoA. *See* Administration on Aging
AONE. *See* American Organization of Nurse
    Executives
AORN. *See* Association of Peri-Operative Nurses
Apartheid, 49
APCs. *See* Ambulatory payment classifications
APHA. *See* American Public Health Association
APNs. *See* Advanced practice nurses
Appearance, 106
Appointments, political, 543-550
    appointed leaders, 614-615
Appropriating committees, 454
Appropriations acts, 529*b*
Arizona State University School of Public Affairs Master
    of Public Administration, 39*b*
Arizona v. Maricopa County Medical Society, 474
Army Aviation Association of America (AAAA), 132*b*
Army Nurse Corps, 24
Arnold, Lynda, 415
Arriving at events, 94
ASA. *See* American Society of Anesthesiologists
Ashley, JoAnn, 28
Asian Americans: health status of, 223, 224
Asian/Pacific Islanders
    health status of, 223, 224, 225
    voter turnout, 567
Asking for what you want, 97
ASPEN. *See* American Society for Parenteral and Enteral
    Nutrition
Aspirin
    market demand for, 230, 230*f*, 230*t*
    market price for, 232, 232*f*
    market supply for, 231, 231*f*, 231*t*
ASPMN. *See* American Society of Pain Management
    Nurses

Assault weapons, 143
Assessment, values, 76-77
Assignments, work, 389
Assisted suicide, 473
Association for Health Services Research (AHSR), 149
Association for Health Services Research and Health
    Policy, 149
Association of Military Surgeons of the United States
    (AMSUS), 132*b*
Association of Nurse Executives, 56
Association of Peri-Operative Nurses (AORN), 642
Association of the United States Army (AUSA), 132*b*
Association of Women's Health, Obstetric and Neonatal
    Nurses (AWHONN), 552, 618
Asthma
    Atlanta Zap Asthma Project, 538-542
    Decatur Community Partnership, 705-706
    Zap Asthma, Inc., 540-541
Atlanta, Georgia
    environmental and health issues in, 539
    Healthy Atlanta Forum, 542
Atlanta Zap Asthma Project, 538-542
ATSDR. *See* Agency for Toxic Substances and Disease
    Registry
Attention, management of, 693-694
Attire, 106
Attitude, 95, 96*b*
AUSA. *See* Association of the United States Army
Authority, 110
Authorization acts, 529*b*
Authorization laws, 528
Authorization process, 454
Authorizing committees, 454
Autonomy, 341
Awareness, 31-32
AWHONN. *See* Association of Women's Health,
    Obstetric and Neonatal Nurses

B

Background, 73-74
    policy issue paper section, 63, 64*b*-65*b*
Balance, 128, 180
Balanced Budget Act (BBA) of 1997, 4, 5, 80, 81, 205,
    245-246, 317, 372, 654
    and Boren Amendment, 477
    child health provision, 251
    Medicare policy spotlight, 273
Balanced Budget and Emergency Deficit Control Act
    (Gramm-Rudman-Hollings Act), 530
Ballenger, Cass, 416, 417
Baltimore, Maryland, 482
Bar Code Medication Administration, 439-440

Bargaining, 618
    collective, 390-393, 604
        definition of, 387
        process of, 393-395
    objectives of, 387
    subjects of work, 604
Bargaining representatives, 393
Bargaining units, all-RN, 394-395
Basic Nurse Education and Practice grants, 522
Baucus, Max, 592
BBA. *See* Balanced Budget Act of 1997
"Be Yourself, Support Yourself" program, 691
Behavior that draws people in, 95, 96*b*
"Behaviors of a Respectful Work Environment"
    (UMHC), 336, 338*f*
Bell, Pam, *678,* 679
Bellevue Hospital (New York City), 21
Ben Casey, 165
Bender, Kaye, 505-509, 549
Benefits. *See also specific programs*
    cost-benefit ratio (B/C), 237
    mandated, 591
    net, 237
Benefits Improvement and Protection Act (BIPA) of
    2000, 274, 317
Bennett, Marshall, 507-508
Bereavement, 689
Bernard, Sister Mary, 277
Betts, Virginia Trotter, 41*b,* 544, 614-615
Bias, inherent, 62
BIDS. *See* Binational infectious disease surveillance
    project
Bill of Rights, 472
Bills, legislative, 454, 455*f*
    criteria for viability, 464
    introduction of, 451-452
    markup, 456
    types of, 452*b*
    voting on, 457
Binational infectious disease surveillance project (BIDS),
    724
Biography, brief, 104, 105*b*
Biohazard waste, 739
Biologic weapons. *See* Chemical, biologic, radiologic,
    nuclear, or high-yield explosive weapons; Nuclear,
    biologic, and chemical (NBC) material
Bioterrorism. *See* Chemical, biologic, radiologic, nuclear,
    or high-yield explosive weapons
Bipartisan Commission on Entitlement and Tax Reform,
    292
Birth control, 27
Black Progress Review, 50

Blacks
  genetic testing of, 444
  health status of, 223, 224, 225
  voter turnout, 566, 566*t*, 567
Blood alcohol levels, 680, 681
Bloodborne Pathogens Standard Compliance Directive
    (OSHA), 414, 415, 416, 417
BLS. *See* Bureau of Labor Statistics
Blue Cross, 241, 635
Blue Cross/Blue Shield, 241, 242
Blue Cross/Blue Shield of Maine, 383
Blue Cross-Blue Shield of Montana, 597
Blue Shield, 241
"Blueprint for Action" (HCCA), 673
Blumenthal, Jackie, 49
Board agendas, 613
Boards
  elected, 487*b*
  policies that support organizational effectiveness, 611
  of supervisors, 487*b*
Body language, 95, 97-98
Bogdanich, Walt, 161
Books, 40
Boren Amendment, 477
Boroughs, 487*b*-488*b*
Boutique plastics recycling efforts, 738
Bowden, Jeanne, 299-310
Bowers, Lynn, 579-583
Boxer, Barbara, 415
Boycotts, 165
Boycr, Chcryl, 622
Bradley, Bill, 634
Brady, Jim, 144
Brady bill, 143
Brainstorming, 117
Breast and Cervical Cancer Treatment Act, 534
Breckenridge, Mary, 590
Brewster, Mary, 26
Breyer, Stephen, 473
Briefing papers, 100, 101*b*
Briefings, 100
Brigner, Sharon, 45*b*, 46, 48-49, 49-50
Bristol-Myers Squibb, 634*b*
Brodin, Rodger, 187, 188, 192-193
Brookings Institute, 545-546
Brown, J. Carter, 192
Brown v. Board of Education, 472
Browner, Carol, 541
Budget Act, 530
Budget and Impoundment Control Act, 530
Budget authority, 529*b*
Budget Enforcement Act, 530

Budget glossary, 529*b*
Budget resolution, 529*b*
Budget surplus, 422
Budget wars, 501
Budgetary process, 531*f*
  federal, 528-530
  timetable, 532*b*
Buerhaus, Peter, 522
Bull, Jan, 40
Bureau of Health Manpower, Health Resources and
    Services Administration (HRSA), 147
Bureau of Health Professions (HRSA), 520, 521
Bureau of Labor Statistics (BLS), 363, 365, 524, 527, 528
Bureau of Primary Health Care (HRSA), 520
Bureau of the Census, 365
Burgess, Ann, 401
Burke, Sheila, 41*b*, 614
Bush, George, *47*, 195
Bush, George W., 161, 168, 292, 429
  ban on human embryo research, 446
  donations from health care interest groups, 634
  opposition to nursing's progress, 5
Bush administration, 275, 284, 285, 426, 432
Business cards, 105
Business etiquette, 106, 106*b*
Business leagues, 613
Business practice, 378
Business Roundtable, 635
Buyer, Steve, 134
Buy-in, 7, 32, 76-77, 78*t*
Bylaws
  of professional organizations, 611
  staff, 388
Byrne, Ethel, 27

C
Cabinet Departments, 516*b*, 517-525
California
  boards of nursing, 510
  Faith-Based Initiative Program, 685
  Genetic Test Disclosure and Genetic Licensure Bill,
    447
  managed care in, 148
  needlestick prevention legislation, 414
  nurse practitioners in, 464
  opportunities for APNs in, 5
  Patient Safety Center of Inquiry (VA), 441
California and Oregon Kaiser System, 284
California Nurses Association (CNA), 329
California Strategic Planning Committee for Nursing,
    122
The Call (Sanger), 27

Call to action, 174
Calling in to talk radio, 159*b,* 172
Cambridge University Judge School of Management
    Studies, 50
Campaign calendars, 574
Campaign finance reform, 632, 633
Campaign management. *See* Political campaigns
Campaign managers, 574
Campaign themes, 580
"Campaign to Insure All Americans," 635
Campaign volunteers, 574-575, 575*b*
Campbell, Bill, 540
Canada, 211
Cancer
    racial and ethnic disparities in, 224
    screening for, case study, 649
Candidates. *See* Political candidates
Canfield, Johanna, *678*
CANS. *See* Children Adjusting to New Situations
Capitation, 59, 234
Capps, Lois, 28, 41*b,* 533-535, 571, 615
Capuzzi, Cecilia, 299-310
Cardiopulmonary resuscitation (CPR), 356-361
Career security, 395-396
Careers, professional, 400
Caribbean Nurses Organization, 719
Caring, 10-11
Carney, Betty, 741
Carondelet St. Joseph's Hospital (Tucson, AZ), 173
Carter, Jimmy, 185, 233
Carve-out managed behavioral health care plan, 220
Carver, John, 611
Case management, 234
    barriers to implementing, 321-322
    community-based, 320
    historical development of, 319-320
    hospital-based, 320
    models for, 322-323
    politics of, 319-324
Case managers, 322
Case mix groups (CMGs), 316
CAT. *See* Computerized adaptive testing
Catastrophic Coverage Act, 256
CBO. *See* Congressional Budget Office
CBOs. *See* Community-based organizations
CBRNE weapons. *See* Chemical, biologic, radiologic,
    nuclear, or high-yield explosive weapons
CCDBG. *See* Child Care and Development Block Grant
CCMC. *See* Committee on the Costs of Medical Care
Cedars-Sinai Medical Center (Los Angeles, CA), 330
Celebrities, 100-102
Cell phones and pagers, 103

Centennial Hospital, Nashville, Tennessee, 139*b*
Center for Beneficiary Choices, 518
Center for Drug Evaluation and Research, 520
Center for Empowered Decisionmaking, 704
Center for Health Economics Research (CHER) report,
    280-281
Center for Health Policy, Research and Ethics, George
    Mason University, 41*b,* 50, 448
Center for Medicaid and State Operations, 518
Center for Medicare Management, 518
Center for Mental Health Services, 219-220, 523
Center for Minority Veterans, 523
Center for Substance Abuse Prevention, 523
Center for Substance Abuse Treatment, 523
Center for Technology in the Public Library, 109
Center for Women Veterans, 523
Centers for Disease Control and Prevention (CDC), 143,
    316, 520
    and childhood asthma, 539
    demographics available from, 660
Centers for Excellence in Hepatitis C Research and
    Education, 249
Centers for Medicare and Medicaid Administration, 59,
    208-209
Centers for Medicare and Medicaid Services (CMS), 81,
    249, 272, 518
    funding, 316, 527
    intervention in supply of RNs, 366
    nurses at, 468
    and physician supervision of CRNAs, 285
    regulatory process, 460, 468, 469
Ceppetelli, Ellen, 740
Certificate of need legislation, 233
Certification, advanced practice, 645-646
Certified nurse midwives (CNMs), 121
Certified registered nurse anesthetists (CRNAs), 277
    Medicare reimbursement for, 278
    physician supervision of, 283-286
Chamber of Commerce, 635
Champions, 339
CHAMPUS. *See* Civilian Health and Medical Program
    for the Uniformed Services
CHAMPVA. *See* Civilian Health and Medical Program of
    the Veterans Administration
Change. *See also* Policy change
    all-or-nothing, 334
    beginning, 349
    courage for, 355-356
    as discrete process, 334
    failure of, 345-346
    in health care organizations, 354-356
    human dynamics of, 339-340, 341-342

Change—cont'd
model for engaging physicians in, 339-340
as normal, 334
Change hardiness, 335
Change theory, 333-335
Chao, Elaine, 47
Chaos theory, 347-349
Chapters of professional organizations, 606
"Characteristics of a Healthy Work Environment"
(UMHC), 336, 337f
Charitable choice, 660
Charles Stewart Mott Foundation, 670
Charlotte/Mecklenburg, North Carolina, 482-483
Chatting, 93-94, 95
Chavez, Linda, 544
Chemical, biologic, radiologic, nuclear, or high-yield
explosive (CBRNE) weapons, 136
Cherry picking, 430
"Chicago Hope," 161
Chicago Tribune, 152
Chief executives, 617
Chief Warrant Officer and Warrant Officer Association
of the United States Coast Guard (CWO & WOA),
132b
Child care, 669-675
"Blueprint for Action" (HCCA), 673
websites on, 674b
Child Care and Development Block Grant (CCDBG),
672-673, 673b, 674
Child Care Bureau (DHHS), 673, 674b
Child health
Atlanta Zap Asthma Project, 538-542
Balanced Budget Act (BBA) of 1997 provision, 251
Zap Asthma, Inc., 540-541
Child Health Insurance Program (CHIP), 57. *See also*
State Children's Health Insurance Program
(S-CHIP)
Child Welfare Services, 527
Child-care centers, 672
Child-care staff, 672
Childhood education policies, 674b
Children, 433-434
"Be Yourself, Support Yourself" program for, 691
Reach Out and Read Program (ROAR) for, 689
school-age, care for, 670
Children Adjusting to New Situations (CANS)
(VNACJ), 689
Children's Defense Fund, 75, 674b
Children's Health Insurance Program (S-CHIP). *See*
State Children's Health Insurance Program
(S-CHIP)

CHIP. *See* Child Health Insurance Program
Choice, charitable, 660
Christopher, Warren, 48
Cigarette warnings, 144n. *See also* Tobacco
Circulating, 96-97
Cisneros, Henry, 48
Cities, 487b-488b
Citizen involvement, 696-697
Citizens, service to, 179
Citizens for Better Medicare, 634
Citizens Petition (AMA), 5, 84, 146, 372, 654-657, 655b
Citizenship, 179, 663
Civera, Mario, 90
Civil Rights Act, 698, 699
Civilian Health and Medical Program for the Uniformed
Services (CHAMPUS), 130, 249
Civilian Health and Medical Program of the Veterans
Administration (CHAMPVA), 249
Clark, Wesley K., 47
Clark University, 539
Clarksburg Veterans Administration Medical Center,
123
Class action suits, 475
Clinical advancement, 314
Clinical economics, 236-238
Clinical efficacy, 295
Clinical Laboratory Improvement Amendments, 161
Clinical Laboratory Improvements Act, 518
*Clinical Nurse Specialist: The Journal for Advanced
Nursing Practice,* 645
Clinical nurse specialists (CNSs)
advocacy for, case study, 644-646
Medicare reimbursement for, 257
Statement on Clinical Nurse Specialist Practice and
Education (NACNS), 645
Clinical practice, 7-8
independent, 269
Clinton, Hillary Rodham, 46, 569, 594
donations from health care interest groups, 634
Zap Asthma, Inc., 541
Clinton, J. Jarrett, 134
Clinton, William Jefferson, 46, 131, 223, 417, *418*
ban on human embryo research, 446
Medicare reform, 426
Presidential Advisory Commission on Consumer
Protection and Quality in the Health Care
Industry, 434-435
Presidential Decision Directive-62 (PDD-62), 136
proposed Health Security Act (HSA), 3, 158, 163, 421
Quality Interagency Coordination Task Force (QuIC),
438

Clinton-Gore ticket (1991), 162
Closing the Gap: Eliminating Racial and Ethnic Disparities, 223
Clothing, 106
CMGs. *See* Case mix groups
CNA. *See* California Nurses Association
CNMs. *See* Certified nurse midwives
CNOs. *See* Community nursing organizations
CNSs. *See* Clinical nurse specialists
COA. *See* Commissioned Officers Association of the United States Public Health Service, Inc.
Coalition for Pain Management, 603-604
Coalition of Nurses in Advanced Practice, 381
Coalitions, 121-140, 560-561, 666
    building, 122-125, 731
    linking with, 308
    participation in, 126, 563
    to tackle childhood asthma, 539-540
Co-creation, 347
Code of Ethics for Nurses with Interpretive Statements (ANA), 178, 180, 183*b*
Codes of ethics, 180
Coding, 297
Coercive power, 79
Coexistence, 335
COLAs. *See* Cost-of-living adjustments
Collaboration, 84-85, 116, 336, 622
    among nursing organizations, 607
    case study, 650-654
    with community, 687-709
    interdisciplinary, 336-339
    lessons learned, 91
    mass casualty, 139
    Military Coalition, 133
    Turning Point: Collaborating for a New Century in Public Health initiative, 701-709
Collaborative Breakthrough Series Model, 440
Colleagues in Caring: Regional Collaboratives for Nursing Work Force Development (Colleagues), 121-122, 313. *See also specific coalitions*
    advocacy by, 128
    decision making, 124
    evaluation of, 126
    RWJF funding, 125
Collective action, 387-397
Collective bargaining, 390-393, 604
    definition of, 387
    process of, 393-395
Collective mentoring, 35
Collective mindset, 690
Collegiality, 374-375

Colorectal cancer screening
    case study, 649
    Coverage for Colorectal Cancer Screening (Virginia S.B. 26), 650
Columbia University, 5, 151
Columbia University School of Nursing, 38*b*, 139*b*
Columbia/HCA Health Care, 262
Columbine High School shootings, 144
COM. *See* Commission on Magnet
Commemorative Works Act (CWA), 188-189, 190
Commerce opportunities, 546*b*
Commission for Women's Equality, 444
Commission municipal governments, 488*b*
Commission of Fine Arts, 190-192, 195
Commission on Magnet (COM), 327
Commission on the Nursing Shortage, 147
Commissioned Officers Association of the United States Public Health Service, Inc. (COA), 132*b*
Commissions
    elected, 487*b*
    nurse appointees to, 549
Committee for the Recognition of Nursing Achievement, 392
Committee on the Costs of Medical Care (CCMC), 202
Committees
    executive, 615
    exploratory, 573-574
    federal, 453
    nurse, 388
    procedures for, 454-457
Common procedure terminology (CPT) codes, 297
Commonwealth Fund, 217*b*
Commonwealth Nurses Federation, 719
Communication, 93
    body language, 97-98
    case study, 650-654
    cultural differences in, 98-99
    disasters, 102
    electronic, 102-104
    expressing gratitude, 99
    gripping and grinning, 94-95
    intercultural, 99
    and leadership, 106
    meeting and greeting, 94-95
    with policymakers and staff, 554-560
    sexual messages, 98
    skills for, 93-111
    by telephone, 554-555
    when arriving at events, 94
Communication accessories, 104-105
Communications technology, new, 665

Communicators, 129
Community
  collaboration with, 687-709
  contemporary issues, 659-685
  definition of, 590, 659-660
  vs individuals, 179-180
  international, 711-735
  organization of, 691-693, 700-701
  vs population, 688
  as sphere of political action, 15-16
Community and migrant health centers, 205-206
Community decision making, 704
Community education, 680
Community faith-based programs, 683-684
Community Health Centers, 692
  funding, 527
  urban nurse-managed, 87-88
Community health workers (CHWs), 540-541
Community nursing organizations (CNOs), 59
Community rating, 242
Community-based case management, 320
Community-based organizations (CBOs), 320
Community-Based Public Health Initiative, 709
Compacts, 339
Compensation. *See also* Reimbursement; *specific programs*
  of child-care staff, 672
  for nurses, 314
  pay-for-performance systems of, 314
Competency, 295-296
Competency-based practice model, 695
Competition, 243-245
Complementary therapies, 293-294
  definition of, 294*b*
  discounted services, 295-296
  increasing use of, 294-295
  reimbursement for, 293-297
  values underlying use, 294-297
Comprehensiveness, 180
Compromise, 116, 181
  principled negotiation, 116-118, 618
Computerized adaptive testing (CAT), 511
Comstock Act, 27
Concurrent Budget Resolution, 529-530, 532
Conditions of Participation, 316
Conferees, 457
Conference action, 457-459
Conference committees, 453
Confidentiality, 317
Confirmation, 547-548
Confirmation hearings, 547-548

Conflict
  contagiousness of, 72
  gender issues and, 71-72
  of interest, 615
  types of, 113-115
Conflict management, 113-119, 118*b*
Conflict resolution, 115-118, 118*b*, 183
  organizational, 618, 619*b*
  principles for, 180-181
Congressional Budget Office (CBO), 530
Congressional committees, 526, 526*b*, 527-528
  joint testimony, 133, 134
  procedures, 454-457
  providing testimony to, 302, 558-560
  ranking minority member, 453
  "Seven Rules for Testifying before Congress," 194
  types of, 453, 526-527
Congressional Detail to the Committee on
      Appropriations Subcommittee on Defense, *51*, 51-53
Congressional Record, 528
Congressional staffers, *51*, 51-53, 561-564
  communication with, 554-560
Congressional Women's Caucus, 415-416
Connecticut Colleagues project, 127
Connecticut League for Nursing, 127
Conrad, Kent, 283
Conservation, 546*b*
Consolidated Appropriations Act of 2001, 252
Consultants, 269, 619
Contemporary issues
  in communities, 659-685
  in context, 660-662
  in government, 421-449
Content, framing for, 169
Continence Coalition, 651-652, 652-653
Continuing education programs, 36, 41*b*
Continuing resolutions, 529*b*
Conversation, 93-96, 96*b*
Conway-Welch, Colleen, 138
Cooperation, 180, 704
Coordinated care plans, 253
Co-participation, 347
Corporation for Public Broadcasting, 162
Corrections, 546*b*
Correspondence, e-mail, 556-557
Cost identification analysis, 236
Cost plans, 253
Cost sharing, 306
Cost-benefit analysis, 152, 216, 236-237
Cost-benefit ratio (B/C), 237

Cost-effectiveness analysis, 237-238
Cost-of-living adjustments (COLAs), 260, 291
Cost-push theory, 233
Costs
    associated with mental illness, 219-220
    containment of, 233-234, 243-249
    direct, 236
    growth factors, 275
    of health care, 232-234, 422
    indirect, 236
    of long-term care, 431-432
    savings with recycling, 736
Council-manager governments, 488b
County executives or county managers, 487b
County government, 487b
County managers, 487b
Couric, Emily, 649
Courts, 471-478
    federal, 532
    state, 532
Coverage for Colorectal Cancer Screening (Virginia S.B. 26), 650
Covering Kids grants (RWJF), 304-305
Cowan, Michael, 130-135
CPOA. See USCG Chief Petty Officers Association
CPS. See Current Population Survey
CPT codes. See Common procedure terminology codes
Credentialing
    Advanced Practice Nurse in Genetics credential (APNGc), 447
    of nurse practitioners, 381
    provider, 296
Crile, George, 277
CRNAs. See Certified registered nurse anesthetists
Crossing the Quality Chasm: A New Health System for the 21st Century (IOM), 311, 435, 525
Crowe, William, 196
Cruzan v. Missouri Dept. of Health, 473
C-SPAN, 41
C-SPAN Radio, 42
Cultural differences, 98-99
Cultural integration, 340
Culture, 335
    organizational, 335
    of safety, 442
Culture/compact, 339, 341
Currency, 110
Current Population Survey (CPS), 365
Curriculum vitae (CV), 104-105
CV. See Curriculum vitae
CWA. See Commemorative Works Act

CWO & WOA. See Chief Warrant Officer and Warrant Officer Association of the United States Coast Guard

D

Daley, Karen A., 412-413, 418
Dallas/Fort Worth, Texas, 482-483
DALYs. See Disability Adjusted Life Years
The Dance of Legislation (Redman), 40
"Dancing With the Chaos" nursing summit, 351
Daschle, Tom, 648
Data, 373-374
    applications of, 270-271
    reporting, 312
Data collection, 563
    case study, 651-652
    selection of site for, 404-406
Davidson, Sue, 645
Davis, Gray, 148
Dayton, Ohio, 488b
DCTC. See Dependent care tax credit
DeAngelis, Catherine, 151n
Decatur Community Partnership, 705-706
Decentralized nursing services, 388
Decertifications, 393-394
Decision agenda, 61
Decision making
    alignment around, 341
    coalition, 124
    community, 704
    ethical political, 182-183
    issue analysis for, 63, 63f
    participatory, 388
    by professional organizations, 605-606
"Defensive" action, 476
Deferrals, 529b
Degree programs
    in policy, public health, and public administration, 39b-40b
    in public health, public administration, and public policy, 36
    in schools of nursing, 36, 37b-38b
DeLaney, Ann, 40
Delaware: nurse practitioners in, 464
Demand, 230-231
    for care, 312-313
    market, 230, 230f, 230t
Demand-pull theory, 232
Democracy, electronic, 571
Democratic Party, 632, 634
Demographic information, 660

Denial, 115

DeParle, Nancy-Ann Min, 283, 653

Dependent care tax credit (DCTC), 671

Devolution, 5-6

DI. *See* Disability Insurance

Diabetes, type 2, 224-225

"Diagnosis: Murder," 161

Diagnosis-related groups (DRGs), 147, 233, 278, 316
    historical development of, 319-320

Dickson, Geri, 123

Dignity
    genetic privacy and, 447-448
    individual, 257

Direct or mandatory spending, 529*b*

Directors at large, 615

Direct-to-consumer (DTC) marketing, 425-426

Disability Adjusted Life Years (DALYs), 219

Disability benefits, 289

Disability group stigma, 444

Disability Insurance (DI) trust fund, 258

Disabled American Veterans, 195

Disaster relief nursing, 138

Disciplinary oversight, 512-513

Discounted services, 295-296

Discretionary funding, 672-673

Discretionary spending, 529, 529*b*, 531*f*

Discrimination, insurance, 443-444, 446

Discrimination and Racism in Health Care position
    statement (ANA), 226

Discussion agenda, 61

Disenrollment, 434

Dissemination of research findings, 408-410

District of Columbia boards of nursing, 510

Districts, special, 489*b*

Diversity
    Nursing Workforce Diversity grants, 522
    of political candidates, 570

Division of Global Migration and Quarantine, 725, 726

Division votes, 457

Dix, Dorothea, 590

DMERCs. *See* Durable Medical Equipment Regional
    Carriers

DNSc in Nursing (Health Policy track), Columbia
    University, 38*b*

Dock, Lavinia, 22

Doctoral programs
    Johns Hopkins University Department of Health
      Policy and Management, 39*b*
    PhD in Nursing (concentration in health care ethics,
      health care administration and health policy),
      George Mason University, 37*b*

Doctoral programs—cont'd
    PhD in Nursing (policy focus on the health of the
      urban family and elderly), University of
      Massachusetts, Boston, 37*b*
    The University of Iowa College of Public Health
      Doctoral Program in Health Management and
      Policy, 40*b*
    The University of Michigan School of Public Health
      program, 40*b*
    The University of South Florida Health Policy and
      Management programs, 40*b*

DoD. *See* U.S. Department of Defense

Dodd, Catherine, 550

DoE. *See* U.S. Department of Education

DoJ. *See* U.S. Department of Justice

DoL. *See* U.S. Department of Labor

Dole, Robert, 614

Domenici, Pete, 221

Dr. Kildare, 165

"Dr. Quinn, Medicine Woman," 161

DRGs. *See* Diagnosis-related groups

Drinking and driving, 676-682

Drugs. *See* Prescription drugs

DTC marketing. *See* Direct-to-consumer marketing

Dual Master's Degree programs, 39*b*

Dues, 604-605

Dukakis, Michael, 677, *678*

Durable Medical Equipment Regional Carriers
    (DMERCs), 643

Durenberger, Dave, 193

Duty to warn, 444-445

E

EANGUS. *See* Enlisted Association of the National
    Guard of the United States

Early childhood education policies, 674*b*

Earned Income Tax Credit (EITC), 661

Ebola virus, 724

Economic analysis, 234-236
    arguments, 742-743
    types of, 236-238

Economic development opportunities, 546*b*

Economic interest groups, 629

Economic Stabilization Program, 233

Economics, 217, 229
    clinical, 236-238
    health, 229-239
    Medicare, 317
    *The Politics of Health Legislation: An Economic
      Perspective* (Feldstein), 40

Editorials, opinion, 165

Education
    Advanced Education Nursing grants, 522
    of APNs, 376-377
    Basic Nurse Education and Practice grants, 522
    community, 680
    early childhood education policies, 674*b*
    federal, 1, 454
    Federal Education Loan program, 523
    for health care personnel, 137
    importance of, 625
    of industry leaders, 296-297
    integration of content into, 296
    of legislators, 296-297
    Nurse Employment and Education Development
        (NEED) Act, 527
    nursing, 1, 137-138, 315, 729
    nursing degree programs, 36
    Nursing Education Loan Repayment Program, 521
    opportunities to serve in, 546*b*
    patient safety lessons, 441*b*
    policy, 708
    professional, 21-22
    of racial and ethnic disparities, 227
    safety, mandatory, 440
    schools of nursing, 21-22
    in UAE, 729
Education for All Handicapped Children Act of 1975
    (PL 94-142), 481
Elderly. *See also* Older adults
    PhD in Nursing (policy focus on the health of the
        urban family and elderly), University of
        Massachusetts, Boston, 37*b*
    Rural Elderly Enhancement Project, 688-689
Elected boards or commissions, 487*b*
Elected leaders, 614-615
Electioneering, 499, 570-571
Elections
    media coverage of, 162
    organizational, 616-617
    to state legislatures, 498-505
    voter turnout in, 566, 566*t*
Electric cars, 740-741
Electronic communication, 102-104
Electronic democracy, 571
Eli Lilly & Co., 634*b*
E-mail (electronic mail), 103-104, 556-557
Embryonic stem cells, 428-429
Emergency Medical Treatment and Active Labor Act
    (EMTALA), 206
Emergency Nurses Association (ENA), 358, 473, 680, 681
Emergency Nurses CARE, 676-682, *678*
Emergency spending, 529*b*

EMILY's List, 537
Emotional intelligence, 93
Empanelment, 268-269
Employee Retirement Income Security Act (ERISA),
    216*n*, 433, 528
Employment
    Nurse Employment and Education Development
        (NEED) Act, 527
    for women out of jail, 684-685
Empowerment, 12-13, 80
EMTALA. *See* Emergency Medical Treatment and Active
    Labor Act
ENA. *See* Emergency Nurses Association
Endorsement
    by PACs, 631
    questions to ask when considering, 573*b*
Engleman, Karl, 624
Enlisted Association of the National Guard of the United
    States (EANGUS), 132*b*
Enterprise, American, 215-216
Entitlement spending, 528-529, 531*f*
Environmental advocacy, case study, 735-744
Environmental health, 688-689, 700
Environmental health policy, 696-701
Environmental justice, 698, 699
Environmental law and regulations, 698
Environmental Protection Agency (EPA), 515, 539, 697,
    741
EPA. *See* Environmental Protection Agency
Epilepsy Foundation of Northeast Ohio, 604
Equal Rights Amendment, 28
Equity or fairness, individual, 257
"ER," 161
ERISA. *See* Employee Retirement Income Security Act
Errors
    health care, 311-312, 437-442
    medication, 497*b*, 513
    nursing, 152
    strategies to reduce, 438-441
Essien, Joyce, 539, 541
Ethical integrity, 182
Ethical issues, 177-184
Ethical political decision making, 182-183
Ethical solutions, viable, 183
Ethics, 181-183
    codes of, 180
    conceptual considerations, 178-180
    health care, 177-178
    PhD in Nursing (concentration in health care ethics,
        health care administration and health policy),
        George Mason University, 37*b*
    values and political ethical conflicts, 180-181

Ethnic and Cultural Diversity Workforce Task Force, Division of Nursing, U.S. Office of Minority Health, 50
Ethnic disparities, 222-228
Ethnic group stigma, 444
Etiquette, 106
    netiquette, 103-104
    protocol, 102
    resources, 106*b*
European Forum of National Nursing and Midwifery Associations, 715, 719
European Union Permanent Committee on Nursing, 719
Evaluation, policy, 62
Evans, Diane Carlson, 185-200
Events, arriving at, 94
"Every Patient Deserves a Nurse" slogan, 160
"Every Patient Deserves an RN—a Real Nurse" campaign, 160
Evidence, practice change based on, 358-359
Evidence-based practice, 152
Examinations, licensure, 511-512
Excellence, achieving, 328-332
Executive agencies, 516*b*, 517-525
Executive branch, 515-525
    organization of, 516*b*
    state, 493-494
Executive committees, 615
Executive Office of the President, 515, 516*b*, 517
Executive Order to Prohibit Discrimination in Federal Government Based on Genetic Information, 428
Expectations of leaders, 341
Experience rating, 242
Experiential learning, 36-42
Expert power, 79
Expertise, 308
Exploratory committees, 573-574
Expressing gratitude, 99

F

Facilitators, 349-350
"Fact Sheet and Reference on Worker Health and Safety for Anthrax Exposure" (OSHA), 524
Fact sheets, 463-464
    leave-behind, 556
Fagin, Claire, 148, 624
Failure to act, 128
Failure to get the right people to participate, 126
Fair Labor Standards Act, 528
Fairness, individual, 257
Fairview Riverside Medical Center (FRMC), 336

Fairview-University Medical Center (FUMC), 336, 340-341
Faith-Based Initiative Program (California), 685
Faith-based programs
    community, 683-684
    for women, 682-685
Families and Work Institute, 674*b*
Family and Medical Leave Act (FMLA), 81, 477, 528
Family health
    PhD in Nursing (policy focus on the health of the urban family and elderly), University of Massachusetts, Boston, 37*b*
    presence at bedside during invasive procedures and CPR, 356-361
Family Health Insurance Assistance Program (FHIAP), 304
Family Health Nurse initiative, 718
Family-centered health, 689
Famous people, encountering, 100-102
Fax, 103
FBI. *See* Federal Bureau of Investigation
FEC. *See* Federal Election Commission
Federal appointments. *See* Political appointments
Federal Bureau of Investigation (FBI) National Domestic Preparedness Office, 139*b*
Federal courts, 532, 533*f*
Federal Department of Nursing (UAE), 729-730
Federal Direct Consolidation loans, 523
Federal Direct PLUS loans, 523
Federal Direct Stafford/Ford loans, 523
Federal Direct Unsubsidized Stafford/Ford loans, 523
Federal Education Loan program, 523
Federal Election Campaign Act, 628
Federal Election Commission (FEC), 551, 632
Federal elections, 566, 566*t*
Federal Emergency Management Agency (FEMA), 136, 515-517
Federal Employees Health Benefit Program (FEHBP), 221, 249
Federal government, 14, 515-542
Federal health care system, 207-208
    financing, 249-260
    programs, 249-250
Federal inmates, health care for, 208
Federal Insurance Contributions Act (FICA), 258
Federal Mental Health Parity Act of 1996, 221
Federal Register, 467-468
Federal Response Plan, 136, 137*b*, 138
Federal spending, 1
    Balanced Budget Amendment (BBA), 4
    budgetary process, 528-530, 531*f*

Federal spending—cont'd
  direct or mandatory, 529*b*
  discretionary, 529, 529*b*, 531*f*
  emergency, 529*b*
  entitlement, 528-529, 531*f*
  health care system financing, 249-260
  health expenditures, 249
Federal Trade Commission (FTC), 376, 474
Federally Qualified Health Center Look-Alikes, 693
Federation of American Health Systems, 284, 635
Feedback, 340, 342, 438
Fee-for-service financing, 245
Fee-for-service Medicare, 253-254
FEHBP. *See* Federal Employees Health Benefit Program
Feingold, Russ, 633
Feldstein, Paul, 40
Fellowships, 36
    White House Fellows (WHF) Program, *46, 46*-51
FEMA. *See* Federal Emergency Management Agency
Female candidates, 568-570
Female veterans, 198-199, 199*b*
Feminism, 9-11, 28
Ferguson, Stephanie, *47*
FHIAP. *See* Family Health Insurance Assistance Program
FICA. *See* Federal Insurance Contributions Act
Fight Crime Invest in Kids, 674*b*
Fikry, Mahmoud, *733*
Final rules, 468
Financing. *See also* Funding
  fee-for-service, 245
  health care, 8, 241-297
  innovative, 262
  Oregon case study, 305-306
FIP. *See* International Pharmaceutical Federation
First impressions, 95
Five-Minute Therapeutic Time, 330
Fixed-pie approach, 117
Flatt, Margaret, 353
Fleet Reserve Association (FRA), 132*b*
Florida
  duty to warn in, 444-445
  Patient Safety Center of Inquiry (VA), 441
125 Flower Estate health project, 692
FMLA. *See* Family and Medical Leave Act
Focus, 621-622
  on core issues, 636
  on interests, 117
Focusing events, 463
Foley, Barbara, 676-682, *678*
Foley, Tom, 159
Food and Agriculture Organization, 724

Food and Drug Administration (FDA), 150, 160, 425, 520, 534
Ford Motor Company, 671
Ford-Roegner, Pat, 3, 538-542
Foreign Medical Program, 249
Forgey, Benjamin, 191
Formula writing, 624
Four on 4 Medical Team of Experts, 173, *175*
FRA. *See* Fleet Reserve Association
Framing, 169-170
Franklin, Eve, 589-599, *592*
Franklin, Martha, 23
Fraud, 316-317
Free media coverage, 171-172
"Free rider" problem, 636-637
Freedom of Information Act, 557
Friends of Biofeedback, 652
Frisa, Daniel, 536, 537
FRMC. *See* Fairview Riverside Medical Center
Front groups, 664
Front page rule for political appointees, 543
FTC. *See* Federal Trade Commission
Full-time equivalents (FTEs), 364
FUMC. *See* Fairview-University Medical Center
Funding
  appropriation of, 453
  authorization of, 453
  coalition, 125
  discretionary, 672-673
  disease-specific, 206
  federal, 531*f*
  Federal Education Loan program, 523
  lessons learned, 91
  mandatory, 672-673
  matching, 673
  of media, 162
  Medicare, 316
  from NIH, 401, 402
  for racial and ethnic disparities research, 227-228
  for research, 401-403
  traditional, 219
Fundraising, 575
  by PACs, 632
  regulation of campaign money trail, 632
  tips for, 576*b*
The Future of Public Health (IOM), 709

G

Gait and Mobility Clinic, 441
Galveston, Texas, 488*b*
"Garbage can" model of policy process, 58

Gardner, John W., 47

Garthwaite, Thomas, 442

Gatekeeping, 234

Bill and Melinda Gates Children's Vaccine Program, 720

GAVI. *See* Global Alliance for Vaccines and
    Immunization

Gejdenson, Sam, 193

Gelsinger, Jesse, 428

Gender gap in voter turnout, 567

Gender issues, 71-72

Gender politics, 71

Gene patenting, 428

General business meeting agendas, 613

General primary care sector, 218

Generation X, 314, 601-602

Generation Y, 314, 601-602

Generational issues, 314-315

Genetic Counselors Licensing Act (Utah), 447

Genetic Information Nondiscrimination in Health
    Insurance Act, 447*t*

Genetic Nondiscrimination in Health Insurance and
    Employment Act, 447*t*

Genetic privacy, 447-448

Genetic Privacy Act, 445

Genetic professionals
    licensure of, 447
    public demand for, 445

Genetic Test Disclosure and Genetic Licensure Bill
    (California), 447

Genetic testing, 427, 443-444
    and duty to warn, 444-445
    "The Potential for Discrimination in Health
        Insurance Based on Predictive Genetic Testing"
        hearing, 446

Genetics, 427-429
    government responses to, 443-449
    proposed legislation regarding, 446, 447*t*

George Mason University (GMU)
    Center for Health Policy, Research and Ethics, 41*b*, 50,
        448
    College of Nursing and Health Science, 37*b*, 50
    Health Policy Institute, 41*b*
    School of Nursing, 139*b*

The George Washington University
    Master of Legislative Affairs program, 40*b*
    Master of Political Management program, 39*b*

Georgia
    boards of nursing, 510
    needlestick prevention legislation, 417

Georgia Southern University School of Nursing, 139*b*

Germany, 201

Gestures, 99

"Get out the vote" (GOTV) strategy, 500

Ghandi, 1

Glaxco Wellcome Inc., 634*b*

Glendening, Parris N., 462, 466

Global Alliance for Vaccines and Immunization (GAVI),
    720

Global nursing peacemaking (GNP), 349

Global Outbreak Alert and Response Network, 724

Global Public Health Information Network, 724

Global Public Health Intelligence Network, 724

Global village (term), 711

Globalization, 711

GMU. *See* George Mason University

GNP. *See* Global nursing peacemaking

Gold Star Wives of America (GSW), 132*b*

Goldfarb v. Virginia State Bar, 474

Goldwater, Marilyn, 462

Goodacre, Glenda, 195, *197*
    Vietnam Women's Memorial, *196*

Gore, Al, 48, 162, 197, 539, 634

Governance
    of professional organizations, 605-606
    shared, 388-389
    strength of, 341

Government
    challenging inappropriate action by, 475-476
    contemporary issues in, 421-449
    county, 487*b*
    historical perspectives on, 421-423
    local, 479-490
    mass casualty directives, 136-137
    municipalities, 487*b*-488*b*
    problem to government phase, 59
    program to government phase, 62
    responses to genetic issues, 443-449
    responsibility for providing guidance in policy, 15
    as sphere of political action, 14-15
    state, 491-513
    strategy for policies, 235-236

Governmental Affairs Program (AAOHN), 642

Government-employed nurses, 583-587

Governo, Margo, 353

Gradison, Willis, 635

Graduate degree programs
    The George Washington University Master of Political
        Management program, 39*b*
    Graduate Program in Nursing/Health Policy,
        University of Maryland, Baltimore, 37*b*
    Johns Hopkins University Department of Health
        Policy and Management, 39*b*

Graduate degree programs—cont'd
  Master of Arts in Public Administration and Policy,
    Rockefeller College State University of New York
    (SUNY) at Albany, 39*b*
  Master of Legislative Affairs program, The George
    Washington University, 40*b*
  Master of Public Administration, Arizona State
    University School of Public Affairs, 39*b*
  Ohio State University, School of Public Policy and
    Management dual Master's Degree program, 39*b*
Grady's Hughes Spalding Children's Hospital, 540
Gramm-Rudman-Hollings Act. *See* Balanced Budget and
    Emergency Deficit Control Act
Grants, 522, 523
Grassroots action, 133, 347-353
  by AAOHN, 642
  engagement and effective use of efforts, 563
  managed care mandated coverage in Maine, 379-385
  mobilizing efforts, 165
  nursing summits, 349
Gratitude
  displaying, 134
  expressing, 99
  saying thanks to media, 165-166
Great Britain: National Health Service, 215
"Great Society," 56
Greenberg, Ellen, 40
Greening up, 739
Grey, Margaret, 87
Grijalva et al v. Shalala, 477
Gripping and grinning, 94-95
Group Health Cooperative, 150
GSW. *See* Gold Star Wives of America
Guam: boards of nursing in, 510
"Guidelines on Shaping Effective Health Policy" (ICN),
    12*b*
Gun control, 143-144
Gun sales, 144*n*

H

Hagel, Charles T., 197
Hager, Gail, 197
Hand, Janet, 353
Handshakes, 94-95, 99
Hanover Insurance, 679
"Harry and Louise" television advertisements, 4, 159,
    635
Hart, Frederick, 186, 191
Harvard School of Public Health Degree Programs in
    Health Policy and Management, 39*b*

Harvard University John F. Kennedy School of
    Government, 39*b*
Hastert, Dennis, 134
Hatch, Carl, 584
Hatch Act. *See* Act to Prevent Pernicious Political
    Activities
Hawaii
  ERISA exemption, 433
  needlestick prevention legislation, 417
Hawaii Colleagues project, 129
Hawaii Nurses Association, 129
Hawkins, Catherine, 730-731
HCCA. *See* Healthy Child Care America
HCFA. *See* Health Care Financing Administration
Head Start, 670
Head Start Bureau, 674*b*
Healing circles, 350*b*
Health
  conceptualization of, 688-690
  definition of, 714*b*
  and environment, 739-740
  environmental, 688-689
  family-centered, 689
  holistic, 689-690
  psychosocial and mental, 689
  racial and ethnic disparities in, 222-228
Health Affairs, 38, 145*n*
Health Alert Network, 724
Health and human services opportunities, 546*b*
Health Canada, 724
Health care
  access to, 301, 303-305, 379, *380,* 708
  demand for, 312-313
  ethical issues in, 177-184
  future possibilities, 210-212
  historical development of, 201-203
  international standards for, 211
  organization of, 201-228
  payors over time, 242, 243*f*
  pollution prevention in, 741-742
  quality of, 434-435
  racial and ethnic disparities in, 222-228
  universal, 215, 309
Health care (term), 302
Health care administration, 37*b*
Health care costs, 232-234
  annual, 422
  containment of, 243-249
Health care delivery, 201-228
Health care errors, 311-312, 437-442

Health care ethics, 177-178
    PhD in Nursing (concentration in health care ethics, health care administration and health policy), George Mason University, 37*b*
Health care financing, 8, 241-297, 305-306
Health Care Financing Administration (HCFA), 59, 81, 146, 205, 272
    approach to decision making, 652
    definition of permanence, 643
    and physician supervision of CRNAs, 284
Health care fraud, 101*b*
Health care information, 110
Health care interest groups, 634
Health care organizations, 354-356
Health care personnel, 137
Health care policy. *See* Health policy
Health care product packaging, 736-737
Health care programs
    federal, 249-250
    military, 249
    Native American, 250
    for rural populations, 250
    for veterans, 249
Health care providers, 270, 296
Health care reform, 3-6, 421
    failure of, 635-636
    modern, 592-596
    in Montana, 592-596, 596-597
    Nursing's Agenda for Health Care Reform, 3
    Peggy Lee, 596-597
    websites of associations interested in, 217*b*
Health Care Security Act, 421
Health care services, 205-206
    public, 206-207
    in UAE, 729
Health care spending, 203-204
    expenditures, 229, 243, 244*t*, 246-247, 249
Health care systems
    federal, 207-208
    national, 214-217
    private, 262
    state-based, 215
Health Care Trust Fund, 507-508
Health Care Without Harm campaign, 740, 740*b*, 742
Health Care Worker Needlestick Prevention Act of 1999, 415
Health care workforce, 708
Health care workplace
    contemporary issues in, 311-332
    nursing's role in, 354
Health economics, 229-239

Health information network, 111
Health Information Portability Data Base (HIPD), 512-513
Health insurance. *See also* Medicaid; Medicare
    coverage, 110
    coverage effects, 232-233
    discrimination in, 443-444, 446
    parity for mental health care, 221
    reimbursement for complementary therapies, 293-297
    uninsured, 432-434
Health Insurance Association of America (HIAA), 164
    "Campaign to Insure All Americans," 4, 158, 635
    "Harry and Louise" television advertisements, 4, 158, 635
Health Insurance Plan of Greater New York, 223
Health Insurance Portability and Accountability Act of 1996 (HIPAA) (Public Law 104-191), 57, 58, 82, 210, 256, 317, 421
    databank, 512
    effects of, 434
    gaps in, 427, 428
    genetic privacy provisions, 445, 446
    protection of personal medical records, 427
Health Leadership Council, 635
Health legislative assistants, 51
Health literacy, 107-111
Health maintenance organizations (HMOs), 208, 209, 662
    closed-panel, 248
    key concepts, 248
    Medicaid, 88
    Medicare, 253
    open-panel, 248
    risk-contract, 253
    "Technical Advisory 95-A," 88
Health Maintenance Organizations (HMOs)—Patient Access to Choice of Provider (Maryland HB 473), 462
    defeat of, 465-466
    fact sheets, 463-464
Health management, 39*b*, 40*b*, 41*b*
Health Network for Rural Schools, 305
Health on the Net Foundation (HON), 110
Health policy, 55
    continuing education programs in, 41*b*
    definition of, 8
    DNSc in Nursing (Health Policy track), Columbia University, 38*b*
    emerging issues, 422-435
    genetics and, 427-429

Health policy—cont'd
    Harvard School of Public Health degree programs in, 39*b*
    how nurses influence, 603
    Johns Hopkins Summer Institute in Health Policy and Management, Johns Hopkins University, 41*b*
    links with health care ethics, 178
    PhD in Nursing (concentration in health care ethics, health care administration and health policy), George Mason University, 37*b*
    promotion of, 618-620
    searching for, 38*b*
    shaping, 26-27
    strategies to influence, 296-297
    The University of Iowa College of Public Health Doctoral Program in Health Management and Policy, 40*b*
    The University of South Florida Health Policy and Management programs, 40*b*
Health Policy Agenda (ONS), 647
Health policy consultants, 619
Health Policy Institute, George Mason University, 41*b*
Health Policy Tool Kit (ONS), 647
Health professionals, 663
Health professionals definition of, 640
Health Resources and Services Administration (HRSA), 139*b*, 520-521, 521*f*, 527
    Bureau of Health Manpower Division of Nursing, 147
    Division of Nursing (DON), 363, 365, 366, 521-522
    National Sample Survey (NSS), 365
Health Security Act (HSA), 3-4, 6, 57, 158, 163
Health Services Research, 527
Healthcare Cost and Utilization Project, 520
healthfinder (DHHS), 110
Healthing circles, 351
HealthMontana (Montana Senate Bill 285), 594-595
Health-promoting organizations, 684-685
Healthy Atlanta Forum, 542
Healthy Child Care America (HCCA), 673
Healthy People 2000, 50, 224
Healthy People 2010, 224, 227, 687
Healthy Work Environment Initiative, 335-336
Hearings, 454-456, 558-559
Heart disease, 224
Heckrotte, Sue, 87
Heide, Wilma Scott, 13, 28
Heinrich, Janet, 148*n*
Helene Fuld Trust, 123, 125
HELP. *See* Senate Committee on Health, Education, Labor, and Pensions
Henderson, Valena, 539

Henry Street Nurses' Settlement (New York City), 26
Hepatitis C virus infection, 412-413, 413-414
Heroines, 16
Heston, Charlton, 143*n*
HIAA. *See* Health Insurance Association of America
Hierarchy, 341
Higher education opportunities, 546*b*
Hill, Martha, 621-625
Hinnegan, Teresita, 89
HIPAA. *See* Health Insurance Portability and Accountability Act
HIPD. *See* Health Information Portability Data Base
Hispanics, 688
    health status of, 223, 224, 225
    voter turnout, 566, 566*t*, 567
Historical perspectives
    early success, 636
    on government, 421-423
    on health care financing, 241-243
    on nurse anesthesia profession, 277-278
    political, 216
    and racial and ethnic disparities, 223-225
Historical precedent, 74
HIV/AIDS, 715-716, 722
    AIDS "Warmline," 690
    in incarcerated men and women, 691
    media coverage, 161
    from needlestick injury, 412-413, 413-414, 415
    post-Apartheid consortium meetings, 49
    prevention of, 141, 142
    racial and ethnic disparities in, 225
HIV/AIDS Bureau (HRSA), 520
HMOs. *See* Health maintenance organizations
Hodgins, Agatha, 277
Holistic health, 689-690
Holistic health care, 294*b*
Holmstrom, Lynda, 401
Home care services
    growth of, 204-205
    Medicare benefits, 255-256
Home site political issues, 406-409
Homeopathy, 294*b*
HON. *See* Health on the Net Foundation
Hope, Persis, 381
Hopper, 451
Horton, Katie, 561-564
Hospice, 689
Hospital evaluation kits, 160
Hospital Insurance (HI) Trust Fund, 245, 254, 258
Hospital Survey and Construction Act (Hill-Burton Act), 202

Hospital-based case management, 320
Hospitals, 328-332
  Conditions of Participation, 316
  horizontal integration of, 203
  magnet, 4-5, 149, 315, 324-327, 388
  PATH (Physician at Teaching Hospital) audits, 317
  patient care outcomes, 325-326
  vertical integration of, 203
Hospital-wide recycling, 735
The House and Senate Explained: The People's Guide to Congress (Greenberg), 40
House Armed Service Committee, 133, 134
House Budget Committee, 527, 530
House Committee on Appropriations
  budgetary process, 529
  Subcommittee on Health and Human Services, and Education, 528
House Committee on Education and the Workforce
  Subcommittee on Employer—Employee Relations, 528
  Subcommittee on Workforce Protections, 528
House Committee on Energy and Commerce, 454
  budgetary process, 529
  nurse appointments to, 534
  Subcommittee on Health, 528
House Committee on Government Reform, 545
House Committee on Veterans' Affairs, 528
The House on Henry Street (Wald), 26
House Subcommittee on Libraries and Memorials, 193
House Ways and Means Committee, 453
  budgetary process, 529
  Subcommittee on Health, 453, 528
Housing for women out of jail, 685
Howard University Division of Nursing, 50
HRSA. *See* Health Resources and Services Administration
HSA. *See* Health Security Act
Hsiao, William, 246
Human embryo research, 446
Human Genome Project, 445
Human Genome Research Institute, 446
Human immunodeficiency virus infection. *See* HIV/AIDS
Human services sector, 218-219
Humanism, 9-11
Humor, 99, 625
Hutchinson, Tim, 134
Hyde, Henry, 646

I

IAET. *See* International Association of Enterostomal Therapy

ICN. *See* International Council of Nurses
Idaho: nurse practitioners in, 464
IDSs. *See* Integrated delivery systems
IFPMA. *See* International Federation of Pharmaceutical Manufacturers Associations
IHI. *See* Institute for Healthcare Improvement
IHS. *See* Indian Health Service
Image, 153
IMF. *See* International Monetary Fund
Immigration policy, 725-726
Impact litigation, 472-473
Impostor complex, 591
Impressions, first, 95
Improvement, 180
Incarceration
  health care for inmates, 208
  with HIV, 691
  transition from, 682-685
  Welcome Home model, 683
  of women, 682-683, 683*b*
Incentives, 340, 342
INC-MCE. *See* International Nursing Coalition on Mass Casualty Education
Income taxes, 291
Incontinence, 651
Incrementalism, 57-58, 216
Independence, 374-375
Independence Foundation, 89
Independent government agencies, 525
Independent practice, 269
Independent practice associations (IPAs), 220, 320
Indian Health Service (IHS), 207-208, 250, 522
Indiana
  campaign management in, 579-583
  local government in, 482
  needlestick prevention legislation, 417
Indianapolis, Indiana, 482
Individual dignity, 257
Individual equity or fairness, 257
Individual versus aggregate focus, 159-160
Individual voter contact, 575-576
Individualism, 179-180
Individuals with Disabilities Education Act, 481
Infant mortality
  approaches to address, 235-236
  racial and ethnic disparities in, 224
Infectious diseases
  binational infectious disease surveillance project (BIDS), 724
  emerging, 722, 723
  reemerging, 723

Influencing, 9, 93

Influenza, 724

Information
    health care, 110
    as member benefit, 602

Information brokers, 161

Information gathering, 182, 483, 552-553. *See also* Data
    collection
    self-knowledge, 624-625
    in UAE, 730-731

Information power, 79

Information sources, 545-546

Information technology
    access to, 108-110
    new, 665

Informing the Future: Critical Issues in Health (IOM), 525

Inglefinger, Franz, 144*n*

Inherent bias, 62

Inherent reasonableness, 643

Initiatives
    inside, 145-146
    outside, 145

Injuries, needlestick, 412-419

Injury prevention, 316

Injury Prevention Institute (ENA), 681

Innovation, 355

Innovative faith-based program for women, 682-685

Inouye, Daniel K., *51,* 146, 146*n*

Inside initiative model for agenda building, 145-146

Inside strategy, 630

The Insider, 144

Institute for Healthcare Improvement (IHI), 440

Institute for Johns Hopkins Nursing, 139*b*

Institute of Medicine (IOM), 6, 525
    Committee on Quality of Health Care, 435
    *Crossing the Quality Chasm: A New Health System for
        the 21st Century,* 311, 435, 525
    To Err is Human: Building a Safer Health System, 15,
        311, 391, 437, 442, 525
    The Future of Public Health, 709
    Informing the Future: Critical Issues in Health, 525
    *Nursing Staff in Hospitals and Nursing Homes: Is It
        Adequate?,* 148-149
    recommendations on access, 430
    recommendations on quality, 431
    recommendations on staffing, 431
    reports, 525
    *The Right Thing to Do, The Smart Thing to Do:
        Enhancing Diversity in Health Professions,* 525

Institutional policies, 8

Insulation, 394

Insurance coverage
    genetic testing and, 443-444
    greater, effects of, 232-233
    mandated benefits, 591
    parity for mental health care, 221
    "The Potential for Discrimination in Health
        Insurance Based on Predictive Genetic Testing"
        hearing, 446
    protecting workers from disenrollment, 434

Integrated delivery systems (IDSs), 211

Integration, 335

Integrative health care, 294*b*

Integrity, ethical, 182

Intelligence, emotional, 93

Interagency Task Force on Environmental Health and
    Safety Risks to Children, 541

Intercultural communication, 99

Interdisciplinary action, case study, 643-644

Interdisciplinary advisory boards, 181-182

Interdisciplinary collaboration, 336-339

Interdisciplinary relationships, 315

Interest groups, 627-638, 630*b*

Interests, focus on, 117

Intergroup conflict, 114-115

Interim Payment System (IPS), 256

International Association of Enterostomal Therapy
    (IAET), 611

International community, 711-735

International Council of Nurses (ICN), 25, 714*b*
    advocates, *712,* 713
    environmental resolutions, 742
    "Guidelines on Shaping Effective Health Policy," 12*b*
    "Participation of Nurses in Health Services Decision
        Making and Policy Development," 12*b*
    partnerships and strategic alliances, 719-720
    and woman suffrage, 26

International Council of Women, 25, 26

International Federation of Pharmaceutical
    Manufacturers Associations (IFPMA), 720

International Health Regulations, 724, 726

International Monetary Fund (IMF), 716*b*

International Nursing Coalition on Mass Casualty
    Education (INC-MCE), 135-140
    organizational members, 139*b*
    website, 140*b*

International Pharmaceutical Federation (FIP), 720

International Society of Nurses in Genetics, 447

International Task Force for Nursing, American Red
    Cross, 50

Internet, 103-104, 109, 602, 665. *See also* Websites
    role in lobbying, 557-558

Internships, 36
  Nurse In Washington Internship (NIWI), 41*b*, 44-45, 642
Interpersonal conflict, 114
Interventions, 159-160
Interviews, 166-168, 547-548
Intrapersonal conflict, 113-114
Invasive procedures, 356-361
Involuntary units, 487*b*
Involved Citizens of Helena, 696, 699-700
IOM. *See* Institute of Medicine
Iowa Intervention Project, 236
IPAs. *See* Independent practice associations
IPS. *See* Interim Payment System
Iron triangles, 627-628
Issue analysis, 63, 63*f*
Issue statements, 63, 65*b*

J

Jackson, Dick, 541
Jacksonville State University College of Nursing and Health Sciences, 139*b*
Jail life, 682-683
Jajuga, James, 680
Japanese Americans, 224
JCAHO. *See* Joint Commission on Accreditation of Healthcare Organizations
Jeffress, Charles, 417
Jenkins, Melinda, 90
Jewish War Veterans of the United States of America (JWW), 132*b*
Jews, 444
Job security, 395-396
"Joe Camel" ads, 161
Johns Hopkins University
  Department of Health Policy and Management programs, 39*b*
  Institute for Johns Hopkins Nursing, 139*b*
  Summer Institute in Health Policy and Management, 41*b*
Johnson, Eddie Bernice, 571, 615
Johnson, Lyndon B., 47, 56
Johnson, Tom, 47
Johnsrud, DuWayne, *503*
Johnston, Patricia, 447
Joint Commission on Accreditation of Healthcare Organizations (JCAHO), 312, 316
Joint committees, 453
Joint congressional testimony, 133, 134
Joint practice committees, 340-341
Joint ventures, 720

Jokes, 99
Journal of Health Politics, Policy and Law, 38
Journal of Professional Nursing, 38
Journal of the American Medical Association (JAMA), 38, 143, 144, 150, 151, 151*n*
Journalists, 100, 163, 165-166
Journals, professional, 38-40
Joyce, Barbara, 347, 351
Judge School of Management Studies, Cambridge University, 50
Judicial branch, 530-532
Judicial system, 471-472
Justice, environmental, 698, 699
JWV. *See* Jewish War Veterans of the United States of America

K

Kaiser Family Foundation (KFF), 217*b*
Kaiser Foundation, 220
Kaiser Permanente, 284
Kansas City (KC) Colleagues, 123
Kansas State Nurses Association, 543
Kassirir, Jerome P., 144*n*
Kellogg, W.K., 702*b*
W.K. Kellogg Foundation, 225, 688, 695, 702*b*, 706
  public health programming tradition, 708-709
  Turning Point: Collaborating for a New Century in Public Health initiative, 701-709
Kemper Insurance, 680
Kennedy, Edward, 190, 417
Kennedy, John F., 168
Kentucky: nurse practitioners in, 464
Kerry, John, 190
Kerry, Robert, 134
Kessler, David, 144, 150
Kidsultants, 705
Kieltyka, Evelyn, 384
King, Angus, 379, *380*
Kingdon's policy streams model, 58-59
Kiser, Kenneth, 48
Kitzhaber, John, 300, 302, 306
Knowledge Development and Application grants, 523
Knowledge gap, 566-567
Koehler, Margie, 380, 381
Koop, C. Everett, 143
Krissovich, Marta, 651

L

Labor unions, 392
Labor-management relations, 390
Land use policy, 698

Landfill applications, 696
Large data set research, 152
Lassman, Janet, 679, 680, 681
Laws. *See* Legislation
Lazio, Rick, 634
Leach, Connie, 736
Leadership, 76-77, 78*t*, 122
 aligned, 339, 340-341
 appointed, 614-615
 communication and, 106
 development of, 708
 elected, 614-615
 exemplary, 378
 expectations of, 341
 nontraditional, 704
 nursing, 565-599
 organizational, 614-617, 621-625
 of professional organizations, 605
 in urban setting, 704
 visionary, 693-694
Leadership U (NSNA), 38
League of Women Voters, 544
LEAP program, 173
Leapfrog Group, 706
Learned professions, 474
Learned skills, 42-43
Learning
 experiential, 36-42
 online, 38
 from others, 118*b*
Learning gap, 625
Learning the ropes, 31-53
Least restrictive setting, 430
Leave-behinds, 556
Leavitt, Patricia ("Patsy"), 379-385
Legal rights. *See also* Rights
 expansion through legislation, 477
Legislation. *See also specific acts*
 AANA-advocated changes, 278-279
 antitrust laws, 474
 appropriations, 454, 529*b*
 authorization, 454, 528, 529, 529*b*
 committee procedures, 454-457
 courts as enforcers of, 473-474
 The Dance of Legislation (Redman), 40
 expansion of legal rights through, 477
 The House and Senate Explained: The People's Guide to Congress (Greenberg), 40
 introduction of bills, 452
 language of, 52, 270
 Master of Legislative Affairs program, The George Washington University, 40*b*

Legislation—cont'd
 needlestick prevention, 415
 The Nurses' Directory of Capitol Connections (Bull, Sharp, and Wakefield), 40
 omnibus bills, 529*b*
 The Politics of Health Legislation: An Economic Perspective (Feldstein), 40
 power of nurses in, 554
 for prevention of needlestick injuries, 416-418
 proposed, regarding genetic information, 446, 447*t*
 reauthorization, 529
 in response to genetic issues, 445-447
 stem cell, 428-429
 Tribes on the Hill: The U.S. Congress Ritual and Realities (Weatherford), 40
 types of bills, 452*b*
Legislative branch, 525-530
Legislative Coalition of Virginia Nurses, 121
Legislative process, 451-470, 455*f*
 federal, 528
 how to influence, 461*b*
 in Maryland, 463-466
 professional organizations in, 603-604
Legislators
 education of, 296-297
 lessons learned, 598-599
 nurses as, 503-504
 term limits for, 598
 transition to, 500-501
 women, 569
Legislatures, state, 492-493
Legitimate (or positional) power, 79
Letter writing, 555-556
Letters of consistency, 696
Letters to the editor, 171-172
Levy, Robert, 624
Liability, product, 474-475
Libraries Online!, 109
Library of Congress, 552
Licensure
 of genetic professionals, 447
 multistate, 513
 of nurses, in UAE, 728-735
Licensure boards, 546*b*
Licensure examinations, 511-512
Lieberman, Joseph I., 543
Life Improving Network to the Community (LINC) program, 691
Life teams, 316
Lin, Maya, 191
LINC program. *See* Life Improving Network to the Community program

Listening, 96, 114
Literacy, health, 107-111
Literature reviews, 152
Litigation
    by AAOHN, 641-642
    class action suits, 475
    impact, 472-473
LN. *See* National League for Nursing
Lobbying. *See also* Advocacy
    for advanced practice nursing statute, 89-90
    inside view, 561-564
    Internet's effect on, 557-558
    rationale for, 552
    strategies for, 551-564
    targets, 553-554
Lobbyists, 91, 551, 562, 619
Local government, 479-490
    case example, 485-486
    decisions made about major issues for society, 14
    forms of, 487*b*-489*b*
    involuntary units, 487*b*
    voluntary units, 487*b*
Local health care systems, 261-262
Locations, 488*b*-489*b*
Longshoremen, 392
Long-term care, 429-432
    custodial, 252
    Medicare benefits, 256-257
Los Angeles Times, 41
Lott, Trent, 134
Louisiana: boards of nursing, 510
Louisiana State University, 139
Low back pain, 149
Lundberg, George, 143-144, 144*n*

M

Maas, Clara, 85
MADD. *See* Mothers Against Drunk Driving
Madison, James, 628
Magaw, Alice, 277
Magnet hospitals, 4-5, 14, 149, 328-332, 388
    characteristics of, 325
    patient care outcomes, 325-326
Magnet Recognition Program for Excellence in Nursing
    Services (ANCC), 315, 324-327, 388
Magnetism, 396
Maine
    "An Act to Increase Access to Primary Health Care
        Services" (PL 296), 379, *380*
    managed care mandated coverage in, 379-385
    municipal governments, 488*b*

Maine—cont'd
    needlestick prevention legislation, 417
    nurse practitioners in, 464
Maine Medical Association (MMA), 381, 383
Maine Nurse Practitioner Association (MNPA), 381
Maine Osteopathic Medical Association (MOA), 383
Majority/minority districts, 570
Mallon, Mary (Typhoid Mary), 722
Managed behavioral health care, 220
Managed care, 57, 234, 247-249
    advanced practice nurses (APNs) and, 146-147
    in California, 148
    continuum of, 247-248, 248*f*
    development of, 208-209, 320
    management of, 265-272
    mandated coverage in Maine, 379-385
    Medicare, 253-254
    mental health care, 218-222
    reimbursement for nurse practitioners, 88-89
    research funding, 402
    types of plans, 220-221
Managed care organizations (MCOs), 207, 209, 662
    cost control strategies, 234
    recognition from, 271
Management
    of attention, 693-694
    labor-management relations, 390
    of meaning, 694
    of self, 694
    of trust, 694
Mandated benefits, 591
Mandatory funding, 672-673
Mandatory patient safety education topics, 440*b*
Mandatory spending, 529*b*
Marbury v. Madison, 472
Marine Corps League (MCL), 132*b*
Marine Corps Reserve Officers Association (MCROA),
    132*b*
Marion Merrill Dow (MMD) Pharmaceuticals, 680
Market demand, 230, 230*f,* 230*t*
Market differentiation, 296
Market nursing, 302
Market price, 232, 232*f*
Market supply, 231, 231*f,* 231*t*
Market systems, 230-232
Marketing
    direct-to-consumer, 425-426
    social, 168, 168*t*
Mark-ups, 456, 529*b,* 530
Marlboro man, 8
Martinez, Ricardo, 680

Maryland
    legislative issues, 462-463
    legislative process, 463-466
    2001 legislative session, 462-466
    local government in, 482
    needlestick prevention legislation, 417
    nurse practitioners in, 462-466
Maryland HB 473. *See* Health Maintenance
        Organizations (HMOs)—Patient Access to Choice
        of Provider
Maryland Medical Chirurgical Society (Med-Chi), 465
Mason, Kathleen, 497*b*
Mass casualty
    government directives, 136-137
    International Nursing Coalition on Mass Casualty
        Education (INC-MCE), 135-140
Massachusetts: needlestick prevention legislation, 417
Massachusetts Advocates for Traffic Safety, 680
Massachusetts General Hospital (Boston,
        Massachusetts), 21
Massachusetts Governor's Highway Safety Bureau
        (MGHSB), 677
Massachusetts Medical Society, 144*n*
Master's Degree programs
    Master of Arts in Public Administration and Policy,
        Rockefeller College State University of New York
        (SUNY) at Albany, 39*b*
    Master of Legislative Affairs, The George Washington
        University, 40*b*
    Master of Political Management, The George
        Washington University, 39*b*
    Master of Public Administration, Arizona State
        University School of Public Affairs, 39*b*
    MSN in Nursing Management and Policy, Yale
        University School of Nursing, 37*b*
    Ohio State University School of Public Policy and
        Management, 39*b*
    University of Michigan School of Public Health, 40*b*
    University of South Florida Health Policy and
        Management, 40*b*
    University of Ulster, 138
Matching funds, 673
Maternal and Child Health Bureau (HRSA), 520, 673
Mayo, Charles, 277
Mayo, William Worrell, 277
Mayor-council municipal governments, 488*b*
Mayor-manager governments, 488*b*
MCA. *See* Military Chaplains Association of the United
        States of America
MCAC. *See* Medicare Coverage Advisory Committee
McCain, John, 633

McCain-Feingold Bill, 633
McCarthy, Carolyn, 75, 536-538, 569, 571
McDonough, John E., 145*n*
McGee, Anita Newcomb, 23
MCL. *See* Marine Corps League
MCOs. *See* Managed care organizations
McRae, Glenn, 739
McRae, Hollie Shaner, 735-744
MCROA. *See* Marine Corps Reserve Officers Association
Meals on Wheels, 519
Meaning, management of, 694
Means testing, 259-260, 291
Measurements, 340, 342
Meatpackers, 392
Med-Chi. *See* Maryland Medical Chirurgical Society
MedCycle, 737-738
MedCycle Depot, 737
Media advocacy, 168-169, 168*t*
Media campaigns, 160
Media coverage, 3, 157-176
    of Emergency Nurses CARE, 677
    front page rule for political appointees, 543
    guidelines for, 166-168
    INC-MCE efforts, 139
    of MedCycle project, 737-738
    political campaigns and, 577
    promoting coalitions, 125
    role and importance of, 563
    tips for, 173-176
    in UAE, 731
    working with, 100
Media events, 162
Medicaid, 202, 250-251
    case management, 319
    cost containment strategies, 246
    eligibility for, 250-251, 481
    enactment of, 56
    expansion of, 206, 432, 433, 508
    financing, 249
    future possibilities, 210-211
    historical perspectives on, 242
    institutional bias, 430
    legislative jurisdiction over, 527
    managed care, 57, 88-89, 247
    mental health spending, 219-220
    nurse-midwifery benefits, 146
    Oregon program, 299-300
    prescription drug coverage, 424
    reimbursement for nurse practitioners, 88-89
    reimbursement rates, 6
    spending reductions, 246

Medicaid—cont'd
  state administration of, 260, 261
  state costs, 57
  waivers, 251
Medicaid HMOs, 88
Medical care (term), 302
Medical errors, 311-312, 437-442
  To Err is Human: Building a Safer Health System
    (IOM), 15, 311, 391, 435, 437
  nursing errors, 152
Medical Information Protection and Research
    Enhancement Act, 447*t*, 448
Medical records, 427
Medical savings accounts (MSAs), 6, 254, 596
Medical waste, 736, 739
Medical-industrial complex, 203-204, 262
Medicare, 202, 251-257, 272-276
  benefits for military retirees, 130, 131-132
  case management, 319
  conditions of participation, 283-286
  diagnosis-related groups, 147
  economics of, 317
  eligibility for, 252
  emerging issues, 422-427
  enactment of, 56
  expansion of, 206, 433
  fee-for-service, 253-254
  financing, 249
  funding, 316
  future possibilities, 210-211
  historical perspectives on, 242
  home care benefits, 255-256
  legislative jurisdiction over, 527
  long-term care benefits, 256-257
  managed care, 247, 253-254
  mental health care, 219-220
  out-of-pocket spending on prescription drugs, 424-
    425
  Part A, hospital insurance (HI), 245, 252, 254-255,
    258, 272, 278
  Part B, supplementary medical insurance (SMI), 245,
    246, 252, 254-255, 258, 273, 278
  Part D, 255
  physician fee schedule, 280*b*-281*b*
  prescription drug benefits, 247, 255, 423-424, 425
    sample criteria/alternatives matrix for, 68*f*
    sample policy issue paper, 64*b*-67*b*
  prospective payment system, 147
  reform, 254-255, 273*b*, 426-427
  reimbursement for APNs, 81, 376
  reimbursement for clinical nurse specialists, 257

Medicare—cont'd
  reimbursement for NPs, 146, 257
  reimbursement for nurse anesthesia practice, 276-287
  reimbursement for nurses, 5, 266-268, 268-271
  reimbursement rates, 6
  spending on, 229, 249
  supplemental insurance coverage, 423-424
Medicare, Medicaid and S-CHIP Benefits Improvement
    and Protection Act of 2000, 251
Medicare Catastrophic Coverage Act, 273*b*
Medicare Coverage Advisory Committee (MCAC), 652,
    653
Medicare Medical Savings Account Plan, 254
Medicare Trust Fund, 317, 422
Medicare+Choice, 209, 247, 253, 254, 272-273, 275
  final rule, 469-470
  implementation of, 468
  prescription drug coverage, 255, 424
Medication errors, 513
  prevention of, 497*b*
Medigap, 253, 272, 275, 424
Meditation, 348*b*
Meehan, Martin T., 633
Meeting and greeting, 94-95
Meetings, coalition, 124
Membership dues, 125
Membership organizations, 601
Memberships, professional, 601-605
Mental health, 689
  specialty, 218
Mental health care
  expansion of services, 508
  managed, 218-222
Mental Health Equitable Treatment Act, 221
Mental Health Parity Act, 221
Mental illness, costs of, 219-220
Mentoring, 33-35
Mentors
  avenues to cultivating, 271
  finding, 34-35, 623-624
Mercury-free facilities, 738
Mergers, 335
Merson, Michael H., 141, 142
Messaging, 174
Metanalyses, 152
Michel, Gracia, 49
Michigan Community Health Project, 708
Michigan Nurses Association, 390
Microsoft Corporation, 109
Microtheories, 333
Midwives. *See* Certified nurse midwives (CNMs)

Migration, 711-714
Milbank Memorial Fund, 148, 217*b*
Military Chaplains Association of the United States of
America (MCA), 132*b*
Military Coalition, 130-135
goals, 133*b*
members, 132*b*
philosophy, 133*b*
Military health programs, 130-135, 249
Military Order of the Purple Heart, 132*b*
Mingling, 97
Mini summits, 351
Minneapolis/St. Paul, Minnesota, 482
Minnesota
local government in, 482
needlestick prevention legislation, 417
nurse practitioners in, 464
Minnesota Nurses Association, 187
Minority health, 223-225
Minority Health and Health Disparities Research and
Education Act of 2000 (Public Law 106-525), 223
Minority Health Initiative, 223
Mission statements, 610-611
Mississippi
opportunities for APNs in, 5
school health nursing in, 508-509
tobacco settlement allocation, 505-509
Mississippi Colleagues, 125
Mississippi Nurses Association, 125
Mississippi State Health Plan, 509
Missouri
independent nurse practitioner practice in, 269
nurse practitioners in, 464
Missouri Nurse Practice Act, 269
Mitsubishi Motors, 680
Mixed county boards, 487*b*
MMA. *See* Maine Medical Association
MNPA. *See* Maine Nurse Practitioner Association
MOA. *See* Maine Osteopathic Medical Association
Mobile Outreach Clinic Program (MOCP) (VNACJ), 689
Mobilization model for agenda building, 145
Mobilization of nurses, 302
MOCP. *See* Mobile Outreach Clinic Program
Money, 632-633
Monroe, James, 539
Montana
modern health care reform in, 592-596
nurse practitioners in, 464
Montana Citizen's Health Care Advisory Group, 594
Montana Health Care Authority, 594, 595, 596, 597
Montana Nurses Association, 598

Montana State Senate, 589-599
Montoya, Patricia, 547
Mood, Lillian H., 697
Moore, Harry, 202
Moore, Mike, 506, 509
Morality policies, 76
Morality policy, 151
Mothers Against Drunk Driving (MADD), 169, 681
Motor voter registration, 568
Moynihan, Daniel Patrick, 562
Mozambique, 49
Multiple payors, 214-215
Multistate practice and licensure, 513
Mundinger, Mary, 151
Municipalities, 487*b*-488*b*
Murdock Trust, 125
Mutual recognition, 513

N

NA. *See* American Nurses Association
NACCHO. *See* National Association of County and City
Health Officials
NACGN. *See* National Association of Colored Graduate
Nurses
NACNS. *See* National Association of Clinical Nurse
Specialists
Narratives, 145*n*
National Academies of Practice, 50
National Academy of Engineering, 525
National Academy of Sciences, 142, 525
National Action Plan on Breast Cancer (NAPBC), 427
National Advisory Council for Nursing Research, 523
National American Woman Suffrage Association, 25
National Association for the Education of Young
Children, 674*b*
National Association of Clinical Nurse Specialists
(NACNS), 639, 644-645
Legislative and Regulatory Committee, 645
Statement on Clinical Nurse Specialist Practice and
Education, 645, 646
National Association of Colored Graduate Nurses
(NACGN), 20, 23-24, 26, 636
National Association of County and City Health
Officials (NACCHO), 703, 704, 705
National Association of Health Underwriters, 635
National Association of Manufacturers, 635
National Bioethics Advisory Commission, 446
National Bipartisan Commission on the Future of
Medicare, 254
National Capital Memorial Commission, 195
National Capital Planning Commission, 195

National Cemetery Administration, 523-524
National Center for Complementary and Alternative
     Medicine (NCCAM), 294-295
National Center for Environmental Health, 541
National Center for Infectious Diseases, 725, 726
National Center for Nursing Research, 80
National Center for Patient Safety (NCPS), 439
National Center on Minority Health and Health
     Disparities (NCMHD), 223-224
National Child Care Information Center, 674b
National Commission on Retirement Policy, 292
National Commission on Social Security Reform, 292
National Conference of State Legislatures (NCSL), 446,
     496b, 674b
National Council of State Boards of Nursing (NCSBN),
     511
National Council of Women, 25
National Council of Women's Organizations (NCWO),
     545
National Database of Nursing Quality Indicators
     (NDNQI), 326
2001 National Defense Authorization Act (NDAA-01)
     (P.L. 106-398), 131-132, 132
National Disaster Medical System (NDMS), 136, 137,
     138
National Disaster Medical System Conference (2001),
     138
National Domestic Preparedness Office, FBI, 139b
National Electronic Disease Surveillance System, 724
National Federation for Specialty Nursing Organizations
     (NFSNO), 642
   Nurse in Washington Internship (NIWI), 41b, 44-45
National Federation of Specialty Nursing Organizations
     (NFSNO), 607
National Governors Association, 477, 496b, 674b, 679
National Guard Association of the United States
     (NGAUS), 132b
National Guideline Clearinghouse, 520
National Health Service (UK), 215
National Health Service Corps, 250, 454, 521, 527
National health systems, 214-217
National Heart, Lung, and Blood Institute (NHLBI), 624
National Highway Traffic Safety Administration
     (NHTSA), 679-680, 681
National Institute for Mental Health (NIMH), 220
National Institute for Occupational Safety and Health
     (NIOSH), 366, 416
National Institute of Nursing Research (NINR), 80, 365,
     454
   funding, 399, 527
   research agenda, 523

National Institute on Out-of-School Time, 674b
National Institutes of Health (NIH), 454, 522, 522b
   Consensus Conference, 142, 150n
   funding, 399, 401, 402, 527, 534
   National Center for Complementary and Alternative
        Medicine (NCCAM), 294-295
   National Center on Minority Health and Health
        Disparities (NCMHD), 223-224
   Office of Alternative Medicine (OAM), 295
   Office of Research on Minority Health (ORMH), 223
National Institutes of Health/Department of Energy
     (NIH/DOE) Ethical, Legal and Social Implications
     (ELSI) Working Group, 427
National Labor Relations Act (NLRA) of 1935, 393, 476,
     528
National Labor Relations Board (NLRB), 393, 476
   and all-RN bargaining units, 394-395
   Epilepsy Foundation of Northeast Ohio, 604
   NLRB v. Health Care & Retirement Corp. of America,
        395, 476
   NLRB v. Kentucky River Community Care Inc. et al,
        395, 476
National League for Nursing (NLN), 20, 22, 25, 365, 636
   Accrediting Commission, 139b
   agenda, 147
   Tri-Council for Nursing, 56
National League of Nursing Education, 22
National Mail Order Pharmacy, 135
National Medical Response Teams, 136
National Military Family Association (NMFA), 132b
National Nosocomial Infections Surveillance, 724
National Nurse Service Corps, 535
National Nursing Centers Consortium (NNCC), 90
National Nursing Council for War Service, 24
National Order of Battlefield Commissions (NOBC),
     132b
National Organization for Women (NOW), 28
National Organization of Public Health Nursing
     (NOPHN), 20, 24, 26, 636
National Organizations for Youth Safety (NOYS), 681
National Patient Safety Partnership (NPSP), 438, 438b
National Patient Safety Registry, 439
National Practitioner Data Bank (NPDB), 512
National Public Radio (NPR), 42, 162
National Research Council, 525
National Resource Center for Health and Safety in Child
     Care, 674b
National Rifle Association (NRA), 143
National Rural Health Association, 284
National Sample Survey (NSS), 365, 522
National Security Forum, 50

National Students Nurses Association (NSNA), 35, 36-37, 38

National Voter Registration Act, 567-568

National Women's Law Center, 674*b*

National Women's Political Caucus (NWPC), 544, 545

Native Americans
   health care programs for, 250
   health status of, 223, 224, 225

Native Hawaiians, 224

Naturopathy, 294*b*

Naval Enlisted Reserve Association (NERA), 132*b*

Naval Reserve Association (NRA), 132*b*

Navy League of the United States (NLUS), 132*b*

NCCAM. *See* National Center for Complementary and Alternative Medicine

NCLEX-PN exam, 511

NCLEX-RN exam, 511

NCMHD. *See* National Center on Minority Health and Health Disparities

NCOA. *See* Non Commissioned Officers Association

NCPS. *See* National Center for Patient Safety

NCSBN. *See* National Council of State Boards of Nursing

NCSL. *See* National Conference of State Legislatures

NCWO. *See* National Council of Women's Organizations

NDAA-01. *See* 2001 National Defense Authorization Act

NDMS. *See* National Disaster Medical System

NDNQI. *See* National Database of Nursing Quality Indicators

NEED Act. *See* Nurse Employment and Education Development Act

Need programs, 243

Needle exchange programs, 141, 142

Needlestick injuries
   case study, 412-419
   prevention of, 415, 416-418

Needlestick Injury Prevention Advisory Committee, 418

Needlestick Safety and Prevention Act, 316, 417, 524, 537, 636

Negotiation, 618
   principled, 116-118, 618

Neighborhood Healing Circles, 702

Neighborhood health centers, 205-206

NEJM. See New England Journal of Medicine

NERA. *See* Naval Enlisted Reserve Association

Netiquette, 103-104

Networking, 83-84, 96, 302
   NIWI, 44-45
   power of, 547

New, Marianne, 444-445

New Christian Right, 628

New England Journal of Medicine (NEJM), 38, 144, 150*n*, 408

New Hampshire, 488*b*-489*b*

New Haven Hospital (New Haven, Connecticut), 21

New Jersey
   demand for RNs in, 366
   duty to warn in, 445
   needlestick prevention legislation, 417
   nurse practitioners in, 464
   Nursing Incentives Reimbursement Program, 367
   prevention of medication errors in, 497*b*
   S-CHIP waivers, 433-434
   state government, *495*

New Jersey Board of Nursing, 123

New Jersey Colleagues project, 123

New Jersey Department of Human Services, 692, 693

New Jersey Medical Society, 497*b*

New Jersey State Nurses Association, 497*b*

New Mexico: nurse practitioners in, 464

New Public Service, 178

New York
   advocacy for expansion of legal rights through legislation, 477
   board of nursing, 510
   demand for RNs in, 366
   diversity and redistricting, 570
   licensure of genetic professionals, 447
   supply of RNs in, 366

New York City Bureau of Child Hygiene, 27

New York State Nurses Association (NYSNA), 160, 351

The New York Times, 41, 161

News teams, TV, 172-176

Newspapers, 40-41, 164*b*

NFSNO. *See* National Federation for Specialty Nursing Organizations

NGAUS. *See* National Guard Association of the United States

NGOs. *See* Nongovernmental organizations

NHLBI. *See* National Heart, Lung, and Blood Institute

NHTSA. *See* National Highway Traffic Safety Administration

Nichols, Barbara, 548-549

Nickles, Don, 646, 647

Nightingale, Florence, 16, 21, 590, 739

Nightingales, 165

NIMH. *See* National Institute for Mental Health

NINR. *See* National Institute of Nursing Research

NIOSH. *See* National Institute for Occupational Safety and Health

NIWI. *See* Nurse In Washington Internship

Nixon, Richard, 233

NLRA. *See* National Labor Relations Act

NLRB. *See* National Labor Relations Board

NLRB v. Health Care & Retirement Corp. of America, 395, 476

NLRB v. Kentucky River Community Care Inc. et al, 395, 476

NLUS. *See* Navy League of the United States

NMFA. *See* National Military Family Association

NMOP. *See* National Mail Order Pharmacy

NNCC. *See* National Nursing Centers Consortium

NOBC. *See* National Order of Battlefield Commissions

Noble Training Center, 139

Non Commissioned Officers Association (NCOA), 132*b*

Nongovernmental organizations (NGOs), 49, 719-720

Nonprofit organizations, 613, 680

NOPHN. *See* National Organization of Public Health Nursing

North American Spine Society, 149

North Carolina
  board of nursing, 510
  licensure of genetic professionals in, 447
  local government, 482

North Central West Virginia Nursing Network, 123

Northern Mariana Islands, 510

Northern Nurses Federation, 719

Northwest Airlines, 190

"Not in my backyard" (NIMBY) category, 484

NOYS. *See* National Organizations for Youth Safety

NPAM. *See* Nurse Practitioner Association of Maryland

NPR. *See* National Public Radio

NPs. *See* Nurse practitioners

NPSP. *See* National Patient Safety Partnership

NRA. *See* National Rifle Association; Naval Reserve Association

NSHG. *See* Nursing Strategic Healthcare Group

NSNA. *See* National Students Nurses Association

NSS. *See* National Sample Survey

N-STAT, 36

Nuclear, biologic, and chemical (NBC) material, 136

The Nurse ("the Lady") (Brodin), 187, 188, 192

Nurse (title), 23

Nurse anesthesia, 5, 277-278
  advocacy issues, 278-279
  certified registered nurse anesthetists (CRNAs), 277
    Medicare reimbursement for, 278
    physician supervision of, 283-286
  historical perspective on, 277-278
  media coverage of, 3
  Medicare payment and reimbursement policies for, 276-287
  prospective outcome study of, 285

Nurse committees, 388

Nurse Day, 385

Nurse Education Act, 454, 527

Nurse Employment and Education Development (NEED) Act, 527

Nurse In Washington Internship (NIWI), 41*b,* 44-45, 642

Nurse Midwifery Associates v. Hibbett et al., 474

Nurse midwives. *See* Certified nurse midwives (CNMs)

Nurse Practice Act (Oklahoma), 473

Nurse Practitioner Association of Maryland (NPAM), 463

Nurse Practitioners: Rx for America's Health campaign, 377-378

Nurse practitioners (NPs), 371
  access to, 463
  credentialing of, 381
  future supply and demand for, 363
  independent practice, 269
  prescriptive authority for, 89-90
  as primary care providers, 463-464
  reimbursement for, 88-89
    managed care, 88-89
    Medicare, 146, 257, 372
  response to Citizens Petition (AMA), 654-657
  in TennCare, 145

Nurse Reinvestment Act, 527, 535

Nurse Staffing and Patient Outcomes in Hospitals, 522

Nurse-activists, 42, 42*b*

Nurse-citizens, 42, 42*b,* 663

Nurse-influentials, 33

Nurse-managed community health centers, urban, 87-88

Nurse-midwifery, 146. *See also* Certified nurse midwives (CNMs)

Nurse-politician, 42-43, 43*b*

Nurses
  access to, 148
  activist, 32, 42, 42*b*
  advanced practice; *See* Advanced practice nurses (APNs)
  African-American, 23, 24
  as appointees, 548-549
  bargaining representatives for, 393
  calls for action, 502-503
  as citizens, 663
  clinical advancement of, 314
  in community, 694-695
  compensation for, 147, 314
  demand for, 147
  ethnic and racial disparities, 225-226
  government-employed, 583-587, 718-719

Nurses—cont'd
  as health professionals, 663
  as heroines, 16
  historic mandate, 16-17
  in international community, 711-735
  leadership in political campaigns, 565-599
  in legislative affairs, 554
  as legislators, 500-501, 503-504
  as members of Congress, 533-535, 571
  mobilization of, 302
  organization of, 24-26, 390-392
  as policy analysts, 468
  policy voice, 717-718
  political clout of, 504-505
  political development of, 7-8, 20, 21, 32-33, 76-77, 78t
  political empowerment of, 12
  as professionals, 390
  progress of, 76-77, 78t
  as radio response squads, 159
  rationing issues of concern to, 300-301, 306-307
  recruitment and retention of, 314
  regulation of, 510-511, 511-513
  respect for, 550
  school health
    in Mississippi, 508-509
    reemergence of, 507
  shortage of, 1, 313-315, 512
    Commission on the Nursing Shortage, 147
    continuing, 148-149
    data on, 147-148, 148n
    media coverage of, 161
  as special interest group, 636-637
  supply of, 147, 313
  on TV news teams, 172-176
  in WHO, 718-719
  in workplace change, 354
Nurses Associated Alumnae of the United States and
    Canada, 20, 22, 23, 636
Nurses Coalition for Action in Politics, 7, 28
The Nurses' Directory of Capitol Connections (Bull, Sharp,
    and Wakefield), 40
"Nurses for Pelosi" effort, 171
Nurse's Pollution Prevention Kit, 741
"Nurses' Toolkit" (ANA), 100
Nurses Week, 2
Nurses-NOW, 28
Nurse-to-patient-day staffing ratios, 367-368
Nursing
  decentralized, 388
  devolution of, 5-6
  marketing, 302

Nursing—cont'd
  modern movement, 21
  policy agenda, 477-478
  political roots, 19-30
  values of, 9-11
Nursing brain drain, 713, 714
Nursing circles, 348, 348b
Nursing Economic$, 38
Nursing education. See also Schools of nursing
  federal, 1, 454
  nurse-training schools, 21-22
  revolution in, 137-138
  in UAE, 729
Nursing Education Loan Repayment Program, 521
Nursing errors, 152
Nursing homes, 204
Nursing Incentives Reimbursement Program (New
    Jersey), 367
"The Nursing Initiatives Program" (UHF), 319
Nursing Organization Alliance (The Alliance), 607
Nursing Organization Coalition, 654b
Nursing Organization Liaison Forum, 607, 646
Nursing organizations, 606-607
  case studies, 639-658
  life cycle of, 613-614
Nursing practice
  change based on evidence, 358-359
  change through research investigation, 358-359
  control of, 387-390
    objectives essential for, 387-388
    through collective bargaining, 390-393
  independent, 269
  multistate, 513
  strategies for change, 357-358
Nursing Practice Act (UAE), 732
Nursing research, 399-411
  questioning of, 151
Nursing scholarships, 508
Nursing Staff in Hospitals and Nursing Homes: Is It
    Adequate? (IOM), 148-149
Nursing Strategic Healthcare Group (NSHG), 524
Nursing students, 36-38
Nursing summits, 350-351
  "Dancing With the Chaos," 351
  grassroots, 349
  mini summits, 351
  process-oriented, 351
  seed questions for, 350b
  suggested ground rules and guidelines for, 352b
  tips for, 351b
Nursing town meetings, 348

Nursing workforce, 313-315, 363-364
  diversity of, 225-226
  politics of, 363-369
Nursing Workforce Development, 527
Nursing Workforce Diversity grants, 522
Nursingmatters, 503
Nursing's Agenda for Healthcare Reform (ANA), 3, 7, 58, 594
Nursing's Social Policy Statement (ANA), 178
Nursism, 19
Nussle, Jim, 283
NWPC. *See* National Women's Political Caucus
NYSNA. *See* New York State Nurses Association

O

OAM. *See* Office of Alternative Medicine
OASI. *See* Old Age and Survivors Insurance
Objective criteria, 117
Objectivity, 110
OBRA. *See* Omnibus Budget Reconciliation Act
O'Brien, Sandy, 353
O'Brien, William, 679
Occupational health nurses. *See* American Association of Occupational Health Nurses (AAOHN)
Occupational Safety and Health Administration (OSHA), 316, 524, 640, 641
  Bloodborne Pathogens Standard Compliance Directive, 414, 415, 416, 417, 524
  Ergonomics Standard, 524
  "Fact Sheet and Reference on Worker Health and Safety for Anthrax Exposure," 524
  "OSHA Recommendations for Handling Suspicious Letters or Packages," 524
  Respiratory Protection Standard, 641
OEP. *See* Office of Emergency Preparedness
Office of Alternative Medicine (OAM), 295
Office of Emergency Preparedness (OEP) (DHHS), 137, 138, 139*b*, 140*b*
Office of Health Affairs (DoD), 523
Office of Management and Budget (OMB), 517
Office of Minority Health (OMH), 50, 223
Office of Occupational Health Nursing, 640
Office of Public Health and Science, 519
Office of Research on Minority Health (ORMH), 223
Office of Special Counsel (OSC), 585
Office of Technology Assessment (OTA), 152
Office of the Air Force Surgeon General, Medical Readiness and Nursing, 139*b*
Office of the Inspector General (OIG), 317
Office of the Secretary of Defense for Health Affairs (OSD/HA), 135

Office of the Special Counsel, 584
Office of the Surgeon General, 519
OHC. *See* Oregon Health Council
Ohio: Patient Safety Center of Inquiry (VA), 441
Ohio State University, 39*b*
OHP. *See* Oregon Health Plan
OIG. *See* Office of the Inspector General
Oklahoma: courts, 473-474
Oklahoma City bombing (1996), 136
Oklahoma Nurses Association, 473-474
Old Age and Survivors Insurance (OASI), 258
Old Dominion Society of Gastroenterology Nurses and Associates, 649-650
Older adults
  PhD in Nursing (policy focus on the health of the urban family and elderly), University of Massachusetts, Boston, 37*b*
  Rural Elderly Enhancement Project, 688-689
  Supportive Services Program for Older Adults, 688
  Your Senior Connection program, 688
Older Americans Act, 518-519
Oligopsony, 147
Olmstead v. L.C., 430
OMB. *See* Office of Management and Budget
OMH. *See* Office of Minority Health
Omnibus bills, 529*b*
Omnibus Budget Reconciliation Act (OBRA) of 1987, 430
Omnibus Budget Reconciliation Act (OBRA) of 1989, 87-88
Omnibus Budget Reconciliation Act (OBRA) of 1997, 257
Oncology Nurses Association (ONA), 604
Oncology Nursing Society (ONS), 611, 616, 646-648
  Health Policy Agenda, 647
  Health Policy Tool Kit, 647
One America in the Twenty-First Century: The President's Initiative on Race, 223
Online learning, 38
Openness, 180
Opinion editorials, 165
Opportunity, 345-346
  taking advantage of, 623, 742
Opportunity cost, 235
Options for mutual gain, 117
Oregon
  health care rationing, case study, 299-310
  impact litigation in, 473
  nurse practitioners in, 464

Oregon Health Council (OHC), 300, 302-303, 304, 305
 "Making Health Policy 2000" meetings, 306
 "Searching for Fairness: Citizen's Values about
  Financing Health Care" meetings, 305-306
Oregon Health Plan (OHP), 299
 current status, 307-308
 implementation of, 300-302, 301*f*
Organizational conflict, 115
 resolving, 618, 619*b*
Organizational elections, 616-617
Organizational leadership, 614-617, 617*b*, 621-625
Organizational policies, 9
Organizational power, 614-617
Organizations
 health-promoting, 684-685
 nonprofit, 613, 680
 nursing, 606-607
  case studies, 639-658
  life cycle of, 613-614
 priorities of, 619-620
 professional, 601-607, 609-625
ORMH. *See* Office of Research on Minority Health
OSC. *See* Office of Special Counsel
OSD/HA. *See* Office of the Secretary of Defense for
  Health Affairs
"OSHA Recommendations for Handling Suspicious
  Letters or Packages," 524
OTA. *See* Office of Technology Assessment
Outdoor Recreation League, 26
Out-of-pocket spending on prescription drugs, 424-425
Outreach
 Mobile Outreach Clinic Program (MOCP) (VNACJ),
  689
 Outreach on the Beach, 741
Outside initiative model for agenda building, 145
Outside strategy, 630-631
Overtime, mandatory, 314, 368
Owens, Major, 417
Oxford Health Plan, 5

P

PAAD program. *See* Pharmaceutical Association for the
  Aged and Disabled program
Packaging, health care product, 736-737
PACs. *See* Political action committees
Pagers, 103
PAHO. *See* Pan-American Health Organization
Pain management, case study, 646-648
Pain Relief Promotion Act, 604, 646-648
Palmer, Sophia, 22
Panama Canal, 49

Pan-American Health Organization (PAHO), 50, 718,
  724
Pap smears, 161
Paperhangers, 392
Paralyzed Veterans of America, 195
Parent, Lisa, 384
Parity for mental health care, 221
Parliamentary procedure, 75
Participation, 720-721
 in coalitions, 563
 in community, 690-691
 joining interest groups, 629
 in local government, 484-485
 long-term, 309
 in political campaigns, 571-577
 public, 697-698
 service in state legislature, case study, 589-599
"Participation of Nurses in Health Services Decision
  Making and Policy Development" (ICN), 12*b*
Participatory decision-making, 388
Participatory research, 540
Partnership for a Healthy Mississippi, 507, 509
Partnerships, 719-720
 with AAOHN, 642
 Decatur Community Partnership, 705-706
 definition of, 690
 Turning Point, 701-709
Pate, Hedi, 444-445
PATH (Physician at Teaching Hospital) audits, 317
Patient advocacy, case study, 643, 650-654
Patient Bill of Rights, 312, 389, 448, 534
Patient care outcomes, 325-326
Patient rights, 312
Patient safety, 312
 education for, 440*b*
 example lessons, 441*b*
 improvement awards program (VHA), 441
 regulation of, 513
 research on, 441
 VHA Handbook 1051/1: Patient Safety Improvement
  (VHA), 439
Patient Safety Act, 312, 389
Patient Safety Centers of Inquiry (VA), 440, 441
Patient Self-Determination Act (PSDA) (P.L. 105-508),
  473
Patients, focus on, 562
Pay-as-you-go, 529*b*, 530
Pay-for-performance systems of compensation, 314
Payments, universal, 214-215
Payors, multiple, 214-215
Payroll taxes, 260, 291

PBS, 41-42

PDD. *See* Presidential Decision Directive

Peer review organizations (PROs), 243

Pell Grants, 523

Pelosi, Nancy, 171

Penn State School of Nursing, 88

Pennsylvania
  Abbottsford Community Health Center, 87-91
  diversity and redistricting, 570
  Medicaid waiver, 88
  prescriptive authority for nurse practitioners in, 89-90
  Regional Nursing Centers Consortium, 90
  "Technical Advisory 95-A," 88

Pennsylvania Association of Nurse Anesthetists, 89

Pennsylvania Coalition of NPs, 89

Pennsylvania Nurses Association, 90

Pennsylvania State Nurses Association, 89

Pentagon attack (September 11, 2001), 1

Permanence, 643

Persistence, 81-82, 91, 639
  case study, 650-654

Personal as political, 31

Personal freedom, 447-448

Personal medical records, 427

Personal Responsibility and Work Opportunities Act of 1996 (Public Law 104-193), 249, 250

Personal Responsibility and Work Opportunity Reconciliation Act (PRWORA) (Public Law [PL] 106-193), 481, 672, 674

Personal space, 99

Personal visits, 556

Personnel. *See also* Staff
  agency, 368

Peters, Lil, 543

Pfizer Inc., 634*b*

Pharmaceutical Association for the Aged and Disabled (PAAD) program, 497*b*

PhD programs. *See* Doctoral programs

Phi Beta Delta International Honor Society, 50

Physician groups, 320

Physician-administrator relationships, 341

Physicians
  model for engaging, 339-340
  opposition to nursing's progress, 5
  supervision of CRNAs by, 283-286

Pima tribe, 225

"2005 Plan," 482

Planned Parenthood of America, 27

Planning
  campaign, 576*b*, 579-581
  formulation of plans, 483-484

Plantations, 488*b*

Plastics recycling efforts, 738

"Plum Book." *See United States Government Policy and Supporting Positions*

Pocket veto, 459, 517

Point-of-service (POS) plans, 208, 220, 234, 248

Policies and procedures manuals, 13

Policy, 1-18, 107-111. *See also* Public policy
  alternatives, 66
    analysis of, 66*b*-67*b*, 67
    comparison of, 67, 68*f*
    sample, 66*b*
  barriers to, in UAE, 734
  child care, 669-675
  courts and, 471-476
  definition of, 8-9
  degree programs in, 39*b*-40*b*
  designing, 661
  development of, 55-69, 347-349, 661
    nursing perspective and, 742
    with tobacco settlement dollars, 508
    in UAE, 730
  ethics and, 181-183
  evaluation of, 62
    criteria for, 66-67, 66*b*
    results of, 67*b*
    sample, 66*b*-67*b*
    in UAE, 732-734
  feasibility of, 73
  health, 55
  helping communities with, 707
  implementation of, in UAE, 731-732
  journals focused on, 38-40
  learning, 31-53
  in Maryland, 464-465
  media influence on, 157-176
  morality, 76, 151
  nursing agenda, 477-478
  pain management by influencing, case study, 646-648
  prevention of, 579-583
  private, 55
  proposed solutions, 73
  range of targets, 705-706
  for regulation of nurses, 730-731
  research design for, 151-152
  searching for, 38*b*
  smoking and, 144
  social, 8
  state boards of nursing and, 510-513
  summary/recommended, 67*b*, 68
  supportive factors in UAE, 733-734

Plantations—cont'd
  technology for making, 377
  and values, 9-13, 10*f*
  workplace, examples, 13
Policy, Politics and Nursing Practice, 38-40
Policy agenda, 60
  setting, 59-61
Policy analysis, 55, 62-63
Policy analysts, 468
Policy and Politics in Nursing and Health Care, 45
Policy change, 708
  agenda setting for, 7
  helping communities through, 706-707
  informing, 706-708
  learning, 35-42
Policy education, 708
Policy issue papers, 63-68, 64*b*-67*b*
Policy issues, 59, 661-662
  framing, 83
Policy leaders, 563
Policy objectives, 63-64, 65*b*
Policy problems
  definition of, 151
  identification of, 59
  U.S. military health, 130-135
Policy process, 58-62
  early involvement in, 308
  "garbage can" model, 58
  government responsibility for providing guidance in, 15
  Kingdon's streams model, 58-59
  stage-sequential model of, 59-62, 60*f*
Policy stream, 58
Policy subsystems, 56-57
Policy venues, 640
Policy wonks, 469
Political action, case studies, 639-658
Political action committees (PACs), 7, 631, 632
Political activism, 228
Political activity, 22-24
  Act to Prevent Pernicious Political Activities (Hatch Act), 583-586
  communication skills for, 93-111
  definition of, 584
  DoD regulations, 586-587
  four spheres of, 13-16, 13*f*
  of government-employed nurses, 583-587
  preparation for, 83
Political analysis, 71-91
Political appointments, 543-550
  opportunities for, 546*b*

Political campaigns, 565-599
  contribution limits, 632
  finance reform, 633
  "get out the vote" (GOTV) strategy, 500
  media and, 162
  plans, 576*b*, 579-581
  staff, 576*b*
  for state elections, 499-500
Political candidates, 568-570
  choosing to support, 572-573
  electability of, 576*b*
  fund raising for, 575
  overall assessment of, 576*b*
  questions to ask when considering, 573*b*
  recruiting, 572
Political consciousness-raising, 31-32
Political contributions, 632-633, 634*b*
Political decision making, ethical, 182-183
Political development, 7-8, 32-33, 76-77, 78*t*
Political empowerment, 12
Political ethical conflicts, 180-181
Political history, 216
Political intelligence, 665
Political nominations, 547
Political nominees, 544
Political parties
  affiliation with, 544
  evolving role of, 633-634
  role in campaigning and electioneering, 570-571
  third, 570-571
Political setting, 74-75
Political sophistication, 7, 33, 76-77, 78*t*
Political strategies, 71-91, 80-82, 82-86
  of Military Coalition, 133
  of Oregon nurses, 301-302
  in UAE, 731-732
Political stream, 58
Political supporters, 548
Politicians, 33
Politics, 1-18, 661
  of case management, 319-324
  case study, 589-599
  coalition work in, 128-129
  definition of, 9
  in dissemination of research findings, 408-410
  ethical issues in, 177-184
  gender, 71
  The George Washington University Master of Political Management program, 39*b*
  The House and Senate Explained: The People's Guide to Congress (Greenberg), 40

Politics—cont'd
  journals focused on, 38-40
  learning, 35-42
  in Maryland, 465-466
  The Nurses' Directory of Capitol Connections (Bull, Sharp, and Wakefield), 40
  of nursing research, 399-411
  of nursing workforce, 363-369
  The Politics of Health Legislation: An Economic Perspective (Feldstein), 40
  of regulation of nurses, 730-731
  of research, 409f-410f, 410
  Tribes on the Hill: The U.S. Congress Ritual and Realities (Weatherford), 40
  values framework for, 9, 10f
Politics (term), 9
Politics for Dummies (DeLaney), 40
The Politics of Health Legislation: An Economic Perspective (Feldstein), 40
Pollution prevention, advocating for, 741-742
Poor, working, 432-433
Portability, 57
PORTs. *See* Practice outcome research teams
POS plans. *See* Point-of-service plans
Position statements, 612
  "Participation of Nurses in Health Services Decision Making and Policy Development" (ICN), 12b
Positional power, 79
"The Potential for Discrimination in Health Insurance Based on Predictive Genetic Testing" hearing, 446
Poverty, 715-716
  levels of, 425n
  working poor, 433
Powell, Colin, 47, 185
Power, 77-80
  of anecdotes, 145n
  of coalitions, 132-134
  control freaks, 127
  devolution of, 491
  empowerment, 12-13
  grabbing, 11
  of listening, 96
  of media, 158-163
  methods of conflict resolution, 116
  in numbers, 133, 560-561
  of one, 651
  organizational, 614-617
  politics and, 11-12
  protecting turf, 127
Power over (term), 11-12
Power with (term), 11-12

PPOs. *See* Preferred provider organizations
PPSs. *See* Prospective payment systems
Practice change
  based on evidence, 358-359
  strategies for, 357-358
  through research investigation, 358-359
Practice guidelines, 149, 150, 234
Practice outcome research teams (PORTs), 149
Practice policies, 234-235
Preauthorization, 234
Preferred provider organizations (PPOs), 208, 220, 248
Premier, Inc., 284
Preparation
  for advocacy, 128-129
  for political action, 83
  for risk taking, 85
Prepared remarks, 559
Prescription drugs
  Bar Code Medication Administration, 439-440
  high-risk, 440
  Medicare benefits, 255, 423, 425
    sample criteria/alternatives matrix for, 68f
    sample policy issue paper, 64b-67b
  out-of-pocket spending on, 424-425
  preventable adverse drug events, 438
  prices of, 425-426
  spending for, 423
  TRICARE Senior Pharmacy Program (TSRx), 134-135
Prescriptive authority, 89-90
  of APNs, 146
  of nurse practitioners, 90
  Wisconsin bills, 501-502
Presidential Advisory Commission on Consumer Protection and Quality in the Health Care Industry, 209, 220, 434-435
Presidential Appointee Initiative (Brookings Institute), 545-546
Presidential Decision Directive-39 (PDD-39), 136
Presidential Decision Directive-62 (PDD-62), 136, 137
Presidential veto
  pocket veto, 459
  types of, 517
President's Commission on White House Fellowships, 50b
Press coverage. *See* Media coverage
Press releases, 167b
Preventable adverse drug events, 438
Preventing Needlestick Injuries in Health Care Settings (NIOSH), 416
Prevention, 742

Price
    determination of, 231-232
    market, 232, 232*f*
Primary care, general, 218
Primary care providers (PCPs)
    nurse practitioners as, 463-464
    of record, 373
Principled negotiation, 116-118, 618
Prioritization, 183
    organizational, 619-620
Prisons
    opportunities to serve in, 546*b*
    women in, 682-683, 683*b*
Privacy, 317
    genetic, 447-448
    genetic testing and, 443
Privacy Commission Act (proposed), 447*t*
Private health care system, 262
Private policy, 55
Privatization, 259, 313
Problem background, 73-74
    policy issue paper section, 63, 64*b*-65*b*
Problem identification, 73, 116-117, 182-183
    framing, 73
    in Maryland, 463-464
    policy issue paper section, 63, 64*b*
Problem stream, 58
Producers, 165
Product liability, 474-475
Product packaging, 736-737
Products, 612
PRO-DUR program. *See* Prospective drug utilization
    review program
Professional associations. *See* Professional organizations
Professional education, 21-22
Professional image, 106, 377-378
Professional journals, 38-40
Professional organizations, 22-24, 609-625
    activities, 36
    advocacy, 603-604
    assessment of, 610
    bylaws, 611
    chapters, 606
    contemporary issues, 601-607
    decision making, 605-606
    dues, 604-605
    generational considerations for, 601-602
    governance of, 605-606
    governance policies, 611
    involvement in, 297
    leaders of, 605

Professional organizations—cont'd
    legislative work, 603-604
    life cycle, 613-614
    member benefits, 602-605
    member needs, 610
    membership, 601-605
    mission statements, 610-611
    multipurpose, 604
    political action, 15
    procedures, 611-613
    processes, 610-613
    regulatory work, 603-604
    research topics, 401
    selection of, 610
    structure of, 605-606, 610-613
    tax-exempt status, 613
Professional practice environments, 315
Professional security, 395-396
Professional standards review organizations (PSROs),
    243
Professionalism, 743
Program implementation, 61
Program to government phase of policy-making, 62
Programs, continuing education, 36
Projects, 612
ProMed, 724
Proposed rules, 468
PROs. *See* Peer review organizations
Prospective drug utilization review (PRO-DUR)
        program, 497*b*
Prospective payment systems (PPSs), 147, 205, 233, 278
    vs fee-for-service financing, 245
    historical development of, 319-320
Protocol, 102, 106*b*
Provider networks, 234
PRWORA. *See* Personal Responsibility and Work
        Opportunity Reconciliation Act
PSDA. *See* Patient Self-Determination Act
PSROs. *See* Professional standards review organizations
Psychosocial and mental health, 689
Public administration degree programs, 36, 39*b*-40*b*
Public broadcasting, 41-42
Public education, 168, 168*t*
Public health, 26-27
    approaches to, 168, 168*t*
    degree programs in, 36, 39*b*-40*b*
    promotion by prevention, 742
    tradition of, 708-709
    Turning Point: Collaborating for a New Century in
        Public Health initiative, 701-709
Public health care financing system, 249-262

Public Health Improvement Act (Public Law [PL] 106-505), 723
Public health nurses (PHNs), 664
Public Health Service, 250
   funding, 527
   Scholarship Training Program and Loan Repayment Program, 521
   travel and immigration policy, 726
Public health services, 206-207
Public interest, 179
Public Law 94-142. *See* Education for All Handicapped Children Act of 1975
Public Law 104-191. *See* Health Insurance Portability and Accountability Act of 1996 (HIPAA)
Public Law 104-193. *See* Personal Responsibility and Work Opportunities Act of 1996
Public Law 105-508. *See* Patient Self-Determination Act (PSDA)
Public Law 106-193. *See* Personal Responsibility and Work Opportunity Reconciliation Act (PRWORA)
Public Law 106-398. *See* 2001 National Defense Authorization Act
Public Law 106-505. *See* Public Health Improvement Act
Public Law 106-525. *See* Minority Health and Health Disparities Research and Education Act of 2000
Public officials, 74
Public opinion
   demand for qualified genetic professionals, 445
   and national health system, 216-217
Public policy, 55, 661
   agendas, 161-162
   definition of, 8
   degree programs in, 36, 39*b*
   development of, case study, 639-640
   ethical issues in, 177-184
   evaluation of, in media, 162
   guidelines for advocating change, 509
   health care, links with health care ethics, 178
   issues, 698
   planning for participation in, 697-698
   to promote child care, 672-674
   and racial and ethnic disparities, 227
   shaping, 26-27
Public policy making, 55-57
   approaches to, 57-58
   definition of, 56
Public recognition, 176
Public relations. *See also* Media coverage
   for coalitions, 125, 129
   for political campaigns, 577
   role and importance of, 563

Public safety opportunities, 546*b*
Public school nurses, 26-27
   case example, 485-486
   in Mississippi, 508-509
   reemergence of, 507
Public service, 179
Public speaking, 99-100
Public-private partnerships, 257
Public/private payors, 219
Puerto Rico: boards of nursing, 510
PulseNet, 724

Q

QISMC. *See* Quality Improvement System for Managed Care
Quad Council of Public Health Nursing Organizations, 228
Qualified genetic professionals, 445
Quality, 311-312
   balancing cost and quality, 216
   "Crossing the Quality Chasm" (IOM), 435
   of health care, 434-435
   IOM recommendations on, 431
   in long-term care, 430-431
Quality Improvement System for Managed Care (QISMC), 470
Quality Interagency Coordination Task Force (QuIC), 311-312, 438
Quality of care, 672
Quality of health care information, 110
Quarantine policy, 725
Questions
   responding to, 95
   seed, 348*b*
Quinlan, Karen Anne, 492

R

Racial and ethnic disparities, 222-228
Racism
   Discrimination and Racism in Health Care position statement (ANA), 226
   genetic testing and, 444
Radio, 42
Radio response squads, 159, 172
Radio talk shows, 172
Radiologic weapons. *See* Chemical, biologic, radiologic, nuclear, or high-yield explosive weapons
Raids, 393-394
Ranking minority member, 453
Rational approach, 57

Rationing health care
    as explicit policy, 300-309
    as implicit policy, 299-300
    issue adoption, 300
    issues of concern to nurses, 300-301, 306-307
    lessons learned, 308-309
    in Oregon, case study, 299-310
    policy implementation, 300-302
    policy realities, 302-305
RBRVS. *See* Resource-based relative value scale
Reach Out and Read Program (ROAR), 689
Reagan, Ronald, 144
Reasonableness, inherent, 643
Reauthorization legislation, 529
Recognition, 175
Recognition appeals, 394
Reconciliation, 529*b*
Recorded teller votes, 457
Recruitment
    of nurses, 314
    of political candidates, 572
    of volunteers, 574, 575*b*
Recycling, 735-736
    boutique plastics, 738
    MedCycle project, 737-738
Red Cross, 694
Redistricting, 570
Redman, Eric, 40
Referent power, 79
Reform
    campaign finance, 633
    health care, 3-6, 421
        failure of, 635-636
        in Montana, 592-596, 596-597
        websites of associations interested in, 217*b*
    Medicare, 254-255, 273*b*, 426-427
Reframing, 169-170
Regier, Darrel, 221
"Registered Nurse/Registered Voter" campaign, 572
Registered nurses (RNs). *See also* Nurses
    Health Security Act and, 4
    National Sample Survey (NSS), 365, 522
    staffing issues, 367-368
    as supervisors, 395
    supply and demand for, 313
        approaches to estimating, 363-364
        government intervention in, 366-367
    vacancy rates, 147
    workforce, 363
        data, 364-365
        research on, 365-366

Regulation, 468
    of advanced practice nursing, 512
    of campaign money trail, 632
    vs competition, 243-245
    of nursing, 510-511
        critical issues in, 511-513
        in UAE, 730-731
    of patient safety, 513
    prescriptive authority via, 90
    for prevention of needlestick injuries, 415, 416-418
    professional organizations and, 603-604
Regulatory boards, 546*b*
Regulatory documents, 468
Regulatory language, 270
Regulatory process, 451, 459-461, 460*f*, 467-470
    how to influence, 461*b*
Regulatory requirements, 316-317
Rehabilitation services, 508
Reid, Harry, 414, 415
Reid, Joe, 539
Reimbursement. *See also specific programs*
    for advanced practice nurses (APNs), 265-272, 375-
        376
    for alternative therapies, 295
    for complementary therapies, 293-297
    for nurse practitioners (NPs), 88-89
    Nursing Incentives Reimbursement Program (New
        Jersey), 367
    third-party, 265-272
Reinhard, Susan, *495*
Reinhard, Tom, *495*
Relationships, 271, 330
    building, 176
Religious motives, 660
Religious practice, 660
Relman, Arnold, 144*n*
Remarks, prepared, 559
Repetition, 129
Reporting, 163
    of data, 312
    newspaper, 164*b*
    of policy, 724-725
    systems for, 724
Reports, 456-457
Republican Party
    donations from health care interest groups, 634
    political contributions to, 632
Requests, making, 97
Rescissions, 529*b*
Research, 296
    aggregating studies, 152
    applications for, 151

Research—cont'd
attacks on messengers of, 150
conduct of, 403-408
data collection site for, 404-406
dissemination of findings, 408-410
federal
appropriating committees for, 454
authorizing committees for, 454
funding for, 401-403
home site political issues, 406-409
human embryo, 446
large data set, 152
on nurse practitioners, 151
nursing, 399
politics of, 399-411
questioning of, 151
participatory, 540
on patient safety, 441
as political, 149
politics of, 409*f*-410*f,* 410
practice change through, 358-359
on racial and ethnic disparities, 227-228
on registered nurse workforce, 365-366
strategies for, 153
as tool, 141-156
topics for, 399-403
utilization of, 296
Research design, 151-152
Research pimps, 403
Research purists, 403
Research realists, 403
Research teams, 403-404
Reservations, 704
Reserve Officers Association (ROA), 132*b*
Resistance
danger of, 354-355
steps for working through, 340
Resolutions, 612
Resource-based relative value scale (RBRVS), 246
Resources, 77
Respect for nurses, 550
Responses, giving, 175
Responsibility, 306
hierarchical diffusion of, 182
Resume, 104-105
Retention of nurses, 314
The Retired Enlisted Association (TREA), 132*b*
The Retired Officers Association (TROA), 132*b*
Retirement age, 291
Retirement benefits, 288-289
Reward power, 79

Rhetoric, 164
Rhode Island: S-CHIP waivers, 433, 434
Richmond, Julius, 144*n*
*The Right Thing to Do, The Smart Thing to Do:
Enhancing Diversity in Health Professions* (IOM),
525
Rights, 180
establishment of, 472-473
legal, 477
Patient Bill of Rights, 312, 389, 448, 534
Right-wing influence, 628
Risk avoidance, 341
Risk sharing, 234
Risk taking, 85
RNs. *See* Registered nurses
ROA. *See* Reserve Officers Association
ROAR. *See* Reach Out and Read Program
Robb, Isabel Hampton, 22, 23, 572
Robert, Henry Martyn, 617
Robert Wood Johnson Foundation (RWJF), 225, 688,
692
Colleagues funding, 125
*Colleagues in Caring: Regional Collaboratives for
Nursing Work Force Development (Colleagues),*
121-122
"Colleagues in Caring" project, 313
Covering Kids grants, 304-305
Turning Point: Collaborating for a New Century in
Public Health initiative, 703
website, 217*b*
Robert's Rules of Order, 613, 617
Robert's Rules of Order Newly Revised, 75
Robson, Judy Biros, 498-505, *503*
Rockefeller College State University of New York
(SUNY) at Albany Master of Arts in Public
Administration and Policy, 39*b*
Rockefeller Foundation, 720
Roe v. Wade, 472-473
Roosevelt, Eleanor, 187, 197
Roukema, Marge, 415
Rules, 468
Rural Elderly Enhancement Project, 688-689
Rural health care programs, 250
Rural health clinics, 205-206, 305
Rural leaders, nontraditional, 704
Rutgers' Center for State Health Policy, 496*b*
RWJF. *See* Robert Wood Johnson Foundation

S

Sabatier's Advocacy Coalition Framework, 58*n*
SADD. *See* Students Against Drunk Driving

Saeed, Mohammad, *733*
Safe Needles Save Lives campaign (ANA), 415
Safer, Morley, 192
Safety, 180, 311-312
    culture of, 442
    mandatory education, 440, 440*b*
    needlestick injuries and, 413
    patient, 312
        improvement awards program (VHA), 441, 441*b*
    workplace, 315-316
Safety net, 662
Safety net providers, 307
Salce, Jane, 141-142
SAMHSA. *See* Substance Abuse and Mental Health
    Services Administration
Samoans, 224
San Francisco State University, 172
Sanger, Margaret, 16, 20, 26, 27, 85, 590
Satcher, David, 223, 540, 541
W.B. Saunders Company, 45
S-CHIP. *See* State Children's Health Insurance Program
Scaccio, Angelo, 679
Schiavone, Terrance, 677, 679
Schiesswohl, Cynthia, 579-583
Scholarships
    Nurse Employment and Education Development
        (NEED) Act, 527
    Nurse In Washington Internship (NIWI), 41*b*, 44-45,
        642
Scholarships for Disadvantaged Students, 454
School board elections, 579-583
School nurses, 26-27
    case example, 485-486
    in Mississippi, 508-509
    reemergence of, 507
School shootings, 144
School-age children, care for, 670
School-Based Youth Services Program (New Jersey
    Department of Human Services), 692, 693
Schools of nursing, 21-22
    degree programs in, 36, 37*b*-38*b*
Schuster, Eleanore, 353
Screening, case study, 648-650
Scruggs, Jan, 190
Scully, Thomas, 460
Searching for policy, health policy, and related subjects,
    38*b*
Seed questions, 348*b*, 350*b*
Seeking Federal Appointment—A 2001 Guide for Nurses
    (ANA), 544-545
Select committees, 453

Self-governance, 388
Self-interest, 7, 26, 32-33, 76-77, 78*t*
Self-knowledge, 624-625
Self-management, 694
Self-promotion opportunities, 559-560
Self-study, 38-42
Senate Armed Service Committee, 133
Senate Budget Committee, 527, 530
Senate Commerce Subcommittee on Commerce, Trade,
    and Consumer Protection, 446
Senate Committee on Agriculture, Nutrition, and
    Forestry, 527
Senate Committee on Appropriations, 527, 529
    Subcommittee on Defense, Congressional Detail to,
        51, 51-53
    Subcommittee on Labor, Health and Human Services,
        and Education, 527
Senate Committee on Government Affairs, 545
Senate Committee on Health, Education, Labor, and
    Pensions (HELP), 527
Senate Committee on Veterans' Affairs, 528
Senate Finance Committee, 527, 529
Senate Health, Education and Labor, and Pensions
    Committee, 221, 529
Senate Labor and Human Resources Committee, 454
Senate Subcommittee on Public Lands, National Parks,
    and Forests, 193
Separation, 335
Sequestration, 529*b*
Serendipity, 122
SERR, Inc., 696
Service(s), 612
    to citizens, 179
    New Public Service, 178, 179
    vs steering, 178-179
Service delivery, 708
Service Employees International Union (SEIU), 392
"Seven Rules for Testifying before Congress," 194
Sexual messages, 98
Shalala, Donna, 48, 49, 50, 142, 283
    Closing the Gap: Eliminating Racial and Ethnic
        Disparities, 223
    respect for nurses, 550
    Zap Asthma, 541
Shared governance, 388-389
A Shared Statement of Ethical Principles for Those Who
    Shape and Give Health Care (Tavistock group),
    180
Sharf, Barbara, 145*n*
Sharp, Nancy, 40
Shays, Christopher, 633

Sheehy, Sue, 680
Shepherd-Towner Act, 201
Shering-Plough Corp., 634*b*
Short Test of Functional Health Literacy in Adults (S-TOFHLA), 108
Shortage of nurses, 512
SHPLs. *See* State health policy liaisons
Sigma Theta Tau International (STTI), 174-175
Signals, body language, 98
60 Minutes, 192
Skilled nursing facilities (SNFs), 256
SLCs. *See* State Legislative Coordinators
Slim Fast Foods/Thompson Medical, 634*b*
"A Small Donation Makes a Monumental Difference" slogan, 189-190
Small talk, 95
SMCAF. *See* Society of Medical Consultants to the Armed Forces
Smiling, 94-95
Smith, Diane, 651
Smoking, 144
Smoothing over, 115
SNFs. *See* Skilled nursing facilities
Social change, 474-475
Social marketing/public education, 168, 168*t*
Social policy, 8
Social Security, 6, 257-260, 287-293
   age to receive full benefits, 289*b*
   legislative jurisdiction over, 527
   website, 288*b*
Social Security Act of 1935, 242, 257
   Title XXI, 492
Social Security Administration, 258, 527
Social Security Trust Funds, 258-259
Social welfare organizations, 613
Socialized medicine, 202
Society of Gastroenterology Nurses and Associates (SGNA), 648-650
Society of Medical Consultants to the Armed Forces (SMCAF), 132*b*
South Africa, 49, 713, 714
South Carolina Colleagues, 126
South Carolina Department of Health and Environmental Control (DHEC), 696-701
South Carolina environmental health policy, 696-701
South Dakota Colleagues, 124, 126
Sox, Harold, 151
Speaker of the House, 525
Special districts, 489*b*
Special interest groups, 627-638
Specialty mental health sector, 218

Spitzer, Walter, 151*n*
Sponsors, 339
The Squad (Brodin), 187
SSI. *See* Supplementary Security Income
St. Francis Hospital (St. Paul, MN), 394
St. John's Hospital (Oklahoma), 473-474
St. Paul Fire and Marine Insurance Company, 284
St. Thomas Hospital (England), 21
Staff
   advocacy, 564
   agency personnel, 368
   campaign, 576*b*
   child-care, 672
   Congressional, *51,* 51-53
      communication with, 554-560
      lessons learned, 562-564
   IOM recommendations on, 431
   professional, 623
   registered nurses (RNs), 367-368
Staff bylaws, 388
Stakeholders, 56-57, 63, 75-76
   engaging, 126
   sample, 65*b*
   styles of, 468-469
Standing committees, 453
Stanford University, 50
Stare decisis (let the decision stand), 472
Starfish, 681-682
Stark, Pete, 415, 562
State appointees, 548-549
State boards of nursing, 510-513
State Children's Health Insurance Program (S-CHIP), 76, 206, 246, 421, 492
   administration of, 260
   Balanced Budget Act (BBA) of 1997 provision, 251
   expansion of, 433
   financing, 249
   match with tobacco settlement funds, 508
   Oregon program, 304
   waivers, 433-434
State courts, 532
State government, 491-513
   decisions made about major issues for society, 14
   resources, 496*b*
   resources on political appointments, 545
   women in, 568-569
State governors, 493-494
State health care systems, 260-261
State health policy liaisons (SHPLs), 647
State Legislative Coordinators (SLCs), 642

State legislatures, 492-493
  election to, 498-505
  service in, case study, 589-599
State nurse associations (SNAs), 572
State policy
  ANA initiatives, 495
  responses to genetic issues, 446-447
State screening policy, case study, 648-650
State-based health systems, 215
*Statement on Clinical Nurse Specialist Practice and
    Education* (NACNS), 645, 646
Statewide trauma networks, 508
Staupers, Mabel, 20
Steering, 178-179
Steering Committee to Eliminate Racial and Ethnic
    Disparities in Health, 226
Stem cell legislation, 428-429
Stephens, Veronica, 137-138
S-TOFHLA. *See* Short Test of Functional Health Literacy
    in Adults
Strategic action fronts, 708
Strategic alliances, 719-720
Strategies, 664-666
  development of, case study, 187-192
  inside, 630
  interest group, 630-631
  new, case study, 192-194
  outside, 630-631
*Strategies for Cost Effective Patient Care through Clinical
    Nurse Specialists* conference, 644
Stroke, 224
Students, nursing, 36-38
Students Against Drunk Driving (SADD), 681
Substance Abuse and Mental Health Services
    Administration (SAMHSA), 219-220, 523
Substitute goods or services, 231
Suffrage, woman, 24-26
Suicide, assisted, 473
Summer Institute in Health Policy and Management,
    Johns Hopkins University, 41*b*
Superintendents, trained, 21
Supervision
  of APNs, 269-270
  of CRNAs, 283-286
  physician, 283-286
Supervisors, 395, 476
Supplementary Medical Insurance (SMI), 258
Supplementary Medical Insurance (SMI) Trust Fund,
    246, 254
Supplementary Security Income (SSI), 250, 289-290

Supply, 231
  market, 231, 231*f,* 231*t*
Support
  capitalizing on all sources of, 134
  political, for INC-MCE, 139
Supportive Services Program for Older Adults, 688
Suppression, 115
Surveillance, 724-725
Surveys, 522
Survivor's Guide for Presidential Nominees (Brookings
    Institute), 545-546
Sweeney, John, 393
Synthroid, 150
System improvement strategies, 705

T

Talk radio, 159*b,* 172
Talking points, 556
TANF. *See* Temporary Assistance for Needy Families
Target audience, 166
Tavistock group, 180
Tax Equity and Fiscal Responsibility Act (TEFRA) of
    1982, 253, 279-282, 282
Taxes
  dependent care tax credit (DCTC), 671
  Earned Income Tax Credit (EITC), 661
  national, 214
  payroll, 260
  tobacco, 662
Tax-exempt status, 613
Taxpayer Team (TPT), 579
Teachable moments, 496
Teamsters, 392
Teamwork, 564
"Technical Advisory 95-A," 88
Technology, 318
  for APN policy and professional decision-making, 377
  information, 108-110
  new, 665
TEFRA. *See* Tax Equity and Fiscal Responsibility Act
Telehealth services, 262
Telenursing, 719
Telephone, 554-555
  calling in to talk radio, 159*b,* 172
  cell phones and pagers, 103
Telepractice, 377
Television (TV), 41, 161
  AMA and, 165
  "Harry and Louise" advertisements, 4, 158-159, 635
  news teams, 172-176

Temporary Assistance for Needy Families (TANF), 249, 250, 541, 673
  block grants, 674
  health impact on communities, 661
TennCare, 145
Tennessee
  antitrust laws in, 474
  needlestick prevention legislation, 414, 417
  state government, 492
Tennessee Department of Health, 139*b*
Tennessee Medical Association (TMA), 145
Tension and remedy, 339, 341
Tepper, Carl, 497*b*
Term limits, 598
Terminology, 294*b*, 297
  budget glossary, 529*b*
  common procedure terminology (CPT) codes, 297
  legislative and regulatory language, 270
  political, 9, 11-12
Terrorist attacks, September 11, 2001, 1, 139-140
Testimony
  joint, 133, 134
  providing, 301-302, 558-560
  "Seven Rules for Testifying before Congress," 194
Texas
  boards of nursing, 510
  local government in, 482
  needlestick prevention legislation, 417
  nurse practitioners in, 464
TFL program. *See* TRICARE for Life program
Therapeutic Time pilot study (UCDMC), 330, 331*f*
Third parties, 570-571
Third-party reimbursement, 265-272
Thomas: Legislative Information on the Internet (website), 448
Thompson, Tommy, 1, 285, 459
Thurm, Kevin, 541
Timing, 84, 174-175, 469
Title V Maternal-Child Block Grant Program, 260
Title XVIII. *See* Medicare
Title XIX. *See* Medicaid
TMA. *See* Tennessee Medical Association; TRICARE Management Activity
To Err is Human: Building a Safer Health System (IOM), 15, 311, 391, 435, 437, 442, 525
Tobacco
  advertisements for, 8, 161
  health effects of, 144
  Mississippi settlement, 505-509
  taxation, 662
Torrisi, Donna, 87

Torts, 474-475
Total parenteral nutrition, home-based, 236
Toughman competitions, 549
Town meetings, 348, 350
  seed questions for, 350*b*
  tips for, 348*b*
Towns and townships, 488*b*-489*b*
TPT. *See* Taxpayer Team
Traditional funding, 219
Trained superintendents, 21
Training schools, 21-22
Transportation opportunities, 546*b*
Trash, 737
Trauma networks, statewide, 508
Travel and immigration policy, 725-726
TREA. *See* The Retired Enlisted Association
Tribes on the Hill: The U.S. Congress Ritual and Realities (Weatherford), 40
TRICARE, 131, 131*f*, 207, 249, 523
  expansion of, 134
TRICARE Extra, 249
TRICARE for Life (TFL) program, 134, 523
TRICARE Management Activity (TMA), 135
TRICARE Prime, 249
TRICARE Senior Pharmacy Program (TSRx), 134-135
Tri-Council for Nursing, 56-57
TROA. *See* The Retired Officers Association
Trust, 28, 694
Truth, Sojourner, 16
TSRx. *See* TRICARE Senior Pharmacy Program
Tu Tu, Desmond, 49
Tubman, Harriet, 85
Turf battles, 323
Turning Point: Collaborating for a New Century in Public Health initiative, 701-709
21st Century Community Learning Centers initiative, 670
Typhoid Mary, 722

U

UAE. *See* United Arab Emirates
UAFA. *See* United Army Forces Association
UAN. *See* United American Nurses
UAPs. *See* Unlicensed assistive personnel
UCDMC
  nursing philosophy, 328*b*
  Therapeutic Time pilot study, 330, 331*f*
UHF. *See* United Hospital Fund of New York
"U-Mass Wants to Keep You Alive, Don't Drink and Drive," 677
Uncertainty, 345-346

UNICEF, 720
Unified strategy, 133
Uniform APRN Licensure/Authority to Practice
    Requirements, 512
Uninsured, 432-434
Unionizing, 390-392
Unit determination, 394-395
United American Nurses (UAN), 393, 604
United Arab Emirates (UAE), 728-729, 728*b*
    licensing and regulation of nurses in, 728-735
United Army Forces Association (UAFA), 132*b*
United Food and Commercial Workers, 392
United Hospital Fund of New York (UHF), 319
United Kingdom, 211, 215
United Mine Workers, 392
United Nations partnerships, 719-720
United Ostomy Association, 650
United States Army Warrant Officers Association
    (USAWOA), 132*b*
United States Government Policy and Supporting Positions
    ("Plum Book"), 545
United States Post Office, 27
United Way, 694
Universal care, 215
    barriers to resolving, 215-216
Universal coverage
    related association websites, 217*b*
    vs universal access, 309
Universal payment, 214-215
University of Chicago, 402
The University of Iowa College of Public Health
    Doctoral Program in Health Management and
    Policy, 40*b*
University of Kentucky School of Nursing, 139*b*
University of Maryland, Baltimore, 37*b*
University of Massachusetts, 139*b*
    PhD in Nursing (policy focus on the health of the
        urban family and elderly), 37*b*
    William Joiner Center, 190
The University of Michigan School of Public Health
    Master's Degree and doctoral programs, 40*b*
University of Minnesota, 237
University of Minnesota Hospital and Clinic (UMHC),
    335
    "Behaviors of a Respectful Work Environment," 336,
        338*f*
    "Characteristics of a Healthy Work Environment,"
        336, 337*f*
University of Nebraska Medical Center, 402
University of Pennsylvania School of Nursing, 90
University of Pittsburgh School of Nursing, 88

The University of South Florida Health Policy and
    Management programs, 40*b*
University of Texas at Austin School of Nursing, 139*b*
University of Ulster, Northern Ireland, 138, 139*b*
University of Washington School of Nursing, 139*b*
Unlicensed assistive personnel (UAPs), 4, 473-474
UPS, 680
Upson, Thomas F., 141
Urban family health, 37*b*
Urban leadership, 704
Urban nurse-managed community health centers, 87-88
U.S. Air Force, 130, 523, 586
U.S. Army, 130, 523, 586
U.S. Child Care Bureau. *See* Child Care Bureau
U.S. Congress, 273*b*
    chief function of, 525
    duties of, 526
    *The House and Senate Explained: The People's Guide to
        Congress* (Greenberg), 40
    introduction of bills to, 451-452
    majority/minority districts, 570
    nurse members of, 533-535, 536-538, 571
    redistricting, 570
    types of bills in, 452*b*
    women in, 569-570
U.S. Constitution, 472
U.S. Department of Defense (DoD), 523
    Directive 1344.10, 586
    Health Program, 130-135, 249
    regulations on political activity, 586-587
    TRICARE health system, 131, 131*f*, 207, 249, 523
        expansion of, 134
U.S. Department of Education (DoE), 523
U.S. Department of Health and Human Services
    (DHHS), 136, 475-476, 518-523. *See also specific
    administrations, offices*
    Child Care Bureau, 673
    healthfinder, 110
    human services operating divisions, 518-519
    mental health spending, 219-220
    organization of, 518, 519*f*
    performance measures for Head Start, 670
    public health service operating divisions, 519-523
    regional directors, 538, 541
    regulatory process, 459, 467
    White House fellowship in, 49
U.S. Department of Justice (DoJ)
    Antitrust Division, 474
    Bureau of Prisons, 208
U.S. Department of Labor (DoL), 366, 524
    Bureau of Labor Statistics (BLS), 363, 365
    Transitional Workforce Stability Provisions, 390

U.S. Department of Veterans Affairs (VA), 139*b*, 523-524
  Civilian Health and Medical Program of the Veterans
      Administration (CHAMPVA), 249
  health care programs, 207, 249, 437
  Patient Safety Centers of Inquiry, 441
U.S. House of Representatives, 525. *See also specific*
      committees under House; *specific Representatives by*
      name
  floor action, 457, 458*b*
  nurses as members of, 533-535, 536-538
  scheduling and raising measures in, 458*b*
  Speaker of the, 525
  standing committees, 526*b*
  women in, 568
U.S. Navy, 130, 523, 586
U.S. Preventive Services Task Force, 520
U.S. Public Health Service, 138, 139*b*, 519
U.S. Senate, 525. *See also specific committees under*
      Senate; *specific Senators by name*
  floor action, 457, 458*b*
  scheduling and raising measures, 458*b*
  standing committees, 526*b*
  women in, 568
U.S. Supreme Court, 472, 530
USA Today, 161, 283
USAWOA. *See* United States Army Warrant Officers
      Association
USCG Chief Petty Officers Association (CPOA), 132*b*
Utah, 447
Utilization review, 234

V

VA. *See* U.S. Department of Veterans Affairs
Vacco v. Quill, 473, 477
Values, 9-13
  analyst, 62
  assessment of, 76-77
  core, 201
  framework for politics and policy process, 9, 10*f*
  health care, 2
  nursing, 9-11
Values conflicts, 180-181
Van der Merwe, Anita Serdyn, 728-735
Vance, Patricia, 89
Vanderbilt University Department of Preventive
      Medicine and Infectious Disease, 139*b*
Vanderbilt University School of Nursing, 138, 139*b*
Vaughan, Bill, 562
Vehicle emissions, 740-741
Vermont, 441
Vermont Agency of Natural Resources (ANR), 737
Vermont State Nurses Association (VSNA), 741

Veterans, health care programs for, 207, 249, 437
Veterans Health Administration (VHA), 123, 437, 523-
      524
  elimination of high-risk drugs, 440
  mandatory safety education, 440
  Medical Centers, 524
  National Center for Patient Safety (NCPS), 438
  National Patient Safety Partnership (NPSP), 438
  National Patient Safety Registry, 439
  patient safety improvement awards program, 441
  systems, 438
  VHA Handbook 1051/1: Patient Safety Improvement,
      439
  Virtual Learning Center (VLC), 440-441
Veterans Health Care Eligibility Reform Act of 1996, 207
Veterans of Foreign Wars (VFW), 132*b*, 195
Veterans' Widows International Network, 132*b*
Vetting, political, 544
VFW. *See* Veterans of Foreign Wars
VHA, Inc., 284
VHA Handbook 1051/1: Patient Safety Improvement
      (VHA), 439
Vice President, 526
Victorelli v. Shadyside Hospital, 477
"Vietnam: In Their Own Words," 198
Vietnam Nurses Memorial Project, 187
Vietnam Veterans Memorial ("the Wall"), 185-186
Vietnam Veterans Memorial Fund (VVMF), 185
Vietnam Veterans of America, 195
Vietnam Veterans Program, 249
Vietnam War, 199*b*
Vietnam Women's Memorial, 185-200, *196, 197*
Vietnam Women's Memorial Project (VWMP), 187,
      193-194, 198
Vietnamese, 224
Villages, 487*b*-488*b*
Violence prevention, 315-316
Virgin Islands: boards of nursing, 510
Virginia
  colon cancer screening policy, case study, 648-650
  Coverage for Colorectal Cancer Screening (S.B. 26),
      650
Virginia Gastroenterological Society, 649
Virginia Legislative Nursing Coalition, 649
Virtual Learning Center (VLC), 440-441
Virtues, 179
Visionary leadership, 693-694
Visiting Nurse Association of Central Jersey (VNACJ),
      688
  community health center, 692
  competency-based practice model, 695

Visiting Nurse Association of Central Jersey (VNACJ)—
cont'd
Hospice Program, 689
Mobile Outreach Clinic Program (MOCP), 689
participation methods, 690-691
Primary Care Centers, 689
visionary leadership, 693-694
Visits, personal, 556
VLC. *See* Virtual Learning Center
VNACJ. *See* Visiting Nurse Association of Central Jersey
Voice votes, 457
Voicemail, 103
Voluntary Effort, 233
Voluntary support network, 219
Voluntary units, 487*b*
Volunteer service, 36, 622-623
Volunteers, campaign, 574-575, 575*b*
Vorce, Susan, 353
Voters, 565-599
"Registered Nurse/Registered Voter" campaign, 572
registration of, 567-568
turnout in federal elections, 566, 566*t*
Votes
on bills, 457
division, 457
recorded teller, 457
voice, 457
Voting patterns, 566-567
Voting Rights Act, 570
Vouchers for child care, 673
VSNA. *See* Vermont State Nurses Association
VVMF. *See* Vietnam Veterans Memorial Fund
VWMP. *See* Vietnam Women's Memorial Project

W

Wakefield, Mary, 40, 547
Wald, Lillian, 15, 16, 20, 26-27, 201, 590
Wall Street Journal, 41, 150, 161
Warmlines, 690
Warner, Joanne Rains, 579-583
Warner, John, 134
Warner-Robbins, Carmen, 683
Washington: nurse practitioners in, 464
Washington Post, 41, 161
Washington v. Glucksberg, 473, 477
Waste, 737
biohazard, 739
medical, 736, 739
Waste management, 739
Health Care Without Harm campaign, 740
Watt, James, 186

W.B. Saunders Company, 45
"We Sea" program, 691
Weapons. *See* Chemical, biologic, radiologic, nuclear, or
high-yield explosive weapons
Weapons of mass destruction (WMDs), 136
Weatherford, J. McIver, 40
Websites, 105, 153, 558
on child care and early childhood education policies,
674*b*
HON code for, 110
state government resources, 496*b*
Weinstein, Beth, 142
Welcome Home incarceration model, 683
contact upon release, 684
needs assessment for, 683-684
Welcome Home Ministries, 684-685
collaboration, 685
recidivism, 684
vignette, 682-685
Welfare reform
health impact on communities, 661
linking with child care, 673-674
Welfare to Work Challenge, 518, 693
Wellstone, Paul, 221
West Nile virus, 723
West Virginia
boards of nursing, 510
needlestick prevention legislation, 417
nurse practitioners in, 464
West Virginia Colleagues, 123
"West Wing," 161
WHCP. *See* Women's Healthcare Partnership, Inc.
Wheeler, Jack, 190
WHF Program. *See* White House Fellows Program
Whinge (term), 142*n*
Whistleblower protection, 389
Whistleblower Protection Act, 537
White House Fellows (WHF) Program, *46,* 46-51
application, 48*b*
application process timeline, 48*b*
contact information, 50*b*
selection criteria, 47*b*
"White-Shoe Army," 500
Whitman, Christine Todd, *495*
Whitner v. South Carolina, 477
WHO. *See* World Health Organization
Widener University, 110
William Joiner Center, University of Massachusetts, 190
Williams, Sharon, 540
Wilson, Catherine A., *51,* 51-53
WIMSA Memorial. *See* Women in Military Service for
America Memorial

Win-lose solutions, 115-116
Win-win solutions, 116-118
Wisconsin
  budget wars, 501
  prescriptive authority bills, 501-502
  S-CHIP waivers, 433, 434
Wisconsin Assembly, 498-505
Wisconsin Federation of Nurses, 504
Wisconsin Nurses Association (WNA), 502, 503, 504
Wisconsin Organization of Nurse Executives, 503
Withdrawal, 115
WMA. *See* World Medical Association
WNA. *See* Wisconsin Nurses Association
Woman Movement, 20-21, 20*n*
Woman Rebel, 27
Women
  in Congress, 569-570
  innovative faith-based program for, 682-685
  political candidates, 568-570
  in prison, 682-683, 683*b*
  voter turnout in federal elections, 567
Women in Government, 544
Women in Military Service for America (WIMSA)
      Memorial, 188
Women's Appointment Project, 545
Women's Healthcare Partnership, Inc. (WHCP), 265,
      266
Women's movement, 20*n,* 27-29
Women's suffrage, 24-26
Woodhull Study on Nursing and the Media, 160
Woolner, Barbara, 653
Work assignments, 389
Work hours, 314
Workers, insured, 434
Workforce, nursing, 313-315
Working a room, 96-97
Working poor, 433
Workplace advocacy, 315, 604, 663-664
Workplace change, 333-361
  case example, 340-343, 343-344
  collective action for, 387-397
  considerations for, 355-356
  nursing's role in, 354
  outcomes, 353
Workplace environments
  "Behaviors of a Respectful Work Environment"
      (UMHC), 336, 338*f*
  "Characteristics of a Healthy Work Environment"
      (UMHC), 336, 337*f*

Workplace environments—cont'd
  Healthy Work Environment Initiative, 335-336
  sphere of, 13-14
Workplace policies
  contemporary issues, 311-332
  examples, 13
  and racial and ethnic disparities, 226-227
  strategy for, 235
Workplace safety, 315-316
  needlestick injuries, case study, 412-419
Worksite Health Promotion Alliance, 642
World Bank, 715*b,* 720
World Bank Group, 720
World Health Organization (WHO), 50, 108, 713, 714*b,*
      720
  functions, 714*b*
  Global Outbreak Alert and Response Network, 724
  Influenza Surveillance Network, 724
  nursing in, 718-719
  public statement on poverty, 715
  reporting infectious diseases to, 724
  travel and immigration policy, 726
World Health Professions Alliance, 720
World Medical Association (WMA), 713, 720
World Trade Center attack (September 11, 2001), 1
World Trade Organization (WTO), 713*b,* 724
World Wide Web (www or "the Web"), 109. *See also*
      Websites
World's Columbian Exposition (Chicago, 1893), 22
Wound, Ostomy, and Continence Nurses Society, 611,
      650
Writing, formula, 624
Writing letters, 555-556
Writing opinion editorials, 165
WTO. *See* World Trade Organization
Wyden, Ron, 648
Wynn, Albert, 633

X

Xers, 314

Y

Yale School of Nursing, 37*b*
Your Senior Connection, 688
Yousif, Enam Abu, 732

Z

Zap Asthma, Inc., 540-541, 540*b*
Zazworsky, Donna, 172-176, *175*